Collectors' Information Bureau

COLLECTIBLES
PRICE GUIDE

&

DIRECTORY TO SECONDARY MARKET DEALERS

Sixth Edition
1996

**More Than
49,000
Collectibles
Listed**

YOUR GUIDE TO CURRENT PRICES
AND SECONDARY MARKET DEALERS
FOR LIMITED EDITION
Figurines ❖ Cottages ❖ Bells ❖ Graphics
Plates ❖ Ornaments ❖ Dolls ❖ Steins

❖ CONTENTS ❖

❖ ACKNOWLEDGMENTS ❖

The staff of the Collectors' Information Bureau would like to express our deep appreciation to our distinguished panel of limited edition retailers and secondary market experts, whose knowledge and dedication to the collectibles industry have helped make this book possible. Although we would like to recognize them by name, they have agreed that to be singled out in this manner may hinder their ability to maintain an unbiased view of the marketplace.

STAFF

Administrative and Editorial Management —
Peggy Veltri   Cindy Zagumny

Research and Development —
Carol Van Elderen   Susan Knappen
Deb Wojtysiak   Deb Ley
Joan Barcal   Arlene Utz

Design and Graphics —
Kristin E. Wiley - Wright Design

Printing —
William C. Brown Communications

Printed in the United States of America.

ISBN: 0-930785-21-5
Collectors' Information Bureau

ISBN: 0-87069-749-8
Wallace-Homestead Book Company

❖ 1996 C.I.B. MEMBERSHIP ❖

Established in 1982, the Collectors' Information Bureau (CIB) is a not-for-profit business league whose mission is to serve and educate collectors, members and dealers, and to provide them with credible, comprehensive and authoritative information on limited edition collectibles and their current values.

Ace Product Management Group
9053 N. Deerbrook Trail
Brown Deer, WI 53223
(800) 294-9007 Ext. 210
Fax: (414) 365-5410

Kurt S. Adler, Inc.
1107 Broadway
New York, NY 10010
(212) 924-0900
Fax: (212) 807-0575

Amaranth Productions
P.O. Box 3505
Huntington Beach, CA
92605-3505
(714) 841-9972
Fax: (714) 847-1090

Amazze Gifts
1030 Sunnyside Road
Vermilion, OH 44089
(800) 543-6759
Fax: (216) 967-5199

Anheuser-Busch, Inc.
2700 South Broadway
St. Louis, MO 63118
(800) 325-1154
Fax: (314) 577-9656

Annalee Mobilitee Dolls, Inc.
P.O. Box 1137
Meredith, NH 03253-1137
(800) 433-6557
Fax: (603) 279-6659

ANRI U.S.
P.O. Box 380760
1126 So. Cedar Ridge,
Ste. 111
Duncanville, TX 75138
(800) 730-ANRI
Fax: (214) 283-3522

G. Armani Society/ Miller Import Corp.
300 Mac Lane
Keasbey, NJ 08832
(800) 3-ARMANI
Fax: (908) 417-0031

The Ashton-Drake Galleries
9200 N. Maryland Avenue
Niles, IL 60714
(800) 634-5164
Fax: (708) 966-3026

Attic Babies
P.O. Box 912
Drumright, OK 74030
(918) 352-4414
Fax: (918) 352-4767

Autom
5226 S. 31st Place
Phoenix, AZ 85040
(602) 243-5200

BAND Creations
28427 N. Ballard
Lake Forest, IL 60045
(800) 535-3242
Fax: (847) 816-3695

The Boyds Collection Ltd.
Somethin' Ta Say Dept.
Gettysburg, PA 17325-4385

The Bradford Exchange
9333 Milwaukee Avenue
Niles, IL 60714
(800) 323-5577

Brandywine Collectibles
104 Greene Dr.
Yorktown, VA 23692
(804) 898-5031
Fax: (804) 898-6895

Byers' Choice Ltd.
P.O. Box 158
Chalfont, PA 18914
(215) 822-6700
Fax: (215) 822-3847

Calabar Creations
1941 S. Vineyard Avenue
Ontario, CA 91761
(909) 930-9978
Fax: (909) 930-9928

Cardew Design
c/o S.P. Skinner Co., Inc.
91 Great Hill Road
P.O. Box 5
Naugatuck, CT 06770
(203) 729-8255

Cast Art Industries, Inc.
1120 California Avenue
Corona, CA 91719
(800) 932-3020
Fax: (909) 270-2852

Cavanagh Group International
1000 Holcomb Woods Pkwy.
#440-B
Roswell, GA 30078
(800) 895-8100
Fax: (404) 643-1172

Christopher Radko
P.O. Box 238
Dobbs Ferry, NY 10522
(800) 71-RADKO
Fax: (914) 693-3770

Crystal World
3 Borinski Road, Suite B
Lincoln Park, NJ 07035
(201) 633-0707
Fax: (201) 633-0102

Department 56, Inc.
P.O. Box 44456
Eden Prairie, MN
55344-1456
(800) 548-8696

The Walt Disney Company
500 South Buena Vista Street
Burbank, CA 91521-6876
(800) WD-CLSIX

Duncan Royale
1141 S. Acacia Avenue
Fullerton, CA 92631
(714) 879-1360
Fax: (714) 879-4611

Enesco Corporation
225 Windsor Drive
Itasca, IL 60143
(708) 875-5300

Ertl Collectibles
P.O. Box 500
Dyersville, IA 52040
(319) 875-2000
Fax: (319) 875-5821

The Fenton Art Glass Company
700 Elizabeth Street
Williamstown, WV 26187
(304) 375-6122
Fax: (304) 375-6459

Fitz and Floyd
13111 N. Central
Dallas, TX 75243
(800) 243-2058

FJ Designs, Inc. Makers of Cat's Meow Village
2163 Great Trails Drive
Wooster, OH 44691-3738
(216) 264-1377
Fax: (216) 263-0219

Flambro Imports
1530 Ellsworth Industrial Dr.
Atlanta, GA 30318
(404) 352-1381
Fax: (404) 352-2150

Forma Vitrum
20414 N. Main Street
Cornelius, NC 28031
(800) 596-9963
Fax: (704) 892-5438

The Franklin Mint
Franklin Center, PA 19091
(800) 225-5836
Fax: (610) 459-6880

Margaret Furlong Designs
210 State Street
Salem, OR 97301
(503) 363-6004
Fax: (503) 371-0676

Ganz
908 Niagara Falls Blvd.
North Tonawanda, NY
14120-2060
(800) 724-5902
Fax: (905) 851-6669

Gartlan USA
575 Rt. 73 North, Ste. A-6
West Berlin, NJ 08091
(609) 753-9229
Fax: (609) 753-9280

Georgetown Collection
P.O. Box 9730
Portland, ME 04104
(800) 626-3330
Fax: (207) 775-6457

Goebel of North America
Goebel Plaza
P.O. Box 10, Rte. 31
Pennington, NJ
08534-0010
(609) 737-8700
Fax: (609) 737-1545

Great American Taylor Collectilbles Corp.
Dept. BIC, P.O. Box 428
Aberdeen, NC 28315
(910) 944-7447
Fax: (910) 944-7449

The Greenwich Workshop
One Greenwich Place
Shelton, CT 06484
(800) 243-4246
Fax: (203) 925-0262

The Hamilton Collection
4810 Executive Park Court
Jacksonville, FL
32216-6069
(800) 228-2945

Hand & Hammer Silversmiths
2610 Morse Lane
Woodbridge, VA 22192
(800) SILVERY
Fax: (703) 491-2031

Harbour Lights
8130 La Mesa Blvd.
La Mesa, CA 91941
(619) 579-1820
Fax: (619) 579-1911

Harmony Kingdom
225 Fifth Avenue, Suite 623
New York, NY 10010
(800) 318-3815
Fax: (212) 684-3686

Hawthorne Architectural Register
9210 N. Maryland Avenue
Niles, IL 60714
(800) 772-4277 customer service
(800) 327-0327 ordering

M.I. Hummel Club
Division of Goebel Art GmbH, Goebel Plaza
P.O. Box 11
Pennington, NJ 08534-0011
(800) 666-2582
Fax: (609) 737-1545

Imperial Graphics
11516 Lake Potomac Dr.
Potomac, MD 20854
(301) 299-5711
Fax: (301) 299-4837

Ladie and Friends, Inc.
220 North Main Street
Sellersville, PA 18960
(800) 76DOLLS
Fax: (215) 453-8155

The Lance Corporation
321 Central Street
Hudson, MA 01749
(508) 568-1401
Fax: (508) 568-8741

Ron Lee's World of Clowns
330 Carousel Pkwy.
Henderson, NV 89014
(800) 829-3928
Fax: (702) 434-4310

George Z. Lefton Co.
3622 S. Morgan St.
Chicago, IL 60609
(800) 628-8492

Legends
2665D Park Center Drive
Simi Valley, CA 93065
(800) 726-9660
Fax: (805) 520-9670

Lenox Collections
1170 Wheeler Way
Langhorne, PA 19047
(800) 225-1779
Fax: (215) 750-7362

Lilliput Lane
P.O. Box 665
Elk Grove Village, IL
60009-0665
(800) 545-5478

Lladro Society
1 Lladro Drive
Moonachie, NJ 07074
(800) 634-9088
Fax: (201) 807-1168

Seymour Mann, Inc.
225 Fifth Avenue
Showroom #102
New York, NY 10010
(212) 683-7262
Fax: (212) 213-4920

Maruri, U.S.A.
7541 Woodman Place
Van Nuys, CA 91405
(800) 5-MARURI
Fax: (818) 780-9871

Media Arts Group
Ten Almaden Blvd. 9th floor
San Jose, CA 95113
(800) 544-4890
Fax: (408) 947-4640

Michael's Limited
P.O. Box 217
Redmond, WA 98052-0217
(800) 835-0181
Fax: (206) 861-0608

Midwest of Cannon Falls
32057 64th Avenue
P.O. Box 20
Cannon Falls, MN
55009-0020
(800) 377-3335
Fax: (507) 263-7752

Miss Martha Originals, Inc.
P.O. Box 5038
Glencoe, AL 35905
(205) 492-0221
Fax: (205) 492-0261

Old World Christmas
P.O. Box 8000
Spokane, WA 99203
(509) 534-9000
Fax: (509) 534-9098

Pacific Rim Import Corp.
5390 4th Avenue South
Seattle, WA 98108
(800) 425-5932
Fax: (206) 767-9179

Possible Dreams
6 Perry Drive
Foxboro, MA 02035
(508) 543-6667
Fax: (508) 543-4255

Precious Art, Inc.
110 E. Ellsworth Road
Ann Arbor, MI 48108
(313) 677-3510
Fax: (313) 677-3412

Pulaski Furniture, Inc.
One Pulaski Square
Pulaski, VA 24301
(800) 287-4625

R.R. Creations
P.O. Box 8707
Pratt, KS 67124
(800) 779-3610
Fax: (316) 672-5850

Reco International
150 Haven Avenue
Port Washington, NY 11050
(516) 767-2400
Fax: (516) 767-2409

Roman, Inc.
555 Lawrence Avenue
Roselle, IL 60172-1599
(708) 529-3000
Fax: (708) 529-1121

Royal Copenhagen/ Bing & Grondahl
27 Holland Avenue
White Plains, NY 10603
(914) 428-8222
Fax: (914) 428-8251

Royal Doulton
701 Cottontail Lane
Somerset, NJ 08873
(800) 68-CHINA
Fax: (908) 356-9467

Sarah's Attic
126-1/2 West Broad
P.O. Box 448
Chesaning, MI 48616
(800) 4-FRIEND
Fax: (517) 845-3477

Shelia's Inc.
P.O. Box 31028
Charleston, SC 29417
(800) 227-6564
Fax: (803) 556-0040

Shube's Manufacturing
600 Moon St. S. E.
Albuquerque, NM 87123
(800) 545-5082
Fax: (505) 275-8182

Swarovski America Limited
2 Slater Road
Cranston, RI 02920
(800) 426-3088
Fax: (401) 463-8459

The Tudor Mint
P.O. Box 431729
Houston, TX 77243-1729
(713) 462-0076
Fax: (713) 462-0170

Glynda Turley Prints, Inc.
P.O. Box 112
Heber Springs, AR 72543
(800) 633-7931

United Design
P.O. Box 1200
Noble, OK 73068
(800) 527-4883
Fax: (405) 360-4442

WACO Products Corp.
I-80 & New Maple Avenue
P.O. Box 898
Pine Brook, NJ 07058-0898
(201) 882-1820
Fax: (201) 882-3661

Walnut Ridge Collectibles
39048 Webb Dr.
Westland, MI 48185
(313) 728-3300
Fax: (313) 728-5950

❖ INTRODUCTION ❖

Welcome to the sixth edition of the *Collectibles Price Guide!* This comprehensive, up-to-date index is published each Spring by the Collectors' Information Bureau and reports on current primary and secondary market retail prices for limited edition figurines, cottages, plates, dolls, bells, Christmas ornaments, graphics and steins.

The Guide is considered one of the most authoritative and comprehensive price guides available today, listing over 49,000 current market prices. It is an ideal resource for collectors to use in establishing the value of their collections for insurance purposes. It is also a useful guide for those collectors who decide to buy or sell a retired collectible on the secondary market.

NEW SECONDARY MARKET DEALER DIRECTORY

This issue of the *Collectibles Price Guide* features a new directory designed to make secondary market transactions more convenient for you. We've added a "Directory to Secondary Market Dealers" at the back of this book to help you find dealers who are secondary market experts in the products that you are looking to buy or sell. And the index, found on pages D11-12, is an easy way to pinpoint the dealer who specializes in particular lines or categories of collectibles. Once you've found the particular dealer that handles your desired products, you're one step closer to a successful secondary market trade!

HOW WE OBTAIN OUR PRICES

The *Collectibles Price Guide* is the result of an extensive cooperative effort between the Collectors' Information Bureau's in-house research and development staff and our national panel of limited edition dealers and secondary market experts. A very systematic procedure for gathering and reporting prices has been developed and refined over the years in order to provide collectors with the most accurate and timely information possible.

The process begins with the C.I.B. research and development staff gathering up-to-date information from collectibles manufacturers on new items as well as those which have been "retired." This information is entered into a computer and copies are mailed to the C.I.B.'s panel of retailers and exchanges across the United States.

Members of this panel are carefully screened by C.I.B. management for their in-depth knowledge of the marketplace, their stature within the collectibles field, and their dedication to meeting the information needs of collectors everywhere. Through mail and telephone surveys, the panel works with our in-house researchers as a cooperative team to report and analyze actual sales transactions.

Based on these findings, which are checked and rechecked, a price is determined for each entry in which there has been trading activity. Where prices for some items may vary throughout the country, we provide a price range showing a "low" and a "high." All prices are for items in mint condition.

The secondary market in collectibles is a vast, ever-changing market. Some collectibles maintain a steady value for years, while prices for others go up and down so quickly it would be impossible to provide a completely up-to-date price in a printed book. That's why it's very important for anyone who uses the *Collectibles Price Guide* — or any of the other price indexes on the market — to think of it as a general guideline only. Also remember that prices quoted are retail prices, which means that they are the prices which these retail stores or secondary market exchanges have confirmed in a sales transaction, including their profit.

❖ 10 Most Frequently Asked Questions ❖
About Buying and Selling Limited Edition Collectibles

Q. How are prices for limited edition collectibles established on the secondary market?

A. As with most items in an open marketplace, prices are established in response to the supply of and demand for each individual item. Since limited edition pieces are, by definition, limited in the number of pieces available, demand for each piece will impact the market value of the item.

Over time, the "supply" of a particular piece may decrease, as natural disasters and home accidents result in damage or breakage. As the supply shrinks, the price may increase again.

Similarly, items that are in relatively large supply and experience small to moderate demand may see modest or low appreciation on the secondary market. Some items with broad distribution and low demand do not appreciate at all on the secondary market.

These fluctuations in the secondary market value of items are tracked by organizations like the COLLECTORS' INFORMATION BUREAU. Twice a year, the CIB surveys over 300 secondary market dealers and asks them to report back on the actual prices collectors have paid for individual pieces. This input is compiled and reported in the COLLECTIBLES PRICE GUIDE (published each May) and the COLLECTIBLES MARKET GUIDE & PRICE INDEX (published each November).

Q. What does a collector need to know if they are planning to buy or sell on the secondary market?

A. There are 4 things to consider when you begin thinking about buying or selling on the secondary market.

1.) *Know the value of the piece you want to buy or sell.* This information can be found by checking reputable price guides like the CIB's COLLECTIBLES PRICE GUIDE. Since these books list actual prices paid by collectors in recent transactions, they represent an excellent starting point for determining the market value of an item.

2.) *Understand the "terms of sale" used by the secondary market dealer that you're considering.* Individual dealers vary greatly in the services they offer the collectors and the fees they charge for these services. Some dealers buy pieces outright, while others provide a listing service or take goods on consignment. Some dealers charge as little as 10% commission while others charge upwards of 30% to 50%. In most cases, the buyer pays the fee, however some dealers will ask the seller to pay all or part of the fee.

3.) *Be realistic about the condition of your piece.* Note any markings, mold numbers, etc. Carefully check your piece for any scratches, blemishes or cracks. If you are upfront with the dealer, you'll save yourself time and aggravation. Gather the original paperwork and box. If you don't have these materials, ask the dealer how this will affect the price of the piece you're selling. If you're looking to buy and have no intention of reselling, let the dealer know that you would accept a piece without the original paperwork. But be sure that you will not want to resell the piece later, since this will have an impact on the price you can demand.

4.) *Ask if the piece will be inspected by the dealer.* Many dealers will suggest that you write your initials or some other "code" on the bottom of the piece in pencil. By doing so, you can be sure that the piece you send in is the piece you get back should the sale fall through. Check with the dealer before putting any markings on the piece to ensure that it will not effect the value of the piece.

Q. Does a factory flaw effect the selling price of a piece?

A. As in most things, "visual perfection" is preferred. Usually, factory flaws are not a problem unless they are very pronounced. That's why it is extremely important to inspect each piece you buy...whether it's on the primary market (through a retailer or direct mail) or on the secondary market (at a "swap & sell" or through a dealer/exchange).

And remember, everyone's definition of "perfection" is different. What one collector may find acceptable, another would reject.

Q. Does the presence of an artist's signature on a piece increase its value?

A. Though the presence of a signature is not as important as it used to be, in some cases the value of a signed piece may be 15% to 25% higher than a comparable unsigned piece. Factors that impact the value of a signature include:

1.) *Age of the artist* — Artists who are reaching the end of their career may be doing fewer signings, making a signed piece more valuable to many collectors.

2.) *Accessibility of an artist* — Signatures from artists that rarely make themselves available for signings are often more coveted and therefore add to the value of a signed piece.

3.) *Buyer's preference* — More and more artists are taking to the road for personal appearances. These events give the collector the chance to share a personal experience with the artist. Some collectors prefer to buy unsigned pieces because they plan to have the artist sign the piece for them personally at an upcoming event.

Q. How important is it to save the original box?

A. Boxes are very important and the absence of an original box will often result in a lower selling price.

If you have a collectible that breaks and you have your original box, you can buy a replacement piece without the box (since you don't need it) and usually save some money.

On a more practical note, the manufacturer designs the box to afford the best possible protection for the piece during shipment. If you and your collectible move, the original box will be your best shot at getting your collection safely to its new home.

Q. What steps should I expect to go through in buying or selling collectibles through a secondary market dealer or exchange?

A. The average secondary market transaction takes about 3 weeks to complete and will usually include the following steps:

1.) *Call the secondary market dealer/exchange and tell them about the piece you want to buy or sell.* Be specific and include the product number if possible.

2.) *If you are looking to buy a piece, the dealer will tell you if they currently have it listed (available from a seller) or in stock, and what the selling price is.* The selling price will usually include a commission or service fee for the dealer/exchange. If you are looking to sell a piece, you should be prepared to tell them your "asking price." This price is the amount of money you expect to clear after the transaction is completed, and should not include the commission. In most cases, the dealer will add the commission on top of your asking price. Keep in mind that you must pay the shipping and insurance charges necessary to get your piece to the dealer/exchange. The buyer will usually pay to have the item shipped to them from the dealer/exchange.

3.) *Once a buyer agrees to pay the price asked, the dealer contacts the seller and has the piece shipped to the dealer for inspection.* At the same time, the buyer sends his/her payment to the dealer.

4.) *After the piece is inspected by the dealer and found to be in acceptable condition, the piece is shipped to the buyer for their inspection.* Before it is shipped, most dealers will put a marking (often invisible) on the bottom of the piece. This is a safeguard to ensure that if the piece is not accepted, the same piece is returned.

5.) *The buyer usually will have a set time-period (3 to 5 days) to either accept or reject the piece.* If the piece is accepted by the buyer, the dealer pays the seller the agreed-upon asking price. If the piece is not acceptable, it is returned to the dealer who can either return it to the seller, or sell it to another buyer for the original asking price.

Q. It seems that there is a wide range of limited edition products being sold today. Has this resulted in a slow-down in secondary market trading?

A. Quite the contrary! The increased vitality of the primary market, as seen in the growing number of manufacturers and lines, has resulted in more vigorous trading on the secondary market. There are more collectors than ever before, they are younger and have more disposable income then their predecessors. In many cases, they're getting started later in a series — after the first few issues have retired — so increased demand for earlier pieces is generated. All of this fuels a very strong secondary market.

Q. Is trading or bartering an option for acquiring limited edition collectibles?

A. Trading and/or bartering is an alternative to buying and selling on the secondary market. Collectors clubs and "swap and sell" events offer the best avenue for trading or bartering, since you have the opportunity to inspect the piece and negotiate right on the spot.

Q. If you have a large collection, is it better to sell it as a "collection" or as single pieces?

A. It is very difficult to sell an entire collection unless it is comprised of all older pieces, since collectors usually have some of the pieces from the collection that they're building. Often, they are looking to supplement their own collection of later issues with some of the earlier pieces that they missed.

It's also typically quite expensive to purchase an entire collection at once, so collectors will add to a collection piece-by-piece as they can afford the investment.

You will usually receive greater value for your collection if you sell it one piece at a time, rather than trying to sell the whole collection at once to one buyer. By listing your collection as individual pieces with a secondary market dealer, you have a better chance of moving all the pieces, though it may take some time.

Q. Do variations in a piece effect its value?

A. Variations are not as uncommon as you may think. Usually they do not effect the value of a piece. The exception to this rule is variations that qualify as "mistakes." Misspelling and other obvious mistakes will usually make a piece more valuable.

❖ Collectors' Information Bureau ❖

PRICE INDEX 1996

Limited Edition
Plates ❖ Figurines ❖ Cottages ❖ Bells ❖ Graphics ❖ Christmas Ornaments ❖ Dolls ❖ Steins

This index includes thousands of the most widely traded limited editions in today's collectibles market. It is based on surveys and interviews with several hundred of the most experienced and informed limited edition dealers in the United States, as well as many independent market advisors.

HOW TO USE THIS INDEX

Listings are set up using the following format:

Enesco Corporation ❶

❷ ❸
Precious Moments Figurines — S. Butcher

❹ ❺ ❻ ❼ ❽ ❾
1979   Praise the Lord Anyhow-E1374B   Retrd.   1982   8.00   75-130

❶ Enesco Corporation = Company Name

❷ Precious Moments Figurines = Series Name

❸ S. Butcher = Artist's Name. The word "Various" may also appear here, meaning that several artists have created pieces within the series. The artist's name then appears after the title of the collectible. In some cases, the artist's name will be indicated after the series name "with exceptions noted." If company staff artists have created the piece, no artist name is listed.

❹ 1979 = Year of Issue

❺ Praise the Lord Anyhow-E1374B = Title of the collectible. Many titles also include the model number for further identification purposes.

❻ Retrd. = Edition Limit. In this case, the collectible is no longer available. The edition limit category generally refers to the number of items created with the same name and decoration. Edition limits may indicate a specific number (i.e. 10,000) or the number of firing days for plates (i.e. 100-day, the capacity of the manufacturer to produce collectibles during a given firing period). Refer to "Open," "Suspd.," "Annual," and "Yr. Iss." under "Terms and Abbreviations" below.

❼ 1982 = Year of Retirement. May also indicate the year the manufacturer ceased production of the collectible. If N/A appears in this column, it indicates the information is not available at this time, but research is continuing.
Note: In the plate section, the year of retirement may not be indicated because many plates are limited to firing days and not years.

❽ 8.00 = Original Issue Price in U.S. Dollars

❾ 75-130 = Current Quote Price listed may show a price or price range. Quotes are based on interviews with retailers across the country, who provide their actual sales transactions. Quotes have been rounded up to the nearest dollar. Quote may also reflect a price increase for pieces that are not retired or closed.

A Special Note to Beatrix Potter, Boyds Bears, Cherished Teddies, Disney Classics, Goebel Miniatures, M.I. Hummel and Precious Moments Collectors: *These collectibles are engraved with a special annual mark. This emblem changes with each production year. The secondary market value for each piece varies because of these distinctive yearly markings. Our pricing reflects an average for all years.*
A Special Note to Hallmark Keepsake Ornament Collectors: *All quotes in this section are for ornaments in mint condition in their original box.*
A Special Note to Department 56 Collectors: *Year of Introduction indicates the year in which the piece was designed, sculpted and copyrighted. It is possible these pieces may not be available to the collectors until the following calendar year.*

TERMS AND ABBREVIATIONS

Annual = Issued once a year.
A/P = Artist Proof.
Closed = An item or series no longer in production.
G/P = Gallery Proof.
N/A = Not available at this time.
Open = Not limited by number or time, available until manufacturer stops production, "retires" or "closes" the item or series.

Retrd. = Retired.
S/N = Signed and Numbered.
S/O = Sold Out.
Set = Refers to two or more items issued together for a single price.
Suspd. = Suspended (not currently being produced: may be produced in the future).

Unkn. = Unknown.
Yr. Iss. = Year of issue (limited to a calendar year).
28-day, 10-day, etc. = Limited to this number of production (or firing) days, usually not consecutive.

BELLS

Ace Product Management Group, Inc.

Harley-Davidson Crystal Christmas Bells - Ace

Year Issue		Edition Limit	Year Retd.	Issue Price	*Quote U.S.$
1988	Crystal Bell 99212-89V	Yr.Iss.	1988	29.95	30
1989	Crystal Bell 99212-90V	Yr.Iss.	1989	29.95	30
1990	Crystal Bell 99212-91V	Yr.Iss.	1990	29.95	30
1991	Crystal Bell 99212-92V	Yr.Iss.	1991	32.95	33
1992	Crystal Bell 99212-93Z	Yr.Iss.	1992	38.00	38

Harley-Davidson Porcelain Holiday Bells - Ace

Year Issue		Edition Limit	Year Retd.	Issue Price	*Quote U.S.$
1993	Checking It Twice 99411-94Z	Yr.Iss.	1993	25.00	25
1994	Santa's Predicament 99439-95Z	Yr.Iss.	1994	25.00	25
1995	Finding The Way 99449-96Z	Yr.Iss.	1995	25.00	25

Artists of the World

DeGrazia Bells - T. DeGrazia

Year Issue		Edition Limit	Year Retd.	Issue Price	*Quote U.S.$
1980	Festival of Lights	5,000	N/A	40.00	85-100
1980	Los Ninos	7,500	N/A	40.00	75-100
1980	Los Ninos (signed)	500	N/A	80.00	200-250

Belleek

Belleek Bells - Belleek

Year Issue		Edition Limit	Year Retd.	Issue Price	*Quote U.S.$
1988	Bell, 1st Ed.	Yr.Iss.		38.00	38
1989	Tower, 2nd Ed.	Yr.Iss.		35.00	35
1990	Leprechaun, 3rd Ed.	Yr.Iss.		30.00	30
1991	Church, 4th Ed.	Yr.Iss.		32.00	32
1992	Cottage, 5th Ed.	Yr.Iss.		30.00	30
1993	Pub, 6th Ed.	Yr.Iss.		30.00	30
1994	Castle, 7th Ed.	Yr.Iss.		30.00	30

Twelve Days of Christmas - Belleek

Year Issue		Edition Limit	Year Retd.	Issue Price	*Quote U.S.$
1991	A Partridge in a Pear Tree	Yr.Iss.		30.00	30
1992	Two Turtle Doves	Yr.Iss.		30.00	30
1993	Three French Hens	Yr.Iss.		30.00	30
1994	Four Calling Birds	Yr.Iss.		30.00	30
1995	Five Golden Rings	Yr.Iss.		30.00	30

Dave Grossman Designs

Norman Rockwell Collection - Rockwell-Inspired

Year Issue		Edition Limit	Year Retd.	Issue Price	*Quote U.S.$
1975	Faces of Christmas NRB-75	Retrd.	N/A	12.50	35
1976	Drum for Tommy NRB-76	Retrd.	N/A	12.00	30
1976	Ben Franklin (Bicentennial)	Retrd.	N/A	12.50	25
1980	Leapfrog NRB-80	Retrd.	N/A	50.00	60

Enesco Corporation

Cherished Teddies - P. Hillman

Year Issue		Edition Limit	Year Retd.	Issue Price	*Quote U.S.$
1992	Angel Bell-906530	Suspd.		20.00	35-60

Memories of Yesterday Bell - M. Attwell

Year Issue		Edition Limit	Year Retd.	Issue Price	*Quote U.S.$
1990	Here Comes the Bride-God Bless Her-523100	Suspd.		25.00	25
1994	Time For Bed-525243	Open		25.00	25

Precious Moments Annual Bells - S. Butcher

Year Issue		Edition Limit	Year Retd.	Issue Price	*Quote U.S.$
1981	Let the Heavens Rejoice-E-5622-	Yr.Iss.	1981	15.00	235-250
1982	I'll Play My Drum for Him-E-2358	Yr.Iss.	1982	17.00	65-75
1983	Surrounded With Joy-E-0522	Yr.Iss.	1983	18.00	70-75
1984	Wishing You a Merry Christmas -E-5393	Yr.Iss.	1984	19.00	45
1985	God Sent His Love-15873	Yr.Iss.	1985	19.00	40-50
1986	Wishing You a Cozy Christmas -102318	Yr.Iss.	1986	20.00	50
1987	Love is the Best Gift of All -109835	Yr.Iss.	1987	22.50	38-45
1988	Time To Wish You a Merry Christmas-115304	Yr.Iss.	1988	25.00	40-45
1989	Oh Holy Night-522821	Yr.Iss.	1989	25.00	30-40
1990	Once Upon A Holy Night-523828	Yr.Iss.	1990	25.00	25-40
1991	May Your Christmas Be Merry-524182	Yr.Iss.	1991	25.00	40
1992	But The Greatest Of These Is Love-527726	Yr.Iss.	1992	25.00	42-50
1993	Wishing You The Sweetest Christmas-530174	Yr.Iss.	1993	25.00	42-50
1994	Your're As Pretty as a Christmas Tree-604216	Yr.Iss.	1994	27.50	37

Precious Moments Various Bells - S. Butcher

Year Issue		Edition Limit	Year Retd.	Issue Price	*Quote U.S.$
1981	Jesus Loves Me (B)-E-5208	Suspd.		15.00	55
1981	Jesus Loves Me (G)-E-5209	Suspd.		15.00	55-65
1981	Prayer Changes Things-E-5210	Suspd.		15.00	55-60
1981	God Understands-E-5211	Retrd.	N/A	15.00	40-60
1981	We Have Seen His Star-E-5620	Suspd.		15.00	50-60
1981	Jesus Is Born-E-5623	Suspd.		15.00	50-65
1982	The Lord Bless You and Keep You-E-7175	Suspd.		17.00	45-55
1982	The Lord Bless You and Keep You-E-7176	Suspd.		17.00	55-65
1982	The Lord Bless You and Keep You-E-7179	Suspd.		22.50	65-85
1982	Mother Sew Dear-E-7181	Suspd.		17.00	45-55
1982	The Purr-fect Grandma-E-7183	Suspd.		17.00	50-60

Fenton Art Glass Company

American Classic Series - M. Dickinson

Year Issue		Edition Limit	Year Retd.	Issue Price	*Quote U.S.$
1986	Jupiter Train, 6 1/2" on Opal Satin	5,000	1986	50.00	50
1986	Studebaker-Garford Car, 6 1/2" on Opal Satin	5,000	1986	50.00	50

Artist Series - Various

Year Issue		Edition Limit	Year Retd.	Issue Price	*Quote U.S.$
1982	After The Snow - D. Johnson	15,000	1982	14.50	15
1983	Winter Chapel - D. Johnson	15,000	1984	15.00	15
1985	Flying Geese - D. Johnson	15,000	1985	15.00	15
1986	The Hummingbird - D. Johnson	15,000	1986	15.00	15
1987	Out in the Country - L. Everson	15,000	1987	15.00	15
1988	Serenity - F. Burton	5,000	1988	16.50	17
1989	Househunting - D. Barbour	5,000	1989	16.50	17

Childhood Treasurers Series - Various

Year Issue		Edition Limit	Year Retd.	Issue Price	*Quote U.S.$
1983	Teddy Bear, 4 1/2" - D. Johnson	15,000	1983	15.00	15
1984	Hobby Horse, 4 1/2" - L. Everson	15,000	1984	15.00	15
1985	Clown, 4 1/2" - L. Everson	15,000	1985	17.50	18
1986	Playful Kitten, 4 1/2" - L. Everson	15,000	1986	15.00	15
1987	Frisky Pup, 4 1/2" - D. Barbour	15,000	1987	15.00	15
1988	Castles in the Air, 4 1/2" - D. Barbour	5,000	1988	16.50	17
1989	A Child's Cuddly Friend, 4 1/2" - D. Johnson	5,000	1989	16.50	17

Christmas - Various

Year Issue		Edition Limit	Year Retd.	Issue Price	*Quote U.S.$
1978	Christmas Morn - M. Dickinson	Yr.Iss.	1978	25.00	25
1979	Nature's Christmas - K. Cunningham	Yr.Iss.	1979	30.00	30
1980	Going Home - D. Johnson	Yr.Iss.	1980	32.50	33
1981	All Is Calm - D. Johnson	Yr.Iss.	1981	35.00	35
1982	Country Christmas - R. Spindler	Yr.Iss.	1982	35.00	35
1983	Anticipation - D. Johnson	7,500	1983	35.00	35
1984	Expectation - D. Johnson	7,500	1984	37.50	38
1985	Heart's Desire - D. Johnson	7,500	1986	37.50	38
1987	Sharing The Spirit - L. Everson	Yr.Iss.	1987	37.50	38
1987	Cardinal in the Churchyard - D. Johnson	4,500	1987	29.50	30
1988	A Chickadee Ballet - D. Johnson	4,500	1988	29.50	30
1989	Downy Pecker - Chisled Song - D. Johnson	4,500	1989	29.50	30
1990	A Blue Bird in Snowfall - D. Johnson	4,500	1990	29.50	30
1990	Sleigh Ride - F. Burton	3,500	1990	39.00	39
1991	Christmas Eve - F. Burton	3,500	1991	35.00	35
1992	Family Tradition - F. Burton	3,500	1992	39.00	39
1993	Family Holiday - F. Burton	3,500	1993	39.50	40
1994	Silent Night - F. Burton	2,500	1994	45.00	45
1995	Our Home Is Blessed - F. Burton	2,500	1995	45.00	45

Christmas Limited Edition - M. Reynolds, unless otherwise noted

Year Issue		Edition Limit	Year Retd.	Issue Price	*Quote U.S.$
1992	Winter on Twilight Blue, 6 1/2"	2,500	1992	29.50	30
1993	Manager Scene on Ruby, 6 1/2"	2,500	1993	39.50	40
1993	Reindeer on Blue, 6 1/2"	2,500	1993	30.00	30
1993	Floral on Green-Musical, 6 1/2"	2,500	1993	39.50	40
1994	Magnolia on Gold, 6 1/2"	1,000	1994	35.00	35
1994	Angel on Ivory, 6 1/2"	1,000	1994	39.50	40
1994	Partridge on Ruby-Musical, 6 1/2"	1,000	1994	48.50	49
1995	Bow & Holly on Ivory, 6 1/2"	900	1995	39.50	40
1995	Chickadee on Gold, 6 1/2"	900	1995	39.50	40
1995	Iced Poinsettia on Ruby, 5 1/2"	900	1995	45.00	45
1995	Angel, Heavenly Bell, 5 3/4" - R. Spindler	1,900	1995	35.00	35

Connoisseur Bell - Various

Year Issue		Edition Limit	Year Retd.	Issue Price	*Quote U.S.$
1983	Bell, Burmese Handpainted - L. Everson	2,000	1983	50.00	95
1983	Craftsman Bell, White Satin Carnival - Fenton	3,500	1983	25.00	50
1984	Bell, Famous Women's Ruby Satin Irid. - Fenton	3,500	1984	25.00	50
1985	Bell, 6 1/2" Burmese, Hndpt. - L. Everson	2,500	1985	55.00	95
1986	Bell, Burmese-Shells, Hndpt. - D. Barbour	2,500	1986	60.00	100
1988	Bell, 7" Wisteria, Hndpt. - L. Everson	4,000	1988	45.00	85
1989	Bell, 7" Handpainted Rosalene Satin - L. Everson	3,500	1989	50.00	75
1991	Bell, 7" Roses on Rosalene, Hndpt. - M. Reynolds	2,000	1991	50.00	60

Designer Bells - Various

Year Issue		Edition Limit	Year Retd.	Issue Price	*Quote U.S.$
1996	Floral Medallion, 6" - M. Reynolds	2,500		60.00	60
1996	Gardenia, 7" - R. Spindler	2,500		55.00	55
1996	Gilded Berry, 6 1/2" - F. Burton	2,500		60.00	60
1996	Wild Rose, 5 1/2" - K. Plauche	2,500		50.00	50

Designer Series - Various

Year Issue		Edition Limit	Year Retd.	Issue Price	*Quote U.S.$
1983	Lighthouse Point, 6" - M. Dickinson	1,000	1983	55.00	55
1983	Down Home, 6" - G. Finn	1,000	1983	55.00	55
1984	Smoke 'N Cinders, 6" - M. Dickinson	1,250	1984	55.00	55
1984	Majestic Flight, 6" - B. Cumberledge	1,250	1984	55.00	55
1985	In Season, 6" - M. Dickinson	1,250	1985	55.00	55
1985	Nature's Grace, 6" - B. Cumberland	1,250	1985	55.00	55
1985	Statue of Liberty, 6" - S. Bryan	1,250	1985	55.00	55
1986	Statue of Liberty, 6" - S. Bryan	1,250	1986	55.00	55

Mary Gregory - M. Reynolds

Year Issue		Edition Limit	Year Retd.	Issue Price	*Quote U.S.$
1993	Bell, 6" Ruby	Closed	1993	49.00	49
1994	Bell, 6" Ruby - Loves Me, Loves Me Not	Closed	1994	49.00	49
1995	Bell, 6 1/2"	Closed	1995	49.00	49

Mother's Day Series - Various

Year Issue		Edition Limit	Year Retd.	Issue Price	*Quote U.S.$
1980	New Born - L. Everson	Closed	1980	25.00	25
1981	Gentle Fawn - L. Everson	Closed	1981	27.50	28
1982	Nature's Awakening - L. Everson	Closed	1982	28.50	29
1983	Where's Mom - L. Everson	Closed	1983	28.50	29
1984	Precious Panda - L. Everson	Closed	1984	28.50	29
1985	Mother's Little Lamb - L. Everson	Closed	1985	35.00	35
1990	White Swan - L. Everson	Closed	1990	35.00	35
1990	White Swan (Musical) - L. Everson	Closed	1990	45.00	45
1991	Mother's Watchful Eye - M. Reynolds	Closed	1991	35.00	35
1992	Let's Play With Mom - M. Reynolds	Closed	1992	37.50	38
1993	Mother Deer - M. Reynolds	Closed	1993	39.50	40
1994	Loving Puppy - M. Reynolds	Closed	1994	39.50	40

Valentine's Day Series - M. Reynolds

Year Issue		Edition Limit	Year Retd.	Issue Price	*Quote U.S.$
1992	Bell, 6" Vining Hearts Hndpt. Opal Irid.	Closed	1992	35.00	35

Goebel/M.I. Hummel

M.I. Hummel Collectibles Annual Bells - M. I. Hummel

Year Issue		Edition Limit	Year Retd.	Issue Price	*Quote U.S.$
1978	Let's Sing 700	Closed	N/A	50.00	50
1979	Farewell 701	Closed	N/A	70.00	70
1980	Thoughtful 702	Closed	N/A	85.00	85
1981	In Tune 703	Closed	N/A	85.00	85
1982	She Loves Me, She Loves Me Not 704	Closed	N/A	90.00	90
1983	Knit One 705	Closed	N/A	90.00	90
1984	Mountaineer 706	Closed	N/A	90.00	90
1985	Sweet Song 707	Closed	N/A	90.00	90
1986	Sing Along 708	Closed	N/A	100.00	100
1987	With Loving Greetings 709	Closed	N/A	110.00	110
1988	Busy Student 710	Closed	N/A	120.00	120
1989	Latest News 711	Closed	N/A	135.00	135
1990	What's New? 712	Closed	N/A	140.00	140
1991	Favorite Pet 713	Closed	N/A	150.00	150
1992	Whistler's Duet 714	Closed	N/A	160.00	160

Gorham

Currier & Ives - Mini Bells - Currier & Ives

Year Issue		Edition Limit	Year Retd.	Issue Price	*Quote U.S.$
1976	Christmas Sleigh Ride	Annual	1976	9.95	35
1977	American Homestead	Annual	1977	9.95	25
1978	Yule Logs	Annual	1978	12.95	20
1979	Sleigh Ride	Annual	1979	14.95	20
1980	Christmas in the Country	Annual	1980	14.95	20
1981	Christmas Tree	Annual	1981	14.95	18
1982	Christmas Visitation	Annual	1982	16.50	18
1983	Winter Wonderland	Annual	1983	16.50	18
1984	Hitching Up	Annual	1984	16.50	18
1985	Skaters Holiday	Annual	1985	17.50	18
1986	Central Park in Winter	Annual	1986	17.50	18
1987	Early Winter	Annual	1987	19.00	19

Mini Bells - N. Rockwell

Year Issue		Edition Limit	Year Retd.	Issue Price	*Quote U.S.$
1981	Tiny Tim	Annual	1981	19.75	20
1982	Planning Christmas Visit	Annual	1982	20.00	20

Various - N. Rockwell

Year Issue		Edition Limit	Year Retd.	Issue Price	*Quote U.S.$
1975	Sweet Song So Young	Annual	1975	19.50	50
1975	Santa's Helpers	Annual	1975	19.50	30
1975	Tavern Sign Painter	Annual	1975	19.50	30
1976	Flowers in Tender Bloom	Annual	1976	19.50	40
1976	Snow Sculpture	Annual	1976	19.50	45
1977	Fondly Do We Remember	Annual	1977	19.50	55
1977	Chilling Chore (Christmas)	Annual	1977	19.50	35
1978	Gaily Sharing Vintage Times	Annual	1978	22.50	23
1978	Gay Blades (Christmas)	Annual	1978	22.50	23
1979	Beguiling Buttercup	Annual	1979	24.50	27
1979	A Boy Meets His Dog (Christmas)	Annual	1979	24.50	30
1980	Flying High	Annual	1980	27.50	28
1980	Chilly Reception (Christmas)	Annual	1980	27.50	28
1981	Sweet Serenade	Annual	1981	27.50	28
1981	Ski Skills (Christmas)	Annual	1981	27.50	28
1982	Young Mans Fancy	Annual	1982	29.50	30
1982	Coal Season's Coming	Annual	1982	29.50	30
1983	Christmas Medley	Annual	1983	29.50	30
1983	The Milkmaid	Annual	1983	29.50	30
1984	Tiny Tim	Annual	1984	29.50	30
1984	Young Love	Annual	1984	29.50	30
1984	Marriage License	Annual	1984	32.50	33
1984	Yarn Spinner	5,000	1984	32.50	33
1985	Yuletide Reflections	5,000	1985	32.50	33
1986	Home For The Holidays	5,000	1986	32.50	33
1986	On Top of the World	5,000	1986	32.50	33
1987	Merry Christmas Grandma	5,000	1987	32.50	33
1987	The Artist	5,000	1987	32.50	33
1988	The Homecoming	15,000	1988	37.50	38

BELLS/CHRISTMAS ORNAMENTS

Kirk Stieff

Bell - Kirk Stieff

YEAR ISSUE		EDITION LIMIT	YEAR RETD.	ISSUE PRICE	*QUOTE U.S.$
1992	Santa's Workshop	3,000		40.00	40
1993	Santa's Reindeer	Closed	N/A	30.00	30

Musical Bells - Kirk Stieff

YEAR ISSUE		EDITION LIMIT	YEAR RETD.	ISSUE PRICE	*QUOTE U.S.$
1977	Annual Bell 1977	Closed	N/A	17.95	75-120
1978	Annual Bell 1978	Closed	N/A	17.95	80-100
1979	Annual Bell 1979	Closed	N/A	17.95	50
1980	Annual Bell 1980	Closed	N/A	19.95	55
1981	Annual Bell 1981	Closed	N/A	19.95	80
1982	Annual Bell 1982	Closed	N/A	19.95	65-95
1983	Annual Bell 1983	Closed	N/A	19.95	55-65
1984	Annual Bell 1984	Closed	N/A	19.95	40
1985	Annual Bell 1985	Closed	N/A	19.95	45
1986	Annual Bell 1986	Closed	N/A	19.95	55
1987	Annual Bell 1987	Closed	N/A	19.95	45
1988	Annual Bell 1988	Closed	N/A	22.50	40-50
1989	Annual Bell 1989	Closed	N/A	25.00	35
1990	Annual Bell 1990	Closed	N/A	27.00	35
1991	Annual Bell 1991	Closed	N/A	28.00	35
1992	Annual Bell 1992	Closed	N/A	30.00	30
1993	Annual Bell 1993	Closed	N/A	30.00	30
1994	Annual Bell 1994	Open	N/A	30.00	30

Lance Corporation

Hudson Pewter Bicentennial Bells - P.W. Baston

YEAR ISSUE		EDITION LIMIT	YEAR RETD.	ISSUE PRICE	*QUOTE U.S.$
1974	Benjamin Franklin	Closed	1977	Unkn.	70-80
1974	George Washington	Closed	1977	Unkn.	30-40
1974	James Madison	Closed	1977	Unkn.	30-40
1974	John Adams	Closed	1977	Unkn.	100-125
1974	Thomas Jefferson	Closed	1977	Unkn.	40-50

Lenox China

Songs of Christmas - Unknown

YEAR ISSUE		EDITION LIMIT	YEAR RETD.	ISSUE PRICE	*QUOTE U.S.$
1991	We Wish You a Merry Christmas	Yr.Iss.	1992	49.00	49
1992	Deck the Halls	Yr.Iss.	1993	53.00	53
1993	Jingle Bells	Yr.Iss.	1994	57.00	57
1994	Silver Bells	Yr.Iss.	1995	62.00	62

Lenox Collections

Bird Bells - Unknown

YEAR ISSUE		EDITION LIMIT	YEAR RETD.	ISSUE PRICE	*QUOTE U.S.$
1991	Bluebird	Open		57.00	57
1991	Chickadee	Open		57.00	57
1991	Hummingbird	Open		57.00	57
1992	Robin Bell	Open		57.00	57

Carousel Bell - Unknown

YEAR ISSUE		EDITION LIMIT	YEAR RETD.	ISSUE PRICE	*QUOTE U.S.$
1992	Carousel Horse	Open		45.00	45

Crystal Christmas Bell - Lenox

YEAR ISSUE		EDITION LIMIT	YEAR RETD.	ISSUE PRICE	*QUOTE U.S.$
1981	Partridge in a Pear Tree	15,000	1981	55.00	55
1982	Holy Family Bell	15,000	1982	55.00	55
1983	Three Wise Men	15,000	1983	55.00	55
1984	Dove Bell	15,000	1984	57.00	57
1985	Santa Claus Bell	15,000	1985	57.00	57
1986	Dashing Through the Snow Bell	15,000	1986	64.00	64
1987	Heralding Angel Bell	15,000	1987	76.00	76
1991	Celestial Harpist	15,000	1991	75.00	75

Lenox Crystal

Annual Bell Series - Lenox

YEAR ISSUE		EDITION LIMIT	YEAR RETD.	ISSUE PRICE	*QUOTE U.S.$
1987	Partridge Bell	Yr.Iss.	1990	45.00	45
1988	Angel Bell	Open	1991	45.00	45
1989	St. Nicholas Bell	Open	1991	45.00	45
1990	Christmas Tree Bell	Open	1993	49.00	49
1991	Teddy Bear Bell	Yr.Iss.	1992	49.00	49
1992	Snowman Bell	Yr.Iss.	1993	49.00	49
1993	Nutcracker Bell	Yr.Iss.	1994	49.00	49
1994	Candle Bell	Yr.Iss.	1995	49.00	49

Lladró

Lladró Bell - Lladró

YEAR ISSUE		EDITION LIMIT	YEAR RETD.	ISSUE PRICE	*QUOTE U.S.$
XX	Crystal Wedding Bell L4500	Closed	N/A	N/A	195

Lladró Christmas Bell - Lladró

YEAR ISSUE		EDITION LIMIT	YEAR RETD.	ISSUE PRICE	*QUOTE U.S.$
1987	Christmas Bell - L5458M	Annual	1987	29.50	60-90
1988	Christmas Bell - L5525M	Annual	1988	32.50	35-50
1989	Christmas Bell - L5616M	Annual	1989	32.50	100-125
1990	Christmas Bell - L5641M	Annual	1990	34.50	60
1991	Christmas Bell - L5803M	Annual	1991	37.50	45
1992	Christmas Bell - L5913M	Annual	1992	37.50	45
1993	Christmas Bell - L6010M	Annual	1993	37.50	45-60
1994	Christmas Bell - L6139M	Annual	1994	39.50	45-55
1995	Christmas Bell - L6206M	Annual	1995	39.50	40-60
1996	Christmas Bell - L6297M	Annual		39.50	40

Lladró Limited Edition Bell - Lladró

YEAR ISSUE		EDITION LIMIT	YEAR RETD.	ISSUE PRICE	*QUOTE U.S.$
1994	Eternal Love 7542M	Annual	1994	95.00	95

Old World Christmas

Porcelain Christmas - E.M. Merck

YEAR ISSUE		EDITION LIMIT	YEAR RETD.	ISSUE PRICE	*QUOTE U.S.$
1988	1st Edition Santa Bell	Retrd.	1988	10.00	10
1989	2nd Edition Santa Bell	Retrd.	1989	10.00	10

Reed & Barton

Noel Musical Bells - Reed & Barton

YEAR ISSUE		EDITION LIMIT	YEAR RETD.	ISSUE PRICE	*QUOTE U.S.$
1980	Bell 1980	Closed	1980	20.00	55-70
1981	Bell 1981	Closed	1981	22.50	50-60
1982	Bell 1982	Closed	1982	22.50	35-50
1983	Bell 1983	Closed	1983	22.50	35-50
1984	Bell 1984	Closed	1984	22.50	40-60
1985	Bell 1985	Closed	1985	25.00	25-50
1986	Bell 1986	Closed	1986	25.00	50-60
1987	Bell 1987	Closed	1987	25.00	25-55
1988	Bell 1988	Closed	1988	25.00	30-50
1989	Bell 1989	Closed	1989	25.00	45-60
1990	Bell 1990	Closed	1990	27.50	35
1991	Bell 1991	Closed	1991	30.00	35
1992	Bell 1992	Closed	1992	30.00	30-40
1993	Bell 1993	Yr.Iss.	1993	30.00	30-40
1994	Bell 1994	Yr.Iss.	1994	30.00	30-40
1995	Bell 1995	Yr.Iss.	1995	30.00	30
1996	Bell 1996	Yr.Iss.		30.00	30

Yuletide Bell - Reed & Barton

YEAR ISSUE		EDITION LIMIT	YEAR RETD.	ISSUE PRICE	*QUOTE U.S.$
1981	Yuletide Holiday	Closed	1981	14.00	14
1982	Little Shepherd	Closed	1982	14.00	14
1983	Perfect Angel	Closed	1983	15.00	15
1984	Drummer Boy	Closed	1984	15.00	15
1985	Caroler	Closed	1985	16.50	20
1986	Night Before Christmas	Closed	1986	16.50	17
1987	Jolly St. Nick	Closed	1987	16.50	17
1988	Christmas Morning	Closed	1988	16.50	17
1989	The Bell Ringer	Closed	1989	16.50	17
1990	The Wreath Bearer	Closed	1990	18.50	20
1991	A Special Gift	Closed	1991	22.50	25
1992	My Special Friend	Closed	1992	22.50	25
1993	My Christmas Present	Yr.Iss.	1993	22.50	25
1994	Holiday Wishes	Yr.Iss.	1994	22.50	25
1995	Christmas Puppy	Yr.Iss.	1995	20.00	20
1996	Yuletide Bell	Yr.Iss.		22.50	23

River Shore

Norman Rockwell Single Issues - N. Rockwell

YEAR ISSUE		EDITION LIMIT	YEAR RETD.	ISSUE PRICE	*QUOTE U.S.$
1981	Grandpa's Guardian	7,000		45.00	45
1981	Looking Out to Sea	7,000		45.00	95
1981	Spring Flowers	347		175.00	175

Rockwell Children Series I - N. Rockwell

YEAR ISSUE		EDITION LIMIT	YEAR RETD.	ISSUE PRICE	*QUOTE U.S.$
1977	First Day of School	7,500		30.00	75
1977	Flowers for Mother	7,500		30.00	60
1977	Football Hero	7,500		30.00	75
1977	School Play	7,500		30.00	75

Rockwell Children Series II - N. Rockwell

YEAR ISSUE		EDITION LIMIT	YEAR RETD.	ISSUE PRICE	*QUOTE U.S.$
1978	Dressing Up	15,000		35.00	50
1978	Five Cents A Glass	15,000		35.00	40
1978	Future All American	15,000		35.00	52
1978	Garden Girl	15,000		35.00	40

Roman, Inc.

Annual Fontanini Christmas Crystal Bell - E. Simonetti

YEAR ISSUE		EDITION LIMIT	YEAR RETD.	ISSUE PRICE	*QUOTE U.S.$
1991	Bell 1991	Closed	1991	30.00	30
1992	Bell 1992	Closed	1992	30.00	30
1993	Bell 1993	Closed	1993	30.00	30

Annual Nativity Bell - I. Spencer

YEAR ISSUE		EDITION LIMIT	YEAR RETD.	ISSUE PRICE	*QUOTE U.S.$
1990	Nativity	Closed	N/A	15.00	15
1991	Flight Into Egypt	Closed	N/A	15.00	15
1992	Gloria in Excelsis Deo	Closed	N/A	15.00	15
1993	Three Kings of Orient	Closed	N/A	15.00	15

F. Hook Bells - F. Hook

YEAR ISSUE		EDITION LIMIT	YEAR RETD.	ISSUE PRICE	*QUOTE U.S.$
1985	Beach Buddies	15,000		25.00	28
1986	Sounds of the Sea	15,000		25.00	28
1987	Bear Hug	15,000		25.00	28

The Masterpiece Collection - Various

YEAR ISSUE		EDITION LIMIT	YEAR RETD.	ISSUE PRICE	*QUOTE U.S.$
1979	Adoration - F. Lippe	Open		20.00	20
1980	Madonna with Grapes - P. Mignard	Open		25.00	25
1981	The Holy Family - G. Notti	Open		25.00	25
1982	Madonna of the Streets - R. Ferruzzi	Open		25.00	25

Schmid

Berta Hummel Christmas Bells - B. Hummel

YEAR ISSUE		EDITION LIMIT	YEAR RETD.	ISSUE PRICE	*QUOTE U.S.$
1972	Angel with Flute	Yr.Iss.	1972	20.00	75
1973	Nativity	Yr.Iss.	1973	15.00	80
1974	The Guardian Angel	Yr.Iss.	1974	17.50	45
1975	The Christmas Child	Yr.Iss.	1975	22.50	45
1976	Sacred Journey	Yr.Iss.	1976	22.50	25
1977	Herald Angel	Yr.Iss.	1977	22.50	50
1978	Heavenly Trio	Yr.Iss.	1978	27.50	40
1979	Starlight Angel	Yr.Iss.	1979	38.00	45
1980	Parade into Toyland	Yr.Iss.	1980	45.00	55
1981	A Time to Remember	Yr.Iss.	1981	45.00	55
1982	Angelic Procession	Yr.Iss.	1982	45.00	50
1983	Angelic Messenger	Yr.Iss.	1983	45.00	55
1984	A Gift from Heaven	Yr.Iss.	1984	45.00	75
1985	Heavenly Light	Yr.Iss.	1985	45.00	75
1986	Tell the Heavens	Yr.Iss.	1986	45.00	45
1987	Angelic Gifts	Yr.Iss.	1987	47.50	48
1988	Cheerful Cherubs	Yr.Iss.	1988	52.50	55
1989	Angelic Musician	Yr.Iss.	1989	53.00	55
1990	Angel's Light	Yr.Iss.	1990	53.00	53
1991	Message From Above	5,000	1991	58.00	58
1992	Sweet Blessings	5,000	1992	65.00	65
1993	Silent Wonder	5,000	1993	58.00	58

Berta Hummel Mother's Day Bells - B. Hummel

YEAR ISSUE		EDITION LIMIT	YEAR RETD.	ISSUE PRICE	*QUOTE U.S.$
1976	Devotion for Mothers	Yr.Iss.	1976	22.50	55
1977	Moonlight Return	Yr.Iss.	1977	22.50	45
1978	Afternoon Stroll	Yr.Iss.	1978	27.50	45
1979	Cherub's Gift	Yr.Iss.	1979	38.00	45
1980	Mother's Little Helper	Yr.Iss.	1980	45.00	45
1981	Playtime	Yr.Iss.	1981	45.00	45
1982	The Flower Basket	Yr.Iss.	1982	45.00	45
1983	Spring Bouquet	Yr.Iss.	1983	45.00	45
1984	A Joy to Share	Yr.Iss.	1984	45.00	45

Disney Annuals - Disney Studios

YEAR ISSUE		EDITION LIMIT	YEAR RETD.	ISSUE PRICE	*QUOTE U.S.$
1985	Snow Biz	10,000	1985	16.50	17
1986	Tree for Two	10,000	1986	16.50	17
1987	Merry Mouse Medley	10,000	1987	17.50	18
1988	Warm Winter Ride	10,000	1988	19.50	20
1989	Merry Mickey Claus	10,000	1989	23.00	23
1990	Holly Jolly Christmas	10,000	1990	26.50	27
1991	Mickey & Minnie's Rockin' Christmas	10,000	1991	26.50	27

RFD Bell - L. Davis

YEAR ISSUE		EDITION LIMIT	YEAR RETD.	ISSUE PRICE	*QUOTE U.S.$
1979	Blossom	Closed	N/A	65.00	300-400
1979	Kate	Closed	N/A	65.00	300-400
1979	Willy	Closed	N/A	65.00	400
1979	Caruso	Closed	N/A	65.00	300
1979	Wilbur	Closed	N/A	65.00	300-350
1979	Old Blue Lead	Closed	N/A	65.00	275-300
1980	Cow Bell "Blossom"	Closed	N/A	65.00	65
1980	Mule Bell "Kate"	Closed	N/A	65.00	65
1980	Goat Bell "Willy"	Closed	N/A	65.00	65
1980	Rooster Bell "Caruso"	Closed	N/A	65.00	65
1980	Pig Bell "Wilbur"	Closed	N/A	65.00	65
1980	Dog Bell "Old Blue and Lead"	Closed	N/A	65.00	65

Seymour Mann, Inc.

Connoisseur Collection - M. Bernini

YEAR ISSUE		EDITION LIMIT	YEAR RETD.	ISSUE PRICE	*QUOTE U.S.$
1995	Bluebird CLT-15	Open		15.00	15
1995	Canary CLT-12	Open		15.00	15
1995	Cardinal CLT-9	Open		15.00	15
1995	Dove CLT-3	Open		15.00	15
1995	Hummingbird CLT-6	Open		15.00	15
1995	Pink Rose CLT-72	Open		15.00	15
1995	Robin CLT-18	Open		15.00	15
1995	Swan CLT-52	Open		15.00	15

CHRISTMAS ORNAMENTS

Ace Product Management Group, Inc.

Harley-Davidson Child's Ornaments - Ace

YEAR ISSUE		EDITION LIMIT	YEAR RETD.	ISSUE PRICE	*QUOTE U.S.$
1991	For The Young At Heart 99433-92Z	Yr.Iss.	1991	14.95	15
1992	The Gift 99466-93Z	Yr.Iss.	1992	15.00	15
1993	First Harley 99429-94Z	Yr.Iss.	1993	15.00	15
1994	Daddy's Boots 99442-95Z	Yr.Iss.	1994	15.00	15
1995	Little Stocking Stuffer 99448-96Z	Yr.Iss.	1995	15.00	15

Harley-Davidson Christmas Ornaments - Ace

YEAR ISSUE		EDITION LIMIT	YEAR RETD.	ISSUE PRICE	*QUOTE U.S.$
1981	Ornament 99407-82V	Yr.Iss.	1981	5.95	5
1983	Ornament 99407-84V	Yr.Iss.	1983	6.50	7
1984	Ornament 99408-85Z	Yr.Iss.	1984	6.95	7
1985	Ornament 99406-86Z	Yr.Iss.	1985	6.95	7
1986	Ornament 99407-87Z	Yr.Iss.	1986	6.95	7
1987	Ornament 99406-88Z	Yr.Iss.	1987	6.95	7
1988	Ornament 99408-89Z	Yr.Iss.	1988	6.95	7
1989	Ornament 99435-90Z	Yr.Iss.	1989	6.95	7
1990	Ornament 99435-91Z	Yr.Iss.	1990	6.95	7
1991	Skating Party 99436-92Z	Yr.Iss.	1991	6.95	7
1992	Surprise Visit 99437-93Z	Yr.Iss.	1992	7.00	7
1993	Xmas Vacation 99427-94Z	Yr.Iss.	1993	8.00	8

Harley-Davidson Holiday Memories - Ace

YEAR ISSUE		EDITION LIMIT	YEAR RETD.	ISSUE PRICE	*QUOTE U.S.$
1994	Under The Mistletoe 99091-95Z	Yr.Iss.	1994	8.00	8
1995	Late Arrival 99495-96Z	Yr.Iss.	1995	8.00	8

Harley-Davidson Mini-Plate Ornaments - Ace

YEAR ISSUE		EDITION LIMIT	YEAR RETD.	ISSUE PRICE	*QUOTE U.S.$
1989	1989 99440-90Z	Yr.Iss.	1989	10.00	10
1990	Santa's Predicament 99442-91Z	Yr.Iss.	1990	9.95	10
1991	Not A Creature 99443-92Z	Yr.Iss.	1991	10.00	10
1992	Finding The Way 99441.93Z	Yr.Iss.	1992	10.00	10
1993	Pulling Together 99416-94Z	Yr.Iss.	1993	10.00	10
1994	Sorry Guys 99445-95Z	Yr.Iss.	1994	10.00	10

*Quotes have been rounded up to nearest dollar

YEAR ISSUE		EDITION LIMIT	YEAR RETD.	ISSUE PRICE	*QUOTE U.S.$
1995	Ratchet The Elf 99480-96Z	Yr.Iss.	1995	10.00	10

Harley-Davidson Pewter Ornaments - Ace

YEAR ISSUE		EDITION LIMIT	YEAR RETD.	ISSUE PRICE	*QUOTE U.S.$
1988	Santa's Secret 99409-89Z	Yr.Iss.	1988	6.95	7
1989	Santa's Workshop 99438-90Z	Yr.Iss.	1989	6.95	7
1990	Stocking Stuffer 99438-91Z	Yr.Iss.	1990	8.95	9
1991	Finishing Touches 99439-92Z	Yr.Iss.	1991	10.95	11
1992	Batteries Not Included 99426-93Z	Yr.Iss.	1992	12.00	12
1993	Joy Ride 99428-94Z	Yr.Iss.	1993	12.00	12
1993	90th Anniversary-"The Reunion" 99430-94Z	7,500	1993	35.00	35
1994	Cleared For Takeoff 99463-95Z	Yr.Iss.	1994	14.00	14
1995	Night Flight 99455-96Z	Yr.Iss.	1995	15.00	15

All God's Children

Angel Dumpling - M. Root

YEAR ISSUE		EDITION LIMIT	YEAR RETD.	ISSUE PRICE	*QUOTE U.S.$
1993	Eric-1570	Retrd.	1994	22.50	40-60
1994	Erica-1578	Retrd.	1995	22.50	35-45

Christmas Ornaments - M. Root

YEAR ISSUE		EDITION LIMIT	YEAR RETD.	ISSUE PRICE	*QUOTE U.S.$
1987	Cameo Ornaments (set/12)-D1912	Retrd.	1988	144.00	1500-2000
1987	Doll Ornaments (set/24) - D1924	Retrd.	1988	336.00	2000-3000
1993	Santa with Scooty-1571	Retrd.	1994	22.50	40-60

Amaranth Productions

Christmas Ornaments - L. West

YEAR ISSUE		EDITION LIMIT	YEAR RETD.	ISSUE PRICE	*QUOTE U.S.$
1994	Mr. Santa 8010	500	1995	110.00	110
1994	St. Nick (burgundy) 8020	500	1995	120.00	120
1994	Angel 8030	500	1995	120.00	120
1994	Jester 8040	500	1995	120.00	120
1995	Mrs. Claus 8015	500	1995	110.00	110
1995	Harlequin 8045	500	1995	110.00	110
1995	St. Nick (white) 8025	500	1995	120.00	120

Anheuser-Busch, Inc.

A & Eagle Collector Ornament Series - A.-Busch, Inc.

YEAR ISSUE		EDITION LIMIT	YEAR RETD.	ISSUE PRICE	*QUOTE U.S.$
1991	Budweiser Girl-Circa 1890's N3178	Open		15.00	15
1992	1893 Columbian Exposition N3649	Open		15.00	15
1993	Greatest Triumph N4089	Open		15.00	15

Christmas Ornaments - Various

YEAR ISSUE		EDITION LIMIT	YEAR RETD.	ISSUE PRICE	*QUOTE U.S.$
1992	Clydesdales Mini Plate Ornaments N3650 - S. Sampson	Open		23.00	23
1993	Budweiser Six-Pack Mini Plate Ornaments N4220 - M. Urdahl	Retrd.	1994	10.00	10

Annalee Mobilitee Dolls, Inc.

Christmas Ornaments - A. Thorndike

YEAR ISSUE		EDITION LIMIT	YEAR RETD.	ISSUE PRICE	*QUOTE U.S.$
1985	Clown Head	5,701	N/A	6.95	175
1986	3" Clown	3,369	1986	11.95	200
1987	3" Elf	1,950	1989	12.95	325
1992	3" Skier	8,332	N/A	14.45	175

ANRI

Disney Four Star Collection - Disney Studios

YEAR ISSUE		EDITION LIMIT	YEAR RETD.	ISSUE PRICE	*QUOTE U.S.$
1989	Maestro Mickey	Yr.Iss.	1989	25.00	40-75
1990	Minnie Mouse	Yr.Iss.	1990	25.00	25

Ferrandiz Message Collection - J. Ferrandiz

YEAR ISSUE		EDITION LIMIT	YEAR RETD.	ISSUE PRICE	*QUOTE U.S.$
1989	Let the Heavens Ring	1,000	1992	215.00	215
1990	Hear The Angels Sing	1,000	1992	225.00	225

Ferrandiz Woodcarvings - J. Ferrandiz

YEAR ISSUE		EDITION LIMIT	YEAR RETD.	ISSUE PRICE	*QUOTE U.S.$
1988	Heavenly Drummer	1,000	1992	175.00	225
1989	Heavenly Strings	1,000	1992	190.00	190

Sarah Kay's First Christmas - S. Kay

YEAR ISSUE		EDITION LIMIT	YEAR RETD.	ISSUE PRICE	*QUOTE U.S.$
1994	Sarah Kay's First Christmas	500		140.00	195
1995	First Xmas Stocking 57502	500		99.00	195
1996	All I Want for Xmas 57503	500		195.00	195

Armani

Christmas - G. Armani

YEAR ISSUE		EDITION LIMIT	YEAR RETD.	ISSUE PRICE	*QUOTE U.S.$
1991	Christmas Ornament 799A	Retrd.	1991	11.50	45
1992	Christmas Ornament 788F	Retrd.	1992	23.50	24
1993	Christmas Ornament 892P	Retrd.	1993	25.00	25
1994	Christmas Ornament 801P	Retrd.	1994	25.00	30
1995	Christmas Ornament 640P	Retrd.	1995	30.00	30
1996	Christmas Ornament A Sweet Christmas 355P	Yr.Iss.		30.00	30

Artists of the World

De Grazia Annual Ornaments - T. De Grazia

YEAR ISSUE		EDITION LIMIT	YEAR RETD.	ISSUE PRICE	*QUOTE U.S.$
1986	Pima Indian Drummer Boy	Yr.Iss.	1986	28.00	400
1987	White Dove	Yr.Iss.	1987	30.00	85-140
1988	Flower Girl	Yr.Iss.	1988	33.00	75-110
1989	Flower Boy	Yr.Iss.	1989	35.00	75-100
1990	Pink Papoose	Yr.Iss.	1990	35.00	80-120
1990	Merry Little Indian	10,000	1990	88.00	100-125
1991	Christmas Prayer (Red)	Yr.Iss.	1991	50.00	75-95
1992	Bearing Gift	Yr.Iss.	1992	55.00	65-95
1993	Lighting the Way	Yr.Iss.	1993	58.00	65-75
1994	Warm Wishes	Yr.Iss.	1994	65.00	65-75
1995	Little Prayer (White)	Yr.Iss.	1995	49.50	50-65
1995	Heavenly Flowers	Yr.Iss.	1995	65.00	65
1995	My Beautiful Rocking Horse	Yr.Iss.	1995	125.00	125
1996	Oh Holy Night	Yr.Iss		69.50	70

Attic Babies

Christmas Decorations- M. Maschino

YEAR ISSUE		EDITION LIMIT	YEAR RETD.	ISSUE PRICE	*QUOTE U.S.$
1993	Raggedy Santa Wreath	Retrd.	1994	101.95	102
1992	Stocking	Retrd.	1994	55.95	56

Wooden Ornaments - M. Maschino

YEAR ISSUE		EDITION LIMIT	YEAR RETD.	ISSUE PRICE	*QUOTE U.S.$
1993	Angel	Retrd.	1994	21.95	22
1993	Snowman	Retrd.	1994	17.95	18
1993	Stocking	Retrd.	1994	25.95	26

Band Creations, Inc.

Best Friends - Angels - Richards/Penfield

YEAR ISSUE		EDITION LIMIT	YEAR RETD.	ISSUE PRICE	*QUOTE U.S.$
1994	4 Assorted Angel Ornaments	Open		5.00	5
1995	Double Angels	Open		8.00	8
1996	4 Assorted Blk Angel Ornaments	Open		6.00	10

Best Friends-A Star is Born - Richards/Penfield

YEAR ISSUE		EDITION LIMIT	YEAR RETD.	ISSUE PRICE	*QUOTE U.S.$
1995	Baseball Boy	Open		6.00	6
1996	Baseball Boy	Open		6.00	6
1995	Baseball Girl	Open		6.00	6
1995	Basketball Boy	Open		6.00	6
1995	Basketball Girl	Open		6.00	6
1996	Biker Boy	Open		6.00	6
1996	Biker Girl	Open		6.00	6
1995	Cheerleader Girl	Open		6.00	6
1996	Fisher Boy	Open		6.00	6
1996	Fisher Girl	Open		6.00	6
1995	Football Boy	Open		6.00	6
1995	Golfer Boy	Open		6.00	6
1995	Golfer Girl	Open		6.00	6
1995	Hockey Boy	Open		6.00	6
1996	Skier Boy	Open		6.00	6
1996	Skier Girl	Open		6.00	6
1995	Soccer Boy	Open		6.00	6
1995	Soccer Girl	Open		6.00	6
1995	Swimmer Boy	Open		6.00	6
1995	Swimmer Girl	Open		6.00	6
1996	Tennis Boy	Open		6.00	6
1996	Tennis Girl	Open		6.00	6

Best Friends-Monthly Angels - Richards/Penfield

YEAR ISSUE		EDITION LIMIT	YEAR RETD.	ISSUE PRICE	*QUOTE U.S.$
1996	January	Open		10.00	10
1996	February	Open		10.00	10
1996	March	Open		10.00	10
1996	April	Open		10.00	10
1996	May	Open		10.00	10
1996	June	Open		10.00	10
1996	July	Open		10.00	10
1996	August	Open		10.00	10
1996	September	Open		10.00	10
1996	October	Open		10.00	10
1996	November	Open		10.00	10
1996	December	Open		10.00	10

Kringle Toppers - Band Creations

YEAR ISSUE		EDITION LIMIT	YEAR RETD.	ISSUE PRICE	*QUOTE U.S.$
1996	America, Santa Claus	Open		10.00	10
1996	Austria, Christkind	Open		10.00	10
1996	England, Father Christmas	Open		10.00	10
1996	France, Pere Noel	Open		10.00	10
1996	Germany, Pelsnickel	Open		10.00	10
1996	Netherlands, St. Nickolas	Open		10.00	10
1996	Russia, Father Frost	Open		10.00	10
1996	Scandinavia, Julnisse	Open		10.00	10

Bing & Grondahl

Christmas - Various

YEAR ISSUE		EDITION LIMIT	YEAR RETD.	ISSUE PRICE	*QUOTE U.S.$
1985	Christmas Eve at the Farmhouse - E. Jensen	Closed	1985	19.50	20
1986	Silent Night, Holy Night - E. Jensen	Closed	1986	19.50	30
1987	The Snowman's Christmas Eve - E. Jensen	Closed	1987	22.50	23
1988	In the King's Garden - E. Jensen	Closed	1988	25.00	25
1989	Christmas Anchorage - E. Jensen	Closed	1989	27.00	27
1990	Changing of the Guards - E. Jensen	Closed	1990	32.50	35
1991	Copenhagen Stock Exchange - E. Jensen	Closed	1991	34.50	35
1992	Christmas at the Rectory - J. Steensen	Closed	1992	36.50	37
1993	Father Christmas in Copenhagen - J. Nielsen	Closed	1993	36.50	37
1994	A Day at the Deer Park - J. Nielsen	Closed	1994	36.50	37
1995	The Towers of Copenhagen - J. Nielsen	Closed	1995	37.50	38
1996	Winter at the Old Mill - J. Nielsen	Yr.Iss.		37.50	38

Christmas In America - J. Woodson

YEAR ISSUE		EDITION LIMIT	YEAR RETD.	ISSUE PRICE	*QUOTE U.S.$
1986	Christmas Eve in Williamsburg	Closed	1986	12.50	40-90
1987	Christmas Eve at the White House	Closed	1987	15.00	25-60
1988	Christmas Eve at Rockefeller Center	Closed	1988	18.50	19
1989	Christmas in New England	Closed	1989	20.00	20
1990	Christmas Eve at the Capitol	Closed	1990	20.00	35
1991	Independence Hall	Closed	1991	23.50	24
1992	Christmas in San Francisco	Closed	1992	25.00	35
1993	Coming Home For Christmas	Closed	1993	25.00	30
1994	Christmas Eve in Alaska	Closed	1994	25.00	45
1995	Christmas Eve in Mississippi	Closed	1995	25.00	25

Santa Around the World - H. Hansen

YEAR ISSUE		EDITION LIMIT	YEAR RETD.	ISSUE PRICE	*QUOTE U.S.$
1995	Santa in Greenland	Yr.Iss.	1995	25.00	25
1996	Santa in Egypt	Yr.Iss.		25.00	25

Santa Claus

YEAR ISSUE		EDITION LIMIT	YEAR RETD.	ISSUE PRICE	*QUOTE U.S.$
1989	Santa's Workshop	Yr.Iss.	1989	20.00	60
1990	Santa's Sleigh	Yr.Iss.	1990	20.00	48
1991	The Journey	Yr.Iss.	1991	24.00	45
1992	Santa's Arrival	Yr.Iss.	1992	25.00	36
1993	Santa's Gifts	Yr.Iss.	1993	25.00	36
1994	Christmas Stories	Yr.Iss.	1994	25.00	25

Boyds Collection Ltd.

The Bearstone Collection™ - G. M. Lowenthal

YEAR ISSUE		EDITION LIMIT	YEAR RETD.	ISSUE PRICE	*QUOTE U.S.$
1994	'Charity'-Angel Bear w/Star 2502	Open		9.45	10-15
1994	'Faith'-Angel Bear w/Trumpet 2500	Open		9.45	10-15
1994	'Hope'-Angel Bear w/Wreath 2501	Open		9.45	10-15
1995	'Edmund'...Believe 2505	Open		9.45	10-15
1995	'Elliot with Tree' 2507	Open		9.45	10-15
1995	'Manheim' the Moose w/Wreath 2506	Open		9.45	10-15

The Folkstone Collection™ - G.M. Lowenthal

YEAR ISSUE		EDITION LIMIT	YEAR RETD.	ISSUE PRICE	*QUOTE U.S.$
1995	Father Christmas 2553	Open		9.45	10
1995	Jean Claude & Jacque...the Skiers 2561	Open		9.45	10
1995	Jingles the Snowman with Wreath 2562	Open		9.45	10
1995	Nicholai with Tree 2550	Open		9.45	10
1995	Nicholas the Giftgiver 2551	Open		9.45	10
1995	Olaf...Let it Snow 2560	Open		9.45	10
1995	Sliknick in the Chimney 2552	Open		9.45	10

Brandywine Collectibles

Custom Collection - M. Whiting

YEAR ISSUE		EDITION LIMIT	YEAR RETD.	ISSUE PRICE	*QUOTE U.S.$
1989	Lorain Lighthouse	Closed	1992	9.00	9
1994	Smithfield Clerk's Office	Open		9.00	9
1991	Smithfield VA. Courthouse	Closed	1992	9.00	9

Williamsburg Ornaments - M. Whiting

YEAR ISSUE		EDITION LIMIT	YEAR RETD.	ISSUE PRICE	*QUOTE U.S.$
1988	Apothocary	Closed	1991	9.00	9
1988	Bootmaker	Closed	1991	9.00	9
1989	Cole Shop	Closed	1991	9.00	9
1988	Finnie Quarter	Closed	1991	9.00	9
1989	Gunsmith	Closed	1991	9.00	9
1994	Gunsmith	360	1994	9.50	10
1989	Music Teacher	Closed	1991	9.00	9
1988	Nicolson Shop	Closed	1991	9.00	9
1988	Tarpley's Store	Closed	1991	9.00	9
1988	Wigmaker	Closed	1991	9.00	9
1989	Windmill	Closed	1991	9.00	9

Calabar Creations

Angelic Pigasus - P. Apsit

YEAR ISSUE		EDITION LIMIT	YEAR RETD.	ISSUE PRICE	*QUOTE U.S.$
1995	Adagio AP75361	Open		5.00	5
1995	Alba AP75351	Open		5.00	5
1995	Ambrose AP75372	Open		5.00	5
1995	Andante AP75381	Open		5.00	5
1995	Angelica AP75312	Open		5.00	5
1995	Anna AP75321	Open		5.00	5
1995	Aria AP75341	Open		5.00	5

Cast Art Industries

Dreamsicles Ornaments - K. Haynes

YEAR ISSUE		EDITION LIMIT	YEAR RETD.	ISSUE PRICE	*QUOTE U.S.$
1992	Bear-DX274	Retrd.	1994	6.00	6
1992	Bunny-DX270	Retrd.	1994	6.00	6
1992	Cherub On Cloud-DX263	Retrd.	1994	6.00	6
1992	Cherub With Moon-DX260	Retrd.	1994	6.00	6
1992	Cherub With Star-DX262	Retrd.	1994	6.00	6
1992	Lamb-DX275	Retrd.	1994	6.00	6
1992	Piggy-DX271	Retrd.	1994	6.00	6
1992	Praying Cherub-DX261	Retrd.	1994	6.00	6
1992	Raccoon-DX272	Retrd.	1994	6.00	6
1992	Squirrel-DX273	Retrd.	1994	6.00	6

The Cat's Meow

1985 Christmas Ornaments - F. Jones

YEAR ISSUE		EDITION LIMIT	YEAR RETD.	ISSUE PRICE	*QUOTE U.S.$
1985	Bancroft House	Retrd.	1986	4.00	40

*Quotes have been rounded up to nearest dollar

YEAR ISSUE		EDITION LIMIT	YEAR RETD.	ISSUE PRICE	*QUOTE U.S.$
1985	Chapel	Retrd.	1986	4.00	N/A
1985	Grayling House	Retrd.	1986	4.00	40
1985	Morton House	Retrd.	1986	4.00	N/A
1985	Rutledge House	Retrd.	1986	4.00	75
1985	School	Retrd.	1986	4.00	N/A

1987 Christmas Ornaments - F. Jones

1987	Blacksmith Shop	Retrd.	1988	5.00	60
1987	District #17 School	Retrd.	1988	5.00	60
1987	Globe Corner Bookstore	Retrd.	1988	5.00	60
1987	Kennedy Birthplace	Retrd.	1988	5.00	26-75
1987	Set/4	Retrd.	1988	20.00	175-200

1995 Christmas Ornaments - F. Jones

1995	Carnegie Library	Retrd.	1995	8.75	9
1995	Holly Hill Farmhouse	Retrd.	1995	8.75	9
1995	North Central School	Retrd.	1995	8.75	9
1995	St. James General Store	Retrd.	1995	8.75	9
1995	Unitarian Church	Retrd.	1995	8.75	9
1995	Yaquina Bay Light	Retrd.	1995	8.75	9

1996 Christmas Ornaments - F. Jones

1996	Christ Church	12/96		9.00	9
1996	Deerfield Post Office	12/96		9.00	9
1996	Gimbel & Sons Country Store	12/96		9.00	9
1996	Hook Windmill	12/96		9.00	9
1996	Maple Manor	12/96		9.00	9
1996	Parsonage	12/96		9.00	9

Cavanagh Group Intl.

Coca-Cola Christmas Collectors Society Members' Only - Sundblom, unless otherwise noted

1993	Ho Ho Ho	Closed	1993	Gift	20-35
1994	Fishing Bear - CGI	Closed	1994	Gift	20-30
1995	Hospitality	Closed	1995	Gift	15-25
1996	Sprite	12/96		Gift	N/A

Coca-Cola Brand Heritage Collection - Sundblom

1995	Christmas Is Love	Open		10.00	10
1995	Santa at the Mantle	Open		10.00	10
1995	Ssshhh!	Open		10.00	10

Coca-Cola Brand Historical Building - CGI

1991	1930's Service Station	Closed	1994	10.00	11-15
1991	Early Coca-Cola Bottling Company	Closed	1994	10.00	11-15
1991	Jacob's Pharmacy	Closed	1994	10.00	11-15
1991	The Pemberton House	Closed	1994	10.00	11-15

Coca-Cola Brand North Pole Bottling Works - CGI

1995	Barrel of Bears	Open		9.00	9
1993	Blast Off	Closed	1995	9.00	9
1993	Delivery for Santa	Open		9.00	9
1993	Fill 'er Up	Closed	1994	9.00	10-20
1995	Fountain Glass Follies	Open		9.00	9
1993	Ice Sculpting	Closed	1995	9.00	9
1993	Long Winter's Nap	Closed	1995	9.00	9
1993	North Pole Express	Closed	1994	9.00	10-25
1995	North Pole Flying School	Open		9.00	9
1994	Power Drive	Open		9.00	9
1996	Refreshing Surprise	Open		9.00	9
1996	Rush Delivery	Open		9.00	9
1994	Santa's Refreshment	Closed	1995	9.00	9
1994	Seltzer Surprise	Closed	1995	9.00	9
1993	Thirsting for Adventure	Closed	1994	9.00	10-15
1996	To: Mrs. Claus	Open		9.00	9
1994	Tops Off Refreshment	Closed	1995	9.00	9
1993	Tops On Refreshment	Closed	1995	9.00	9

Coca-Cola Brand Polar Bear - CGI

1996	The Christmas Star	Open		9.00	9
1994	Downhill Sledder	Open		9.00	9
1996	Hollywood	Open		9.00	9
1994	North Pole Delivery	Closed	1995	9.00	9
1995	Polar Bear in Bottle Opener	Open		9.00	9
1994	Skating Coca-Cola Polar Bear	Closed	1995	9.00	9
1995	Snowboardin' Bear	Open		9.00	9
1994	Vending Machine Mischief	Open		9.00	9

Coca-Cola Brand Trim A Tree Collection - Sundblom

1990	Away with a Tired and Thirsty Face	Closed	1993	10.00	25
1994	Busy Man's Pause	Open		10.00	10
1991	Christmas Is Love	Closed	1992	10.00	15
1993	Decorating the Tree	Closed	1994	10.00	15-20
1993	Extra Bright Refreshment	Closed	1994	10.00	15-20
1994	For Sparkling Holidays	Closed	1995	10.00	10
1992	Happy Holidays	Closed	1992	10.00	10
1990	Hospitality	Closed	1993	10.00	15
1995	It Will Refresh You Too	Open		10.00	10
1990	Merry Christmas and a Happy New Year	Closed	1991	10.00	30
1996	The Pause That Refreshes	Open		10.00	10
1995	Please Pause Here	Open		10.00	10
1990	Santa on Stool	Closed	1993	10.00	15-20
1990	Season's Greetings	Closed	1991	10.00	15
1992	Sshhh!	Closed	1993	10.00	20-35
1996	They Remembered Me	Open		10.00	10
1994	Things Go Better with Coke	Open		10.00	10
1991	A Time to Share	Closed	1993	10.00	15-25

YEAR ISSUE		EDITION LIMIT	YEAR RETD.	ISSUE PRICE	*QUOTE U.S.$
1993	Travel Refreshed	Closed	1995	10.00	10

Christopher Radko

Christopher Radko Family of Collectors - C. Radko

1993	Angels We Have Heard on High SP1	Retrd.	1993	50.00	450-575
1994	Starbuck Santa SP3	Retrd.	1994	75.00	180-300
1995	Dash Away All SP7	Retrd.	1995	34.00	34
1995	Purrfect Present SP8	Retrd.	1995	Gift	N/A
1996	Christmas Magic SP13	Yr.Iss.		50.00	50
1996	Frosty Weather SP14	Yr.Iss.		Gift	N/A

10 Year Anniversary - C. Radko

1995	On Top of the World SP6	Yr.Iss.	1995	32.00	35-55

1987 Holiday Collection - C. Radko

1987	Memphis 18	Retrd.	N/A	15.00	125

1988 Holiday Collection - C. Radko

1988	Alpine Flowers 8822	Retrd.	N/A	16.00	30
1988	Baby Balloon 8832	Retrd.	N/A	7.95	125
1988	Birdhouse 8873	Retrd.	1987	10.00	110
1988	Buds in Bloom (pink) 8824	Retrd.	N/A	16.00	125
1988	Celestial 884	Retrd.	N/A	15.00	35
1988	Christmas Fanfare 8850	Retrd.	1988	15.00	125
1988	Circle of Santas 8811	Retrd.	N/A	16.95	100
1988	Crown Jewels 8874	Retrd.	1993	15.00	175
1988	Double Royal Star 8856	Retrd.	1991	23.00	150
1988	Exclamation Flask 8871	Retrd.	N/A	7.50	95
1988	Faberge Oval 883	Retrd.	N/A	15.00	30
1988	Gilded Leaves 8813	Retrd.	N/A	16.00	125
1988	Grecian Column 8842	Retrd.	1990	9.95	95
1988	Hot Air Balloon 885	Retrd.	N/A	15.00	125
1988	Lilac Sparkle 1814	Retrd.	N/A	15.00	125
1988	Mushroom in Winter 8862	Retrd.	1993	12.00	85
1988	Ripples on Oval 8844	Retrd.	1987	6.00	85
1988	Royal Diadem 8860	Retrd.	1987	25.00	135
1988	Royal Porcelain 8812	Retrd.	1991	16.00	187
1988	Russian St. Nick 8823	Retrd.	N/A	15.00	125
1988	Satin Scepter 8847	Retrd.	1987	8.95	110
1988	Simply Cartiere 8817	Retrd.	N/A	16.95	125
1988	Stained Glass 8816	Retrd.	1990	16.00	125
1988	Striped Balloon 8877	Retrd.	N/A	16.95	60
1988	Tree on Ball 8864	Retrd.	N/A	9.00	95
1988	Twin Finial 8857	Retrd.	N/A	23.50	135
1988	Zebra - Tiger 886	Retrd.	N/A	15.00	60

1989 Holiday Collection - C. Radko

1989	Alpine Flowers 9-43	Retrd.	N/A	17.00	30
1989	Baroque Angel 9-11	Retrd.	1989	17.00	95
1989	Charlie Chaplin (blue hat) 9-55	Retrd.	1990	8.50	50-75
1989	Double Top 9-71	Retrd.	1989	7.00	40
1989	Elf on Ball (matte) 9-62	Retrd.	1990	9.50	45
1989	Fisher Frog 9-65	Retrd.	1991	7.00	40
1989	Grecian Urn 9-69	Retrd.	1989	9.00	35
1989	The Holly 9-49	Retrd.	N/A	17.00	90
1989	Hurricane Lamp 9-67	Retrd.	1989	7.00	45
1989	Joey Clown (light pink) 9-58	Retrd.	1992	9.00	60
1989	Kim Ono 9-57	Retrd.	1990	6.50	45
1989	King Arthur (Lt. Blue) 9-103	Retrd.	1991	12.00	45
1989	Lilac Sparkle 9-7	Retrd.	1989	17.00	30
1989	Lucky Fish 9-73	Retrd.	1989	6.50	30
1989	Parachute 9-68	Retrd.	1989	6.50	20
1989	Royal Rooster 9-18	Retrd.	1993	17.00	20
1989	Royal Star Tree Finial 108	Retrd.	N/A	42.00	95
1989	Seahorse 9-54	Retrd.	1992	10.00	145
1989	Serpent 9-72	Retrd.	N/A	7.00	18
1989	Shy Kitten 9-66	Retrd.	N/A	7.00	45
1989	Shy Rabbit 9-61	Retrd.	N/A	7.00	50
1989	Small Reflector 9-76	Retrd.	N/A	7.50	32
1989	Smiling Sun 9-59	Retrd.	N/A	7.00	45
1989	Tiffany 44	Retrd.	N/A	17.00	500-650
1989	Vineyard 9-51	Retrd.	N/A	17.00	115
1989	Walrus 9-63	Retrd.	1990	8.00	50-90
1989	Zebra 9-10	Retrd.	1991	17.50	95

1990 Holiday Collection - C. Radko

1990	Angel on Harp 46	Retrd.	1990	9.00	65
1990	Ballooning Santa 87	Retrd.	1991	20.00	95-145
1990	Bathing Baby 70	Retrd.	N/A	11.00	65
1990	Calla Lilly 38	Retrd.	N/A	7.00	50
1990	Carmen Miranda 18	Retrd.	1991	19.00	125
1990	Christmas Cardinals 16	Retrd.	1992	18.00	125
1990	Conch Shell 65	Retrd.	1991	9.00	100
1990	Crowned Prince 56	Retrd.	1990	14.00	45
1990	Dublin Pipe 40	Retrd.	1990	14.00	50
1990	Eagle Medallion 67	Retrd.	1990	9.00	85
1990	Early Winter 24	Retrd.	1990	10.00	40
1990	Emerald City 92	Retrd.	1990	7.50	95
1990	Fat Lady 35	Retrd.	N/A	7.00	35
1990	Father Christmas 76	Retrd.	N/A	7.00	45
1990	Frog Under Balloon 58	Retrd.	1991	14.00	45
1990	Golden Puppy 53	Retrd.	1990	8.00	95
1990	Google Eyes 44	Retrd.	1990	9.00	45
1990	Happy Gnome 77	Retrd.	1991	8.00	40
1990	Holly Ball 4	Retrd.	N/A	19.00	125
1990	Joey Clown (red striped) 55	Retrd.	N/A	14.00	40-75
1990	Kim Ono 79	Retrd.	1990	6.00	55
1990	King Arthur (Red) 72	Retrd.	N/A	16.00	95
1990	Lullaby 47	Retrd.	1990	9.00	65

YEAR ISSUE		EDITION LIMIT	YEAR RETD.	ISSUE PRICE	*QUOTE U.S.$
1990	Maracca 94	Retrd.	1990	9.00	125
1990	Mother Goose (blue bonnet/pink shawl) 52	Retrd.	N/A	10.00	65
1990	Nativity 36	Retrd.	1990	6.00	25
1990	Peacock (on snowball) 74	Retrd.	N/A	18.00	50
1990	Pierre Le Berry	Retrd.	N/A	10.00	60
1990	Polish Folk Dance 13	Retrd.	N/A	19.00	150
1990	Proud Peacock 74	Retrd.	N/A	18.00	50
1990	Roly Poly Santa (Red bottom) 69	Retrd.	N/A	13.00	60
1990	Rose Lamp 96	Retrd.	1990	14.00	95
1990	Santa on Ball 80	Retrd.	1991	16.00	75
1990	Silent Movie (black hat) 75	Retrd.	1990	8.50	75
1990	Small Nautilus Shell 78	Retrd.	N/A	7.00	22
1990	Smiling Kite 63	Retrd.	1990	14.00	45
1990	Snowball Tree 71	Retrd.	1990	17.00	100
1990	Snowman on Ball 45	Retrd.	1990	14.00	75
1990	Spin Top 90	Retrd.	N/A	11.00	95
1990	Sunburst Fish (green/yellow) 68	Retrd.	N/A	13.00	28
1990	Trumpet Player 85	Retrd.	N/A	18.00	100
1990	Tuxedo Penguin 57	Retrd.	1990	8.00	300-325
1990	Walrus 59	Retrd.	1990	8.50	45
1990	Yarn Fight 23	Retrd.	N/A	17.00	125-150

1991 Holiday Collection - C. Radko

1991	All Weather Santa 137	Retrd.	1992	32.00	275
1991	Altar Boy 18	Retrd.	1992	16.00	35
1991	Anchor America 65	Retrd.	1992	21.50	65
1991	Apache 42	Retrd.	N/A	8.50	50
1991	Aspen 76	Retrd.	1992	20.50	95
1991	Aztec 141	Retrd.	1991	21.50	95
1991	Aztec Bird 41	Retrd.	1992	20.00	85
1991	Ballooning Santa 110	Retrd.	1991	23.00	250
1991	Barnum Clown 56	Retrd.	1991	15.00	85
1991	Bishop 22	Retrd.	N/A	15.00	40
1991	Blue Rainbow 136	Retrd.	1992	21.50	150
1991	Bowery Kid 50	Retrd.	1991	14.50	70
1991	By the Nile 124	Retrd.	1992	21.50	50
1991	Chance Encounter 104	Retrd.	1992	13.50	40
1991	Chimney Santa 12	Retrd.	N/A	14.50	65
1991	Clown Drum 33	Retrd.	1991	14.00	40
1991	Comet 62	Retrd.	1991	9.00	75
1991	Cosette 16	Retrd.	1991	16.00	60-100
1991	Dapper Shoe 89	Retrd.	1991	10.00	55
1991	Dawn & Dust 34	Retrd.	N/A	14.00	24-35
1991	Deco Floral 133	Retrd.	1991	22.00	60
1991	Deco Sparkle 134	Retrd.	1992	21.00	95
1991	Dutch Boy 27	Retrd.	1991	11.00	45-75
1991	Dutch Girl 28	Retrd.	1991	11.00	45-75
1991	Edwardian Lace 82	Retrd.	1991	21.50	60
1991	Einstein Kite 98	Retrd.	N/A	20.00	75
1991	Elf Reflector 135	Retrd.	1992	23.00	50
1991	Fanfare 126	Retrd.	1992	21.50	98
1991	Fisher Frog 44	Retrd.	1991	11.00	65-125
1991	Florentine 83	Retrd.	N/A	22.00	40
1991	Flower Child 90	Retrd.	1991	13.00	40
1991	Frog Under Balloon 53	Retrd.	N/A	16.00	45
1991	Fruit in Balloon 40	Retrd.	N/A	22.00	95-135
1991	Fu Manchu 11	Retrd.	N/A	15.00	75
1991	Galaxy 120	Retrd.	1991	21.50	75
1991	Grapefruit Tree 113	Retrd.	N/A	23.00	150-250
1991	Harvest 3	Retrd.	N/A	13.50	25
1991	Hatching Duck 35	Retrd.	1991	14.00	50
1991	Hearts & Flowers Finial 158	Retrd.	1993	53.00	95
1991	Her Majesty 39	Retrd.	1991	21.00	100
1991	Her Purse 88	Retrd.	N/A	10.00	55-65
1991	Holly Ball 156	Retrd.	N/A	22.00	60
1991	Irish Laddie 10	Retrd.	1991	12.00	60
1991	Jemima's Child 111	Retrd.	1991	16.00	60-75
1991	King Arthur (Blue) 95	Retrd.	N/A	18.50	95
1991	Lion's Head 31	Retrd.	N/A	16.00	35
1991	Madonna & Child 103	Retrd.	N/A	15.00	85
1991	Melon Slice 99	Retrd.	N/A	18.00	31
1991	Mother Goose 57	Retrd.	N/A	11.00	40
1991	Olympiad 125	Retrd.	1992	22.00	85-95
1991	Peruvian 74	Retrd.	1991	21.50	60
1991	Pierre Le Berry 2	Retrd.	1993	14.00	75
1991	Pink Elephants 70	Retrd.	N/A	21.50	130
1991	Pipe Smoking Monkey 54	Retrd.	1991	11.00	75
1991	Polish Folk Art 116	Retrd.	N/A	20.50	45
1991	Prince on Ball (pink/blue/green) 51	Retrd.	1991	15.00	50
1991	Prince Umbrella 21	Retrd.	1991	15.00	70
1991	Proud Peacock 37	Retrd.	N/A	23.00	37
1991	Rainbow Bird 92	Retrd.	1991	16.00	45
1991	Raspberry & Lime 96	Retrd.	1991	12.00	50
1991	Red Star 129	Retrd.	1992	21.50	40
1991	Sally Ann 43	Retrd.	1991	8.00	40
1991	Santa Bootie 55	Retrd.	1993	10.00	35
1991	Shirley 15	Retrd.	1991	16.00	95-125
1991	Shy Elf 1	Retrd.	1991	10.00	40-70
1991	Sitting Bull 107	Retrd.	1992	16.00	75
1991	Sleepy Time Santa 52	Retrd.	N/A	15.00	60-120
1991	Star Quilt 139	Retrd.	1991	21.50	40
1991	Sunburst Fish 108	Retrd.	N/A	15.00	28
1991	Sunshine 67	Retrd.	N/A	22.00	40
1991	Tabby 46	Retrd.	1991	8.00	30-50
1991	Tiffany 68	Retrd.	1991	22.00	50
1991	Tiger 5	Retrd.	N/A	15.00	35
1991	Trigger 114	Retrd.	1991	15.00	100
1991	Trumpet Man 100	Retrd.	1992	21.00	35
1991	Tulip Fairy 63	Retrd.	1992	16.00	65
1991	Vienna 1901 127	Retrd.	1992	21.50	N/A
1991	Villandry 87	Retrd.	1991	21.00	144

*Quotes have been rounded up to nearest dollar

YEAR ISSUE		EDITION LIMIT	YEAR RETD.	ISSUE PRICE	*QUOTE U.S.$
1991	Woodland Santa 38	Retrd.	N/A	14.00	55
1991	Zebra (glittered) 79	Retrd.	1991	22.00	60

1992 Holiday Collection - C. Radko

YEAR ISSUE		EDITION LIMIT	YEAR RETD.	ISSUE PRICE	*QUOTE U.S.$
1992	Alpine Flowers 162	Retrd.	1992	28.00	36
1992	Alpine Village 105	Retrd.	N/A	24.00	65
1992	Aspen 120	Retrd.	1992	26.00	50
1992	Barbie's Mom 69	Retrd.	1992	18.00	60
1992	Benjamin's Nutcrackers 185	Retrd.	N/A	58.00	95-150
1992	Butterfly Bouquet 119	Retrd.	1992	26.50	33
1992	By the Nile 139	Retrd.	1992	27.00	33-40
1992	Cabaret (see-through) 159	Retrd.	1993	28.00	60
1992	Candy Trumpet Men (pink/blue) 98	Retrd.	N/A	27.00	52
1992	Candy Trumpet Men (red) w/ white glitter 98	Retrd.	1992	27.00	95
1992	Celestial 129	Retrd.	N/A	26.00	40
1992	Cheerful Sun 50	Retrd.	N/A	18.00	25
1992	Chevron 160	Retrd.	1992	28.00	40
1992	Choir Boy 114	Retrd.	1992	24.00	30
1992	Christmas Cardinals 123	Retrd.	1992	26.00	95
1992	Christmas Rose 143	Retrd.	1992	25.50	60
1992	Circus lady 54	Retrd.	1992	12.00	15
1992	Clown Snake 62	Retrd.	N/A	22.00	35
1992	Country Star Quilt 176	Retrd.	N/A	12.00	20
1992	Cowboy Santa 94	Retrd.	N/A	24.00	N/A
1992	Delft Design 124	Retrd.	1992	26.50	170
1992	Diva 73	Retrd.	1992	17.00	65
1992	Dolly Madison 115	Retrd.	1992	17.00	65
1992	Downhill Racer 76	Retrd.	1992	34.00	80
1992	Elephant on Parade 141	Retrd.	1992	26.00	75
1992	Elephant Reflector 181	Retrd.	N/A	17.00	50
1992	Elf Reflectors 136	Retrd.	1992	28.00	36
1992	Faberge 148	Retrd.	N/A	26.50	55
1992	Faith, Hope & Love 183	Retrd.	1992	12.00	30
1992	Festive Smitty	Retrd.	N/A	N/A	75
1992	Floral Cascade Tier Drop 175	Retrd.	1992	32.00	41-45
1992	Florentine 131	Retrd.	N/A	27.00	40
1992	Flutter By's 201(Set/4)	Retrd.	N/A	11.00	40
1992	Folk Art Set 95	Retrd.	1992	10.00	13
1992	Forest Friends 103	Retrd.	1992	14.00	18
1992	French Country 121	Retrd.	N/A	26.00	65
1992	Fruit in Balloon 83	Retrd.	N/A	28.00	150-250
1992	Gabriel's Trumpets 188	Retrd.	N/A	20.00	25
1992	Harlequin Tier Drop 74	Retrd.	1992	36.00	65
1992	Harold Lloyd Reflector 218	Retrd.	1992	70.00	110
1992	Her Purse 43	Retrd.	N/A	20.00	65
1992	Her Slipper 56	Retrd.	1992	17.00	22
1992	Holly Finial 200	Retrd.	N/A	70.00	83
1992	Ice Pear 241	Retrd.	N/A	20.00	30-50
1992	Ice Poppies 127	Retrd.	1992	26.00	60
1992	Jumbo 99	Retrd.	N/A	31.00	45
1992	King of Prussia 149	Retrd.	1992	27.00	33-35
1992	Kitty Rattle 166	Retrd.	1993	18.00	85
1992	Little League 53	Retrd.	1992	20.00	35
1992	Merry Christmas Maiden 137	Retrd.	1992	26.00	N/A
1992	Mother Goose 37	Retrd.	N/A	15.00	25
1992	Mr. & Mrs. Claus 59	Retrd.	N/A	18.00	200
1992	Mushroom Elf 87	Retrd.	N/A	18.00	58
1992	Neopolitan Angels 152 (Set/3)	Retrd.	1992	27.00	200
1992	Norweigian Princess 170	Retrd.	1992	15.00	25
1992	Pierre Winterberry 64	Retrd.	1993	17.00	45-85
1992	Pink Lace Ball (See Through) 158	Retrd.	1992	28.00	60
1992	Polar Bear 184	Retrd.	N/A	16.00	50
1992	Primary Colors 108	Retrd.	1992	30.00	43
1992	Quilted Hearts (Old Salem Museum) 194	Retrd.	N/A	27.50	60
1992	Rainbow Parasol 90	Retrd.	1992	30.00	30
1992	Royal Scepter 77	Retrd.	1992	36.00	95
1992	Russian Imperial 112	Retrd.	1992	25.00	45
1992	Russian Jewel Hearts 146	Retrd.	N/A	27.00	90
1992	Russian Star 130	Retrd.	1992	26.00	32-40
1992	Sail Away 215	Retrd.	N/A	22.00	50
1992	Santa in Winter White 106	Retrd.	N/A	28.00	65
1992	Seahorse (pink) 92	Retrd.	1992	20.00	86
1992	Serpents of Paradise 97	Retrd.	N/A	13.00	30
1992	Siberian Sleighride (pink) 154	Retrd.	N/A	27.00	75
1992	Sitting Bull 93	Retrd.	1992	26.00	75
1992	Sleepytime Santa (pink) 81	Retrd.	N/A	18.00	40
1992	Sloopy Snowman 328	Retrd.	N/A	19.90	60-75
1992	Snowflakes 209	Retrd.	N/A	10.00	40
1992	Sputniks 134	Retrd.	1992	25.50	32
1992	St. Nickcicle 107	Retrd.	N/A	26.00	35
1992	Star of Wonder 177	Retrd.	1992	27.00	35
1992	Starbursts 214	Retrd.	N/A	12.00	40
1992	Stardust Joey 110	Retrd.	1992	16.00	60-75
1992	Starlight Santa (powder blue) 180	Retrd.	N/A	18.00	50
1992	Talking Pipe (black stem) 104	Retrd.	N/A	26.00	60
1992	Thunderbolt 178	Retrd.	1993	60.00	75
1992	Tiffany Bright Harlequin 161	Retrd.	1992	28.00	45-95
1992	Tiffany Pastel Harlequin 163	Retrd.	N/A	28.00	45-95
1992	To Grandma's House 239	Retrd.	N/A	20.00	N/A
1992	Topiary 117	Retrd.	N/A	30.00	175-250
1992	Tropical Fish 109	Retrd.	N/A	17.00	60
1992	Tulip Fairy 57	Retrd.	1992	18.00	45
1992	Tuxedo Santa 88	Retrd.	1993	22.00	125
1992	Two Sided Santa Reflector 102	Retrd.	1992	28.00	125
1992	Umbrella Santa 182	Retrd.	N/A	60.00	175
1992	Victorian Santa & Angel Balloon 122	Retrd.	1992	68.00	200-250
1992	Vienna 1901 128	Retrd.	1992	27.00	40
1992	Virgin Mary 46	Retrd.	1992	20.00	29
1992	Wacko's Brother, Doofus 55	Retrd.	N/A	20.00	65-120
1992	Water Lilies 133	Retrd.	1992	26.00	50
1992	Wedding Bells 217	Retrd.	N/A	40.00	165
1992	Winter Wonderland 156	Retrd.	1992	26.00	110
1992	Woodland Santa 111	Retrd.	N/A	20.00	55
1992	Ziegfeld Follies 126	Retrd.	1992	27.00	56

1993 Holiday Collection - C. Radko

YEAR ISSUE		EDITION LIMIT	YEAR RETD.	ISSUE PRICE	*QUOTE U.S.$
1993	1939 World's Fair 149	Retrd.	N/A	26.80	85
1993	Accordian Elf 189	Retrd.	N/A	21.00	65
1993	Aladdin's Lamp 237	Retrd.	N/A	20.00	30-45
1993	Alpine Village 420	Retrd.	1993	23.80	35
1993	Anassazi 172	Retrd.	N/A	26.60	75
1993	Angel of Peace 132	Retrd.	1993	17.00	24
1993	Apache 357	Retrd.	1993	13.90	40
1993	Auld Lang Syne 246	Retrd.	N/A	15.00	40
1993	Bedtime Buddy 239	Retrd.	N/A	29.00	65-85
1993	Bell House Boy 291	Retrd.	1993	21.00	28
1993	Beyond the Stars 108	Retrd.	1993	18.50	20
1993	Bishop of Myra 327	Retrd.	1993	19.90	50
1993	Blue Top 114	Retrd.	1993	16.00	16
1993	Bowzer 228	Retrd.	N/A	22.80	140
1993	By Jiminy 285	Retrd.	N/A	16.40	85
1993	Calla Lilly 314	Retrd.	N/A	12.90	23
1993	Carnival Rides 303	Retrd.	N/A	18.00	95
1993	Celeste 271	Retrd.	N/A	26.00	60
1993	Celestial Peacock Finial 322	Retrd.	N/A	69.00	200-295
1993	Center Ring (Exclusive) 192	Retrd.	1993	30.80	38
1993	Centurian 224	Retrd.	1993	25.50	200
1993	Chimney Sweep Bell 294	Retrd.	1993	26.00	150
1993	Christmas Express 394 (Garland)	Retrd.	N/A	58.00	200
1993	Christmas Stars 342	Retrd.	N/A	14.00	21
1993	Cinderella's Bluebirds 145	Retrd.	1993	25.90	40
1993	Circle of Santas Finial 413	Retrd.	N/A	69.00	163
1993	Circus Seal 249	Retrd.	1993	28.00	60
1993	Class Clown 332	Retrd.	N/A	21.00	65
1993	Clowning Around 84	Retrd.	N/A	42.50	65
1993	Confucius 363	Retrd.	1993	19.00	28
1993	Cool Cat 184	Retrd.	N/A	21.00	45
1993	Copenhagen 166	Retrd.	1993	26.80	55
1993	Crowned Passion 299	Retrd.	1993	23.00	60
1993	Crystal Rainbow 308	Retrd.	N/A	29.90	60
1993	Deco Snowfall 147	Retrd.	1993	26.80	33
1993	Deer Drop 304	Retrd.	N/A	34.00	150
1993	Downhill Racer 195	Retrd.	1993	30.00	36
1993	Emerald Wizard 279	Retrd.	N/A	18.00	65
1993	Emperor's Pet 253	Retrd.	1993	22.00	100-150
1993	Enchanted Gardens 341	Retrd.	1993	5.50	13
1993	English Kitchen 234	Retrd.	1993	26.00	28
1993	Epiphany 421	Retrd.	N/A	29.00	90
1993	Evening Star Santa 409	Retrd.	1993	59.00	95
1993	Fiesta Ball 316	Retrd.	N/A	26.40	85
1993	Flora Dora 255	Retrd.	N/A	25.00	75
1993	Forest Friends 250	Retrd.	1993	28.00	35
1993	French Rose 152	Retrd.	1993	26.60	27-33
1993	Fruit in Balloon 115	Retrd.	N/A	27.90	100
1993	Geisha Girls 261	Retrd.	1993	11.90	12-19
1993	Gold Fish 158	Retrd.	1993	25.80	26
1993	Goofy Garden 191 (Set/4)	Retrd.	N/A	15.00	150-200
1993	Grandpa Bear 260	Retrd.	1993	12.80	13-20
1993	Grecian Urn 231	Retrd.	1993	23.00	23
1993	Gypsy Girl 371	Retrd.	1993	16.00	35
1993	Holiday Spice 422	Retrd.	1993	24.00	24
1993	Honey Bear 352	Retrd.	1993	13.90	55
1993	Ice Star Santa 405	Retrd.	1993	38.00	145-225
1993	Jack Frost (blue) 333	Retrd.	N/A	23.00	30
1993	Jaques Le Berry 356	Retrd.	N/A	16.90	70
1993	Joey B. Clown 135	Retrd.	N/A	26.00	55-75
1993	Just Like Grandma Lg. 200	Retrd.	N/A	7.20	25
1993	Just Like Grandmas Sm. 200	Retrd.	N/A	7.20	20
1993	Kissing Cousins 245 (Pair)	Retrd.	N/A	30.00	200-250
1993	Kitty Rattle 374	Retrd.	1993	17.80	30-45
1993	Letter to Santa 188	Retrd.	N/A	22.00	55
1993	Light in the Windows 229	Retrd.	1994	24.50	30
1993	Little Doggie 180	Retrd.	1993	7.00	30
1993	Little Eskimo 355	Retrd.	N/A	13.90	21
1993	Majestic Reflector 312	Retrd.	1993	70.00	165
1993	Mediterranean Sunshine 156	Retrd.	N/A	26.90	65
1993	Midas Touch 162	Retrd.	N/A	27.80	50-70
1993	Monkey Man 97	Retrd.	1993	16.00	65
1993	Monterey 290	Retrd.	1993	15.00	35
1993	Mr. & Mrs. Claus 121	Retrd.	1993	17.90	25-75
1993	Mushroom Elf 267	Retrd.	N/A	17.90	35
1993	Nellie (Italian ornament) 225	Retrd.	1993	27.50	200
1993	North Woods 317	Retrd.	1993	26.80	40-90
1993	One Small Leap 222	Retrd.	N/A	26.00	75
1993	Pagoda 258	Retrd.	1993	8.00	15
1993	Pennsylvania Dutch 146	Retrd.	1993	26.80	33
1993	Piggly Wiggly 101	Retrd.	N/A	11.00	40
1993	Pineapple Quilt 150	Retrd.	N/A	26.80	85
1993	Pixie Santa 186	Retrd.	N/A	16.00	50
1993	Poinsetta Santa 269	Retrd.	N/A	19.80	76
1993	Polar Bears 112A	Retrd.	1993	15.50	15
1993	Pompadour 344	Retrd.	1993	8.80	18
1993	Prince Albert 263	Retrd.	N/A	23.00	40-60
1993	Purse 389	Retrd.	1993	15.60	16
1993	Quartet 392	Retrd.	1993	3.60	11
1993	Rainbow Reflector 154	Retrd.	1993	26.60	30-40
1993	Rainbow Shark 277	Retrd.	N/A	18.00	40
1993	Rainy Day Friend 206	Retrd.	N/A	22.00	50-75
1993	Regal Rooster 177	Retrd.	N/A	25.80	50
1993	Rose Pointe Finial 323	Retrd.	1993	34.00	40
1993	Sail by Starlight 339	Retrd.	1993	11.80	14-19
1993	Santa in Space 127	Retrd.	N/A	39.00	100-125
1993	Santa Tree 320	Retrd.	N/A	66.00	200-250
1993	Saraband 140	Retrd.	1993	27.80	75-125
1993	Serenade Pink 157	Retrd.	1993	26.80	55
1993	Shy Rabbit 280	Retrd.	N/A	14.00	45
1993	Silent Night 120	Retrd.	N/A	18.00	55
1993	The Skating Bettinas 242	Retrd.	N/A	29.00	60
1993	Ski Baby 99	Retrd.	N/A	21.00	60
1993	Sloopy Snowman 328	Retrd.	1993	19.90	55
1993	Smitty 378	Retrd.	N/A	17.90	25
1993	Snow Dance 247	Retrd.	N/A	29.00	125
1993	Snowday Santa 98	Retrd.	1993	20.00	70
1993	Snowman by Candlelight 155	Retrd.	N/A	26.50	60
1993	Southern Colonial 171	Retrd.	N/A	26.90	120
1993	Spider & the Fly 393	Retrd.	1993	6.40	14
1993	St. Nick's Pipe 330	Retrd.	N/A	4.40	30-75
1993	Star Children 208	Retrd.	1993	18.00	75
1993	Star Fire 175	Retrd.	N/A	26.80	60
1993	Starlight Santa 348	Retrd.	N/A	11.90	19
1993	Stocking Stuffers 236	Retrd.	1993	16.00	23
1993	Sweetheart 202	Retrd.	1993	16.00	40
1993	Talking Pipe 373	Retrd.	N/A	26.00	40-55
1993	Texas Star 338	Retrd.	1993	7.50	8
1993	Tuxedo Santa 117	Retrd.	1993	21.90	65-125
1993	Tweeter 94	Retrd.	1993	3.20	6
1993	Twinkle Tree 254	Retrd.	N/A	15.50	45
1993	U-Boat 353	Retrd.	1993	15.50	50
1993	V.I.P. 230	Retrd.	1993	23.00	150
1993	Waddles 95	Retrd.	1993	3.80	20-60
1993	Winterbirds 164	Retrd.	1993	26.80	30-45

1994 Holiday Collection - C. Radko

YEAR ISSUE		EDITION LIMIT	YEAR RETD.	ISSUE PRICE	*QUOTE U.S.$
1994	Andy Gump 48	Retrd.	N/A	18.00	32-45
1994	Baby Booties (pink) 236	Retrd.	N/A	17.00	35
1994	Bird Brain 254	Retrd.	N/A	33.00	95
1994	Bright Heavens Above 136	Retrd.	N/A	56.00	65-95
1994	Corn Husk 336	Retrd.	N/A	13.00	20
1994	Crescent Moons 195	Retrd.	N/A	29.00	75
1994	Einstein's Kite 375	Retrd.	N/A	29.90	45
1994	Elephant Prince 170	Retrd.	N/A	14.50	25
1994	Fleet's In 281	Retrd.	N/A	38.00	75
1994	French Country 192	Retrd.	N/A	29.00	40
1994	Golden Crescendo Finial 384	Retrd.	N/A	42.00	225
1994	Hieroglyph 194	Retrd.	N/A	29.00	55
1994	Honey Belle 156	Retrd.	N/A	74.00	95
1994	House Sitting Santa 240	Retrd.	N/A	26.00	30
1994	Jockey Pipe 51	Retrd.	N/A	36.00	50-95
1994	Just Like Us 324	Retrd.	N/A	29.50	50
1994	Kayo 165	Retrd.	N/A	14.00	25
1994	King of Kings 18	Retrd.	N/A	22.00	45
1994	Kitty Tamer 331	Retrd.	N/A	65.00	185
1994	Leader of the Band 94-915D (wh pants) - signed	Retrd.	1994	25.00	360
1994	Leader of the Band 94-915D (wh pants) - unsigned	Retrd.	1994	25.00	85
1994	Lemon Twist 28	Retrd.	N/A	14.00	25
1994	The Los Angeles 155	Retrd.	N/A	26.00	40
1994	Martian Holiday 326	Retrd.	N/A	42.00	60
1994	Masquerade 45	Retrd.	N/A	16.00	25
1994	Medium Nautilus (gold) 103	Retrd.	N/A	16.00	25
1994	Moon Martian 298	Retrd.	N/A	26.00	60-120
1994	Moon Mullins 230	Retrd.	N/A	18.00	45
1994	Mr. Smedley Drysdale 37	Retrd.	N/A	44.00	120-175
1994	Nighty Night 299	Retrd.	N/A	36.00	125
1994	On The Run (Original) 247	Retrd.	N/A	45.00	60-75
1994	Owl Reflector 40	Retrd.	N/A	54.00	75
1994	Party Hopper 274	Retrd.	N/A	37.00	200
1994	Pickled 317	Retrd.	N/A	26.00	55
1994	Pinecone Santa 118	Retrd.	N/A	29.50	30
1994	President Taft 74	Retrd.	N/A	18.00	50
1994	Prince Philip 909	Retrd.	N/A	N/A	150
1994	Private Eye 163	Retrd.	N/A	18.00	35
1994	Quick Draw 330	Retrd.	N/A	65.00	185
1994	Santa's Helper 131	Retrd.	N/A	19.90	25
1994	Shivers 262	Retrd.	N/A	25.00	140
1994	Smiley 52	Retrd.	N/A	16.00	35
1994	Soldier Boy 142	Retrd.	N/A	19.00	100-125
1994	Stocking Sam 108	Retrd.	N/A	23.00	35
1994	Swami 128	Retrd.	N/A	18.00	25
1994	Sweet Pear 59	Retrd.	N/A	24.00	60-75
1994	Terrance 53	Retrd.	N/A	16.00	45
1994	Tiny Nautilus (gold) 100	Retrd.	N/A	12.00	20
1994	Vaudeville Sam 57	Retrd.	N/A	18.00	30
1994	Wedded Bliss 94	Retrd.	N/A	88.00	195
1994	Wednesday 120	Retrd.	N/A	42.00	63
1994	White Nights 197	Retrd.	N/A	26.00	65-75
1994	Xenon 304	Retrd.	N/A	38.00	150-200

Aids Awareness - C. Radko

YEAR ISSUE		EDITION LIMIT	YEAR RETD.	ISSUE PRICE	*QUOTE U.S.$
1993	A Shy Rabbit's Heart 462	Retrd.	1993	15.00	75-150
1994	Frosty Cares SP5	Retrd.	1994	25.00	50-65
1995	On Wings of Hope SP10	Retrd.	1995	30.00	30
1996	A Winter Bear's Heart SP15	Yr.Iss.		34.00	34

Disney Gallery Ornaments - C. Radko

YEAR ISSUE		EDITION LIMIT	YEAR RETD.	ISSUE PRICE	*QUOTE U.S.$
1995	Mickey's Tree DIS1	2,500	1995	45.00	230-250
1995	Pooh's Favorite Gift DIS2	2,500	1995	45.00	230-250

*Quotes have been rounded up to nearest dollar

CHRISTMAS ORNAMENTS

Event Only - C. Radko

YEAR ISSUE		EDITION LIMIT	YEAR RETD.	ISSUE PRICE	*QUOTE U.S.$
1993	Littlest Snowman 347S	Retrd.	1993	15.00	55
1994	Roly Poly 94125E	Retrd.	1994	22.00	45-70
1995	Forever Lucy 91075E	Retrd.	1995	32.00	35
1996	Poinsettia Elegance 287E	Yr.Iss.		32.00	32

Limited Edition Ornaments - C. Radko

YEAR ISSUE		EDITION LIMIT	YEAR RETD.	ISSUE PRICE	*QUOTE U.S.$
1995	And Snowy Makes Eight 169 (Set/8)	15,000		125.00	125
1996	Russian Rhapsody RUS (Set/6)	7,500		150.00	150

Matt Berry Memorial Soccer Fund - C. Radko

YEAR ISSUE		EDITION LIMIT	YEAR RETD.	ISSUE PRICE	*QUOTE U.S.$
1995	Matthew's Game 158-0	Open		12.00	12

Nativity Series - C. Radko

YEAR ISSUE		EDITION LIMIT	YEAR RETD.	ISSUE PRICE	*QUOTE U.S.$
1996	Holy Family HF (Set/3)	15,000		70.00	70
1995	Three Wise Men WM (Set/3)	15,000		90.00	90

Nutcracker Series - C. Radko

YEAR ISSUE		EDITION LIMIT	YEAR RETD.	ISSUE PRICE	*QUOTE U.S.$
1995	Nutcracker Suite I NC1 (Set/3)	15,000		90.00	90
1996	Nutcracker Suite II NC2 (Set/3)	15,000		90.00	90

Pediatrics Cancer Research - C. Radko

YEAR ISSUE		EDITION LIMIT	YEAR RETD.	ISSUE PRICE	*QUOTE U.S.$
1994	A Gifted Santa 70	Retrd.	1994	25.00	35-65
1995	Christmas Puppy Love SP11	Retrd.	1995	30.00	40
1996	Bearly Awake SP16	Yr.Iss.		34.00	34

South Bend Special - C. Radko

YEAR ISSUE		EDITION LIMIT	YEAR RETD.	ISSUE PRICE	*QUOTE U.S.$
1995	Polar Express (lilac) 950-76-SB	Retrd.	1995	24.95	45-75

Sunday Brunch - C. Radko

YEAR ISSUE		EDITION LIMIT	YEAR RETD.	ISSUE PRICE	*QUOTE U.S.$
1996	Hansel & Gretel and Witch HG1	7,500		50.00	50

Twelve Days of Christmas - C. Radko

YEAR ISSUE		EDITION LIMIT	YEAR RETD.	ISSUE PRICE	*QUOTE U.S.$
1993	Partridge in a Pear Tree SP2	5,000	1993	35.00	750-1000
1994	Two Turtle Doves SP4	10,000	1994	28.00	100-200
1995	Three French Hens SP9	10,000	1995	34.00	40-65
1996	Four Calling Birds SP12	10,000		44.00	44

Warner Brothers - C. Radko

YEAR ISSUE		EDITION LIMIT	YEAR RETD.	ISSUE PRICE	*QUOTE U.S.$
1995	Santa's Bugs Bunny WB1	Retrd.	1995	45.00	90-145
1995	Taz Angel WB2	Retrd.	1995	40.00	90-145
1995	Tweety's Sprite WB3	Retrd.	1995	45.00	90-145

Dave Grossman Creations

Gone With the Wind Ornaments - Various

YEAR ISSUE		EDITION LIMIT	YEAR RETD.	ISSUE PRICE	*QUOTE U.S.$
1987	Ashley - D. Geenty	Closed	N/A	15.00	45
1994	Gold Plated GWO-00 - Unknown	Open		13.00	13
1994	Limited Edition GWO-94 - Unknown	Yr.Iss.		25.00	25
1989	Mammy - D. Geenty	Closed	N/A	20.00	20
1991	Prissy - Unknown	Closed	N/A	20.00	20
1993	Rhett (White Suit) GWO-93 - Unknown	Closed	N/A	20.00	20
1987	Rhett - D. Geenty	Closed	N/A	15.00	45
1988	Rhett and Scarlett - D. Geenty	Closed	N/A	20.00	40
1992	Scarlett (Green Dress) - Unknown	Closed	N/A	20.00	20
1990	Scarlett (Red Dress) - D. Geenty	Closed	N/A	20.00	20
1987	Scarlett - D. Geenty	Closed	N/A	15.00	45
1994	Scarlett GWO-94 - Unknown	Yr.Iss.		20.00	20
1987	Tara - D. Geenty	Closed	N/A	15.00	45

Rockwell Collection-Annual Rockwell Ball - Rockwell-Inspired

YEAR ISSUE		EDITION LIMIT	YEAR RETD.	ISSUE PRICE	*QUOTE U.S.$
1975	Santa with Feather Quill NRO-01	Retrd.	N/A	3.50	25
1976	Santa at Globe NRO-02	Retrd.	N/A	4.00	25
1977	Grandpa on Rocking Horse NRO-03	Retrd.	N/A	4.00	12
1978	Santa with Map NRO-04	Retrd.	N/A	4.50	12
1979	Santa at Desk with Mail Bag NRO-05	Retrd.	N/A	5.00	12
1980	Santa Asleep with Toys NRO-06	Retrd.	N/A	5.00	10
1981	Santa w/Boy on Finger NRO-07	Retrd.	N/A	5.00	10
1982	Santa Face on Winter Scene NRO-08	Retrd.	N/A	5.00	10
1983	Coachman with Whip NRO-9	Retrd.	N/A	5.00	10
1984	Christmas Bounty Man NRO-10	Retrd.	N/A	5.00	10
1985	Old English Trio NRO-11	Retrd.	N/A	5.00	10
1986	Tiny Tim on Shoulder NRO-12	Retrd.	N/A	5.00	10
1987	Skating Lesson NRO-13	Retrd.	N/A	5.00	10
1988	Big Moment NRO-14	Retrd.	N/A	5.50	6
1989	Discovery NRO-15	Retrd.	N/A	6.00	6
1990	Bringing Home The Tree NRO-16	Retrd.	N/A	6.00	6
1991	Downhill Daring NRO-17	Retrd.	N/A	6.00	6
1992	On The Ice NRO-18	Retrd.	N/A	6.00	6
1993	Granps NRO-19	Retrd.	N/A	6.00	6
1994	Triple Self Portrait - Commemorative NRO-20	Yr.Iss.		6.00	6

Rockwell Collection-Annual Rockwell Figurine Ornaments - Rockwell-Inspired

YEAR ISSUE		EDITION LIMIT	YEAR RETD.	ISSUE PRICE	*QUOTE U.S.$
1978	Caroler NRX-03	Retrd.	N/A	15.00	45
1979	Drum for Tommy NRX-24	Retrd.	N/A	20.00	30
1980	Santa's Good Boys NRX-37	Retrd.	N/A	20.00	30
1981	Letters to Santa NRX-39	Retrd.	N/A	20.00	30
1982	Cornettist NRX-32	Retrd.	N/A	20.00	30
1983	Fiddler NRX-83	Retrd.	N/A	20.00	30
1984	Christmas Bounty NRX-84	Retrd.	N/A	20.00	30
1985	Jolly Coachman NRX-85	Retrd.	N/A	20.00	30
1986	Grandpa on Rocking Horse NRX-86	Retrd.	N/A	20.00	30
1987	Skating Lesson NRX-87	Retrd.	N/A	20.00	30
1988	Big Moment NRX-88	Retrd.	N/A	20.00	25
1989	Discovery NRX-89	Retrd.	N/A	20.00	20
1990	Bringing Home The Tree NRX-90	Retrd.	N/A	20.00	20
1991	Downhill Daring B NRX-91	Retrd.	N/A	20.00	20
1992	On The Ice	Retrd.	N/A	20.00	20
1993	Granps NRX-93	Retrd.	N/A	24.00	24
1993	Marriage License First Christmas Together NRX-m1	Retrd.	N/A	30.00	30
1994	Merry Christmas NRX-94	Yr.Iss.		24.00	24

Department 56

Bisque Light-Up, Clip-on Ornaments - Department 56

YEAR ISSUE		EDITION LIMIT	YEAR RETD.	ISSUE PRICE	*QUOTE U.S.$
1986	Angelic Lite-up 8260-0	Open		4.00	4
1987	Anniversary Love Birds, (pair) w/brass ribbon 8353-4	Closed	1988	4.00	4
1986	Dessert, 6 asst. 7100-5	Closed	1987	5.00	5
1985	Humpty Dumpty 3525-4	Closed	1986	4.50	5
1990	Owl w/clip 8344-5	Closed	1994	5.00	14
1986	Plum Pudding 7101-3	Closed	1987	4.50	5
1989	Pond-Frog w/clip 8347-0	Closed	1991	5.00	5
1989	Pond-Snail w/clip 8347-0	Closed	1991	5.00	55
1988	Rabbit w/clip 8350-0	Open		4.00	17
1987	Shells, set/4 8349-6	Closed	1991	14.00	14
1986	Shooting Star 7106-4	Closed	1987	5.50	6
1985	Snowbirds, (pair) w/clip 8357-7	Open		5.00	5
1985	Snowbirds, set/6 8367-4	Closed	1988	15.00	15
1985	Snowbirds, set/8 8358-5	Closed	1988	20.00	20
1985	Snowmen, 3 asst. 8360-7	Closed	1988	10.50	11
1986	Teddy Bear w/clip 8262-7	Closed	1991	5.00	5
1986	Truffles Sampler, set/4 7102-1	Closed	1987	17.50	18
1986	Winged Snowbird 8261-9	Closed	1988	2.50	3
1989	Woodland-Field Mouse w/clip 8348-8	Closed	1991	5.00	55
1989	Woodland-Squirrel w/clip 8348-8	Closed	1991	5.00	55

CCP Ornaments-Flat -Department 56

YEAR ISSUE		EDITION LIMIT	YEAR RETD.	ISSUE PRICE	*QUOTE U.S.$
1986	Christmas Carol Houses, set/3 (6504-8)	Closed	1989	13.00	45-70
1986	•The Cottage of Bob Cratchit & Tiny Tim	Closed	1989	4.35	N/A
1986	•Fezziwig's Warehouse	Closed	1989	4.35	N/A
1986	•Scrooge and Marley Countinghouse	Closed	1989	4.35	N/A
1986	New England Village, set/7 (6536-6)	Closed	1989	25.00	300
1986	•Apothecary Shop	Closed	1989	3.50	40
1986	•Brick Town Hall	Closed	1989	3.50	50
1986	•General Store	Closed	1989	3.50	55
1986	•Livery Stable & Boot Shop	Closed	1989	3.50	40-50
1986	•Nathaniel Bingham Fabrics	Closed	1989	3.50	20-55
1986	•Red Schoolhouse	Closed	1989	3.50	40-70
1986	•Steeple Church	Closed	1989	3.50	150-225

Christmas Carol Character Ornaments-Flat -Department 56

YEAR ISSUE		EDITION LIMIT	YEAR RETD.	ISSUE PRICE	*QUOTE U.S.$
1986	Christmas Carol Characters, set/3 (6505-6)	Closed	1987	13.00	40-60
1986	•Bob Cratchit & Tiny Tim	Closed	1987	4.35	35-75
1986	•Poulterer	Closed	1987	4.35	30
1986	•Scrooge	Closed	1987	4.35	35-75

Merry Makers - Department 56

YEAR ISSUE		EDITION LIMIT	YEAR RETD.	ISSUE PRICE	*QUOTE U.S.$
1992	Tolland The Toller 9369-6	Closed	1995	11.00	11

Miscellaneous Ornaments - Department 56

YEAR ISSUE		EDITION LIMIT	YEAR RETD.	ISSUE PRICE	*QUOTE U.S.$
1983	Snow Village Wood Ornaments, set/6, 5099-7	Closed	1984	30.00	N/A
1983	•Carriage House	Closed	1984	5.00	50
1983	•Centennial House	Closed	1984	5.00	100
1983	•Countryside Church	Closed	1984	5.00	125
1983	•Gabled House	Closed	1984	5.00	75
1983	•Pioneer Church	Closed	1984	5.00	75-125
1983	•Swiss Chalet	Closed	1984	5.00	75
1984	Dickens 2-sided Tin Ornaments, set/6, 6522-6	Closed	1985	12.00	440
1984	•Abel Beesley Butcher	Closed	1985	2.00	45
1984	•Bean and Son Smithy Shop	Closed	1985	2.00	45
1984	•Crowntree Inn	Closed	1985	2.00	45
1984	•Golden Swan Baker	Closed	1985	2.00	45
1984	•Green Grocer	Closed	1985	2.00	45
1984	•Jones & Co. Brush & Basket Shop	Closed	1985	2.00	45
1986	Cherub on Brass Ribbon, 8248-1	Closed	1988	8.00	66
1986	Teddy Bear on Brass Ribbon, 8263-5	Closed	1988	7.00	70
1988	Balsam Bell Brass Dickens' Candlestick, 6244-8	Closed	1989	3.00	15
1988	Christmas Carol- Bob & Mrs. Cratchit, 5914-5	Closed	1989	18.00	36-45
1988	Christmas Carol- Scrooge's Head, 5912-9	Closed	1989	13.00	30-35
1988	Christmas Carol- Tiny Tim's Head, 5913-7	Closed	1989	10.00	25-35
1994	Dickens Village Dedlock Arms 9872-8, (porcelain, gift boxed)	Closed	1994	12.50	15-25
1995	Sir John Falstaff 9870-1 (Charles Dickens' Signature Series)	Closed	1995	15.00	15

Snowbabies Ornaments - Department 56

YEAR ISSUE		EDITION LIMIT	YEAR RETD.	ISSUE PRICE	*QUOTE U.S.$
1994	Be My Baby 6866-7	Open		15.00	25
1986	Crawling, Lite-Up, Clip-On, 7953-7	Closed	1992	7.00	28
1994	First Star Jinglebaby, 6858-6	Open		10.00	11
1994	Gathering Stars in the Sky, 6855-1	Open		12.50	13
1995	Joy 68807, set/3	Open		32.50	33
1994	Juggling Stars in the Sky 6867-5	Open		15.00	15
1994	Just For You Jinglebaby 6869-1	Open		11.00	11
1994	Little Drummer Jinglebaby, 6859-4	Open		10.00	11
1987	Mini, Winged Pair, Lite-Up, Clip-On, 7976-6	Open		9.00	12
1987	Moon Beams, 7951-0	Open		7.50	9
1991	My First Star, 6811-0	Open		7.00	8
1989	Noel, 7988-0	Open		7.50	8
1995	One Little Candle Jinglebaby 68806	Open		11.00	11
1995	Overnight Delivery, 759-5 (Event Piece)	Open		10.00	10
1995	Overnight Delivery, 68808	Open		10.00	10
1990	Penguin, Lite-Up, Clip-On, 7940-5	Closed	1992	5.00	15-25
1990	Polar Bear, Lite-Up, Clip-On, 7941-3	Closed	1992	5.00	15-20
1990	Rock-A-Bye Baby, 7939-1	Closed	1995	7.00	8
1986	Sitting, Lite-Up, Clip-On, 7952-9	Closed	1990	7.00	30-50
1992	Snowbabies Icicle w/Star, 6825-0	Closed	1995	16.00	16
1987	Snowbaby Adrift Lite-Up, Clip-On, 7969-3	Closed	1990	8.50	100-150
1986	Snowbaby on Brass Ribbon, 7961-8	Closed	1989	8.00	145-180
1993	Sprinkling Stars in the Sky, 6848-9	Open		12.50	13
1989	Star Bright, 7990-1	Open		7.50	8
1992	Starry, Starry Night, 6830-6	Open		12.50	13
1994	Stars in My Stocking Jinglebaby 6868-3	Open		11.00	11
1989	Surprise, 7989-8	Closed	1994	12.00	15-25
1991	Swinging On a Star, 6810-1	Open		9.50	10
1988	Twinkle Little Star, 7980-4	Closed	1990	7.00	80-120
1993	Wee...This is Fun!, 6847-0	Open		13.50	14
1986	Winged, Lite-Up, Clip-On, 7954-5	Closed	1990	7.00	35-45

Village Light-Up Ornaments - Department 56

YEAR ISSUE		EDITION LIMIT	YEAR RETD.	ISSUE PRICE	*QUOTE U.S.$
1987	Christmas Carol Cottages, set/3 (6513-7)	Closed	1989	17.00	50-65
1987	•The Cottage of Bob Cratchit & Tiny Tim	Closed	1989	6.00	20-28
1987	•Fezziwig's Warehouse	Closed	1989	6.00	25-30
1987	•Scrooge & Marley Countinghouse	Closed	1989	6.00	15-25
1987	Dickens' Village, set/14 (6521-8, 6520-0)	Closed	1989	84.00	400
1987	Dickens' Village, set/6 (6520-0)	Closed	1989	36.00	85-175
1987	•Barley Bree Farmhouse	Closed	1989	6.00	20-40
1987	•Blythe Pond Mill House	Closed	1989	6.00	40
1987	•Brick Abbey	Closed	1989	6.00	90
1987	•Chesterton Manor House	Closed	1989	6.00	45
1987	•Kenilworth Castle	Closed	1989	6.00	60
1987	•The Old Curiosity Shop	Closed	1989	6.00	45
1985	Dickens' Village, set/8 (6521-8)	Closed	1989	48.00	200
1985	•Abel Beesley Butcher	Closed	1989	6.00	25
1985	•Bean and Son Smithy Shop	Closed	1989	6.00	20-35
1985	•Candle Shop	Closed	1989	6.00	25-35
1985	•Crowntree Inn	Closed	1989	6.00	65
1985	•Dickens' Village Church	Closed	1989	6.00	40-50
1985	•Golden Swan Baker	Closed	1989	6.00	20-30
1985	•Green Grocer	Closed	1989	6.00	20-30
1985	•Jones & Co. Brush & Basket Shop	Closed	1989	6.00	30-40
1987	New England Village, set/13 (6533-1, 6534-0)	Closed	1989	78.00	700-750
1987	New England Village, set/6 (6534-0)	Closed	1989	36.00	200-275
1987	•Craggy Cove Lighthouse	Closed	1989	6.00	125-140
1987	•Jacob Adams Barn	Closed	1989	6.00	60
1987	•Jacob Adams Farmhouse	Closed	1989	6.00	60
1987	•Smythe Woolen Mill	Closed	1989	6.00	135-145
1987	•Timber Knoll Log Cabin	Closed	1989	6.00	115-125
1987	•Weston Train Station	Closed	1989	6.00	35-65
1986	New England Village, set/7 (6533-1)	Closed	1989	42.00	325
1986	•Apothecary Shop	Closed	1989	6.00	20
1986	•Brick Town Hall	Closed	1989	6.00	40
1986	•General Store	Closed	1989	6.00	38
1986	•Livery Stable & Boot Shop	Closed	1989	6.00	30
1986	•Nathaniel Bingham Fabrics	Closed	1989	6.00	38
1986	•Red Schoolhouse	Closed	1989	6.00	70-80
1986	•Steeple Church	Closed	1989	6.00	135

Duncan Royale

History Of Santa Claus - Duncan Royale

YEAR ISSUE		EDITION LIMIT	YEAR RETD.	ISSUE PRICE	*QUOTE U.S.$
1992	Santa I (set of 12)	Open		144.00	144
1992	Santa II (set of 12)	Open		144.00	144

Enesco Corporation

Cherished Teddies - P. Hillman

YEAR ISSUE		EDITION LIMIT	YEAR RETD.	ISSUE PRICE	*QUOTE U.S.$
1995	Cupid Bear Flying-103608	Suspd.		13.00	15
1995	Girl Flying Cupid-103616	Suspd.		13.00	15
1995	Teddy with Ice Skates dated 95-141232	Open		12.50	13
1995	Baby Angel on Cloud-141240	Open		13.50	14
1995	Boy/Girl with Banner-141259	Open		13.50	14
1996	Toy Soldier (dated)-176052	Yr.Iss.		12.50	13
1996	Santa Bear 2 asst.-176168	Open		12.50	13

*Quotes have been rounded up to nearest dollar

YEAR ISSUE		EDITION LIMIT	YEAR RETD.	ISSUE PRICE	*QUOTE U.S. $
1996	Bear w/Dangling Mittens-177768	Open		12.50	13
1994	Bundled Up For The Holidays -617229	Open		15.00	15
1994	Beary Christmas Dated 1994 -617253	Yr.Iss.		15.00	18-30
1995	Mrs Claus Xmas Holding Tray/ Cookies-625426	Yr.Iss.	1995	12.50	13-25
1995	Elf Bear W/Doll-625434	Open		12.50	13
1995	Elf Bear W/Stuffed Reindeer -625442	Open		12.50	13
1995	Teddies Santa Bear-651370	Open		12.50	13
1995	Elf Bears/Candy Cane-651389	Open		12.50	13
1993	Girl w/Muff (Alice) dated 1993-912832	Yr.Iss.		13.50	25-50
1994	Drummer Boy Dated 1994 -912891	Yr.Iss.		10.00	20-30
1993	3 Asst. Angel-912980	Open		12.50	13
1993	Baby Girl dated 1993-913006	Yr.Iss.		12.50	25
1993	Baby Boy dated 1993-913014	Yr.Iss.		12.50	25
1993	Jointed Teddy Bear -914894	Suspd.		12.50	13-23
1992	Bear In Stocking, dated 1992 -950653	Yr.Iss.		16.00	25-60
1992	Angel-950777	Suspd.		12.50	50-65
1992	Beth On Rocking Reindeer -950793	Suspd.		20.00	35-65
1992	3 Asst. Christmas Sister Bears -951226	Suspd.		12.50	13-20

Enesco Treasury of Christmas Ornaments - Various

YEAR ISSUE		EDITION LIMIT	YEAR RETD.	ISSUE PRICE	*QUOTE U.S. $
1983	Wide Open Throttle-E-0242	3-Yr.	1985	12.00	35
1983	Baby's First Christmas-E-0271	Yr.Iss.	1983	6.00	N/A
1983	Grandchild's First Christmas-E-0272	Yr.Iss.	1983	5.00	N/A
1983	Baby's First Christmas-E-0273	3-Yr.	1985	9.00	N/A
1983	Toy Drum Teddy-E-0274	4-Yr.	1986	9.00	N/A
1983	Watching At The Window-E-0275	3-Yr.	1985	13.00	N/A
1983	To A Special Teacher-E-0276	7-Yr.	1989	5.00	15
1983	Toy Shop-E-0277	7-Yr.	1989	8.00	50
1983	Carousel Horse-E-0278	7-Yr.	1989	9.00	20
1981	Look Out Below-E-6135	2-Yr.	1982	6.00	N/A
1982	Flyin' Santa Christmas Special 1982-E-6136	Yr.Iss.	1982	9.00	75
1981	Flyin' Santa Christmas Special 1981-E-6136	Yr.Iss.	1981	9.00	N/A
1981	Sawin' Elf Helper-E-6138	2-Yr.	1982	6.00	40
1981	Snow Shoe-In Santa-E-6139	2-Yr.	1982	6.00	35
1981	Baby's First Christmas 1981-E-6145	Yr.Iss.	1981	6.00	N/A
1981	Our Hero-E-6146	2-Yr.	1982	4.00	N/A
1981	Whoops-E-6147	2-Yr.	1982	3.50	N/A
1981	Whoops, It's 1981-E-6148	Yr.Iss.	1981	7.50	75
1981	Not A Creature Was Stirring-E-6149	2-Yr.	1982	4.00	25
1984	Joy To The World-E-6209	2-Yr.	1985	9.00	35
1984	Letter To Santa-E-6210	2-Yr.	1985	5.00	30
1984	Lucy & Me Photo Frames-E-6211	3-Yr.	1986	5.00	N/A
1984	Lucy & Me Photo Frames-E-6211	3-Yr.	1986	5.00	N/A
1984	Lucy & Me Photo Frames-E-6211	3-Yr.	1986	5.00	N/A
1984	Lucy & Me Photo Frames-E-6211	3-Yr.	1986	5.00	N/A
1984	Lucy & Me Photo Frames-E-6211	3-Yr.	1986	5.00	N/A
1984	Lucy & Me Photo Frames-E-6211	3-Yr.	1986	5.00	N/A
1984	Baby's First Christmas 1984-E-6212 - Gilmore	Yr.Iss.	1984	10.00	30
1984	Merry Christmas Mother-E-6213	3-Yr.	1986	10.00	30
1984	Baby's First Christmas 1984-E-6215	Yr.Iss.	1984	6.00	N/A
1984	Ferris Wheel Mice-E-6216	2-Yr.	1985	9.00	30
1984	Cuckoo Clock-E-6217	2-Yr.	1985	8.00	40
1984	Muppet Babies Baby's First Christmas-E6222 - J. Henson	Yr.Iss.	1984	10.00	45
1984	Muppet Babies Baby's First Christmas-E6223 -J. Henson	Yr.Iss.	1984	10.00	45
1984	Garfield Hark! The Herald Angel-E-6224 - J. Davis	2-Yr.	1985	7.50	35
1984	Fun in Santa's Sleigh-E-6225 - J. Davis	2-Yr.	1985	12.00	35
1984	Deer! Odie-E-6226 -J. Davis	2-Yr.	1985	6.00	30
1984	Garfield The Snow Cat-E-6227 - J. Davis	2-Yr.	1985	12.00	35
1984	Peek-A-Bear Baby's First Christmas-E-6228	3-Yr.	1986	10.00	N/A
1984	Peek-A-Bear Baby's First Christmas-E-6229	3-Yr.	1986	9.00	N/A
1984	Owl Be Home For Christmas -E-6230	2-Yr.	1985	10.00	23
1984	Santa's Trolley-E-6231	3-Yr.	1986	11.00	50
1984	Holiday Penguin-E-6240	3-Yr.	1986	1.50	15-20
1984	Little Drummer-E-6241	5-Yr.	1988	2.00	N/A
1984	Happy Holidays-E-6248	2-Yr.	1985	2.00	N/A
1984	Christmas Nest-E-6249	2-Yr.	1985	3.00	25
1984	Bunny's Christmas Stocking -E-6251	Yr.Iss.	1984	2.00	15
1984	Santa On Ice-E-6252	3-Yr.	1986	2.50	25
1984	Treasured Memories The New Sled-E-6256	2-Yr.	1985	7.00	N/A
1984	Penguins On Ice-E-6280	2-Yr.	1985	7.50	N/A
1984	Up On The House Top-E-6281	6-Yr.	1989	9.00	N/A
1984	Grandchild's First Christmas 1984-E-6286	Yr.Iss.	1984	5.00	N/A
1984	Grandchild's First Christmas 1984-E-6286	Yr.Iss.	1984	5.00	N/A
1984	Godchild's First Christmas -E-6287	3-Yr.	1986	7.00	N/A
1984	Santa In The Box-E-6292	2-Yr.	1985	6.00	N/A
1984	Carousel Horse-E-6913	2-Yr.	1985	1.50	N/A
1983	Arctic Charmer-E-6945	2-Yr.	1984	7.00	N/A
1982	Victorian Sleigh-E-6946	4-Yr.	1985	9.00	15
1983	Wing-A-Ding Angel-E-6948	3-Yr.	1985	7.00	50
1982	A Saviour Is Born This Day -E-6949	8-Yr.	1989	4.00	18
1982	Crescent Santa-E-6950 - Gilmore	4-Yr.	1985	10.00	50
1982	Baby's First Christmas 1982 -E-6952	Yr.Iss.	1982	10.00	N/A
1982	Polar Bear Fun Whoops, It's 1982-E-6953	Yr.Iss.	1982	10.00	75
1982	Holiday Skier-E-6954 - J. Davis	5-Yr.	1986	7.00	N/A
1982	Toy Soldier 1982-E-6957	Yr.Iss.	1982	6.50	N/A
1982	Merry Christmas Grandma -E-6975	3-Yr.	1984	5.00	N/A
1982	Carousel Horses-E-6958	3-Yr.	1984	8.00	20-40
1982	Dear Santa-E-6959 - Gilmore	8-Yr.	1989	10.00	25
1982	Penguin Power-E-6977	2-Yr.	1983	6.00	15
1982	Bunny Winter Playground 1982-E-6978	Yr.Iss.	1982	10.00	N/A
1982	Baby's First Christmas 1982 -E-6979	Yr.Iss.	1982	10.00	N/A
1983	Carousel Horses-E-6980	4-Yr.	1986	8.00	N/A
1982	Grandchild's First Christmas 1982-E-6983	Yr.Iss.	1982	5.00	73
1982	Merry Christmas Teacher-E-6984	4-Yr.	1985	7.00	N/A
1983	Garfield Cuts The Ice-E-8771 - J. Davis	3-Yr.	1985	6.00	45
1984	A Stocking Full For 1984-E-8773 - J. Davis	Yr.Iss.	1984	6.00	N/A
1983	Stocking Full For 1983-E-8773 - J. Davis	Yr.Iss.	1983	6.00	N/A
1985	Santa Claus Balloon-55794	Yr.Iss.	1985	8.50	20
1985	Carousel Reindeer-55808	4-Yr.	1988	12.00	33
1985	Angel In Flight-55816	4-Yr.	1988	8.00	23
1985	Christmas Penguin-55824	4-Yr.	1988	7.50	43
1985	Merry Christmas Godchild-55832 - Gilmore	5-Yr.	1989	8.00	N/A
1985	Baby's First Christmas-55840	2-Yr.	1986	15.00	N/A
1985	Old Fashioned Rocking Horse-55859	2-Yr.	1986	10.00	15
1985	Child's Second Christmas-55867	5-Yr.	1989	11.00	N/A
1985	Fishing For Stars-55875	5-Yr.	1989	9.00	25
1985	Baby Blocks-55883	2-Yr.	1986	12.00	N/A
1985	Christmas Toy Chest-55891	5-Yr.	1989	10.00	N/A
1985	Grandchild's First Ornament-55921	5-Yr.	1989	7.00	30
1985	Joy Photo Frame-55956	Yr.Iss.	1985	6.00	N/A
1985	We Three Kings-55964	Yr.Iss.	1985	4.50	20
1985	The Night Before Christmas-55972	2-Yr.	1986	5.00	N/A
1985	Baby's First Christmas 1985-55980	Yr.Iss.	1985	6.00	N/A
1985	Baby Rattle Photo Frame-56006	2-Yr.	1986	5.00	N/A
1985	Baby's First Christmas 1985 -56014 - Gilmore	Yr.Iss.	1985	10.00	N/A
1985	Christmas Plane Ride-56049 - L. Rigg	6-Yr.	1990	10.00	N/A
1985	Scottie Celebrating Christmas -56065	5-Yr.	1989	7.50	25
1985	North Pole Native-56073	2-Yr.	1986	9.00	N/A
1985	Skating Walrus-56081	2-Yr.	1986	9.00	20
1985	Ski Time-56111 - J. Davis	Yr.Iss.	1985	13.00	N/A
1985	North Pole Express-56138 - J. Davis	Yr.Iss.	1985	12.00	N/A
1985	Merry Christmas Mother-56146 - J. Davis	Yr.Iss.	1985	8.50	N/A
1985	Hoppy Christmas-56154 - J. Davis	Yr.Iss.	1985	8.50	N/A
1985	Merry Christmas Teacher-56170 - J. Davis	Yr.Iss.	1985	6.00	N/A
1985	Garfield-In-The-Box-56189 - J. Davis	Yr.Iss.	1985	6.50	25
1985	Merry Christmas Grandma -56197	Yr.Iss.	1985	7.00	N/A
1985	Christmas Lights-56200	2-Yr.	1986	8.00	N/A
1985	Victorian Doll House-56251	Yr.Iss.	1985	13.00	40
1985	Tobaoggan Ride-56286	4-Yr.	1988	6.00	15
1985	Look Out Below-56375	Yr.Iss.	1985	8.50	40
1985	Flying Santa Christmas Special -56383	2-Yr.	1986	10.00	N/A
1985	Sawin Elf Helper-56391	Yr.Iss.	1985	8.00	N/A
1985	Snow Shoe-In Santa-56405	Yr.Iss.	1985	8.00	50
1985	Our Hero-56413	Yr.Iss.	1985	5.50	N/A
1985	Not A Creature Was Stirring -56421	2-Yr.	1986	4.00	N/A
1985	Merry Christmas Teacher-56448	Yr.Iss.	1985	9.00	N/A
1985	A Stocking Full For 1985-56464 - J. Davis	Yr.Iss.	1985	6.00	25
1985	St. Nicholas Circa 1910-56659	5-Yr.	1989	6.00	15
1985	Christmas Tree Photo Frame-56871	4-Yr.	1988	10.00	N/A
1988	Making A Point-489212 - G.G. Santiago	3-Yr.	1990	10.00	N/A
1988	Mouse Upon A Pipe-489220 - G.G. Santiago	2-Yr.	1989	10.00	12
1988	North Pole Deadline-489387	3-Yr.	1990	13.50	25
1988	Christmas Pin-Up-489409	2-Yr.	1989	11.00	30
1988	Airmail For Teacher-489425 - Gilmore	3-Yr.	1990	13.50	N/A
1986	1st Christmas Together 1986 -551171	Yr.Iss.	1986	9.00	15-35
1986	Elf Stringing Popcorn-551198	4-Yr.	1989	10.00	20-30
1986	Christmas Scottie-551201	4-Yr.	1989	7.00	15-30
1986	Santa and Child-551236	4-Yr.	1989	13.50	25-50
1986	The Christmas Angel-551244	4-Yr.	1989	22.50	75
1986	Carousel Unicorn-551252 - Gilmore	4-Yr.	1989	12.00	38
1986	Have a Heavenly Holiday -551260	4-Yr.	1989	9.00	N/A
1986	Siamese Kitten-551279	4-Yr.	1989	9.00	36
1986	Old Fashioned Doll House -551287	4-Yr.	1989	15.00	N/A
1986	Holiday Fisherman-551309	3-Yr.	1988	8.00	40
1986	Antique Toy-551317	3-Yr.	1988	9.00	N/A
1986	Time For Christmas-551325 - Gilmore	4-Yr.	1989	13.00	N/A
1986	Christmas Calendar-551333	2-Yr.	1987	7.00	N/A
1986	Merry Christmas-551341 - Gilmore	3-Yr.	1988	8.00	98
1986	The Santa Claus Shoppe Circa 1905-551562 - J. Grossman	4-Yr.	1989	8.00	15
1986	Baby Bear Sleigh-551651 - Gilmore	3-Yr.	1988	9.00	30
1986	Baby's First Christmas 1986 -551678 - Gilmore	Yr.Iss.	1986	10.00	20
1986	First Christmas Together-551708	3-Yr.	1988	6.00	10
1986	Baby's First Christmas-551716	3-Yr.	1988	5.50	10
1986	Baby's First Christmas 1986 -551724	Yr.Iss.	1986	6.50	30
1986	Peek-A-Bear Grandchild's First Christmas	Yr.Iss.	1986	6.00	23
1986	Peek-A-Bear Present-552089	4-Yr.	1989	2.50	N/A
1986	Peek-A-Bear Present-552089	4-Yr.	1989	2.50	N/A
1986	Peek-A-Bear Present-552089	4-Yr.	1989	2.50	N/A
1986	Peek-A-Bear Present-552089	4-Yr.	1989	2.50	N/A
1986	Merry Christmas 1986-552186 - L. Rigg	Yr.Iss.	1986	8.00	N/A
1986	Merry Christmas 1986-552534 - L. Rigg	Yr.Iss.	1986	8.00	N/A
1986	Lucy & Me Christmas Tree-552542 - L. Rigg	3-Yr.	1988	7.00	25
1986	Santa's Helpers-552607	3-Yr.	1988	2.50	N/A
1986	My Special Friend-552615	3-Yr.	1988	6.00	N/A
1986	Christmas Wishes From Panda-552623	3-Yr.	1988	6.00	N/A
1986	Lucy & Me Ski Time-552658 - L. Rigg	2-Yr.	1987	6.50	30
1986	Merry Christmas Teacher-552666	3-Yr.	1988	6.50	N/A
1986	Country Cousins Merry Christmas, Mom	3-Yr.	1988	7.00	23
1986	Country Cousins Merry Christmas, Dad	3-Yr.	1988	7.00	23
1986	Country Cousins Merry Christmas, Mom-552712	4-Yr.	1989	7.00	23
1986	Country Cousins Merry Christmas, Dad-552712	4-Yr.	1989	7.00	25
1986	Grandmother's Little Angel -552747	4-Yr.	1989	8.00	N/A
1987	Puppy's 1st Christmas-552909	2-Yr.	1988	4.00	N/A
1987	Kitty's 1st Christmas-552917	2-Yr.	1988	4.00	25
1987	Merry Christmas Puppy-552925	2-Yr.	1988	3.50	N/A
1987	Merry Christmas Kitty-552933	2-Yr.	1988	3.50	N/A
1986	I Love My Grandparents-553263	Yr.Iss.	1986	6.00	N/A
1986	Merry Christmas Mom & Dad -553271	Yr.Iss.	1986	6.00	N/A
1986	S. Claus Hollycopter-553344	4-Yr.	1989	13.50	35
1986	From Our House To Your House -553360	3-Yr.	1988	15.00	40
1986	Christmas Rattle-553379	3-Yr.	1988	8.00	35
1986	Bah, Humbug!-553387	4-Yr.	1989	9.00	N/A
1986	God Bless Us Everyone-553395	4-Yr.	1989	10.00	15
1987	Carousel Mobile-553409	3-Yr.	1989	15.00	50
1986	Holiday Train-553417	4-Yr.	1989	10.00	N/A
1986	Lighten Up!-553603 - J. Davis	5-Yr.	1990	10.00	N/A
1986	Gift Wrap Odie-553611 - J. Davis	Yr.Iss.	1986	7.00	20
1986	Merry Christmas-553646	4-Yr.	1989	8.00	N/A
1987	M.V.B. (Most Valuable Bear) -554219	2-Yr.	1988	3.00	N/A
1987	M.V.B. (Most Valuable Bear) -554219	2-Yr.	1988	3.00	N/A
1987	M.V.B. (Most Valuable Bear) -554219	2-Yr.	1988	3.00	N/A
1987	M.V.B. (Most Valuable Bear) -554219	2-Yr.	1988	3.00	N/A
1988	1st Christmas Together-554537 - Gilmore	3-Yr.	1990	15.00	N/A
1988	An Eye On Christmas-554545 - Gilmore	3-Yr.	1990	22.50	60
1988	A Mouse Check-554553 - Gilmore	3-Yr.	1990	13.50	45
1988	Merry Christmas Engine-554561	2-Yr.	1989	22.50	35
1989	Sardine Express-554588 - Gilmore	2-Yr.	1990	17.50	30
1988	1st Christmas Together 1988 -554596	Yr.Iss.	1988	10.00	N/A
1988	Forever Friends-554626 - Gilmore	2-Yr.	1989	12.00	27
1988	Santa's Survey-554642	2-Yr.	1989	35.00	75-100
1989	Old Town's Church-554871 - Gilmore	2-Yr.	1990	17.50	20
1988	A Chipmunk Holiday-554898 - Gilmore	3-Yr.	1990	11.00	25
1988	Christmas Is Coming-554901	3-Yr.	1990	12.00	12
1988	Baby's First Christmas 1988 -554928	Yr.Iss.	1988	7.50	N/A
1988	Baby's First Christmas 1988 -554936 - Gilmore	Yr.Iss.	1988	10.00	25
1988	The Christmas Train-554944	3-Yr.	1990	15.00	N/A
1988	Li'l Drummer Bear-554952 - Gilmore	3-Yr.	1990	12.00	12
1987	Baby's First Christmas-555061	3-Yr.	1989	12.00	N/A
1987	Baby's First Christmas-555088	3-Yr.	1989	7.50	N/A

*Quotes have been rounded up to nearest dollar

Collectors' Information Bureau

13

CHRISTMAS ORNAMENTS

YEAR ISSUE		EDITION LIMIT	YEAR RETD.	ISSUE PRICE	*QUOTE U.S.$
1987	Baby's First Christmas-555118	3-Yr.	1989	6.00	N/A
1987	Sugar Plum Bearies-555193	2-Yr.	1988	4.50	N/A
1987	Garfield Merry Kissmas-555215 - J. Davis	3-Yr.	1989	8.50	30
1987	Sleigh Away-555401	3-Yr.	1989	12.00	N/A
1987	Merry Christmas 1987-555428 - L. Rigg	Yr.Iss.	1987	8.00	N/A
1987	Merry Christmas 1987-555436 - L. Rigg	Yr.Iss.	1987	8.00	N/A
1987	Lucy & Me Storybook Bear-555444 - L. Rigg	3-Yr.	1989	6.50	N/A
1987	Time For Christmas-555452 - L. Rigg	3-Yr.	1989	12.00	20
1987	Lucy & Me Angel On A Cloud -555487 - L. Rigg	3-Yr.	1989	8.00	35
1987	Teddy's Stocking-555940 - Gilmore	3-Yr.	1989	10.00	N/A
1987	Kitty's Jack-In-The-Box-555959	3-Yr.	1989	11.00	30
1987	Merry Christmas Teacher -555967	3-Yr.	1989	7.50	N/A
1987	Mouse In A Mitten-555975	3-Yr.	1989	7.50	N/A
1987	Boy On A Rocking Horse-555983	3-Yr.	1989	12.00	18
1987	Peek-A-Bear Letter To Santa -555991	2-Yr.	1988	8.00	30
1987	Garfield Sugar Plum Fairy -556009 - J. Davis	3-Yr.	1989	8.50	20
1987	Garfield The Nutcracker-556017 - J. Davis	4-Yr.	1990	8.50	35
1987	Carousel Lion-556025 - Gilmore	3-Yr.	1989	12.00	25
1987	Home Sweet Home-556033 - Gilmore	3-Yr.	1989	15.00	40
1987	Baby's First Christmas-556041	4-Yr.	1990	10.00	20
1990	Deck The Halls-566063	3-Yr.	1992	12.50	N/A
1987	Little Sailor Elf-556068	3-Yr.	1989	10.00	28
1987	Carousel Goose-556076	3-Yr.	1989	17.00	40
1987	Night Caps-556084	2-Yr.	1988	5.50	N/A
1987	Night Caps-556084	2-Yr.	1988	5.50	N/A
1987	Night Caps-556084	2-Yr.	1988	5.50	N/A
1987	Night Caps-556084	2-Yr.	1988	5.50	N/A
1987	Rocking Horse Past Joys -556157	3-Yr.	1989	10.00	20
1987	Partridge In A Pear Tree -556173 - Gilmore	3-Yr.	1989	9.00	35
1987	Skating Santa 1987-556211	Yr.Iss.	1987	13.50	75
1987	Baby's First Christmas 1987 -556238 - Gilmore	Yr.Iss.	1987	10.00	25
1987	Baby's First Christmas 1987 -556254	Yr.Iss.	1987	7.00	25
1987	Teddy's Suspenders-556262	4-Yr.	1990	8.50	22
1987	Baby's First Christmas 1987 -556297	Yr.Iss.	1987	2.00	N/A
1987	Baby's First Christmas 1987 -556297	Yr.Iss.	1987	2.00	N/A
1987	Beary Christmas Family-556300	2-Yr.	1988	2.00	N/A
1987	Beary Christmas Family-556300	2-Yr.	1988	2.00	N/A
1987	Beary Christmas Family-556300	2-Yr.	1988	2.00	N/A
1987	Beary Christmas Family-556300	2-Yr.	1988	2.00	N/A
1987	Beary Christmas Family-556300	2-Yr.	1988	2.00	N/A
1987	Beary Christmas Family-556300	2-Yr.	1988	2.00	N/A
1987	Merry ChristmasTeacher-556319	2-Yr.	1988	2.00	N/A
1987	Merry ChristmasTeacher-556319	2-Yr.	1988	2.00	N/A
1987	Merry ChristmasTeacher-556319	2-Yr.	1988	2.00	N/A
1987	Merry ChristmasTeacher-556319	2-Yr.	1988	2.00	N/A
1987	1st ChristmasTogether 1987 -556335	Yr.Iss.	1987	9.00	18
1987	Country Cousins Katie Goes Ice Skating	3-Yr.	1989	8.00	30
1987	Country Cousins Scooter Snowman-556386	3-Yr.	1989	8.00	30
1987	Santa's List-556394	3-Yr.	1989	7.00	23
1987	Kitty's Bed-556408	3-Yr.	1989	12.00	30
1987	Grandchild's First Christmas -556416	3-Yr.	1989	10.00	N/A
1987	Two Turtledoves-556432 - Gilmore	3-Yr.	1989	9.00	30
1987	Three French Hens-556440 - Gilmore	3-Yr.	1989	9.00	30
1988	Four Calling Birds-556459 - Gilmore	3-Yr.	1990	11.00	30
1987	Teddy Takes A Spin-556467	4-Yr.	1990	13.00	35
1987	Tiny Toy Thimble Mobile-556475	2-Yr.	1988	12.00	35
1987	Bucket O'Love-556491	2-Yr.	1988	2.50	N/A
1987	Bucket O'Love-556491	2-Yr.	1988	2.50	N/A
1987	Puppy Love-556505	3-Yr.	1989	6.00	N/A
1987	Peek-A-Bear My Special Friend -556513	4-Yr.	1990	6.00	30
1987	Our First Christmas Together -556548	3-Yr.	1989	13.00	20
1987	Three Little Bears-556556	3-Yr.	1989	7.50	15
1987	Lucy & Me Mailbox Bear-556564 - L. Rigg	4-Yr.	1990	3.00	N/A
1987	Twinkle Bear-556572 - Gilmore	3-Yr.	1989	8.00	N/A
1987	I'm Dreaming Of A Bright Christmas-556602	2-Yr.	1988	2.50	N/A
1987	I'm Dreaming Of A Bright Christmas-556602	2-Yr.	1988	2.50	N/A
1987	Christmas Train-557196	3-Yr.	1989	10.00	N/A
1988	Dairy Christmas-557501 - M. Cook	2-Yr.	1989	10.00	30
1988	Merry Christmas 1988-557595 - L. Rigg	Yr.Iss.	1988	10.00	N/A
1988	Merry Christmas 1988-557609 - L. Rigg	Yr.Iss.	1988	10.00	N/A
1988	Toy Chest Keepsake-558206 - L. Rigg	3-Yr.	1990	12.50	30
1988	Teddy Bear Greetings-558214 - L. Rigg	3-Yr.	1990	8.00	30
1988	Jester Bear-558222 - L. Rigg	2-Yr.	1989	8.00	N/A
1988	Night-Watch Cat-558362 - J. Davis	3-Yr.	1990	13.00	35
1988	Christmas Thim-bell-558389	Yr.Iss.	1988	4.00	30
1988	Christmas Thim-bell-558389	Yr.Iss.	1988	4.00	N/A
1988	Christmas Thim-bell-558389	Yr.Iss.	1988	4.00	N/A
1988	Christmas Thim-bell-558389	Yr.Iss.	1988	4.00	N/A
1988	Baby's First Christmas-558397 - D. Parker	3-Yr.	1990	16.00	30
1988	Christmas Tradition-558400 - Gilmore	2-Yr.	1989	10.00	25
1988	Stocking Story-558419 - G.G. Santiago	3-Yr.	1990	10.00	23
1988	Winter Tale-558427 - G.G. Santiago	2-Yr.	1989	6.00	N/A
1988	Party Mouse-558435 - G.G. Santiago	3-Yr.	1990	12.00	30
1988	Christmas Watch-558443 - G.G. Santiago	2-Yr.	1989	11.00	32
1988	Christmas Vacation-558451 - G.G. Santiago	3-Yr.	1990	8.00	23
1988	Sweet Cherub-558478 - G.G. Santiago	3-Yr.	1990	7.00	8
1988	Time Out-558486 - G.G. Santiago	2-Yr.	1989	11.00	N/A
1988	The Ice Fairy-558516 - G.G. Santiago	3-Yr.	1990	23.00	45-55
1988	Santa Turtle-558559	2-Yr.	1989	10.00	35
1988	The Teddy Bear Ball-558567	3-Yr.	1990	10.00	25
1988	Turtle Greetings-558583	2-Yr.	1989	8.50	25
1988	Happy Howladays-558605	Yr.Iss.	1988	7.00	15
1988	Special Delivery-558699 - J. Davis	3-Yr.	1990	9.00	30
1988	Deer Garfield-558702 - J. Davis	3-Yr.	1990	12.00	30
1988	Garfield Bags O' Fun-558761 - J. Davis	Yr.Iss.	1988	3.30	N/A
1988	Gramophone Keepsake-558818	2-Yr.	1989	13.00	20
1988	North Pole Lineman-558834 - Gilmore	2-Yr.	1989	10.00	50
1988	Five Golden Rings-559121 - Gilmore	3-Yr.	1990	11.00	25
1988	Six Geese A-Laying-559148 - Gilmore	3-Yr.	1990	11.00	25
1988	Pretty Baby-559156 - R. Morehead	3-Yr.	1990	12.50	25
1988	Old Fashioned Angel-559164 - R. Morehead	3-Yr.	1990	12.50	20
1988	Two For Tea-559776 - Gilmore	3-Yr.	1990	20.00	35-40
1988	Merry Christmas Grandpa -560065	3-Yr.	1990	8.00	N/A
1990	Reeling In The Holidays-560405 - M. Cook	2-Yr.	1991	8.00	15
1991	Walkin' With My Baby-561029 - M. Cook	2-Yr.	1992	10.00	N/A
1989	Scrub-A-Dub Chipmunk-561037 - M. Cook	2-Yr.	1990	8.00	20
1989	Christmas Cook-Out-561045 - M. Cook	2-Yr.	1990	9.00	20
1989	Bunkie-561835 - S. Zimnicki	3-Yr.	1991	22.50	30
1989	Sparkles-561843 - S. Zimnicki	3-Yr.	1991	17.50	25-28
1992	Sparky & Buffer-561851 - S. Zimnicki	3-Yr.	1994	25.00	25
1989	Popper-561878 - S. Zimnicki	3-Yr.	1991	12.00	25
1989	Seven Swans A-Swimming -562742 - Gilmore	3-Yr.	1991	12.00	23
1989	Eight Maids A-Milking-562750 - Gilmore	3-Yr.	1991	12.00	23
1989	Nine Dancers Dancing-562769 - Gilmore	3-Yr.	1991	15.00	23
1989	Baby's First Christmas 1989 -562807	Yr.Iss.	1989	8.00	20
1989	Baby's First Christmas 1989 -562815 - Gilmore	Yr.Iss.	1989	10.00	N/A
1989	First Christmas Together 1989 -562823	Yr.Iss.	1989	11.00	N/A
1989	Travelin' Trike-562882 - Gilmore	3-Yr.	1991	15.00	15
1989	Victorian Sleigh Ride-562890	3-Yr.	1991	22.50	23
1991	Santa Delivers Love-562904 - Gilmore	2-Yr.	1992	17.50	18
1989	Chestnut Roastin'-562912 - Gilmore	2-Yr.	1990	13.00	13
1990	Th-Ink-In' Of You-562920 - Gilmore	2-Yr.	1991	20.00	30
1989	Ye Olde Puppet Show-562939	2-Yr.	1990	17.50	34
1989	Static In The Attic-562947	2-Yr.	1990	13.00	25
1989	Mistle-Toast 1989-562963 - Gilmore	Yr.Iss.	1989	15.00	25
1989	Merry Christmas Pops-562971 - Gilmore	3-Yr.	1991	12.00	12
1990	North Pole Or Bust-562998 - Gilmore	2-Yr.	1991	25.00	25
1989	By The Light Of The Moon -563005 - Gilmore	3-Yr.	1991	12.00	24
1989	Stickin' To It-563013 - Gilmore	2-Yr.	1990	10.00	12
1989	Christmas Cookin'-563048 - Gilmore	3-Yr.	1991	22.50	25
1989	All Set For Santa-563080 -Gilmore	3-Yr.	1991	17.50	25
1990	Santa's Sweets-563196 - Gilmore	2-Yr.	1991	20.00	20
1990	Purr-Fect Pals-563218	2-Yr.	1991	8.00	8
1989	The Pause That Refreshes -563226	3-Yr.	1991	15.00	75-100
1989	Ho-Ho Holiday Scrooge-563234 - J. Davis	3-Yr.	1991	13.50	30
1989	God Bless Us Everyone-563242 - J. Davis	3-Yr.	1991	13.50	30
1989	Scrooge With The Spirit-563250 - J. Davis	3-Yr.	1991	13.50	30
1989	A Chains Of Pace For Odie -563269 - J. Davis	3-Yr.	1991	12.00	25
1990	Jingle Bell Rock 1990-563390 - G. Armgardt	Yr.Iss.	1990	13.50	30
1989	Joy Ridin'-563463 - J. Davis	2-Yr.	1990	15.00	30
1989	Just What I Wanted-563668 - M. Peters	3-Yr.	1991	13.50	14
1990	Pucker Up!-563676 - M. Peters	3-Yr.	1992	11.00	11
1989	What's The Bright Idea-563684 - M. Peters	3-Yr.	1991	13.50	14
1990	Fleas Navidad-563978 - M. Peters	3-Yr.	1992	13.50	25
1990	Tweet Greetings-564044 - J. Davis	2-Yr.	1991	15.00	30
1990	Trouble On 3 Wheels-564052 - J. Davis	3-Yr.	1992	20.00	35
1989	Mine, All Mine!-564079 - J. Davis	Yr.Iss.	1989	15.00	40
1989	Star of Stars-564389 - J. Jonik	3-Yr.	1991	9.00	15
1990	Hang Onto Your Hat-564397 - J. Jonik	3-Yr.	1992	8.00	15
1990	Fireplace Frolic-564435 - N. Teiber	2-Yr.	1991	25.00	32
1989	Hoe! Hoe! Hoe!-564761	Yr.Iss.	1989	20.00	35
1991	Double Scoop Snowmouse -564796 - M. Cook	3-Yr.	1993	13.50	14
1990	Christmas Is Magic-564826 - M. Cook	2-Yr.	1991	10.00	10
1990	Lighting Up Christmas-564834 - M. Cook	2-Yr.	1991	10.00	10
1989	Feliz Navidad! 1989-564842 - M. Cook	Yr.Iss.	1989	11.00	40
1989	Spreading Christmas Joy -564850 - M. Cook	3-Yr.	1991	10.00	10
1989	Yuletide Tree House-564915 - J. Jonik	3-Yr.	1991	20.00	20
1990	Brewing Warm Wishes-564974	2-Yr.	1991	10.00	10
1990	Yippie-I-Yuletide-564982 - Hahn	3-Yr.	1992	15.00	15
1990	Coffee Break-564990 - Hahn	3-Yr.	1992	15.00	15
1990	You're Sew Special-565008 - Hahn	Yr.Iss.	1990	20.00	35
1989	Full House Mouse-565016 - Hahn	2-Yr.	1990	13.50	25
1989	I Feel Pretty-565024 - Hahn	3-Yr.	1991	20.00	30
1990	Warmest Wishes-565032 - Hahn	3-Yr.	1992	15.00	15
1990	Baby's Christmas Feast-565040 - Hahn	3-Yr.	1992	13.50	14
1990	Bumper Car Santa-565083 - G.G. Santiago	Yr.Iss.	1990	20.00	40
1989	Special Delivery (Proof Ed.) -565091 - G.G. Santiago	Yr.Iss.	1989	12.00	15
1990	Ho! Ho! Yo-Yo! (Proof Ed.) -565105 - G.G. Santiago	Yr.Iss.	1990	12.00	15
1989	Weightin' For Santa-565148 - G.G. Santiago	3-Yr.	1991	7.50	8
1989	Holly Fairy-565199 - C.M. Baker	Yr.Iss.	1989	15.00	45
1990	The Christmas Tree Fairy -565202 - C.M. Baker	Yr.Iss.	1990	15.00	40
1989	Christmas 1989-565210 - L. Rigg	Yr.Iss.	1989	12.00	38
1989	Top Of The Class-565237 - L. Rigg	3-Yr.	1991	11.00	11
1989	Deck The Hogs-565490 - M. Cook	2-Yr.	1990	12.00	14
1989	Pinata Ridin'-565504 - M. Cook	2-Yr.	1990	11.00	N/A
1989	Hangin' In There 1989-565598 - K. Wise	Yr.Iss.	1989	10.00	20
1990	Meow-y Christmas 1990-565601 - K. Wise	Yr.Iss.	1990	10.00	25
1990	Seaman's Greetings-566047	2-Yr.	1991	11.00	24
1990	Hang In There-566055	3-Yr.	1992	13.50	14
1991	Pedal Pushin' Santa-566071	Yr.Iss.	1991	20.00	30
1990	Merry Christmas Teacher -566098	2-Yr.	1991	11.00	11
1990	Festive Flight-566101	2-Yr.	1991	11.00	11
1993	I'm Dreaming of a White-Out Christmas-566144	2-Yr.	1994	22.50	23
1990	Santa's Suitcase-566160	3-Yr.	1992	25.00	25
1989	The Purr-Fect Fit!-566462	3-Yr.	1991	15.00	35
1990	Tumbles 1990-566519 - S. Zimnicki	Yr.Iss.	1990	16.00	25
1990	Twiddles-566551 - S. Zimnicki	3-Yr.	1992	15.00	30
1991	Snuffy-566578 - S. Zimnicki	3-Yr.	1993	17.50	18
1990	All Aboard-567671 - Gilmore	2-Yr.	1991	17.50	18
1989	Gone With The Wind-567698	Yr.Iss.	1989	13.50	30
1989	Dorothy-567760	Yr.Iss.	1989	12.00	35
1989	The Tin Man-567779	Yr.Iss.	1989	12.00	25
1989	The Cowardly Lion-567787	Yr.Iss.	1989	12.00	25
1989	The Scarecrow-567795	Yr.Iss.	1989	12.00	25
1990	Happy Holiday Readings-568104	2-Yr.	1991	8.00	8
1989	Christmas 1989-568325 - L. Rigg	Yr.Iss.	1989	12.00	N/A
1991	Holiday Ahoy-568368	2-Yr.	1992	12.50	13
1991	Christmas Countdown-568376	3-Yr.	1993	20.00	20
1989	Clara-568406	Yr.Iss.	1989	12.50	20
1990	The Nutcracker-568414	Yr.Iss.	1990	12.50	30
1991	Clara's Prince-568422	Yr.Iss.	1991	12.50	18
1989	Santa's Little Reindear-568430	2-Yr.	1990	15.00	25
1991	Tuba Totin' Teddy-568449	3-Yr.	1993	15.00	15
1990	A Calling Home At Christmas -568457	2-Yr.	1991	15.00	15
1991	Love Is The Secret Ingredient-568562 - L. Rigg	2-Yr.	1992	15.00	1
1990	A Spoonful of Love-568570 - L. Rigg	2-Yr.	1991	10.00	1
1990	Christmas Swingtime 1990 -568597 - L. Rigg	Yr.Iss.	1990	13.00	N/A
1990	Christmas Swingtime 1990 -568600 - L. Rigg	Yr.Iss.	1990	13.00	N/A
1990	Bearing Holiday Wishes-568619 - L. Rigg	3-Yr.	1992	22.50	2
1992	Moonlight Swing-568627 - L. Rigg	3-Yr.	1994	15.00	1
1990	Smitch-570184 - S. Zimnicki	3-Yr.	1992	22.50	2
1992	Carver-570192 - S. Zimnicki	Yr.Iss.	1992	17.50	1
1991	Twinkle & Sprinkle-570206 - S. Zimnicki	3-Yr.	1993	22.50	2
1990	Blinkie-570214 - S. Zimnicki	3-Yr.	1992	15.00	1
1990	Have A Coke And A Smile™ -571512	3-Yr.	1992	15.00	2

*Quotes have been rounded up to nearest dollar

YEAR ISSUE		EDITION LIMIT	YEAR RETD.	ISSUE PRICE	*QUOTE U.S.$
1990	Fleece Navidad-571903 - M. Cook	2-Yr.	1991	13.50	25
1990	Have a Navaho-Ho-Ho 1990 -571970 - M. Cook	Yr.Iss.	1990	15.00	35
1990	Cheers 1990-572411 - T. Wilson	Yr.Iss.	1990	13.50	22
1990	A Night Before Christmas -572438 - T. Wilson	2-Yr.	1991	17.50	18
1990	Merry Kissmas-572446 - T. Wilson	2-Yr.	1991	10.00	30
1992	A Rockin' GARFIELD Christmas -572527 - J. Davis	2-Yr.	1993	17.50	18
1991	Here Comes Santa Paws -572535 - J. Davis	3-Yr.	1993	20.00	20
1990	Frosty Garfield 1990-572551 - J. Davis	Yr.Iss.	1990	13.50	35
1990	Pop Goes The Odie-572578 - J. Davis	2-Yr.	1991	15.00	30
1991	Sweet Beams-572586 - J. Davis	2-Yr.	1992	13.50	14
1990	An Apple A Day-572594 - J. Davis	2-Yr.	1991	12.00	12
1990	Dear Santa-572608 - J. Davis	3-Yr.	1992	17.00	17
1991	Have A Ball This Christmas -572616 - J. Davis	Yr.Iss.	1991	15.00	15
1990	Oh Shoosh!-572624 - J. Davis	3-Yr.	1992	17.00	17
1990	Little Red Riding Cat-572632 - J. Davis	Yr.Iss.	1990	13.50	33
1991	All Decked Out-572659 - J. Davis	2-Yr.	1992	13.50	14
1990	Over The Rooftops-572721 - J. Davis	2-Yr.	1991	17.50	28-35
1990	Garfield NFL Los Angeles Rams -572764 - J. Davis	2-Yr.	1991	12.50	13
1993	Born To Shop-572942	Yr.Iss.	1993	26.50	35
1990	Garfield NFL Cincinnati Bengals -573000 - J. Davis	2-Yr.	1991	12.50	13
1990	Garfield NFL Cleveland Browns -573019 - J. Davis	2-Yr.	1991	12.50	13
1990	Garfield NFL Houston Oilers -573027 - J. Davis	2-Yr.	1991	12.50	13
1990	Garfield NFL Pittsburg Steelers -573035 - J. Davis	2-Yr.	1991	12.50	13
1990	Garfield NFL Denver Broncos -573043 - J. Davis	2-Yr.	1991	12.50	13
1990	Garfield NFL Kansas City Chiefs -573051 - J. Davis	2-Yr.	1991	12.50	13
1990	Garfield NFL Los Angeles Raiders-573078 - J. Davis	2-Yr.	1991	12.50	13
1990	Garfield NFL San Diego Chargers-573086 - J. Davis	2-Yr.	1991	12.50	13
1990	Garfield NFL Seattle Seahawks -573094 - J. Davis	2-Yr.	1991	12.50	13
1990	Garfield NFL Buffalo Bills -573108 - J. Davis	2-Yr.	1991	12.50	13
1990	Garfield NFL Indianapolis Colts -573116 - J. Davis	2-Yr.	1991	12.50	13
1990	Garfield NFL Miami Dolphins -573124 - J. Davis	2-Yr.	1991	12.50	13
1990	Garfield NFL New England Patriots-573132 - J. Davis	2-Yr.	1991	12.50	13
1990	Garfield NFL New York Jets -573140 - J. Davis	2-Yr.	1991	12.50	13
1990	Garfield NFL Atlanta Falcons -573159 - J. Davis	2-Yr.	1991	12.50	13
1990	Garfield NFL New Orleans Saints-573167 - J. Davis	2-Yr.	1991	12.50	13
1990	Garfield NFL San Francisco 49ers-573175 - J. Davis	2-Yr.	1991	12.50	13
1990	Garfield NFL Dallas Cowboys-573183 - J. Davis	2-Yr.	1991	12.50	13
1990	Garfield NFL New York Giants -573191 - J. Davis	2-Yr.	1991	12.50	13
1990	Garfield NFL Philadelphia Eagles-573205 - J. Davis	2-Yr.	1991	12.50	13
1990	Garfield NFL Phoenix Cardinals -573213 - J. Davis	2-Yr.	1991	12.50	13
1990	Garfield NFL Washington Redskins-573221 - J. Davis	2-Yr.	1991	12.50	13
1990	Garfield NFL Chicago Bears -573248 - J. Davis	2-Yr.	1991	12.50	13
1990	Garfield NFL Detroit Lions -573256 - J. Davis	2-Yr.	1991	12.50	13
1990	Garfield NFL Green Bay Packers-573264 - J. Davis	2-Yr.	1991	12.50	13
1990	Garfield NFL Minnesota Vikings -573272 - J. Davis	2-Yr.	1991	12.50	13
1990	Garfield NFL Tampa Bay Buccaneers-573280 - J. Davis	2-Yr.	1991	12.50	13
1991	Tea For Two-573299 - Hahn	3-Yr.	1993	30.00	50
1991	Hot Stuff Santa-573523	Yr.Iss.	1991	25.00	30
1990	Merry Moustronauts-573558 - M. Cook	3-Yr.	1992	20.00	40
1991	Santa Wings It-573612 - J. Jonik	3-Yr.	1993	13.00	13
1990	All Eye Want For Christmas -573647 - Gilmore	3-Yr.	1992	27.50	32
1990	Stuck On You-573655 - Gilmore	2-Yr.	1991	12.50	13
1990	Professor Michael Bear, The One Bear Band-573663 - Gilmore	3-Yr.	1992	22.50	28
1990	A Caroling Wee Go-573671 - Gilmore	3-Yr.	1992	12.00	12
1990	Merry Mailman-573698 - Gilmore	2-Yr.	1991	15.00	30
1990	Deck The Halls-573701 - Gilmore	3-Yr.	1992	22.50	30
1992	Sundae Ride-583707	2-Yr.	1993	20.00	20
1990	You're Wheel Special-573728 - Gilmore	3-Yr.	1992	15.00	15
1991	Come Let Us Adore Him -573736 - Gilmore	2-Yr.	1992	9.00	9
1991	Moon Beam Dreams-573760 - Gilmore	3-Yr.	1993	12.00	12
1991	A Song For Santa-573779 - Gilmore	3-Yr.	1993	25.00	25
1990	Warmest Wishes-573825 - Gilmore	Yr.Iss.	1990	17.50	25
1991	Kurious Kitty-573868 - Gilmore	3-Yr.	1993	17.50	18
1990	Old Mother Mouse-573922 - Gilmore	2-Yr.	1991	17.50	20-32
1990	Railroad Repairs-573930 - Gilmore	2-Yr.	1991	12.50	25
1990	Ten Lords A-Leaping-573949 - Gilmore	3-Yr.	1992	15.00	25
1990	Eleven Drummers Drumming -573957 - Gilmore	3-Yr.	1992	15.00	25
1990	Twelve Pipers Piping-573965 - Gilmore	3-Yr.	1992	15.00	25
1990	Baby's First Christmas 1990 -573973 - Gilmore	Yr.Iss.	1990	10.00	N/A
1990	Baby's First Christmas 1990 -573981 - Gilmore	Yr.Iss.	1990	12.00	N/A
1991	Peter, Peter Pumpkin Eater -574015 - Gilmore	2-Yr.	1992	20.00	30
1992	The Nutcracker-574023 - Gilmore	3-Yr.	1994	25.00	25
1990	Little Jack Horner-574058 - Gilmore	2-Yr.	1991	17.50	35
1991	Mary, Mary Quite Contrary -574066 - Gilmore	2-Yr.	1992	22.50	33
1992	Humpty Dumpty-574244 - Gilmore	2-Yr.	1993	25.00	25
1991	Through The Years-574252 - Gilmore	Yr.Iss.	1991	17.50	18
1991	Holiday Wing Ding-574333	3-Yr.	1993	22.50	23
1991	North Pole Here I Come-574597	3-Yr.	1993	10.00	10
1991	Christmas Caboose-574856 - Gilmore	2-Yr.	1992	25.00	30
1990	Bubble Trouble-575038 - Hahn	3-Yr.	1992	20.00	35
1991	Merry Mother-To-Be-575046 - Hahn	3-Yr.	1993	13.50	14
1990	A Holiday 'Scent' Sation-575054 - Hahn	3-Yr.	1992	15.00	30
1990	Catch Of The Day-575070 - Hahn	3-Yr.	1992	25.00	25
1990	Don't Open 'Til Christmas -575089 - Hahn	3-Yr.	1992	17.50	18
1990	I Can't Weight 'Til Christmas -575119 - Hahn	3-Yr.	1992	16.50	30
1991	Deck The Halls-575127 - Hahn	2-Yr.	1992	15.00	25
1992	Music Mice-Trol-575143	2-Yr.	1993	12.00	12
1990	Mouse House-575186	3-Yr.	1992	16.00	16
1991	Dream A Little Dream-575593	2-Yr.	1992	17.50	18
1991	Christmas Two-gether-575615 - L. Rigg	3-Yr.	1993	22.50	23
1992	On Target Two-Gether-575623	Yr.Iss.	1992	17.00	17
1991	Christmas Trimmings-575631	2-Yr.	1992	17.00	17
1991	Gumball Wizard-575658 - Gilmore	2-Yr.	1992	13.00	13
1991	Crystal Ball Christmas-575666 - Gilmore	2-Yr.	1992	22.50	23
1990	Old King Cole-575682 - Gilmore	2-Yr.	1991	20.00	29
1991	Tom, Tom The Piper's Son -575690 - Gilmore	2-Yr.	1992	15.00	33
1992	Rock-A-Bye Baby-575704 - Gilmore	2-Yr.	1993	13.50	14
1992	Queen of Hearts-575712 - Gilmore	2-Yr.	1992	17.50	18
1993	Toy To The World-575763	2-Yr.	1994	25.00	25
1992	Tasty Tidings-575836 - L. Rigg	Yr.Iss.	1992	13.50	14
1991	Tire-d Little Bear-575852 - L. Rigg	Yr.Iss.	1991	12.50	13
1990	Baby Bear Christmas 1990 - 575860 - L. Rigg	Yr.Iss.	1990	12.00	28
1991	Crank Up The Carols-575887 - L. Rigg	2-Yr.	1992	17.50	18
1990	Beary Christmas 1990-576158 - L. Rigg	Yr.Iss.	1990	12.00	12
1991	Christmas Swingtime 1991 -576166 - L. Rigg	Yr.Iss.	1991	13.00	13
1991	Christmas Swingtime 1991 -576174 - L. Rigg	Yr.Iss.	1991	13.00	13
1991	Christmas Cutie-576182	3-Yr.	1993	13.50	14
1991	Meow Mates-576220	3-Yr.	1993	12.00	12
1991	Frosty The Snowmant-576425	3-Yr.	1993	15.00	15
1991	Ris-ski Business-576719 - T. Wilson	2-Yr.	1992	10.00	10
1991	Pinocchio-577391 - J. Davis	3-Yr.	1993	15.00	15
1990	Yuletide Ride 1990-577502 - Gilmore	Yr.Iss.	1990	13.50	50
1990	Tons of Toys-577510	Yr.Iss.	1990	13.00	30
1990	McHappy Holidays-577529	2-Yr.	1991	17.50	25
1990	Heading For Happy Holidays - 577537	3-Yr.	1992	17.50	18
1990	'Twas The Night Before Christmas-577545	3-Yr.	1992	17.50	18
1990	Over One Million Holiday Wishes!-577553	Yr.Iss.	1990	17.50	30
1990	You Malt My Heart-577596	2-Yr.	1991	25.00	25
1991	All I Want For Christmas-577618	2-Yr.	1992	20.00	20
1992	Bearly Sleepy-578029 - Gilmore	Yr.Iss.	1992	17.50	18
1992	Spreading Sweet Joy-580465	Yr.Iss.	1992	13.50	14
1991	Things Go Better With Coke™ -580597	3-Yr.	1993	17.00	25
1991	Christmas To Go-580600 - M. Cook	Yr.Iss.	1991	22.50	23
1991	Have A Mariachi Christmas -580619 - M. Cook	2-Yr.	1992	13.50	14
1993	Bearly Balanced-580724	Yr.Iss.	1993	15.00	15
1992	Ring My Bell-580740 - J. Davis	Yr.Iss.	1992	13.50	14
1992	4 x 4 Holiday Fun-580783 - J. Davis	2-Yr.	1993	20.00	20
1991	Christmas Is In The Air-581453	Yr.Iss.	1991	15.00	15
1991	Holiday Treats-581542	Yr.Iss.	1991	17.50	18
1991	Christmas Is My Goal-581550	2-Yr.	1992	17.50	18
1991	A Quarter Pounder With Cheerr -581569	3-Yr.	1993	20.00	20
1992	The Holidays Are A Hit-581577	2-Yr.	1993	17.50	18
1991	From The Same Mold-581798 - Gilmore	3-Yr.	1993	17.00	17
1991	The Glow Of Christmas-581801	2-Yr.	1992	20.00	20
1992	Tip Top Tidings-581828	2-Yr.	1993	13.00	13
1992	Christmas Lifts The Spirits -582018	2-Yr.	1993	25.00	25
1993	Joyeux Noel-582026	2-Yr.	1994	24.50	25
1992	A Pound Of Good Cheers -582034	2-Yr.	1993	17.50	18
1993	Holiday Mew-Sic-582107	2-Yr.	1994	20.00	20
1993	Santa's Magic Ride-582115	2-Yr.	1994	24.00	24
1993	Warm And Hearty Wishes -582344	Yr.Iss.	1993	17.50	18
1993	Cool Yule-582352	Yr.Iss.	1993	12.00	12
1993	Have A Holly Jell-O Christmas -582387	Yr.Iss.	1993	45.00	45
1993	Festive Firemen-582565 - Gilmore	2-Yr.	1994	17.00	17
1991	All Caught Up In Christmas -583537	2-Yr.	1992	10.00	10
1991	Lights..Camera..Kissmas!-583626 - Gilmore	Yr.Iss.	1991	15.00	35
1991	Sweet Steed-583634 - Gilmore	3-Yr.	1993	15.00	15
1992	Sweet as Cane Be-583642 - Gilmore	3-Yr.	1994	15.00	15
1991	Dreamin' Of A White Christmas -583669 - Gilmore	2-Yr.	1992	15.00	15
1991	Merry Millimeters-583677 - Gilmore	3-Yr.	1993	17.00	17
1991	Here's The Scoop-583693	2-Yr.	1992	13.50	20
1991	Happy Mealr On Wheels-583715	3-Yr.	1993	22.50	23
1991	Christmas Kayak-583723	2-Yr.	1992	13.50	14
1993	Light Up Your Holidays With Coke-583758	Yr.Iss.	1993	27.50	28
1992	The Cold, Crisp Taste Of Coke -583766	3-Yr.	1994	17.00	17
1991	Marilyn Monroe-583774	Yr.Iss.	1991	20.00	20
1992	Sew Christmasy-583820	3-Yr.	1994	25.00	25
1991	A Christmas Carol-583928 - Gilmore	3-Yr.	1993	22.50	23
1991	Checking It Twice-583936	2-Yr.	1992	25.00	25
1992	Catch A Falling Star-583944 - Gilmore	2-Yr.	1993	15.00	15
1992	Swingin' Christmas-584096	2-Yr.	1993	15.00	15
1993	Pool Hall-idays-584851	2-Yr.	1994	19.90	20
1992	Mc Ho, Ho, Ho-585181	3-Yr.	1994	22.50	23
1991	Merry Christmas Go-Round -585203 - J. Davis	3-Yr.	1993	20.00	20
1992	Holiday On Ice-585254 - J. Davis	3-Yr.	1994	17.50	18
1991	Holiday Hideout-585270 - J. Davis	2-Yr.	1992	15.00	15
1992	Fast Track Cat-585289 - J. Davis	3-Yr.	1994	17.50	18
1992	Holiday Cat Napping-585319 - J. Davis	2-Yr.	1993	20.00	20
1993	Bah Humbug-585394 - Davis	Yr.Iss.	1993	15.00	15
1992	The Finishing Touches-585610 - T. Wilson	2-Yr.	1993	17.50	18
1992	Jolly Ol' Gent-585645 - J. Jonik	3-Yr.	1994	13.50	14
1991	Our Most Precious Gift-585726	Yr.Iss.	1991	17.50	18
1991	Christmas Cheer-585769	2-Yr.	1992	13.50	14
1993	Chimer-585777 - Zimnicki	Yr.Iss.	1993	25.00	25
1993	Sweet Whiskered Wishes -585807	Yr.Iss.	1993	17.00	17
1993	Grade "A" Wishes From Garfield -585823 - Davis	2-Yr.	1994	20.00	20
1993	Baby's First Christmas 1993- 585823 - Gilmore	Yr.Iss.	1993	17.50	18
1992	A Child's Christmas-586358	3-Yr.	1994	25.00	25
1992	Festive Fiddlers-586501	Yr.Iss.	1992	20.00	25
1992	La Luminaria-586579 - M. Cook	2-Yr.	1993	13.50	14
1991	Fired Up For Christmas-586587 - Gilmore	2-Yr.	1992	32.50	33
1991	One Foggy Christmas Eve -586625 - Gilmore	3-Yr.	1993	30.00	30
1991	For A Purr-fect Mom-586641 - Gilmore	Yr.Iss.	1991	12.00	12
1991	For A Special Dad-586668 - Gilmore	Yr.Iss.	1991	17.50	18
1991	With Love-586676 - Gilmore	Yr.Iss.	1991	13.00	13
1991	For A Purr-fect Aunt-586692 - Gilmore	Yr.Iss.	1991	12.00	12
1991	For A Dog-Gone Great Uncle -586706 - Gilmore	Yr.Iss.	1991	12.00	12
1991	Peddling Fun-586714 - Gilmore	Yr.Iss.	1991	16.00	16
1991	Special Keepsakes-586722 - Gilmore	Yr.Iss.	1991	13.50	14
1992	Cozy Chrismas Carriage -586730 - Gilmore	2-Yr.	1993	22.50	23
1992	Small Fry's First Christmas - 586749	2-Yr.	1993	17.00	17
1991	Hats Off To Christmas-586757 - Hahn	Yr.Iss.	1991	22.50	23
1992	Friendships Preserved-586765 - Hahn	Yr.Iss.	1992	22.50	23
1993	Tree For Two-586781 - Gilmore	2-Yr.	1994	17.50	18
1993	A Bright Idea-586803 - Gilmore	2-Yr.	1994	22.50	23
1992	Window Wish List-586854 - Gilmore	2-Yr.	1993	30.00	30
1992	Through The Years-586862 - Gilmore	Yr.Iss.	1992	17.50	18
1993	My Special Christmas-586900 - Gilmore	Yr.Iss.	1993	17.50	18
1991	Baby's First Christmas 1991 -586935	Yr.Iss.	1991	12.50	13
1992	Baby's First Christmas 1992 -586943	Yr.Iss.	1992	12.50	13
1992	Firehouse Friends-586951 - Gilmore	Yr.Iss.	1992	22.50	23
1992	Bubble Buddy-586978 - Gilmore	2-Yr	1993	13.50	14

*Quotes have been rounded up to nearest dollar

CHRISTMAS ORNAMENTS

YEAR ISSUE		EDITION LIMIT	YEAR RETD.	ISSUE PRICE	*QUOTE U.S.$
1992	The Warmth Of The Season -586994	2-Yr.	1993	20.00	20
1993	Baby's First Christmas Dinner -587001	Yr.Iss.	1993	12.00	12
1991	Jugglin' The Holidays-587028	2-Yr.	1992	13.00	13
1991	Santa's Steed-587044	Yr.Iss.	1991	15.00	15
1991	A Decade of Treasures-587052 - Gilmore	Yr.Iss.	1991	37.50	75
1992	It's A Go For Christmas-587095 - Gilmore	2-Yr.	1993	15.00	15
1991	Mr. Mailmouse-587109 - Gilmore	2-Yr.	1992	17.00	17
1992	Post-Mouster General-587117 - Gilmore	2-Yr.	1993	20.00	20
1992	To A Deer Baby-587168	Yr.Iss.	1992	18.50	19
1991	Starry Eyed Santa-587176	2-Yr.	1992	15.00	15
1992	Moon Watch-587184	2-Yr.	1993	20.00	20
1992	Guten Cheers-587192	Yr.Iss.	1992	22.50	23
1992	Put On A Happy Face-588237	2-Yr.	1993	15.00	15
1992	Beginning To Look A Lot Like Christmas-588253	2-Yr.	1993	15.00	15
1992	A Christmas Toast-588261	2-Yr.	1993	20.00	20
1992	Merry Mistle-Toad-588288	2-Yr.	1993	15.00	15
1992	Tic-Tac-Mistle-Toe-588296	3-Yr.	1994	23.00	23
1993	A Pause For Claus-588318	2-Yr.	1994	22.50	23
1992	Heaven Sent-588423 - J. Penchoff	2-Yr.	1993	12.50	13
1992	Holiday Happenings-588555 - Gilmore	3-Yr.	1994	30.00	30
1992	Seed-son's Greetings-588571 - Gilmore	3-Yr.	1994	27.00	27
1992	Santa's Midnight Snack-588598 - Gilmore	2-Yr.	1993	20.00	20
1992	Trunk Of Treasures-588636	Yr.Iss.	1992	30.00	30
1993	Terrific Toys-588644	Yr.Iss.	1993	20.00	20
1993	Christmas Dancer-588652	Yr.Iss.	1993	15.00	15
1993	Not A Creature Was Stirring... -588663 - Gilmore	2-Yr.	1994	27.50	28
1991	Lighting The Way-588776	2-Yr.	1992	20.00	20
1991	Rudolph-588784	2-Yr.	1992	17.50	18
1992	Festive Newsflash-588792	2-Yr.	1993	17.50	18
1992	A-B-C-Son's Greetings-588806	2-Yr.	1993	16.50	17
1992	Hoppy Holidays-588814	Yr.Iss.	1992	13.50	14
1992	Fireside Friends-588830	2-Yr.	1993	20.00	20
1992	Christmas Eve-mergency -588849	2-Yr.	1993	27.00	27
1992	A Sure Sign Of Christmas -588857	2-Yr.	1993	22.50	23
1992	Holidays Give Me A Lift-588865	2-Yr.	1993	30.00	30
1992	Yule Tide Together-588903	2-Yr.	1993	20.00	20
1992	Have A Soup-er Christmas -588911	2-Yr.	1993	17.50	18
1992	Christmas Cure-Alls-588938	2-Yr.	1993	20.00	20
1993	Countin' On A Merry Christmas -588954	2-Yr.	1994	22.50	23
1993	To My Gem-589004	Yr.Iss.	1993	27.50	28
1993	Christmas Mall Call-589012	2-Yr.	1994	20.00	20
1993	Spreading Joy-589047	2-Yr.	1994	27.50	28
1993	Pitter-Patter Post Office-589055	2-Yr.	1994	20.00	20
1993	Happy Haul-idays-589098	2-Yr.	1994	30.00	30
1993	Hot Off ThePress-589292	2-Yr.	1994	27.50	28
1993	Designed With You In Mind -589306	2-Yr.	1994	16.00	16
1992	Dial 'S' For Santa-589373	2-Yr.	1993	25.00	25
1993	Seeing Is Believing-589381 - Gilmore	2-Yr.	1994	20.00	20
1992	Joy To The Whirled-589551 - Hahn	2-Yr.	1993	20.00	20
1992	Merry Make-Over-589586 - Hahn	3-Yr.	1994	20.00	20
1992	Campin' Companions-590282 - Hahn	3-Yr.	1994	20.00	20
1992	Fur-Ever Friends-590797 - Gilmore	2-Yr.	1993	13.50	14
1993	Roundin' Up Christmas Together-590800	Yr.Iss.	1993	25.00	25
1992	Tee-rific Holidays-590827	3-Yr.	1994	25.00	25
1992	Spinning Christmas Dreams -590908 - Hahn	3-Yr.	1994	22.50	23
1992	Christmas Trimmin'-590932	3-Yr.	1994	17.00	17
1993	Toasty Tidings-590940	2-Yr.	1994	20.00	20
1993	Focusing On Christmas-590983 - Gilmore	2-Yr.	1994	27.50	28
1993	Dunk The Halls-591009	2-Yr.	1994	18.50	19
1993	Mice Capades-591386 - Hahn	2-Yr.	1994	26.50	27
1993	25 Points For Christmas-591750	Yr.Iss.	1993	25.00	25
1993	Carving Christmas Wishes-592625 - Gilmore	2-Yr.	1994	25.00	25
1993	Celebrating With A Splash -592692	Yr.Iss.	1993	17.00	17
1993	Slimmin' Santa-592722	Yr.Iss.	1993	18.50	24
1993	Plane Ol' Holiday Fun-592773	Yr.Iss.	1993	27.50	28
1992	Wrappin' Up Warm Wishes -593141	Yr.Iss.	1992	17.50	18
1992	Christmas Biz-593168	2-Yr.	1993	22.50	23
1993	Smooth Move, Mom-593176	Yr.Iss.	1993	20.00	20
1993	Tool TIme, Yule TIme-593192	Yr.Iss.	1993	18.50	19
1993	Speedy-593370 - Zimnicki	2-Yr.	1994	25.00	25
1992	Holiday Take-Out-593508	Yr.Iss.	1992	17.50	18
1992	A Christmas Yarn-593516 - Gilmore	Yr.Iss.	1992	20.00	20
1993	On Your Mark, Set, Is That To Go?-593524	Yr.Iss.	1993	13.50	14
1993	Do Not Open 'Til Christmas -593737 - Hahn	2-Yr.	1994	15.00	15
1993	Greetings In Stereo-593745 - Hahn	Yr.Iss.	1993	19.50	20
1992	Treasure The Earth-593826 - Hahn	2-Yr.	1993	25.00	25
1993	Tangled Up For Christmas -593974	2-Yr.	1994	14.50	15

YEAR ISSUE		EDITION LIMIT	YEAR RETD.	ISSUE PRICE	*QUOTE U.S.$
1992	Toyful' Rudolph-593982	2-Yr.	1993	22.50	23
1992	Take A Chance On The Holidays-594075	3-Yr.	1994	20.00	20
1993	Sweet Season's Eatings-594202	Yr.Iss.	1993	22.50	23
1993	Have A Darn Good Christmas -594229 - Gilmore	2-Yr.	1994	21.00	21
1993	The Sweetest Ride-594253 - Gilmore	2-Yr.	1994	18.50	19
1992	Lights..Camera..Christmas! -594369	3-Yr.	1994	20.00	20
1993	Lights...Camera...Christmas -594369	Yr.Iss.	1993	20.00	20
1992	Spirited Stallion-594407	Yr.Iss.	1992	15.00	15
1993	Have A Cheery Christmas, Sister-594687	Yr.Iss.	1993	13.50	14
1993	Say Cheese-594962 - Gilmore	2-Yr.	1994	13.50	14
1993	Christmas Kicks-594989	Yr.Iss.	1993	17.50	18
1993	Time For Santa-594997 - Gilmore	2-Yr.	1994	17.50	18
1993	Holiday Orders-595004	Yr.Iss.	1993	20.00	20
1993	T'Was The Night Before Christmas-595012	Yr.Iss.	1993	22.50	23
1993	Sugar Chef Shoppe-595055 - Gilmore	2-Yr.	1994	23.50	24
1993	Merry Mc-Choo-Choo-595063	Yr.Iss.	1993	30.00	30
1993	Basketful Of Friendship-595098	Yr.Iss.	1993	20.00	20
1993	Rockin' With Santa-595195	2-Yr.	1994	13.50	14
1993	Christmas-To-Go-595217	Yr.Iss.	1993	25.50	26
1993	Sleddin' Mr. Snowman-595275	2-Yr.	1994	13.00	13
1993	A Kick Out Of Christmas-595373	2-Yr.	1994	10.00	10
1993	Friends Through Thick And Thin -595381	2-Yr.	1994	10.00	10
1993	See-Saw Sweethearts-595403	2-Yr.	1994	10.00	10
1993	Special Delivery For Santa -595411	2-Yr.	1994	10.00	10
1993	Top Marks For Teacher-595438	2-Yr.	1994	10.00	10
1993	Home Tweet Home-595446	2-Yr.	1994	10.00	10
1993	Clownin' Around-595454	2-Yr.	1994	10.00	10
1993	Heart Filled Dreams-595462	2-Yr.	1994	10.00	10
1993	Merry Christmas Baby-595470	2-Yr.	1994	10.00	10
1993	Your A Hit With Me, Brother -595535 - Hahn	Yr.Iss.	1993	10.00	10
1993	For A Sharp Uncle-595543	Yr.Iss.	1993	10.00	10
1993	Paint Your Holidays Bright- 595551 - Hahn	2-Yr.	1994	10.00	10
1992	A Watchful Eye-595713	Yr.Iss.	1992	15.00	15
1992	Good Catch-595721	Yr.Iss.	1992	12.50	13
1993	You Got To Treasure The Holidays, Man'-596051	Yr.Iss.	1993	22.50	23
1992	Squirrelin' It Away-595748 - Hahn	Yr.Iss.	1992	12.00	12
1992	Checkin' His List-595756	Yr.Iss.	1992	12.50	13
1992	Christmas Cat Nappin'	Yr.Iss.	1992	12.00	12
1992	Bless Our Home-595772	Yr.Iss.	1992	12.00	12
1992	Salute the Season-595780 - Hahn	Yr.Iss.	1992	12.00	12
1992	Fired Up For Christmas-595799	Yr.Iss.	1992	12.00	12
1992	Speedin' Mr. Snowman-595802 - M. Rhyner	Yr.Iss.	1992	12.00	12
1992	Merry Christmas Mother Earth -595810 - Hahn	Yr.Iss.	1992	11.00	11
1992	Wear The Season With A Smile -595829	Yr.Iss.	1992	10.00	10
1992	Jesus Loves Me-595837 - Hahn	Yr.Iss.	1992	10.00	10
1989	Bottom's Up 1989-830003	Yr.Iss.	1989	11.00	32
1990	Sweetest Greetings 1990- 830011 - Gilmore	Yr.Iss.	1990	10.00	27
1990	First Class Christmas-830038 - Gilmore	3-Yr.	1992	10.00	10
1989	Caught In The Act-830046 - Gilmore	3-Yr.	1991	12.50	13
1989	Readin' & Ridin'-830054 - Gilmore	3-Yr.	1991	13.50	34
1991	Beary Merry Mailman-830151 - L. Rigg	3-Yr.	1993	13.50	14
1990	Here's Looking at You!-830259 - Gilmore	2-Yr.	1991	17.50	18
1991	Stamper-830267 - S. Zimnicki	Yr.Iss.	1991	13.50	14
1991	Santa's Key Man-830461 - Gilmore	2-Yr.	1992	11.00	11
1991	Tie-dings Of Joy-830488 - Gilmore	Yr.Iss.	1991	12.00	12
1990	Have a Cool Yule-830496 - Gilmore	3-Yr.	1992	12.00	27
1990	Slots of Luck-830518 - Hahn	2-Yr.	1991	13.50	45-60
1991	Straight To Santa-830534 - J. Davis	2-Yr.	1992	13.50	14
1991	Letters To Santa-830925 - Gilmore	2-Yr.	1992	15.00	15
1991	Sneaking Santa's Snack-830933 - Gilmore	3-Yr.	1993	13.00	13
1991	Aiming For The Holidays -830941 - Gilmore	2-Yr.	1992	12.00	12
1991	Ode To Joy-830968 - Gilmore	3-Yr.	1993	10.00	10
1991	Fittin' Mittens-830976 - Gilmore	3-Yr.	1993	12.00	12
1992	Merry Kisses-831166	2-Yr.	1993	17.50	18
1992	Christmas Is In The Air-831174	2-Yr.	1993	25.00	25
1992	To The Point-831182	2-Yr.	1993	13.50	14
1992	Poppin' Hoppin' Holidays -831263 - Gilmore	Yr.Iss.	1992	25.00	25
1992	Tankful Tidings-831271 - Gilmore	2-Yr.	1993	30.00	30
1991	The Finishing Touch-831530 - Gilmore	Yr.Iss.	1991	10.00	10
1992	Ginger-Bred Greetings-831581 - Gilmore	Yr.Iss.	1992	12.00	12
1991	A Real Classic-831603 - Gilmore	Yr.Iss.	1991	10.00	10
1991	Christmas Fills The Air-831921 - Gilmore	3-Yr.	1993	12.00	12
1992	A Gold Star For Teacher -831948 - Gilmore	3-Yr.	1994	15.00	15

YEAR ISSUE		EDITION LIMIT	YEAR RETD.	ISSUE PRICE	*QUOTE U.S.$
1992	A Tall Order-832758 - Gilmore	3-Yr.	1994	12.00	12
1992	Candlelight Serenade-832766 - Gilmore	2-Yr.	1993	12.00	12
1992	Holiday Glow Puppet Show -832774 - Gilmore	3-Yr.	1994	15.00	15
1992	Christopher Columouse-832782 - Gilmore	Yr.Iss.	1992	12.00	12
1992	Cartin' Home Holiday Treats -832790	2-Yr.	1993	13.50	14
1992	Making Tracks To Santa-832804 - Gilmore	2-Yr.	1993	15.00	15
1992	Special Delivery-832812	2-Yr.	1993	12.00	12
1992	A Mug Full Of Love-832928 - Gilmore	Yr.Iss.	1992	13.50	14
1992	Have A Cool Christmas-832944 - Gilmore	Yr.Iss.	1992	13.50	14
1992	Knitten' Kittens-832952 - Gilmore	Yr.Iss.	1992	17.50	18
1992	Holiday Honors-833029 - Gilmore	Yr.Iss.	1992	15.00	15
1992	Christmas Nite Cap-834424 - Gilmore	3-Yr.	1994	13.50	14
1992	North Pole Peppermint Patro l-840157 - Gilmore	2-Yr.	1993	25.00	25
1992	A Boot-iful Christmas-840165 - Gilmore	Yr.Iss.	1992	20.00	20
1992	Watching For Santa-840432	2-Yr.	1993	25.00	25
1992	Special Delivery-840440	Yr.Iss.	1992	22.50	23
1991	Deck The Halls-860573 - M. Peters	3-Yr.	1993	12.00	12
1991	Bathing Beauty-860581 - Hahn	3-Yr.	1993	13.50	35
1993	Ariel's Under-The-Sea Tree -596078	Yr.Iss.	1993	20.00	20
1993	Here Comes Santa Claws -596086	Yr.Iss.	1993	22.50	35
1993	You're Tea-Lighting, Mom! -596094	Yr.Iss.	1993	17.50	18
1993	Hearts A Glow-596108	Yr.Iss.	1993	18.50	35
1993	Love's Sweet Dance-596116	Yr.Iss.	1993	25.00	25
1993	Holiday Wishes-596124	Yr.Iss.	1993	15.00	15
1993	Hangin Out For The Holidays -596132	Yr.Iss.	1993	15.00	35
1993	Magic Carpet Ride-596140	Yr.Iss.	1993	20.00	20
1993	Holiday Treasures-596159	Yr.Iss.	1993	18.50	35
1993	Happily Ever After-596167	Yr.Iss.	1993	22.50	23
1993	The Fairest Of Them All-596175	Yr.Iss.	1993	18.50	19
1993	December 25...Dear Diary -596809 - Hahn	2-Yr.	1994	10.00	10
1993	Wheel Merry Wishes-596930 - Hahn	2-Yr.	1994	15.00	15
1993	Good Grounds For Christmas -596957 - Hahn	Yr.Iss.	1993	24.50	25
1993	Ducking The Season's Rush -597597	Yr.Iss.	1993	17.50	18
1993	Here Comes Rudolph® 597686	2-Yr.	1994	17.50	18
1993	It's Beginning To Look A Lot Like Christmas-597694	Yr.Iss.	1993	22.50	23
1993	Christmas In The Making-597716	Yr.Iss.	1993	20.00	20
1993	Mickey's Holiday Treasure -597759	Yr.Iss.	1993	12.00	12
1993	Dream Wheels-597856	Yr.Iss.	1993	29.50	50-75
1993	All You Add Is Love-598429	Yr.Iss.	1993	18.50	19
1993	Goofy About Skiing-598631	Yr.Iss.	1993	22.50	23
1989	Tea For Two-693758 - N. Teiber	2-Yr.	1990	12.50	30
1990	Holiday Tea Toast-694770 - N. Teiber	2-Yr.	1991	13.50	14
1991	It's Tea-lightful-694789	2-Yr.	1992	13.50	14
1989	Tea Time-694797 - N. Teiber	2-Yr.	1990	12.50	30
1993	A Toast Ladled With Love - 830828 - Hahn	2-Yr.	1994	15.00	15
1993	Christmas Is In The Air-831174	2-Yr.	1994	25.00	35
1993	Delivered to The Nick In Time -831808 - Gilmore	2-Yr.	1994	13.50	14
1993	Sneaking A Peek-831840 - Gilmore	2-Yr.	1994	10.00	10
1993	Jewel Box Ballet-831859 - Hahn	2-Yr.	1994	20.00	20
1993	A Mistle-Tow-831867 - Gilmore	2-Yr.	1994	15.00	15
1993	Grandma's Liddle Griddle -832936 - Gilmore	Yr.Iss.	1993	10.00	10
1993	To A Grade "A" Teacher-833037 - Gilmore	2-Yr.	1994	10.00	10
1993	Have A Cool Christmas-834467 - Gilmore	2-Yr.	1994	10.00	10
1993	For A Star Aunt-834556 - Gilmore	Yr.Iss.	1993	12.00	12
1993	Watching For Santa-840432	2-Yr.	1994	25.00	30
1994	Sending You A Season's Greetings-550140 - Butcher	Yr.Iss.	1994	25.00	25
1994	Goofy Delivery-550639	Yr.Iss.	1994	22.50	23
1994	Happy Howl-idays-550647	Yr.Iss.	1994	22.50	23
1994	Christmas Crusin'-550655	Yr.Iss.	1994	22.50	23
1994	Holiday Honeys-550663	Yr.Iss.	1994	20.00	20
1994	May Your Holiday Be Brightened With Love-550698 - Butcher	Yr.Iss.	1994	15.00	15
1994	May All Your Wishes Come True-550701 - Butcher	Yr.Iss.	1994	20.00	20
1994	Baby's First Christmas-550728 - Butcher	Yr.Iss.	1994	20.00	20
1994	Baby's First Christmas-550736 - Butcher	Yr.Iss.	1994	20.00	20
1994	Our First Christmas Together -550744 - Butcher	Yr.Iss.	1994	25.00	25
1994	Drumming Up A Season Of Joy -550752 - Butcher	Yr.Iss.	1994	18.50	19
1994	Friendships Warm The Holidays -550760 - Butcher	Yr.Iss.	1994	20.00	20
1994	Dropping In For The Holidays -550779 - Butcher	Yr.Iss.	1994	20.00	20
1994	Ringing Up Holiday Wishes -550787 - Butcher	Yr.Iss.	1994	18.50	19
1994	A Child Is Born-550795 - Butcher	Yr.Iss.	1995	25.00	25
1994	Tis The Season To Go Shopping-550817 - Butcher	Yr.Iss.	1994	22.50	23

*Quotes have been rounded up to nearest dollar

YEAR ISSUE		EDITION LIMIT	YEAR RETD.	ISSUE PRICE	*QUOTE U.S.$
1994	The Way To A Mouse's Heart -550922	Yr.Iss.	1994	15.00	15
1994	Teed-Off Donald-550930	Yr.Iss.	1994	15.00	15
1994	Holiday Show-Stopper-550949	Yr.Iss.	1995	15.00	15
1994	Answering Christmas Wishes -551023	Yr.Iss.	1994	17.50	18
1994	Pure Christmas Pleasure-551066	Yr.Iss.	1995	20.00	20
1994	Good Tidings, Tidings, Tidings, Tidings-551333	Yr.Iss.	1995	20.00	20
1994	From Our House To Yours -551384 - Gilmore	Yr.Iss.	1994	25.00	25
1994	Sugar 'N' Spice For Someone Nice-551406 - Gilmore	Yr.Iss.	1994	30.00	30
1994	Picture Perfect Christmas -551465	Yr.Iss.	1994	15.00	15
1994	Toodles-551503 - Zimnicki	Yr.Iss.	1994	25.00	25
1994	A Bough For Belle!-551554	Yr.Iss.	1995	18.50	19
1994	Ariel's Christmas Surprise! -551570	Yr.Iss.	1994	20.00	20
1994	Merry Little Two-Step-551589	Yr.Iss.	1995	12.50	13
1994	Sweets For My Sweetie-551600	Yr.Iss.	1994	15.00	15
1994	Friends Are The Spice of Life - 551619 - Hahn	Yr.Iss.	1995	20.00	20
1994	Cool Cruise-551635	19,640	1994	20.00	20
1994	A Christmas Tail-551759	Yr.Iss.	1995	20.00	20
1994	Merry Mischief- 551767	Yr.Iss.	1994	15.00	15
1994	L'il Stocking Stuffer-551791	Yr.Iss.	1994	17.50	18
1994	Once Upon A Time-551805	Yr.Iss.	1994	15.00	15
1994	Wishing Upon A Star-551813	Yr.Iss.	1994	18.50	19
1994	A Real Boy For Christmas -551821	Yr.Iss.	1995	15.00	15
1994	Minnie's Holiday Treasure -552216	Yr.Iss.	1994	12.00	12
1994	Sweet Holidays-552259 - Butcher	Yr.Iss.	1994	11.00	11
1994	Special Delivery-561657	Yr.Iss.	1994	20.00	20
1994	Merry Miss Merry-564508 - Hahn	Yr.Iss.	1994	12.00	12
1994	Santa Delivers-564567	Yr.Iss.	1994	12.00	12
1994	Buttons 'N' Bow Boutique -578363 - Gilmore	Yr.Iss.	1995	22.50	23
1994	A Sign of Peace-581992	Yr.Iss.	1994	18.50	19
1994	Wishing You Well At Christmas -582050	Yr.Iss.	1994	25.00	25
1994	Ahoy Joy!-582085	Yr.Iss.	1994	20.00	20
1994	Santa...Phone Home-582166	Yr.Iss.	1994	25.00	25
1994	Christmas Swishes-582379	Yr.Iss.	1994	17.50	18
1994	The Latest Scoop From Santa -582395 - Gilmore	Yr.Iss.	1994	18.50	19
1994	Chimny Cheer-582409 - Gilmore	Yr.Iss.	1994	22.50	23
1994	Cozy Candlelight Dinner-582417 - Gilmore	Yr.Iss.	1994	25.00	25
1994	Fine Feathered Festivities -582425 - Gilmore	Yr.Iss.	1994	22.50	23
1994	Joy From Head To Hose -582433 - Gilmore	Yr.Iss.	1994	15.00	15
1994	Yuletide Yummies-584835 - Gilmore	Yr.Iss.	1994	20.00	20
1994	Merry Christmas Tool You, Dad -584886	Yr.Iss.	1994	22.50	23
1994	Exercising Good Taste-584967	Yr.Iss.	1994	17.50	18
1994	Holiday Chew-Chew-584983 - Gilmore	Yr.Iss.	1994	22.50	23
1994	Mine, Mine, Mine-585815 - Davis	Yr.Iss.	1994	20.00	20
1994	To The Sweetest Baby-588725 - Gilmore	Yr.Iss.	1994	18.50	19
1994	Rockin' Ranger-588970	Yr.Iss.	1994	25.00	25
1994	Peace On Earthworm-588989	Yr.Iss.	1994	20.00	20
1994	Good Things Crop Up At Christmas-589071	Yr.Iss.	1994	25.00	25
1994	Christmas Crossroads-589128	Yr.Iss.	1994	20.00	20
1994	Have A Ball At Christmas -590673	Yr.Iss.	1994	15.00	15
1994	Have A Totem-ly Terrific Christmas-590819	Yr.Iss.	1994	30.00	30
1994	Cocoa 'N' Kisses For Santa - 591939	Yr.Iss.	1995	22.50	23
1994	On The Road With Coke™ -592528	Yr.Iss.	1995	25.00	25
1994	What's Shakin' For Christmas -592668	Yr.Iss.	1994	18.50	19
1994	"A" For Santa-592676	Yr.Iss.	1994	17.50	18
1994	Christmas Fly-By-592714	Yr.Iss.	1994	15.00	15
1994	Santa...You're The Pops! -593761	Yr.Iss.	1994	22.50	23
1994	Purdy Packages, Pardner! -593834	Yr.Iss.	1994	20.00	20
1994	Handle With Care-593842	Yr.Iss.	1994	20.00	20
1994	To Coin A Phrase, Merry Christmas-593877	Yr.Iss.	1994	20.00	20
1994	Featured Presentation-593885	Yr.Iss.	1994	20.00	20
1994	Christmas Fishes From Santa Paws-593893	Yr.Iss.	1994	18.50	19
1994	Melted My Heart-594237 - Gilmore	Yr.Iss.	1994	15.00	15
1994	Finishing First-594342 - Gilmore	Yr.Iss.	1994	20.00	20
1994	Yule Fuel-594385	Yr.Iss.	1994	20.00	20
1994	Toy Tinker Topper-595047 - Gilmore	Yr.Iss.	1994	20.00	20
1994	Santa Claus Is Comin'-595209	Yr.Iss.	1994	20.00	20
1994	Seasoned With Love-595268	Yr.Iss.	1994	22.50	23
1994	Sweet Dreams-595489	Yr.Iss.	1994	12.50	13
1994	Peace On Earth-595497	Yr.Iss.	1994	12.50	13
1994	Christmas Two-gether-595500	Yr.Iss.	1994	12.50	13
1994	Santa's L'il Helper-595519	Yr.Iss.	1994	12.50	13
1994	Expecting Joy-595527 - Hahn	Yr.Iss.	1994	12.50	13
1994	Sweet Greetings-595578	Yr.Iss.	1994	12.50	13
1994	Ring In The Holidays-595586 - Hahn	Yr.Iss.	1994	12.50	13
1994	Grandmas Are Sew Special -595594	Yr.Iss.	1994	12.50	13
1994	Holiday Catch-595608 - Hahn	Yr.Iss.	1994	12.50	13
1994	Bubblin' with Joy-595616	Yr.Iss.	1994	12.50	13
1994	Good Friends Are Forever -595950 - Gilmore	Yr.Iss.	1994	13.50	14
1994	Christmas Tee Time-596256	Yr.Iss.	1995	25.00	25
1994	Have a Merry Dairy Christmas -596264	Yr.Iss.	1994	22.50	23
1994	Happy Holi-date-596272 - Hahn	Yr.Iss.	1995	22.50	23
1994	O' Come All Ye Faithful-596280 - Hahn	Yr.Iss.	1994	15.00	15
1994	One Small Step...-596299 - Hahn	19,690	1994	25.00	30
1994	To My Favorite V.I.P.-596698	Yr.Iss.	1994	20.00	20
1994	Building Memories-596876 - Hahn	Yr.Iss.	1994	25.00	25
1994	Open For Business-596906 - Hahn	Yr.Iss.	1994	17.50	18
1994	Twas The Nite Before Christmas -597643 - Gilmore	Yr.Iss.	1994	18.50	19
1994	I Can Bear-ly Wait For A Coke™ -597724	Yr.Iss.	1995	18.50	19
1994	Gallant Greeting- 598313	Yr.Iss.	1994	15.00	20
1994	Merry Menage-598321	Yr.Iss.	1994	20.00	20
1994	Bundle Of Joy-598992	Yr.Iss.	1994	10.00	10
1994	Bundle Of Joy-599018	Yr.Iss.	1994	10.00	10
1994	Have A Dino-mite Christmas -599026 - Hahn	Yr.Iss.	1994	18.50	19
1994	Good Fortune To You-599034	Yr.Iss.	1994	25.00	25
1994	Building a Sew-man-599042	Yr.Iss.	1994	18.50	19
1994	Merry Memo-ries-599050	Yr.Iss.	1994	22.50	23
1994	Ski-son's Greetings-599069	Yr.Iss.	1994	20.00	20
1994	Holiday Freezer Teaser-599085 - Gilmore	Yr.Iss.	1994	25.00	25
1994	Almost Time For Santa-599093 - Gilmore	Yr.Iss.	1994	25.00	25
1994	Santa's Secret Test Drive -599107 - Gilmore	Yr.Iss.	1994	20.00	20
1994	You're A Wheel Cool Brother -599115 - Gilmore	Yr.Iss.	1994	22.50	23
1994	Hand-Tossed Tidings-599166	Yr.Iss.	1994	17.50	18
1994	Tasty Take Off-599174	Yr.Iss.	1994	20.00	20
1994	Formula For Love-599530 - Olsen	Yr.Iss.	1994	10.00	10
1994	Santa's Ginger-bred Doe -599697 - Gilmore	Yr.Iss.	1994	15.00	15
1994	Nutcracker Sweetheart-599700	Yr.Iss.	1994	15.00	15
1994	Merry Reindeer Ride-599719	Yr.Iss.	1994	20.00	20
1994	Santa's Sing-A-Long-599727 - Gilmore	Yr.Iss.	1994	20.00	20
1994	A Holiday Opportunity-599735	Yr.Iss.	1995	20.00	20
1994	Holiday Stars-599743	Yr.Iss.	1994	20.00	20
1994	The Latest Mews From Home -653977	Yr.Iss.	1994	16.00	16
1994	You're A Winner Son!-834564 - Gilmore	Yr.Iss.	1994	18.50	19
1994	Especially For You-834580 - Gilmore	Yr.Iss.	1994	27.50	28
1995	How...Do I Love Thee-104949	Yr.Iss.	1995	22.50	23
1995	Swishing You Sweet Greetings -105201	Yr.Iss.	1995	20.00	20
1995	Planely Delicious-109665	Yr.Iss.		20.00	20
1996	Spice Up The Season-111724	Yr. Iss.		20.00	20
1995	Home For The Howl-i-days -111732	Yr.Iss.	1995	20.00	20
1995	Time For Refreshment-111872	Yr.Iss.	1995	20.00	20
1995	Holiday Bike Hike 111937	Yr.Iss.	1995	20.00	20
1996	Santa's Sacks-111945 - Hahn	Yr. Iss.		17.50	18
1995	Ho, Ho, Hole in One!-111953	Yr.Iss.	1995	20.00	20
1995	No Time To Spare at Christmas -111961	Yr.Iss.	1995	20.00	20
1995	Hustling Up Some Cheer-112038	Yr.Iss.	1995	20.00	20
1995	Scoring Big at Christmas-112046	Yr.Iss.	1995	20.00	20
1995	Serving Up the Best 112054	Yr.Iss.	1995	17.50	18
1995	Sea-sons Greetings, Teacher 112070 - Gilmore	Yr.Iss.		17.50	18
1995	Siesta Santa-112089 - Gilmore	Yr.Iss.	1995	25.00	25
1995	We've Shared Sew Much -112097 - Gilmore	Yr.Iss.	1995	25.00	25
1995	Toys To Treasure-112119	Yr.Iss.	1995	20.00	20
1995	To Santa, Post Haste-112151 - Gilmore	Yr.Iss.	1995	15.00	15
1995	Yule Logon For Christmas Cheer - 122513	Yr.Iss.	1995	20.00	20
1995	Pretty Up For The Holidays -125830 - Butcher	Yr.Iss.	1995	20.00	20
1995	You Bring The Love to Christmas-125849 - Butcher	Yr.Iss.	1995	15.00	15
1995	Happy Birthday Jesus-125857 - Butcher	Yr.Iss.	1995	15.00	15
1995	Let's Snuggle Together For Christmas-125865 - Butcher	Yr.Iss.	1995	15.00	15
1995	I'm In A Spin Over You-125873 - Butcher	Yr.Iss.	1995	15.00	15
1995	Our First Christmas Together -125881 - Butcher	Yr.Iss.	1995	22.50	23
1995	Twinkle, Twinkle Christmas Star -125903 - Butcher	Yr.Iss.	1995	17.50	18
1995	Bringing Holiday Wishes To You -125911 - Butcher	Yr.Iss.	1995	22.50	23
1995	You Pull The Strings To My Heart-125938 - Butcher	Yr.Iss.	1995	20.00	20
1995	Baby's First Christmas-125946 - Butcher	Yr.Iss.	1995	15.00	15
1995	Baby's First Christmas-125954 - Butcher	Yr.Iss.	1995	15.00	15
1995	Friends Are The Greatest Treasure-125962 - Butcher	20,000	1995	25.00	25
1995	4-Alarm Christmas-128767 - Gilmore	Yr.Iss.	1995	17.50	18
1995	Truckin'-128813	Yr.Iss.	1995	25.00	25
1995	T-Bird-128821	19,550	1995	20.00	20
1995	57 HVN-128848	Yr.Iss.	1995	20.00	20
1995	Corvette-128856	Yr.Iss.	1995	20.00	20
1995	Mom's Taxi-128872	Yr.Iss.	1995	25.00	25
1995	Choc Full of Wishes-128945	Yr.Iss.	1995	20.00	20
1995	Have a Coke and a Smile™ -128953	Yr.Iss.	1995	22.50	23
1995	Trunk Full of Treasures-128961	20,000	1995	25.00	25
1995	Make Mine a Coke™-128988	Yr.Iss.	1995	25.00	25
1995	Dashing Through the Snow -128996	Yr.Iss.	1995	20.00	20
1995	Happy Yuleglide-129003	Yr.Iss.	1995	17.50	18
1995	Santa's Speedway-129011	Yr.Iss.	1995	20.00	20
1995	You're My Cup of Tea-129038	Yr.Iss.		20.00	20
1995	Crackin' a Smile-129046	Yr.Iss.	1995	17.50	18
1995	Rx:Mas Greetings-129054	Yr.Iss.	1995	17.50	18
1996	Special Bear-Livery-129062	Yr.Iss.		15.00	15
1995	Merry McMeal-129070	Yr.Iss.	1995	17.50	18
1995	Above the Crowd-129089	Yr.Iss.	1995	20.00	20
1995	Mickey at the Helm-132063	Yr.Iss.	1995	17.50	18
1995	Caddy-132705	Yr.Iss.	1995	20.00	20
1996	Catch Of The Holiday-132888 - Hahn	Yr.Iss.		20.00	20
1995	Jackpot Joy!-132896 - Hahn	Yr.Iss.	1995	17.50	18
1995	Get in the Spirit...Recycle -132918 - Hahn	Yr.Iss.		17.50	18
1995	Miss Merry's Secret-132934 - Hahn	Yr.Iss.	1995	20.00	20
1995	...Good Will Toward Men -132942 - Hahn	19,450	1995	25.00	25
1995	Friendships Bloom Through All Seasons-132950 - Hahn	Yr.Iss.	1995	22.50	23
1995	Merry Monopoly-132969	Yr.Iss.		22.50	23
1995	The Night B 4 Christmas -134848 - Hahn	Yr.Iss.	1995	20.00	20
1996	A Cup Of Cheer-135070 - Gilmore	Yr.Iss.		25.00	25
1995	Bubblin' With Joy-136581	Yr.Iss.	1995	15.00	15
1996	Steppin' With Minnie-136603	Yr.Iss.		13.50	14
1995	Minnie's Merry Christmas -136611	Yr.Iss.	1995	20.00	20
1996	Motorcycle Mickey-136654	Yr.Iss.		25.00	25
1995	Makin' Tracks With Mickey -136662	Yr.Iss.	1995	20.00	20
1995	Mickey's Airmail-136670	Yr.Iss.		20.00	20
1995	Holiday Bound-136689	Yr.Iss.		20.00	20
1995	Goofed-Up-136697	Yr.Iss.		20.00	20
1995	On The Ball At Christmas -136700	Yr.Iss.		15.00	15
1995	Sweet on You-136719	Yr.Iss.	1995	22.50	23
1995	Nutty About Christmas-137030	Yr.Iss.	1995	22.50	23
1995	Tinkertoy Joy-137049	Yr.Iss.		20.00	20
1995	Starring Roll At Christmas -137057	Yr.Iss.	1995	17.50	18
1995	A Thimble of the Season -137243 - Gilmore	Yr.Iss.		22.50	23
1995	A Little Something Extra...Extra -137251	10,000	1995	25.00	25
1995	The Maze Of Our Lives-139599 - Hahn	Yr.Iss.	1995	17.50	18
1995	A Sip For Good Measure-139610	Yr.Iss.	1995	17.50	18
1995	Christmas Fishes, Dad-139629 - Hahn	Yr.Iss.		17.50	18
1995	Christmas Is In The Bag-139645	Yr.Iss.	1995	17.50	18
1995	Gotta Have a Clue-139653	Yr.Iss.	1995	20.00	20
1995	Fun In Hand-139661	Yr.Iss.	1995	17.50	18
1995	Christmas Cuddle-139688	Yr.Iss.		20.00	20
1995	Dreamin Of the One I Love -139696	Yr.Iss.		25.00	25
1995	Sneaking a Peek-139718	Yr.Iss.		22.50	23
1995	Christmas Eve Mischief-139726	Yr.Iss.	1995	17.50	18
1995	All Tucked In-139734	Yr.Iss.	1995	15.00	15
1995	Merry Christmas To Me-139742	Yr.Iss.	1995	20.00	20
1995	Looking Our Holiday Best -139750	Yr.Iss.	1995	25.00	25
1995	Christmas Vacation-142158	Yr.Iss.		20.00	20
1995	Just Fore Christmas-142174	Yr.Iss.		15.00	15
1995	Christmas Belle-142182	Yr.Iss.		20.00	20
1995	Tail Waggin' Wishes-142190	Yr.Iss.	1995	17.50	18
1995	Holiday Ride-142204	Yr.Iss.	1995	17.50	18
1995	A Carousel For Ariel-142212	Yr.Iss.	1995	17.50	18
1995	On The Move At Christmas 142220 - Hahn	Yr.Iss.	1995	17.50	18
1995	T-Bird-146838	Yr.Iss.	1995	20.00	20
1996	Swinging On A Star-166642	Yr.Iss.		20.00	20
1996	A-Joy Matie, Throw Me A Lifesaver-166677	Yr.Iss.		20.00	20
1996	It's Plane To See...Coke Is It -166723	Yr.Iss.		25.00	25
1996	A Century Of Good Taste-166774	Yr.Iss.		25.00	25
1996	Servin' Up Joy-166847	Yr.Iss.		20.00	20
1996	In-Line To Help Santa-166855	Yr.Iss.		20.00	20
1996	I Love My Daughter-166863	Yr.Iss.		9.00	9
1996	I Love Grandma-166898	Yr.Iss.		9.00	9
1996	I Love Dad-166901	Yr.Iss.		9.00	9
1996	I Love Mom-166928	Yr.Iss.		9.00	9
1996	I Love My Godchild-166936	Yr.Iss.		9.00	9
1996	Baby's 1st Christmas-166944	Yr.Iss.		9.00	9
1996	A Boot Full Of Cheer-166952	Yr.Iss.		20.00	20
1996	Summons For A Merry Christmas-166960	Yr.Iss.		22.50	23
1996	An Appointment With Santa -166979	Yr.Iss.		20.00	20

*Quotes have been rounded up to nearest dollar

CHRISTMAS ORNAMENTS

YEAR ISSUE		EDITION LIMIT	YEAR RETD.	ISSUE PRICE	*QUOTE U.S.$
1996	Play It Again, Nick-166987	Yr.Iss.		17.50	18
1996	Holiday Tinkertoy Tree-166995	Yr.Iss.		17.50	18
1996	A Picture Perfect Pair-167002	Yr.Iss.		25.00	25
1996	Santa's On The Line-167037	Yr.Iss.		25.00	25
1996	Downhill Delivery-167053	Yr.Iss.		25.00	25
1996	On A Roll With Diet Coke -167061	Yr.Iss.		20.00	20
1996	Hold On, Santa!-167088	Yr.Iss.		25.00	25
1996	There's A Friendship Brewing -167096 - Hahn	Yr.Iss.		25.00	25
1996	Tails A' Wagon-167126	Yr.Iss.		20.00	20
1996	In Store For More-167134	15,000		25.00	25
1996	Jeep Grand Cherokee-167215	Yr.Iss.		22.50	23
1996	Chevy Blazer-167223	Yr.Iss.		22.50	23
1996	Ford Explorer-167231	Yr.Iss.		22.50	23
1996	Dodge Ram Truck-167258	Yr.Iss.		22.50	23
1996	Trees To Please-168378	Yr.Iss.		25.00	25
1996	Plane Crazy-168386	Yr.Iss.		22.50	23
1996	I Love My Son-168432	Yr.Iss.		9.00	9
1996	#1 Coach-168440	Yr.Iss.		9.00	9
1996	Goin' Fishin'-168459	Yr.Iss.		22.50	23
1996	Gifts From Mickey-168467	Yr.Iss.		20.00	20
1996	All Fired Up For Christmas -168475	Yr.Iss.		25.00	25
1996	Minnie's Mall Haul-168491	Yr.Iss.		25.00	25
1996	A Magic Moment-172197	Yr.Iss.		17.50	18
1996	Happy's Holiday-172200	Yr.Iss.		17.50	18
1996	Beauty For The Beast-172219	Yr.Iss.		17.50	18
1996	Life's Sweet Choices-172634	Yr.Iss.		25.00	25
1996	Holiday In Bloom-172669	Yr.Iss.		25.00	25
1996	Have A Cracker Jack Christmas -172979	Yr.Iss.		25.00	25
1996	Hair's The Place-173029 - Hahn	Yr.Iss.		25.00	25
1996	Merry Manicure-173339 - Hahn	Yr.Iss.		25.00	25
1996	100 Years...And Still On A Roll 173770	19,960		17.50	18
1996	Tracking Reindeer Pause -173789 - Hahn	Yr.Iss.		25.00	25
1996	Holiday Dreams Of Green -173797 - Hahn	Yr.Iss.		15.00	15
1996	1965 Ford Mustang-173800	Yr.Iss.		22.50	23
1996	Toyland, Joyland-173878	Yr.Iss.		20.00	20
1996	Tobin's Debut Dancer-173886 - Fraley	20,000		20.00	20
1996	Thou Art My Lamp, O Lord -173894 - Hahn	Yr.Iss.		25.00	25
1996	'Tis The Season To Be Nutty -175234	Yr.Iss.		17.50	18
1996	1956 Chevy Corvette-175269	19,560		22.50	23
1996	A World Of Good Taste-175420	18,600		20.00	20
1996	It's Time For Christmas-175455	Yr.Iss.		25.00	25
1996	15 Years Of Hits-175463	10,000		25.00	25
1996	Sew Darn Cute-176761 - Hahn	Yr.Iss.		25.00	25
1996	Decked Out For Christmas -176796 - Hahn	Yr.Iss.		25.00	25
1996	Campaign For Christmas-176818	19,960		17.50	18
1996	Delivering Holiday Cheers -177318	Yr.Iss.		25.00	25
1996	A Splash Of Cool Yule-213713	Yr.Iss.		20.00	20
1995	Sweet Harmony-586773 - Gilmore	Yr.Iss.	1995	17.50	18
1995	Yule Tide Prancer-588660	Yr.Iss.	1995	15.00	15
1995	Baby's Sweet Feast-588733 - Gilmore	Yr.Iss.		18.50	19
1995	A Well, Balanced Meal For Santa-592633	Yr.Iss.	1995	17.50	18
1995	Salute-593133	Yr.Iss.	1995	22.50	23
1995	Filled To The Brim-595039 - Gilmore	Yr.Iss.	1995	25.00	25

Enesco Treasury of Christmas Ornaments Collectors' Club - Various

YEAR ISSUE		EDITION LIMIT	YEAR RETD.	ISSUE PRICE	*QUOTE U.S.$
1993	The Treasury Card (Club) -T0001 - Gilmore	Yr.Iss.	1993	20.00	20
1993	Together We Can Shoot For The Stars (Club)-TR931 - Hahn	Yr.Iss.	1993	17.50	18
1993	Can't Weights For The Holidays (Club)-TR932	Yr.Iss.	1993	18.50	19
1994	Seedlings Greetings (Club) -TR933 - Hahn	Yr.Iss.	1994	22.50	23
1994	Spry Fry (Club)-TR934	Yr.Iss.	1994	15.00	15
1995	You're the Perfect Fit-T0002 - Hahn	Yr.Iss.	1995	Gift	N/A
1995	You're the Perfect Fit-T0102 (Charter Members) - Hahn	Yr.Iss.	1995	Gift	N/A
1995	Things Go Better With Coke™ - TR951	Yr.Iss.	1995	15.00	15
1995	Buttoning Up Our Holiday Best - TR952 - Gilmore	Yr.Iss.	1995	22.50	23
1995	Holiday High-Light- TR953 - Gilmore	Yr.Iss.	1995	15.00	15
1995	First Class Christmas- TR954 - Gilmore	Yr.Iss.	1995	22.50	23

Memories of Yesterday - M. Attwell

YEAR ISSUE		EDITION LIMIT	YEAR RETD.	ISSUE PRICE	*QUOTE U.S.$
1988	Baby's First Christmas 1988 - 520373	Yr.Iss.		13.50	40-60
1988	Special Delivery! 1988-520381	Yr.Iss.		13.50	35-45
1989	Baby's First Christmas-522465	Open		15.00	15-20
1989	A Surprise for Santa-522473	Yr.Iss.		13.50	15-25
1989	Christmas Together-522562	Open		15.00	15-25
1995	Happy Landings (Dated 1995) 522619	Yr.Iss.		16.00	16
1990	Time For Bed-524638	Yr.Iss.		15.00	15-30
1990	New Moon-524646	Suspd.		15.00	15-25
1994	Just Dreaming of You-524786	Open		16.00	16
1990	Moonstruck-524794	Retrd.	1992	15.00	15-25
1991	Just Watchin' Over You-525421	Retrd.	1994	17.50	18
1991	Lucky Me-525448	Retrd.	1993	16.00	20
1993	Wish I Could Fly To You-525790	Yr.Iss.		16.00	16
1992	I'll Fly Along To See You Soon-525804 (Bisque)	Yr.Iss.		16.00	16
1991	Star Fishin'-525820	Open		16.00	16
1993	May All Your Finest Dreams Come True-528811	Open		16.00	16
1991	Lucky You-525847	Retrd.	1993	16.00	16
1995	Now I Lay Me Down to Sleep 527009	Open		15.00	15
1995	I Pray the Lord My Soul to Keep 527017	Open		15.00	15
1992	Mommy, I Teared It-527041 (Five Year Anniversary Limited Ed.	Yr.Iss.		15.00	20
1991	S'no Use Lookin' Back Now!-527181(dated)	Yr.Iss.		17.50	28
1992	Merry Christmas, Little Boo-Boo-528803	Open		37.50	38
1992	Star Light. Star Bright-528838	Open		16.00	16
1994	Give Yourself a Hug From Me!-529109 ('94 Dated)	Yr. Iss.		17.50	18
1992	Swinging Together -580481(1992 Dated Artplas)	Yr.Iss.		17.50	22
1992	Sailin' With My Friends-587575 (Artplas)	Open		25.00	25
1993	Bringing Good Wishes Your Way-592846 (Artplas)	Open		25.00	25
1994	Bout Time I Came Along to See You-592854 (Artplas)	Open		17.50	18

Memories of Yesterday Event Item Only - Enesco

YEAR ISSUE		EDITION LIMIT	YEAR RETD.	ISSUE PRICE	*QUOTE U.S.$
1993	How 'Bout A Little Kiss?-527068	Closed	1993	16.50	50
1996	Hoping To See You Soon-527033	Yr.Iss.		15.00	15

Memories of Yesterday Friendship - Enesco

YEAR ISSUE		EDITION LIMIT	YEAR RETD.	ISSUE PRICE	*QUOTE U.S.$
1996	I Love You This Much!-185809	Open		13.50	14

Memories of Yesterday Peter Pan - Enesco

YEAR ISSUE		EDITION LIMIT	YEAR RETD.	ISSUE PRICE	*QUOTE U.S.$
1996	Tinkerbell-164682	Open		20.00	20

Memories of Yesterday Society Member's Only - M. Attwell

YEAR ISSUE		EDITION LIMIT	YEAR RETD.	ISSUE PRICE	*QUOTE U.S.$
1992	With Luck And A Friend, I's In Heaven-MY922	Yr.Iss.		16.00	20
1993	I'm Bringing Good Luck-Wherever You Are	Yr.Iss.		16.00	22

Miss Martha's Collection - M. Holcombe

YEAR ISSUE		EDITION LIMIT	YEAR RETD.	ISSUE PRICE	*QUOTE U.S.$
1993	Caroline - Always Someone Watching Over Me-350532	Closed	1994	25.00	50
1993	Arianna - Heavenly Sounds H/O-350567	Closed	1994	25.00	50
1992	Baby in Basket-369454	Closed	1994	25.00	31
1992	Baby In Swing-421480	Retrd.	1993	25.00	50
1992	Girl Holding Stocking DTD 1992-421499	Closed	1994	25.00	30-50
1992	Girl/Bell In Hand-421502	Retrd.	1993	25.00	50

Precious Moments - S. Butcher

YEAR ISSUE		EDITION LIMIT	YEAR RETD.	ISSUE PRICE	*QUOTE U.S.$
1983	Surround Us With Joy-E-0513	Yr.Iss.		9.00	50-60
1983	Mother Sew Dear-E-0514	Open		9.00	17-32
1983	To A Special Dad-E-0515	Suspd.		9.00	30-54
1983	The Purr-fect Grandma-E-0516	Open		9.00	17-32
1983	The Perfect Grandpa-E-0517	Suspd.		9.00	30-39
1983	Blessed Are The Pure In Heart -E-0518	Yr.Iss.		9.00	45
1983	O Come All Ye Faithful-E-0531	Suspd.		10.00	55
1983	Let Heaven And Nature Sing-E-0532	Retrd.	1986	9.00	24-35
1983	Tell Me The Story Of Jesus-E-0533	Suspd.		9.00	36-57
1983	To Thee With Love-E-0534	Retrd.	1989	9.00	25-55
1983	Love Is Patient-E-0535	Suspd.		9.00	46-52
1983	Love Is Patient-E-0536	Suspd.		9.00	60
1983	Jesus Is The Light That Shines - E-0537	Suspd.		9.00	60-70
1982	Joy To The World-E-2343	Suspd.		9.00	40-66
1982	I'll Play My Drum For Him-E-2359	Yr.Iss.		9.00	100
1982	Baby's First Christmas-E-2362	Suspd.		9.00	33-70
1982	The First Noel-E-2367	Suspd.		9.00	66
1982	The First Noel-E-2368	Retrd.	1984	9.00	36-68
1982	Dropping In For Christmas -E-2369	Retrd.	1986	9.00	36-55
1982	Unicorn-E-2371	Retrd.	1988	10.00	40-60
1982	Baby's First Christmas-E-2372	Suspd.		9.00	35-45
1982	Dropping Over For Christmas -E-2376	Retrd.	1985	9.00	29-60
1982	Mouse With Cheese-E-2381	Suspd.		9.00	100-125
1982	Our First Christmas Together -E-2385	Suspd.		10.00	26-55
1982	Camel, Donkey & Cow (3 pc. set)-E2386	Suspd.		25.00	65-105
1984	Wishing You A Merry Christmas -E-5387	Yr.Iss.		10.00	50-60
1984	Joy To The World-E-5388	Retrd.	1987	10.00	40-55
1984	Peace On Earth-E-5389	Suspd.		10.00	30-45
1984	May God Bless You With A Perfect Holiday Season-E-5390	Suspd.		10.00	20-30
1984	Love Is Kind-E-5391	Suspd.		10.00	24-35
1984	Blessed Are The Pure In Heart -E-5392	Yr.Iss.		10.00	40
1981	But Love Goes On Forever -E-5627	Suspd.		6.00	90-155
1981	But Love Goes On Forever E-5628	Suspd.		6.00	80-125
1981	Let The Heavens Rejoice-E-5629	Yr.Iss.		6.00	200
1981	Unto Us A Child Is Born-E-5630	Suspd.		6.00	40-70
1981	Baby's First Christmas-E-5631	Suspd.		6.00	45-60
1981	Baby's First Christmas-E-5632	Suspd.		6.00	45-85
1981	Come Let Us Adore Him (4pc. set)-E-5633	Suspd.		22.00	115-150
1981	Wee Three Kings (3pc. set) -E-5634	Suspd.		19.00	100-129
1981	We Have Seen His Star-E-6120	Retrd.	1984	6.00	40-60
1985	Have A Heavenly Christmas-12416	Open		12.00	19-30
1995	He Covers The Earth With His Beauty-142689	Yr.Iss.		30.00	30
1995	He Covers The Earth With His Beauty-142662	Yr.Iss.		17.00	17
1995	Our First Christmas Together - 142700	Yr.Iss.		18.50	19
1995	Baby's First Christmas-142719	Yr.Iss.		17.50	50
1995	Baby's First Christmas-142727	Yr.Iss.		17.50	50
1985	God Sent His Love-15768	Yr.Iss.		10.00	35
1985	May Your Christmas Be Happy - 15822	Suspd.		10.00	30-48
1985	Happiness Is The Lord-15830	Suspd.		10.00	20-37
1985	May Your Christmas Be Delightful-15849	Suspd.		10.00	15-35
1985	Honk If You Love Jesus-15857	Suspd.		10.00	23-35
1985	Baby's First Christmas-15903	Yr.Iss.		10.00	42
1985	Baby's First Christmas-15911	Yr.Iss.		10.00	30-45
1986	Shepherd of Love-102288	Suspd.		10.00	35
1986	Wishing You A Cozy Christmas -102326	Yr.Iss.		10.00	40
1986	Our First Christmas Together -102350	Yr.Iss.		10.00	15-39
1986	Trust And Obey-102377	Open		10.00	17-30
1986	Love Rescued Me-102385	Open		10.00	17-23
1986	Angel Of Mercy-102407	Open		10.00	17-30
1986	It's A Perfect Boy-102415	Suspd.		10.00	30
1986	Lord Keep Me On My Toes - 102423	Retrd.	1990	10.00	30-50
1986	Serve With A Smile-102431	Suspd.		10.00	20-30
1986	Serve With A Smile-102458	Suspd.		10.00	30
1986	Reindeer-102466	Yr.Iss.		11.00	160-250
1986	Rocking Horse-102474	Suspd.		10.00	25
1986	Baby's First Christmas-102504	Yr.Iss.		10.00	25
1986	Baby's First Christmas-102512	Yr.Iss.		10.00	25
1987	Bear The Good News Of Christmas-104515	Yr.Iss.		12.50	45
1987	Baby's First Christmas-109401	Yr.Iss.		12.00	40
1987	Baby's First Christmas-109428	Yr.Iss.		12.00	40
1987	Love Is The Best Gift Of All -109770	Yr.Iss.		11.00	35
1987	I'm A Possibility-111120	Suspd.		11.00	25
1987	You Have Touched So Many Hearts-112356	Open		11.00	17-30
1987	Waddle I Do Without You -112364	Open		11.00	17-30
1987	I'm Sending You A White Christmas-112372	Suspd.		11.00	20-25
1987	He Cleansed My Soul-112380	Open		12.00	17-25
1987	Our First Christmas Together -112399	Yr.Iss.		11.00	25-35
1988	To My Forever Friend-113956	Open		16.00	19-35
1988	Smile Along The Way-113964	Suspd.		15.00	30
1988	God Sent You Just In Time -113972	Suspd.		13.50	30
1988	Rejoice O Earth-113980	Retrd.	1991	13.50	30-40
1988	Cheers To The Leader-113999	Suspd.		13.50	30-40
1988	My Love Will Never Let You Go -114006	Suspd.		13.50	32
1988	Baby's First Christmas-115282	Yr.Iss.		15.00	17-25
1988	Time To Wish You A Merry Christmas-115320	Yr.Iss.		13.00	42
1996	Owl Be Home For Christmas -128708	Yr.Iss.		18.50	19
1995	He Covers The Earth With His Beauty (ball)-142489	Yr.Iss.		30.00	30
1995	He Covers The Earth With His Beauty-142662	Yr.Iss.		17.00	17
1995	Our First Christmas Together -142700	Yr.Iss.		18.50	19
1995	Baby's First Christmas-142719	Yr.Iss.		17.50	18
1995	Baby's First Christmas-142727	Yr.Iss.		17.50	18
1995	Joy From Head To Mistletoe -150126	Open		18.50	19
1995	You're "A" Number One In My Book, Teacher-150142	Open		18.50	19
1995	Joy To The World-150320	Open		20.00	20
1996	Joy To The World-153338	Open		20.00	20
1996	Peace On Earth...Anyway (Ball)-183350	Yr.Iss.		30.00	30
1996	Peace On Earth...Anyway - 183369	Yr.Iss.		18.50	19
1996	God's Precious Gift-183881	Open		20.00	20
1996	Puppy In Ice Skate-183903	Open		18.50	19
1996	Our First Christmas Together -183911	Open		22.50	23
1996	Baby's First Christmas-183938	Open		17.50	18
1996	Baby's First Christmas-183946	Open		17.50	18
1988	Our First Christmas Together -520233	Yr.Iss.		13.00	21
1988	Baby's First Christmas-520241	Yr.Iss.		15.00	22
1988	You Are My Gift Come True -520276	Yr.Iss.		12.50	50-60
1988	Hang On For The Holly Days -520292	Yr.Iss.		13.00	50-55
1992	I'm Nuts About You-520411	Yr.Iss.		15.00	15-25
1995	Hippo Holidays-520403	Yr.Iss.		17.00	17
1991	Sno-Bunny Falls For You Like I Do-520438	Yr.Iss.		15.00	50-52
1989	Christmas is Ruff Without You -520462	Yr.Iss.		13.00	13-30
1993	Slow Down & Enjoy The Holidays-520489	Yr.Iss.		16.00	16

*Quotes have been rounded up to nearest dollar

YEAR	ISSUE	EDITION LIMIT	YEAR RETD.	ISSUE PRICE	*QUOTE U.S.$
1990	Wishing You A Purr-fect Holiday -520497	Yr.Iss.		15.00	35-45
1989	May All Your Christmases Be White-521302 (dated)	Suspd.		15.00	25-35
1989	Our First Christmas Together -521558	Yr.Iss.		17.50	30
1990	Glide Through the Holidays -521566	Retrd.	1992	13.50	25-40
1990	Dashing Through the Snow 521574	Suspd.		15.00	15-25
1990	Don't Let the Holidays Get You Down-521590	Retrd.	1994	15.00	45-50
1989	Oh Holy Night-522848	Yr.Iss.		13.50	40-55
1989	Make A Joyful Noise-522910	Open		15.00	17
1989	Love One Another-522929	Open		17.50	19-25
1990	Friends Never Drift Apart-522937	Retrd.	1995	17.50	19-27
1991	Our First Christmas Together -522945	Yr.Iss.		17.50	18-25
1989	I Believe In The Old Rugged Cross-522953	Suspd.		15.00	30
1989	Peace On Earth-523062	Yr.Iss.		25.00	60-70
1989	Baby's First Christmas-523194	Yr.Iss.		15.00	25
1989	Baby's First Christmas-523208	Yr.Iss.		15.00	32
1991	Happy Trails Is Trusting Jesus -523224	Suspd.		15.00	16-30
1990	May Your Christmas Be A Happy Home-523704	Yr.Iss.		27.50	35
1990	Baby's First Christmas-523798	Yr.Iss.		15.00	20
1990	Baby's First Christmas-523771	Yr.Iss.		15.00	20
1990	Once Upon A Holy Night-523852	Yr.Iss.		15.00	25
1992	Good Friends Are For Always -524131	Open		15.00	17
1991	May Your Christmas Be Merry -524174	Yr.Iss.		15.00	25
1990	Bundles of Joy-525057	Yr.Iss.		15.00	25-35
1990	Our First Christmas Together -525324	Yr.Iss.		17.50	18-25
1992	Lord, Keep Me On My Toes -525332	Open		15.00	17-18
1991	May Your Christmas Be Merry (on Base)-526940	Yr.Iss.		30.00	35
1991	Baby's First Christmas (Boy) -527084	Yr.Iss.		15.00	25
1991	Baby's First Christmas (Girl) -527092	Yr.Iss.		15.00	25
1991	The Good Lord Always Delivers -527165	Suspd.		15.00	25
1993	Share in The Warmth of Christmas-527211	Open		15.00	17
1994	Onward Christmas Soldiers -527327	Open		16.00	16
1992	Baby's First Christmas-527475	Yr.Iss.		15.00	17
1992	Baby's First Christmas-527483	Yr.Iss.		15.00	17
1992	But The Greatest of These Is Love-527696	Yr.Iss.		15.00	30
1992	But The Greatest of These Is Love-527734 (on Base)	Yr.Iss.		30.00	35
1994	Sending You A White Christmas -528218	Open		16.00	16
1994	Bringing You A Merry Christmas -528226	Open		16.00	16
1993	It's So Uplifting to Have a Friend Like You-528846	Open		16.00	17
1992	Our First Christmas-528870	Yr.Iss.		17.50	18-25
1994	Our 1st Christmas Together -529206	Yr.Iss.		18.50	19-27
1993	Wishing You the Sweetest Christmas-530190	Yr.Iss.		30.00	30-45
1993	Wishing You the Sweetest Christmas-530212	Yr.Iss.		15.00	15-28
1994	Baby's First Christmas-530255	Yr.Iss.		16.00	16
1994	Baby's First Christmas-530263	Yr.Iss.		16.00	16
1994	You're As Pretty As A Christmas Tree-530387	Yr.Iss.		30.00	30
1994	You're As Pretty As A Christmas Tree-530395	Yr.Iss.		16.00	16
1993	Our First Christmas Together -530506	Yr.Iss.		17.50	18
1993	Baby's First Christmas-530859	Yr.Iss.		15.00	15
1993	Baby's First Christmas-530867	Yr.Iss.		15.00	15
1994	You Are Always In My Heart -530972	Yr.Iss.		16.00	16-28

Precious Moments Club 15th Anniversary Commemorative Edition - S. Butcher

YEAR	ISSUE	EDITION LIMIT	YEAR RETD.	ISSUE PRICE	*QUOTE U.S.$
1993	15 Years Tweet Music Together -530840	Yr.Iss.		15.00	18-50

Precious Moments DSR Open House Weekend Ornaments - S. Butcher

YEAR	ISSUE	EDITION LIMIT	YEAR RETD.	ISSUE PRICE	*QUOTE U.S.$
1992	The Magic Starts With You -529648	Yr.Iss.		16.00	30
1993	An Event For All Seasons -529974	Yr.Iss.		15.00	20
1994	Take A Bow Cuz You're My Christmas Star-520470	Yr.Iss.	1994	16.00	22
1995	Merry Chrismoose-150134	Yr.Iss.		17.00	17

Precious Moments Easter Seal Commemorative Ornaments - S. Butcher

YEAR	ISSUE	EDITION LIMIT	YEAR RETD.	ISSUE PRICE	*QUOTE U.S.$
1994	It's No Secret What God Can Do -244570	Yr.Iss.		6.50	7
1995	Take Time To Smell The Flowers-128899	Yr.Iss.		7.50	8
1996	You Can Always Count on Me -152579	Yr.Iss.		6.50	7

Precious Moments Special Edition Members' Only - S. Butcher

YEAR	ISSUE	EDITION LIMIT	YEAR RETD.	ISSUE PRICE	*QUOTE U.S.$
1993	Loving, Caring And Sharing Along The Way-PM040 (Club Appreciation)	Yr.Iss.		12.50	20
1994	You Are The End of My Rainbow-PM041	Yr.Iss.		15.00	15

Precious Moments Sugartown - S. Butcher

YEAR	ISSUE	EDITION LIMIT	YEAR RETD.	ISSUE PRICE	*QUOTE U.S.$
1993	Sugartown Chapel-530484	Yr.Iss.		17.50	18
1994	Sam's House-530468	Yr.Iss.		17.50	18
1995	Dr. Sugar's Office-530441	Yr.Iss.		8.75	9
1996	Train Station-184101	Yr.Iss.		18.50	19

Flambro Imports

Emmett Kelly Jr. Christmas Ornaments - Undis.

YEAR	ISSUE	EDITION LIMIT	YEAR RETD.	ISSUE PRICE	*QUOTE U.S.$
1989	65th Birthday	Yr.Iss.	1989	24.00	90-125
1990	30 Years Of Clowning	Yr.Iss.	1990	30.00	125-150
1991	EKJ With Stocking And Toys	Yr.Iss.	1991	30.00	30
1992	Home For Christmas	Yr.Iss.	1992	24.00	65
1993	Christmas Mail	Yr.Iss.	1993	25.00	65
1994	'70 Birthday Commemorative	Yr.Iss.	1994	24.00	40-55
1995	20th Anniversary All Star Circus	Yr.Iss.	1995	25.00	25
1996	Christmas Pageant	Yr.Iss.		29.00	29

Little Emmett Ornaments - M. Wu

YEAR	ISSUE	EDITION LIMIT	YEAR RETD.	ISSUE PRICE	*QUOTE U.S.$
1995	Little Emmett Christmas Wrap	Open		11.50	12
1995	Little Emmett Deck the Neck	Open		11.50	12
1996	Little Emmett Singing Carols	Open		13.00	13
1996	Little Emmett Your Present	Open		13.00	13
1996	Little Emmett Baby 1st Christmas	Open		13.00	13
1996	Little Emmett on Rocking Horse	Open		25.00	25

Ganz

Cowtown/The Christmas Collection - C. Thammavongsa

YEAR	ISSUE	EDITION LIMIT	YEAR RETD.	ISSUE PRICE	*QUOTE U.S.$
1995	Bells on Cowtail Ring	Open		11.50	12
1994	Bronco Bully	Open		13.00	13
1995	Buckets of Joy	Open		12.00	12
1994	Calf-in-the Box	Open		12.50	13
1994	Christmoos Eve	Open		12.00	12
1995	Dairy Christmas	Open		11.50	12
1994	Downhill Dare Debull	Open		12.00	12
1994	Hallemooah	Open		12.00	12
1995	Holy Cow	Open		12.00	12
1994	Jingle Bull	Open		15.50	16
1994	Li'l Red Gliding Hoof	Open		12.00	12
1994	Little Drummer Calf	Open		12.00	12
1995	Moo, Moo, Moo	Open		11.50	12

Little Cheesers/The Christmas Collection - C. Thammavongsa, unless otherwise noted

YEAR	ISSUE	EDITION LIMIT	YEAR RETD.	ISSUE PRICE	*QUOTE U.S.$
1992	Abner Appleton Ornament - GDA/Thammavongsa	Open		15.00	15
1994	All I Want For Christmas	Closed	1994	13.50	14
1994	Angel	Open		8.00	8
1995	Annual Angel 1995	Open		10.50	11
1993	Baby's First X'mas Ornament	Retrd.	1995	12.50	13
1994	Candy Cane Caper	Open		9.00	9
1994	Cheeser Snowman	Closed	1994	5.00	5
1994	Chelsea's Stocking Bell	Open		15.50	16
1994	Cousin Woody Playing Flute	Closed	1994	10.00	10
1993	Dashing Through the Snow	Open		11.00	11
1994	Grandpa Blowing Horn	Closed	1994	10.00	10
1994	Hickory Playing Cello	Closed	1994	10.00	10
1992	Jenny Butterfield Ornament - GDA/Thammavongsa	Open		17.00	17
1992	Jeremy With Teddy Bear - GDA/Thammavongsa	Open		13.00	13
1995	Light of the World Bell	Open		16.00	16
1993	Little Stocking Stuffer Ornament	Open		10.50	11
1992	Little Truffle Ornament - GDA/Thammavongsa	Open		9.50	10
1995	Mama Claus' Special Recipe	Open		11.50	12
1993	Medley Meadowmouse X'mas Bell Ornament	Open		17.00	17
1994	Medley Playing Drum	Closed	1994	5.50	6
1992	Myrtle Meadowmouse GDA/Thammavongsa	Open		15.00	15
1995	Noel	Open		10.50	11
1993	Our First Christmas Together	Open		18.50	19
1994	Peace on Earth	Open		8.00	8
1992	Santa Cheeser Ornament - GDA/Thammavongsa	Open		14.00	14
1993	Santa's Little Helper Ornament	Open		11.00	11
1994	Santa's Workshop	Open		10.00	10
1993	Skating Into Your Heart	Open		10.00	10
1995	Skiing Santa	Open		10.00	10
1994	Sleigh Ride	Closed	1994	9.00	9
1995	Snow Cheeser II	Open		6.50	7
1994	Swinging Into the Season	Open		11.00	11
1996	Swinging on the Moon - Chiemlowski	Open		10.00	10
1994	Violet With Snowball	Closed	1994	5.50	6

Little Cheesers/The Silverwoods - C. Thammavongsa

YEAR	ISSUE	EDITION LIMIT	YEAR RETD.	ISSUE PRICE	*QUOTE U.S.$
1995	Angel Above	Open		8.50	9
1994	Christmas Surprise	Open		8.50	9
1994	Comfort and Joy	Open		6.00	6
1994	Deck the Halls	Open		9.50	10
1994	Giddy Up!	Open		8.50	9
1995	Harps of Gold	Open		8.50	9
1994	Hickory Dickory Dock	Open		9.50	10
1995	Joyful Sounds	Open		8.50	9
1994	Mrs. Claus	Open		9.00	9
1995	Over The Hills	Open		8.50	9
1994	Santa Silverwood	Open		9.00	9
1994	Xmas Express	Open		8.50	9

Perfect Little Place/Christmas Collection - C.Thammavongsa

YEAR	ISSUE	EDITION LIMIT	YEAR RETD.	ISSUE PRICE	*QUOTE U.S.$
1995	Angel of Light	Open		12.00	12

Pigsville/The Christmas Collection - C. Thammavongsa

YEAR	ISSUE	EDITION LIMIT	YEAR RETD.	ISSUE PRICE	*QUOTE U.S.$
1994	Caroler	Open		10.00	10
1994	Christmas Treats	Open		9.00	9
1994	Drummer Pig	Open		10.00	10
1995	Fa-La-La-La-La	Open		9.50	10
1995	Heaven Sent	Open		10.50	11
1994	Joy to the World	Open		10.00	10
1994	Lovestruck	Open		10.50	11
1994	Santa Pig	Open		11.00	11
1994	Wheeeeeel Piggy	Open		9.00	9

The Precious Steeples Collection - Ganz/L. Sunarth

YEAR	ISSUE	EDITION LIMIT	YEAR RETD.	ISSUE PRICE	*QUOTE U.S.$
1995	Florence Cathedral	Open		11.00	11
1995	Notre-Dame Cathedral	Open		11.00	11
1995	St. Patrick's Cathedral	Open		11.00	11
1995	St. Paul's Cathedral	Open		11.00	11
1995	St. Peter's Basilica	Open		11.00	11
1995	Westminster Abbey	Open		11.00	11

Trains Gone By/Christmas Collection - Ganz

YEAR	ISSUE	EDITION LIMIT	YEAR RETD.	ISSUE PRICE	*QUOTE U.S.$
1996	C.P. Huntington Train	4,896		10.00	10
1996	General Train	4,896		10.00	10
1996	New York Central Train	4,896		10.00	10
1996	Pennsylvania Train	4,896		10.00	10

Goebel of North America

Angel Bell 3" - Goebel

YEAR	ISSUE	EDITION LIMIT	YEAR RETD.	ISSUE PRICE	*QUOTE U.S.$
1994	Angel w/Clarinet - Red	Closed	1994	17.50	18
1995	Angel w/Harp - Blue	Closed	1995	17.50	18
1996	Angel w/Mandolin - Champagne	Yr.Iss.		18.00	18

Angel Bells - 3 Asst. Colors - Goebel

YEAR	ISSUE	EDITION LIMIT	YEAR RETD.	ISSUE PRICE	*QUOTE U.S.$
1976	Angel Bell w/Clarinet (3 colors)	Closed	1976	8.00	8
1976	Angel Bell w/Clarinet (wh. bisque)	Closed	1976	6.00	6
1977	Angel Bell w/Mandolin (3 colors)	Closed	1977	8.50	9
1977	Angel Bell w/Mandolin (wh. bisque)	Closed	1977	6.50	7
1978	Angel Bell w/Harp (3 colors)	Closed	1978	9.00	9
1978	Angel Bell w/Harp (white bisque)	Closed	1978	7.00	7
1979	Angel Bell w/Accordion (3 colors)	Closed	1979	9.50	10
1979	Angel Bell w/Accordion (wh. bisque)	Closed	1979	7.50	8
1980	Angel Bell w/Saxaphone (3 colors)	Closed	1980	10.00	10
1980	Angel Bell w/Saxaphone (white bisque)	Closed	1980	8.00	8
1981	Angel Bell w/Music (3 colors)	Closed	1981	11.00	11
1981	Angel Bell w/Music (wh. bisque)	Closed	1981	9.00	9
1982	Angel Bell w/French Horn (3 colors)	Closed	1982	11.75	12
1982	Angel Bell w/French Horn (white bisque)	Closed	1982	9.75	10
1983	Angel Bell w/Flute (3 colors)	Closed	1983	12.50	13
1983	Angel Bell w/Flute (white bisque)	Closed	1983	10.50	11
1984	Angel Bell w/Drum (3 colors)	Closed	1984	14.00	14
1984	Angel Bell w/Drum (white bisque)	Closed	1984	12.00	12
1985	Angel Bell w/Trumpet (3 colors)	Closed	1985	14.00	14
1985	Angel Bell w/Trumpet (white bisque)	Closed	1985	12.00	12
1986	Angel Bell w/Bells (3 colors)	Closed	1986	15.00	15
1986	Angel Bell w/Bells (white bisque)	Closed	1986	12.50	13
1987	Angel Bell w/Conductor (3 colors)	Closed	1987	16.50	17
1987	Angel Bell w/Conductor (white bisque)	Closed	1987	13.50	14
1988	Angel Bell w/Candle (3 colors)	Closed	1988	17.50	18
1988	Angel Bell w/Candle(wh. bisque)	Closed	1988	15.00	15
1989	Angel Bell w/Star (3 colors)	Closed	1989	20.00	20
1989	Angel Bell w/Star (white bisque)	Closed	1989	17.50	18
1990	Angel Bell w/Lantern (3 colors)	Closed	1990	22.50	23
1990	Angel Bell w/Lantern (wh. bisque)	Closed	1990	20.00	20
1991	Angel Bell w/Teddy (3 colors)	Closed	1991	25.00	25
1991	Angel Bell w/Teddy (wh. bisque)	Closed	1991	22.50	23
1992	Angel Bell w/Doll (3 colors)	Closed	1992	27.50	28
1992	Angel Bell w/Doll (white bisque)	Closed	1992	25.00	25
1993	Angel Bell w/Rocking Horse (3 colors)	Closed	1993	30.00	30
1993	Angel Bell w/Rocking Horse (white bisque)	Closed	1993	27.50	28
1994	Angel Bell w/Clown (3 colors)	Closed	1994	34.50	35
1994	Angel Bell w/Clown (wh. bisque)	Closed	1994	29.50	30
1995	Angel Bell w/Train (3 colors)	Closed	1995	37.00	37
1995	Angel Bell w/Train (white bisque)	Closed	1995	30.50	31
1996	Angel Bell w/Puppy (3 colors)	Open		40.00	40
1996	Angel Bell w/Puppy (wh. bisque)	Open		32.00	32

Goebel/M.I. Hummel

M.I. Hummel Annual Figurine Ornaments - M.I. Hummel

YEAR	ISSUE	EDITION LIMIT	YEAR RETD.	ISSUE PRICE	*QUOTE U.S.$
1988	Flying High 452	Closed	N/A	75.00	125
1989	Love From Above 481	Closed	N/A	75.00	100
1990	Peace on Earth 484	Closed	N/A	80.00	85-100
1991	Angelic Guide 571	Closed	N/A	95.00	95-125

CHRISTMAS ORNAMENTS

YEAR ISSUE		EDITION LIMIT	YEAR RETD.	ISSUE PRICE	*QUOTE U.S.$
1992	Light Up The Night 622	Closed	N/A	100.00	95-125
1993	Herald on High 623	Closed	N/A	155.00	180

M.I. Hummel Collectibles Christmas Bell Ornaments - M.I. Hummel

1989	Ride Into Christmas 775	Closed	1989	35.00	70
1990	Letter to Santa Claus 776	Closed	1990	37.50	50
1991	Hear Ye, Hear Ye 777	Closed	1991	40.00	40
1992	Harmony in Four Parts 778	Closed	1992	50.00	50
1993	Celestial Musician 779	Closed	1993	50.00	50
1994	Festival Harmony w/Mandolin 780	Closed	1994	50.00	50
1995	Festival Harmony w/Flute 781	Closed	1995	55.00	50
1996	Christmas Song 782	Yr.Iss.		65.00	65

M.I. Hummel Collectibles Miniature Ornaments - M.I. Hummel

1993	Celestial Musician 646	Open		90.00	110
1994	Festival Harmony w/Mandolin 647	Open		95.00	110
1995	Festival Harmony w/Flute 648	Open		100.00	110
1996	Christmas Song 645	Open		115.00	115

Gorham

Annual Crystal Ornaments - Gorham

1985	Crystal Ornament	Closed	1985	22.00	22
1986	Crystal Ornament	Closed	1986	25.00	25
1987	Crystal Ornament	Closed	1987	25.00	25
1988	Crystal Ornament	Closed	1988	28.00	28
1989	Crystal Ornament	Closed	1989	28.00	28
1990	Crystal Ornament	Closed	1990	30.00	30
1991	Crystal Ornament	Closed	1991	35.00	35
1992	Crystal Ornament	Closed	1992	32.50	33
1993	Crystal Ornament	Closed	1993	32.50	33

Annual Snowflake Ornaments - Gorham

1970	Sterling Snowflake	Closed	1970	10.00	300-600
1971	Sterling Snowflake	Closed	1971	10.00	75-125
1972	Sterling Snowflake	Closed	1972	10.00	75-125
1973	Sterling Snowflake	Closed	1973	11.00	75-130
1974	Sterling Snowflake	Closed	1974	18.00	70-110
1975	Sterling Snowflake	Closed	1975	18.00	35-85
1976	Sterling Snowflake	Closed	1976	20.00	45-100
1977	Sterling Snowflake	Closed	1977	23.00	35-80
1978	Sterling Snowflake	Closed	1978	23.00	50-80
1979	Sterling Snowflake	Closed	1979	33.00	50-95
1980	Silverplated Snowflake	Closed	1980	15.00	125-150
1981	Sterling Snowflake	Closed	1981	50.00	150-225
1982	Sterling Snowflake	Closed	1982	38.00	55-90
1983	Sterling Snowflake	Closed	1983	45.00	65-100
1984	Sterling Snowflake	Closed	1984	45.00	55-95
1985	Sterling Snowflake	Closed	1985	45.00	65-125
1986	Sterling Snowflake	Closed	1986	45.00	55-85
1987	Sterling Snowflake	Closed	1987	50.00	55-75
1988	Sterling Snowflake	Closed	1988	50.00	60
1989	Sterling Snowflake	Closed	1989	50.00	60
1990	Sterling Snowflake	Closed	1990	50.00	60
1991	Sterling Snowflake	Closed	1991	55.00	60
1992	Sterling Snowflake	Closed	1992	50.00	55-65
1993	Sterling Snowflake	Closed	1993	50.00	50
1994	Sterling Snowflake	Closed	1994	50.00	50
1995	Sterling Snowflake	Closed	1995	50.00	50

Archive Collectible - Gorham

1988	Victorian Heart	Closed	1988	50.00	55-75
1989	Victorian Wreath	Closed	1989	50.00	65
1990	Elizabethan Cupid	Closed	1990	60.00	60
1991	Baroque Angels	Closed	1991	55.00	65
1992	Madonna and Child	Closed	1992	50.00	55
1993	Angel With Mandolin	Closed	1993	50.00	55

Baby's First Christmas Crystal - Gorham

1991	Baby's First Rocking Horse	Closed	1994	35.00	35

Greenwich Workshop

Christensen - J. Christensen

1995	The Angel's Gift	Yr.Iss	1995	50.00	50

Hallmark Keepsake Ornaments

1973 Hallmark Keepsake Collection - Keepsake

1973	Betsey Clark XHD100-2	Yr.Iss.	1973	2.50	60-85
1973	Betsey Clark-(1st Ed.) XHD 110-2	Yr.Iss.	1973	2.50	125
1973	Christmas Is Love XHD106-2	Yr.Iss.	1973	2.50	80
1973	Elves XHD103-5	Yr.Iss.	1973	2.50	75
1973	Manger Scene XHD102-2	Yr.Iss.	1973	2.50	85-125
1973	Santa with Elves XHD101-5	Yr.Iss.	1973	2.50	85

1973 Keepsake Yarn Ornaments - Keepsake

1973	Angel XHD78-5	Yr.Iss.	1973	1.25	23
1973	Blue Girl XHD85-2	Yr.Iss.	1973	1.25	23
1973	Boy Caroler XHD83-2	Yr.Iss.	1973	1.25	30
1973	Choir Boy XHD80-5	Yr.Iss.	1973	1.25	28
1973	Elf XHD79-2	Yr.Iss.	1973	1.25	25
1973	Green Girl XHD84-5	Yr.Iss.	1973	1.25	25
1973	Little Girl XHD82-5	Yr.Iss.	1973	1.25	20
1973	Mr. Santa XHD74-5	Yr.Iss.	1973	1.25	25
1973	Mr. Snowman XHD76-5	Yr.Iss.	1973	1.25	25
1973	Mrs. Santa XHD75-2	Yr.Iss.	1973	1.25	23
1973	Mrs. Snowman XHD77-2	Yr.Iss.	1973	1.25	23
1973	Soldier XHD81-2	Yr.Iss.	1973	1.00	22

1974 Hallmark Keepsake Collection - Keepsake

1974	Angel QX110-1	Yr.Iss.	1974	2.50	75
1974	Betsey Clark-(2nd Ed.) QX 108-1	Yr.Iss.	1974	2.50	47-85
1974	Buttons & Bo (Set/2) QX113-1	Yr.Iss.	1974	3.50	50
1974	Charmers QX109-1	Yr.Iss.	1974	2.50	23-45
1974	Currier & Ives (Set/2) QX112-1	Yr.Iss.	1974	3.50	42-55
1974	Little Miracles (Set/4) QX115-1	Yr.Iss.	1974	4.50	55
1974	Norman Rockwell QX106-1	Yr.Iss.	1974	2.50	45-95
1974	Norman Rockwell QX111-1	Yr.Iss.	1974	2.50	85
1974	Raggedy Ann and Andy(4/set) QX114-1	Yr.Iss.	1974	4.50	75
1974	Snowgoose QX107-1	Yr.Iss.	1974	2.50	75

1974 Keepsake Yarn Ornaments - Keepsake

1974	Angel QX103-1	Yr.Iss.	1974	1.50	28
1974	Elf QX101-1	Yr.Iss.	1974	1.50	23
1974	Mrs. Santa QX100-1	Yr.Iss.	1974	1.50	23
1974	Santa QX105-1	Yr.Iss.	1974	1.50	25
1974	Snowman QX104-1	Yr.Iss.	1974	1.50	23
1974	Soldier QX102-1	Yr.Iss.	1974	1.50	23

1975 Handcrafted Ornaments: Adorable - Keepsake

1975	Betsey Clark QX157-1	Yr.Iss.	1975	2.50	225
1975	Drummer Boy QX161-1	Yr.Iss.	1975	2.50	295
1975	Mrs. Santa QX156-1	Yr.Iss.	1975	2.50	275
1975	Raggedy Andy QX160-1	Yr.Iss.	1975	2.50	375
1975	Raggedy Ann QX159-1	Yr.Iss.	1975	2.50	295
1975	Santa QX155-1	Yr.Iss.	1975	2.50	250

1975 Handcrafted Ornaments: Nostalgia - Keepsake

1975	Drummer Boy QX130-1	Yr.Iss.	1975	3.50	115-175
1975	Joy QX132-1	Yr.Iss.	1975	3.50	125-175
1975	Locomotive (dated) QX127-1	Yr.Iss.	1975	3.50	110-175
1975	Peace on Earth (dated) QX131-1	Yr.Iss.	1975	3.50	95-165
1975	Rocking Horse QX128-1	Yr.Iss.	1975	3.50	115
1975	Santa & Sleigh QX129-1	Yr.Iss.	1975	3.50	125

1975 Keepsake Property Ornaments - Keepsake

1975	Betsey Clark (Set/2) QX167-1	Yr.Iss.	1975	3.50	25-45
1975	Betsey Clark (Set/4) QX168-1	Yr.Iss.	1975	4.50	50
1975	Betsey Clark QX163-1	Yr.Iss.	1975	2.50	40
1975	Betsey Clark-(3rd Ed.) QX133-1	Yr.Iss.	1975	3.00	30-60
1975	Buttons & Bo (Set/4) QX139-1	Yr.Iss.	1975	5.00	50
1975	Charmers QX135-1	Yr.Iss.	1975	3.00	30-40
1975	Currier & Ives (Set/2) QX137-1	Yr.Iss.	1975	4.00	40
1975	Currier & Ives (Set/2) QX164-1	Yr.Iss.	1975	2.50	35-40
1975	Little Miracles (Set/4) QX140-1	Yr.Iss.	1975	5.00	40
1975	Marty Links QX136-1	Yr.Iss.	1975	3.00	50
1975	Norman Rockwell QX134-1	Yr.Iss.	1975	3.00	40-55
1975	Norman Rockwell QX166-1	Yr.Iss.	1975	2.50	37-55
1975	Raggedy Ann and Andy(2/set) QX138-1	Yr.Iss.	1975	4.00	65
1975	Raggedy Ann QX165-1	Yr.Iss.	1975	2.50	50-65

1975 Keepsake Yarn Ornaments - Keepsake

1975	Drummer Boy QX123-1	Yr.Iss.	1975	1.75	25
1975	Little Girl QX126-1	Yr.Iss.	1975	1.75	20
1975	Mrs. Santa QX125-1	Yr.Iss.	1975	1.75	22
1975	Raggedy Andy QX122-1	Yr.Iss.	1975	1.75	40
1975	Raggedy Ann QX121-1	Yr.Iss.	1975	1.75	35
1975	Santa QX124-1	Yr.Iss.	1975	1.75	22

1976 Bicentennial Commemoratives - Keepsake

1976	Bicentennial '76 Commemorative QX211-1	Yr.Iss.	1976	2.50	45-60
1976	Bicentennial Charmers QX198-1	Yr.Iss.	1976	3.00	60
1976	Colonial Children (Set/2) 4 QX208-1	Yr.Iss.	1976	4.00	40-65

1976 Decorative Ball Ornaments - Keepsake

1976	Cardinals QX205-1	Yr.Iss.	1976	2.30	50
1976	Chickadees QX204-1	Yr.Iss.	1976	2.30	50-65

1976 First Commemorative Ornament - Keepsake

1976	Baby's First Christmas QX211-1	Yr.Iss.	1976	2.50	150

1976 Handcrafted Ornaments: Nostalgia - Keepsake

1976	Drummer Boy QX130-1	Yr.Iss.	1976	3.50	160-175
1976	Locomotive QX222-1	Yr.Iss.	1976	3.50	165
1976	Peace on Earth QX223-1	Yr.Iss.	1976	3.50	95-175
1976	Rocking Horse QX128-1	Yr.Iss.	1976	3.50	165

1976 Handcrafted Ornaments: Tree Treats - Keepsake

1976	Angel QX176-1	Yr.Iss.	1976	3.00	150-195
1976	Reindeer QX 178-1	Yr.Iss.	1976	3.00	115
1976	Santa QX177-1	Yr.Iss.	1976	3.00	200-225
1976	Shepherd QX175-1	Yr.Iss.	1976	3.00	95-115

1976 Handcrafted Ornaments: Twirl-Abouts - Keepsake

1976	Angel QX171-1	Yr.Iss.	1976	4.50	132-165
1976	Partridge QX174-1	Yr.Iss.	1976	4.50	195
1976	Santa QX172-1	Yr.Iss.	1976	4.50	103-125
1976	Soldier QX173-1	Yr.Iss.	1976	4.50	95

1976 Handcrafted Ornaments: Yesteryears - Keepsake

1976	Drummer Boy QX184-1	Yr.Iss.	1976	5.00	122-150
1976	Partridge QX183-1	Yr.Iss.	1976	5.00	115
1976	Santa QX182-1	Yr.Iss.	1976	5.00	165
1976	Train QX181-1	Yr.Iss.	1976	5.00	135-160

1976 Property Ornaments - Keepsake

1976	Betsey Clark (Set/3) QX218-1	Yr.Iss.	1976	4.50	50
1976	Betsey Clark QX210-1	Yr.Iss.	1976	2.50	38-42
1976	Betsey Clark-(4th Ed.)QX 195-1	Yr.Iss.	1976	3.00	75-100
1976	Charmers (Set/2) QX215-1	Yr.Iss.	1976	3.50	55
1976	Currier & Ives QX197-1	Yr.Iss.	1976	3.00	50
1976	Currier & Ives QX209-1	Yr.Iss.	1976	2.50	50
1976	Happy the Snowman (Set/2) QX216-1	Yr.Iss.	1976	3.50	55
1976	Marty Links (Set/2) QX207-1	Yr.Iss.	1976	4.00	45
1976	Norman Rockwell QX196-1	Yr.Iss.	1976	3.00	65
1976	Raggedy Ann QX212-1	Yr.Iss.	1976	2.50	65
1976	Rudolph and Santa QX213-1	Yr.Iss.	1976	2.50	75

1976 Yarn Ornaments - Keepsake

1976	Caroler QX126-1	Yr.Iss.	1976	1.75	28
1976	Drummer Boy QX123-1	Yr.Iss.	1976	1.75	23
1976	Mrs. Santa QX125-1	Yr.Iss.	1976	1.75	22
1976	Raggedy Andy QX122-1	Yr.Iss.	1976	1.75	40
1976	Raggedy Ann QX121-1	Yr.Iss.	1976	1.75	35
1976	Santa QX124-1	Yr.Iss.	1976	1.75	24

1977 Christmas Expressions Collection - Keepsake

1977	Bell QX154-2	Yr.Iss.	1977	3.50	35
1977	Mandolin QX157-5	Yr.Iss.	1977	3.50	65
1977	Ornaments QX155-5	Yr.Iss.	1977	3.50	65
1977	Wreath QX156-2	Yr.Iss.	1977	3.50	65

1977 Cloth Doll Ornaments - Keepsake

1977	Angel QX220-2	Yr.Iss.	1977	1.75	40-50
1977	Santa QX221-5	Yr.Iss.	1977	1.75	55-80

1977 Colors of Christmas - Keepsake

1977	Bell QX200-2	Yr.Iss.	1977	3.50	35-45
1977	Candle QX203-5	Yr.Iss.	1977	3.50	55
1977	Joy QX201-5	Yr.Iss.	1977	3.50	45
1977	Wreath QX202-2	Yr.Iss.	1977	3.50	35-55

1977 Commemoratives - Keepsake

1977	Baby's First Christmas QX131-5	Yr.Iss.	1977	3.50	55-75
1977	First Christmas Together QX132-2	Yr.Iss.	1977	3.50	65
1977	For Your New Home QX263-5	Yr.Iss.	1977	3.50	120
1977	Granddaughter QX208-2	Yr.Iss.	1977	3.50	150
1977	Grandmother QX260-2	Yr.Iss.	1977	3.50	150
1977	Grandson QX209-5	Yr.Iss.	1977	3.50	150
1977	Love QX262-2	Yr.Iss.	1977	3.50	95
1977	Mother QX261-5	Yr.Iss.	1977	3.50	75

1977 Decorative Ball Ornaments - Keepsake

1977	Christmas Mouse QX134-2	Yr.Iss.	1977	3.50	65
1977	Rabbit QX139-5	Yr.Iss.	1977	2.50	95
1977	Squirrel QX138-2	Yr.Iss.	1977	2.50	95
1977	Stained Glass QX152-2	Yr.Iss.	1977	3.50	40-70

1977 Holiday Highlights - Keepsake

1977	Drummer Boy QX312-2	Yr.Iss.	1977	3.50	45-65
1977	Joy QX310-2	Yr.Iss.	1977	3.50	45
1977	Peace on Earth QX311-5	Yr.Iss.	1977	3.50	65
1977	Star QX313-5	Yr.Iss.	1977	3.50	50

1977 Metal Ornaments - Keepsake

1977	Snowflake Collection (Set/4) QX 210-2	Yr.Iss.	1977	5.00	95

1977 Nostalgia Collection - Keepsake

1977	Angel QX182-2	Yr.Iss.	1977	5.00	95-125
1977	Antique Car QX180-2	Yr.Iss.	1977	5.00	65
1977	Nativity QX181-5	Yr.Iss.	1977	5.00	137
1977	Toys QX183-5	Yr.Iss.	1977	5.00	155

1977 Peanuts Collection - Keepsake

1977	Peanuts (Set/2) QX163-5	Yr.Iss.	1977	4.00	75
1977	Peanuts QX135-5	Yr.Iss.	1977	3.50	60
1977	Peanuts QX162-2	Yr.Iss.	1977	2.50	60

1977 Property Ornaments - Keepsake

1977	Betsey Clark -(5th Ed.) QX264-2	Yr.Iss.	1977	3.50	465-485
1977	Charmers QX153-5	Yr.Iss.	1977	3.50	50
1977	Currier & Ives QX130-2	Yr.Iss.	1977	3.50	55
1977	Disney (Set/2) QX137-5	Yr.Iss.	1977	4.00	75
1977	Disney QX133-5	Yr.Iss.	1977	3.50	45
1977	Grandma Moses QX150-2	Yr.Iss.	1977	3.50	100-175
1977	Norman Rockwell QX151-5	Yr.Iss.	1977	3.50	70

1977 The Beauty of America Collection - Keepsake

1977	Desert QX159-5	Yr.Iss.	1977	2.50	25
1977	Mountains QX158-2	Yr.Iss.	1977	2.50	15
1977	Seashore QX160-2	Yr.Iss.	1977	2.50	50
1977	Wharf QX161-5	Yr.Iss.	1977	2.50	30-50

1977 Twirl-About Collection - Keepsake

1977	Bellringer QX192-2	Yr.Iss.	1977	6.00	45-55
1977	Della Robia Wreath QX193-5	Yr.Iss.	1977	4.50	90-115
1977	Snowman QX190-2	Yr.Iss.	1977	4.50	60-75
1977	Weather House QX191-5	Yr.Iss.	1977	6.00	85-95

1977 Yesteryears Collection - Keepsake

1977	Angel QX172-2	Yr.Iss.	1977	6.00	85
1977	House QX170-2	Yr.Iss.	1977	6.00	100-125
1977	Jack-in-the-Box QX171-5	Yr.Iss.	1977	6.00	100-125
1977	Reindeer QX173-5	Yr.Iss.	1977	6.00	110-140

*Quotes have been rounded up to nearest dollar

CHRISTMAS ORNAMENTS

1978 Colors of Christmas - Keepsake

YEAR ISSUE	EDITION LIMIT	YEAR RETD.	ISSUE PRICE	*QUOTE U.S.$
1978 Angel QX354-3	Yr.Iss.	1978	3.50	40
1978 Candle QX357-6	Yr.Iss.	1978	3.50	85
1978 Locomotive QX356-3	Yr.Iss.	1978	3.50	47
1978 Merry Christmas QX355-6	Yr.Iss.	1978	3.50	50

1978 Commemoratives - Keepsake

YEAR ISSUE	EDITION LIMIT	YEAR RETD.	ISSUE PRICE	*QUOTE U.S.$
1978 25th Christmas Together QX269-3	Yr.Iss.	1978	3.50	35
1978 Baby's First Christmas QX200-3	Yr.Iss.	1978	3.50	65-85
1978 First Christmas Together QX218-3	Yr.Iss.	1978	3.50	45
1978 For Your New Home QX217-6	Yr.Iss.	1978	3.50	75
1978 Granddaughter QX216-3	Yr.Iss.	1978	3.50	55
1978 Grandmother QX267-6	Yr.Iss.	1978	3.50	50
1978 Grandson QX215-6	Yr.Iss.	1978	3.50	45
1978 Love QX268-3	Yr.Iss.	1978	3.50	55
1978 Mother QX266-3	Yr.Iss.	1978	3.50	25-35

1978 Decorative Ball Ornaments - Keepsake

YEAR ISSUE	EDITION LIMIT	YEAR RETD.	ISSUE PRICE	*QUOTE U.S.$
1978 Drummer Boy QX252-3	Yr.Iss.	1978	3.50	35-45
1978 Hallmark's Antique Card Collection Design QX220-3	Yr.Iss.	1978	3.50	40
1978 Joy QX254-3	Yr.Iss.	1978	3.50	20-40
1978 Merry Christmas (Santa) QX202-3	Yr.Iss.	1978	3.50	45-55
1978 Nativity QX253-6	Yr.Iss.	1978	3.50	150
1978 The Quail QX251-6	Yr.Iss.	1978	3.50	45
1978 Yesterday's Toys QX250-3	Yr.Iss.	1978	3.50	55

1978 Handcrafted Ornaments - Keepsake

YEAR ISSUE	EDITION LIMIT	YEAR RETD.	ISSUE PRICE	*QUOTE U.S.$
1978 Angel QX139-6	Yr.Iss.	1981	4.50	85-95
1978 Angels QX150-3	Yr.Iss.	1978	8.00	345
1978 Animal Home QX149-6	Yr.Iss.	1978	6.00	125-175
1978 Calico Mouse QX137-6	Yr.Iss.	1978	4.50	95
1978 Carrousel Series-(1st Ed.) QX146-3	Yr.Iss.	1978	6.00	400
1978 Dough Angel QX139-6	Yr.Iss.	1981	5.50	65-95
1978 Dove QX190-3	Yr.Iss.	1978	4.50	65-85
1978 Holly and Poinsettia Ball QX147-6	Yr.Iss.	1978	6.00	85
1978 Joy QX138-3	Yr.Iss.	1978	4.50	75-85
1978 Panorama Ball QX145-6	Yr.Iss.	1978	6.00	135
1978 Red Cardinal QX144-3	Yr.Iss.	1978	4.50	152-175
1978 Rocking Horse QX148-3	Yr.Iss.	1978	6.00	85
1978 Schneeberg Bell QX152-3	Yr.Iss.	1978	8.00	190
1978 Skating Raccoon QX142-3	Yr.Iss.	1978	6.00	85-95

1978 Holiday Chimes - Keepsake

YEAR ISSUE	EDITION LIMIT	YEAR RETD.	ISSUE PRICE	*QUOTE U.S.$
1978 Reindeer Chimes QX320-3	Yr.Iss.	1980	4.50	60

1978 Holiday Highlights - Keepsake

YEAR ISSUE	EDITION LIMIT	YEAR RETD.	ISSUE PRICE	*QUOTE U.S.$
1978 Dove QX310-3	Yr.Iss.	1978	3.50	125
1978 Nativity QX309-6	Yr.Iss.	1978	3.50	70-80
1978 Santa QX307-6	Yr.Iss.	1978	3.50	75
1978 Snowflake QX308-3	Yr.Iss.	1978	3.50	65

1978 Little Trimmers - Keepsake

YEAR ISSUE	EDITION LIMIT	YEAR RETD.	ISSUE PRICE	*QUOTE U.S.$
1978 Drummer Boy QX136-3	Yr.Iss.	1978	2.50	55-75
1978 Praying Angel QX134-3	Yr.Iss.	1978	2.50	90
1978 Santa QX135-6	Yr.Iss.	1978	2.50	58-65
1978 Set/4 - QX355-6	Yr.Iss.	1978	10.00	400-425
1978 Thimble Series (Mouse) -(1st Ed.) QX133-6	Yr.Iss.	1978	2.50	265-295

1978 Peanuts Collection - Keepsake

YEAR ISSUE	EDITION LIMIT	YEAR RETD.	ISSUE PRICE	*QUOTE U.S.$
1978 Peanuts QX203-6	Yr.Iss.	1978	2.50	50
1978 Peanuts QX204-3	Yr.Iss.	1978	2.50	60
1978 Peanuts QX205-6	Yr.Iss.	1978	3.50	65
1978 Peanuts QX206-3	Yr.Iss.	1978	3.50	50

1978 Property Ornaments - Keepsake

YEAR ISSUE	EDITION LIMIT	YEAR RETD.	ISSUE PRICE	*QUOTE U.S.$
1978 Betsey Clark-(6th Ed.) QX201-6	Yr.Iss.	1978	3.50	60
1978 Disney QX207-6	Yr.Iss.	1978	3.50	60
1978 Joan Walsh Anglund QX221-6	Yr.Iss.	1978	3.50	65
1978 Spencer Sparrow QX219-6	Yr.Iss.	1978	3.50	50

1978 Yarn Collection - Keepsake

YEAR ISSUE	EDITION LIMIT	YEAR RETD.	ISSUE PRICE	*QUOTE U.S.$
1978 Green Boy QX123-1	Yr.Iss.	1979	2.00	25
1978 Green Girl QX126-1	Yr.Iss.	1979	2.00	20
1978 Mr. Claus QX340-3	Yr.Iss.	1979	2.00	23
1978 Mrs. Claus QX125-1	Yr.Iss.	1979	2.00	22

1979 Collectible Series - Keepsake

YEAR ISSUE	EDITION LIMIT	YEAR RETD.	ISSUE PRICE	*QUOTE U.S.$
1979 Bellringer-(1st Ed.) QX147-9	Yr.Iss.	1979	10.00	400
1979 Carousel-(2nd Ed.) QX146-7	Yr.Iss.	1979	6.50	165-185
1979 Here Comes Santa-(1st Ed.) QX155-9	Yr.Iss.	1979	9.00	425-550
1979 Snoopy and Friends QX141-9	Yr.Iss.	1979	8.00	95-120
1979 Thimble-(2nd Ed.) QX131-9	Yr.Iss.	1980	3.00	150-175

1979 Colors of Christmas - Keepsake

YEAR ISSUE	EDITION LIMIT	YEAR RETD.	ISSUE PRICE	*QUOTE U.S.$
1979 Holiday Wreath QX353-9	Yr.Iss.	1979	3.50	35-45
1979 Partridge in a Pear Tree QX351-9	Yr.Iss.	1979	3.50	35-45
1979 Star Over Bethlehem QX352-7	Yr.Iss.	1979	3.50	75
1979 Words of Christmas QX350-7	Yr.Iss.	1979	3.50	85

1979 Commemoratives - Keepsake

YEAR ISSUE	EDITION LIMIT	YEAR RETD.	ISSUE PRICE	*QUOTE U.S.$
1979 Baby's First Christmas QX154-7	Yr.Iss.	1979	8.00	175
1979 Baby's First Christmas QX208-7	Yr.Iss.	1979	3.50	22-30
1979 Friendship QX203-9	Yr.Iss.	1979	3.50	18
1979 Granddaughter QX211-9	Yr.Iss.	1979	3.50	20-35
1979 Grandmother QX252-7	Yr.Iss.	1979	3.50	10
1979 Grandson QX210-7	Yr.Iss.	1979	3.50	35
1979 Love QX258-7	Yr.Iss.	1979	3.50	17-25
1979 Mother QX251-9	Yr.Iss.	1979	3.50	15-23
1979 New Home QX212-7	Yr.Iss.	1979	3.50	45
1979 Our First Christmas Together QX209-9	Yr.Iss.	1979	3.50	50-75
1979 Our Twenty-Fifth Anniversary QX 250-7	Yr.Iss.	1979	3.50	17-28
1979 Teacher QX213-9	Yr.Iss.	1979	3.50	15

1979 Decorative Ball Ornaments - Keepsake

YEAR ISSUE	EDITION LIMIT	YEAR RETD.	ISSUE PRICE	*QUOTE U.S.$
1979 Behold the Star QX255-9	Yr.Iss.	1979	3.50	40
1979 Black Angel QX207-9	Yr.Iss.	1979	3.50	25
1979 Christmas Chickadees QX204-7	Yr.Iss.	1979	3.50	30
1979 Christmas Collage QX257-9	Yr.Iss.	1979	3.50	16-35
1979 Christmas Traditions QX253-9	Yr.Iss.	1979	3.50	35
1979 The Light of Christmas QX256-7	Yr.Iss.	1979	3.50	18-30
1979 Night Before Christmas QX214-7	Yr.Iss.	1979	3.50	40

1979 Handcrafted Ornaments - Keepsake

YEAR ISSUE	EDITION LIMIT	YEAR RETD.	ISSUE PRICE	*QUOTE U.S.$
1979 Christmas Eve Surprise QX157-9	Yr.Iss.	1979	6.50	65
1979 Christmas Heart QX140-7	Yr.Iss.	1979	6.50	105-115
1979 Christmas is for Children QX135-9	Yr.Iss.	1980	5.00	83-95
1979 A Christmas Treat QX134-7	Yr.Iss.	1980	5.00	85
1979 The Downhill Run QX145-9	Yr.Iss.	1979	6.50	135-175
1979 The Drummer Boy QX143-9	Yr.Iss.	1979	8.00	90-125
1979 Holiday Scrimshaw QX152-7	Yr.Iss.	1979	4.00	225
1979 Outdoor Fun QX150-7	Yr.Iss.	1979	8.00	125-135
1979 Raccoon QX142-3	Yr.Iss.	1979	6.50	85
1979 Ready for Christmas QX133-9	Yr.Iss.	1979	6.50	95-150
1979 Santa's Here QX138-7	Yr.Iss.	1979	5.00	55-75
1979 The Skating Snowman QX139-9	Yr.Iss.	1980	5.00	65-80

1979 Holiday Chimes - Keepsake

YEAR ISSUE	EDITION LIMIT	YEAR RETD.	ISSUE PRICE	*QUOTE U.S.$
1979 Reindeer Chimes QX320-3	Yr.Iss.	1980	4.50	75
1979 Star Chimes QX137-9	Yr.Iss.	1979	4.50	75-85

1979 Holiday Highlights - Keepsake

YEAR ISSUE	EDITION LIMIT	YEAR RETD.	ISSUE PRICE	*QUOTE U.S.$
1979 Christmas Angel QX300-7	Yr.Iss.	1979	3.50	95
1979 Christmas Cheer QX303-9	Yr.Iss.	1979	3.50	95
1979 Christmas Tree QX302-7	Yr.Iss.	1979	3.50	75
1979 Love QX304-7	Yr.Iss.	1979	3.50	88
1979 Snowflake QX301-9	Yr.Iss.	1979	3.50	40

1979 Little Trimmer Collection - Keepsake

YEAR ISSUE	EDITION LIMIT	YEAR RETD.	ISSUE PRICE	*QUOTE U.S.$
1979 Angel Delight QX130-7	Yr.Iss.	1979	3.00	80-95
1979 A Matchless Christmas QX132-7	Yr.Iss.	1979	4.00	65-85
1979 Santa QX135-6	Yr.Iss.	1979	3.00	55
1979 Thimble Series-Mouse QX133-6	Yr.Iss.	1979	3.00	150-225

1979 Property Ornaments - Keepsake

YEAR ISSUE	EDITION LIMIT	YEAR RETD.	ISSUE PRICE	*QUOTE U.S.$
1979 Betsey Clark-(7th Ed.) QX 201-9	Yr.Iss.	1979	3.50	33-40
1979 Joan Walsh Anglund QX205-9	Yr.Iss.	1979	3.50	35
1979 Mary Hamilton QX254-7	Yr.Iss.	1979	3.50	25
1979 Peanuts (Time to Trim) QX202-7	Yr.Iss.	1979	3.50	40
1979 Spencer Sparrow QX200-7	Yr.Iss.	1979	3.50	25-40
1979 Winnie-the-Pooh QX206-7	Yr.Iss.	1979	3.50	40

1979 Sewn Trimmers - Keepsake

YEAR ISSUE	EDITION LIMIT	YEAR RETD.	ISSUE PRICE	*QUOTE U.S.$
1979 Angel Music QX343-9	Yr.Iss.	1980	2.00	20
1979 Merry Santa QX342-7	Yr.Iss.	1980	2.00	20
1979 The Rocking Horse QX340-7	Yr.Iss.	1980	2.00	23
1979 Stuffed Full Stocking QX341-9	Yr.Iss.	1980	2.00	18-25

1979 Yarn Collection - Keepsake

YEAR ISSUE	EDITION LIMIT	YEAR RETD.	ISSUE PRICE	*QUOTE U.S.$
1979 Green Boy QX123-1	Yr.Iss.	1979	2.00	20
1979 Green Girl QX126-1	Yr.Iss.	1979	2.00	18
1979 Mr. Claus QX340-3	Yr.Iss.	1979	2.00	20
1979 Mrs. Claus QX125-1	Yr.Iss.	1979	2.00	20

1980 Collectible Series - Keepsake

YEAR ISSUE	EDITION LIMIT	YEAR RETD.	ISSUE PRICE	*QUOTE U.S.$
1980 The Bellringers-(2nd Ed.) QX157-4	Yr.Iss.	1980	15.00	60-85
1980 Carrousel-(3rd Ed.) QX141-4	Yr.Iss.	1980	7.50	140-165
1980 Frosty Friends-(1st Ed.)QX 137-4	Yr.Iss.	1980	6.50	625
1980 Here Comes Santa-(2nd Ed.) QX 143-4	Yr.Iss.	1980	12.00	170
1980 Norman Rockwell-(1st Ed.) QX306-1	Yr.Iss.	1980	6.50	250
1980 Snoopy & Friends-(2nd Ed.) QX154-1	Yr.Iss.	1980	9.00	100-125
1980 Thimble-(3rd Ed.) QX132-1	Yr.Iss.	1980	4.00	175

1980 Colors of Christmas - Keepsake

YEAR ISSUE	EDITION LIMIT	YEAR RETD.	ISSUE PRICE	*QUOTE U.S.$
1980 Joy QX350-1	Yr.Iss.	1980	4.00	20

1980 Commemoratives - Keepsake

YEAR ISSUE	EDITION LIMIT	YEAR RETD.	ISSUE PRICE	*QUOTE U.S.$
1980 25th Christmas Together QX206-1	Yr.Iss.	1980	4.00	20
1980 Baby's First Christmas QX156-1	Yr.Iss.	1980	12.00	50
1980 Baby's First Christmas QX200-1	Yr.Iss.	1980	4.00	22-30
1980 Beauty of Friendship QX303-4	Yr.Iss.	1980	4.00	60
1980 Black Baby's First Christmas QX229-4	Yr.Iss.	1980	4.00	30
1980 Christmas at Home QX210-1	Yr.Iss.	1980	4.00	35
1980 Christmas Love QX207-4	Yr.Iss.	1980	4.00	40
1980 Dad QX214-1	Yr.Iss.	1980	4.00	9-18
1980 Daughter QX212-1	Yr.Iss.	1980	4.00	40
1980 First Christmas Together QX205-4	Yr.Iss.	1980	4.00	25-40
1980 First Christmas Together QX305-4	Yr.Iss.	1980	4.00	30-55
1980 Friendship QX208-1	Yr.Iss.	1980	4.00	10-20
1980 Granddaughter QX202-1	Yr.Iss.	1980	4.00	35
1980 Grandfather QX231-4	Yr.Iss.	1980	4.00	10-20
1980 Grandmother QX204-1	Yr.Iss.	1980	4.00	20
1980 Grandparents QX213-4	Yr.Iss.	1980	4.00	40
1980 Grandson QX201-4	Yr.Iss.	1980	4.00	20-35
1980 Love QX302-1	Yr.Iss.	1980	4.00	65
1980 Mother and Dad QX230-1	Yr.Iss.	1980	4.00	11-20
1980 Mother QX203-4	Yr.Iss.	1980	4.00	11-23
1980 Mother QX304-1	Yr.Iss.	1980	4.00	35
1980 Son QX211-4	Yr.Iss.	1980	4.00	27-35
1980 Teacher QX209-4	Yr.Iss.	1980	4.00	10-20

1980 Decorative Ball Ornaments - Keepsake

YEAR ISSUE	EDITION LIMIT	YEAR RETD.	ISSUE PRICE	*QUOTE U.S.$
1980 Christmas Cardinals QX224-1	Yr.Iss.	1980	4.00	35
1980 Christmas Choir QX228-1	Yr.Iss.	1980	4.00	85
1980 Christmas Time QX226-1	Yr.Iss.	1980	4.00	30
1980 Happy Christmas QX222-1	Yr.Iss.	1980	4.00	30
1980 Jolly Santa QX227-4	Yr.Iss.	1980	4.00	30
1980 Nativity QX225-4	Yr.Iss.	1980	4.00	125
1980 Santa's Workshop QX223-4	Yr.Iss.	1980	4.00	15-30

1980 Frosted Images - Keepsake

YEAR ISSUE	EDITION LIMIT	YEAR RETD.	ISSUE PRICE	*QUOTE U.S.$
1980 Dove QX308-1	Yr.Iss.	1980	4.00	30-40
1980 Drummer Boy QX309-4	Yr.Iss.	1980	4.00	25
1980 Santa QX310-1	Yr.Iss.	1980	4.00	22

1980 Handcrafted Ornaments - Keepsake

YEAR ISSUE	EDITION LIMIT	YEAR RETD.	ISSUE PRICE	*QUOTE U.S.$
1980 The Animals' Christmas QX150-1	Yr.Iss.	1980	8.00	40-65
1980 Caroling Bear QX140-1	Yr.Iss.	1980	7.50	120-150
1980 Christmas is for Children QX135-9	Yr.Iss.	1980	5.50	95
1980 A Christmas Treat QX134-7	Yr.Iss.	1980	5.50	75
1980 A Christmas Vigil QX144-1	Yr.Iss.	1980	9.00	185
1980 Drummer Boy QX147-4	Yr.Iss.	1980	5.50	75-95
1980 Elfin Antics QX142-1	Yr.Iss.	1980	9.00	225
1980 A Heavenly Nap QX139-4	Yr.Iss.	1981	6.50	40
1980 Heavenly Sounds QX152-1	Yr.Iss.	1980	7.50	72-95
1980 Santa 1980 QX146-1	Yr.Iss.	1980	5.50	95
1980 Santa's Flight QX138-1	Yr.Iss.	1980	5.50	105-115
1980 Skating Snowman QX139-9	Yr.Iss.	1980	5.50	80
1980 The Snowflake Swing QX133-4	Yr.Iss.	1980	4.00	45
1980 A Spot of Christmas Cheer QX153-4	Yr.Iss.	1980	8.00	145

1980 Holiday Chimes - Keepsake

YEAR ISSUE	EDITION LIMIT	YEAR RETD.	ISSUE PRICE	*QUOTE U.S.$
1980 Reindeer Chimes QX320-3	Yr.Iss.	1980	5.50	25
1980 Santa Mobile QX136-1	Yr.Iss.	1981	5.50	25-50
1980 Snowflake Chimes QX165-4	Yr.Iss.	1981	5.50	33

1980 Holiday Highlights - Keepsake

YEAR ISSUE	EDITION LIMIT	YEAR RETD.	ISSUE PRICE	*QUOTE U.S.$
1980 Three Wise Men QX300-1	Yr.Iss.	1980	4.00	30
1980 Wreath QX301-4	Yr.Iss.	1980	4.00	85

1980 Little Trimmers - Keepsake

YEAR ISSUE	EDITION LIMIT	YEAR RETD.	ISSUE PRICE	*QUOTE U.S.$
1980 Christmas Owl QX131-4	Yr.Iss.	1982	4.00	43
1980 Christmas Teddy QX135-4	Yr.Iss.	1980	2.50	80-135
1980 Clothespin Soldier QX134-1	Yr.Iss.	1980	3.50	40
1980 Merry Redbird QX160-1	Yr.Iss.	1980	3.50	50-65
1980 Swingin' on a Star QX130-1	Yr.Iss.	1980	4.00	75-85
1980 Thimble Series-A Christmas Salute QX131-9	Yr.Iss.	1980	4.00	175

1980 Old-Fashioned Christmas Collection - Keepsake

YEAR ISSUE	EDITION LIMIT	YEAR RETD.	ISSUE PRICE	*QUOTE U.S.$
1980 In a Nutshell QX469-7	Yr.Iss.	1988	5.50	24-33

1980 Property Ornaments - Keepsake

YEAR ISSUE	EDITION LIMIT	YEAR RETD.	ISSUE PRICE	*QUOTE U.S.$
1980 Betsey Clark QX307-4	Yr.Iss.	1980	6.50	55
1980 Betsey Clark's Christmas QX194-4	Yr.Iss.	1980	7.50	35
1980 Betsey Clark-(8th Ed.) QX 215-4	Yr.Iss.	1980	4.00	24-30
1980 Disney QX218-1	Yr.Iss.	1980	4.00	30
1980 Joan Walsh Anglund QX217-4	Yr.Iss.	1980	4.00	23-25
1980 Marty Links QX221-4	Yr.Iss.	1980	4.00	11-23
1980 Mary Hamilton QX219-4	Yr.Iss.	1980	4.00	23
1980 Muppets QX220-1	Yr.Iss.	1980	4.00	40
1980 Peanuts QX216-1	Yr.Iss.	1980	4.00	30

1980 Sewn Trimmers - Keepsake

YEAR ISSUE	EDITION LIMIT	YEAR RETD.	ISSUE PRICE	*QUOTE U.S.$
1980 Angel Music QX343-9	Yr.Iss.	1980	2.00	20
1980 Merry Santa QX342-7	Yr.Iss.	1980	2.00	20
1980 The Rocking Horse QX340-7	Yr.Iss.	1980	2.00	22
1980 Stuffed Full Stocking QX341-9	Yr.Iss.	1980	2.00	25

1980 Special Editions - Keepsake

YEAR ISSUE	EDITION LIMIT	YEAR RETD.	ISSUE PRICE	*QUOTE U.S.$
1980 Checking it Twice QX158-4	Yr.Iss.	1981	20.00	175-195
1980 Heavenly Minstrel QX156-7	Yr.Iss.	1980	15.00	345

1980 Yarn Ornaments - Keepsake

YEAR ISSUE	EDITION LIMIT	YEAR RETD.	ISSUE PRICE	*QUOTE U.S.$
1980 Angel QX162-1	Yr.Iss.	1981	3.00	10
1980 Santa QX161-4	Yr.Iss.	1981	3.00	9
1980 Snowman QX163-4	Yr.Iss.	1981	3.00	9
1980 Soldier QX164-1	Yr.Iss.	1981	3.00	9

1981 Collectible Series - Keepsake

YEAR ISSUE	EDITION LIMIT	YEAR RETD.	ISSUE PRICE	*QUOTE U.S.$
1981 Bellringer-(3rd Ed.) QX441-5	Yr.Iss.	1981	15.00	70-95
1981 Carrousel-(4th Ed.) QX427-5	Yr.Iss.	1981	9.00	95
1981 Frosty Friends-(2nd Ed.) QX433-5	Yr.Iss.	1981	8.00	365-425
1981 Here Comes Santa-(3rd Ed.) QX438-2	Yr.Iss.	1981	13.00	205-295

*Quotes have been rounded up to nearest dollar

CHRISTMAS ORNAMENTS

YEAR ISSUE		EDITION LIMIT	YEAR RETD.	ISSUE PRICE	*QUOTE U.S.$
1981	Norman Rockwell-(2nd Ed.) QX 511-5	Yr.Iss.	1981	8.50	31-51
1981	Rocking Horse-(1st Ed.) QX 422-2	Yr.Iss.	1981	9.00	625
1981	Snoopy and Friends-(3rd Ed.) QX436-2	Yr.Iss.	1981	12.00	95
1981	Thimble-(4th Ed.) QX413-5	Yr.Iss.	1981	4.50	150

1981 Commemoratives - Keepsake

YEAR ISSUE		EDITION LIMIT	YEAR RETD.	ISSUE PRICE	*QUOTE U.S.$
1981	25th Christmas Together QX504-2	Yr.Iss.	1981	5.50	10-22
1981	25th Christmas Together QX707-5	Yr.Iss.	1981	4.50	10-22
1981	50th Christmas QX708-2	Yr.Iss.	1981	4.50	20
1981	Baby's First Christmas QX440-2	Yr.Iss.	1981	13.00	37
1981	Baby's First Christmas QX513-5	Yr.Iss.	1981	8.50	11-20
1981	Baby's First Christmas QX516-2	Yr.Iss.	1981	5.50	30
1981	Baby's First Christmas-Black QX602-2	Yr.Iss.	1981	4.50	25
1981	Baby's First Christmas-Boy QX 601-5	Yr.Iss.	1981	4.50	20-30
1981	Baby's First Christmas-Girl QX 600-2	Yr.Iss.	1981	4.50	16-30
1981	Daughter QX607-5	Yr.Iss.	1981	4.50	20-30
1981	Father QX609-5	Yr.Iss.	1981	4.50	10-40
1981	First Christmas Together QX505-5	Yr.Iss.	1981	5.50	15-30
1981	First Christmas Together QX706-2	Yr.Iss.	1981	4.50	25
1981	Friendship QX503-5	Yr.Iss.	1981	5.50	30
1981	Friendship QX704-2	Yr.Iss.	1981	4.50	17-30
1981	The Gift of Love QX705-5	Yr.Iss.	1981	4.50	14-20
1981	Godchild QX603-5	Yr.Iss.	1981	4.50	10-20
1981	Granddaughter QX605-5	Yr.Iss.	1981	4.50	13-30
1981	Grandfather QX701-5	Yr.Iss.	1981	4.50	20
1981	Grandmother QX702-2	Yr.Iss.	1981	4.50	10-20
1981	Grandparents QX703-5	Yr.Iss.	1981	4.50	15-20
1981	Grandson QX604-2	Yr.Iss.	1981	4.50	13-30
1981	Home QX709-5	Yr.Iss.	1981	4.50	20
1981	Love QX502-2	Yr.Iss.	1981	5.50	40-50
1981	Mother and Dad QX700-2	Yr.Iss.	1981	4.50	6-16
1981	Mother QX608-2	Yr.Iss.	1981	4.50	11-18
1981	Son QX606-2	Yr.Iss.	1981	4.50	14-30
1981	Teacher QX800-2	Yr.Iss.	1981	4.50	7-15

1981 Crown Classics - Keepsake

YEAR ISSUE		EDITION LIMIT	YEAR RETD.	ISSUE PRICE	*QUOTE U.S.$
1981	Angel QX507-5	Yr.Iss.	1981	4.50	11-20
1981	Tree Photoholder QX515-5	Yr.Iss.	1981	5.50	17-30
1981	Unicorn QX516-5	Yr.Iss.	1981	8.50	15-25

1981 Decorative Ball Ornaments - Keepsake

YEAR ISSUE		EDITION LIMIT	YEAR RETD.	ISSUE PRICE	*QUOTE U.S.$
1981	Christmas 1981 QX809-5	Yr.Iss.	1981	4.50	15-25
1981	Christmas in the Forest QX813-5	Yr.Iss.	1981	4.50	145
1981	Christmas Magic QX810-2	Yr.Iss.	1981	4.50	15-25
1981	Let Us Adore Him QX811-5	Yr.Iss.	1981	4.50	30-60
1981	Merry Christmas QX814-2	Yr.Iss.	1981	4.50	10-20
1981	Santa's Coming QX812-2	Yr.Iss.	1981	4.50	12-27
1981	Santa's Surprise QX815-5	Yr.Iss.	1981	4.50	25
1981	Traditional (Blk.Santa) QX801-5	Yr.Iss.	1981	4.50	45-90

1981 Fabric Ornaments - Keepsake

YEAR ISSUE		EDITION LIMIT	YEAR RETD.	ISSUE PRICE	*QUOTE U.S.$
1981	Calico Kitty QX403-5	Yr.Iss.	1981	3.00	20
1981	Cardinal Cutie QX400-2	Yr.Iss.	1981	3.00	10-22
1981	Gingham Dog QX402-2	Yr.Iss.	1981	3.00	11-20
1981	Peppermint Mouse QX401-5	Yr.Iss.	1981	3.00	35

1981 Frosted Images - Keepsake

YEAR ISSUE		EDITION LIMIT	YEAR RETD.	ISSUE PRICE	*QUOTE U.S.$
1981	Angel QX509-5	Yr.Iss.	1981	4.00	50-65
1981	Mouse QX508-2	Yr.Iss.	1981	4.00	25
1981	Snowman QX510-2	Yr.Iss.	1981	4.00	25

1981 Hand Crafted Ornaments - Keepsake

YEAR ISSUE		EDITION LIMIT	YEAR RETD.	ISSUE PRICE	*QUOTE U.S.$
1981	Candyville Express QX418-2	Yr.Iss.	1981	7.50	83-95
1981	Checking It Twice QX158-4	Yr.Iss.	1981	23.00	195
1981	Christmas Dreams QX437-5	Yr.Iss.	1981	12.00	200-225
1981	Christmas Fantasy QX155-4	Yr.Iss.	1982	13.00	68-85
1981	Dough Angel QX139-6	Yr.Iss.	1981	5.50	80
1981	Drummer Boy QX148-1	Yr.Iss.	1981	2.50	43
1981	The Friendly Fiddler QX434-2	Yr.Iss.	1981	8.00	75
1981	A Heavenly Nap QX139-4	Yr.Iss.	1981	6.50	50
1981	Ice Fairy QX431-5	Yr.Iss.	1981	6.50	85-100
1981	The Ice Sculptor QX432-2	Yr.Iss.	1982	8.00	90-100
1981	Love and Joy QX425-2	Yr.Iss.	1981	9.00	75-95
1981	Mr. & Mrs. Claus QX448-5	Yr.Iss.	1981	12.00	120-135
1981	Sailing Santa QX439-5	Yr.Iss.	1981	13.00	225-290
1981	Space Santa QX430-2	Yr.Iss.	1981	6.50	75-110
1981	St. Nicholas QX446-2	Yr.Iss.	1981	5.50	40-50
1981	Star Swing QX421-5	Yr.Iss.	1981	5.50	60
1981	Topsy-Turvy Tunes QX429-5	Yr.Iss.	1981	7.50	66-80
1981	A Well-Stocked Stocking QX154-7	Yr.Iss.	1981	9.00	85

1981 Holiday Chimes - Keepsake

YEAR ISSUE		EDITION LIMIT	YEAR RETD.	ISSUE PRICE	*QUOTE U.S.$
1981	Santa Mobile QX136-1	Yr.Iss.	1981	5.50	40
1981	Snowflake Chimes QX165-4	Yr.Iss.	1981	5.50	25
1981	Snowman Chimes QX445-5	Yr.Iss.	1981	5.50	25-30

1981 Holiday Highlights - Keepsake

YEAR ISSUE		EDITION LIMIT	YEAR RETD.	ISSUE PRICE	*QUOTE U.S.$
1981	Christmas Star QX501-5	Yr.Iss.	1981	5.50	17-30
1981	Shepherd Scene QX500-2	Yr.Iss.	1981	5.50	16-27

1981 Little Trimmers - Keepsake

YEAR ISSUE		EDITION LIMIT	YEAR RETD.	ISSUE PRICE	*QUOTE U.S.$
1981	Clothespin Drummer Boy QX408-2	Yr.Iss.	1981	4.50	30-45
1981	Jolly Snowman QX407-5	Yr.Iss.	1981	3.50	40-60
1981	Perky Penguin QX409-5	Yr.Iss.	1982	3.50	45-60
1981	Puppy Love QX406-2	Yr.Iss.	1981	3.50	25-40
1981	The Stocking Mouse QX412-2	Yr.Iss.	1981	4.50	85-100

1981 Plush Animals - Keepsake

YEAR ISSUE		EDITION LIMIT	YEAR RETD.	ISSUE PRICE	*QUOTE U.S.$
1981	Christmas Teddy QX404-2	Yr.Iss.	1981	5.50	22
1981	Raccoon Tunes QX405-5	Yr.Iss.	1981	5.50	15-23

1981 Property Ornaments - Keepsake

YEAR ISSUE		EDITION LIMIT	YEAR RETD.	ISSUE PRICE	*QUOTE U.S.$
1981	Betsey Clark Cameo QX512-2	Yr.Iss.	1981	8.50	20-30
1981	Betsey Clark QX423-5	Yr.Iss.	1981	9.00	50-75
1981	Betsey Clark-(9th Ed.)QX 802-2	Yr.Iss.	1981	4.50	23-35
1981	Disney QX805-5	Yr.Iss.	1981	4.50	15-30
1981	The Divine Miss Piggy QX425-5	Yr.Iss.	1982	12.00	80-95
1981	Joan Walsh Anglund QX804-2	Yr.Iss.	1981	4.50	11-25
1981	Kermit the Frog QX424-2	Yr.Iss.	1981	9.00	80-95
1981	Marty Links QX808-2	Yr.Iss.	1981	4.50	23
1981	Mary Hamilton QX806-2	Yr.Iss.	1981	4.50	10-20
1981	Muppets QX807-5	Yr.Iss.	1981	4.50	15-30
1981	Peanuts QX803-5	Yr.Iss.	1981	4.50	15-40

1982 Brass Ornaments - Keepsake

YEAR ISSUE		EDITION LIMIT	YEAR RETD.	ISSUE PRICE	*QUOTE U.S.$
1982	Brass Bell QX460-6	Yr.Iss.	1982	12.00	18-25
1982	Santa and Reindeer QX467-6	Yr.Iss.	1982	9.00	40-50
1982	Santa's Sleigh QX478-6	Yr.Iss.	1982	9.00	15-30

1982 Collectible Series - Keepsake

YEAR ISSUE		EDITION LIMIT	YEAR RETD.	ISSUE PRICE	*QUOTE U.S.$
1982	The Bellringer-(4th Ed.) QX455-6	Yr.Iss.	1982	15.00	80-95
1982	Carrousel Series-(5th Ed.) QX478-3	Yr.Iss.	1982	10.00	90
1982	Clothespin Soldier-(1st Ed.) QX458-3	Yr.Iss.	1982	5.00	115-125
1982	Frosty Friends-(3rd Ed.) QX452-3	Yr.Iss.	1982	8.00	200-300
1982	Here Comes Santa-(4th Ed.) QX464-3	Yr.Iss.	1982	15.00	105-145
1982	Holiday Wildlife-(1st Ed.) QX313-3	Yr.Iss.	1982	7.00	375-450
1982	Rocking Horse-(2nd Ed.) QX 502-3	Yr.Iss.	1982	10.00	425
1982	Snoopy and Friends-(4th Ed.) QX478-3	Yr.Iss.	1982	13.00	85-125
1982	Thimble-(5th Ed.) QX451-3	Yr.Iss.	1982	5.00	60-75
1982	Tin Locomotive-(1st Ed.) QX460-3	Yr.Iss.	1982	13.00	500-600

1982 Colors of Christmas - Keepsake

YEAR ISSUE		EDITION LIMIT	YEAR RETD.	ISSUE PRICE	*QUOTE U.S.$
1982	Nativity QX308-3	Yr.Iss.	1982	4.50	37-50
1982	Santa's Flight QX308-6	Yr.Iss.	1982	4.50	47

1982 Commemoratives - Keepsake

YEAR ISSUE		EDITION LIMIT	YEAR RETD.	ISSUE PRICE	*QUOTE U.S.$
1982	25th Christmas Together QX211-6	Yr.Iss.	1982	4.50	6-20
1982	50th Christmas Together QX212-3	Yr.Iss.	1982	4.50	6-20
1982	Baby's First Christmas (Boy) QX 216-3	Yr.Iss.	1982	4.50	25
1982	Baby's First Christmas (Girl) QX 207-3	Yr.Iss.	1982	4.50	20-28
1982	Baby's First Christmas QX302-3	Yr.Iss.	1982	5.50	20-40
1982	Baby's First Christmas QX455-3	Yr.Iss.	1982	13.00	38-50
1982	Baby's First Christmas -Photoholder QX312-6	Yr.Iss.	1982	6.50	22
1982	Christmas Memories QX311-6	Yr.Iss.	1982	6.50	20
1982	Daughter QX204-6	Yr.Iss.	1982	4.50	20-35
1982	Father QX205-6	Yr.Iss.	1982	4.50	8-20
1982	First Christmas Together QX211-3	Yr.Iss.	1982	4.50	35
1982	First Christmas Together QX302-6	Yr.Iss.	1982	5.50	10-20
1982	First Christmas Together QX306-6	Yr.Iss.	1982	8.50	15-40
1982	First Christmas Together-Locket QX456-3	Yr.Iss.	1982	15.00	25-40
1982	Friendship QX208-6	Yr.Iss.	1982	4.50	8-18
1982	Friendship QX304-6	Yr.Iss.	1982	5.50	15-25
1982	Godchild QX222-6	Yr.Iss.	1982	4.50	11-22
1982	Granddaughter QX224-3	Yr.Iss.	1982	4.50	12-28
1982	Grandfather QX207-6	Yr.Iss.	1982	4.50	8-20
1982	Grandmother QX200-3	Yr.Iss.	1982	4.50	7-18
1982	Grandparents QX214-6	Yr.Iss.	1982	4.50	12-18
1982	Grandson QX224-6	Yr.Iss.	1982	4.50	11-30
1982	Love QX209-6	Yr.Iss.	1982	4.50	8-20
1982	Love QX304-3	Yr.Iss.	1982	5.50	30
1982	Moments of Love QX209-3	Yr.Iss.	1982	4.50	7-17
1982	Mother and Dad QX222-3	Yr.Iss.	1982	4.50	8-20
1982	Mother QX205-3	Yr.Iss.	1982	4.50	7-17
1982	New Home QX212-6	Yr.Iss.	1982	4.50	8-22
1982	Sister QX208-3	Yr.Iss.	1982	4.50	13-30
1982	Son QX204-3	Yr.Iss.	1982	4.50	11-30
1982	Teacher QX214-3	Yr.Iss.	1982	4.50	6-15
1982	Teacher QX312-3	Yr.Iss.	1982	6.50	10-18
1982	Teacher-Apple QX301-6	Yr.Iss.	1982	5.50	8-14

1982 Decorative Ball Ornaments - Keepsake

YEAR ISSUE		EDITION LIMIT	YEAR RETD.	ISSUE PRICE	*QUOTE U.S.$
1982	Christmas Angel QX220-6	Yr.Iss.	1982	4.50	10-25
1982	Currier & Ives QX201-3	Yr.Iss.	1982	4.50	10-25
1982	Santa QX221-6	Yr.Iss.	1982	4.50	12-20
1982	Season for Caring QX221-3	Yr.Iss.	1982	4.50	23

1982 Designer Keepsakes - Keepsake

YEAR ISSUE		EDITION LIMIT	YEAR RETD.	ISSUE PRICE	*QUOTE U.S.$
1982	Merry Christmas QX225-6	Yr.Iss.	1982	4.50	10-22
1982	Old Fashioned Christmas QX227-6	Yr.Iss.	1982	4.50	40
1982	Old World Angels QX226-3	Yr.Iss.	1982	4.50	23
1982	Patterns of Christmas QX226-6	Yr.Iss.	1982	4.50	15-22
1982	Stained Glass QX228-3	Yr.Iss.	1982	4.50	12-22
1982	Twelve Days of Christmas QX203-6	Yr.Iss.	1982	4.50	30

1982 Handcrafted Ornaments - Keepsake

YEAR ISSUE		EDITION LIMIT	YEAR RETD.	ISSUE PRICE	*QUOTE U.S.$
1982	Baroque Angel QX456-6	Yr.Iss.	1982	15.00	175
1982	Christmas Fantasy QX155-4	Yr.Iss.	1982	13.00	59
1982	Cloisonne Angel QX145-4	Yr.Iss.	1982	12.00	95
1982	Cowboy Snowman QX480-6	Yr.Iss.	1982	8.00	53
1982	Cycling Santa QX435-5	Yr.Iss.	1983	20.00	120-150
1982	Elfin Artist QX457-3	Yr.Iss.	1982	9.00	42-50
1982	Embroidered Tree - QX494-6	Yr.Iss.	1982	6.50	40
1982	Ice Sculptor QX432-2	Yr.Iss.	1982	8.00	75
1982	Jogging Santa QX457-6	Yr.Iss.	1982	8.00	32-50
1982	Jolly Christmas Tree QX465-3	Yr.Iss.	1982	6.50	80
1982	Peeking Elf QX419-5	Yr.Iss.	1982	6.50	24-40
1982	Pinecone Home QX461-3	Yr.Iss.	1982	8.00	160-175
1982	Raccoon Surprises QX479-3	Yr.Iss.	1982	9.00	125-145
1982	Santa Bell QX148-7	Yr.Iss.	1982	15.00	45-60
1982	Santa's Workshop QX450-3	Yr.Iss.	1983	10.00	78-85
1982	The Spirit of Christmas QX452-6	Yr.Iss.	1982	10.00	107-125
1982	Three Kings QX307-3	Yr.Iss.	1982	8.50	17-27
1982	Tin Soldier QX483-6	Yr.Iss.	1982	6.50	30-50

1982 Holiday Chimes - Keepsake

YEAR ISSUE		EDITION LIMIT	YEAR RETD.	ISSUE PRICE	*QUOTE U.S.$
1982	Bell Chimes QX494-3	Yr.Iss.	1982	5.50	30
1982	Tree Chimes QX484-6	Yr.Iss.	1982	5.50	50

1982 Holiday Highlights - Keepsake

YEAR ISSUE		EDITION LIMIT	YEAR RETD.	ISSUE PRICE	*QUOTE U.S.$
1982	Angel QX309-6	Yr.Iss.	1982	5.50	16-35
1982	Christmas Magic QX311-3	Yr.Iss.	1982	5.50	22-30
1982	Christmas Sleigh QX309-3	Yr.Iss.	1982	5.50	55-75

1982 Ice Sculptures - Keepsake

YEAR ISSUE		EDITION LIMIT	YEAR RETD.	ISSUE PRICE	*QUOTE U.S.$
1982	Arctic Penguin QX300-3	Yr.Iss.	1982	4.00	8-20
1982	Snowy Seal QX300-6	Yr.Iss.	1982	4.00	13-20

1982 Little Trimmers - Keepsake

YEAR ISSUE		EDITION LIMIT	YEAR RETD.	ISSUE PRICE	*QUOTE U.S.$
1982	Christmas Kitten QX454-3	Yr.Iss.	1983	4.00	38
1982	Christmas Owl QX131-4	Yr.Iss.	1982	4.50	35
1982	Cookie Mouse QX454-6	Yr.Iss.	1982	4.50	49-60
1982	Dove Love QX462-3	Yr.Iss.	1982	4.50	47-55
1982	Jingling Teddy QX477-6	Yr.Iss.	1982	4.00	23-40
1982	Merry Moose QX415-5	Yr.Iss.	1982	5.50	38-60
1982	Musical Angel QX459-6	Yr.Iss.	1982	5.50	112-125
1982	Perky Penguin QX409-5	Yr.Iss.	1982	4.00	35

1982 Property Ornaments - Keepsake

YEAR ISSUE		EDITION LIMIT	YEAR RETD.	ISSUE PRICE	*QUOTE U.S.$
1982	Betsey Clark QX305-6	Yr.Iss.	1982	8.50	17-25
1982	Betsey Clark-(10th Ed.) QX215-6	Yr.Iss.	1982	4.50	24-34
1982	Disney QX217-3	Yr.Iss.	1982	4.50	20-35
1982	The Divine Miss Piggy QX425-5	Yr.Iss.	1982	12.00	125
1982	Joan Walsh Anglund QX219-3	Yr.Iss.	1982	4.50	8-20
1982	Kermit the Frog QX495-6	Yr.Iss.	1982	11.00	62-95
1982	Mary Hamilton QX217-6	Yr.Iss.	1982	4.50	10-22
1982	Miss Piggy and Kermit QX218-3	Yr.Iss.	1982	4.50	28-40
1982	Muppets Party QX218-6	Yr.Iss.	1982	4.50	21-40
1982	Norman Rockwell QX202-3	Yr.Iss.	1982	4.50	10-28
1982	Norman Rockwell-(3rd Ed.) QX305-3	Yr.Iss.	1982	8.50	28
1982	Peanuts QX200-6	Yr.Iss.	1982	4.50	15-30

1983 Collectible Series - Keepsake

YEAR ISSUE		EDITION LIMIT	YEAR RETD.	ISSUE PRICE	*QUOTE U.S.$
1983	The Bellringer-(5th Ed.)QX 403-9	Yr.Iss.	1983	15.00	95-135
1983	Carrousel-(6th Ed.) QX401-9	Yr.Iss.	1983	11.00	49
1983	Clothespin Soldier-(2nd Ed.) QX402-9	Yr.Iss.	1983	5.00	34-50
1983	Frosty Friends-(4th Ed.) QX400-7	Yr.Iss.	1983	8.00	215-295
1983	Here Comes Santa-(5th Ed.) QX 403-7	Yr.Iss.	1983	13.00	250-295
1983	Holiday Wildlife-(2nd Ed.) QX 309-9	Yr.Iss.	1983	7.00	51-75
1983	Porcelain Bear-(1st Ed.) QX428-9	Yr.Iss.	1983	7.00	50-75
1983	Rocking Horse-(3rd Ed.) QX417-7	Yr.Iss.	1983	10.00	298
1983	Snoopy and Friends-(5th Ed.) QX416-9	Yr.Iss.	1983	13.00	85
1983	Thimble-(6th Ed.) QX401-7	Yr.Iss.	1983	5.00	30
1983	Tin Locomotive-(2nd Ed.) QX404-9	Yr.Iss.	1983	13.00	275-295

1983 Commemoratives - Keepsake

YEAR ISSUE		EDITION LIMIT	YEAR RETD.	ISSUE PRICE	*QUOTE U.S.$
1983	25th Christmas Together QX224-7	Yr.Iss.	1983	4.50	18
1983	Baby's First Christmas QX200-7	Yr.Iss.	1983	4.50	20-30
1983	Baby's First Christmas QX200-9	Yr.Iss.	1983	4.50	20-28
1983	Baby's First Christmas QX301-9	Yr.Iss.	1983	7.50	8-18
1983	Baby's First Christmas QX302-9	Yr.Iss.	1983	7.00	10-30
1983	Baby's First Christmas QX402-7	Yr.Iss.	1983	14.00	30-40
1983	Baby's Second Christmas QX226-7	Yr.Iss.	1983	4.50	20-35
1983	Child's Third Christmas QX226-9	Yr.Iss.	1983	4.50	25
1983	Daughter QX203-7	Yr.Iss.	1983	4.50	25-43
1983	First Christmas Together QX208-9	Yr.Iss.	1983	4.50	28
1983	First Christmas Together QX301-7	Yr.Iss.	1983	7.50	20-40
1983	First Christmas Together QX306-9	Yr.Iss.	1983	6.00	10-25
1983	First Christmas Together QX310-7	Yr.Iss.	1983	6.00	12-25

*Quotes have been rounded up to nearest dollar

YEAR	ISSUE	EDITION LIMIT	YEAR RETD.	ISSUE PRICE	*QUOTE U.S.$
1983	First Christmas Together-Brass Locket QX 432-9	Yr.Iss.	1983	15.00	20-30
1983	Friendship QX207-7	Yr.Iss.	1983	4.50	20
1983	Friendship QX305-9	Yr.Iss.	1983	6.00	8-20
1983	Godchild QX201-7	Yr.Iss.	1983	4.50	12-18
1983	Grandchild's First Christmas QX 312-9	Yr.Iss.	1983	6.00	10-23
1983	Grandchild's First Christmas QX430-9	Yr.Iss.	1983	14.00	21-38
1983	Granddaughter QX202-7	Yr.Iss.	1983	4.50	30
1983	Grandmother QX205-7	Yr.Iss.	1983	4.50	19
1983	Grandparents QX429-9	Yr.Iss.	1983	6.50	11-22
1983	Grandson QX201-9	Yr.Iss.	1983	4.50	12-30
1983	Love Is a Song QX223-9	Yr.Iss.	1983	4.50	30
1983	Love QX207-9	Yr.Iss.	1983	4.50	43
1983	Love QX305-7	Yr.Iss.	1983	6.00	9-19
1983	Love QX310-9	Yr.Iss.	1983	6.00	40
1983	Love QX422-7	Yr.Iss.	1983	13.00	16-40
1983	Mom and Dad QX429-7	Yr.Iss.	1983	6.50	14-24
1983	Mother QX306-7	Yr.Iss.	1983	6.00	20
1983	New Home QX210-7	Yr.Iss.	1983	4.50	15-30
1983	Sister QX206-9	Yr.Iss.	1983	4.50	23
1983	Son QX202-9	Yr.Iss.	1983	4.50	25-35
1983	Teacher QX224-9	Yr.Iss.	1983	4.50	8-17
1983	Teacher QX304-9	Yr.Iss.	1983	6.00	13
1983	10thChristmas Together QX430-7	Yr.Iss.	1983	6.50	12-24

1983 Crown Classics - Keepsake

YEAR	ISSUE	EDITION LIMIT	YEAR RETD.	ISSUE PRICE	*QUOTE U.S.$
1983	Enameled Christmas Wreath QX 311-9	Yr.Iss.	1983	9.00	7-15
1983	Memories to Treasure QX303-7	Yr.Iss.	1983	7.00	25
1983	Mother and Child QX302-7	Yr.Iss.	1983	7.50	20-40

1983 Decorative Ball Ornaments - Keepsake

YEAR	ISSUE	EDITION LIMIT	YEAR RETD.	ISSUE PRICE	*QUOTE U.S.$
1983	1983 QX220-9	Yr.Iss.	1983	4.50	17-30
1983	Angels QX219-7	Yr.Iss.	1983	5.00	24
1983	The Annunciation QX216-7	Yr.Iss.	1983	4.50	30
1983	Christmas Joy QX216-9	Yr.Iss.	1983	4.50	15-30
1983	Christmas Wonderland QX221-9	Yr.Iss.	1983	4.50	95
1983	Currier & Ives QX215-9	Yr.Iss.	1983	4.50	8-19
1983	Here Comes Santa QX217-7	Yr.Iss.	1983	4.50	38
1983	An Old Fashioned Christmas QX2217-9	Yr.Iss.	1983	4.50	30
1983	Oriental Butterflies QX218-7	Yr.Iss.	1983	4.50	30
1983	Season's Greeting QX219-9	Yr.Iss.	1983	4.50	10-22
1983	The Wise Men QX220-7	Yr.Iss.	1983	4.50	30-40

1983 Handcrafted Ornaments - Keepsake

YEAR	ISSUE	EDITION LIMIT	YEAR RETD.	ISSUE PRICE	*QUOTE U.S.$
1983	Angel Messenger QX408-7	Yr.Iss.	1983	6.50	75-95
1983	Baroque Angels QX422-9	Yr.Iss.	1983	13.00	130
1983	Bell Wreath QX420-9	Yr.Iss.	1983	6.50	35
1983	Brass Santa QX423-9	Yr.Iss.	1983	9.00	23
1983	Caroling Owl QX411-7	Yr.Iss.	1983	4.50	25-40
1983	Christmas Kitten QX454-3	Yr.Iss.	1983	4.00	35
1983	Christmas Koala QX419-9	Yr.Iss.	1983	4.00	20-33
1983	Cycling Santa QX435-5	Yr.Iss.	1983	20.00	195
1983	Embroidered Heart QX421-7	Yr.Iss.	1983	6.50	25
1983	Embroidered Stocking QX479-6	Yr.Iss.	1983	6.50	10-22
1983	Hitchhiking Santa QX424-7	Yr.Iss.	1983	8.00	40
1983	Holiday Puppy QX412-7	Yr.Iss.	1983	3.50	16-30
1983	Jack Frost QX407-9	Yr.Iss.	1983	9.00	60
1983	Jolly Santa QX425-9	Yr.Iss.	1983	3.50	21-35
1983	Madonna and Child QX428-7	Yr.Iss.	1983	12.00	26-45
1983	Mailbox Kitten QX415-7	Yr.Iss.	1983	6.50	40-60
1983	Mountain Climbing Santa QX407-7	Yr.Iss.	1984	6.50	22-40
1983	Mouse in Bell QX419-7	Yr.Iss.	1983	10.00	65
1983	Mouse on Cheese QX413-7	Yr.Iss.	1983	6.50	30-50
1983	Old-Fashioned Santa QX409-9	Yr.Iss.	1983	11.00	54-65
1983	Peppermint Penguin QX408-9	Yr.Iss.	1983	6.50	29-49
1983	Porcelain Doll, Diana QX423-7	Yr.Iss.	1983	9.00	16-32
1983	Rainbow Angel QX416-7	Yr.Iss.	1983	5.50	112-125
1983	Santa's Many Faces QX311-6	Yr.Iss.	1983	6.00	30
1983	Santa's on His Way QX426-9	Yr.Iss.	1983	10.00	35
1983	Santa's Workshop QX450-3	Yr.Iss.	1983	10.00	60
1983	Scrimshaw Reindeer QX424-9	Yr.Iss.	1983	8.00	17-35
1983	Skating Rabbit QX409-7	Yr.Iss.	1983	8.00	55
1983	Ski Lift Santa QX418-7	Yr.Iss.	1983	8.00	50-75
1983	Skiing Fox QX420-7	Yr.Iss.	1983	8.00	30-40
1983	Sneaker Mouse QX400-9	Yr.Iss.	1983	4.50	23-40
1983	Tin Rocking Horse QX414-9	Yr.Iss.	1983	6.50	50
1983	Unicorn QX426-7	Yr.Iss.	1983	10.00	40-65

1983 Holiday Highlights - Keepsake

YEAR	ISSUE	EDITION LIMIT	YEAR RETD.	ISSUE PRICE	*QUOTE U.S.$
1983	Christmas Stocking QX303-9	Yr.Iss.	1983	6.00	15-40
1983	Star of Peace QX304-7	Yr.Iss.	1983	6.00	20
1983	Time for Sharing QX307-7	Yr.Iss.	1983	6.00	40

1983 Holiday Sculptures - Keepsake

YEAR	ISSUE	EDITION LIMIT	YEAR RETD.	ISSUE PRICE	*QUOTE U.S.$
1983	Heart QX307-9	Yr.Iss.	1983	4.00	50
1983	Santa QX308-7	Yr.Iss.	1983	4.00	17-35

1983 Property Ornaments - Keepsake

YEAR	ISSUE	EDITION LIMIT	YEAR RETD.	ISSUE PRICE	*QUOTE U.S.$
1983	Betsey Clark QX404-7	Yr.Iss.	1983	6.50	35
1983	Betsey Clark QX440-1	Yr.Iss.	1983	9.00	35
1983	Betsey Clark-(11th Ed.) QX211-9	Yr.Iss.	1983	4.50	30
1983	Disney QX212-9	Yr.Iss.	1983	4.50	45
1983	Kermit the Frog QX495-6	Yr.Iss.	1983	11.00	35
1983	Mary Hamilton QX213-7	Yr.Iss.	1983	4.50	40
1983	Miss Piggy QX405-7	Yr.Iss.	1983	13.00	225
1983	The Muppets QX214-7	Yr.Iss.	1983	4.50	40-50
1983	Norman Rockwell QX215-7	Yr.Iss.	1983	4.50	50
1983	Norman Rockwell-(4th Ed.) QX 300-7	Yr.Iss.	1983	7.50	35
1983	Peanuts QX212-7	Yr.Iss.	1983	4.50	14-38
1983	Shirt Tales QX214-9	Yr.Iss.	1983	4.50	25

1984 Collectible Series - Keepsake

YEAR	ISSUE	EDITION LIMIT	YEAR RETD.	ISSUE PRICE	*QUOTE U.S.$
1984	Art Masterpiece-(1st Ed.) QX349-4	Yr.Iss.	1984	6.50	18
1984	The Bellringer-(6th & Final Ed.) QX438-4	Yr.Iss.	1984	15.00	30-45
1984	Betsey Clark-(12th Ed.) QX249-4	Yr.Iss.	1984	5.00	24-34
1984	Clothespin Soldier-(3rd Ed.) QX447-1	Yr.Iss.	1984	5.00	20-30
1984	Frosty Friends-(5th Ed.) QX437-1	Yr.Iss.	1984	8.00	60-85
1984	Here Comes Santa-(6th Ed.) QX438-4	Yr.Iss.	1984	13.00	60-90
1984	Holiday Wildlife-(3rd Ed.) QX 347-4	Yr.Iss.	1984	7.25	20-30
1984	Norman Rockwell-(5th Ed.) QX341-1	Yr.Iss.	1984	7.50	24-34
1984	Nostalgic Houses and Shops-(1st Ed.) QX 448-1	Yr.Iss.	1984	13.00	155-195
1984	Porcelain Bear-(2nd Ed.) QX454-1	Yr.Iss.	1984	7.00	34-50
1984	Rocking Horse-(4th Ed.) QX435-4	Yr.Iss.	1984	10.00	58-95
1984	Thimble-(7th Ed.) QX430-4	Yr.Iss.	1984	5.00	40-60
1984	Tin Locomotive-(3rd Ed.) QX440-4	Yr.Iss.	1984	14.00	63-90
1984	The Twelve Days of Christmas (1st Ed.) QX 3484	Yr.Iss.	1984	6.00	300
1984	Wood Childhood Ornaments (1st Ed.) QX 439-4	Yr.Iss.	1984	6.50	45

1984 Commemoratives - Keepsake

YEAR	ISSUE	EDITION LIMIT	YEAR RETD.	ISSUE PRICE	*QUOTE U.S.$
1984	Baby's First Christmas QX300-1	Yr.Iss.	1984	7.00	10-25
1984	Baby's First Christmas QX340-1	Yr.Iss.	1984	6.00	20-40
1984	Baby's First Christmas QX438-1	Yr.Iss.	1984	14.00	30-50
1984	Baby's First Christmas QX904-1	Yr.Iss.	1984	16.00	50
1984	Baby's First Christmas-Boy QX240-4	Yr.Iss.	1984	4.50	20-28
1984	Baby's First Christmas-Girl QX340-1	Yr.Iss.	1984	4.50	20-40
1984	Baby's Second Christmas QX241-1	Yr.Iss.	1984	4.50	25-35
1984	Baby-sitter QX253-1	Yr.Iss.	1984	4.50	6-14
1984	Child's Third Christmas QX261-1	Yr.Iss.	1984	4.50	16-23
1984	Daughter QX244-4	Yr.Iss.	1984	4.50	25-35
1984	Father QX257-1	Yr.Iss.	1984	6.00	20
1984	First Christmas Together QX245-1	Yr.Iss.	1984	4.50	15-25
1984	First Christmas Together QX340-4	Yr.Iss.	1984	7.50	15-30
1984	First Christmas Together QX342-1	Yr.Iss.	1984	6.00	15-25
1984	First Christmas Together QX436-4	Yr.Iss.	1984	15.00	15-40
1984	First Christmas Together QX904-4	Yr.Iss.	1984	16.00	41
1984	Friendship QX248-1	Yr.Iss.	1984	4.50	15
1984	From Our Home to Yours QX248-4	Yr.Iss.	1984	4.50	50
1984	The Fun of Friendship QX343-1	Yr.Iss.	1984	6.00	10-30
1984	A Gift of Friendship QX260-4	Yr.Iss.	1984	4.50	25
1984	Godchild QX242-1	Yr.Iss.	1984	4.50	20
1984	Grandchild's First Christmas QX257-4	Yr.Iss.	1984	4.50	7-17
1984	Grandchild's First Christmas QX460-1	Yr.Iss.	1984	11.00	30
1984	Granddaughter QX243-1	Yr.Iss.	1984	4.50	30
1984	Grandmother QX244-1	Yr.Iss.	1984	4.50	13-18
1984	Grandparents QX256-1	Yr.Iss.	1984	4.50	18
1984	Grandson QX242-4	Yr.Iss.	1984	4.50	18-30
1984	Gratitude QX344-4	Yr.Iss.	1984	6.00	12
1984	Heartful of Love QX443-4	Yr.Iss.	1984	10.00	45
1984	Love QX255-4	Yr.Iss.	1984	4.50	25
1984	Love...the Spirit of Christmas QX247-4	Yr.Iss.	1984	4.50	15-40
1984	The Miracle of Love QX342-4	Yr.Iss.	1984	6.00	33
1984	Mother and Dad QX258-1	Yr.Iss.	1984	6.50	18
1984	Mother QX343-4	Yr.Iss.	1984	6.00	12-25
1984	New Home QX245-4	Yr.Iss.	1984	4.50	85
1984	Sister QX259-4	Yr.Iss.	1984	6.50	20-32
1984	Son QX243-4	Yr.Iss.	1984	4.50	10-30
1984	Teacher QX249-1	Yr.Iss.	1984	4.50	6-15
1984	Ten Years Together QX258-4	Yr.Iss.	1984	6.50	11-25
1984	Twenty Five Years Together QX259-1	Yr.Iss.	1984	6.50	20

1984 Holiday Humor - Keepsake

YEAR	ISSUE	EDITION LIMIT	YEAR RETD.	ISSUE PRICE	*QUOTE U.S.$
1984	Bell Ringer Squirrel QX443-1	Yr.Iss.	1984	10.00	20-40
1984	Christmas Owl QX444-1	Yr.Iss.	1984	6.00	20-33
1984	A Christmas Prayer QX246-1	Yr.Iss.	1984	4.50	10-23
1984	Flights of Fantasy QX256-4	Yr.Iss.	1984	4.50	20
1984	Fortune Cookie Elf QX452-4	Yr.Iss.	1984	4.50	37
1984	Frisbee Puppy QX444-4	Yr.Iss.	1984	5.00	40-50
1984	Marathon Santa QX456-4	Yr.Iss.	1984	8.00	43
1984	Mountain Climbing Santa QX407-7	Yr.Iss.	1984	6.50	35
1984	Musical Angel QX434-4	Yr.Iss.	1984	5.50	70
1984	Napping Mouse QX435-1	Yr.Iss.	1984	5.50	38-50
1984	Peppermint 1984 QX452-1	Yr.Iss.	1984	4.50	52
1984	Polar Bear Drummer QX430-1	Yr.Iss.	1984	4.50	30
1984	Raccoon's Christmas QX447-7	Yr.Iss.	1984	9.00	34-55
1984	Reindeer Racetrack QX254-4	Yr.Iss.	1984	4.50	10-23
1984	Roller Skating Rabbit QX457-1	Yr.Iss.	1985	5.00	18-35
1984	Santa Mouse QX433-4	Yr.Iss.	1984	4.50	47
1984	Santa Star QX450-4	Yr.Iss.	1984	5.50	33-40
1984	Snowmobile Santa QX431-4	Yr.Iss.	1984	6.50	35-40
1984	Snowshoe Penguin QX453-1	Yr.Iss.	1984	6.50	50-60
1984	Snowy Seal QX450-1	Yr.Iss.	1985	4.00	12-24
1984	Three Kittens in a Mitten QX431-1	Yr.Iss.	1985	8.00	32-50

1984 Keepsake Magic Ornaments - Keepsake

YEAR	ISSUE	EDITION LIMIT	YEAR RETD.	ISSUE PRICE	*QUOTE U.S.$
1984	All Are Precious QLX704-1	Yr.Iss.	1985	8.00	13-25
1984	Brass Carrousel QLX707-1	Yr.Iss.	1984	9.00	95
1984	Christmas in the Forest QLX703-4	Yr.Iss.	1984	8.00	15
1984	City Lights QLX701-4	Yr.Iss.	1984	10.00	47-53
1984	Nativity QLX700-1	Yr.Iss.	1985	12.00	18-30
1984	Santa's Arrival QLX702-4	Yr.Iss.	1984	13.00	47-65
1984	Santa's Workshop QLX700-4	Yr.Iss.	1985	13.00	45-62
1984	Stained Glass QLX703-1	Yr.Iss.	1984	8.00	20
1984	Sugarplum Cottage QLX701-1	Yr.Iss.	1986	11.00	40
1984	Village Church QLX702-1	Yr.Iss.	1985	15.00	35-50

1984 Limited Edition - Keepsake

YEAR	ISSUE	EDITION LIMIT	YEAR RETD.	ISSUE PRICE	*QUOTE U.S.$
1984	Classical Angel QX459-1	Yr.Iss.	1984	28.00	65-100

1984 Property Ornaments - Keepsake

YEAR	ISSUE	EDITION LIMIT	YEAR RETD.	ISSUE PRICE	*QUOTE U.S.$
1984	Betsey Clark Angel QX462-4	Yr.Iss.	1984	9.00	19-35
1984	Currier & Ives QX250-1	Yr.Iss.	1984	4.50	23
1984	Disney QX250-4	Yr.Iss.	1984	4.50	23-43
1984	Katybeth QX463-1	Yr.Iss.	1984	9.00	17-33
1984	Kit QX453-4	Yr.Iss.	1984	5.50	28
1984	Muffin QX442-1	Yr.Iss.	1984	5.50	25-33
1984	The Muppets QX251-4	Yr.Iss.	1984	4.50	20-35
1984	Norman Rockwell QX251-4	Yr.Iss.	1984	4.50	33
1984	Peanuts QX252-1	Yr.Iss.	1984	4.50	20-33
1984	Shirt Tales QX252-4	Yr.Iss.	1984	4.50	17
1984	Snoopy and Woodstock QX439-1	Yr.Iss.	1984	7.50	95

1984 Traditional Ornaments - Keepsake

YEAR	ISSUE	EDITION LIMIT	YEAR RETD.	ISSUE PRICE	*QUOTE U.S.$
1984	Alpine Elf QX452-1	Yr.Iss.	1984	6.00	32-40
1984	Amanda QX432-1	Yr.Iss.	1984	9.00	20-30
1984	Chickadee QX451-4	Yr.Iss.	1984	6.00	33-40
1984	Christmas Memories Photoholder QX300-4	Yr.Iss.	1984	6.50	25
1984	Cuckoo Clock QX455-1	Yr.Iss.	1984	10.00	47
1984	Gift of Music QX451-1	Yr.Iss.	1984	15.00	62-95
1984	Holiday Friendship QX445-1	Yr.Iss.	1984	13.00	30
1984	Holiday Jester QX437-4	Yr.Iss.	1984	11.00	20-35
1984	Holiday Starburst QX253-4	Yr.Iss.	1984	5.00	20
1984	Madonna and Child QX344-1	Yr.Iss.	1984	6.00	50
1984	Needlepoint Wreath QX459-4	Yr.Iss.	1984	6.50	13
1984	Nostalgic Sled QX442-4	Yr.Iss.	1984	6.00	12-30
1984	Old Fashioned Rocking Horse QX346-4	Yr.Iss.	1984	7.50	10-20
1984	Peace on Earth QX341-4	Yr.Iss.	1984	7.50	30
1984	Santa QX458-4	Yr.Iss.	1984	7.50	10-20
1984	Santa Sulky Driver QX436-1	Yr.Iss.	1984	9.00	20-35
1984	A Savior is Born QX254-1	Yr.Iss.	1984	4.50	33
1984	Twelve Days of Christmas QX 415-9	Yr.Iss.	1984	15.00	95
1984	Uncle Sam QX449-1	Yr.Iss.	1984	6.00	50
1984	White Christmas QX905-1	Yr.Iss.	1984	16.00	70-95

1985 Collectible Series - Keepsake

YEAR	ISSUE	EDITION LIMIT	YEAR RETD.	ISSUE PRICE	*QUOTE U.S.$
1985	Art Masterpiece-(2nd Ed.) QX377-2	Yr.Iss.	1985	6.75	15
1985	Betsey Clark-(13th & final Ed.) QX263-2	Yr.Iss.	1985	5.00	24-35
1985	Clothespin Soldier-(4th Ed.) QX471-5	Yr.Iss.	1985	5.50	20-30
1985	Frosty Friends-(6th Ed.) QX482-2	Yr.Iss.	1985	8.50	45-65
1985	Here Comes Santa-(7th Ed.) QX496-5	Yr.Iss.	1985	14.00	43-63
1985	Holiday Wildlife-(4th Ed.) QX376-5	Yr.Iss.	1985	7.50	20-30
1985	Miniature Creche-(1st Ed.) QX482-5	Yr.Iss.	1985	8.75	20-40
1985	Norman Rockwell-(6th Ed.) QX374-5	Yr.Iss.	1985	7.50	20-29
1985	Nostalgic Houses and Shops-(2nd Ed.) QX497-5	Yr.Iss.	1985	13.75	90-130
1985	Porcelain Bear-(3rd Ed.) QX479-2	Yr.Iss.	1985	7.50	36-60
1985	Rocking Horse-(5th Ed.) QX493-2	Yr.Iss.	1985	10.75	50-80
1985	Thimble-(8th Ed.) QX472-5	Yr.Iss.	1985	5.50	24-35
1985	Tin Locomotive-(4th Ed.) QX497-2	Yr.Iss.	1985	14.75	50-80
1985	Twelve Days of Christmas -(2nd Ed.) QX371-2	Yr.Iss.	1985	6.50	50-70
1985	Windows of the World-(1st Ed.) QX490-2	Yr.Iss.	1985	9.75	82-97
1985	Wood Childhood Ornaments-(2nd Ed.) QX472-2	Yr.Iss.	1985	7.00	34-50

1985 Commemoratives - Keepsake

YEAR	ISSUE	EDITION LIMIT	YEAR RETD.	ISSUE PRICE	*QUOTE U.S.$
1985	Baby Locket QX401-2	Yr.Iss.	1985	16.00	35-38
1985	Baby's First Christmas QX260-2	Yr.Iss.	1985	5.00	19-25
1985	Baby's First Christmas QX370-2	Yr.Iss.	1985	5.75	22
1985	Baby's First Christmas QX478-2	Yr.Iss.	1985	7.00	18
1985	Baby's First Christmas QX499-2	Yr.Iss.	1985	15.00	40-50
1985	Baby's First Christmas QX499-5	Yr.Iss.	1985	16.00	43
1985	Baby's Second Christmas QX478-5	Yr.Iss.	1985	6.00	25-38
1985	Baby-sitter QX264-2	Yr.Iss.	1985	4.75	13

*Quotes have been rounded up to nearest dollar

YEAR ISSUE		EDITION LIMIT	YEAR RETD.	ISSUE PRICE	*QUOTE U.S.$
1985	Child's Third Christmas QX475-5	Yr.Iss.	1985	6.00	20
1985	Daughter QX503-2	Yr.Iss.	1985	5.50	15-25
1985	Father QX376-2	Yr.Iss.	1985	6.50	10
1985	First Christmas Together QX261-2	Yr.Iss.	1985	4.75	28
1985	First Christmas Together QX370-5	Yr.Iss.	1985	6.75	30
1985	First Christmas Together QX400-5	Yr.Iss.	1985	16.75	23
1985	First Christmas Together QX493-5	Yr.Iss.	1985	13.00	23
1985	First Christmas Together QX507-2	Yr.Iss.	1985	8.00	17
1985	Friendship QX378-5	Yr.Iss.	1985	6.75	18
1985	Friendship QX506-2	Yr.Iss.	1985	7.75	15
1985	From Our House to Yours QX520-2	Yr.Iss.	1985	7.75	15
1985	Godchild QX380-2	Yr.Iss.	1985	6.75	15
1985	Good Friends QX265-2	Yr.Iss.	1985	4.75	15-30
1985	Grandchild's First Christmas QX260-5	Yr.Iss.	1985	5.00	15
1985	Grandchild's First Christmas QX495-5	Yr.Iss.	1985	11.00	20
1985	Granddaughter QX263-5	Yr.Iss.	1985	4.75	30
1985	Grandmother QX262-5	Yr.Iss.	1985	4.75	18
1985	Grandparents QX380-5	Yr.Iss.	1985	7.00	10
1985	Grandson QX262-2	Yr.Iss.	1985	4.75	10-25
1985	Heart Full of Love QX378-2	Yr.Iss.	1985	6.75	10-20
1985	Holiday Heart QX498-2	Yr.Iss.	1985	8.00	10-20
1985	Love at Christmas QX371-5	Yr.Iss.	1985	5.75	25-40
1985	Mother and Dad QX509-2	Yr.Iss.	1985	7.75	15
1985	Mother QX372-2	Yr.Iss.	1985	6.75	10-20
1985	New Home QX269-5	Yr.Iss.	1985	4.75	30
1985	Niece QX520-5	Yr.Iss.	1985	5.75	11
1985	Sister QX506-5	Yr.Iss.	1985	7.25	20
1985	Son QX502-5	Yr.Iss.	1985	5.50	37
1985	Special Friends QX372-5	Yr.Iss.	1985	5.75	10
1985	Teacher QX505-2	Yr.Iss.	1985	6.00	20
1985	Twenty-Five Years Together QX500-5	Yr.Iss.	1985	8.00	20
1985	With Appreciation QX375-2	Yr.Iss.	1985	6.75	10

1985 Country Christmas Collection - Keepsake

YEAR ISSUE		EDITION LIMIT	YEAR RETD.	ISSUE PRICE	*QUOTE U.S.$
1985	Country Goose QX518-5	Yr.Iss.	1985	7.75	14
1985	Old-Fashioned Doll QX519-5	Yr.Iss.	1985	15.00	40
1985	Rocking Horse Memories QX518-2	Yr.Iss.	1985	10.00	14
1985	Sheep at Christmas QX517-5	Yr.Iss.	1985	8.25	30
1985	Whirligig Santa QX519-2	Yr.Iss.	1985	13.00	25

1985 Heirloom Christmas Collection - Keepsake

YEAR ISSUE		EDITION LIMIT	YEAR RETD.	ISSUE PRICE	*QUOTE U.S.$
1985	Charming Angel QX512-5	Yr.Iss.	1985	9.75	10-25
1985	Keepsake Basket QX514-5	Yr.Iss.	1985	15.00	15
1985	Lacy Heart QX511-2	Yr.Iss.	1985	8.75	15-30
1985	Snowflake QX510-5	Yr.Iss.	1985	6.50	18
1985	Victorian Lady QX513-2	Yr.Iss.	1985	9.50	25

1985 Holiday Humor - Keepsake

YEAR ISSUE		EDITION LIMIT	YEAR RETD.	ISSUE PRICE	*QUOTE U.S.$
1985	Baker Elf QX491-2	Yr.Iss.	1985	5.75	30
1985	Beary Smooth Ride QX480-5	Yr.Iss.	1986	6.50	23
1985	Bottlecap Fun Bunnies QX481-5	Yr.Iss.	1985	7.75	33
1985	Candy Apple Mouse QX470-5	Yr.Iss.	1985	6.50	63
1985	Children in the Shoe QX490-5	Yr.Iss.	1985	9.50	45
1985	Dapper Penguin QX477-2	Yr.Iss.	1985	5.00	30
1985	Do Not Disturb Bear QX481-2	Yr.Iss.	1986	7.75	16-33
1985	Doggy in a Stocking QX474-2	Yr.Iss.	1985	5.50	25-40
1985	Engineering Mouse QX473-5	Yr.Iss.	1985	5.50	15-25
1985	Ice-Skating Owl QX476-5	Yr.Iss.	1985	5.00	15-25
1985	Kitty Mischief QX474-5	Yr.Iss.	1986	5.00	15-25
1985	Lamb in Legwarmers QX480-2	Yr.Iss.	1985	7.00	15-25
1985	Merry Mouse QX403-2	Yr.Iss.	1986	4.50	20-30
1985	Mouse Wagon QX476-2	Yr.Iss.	1985	5.75	37-60
1985	Nativity Scene QX264-5	Yr.Iss.	1985	4.75	30
1985	Night Before Christmas QX449-4	Yr.Iss.	1985	13.00	20-40
1985	Roller Skating Rabbit QX457-1	Yr.Iss.	1985	5.00	19
1985	Santa's Ski Trip QX496-2	Yr.Iss.	1985	12.00	41-60
1985	Skateboard Raccoon QX473-2	Yr.Iss.	1986	6.50	25-43
1985	Snow-Pitching Snowman QX470-2	Yr.Iss.	1986	4.50	25
1985	Snowy Seal QX450-1	Yr.Iss.	1985	4.00	16
1985	Soccer Beaver QX477-5	Yr.Iss.	1986	6.50	15-25
1985	Stardust Angel QX475-2	Yr.Iss.	1985	5.75	35
1985	Sun and Fun Santa QX492-2	Yr.Iss.	1985	7.75	40
1985	Swinging Angel Bell QX492-5	Yr.Iss.	1985	11.00	40
1985	Three Kittens in a Mitten QX431-1	Yr.Iss.	1985	8.00	35
1985	Trumpet Panda QX471-2	Yr.Iss.	1985	4.50	15-25

1985 Keepsake Magic Ornaments - Keepsake

YEAR ISSUE		EDITION LIMIT	YEAR RETD.	ISSUE PRICE	*QUOTE U.S.$
1985	All Are Precious QLX704-1	Yr.Iss.	1985	8.00	12-25
1985	Baby's First Christmas QLX700-5	Yr.Iss.	1985	17.00	30-40
1985	Chris Mouse-1st Ed.) QLX703-2	Yr.Iss.	1985	13.00	88
1985	Christmas Eve Visit QLX710-5	Yr.Iss.	1985	12.00	33
1985	Katybeth QLX710-2	Yr.Iss.	1985	10.75	30-43
1985	Little Red Schoolhouse QLX711-2	Yr.Iss.	1985	15.75	70-95
1985	Love Wreath QLX702-5	Yr.Iss.	1985	8.50	19-30
1985	Mr. and Mrs. Santa QLX705-2	Yr.Iss.	1986	15.00	73-90
1985	Nativity 1200 QLX700-1	Yr.Iss.	1985	12.00	18-30
1985	Santa's Workshop QLX700-4	Yr.Iss.	1985	13.00	58
1985	Season of Beauty QLX712-2	Yr.Iss.	1985	8.00	19-29
1985	Sugarplum Cottage QLX701-1	Yr.Iss.	1985	11.00	45
1985	Swiss Cheese Lane QLX706-5	Yr.Iss.	1985	13.00	34-50
1985	Village Church QLX702-1	Yr.Iss.	1985	15.00	35-50

1985 Limited Edition - Keepsake

YEAR ISSUE		EDITION LIMIT	YEAR RETD.	ISSUE PRICE	*QUOTE U.S.$
1985	Heavenly Trumpeter QX405-2	Yr.Iss.	1985	28.00	75-100

1985 Property Ornaments - Keepsake

YEAR ISSUE		EDITION LIMIT	YEAR RETD.	ISSUE PRICE	*QUOTE U.S.$
1985	Betsey Clark QX508-5	Yr.Iss.	1985	8.50	30
1985	A Disney Christmas QX271-2	Yr.Iss.	1985	4.75	30
1985	Fraggle Rock Holiday QX265-5	Yr.Iss.	1985	4.75	23
1985	Hugga Bunch QX271-5	Yr.Iss.	1985	5.00	15-30
1985	Kit the Shepherd QX484-5	Yr.Iss.	1985	5.75	28
1985	Merry Shirt Tales QX267-2	Yr.Iss.	1985	4.75	20
1985	Muffin the Angel QX483-5	Yr.Iss.	1985	5.75	24
1985	Norman Rockwell QX266-2	Yr.Iss.	1985	4.75	30
1985	Peanuts QX266-5	Yr.Iss.	1985	4.75	35
1985	Rainbow Brite and Friends QX 268-2	Yr.Iss.	1985	4.75	10-20
1985	Snoopy and Woodstock QX491-5	Yr.Iss.	1985	7.50	65

1985 Traditional Ornaments - Keepsake

YEAR ISSUE		EDITION LIMIT	YEAR RETD.	ISSUE PRICE	*QUOTE U.S.$
1985	Candle Cameo QX374-2	Yr.Iss.	1985	6.75	15
1985	Christmas Treats QX507-5	Yr.Iss.	1985	5.50	10-18
1985	Nostalgic Sled QX442-4	Yr.Iss.	1985	6.00	20
1985	Old-Fashioned Wreath QX373-5	Yr.Iss.	1985	7.50	25
1985	Peaceful Kingdom QX373-2	Yr.Iss.	1985	5.75	20-30
1985	Porcelain Bird QX479-5	Yr.Iss.	1985	6.50	20-30
1985	Santa Pipe QX494-2	Yr.Iss.	1985	9.50	15-25
1985	Sewn Photoholder QX379-5	Yr.Iss.	1985	7.00	10-25
1985	The Spirit of Santa Claus -(Special Ed.) QX 498-5	Yr.Iss.	1985	23.00	75-95

1986 Christmas Medley Collection - Keepsake

YEAR ISSUE		EDITION LIMIT	YEAR RETD.	ISSUE PRICE	*QUOTE U.S.$
1986	Christmas Guitar QX512-6	Yr.Iss.	1986	7.00	10-20
1986	Favorite Tin Drum QX514-3	Yr.Iss.	1986	8.50	30
1986	Festive Treble Clef QX513-3	Yr.Iss.	1986	8.75	10-28
1986	Holiday Horn QX514-6	Yr.Iss.	1986	8.00	17-33
1986	Joyful Carolers QX513-6	Yr.Iss.	1986	9.75	30-40

1986 Collectible Series - Keepsake

YEAR ISSUE		EDITION LIMIT	YEAR RETD.	ISSUE PRICE	*QUOTE U.S.$
1986	Art Masterpiece-(3rd & Final Ed.) QX350-6	Yr.Iss.	1986	6.75	23
1986	Betsey Clark: Home for Christmas-(1st Ed.) QX277-6	Yr.Iss.	1986	5.00	20-35
1986	Clothespin Soldier-(5th Ed.) QX406-3	Yr.Iss.	1986	5.50	23
1986	Frosty Friends-(7th Ed.) QX405-3	Yr.Iss.	1986	8.50	62-70
1986	Here Comes Santa-(8th Ed.) QX404-3	Yr.Iss.	1986	14.00	43-65
1986	Holiday Wildlife-(5th Ed.) QX321-6	Yr.Iss.	1986	7.50	20-30
1986	Miniature Creche-(2nd Ed.) QX407-6	Yr.Iss.	1986	9.00	40-55
1986	Mr. and Mrs. Claus-(1st Ed.) QX402-6	Yr.Iss.	1986	13.00	85-100
1986	Norman Rockwell-(7th Ed.) QX321-3	Yr.Iss.	1986	7.75	20-28
1986	Nostalgic Houses and Shops-(3rd Ed.) QX403-3	Yr.Iss.	1986	13.75	200-300
1986	Porcelain Bear-(4th Ed.) QX405-6	Yr.Iss.	1986	7.75	35-45
1986	Reindeer Champs-(1st Ed.) QX422-3	Yr.Iss.	1986	7.50	125-150
1986	Rocking Horse-(6th Ed.) QX401-6	Yr.Iss.	1986	10.75	60-75
1986	Thimble-(9th Ed.) QX406-6	Yr.Iss.	1986	5.75	20-30
1986	Tin Locomotive-(5th Ed.) QX403-6	Yr.Iss.	1986	14.75	50-75
1986	Twelve Days of Christmas -(3rd Ed.) QX378-6	Yr.Iss.	1986	6.50	33-44
1986	Windows of the World-(2nd Ed.) QX408-3	Yr.Iss.	1986	10.00	20-55
1986	Wood Childhood Ornaments-(3rd Ed.) QX407-3	Yr.Iss.	1986	7.50	21-33

1986 Commemoratives - Keepsake

YEAR ISSUE		EDITION LIMIT	YEAR RETD.	ISSUE PRICE	*QUOTE U.S.$
1986	Baby Locket QX412-3	Yr.Iss.	1986	16.00	19-27
1986	Baby's First Christmas Photoholder QX379-2	Yr.Iss.	1986	8.00	20
1986	Baby's First Christmas QX271-3	Yr.Iss.	1986	5.50	15-25
1986	Baby's First Christmas QX380-3	Yr.Iss.	1986	6.00	22
1986	Baby's First Christmas QX412-6	Yr.Iss.	1986	9.00	35
1986	Baby's Second Christmas QX413-3	Yr.Iss.	1986	6.50	27
1986	Baby-Sitter QX275-6	Yr.Iss.	1986	4.75	7-12
1986	Child's Third Christmas QX413-6	Yr.Iss.	1986	6.50	20-26
1986	Daughter QX430-6	Yr.Iss.	1986	5.75	32-50
1986	Father QX431-3	Yr.Iss.	1986	6.50	8-15
1986	Fifty Years Together QX400-6	Yr.Iss.	1986	10.00	20
1986	First Christmas Together QX270-3	Yr.Iss.	1986	4.75	30
1986	First Christmas Together QX379-3	Yr.Iss.	1986	7.00	20
1986	First Christmas Together QX400-3	Yr.Iss.	1986	16.00	28
1986	First Christmas Together QX409-6	Yr.Iss.	1986	12.00	20
1986	Friends Are Fun QX272-3	Yr.Iss.	1986	4.75	40
1986	Friendship Greeting QX427-3	Yr.Iss.	1986	8.00	15
1986	Friendship's Gift QX381-6	Yr.Iss.	1986	6.00	15
1986	From Our Home to Yours QX383-3	Yr.Iss.	1986	6.00	15
1986	Godchild QX271-6	Yr.Iss.	1986	4.75	15
1986	Grandchild's First Christmas QX411-6	Yr.Iss.	1986	10.00	15
1986	Granddaughter QX273-6	Yr.Iss.	1986	4.75	25
1986	Grandmother QX274-3	Yr.Iss.	1986	4.75	8-16
1986	Grandparents QX432-3	Yr.Iss.	1986	7.50	10-23
1986	Grandson QX273-3	Yr.Iss.	1986	4.75	25
1986	Gratitude QX432-6	Yr.Iss.	1986	6.00	10
1986	Husband QX383-6	Yr.Iss.	1986	8.00	14-25
1986	Joy of Friends QX382-3	Yr.Iss.	1986	6.75	18
1986	Loving Memories QX409-3	Yr.Iss.	1986	9.00	35
1986	Mother and Dad QX431-6	Yr.Iss.	1986	7.50	18
1986	Mother QX382-6	Yr.Iss.	1986	7.00	10-20
1986	Nephew QX381-3	Yr.Iss.	1986	6.25	10
1986	New Home QX274-6	Yr.Iss.	1986	4.75	65
1986	Niece QX426-6	Yr.Iss.	1986	6.00	10
1986	Season of the Heart QX270-6	Yr.Iss.	1986	4.75	10-18
1986	Sister QX380-6	Yr.Iss.	1986	6.75	15
1986	Son QX430-3	Yr.Iss.	1986	5.75	25-35
1986	Sweetheart QX408-6	Yr.Iss.	1986	11.00	50-70
1986	Teacher QX275-3	Yr.Iss.	1986	4.75	6-12
1986	Ten Years Together QX401-3	Yr.Iss.	1986	7.50	25
1986	Timeless Love QX379-6	Yr.Iss.	1986	6.00	30
1986	Twenty-Five Years Together QX410-3	Yr.Iss.	1986	8.00	25

1986 Country Treasures Collection - Keepsake

YEAR ISSUE		EDITION LIMIT	YEAR RETD.	ISSUE PRICE	*QUOTE U.S.$
1986	Country Sleigh QX511-3	Yr.Iss.	1986	10.00	25
1986	Little Drummers QX511-6	Yr.Iss.	1986	12.50	18-35
1986	Nutcracker Santa QX512-3	Yr.Iss.	1986	10.00	25-50
1986	Remembering Christmas QX510-6	Yr.Iss.	1986	8.75	30
1986	Welcome, Christmas QX510-3	Yr.Iss.	1986	8.25	20-35

1986 Holiday Humor - Keepsake

YEAR ISSUE		EDITION LIMIT	YEAR RETD.	ISSUE PRICE	*QUOTE U.S.$
1986	Acorn Inn QX424-3	Yr.Iss.	1986	8.50	28
1986	Beary Smooth Ride QX480-5	Yr.Iss.	1986	6.50	20
1986	Chatty Penguin QX417-6	Yr.Iss.	1986	5.75	15-25
1986	Cookies for Santa QX414-6	Yr.Iss.	1986	4.50	17-30
1986	Do Not Disturb Bear QX481-2	Yr.Iss.	1986	7.75	15-25
1986	Happy Christmas to Owl QX418-3	Yr.Iss.	1986	6.00	15-25
1986	Heavenly Dreamer QX417-3	Yr.Iss.	1986	5.75	22-35
1986	Jolly Hiker QX483-2	Yr.Iss.	1987	5.00	20-30
1986	Kitty Mischief QX474-5	Yr.Iss.	1986	5.00	25
1986	Li'l Jingler QX419-3	Yr.Iss.	1987	6.75	22-40
1986	Merry Koala QX415-3	Yr.Iss.	1987	5.00	23
1986	Merry Mouse QX403-2	Yr.Iss.	1986	4.50	22
1986	Mouse in the Moon QX416-6	Yr.Iss.	1987	5.50	23
1986	Open Me First QX422-6	Yr.Iss.	1986	7.25	15-30
1986	Playful Possum QX425-3	Yr.Iss.	1986	11.00	33
1986	Popcorn Mouse QX421-3	Yr.Iss.	1986	6.75	40-55
1986	Puppy's Best Friend QX420-3	Yr.Iss.	1986	6.50	17-30
1986	Rah Rah Rabbit QX421-6	Yr.Iss.	1986	7.00	40
1986	Santa's Hot Tub QX426-3	Yr.Iss.	1986	12.00	58
1986	Skateboard Raccoon QX473-2	Yr.Iss.	1986	6.50	40
1986	Ski Tripper QX420-6	Yr.Iss.	1986	6.75	12-22
1986	Snow Buddies QX423-6	Yr.Iss.	1986	8.00	38
1986	Snow-Pitching Snowman QX470-2	Yr.Iss.	1986	4.50	23
1986	Soccer Beaver QX477-5	Yr.Iss.	1986	6.50	25
1986	Special Delivery QX415-6	Yr.Iss.	1986	5.00	17-30
1986	Tipping the Scales QX418-6	Yr.Iss.	1986	6.75	15-30
1986	Touchdown Santa QX423-3	Yr.Iss.	1986	8.00	42
1986	Treetop Trio QX424-6	Yr.Iss.	1987	11.00	32
1986	Walnut Shell Rider QX419-6	Yr.Iss.	1987	6.00	18-30
1986	Wynken, Blynken and Nod QX424-6	Yr.Iss.	1986	9.75	42

1986 Lighted Ornament Collection - Keepsake

YEAR ISSUE		EDITION LIMIT	YEAR RETD.	ISSUE PRICE	*QUOTE U.S.$
1986	Baby's First Christmas QLX710-3	Yr.Iss.	1986	19.50	45
1986	Chris Mouse-(2nd Ed.) QLX705-6	Yr.Iss.	1986	13.00	75
1986	Christmas Classics-(1st Ed.) QLX704-3	Yr.Iss.	1986	17.50	85
1986	Christmas Sleigh Ride QLX701-2	Yr.Iss.	1986	24.50	120-145
1986	First Christmas Together QLX707-3	Yr.Iss.	1986	14.00	43
1986	General Store QLX705-3	Yr.Iss.	1986	15.75	43-60
1986	Gentle Blessings QLX708-3	Yr.Iss.	1986	15.00	110-175
1986	Keep on Glowin' QLX707-6	Yr.Iss.	1987	10.00	37-50
1986	Merry Christmas Bell QLX709-3	Yr.Iss.	1986	8.50	15-25
1986	Mr. and Mrs. Santa QLX705-2	Yr.Iss.	1986	14.50	65-95
1986	Santa and Sparky-(1st Ed.) QLX703-3	Yr.Iss.	1986	22.00	95
1986	Santa's On His Way QLX711-5	Yr.Iss.	1986	15.00	63-75
1986	Santa's Snack QLX706-6	Yr.Iss.	1986	10.00	58
1986	Sharing Friendship QLX706-3	Yr.Iss.	1986	8.50	16
1986	Sugarplum Cottage QLX701-1	Yr.Iss.	1986	11.00	45
1986	Village Express QLX707-2	Yr.Iss.	1987	24.50	87-125

1986 Limited Edition - Keepsake

YEAR ISSUE		EDITION LIMIT	YEAR RETD.	ISSUE PRICE	*QUOTE U.S.$
1986	Magical Unicorn QX429-3	Yr.Iss.	1986	27.50	85

1986 Property Ornaments - Keepsake

YEAR ISSUE		EDITION LIMIT	YEAR RETD.	ISSUE PRICE	*QUOTE U.S.$
1986	Heathcliff QX436-3	Yr.Iss.	1986	7.50	20-33
1986	Katybeth QX435-3	Yr.Iss.	1986	7.00	25
1986	Norman Rockwell QX276-3	Yr.Iss.	1986	4.75	33
1986	Paddington Bear QX435-6	Yr.Iss.	1986	6.00	30-40
1986	Peanuts QX276-6	Yr.Iss.	1986	4.75	30
1986	Shirt Tales Parade QX277-3	Yr.Iss.	1986	4.75	18
1986	Snoopy and Woodstock QX434-6	Yr.Iss.	1986	8.00	45-60
1986	The Statue of Liberty QX384-3	Yr.Iss.	1986	6.00	10-25

1986 Special Edition - Keepsake

YEAR ISSUE		EDITION LIMIT	YEAR RETD.	ISSUE PRICE	*QUOTE U.S.$
1986	Jolly St. Nick QX429-6	Yr.Iss.	1986	22.50	50-75

1986 Traditional Ornaments - Keepsake

YEAR ISSUE		EDITION LIMIT	YEAR RETD.	ISSUE PRICE	*QUOTE U.S.$
1986	Bluebird QX428-3	Yr.Iss.	1986	7.25	40-50

*Quotes have been rounded up to nearest dollar

YEAR	ISSUE	EDITION LIMIT	YEAR RETD.	ISSUE PRICE	*QUOTE U.S.$
1986	Christmas Beauty QX322-3	Yr.Iss.	1986	6.00	10
1986	Glowing Christmas Tree QX428-6	Yr.Iss.	1986	7.00	15
1986	Heirloom Snowflake QX515-3	Yr.Iss.	1986	6.75	10-22
1986	Holiday Jingle Bell QX404-6	Yr.Iss.	1986	16.00	30-55
1986	The Magi QX272-6	Yr.Iss.	1986	4.75	19
1986	Mary Emmerling:American Country Collection QX275-2	Yr.Iss.	1986	7.95	25
1986	Memories to Cherish QX427-6	Yr.Iss.	1986	7.50	25
1986	Star Brighteners QX322-6	Yr.Iss.	1986	6.00	17

1987 Artists' Favorites - Keepsake

YEAR	ISSUE	EDITION LIMIT	YEAR RETD.	ISSUE PRICE	*QUOTE U.S.$
1987	Beary Special QX455-7	Yr.Iss.	1987	4.75	15-30
1987	December Showers QX448-7	Yr.Iss.	1987	5.50	36
1987	Three Men in a Tub QX454-7	Yr.Iss.	1987	8.00	17-30
1987	Wee Chimney Sweep QX451-9	Yr.Iss.	1987	6.25	15-30

1987 Christmas Pizzazz Collection Keepsake

YEAR	ISSUE	EDITION LIMIT	YEAR RETD.	ISSUE PRICE	*QUOTE U.S.$
1987	Christmas Fun Puzzle QX467-9	Yr.Iss.	1987	8.00	15-30
1987	Doc Holiday QX467-7	Yr.Iss.	1987	8.00	43
1987	Happy Holidata QX471-7	Yr.Iss.	1988	6.50	15-30
1987	Holiday Hourglass QX470-7	Yr.Iss.	1987	8.00	25
1987	Jolly Follies QX466-9	Yr.Iss.	1987	8.50	40
1987	Mistletoad QX468-7	Yr.Iss.	1988	7.00	30
1987	St. Louie Nick QX453-9	Yr.Iss.	1988	7.75	16-33

1987 Collectible Series - Keepsake

YEAR	ISSUE	EDITION LIMIT	YEAR RETD.	ISSUE PRICE	*QUOTE U.S.$
1987	Betsey Clark:Home for Christmas-(2nd Ed.) QX272-7	Yr.Iss.	1987	5.00	17-25
1987	Clothespin Soldier-(6th & Final Ed.) QX480-7	Yr.Iss.	1987	5.50	20-30
1987	Collector's Plate-(1st Ed.) QX481-7	Yr.Iss.	1987	8.00	75
1987	Frosty Friends-(8th Ed.) QX440-9	Yr.Iss.	1987	8.50	43-60
1987	Here Comes Santa-(9th Ed.) QX484-7	Yr.Iss.	1987	14.00	45-75
1987	Holiday Heirloom-(1st Ed./ limited Ed.)QX485-7	Yr.Iss.	1987	25.00	48
1987	Holiday Wildlife-(6th Ed.) QX371-7	Yr.Iss.	1987	7.50	15-25
1987	Miniature Creche-(3rd Ed.) QX481-9	Yr.Iss.	1987	9.00	24-38
1987	Mr. and Mrs. Claus-(2nd Ed.) QX483-7	Yr.Iss.	1987	13.25	42-65
1987	Norman Rockwell-(8th Ed.) QX370-7	Yr.Iss.	1987	7.75	15-25
1987	Nostalgic Houses and Shops-(4th Ed.) QX483-9	Yr.Iss.	1987	14.00	57-75
1987	Porcelain Bear-(5th Ed.) QX442-7	Yr.Iss.	1987	7.75	25-40
1987	Reindeer Champs-(2nd Ed.) QX480-9	Yr.Iss.	1987	7.50	35-55
1987	Rocking Horse-(7th Ed.) QX482-9	Yr.Iss.	1987	10.75	41-70
1987	Thimble-(10th Ed.) QX441-9	Yr.Iss.	1987	5.75	20-30
1987	Tin Locomotive-(6th Ed.) QX484-9	Yr.Iss.	1987	14.75	45-65
1987	Twelve Days of Christmas -(4th Ed.) QX370-9	Yr.Iss.	1987	6.50	27-35
1987	Windows of the World-(3rd Ed.) QX482-7	Yr.Iss.	1987	10.00	25
1987	Wood Childhood Ornaments-(4th Ed.) QX441-7	Yr.Iss.	1987	7.50	17-27

1987 Commemoratives - Keepsake

YEAR	ISSUE	EDITION LIMIT	YEAR RETD.	ISSUE PRICE	*QUOTE U.S.$
1987	Baby Locket QX461-7	Yr.Iss.	1987	15.00	15-30
1987	Baby's First Christmas Photoholder QX4661-9	Yr.Iss.	1987	7.50	30
1987	Baby's First Christmas QX372-9	Yr.Iss.	1987	6.00	20
1987	Baby's First Christmas QX411-3	Yr.Iss.	1987	9.75	27
1987	Baby's First Christmas-Baby Boy QX274-9	Yr.Iss.	1987	4.75	25
1987	Baby's First Christmas-Baby Girl QX274-7	Yr.Iss.	1987	4.75	25
1987	Baby's Second Christmas QX460-7	Yr.Iss.	1987	5.75	32
1987	Babysitter QX279-7	Yr.Iss.	1987	4.75	10-20
1987	Child's Third Christmas QX459-9	Yr.Iss.	1987	5.75	30
1987	Dad QX462-9	Yr.Iss.	1987	6.00	40
1987	Daughter QX463-7	Yr.Iss.	1987	5.75	26
1987	Fifty Years Together QX443-7	Yr.Iss.	1987	8.00	25
1987	First Christmas Together QX272-9	Yr.Iss.	1987	4.75	23
1987	First Christmas Together QX371-9	Yr.Iss.	1987	6.50	20
1987	First Christmas Together QX445-9	Yr.Iss.	1987	8.00	20-38
1987	First Christmas Together QX446-7	Yr.Iss.	1987	9.50	30
1987	First Christmas Together QX446-9	Yr.Iss.	1987	15.00	30
1987	From Our Home to Yours QX279-9	Yr.Iss.	1987	4.75	50
1987	Godchild QX276-7	Yr.Iss.	1987	4.75	20
1987	Grandchild's First Christmas QX460-9	Yr.Iss.	1987	9.00	25
1987	Granddaughter QX374-7	Yr.Iss.	1987	6.00	15-25
1987	Grandmother QX277-9	Yr.Iss.	1987	4.75	15
1987	Grandparents QX277-7	Yr.Iss.	1987	4.75	18
1987	Grandson QX276-9	Yr.Iss.	1987	4.75	30
1987	Heart in Blossom QX372-7	Yr.Iss.	1987	6.00	25
1987	Holiday Greetings QX375-7	Yr.Iss.	1987	6.00	13
1987	Husband QX373-9	Yr.Iss.	1987	7.00	12
1987	Love is Everywhere QX278-7	Yr.Iss.	1987	4.75	25
1987	Mother and Dad QX462-7	Yr.Iss.	1987	7.00	20
1987	Mother QX373-7	Yr.Iss.	1987	6.50	25
1987	New Home QX376-7	Yr.Iss.	1987	6.00	30
1987	Niece QX275-9	Yr.Iss.	1987	4.75	13
1987	Sister QX474-7	Yr.Iss.	1987	6.00	15
1987	Son QX463-9	Yr.Iss.	1987	5.75	45
1987	Sweetheart QX447-9	Yr.Iss.	1987	11.00	15-30
1987	Teacher QX466-7	Yr.Iss.	1987	5.75	21
1987	Ten Years Together QX444-7	Yr.Iss.	1987	7.00	25
1987	Time for Friends QX280-7	Yr.Iss.	1987	4.75	22
1987	Twenty-Five Years Together QX443-9	Yr.Iss.	1987	7.50	15-30
1987	Warmth of Friendship QX375-9	Yr.Iss.	1987	6.00	12
1987	Word of Love QX447-7	Yr.Iss.	1987	8.00	10-22

1987 Holiday Humor - Keepsake

YEAR	ISSUE	EDITION LIMIT	YEAR RETD.	ISSUE PRICE	*QUOTE U.S.$
1987	Bright Christmas Dreams QX440-7	Yr.Iss.	1987	7.25	75-85
1987	Chocolate Chipmunk QX456-7	Yr.Iss.	1987	6.00	50
1987	Christmas Cuddle QX453-7	Yr.Iss.	1987	5.75	25-35
1987	Dr. Seuss:The Grinch's Christmas QX278-3	Yr.Iss.	1987	4.75	50-60
1987	Fudge Forever QX449-7	Yr.Iss.	1987	5.00	25-40
1987	Happy Santa QX456-9	Yr.Iss.	1987	4.75	30
1987	Hot Dogger QX471-9	Yr.Iss.	1987	6.50	25-30
1987	Icy Treat QX450-9	Yr.Iss.	1987	4.50	20-30
1987	Jack Frosting QX449-9	Yr.Iss.	1987	7.00	30-50
1987	Jammie Pies QX283-9	Yr.Iss.	1987	4.75	18
1987	Jogging Through the Snow QX457-7	Yr.Iss.	1987	7.25	25-40
1987	Jolly Hiker QX483-2	Yr.Iss.	1987	5.00	18
1987	Joy Ride QX440-7	Yr.Iss.	1987	11.50	45-55
1987	Let It Snow QX458-9	Yr.Iss.	1987	6.50	15-25
1987	Li'l Jingler QX419-3	Yr.Iss.	1987	6.75	22-36
1987	Merry Koala QX415-3	Yr.Iss.	1987	5.00	17
1987	Mouse in the Moon QX416-6	Yr.Iss.	1987	5.50	21
1987	Nature's Decorations QX273-9	Yr.Iss.	1987	4.75	35
1987	Night Before Christmas QX451-7	Yr.Iss.	1988	6.50	19-33
1987	Owliday Wish QX455-9	Yr.Iss.	1988	6.50	14-25
1987	Paddington Bear QX472-7	Yr.Iss.	1987	5.50	30-35
1987	Peanuts QX281-9	Yr.Iss.	1987	4.75	34
1987	Pretty Kitten QX448-9	Yr.Iss.	1987	11.00	35
1987	Raccoon Biker QX458-7	Yr.Iss.	1987	7.00	15-30
1987	Reindoggy QX452-7	Yr.Iss.	1988	5.75	20-35
1987	Santa at the Bat QX457-9	Yr.Iss.	1987	7.75	20-30
1987	Seasoned Greetings QX454-9	Yr.Iss.	1987	6.25	15-30
1987	Sleepy Santa QX450-7	Yr.Iss.	1987	6.25	35-40
1987	Snoopy and Woodstock QX472-9	Yr.Iss.	1987	7.25	40-50
1987	Spots 'n Stripes QX452-9	Yr.Iss.	1987	5.50	15-25
1987	Treetop Dreams QX459-7	Yr.Iss.	1988	6.75	15-30
1987	Treetop Trio QX425-6	Yr.Iss.	1987	11.00	25
1987	Walnut Shell Rider QX419-6	Yr.Iss.	1987	6.00	18

1987 Keepsake Collector's Club - Keepsake

YEAR	ISSUE	EDITION LIMIT	YEAR RETD.	ISSUE PRICE	*QUOTE U.S.$
1987	Carrousel Reindeer QXC580-7	Yr.Iss.	1987	Unkn.	55-65
1987	Wreath of Memories QXC580-9	Yr.Iss.	1988	Unkn.	55

1987 Keepsake Magic Ornaments - Keepsake

YEAR	ISSUE	EDITION LIMIT	YEAR RETD.	ISSUE PRICE	*QUOTE U.S.$
1987	Angelic Messengers QLX711-3	Yr.Iss.	1987	18.75	53-60
1987	Baby's First Christmas QLX704-9	Yr.Iss.	1987	13.50	38
1987	Bright Noel QLX705-9	Yr.Iss.	1987	7.00	18-33
1987	Chris Mouse-(3rd Ed.) QLX705-7	Yr.Iss.	1987	11.00	60
1987	Christmas Classics-(2nd Ed.) QLX702-9	Yr.Iss.	1987	16.00	50-75
1987	Christmas Morning QLX701-3	Yr.Iss.	1988	24.50	33-50
1987	First Christmas Together QLX708-7	Yr.Iss.	1987	11.50	40-50
1987	Good Cheer Blimp QLX704-6	Yr.Iss.	1987	16.00	52-59
1987	Keeping Cozy QLX704-7	Yr.Iss.	1987	11.75	30-37
1987	Lacy Brass Snowflake QLX709-7	Yr.Iss.	1987	11.50	20
1987	Loving Holiday QLX701-6	Yr.Iss.	1987	22.00	38-55
1987	Memories are Forever Photoholder QLX706-7	Yr.Iss.	1987	8.50	33
1987	Meowy Christmas QLX708-9	Yr.Iss.	1987	10.00	45-63
1987	Santa and Sparky-(2nd Ed.) QLX701-9	Yr.Iss.	1987	19.50	65-75
1987	Season for Friendship QLX706-9	Yr.Iss.	1987	8.50	11-20
1987	Train Station QLX703-9	Yr.Iss.	1987	12.75	50

1987 Lighted Ornament Collection - Keepsake

YEAR	ISSUE	EDITION LIMIT	YEAR RETD.	ISSUE PRICE	*QUOTE U.S.$
1987	Keep on Glowin' QLX707-6	Yr.Iss.	1987	10.00	37
1987	Village Express QLX707-2	Yr.Iss.	1987	24.50	87-120

1987 Limited Edition - Keepsake

YEAR	ISSUE	EDITION LIMIT	YEAR RETD.	ISSUE PRICE	*QUOTE U.S.$
1987	Christmas is Gentle QX444-9	Yr.Iss.	1987	17.50	45-85
1987	Christmas Time Mime QX442-9	Yr.Iss.	1987	27.50	45-55

1987 Old-Fashioned Christmas Collection - Keepsake

YEAR	ISSUE	EDITION LIMIT	YEAR RETD.	ISSUE PRICE	*QUOTE U.S.$
1987	Country Wreath QX470-9	Yr.Iss.	1987	5.75	30
1987	Folk Art Santa QX474-9	Yr.Iss.	1987	5.25	20-33
1987	In a Nutshell QX469-7	Yr.Iss.	1988	5.50	24-34
1987	Little Whittler QX469-9	Yr.Iss.	1987	6.00	25-33
1987	Nostalgic Rocker QX468-9	Yr.Iss.	1987	6.50	26-33

1987 Special Edition - Keepsake

YEAR	ISSUE	EDITION LIMIT	YEAR RETD.	ISSUE PRICE	*QUOTE U.S.$
1987	Favorite Santa QX445-7	Yr.Iss.	1987	22.50	35-45

1987 Traditional Ornaments - Keepsake

YEAR	ISSUE	EDITION LIMIT	YEAR RETD.	ISSUE PRICE	*QUOTE U.S.$
1987	Christmas Keys QX473-9	Yr.Iss.	1987	5.75	20-33
1987	Currier & Ives: American Farm Scene QX282-9	Yr.Iss.	1987	4.75	30
1987	Goldfinch QX464-9	Yr.Iss.	1987	7.00	55-85
1987	Heavenly Harmony QX465-9	Yr.Iss.	1987	15.00	33
1987	I Remember Santa QX278-9	Yr.Iss.	1987	4.75	33
1987	Joyous Angels QX465-7	Yr.Iss.	1987	7.75	15-25
1987	Norman Rockwell:Christmas Scenes QX282-7	Yr.Iss.	1987	4.75	30
1987	Promise of Peace QX374-9	Yr.Iss.	1987	6.50	17-25
1987	Special Memories Photoholder QX464-7	Yr.Iss.	1987	6.75	15-27

1988 Artist Favorites - Keepsake

YEAR	ISSUE	EDITION LIMIT	YEAR RETD.	ISSUE PRICE	*QUOTE U.S.$
1988	Baby Redbird QX410-1	Yr.Iss.	1988	5.00	20
1988	Cymbals of Christmas QX411-1	Yr.Iss.	1988	5.50	17-30
1988	Little Jack Horner QX408-1	Yr.Iss.	1988	8.00	14-28
1988	Merry-Mint Unicorn QX423-4	Yr.Iss.	1988	8.50	12-22
1988	Midnight Snack QX410-4	Yr.Iss.	1988	6.00	21
1988	Very Strawbeary QX409-1	Yr.Iss.	1988	4.75	20

1988 Christmas Pizzazz Collection - Keepsake

YEAR	ISSUE	EDITION LIMIT	YEAR RETD.	ISSUE PRICE	*QUOTE U.S.$
1988	Happy Holidata QX471-7	Yr.Iss.	1988	6.50	15-30
1988	Mistletoad QX468-7	Yr.Iss.	1988	7.00	20-30
1988	St. Louie Nick QX453-9	Yr.Iss.	1988	7.75	15-22

1988 Collectible Series - Keepsake

YEAR	ISSUE	EDITION LIMIT	YEAR RETD.	ISSUE PRICE	*QUOTE U.S.$
1988	Betsey Clark: Home for Christmas-(3rd Ed.) QX271-4	Yr.Iss.	1988	5.00	18-25
1988	Collector's Plate-(2nd Ed.) QX406-1	Yr.Iss.	1988	8.00	50
1988	Five Golden Rings-(5th Ed.) QX371-4	Yr.Iss.	1988	6.50	20
1988	Frosty Friends-(9th Ed.) QX403-1	Yr.Iss.	1988	8.75	45-65
1988	Here Comes Santa-(10th Ed.) QX400-1	Yr.Iss.	1988	14.00	47
1988	Holiday Heirloom-(2nd Ed.) QX406-4	Yr.Iss.	1988	25.00	24
1988	Holiday Wildlife-(7th Ed.) QX371-1	Yr.Iss.	1988	7.75	16-25
1988	Mary's Angels-(1st Ed.) QX407-4	Yr.Iss.	1988	5.00	43-55
1988	Miniature Creche-(4th Ed.) QX403-4	Yr.Iss.	1988	8.50	21
1988	Mr. and Mrs. Claus-(3rd Ed.)QX401-1	Yr.Iss.	1988	13.00	40-55
1988	Norman Rockwell-(9th Ed.) QX370-4	Yr.Iss.	1988	7.75	17
1988	Nostalgic Houses and Shops-(5th Ed.) QX401-4	Yr.Iss.	1988	14.50	50-60
1988	Porcelain Bear-(6th Ed.) QX404-4	Yr.Iss.	1988	8.00	25-40
1988	Reindeer Champs-(3rd Ed.) QX405-1	Yr.Iss.	1988	7.50	37
1988	Rocking Horse-(8th Ed.) QX402-4	Yr.Iss.	1988	10.75	25-60
1988	Thimble-(11th Ed.) QX405-4	Yr.Iss.	1988	5.75	25
1988	Tin Locomotive-(7th Ed.) QX400-4	Yr.Iss.	1988	14.75	38-60
1988	Windows of the World-(4th Ed.) QX402-1	Yr.Iss.	1988	10.00	22-35
1988	Wood Childhood-(5th Ed.) QX404-1	Yr.Iss.	1988	7.50	23

1988 Commemoratives - Keepsake

YEAR	ISSUE	EDITION LIMIT	YEAR RETD.	ISSUE PRICE	*QUOTE U.S.$
1988	Baby's First Christmas (Boy) QX272-1	Yr.Iss.	1988	4.75	17-25
1988	Baby's First Christmas (Girl) QX272-4	Yr.Iss.	1988	4.75	23
1988	Baby's First Christmas QX372-1	Yr.Iss.	1988	6.00	18
1988	Baby's First Christmas QX470-1	Yr.Iss.	1988	9.75	30-40
1988	Baby's First Christmas QX470-4	Yr.Iss.	1988	7.50	28
1988	Baby's Second Christmas QX471-1	Yr.Iss.	1988	6.00	33
1988	Babysitter QX279-1	Yr.Iss.	1988	4.75	10
1988	Child's Third Christmas QX471-4	Yr.Iss.	1988	6.00	23-30
1988	Dad QX414-1	Yr.Iss.	1988	7.00	25
1988	Daughter QX415-1	Yr.Iss.	1988	5.75	50
1988	Fifty Years Together QX374-1	Yr.Iss.	1988	6.75	10-20
1988	First Christmas Together QX274-1	Yr.Iss.	1988	4.75	23
1988	First Christmas Together QX373-1	Yr.Iss.	1988	6.75	20-30
1988	First Christmas Together QX489-4	Yr.Iss.	1988	9.00	27
1988	Five Years Together QX274-4	Yr.Iss.	1988	4.75	6-20
1988	From Our Home to Yours QX279-4	Yr.Iss.	1988	4.75	17
1988	Godchild QX278-4	Yr.Iss.	1988	4.75	10-20
1988	Granddaughter QX277-4	Yr.Iss.	1988	4.75	10-25
1988	Grandmother QX276-4	Yr.Iss.	1988	4.75	20
1988	Grandparents QX277-1	Yr.Iss.	1988	4.75	17
1988	Grandson QX278-1	Yr.Iss.	1988	4.75	15-25
1988	Gratitude QX375-4	Yr.Iss.	1988	6.00	12
1988	Love Fills the Heart QX374-4	Yr.Iss.	1988	6.00	25
1988	Love Grows QX275-4	Yr.Iss.	1988	4.75	31
1988	Mother and Dad QX414-4	Yr.Iss.	1988	8.00	18
1988	Mother QX375-1	Yr.Iss.	1988	6.50	20
1988	New Home QX376-1	Yr.Iss.	1988	6.00	25
1988	Sister QX499-4	Yr.Iss.	1988	8.00	15-32
1988	Son QX415-4	Yr.Iss.	1988	5.75	40-50
1988	Spirit of Christmas QX276-1	Yr.Iss.	1988	4.75	22
1988	Sweetheart QX490-1	Yr.Iss.	1988	9.75	11-22
1988	Teacher QX417-1	Yr.Iss.	1988	6.25	20
1988	Ten Years Together QX275-1	Yr.Iss.	1988	4.75	10-21
1988	Twenty-Five Years Together QX373-4	Yr.Iss.	1988	6.75	10-20
1988	Year to Remember QX416-4	Yr.Iss.	1988	7.00	25

1988 Hallmark Handcrafted Ornaments - Keepsake

YEAR	ISSUE	EDITION LIMIT	YEAR RETD.	ISSUE PRICE	*QUOTE U.S.$
1988	Americana Drum QX488-1	Yr.Iss.	1988	7.75	15-25
1988	Arctic Tenor QX472-1	Yr.Iss.	1988	4.00	10-20
1988	Christmas Cardinal QX494-1	Yr.Iss.	1988	4.75	10-20

*Quotes have been rounded up to nearest dollar

CHRISTMAS ORNAMENTS

YEAR ISSUE		EDITION LIMIT	YEAR RETD.	ISSUE PRICE	*QUOTE U.S.$
1988	Christmas Cuckoo QX480-1	Yr.Iss.	1988	8.00	30
1988	Christmas Memories QX372-4	Yr.Iss.	1988	6.50	25
1988	Christmas Scenes QX273-1	Yr.Iss.	1988	4.75	18
1988	Cool Juggler QX487-4	Yr.Iss.	1988	6.50	20
1988	Feliz Navidad QX416-1	Yr.Iss.	1988	6.75	18-33
1988	Filled with Fudge QX419-1	Yr.Iss.	1988	4.75	16-33
1988	Glowing Wreath QX492-1	Yr.Iss.	1988	6.00	15
1988	Go For The Gold QX417-4	Yr.Iss.	1988	8.00	16-30
1988	Goin' Cross-Country QX476-4	Yr.Iss.	1988	8.50	26
1988	Gone Fishing QX479-4	Yr.Iss.	1989	5.00	16
1988	Hoe-Hoe-Hoe! QX422-1	Yr.Iss.	1988	5.00	11-20
1988	Holiday Hero QX423-1	Yr.Iss.	1988	5.00	20
1988	Jingle Bell Clown QX477-4	Yr.Iss.	1988	15.00	20-37
1988	Jolly Walrus QX473-1	Yr.Iss.	1988	4.50	23
1988	Kiss from Santa QX482-1	Yr.Iss.	1989	4.50	23
1988	Kiss the Claus QX486-1	Yr.Iss.	1988	5.00	10-18
1988	Kringle Moon QX495-1	Yr.Iss.	1988	5.00	35
1988	Kringle Portrait QX496-1	Yr.Iss.	1988	7.50	25-40
1988	Kringle Tree QX495-4	Yr.Iss.	1988	6.50	35-40
1988	Love Santa QX486-4	Yr.Iss.	1988	5.00	20
1988	Loving Bear QX493-4	Yr.Iss.	1988	4.75	18
1988	Nick the Kick QX422-4	Yr.Iss.	1988	5.00	23
1988	Noah's Ark QX490-4	Yr.Iss.	1988	8.50	20
1988	Old-Fashioned Church QX498-1	Yr.Iss.	1988	4.00	24
1988	Old-Fashioned School House QX497-1	Yr.Iss.	1988	4.00	23
1988	Oreo QX481-4	Yr.Iss.	1989	4.00	17
1988	Par for Santa QX479-1	Yr.Iss.	1988	5.00	20
1988	Party Line QX476-1	Yr.Iss.	1989	8.75	20-30
1988	Peanuts QX280-1	Yr.Iss.	1988	4.75	35-50
1988	Peek-a-boo Kittens QX487-1	Yr.Iss.	1989	7.50	22
1988	Polar Bowler QX478-4	Yr.Iss.	1989	5.00	10-20
1988	Purrfect Snuggle QX474-4	Yr.Iss.	1988	6.25	20-30
1988	Sailing! Sailing! QX491-1	Yr.Iss.	1988	8.50	27
1988	Santa Flamingo QX483-4	Yr.Iss.	1988	4.75	16-33
1988	Shiny Sleigh QX492-4	Yr.Iss.	1988	5.75	20
1988	Slipper Spaniel QX472-4	Yr.Iss.	1988	4.50	17
1988	Snoopy and Woodstock QX474-1	Yr.Iss.	1988	6.00	35-46
1988	Soft Landing QX475-1	Yr.Iss.	1988	7.00	15-25
1988	Sparkling Tree QX483-1	Yr.Iss.	1988	6.00	19
1988	Squeaky Clean QX475-4	Yr.Iss.	1988	6.75	22
1988	Starry Angel QX494-4	Yr.Iss.	1988	4.75	20
1988	Sweet Star QX418-4	Yr.Iss.	1988	5.00	20-32
1988	Teeny Taster QX418-1	Yr.Iss.	1989	4.75	27
1988	The Town Crier QX473-4	Yr.Iss.	1988	5.50	15-25
1988	Travels with Santa QX477-1	Yr.Iss.	1988	10.00	26-40
1988	Uncle Sam Nutcracker QX488-4	Yr.Iss.	1988	7.00	20-40
1988	Winter Fun QX478-1	Yr.Iss.	1988	8.50	17-27

1988 Hallmark Keepsake Ornament Collector's Club - Keepsake

YEAR ISSUE		EDITION LIMIT	YEAR RETD.	ISSUE PRICE	*QUOTE U.S.$
1988	Angelic Minstrel QXC408-4	Yr.Iss.	1988	27.50	39-59
1988	Christmas is Sharing QXC407-1	Yr.Iss.	1988	17.50	31-49
1988	Hold on Tight QXC570-4	Yr.Iss.	1988	Unkn.	75
1988	Holiday Heirloom-(2nd Ed.) QXC406-4	Yr.Iss.	1988	25.00	23-37
1988	Our Clubhouse QXC580-4	Yr.Iss.	1988	Unkn.	40-50
1988	Sleighful of Dreams QC580-1	Yr.Iss.	1988	8.00	50-75

1988 Holiday Humor - Keepsake

YEAR ISSUE		EDITION LIMIT	YEAR RETD.	ISSUE PRICE	*QUOTE U.S.$
1988	Night Before Christmas QX451-7	Yr.Iss.	1988	6.50	18-33
1988	Owliday Wish QX455-9	Yr.Iss.	1988	6.50	14-25
1988	Reindoggy QX452-7	Yr.Iss.	1988	5.75	20-25
1988	Treetop Dreams QX459-7	Yr.Iss.	1988	6.75	15-25

1988 Keepsake Magic Ornaments - Keepsake

YEAR ISSUE		EDITION LIMIT	YEAR RETD.	ISSUE PRICE	*QUOTE U.S.$
1988	Baby's First Christmas QLX718-4	Yr.Iss.	1988	24.00	40-60
1988	Bearly Reaching QLX715-1	Yr.Iss.	1988	9.50	40
1988	Chris Mouse-(4th Ed.) QLX715-4	Yr.Iss.	1988	8.75	60
1988	Christmas Classics-(3rd Ed.) QLX716-1	Yr.Iss.	1988	15.00	30
1988	Christmas is Magic QLX717-1	Yr.Iss.	1988	12.00	35-55
1988	Christmas Morning QLX701-3	Yr.Iss.	1988	24.50	33-50
1988	Circling the Globe QLX712-4	Yr.Iss.	1988	10.50	45
1988	Country Express QLX721-1	Yr.Iss.	1988	24.50	67-75
1988	Festive Feeder QLX720-4	Yr.Iss.	1988	11.50	45
1988	First Christmas Together QLX702-7	Yr.Iss.	1988	12.00	37
1988	Heavenly Glow QLX711-4	Yr.Iss.	1988	11.75	19-29
1988	Kitty Capers QLX716-4	Yr.Iss.	1988	13.00	45
1988	Kringle's Toy Shop QLX701-7	Yr.Iss.	1988	25.00	35-65
1988	Last-Minute Hug QLX718-1	Yr.Iss.	1988	19.50	47
1988	Moonlit Nap QLX713-4	Yr.Iss.	1988	8.75	21-30
1988	Parade of the Toys QLX719-4	Yr.Iss.	1988	22.00	53
1988	Radiant Tree QLX712-1	Yr.Iss.	1988	11.75	24
1988	Santa and Sparky-(3rd Ed.) QLX719-1	Yr.Iss.	1988	19.50	43
1988	Skater's Waltz QLX720-1	Yr.Iss.	1988	19.50	36-62
1988	Song of Christmas QLX711-1	Yr.Iss.	1988	8.50	15-30
1988	Tree of Friendship QLX710-4	Yr.Iss.	1988	8.50	25

1988 Keepsake Miniature Ornaments - Keepsake

YEAR ISSUE		EDITION LIMIT	YEAR RETD.	ISSUE PRICE	*QUOTE U.S.$
1988	Baby's First Christmas	Yr.Iss.	1988	6.00	12
1988	Brass Angel	Yr.Iss.	1988	1.50	20
1988	Brass Star	Yr.Iss.	1988	1.50	20
1988	Brass Tree	Yr.Iss.	1988	1.50	20
1988	Candy Cane Elf	Yr.Iss.	1988	3.00	20
1988	Country Wreath	Yr.Iss.	1988	4.00	11
1988	Family Home-(1st Ed.)	Yr.Iss.	1988	8.50	45
1988	First Christmas Together	Yr.Iss.	1988	4.00	11
1988	Folk Art Lamb	Yr.Iss.	1988	2.50	14-23
1988	Folk Art Reindeer	Yr.Iss.	1988	2.50	13-20
1988	Friends Share Joy	Yr.Iss.	1988	2.00	15
1988	Gentle Angel	Yr.Iss.	1988	2.00	15
1988	Happy Santa	Yr.Iss.	1988	4.50	19
1988	Holy Family	Yr.Iss.	1988	8.50	13
1988	Jolly St. Nick	Yr.Iss.	1988	8.00	33
1988	Joyous Heart	Yr.Iss.	1988	3.50	23-30
1988	Kittens in Toyland-(1st Ed.)	Yr.Iss.	1988	5.00	20-30
1988	Little Drummer Boy	Yr.Iss.	1988	4.50	20-27
1988	Love is Forever	Yr.Iss.	1988	2.00	15
1988	Mother	Yr.Iss.	1988	3.00	12
1988	Penguin Pal-(1st Ed.)	Yr.Iss.	1988	3.75	20-28
1988	Rocking Horse-(1st Ed.)	Yr.Iss.	1988	4.50	35-45
1988	Skater's Waltz	Yr.Iss.	1988	7.00	14-22
1988	Sneaker Mouse	Yr.Iss.	1988	4.00	14-20
1988	Snuggly Skater	Yr.Iss.	1988	4.50	27
1988	Sweet Dreams	Yr.Iss.	1988	7.00	16-23
1988	Three Little Kitties	Yr.Iss.	1988	6.00	13-19

1988 Old Fashioned Christmas Collection - Keepsake

YEAR ISSUE		EDITION LIMIT	YEAR RETD.	ISSUE PRICE	*QUOTE U.S.$
1988	In A Nutshell QX469-7	Yr.Iss.	1988	5.50	24-33

1988 Special Edition - Keepsake

YEAR ISSUE		EDITION LIMIT	YEAR RETD.	ISSUE PRICE	*QUOTE U.S.$
1988	The Wonderful Santacycle QX411-4	Yr.Iss.	1988	22.50	34-45

1989 Artists' Favorites - Keepsake

YEAR ISSUE		EDITION LIMIT	YEAR RETD.	ISSUE PRICE	*QUOTE U.S.$
1989	Baby Partridge QX452-5	Yr.Iss.	1989	6.75	10-15
1989	Bear-i-Tone QX454-2	Yr.Iss.	1989	4.75	10-20
1989	Carousel Zebra QX451-5	Yr.Iss.	1989	9.25	15-20
1989	Cherry Jubilee QX453-2	Yr.Iss.	1989	5.00	15-27
1989	Mail Call QX452-2	Yr.Iss.	1989	8.75	12-20
1989	Merry-Go-Round Unicorn QX447-2	Yr.Iss.	1989	10.75	16
1989	Playful Angel QX453-5	Yr.Iss.	1989	6.75	15-25

1989 Collectible Series - Keepsake

YEAR ISSUE		EDITION LIMIT	YEAR RETD.	ISSUE PRICE	*QUOTE U.S.$
1989	Betsey Clark:Home for Christmas-(4th Ed.) QX230-2	Yr.Iss.	1989	5.00	20-28
1989	Christmas Kitty (1st Ed.) QX544-5	Yr.Iss.	1989	14.75	20-32
1989	Collector's Plate-(3rd Ed.) QX461-2	Yr.Iss.	1989	8.25	20-35
1989	Crayola Crayon (1st Ed.) QX435-2	Yr.Iss.	1989	8.75	45
1989	Frosty Friends-(10th Ed.) QX457-2	Yr.Iss.	1989	9.25	35-50
1989	The Gift Bringers (1st Ed.) QX279-5	Yr.Iss.	1989	5.00	20
1989	Hark! It's Herald (1st Ed.) QX455-5	Yr.Iss.	1989	6.75	20-30
1989	Here Comes Santa (11th Ed.) QX458-5	Yr.Iss.	1989	14.75	31-50
1989	Mary's Angels-(2nd Ed.) QX454-5	Yr.Iss.	1989	5.75	65
1989	Miniature Creche (5th Ed.) QX459-2	Yr.Iss.	1989	9.25	17
1989	Mr. and Mrs. Claus-(4th Ed.) QX 457-5	Yr.Iss.	1989	13.25	33-50
1989	Nostalgic Houses and Shops-(6th Ed.) QX458-2	Yr.Iss.	1989	14.25	57
1989	Porcelain Bear (7th Ed.) QX461-5	Yr.Iss.	1989	8.75	20-40
1989	Reindeer Champs-(4th Ed.) QX456-2	Yr.Iss.	1989	7.75	17-27
1989	Rocking Horse (9th Ed.) QX462-2	Yr.Iss.	1989	10.75	22-45
1989	Thimble (12th Ed.) QX455-2	Yr.Iss.	1989	5.75	13-25
1989	Tin Locomotive (8th Ed.) QX460-2	Yr.Iss.	1989	14.75	31-60
1989	Twelve Days of Christmas (6th Ed.) QX381-2	Yr.Iss.	1989	6.75	16
1989	Windows of the World (5th Ed.) QX462-5	Yr.Iss.	1989	10.75	21-33
1989	Winter Surprise (1st Ed.) QX427-2	Yr.Iss.	1989	10.75	25-33
1989	Wood Childhood Ornaments-(6th Ed.) QX459-5	Yr.Iss.	1989	7.75	15-25

1989 Commemoratives - Keepsake

YEAR ISSUE		EDITION LIMIT	YEAR RETD.	ISSUE PRICE	*QUOTE U.S.$
1989	Baby's Fifth Christmas QX543-5	Yr.Iss.	1989	6.75	20
1989	Baby's First Christmas Photoholder QX468-2	Yr.Iss.	1989	6.25	50
1989	Baby's First Christmas QX381-5	Yr.Iss.	1989	6.75	10-20
1989	Baby's First Christmas QX449-2	Yr.Iss.	1989	7.25	65
1989	Baby's First Christmas-Baby Boy QX272-5	Yr.Iss.	1989	4.75	18
1989	Baby's First Christmas-Baby Girl QX272-2	Yr.Iss.	1989	4.75	18
1989	Baby's Fourth Christmas QX543-2	Yr.Iss.	1989	6.75	20
1989	Baby's Second Christmas QX449-5	Yr.Iss.	1989	6.75	27
1989	Baby's Third Christmas QX469-5	Yr.Iss.	1989	6.75	25
1989	Brother QX445-2	Yr.Iss.	1989	6.25	17
1989	Dad QX442-5	Yr.Iss.	1989	7.25	12-20
1989	Daughter QX443-2	Yr.Iss.	1989	6.25	20-30
1989	Festive Year QX384-2	Yr.Iss.	1989	7.75	10-20
1989	Fifty Years Together Photoholder QX486-2	Yr.Iss.	1989	8.75	17
1989	First Christmas Together QX273-2	Yr.Iss.	1989	4.75	10-25
1989	First Christmas Together QX383-2	Yr.Iss.	1989	6.75	23
1989	First Christmas Together QX485-2	Yr.Iss.	1989	9.75	15-25
1989	Five Years Together QX273-5	Yr.Iss.	1989	4.75	14-23
1989	Forty Years Together Photoholder QX545-2	Yr.Iss.	1989	8.75	15
1989	Friendship Time QX413-2	Yr.Iss.	1989	9.75	25-33
1989	From Our Home to Yours QX384-5	Yr.Iss.	1989	6.25	15
1989	Godchild QX311-2	Yr.Iss.	1989	6.25	14
1989	Granddaughter QX278	Yr.Iss.	1989	4.75	23
1989	Granddaughter's First Christmas QX382-2	Yr.Iss.	1989	6.75	10-23
1989	Grandmother QX277-5	Yr.Iss.	1989	4.75	18
1989	Grandparents QX277-2	Yr.Iss.	1989	4.75	18
1989	Grandson QX278-5	Yr.Iss.	1989	4.75	17
1989	Grandson's First Christmas QX382-5	Yr.Iss.	1989	6.75	10-18
1989	Gratitude QX385-2	Yr.Iss.	1989	6.75	14
1989	Language of Love QX383-5	Yr.Iss.	1989	6.25	22
1989	Mom and Dad QX442-5	Yr.Iss.	1989	9.75	15-24
1989	Mother QX440-5	Yr.Iss.	1989	9.75	20-30
1989	New Home QX275-5	Yr.Iss.	1989	4.75	15
1989	Sister QX279-2	Yr.Iss.	1989	4.75	17
1989	Son QX444-5	Yr.Iss.	1989	6.25	20-33
1989	Sweetheart QX486-5	Yr.Iss.	1989	9.75	33
1989	Teacher QX412-5	Yr.Iss.	1989	5.75	14-24
1989	Ten Years Together QX274-2	Yr.Iss.	1989	4.75	30
1989	Twenty-five Years Together Photoholder QX485-5	Yr.Iss.	1989	8.75	17
1989	World of Love QX274-5	Yr.Iss.	1989	4.75	35

1989 Hallmark Handcrafted Ornaments - Keepsake

YEAR ISSUE		EDITION LIMIT	YEAR RETD.	ISSUE PRICE	*QUOTE U.S.$
1989	Peek-a-boo Kittens QX487-1	Yr.Iss.	1989	7.50	21

1989 Hallmark Keepsake Ornament Collector's Club - Keepsake

YEAR ISSUE		EDITION LIMIT	YEAR RETD.	ISSUE PRICE	*QUOTE U.S.$
1989	Christmas is Peaceful QXC451-2	Yr.Iss.	1989	18.50	45
1989	Collect a Dream QXC428-5	Yr.Iss.	1989	9.00	55-65
1989	Holiday Heirloom-(3rd Ed.) QXC460-5	Yr.Iss.	1989	25.00	35
1989	Noelle QXC448-3	Yr.Iss.	1989	19.75	50-60
1989	Sitting Purrty QXC581-2	Yr.Iss.	1989	Unkn.	45
1989	Visit from Santa QXC580-2	Yr.Iss.	1989	Unkn.	45-55

1989 Holiday Traditions - Keepsake

YEAR ISSUE		EDITION LIMIT	YEAR RETD.	ISSUE PRICE	*QUOTE U.S.$
1989	Camera Claus QX546-5	Yr.Iss.	1989	5.75	15
1989	A Charlie Brown Christmas QX276-5	Yr.Iss.	1989	4.75	30-40
1989	Cranberry Bunny QX426-2	Yr.Iss.	1989	5.75	11-18
1989	Deer Disguise QX426-5	Yr.Iss.	1989	5.75	17-25
1989	Feliz Navidad QX439-2	Yr.Iss.	1989	6.75	20-30
1989	The First Christmas QX547-5	Yr.Iss.	1989	7.75	14-16
1989	Gentle Fawn QX548-5	Yr.Iss.	1989	7.75	13-20
1989	George Washington Bicentennial QX386-2	Yr.Iss.	1989	6.75	9-20
1989	Gone Fishing QX479-4	Yr.Iss.	1989	5.75	17
1989	Gym Dandy QX418-5	Yr.Iss.	1989	5.75	15
1989	Hang in There QX430-5	Yr.Iss.	1989	5.25	25-35
1989	Here's the Pitch QX545-5	Yr.Iss.	1989	5.75	15
1989	Hoppy Holidays QX469-2	Yr.Iss.	1989	7.75	13-24
1989	Joyful Trio QX437-2	Yr.Iss.	1989	9.75	15
1989	A Kiss™ From Santa QX482-1	Yr.Iss.	1989	4.50	20
1989	Kristy Claus QX424-5	Yr.Iss.	1989	5.75	12
1989	Norman Rockwell QX276-2	Yr.Iss.	1989	4.75	20
1989	North Pole Jogger QX546-2	Yr.Iss.	1989	5.75	15
1989	Old-World Gnome QX434-5	Yr.Iss.	1989	7.75	15-30
1989	On the Links QX419-2	Yr.Iss.	1989	5.75	17
1989	Oreo ® Chocolate Sandwich Cookies QX481-4	Yr.Iss.	1989	4.00	15
1989	Owliday Greetings QX436-5	Yr.Iss.	1989	4.00	15
1989	Paddington Bear QX429-2	Yr.Iss.	1989	5.75	15-30
1989	Party Line QX476-1	Yr.Iss.	1989	8.75	27
1989	Peek-a-Boo Kitties QX487-1	Yr.Iss.	1989	7.50	16-22
1989	Polar Bowler QX478-4	Yr.Iss.	1989	5.75	17
1989	Sea Santa QX415-2	Yr.Iss.	1989	5.75	15
1989	Snoopy and Woodstock QX433-2	Yr.Iss.	1989	6.75	30-40
1989	Snowplow Santa QX420-5	Yr.Iss.	1989	5.75	12-22
1989	Special Delivery QX432-5	Yr.Iss.	1989	5.25	12-25
1989	Spencer Sparrow, Esq. QX431-2	Yr.Iss.	1990	6.75	14-23
1989	Stocking Kitten QX456-5	Yr.Iss.	1990	6.75	15
1989	Sweet Memories Photoholder QX438-5	Yr.Iss.	1989	6.75	25
1989	Teeny Taster QX418-1	Yr.Iss.	1989	4.75	17

1989 Keepsake Magic Collection - Keepsake

YEAR ISSUE		EDITION LIMIT	YEAR RETD.	ISSUE PRICE	*QUOTE U.S.$
1989	Angel Melody QLX720-2	Yr.Iss.	1989	9.50	25
1989	The Animals Speak QLX723-2	Yr.Iss.	1989	13.50	78-100
1989	Baby's First Christmas QLX727-2	Yr.Iss.	1989	30.00	47-65
1989	Backstage Bear QLX721-5	Yr.Iss.	1989	13.50	30
1989	Busy Beaver QLX724-5	Yr.Iss.	1989	17.50	35-45
1989	Chris Mouse-(5th Ed.) QLX722-5	Yr.Iss.	1989	9.50	50-60
1989	Christmas Classics-(4th Ed.) QLX724-2	Yr.Iss.	1989	13.50	27-43
1989	First Christmas Together QLX734-2	Yr.Iss.	1989	17.50	35-45
1989	Forest Frolics-(1st Ed.) QLX728-2	Yr.Iss.	1989	24.50	85
1989	Holiday Bell QLX722-2	Yr.Iss.	1989	17.50	29-35
1989	Joyous Carolers QLX729-5	Yr.Iss.	1989	30.00	47-70
1989	Kringle's Toy Shop QLX701-7	Yr.Iss.	1989	24.50	40-60
1989	Loving Spoonful QLX726-2	Yr.Iss.	1989	19.50	35
1989	Metro Express QLX727-5	Yr.Iss.	1989	28.00	75
1989	Moonlit Nap QLX713-4	Yr.Iss.	1989	8.75	23
1989	Rudolph the Red-Nosed Reindeer QLX725-2	Yr.Iss.	1989	19.50	50-70
1989	Spirit of St. Nick QLX728-5	Yr.Iss.	1989	24.50	72
1989	Tiny Tinker QLX717-4	Yr.Iss.	1989	19.50	63
1989	Unicorn Fantasy QLX723-5	Yr.Iss.	1989	9.50	20

*Quotes have been rounded up to nearest dollar

1989 Keepsake Miniature Ornaments - Keepsake

YEAR	ISSUE	EDITION LIMIT	YEAR RETD.	ISSUE PRICE	*QUOTE U.S.$
1989	Acorn Squirrel QXM568-2	Yr.Iss.	1989	4.50	9
1989	Baby's First Christmas QXM573-2	Yr.Iss.	1989	6.00	13
1989	Brass Partridge QXM572-5	Yr.Iss.	1989	3.00	10
1989	Brass Snowflake QXM570-2	Yr.Iss.	1989	4.50	13
1989	Bunny Hug QXM577-5	Yr.Iss.	1989	3.00	8
1989	Country Wreath QXM573-1	Yr.Iss.	1989	4.50	12
1989	Cozy Skater QXM573-5	Yr.Iss.	1989	4.50	11
1989	First Christmas Together QXM564-2	Yr.Iss.	1989	8.50	10
1989	Folk Art Bunny QXM569-2	Yr.Iss.	1989	4.50	10
1989	Happy Bluebird QXM566-2	Yr.Iss.	1989	4.50	13
1989	Holiday Deer QXM577-2	Yr.Iss.	1989	3.00	12
1989	Holy Family QXM561-1	Yr.Iss.	1989	8.50	15
1989	Kittens in Toyland-(2nd Ed.) QXM561-2	Yr.Iss.	1989	4.50	17
1989	Kitty Cart QXM572-2	Yr.Iss.	1989	3.00	7
1989	The Kringles-(1st Ed.) QXM562-2	Yr.Iss.	1989	6.00	23-33
1989	Little Soldier QXM567-5	Yr.Iss.	1989	4.50	10
1989	Little Star Bringer QXM562-2	Yr.Iss.	1989	6.00	18
1989	Load of Cheer QXM574-5	Yr.Iss.	1989	6.00	15
1989	Lovebirds QXM563-5	Yr.Iss.	1989	6.00	11
1989	Merry Seal QXM575-5	Yr.Iss.	1989	6.00	13
1989	Mother QXM564-5	Yr.Iss.	1989	6.00	11
1989	Noel R.R.-(1st Ed.) QXM576-2	Yr.Iss.	1989	8.50	35-43
1989	Old English Village-(2nd Ed.) QXM561-5	Yr.Iss.	1989	8.50	30-38
1989	Old-World Santa QXM569-5	Yr.Iss.	1989	3.00	8
1989	Penguin Pal-(2nd Ed.) QXM560-2	Yr.Iss.	1989	4.50	19
1989	Pinecone Basket QXM573-4	Yr.Iss.	1989	4.50	7
1989	Puppy Cart QXM571-5	Yr.Iss.	1989	3.00	9-20
1989	Rejoice QXM578-2	Yr.Iss.	1989	3.00	9
1989	Rocking Horse-(2nd Ed.) QXM560-5	Yr.Iss.	1989	4.50	20-30
1989	Roly-Poly Pig QXM571-2	Yr.Iss.	1989	3.00	15
1989	Roly-Poly Ram QXM570-5	Yr.Iss.	1989	3.00	13
1989	Santa's Magic Ride QXM563-2	Yr.Iss.	1989	8.50	17
1989	Santa's Roadster QXM566-5	Yr.Iss.	1989	6.00	17
1989	Scrimshaw Reindeer QXM568-5	Yr.Iss.	1989	4.50	8
1989	Sharing a Ride QXM576-5	Yr.Iss.	1989	8.50	14
1989	Slow Motion QXM575-2	Yr.Iss.	1989	6.00	14
1989	Special Friend QXM565-2	Yr.Iss.	1989	4.50	13
1989	Starlit Mouse QXM565-5	Yr.Iss.	1989	4.50	14
1989	Stocking Pal QXM567-2	Yr.Iss.	1989	4.50	10
1989	Strollin' Snowman QXM574-2	Yr.Iss.	1989	4.50	15
1989	Three Little Kitties QXM569-4	Yr.Iss.	1989	6.00	19

1989 New Attractions - Keepsake

YEAR	ISSUE	EDITION LIMIT	YEAR RETD.	ISSUE PRICE	*QUOTE U.S.$
1989	Balancing Elf QX489-5	Yr.Iss.	1989	6.75	21
1989	Cactus Cowboy QX411-2	Yr.Iss.	1989	6.75	33-44
1989	Claus Construction QX488-5	Yr.Iss.	1990	7.75	25-35
1989	Cool Swing QX487-5	Yr.Iss.	1989	6.25	31
1989	Country Cat QX467-2	Yr.Iss.	1989	6.25	16
1989	Festive Angel QX463-5	Yr.Iss.	1989	6.75	20
1989	Goin' South QX410-5	Yr.Iss.	1989	4.25	18-25
1989	Graceful Swan QX464-2	Yr.Iss.	1989	6.75	20
1989	Horse Weathervane QX463-2	Yr.Iss.	1989	5.75	15
1989	Let's Play QX488-2	Yr.Iss.	1989	7.25	25
1989	Nostalgic Lamb QX466-5	Yr.Iss.	1989	6.75	11
1989	Nutshell Dreams QX465-5	Yr.Iss.	1989	5.75	14-23
1989	Nutshell Holiday QX465-2	Yr.Iss.	1990	5.75	17-27
1989	Nutshell Workshop QX487-2	Yr.Iss.	1989	5.75	15-23
1989	Peppermint Clown QX450-5	Yr.Iss.	1989	24.75	25
1989	Rodney Reindeer QX407-2	Yr.Iss.	1989	6.75	12
1989	Rooster Weathervane QX467-5	Yr.Iss.	1989	5.75	18-24
1989	Sparkling Snowflake QX547-2	Yr.Iss.	1989	7.75	25
1989	TV Break QX409-2	Yr.Iss.	1989	6.25	17
1989	Wiggly Snowman QX489-2	Yr.Iss.	1989	6.75	25-35

1989 Special Edition - Keepsake

YEAR	ISSUE	EDITION LIMIT	YEAR RETD.	ISSUE PRICE	*QUOTE U.S.$
1989	The Ornament Express QX580-5	Yr.Iss.	1989	22.00	45

1990 Artists' Favorites - Keepsake

YEAR	ISSUE	EDITION LIMIT	YEAR RETD.	ISSUE PRICE	*QUOTE U.S.$
1990	Angel Kitty QX4746	Yr.Iss.	1990	8.75	15-25
1990	Donder's Diner QX4823	Yr.Iss.	1990	13.75	22
1990	Gentle Dreamers QX4756	Yr.Iss.	1990	8.75	17-30
1990	Happy Woodcutter QX4763	Yr.Iss.	1990	9.75	17-25
1990	Mouseboat QX4753	Yr.Iss.	1990	7.75	15
1990	Welcome, Santa QX4773	Yr.Iss.	1990	11.75	19-30

1990 Collectible Series - Keepsake

YEAR	ISSUE	EDITION LIMIT	YEAR RETD.	ISSUE PRICE	*QUOTE U.S.$
1990	Betsey Clark: Home for Christmas-(5th Ed.) QX2033	Yr.Iss.	1990	5.00	15-25
1990	Christmas Kitty-(2nd Ed.) QX4506	Yr.Iss.	1990	14.75	15-30
1990	Cinnamon Bear-(8th Ed.) QX4426	Yr.Iss.	1990	8.75	20-33
1990	Cookies for Santa-(4th Ed.) QX4436	Yr.Iss.	1990	8.75	22-35
1990	CRAYOLA Crayon-Bright Moving Colors-(2nd Ed.) QX4586	Yr.Iss.	1990	8.75	35-43
1990	Fabulous Decade-(1st Ed.) QX4466	Yr.Iss.	1990	7.75	20-45
1990	Festive Surrey-(12th Ed.) QX4923	Yr.Iss.	1990	14.75	33
1990	Frosty Friends-(11th Ed.) QX4396	Yr.Iss.	1990	9.75	21-33
1990	The Gift Bringers-St. Lucia-(2nd Ed.) QX2803	Yr.Iss.	1990	5.00	14-23
1990	Greatest Story-(1st Ed.) QX4656	Yr.Iss.	1990	12.75	15-35
1990	Hark! It's Herald-(2nd Ed.) QX4463	Yr.Iss.	1990	6.75	17-27
1990	Heart of Christmas-(1st Ed.) QX4726	Yr.Iss.	1990	13.75	45-80
1990	Holiday Home-(7th Ed.) QX4696	Yr.Iss.	1990	14.75	50
1990	Irish-(6th Ed.) QX4636	Yr.Iss.	1990	10.75	23
1990	Mary's Angels-Rosebud-(3rd Ed.) QX4423	Yr.Iss.	1990	5.75	30-45
1990	Merry Olde Santa-(1st Ed.) QX4736	Yr.Iss.	1990	14.75	65-75
1990	Popcorn Party-(5th Ed.) QX4393	Yr.Iss.	1990	13.75	45-75
1990	Reindeer Champs-Comet-(5th Ed.) QX4433	Yr.Iss.	1990	7.75	20-30
1990	Rocking Horse-(10th Ed.) QX4646	Yr.Iss.	1990	10.75	60-95
1990	Seven Swans A-Swimming-(7th Ed.) QX3033	Yr.Iss.	1990	6.75	19-32
1990	Winter Surprise-(2nd Ed.) QX4443	Yr.Iss.	1990	10.75	19-29

1990 Commemoratives - Keepsake

YEAR	ISSUE	EDITION LIMIT	YEAR RETD.	ISSUE PRICE	*QUOTE U.S.$
1990	Across The Miles QX3173	Yr.Iss.	1990	6.75	15
1990	Baby's First Christmas QX3036	Yr.Iss.	1990	6.75	13
1990	Baby's First Christmas QX4853	Yr.Iss.	1990	9.75	19
1990	Baby's First Christmas QX4856	Yr.Iss.	1990	7.75	28
1990	Baby's First Christmas-Baby Boy QX2063	Yr.Iss.	1990	4.75	18
1990	Baby's First Christmas-Baby Girl QX2066	Yr.Iss.	1990	4.75	17
1990	Baby's First Christmas-Photo Holder QX4843	Yr.Iss.	1990	7.75	23-30
1990	Baby's Second Christmas QX4683	Yr.Iss.	1990	6.75	25-33
1990	Brother QX4493	Yr.Iss.	1990	5.75	12
1990	Child Care Giver QX3166	Yr.Iss.	1990	6.75	13
1990	Child's Fifth Christmas QX4876	Yr.Iss.	1990	6.75	17
1990	Child's Fourth Christmas QX4873	Yr.Iss.	1990	6.75	15-25
1990	Child's Third Christmas QX4866	Yr.Iss.	1990	6.75	18-25
1990	Copy of Cheer QX4486	Yr.Iss.	1990	7.75	17
1990	Dad QX4533	Yr.Iss.	1990	6.75	18
1990	Dad-to-Be QX4913	Yr.Iss.	1990	5.75	18
1990	Daughter QX4496	Yr.Iss.	1990	5.75	15-25
1990	Fifty Years Together QX4906	Yr.Iss.	1990	9.75	19
1990	Five Years Together QX2103	Yr.Iss.	1990	4.75	19
1990	Forty Years Together QX4903	Yr.Iss.	1990	9.75	20
1990	Friendship Kitten QX4142	Yr.Iss.	1990	6.75	17-25
1990	From Our Home to Yours QX2166	Yr.Iss.	1990	4.75	20
1990	Godchild QX3167	Yr.Iss.	1990	6.75	11-20
1990	Granddaughter QX2286	Yr.Iss.	1990	4.75	15
1990	Granddaughter's First Christmas QX3106	Yr.Iss.	1990	6.75	15-23
1990	Grandmother QX2236	Yr.Iss.	1990	4.75	17
1990	Grandparents QX2253	Yr.Iss.	1990	4.75	15
1990	Grandson QX2293	Yr.Iss.	1990	4.75	15
1990	Grandson's First Christmas QX3063	Yr.Iss.	1990	6.75	17
1990	Jesus Loves Me QX3156	Yr.Iss.	1990	6.75	11
1990	Mom and Dad QX4593	Yr.Iss.	1990	8.75	20
1990	Mom-to-Be QX4916	Yr.Iss.	1990	5.75	25
1990	Mother QX4536	Yr.Iss.	1990	8.75	30
1990	New Home QX4343	Yr.Iss.	1990	6.75	18
1990	Our First Christmas Together QX2136	Yr.Iss.	1990	4.75	20
1990	Our First Christmas Together QX3146	Yr.Iss.	1990	6.75	20
1990	Our First Christmas Together QX4883	Yr.Iss.	1990	9.75	30
1990	Our First Christmas Together-Photo Holder QX4886	Yr.Iss.	1990	7.75	15
1990	Peaceful Kingdom QX2106	Yr.Iss.	1990	4.75	20
1990	Sister QX2273	Yr.Iss.	1990	4.75	19
1990	Son QX4516	Yr.Iss.	1990	5.75	15-25
1990	Sweetheart QX4893	Yr.Iss.	1990	11.75	20
1990	Teacher QX4483	Yr.Iss.	1990	7.75	13
1990	Ten Years Together QX2153	Yr.Iss.	1990	4.75	19
1990	Time for Love QX2133	Yr.Iss.	1990	4.75	10-22
1990	Twenty-Five Years Together QX4896	Yr.Iss.	1990	9.75	18

1990 Holiday Traditions - Keepsake

YEAR	ISSUE	EDITION LIMIT	YEAR RETD.	ISSUE PRICE	*QUOTE U.S.$
1990	Spencer Sparrow, Esq. QX431-2	Yr.Iss.	1990	6.75	15
1990	Stocking Kitten QX456-5	Yr.Iss.	1990	6.75	11-15

1990 Keepsake Collector's Club - Keepsake

YEAR	ISSUE	EDITION LIMIT	YEAR RETD.	ISSUE PRICE	*QUOTE U.S.$
1990	Armful of Joy QXC445-3	Yr.Iss.	1990	8.00	42
1990	Christmas Limited 1975 QXC476-6	38700	1990	19.75	75-125
1990	Club Hollow QXC445-6	Yr.Iss.	1990	Unkn.	35-40
1990	Crown Prince QXC560-3	Yr.Iss.	1990	Unkn.	39
1990	Dove of Peace QXC447-6	25400	1990	24.75	75
1990	Sugar Plum Fairy QXC447-3	25400	1990	27.75	60

1990 Keepsake Magic Ornaments - Keepsake

YEAR	ISSUE	EDITION LIMIT	YEAR RETD.	ISSUE PRICE	*QUOTE U.S.$
1990	Baby's First Christmas QLX7246	Yr.Iss.	1990	28.00	50-60
1990	Beary Short Nap QLX7326	Yr.Iss.	1990	10.00	24-30
1990	Blessings of Love QLX7363	Yr.Iss.	1990	14.00	47
1990	Children's Express QLX7243	Yr.Iss.	1990	28.00	65-75
1990	Chris Mouse Wreath QLX7296	Yr.Iss.	1990	10.00	30-45
1990	Christmas Memories QLX7276	Yr.Iss.	1990	25.00	47
1990	Deer Crossing QLX7213	Yr.Iss.	1990	18.00	40-50
1990	Elf of the Year QLX7356	Yr.Iss.	1990	10.00	16-25
1990	Elfin Whittler QLX7265	Yr.Iss.	1990	20.00	40-55
1990	Forest Frolics QLX7236	Yr.Iss.	1990	25.00	75
1990	Holiday Flash QLX7333	Yr.Iss.	1990	18.00	25-40
1990	Hop 'N Pop Popper QLX7353	Yr.Iss.	1990	20.00	85-95
1990	Letter to Santa QLX7226	Yr.Iss.	1990	14.00	28-35
1990	The Littlest Angel QLX7303	Yr.Iss.	1990	14.00	28-40
1990	Mrs. Santa's Kitchen QLX7263	Yr.Iss.	1990	25.00	50-80
1990	Our First Christmas Together QLX7255	Yr.Iss.	1990	18.00	27-47
1990	Partridges in a Pear QLX7212	Yr.Iss.	1990	14.00	30
1990	Santa's Ho-Ho-Hoedown QLX7256	Yr.Iss.	1990	25.00	90
1990	Song and Dance QLX7253	Yr.Iss.	1990	20.00	60-95
1990	Starlight Angel QLX7306	Yr.Iss.	1990	14.00	27-37
1990	Starship Christmas QLX7336	Yr.Iss.	1990	18.00	35-55

1990 Keepsake Miniature Ornaments - Keepsake

YEAR	ISSUE	EDITION LIMIT	YEAR RETD.	ISSUE PRICE	*QUOTE U.S.$
1990	Acorn Wreath QXM5686	Yr.Iss.	1990	6.00	10
1990	Air Santa QXM5656	Yr.Iss.	1990	4.50	10
1990	Baby's First Christmas QXM5703	Yr.Iss.	1990	8.50	16
1990	Basket Buddy QXM5696	Yr.Iss.	1990	6.00	10
1990	Bear Hug QXM5633	Yr.Iss.	1990	6.00	12
1990	Brass Bouquet 600QMX5776	Yr.Iss.	1990	6.00	6
1990	Brass Horn QXM5793	Yr.Iss.	1990	3.00	8
1990	Brass Peace QXM5796	Yr.Iss.	1990	3.00	8
1990	Brass Santa QXM5786	Yr.Iss.	1990	3.00	7
1990	Brass Year QXM5833	Yr.Iss.	1990	3.00	8
1990	Busy Carver QXM5673	Yr.Iss.	1990	4.50	9
1990	Christmas Dove QXM5636	Yr.Iss.	1990	4.50	12
1990	Cloisonne Poinsettia QMX5533	Yr.Iss.	1990	10.75	22-30
1990	Coal Car QXM5756	Yr.Iss.	1990	8.50	23
1990	Country Heart QXM5693	Yr.Iss.	1990	4.50	9
1990	First Christmas Together QXM5536	Yr.Iss.	1990	6.00	12
1990	Going Sledding QXM5683	Yr.Iss.	1990	4.50	12
1990	Grandchild's First Christmas QXM5723	Yr.Iss.	1990	6.00	11
1990	Holiday Cardinal QXM5526	Yr.Iss.	1990	3.00	10
1990	Kittens in Toyland QXM5736	Yr.Iss.	1990	4.50	18
1990	The Kringles QXM5753	Yr.Iss.	1990	6.00	22
1990	Lion and Lamb QXM5676	Yr.Iss.	1990	4.50	8
1990	Loving Hearts QXM5523	Yr.Iss.	1990	3.00	8
1990	Madonna and Child QXM5643	Yr.Iss.	1990	6.00	10
1990	Mother QXM5716	Yr.Iss.	1990	4.50	15
1990	Nativity QXM5706	Yr.Iss.	1990	4.50	15
1990	Nature's Angels QMX5733	Yr.Iss.	1990	4.50	23
1990	Panda's Surprise QXM5616	Yr.Iss.	1990	4.50	12
1990	Penguin Pal QXM5746	Yr.Iss.	1990	4.50	10-20
1990	Perfect Fit QXM5516	Yr.Iss.	1990	4.50	10
1990	Puppy Love QXM5666	Yr.Iss.	1990	6.00	12
1990	Rocking Horse QXM5743	Yr.Iss.	1990	4.50	17-25
1990	Ruby Reindeer QXM5816	Yr.Iss.	1990	6.00	11
1990	Santa's Journey QXM5826	Yr.Iss.	1990	8.50	18
1990	Santa's Streetcar QXM5766	Yr.Iss.	1990	8.50	15
1990	School QXM5763	Yr.Iss.	1990	8.50	16-25
1990	Snow Angel QXM5773	Yr.Iss.	1990	6.00	12
1990	Special Friends QXM5726	Yr.Iss.	1990	6.00	12
1990	Stamp Collector QXM5623	Yr.Iss.	1990	4.50	9
1990	Stringing Along QXM5606	Yr.Iss.	1990	8.50	16
1990	Sweet Slumber QXM5663	Yr.Iss.	1990	4.50	10
1990	Teacher QXM5653	Yr.Iss.	1990	4.50	8
1990	Thimble Bells QXM5543	Yr.Iss.	1990	6.00	19-28
1990	Type of Joy QXM5646	Yr.Iss.	1990	4.50	8
1990	Warm Memories QXM5713	Yr.Iss.	1990	4.50	10
1990	Wee Nutcracker QXM5843	Yr.Iss.	1990	8.50	14

1990 New Attractions - Keepsake

YEAR	ISSUE	EDITION LIMIT	YEAR RETD.	ISSUE PRICE	*QUOTE U.S.$
1990	Baby Unicorn QX5486	Yr.Iss.	1990	9.75	12
1990	Bearback Rider QX5483	Yr.Iss.	1990	9.75	25-32
1990	Beary Good Deal QX4733	Yr.Iss.	1990	6.75	12
1990	Billboard Bunny QX5196	Yr.Iss.	1990	7.75	15
1990	Born to Dance QX5043	Yr.Iss.	1990	7.75	17
1990	Chiming In QX4366	Yr.Iss.	1990	9.75	20
1990	Christmas Croc QX4373	Yr.Iss.	1990	7.75	15
1990	Christmas Partridge QX5246	Yr.Iss.	1990	7.75	13-23
1990	Claus Construction QX4885	Yr.Iss.	1990	7.75	15-20
1990	Country Angel QX5046	Yr.Iss.	1990	6.75	75-125
1990	Coyote Carols QX4993	Yr.Iss.	1990	8.75	20
1990	Cozy Goose QX4966	Yr.Iss.	1990	5.75	14
1990	Feliz Navidad QX5173	Yr.Iss.	1990	6.75	20
1990	Garfield QX2303	Yr.Iss.	1990	4.75	20
1990	Gingerbread Elf QX5033	Yr.Iss.	1990	5.75	17
1990	Goose Cart QX5236	Yr.Iss.	1990	7.75	14
1990	Hang in There QX4713	Yr.Iss.	1990	6.75	17
1990	Happy Voices QX4645	Yr.Iss.	1990	6.75	14
1990	Holiday Cardinals QX5243	Yr.Iss.	1990	7.75	14-23
1990	Home for the Owlidays QX5183	Yr.Iss.	1990	6.75	11
1990	Hot Dogger QX4976	Yr.Iss.	1990	7.75	16
1990	Jolly Dolphin QX4683	Yr.Iss.	1990	6.75	23
1990	Joy is in the Air QX5503	Yr.Iss.	1990	7.75	23
1990	King Klaus QX4106	Yr.Iss.	1990	7.75	15
1990	Kitty's Best Pal QX4716	Yr.Iss.	1990	6.75	17
1990	Little Drummer Boy QX5233	Yr.Iss.	1990	7.75	19
1990	Long Winter's Nap QX4703	Yr.Iss.	1990	6.75	14-25
1990	Lovable Dears QX5476	Yr.Iss.	1990	8.75	15
1990	Meow Mart QX4446	Yr.Iss.	1990	7.75	16
1990	Mooy Christmas QX4933	Yr.Iss.	1990	6.75	25
1990	Norman Rockwell Art QX2296	Yr.Iss.	1990	4.75	20
1990	Nutshell Chat QX5193	Yr.Iss.	1990	6.75	20
1990	Nutshell Holiday QX465-2	Yr.Iss.	1990	5.75	17-28
1990	Peanuts QX2233	Yr.Iss.	1990	4.75	25
1990	Pepperoni Mouse QX4973	Yr.Iss.	1990	6.75	15
1990	Perfect Catch QX4693	Yr.Iss.	1990	7.75	13
1990	Polar Jogger QX4666	Yr.Iss.	1990	5.75	9

*Quotes have been rounded up to nearest dollar

YEAR ISSUE		EDITION LIMIT	YEAR RETD.	ISSUE PRICE	*QUOTE U.S.$
1990	Polar Pair QX4626	Yr.Iss.	1990	5.75	15
1990	Polar Sport QX5156	Yr.Iss.	1990	7.75	12
1990	Polar TV QX5166	Yr.Iss.	1990	7.75	12
1990	Polar V.I.P. QX4663	Yr.Iss.	1990	5.75	12
1990	Polar Video QX4633	Yr.Iss.	1990	5.75	9
1990	Poolside Walrus QX4986	Yr.Iss.	1990	7.75	15
1990	S. Claus Taxi QX4686	Yr.Iss.	1990	11.75	25
1990	Santa Schnoz QX4983	Yr.Iss.	1990	6.75	30
1990	Snoopy and Woodstock QX4723	Yr.Iss.	1990	6.75	31-40
1990	Spoon Rider QX5496	Yr.Iss.	1990	9.75	15
1990	Stitches of Joy QX5186	Yr.Iss.	1990	7.75	13-25
1990	Stocking Kitten QX456-5	Yr.Iss.	1990	6.75	7
1990	Stocking Pals QX5493	Yr.Iss.	1990	10.75	18
1990	Three Little Piggies QX4996	Yr.Iss.	1990	7.75	15
1990	Two Peas in a Pod QX4926	Yr.Iss.	1990	4.75	22

1990 Special Edition - Keepsake

1990	Dickens Caroler Bell-Mr. Ashbourne QX5056	Yr.Iss.	1990	21.75	25-55

1991 Artists' Favorites - Keepsake

1991	Fiddlin' Around QX4387	Yr.Iss.	1991	7.75	17
1991	Hooked on Santa QX4109	Yr.Iss.	1991	7.75	21
1991	Noah's Ark QX4867	Yr.Iss.	1991	13.75	45
1991	Polar Circus Wagon QX4399	Yr.Iss.	1991	13.75	15-30
1991	Santa Sailor QX4389	Yr.Iss.	1991	9.75	22
1991	Tramp and Laddie QX4397	Yr.Iss.	1991	7.75	25-30

1991 Club Limited Editions - Keepsake

1991	Galloping Into Christmas QXC4779	28,400	1991	19.75	75-100
1991	Secrets for Santa QXC4797	28,700	1991	23.75	35-48

1991 Collectible Series - Keepsake

1991	1957 Corvette-(1st Ed.) QX4319	Yr.Iss.	1991	12.75	175-195
1991	Betsey Clark: Home for Christmas (6th Ed.) QX2109	Yr.Iss.	1991	5.00	15-25
1991	Checking His List (6th Ed.) QX4339	Yr.Iss.	1991	13.75	25-40
1991	Christmas Kitty-(3rd Ed.) QX4377	Yr.Iss.	1991	14.75	20-30
1991	CRAYOLA CRAYON-Bright Vibrant Carols-(3rd Ed.) QX4219	Yr.Iss.	1991	9.75	25-35
1991	Eight Maids A-Milking-(8th Ed.) QX3089	Yr.Iss.	1991	6.75	19-29
1991	Fabulous Decade-(2nd Ed.) QX4119	Yr.Iss.	1991	7.75	15-30
1991	Fire Station-(8th Ed.) QX4139	Yr.Iss.	1991	14.75	45
1991	Frosty Friends-(12th Ed.) QX4327	Yr.Iss.	1991	9.75	30-40
1991	The Gift Bringers-Christkind (3rd Ed.) QX2117	Yr.Iss.	1991	5.00	15
1991	Greatest Story-(2nd Ed.) QX4129	Yr.Iss.	1991	12.75	10-25
1991	Hark! It's Herald (3rd Ed.) QX4379	Yr.Iss.	1991	6.75	10-25
1991	Heart of Christmas-(2nd Ed.) QX4357	Yr.Iss.	1991	13.75	15-35
1991	Heavenly Angels-(1st Ed.) QX4367	Yr.Iss.	1991	7.75	15-35
1991	Let It Snow! (5th Ed.) QX4369	Yr.Iss.	1991	8.75	17
1991	Mary's Angels-Iris (4th Ed.) QX4279	Yr.Iss.	1991	6.75	15-30
1991	Merry Olde Santa-(2nd Ed.) QX4359	Yr.Iss.	1991	14.75	65-80
1991	Peace on Earth-Italy (1st Ed.) QX5129	Yr.Iss.	1991	11.75	15-25
1991	Puppy Love-(1st Ed.) QX5379	Yr.Iss.	1991	7.75	35-50
1991	Reindeer Champ-Cupid -(6th Ed.) QX4347	Yr.Iss.	1991	7.75	15-25
1991	Rocking Horse-(11th Ed.) QX4147	Yr.Iss.	1991	10.75	25-40
1991	Santa's Antique Car-(13th Ed.) QX4349	Yr.Iss.	1991	14.75	27
1991	Winter Surprise-(3rd Ed.) QX4277	Yr.Iss.	1991	10.75	20-35

1991 Commemoratives - Keepsake

1991	Across the Miles QX3157	Yr.Iss.	1991	6.75	13
1991	Baby's First Christmas QX4889	Yr.Iss.	1991	7.75	30
1991	Baby's First Christmas QX5107	Yr.Iss.	1991	17.75	33
1991	Baby's First Christmas-Baby Boy QX2217	Yr.Iss.	1991	4.75	15
1991	Baby's First Christmas-Baby Girl QX2227	Yr.Iss.	1991	4.75	15
1991	Baby's First Christmas-Photo Holder QX4869	Yr.Iss.	1991	7.75	17
1991	Baby's Second Christmas QX4897	Yr.Iss.	1991	6.75	27
1991	The Big Cheese QX5327	Yr.Iss.	1991	6.75	18
1991	Brother QX5479	Yr.Iss.	1991	6.75	18
1991	A Child's Christmas QX4887	Yr.Iss.	1991	9.75	15
1991	Child's Fifth Christmas QX4909	Yr.Iss.	1991	6.75	18
1991	Child's Fourth Christmas QX4907	Yr.Iss.	1991	6.75	18
1991	Child's Third Christmas QX4899	Yr.Iss.	1991	6.75	23
1991	Dad QX5127	Yr.Iss.	1991	7.75	19
1991	Dad-to-Be QX4879	Yr.Iss.	1991	5.75	14
1991	Daughter QX5477	Yr.Iss.	1991	5.75	24
1991	Extra-Special Friends QX2279	Yr.Iss.	1991	4.75	15
1991	Fifty Years Together QX4947	Yr.Iss.	1991	8.75	18
1991	Five Years Together QX4927	Yr.Iss.	1991	7.75	16
1991	Forty Years Together QX4939	Yr.Iss.	1991	7.75	18
1991	Friends Are Fun QX5289	Yr.Iss.	1991	9.75	33
1991	From Our Home to Yours QX2287	Yr.Iss.	1991	4.75	15
1991	Gift of Joy QX5319	Yr.Iss.	1991	8.75	20
1991	Godchild QX5489	Yr.Iss.	1991	6.75	19
1991	Granddaughter QX2299	Yr.Iss.	1991	4.75	20
1991	Granddaughter's First Christmas QX5119	Yr.Iss.	1991	6.75	18
1991	Grandmother QX2307	Yr.Iss.	1991	4.75	15-20
1991	Grandparents QX2309	Yr.Iss.	1991	4.75	14
1991	Grandson QX2297	Yr.Iss.	1991	4.75	14
1991	Grandson's First Christmas QX5117	Yr.Iss.	1991	6.75	14
1991	Jesus Loves Me QX3147	Yr.Iss.	1991	7.75	14
1991	Mom and Dad QX5467	Yr.Iss.	1991	9.75	21
1991	Mom-to-Be QX4877	Yr.Iss.	1991	5.75	16
1991	Mother QX5457	Yr.Iss.	1991	9.75	25-35
1991	New Home QX5449	Yr.Iss.	1991	6.75	20
1991	Our First Christmas Together QX2229	Yr.Iss.	1991	4.75	15
1991	Our First Christmas Together QX3139	Yr.Iss.	1991	6.75	15
1991	Our First Christmas Together QX4919	Yr.Iss.	1991	8.75	25
1991	Our First Christmas Together-Photo Holder QX4917	Yr.Iss.	1991	8.75	20
1991	Sister QX5487	Yr.Iss.	1991	6.75	18
1991	Son QX5469	Yr.Iss.	1991	5.75	14-25
1991	Sweetheart QX4957	Yr.Iss.	1991	9.75	18
1991	Teacher QX2289	Yr.Iss.	1991	4.75	12
1991	Ten Years Together QX4929	Yr.Iss.	1991	7.75	15
1991	Terrific Teacher QX5309	Yr.Iss.	1991	6.75	16
1991	Twenty -Five Years Together QX4937	Yr.Iss.	1991	8.75	16
1991	Under the Mistletoe QX4949	Yr.Iss.	1991	8.75	19

1991 Keepsake Collector's Club - Keepsake

1991	Beary Artistic QXC7259	Yr.Iss.	1991	10.00	32-40
1991	Hidden Treasure/Li'l Keeper QXC4769	Yr.Iss.	1991	15.00	38

1991 Keepsake Magic Ornaments - Keepsake

1991	Angel of Light QLT7239	Yr.Iss.	1991	30.00	60
1991	Arctic Dome QLX7117	Yr.Iss.	1991	25.00	45-55
1991	Baby's First Christmas QLX7247	Yr.Iss.	1991	30.00	45-85
1991	Bringing Home the Tree-QLX7249	Yr.Iss.	1991	28.00	51-65
1991	Chris Mouse Mail QLX7207	Yr.Iss.	1991	10.00	25-40
1991	Elfin Engineer QLX7209	Yr.Iss.	1991	10.00	25
1991	Father Christmas QLX7147	Yr.Iss.	1991	14.00	29-39
1991	Festive Brass Church QLX7179	Yr.Iss.	1991	14.00	30
1991	Forest Frolics QLX7219	Yr.Iss.	1991	25.00	68
1991	Friendship Tree QLX7169	Yr.Iss.	1991	10.00	24
1991	Holiday Glow QLX7177	Yr.Iss.	1991	14.00	30
1991	It's A Wonderful Life QLX7237	Yr.Iss.	1991	20.00	60-75
1991	Jingle Bears QLX7323	Yr.Iss.	1991	25.00	45-55
1991	Kringles's Bumper Cars -QLX7119	Yr.Iss.	1991	25.00	45-55
1991	Mole Family Home QLX7149	Yr.Iss.	1991	20.00	35-50
1991	Our First Christmas Together QXL7137	Yr.Iss.	1991	25.00	40-60
1991	PEANUTS QLX7229	Yr.Iss.	1991	18.00	65-75
1991	Salvation Army Band QLX7273	Yr.Iss.	1991	30.00	55-75
1991	Santa Special QLX7167	Yr.Iss.	1992	40.00	55-80
1991	Santa's Hot Line QLX7159	Yr.Iss.	1991	18.00	32-42
1991	Ski Trip QLX7266	Yr.Iss.	1991	28.00	50-60
1991	Sparkling Angel QLX7157	Yr.Iss.	1991	18.00	27-37
1991	Toyland Tower QLX7129	Yr.Iss.	1991	20.00	37-45

1991 Keepsake Miniature Ornaments - Keepsake

1991	All Aboard QXM5869	Yr.Iss.	1991	4.50	17
1991	Baby's First Christmas QXM5799	Yr.Iss.	1991	6.00	20
1991	Brass Church QXM5979	Yr.Iss.	1991	3.00	9
1991	Brass Soldier QXM5987	Yr.Iss.	1991	3.00	9
1991	Bright Boxers QXM5877	Yr.Iss.	1991	4.50	17
1991	Busy Bear QXM5939	Yr.Iss.	1991	4.50	12
1991	Cardinal Cameo QXM5957	Yr.Iss.	1991	6.00	17
1991	Caring Shepherd QXM5949	Yr.Iss.	1991	6.00	17
1991	Cool 'n' Sweet QXM5867	Yr.Iss.	1991	4.50	20
1991	Country Sleigh QXM5999	Yr.Iss.	1991	4.50	14
1991	Courier Turtle QXM5857	Yr.Iss.	1991	4.50	14
1991	Fancy Wreath QXM5917	Yr.Iss.	1991	4.50	14
1991	Feliz Navidad QXM5887	Yr.Iss.	1991	6.00	15
1991	Fly By QXM5859	Yr.Iss.	1991	4.50	17
1991	Friendly Fawn QXM5947	Yr.Iss.	1991	6.00	17
1991	Grandchild's First Christmas QXM5697	Yr.Iss.	1991	4.50	14
1991	Heavenly Minstrel QXM5687	Yr.Iss.	1991	9.75	21-30
1991	Holiday Snowflake QXM5997	Yr.Iss.	1991	3.00	12
1991	Inn-(4th Ed.) QXM5627	Yr.Iss.	1991	8.50	20-30
1991	Key to Love QXM5689	Yr.Iss.	1991	4.50	16
1991	Kittens in Toyland-(4th Ed.) QXM5639	Yr.Iss.	1991	4.50	15
1991	Kitty in a Mitty QXM5879	Yr.Iss.	1991	4.50	13
1991	The Kringles-(3rd Ed.) QXM5647	Yr.Iss.	1991	6.00	20
1991	Li'l Popper QXM5897	Yr.Iss.	1991	4.50	16
1991	Love Is Born QXM5959	Yr.Iss.	1991	6.00	18
1991	Lulu & Family QXM5677	Yr.Iss.	1991	6.00	20
1991	Mom QXM5699	Yr.Iss.	1991	6.00	17
1991	N. Pole Buddy QXM5927	Yr.Iss.	1991	4.50	18
1991	Nature's Angels-(2nd Ed.) QXM5657	Yr.Iss.	1991	4.50	20
1991	Noel QXM5989	Yr.Iss.	1991	3.00	12
1991	Our First Christmas Together QXM5819	Yr.Iss.	1991	6.00	15
1991	Passenger Car-(3rd Ed.) QXM5649	Yr.Iss.	1991	8.50	25
1991	Penquin Pal-(4th Ed.) QXM5629	Yr.Iss.	1991	4.50	17
1991	Ring-A-Ding Elf QXM5669	Yr.Iss.	1991	8.50	18
1991	Rocking Horse-(4th Ed.) QXM5637	Yr.Iss.	1991	4.50	15-25
1991	Seaside Otter QXM5909	Yr.Iss.	1991	4.50	13
1991	Silvery Santa QXM5679	Yr.Iss.	1991	9.75	22
1991	Special Friends QXM5797	Yr.Iss.	1991	8.50	18
1991	Thimble Bells-(2nd Ed.) QXM5659	Yr.Iss.	1991	6.00	23
1991	Tiny Tea Party (set/6) QXM5827	Yr.Iss.	1991	29.00	142-160
1991	Top Hatter QXM5889	Yr.Iss.	1991	6.00	16
1991	Treeland Trio QXM5899	Yr.Iss.	1991	8.50	17
1991	Upbeat Bear QXM5907	Yr.Iss.	1991	6.00	16
1991	Vision of Santa QXM5937	Yr.Iss.	1991	4.50	14
1991	Wee Toymaker QXM5967	Yr.Iss.	1991	8.50	15
1991	Woodland Babies QXM5667	Yr.Iss.	1991	6.00	12-22

1991 New Attractions - Keepsake

1991	All-Star QX5329	Yr.Iss.	1991	6.75	17
1991	Basket Bell Players QX5377	Yr.Iss.	1991	7.75	21
1991	Bob Cratchit QX4997	Yr.Iss.	1991	13.75	22-32
1991	Chilly Chap QX5339	Yr.Iss.	1991	6.75	17
1991	Christmas Welcome QX5299	Yr.Iss.	1991	9.75	21
1991	Christopher Robin QX5579	Yr.Iss.	1991	9.75	25-35
1991	Cuddly Lamb QX5199	Yr.Iss.	1991	6.75	20
1991	Dinoclaus QX5277	Yr.Iss.	1991	7.75	16
1991	Ebenezer Scrooge QX4989	Yr.Iss.	1991	13.75	30
1991	Evergreen Inn QX5389	Yr.Iss.	1991	8.75	15
1991	Fanfare Bear QX5337	Yr.Iss.	1991	8.75	19
1991	Feliz Navidad QX5279	Yr.Iss.	1991	6.75	15
1991	Folk Art Reindeer QX5359	Yr.Iss.	1991	8.75	14
1991	GARFIELD QX5177	Yr.Iss.	1991	7.75	25
1991	Glee Club Bears QX4969	Yr.Iss.	1991	8.75	18
1991	Holiday Cafe QX5399	Yr.Iss.	1991	8.75	14
1991	Jolly Wolly Santa QX5419	Yr.Iss.	1991	7.75	21
1991	Jolly Wolly Snowman QX5427	Yr.Iss.	1991	7.75	21
1991	Jolly Wolly Soldier QX5429`	Yr.Iss.	1991	7.75	20
1991	Joyous Memories-Photoholder QX5369	Yr.Iss.	1991	6.75	20
1991	Kanga and Roo QX5617	Yr.Iss.	1991	9.75	35-50
1991	Look Out Below QX4959	Yr.Iss.	1991	8.75	18
1991	Loving Stitches QX4987	Yr.Iss.	1991	8.75	30
1991	Mary Engelbreit QX2237	Yr.Iss.	1991	4.75	28
1991	Merry Carolers QX4799	Yr.Iss.	1991	29.75	95
1991	Mrs. Cratchit QX4999	Yr.Iss.	1991	13.75	30
1991	Night Before Christmas QX5307	Yr.Iss.	1991	9.75	21
1991	Norman Rockwell Art QX2259	Yr.Iss.	1991	5.00	20
1991	Notes of Cheer QX5357	Yr.Iss.	1991	5.75	14
1991	Nutshell Nativity QX5176	Yr.Iss.	1991	6.75	20
1991	Nutty Squirrel QX4833	Yr.Iss.	1991	5.75	14
1991	Old-Fashioned Sled QX4317	Yr.Iss.	1991	8.75	18
1991	On a Roll QX5347	Yr.Iss.	1991	6.75	18
1991	Partridge in a Pear Tree QX5297	Yr.Iss.	1991	9.75	18
1991	PEANUTS QX2257	Yr.Iss.	1991	5.00	15-25
1991	Piglet and Eeyore QX5577	Yr.Iss.	1991	9.75	20-40
1991	Plum Delightful QX4977	Yr.Iss.	1991	8.75	19
1991	Polar Classic QX5287	Yr.Iss.	1991	6.75	18
1991	Rabbit QX5607	Yr.Iss.	1991	9.75	20-30
1991	Santa's Studio QX5397	Yr.Iss.	1991	8.75	15
1991	Ski Lift Bunny QX5447	Yr.Iss.	1991	6.75	17
1991	Snoopy and Woodstock QX5197	Yr.Iss.	1991	6.75	32
1991	Snow Twins QX4979	Yr.Iss.	1991	8.75	20
1991	Snowy Owl QX5269	Yr.Iss.	1991	7.75	18
1991	Sweet Talk QX5367	Yr.Iss.	1991	8.75	17
1991	Tigger QX5609	Yr.Iss.	1991	9.75	95-105
1991	Tiny Tim QX5037	Yr.Iss.	1991	10.75	24-40
1991	Up 'N'Down Journey QX5047	Yr.Iss.	1991	9.75	20
1991	Winnie-the Pooh QX5569	Yr.Iss.	1991	9.75	55
1991	Yule Logger QX4967	Yr.Iss.	1991	8.75	17-27

1991 Special Edition - Keepsake

1991	Dickens Caroler Bell-Mrs. Beaumont QX5039	Yr.Iss.	1991	21.75	45-50
1991	Starship Enterprise QLX7199	Yr.Iss.	1991	20.00	250-500

1992 Artists' Favorites - Keepsake

1992	Elfin Marionette QX5931	Yr.Iss.	1992	11.75	23
1992	Mother Goose QX4984	Yr.Iss.	1992	13.75	27
1992	Polar Post QX4914	Yr.Iss.	1992	8.75	18
1992	Stocked With Joy QX5934	Yr.Iss.	1992	7.75	20
1992	Turtle Dreams QX4991	Yr.Iss.	1992	8.75	20-28
1992	Uncle Art's Ice Cream QX5001	Yr.Iss.	1992	8.75	22-30

1992 Collectible Series - Keepsake

1992	1966 Mustang-(2nd Ed.) QX4284	Yr.Iss.	1992	12.75	45-55
1992	Betsey's Country Christmas -(1st Ed.) QX2104	Yr.Iss.	1992	5.00	20-30
1992	CRAYOLA CRAYON-Bright Colors (4th Ed.) QX4264	Yr.Iss.	1992	9.75	25-35
1992	Fabulous Decade-(3rd Ed.) QX4244	Yr.Iss.	1992	7.75	35
1992	Five-and-Ten-Cent Store (9th Ed.) QX4254	Yr.Iss.	1992	14.75	30
1992	Frosty Friends (13th Ed.) QX4291	Yr.Iss.	1992	9.75	30
1992	The Gift Bringers-Kolyada (4th Ed.) QX2124	Yr.Iss.	1992	5.00	15
1992	Gift Exchange (7th Ed.) QX4294	Yr.Iss.	1992	14.75	33
1992	Greatest Story (3rd Ed.) QX4251	Yr.Iss.	1992	12.75	15-25
1992	Hark! It's Herald (4th Ed.) QX4464	Yr.Iss.	1992	7.75	17-25
1992	Heart of Christmas (3rd Ed.) QX4411	Yr.Iss.	1992	13.75	30
1992	Heavenly Angels (2nd Ed.) QX4454	Yr.Iss.	1992	7.75	10-25
1992	Kringle Tours (14th Ed.) QX4341	Yr.Iss.	1992	14.75	27-35
1992	Mary's Angels-Lily (5th Ed.) QX4274	Yr.Iss.	1992	6.75	4

*Quotes have been rounded up to nearest dollar

YEAR ISSUE	EDITION LIMIT	YEAR RETD.	ISSUE PRICE	*QUOTE U.S.$
1992 Merry Olde Santa (3rd Ed.) QX4414	Yr.Iss.	1992	14.75	37
1992 Nine Ladies Dancing (9th Ed.) QX3031	Yr.Iss.	1992	6.75	18-24
1992 Owliver (1st Ed.) QX4544	Yr.Iss.	1992	7.75	17
1992 Peace On Earth-Spain (2nd Ed.) QX5174	Yr.Iss.	1992	11.75	25
1992 Puppy Love (2nd Ed.) QX4484	Yr.Iss.	1992	7.75	25-40
1992 Reindeer Champs-Donder -(7th Ed.) QX5284	Yr.Iss.	1992	8.75	20-33
1992 Rocking Horse (12th Ed.) QX4261	Yr.Iss.	1992	10.75	25-40
1992 Sweet Holiday Harmony -(6th Ed.) QX4461	Yr.Iss.	1992	8.75	19
1992 Tobin Fraley Carousel (1st Ed.) QX4891	Yr.Iss.	1992	28.00	45-75
1992 Winter Surprise (4th Ed.) QX4271	Yr.Iss.	1992	11.75	27-33

1992 Collectors' Club - Keepsake

YEAR ISSUE	EDITION LIMIT	YEAR RETD.	ISSUE PRICE	*QUOTE U.S.$
1992 Chipmunk Parcel Service QXC5194	Yr.Iss.	1992	6.75	21
1992 Rodney Takes Flight QXC5081	Yr.Iss.	1992	9.75	22
1992 Santa's Club List QXC7291	Yr.Iss.	1992	15.00	36

1992 Commemoratives - Keepsake

YEAR ISSUE	EDITION LIMIT	YEAR RETD.	ISSUE PRICE	*QUOTE U.S.$
1992 Across the Miles QX3044	Yr.Iss.	1992	6.75	14
1992 Anniversary Year QX4851	Yr.Iss.	1992	9.75	18-25
1992 Baby's First Christmas QX4641	Yr.Iss.	1992	7.75	18
1992 Baby's First Christmas QX4644	Yr.Iss.	1992	7.75	23
1992 Baby's First Christmas-Baby Boy QX2191	Yr.Iss.	1992	4.75	13
1992 Baby's First Christmas-Baby Girl QX2204	Yr.Iss.	1992	4.75	13
1992 Baby's First ChristmasQX4581	Yr.Iss.	1992	18.75	25-38
1992 Baby's Second Christmas QX4651	Yr.Iss.	1992	6.75	20-40
1992 Brother QX4684	Yr.Iss.	1992	6.75	14
1992 A Child's Christmas QX4574	Yr.Iss.	1992	9.75	18
1992 Child's Fifth Christmas QX4664	Yr.Iss.	1992	6.75	15
1992 Child's Fourth Christmas QX4661	Yr.Iss.	1992	6.75	20
1992 Child's Third Christmas QX4654	Yr.Iss.	1992	6.75	22
1992 Dad QX4674	Yr.Iss.	1992	7.75	18
1992 Dad-to-Be QX4611	Yr.Iss.	1992	6.75	17
1992 Daughter QX5031	Yr.Iss.	1992	6.75	20
1992 For My Grandma QX5184	Yr.Iss.	1992	7.75	15
1992 For The One I Love QX4884	Yr.Iss.	1992	9.75	20
1992 Friendly Greetings QX5041	Yr.Iss.	1992	7.75	16
1992 Friendship Line QX5034	Yr.Iss.	1992	9.75	27
1992 From Our Home To Yours QX2131	Yr.Iss.	1992	4.75	15
1992 Godchild QX5941	Yr.Iss.	1992	6.75	18
1992 Grandaughter QX5604	Yr.Iss.	1992	6.75	15
1992 Grandaughter's First Christmas QX4634	Yr.Iss.	1992	6.75	14
1992 Grandmother QX2011	Yr.Iss.	1992	4.75	15
1992 Grandparents QX2004	Yr.Iss.	1992	4.75	17
1992 Grandson QX5611	Yr.Iss.	1992	6.75	16
1992 Grandson's First Christmas QX4621	Yr.Iss.	1992	6.75	20
1992 Holiday Memo QX5044	Yr.Iss.	1992	7.75	14
1992 Love To Skate QX4841	Yr.Iss.	1992	8.75	14
1992 Mom and Dad QX4671	Yr.Iss.	1992	9.75	35
1992 Mom QX5164	Yr.Iss.	1992	7.75	18
1992 Mom-to-Be QX4614	Yr.Iss.	1992	6.75	16
1992 New Home QX5191	Yr.Iss.	1992	8.75	18
1992 Our First Christmas Together QX4694	Yr.Iss.	1992	8.75	20
1992 Our First Christmas Together QX3011	Yr.Iss.	1992	6.75	16
1992 Our First Christmas Together QX5061	Yr.Iss.	1992	9.75	20
1992 Secret Pal QX5424	Yr.Iss.	1992	7.75	15
1992 Sister QX4681	Yr.Iss.	1992	6.75	15
1992 Son QX5024	Yr.Iss.	1992	6.75	17-25
1992 Special Cat QX5414	Yr.Iss.	1992	7.75	17
1992 Special Dog QX5421	Yr.Iss.	1992	7.75	30
1992 Teacher QX2264	Yr.Iss.	1992	4.75	17
1992 V. P. of Important Stuff QX5051	Yr.Iss.	1992	6.75	14
1992 World-Class Teacher QX5054	Yr.Iss.	1992	7.75	20

1992 Easter Ornaments - Keepsake

YEAR ISSUE	EDITION LIMIT	YEAR RETD.	ISSUE PRICE	*QUOTE U.S.$
1992 Easter Parade (1st Ed.) 675QEO8301	Yr.Iss.	1992	6.75	28
1992 Egg in Sports (1st Ed.) 675QEO9341	Yr.Iss.	1992	6.75	25-35

1992 Limited Edition Ornaments - Keepsake

YEAR ISSUE	EDITION LIMIT	YEAR RETD.	ISSUE PRICE	*QUOTE U.S.$
1992 Christmas Treasures QXC5464	15,500	1992	22.00	22
1992 Victorian Skater (w/ base) QXC4067	14,700	1992	25.00	35

1992 Magic Ornaments - Keepsake

YEAR ISSUE	EDITION LIMIT	YEAR RETD.	ISSUE PRICE	*QUOTE U.S.$
1992 Angel Of Light QLT7239	Yr.Iss.	1992	30.00	30
1992 Baby's First Christmas QLX7281	Yr.Iss.	1992	22.00	90
1992 Chris Mouse Tales (8th Ed.) QLX7074	Yr.Iss.	1992	12.00	27
1992 Christmas Parade QLX7271	Yr.Iss.	1992	30.00	55
1992 Continental Express QLX7264	Yr.Iss.	1992	32.00	58-70
1992 The Dancing Nutcracker QLX7261	Yr.Iss.	1992	30.00	40-60
1992 Enchanted Clock QLX7274	Yr.Iss.	1992	30.00	60
1992 Feathered Friends QLX7091	Yr.Iss.	1992	14.00	29
1992 Forest Frolics-(4th Ed.) QLX7254	Yr.Iss.	1992	28.00	50-65
1992 Good Sledding Ahead QLX7244	Yr.Iss.	1992	28.00	55
1992 Lighting the Way QLX7231	Yr.Iss.	1992	18.00	39-49
1992 Look! It's Santa QLX7094	Yr.Iss.	1992	14.00	30-40
1992 Nut Sweet Nut QLX7081	Yr.Iss.	1992	10.00	22
1992 Out First Christmas Together QLX7221	Yr.Iss.	1992	20.00	40-45
1992 PEANUTS (2nd Ed.) QLX7214	Yr.Iss.	1992	18.00	52
1992 Santa Special QLX7167	Yr.Iss.	1992	40.00	80
1992 Santa Sub QLX7321	Yr.Iss.	1992	18.00	34-40
1992 Santa's Answering Machine QLX7241	Yr.Iss.	1992	22.00	43
1992 Under Construction QLX7324	Yr.Iss.	1992	18.00	37
1992 Watch Owls QLX7084	Yr.Iss.	1992	12.00	26
1992 Yuletide Rider QLX7314	Yr.Iss.	1992	28.00	55

1992 Miniature Ornaments - Keepsake

YEAR ISSUE	EDITION LIMIT	YEAR RETD.	ISSUE PRICE	*QUOTE U.S.$
1992 A+ Teacher QXM5511	Yr.Iss.	1992	3.75	8
1992 Angelic Harpist QXM5524	Yr.Iss.	1992	4.50	13
1992 Baby's First Christmas QXM5494	Yr.Iss.	1992	4.50	18
1992 The Bearymores(1st Ed.) QXM5544	Yr.Iss.	1992	5.75	15-20
1992 Black-Capped Chickadee QXM5484	Yr.Iss.	1992	3.00	15
1992 Box Car (4th Ed.) Noel R.R. QXM5441	Yr.Iss.	1992	7.00	20
1992 Bright Stringers QXM5841	Yr.Iss.	1992	3.75	14
1992 Buck-A-Roo QXM5814	Yr.Iss.	1992	4.50	13
1992 Christmas Bonus QXM5811	Yr.Iss.	1992	3.00	8
1992 Christmas Copter QXM5844	Yr.Iss.	1992	5.75	15
1992 Church (5th Ed.) Old English V. QXM5384	Yr.Iss.	1992	7.00	20-30
1992 Coca-Cola Santa QXM5884	Yr.Iss.	1992	5.75	16
1992 Cool Uncle Sam QXM5561	Yr.Iss.	1992	3.00	14
1992 Cozy Kayak QXM5551	Yr.Iss.	1992	3.75	12
1992 Fast Finish QXM5301	Yr.Iss.	1992	3.75	12
1992 Feeding Time QXM5481	Yr.Iss.	1992	5.75	16
1992 Friendly Tin Soldier QXM5874	Yr.Iss.	1992	4.50	15
1992 Friends Are Tops QXM5521	Yr.Iss.	1992	4.50	10
1992 Gerbil Inc. QXM5924	Yr.Iss.	1992	3.75	11
1992 Going Places QXM5871	Yr.Iss.	1992	3.75	10
1992 Grandchild's First Christmas QXM5501	Yr.Iss.	1992	5.75	13
1992 Grandma QXM5514	Yr.Iss.	1992	4.50	15
1992 Harmony Trio-Set/3 QXM5471	Yr.Iss.	1992	11.75	20
1992 Hickory, Dickory, Dock QXM5861	Yr.Iss.	1992	3.75	13
1992 Holiday Holly QXM5364	Yr.Iss.	1992	9.75	20
1992 Holiday Splash QXM5834	Yr.Iss.	1992	5.75	12
1992 Hoop It Up QXM5831	Yr.Iss.	1992	4.50	11
1992 Inside Story QXM5881	Yr.Iss.	1992	7.25	17
1992 Kittens in Toyland (5th Ed.) QXM5391	Yr.Iss.	1992	4.50	15
1992 The Kringles-(4th Ed.) QXM5381	Yr.Iss.	1992	6.00	15-22
1992 Little Town of Bethlehem QXM5864	Yr.Iss.	1992	3.00	18
1992 Minted For Santa QXM5854	Yr.Iss.	1992	3.75	14
1992 Mom QXM5504	Yr.Iss.	1992	4.50	14
1992 Nature's Angels (3rd Ed.) QXM5451	Yr.Iss.	1992	4.50	10-20
1992 The Night Before Christmas QXM5541	Yr.Iss.	1992	13.75	25-35
1992 Perfect Balance QXM5571	Yr.Iss.	1992	3.00	12
1992 Polar Polka QXM5534	Yr.Iss.	1992	4.50	14
1992 Puppet Show QXM5574	Yr.Iss.	1992	3.00	12
1992 Rocking Horse (5th Ed.) QXM5454	Yr.Iss.	1992	4.50	17
1992 Sew Sew Tiny (set/6) QXM5794	Yr.Iss.	1992	29.00	55
1992 Ski For Two QXM5821	Yr.Iss.	1992	4.50	14
1992 Snowshoe Bunny QXM5564	Yr.Iss.	1992	3.75	12
1992 Snug Kitty QXM5554	Yr.Iss.	1992	3.75	13
1992 Spunky Monkey QXM5921	Yr.Iss.	1992	3.00	13
1992 Thimble Bells (3rd Ed.) QXM5461	Yr.Iss.	1992	6.00	18
1992 Visions Of Acorns QXM5851	Yr.Iss.	1992	4.50	15
1992 Wee Three Kings QXM5531	Yr.Iss.	1992	5.75	18
1992 Woodland Babies (2nd Ed.) QXM5444	Yr.Iss.	1992	6.00	14

1992 New Attractions - Keepsake

YEAR ISSUE	EDITION LIMIT	YEAR RETD.	ISSUE PRICE	*QUOTE U.S.$
1992 Bear Bell Champ QX5071	Yr.Iss.	1992	7.75	16
1992 Caboose QX5321	Yr.Iss.	1992	9.75	20
1992 Cheerful Santa QX5154	Yr.Iss.	1992	9.75	30
1992 Coal Car QX5401	Yr.Iss.	1992	9.75	19
1992 Cool Fliers QX5474	Yr.Iss.	1992	10.75	20
1992 Deck the Hogs QX5204	Yr.Iss.	1992	8.75	20
1992 Down-Under Holiday QX5144	Yr.Iss.	1992	7.75	18
1992 Egg Nog Nest QX5121	Yr.Iss.	1992	7.75	14
1992 Eric the Baker QX5244	Yr.Iss.	1992	8.75	18
1992 Feliz Navidad QX5181	Yr.Iss.	1992	6.75	16
1992 Franz the Artist QX5261	Yr.Iss.	1992	8.75	18
1992 Freida the Animals' Friend QX5264	Yr.Iss.	1992	8.75	16-25
1992 Fun on a Big Scale QX5134	Yr.Iss.	1992	10.75	21
1992 GARFIELD QX5374	Yr.Iss.	1992	7.75	18
1992 Genius at Work QX5371	Yr.Iss.	1992	10.75	20
1992 Golf's a Ball QX5984	Yr.Iss.	1992	6.75	28
1992 Gone Wishin' QX5171	Yr.Iss.	1992	8.75	19
1992 Green Thumb Santa QX5101	Yr.Iss.	1992	7.75	15
1992 Hello-Ho-Ho QX5141	Yr.Iss.	1992	9.75	16-23
1992 Holiday Teatime QX5431	Yr.Iss.	1992	14.75	25
1992 Holiday Wishes QX5131	Yr.Iss.	1992	7.75	17
1992 Honest George QX5064	Yr.Iss.	1992	7.75	18
1992 Jesus Loves Me QX3024	Yr.Iss.	1992	7.75	15
1992 Locomotive QX5311	Yr.Iss.	1992	9.75	43-60
1992 Loving Shepherd QX5151	Yr.Iss.	1992	7.75	15
1992 Ludwig the Musician QX5281	Yr.Iss.	1992	8.75	15-20
1992 Mary Engelbreit Santa Jolly Wolly QX5224	Yr.Iss.	1992	7.75	8
1992 Max the Tailor QX5251	Yr.Iss.	1992	8.75	20
1992 Memories to Cherish QX5161	Yr.Iss.	1992	10.75	20
1992 Merry "Swiss" Mouse QX5114	Yr.Iss.	1992	7.75	15
1992 Norman Rockwell Art QX2224	Yr.Iss.	1992	5.00	19
1992 North Pole Fire Fighter QX5104	Yr.Iss.	1992	9.75	21
1992 Otto the Carpenter QX5254	Yr.Iss.	1992	8.75	21
1992 Owl QX5614	Yr.Iss.	1992	9.75	20
1992 Partridge In a Pear Tree QX5234	Yr.Iss.	1992	8.75	19
1992 PEANUTS® QX2244	Yr.Iss.	1992	5.00	20-30
1992 Please Pause Here QX5291	Yr.Iss.	1992	14.75	30-40
1992 Rapid Delivery QX5094	Yr.Iss.	1992	8.75	21
1992 Santa's Hook Shot QX5434	Yr.Iss.	1992	12.75	28
1992 Santa's Roundup QX5084	Yr.Iss.	1992	8.75	20
1992 A Santa-Full! QX5991	Yr.Iss.	1992	9.75	30-40
1992 Silver Star QX5324	Yr.Iss.	1992	28.00	45-53
1992 Skiing 'Round QX5214	Yr.Iss.	1992	8.75	18
1992 SNOOPY® and WOODSTOCK QX5954	Yr.Iss.	1992	8.75	25-40
1992 Spirit of Christmas Stress QX5231	Yr.Iss.	1992	8.75	18
1992 Stock Car QX5314	Yr.Iss.	1992	9.75	19
1992 Tasty Christmas QX5994	Yr.Iss.	1992	9.75	19
1992 Toboggan Tail QX5459	Yr.Iss.	1992	7.75	16
1992 Tread Bear QX5091	Yr.Iss.	1992	8.75	23

1992 Special Edition - Keepsake

YEAR ISSUE	EDITION LIMIT	YEAR RETD.	ISSUE PRICE	*QUOTE U.S.$
1992 Dickens Caroler Bell-Lord Chadwick (3rd Ed.) QX4554	Yr.Iss.	1992	21.75	38-50

1992 Special Issues - Keepsake

YEAR ISSUE	EDITION LIMIT	YEAR RETD.	ISSUE PRICE	*QUOTE U.S.$
1992 Elvis QX562-4	Yr.Iss.	1992	14.75	33
1992 Santa Maria QX5074	Yr.Iss.	1992	12.75	20-30
1992 Shuttlecraft Galileo 2400QLX733-1	Yr.Iss.	1992	24.00	41-60

1993 Anniversary Edition - Keepsake

YEAR ISSUE	EDITION LIMIT	YEAR RETD.	ISSUE PRICE	*QUOTE U.S.$
1993 Frosty Friends QX5682	Yr.Iss.	1993	20.00	20-50
1993 Glowing Pewter Wreath QX5302	Yr.Iss.	1993	18.75	38
1993 Shopping With Santa QX5675	Yr.Iss.	1993	24.00	25-50
1993 Tannenbaum's Dept. Store QX5612	Yr.Iss.	1993	26.00	54-60

1993 Artists' Favorites - Keepsake

YEAR ISSUE	EDITION LIMIT	YEAR RETD.	ISSUE PRICE	*QUOTE U.S.$
1993 Bird Watcher QX5252	Yr.Iss.	1993	9.75	15-20
1993 Howling Good Time QX5255	Yr.Iss.	1993	9.75	18
1993 On Her Toes QX5265	Yr.Iss.	1993	8.75	18
1993 Peek-a-Boo Tree QX5245	Yr.Iss.	1993	10.75	25
1993 Wake-Up Call QX5262	Yr.Iss.	1993	8.75	18

1993 Collectible Series - Keepsake

YEAR ISSUE	EDITION LIMIT	YEAR RETD.	ISSUE PRICE	*QUOTE U.S.$
1993 1956 Ford Thunderbird (3rd Ed.) QX5275	Yr.Iss.	1993	12.75	32-40
1993 Betsey's Country Christmas (2nd Ed.) QX2062	Yr.Iss.	1993	5.00	20
1993 Cozy Home (10th Ed.) QX4175	Yr.Iss.	1993	14.75	33
1993 CRAYOLA CRAYON-Bright Shining Castle (5th Ed.) QX4422	Yr.Iss.	1993	11.00	33
1993 Fabulous Decade (4th Ed.) QX4475	Yr.Iss.	1993	7.75	17
1993 A Fitting Moment (8th Ed.) QX4202	Yr.Iss.	1993	14.75	30
1993 Frosty Friends (14th Ed.) QX4142	Yr.Iss.	1993	9.75	22-40
1993 The Gift Bringers-The Magi (5th Ed.) QX2065	Yr.Iss.	1993	5.00	16
1993 Happy Haul-idays (15th Ed.) QX4102	Yr.Iss.	1993	14.75	30
1993 Heart Of Christmas-(4th Ed.) QX4482	Yr.Iss.	1993	14.75	28
1993 Heavenly Angels (3rd Ed.) QX4945	Yr.Iss.	1993	7.75	18
1993 Humpty-Dumpty (1st Ed.) QX5282	Yr.Iss.	1993	13.75	35
1993 Mary's Angels-Ivy (6th Ed.) QX4282	Yr.Iss.	1993	6.75	15-25
1993 Merry Olde Santa (4th Ed.) QX4842	Yr.Iss.	1993	14.75	27-35
1993 Owliver (2nd Ed.) QX5425	Yr.Iss.	1993	7.75	17
1993 Peace On Earth-Poland (3rd Ed.) QX5242	Yr.Iss.	1993	11.75	22
1993 Peanuts (1st Ed.) QX5315	Yr.Iss.	1993	9.75	40-65
1993 Puppy Love (3rd Ed.) QX5045	Yr.Iss.	1993	7.75	20-27
1993 Reindeer Champs-Blitzen (8th Ed.) QX4331	Yr.Iss.	1993	8.75	21
1993 Rocking Horse (13th Ed.) QX4162	Yr.Iss.	1993	10.75	30-40
1993 Ten Lords A-Leaping (10th Ed.) QX3012	Yr.Iss.	1993	6.75	15-25
1993 Tobin Fraley Carousel (2nd Ed.) QX5502	Yr.Iss.	1993	28.00	35-55
1993 U.S. Christmas Stamps (1st Ed.) QX5292	Yr.Iss.	1993	10.75	32-42

1993 Commemoratives - Keepsake

YEAR ISSUE	EDITION LIMIT	YEAR RETD.	ISSUE PRICE	*QUOTE U.S.$
1993 Across the Miles QX5912	Yr.Iss.	1993	8.75	18
1993 Anniversary Year QX5972	Yr.Iss.	1993	9.75	18
1993 Apple for Teacher QX5902	Yr.Iss.	1993	7.75	16
1993 Baby's First Christmas QX5512	Yr.Iss.	1993	18.75	40
1993 Baby's First Christmas QX5515	Yr.Iss.	1993	10.75	21
1993 Baby's First Christmas QX5522	Yr.Iss.	1993	7.75	21
1993 Baby's First Christmas QX5525	Yr.Iss.	1993	7.75	27
1993 Baby's First Christmas-Baby Boy QX2105	Yr.Iss.	1993	4.75	13

CHRISTMAS ORNAMENTS

YEAR ISSUE		EDITION LIMIT	YEAR RETD.	ISSUE PRICE	*QUOTE U.S.$
1993	Baby's First Christmas-Baby Girl QX2092	Yr.Iss.	1993	4.75	12
1993	Baby's Second Christmas QX5992	Yr.Iss.	1993	6.75	16-25
1993	Brother QX5542	Yr.Iss.	1993	6.75	13
1993	A Child's Christmas QX5882	Yr.Iss.	1993	9.75	20
1993	Child's Fifth Christmas QX5222	Yr.Iss.	1993	6.75	17
1993	Child's Fourth Christmas QX5215	Yr.Iss.	1993	6.75	14-25
1993	Child's Third Christmas QX5995	Yr.Iss.	1993	6.75	20
1993	Coach QX5935	Yr.Iss.	1993	6.75	15
1993	Dad QX5855	Yr.Iss.	1993	7.75	17
1993	Dad-to-Be QX5532	Yr.Iss.	1993	6.75	15
1993	Daughter QX5872	Yr.Iss.	1993	6.75	17
1993	Godchild QX5875	Yr.Iss.	1993	8.75	18
1993	Grandchild's First Christmas QX5552	Yr.Iss.	1993	6.75	13
1993	Granddaughter QX5635	Yr.Iss.	1993	6.75	13
1993	Grandmother QX5665	Yr.Iss.	1993	6.75	13
1993	Grandparents QX2085	Yr.Iss.	1993	4.75	15
1993	Grandson QX5632	Yr.Iss.	1993	6.75	13
1993	Mom and Dad QX5845	Yr.Iss.	1993	9.75	17
1993	Mom QX5852	Yr.Iss.	1993	7.75	17
1993	Mom-to-Be QX5535	Yr.Iss.	1993	6.75	14
1993	Nephew QX5735	Yr.Iss.	1993	6.75	13
1993	New Home QX5905	Yr.Iss.	1993	7.75	37
1993	Niece QX5732	Yr.Iss.	1993	6.75	14
1993	Our Christmas Together QX5942	Yr.Iss.	1993	10.75	22
1993	Our Family QX5892	Yr.Iss.	1993	7.75	17
1993	Our First Christmas Together QX3015	Yr.Iss.	1993	6.75	17
1993	Our First Christmas Together QX5642	Yr.Iss.	1993	9.75	15-25
1993	Our First Christmas Together QX5952	Yr.Iss.	1993	8.75	20
1993	Our First Christmas Together QX5955	Yr.Iss.	1993	18.75	45
1993	People Friendly QX5932	Yr.Iss.	1993	8.75	16
1993	Sister QX5545	Yr.Iss.	1993	6.75	16-23
1993	Sister to Sister QX5885	Yr.Iss.	1993	9.75	35
1993	Son QX5865	Yr.Iss.	1993	6.75	13-20
1993	Special Cat QX5235	Yr.Iss.	1993	7.75	14
1993	Special Dog QX5962	Yr.Iss.	1993	7.75	15
1993	Star Teacher QX5645	Yr.Iss.	1993	5.75	13
1993	Strange and Wonderful Love QX5965	Yr.Iss.	1993	8.75	16
1993	To My Grandma QX5555	Yr.Iss.	1993	7.75	16
1993	Top Banana QX5925	Yr.Iss.	1993	7.75	18
1993	Warm and Special Friends QX5895	Yr.Iss.	1993	10.75	23

1993 Easter Ornaments - Keepsake

1993	Easter Parade (2nd Ed.) QEO8325	Yr.Iss.	1993	6.75	17
1993	Egg in Sports (2nd Ed.) QEO8332	Yr.Iss.	1993	6.75	17
1993	Springtime Bonnets (1st Ed.) QEO8322	Yr.Iss.	1993	7.75	25

1993 Keepsake Collector's Club - Keepsake

1993	It's In The Mail QXC5272	Yr.Iss.	1993	10.00	22
1993	Trimmed With Memories QXC5432	Yr.Iss.	1993	12.00	38

1993 Keepsake Magic Ornaments - Keepsake

1993	Baby's First Christmas QLX7365	Yr.Iss.	1993	22.00	43
1993	Bells Are Ringing QLX7402	Yr.Iss.	1993	28.00	54-65
1993	Chris Mouse Flight (9th Ed.) QLX7152	Yr.Iss.	1993	12.00	26-33
1993	Dog's Best Friend QLX7172	Yr.Iss.	1993	12.00	23
1993	Dollhouse Dreams QLX7372	Yr.Iss.	1993	22.00	35-50
1993	Forest Frolics (5th Ed.) QLX7165	Yr.Iss.	1993	25.00	45-53
1993	Home On The Range QLX7395	Yr.Iss.	1993	32.00	63-75
1993	The Lamplighter QLX7192	Yr.Iss.	1993	18.00	36
1993	Last-Minute Shopping QLX7385	Yr.Iss.	1993	28.00	40-60
1993	North Pole Merrython QLX7392	Yr.Iss.	1993	25.00	48
1993	Our First Christmas Together QLX7355	Yr.Iss.	1993	20.00	38
1993	PEANUTS (3rd Ed.) QLX7155	Yr.Iss.	1993	18.00	38-50
1993	Radio News Flash QLX7362	Yr.Iss.	1993	22.00	40-50
1993	Raiding The Fridge QLX7185	Yr.Iss.	1993	16.00	37
1993	Road Runner and Wile E. Coyote QLX7415	Yr.Iss.	1993	30.00	70
1993	Santa's Snow-Getter QLX7352	Yr.Iss.	1993	18.00	39
1993	Santa's Workshop QLX7375	Yr.Iss.	1993	28.00	60
1993	Song Of The Chimes QLX7405	Yr.Iss.	1993	25.00	52
1993	Winnie The Pooh QLX7422	Yr.Iss.	1993	24.00	50

1993 Limited Edition Ornaments - Keepsake

1993	Gentle Tidings QXC5442	17,500	1993	25.00	50
1993	Sharing Christmas QXC5435	16,500	1993	20.00	45

1993 Miniature Ornaments - Keepsake

1993	'Round The Mountain QXM4025	Yr.Iss.	1993	7.25	17
1993	Baby's First Christmas QXM5145	Yr.Iss.	1993	5.75	14
1993	The Bearymores (2nd Ed.). QXM5125	Yr.Iss.	1993	5.75	17
1993	Cheese Please QXM4072	Yr.Iss.	1993	3.75	7
1993	Christmas Castle QXM4085	Yr.Iss.	1993	5.75	12
1993	Cloisonne Snowflake QXM4012	Yr.Iss.	1993	9.75	19
1993	Country Fiddling QXM4062	Yr.Iss.	1993	3.75	9
1993	Crystal Angel QXM4015	Yr.Iss.	1993	9.75	54-75
1993	Ears To Pals QXM4075	Yr.Iss.	1993	3.75	8
1993	Flatbed Car (5th Ed.) QXM5105	Yr.Iss.	1993	7.00	15
1993	Grandma QXM5162	Yr.Iss.	1993	4.50	12
1993	I Dream Of Santa QXM4055	Yr.Iss.	1993	3.75	11
1993	Into The Woods QXM4045	Yr.Iss.	1993	3.75	7
1993	The Kringles (5th Ed.) QXM5135	Yr.Iss.	1993	5.75	14
1993	Learning To Skate QXM4122	Yr.Iss.	1993	3.00	8
1993	Lighting A Path QXM4115	Yr.Iss.	1993	3.00	9
1993	March Of The Teddy Bears (1st Ed.) QX2403	Yr.Iss.	1993	4.50	16
1993	Merry Mascot QXM4042	Yr.Iss.	1993	3.75	9
1993	Mom QXM5155	Yr.Iss.	1993	4.50	11
1993	Monkey Melody QXM4092	Yr.Iss.	1993	5.75	13
1993	Nature's Angels (4th Ed.) QXM5122	Yr.Iss.	1993	4.50	13
1993	The Night Before Christmas (2nd Ed.) QXM5115	Yr.Iss.	1993	4.50	15
1993	North Pole Fire Truck QXM4105	Yr.Iss.	1993	4.75	10
1993	On The Road (1st Ed.) QXM4002	Yr.Iss.	1993	5.75	14
1993	Pear-Shaped Tones QXM4052	Yr.Iss.	1993	3.75	7
1993	Pull Out A Plum QXM4095	Yr.Iss.	1993	5.75	12
1993	Refreshing Flight QXM4112	Yr.Iss.	1993	5.75	14
1993	Rocking Horse (6th Ed.) QXM5112	Yr.Iss.	1993	4.50	15
1993	Secret Pals QXM5172	Yr.Iss.	1993	3.75	10
1993	Snuggle Birds QXM5182	Yr.Iss.	1993	5.75	13
1993	Special Friends QXM5165	Yr.Iss.	1993	4.50	9
1993	Thimble Bells (4th Ed.) QXM5142	Yr.Iss.	1993	5.75	14
1993	Tiny Green Thumbs, set/6, QXM4032	Yr.Iss.	1993	29.00	38-55
1993	Toy Shop (6th Ed.) QXM5132	Yr.Iss.	1993	7.00	15
1993	Visions Of Sugarplums QXM4022	Yr.Iss.	1993	7.25	15
1993	Woodland Babies (3rd Ed.) QXM5102	Yr.Iss.	1993	5.75	13

1993 New Attractions - Keepsake

1993	Beary Gifted QX5762	Yr.Iss.	1993	7.75	18
1993	Big on Gardening QX5842	Yr.Iss.	1993	9.75	18
1993	Big Roller QX5352	Yr.Iss.	1993	8.75	16
1993	Bowling For ZZZ's QX5565	Yr.Iss.	1993	7.75	18
1993	Bugs Bunny QX5412	Yr.Iss.	1993	8.75	23
1993	Caring Nurse QX5785	Yr.Iss.	1993	6.75	18
1993	Christmas Break QX5825	Yr.Iss.	1993	7.75	18
1993	Clever Cookie QX5662	Yr.Iss.	1993	7.75	16
1993	Curly 'n' Kingly QX5285	Yr.Iss.	1993	10.75	21
1993	Dunkin' Roo QX5575	Yr.Iss.	1993	7.75	15
1993	Eeyore QX5712	Yr.Iss.	1993	9.75	19
1993	Elmer Fudd QX5495	Yr.Iss.	1993	8.75	18
1993	Faithful Fire Fighter QX5782	Yr.Iss.	1993	7.75	19
1993	Feliz Navidad QX5365	Yr.Iss.	1993	9.75	18
1993	Fills the Bill QX5572	Yr.Iss.	1993	8.75	17
1993	Great Connections QX5402	Yr.Iss.	1993	10.75	22
1993	He Is Born QX5362	Yr.Iss.	1993	9.75	35
1993	High Top-Purr QX5332	Yr.Iss.	1993	8.75	22
1993	Home For Christmas QX5562	Yr.Iss.	1993	7.75	15
1993	Icicle Bicycle QX5835	Yr.Iss.	1993	9.75	18
1993	Kanga and Roo QX5672	Yr.Iss.	1993	9.75	21
1993	Little Drummer Boy QX5372	Yr.Iss.	1993	8.75	21
1993	Look For Wonder QX5685	Yr.Iss.	1993	12.75	25
1993	Lou Rankin Polar Bear QX5745	Yr.Iss.	1993	9.75	21
1993	Makin' Music QX5325	Yr.Iss.	1993	9.75	18
1993	Making Waves QX5775	Yr.Iss.	1993	9.75	22
1993	Mary Engelbreit QX2075	Yr.Iss.	1993	5.00	20
1993	Maxine QX5385	Yr.Iss.	1993	8.75	19
1993	One-Elf Marching Band QX5342	Yr.Iss.	1993	12.75	25
1993	Owl QX5695	Yr.Iss.	1993	9.75	19
1993	PEANUTS QX2072	Yr.Iss.	1993	5.00	20-30
1993	Peep Inside QX5322	Yr.Iss.	1993	13.75	22
1993	Perfect Match QX5772	Yr.Iss.	1993	8.75	18
1993	The Pink Panther QX5755	Yr.Iss.	1993	12.75	25
1993	Playful Pals QX5742	Yr.Iss.	1993	14.75	28
1993	Popping Good Times QX5392	Yr.Iss.	1993	14.75	27
1993	Porky Pig QX5652	Yr.Iss.	1993	8.75	19
1993	Putt-Putt Penguin QX5795	Yr.Iss.	1993	9.75	18
1993	Quick As A Fox QX5792	Yr.Iss.	1993	8.75	16
1993	Rabbit QX5702	Yr.Iss.	1993	9.75	19
1993	Ready For Fun QX5124	Yr.Iss.	1993	7.75	16
1993	Room For One More QX5382	Yr.Iss.	1993	8.75	45
1993	Silvery Noel QX5305	Yr.Iss.	1993	12.75	20-30
1993	Smile! It's Christmas QX5335	Yr.Iss.	1993	9.75	18
1993	Snow Bear Angel QX5355	Yr.Iss.	1993	7.75	16
1993	Snowbird QX5765	Yr.Iss.	1993	7.75	15
1993	Snowy Hideaway QX5312	Yr.Iss.	1993	9.75	15-20
1993	Star Of Wonder QX5982	Yr.Iss.	1993	6.75	32
1993	Superman QX5752	Yr.Iss.	1993	12.75	35-50
1993	The Swat Team QX5395	Yr.Iss.	1993	12.75	27
1993	Sylvester and Tweety QX5405	Yr.Iss.	1993	9.75	32
1993	That's Entertainment QX5345	Yr.Iss.	1993	8.75	18
1993	Tigger and Piglet QX5705	Yr.Iss.	1993	9.75	25-50
1993	Tin Airplane QX5622	Yr.Iss.	1993	7.75	27
1993	Tin Blimp QX5625	Yr.Iss.	1993	7.75	15
1993	Tin Hot Air Balloon QX5615	Yr.Iss.	1993	7.75	15
1993	Water Bed Snooze QX5375	Yr.Iss.	1993	9.75	21
1993	Winnie the Pooh QX5715	Yr.Iss.	1993	9.75	27

1993 Showcase Folk Art Americana - Keepsake

1993	Angel in Flight QK1052	Yr.Iss.	1993	15.75	45
1993	Polar Bear Adventure QK1055	Yr.Iss.	1993	15.00	60
1993	Riding in the Woods QK1065	Yr.Iss.	1993	15.75	60
1993	Riding the Wind QK1045	Yr.Iss.	1993	15.75	42
1993	Santa Claus QK1072	Yr.Iss.	1993	16.75	225

1993 Showcase Holiday Enchantment - Keepsake

1993	Angelic Messengers QK1032	Yr.Iss.	1993	13.75	40
1993	Bringing Home the Tree QK1042	Yr.Iss.	1993	13.75	35
1993	Journey to the Forest QK1012	Yr.Iss.	1993	13.75	32
1993	The Magi QK1025	Yr.Iss.	1993	13.75	37
1993	Visions of Sugarplums QK1005	Yr.Iss.	1993	13.75	35

1993 Showcase Old-World Silver - Keepsake

1993	Silver Dove of Peace QK1075	Yr.Iss.	1993	24.75	35
1993	Silver Santa QK1092	Yr.Iss.	1993	24.75	30-55
1993	Silver Sleigh QK1082	Yr.Iss.	1993	24.75	33
1993	Silver Stars and Holly QK1085	Yr.Iss.	1993	24.75	33

1993 Showcase Portraits in Bisque - Keepsake

1993	Christmas Feast QK1152	Yr.Iss.	1993	15.75	34
1993	Joy of Sharing QK1142	Yr.Iss.	1993	15.75	34
1993	Mistletoe Kiss QK1145	Yr.Iss.	1993	15.75	32
1993	Norman Rockwell-Filling the Stockings QK1155	Yr.Iss.	1993	15.75	36
1993	Norman Rockwell-Jolly Postman QK1142	Yr.Iss.	1993	15.75	36

1993 Special Editions - Keepsake

1993	Dickens Caroler Bell-Lady Daphne-(4th Ed.) QX5505	Yr.Iss.	1993	21.75	40-50
1993	Julianne and Teddy QX5295	Yr.Iss.	1993	21.75	35-55

1993 Special Issues - Keepsake

1993	Holiday Barbie-(1st Ed.) QX572-5	Yr.Iss.	1993	14.75	100-155
1993	Messages of Christmas QLX747-6	Yr.Iss.	1993	35.00	45-55
1993	Star Trek: The Next Generation QLX741-2	Yr.Iss.	1993	24.00	50-65

1994 Artists' Favorites - Keepsake

1994	Cock-a-Doodle Christmas QX5396	Yr.Iss.	1994	8.95	20
1994	Happy Birthday Jesus QX5423	Yr.Iss.	1994	12.95	23
1994	Keep on Mowin' QX5413	Yr.Iss.	1994	8.95	17
1994	Kitty's Catamaran QX5416	Yr.Iss.	1994	10.95	17
1994	Making It Bright QX5403	Yr.Iss.	1994	8.95	15

1994 Collectible Series - Keepsake

1994	1957 Chevy (4th Ed.) QX5422	Yr.Iss.	1994	12.95	30
1994	Baseball Heroes-Babe Ruth (1st Ed.) QX5323	Yr.Iss.	1994	12.95	40-65
1994	Betsey's Country Christmas (3rd Ed.) QX2403	Yr.Iss.	1994	5.00	15
1994	Cat Naps (1st Ed.) QX5313	Yr.Iss.	1994	7.95	25
1994	CRAYOLA CRAYON-Bright Playful Colors-(6th Ed.) QX5273	Yr.Iss.	1994	10.95	25
1994	Fabulous Decade-(5th Ed.) QX5263	Yr.Iss.	1994	7.95	15-25
1994	Frosty Friends (15th Ed.) QX5293	Yr.Iss.	1994	9.95	22-30
1994	Handwarming Present (9th Ed.) QX5283	Yr.Iss.	1994	14.95	26
1994	Heart of Christmas-(5th Ed.) QX5266	Yr.Iss.	1994	14.95	28
1994	Hey Diddle Diddle-(2nd Ed.) QX5213	Yr.Iss.	1994	13.95	30-40
1994	Makin' Tractor Tracks (16th Ed.) QX5296	Yr.Iss.	1994	14.95	50
1994	Mary's Angels-Jasmine-(7th Ed.) QX5276	Yr.Iss.	1994	6.95	20
1994	Merry Olde Santa-(5th Ed.) QX5256	Yr.Iss.	1994	14.95	25-33
1994	Murray Blue Champion-(1st Ed.) QX5426	Yr.Iss.	1994	13.95	40-60
1994	Neighborhood Drugstore -(11th Ed.) QX5286	Yr.Iss.	1994	14.95	27-35
1994	Owliver-(3rd Ed.) QX5226	Yr.Iss.	1994	7.95	19
1994	PEANUTS-Lucy-(2nd Ed.) QX5203	Yr.Iss.	1994	9.95	25-39
1994	Pipers Piping-(11th Ed.) QX3183	Yr.Iss.	1994	6.95	18
1994	Puppy Love-(4th Ed.) QX5253	Yr.Iss.	1994	7.95	19
1994	Rocking Horse-(14th Ed.) QX5016	Yr.Iss.	1994	10.95	22-30
1994	Tobin Fraley Carousel-(3rd Ed.) QX5223	Yr.Iss.	1994	28.00	55-70
1994	Xmas Stamp-(2nd Ed.) QX5206	Yr.Iss.	1994	10.95	2[illegible]
1994	Yuletide Central-(1st Ed.) QX5316	Yr.Iss.	1994	18.95	45-55

1994 Commemoratives - Keepsake

1994	Across the Miles QX5656	Yr.Iss.	1994	8.95	17
1994	Anniversary Year QX5683	Yr.Iss.	1994	10.95	2[illegible]
1994	Baby's First Christmas Photo QX5636	Yr.Iss.	1994	7.95	1[illegible]
1994	Baby's First Christmas QX5633	Yr.Iss.	1994	18.95	25-3[illegible]
1994	Baby's First Christmas QX5713	Yr.Iss.	1994	7.95	2[illegible]
1994	Baby's First Christmas QX5743	Yr.Iss.	1994	12.95	2[illegible]
1994	Baby's First Christmas-Baby Boy QX2436	Yr.Iss.	1994	5.00	1[illegible]
1994	Baby's First Christmas-Baby Girl QX2433	Yr.Iss.	1994	5.00	1[illegible]
1994	Baby's Second Christmas QX5716	Yr.Iss.	1994	7.95	1[illegible]
1994	Brother QX5516	Yr.Iss.	1994	6.95	1[illegible]
1994	Child's Fifth Christmas QX5733	Yr.Iss.	1994	6.95	1[illegible]
1994	Child's Fourth Christmas QX5726	Yr.Iss.	1994	6.95	1[illegible]
1994	Child's Third Christmas QX5723	Yr.Iss.	1994	6.95	1[illegible]
1994	Dad QX5463	Yr.Iss.	1994	7.95	1[illegible]
1994	Dad-To-Be QX5473	Yr.Iss.	1994	7.95	[illegible]
1994	Daughter QX5623	Yr.Iss.	1994	6.95	[illegible]
1994	Friendly Push QX5686	Yr.Iss.	1994	8.95	1[illegible]
1994	Godchild QX4453	Yr.Iss.	1994	8.95	2[illegible]
1994	Godparents QX2423	Yr.Iss.	1994	5.00	[illegible]
1994	Grandchild's First Christmas QX5676	Yr.Iss.	1994	7.95	[illegible]

*Quotes have been rounded up to nearest dollar

CHRISTMAS ORNAMENTS

YEAR	ISSUE	EDITION LIMIT	YEAR RETD.	ISSUE PRICE	*QUOTE U.S.$
1994	Granddaughter QX5523	Yr.Iss.	1994	6.95	15
1994	Grandma Photo QX5613	Yr.Iss.	1994	6.95	7
1994	Grandmother QX5673	Yr.Iss.	1994	7.95	18
1994	Grandpa QX5616	Yr.Iss.	1994	7.95	17
1994	Grandparents QX2426	Yr.Iss.	1994	5.00	13
1994	Grandson QX5526	Yr.Iss.	1994	6.95	15
1994	Mom and Dad QX5666	Yr.Iss.	1994	9.95	16
1994	Mom QX5466	Yr.Iss.	1994	7.95	20
1994	Mom-To-Be QX5506	Yr.Iss.	1994	7.95	16
1994	Nephew QX5546	Yr.Iss.	1994	7.95	15
1994	New Home QX5663	Yr.Iss.	1994	8.95	17
1994	Niece QX5543	Yr.Iss.	1994	7.95	15
1994	Our Family QX5576	Yr.Iss.	1994	7.95	17
1994	Our First Christmas Together Photo QX5653	Yr.Iss.	1994	8.95	18
1994	Our First Christmas Together QX3186	Yr.Iss.	1994	6.95	15
1994	Our First Christmas Together QX4816	Yr.Iss.	1994	9.95	25
1994	Our First Christmas Together QX5643	Yr.Iss.	1994	9.95	25
1994	Our First Christmas Together QX5706	Yr.Iss.	1994	18.95	35
1994	Secret Santa QX5736	Yr.Iss.	1994	7.95	18
1994	Sister QX5513	Yr.Iss.	1994	6.95	16
1994	Sister to Sister QX5533	Yr.Iss.	1994	9.95	21
1994	Son QX5626	Yr.Iss.	1994	6.95	15
1994	Special Cat QX5606	Yr.Iss.	1994	7.95	16
1994	Special Dog QX5603	Yr.Iss.	1994	7.95	16
1994	Thick 'N' Thin QX5693	Yr.Iss.	1994	10.95	23
1994	Tou Can Love QX5646	Yr.Iss.	1994	8.95	18

1994 Easter Ornaments - Keepsake

YEAR	ISSUE	EDITION LIMIT	YEAR RETD.	ISSUE PRICE	*QUOTE U.S.$
1994	Baby's First Easter QEO8153	Yr.Iss.	1994	6.75	18
1994	Carrot Trimmers QEO8226	Yr.Iss.	1994	5.00	5
1994	CRAYOLA CRAYON-Colorful Spring QEO8166	Yr.Iss.	1994	7.75	20-28
1994	Daughter QEO8156	Yr.Iss.	1994	5.75	15
1994	Divine Duet QEO8183	Yr.Iss.	1994	6.75	15
1994	Easter Art Show QEO8193	Yr.Iss.	1994	7.75	16
1994	Egg Car-(1st Ed.) QEO8093	Yr.Iss.	1994	7.75	26
1994	Golf-(3rd Ed.) QEO8133	Yr.Iss.	1994	6.75	18
1994	Horn-(3rd Ed.) QEO8136	Yr.Iss.	1994	6.75	18
1994	Joyful Lamb QEO8206	Yr.Iss.	1994	5.75	14
1994	PEANUTS QEO8176	Yr.Iss.	1994	7.75	20-45
1994	Peeping Out QEO8203	Yr.Iss.	1994	6.75	14
1994	Riding a Breeze QEO8213	Yr.Iss.	1994	5.75	14
1994	Son QEO8163	Yr.Iss.	1994	5.75	15
1994	Springtime Bonnets-(2nd Ed.) QEO8096	Yr.Iss.	1994	7.75	15-25
1994	Sunny Bunny Garden, (Set/3) QEO8146	Yr.Iss.	1994	15.00	28
1994	Sweet as Sugar QEO8086	Yr.Iss.	1994	8.75	19
1994	Sweet Easter Wishes Tender Touches QEO8196	Yr.Iss.	1994	8.75	23
1994	Treetop Cottage QEO8186	Yr.Iss.	1994	9.75	19
1994	Yummy Recipe QEO8143	Yr.Iss.	1994	7.75	20

1994 Keepsake Collector's Club - Keepsake

YEAR	ISSUE	EDITION LIMIT	YEAR RETD.	ISSUE PRICE	*QUOTE U.S.$
1994	First Hello QXC4846	Yr.Iss.	1994	5.00	15
1994	Happy Collecting QXC4803	Yr.Iss.	1994	3.00	25
1994	Holiday Pursuit QXC4823	Yr.Iss.	1994	11.75	23
1994	Mrs. Claus' Cupboard QXC4843	Yr.Iss.	1994	55.00	210
1994	On Cloud Nine QXC4853	Yr.Iss.	1994	12.00	28
1994	Sweet Bouquet QXC4806	Yr.Iss.	1994	8.50	23
1994	Tilling Time QXC8256	Yr.Iss.	1994	5.00	20-50

1994 Keepsake Magic Ornaments - Keepsake

YEAR	ISSUE	EDITION LIMIT	YEAR RETD.	ISSUE PRICE	*QUOTE U.S.$
1994	Away in a Manager QLX7383	Yr.Iss.	1994	16.00	25-40
1994	Baby's First Christmas QLX7466	Yr.Iss.	1994	20.00	35-43
1994	Candy Cane Lookout QLX7376	Yr.Iss.	1994	18.00	46-65
1994	Chris Mouse Jelly-(10th Ed.) QLX7393	Yr.Iss.	1994	12.00	16-29
1994	Conversations With Santa QLX7426	Yr.Iss.	1994	28.00	53
1994	Country Showtime QLX7416	Yr.Iss.	1994	22.00	45
1994	The Eagle Has Landed QLX7486	Yr.Iss.	1994	24.00	40
1994	Feliz Navidad QLX7433	Yr.Iss.	1994	28.00	53
1994	Forest Frolics-(6th Ed.) QLX7436	Yr.Iss.	1994	28.00	55
1994	Gingerbread Fantasy-(Sp. Ed.) QLX7382	Yr.Iss.	1994	44.00	97
1994	Kringle Trolley QLX7413	Yr.Iss.	1994	20.00	47
1994	Maxine QLX7503	Yr.Iss.	1994	20.00	40
1994	PEANUTS-(4th Ed.) QLX7406	Yr.Iss.	1994	20.00	35-45
1994	Peekaboo Pup QLX7423	Yr.Iss.	1994	20.00	40
1994	Rock Candy Miner QLX7403	Yr.Iss.	1994	20.00	38
1994	Santa's Sing-Along QLX7473	Yr.Iss.	1994	24.00	55
1994	Tobin Fraley-(1st Ed.) QLX7496	Yr.Iss.	1994	32.00	60-68
1994	Very Merry Minutes QLX7443	Yr.Iss.	1994	24.00	45
1994	White Christmas QLX7463	Yr.Iss.	1994	28.00	40-54
1994	Winnie the Pooh Parade QLX7493	Yr.Iss.	1994	32.00	45-65

1994 Limited Editions - Keepsake

YEAR	ISSUE	EDITION LIMIT	YEAR RETD.	ISSUE PRICE	*QUOTE U.S.$
1994	Jolly Holly Santa QXC4833	N/A	1994	22.00	22
1994	Majestic Deer QXC4836	N/A	1994	25.00	25

1994 Miniature Ornaments - Keepsake

YEAR	ISSUE	EDITION LIMIT	YEAR RETD.	ISSUE PRICE	*QUOTE U.S.$
1994	Babs Bunny QXM4116	Yr.Iss.	1994	5.75	12
1994	Baby's First Christmas QXM4003	Yr.Iss.	1994	5.75	12
1994	Baking Tiny Treats, (Set/6) QXM4033	Yr.Iss.	1994	29.00	58
1994	Beary Perfect Tree QXM4076	Yr.Iss.	1994	4.75	9
1994	The Bearymores-(3rd Ed.) QXM5133	Yr.Iss.	1994	5.75	13
1994	Buster Bunny QXM5163	Yr.Iss.	1994	5.75	12
1994	Centuries of Santa-(1st Ed.) QXM5153	Yr.Iss.	1994	6.00	20
1994	Corny Elf QXM4063	Yr.Iss.	1994	4.50	9
1994	Cute as a Button QXM4103	Yr.Iss.	1994	3.75	11
1994	Dazzling Reindeer-(Pr. Ed.) QXM4026	Yr.Iss.	1994	9.75	19
1994	Dizzy Devil QXM4133	Yr.Iss.	1994	5.75	13
1994	Friends Need Hugs QXM4016	Yr.Iss.	1994	4.50	12
1994	Graceful Carousel QXM4056	Yr.Iss.	1994	7.75	16
1994	Hamton QXM4126	Yr.Iss.	1994	5.75	12
1994	Hat Shop (7th Ed.) QXM5143	Yr.Iss.	1994	7.00	15
1994	Have a Cookie QXM5166	Yr.Iss.	1994	5.75	15
1994	Hearts A-Sail QXM4006	Yr.Iss.	1994	5.75	13
1994	Jolly Visitor QXM4053	Yr.Iss.	1994	5.75	15
1994	Jolly Wolly Snowman QXM4093	Yr.Iss.	1994	3.75	11
1994	Journey to Bethlehem QXM4036	Yr.Iss.	1994	5.75	12
1994	Just My Size QXM4086	Yr.Iss.	1994	3.75	10
1994	Love Was Born QXM4043	Yr.Iss.	1994	4.50	13
1994	March of the Teddy Bears -(2nd Ed.) QXM5106	Yr.Iss.	1994	4.50	14
1994	Melodic Cherub QXM4066	Yr.Iss.	1994	3.75	9
1994	A Merry Flight QXM4073	Yr.Iss.	1994	5.75	12
1994	Mom QXM4013	Yr.Iss.	1994	4.50	10
1994	Nature's Angels-(5th Ed.) QXM5126	Yr.Iss.	1994	4.50	12
1994	Night Before Christmas -(3rd Ed.) QXM5123	Yr.Iss.	1994	4.50	13
1994	Noah's Ark (Sp. Ed.)) QXM4106	Yr.Iss.	1994	24.50	48-60
1994	Nutcracker Guild-(1st Ed.) QXM5146	Yr.Iss.	1994	5.75	13-20
1994	On the Road-(2nd Ed.) QXM5103	Yr.Iss.	1994	5.75	12-17
1994	Plucky Duck QXM4123	Yr.Iss.	1994	5.75	12
1994	Pour Some More QXM5156	Yr.Iss.	1994	5.75	12
1994	Rocking Horse-(7th Ed.) QXM5116	Yr.Iss.	1994	4.50	15
1994	Scooting Along QXM5173	Yr.Iss.	1994	6.75	14
1994	Stock Car-(6th Ed.) QXM5113	Yr.Iss.	1994	7.00	15
1994	Sweet Dreams QXM4096	Yr.Iss.	1994	3.00	14
1994	Tea With Teddy QXM4046	Yr.Iss.	1994	7.25	15

1994 New Attractions - Keepsake

YEAR	ISSUE	EDITION LIMIT	YEAR RETD.	ISSUE PRICE	*QUOTE U.S.$
1994	All Pumped Up QX5923	Yr.Iss.	1994	8.95	18
1994	Angel Hare QX5896	Yr.Iss.	1994	8.95	18
1994	Batman QX5853	Yr.Iss.	1994	12.95	27
1994	Beatles Gift Set QX5373	Yr.Iss.	1994	48.00	103
1994	BEATRIX POTTER The Tale of Peter Rabbit QX2443	Yr.Iss.	1994	5.00	13-20
1994	Big Shot QX5873	Yr.Iss.	1994	7.95	17
1994	Busy Batter QX5876	Yr.Iss.	1994	7.95	16
1994	Candy Caper QX5776	Yr.Iss.	1994	8.95	18
1994	Caring Doctor QX5823	Yr.Iss.	1994	8.95	18
1994	Champion Teacher QX5836	Yr.Iss.	1994	6.95	16
1994	Cheers to You! QX5796	Yr.Iss.	1994	10.95	23
1994	Cheery Cyclists QX5786	Yr.Iss.	1994	12.95	27
1994	Child Care Giver QX5906	Yr.Iss.	1994	7.95	16
1994	Coach QX5933	Yr.Iss.	1994	7.95	18
1994	Colors of Joy QX5893	Yr.Iss.	1994	7.95	18
1994	Cowardly Lion QX5446	Yr.Iss.	1994	9.95	33
1994	Daffy Duck QX5415	Yr.Iss.	1994	8.95	21
1994	Daisy Days QX5986	Yr.Iss.	1994	9.95	10
1994	Deer Santa Mouse (2) QX5806	Yr.Iss.	1994	14.95	27
1994	Dorothy and Toto QX5433	Yr.Iss.	1994	10.95	53
1994	Extra-Special Delivery QX5833	Yr.Iss.	1994	7.95	16
1994	Feelin' Groovy QX5953	Yr.Iss.	1994	7.95	21
1994	A Feline of Christmas QX5816	Yr.Iss.	1994	8.95	25
1994	Feliz Navidad QX5793	Yr.Iss.	1994	8.95	20
1994	Follow the Sun QX5846	Yr.Iss.	1994	8.95	18
1994	Fred and Barney QX5003	Yr.Iss.	1994	14.95	28-40
1994	Friendship Sundae QX4766	Yr.Iss.	1994	10.95	21
1994	GARFIELD QX5753	Yr.Iss.	1994	12.95	27
1994	Gentle Nurse QX5973	Yr.Iss.	1994	6.95	18
1994	Harvest Joy QX5993	Yr.Iss.	1994	9.95	10
1994	Hearts in Harmony QX4406	Yr.Iss.	1994	10.95	21
1994	Helpful Shepherd QX5536	Yr.Iss.	1994	8.95	18
1994	Holiday Patrol QX5826	Yr.Iss.	1994	8.95	18
1994	Ice Show QX5946	Yr.Iss.	1994	7.95	17
1994	In the Pink QX5763	Yr.Iss.	1994	9.95	20
1994	It's a Strike QX5856	Yr.Iss.	1994	8.95	18
1994	Jingle Bell Band QX5783	Yr.Iss.	1994	10.95	25
1994	Joyous Song QX4473	Yr.Iss.	1994	8.95	17
1994	Jump-along Jackalope QX5756	Yr.Iss.	1994	8.95	18
1994	Kickin' Roo QX5916	Yr.Iss.	1994	7.95	16
1994	Kringle's Kayak QX5886	Yr.Iss.	1994	7.95	17
1994	LEGO'S QX5453	Yr.Iss.	1994	10.95	21
1994	Lou Rankin Seal QX5456	Yr.Iss.	1994	9.95	19
1994	Magic Carpet Ride QX5883	Yr.Iss.	1994	7.95	21
1994	Mary Engelbreit QX2416	Yr.Iss.	1994	5.00	15
1994	Merry Fishmas QX5913	Yr.Iss.	1994	8.95	16
1994	Mistletoe Surprise (2)QX5996	Yr.Iss.	1994	12.95	26
1994	Norman Rockwell QX2413	Yr.Iss.	1994	5.00	15
1994	Open-and-Shut Holiday QX5696	Yr.Iss.	1994	9.95	20
1994	Out of This World Teacher QX5766	Yr.Iss.	1994	7.95	19
1994	Practice Makes Perfect QX5863	Yr.Iss.	1994	7.95	17
1994	Red Hot Holiday QX5843	Yr.Iss.	1994	7.95	16
1994	Reindeer Pro QX5926	Yr.Iss.	1994	7.95	16
1994	Relaxing Moment QX5356	Yr.Iss.	1994	14.95	29
1994	Road Runner and Wile E. Coyote QX5602	Yr.Iss.	1994	12.95	20-28
1994	Scarecrow QX5436	Yr.Iss.	1994	9.95	36
1994	A Sharp Flat QX5773	Yr.Iss.	1994	10.95	23
1994	Speedy Gonzales QX5343	Yr.Iss.	1994	8.95	17
1994	Stamp of Approval QX5703	Yr.Iss.	1994	7.95	16
1994	Sweet Greeting (2) QX5803	Yr.Iss.	1994	10.95	21
1994	Tasmanian Devil QX5605	Yr.Iss.	1994	8.95	45-60
1994	Thrill a Minute QX5866	Yr.Iss.	1994	8.95	18
1994	Time of Peace QX5813	Yr.Iss.	1994	7.95	15
1994	Tin Man QX5443	Yr.Iss.	1994	9.95	51
1994	Tulip Time QX5983	Yr.Iss.	1994	9.95	10
1994	Winnie the Pooh/Tigger QX5746	Yr.Iss.	1994	12.95	25-33
1994	Yosemite Sam QX5346	Yr.Iss.	1994	8.95	18
1994	Yuletide Cheer QX5976	Yr.Iss.	1994	9.95	10

1994 Premiere Event - Keepsake

YEAR	ISSUE	EDITION LIMIT	YEAR RETD.	ISSUE PRICE	*QUOTE U.S.$
1994	Eager for Christmas QX5336	Yr.Iss.	1994	15.00	15

1994 Showcase Christmas Lights - Keepsake

YEAR	ISSUE	EDITION LIMIT	YEAR RETD.	ISSUE PRICE	*QUOTE U.S.$
1994	Home for the Holidays QK1123	Yr.Iss.	1994	15.75	16
1994	Moonbeams QK1116	Yr.Iss.	1994	15.75	16
1994	Mother and Child QK1126	Yr.Iss.	1994	15.75	16
1994	Peaceful Village QK1106	Yr.Iss.	1994	15.75	16

1994 Showcase Folk Art Americana Collection - Keepsake

YEAR	ISSUE	EDITION LIMIT	YEAR RETD.	ISSUE PRICE	*QUOTE U.S.$
1994	Catching 40 Winks QK1183	Yr.Iss.	1994	16.75	32
1994	Going to Town QK1166	Yr.Iss.	1994	15.75	35
1994	Racing Through the Snow QK1173	Yr.Iss.	1994	15.75	50
1994	Rarin' to Go QK1193	Yr.Iss.	1994	15.75	35
1994	Roundup Time QK1176	Yr.Iss.	1994	16.75	35

1994 Showcase Holiday Favorites - Keepsake

YEAR	ISSUE	EDITION LIMIT	YEAR RETD.	ISSUE PRICE	*QUOTE U.S.$
1994	Dapper Snowman QK1053	Yr.Iss.	1994	13.75	14
1994	Graceful Fawn QK1033	Yr.Iss.	1994	11.75	12
1994	Jolly Santa QK1046	Yr.Iss.	1994	13.75	14
1994	Joyful Lamb QK1036	Yr.Iss.	1994	11.75	12
1994	Peaceful Dove QK1043	Yr.Iss.	1994	11.75	12

1994 Showcase Old World Silver Collection - Keepsake

YEAR	ISSUE	EDITION LIMIT	YEAR RETD.	ISSUE PRICE	*QUOTE U.S.$
1994	Silver Bells QK1026	Yr.Iss.	1994	24.75	40
1994	Silver Bows QK1023	Yr.Iss.	1994	24.75	40
1994	Silver Poinsettias QK1006	Yr.Iss.	1994	24.75	59
1994	Silver Snowflakes QK1016	Yr.Iss.	1994	24.75	40

1994 Special Edition - Keepsake

YEAR	ISSUE	EDITION LIMIT	YEAR RETD.	ISSUE PRICE	*QUOTE U.S.$
1994	Lucinda and Teddy QX4813	Yr.Iss.	1994	21.75	30-43

1994 Special Issues - Keepsake

YEAR	ISSUE	EDITION LIMIT	YEAR RETD.	ISSUE PRICE	*QUOTE U.S.$
1994	Barney QLX7506	Yr.Iss.	1994	24.00	27-50
1994	Barney QX5966	Yr.Iss.	1994	9.95	22
1994	Holiday Barbie™-(2nd Ed.) QX5216	Yr.Iss.	1994	14.95	40-55
1994	Klingon Bird of Prey™ QLX7386	Yr.Iss.	1994	24.00	40-50
1994	Mufasa/Simba-Lion King QX5406	Yr.Iss.	1994	14.95	30
1994	Nostalgic-Barbie™-(1st Ed.) QX5006	Yr.Iss.	1994	14.95	30-50
1994	Simba/Nala-Lion King (2) QX5303	Yr.Iss.	1994	12.95	28
1994	Simba/Sarabi/Mufasa the Lion King QLX7513	Yr.Iss.	1994	20.00	41-70
1994	Simba/Sarabi/Mufasa the Lion King QLX7513	Yr.Iss.	1994	32.00	41-70
1994	Timon/Pumbaa-Lion King QX5366	Yr.Iss.	1994	8.95	23-30

1995 Anniversary Edition - Keepsake

YEAR	ISSUE	EDITION LIMIT	YEAR RETD.	ISSUE PRICE	*QUOTE U.S.$
1995	Pewter Rocking Horse QX6167	Yr.Iss.		20.00	50

1995 Artists' Favorite - Keepsake

YEAR	ISSUE	EDITION LIMIT	YEAR RETD.	ISSUE PRICE	*QUOTE U.S.$
1995	Barrel-Back Rider QX5189	Yr.Iss.		9.95	28
1995	Our Little Blessings QX5209	Yr.Iss.		12.95	26

1995 Collectible Series - Keepsake

YEAR	ISSUE	EDITION LIMIT	YEAR RETD.	ISSUE PRICE	*QUOTE U.S.$
1995	1956 Ford Truck-(1st Ed.) QX5527	Yr.Iss.		13.95	33
1995	1969 Chevrolet Camaro -(5th Ed.) QX5239	Yr.Iss.		12.95	27
1995	Bright 'n' Sunny Tepee (7th Ed.) QX5247	Yr.Iss.		10.95	11
1995	Camellia - Mary's Angels (8th Ed.) QX5149	Yr.Iss.		6.95	15
1995	Cat Naps-(2nd Ed.) QX5097	Yr.Iss.		7.95	20
1995	A Celebration of Angels -(1st Ed.) QX5077	Yr.Iss.		12.95	13
1995	Christmas Eve Kiss (10th Ed.) QX5157	Yr.Iss.		14.95	25
1995	Fabulous Decade (6th Ed.) QX5147	Yr.Iss.		7.95	18
1995	Frosty Friends (16th Ed.) QX5169	Yr.Iss.		10.95	20-28
1995	Jack and Jill-(3rd Ed.) QX5099	Yr.Iss.		13.95	14
1995	Lou Gehrig -(2nd Ed.) QX5029	Yr.Iss.		12.95	13
1995	Merry Olde Santa (6th Ed.) QX5139	Yr.Iss.		14.95	30
1995	Murrayr Fire Truck -(2nd Ed.) QX5027	Yr.Iss.		13.95	25
1995	The PEANUTS® Gang -(3rd Ed.) QX5059	Yr.Iss.		9.95	20
1995	Puppy Love -(5th Ed.) QX5137	Yr.Iss.		7.95	18
1995	Rocking Horse -(15th Ed.) QX5167	Yr.Iss.		10.95	29-55
1995	Santa's Roadster -(17th Ed.) QX5179	Yr.Iss.		14.95	15

*Quotes have been rounded up to nearest dollar

CHRISTMAS ORNAMENTS

YEAR ISSUE		EDITION LIMIT	YEAR RETD.	ISSUE PRICE	*QUOTE U.S.$
1995	St. Nicholas -(1st Ed.) QX5087	Yr.Iss.		14.95	15
1995	Tobin Fraley Carousel (4th Ed.) QX5069	Yr.Iss.		28.00	50
1995	Town Church -(12th Ed.) QX5159	Yr.Iss.		14.95	30
1995	Twelve Drummers Drumming -(12th Ed.) QX3009	Yr.Iss.		6.95	17
1995	U.S. Christmas Stamps (3rd Ed.) QX5067	Yr.Iss.		10.95	23
1995	Yuletide Central-(2nd Ed.) QX5079	Yr.Iss.		18.95	35

1995 Commemoratives - Keepsake

1995	Across the Miles QX5847	Yr.Iss.		8.95	9
1995	Air Express QX5977	Yr.Iss.		7.95	8
1995	Anniversary Year QX5819	Yr.Iss.		8.95	9
1995	Baby's First Christmas QX5547	Yr.Iss.		18.95	37
1995	Baby's First Christmas QX5549	Yr.Iss.		7.95	18
1995	Baby's First Christmas QX5557	Yr.Iss.		9.95	10
1995	Baby's First Christmas QX5559	Yr.Iss.		7.95	8
1995	Baby's First Christmas-Baby Boy QX2319	Yr.Iss.		5.00	5
1995	Baby's First Christmas-Baby Girl QX2317	Yr.Iss.		5.00	5
1995	Baby's Second Christmas QX5567	Yr.Iss.		7.95	15
1995	Brother QX5679	Yr.Iss.		6.95	7
1995	Child's Fifth Christmas QX5637	Yr.Iss.		6.95	7
1995	Child's Fourth Christmas QX5629	Yr.Iss.		6.95	7
1995	Child's Third Christmas QX5627	Yr.Iss.		7.95	8
1995	Christmas Fever QX5967	Yr.Iss.		7.95	8
1995	Christmas Patrol QX5959	Yr.Iss.		7.95	8
1995	Dad QX5649	Yr.Iss.		7.95	8
1995	Dad-to-Be QX5667	Yr.Iss.		7.95	8
1995	Daughter QX5677	Yr.Iss.		6.95	7
1995	For My Grandma QX5729	Yr.Iss.		6.95	7
1995	Friendly Boost QX5827	Yr.Iss.		8.95	9
1995	Godchild QX5707	Yr.Iss.		7.95	8
1995	Godparent QX2417	Yr.Iss.		5.00	5
1995	Grandchild's First Christmas QX5777	Yr.Iss.		7.95	8
1995	Granddaughter QX5779	Yr.Iss.		6.95	7
1995	Grandmother QX5767	Yr.Iss.		7.95	8
1995	Grandpa QX5769	Yr.Iss.		8.95	9
1995	Grandparents QX2419	Yr.Iss.		5.00	5
1995	Grandson QX5787	Yr.Iss.		6.95	7
1995	Important Memo QX5947	Yr.Iss.		8.95	9
1995	In a Heartbeat QX5817	Yr.Iss.		8.95	9
1995	Mom and Dad QX5657	Yr.Iss.		9.95	10
1995	Mom QX5647	Yr.Iss.		7.95	8
1995	Mom-to-Be QX5659	Yr.Iss.		7.95	8
1995	New Home QX5839	Yr.Iss.		8.95	9
1995	North Pole 911 QX5957	Yr.Iss.		10.95	11
1995	Number One Teacher QX5949	Yr.Iss.		7.95	8
1995	Our Christmas Together QX5809	Yr.Iss.		9.95	10
1995	Our Family QX5709	Yr.Iss.		7.95	8
1995	Our First Christmas Together QX3177	Yr.Iss.		6.95	7
1995	Our First Christmas Together QX5797	Yr.Iss.		16.95	17
1995	Our First Christmas Together QX5799	Yr.Iss.		8.95	9
1995	Our First Christmas Together QX5807	Yr.Iss.		8.95	9
1995	Packed With Memories QX5639	Yr.Iss.		7.95	8
1995	Sister QX5687	Yr.Iss.		6.95	7
1995	Sister to Sister QX5689	Yr.Iss.		8.95	9
1995	Son QX5669	Yr.Iss.		6.95	7
1995	Special Cat QX5717	Yr.Iss.		7.95	8
1995	Special Dog QX5719	Yr.Iss.		7.95	8
1995	Two for Tea QX5829	Yr.Iss.		9.95	10

1995 Easter Ornaments - Keepsake

1995	3 Flowerpot Friends 1495QEO8229	Yr.Iss.		14.95	25
1995	Baby's First Easter QEO8237	Yr.Iss.		7.95	16
1995	Bugs Bunny (Looney Tunes) QEO8279	Yr.Iss.		8.95	17
1995	Bunny w/Crayons (Crayola) QEO8249	Yr.Iss.		7.95	19-26
1995	Bunny w/Seed Packets (Tender Touches) QEO8259	Yr.Iss.		8.95	20
1995	Bunny w/Water Bucket QEO8253	Yr.Iss.		6.95	14
1995	Collector's Plate-(2nd Ed.) QEO8217	Yr.Iss.		7.95	15
1995	Daughter Duck QEO8239	Yr.Iss.		5.95	14
1995	Easter Beagle (Peanuts) QEO8257	Yr.Iss.		7.95	20-25
1995	Easter Egg Cottages-(1st Ed.) QEO8207	Yr.Iss.		8.95	20
1995	Garden Club-(1st Ed.) QEO8209	Yr.Iss.		7.95	19
1995	Ham n Eggs QEO8277	Yr.Iss.		7.95	16
1995	Here Comes Easter-(2nd Ed.) QEO8217	Yr.Iss.		7.95	20-25
1995	Lily (Religious) QEO8267	Yr.Iss.		6.95	12
1995	Miniature Train QEO8269	Yr.Iss.		4.95	13
1995	Son Duck QEO8247	Yr.Iss.		5.95	16
1995	Springtime Barbie-(1st Ed.) QEO8069	Yr.Iss.		12.95	25-37
1995	Springtime Bonnets-(3rd Ed.) QEO8227	Yr.Iss.		7.95	15-20

1995 Keepsake Collector's Club - Keepsake

1995	1958 Ford Edsel Citation Convertible QXC4167	Yr.Iss.		12.95	13
1995	Brunette Debut-1959 QXC5397	Yr.Iss.		14.95	15
1995	Christmas Eve Bake-Off QXC4049	Yr.Iss.		55.00	110-170
1995	Cinderella's Stepsisters QXC4159	Yr.Iss.		3.75	4
1995	Collecting Memories QXC4117	Yr.Iss.		12.00	12
1995	Cool Santa QXC4457	Yr.Iss.		5.75	6
1995	Cozy Christmas QXC4119	Yr.Iss.		8.50	9
1995	Fishing for Fun QXC5207	Yr.Iss.		10.95	17
1995	A Gift From Rodney QXC4129	Yr.Iss.		5.00	5
1995	Home From the Woods QXC1059	Yr.Iss.		15.95	16
1995	May Flower QXC8246	Yr.Iss.		4.95	25

1995 Keepsake Magic Ornaments - Keepsake

1995	Baby's First Christmas QLX7317	Yr.Iss.		22.00	45
1995	Chris Mouse Tree (11th Ed.) QLX7307	Yr.Iss.		12.50	30
1995	Coming to See Santa QLX7369	Yr.Iss.		32.00	50-65
1995	Forest Frolics (7th Ed.) QLX7299	Yr.Iss.		28.00	55
1995	Fred and Dino QLX7289	Yr.Iss.		28.00	55
1995	Friends Share Fun QLX7349	Yr.Iss.		16.50	35
1995	Goody Gumballs! QLX7367	Yr.Iss.		12.50	30
1995	Headin' Home QLX7327	Yr.Iss.		22.00	45
1995	Holiday Swim QLX7319	Yr.Iss.		18.50	35
1995	Jukebox Party QLX7339	Yr.Iss.		24.50	25
1995	Jumping for Joy QLX7347	Yr.Iss.		28.00	55
1995	My First HOT WHEELS™ QLX7279	Yr.Iss.		28.00	55
1995	PEANUTS®- (5th Ed.) QLX7277	Yr.Iss.		24.50	45
1995	Santa's Diner QLX7337	Yr.Iss.		24.50	45
1995	Space Shuttle QLX7396	Yr.Iss.		24.50	45
1995	Superman™ QLX7309	Yr.Iss.		28.00	52
1995	Tobin Fraley Holiday Carousel -(2nd Ed.) QLX7269	Yr.Iss.		32.00	60
1995	Victorian Toy Box -Special Ed. QLX7357	Yr.Iss.		42.00	80
1995	Wee Little Christmas QLX7329	Yr.Iss.		22.00	40
1995	Winnie the Pooh Too Much Hunny QLX7297	Yr.Iss.		24.50	45

1995 Miniature Ornaments - Keepsake

1995	Alice in Wonderland- (1st Ed.) QXM4777	Yr.Iss.		6.75	15
1995	Baby's First Christmas QXM4027	Yr.Iss.		4.75	14
1995	Calamity Coyote QXM4467	Yr.Iss.		6.75	15
1995	Centuries of Santa- (2nd Ed.) QXM4789	Yr.Iss.		5.75	14
1995	Christmas Bells- (1st Ed.) QXM4007	Yr.Iss.		4.75	15
1995	Christmas Wishes QXM4087	Yr.Iss.		3.75	13
1995	Cloisonne Partridge QXM4017	Yr.Iss.		9.75	19
1995	Downhill Double QXM4837	Yr.Iss.		4.75	13
1995	Friendship Duet QXM4019	Yr.Iss.		4.75	13
1995	Furrball QXM4459	Yr.Iss.		5.75	15
1995	Grandpa's Gift QXM4829	Yr.Iss.		5.75	13
1995	Heavenly Praises QXM4037	Yr.Iss.		5.75	13
1995	Joyful Santa QXM4089	Yr.Iss.		4.75	13
1995	Little Beeper QXM4469	Yr.Iss.		5.75	15
1995	March of the Teddy Bears -(3rd Ed.) QXM4799	Yr.Iss.		4.75	13
1995	Merry Walruses QXM4057	Yr.Iss.		5.75	14
1995	Milk Tank Car -(7th Ed.) QXM4817	Yr.Iss.		6.75	15
1995	Miniature Clothespin Soldier -(1st Ed.) QXM4097	Yr.Iss.		3.75	13
1995	A Moustershire Christmas QXM4839	Yr.Iss.		24.50	48
1995	Murray® "Champion" -(1st Ed.) QXM4079	Yr.Iss.		5.75	15
1995	Nature's Angels (6th Ed.) QXM4809	Yr.Iss.		4.75	14
1995	The Night Before Christmas- (4th Ed.) QXM4807	Yr.Iss.		4.75	12-18
1995	Nutcracker Guild -(2nd Ed.) QXM4787	Yr.Iss.		5.75	15
1995	On the Road -(3rd Ed.) QXM4797	Yr.Iss.		5.75	14
1995	Pebbles and Bamm-Bamm QXM4757	Yr.Iss.		9.75	19
1995	Playful Penguins QXM4059	Yr.Iss.		5.75	12-20
1995	Precious Creations QXM4077	Yr.Iss.		9.75	19
1995	Rocking Horse -(8th Ed.) QXM4827	Yr.Iss.		4.75	13
1995	Santa's Little Big Top- (1st Ed.) QXM4779	Yr.Iss.		6.75	15
1995	Santa's Visit QXM4047	Yr.Iss.		7.75	17
1995	Starlit Nativity QXM4039	Yr.Iss.		7.75	19
1995	Sugarplum Dreams QXM4099	Yr.Iss.		4.75	11
1995	Tiny Treasures (set of 6) QXM4009	Yr.Iss.		29.00	48
1995	Tudor House- (8th Ed.) QXM4819	Yr.Iss.		6.75	15
1995	Tunnel of Love QXM4029	Yr.Iss.		4.75	12

1995 New Attractions - Keepsake

1995	Acorn 500 QX5929	Yr.Iss.		10.95	11
1995	Batmobile QX5739	Yr.Iss.		14.95	30
1995	Betty and Wilma QX5417	Yr.Iss.		14.95	30
1995	Bingo Bear QX5919	Yr.Iss.		7.95	8
1995	Bobbin' Along QX5879	Yr.Iss.		8.95	9
1995	Bugs Bunny QX5019	Yr.Iss.		8.95	18
1995	Catch the Spirit QX5899	Yr.Iss.		7.95	8
1995	Christmas Morning QX5997	Yr.Iss.		10.95	11
1995	Colorful World QX5519	Yr.Iss.		10.95	11
1995	Cows of Bali QX5999	Yr.Iss.		8.95	9
1995	Delivering Kisses QX4107	Yr.Iss.		10.95	11
1995	Dream On QX6007	Yr.Iss.		10.95	11
1995	Dudley the Dragon QX6209	Yr.Iss.		10.95	11
1995	Faithful Fan QX5897	Yr.Iss.		8.95	9
1995	Feliz Navidad QX5869	Yr.Iss.		7.95	8
1995	Forever Friends Bear QX5258	Yr.Iss.		8.95	9
1995	GARFIELD QX5007	Yr.Iss.		10.95	25
1995	Glinda, Witch of the North QX5749	Yr.Iss.		13.95	30
1995	Gopher Fun QX5887	Yr.Iss.		9.95	10
1995	Happy Wrappers QX6037	Yr.Iss.		10.95	11
1995	Heaven's Gift QX6057	Yr.Iss.		20.00	20
1995	Hockey Pup QX5917	Yr.Iss.		9.95	10
1995	In Time With Christmas QX6049	Yr.Iss.		12.95	13
1995	Joy to the World QX5867	Yr.Iss.		8.95	9
1995	LEGO® Fireplace With Santa QX4769	Yr.Iss.		10.95	25
1995	Lou Rankin Bear QX4069	Yr.Iss.		9.95	20
1995	The Magic School Bus™ QX5849	Yr.Iss.		10.95	11
1995	Mary Engelbreit QX2409	Yr.Iss.		5.00	5
1995	Merry RV QX6027	Yr.Iss.		12.95	13
1995	Muletide Greetings QX6009	Yr.Iss.		7.95	8
1995	The Olympic Spirit QX3169	Yr.Iss.		7.95	8
1995	On the Ice QX6047	Yr.Iss.		7.95	8
1995	Perfect Balance QX5927	Yr.Iss.		7.95	8
1995	PEZ® Santa QX5267	Yr.Iss.		7.95	16
1995	Polar Coaster QX6117	Yr.Iss.		8.95	9
1995	Popeyer QX5257	Yr.Iss.		10.95	23
1995	Refreshing Gift QX4067	Yr.Iss.		14.95	15
1995	Rejoice! QX5987	Yr.Iss.		10.95	11
1995	Roller Whiz QX5937	Yr.Iss.		7.95	8
1995	Santa in Paris QX5877	Yr.Iss.		8.95	9
1995	Santa's Serenade QX6017	Yr.Iss.		8.95	9
1995	Santa's Visitors QX2407	Yr.Iss.		5.00	5
1995	Simba, Pumbaa and Timon QX6159	Yr.Iss.		12.95	27
1995	Ski Hound QX5909	Yr.Iss.		8.95	9
1995	Surfin' Santa QX6019	Yr.Iss.		9.95	21-30
1995	Sylvester and Tweety QX5017	Yr.Iss.		13.95	14
1995	Takin' a Hike QX6029	Yr.Iss.		7.95	8
1995	Tennis, Anyone? QX5907	Yr.Iss.		7.95	8
1995	Thomas the Tank Engine-No. 1 QX5857	Yr.Iss.		9.95	22
1995	Three Wishes QX5979	Yr.Iss.		7.95	8
1995	Vera the Mouse QX5537	Yr.Iss.		8.95	9
1995	Waiting Up for Santa QX6106	Yr.Iss.		8.95	9
1995	Water Sports QX6039	Yr.Iss.		14.95	15
1995	Wheel of Fortune® QX6187	Yr.Iss.		12.95	28
1995	Winnie the Pooh and Tigger QX5009	Yr.Iss.		12.95	25-30
1995	The Winning Play QX5889	Yr.Iss.		7.95	8

1995 Premiere Event - Keepsake

1995	Wish List QX5859	Yr.Iss.		15.00	15

1995 Showcase All Is Bright Collection - Keepsake

1995	Angel of Light QK1159	Yr.Iss.		11.95	25
1995	Gentle Lullaby QK1157	Yr.Iss.		11.95	25

1995 Showcase Angel Bells Collection - Keepsake

1995	Carole QK1147	Yr.Iss.		12.95	30
1995	Joy QK1137	Yr.Iss.		12.95	27
1995	Noelle QK1139	Yr.Iss.		12.95	27

1995 Showcase Folk Art Americana Collection - Keepsake

1995	Fetching the Firewood QK1057	Yr.Iss.		15.95	35
1995	Fishing Party QK1039	Yr.Iss.		15.95	35
1995	Guiding Santa QK1037	Yr.Iss.		18.95	45
1995	Learning to Skate QK1047	Yr.Iss.		14.95	37

1995 Showcase Holiday Enchantment Collection - Keepsake

1995	Away in a Manger QK1097	Yr.Iss.		13.95	30
1995	Following the Star QK1099	Yr.Iss.		13.95	30

1995 Showcase Invitation to Tea Collection - Keepsake

1995	Cozy Cottage Teapot QK1127	Yr.Iss.		15.95	30
1995	European Castle Teapot QK1129	Yr.Iss.		15.95	30
1995	Victorian Home Teapot QK1119	Yr.Iss.		15.95	30

1995 Showcase Nature's Sketchbook Collection - Keepsake

1995	Backyard Orchard QK1069	Yr.Iss.		18.95	40
1995	Christmas Cardinal QK1077	Yr.Iss.		18.95	50
1995	Raising a Family QK1067	Yr.Iss.		18.95	40
1995	Violets and Butterflies QK1079	Yr.Iss.		16.95	40

1995 Showcase Symbols of Christmas Collection - Keepsake

1995	Jolly Santa QK1087	Yr.Iss.		15.95	35
1995	Sweet Song QK1089	Yr.Iss.		15.95	32

1995 Showcase Turn-of-the-Century Parade - Keepsake

1995	The Fireman QK1027	Yr.Iss.		16.95	40

1995 Special Edition - Keepsake

1995	Beverly and Teddy QX5259	Yr.Iss.		21.75	43

1995 Special Issues - Keepsake

1995	Captain Jean-Luc Picard QXI5737	Yr.Iss.		13.95	29
1995	Captain James T. Kirk QXI5539	Yr.Iss.		13.95	29

*Quotes have been rounded up to nearest dollar

CHRISTMAS ORNAMENTS

YEAR ISSUE		EDITION LIMIT	YEAR RETD.	ISSUE PRICE	*QUOTE U.S.$
1995	Captain John Smith and Meeko QXI6169	Yr.Iss.		12.95	25
1995	Holiday Barbie™ -(3rd Ed.) QXI5057	Yr.Iss.		14.95	25-45
1995	Hoop Stars -(1st Ed.) QXI5517	Yr.Iss.		14.95	50
1995	Joe Montana -(1st Ed.) QXI5759	Yr.Iss.		14.95	25-50
1995	Percy, Flit and Meeko QXI6179	Yr.Iss.		9.95	20
1995	Pocahontas and Captain John Smith QXI6197	Yr.Iss.		14.95	30
1995	Pocahontas QXI6177	Yr.Iss.		12.95	25
1995	Romulan Warbird™ QXI7267	Yr.Iss.		24.00	30-40
1995	The Ships of Star Trek®QXI4109	Yr.Iss.		19.95	21-35
1995	Solo in the Spotlight-Barbie™ -(2nd Ed.) QXI5049	Yr.Iss.		14.95	32-45

1995 Special Offer - Keepsake

1995	Charlie Brown QRP4207	Yr.Iss.		3.95	23
1995	Linus QRP4217	Yr.Iss.		3.95	8-15
1995	Lucy QRP4209	Yr.Iss.		3.95	8-15
1995	SNOOPY QRP4219	Yr.Iss.		3.95	20
1995	Snow Scene QRP4227	Yr.Iss.		3.95	5-15
1995	5-Pc. Set	Yr.Iss.		19.95	50-75

Hamilton Collection

Christmas Angels - S. Kuck

1994	Angel of Charity	Open		19.50	20
1995	Angel of Joy	Open		19.50	20
1995	Angel of Grace	Open		19.50	20
1995	Angel of Faith	Open		19.50	20
1995	Angel of Patience	Open		19.50	20
1995	Angel of Glory	Open		19.50	20
1996	Angel of Gladness	Open		19.50	20
1996	Angel of Innocence	Open		19.50	20
1996	Angel of Beauty	Open		19.50	20
1996	Angel of Purity	Open		19.50	20
1996	Angel of Charm	Open		19.50	20
1996	Angel of Kindness	Open		19.50	20

Derek Darlings - N/A

1995	Jessica, Sara, Chelsea (set)	Open		29.85	30

Hand & Hammer

Annual Ornaments - De Matteo

1987	Silver Bells 737	2,700	1987	38.00	66
1988	Silver Bells 792	3,150	1988	39.50	60
1989	Silver Bells 843	3,150	1989	39.50	63
1990	Silver Bells 865	3,615	1990	39.00	50
1990	Silver Bells Rev. 964	4,490	1990	39.00	40
1991	Silver Bells 1080	4,100	1991	39.50	40
1992	Silver Bells 1148	4,100	1992	39.50	40
1993	Silver Bells 1311	Retrd.	1993	39.50	40
1994	Silver Bells 1463	Retrd.	1994	39.50	40
1995	Silver Bells 1597	Retrd.	1995	39.50	40
1996	Silver Bells 1795	Yr.Iss.		39.50	40

Hand & Hammer Ornaments - De Matteo

1985	Abigail 613	Suspd.		32.00	50
1991	Alice 1119	Open		39.00	39
1991	Alice in Wonderland 1159	Open		140.00	140
1992	America At Peace 1245	2,000		85.00	100
1992	Andrea 1163	Retrd.	1994	36.00	40
1992	Angel 1213	2,000		39.00	50
1993	Angel 1342	Suspd.		38.00	38
1993	Angel 1993 1405	Suspd.		45.00	50
1985	Angel 607	225	1989	36.00	50
1985	Angel 612	217	1989	32.00	75
1988	Angel 797 (sp)	Unkn.		13.00	13
1988	Angel 818	Suspd.		32.00	45
1993	Angel Bell 1312	Retrd.	1994	38.00	40
1992	Angel with Double Horn 1212	2,000		39.00	50
1991	Angel with Horn 1026	Open		32.00	40
1987	Angel with Lyre 750	Retrd.	1991	32.00	44
1994	Angel with Star 1480	Open		38.00	40
1990	Angel with Star 871	Suspd.		38.00	38
1990	Angel with Violin 1024	Suspd.		39.00	60
1990	Angels 1039	Retrd.	1992	36.00	47
1991	Appley Dapply 1091	Open		39.50	40
1986	Archangel 684	Retrd.	1990	29.00	60
1987	Art Deco Angel 765	Retrd.	1992	38.00	56
1985	Art Deco Deer 620	Suspd.		34.00	55
1985	Audubon Bluebird 615	Suspd.		48.00	125
1985	Audubon Swallow 614	Suspd.		48.00	125
1995	Augusta Golf 1653	Open		39.00	39
1988	Bank 812	400	1989	40.00	100
1989	Barnesville Buggy 1989 950 (sp)	Unkn.		13.00	13
1993	Beantown 1344	Suspd.		38.00	50
1986	Bear Claus 692 (sp)	Unkn.		13.00	13
1990	Beardsley Angel 1040	Retrd.	1991	34.00	70
1984	Beardsley Angel 398	Open		28.00	48
1994	Beatrix Potter Noel 1438	Open		39.50	40
1985	Bicycle 669 (sp)	Unkn.		13.00	30
1984	Bird & Cherub 588 (sp)	Unkn.		13.00	30
1995	Bird Swirl 1502	Open		39.00	39
1990	Blake Angel 961	Suspd.		36.00	40
1992	Bob & Tiny Tim 1242	Open		36.00	40
1990	The Boston Light 1032	Suspd.		39.50	50
1988	Boston State House 819	Open		34.00	40
1987	Buffalo 777	Suspd.		36.00	48
1988	Buggy 817 (sp)	Unkn.		13.00	13
1989	Bugle Bear 935 (sp)	Unkn.		12.00	12
1996	Bugs Bunny 1797	2,500		39.50	40
1984	Bunny 582 (sp)	Unkn.		13.00	30
1985	Butterfly 646	Suspd.		39.00	56
1988	Cable Car 848	Suspd.		38.00	75
1993	Cable Car to the Stars 1363	Suspd.		39.00	50
1983	Calligraphic Deer 511	Suspd.		25.00	38
1985	Camel 655 (sp)	Unkn.		13.00	30
1994	Canterbury Star 1441	Suspd.		35.00	35
1994	Cardinal & Holly 1445	Open		38.00	40
1990	Cardinals 870	Retrd.	1994	39.00	40
1990	Carousel Horse 866	1,915	1992	38.00	40
1991	Carousel Horse 1025	Retrd.	1993	38.00	40
1993	Carousel Horse 1993 1321	Retrd.	1993	38.00	40
1989	Carousel Horse 811	2,150	1990	34.00	43
1985	Carousel Pony 618 (sp)	Unkn.		13.00	13
1990	Carriage 960 (sp)	Unkn.		13.00	13
1982	Carved Heart 425	Suspd.		29.00	70
1995	Cat & Fiddle 1658	Open		39.00	39
1987	Cat 754	Suspd.		37.00	37
1990	Cat on Pillow 915 (sp)	Unkn.		13.00	13
1993	Celebrate America 1352	Retrd.	1994	38.00	38
1993	Cheer Mouse 1359	Retrd.	1994	39.00	39
1983	Cherub 528	295	1987	29.00	56
1985	Cherub 642	815	1989	37.00	60
1992	Chocolate Pot 1208	Retrd.	1994	49.50	75
1990	Christmas Seal 931	Unkn.		25.00	25
1986	Christmas Tree 708 (sp)	Unkn.		13.00	13
1988	Christmas Tree 798 (sp)	Unkn.		13.00	13
1990	Church 921	Retrd.	1994	37.00	40
1993	Clara with Nutcracker 1316	Suspd.		38.00	50
1987	Clipper Ship 756	Suspd.		35.00	55
1990	Clown w/Dog 958 (sp)	Unkn.		13.00	13
1990	Cockatoo 969 (sp)	Unkn.		13.00	13
1990	Colonial Capitol 965	Suspd.		39.00	75
1991	Columbus 1140	1,500	1993	39.00	50
1990	Conestoga Wagon 1027	Suspd.		38.00	45
1988	Conn. State House 833	Open		38.00	38
1988	Coronado 864	Suspd.		38.00	75
1990	Covered Bridge 920	Retrd.	1994	37.00	40
1995	Cow & Moon 1660	Open		39.00	39
1991	Cow Jumped Over The Moon 1055	Suspd.		38.00	38
1992	Cowardly Lion 1287	Retrd.	1993	36.00	50
1985	Crane 606	Suspd.		38.00	65
1993	Creche 1351	Open		38.00	40
1984	Crescent Angel 559	Suspd.		30.00	60
1995	Cross 1622	Open		39.00	40
1990	Currier & Ives Set -Victorian Village 923	2,000	1994	140.00	160
1995	Degas Dancer 1650	Open		39.00	39
1992	Della Robbia Ornament 1219	Retrd.	1994	39.00	44
1992	Dorothy 1284	Retrd.	1993	36.00	50
1983	Dove 522 (sp)	Unkn.		13.00	13
1987	Dove 747 (sp)	Unkn.		13.00	13
1988	Dove 786	112	1991	36.00	60
1988	Drummer Bear 773 (sp)	Unkn.		13.00	13
1990	Ducklings 1114	Suspd.		38.00	50
1985	Eagle 652	375	1989	30.00	125
1983	Egyptian Cat 521 (sp)	Unkn.		13.00	13
1988	Eiffel Tower 861	225	1989	38.00	100
1990	Elk 1023 (sp)	Unkn.		13.00	13
1990	Ember 1124	120		N/A	350
1994	Emperor 1439	Retrd.	1995	38.00	50
1994	Esplanade 1523	Open		39.00	39
1995	Esplanade 1667	Open		39.00	39
1995	Faberge Egg 1618	Open		39.00	40
1996	Faberge Egg 1725	Yr.Iss.		39.50	40
1992	Fairy-Tale Angel 1222	Open		36.00	36
1985	Family 659	915	1989	32.00	53
1993	Faneuil Hall 1399	Suspd.		39.00	50
1993	Faneuil Hall 1412	Open		39.50	40
1990	Farmhouse 919	Retrd.	1994	37.00	40
1995	Father Christmas 1715	Open		39.00	39
1990	Father Christmas 970	Open		36.00	40
1990	Ferrel's Angel 1990 1084 (sp)	Unkn.		15.00	15
1991	Fir Tree 1145	Retrd.	1995	39.00	50
1983	Fire Angel 473	315	1985	25.00	53
1990	First Baptist Angel 997	200	1992	35.00	75
1987	First Christmas 771 (sp)	Unkn.		13.00	13
1989	First Christmas 842 (sp)	Unkn.		13.00	13
1990	First Christmas Bear 940	Suspd.		35.00	40
1982	Fleur de Lys Angel 343	320	1985	28.00	75
1990	Flopsy Bunnies 995	Suspd.		39.50	40
1990	Florida State Capitol 1044	2,000		39.50	40
1996	Four Calling Birds 1789	Open		39.50	40
1984	Freer Star 553 (sp)	Unkn.		13.00	30
1985	French Quarter Heart 647	Open		37.00	38
1981	Gabriel 320	Suspd.		25.00	60
1981	Gabriel with Liberty Cap 301	275	1986	25.00	60
1985	George Washington 629	Suspd.		35.00	50
1990	Georgia State Capitol 1042	2,000		39.50	40
1994	Golden Gate Bridge 1429	Suspd.		39.50	50
1990	Goose & Wreath 868	Retrd.	1993	37.00	40
1989	Goose 857	650	1993	37.00	55
1990	Governor's Palace 966	Suspd.		39.00	75
1985	Grasshopper 634	Suspd.		32.00	50
1985	Guardian Angel 616	Suspd.		35.00	48
1993	Gurgling Cod 1397	Open		50.00	50
1991	Gus 1195	200		N/A	150
1986	Hallelujah 686	Suspd.		38.00	56
1985	Halley's Comet 621	432	1990	35.00	75
1995	Hart 1501	Open		38.00	38
1990	Heart Angel 959	Suspd.		39.00	39
1992	Heart of Christmas 1301	500		39.00	60
1994	Heart of Christmas 1440	500		39.00	50
1994	Heart of Christmas 1537	500		39.00	39-50
1995	Heart of Christmas 1682	Yr.Iss.		39.00	39
1996	Heavenly Music 1791	Open		39.50	40
1985	Herald Angel 641	Retrd.	1989	36.00	60
1994	Heralding Angel 1481	Open		39.00	40
1994	Holly 1472	Open		38.00	40
1985	Hosanna 635	715	1988	32.00	64
1995	Hummingbird 1631	Open		39.00	40
1987	Hunting Horn 738	Suspd.		37.00	40
1991	I Love Santa 998	Open		36.00	40
1984	Ibex 584	400	1988	29.00	75
1980	Icicle 009	490	1985	25.00	60
1989	Independence Hall 908	Suspd.		38.00	45
1983	Indian 494	190	1985	29.00	58
1988	Jack in the Box 789	Retrd.	1991	39.50	60
1989	Jack in the Box Bear 936 (sp)	Unkn.		12.00	12
1983	Japanese Snowflake 534	350	1989	29.00	60
1994	Jefferson Hotel 1594	Open		39.00	39
1990	Jemima Puddleduck 1020	Unkn.		30.00	30
1992	Jemima Puddleduck 1992 1167	Retrd.	1992	39.50	40
1990	Jeremy Fisher 992	Open		39.50	40
1990	Joy 1047	Retrd.	1992	39.00	55
1992	Joy 1164	Open		39.50	40
1990	Joy 867	1,140	1993	36.00	40
1995	Kate Greenaway Joy 1651	Open		39.00	39
1995	Kate Greenaway Noel 1515	Open		39.00	39
1995	Kermit Joy 1596	Open		36.00	40
1990	Koala San Diego Zoo 1095	Suspd.		36.00	40
1986	Kringle Bear 723 (sp)	Unkn.		13.00	30
1995	L&T Santa 1700	Yr.Iss.		39.00	39
1989	L&T Ugly Duckling 917	Retrd.	1995	38.00	75
1985	Lafarge Angel 658	Suspd.		32.00	45
1986	Lafarge Angel 710	Suspd.		31.00	45
1990	Landing Duck 1021 (sp)	Unkn.		13.00	13
1991	Large Jemima Puddleduck 1083	Open		49.50	50
1991	Large Peter Rabbit 1116	Open		49.50	50
1991	Large Tailor of Gloucester 1117	Open		49.50	50
1990	Liberty Bell 1028	Suspd.		38.00	45
1985	Liberty Bell 611	Suspd.		32.00	50
1993	Lion and Lamb 1322	Open		38.00	40
1989	Locket Bear 844	Unkn.		25.00	25
1990	Locomotive 1100	Suspd.		39.00	50
1994	Loudoun County C.H. 1611	Open		39.00	39
1994	Lyre 1505	Open		39.00	39
1991	Mad Tea Party 1120	Open		39.00	39
1982	Madonna & Child 388	175	1985	28.00	75
1996	Madonna 1790	Open		39.50	40
1985	Madonna 666	227	1990	35.00	75
1988	Madonna 787	600	1992	35.00	60
1988	Madonna 809	Suspd.		39.00	50
1988	Madonna 815	Suspd.		39.00	75
1988	Magi 788	Suspd.		39.50	50
1994	Mandoline 1506	Open		39.00	39
1984	Manger 601	Retrd.	1988	29.00	48
1994	Marengo 1482	Open		39.00	39
1992	Marley's Ghost 1243	Open		36.00	40
1994	Marmion Angels 1443	Suspd.		50.00	75
1994	Mass State House 1540	Open		39.00	39
1985	Mermaid 622	Retrd.	1995	35.00	75
1990	Merry Christmas Locket 948	Unkn.		25.00	25
1989	MFA Angel with Tree 906	Suspd.		36.00	55
1989	MFA Durer Snowflake 907	Suspd.		36.00	44
1989	MFA LaFarge Angel set 937	Suspd.		98.00	110
1989	MFA Noel 905	Suspd.		36.00	44
1992	MFA Snowflake 1246	Retrd.	1993	39.00	44
1991	MFA Snowflake 1991 1143	Retrd.	1991	36.00	44
1985	Militiaman 608	Suspd.		25.00	38
1990	Mill 922	Retrd.	1994	37.00	40
1987	Minuteman 776	Suspd.		35.00	100
1985	Model A Ford 604 (sp)	Unkn.		13.00	30
1990	Mole & Rat Wind in Will 944	Suspd.		36.00	36
1991	Mommy & Baby Kangaroo 1078	Retrd.	1993	36.00	36
1991	Mommy & Baby Koala Bear 1077	Retrd.	1993	36.00	36
1991	Mommy & Baby Panda Bear 1079	Retrd.	1993	36.00	40
1991	Mommy & Baby Seal 1075	Retrd.	1993	36.00	36
1991	Mommy & Baby Wolves 1076	Retrd.	1993	36.00	36
1990	Montpelier 1113	Suspd.		36.00	75
1984	Moravian Star 595	Suspd.		38.00	100
1986	Mother Goose 719	Open		34.00	40
1993	Mouse King 1398	Suspd.		38.00	50
1990	Mouse with Candy Cane 916 (sp)	Unkn.		13.00	13
1992	Mrs. Cratchit 1244	Open		36.00	40
1992	Mrs. Rabbit 1181	Open		39.50	40
1991	Mrs. Rabbit 1991 1086	Retrd.	1991	39.50	40
1993	Mrs. Rabbit 1993 1325	Retrd.	1993	39.50	40
1990	Mrs. Rabbit 991	Open		39.50	40
1984	Mt. Vernon Weathervane 602	Suspd.		32.00	50
1990	N. Carolina State Capitol 1043	2,000		39.50	40
1987	Naptime 732	Retrd.	1991	32.00	48
1991	Nativity 1118	Open		38.00	40
1986	Nativity 679	Retrd.	1991	36.00	55
1988	Nativity 821	Suspd.		32.00	75
1995	Night Before Christmas 1600	Open		160.00	160
1988	Night Before Xmas Col. 841	10,000		160.00	275
1986	Nightingale 716	Retrd.	1995	35.00	75

CHRISTMAS ORNAMENTS

YEAR ISSUE		EDITION LIMIT	YEAR RETD.	ISSUE PRICE	*QUOTE U.S.$
1984	Nine Hearts 572	275	1985	34.00	66
1992	Noah's Ark 1166	Open		36.00	40
1994	Noel 1477	Open		38.00	40
1987	Noel 731	Suspd.		38.00	40
1991	Nutcracker 1151	Open		49.50	50
1991	Nutcracker 1183	Open		38.00	38
1989	Nutcracker 1989 872	1,790	1990	38.00	75
1985	Nutcracker 609	510	1989	30.00	55
1986	Nutcracker 681	1,356	1988	37.00	61
1991	Nutrcracker Suite 1184	Suspd.		38.00	100
1990	Old Fashioned Santa 971	Suspd.		36.00	40
1987	Old Ironsides 767	Suspd.		35.00	45
1988	Old King Cole 824	Retrd.	1990	34.00	43
1985	Old North Church 661	Open		35.00	39
1991	Olivers Rocking Horse 1085	Retrd.	1993	37.00	40
1994	Palace of Fine Arts 1522	Open		39.50	40
1992	Parrot 1233	Open		37.00	37
1993	Partridge & Pear 1328	Open		38.00	40
1990	Patriotic Santa 972	Suspd.		36.00	40
1991	Paul Revere 1158	Open		39.00	39
1994	Paul Revere Lantern 1541	Open		39.00	39
1993	Peace 1327	Suspd.		36.00	36
1995	Peace on Earth 1503	Open		36.00	36
1994	Peachtree Swan 1612	Open		39.00	39
1985	Peacock 603	470	1989	34.00	65
1990	Pegasus 1037	Retrd.	1991	35.00	40
1987	Pegasus 745 (sp)	Unkn.		13.00	13
1995	Peter Rabbit & B Bunny 1492	Open		39.50	40
1993	Peter Rabbit 100th 1383	Retrd.	1993	39.50	45
1990	Peter Rabbit 1990 1018	4,315	1990	39.50	40
1994	Peter Rabbit 1994 1444	Retrd.	1994	39.50	40
1995	Peter Rabbit 1995 1598	Yr.Iss.		39.50	40
1996	Peter Rabbit 1996 1699	Yr.Iss.		39.50	40
1990	Peter Rabbit 993	Open		39.50	40
1990	Peter Rabbit Locket 1019	Unkn.		30.00	30
1991	Peter Rabbit with Book 1093	Open		39.50	40
1990	Peter's First Christmas 994	Suspd.		39.50	40
1986	Phaeton 683 (sp)	Unkn.		13.00	13
1985	Piazza 653	Suspd.		32.00	55
1991	Pig Robinson 1090	Open		39.50	40
1984	Pineapple 558	Suspd.		30.00	53
1995	Plate & Spoon 1659	Open		39.00	39
1983	Pollock Angel 502	Suspd.		35.00	75
1995	Pooh & Christopher Robin 1668	Open		39.00	39
1995	Pooh Hunny Pot 1663	Open		39.50	40
1995	Pooh with Balloon 1664	Open		39.50	40
1986	Prancer 698	Open		38.00	40
1984	Praying Angel 576	Suspd.		29.00	45
1991	Precious Planet 1142	2,000		120.00	200
1990	Presidential Homes 990	Suspd.		350.00	400
1989	Presidential Seal 858	Suspd.		39.00	150
1992	Princess & The Pea 1247	Retrd.	1995	39.00	50
1993	Public Garden 1370	Suspd.		38.00	50
1995	Public Garden Angel 1701	Open		39.00	39
1993	Puss In Boots 1396	Suspd.		40.00	44
1994	Quatrefoil 1542	Open		50.00	50
1991	Queen of Hearts 1122	Open		39.00	39
1994	R.E. Lee Monument 1446	Open		39.00	39
1988	Rabbit 816 (sp)	Unkn.		13.00	13
1985	Reindeer 656 (sp)	Unkn.		13.00	30
1987	Reindeer 752	Retrd.	1991	38.00	45
1992	Revere Teapot 1207	Retrd.	1994	49.50	75
1987	Ride a Cock Horse 757	Retrd.	1991	34.00	43
1984	Rocking Horse 581 (sp)	Unkn.		13.00	13
1996	Rose Window Collection 1751	Open		160.00	160
1984	Rosette 571	220	1988	32.00	65
1992	Round Teapot 1206	Retrd.	1994	49.50	55
1981	Roundel 109	220	1985	25.00	60
1990	S. Carolina State Capitol 1045	2,000		39.50	40
1986	Salem Lamb 712	Retrd.	1989	32.00	75
1985	Samantha 648	Suspd.		35.00	46
1991	San Francisco Heart 1196	Open		39.00	39
1995	San Francisco House 1685	Open		39.00	39
1990	San Francisco Row House 1071	Suspd.		39.50	50
1990	Santa & Reindeer 929	395	1991	39.00	50
1989	Santa 1989 856	1,715	1989	35.00	60
1990	Santa 1990 869	2,250	1990	38.00	42
1991	Santa 1991 1056	3,750	1992	38.00	40
1987	Santa 741 (sp)	Unkn.		13.00	13
1987	Santa and Sleigh 751	Retrd.	1989	32.00	100
1990	Santa in Balloon 973	Open		36.00	40
1990	Santa in the Moon 941	Suspd.		38.00	40
1990	Santa on Reindeer 974	Suspd.		36.00	100
1986	Santa Skates 715	Suspd.		36.00	45
1987	Santa Star 739	Retrd.	1991	32.00	48
1990	Santa UpTo Date 975	Suspd.		36.00	40
1988	Santa with Scroll 814	250	1991	34.00	44
1983	Sargent Angel 523	690	1987	29.00	56
1992	Scarecrow 1286	Retrd.	1993	36.00	50
1995	Schwarzschild Carillon 1738	Open		39.00	39
1992	Scrooge 1241	Open		36.00	40
1985	Shepherd 617	1,770	1990	35.00	60
1994	Shepherdstown House 1630	Open		39.00	39
1995	SI Angel 1691	Open		39.00	39
1995	SI Teddy Bear 1687	Open		39.00	39
1988	Skaters 790	Retrd.	1991	39.50	50
1994	Skaters in the Park 1617	Open		39.00	40
1995	Skating in the Park 1705	Open		39.00	39
1988	Sleigh 834	Open		34.00	40
1994	Smithsonian Angel 1534	Retrd.	1994	39.00	39
1987	Snow Queen 746	Retrd.	1995	35.00	75
1995	Snowflake 1574	Open		38.00	38
1990	Snowflake 1990 1033	1,415	1990	36.00	45
1993	Snowflake 1993 1394	Retrd.	1993	40.00	44
1994	Snowflake 1994 1486	Retrd.	1994	39.00	39
1995	Snowflake 1995 1652	Yr.Iss.		39.00	40
1986	Snowflake 713	Retrd.	1990	36.00	55
1994	Snowman 1572	Retrd.	1995	39.00	50
1987	Snowman 753	825	1991	38.00	56
1992	St. John Angel 1236	10,000		39.00	50
1992	St. John Lion 1235	10,000		39.00	50
1985	St. Nicholas 670 (sp)	Unkn.		13.00	30
1995	Star 1591	Open		40.00	40
1994	Star 1994 1462	Retrd.	1994	39.50	40
1996	Star 1996 1796	Open		39.50	40
1988	Star 806	311	1990	50.00	200
1988	Star 854	275	1990	32.00	75
1988	Star of the East 785	Retrd.	1992	35.00	48
1990	Steadfast Tin Soldier 1050	Retrd.	1995	36.00	75
1987	Stocking 772 (sp)	Unkn.		13.00	13
1988	Stocking 774 (sp)	Unkn.		13.00	13
1988	Stocking 827 (sp)	Unkn.		13.00	13
1989	Stocking Bear 835 (sp)	Unkn.		13.00	13
1989	Stocking Bear 955 (sp)	Unkn.		12.00	12
1989	Stocking with Toys 956 (sp)	Unkn.		12.00	12
1982	Straw Star 448	590	1986	25.00	50
1983	Sunburst 543	Unkn.		13.00	50
1989	Swan Boat 904	Suspd.		38.00	50
1987	Sweetheart Star 740	Retrd.	1991	39.50	58
1991	Tailor of Gloucester 1087	Open		39.50	40
1985	Teddy 637	Suspd.		37.00	47
1986	Teddy 707	Unkn.		13.00	30
1986	Teddy Bear 685	Retrd.	1991	38.00	58
1990	Teddy Bear Locket 949	Unkn.		25.00	25
1990	Teddy Bear with Heart 957 (sp)	Unkn.		13.00	13
1995	Three Angels 1683	Open		39.50	40
1995	Three French Hens 1621	Open		39.00	40
1988	Thumbelina 803	Retrd.	1995	35.00	75
1992	Tin Man 1285	Retrd.	1993	36.00	50
1990	Toad Wind in Willows 945	Suspd.		38.00	38
1994	Trumpet 1504	Open		39.00	39
1994	Two Turtle Doves 1478	Open		38.00	40
1992	Unicorn 1165	Retrd.	1994	36.00	36
1985	Unicorn 660	Retrd.	1990	37.00	55
1988	US Capitol 820	Open		38.00	40
1984	USHS 1984 Angel 574	Suspd.		35.00	75
1989	USHS Angel 1989 901	Suspd.		38.00	75
1990	USHS Angel 1990 1061	Suspd.		39.00	39
1991	USHS Angel 1991 1139	Suspd.		38.00	50
1995	USHS Angel 1995 1703	Yr.Iss.		39.00	39
1986	USHS Angel 703	Suspd.		35.00	75
1985	USHS Bluebird 631	Suspd.		29.00	38
1994	USHS Dove 1521	Open		39.00	39
1987	USHS Gloria Angel 748	Suspd.		39.00	75
1985	USHS Madonna 630	Suspd.		35.00	75
1985	USHS Swallow 632	Suspd.		29.00	38
1989	Victorian Heart 954 (sp)	Unkn.		13.00	13
1986	Victorian Santa 724	250	1988	32.00	45
1993	Violin 1340	Retrd.	1993	38.00	90
1991	The Voyages Of Columbus 1141	1,500	1993	39.00	50
1991	Waiting For Santa 1123	Retrd.	1993	38.00	38
1994	Weld Boathouse 1447	Open		39.00	39
1991	White Rabbit 1121	Open		39.00	39
1990	White Tail Deer 1022 (sp)	Unkn.		13.00	13
1984	Wild Swan 592	Retrd.	1995	35.00	75
1993	Window 1360	Retrd.	1994	38.00	38
1986	Winged Dove 680	Retrd.	1993	35.00	54
1983	Wise Man 549	Retrd.	1988	29.00	56
1984	Wreath 575 (sp)	Unkn.		13.00	30
1986	Wreath 714	Suspd.		36.00	38
1992	Xmas Tree & Heart 1162	Retrd.	1994	36.00	36
1993	Xmas Tree 1395	Suspd.		40.00	44
1993	Zig Zag Tree 1343	Suspd.		39.00	39

John Hine N.A. Ltd.

David Winter Ornaments - Various

YEAR ISSUE		EDITION LIMIT	YEAR RETD.	ISSUE PRICE	*QUOTE U.S.$
1991	Christmas Carol - D. Winter	Closed	1991	15.00	15
1991	Christmas in Scotland & Hogmanay - D. Winter	Closed	1991	15.00	15
1991	Mr. Fezziwig's Emporium - D. Winter	Closed	1991	15.00	15
1991	Ebenezer Scrooge's Counting House - D. Winter	Closed	1991	15.00	15
1992	Fairytale Castle - D. Winter	Closed	1992	15.00	15
1992	Fred's Home - D. Winter	Closed	1992	15.00	15
1992	Suffolk House - D. Winter	Closed	1992	15.00	15
1992	Tudor Manor - D. Winter	Closed	1992	15.00	15
1993	The Grange - J. Hine Studios	Closed	1993	15.00	15
1993	Scrooge's School - J. Hine Studios	Closed	1993	15.00	15
1993	Tomfool's Cottage - J. Hine Studios	Closed	1993	15.00	15
1993	Will-O The Wisp - J. Hine Studios	Closed	1993	15.00	15
1994	Old Joe's Beetling Shop - J. Hine Studios	Closed	1994	17.50	18
1994	Scrooge's Family Home - J. Hine Studios	Closed	1994	17.50	18
1994	What Cottage - J. Hine Studios	Closed	1994	17.50	18
1995	Buttercup Cottage - J. Hine Studios	Open		17.50	18
1995	The Flowershop - J. Hine Studios	Open		17.50	18
1995	Looking for Santa - J. Hine Studios	Open		17.50	18
1995	Miss Belle's Cottage - J. Hine Studios	Closed	1995	17.50	18
1995	Robin's Merry Mouse - J. Hine Studios	Open		17.50	18
1995	Season's Greetings - J. Hine Studios	Open		17.50	18

June McKenna Collectibles, Inc.

Flatback Ornaments - J. McKenna

YEAR ISSUE		EDITION LIMIT	YEAR RETD.	ISSUE PRICE	*QUOTE U.S.$
1988	1776 Santa	Closed	1991	17.00	45-60
1986	Amish Boy, blue	Closed	1989	13.00	100
1986	Amish Boy, pink	Closed	1986	13.00	200-300
1986	Amish Girl, blue	Closed	1989	13.00	100-250
1986	Amish Girl, pink	Closed	1986	13.00	300
1985	Amish Man	Closed	1989	13.00	105
1985	Amish Woman	Closed	1989	13.00	100-140
1993	Angel of Peace, white or pink	Closed	1994	30.00	50
1984	Angel with Horn	Closed	1988	14.00	150
1982	Angel With Toys	Closed	1988	14.00	155
1994	Angel, Guiding Light ,green, pink & white	Closed	1995	30.00	30
1983	Baby Bear in Vest, 5 colors	Closed	1988	11.00	60
1982	Baby Bear, Teeshirt	Closed	1984	11.00	85
1985	Baby Pig	Closed	1988	11.00	105
1983	Baby, blue trim	Closed	1988	11.00	110
1983	Baby, pink trim	Closed	1988	11.00	60-75
1991	Boy Angel, white	Closed	1992	20.00	88-120
1982	Candy Cane	Closed	1984	10.00	375
1982	Colonial Man, 3 colors	Closed	1984	12.00	175
1982	Colonial Woman, 3 colors	Closed	1984	12.00	95
1984	Country Boy, 2 colors	Closed	1988	12.00	65
1984	Country Girl, 2 colors	Closed	1988	12.00	65
1993	Elf Bernie	Closed	1994	30.00	30
1990	Elf Jeffrey	Closed	1992	17.00	40
1991	Elf Joey	Closed	1993	20.00	20
1992	Elf Scotty	Closed	1993	25.00	30
1994	Elf-Ricky	Closed	1995	30.00	30
1994	Elf-Tammy	Closed	1995	30.00	30
1988	Elizabeth, sill sitter	Closed	1989	20.00	100-200
1983	Father Bear in Suit, 3 colors	Closed	1988	12.00	60-70
1985	Father Pig	Closed	1988	12.00	120-180
1993	Final Notes	Closed	1994	30.00	30
1991	Girl Angel, white	Closed	1993	20.00	88-130
1983	Gloria Angel	Closed	1984	14.00	400-550
1989	Glorious Angel	Closed	1992	17.00	17
1983	Grandma, 4 colors	Closed	1988	12.00	80
1983	Grandpa, 4 colors	Closed	1988	12.00	105
1988	Guardian Angel	Closed	1991	16.00	40
1990	Harvest Santa	Closed	1992	17.00	40
1990	Ho Ho Ho	Closed	1992	17.00	65
1982	Kate Greenaway Boy, 3 colors	Closed	1983	12.00	155
1982	Kate Greenaway Girl, 3 colors	Closed	1983	12.00	125
1982	Mama Bear, Blue Cape	Closed	1984	12.00	75
1983	Mother Bear in Dress, 3 colors	Closed	1988	12.00	73
1985	Mother Pig	Closed	1988	12.00	100-130
1984	Mr. Claus	Closed	1988	14.00	75
1984	Mrs. Claus	Closed	1988	14.00	75
1992	Northpole News	Closed	1993	25.00	30
1994	Nutcracker	Closed	1995	30.00	30
1993	Old Lamplighter	Closed	1994	30.00	30
1984	Old World Santa, 3 colors	Closed	1989	14.00	75-200
1984	Old World Santa, gold	Closed	1986	14.00	200-275
1982	Papa Bear, Red Cape	Closed	1984	12.00	85
1992	Praying Angel	Closed	1993	25.00	30
1985	Primitive Santa	Closed	1989	17.00	130-150
1983	Raggedy Andy, 2 colors	Closed	1983	12.00	250
1983	Raggedy Ann, 2 colors	Closed	1983	12.00	325
1994	Ringing in Christmas	Closed	1995	30.00	30
1986	Santa with Bag	Closed	1989	16.00	75
1991	Santa with Banner	Closed	1992	20.00	20
1992	Santa with Basket	Closed	1993	25.00	30
1986	Santa with Bear	Closed	1991	14.00	65
1986	Santa with Bells, blue	Closed	1989	14.00	75
1986	Santa with Bells, green	Closed	1987	14.00	400
1988	Santa with Book, blue & red	Closed	1988	17.00	250-275
1991	Santa with Lights, black or white	Closed	1992	20.00	60
1992	Santa with Sack	Closed	1993	25.00	30
1989	Santa with Staff	Closed	1991	17.00	40
1982	Santa with Toys	Closed	1988	14.00	75-100
1988	Santa with Toys	Closed	1991	17.00	150
1989	Santa with Tree	Closed	1991	17.00	45
1988	Santa with Wreath	Closed	1991	17.00	40
1983	St. Nick with Lantern (wooden)	Closed	1988	14.00	70-120
1989	Winking Santa	Closed	1991	17.00	50

Kirk Stieff

Colonial Williamsburg - D. Bacorn

YEAR ISSUE		EDITION LIMIT	YEAR RETD.	ISSUE PRICE	*QUOTE U.S.$
1992	Court House	Open		10.00	10
1989	Doll ornament, silverplate	Closed	N/A	22.00	30
1993	Governors Palace	Open		10.00	10
1988	Lamb, silverplate	Closed	N/A	20.00	22
1992	Prentis Store	Open		10.00	10
1987	Rocking Horse, silverplate	Closed	N/A	20.00	30
1987	Tin Drum, silverplate	Closed	N/A	20.00	25
1983	Tree Top Star, silverplate	Closed	N/A	29.50	35
1984	Unicorn, silverplate	Closed	N/A	22.00	30
1992	Wythe House	Open		10.00	10

Kirk Stieff Ornaments - Various

YEAR ISSUE		EDITION LIMIT	YEAR RETD.	ISSUE PRICE	*QUOTE U.S.$
1994	Angel with Star - J. Ferraioli	Open		8.00	8

*Quotes have been rounded up to nearest dollar

YEAR ISSUE	EDITION LIMIT	YEAR RETD.	ISSUE PRICE	*QUOTE U.S.$
1993 Baby's Christmas - D. Bacorn	Open		12.00	12
1993 Bell with Ribbon - D. Bacorn	Open		12.00	12
1992 Cat and Ornament - D. Bacorn	Closed	N/A	10.00	10
1993 Cat with Ribbon - D. Bacorn	Open		12.00	12
1983 Charleston Locomotive - D. Bacorn	Closed	N/A	18.00	20
1993 First Christmas Together - D. Bacorn	Closed	N/A	10.00	10
1993 French Horn - D. Bacorn	Closed	N/A	12.00	12
1992 Guardian Angel - J. Ferraioli	Closed	N/A	13.00	13
1986 Icicle, sterling silver - D. Bacorn	Closed	N/A	35.00	65
1994 Kitten with Tassel - J. Ferraioli	Open		12.00	12
1993 Mouse and Ornament - D. Bacorn	Closed	N/A	10.00	10
1992 Repoussé Angel - J. Ferraioli	Open		13.00	13
1992 Repoussé Wreath - J. Ferraioli	Open		13.00	13
1994 Santa with Tassel - J. Ferraioli	Open		12.00	12
1989 Smithsonian Carousel Horse - Kirk Stieff	Closed	N/A	50.00	50
1989 Smithsonian Carousel Seahorse - Kirk Stieff	Closed	N/A	50.00	50
1994 Teddy Bear - D. Bacorn	Open		8.00	8
1990 Toy Ship - Kirk Stieff	Closed	N/A	23.00	25
1984 Unicorn - D. Bacorn	Closed	N/A	18.00	20
1994 Unicorn - D. Bacorn	Open		8.00	8
1994 Victorian Skaters - D. Bacorn	Open		8.00	8
1994 Williamsburg Wreath - D. Bacorn	Open		15.00	15
1993 Wreath with Ribbon - D. Bacorn	Open		12.00	12

Kurt S. Adler, Inc.

Children's Hour - J. Mostrom

YEAR ISSUE	EDITION LIMIT	YEAR RETD.	ISSUE PRICE	*QUOTE U.S.$
1995 Alice in Wonderland J5751	Open		22.50	23
1995 Bow Peep J5753	Open		27.00	27
1995 Cinderella J5752	Open		28.00	28
1995 Little Boy Blue J5755	Retrd.	1995	18.00	18
1995 Miss Muffet J5753	Open		27.00	27
1995 Mother Goose J5754	Open		27.00	27
1995 Red Riding Hood J5751	Open		22.50	23

Christmas in Chelsea Collection - J. Mostrom

YEAR ISSUE	EDITION LIMIT	YEAR RETD.	ISSUE PRICE	*QUOTE U.S.$
1994 Alice, Marguerite W2973	Open		28.00	28
1992 Allison Sitting in Chair W2812	Retrd.	1994	25.50	26
1992 Allison W2729	Retrd.	1993	21.00	21
1992 Amanda W2709	Retrd.	1994	21.00	21
1992 Amy W2729	Retrd.	1993	21.00	21
1992 Christina W2812	Retrd.	1994	25.50	26
1992 Christopher W2709	Retrd.	1994	21.00	21
1992 Delphinium W2728	Open		20.00	20
1995 Edmond With Violin W3078	Open		32.00	32
1994 Guardian Angel With Baby W2974	Retrd.	1995	31.00	31
1992 Holly Hock W2728	Open		20.00	20
1992 Holly W2709	Retrd.	1994	21.00	21
1995 Jose With Violin W3078	Open		32.00	32
1995 Pauline With Violin W3078	Open		32.00	32
1992 Peony W2728	Open		20.00	20
1992 Rose W2728	Open		20.00	20

Cornhusk Mice Ornament Series - M. Rothenberg

YEAR ISSUE	EDITION LIMIT	YEAR RETD.	ISSUE PRICE	*QUOTE U.S.$
1994 3" Father Christmas W2976	Open		18.00	18
1994 9" Father Christmas W2982	Open		25.00	25
1995 Angel Mice W3088	Open		10.00	10
1995 Baby's First Mouse W3087	Open		10.00	10
1993 Ballerina Cornhusk Mice W2700	Retrd.	1994	13.50	14
1994 Clara, Prince W2948	Open		16.00	16
1994 Cowboy W2951	Open		18.00	18
1994 Drosselmeir Fairy, Mouse King W2949	Open		16.00	16
1994 Little Pocahontas, Indian Brave W2950	Open		18.00	18
1995 Miss Tammie Mouse W3086	Open		17.00	17
1995 Mr. Jamie Mouse W3086	Open		17.00	17
1995 Mrs. Molly Mouse W3086	Open		17.00	17
1993 Nutcracker Suite Fantasy Cornhusk Mice W2885	Retrd.	1994	15.50	16

Fabriche™ Ornament Series - KS. Adler, unless otherwise noted

YEAR ISSUE	EDITION LIMIT	YEAR RETD.	ISSUE PRICE	*QUOTE U.S.$
1994 All Star Santa W1665	Open		27.00	27
1992 An Apron Full of Love W1594 - M. Rothenberg	Open		27.00	27
1995 Captain Claus W1711	Open		25.00	25
1994 Checking His List W1634	Open		23.50	24
1992 Christmas in the Air W1593	Open		35.50	36
1994 Cookies For Santa W1639	Open		28.00	28
1994 Firefighting Friends W1668	Open		28.00	28
1992 Hello Little One! W1561	Open		22.00	22
1994 Holiday Flight W1637 - Smithsonian	Open		40.00	40
1993 Homeward Bound W1596	Open		27.00	27
1992 Hugs And Kisses W1560	Open		22.00	22
1993 Master Toymaker W1595	Open		27.00	27
1992 Merry Chrismouse W1565	Retrd.	1994	10.00	10
1992 Not a Creature Was Stirring W1563	Open		22.00	22
1993 Par For the Claus W1625	Open		27.00	27
1993 Santa With List W1510	Open		20.00	20
1994 Santa's Fishtales W1666	Open		29.00	29
1995 Strike Up The Band W1710	Open		25.00	25

Holly Bearies - H. Adler

YEAR ISSUE	EDITION LIMIT	YEAR RETD.	ISSUE PRICE	*QUOTE U.S.$
1996 Angel Starcatcher (Starlight Foundation) J7222	Open		20.00	20

International Christmas - J. Mostrom

YEAR ISSUE	EDITION LIMIT	YEAR RETD.	ISSUE PRICE	*QUOTE U.S.$
1994 Cathy, Johnny W2945	Open		24.00	24
1994 Eskimo-Atom, Ukpik W2967	Open		28.00	28
1994 Germany-Katerina, Hans W2969	Open		27.00	27
1994 Native American-White Dove, Little Wolf W2970	Retrd.	1994	28.00	28
1994 Poland-Marissa, Hedwig W2965	Open		27.00	27
1994 Scotland-Bonnie, Douglas W2966	Open		27.00	27
1994 Spain-Maria, Miguel W2968	Open		27.00	27

Little Dickens - J. Mostrom

YEAR ISSUE	EDITION LIMIT	YEAR RETD.	ISSUE PRICE	*QUOTE U.S.$
1994 Little Bob Crachit W2961	Open		30.00	30
1994 Little Marley's Ghost W2964	Open		33.50	34
1994 Little Mrs. Crachit W2962	Open		27.00	27
1994 Little Scrooge in Bathrobe W2959	Open		30.00	30
1994 Little Scrooge in Overcoat W2960	Open		30.00	30
1994 Little Tiny Tim W2963	Open		22.50	23

Polonaise™ by Komozja - KSA/Komozja, unless otherwise noted

YEAR ISSUE	EDITION LIMIT	YEAR RETD.	ISSUE PRICE	*QUOTE U.S.$
1995 Alarm Clock GP452	Open		25.00	25
1994 Angel Head GP372	Open		18.00	18
1994 Angel w/Bear GP396	Retrd.	1995	20.20	21
1996 Antique Cars boxed set GP522	Open		124.00	124
1994 Beer Glass GP366	Open		18.00	18
1996 Bette Boop GP624 - King Features	Open		32.00	32
1995 Blessed Mother GP413	Open		22.50	23
1996 Candleholder GP450	Open		20.00	20
1994 Cardinal GP420	Open		18.00	18
1995 Cat in Boot GP478 - Rothenberg	Open		28.00	28
1994 Cat w/Ball GP390	Open		23.00	23
1995 Cat w/Bow GP446	Open		22.50	23
1995 Ceasar GP422	Open		25.00	25
1995 Christ Child GP414	Open		20.00	20
1995 Christmas Tree GP461	Open		22.50	23
1996 Cinderella 4 pc boxed set GP512	Open		134.00	134
1996 Cinderella 6 pc boxed set GP511	7,500		190.00	190
1996 Cinderella Coach GP487	Open		33.00	33
1996 Cinderella GP488	Open		28.00	28
1995 Clara GP408	Open		20.00	20
1995 Clown Head 4.5" GP460	Open		25.00	25
1996 Coca Cola 4 pc boxed set GP517	Open		135.00	135
1996 Coca Cola Bear GP630 - Coca Cola	Open		37.00	37
1996 Coca Cola Bottle GP631 - Coca Cola	Open		33.00	33
1996 Coca Cola Bottle Top GP633 - Coca Cola	Open		27.00	27
1996 Coca Cola Disk GP632 - Coca Cola	Open		26.00	26
1996 Coca Cola Vending Machine GP634 - Coca Cola	Open		37.00	37
1996 Cossack GP604	Open		35.00	35
1995 Cowboy Head GP462	Open		30.00	30
1995 Creche GP458 - Stefan	Open		28.00	28
1995 Crocodile GP468	Open		28.00	28
1996 Dice boxed set GP509	Open		60.00	60
1994 Dinosaurs GP397	Open		22.50	23
1994 Dinosaurs-brown GP397	Retrd.	1995	22.50	35-50
1995 Dove on Ball GP472 - Stefan	Open		30.00	30
1995 Eagle GP453	Open		28.00	28
1994 Egyptian (12 pc boxed set) GP500	Retrd.	1995	200.00	200
1996 Egyptian Cat GP351	Open		30.00	30
1996 Egyptian II boxed set GP510	Open		170.00	170
1996 Egyptian Princess GP482	Open		33.00	33
1995 Egyptiant (4 pc. boxed set) GP500/4	Open		110.00	110
1995 Elephant GP 464	Open		28.00	28
1996 Elves GP611/23	Open		30.00	30
1996 Emerald City GP623	Open		32.00	32
1996 Fire Engine GP605	Open		30.00	30
1995 Fish 4 pc. boxed GP506	Open		110.00	110
1996 French Hen GP626 - Stefan	Open		33.00	33
1996 Gift Boxes GP614	Open		25.00	25
1994 Glass Acorn GP342	Retrd.	1995	11.00	150
1994 Glass Angel GP309	Open		18.00	18
1994 Glass Apple GP339	Open		11.00	11
1994 Glass Church GP369	Open		18.00	18
1994 Glass Clown 4" GP301	Retrd.	1995	13.50	35
1994 Glass Clown 6" GP303	Retrd.	1995	22.50	35
1994 Glass Clown 6.5" GP302	Open		22.50	23
1994 Glass Dice (original-square) GP363	Retrd.	1994	18.00	35
1994 Glass Dice GP363	Open		18.00	18
1994 Glass Doll GP377	Retrd.	1995	13.50	14
1994 Glass Gnome GP347	Open		18.00	18
1994 Glass Knight GP304	Open		18.00	18
1994 Glass Owl GP328	Open		20.00	20
1996 Glass Slipper GP490	Open		20.00	20
1994 Glass Top GP359	Retrd.	1995	9.00	25
1994 Glass Turkey GP326	Open		20.00	20
1996 Glinda the Good Witch GP621	Open		32.00	32
1994 Golden Cherub Head GP372	Retrd.	1994	18.00	125
1994 Golden Rocking Horse GP355	Retrd.	1994	22.50	75-100
1995 Goose w/Wreath GP475 - Stefan	Open		30.00	30
1996 Gramophone GP446	Open		22.50	23
1994 Guardman GP407	Retrd.	1995	15.50	35-40
1995 Herr Drosselmeir GP465 - Rothenberg	Open		30.00	30
1995 Holy Family 3 pc. GP504	Open		84.00	84
1994 Holy Family GP371	Open		28.00	28
1996 Horus GP484	Open		33.00	33
1995 Humpty Dumpty GP477 - Stefan	Open		30.00	30
1995 Icicle Santa GP474 - Stefan	Open		25.00	25
1995 Indian GP463	Open		30.00	30
1996 King Balthazar GP607	Open		30.00	30
1996 King Neptune GP496	Open		35.00	35
1996 Light Bulb GP449	Open		20.00	20
1996 Little Mermaid GP492	Open		28.00	28
1994 Locomotive GP353	Open		22.50	23
1995 Locomotive GP447	Open		28.00	28
1994 Madonna w/Child GP370	Open		22.50	23
1996 Medieval boxed set GP519	Open		160.00	160
1996 Medieval Dragon GP642	Open		35.00	35
1996 Medieval Knight GP641	Open		35.00	35
1996 Medieval Lady GP643	Open		35.00	35
1994 Merlin GP373	Retrd.	1995	20.00	30
1994 Mickey Mouse GP392	Retrd.	1995	33.00	125
1994 Minnie Mouse GP391	Retrd.	1995	33.00	75
1994 Moose King GP406	Open		20.00	20
1996 Mummy GP483	Open		33.00	33
1996 Neferitti 96 GP485	Open		33.00	33
1994 Nefertiti GP349	Open		25.00	25
1994 Night & Day GP307	Open		22.50	23
1995 Noah's Ark GP469	Open		28.00	28
1994 Nutcracker GP404	Open		20.00	20
1995 Nutcracker Suite 4 pc. boxed GP507	Open		110.00	110
1994 Old Fashion Car GP380	Retrd.	1995	13.50	14
1994 Parrott GP332	Open		15.50	16
1995 Partridge GP467 - Stefan	Open		33.50	34
1994 Peacock 5" GP324	Open		18.00	18
1994 Peacock 7.5" GP323	Open		28.00	28
1995 Peter Pan 4 pc. boxed set GP503	Open		124.00	124
1995 Peter Pan GP419	Open		22.50	23
1996 Pharaoh GP481	Open		35.00	35
1994 Pierrot Clown GP405	Retrd.	1995	18.00	35
1996 Polanaise Medieval Horse GP640	Open		35.00	35
1995 Polonaise Afro-American Santa GP389/1	Open		25.00	25
1995 Polonaise Cardinal GP473 - Stefan	Open		30.00	30
1995 Polonaise House GP455	Open		25.00	25
1995 Polonaise Santa GP389	Open		25.00	25
1996 Prince Charming GP489	Open		28.00	28
1994 Puppy (gold) GP333	Retrd.	1994	15.50	28
1994 Puppy GP333	Open		15.50	16
1994 Pyramid GP352	Open		22.50	23
1996 Raggedy Ann GP321	Open		28.00	28
1994 Rocking Horse 4" GP355	Open		22.50	23
1994 Rocking Horse 5" GP356	Open		22.50	23
1995 Roman 7 pc. boxed set GP402	Open		164.00	164
1995 Roman Centurian GP427	Open		22.50	23
1995 Roman set 4 pc. boxed GP402/4	Open		110.00	110
1996 Russian 5 pc boxed set GP514	Open		190.00	190
1996 Russian Bishop GP603	Open		35.00	35
1996 Russian Woman GP602	Open		35.00	35
1995 Sailing Ship GP415	Open		30.00	30
1994 Saint Nick GP316	Open		28.00	28
1994 Santa Boot GP375	Open		20.00	20
1996 Santa Car GP367	Open		33.00	33
1994 Santa GP317	Open		22.50	23
1995 Santa GP442	Open		25.00	25
1994 Santa Head 4" GP315	Open		13.50	14
1994 Santa Head 4.5" GP374	Open		18.00	18
1995 Santa Moon GP454 - Stefan	Open		28.00	28
1995 Santa on Goose on Sled GP479	Open		30.00	30
1996 Santa Pilot GP365	Open		33.00	33
1996 Sea Horse GP494	Open		25.00	25
1995 Shark GP417	Open		18.00	18
1994 Snowman w/Parcel GP313	Open		22.50	23
1994 Snowman w/Specs GP312	Retrd.	1995	20.00	25-35
1994 Sparrow GP 329	Open		15.50	16
1994 Sphinx GP350	Retrd.	1995	22.50	23
1996 Sphinx GP480	Open		33.00	33
1996 St. Basils Cathedral GP600	Open		35.00	35
1995 St. Joseph GP412	Open		22.50	23
1995 Star Santa GP470 - Stefan	Open		25.00	25
1996 Star Snowman GP625 - Stefan	Open		32.00	32
1996 Sting Ray GP495	Open		28.00	28
1994 Swan GP325	Open		20.00	20
1994 Teddy Bear (gold) GP338	Retrd.	1994	15.50	35-50
1994 Teddy Bear GP338	Open		15.50	16
1995 Telephone GP448	Open		25.00	25
1996 Three Kings boxed set GP516	Open		144.00	144
1994 Train Coaches GP354	Open		15.50	16
1994 Train Set (boxed) GP501	Open		90.00	90
1995 Treasure Chest GP416	Open		20.00	20
1994 Tropical Fish GP409	Open		22.50	23
1996 Tsar Ivan GP601	Open		35.00	35
1995 Turtle Doves GP471 - Stefan	Open		25.00	25
1996 Tutenkhamen #2 GP476	Open		35.00	35
1994 Tutenkhamen GP348	Open		25.00	25

*Quotes have been rounded up to nearest dollar

CHRISTMAS ORNAMENTS

YEAR ISSUE		EDITION LIMIT	YEAR RETD.	ISSUE PRICE	*QUOTE U.S.$
1996	Wicked Witch GP606	Open		32.00	32
1996	Winter Boy GP615	Open		22.50	23
1996	WinterGirl GP615	Open		22.50	23
1996	Wizard in Balloon GP622	Open		32.00	32
1995	Wizard of Oz 4 pc. boxed GP505	Open		124.00	124
1995	Wizard of Oz 6 pc. boxed GP508	5,000	1995	170.00	200-400
1995	Wizard of Oz Dorothy GP434	Open		25.00	25
1996	Wizard of Oz II boxed set GP518	Open		164.00	164
1995	Wizard of Oz Lion GP433	Open		22.50	23
1995	Wizard of Oz Scarecrow GP435	Open		25.00	25
1995	Wizard of Oz Tinman GP436	Open		25.00	25
1994	Zodiac Sun GP381	Open		22.50	23

Polonaise™ Vatican Library Collection - Vatican Library

1996	Cherub Bust Glass GP651	Open		N/A	N/A
1996	Cherubum boxed set, GP 521	Open		N/A	N/A
1996	Dancing Cherubs on Ball GP652	Open		N/A	N/A
1996	Full Body Cherub GP 650	Open		N/A	N/A
1996	Garden of Mary boxed set, GP 520	Open		N/A	N/A
1996	Lily Glass GP655	Open		N/A	N/A
1996	Madonna & Child GP653	Open		N/A	N/A
1996	Rose Glass GP654	Open		N/A	N/A

Royal Heritage Collection - J. Mostrom

1993	Anastasia W2922	Retrd.	1994	28.00	28
1996	Angelique Angel Baby W3278	Open		25.00	25
1995	Benjamin J5756	Open		24.50	25
1995	Blythe J5756	Open		24.50	25
1996	Brianna Ivory W7663	Open		25.00	25
1996	Brianna Pink W7663	Open		25.00	25
1993	Caroline W2924	Retrd.	1995	25.50	26
1993	Charles W2924	Retrd.	1995	25.50	26
1993	Elizabeth W2924	Retrd.	1995	25.50	26
1996	Etoile Angel Baby W3278	Open		25.00	25
1996	Francis Winter Boy W3279	Open		28.00	28
1996	Gabrielle in Pink Coat W3276	Open		28.00	28
1996	Giselle w/Bow W3277	Open		28.00	28
1996	Giselle Winter Girl w/Package W3279	Open		28.00	28
1994	Ice Fairy, Winter Fairy W2972	Open		25.50	26
1993	Joella W2979	Retrd.	1993	27.00	27
1993	Kelly W2979	Retrd.	1993	27.00	27
1996	Lady Colette in Sled W3301	Open		32.00	32
1996	Laurielle Lady Skater W3281	Open		36.00	36
1996	Miniotte w/Muff W3279	Open		28.00	28
1996	Monique w/Hat Box W3277	Open		28.00	28
1993	Nicholas W2923	Open		25.50	26
1996	Nicole w/Balloon W3277	Open		28.00	28
1993	Patina W2923	Open		25.50	26
1996	Rene Victorian Lady W3280	Open		36.00	36
1993	Sasha W2923	Open		25.50	26
1994	Snow Princess W2971	Open		28.00	28

Smithsonian Museum Carousel - KSA/Smithsonian

1987	Antique Bunny S3027/2	Retrd.	1992	14.50	15
1992	Antique Camel S3027/12	Open		15.00	15
1989	Antique Cat S3027/6	Retrd.	1995	14.50	15
1992	Antique Elephant S3027/11	Open		14.50	15
1995	Antique Frog S32027/18	Open		15.50	16
1988	Antique Giraffe S3027/4	Retrd.	1993	14.50	15
1987	Antique Goat S3027/1	Retrd.	1992	14.50	15
1991	Antique Horse S3027/10	Open		14.50	15
1993	Antique Horse S3027/14	Open		15.00	15
1988	Antique Horse S3027/3	Retrd.	1993	14.50	15
1989	Antique Lion S3027/5	Retrd.	1994	14.50	15
1994	Antique Pig S3027/16	Open		15.50	16
1994	Antique Reindeer S3027/15	Open		15.50	16
1991	Antique Rooster S3027/9	Retrd.	1994	14.50	15
1990	Antique Seahorse S3027/8	Open		14.50	15
1993	Antique Tiger S3027/13	Open		15.00	15
1990	Antique Zebra S3027/7	Open		14.50	15
1995	Armored Horse S3027/17	Open		15.50	16

Smithsonian Museum Fabriché™ - KSA/Smithsonian

1992	Holiday Drive W1580	Retrd.	1995	38.00	38
1992	Santa On a Bicycle W1547	Open		31.00	31

Steinbach Ornament Series - KS. Adler

1992	The King's Guards ES300	Open		27.00	27

Lance Corporation

Sebastian Christmas Ornaments - P.W. Baston Jr., unless otherwise noted

1943	Madonna of the Chair - P.W. Baston	25	1943	2.00	150-200
1981	Santa Claus - P.W. Baston	5,000	1981	28.50	30
1982	Madonna of the Chair (Reissue of '43) - P.W. Baston	2,165	1982	15.00	30-45
1985	Home for the Holidays	Closed	1993	10.00	13
1986	Holiday Sleigh Ride	Closed	1993	10.00	13
1987	Santa	Closed	1993	10.00	13
1988	Decorating the Tree	Closed	1993	12.50	13
1989	Final Preparations for Christmas	Closed	1993	13.90	14
1990	Stuffing the Stockings	Closed	1993	14.00	14
1990	Christmas Rose-Red on White (Blossom Shop)	Closed		22.00	25-35
1991	Merry Christmas	Closed	1993	14.50	15
1992	Final Check	Closed	1993	14.50	15
1993	Ethnic Santa	Closed	1993	12.50	25-30
1993	Caroling With Santa	Closed	1993	15.00	15

YEAR ISSUE		EDITION LIMIT	YEAR RETD.	ISSUE PRICE	*QUOTE U.S.$
1994	Victorian Christmas Skaters	Closed	1994	17.00	17
1995	Midnight Snacks	Closed	1995	17.00	17

Lenox China

Yuletide - Lenox

1994	Cat	Open		19.50	20

Lenox Collections

The Christmas Carousel - Lenox

1989	Cat	Open		19.50	20
1989	Elephant	Open		19.50	20
1989	Goat	Open		19.50	20
1989	Hare	Open		19.50	20
1989	Lion	Open		19.50	20
1989	Palomino	Open		19.50	20
1989	Pinto	Open		19.50	20
1989	Polar Bear	Open		19.50	20
1989	Reindeer	Open		19.50	20
1989	Sea Horse	Open		19.50	20
1989	Swan	Open		19.50	20
1989	Tiger	Open		19.50	20
1989	Unicorn	Open		19.50	20
1989	White Horse	Open		19.50	20
1989	Zebra	Open		19.50	20
1989	Black Horse	Open		19.50	20
1990	Camel	Open		19.50	20
1990	Frog	Open		19.50	20
1990	Giraffe	Open		19.50	20
1990	Medieval Horse	Open		19.50	20
1990	Panda	Open		19.50	20
1990	Pig	Open		19.50	20
1990	Rooster	Open		19.50	20
1990	St. Bernard	Open		19.50	20
1990	Set of 24	Open		468.00	468

Lilliput Lane Ltd.

Christmas Ornaments - Lilliput Lane

1992	Mistletoe Cottage	Retrd.	1992	27.50	35-45
1993	Robin Cottage	Retrd.	1993	35.00	45
1994	Ivy House	Retrd.	1994	35.00	40
1995	Plum Cottage	Retrd.	1995	30.00	30
1996	Fir Tree Cottage	Yr.Iss.		30.00	30

Coca Cola Country - R. Day

1996	Corner Cafe	19,960		35.00	35

Lladró

Angels - Lladró

1994	Joyful Offering L6125G	Yr.Iss.	1994	245.00	265
1995	Angel of the Stars L6132G	Yr.Iss.	1995	195.00	195
1996	Rejoice L6321G	Yr.Iss.		220.00	220

Annual Ornaments - Lladró

1988	Christmas Ball-L1603M	Yr.Iss.	1988	60.00	60-80
1989	Christmas Ball-L5656M	Yr.Iss.	1989	65.00	65
1990	Christmas Ball-L5730M	Yr Iss.	1990	70.00	70
1991	Christmas Ball-L5829M	Yr.Iss.	1991	52.00	68
1992	Christmas Ball-L5914M	Yr.Iss.	1992	52.00	55
1993	Christmas Ball-L6009M	Yr.Iss.	1993	54.00	55
1994	Christmas Ball-L6105M	Yr.Iss.	1994	55.00	55
1995	Christmas Ball-L6207M	Yr.Iss.	1995	55.00	55
1996	Christmas Ball-L6298M	Yr.Iss.		55.00	55

Cherub Ornaments - Lladró

1995	Surprised Cherub L6253G	Open		120.00	120
1995	Playing Cherub L6254G	Open		120.00	120
1995	Thinking Cherub L6255G	Open		120.00	120

Dove Ornaments - Lladró

1995	Landing Dove L6266G	Open		49.00	49
1995	Flying Dove L6267G	Open		49.00	49

Miniature Ornaments - Lladró

1988	Miniature Angels-L1604G, Set/3	Yr.Iss.	1988	75.00	175
1989	Holy Family-L5657G, Set/3	Yr.Iss.	1990	79.50	100
1990	Three Kings-L5729G, Set/3	Yr Iss.	1991	87.50	100-150
1991	Holy Shepherds-L5809G	Yr.Iss.	1991	97.50	100-125
1993	Nativity Trio-L6095G	Yr.Iss.	1993	115.00	115-140

Ornaments - Lladró

1991	Our First-1991-L5840G	Yr.Iss.	1991	50.00	57
1992	Snowman-L5841G	Yr.Iss.	1994	50.00	60
1992	Santa-L5842G	Yr.Iss.	1994	55.00	60
1992	Baby's First-1992-L5922G	Yr.Iss.	1992	55.00	55
1992	Our First-1992-L5923G	Yr.Iss.	1992	50.00	50
1992	Elf Ornament-L5938G	Yr.Iss.	1994	50.00	57-75
1992	Mrs. Claus-L5939G	Yr.Iss.	1994	55.00	57
1992	Christmas Morning-L5940G	Yr.Iss.	1992	97.50	100
1993	Nativity Lamb-L5969G	Yr.Iss.	1994	85.00	85
1993	Baby's First 1993-L6037G	Yr.Iss.	1993	57.00	57
1993	Our First-L6038G	Yr.Iss.	1993	52.00	57

Toy Ornaments - Lladró

1995	Christmas Tree L6261G	Open		75.00	75
1995	Rocking Horse L6262G	Open		69.00	69

YEAR ISSUE		EDITION LIMIT	YEAR RETD.	ISSUE PRICE	*QUOTE U.S.$
1995	Doll L6263G	Open		69.00	69
1995	Train L6264G	Open		69.00	69

Tree Topper Ornaments - Lladró

1990	Angel Tree Topper-L5719G-Blue	Yr.Iss.	1990	115.00	225-250
1991	Angel Tree Topper-L5831G-Pink	Yr.Iss.	1991	115.00	145-175
1992	Angel Tree Topper -L5875G -Green	Yr.Iss.	1992	120.00	145-150
1993	Angel Tree Topper -L5962G -Lavender	Yr.Iss.	1993	125.00	150

Margaret Furlong Designs

Annual Ornaments - M. Furlong

1980	3" Trumpeter Angel	Closed	1994	12.00	50-100
1980	4" Trumpeter Angel	Closed	1994	21.00	50-125
1982	3" Star Angel	Closed	1994	12.00	50-100
1982	4" Star Angel	Closed	1994	21.00	50-125
1984	3" Dove Angel	Closed	1995	12.00	50-75
1988	3" Butterfly Angel	Closed	1996	12.00	12
1988	4" Butterfly Angel	Closed	1996	21.00	21
1984	4" Dove Angel	Closed	1995	21.00	25-75
1996	4" Sunflower Angel	Yr.Iss.		21.00	21

Flora Angelica - M. Furlong

1995	Faith Angel	10,000	1995	45.00	100
1996	Hope Angel	10,000	1996	45.00	50-90

Gifts from God - M. Furlong

1985	1985 The Charis Angel	3,000	1985	45.00	400-500
1986	1986 The Hallelujah Angel	3,000	1986	45.00	700-1000
1987	1987 The Angel of Light	3,000	1987	45.00	100-300
1988	1988 The Celestial Angel	3,000	1988	45.00	150-200
1989	1989 Coronation Angel	3,000	1989	45.00	100-500

Joyeux Noel - M. Furlong

1990	1990 Celebration Angel	10,000	1994	45.00	100-300
1991	1991 Thanksgiving Angel	10,000	1994	45.00	100-300
1992	1992 Joyeux Noel Angel	10,000	1994	45.00	100-250
1993	1993 Star of Bethlehem Angel	10,000	1994	45.00	100-250
1994	1994 Messiah Angel	10,000	1994	45.00	250-800

Musical Series - M. Furlong

1980	1980 The Caroler	3,000	1980	50.00	200-600
1981	1981 The Lyrist	3,000	1981	45.00	100-300
1982	1982 The Lutist	3,000	1982	45.00	100-300
1983	1983 The Concertinist	3,000	1983	45.00	100-300
1984	1984 The Herald Angel	3,000	1984	45.00	100-300

Midwest of Cannon Falls

Leo R. Smith III Collection - L.R. Smith

1996	Angel of Heaven & Earth 18396-0	3,500		33.00	33
1996	Angel of Light 18076-1	4,000		33.00	33
1996	Angel of Music 18073-4	3,500		33.00	33
1996	Belsnickle Santa 18074-7	4,000		39.00	39
1994	Flying Woodsman Santa 11921-1	2,500	1994	35.00	200-450
1995	Angel of Love 16123-4	3,500		32.00	32
1995	Angel of Peace 16199-9	3,500		32.00	32
1995	Angel of Your Dreams 16130-2	3,500		32.00	32
1995	Partridge Angel 13994-3	3,500		30.00	30
1995	Santa on Reindeer 13780-2	3,500	1996	35.00	50

Wendt and Kuhn Ornaments - Wendt/Kuhn

1978	Angel Clip-on Ornament 00729-7	Open		20.00	24
1989	Trumpeting Angel, 2 asst. 09402-0	Retrd.	1995	14.00	17
1991	Angel in Ring Ornament 01208-6	Open		12.00	15
1994	Angel on Moon, Star, 12 asst. 12945-6	Open		20.00	22

Old World Christmas

Collector Club - E.M. Merck, unless otherwise noted

1993	Mr. & Mrs. Claus set 1490	Retrd.	1993	Gift	90-200
1993	Glass Christmas Maidens, Set/4, 1491	Retrd.	1993	35.00	85-150
1993	Dresdener Drummer Nutcracker 7258	Retrd.	1993	110.00	160-300
1994	Santa in Moon 1492	Retrd.	1994	Gift	50-75
1994	Large Santa in Chimney 1493	Retrd.	1994	42.50	65-85
1995	Large Christmas Carousel 1587 - Inge-Glas	Retrd.	1995	79.50	90
1995	The Konigsee Nutcracker 7284	Retrd.	1995	125.00	125
1995	Cherub on Reflector 1545 - Inge-Glas	Retrd.	1995	Gift	N/A

Angel & Female - E.M. Merck, unless otherwise noted

1991	Angel of Peace 1033	Retrd.	1995	9.25	10
1990	Angel on Disc 1028	Retrd.	1993	11.70	16
1992	Angel on Form 1044	Retrd.	1995	9.70	10
1987	Baby 1009	Retrd.	1995	5.25	6
1988	Baby in Bunting 1015	Retrd.	1990	7.70	14
1991	Baby Jesus 1036	Retrd.	1995	9.25	10
1991	Baroque Angel 1031	Retrd.	1995	12.95	13
1985	Caroling Girl 101062	Retrd.	1990	6.65	19
1985	Doll Head 103209	Retrd.	1989	6.40	11
1993	Frau Schneemann 1059	Retrd.	1995	16.90	17
1987	Girl in Grapes 1010	Retrd.	1989	8.45	20
1987	Girl on Snowball w/Teddy 1007	Retrd.	1995	9.25	15
1988	Girl Under Tree 1014	Retrd.	1995	7.80	8
1985	Girl with Flowers 101069	Retrd.	1993	7.50	13

*Quotes have been rounded up to nearest dollar

YEAR ISSUE	EDITION LIMIT	YEAR RETD.	ISSUE PRICE	*QUOTE U.S.$
1985 Gold Girl with Tree 1010306	Retrd.	1995	8.25	12
1992 Guardian Angel 1043	Retrd.	1995	8.25	9
1992 Honey Child 1042	Retrd.	1995	7.45	8
1988 Large Blue Angel 1012	Retrd.	1994	13.40	17
1988 Large Doll Head 1013	Retrd.	1995	11.60	12
1985 Light Blue Angel w/Wings 101052	Retrd.	1994	9.25	14
1986 Little Red Riding Hood 1001	Retrd.	1993	9.90	16
1990 Miniature Mrs. Claus 1027	Retrd.	1995	4.95	5
1986 Mrs. Santa Claus 1003	Retrd.	1989	8.90	24
1987 Mushroom Girl 1006	Retrd.	1994	9.25	12
1986 Pink Angel with Wings 1002	Retrd.	1988	8.90	16
1990 Praying Girl 1025	Retrd.	1993	7.80	12
1985 Red Girl with Tree 1010309	Retrd.	1995	8.25	13
1985 Small Girl with Tree 101029	Retrd.	1995	5.85	6
1985 Victorian Girl 101035	Retrd.	1989	5.30	16

Animals - E.M. Merck, unless otherwise noted

YEAR ISSUE	EDITION LIMIT	YEAR RETD.	ISSUE PRICE	*QUOTE U.S.$
1993 Bear Above Reflector 1279	Retrd.	1995	33.75	36
1986 Bear in Crib 1203	Retrd.	1994	9.00	12
1985 Butterfly on Form 1237447	Retrd.	1995	7.80	8
1989 Cat and the Fiddle 1221	Retrd.	1994	7.80	11
1986 Cat in Bag 1204	Retrd.	1995	9.00	9
1985 Cat in Show 121103	Retrd.	1994	7.80	11
1991 Christmas Butterfly 1247	Retrd.	1994	7.00	9
1984 Circus Dog 121021	Retrd.	1994	9.00	12
1989 Fat Fish 1223	Retrd.	1995	5.85	6
1985 Grey Elephant 123420	Retrd.	1995	7.00	7
1993 Grizzly Bear 1265	Retrd.	1995	8.35	9
1988 Jumbo Elephant 1213	Retrd.	1995	9.25	10
1989 King Charles Spaniel 1222	Retrd.	1995	9.90	10
1984 Kitten 121004	Retrd.	1995	7.00	7
1989 Large Fish 1214	Retrd.	1993	6.70	14
1991 Large Puppy with Basket 1241	Retrd.	1993	13.25	22
1985 Large Teddy Bear 121089	Retrd.	1988	13.00	18
1985 Large Three-Sided Head 121088	Retrd.	1994	12.95	23
1986 Monkey 1205	Retrd.	1994	5.85	11
1987 Mouse 1211	Retrd.	1995	9.90	10
1993 My Darling 1276	Retrd.	1995	6.30	7
1993 Pastel Butterfly 1268	Retrd.	1995	8.45	9
1990 Pink Poodle 1227	Retrd.	1994	8.80	11
1986 Playing Cat 1202	Retrd.	1994	8.80	10
1984 Puppy 121010	Retrd.	1994	7.00	9
1989 Rabbit in Tree 1219	Retrd.	1995	8.35	9
1991 Rabbit on Heart 1244	Retrd.	1995	8.00	8
1990 Red Butterfly on Form 1231	Retrd.	1994	8.55	9
1990 Sitting Black Cat 1228	Retrd.	1995	7.00	7
1986 Sitting Dog with Pipe 1206	Retrd.	1995	7.80	11
1991 Sitting Puppy 1246	Retrd.	1994	6.75	9
1985 Small Bunny 121090	Retrd.	1994	5.20	8
1986 Smiling Dog 1207	Retrd.	1994	7.80	10
1985 Snail 121041	Retrd.	1993	6.70	18
1989 Teddy Bear with Bow 1218	Retrd.	1990	6.65	17
1984 Three-Sided: Owl, Dog, Cat 121009	Retrd.	1994	8.55	13
1990 West Highland Terrier 1232	Retrd.	1993	7.45	15
1989 White Kitty 1220	Retrd.	1990	7.45	10
1994 Woodland Squirrel 1291	Retrd.	1995	21.00	21

Bead Garlands - E.M. Merck

YEAR ISSUE	EDITION LIMIT	YEAR RETD.	ISSUE PRICE	*QUOTE U.S.$
1993 Angel Garland 1306	Retrd.	1993	55.00	85
1993 Celestial Garland 1303	Retrd.	1993	55.00	80
1993 Clown & Drum Garland 1301	Retrd.	1993	55.00	65
1993 Frog and Fish Garland 1305	Retrd.	1995	55.00	95
1993 Fruit Garland 1302	Retrd.	1993	55.00	70
1993 Pickle Garland 1304	Retrd.	1993	55.00	110
1993 Santa Garland 1308	Retrd.	1995	55.00	80-110
1993 Teddy Bear & Heart Garland 1307	Retrd.	1993	55.00	100

Butterflies - E.M. Merck

YEAR ISSUE	EDITION LIMIT	YEAR RETD.	ISSUE PRICE	*QUOTE U.S.$
1987 Butterfly, Blue with Blue 1905	Retrd.	1991	20.95	30
1987 Butterfly, Gold with Gold 1906	Retrd.	1991	20.95	30
1987 Butterfly, Orange w/Orange 1904	Retrd.	1991	20.95	30
1987 Butterfly, Red with Cream 1903	Retrd.	1991	20.95	30
1987 Butterfly, White with Blue 1902	Retrd.	1991	20.95	30
1987 Butterfly, White with Red 1901	Retrd.	1991	20.95	30

Celestial Figures - E.M. Merck

YEAR ISSUE	EDITION LIMIT	YEAR RETD.	ISSUE PRICE	*QUOTE U.S.$
1985 Large Gold Star with Glitter 2237139	Retrd.	1993	7.00	10
1986 Shooting Star on Ball 2201	Retrd.	1993	6.65	12
1985 Sun/Moon 221027	Retrd.	1993	7.00	10

Churches & Houses - E.M. Merck

YEAR ISSUE	EDITION LIMIT	YEAR RETD.	ISSUE PRICE	*QUOTE U.S.$
1985 Bavarian House 201059	Retrd.	1994	8.00	13
1990 Christmas Chalet 2014	Retrd.	1995	8.00	8
1991 Christmas Shop 2020	Retrd.	1995	9.45	10
1990 Church on Disc 2018	Retrd.	1995	12.50	13
1988 Church/Tree on Form 2008	Retrd.	1995	8.35	9
1990 Garden House with Gnome 2011	Retrd.	1993	7.80	14
1986 Gingerbread House (A) 2001	Retrd.	1989	6.55	16
1986 House with Peacock 2004	Retrd.	1987	7.45	16
1991 Large Lighthouse/Mill 2023	Retrd.	1995	11.00	11
1985 Matte Cream Church 206790-2	Retrd.	1993	6.45	11
1985 Mill 201094	Retrd.	1990	9.45	25
1985 Rathaus 201051	Retrd.	1989	7.00	14
1985 Square House 201040	Retrd.	1995	7.80	8
1991 Thatched Cottage 2019	Retrd.	1995	7.35	8
1986 Windmill on Form 2006	Retrd.	1988	7.45	22

Clip-On Birds - E.M. Merck

YEAR ISSUE	EDITION LIMIT	YEAR RETD.	ISSUE PRICE	*QUOTE U.S.$
1991 Advent Bird 1837	Retrd.	1995	8.00	8
1986 Bird in Nest 1801	Retrd.	1995	10.35	11
1985 Bird of Paradise 181101	Retrd.	1994	7.80	10
1985 Blue Bird 181078	Retrd.	1995	6.65	7
1992 Brilliant Songbird 1841	Retrd.	1995	7.35	8
1991 Canary 1834	Retrd.	1994	7.35	10
1990 Cardinal 1822	Retrd.	1995	9.90	10
1990 Christmas Bird 1824	Retrd.	1995	7.00	7
1992 Christmas Finch 1843	Retrd.	1995	7.65	8
1986 Clip-On Rooster 1802	Retrd.	1989	8.00	31
1991 Cockatiel 1838	Retrd.	1995	9.25	10
1985 Cockatoo 181077	Retrd.	1995	8.55	9
1985 Fancy Peacock 181073	Retrd.	1993	13.50	16
1985 Fancy Pink Peacock 181096	Retrd.	1995	13.95	14
1985 Fantasy Bird with Tinsel Tail 181075	Retrd.	1995	8.00	8
1987 Fat Burgundy Bird 1813	Retrd.	1995	7.80	8
1991 Festive Bird 1832	Retrd.	1995	7.00	7
1993 Festive Sparrow 1853	Retrd.	1995	6.00	6
1992 Forest Finch 1840	Retrd.	1995	8.00	8
1986 Gold Bird with Tinsel Tail 1803	Retrd.	1994	7.45	8
1985 Gold Peacock, Tinsel Tail 1872016	Retrd.	1995	8.25	9
1984 Large Cockatoo 181025	Retrd.	1994	13.95	16
1985 Large Goldfinch 181085	Retrd.	1994	9.25	11
1991 Large Peacock with Crown 1830	Retrd.	1994	13.95	19
1987 Lilac Bird 1811	Retrd.	1995	8.70	9
1985 Magnificent Songbird 181086	Retrd.	1994	13.95	16
1985 Medium Peacock with Tinsel Tail 187215	Retrd.	1995	9.00	9
1990 Miniature Parrot 1828	Retrd.	1995	8.45	9
1990 Miniature Peacock 1825	Retrd.	1994	8.35	12
1985 Nuthatch 181076	Retrd.	1995	7.00	7
1987 Partridge 1814	Retrd.	1994	8.80	11
1985 Pink Bird w/Blue Wings 181082	Retrd.	1994	5.55	8
1985 Pink Snowbird 181079	Retrd.	1994	7.25	8
1987 Red Breasted Songbird 1812	Retrd.	1995	9.25	10
1987 Red Snowbird 1810	Retrd.	1993	8.70	13
1987 Robin 1819	Retrd.	1993	8.80	13
1987 Shiny Gold Bird 1807	Retrd.	1995	5.55	6
1991 Silly Bird 1833	Retrd.	1994	6.75	12
1987 Small Purple Bird 1809	Retrd.	1995	7.00	7
1990 Small Red-Headed Songbird 1823	Retrd.	1995	7.00	7
1987 Snow Owl 1816	Retrd.	1994	9.90	13
1985 Snowbird 181080	Retrd.	1993	8.00	14
1990 Tropical Parrot 1826	Retrd.	1994	10.35	13
1987 White Cockatoo 1805	Retrd.	1995	7.80	8

Clowns & Male Figures - E.M. Merck, unless otherwise noted

YEAR ISSUE	EDITION LIMIT	YEAR RETD.	ISSUE PRICE	*QUOTE U.S.$
1984 'Shorty Clown' 241011	Retrd.	1988	5.65	14
1984 'Stop' Keystone Cop 241019	Retrd.	1989	6.65	26
1986 Aviator 2402	Retrd.	1994	7.80	11
1986 Baby 2405	Retrd.	1989	6.75	19
1990 Black Boy 2439	Retrd.	1995	9.00	12
1986 Boy Head w/Stocking Cap 2411	Retrd.	1993	5.30	13
1985 Boy in Yellow Sweater 241032	Retrd.	1988	7.00	15
1995 Charlie Chaplin 2487 - Inge-Glas	Retrd.	1995	25.00	25
1986 Clip-on Boy Head 2416	Retrd.	1989	6.45	13
1993 Clown Above Ball 2470	Retrd.	1994	42.00	45
1986 Clown Head w/Burgundy Hat 2418	Retrd.	1994	7.00	10
1984 Clown in Stocking 241006	Retrd.	1988	6.65	14
1986 Clown with Accordion 2409	Retrd.	1995	10.35	11
1986 Clown with Banjo 2407	Retrd.	1995	7.00	7
1986 Clown with Drum 2408	Retrd.	1995	10.35	11
1985 Dutch Boy 243321	Retrd.	1993	7.55	16
1990 English Bobby 2442	Retrd.	1994	8.80	12
1986 Farm Boy 2414	Retrd.	1989	4.95	17
1985 Fat Boy with Sweater & Cap 2442265	Retrd.	1994	5.85	9
1986 Gnome Under Mushroom 2417	Retrd.	1993	7.00	12
1988 Harpo 2432	Retrd.	1991	6.20	26
1986 Jester 2419	Retrd.	1995	7.45	8
1987 Jolly Clown Head 2429	Retrd.	1994	12.95	13
1984 Keystone Cop 241003	Retrd.	1994	9.90	19
1987 King 2421	Retrd.	1995	10.60	11
1989 Leprechaun 2435	Retrd.	1994	7.65	10
1993 Miniature Clown 2464	Retrd.	1995	6.00	6
1993 Monk 2467	Retrd.	1994	7.90	10
1987 Mr. Big Nose 2426	Retrd.	1993	8.00	19
1995 Mr. Sci-Fi 2492 - Inge-Glas	Retrd.	1995	29.50	30
1988 Mushroom Gnome 2430	Retrd.	1989	6.20	13
1986 Pixie with Accordion 2406	Retrd.	1989	4.95	16
1984 Roly-Poly Keystone Cop 241015	Retrd.	1988	9.90	26
1986 Sailor Head 2404	Retrd.	1990	7.45	29
1986 School Boy 2415	Retrd.	1989	4.95	13
1984 Scotsman 241017	Retrd.	1988	6.20	20
1990 Scout 2440	Retrd.	1995	9.25	10
1987 Scrooge 2427	Retrd.	1995	8.55	11
1989 Small Clown Head 2436	Retrd.	1993	6.65	11
1990 Snowman on Reflector 2445	Retrd.	1993	10.35	15
1985 Waiter in Tuxedo 241047	Retrd.	1989	7.00	24

Collector's Editions - E.M. Merck, unless otherwise noted

YEAR ISSUE	EDITION LIMIT	YEAR RETD.	ISSUE PRICE	*QUOTE U.S.$
1994 '94 Santa/Moon on Disc 1512	Retrd.	1994	32.50	33
1992 Angel with Tinsel Wire 1522	Retrd.	1993	55.00	79
1993 Angel with Wings 1556	Retrd.	1993	12.50	50
1993 Christmas Heart 1593	Retrd.	1993	10.00	20
1995 Christmas Tree above Star Reflector 1513	2,400	1995	53.00	53
1995 Devil Bell 1599	Retrd.	1995	34.95	35
1992 Flying Peacock with Wings 1550	Retrd.	1995	22.50	23
1992 Flying Songbird with Wings 1551	Retrd.	1995	21.75	22
1993 Hansel and Gretal 1511	2,400	1995	45.00	100-125
1993 Heavenly Angel 1563	Retrd.	1995	20.00	20
1990 Night Before Christmas Ball 1501	500	1993	72.50	115
1992 Nutcracker Ornament 1510	Retrd.	1993	33.75	115-175
1995 Parachuting Santa 1547	Retrd.	1995	59.50	60
1993 Santa with Hot Air Balloon 1570	Retrd.	1995	38.85	39
1992 Santa with Tinsel Wire 1521	Retrd.	1993	55.00	72
1992 Santa's Departure 1503	500	1994	72.50	76
1991 Santa's Visit 1502	500	1994	72.50	82
1992 Snowman with Tinsel Wire 1523	Retrd.	1993	32.50	43
1995 Special Event Santa 1560	5,000	1995	15.00	15
1995 Witch 1582	Retrd.	1995	34.95	35

Easter - E.M. Merck

YEAR ISSUE	EDITION LIMIT	YEAR RETD.	ISSUE PRICE	*QUOTE U.S.$
1988 Gentleman Chick 9311	Retrd.	1993	22.50	23
1988 Gentleman Rabbit 9301	Retrd.	1993	25.00	25
1988 Lady Chick 9312	Retrd.	1993	22.50	23

Easter Light Covers - E.M. Merck

YEAR ISSUE	EDITION LIMIT	YEAR RETD.	ISSUE PRICE	*QUOTE U.S.$
1988 Assorted Easter Egg 9331-1	Retrd.	1993	3.95	7
1988 Assorted Pastel Egg 9335-1	Retrd.	1994	2.95	3
1988 Bunny 9333-4	Retrd.	1994	4.20	8
1988 Bunny in Basket 9333-6	Retrd.	1994	4.20	8
1988 Chick 9333-3	Retrd.	1994	4.20	8
1988 Chick in Egg 9333-5	Retrd.	1994	4.20	8
1988 Hen in Basket 9333-1	Retrd.	1994	4.20	8
1988 Rabbit in Egg 9333-2	Retrd.	1994	4.20	8

Fruits & Vegetables - E.M. Merck, unless otherwise noted

YEAR ISSUE	EDITION LIMIT	YEAR RETD.	ISSUE PRICE	*QUOTE U.S.$
1990 Apricot 2831	Retrd.	1995	6.55	7
1990 Cherries on Form 2825	Retrd.	1993	9.00	12
1989 Cucumber 2820	Retrd.	1989	6.65	15
1985 Grapes on Form 281038	Retrd.	1987	7.00	14
1987 Green Pepper 2812	Retrd.	1995	8.00	8
1985 Large Basket of Grapes 281053	Retrd.	1995	10.35	11
1991 Large Fruit Basket 2849	Retrd.	1995	12.50	13
1984 Large Matte Corn 281033	Retrd.	1995	9.25	10
1985 Large Strawberry 2841432	Retrd.	1993	4.20	10
1990 Large Strawberry w/Flower 2841	Retrd.	1993	10.50	19
1985 Mr. Apple 281071	Retrd.	1988	6.20	20
1984 Mr. Pear 281023	Retrd.	1993	6.75	7
1987 Onion 2810	Retrd.	1989	8.25	80
1986 Pear with Face 2805	Retrd.	1995	7.00	7
1990 Raspberry 2835	Retrd.	1993	6.20	9
1991 Strawberries/Flower on Form 2851	Retrd.	1994	8.55	10
1990 Strawberry Cluster 2836	Retrd.	1995	5.20	6
1991 Very Large Apple 2848	Retrd.	1993	10.60	15
1991 Very Large Pear 2847	Retrd.	1993	10.60	15

Halloween Light Covers - E.M. Merck

YEAR ISSUE	EDITION LIMIT	YEAR RETD.	ISSUE PRICE	*QUOTE U.S.$
1989 Dancing Scarecrow 9241-3	Retrd.	1994	7.65	9
1987 Devil 9223-5	Retrd.	1993	3.95	8
1987 Ghost w/Pumpkin 9221-2	Retrd.	1994	3.95	8
1987 Haunted House 9223-1	Retrd.	1994	3.95	8
1987 Jack O'Lantern 9221-1	Retrd.	1993	3.95	7
1989 Man in the Moon 9241-5	Retrd.	1993	7.65	20
1989 Pumpkin Face 9241-6	Retrd.	1994	7.65	9
1987 Pumpkin w/Top Hat 9223-6	Retrd.	1994	3.95	7
1987 Sad Pumpkin 9221-5	Retrd.	1993	3.95	7
1987 Scarecrow 9221-3	Retrd.	1993	3.95	7
1987 Six Halloween Light Covers 9221	Retrd.	1994	25.00	36
1987 Six Halloween Light Covers 9223	Retrd.	1993	25.90	36
1987 Skull 9221-6	Retrd.	1994	3.95	8
1987 Smiling Cat 9223-2	Retrd.	1993	3.95	7
1987 Smiling Ghost 9223-4	Retrd.	1994	3.95	7
1989 Spider 9241-1	Retrd.	1994	7.65	8
1987 Standing Witch 9223-3	Retrd.	1994	3.95	7
1987 Witch Head 9221-4	Retrd.	1993	3.95	7
1989 Witch Head 9241-2	Retrd.	1994	7.65	10
1989 Wizard 9241-4	Retrd.	1993	7.65	23

Hanging Birds - E.M. Merck

YEAR ISSUE	EDITION LIMIT	YEAR RETD.	ISSUE PRICE	*QUOTE U.S.$
1988 Bird House 1611	Retrd.	1995	10.35	11
1985 Blue Bird with Wings 161100	Retrd.	1991	7.65	10
1985 Cardinal with Wings 161098	Retrd.	1994	10.95	11
1991 Chick on Form 1619	Retrd.	1993	8.00	12
1984 Cock Robin 161012	Retrd.	1995	7.00	7
1990 Duck 1613	Retrd.	1995	6.20	7
1985 Fancy Peacock 161066	Retrd.	1995	9.25	10
1987 Fat Rooster 1610	Retrd.	1995	10.35	11
1986 Large Owl with Stein 1604	Retrd.	1989	10.00	45
1991 Large Parrot on Ball 1617	Retrd.	1995	11.00	11
1986 Owl on Form 1601	Retrd.	1995	11.00	11
1993 Rooster at Hen House 1629	Retrd.	1995	10.25	12
1986 Rooster on Form 1603	Retrd.	1989	6.65	9
1990 Songbird on Form 1614	Retrd.	1994	8.80	10
1991 Songbird on Heart (A) 1618	Retrd.	1993	8.25	11
1986 Songbirds on Ball 1602	Retrd.	1994	9.25	11
1986 Swan on Form 1605	Retrd.	1995	8.35	9
1988 Swans on Lake 1612	Retrd.	1995	7.80	8
1985 Turkey 161058	Retrd.	1989	8.00	13

Hearts - E.M. Merck

YEAR ISSUE	EDITION LIMIT	YEAR RETD.	ISSUE PRICE	*QUOTE U.S.$
1987 Burgundy Heart with Glitter 3004	Retrd.	1995	6.75	7
1992 Heart with Flowers 3010	Retrd.	1993	9.50	13
1985 Large Matte Red Heart 306925	Retrd.	1995	5.30	6
1985 Pink Heart with Glitter 306767	Retrd.	1995	6.75	7

*Quotes have been rounded up to nearest dollar

CHRISTMAS ORNAMENTS

YEAR ISSUE		EDITION LIMIT	YEAR RETD.	ISSUE PRICE	*QUOTE U.S.$
1986	Small Gold Heart with Star 3001	Retrd.	1993	2.85	9
1988	Valentine 3005	Retrd.	1995	5.75	6

Household Items - E.M. Merck

YEAR ISSUE		EDITION LIMIT	YEAR RETD.	ISSUE PRICE	*QUOTE U.S.$
1986	Black Stocking 3203	Retrd.	1993	9.45	36
1985	Clip-On Candle 321063	Retrd.	1995	12.95	13
1991	Money Bag 3206	Retrd.	1994	7.00	10
1985	Pastel Umbrella (A) 321091	Retrd.	1993	11.00	15
1985	Pocket Watch 326729	Retrd.	1995	5.85	6
1986	Red Stocking 3201	Retrd.	1987	9.00	19
1991	Small Cuckoo Clock 3209	Retrd.	1995	7.00	7
1991	Small Wine Barrel 3210	Retrd.	1993	6.30	10
1985	Very Large Pink Umbrella 321103	Retrd.	1986	29.50	49
1985	Wall Clock 321060	Retrd.	1995	11.00	11
1988	Wine Barrel 3204	Retrd.	1990	7.00	13

Icicles - E.M. Merck

YEAR ISSUE		EDITION LIMIT	YEAR RETD.	ISSUE PRICE	*QUOTE U.S.$
1988	Long Champagne Icicle 3401	Retrd.	1988	7.25	15

Light Covers - E.M. Merck

YEAR ISSUE		EDITION LIMIT	YEAR RETD.	ISSUE PRICE	*QUOTE U.S.$
1984	3 Men in a Tub 529007-1	Retrd.	1986	1.60	12
1986	Angel on Bell 529023-5	Retrd.	1991	3.95	11
1985	Apple 529011-5	Retrd.	1989	3.00	10
1986	Assorted Alphabet Blocks 529043-1	Retrd.	1991	4.50	12
1984	Assorted Animals, set /6 529003	Retrd.	1987	10.35	48
1986	Assorted Bells, set /6 529023	Retrd.	1993	22.50	48
1988	Assorted Birds 529057-1	Retrd.	1990	3.95	9
1986	Assorted Easter Eggs 529031-1	Retrd.	1993	3.00	8
1988	Assorted Fast Food 529055-1	Retrd.	1991	3.95	12
1984	Assorted Figurals, set /6 529005	Retrd.	1987	10.35	54
1989	Assorted Fir Cone 529209-1	Retrd.	1991	2.85	8
1993	Assorted Frosty Bell 5275	Retrd.	1993	5.65	8
1985	Assorted Fruit, set of 6 529011	Retrd.	1989	20.00	48
1985	Assorted Heads, set of 6 529009	Retrd.	1988	10.35	54
1986	Assorted Peach Roses 529045-4	Retrd.	1990	3.95	27
1986	Assorted Roses, set of 6 529045	Retrd.	1991	22.50	48
1985	Assorted Santas, set of 6 529015	Retrd.	1992	20.00	54
1989	Assorted Sea Shells 529301-1	Retrd.	1992	3.50	12
1991	Assorted Snowmen 529305-1	Retrd.	1993	5.55	10
1986	Assorted Yellow Roses 529045-2	Retrd.	1990	3.95	9
1985	Automobile 529019-3	Retrd.	1988	2.70	12
1985	Balloon 529019-2	Retrd.	1988	2.70	12
1984	Bear 519003-3	Retrd.	1987	2.50	12
1986	Blue Father Christmas 529047-3	Retrd.	1992	3.95	13
1993	Blue Man in the Moon 5206	Retrd.	1993	5.50	6
1986	Bunny 529033-4	Retrd.	1993	3.60	10
1986	Bunny in Basket 529033-6	Retrd.	1993	3.60	8
1985	Cable Car 529019-5	Retrd.	1988	2.70	12
1984	Carousel 529005-3	Retrd.	1987	2.70	12
1986	Chick 529033-3	Retrd.	1993	3.60	8
1986	Chick in Egg 529033-5	Retrd.	1993	3.60	8
1988	Christmas Carol 529053	Retrd.	1991	25.00	54
1993	Christmas House 5205	Retrd.	1993	5.50	6
1988	Christmas Tree 529051-4	Retrd.	1992	3.95	9
1984	Church on Ball 529005-6	Retrd.	1987	2.50	12
1985	Clara-The Doll 529017-1	Retrd.	1989	2.70	10
1985	Clear Icicles, set of 6 529205	Retrd.	1989	20.00	48
1984	Clown 529001-5	Retrd.	1986	1.60	12
1988	Clown 529051-6	Retrd.	1991	3.95	9
1985	Clown Head 529009-1	Retrd.	1988	1.60	10
1988	Cornucopia 529049-1	Retrd.	1992	3.95	10
1988	Doll 529051-2	Retrd.	1993	3.95	10
1993	Doll Head 5202	Retrd.	1993	5.65	10
1985	Doll Head 529009-4	Retrd.	1988	1.60	9
1988	Drum 529051-1	Retrd.	1992	3.95	9
1988	Ear of Corn 529049-6	Retrd.	1992	3.95	10
1984	Elephant 529003-4	Retrd.	1987	1.60	10
1985	Father Christmas 529009-5	Retrd.	1990	3.00	8
1986	Father Christmas Set 529047	Retrd.	1992	25.00	48
1984	Flower Basket 529005-1	Retrd.	1987	1.60	12
1989	Frog 529303-6	Retrd.	1993	6.45	10
1993	Frosty Acorn 5276	Retrd.	1994	5.65	8
1993	Frosty Cone 5271	Retrd.	1994	5.65	8
1993	Frosty Icicle 5272	Retrd.	1993	5.65	8
1993	Frosty Red Rose 5277	Retrd.	1993	5.65	9
1993	Frosty Snowman 5270	Retrd.	1993	5.65	9
1993	Frosty Tree 5273	Retrd.	1993	5.65	8
1984	Gnome 529001-1	Retrd.	1986	1.60	8
1985	Grapes 529011-3	Retrd.	1989	3.00	8
1986	Green Father Christmas 529047-2	Retrd.	1992	3.95	12
1984	Hedgehog 529003-5	Retrd.	1987	1.60	12
1986	Hen in Basket 529033-1	Retrd.	1993	3.60	8
1984	House 529005-2	Retrd.	1987	1.60	12
1988	Indian 529049-5	Retrd.	1992	3.95	10
1993	Jolly Santa Head 5201	Retrd.	1993	5.50	6
1985	King 529013-3	Retrd.	1988	2.70	12
1989	Kitten 529303-3	Retrd.	1993	6.45	10
1984	Lil' Boy Blue 529007-5	Retrd.	1986	1.60	12
1985	Lil' Rascal Head 529009-6	Retrd.	1988	1.60	12
1985	Locomotive 529019-4	Retrd.	1988	2.70	12
1993	Man in the Moon 5204	Retrd.	1993	5.50	6
1985	Marie-The Girl 529017-3	Retrd.	1989	2.70	12
1985	Mouse King 529017-5	Retrd.	1989	2.70	12
1984	Mrs. Claus 529001-4	Retrd.	1986	1.60	12
1985	Nutcracker 529017-4	Retrd.	1989	2.70	10
1986	Nutcracker on Bell 529023-6	Retrd.	1993	3.95	9
1985	Nutcracker Suite Figures, set/6 529017	Retrd.	1989	19.00	54
1985	Orange 529011-6	Retrd.	1989	3.00	7
1984	Owl 529003-2	Retrd.	1987	1.60	10
1989	Panda 529303-1	Retrd.	1994	6.45	9
1985	Pastel Icicles 529207	Retrd.	1989	N/A	N/A
1984	Peacock 519003-6	Retrd.	1987	2.70	10
1993	Peacock 5203	Retrd.	1993	5.65	11
1985	Pear 529011-1	Retrd.	1989	3.00	9
1988	Pilgrim Boy 529049-3	Retrd.	1992	3.95	12
1988	Pilgrim Girl 529049-4	Retrd.	1992	3.95	12
1985	Pineapple 529011-4	Retrd.	1989	3.00	10
1985	Pink Heart 529201-3	Retrd.	1989	2.85	9
1989	Puppy 529303-4	Retrd.	1994	6.45	10
1986	Purple Father Christmas 529047-6	Retrd.	1992	3.95	12
1984	Queen of Heart 529007-3	Retrd.	1986	2.70	12
1986	Rabbit in Egg 529033-2	Retrd.	1993	3.60	9
1986	Red Father Christmas 529047-1	Retrd.	1992	3.95	12
1986	Red Father Christmas 529047-4	Retrd.	1992	3.95	12
1985	Red Heart 529201-1	Retrd.	1990	2.85	9
1985	Red Riding Hood 529009-2	Retrd.	1988	1.60	10
1986	Rocking Horse on Bell 529023-4	Retrd.	1990	3.95	9
1985	Roly-Poly Santa 529015-6	Retrd.	1989	3.00	12
1984	Santa Head 529005-4	Retrd.	1987	2.70	12
1985	Santa Head 529009-3	Retrd.	1988	3.00	10
1986	Santa on Bell 529023-3	Retrd.	1990	3.95	12
1984	Santa on Heart 529005-5	Retrd.	1987	3.00	10
1993	Santa with Tree 5207	Retrd.	1993	5.50	6
1985	Santa with Tree 529015-3	Retrd.	1992	3.00	10
1985	School Bus 529019-6	Retrd.	1991	2.70	13
1985	Six Red & White Hearts 529201	Retrd.	1989	15.00	16
1992	Six Snowmen 529305	Retrd.	1993	29.00	54
1984	Snowman 519001-2	Retrd.	1986	2.50	10
1985	Soldier with Drum 529013-1	Retrd.	1988	2.70	10
1985	Soldier with Gun 529013-2	Retrd.	1988	2.70	10
1985	Soldiers, set of 6 529013	Retrd.	1988	17.95	54
1989	Squirrel 529303-2	Retrd.	1994	6.45	9
1984	Standing Santa 529001-3	Retrd.	1987	3.00	10
1988	Stocking 529051-3	Retrd.	1992	3.95	10
1985	Strawberry 529011-2	Retrd.	1989	3.00	9
1993	Sugar Apple 5254	Retrd.	1993	5.50	6
1993	Sugar Fruit Basket 5256	Retrd.	1994	5.65	8
1993	Sugar Grapes 5252	Retrd.	1993	5.50	6
1993	Sugar Pear 5255	Retrd.	1993	5.50	6
1993	Sugar Plum 5253	Retrd.	1993	5.65	8
1985	Sugar Plum Fairy 529017-6	Retrd.	1989	2.70	10
1993	Sugar Strawberry 5251	Retrd.	1993	5.65	8
1989	Swan 529303-5	Retrd.	1994	6.45	12
1986	Teddy Bear 529023-2	Retrd.	1990	3.95	10
1988	Teddy Bear 529051-5	Retrd.	1992	3.95	9
1986	Teddy Bear with Ball 529041-5	Retrd.	1994	3.95	6
1986	Teddy Bear w/Candy Cane 529041-1	Retrd.	1992	3.95	8
1986	Teddy Bear w/Nightshirt 529041-4	Retrd.	1994	3.95	9
1986	Teddy Bear w/Red Heart 529041-2	Retrd.	1992	3.95	8
1986	Teddy Bear with Tree 529041-3	Retrd.	1992	3.95	10
1986	Teddy Bear with Vest 529041-6	Retrd.	1992	3.95	6
1986	Teddy Bears, set of 6 529041	Retrd.	1991	25.00	54
1988	Thanksgiving, set of 6 529049	Retrd.	1992	25.00	54
1988	Toy, set of 6 529051	Retrd.	1992	25.00	58
1985	Transportation Set 529019	Retrd.	1988	17.90	58
1986	Tree on Bell 529023-1	Retrd.	1991	3.95	9
1985	Tug Boat 529019-1	Retrd.	1988	2.70	12
1988	Turkey 529049-2	Retrd.	1992	3.95	8
1986	White Father Christmas 529047-5	Retrd.	1992	3.95	12
1985	White Heart 529201-2	Retrd.	1989	2.85	8

Miscellaneous Forms - E.M. Merck, unless otherwise noted

YEAR ISSUE		EDITION LIMIT	YEAR RETD.	ISSUE PRICE	*QUOTE U.S.$
1990	Assorted Christmas Flowers 3626	Retrd.	1994	8.00	9
1990	Assorted Christmas Stars 3620	Retrd.	1995	7.00	7
1993	Assorted Fantasy Form with Wire 3650	Retrd.	1994	20.00	23
1992	Assorted Northern Stars 3640	Retrd.	1995	6.20	7
1992	Assorted Spirals 3636	Retrd.	1995	8.25	9
1992	Christmas Ball with Roses 3634	Retrd.	1995	9.45	10
1990	Clip-On Pink Rose 3628	Retrd.	1995	9.25	10
1988	Clip-On Tulip (A) 3605	Retrd.	1995	8.70	9
1990	Edelweiss on Form 3618	Retrd.	1995	8.25	9
1986	Flower Basket 3601	Retrd.	1995	10.25	11
1989	Flower with Butterfly 3609	Retrd.	1993	9.75	13
1985	Ice Cream Cone 3637164	Retrd.	1988	14.50	24
1990	Large Conical Shell 3629	Retrd.	1993	8.70	12
1990	Large Sea Shell 3625	Retrd.	1995	8.35	9
1990	Large Snowflake 3622	Retrd.	1995	13.00	13
1993	Lucky Shamrock 3643	Retrd.	1993	7.80	23
1989	Morning Glories 3608	Retrd.	1995	8.90	9
1990	Poinsettias 3619	Retrd.	1995	9.90	10
1989	Red Rose on Form 3607	Retrd.	1995	5.85	6
1990	Shamrock on Form 3621	Retrd.	1995	5.55	6
1989	Shiny Red Clip-On Tulip 3617	Retrd.	1990	7.45	8
1988	Skull 3606	Retrd.	1995	7.35	8
1990	Sunburst 3624	Retrd.	1993	8.00	8
1994	Victorian Floral Drop 3659	Retrd.	1995	22.00	22

Musical Instruments - E.M. Merck

YEAR ISSUE		EDITION LIMIT	YEAR RETD.	ISSUE PRICE	*QUOTE U.S.$
1989	Bell with Flowers 3805	Retrd.	1995	5.85	6
1986	Cello 3801	Retrd.	1995	6.65	7
1989	Christmas Bells on From 3806	Retrd.	1995	8.35	9
1988	Clip-On Drum 383534	Retrd.	1994	8.00	10
1987	Guitar 3802	Retrd.	1995	6.65	7
1988	Large Bell with Acorns 3804	Retrd.	1994	9.00	12
1990	Large Christmas Bell 3808	Retrd.	1995	10.35	11
1990	Lyre 3809	Retrd.	1995	8.35	9
1990	Small Fancy Drum 3815	Retrd.	1995	7.80	8

Porcelain Christmas - E.M. Merck

YEAR ISSUE		EDITION LIMIT	YEAR RETD.	ISSUE PRICE	*QUOTE U.S.$
1989	Angel 9435	Retrd.	1994	6.65	12
1995	Angelic Gifts 9712	Retrd.	1995	11.25	12
1988	Bear on Skates 9495	Retrd.	1988	10.00	19
1988	Bunnies on Skies 9494	Retrd.	1988	10.00	19
1987	Father Christmas (A) 9404	Retrd.	1988	11.00	13
1987	Father Christmas w/Cape 9405	Retrd.	1988	11.00	14
1987	Father Christmas w/Toys 9406	Retrd.	1988	11.00	12
1989	Hummingbird 9433	Retrd.	1994	6.65	9
1987	Lighted Angel Tree Top 9420	Retrd.	1992	29.50	37
1989	Nutcracker 9436	Retrd.	1994	6.65	12
1988	Penguin w/Gifts 9496	Retrd.	1988	10.00	19
1989	Rocking Horse 9431	Retrd.	1994	6.65	11
1987	Roly-Poly Santa 9441	Retrd.	1988	6.75	14
1989	Santa 9432	Retrd.	1994	6.65	7
1987	Santa Head 9410	Retrd.	1988	6.55	12
1989	Teddy Bear 9434	Retrd.	1994	6.65	10
1995	Toys Ahoy 9713	Retrd.	1995	11.25	12
1995	Wish Upon a Star 9711	Retrd.	1995	11.25	12

Reflectors - E.M. Merck, unless otherwise noted

YEAR ISSUE		EDITION LIMIT	YEAR RETD.	ISSUE PRICE	*QUOTE U.S.$
1990	Assorted 6 cm Reflectors 4207	Retrd.	1995	7.00	7
1990	Assorted Reflectors with Diamonds 4206	Retrd.	1995	9.95	12
1992	Flower in Reflector 4212	Retrd.	1995	9.25	10
1986	Horseshoe Reflector 4203	Retrd.	1989	7.80	15
1987	Large Drop with Indents (A) 4204	Retrd.	1994	12.85	17
1986	Pink Reflector 4202	Retrd.	1995	9.50	10
1993	Reflector with Tinsel Wire 4215	Retrd.	1995	20.00	20
1992	Scrap Santa in Reflector 4214	Retrd.	1993	8.80	18
1986	Star Pattern Reflector (A) 4201	Retrd.	1994	9.25	14

Santas - E.M. Merck, unless otherwise noted

YEAR ISSUE		EDITION LIMIT	YEAR RETD.	ISSUE PRICE	*QUOTE U.S.$
1985	Blue Father Christmas 4010498	Retrd.	1995	8.00	8
1990	Blue Victorian St. Nick 4028	Retrd.	1993	9.95	14
1987	Burgundy Father Christmas 4013	Retrd.	1995	7.80	16
1987	Burgundy Santa Claus 4014	Retrd.	1994	13.95	14
1990	Clip-On Victorian St. Nick 4030	Retrd.	1995	11.00	11
1986	Father Christmas Head 4006	Retrd.	1995	7.80	8
1985	Father Christmas Head 403223	Retrd.	1994	7.80	10
1985	Father Christmas with Basket 403224	Retrd.	1994	7.80	10
1985	Father Christmas w/Tree 401039	Retrd.	1995	8.00	8
1990	Festive Santa Head 4039	Retrd.	1995	11.00	11
1985	Gold Father Christmas 401045	Retrd.	1995	7.45	8
1986	Green Clip-On Santa 4007	Retrd.	1995	7.80	8
1985	Jolly Father Christmas 401043	Retrd.	1995	7.00	7
1993	Large Father Christmas Head 4066	Retrd.	1995	22.50	23
1984	Large Santa In Basket 401001	Retrd.	1995	12.95	13
1985	Large Santa with Tree 401055	Retrd.	1995	12.60	13
1990	Light Blue St. Nicholas 4029	Retrd.	1994	6.45	10
1987	Matte Red Roly-Poly Santa 4012	Retrd.	1995	7.90	8
1984	Old Father Christmas Head 401007	Retrd.	1994	7.00	10
1989	Old-Fashioned Santa (A) 4019	Retrd.	1995	5.75	6
1986	Pink Clip-On Santa 4011	Retrd.	1994	8.35	10
1985	Pink Father Christmas 4010499	Retrd.	1995	8.00	8
1984	Roly-Poly Santa 401002	Retrd.	1994	7.90	11
1990	Round Jolly Santa Head 4035	Retrd.	1995	11.00	11
1987	Santa Above Ball 4018	Retrd.	1995	13.95	14
1985	Santa and Tree on Form 401026	Retrd.	1995	9.25	10
1987	Santa in Airplane 4017	Retrd.	1995	13.95	14
1986	Santa In Chimney 4005	Retrd.	1995	8.70	18
1985	Santa in Chimney 406912	Retrd.	1989	11.00	17
1985	Santa in Tree 401054	Retrd.	1995	7.45	8
1986	Santa On Carriage 4003	Retrd.	1988	10.00	29
1986	Santa On Cone 4002	Retrd.	1993	7.90	16
1986	Santa with Glued-On Tree 4009	Retrd.	1995	9.00	9
1986	Small Blue Santa 4010	Retrd.	1995	5.40	6
1984	Small Old-Fashioned Santa 401022	Retrd.	1994	6.65	9
1985	Small Santa in Basket 401105	Retrd.	1995	9.25	10
1985	Small Santa with Pack 401065	Retrd.	1995	5.40	6
1989	St. Nicholas 4020	Retrd.	1995	10.00	10
1986	St. Nicholas Head 4008	Retrd.	1995	6.65	7
1987	Very Large Santa Head 4015	Retrd.	1995	13.95	14
1989	Victorian Santa 4021	Retrd.	1995	8.45	9
1990	Victorian Scrap Santa 4043	Retrd.	1993	9.70	14
1990	Weihnachtsmann 4034	Retrd.	1995	9.00	9
1990	White Clip-On Santa 4026	Retrd.	1995	7.35	8

Toys - E.M. Merck

YEAR ISSUE		EDITION LIMIT	YEAR RETD.	ISSUE PRICE	*QUOTE U.S.$
1995	Bowling Pin 4413	Retrd.	1995	12.75	13
1985	Doll Buggy with Doll 4437138	Retrd.	1994	7.00	9
1986	Dumb-Dumb 4403	Retrd.	1988	6.45	24
1990	Large Doll Buggy with Doll 4409	Retrd.	1995	11.50	12
1986	Large Nutcracker 4401	Retrd.	1995	13.50	14
1985	Matte Dice 443793	Retrd.	1993	5.75	6
1988	Nutcracker Guard 4405	Retrd.	1995	8.50	9
1985	Small Carousel 446836	Retrd.	1995	7.00	7
1986	Small Nutcracker 4402	Retrd.	1995	10.00	10

Transportation - E.M. Merck, unless otherwise noted

YEAR ISSUE		EDITION LIMIT	YEAR RETD.	ISSUE PRICE	*QUOTE U.S.$
1988	Cable Car 4602	Retrd.	1989	8.45	26
1985	Cable Car 461067	Retrd.	1988	14.95	25
1990	Large Zeppelin 4605	Retrd.	1995	8.25	9
1985	Locomotive 461069	Retrd.	1993	7.00	18
1985	Old-Fashioned Car 463747	Retrd.	1989	6.25	24
1992	Race Car 4609	Retrd.	1995	7.00	7
1986	Rolls Royce 4601	Retrd.	1989	7.90	24

*Quotes have been rounded up to nearest dollar

Tree Tops - E.M. Merck, unless otherwise noted

YEAR ISSUE		EDITION LIMIT	YEAR RETD.	ISSUE PRICE	*QUOTE U.S. $
1987	Angel in Indent Tree Top 5009	Retrd.	1995	27.00	27
1987	Angel w/Crown 5007	Retrd.	1993	50.00	72
1986	Blue Santa 5002	Retrd.	1995	37.50	38
1985	Fancy Gold Spire w/Bells 506266	Retrd.	1993	32.00	46
1985	Fancy Red Spire w/Bells 506269	Retrd.	1993	32.00	46
1987	Santa in Indent 5008	Retrd.	1995	25.00	25

Trees & Cones - E.M. Merck, unless otherwise noted

YEAR ISSUE		EDITION LIMIT	YEAR RETD.	ISSUE PRICE	*QUOTE U.S. $
1988	Large Mauve & Champagne Cone 4802	Retrd.	1993	11.85	17
1985	Medium Gold Cone w/Glitter 486712-5	Retrd.	1995	3.85	4
1990	Multi-Colored Tree 4812	Retrd.	1994	5.55	9
1985	Very Large Red & Gold Cones 483612	Retrd.	1995	7.00	7

Orrefors

Christmas Ornaments - E. Lagerbielke

YEAR ISSUE		EDITION LIMIT	YEAR RETD.	ISSUE PRICE	*QUOTE U.S. $
1996	Snow Star	Yr.Iss.		45.00	45

Pacific Rim Import Corp.

Bristol Waterfront - P. Sebern

YEAR ISSUE		EDITION LIMIT	YEAR RETD.	ISSUE PRICE	*QUOTE U.S. $
1995	Portshead Lighthouse	Open		10.00	10

Possible Dreams

Clothtique® Pepsi® Santa Collection - B. Prata

YEAR ISSUE		EDITION LIMIT	YEAR RETD.	ISSUE PRICE	*QUOTE U.S. $
1995	Yule Pop The Top	Open		7.90	8
1995	Christmas Bells & Bubbles	Open		7.40	8
1995	Holiday Cheer on Top	Open		12.20	13
1995	Get Into The Swing	Open		9.90	10
1995	Unfurl The Fun	Open		7.40	8

Crinkle Claus - Staff

YEAR ISSUE		EDITION LIMIT	YEAR RETD.	ISSUE PRICE	*QUOTE U.S. $
1996	Bishop of Maya-659702	Open		7.80	8
1996	Black Forest Santa-659706	Open		7.80	8
1996	Father Christmas-659703	Open		7.80	8
1996	German Santa-659701	Open		7.80	8
1996	Pere Noel Santa-659705	Open		7.80	8
1996	St. Nicholas-659704	Open		7.80	8

The Thickets at Sweetbriar®- B. Ross

YEAR ISSUE		EDITION LIMIT	YEAR RETD.	ISSUE PRICE	*QUOTE U.S. $
1995	Christmas Whiskers-350400	Closed	1996	11.50	12
1995	Jingle Bells-350407	Closed	1996	12.00	12
1996	Snuggles-350416	Open		11.70	12
1996	Nibbley-Do-350415	Open		10.50	11

Rawcliffe Corporation

Bubble Fairy™ Ornaments - J. deStefano

YEAR ISSUE		EDITION LIMIT	YEAR RETD.	ISSUE PRICE	*QUOTE U.S. $
1993	Blessing Hanging Baby Bubble Fairy	Open		40.00	40
1992	Holly Hanging Baby Bubble Fairy	Open		40.00	40
1993	Joy Hanging Baby Bubble Fairy	Open		40.00	40
1993	Sweetness Hanging Baby Bubble Fairy	Open		40.00	40
1993	Wonder Hanging Baby Bubble Fairy	Open		40.00	40

Reed & Barton

12 Days of Christmas Sterling and Lead Crystal - Reed & Barton

YEAR ISSUE		EDITION LIMIT	YEAR RETD.	ISSUE PRICE	*QUOTE U.S. $
1988	Partridge in a Pear Tree	Yr.Iss.		25.00	40
1989	Two Turtle Doves	Yr.Iss.		25.00	28
1990	Three French Hens	Yr.Iss.		27.50	30
1991	Four Colly birds	Yr.Iss.		27.50	30
1992	Five Golden Rings	Yr.Iss.		27.50	28
1993	Six Geese A Laying	Yr.Iss.		27.50	35
1994	Seven Swans A 'Swimming	Yr.Iss.		27.50	35
1995	Eight Maids A Milking	Yr.Iss.		30.00	28
1996	Nine Ladies Dancing	Yr.Iss.		30.00	30

Carousel Horse - Reed & Barton

YEAR ISSUE		EDITION LIMIT	YEAR RETD.	ISSUE PRICE	*QUOTE U.S. $
1988	Silverplate-1988	Closed	1988	13.50	14
1988	Gold-covered-1988	Closed	1988	15.00	15
1989	Silverplate-1989	Closed	1989	13.50	14
1989	Gold-covered-1989	Closed	1989	15.00	15
1990	Silverplate-1990	Closed	1990	13.50	14
1990	Gold-covered-1990	Closed	1990	15.00	15
1991	Silverplate-1991	Closed	1991	13.50	14
1991	Gold-covered-1991	Closed	1991	15.00	15
1992	Silverplate-1992	Closed	1992	13.50	14
1992	Gold-covered-1992	Closed	1992	15.00	15
1993	Silverplate-1993	Closed	1993	13.50	14
1993	Gold-covered-1993	Closed	1993	15.00	15
1994	Silverplate-1994	Yr.Iss.	1994	13.50	14
1994	Gold-covered-1994	Yr.Iss.	1994	15.00	15
1995	Silverplate-1995	Yr.Iss.		13.50	14
1995	Gold-covered-1995	Yr.Iss.		15.00	15

Christmas Cross - Reed & Barton

YEAR ISSUE		EDITION LIMIT	YEAR RETD.	ISSUE PRICE	*QUOTE U.S. $
1971	Sterling Silver-1971	Closed	1971	10.00	140-300
1971	24Kt. Gold over Sterling-V1971	Closed	1971	17.50	300
1972	Sterling Silver-1972	Closed	1972	10.00	75-175
1972	24Kt. Gold over Sterling-V1972	Closed	1972	17.50	75-175
1973	Sterling Silver-1973	Closed	1973	10.00	60-85
1973	24Kt. Gold over Sterling-V1973	Closed	1973	17.50	60-85
1974	Sterling Silver-1974	Closed	1974	12.95	45-75
1974	24Kt. Gold over Sterling-V1974	Closed	1974	20.00	45-75
1975	Sterling Silver-1975	Closed	1975	12.95	35-60
1975	24Kt. Gold over Sterling-V1975	Closed	1975	20.00	50-60
1976	Sterling Silver-1976	Closed	1976	13.95	45-75
1976	24Kt. Gold over Sterling-V1976	Closed	1976	19.95	45-50
1977	Sterling Silver-1977	Closed	1977	15.00	35-60
1977	24Kt. Gold over Sterling-V1977	Closed	1977	18.50	45-50
1978	Sterling Silver-1978	Closed	1978	16.00	45-85
1978	24Kt. Gold over Sterling-V1978	Closed	1978	20.00	45-55
1979	Sterling Silver-1979	Closed	1979	20.00	45-90
1979	24Kt. Gold over Sterling-V1979	Closed	1979	24.00	32-57
1980	Sterling Silver-1980	Closed	1980	35.00	125
1980	24Kt. Gold over Sterling-V1980	Closed	1980	40.00	45-50
1981	Sterling Silver-1981	Closed	1981	35.00	95-125
1981	24Kt. Gold over Sterling-V1981	Closed	1981	40.00	45
1982	Sterling Silver-1982	Closed	1982	35.00	45-90
1982	24Kt. Gold over Sterling-V1982	Closed	1982	40.00	45
1983	Sterling Silver-1983	Closed	1983	35.00	100-150
1983	24Kt. Gold over Sterling-V1983	Closed	1983	40.00	40-45
1984	Sterling Silver-1984	Closed	1984	35.00	50-90
1984	24Kt. Gold over Sterling-V1984	Closed	1984	45.00	45
1985	Sterling Silver-1985	Closed	1985	35.00	50-80
1985	24Kt. Gold over Sterling-V1985	Closed	1985	40.00	40
1986	Sterling Silver-1986	Closed	1986	38.50	50-80
1986	24Kt. Gold over Sterling-V1986	Closed	1986	40.00	40
1987	Sterling Silver-1987	Closed	1987	35.00	45-70
1987	24Kt. Gold over Sterling-V1987	Closed	1987	40.00	40
1988	Sterling Silver-1988	Closed	1988	35.00	45-70
1988	24Kt. Gold over Sterling-V1988	Closed	1988	40.00	40
1989	Sterling Silver-1989	Closed	1989	35.00	40-80
1989	24Kt. Gold over Sterling-V1989	Closed	1989	40.00	40
1990	Sterling Silver-1990	Closed	1990	40.00	40-65
1990	24Kt. Gold over Sterling-1990	Closed	1990	45.00	45
1991	Sterling Silver-1991	Closed	1991	40.00	40-65
1991	24Kt. Gold over Sterling-1991	Closed	1991	45.00	45
1992	Sterling Silver-1992	Closed	1992	40.00	55
1992	24Kt. Gold over Sterling-1992	Closed	1992	45.00	45
1993	Sterling Silver-1993	Closed	1993	40.00	65
1993	24Kt. Gold over Sterling-1993	Closed	1993	45.00	45
1994	Sterling Silver-1994	Closed	1994	40.00	28-45
1994	24Kt. Gold over Sterling-1994	Closed	1994	45.00	45
1995	Sterling Silver-1995	Closed	1995	40.00	40
1995	24Kt. Gold over Sterling-1995	Closed	1995	45.00	45
1996	Sterling Silver-1996	Yr.Iss.		40.00	40
1996	Gold Vermiel-1996	Yr.Iss.		45.00	45

Holly Ball - Reed & Barton

YEAR ISSUE		EDITION LIMIT	YEAR RETD.	ISSUE PRICE	*QUOTE U.S. $
1976	1976 Silver plated	Closed	1976	14.00	50
1977	1977 Silver plated	Closed	1977	15.00	50-65
1978	1978 Silver plated	Closed	1978	15.00	30-65
1979	1979 Silver plated	Closed	1979	15.00	45

Holly Bell - Reed & Barton

YEAR ISSUE		EDITION LIMIT	YEAR RETD.	ISSUE PRICE	*QUOTE U.S. $
1980	1980 Bell	Closed	1980	22.50	25-45
1980	Bell, gold plate, V1980	Closed	1980	25.00	45
1981	1981 Bell	Closed	1981	22.50	50
1981	Bell, gold plate, V1981	Closed	1981	27.50	35
1982	1982 Bell	Closed	1982	22.50	75
1982	Bell, gold plate, V1982	Closed	1982	27.50	50
1983	1983 Bell	Closed	1983	23.50	45-75
1983	Bell, gold plate, V1983	Closed	1983	30.00	75
1984	1984 Bell	Closed	1984	25.00	80
1984	Bell, gold plate, V1984	Closed	1984	28.50	50
1985	1985 Bell	Closed	1985	25.00	75
1985	Bell, gold plate, V1985	Closed	1985	28.50	50
1986	1986 Bell	Closed	1986	25.00	75
1986	Bell, gold plate, V1986	Closed	1986	28.50	50
1987	1987 Bell	Closed	1987	27.50	70
1987	Bell, gold plate, V1987	Closed	1987	30.00	50
1988	1988 Bell	Closed	1988	27.50	65
1988	Bell, gold plate, V1988	Closed	1988	30.00	30
1989	1989 Bell	Closed	1989	27.50	55
1989	Bell, gold plate, V1989	Closed	1989	30.00	30
1990	Bell, gold plate, V1990	Closed	1990	30.00	30
1990	1990 Bell	Closed	1990	27.50	55
1991	Bell, gold plate, V1991	Closed	1991	30.00	30
1991	1991 Bell	Closed	1991	27.50	50
1992	Bell, gold plate, V1992	Closed	1992	30.00	30
1992	Bell, silver plate, 1992	Closed	1992	27.50	45
1993	Bell, gold plate, V1993	Closed	1993	27.50	28
1993	Bell, silver plate, 1993	Closed	1993	30.00	45
1994	Bell, gold plate, 1994	Closed	1994	30.00	30
1994	Bell, silver plate, 1994	Closed	1994	27.50	30
1995	Bell, gold plate, 1995	Closed	1995	30.00	30
1995	Bell, silver plate, 1995	Closed	1995	27.50	28
1996	Bell, gold plate, 1996	Yr.Iss.		30.00	30
1996	Bell, silver plate, 1996	Yr.Iss.		27.50	28

Roman, Inc.

Catnippers - I. Spencer

YEAR ISSUE		EDITION LIMIT	YEAR RETD.	ISSUE PRICE	*QUOTE U.S. $
1989	Bow Brummel	Open		15.00	15
1991	Christmas Knight	Open		15.00	15
1988	Christmas Mourning	Open		15.00	15
1991	Faux Paw	Open		15.00	15
1990	Felix Navidad	Open		15.00	15
1989	Happy Holidaze	Open		15.00	15
1991	Holly Days Are Happy Days	Open		15.00	15
1991	Meowy Christmas	Open		15.00	15
1991	Pawtridge in a Purr Tree	Open		15.00	15
1988	Puss in Berries	Open		15.00	15
1988	Ring A Ding-Ding	Open		15.00	15
1989	Sandy Claws	Open		15.00	15
1991	Snow Biz	Open		15.00	15
1990	Sock It to Me Santa	Open		15.00	15
1990	Stuck on Christmas	Open		15.00	15

The Discovery of America - I. Spencer

YEAR ISSUE		EDITION LIMIT	YEAR RETD.	ISSUE PRICE	*QUOTE U.S. $
1991	Kitstopher Kolumbus	1,992		15.00	15
1991	Queen Kitsabella	1,992		15.00	15

Fontanini Annual Christmas Ornaments - E. Simonetti

YEAR ISSUE		EDITION LIMIT	YEAR RETD.	ISSUE PRICE	*QUOTE U.S. $
1991	1991 Annual (Girl)	Yr.Iss.	1991	8.50	9
1991	1991 Annual (Boy)	Yr.Iss.	1991	8.50	9
1992	1992 Annual (Girl)	Yr.Iss.	1992	8.50	9
1992	1992 Annual (Boy)	Yr.Iss.	1992	8.50	9
1993	1993 Annual (Girl)	Yr.Iss.	1993	8.50	9
1993	1993 Annual (Boy)	Yr.Iss.	1993	8.50	9

Fontanini Limited Edition Ornaments - E. Simonetti

YEAR ISSUE		EDITION LIMIT	YEAR RETD.	ISSUE PRICE	*QUOTE U.S. $
1995	The Annunciation	20,000		20.00	20
1996	Journey to Bethlehem	20,000		20.00	20

Millenium™ Ornament - A. Lucchesi

YEAR ISSUE		EDITION LIMIT	YEAR RETD.	ISSUE PRICE	*QUOTE U.S. $
1992	Silent Night	20,000	1992	20.00	20
1993	The Annunciation	20,000	1993	20.00	20
1994	Peace On Earth	20,000	1994	20.00	20
1995	Cause of Our Joy	20,000	1995	20.00	20
1996	Prince of Peace	30,000		20.00	20

Museum Collection of Angela Tripi - A. Tripi

YEAR ISSUE		EDITION LIMIT	YEAR RETD.	ISSUE PRICE	*QUOTE U.S. $
1994	1994 Annual Angel Ornament	2,500	1994	49.50	50
1995	1995 Annual Angel Ornament	2,500		49.50	50

Seraphim Classics™ - Seraphim Studios

YEAR ISSUE		EDITION LIMIT	YEAR RETD.	ISSUE PRICE	*QUOTE U.S. $
1995	Isabel - Gentle Spirit	Open		15.00	15
1995	Iris - Rainbow's End	Open		15.00	15
1995	Lydia - Winged Poet	Open		15.00	15
1995	Cymbeline - Peacemaker	Open		15.00	15
1995	Ophelia - Heart Seeker	Open		15.00	15
1995	Evangeline - Angel of Mercy	Open		15.00	15
1996	Laurice - Wisdom's Child	Open		15.00	15
1996	Felicia - Adoring Maiden	Open		15.00	15
1996	Priscilla - Benevolent Guide	Open		15.00	15
1996	Seraphina - Heaven's Helper	Open		15.00	15

Seraphim Collection by Faro - Faro

YEAR ISSUE		EDITION LIMIT	YEAR RETD.	ISSUE PRICE	*QUOTE U.S. $
1994	Rarest of Heaven	20,000		25.00	25
1995	Heaven's Herald	20,000		25.00	25
1996	Flora, Flower of Heaven	20,000		25.00	25

Vernon Wilson Signature Series - V. Wilson

YEAR ISSUE		EDITION LIMIT	YEAR RETD.	ISSUE PRICE	*QUOTE U.S. $
1995	We Three Kings	Open		34.00	34

Royal Doulton

Bunnykins - Unknown

YEAR ISSUE		EDITION LIMIT	YEAR RETD.	ISSUE PRICE	*QUOTE U.S. $
1992	Caroling	N/A		19.00	19
1991	Santa Bunny	N/A		19.00	19

Christmas Ornaments - Unknown

YEAR ISSUE		EDITION LIMIT	YEAR RETD.	ISSUE PRICE	*QUOTE U.S. $
1993	Together for Christmas	Yr.Iss.		20.00	20
1994	Home For Christmas	Yr.Iss.		20.00	20

Seymour Mann, Inc.

Christmas Collection - Various

YEAR ISSUE		EDITION LIMIT	YEAR RETD.	ISSUE PRICE	*QUOTE U.S. $
1985	Angel Wall XMAS-523 - J. White	Closed	1988	12.00	12
1989	Christmas Cat in Teacup XMAS-660 - J. White	Closed	1992	13.50	14
1990	Cupid CPD-5 - J. White	Closed	1993	13.50	14
1990	Cupid CPD-6 - J. White	Closed	1993	13.50	14
1986	Cupid Head XMAS-53 - J. White	Closed	1988	25.00	25
1990	Doll Tree Topper OM-124 - J. White	Closed	1993	85.00	85
1991	Elf w/ Reindeer CJ-422 - Jaimy	Closed	1993	9.00	9
1991	Elves w/ Mail CJ-464 - J. White	Closed	1993	30.00	30
1991	Flat Red Santa CJ-115R - Jaimy	Closed	1993	2.88	3
1991	Flat Santa CJ-115 - Jaimy	Closed	1993	7.50	8
1991	Floral Plaque XMAS-911 - J. White	Closed	1993	10.00	10
1991	Flower Basket XMAS-912 - J. White	Closed	1993	10.00	10
1990	Hat w/ Streamers OM-116 - J. White	Closed	1993	20.00	20
1990	Heartlace OM-119 - J. White	Closed	1993	12.00	12
1990	Lace Ball OM-120 - J. White	Closed	1993	10.00	10
1994	Santa w/ Candle CBU-300 - J. White	Open		40.00	40
1994	Santa w/ Child CBU-305 - J. White	Open		40.00	40
1994	Santa w/ Children CBU-304 - J. White	Open		40.00	40
1994	Santa w/ Lamb CBU-301 - J. White	Open		40.00	40
1994	Santa w/ Lantern CBU-303 - J. White	Open		40.00	40
1994	Santa w/ List CBU-307 - J. White	Open		40.00	40

*Quotes have been rounded up to nearest dollar

CHRISTMAS ORNAMENTS

YEAR ISSUE		EDITION LIMIT	YEAR RETD.	ISSUE PRICE	*QUOTE U.S.$
1994	Santa w/ Sled CBU-306 - J. White	Open		40.00	40
1994	Santa w/ Stick CBU-302 - J. White	Open		40.00	40
1986	Santa XMAS-384 - J. White	Closed	1989	7.50	8
1991	Santas, set of 6 CJ-12 - Jaimy	Closed	1993	60.00	60
1990	Tassel OM-118 - J. White	Closed	1993	7.50	8

Christmas Lite-Up Houses - L. Sciola

YEAR ISSUE		EDITION LIMIT	YEAR RETD.	ISSUE PRICE	*QUOTE U.S.$
1994	Lite-up Church XMR-21	Open		30.00	30
1994	Lite-up Country House	Open		30.00	30
1994	Lite-up Library XMR-24	Open		30.00	30
1994	Lite-up Mansion XMR-23	Open		30.00	30
1994	Lite-up Restaurant XMR-20	Open		30.00	30
1994	Set/10 Lite-up Houses XMR-10	Open		95.00	95
1994	Set/10 Lite-up Houses XMR-11	Open		95.00	95

Gingerbread Christmas - J. Sauerbrey

YEAR ISSUE		EDITION LIMIT	YEAR RETD.	ISSUE PRICE	*QUOTE U.S.$
1991	Gingerbread Angel CJ-411	Closed	1992	7.50	8
1991	Gingerbread House CJ-416	Closed	1992	7.50	8
1991	Gingerbread Man CJ-415	Closed	1992	7.50	8
1991	Gingerbread Mouse/Boot CJ-409	Closed	1992	7.50	8
1991	Gingerbread Mrs. Claus CJ-414	Closed	1992	7.50	8
1991	Gingerbread Reindeer CJ-410	Closed	1992	7.50	8
1991	Gingerbread Santa CJ-408	Closed	1992	7.50	8
1991	Gingerbread Sleigh CJ-406	Closed	1992	7.50	8
1991	Gingerbread Snowman CJ-412	Closed	1992	7.50	8
1991	Gingerbread Tree CJ-407	Closed	1992	7.50	8

Victorian Christmas Collection - Jaimy

YEAR ISSUE		EDITION LIMIT	YEAR RETD.	ISSUE PRICE	*QUOTE U.S.$
1991	Couple Against Wind CJ-420	Closed	1993	15.00	15

Shelia's Collectibles

Historical Ornament Collection - S. Thompson

YEAR ISSUE		EDITION LIMIT	YEAR RETD.	ISSUE PRICE	*QUOTE U.S.$
1995	Blue Cottage (1st ed.) OR001	7/96		15.00	15
1995	Cape Hatteras Light (1st ed.) OR007	7/96		15.00	15
1995	Chestnut House (1st ed.) OR002	7/96		15.00	15
1995	Drayton House (1st ed.) OR003	7/96		15.00	15
1995	East Brother Lighthouse (1st ed.) OR008	7/96		15.00	15
1995	Eclectic Blue (1st ed.) OR004	7/96		15.00	15
1995	Goeller House (1st ed.) OR005	7/96		15.00	15
1995	Point Fermin Light (1st ed.) OR009	7/96		15.00	15
1996	Artist House OR015	Open		19.00	19
1996	Capital OR018	Open		19.00	19
1996	Dragon OR010	Open		19.00	19
1996	E.B. Hall House OR011	Open		19.00	19
1996	Mail Pouch Barn OR016	Open		19.00	19
1996	Market OR013	Open		19.00	19
1996	Pink House OR020	Open		19.00	19
1996	Rutledge OR012	Open		19.00	19
1996	St. Philips Church OR022	Open		19.00	19
1995	Stockton Row (1st ed.) OR006	7/96		15.00	15
1996	Thomas Point Light OR019	Open		19.00	19
1996	Titman House OR021	Open		19.00	19
1996	Victoria OR014	Open		19.00	19
1996	White Cottage OR017	Open		19.00	19

Swarovski America Limited

Holiday Ornaments - Swarovski

YEAR ISSUE		EDITION LIMIT	YEAR RETD.	ISSUE PRICE	*QUOTE U.S.$
1981	1981 Snowflake 7563NR35	Yr.Iss.		30.00	300-400
1987	1987 Holiday Etching-Candle	Yr.Iss.		20.00	200-315
1988	1988 Holiday Etching-Wreath	Yr.Iss.		25.00	65-95
1989	1989 Holiday Etching-Dove	Yr.Iss.		35.00	175-225
1990	1990 Holiday Etching-Merry Christmas	Yr.Iss.		25.00	150-225
1991	1991 Holiday Ornament-Star	Yr.Iss.		35.00	75-100
1992	1992 Holiday Ornament-Star	Yr.Iss.		37.50	85-175
1993	1993 Holiday Ornament-Star	Yr.Iss.		37.50	125-225
1994	1994 Holiday Ornament-Star	Yr.Iss.		37.50	50-100
1995	1995 Holiday Ornament-Star	Yr.Iss.		40.00	50-100

Towle Silversmiths

Christmas Angel Medallions - Towle

YEAR ISSUE		EDITION LIMIT	YEAR RETD.	ISSUE PRICE	*QUOTE U.S.$
1991	1991 Angel	Closed	1991	45.00	75
1992	1992 Angel	Closed	1992	45.00	70
1993	1993 Angel	Closed	1993	45.00	50
1994	1994 Angel	Closed	1994	50.00	50
1995	1995 Angel	Closed	1995	50.00	50

Remembrance Collection - Towle

YEAR ISSUE		EDITION LIMIT	YEAR RETD.	ISSUE PRICE	*QUOTE U.S.$
1990	1990 - Old Master Snowflake	Closed	1990	40.00	55-75
1991	1991 - Old Master Snowflake	Closed	1991	40.00	50-70
1992	1992 - Old Master Snowflake	Closed	1992	40.00	45-65
1993	1993 - Old Master Snowflake	Closed	1993	40.00	45-65
1994	1994 - Old Master Snowflake	Closed	1994	50.00	60
1995	1995 - Old Master Snowflake	Closed	1995	50.00	50

Songs of Christmas Medallions - Towle

YEAR ISSUE		EDITION LIMIT	YEAR RETD.	ISSUE PRICE	*QUOTE U.S.$
1978	Silent Night Medallion	Closed	1978	35.00	45-75
1979	Deck The Halls	Closed	1979	35.00	60-75
1980	Jingle Bells	Closed	1980	53.00	75
1981	Hark the Hearld Angels Sing	Closed	1981	53.00	100
1982	O Christmas Tree	Closed	1982	35.00	75-100
1983	Silver Bells	Closed	1983	40.00	55-65
1984	Let It Snow	Closed	1984	30.00	55-70
1985	Chestnuts Roasting on Open Fire	Closed	1985	35.00	55-70
1986	It Came Upon a Midnight Clear	Closed	1986	35.00	45-70
1987	White Christmas	Closed	1987	35.00	45-70

Sterling Cross - Towle

YEAR ISSUE		EDITION LIMIT	YEAR RETD.	ISSUE PRICE	*QUOTE U.S.$
1994	Sterling Cross	Closed	1994	50.00	50
1995	Christmas Cross	Closed	1995	50.00	50

Sterling Floral Medallions - Towle

YEAR ISSUE		EDITION LIMIT	YEAR RETD.	ISSUE PRICE	*QUOTE U.S.$
1983	Christmas Rose	Closed	1983	40.00	55
1984	Hawthorn/Glastonbury Thorn	Closed	1984	40.00	50
1985	Poinsettia	Closed	1985	35.00	50-60
1986	Laurel Bay	Closed	1986	35.00	45-70
1987	Mistletoe	Closed	1987	35.00	55-75
1988	Holly	Closed	1988	40.00	55-70
1989	Ivy	Closed	1989	35.00	55-65
1990	Christmas Cactus	Closed	1990	40.00	55
1991	Chrysanthemum	Closed	1991	40.00	55
1992	Star of Bethlehem	Closed	1992	40.00	45

Sterling Nativity Medallions - Towle

YEAR ISSUE		EDITION LIMIT	YEAR RETD.	ISSUE PRICE	*QUOTE U.S.$
1988	The Angel Appeared	Closed	1988	40.00	80-135
1989	The Journey	Closed	1989	40.00	60-80
1990	No Room at the Inn	Closed	1990	40.00	45-60
1991	Tidings of Joy	Closed	1991	40.00	45-55
1992	Star of Bethlehem	Closed	1992	40.00	45-70
1993	Mother and Child	Closed	1993	40.00	55
1994	Three Wisemen	Closed	1994	40.00	45
1995	Newborn King	Closed	1995	40.00	40

Sterling Twelve Days of Christmas Medallions - Towle

YEAR ISSUE		EDITION LIMIT	YEAR RETD.	ISSUE PRICE	*QUOTE U.S.$
1971	Partridge in A Pear Tree	Closed	1971	20.00	500
1972	Two Turtle Doves	Closed	1972	20.00	125-250
1973	Three French Hens	Closed	1973	20.00	50-90
1974	Four Calling Birds	Closed	1974	30.00	80-150
1975	Five Golden Rings	Closed	1975	30.00	90-100
1975	Five Golden Rings (vermeil)	Closed	1975	30.00	200-300
1976	Six Geese-a-Laying	Closed	1976	30.00	90-150
1977	Seven Swans-a-Swimming	Closed	1977	35.00	90
1977	Seven Swans-a-Swimming (turquoise)	Closed	1977	35.00	200-300
1978	Eight Maids-a-Milking	Closed	1978	37.00	80-100
1979	Nine Ladies Dancing	Closed	1979	37.00	80-100
1980	Ten Lords-a-Leaping	Closed	1980	76.00	80-100
1981	Eleven Pipers Piping	Closed	1981	50.00	80-100
1982	Twelve Drummers Drumming	Closed	1982	35.00	80-100

Twelve Days of Christmas - Towle

YEAR ISSUE		EDITION LIMIT	YEAR RETD.	ISSUE PRICE	*QUOTE U.S.$
1991	Partridge in A Pear Tree In A Wreath	Closed	1991	50.00	85
1992	Two Turtle Doves In A Wreath	Closed	1992	50.00	55
1993	Three French Hens In A Wreath	Closed	1993	50.00	60
1994	Four Calling Birds In A Wreath	Closed	1995	50.00	50

United Design Corp.

Angels Collection-Tree Ornaments™ - P.J. Jonas, unless otherwise noted

YEAR ISSUE		EDITION LIMIT	YEAR RETD.	ISSUE PRICE	*QUOTE U.S.$
1992	Angel and Tambourine IBO-422 - S. Bradford	Open		20.00	20
1992	Angel and Tambourine, ivory IBO-425 - S. Bradford	Open		20.00	20
1993	Angel Baby w/ Bunny IBO-426 - D. Newburn	Open		23.00	24
1991	Angel Waif, ivory IBO-411	Open		15.00	20
1993	Angel Waif, plum IBO-437	Open		20.00	20
1995	Autumn's Bounty IBO-460	Open		32.00	32
1995	Autumn's Bounty, light IBO-454	Open		32.00	32
1995	Birds of a Feather IBO-457	Open		27.00	27
1990	Crystal Angel IBO-401	Retrd.	1993	20.00	20
1993	Crystal Angel, emerald IBO-446	Open		20.00	20
1990	Crystal Angel, ivory IBO-405	Open		20.00	20
1991	Fra Angelico Drummer, blue IBO-414 - S. Bradford	Open		20.00	20
1991	Fra Angelico Drummer, ivory IBO-420 - S. Bradford	Open		20.00	20
1991	Girl Cupid w/Rose, ivory IBO-413 - S. Bradford	Open		15.00	20
1995	Heavenly Blossoms IBO-458	Open		27.00	27
1993	Heavenly Harmony IBO-428	Open		25.00	30
1993	Heavenly Harmony, crimson IBO-433	Open		22.00	30
1993	Little Angel IBO-430 - D. Newburn	Open		18.00	20
1993	Little Angel, crimson IBO-445 - D. Newburn	Open		18.00	20
1992	Mary and Dove IBO-424 - S. Bradford	Open		20.00	20
1994	Music and Grace IBO-448	Open		24.00	24
1994	Music and Grace, crimson IBO-449	Open		24.00	24
1994	Musical Flight IBO-450	Open		28.00	28
1994	Musical Flight, crimson IBO-451	Open		28.00	28
1991	Peace Descending, ivory IBO-412	Open		20.00	20
1993	Peace Descending, crimson IBO-436	Open		20.00	20
1993	Renaissance Angel IBO-429	Open		24.00	24
1993	Renaissance Angel, crimson IBO-431	Open		24.00	24
1990	Rose of Sharon IBO-402	Retrd.	1993	20.00	20
1993	Rose of Sharon, crimson IBO-439	Open		20.00	20
1990	Rose of Sharon, ivory IBO-406	Open		20.00	20
1993	Rosetti Angel, crimson IBO-434	Open		20.00	24
1991	Rosetti Angel, ivory IBO-410	Open		20.00	24
1995	Special Wishes IBO-456 - D. Newburn	Open		27.00	27
1995	Spring's Rebirth IBO-452	Open		32.00	32
1992	St. Francis and Critters IBO-423 - S. Bradford	Open		20.00	20
1994	Star Flight IBO-447	Open		20.00	20
1990	Star Glory IBO-403	Retrd.	1993	15.00	15
1993	Star Glory, crimson IBO-438	Open		20.00	20
1990	Star Glory, ivory IBO-407	Open		15.00	20
1993	Stars & Lace IBO-427	Open		18.00	20
1993	Stars & Lace, Emerald IBO-432	Open		18.00	20
1995	Summer's Glory IBO-453	Open		32.00	32
1995	Tender Time IBO-459	Open		27.00	27
1990	Victorian Angel IBO-404	Retrd.	1993	15.00	15
1990	Victorian Angel, ivory IBO-408	Open		15.00	20
1993	Victorian Angel, plum IBO-435	Open		18.00	20
1993	Victorian Cupid, crimson IBO-440	Open		15.00	20
1991	Victorian Cupid, ivory IBO-409	Open		15.00	20
1995	Winter's Light IBO-455	Open		32.00	32

Teddy Angels™ - P.J. Jonas

YEAR ISSUE		EDITION LIMIT	YEAR RETD.	ISSUE PRICE	*QUOTE U.S.$
1995	Casey "You're a bright & shining star." BA-017	Open		13.00	13
1995	Ivy "Enchantment glows in winter snows." BA-018	Open		13.00	13

Wallace Silversmiths

Annual Pewter Bells - Wallace

YEAR ISSUE		EDITION LIMIT	YEAR RETD.	ISSUE PRICE	*QUOTE U.S.$
1992	Angel	Closed	1992	25.00	30
1993	Santa Holding List	Closed	1993	25.00	25
1994	Large Santa Bell	Closed	1994	25.00	25
1995	Santa Bell	Yr.Iss.		25.00	25

Annual Silverplated Sleigh Bells - Wallace

YEAR ISSUE		EDITION LIMIT	YEAR RETD.	ISSUE PRICE	*QUOTE U.S.$
1971	1st Edition Sleigh Bell	Closed	1971	12.95	600-1000
1972	2nd Edition Sleigh Bell	Closed	1972	12.95	500-620
1973	3rd Edition Sleigh Bell	Closed	1973	12.95	450-575
1974	4th Edition Sleigh Bell	Closed	1974	13.95	200-350
1975	5th Edition Sleigh Bell	Closed	1975	13.95	150-275
1976	6th Edition Sleigh Bell	Closed	1976	13.95	200-375
1977	7th Edition Sleigh Bell	Closed	1977	14.95	125-225
1978	8th Edition Sleigh Bell	Closed	1978	14.95	85-120
1979	9th Edition Sleigh Bell	Closed	1979	15.95	120-170
1980	10th Edition Sleigh Bell	Closed	1980	18.95	50-75
1981	11th Edition Sleigh Bell	Closed	1981	18.95	80-100
1982	12th Edition Sleigh Bell	Closed	1982	19.95	100-125
1983	13th Edition Sleigh Bell	Closed	1983	19.95	100-125
1984	14th Edition Sleigh Bell	Closed	1984	21.95	90
1985	15th Edition Sleigh Bell	Closed	1985	21.95	75-100
1986	16th Edition Sleigh Bell	Closed	1986	21.95	40-75
1987	17th Edition Sleigh Bell	Closed	1987	21.99	35-60
1988	18th Edition Sleigh Bell	Closed	1988	21.99	40-60
1989	19th Edition Sleigh Bell	Closed	1989	24.99	50-75
1990	20th Edition Sleigh Bell	Closed	1990	25.00	40-55
1990	Special Edition Sleigh Bell, gold	Closed	1990	35.00	75
1991	21st Edition Sleigh Bell	Closed	1991	25.00	40
1992	22th Edition Sleigh Bell	Closed	1992	25.00	45
1993	23rd Edition Sleigh Bell	Closed	1993	25.00	40
1994	24th Edition Sleigh Bell	Closed	1994	25.00	35
1994	Sleigh Bell, gold	Closed	1994	35.00	45
1995	25th Edition Sleigh Bell	Closed	1995	30.00	30
1995	Sleigh Bell, gold	Closed	1995	35.00	35

Candy Canes - Wallace

YEAR ISSUE		EDITION LIMIT	YEAR RETD.	ISSUE PRICE	*QUOTE U.S.$
1981	Peppermint	Closed	1981	8.95	125-250
1982	Wintergreen	Closed	1982	9.95	60-110
1983	Cinnamon	Closed	1983	10.95	50-75
1984	Clove	Closed	1984	10.95	50-60
1985	Dove Motif	Closed	1985	11.95	50-70
1986	Bell Motif	Closed	1986	11.95	80-120
1987	Teddy Bear Motif	Closed	1987	12.95	70-110
1988	Christmas Rose	Closed	1988	13.99	45-75
1989	Christmas Candle	Closed	1989	14.99	45
1990	Reindeer	Closed	1990	16.00	30
1991	Christmas Goose	Closed	1991	16.00	35
1992	Angel	Closed	1992	16.00	30
1993	Snowmen	Closed	1993	16.00	30
1994	Canes	Closed	1994	17.00	20
1995	Santa	Closed	1995	18.00	20

Cathedral Ornaments - Wallace

YEAR ISSUE		EDITION LIMIT	YEAR RETD.	ISSUE PRICE	*QUOTE U.S.$
1988	1988-1st Edition	Closed	1988	24.99	45
1989	1989-2nd Edition	Closed	1989	24.99	30
1990	1990-3rd Edition	Closed	1990	25.00	25

Grande Baroque 12 Day Series - Wallace

YEAR ISSUE		EDITION LIMIT	YEAR RETD.	ISSUE PRICE	*QUOTE U.S.$
1988	Partridge	Closed	1988	39.99	75
1989	Two Turtle Doves	Closed	1989	39.99	60-100
1990	Three French Hens	Closed	1990	40.00	60-100
1991	Four Colly Birds	Closed	1991	40.00	150
1992	Five Golden Rings	Closed	1992	40.00	40-60
1993	Six Geese-a-Laying	Closed	1993	40.00	50
1994	Seven Swans-a-Swimming	Closed	1994	40.00	50
1995	Eight Maids-a-Milking	Open		40.00	40

*Quotes have been rounded up to nearest dollar

Walnut Ridge Collectibles

Gossamer Wings - K. Bejma

YEAR ISSUE		EDITION LIMIT	YEAR RETD.	ISSUE PRICE	*QUOTE U.S.$
1996	Charity Piece - Glimmer of Hope I	Open		40.00	40

Limited Edition Christmas Ornament - K. Bejma

YEAR ISSUE		EDITION LIMIT	YEAR RETD.	ISSUE PRICE	*QUOTE U.S.$
1996	Snowy, Snowy Night-703	Yr. Iss.		56.00	56

Ornament Collection - K. Bejma

YEAR ISSUE		EDITION LIMIT	YEAR RETD.	ISSUE PRICE	*QUOTE U.S.$
1994	Angel Bunny-21	Open		26.00	26
1995	Angel Donkey-24	Open		26.00	26
1995	Angel Elephant-23	Open		26.00	26
1993	Angel Icicle-9	Open		22.00	22
1994	Angel Kitty-20	Open		26.00	26
1994	Angel Pig-22	Open		26.00	26
1996	Angel w/Star on Wand-35	Open		24.00	24
1994	Angels, Set/3-15	Open		66.00	66
1995	Angels, Set/3-18	Open		66.00	66
1993	Baby Snowman Icicle-12	Open		22.00	22
1996	Baby's First-33	Open		30.00	30
1996	Black and White Bunny-28	Open		26.00	26
1996	Calico Cat-27	Open		26.00	26
1995	Carrot-cicle-17	Open		22.00	22
1996	Cat-cicle w/Stocking-37	Open		22.00	22
1996	Cat-cicle-36	Open		22.00	22
1993	Cherub Icicle-8	Open		22.00	22
1996	Crescent Santa-29	Open		28.00	28
1993	Father Christmas Icicle-13	Open		22.00	22
1994	Father Christmas, Set/3-16	Open		66.00	66
1993	Father Snowman Icicle-10	Open		22.00	22
1996	Golden Father Christmas-38	Open		24.00	24
1996	Kitty Angel-34	Open		24.00	24
1993	Mother Snowman Icicle-11	Open		22.00	22
1994	Nutcracker-30	Open		22.00	22
1995	Nutcracker-31	Open		22.00	22
1996	Nutcracker-32	Open		22.00	22
1995	Reindeer-26	Open		22.00	22
1993	Santa Icicle-14	Open		22.00	22
1995	Snow Family, Set/3-19	Open		66.00	66
1995	Tabby/Holly Bunch-25	Open		22.00	22

Walt Disney

Classics Collection-Holiday Series - Disney Studios

YEAR ISSUE		EDITION LIMIT	YEAR RETD.	ISSUE PRICE	*QUOTE U.S.$
1995	Presents For My Pals 41087	Closed	1995	50.00	75
1995	Tinkerbell	Open		50.00	50

DOLLS

Annalee Mobilitee Dolls, Inc.

Doll Society-Animals - A. Thorndike

YEAR ISSUE		EDITION LIMIT	YEAR RETD.	ISSUE PRICE	*QUOTE U.S.$
1985	10" Penguin and Chick	3,000	N/A	29.95	225
1986	10" Unicorn	3,000	N/A	36.95	350
1987	7" Kangaroo	3,000	N/A	37.45	450
1988	5" Owl	3,000	N/A	37.45	300
1989	7" Polar Bear	3,000	N/A	37.50	300
1990	10" Thorndike Chicken	3,000	N/A	37.50	275

Doll Society-Folk Heroes - A. Thorndike

YEAR ISSUE		EDITION LIMIT	YEAR RETD.	ISSUE PRICE	*QUOTE U.S.$
1984	10" Johnny Appleseed	1,500	N/A	80.00	1000
1984	10" Robin Hood	1,500	N/A	90.00	850
1985	10" Annie Oakley	1,500	N/A	95.00	700
1986	10" Mark Twain	2,500	N/A	117.50	500
1987	10" Ben Franklin	2,500	N/A	119.50	525
1988	10" Sherlock Holmes	2,500	N/A	119.50	500
1989	10" Abraham Lincoln	2,500	N/A	119.50	500
1990	10" Betsy Ross	2,500	N/A	119.50	450
1991	10" Christopher Columbus	1,132	N/A	119.50	300
1992	10" Uncle Sam	1,034	N/A	87.50	N/A
1993	10" Pony Express Rider	Yr.Iss.	N/A	97.50	N/A
1994	10" Bean Nose Santa	Yr.Iss.	1994	119.50	N/A
1995	10" Pocahontas	Yr.Iss.		87.50	88

Doll Society-Logo Kids - A. Thorndike

YEAR ISSUE		EDITION LIMIT	YEAR RETD.	ISSUE PRICE	*QUOTE U.S.$
1985	Christmas Logo w/Cookie	3,562	1986	N/A	675
1986	Sweetheart Logo	6,271	1987	N/A	275
1987	Naughty Logo	1,100	1988	N/A	425
1988	Raincoat Logo	13,646	1989	N/A	200
1989	Christmas Morning Logo	16,641	1990	N/A	150
1990	Clown	20,049	1991	N/A	150
1991	Reading Logo	26,516	1992	N/A	125
1992	Back to School Logo	17,524	1993	N/A	90
1993	Ice Cream Logo	Yr.Iss.	1994	N/A	N/A
1994	Dress Up Santa Logo	Yr.Iss	1995	N/A	N/A
1995	Goin' Fishin' Logo	Yr.Iss		29.95	30

Assorted Dolls - A. Thorndike

YEAR ISSUE		EDITION LIMIT	YEAR RETD.	ISSUE PRICE	*QUOTE U.S.$
1987	3" Baby Witch	3,645	1987	13.95	275
1987	3" Bride and Groom	1,053	1987	38.95	375
1983	3" PJ Kid (designer series)	2,360	1983	10.95	200
1971	3" Reindeer Head	N/A	1976	1.00	200
1991	3" Water Baby in Pond Lily	3,720	1991	14.95	175
1984	5" E.P. Boy Bunny	2,583	1984	11.95	200
1984	5" E.P. Girl Bunny	2,790	1984	11.95	200
1983	5" Easter Parade Girl Bunny w/ Music Box	1,167	1983	29.95	400
1963	5" Elf (Lilac)	N/A	1963	2.50	325
1959	5" Man (Special Order)	N/A	1959	N/A	1525
1960	5" Wee Skis	N/A	N/A	3.95	325
1978	7" Airplane Pilot Mouse	2,308	1981	6.95	425
1964	7" Angel in a Blanket	N/A	1964	2.45	325
1984	7" Angel on Star	772	1984	32.95	475
1983	7" Angel w/ Musical Instrument on Music Box	N/A	1983	29.95	425
1960	7" Angel w/ Paper Wings	N/A	1966	N/A	400
1970	7" Artist Mouse	298	1974	3.95	400
1950	7" Baby Angel	N/A	1950	2.45	1650
1960	7" Baby Angel (yellow feather hair)	N/A	1962	N/A	350
1962	7" Baby Angel on Cloud	N/A	1963	2.45	500-700
1962	7" Baby Angel w/ Star	N/A	1962	2.00	225
1980	7" Baby in Bassinet	12,215	1983	13.95	275
1968	7" Baby in Christmas Bag	N/A	1968	2.95	350
1968	7" Baby in Santa's Hat	N/A	1969	2.95	500
1975	7" Baby Mouse	N/A	1975	5.50	150
1971	7" Baby w/ Bottle	N/A	1971	N/A	300
1965	7" Baby w/ Bow	N/A	1965	N/A	325
1979	7" Ballerina	4,700	1979	7.45	275
1967	7" Ballerina Mouse	N/A	1968	3.95	450
1980	7" Ballooning Santa	N/A	1983	49.95	350
1970	7" Bartender Mouse	289	1973	3.95	400
1971	7" Baseball Player Mouse	1,085	1975	5.50	175
1987	7" BBQ Mouse	1,798	1987	17.95	300
1974	7" Black Santa w/Oversized Bag	1,638	1975	5.45	550
1977	7" Boating Mouse	1,186	1977	5.95	175
1964	7" Boudoir Puff Baby Angel	N/A	1965	3.95	400
1984	7" Boy w/ Firecracker	1,893	1984	19.95	400
1966	7" Bride & Groom Mice	N/A	1966	3.95	600
1979	7" Bunny	3,125	1979	6.95	175
1970	7" Bunny (yellow)	3,215	1973	3.95	375
1987	7" Bunny in 10" Carrot Balloon	624	1987	49.95	375
1974	7" Camper in Tent Mouse	468	1974	5.45	325
1976	7" Card Playing Girl Mouse	2,878	1977	5.50	275
1968	7" Caroller Boy Mouse w/ Music	N/A	1969	4.45	400
1974	7" Carpenter Mouse	2,687	1978	5.45	275
1978	7" Carpenter Mouse	1,494	1978	6.95	350
1970	7" Christmas Baby on Hat Box	1,894	1971	2.95	350
1965	7" Christmas Dumb Bunny	N/A	1965	3.95	775
1975	7" Christmas Mouse in Santa Mitten	3,959	1976	5.45	375
1977	7" Christmas Mouse in Santa's Mitten	15,916	1979	7.95	175
1975	7" Colonial Boy Mouse	12,739	1976	5.45	350
1975	7" Colonial Girl Mouse	9,338	1976	5.45	350
1965	7" Colored Mouse (Peek)	N/A	1965	3.95	550
1982	7" Cowboy Mouse	3,776	1983	12.95	300
1982	7" Cowgirl Mouse	3,116	1983	12.95	300
1984	7" Cupid in Hanging Heart	2,445	1985	32.95	375
1984	7" Dentist Mouse	2,362	1985	14.95	400
1976	7" Diet Time Mouse	3,399	1977	6.00	200
1992	7" Disney Kid	300	1992	59.95	400
1985	7" Dress-Up Boy	1,174	1985	18.95	225
1985	7" Dress-Up Girl	1,536	1985	18.95	225
1993	7" Eric & Shane Boating in Hawaii	100	1993	105.00	750
1979	7" Fishing Mouse	N/A	1979	7.95	275
1972	7" Football Mouse	744	1974	3.95	300
1991	7" Fun in the Sun Kid	300	1991	80.00	300
1962	7" Furcapped Baby	N/A	1962	2.45	400
1967	7" Garden Club Baby	N/A	1969	2.95	575
1974	7" Gardener Mouse	485	1980	5.45	400
1979	7" Gardener Mouse	1,939	1980	7.95	325
1969	7" Gardener Mouse	N/A	1973	4.45	300
1992	7" Gnome w/ Mushroom	1,691	1992	35.95	350
1967	7" Gnome w/ Pajama Suit	N/A	1970	2.95	375
1965	7" Gnome w/ Vest	N/A	1965	2.45	675
1965	7" Hangover Mouse	N/A	1987	3.95	375
1987	7" Hangover Mouse	1,548	1987	13.95	175
1977	7" Hobo Mouse	1,004	1977	5.95	275
1980	7" Hockey Mouse	2,477	1981	9.95	250
1985	7" Hockey Player Kid	1,578	1985	18.95	400
1974	7" Hunter Mouse w/ Bird	690	1975	5.45	325
1981	7" I'm Late Bunny	100	1981	N/A	475
1985	7" Kid w/ Kite	1,084	1985	17.95	300
1965	7" Lawyer Mouse	N/A	1965	3.95	350
1965	7" M/M Indoor Santa	N/A	1966	5.95	500
1970	7" M/M Santa on Ski Bob	N/A	1970	5.95	600
1983	7" M/M Santa w/ Basket	5,105	1983	25.95	300
1980	7" M/M Santa w/ Pot Belly Stove	6,552	1980	20.94	325
1970	7" M/M Tuckered Santa w/ Hot Water Bottle	1,761	1971	6.45	200
1959	7" Man (special order)	N/A	1959	N/A	1200
1993	7" Mississippi Levee Mouse	341	1993	N/A	400
1982	7" Mouse w/ Strawberry	10,267	1985	12.95	175
1982	7" Mr. A.M. Mouse	3,724	1983	11.95	150
1970	7" Mr. Holly Mouse	1,726	1970	3.95	225
1977	7" Mr. Santa Mouse	7,197	1979	6.00	300
1967	7" Mrs. Holly Mouse	N/A	1976	3.95	350
1967	7" Mrs. Santa w/ Fur-Trimmed Cape	N/A	1973	2.95	450
1971	7" Naughty Angel	12,359	1971	10.95	275
1976	7" Needlework Mouse	3,566	1978	6.95	400
1964	7" Nude Angel Bath Puff	N/A	1965	3.95	275
1968	7" Patches Pam	N/A	1968	2.95	850
1979	7" Quilting Mouse	213	1979	N/A	375
1991	7" Santa in Tub w/ Rubber Duckie	5,373	1991	33.95	200
1971	7" Santa Mailman	8,296	1974	5.50	375
1972	7" Santa on Ski-Bob w/ Oversized Bag	7,590	1974	7.95	400
1978	7" Santa w/ 10" Reindeer Trimming Christmas Tree	1,621	1978	18.45	425
1981	7" Santa w/ 18" Moon	N/A	1981	6.95	200
1963	7" Santa w/ Fur Trimmed Suit	N/A	1967	2.95	400
1969	7" Santa w/ Oversized Bag	N/A	1970	3.95	350
1971	7" Santa w/ Skis and Poles	N/A	1978	5.45	300
1989	7" Science Center Mouse	500	1989	75.00	525
1972	7" Secretary Mouse	727	1974	3.95	500
1970	7" Secretary Mouse	727	1972	3.95	150
1970	7" Sherriff Mouse	11	1970	3.95	650
1991	7" Sherriff Mouse #92	1,191	1992	49.50	700
1965	7" Singing Mouse	N/A	1965	3.95	450
1979	7" Skateboard Mouse	1,821	1979	7.95	275
1978	7" Skateboard Mouse	3,733	1979	7.00	200
1976	7" Ski Mouse	10,375	1981	6.95	225
1974	7" Ski Mouse	1,603	1974	5.45	225
1974	7" Sloppy Painter Mouse	349	1974	5.45	550
1971	7" Swimmer Mouse w/ Inner Tube	267	1971	3.95	325
1967	7" Tuckered Mr. & Mrs. Santa Water Bottle	N/A	1969	5.95	400
1973	7" Vacationer Girl Mouse	1,017	1974	4.45	325
1986	7" Witch Mouse w/ Pumpkin Balloon	868	1987	59.95	300
1982	7" Wood Chopper Mouse	1,910	1982	11.95	375
1992	7" Workshop Mouse	6,618	1992	21.95	275
1971	7" Yachtsman Mouse w/ Binnacle	249	1974	3.95	400
1966	7" Yum Yum Bunny	N/A	1966	3.95	700
1968	8" Elephant (Tubby)	N/A	1969	4.95	450
1980	8" Girl BBQ Pig	3,854	1981	9.95	175
1975	8" Lamb	234	1975	8.95	450
1977	8" Rooster	1,642	1977	5.95	350
1959	10" 4th of July Doll	N/A	1959	N/A	1525
1959	10" Architect	N/A	1959	19.95	1250
1991	10" Aviator Frog w/ Flag	2,110	1991	19.95	425
1957	10" Baby Angel	N/A	1958	8.95	525
1963	10" Ballerina	N/A	1963	5.95	1350
1980	10" Balloon w/ Two 10" Frogs	837	1980	49.95	850
1968	10" Bather (Skinny Minnie w/ Towel)	N/A	1968	5.95	950
1966	10" Bathersome Chick w/ Flippers	N/A	1966	5.95	650
1959	10" Bathing Girl	N/A	1959	7.95	850
1957	10" Bathing Girl	N/A	1957	N/A	1300
1989	10" BBQ Pig	2,471	1989	27.95	325
1964	10" Black (Monk)	N/A	1965	2.95	375
1994	10" Boston Bruins Hockey Player (Signed by team)	2	1994	N/A	500
1966	10" Boy & Girl on Tandem Bike	N/A	1966	20.95	1350
1956	10" Boy Building Boat	N/A	1969	N/A	1550
1950	10" Boy Building Boat	N/A	1950	9.95	1200
1960	10" Boy Building Boat	N/A	1968	12.95	1600
1976	10" Boy in Tire Swing	358	1976	6.95	350
1965	10" Boy on Bike	N/A	1965	N/A	600
1980	10" Boy on Raft	1,087	1981	28.95	325
1969	10" Bride & Groom Set	N/A	1969	11.95	800
1967	10" Brown Nun	N/A	1967	2.95	375
1950	10" Calypso Dancer	N/A	1950	N/A	1350
1967	10" Carnaby Street Boy	N/A	1967	3.95	400
1960	10" Carpenter	N/A	1965	N/A	575
1987	10" Carrot Balloon w / 7" Bunny in Basket	624	1987	49.95	500
1970	10" Casualty Ski Elf w/ Crutch & Leg in Cast	2,818	1972	4.50	600
1967	10" Choir Boy (set/3)	N/A	1967	2.95	725
1950	10" Christmas Girl	N/A	1957	N/A	2350
1970	10" Christmas Mushroom w/ 7" Mouse	198	1970	7.95	400
1987	10" Clown	2,699	1987	17.95	425
1981	10" Clown	6,479	1981	9.95	200
1971	10" Clown (black & white)	N/A	1971	2.00	300
1969	10" Clown (bright stripes)	N/A	1971	3.95	350
1969	10" Clown (pink w/green polka dots)	N/A	1969	3.95	525
1971	10" Clown w/ Mushroom	45	1971	7.95	850
1975	10" Colonial Drummer Boy	1,846	1976	5.95	375
1989	10" Country Boy Pig	2,566	1989	25.95	175
1989	10" Country Girl Pig	2,367	1989	25.95	175
1968	10" Cross Country Skier	N/A	1968	7.95	700
1982	10" Cyrano de Bergerac	35	1982	N/A	2300
1961	10" Dalmation	N/A	1961	N/A	1500
1972	10" Democratic Donkey	861	1972	3.95	450
1960	10" Elf	N/A	1966	N/A	400
1950	10" Elf	N/A	N/A	N/A	900
1963	10" Elf	N/A	1963	N/A	350
1954	10" Elf w/ Cap	N/A	1954	N/A	1150
1978	10" Elf w/ Planter	1,978	1978	6.95	275
1967	10" Elf w/ Skis and Poles	48	1971	2.95	425-900
1988	10" Fall Elf	3,183	1988	13.95	125
1959	10" Fisherman & Girl in Boat	N/A	1959	N/A	2550
1963	10" Friar	N/A	1963	2.95	500
1959	10" Girl & Boy on Tandem Bike	N/A	1959	20.95	2200
1965	10" Girl on Bike	N/A	1965	N/A	600
1966	10" Go-Go Boy	N/A	1966	3.95	350
1967	10" Golfer Boy	N/A	1968	5.95	925
1965	10" Golfer Boy Doll	N/A	1965	9.95	700
1966	10" Golfer-Girl Putter	N/A	1968	5.95	925
1957	10" Halloween Girl	N/A	1959	9.95	3200
1965	10" Hiking Doll	N/A	1965	9.95	750
1987	10" Huck Finn (#62)	800	1988	102.95	700
1991	10" Husky w/ 5" Puppy in Dog Sled	2,860	1991	54.95	350
1960	10" Impski	N/A	1966	3.95	500
1960	10" Impski (red)	N/A	1966	3.95	325
1960	10" Impski (white)	N/A	1966	3.95	350
1977	10" Jack Frost Elf	5,580	1977	6.00	225
1982	10" Jack Frost Elf w/ 10" Snowflake	N/A	1982	13.50	150

*Quotes have been rounded up to nearest dollar

YEAR ISSUE		EDITION LIMIT	YEAR RETD.	ISSUE PRICE	*QUOTE U.S.$
1981	10" Jack Frost Elf w/ 5" Snowflake	5,950	1981	31.95	325
1974	10" Leprechaun w/ Sack	8,834	1974	5.45	350
1959	10" Man (special Order)	N/A	1959	N/A	1400
1964	10" Monk (red robe)	N/A	1965	2.95	800
1965	10" Monk w/ Christmas Tree Planting	N/A	1967	2.95	450
1967	10" Monk w/ Jug	N/A	1969	2.95	375
1970	10" Monk w/ Skis and Poles	1,386	1972	3.95	350
1970	10" Mushroom w/ 7" Santa	1,535	1971	7.95	250
1967	10" Nun (green)	N/A	1967	42.95	700
1994	10" Piper Bear	200	1994	130.00	650
1974	10" Polly Frog Spring Cleaning	580	1974	5.50	325
1965	10" Reindeer	N/A	1965	4.95	425
1975	10" Reindeer w/ 7" Santa	2,429	1976	10.50	400
1964	10" Robin Hood Elf	N/A	1965	2.50	500
1988	10" Scrooge Head	N/A	1988	N/A	325
1984	10" Shriner (special order)	1,000	1984	N/A	875
1987	10" Sitting Frog w/Instrument	2,162	1987	19.95	525
1987	10" Ski Elf	N/A	1987	19.95	350
1971	10" Ski Elf	1,262	1971	3.95	275
1985	10" Skier (Cross Country)	1,076	1985	33.50	225
1956	10" Skier Girl w/ Broken Leg in Cast	N/A	1957	14.95	1550
1990	10" Spirit of '76	1,080	1990	175.00	550
1992	10" Spring Chicken w/ Boa	N/A	1992	34.95	150
1965	10" Spring Elf	N/A	1965	2.50	375
1954	10" Spring Girl	N/A	1954	N/A	2350
1957	10" Square Dancer (Girl)	N/A	1959	9.95	900
1950	10" Square Dancers (Boy & Girl)	N/A	1959	9.95	2100
1956	10" Square Dancers (set/8)	N/A	1956	59.95	5200
1987	10" State Trooper (#642)	511	1988	134.00	500
1991	10" Summer Santa #1663	1,926	1991	59.95	425
1967	10" Surfer Boy	N/A	1968	5.95	525
1967	10" Surfer Girl	N/A	1968	5.95	625
1989	10" Three Bunnies w/ Maypole	647	1989	190.00	600
1976	10" Uncle Sam	1,095	1976	5.95	500
1957	10" Valentine Doll	N/A	1957	9.95	1800
1991	10" Victory Ski Doll	1,192	1991	49.50	350
1959	10" Wood Sprite	N/A	1967	N/A	750
1966	10" Workshop Elf	N/A	1966	N/A	425
1976	12" Angel	13,338	1979	10.95	350
1960	12" Baby in Green	N/A	1960	N/A	550
1992	12" Bat	2,107	1992	31.95	225
1965	12" Christmas Bonnet Lady Mouse	N/A	1965	9.95	400
1967	12" Country Cousin Boy Mouse	N/A	1967	9.95	500
1990	12" Easter Parade Duck w/ Watering Can	2,891	1990	49.95	300
1967	12" Fancy Nancy Cat	N/A	1967	6.95	1950
1968	12" Gnome w/ Gay Apron	N/A	1968	5.95	900
1968	12" Laura May Cat	N/A	1971	7.95	900
1981	12" Monkey Boy w/ Banana	N/A	1971	23.95	225
1970	12" Mr. Santa Mouse w/ Toybag	N/A	1971	10.95	525
1967	12" Mrs. Santa w/ Muff	N/A	1969	9.95	550
1968	12" Myrtle Turtle	N/A	1969	6.95	2600
1969	12" Myrtle Turtle	N/A	1969	6.95	800
1969	12" Nightshirt Boy Mouse	N/A	1976	9.95	550
1957	12" Santa	N/A	1957	N/A	925
1954	12" Santa (Bean Nose)	N/A	1957	19.95	1000
1990	12" Santa Duck	506	1991	49.95	300
1982	12" Skunk Boy	935	1982	27.95	225
1982	12" Skunk Girl	936	1982	27.95	225
1967	12" Sneaky Peaky Boy Cat	N/A	1967	6.95	375
1992	12" Spider	3,461	1992	38.95	200
1967	12" Yum-Yum Bunny	N/A	1968	9.95	850
1980	14" Dragon w/ Bush Boy	2,130	1982	32.95	300
1955	14" Fireman	N/A	1955	N/A	4750
1990	15" Christmas Dragon	448	1990	49.95	400
1970	16" Christmas Wreath w/ Santa Head	1,662	1974	9.95	375
1972	16" Democratic Donkey	219	1972	12.95	1600
1972	16" Elephant (Republican)	230	1972	12.95	800
1984	18" Aerobic Girl	622	1984	35.95	375
1988	18" Americana Couple #82	7,258	1988	169.95	700
1990	18" Angel w/ Instrument	398	1990	51.95	325
1978	18" Artist Bunny w/ Brush & Palette	2,023	1979	14.00	300
1985	18" Ballerina Bear	918	1985	39.95	275
1980	18" Ballerina Bunny	7,069	1982	27.95	425
1979	18" Ballerina Bunny	2,315	1982	15.95	450
1984	18" Bear w/ Brush	1,392	1984	39.95	250
1985	18" Bear w/ Honey Pot & Bee	2,032	1986	41.50	600
1974	18" Bell Hop (special order)	3	1974	N/A	1000
1974	18" Bob Cratchet w/ 7" Tiny Tim	984	1974	11.95	425
1977	18" Boy Bunny w/Carrot	1,159	1977	13.50	250
1979	18" Boy Frog	3,524	1981	22.95	175
1977	18" Bunny w/Egg	1,172	1977	13.50	300
1981	18" Butterfly w/ 10" Elf	2,507	1982	27.95	500
1972	18" Candy Kid Boy	4,350	1973	11.95	775
1972	18" Candy Kid Girl	4,350	1973	11.95	775
1975	18" Caroller Boy	1,024	1975	12.00	400
1963	18" Choir Boy	1,470	1963	7.45	550
1973	18" Christmas Panda	437	1973	10.50	600
1975	18" Clown	166	1975	N/A	450
1983	18" Country Girl Bunny w/ Basket	2,905	1983	29.95	400
1984	18" E.P. Girl Bunny	2,952	1984	35.95	350
1976	18" Elephant "Vote '76"	806	1976	8.50	500
1984	18" Fawn w/ Wreath	2,080	1984	32.95	375
1979	18" Girl Frog	3,677	1981	22.95	175
1979	18" Gnome	15,851	1980	19.95	350
1975	18" Horse	221	1976	16.95	375
1974	18" Martha Cratchet	1,043	1974	11.95	425

YEAR ISSUE		EDITION LIMIT	YEAR RETD.	ISSUE PRICE	*QUOTE U.S.$
1970	18" Mr. & Mrs. Fireside Couple	N/A	1971	7.45	300
1968	18" Mrs. Santa w/ Boudoir Cap & Apron	N/A	1968	7.45	250
1968	18" Mrs. Santa w/ Hot Water Bottle	N/A	1968	7.45	525
1990	18" Naughty Kid	1,454	1991	69.95	525
1970	18" Patchwork Kid	496	1970	7.45	450
1978	18" Pilgrim Boy	1,213	1978	14.95	275
1964	18" PJ Kid	N/A	1964	6.95	500
1980	18" Santa Frog w/ Toybag	2,126	1980	24.95	450
1971	18" Santa Fur Kid	1,191	1972	7.45	250
1964	18" Santa Kid	N/A	1965	6.95	450
1990	18" Santa Playing w/ Electric Train	168	1990	119.00	350
1987	18" Special Mrs. Santa (special order)	341	1987	N/A	400
1976	18" Uncle Sam	345	1976	16.95	500
1985	18" Valentine Bear	2,439	1986	41.50	275
1987	18" Workshop Santa (special order)	1,001	1987	N/A	450
1975	18" Yankee Doodle Dandy w/ 18" Horse	437	1976	28.95	900
1981	22" Christmas Giraffe w/ 10" Elf	1,377	1982	36.95	500
1974	22" Christmas Stocking	8,536	1974	4.95	150
1974	22" Leprchaun	199	1974	11.45	650
1970	22" Monkey (chartreuse)	70	1970	10.95	725
1990	22" Spring Elf (yellow)	1,636	1990	34.95	325
1981	22" Sun Mobile	3,003	1985	36.95	475
1975	25" Lad w/ Kite	95	1975	28.95	400
1975	25" Lass w/ Flowers	92	1975	28.95	450
1954	26" Elf	N/A	1956	9.95	550
1963	26" Friar	N/A	1963	14.95	2500
1979	29" Artist Bunny w/ Brush & Palette	179	1979	42.95	350
1974	29" Bell Hop (special order)	3	1974	29.00	1200
1978	29" Caroller Mouse	658	1978	49.95	475
1976	29" Clown (blue w/wh. polka dots)	466	1976	29.95	925
1981	29" Dragon w/ 12 Bush Boy	151	1982	69.95	700
1960	29" Fur Trim Santa	N/A	1979	N/A	1000
1971	29" M/M Tuckered w/ 2 18" Kids	811	1972	51.95	800
1974	29" Motorized See-Saw Bunny Set	43	1975	250.00	1600
1977	29" Mr. Santa Mouse w/ Sack	704	1977	49.95	800
1968	29" Mrs. Indoor Santa	N/A	1968	16.95	475
1977	29" Mrs. Santa Mouse w/ Muff	571	1977	49.95	800
1969	29" Mrs. Santa w/ Wired Cardholder Skirt	N/A	1969	18.95	250
1972	29" Mrs. Snow Woman w/ Cardholder Skirt	331	1972	19.95	700
1990	30" Clown	530	1990	99.95	350
1984	30" Santa in Chair w/ 2 18" Kids	940	1984	169.95	1200
1984	30" Snowgirl w/ Muff	685	1984	79.50	1000
1984	32" Monk w/ Grapes	416	1984	78.50	450
1959	33" Boy & Girl on Tandem Bike	N/A	1959	N/A	4500
1960	36" PJ Kid	N/A	1960	N/A	1200
1980	42" Clown	224	1980	74.95	700
1977	42" Scarecrow	365	1978	61.95	2050
1986	48" Velour Santa	410	1988	269.95	750
1963	Baby Angel Head w/ Santa Hat	N/A	1963	1.00	350
1965	The Bang Hat (red)	N/A	1965	N/A	175
1963	Bath Puff (yellow)	N/A	1965	1.95	325
1968	Bunny Head Pin On	N/A	1968	1.00	400
1950	Cellist	N/A	N/A	N/A	5250
1976	Colonial Boy Head Pin On	N/A	1976	1.50	275
1976	Colonial Girl Head Pin On	N/A	1976	1.50	275
1972	Donkey Head Pin On	1,371	1972	1.00	300
1972	Elephant Head Pin On	1,384	1972	1.00	325
1962	Fur-Capped Baby on Cloud	N/A	1962	N/A	350
1961	Fur-Capped Head Pin-On	N/A	1962	1.00	225
1960	Head Pin	N/A	N/A	N/A	200
1968	Hippy Head (Boy)	N/A	1969	1.00	350
1968	Hippy Head (Girl)	N/A	1969	1.00	350
1960	Man Head Pin-on	N/A	N/A	N/A	800
1970	Monkey Head Pin-on (boy)	153	1973	1.00	275
1970	Monkey Head Pin-on (girl)	153	1973	1.00	275
1971	Monkey Head Pin-on (hot pink)	N/A	1971	1.00	450
1960	Mouse Head Pin-On	N/A	1976	1.00	250
1970	Mouse Pin	N/A	1970	1.45	150
1971	Snowman Head Pin-on	4,040	1972	1.00	200
1971	Snowman Kid	1,374	1971	3.95	450
1985	Tree Skirt	1,332	1985	24.95	350
1989	Two Bunnies on Flexible Flyer Sled	4,104	1990	52.95	325

ANRI

Disney Dolls - Disney Studios

1990	Daisy Duck, 14"	2,500	1991	895.00	895
1990	Donald Duck, 14"	2,500	1991	895.00	895
1989	Mickey Mouse, 14"	2,500	1991	850.00	895
1989	Minnie Mouse, 14"	2,500	1991	850.00	895
1989	Pinocchio, 14"	2,500	1991	850.00	895

Ferrandiz Dolls - J. Ferrandiz

1991	Carmen, 14"	1,000	1992	730.00	730
1991	Fernando, 14"	1,000	1992	730.00	730
1989	Gabriel, 14"	1,000	1991	550.00	575
1991	Juanita, 7"	1,500	1992	300.00	300
1990	Margarite, 14"	1,000	1992	575.00	730
1989	Maria, 14"	1,000	1991	550.00	575
1991	Miguel, 7"	1,500	1992	300.00	300
1990	Philipe, 14"	1,000	1992	575.00	680

Sarah Kay Dolls - S. Kay

YEAR ISSUE		EDITION LIMIT	YEAR RETD.	ISSUE PRICE	*QUOTE U.S.$
1991	Annie, 7"	1,500	1993	300.00	300
1989	Bride to Love And To Cherish	750	1992	750.00	790
1989	Charlotte (Blue)	1,000	1991	550.00	575
1990	Christina, 14"	1,000	1993	575.00	730
1989	Eleanor (Floral)	1,000	1991	550.00	575
1989	Elizabeth (Patchwork)	1,000	1991	550.00	575
1988	Emily, 14"	Closed	1989	500.00	500
1990	Faith, 14"	1,000	1993	575.00	685
1989	Groom With This Ring Doll, 14"	750	1992	550.00	730
1989	Helen (Brown), 14"	1,000	1991	550.00	575
1989	Henry, 14"	1,000	1991	550.00	575
1991	Janine, 14"	1,000	1993	750.00	750
1988	Jennifer, 14"	Closed	1989	500.00	500
1991	Jessica, 7"	1,500	1993	300.00	300
1991	Julie, 7"	1,500	1993	300.00	300
1988	Katherine, 14"	Closed	1989	500.00	500
1988	Martha, 14"	Closed	1989	500.00	500
1989	Mary (Red)	1,000	1991	550.00	575
1991	Michelle, 7"	1,500	1993	300.00	300
1991	Patricia, 14"	1,000	1993	730.00	730
1991	Peggy, 7"	1,500	1993	300.00	300
1990	Polly, 14"	1,000	1993	575.00	680
1988	Rachael, 14"	Closed	1989	500.00	500
1988	Rebecca, 14"	Closed	1989	500.00	500
1988	Sarah, 14"	Closed	1989	500.00	500
1990	Sophie, 14"	1,000	1993	575.00	660
1991	Susan, 7"	1,500	1993	300.00	300
1988	Victoria, 14"	Closed	1989	500.00	500

Ashton-Drake Galleries

All I Wish For You - Good-Kruger

1994	I Wish You Love	Closed	1995	79.95	80
1995	I Wish You Faith	12/98		79.95	80

America the Beautiful - Y. Bello

1995	Billy	12/96		49.95	50
1995	Bobby	12/96		49.95	50

The American Dream - J. Kovacik

1994	Patience	Closed	1995	79.95	80
1994	Hope	Closed	1995	79.95	80

Amish Blessings - J. Good-Kruger

1990	Rebeccah	Closed	1993	68.00	100-125
1991	Rachel	Closed	1993	69.00	125-150
1991	Adam	Closed	1993	75.00	175-200
1992	Ruth	Closed	1993	75.00	125
1992	Eli	Closed	1993	79.95	125
1993	Sarah	Closed	1994	79.95	125

Amish Inspirations - J. Ibarolle

1994	Ethan	Closed	1995	69.95	70
1994	Mary	Closed	1995	69.95	70
1995	Seth	12/96		74.95	75
1995	Anna	12/96		74.95	75

Anne of Green Gables - J. Kovacik

1995	Anne	12/98		69.95	70

As Cute As Can Be - D. Effner

1993	Sugar Plum	Closed	1994	49.95	60-95
1994	Puppy Love	Closed	1995	49.95	50
1994	Angel Face	Closed	1995	49.95	50
1995	Patty Cake	12/98		49.95	50

Baby Book Treasures - K. Barry-Hippensteel

1990	Elizabeth's Homecoming	Closed	1993	58.00	58
1991	Catherine's Christening	Closed	1994	58.00	58
1991	Christopher's First Smile	Closed	1992	63.00	63-80

Baby Talk - Good-Kruger

1994	All Gone	Closed	1995	49.95	60-95
1994	Bye-Bye	Closed	1995	49.95	50
1994	Night, Night	Closed	1995	49.95	50

Barely Yours - T. Tomescu

1994	Cute as a Button	Closed	1994	69.95	70
1994	Snug as a Bug in a Rug	Closed	1995	75.00	75
1995	Clean as a Whistle	12/96		75.00	75
1995	Pretty as a Picture	12/96		75.00	75
1995	Good as Gold	12/96		75.00	75
1996	Cool As A Cucumber	12/99		75.00	75

Beautiful Dreamers - G. Rademann

1992	Katrina	Closed	1993	89.00	100-125
1992	Nicolette	Closed	1994	89.95	95
1993	Brigitte	Closed	1994	94.00	100
1993	Isabella	Closed	1994	94.00	100
1993	Gabrielle	Closed	1994	94.00	100

Born To Be Famous - K. Barry-Hippensteel

1989	Little Sherlock	Closed	1991	87.00	87
1990	Little Florence Nightingale	Closed	1991	87.00	90
1991	Little Davey Crockett	Closed	1994	92.00	92-100
1992	Little Christopher Columbus	Closed	1993	95.00	95-100

Calendar Babies - Ashton-Drake

1995	New Year	Open		24.95	25

*Quotes have been rounded up to nearest dollar

YEAR ISSUE		EDITION LIMIT	YEAR RETD.	ISSUE PRICE	*QUOTE U.S.$
1995	Cupid	Open		24.95	25
1995	Leprechaun	Open		24.95	25
1995	April Showers	Open		24.95	25
1995	May Flowers	Open		24.95	25
1995	June Bride	Open		24.95	25
1995	Uncle Sam	Open		24.95	25
1995	Sun & Fun	Open		24.95	25
1995	Back to School	Open		24.95	25
1995	Happy Haunting	Open		24.95	25
1995	Thanksgiving Turkey	Open		24.95	25
1995	Jolly Santa	Open		24.95	25

Caught In The Act - M. Tretter

1992	Stevie, Catch Me If You Can	Closed	1994	49.95	125-145
1993	Kelly, Don't I Look Pretty?	Closed	1994	49.95	85-95
1994	Mikey (Look It Floats)	Closed	1994	55.00	55
1994	Nickie (Cookie Jar)	Closed	1995	59.95	60
1994	Becky (Kleenex Box)	Closed	1995	59.95	60
1994	Sandy	Closed	1995	59.95	60

Children of Christmas - M. Sirko

1994	The Little Drummer Boy	Closed	1995	79.95	80
1994	The Littlest Angel	Closed	1995	79.95	80
1995	O Christmas Tree	12/98		79.95	80

Children of Mother Goose - Y. Bello

1987	Little Bo Peep	Closed	1988	58.00	125
1987	Mary Had a Little Lamb	Closed	1989	58.00	125
1988	Little Jack Horner	Closed	1989	63.00	125
1989	Miss Muffet	Closed	1991	63.00	63

Children Of The Sun - M. Severino

1993	Little Flower	Closed	1994	69.95	70
1993	Desert Star	Closed	1995	69.95	70

A Children's Circus - J. McClelland

1990	Tommy The Clown	Closed	1993	78.00	78
1991	Katie The Tightrope Walker	Closed	1993	78.00	78
1991	Johnnie The Strongman	Closed	1994	83.00	83
1992	Maggie The Animal Trainer	Closed	1994	83.00	83

Christmas Memories - Y. Bello

1994	Christopher	Closed	1995	59.95	60
1994	Joshua	Closed	1995	59.95	60
1994	Stephanie	Closed	1995	59.95	60

Cindy's Playhouse Pals - C. McClure

1989	Meagan	Closed	1990	87.00	88
1989	Shelly	Closed	1993	87.00	87
1990	Ryan	Closed	1993	89.00	89
1991	Samantha	Closed	1993	89.00	89

Classic Brides of The Century - E. Williams

1990	Flora, The 1900s Bride	Closed	1993	145.00	145
1991	Jennifer, The 1980s Bride	Closed	1992	149.00	149
1993	Kathleen, The 1930s Bride	Closed	1993	149.95	150

Classic Collection - D. Effner

1995	Hilary	12/98		79.95	80

Cuddle Chums - K. Barry-Hippensteel

1995	Heather	12/98		59.95	60
1995	Jeffrey	12/98		59.95	60

Days of the Week - K. Barry-Hippensteel

1994	Monday	Closed	1995	49.95	50
1995	Tuesday	12/96		49.95	50
1995	Wednesday	12/96		49.95	50
1995	Thursday	12/96		49.95	50
1995	Friday	12/96		49.95	50
1995	Saturday	12/96		49.95	50
1995	Sunday	12/96		49.95	50

Dianna Effner's Mother Goose - D. Effner

1990	Mary, Mary, Quite Contrary	Closed	1992	78.00	200
1991	The Little Girl With The Curl (Horrid)	Closed	1992	79.00	125-195
1991	The Little Girl With The Curl (Good)	Closed	1993	79.00	85-125
1992	Little Boy Blue	Closed	1993	85.00	85
1993	Snips & Snails	Closed	1994	85.00	125-195
1993	Sugar & Spice	Closed	1994	89.95	125
1993	Curly Locks	Closed	1995	89.95	90

Down The Garden Path - P. Coffer

1991	Rosemary	Closed	1994	79.00	79
1991	Angelica	Closed	1994	85.00	85

Elvis: Lifetime Of A Legend - L. Di Leo

1992	'68 Comeback Special	Closed	1994	99.95	100
1994	King of Las Vegas	Closed	1994	99.95	100

European Fairytales - G. Rademann

1994	Little Red Riding Hood	Closed	1995	79.95	80
1995	Snow White	12/96		79.95	80

Family Ties - M. Tretter

1994	Welcome Home Baby Brother	Closed	1995	79.95	80
1995	Kiss and Make it Better	12/96		89.95	90
1995	Happily Ever Better	12/96		89.95	90

Father's Touch - L. Di Leo

1993	2 A.M. Feeding	Closed	1994	99.95	100

From The Heart - T. Menzenbach

1992	Carolin	Closed	1994	79.95	80-95
1992	Erik	Closed	1994	79.95	80-95

From This Day Forward - P. Tumminio

1994	Elizabeth	Closed	1995	89.95	90
1995	Betty	12/96		89.95	90
1995	Beth	12/96		89.95	90
1995	Lisa	12/96		89.95	90

Garden of Inspirations - B. Hanson

1994	Gathering Violets	Closed	1995	69.95	70
1994	Daisy Chain	Closed	1995	69.95	70
1995	Heart's Bouquet	12/96		74.95	75
1995	Garden Prayer	12/96		74.95	75

Gene - M. Odom

1995	Premiere	12/96		69.95	70
1995	Red Venus	12/96		69.95	70
1995	Monaco	12/96		69.95	70

Gingham & Bows - S. Freeman

1995	Gwendolyn	12/98		69.95	70

God Hears the Children - B. Conner

1995	Now I Lay Me Down	12/98		79.95	80
1996	God Is Great, God Is Good	12/99		79.95	80

Growing Young Minds - K. Barry-Hippensteel

1991	Alex	Closed	1992	79.00	80-120

Happiness Is... - K. Barry-Hippensteel

1991	Patricia (My First Tooth)	Closed	1993	69.00	100-125
1992	Crystal (Feeding Myself)	Closed	1994	69.95	100
1993	Brittany (Blowing Kisses)	Closed	1993	69.95	100
1993	Joy (My First Christmas)	Closed	1993	69.95	70
1994	Candy Cane (Holly)	Closed	1994	69.95	70
1994	Patrick (My First Playmate)	Closed	1994	69.95	70-85

Happy Thoughts - K. Barry-Hippensteel

1994	Laughter is the Best Medicine	Closed	1995	59.95	60

Heavenly Inspirations - C. McClure

1992	Every Cloud Has a Silver Lining	Closed	1994	59.95	60-95
1993	Wish Upon A Star	Closed	1994	59.95	60-95
1994	Sweet Dreams	Closed	1994	65.00	65-95
1994	Luck at the End of Rainbow	Closed	1994	65.00	65
1994	Sunshine	Closed	1994	69.95	70
1994	Pennies From Heaven	Closed	1995	69.95	70

Heritage of American Quilting - J. Lundy

1994	Eleanor	Closed	1995	79.95	80
1995	Abigail	12/96		79.95	80
1995	Louisa	12/96		84.95	85
1995	Ruth Anne	12/96		84.95	85

Heroines from the Fairy Tale Forests - D. Effner

1988	Little Red Riding Hood	Closed	1990	68.00	200
1989	Goldilocks	Closed	1991	68.00	70-95
1990	Snow White	Closed	1992	73.00	175
1991	Rapunzel	Closed	1993	79.00	150-175
1992	Cinderella	Closed	1993	79.00	150-200
1993	Cinderella (Ballgown)	Closed	1994	79.95	150-200

How Little Was I? - K. Barry-Hippensteel

1995	Brittany	12/96		59.95	60
1995	Claire	12/96		59.95	60

I Want Mommy - K. Barry-Hippensteel

1993	Timmy (Mommy I'm Sleepy)	Closed	1994	59.95	175
1993	Tommy (Mommy I'm Sorry)	Closed	1994	59.95	125
1994	Up Mommy (Tammy)	Closed	1994	65.00	90-125

I'm Just Little - K. Barry-Hippensteel

1995	I'm a Little Angel	12/96		49.95	50
1995	I'm a Little Devil	12/96		49.95	50

International Festival of Toys and Tots - K. Barry-Hippensteel

1989	Chen, a Little Boy of China	Closed	1990	78.00	85-125
1989	Natasha	Closed	1992	78.00	78
1990	Molly	Closed	1993	83.00	83
1991	Hans	Closed	1993	88.00	88
1992	Miki, Eskimo	Closed	1994	88.00	88

Joys of Summer - K. Barry-Hippensteel

1993	Tickles	Closed	1994	49.95	75-125
1993	Little Squirt	Closed	1994	49.95	50-75
1994	Yummy	Closed	1994	55.00	55-75
1994	Havin' A Ball	Closed	1994	55.00	65-75
1994	Lil' Scoop	Closed	1994	55.00	65-75

The King & I - P. Ryan Brooks

1991	Shall We Dance?	Closed	1992	175.00	395

Lasting Traditions - W. Hanson

1993	Something Old	Closed	1993	69.95	70
1994	Finishing Touch	Closed	1994	69.95	70
1994	Mother's Pearls	Closed	1994	85.00	85
1994	Her Traditional Garter	Closed	1995	85.00	85

Lawton's Nursery Rhymes - W. Lawton

1994	Little Bo Peep	Closed	1995	79.95	80
1994	Little Miss Muffet	Closed	1995	79.95	80
1994	Mary, Mary	Closed	1995	85.00	85
1994	Mary/Lamb	Closed	1995	85.00	85

The Legends of Baseball - Various

1994	Babe Ruth - T. Tomescu	Closed	1995	79.95	80
1994	Lou Gehrig - T. Tomescu	Closed	1995	79.95	80
1995	Ty Cobb - E. Shelton	12/96		79.95	80

Let's Play Mother Goose - K. Barry-Hippensteel

1994	Cow Jumped Over the Moon	Closed	1995	69.95	70
1994	Hickory, Dickory, Dock	Closed	1995	69.95	70-95

Little Bits - G. Rademan

1993	Lil Bit of Sunshine	Closed	1993	39.95	40
1993	Lil Bit of Love	Closed	1994	39.95	40
1994	Lil Bit of Tenderness	Closed	1994	39.95	40
1994	Lil Bit of Innocence	Closed	1994	39.95	40

Little Girls of Classic Literature - W. Lawton

1995	Pollyanna	12/98		79.95	80

Little Handfuls - M. Severino

1993	Ricky	Closed	1994	39.95	40
1993	Abby	Closed	1995	39.95	40
1993	Josie	Closed	1995	39.95	40

Little House On The Prairie - J. Ibarolle

1992	Laura	Closed	1993	79.95	80-100
1993	Mary Ingalls	Closed	1993	79.95	275-395
1993	Nellie Olson	Closed	1994	85.00	95
1993	Almanzo	Closed	1994	85.00	95
1994	Carrie	Closed	1994	85.00	85
1994	Ma Ingalls	Closed	1995	85.00	85
1994	Pa Ingalls	Closed	1995	85.00	85
1995	Baby Grace	12/96		69.95	70

Little Women - W. Lawton

1994	Jo	Closed	1995	59.95	60
1994	Meg	Closed	1995	59.95	60
1994	Beth	12/96		59.95	60
1994	Amy	12/96		59.95	60
1995	Marmie	12/96		59.95	60

The Littlest Clowns - M. Tretter

1991	Sparkles	Closed	1992	63.00	63
1991	Bubbles	Closed	1992	65.00	65
1991	Smooch	Closed	1992	69.00	69
1992	Daisy	Closed	1993	69.95	70

Look At Me - L. Di Leo

1993	Rose Marie	Closed	1994	49.95	50
1994	Ann Marie	Closed	1994	49.95	50
1994	Lisa Marie	Closed	1995	55.00	55

Lots Of Love - T. Menzenbach

1993	Hannah Needs A Hug	Closed	1994	49.95	60-110
1993	Kaitlyn	Closed	1994	49.95	95
1994	Nicole	Closed	1995	55.00	55
1995	Felicia	12/98		55.00	55

Lucky Charmers - C. McClure

1995	Lucky Star	12/98		69.95	70

Magical Moments of Summer - Y. Bello

1995	Whitney	12/98		59.95	60
1996	Zoe	12/99		59.95	60

Mainstreet Saturday Morning - M. Tretter

1994	Kenny	Closed	1995	69.95	70
1995	Betty	12/96		69.95	70
1995	Donny	12/96		69.95	70

Memories of Yesterday - M. Attwell

1994	A Friend in Need	Closed	1995	59.95	60
1994	Tomorrow is Another Day	Closed	1995	59.95	60
1995	Beauty is in the Eye of the Beholder	12/96		59.95	60

Messages of Hope - T. Tomescu

1994	Let the Little Children Come to Me	Closed	1995	129.95	130
1995	Good Shepherd	12/96		129.95	130
1995	I Stand at the Door	12/96		129.95	130

Moments To Remember - Y. Bello

1991	Justin	Closed	1994	75.00	75-100
1992	Jill	Closed	1993	75.00	75-100
1993	Brandon (Ring Bearer)	Closed	1994	79.95	80
1993	Suzanne (Flower Girl)	Closed	1994	79.95	80

*Quotes have been rounded up to nearest dollar

Column 1

YEAR ISSUE	EDITION LIMIT	YEAR RETD.	ISSUE PRICE	*QUOTE U.S.$
My Closest Friend - J. Goodyear				
1991 Boo Bear 'N Me	Closed	1992	78.00	125-200
1991 Me and My Blankie	Closed	1993	79.00	95
1992 My Secret Pal (Robbie)	Closed	1993	85.00	85
1992 My Beary Best Friend	Closed	1993	79.95	80
My Fair Lady - P. Ryan Brooks				
1991 Eliza at Ascot	Closed	1992	125.00	395
My Heart Belongs To Daddy - J. Singer				
1992 Peanut	Closed	1994	49.95	95
1992 Pumpkin	Closed	1994	49.95	50-75
1994 Princess	Closed	1994	59.95	60
My Little Ballerina - K. Barry-Hippensteel				
1994 My Little Ballerina	Closed	1995	69.95	60
Nursery Newborns - J. Wolf				
1994 It's A Boy	Closed	1995	79.95	80
1994 It's A Girl	Closed	1995	79.95	80
Oh Holy Night - Good-Krüger				
1994 The Holy Family (Jesus, Mary, Joseph)	Closed	1995	129.95	130
1995 The Kneeling King	Closed	1995	59.95	60
1995 The Purple King	Closed	1995	59.95	60
1995 The Blue King	Closed	1995	59.95	60
1995 Shepherd with Pipes	Closed	1995	59.95	60
1995 Shepherd with Lamb	Closed	1995	59.95	60
1995 Angel	Closed	1995	59.95	60
Parade of American Fashion - Stevens/Siegel				
1987 The Glamour of the Gibson Girl	Closed	1989	77.00	125
1988 The Southern Belle	Closed	1989	77.00	125
1990 Victorian Lady	Closed	1991	82.00	82
1991 Romantic Lady	Closed	1993	85.00	85
Passports to Friendship - J. Ibarolle				
1995 Serena	12/98		79.95	80
1996 Kali	12/99		79.95	80
Patchwork of Love - Good-Krüger				
1995 Warmth of the Heart	12/98		59.95	60
Perfect Pairs - B. Bambina				
1995 Amber	12/96		59.95	60
1995 Tiffany	12/96		59.95	60
1995 Carmen	12/96		59.95	60
Petting Zoo - Y. Bello				
1995 Andy	12/96		59.95	60
1995 Kendra	12/96		59.95	60
1995 Cory	12/96		59.95	60
1995 Maddie	12/96		59.95	60
Polly's Tea Party - S. Krey				
1990 Polly	Closed	1992	78.00	125
1991 Lizzie	Closed	1992	79.00	79
1992 Annie	Closed	1993	83.00	83
Potpourri Babies - A. Brown				
1995 Bubble Trouble	12/98		79.95	80
Precious Memories of Motherhood - S. Kuck				
1989 Loving Steps	Closed	1991	125.00	125-175
1990 Lullaby	Closed	1993	125.00	125
1991 Expectant Moments	Closed	1993	149.00	195
1992 Bedtime	Closed	1993	150.00	150
Precious Papooses - S. Housely				
1995 Sleeping Bear	12/98		79.95	80
Pretty in Pastels - J. Goodyear				
1994 Precious in Pink	Closed	1995	79.95	80
Rainbow of Love - Y. Bello				
1994 Blue Sky	Closed	1995	59.95	60
1994 Yellow Sunshine	Closed	1995	59.95	60
1994 Green Earth	Closed	1995	59.95	60
1994 Pink Flower	12/96		59.95	60
1994 Purple Mountain	12/96		59.95	60
1994 Orange Sunset	12/96		59.95	60
Rockwell Christmas - Rockwell-Inspired				
1990 Scotty Plays Santa	Closed	1991	48.00	48
1991 Scotty Gets His Tree	Closed	1992	59.95	59
1993 Merry Christmas Grandma	Closed	1993	59.95	60
Romantic Flower Maidens - M. Roderick				
1988 Rose, Who is Love	Closed	1990	87.00	87
1989 Daisy	Closed	1993	87.00	87
1990 Violet	Closed	1993	92.00	92
1990 Lily	Closed	1991	92.00	92
Season of Dreams - G. Rademann				
1994 Autumn Breeze	Closed	1995	79.95	80
Secret Garden - J. Kovacik				
1994 Mary	Closed	1995	69.95	70
1995 Colin	12/96		69.95	70

Column 2

YEAR ISSUE	EDITION LIMIT	YEAR RETD.	ISSUE PRICE	*QUOTE U.S.$
1995 Martha	12/96		69.95	70
1995 Dickon	12/96		69.95	70
A Sense of Discovery - K. Barry-Hippensteel				
1993 Sweetie (Sense of Discovery)	Closed	1994	59.95	60
Siblings Through Time - C. McClure				
1995 Alexandra	12/96		69.95	70
1995 Gracie	12/96		59.95	60
Snow Babies - T. Tomescu				
1995 Beneath the Mistletoe	Closed	1995	69.95	70
1995 Follow the Leader	12/96		75.00	75
1995 Snow Baby Express	12/96		75.00	75
Someone to Watch Over Me - K. Barry-Hippensteel				
1994 Sweet Dreams	Closed	1995	69.95	70
1995 Night-Night Angel	Closed	1995	24.95	25
1995 Lullaby Angel	Closed	1995	24.95	25
1995 Sleepyhead Angel	12/96		24.95	25
1995 Stardust Angel	12/96		24.95	25
1995 Tuck-Me-In Angel	12/96		24.95	25
Sooo Big - M. Tretter				
1993 Jimmy	Closed	1994	59.95	60
1994 Kimmy	Closed	1995	59.95	60
Special Edition Tour 1993 - Y. Bello				
1993 Miguel	Closed	1993	69.95	70
1993 Rosa	Closed	1993	69.95	70
Stepping Out - Akers/Girardi				
1991 Millie	Closed	1992	99.00	125
Tender Moments - L. Tierney				
1995 Tender Love	12/96		49.95	50
1995 Tender Heart	12/96		49.95	50
1995 Tender Care	12/96		49.95	50
Together Forever - S. Krey				
1994 Kirsten	Closed	1995	59.95	60
1994 Courtney	Closed	1995	59.95	60
1994 Kim	Closed	1995	59.95	60
Treasured Togetherness - M. Tretter				
1994 Tender Touch	Closed	1995	99.95	100
1994 Touch of Love	Closed	1995	99.95	100
Tumbling Tots - K. Barry-Hippensteel				
1993 Roly Poly Polly	Closed	1994	69.95	70
1994 Handstand Harry	Closed	1995	69.95	70
Two Much To Handle - K. Barry-Hippensteel				
1993 Julie (Flowers For Mommy)	Closed	1994	59.95	60
1993 Kevin (Clean Hands)	Closed	1995	59.95	100-125
Under Her Wings - P. Bomar				
1995 Guardian Angel	12/98		79.95	80
Victorian Dreamers - K. Barry-Hippensteel				
1995 Rock-A-Bye/Good Night	12/96		49.95	50
1995 Victorian Storytime	12/96		49.95	50
Victorian Lace - C. Layton				
1993 Alicia	Closed	1994	79.95	100-125
1994 Colleen	Closed	1995	79.95	80
1994 Olivia	Closed	1995	79.95	80
Victorian Nursery Heirloom - C. McClure				
1994 Victorian Lullaby	Closed	1995	129.95	130
1995 Victorian Highchair	12/96		129.95	130
1995 Victorian Playtime	12/96		139.95	140
1995 Victorian Bunny Buggy	12/96		139.95	140
What Little Girls Are Made Of - D. Effner				
1994 Peaches and Cream	Closed	1995	69.95	70
1995 Lavender & Lace	12/98		69.95	70
1995 Sunshine & Lollipops	12/98		69.95	70
Winter Wonderland - K. Barry-Hippensteel				
1994 Annie	Closed	1995	59.95	60
1994 Bobby	Closed	1995	59.95	60
Winterfest - S. Sherwood				
1991 Brian	Closed	1992	89.00	100-125
1992 Michelle	Closed	1993	89.95	125
1993 Bradley	Closed	1993	89.95	90
The Wonderful Wizard of Oz - M. Tretter				
1994 Dorothy	Closed	1995	79.95	80
1994 Scarecrow	Closed	1995	79.95	80
1994 Tin Man	Closed	1995	79.95	80
1994 The Cowardly Lion	12/96		79.95	80
Year Book Memories - Akers/Girardi				
1991 Peggy Sue	Closed	1992	87.00	95
1993 Going Steady (Patty Jo)	Closed	1994	89.95	90
1993 Prom Queen (Betty Jean)	Closed	1993	92.00	92
Yesterday's Dreams - M. Oldenburg				
1990 Andy	Closed	1993	68.00	68

Column 3

YEAR ISSUE	EDITION LIMIT	YEAR RETD.	ISSUE PRICE	*QUOTE U.S.$
1991 Janey	Closed	1993	69.00	69
Yolanda's Heaven Scent Babies - Y. Bello				
1993 Meagan Rose	Closed	1994	49.95	75
1993 Daisy Anne	Closed	1994	49.95	50
1993 Morning Glory	Closed	1995	49.95	50
1993 Sweet Carnation	Closed	1995	54.95	55
1993 Lily	Closed	1995	54.95	55
1993 Cherry Blossom	Closed	1995	54.95	55
Yolanda's Lullaby Babies - Y. Bello				
1991 Christy (Rock-a-Bye)	Closed	1993	69.00	70-90
1992 Joey (Twinkle, Twinkle)	Closed	1994	69.00	70-85
1993 Amy (Brahms Lullaby)	Closed	1994	75.00	75
1993 Eddie (Teddy Bear Lullaby)	Closed	1994	75.00	75
1993 Jacob (Silent Night)	Closed	1994	75.00	75
1994 Bonnie (You Are My Sunshine)	Closed	1994	80.00	80
Yolanda's Picture - Perfect Babies - Y. Bello				
1985 Jason	Closed	1988	48.00	700
1986 Heather	Closed	1988	48.00	225-450
1987 Jennifer	Closed	1989	58.00	225-325
1987 Matthew	Closed	1990	58.00	195
1987 Sarah	Closed	1990	58.00	100-175
1988 Amanda	Closed	1990	63.00	125
1989 Jessica	Closed	1993	63.00	75-95
1990 Michael	Closed	1992	63.00	125
1990 Lisa	Closed	1992	63.00	95
1991 Emily	Closed	1992	63.00	100-125
1991 Danielle	Closed	1993	69.00	95-125
Yolanda's Playtime Babies - Y. Bello				
1993 Todd	Closed	1994	59.95	60
1993 Lindsey	Closed	1994	59.95	65
1993 Shawna	Closed	1994	59.95	60
Yolanda's Precious Playmates - Y. Bello				
1992 David	Closed	1994	69.95	125
1993 Paul	Closed	1994	69.95	125
1994 Johnny	Closed	1994	69.95	70
Young Love - J.W. Smith				
1993 First Kiss	Closed	1993	118.00	118
1993 Buttercups	Closed	1994	Set	Set

Attic Babies

YEAR ISSUE	EDITION LIMIT	YEAR RETD.	ISSUE PRICE	*QUOTE U.S.$
Attic Babies' Collector Club - M. Maschino				
1992 Burtie Buzbee, SNL		Retrd. 1992	40.00	40
1993 Izzie B. Ruebottom, SNL	277	1993	35.00	35
1994 Sunflower Flossie, SNL		Retrd. 1994	42.00	42
1995 Tricia Kay Yum-Yum, SNL		Retrd. 1995	40.00	40
Baggie Collection - M. Maschino				
1991 Americana Baggie Bear		Retrd. 1994	19.95	22
1991 Americana Baggie Girl		Retrd. 1994	19.95	22
1991 Americana Baggie Rabbit		Retrd. 1994	19.95	22
1991 Americana Baggie Santa		Retrd. 1994	19.95	22
1991 Christmas Baggie Bear		Retrd. 1994	19.95	22
1991 Christmas Baggie Girl		Retrd. 1994	19.95	22
1991 Christmas Baggie Rabbit		Retrd. 1994	19.95	22
1991 Christmas Baggie Santa		Retrd. 1994	19.95	22
1991 Country Baggie Bear		Retrd. 1994	19.95	22
1991 Country Baggie Girl		Retrd. 1994	19.95	22
1991 Country Baggie Rabbit		Retrd. 1994	19.95	22
Mother's Day Angels - M. Maschino				
1994 Nattie Fae Tucker, SNL	757	1994	64.95	65
Retired Dolls - M. Maschino				
1994 Abner Abernathy		Retrd. 1995	55.95	56
1994 Addie Abernathy		Retrd. 1995	61.95	62
1992 Americana Raggedy Santa (1st ed.), SNL		Retrd. 1992	85.95	150
1992 Americana Raggedy Santa (2nd ed.), SNL		Retrd. 1992	89.95	90
1989 Annie Fannie		Retrd. 1992	43.95	70-110
1992 Artilma Hunnicut		Retrd. 1995	73.95	74
1990 Beary Harriete Bear		Retrd. 1995	87.95	88
1990 Beary Harry Bear		Retrd. 1995	87.95	88
1987 Bessie Jo		Retrd. 1995	31.95	98
1987 Beth Sue		Retrd. 1991	27.95	75
1989 Bouncing Baby Roy		Retrd. 1995	49.95	50
1988 Bunnifer		Retrd. 1995	39.95	82
1988 Buttons		Retrd. 1991	27.95	28
1992 Candy Applebee		Retrd. 1994	15.95	18
1992 Christopher Columbus SNL		Retrd. 1992	79.95	200-250
1989 Cloddy Clyde		Retrd. 1995	69.95	70
1989 Cotton Pickin' Ninny		Retrd. 1994	47.95	100
1987 Country Clyde		Retrd. 1988	27.95	28
1992 Daddy's Lil Punkin Patty, SNL		Retrd. 1993	79.95	175
1992 Darcie Duckworth		Retrd. 1995	59.95	60
1987 Dirty Harry		Retrd. 1991	27.95	55-100
1994 Dollie Boots (1st ed.)	100	1994	79.95	80
1995 Dollie Boots (2nd ed.)	2,000	1995	84.95	85
1990 Duckie Dinkle		Retrd. 1991	95.95	96
1992 Durwin Duckworth		Retrd. 1995	59.95	60
1988 Fester Chester		Retrd. 1994	39.95	50
1989 Flakey Jakey		Retrd. 1995	59.95	60
1990 Frannie Farkle		Retrd. 1991	129.95	130
1990 Frizzy Lizzy		Retrd. 1992	95.95	25

YEAR	ISSUE	EDITION LIMIT	YEAR RETD.	ISSUE PRICE	*QUOTE U.S.$
1995	Fuzzy Sweezy (1st ed.)	2,000	1995	77.95	78
1990	Gabbie Abbie	Retrd.	1995	109.95	110
1988	Hannah Lou	Retrd.	1994	39.95	50
1990	Happy Huck	Retrd.	1992	47.95	102
1993	Happy Pappy Claus SNL	805	1994	73.95	74
1987	Harold	Retrd.	1990	27.95	80
1995	Hazel Lynora Grimsley	2,000	1995	68.95	69
1989	Heavenly Heather	Retrd.	1992	59.95	100
1988	Hefty Cheffy	Retrd.	1994	75.95	125
1990	Homer Hare	Retrd.	1995	147.95	148
1990	Hunnie Bunnie	Retrd.	1995	147.95	148
1989	Itsy Bitsy Mitzy	Retrd.	1995	49.95	50
1993	Itty Bitty Santa	Retrd.	1993	5.95	6
1990	Ivan Ivie	Retrd.	1991	129.95	230
1987	Jacob	Retrd.	1988	27.95	100
1993	Jammy Mammy Claus SNL	653	1994	67.95	68
1987	Jenny Lou	Retrd.	1992	35.95	36
1989	Jingle Jangle Jo	Retrd.	1995	69.95	70
1989	Jolly Jim	Retrd.	1992	31.95	32
1990	Jumpin Pumkin Jill	Retrd.	1994	55.95	56
1988	Katy	Retrd.	1995	59.95	60
1990	Lampsie Divie Ivie	Retrd.	1991	129.95	230
1995	Lani Frumpet 1st ed.	2,000	1995	56.95	57
1988	Lazy Daisy	Retrd.	1992	39.95	60
1988	Lazy Liza Jane	Retrd.	1991	47.95	48
1995	Lily Lumpbucket	2,000	1995	61.95	62
1988	Little Dove	Retrd.	1988	39.95	40
1994	Lollie Ann	Retrd.	1994	39.95	40
1987	Maggie Mae	Retrd.	1991	25.95	28
1991	Maizie Mae	Retrd.	1994	51.95	52
1991	Mandi Mae	Retrd.	1994	51.95	52
1991	Memsie Mae	Retrd.	1994	51.95	52
1993	Merry Beary Raggady Santy	1,000	1995	113.95	114
1994	Merry Ole Farley Fagan Dooberry, SNL	Retrd.	1994	131.95	132
1987	Messy Tessy	Retrd.	1995	43.95	44
1993	Millie Wilset	2,000	1994	39.95	40
1987	Miss Pitty Pat	Retrd.	1988	27.95	100
1988	Molly Bea	Retrd.	1990	39.95	45-80
1995	Monty Thumpet	2,000	1995	56.95	57
1988	Moosey Matilda	Retrd.	1990	39.95	150-300
1989	Mr. Gardner	Retrd.	1995	109.95	110
1993	Mr. Kno Mo Sno, SNL	1,800	1994	51.95	52
1991	Mr. Raggedy Claus, SNL	Retrd.	1992	69.95	120
1989	Mrs. Gardner	Retrd.	1995	109.95	110
1991	Mrs. Raggedy Claus, SNL	Retrd.	1992	69.95	120
1989	Ms. Waddles	Retrd.	1990	47.95	48
1987	Muslin Bunny	Retrd.	1993	7.95	8
1987	Muslin Teddy	Retrd.	1993	7.95	8
1988	Nathan	Retrd.	1995	59.95	60
1988	Naughty Nellie	Retrd.	1990	31.95	85
1990	Nerdie Nelda	Retrd.	1995	69.95	70
1994	Old Raggady Noah	2,500	1995	139.95	140
1993	Old St. Knickerbocker, SNL	Retrd.	1993	79.95	80
1992	Old St. Nick, SNL	Retrd.	1993	95.95	130
1989	Old Tyme Santy	Retrd.	1989	79.95	80
1995	Pea Pod Sweezy (1st ed.)	2,000	1995	74.95	75
1990	Phylbert Farkle	Retrd.	1991	129.95	225
1991	Pippy Pat	Retrd.	1994	47.95	52
1988	Prissy Missy	Retrd.	1990	31.95	32
1987	Rachel	Retrd.	1988	29.95	85
1987	Raggady Kitty	Retrd.	1988	29.95	30
1995	Raggady Old Wooly Tackitt	2,000	1995	46.95	47
1990	Raggady Ole Chris Cringle (1st ed.)	Retrd.	1990	189.95	262
1990	Raggady Ole Chris Cringle (2nd ed.)	Retrd.	1991	189.95	190
1994	Raggady P. Shagnasty	Retrd.	1995	139.95	140
1988	Raggady Sam (1st ed.)	Retrd.	1991	55.95	115
1991	Raggady Sam (2nd ed.)	500	1995	399.95	400
1987	Raggady Santy (1st ed.)	Retrd.	1988	75.95	200
1990	Raggady Santy (2nd ed.)	Retrd.	1991	89.95	90
1987	Raggady Teddy	Retrd.	1995	9.95	10
1989	Rammy Sammy	Retrd.	1990	43.95	44
1987	Rose Ann	Retrd.	1991	39.95	40
1988	Rotten Wilber	Retrd.	1990	35.95	140
1988	Rufus	Retrd.	1992	35.95	70-80
1987	Sally Francis	Retrd.	1993	35.95	62
1987	Sara	Retrd.	1992	39.95	86
1992	Scary Larry Scarecrow, SNL	Retrd.	1994	79.95	80
1988	Silly Willie	Retrd.	1990	39.95	76
1989	Skitty Kitty	Retrd.	1991	43.95	140
1990	Sollie Ollie Otis	Retrd.	1991	129.95	130
1995	Spirit of Christmas Santy	Retrd.	1995	87.95	88
1988	Spring Santy	Retrd.	1989	47.95	48
1988	Sweet William	Retrd.	1989	35.95	152
1992	Teeny Weenie Christmas Angel	Retrd.	1994	9.95	12
1992	Teeny Weenie Country Angel	Retrd.	1994	9.95	12
1987	Toddy Sue	Retrd.	1990	27.95	87
1995	Tootie Twinkles (1st ed.)	5,000	1995	59.95	60
1990	Verlie Mae	Retrd.	1995	49.95	50
1988	Wacky Jackie	Retrd.	1990	39.95	40
1995	Willa Thumpet	2,000	1995	73.95	74
1991	Winkie Binkie	Retrd.	1993	53.95	54
1992	Witchy Wanda, SNL	Retrd.	1994	79.95	80
1989	Wood Doll, black-large	Retrd.	1991	36.00	36
1989	Wood Doll, white-large	Retrd.	1991	36.00	36
1989	Wood Doll-medium	Retrd.	1991	31.95	32
1989	Wood Doll-small	Retrd.	1991	23.95	24
1990	Yankee Doodle Debbie	Retrd.	1993	95.95	150
1990	Zitty Zelda, SNL	Retrd.	1993	89.95	176

Tour Babies - M. Maschino

YEAR	ISSUE	EDITION LIMIT	YEAR RETD.	ISSUE PRICE	*QUOTE U.S.$
1992	Tour Baby-old man 1992	Retrd.	1992	19.95	20
1992	Tour Baby-old woman 1992	Retrd.	1992	19.95	20
1992	Tour Baby-young boy 1992	Retrd.	1992	19.95	20
1992	Tour Baby-young girl 1992	Retrd.	1992	19.95	20
1993	Tour Baby 1993	Retrd.	1993	19.95	22
1994	Tour Baby 1994	Retrd.	1994	24.95	25
1995	Tour Baby 1995	Retrd.	1995	26.95	27

Valentine Collection - M. Maschino

YEAR	ISSUE	EDITION LIMIT	YEAR RETD.	ISSUE PRICE	*QUOTE U.S.$
1993	Valentine Bear-Girl	Retrd.	1993	39.95	40
1993	Valentine Bear-Boy	Retrd.	1993	39.95	40
1994	Herwin Heaps-O Hugs	613	1994	39.95	40
1994	Lottie Lots-A Hugs	825	1994	39.95	40
1995	Ruthie Claire	Retrd.	1995	39.95	40

The Collectables Inc.

Collector's Club Doll - P. Parkins

YEAR	ISSUE	EDITION LIMIT	YEAR RETD.	ISSUE PRICE	*QUOTE U.S.$
1991	Mandy	Closed	1991	360.00	360
1992	Kallie	Closed	1992	410.00	410
1993	Mommy and Me	Closed	1993	810.00	810
1994	Krystal	Closed	1994	380.00	380
1995	Taylor	Closed	1995	380.00	380

Angel Series - P. Parkins

YEAR	ISSUE	EDITION LIMIT	YEAR RETD.	ISSUE PRICE	*QUOTE U.S.$
1992	Angel on My Shoulder	Closed	1993	530.00	530
1994	Guarding the Way	500	1995	950.00	950
1993	My Guardian Angel	500	1993	590.00	590

Butterfly Babies - P. Parkins

YEAR	ISSUE	EDITION LIMIT	YEAR RETD.	ISSUE PRICE	*QUOTE U.S.$
1989	Belinda	S/O	1990	270.00	375
1992	Laticia	Closed	1993	320.00	320
1990	Willow	Closed	1991	240.00	375

Cherished Memories - P. Parkins, unless otherwise noted

YEAR	ISSUE	EDITION LIMIT	YEAR RETD.	ISSUE PRICE	*QUOTE U.S.$
1986	Amy and Andrew	S/O	1986	220.00	325
1988	Brittany	Closed	1988	240.00	300
1990	Cassandra	Closed	1990	500.00	550
1989	Generations	Closed	1989	480.00	500
1988	Heather	Closed	1988	280.00	300-350
1988	Jennifer	Closed	1988	380.00	500-600
1988	Leigh Ann And Leland	Closed	1988	250.00	250-300
1988	Tea Time - D. Effner	S/O	1986	380.00	450
1990	Twinkles	Closed	1991	170.00	275

The Collectibles Inc. Dolls - P. Parkins, unless otherwise noted

YEAR	ISSUE	EDITION LIMIT	YEAR RETD.	ISSUE PRICE	*QUOTE U.S.$
1991	Adrianna	Closed	1992	1350.00	1350
1994	Afternoon Delight	500	1995	410.00	410
1995	Alexus	150		770.00	770
1993	Amber	500	1994	330.00	330
1994	Amber Hispanic	500	1994	340.00	340
1992	Angel on My Shoulder (Lillianne w/CeCe)	500	1993	530.00	530
1990	Bassinet Baby	2,000	1990	130.00	375-425
1991	Bethany	Closed	1992	450.00	450
1995	Brianna	150	1995	590.00	590
1995	Christine	350		390.00	390
1990	Danielle	1,000	1990	400.00	475
1994	Earth Angel	500		195.00	195
1993	Haley	500	1994	330.00	330
1990	In Your Easter Bonnet	1,000	1990	350.00	350
1992	Karlie	500	1992	380.00	380
1991	Kelsie	500	1991	320.00	320
1991	Lauren	S/O	1991	490.00	490
1993	Little Dumpling (Black)	500	1994	190.00	190
1993	Little Dumpling (White)	500	1994	190.00	190
1990	Lizbeth Ann - D. Effner	1,000	1990	420.00	420
1994	Madison	250		350.00	350
1994	Madison Sailor	250	1995	370.00	370
1993	Maggie	500	1994	330.00	330
1992	Marissa	300	1992	350.00	350
1992	Marty	250	1992	190.00	190
1992	Matia	250	1992	190.00	190
1989	Michelle	250	1990	270.00	400-450
1992	Missy	Open		59.00	59
1992	Molly	450	1993	350.00	350
1994	Morgan	250	1995	390.00	390
1994	Morgan in Red	250	1995	390.00	390
1995	A Mother's Love	450		770.00	770
1995	My Little Angel Boy	250		450.00	450
1995	My Little Angel Girl	250		450.00	450
1991	Natasha	Closed	1992	510.00	510
1992	Shelley	300	1992	450.00	450
1987	Storytime By Sarah Jane	S/O	1990	330.00	475-525
1994	Sugar Plum Fairy	500		250.00	250
1987	Tasha	S/O	1987	290.00	1400
1986	Tatiana	S/O	1986	270.00	1000
1989	Welcome Home - D. Effner	1,000	1990	330.00	475-675
1991	Yvette	300	1992	580.00	580

Enchanted Children - P. Parkins

YEAR	ISSUE	EDITION LIMIT	YEAR RETD.	ISSUE PRICE	*QUOTE U.S.$
1990	Kara	Closed	1991	550.00	550
1990	Katlin	Closed	1991	550.00	550
1990	Kristin	S/O	1991	550.00	650
1990	Tiffy	S/O	1991	370.00	500

Fairy - P. Parkins

YEAR	ISSUE	EDITION LIMIT	YEAR RETD.	ISSUE PRICE	*QUOTE U.S.$
1988	Tabatha	1,500	1989	370.00	400-450

Mother's Little Treasures - D. Effner

YEAR	ISSUE	EDITION LIMIT	YEAR RETD.	ISSUE PRICE	*QUOTE U.S.$
1985	1st Edition	S/O	1985	380.00	1000
1990	2nd Edition	S/O	1990	440.00	475-595

Storybook Series - P. Parkins

YEAR	ISSUE	EDITION LIMIT	YEAR RETD.	ISSUE PRICE	*QUOTE U.S.$
1995	Jack	300		170.00	170
1995	Jill	300		170.00	170
1995	Little Bo Peep	300		220.00	220
1995	Little Boy Blue	300		170.00	170
1995	Little Red Riding Hood	300		210.00	210
1995	Twinkle, Twinkle Little Star	300		170.00	170

Yesterday's Child - D. Effner, unless otherwise noted

YEAR	ISSUE	EDITION LIMIT	YEAR RETD.	ISSUE PRICE	*QUOTE U.S.$
1986	Ashley - P. Parkins	Closed	1987	220.00	275
1983	Chad And Charity	Closed	1984	190.00	190
1982	Cleo	Closed	1983	180.00	250
1982	Columbine	Closed	1983	180.00	250
1982	Jason And Jessica	Closed	1983	150.00	300
1984	Kevin And Karissa	Closed	1985	190.00	250-300
1983	Noel	Closed	1984	190.00	240
1984	Rebecca	Closed	1985	250.00	250-300
1986	Todd And Tiffany	Closed	1987	220.00	250

Department 56

Heritage Village Doll Collection - Department 56

YEAR	ISSUE	EDITION LIMIT	YEAR RETD.	ISSUE PRICE	*QUOTE U.S.$
1987	Christmas Carol Dolls 1000-6 set/4 (Tiny Tim, Bob Crachet, Mrs. Crachet, Scrooge)	250	1988	1500.00	1500
1987	Christmas Carol Dolls 5907-2 set/4 (Tiny Tim, Bob Crachet, Mrs. Crachet, Scrooge)	Closed	1993	250.00	265-300
1988	Christmas Carol Dolls 1001-4 set/4 (Tiny Tim, Bob Crachet, Mrs. Crachet, Scrooge)	350	1989	1600.00	1600
1988	Mr. & Mrs. Fezziwig 5594-8 set/2	Open		172.00	172

Snowbabies Dolls - Department 56

YEAR	ISSUE	EDITION LIMIT	YEAR RETD.	ISSUE PRICE	*QUOTE U.S.$
1988	Allison & Duncan-Set /2, 7730-5	Closed	1989	200.00	750-795

Dolls by Jerri

Dolls by Jerri - J. McCloud

YEAR	ISSUE	EDITION LIMIT	YEAR RETD.	ISSUE PRICE	*QUOTE U.S.$
1986	Alfalfa	1,000		350.00	350
1986	Allison	1,000		350.00	450
1986	Amber	1,000		350.00	850
1986	Annabelle	300		600.00	585
1986	Ashley	1,000		350.00	500
1986	Audrey	300		550.00	550
1982	Baby David	538		290.00	2000
XX	Boy	1,000		350.00	425
1985	Bride	1,000		350.00	400
1986	Bridgette	300		500.00	500
1985	Candy	1,000		340.00	2000
1986	Cane	1,000		350.00	1200
1986	Charlotte	1,000		330.00	450
1984	Clara	1,000		320.00	1200-1500
1986	Clown-David 3 Yrs. Old	1,000		340.00	450
1986	Danielle	1,000		350.00	500
1986	David-2 Years Old	1,000		330.00	550
1986	David-Magician	1,000		350.00	450
XX	Denise	1,000		380.00	550
1986	Elizabeth	1,000		340.00	350
1984	Emily	1,000		330.00	2500
1986	The Fool	1,000		350.00	350
XX	Gina	1,000		350.00	475
XX	Goldilocks	1,000		370.00	600-750
1989	Goose Girl, Guild	Closed		300.00	700
1986	Helenjean	1,000		350.00	500-650
1988	Holly	1,000		370.00	825
1986	Jacqueline	300		500.00	500
XX	Jamie	800		380.00	450
1986	Joy	1,000		350.00	350
XX	Laura	1,000		350.00	500
1989	Laura Lee	1,000		370.00	575
XX	Little Bo Peep	1,000		340.00	450
XX	Little Miss Muffet	1,000		340.00	450
1986	Lucianna	300		500.00	500
1986	Mary Beth	1,000		350.00	350
XX	Megan	750		420.00	550
XX	Meredith	750		430.00	600
1985	Miss Nanny	1,000		160.00	275
1986	Nobody	1,000		350.00	550-650
1986	Princess and the Unicorn	1,000		370.00	400
1986	Samantha	1,000		350.00	550
1985	Scotty	1,000		340.00	1800
1986	Somebody	1,000		350.00	550-750
1986	Tammy	1,000		350.00	900
1985	Uncle Joe	1,000		160.00	250-300
XX	Uncle Remus	500		290.00	450
1986	Yvonne	300		500.00	500

Dynasty Doll

Annual - Various

YEAR	ISSUE	EDITION LIMIT	YEAR RETD.	ISSUE PRICE	*QUOTE U.S.$
1989	Amber - Unknown	Yr.Iss.		90.00	90

*Quotes have been rounded up to nearest dollar

YEAR ISSUE	EDITION LIMIT	YEAR RETD.	ISSUE PRICE	*QUOTE U.S.$
1990 Marcella - Unknown	Yr.Iss.		90.00	90
1991 Butterfly Princess - Unknown	Yr.Iss.		110.00	110
1993 Annual Bride - H. Tertsakian	Yr.Iss.		190.00	190
1993 Ariel - Unknown	Yr.Iss.		120.00	120
1994 Annual Bride - H. Tertsakian	Yr.Iss.		200.00	200
1994 Janie '94 - Unknown	Yr.Iss.		120.00	120
1995 Victoria Jane - H. Tertsakian	Yr.Iss.		160.00	160
1995 Annual Bride - B. Lee	Yr.Iss.		210.00	210

Christmas - Unknown

YEAR ISSUE	EDITION LIMIT	YEAR RETD.	ISSUE PRICE	*QUOTE U.S.$
1987 Merrie	Retrd.	N/A	60.00	60
1988 Noel	Retrd.	N/A	80.00	80
1990 Faith	Retrd.	N/A	110.00	110
1991 Joy	Retrd.	N/A	125.00	125
1993 Genevieve	Retrd.	N/A	164.00	164
1994 Gloria '94	5,000	1994	170.00	170
1995 Sparkle	3,500		160.00	150

Dynasty Collection - Various

YEAR ISSUE	EDITION LIMIT	YEAR RETD.	ISSUE PRICE	*QUOTE U.S.$
1993 Amanda - Unknown	3,000	1994	195.00	195
1994 Amelia - G. Hoyt	1,500	1995	170.00	170
1994 Amy - Unknown	1,500		175.00	175
1993 Angela - Unknown	1,500		195.00	195
1993 Antoinette - H. Tertsakian	5,000	1995	190.00	190
1993 Carley - G. Hoyt	Retrd.	1995	120.00	120
1993 Catherine - H. Tertsakian	5,000	1995	190.00	190
1994 Christina - Unknown	3,500		200.00	200
1994 Gabrielle - S. Kelsey	1,500		180.00	180
1993 Heather - G. Tepper	Retrd.	N/A	160.00	160
1993 Julie - K. Henderson	Retrd.	N/A	175.00	175
1993 Juliet - G. Tepper	Retrd.	N/A	160.00	160
1993 Kadyrose - M. Cohen	Retrd.	1995	145.00	145
1993 Katy - M. Cohen	Retrd.	N/A	135.00	135
1994 Kelsey - S. Kelsey	1,500	1995	225.00	225
1991 Lana - Unknown	Open		85.00	85
1994 Laurelyn - Unknown	2,000	1995	180.00	180
1993 Megan - Unknown	3,500	1994	150.00	150
1993 Nicole - Unknown	Retrd.	N/A	135.00	135
1993 Patricia - Unknown	Open		160.00	160
1994 Rebecca - Unknown	1,500		175.00	175
1993 Shannon - Unknown	1,500		195.00	195
1993 Tami - M. Cohen	7,500	1995	190.00	190
1993 Tory - M. Cohen	7,500	1995	190.00	190

Elke's Originals, Ltd.
Elke Hutchens - E. Hutchens

YEAR ISSUE	EDITION LIMIT	YEAR RETD.	ISSUE PRICE	*QUOTE U.S.$
1991 Alicia	250		595.00	700-995
1989 Annabelle	250		575.00	1300-1600
1990 Aubra	250		575.00	850-995
1990 Aurora	250		595.00	850-995
1991 Bellinda	400		595.00	800-895
1992 Bethany	400		595.00	700-895
1991 Braelyn	400		595.00	1300-1700
1991 Brianna	400		595.00	895
1992 Cecilia	435		635.00	750-895
1992 Charles	435		635.00	450-800
1992 Cherie	435		635.00	900
1992 Clarissa	435		635.00	800-895
1993 Daphne	435		675.00	500-895
1993 Deidre	435		675.00	500-800
1993 Desirée	435		675.00	550-800
1990 Kricket	500		575.00	400
1992 Laurakaye	435		550.00	550
1990 Little Liebchen	250		475.00	1000
1990 Victoria	500		645.00	645

Enesco Corporation
Precious Moments Dolls - S. Butcher

YEAR ISSUE	EDITION LIMIT	YEAR RETD.	ISSUE PRICE	*QUOTE U.S.$
1981 Mikey, 18"- E-6214B	Suspd.		150.00	225
1981 Debbie, 18"- E-6214G	Suspd.		150.00	230
1982 Cubby, 18"- E-7267B	5,000		200.00	350-450
1982 Tammy, 18"- E-7267G	5,000		300.00	500-600
1983 Katie Lynne, 16"- E-0539	Suspd.		165.00	175
1984 Mother Sew Dear, 18"- E-2850	Retrd.	1985	350.00	350
1984 Kristy, 12"- E-2851	Suspd.		150.00	175
1984 Timmy, 12"- E-5397	Suspd.		125.00	160
1985 Aaron, 12"- 12424	Suspd.		135.00	150
1985 Bethany, 12"- 12432	Suspd.		135.00	150
1985 P.D., 7"- 12475	Suspd.		50.00	75
1985 Trish, 7"-12483	Suspd.		50.00	75
1986 Bong Bong, 13"-100455	12,000		150.00	265
1986 Candy, 13"-100463	12,000		150.00	275
1986 Connie, 12"-102253	7,500		160.00	240
1987 Angie, The Angel of Mercy-12491	12,500		160.00	275
1990 The Voice of Spring-408786	2-Yr.		150.00	150
1990 Summer's Joy-408794	2-Yr.		150.00	150
1990 Autumn's Praise-408808	2-Yr.		150.00	150
1990 Winter's Song-408816	2-Yr.		150.00	170
1991 You Have Touched So Many Hearts-427527	2-Yr.		90.00	90
1991 May You Have An Old Fashioned Christmas-417785	2-Yr.		150.00	175
1991 The Eyes Of The Lord Are Upon You (Boy Action Musical) 429570	Suspd.		65.00	65
1991 The Eyes Of The Lord Are Upon You (Girl Action Musical)-429589	Suspd.		65.00	65

Precious Moments-Jack-In-The-Boxes - S. Butcher

YEAR ISSUE	EDITION LIMIT	YEAR RETD.	ISSUE PRICE	*QUOTE U.S.$
1991 You Have Touched So Many Hearts-422282	2-Yr.		175.00	175
1991 May You Have An Old Fashioned Christmas-417777	2-Yr.		200.00	200

Precious Moments-Jack-In-The-Boxes-4 Seasons - S. Butcher

YEAR ISSUE	EDITION LIMIT	YEAR RETD.	ISSUE PRICE	*QUOTE U.S.$
1990 Voice of Spring-408735	2-Yr.		200.00	200
1990 Summer's Joy-408743	2-Yr.		200.00	200
1990 Autumn's Praise-408751	2-Yr.		200.00	200
1990 Winter's Song-408778	2-Yr.		200.00	200

Ganz
Cowtown - C. Thammavongsa

YEAR ISSUE	EDITION LIMIT	YEAR RETD.	ISSUE PRICE	*QUOTE U.S.$
1994 Buffalo Bull Cody	Open		20.00	20
1994 Old MooDonald	Open		20.00	20
1994 Santa Cows	Open		25.00	25

Little Cheesers/Cheeserville Picnic Collection - G.D.A. Group

YEAR ISSUE	EDITION LIMIT	YEAR RETD.	ISSUE PRICE	*QUOTE U.S.$
1992 Sweet Cicely Musical Doll In Basket	Open		85.00	85

Georgetown Collection, Inc.
Age of Romance - J. Reavey

YEAR ISSUE	EDITION LIMIT	YEAR RETD.	ISSUE PRICE	*QUOTE U.S.$
1994 Catherine	100-day		150.00	150

American Diary Dolls - L. Mason

YEAR ISSUE	EDITION LIMIT	YEAR RETD.	ISSUE PRICE	*QUOTE U.S.$
1991 Bridget Quinn	100-day		129.25	130
1991 Christina Merovina	100-day		129.25	130
1990 Jennie Cooper	100-day		129.25	130-155
1994 Lian Ying	100-day		130.00	130
1991 Many Stars	100-day		129.25	130
1992 Rachel Williams	100-day		129.25	130
1993 Sarah Turner	100-day		130.00	130
1992 Tulu	100-day		129.25	130

Baby Kisses - T. DeHetre

YEAR ISSUE	EDITION LIMIT	YEAR RETD.	ISSUE PRICE	*QUOTE U.S.$
1992 Michelle	100-day		118.60	119

Best Friends - K. Murawska

YEAR ISSUE	EDITION LIMIT	YEAR RETD.	ISSUE PRICE	*QUOTE U.S.$
1995 Christina	100-day		130.00	130

Blessed Are The Children - J. Reavey

YEAR ISSUE	EDITION LIMIT	YEAR RETD.	ISSUE PRICE	*QUOTE U.S.$
1994 Faith	100-day		83.00	83

Boys Will Be Boys - J. Reavey

YEAR ISSUE	EDITION LIMIT	YEAR RETD.	ISSUE PRICE	*QUOTE U.S.$
1996 Just Like Dad	100-day		96.00	96
1994 Mr. Mischief	100-day		96.00	96

Children of the Great Spirit - C. Theroux

YEAR ISSUE	EDITION LIMIT	YEAR RETD.	ISSUE PRICE	*QUOTE U.S.$
1993 Buffalo Child	100-day		140.00	140
1994 Golden Flower	100-day		130.00	130
1994 Little Fawn	100-day		114.00	114
1993 Winter Baby	100-day		160.00	160

Class Portraits - J. Kissling

YEAR ISSUE	EDITION LIMIT	YEAR RETD.	ISSUE PRICE	*QUOTE U.S.$
1995 Anna	100-day		140.00	140

Country Quilt Babies - B. Prusseit

YEAR ISSUE	EDITION LIMIT	YEAR RETD.	ISSUE PRICE	*QUOTE U.S.$
1996 Hannah	100-day		104.00	104

Dreams Come True - M. Sirko

YEAR ISSUE	EDITION LIMIT	YEAR RETD.	ISSUE PRICE	*QUOTE U.S.$
1995 Amanda	100-day		120.00	120

Faerie Princess - B. Deval

YEAR ISSUE	EDITION LIMIT	YEAR RETD.	ISSUE PRICE	*QUOTE U.S.$
1989 Faerie Princess	Closed	N/A	248.00	248

Fanciful Dreamers - A. Timmerman

YEAR ISSUE	EDITION LIMIT	YEAR RETD.	ISSUE PRICE	*QUOTE U.S.$
1995 Sweetdreams & Moonbeams	100-day		130.00	130

Faraway Friends - S. Skille

YEAR ISSUE	EDITION LIMIT	YEAR RETD.	ISSUE PRICE	*QUOTE U.S.$
1994 Dara	100-day		140.00	140
1993 Kristin	100-day		140.00	140
1994 Mariama	100-day		140.00	140

Georgetown Collection - Various

YEAR ISSUE	EDITION LIMIT	YEAR RETD.	ISSUE PRICE	*QUOTE U.S.$
1995 Buffalo Boy - C. Theroux	100-day		130.00	130
1993 Quick Fox - L. Mason	100-day		138.95	139
1994 Silver Moon - L. Mason	100-day		140.00	140

Gifts From Heaven - B. Prusseit

YEAR ISSUE	EDITION LIMIT	YEAR RETD.	ISSUE PRICE	*QUOTE U.S.$
1994 Good as Gold	100-day		88.00	88
1995 Sweet Pea	100-day		88.00	88

Hearts in Song - J. Galperin

YEAR ISSUE	EDITION LIMIT	YEAR RETD.	ISSUE PRICE	*QUOTE U.S.$
1994 Angelique	100-day		150.00	150
1992 Grace	100-day		149.60	150
1993 Michael	100-day		150.00	150

Heavenly Messages - M. Sirko

YEAR ISSUE	EDITION LIMIT	YEAR RETD.	ISSUE PRICE	*QUOTE U.S.$
1996 David	100-day		104.00	104
1995 Gabrielle	100-day		104.00	104

Kindergarten Kids - V. Walker

YEAR ISSUE	EDITION LIMIT	YEAR RETD.	ISSUE PRICE	*QUOTE U.S.$
1992 Nikki	100-day		129.60	130

Let's Play - T. DeHetre

YEAR ISSUE	EDITION LIMIT	YEAR RETD.	ISSUE PRICE	*QUOTE U.S.$
1992 Eentsy Weentsy Willie	100-day		118.60	119
1992 Peek-A-Boo Beckie	100-day		118.60	119

Linda's Little Ladies - L. Mason

YEAR ISSUE	EDITION LIMIT	YEAR RETD.	ISSUE PRICE	*QUOTE U.S.$
1993 Shannon's Holiday	100-day		169.95	170

Little Bit of Heaven - A. Timmerman

YEAR ISSUE	EDITION LIMIT	YEAR RETD.	ISSUE PRICE	*QUOTE U.S.$
1994 Arielle	100-day		130.00	130
1995 Cupid	100-day		135.00	135
1995 Noelle	100-day		130.00	130

Little Bloomers - J. Reavey

YEAR ISSUE	EDITION LIMIT	YEAR RETD.	ISSUE PRICE	*QUOTE U.S.$
1995 Darling Daisy	100-day		104.00	104

Little Dreamers - A. DiMartino

YEAR ISSUE	EDITION LIMIT	YEAR RETD.	ISSUE PRICE	*QUOTE U.S.$
1994 Beautiful Buttercup	100-day		130.00	130
1995 Julie	100-day		130.00	130
1996 Nicole	100-day		130.00	130

Little Loves - B. Deval

YEAR ISSUE	EDITION LIMIT	YEAR RETD.	ISSUE PRICE	*QUOTE U.S.$
1988 Emma	Closed	N/A	139.20	140
1989 Katie	Closed	N/A	139.20	140
1990 Laura	Closed	N/A	139.20	140
1989 Megan	Closed	N/A	138.00	160

Little Performers - M. Sirko

YEAR ISSUE	EDITION LIMIT	YEAR RETD.	ISSUE PRICE	*QUOTE U.S.$
1996 Tickled Pink	100-day		100.00	100

Maud Humphrey's Little Victorians - M. Humphrey

YEAR ISSUE	EDITION LIMIT	YEAR RETD.	ISSUE PRICE	*QUOTE U.S.$
1996 Papa's Little Sailor	100-day		130.00	130

Messengers of the Great Spirit - Various

YEAR ISSUE	EDITION LIMIT	YEAR RETD.	ISSUE PRICE	*QUOTE U.S.$
1994 Noatak - L. Mason	100-day		150.00	150
1994 Prayer for the Buffalo - C. Theroux	100-day		120.00	120

Miss Ashley - P. Thompson

YEAR ISSUE	EDITION LIMIT	YEAR RETD.	ISSUE PRICE	*QUOTE U.S.$
1989 Miss Ashley	Closed	N/A	228.00	228

Naturally Curious Kids - A. Hollis

YEAR ISSUE	EDITION LIMIT	YEAR RETD.	ISSUE PRICE	*QUOTE U.S.$
1996 Jennifer	100-day		100.00	100

Nursery Babies - T. DeHetre

YEAR ISSUE	EDITION LIMIT	YEAR RETD.	ISSUE PRICE	*QUOTE U.S.$
1990 Baby Bunting	Closed	N/A	118.20	150
1991 Diddle, Diddle	Closed	N/A	118.20	119
1991 Little Girl	100-day		118.20	119
1990 Patty Cake	Closed	N/A	118.20	119
1991 Rock-A-Bye Baby	100-day		118.20	119
1991 This Little Piggy	100-day		118.20	119

Nutcracker Sweethearts - S. Skille

YEAR ISSUE	EDITION LIMIT	YEAR RETD.	ISSUE PRICE	*QUOTE U.S.$
1995 Sugar Plum	100-day		130.00	13

Pictures of Innocence - J. Reavey

YEAR ISSUE	EDITION LIMIT	YEAR RETD.	ISSUE PRICE	*QUOTE U.S.$
1994 Clarissa	100-day		137.50	13

Portraits of Enchantment - A. Timmerman

YEAR ISSUE	EDITION LIMIT	YEAR RETD.	ISSUE PRICE	*QUOTE U.S.$
1996 Sleeping Beauty	100-day		150.00	15

Portraits of Perfection - A. Timmerman

YEAR ISSUE	EDITION LIMIT	YEAR RETD.	ISSUE PRICE	*QUOTE U.S.$
1993 Apple Dumpling	100-day		149.60	15
1994 Blackberry Blossom	100-day		149.60	15
1993 Peaches & Cream	100-day		149.60	15
1993 Sweet Strawberry	100-day		149.60	15

Prayers From The Heart - S. Skille

YEAR ISSUE	EDITION LIMIT	YEAR RETD.	ISSUE PRICE	*QUOTE U.S.$
1995 Hope	100-day		115.00	11

Russian Fairy Tales Dolls - B. Deval

YEAR ISSUE	EDITION LIMIT	YEAR RETD.	ISSUE PRICE	*QUOTE U.S.$
1993 Vasilisa	100-day		190.00	19

Small Wonders - B. Deval

YEAR ISSUE	EDITION LIMIT	YEAR RETD.	ISSUE PRICE	*QUOTE U.S.$
1991 Abbey	100-day		97.60	
1990 Corey	100-day		97.60	
1992 Sarah	100-day		97.60	

Songs of Innocence - J. Reavey

YEAR ISSUE	EDITION LIMIT	YEAR RETD.	ISSUE PRICE	*QUOTE U.S.$
1995 Kelsey	100-day		104.00	10
1996 Meagan	100-day		104.00	10

Sugar & Spice - L. Mason

YEAR ISSUE	EDITION LIMIT	YEAR RETD.	ISSUE PRICE	*QUOTE U.S.$
1992 Little Sunshine	100-day		141.10	14
1991 Little Sweetheart	100-day		118.25	11
1991 Red Hot Pepper	100-day		118.25	1

Sweethearts of Summer - P. Phillips

YEAR ISSUE	EDITION LIMIT	YEAR RETD.	ISSUE PRICE	*QUOTE U.S.$
1994 Caroline	100-day		140.00	1
1995 Jessica	100-day		140.00	1
1995 Madeleine & Harry	100-day		140.00	1

Tansie - P. Coffer

YEAR ISSUE	EDITION LIMIT	YEAR RETD.	ISSUE PRICE	*QUOTE U.S.$
1988 Tansie	Closed	N/A	81.00	

Victorian Fantasies - L. Mason

YEAR ISSUE	EDITION LIMIT	YEAR RETD.	ISSUE PRICE	*QUOTE U.S.$
1995 Amber Afternoon	100-day		150.00	1
1995 Lavender Dreams	100-day		150.00	1

Victorian Innocence - L. Mason

YEAR ISSUE	EDITION LIMIT	YEAR RETD.	ISSUE PRICE	*QUOTE U.S.$
1994 Annabelle	100-day		130.00	1

Victorian Splendor - J. Reavey

YEAR ISSUE	EDITION LIMIT	YEAR RETD.	ISSUE PRICE	*QUOTE U.S.$
1994 Emily	100-day		130.00	130

What a Beautiful World - R. Hockh

YEAR ISSUE	EDITION LIMIT	YEAR RETD.	ISSUE PRICE	*QUOTE U.S.$
1996 Marisa	100-day		130.00	130

Yesterday's Dreams - P. Phillips

YEAR ISSUE	EDITION LIMIT	YEAR RETD.	ISSUE PRICE	*QUOTE U.S.$
1994 Mary Elizabeth	100-day		130.00	130
1996 Sophie	100-day		130.00	130

Goebel of North America

Bob Timberlake Dolls - B. Ball

YEAR ISSUE	EDITION LIMIT	YEAR RETD.	ISSUE PRICE	*QUOTE U.S.$
1996 Abby Liz	2,000		195.00	195
1996 Ann	2,000		195.00	195
1996 Carter	2,000		195.00	195
1996 Kate	2,000		195.00	195

Cindy Guyer Romance Dolls - B. Ball

YEAR ISSUE	EDITION LIMIT	YEAR RETD.	ISSUE PRICE	*QUOTE U.S.$
1996 Cordelia	1,000		225.00	225
1996 Mackenzie	1,000		225.00	225

Dolly Dingle - B. Ball

YEAR ISSUE	EDITION LIMIT	YEAR RETD.	ISSUE PRICE	*QUOTE U.S.$
1995 Melvis Bumps	1,000		99.00	99

Goebel Dolls - B. Ball

YEAR ISSUE	EDITION LIMIT	YEAR RETD.	ISSUE PRICE	*QUOTE U.S.$
1995 Brother Murphy	2,000		125.00	125

United States Historical Society - B. Ball

YEAR ISSUE	EDITION LIMIT	YEAR RETD.	ISSUE PRICE	*QUOTE U.S.$
1995 Mary	1,500		195.00	195

Victoria Ashlea® Birthstone Dolls - K. Kennedy

YEAR ISSUE	EDITION LIMIT	YEAR RETD.	ISSUE PRICE	*QUOTE U.S.$
1995 January-Garnet-912471	2,500		29.50	30
1995 February-Amethyst-912472	2,500		29.50	30
1995 March-Aquamarine-912473	2,500		29.50	30
1995 April-Diamond-912474	2,500		29.50	30
1995 May-Emerald-912475	2,500		29.50	30
1995 June -Lt. Amethyst-912476	2,500		29.50	30
1995 July-Ruby-912477	2,500		29.50	30
1995 August-Peridot-912478	2,500		29.50	30
1995 September-Sapphire-912479	2,500		29.50	30
1995 October-Rosestone-912480	2,500		29.50	30
1995 November-Topaz-912481	2,500		29.50	30
1995 December-Zircon-912482	2,500		29.50	30

Victoria Ashlea® Originals - B. Ball, unless otherwise noted

YEAR ISSUE	EDITION LIMIT	YEAR RETD.	ISSUE PRICE	*QUOTE U.S.$
1985 Adele-901172	Closed	1989	145.00	275
1989 Alexa-912214	Closed	1991	195.00	195
1989 Alexandria-912273	Closed	1991	275.00	275
1987 Alice-901212	Closed	1991	95.00	135
1990 Alice-912296 - K. Kennedy	Closed	1992	65.00	65
1992 Alicia-912388	500	1994	135.00	135
1992 Allison-912358	Closed	1993	160.00	165
1987 Amanda Pouty-901209	Closed	1991	150.00	215
1988 Amanda-912246	Closed	1991	180.00	180
1993 Amanda-912409	2,000	1995	40.00	40
1984 Amelia-933006	Closed	1988	100.00	100
1990 Amie-912313 - K. Kennedy	Closed	1991	150.00	150
1990 Amy-901262	Closed	1993	110.00	110
1990 Angela-912324 - K. Kennedy	Closed	1994	130.00	135
1988 Angelica-912204	Closed	1991	150.00	150
1992 Angelica-912339	1,000	1995	145.00	145
1990 Annabelle-912278	Closed	1992	200.00	200
1988 Anne-912213	Closed	1991	130.00	150
1990 Annette-912333 - K. Kennedy	Closed	1993	85.00	85
1988 April-901239	Closed	1992	225.00	225
1989 Ashlea-901250	Closed	1992	550.00	550
1988 Ashley-901235	Closed	1991	110.00	110
1992 Ashley-911004	Closed	1994	99.00	105
1986 Ashley-912147	Closed	1989	125.00	125
1986 Baby Brook Beige Dress-912103	Closed	1989	60.00	60
1986 Baby Courtney-912124	Closed	1990	120.00	120
1988 Baby Daryl-912200	Closed	1991	85.00	85
1987 Baby Doll-912184	Closed	1990	75.00	75
1988 Baby Jennifer-912210	Closed	1992	75.00	75
1988 Baby Katie-912222	Closed	1993	70.00	70
1986 Baby Lauren Pink-912086	Closed	1991	120.00	120
1987 Baby Lindsay-912190	Closed	1990	80.00	80
1984 Barbara-901108	Closed	1987	57.00	110
1990 Baryshnicat-912298 - K. Kennedy	Closed	1991	25.00	25
1988 Bernice-901245	Closed	1991	90.00	90
1993 Beth-912430 - K. Kennedy	2,000		45.00	45
1992 Betsy-912390	500	1994	150.00	150
1990 Bettina-912310	Closed	1993	100.00	105
1988 Betty Doll-912220	Closed	1993	90.00	90
1987 Bonnie Pouty-901207	Closed	1992	100.00	100
1988 Brandon-901234	Closed	1992	90.00	90
1990 Brandy-912304 - K. Kennedy	Closed	1992	150.00	150
1987 Bride Allison-901218	Closed	1993	180.00	180
1988 Brittany-912207	Closed	1990	130.00	145
1992 Brittany-912365 - K. Kennedy	Closed	1993	140.00	145
1987 Caitlin-901228	Closed	1991	260.00	260
1988 Campbell Kid-Boy-758701	Closed	1988	13.80	14
1988 Campbell Kid-Girl-758700	Closed	1988	13.80	14
1989 Candace-912288 - K. Kennedy	Closed	1992	70.00	70
1992 Carol-912387 - K. Kennedy	1,000		140.00	140
1987 Caroline-912191	Closed	1990	80.00	80
1990 Carolyn-901261 - K. Kennedy	Closed	1993	200.00	200
1992 Cassandra-912355 - K. Kennedy	1,000		165.00	165
1988 Cat Maude-901247	Closed	1993	85.00	85
1986 Cat/Kitty Cheerful Gr Dr-901179	Closed	1990	60.00	60
1987 Catanova-901227	Closed	1991	75.00	75
1988 Catherine-901242	Closed	1992	240.00	240
XX Charity-912244	Closed	1990	70.00	70
1982 Charleen-912094	Closed	1986	65.00	65
1985 Chauncey-912085	Closed	1988	75.00	110
1988 Christina-901229	Closed	1991	350.00	400
1987 Christine-912168	Closed	1989	75.00	75
1992 Cindy-912384	1,000	1994	185.00	190
1985 Claire-901158	Closed	1988	115.00	160
1984 Claude-901032	Closed	1987	110.00	225
1984 Claudette-901033	Closed	1987	110.00	225
1989 Claudia-901257 - K. Kennedy	Closed	1993	225.00	225
1987 Clementine-901226	Closed	1991	75.00	75
1986 Clown Calypso-912104	Closed	1990	70.00	70
1985 Clown Casey-912078	Closed	1988	40.00	40
1986 Clown Cat Cadwalader-912132	Closed	1988	55.00	55
1987 Clown Champagne-912180	Closed	1989	95.00	95
1986 Clown Christabel-912095	Closed	1988	100.00	150
1985 Clown Christie-912084	Closed	1988	60.00	90
1986 Clown Clarabella-912096	Closed	1989	70.00	80
1986 Clown Clarissa-912123	Closed	1990	75.00	110
1988 Clown Cotton Candy-912199	Closed	1990	67.00	67
1986 Clown Cyd-912093	Closed	1988	70.00	70
1985 Clown Jody-912079	Closed	1988	100.00	150
1982 Clown Jolly-912181	Closed	1991	70.00	70
1986 Clown Kitten-Cleo-912133	Closed	1989	50.00	50
1986 Clown Lollipop-912127	Closed	1989	125.00	225
1984 Clown-901136	Closed	1988	90.00	120
1988 Crystal-912226	Closed	1992	75.00	75
1983 Deborah-901107	Closed	1987	220.00	400
1990 Debra-912319 - K. Kennedy	Closed	1992	120.00	120
1992 Denise-912362 - K. Kennedy	1,000	1994	145.00	175-225
1989 Diana Bride-912277	Closed	1992	180.00	180
1984 Diana-901119	Closed	1987	55.00	135
1988 Diana-912218	Closed	1992	270.00	270
1987 Dominique-901219	Closed	1991	170.00	225
1987 Doreen-912198	Closed	1990	75.00	75
1985 Dorothy-901157	Closed	1988	130.00	275
1992 Dottie-912393 - K. Kennedy	1,000		160.00	160
1988 Elizabeth-901214	Closed	1991	90.00	90
1988 Ellen-901246	Closed	1991	100.00	100
1990 Emily-912303	Closed	1992	150.00	150
1988 Erin-901241	Closed	1991	170.00	170
1990 Fluffer-912293	Closed	1994	135.00	150-225
1985 Garnet-901183	Closed	1988	160.00	295
1990 Gigi-912306 - K. Kennedy	Closed	1994	150.00	150
1986 Gina-901176	Closed	1989	300.00	300
1989 Ginny-912287 - K. Kennedy	Closed	1993	140.00	140
1986 Girl Frog Freda-912105	Closed	1989	20.00	20
1988 Goldilocks-912234 - K. Kennedy	Closed	1992	65.00	65
1986 Googley German Astrid-912109	Closed	1989	60.00	60
1988 Heather-912247	Closed	1990	135.00	150
1990 Heather-912322	Closed	1992	150.00	150
1990 Heidi-901266	2,000	1995	150.00	150
1990 Helene-901249 - K. Kennedy	Closed	1991	160.00	160
1990 Helga-912337	Closed	1994	325.00	325
1984 Henri-901035	Closed	1986	100.00	200
1984 Henrietta-901036	Closed	1986	100.00	200
1992 Hilary-912353	Closed	1993	130.00	135
1992 Holly Belle-912380	500	1994	125.00	125
1982 Holly-901233	Closed	1985	160.00	200
1989 Holly-901254	Closed	1992	180.00	180
1989 Hope Baby w/ Pillow-912292	Closed	1992	110.00	110
1992 Iris-912389 - K. Kennedy	500	1995	165.00	165
1987 Jacqueline-912192	Closed	1990	80.00	80
1990 Jacqueline-912329 - K. Kennedy	Closed	1993	136.00	150-225
1984 Jamie-912061	Closed	1987	65.00	100
1984 Jeannie-901062	Closed	1987	200.00	550
1988 Jennifer-901248	Closed	1991	150.00	150
1988 Jennifer-912221	Closed	1990	80.00	80
1992 Jenny-912374 - K. Kennedy	Closed	1993	150.00	150
1988 Jesse-912231	Closed	1994	110.00	115
1987 Jessica-912195	Closed	1990	120.00	135
1993 Jessica-912410	2,000	1994	40.00	40
1990 Jillian-912323	Closed	1993	150.00	150
1989 Jimmy Baby w/ Pillow-912291 - K. Kennedy	Closed	1992	165.00	165
1989 Jingles-912271	Closed	1991	60.00	60
1990 Joanne-912307 - K. Kennedy	Closed	1991	165.00	165
1987 Joy-912155	Closed	1989	50.00	50
1989 Joy-912289 - K. Kennedy	Closed	1992	110.00	110
1987 Julia-912174	Closed	1989	80.00	80
1990 Julia-912334 - K. Kennedy	Closed	1993	85.00	85
1993 Julie-912435 - K. Kennedy	2,000	1995	45.00	45
1990 Justine-901256	Closed	1992	200.00	200
1988 Karen-912205	Closed	1991	200.00	250
1993 Katie-912412	2,000		40.00	40
1993 Kaylee-912433 - K. Kennedy	2,000	1994	45.00	45
1992 Kelli-912361	1,000	1995	160.00	165
1990 Kelly-912331	Closed	1991	95.00	95
1990 Kimberly-912341	1,000		140.00	145
1987 Kittie Cat-912167	Closed	1989	55.00	55
1987 Kitty Cuddles-901201	Closed	1990	65.00	65
1992 Kris-912345 - K. Kennedy	Closed	1992	160.00	160
1989 Kristin-912285 - K. Kennedy	Closed	1994	90.00	95
1984 Laura-901106	Closed	1987	300.00	575
1988 Laura-912225	Closed	1991	135.00	135
1988 Lauren-912212	Closed	1991	110.00	110
1992 Lauren-912363 - K. Kennedy	1,000		190.00	195
1993 Lauren-912413	2,000		40.00	40
1993 Leslie-912432 - K. Kennedy	2,000	1994	45.00	45
1989 Licorice-912290	Closed	1991	75.00	75
1987 Lillian-901199	Closed	1990	85.00	100
1989 Lindsey-901263	Closed	1991	100.00	100
1989 Lisa-912275	Closed	1991	160.00	160
1989 Loni-912276	Closed	1993	125.00	150-185
1985 Lynn-912144	Closed	1988	90.00	135
1992 Margaret-912354 - K. Kennedy	1,000	1994	150.00	150
1989 Margot-912269	Closed	1991	110.00	110
1989 Maria-912265	Closed	1990	90.00	90
1982 Marie-901231	Closed	1985	95.00	95
1989 Marissa-901252 - K. Kennedy	Closed	1993	225.00	225
1988 Maritta Spanish-912224	Closed	1990	140.00	140
1992 Marjorie-912357	Closed	1993	135.00	135
1990 Marshmallow-912294 - K. Kennedy	Closed	1992	75.00	75
1985 Mary-912126	Closed	1988	60.00	90
1990 Matthew-901251	Closed	1993	100.00	100
1989 Megan-901260	Closed	1993	120.00	120
1987 Megan-912148	Closed	1989	70.00	70
1989 Melanie-912284 - K. Kennedy	Closed	1992	135.00	135
1990 Melinda-912309 - K. Kennedy	Closed	1991	70.00	70
1988 Melissa-901230	Closed	1991	110.00	110
1988 Melissa-912208	Closed	1990	125.00	125
1989 Merry-912249	Closed	1990	200.00	200
1987 Michelle-901222	Closed	1991	90.00	90
1985 Michelle-912066	Closed	1989	100.00	225
1992 Michelle-912381 - K. Kennedy	Closed	1992	175.00	175
1985 Millie-912135	Closed	1988	70.00	125
1989 Missy-912283	Closed	1993	110.00	115
1988 Molly-912211 - K. Kennedy	Closed	1992	75.00	75
1990 Monica-912336 - K. Kennedy	Closed	1993	100.00	105
1990 Monique-912335 - K. Kennedy	Closed	1993	85.00	85
1988 Morgan-912239 - K. Kennedy	Closed	1992	75.00	75
1990 Mrs. Katz-912301	Closed	1993	140.00	145
1993 Nadine-912431 - K. Kennedy	2,000	1995	45.00	45
1989 Nancy-912266	Closed	1990	110.00	110
1987 Nicole-901225	Closed	1991	575.00	575
1993 Nicole-912411	2,000		40.00	40
1987 Noel-912170	Closed	1989	125.00	125
1992 Noelle-912360 - K. Kennedy	1,000	1994	165.00	170
1990 Pamela-912302	Closed	1991	95.00	95
1986 Patty Artic Flower Print-901185	Closed	1990	140.00	140
1990 Paula-912316	Closed	1992	100.00	100
1988 Paulette-901244	Closed	1991	90.00	90
1990 Penny-912325 - K. Kennedy	Closed	1993	130.00	150-225
1986 Pepper Rust Dr/Appr-901184	Closed	1990	125.00	200
1985 Phyllis-912067	Closed	1989	60.00	60
1989 Pinky Clown-912268 - K. Kennedy	Closed	1993	70.00	75
1988 Polly-912206	Closed	1990	100.00	125
1990 Priscilla-912300	Closed	1993	185.00	190
1990 Rebecca-901258	Closed	1992	250.00	250
1988 Renae-912245	Closed	1990	120.00	120
1990 Robin-912321	Closed	1993	160.00	165
1985 Rosalind-912087	Closed	1988	145.00	225
1985 Roxanne-901174	Closed	1988	155.00	275
1984 Sabina-901155	Closed	1988	75.00	N/A
1990 Samantha-912314	Closed	1993	185.00	190
1988 Sandy-901240 - K. Kennedy	Closed	1993	115.00	115
1989 Sara-912279	Closed	1991	175.00	175
1988 Sarah w/Pillow-912219	Closed	1991	105.00	105
1987 Sarah-901220	Closed	1992	350.00	350
1993 Sarah-912408	2,000		40.00	40
1993 Shannon-912434 - K. Kennedy	2,000		45.00	45
1990 Sheena-912338	Closed	1992	115.00	115
1984 Sheila-912060	Closed	1988	75.00	135
1990 Sheri-912305 - K. Kennedy	Closed	1992	115.00	115
1992 Sherise-912383 - K. Kennedy	Closed	1992	145.00	145
1989 Sigrid-912282	Closed	1992	145.00	145
1988 Snow White-912235 - K. Kennedy	Closed	1992	65.00	65
1987 Sophia-912173	Closed	1989	40.00	40
1988 Stephanie-912238	Closed	1992	200.00	200
1990 Stephanie-912312	Closed	1993	150.00	150
1984 Stephanie-933012	Closed	1988	115.00	115
1988 Susan-901243	Closed	1991	100.00	100
1990 Susie-912328	Closed	1993	115.00	120
1987 Suzanne-901200	Closed	1990	85.00	100
1989 Suzanne-912286	Closed	1992	120.00	120
1989 Suzy-912295	Closed	1991	110.00	110
1992 Tamika-912382	500	1994	185.00	185
1989 Tammy-912264	Closed	1990	110.00	110
1987 Tasha-901221	Closed	1990	115.00	130
1990 Tasha-912299 - K. Kennedy	Closed	1992	25.00	25
1989 Terry-912281	Closed	1994	125.00	130
1987 Tiffany Pouty-901211	Closed	1991	120.00	160
1990 Tiffany-912326 - K. Kennedy	Closed	1992	180.00	180
1984 Tobie-912023	Closed	1987	30.00	30
1992 Toni-912367 - K. Kennedy	Closed	1993	120.00	120
1990 Tracie-912315	Closed	1993	125.00	125
1992 Trudie-912391	500		135.00	135
1982 Trudy-901232	Closed	1985	100.00	100
1992 Tulip-912385 - K. Kennedy	500	1994	145.00	145
1989 Valerie-901255	Closed	1994	175.00	175
1989 Vanessa-912272	Closed	1991	110.00	110
1984 Victoria-901068	Closed	1987	200.00	1500
1992 Wendy-912330 - K. Kennedy	1,000	1995	125.00	130

*Quotes have been rounded up to nearest dollar

DOLLS

YEAR ISSUE		EDITION LIMIT	YEAR RETD.	ISSUE PRICE	*QUOTE U.S.$
1988	Whitney Blk-912232	Closed	1994	62.50	65

Victoria Ashlea® Originals-Birthday Babies - K. Kennedy

1996	January	2,500		30.00	30
1996	February	2,500		30.00	30
1996	March	2,500		30.00	30
1996	April	2,500		30.00	30
1996	May	2,500		30.00	30
1996	June	2,500		30.00	30
1996	July	2,500		30.00	30
1996	August	2,500		30.00	30
1996	September	2,500		30.00	30
1996	October	2,500		30.00	30
1996	November	2,500		30.00	30
1996	December	2,500		30.00	30

Victoria Ashlea® Originals-Collectible Cats - K. Kennedy

1996	Charmer	2,000		39.50	40
1996	Copper	2,000		39.50	40
1996	Cuddles	2,000		39.50	40
1996	Fluffy	2,000		39.50	40
1996	Lollipop	2,000		39.50	40
1996	Mittens	2,000		39.50	40
1996	Patches	2,000		39.50	40
1996	Pebbles	2,000		39.50	40
1996	Pepper	2,000		39.50	40
1996	Ruffles	2,000		39.50	40
1996	Tumbles	2,000		39.50	40
1996	Whiskers	2,000		39.50	40

Victoria Ashlea® Originals-Holiday Babies - K. Kennedy

1996	Boo!	1,000		30.00	30
1996	Happy Easter	1,000		30.00	30
1996	Happy Holidays	1,000		30.00	30
1996	I Love You	1,000		30.00	30

Victoria Ashlea® Originals-Tiny Tot Clowns - K. Kennedy

1994	Danielle-912461	2,000		45.00	45
1994	Lindsey-912463	2,000		45.00	45
1994	Lisa-912458	2,000		45.00	45
1994	Marie-912462	2,000		45.00	45
1994	Megan-912460	2,000		45.00	45
1994	Stacy-912459	2,000		45.00	45

Victoria Ashlea® Originals-Tiny Tot School Girls - K. Kennedy

1994	Andrea- 912456	2,000		47.50	48
1994	Christine- 912450	2,000		47.50	48
1994	Monique- 912455	2,000		47.50	48
1994	Patricia- 912453	2,000		47.50	48
1994	Shawna- 912449	2,000		47.50	48
1994	Susan- 912457	2,000		47.50	48

Goebel/M.I. Hummel

M. I. Hummel Collectible Dolls - M. I. Hummel

1964	Chimney Sweep 1908	Closed	N/A	55.00	110
1964	For Father 1917	Closed	N/A	55.00	90
1964	Goose Girl 1914	Closed	N/A	55.00	80
1964	Gretel 1901	Closed	N/A	55.00	125
1964	Hansel 1902	Closed	N/A	55.00	110
1964	Little Knitter 1905	Closed	N/A	55.00	75
1964	Lost Stocking 1926	Closed	N/A	55.00	75
1964	Merry Wanderer 1906	Closed	N/A	55.00	90
1964	Merry Wanderer 1925	Closed	N/A	55.00	110
1964	On Secret Path 1928	Closed	N/A	55.00	80
1964	Rosa-Blue Baby 1904/B	Closed	N/A	45.00	85
1964	Rosa-Pink Baby 1904/P	Closed	N/A	45.00	75
1964	School Boy 1910	Closed	N/A	55.00	80
1964	School Girl 1909	Closed	N/A	55.00	75
1964	Visiting and Invalid 1927	Closed	N/A	55.00	75

M. I. Hummel Porcelain Dolls - M. I. Hummel

1984	Birthday Serenade/Boy	Closed	N/A	225.00	250-300
1984	Birthday Serenade/Girl	Closed	N/A	225.00	250-300
1985	Carnival	Closed	N/A	225.00	250-300
1985	Easter Greetings	Closed	N/A	225.00	250-300
1985	Lost Sheep	Closed	N/A	225.00	250-300
1984	On Holiday	Closed	N/A	225.00	250-300
1984	Postman	Closed	N/A	225.00	250-300
1985	Signs of Spring	Closed	N/A	225.00	250-300

Good-Krüger

Limited Edition - J. Good-Krüger

1990	Alice	Retrd.	1991	250.00	250
1992	Anne with an E	Retrd.	1992	240.00	500
1990	Annie-Rose	Retrd.	1990	219.00	425
1994	Christmas Carols	1,000	1995	240.00	240
1990	Christmas Cookie	Retrd.	1993	199.00	225
1995	Circus Trainer	500	1995	250.00	250
1990	Cozy	Retrd.	1992	179.00	275-375
1990	Daydream	Retrd.	1990	199.00	350
1994	Heidi	1,000	1994	250.00	250
1992	Jeepers Creepers (Porcelain)	Retrd.	1992	725.00	800
1991	Johnny-Lynn	Retrd.	1991	240.00	500
1995	Letter to Santa	1,000	1995	250.00	250
1995	Little Princess	1,500	1995	250.00	250
1991	Moppett	Retrd.	1991	179.00	275
1994	Mother's Love	1,000	1994	275.00	275
1994	Stuffed Animal Zoo	1,000	1994	189.00	189
1990	Sue-Lynn	Retrd.	1990	240.00	300
1991	Teachers Pet	Retrd.	1991	199.00	250
1995	Tiny Newborns	500	1995	225.00	225
1991	Victorian Christmas	Retrd.	1992	219.00	275

Gorham

Beverly Port Designer Collection - B. Port

1988	The Amazing Calliope Merriweather 17"	Closed	1990	275.00	1000-1500
1988	Baery Mab 9-1/2"	Closed	1990	110.00	300
1987	Christopher Paul Bearkin 10"	Closed	1990	95.00	450
1988	Hollybeary Kringle 15"	Closed	1990	350.00	500
1987	Kristobear Kringle 17"	Closed	1990	200.00	500
1988	Miss Emily 18"	Closed	1990	350.00	1500
1987	Molly Melinda Bearkin 10"	Closed	1990	95.00	300
1987	Silver Bell 17"	Closed	1990	175.00	350
1988	T.R. 28-1/2"	Closed	1990	400.00	600
1987	Tedward Jonathan Bearkin 10"	Closed	1990	95.00	350
1987	Tedwina Kimelina Bearkin 10"	Closed	1990	95.00	350
1988	Theodore B. Bear 14"	Closed	1990	175.00	550

Bonnet Babies - M. Sirko

1993	Chelsea's Bonnet	Closed	1994	95.00	95

Bonnets & Bows - B. Gerardi

1988	Belinda	Closed	1990	195.00	450
1988	Annemarie	Closed	1990	195.00	450
1988	Allessandra	Closed	1990	195.00	350
1988	Lisette	Closed	1990	285.00	495
1988	Bettina	Closed	1994	285.00	495
1988	Ellie	Closed	1994	285.00	495
1988	Alicia	Closed	1994	385.00	700
1988	Bethany	Closed	1994	385.00	1350
1988	Jesse	Closed	1994	525.00	675
1988	Francie	Closed	1994	625.00	800

Bride Dolls - D. Valenza

1993	Susannah's Wedding Day	9,500	1994	295.00	295

Carousel Dolls - C. Shafer

1993	Ribbons And Roses	Closed	1994	119.00	119

Celebrations Of Childhood - L. Di Leo

1992	Happy Birthday Amy	Closed	1994	160.00	225

Childhood Memories - D. Valenza

1991	Amanda	Closed	1994	98.00	98
1991	Jennifer	Closed	1994	98.00	98
1991	Jessica Anne's Playtime	Closed	1994	98.00	98
1991	Kimberly	Closed	1994	98.00	98

Children Of Christmas - S. Stone Aiken

1989	Clara, 16"	Closed	1994	325.00	650
1990	Natalie, 16"	1,500	1994	350.00	500
1991	Emily	1,500	1994	375.00	400
1992	Virginia	1,500	1994	375.00	400

Christmas Traditions - S. Stone Aiken

1993	Trimming the Tree	2,500	1994	295.00	295
1993	Chrissy	Closed	1994	150.00	150

Daydreamer Dolls - S. Stone Aiken

1992	Heather's Daydream	Closed	1994	119.00	119

Days Of The Week - R./L. Schrubbe

1992	Monday's Child	Closed	1994	98.00	98
1992	Tuesday's Child	Closed	1994	98.00	98
1992	Wednesday's Child	Closed	1994	98.00	98
1992	Thurday's Child	Closed	1994	98.00	98
1992	Friday's Child	Closed	1994	98.00	98
1992	Saturday's Child	Closed	1994	98.00	98
1992	Sunday's Child	Closed	1994	98.00	98

Dollie And Me - J. Pilallis

1991	Dollie's First Steps	Closed	1994	160.00	225

Dolls of the Month - Gorham

1991	Miss January	Closed	1994	79.00	79
1991	Miss February	Closed	1994	79.00	79
1991	Miss March	Closed	1994	79.00	79
1991	Miss April	Closed	1994	79.00	79
1991	Miss May	Closed	1994	79.00	79
1991	Miss June	Closed	1994	79.00	79
1991	Miss July	Closed	1994	79.00	79
1991	Miss August	Closed	1994	79.00	79
1991	Miss September	Closed	1994	79.00	79
1991	Miss October	Closed	1994	79.00	79
1991	Miss November	Closed	1994	79.00	79
1991	Miss December	Closed	1994	79.00	79

The Friendship Dolls - Various

1991	Angela-The Italian Traveler - S. Nappo	Closed	1994	98.00	98
1991	Kinuko-The Japanese Traveler - S. Ueki	Closed	1994	98.00	98
1991	Meagan-The Irish Traveler - L. O'Connor	Closed	1994	98.00	98
1991	Peggy-The American Traveler - P. Seaman	Closed	1994	98.00	98

Gift of Dreams - Young/Gerardi

1991	Christina (Christmas)	Closed	1994	695.00	695
1991	Elizabeth	Closed	1994	495.00	495
1991	Katherine	Closed	1994	495.00	495
1991	Melissa	Closed	1994	495.00	495
1991	Samantha	Closed	1994	495.00	495

Gifts of the Garden - S. Stone Aiken

1991	Alisa	Closed	1994	125.00	250
1991	Deborah	Closed	1994	125.00	250
1991	Holly (Christmas)	Closed	1994	150.00	250
1991	Irene	Closed	1994	125.00	250
1991	Joelle (Christmas)	Closed	1994	150.00	250
1991	Lauren	Closed	1994	125.00	250
1991	Maria	Closed	1994	125.00	250
1991	Priscilla	Closed	1994	125.00	250
1991	Valerie	Closed	1994	125.00	250

Gorham Baby Doll Collection - Aiken/Matthews

1987	Christening Day	Closed	1990	245.00	350
1987	Leslie	Closed	1990	245.00	350
1987	Matthew	Closed	1990	245.00	350

Gorham Dolls - S. Stone Aiken, unless otherwise noted

1985	Alexander, 19"	Closed	1990	275.00	400
1981	Alexandria, 18"	Closed	1990	250.00	500
1986	Alissa	Closed	1990	245.00	300
1985	Amelia, 19"	Closed	1990	275.00	325
1982	Baby in Apricot Dress, 16"	Closed	1990	175.00	375
1982	Baby in Blue Dress, 12"	Closed	1990	150.00	300
1982	Baby in Wh. Dress, 18" - Gorham	Closed	1990	250.00	350
1982	Benjamin, 18"	Closed	1990	200.00	600
1981	Cecile, 16"	Closed	1990	200.00	800
1981	Christina, 16"	Closed	1990	200.00	425
1981	Christopher, 19"	Closed	1990	250.00	500
1982	Corrine, 21"	Closed	1990	250.00	500
1981	Danielle, 14"	Closed	1990	150.00	300
1981	Elena, 14"	Closed	1990	150.00	650
1982	Ellice, 18"	Closed	1990	200.00	400
1986	Emily, 14"	Closed	1990	175.00	395
1986	Fleur, 19"	Closed	1990	300.00	450
1985	Gabrielle, 19"	Closed	1990	225.00	350
1983	Jennifer, 19" Bridal Doll	Closed	1990	325.00	750
1982	Jeremy, 23"	Closed	1990	300.00	700
1986	Jessica	Closed	1990	195.00	275
1981	Jillian, 16"	Closed	1990	200.00	400
1986	Julia, 16"	Closed	1990	225.00	350
1987	Juliet	Closed	1990	325.00	400
1982	Kristin, 23"	Closed	1990	300.00	575
1986	Lauren, 14"	Closed	1990	175.00	350
1985	Linda, 19"	Closed	1990	275.00	600
1982	M. Anton, 12" - Unknown	Closed	1990	125.00	175
1982	Melanie, 23"	Closed	1990	300.00	600
1981	Melinda, 14"	Closed	1990	150.00	300
1986	Meredith	Closed	1990	295.00	350
1982	Mlle. Jeanette, 12"	Closed	1990	125.00	175
1982	Mlle. Lucille, 12"	Closed	1990	125.00	375
1982	Mlle. Marsella, 12" - Unknown	Closed	1990	125.00	275
1982	Mlle. Monique, 12"	Closed	1990	125.00	275
1982	Mlle. Yvonne, 12" - Unknown	Closed	1990	125.00	375
1985	Nanette, 19"	Closed	1990	275.00	325
1985	Odette, 19"	Closed	1990	250.00	450
1981	Rosemond, 18"	Closed	1990	250.00	750
1981	Stephanie, 18"	Closed	1990	250.00	2000

Gorham Holly Hobbie Childhood Memories - Holly Hobbie

1985	Mother's Helper	Closed	1990	45.00	175
1985	Best Friends	Closed	1994	45.00	175
1985	First Day of School	Closed	1994	45.00	175
1985	Christmas Wishes	Closed	1994	45.00	175

Gorham Holly Hobbie For All Seasons - Holly Hobbie

1984	Summer Holly 12"	Closed	1994	42.50	195
1984	Fall Holly 12"	Closed	1994	42.50	195
1984	Winter Holly 12"	Closed	1994	42.50	195
1984	Spring Holly 12"	Closed	1994	42.50	195
1984	Set of 4	Closed	1994	170.00	750

Holly Hobbie - Holly Hobbie

1983	Blue Girl, 14"	Closed	1994	80.00	245
1983	Blue Girl, 18"	Closed	1994	115.00	295
1983	Christmas Morning, 14"	Closed	1994	80.00	245
1983	Heather, 14"	Closed	1994	80.00	275
1983	Little Amy, 14"	Closed	1994	80.00	245
1983	Robbie, 14"	Closed	1994	80.00	275
1983	Sunday Best, 18"	Closed	1994	115.00	295
1983	Sweet Valentine, 16"	Closed	1994	100.00	295
1983	Yesterday's Memories, 18"	Closed	1994	125.00	375

Imaginary People - R. Tonner

1993	Melinda, The Tooth Fairy	2,900	1994	95.00	95

International Babies - R. Tonner

1993	Natalia's Matrioshka	Closed	1994	95.00	9[illegible]

Joyful Years - B. Gerardi

1989	Katrina	Closed	1994	295.00	37[illegible]
1989	William	Closed	1994	295.00	37[illegible]

Kezi Doll For All Seasons - Kezi

1985	Ariel 16"	Closed	1994	135.00	50[illegible]

*Quotes have been rounded up to nearest dollar

YEAR ISSUE	EDITION LIMIT	YEAR RETD.	ISSUE PRICE	*QUOTE U.S.$
1985 Aubrey 16"	Closed	1994	135.00	500
1985 Amber 16"	Closed	1994	135.00	500
1985 Adrienne 16"	Closed	1994	135.00	500
1985 Set of 4	Closed	1994	540.00	1900

Kezi Golden Gifts - Kezi

1984 Charity 16"	Closed	1990	85.00	175
1984 Faith 18"	Closed	1990	95.00	195
1984 Felicity 18"	Closed	1990	95.00	195
1984 Grace 16"	Closed	1990	85.00	175
1984 Hope 16"	Closed	1990	85.00	175
1984 Merrie 16"	Closed	1990	85.00	175
1984 Patience 18"	Closed	1990	95.00	195
1984 Prudence 18"	Closed	1990	85.00	195

Legendary Heroines - S. Stone Aiken

1991 Guinevere	1,500	1994	245.00	245
1991 Jane Eyre	1,500	1994	245.00	245
1991 Juliet	1,500	1994	245.00	245
1991 Lara	1,500	1994	245.00	245

Les Belles Bebes Collection - S. Stone Aiken

1993 Camille	1,500	1994	375.00	395
1991 Cherie	1,500	1994	375.00	475
1991 Desiree	1,500	1994	375.00	395

Limited Edition Dolls - S. Stone Aiken

1982 Allison, 19"	Closed	1990	300.00	4500
1983 Ashley, 19"	Closed	1990	350.00	1000
1984 Nicole, 19"	Closed	1990	350.00	875
1984 Holly (Christmas), 19"	Closed	1990	300.00	850
1985 Lydia,19"	Closed	1990	550.00	1800
1985 Joy (Christmas), 19"	Closed	1990	350.00	695
1986 Noel (Christmas), 19"	Closed	1990	400.00	750
1987 Jacqueline, 19"	Closed	1994	500.00	700
1987 Merrie (Christmas), 19"	Closed	1994	500.00	750
1988 Andrew, 19"	Closed	1994	475.00	750
1988 Christa (Christmas), 19"	Closed	1994	550.00	1500
1990 Amey (10th Anniversary Edition)	Closed	1994	650.00	1100

Limited Edition Sister Set - S. Stone Aiken

1988 Kathleen	Closed	1994	550.00	750
1988 Katelin	Set	1994	Set	Set

Little Women - S. Stone Aiken

1983 Amy, 16"	Closed	1994	225.00	500
1983 Beth, 16"	Closed	1994	225.00	500
1983 Jo, 19"	Closed	1994	275.00	575
1983 Meg, 19"	Closed	1994	275.00	650

Littlest Angel Dolls - L. Di Leo

1992 Merriel	Closed	1994	49.50	50

Nature's Bounty - R. Tonner

1993 Jamie's Fruitful Harvest	Closed	1994	95.00	95

Pillow Baby Dolls - L. Gordon

1993 On the Move	Closed	1994	39.00	39
1993 Sitting Pretty	Closed	1994	39.00	39
1993 Tickling Toes	Closed	1994	39.00	39

Portrait Perfect Victorian Dolls - R. Tonner

1993 Pretty in Peach	2,900	1994	119.00	119

Precious as Pearls - S. Stone Aiken

1986 Colette	Closed	1994	400.00	1500
1987 Charlotte	Closed	1994	425.00	750
1988 Chloe	Closed	1994	525.00	850
1989 Cassandra	Closed	1994	525.00	1250
XX Set	Closed	1994	1875.00	4000

Puppy Love Dolls - R./ L. Schrubbe

1992 Katie And Kyle	Closed	1994	119.00	119

Small Wonders - B. Gerardi

1988 Madeline	Closed	1990	365.00	365
1988 Marguerite	Closed	1990	425.00	425
1988 Patina	Closed	1990	265.00	265

Southern Belles - S. Stone Aiken

1985 Amanda, 19"	Closed	1990	300.00	1400
1986 Veronica, 19"	Closed	1990	325.00	750
1987 Rachel, 19"	Closed	1990	375.00	800
1988 Cassie, 19"	Closed	1990	500.00	875

Special Moments - E. Worrell

1991 Baby's First Christmas	Closed	1994	135.00	235
1992 Baby's First Steps	Closed	1994	135.00	135

Sporting Kids - R. Schrubbe

1993 Up At Bat	Closed	1994	49.50	80

Tender Hearts - M. Murphy

1993 Saying Grace	Closed	1994	119.00	119

Times To Treasure - L. Di Leo

1991 Bedtime	Closed	1994	195.00	250
1993 Playtime	Closed	1994	195.00	250
1990 Storytime	Closed	1994	195.00	250

Valentine Ladies - P. Valentine

YEAR ISSUE	EDITION LIMIT	YEAR RETD.	ISSUE PRICE	*QUOTE U.S.$
1987 Anabella	Closed	1994	145.00	395
1987 Elizabeth	Closed	1994	145.00	450
1988 Felicia	Closed	1994	225.00	325
1987 Jane	Closed	1994	145.00	350
1988 Judith Anne	Closed	1994	195.00	325
1989 Julianna	Closed	1994	225.00	275
1987 Lee Ann	Closed	1994	145.00	325
1988 Maria Theresa	Closed	1994	225.00	350
1987 Marianna	Closed	1994	160.00	400
1987 Patrice	Closed	1994	145.00	325
1988 Priscilla	Closed	1994	195.00	325
1987 Rebecca	Closed	1994	145.00	325
1987 Rosanne	Closed	1994	145.00	325
1989 Rose	Closed	1994	225.00	275
1987 Sylvia	Closed	1994	160.00	350

Victorian Cameo Collection - B. Gerardi

1990 Victoria	1,500	1994	375.00	425
1991 Alexandra	1,500	1994	375.00	425

Victorian Children - S. Stone Aiken

1992 Sara's Tea Time	1,000	1994	495.00	750
1993 Catching Butterflies	1,000	1994	495.00	495

The Victorian Collection - E. Woodhouse

1992 Victoria's Jubilee	Yr.Iss.	1994	295.00	350

Victorian Flower Girls - J. Pillalis

1993 Rose	Closed	1994	95.00	95

H & G Studios

Brenda Burke Dolls - B. Burke

1989 Adelaine	25		1795.00	3600
1989 Alexandra	125		995.00	2000
1989 Alicia	125		895.00	1800
1989 Amanda	25		1995.00	6000
1989 Angelica	50		1495.00	3000
1989 Arabelle	500		695.00	1400
1989 Beatrice	85		2395.00	2395
1990 Belinda	12		3695.00	3695
1989 Bethany	45		2995.00	2995
1989 Brittany	75		2695.00	2695
1991 Charlotte	20		2395.00	2395
1991 Clarissa	15		3595.00	3595
1992 Dorothea	500		395.00	395
1993 Giovanna	1		7800.00	7800
1993 Melissa	1		7750.00	7750
1991 Sleigh Ride	20		3695.00	3695
1991 Tender Love	25		3295.00	3295

Hallmark

Special Edition Hallmark Barbie Dolls

1994 Victorian Elegance Barbie	Yr.Iss.	1994	40.00	110-150
1995 Holiday Memories Barbie	Yr.Iss.	1995	45.00	45

Hamilton Collection

Abbie Williams Doll Collection - A. Williams

1992 Molly	Closed	N/A	155.00	200

Annual Connossieur Doll - N/A

1992 Lara	7,450		295.00	295

The Antique Doll Collection - Unknown

1989 Nicole	Closed	N/A	195.00	300
1990 Colette	Open		195.00	195
1991 Lisette	Open		195.00	225
1991 Katrina	Open		195.00	195

Baby Portrait Dolls - B. Parker

1991 Melissa	Closed	1993	135.00	175-200
1992 Jenna	Closed	N/A	135.00	200-250
1992 Bethany	Open		135.00	135
1993 Mindy	Open		135.00	135

Belles of the Countryside - C. Heath Orange

1992 Erin	Open		135.00	135
1992 Rose	Open		135.00	135
1993 Lorna	Open		135.00	135
1994 Gwyn	Open		135.00	135

The Bessie Pease Gutmann Doll Collection - B.P. Gutmann

1989 Love is Blind	Closed	N/A	135.00	220
1989 He Won't Bite	Closed	N/A	135.00	135
1991 Virginia	Open		135.00	135
1991 First Dancing Lesson	Open		195.00	195
1991 Good Morning	Open		195.00	195
1991 Love At First Sight	Open		195.00	195

Best Buddies - C.M. Rolfe

1994 Jodie	Open		69.00	69
1994 Brandy	Open		69.00	69
1995 Joey	Open		69.00	69

Boehm Christening - Boehm Studio

YEAR ISSUE	EDITION LIMIT	YEAR RETD.	ISSUE PRICE	*QUOTE U.S.$
1994 Elena's First Portrait	Open		155.00	155

Boehm Dolls - N/A

1994 Elena	Open		155.00	155

Bridal Elegance - Boehm

1994 Camille	Open		195.00	195

Bride Dolls - Unknown

1991 Portrait of Innocence	Open		195.00	195
1992 Portrait of Loveliness	Open		195.00	195

Brooks Wooden Dolls - P. Ryan Brooks

1993 Waiting For Santa	15,000	1994	135.00	200-250
1993 Are You the Easter Bunny?	15,000		135.00	135
1994 Be My Valentine	Open		135.00	135
1995 Shhl I Only Wanna Peek	Open		135.00	135

Catherine Mather Dolls - C. Mather

1993 Justine	15,000		155.00	155

Central Park Skaters - Unknown

1991 Central Park Skaters	Open		245.00	245

A Child's Menagerie - B. Van Boxel

1993 Becky	Open		69.00	69
1993 Carrie	Open		69.00	69
1994 Mandy	Open		69.00	69
1994 Terry	Open		69.00	69

Children To Cherish - N/A

1991 A Gift of Innocence	Yr.Iss.		135.00	135
1991 A Gift of Beauty	Open		135.00	135

Cindy Marschner Rolfe Dolls - C. M. Rolfe

1993 Shannon	Open		95.00	95
1993 Julie	Open		95.00	95
1993 Kayla	Open		95.00	95
1994 Janey	Open		95.00	95

Cindy Marschner Rolfe Twins - C. M. Rolfe

1995 Shelby & Sydney	Open		190.00	190

Connie Walser Derek Baby Dolls - C.W. Derek

1990 Jessica	Closed	1993	155.00	300-500
1991 Sara	Closed	N/A	155.00	180
1991 Andrew	Open		155.00	155
1991 Amanda	Open		155.00	155
1992 Samantha	Open		155.00	155

Connie Walser Derek Baby Dolls II - C. W. Derek

1992 Stephanie	Open		95.00	95
1992 Beth	Open		95.00	95

Connie Walser Derek Baby Dolls III - C. W. Derek

1994 Chelsea	Open		79.00	79
1995 Tina	Open		79.00	79
1995 Tabitha	Open		79.00	79
1995 Ginger	Open		79.00	79

Connie Walser Derek Dolls - C. W. Derek

1992 Baby Jessica	Open		75.00	75
1993 Baby Sara	Open		75.00	75

Connie Walser Derek Toddlers - C. W. Derek

1994 Jessie	Open		79.00	79
1994 Casey	Open		79.00	79

Daddy's Little Girls - M. Snyder

1992 Lindsay	Open		95.00	95
1993 Cassie	Open		95.00	95
1993 Dana	Open		95.00	95
1994 Tara	Open		95.00	95

Dolls by Autumn Berwick - A. Berwick

1993 Laura	Open		135.00	135

Dolls By Kay McKee - K. McKee

1992 Shy Violet	Closed	1993	135.00	250-300
1992 Robin	Open		135.00	135
1993 Katie Did It!	Open		135.00	135
1993 Ryan	Open		135.00	135

Dolls of America's Colonial Heritage - A. Elekfy

1986 Katrina	Open		55.00	55
1986 Nicole	Open		55.00	55
1987 Maria	Open		55.00	55
1987 Priscilla	Open		55.00	55
1987 Colleen	Open		55.00	55
1988 Gretchen	Open		55.00	55

Elaine Campbell Dolls - E. Campbell

1994 Emma	Open		95.00	95
1995 Abby	Open		95.00	95
1995 Jana	Open		95.00	95
1995 Molly	Open		95.00	95

DOLLS

YEAR ISSUE		EDITION LIMIT	YEAR RETD.	ISSUE PRICE	*QUOTE U.S.$
First Recital - N/A					
1993	Hillary	Open		135.00	135
1994	Olivia	Open		135.00	135
Grobben Ethnic Babies - J. Grobben					
1994	Jasmine	Open		135.00	135
1995	Taiya	Open		135.00	135
Grothedde Dolls - N. Grothedde					
1993	Cindy	Open		69.00	69
Hargrave Dolls - M. Hargrave					
1994	Angela	Open		79.00	79
Heath Babies - C. Heath Orange					
1995	Hayley	Open		95.00	95
1996	Ellie	Open		95.00	95
Helen Carr Dolls - H. Carr					
1994	Claudia	Open		135.00	135
Helen Kish II Dolls - H. Kish					
1992	Vanessa	Open		135.00	135
1994	Jordan	Open		95.00	95
Holiday Carollers - U. Lepp					
1992	Joy	Open		155.00	155
1993	Noel	Open		155.00	155
Huckleberry Hill Kids - B. Parker					
1994	Gabrielle	Open		95.00	95
1994	Alexandra	Open		95.00	95
I Love Lucy (Porcelain) - Unknown					
1990	Lucy	Closed	N/A	95.00	240-300
1991	Ricky	Closed	N/A	95.00	350
1992	Queen of the Gypsies	Closed	N/A	95.00	245
1992	Vitameatavegamin	Closed	N/A	95.00	200-300
I Love Lucy (Vinyl) - Unknown					
1988	Ethel	Closed	N/A	40.00	100
1988	Fred	Closed	N/A	40.00	100
1990	Lucy	Closed	N/A	40.00	100
1991	Ricky	Closed	N/A	40.00	150
1992	Queen of the Gypsies	Open		40.00	40
1992	Vitameatavegamin	Open		40.00	40
I'm So Proud Doll Collection - L. Cobabe					
1992	Christina	Open		95.00	95
1993	Jill	Open		95.00	95
1994	Tammy	Open		95.00	95
1994	Shelly	Open		95.00	95
Inga Manders - I. Manders					
1995	Miss Priss	Open		79.00	79
1995	Miss Hollywood	Open		79.00	79
1995	Miss Glamour	Open		79.00	79
International Children - C. Woodie					
1991	Miko	Closed	N/A	49.50	80
1991	Anastasia	Open		49.50	50
1991	Angelina	Open		49.50	50
1992	Lian	Open		49.50	50
1992	Monique	Open		49.50	50
1992	Lisa	Open		49.50	50
Jane Zidjunas Party Dolls - J. Zidjunas					
1991	Kelly	Open		135.00	135
1992	Katie	Open		135.00	135
1993	Meredith	Open		135.00	135
Jane Zidjunas Toddler Dolls - J. Zidjunas					
1991	Jennifer	Open		135.00	135
1991	Megan	Open		135.00	160
1992	Kimberly	Open		135.00	135
1992	Amy	Open		135.00	135
Jane Zidjunas Victorian - J. Zidjunas					
1996	Constance	9,500		195.00	195
Jeanne Wilson Dolls - J. Wilson					
1994	Priscilla	Open		155.00	155
Johnston Cowgirls - C. Johnston					
1994	Savannah	Open		79.00	79
1994	Skyler	Open		79.00	79
Join The Parade - N/A					
1992	Betsy	Open		49.50	50
1994	Peggy	Open		55.00	55
1994	Sandy	Open		55.00	55
Joke Grobben Dolls - J. Grobben					
1992	Heather	Open		69.00	69
1993	Kathleen	Open		69.00	69
1993	Brianna	Open		69.00	69
1994	Bridget	Open		69.00	69
Joke Grobben Tall Dolls - J. Grobben					
1995	Jade	Open		135.00	135

YEAR ISSUE		EDITION LIMIT	YEAR RETD.	ISSUE PRICE	*QUOTE U.S.$
Just Like Mom - H. Kish					
1991	Ashley	Closed	1993	135.00	250-300
1992	Elizabeth	Open		135.00	135
1992	Hannah	Open		135.00	135
1993	Margaret	Open		135.00	135
Kay McKee Klowns - K. McKee					
1993	The Dreamer	15,000		155.00	155
1994	The Entertainer	15,000		155.00	155
Kuck Fairy - S. Kuck					
1994	Tooth Fairy	Open		135.00	135
Laura Cobabe Dolls - L. Cobabe					
1992	Amber	Open		195.00	195
1992	Brooke	Open		195.00	195
Laura Cobabe Dolls II - L. Cobabe					
1993	Kristen	Open		75.00	75
Laura Cobabe Ethnic - L. Cobabe					
1995	Nica	Open		95.00	95
1996	Kenu	Open		95.00	95
Laura Cobabe Indians - L. Cobabe					
1994	Snowbird	Open		135.00	135
Laura Cobabe Tall Dolls - L. Cobabe					
1994	Cassandra	Open		195.00	195
1994	Taylor	Open		195.00	195
Laura Cobabe's Costume Kids - L. Cobabe					
1994	Lil' Punkin	Open		79.00	79
1994	Little Ladybug	Open		79.00	79
1995	Miss Dinomite	Open		79.00	79
Little Gardners - J. Galperin					
1996	Daisy	Open		95.00	95
Little Rascals™ - S./J. Hoffman					
1992	Spanky	Open		75.00	75
1993	Alfalfa	Open		75.00	75
1994	Darla	Open		75.00	75
1994	Buckwheat	Open		75.00	75
1994	Stymie	Open		75.00	75
Littlest Members of the Wedding - J. Esteban					
1993	Matthew & Melanie	Open		195.00	195
Maud Humphrey Bogart Dolls - Unknown					
1992	Playing Bridesmaid	Closed	N/A	195.00	225
Maud Humphrey Bogart Doll Collection - M.H. Bogart					
1989	Playing Bride	Closed	N/A	135.00	225
1990	First Party	Closed	N/A	135.00	150
1990	The First Lesson	Closed	N/A	135.00	149
1991	Seamstress	Closed	N/A	135.00	149
1991	Little Captive	Open		135.00	135
1992	Kitty's Bath	Open		135.00	135
Mavis Snyder Dolls - M. Snyder					
1994	Tara	Open		95.00	95
Parker-Levi Toddlers - B. Parker					
1992	Courtney	Open		135.00	135
1992	Melody	Open		135.00	135
Parkins Connisseur - S. Kuck					
1993	Faith	Open		135.00	135
Parkins Portraits - P. Parkins					
1993	Lauren	Open		79.00	79
1993	Kelsey	Open		79.00	79
1994	Morgan	Open		79.00	79
1994	Cassidy	Open		79.00	79
Parkins Treasures - P. Parkins					
1992	Tiffany	Closed	1994	55.00	95-120
1992	Dorothy	Closed	N/A	55.00	55
1993	Charlotte	Open		55.00	55
1993	Cynthia	Open		55.00	55
Phyllis Parkins Dolls - P. Parkins					
1992	Swan Princess	9,850		195.00	220-250
Picnic In The Park - J. Esteban					
1991	Rebecca	Open		155.00	155
1992	Emily	Open		155.00	155
1992	Victoria	Open		155.00	155
1993	Benjamin	Open		155.00	155
Precious Moments - S. Butcher					
1994	Tell Me the Story of Jesus	Open		79.00	79
Proud Indian Nation - N/A					
1992	Navajo Little One	Closed	1993	95.00	200
1993	Dressed Up For The Pow Wow	Open		95.00	95
1993	Autumn Treat	Open		95.00	95
1994	Out with Mama's Flock	Open		95.00	95

YEAR ISSUE		EDITION LIMIT	YEAR RETD.	ISSUE PRICE	*QUOTE U.S.$
Rachel Cold Toddlers - R. Cold					
1995	Jenny	Open		95.00	95
The Royal Beauty Dolls - Unknown					
1991	Chen Mai	Open		195.00	195
Russian Czarra Dolls - Unknown					
1991	Alexandra	Closed	N/A	295.00	350
Sandra Kuck Dolls - S. Kuck					
1993	A Kiss Goodnight	Open		79.00	79
1994	Teaching Teddy	Open		79.00	79
Santa's Little Helpers - C.W. Derek					
1992	Nicholas	Open		155.00	155
1993	Hope	Open		155.00	155
Schmidt Dolls - J. Schmidt					
1994	Kaitlyn	Open		79.00	79
Schrubbe Santa Dolls - R. Schrubbe					
1994	Jolly Old St. Nick	Open		135.00	135
Simon Indians - S. Simon					
1994	Meadowlark	Open		95.00	95
Songs of the Seasons Hakata Doll Collection - T. Murakami					
1985	Winter Song Maiden	9,800		75.00	75
1985	Spring Song Maiden	9,800		75.00	75
1985	Summer Song Maiden	9,800		75.00	75
1985	Autumn Song Maiden	9,800		75.00	75
Star Trek Doll Collection - E. Daub					
1988	Mr. Spock	Closed	N/A	75.00	150
1988	Captain Kirk	Closed	N/A	75.00	120
1989	Dr. Mc Coy	Closed	N/A	75.00	120
1989	Scotty	Closed	N/A	75.00	120
1990	Sulu	Closed	N/A	75.00	120
1990	Chekov	Closed	N/A	75.00	120
1991	Uhura	Closed	N/A	75.00	120
Storybook Dolls - L. Di Leo					
1991	Alice in Wonderland	Open		75.00	75
Summertime Beauties - C. Marschner					
1995	Sally	Open		95.00	95
Through The Eyes of Virginia Turner - V. Turner					
1992	Michelle	Closed	1993	95.00	130-180
1992	Danielle	Open		95.00	95
1993	Wendy	Closed	1995	95.00	95
1994	Dawn	Open		95.00	95
Toddler Days Doll Collection - D. Schurig					
1992	Erica	Open		95.00	95
1993	Darlene	Open		95.00	95
1994	Karen	Open		95.00	95
1995	Penny	Open		95.00	95
Treasured Toddlers - V. Turner					
1992	Whitney	Open		95.00	95
1993	Natalie	Open		95.00	95
Vickie Walker 1st's - V. Walker					
1995	Leah	Open		79.00	79
Victorian Treasures - C.W. Derek					
1992	Katherine	Open		155.00	155
1993	Madeline	Open		155.00	155
Wooden Dolls - N/A					
1991	Gretchen	9,850	1995	225.00	280
1991	Heidi	9,850	1995	225.00	200-250
Wright Indian Dolls - D. Wright					
1994	Sacajawea	Open		135.00	135
1994	Minnehaha	Open		135.00	135
1995	Pine Leaf	Open		135.00	135
1995	Lozen	Open		135.00	135
Year Round Fun - D. Schurig					
1992	Allison	Open		95.00	95
1993	Christy	Open		95.00	95
1993	Paula	Open		95.00	95
1994	Kaylie	Open		95.00	95
Zolan Dolls - D. Zolan					
1991	A Christmas Prayer	Closed	1993	95.00	250-280
1992	Winter Angel	Open		95.00	95
1992	Rainy Day Pals	Open		95.00	95
1992	Quiet Time	Open		95.00	95
1993	For You	Open		95.00	95
1993	The Thinker	Open		95.00	95
Zolan Double Dolls - D. Zolan					
1993	First Kiss	Closed	1995	155.00	155
1994	New Shoes	Open		155.00	155

*Quotes have been rounded up to nearest dollar

Jan McLean Originals

Flowers of the Heart Collection - J. McLean

YEAR ISSUE	EDITION LIMIT	YEAR RETD.	ISSUE PRICE	*QUOTE U.S.$
1991 Marigold	100		2400.00	2800-3200
1990 Pansy	100		2200.00	2800-3400
1990 Pansy (bobbed blonde)	Retrd.	N/A	2200.00	2800-3800
1990 Pansy A/P	Retrd.	N/A	4300	4800
1990 Poppy	100		2200.00	2600-2800
1991 Primrose	100		2500.00	2600-2800

Jan McLean Originals - J. McLean

YEAR ISSUE	EDITION LIMIT	YEAR RETD.	ISSUE PRICE	*QUOTE U.S.$
1991 Lucrezia	15		6000.00	6000
1990 Phoebe I	25		2700.00	3200

Kurt S. Adler, Inc.

Royal Heritage Collection - J. Mostrom

YEAR ISSUE	EDITION LIMIT	YEAR RETD.	ISSUE PRICE	*QUOTE U.S.$
1993 Anastasia J5746	3,000		125.00	125
1993 Good King Wenceslas W2928	2,000		130.00	130
1993 Medieval King of Christmas W2981	2,000	1994	390.00	390
1994 Nicholas on Skates J5750	3,000		120.00	120
1994 Sasha on Skates J5749	3,000		130.00	130

Small Wonders - J. Mostrom

YEAR ISSUE	EDITION LIMIT	YEAR RETD.	ISSUE PRICE	*QUOTE U.S.$
1995 America-Hollie Blue W3162	Open		30.00	30
1995 America-Texas Tyler W3162	Open		30.00	30
1995 Ireland-Cathleen W3082	Open		28.00	28
1995 Ireland-Michael W3082	Open		28.00	28
1995 Kwanza-Mufaro W3161	Open		28.00	28
1995 Kwanza-Shani W3161	Open		28.00	28

When I Grow Up - J. Mostrom

YEAR ISSUE	EDITION LIMIT	YEAR RETD.	ISSUE PRICE	*QUOTE U.S.$
1995 Dr. Brown W3079	Open		27.00	27
1995 Freddy the Fireman W3163	Open		28.00	28
1995 Melissa the Teacher W3081	Open		28.00	28
1995 Nurse Nancy W3079	Open		27.00	27
1995 Scott the Golfer W3080	Open		28.00	28

Ladie and Friends

Lizzie High Society™ Members-Only Dolls - B.K. Wisber

YEAR ISSUE	EDITION LIMIT	YEAR RETD.	ISSUE PRICE	*QUOTE U.S.$
1993 Audrey High-1301	Closed	1992	59.00	300
1993 Becky High-1330	Closed	1994	96.00	275
1994 Chloe Valentine-1351	Closed	1995	79.00	79
1996 Dottie Bowman-1371	Yr.Iss.		78.00	78

The Christmas Concert - B.K. Wisber

YEAR ISSUE	EDITION LIMIT	YEAR RETD.	ISSUE PRICE	*QUOTE U.S.$
1990 Claire Valentine-1262	Open		56.00	60
1993 James Valentine-1310	Open		60.00	63
1992 Judith High-1292	Open		70.00	74
1993 Stephanie Bowman-1309	Open		74.00	77

The Christmas Pageant™ - B.K. Wisber

YEAR ISSUE	EDITION LIMIT	YEAR RETD.	ISSUE PRICE	*QUOTE U.S.$
1985 "Earth" Angel-1122	Closed	1989	30.00	100
1985 "Noel" Angel (1st Ed.)-1126	Closed	1989	30.00	100
1989 "Noel" Angel (2nd Ed.)-1126	Open		48.00	52
1985 "On" Angel-1121	Closed	1989	30.00	100
1985 "Peace" Angel (1st Ed.)-1120	Closed	1989	30.00	100
1989 "Peace" Angel (2nd Ed.)-1120	Open		48.00	52
1985 Christmas Wooly Lamb-1133	Closed	1991	11.00	35
1985 Joseph and Donkey-1119	Open		30.00	39
1985 Mary and Baby Jesus-1118	Open		30.00	39
1986 Shepherd-1193	Open		32.00	39
1985 Wiseman #1-1123	Open		30.00	39
1985 Wiseman #2-1124	Open		30.00	39
1985 Wiseman #3-1125	Open		30.00	39
1985 Wooden Creche-1132	Open		28.00	33

The Family and Friends of Lizzie High® - B.K. Wisber

YEAR ISSUE	EDITION LIMIT	YEAR RETD.	ISSUE PRICE	*QUOTE U.S.$
1987 Abigail Bowman-1199	Closed	1994	40.00	90
1987 Addie High-1202	Open		37.00	43
1990 Albert Valentine-1260	Closed	1995	42.00	45
1986 Alice Valentine (1st Ed.)-1148	Closed	1987	32.00	100
1995 Alice Valentine (2nd Ed.)-1148	Open		56.00	58
1988 Allison Bowman-1229	Closed	1996	56.00	62
1985 Amanda High (1st Ed.)-1111	Closed	1988	30.00	100
1990 Amanda High (2nd Ed.)-1111	Closed	1995	54.00	58
1989 Amelia High-1248	Open		45.00	50
1987 Amy Bowman-1201	Closed	1994	37.00	82
1986 Andrew Brown-1157	Closed	1988	45.00	125
1991 Annabelle Bowman-1267	Open		68.00	72
1986 Annie Bowman (1st Ed.)-1150	Closed	1989	32.00	100
1993 Annie Bowman (2nd Ed.)-1150	Open		68.00	71
1993 Ashley Bowman-1304	Open		48.00	50
1992 Barbara Helen-1274	Open		58.00	62
1985 Benjamin Bowman (Santa)-1134	Open		34.00	42
1985 Benjamin Bowman-1129	Closed	1987	30.00	100
1988 Bess High-1241	Open		45.00	50
1988 Betsy Valentine-1245	Open		42.00	46
1994 Bonnie Valentine-1323	Open		35.00	37
1987 Bridget Bowman-1222	Closed	1994	40.00	95
1992 Carol Anne Bowman-1282	Closed	1994	70.00	142
1986 Carrie High (1st Ed.)-1190	Closed	1989	45.00	100
1989 Carrie High (2nd Ed.)-1190	Open		46.00	50
1986 Cassie Yocum (1st Ed.)-1179	Closed	1988	36.00	100
1993 Cassie Yocum (2nd Ed.)-1179	Open		80.00	83
1987 Cat on Chair-1217	Closed	1991	16.00	35
1996 Cecelia Brown (alone)-1366A	Open		27.50	28
1996 Cecelia Brown (w/Mother)-1366	Open		101.00	101
1987 Charles Bowman (1st Ed.)-1221	Closed	1990	34.00	100
1992 Charles Bowman (2nd Ed.)-1221	Closed	1995	46.00	48
1996 Charlotte High-1370	Open		73.50	74
1985 Christian Bowman-1110	Closed	1987	30.00	100
1994 Christine Bowman-1332	Open		62.00	65
1993 Christmas Tree w/Cats-1293A	Open		42.00	44
1986 Christopher High-1182	Closed	1992	34.00	72
1985 Cora High-1115	Closed	1987	30.00	110
1991 Cynthia High-1127A	Closed	1995	60.00	62
1996 Daniel Brown (alone)-1367A	Open		27.50	28
1996 Daniel Brown (w/Mother)-1367	Open		101.00	101
1988 Daphne Bowman-1235	Closed	1994	38.00	40
1996 Darlene Bowman-1368	Open		77.50	78
1986 David Yocum-1195	Closed	1995	33.00	37
1986 Delia Valentine-1153	Closed	1988	32.00	100
1991 The Department Store Santa-1270	Open		76.00	80
1986 Dora Valentine (1st Ed.)-1152	Closed	1989	30.00	100
1992 Dora Valentine (2nd Ed.)-1152	Open		48.00	51
1986 Edward Bowman (1st Ed.)-1158	Closed	1988	45.00	125
1994 Edward Bowman (2nd Ed.)-1158	Open		76.00	79
1992 Edwin Bowman-1281	Closed	1994	70.00	71
1995 Edwina High-1343	Open		56.00	58
1985 Elizabeth Sweetland (1st Ed.)-1109	Closed	1987	30.00	100
1991 Elizabeth Sweetland (2nd Ed.)-1109	Closed	1996	56.00	60
1994 Elsie Bowman-1325	Open		64.00	67
1986 Emily Bowman (1st Ed.)-1185	Closed	1990	34.00	100
1990 Emily Bowman (2nd Ed.)-1185	Open		48.00	51
1985 Emma High-1103	Closed	1988	30.00	100
1989 Emmy Lou Valentine-1251	Open		45.00	49
1985 Esther Dunn (1st Ed.)-1127	Closed	1987	45.00	N/A
1991 Esther Dunn (2nd Ed.)-1127	Closed	1995	60.00	62
1988 Eunice High-1240	Closed	1994	56.00	58
1985 Flossie High (1st Ed.)-1128	Closed	1988	45.00	100-125
1989 Flossie High (2nd Ed.)-1128	Open		54.00	59
1987 The Flower Girl-1204	Closed	1995	17.00	24
1993 Francis Bowman-1305	Open		48.00	50
1994 Gilbert High-1335	Open		65.00	68
1986 Grace Valentine (1st Ed.)-1146	Closed	1989	32.00	100
1991 Grace Valentine (2nd Ed.)-1146	Open		48.00	51
1987 Gretchen High-1216	Closed	1994	40.00	44
1994 Gwendolyn High-1342	Open		56.00	59
1985 Hannah Brown-1131	Closed	1988	45.00	125
1988 Hattie Bowman-1239	Open		40.00	46
1985 Ida Valentine-1116	Closed	1988	30.00	80
1987 Imogene Bowman-1206	Closed	1994	37.00	80
1988 Jacob High-1230	Closed	1994	44.00	46
1994 Jamie Bowman-1324	Open		35.00	37
1988 Janie Valentine-1231	Open		37.00	43
1989 Jason High (alone)-1254A	Closed	1996	20.00	25
1989 Jason High (with Mother)-1254	Closed	1996	58.00	63
1986 Jenny Valentine-1181	Closed	1989	34.00	110
1986 Jeremy Bowman-1192	Closed	1991	36.00	80
1989 Jessica High (alone)-1253A	Closed	1996	20.00	25
1989 Jessica High (with Mother)-1253	Closed	1996	58.00	63
1995 Jillian Bowman ((2nd Ed.))-1180	Open		90.00	92
1986 Jillian Bowman (1st Ed.)-1180	Closed	1990	34.00	110
1992 Joanie Valentine-1295	Open		48.00	51
1989 Johann Bowman-1250	Open		40.00	44
1987 Johanna Valentine-1198	Closed	1988	37.00	100
1992 Joseph Valentine-1283	Closed	1995	62.00	64
1994 Josie Valentine-1322	Open		76.00	79
1986 Juliet Valentine (1st Ed.)-1147	Closed	1988	32.00	100
1990 Juliet Valentine (2nd Ed.)-1147	Open		48.00	52
1993 Justine Valentine-1302	Open		84.00	87
1986 Karl Valentine (1st Ed.)-1161	Closed	1988	30.00	100
1994 Karl Valentine (2nd Ed.)-1161	Open		54.00	57
1987 Katie and Barney-1219	Closed	1996	38.00	43
1986 Katie Bowman-1178	Closed	1994	36.00	82
1985 Katrina Valentine-1135	Closed	1989	30.00	100
1988 Kinch Bowman-1237	Closed	1996	47.00	51
1987 Laura Valentine-1223	Closed	1994	36.00	80
1995 Leona High-1355	Open		68.00	70
1986 Little Ghosts-1197	Open		15.00	20
1987 Little Witch-1225	Open		17.00	24
1985 Lizzie High® (1st Ed.)-1100	Closed	1995	30.00	45
1996 Lizzie High® (2nd Ed.)-1100	Open		92.00	92
1985 Louella Valentine-1112	Closed	1991	30.00	100
1989 Lucy Bowman-1255	Open		45.00	49
1985 Luther Bowman (1st Ed.)-1108	Closed	1987	30.00	100
1993 Luther Bowman (2nd Ed.)-1108	Open		60.00	63
1995 Lydia Bowman-1347	Open		54.00	55
1986 Madaleine Valentine (1st Ed.)-1187	Closed	1989	34.00	90
1989 Madaleine Valentine (2nd Ed.)-1187	Open		37.00	41
1986 Maggie High-1160	Closed	1988	30.00	100
1987 Margaret Bowman-1213	Open		35.00	43
1986 Marie Valentine (1st Ed.)-1184	Closed	1990	47.00	125
1992 Marie Valentine (2nd Ed.)-1184	Open		68.00	72
1986 Marisa Valentine (alone)-1194A	Open		33.00	40
1986 Marisa Valentine (w/ Brother Petey)-1194	Open		45.00	51
1994 Marisa Valentine-1333	Open		58.00	61
1986 Marland Valentine-1183	Closed	1990	33.00	100
1990 Marlene Valentine-1259	Closed	1995	48.00	51
1986 Martha High-1151	Closed	1989	32.00	75-100
1985 Martin Bowman-1117	Closed	1992	30.00	43-85
1988 Mary Ellen Valentine-1236	Open		40.00	45
1985 Mary Valentine-1105	Closed	1988	30.00	88-100
1986 Matthew Yocum-1186	Closed	1988	33.00	100
1995 Mattie Dunn-1344	Open		56.00	58
1988 Megan Valentine-1227	Closed	1994	44.00	94
1987 Melanie Bowman (1st Ed.)-1220	Closed	1990	36.00	125
1992 Melanie Bowman (2nd Ed.)-1220	Closed	1995	46.00	48
1991 Michael Bowman-1268	Open		52.00	55
1994 Minnie Valentine-1336	Open		64.00	67
1989 Miriam High-1256	Open		46.00	50
1986 Molly Yocum (1st Ed.)-1189	Closed	1989	34.00	80-100
1989 Molly Yocum (2nd Ed.)-1189	Open		39.00	43
1993 Mommy-1312	Open		48.00	50
1989 Mrs. Claus-1258	Open		42.00	46
1990 Nancy Bowman-1261	Open		48.00	52
1987 Naomi Valentine-1200	Closed	1993	40.00	88
1992 Natalie Valentine-1284	Closed	1995	62.00	64
1995 Nathan Bowman-1354	Open		70.00	72
1985 Nettie Brown (1st Ed.)-1102	Closed	1987	30.00	100
1988 Nettie Brown (2nd Ed.)-1102	Closed	1995	36.00	39
1985 Nettie Brown (Christmas)-1114	Closed	1987	30.00	100
1996 Nicholas Valentine (alone)-1365A	Open		27.50	28
1996 Nicholas Valentine (w/Mother) -1365	Open		101.00	101
1987 Olivia High-1205	Open		37.00	43
1987 Patsy Bowman-1214	Closed	1995	50.00	53
1988 Pauline Bowman-1228	Closed	1996	44.00	50
1993 Pearl Bowman-1303	Open		56.00	59
1989 Peggy Bowman-1252	Closed	1995	58.00	70
1987 Penelope High-1208	Closed	1991	40.00	100
1993 Penny Valentine-1308	Open		60.00	63
1985 Peter Valentine (1st Ed.)-1113	Closed	1991	30.00	75
1995 Peter Valentine (2nd Ed.)-1113	Open		55.00	57
1988 Phoebe High-1246	Closed	1992	48.00	90
1987 Priscilla High-1226	Closed	1995	56.00	62
1986 Rachel Bowman (1st Ed.)-1188	Closed	1989	34.00	100
1989 Rachel Bowman (2nd Ed.)-1188	Open		34.00	39
1987 Ramona Brown-1215	Closed	1989	40.00	50
1985 Rebecca Bowman (1st Ed.)-1104	Closed	1988	30.00	100
1989 Rebecca Bowman (2nd Ed.)-1104	Open		56.00	62
1987 Rebecca's Mother-1207	Closed	1995	37.00	54
1995 Regina Bowman-1353	Open		70.00	72
1995 Robert Bowman-1348	Open		64.00	66
1985 Russell Dunn-1107	Closed	1987	30.00	100
1988 Ruth Anne Bowman-1232	Closed	1994	44.00	92
1985 Sabina Valentine (1st Ed.)-1101	Closed	1987	30.00	100
1988 Sabina Valentine (2nd Ed.)-1101	Closed	1996	40.00	44
1986 Sadie Valentine-1163	Closed	1996	45.00	50
1986 Sally Bowman (1st Ed.)-1155	Closed	1991	32.00	110
1996 Sally Bowman (2nd Ed.)-1155	Open		75.50	76
1988 Samantha Bowman-1238	Closed	1996	47.00	51
1989 Santa (with Tub)-1257	Open		58.00	64
1987 Santa Claus (sitting)-1224	Closed	1991	50.00	61
1993 Santa Claus-1311	Open		48.00	50
1991 Santa's Helper-1271	Open		52.00	55
1986 Sara Valentine-1154	Closed	1994	32.00	38-76
1994 Shirley Bowman-1334	Open		63.00	66
1986 Sophie Valentine (1st Ed.)-1164	Closed	1991	45.00	125
1996 Sophie Valentine (alone)-1164A	Open		27.50	28
1996 Sophie Valentine (w/Mother) (2nd Ed.)-1164	Open		101.00	101
1995 St. Nicholas-1356	Open		98.00	100
1986 Susanna Bowman-1149	Closed	1988	45.00	125
1986 Thomas Bowman-1159	Closed	1987	30.00	100
1986 Tillie Brown-1156	Closed	1988	32.00	100
1992 Timothy Bowman-1294	Open		56.00	60
1991 Trudy Valentine-1269	Open		64.00	68
1996 Tucker Bowman-1369	Open		77.50	78
1989 Vanessa High-1247	Open		45.00	50
1989 Victoria Bowman-1249	Open		40.00	44
1987 The Wedding (Bride)-1203	Closed	1995	37.00	50
1987 The Wedding (Groom)-1203A	Closed	1995	34.00	37
1985 Wendel Bowman (1st Ed.)-1106	Closed	1987	30.00	100
1992 Wendel Bowman (2nd Ed.)-1106	Open		60.00	64
1992 Wendy Bowman-1293	Open		78.00	82
1986 William Valentine-1191	Closed	1992	36.00	72
1986 Willie Bowman-1162	Closed	1992	30.00	60

The Grummels of Log Hollow™ - B.K. Wisber

YEAR ISSUE	EDITION LIMIT	YEAR RETD.	ISSUE PRICE	*QUOTE U.S.$
1986 Aunt Gertie Grummel™ -1171	Closed	1988	34.00	70-110
1986 Aunt Hilda Grummel™ -1174	Closed	1988	34.00	70-110
1986 Aunt Polly Grummel ™ -1169	Closed	1988	36.00	70-110
1986 Cousin Lottie Grummel™ -1170	Closed	1988	36.00	70-110
1986 Cousin Miranda Grummel™ -1165	Closed	1988	47.00	70-110
1986 Grandma Grummel™ -1173	Closed	1988	45.00	70-110
1986 Grandpa Grummel ™ -1176	Closed	1988	36.00	180
1986 The Little Ones-Grummels™ (boy/girl)-1196	Closed	1988	15.00	40
1986 Ma Grummel™ -1167	Closed	1988	36.00	70-110
1986 Pa Grummel™ -1172	Closed	1988	34.00	70-110
1986 Sister Nora Grummel™ -1177	Closed	1988	34.00	70-110
1986 Teddy Bear Bed-1168	Closed	1988	15.00	70-100
1986 Uncle Hollis Grummel™ -1166	Closed	1988	34.00	70-110
1986 Washline-1175	Closed	1988	15.00	70-100

The Little Ones™ at Christmas-Nativity™ - B.K. Wisber

YEAR ISSUE	EDITION LIMIT	YEAR RETD.	ISSUE PRICE	*QUOTE U.S.$
1995 Donkey-1362	Open		17.00	18
1995 Little Angel-1359	Open		36.00	37
1995 Little Joseph-1358	Open		31.00	32
1995 Little Mary w/Baby in Manger-1357	Open		33.00	34

*Quotes have been rounded up to nearest dollar

DOLLS

YEAR ISSUE		EDITION LIMIT	YEAR RETD.	ISSUE PRICE	*QUOTE U.S.$
1995	Little Ones' Creche-1361	Open		24.00	25
1995	Little Shepherd w/Lamb-1360	Open		45.00	46

The Little Ones™ at Christmas™ - B.K. Wisber

YEAR ISSUE		EDITION LIMIT	YEAR RETD.	ISSUE PRICE	*QUOTE U.S.$
1990	Girl (black) w/Basket of Greens-1263	Open		22.00	27
1990	Girl (white) w/Cookie-1264	Open		22.00	27
1990	Girl (white) w/Gift-1266	Open		22.00	27
1990	Girl (white) w/Tree Garland-1265	Open		22.00	27
1991	Boy (black) w/Santa Photo-1273A	Open		24.00	29
1991	Boy (white) w/Santa Photo-1273	Open		24.00	29
1991	Girl (black) w/Santa Photo-1272A	Open		24.00	29
1991	Girl (white) w/Santa Photo-1272	Open		24.00	29
1993	Boy Peeking (Alone)-1314	Open		22.00	24
1993	Boy Peeking w/Tree-1313	Open		60.00	63
1993	Girl w/Baking Table-1317	Open		38.00	40
1993	Girl w/Note for Santa-1318	Open		36.00	38
1993	Girl Peeking (Alone)-1316	Open		22.00	24
1993	Girl Peeking w/Tree-1315	Open		60.00	63
1994	Girl w/Greens on Table-1337	Open		46.00	48
1995	Little Santa-1364	Open		50.00	51

The Little Ones™ - B.K. Wisber

YEAR ISSUE		EDITION LIMIT	YEAR RETD.	ISSUE PRICE	*QUOTE U.S.$
1985	Boy (black) (1st Ed.)-1130	Closed	1989	15.00	45-65
1985	Boy (white) (1st Ed.)-1130	Closed	1989	15.00	45-65
1985	Girl (black) (1st Ed.)-1130	Closed	1989	15.00	45-65
1985	Girl (white) (1st Ed.)-1130	Closed	1989	15.00	45-65
1989	Boy (black) (2nd Ed.)-1130I	Closed	1994	20.00	23
1989	Boy (white) (2nd Ed.)-1130H	Closed	1994	20.00	23
1989	Girl (black)-country color (2nd Ed.)-1130G	Closed	1994	20.00	23
1989	Girl (black)-pastels (2nd Ed.)-1130E	Closed	1994	20.00	23
1989	Girl (white)-country color (2nd Ed.)-1130F	Closed	1994	20.00	23
1989	Girl (white)-pastels (2nd Ed.)-1130H	Closed	1994	20.00	23
1992	Boy w/Sled-1289	Open		30.00	33
1992	Clown-1290	Open		32.00	35
1992	Girl Reading-1286	Open		36.00	39
1992	Girl w/Apples-1277	Open		26.00	29
1992	Girl w/Beach Bucket-1275	Open		26.00	29
1992	Girl w/Birthday Gift-1279	Open		26.00	29
1992	Girl w/Christmas Lights-1287	Open		34.00	37
1992	Girl w/Easter Eggs-1276	Open		26.00	29
1992	Girl w/Kitten and Milk-1280	Open		32.00	35
1992	Girl w/Kitten and Yarn-1278	Open		34.00	37
1992	Girl w/Snowman-1288	Open		36.00	39
1992	Girl w/Valentine-1291	Open		30.00	33
1993	4th of July Boy-1307	Open		28.00	30
1993	Ballerina-1321	Open		40.00	42
1993	Boy w/Easter Flowers-1306	Open		30.00	32
1993	Bunny-1297	Open		36.00	38
1993	Girl Picnicking w/ Teddy Bear-1320	Open		34.00	36
1993	Girl w/Easter Flowers-1296	Open		34.00	36
1993	Girl w/Mop-1300	Open		36.00	38
1993	Girl w/Spinning Wheel-1299	Open		36.00	38
1993	Girl w/Violin-1319	Open		28.00	30
1993	4th of July Girl-1298	Open		30.00	32
1994	Boy Dyeing Eggs-1327	Open		30.00	32
1994	Boy w/Pumpkin-1341	Open		29.00	31
1994	Girl Dyeing Eggs-1326	Open		30.00	32
1994	Girl w/Laundry Basket-1338	Open		38.00	40
1994	Girl w/Puppy in Tub-1339	Open		43.00	45
1994	Girl w/Pumpkin Wagon-1340	Open		42.00	44
1994	Nurse-1328	Open		40.00	42
1994	Teacher-1329	Open		38.00	40
1995	Basketweaver-1363	Open		48.00	49
1996	Girl w/Sunflower-1373	Open		37.00	37
1996	Bride-1374	Open		41.50	42
1996	Groom-1375	Open		23.50	24
1996	White Girl Rollerskating-1376	Open		40.00	40
1996	Black Girl Rollerskating-1377	Open		40.00	40

The Pawtuckets of Sweet Briar Lane™ - B.K. Wisber

YEAR ISSUE		EDITION LIMIT	YEAR RETD.	ISSUE PRICE	*QUOTE U.S.$
1994	Aunt Lillian Pawtucket™ (2nd Ed.)-1141	Open		58.00	61
1986	Aunt Lillian Pawtucket™ (1st Ed.)-1141	Closed	1989	32.00	110
1987	Aunt Mabel Pawtucket™ -212	Closed	1989	45.00	130
1986	Aunt Minnie Pawtucket ™ (1st Ed.)-1136	Closed	1989	45.00	110
1994	Aunt Minnie Pawtucket ™ (2nd Edi)-1136	Open		72.00	75
1986	Brother Noah Pawtucket ™-1140	Closed	1989	32.00	110
1987	Bunny Bed-1218	Closed	1989	16.00	110
1987	Cousin Alberta Pawtucket ™ -1210	Closed	1989	36.00	110
1986	Cousin Clara Pawtucket ™ (1st Ed.)-1144	Closed	1989	32.00	110
1987	Cousin Isabel Pawtucket™ -1209	Closed	1989	36.00	110
1988	Cousin Jed Pawtucket ™-1234	Closed	1990	34.00	110
1988	Cousin Winnie Pawtucket ™-1233	Closed	1990	49.00	110
1994	Flossie Pawtucket ™-1136A	Open		33.00	35
1986	Grammy Pawtucket™ (1st Ed.)-1137	Closed	1989	32.00	110
1994	Grammy Pawtucket™ (2nd Edi.)-1137	Open		68.00	71
1995	The Little One Bunnies (1995)-female w/ laundry basket-1211A	Open		33.00	34
1986	The Little One Bunnies-boy (1st Ed.)-1145	Closed	1989	15.00	20
1994	The Little One Bunnies-boy (2nd Ed.)-1145A	Open		33.00	35
1986	The Little One Bunnies-girl (1st Ed.)-1145	Closed	1989	15.00	50
1994	The Little One Bunnies-girl (2nd Ed.)-1145	Open		33.00	35
1986	Mama Pawtucket ™ (1st Ed.)-1142	Closed	1989	34.00	110
1994	Mama Pawtucket™(2nd Ed.)-1142	Open		86.00	89
1986	Pappy Pawtucket ™(1st Ed.)-1143	Closed	1989	32.00	110
1995	Pappy Pawtucket ™(2nd Ed.)-1143	Open		56.00	58
1994	Pawtucket™ Bunny Hutch-1141A	Open		38.00	40
1995	Pawtucket™ Wash Line-1211B	Open		20.00	21
1987	Sister Clemmie Pawtucket™ (1st Ed.)-1211	Closed	1989	34.00	110
1995	Sister Clemmie Pawtucket™ (2nd Ed.)-1211	Open		60.00	62
1986	Sister Flora Pawtucket™ (1st Ed.)-1139	Closed	1989	32.00	110
1996	Sister Flora Pawtucket™ (2nd Ed.)-1139	Open		63.50	64
1986	Uncle Harley Pawtucket™ (1st Ed.)-1138	Closed	1989	32.00	110
1994	Uncle Harley Pawtucket™ (2nd Ed.)-1138	Open		74.00	77

Special Editions - B.K. Wisber

YEAR ISSUE		EDITION LIMIT	YEAR RETD.	ISSUE PRICE	*QUOTE U.S.$
1992	Kathryn Bowman (Limited Edition)-1285	3,000	1992	140.00	500
1994	Prudence Valentine-1331	4,000	1994	180.00	180
1995	Little Lizzie High® Anniversay Special Event Edition	Yr.Iss.	1995	40.00	40
1995	Lizzie High®-10th Anniversary Signature Edition-1100A	Yr.Iss.	1995	90.00	90
1996	Little Rebecca Bowman™-1996 Special Event Edition-1372	Yr.Iss.		37.00	37

The Thanksgiving Play - B.K. Wisber

YEAR ISSUE		EDITION LIMIT	YEAR RETD.	ISSUE PRICE	*QUOTE U.S.$
1988	Indian Squaw-1244	Closed	1995	36.00	39
1988	Pilgrim Boy-1242	Closed	1995	40.00	45
1988	Pilgrim Girl-1243	Closed	1995	48.00	51

Lawtons

Guild Dolls - W. Lawton

YEAR ISSUE		EDITION LIMIT	YEAR RETD.	ISSUE PRICE	*QUOTE U.S.$
1989	Baa Baa Black Sheep	1,003	1989	395.00	650
1990	Lavender Blue	781	1990	395.00	400
1991	To Market, To Market	683	1991	495.00	495
1992	Little Boy Blue	510	1992	395.00	395
1993	Lawton Logo Doll	575	1993	350.00	500
1994	Wee Handful	540	1994	250.00	250
1995	Uniquely Yours	12/95		395.00	395

Cherished Customs - W. Lawton

YEAR ISSUE		EDITION LIMIT	YEAR RETD.	ISSUE PRICE	*QUOTE U.S.$
1990	The Blessing/Mexico	500	1990	395.00	1000
1992	Carnival/Brazil	750	1992	425.00	425
1992	Cradleboard/Navajo	750	1993	425.00	425
1991	Frolic/Amish	500	1991	395.00	395
1990	Girl's Day/Japan	500	1990	395.00	395
1990	High Tea/Great Britain	500	1990	395.00	450-550
1994	Kwanzaa/Africa	500	1994	425.00	425
1990	Midsommar/Sweden	500	1990	395.00	395
1993	Nalauqataq-Eskimo	500	1993	395.00	395
1991	Ndeko/Zaire	500	1991	395.00	550
1992	Pascha/Ukraine	750	1992	495.00	495
1995	Piping the Haggis	350		495.00	495
1993	Topeng Klana-Java	250	1993	495.00	495

Childhood Classics® - W. Lawton

YEAR ISSUE		EDITION LIMIT	YEAR RETD.	ISSUE PRICE	*QUOTE U.S.$
1983	Alice In Wonderland	100	1983	225.00	2000
1986	Anne Of Green Gables	250	1986	325.00	1600-2400
1991	The Bobbsey Twins: Flossie	350	1991	364.50	500
1991	The Bobbsey Twins: Freddie	350	1991	364.50	500
1985	Hans Brinker	250	1985	325.00	1800
1984	Heidi	250	1984	325.00	650
1991	Hiawatha	500	1991	395.00	500
1989	Honey Bunch	250	1989	350.00	550
1987	Just David	250	1987	325.00	700
1986	Laura Ingalls	250	1986	325.00	500
1991	Little Black Sambo	500	1991	395.00	650
1988	Little Eva	250	1988	350.00	500-1000
1989	Little Princess	250	1989	395.00	600
1990	Mary Frances	350	1990	350.00	350
1987	Mary Lennox	250	1987	325.00	500
1987	Polly Pepper	250	1987	325.00	450
1986	Pollyanna	250	1986	325.00	1600
1990	Poor Little Match Girl	350	1990	350.00	500
1988	Rebecca	250	1988	350.00	450
1988	Topsy	250	1988	350.00	750

The Children's Hour - W. Lawton

YEAR ISSUE		EDITION LIMIT	YEAR RETD.	ISSUE PRICE	*QUOTE U.S.$
1991	Edith With Golden Hair	500	1991	395.00	475
1991	Grave Alice	500	1991	395.00	475
1991	Laughing Allegra	500	1991	395.00	475

Newcomer Collection - W. Lawton

YEAR ISSUE		EDITION LIMIT	YEAR RETD.	ISSUE PRICE	*QUOTE U.S.$
1987	Ellin Elizabeth, Eyes Closed	49	1987	335.00	750-1000
1987	Ellin Elizabeth, Eyes Open	19	1987	335.00	900-1200

Playthings Past - W. Lawton

YEAR ISSUE		EDITION LIMIT	YEAR RETD.	ISSUE PRICE	*QUOTE U.S.$
1989	Edward And Dobbin	500	1989	395.00	495-600
1989	Elizabeth And Baby	500	1989	395.00	495-650
1989	Victoria And Teddy	500	1989	395.00	395

Special Edition - W. Lawton

YEAR ISSUE		EDITION LIMIT	YEAR RETD.	ISSUE PRICE	*QUOTE U.S.$
1993	Flora McFlimsey	250	1993	895.00	1000
1988	Marcella And Raggedy Ann	2,500	1988	395.00	700-750
1994	Mary Chilton	350	1994	395.00	395

Special Occasion - W. Lawton

YEAR ISSUE		EDITION LIMIT	YEAR RETD.	ISSUE PRICE	*QUOTE U.S.$
1990	First Birthday	500	1990	295.00	350
1989	First Day Of School	500	1989	325.00	525
1988	Nanthy	500	1988	325.00	525

Sugar 'n' Spice - W. Lawton

YEAR ISSUE		EDITION LIMIT	YEAR RETD.	ISSUE PRICE	*QUOTE U.S.$
1987	Ginger	454	1987	275.00	395-550
1986	Jason	27	1986	250.00	800-1700
1986	Jessica	30	1986	250.00	800-1700
1986	Kersten	103	1986	250.00	550-800
1986	Kimberly	87	1986	250.00	550-800
1987	Marie	208	1987	275.00	450

Timeless Ballads® - W. Lawton

YEAR ISSUE		EDITION LIMIT	YEAR RETD.	ISSUE PRICE	*QUOTE U.S.$
1987	Annabel Lee	250	1987	550.00	600-695
1987	Highland Mary	250	1987	550.00	600-875
1988	She Walks In Beauty	250	1988	550.00	600-800
1987	Young Charlotte	250	1987	550.00	850-900

Wee Bits - W. Lawton

YEAR ISSUE		EDITION LIMIT	YEAR RETD.	ISSUE PRICE	*QUOTE U.S.$
1989	Wee Bit O'Bliss	250	1989	295.00	350
1988	Wee Bit O'Heaven	250	1988	295.00	350
1988	Wee Bit O'Sunshine	250	1988	295.00	350
1988	Wee Bit O'Woe	250	1988	295.00	350
1989	Wee Bit O'Wonder	250	1989	295.00	350

Lenox Collections

Bolshoi Nutcracker Dolls - Unknown

YEAR ISSUE		EDITION LIMIT	YEAR RETD.	ISSUE PRICE	*QUOTE U.S.$
1991	Clara	Closed	1993	195.00	195

Children of the World - Unknown

YEAR ISSUE		EDITION LIMIT	YEAR RETD.	ISSUE PRICE	*QUOTE U.S.$
1991	Amma-The African Girl	Closed	1993	119.00	119
1992	Gretchen, German Doll	Closed	1993	119.00	119
1989	Hannah, The Little Dutch Maiden	Closed	1993	119.00	119
1990	Heather, Little Highlander	Closed	1993	119.00	119
1991	Sakura-The Japanese Girl	Closed	1993	119.00	119

Children With Toys Dolls - Unknown

YEAR ISSUE		EDITION LIMIT	YEAR RETD.	ISSUE PRICE	*QUOTE U.S.$
1991	Tea For Teddy	Closed	1993	136.00	136

China Dolls - Cloth Bodies - J. Grammer

YEAR ISSUE		EDITION LIMIT	YEAR RETD.	ISSUE PRICE	*QUOTE U.S.$
1985	Amy, 14"	Closed	1990	250.00	N/A
1985	Annabelle, 14"	Closed	1990	250.00	N/A
1985	Elizabeth, 14"	Closed	1990	250.00	N/A
1985	Jennifer, 14"	Closed	1990	250.00	N/A
1985	Miranda, 14"	Closed	1990	250.00	N/A
1985	Sarah, 14"	Closed	1990	250.00	N/A

Country Decor Dolls - Unknown

YEAR ISSUE		EDITION LIMIT	YEAR RETD.	ISSUE PRICE	*QUOTE U.S.$
1991	Molly	Closed	1994	150.00	150

Ellis Island Dolls - P. Thompson

YEAR ISSUE		EDITION LIMIT	YEAR RETD.	ISSUE PRICE	*QUOTE U.S.$
1992	Angelina	Closed	1994	150.00	150
1992	Anna	Closed	1994	152.00	152
1992	Catherine	Closed	1994	152.00	152
1991	Megan	Closed	1994	150.00	150
1991	Stefan	Closed	1994	150.00	150

First Collector Doll - Unknown

YEAR ISSUE		EDITION LIMIT	YEAR RETD.	ISSUE PRICE	*QUOTE U.S.$
1992	Lauren	Closed	1993	152.00	152

Inspirational Doll - Unknown

YEAR ISSUE		EDITION LIMIT	YEAR RETD.	ISSUE PRICE	*QUOTE U.S.$
1992	Blessed Are The Peacemakers	Closed	1993	119.00	119

International Baby Doll - Unknown

YEAR ISSUE		EDITION LIMIT	YEAR RETD.	ISSUE PRICE	*QUOTE U.S.$
1992	Natalia, Russian Baby	Closed	1993	119.00	119

Lenox China Dolls - J. Grammer

YEAR ISSUE		EDITION LIMIT	YEAR RETD.	ISSUE PRICE	*QUOTE U.S.$
1984	Abigail, 20"	Closed	1990	425.00	N/A
1984	Amanda, 16"	Closed	1990	385.00	N/A
1984	Jessica, 20"	Closed	1990	450.00	N/A
1984	Maggie, 16"	Closed	1990	375.00	N/A
1984	Maryanne, 20"	Closed	1990	425.00	N/A
1984	Melissa, 16"	Closed	1990	450.00	N/A
1984	Rebecca, 16"	Closed	1990	375.00	N/A
1984	Samantha, 16"	Closed	1990	500.00	N/A

Lenox Victorian Dolls - Unknown

YEAR ISSUE		EDITION LIMIT	YEAR RETD.	ISSUE PRICE	*QUOTE U.S.$
1990	Christmas Doll, Elizabeth	Closed	1993	195.00	195
1992	Lady at Gala	Closed	1993	295.00	295
1989	The Victorian Bride	Closed	1993	295.00	295
1991	Victorian Christening Doll	Closed	1993	295.00	295

Little Women - Unknown

YEAR ISSUE		EDITION LIMIT	YEAR RETD.	ISSUE PRICE	*QUOTE U.S.$
1992	Amy, The Inspiring Artist	Closed	1993	152.00	152

Musical Baby Dolls - Unknown

YEAR ISSUE		EDITION LIMIT	YEAR RETD.	ISSUE PRICE	*QUOTE U.S.$
1991	Patrick's Lullabye	Closed	1993	95.00	95

Nutcracker Dolls - Unknown

YEAR ISSUE		EDITION LIMIT	YEAR RETD.	ISSUE PRICE	*QUOTE U.S.$
1993	Nutcracker	Closed	1993	195.00	195
1992	Sugarplum	Closed	1993	195.00	195

*Quotes have been rounded up to nearest dollar

Prima Ballerina Collection - Unknown

YEAR	ISSUE	EDITION LIMIT	YEAR RETD.	ISSUE PRICE	*QUOTE U.S.$
1992	Odette, Queen of the Swans	Closed	1992	195.00	195

Sibling Dolls - A. Lester

YEAR	ISSUE	EDITION LIMIT	YEAR RETD.	ISSUE PRICE	*QUOTE U.S.$
1991	Skating Lesson	Closed	1993	195.00	195

Mattel

35th Anniversary Dolls by Mattel - Mattel

YEAR	ISSUE	EDITION LIMIT	YEAR RETD.	ISSUE PRICE	*QUOTE U.S.$
1994	Blonde	Retrd.	1994	39.99	40-50
1994	Brunette	Retrd.	1994	39.99	50-75
1994	Gift Pack	Retrd.	1994	79.97	125-150

Annual Holiday (white) Barbie Dolls - Mattel

YEAR	ISSUE	EDITION LIMIT	YEAR RETD.	ISSUE PRICE	*QUOTE U.S.$
1988	Holiday Barbie	Retrd.	1990	24.95	600-900
1989	Holiday Barbie	Retrd.	1991	N/A	200-300
1990	Holiday Barbie	Retrd.	1991	N/A	175-275
1991	Holiday Barbie	Retrd.	1993	N/A	200-300
1992	Holiday Barbie	Retrd.	1992	N/A	125-150
1993	Holiday Barbie	Retrd.	1993	N/A	120-175
1994	Holiday Barbie	Retrd.	1994	44.95	150-225
1995	Holiday Barbie	Retrd.	1995	44.95	75-125

Bob Mackie Barbie Dolls - B. Mackie

YEAR	ISSUE	EDITION LIMIT	YEAR RETD.	ISSUE PRICE	*QUOTE U.S.$
1992	Empress Bride Barbie 4247	Retrd.	1992	232.00	900-1200
1990	Gold Barbie 5405	Retrd.	1990	120.00	650-850
1993	Masquerade	Retrd.	1993	175.00	425-500
1992	Neptune Fantasy Barbie 4248	Retrd.	1993	160.00	800-1100
1991	Platinum Barbie 2703	Retrd.	1991	153.00	650-850
1994	Queen of Hearts	Retrd.	1994	175.00	225-300
1991	Starlight Splendor Barbie 2704	Retrd.	1991	135.00	750-950

Classique Collection - Various

YEAR	ISSUE	EDITION LIMIT	YEAR RETD.	ISSUE PRICE	*QUOTE U.S.$
1992	Benefit Ball - C. Spencer	Retrd.	1994	59.95	175-225
1993	City Style - J. Goldblatt	Retrd.	1994	59.95	100-125
1993	Opening Night - J. Goldblatt	Retrd.	1994	59.95	100-125

Golden Jubilee - C. Spencer

YEAR	ISSUE	EDITION LIMIT	YEAR RETD.	ISSUE PRICE	*QUOTE U.S.$
1994	Golden Jubliee	Retrd.	1994	299.00	700-1100

Great Eras - Mattel

YEAR	ISSUE	EDITION LIMIT	YEAR RETD.	ISSUE PRICE	*QUOTE U.S.$
1993	Flapper	Retrd.	1995	54.00	125-175
1993	Gibson Girl	Retrd.	1995	54.00	75-100

Nostalgic Porcelain Barbie Dolls - Mattel

YEAR	ISSUE	EDITION LIMIT	YEAR RETD.	ISSUE PRICE	*QUOTE U.S.$
1990	Solo in the Spotlight 7613	Retrd.	1990	198.00	200-250
1990	Sophisticated Lady 5313	Retrd.	1990	198.00	200-275
1989	Wedding Day Barbie 2641	Retrd.	1989	198.00	500-600

The Winter Princess Collection - Mattel

YEAR	ISSUE	EDITION LIMIT	YEAR RETD.	ISSUE PRICE	*QUOTE U.S.$
1994	Evergreen Princess	Retrd.	1994	59.95	120-175
1994	Evergreen Princess (Red Head)	Retrd.	1994	59.95	400-450
1995	Peppermint Princess	Retrd.	1995	59.95	65
1993	Winter Princess	Retrd.	1993	59.95	400-550

Middleton Doll Company

Christmas Angel Collection - L. Middleton

YEAR	ISSUE	EDITION LIMIT	YEAR RETD.	ISSUE PRICE	*QUOTE U.S.$
1987	Christmas Angel 1987	4,174	1987	130.00	400-500
1988	Christmas Angel 1988	8,969	1988	130.00	200-250
1989	Christmas Angel 1989	7,500	1991	150.00	190
1990	Christmas Angel 1990	5,000	1991	150.00	190
1991	Christmas Angel 1991	5,000	1992	180.00	200
1992	Christmas Angel 1992	5,000	1995	190.00	190
1993	Christmas Angel 1993-Girl	3,144	1995	190.00	190
1993	Christmas Angel 1993 (set)	1,000	1993	390.00	500
1994	Christmas Angel 1994	5,000		190.00	190
1995	Christmas Angel 1995 (white or black)	3,000		190.00	190

First Moments Series - L. Middleton

YEAR	ISSUE	EDITION LIMIT	YEAR RETD.	ISSUE PRICE	*QUOTE U.S.$
1984	First Moments (Sleeping)	40,861	1990	69.00	200
1992	First Moments Awake in Blue	1,230	1994	170.00	170
1992	First Moments Awake in Pink	856	1994	170.00	170
1986	First Moments Blue Eyes	14,494	1990	120.00	150
1987	First Moments Boy	6,075	1989	130.00	160
1986	First Moments Brown Eyes	5,324	1989	120.00	150
1987	First Moments Christening (Asleep)	9,377	1992	160.00	250
1987	First Moments Christening (Awake)	16,384	1992	160.00	180
1993	First Moments Heirloom	1,372	1995	190.00	190
1991	First Moments Sweetness	6,323	1995	180.00	180
1994	Sweetness-Newborn	Retrd.	1995	190.00	190

Porcelain Collector Series - L. Middleton

YEAR	ISSUE	EDITION LIMIT	YEAR RETD.	ISSUE PRICE	*QUOTE U.S.$
1992	Beloved & Bé Bé	362	1994	590.00	590
1993	Cherish - Lilac & Lace	141	1994	500.00	500
1992	Sencerity II - Country Fair	253	1994	500.00	500

Porcelain Limited Edition Series - L. Middleton

YEAR	ISSUE	EDITION LIMIT	YEAR RETD.	ISSUE PRICE	*QUOTE U.S.$
1990	Baby Grace	500	1990	500.00	500
1994	Blossom	86	1995	500.00	500
1994	Bride	200	1994	1390.00	1390
1988	Cherish -1st Edition	750	1988	350.00	500
1989	Devan	543	1991	500.00	500
1995	Elise - 1860's Fashion	200		1790.00	1790
1991	Johanna	381	1992	500.00	500
1991	Molly Rose	500	1991	500.00	500
1989	My Lee	655	1991	500.00	500
1988	Sincerity -1st Edition -Nettie/Simplicity	750	1988	330.00	350-600
1995	Tenderness - Baby Clown	250		590.00	590
1994	Tenderness-Petite Pierrot	250	1994	500.00	500

Vinyl Collectors Series - L. Middleton

YEAR	ISSUE	EDITION LIMIT	YEAR RETD.	ISSUE PRICE	*QUOTE U.S.$
1987	Amanda - 1st Edition	3,778	1989	140.00	160
1985	Angel Face	20,200	1989	90.00	150
1994	Angel Kisses Boy	Open		98.00	98
1994	Angel Kisses Girl	Open		98.00	98
1992	Beth	1,414	1994	160.00	160
1986	Bubba Chubbs	5,550	1988	100.00	150-200
1988	Bubba Chubbs Railroader	7,925	1994	140.00	170
1988	Cherish	14,790	1992	160.00	250
1994	Country Boy	Open		118.00	118
1994	Country Boy (Dark Flesh)	Open		118.00	118
1994	Country Girl	Open		118.00	118
1994	Country Girl (Dark Flesh)	Open		118.00	118
1986	Dear One - 1st Edition	4,935	1988	90.00	250
1989	Devan	8,336	1991	170.00	170
1993	Echo	Open		180.00	180
1995	Hershey's Kisses - Gold	Open		99.50	100
1994	Hershey's Kisses - Silver	Open		99.50	100
1986	Little Angel - 3rd Edition	15,158	1992	90.00	110
1992	Little Angel Boy	Open		130.00	130
1992	Little Angel Girl	Open		130.00	130
1987	Missy	11,855	1991	100.00	120
1989	My Lee	3,794	1991	170.00	170
1992	Polly Esther	2,137	1994	160.00	160
1995	Polly Esther - Hershey's Country Girl	Open		130.00	130
1988	Sincerity - Limited 1st Ed. - Nettie/Simplicity	3,711	1989	160.00	200-250
1989	Sincerity-Schoolgirl	6,622	1992	180.00	200
1994	Town Boy	Open		118.00	118
1994	Town Boy (Dark Flesh)	Open		118.00	118
1994	Town Girl	Open		118.00	118
1994	Town Girl (Dark Flesh)	Open		118.00	118

Original Appalachian Artworks

Collectors Club Editions - X. Roberts

YEAR	ISSUE	EDITION LIMIT	YEAR RETD.	ISSUE PRICE	*QUOTE U.S.$
1987	Baby Otis	Closed	1987	250.00	500
1989	Anna Ruby	Closed	1989	250.00	350-500
1990	Lee Ann	Closed	1990	250.00	400-500
1991	Richard Russell	Closed	1991	250.00	350-500
1992	Baby Dodd	Closed	1992	250.00	300-500
1993	Patti w/ Cabbage Bud Boutonnier	Closed	1993	280.00	280
1994	Mother Cabbage	Closed	1995	150.00	150
1995	Rosie	Closed	1996	275.00	275

Cabbage Patch Kids - X. Roberts

YEAR	ISSUE	EDITION LIMIT	YEAR RETD.	ISSUE PRICE	*QUOTE U.S.$
1982	Amy	Closed	1982	125.00	500-700
1983	Andre/Madeira	Closed	1982	250.00	1200
1982	Billie	Closed	1982	125.00	450-700
1982	Bobbie	Closed	1982	125.00	450-700
1984	Daddy's Darlins' Kitten	Closed	1984	300.00	400-500
1984	Daddy's Darlins' Princess	Closed	1984	300.00	500-750
1984	Daddy's Darlins' Pun'kin	Closed	1983	300.00	400-500
1984	Daddy's Darlins' Tootsie	Closed	1984	300.00	400-500
1984	Daddy's Darlins', set of 4	Closed	1984	1600.00	1000-2000
1982	Dorothy	Closed	1982	125.00	700
1982	Gilda	Closed	1982	125.00	700-2500
1994	Little People 27" (Boy)	Closed	1994	325.00	700-850
1993	Little People 27" (Girl)	Closed	1993	325.00	750-1000
1982	Marilyn	Closed	1982	125.00	700-800
1994	Mountain Laurel 'Kids'™	Closed	1994	210.00	210
1994	Mountain Laurel Baby Sidney & Baby Lanier	100	1994	390.00	390
1994	Mountain Laurel Easter	200	1994	210.00	210
1994	Mountain Laurel Mysterious Barry	Closed	1994	225.00	375
1994	Mountain Laurel Norma Jean	Closed	1994	225.00	425
1994	Mountain Laurel-St. Patrick Boys	100	1994	210.00	210
1994	Mountain Laurel-St. Patrick Girls	200	1994	210.00	210
1995	Mt. Yonah	Closed	1995	210.00	210
1995	Mt. Yonah Easter	Closed	1995	215.00	215
1995	Mt. Yonah Valentine	Closed	1995	200.00	200
1982	Otis	Closed	1982	125.00	700
1982	Rebecca	Closed	1982	125.00	700
1982	Sybil	Closed	1982	125.00	450-700
1989	Tiger's Eye-Mother's Day	Closed	1989	150.00	300-375
1988	Tiger's Eye-Valentine's Day	Closed	1984	150.00	300-375
1982	Tyler	Closed	1982	125.00	2000-3000
1993	Unicoi Edition	Closed	1993	210.00	210

Cabbage Patch Kids Circus Parade - X. Roberts

YEAR	ISSUE	EDITION LIMIT	YEAR RETD.	ISSUE PRICE	*QUOTE U.S.$
1987	Big Top Clown-Baby Cakes	2,000	1987	180.00	450-600
1989	Happy Hobo-Bashful Billy	1,000	1989	180.00	350
1991	Mitzi	1,000	1991	220.00	250-350

Cabbage Patch Kids International - X. Roberts

YEAR	ISSUE	EDITION LIMIT	YEAR RETD.	ISSUE PRICE	*QUOTE U.S.$
1983	American Indian/Pair	Closed	1983	300.00	1200
1984	Bavarian/Pair	Closed	1984	300.00	450-800
1983	Hispanic/Pair	Closed	1983	300.00	400
1983	Irish/Pair	Closed	1985	320.00	320
1983	Oriental/Pair	Closed	1983	300.00	1000

Christmas Collection - X. Roberts

YEAR	ISSUE	EDITION LIMIT	YEAR RETD.	ISSUE PRICE	*QUOTE U.S.$
1979	X Christmas/Pair	Closed	1979	300.00	5500
1980	Christmas-Nicholas/Noel	Closed	1980	400.00	2600
1982	Christmas-Baby Rudy/Christy Nicole	Closed	1982	400.00	1600
1983	Christmas-Holly/Berry	Closed	1983	400.00	800
1984	Christmas-Carole/Chris	Closed	1984	400.00	600
1985	Christmas-Baby Sandy/Claude	Closed	1985	400.00	400
1986	Christmas-Hilliary/Nigel	Closed	1986	400.00	400
1987	Christmas-Katrina/Misha	Closed	1987	500.00	500
1988	Christmas-Kelly/Kane	Closed	1988	500.00	500-600
1989	Christmas-Joy	Closed	1989	250.00	600
1990	Christmas-Krystina	Closed	1990	250.00	250
1991	Christmas-Nick	Closed	1991	275.00	275
1992	Christmas-Christy Claus	Closed	1992	285.00	285
1993	Christmas-Rudolph	Closed	1993	275.00	275
1994	Christmas-Natalie	Closed	1994	275.00	275
1995	Christmas-Treena	Closed	1995	275.00	275

Convention Baby - X. Roberts

YEAR	ISSUE	EDITION LIMIT	YEAR RETD.	ISSUE PRICE	*QUOTE U.S.$
1989	Ashley	Closed	1989	150.00	500
1990	Bradley	Closed	1990	175.00	500-600
1991	Caroline	Closed	1991	200.00	300
1992	Duke	Closed	1992	225.00	400-500
1993	Ellen	Closed	1993	225.00	300-400
1994	Justin	Closed	1994	238.50	300-400
1995	Fifi	Closed	1995	250.00	350-500

Happily Ever After - X. Roberts

YEAR	ISSUE	EDITION LIMIT	YEAR RETD.	ISSUE PRICE	*QUOTE U.S.$
1993	Bride	Closed	1993	230.00	275
1993	Groom	Closed	1993	230.00	275

Little People - X. Roberts

YEAR	ISSUE	EDITION LIMIT	YEAR RETD.	ISSUE PRICE	*QUOTE U.S.$
1978	"A" Blue	Closed	1978	125.00	7000-8500
1978	"B" Red	Closed	1978	100.00	4500-6000
1978	"C" Burgundy	Closed	1978	100.00	1500-1800
1979	"D" Purple	Closed	1979	100.00	1000-1500
1979	"E" Bronze	Closed	1979	125.00	750-850
1982	"PE" New 'Ears Preemie	Closed	1982	140.00	300-450
1981	"PR II" Preemie	Closed	1981	130.00	350-450
1980	"SP" Preemie	Closed	1980	100.00	600-800
1982	"U" Unsigned	Closed	1982	125.00	250-450
1980	"U" Unsigned	Closed	1981	125.00	250-450
1980	Celebrity	Closed	1980	200.00	550-750
1980	Grand Edition	Closed	1986	1000.00	1000
1978	Helen Blue	Closed	1978	150.00	800-1100
1981	New 'Ears	Closed	1981	125.00	250
1981	Standing Edition	Closed	1986	300.00	350-400

Reco International

Childhood Doll Collection - S. Kuck

YEAR	ISSUE	EDITION LIMIT	YEAR RETD.	ISSUE PRICE	*QUOTE U.S.$
1994	A Kiss Goodnight	Retrd.	1995	79.00	79
1995	Reading With Teddy	Retrd.	1995	79.00	79
1994	Teaching Teddy His Prayers	Open		79.00	79
1996	Teddy's Picnic	Open		79.00	79

Children's Circus Doll Collection - J. McClelland

YEAR	ISSUE	EDITION LIMIT	YEAR RETD.	ISSUE PRICE	*QUOTE U.S.$
1991	Johnny The Strongman	Yr.Iss.		83.00	83
1991	Katie The Tightrope Walker	Yr.Iss.		78.00	78
1992	Maggie The Animal Trainer	Yr.Iss.		83.00	83
1991	Tommy The Clown	Yr.Iss.		78.00	78

Precious Memories of Motherhood - S. Kuck

YEAR	ISSUE	EDITION LIMIT	YEAR RETD.	ISSUE PRICE	*QUOTE U.S.$
1993	Bedtime	Retrd.	1994	149.00	149
1992	Expectant Moments	Retrd.	1993	149.00	149
1990	Loving Steps	Retrd.	1993	125.00	150-195
1991	Lullaby	Retrd.	1995	125.00	125

Roman, Inc.

Abbie Williams Collection - E. Williams

YEAR	ISSUE	EDITION LIMIT	YEAR RETD.	ISSUE PRICE	*QUOTE U.S.$
1991	Molly	5,000		155.00	155

A Christmas Dream - E. Williams

YEAR	ISSUE	EDITION LIMIT	YEAR RETD.	ISSUE PRICE	*QUOTE U.S.$
1990	Carole	5,000		125.00	125
1990	Chelsea	5,000		125.00	125

Classic Brides of the Century - E. Williams

YEAR	ISSUE	EDITION LIMIT	YEAR RETD.	ISSUE PRICE	*QUOTE U.S.$
1991	Flora-The 1900's Bride	Yr.Iss.	1991	145.00	145
1992	Jennifer-The 1980's Bride	Yr.Iss.	1992	149.00	149
1993	Kathleen-The 1930's Bride	Yr.Iss.	1993	149.00	149

Ellen Williams Doll - E. Williams

YEAR	ISSUE	EDITION LIMIT	YEAR RETD.	ISSUE PRICE	*QUOTE U.S.$
1989	Noelle	5,000		125.00	125
1989	Rebecca 999	7,500		195.00	195

Sarah's Attic, Inc.

Heirlooms from the Attic - Sarah's Attic

YEAR	ISSUE	EDITION LIMIT	YEAR RETD.	ISSUE PRICE	*QUOTE U.S.$
1991	Adora 1823	500	1991	90.00	200
1991	All Cloth Muffin Bl. Doll 1820	Closed	1991	90.00	200
1991	All Cloth Puffin Bl. Doll 1821	Closed	1991	90.00	200
1992	Angelle Guardian Angel 3569	2,000	1993	170.00	170
1986	Cupcake Doll 0039B	Closed	1986	32.00	32
1991	Enos 1822	500	1991	90.00	200
1993	Granny Quilting Lady Doll 3576	Closed	1993	130.00	150
1992	Harpster w/Banjo 3591	Closed	1992	250.00	250

Sarah's Attic, Inc.
to Seymour Mann, Inc.

DOLLS

YEAR ISSUE		EDITION LIMIT	YEAR RETD.	ISSUE PRICE	*QUOTE U.S.$
1990	Hickory-Americana 1771	Closed	1993	150.00	170
1990	Hickory-Beachtime 1769	2,000	1993	140.00	150-175
1991	Hickory-Christmas 1810	2,000	1993	150.00	150-175
1990	Hickory-Playtime 1768	2,000	1993	140.00	175
1990	Hickory-School Days 1766	2,000	1993	140.00	175
1991	Hickory-Springtime 1814	2,000	1993	150.00	195
1990	Hickory-Sunday's Best 1770	2,000	1993	150.00	195
1990	Hickory-Sweet Dreams 1767	2,000	1993	140.00	175
1986	Holly Bl. Angel 0410	Retrd.	1986	34.00	200
1993	Jack Boy Doll 3893	500	1995	130.00	130
1986	Katie Doll 0039F	Closed	1986	32.00	32
1992	Kiah Guardian Angel 3570	2,000	1993	170.00	200
1993	Lilla Quilting Lady Doll 3581	Closed	1993	130.00	150
1986	Maggie Cloth Doll 0012	Closed	1989	70.00	120
1986	Maggie Cloth Doll 0039 D	Closed	1986	32.00	32
1986	Matt Cloth Doll 0011	Closed	1989	70.00	120
1986	Matt Cloth Doll 0039 C	Closed	1986	32.00	32
1993	Millie Quilting Lady Doll 3586	Closed	1993	130.00	130
1992	Peace on Earth Santa 3564	200	1992	175.00	350
1986	Priscilla Doll 0030	Closed	1989	140.00	300
1993	Sally Booba Doll 3890	500	1995	130.00	130
1990	Sassafras-Americana 1685	2,000	1993	150.00	175
1990	Sassafras-Beachtime 1683	2,000	1993	140.00	175
1991	Sassafras-Christmas 1809	2,000	1993	150.00	150-175
1990	Sassafras-Playtime 1682	2,000	1993	140.00	175
1989	Sassafras-School Days 1680	2,000	1993	140.00	175
1991	Sassafras-Springtime 1813	2,000	1993	150.00	195
1990	Sassafras-Sunday's Best 1684	2,000	1993	150.00	175
1990	Sassafras-Sweet Dreams 1681	2,000	1993	140.00	195
1988	Smiley Clown Doll 3050	Closed	1988	126.00	126
1986	Tillie Doll 0039J	Closed	1986	32.00	32
1987	Tillie Rag Doll 0344	Closed	1987	32.00	32
1994	Tillie-Clown 9601	1,000	1995	120.00	120
1986	Twinkie Doll 0039A	Closed	1986	32.00	32
1986	Whimpy Doll 0039E	Closed	1986	32.00	32
1992	Whoopie 3597	Closed	1992	200.00	200
1986	Willie Doll 0039I	Closed	1986	32.00	32
1995	Willie Doll 433	150		300.00	300
1994	Willie-Clown Doll 9601	1,000	1995	120.00	120
1992	Wooster 3602	Closed	1992	160.00	160

Seymour Mann, Inc.

Connoisseur Doll Collection - E. Mann

YEAR ISSUE		EDITION LIMIT	YEAR RETD.	ISSUE PRICE	*QUOTE U.S.$
1991	Abby 16" Pink Dress-C3145	Closed	1993	100.00	100
1995	Abby C-3229	2,500		30.00	30
1994	Abby YK-4533	3,500		135.00	135
1991	Abigail-EP-3	Closed	1993	100.00	100
1991	Abigail-WB-72WM	Closed	1993	75.00	75
1994	Adak PS-412	2,500		150.00	150
1993	Adrienne C-3162	Closed	1994	135.00	135
1995	Aggie PS-435	2,500		80.00	80
1991	Alexis 24" Beige Lace-EP32	Closed	1993	220.00	220
1995	Alice GU-32	2,500		150.00	150
1994	Alice IND-508	2,500	1995	115.00	115
1992	Alice-JNC-4013	Open	1993	90.00	90
1995	Alicia C-3235	2,500		65.00	65
1991	Alicia-YK-4215	Closed	1993	90.00	90
1995	Allison CD-18183	2,500		35.00	35
1995	Allison TR-92	2,500		125.00	125
1994	Ally FH-556	2,500	1995	115.00	115
1994	Alyssa C-3201	2,500	1995	110.00	110
1994	Alyssa PP-1	2,500		275.00	275
1991	Amanda Toast-OM-182	Closed	1993	260.00	260
1995	Amanda TR-96	2,500		135.00	135
1989	Amber-DOM-281A	Closed	1993	85.00	85
1991	Amelia-TR-47	Closed	1993	105.00	105
1991	Amy C-3147	Closed	1993	135.00	135
1995	Amy GU-300A	2,500	1995	30.00	30
1994	Amy OC-43M	2,500		115.00	115
1992	Amy OM-06	2,500	1993	150.00	150
1990	Anabelle C-3080	Closed	1992	85.00	85
1990	Angel DOM-335	Closed	1992	105.00	105
1995	Angel FH-291DP	2,500		70.00	70
1994	Angel LL-956	2,500		90.00	90
1994	Angel SP-460	2,500		140.00	140
1990	Angela C-3084	Closed	1992	105.00	105
1990	Angela C-3084M	Closed	1992	115.00	115
1995	Angela Doll 556	2,500		35.00	35
1995	Angela FH-511	2,500		85.00	85
1995	Angela OM-87	2,500		150.00	150
1995	Angelica FH-291B	2,500		70.00	70
1994	Angelica FH-291E	2,500		85.00	85
1995	Angelica FH-511B	2,500		85.00	85
1994	Angelina FH-291S	2,500		85.00	85
1995	Angelina FH-291S	2,500		70.00	70
1995	Angeline FH-291WG	2,500		75.00	75
1994	Angeline FH-291WG	2,500		85.00	85
1995	Angeline OM-84	2,500		100.00	100
1995	Angelique	2,500		150.00	150
1995	Angelita FH-291G	2,500		70.00	70
1994	Angelita FH-291G	2,500		85.00	85
1994	Angelo OC-57	2,500		135.00	135
1990	Anita FH-277G	Closed	1992	65.00	65
1991	Ann TR-52	Closed	1993	135.00	135
1995	Anna Doll 550	2,500		60.00	60
1995	Annette FH-635	2,500		110.00	110
1991	Annette-TR-59	Closed	1993	130.00	130
1991	Annie YK-4214	Closed	1993	145.00	145
1991	Antoinette FH-452	Closed	1993	100.00	100
1993	Antonia OM-227	2,500	1993	350.00	350

YEAR ISSUE		EDITION LIMIT	YEAR RETD.	ISSUE PRICE	*QUOTE U.S.$
1994	Antonia OM-42	2,500		150.00	150
1995	April CD-2212B	2,500		50.00	50
1991	Arabella-C-3163	Closed	1993	135.00	135
1991	Ariel 34" Blue/White-EP-33	Closed	1993	175.00	175
1995	Ariel OM-81	2,500		185.00	185
1994	Arilene LL-940	2,500	1994	90.00	90
1993	Arlene SP-421	Closed	1993	100.00	100
1988	Ashley C-278	Closed	1990	80.00	80
1989	Ashley C-278	Closed	1993	80.00	80
1990	Ashley FH-325	Closed	1993	75.00	75
1995	Ashley OC-76	2,500		40.00	40
1995	Ashley PS-433	2,500		110.00	110
1994	Atanak PS-414	2,500	1994	150.00	150
1991	Audrey FH-455	2,500	1993	125.00	125
1990	Audrey YK-4089	Closed	1992	125.00	125
1987	Audrina YK-200	Closed	1986	85.00	140
1991	Aurora Gold 22"-OM-181	2,500	1993	260.00	260
1991	Azure AM-15	2,500	1993	176.00	175
1994	Baby Belle C-3193	2,500	1994	150.00	150
1991	Baby Beth-DOLL-406P	2,500	1993	27.50	28
1995	Baby Betsy Doll 336	2,500		75.00	75
1990	Baby Betty YK-4087	Closed	1991	125.00	125
1990	Baby Bonnie SP-341	Closed	1991	55.00	55
1991	Baby Bonnie SP-341	Closed	1993	55.00	55
1991	Baby Bonnie w/Walker Music-DOLL-409	2,500	1993	40.00	40
1990	Baby Brent EP-15	Closed	1991	85.00	85
1991	Baby Brent EP-15	Closed	1993	85.00	85
1991	Baby Carrie DOLL-402P	2,500	1993	27.50	28
1990	Baby Ecru WB-17	Closed	1991	65.00	65
1991	Baby Ecru WB-17	Closed	1993	65.00	65
1991	Baby Ellie Ecru Musical DOLL-402E	2,500	1993	27.50	28
1991	Baby Gloria Black Baby PS-289	Closed	1993	75.00	75
1991	Baby John PS-498	Closed	1993	85.00	85
1989	Baby John PS-49B	Closed	1991	85.00	85
1990	Baby Kate WB-19	Closed	1991	85.00	85
1991	Baby Linda-DOLL-406E	2,500	1993	27.50	28
1990	Baby Nelly-PS-163	Closed	1991	95.00	95
1994	Baby Scarlet C-3194	2,500	1994	115.00	115
1991	Baby Sue-DOLL-402B	2,500	1993	27.50	28
1990	Baby Sue-DOLL-402B	Closed	1992	27.50	28
1990	Baby Sunshine-C-3055	Closed	1992	90.00	90
1995	Barbara PS-439	2,500		65.00	65
1995	Beige Angel FH-291E	2,500		70.00	70
1991	Belinda-C-3164	Closed	1993	150.00	150
1991	Bernetta-EP-40	Closed	1993	115.00	115
1995	Beth OC-74	2,500		40.00	40
1992	Beth-OM-05	Closed	1993	135.00	135
1990	Beth-YK-4099A/B	Closed	1992	125.00	125
1995	Betsy C-3224	2,500		45.00	45
1995	Betsy OM-89B	2,500		125.00	125
1995	Betsy RDK-230	2,500		35.00	35
1991	Betsy-AM-6	Closed	1993	105.00	105
1992	Bette-OM-01	2,500	1993	115.00	115
1990	Bettina-TR-4	Closed	1991	125.00	125
1991	Bettina-YK-4144	Closed	1993	105.00	105
1995	Betty LL-996	2,500		115.00	115
1989	Betty-PS27G	Closed	1993	65.00	125
1990	Beverly-DOLL-335	Closed	1992	110.00	110
1995	Bianca CD-1450C	2,500		35.00	35
1990	Billie-YK-4056V	Closed	1992	65.00	65
1993	Blaine C-3167	Closed	1993	100.00	100
1991	Blaine-TR-61	Closed	1993	115.00	115
1994	Blair YK-4532	3,500	1994	150.00	150
1991	Blythe-CH-15V	Closed	1993	135.00	135
1991	Bo-Peep w/Lamb-C-3128	Closed	1993	105.00	105
1994	Bobbi NM-30	2,500	1994	135.00	135
1994	Brandy YK-4537	3,500	1995	165.00	165
1995	Brenda Doll 551	2,500		60.00	60
1989	Brett-PS27B	Closed	1992	65.00	125
1995	Brianna GU-300B	2,500		30.00	30
1991	Bridget-SP-379	2,500	1993	105.00	105
1995	Brie C-3230	2,500		30.00	30
1995	Brie CD-16310C	2,500		30.00	30
1995	Brie OM-89W	2,500		125.00	125
1995	Britt OC-77	2,500		40.00	40
1995	Brittany Doll 558	2,500		35.00	35
1989	Brittany-TK-4	Closed	1990	150.00	150
1988	Brittany-TK-5	Closed	1990	120.00	120
1994	Bronwyn IND-517	2,500	1994	140.00	140
1991	Brooke-FH-461	2,500	1993	115.00	115
1995	Bryna Doll 555	2,500		35.00	35
1991	Bryna-AM-100B	2,500	1993	70.00	70
1995	Bunny TR-97	2,500		85.00	85
1995	Burgundy Angel FH-291D	2,500		75.00	75
1994	Cactus Flower Indian LL-944	2,500	1994	105.00	105
1990	Caillin-DOLL-11PH	Closed	1992	60.00	60
1995	Caitlin LL-997	2,500		115.00	115
1990	Caitlin-YK-4051V	Closed	1992	90.00	90
1994	Callie TR-76	2,500	1994	140.00	140
1994	Calypso LL-942	2,500	1994	150.00	150
1991	Camellia-FH-457	2,500	1993	100.00	100
1986	Camelot Fairy-C-84	Closed	1988	75.00	225
1993	Camille OM-230	2,500	1994	250.00	250
1995	Candice TR-94	2,500	1995	135.00	135
1995	Carmel TR-93	2,500		125.00	125
1994	Carmen PS-408	2,500	1994	150.00	150
1990	Carole-YK-4085W	Closed	1992	125.00	125
1991	Caroline-LL-838	2,500	1993	110.00	110
1991	Caroline-LL-905	2,500	1993	110.00	110
1995	Carolotta OM-80	2,500		175.00	175

YEAR ISSUE		EDITION LIMIT	YEAR RETD.	ISSUE PRICE	*QUOTE U.S.$
1995	Carrie C-3231	2,500		30.00	30
1994	Casey C-3197	2,500		140.00	140
1995	Catherine RDK-231	2,500		30.00	30
1994	Cathy GU-41	2,500	1994	140.00	140
1995	Cecily Doll 552	2,500		60.00	60
1995	Celene FH-618	2,500		120.00	120
1995	Celestine LL-982	2,500		100.00	100
1990	Charlene-YK-4112	Closed	1992	90.00	90
1992	Charlotte-FH-484	2,500	1993	115.00	115
1995	Chelsea Doll 560	2,500		35.00	35
1992	Chelsea-IND-397	Open	1993	85.00	85
1995	Cherry FH-616	2,500	1994	100.00	100
1991	Cheryl-TR-49	2,500	1993	120.00	120
1991	Chin Chin-YK-4211	Closed	1993	85.00	85
1990	Chin Fa-C-3061	Closed	1992	95.00	95
1990	Chinook-WB-24	Closed	1992	85.00	85
1994	Chris FH-561	2,500	1994	85.00	85
1994	Chrissie FH-562	2,500	1994	85.00	85
1990	Chrissie-WB-2	Closed	1992	75.00	75
1991	Christina-PS-261	Closed	1993	115.00	115
1985	Christmas Cheer-125	Closed	1988	40.00	100
1995	Christmas Kitten IND-530	2,500		100.00	100
1991	Cindy Lou-FH-464	2,500	1993	85.00	85
1994	Cindy OC-58	2,500	1994	140.00	140
1993	Cinnamon JNC-4014	Closed	1993	90.00	90
1988	Cissie-DOM263	Closed	1990	65.00	135
1991	Cissy-EP-56	2,500	1993	95.00	95
1995	Clancy GU-54	2,500	1995	80.00	80
1994	Clara IND-518	2,500	1994	140.00	140
1994	Clara IND-524	2,500	1994	150.00	150
1993	Clare FH-497	2,500	1993	100.00	100
1991	Clare-DOLL-465	Open	1993	100.00	100
1994	Claudette TR-81	2,500	1995	150.00	150
1991	Claudine-C-3146	Closed	1993	95.00	95
1993	Clothilde FH-469	2,500	1993	125.00	125
1995	Cody FH-629	2,500	1995	120.00	120
1991	Colette-WB-7	Closed	1993	65.00	65
1991	Colleen-YK-4163	Closed	1993	120.00	120
1991	Cookie-GU-6	2,500	1993	110.00	110
1994	Copper YK-4546C	3,500		150.00	150
1994	Cora FH-565	2,500		140.00	140
1992	Cordelia-OM-009	2,500	1993	250.00	250
1992	Cordelia-OM-09	2,500	1993	250.00	250
1994	Cory FH-564	2,500	1994	115.00	115
1991	Courtney-LL-859	2,500	1993	150.00	150
1991	Creole-AM-17	2,500	1993	160.00	160
1989	Crying Courtney-PS-75	Closed	1992	115.00	115
1988	Crying Courtney-PS75	Closed	1990	115.00	115
1991	Crystal-YK-4237	3,500	1993	125.00	125
1995	Cynthia GU-300C	2,500		30.00	30
1987	Cynthia-DOM-211	Closed	1986	85.00	85
1988	Cynthia-DOM-211	3,500	1990	85.00	85
1990	Daisy-EP-6	Closed	1992	90.00	90
1994	Dallas PS-403	2,500	1994	150.00	150
1995	Danielle MER-808	2,500		65.00	65
1995	Danielle PS-432	2,500		100.00	100
1991	Danielle-AM-5	Closed	1993	125.00	125
1990	Daphne Ecru-C-3025	Closed	1992	85.00	85
1989	Daphne Ecru/Mint Green-C3025	Closed	1990	85.00	85
1995	Darcy FH-636	2,500		80.00	80
1995	Darcy LL-986	2,500		110.00	110
1991	Darcy-EP-47	Closed	1993	110.00	110
1991	Darcy-FH-451	2,500	1993	105.00	105
1991	Daria-C-3122	Closed	1993	110.00	110
1995	Darla LL-988	2,500		100.00	100
1991	Darlene-DOLL-444	2,500	1993	75.00	75
1994	Daryl LL-947	2,500	1994	150.00	150
1991	Dawn-C-3135	Closed	1993	130.00	130
1987	Dawn-C185	Closed	1986	75.00	175
1992	Debbie-JNC-4006	Open	1993	90.00	90
1994	Dee LL-948	2,500	1994	110.00	110
1992	Deidre-FH-473	2,500	1993	115.00	115
1992	Deidre-YK-4083	Closed	1993	95.00	95
1994	Delilah C-3195	2,500	1994	150.00	150
1995	Denise LL-994	2,500		105.00	105
1991	Denise-LL-852	2,500	1993	105.00	105
1991	Dephine-SP-308	Closed	1993	135.00	135
1991	Desiree-LL-898	2,500	1993	120.00	120
1995	Diana RDK-221A	2,500		35.00	35
1995	Diane PS-444	2,500		110.00	110
1990	Diane-FH-275	Closed	1992	90.00	90
1990	Dianna-TK-31	Closed	1992	175.00	175
1995	Dinah OC-79	2,500		40.00	40
1988	Doll Oliver-FH392	Closed	1990	100.00	100
1990	Domino-C-3050	Closed	1992	145.00	200
1992	Dona-FH-494	2,500	1993	100.00	100
1993	Donna DOLL-447	2,500	1993	85.00	85
1995	Donna GU-300D	2,500		30.00	30
1990	Dorothy-TR-10	Closed	1992	135.00	150
1990	Dorri-DOLL-16PH	Closed	1992	85.00	85
1991	Duanane-SP-366	Closed	1993	85.00	85
1995	Dulcie FH-622	2,500		110.00	110
1991	Dulcie-YK-4131V	Closed	1993	100.00	100
1991	Dwayne-C-3123	Closed	1993	120.00	120
1991	Edie -YK-4177	Closed	1993	115.00	115
1990	Eileen-FH-367	Closed	1992	100.00	100
1995	Elaine CD-02210	2,500		50.00	50
1995	Eleanor C16669	2,500		35.00	35
1991	Elisabeth and Lisa-C-3095	2,500	1993	195.00	195
1989	Elisabeth-OM-32	Closed	1990	120.00	120
1991	Elise -PS-259	Closed	1993	105.00	105
1995	Elizabeth Doll 553	2,500		35.00	35

*Quotes have been rounded up to nearest dollar

DOLLS

YEAR ISSUE		EDITION LIMIT	YEAR RETD.	ISSUE PRICE	*QUOTE U.S.$
1991	Elizabeth-AM-32	2,500	1993	105.00	105
1989	Elizabeth-C-246P	Closed	1990	150.00	200
1993	Ellen YK-4223	3,500	1994	150.00	150
1995	Ellie FH-621	2,500		125.00	125
1989	Emily-PS-48	Closed	1990	110.00	110
1988	Emily-YK-243V	Closed	1990	70.00	70
1995	Emma Doll 559	2,500		35.00	35
1995	Emma GU-300E	2,500		30.00	30
1991	Emmaline Beige/Lilac-OM-197	Closed	1993	300.00	300
1991	Emmaline-OM-191	2,500	1993	300.00	300
1991	Emmy-C-3099	Closed	1993	125.00	125
1995	Erin RDK-223	2,500		30.00	30
1991	Erin-DOLL-4PH	Closed	1993	60.00	60
1992	Eugenie-OM-225	2,500	1993	300.00	300
1991	Evalina-C-3124	Closed	1993	135.00	135
1994	Faith IND-522	2,500	1994	135.00	135
1994	Faith OC-60	2,500	1994	115.00	115
1995	Fawn C-3228	2,500		55.00	55
1995	Felicia GU-300F	2,500		30.00	30
1990	Felicia-TR-9	Closed	1992	115.00	115
1991	Fifi-AM-100F	Closed	1993	70.00	70
1995	Fleur C16415	2,500		30.00	30
1991	Fleurette-PS-286	2,500	1993	75.00	75
1994	Flora FH-583	2,500	1994	115.00	115
1991	Flora-TR-46	Closed	1993	125.00	125
1994	Florette IND-519	2,500	1994	140.00	140
1988	Frances-C-233	Closed	1990	80.00	125
1989	Frances-C233	Closed	1990	80.00	125
1991	Francesca-AM-14	2,500	1993	175.00	175
1990	Francesca-C-3021	Closed	1992	100.00	175
1994	Gardiner PS-405	2,500		150.00	150
1993	Gena OM-229	Closed	1994	250.00	250
1994	Georgia IND-510	2,500	1995	220.00	220
1995	Georgia IND-528	2,500		125.00	125
1994	Georgia SP-456	2,500		115.00	115
1991	Georgia-YK-4131	Closed	1993	100.00	100
1991	Georgia-YK-4143	Closed	1993	150.00	150
1990	Gerri Beige-YK4094	Closed	1992	95.00	140
1991	Gigi-C-3107	Closed	1993	135.00	135
1991	Ginger-LL-907	Closed	1993	115.00	115
1995	Ginnie FH-619	2,500		110.00	110
1990	Ginny-YK-4119	Closed	1995	100.00	100
1988	Giselle on Goose-FH176	Closed	1990	105.00	225
1992	Giselle-OM-02	Closed	1993	90.00	90
1991	Gloria-AM-100G	2,500	1993	70.00	70
1991	Gloria-YK-4166	Closed	1993	105.00	105
1995	Gold Angel FH-511G	2,500		85.00	85
1995	Green Angel FH-511C	2,500		85.00	85
1995	Gretchen FH-620	2,500	1995	120.00	120
1991	Gretchen-DOLL-446	Open	1993	45.00	45
1991	Gretel-DOLL-434	Closed	1993	60.00	60
1995	Guardian Angel TR-98	2,500		85.00	85
1995	Guardian Angel OM-91	2,500		150.00	150
1991	Hansel and Gretel-DOLL-448V	Closed	1993	60.00	60
1989	Happy Birthday-C3012	Closed	1990	80.00	125
1993	Happy FH-479	2,500	1994	105.00	105
1995	Happy RDK-238	2,500		25.00	25
1994	Hatty/Matty IND-514	2,500		165.00	165
1995	Heather LL-991	2,500		115.00	115
1995	Heather PS-436	2,500		115.00	115
1994	Heather YK-4531	3,500		165.00	165
1993	Hedy FH-449	Closed	1994	95.00	95
1989	Heidi-260	Closed	1990	50.00	95
1991	Helene-AM-29	2,500	1993	150.00	150
1995	Holly CD-16526	2,500		30.00	30
1991	Holly-CH-6	Closed	1993	100.00	100
1991	Honey Bunny-WB-9	Closed	1993	70.00	70
1994	Honey LL-945	2,500		150.00	150
1991	Honey-FH-401	Closed	1993	100.00	100
1991	Hope-FH-434	2,500	1993	90.00	90
1990	Hope-YK-4118	Closed	1992	90.00	90
1995	Hyacinth C-3227	2,500		130.00	130
1994	Hyacinth LL-941	2,500	1995	90.00	90
1990	Hyacinth-DOLL-15PH	Closed	1992	85.00	85
1990	Indian Doll-FH-295	Closed	1992	60.00	60
1994	Indian IND-520	2,500		115.00	115
1991	Indira-AM-4	2,500	1993	125.00	125
1995	Irene GU-56	2,500		85.00	85
1995	Irina RDK-237	2,500		35.00	35
1993	Iris FH-483	2,500	1994	95.00	95
1991	Iris-TR-58	Closed	1993	120.00	120
1995	Ivana RDK-233	2,500		35.00	35
1994	Ivy C-3203	2,500		85.00	85
1991	Ivy-PS-307	Closed	1993	75.00	75
1994	Jacqueline C-3202	2,500		150.00	150
1995	Jamaica LL-989	2,500		75.00	75
1993	Jan Dress-Up OM-12	2,500	1994	135.00	135
1994	Jan FH-584R	2,500		115.00	115
1992	Jan-OM-012	9,200	1993	135.00	135
1991	Jane-PS-243L	Closed	1993	115.00	115
1992	Janet-FH-496	2,500	1993	120.00	120
1990	Janette-DOLL-385	Closed	1992	85.00	85
1991	Janice-OM-194	2,500	1993	300.00	300
1994	Janis FH-584B	2,500		115.00	115
1989	Jaqueline-DOLL-254M	Closed	1990	85.00	85
1995	Jennifer PS-446	2,500		145.00	145
1995	Jenny CD-16673B	2,500		35.00	35
1994	Jenny OC-36M	2,500		115.00	115
1995	Jerri PS-434	2,500		100.00	100
1995	Jessica RDK-225	2,500		30.00	30
1988	Jessica-DOM-267	Closed	1990	90.00	90
1991	Jessica-FH-423	2,500	1993	95.00	95
1992	Jet-FH-478	2,500	1993	115.00	115
1995	Jewel TR-100	2,500		110.00	110
1994	Jillian C-3196	2,500		150.00	150
1993	Jillian SP-428	Closed	1994	165.00	165
1990	Jillian-DOLL-41PH	Closed	1992	90.00	90
1994	Jo YK-4539	3,500	1995	150.00	150
1988	Joanne Cry Baby-PS-50	Closed	1990	100.00	100
1989	Joanne Cry Baby-PS-50	2,500	1991	100.00	100
1990	Joanne-TR-12	Closed	1992	175.00	175
1992	Jodie-FH-495	2,500	1993	115.00	115
1995	Joella CD-16779	2,500		35.00	35
1988	Jolie-C231	Closed	1990	65.00	150
1994	Jordan SP-455	2,500		150.00	150
1995	Joy CD-1450A	2,500		35.00	35
1995	Joy TR-99	2,500		85.00	135
1991	Joy-EP-23V	Closed	1993	130.00	130
1991	Joyce-AM-100J	2,500	1993	35.00	35
1995	Julia C-3234	2,500		100.00	100
1995	Julia RDK-222	2,500		35.00	35
1991	Julia-C-3102	Closed	1993	135.00	135
1988	Julie-C245A	Closed	1990	65.00	160
1990	Julie-WB-35	Closed	1992	70.00	70
1988	Juliette Bride Musical-C246LTM	Closed	1990	150.00	200
1993	Juliette OM-8	2,500	1994	175.00	175
1992	Juliette-OM-08	2,500	1993	175.00	175
1991	Juliette-OM-192	2,500	1993	300.00	300
1995	June CD-2212	2,500		50.00	50
1991	Karen-EP-24	Closed	1993	115.00	115
1990	Karen-PS-198	Closed	1992	150.00	150
1991	Karmela-EP-57	2,500	1993	120.00	120
1995	Karyn RDK-224	2,500		35.00	35
1994	Kate OC-55	2,500		150.00	150
1990	Kate-C-3060	Closed	1992	95.00	95
1990	Kathy w/Bear-TE1	Closed	1992	70.00	70
1994	Katie IND-511	2,500		110.00	110
1989	Kayoko-PS-24	Closed	1991	75.00	175
1994	Kelly YK-4536	3,500		150.00	150
1991	Kelly-AM-8	Closed	1993	125.00	125
1995	Kelsey Doll 561	2,500		35.00	35
1993	Kendra FH-481	2,500	1994	115.00	115
1991	Kerry-FH-396	Closed	1993	100.00	100
1994	Kevin MS-25	2,500		150.00	150
1994	Kevin YK-4543	3,500		140.00	140
1990	Kiku-EP-4	Closed	1992	100.00	100
1991	Kim-AM-100K	2,500	1993	70.00	70
1995	Kimmie CD-15816	2,500		30.00	30
1991	Kinesha-SP-402	2,500	1993	110.00	110
1988	Kirsten-PS-40G	Closed	1990	70.00	70
1989	Kirsten-PS-40G	Closed	1991	70.00	70
1993	Kit SP-426	Closed	1994	55.00	55
1994	Kit YK-4547	3,500		115.00	115
1994	Kitten IND-512	2,500		110.00	110
1995	Kitty IND-527	2,500		40.00	40
1991	Kristi-FH-402	Closed	1993	100.00	100
1991	Kyla-YK-4137	Closed	1993	95.00	95
1994	Lady Caroline LL-938	2,500		120.00	120
1994	Lady Caroline LL-939	2,500		120.00	120
1994	Laughing Waters PS-410	2,500		150.00	150
1990	Laura-DOLL-25PH	Closed	1992	55.00	55
1992	Laura-OM-010	2,500	1993	250.00	250
1991	Laura-WB-110P	Closed	1993	85.00	85
1994	Lauren SP-458	2,500		125.00	125
1990	Lauren-SP-300	Closed	1992	85.00	85
1992	Laurie-JNC-4004	Open	1993	90.00	90
1990	Lavender Blue-YK-4024	Closed	1992	95.00	135
1991	Leigh-DOLL-457	2,500	1993	95.00	95
1991	Leila-AM-2	Closed	1993	125.00	125
1995	Lenore FH-617	2,500		120.00	120
1995	Lenore RDK-229	2,500		50.00	50
1991	Lenore-LL-911	2,500	1993	105.00	105
1991	Lenore-YK-4218	3,500	1995	135.00	135
1995	Leslie LL-983	2,500		105.00	105
1995	Leslie MER-809	2,500		65.00	65
1991	Libby-EP-18	Closed	1993	85.00	85
1990	Lien Wha-YK-4092	Closed	1992	100.00	100
1995	Lila GU-55	2,500		55.00	55
1991	Lila-AM-10	2,500	1993	125.00	125
1991	Lila-FH-404	2,500	1993	100.00	100
1995	Lili CD-16888	2,500		30.00	30
1995	Lily FH-630	2,500		120.00	120
1995	Lily in pink stripe IND-533	2,500	1995	85.00	85
1993	Linda SP-435	Closed	1994	95.00	95
1987	Linda-C190	Closed	1986	60.00	120
1995	Lindsay PS-442	2,500		175.00	175
1994	Lindsay SP-462	2,500		150.00	150
1991	Lindsey-C-3127	Closed	1993	135.00	135
1991	Linetta-C-3166	Closed	1993	135.00	135
1990	Ling-Ling-DOLL	Closed	1992	50.00	50
1989	Ling-Ling-PS-87G	Closed	1991	90.00	90
1988	Lionel-FH206B	Closed	1990	50.00	120
1990	Lisa Beige Accordion Pleat-YK4093	Closed	1992	125.00	125
1991	Lisa-AM-100L	2,500	1993	70.00	70
1990	Lisa-FH-379	Closed	1992	100.00	100
1995	Lisette LL-993	2,500		105.00	105
1995	Little Bobby RDK-235	2,500		25.00	25
1991	Little Boy Blue-C-3159	Closed	1993	100.00	100
1995	Little Lisa OM-86	2,500		125.00	125
1995	Little Lori RDK-228	2,500		20.00	20
1995	Little Lou RDK-227	2,500		20.00	20
1995	Little Mary RDK-234	2,500		25.00	25
1995	Little Patty PS-429	2,500		50.00	50
1994	Little Red Riding Hood FH-557	2,500		140.00	140
1989	Liz -YK-269	Closed	1991	70.00	100
1991	Liz-C-3150	2,500	1993	100.00	100
1990	Liza-C-3053	Closed	1992	100.00	100
1991	Liza-YK-4226	3,500	1993	35.00	35
1991	Lola-SP-363	2,500	1993	90.00	90
1990	Lola-SP-79	Closed	1992	105.00	105
1991	Loni-FH-448	2,500	1993	100.00	100
1994	Loretta SP-457	2,500		140.00	140
1990	Loretta-FH-321	Closed	1992	90.00	90
1991	Lori-EP-52	2,500	1993	95.00	95
1990	Lori-WB-72BM	Closed	1992	75.00	75
1991	Louise-LL-908	2,500	1993	105.00	105
1995	Lucie MER-607	2,500		65.00	65
1989	Lucinda -DOM-293	Closed	1990	90.00	90
1994	Lucinda PS-406	2,500		150.00	150
1988	Lucinda-DOM-293	Closed	1990	90.00	90
1991	Lucy-LL-853	Closed	1993	80.00	80
1992	Lydia-OM-226	2,500	1993	250.00	250
1993	Lynn FH-498	2,500	1994	120.00	120
1995	Lynn LL-995	2,500		105.00	105
1990	Madame De Pompadour-C-3088	Closed	1992	250.00	250
1991	Madeleine-C-3106	Closed	1993	95.00	95
1995	Mae PS-431	2,500		70.00	70
1995	Maggie IND-532	2,500		80.00	80
1992	Maggie-FH-505	Closed	1993	125.00	125
1990	Maggie-PS-151P	Closed	1992	90.00	90
1990	Maggie-WB-51	Closed	1992	105.00	105
1994	Magnolia FH-558	2,500		150.00	150
1989	Mai-Ling-PS-79	2,500	1991	100.00	100
1994	Maiden PS-409	2,500	1995	150.00	150
1994	Mandy YK-4548	3,500		115.00	115
1989	Marcey-YK-4005	3,500	1995	90.00	90
1991	Marcy-TR-55	Closed	1993	135.00	135
1987	Marcy-YK122	Closed	1986	55.00	100
1994	Margaret C-3204	2,500		150.00	150
1989	Margaret-245	Closed	1991	100.00	150
1994	Maria GU-35	2,500		115.00	115
1990	Maria-YK-4116	Closed	1992	85.00	85
1993	Mariah LL-909	Closed	1993	135.00	135
1991	Mariel 18" Ivory-C-3119	Closed	1993	125.00	125
1995	Marielle PS-443	2,500		175.00	175
1995	Marla PS-437	2,500		125.00	125
1995	Martina RDK-232	2,500		35.00	35
1995	Mary Ann FH-633	2,500		110.00	110
1994	Mary Ann TR-79	2,500		125.00	125
1995	Mary Elizabeth OC-51	2,500		50.00	50
1994	Mary Jo FH-552	2,500		150.00	150
1994	Mary Lou FH-565	2,500		135.00	135
1994	Mary OC-56	2,500		135.00	135
1991	Maude-AM-100M	2,500	1993	70.00	70
1989	Maureen-PS-84	Closed	1990	90.00	90
1995	Maxine C-3225	2,500		125.00	125
1995	Mc Kenzie LL-987	2,500		100.00	100
1994	Megan C-3192	2,500		150.00	150
1995	Megan RDK-220	2,500		30.00	30
1989	Meimei-PS22	Closed	1990	75.00	225
1990	Melanie-YK-4115	Closed	1992	80.00	80
1991	Melissa-AM-9	Closed	1993	120.00	120
1991	Melissa-CH-3	Closed	1993	110.00	110
1990	Melissa-DOLL-390	Closed	1992	75.00	75
1989	Melissa-LL-794	Closed	1990	95.00	95
1991	Melissa-LL-901	Closed	1993	135.00	135
1992	Melissa-OM-03	2,500	1993	135.00	135
1995	Meredith MER-806	2,500		65.00	65
1991	Meredith-FH-391-P	Closed	1993	95.00	95
1995	Merri MER-810	2,500		65.00	65
1990	Merry Widow 20"-C-3040M	Closed	1992	140.00	140
1990	Merry Widow-C-3040	Closed	1992	145.00	145
1991	Meryl-FH-463	2,500	1993	95.00	95
1991	Michael w/School Books-FH-439B	2,500	1993	95.00	95
1988	Michelle & Marcel-YK176	Closed	1990	70.00	150
1991	Michelle Lilac/Green-EP36	Closed	1993	95.00	95
1991	Michelle w/School Books-FH-439G	Closed	1993	95.00	95
1995	Mindi PS-441	2,500	1995	125.00	125
1995	Mindy LL-990	2,500		75.00	75
1995	Miranda C16456B	2,500		30.00	30
1995	Miranda TR-91	2,500		135.00	135
1991	Miranda-DOLL-9PH	Closed	1993	75.00	75
1984	Miss Debutante Debi	Closed	1987	75.00	180
1994	Miss Elizabeth SP-459	2,500		150.00	150
1989	Miss Kim-PS-25	Closed	1990	75.00	175
1994	Missy FH-567	2,500		140.00	140
1991	Missy-DOLL-464	Closed	1993	70.00	70
1991	Missy-PS-258	Closed	1993	90.00	90
1991	Mon Yun w/Parasol-TR33	2,500	1993	115.00	115
1995	Monica TR-95	2,500		135.00	135
1994	Morning Dew Indian PS-404	2,500		150.00	150
1994	Musical Doll OC-45M	2,500		140.00	140
1991	Nancy -WB-73	2,500	1993	65.00	65
1991	Nancy 21" Pink w/Rabbit-EP-31	Closed	1993	165.00	165
1995	Nancy FH-615	2,500		100.00	100
1992	Nancy-JNC-4001	Open	1993	90.00	90
1990	Nanook-WB-23	Closed	1992	75.00	75
1994	Natalie PP-2	2,500		275.00	275
1995	Natasha TR-90	2,500		125.00	125
1990	Natasha-PS-102	Closed	1992	100.00	100

*Quotes have been rounded up to nearest dollar

YEAR ISSUE		EDITION LIMIT	YEAR RETD.	ISSUE PRICE	*QUOTE U.S.$
1991	Nellie-EP-1B	Closed	1993	75.00	75
1991	Nicole-AM-12	Closed	1993	135.00	135
1994	Nikki PS-401	2,500	1995	150.00	150
1994	Nikki SP-461	2,500		150.00	150
1993	Nina YK-4232	3,500	1993	135.00	135
1987	Nirmala-YK-210	Closed	1995	50.00	50
1994	Noel MS-27	2,500		150.00	150
1994	Noelle C-3199	2,500		195.00	195
1994	Noelle MS-28	2,500		150.00	150
1991	Noelle-PS-239V	Closed	1993	95.00	95
1995	Norma C-3226	2,500		135.00	135
1990	Odessa-FH-362	Closed	1992	65.00	65
1994	Odetta IND-521	2,500	1995	140.00	140
1993	Oona TR-57	Closed	1993	135.00	135
1994	Oriana IND-515	2,500		140.00	140
1995	Our First Skates RDK-226/BG	2,500		50.00	50
1994	Paige GU-33	2,500		150.00	150
1995	Paige IND-529	2,500		80.00	80
1994	Pamela LL-949	2,500		115.00	115
1995	Pan Pan GU-52	2,500		60.00	60
1994	Panama OM-43	2,500		195.00	195
1989	Patricia/Patrick-215GBB	Closed	1990	105.00	135
1991	Patti-DOLL-440	2,500	1993	65.00	65
1995	Patty C-3220	2,500		60.00	60
1994	Patty GU-34	2,500		115.00	115
1991	Patty-YK-4221	3,500	1993	125.00	125
1989	Paula-PS-56	Closed	1990	75.00	75
1995	Paulette PS-430	2,500		80.00	80
1989	Pauline Bonaparte-OM68	Closed	1990	120.00	120
1995	Pauline PS-440	2,500		65.00	65
1988	Pauline-YK-230	Closed	1990	90.00	90
1994	Payson YK-4541	3,500		135.00	135
1994	Payton PS-407	2,500	1995	150.00	150
1995	Peaches IND-531	2,500		80.00	80
1994	Pearl IND-523	2,500		275.00	275
1994	Pegeen C-3205	2,500		150.00	150
1994	Peggy TR-75	2,500		185.00	185
1991	Pepper-PS-277	Closed	1993	130.00	130
1994	Petula C-3191	2,500		140.00	140
1991	Pia-PS-246L	Closed	1993	115.00	115
1990	Ping-Ling-DOLL-363RV	Closed	1992	50.00	50
1990	Polly-DOLL-22PH	Closed	1992	90.00	90
1990	Princess Fair Skies-FH-268B	Closed	1992	75.00	75
1994	Princess Foxfire PS-411	2,500		150.00	150
1994	Princess Moonrise YK-4542	3,500		140.00	140
1990	Princess Red Feather-PS-189	Closed	1992	90.00	90
1994	Princess Snow Flower PS-402	2,500	1995	150.00	150
1991	Princess Summer Winds-FH-427	2,500	1993	120.00	120
1994	Priscilla YK-4538	3,500		135.00	135
1990	Priscilla-WB-50	Closed	1992	105.00	105
1991	Prissy White/Blue-C-3140	Closed	1993	100.00	100
1995	Rainie LL-984	2,500		125.00	125
1989	Ramona-PS-31B	Closed	1992	80.00	80
1991	Rapunzel-C-3157	2,500	1993	150.00	150
1987	Rapunzel-C158	Closed	1986	95.00	165
1994	Rebecca C-3177	2,500		135.00	135
1993	Rebecca C-3177	2,500	1993	135.00	135
1989	Rebecca-PS-34V	Closed	1992	45.00	45
1991	Red Wing-AM-30	2,500	1993	165.00	165
1994	Regina OM-41	2,500		150.00	150
1994	Rita FH-553	2,500		115.00	115
1994	Robby NM-29	2,500		135.00	135
1995	Robin C-3236	2,500		60.00	60
1991	Robin-AM-22	Closed	1993	120.00	120
1991	Rosalind-C-3090	Closed	1992	150.00	150
1989	Rosie-290M	Closed	1992	55.00	85
1995	Rusty CD-1450B	2,500		35.00	35
1988	Sabrina -C-208	Closed	1990	65.00	95
1987	Sabrina-C208	Closed	1986	65.00	95
1990	Sabrina-C3050	Closed	1992	105.00	105
1987	Sailorette-DOM217	Closed	1986	70.00	150
1992	Sally-FH-492	2,500	1993	105.00	105
1990	Sally-WB-20	Closed	1992	95.00	95
1991	Samantha-GU-3	Closed	1992	100.00	100
1995	San San GU-53	2,500		60.00	60
1991	Sandra-DOLL-6-PHE	2,500	1992	65.00	65
1992	Sapphires-OM-223	2,500	1993	250.00	250
1992	Sara Ann-FH-474	2,500	1993	115.00	115
1995	Sarah C-3214	2,500		110.00	110
1994	Saretta SP-423	2,500		100.00	100
1993	Saretta SP-423	2,500	1993	100.00	100
1995	Sasha GU-57	2,500		75.00	75
1991	Scarlett-FH-399	2,500	1992	100.00	100
1991	Scarlett-FH-436	2,500	1992	135.00	135
1992	Scarlett-FH-471	2,500	1993	120.00	120
1993	Shaka TR-45	2,500	1993	100.00	100
1994	Shaka TR-45	2,500		100.00	100
1991	Shaka-SP-401	2,500	1992	110.00	110
1991	Sharon 21" Blue-EP-34	Closed	1992	120.00	120
1995	Sharon C-3237	2,500		95.00	95
1991	Shau Chen-GU-2	2,500	1992	85.00	85
1991	Shelley-CH-1	2,500	1992	110.00	110
1995	Shimmering Caroline LL-992	2,500		115.00	115
1990	Shirley-WB-37	Closed	1992	65.00	65
1988	Sister Agnes 14"-C250	Closed	1990	75.00	75
1988	Sister Ignatius Notre Dame-FH184	Closed	1990	75.00	75
1989	Sister Mary-C-249	Closed	1992	75.00	125
1990	Sister Mary-WB-15	Closed	1992	70.00	70
1994	Sister Suzie IND-509	2,500	1995	95.00	95
1988	Sister Teresa-FH187	Closed	1990	80.00	80
1995	Sleeping Beauty OM-88	2,500		115.00	115

YEAR ISSUE		EDITION LIMIT	YEAR RETD.	ISSUE PRICE	*QUOTE U.S.$
1992	Sonja-FH-486	2,500	1994	125.00	125
1995	Sophia PS-445	2,500		125.00	125
1990	Sophie-OM-1	Closed	1992	65.00	65
1991	Sophie-TR-53	2,500	1992	135.00	135
1995	Southern Belle Bride FH-637	2,500		160.00	160
1994	Southern Belle FH-570	2,500		140.00	140
1994	Sparkle OM-40	2,500		150.00	150
1995	Stacy FH-634	2,500		110.00	110
1995	Stacy OC-75	2,500		40.00	40
1991	Stacy-DOLL-6PH	Closed	1992	65.00	65
1990	Stacy-TR-5	Closed	1992	105.00	105
1991	Stephanie Pink & White-OM-196	Closed	1992	300.00	300
1991	Stephanie-AM-11	Closed	1992	105.00	105
1991	Stephanie-FH-467	Closed	1992	95.00	95
1994	Stephie OC-41M	2,500		115.00	115
1990	Sue Chuen-C-3061G	Closed	1992	95.00	95
1994	Sue Kwei TR-73	2,500		110.00	110
1992	Sue-JNC-4003	Closed	1994	90.00	90
1994	Sugar Plum Fairy OM-39	2,500		150.00	150
1991	Summer-AM-33	Closed	1992	200.00	200
1990	Sunny-FH-331	Closed	1992	70.00	70
1989	Sunny-PS-59V	Closed	1992	71.00	71
1990	Susan-DOLL-364MC	Closed	1992	75.00	75
1995	Suzanna Doll 554	2,500		35.00	35
1994	Suzanne LL-943	2,500		105.00	105
1994	Suzie GU-38	2,500		135.00	135
1995	Suzie OC-80	2,500		50.00	50
1993	Suzie SP-422	2,500	1993	164.00	164
1994	Suzie SP-422	2,500		164.00	164
1989	Suzie-PS-32	Closed	1992	80.00	80
1995	Sweet Pea LL-981	2,500		90.00	90
1991	Sybil 20" Beige-C-3131	Closed	1992	135.00	135
1991	Sybil Pink-DOLL-12PHMC	2,500	1992	75.00	75
1995	Sylvie CD-16634B	2,500		35.00	35
1995	Tabitha C-3233	2,500		50.00	50
1994	Taffey TR-80	2,500		150.00	150
1994	Tallulah OM-44	2,500		275.00	275
1991	Tamara-OM-187	Closed	1992	135.00	135
1990	Tania-DOLL-376P	Closed	1992	65.00	65
1989	Tatiana Pink Ballerina-OM-60	Closed	1991	120.00	175
1994	Teresa C-3198	2,500	1995	110.00	110
1995	Terri OM-78	2,500		150.00	150
1989	Terri-PS-104	Closed	1991	85.00	85
1991	Terri-TR-62	Closed	1992	75.00	75
1991	Tessa-AM-19	Closed	1992	135.00	135
1994	Tiffany OC-44M	2,500		140.00	140
1992	Tiffany-OM-014	2,500	1994	150.00	150
1995	Tina OM-79	2,500		150.00	150
1991	Tina-AM-16	Closed	1992	130.00	130
1990	Tina-DOLL-371	Closed	1992	85.00	85
1990	Tina-WB-32	Closed	1992	65.00	65
1994	Tippy LL-946	2,500	1995	110.00	110
1995	Tobey C-3232	2,500		50.00	50
1994	Todd YK-4540	3,500		45.00	45
1990	Tommy-C-3064	Closed	1992	75.00	75
1994	Topaz TR-74	2,500	1995	195.00	195
1988	Tracy-C-3006	Closed	1990	95.00	150
1992	Trina-OM-011	Closed	1994	165.00	165
1994	Trixie TR-77	2,500		110.00	110
1991	Vanessa-AM-34	Closed	1992	90.00	90
1991	Vicki-C-3101	Closed	1992	200.00	200
1991	Violet-EP-41	Closed	1992	135.00	135
1991	Violet-OM-186	2,500	1992	270.00	270
1992	Violette-FH-503	2,500	1994	120.00	120
1994	Virginia TR-78	2,500		195.00	195
1991	Virginia-SP-359	Closed	1992	120.00	120
1987	Vivian-C-201P	Closed	1986	80.00	80
1988	Vivian-C201P	Closed	1990	80.00	80
1991	Wah-Ching Watching Oriental Toddler YK-4175	Closed	1992	110.00	110
1995	Wei Lin GU-44	2,500		70.00	70
1994	Wendy MS-26	2,500		150.00	150
1985	Wendy-C120	Closed	1987	45.00	150
1989	Wendy-PS-51	Closed	1991	105.00	105
1990	Wendy-TE-3	Closed	1992	75.00	75
1990	Wilma-PS-174	Closed	1992	75.00	75
1995	Windy in Rose Print FH-626	2,500	1995	200.00	200
1995	Winnie LL-985	2,500		75.00	75
1995	Winter Wonderland RDK-301	2,500		35.00	35
1995	Woodland Sprite OM-90	2,500		100.00	100
1995	Yelena RDK-236	2,500		35.00	35
1990	Yen Yen-YK-4091	Closed	1992	95.00	95
1992	Yvette-OM-015	2,500	1994	150.00	150

Signature Doll Series - Various

YEAR ISSUE		EDITION LIMIT	YEAR RETD.	ISSUE PRICE	*QUOTE U.S.$
1992	Abigail-MS-11 - M. Severino	5,000	1994	125.00	125
1995	Adak PPA-21 - P. Phillips	5,000		110.00	110
1992	Adora-MS-14 - M. Severino	5,000	1994	185.00	185
1995	Alain PPA-19 - P. Phillips	2,500		100.00	100
1992	Alexandria-PAC-19 - P. Aprile	5,000	1995	300.00	300
1991	Alice-MS-7 - M. Severino	5,000		120.00	120
1995	Amanda KSFA-1 - K. Fitzpatrick	5,000		175.00	175
1991	Amber-MS-1 - M. Severino	Closed	1994	95.00	95
1995	Amelia PAC-28 - P. Aprile	5,000		130.00	130
1995	Amy Rose HKHF-200 - H.K. Hyland	5,000		125.00	125
1992	Baby Cakes Crumbs - PK-CRUMBS - P. Kolesar	5,000		17.50	18
1992	Baby Cakes Crumbs/Black - PK-CRUMBS/B - P. Kolesar	5,000		17.50	18
1991	Becky-MS-2 - M. Severino	5,000	1994	95.00	95
1991	Bianca-PK-101 - P. Kolesar	Closed	1994	120.00	120
1993	Bonnett Baby MS-17W - M. Severino	5,000		175.00	175
1995	Brad HKH-15 - H.K. Hyland	5,000		85.00	85
1992	Bride & Flower Girl-PAC-6 - P. Aprile	5,000		600.00	600
1991	Bridgette-PK-104 - P. Kolesar	Closed	1994	120.00	120
1995	Brie PPA-26 - P. Aprile	5,000		180.00	180
1995	Cara DALI-1 - E. Dali	5,000		400.00	400
1995	Casey PPA-23 - P. Phillips	5,000		85.00	85
1992	Cassandra-PAC-8 - P. Aprile	Closed	N/A	450.00	450
1992	Cassie Flower Girl-PAC-9 - P. Aprile	Closed	N/A	175.00	175
1992	Celine-PAC-11 - P. Aprile	5,000	1995	165.00	165
1991	Clair-Ann-PK-252 - P. Kolesar	5,000		100.00	100
1992	Clarissa-PAC-3 - P. Aprile	5,000		165.00	165
1992	Cody-MS-19 - M. Severino	Closed	1993	120.00	120
1992	Creole Black-HP-202 - H. Payne	Closed	1993	250.00	250
1992	Cynthia-PAC-10 - P. Aprile	Closed	1993	165.00	165
1991	Daddy's Little Darling-MS-8 - M. Severino	5,000		165.00	165
1992	Darla-HP-204 - H. Payne	5,000		250.00	250
1991	Dozy Elf w/ Featherbed - MAB-100 - M.A. Byerly	Closed	1991	110.00	110
1991	Duby Elf w/ Featherbed -MAB-103 - M.A. Byerly	Closed	1991	110.00	110
1991	Dudley Elf w/ Featherbed - MAB-101 - M.A. Byerly	Closed	1991	110.00	110
1991	Duffy Elf w/ Featherbed-MAB-102 - M.A. Byerly	Closed	1991	110.00	110
1992	Dulcie-HP-200 - H. Payne	Closed	1993	250.00	250
1992	Dustin-HP-201 - H. Payne	5,000	1993	250.00	250
1995	Eleanore GMNA-100 - G. McNeil	5,000		225.00	225
1991	Enoc-PK-100 - P. Kolesar	5,000		100.00	100
1992	Eugenie Bride-PAC-1 - P. Aprile	5,000		165.00	165
1992	Evening Star-PAC-5 - P. Aprile	Closed	1993	500.00	500
1995	Ginny LR-2 - L. Randolph	5,000		360.00	360
1993	Grace HKH-2 - H. Kahl-Hyland	5,000		250.00	250
1995	Happy JFC-100 - K. Fitzpatrick	5,000		120.00	120
1993	Helene HKH-1 - H. Kahl-Hyland	5,000		250.00	250
1995	Holly GMN-202 - G. McNeil	5,000		150.00	150
1995	Iman PPA-24 - P. Aprile	5,000		110.00	110
1992	Kate-MS-15 - M. Severino	Closed	1993	190.00	190
1995	Latisha PPA-25 - P. Phillips	5,000		110.00	110
1995	Laurel HKH-17R - H.K. Hyland	5,000		110.00	110
1995	Lauren HKH-202 - H.K. Hyland	5,000		150.00	150
1995	Lena PPA-20 - P. Phillips	5,000		120.00	120
1995	Lenore LRC-100 - L. Randolph	5,000		140.00	140
1992	Little Match Girl-HP-205 - H. Payne	Closed	1994	150.00	150
1992	Little Turtle Indian-PK-110 - P. Kolesar	Closed	1993	150.00	150
1995	Lucy HKH-14 - H.K. Hyland	5,000		105.00	105
1992	Megan-MS-12 - M. Severino	5,000	1995	125.00	125
1992	Melanie-PAC-14 - P. Aprile	Closed	1993	300.00	300
1995	Meredith LR-3 - L. Randolph	5,000		375.00	375
1991	Mikey-MS-3 - M. Severino	5,000	1994	95.00	95
1991	Mommy's Rays of Sunshine -MS-9 - M. Severino	5,000		165.00	165
1992	Nadia-PAC-18 - P. Aprile	Closed	1993	175.00	175
1995	Natasha HKH-17P - H.K. Hyland	5,000		110.00	110
1995	Nikki HKHF-20 - H.K. Hyland	5,000		125.00	125
1992	Olivia-PAC-12 - P. Aprile	Closed	1993	300.00	300
1995	Patricia DALI-3 - E. Dali	5,000		280.00	280
1991	Paulette-PAC-2 - P. Aprile	5,000		250.00	250
1991	Paulette-PAC-4 - P. Aprile	5,000		250.00	250
1992	Pavlova-PAC-17 - P. Aprile	5,000	1994	145.00	145
1992	Polly-HP-206 - H. Payne	5,000		120.00	120
1991	Precious Baby-SB-100 - S. Bilotto	5,000		250.00	250
1991	Precious Pary Time-SB-102 - S. Bilotto	5,000		250.00	250
1991	Precious Spring Time-SB-104 - S. Bilotto	Closed	N/A	250.00	250
1992	Raven Eskimo-PK-106 - P. Kolesar	Closed	1993	130.00	130
1992	Rebecca Beige Bonnet-MS-17B - M. Severino	5,000	1995	175.00	175
1993	Reilly HKH-3 - H. Kahl-Hyland	5,000		260.00	260
1992	Ruby-MS-18 - M. Severino	5,000		135.00	135
1992	Sally-MS-25 - M. Severino	5,000	1993	110.00	110
1995	Shao Ling PPA-22 - P. Phillips	5,000		110.00	110
1991	Shun Lee-PK-102 - P. Kolesar	Closed	N/A	120.00	120
1994	Sis JAG-110 - J. Grammer	5,000	1994	110.00	110
1992	Spanky-HP-25 - H. Payne	5,000	1994	250.00	250
1991	Sparkle-PK-250 - P. Kolesar	5,000		100.00	100
1995	Stacy DALI-2 - E. Dali	5,000		360.00	360
1992	Stacy-MS-24 - M. Severino	Closed	1993	110.00	110
1991	Stephie-MS-6 - M. Severino	Closed	1994	125.00	125
1991	Su Lin-MS-5 - M. Severino	5,000	1994	105.00	105
1991	Susan Marie-PK-103 - P. Kolesar	Closed	1991	120.00	120
1995	Suzie HKH-16 - H.K. Hyland	5,000		100.00	100
1991	Sweet Pea-PK-251 - P. Kolesar	Closed		100.00	100
1995	Tammy LR-4 - L. Randolph	5,000		325.00	325
1994	Tex JAG-114 - J. Grammer	5,000		110.00	110
1995	Tiffany LR-1 - L. Randolph	5,000		370.00	370
1994	Tracy JAG-111 - J. Grammer	5,000		150.00	150
1994	Trevor JAG-112 - J. Grammer	5,000		115.00	115
1992	Vanessa-PAC-15 - P. Aprile	Closed	1993	300.00	300
1992	Victoria w/Blanket-MS-10 - M. Severino	Closed	1993	110.00	110
1992	Violetta-PAC-16 - P. Aprile	5,000	1994	165.00	165
1991	Yawning Kate-MS-4 - M. Severino	Closed	1994	105.00	105

*Quotes have been rounded up to nearest dollar

Susan Wakeen Doll Co. Inc.

The Littlest Ballet Company - S. Wakeen

Year	Issue	Edition Limit	Year Retd.	Issue Price	*Quote U.S.$
1985	Cynthia	375		198.00	350
1987	Elizabeth	250		425.00	1000
1985	Jeanne	375		198.00	800
1985	Jennifer	250		750.00	750
1987	Marie Ann	50		1000.00	1000
1985	Patty	375		198.00	400-500

Timeless Creations

Barefoot Children - A. Himstedt

Year	Issue	Edition Limit	Year Retd.	Issue Price	*Quote U.S.$
1987	Bastian	Closed	1989	329.00	700-850
1987	Beckus	Closed	1989	329.00	1100
1987	Ellen	Closed	1989	329.00	750-900
1987	Fatou	Closed	1989	329.00	850-1100
1987	Fatou (Cornroll)	Closed	1989	329.00	1100-1200
1987	Kathe	Closed	1989	329.00	750-900
1987	Lisa	Closed	1989	329.00	700-900
1987	Paula	Closed	1989	329.00	650-900

Blessed Are The Children - A. Himstedt

Year	Issue	Edition Limit	Year Retd.	Issue Price	*Quote U.S.$
1988	Friederike	Closed	1990	499.00	1200-1800
1988	Kasimir	Closed	1990	499.00	1200-1700
1988	Makimura	Closed	1990	499.00	1000-1400
1988	Malin	Closed	1990	499.00	1300-1700
1988	Michiko	Closed	1990	499.00	1100-1400

Faces of Friendship - A. Himstedt

Year	Issue	Edition Limit	Year Retd.	Issue Price	*Quote U.S.$
1991	Liliane (Netherlands)	2-Yr.	1993	598.00	575-700
1991	Neblina (Switzerland)	2-Yr.	1993	598.00	598
1991	Shireem (Bali)	2-Yr.	1993	598.00	598

Fiene And The Barefoot Babies - A. Himstedt

Year	Issue	Edition Limit	Year Retd.	Issue Price	*Quote U.S.$
1990	Annchen-German Baby Girl	2-Yr.	1992	498.00	600-800
1990	Fiene-Belgian Girl	2-Yr.	1992	598.00	700-800
1990	Mo-American Baby Boy	2-Yr.	1992	498.00	500-600
1990	Taki-Japanese Baby Girl	2-Yr.	1992	498.00	600-900

Heartland Series - A. Himstedt

Year	Issue	Edition Limit	Year Retd.	Issue Price	*Quote U.S.$
1988	Timi	Closed		329.00	500
1988	Toni	Closed		329.00	500

Images of Childhood - A. Himstedt

Year	Issue	Edition Limit	Year Retd.	Issue Price	*Quote U.S.$
1993	Kima (Greenland)	2-Yr.	1995	599.00	599
1993	Lona (California)	2-Yr.	1995	599.00	599
1993	Tara (Germany)	2-Yr.	1995	599.00	599

Reflection of Youth - A. Himstedt

Year	Issue	Edition Limit	Year Retd.	Issue Price	*Quote U.S.$
1989	Adrienne (France)	Closed	1991	558.00	795-850
1989	Ayoka (Africa)	Closed	1991	558.00	950-1200
1989	Janka (Hungry)	Closed	1991	558.00	750-800
1989	Kai (German)	Closed	1991	558.00	675-800

Summer Dreams - A. Himstedt

Year	Issue	Edition Limit	Year Retd.	Issue Price	*Quote U.S.$
1992	Enzo	2-Yr.	1994	599.00	599
1992	Jule	2-Yr.	1994	599.00	599
1992	Pemba	2-Yr.	1994	599.00	599
1992	Sanga	2-Yr.	1994	599.00	599

The Wimbledon Collection

The Wimbledon Collection - Various

Year	Issue	Edition Limit	Year Retd.	Issue Price	*Quote U.S.$
1992	Abigail (signed) A-104-S - G.F. Wolff	600	1994	200.00	200
1992	Abigail A-104 - G.F. Wolff	Retrd.	1994	170.00	170
1992	Alexandra (signed) A-118-S - G.F. Wolff	600	1994	254.00	254
1992	Alexandra A-118 - G.F. Wolff	Retrd.	1994	224.00	224
1990	Alexis A-048 - Gr. M. Wolff	1,200	1991	200.00	200
1989	Alicia A-4089 - G.&G. Wolff	1,000	1991	65.00	65
1993	Alliston A-3002 - G.&G. Wolff	360	1994	120.00	120
1989	Alyson A-047 - G.&G. Wolff	1,000	1991	80.00	80
1990	Amanda A-051 - Gr. M. Wolff	1,000	1991	200.00	200
1989	Amber A-5014 - G.&G. Wolff	1,000	1991	77.00	77
1992	American Beauty (signed) A-111-S - G.F. Wolff	600	1992	255.00	255
1992	American Beauty A-111 - G.F. Wolff	Retrd.	1994	224.00	224
1989	Amy A-4070 - G.&G. Wolff	1,000	1990	45.00	45
1989	Anastasia A-011 - G.&G. Wolff	1,000	1993	150.00	150
1989	Andrea A-4092 - G.&G. Wolff	1,000	1990	65.00	65
1989	Angela A-5016 - G.&G. Wolff	1,000	1990	115.00	115
1989	Annessa A-019 - G.&G. Wolff	1,000	1992	85.00	85
1994	April A-098 - G.&G. Wolff	360	1994	80.00	80
1989	Ashley A-4039 - G.&G. Wolff	1,000	1990	48.00	48
1991	Autumn A-065 - G.&G. Wolff	1,000	1993	140.00	140
1989	Becky A-4057 - G.&G. Wolff	1,000	1990	48.00	48
1989	Belinda A-029 - G.&G. Wolff	1,000	1992	55.00	55
1992	Berkeley (signed) A-112-S - G.F. Wolff	600	1994	360.00	360
1992	Berkeley A-112 - G.F. Wolff	Retrd.	1994	330.00	330
1989	Bethany A-5013 - G.&G. Wolff	1,000	1991	75.00	75
1989	Bo Peep A-003 - G.&G. Wolff	1,000	1991	95.00	95
1989	Bobbie A-4083 - G.&G. Wolff	1,000	1991	40.00	40
1989	Bonnie A-031 - G.&G. Wolff	1,000	1992	50.00	50
1991	Brandi A-078 - G.&G. Wolff	1,000	1994	130.00	130
1989	Brenda A-027 - G.&G. Wolff	1,000	1991	55.00	55
1994	Brianna A-3012 - G.&G. Wolff	360	1994	120.00	120
1989	Brittany A-5011 - G.&G. Wolff	1,000	1991	70.00	70
1989	Brooke A-5002 - G.&G. Wolff	1,000	1990	46.00	46
1989	Caitlin A-4088 - G.&G. Wolff	1,000	1991	75.00	75
1989	Camille A-038 - G.&G. Wolff	1,000	1992	100.00	100
1991	Candi A-090 - G.&G. Wolff	1,000	1992	90.00	90
1989	Carla A-5023 - G.&G. Wolff	1,000	1990	89.00	89
1989	Carole A-015 - G.&G. Wolff	1,000	1991	21.00	21
1989	Caroline A-002 - G.&G. Wolff	1,000	1992	90.00	90
1989	Cassie A-016 - G.&G. Wolff	1,000	1992	130.00	130
1989	Cecilia A-006 - G.&G. Wolff	1,000	1991	70.00	70
1989	Charlotte A-039 - G.&G. Wolff	1,000	1993	100.00	100
1992	Chelsey (signed) A-110-S - G.F. Wolff	600	1993	255.00	255
1992	Chelsey A-110 G.F. Wolff	Retrd.	1994	224.00	224
1991	Christa A-091 - G.&G. Wolff	1,000	1992	230.00	230
1989	Christina A-4086 - G.&G. Wolff	1,000	1991	65.00	65
1989	Christmas Doll A-046 - G.&G. Wolff	1,000	1990	N/A	N/A
1989	Christopher A-4087 - G.&G. Wolff	1,000	1990	65.00	65
1989	Cindy A-4085 - G.&G. Wolff	1,000	1990	43.00	43
1989	Colleen (blue) A-4030-B - G.&G. Wolff	1,000	1991	40.00	40
1989	Colleen (pink) A-4030-P - G.&G. Wolff	1,000	1991	40.00	40
1989	Corey A-004 - G.&G. Wolff	1,000	1991	72.00	72
1991	Cricket A-066 - G.&G. Wolff	1,000	1992	100.00	100
1992	Crissie (signed) A-102-S - Gr. M. Wolff	600	1993	170.00	170
1992	Crissie A-102 - Gr. M. Wolff	Retrd.	1994	140.00	140
1989	Dana A-035 - G.&G. Wolff	1,000	1991	98.00	98
1989	Dee A-5007 - G.&G. Wolff	1,000	1991	60.00	60
1991	Denise A-087 - G.&G. Wolff	1,000	1992	90.00	90
1994	Devon A-3020 - G.&G. Wolff	360	1994	120.00	120
1989	Diane A-045 - G.&G. Wolff	1,000	1992	75.00	75
1992	Don't Cry Over Spilt Milk (signed) A-101-S - G.F. Wolff	600	1992	190.00	190
1991	Elise A-077 - G.&G. Wolff	1,000	1993	100.00	100
1989	Elizabeth A-5015 - G.&G. Wolff	1,000	1991	80.00	80
1991	Emma A-073 - G.&G. Wolff	1,000	1992	100.00	100
1992	Erika (signed) A-105-S - Gr. M. Wolff	600	1993	200.00	200
1992	Erika A-105 - Gr. M. Wolff	Retrd.	1994	170.00	170
1989	Erika A-4090 - G.&G. Wolff	1,000	1990	65.00	65
1989	Erin A-4033 - G.&G. Wolff	1,000	1991	40.00	40
1989	Faith A-014 - G.&G. Wolff	1,000	1991	50.00	50
1991	Fran A-064 - G.&G. Wolff	1,000	1992	150.00	150
1990	Franz A-053 - G. F. Wolff	1,000	1992	200.00	200
1990	Grandma's Attic A-052 - Gr. M. Wolff	1,000	1991	170.00	170
1989	Gretchen A-4032 - G.&G. Wolff	1,000	1991	37.00	37
1991	Hannah A-076 - G.&G. Wolff	1,000	1992	150.00	150
1989	Heather A-5003 - G.&G. Wolff	1,000	1990	53.00	53
1989	Heidi A-010 - G.&G. Wolff	1,000	1991	80.00	80
1989	Hillary A-5021 - G.&G. Wolff	1,000	1991	90.00	90
1989	Holly A-4080 - G.&G. Wolff	1,000	1990	36.00	36
1994	Hunter A-3011 - G.&G. Wolff	360	1994	100.00	100
1989	Jackie A-022 - G.&G. Wolff	1,000	1991	80.00	80
1989	Jamie (lavender) A-4088-L - G.&G. Wolff	1,000	1991	38.00	38
1989	Jamie (pink) A-4088-P - G.&G. Wolff	1,000	1990	37.00	37
1991	Jeanine A-070 - G.&G. Wolff	1,000	1993	110.00	110
1989	Jennifer A-4058 - G.&G. Wolff	1,000	1991	40.00	40
1991	Jill A-056 - G.&G. Wolff	1,000	1991	90.00	90
1994	Jill A-094 - G.&G. Wolff	360	1994	70.00	70
1989	Jill A-4031 - G.&G. Wolff	1,000	1991	38.00	38
1989	Joanne A-4037 - G.&G. Wolff	1,000	1990	43.00	43
1989	Jodi A-4055 - G.&G. Wolff	1,000	1990	27.00	27
1992	Johnny (signed) A-117-S - G.F. Wolff	600	1994	254.00	254
1989	Julie A-4081 - G.&G. Wolff	1,000	1990	35.00	35
1993	Kariss (signed) A-125-S - Gr. M. Wolff	600	1994	329.00	329
1993	Kariss A-125 - Gr. M. Wolff	Retrd.	1994	300.00	300
1989	Kate A-5001 - G.&G. Wolff	1,000	1990	46.00	46
1989	Kathy A-036 - G.&G. Wolff	1,000	1993	95.00	95
1989	Katrina A-017 - G.&G. Wolff	1,000	1992	77.00	77
1992	Kayla (signed) A-107-S - Gr. M. Wolff	600	1993	200.00	200
1992	Kayla A-107 - Gr. M. Wolff	Retrd.	1994	170.00	170
1993	Keightley (signed) A-123-S - Gr. M. Wolff	600	1993	254.00	254
1993	Keightley A-123 - Gr. M. Wolff	Retrd.	1993	224.00	224
1989	Kelly A-5018 - G.&G. Wolff	1,000	1990	56.00	56
1989	Kimberly A-5006 - G.&G. Wolff	1,000	1991	64.00	64
1993	Krista (signed) A-124-S - G.F. Wolff	600	1994	276.00	276
1989	Kristin (blue) A-4040-B - G.&G. Wolff	1,000	1990	45.00	45
1989	Kristin (pink) A-4040-P - G.&G. Wolff	1,000	1990	45.00	45
1989	Kristy A-001 - G.&G. Wolff	1,000	1992	90.00	90
1989	Kyle A-018 - G.&G. Wolff	1,000	1992	77.00	77
1994	Larkin (signed) A-130-S - G.F. Wolff	600	1994	254.00	254
1990	Laurel A-049 - Gr. M. Wolff	1,200	1991	200.00	200
1989	Laurie A-030 - G.&G. Wolff	1,000	1992	55.00	55
1992	Leigh Ann (signed) A-108-S - Gr. M. Wolff	600	1995	255.00	255
1992	Leigh Ann A-108 - Gr. M. Wolff	Retrd.	1995	224.00	224
1989	Leslie A-007 - G.&G. Wolff	1,000	1991	80.00	80
1989	Libby A-008 - G.&G. Wolff	1,000	1991	70.00	70
1989	Lindsey A-4093 - G.&G. Wolff	1,000	1991	65.00	65
1994	Lloyd A-3013 - G.&G. Wolff	360	1994	120.00	120
1989	Loving Care A-009 - G.&G. Wolff	1,000	1991	150.00	150
1989	Lucy A-5017 - G.&G. Wolff	1,000	1991	70.00	70
1989	Lydia A-043 - Gr. M. Wolff	3,000	1992	120.00	120
1991	Maggie A-071 - G.&G. Wolff	1,000	1993	100.00	100
1989	Mandy A-4082 - G.&G. Wolff	1,000	1991	40.00	40
1989	Marcy A-021 - G.&G. Wolff	1,000	1991	150.00	150
1989	Marla A-5012 - G.&G. Wolff	1,000	1991	75.00	75
1991	Martina A-069 - G.&G. Wolff	1,000	1992	130.00	130
1989	Mary A-020 - G.&G. Wolff	1,000	1991	85.00	85
1989	Mattie A-026 - G.&G. Wolff	1,000	1992	50.00	50
1992	McKenzie (signed) A-106-S - G.F. Wolff	600	1992	220.00	220
1992	McKenzie A-106 - G.F. Wolff	Retrd.	1994	190.00	190
1989	Megan A-032 - G.&G. Wolff	1,000	1992	100.00	100
1989	Melissa A-042 - G.&G. Wolff	1,000	1992	150.00	150
1989	Michelle A-037 - G.&G. Wolff	1,000	1992	90.00	90
1989	Mindy A-5005 - G.&G. Wolff	1,000	1991	60.00	60
1989	Missy A-5010 - G.&G. Wolff	1,000	1990	70.00	70
1992	Morgan (signed) A-10S - Gr. M. Wolff	600	1992	200.00	200
1992	Morgan A-100 - Gr. M. Wolff	Retrd.	1993	170.00	170
1989	Nancy A-4084 - G.&G. Wolff	1,000	1991	45.00	45
1989	Natalie A-023 - G.&G. Wolff	1,000	1991	95.00	95
1989	Natasha A-005 - G.&G. Wolff	1,000	1991	60.00	60
1993	Noel A-096 - G.&G. Wolff	600	1993	80.00	80
1994	Paige (signed) A-133-S - G.F. Wolff	600	1995	254.00	254
1993	Palmer A-3007 - G.&G. Wolff	360	1994	150.00	150
1993	Parker A-3001 - G.&G. Wolff	700	1994	120.00	120
1989	Paula A-4068 - G.&G. Wolff	1,000	1990	35.00	35
1991	Penny A-063 - G.&G. Wolff	1,000	1992	150.00	150
1992	Peyton (signed) A-115-S - G.F. Wolff	600	1994	255.00	255
1992	Peyton A-115 - G.F. Wolff	Retrd.	1994	224.00	224
1991	Rachel A-085 - G.&G. Wolff	1,000	1992	90.00	90
1989	Rebecca (blue) A-4051 -B - G.&G. Wolff	1,000	1991	37.00	37
1989	Rebecca (pink) A-4051 -P - G.&G. Wolff	1,000	1991	37.00	37
1989	Robin A5004 - G.&G. Wolff	1,000	1991	60.00	60
1989	Rose A-033 - G.&G. Wolff	1,000	1991	45.00	45
1991	Roxanne A-088 - G.&G. Wolff	1,000	1992	90.00	90
1989	Ryan A-034 - G.&G. Wolff	1,000	1991	45.00	45
1989	Sabrina A-4015 - G.&G. Wolff	1,000	1990	75.00	75
1991	Samantha A-062 - G.&G. Wolff	1,000	1992	150.00	150
1989	Samuel A-4014 - G.&G. Wolff	1,000	1991	75.00	75
1989	Sandy A-4056 - G.&G. Wolff	1,000	1991	42.00	42
1991	Sarah A-075 - G.&G. Wolff	1,000	1992	200.00	200
1990	Savannah A-050 - G.F. Wolff	1,200	1991	200.00	200
1990	Shelly A-054 - G.&G. Wolff	1,000	1991	90.00	90
1991	Snow Queen A-074 - G.&G. Wolff	1,000	1992	250.00	250
1989	Sondra A-4054 - G.&G. Wolff	1,000	1990	54.00	54
1989	Sophia A-044 - G.&G. Wolff	1,000	1991	80.00	80
1990	Stacey A-055 - G.&G. Wolff	1,000	1990	80.00	80
1989	Stephanie A-028 - G.&G. Wolff	1,000	1991	55.00	55
1989	Susan A-4052 - G.&G. Wolff	1,000	1991	25.00	25
1992	Susie (signed) A-103-S - G.F. Wolff	600	1992	200.00	200
1989	Suzanne A-012 - G.&G. Wolff	1,000	1993	100.00	100
1992	Sydney (signed) A-114-S - Gr. M. Wolff	600	1994	255.00	255
1992	Sydney A-114 - Gr. M. Wolff	Retrd.	1994	224.00	224
1992	Sylvia (signed) A-119-S - Gr. M. Wolff	600	1993	254.00	254
1992	Sylvia A-119 - Gr. M. Wolff	Retrd.	1994	224.00	224
1989	Tamara A-025 - Gr. M. Wolff	1,000	1991	200.00	200
1989	Tara A-041 - G.&G. Wolff	1,000	1991	105.00	105
1991	Taylor A-094 - G.&G. Wolff	1,000	1992	150.00	150
1989	Terri A-013 - G.&G. Wolff	1,000	1991	80.00	80
1989	Tessa A-5020 - G.&G. Wolff	1,000	1991	90.00	90
1989	Tiffany A-040 - G.&G. Wolff	1,000	1991	150.00	150
1994	Tina A-097 - G.&G. Wolff	360	1994	70.00	70
1991	Tonya A-089 - G.&G. Wolff	1,000	1992	90.00	90
1989	Tracy A-024 - G.&G. Wolff	1,000	1992	70.00	70
1991	Tricia A-086 - G.&G. Wolff	1,000	1992	90.00	90
1989	Tricia A-5022 - G.&G. Wolff	1,000	1990	89.00	89
1991	Victoria A-061 - G.&G. Wolff	1,000	1992	200.00	200
1991	Wendy A-068 - G.&G. Wolff	1,000	1992	130.00	130
1989	Whitney A-5009 - G.&G. Wolff	1,000	1990	60.00	60

FIGURINES/COTTAGES

Ace Product Management Group, Inc.

Harley-Davidson Archive Pewter Figurines - Ace

Year	Issue	Edition Limit	Year Retd.	Issue Price	*Quote U.S.$
1994	Catch Of The Day 99450-93Z	1,500		150.00	150

Harley-Davidson Christmas Figurines - Ace

Year	Issue	Edition Limit	Year Retd.	Issue Price	*Quote U.S.$
1989	Perfect Tree 99420-90Z	3,000	1989	99.95	100
1990	Mainstreet U.S.A. 99421-91Z	3,000	1990	129.95	130
1991	Joy Of Giving 99423-92Z	3,000	1991	134.95	135
1992	Home For The Holidays 99422-93Z	3,000	1992	145.00	145
1993	Rural Delivery 99423-94Z	3,000	1993	155.00	155
1994	29 Days 'Til Christmas 99089-95Z	3,000	1994	170.00	170
1995	Skating Party 99417-96Z	3,000	1995	185.00	185

Harley-Davidson Mini-Plate Figurines - Ace

Year	Issue	Edition Limit	Year Retd.	Issue Price	*Quote U.S.$
1992	Letters To Santa 99415-93Z	Yr.Iss	1992	25.00	25
1993	Santa's Predicament 99420-94Z	Yr.Iss.	1993	18.00	18
1994	Not A Creature Was Stirring 99447-95Z	Yr.Iss.	1994	20.00	20

*Quotes have been rounded up to nearest dollar

FIGURINES/COTTAGES

YEAR ISSUE		EDITION LIMIT	YEAR RETD.	ISSUE PRICE	*QUOTE U.S.$
1995	Planning The Route 99476-96Z	Yr.Iss.	1995	22.00	22

Harley-Davidson Sculptures - M. Patrick

YEAR ISSUE		EDITION LIMIT	YEAR RETD.	ISSUE PRICE	*QUOTE U.S.$
1993	90th Anniversary -The Reunion 99215-93Z	2,500	1993	495.00	495
1993	90th Anniversary-Bronze The Reunion 99216-93ZB	90	1993	3495.00	3495
1993	Milwaukee Ride 99497-94Z	1,500	1995	350.00	350
1994	Old Soldier 99403-95Z	1,500	1995	350.00	350
1995	Just Hitched 99079-96Z	1,500	1995	350.00	350

Harley-Davidson Young Rider Figurines - Ace

YEAR ISSUE		EDITION LIMIT	YEAR RETD.	ISSUE PRICE	*QUOTE U.S.$
1992	The Jacket 99370-93Z	3,000	1994	25.00	25
1993	Free Wheelin' 99371-93Z	3,000	1995	25.00	25
1993	The Enthusiast 99372-94Z	3,000	1995	25.00	25
1994	Engine Lesson 99376-95Z	3,000		28.00	28
1995	Harley Rides-5 Cents 99377-95Z	3,000		28.00	28
1995	Treehouse Christening 99296-96Z	3,000		32.00	32

All God's Children

Collectors' Club - M. Root

YEAR ISSUE		EDITION LIMIT	YEAR RETD.	ISSUE PRICE	*QUOTE U.S.$
1989	Molly -1524	Retrd.	1990	38.00	425-600
1990	Joey -1539	Retrd.	1991	32.00	275-450
1991	Mandy -1540	Retrd.	1992	36.00	200-280
1992	Olivia -1562	Retrd.	1993	36.00	175-220
1993	Garrett -1567	Retrd.	1994	36.00	100-180
1993	Peek-a-Boo	Retrd.	1994	Gift	35-63
1994	Alexandria -1575	Retrd.	1995	36.00	90
1994	Lindy	Retrd.	1995	Gift	30-53
1995	Zamika -1581	5/96		36.00	36
1995	Zizi	5/96		Gift	N/A

All God's Children - M. Root

YEAR ISSUE		EDITION LIMIT	YEAR RETD.	ISSUE PRICE	*QUOTE U.S.$
1985	Abe -1357	Retrd.	1988	25.00	1450
1989	Adam - 1526	Open		36.00	37
1987	Amy - 1405W	Retrd.	1996	22.00	27
1987	Angel - 1401W	Retrd.	1995	20.00	40-55
1986	Annie Mae 6" -1311	Retrd.	1989	19.00	80-175
1986	Annie Mae 8 1/2" -1310	Retrd.	1989	27.00	150-250
1987	Aunt Sarah - blue -1440	Retrd.	1989	45.00	150-250
1987	Aunt Sarah - red-1440	Retrd.	1989	45.00	250-385
1992	Barney - 1557	Retrd.	1995	32.00	75
1988	Bean (Clear Water)-1521	Retrd.	1992	36.00	250-350
1992	Bean (Painted Water)-1521	Retrd.	1993	36.00	125
1987	Becky - 1402W	Retrd.	1995	22.00	55
1987	Becky with Patch - 1402W	Retrd.	N/A	19.00	200-230
1987	Ben - 1504	Retrd.	1988	22.00	300-425
1991	Bessie & Corkie - 1547	Open		70.00	70
1992	Beth - 1558	Retrd.	1995	32.00	70
1988	Betsy (Clear Water)- 1513	Retrd.	1992	36.00	250-350
1992	Betsy (Painted Water)- 1513	Retrd.	1993	36.00	130
1989	Beverly (sm.)- 1525	Retrd.	1990	50.00	400-600
1991	Billy (lg. stars raised)- 1545	Retrd.	1993	36.00	100-150
1991	Billy (stars imprinted)- 1545	Retrd.	1993	36.00	150-175
1987	Blossom - blue - 1500	Retrd.	1989	60.00	225-385
1987	Blossom - red - 1500	Retrd.	1989	60.00	750-790
1989	Bo - 1530	Retrd.	1994	22.00	40-80
1987	Bonnie & Buttons - 150	Retrd.	1992	24.00	75-150
1985	Booker T - 1320	Retrd.	1988	19.00	1200-1400
1987	Boone - 1510	Retrd.	1989	16.00	95-160
1989	Bootsie - 1529	Retrd.	1994	22.00	55-75
1992	Caitlin - 1554	Retrd.	1994	36.00	75-95
1985	Callie 2 1/4" - 1362	Retrd.	1988	12.00	250-280
1985	Callie 4 1/2" - 1361	Retrd.	1988	19.00	500
1988	Calvin - 777	Retrd.	1988	200.00	1500-2000
1987	Cassie - 1503	Retrd.	1989	22.00	85-175
1994	Chantel 1573	Open		39.00	39
1987	Charity - 1408	Retrd.	1994	28.00	70-110
1994	Cheri 1574	Open		38.00	38
1989	David - 1528	Open		28.00	30
1996	Debi - 1584	Open		N/A	N/A
1991	Dori (green dress) - 1544	Retrd.	N/A	30.00	250-390
1991	Dori (peach dress) - 1544	Open		28.00	30
1987	Eli - 1403W	Open		26.00	28
1985	Emma - 1322	Retrd.	1988	27.00	1650-1950
1992	Faith - 1555	Retrd.	1993	32.00	80-100
1995	Gina - 1579	Open		38.00	38
1987	Ginnie - 1508	Retrd.	1988	22.00	375-435
1986	Grandma - 1323	Retrd.	1987	30.00	3200-3675
1988	Hannah - 1515	Open		36.00	37
1988	Hope - 1519	Open		36.00	37
1987	Jacob - 1407W	Retrd.	1996	26.00	28
1989	Jeremy - 1523	800	1993	195.00	750-895
1989	Jerome - 1532	Open		30.00	32
1989	Jessica - 1522	800	1993	195.00	700-890
1989	Jessica and Jeremy -1522-1523	Retrd.	1993	390.00	1800
1987	Jessie (no base) -1501W	Retrd.	1989	19.00	250-425
1989	Jessie - 1501	Open		30.00	32
1988	John -1514	Retrd.	1990	30.00	140-225
1989	Joseph - 1537	Open		30.00	30
1991	Joy - 1548	Open		30.00	30
1994	Justin - 1576	Open		37.00	37
1989	Kacie - 1533	Open		38.00	38
1988	Kezia - 1518	Open		36.00	37
1986	Lil' Emmie 3 1/2"-1345	Retrd.	1989	14.00	100-155
1986	Lil' Emmie 4 1/2" -1344	Retrd.	1989	18.00	115-175
1988	Lisa-1512	Retrd.	1991	36.00	175-235
1989	Mary - 1536	Open		30.00	30
1988	Maya - 1520	Retrd.	1993	36.00	75-135
1987	Meg (beige dress) -1505	Retrd.	1988	21.00	950-1125
1988	Meg (blue dress, long hair) -1505	Retrd.	1988	21.00	440
1988	Meg (blue dress, short hair) -1505	Retrd.	1988	21.00	800-925
1992	Melissa - 1556	Retrd.	1995	32.00	55-75
1992	Merci - 1559	Open		36.00	37
1986	Michael & Kim - 1517	Open		36.00	38
1988	Moe & Pokey - 1552	Retrd.	1993	16.00	50-80
1987	Moses - 1506	Retrd.	1992	30.00	95-155
1993	Nathaniel-11569	Open		36.00	36
1991	Nellie - 1546	Retrd.	1993	36.00	125-150
1994	Niambi- 1577	Open		34.00	34
1987	Paddy Paw & Lucy - 1553	Suspd.		24.00	50-73
1987	Paddy Paw & Luke - 1551	Suspd.		24.00	50-70
1988	Peanut -1509	Retrd.	1990	16.00	100-170
1989	Preshus - 1538	Open		24.00	24
1987	Primas Jones (w/base) -1377	Retrd.	1988	40.00	700-820
1987	Primas Jones -1377	Retrd.	1988	40.00	700-820
1986	Prissy (Bear) - 1558	Open		18.00	25
1986	Prissy (Moon Pie) - 1557	Open		20.00	32
1986	Prissy with Basket -1346	Retrd.	1989	16.00	110-160
1986	Prissy with Yarn Hair (6 strands) -1343	Retrd.	1989	19.00	225-275
1986	Prissy with Yarn Hair (9 strands) -1343	Retrd.	1989	19.00	400-430
1987	Pud - 1550	Retrd.	1988	11.00	1200-1300
1987	Rachel - 1404W	Open		20.00	28
1992	Rakiya - 1561	Open		36.00	36
1988	Sally -1507	Retrd.	1989	19.00	125-185
1991	Samantha - 1542	Retrd.	1994	38.00	75-110
1991	Samuel - 1541	Retrd.	1994	32.00	95
1989	Sasha - 1531	Open		30.00	32
1986	Selina Jane (6 strands) -1338	Retrd.	1989	21.95	255-295
1986	Selina Jane (9 strands) -1338	Retrd.	1989	21.95	500-600
1995	Shani - 1583	Open		33.00	33
1986	St. Nicholas-B -1316	Retrd.	1990	30.00	120-150
1986	St. Nicholas-W -1315	Retrd.	1990	30.00	135-150
1992	Stephen (Nativity Shepherd) - 1563	Open		36.00	36
1988	Sunshine - 1535	Open		38.00	38
1993	Sylvia - 1564	Open		36.00	37
1988	Tansi & Tedi (green socks, collar, cuffs)-1516	Retrd.	N/A	30.00	200-295
1988	Tansy & Tedi - 1516	Open		N/A	37
1989	Tara - 1527	Open		36.00	37
1989	Tess - 1534	Open		30.00	32
1990	Thaliyah-778	Retrd.	1990	200.00	1600-1825
1991	Thomas - 1549	Open		30.00	32
1987	Tiffany - 1511	Open		32.00	33
1994	Tish 1572	Open		38.00	38
1986	Toby 3 1/2"- 1332	Retrd.	1989	13.00	100-160
1986	Toby 4 1/2"- 1331	Retrd.	1989	16.00	115-185
1985	Tom- 1353	Retrd.	1988	16.00	325-425
1986	Uncle Bud 6"- 1304	Retrd.	1991	19.00	155-175
1986	Uncle Bud 8 1/2"- 1303	Retrd.	1991	27.00	350-385
1992	Valerie - 1560	Open		36.00	37
1995	William - 1580	Open		38.00	38
1987	Willie - 1406W	Open		22.00	28
1993	Zack - 1566	Open		34.00	34

All God's Children Ragbabies - M. Root

YEAR ISSUE		EDITION LIMIT	YEAR RETD.	ISSUE PRICE	*QUOTE U.S.$
1995	Honey - 4005	Open		33.00	33
1995	Issie - 4004	Open		33.00	33
1995	Ivy - 4008	Open		33.00	33
1995	Josie - 4003	Open		33.00	33
1995	Mitzi - 4000	Open		33.00	33
1995	Muffin - 4001	Open		33.00	33
1995	Puddin - 4006	Open		33.00	33
1995	Punkin - 4007	Open		33.00	33
1995	Sweetie - 4002	Open		33.00	33

Angelic Messengers - M. Root

YEAR ISSUE		EDITION LIMIT	YEAR RETD.	ISSUE PRICE	*QUOTE U.S.$
1994	Cieara 2500	Open		38.00	38
1994	Mariah 2501	Open		38.00	38
1995	Sabrina - 2502	Open		38.00	38

Christmas - M. Root

YEAR ISSUE		EDITION LIMIT	YEAR RETD.	ISSUE PRICE	*QUOTE U.S.$
1987	1987 Father Christmas-W -1750	Retrd.	N/A	145.00	600-700
1987	1987 Father Christmas-B -1751	Retrd.	N/A	145.00	600-700
1988	1988 Father Christmas-W -1757	Retrd.	N/A	195.00	450-595
1988	1988 Father Christmas-B -1758	Retrd.	N/A	195.00	450-595
1988	Santa Claus-W -1767	Retrd.	N/A	185.00	450-625
1988	Santa Claus-B -1768	Retrd.	N/A	185.00	450-625
1989	1989 Father Christmas-W -1769	Retrd.	N/A	195.00	550-675
1989	1989 Father Christmas-B -1770	Retrd.	N/A	195.00	550-675
1990	1990-91 Father Christmas-W -1771	Retrd.	N/A	195.00	500-625
1990	1990-91 Father Christmas-B -1772	Retrd.	N/A	195.00	500-625
1991	1991-92 Father Christmas-W -1773	Retrd.	N/A	195.00	465
1991	1991-92 Father Christmas-B -1774	Retrd.	N/A	195.00	465
1992	Father Christmas Bust-W -1775	Retrd.	N/A	145.00	300-350
1992	Father Christmas Bust-B -1776	Retrd.	N/A	145.00	300-350

Event Piece - M. Root

YEAR ISSUE		EDITION LIMIT	YEAR RETD.	ISSUE PRICE	*QUOTE U.S.$
1994	Uriel 2000	Yr.Iss.	1994	45.00	100-130
1995	Jane - 2001 (10 year Anniversary)	Yr.Iss.	1995	45.00	75-90
1996	Patti - 2002	Yr.Iss.		45.00	45

Historical Series - M. Root

YEAR ISSUE		EDITION LIMIT	YEAR RETD.	ISSUE PRICE	*QUOTE U.S.$
1994	Augustus Walley (Buffalo Soldier) - 1908	Retrd.	1995	95.00	175-200
1994	Bessie Smith- 1909	Open		70.00	70
1992	Dr. Daniel Williams - 1903	Retrd.	1995	70.00	100-140
1992	Frances Harper - 1905	Open		70.00	70
1991	Frederick Douglass - 1902	Open		70.00	70
1992	George Washington Carver - 1907	Open		70.00	70
1989	Harriet Tubman - 1900	Retrd.	1994	65.00	150-200
1992	Ida B. Wells - 1906	Open		70.00	70
1992	Mary Bethune (misspelled) - 1904	Retrd.	1992	70.00	245
1992	Mary Bethune - 1904	Open		70.00	70
1995	Mary Mahoney - 1911	Open		65.00	65
1995	Richard Allen - 1910	Open		70.00	70
1990	Sojourner Truth - 1901	Open		65.00	65

International Series - M. Root

YEAR ISSUE		EDITION LIMIT	YEAR RETD.	ISSUE PRICE	*QUOTE U.S.$
1987	Juan - 1807	Retrd.	1993	26.00	135
1987	Kameko - 1802	Open.		26.00	28
1987	Karl - 1808	Open.		26.00	28
1987	Katrina - 1803	Retrd.	1993	26.00	115-145
1987	Kelli - 1805	Open		30.00	30
1987	Little Chief - 1804	Open		32.00	32
1993	Minnie - 1568	Open		36.00	36
1987	Pike - 1806	Open		30.00	32
1987	Tat - 1801	Retrd.	1996	30.00	32

Little Missionary Series - M. Root

YEAR ISSUE		EDITION LIMIT	YEAR RETD.	ISSUE PRICE	*QUOTE U.S.$
1994	Nakia 3500	Retrd.	1995	40.00	85

Sugar And Spice - M. Root

YEAR ISSUE		EDITION LIMIT	YEAR RETD.	ISSUE PRICE	*QUOTE U.S.$
1987	Blessed are the Peacemakers (Eli) -1403	Retrd.	1988	22.00	525
1987	Friend Show Love (Becky) -1402	Retrd.	1988	22.00	525
1987	Friendship Warms the Heart (Jacob) -1407	Retrd.	1988	22.00	525
1987	God is Love (Angel) -1401	Retrd.	1988	22.00	525
1987	Jesus Loves Me (Amy) -1405	Retrd.	1989	22.00	525
1987	Old Friends are Best (Rachel) -1404	Retrd.	1988	22.00	525
1987	Sharing with Friends (Willie) -1406	Retrd.	1988	22.00	525

Through His Eyes - M. Root

YEAR ISSUE		EDITION LIMIT	YEAR RETD.	ISSUE PRICE	*QUOTE U.S.$
1993	Simon & Andrew - 1565	Open		45.00	45
1995	Jewel & Judy - 1582	Open		45.00	45

Amaranth Productions

Angels - L. West

YEAR ISSUE		EDITION LIMIT	YEAR RETD.	ISSUE PRICE	*QUOTE U.S.$
1995	Andre-Victorian 4261	250		590.00	590
1995	Anna- Victorian 4262	250		590.00	590
1996	Katherine-Caroler 4267	250		590.00	590
1996	Naathanael, Caroler 4266	250		590.00	590

Bears - L. West

YEAR ISSUE		EDITION LIMIT	YEAR RETD.	ISSUE PRICE	*QUOTE U.S.$
1991	Ashley Bearsley 5005	300	1991	500.00	500
1990	Duchess Tinchin 4900	100	1990	750.00	750
1991	Mr. Santa B. Claws 5000	300	1991	500.00	500
1991	Mrs. Santa B. Claws 5001	300	1991	500.00	500
1989	Princess Simsong and PI 3100	150	1989	750.00	750
1989	Sara Bearsley 5006	300	1991	500.00	500
1994	Su-Lin and Son 9001	Retrd.	1994	300.00	300
1989	Wee Woo Wong 2500	Retrd.	1988	750.00	750

Christmas Elves - L. West

YEAR ISSUE		EDITION LIMIT	YEAR RETD.	ISSUE PRICE	*QUOTE U.S.$
1988	Bayberry 2304	300	1988	250.00	250
1989	Bayberry 3503	300	1989	278.00	278
1994	Brandy 8103	150	1994	230.00	230
1991	D'Light 4505	350	1992	500.00	50[illegible]
1993	Dominick 4531	350	1994	420.00	420
1994	Forrest 8101	150	1994	210.00	210
1995	Giuseppe-Christmas Elf 4515	150		900.00	90[illegible]
1995	Goldwin 4525	150	1995	950.00	95[illegible]
1990	Half Note 4603	500	1992	278.00	27[illegible]
1988	Holly 1988 2302	300	1988	230.00	230
1989	Holly 3501	300	1989	250.00	250
1994	Jolly Holiday 4540	200		950.00	95[illegible]
1994	Krister 4541	250		510.00	51[illegible]
1994	Nate 8102	150	1994	220.00	22[illegible]
1992	Oliver 2452	200	1993	470.00	47[illegible]
1992	Patches 4605	500	1993	278.00	27[illegible]
1992	Pepe Mint 4510	350	1992	850.00	85[illegible]
1993	Raffael 4530	350	1994	390.00	39[illegible]
1990	Rocky 4602	500	1992	278.00	27[illegible]
1991	Rump-Papa-Pum 4604	500	1992	278.00	27[illegible]
1990	Russell The Wrapper 4500	350	1992	480.00	48[illegible]
1990	Skeeter 4601	500	1992	278.00	27[illegible]
1993	T'Winkle 4520	200	1994	950.00	95[illegible]
1992	Timothy 2453	200	1994	590.00	59[illegible]
1988	Wassail 2303	300	1988	250.00	25[illegible]
1989	Wassail 3502	300	1989	250.00	25[illegible]
1993	Wolfie 4532	350	1995	390.00	39[illegible]

Christmas Scenes - L. West

YEAR ISSUE		EDITION LIMIT	YEAR RETD.	ISSUE PRICE	*QUOTE U.S.$
1993	Checking It Twice 2350	150	1995	3590.00	359[illegible]
1992	Christmas Memories Set 2450	200	1994	2390.00	239[illegible]
1991	Merry Little Christmas 2400	200	1993	1990.00	199[illegible]
1989	Tree Top Angel 3600	Retrd.	1989	500.00	50[illegible]
1989	Up On The Roof Top 2305	100	1991	1300.00	130[illegible]

Faeries - L. West

YEAR ISSUE		EDITION LIMIT	YEAR RETD.	ISSUE PRICE	*QUOTE U.S.$
1994	Asteroid 4221	300	1995	284.00	28[illegible]
1992	Baubles 4211	500	1993	284.00	28[illegible]
1990	Berry 4201	500	1991	278.00	27[illegible]
1990	Blueberry 4101	500	1990	270.00	27[illegible]
1995	Borealis 4224	300	1995	310.00	31[illegible]
1994	Cadence 4222	300	1995	284.00	28[illegible]

*Quotes have been rounded up to nearest dollar

YEAR ISSUE		EDITION LIMIT	YEAR RETD.	ISSUE PRICE	*QUOTE U.S.$
1992	Cardinal 4213	500	1993	284.00	284
1996	Dreamweaver 4230	110		330.00	330
1990	Dusty 4103	500	1991	270.00	270
1991	Eggburt 4112	500	1993	278.00	278
1990	Emerald 4102	500	1992	270.00	270
1993	Evergreen 4219	300	1994	284.00	284
1992	Fiddler 4210	500	1993	284.00	284
1995	Figaro 4225	300	1995	310.00	310
1996	Gardino 4232	250		330.00	330
1992	Golden Frost 4214	500	1993	284.00	284
1996	Gumdrop 4233	250		330.00	330
1993	Jack 4218	300	1994	284.00	284
1990	Jingles 4202	500	1992	278.00	278
1996	Jubilee 4231	250		330.00	330
1992	Ludwig 4216	500	1993	284.00	284
1994	Mendicino 7020	200	1995	510.00	510
1991	Mistletoe 4205	500	1993	284.00	284
1991	Raddish 4111	500	1992	278.00	278
1995	Sean-Custom Faerie/Neiman Marcus 101	38	1995	310.00	310
1995	Serenade 4223	300	1995	310.00	310
1990	Snowflake 4203	500	1991	278.00	278
1992	Spring Mist 4215	500	1993	284.00	284
1992	Tealberry 4217	500	1994	284.00	284
1994	Timber 4220	300	1995	284.00	284
1991	Tweetle Berry 4204	500	1992	284.00	284
1995	Winsor-Custom Faerie/Neiman Marcus 100	38	1995	310.00	310
1992	Woodie 4212	500	1993	284.00	284

Father Christmas - L. West

1994	Anniversary Father Christmas 4330	300	1995	750.00	750
1992	Christmas Glory 4310	350	1993	750.00	750
1989	Christmas Majesty 2300	250	1988	750.00	750
1993	Christmas Majesty Special Ed. 4270	100	1993	1590.00	1590
1994	Christmas Peace 4275	100	1995	1450.00	1450
1993	Father Christmas with Staff 4250	200	1994	1300.00	1300
1991	Father Nikolai 4305	500	1993	750.00	750
1989	Grand Father Christmas 3520	300	1991	750.00	750
1996	Old World Santa 4340	250		750.00	750
1993	Special Delivery 4320	350	1993	750.00	750
1994	Victorian Saint Nicholas 4255	150	1995	1300.00	1300
1995	Victorian Winter Father Christmas 4260	250		1450.00	1450
1990	Winter Majesty 4300	350	1992	750.00	750
1996	Yuletide Saint Nick 4265	250		1450.00	1450

Forest Fantasies - L. West

1994	Captain Surewood 7025	200	1995	950.00	950
1992	Father Earth 7000	350	1993	830.00	830
1995	Frederick-Music School 7006	100	1995	490.00	490
1993	Hermes 7010	200	1993	790.00	790
1992	Leopole 7002	350	1993	470.00	470
1995	Professer Wind Chime 7005	100	1995	1190.00	1190
1991	Sullivan 4110	350	1992	480.00	480
1990	Telltale and Teabu 7001	350	1993	670.00	670
1990	Wee Willie 4000	350	1991	480.00	480
1993	Whiskers and Wink 7015	200	1993	590.00	590

Home Bred Folks - L. Gill

1995	Aunt Ruthie with Quilt 1000	250	1995	430.00	430
1996	Belle, HomeBred Angel 1007	250		350.00	350
1995	Dottie Ellen with Bread 1006	250	1995	430.00	430
1995	Hazel Jane with Birds 1001	250	1995	430.00	430
1995	Jake and His Dog 1003	250	1995	430.00	430
1995	Margaret with Vegetables 1004	250	1995	430.00	430
1995	Marie And Her Dog 1002	250	1995	430.00	430
1995	Miss Henrieta with Eggs 1005	250	1995	430.00	430

Lynniputs - L. West

1994	Chestnut-Lynniputs 7032	350	1995	450.00	450
1995	Fern-Lynniputs 7035	350	1995	450.00	450
1995	Frostie-Lynniputs 7034	350		450.00	450
1994	Nester-Lynniputs 7030	350	1995	450.00	450
1994	Noel-Lynniputs 7033	350	1995	450.00	450
1994	Pops-Lynniputs 7031	350	1995	450.00	450

Old Time Santa Series - L. West

1992	Old Time Santa-1st in Series 3540	300	1993	530.00	530
1993	Still Fits-2nd in Series 3545	300	1993	700.00	700
1994	Old Time Santa and Tree-3rd in Series 3546	250	1995	650.00	650

Santa Elves Series - L. West

1995	Franz, Santa's Helper 3555	300	1995	330.00	330
1996	Herbie, Holiday Helper 3602	250		350.00	350

Santas - L. West

1992	Classic Santa With Chair 2451	200	1993	1450.00	1450
1988	Kris Kringle Special Edition 1115	50	1988	2000.00	2000
1990	Large Santa 4400	250	1993	700.00	700
1991	Last Minute Details w/ Beard 6005BRD	950	1992	550.00	550
1991	Last Minute Details-M.B. 6005	950	1992	430.00	430
1995	Lynn West's Santa Claus 3550	250		550.00	550
1991	Saint Nick 6000	950	1991	370.00	370
1989	Santa At The North Pole 3535	300	1991	450.00	450
1988	Spencer 2301	150	1991	850.00	850
1994	Standing Santa w/Toypack 9002	Retrd.	1994	450.00	450

YEAR ISSUE		EDITION LIMIT	YEAR RETD.	ISSUE PRICE	*QUOTE U.S.$
1996	Woodland Santa & Herbie 3600	250		1650.00	1650
1996	Woodland Santa on wooden base 3601	250		690.00	690

Toys With Affection - D. Thibault

1995	Father Folk Art 2004	250	1995	260.00	260
1995	Good Tidings Santa 2003	250	1995	380.00	380
1995	Jolly Jack 2002	250	1995	290.00	290
1995	The Melon Man 2001	250	1995	290.00	290
1995	Santa And His Sled 2005	250	1995	380.00	380
1995	True Blue Santa 2000	250	1995	250.00	250

Amazze Gifts, Inc.

Century Lights - S.N. Meyers

1994	Admiralty Head, WA	3,995		66.00	66
1995	Assateague, VA	4,975		62.00	62
1994	Barnegat, NJ	10,000		58.00	58
1995	Block Island, RI	4,896		86.00	86
1994	Boston Harbor, MA	3,475		58.00	58
1994	Buffalo, NY	3,475		54.00	54
1994	Burrows Island, WA	2,995		66.00	66
1994	Cape Blanco, OR	2,995	1996	58.00	58
1994	Cape Hatteras, NC	10,000		58.00	58
1995	Cape May, NJ	4,975		58.00	58
1994	Charlotte-Genesee, NY	3,475		40.00	40
1995	Chicago Harbor, IL	4,250		66.00	66
1994	Coquille River, OR	2,995		66.00	66
1994	Diamond Head, HI	10,000		54.00	54
1995	East Quoddy Head, Canada	2,475		58.00	58
1994	Fort Gratiot, MI	3,475		58.00	58
1994	Great Point, MA	2,475		58.00	58
1994	Hilton Head, SC	10,000		54.00	54
1994	Holland, MI	4,975		66.00	66
1995	Jupiter Inlet, FL	7,500		58.00	58
1995	Lorain Light, OH	3,195		66.00	66
1994	Marblehead, OH	7,500		54.00	54
1994	Montauk Point, NY	3,475		54.00	54
1995	Nauset Beach, MA	4,995		56.00	56
1994	Ned Point, MA	2,475	1996	40.00	40
1994	North Head, WA	2,995		58.00	58
1995	Ocracoke Island Light, NC	3,975		54.00	54
1994	Old Point Loma, CA	4,550		66.00	66
1994	Plymouth, MA	3,475		58.00	58
1994	Ponce De Leon, FL	3,475		54.00	54
1995	Port Isabel, TX	3,975		58.00	58
1995	Rose Island, RI	4,111		68.00	68
1994	Sand Point, MI	3,475		66.00	66
1995	Sandy Hook, NJ	4,975		58.00	58
1995	Split Rock, MN	4,449		66.00	66
1995	St. Augustine, FL	10,000		62.00	62
1995	St. George Reef, CA	4,500		62.00	62
1995	St. Simmons, GA	3,975		56.00	56
1994	Tybee Island, GA	3,475		58.00	58
1994	Umpqua, OR	2,995		58.00	58
1995	West Quoddy Head, ME	4,995		66.00	66
1995	Yaquina Head, OR	4,500		60.00	60

Centuryville - S.N. Meyers

1995	Bed & Breakfast	1,975		56.00	56
1994	Cathedral	2,950	1995	70.00	70
1994	Centuryville B&O	3,250		56.00	56
1994	Cranes Eye Point	3,750		50.00	50
1995	Fire Station	1,975		60.00	60
1994	Foggy Point	4,998	1995	50.00	50
1994	Gothic Church	3,436		60.00	60
1995	Lawrence Keith	1,975		64.00	64
1994	Mr. John Johnson	2,960		50.00	50
1994	Mr. Lyle E. Wilson	2,960		50.00	50
1994	Ms. Hilda Grant	2,960		50.00	50
1995	Ms. Marv William	1,975		60.00	60
1994	Ms. Mary Thompson	2,342		50.00	50
1994	Richard & Jan Smith	2,960		50.00	50
1994	Schoolhouse	3,250	1995	56.00	56
1995	Ship Island Miss	1,975	1995	48.00	48
1995	Sweet Shoppe	1,975		56.00	56
1994	Village Church	3,250		60.00	60

Evergreen Village - S.N. Meyers

1994	Candymakers	2,475		36.00	36
1994	Carpenters	2,475		36.00	36
1994	Cobblers	2,475		36.00	36
1994	Cottage Point	2,675	1995	36.00	36
1994	Evergreen Church	2,475	1995	50.00	50
1994	Train Conductors	2,475		36.00	36

American Artists

Fred Stone Figurines - F. Stone

1986	Arab Mare & Foal	2,500		150.00	225
1985	The Black Stallion, bronze	1,500		150.00	175
1985	The Black Stallion, porcelain	2,500		125.00	260
1987	Rearing Black Stallion (Bronze)	1,250		175.00	195
1987	Rearing Black Stallion (Porcelain)	3,500		150.00	175
1986	Tranquility	2,500		175.00	275

Anheuser-Busch, Inc.

Anheuser-Busch Collectible Figurines - Various

YEAR ISSUE		EDITION LIMIT	YEAR RETD.	ISSUE PRICE	*QUOTE U.S.$
1994	Buddies N4575 - M. Urdahl	7,500		65.00	65
1995	Horseplay F1 - P. Radtke	7,500		65.00	65
1995	"Bud-weis-er Frogs" F4 - A. Busch, Inc.	Open		30.00	30

ANRI

Club ANRI - Various

1983	Welcome, 4" J. Ferrandiz	Yr.Iss.	1984	110.00	395
1984	My Friend, 4" - J. Ferrandiz	Yr.Iss.	1985	110.00	400
1984	Apple of My Eye, 4 1/2" - S. Kay	Yr.Iss.	1985	135.00	385
1985	Harvest Time, 4" - J. Ferrandiz	Yr.Iss.	1986	125.00	175-385
1985	Dad's Helper, 4 1/2" - S. Kay	Yr.Iss.	1986	135.00	150-375
1986	Harvest's Helper, 4" - J. Ferrandiz	Yr.Iss.	1987	135.00	175-335
1986	Romantic Notions, 4" - S. Kay	Yr.Iss.	1987	135.00	175-310
1986	Celebration March, 5" - J. Ferrandiz	Yr.Iss.	1987	165.00	225-295
1987	Will You Be Mine, 4" - J. Ferrandiz	Yr.Iss.	1988	135.00	175-310
1987	Make A Wish, 4" - S. Kay	Yr.Iss.	1988	165.00	215-325
1987	A Young Man's Fancy, 4" - S. Kay	Yr.Iss.	1988	135.00	165-265
1988	Forever Yours, 4" - J. Ferrandiz	Yr.Iss.	1989	170.00	250
1988	I've Got a Secret, 4" - S. Kay	Yr.Iss.	1989	170.00	205
1988	Maestro Mickey, 4 1/2" - Disney Studio	Yr.Iss.	1989	170.00	175
1989	Diva Minnie, 4 1/2" - Disney Studio	Yr.Iss.	1990	190.00	190
1989	I'll Never Tell, 4" - S. Kay	Yr.Iss.	1990	190.00	190
1989	Twenty Years of Love, 4" - J. Ferrandiz	Yr.Iss.	1990	190.00	190
1990	You Are My Sunshine, 4" - J. Ferrandiz	Yr.Iss.	1991	220.00	220
1990	A Little Bashful, 4" - S. Kay	Yr.Iss.	1991	220.00	220
1990	Dapper Donald, 4" - Disney Studio	Yr.Iss.	1991	199.00	199
1991	With All My Heart, 4" - J. Ferrandiz	Yr.Iss.	1992	250.00	250
1991	Kiss Me, 4" - S. Kay	Yr.Iss.	1992	250.00	250
1991	Daisy Duck, 4 1/2" - Disney Studio	Yr.Iss.	1992	250.00	250

ANRI Club - Various

1992	You Are My All, 4" - J. Ferrandiz	Yr.Iss.	1993	260.00	260
1992	My Present For You, 4" - S. Kay	Yr.Iss.	1993	270.00	270
1992	Gift of Love - S. Kay	Yr.Iss.	1993	Gift	N/A
1993	Truly Yours, 4" - J. Ferrandiz	Yr.Iss.	1994	290.00	290
1993	Sweet Thoughts, 4" - S. Kay	Yr.Iss.	1994	300.00	300
1993	Just For You - S. Kay	Yr.Iss.	1994	Gift	N/A
1994	Sweet 'N Shy, 4" - J. Ferrandiz	Yr.Iss.	1994	250.00	250
1994	Snuggle Up, 4" - S. Kay	Yr.Iss.	1994	300.00	300
1994	Dapper 'N Dear, 4" - J. Ferrandiz	Yr.Iss.	1994	250.00	250

ANRI Collectors' Society- Various

1995	On My Own, 4" - S. Kay	Yr.Iss.	1996	175.00	175
1995	Sealed With A Kiss - J. Ferrandiz	Yr.Iss.		275.00	275
1995	ANRI Artists' Tree House - ANRI	Yr.Iss.		695.00	695
1996	On Cloud Nine - J. Ferrandiz	Yr.Iss.		275.00	275
1996	Sweet Tooth - S. Kay	Yr.Iss.		199.50	200

Bernardi Reflections - U. Bernardi

1994	Master Carver, 4"	500		350.00	350
1994	Master Carver, 6"	250	1995	600.00	600
1995	Planning the Tour, 4"	500		450.00	450
1995	Planning the Tour, 6"	250		300.00	300

Disney Studios Mickey Mouse Thru The Ages - Disney Studios

1991	The Mad Dog, 4"	1,000	1991	500.00	375-500
1990	Steam Boat Willie, 4"	1,000	1990	295.00	450-550

Disney Woodcarving - Disney Studio

1991	Bell Boy Donald, 4" 656029	Closed	1991	250.00	250
1991	Bell Boy Donald, 6" 656110	500	1991	400.00	400
1990	Chef Goofy, 2 1/2" 656222	Closed	1991	125.00	150-175
1990	Chef Goofy, 5" 656227	Closed	1991	265.00	265
1989	Daisy, 4" 656021	Closed	1991	190.00	225
1990	Donald & Daisy, 6" 656108	500	1991	700.00	700
1988	Donald Duck, 1 3/4" 656209	Closed	1990	80.00	125
1988	Donald Duck, 2" 656204	Closed	1990	85.00	100-135
1987	Donald Duck, 4" 656004	Closed	1989	150.00	200-265
1988	Donald Duck, 4" 656014	Closed	1990	180.00	200-295
1988	Donald Duck, 6" 656102	500	1988	350.00	500
1989	Donald, 4" 656020	Closed	1991	190.00	200-250
1988	Goofy, 1 3/4" 656210	Closed	1990	80.00	100-150
1988	Goofy, 2" 656205	Closed	1990	85.00	100-150
1987	Goofy, 4" 656005	Closed	1989	150.00	200-250
1988	Goofy, 4" 656015	Closed	1990	180.00	200-250
1989	Goofy, 4" 656022	Closed	1991	190.00	200-250
1988	Goofy, 6" 656103	500	1988	380.00	575
1988	Goofy, 6" 656105	500	1991	350.00	400-500
1989	Mickey & Minnie Set, 6" 656106	500	1991	700.00	750-950
1989	Mickey & Minnie, 20" matched set	50	1991	7000.00	7000
1987	Mickey & Minnie, 6" 656101	500	1987	625.00	1000
1988	Mickey Mouse, 1 3/4" 656206	Closed	1990	80.00	200-250
1988	Mickey Mouse, 2" 656201	Closed	1990	85.00	100-150
1990	Mickey Mouse, 2" 656220	Closed	1991	100.00	200-400

*Quotes have been rounded up to nearest dollar

FIGURINES/COTTAGES

YEAR ISSUE		EDITION LIMIT	YEAR RETD.	ISSUE PRICE	*QUOTE U.S.$
1987	Mickey Mouse, 4" 656001	Closed	1989	150.00	200-300
1988	Mickey Mouse, 4" 656011	Closed	1990	180.00	200-300
1990	Mickey Mouse, 4" 656025	Closed	1991	199.00	250-295
1991	Mickey Skating, 2" 656224	Closed	1991	120.00	250-295
1991	Mickey Skating, 4" 656030	Closed	1991	250.00	150
1988	Mickey Sorcerer's Apprentice, 2" 656211	Closed	1991	80.00	200
1988	Mickey Sorcerer's Apprentice, 4" 656016	Closed	1991	180.00	199
1988	Mickey Sorcerer's Apprentice, 6" 656109	500	1991	350.00	650
1989	Mickey, 10" 656800	250	1991	700.00	850-1000
1989	Mickey, 20" 656850	50	1991	3500.00	3500
1989	Mickey, 4" 656018	Closed	1991	190.00	250-350
1988	Mini Donald, 1 3/4" 656204	Closed	1991	85.00	150
1989	Mini Donald, 2" 656215	Closed	1991	85.00	150
1988	Mini Goofy, 1 3/4" 656205	Closed	1991	85.00	175
1989	Mini Goofy, 2" 656217	Closed	1991	85.00	175
1988	Mini Mickey, 1 3/4" 656201	Closed	1991	85.00	185
1989	Mini Mickey, 2" 656213	Closed	1991	85.00	185
1988	Mini Minnie, 1 3/4" 656202	Closed	1991	85.00	185
1989	Mini Minnie, 2" 656214	Closed	1991	85.00	185
1989	Mini Pluto, 2" 656218	Closed	1991	85.00	100-125
1989	Minnie Daisy, 2" 656216	Closed	1991	85.00	100-125
1988	Minnie Mouse, 2" 656202	Closed	1990	85.00	100-125
1990	Minnie Mouse, 2" 656221	Closed	1991	100.00	100-125
1987	Minnie Mouse, 4" 656002	Closed	1989	150.00	250
1990	Minnie Mouse, 4" 656026	Closed	1991	199.00	200
1988	Minnie Pinocchio, 1 3/4" 656203	Closed	1991	85.00	200-300
1991	Minnie Skating, 2" 656225	Closed	1991	120.00	125
1991	Minnie Skating, 4" 656031	Closed	1991	250.00	350
1989	Minnie, 10" 656801	250	1991	700.00	900-1100
1989	Minnie, 20" 656851	50	1991	3500.00	3500
1989	Minnie, 4" 656019	Closed	1991	190.00	250
1988	Pinocchio, 1 3/4" 656208	Closed	1990	80.00	200-300
1989	Pinocchio, 10" 656802	250	1991	700.00	1000
1988	Pinocchio, 2" 656203	Closed	1990	85.00	85
1989	Pinocchio, 2" 656219	Closed	1991	85.00	100
1989	Pinocchio, 20" 656851	50	1991	3500.00	3500
1987	Pinocchio, 4" 656003 (apple)	Closed	1989	150.00	300
1988	Pinocchio, 4" 656013	Closed	1990	180.00	199
1989	Pinocchio, 4" 656024	Closed	1991	190.00	199
1989	Pinocchio, 6" 656107	500	1991	350.00	350
1988	Pluto, 1 3/4" 656207	Closed	1990	80.00	100-135
1988	Pluto, 4" 656012	Closed	1990	180.00	225
1989	Pluto, 4" 656023	Closed	1991	190.00	225
1988	Pluto, 6" 656104	500	1991	350.00	350
1990	Sorcerer's Apprentice w/ crystal, 2" 656223	Closed	1991	125.00	300-450
1990	Sorcerer's Apprentice w/ crystal, 4" 656028	Closed	1991	265.00	350
1990	Sorcerer's Apprentice w/ crystal, 6" 656109	1,000	1991	475.00	500-650
1990	Sorcerer's Apprentice w/ crystal, 8" 656803	350	1991	790.00	800-900
1990	Sorcerer's Apprentice w/ crystal,16" 656853	100	1991	3500.00	3500

Ferrandiz Boy and Girl - J. Ferrandiz

YEAR ISSUE		EDITION LIMIT	YEAR RETD.	ISSUE PRICE	*QUOTE U.S.$
1983	Admiration, 6"	2,250	1983	220.00	295
1990	Alpine Friend, 3"	1,500	1990	225.00	365
1990	Alpine Friend, 6"	1,500	1990	450.00	610
1990	Alpine Music, 3"	1,500	1990	225.00	225
1990	Alpine Music, 6"	1,500	1990	450.00	580
1989	Baker Boy, 3"	1,500	1989	170.00	170
1989	Baker Boy, 6"	1,500	1989	340.00	340
1978	Basket of Joy, 6"	1,500	1978	140.00	350-450
1983	Bewildered, 6"	2,250	1983	196.00	295
1991	Catalonian Boy, 3"	1,500	1993	227.50	228
1991	Catalonian Boy, 6"	1,500	1993	500.00	500
1991	Catalonian Girl, 3"	1,500	1993	227.50	228
1991	Catalonian Girl, 6"	1,500	1993	500.00	500
1976	Cowboy, 6"	1,500	1976	75.00	500-600
1987	Dear Sweetheart, 3"	2,250	1989	130.00	130
1987	Dear Sweetheart, 6"	2,250	1989	250.00	250
1988	Extra, Extra!, 3"	1,500	1988	145.00	145
1988	Extra, Extra!, 6"	1,500	1988	320.00	320
1979	First Blossom, 6"	2,250	1979	135.00	345-375
1987	For My Sweetheart, 3"	2,250	1989	130.00	130
1987	For My Sweetheart, 6"	2,250	1989	250.00	250
1984	Friendly Faces, 3"	2,250	1984	93.00	110
1984	Friendly Faces, 6"	2,250	1984	210.00	225-295
1980	Friends, 6"	2,250	1980	200.00	300-350
1986	Golden Sheaves, 3"	2,250	1986	125.00	125
1986	Golden Sheaves, 6"	2,250	1986	245.00	245
1982	Guiding Light, 6"	2,250	1982	225.00	275-350
1979	Happy Strummer, 6"	2,250	1979	160.00	395
1976	Harvest Girl, 6"	1,500	1976	75.00	400-800
1977	Leading the Way, 6"	1,500	1977	100.00	300-375
1992	May I, Too?, 3"	1,000	1993	230.00	230
1992	May I, Too?, 6"	1,000	1993	440.00	440
1980	Melody for Two, 6"	2,250	1980	200.00	350
1981	Merry Melody, 6"	2,250	1981	210.00	300-350
1989	Pastry Girl, 3"	1,500	1989	170.00	170
1989	Pastry Girl, 6"	1,500	1989	340.00	340
1978	Peace Pipe, 6"	1,500	1978	140.00	325-450
1985	Peaceful Friends, 3"	2,250	1985	120.00	120
1985	Peaceful Friends, 6"	2,250	1985	250.00	295
1986	Season's Bounty, 3"	2,250	1986	125.00	125
1986	Season's Bounty, 6"	2,250	1986	245.00	245
1988	Sunny Skies, 3"	1,500	1988	145.00	145
1988	Sunny Skies, 6"	1,500	1988	320.00	320
1985	Tender Love, 3"	2,250	1985	100.00	125
1985	Tender Love, 6"	2,250	1985	225.00	250

YEAR ISSUE		EDITION LIMIT	YEAR RETD.	ISSUE PRICE	*QUOTE U.S.$
1981	Tiny Sounds, 6"	2,250	1981	210.00	300-350
1982	To Market, 6"	1,500	1982	220.00	295
1977	Tracker, 6"	1,500	1977	100.00	400
1984	Wanderer's Return, 3"	2,250	1984	93.00	135
1984	Wanderer's Return, 6"	2,250	1984	196.00	250
1992	Waste Not, Want Not, 3"	1,000	1993	190.00	200
1992	Waste Not, Want Not, 6"	1,000	1993	430.00	430

Ferrandiz Message Collection - J. Ferrandiz

YEAR ISSUE		EDITION LIMIT	YEAR RETD.	ISSUE PRICE	*QUOTE U.S.$
1990	Christmas Carillon, 4 1/2"	2,500	1992	299.00	299
1990	Count Your Blessings, 4 1/2"	5,000	1992	300.00	300
1990	God's Creation, 4 1/2"	5,000	1992	300.00	300
1989	God's Miracle, 4 1/2"	5,000	1991	300.00	300
1989	God's Precious Gift, 4 1/2"	5,000	1991	300.00	300
1989	He Guides Us, 4 1/2"	5,000	1991	300.00	300
1989	He is the Light, 4 1/2"	5,000	1991	300.00	300
1989	He is the Light, 9"	5,000	1991	600.00	600
1989	Heaven Sent, 4 1/2"	5,000	1991	300.00	300
1989	Light From Within, 4 1/2"	5,000	1991	300.00	300
1989	Love Knows No Bounds, 4 1/2"	5,000	1991	300.00	300
1989	Love So Powerful, 4 1/2"	5,000	1991	300.00	300

Ferrandiz Mini Nativity Set - J. Ferrandiz

YEAR ISSUE		EDITION LIMIT	YEAR RETD.	ISSUE PRICE	*QUOTE U.S.$
1985	Baby Camel, 1 1/2"	Closed	1993	45.00	53
1985	Camel Guide, 1 1/2"	Closed	1993	45.00	53
1985	Camel, 1 1/2"	Closed	1993	45.00	53
1988	Devotion, 1 1/2"	Closed	1993	53.00	53
1985	Harmony, 1 1/2"	Closed	1993	45.00	53
1984	Infant, 1 1/2"	Closed	1993	Set	Set
1988	Jolly Gift, 1 1/2"	Closed	1992	53.00	53
1984	Joseph, 1 1/2"	Closed	1993	Set	Set
1984	Leading the Way, 1 1/2"	Closed	1993	Set	Set
1988	Long Journey, 1 1/2"	Closed	1993	53.00	53
1984	Mary, 1 1/2"	Closed	1993	300.00	540
1986	Mini Angel, 1 1/2"	Closed	1993	45.00	53
1986	Mini Balthasar, 1 1/2"	Closed	1993	45.00	53
1986	Mini Caspar, 1 1/2"	Closed	1993	45.00	53
1986	Mini Free Ride, plus Mini Lamb, 1 1/2"	Closed	1993	45.00	53
1986	Mini Melchoir, 1 1/2"	Closed	1993	45.00	53
1986	Mini Star Struck, 1 1/2"	Closed	1993	45.00	53
1986	Mini The Hiker, 1 1/2"	Closed	1993	45.00	53
1986	Mini The Stray, 1 1/2"	Closed	1993	45.00	53
1986	Mini Weary Traveller, 1 1/2"	Closed	1993	45.00	53
1984	Ox Donkey, 1 1/2"	Closed	1993	Set	Set
1985	Rest, 1 1/2"	Closed	1993	45.00	53
1985	Reverence, 1 1/2"	Closed	1993	45.00	53
1984	Sheep Kneeling, 1 1/2"	Closed	1993	Set	Set
1984	Sheep Standing, 1 1/2"	Closed	1993	Set	Set
1985	Small Talk, 1 1/2"	Closed	1993	45.00	53
1988	Sweet Dreams, 1 1/2"	Closed	1993	53.00	53
1988	Sweet Inspiration, 1 1/2"	Closed	1992	53.00	53
1985	Thanksgiving, 1 1/2"	Closed	1993	45.00	53

Ferrandiz Shepherds of the Year - J. Ferrandiz

YEAR ISSUE		EDITION LIMIT	YEAR RETD.	ISSUE PRICE	*QUOTE U.S.$
1982	Companions, 6"	2,250	1982	220.00	275-300
1984	Devotion, 3"	2,250	1984	82.50	125
1984	Devotion, 6"	2,250	1984	180.00	200-250
1979	Drummer Boy, 3"	Yr.Iss.	1979	80.00	250
1979	Drummer Boy, 6"	Yr.Iss.	1979	220.00	400-425
1980	Freedom Bound, 3"	Yr.Iss.	1980	90.00	225
1980	Freedom Bound, 6"	Yr.Iss.	1980	225.00	400
1977	Friendship, 3"	Yr.Iss.	1977	53.50	330
1977	Friendship, 6"	Yr.Iss.	1977	110.00	500-675
1983	Good Samaritan, 6"	2,250	1983	220.00	300-320
1981	Jolly Piper, 6"	2,250	1981	225.00	375
1978	Spreading the Word, 3"	Yr.Iss.	1978	115.00	250-275
1978	Spreading the Word, 6"	Yr.Iss.	1978	270.50	500

Ferrandiz Woodcarvings - J. Ferrandiz

YEAR ISSUE		EDITION LIMIT	YEAR RETD.	ISSUE PRICE	*QUOTE U.S.$
1988	Abracadabra, 3"	1,500	1991	145.00	165
1988	Abracadabra, 6"	1,500	1991	315.00	345
1976	Adoration, 12"	Closed	1987	350.00	350
1981	Adoration, 20"	250	1987	3200.00	3200
1976	Adoration, 3"	Closed	1987	45.00	45
1976	Adoration, 6"	Closed	1987	100.00	100
1987	Among Friends, 3"	3,000	1990	125.00	151
1987	Among Friends, 6"	3,000	1990	245.00	291
1969	Angel Sugar Heart, 6"	Closed	1973	25.00	2500
1974	Artist, 3"	Closed	1981	30.00	195
1970	Artist, 6"	Closed	1981	25.00	350
1982	Bagpipe, 3"	Closed	1983	80.00	95
1982	Bagpipe, 6"	Closed	1983	175.00	190
1978	Basket of Joy, 3"	Closed	1984	65.00	120
1984	Bird's Eye View, 3"	Closed	1989	88.00	129
1984	Bird's Eye View, 6"	Closed	1989	216.00	700
1987	Black Forest Boy, 3"	3,000	1990	125.00	151
1987	Black Forest Boy, 6"	3,000	1990	250.00	301
1987	Black Forest Girl, 3"	3,000	1990	125.00	151
1987	Black Forest Girl, 6"	3,000	1990	250.00	300-350
1977	The Blessing, 3"	Closed	1982	45.00	150
1977	The Blessing, 6"	Closed	1982	125.00	250
1988	Bon Appetit, 3"	500	1991	175.00	195
1988	Bon Appetit, 6"	500	1991	395.00	440
1974	The Bouquet, 3"	Closed	1981	35.00	175
1974	The Bouquet, 6"	Closed	1981	75.00	325
1982	Bundle of Joy, 3"	Closed	1990	100.00	300
1982	Bundle of Joy, 6"	Closed	1990	225.00	323
1985	Butterfly Boy, 3"	Closed	1990	95.00	140
1985	Butterfly Boy, 6"	Closed	1990	220.00	322
1976	Catch a Falling Star, 3"	Closed	1983	35.00	150
1976	Catch a Falling Star, 6"	Closed	1983	75.00	250
1982	The Champion, 3"	Closed	1985	98.00	110
1982	The Champion, 6"	Closed	1985	225.00	250
1975	Cherub, 2"	Open		32.00	90
1975	Cherub, 4"	Open		32.00	275
1993	Christmas Time, 5"	750		360.00	420
1982	Circus Serenade, 3"	Closed	1988	100.00	160
1982	Circus Serenade, 6"	Closed	1988	220.00	220
1982	Clarinet, 3"	Closed	1983	80.00	100
1982	Clarinet, 6"	Closed	1983	175.00	200
1982	Companions, 3"	Closed	1984	95.00	115
1975	Courting, 3"	Closed	1982	70.00	235
1975	Courting, 6"	Closed	1982	150.00	450
1984	Cowboy, 10"	Closed	1989	370.00	500
1983	Cowboy, 20"	250	1989	2100.00	2100
1976	Cowboy, 3"	Closed	1989	35.00	140-160
1994	Donkey Driver, 3"	Open		160.00	160
1994	Donkey Driver, 6"	Open		360.00	360
1994	Donkey, 3"	Open		200.00	200
1994	Donkey, 6"	Open		450.00	450
1980	Drummer Boy, 3"	Closed	1988	130.00	200
1980	Drummer Boy, 6"	Closed	1988	300.00	400
1970	Duet, 3"	Closed	1991	36.00	165
1970	Duet, 6"	Closed	1991	Unkn.	355
1986	Edelweiss, 10"	Open		500.00	1000
1986	Edelweiss, 20"	250		3300.00	5420
1983	Edelweiss, 3"	Open		95.00	205
1983	Edelweiss, 6"	Open		220.00	500
1982	Encore, 3"	Closed	1984	100.00	115
1982	Encore, 6"	Closed	1984	225.00	235
1979	First Blossom, 3"	Closed	1985	70.00	110
1974	Flight Into Egypt, 3"	Closed	1986	35.00	125
1974	Flight Into Egypt, 6"	Closed	1986	70.00	500
1976	Flower Girl, 3"	Closed	1988	40.00	40
1976	Flower Girl, 6"	Closed	1988	90.00	310
1982	Flute, 3"	Closed	1983	80.00	95
1982	Flute, 6"	Closed	1983	175.00	190
1976	Gardener, 3"	Closed	1984	32.00	195
1976	Gardener, 6"	Closed	1985	65.00	275-350
1975	The Gift, 3"	Closed	1982	40.00	195
1975	The Gift, 6"	Closed	1982	70.00	295
1973	Girl in the Egg, 3"	Closed	1988	30.00	127
1973	Girl in the Egg, 6"	Closed	1988	60.00	272
1973	Girl with Dove, 3"	Closed	1984	30.00	110
1973	Girl with Dove, 6"	Closed	1984	50.00	175-200
1976	Girl with Rooster, 3"	Closed	1982	32.50	175
1976	Girl with Rooster, 6"	Closed	1982	60.00	275
1986	God's Little Helper, 2"	3,500	1991	170.00	255
1986	God's Little Helper, 4"	2,000	1991	425.00	550
1975	Going Home, 3"	Closed	1988	40.00	175
1975	Going Home, 6"	Closed	1988	70.00	325
1986	Golden Blossom, 10"	Open		500.00	1000
1986	Golden Blossom, 20"	250		3300.00	5420
1983	Golden Blossom, 3"	Open		95.00	205
1986	Golden Blossom, 40"	50	1994	8300.00	12950
1983	Golden Blossom, 6"	Open		220.00	500
1982	The Good Life, 3"	Closed	1984	100.00	200
1982	The Good Life, 6"	Closed	1984	225.00	295
1969	The Good Sheperd, 3"	Closed	1988	12.50	121
1971	The Good Shepherd, 10"	Closed	1988	90.00	90
1969	The Good Shepherd, 6"	Closed	1988	25.00	237
1974	Greetings, 3"	Closed	1976	30.00	300
1974	Greetings, 6"	Closed	1976	55.00	475
1982	Guiding Light, 3"	Closed	1984	100.00	115-140
1982	Guitar, 3"	Closed	1983	80.00	95
1982	Guitar, 6"	Closed	1983	175.00	190
1979	Happy Strummer, 3"	Closed	1986	75.00	110
1973	Happy Wanderer, 10"	Closed	1985	120.00	500
1974	Happy Wanderer, 3"	Closed	1986	40.00	105
1974	Happy Wanderer, 6"	Closed	1986	70.00	200
1982	Harmonica, 3"	Closed	1983	80.00	95
1982	Harmonica, 3"	Closed	1983	80.00	95
1982	Harmonica, 6"	Closed	1983	175.00	190
1978	Harvest Girl, 3"	Closed	1986	75.00	110-140
1979	He's My Brother, 3"	Closed	1984	70.00	130
1979	He's My Brother, 6"	Closed	1984	155.00	240
1987	Heavenly Concert, 2"	3,000	1991	200.00	200
1987	Heavenly Concert, 4"	2,000	1991	450.00	550
1969	Heavenly Gardener, 6"	Closed	1973	25.00	2000
1969	Heavenly Quintet, 6"	Closed	1973	25.00	2000
1974	Helping Hands, 3"	Closed	1976	30.00	350
1974	Helping Hands, 6"	Closed	1976	55.00	70
1984	High Hopes, 3"	Closed	1986	81.00	81-10
1984	High Hopes, 6"	Closed	1986	170.00	25
1979	High Riding, 3"	Closed	1984	145.00	20
1979	High Riding, 6"	Closed	1984	340.00	47
1974	The Hiker, 3"	Closed	1993	36.00	3
1974	The Hiker, 6"	Closed	1993	80.00	8
1982	Hitchhiker, 3"	Closed	1986	98.00	85-11
1982	Hitchhiker, 6"	Closed	1986	125.00	23
1993	Holiday Greetings, 3"	1,000	1993	200.00	20
1993	Holiday Greetings, 6"	1,000	1993	450.00	45
1975	Holy Family, 3"	Closed	1988	75.00	25
1975	Holy Family, 6"	Closed	1988	200.00	67
1977	Hurdy Gurdy, 3"	Closed	1988	53.00	15
1977	Hurdy Gurdy, 6"	Closed	1988	112.00	39
1975	Inspector, 3"	Closed	1981	40.00	25
1975	Inspector, 6"	Closed	1981	80.00	39
1988	Jolly Gift, 3"	Closed	1991	129.00	12
1988	Jolly Gift, 6"	Closed	1991	296.00	29
1981	Jolly Piper, 3"	Closed	1984	100.00	12
1977	Journey, 3"	Closed	1983	67.50	17
1977	Journey, 6"	Closed	1983	120.00	40

*Quotes have been rounded up to nearest dollar

FIGURINES/COTTAGES

YEAR ISSUE		EDITION LIMIT	YEAR RETD.	ISSUE PRICE	*QUOTE U.S.$
1977	Leading the Way, 3"	Closed	1984	62.50	120
1976	The Letter, 3"	Closed	1988	40.00	40
1976	The Letter, 6"	Closed	1988	90.00	600
1982	Lighting the Way, 3"	Closed	1984	105.00	150
1982	Lighting the Way, 6"	Closed	1984	225.00	295
1974	Little Mother, 3"	Closed	1981	136.00	290
1974	Little Mother, 6"	Closed	1981	85.00	285
1989	Little Sheep Found, 3"	Open		120.00	120
1989	Little Sheep Found, 6"	Open		275.00	275
1993	Lots of Gifts, 3"	1,000	1993	200.00	200
1993	Lots of Gifts, 6"	1,000	1993	450.00	450
1975	Love Gift, 3"	Closed	1982	40.00	175
1975	Love Gift, 6"	Closed	1982	70.00	295
1969	Love Letter, 3"	Closed	1982	12.50	150
1969	Love Letter, 6"	Closed	1982	25.00	250
1983	Love Message, 3"	Closed	1990	105.00	151
1983	Love Message, 6"	Closed	1990	240.00	366
1969	Love's Messenger, 6"	Closed	1973	25.00	2000
1992	Madonna With Child, 3"	1,000	1994	190.00	190
1992	Madonna With Child, 6"	1,000	1994	370.00	370
1981	Merry Melody, 3"	Closed	1984	90.00	115
1989	Mexican Boy, 3"	1,500	1993	170.00	175
1989	Mexican Boy, 6"	1,500	1993	340.00	350
1989	Mexican Girl, 3"	1,500	1993	170.00	175
1989	Mexican Girl, 6"	1,500	1993	340.00	350
1975	Mother and Child, 3"	Closed	1983	45.00	150
1975	Mother and Child, 6"	Closed	1983	90.00	295
1981	Musical Basket, 3"	Closed	1984	90.00	115
1981	Musical Basket, 6"	Closed	1984	200.00	225
1986	A Musical Ride, 4"	Closed	1990	165.00	237
1986	A Musical Ride, 8"	Closed	1990	395.00	559
1973	Nature Girl, 3"	Closed	1988	30.00	30
1973	Nature Girl, 6"	Closed	1988	60.00	272
1987	Nature's Wonder, 3"	3,000	1990	125.00	151
1987	Nature's Wonder, 6"	3,000	1990	245.00	291
1974	New Friends, 3"	Closed	1976	30.00	275
1974	New Friends, 6"	Closed	1976	55.00	550
1977	Night Night, 3"	Closed	1983	45.00	120
1977	Night Night, 6"	Closed	1983	67.50	250-315
1992	Pascal Lamb, 3"	1,000	1993	210.00	210
1992	Pascal Lamb, 6"	1,000	1993	460.00	460
1988	Peace Maker, 3"	1,500	1991	180.00	200
1988	Peace Maker, 6"	1,500	1991	360.00	395
1983	Peace Pipe, 10"	Closed	1986	460.00	495
1984	Peace Pipe, 20"	250	1986	2200.00	3500
1979	Peace Pipe, 3"	Closed	1986	85.00	120
1988	Picnic for Two, 3"	500	1991	190.00	210
1988	Picnic for Two, 6"	500	1991	425.00	465
1982	Play It Again, 3"	Closed	1984	100.00	120
1982	Play It Again, 6"	Closed	1984	250.00	255
1977	Poor Boy, 3"	Closed	1986	50.00	110
1977	Poor Boy, 6"	Closed	1986	125.00	215
1977	Proud Mother, 3"	Closed	1988	52.50	150
1977	Proud Mother, 6"	Closed	1988	130.00	350
1971	The Quintet, 10"	Closed	1990	100.00	750
1971	The Quintet, 20"	Closed	1990	Unkn.	4750
1969	The Quintet, 3"	Closed	1990	12.50	175
1969	The Quintet, 6"	Closed	1990	25.00	395
1977	Riding Thru the Rain, 10"	Open		400.00	1190
1985	Riding Thru the Rain, 20"	100	1988	3950.00	3950
1977	Riding Thru the Rain, 5"	Open		145.00	470
1974	Romeo, 3"	Closed	1981	50.00	250
1974	Romeo, 6"	Closed	1981	85.00	395
1993	Santa and Teddy, 5"	750		360.00	380
1994	Santa Resting on Bag, 5"	750		400.00	400
1987	Serenity, 3"	3,000	1989	125.00	151
1987	Serenity, 6"	3,000	1989	245.00	291
1976	Sharing, 3"	Closed	1983	32.50	130
1976	Sharing, 6"	Closed	1983	32.50	225-275
1984	Shipmates, 3"	Closed	1989	81.00	119
1984	Shipmates, 6"	Closed	1989	170.00	248
1978	Spreading the Word, 3"	Closed	1989	115.00	194
1978	Spreading the Word, 6"	Closed	1989	270.00	495
1980	Spring Arrivals, 10"	Open		435.00	770
1980	Spring Arrivals, 20"	250		2000.00	3360
1973	Spring Arrivals, 3"	Open		30.00	160
1973	Spring Arrivals, 6"	Open		50.00	350
1978	Spring Dance, 12"	Closed	1984	950.00	1750
1978	Spring Dance, 24"	Closed	1984	4750.00	6200
1974	Spring Outing, 3"	Closed	1976	30.00	625
1974	Spring Outing, 6"	Closed	1976	55.00	900
1982	Star Bright, 3"	Closed	1984	110.00	125
1982	Star Bright, 6"	Closed	1984	250.00	295
1982	Star Struck, 10"	Closed	1987	490.00	490
1982	Star Struck, 20"	250	1987	2400.00	2400
1974	Star Struck, 3"	Closed	1987	97.50	98
1974	Star Struck, 6"	Closed	1987	210.00	210
1981	Stepping Out, 3"	Closed	1984	95.00	110-145
1981	Stepping Out, 6"	Closed	1984	220.00	275
1979	Stitch in Time, 3"	Closed	1984	75.00	125
1979	Stitch in Time, 6"	Closed	1984	150.00	235
1969	Sugar Heart, 3"	Closed	1973	12.50	450
1969	Sugar Heart, 6"	Closed	1973	25.00	525
1975	Summertime, 3"	Closed	1989	35.00	35
1975	Summertime, 6"	Closed	1989	70.00	258
1982	Surprise, 3"	Closed	1988	100.00	150
1982	Surprise, 6"	Closed	1988	225.00	325
1973	Sweeper, 3"	Closed	1981	35.00	130
1973	Sweeper, 6"	Closed	1981	75.00	425
1981	Sweet Arrival Blue, 3"	Closed	1985	105.00	110
1981	Sweet Arrival Blue, 6"	Closed	1985	225.00	255
1981	Sweet Arrival Pink, 3"	Closed	1985	105.00	110
1981	Sweet Arrival Pink, 6"	Closed	1985	225.00	225
1981	Sweet Dreams, 3"	Closed	1990	100.00	140
1982	Sweet Dreams, 6"	Closed	1990	225.00	330
1982	Sweet Melody, 3"	Closed	1985	80.00	90
1982	Sweet Melody, 6"	Closed	1985	198.00	210
1989	Swiss Boy, 3"	Closed	1993	180.00	180
1986	Swiss Boy, 3"	Closed	1993	122.00	162
1986	Swiss Boy, 6"	Closed	1993	245.00	324
1989	Swiss Boy, 6"	Closed	1993	380.00	380
1989	Swiss Girl, 3"	Closed	1993	200.00	200
1986	Swiss Girl, 3"	Closed	1993	122.00	122
1986	Swiss Girl, 6"	Closed	1993	245.00	304
1989	Swiss Girl, 6"	Closed	1993	470.00	470
1971	Talking to Animals, 20"	Closed	1989	Unkn.	3000
1971	Talking to the Animals, 10"	Closed	1989	90.00	600
1969	Talking to the Animals, 3"	Closed	1989	12.50	125
1969	Talking to the Animals, 6"	Closed	1989	45.00	250
1995	Tender Care, 3" 55710/52	Open		125.00	135
1995	Tender Care, 6" 55700/52	Open		275.00	275
1974	Tender Moments, 3"	Closed	1976	30.00	375
1974	Tender Moments, 6"	Closed	1976	55.00	575
1981	Tiny Sounds, 3"	Closed	1984	90.00	105
1982	To Market, 3"	Closed	1984	95.00	115
1977	Tracker, 3"	Closed	1984	70.00	120-200
1980	Trumpeter, 10"	Closed	1986	500.00	500
1984	Trumpeter, 20"	250	1986	2350.00	3050
1973	Trumpeter, 3"	Closed	1986	69.00	115
1973	Trumpeter, 6"	Closed	1986	120.00	240
1980	Umpapa, 4"	Closed	1984	125.00	140
1982	Violin, 3"	Closed	1983	80.00	95
1982	Violin, 6"	Closed	1983	175.00	195
1976	Wanderlust, 3"	Closed	1983	32.50	125
1975	Wanderlust, 6"	Closed	1983	70.00	450
1972	The Weary Traveler, 3"	Closed	1989	24.00	24
1972	The Weary Traveler, 6"	Closed	1989	48.00	48
1988	Winter Memories, 3"	1,500	1991	180.00	195
1988	Winter Memories, 6"	1,500	1991	398.00	440

Limited Edition Couples - J. Ferrandiz

YEAR ISSUE		EDITION LIMIT	YEAR RETD.	ISSUE PRICE	*QUOTE U.S.$
1985	First Kiss, 8"	750	1985	590.00	950
1987	Heart to Heart, 8"	750	1991	590.00	850
1988	A Loving Hand, 8"	750	1991	795.00	850
1986	My Heart Is Yours, 8"	750	1991	590.00	850
1985	Springtime Stroll, 8"	750	1990	590.00	950
1986	A Tender Touch, 8"	750	1990	590.00	850

Sarah Kay Christmas Firsts - S. Kay

YEAR ISSUE		EDITION LIMIT	YEAR RETD.	ISSUE PRICE	*QUOTE U.S.$
1994	Sarah Kay's First Christmas, 4"	500		350.00	350
1994	Sarah Kay's First Christmas, 6"	250	1995	600.00	600
1995	First Christmas Stocking, 4" 57553	500		250.00	250
1995	First Christmas Stocking, 6" 57554	250		395.00	395
1996	All I Want For Christmas, 4" 57555	500		325.00	325
1996	All I Want For Christmas, 6" 57556	250		550.00	550

Sarah Kay Figurines - S. Kay

YEAR ISSUE		EDITION LIMIT	YEAR RETD.	ISSUE PRICE	*QUOTE U.S.$
1985	Afternoon Tea, 11"	750	1993	650.00	770
1985	Afternoon Tea, 20"	100	1993	3100.00	3500
1985	Afternoon Tea, 4"	4,000	1990	95.00	185
1985	Afternoon Tea, 6"	4,000	1990	195.00	325-365
1987	All Aboard, 1 1/2"	7,500	1990	50.00	90
1987	All Aboard, 4"	4,000	1990	130.00	185
1987	All Aboard, 6"	2,000	1990	265.00	355
1987	All Mine, 1 1/2"	7,500	1988	49.50	95
1987	All Mine, 4"	4,000	1988	130.00	225
1987	All Mine, 6"	4,000	1988	245.00	465
1986	Always By My Side, 1 1/2"	7,500	1988	45.00	95
1986	Always By My Side, 4"	4,000	1988	95.00	195
1986	Always By My Side, 6"	4,000	1988	195.00	375
1990	Batter Up, 1 1/2"	3,750	1991	90.00	95
1990	Batter Up, 4"	2,000		220.00	265
1990	Batter Up, 6"	2,000		440.00	515
1983	Bedtime, 1 1/2"	7,500	1984	45.00	110
1983	Bedtime, 4"	Closed	1987	95.00	230
1983	Bedtime, 6"	4,000	1987	195.00	435
1994	Bubbles & Bows, 4"	1,000		300.00	300
1994	Bubbles & Bows, 6"	1,000		600.00	600
1986	Bunny Hug, 1 1/2"	7,500	1989	45.00	85
1986	Bunny Hug, 4"	4,000	1989	95.00	172
1986	Bunny Hug, 6"	2,000	1989	210.00	395
1989	Cherish, 1 1/2"	Closed	1991	80.00	95
1989	Cherish, 4"	2,000	1994	199.00	290
1989	Cherish, 6"	2,000	1994	398.00	560
1993	Christmas Basket, 4"	1,000		310.00	290
1993	Christmas Basket, 6"	1,000		600.00	580
1994	Christmas Wonder, 4"	1,000		370.00	370
1994	Christmas Wonder, 6"	1,000		700.00	700
1994	Clowning Around, 4"	1,000		300.00	300
1994	Clowning Around, 6"	1,000		550.00	550
1987	Cuddles, 1 1/2"	7,500	1988	49.50	95
1987	Cuddles, 4"	4,000	1988	130.00	225
1987	Cuddles, 6"	4,000	1988	245.00	465
1984	Daydreaming, 1 1/2"	7,500	1984	45.00	125
1984	Daydreaming, 4"	4,000	1988	95.00	235
1984	Daydreaming, 6"	4,000	1988	195.00	445
1991	Dress Up, 1 1/2"	3,750	1991	110.00	110
1991	Dress Up, 4"	2,000	1993	270.00	270
1991	Dress Up, 6"	2,000	1993	550.00	570
1983	Feeding the Chickens, 1 1/2"	7,500	1984	45.00	110
1983	Feeding the Chickens, 4"	Closed	1987	95.00	250
1983	Feeding the Chickens, 6"	4,000	1987	195.00	450
1991	Figure Eight, 1 1/2"	3,750	1991	110.00	110
1991	Figure Eight, 4"	2,000		270.00	365
1991	Figure Eight, 6"	2,000		550.00	660
1984	Finding Our Way, 1 1/2"	7,500	1984	45.00	135
1984	Finding Our Way, 4"	4,000	1988	95.00	245
1984	Finding Our Way, 6"	2,000	1984	210.00	495
1986	Finishing Touch, 1 1/2"	7,500	1989	45.00	85
1986	Finishing Touch, 4"	4,000	1989	95.00	172
1986	Finishing Touch, 6"	4,000	1989	195.00	312
1989	First School Day, 1 1/2"	Closed	1991	85.00	95
1989	First School Day, 4"	2,000	1993	290.00	350
1989	First School Day, 6"	2,000	1993	550.00	650
1989	Fisherboy, 1 1/2"	Closed	1991	85.00	95
1989	Fisherboy, 4"	2,000	1994	220.00	250
1989	Fisherboy, 6"	1,000	1994	440.00	475
1984	Flowers for You, 1 1/2"	7,500	1984	45.00	125
1984	Flowers for You, 4"	4,000	1988	95.00	250
1984	Flowers for You, 6"	4,000	1988	195.00	450
1991	Forell, 1 1/2"	3,750	1991	110.00	115
1991	Forell, 4"	2,000		270.00	325
1991	Forell, 6"	2,000		550.00	580
1992	Free Skating, 4"	1,000		310.00	325
1992	Free Skating, 6"	1,000		590.00	620
1983	From the Garden, 1 1/2"	7,500	1984	45.00	110
1983	From the Garden, 4"	Closed	1987	95.00	235
1983	From the Garden, 6"	4,000	1987	195.00	450
1989	Garden Party, 1 1/2"	Closed	1991	85.00	95
1989	Garden Party, 4"	2,000	1993	220.00	240
1989	Garden Party, 6"	2,000	1993	440.00	475
1985	Giddyapl, 4"	4,000	1990	95.00	250
1985	Giddyapl, 6"	4,000	1990	195.00	325
1988	Ginger Snap, 1 1/2"	Closed	1990	70.00	90
1988	Ginger Snap, 4"	2,000	1990	150.00	185
1988	Ginger Snap, 6"	1,000	1990	300.00	355
1986	Good As New, 1 1/2"	7,500	1991	45.00	90
1986	Good As New, 4"	4,000	1994	95.00	290
1986	Good As New, 6"	4,000	1994	195.00	500
1996	Head of the Class, 4"	500		295.00	295
1996	Head of the Class, 6"	250		495.00	495
1983	Helping Mother, 1 1/2"	7,500	1983	45.00	110
1983	Helping Mother, 4"	Closed	1983	95.00	300
1983	Helping Mother, 6"	2,000	1983	210.00	495
1988	Hidden Treasures, 1 1/2"	Closed	1990	70.00	90
1988	Hidden Treasures, 4"	2,000	1990	150.00	185
1988	Hidden Treasures, 6"	1,000	1990	300.00	355
1990	Holiday Cheer, 1 1/2"	3,750	1991	90.00	95
1990	Holiday Cheer, 4"	2,000		225.00	320
1990	Holiday Cheer, 6"	1,000		450.00	610
1989	House Call, 1 1/2"	Closed	1991	85.00	95
1989	House Call, 4"	2,000	1991	190.00	195
1989	House Call, 6"	2,000	1991	390.00	390
1995	I Know, I Know, 4" 57701	500		250.00	275
1995	I Know, I Know, 6" 57702	250		395.00	450
1993	Innocence, 4"	1,000		345.00	315
1993	Innocence, 6"	1,000		630.00	630
1994	Jolly Pair, 4"	1,000		350.00	350
1994	Jolly Pair, 6"	1,000		650.00	650
1993	Joy to the World, 4"	1,000		310.00	290
1993	Joy to the World, 6"	1,000		600.00	580
1987	Let's Play, 1 1/2"	7,500	1990	49.50	90
1987	Let's Play, 4"	4,000	1990	130.00	185
1987	Let's Play, 6"	2,000	1990	265.00	355
1994	Little Chimney Sweep, 4"	1,000		300.00	310
1994	Little Chimney Sweep, 6"	1,000		600.00	600
1987	Little Nanny, 1 1/2"	7,500	1990	49.50	90
1987	Little Nanny, 4"	4,000	1990	150.00	200
1987	Little Nanny, 6"	4,000	1990	295.00	400
1987	A Loving Spoonful, 1 1/2"	7,500	1991	49.50	90
1987	A Loving Spoonful, 4"	4,000	1994	150.00	290
1987	A Loving Spoonful, 6"	4,000	1994	295.00	550
1992	Merry Christmas, 1 1/2"	3,750	1994	110.00	115
1992	Merry Christmas, 4"	1,000	1994	350.00	350
1992	Merry Christmas, 6"	1,000	1994	580.00	580
1995	Mom's Joy, 5" 57902	250	1995	297.00	297
1983	Morning Chores, 1 1/2"	7,500	1983	45.00	110
1983	Morning Chores, 4"	Closed	1983	95.00	300
1983	Morning Chores, 6"	2,000	1983	210.00	550
1993	Mr. Santa, 4"	750		375.00	390
1993	Mr. Santa, 6"	750		695.00	730
1993	Mrs. Santa, 4"	750		375.00	390
1993	Mrs. Santa, 6"	750		695.00	730
1993	My Favorite Doll, 4"	1,000		315.00	315
1993	My Favorite Doll, 6"	1,000		600.00	600
1988	My Little Brother, 1 1/2"	Closed	1991	70.00	90
1988	My Little Brother, 4"	2,000	1991	195.00	225
1988	My Little Brother, 6"	2,000	1991	375.00	450
1988	New Home, 1 1/2"	Closed	1991	70.00	90
1988	New Home, 4"	2,000	1991	185.00	240
1988	New Home, 6"	2,000	1991	365.00	500
1985	Nightie Night, 4"	4,000	1990	95.00	185
1985	Nightie Night, 6"	4,000	1990	195.00	325
1984	Off to School, 1 1/2"	7,500	1984	45.00	125
1984	Off to School, 11"	750		590.00	880
1984	Off to School, 20"	100		2900.00	4200
1984	Off to School, 4"	4,000		95.00	240
1984	Off to School, 6"	4,000		195.00	450
1986	Our Puppy, 1 1/2"	7,500	1990	45.00	90
1986	Our Puppy, 4"	4,000	1990	95.00	185
1986	Our Puppy, 6"	2,000	1990	210.00	355
1988	Penny for Your Thoughts, 1 1/2"	Closed	1991	70.00	90

*Quotes have been rounded up to nearest dollar

FIGURINES/COTTAGES

YEAR ISSUE		EDITION LIMIT	YEAR RETD.	ISSUE PRICE	*QUOTE U.S.$
1988	Penny for Your Thoughts, 4"	2,000		185.00	275
1988	Penny for Your Thoughts, 6"	2,000		365.00	570
1983	Playtime, 1 1/2"	7,500	1984	45.00	110
1983	Playtime, 4"	Closed	1987	95.00	250
1983	Playtime, 6"	4,000	1987	195.00	495
1988	Purrfect Day, 4"	2,000	1991	184.00	215
1988	Purrfect Day, 1 1/2"	Closed	1991	70.00	90
1988	Purrfect Day, 6"	2,000	1991	265.00	455
1992	Raindrops, 1 1/2"	3,750	1994	110.00	110
1992	Raindrops, 4"	1,000	1994	350.00	350
1992	Raindrops, 6"	1,000	1994	640.00	640
1988	School Marm, 6"	2,000	1988	398.00	398
1991	Season's Joy, 1 1/2"	3,750	1991	110.00	115
1991	Season's Joy, 4"	2,000		270.00	350
1991	Season's Joy, 6"	1,000		550.00	690
1990	Seasons Greetings, 1 1/2"	3,750	1991	90.00	95
1990	Seasons Greetings, 4"	2,000		225.00	285
1990	Seasons Greetings, 6"	1,000		450.00	610
1990	Shootin' Hoops, 4"	2,000	1993	220.00	250
1990	Shootin' Hoops, 6"	2,000	1993	440.00	450
1990	Shootin' Hoops,1 1/2"	3,750	1991	90.00	95
1985	A Special Day, 4"	4,000	1990	95.00	195
1985	A Special Day, 6"	4,000	1990	195.00	325
1984	Special Delivery, 1 1/2"	7,500	1984	45.00	125
1984	Special Delivery, 4"	4,000	1989	95.00	187
1984	Special Delivery, 6"	4,000	1989	195.00	312-350
1990	Spring Fever, 1 1/2"	3,750	1991	90.00	95
1990	Spring Fever, 4"	2,000		225.00	325
1990	Spring Fever, 6"	2,000		450.00	610
1983	Sweeping, 1 1/2"	7,500	1984	45.00	110
1983	Sweeping, 4"	Closed	1987	95.00	230
1983	Sweeping, 6"	4,000	1987	195.00	435
1986	Sweet Treat, 1 1/2"	7,500	1989	45.00	85
1986	Sweet Treat, 4"	4,000	1989	95.00	172
1986	Sweet Treat, 6"	4,000	1989	195.00	312
1996	Sweets for My Sweet, 6"	250		399.00	399
1984	Tag Along, 4"	4,000	1988	95.00	225
1984	Tag Along, 6"	4,000	1988	195.00	290
1984	Tag Along,1 1/2"	7,500	1984	45.00	130
1989	Take Me Along, 1 1/2"	Closed	1991	85.00	95
1992	Take Me Along, 11"	400		950.00	950
1992	Take Me Along, 20"	100		4550.00	4550
1989	Take Me Along, 4"	2,000		220.00	285
1989	Take Me Along, 6"	1,000		440.00	565
1993	Ten Roses For You, 4"	1,000		290.00	290
1993	Ten Roses For You, 6"	1,000		525.00	525
1990	Tender Loving Care, 1 1/2"	3,750	1991	90.00	95
1990	Tender Loving Care, 4"	2,000	1993	220.00	240
1990	Tender Loving Care, 6"	2,000	1993	440.00	475
1985	Tis the Season, 4"	4,000	1993	95.00	250
1985	Tis the Season, 6"	2,000	1985	210.00	425
1986	To Love And To Cherish, 1 1/2"	7,500	1989	45.00	85
1986	To Love and To Cherish, 11"	1,000	1989	Unkn.	667
1986	To Love and To Cherish, 20"	200	1989	Unkn.	3600
1986	To Love And To Cherish, 4"	4,000	1989	95.00	172
1986	To Love And To Cherish, 6"	4,000	1989	195.00	312
1991	Touch Down, 1 1/2"	3,750	1994	110.00	110
1991	Touch Down, 4"	2,000	1994	270.00	310
1991	Touch Down, 6"	2,000	1994	550.00	550
1992	Tulips For Mother, 4"	1,000		310.00	325
1992	Tulips For Mother, 6"	1,000		590.00	620
1983	Waiting for Mother, 1 1/2"	7,500	1984	45.00	110
1983	Waiting for Mother, 11"	750	1987	495.00	795
1983	Waiting for Mother, 4"	Closed	1987	95.00	230
1983	Waiting for Mother, 6"	4,000	1987	195.00	445
1984	Wake Up Kiss, 1 1/2"	7,500	1984	45.00	550
1984	Wake Up Kiss, 4"	4,000	1993	95.00	195
1983	Wake Up Kiss, 6"	2,000	1984	210.00	550
1984	Watchful Eye, 4"	4,000	1988	95.00	235
1984	Watchful Eye, 6"	4,000	1988	195.00	445
1984	Watchful Eye,1 1/2"	7,500	1984	45.00	125
1992	Winter Cheer, 4"	2,000	1993	300.00	300
1992	Winter Cheer, 6"	1,000	1993	580.00	580
1991	Winter Surprise, 1 1/2"	3,750	1994	110.00	110
1991	Winter Surprise, 4"	2,000	1994	270.00	290
1991	Winter Surprise, 6"	1,000	1994	550.00	570
1986	With This Ring, 1 1/2"	7,500	1989	45.00	85
1986	With This Ring, 11"	1,000	1989	Unkn.	668
1986	With This Ring, 20"	200	1989	Unkn.	3600
1986	With This Ring, 4"	4,000	1989	95.00	172
1986	With This Ring, 6"	4,000	1989	195.00	312
1989	Yearly Check-Up, 1 1/2"	Closed	1991	85.00	95
1989	Yearly Check-Up, 4"	2,000	1991	190.00	195
1989	Yearly Check-Up, 6"	2,000	1991	390.00	390
1985	Yuletide Cheer, 4"	4,000	1993	95.00	250
1985	Yuletide Cheer, 6"	Closed	1985	210.00	435

Sarah Kay Mini Santas - S. Kay

1992	Father Christmas, 1 1/2"	2,500	1993	110.00	110
1992	A Friend to All, 1 1/2"	2,500	1993	110.00	110
1991	Jolly Santa, 1 1/2"	2,500	1993	110.00	110
1991	Jolly St. Nick, 1 1/2"	2,500	1993	110.00	110
1991	Kris Kringle, 1 1/2"	2,500	1993	110.00	110
1991	Sarah Kay Santa, 1 1/2"	2,500	1993	110.00	110

Sarah Kay Santas - S. Kay

1995	Checking It Twice, 4" 57709	500		250.00	250
1995	Checking It Twice, 6" 57710	250		395.00	395
1992	Father Christmas, 4"	750	1994	350.00	350
1992	Father Christmas, 6"	750	1994	590.00	590
1991	A Friend To All, 4"	750	1994	300.00	300
1991	A Friend To All, 6"	750	1994	590.00	590
1989	Jolly Santa, 12"	150	1990	1300.00	1300
1988	Jolly Santa, 4"	750	1989	235.00	300-350
1988	Jolly Santa, 6"	750	1989	480.00	600
1988	Jolly St. Nick, 4"	750	1989	199.00	300-550
1988	Jolly St. Nick, 6"	750	1989	398.00	850
1990	Kris Kringle Santa, 4"	750	1990	275.00	350
1990	Kris Kringle Santa, 6"	750	1990	550.00	550
1989	Santa, 4"	750	1990	235.00	350
1989	Santa, 6"	750	1990	480.00	480
1996	Workshop Santa, 4"	500		295.00	295
1996	Workshop Santa, 6"	250		495.00	495

Armani

G. Armani Society Members Only Figurine - G. Armani

1990	Awakening 591C	Closed	1990	137.50	1100-1400
1991	Ruffles 745E	Closed	1991	139.00	300-525
1992	Ascent 866C	Closed	1992	195.00	300-425
1993	Venus 881C	Closed	1993	225.00	400-650
1993	Lady Rose (Bonus) 197C	Closed	1993	125.00	200
1993	Julie (Bonus) 293P	Closed	1993	90.00	135-200
1993	Juliette (Bonus) 294P	Closed	1994	90.00	200-250
1994	Flora 212C	Closed	1994	225.00	275-400
1994	Aquarius (Bonus) 248C	Closed	1994	125.00	125-155
1994	Harlequin (Bonus) 490C	Closed	1994	300.00	350-450
1995	Melody 656C	Closed	1995	250.00	300
1995	Scarlett (Bonus) 698C	Closed	1995	200.00	200
1995	Lady w/Doves mini 546C	Closed	1995	Gift	N/A
1996	Arianna (Bonus) 400C	Yr.Iss.		125.00	125
1996	Allegra 345C	Yr.Iss.		250.00	250
1996	Lady Jane (Figurine of the Year) 390C	Yr.Iss.		200.00	200

G. Armani Society Members Only Event - G. Armani

1990	My Fine Feathered Friends (Bonus)122S	Closed	1991	175.00	350
1991	Peace & Harmony (Bonus) 824C	7,500	1992	300.00	325-360
1992	Springtime 961C	Closed	1992	250.00	395-500
1992	Boy with Dog (Bonus) 407S	Closed	1992	200.00	200
1993	Loving Arms 880E	Closed	1993	250.00	350
1994	Daisy 202E	Closed	1994	250.00	325-450
1995	Iris 628E	Closed	1995	250.00	275
1996	Rose 678C	Yr.Iss.		250.00	250

Can-Can Dancers - G. Armani

1989	Two Can-Can Dancers 516C	Closed	1994	820.00	975

Capodimonte - G. Armani

1995	Easy Ride 334C	Open		350.00	350
1995	Easy Ride 334F	Open		220.00	220
1995	Flowers For Sale 333C	Open		500.00	500
1995	Flowers For Sale 333F	Open		300.00	300
1995	Gentle Swing 335C	Open		550.00	550
1995	Gentle Swing 335F	Open		350.00	350
1995	Spring Water 381C	Open		300.00	300
1995	Spring Water 381F	Open		170.00	170
1995	Sweet Apple 369C	Open		600.00	600
1995	Sweet Apple 369F	Open		420.00	420
1995	Wild Flower 367C	Open		560.00	560
1995	Wild Flower 367F	Open		400.00	400
1995	Young Hearts 679C	1,500		900.00	900

Clown Series - G. Armani

1991	Bust of Clown 725E	5,000		500.00	550
1995	Charlie 644C	Open		175.00	175
1994	The Happy Fiddler 478C	Open		360.00	360
1995	Jerry 643C	Open		200.00	200
1994	Sound the Trumpet 476C	Open		300.00	300

Country Series - G. Armani

1994	Back From the Fields 473F	Open		360.00	360
1993	Boy With Accordion 177C	Open		170.00	170
1993	Boy With Accordion 177F	Open		75.00	75
1993	Boy With Flute 890C	Open		175.00	175
1993	Boy With Flute 890F	Open		90.00	90
1994	Country Girl with Grapes 215C	Open		230.00	230
1994	Country Girl with Grapes 215F	Open		120.00	120
1994	Fresh Fruits 471F	Open		250.00	250
1993	Girl Tending Flowers 466C	Open		210.00	210
1993	Girl With Chicks 889C	Open		155.00	155
1993	Girl With Chicks 889F	Open		75.00	75
1993	Girl With Sheep 178C	Open		150.00	150
1993	Girl With Sheep 178F	Open		65.00	65
1993	Girl With Wheelbarrow /Flowers 468C	Open		240.00	240
1994	Laundry Girl 214C	Open		230.00	230
1994	Laundry Girl 214F	Open		120.00	120

Etruscan - G. Armani

1993	Lady with Bag 2149E	Retrd.	1996	350.00	365

Florentine Garden - G. Armani

1995	Wisteria 626C	Open		350.00	350
1995	Wisteria 626F	Open		275.00	275

Four Seasons - G. Armani

1990	Lady on Seashore (Summer) 540C	Open		440.00	440
1990	Lady With Bicycle (Spring) 539C	Open		550.00	550
1992	Lady With Fruit (Summer) 182B	Open		135.00	135
1992	Lady With Fruit (Summer) 182C	Open		275.00	275
1992	Lady With Grapes (Fall) 183C	Open		275.00	275
1992	Lady With Grapes (Fall)182B	Open		135.00	135
1990	Lady W/Ice Skates (Winter) 542C	Open		400.00	400
1992	Lady With Roses (Spring)181B	Open		135.00	135
1992	Lady With Roses (Spring)181C	Open		275.00	275
1990	Lady With Umbrella (Fall) 541C	Open		475.00	475
1992	Lady With Vegetables (Winter)183B	Open		135.00	135
1992	Lady With Vegetables (Winter)183C	Open		275.00	275

Galleria Collection: Distinguished Dealers - G. Armani

1996	Eros 406T	1,500		750.00	750
1994	The Falconer 224S	3,000		1000.00	1000
1994	Leda & The Swan 1012T	1,500		500.00	650
1993	The Sea Wave 1006T	1,500	1994	500.00	500
1993	Spring Herald 1009T	1,500	1994	500.00	500
1993	Spring Water 1007T	1,500	1994	500.00	500
1993	Zephyr 1010T	1,500	1994	500.00	500

Garden Series - G. Armani

1994	Lady At Well 222C	Open		275.00	275
1994	Lady At Well 222F	Open		150.00	150
1991	Lady with Cornucopie 870C	10,000		600.00	600
1991	Lady with Harp 874C	10,000		500.00	500
1991	Lady with Peacock 871C	10,000		585.00	585
1991	Lady with Violin 872C	10,000		560.00	560

Golden Age - G. Armani

1995	Christine 348C	Open		300.00	300
1995	Christine 348F	Open		200.00	200
1995	Claire 654C	Open		250.00	250
1995	Claire 654F	Open		100.00	100
1995	Dear Friends 532F	Open		100.00	100
1995	Eloise 350C	Open		285.00	285
1995	Eloise 350F	Open		170.00	170
1995	Florence 535C	Open		250.00	250
1995	Florence 535F	Open		155.00	155
1996	Fragrance 340C	3,000		500.00	500
1996	Fragrance 340F	Open		300.00	300
1995	Gloria 655C	Open		250.00	250
1995	Gloria 655F	Open		100.00	100
1995	Love and Peace 538C	Open		125.00	125
1996	Promenade 339C	3,000		600.00	600
1996	Promenade 339F	Open		400.00	400
1995	Serena 349C	Open		300.00	300
1995	Serena 349F	Open		200.00	200
1996	Soiree 338C	3,000		600.00	600
1996	Soiree 338F	Open		350.00	350
1996	Spring Morning 337C	3,000		600.00	600
1996	Spring Morning 337F	Open		370.00	370
1995	Stormy Weather 533C	Open		260.00	260
1995	Stormy Weather 533F	Open		135.00	135
1995	Sunday Drive 531C	Open		275.00	275
1995	Sunday Drive 531F	Open		140.00	140
1995	Sunshine Dream 529C	Open		165.00	165
1995	Sunshine Dream 529F	Open		90.00	90
1995	Sweet Dreams 536C	Open		225.00	225
1995	Sweet Dreams 536F	Open		135.00	135
1995	Vanessa 347C	Open		350.00	350
1995	Vanessa 347F	Open		220.00	220

Gulliver's World - G. Armani

1994	The Barrel 659T	1,000		225.00	225
1994	Cowboy 657T	1,000	1995	125.00	125
1994	Getting Clean 661T	1,000		130.00	130
1994	Ray of Moon 658T	1,000		100.00	100
1994	Serenade 660T	1,000		200.00	200

Gypsy Series - G. Armani

1994	Esmeralda-Gypsy Girl 198C	Open		400.00	400
1994	Esmeralda-Gypsy Girl 198F	Open		215.00	215

Impressions - G. Armani

1990	Bittersweet 528P	Retrd.	1993	275.00	31
1990	Masquerade 527P	Retrd.	1993	300.00	32

Little Treasures - G. Armani

1994	Bathtime 357T	Open		50.00	5
1994	Clean Sweep 373T	Open		50.00	5
1994	Girl at the Telephone 364T	Open		50.00	5
1994	Girl with Ice Cream 365T	Open		50.00	5
1994	Little Fisher Boy 362T	Open		37.00	3
1994	Playing the Piano 376T	Open		50.00	5
1994	Sweet Dreams 360T	Open		35.00	3
1994	A Woman's Work 363T	Open		50.00	5

Masterworks - G. Armani

1996	Aurora 680C	1,500		3500.00	350

Moonlight Masquerade - G. Armani

1990	Harlequin Lady 740C	7,500	1994	450.00	46
1990	Lady Clown with Cane 742C	7,500	1994	390.00	41
1990	Lady Clown with Doll 743C	7,500	1994	410.00	41
1990	Lady Pierrot 741C	7,500	1994	390.00	49
1990	Queen of Hearts 744C	7,500	1994	450.00	46

Motherhood - G. Armani

1994	Black Maternity 502C	5,000		500.00	50
1994	Black Maternity 502F	Open		335.00	33
1993	Garden Maternity 188C	Open		210.00	21
1993	Garden Maternity 188F	Open		115.00	11
1994	Kneeling Maternity 216C	Open		275.00	27

*Quotes have been rounded up to nearest dollar

YEAR ISSUE		EDITION LIMIT	YEAR RETD.	ISSUE PRICE	*QUOTE U.S.$
1994	Kneeling Maternity 216F	Open		135.00	135
1993	Maternity Embracing 190C	Open		250.00	250
1993	Maternity Embracing 190F	Open		160.00	160
1994	Mother & Child 470F	Open		150.00	150
1992	Mother with Child (Mother's Day) 185B	Open		235.00	235
1992	Mother with Child (Mother's Day) 185C	Open		400.00	400
1994	Mother's Hand 479F	Open		215.00	215
1993	Mother/Child 792C	Open		385.00	385
1993	Mother/Child 792F	Open		250.00	250
1995	Perfect Love 652C	3,000		1200.00	1200
1995	Perfect Love 652F	Open		800.00	800

My Fair Ladies™ - G. Armani

YEAR ISSUE		EDITION LIMIT	YEAR RETD.	ISSUE PRICE	*QUOTE U.S.$
1995	At Ease 634C	5,000		650.00	650
1995	At Ease 634F	Open		400.00	400
1995	Awaiting 631C	Open		170.00	170
1995	Awaiting 631F	Open		90.00	90
1993	Elegance 195C	5,000	1996	525.00	525
1993	Elegance 195F	Open		300.00	300
1993	Fascination 192C	5,000		500.00	500
1993	Fascination 192F	Open		250.00	250
1987	Flamenco Dancer 389C	5,000		400.00	500
1996	Georgia 414C	5,000		550.00	550
1996	Grace 383C	5,000		475.00	475
1996	In Love 382C	5,000		450.00	450
1995	Isadora 633C	3,000		920.00	920
1995	Isadora 633F	Open		500.00	500
1987	Lady with Book 384C	5,000		300.00	450
1987	Lady with Compact 386C	Retrd.	1993	300.00	750-950
1987	Lady with Fan 387C	5,000		300.00	400
1987	Lady with Fan 387E	Retrd.	1995	400.00	420
1987	Lady with Great Dane 429C	5,000	1996	365.00	475
1987	Lady with Muff 388C	5,000		250.00	450
1989	Lady with Parrot 616C	5,000	1996	400.00	475
1987	Lady with Peacock 385C	Retrd.	1992	380.00	2000-3000
1994	Lady with Umbrella 196C	5,000		335.00	335
1994	Lady with Umbrella 196F	Open		200.00	200
1996	Lara 333C	5,000		450.00	450
1993	Mahogany 194C	5,000	1995	500.00	550-600
1993	Mahogany 194F	Open		360.00	360
1993	Morning Rose 193C	5,000		450.00	450
1993	Morning Rose 193F	Open		225.00	225
1987	Mother & Child 405C	5,000		410.00	550
1995	Promenade 630C	Open		185.00	185
1995	Promenade 630F	Open		90.00	90
1995	Starry Night 632C	Open		185.00	185
1995	Starry Night 632F	Open		90.00	90

Pearls Of The Orient - G. Armani

YEAR ISSUE		EDITION LIMIT	YEAR RETD.	ISSUE PRICE	*QUOTE U.S.$
1989	Chu Chu San 612C	10,000	1994	500.00	550
1989	Lotus Blossom 613C	10,000	1994	450.00	475
1989	Madame Butterfly 610C	10,000	1994	450.00	500
1989	Turnadot 611C	10,000	1994	475.00	500

Premiere Ballerina - G. Armani

YEAR ISSUE		EDITION LIMIT	YEAR RETD.	ISSUE PRICE	*QUOTE U.S.$
1988	Ballerina 508C	10,000	1994	430.00	530
1988	Ballerina 517C	10,000	1994	325.00	385
1988	Ballerina Group in Flight 518C	7,500	1994	810.00	1000-1200
1988	Ballerina in Flight 503C	Retrd.	1994	420.00	500
1988	Ballerina with Drape 504C	10,000	1994	450.00	575
1991	Dancer w/Peacock 727C	Retrd.	1993	460.00	510
1990	Fly Dancer 585F	7,500	1993	190.00	210
1988	Two Ballerinas 515C	Retrd.	1994	620.00	775

Professionals - G. Armani

YEAR ISSUE		EDITION LIMIT	YEAR RETD.	ISSUE PRICE	*QUOTE U.S.$
1995	Nurse 693C	Open		250.00	250
1995	Nurse 693F	Open		175.00	175
1995	Teacher 694C	Open		310.00	310
1995	Teacher 694F	Open		175.00	175

Religious - G. Armani

YEAR ISSUE		EDITION LIMIT	YEAR RETD.	ISSUE PRICE	*QUOTE U.S.$
1995	The Assumption 697C	5,000		675.00	675
1994	Baby Jesus 1020C	1,000		175.00	175
1987	Choir Boys 900	5,000		350.00	620
1990	Crucifix Plaque 711C	15,000		265.00	265
1987	Crucifix 1158C	10,000	1990	155.00	600-895
1993	Crucifix 786C	7,500		250.00	250
1991	Crucifix 790C	15,000		180.00	180
1996	The Crucifixion 780C	5,000		500.00	500
1994	Donkey 1027C	1,000		185.00	185
1996	The Holy Family 788C	5,000		1000.00	1000
1994	Joseph 1021C	1,000		500.00	500
1994	La Pieta 802C	5,000		950.00	950
1994	La Pieta 802F	Open		550.00	550
1992	Madonna with Child 787B	Open		260.00	260
1992	Madonna with Child 787C	Open		425.00	425
1992	Madonna with Child 787F	Open		265.00	265
1994	Magi King Gold 1023C	1,000		600.00	600
1994	Magi King Incense 1024C	1,000		600.00	600
1994	Magi King Myrrh 1025C	1,000		450.00	450
1994	Mary 1022C	1,000		365.00	365
1995	Moses 606C	2,500		365.00	365
1994	Moses 812C	Open		220.00	220
1994	Moses 812F	Open		115.00	115
1994	Ox 1026C	1,000		300.00	300
1994	Renaissance Crucifix 1017T	5,000		250.00	250

Renaissance - G. Armani

YEAR ISSUE		EDITION LIMIT	YEAR RETD.	ISSUE PRICE	*QUOTE U.S.$
1992	Abundance 870C	5,000		600.00	600
1992	Abundance 870F	Retrd.	1994	420.00	420
1994	Ambrosia 482C	5,000		435.00	435
1994	Angelica 484C	5,000		575.00	575
1992	Aurora-Girl With Doves 884B	Open		220.00	220
1992	Aurora-Girl With Doves 884C	7,500		370.00	370
1991	Bust of Eve 590T	1,000	1991	250.00	500-850
1992	Dawn 874C	5,000		500.00	500
1996	Ebony 372C	5,000		550.00	550
1993	Freedom-Man And Horse 906C	3,000		850.00	850
1992	Liberty-Girl On Horse 903B	Open		450.00	450
1992	Liberty-Girl On Horse 903C	5,000		750.00	750
1992	Lilac & Roses-Girl w/Flowers 882B	Open		220.00	220
1992	Lilac & Roses-Girl w/Flowers 882C	7,500		410.00	410
1992	Twilight 872C	5,000		560.00	560
1992	Vanity 871C	5,000		585.00	585
1993	Wind Song-Girl With Sail 904C	5,000		520.00	520

Romantic - G. Armani

YEAR ISSUE		EDITION LIMIT	YEAR RETD.	ISSUE PRICE	*QUOTE U.S.$
1994	The Embrace 480C	3,000	1996	1450.00	1450
1993	Girl w/Dog At Fence 886C	Open		350.00	350
1993	Girl w/Dog At Fence 886F	Open		175.00	175
1993	Girl With Ducks 887C	Open		320.00	320
1993	Girl With Ducks 887F	Open		160.00	160
1992	Lady with Doves 858E	1,000	1993	250.00	450
1993	Lovers 191C	3,000	1996	450.00	450
1993	Lovers 879C	3,000		570.00	570
1993	Lovers 879F	Open		325.00	325
1993	Lovers On A Swing 942C	Open		410.00	410
1993	Lovers On A Swing 942F	Open		265.00	265
1993	Lovers With Roses 888C	Open		300.00	300
1993	Lovers With Roses 888F	Open		155.00	155
1993	Lovers With Wheelbarrow 891C	Open		370.00	370
1993	Lovers With Wheelbarrow 891F	Open		190.00	190

Romantic Motherhood - G. Armani

YEAR ISSUE		EDITION LIMIT	YEAR RETD.	ISSUE PRICE	*QUOTE U.S.$
1993	Maternity On Swing 941C	Open		360.00	360
1993	Maternity On Swing 941F	Open		220.00	220

Siena Collection - G. Armani

YEAR ISSUE		EDITION LIMIT	YEAR RETD.	ISSUE PRICE	*QUOTE U.S.$
1993	Back From The Fields 1002T	1,000	1995	400.00	450
1994	Country Boy 1014T	2,500		135.00	135
1993	Encountering 1003T	1,000	1995	350.00	370
1993	Fresh Fruit 1001T	2,500	1995	155.00	350
1993	Happy Fiddler 1005T	1,000		225.00	225
1993	Mother's Hand 1008T	2,500		250.00	300-400
1996	Pearl 1019T	1,000		550.00	550
1993	Soft Kiss 1000T	2,500	1995	155.00	250
1993	Sound The Trumpet 1004T	1,000	1995	225.00	250

Special Issues - G. Armani

YEAR ISSUE		EDITION LIMIT	YEAR RETD.	ISSUE PRICE	*QUOTE U.S.$
1991	Discovery of America Plaque 867C	Closed	1994	400.00	400
1993	Mother's Day Plaque 899C	Closed	1993	100.00	100
1994	Mother's Day Plaque-The Swing 254C	Closed	1994	120.00	120
1995	Mother's Day Plaque - Love/Peace 538C	Closed	1995	125.00	125
1996	Mother's Day Plaque/Mother's Rosebud 341C	Yr.Iss.		150.00	150

Special Times - G. Armani

YEAR ISSUE		EDITION LIMIT	YEAR RETD.	ISSUE PRICE	*QUOTE U.S.$
1982	Card Players (Cheaters) 3280	Open		400.00	1200
1991	Couple in Car 862C	5,000		1000.00	1000
1991	Doctor in Car 848C	2,000		800.00	800
1994	The Encounter 472F	Open		315.00	315
1994	The Fairy Tale 219C	Open		335.00	335
1994	The Fairy Tale 219F	Open		175.00	175
1982	Girl with Chicks 5122E	Suspd.		95.00	165
1982	Girl with Sheep Dog 5117E	Retrd.	1992	100.00	210
1994	Grandpa's Nap 251C	Open		225.00	225
1994	Lady Doctor 249C	Open		200.00	200
1994	Lady Doctor 249F	Open		105.00	105
1994	Lady Graduate-Lawyer 253C	Open		225.00	225
1994	Lady Graduate-Lawyer 253F	Open		120.00	120
1991	Lady with Car 861C	3,000	1995	900.00	900
1994	Old Acquaintance 252C	Open		275.00	275
1982	Shy Kiss 5138E	Retrd.	1992	125.00	285
1982	Sledding 5111E	Retrd.	1992	115.00	250
1982	Soccer Boy 5109	Open		75.00	180
1994	Story Time 250C	Open		275.00	275

Special Walt Disney Production - G. Armani

YEAR ISSUE		EDITION LIMIT	YEAR RETD.	ISSUE PRICE	*QUOTE U.S.$
1992	Cinderella	Retrd.	1992	500.00	3300-4500
1993	Dopey	Retrd.	1993	125.00	190-300
1993	Snow White 199C	Retrd.	1993	750.00	1000-1800
1994	Ariel (Little Mermaid) 505C	1,500	1994	750.00	1200-1500
1995	Beauty and the Beast	2,000	1995	975.00	1000-1200

Sports - G. Armani

YEAR ISSUE		EDITION LIMIT	YEAR RETD.	ISSUE PRICE	*QUOTE U.S.$
1992	Lady Equestrian 910C	Open		315.00	315
1992	Lady Equestrian 910F	Open		155.00	155
1992	Lady Golfer 911C	Open		325.00	325
1992	Lady Golfer 911F	Open		170.00	170
1992	Lady Skater 913C	Open		300.00	300
1992	Lady Skater 913F	Open		170.00	170
1992	Lady Tennis 912C	Open		275.00	275
1992	Lady Tennis 912F	Open		175.00	175

Terra Cotta - G. Armani

YEAR ISSUE		EDITION LIMIT	YEAR RETD.	ISSUE PRICE	*QUOTE U.S.$
1994	Ambrosia 1013T	Open		275.00	275
1994	Angelica 1016T	Open		450.00	450
1994	Country Boy W/Mushrooms 1014T	2,500		135.00	135
1994	The Embrace 1011T	Open		930.00	930
1994	La Pieta 1015T	Open		550.00	550

Vanity - G. Armani

YEAR ISSUE		EDITION LIMIT	YEAR RETD.	ISSUE PRICE	*QUOTE U.S.$
1992	Beauty at the Mirror 850P	Retrd.	1994	300.00	325
1992	Beauty w/Perfume 853P	Retrd.	1994	370.00	380

Via Veneto - G. Armani

YEAR ISSUE		EDITION LIMIT	YEAR RETD.	ISSUE PRICE	*QUOTE U.S.$
1995	Alessandra 648C	5,000		370.00	370
1995	Marina 649C	5,000		475.00	475
1995	Nicole 651C	5,000		515.00	515
1995	Valentina 647C	5,000		420.00	420

Wedding - G. Armani

YEAR ISSUE		EDITION LIMIT	YEAR RETD.	ISSUE PRICE	*QUOTE U.S.$
1994	Black Bride 500C	Open		170.00	170
1994	Black Bride 500F	Open		115.00	115
1994	Black Wedding Waltz 501C	3,000		750.00	750
1994	Black Wedding Waltz 501F	Open		450.00	450
1988	Bride & Groom Wedding 475P	Open		270.00	285
1994	Bride With Column & Vase 488C	Open		260.00	260
1994	Bride With Column & Vase 488F	Open		200.00	200
1992	Bride With Doves 885C	Open		280.00	280
1992	Bride With Doves 885F	Open		220.00	220
1994	Bride With Flower Vase 489C	Open		135.00	135
1994	Bride With Flower Vase 489F	Open		90.00	90
1993	Carriage Wedding 902C	2,500		1000.00	1000
1993	Carriage Wedding 902F	Open		500.00	500
1993	Garden Wedding 189C	Open		225.00	225
1993	Garden Wedding 189F	Open		120.00	120
1989	Just Married 827C	5,000		950.00	1000
1996	Tenderness 418C	5,000		950.00	950
1996	Tomorrow's Dream 336C	5,000		700.00	700
1987	Wedding Couple 407C	Open		525.00	550
1982	Wedding Couple 5132	Open		110.00	190
1991	Wedding Couple At Threshold 813C	7,500		400.00	400
1993	Wedding Couple At Wall 201C	Open		225.00	225
1993	Wedding Couple At Wall 201F	Open		115.00	115
1993	Wedding Couple Forever 791F	Open		250.00	250
1991	Wedding Couple Kissing 815C	7,500		500.00	500
1991	Wedding Couple W/Bicycle 814C	7,500		600.00	600
1993	Wedding Flowers To Mary 187C	Open		225.00	225
1993	Wedding Flowers To Mary 187F	Open		115.00	115
1994	Wedding Waltz 493C	3,000		750.00	750
1994	Wedding Waltz 493F	Open		450.00	450

Wildlife - G. Armani

YEAR ISSUE		EDITION LIMIT	YEAR RETD.	ISSUE PRICE	*QUOTE U.S.$
1988	Bird Of Paradise 454S	5,000		475.00	500
1990	Bird of Paradise 718S	5,000		550.00	575
1996	Companions (2 Collies) 302S	3,000		900.00	900
1993	Doves With Vase 204S	3,000		375.00	375
1983	Eagle Bird of Prey 3213	Open		210.00	425
1995	Elegance in Nature (Herons) 226S	3,000		1000.00	1000
1996	Feed Us! (Mother/Baby Owls) 305S	1,500		950.00	950
1991	Flamingo 713S	5,000		420.00	420
1991	Flying Duck 839S	5,000		470.00	470
1993	Galloping Horse 905S	7,500		465.00	465
1991	Great Argus Pheasant 717S	3,000		600.00	600
1993	Horse Head 205S	Open		140.00	140
1996	The Hunt 290S	3,000		850.00	850
1991	Large Owl 842S	5,000		520.00	520
1996	Lone Wolf 284S	3,000		600.00	600
1996	Mid Night (Wolf) 285S	3,000		550.00	550
1995	Midnight 284S	3,000		600.00	600
1996	Night Vigil (Owl) 306S	3,000		1050.00	1050
1996	Nocturne 976S	1,500		1000.00	1000
1993	Parrot With Vase 736S	3,000		460.00	460
1988	Peacock 455S	5,000		600.00	675
1988	Peacock 458S	5,000		630.00	700
1993	Peacock With Vase 735S	3,000		375.00	375
1996	Proud Watch (Lion) 278S	1,500		700.00	700
1993	Rearing Horse 909S	7,500		515.00	515
1983	Royal Eagle with Babies 3553	Open		215.00	400
1993	Show Horse 907S	7,500		550.00	550
1996	Silent Watch (Mtn. Lion) 291S	1,500		700.00	700
1982	Snow Bird 5548	Open		100.00	180
1990	Soaring Eagle 970S	5,000	1996	620.00	700
1991	Swan 714S	5,000		550.00	550
1990	Three Doves 996S	5,000		670.00	750
1996	Vantage Point (Eagle) 270S	3,000		600.00	600
1996	Wild Hearts (Horses) 282S	3,000		2000.00	2000
1996	Wisdom (Owl) 281S	3,000		1250.00	1250
1995	Wisdom 281S	3,000		1250.00	1250

Yesteryears - G. Armani

YEAR ISSUE		EDITION LIMIT	YEAR RETD.	ISSUE PRICE	*QUOTE U.S.$
1993	Country Doctor In Car 848C	2,000	1995	800.00	800
1994	Summertime-Lady on Swing 485C	5,000		650.00	650
1994	Summertime-Lady on Swing 485F	Open		450.00	450

Zodiac Collection - G. Armani

YEAR ISSUE		EDITION LIMIT	YEAR RETD.	ISSUE PRICE	*QUOTE U.S.$
1996	Aquarius 426C	5,000		600.00	600
1996	Gemini 427C	5,000		600.00	600
1996	Virgo 425C	5,000		600.00	600

*Quotes have been rounded up to nearest dollar

Armstrong's

Armstrong's/Ron Lee - R. Skelton

YEAR ISSUE		EDITION LIMIT	YEAR RETD.	ISSUE PRICE	*QUOTE U.S.$
1984	Captain Freddie	7,500		85.00	325-425
1984	Freddie the Torchbearer	7,500		110.00	375-450

Happy Art - W. Lantz

YEAR ISSUE		EDITION LIMIT	YEAR RETD.	ISSUE PRICE	*QUOTE U.S.$
1982	Woody's Triple Self-Portrait	5,000		95.00	325

Pro Autographed Ceramic Baseball Card Plaque - Unknown

YEAR ISSUE		EDITION LIMIT	YEAR RETD.	ISSUE PRICE	*QUOTE U.S.$
1985	Brett, Garvey, Jackson, Rose, Seaver, auto, 3-1/4X5	1,000		150.00	250

The Red Skelton Collection - R. Skelton

YEAR ISSUE		EDITION LIMIT	YEAR RETD.	ISSUE PRICE	*QUOTE U.S.$
1981	Clem Kadiddlehopper	7,500		75.00	150
1981	Freddie in the Bathtub	7,500		80.00	85-100
1981	Freddie on the Green	7,500		00.00	150
1981	Freddie the Freeloader	7,500		70.00	150
1981	Jr., The Mean Widdle Kid	7,500		75.00	150
1981	San Fernando Red	7,500		75.00	150
1981	Sheriff Deadeye	7,500		75.00	150

The Red Skelton Porcelain Plaque - R. Skelton

YEAR ISSUE		EDITION LIMIT	YEAR RETD.	ISSUE PRICE	*QUOTE U.S.$
1991	All American	1,500		495.00	1500
1994	Another Day	1,994		675.00	675
1992	Independance Day?	1,500		525.00	1000
1993	Red & Freddie Both Turned 80	1,993		595.00	1200-1500

Artaffects

Members Only Limited Edition Redemption Offerings - G. Perillo

YEAR ISSUE		EDITION LIMIT	YEAR RETD.	ISSUE PRICE	*QUOTE U.S.$
1983	Apache Brave (Bust)	Closed		50.00	150
1986	Painted Pony	Closed		125.00	175
1991	Chief Crazy Horse	Closed		195.00	250

Limited Edition Free Gifts to Members - G. Perillo

YEAR ISSUE		EDITION LIMIT	YEAR RETD.	ISSUE PRICE	*QUOTE U.S.$
1986	Dolls	Closed		Gift	35
1991	Sunbeam	Closed		Gift	35
1992	Little Shadow	Closed		Gift	35

The Chieftains - G. Perillo

YEAR ISSUE		EDITION LIMIT	YEAR RETD.	ISSUE PRICE	*QUOTE U.S.$
1983	Crazy Horse	5,000		65.00	200
1983	Geronimo	5,000		65.00	135
1983	Joseph	5,000		65.00	250
1983	Red Cloud	5,000		65.00	275
1983	Sitting Bull	5,000		65.00	200

Pride of America's Indians - G. Perillo

YEAR ISSUE		EDITION LIMIT	YEAR RETD.	ISSUE PRICE	*QUOTE U.S.$
1988	Brave and Free	10-day		50.00	150
1989	Dark Eyed Friends	10-day		45.00	75
1989	Kindred Spirits	10-day		45.00	50
1989	Loyal Alliance	10-day		45.00	75
1989	Noble Companions	10-day		45.00	50
1989	Peaceful Comrades	10-day		45.00	50
1989	Small & Wise	10-day		45.00	50
1989	Winter Scouts	10-day		45.00	50

Special Issue - G. Perillo

YEAR ISSUE		EDITION LIMIT	YEAR RETD.	ISSUE PRICE	*QUOTE U.S.$
1984	Apache Boy Bust	Closed	N/A	40.00	75
1984	Apache Girl Bust	Closed	N/A	40.00	75
1985	Lovers	Closed	N/A	70.00	125
1984	Papoose	325		500.00	500
1982	The Peaceable Kingdom	950		750.00	750

The Storybook Collection - G. Perillo

YEAR ISSUE		EDITION LIMIT	YEAR RETD.	ISSUE PRICE	*QUOTE U.S.$
1981	Cinderella	10,000		65.00	95
1982	Goldilocks & 3 Bears	10,000		80.00	110
1982	Hansel and Gretel	10,000		80.00	110
1980	Little Red Ridinghood	10,000		65.00	95

The Tribal Ponies - G. Perillo

YEAR ISSUE		EDITION LIMIT	YEAR RETD.	ISSUE PRICE	*QUOTE U.S.$
1984	Arapaho	1,500		65.00	175-200
1984	Comanche	1,500		65.00	175-200
1984	Crow	1,500		65.00	175-200

The War Pony - G. Perillo

YEAR ISSUE		EDITION LIMIT	YEAR RETD.	ISSUE PRICE	*QUOTE U.S.$
1983	Apache War Pony	495		150.00	175-200
1983	Nez Perce War Pony	495		150.00	175-200
1983	Sioux War Pony	495		150.00	175-200

Artists of the World

DeGrazia Annual Christmas Collection - T. DeGrazia

YEAR ISSUE		EDITION LIMIT	YEAR RETD.	ISSUE PRICE	*QUOTE U.S.$
1992	Feliz Navidad	1,992		195.00	225
1993	Fiesta Angels	1,993	1995	295.00	350-400
1994	Littlest Angel	1,994		165.00	165
1995	Bethlehem Bound	1,995		195.00	195
1996	Christmas Serenade	1,996		145.00	145

DeGrazia Figurine - T. DeGrazia

YEAR ISSUE		EDITION LIMIT	YEAR RETD.	ISSUE PRICE	*QUOTE U.S.$
1990	Alone	S/O	N/A	395.00	395-595
1995	Apache Mother	3,500		165.00	195
1994	Bearing Gifts	Open		145.00	145
1988	Beautiful Burden	Closed	1990	175.00	250-300
1990	Biggest Drum	Closed	1992	110.00	135
1996	Blessed Madonna	2,500		195.00	195
1986	The Blue Boy	Suspd.		70.00	125
1992	Coming Home	3,500		165.00	175
1990	Crucifixion	S/O	1995	295.00	300-425
1990	Desert Harvest	S/O	N/A	135.00	150
1986	Festival Lights	Suspd.		75.00	110
1994	Festive Flowers	Open		145.00	145
1994	Fiesta Flowers	3,500		197.50	198
1995	Floral Harvest	Open		175.00	185
1984	Flower Boy	Closed	1992	65.00	250-300
1988	Flower Boy Plaque	Closed	1990	80.00	85
1984	Flower Girl	Suspd.		65.00	250
1984	Flower Girl Plaque	Closed	1985	45.00	85
1993	Flowers For Mother	Open		145.00	145
1996	Homeward Bound	2,500		195.00	195
1995	Little Farm Boy	Open		145.00	165
1995	Little Helper	3,500		165.00	185
1995	Little Hopi Girl	Open		97.50	110
1985	Little Madonna	Closed	1993	80.00	250-300
1993	Little Medicine Man	Open		175.00	185
1996	Little Navajo Shepherd Boy	Open		165.00	165
1988	Los Ninos	S/O	N/A	595.00	1200-1500
1989	Los Ninos (Artist's Edition)	S/O	N/A	695.00	2000-3500
1987	Love Me	Closed	1992	95.00	200-350
1994	Loving Mother	3,500		165.00	165
1988	Merrily, Merrily, Merrily	Closed	1991	95.00	220-250
1986	Merry Little Indian	S/O	N/A	175.00	275-300
1993	Mother Silently Prays	3,500		345.00	345
1996	Mother's Warmth	950		295.00	295
1996	My Beautiful Balloon	Open		135.00	135
1989	My Beautiful Rocking Horse	Suspd.		225.00	350
1995	My Blue Balloon	Open		110.00	115
1996	My Christmas Pony	Open		165.00	165
1989	My First Arrow	Closed	1992	95.00	250-300
1984	My First Horse	Closed	1990	65.00	250-300
1990	Navajo Boy	Closed	1992	110.00	150-300
1992	Navajo Madonna	Closed	1993	135.00	200
1991	Navajo Mother	3,500		295.00	325
1994	Pedro	Open		145.00	145
1985	Pima Drummer Boy	Closed	1991	65.00	200-300
1994	Rio Grande Dancer	Open		97.50	98
1993	Saddle Up	5,000		195.00	215
1994	Saguaro Dance	2,500		495.00	495
1994	Spring Blossoms	5,000		170.00	170
1996	Spring Bouquet	Open		195.00	195
1992	Sun Showers	5,000		195.00	225
1984	Sunflower Boy	Closed	1985	65.00	300
1990	Sunflower Girl	Closed	1993	95.00	220
1993	Water Wagon	Open		295.00	295
1995	Wedding Party	Open		175.00	175
1995	Wedding Party Children	Open		75.00	75
1987	Wee Three	Closed	1990	180.00	200-300
1984	White Dove	Closed	1992	45.00	150
1984	Wondering	Closed	1987	85.00	280

DeGrazia Nativity Collection - T. DeGrazia

YEAR ISSUE		EDITION LIMIT	YEAR RETD.	ISSUE PRICE	*QUOTE U.S.$
1993	Balthasar	Open		135.00	135
1988	Christmas Prayer Angel (red)	Closed	1991	70.00	295
1990	El Burrito	Closed	N/A	60.00	90-125
1993	El Toro	Open		95.00	98
1993	Gaspar	Open		135.00	135
1985	Jesus	Open		55.00	65
1985	Joseph	Open		100.00	110
1990	Little Prayer Angel (white)	Closed	1992	85.00	295-395
1985	Mary	Open		90.00	100
1993	Melchoir	Open		135.00	135
1996	Music For Baby Jesus	Open		145.00	145
1985	Nativity Set-3 pc. (Mary, Joseph, Jesus)	Open		275.00	275
1995	Pima Indian Drummer Boy	Open		135.00	135
1991	Shepherd's Boy	Open		95.00	135
1989	Two Little Lambs	Closed	1992	70.00	220-295

DeGrazia Pendants - R. Olszewski

YEAR ISSUE		EDITION LIMIT	YEAR RETD.	ISSUE PRICE	*QUOTE U.S.$
1987	Festival of Lights 562-P	Suspd.		90.00	275
1985	Flower Girl Pendant 561-P	Suspd.		125.00	200

DeGrazia Platinum Figurine - T. DeGrazia

YEAR ISSUE		EDITION LIMIT	YEAR RETD.	ISSUE PRICE	*QUOTE U.S.$
1996	Little Hunter	950		165.00	165
1995	Little Navajo Music Man	950		165.00	175

DeGrazia Village Collection - T. DeGrazia

YEAR ISSUE		EDITION LIMIT	YEAR RETD.	ISSUE PRICE	*QUOTE U.S.$
1993	Let's Compromise	Open		65.00	65
1992	The Listener	Closed	1992	48.00	75
1993	Peace Pipe	Open		65.00	65
1992	Telling Tales	Closed	1992	48.00	75
1993	Three Feathers	Open		65.00	65

DeGrazia: Goebel Miniatures - R. Olszewski

YEAR ISSUE		EDITION LIMIT	YEAR RETD.	ISSUE PRICE	*QUOTE U.S.$
1988	Adobe Display 948D	Suspd.		45.00	75-100
1990	Adobe Hacienda (large) Display 958-D	Suspd.		85.00	125-175
1989	Beautiful Burden 554-P	Suspd.		110.00	150-200
1990	Chapel Display 971-D	Suspd.		95.00	125
1986	Festival of Lights 507-P	Suspd.		85.00	150-300
1985	Flower Boy 502-P	Suspd.		85.00	100-200
1985	Flower Girl 501-P	Suspd.		85.00	100-200
1986	Little Madonna 552-P	Suspd.		93.00	175-225
1989	Merry Little Indian 508-P (new style)	Suspd.		110.00	150-200
1987	Merry Little Indian 508-P (old style)	Closed		95.00	250-300
1991	My Beautiful Rocking Horse 555-P	Suspd.		110.00	165-200
1985	My First Horse 503-P	Suspd.		85.00	100-165
1986	Pima Drummer Boy 506-P	Suspd.		85.00	200-300
1985	Sunflower Boy 551- P	Suspd.		93.00	125-165
1985	White Dove 504-P	Suspd.		80.00	100-150
1985	Wondering 505-P	Suspd.		93.00	100-175

Autom

Lisi Martin Resin - L. Martin

YEAR ISSUE		EDITION LIMIT	YEAR RETD.	ISSUE PRICE	*QUOTE U.S.$
1995	Barefoot Buddies	Open		38.00	38
1995	Celebrate The Season	Open		29.00	29
1995	Come Let Us Adore Him	Open		36.00	36
1995	Dress Rehearsal	Open		32.00	32
1995	First Love	Open		38.00	38
1995	Garden Secrets	Open		38.00	38
1995	Gifts Galore	Open		38.00	38
1995	Greetings	Open		34.00	34
1995	Just Friends	Open		38.00	38
1995	Mother's Little Helper	Open		36.00	36
1995	My First Kitten	Open		29.00	29
1995	Nap Time	Open		36.00	36
1996	Newborn Baby	1996		49.00	49
1995	Pampered Puppies	Open		38.00	38
1995	Peaceful Glow	Open		34.00	34
1995	Playful Pals	Open		36.00	36
1995	Sing A Song Of Joy	Open		29.00	29
1995	Snowy Sleigh Ride	Open		34.00	34
1995	Springtime Friends	Open		14.50	15
1995	Study Break	Open		36.00	36
1995	Wrapped In Love	Open		36.00	36

Lisi Martin Wood - L. Martin

YEAR ISSUE		EDITION LIMIT	YEAR RETD.	ISSUE PRICE	*QUOTE U.S.$
1990	Come Let Us Adore Him	5,000		240.00	240
1990	Garden Secrets	5,000		195.00	195
1990	Littlest Santa	5,000		195.00	195
1990	Mother's Little Helper	5,000		195.00	195
1990	My First Kitten	5,000		220.00	220
1990	Peaceful Glow	5,000		195.00	195
1990	Sleepyhead	5,000		220.00	220
1990	Snowy Sleigh Ride	5,000		220.00	220
1990	Springtime Friends	5,000		195.00	195
1990	Springtime Shower	5,000		195.00	195
1990	Study Break	5,000		220.00	220
1990	Wrapped In Love	5,000		220.00	220

Lisi Water Globes - L. Martin

YEAR ISSUE		EDITION LIMIT	YEAR RETD.	ISSUE PRICE	*QUOTE U.S.$
1995	Birdland Cafe	Open		39.00	39
1995	Littlest Santa	Open		39.00	39
1995	My First Kitten	Open		39.00	39
1995	Pampered Puppies	Open		39.00	39
1995	Playful Pals	Open		39.00	39
1995	Snowy Sleigh Ride	Open		39.00	39

Matteo Nativity Resin - Matteo Comploi

YEAR ISSUE		EDITION LIMIT	YEAR RETD.	ISSUE PRICE	*QUOTE U.S.$
1995	Baby Jesus	Open		14.95	15
1995	Black Wise Man	Open		29.95	30
1995	Camel	Open		39.95	40
1995	Camel Driver	Open		29.95	30
1995	Gloria Angel	Open		29.95	30
1995	Gray Donkey	Open		29.95	30
1995	Joseph	Open		29.95	30
1995	Kneeling Shepherd	Open		29.95	30
1995	Kneeling Wise Man	Open		29.95	30
1995	Mary	Open		29.95	30
1995	Ox	Open		14.95	15
1995	Ram	Open		14.95	15
1995	Shepherd w/ Bagpipes	Open		29.95	30
1995	Shepherd w/ Ducks	Open		29.95	30
1995	Shepherd w/Hat	Open		29.95	30
1995	Shepherdess w/ Basket	Open		29.95	30
1995	Shepherdess w/Boy	Open		29.95	30
1995	Standing Sheep	Open		14.95	15
1995	Wise Man	Open		29.95	30

Band Creations, Inc.

America's Farmland Collection-Barns - Band Creations

YEAR ISSUE		EDITION LIMIT	YEAR RETD.	ISSUE PRICE	*QUOTE U.S.$
1996	Double Crib Barn	Open		29.95	30
1996	Dutch Barn	Open		29.95	30
1996	English Barn	Open		29.95	30
1996	Gambrel Roof Barn	Open		29.95	30
1996	Log Barn	Open		29.95	30
1996	Pennsylvania Dutch Barn	Open		29.95	30
1996	Polygonal Barn	Open		29.95	30
1996	Round Barn	Open		29.95	30

America's Farmland Collection-Covered Bridges - Band Creations

YEAR ISSUE		EDITION LIMIT	YEAR RETD.	ISSUE PRICE	*QUOTE U.S.$
1995	Billie Creek, Parke County, IN	Open		29.95	30
1995	Bridge at the Green, Bennington County, VT	Open		29.95	30
1996	Bridgton, Indiana	Open		29.95	30
1995	Bunker Hill, Catawba County, NC	Open		29.95	30
1995	Burfordville, Cape Giradeai County, MO	Open		39.95	40
1995	Cedar Creek, Ozaukee County, WI	Open		29.95	30
1995	Chiselville, Bennington County, VT	Open		29.95	30
1995	Elder's Mill, Oconee County, GA	Open		29.95	30
1995	Elizabethton, Carter County, TN	Open		29.95	30
1995	Fallasburg, Kent County, MI	Open		29.95	30
1995	Gilliland, Etowah County, AL	Open		29.95	30
1995	Humpback, Allegheny County, VA	Open		29.95	30
1996	Knoebel's Grove Amusement Park, Pennsylvania	Open		29.95	30

*Quotes have been rounded up to nearest dollar

Year Issue		Edition Limit	Year Retd.	Issue Price	*Quote U.S.$
1995	Knox, Chester County, PA	Open		29.95	30
1995	Narrows, Parke County, IN	Open		29.95	30
1995	Old Blenheim, Schoharie County, NY	Open		39.95	40
1996	Olins, Ohio	Open		29.95	30
1995	Philippi, Barbour County, WV	Open		39.95	40
1995	Roberts, Preble County, OH	Open		29.95	30
1995	Robyville, Penobscot County, ME	Open		29.95	30
1995	Roseman, Madison County, IA	Open		29.95	30
1995	Shimenak, Linn County, OR	Open		29.95	30
1995	Thompson Mill, Shelly County, IL	Open		29.95	30
1995	Wawona, Mariposa County, CA	Open		29.95	30
1995	Zumbrota, Goodhue County, MN	Open		29.95	30

Best Friends Angel Pins - Richards/Penfield

Year Issue		Edition Limit	Year Retd.	Issue Price	*Quote U.S.$
1996	Angel on Your Shoulder	Open		5.00	5
1995	Daughter	Open		5.00	5
1995	Friend	Open		5.00	5
1995	Grandmother	Open		5.00	5
1995	Mother	Open		5.00	5
1995	Nurse	Open		5.00	5
1996	Secret Pal	Open		5.00	5
1995	Sister	Open		5.00	5
1996	Sweetheart	Open		5.00	5
1995	Teacher	Open		5.00	5
1995	Teammate	Open		5.00	5

Best Friends-Angel Wishes - Richards/Penfield

Year Issue		Edition Limit	Year Retd.	Issue Price	*Quote U.S.$
1994	Anniversary	Open		12.00	12
1994	Best Wishes	Open		12.00	12
1994	Bride and Groom	Open		12.00	12
1994	Congratulations	Open		12.00	12
1994	Create A Wish	Open		12.00	12
1994	Get Well	Open		12.00	12
1994	Good Luck	Open		12.00	12
1994	Happy Birthday	Open		12.00	12
1994	Inspirational	Open		12.00	12
1994	New Baby	Open		12.00	12

Best Friends-Angels Of The Month - Richards/Penfield

Year Issue		Edition Limit	Year Retd.	Issue Price	*Quote U.S.$
1993	January	Open		10.00	10
1993	February	Open		10.00	10
1993	March	Open		10.00	10
1993	April	Open		10.00	10
1993	May	Open		10.00	10
1993	June	Open		10.00	10
1993	July	Open		10.00	10
1993	August	Open		10.00	10
1993	September	Open		10.00	10
1993	October	Open		10.00	10
1993	November	Open		10.00	10
1993	December	Open		10.00	10

Best Friends-Celebrate Around the World Santas - Richards/Penfield

Year Issue		Edition Limit	Year Retd.	Issue Price	*Quote U.S.$
1996	England	Open		12.00	12
1996	Germany	Open		12.00	12
1996	Mexico	Open		12.00	12
1996	Norway	Open		12.00	12
1996	Russia	Open		12.00	12
1996	United States (black)	Open		12.00	12
1996	United States (white)	Open		12.00	12

Best Friends-Celebrate Around the World Trees - Richards/Penfield

Year Issue		Edition Limit	Year Retd.	Issue Price	*Quote U.S.$
1996	Around the World Tree	Open		18.00	18
1996	British Tree	Open		19.50	20
1996	Germany Tree	Open		19.50	20
1996	Scandinavian Tree	Open		19.50	20
1996	United States Tree	Open		19.50	20

Best Friends-Christmas Pageant - Richards/Penfield

Year Issue		Edition Limit	Year Retd.	Issue Price	*Quote U.S.$
1996	Angel-peace/joy	Open		6.00	6
1996	Bench	Open		4.00	4
1996	Boy with Star	Open		6.00	6
1996	Donkey	Open		4.00	4
1996	Girl with Tree	Open		6.00	6
1996	Joseph	Open		6.00	6
1996	Mary and Baby Jesus	Open		6.00	6
1996	Sheep	Open		4.00	4
1996	Sign	Open		4.00	4
1996	Stage	Open		14.00	14
1996	Christmas Pageant 10 pc set	Open		60.00	60

Best Friends-Earth Angels - Richards/Penfield

Year Issue		Edition Limit	Year Retd.	Issue Price	*Quote U.S.$
1996	Angel Potsitter Bird Nest	Open		10.00	10
1996	Angel Potsitter Front	Open		8.00	8
1996	Angel Potsitter Left	Open		9.00	9
1996	Angel with Aster	Open		10.00	10
1996	Angel with Calendula	Open		10.00	10
1996	Angel with Carnation	Open		10.00	10
1996	Angel with Chrysanthemum	Open		10.00	10
1996	Angel with Gladiolous	Open		10.00	10
1996	Angel with Jonquil	Open		10.00	10
1996	Angel with Larkspur	Open		10.00	10
1996	Angel with Lily of the Valley	Open		10.00	10
1996	Angel with Narcissus	Open		10.00	10
1996	Angel with Rose	Open		10.00	10
1996	Angel with Sunflower	Open		10.00	10
1996	Angel with Sweet Pea	Open		10.00	10
1996	Angel with Violet	Open		10.00	10

Best Friends-First Friends Begin At Childhood - Richards/Penfield

Year Issue		Edition Limit	Year Retd.	Issue Price	*Quote U.S.$
1993	Castles In The Sand (4 pc set)	Open		16.00	16
1993	Checking It Twice (2 pc set)	Open		15.00	15
1993	Dad's Best Pal	Open		15.00	15
1993	Feathered Friends	Open		13.00	13
1993	Fishing Friends	Open		18.00	18
1993	Grandma's Favorite	Open		15.00	15
1993	My "Beary" Best Friend	Open		12.00	12
1993	My Best Friend (2 pc set)	Open		24.00	24
1993	Oh So Pretty	Open		14.00	14
1993	Purr-Fit Friends	Open		12.00	12
1993	Quiet Time	Open		15.00	15
1993	Rainbow Of Friends	Open		24.00	24
1993	Santa's First Visit	Open		15.00	15
1993	Santa's Surprise	Open		14.00	14
1993	Sharing Is Caring	Open		12.00	12
1993	A Wagon Full Of Fun (2 pc set)	Open		15.00	15

Best Friends-Happy Hearts - Richards/Penfield

Year Issue		Edition Limit	Year Retd.	Issue Price	*Quote U.S.$
1996	Angels in the Snow	Open		35.00	35
1996	Best Friends	Open		35.00	35
1996	A Guiding Star	Open		35.00	35
1996	Just Married	Open		35.00	35
1996	Making New Friends	Open		35.00	35
1996	Thanksgiving Friends	Open		35.00	35

Best Friends-Heavenly Helpers - Richards/Penfield

Year Issue		Edition Limit	Year Retd.	Issue Price	*Quote U.S.$
1996	Childcare	Open		12.00	12
1996	Emergency Medical Team	Open		12.00	12
1996	Fireman	Open		12.00	12
1996	Nurse	Open		12.00	12
1996	Policeman	Open		12.00	12
1996	Teacher	Open		12.00	12
1996	Volunteer	Open		12.00	12

Best Friends-Noah's Ark - Richards/Penfield

Year Issue		Edition Limit	Year Retd.	Issue Price	*Quote U.S.$
1995	Animals (set of 10)	Open		20.00	20
1995	Noah's Ark & Raft	Open		42.00	42

Best Friends Joyful Night Nativity - Richards/Penfield

Year Issue		Edition Limit	Year Retd.	Issue Price	*Quote U.S.$
1994	3 Kings (set/3)	Open		24.00	24
1994	Angel on Stable (wall)	Open		16.00	16
1994	Camel and Donkey (set/2)	Open		8.00	8
1995	Camel Standing	Open		6.00	6
1994	Holy Family (Joseph, Mary & Jesus)	Open		16.00	16
1994	Shepard Boy	Open		8.00	8
1995	Shepherd with Sheep (set/7)	Open		8.00	8

Best Friends-Rainbow of Friends - Richards/Penfield

Year Issue		Edition Limit	Year Retd.	Issue Price	*Quote U.S.$
1996	Rainbow of Friends	Open		24.00	24
1996	Rainbow of Friends, music Box	Open		17.50	18

Best Friends-RiverSong - Richards/Penfield

Year Issue		Edition Limit	Year Retd.	Issue Price	*Quote U.S.$
1994	3 Assorted Carolers	Open		22.00	22
1995	Brick House	Open		19.95	20
1993	Carolers Set UF14 set/5 (3 carolers, 1 lamp post, 1 dog)	Open		30.00	30
1995	Church	Open		19.95	20
1995	Double Angels	Open		8.00	8
1995	Gingerbread House	Open		19.95	20
1995	Skaters Sitting (set/2)	Open		12.00	12
1995	Skaters Standing (set/2)	Open		12.00	12
1995	Snowball Fight (set/3)	Open		15.00	15
1995	Snowmen (set/3)	Open		12.95	13
1995	Stucco House	Open		19.95	20
1995	Wood House	Open		19.95	20

Best Friends-Winter Wonderland - Richards/Penfield

Year Issue		Edition Limit	Year Retd.	Issue Price	*Quote U.S.$
1994	3 Assorted White Trees & 3 presents	Open		18.00	18
1994	Accessories; rabbits, teddies, presents (set/3)	Open		4.00	4
1994	Mr. Santa	Open		9.00	9
1994	Mrs. Santa	Open		9.00	9
1994	Reindeer (1 standing, 1 sitting) (set/2)	Open		10.00	10

Dream Pots - Amy S.

Year Issue		Edition Limit	Year Retd.	Issue Price	*Quote U.S.$
1996	Aster	Open		8.00	8
1996	Calendula	Open		8.00	8
1996	Carnation	Open		8.00	8
1996	Chrysanthemum	Open		8.00	8
1996	Gladiolous	Open		8.00	8
1996	Jonquil	Open		8.00	8
1996	Larkspur	Open		8.00	8
1996	Lily of the Valley	Open		8.00	8
1996	Narcissus	Open		8.00	8
1996	Rose	Open		8.00	8
1996	Sunflower	Open		8.00	8
1996	Sweet Pea	Open		8.00	8
1996	Violet	Open		8.00	8

Bing & Grondahl

Centennial Anniversary Commemoratives - F.A. Hallin

Year Issue		Edition Limit	Year Retd.	Issue Price	*Quote U.S.$
1995	Centennial Vase: Behind the Frozen Window	1,250	1995	295.00	295

Boyds Collection Ltd.

The Bearstone Collection™ - G.M. Lowenthal

Year Issue		Edition Limit	Year Retd.	Issue Price	*Quote U.S.$
1994	Agatha & Shelly-'Scardy Cat' 2246	Open		16.25	17-75
1995	Amelia's Enterprise 'Carrot Juice' 2258	Open		16.25	17-50
1995	Angelica...'the Guardian' 2266	Open		17.95	18-65
1995	Angelica...the Guardian Angel Water Globe 2702	Open		37.50	38-55
1993	Arthur...with Red Scarf 2003-03	Retrd.	1994	10.50	50-110
1994	Bailey & Emily...'Forever Friends' 2018	Open		34.00	34-125
1994	Bailey & Wixie 'To Have and To Hold' 2017	Open		15.75	16-125
1994	Bailey at the Beach 2020-09	Retrd.	1995	15.75	40-115
1993	Bailey Bear with Suitcase (old version) 2000	Retrd.	1993	14.20	100-190
1993	Bailey Bear with Suitcase (revised version) 2000	Open		14.20	15-75
1994	Bailey's Birthday 2014	Open		15.95	16-100
1995	Bailey...'The Baker with Sweetie Pie' 2254	Open		12.50	13-50
1995	Bailey...'The Baker with Sweetie Pie' 2254CL	3,600	1995	15.00	150-250
1995	Bailey...'the Cheerleader' 2268	Open		15.95	16-55
1995	Bailey...'The Honeybear' 2260	Open		15.75	16-65
1996	Bailey...Heart's Desire 2272	Open		15.00	15
1993	Bailey...in the Orchard 2006	Open		14.20	15-125
1995	Baldwin...as the Child 2403	Open		14.95	15
1994	Bessie the Santa Cow 2239	Open		15.75	16-70
1993	Byron & Chedda w/Catmint 2010	Retrd.	1994	14.20	50-100
1994	Celeste...'The Angel Rabbit' 2230	Open		16.25	17-125
1994	Charlotte & Bebe...'The Gardeners' 2229	Retrd.	1995	15.75	65-120
1993	Christian by the Sea 2012	Open		14.20	15-75
1994	Christmas Big Pig, Little Pig BC2256	Retrd.	N/A	12.50	50-100
1994	Clara...'The Nurse' 2231	Open		16.25	17-200
1994	Clarence Angel Bear (rust) 2029-11	Retrd.	1995	12.60	50-125
1995	Cookie Catberg...'Knittin' Kitten' 2250	Open		18.75	19-45
1994	Cookie the Santa Cat 2237	Retrd.	1995	15.25	45-65
1995	Daphne and Eloise...'Women's Work' 2251	Open		18.00	18-47
1993	Daphne Hare & Maisey Ewe 2011	Retrd.	1995	14.20	100-125
1994	Daphne...The Reader Hare 2226	Open		14.20	15-90
1994	Edmond & Bailey...'Gathering Holly' 2240	Open		24.25	25-110
1994	Elf Bear with List BC2252	1,865	1994	12.50	200-400
1994	Elgin the Elf Bear 2236	Open		14.20	15-80
1994	Elliot & Snowbeary 2242	Open		15.25	16-65
1994	Elliot & The Tree 2241	Open		16.25	17-120
1995	Elliot & the Tree Water Globe 2704	Open		35.00	35-65
1996	Emma & Bailey...Afternoon Tea 2277	Open		18.00	18
1995	Emma...'the Witchy Bear' 2269	Open		16.75	17-45
1993	Father Chrisbear and Son 2008	Retrd.	1993	15.00	220-300
1994	Grenville & Beatrice...'Best Friends' 2016	Open		26.25	27-150
1996	Grenville & Beatrice...True Love 2274	Open		36.00	36
1995	Grenville & Knute...Football Buddies 2255	Open		19.95	20-55
1993	Grenville & Neville...'The Sign' (prototype) 2099	Retrd.	1993	15.75	60-100
1993	Grenville & Neville...'The Sign' 2099	Open		15.75	16-60
1994	Grenville the Santabear 2030	Open		14.20	15-325
1994	Grenville the Santabear Musical Waterball 2700	Open		35.75	36-95
1994	Grenville...'The Graduate' 2233	12/96		16.25	17-70
1995	Grenville...'The Storyteller' 2265	Retrd.	1995	50.00	50-125
1993	Grenville...with Green Scarf 2003-04	Retrd.	1994	10.50	200-285
1993	Grenville...with Red Scarf 2003-08	Retrd.	1995	10.50	50-100
1994	Homer on the Plate 2225	Open		15.75	16-75
1994	Homer on the Plate BC2218	Retrd.	N/A	12.50	60-100
1995	Hop-a-Long...'The Deputy' 2247	Open		14.00	14-60
1994	Juliette Angel Bear (ivory) 2029-10	Retrd.	1995	12.60	75-125
1994	Justina & M. Harrison...'Sweetie Pie' 2015	Open		26.25	27-75
1996	Justina...The Message "Bearer" 2273	Open		16.00	16
1994	Knute & The Gridiron 2245	Open		16.25	17-70
1994	Kringle & Bailey with List 2235	Open		14.20	15-65
1995	Lefty...'On the Mound' 2253	Open		15.00	15-80
1995	Lefty...'On the Mound' BC2056	Retrd.	N/A	12.50	50-80
1996	M. Harrison's Birthday 2275	Open		17.00	17
1994	Manheim the 'Eco-Moose' 2243	Open		15.25	16-75
1994	Maynard the Santa Moose 2238	Open		15.25	16-60
1995	Miss Bruin & Bailey 'The Lesson' 2259	Open		18.45	19-60
1993	Moriarty-'The Bear in the Cat Suit' 2005	Retrd.	1995	13.75	60-110
1996	Ms. Griz...Monday Morning 2276	Open		34.00	34
1995	Neville...as Joseph 2401	Open		14.95	15
1993	Neville...The 'Bedtime Bear' 2002	12/96		14.20	15-110
1996	Noah & Co...Art Builders 2278	12/96		61.00	61
1995	Otis...'Taxtime' 2262	Open		18.75	19-60
1995	Otis...'The Fisherman' 2249-06	Open		15.75	16-50
1994	Sebastian's Prayer 2227	12/96		16.25	17-70
1994	Sherlock & Watson-In Disguise 2019	7/96		15.75	16-65

*Quotes have been rounded up to nearest dollar

YEAR ISSUE		EDITION LIMIT	YEAR RETD.	ISSUE PRICE	*QUOTE U.S.$
1995	Simone & Bailey...'Helping Hands' 2267	Open		25.95	26-50
1993	Simone De Bearvoire and Her Mom 2001	12/96		14.20	15-115
1995	The Stage...the School Pagent 2425	Open		34.95	35
1994	Ted & Teddy 2223	Open		15.75	16-75
1995	Theresa...as Mary 2402	Open		14.95	15
1995	Union Jack...'Love Letters' 2263	Open		18.95	19-45
1993	Victoria...'The Lady' 2004	Open		18.40	19-120
1994	Wilson at the Beach 2020-06	Open		15.75	16-80
1994	Wilson the "Perfesser" 2222	Open		16.25	17-65
1993	Wilson with Love Sonnets 2007	Open		12.60	13-325
1995	Wilson...'the Wonderful Wizard of Wuz' 2261	Open		15.95	16-55

The Dollstone Collection™ - G.M. Lowenthal

YEAR ISSUE		EDITION LIMIT	YEAR RETD.	ISSUE PRICE	*QUOTE U.S.$
1995	Betsy & Edmund 3503PE	Retrd.	1995	19.50	set
1995	Katherine, Amanda & Edmund 3505PE	Retrd.	1995	19.50	set
1995	Meagan 3504PE	Retrd.	1995	19.50	set
1995	Victoria with Samantha 3502PE	Retrd.	1995	19.50	set
1995	Set of 4 PE	Retrd.	1995	78.00	285-315
1996	Ashley with Chrissie...Dress Up 3506	Open		20.50	21
1996	Betsy with Edmond...The Patriots 3503	Open		20.00	20
1996	Emily with Kathleen & Otis...The Future 3508	Open		30.00	30
1996	Jennifer with Priscilla...The Doll in the Attic 3500	Open		20.50	21
1996	Katherine with Amanda & Edmond...Kind Hearts 3505	Open		20.00	20
1996	Priscilla with Molly...Attic Treasures 3501	Open		14.00	14
1996	Rebecca w/ Elliot...Birthday 3509	Open		20.50	21
1996	Sara & Heather with Elliot & Amelia...Tea for Four 3507	12/96		46.00	46
1996	Victoria with Samantha...Victorian Ladies 3502	Open		20.00	20

The Folkstone Collection™ - G.M. Lowenthal

YEAR ISSUE		EDITION LIMIT	YEAR RETD.	ISSUE PRICE	*QUOTE U.S.$
1995	Abigail...Peaceable Kingdom 2829	Open		18.95	19-30
1996	Alvin T. Mac Barker...Dogface 2872	Open		19.00	19
1994	Angel of Freedom 2820	Open		16.75	17-55
1994	Angel of Love 2821	Open		16.75	17-55
1994	Angel of Peace 2822	Open		16.75	17-65
1996	Athena...The Wedding Angel 28202	Open		19.00	19
1994	Beatrice-Birthday Angel 2825	Open		20.00	20-30
1995	Beatrice...the Giftgiver 2836	Open		17.95	18-25
1996	Betty Cocker 2870	Open		19.00	19
1995	Boowinkle Vonhindenmoose ...2831	Open		17.95	18-25
1996	Buster Goes A' Courtin' 2844	Open		19.00	19
1994	Chilly & Son with Dove 2811	Open		17.75	18-40
1996	Cosmos...The Gardening Angel 28201	Open		19.00	19
1994	Elmer-Cow on Haystacks 2851	Open		19.00	19
1996	Elmo "Tex" Beefcake...On the Range 2853	Open		19.00	19
1995	Ernest Hemmingmoose...the Hunter 2835	Open		17.95	18-35
1995	Esmeralda...the Wonderful Witch 2860	Open		17.95	18-30
1996	Flora & Amelia...The Gardeners 2843	Open		19.00	19
1996	Flora, Amelia & Eloise...The Tea Party 2846	Open		19.00	19
1994	Florence-Kitchen Angel 2824	Open		20.00	20-38
1995	Icabod Mooselman...the Pilgrim 2833	Open		17.95	18-28
1994	Ida & Bessie-The Gardeners 2852	Open		19.00	19-30
1995	Jean Claude & Jacques...the Skiers 2815	Open		16.95	17
1994	Jill-Language of Love 2842	Open		19.00	19-60
1994	Jingle Moose 2830	Open		17.75	18
1994	Jingles & Son withWreath 2812	Open		17.75	18
1994	Lizzie Shopping Angel 2827	Open		20.00	20-28
1996	Loretta Moostein..."Yer Cheatin' Heart" 2854	Open		19.00	19
1994	Minerva-Baseball Angel 2826	Open		20.00	20-28
1994	Myrtle-Believe 2840	Open		20.00	20
1995	Na-Nick of the North 2804	Open		17.95	18
1994	Nicholai with Tree 2800	Open		17.75	18-40
1994	Nicholas with Book 2802	Open		17.75	18
1994	Nick on Ice (1st ed. GCC) 3001	3,600	1995	49.95	75
1994	Nick on Ice 3001	Open		32.95	33
1994	Nikki with Candle 2801	Open		17.75	18-45
1995	Northbound Wille 2814	Open		16.95	17
1994	Oceana-Ocean Angel 2823	Open		16.75	17-60
1994	Peter-The Whopper 2841	Open		19.00	19
1995	Prudence Mooselmaid...the Pilgrim 2834	Open		17.95	18
1994	Rufus-Hoedown 2850	Open		19.00	19-28
1994	Santa's Challenge (1st ed. GCC) 3002	3,600	1995	49.95	75
1994	Santa's Challenge 3002	Open		32.95	33
1994	Santa's Flight Plan (1st ed. GCC) 3000	3,600	1995	49.95	75
1994	Santa's Flight Plan 3000	Open		32.95	33
1995	Seraphina with Jacob & Rachael...the Choir Angels 2828	Open		19.95	20-30
1995	Siegfried and Egon...the Sign 2899	Open		18.95	19-45
1995	Sliknick the Chimney Sweep 2803	Open		17.95	18
1996	Sparky McPlug 2871	Open		19.00	19
1996	Too Loose Lapin...The Arteest 2845	Open		19.00	19
1994	Windy with Book 2810	Open		17.75	18-45

Brandywine Collectibles

Accessories - M. Whiting

YEAR ISSUE		EDITION LIMIT	YEAR RETD.	ISSUE PRICE	*QUOTE U.S.$
1992	Apple Tree/Tire Swing	Open		10.00	10
1991	Baggage Cart	Open		10.50	11
1990	Bandstand	Closed	1992	10.50	11
1994	Elm Tree with Benches	Open		16.00	16
1988	Flag	Open		10.00	10
1990	Flower Cart	Open		13.00	13
1990	Gate & Arbor	Closed	1992	9.00	9
1990	Gooseneck Lamp	Open		7.50	8
1989	Horse & Carriage	Open		13.00	13
1994	Lamp with Barber Pole	Open		10.50	11
1988	Lampost, Wall & Fence	Open		11.00	11
1989	Mailbox, Tree & Fence	Open		10.00	10
1989	Pumpkin Wagon	Open		11.50	12
1991	Street Sign	Open		8.00	8
1987	Summer Tree with Fence	Open		7.00	7
1991	Town Clock	Open		7.50	8
1992	Tree with Birdhouse	Open		10.00	10
1989	Victorian Gas Light	Open		6.50	7
1990	Wishing Well	Open		10.00	10

Barnsville Collection - M. Whiting

YEAR ISSUE		EDITION LIMIT	YEAR RETD.	ISSUE PRICE	*QUOTE U.S.$
1991	B & O Station	Open		28.00	28
1992	Barnesville Church	Open		44.00	44
1991	Bradfield House	Open		32.00	32
1990	Candace Bruce House	Closed	1996	30.00	30
1990	Gay 90's Mansion	Closed	1996	32.00	32
1992	Plumtree Bed & Breakfast	Open		44.00	44
1990	Thompson House	Closed	1996	32.00	32
1990	Treat-Smith House	Open		32.00	32
1991	Whiteley House	Open		32.00	32

Country Lane - M. Whiting

YEAR ISSUE		EDITION LIMIT	YEAR RETD.	ISSUE PRICE	*QUOTE U.S.$
1995	Berry Farm	Open		30.00	30
1995	Country School	Open		30.00	30
1995	Dairy Farm	Open		30.00	30
1995	Farm House	Open		30.00	30
1995	The General Store	Open		30.00	30

Country Lane II - M. Whiting

YEAR ISSUE		EDITION LIMIT	YEAR RETD.	ISSUE PRICE	*QUOTE U.S.$
1995	Antiques & Crafts	Open		30.00	30
1995	Basketmaker	Open		30.00	30
1995	Country Church	Open		30.00	30
1995	Fishing Lodge	Open		30.00	30
1995	Herb Farm	Open		30.00	30
1995	Olde Mill	Open		30.00	30
1995	Spinners & Weavers	Open		30.00	30

Country Lane III - M. Whiting

YEAR ISSUE		EDITION LIMIT	YEAR RETD.	ISSUE PRICE	*QUOTE U.S.$
1996	Airport	Open		30.00	30
1996	Country Club	Open		30.00	30
1996	Country Fair	Open		30.00	30
1996	Firehouse	Open		30.00	30
1996	Old Orchard	Open		30.00	30
1996	Post Office	Open		30.00	30

Custom Collection - M. Whiting

YEAR ISSUE		EDITION LIMIT	YEAR RETD.	ISSUE PRICE	*QUOTE U.S.$
1988	Burgess Museum	Open		15.50	16
1992	Cumberland County Courthouse	Open		15.00	15
1990	Doylestown Public School	Open		32.00	32
1991	Jamestown Tower	Closed	1991	9.00	9
1990	Jared Coffin House	Open		32.00	32
1989	Lorain Lighthouse	Closed	1992	11.00	11
1992	Loudon County Courthouse	Open		15.00	15
1988	Princetown Monument	Closed	1989	9.70	10
1991	Smithfield VA. Courthouse	Closed	1992	12.00	12
1989	Yankee Candle Co.	Open		13.50	14

Hilton Village - M. Whiting

YEAR ISSUE		EDITION LIMIT	YEAR RETD.	ISSUE PRICE	*QUOTE U.S.$
1987	Dutch House	Closed	1991	8.50	9
1987	English House	Closed	1991	8.50	9
1987	Georgian House	Closed	1991	8.50	9
1987	Gwen's House	Closed	1991	8.50	9
1987	Hilton Firehouse	Closed	1991	8.50	9

Hometown I - M. Whiting

YEAR ISSUE		EDITION LIMIT	YEAR RETD.	ISSUE PRICE	*QUOTE U.S.$
1990	Barber Shop	Closed	1992	14.00	14
1990	General Store	Closed	1992	14.00	14
1990	School	Closed	1992	14.00	14
1990	Toy Store	Closed	1992	14.00	14

Hometown II - M. Whiting

YEAR ISSUE		EDITION LIMIT	YEAR RETD.	ISSUE PRICE	*QUOTE U.S.$
1991	Church	Closed	1993	14.00	14
1991	Dentist	Closed	1993	14.00	14
1991	Ice Cream Shop	Closed	1993	14.00	14
1991	Stitch-N-Sew	Closed	1993	14.00	14

Hometown III - M. Whiting

YEAR ISSUE		EDITION LIMIT	YEAR RETD.	ISSUE PRICE	*QUOTE U.S.$
1991	Basket Shop	Closed	1993	15.50	16
1991	Dairy	Closed	1993	15.50	16
1991	Firehouse	Closed	1993	15.50	16
1991	Library	Closed	1993	15.50	16

Hometown IV - M. Whiting

YEAR ISSUE		EDITION LIMIT	YEAR RETD.	ISSUE PRICE	*QUOTE U.S.$
1992	Bakery	Closed	1994	21.00	21
1992	Country Inn	Closed	1994	21.50	22
1992	Courtnhouse	Closed	1994	21.50	22
1992	Gas Station	Closed	1994	21.00	21

Hometown V - M. Whiting

YEAR ISSUE		EDITION LIMIT	YEAR RETD.	ISSUE PRICE	*QUOTE U.S.$
1992	Antiques Shop	Closed	1995	22.00	22
1992	Gift Shop	Closed	1995	22.00	22
1992	Pharmacy	Closed	1995	22.00	22
1992	Sporting Goods	Closed	1995	22.00	22
1992	Tea Room	Closed	1995	22.00	22

Hometown VI - M. Whiting

YEAR ISSUE		EDITION LIMIT	YEAR RETD.	ISSUE PRICE	*QUOTE U.S.$
1993	Church	Closed	1995	24.00	24
1993	Diner	Closed	1995	24.00	24
1993	General Store	Closed	1995	24.00	24
1993	School	Closed	1995	24.00	24
1993	Train Station	Closed	1995	24.00	24

Hometown VII - M. Whiting

YEAR ISSUE		EDITION LIMIT	YEAR RETD.	ISSUE PRICE	*QUOTE U.S.$
1993	Candy Shop	Closed	1996	24.00	24
1993	Dress Shop	Closed	1996	24.00	24
1993	Flower Shop	Closed	1996	24.00	24
1993	Pet Shop	Closed	1996	24.00	24
1993	Post Office	Closed	1996	24.00	24
1993	Quilt Shop	Closed	1996	24.00	24

Hometown VIII - M. Whiting

YEAR ISSUE		EDITION LIMIT	YEAR RETD.	ISSUE PRICE	*QUOTE U.S.$
1994	Barber Shop	Open		28.00	28
1994	Country Store	Open		28.00	28
1994	Fire Company	Open		28.00	28
1994	Professional Building	Open		28.00	28
1994	Sewing Shop	Open		26.00	26

Hometown IX - M. Whiting

YEAR ISSUE		EDITION LIMIT	YEAR RETD.	ISSUE PRICE	*QUOTE U.S.$
1994	Bed & Breakfast	Open		29.00	29
1994	Cafe/Deli	Open		29.00	29
1994	Hometown Bank	Open		29.00	29
1994	Hometown Gazette	Open		29.00	29
1994	Teddys & Toys	Open		29.00	29

Hometown X - M. Whiting

YEAR ISSUE		EDITION LIMIT	YEAR RETD.	ISSUE PRICE	*QUOTE U.S.$
1995	Brick Church	Open		29.00	29
1995	The Doll Shoppe	Open		29.00	29
1995	General Hospital	Open		29.00	29
1995	The Gift Box	Open		29.00	29
1995	Police Station	Open		29.00	29

Hometown XI - M. Whiting

YEAR ISSUE		EDITION LIMIT	YEAR RETD.	ISSUE PRICE	*QUOTE U.S.$
1995	Antiques	Open		29.00	29
1995	Church II	Open		29.00	29
1995	Grocer	Open		29.00	29
1995	Pharmacy	Open		29.00	29
1995	School II	Open		29.00	29

Hometown XII - M. Whiting

YEAR ISSUE		EDITION LIMIT	YEAR RETD.	ISSUE PRICE	*QUOTE U.S.$
1996	Bridal & Dress Shoppe	Open		29.00	29
1996	Five & Dime	Open		29.00	29
1996	Hometown Theater	Open		29.00	29
1996	Post Office	Open		29.00	29
1996	Travel Agency	Open		29.00	29

North Pole Collection - M. Whiting, unless otherwise noted

YEAR ISSUE		EDITION LIMIT	YEAR RETD.	ISSUE PRICE	*QUOTE U.S.$
1992	3 Winter Trees - D. Whiting	Open		10.50	11
1993	Candy Cane Factory	Open		24.00	24
1991	Claus House	Open		24.00	24
1993	Elf Club	Open		24.00	24
1992	Elves Workshop	Open		24.00	24
1991	Gingerbread House	Open		24.00	24
1995	New Reindeer Barn	Open		24.00	24
1994	Post Office	Open		25.00	25
1991	Reindeer Barn	Closed	1996	24.00	24
1992	Snowflake Lodge	Open		24.00	24
1992	Snowman with St. Sign	Open		11.50	12
1995	Stocking Shop	Open		24.00	24
1992	Sugarplum Bakery	Open		24.00	24
1993	Teddybear Factory	Open		24.00	24
1993	Town Christmas Tree	Open		20.00	20
1994	Town Hall	Open		25.00	25

Old Salem Collection - M. Whiting

YEAR ISSUE		EDITION LIMIT	YEAR RETD.	ISSUE PRICE	*QUOTE U.S.$
1987	Boys School	Open		18.50	19
1987	First House	Open		12.80	13
1987	Home Moravian Church	Open		18.50	19
1987	Miksch Tobacco Shop	Closed	1993	12.00	12
1987	Salem Tavern	Open		20.50	21
1987	Schultz Shoemaker	Open		10.50	11
1987	Vogler House	Open		20.50	21
1987	Winkler Bakery	Open		20.50	21

Patriots Collection - M. Whiting

YEAR ISSUE		EDITION LIMIT	YEAR RETD.	ISSUE PRICE	*QUOTE U.S.$
1992	Betsy Ross House	Open		17.50	18
1992	Washingtons Headquarters	Open		24.00	24

Seymour Collection - M. Whiting

YEAR ISSUE		EDITION LIMIT	YEAR RETD.	ISSUE PRICE	*QUOTE U.S.$
1991	Anderson House	Open		20.00	20
1991	Blish Home	Open		20.00	20
1992	Majestic Theater	Open		22.00	22
1991	Seymour Church	Open		19.00	19
1991	Seymour Library	Open		20.00	20

*Quotes have been rounded up to nearest dollar

Treasured Times - M. Whiting

YEAR ISSUE		EDITION LIMIT	YEAR RETD.	ISSUE PRICE	*QUOTE U.S.$
1994	Birthday House	750		32.00	32
1994	Halloween House	750		32.00	32
1994	Mother's Day House	750		32.00	32
1994	New Baby Boy House	750		32.00	32
1994	New Baby Girl House	750		32.00	32
1994	Valentine House	750		32.00	32

Victorian Collection - M. Whiting

YEAR ISSUE		EDITION LIMIT	YEAR RETD.	ISSUE PRICE	*QUOTE U.S.$
1989	Broadway House	Closed	1994	22.00	22
1989	Elm House	Closed	1994	25.00	25
1989	Fairplay Church	Closed	1994	19.50	20
1989	Hearts Ease Cottage	Closed	1994	15.30	16
1989	Old Star Hook & Ladder	Closed	1994	23.00	23
1989	Peachtree House	Closed	1994	22.50	23
1989	Seabreeze Cottage	Closed	1994	15.30	16
1989	Serenity Cottage	Closed	1994	15.30	16
1989	Skippack School	Closed	1994	22.50	23

Williamsburg Collection -M. Whiting

YEAR ISSUE		EDITION LIMIT	YEAR RETD.	ISSUE PRICE	*QUOTE U.S.$
1993	Campbell's Tavern	Open		28.00	28
1988	Colonial Capitol	Open		43.50	44
1988	Court House of 1770	Open		26.50	27
1988	Governor's Palace	Open		37.50	38
1993	Kings Arms Tavern	Open		25.00	25
1988	The Magazine	Open		23.50	24
1988	Wythe House	Open		25.00	25

Yorktown Collection - M. Whiting

YEAR ISSUE		EDITION LIMIT	YEAR RETD.	ISSUE PRICE	*QUOTE U.S.$
1987	Custom House	Open		17.50	18
1993	Digges House	Open		22.00	22
1987	Grace Church	Open		19.00	19
1987	Medical Shop	Open		13.00	13
1987	Moore House	Open		22.00	22
1987	Nelson House	Open		22.00	22
1987	Pate House	Open		19.00	19
1987	Swan Tavern	Open		22.00	22

Byers' Choice Ltd.

Accessories - J. Byers

YEAR ISSUE		EDITION LIMIT	YEAR RETD.	ISSUE PRICE	*QUOTE U.S.$
1995	Cat in Hat	Open		10.00	10
1996	Dog with Hat	Open		18.50	19
1995	Dog with Sausages	Closed	1995	18.00	20

Carolers - J. Byers

YEAR ISSUE		EDITION LIMIT	YEAR RETD.	ISSUE PRICE	*QUOTE U.S.$
1988	Children with Skates	Open		40.00	49
1988	Singing Cats	Open		13.50	16
1986	Singing Dogs	Open		13.00	16
1996	Teenagers (Traditional)	Open		46.00	46
1996	Teenagers (Victorian)	Open		49.00	49
1976	Traditional Adult (1976-80)	Closed	1980	N/A	475
1981	Traditional Adult (1981-current)	Open		45.00	45-300
XX	Traditional Adult (undated)	Closed	N/A	N/A	400-700
1978	Traditional Colonial Lady (w/ hands)	Closed	1978	N/A	1500
1986	Traditional Grandparents	Open		35.00	45
1982	Victorian Adult (1st ed.)	Closed	1982	32.00	400
1982	Victorian Adult (2nd ed./dressed alike)	Closed	1983	46.00	300-400
1983	Victorian Adult (assorted) (2nd ed.)	Open		35.00	48
1982	Victorian Child (1st ed. w/floppy hats)	Closed	1982	32.00	300-375
1983	Victorian Child (2nd ed./sailor suit)	Closed	1983	33.00	300-400
1983	Victorian Child (assorted)	Open		33.00	48
1988	Victorian Grand Parent	Open		40.00	48

Children of The World - J. Byers

YEAR ISSUE		EDITION LIMIT	YEAR RETD.	ISSUE PRICE	*QUOTE U.S.$
1993	Bavarian Boy	Closed	1993	50.00	175-250
1992	Dutch Boy	Closed	1992	50.00	225-300
1992	Dutch Girl	Closed	1992	50.00	225-300
1994	Irish Girl	Closed	1994	50.00	150-250
1996	Saint Lucia	Open		52.00	52

Cries Of London - J. Byers

YEAR ISSUE		EDITION LIMIT	YEAR RETD.	ISSUE PRICE	*QUOTE U.S.$
1991	Apple Lady (red stockings)	Closed	1991	80.00	800-1100
1991	Apple Lady (red/wh stockings)	Closed	1991	80.00	900-1200
1992	Baker	Closed	1992	62.00	150-225
1993	Chestnut Roaster	Closed	1993	64.00	175-300
1996	Children Buying Gingerbread	Open		46.00	46
1995	Dollmaker	Closed	1995	64.00	64
1994	Flower Vendor	Closed	1994	64.00	150-200
1996	Gingerbread Vendor	Open		75.00	75
1995	Girl Holding Doll	Closed	1995	48.00	50-90

Dickens Series - J. Byers

YEAR ISSUE		EDITION LIMIT	YEAR RETD.	ISSUE PRICE	*QUOTE U.S.$
1990	Bob Cratchit & Tiny Tim (1st ed.)	Closed	1990	84.00	150-275
1991	Bob Cratchit & Tiny Tim (2nd ed.)	Open		86.00	89
1991	Happy Scrooge (1st ed.)	Closed	1991	50.00	225-325
1992	Happy Scrooge (2nd ed.)	Closed	1992	50.00	225
1986	Marley's Ghost (1st ed.)	Closed	1986	40.00	350-500
1987	Marley's Ghost (2nd ed.)	Closed	1992	42.00	250-325
1985	Mr. Fezziwig (1st ed.)	Closed	1985	43.00	750
1986	Mr. Fezziwig (2nd ed.)	Closed	1990	43.00	400-600
1984	Mrs. Cratchit (1st ed.)	Closed	1984	38.00	900-1200
1985	Mrs. Cratchit (2nd ed.)	Open		39.00	49
1985	Mrs. Fezziwig (1st ed.)	Closed	1985	43.00	600-750
1986	Mrs. Fezziwig (2nd ed.)	Closed	1990	43.00	250-400
1983	Scrooge (1st ed.)	Closed	1983	36.00	1100-1500
1984	Scrooge (2nd ed.)	Open		38.00	49
1989	Spirit of Christmas Future (1st ed.)	Closed	1989	46.00	300-350
1990	Spirit of Christmas Future (2nd ed.)	Closed	1991	48.00	300-345
1987	Spirit of Christmas Past (1st ed.)	Closed	1987	42.00	315-365
1988	Spirit of Christmas Past (2nd ed.)	Closed	1991	46.00	275-300
1988	Spirit of Christmas Present (1st ed.)	Closed	1988	44.00	300-400
1989	Spirit of Christmas Present (2nd ed.)	Closed	1991	48.00	250-350

Display Figures - J. Byers

YEAR ISSUE		EDITION LIMIT	YEAR RETD.	ISSUE PRICE	*QUOTE U.S.$
1986	Display Adults	Closed	1987	170.00	500
1983	Display Carolers	Closed	1983	200.00	500
1985	Display Children (Boy & Girl)	Closed	1987	140.00	1200-1400
1982	Display Drummer Boy-1st	Closed	1983	96.00	800-1200
1985	Display Drummer Boy-2nd	Closed	1986	160.00	400-600
1981	Display Lady	Closed	1981	N/A	2000
1981	Display Man	Closed	1981	N/A	2000
1985	Display Old World Santa	Closed	1985	260.00	500
1982	Display Santa	Closed	1983	96.00	600
1990	Display Santa-bayberry	Closed	1990	250.00	450-500
1990	Display Santa-red	Closed	1990	250.00	425-475
1984	Display Working Santa	Closed	1985	260.00	500
1987	Mechanical Boy with Drum	Closed	1987	N/A	600-800
1987	Mechanical Girl with Bell	Closed	1987	N/A	600-800

Musicians - J. Byers

YEAR ISSUE		EDITION LIMIT	YEAR RETD.	ISSUE PRICE	*QUOTE U.S.$
1991	Boy with Mandolin	Closed	1991	48.00	200-300
1985	Horn Player	Closed	1985	38.00	500-700
1985	Horn Player, chubby face	Closed	1985	37.00	900-1200
1991	Musician with Accordian	Closed	1991	48.00	225-250
1989	Musician with Clarinet	Closed	1989	44.00	500-600
1992	Musician with French Horn	Closed	1992	52.00	100-200
1990	Musician with Mandolin	Closed	1990	46.00	100-200
1986	Victorian Girl with Violin	Closed	1986	39.00	300-400
1983	Violin Player Man (1st ed.)	Closed	1983	38.00	1500
1984	Violin Player Man (2nd ed.)	Closed	1984	38.00	1500

Nativity - J. Byers

YEAR ISSUE		EDITION LIMIT	YEAR RETD.	ISSUE PRICE	*QUOTE U.S.$
1989	Angel Gabriel	Closed	1991	37.00	150-200
1987	Angel-Great Star (Blonde)	Closed	1991	40.00	250
1987	Angel-Great Star (Brunette)	Closed	1991	40.00	250
1987	Angel-Great Star (Red Head)	Closed	1991	40.00	225-275
1987	Black Angel	Closed	1987	36.00	225-310
1990	Holy Family with stable	Closed	1991	119.00	225-375
1989	King Balthasar	Closed	1991	40.00	95
1989	King Gaspar	Closed	1991	40.00	100
1989	King Melchior	Closed	1991	40.00	95
1988	Shepherds	Closed	1991	37.00	95

The Nutcracker - J. Byers

YEAR ISSUE		EDITION LIMIT	YEAR RETD.	ISSUE PRICE	*QUOTE U.S.$
1996	Drosselmeier w/Music Box (1st ed.)	Open		83.00	83
1994	Fritz (1st ed.)	Closed	1994	56.00	100-150
1995	Fritz (2nd ed.)	Open		57.00	57
1995	Louise Playing Piano (1st ed.)	Closed	1995	82.00	125
1996	Louise Playing Piano (2nd ed.)	Open		83.00	83
1993	Marie (1st ed.)	Closed	1993	52.00	150-275
1994	Marie (2nd ed.)	Open		53.00	54

Salvation Army Band - J. Byers

YEAR ISSUE		EDITION LIMIT	YEAR RETD.	ISSUE PRICE	*QUOTE U.S.$
1995	Girl with War Cry	Open		55.00	55
1996	Man with Bass Drum	Open		60.00	60
1993	Man with Cornet	Open		54.00	56
1992	Woman with Kettle	Open		64.00	67
1992	Woman with Kettle (1st ed.)	Closed	1992	64.00	175
1993	Woman with Tambourine	Closed	1995	58.00	59

Santas - J. Byers

YEAR ISSUE		EDITION LIMIT	YEAR RETD.	ISSUE PRICE	*QUOTE U.S.$
1991	Father Christmas	Closed	1992	48.00	150-200
1988	Knecht Ruprecht (Black Peter)	Closed	1989	38.00	150-160
1996	Knickerbocker Santa	Open		58.00	58
1984	Mrs. Claus	Closed	1991	38.00	250-350
1992	Mrs. Claus (2nd ed.)	Closed	1993	50.00	135-150
1986	Mrs. Claus on Rocker	Closed	1986	73.00	600
1995	Mrs. Claus' Needlework	Closed	1995	70.00	100-150
1994	Old Befana	Open		53.00	54
1978	Old World Santa	Closed	1986	33.00	375-440
1989	Russian Santa	Closed	1989	85.00	350-650
1988	Saint Nicholas	Closed	1992	44.00	165-200
1982	Santa in a Sleigh (1st ed.)	Closed	1983	46.00	800
1984	Santa in Sleigh (2nd ed.)	Closed	1985	70.00	750
1993	Skating Santa	Closed	1993	60.00	100-125
1987	Velvet Mrs. Claus	Open		44.00	53
1987	Velvet Mrs. Claus (1st ed.)	Closed	1987	44.00	115
1978	Velvet Santa	Closed	1993	Unkn.	300
1994	Velvet Santa w/Stocking (2nd ed.)	Open		47.00	51
1986	Victorian Santa	Closed	1989	39.00	250-300
1990	Weihnachtsmann (German Santa)	Closed	1990	56.00	160-190
1983	Working Santa (1st ed.)	Closed	1991	38.00	150-250
1992	Working Santa (1st ed.)	Closed	1992	52.00	115
1992	Working Santa (2nd ed.)	Open		52.00	55

Skaters - J. Byers

YEAR ISSUE		EDITION LIMIT	YEAR RETD.	ISSUE PRICE	*QUOTE U.S.$
1991	Adult Skaters	Closed	1994	50.00	75
1991	Adult Skaters (1991 ed.)	Closed	1991	50.00	115-130
1993	Boy Skater on Log	Closed	1993	55.00	125
1992	Children Skaters	Open		50.00	52
1992	Children Skaters (1992 ed.)	Closed	1992	50.00	150
1993	Grandparent Skaters	Closed	1993	50.00	60
1993	Grandparent Skaters (1993 ed.)	Closed	1993	50.00	145
1995	Man Holding Skates	Open		52.00	52
1995	Woman Holding Skates	Open		52.00	52

Special Characters - J. Byers

YEAR ISSUE		EDITION LIMIT	YEAR RETD.	ISSUE PRICE	*QUOTE U.S.$
1996	Actress	Open		52.00	52
1979	Adult Male "Icabod"	Closed	1979	32.00	2400-2600
1988	Angel Tree Top	100	1988	Unkn.	275-375
1994	Baby in Basket	Closed	1994	7.50	10-20
1989	Black Boy w/skates	Closed	N/A	N/A	400-450
1989	Black Drummer Boy	Closed	N/A	N/A	500
1989	Black Girl w/skates	Closed	N/A	N/A	400-450
1983	Boy on Rocking Horse	300	1983	85.00	2500-2900
1987	Boy on Sled	Closed	1987	50.00	350
1991	Boy with Apple	Closed	1991	41.00	125-275
1994	Boy with Goose	Closed	1995	49.50	50
1995	Boy with Skis	Open		49.50	50
1991	Boy with Tree	Closed	1994	49.00	95-125
1995	Butcher	Closed	1995	54.00	110
1987	Caroler with Lamp	Closed	1987	40.00	175-200
1984	Chimney Sweep-Adult	Closed	1984	36.00	1200-1500
1991	Chimney Sweep-Child	Closed	1994	50.00	125
1982	Choir Children, boy and girl set	Closed	1986	32.00	600-700
1993	Choir Director,lady/music stand	Closed	1995	56.00	58
1982	Conductor	Closed	1992	32.00	155
1994	Constable	Open		53.00	54
1995	Couple in Sleigh	Closed	1995	110.00	110
1982	Drummer Boy	Closed	1992	34.00	150
1982	Easter Boy	Closed	1983	32.00	450-550
1982	Easter Girl	Closed	1983	32.00	450-550
1991	Girl with Apple	Closed	1991	41.00	150-250
1991	Girl with Apple/coin purse	Closed	1991	41.00	350-500
1989	Girl with Hoop	Closed	1990	44.00	185
1995	Girl with Skis	Open		49.50	50
1982	Icabod	Closed	1982	32.00	1150
1993	Lamplighter	Open		48.00	50
1993	Lamplighter (1st ed.)	Closed	1993	48.00	100-220
1982	Leprechauns	Closed	1982	34.00	1200-2000
1988	Mother Holding Baby	Closed	1993	40.00	100-250
1987	Mother's Day	225	1987	125.00	265-400
1988	Mother's Day (Daughter)	Closed	1988	125.00	450
1988	Mother's Day (Son)	Closed	1988	125.00	450-575
1989	Mother's Day (with Carriage)	3,000	1989	75.00	420
1994	Nanny	Open		66.00	67
1989	Newsboy with Bike	Closed	1992	78.00	175-225
1985	Pajama Children (painted flannel)	Closed	1989	35.00	285-350
1985	Pajama Children (red flannel)	Closed	1989	35.00	320
1990	Parson	Closed	1993	44.00	125-225
1996	Pilgrims	Open		53.00	53
1990	Postman	Closed	1993	45.00	125-175
1996	Puppeteer	Open		54.00	54
1994	Sandwich Board Man (red board)	Closed	1994	52.00	100
1994	Sandwich Board Man (wh. board)	Open		52.00	53
1993	School Kids	Closed	1994	48.00	75-125
1992	Schoolteacher	Closed	1994	48.00	125
1995	Shopper-Man	Closed	1995	56.00	75
1995	Shopper-Woman	Closed	1995	56.00	75
1996	Shoppers - Grandparents	Open		56.00	56
1981	Thanksgiving Lady (Clay Hands)	Closed	1981	Unkn.	2000
1981	Thanksgiving Man (Clay Hands)	Closed	1981	Unkn.	2000
1994	Treetop Angel	Open		50.00	50
1982	Valentine Boy	Closed	1983	32.00	450-550
1982	Valentine Girl	Closed	1983	32.00	450-550
1990	Victorian Girl On Rocking Horse (blonde)	Closed	1991	70.00	175-200
1990	Victorian Girl On Rocking Horse (brunette)	Closed	1991	70.00	185-275
1992	Victorian Mother with Toddler (Fall/Win-green)	Closed	1993	60.00	125-175
1993	Victorian Mother with Toddler (Spr/Sum-blue)	Closed	1993	61.00	125-150
1992	Victorian Mother with Toddler (Spr/Sum-white)	Closed	1993	60.00	125-150

Store Exclusives-Christmas Loft - J. Byers

YEAR ISSUE		EDITION LIMIT	YEAR RETD.	ISSUE PRICE	*QUOTE U.S.$
1991	Russian Santa	40	1991	100.00	500-700

Store Exclusives-Country Christmas - J. Byers

YEAR ISSUE		EDITION LIMIT	YEAR RETD.	ISSUE PRICE	*QUOTE U.S.$
1988	Toymaker	600	1988	59.00	850-1000

Store Exclusives-Foster's Exclusives - J. Byers

YEAR ISSUE		EDITION LIMIT	YEAR RETD.	ISSUE PRICE	*QUOTE U.S.$
1995	American Boy	100	1995	50.00	500

Store Exclusives-Long's Jewelers - J. Byers

YEAR ISSUE		EDITION LIMIT	YEAR RETD.	ISSUE PRICE	*QUOTE U.S.$
1981	Leprechaun (with bucket)	Closed	N/A	N/A	2500

Store Exclusives-Port-O-Call - J. Byers

YEAR ISSUE		EDITION LIMIT	YEAR RETD.	ISSUE PRICE	*QUOTE U.S.$
1986	Cherub Angel-blue	Closed	1987	N/A	275-400
1986	Cherub Angel-cream	Closed	1987	N/A	400
1986	Cherub Angel-pink	Closed	1987	N/A	275-400
1987	Cherub Angel-rose	Closed	1987	N/A	275-400

Store Exclusives-Snow Goose - J. Byers

YEAR ISSUE		EDITION LIMIT	YEAR RETD.	ISSUE PRICE	*QUOTE U.S.$
1988	Man with Goose	600	1988	60.00	300

Store Exclusives-Stacy's Gifts & Collectibles - J. Byers

YEAR ISSUE		EDITION LIMIT	YEAR RETD.	ISSUE PRICE	*QUOTE U.S.$
1987	Santa in Rocking Chair with Boy	100	1987	130.00	1000-1500
1987	Santa in Rocking Chair with Girl	100	1987	130.00	1000-1500

Store Exclusives-Talbots - J. Byers

YEAR ISSUE		EDITION LIMIT	YEAR RETD.	ISSUE PRICE	*QUOTE U.S.$
1990	Victorian Family of Four	Closed	N/A	N/A	375-450
1993	Skating Girl/Boy	Retrd.	N/A	N/A	450
1994	Man w/Log Carrier	Closed	N/A	N/A	130-150
1994	Family of Four/Sweaters	Retrd.	N/A	N/A	500
1995	Santa in Sleigh	1,625	1995	88.00	150

*Quotes have been rounded up to nearest dollar

FIGURINES/COTTAGES

Store Exclusives-Wayside Country Store Exclusives - J. Byers

YEAR ISSUE		EDITION LIMIT	YEAR RETD.	ISSUE PRICE	*QUOTE U.S.$
1988	Colonial Lady s/n	600	1988	49.00	450-500
1986	Colonial Lamplighter s/n	600	1986	46.00	750-900
1987	Colonial Watchman s/n	600	1987	49.00	675-750
1995	Sunday School Boy	300	1995	52.00	200
1995	Sunday School Girl	300	1995	52.00	200

Store Exclusives-Wooden Soldier - J. Byers

YEAR ISSUE		EDITION LIMIT	YEAR RETD.	ISSUE PRICE	*QUOTE U.S.$
XX	Victorian Lamp Lighter	Closed	N/A	N/A	175-200

Store Exclusives-Woodstock Inn - J. Byers

YEAR ISSUE		EDITION LIMIT	YEAR RETD.	ISSUE PRICE	*QUOTE U.S.$
1987	Skier Boy	200	1987	40.00	250-350
1987	Skier Girl	200	1987	40.00	250-350
1991	Sugarin Kids (Woodstock)	Closed	1991	41.00	300
1988	Woodstock Lady	Closed	1988	41.00	350
1988	Woodstock Man	Closed	1988	41.00	350

Toddlers - J. Byers

YEAR ISSUE		EDITION LIMIT	YEAR RETD.	ISSUE PRICE	*QUOTE U.S.$
1996	Book - "Night Before Christmas"	Open		20.00	20
1996	Doll - "Night Before Christmas"	Open		20.00	20
1993	Gingerbread Boy	Closed	1994	18.50	25
1993	Package	Closed	1993	18.50	35
1992	Shovel	Closed	1993	17.00	35
1994	Skis	Open		19.00	20
1994	Sled (black toddler)	Closed	1994	19.00	19
1992	Sled (white toddler)	Closed	1993	17.00	20
1995	Sled (white toddler-2nd ed.)	Open		19.00	20
1991	Sled with Dog/toddler	Closed	1991	30.00	125-200
1992	Snowball	Closed	1994	17.00	35
1994	Snowflake	Closed	1994	18.00	18
1993	Teddy Bear	Closed	1993	18.50	35
1995	Toddler with Wagon	Open		19.50	20
1994	Tree	Open		18.00	20
1996	Tricycle	Open		20.00	20
1995	Victorian Boy Toddler	Open		19.50	20
1995	Victorian Girl Toddler	Open		19.50	20

Calabar Creations

Angelic Pigasus - P. Apsit

YEAR ISSUE		EDITION LIMIT	YEAR RETD.	ISSUE PRICE	*QUOTE U.S.$
1996	Acapella & Atto AP75424	Open		25.00	25
1995	Adagio AP75364	Open		18.00	18
1996	Adagio Mini Waterglobe AP76053	Open		8.50	9
1994	Alba AP75353	6/96		12.00	12
1995	Allegria AP75395	Open		24.00	24
1996	Allegria Mini Waterglobe AP76033	Open		8.50	9
1995	Ambrose AP75374	Open		22.00	22
1996	Ambrose Mini Waterglobe AP76043	Open		8.50	9
1995	Andante AP75384	Open		18.00	18
1994	Angelica AP75315	Open		24.00	24
1996	Angelica Mini Waterglobe AP76063	Open		8.50	9
1995	Angelo AP75335	Open		5.00	5
1994	Angelo AP75335	Open		24.00	24
1996	Angelo Mini Waterglobe AP76083	Open		8.50	9
1996	Anna & Allegria Mini Waterglobe AP76094	Open		20.00	20
1994	Anna AP75324	Retrd.	1995	22.00	22
1996	Anna Mini Waterglobe AP76073	Open		8.50	9
1994	Aria AP75343	Retrd.	1996	12.00	12
1996	Arpeggio AP75414	Open		22.00	22
1995	Signature Piece AP75405	Open		24.00	24

Daddy's Girl - P. Apsit

YEAR ISSUE		EDITION LIMIT	YEAR RETD.	ISSUE PRICE	*QUOTE U.S.$
1994	All Aboard! DA74804	5,000		20.00	20
1994	Discovery DA74816	5,000		28.00	28
1994	Moi! DA74834	5,000		20.00	20
1994	Peek-A-Boo DA74843	5,000		20.00	20
1994	Spring Harvest DA74856	5,000		28.00	28
1995	Summer DA74866	5,000		34.00	34
1994	Teddy Talks DA74826	5,000		40.00	40

Days of Innocence - P. Apsit

YEAR ISSUE		EDITION LIMIT	YEAR RETD.	ISSUE PRICE	*QUOTE U.S.$
1995	Dear God DI74975	5,000		28.00	28
1995	A Letter From Grandma DI74966	5,000		40.00	40
1995	To Grandma's DI74956	5,000		28.00	28

Grandpions - P. Apsit

YEAR ISSUE		EDITION LIMIT	YEAR RETD.	ISSUE PRICE	*QUOTE U.S.$
1995	Alex the Great OM77144	Open		13.00	13
1995	Alley King OM77313	Open		13.00	13
1995	Blue Baron OM77294	Open		13.00	13
1995	Chained OM77234	Open		13.00	13
1995	Doc OM77184	Open		13.00	13
1996	Dr. Tooth OM 77544	Open		13.00	13
1995	The Finest OM77174	Open		13.00	13
1995	Harleyson OM77164	Open		15.00	15
1996	Hazel (Waitress) OM 77384	Open		13.00	13
1995	Ice Proof OM77133	Open		13.00	13
1995	Lady Hope OM77304	Open		13.00	13
1995	Marathon Man OM77224	Open		13.00	13
1995	Martiny OM77264	Open		13.00	13
1995	Mazuma OM77244	Open		13.00	13
1996	Ms. Brown (Teacher) OM 77374	Open		13.00	13
1996	Ms. Ellie S. Crow (Real Estate Agent) OM 77394	Open		13.00	13
1996	Ms. Will Do (Secretary) OM 77404	Open		13.00	13
1995	Oh Gee! OM77203	Open		13.00	13
1995	Old Red OM77154	Open		13.00	13
1995	Peleman OM77274	Open		13.00	13
1995	Ratchet OM77254	Open		13.00	13
1995	Rocky Road OM77283	Open		13.00	13
1995	See The Birdy OM77193	Open		13.00	13
1995	Struck OM77214	Open		13.00	13
1995	Weed Child OM77323	Open		13.00	13

Junior Murphy's Law - P. Apsit

YEAR ISSUE		EDITION LIMIT	YEAR RETD.	ISSUE PRICE	*QUOTE U.S.$
1995	Extra Topping JM75216	5,000		40.00	40
1995	Fast Food JM75196	5,000		46.00	46
1995	Lucky Me! JM75176	5,000		40.00	40
1995	Milk Fan JM75205	5,000		44.00	44
1995	Robin Tell JM75226	5,000		40.00	40

Little Farmers - P. Apsit

YEAR ISSUE		EDITION LIMIT	YEAR RETD.	ISSUE PRICE	*QUOTE U.S.$
1994	Apple Delivery LF73127	5,000		54.00	54
1993	Between Chores LF73105	5,000		40.00	40
1993	Caring Friend LF73066	5,000		57.00	57
1993	Going Home LF73027	5,000		64.00	64
1993	It's Not For You LF73038	5,000		64.00	64
1994	LF Signature Piece LF73147	Open		40.00	40
1993	Little Lumber Joe LF73077	5,000		64.00	64
1994	Lunch Express LF73117	5,000		76.00	76
1993	Oops! LF73058	5,000		64.00	64
1993	Piggy Ride LF73097	5,000		45.00	45
1993	Playful Kittens LF73016	5,000		64.00	64
1993	Surprise! LF73046	5,000		60.00	60
1993	True Love LF73087	5,000		45.00	45
1994	Vita-Veggie Vendor LF73137	5,000		62.00	62

Little Professionals - P. Apsit

YEAR ISSUE		EDITION LIMIT	YEAR RETD.	ISSUE PRICE	*QUOTE U.S.$
1994	Little Angelo LP75057	5,000		38.00	38
1995	Little Count LP75084	5,000		36.00	36
1995	Little Desi LP75135	5,000		18.00	18
1994	Little Florence LP75065	5,000		44.00	44
1995	Little Gypsy LP75115	5,000		18.00	18
1995	Little Louis LP75106	5,000		18.00	18
1994	Little Miss Market LP75046	5,000		40.00	40
1995	Little Red LP75075	5,000		38.00	38
1995	Little Ringo LP75094	5,000		18.00	18

Pig Hollow - P. Apsit

YEAR ISSUE		EDITION LIMIT	YEAR RETD.	ISSUE PRICE	*QUOTE U.S.$
1994	The After Picture PH75544	Open		12.00	12
1995	Armchair/buttons PH75752	Open		7.00	7
1994	Barn Fun PH75474	Open		15.00	15
1995	Bathroom Vanity PH75703	Open		6.00	6
1995	Double Bed PH75722	Open		9.00	9
1995	Dresser/2-drawer PH75714	Open		8.00	8
1994	Going South PH75533	Open		11.00	11
1994	Just Cute PH75442	Open		9.00	9
1995	Kitchen Counter PH75684	Open		19.00	19
1995	Large Armchair PH75742	Open		8.00	8
1994	Mary Pig PH75524	Open		11.00	11
1994	Move Please PH75462	Open		11.00	11
1994	Nap Time PH75492	Open		11.00	11
1994	Old McPig PH75513	Open		11.00	11
1995	Par PH75674	Open		15.00	15
1995	Pauline PH75873	Open		9.00	9
1995	Pelota PH75612	Open		8.00	8
1995	Pendleton PH75822	Open		10.00	10
1995	Pepin PH75842	Open		9.00	9
1995	Pieball PH75633	Open		9.00	9
1995	Pig Kahuna PH75602	Open		9.00	9
1995	Pigmobile PH75853	Open		34.00	34
1995	Pilar PH75832	Open		9.00	9
1994	Pillow Talk PH75453	Open		12.00	12
1995	Plopsy PH75642	Open		8.00	8
1995	Pluckster PH75812	Open		9.00	9
1995	Poirot PH75622	Open		8.00	8
1995	Poof PH75592	Open		8.00	8
1995	Pot Belly PH75883	Open		12.00	12
1995	Pristine Pig PH75573	Open		10.00	10
1995	Prof PH75583	Open		9.00	9
1995	Proof PH75862	Open		12.00	12
1995	Prude Jr. PH75652	Open		8.00	8
1995	Prude PH75663	Open		9.00	9
1994	Reddie PH75554	Open		12.00	12
1995	Sidetable/1 book PH75773	Open		8.00	8
1995	Sidetable/2 doors PH75782	Open		6.00	6
1994	Signature Piece PH75565	Open		19.00	19
1995	Sofa PH75762	Open		14.00	14
1995	Stove/Oven PH75693	Open		7.00	7
1994	Sweet Corn PH75503	Open		9.00	9
1994	Time For School PH75484	Open		15.00	15
1995	TV Console PH75793	Open		7.00	7
1995	Twin Bed PH75732	Open		9.00	9

Santaventure - P. Apsit

YEAR ISSUE		EDITION LIMIT	YEAR RETD.	ISSUE PRICE	*QUOTE U.S.$
1994	Almost Done SV73836	5,000		50.00	50
1993	Cart O' Plenty SV73737	5,000		66.00	66
1993	Hooray For Santa SV73757	5,000		59.00	59
1994	In His Dream SV73816	5,000		78.00	78
1994	The Last Mile SV73806	5,000		54.00	54
1993	Nuts For You SV73787	5,000		59.00	59
1993	Pilgrim Santa SV73748	5,000		59.00	59
1993	A Pinch of Advice SV73768	5,000		68.00	68
1994	Reindeer's Strike SV73827	5,000		54.00	54
1993	Santa Tested SV73778	5,000		68.00	68
1993	Santa's Sack Attack SV73796	5,000		60.00	60
1994	Signature Piece SV73577	5,000		60.00	60
1994	Viola! SV73847	5,000		50.00	50

Tee Club - P. Apsit

YEAR ISSUE		EDITION LIMIT	YEAR RETD.	ISSUE PRICE	*QUOTE U.S.$
1993	Certain-Tee TC73898	5,000		100.00	100
1993	Naugh-Tee TC73908	5,000		56.00	56
1993	Old Tee-Mer TC73887	5,000		78.00	78
1993	Prac-Tees TC73858	5,000		66.00	66
1993	Putt-Teeing TC73868	5,000		66.00	66
1993	Teed-Off TC73877	5,000		60.00	60

Yesterday's Friends - P. Apsit

YEAR ISSUE		EDITION LIMIT	YEAR RETD.	ISSUE PRICE	*QUOTE U.S.$
1993	Bayou Boys RW74456	3,500		80.00	80
1993	Bluester RW74446	7,500		44.00	44
1993	Buddies RW74466	7,500		50.00	50
1994	Caddie Chris RW74527	7,500		34.00	34
1994	Cornered RW74707	7,500		54.00	54
1993	Dinner For Two RW74496	7,500		38.00	38
1994	Equipment Manager RW74596	7,500		34.00	34
1994	Excess RW74726	7,500		50.00	50
1993	Freewheeling RW74436	7,500		48.00	48
1994	Funny Frog RW74745	7,500		44.00	44
1994	Goose Loose RW74635	7,500		40.00	40
1995	High Fly RW74795	7,500		28.00	28
1993	Hop-a-Long Pete RW74539	3,500		80.00	80
1993	Interference RW74506	7,500		42.00	42
1993	Jazzy Bubble RW74486	7,500		37.00	37
1993	Me Big Chief RW74548	7,500		56.00	56
1993	Mike's Magic RW74475	7,500		37.00	37
1995	Out! RW74766	7,500		34.00	34
1994	Parade RW74716	7,500		60.00	60
1995	Pop Up! RW74755	7,500		34.00	34
1994	Read All About It RW74616	7,500		70.00	70
1994	Read-A-Thon RW74694	7,500		40.00	40
1994	Scrub-a-Swine RW74606	7,500		48.00	48
1994	Signature Piece RW74737	Open		54.00	54
1993	Strike So Sweet RW74517	7,500		42.00	42
1994	Tuba Notes RW74688	7,500		54.00	54
1993	Tug-a-Leg RW74557	7,500		56.00	56
1994	What A Smile RW74626	7,500		40.00	40

Cardew Design

"English Bettys" - P. Cardew

YEAR ISSUE		EDITION LIMIT	YEAR RETD.	ISSUE PRICE	*QUOTE U.S.$
1995	Cat Got the Cream-Brown Betty	Open		50.00	50
1996	Chess-Black Betty	Open		50.00	50
1996	Gardening-Green Betty	Open		50.00	50
1996	Golf-White Betty	Open		50.00	50
1995	Harvest Pies-Brown Betty	Open		50.00	50
1996	London Touring-Black Betty	Open		50.00	50
1996	Magician-Black Betty	Open		50.00	50
1995	Ploughman's Lunch-Brown Betty	Open		50.00	50
1995	Rise & "Shoe" Shine-Brown Betty	Open		50.00	50
1995	Summer Picnic-Brown Betty	Open		50.00	50
1995	Tea Table-Brown Betty	Open		50.00	50
1996	Teddy Bear's Picnic-Yellow Betty	Open		50.00	50

Event Piece - P. Cardew

YEAR ISSUE		EDITION LIMIT	YEAR RETD.	ISSUE PRICE	*QUOTE U.S.$
1996	"Travellers Return"	5,000		45.00	45

Limited Edition Full Sized Teapots - P. Cardew

YEAR ISSUE		EDITION LIMIT	YEAR RETD.	ISSUE PRICE	*QUOTE U.S.$
1995	Kitchen Sink	5,000		175.00	175
1995	Ladies Dressing Table	5,000		175.00	175
1996	Lilliput Lane Market Stall	Yr.Iss.		250.00	250
1996	Moving Day	5,000		175.00	175
1995	Refrigerator	5,000		175.00	175
1995	Teapot Market Stall	5,000	1996	199.00	199
1996	Teddy Bear's Picnic	5,000		175.00	175
1995	Washing Machine	5,000		175.00	175

Market Stall Series - P. Cardew

YEAR ISSUE		EDITION LIMIT	YEAR RETD.	ISSUE PRICE	*QUOTE U.S.$
1993	Antiques Market Stall	Open		160.00	160
1993	China Market Stall	Open		160.00	160
1993	Hardware Market Stall	Open		160.00	160
1995	Shoe Market Stall	Open		160.00	160

One-Cup Teapot Collection - P. Cardew

YEAR ISSUE		EDITION LIMIT	YEAR RETD.	ISSUE PRICE	*QUOTE U.S.$
1995	China Stall	Open		45.00	45
1995	Christmas Presents	Open		45.00	45
1996	Christmas Tree	Open		45.00	45
1996	Fireplace	Open		45.00	45
1996	Gardening	Open		45.00	45
1996	Golf Bag	Open		45.00	45
1996	Grandfather Clock	Open		45.00	45
1995	Kitchen Sink	Open		45.00	45
1995	Lady's Dressing Table	Open		45.00	45
1995	Moving Day	Open		45.00	45
1996	Outward Bound	Open		45.00	45
1995	Refrigerator	Open		45.00	45
1996	Romance/Heart	Open		45.00	45
1996	Santa Claus	Open		45.00	45
1995	Sewing Machine	Open		45.00	45
1995	Tea Chest	Open		45.00	45
1995	Tea Shop Counter	Open		45.00	45
1995	Teddy Bear's Picnic	Open		45.00	45
1995	Toy Box	Open		45.00	45
1995	Victorian Tea Table	Open		45.00	45
1995	Washing Machine	Open		45.00	45
1995	Washing Mangle	Open		45.00	45
1995	Welsh Dresser	Open		45.00	45

Standard Teapots - P. Cardew

YEAR ISSUE		EDITION LIMIT	YEAR RETD.	ISSUE PRICE	*QUOTE U.S.$
1991	50's Stove	Open		140.00	140

*Quotes have been rounded up to nearest dollar

YEAR	ISSUE	EDITION LIMIT	YEAR RETD.	ISSUE PRICE	*QUOTE U.S.$
1992	Baking Day	Open		140.00	140
1992	Crime Writer's Desk	Open		140.00	140
1992	Sewing Machine	Open		140.00	140
1991	Toy Box	Open		140.00	140
1992	Victorian Tea Table	Open		140.00	140
1992	Washing Mangle	Open		140.00	140

Tiny Teapots - P. Cardew

YEAR	ISSUE	EDITION LIMIT	YEAR RETD.	ISSUE PRICE	*QUOTE U.S.$
1995	50's Stove	Open		12.00	12
1995	Baking Day	Open		12.00	12
1995	Crime Writer's Desk	Open		12.00	12
1995	Kitchen Sink	Open		12.00	12
1995	Refrigerator	Open		12.00	12
1995	Sewing Machine	Open		12.00	12
1995	Tea Shop Counter	Open		12.00	12
1995	Teddy Bear's Picnic	Open		12.00	12
1995	Toy Box	Open		12.00	12
1995	Victorian Wash Stand	Open		12.00	12
1995	Washing Machine	Open		12.00	12
1995	Washing Mangle	Open		12.00	12
1996	Golf Trolley	Open		12.00	12
1996	Petrol Pump	Open		12.00	12
1996	Heart	Open		12.00	12
1996	Radio	Open		12.00	12
1996	Safe	Open		12.00	12
1996	50's TV	Open		12.00	12
1996	Fireplace	Open		12.00	12
1996	Grandfather's Clock	Open		12.00	12
1996	Lady's Dressing Table	Open		12.00	12
1996	Night Stand	Open		12.00	12
1996	Victorian Tea Table	Open		12.00	12
1996	Welsh Dresser	Open		12.00	12

Cast Art Industries

Dreamsicles Collectors Club - K. Haynes

YEAR	ISSUE	EDITION LIMIT	YEAR RETD.	ISSUE PRICE	*QUOTE U.S.$
1993	A Star is Born-CD001	Retrd.	1993	Gift	100
1994	Daydream Believer-CD100	Retrd.	1994	29.95	60
1994	Join The Fun-CD002	Retrd.	1994	Gift	35
1994	Makin' A List-CD101	Retrd.	1994	47.95	75
1995	Three Cheers-CD003	Retrd.	1995	Gift	30
1995	Town Crier-CD102	Retrd.	1995	24.95	25
1995	Snowbound-CD103	Yr.Iss.		24.95	25
1996	Star Shower-CD004	Yr.Iss.		Gift	N/A

Dreamsicles - K. Haynes

YEAR	ISSUE	EDITION LIMIT	YEAR RETD.	ISSUE PRICE	*QUOTE U.S.$
1995	The 1995 International Collectible Exposition Commemorative Figurine	Retrd.	1995	34.95	150-200
1992	Baby Love-DC147	Retrd.	1995	7.00	7
1991	Best Pals-DC103	Retrd.	1994	15.00	30
1994	Birthday Party-DC171	Suspd.		13.50	14
1992	Bluebird On My Shoulder-DC115	Retrd.	1995	19.00	19
1994	Boxful of Stars-DC224	Suspd.		16.00	16
1992	Bundle of Joy-DC142	Retrd.	1995	7.00	7
1992	Bunny Wall Plaque-5018	Suspd.		22.00	22
1992	Bunny Wall Plaque-5019	Suspd.		22.00	22
1993	By the Silvery Moon-DC253	10,000	1994	100.00	350
1992	Caroler - Center Scroll-DC216	Retrd.	1995	19.00	22
1992	Caroler - Left Scroll-DC218	Retrd.	1995	19.00	22
1992	Caroler - Right Scroll-DC217	Retrd.	1995	19.00	22
1991	Cherub and Child-DC100	Retrd.	1995	15.00	30
1992	Cherub For All Seasons-DC114	Retrd.	1995	23.00	50
1991	Cherub Wall Plaque-5130	Suspd.		15.00	15
1991	Cherub Wall Plaque-5131	Suspd.		15.00	15
1992	Cherub-DC111	10,000	1992	50.00	75
1992	Cherub-DC112	10,000	1993	50.00	75
1996	A Child Is Born-DC256	10,000		95.00	95
1992	A Child's Prayer-DC145	Retrd.	1995	7.00	7
1994	Cuddle Blanket-DC153	Retrd.	1995	6.50	7
1992	Cupid's Bow-DC202	Suspd.		27.00	27
1992	Dance Ballerina Dance-DC140	Retrd.	1995	37.00	42
1992	Dream A Little Dream-DC144	Retrd.	1995	7.00	7
1994	Eager to Please-DC154	Retrd.	1995	6.50	7
1992	Flying Lesson-DC251	10,000	1993	80.00	370
1991	Forever Friends-DC102	Retrd.	1994	15.00	30
1991	Forever Yours-DC110	Retrd.	1995	44.00	44
1994	Happy Birthday w/hat-DC133	Suspd.		13.50	14
1994	Here's Looking at You-DC172	Retrd.	1995	25.00	27
1994	I Can Read-DC151	Retrd.	1995	6.50	9
1991	King Heart "I Love You" Box -5850	Suspd.		37.50	38
1991	King Oval Cow Box-5860	Suspd.		55.00	55
1993	Lg. Candle Holder Boy-DC138	Suspd.		20.00	22
1993	Lg. Candle Holder Girl-DC139	Suspd.		20.00	22
1992	Little Darlin'-DC146	Retrd.	1995	7.00	7
1993	Little Dickens-DC127	Retrd.	1995	24.00	24
1992	Littlest Angel-DC143	Retrd.	1995	7.00	7
1993	Long Fellow-DC126	Retrd.	1995	24.00	24
1991	Medium Heart Cherub Box-5751	Suspd.		14.00	14
1991	Musician w/Cymbals-5154	Suspd.		22.00	22
1991	Musician w/Drums-5152	Suspd.		22.00	22
1991	Musician w/Flute-5153	Suspd.		22.00	22
1991	Musician w/Trumpet-5151	Suspd.		22.00	22
1992	My Funny Valentine-DC201	Suspd.		17.00	28
1995	Nursery Rhyme-DC229	Suspd.		42.00	50
1991	Octagonal Ballerina Box-5700	Suspd.		9.00	9
1995	Picture Perfect-DC255	10,000	1995	100.00	112
1991	Queen Octagonal Cherub Box -5804	Suspd.		26.00	26
1991	Queen Rectangle Cat Box-5800	Suspd.		28.75	29
1991	Queen Round Bears Box-5801	Suspd.		28.75	29
1994	The Recital-DC254	10,000	1994	135.00	175-250
1994	Side By Side-DC169	Retrd.	1995	31.50	32
1992	Sleigh Ride-DC122	Suspd.		15.50	16
1991	Small Cherub with Hanging Ribbon-5104	Suspd.		10.00	10
1991	Small Heart "I Love You" Box -5701	Suspd.		9.00	9
1991	Small Rectangle "Dicky Duck" Box-5703	Suspd.		9.00	9
1991	Small Square Dinosaur Box-5702	Suspd.		9.00	9
1994	Sock Hop-DC222	Suspd.		16.00	16
1991	Speed Racer Box-5750	Suspd.		14.00	14
1994	Sucking My Thumb-DC156	Retrd.	1995	6.50	7
1994	Surprise Gift-DC152	Retrd.	1995	6.50	7
1993	Sweet Dreams-DC125	Retrd.	1995	29.00	29
1994	Sweet Gingerbread-DC223	Suspd.		16.00	16
1993	Teeter Tots-DC252	10,000	1993	100.00	175-295
1991	Train Box-5803	Suspd.		28.75	29
1994	Up All Night-DC155	Retrd.	1995	6.50	7
1991	You're Special Box-5802	Suspd.		28.75	29

Dreamsicles Animals - K. Haynes

YEAR	ISSUE	EDITION LIMIT	YEAR RETD.	ISSUE PRICE	*QUOTE U.S.$
1991	Armadillo-5176	Suspd.		14.00	14
1992	Beach Baby-DA615	Suspd.		26.00	26
1992	Blowfish-DA608	Suspd.		10.00	10
1991	Buddy Bear-DA451	Suspd.		7.50	8
1992	Bunny Bookends-DA122	Suspd.		44.00	44
1991	Bunny Hop-DA105	Retrd.	1995	19.50	20
1992	Cat Nap-DA551	Suspd.		10.00	10
1992	The Cat's Meow-DA552	Suspd.		10.00	10
1992	Crabby-DA607	Suspd.		8.00	8
1992	Cute As A Button-DA553	Suspd.		10.00	10
1991	Dairy Delight-DA381	Retrd.	1995	28.00	30
1991	Dimples (girl)-DA100	Retrd.	1995	6.00	6
1992	Dino-DA480	Suspd.		14.00	14
1992	Dodo-DA482	Suspd.		9.00	9
1992	Double fish-DA611	Suspd.		8.00	8
1992	Fat Cat-DA555	Suspd.		26.00	26
1991	Gathering Flowers-DA320	Retrd.	1995	18.00	18
1992	Helga-DA112	Retrd.	1995	8.00	8
1991	Hippity Hop- DA106	Suspd.		31.00	31
1991	Honey Bun (boy)-DA101	Retrd.	1995	6.00	6
1992	Hound Dog-DA568	Suspd.		11.00	11
1991	King Rabbit-DA124	Suspd.		66.00	66
1991	Kitchen Pig-DA345	Suspd.		31.50	32
1991	Lambie Pie-DA328	Suspd.		9.00	9
1992	Largemouth-DA609	Suspd.		8.00	8
1992	Lazy Bones-DA605	Suspd.		14.00	14
1993	Li'l Chick-DA385	Suspd.		7.00	7
1993	Li'l Duck-DA388	Suspd.		7.00	7
1991	Mama Bear-DA452	Suspd.		9.00	9
1992	Man's Best Friend-DA560	Suspd.		11.00	11
1991	Mother Mouse-DA477	Suspd.		10.00	10
1991	Mouse on Skis-DA475	Suspd.		17.00	17
1991	Mr. Bunny- DA107	Suspd.		27.00	27
1991	Mrs. Bunny- DA108	Suspd.		27.00	27
1991	Mutton Chops-DA326	Suspd.		7.50	8
1992	Needlenose-DA610	Suspd.		8.00	8
1992	Octopus' Garden-DA606	Suspd.		10.00	10
1991	P.J. Mouse-DA476	Suspd.		10.00	10
1993	Pal Joey-DA104	Retrd.	1995	13.50	14
1992	Papa Pelican-DA602	Suspd.		22.00	22
1993	Party Bunny-DA116	Suspd.		19.00	19
1991	Pigmalion-DA340	Retrd.	1995	6.00	6
1991	Pigtails-DA341	Retrd.	1995	6.00	6
1992	Pretty Kitty-DA554	Suspd.		15.00	15
1992	Pumpkin Harvest-DA322	Suspd.		19.00	19
1992	Puppy Love-DA562	Suspd.		12.00	12
1992	Red Rover-DA566	Suspd.		17.00	17
1992	Rhino-DA481	Suspd.		14.00	14
1991	Ricky Raccoon-5170	Suspd.		27.00	27
1992	Sarge-DA111	Retrd.	1995	8.00	8
1992	Scooter-DA567	Suspd.		11.00	11
1992	Slow Poke-DA630	Suspd.		13.00	13
1991	Soap Box Bunny-DA221	Retrd.	1995	15.00	15
1991	Socrates the Sheep-5029	Suspd.		18.00	18
1992	Splash-DA616	Suspd.		26.00	26
1992	St. Peter Rabbit-DA243	Suspd.		29.00	29
1992	Teddy Bear-DA456	Suspd.		14.00	14
1991	Tiny Bunny-DA102	Retrd.	1995	7.50	10
1992	Winter's Comin'-DA471	Suspd.		10.00	15
1991	Wooly Bully-DA327	Suspd.		9.00	9

Dreamsicles Calendar Collection - K. Haynes

YEAR	ISSUE	EDITION LIMIT	YEAR RETD.	ISSUE PRICE	*QUOTE U.S.$
1994	Winter Wonderland (January) -DC180	Retrd.	1995	24.00	24
1994	Special Delivery (February) -DC181	Retrd.	1995	24.00	27
1994	Ride Like The Wind (March) -DC182	Retrd.	1995	24.00	24
1994	Springtime Frolic (April)-DC183	Retrd.	1995	24.00	27
1994	Love In Bloom (May)-DC184	Retrd.	1995	24.00	24
1994	Among Friends (June)-DC185	Retrd.	1995	24.00	24
1994	Pool Pals (July)-DC186	Retrd.	1995	24.00	24
1994	Nature's Bounty (August)-DC187	Retrd.	1995	24.00	24
1994	School Days (September) -DC188	Retrd.	1995	24.00	27
1994	Autumn Leaves (October) -DC189	Retrd.	1995	24.00	27
1994	Now Give Thanks (November) -DC190	Retrd.	1995	24.00	24
1994	Holiday Magic (December) -DC191	Retrd.	1995	24.00	27

Dreamsicles Christmas - K. Haynes

YEAR	ISSUE	EDITION LIMIT	YEAR RETD.	ISSUE PRICE	*QUOTE U.S.$
1992	Baby Love-DX147	Retrd.	1995	7.00	7
1992	Bluebird On My Shoulder-DX115	Retrd.	1995	19.00	19
1992	Bundle of Joy-DX142	Retrd.	1995	7.00	7
1992	Caroler - Center Scroll-DX216	Retrd.	1995	19.00	22
1992	Caroler - Left Scroll-DX218	Retrd.	1995	19.00	22
1992	Caroler - Right Scroll-DX217	Retrd.	1995	19.00	22
1991	Cherub and Child-DX100	Retrd.	1995	14.00	30
1992	A Child's Prayer-DX145	Retrd.	1995	7.00	7
1992	Dream A Little Dream-DX144	Retrd.	1995	7.00	7
1993	The Finishing Touches-DX248 (2nd Ed.)	Retrd.	1994	85.00	100
1991	Forever Yours-DX110	Retrd.	1995	44.00	44
1994	Here's Looking at You-DX172	Retrd.	1995	25.00	28
1994	Holiday on Ice-DX249 (3rd Ed.)	Retrd.	1995	85.00	100
1992	Little Darlin'-DX146	Retrd.	1995	7.00	7
1993	Little Dickens-DX127	Retrd.	1995	24.00	24
1992	Littlest Angel-DX143	Retrd.	1995	7.00	7
1993	Long Fellow-DX126	Retrd.	1995	24.00	24
1991	Santa Bunny-DX203	Retrd.	1994	32.00	32
1992	Santa In Dreamsicle Land-DX247 (1st Ed.)	Retrd.	1993	85.00	225-350
1995	Santa's Kingdom-DX250 (4th Ed.)	Yr.Iss.		80.00	90
1994	Side By Side-DX169	Retrd.	1995	31.50	32
1993	Sweet Dreams-DX125	Retrd.	1995	29.00	29

Dreamsicles Day Event- K. Haynes

YEAR	ISSUE	EDITION LIMIT	YEAR RETD.	ISSUE PRICE	*QUOTE U.S.$
1995	1995 Dreamsicles Event Figurine-DC075	Retrd.	1995	20.00	25
1996	Glad Tidings-DD100	Yr.Iss.		20.00	20

Dreamsicles Heavenly Classics - K. Haynes & S. Hackett

YEAR	ISSUE	EDITION LIMIT	YEAR RETD.	ISSUE PRICE	*QUOTE U.S.$
1995	The Dedication-DC351	10,000	1995	118.00	125

The Cat's Meow

Collector Club Gift - Houses - F. Jones

YEAR	ISSUE	EDITION LIMIT	YEAR RETD.	ISSUE PRICE	*QUOTE U.S.$
1989	1989 Betsy Ross House	Retrd.	1989	Gift	200
1990	1990 Amelia Earhart	Retrd.	1990	Gift	100
1991	1991 Limberlost Cabin	Retrd.	1991	Gift	50
1992	1992 Abigail Adams Birthplace	Retrd.	1992	Gift	50
1993	1993 Pearl S. Buck House	Retrd.	1993	Gift	50
1993	Set of '89-'93	Retrd.	1993	Gift	450
1994	1994 Lillian Gish	Retrd.	1994	Gift	30
1995	1995 Eleanor Roosevelt	Retrd.	1995	Gift	N/A
1996	1996 Mother's Day Church	12/96		Gift	N/A

Collector Club - Famous Authors - F. Jones

YEAR	ISSUE	EDITION LIMIT	YEAR RETD.	ISSUE PRICE	*QUOTE U.S.$
1989	Harriet Beecher Stowe	Retrd.	1989	8.75	N/A
1989	Orchard House	Retrd.	1989	8.75	N/A
1989	Longfellow House	Retrd.	1989	8.75	N/A
1989	Herman Melville's Arrowhead	Retrd.	1989	8.75	800
1989	Set	Retrd.	1989	35.00	800

Collector Club - Great Inventors - F. Jones

YEAR	ISSUE	EDITION LIMIT	YEAR RETD.	ISSUE PRICE	*QUOTE U.S.$
1990	Thomas Edison	Retrd.	1990	9.25	N/A
1990	Ford Motor Co.	Retrd.	1990	9.25	N/A
1990	Seth Thomas Clock Co.	Retrd.	1990	9.25	75
1990	Wright Cycle Co.	Retrd.	1990	9.25	N/A
1990	Set	Retrd.	1990	37.00	400-500

Collector Club - American Songwriters - F. Jones

YEAR	ISSUE	EDITION LIMIT	YEAR RETD.	ISSUE PRICE	*QUOTE U.S.$
1991	Benjamin R. Hanby House	Retrd.	1991	9.25	N/A
1991	Anna Warner House	Retrd.	1991	9.25	N/A
1991	Stephen Foster Home	Retrd.	1991	9.25	22
1991	Oscar Hammerstein House	Retrd.	1991	9.25	22
1991	Set	Retrd.	1991	37.00	200

Collector Club - Signers of the Declaration - F. Jones

YEAR	ISSUE	EDITION LIMIT	YEAR RETD.	ISSUE PRICE	*QUOTE U.S.$
1992	Josiah Bartlett Home	Retrd.	1992	9.75	N/A
1992	George Clymer Home	Retrd.	1992	9.75	N/A
1992	Stephen Hopkins Home	Retrd.	1992	9.75	N/A
1992	John Witherspoon Home	Retrd.	1992	9.75	N/A
1992	Set	Retrd.	1992	39.00	250

Collector Club -19th Century Master Builders - F. Jones

YEAR	ISSUE	EDITION LIMIT	YEAR RETD.	ISSUE PRICE	*QUOTE U.S.$
1993	Henry Hobson Richardson	Retrd.	1993	10.25	N/A
1993	Samuel Sloan	Retrd.	1993	10.25	N/A
1993	Alexander Jackson Davis	Retrd.	1993	10.25	N/A
1993	Andrew Jackson Downing	Retrd.	1993	10.25	N/A
1993	Set	Retrd.	1993	41.00	100

Collector Club - Williamsburg Merchants - F. Jones

YEAR	ISSUE	EDITION LIMIT	YEAR RETD.	ISSUE PRICE	*QUOTE U.S.$
1994	East Carlton Wigmaker	Retrd.	1994	11.15	12
1994	J. Geddy Silversmith	Retrd.	1994	11.15	12
1994	Craig Jeweler	Retrd.	1994	11.15	12
1994	M. Hunter Millinery	Retrd.	1994	11.15	12
1994	Set	Retrd.	1994	44.60	75

Collector Club - Mt. Rushmore Presidential Series - F. Jones

YEAR	ISSUE	EDITION LIMIT	YEAR RETD.	ISSUE PRICE	*QUOTE U.S.$
1995	George Washington Birthplace	Retrd.	1995	12.00	12
1995	Metamora Courthouse	Retrd.	1995	12.00	12
1995	Theodore Roosevelt Birthplace	Retrd.	1995	12.00	12
1995	Tuckahoe Plantation	Retrd.	1995	12.00	12
1995	Set	Retrd.	1995	48.00	48

Collector Club - American Holiday Series - F. Jones

YEAR	ISSUE	EDITION LIMIT	YEAR RETD.	ISSUE PRICE	*QUOTE U.S.$
1996	And to all a Goodnight	12/96		11.00	11

*Quotes have been rounded up to nearest dollar

YEAR ISSUE		EDITION LIMIT	YEAR RETD.	ISSUE PRICE	*QUOTE U.S.$
1996	Boo to You	12/96		11.00	11
1996	Easter's On Its Way	12/96		11.00	11
1996	Let Freedom Ring	12/96		11.00	11

Accessories - F. Jones

YEAR ISSUE		EDITION LIMIT	YEAR RETD.	ISSUE PRICE	*QUOTE U.S.$
1990	1909 Franklin Limousine	Retrd.	1995	4.00	7
1990	1913 Peerless Touring Car	Retrd.	1995	4.00	7
1990	1914 Fire Pumper	Retrd.	1995	4.00	7
1983	5" Hedge	Retrd.	1988	3.00	30-50
1983	5" Iron Fence	Retrd.	1988	3.00	30-50
1987	5" Picket Fence	Retrd.	1992	3.00	18
1990	5" Wrought Iron Fence	Retrd.	1995	3.00	6
1983	8" Hedge	Retrd.	1988	3.25	40-50
1983	8" Iron Fence	Retrd.	1988	3.25	50-65
1983	8" Picket Fence	Retrd.	1988	3.25	40
1989	Ada Belle	Retrd.	1994	4.00	11
1990	Amish Buggy	Retrd.	1995	4.00	8
1991	Amish Garden	5-Yr.		4.00	5
1994	Amish Milk Wagon	5-Yr.		4.50	5
1994	Amish Produce Wagon	5-Yr.		4.50	5
1994	Apple Tree	5-Yr.		4.50	5
1987	Band Stand	Retrd.	1992	6.50	18
1991	Barnyard	5-Yr.		4.00	5
1995	Beech & Cherry Tree Row	5-Yr.		4.50	5
1995	Bennington Flag	5-Yr.		4.50	5
1994	Berries & Sheep	5-Yr.		4.50	5
1990	Blue Spruce	Retrd.	1995	4.00	7
1994	Booker T. Washington Monument	5-Yr.		4.50	5
1996	Bow Bridge	5-Yr.		5.00	5
1995	Burma-Shave Signs	5-Yr.		4.50	5
1990	Bus Stop	Retrd.	1995	4.00	7
1987	Butch & T.J.	Retrd.	1992	4.00	10-20
1986	Cable Car	Retrd.	1991	4.00	9-18
1993	Cannonball Express	5-Yr.		4.00	5
1986	Carolers	Retrd.	1991	4.00	12-20
1994	Cat & The Fiddle S/2	5-Yr.		4.50	5
1995	Central Park Skaters	5-Yr.		4.50	5
1995	Charles & Lady	5-Yr.		4.50	5
1987	Charlie & Co.	Retrd.	1992	4.00	10-18
1985	Cherry Tree	Retrd.	1990	4.00	40-50
1991	Chessie Hopper Car	5-Yr.		4.00	5
1986	Chickens	Retrd.	1991	3.25	12-24
1993	Chippewa Lake Billboard	5-Yr.		4.00	5
1990	Christmas Tree Lot	Retrd.	1995	4.00	7
1989	Clothesline	Retrd.	1994	4.00	9
1988	Colonial Bread Wagon	Retrd.	1993	4.00	10-15
1991	Concert in the Park	5-Yr.		4.00	5
1994	Cornstalks & Turkeys	5-Yr.		4.50	5
1986	Cows	Retrd.	1991	4.00	15-25
1994	Daily Business (wlbg. people)	5-Yr.		4.50	5
1986	Dairy Wagon	Retrd.	1991	4.00	12-20
1995	Dancing Cat & Clipper Ship	5-Yr.		9.00	9
1994	Deer	5-Yr.		4.50	5
1992	Delivery Truck	5-Yr.		4.00	5
1995	Directional Sign	5-Yr.		5.00	5
1986	Ducks	Retrd.	1991	3.25	12-20
1990	Eugene	Retrd.	1995	4.00	7
1985	Fall Tree	Retrd.	1990	4.00	25-35
1995	Father Serra & Indians	5-Yr.		4.50	5
1987	FJ Express	Retrd.	1992	4.00	18
1986	FJ Real Estate Sign	Retrd.	1991	3.00	24
1988	Flower Pots	Retrd.	1993	4.00	9-15
1992	Forsythia Bush	5-Yr.		4.00	5
1993	Garden House	5-Yr.		3.25	5
1994	Garden Wall	5-Yr.		4.50	5
1988	Gas Light	Retrd.	1993	4.00	9-15
1990	Gerstenslager Buggy	Retrd.	1995	4.00	7
1993	Getting Directions	5-Yr.		4.00	5
1994	Good Humor Man	5-Yr.		4.50	5
1994	Gracie (in carriage)	5-Yr.		4.50	5
1993	Grape Arbor	5-Yr.		4.00	5
1989	Harry's Hotdogs	Retrd.	1994	4.00	7-11
1986	Horse & Carriage	Retrd.	1991	4.00	10-20
1987	Horse & Sleigh	Retrd.	1992	4.00	10
1996	Hot Air Balloon	5-Yr.		5.00	5
1995	Humpty Dumpty	5-Yr.		9.00	9
1986	Ice Wagon	Retrd.	1991	4.00	12-22
1983	Iron Gate	Retrd.	1988	3.00	50-75
1991	Jack The Postman	5-Yr.		3.25	5
1994	Jacob, Atlee & Noah	5-Yr.		4.50	5
1993	Jennie & George's Wedding	5-Yr.		4.00	5
1993	Johnny Appleseed Statue	5-Yr.		4.00	5
1994	Kearsarge Fire Pumper	5-Yr.		4.50	5
1995	Knickerbockers Ball Team	5-Yr.		4.50	5
1994	Lemonade Stand	5-Yr.		4.50	5
1986	Liberty St. Sign	Retrd.	1991	3.25	10-20
1994	Light Ship	5-Yr.		4.50	5
1983	Lilac Bushes	Retrd.	1988	3.00	200-400
1995	Lion Circus Wagon	5-Yr.		4.50	5
1993	Little Marine	5-Yr.		4.00	5
1990	Little Red Caboose	Retrd.	1995	4.00	8
1996	Little Red Riding Hood	5-Yr.		5.00	5
1994	Lunch Wagon	5-Yr.		4.50	5
1995	Magnolia Tree	5-Yr.		4.50	5
1988	Mail Wagon	Retrd.	1993	4.00	10
1988	Main St. Sign	Retrd.	1993	3.25	8-15
1991	Marble Game	5-Yr.		4.00	5
1986	Market St. Sign	Retrd.	1991	3.25	12-22
1993	Market Wagon	5-Yr.		4.00	5
1991	Martin House	5-Yr.		3.25	5
1994	Moving Truck	5-Yr.		4.50	5
1994	Moving Truck	5-Yr.		4.50	5
1992	Mr. Softee Truck	5-Yr.		4.00	5
1995	Mt. Rushmore	5-Yr.		9.00	9
1987	Nanny	Retrd.	1992	4.00	10
1994	Nativity	5-Yr.		15.00	17
1994	Nativity Visitors Trio Set	5-Yr.		19.00	19
1995	Noah's Ark Trio Set	5-Yr.		21.00	21
1996	Noah's Sons Trio Set	5-Yr.		5.00	5
1992	Nutcracker Billboard	5-Yr.		4.00	5
1991	On Vacation	5-Yr.		4.00	5
1996	Owl & PussyCat Went to Sea	5-Yr.		5.00	5
1995	Palm Trees	5-Yr.		9.00	9
1989	Passenger Train Car	Retrd.	1994	4.00	9
1996	Peachtree Street Sign	5-Yr.		5.00	5
1985	Pine Tree	Retrd.	1990	4.00	30
1992	Police Car	5-Yr.		4.00	5
1988	Pony Express Rider	Retrd.	1993	4.00	11-15
1991	Popcorn Wagon	5-Yr.		4.00	5
1985	Poplar Tree	Retrd.	1990	4.00	40-50
1989	Pumpkin Wagon	Retrd.	1994	3.25	9
1989	Quaker Oats Train Car	Retrd.	1994	4.00	9
1987	Railroad Sign	Retrd.	1992	3.00	12-20
1990	Red Maple Tree	Retrd.	1995	4.00	8
1995	Rose Arbor	5-Yr.		4.50	5
1989	Rose Trellis	Retrd.	1994	3.25	9
1995	Rubbermaid Train Car	5-Yr.		4.50	5
1989	Rudy & Aldine	Retrd.	1994	4.00	8
1993	Rustic Fence	5-Yr.		4.00	5
1994	Salvation Army Band	5-Yr.		4.50	5
1995	San Juan Capistrano Bells	5-Yr.		9.00	9
1990	Santa & Reindeer	Retrd.	1995	4.00	7
1991	Scarey Harry (Scarecrow)	5-Yr.		4.00	5
1991	School Bus	5-Yr.		4.00	5
1992	School Crossing	5-Yr.		4.00	5
1996	Seagulls	5-Yr.		5.00	5
1992	Silo	5-Yr.		4.00	5
1991	Ski Party	5-Yr.		4.00	5
1988	Skipjack	Retrd.	1993	6.50	15
1996	Smucker Train Car	5-Yr.		5.00	5
1989	Snowmen	Retrd.	1994	4.00	9
1996	Soccer Game	5-Yr.		5.00	5
1992	Springhouse	5-Yr.		3.25	5
1994	Stock Train Car	5-Yr.		4.50	5
1988	Street Clock	Retrd.	1993	4.00	10
1994	Street Lamp	5-Yr.		4.50	5
1985	Summer Tree	Retrd.	1990	4.00	35
1989	Tad & Toni	Retrd.	1994	4.00	9
1996	Tea For Two	5-Yr.		5.00	5
1988	Telephone Booth	Retrd.	1993	4.00	9-15
1986	Touring Car	Retrd.	1991	4.00	10-20
1996	Treehouse	5-Yr.		5.00	5
1994	Trick or Treat	5-Yr.		4.50	5
1990	Tulip Tree	Retrd.	1995	4.00	9-15
1994	U.S. Flag	5-Yr.		4.50	5
1988	U.S. Flag	Retrd.	1993	4.00	7
1995	Ulric the Undertaker	5-Yr.		4.50	5
1991	USMC War Memorial	5-Yr.		6.50	7
1990	Veterinary Wagon	Retrd.	1995	4.00	7
1990	Victorian Outhouse	Retrd.	1995	4.00	7
1991	Village Entrance Sigh	5-Yr.		6.50	7
1995	Vineyard Fence	5-Yr.		4.50	5
1995	Watermelon Wagon	5-Yr.		4.50	5
1990	Watkins Wagon	Retrd.	1995	4.00	7
1994	Weeping Willow Tree	5-Yr.		4.50	5
1986	Wells, Fargo Wagon	Retrd.	1991	4.00	15
1994	Wharf	5-Yr.		4.50	5
1987	Windmill	Retrd.	1992	3.25	12
1995	Winter Tree	5-Yr.		4.50	5
1986	Wishing Well	Retrd.	1991	3.25	23
1987	Wooden Gate (two-sided)	Retrd.	1992	3.00	10-25
1985	Xmas Pine Tree	Retrd.	1990	4.00	30-50
1985	Xmas Pine Tree w/Red Bows	Retrd.	1990	3.00	100-200
1990	Xmas Spruce	Retrd.	1995	4.00	5
1994	Yule Tree S/2	5-Yr.		4.50	5

American Barns - F. Jones

YEAR ISSUE		EDITION LIMIT	YEAR RETD.	ISSUE PRICE	*QUOTE U.S.$
1992	Bank Barn	5-Yr.		8.50	10
1992	Crib Barn	5-Yr.		8.50	10
1992	Ohio Barn	5-Yr.		8.50	10
1992	Vermont Barn	5-Yr.		8.50	10

Bed & Breakfast Series - F. Jones

YEAR ISSUE		EDITION LIMIT	YEAR RETD.	ISSUE PRICE	*QUOTE U.S.$
1995	Glen Iris	5-Yr.		10.00	10
1995	Kinter House Inn	5-Yr.		10.00	10
1995	Southmoreland	5-Yr.		10.00	10
1995	Victorian Mansion	5-Yr.		10.00	10

Black Heritage Series - F. Jones

YEAR ISSUE		EDITION LIMIT	YEAR RETD.	ISSUE PRICE	*QUOTE U.S.$
1994	Dexter Avenue Baptist Church	5-Yr.		8.00	8
1994	Frederick Douglass Home	5-Yr.		8.00	8
1994	George Washington Carver Museum	5-Yr.		8.00	8
1994	Martin Luther King Birthplace	Retrd.	1994	8.00	45

California Mission Series - F. Jones

YEAR ISSUE		EDITION LIMIT	YEAR RETD.	ISSUE PRICE	*QUOTE U.S.$
1995	Mission Dolores	5-Yr.		10.00	10
1995	Mission San Buenaventura	5-Yr.		10.00	10
1995	Mission San Juan Bautista	5-Yr.		10.00	10
1995	Mission San Luis Rey	5-Yr.		10.00	10

Chippewa Amusement Park - F. Jones

YEAR ISSUE		EDITION LIMIT	YEAR RETD.	ISSUE PRICE	*QUOTE U.S.$
1993	Ballroom	5-Yr.		9.00	10
1993	Bath House	5-Yr.		9.00	10
1993	Midway	5-Yr.		9.00	10
1993	Pavilion	5-Yr.		9.00	10

Christmas '83-Williamsburg - F. Jones

YEAR ISSUE		EDITION LIMIT	YEAR RETD.	ISSUE PRICE	*QUOTE U.S.$
1983	Christmas Church	Retrd.	1983	6.00	N/A
1983	Federal House	Retrd.	1983	6.00	N/A
1983	Garrison House	Retrd.	1983	6.00	N/A
1983	Georgian House	Retrd.	1983	6.00	450
1983	Set	Retrd.	1983	24.00	N/A

Christmas '84-Nantucket - F. Jones

YEAR ISSUE		EDITION LIMIT	YEAR RETD.	ISSUE PRICE	*QUOTE U.S.$
1984	Christmas Shop	Retrd.	1984	6.50	N/A
1984	Powell House	Retrd.	1984	6.50	350
1984	Shaw House	Retrd.	1984	6.50	350
1984	Wintrop House	Retrd.	1984	6.50	250
1984	Set	Retrd.	1984	26.00	1600

Christmas '85-Ohio Western Reserve - F. Jones

YEAR ISSUE		EDITION LIMIT	YEAR RETD.	ISSUE PRICE	*QUOTE U.S.$
1985	Bellevue House	Retrd.	1985	7.00	175
1985	Gates Mills Church	Retrd.	1985	7.00	200
1985	Olmstead House	Retrd.	1985	7.00	175
1985	Western Reserve Academy	Retrd.	1985	7.00	175
1985	Set	Retrd.	1985	27.00	600-975

Christmas '86-Savannah - F. Jones

YEAR ISSUE		EDITION LIMIT	YEAR RETD.	ISSUE PRICE	*QUOTE U.S.$
1986	J.J. Dale Row House	Retrd.	1986	7.25	150
1986	Lafayette Square House	Retrd.	1986	7.25	140-150
1986	Liberty Inn	Retrd.	1986	7.25	200
1986	Simon Mirault Cottage	Retrd.	1986	7.25	200
1986	Set	Retrd.	1986	29.00	850-925

Christmas '87-Maine - F. Jones

YEAR ISSUE		EDITION LIMIT	YEAR RETD.	ISSUE PRICE	*QUOTE U.S.$
1987	Cappy's Chowder House	Retrd.	1987	7.75	250
1987	Captain's House	Retrd.	1987	7.75	250
1987	Damariscotta Church	Retrd.	1987	7.75	250
1987	Portland Head Lighthouse	Retrd.	1987	7.75	250
1987	Set	Retrd.	1987	31.00	800-1050

Christmas '88-Philadelphia - F. Jones

YEAR ISSUE		EDITION LIMIT	YEAR RETD.	ISSUE PRICE	*QUOTE U.S.$
1988	Elfreth's Alley	Retrd.	1988	7.75	150-200
1988	Graff House	Retrd.	1988	7.75	150-200
1988	The Head House	Retrd.	1988	7.75	150-200
1988	Hill-Physick-Keith House	Retrd.	1988	7.75	150-200
1988	Set	Retrd.	1988	31.00	500-725

Christmas '89-In New England - F. Jones

YEAR ISSUE		EDITION LIMIT	YEAR RETD.	ISSUE PRICE	*QUOTE U.S.$
1989	Hunter House	Retrd.	1989	8.00	80-125
1989	The Old South Meeting House	Retrd.	1989	8.00	80-125
1989	Sheldon's Tavern	Retrd.	1989	8.00	125
1989	The Vermont Country Store	Retrd.	1989	8.00	80-125
1989	Set	Retrd.	1989	32.00	250-450

Christmas '90-Colonial Virginia - F. Jones

YEAR ISSUE		EDITION LIMIT	YEAR RETD.	ISSUE PRICE	*QUOTE U.S.$
1990	Dulany House	Retrd.	1990	8.00	50-100
1990	Rising Sun Tavern	Retrd.	1990	8.00	70-100
1990	Shirley Plantation	Retrd.	1990	8.00	40-100
1990	St. John's Church	Retrd.	1990	8.00	100
1990	St. John's Church (blue)	Retrd.	1990	8.00	150-200
1990	Set	Retrd.	1990	32.00	400-600

Christmas '91-Rocky Mountain - F. Jones

YEAR ISSUE		EDITION LIMIT	YEAR RETD.	ISSUE PRICE	*QUOTE U.S.$
1991	First Presbyterian Church	Retrd.	1991	8.20	55
1991	Tabor House	Retrd.	1991	8.20	55-75
1991	Western Hotel	Retrd.	1991	8.20	25-55
1991	Wheller-Stallard House	Retrd.	1991	8.20	25-55
1991	Set	Retrd.	1991	32.80	125-260

Christmas '92-Hometown - F. Jones

YEAR ISSUE		EDITION LIMIT	YEAR RETD.	ISSUE PRICE	*QUOTE U.S.$
1992	August Imgard House	Retrd.	1992	8.50	30-50
1992	Howey House	Retrd.	1992	8.50	30-50
1992	Overholt House	Retrd.	1992	8.50	30-50
1992	Wayne Co. Courthouse	Retrd.	1992	8.50	30-50
1992	Set	Retrd.	1992	34.00	150-200

Christmas '93-St. Charles - F. Jones

YEAR ISSUE		EDITION LIMIT	YEAR RETD.	ISSUE PRICE	*QUOTE U.S.$
1993	Lewis & Clark Center	Retrd.	1993	9.00	15-20
1993	Newbill-McElhiney House	Retrd.	1993	9.00	15-20
1993	St. Peter's Catholic Church	Retrd.	1993	9.00	15-20
1993	Stone Row	Retrd.	1993	9.00	15-20
1993	Set	Retrd.	1993	36.00	60-100

Christmas '94-New Orleans Series - F. Jones

YEAR ISSUE		EDITION LIMIT	YEAR RETD.	ISSUE PRICE	*QUOTE U.S.$
1994	Beauregard-Keyes House	Retrd.	1994	10.00	14-20
1994	Gallier House	Retrd.	1994	10.00	14-20
1994	Hermann-Grima House	Retrd.	1994	10.00	14-20
1994	St. Patrick's Church	Retrd.	1994	10.00	14-20
1994	Set	Retrd.	1994	40.00	50

Christmas '95-New York Series - F. Jones

YEAR ISSUE		EDITION LIMIT	YEAR RETD.	ISSUE PRICE	*QUOTE U.S.$
1995	Clement C. Moore House	Retrd.	1995	10.00	10-15
1995	Fraunces Taver	Retrd.	1995	10.00	10-15
1995	Fulton Market	Retrd.	1995	10.00	10-15
1995	St. Marks-In-the-Bowery	Retrd.	1995	10.00	10-15
1995	Set	Retrd.	1995	40.00	55

Christmas '96-Atlanta Series - F. Jones

YEAR ISSUE		EDITION LIMIT	YEAR RETD.	ISSUE PRICE	*QUOTE U.S.$
1996	Callanwolde	12/96		11.00	11
1996	First Baptist Church	12/96		11.00	11
1996	Fox Theatre	12/96		11.00	11
1996	Margaret Mitchell House	12/96		11.00	11

*Quotes have been rounded up to nearest dollar

YEAR ISSUE		EDITION LIMIT	YEAR RETD.	ISSUE PRICE	*QUOTE U.S.$

Circus Series - F. Jones

1996	Ferris Wheel	12/96		10.00	10
1995	Sideshow	Retrd.	1995	10.00	10-15

Covered Bridge Series - F. Jones

1995	Creamery Bridge	Retrd.	1995	10.00	10-15
1996	Kennedy Bridge	12/96		10.00	10

Daughters of the Painted Lady Series - F. Jones

1995	Barber Cottage	5-Yr.		10.00	10
1995	The Fan House	5-Yr.		10.00	10
1995	Hall Cottage	5-Yr.		10.00	10
1995	The Painted Lady	5-Yr.		10.00	10

Duke of Gloucester Series - F. Jones

1994	Cole Shop	5-Yr.		10.00	10
1994	Nicolson Store	5-Yr.		10.00	10
1994	Pasteur & Galt Apothecary	5-Yr.		10.00	10
1994	Prentis Shop	5-Yr.		10.00	10

Elm Street Series - F. Jones

1994	Blumenthal's	5-Yr.		10.00	10
1994	Clyde's Shoe Repair	5-Yr.		10.00	10
1994	First Congregational Church	5-Yr.		10.00	10
1994	Jim's Hunting & Fishing	5-Yr.		10.00	10

Fairy Tale Series - F. Jones

1996	Gingerbread House	5-Yr.		10.00	10
1996	Grandmother's House	5-Yr.		10.00	10
1996	Seven Dwarf's House	5-Yr.		10.00	10
1996	Three Bear's House	5-Yr.		10.00	10

Fall - F. Jones

1986	Golden Lamb Buttery	Retrd.	1991	8.00	35-65
1986	Grimm's Farmhouse	Retrd.	1991	8.00	45
1986	Mail Pouch Barn	Retrd.	1991	8.00	45-75
1986	Vollant Mills	Retrd.	1991	8.00	35-65
1986	Set	Retrd.	1991	32.00	135-180

Firehouse Series - F. Jones

1994	David Crockett No. 1	5-Yr.		10.00	10
1994	Denver No. 1	5-Yr.		10.00	10
1994	Toledo No. 18	5-Yr.		10.00	10
1994	Vigilant 1891	5-Yr.		10.00	10

Galveston Series - F. Jones

1996	Ashton Villa	5-Yr.		10.00	10
1996	Lemuel Burr House	5-Yr.		10.00	10
1996	Sacred Heart Church	5-Yr.		10.00	10
1996	Trueheart - Adriance Building	5-Yr.		10.00	10

General Store Series - F. Jones

1993	Calef's Country Store	5-Yr.		10.00	10
1993	Davoll's General Store	5-Yr.		10.00	10
1993	Peltier's Market	5-Yr.		10.00	10
1993	S. Woodstock Country Store	5-Yr.		10.00	10

Great Americans Series - F. Jones

1996	Daniel Boone Home	12/96		10.00	10

Green Gables Series - F. Jones

1996	Green Gables House	12/96		10.00	10

Greenwich Village Series - F. Jones

1996	Hudson Gormet	5-Yr.		10.00	10
1996	Mc Nulty's Tea & Coffee	5-Yr.		10.00	10
1996	Three Lives Books	5-Yr.		10.00	10
1996	Vesuvio Bakery	5-Yr.		10.00	10

Hagerstown - F. Jones

1988	J Hager House	Retrd.	1993	8.00	17-32
1988	Miller House	Retrd.	1993	8.00	17-32
1988	Woman's Club	Retrd.	1993	8.00	17-35
1988	The Yule Cupboard	Retrd.	1993	8.00	17-35
1988	Set	Retrd.	1993	32.00	100

Historic Nauvoo Series - F. Jones

1995	Cultural Hall	5-Yr.		10.00	10
1995	J. Browning Gunsmith	5-Yr.		10.00	10
1995	Printing Office	5-Yr.		10.00	10
1995	Stoddard Home & Tinsmith	5-Yr.		10.00	10

Liberty St. - F. Jones

1988	County Courthouse	Retrd.	1993	8.00	17-31
1988	Graf Printing Co.	Retrd.	1993	8.00	17-31
1988	Wilton Railway Depot	Retrd.	1993	8.00	17-31
1988	Z. Jones Basketmaker	Retrd.	1993	8.00	20-40

Lighthouse - F. Jones

1990	Admiralty Head	Retrd.	1995	8.00	11
1990	Cape Hatteras Lighthouse	Retrd.	1995	8.00	11-22
1990	Sandy Hook Lighthouse	Retrd.	1995	8.00	11
1990	Split Rock Lighthouse	Retrd.	1995	8.00	11-22

Limited Edition Promotional Items - F. Jones

1993	Convention Museum	Retrd.	1993	12.95	13
1993	FJ Factory	Open		12.95	13
1994	FJ Factory/5 Yr. Banner	Retrd.	1994	10.00	18
1993	FJ Factory/Gold Cat Edition	Retrd.	1993	12.95	490
1994	FJ Factory/Home Banner	Retrd.	1994	10.00	10
1990	Frycrest Farm Homestead	Retrd.	1991	10.00	125
1992	Glen Pine	Retrd.	1993	10.00	27
1993	Nativity Cat on the Fence	Retrd.	1993	19.95	30

Main St. - F. Jones

1987	Franklin Library	Retrd.	1992	8.00	25
1987	Garden Theatre	Retrd.	1992	8.00	25
1987	Historical Museum	Retrd.	1992	8.00	25-45
1987	Telegraph/Post Office	Retrd.	1992	8.00	25-45
1987	Set	Retrd.	1992	32.00	70-150

Mark Twain's Hannibal Series - F. Jones

1995	Becky Thatcher House	Retrd.	1995	10.00	10-15
1996	Hickory Stick	12/96		10.00	10

Market St. - F. Jones

1989	Schumacher Mills	Retrd.	1993	8.00	17-31
1989	Seville Hardware Store	Retrd.	1993	8.00	17-31
1989	West India Goods Store	Retrd.	1993	8.00	17-31
1989	Yankee Candle Company	Retrd.	1993	8.00	17-31

Martha's Vineyard Series - F. Jones

1995	John Coffin House	Retrd.	1995	10.00	10-15
1996	West Chop Lighthouse	12/96		10.00	10

Miscellaneous - F. Jones

1985	Pencil Holder	Retrd.	1988	3.95	210
1985	Recipe Holder	Retrd.	1988	3.95	250
1986	School Desk-blue	Retrd.	1988	12.00	N/A
1986	School Desk-red	Retrd.	1988	12.00	175

Nantucket - F. Jones

1987	Jared Coffin House	Retrd.	1992	8.00	24-45
1987	Maria Mitchell House	Retrd.	1992	8.00	24-45
1987	Nantucket Atheneum	Retrd.	1992	8.00	24-45
1987	Unitarian Church	Retrd.	1992	8.00	24-45
1987	Set	Retrd.	1992	32.00	70-100

Nautical - F. Jones

1987	H & E Ships Chandlery	Retrd.	1992	8.00	24-40
1987	Lorain Lighthouse	Retrd.	1992	8.00	24-40
1987	Monhegan Boat Landing	Retrd.	1992	8.00	24-40
1987	Yacht Club	Retrd.	1992	8.00	24-40
1987	Set	Retrd.	1992	32.00	70-140

Neighborhood Event Series - F. Jones

1995	Peter Seitz Tavern & Stagecoach	Retrd.	1995	12.95	18
1995	Birely Place	Retrd.	1995	12.95	18
1996	Sea-Chimes	12/96		12.95	13
1996	Bailey-Gombert House	12/96		12.95	13

Nursery Rhyme Series - F. Jones

1994	Crooked House	5-Yr.		10.00	10
1994	House That Jack Built	5-Yr.		10.00	10
1994	Old Woman in the Shoe	5-Yr.		10.00	10
1994	Peter, Peter Pumpkin Eater	5-Yr.		10.00	10

Ohio Amish - F. Jones

1991	Ada Mae's Quilt Barn	5-Yr.		8.00	10
1991	Brown School	5-Yr.		8.00	10
1991	Eli's Harness Shop	5-Yr.		8.00	10
1991	Jonas Troyer Home	5-Yr.		8.00	10

Painted Ladies - F. Jones

1988	Andrews Hotel	Retrd.	1993	8.00	17-31
1988	Lady Amanda	Retrd.	1993	8.00	17-31
1988	Lady Elizabeth	Retrd.	1993	8.00	17-31
1988	Lady Iris	Retrd.	1993	8.00	17-31
1988	Set	Retrd.	1993	32.00	60

Roscoe Village - F. Jones

1986	Canal Company	Retrd.	1991	8.00	45-65
1986	Jackson Twp. Hall	Retrd.	1991	8.00	45-65
1986	Old Warehouse Rest.	Retrd.	1991	8.00	45-65
1986	Roscoe General Store	Retrd.	1991	8.00	45-65
1986	Set	Retrd.	1991	32.00	150

Series I - F. Jones

1983	Antique Shop	Retrd.	1988	8.00	100-125
1983	Apothecary	Retrd.	1988	8.00	100-125
1983	Barbershop	Retrd.	1988	8.00	80-125
1983	Book Store	Retrd.	1988	8.00	50-125
1983	Cherry Tree Inn	Retrd.	1988	8.00	N/A
1983	Federal House	Retrd.	1988	8.00	60-125
1983	Florist Shop	Retrd.	1988	8.00	60-125
1983	Garrison House	Retrd.	1988	8.00	125
1983	Red Whale Inn	Retrd.	1988	8.00	N/A
1983	School	Retrd.	1988	8.00	80-125
1983	Sweetshop	Retrd.	1988	8.00	125
1983	Toy Shoppe	Retrd.	1988	8.00	125
1983	Victorian House	Retrd.	1988	8.00	50-125
1983	Wayside Inn	Retrd.	1988	8.00	N/A
1983	Set of 12 w/1 Inn	Retrd.	1988	96.00	800-1500
1983	Set of 14 w/ 3 Inns	Retrd.	1988	112.00	2000-3000

Series II - F. Jones

1984	Attorney/Bank	Retrd.	1989	8.00	95-150
1984	Brocke House	Retrd.	1989	8.00	95-150
1984	Church	Retrd.	1989	8.00	95-150
1984	Eaton House	Retrd.	1989	8.00	150-175
1984	Grandinere House	Retrd.	1989	8.00	95-150
1984	Millinery/Quilt	Retrd.	1989	8.00	150-200
1984	Music Shop	Retrd.	1989	8.00	150
1984	S&T Clothiers	Retrd.	1989	8.00	150-175
1984	Tobacconist/Shoemaker	Retrd.	1989	8.00	95-150
1984	Town Hall	Retrd.	1989	8.00	150
1984	Set	Retrd.	1989	96.00	750

Series III - F. Jones

1985	Allen-Coe House	Retrd.	1990	8.00	60
1985	Connecticut Ave. FireHouse	Retrd.	1990	8.00	40-75
1985	Dry Goods Store	Retrd.	1990	8.00	50-75
1985	Edinburgh Times	Retrd.	1990	8.00	40-75
1985	Fine Jewelers	Retrd.	1990	8.00	40-50
1985	Hobart-Harley House	Retrd.	1990	8.00	50-75
1985	Kalorama Guest House	Retrd.	1990	8.00	40-50
1985	Main St. Carriage Shop	Retrd.	1990	8.00	50-75
1985	Opera House	Retrd.	1990	8.00	50-75
1985	Ristorante	Retrd.	1990	8.00	50-75
1985	Set	Retrd.	1990	80.00	500-675

Series IV - F. Jones

1986	Bennington-Hull House	Retrd.	1991	8.00	30-65
1986	Chagrin Falls Popcorn Shop	Retrd.	1991	8.00	30-65
1986	Chepachet Union Church	Retrd.	1991	8.00	30-65
1986	John Belville House	Retrd.	1991	8.00	30-65
1986	Jones Bros. Tea Co.	Retrd.	1991	8.00	30-65
1986	The Little House Giftables	Retrd.	1991	8.00	30-65
1986	O'Malley's Livery Stable	Retrd.	1991	8.00	30-65
1986	Vandenberg House	Retrd.	1991	8.00	30-65
1986	Village Clock Shop	Retrd.	1991	8.00	30-65
1986	Westbrook House	Retrd.	1991	8.00	30-65
1986	Set	Retrd.	1991	80.00	450-550

Series V - F. Jones

1987	Amish Oak/Dixie Shoe	Retrd.	1992	8.00	20-30
1987	Architect/Tailor	Retrd.	1992	8.00	20-45
1987	Congruity Tavern	Retrd.	1992	8.00	20-45
1987	Creole House	Retrd.	1992	8.00	20-45
1987	Dentist/Physician	Retrd.	1992	8.00	20-45
1987	M. Washington House	Retrd.	1992	8.00	20-45
1987	Markethouse	Retrd.	1992	8.00	20-45
1987	Murray Hotel	Retrd.	1992	8.00	20-45
1987	Police Department	Retrd.	1992	8.00	20-45
1987	Southport Bank	Retrd.	1992	8.00	20-45
1987	Set	Retrd.	1992	80.00	350

Series VI - F. Jones

1988	Burton Lancaster House	Retrd.	1993	8.00	17-31
1988	City Hospital	Retrd.	1993	8.00	17-31
1988	First Baptist Church	Retrd.	1993	8.00	17-31
1988	Fish/Meat Market	Retrd.	1993	8.00	17-31
1988	Lincoln School	Retrd.	1993	8.00	17-31
1988	New Masters Gallery	Retrd.	1993	8.00	17-31
1988	Ohliger House	Retrd.	1993	8.00	17-31
1988	Pruyn House	Retrd.	1993	8.00	17-31
1988	Stiffenbody Funeral Home	Retrd.	1993	8.00	17-31
1988	Williams & Sons	Retrd.	1993	8.00	17-31
1988	Set	Retrd.	1993	80.00	200-300

Series VII - F. Jones

1989	Black Cat Antiques	Retrd.	1994	8.00	16
1989	Hairdressing Parlor	Retrd.	1994	8.00	15-22
1989	Handcrafted Toys	Retrd.	1994	8.00	15-22
1989	Justice of the Peace	Retrd.	1994	8.00	15-22
1989	Octagonal School	Retrd.	1994	8.00	15-22
1989	Old Franklin Book Shop	Retrd.	1994	8.00	15-22
1989	Thorpe House Bed & Breakfast	Retrd.	1994	8.00	15-22
1989	Village Tinsmith	Retrd.	1994	8.00	15-22
1989	Williams Apothecary	Retrd.	1994	8.00	15-22
1989	Winkler Bakery	Retrd.	1994	8.00	15-22

Series VIII - F. Jones

1990	FJ Realty Company	Retrd.	1995	8.00	15
1990	Globe Corner Bookstore	Retrd.	1995	8.00	15
1990	Haberdashers	Retrd.	1995	8.00	15
1990	Medina Fire Department	Retrd.	1995	8.00	15
1990	Nell's Stems & Stitches	Retrd.	1995	8.00	15
1990	Noah's Ark Veterinary	Retrd.	1995	8.00	15
1990	Piccadilli Pipe & Tobacco	Retrd.	1995	8.00	15
1990	Puritan House	Retrd.	1995	8.00	15
1990	Victoria's Parlour	Retrd.	1995	8.00	15
1990	Walldorff Furniture	Retrd.	1995	8.00	15

Series IX - F. Jones

1991	All Saints Chapel	5-Yr.		8.00	10
1991	American Red Cross	5-Yr.		8.00	10
1991	Central City Opera House	5-Yr.		8.00	10
1991	City Hall	5-Yr.		8.00	10
1991	CPA/Law Office	5-Yr.		8.00	10
1991	Gov. Snyder Mansion	5-Yr.		8.00	10
1991	Jeweler/Optometrist	5-Yr.		8.00	10
1991	Osbahr's Upholstery	5-Yr.		8.00	10
1991	Spanky's Hardware Co.	5-Yr.		8.00	10
1991	The Treble Clef	5-Yr.		8.00	10

Series X - F. Jones

1992	City News	5-Yr.		8.50	10
1992	Fudge Kitchen	5-Yr.		8.50	10

*Quotes have been rounded up to nearest dollar

YEAR ISSUE		EDITION LIMIT	YEAR RETD.	ISSUE PRICE	*QUOTE U.S.$
1992	Grand Haven	5-Yr.		8.50	10
1992	Henyan's Athletic Shop	5-Yr.		8.50	10
1992	Leppert's 5 &10	5-Yr.		8.50	10
1992	Madeline's Dress Shop	5-Yr.		8.50	10
1992	Owl And The Pussycat	5-Yr.		8.50	10
1992	Pickles Pub	5-Yr.		8.50	10
1992	Pure Gas Station	5-Yr.		8.50	10
1993	Shrimplin & Jones Produce	5-Yr.		9.00	10
1992	United Church of Acworth	5-Yr.		8.50	10

Series XI - F. Jones

1993	Barbershop/Gallery	5-Yr.		9.00	10
1993	Haddonfield Bank	5-Yr.		9.00	10
1993	Immanuel Church	5-Yr.		9.00	10
1993	Johann Singer Boots & Shoes	5-Yr.		9.00	10
1993	Pet Shop/Gift Shop	5-Yr.		9.00	10
1993	Police-Troop C	5-Yr.		9.00	10
1993	Stone's Restaurant	5-Yr.		9.00	10
1993	U.S. Armed Forces	5-Yr.		9.00	10
1993	U.S. Post Office	5-Yr.		9.00	10

Series XII - F. Jones

1994	Arnold-Lynch Funeral Home	5-Yr.		10.00	10
1994	Bedford County Courthouse	5-Yr.		10.00	10
1994	Boyd's Drug Strore	5-Yr.		10.00	10
1994	Christmas Tree Hill Gifts	5-Yr.		10.00	10
1994	Foorman-Morrison House	5-Yr.		10.00	10
1994	Haddon Hts. Train Depot	5-Yr.		10.00	10
1994	Historical Society	5-Yr.		10.00	10
1994	Masonic Temple	5-Yr.		10.00	10
1994	Ritz Theater	5-Yr.		10.00	10
1994	Spread Eagle Tavern	5-Yr.		10.00	10

Series XIII - F. Jones

1995	Alvanas & Coe Barbers	5-Yr.		10.00	10
1995	Cedar School	5-Yr.		10.00	10
1995	Hospital	5-Yr.		10.00	10
1995	Needleworker	5-Yr.		10.00	10
1995	Public Library	5-Yr.		10.00	10
1995	Schneider's Bakery	5-Yr.		10.00	10
1995	Susquehanna Antiques	5-Yr.		10.00	10
1995	YMCA	5-Yr.		10.00	10

Series XIV - F. Jones

1996	3 Guys Pizzeria	5-Yr.		10.00	10
1996	Dr. Goodbody III	5-Yr.		10.00	10
1996	Mc Auley School	5-Yr.		10.00	10
1996	Rosie's Fish & Chips	5-Yr.		10.00	10
1996	Stabler Apothecary	5-Yr.		10.00	10
1996	Wayside Inn Grist Mill	5-Yr.		10.00	10
1996	Willa Cather Home	5-Yr.		10.00	10
1996	Winter Clove Inn	5-Yr.		10.00	10

Shaker Village Series - F. Jones

1995	Great Stone Dwelling	5-Yr.		10.00	10
1995	Meetinghouse	5-Yr.		10.00	10
1995	Round Barn	5-Yr.		10.00	10
1995	Trustees Office	5-Yr.		10.00	10

Southern Belles Series - F. Jones

1996	Auburn	12/96		10.00	10

Special Item - F. Jones

1995	Smokey Bear	Retrd.	1995	8.95	13
1994	Smokey Bear w/ 50th stamp	Retrd.	1994	8.95	10

Tradesman - F. Jones

1988	Buckeye Candy & Tobacco	Retrd.	1993	8.00	17-31
1988	C.O. Wheel Company	Retrd.	1993	8.00	17-31
1988	Hermannhof Winery	Retrd.	1993	8.00	17-31
1988	Jenney Grist Mill	Retrd.	1993	8.00	15-50

Washington - F. Jones

1991	National Archives	5-Yr.		8.00	10
1991	U.S. Capitol	5-Yr.		8.00	10
1991	U.S. Supreme Court	5-Yr.		8.00	10
1991	White House	5-Yr.		8.00	10

Waterfront Series - F. Jones

1994	Arnold Transit Company	5-Yr.		10.00	10
1994	Lowell's Boat Shop	5-Yr.		10.00	10
1994	Sand Island Lighthouse	5-Yr.		10.00	10
1994	Seaside Market	5-Yr.		10.00	10

West Coast Lighthouse Series - F. Jones

1994	East Brother Lighthouse	5-Yr.		10.00	10
1994	Heceta Head Light	5-Yr.		10.00	10
1994	Mukilteo Light	5-Yr.		10.00	10
1994	Point Pinos Light	5-Yr.		10.00	10

Wild West - F. Jones

1989	Drink 'em up Saloon	Retrd.	1993	8.00	17-31
1989	F.C. Zimmermann's Gun Shop	Retrd.	1993	8.00	17-31
1989	Marshal's Office	Retrd.	1993	8.00	17-31
1989	Wells, Fargo & Co.	Retrd.	1993	8.00	17-31

Williamsburg Series - F. Jones

1993	Bruton Parish	5-Yr.		10.00	10
1993	Governor's Palace	5-Yr.		10.00	10
1993	Grissell Hay Lodging House	5-Yr.		10.00	10
1993	Raleigh Tavern	5-Yr.		10.00	10

Wine Country Series - F. Jones

1996	Charles Krug Winery	12/96		10.00	10

Cavanagh Group Intl.

Coca-Cola Brand Heritage Collection - Various

1995	Always - CGI	Open		30.00	30
1995	Always-Musical - CGI	Open		50.00	50
1995	Boy at Well - N. Rockwell	5,000		60.00	60
1995	Boy Fishing - N. Rockwell	5,000		60.00	60
1996	Busy Man's Pause - Sundblom	Open		80.00	80
1994	Calendar Girl 1916-Music Box - CGI	500		60.00	60
1996	Coca-Cola Stand - CGI	Open		45.00	45
1996	Cool Break - CGI	Open		40.00	45
1994	Dear Santa, Please Pause Here - Sundblom	2,500	1995	80.00	80
1994	Dear Santa, Please Pause Here-Musical - Sundblom	2,500	1995	100.00	100
1996	Decorating The Tree - CGI	Open		45.00	45
1994	Eight Polar Bears on Wood - CGI	5,000		100.00	100
1994	Eight Polar Bears on Wood-Musical - CGI	10,000		150.00	150
1995	Elaine - CGI	2,500		100.00	100
1994	Extra Bright Refreshment - Snowglobe - Sundblom	2,500		50.00	50
1996	For Me - Sundblom	Open		40.00	40
1995	Girl on Swing - CGI	2,500		80.00	80
1996	Gone Fishing - CGI	Open		40.00	40
1994	Good Boys and Girl - Sundblom	2,500	1995	80.00	80
1994	Good Boys and Girls-Musical - Sundblom	2,500	1995	100.00	100
1994	Good Boys and Girls-Snowglobe - Sundblom	2,000	1995	45.00	45
1994	Hilda Clark 1901-Music Box - CGI	500		60.00	60
1994	Hilda Clark 1903-Music Box - CGI	500		60.00	60
1996	Hollywood-Snowglobe - CGI	Open		50.00	50
1996	The Homecoming - S. Stearman	2,000	1995	125.00	125
1995	Hospitality - Sundblom	5,000		35.00	35
1995	Playing with Dad - CGI	Open		40.00	40
1996	A Refreshing Break - N. Rockwell	Open		60.00	60
1996	Refreshing Treat - CGI	Open		45.00	45
1994	Santa at His Desk - Sundblom	5,000		80.00	80
1994	Santa at His Desk-Musical - Sundblom	5,000		100.00	100
1994	Santa at His Desk-Snowglobe - Sundblom	Open		45.00	45
1994	Santa at the Fireplace - Sundblom	5,000		80.00	80
1994	Santa at the Fireplace-Musical - Sundblom	5,000		100.00	100
1994	Santa at the Lamppost - Snowglobe - Sundblom	Open		50.00	50
1996	Santa with Polar Bear-Snowglobe - CGI	Open		50.00	50
1996	Say Uncle-Snowglobe - CGI	Open		50.00	50
1994	Single Polar Bear on Ice-Snowglobe - CGI	Open		40.00	40
1996	Sshh!-Musical - Sundblom	Open		55.00	55
1995	They Remember Me-Musical - Sundblom	5,000		50.00	50
1994	Two Polar Bears on Ice - CGI	Open		25.00	25
1994	Two Polar Bears on Ice-Musical -CGI	Open		45.00	45

Coca-Cola Brand Heritage Collection Polar Bear Cubs - CGI

1996	Balancing Act	Open		16.00	16
1996	The Bear Cub Club	Open		20.00	20
1996	The Big Catch	Open		16.00	16
1996	A Christmas Wish	Open		10.00	10
1996	Friends Are Forever	Open		16.00	16
1996	Giving Is Better Than Receiving	Open		12.00	12
1996	A Helping Hand	Open		20.00	20
1996	I'm Not Sleepy...Really	Open		10.00	10
1996	It's My Turn to Hide	Open		12.00	12
1996	Look What I Can Do	Open		12.00	12
1996	Ride 'em Cowboy	Open		20.00	20
1996	Skating Rink Romance	Open		16.00	16
1996	Snowday Adventure	Open		12.00	12
1996	Sweet Dreams	Open		12.00	12
1996	To Grandmother's House We Go	Open		12.00	12
1996	Who Says Girls Can't Throw	Open		16.00	16

Coca-Cola Brand Musical - Various

1993	Dear Santa, Please Pause Here - Sundblom	Open		50.00	50
1994	Santa's Soda Shop - CGI	Open		50.00	50

Coca-Cola Brand North Pole Bottling Works - CGI

1995	All in a Day's Work	Open		25.00	25
1996	Art Department	Open		50.00	50
1996	An Artist's Touch	Open		25.00	25
1996	Big Ambitions	Open		25.00	25
1995	Checking His List	Open		30.00	30
1996	Delivery for Mrs. Claus	Open		25.00	25
1996	Elf in Training	Open		25.00	25
1995	An Elf's Favorite Chore	Open		30.00	30
1995	Filling Operations	Open		45.00	45
1995	Front Office	Open		50.00	50
1995	The Kitchen Corner	Open		55.00	55
1995	Maintenance Mischief	Open		25.00	25
1995	Making the Secret Syrup	Open		30.00	30
1996	Oops!	Open		25.00	25
1996	Order Department	Open		55.00	55
1996	Precious Cargo	Open		25.00	25
1995	Quality Control	Open		25.00	25
1996	Shipping Department	Open		55.00	55
1996	Special Delivery	Open		25.00	25
1996	A Stroke of Genius	Open		50.00	50
1995	Top Secret	Open		30.00	30

Coca-Cola Brand Santa Animations - Sundblom

1991	Ssshh! (1st Ed.)	Closed	1992	99.99	135-285
1992	Santa's Pause for Refreshment (2nd Ed.)	Closed	1993	99.99	135-235
1993	Trimming the Tree (3rd Ed.)	Closed	1994	99.99	135-250
1995	Santa at the Lamppost (4th Ed.)	Open		110.00	110

Coca-Cola Brand Town Square Collection - CGI

1992	Candler's Drugs	Closed	1993	40.00	50-70
1996	Chandler's Ski Resort	Open		40.00	40
1993	City Hall	Closed	1994	40.00	60-70
1996	Clara's Christmas Shop	Open		40.00	40
1995	Coca-Cola Bottling Works	Closed	1995	40.00	50
1996	Cooper's Tree Farm	Open		20.00	20
1992	Dee's Boarding House	Closed	1993	40.00	300-500
1992	Dick's Luncheonette	Closed	1993	40.00	45-70
1994	Flying "A" Service Station	Open		40.00	40
1992	Gilbert's Grocery	Closed	1993	40.00	50-90
1995	Grist Mill	Closed	1995	40.00	50
1992	Howard Oil	Closed	1993	40.00	125-175
1993	Jacob's Pharmacy	5,000	1993	25.00	300-500
1995	Jenny's Sweet Shoppe	Closed	1995	40.00	50
1995	Lighthouse Point Snack Bar	Open		40.00	40
1994	McMahon's General Store	Closed	1995	40.00	50
1993	Mooney's Antique Barn	Closed	1994	40.00	45-90
1994	Plaza Drugs	Closed	1995	20.00	50
1993	Route 93 Covered Bridge	Closed	1995	20.00	25
1996	Scooter's Drive In	Open		40.00	40
1994	Station #14 Firehouse	Open		40.00	40
1994	Strand Theatre	Open		40.00	40
1993	T. Taylor's Emporium	Closed	1994	40.00	45-70
1993	The Tick Tock Diner	Closed	1995	40.00	50
1996	Town Barber Shop	Open		40.00	40
1994	Town Gazebo	Closed	1995	20.00	20
1992	Train Depot	Closed	1993	40.00	200-300

Coca-Cola Brand Town Square Collection Accessories - CGI

1992	Ad Car "Coca-Cola"	Closed	1993	9.00	25
1992	After Skating	Closed	1993	8.00	12
1995	Boys with Snowballs	Closed	1995	11.00	11
1992	Bringing It Home	Closed	1993	8.00	13
1994	Checker Players	Closed	1995	15.00	20
1994	Crowley Cab Co.	Closed	1995	11.00	11
1992	Delivery Man	Closed	1993	8.00	15-25
1992	Delivery Truck "Coca-Cola"	Closed	1993	15.00	28
1993	Extra! Extra!	Closed	1994	7.00	10
1992	Gil the Grocer	Closed	1993	8.00	13
1993	Gone Fishing	Closed	1994	11.00	11
1994	Homeward Bound	Closed	1995	8.00	8
1992	Horse-Drawn Wagon	Closed	1993	12.00	25-50
1995	Lunch Wagon	Closed	1995	15.00	15
1993	Officer Pat	Closed	1995	7.00	7
1993	Old Number Seven	Closed	1995	15.00	25
1994	Sledders	Closed	1995	11.00	11
1994	Sleigh Ride	Closed	1995	15.00	15
1993	Soda Jerk	Closed	1995	7.00	10
1993	Street Vendor	Closed	1994	11.00	11
1992	Thirsty the Snowman	Closed	1993	9.00	17

Classic Collectables by Uniquely Yours

Dicken's-A Christmas Carol (Miniatures) - E. Tisa

1987	Belle	Closed	1989	40.00	40
1987	Christmas Past	Closed	1989	40.00	40
1987	Christmas Present	Closed	1989	40.00	40
1987	Christmas Yet to Be	Closed	1989	32.00	32
1987	Father Christmas	Closed	1989	40.00	40
1987	Marley's Ghost	Closed	1989	40.00	40
1987	Mr. Fezzziwig	Closed	1989	40.00	40
1987	Mrs. Cratchit	Closed	1989	42.00	42
1987	Mrs. Fezziwig	Closed	1989	40.00	40
1987	Scrooge	Closed	1989	40.00	40
1987	Tiny Tim & Bob	Closed	1989	60.00	60

Dicken's-A Christmas Carol - E. Tisa

1989	Adult Carolers	Open		78.00	125
1988	Bob Cratchit and Tiny Tim	Open		68.00	122
1988	Boy on Sled	Open		32.00	63
1989	Children Carolers	Open		68.00	119
1989	Christmas Present (vingette w/feast)	Closed	1990	90.00	90
1988	Ghost of Christmas Past	Open		36.00	68
1988	Ghost of Christmas Present	Open		68.00	122
1988	Ghost of Christmas Yet To Be	Open		48.00	102
1988	Girl in a Sleigh	Open		36.00	74
1990	Lighting the Menorrah	Closed	1990	96.00	96
1988	Marley's Ghost	Open		36.00	77
1988	Match Girl w/ Lamppost	Closed	1992	68.00	68
1988	Mr. & Mrs. Fezziwig	Open		78.00	125
1988	Mrs. Crachit	Open		36.00	68
1988	Scrooge	Open		36.00	68
1989	Scrooge & Marley	Closed	1991	78.00	78
1989	Senior Carolers	Open		78.00	125
1986	Single Boy Caroler	Closed	1989	N/A	N/A
1986	Single Girl Caroler	Closed	1989	N/A	N/A
1986	Single Man Caroler	Closed	1989	N/A	N/A
1986	Single Woman Caroler	Closed	1989	N/A	N/A

*Quotes have been rounded up to nearest dollar

YEAR	ISSUE	EDITION LIMIT	YEAR RETD.	ISSUE PRICE	*QUOTE U.S.$
1989	Victorian Band	Closed	1989	144.00	144

Limited Edition Santas - E. Tisa

YEAR	ISSUE	EDITION LIMIT	YEAR RETD.	ISSUE PRICE	*QUOTE U.S.$
1994	Black Santa on Tricycle	600		160.00	228
1995	Countryside Santa	300		396.00	396
1991	European Santa w/Little Girl	1,000		118.00	205
1989	Father Christmas	Closed	1992	138.00	190
1989	Father Christmas-sm.	Closed	1992	48.00	56
1990	Jolly St. Nick	250		104.00	184
1989	Kris Kringle	Closed	1992	178.00	230
1989	Olde World Santa	Closed	1992	48.00	56
1993	Olde World Santa	300		270.00	383
1993	Pere Noel	500		350.00	496
1993	Renaissance Santa	450		210.00	326
1994	Santa on Tricycle	600		160.00	228
1993	Traditional Santa in Sleigh	400		160.00	241
1991	Victorian Santa	1,500		196.00	326

Cody

The American Spirits Collection - B. Austin

YEAR	ISSUE	EDITION LIMIT	YEAR RETD.	ISSUE PRICE	*QUOTE U.S.$
1996	Spirit of the Antelope	2,500		150.00	150
1996	Spirit of the Bear	2,500		130.00	130
1996	Spirit of the Buffalo	2,500		130.00	130
1996	Spirit of the Eagle	2,500		130.00	130
1996	Spirit of the Wolf	2,500		130.00	130

The Animal Tracks Collection - K. Cantrell

YEAR	ISSUE	EDITION LIMIT	YEAR RETD.	ISSUE PRICE	*QUOTE U.S.$
1995	Cougar	3,500		125.00	125
1995	Eagle	3,500		125.00	125
1995	Grizzly Bear	3,500		125.00	125
1995	Wolf	3,500		125.00	125

The Canine Collection - K. Cantrell

YEAR	ISSUE	EDITION LIMIT	YEAR RETD.	ISSUE PRICE	*QUOTE U.S.$
1996	Cocker Spaniel	2,500		140.00	140
1996	Dalmation	2,500		140.00	140
1996	German Shepherd	2,500		140.00	140
1996	Golden Retriever	2,500		140.00	140
1996	Labrador Retriever (black)	2,500		140.00	140
1996	Labrador Retriever (yellow)	2,500		140.00	140
1996	Rottweiler	2,500		140.00	140

The Equinus Collection - K. Cantrell

YEAR	ISSUE	EDITION LIMIT	YEAR RETD.	ISSUE PRICE	*QUOTE U.S.$
1995	Arabian	2,500		150.00	150
1995	Arabian Mare and Foal	2,500		190.00	190
1995	Clydesdale	2,500		190.00	190
1995	Quarterhorse	2,500		150.00	150
1995	Thoroughbred	2,500		150.00	150

Native American Spirits - W. Whitten

YEAR	ISSUE	EDITION LIMIT	YEAR RETD.	ISSUE PRICE	*QUOTE U.S.$
1996	Buffalo Dreamer	1,250		250.00	250
1996	Calling the Buffalo	1,250		250.00	250
1996	Cheyenne War Shield	1,250		250.00	250
1996	Flying Shield	1,250		250.00	250
1996	Peace Pipe	1,250		250.00	250
1996	War Bonnet	1,250		250.00	250
1996	Wolf Headdress	1,250		290.00	290

The Noble Americans Collection - C. Pardell

YEAR	ISSUE	EDITION LIMIT	YEAR RETD.	ISSUE PRICE	*QUOTE U.S.$
1995	Crazy Horse	2,500		150.00	150
1995	Pocahontas	2,500		150.00	150
1995	Red Cloud	2,500		150.00	150
1995	Sacajewca	2,500		150.00	150
1995	Sitting Bull	2,500		190.00	190

The North American Collection - K. Cantrell

YEAR	ISSUE	EDITION LIMIT	YEAR RETD.	ISSUE PRICE	*QUOTE U.S.$
1995	Artful Dodger	2,500		160.00	160
1995	Buffalo Spirit	2,500		160.00	160
1995	Eagles Realm	2,500		160.00	160
1995	Elusive	2,500		160.00	160
1995	Northern Express	2,500		160.00	160
1995	Spirit of the Wolf	2,500		160.00	160
1995	Wild Music	2,500		160.00	160
1995	Wind Blown	2,500		160.00	160

The Western Hats Collection - D. Lemon

YEAR	ISSUE	EDITION LIMIT	YEAR RETD.	ISSUE PRICE	*QUOTE U.S.$
1996	The Plainsman-1860's	2,500		150.00	150
1996	The Plainsman-1870's	2,500		150.00	150
1996	The Montana Peak-1880's	2,500		150.00	150
1996	The Bowler-1890's	2,500		150.00	150
1996	The Sombrero-1900's	2,500		150.00	150
1996	The Tom Mix-1920's	2,500		150.00	150
1996	The Buckaroo-1980's	2,500		150.00	150
1996	The Stetson-1990's	2,500		150.00	150

Creart

African Wildlife - Various

YEAR	ISSUE	EDITION LIMIT	YEAR RETD.	ISSUE PRICE	*QUOTE U.S.$
1987	African Elephant With Leaf-22 - Martinez	2,500	1996	230.00	298
1987	African Elephant-10 - Perez	2,500	1993	410.00	575
1987	African Lion-61 - Martinez	2,500	1996	260.00	338
1991	Breaking Away Gazelles-256 - Quesada	1,500		650.00	698
1993	Cape Buffalo-412 - Contreras	1,500		278.00	278
1987	Cob Antelope-46 - Perez	2,500	1996	310.00	398
1995	Elephant Tracks-472 - Perez	1,500		350.00	358
1987	Giraffe-43 - Perez	2,500	1996	250.00	338
1994	Grumbler Cape Buffalo-451 - Martinez	1,500		398.00	398
1990	Hippopotamus-55 - Quesada	Suspd.		420.00	438
1995	Lion-448 - Contreras	1,500		260.00	260
1996	Necking Signs Giraffes-909 - Estevez	950		198.00	198
1994	Numa Lion's Head-433 - Contreras	2,500		298.00	298
1986	Running Elephant-73 - Perez	2,500	1996	260.00	338
1992	Small African Elephant-271 - Perez	2,500	1993	320.00	320
1991	Sound of Warning Elephant-268 - Perez	2,500		500.00	518
1990	Symbol of Power Lion-40 - Quesada	2,500		398.00	398
1993	Travieso-358 - Perez	1,500		158.00	158
1987	White Rhinoceros-136 - Perez	2,500	1995	330.00	438
1987	Zebra-67 - Perez	Suspd.		305.00	398

American Wildlife - Various

YEAR	ISSUE	EDITION LIMIT	YEAR RETD.	ISSUE PRICE	*QUOTE U.S.$
1994	Ambushing Puma-508 - Nelson	1,950		150.00	150
1986	American Bison-121 - Perez	Susp.		400.00	498
1986	Bald Eagle-70 - Martinez	Susp.		730.00	900
1994	Briefly Rest Pumas-526 - Nelson	1,950		250.00	250
1993	Buenos Dias Jack Rabbit-229 - Martinez	1,500		158.00	158
1992	California Grizzly-238 - Perez	2,500	1996	270.00	278
1995	Canvasback Duck-902 - Nelson	2,500		95.00	95
1994	Catamountain-505 - Estevez	2,500	1996	118.00	118
1990	The Challenge, Rams-82 - Gonzalez	1,500		698.00	738
1995	Dall Sheep-295 - Martinez	950		240.00	270
1990	Dolphin, Back-148 - Perez	2,500	1996	210.00	250
1990	Dolphin, Front-142 - Perez	2,500	1996	210.00	250
1990	Dolphin, Middle-145 - Perez	2,500	1996	210.00	250
1988	Flamingo Flapping-175 - Perez	2,500	1996	230.00	298
1988	Flamingo Head Down-172 - Perez	2,500	1996	230.00	298
1988	Flamingo Upright-169 - Perez	2,500	1996	230.00	298
1994	Freedom Eagle-430 - Martinez	1,500		398.00	398
1990	Gray Wolf-88 - Quesada	2,500	1995	365.00	378
1987	Grizzley Bear-31 - Perez	2,500		210.00	278
1993	Howling Coyote-217 - Martinez	1,500	1995	199.00	218
1989	Jaguar-79 - Gonzalez	500		640.00	640
1988	Mammoth-112 - Martinez	2,500	1996	450.00	578
1991	Mischievous Raccoon-262 - Quesada	2,500		278.00	278
1995	Moose-478 - Contreras	1,500		298.00	298
1995	Mourning Dove-535 - Nelson	1,500		98.00	98
1994	Out of the Den Puma-523 - Estevez	1,500		130.00	130
1990	Over the Clouds Falcon-85 - Martinez	2,500		520.00	538
1994	Over the Top Puma-445 - Perez	1,500		398.00	398
1989	Penguins-R76 - Del Valle	Closed	1992	175.00	175
1995	Pheasant-903 - Nelson	2,500		95.00	95
1985	Pigeons-64 - Perez	Closed	1991	265.00	265
1991	Playmates Sparrows-265 - Martinez	2,500	1996	500.00	518
1986	Polar Bear-58 - Martinez	2,500	1995	200.00	258
1994	Puffins-511 - Estevez	1,500		258.00	258
1987	Puma-130 - Perez	2,500	1994	370.00	470
1993	The Red Fox-220 - Contreras	Suspd.		199.00	218
1994	Red Tail Hawk-520 - Nelson	1,950		58.00	58
1989	Rooster-R40 - Martinez	Closed	1990	290.00	290
1991	Royal Eagle With Snake-259 - Martinez	2,500		700.00	738
1987	Royal Eagle-49 - Martinez	Closed	1992	545.00	598
1993	Scent of Honey Bear-223 - Perez	1,500		358.00	358
1994	Singing to the Moon I Wolf-439 - Perez	1,500		398.00	398
1994	Singing to the Moon II Wolf-442 - Perez	1,500		358.00	358
1992	Soaring Royal Eagle-52 - Martinez	2,500		580.00	598
1992	Standing Whitetail Deer-109 - Martinez	2,500		364.00	378
1991	White Hunter Polar Bear-250 - Gonzalez	2,500		380.00	398
1990	White Tail Deer-151 - Martinez	2,500		380.00	478
1990	White Tail Doe-154 - Martinez	2,500		398.00	398
1990	White Tail Fawn-157 - Martinez	2,500		250.00	250

From Asia & Europe - Various

YEAR	ISSUE	EDITION LIMIT	YEAR RETD.	ISSUE PRICE	*QUOTE U.S.$
1988	Bengal Tiger-115 - Perez	Suspd.		440.00	520
1986	Deer-4 - Martinez	Closed	1992	560.00	600
1987	Drover of Camels-124 - Martinez	2,500	1996	650.00	718
1990	Giant Panda-244 - Martinez	Suspd.		280.00	298
1986	Indian Elephant Baby-16 - Perez	Closed	1995	200.00	200
1985	Indian Elephant Mother-25 - Perez	Closed	1995	485.00	538
1985	Marco Polo Sheep-37 - Martinez	2,500	1995	270.00	318
1996	Ranthambhore King Tiger-906 - Estevez	950		198.00	198
1987	Royal Owl-133 - Perez	Closed	1992	340.00	370
1995	Striking Power-292 - Perez	950		338.00	378
1985	Tiger-R55 - Martinez	Closed	1990	200.00	200

Crystal World

Animal Friends Collection - R. Nakai, unless otherwise noted

YEAR	ISSUE	EDITION LIMIT	YEAR RETD.	ISSUE PRICE	*QUOTE U.S.$
1983	Alligator	Closed	N/A	46.00	46
1990	Baby Dinosaur - T. Suzuki	Closed	N/A	50.00	50
1990	Barney Dog - T. Suzuki	Closed	N/A	32.00	32
1984	Beaver	Closed	N/A	30.00	30
1990	Betsy Bunny - T. Suzuki	Closed	N/A	32.00	32
1984	Butterfly	Closed	N/A	36.00	36
1994	Cheese Mouse	Open		53.00	53
1990	Clara Cow - T. Suzuki	Closed	N/A	32.00	32
1984	Dachshund	Closed	N/A	28.00	28
1984	Dog	Closed	N/A	28.00	28
1984	Donkey	Closed	N/A	40.00	40
1987	Duckling - T. Suzuki	Closed	N/A	60.00	60
1983	Elephant	Closed	N/A	40.00	40
1995	Fido the Dog - T. Suzuki	Open		27.00	27
1995	Frisky Fido - T. Suzuki	Closed	1996	27.00	27
1990	Georgie Giraffe - T. Suzuki	Closed	N/A	32.00	32
1990	Henry Hippo - T. Suzuki	Closed	N/A	32.00	32
1990	Jumbo Elephant - T. Suzuki	Open		32.00	32
1984	Koala Bear	Closed	N/A	50.00	50
1987	Large Circus Puppy	Closed	N/A	50.00	50
1985	Large Elephant	Closed	N/A	54.00	54
1984	Large Hippo	Closed	N/A	50.00	50
1984	Large Kangaroo	Closed	N/A	50.00	50
1985	Large Lion	Closed	N/A	60.00	60
1983	Large Mouse	Closed	N/A	36.00	36
1987	Large Panda	Closed	1995	45.00	45
1983	Large Pig	Closed	N/A	50.00	50
1987	Large Playful Pup	Closed	N/A	85.00	85
1987	Large Poodle	Closed	N/A	64.00	64
1983	Large Rabbit	Closed	N/A	50.00	50
1987	Large Rabbit with Carrot	Closed	N/A	55.00	55
1984	Large Racoon	Closed	N/A	44.00	44
1987	Large Snowbunny	Closed	N/A	45.00	45
1983	Large Turtle	Closed	N/A	56.00	56
1995	Ling Ling - T. Suzuki	Open		53.00	53
1983	Medium Mouse	Closed	N/A	28.00	28
1983	Medium Pig	Closed	N/A	32.00	32
1983	Medium Turtle	Closed	N/A	38.00	38
1990	Mikey Monkey - T. Suzuki	Closed	N/A	32.00	32
1986	Mini Butterfly - N. Mulargia	Closed	N/A	15.00	15
1986	Mini Dachshund - N. Mulargia	Closed	N/A	15.00	15
1986	Mini Frog Mushroom - N. Mulargia	Closed	N/A	15.00	15
1986	Mini Koala - N. Mulargia	Closed	N/A	15.00	15
1986	Mini Mouse - N. Mulargia	Closed	N/A	15.00	15
1986	Mini Rabbit - N. Mulargia	Closed	N/A	15.00	15
1989	Mini Rainbow Dog	Closed	N/A	25.00	25
1989	Mini Rainbow Owl	Closed	N/A	25.00	25
1989	Mini Rainbow Penguin	Closed	N/A	25.00	25
1989	Mini Rainbow Squirrel	Closed	N/A	25.00	25
1986	Mini Swan - N. Mulargia	Open		15.00	28
1984	Mini Turtle	Closed	N/A	18.00	18
1987	Mother Koala and Cub	Closed	N/A	55.00	55
1983	Mouse Standing	Closed	N/A	34.00	34
1994	Mozart - T. Suzuki	Open		48.00	48
1994	Owls - N. Mulargia	Open		53.00	53
1984	Peacock	Closed	N/A	50.00	50
1984	Penguin	Closed	N/A	34.00	34
1987	Penguin On Cube	Closed	1996	30.00	30
1995	Percy Piglet - T. Suzuki	Open		19.00	19
1993	Pig - N. Mulargia	Closed	1995	50.00	50
1994	Playful Pup - T. Suzuki	Open		53.00	53
1993	Playful Seal - T. Suzuki	Open		42.00	42
1984	Poodle	Closed	N/A	30.00	30
1984	Porcupine	Closed	N/A	42.00	42
1987	Posing Penguin	Closed	N/A	85.00	85
1990	Puppy Love - T. Suzuki	Closed	N/A	45.00	45
1993	Puppy-Gram - T. Suzuki	Open		58.00	58
1985	Racoon	Closed	N/A	50.00	50
1987	Rhinoceros	Closed	N/A	55.00	55
1994	Seal	Closed	1996	46.00	46
1987	Small Circus Puppy	Closed	N/A	28.00	28
1984	Small Hippo	Closed	N/A	30.00	30
1984	Small Kangaroo	Closed	N/A	34.00	34
1984	Small Koala	Closed	N/A	28.00	28
1985	Small Lion	Closed	N/A	36.00	36
1983	Small Mouse	Closed	N/A	20.00	20
1987	Small Panda	Closed	N/A	30.00	30
1983	Small Pig	Closed	N/A	22.00	22
1987	Small Playful Pup	Closed	1995	32.00	32
1987	Small Poodle	Closed	1994	35.00	35
1983	Small Rabbit	Closed	N/A	28.00	28
1987	Small Rabbit with Carrot	Closed	N/A	32.00	32
1984	Small Racoon	Closed	N/A	30.00	30
1987	Small Racoon	Closed	N/A	30.00	30
1987	Small Snowbunny	Closed	N/A	25.00	25
1983	Small Turtle	Closed	N/A	28.00	28
1987	Small Walrus - T. Suzuki	Closed	N/A	60.00	60
1991	Spike	Closed	N/A	50.00	50
1991	Spot	Closed	N/A	50.00	50
1985	Squirrel	Closed	1994	30.00	30
1994	Sweetie - T. Suzuki	Open		28.00	28
1995	Tea Time	Open		50.00	50
1992	Trumpeting Elephant - T. Suzuki	Closed	1996	50.00	50
1993	Turtle	Closed	1996	65.00	65
1986	Unicorn	Closed	1994	110.00	110
1987	Walrus	Closed	N/A	70.00	70
1995	Wilbur in Love - N. Mulargia	Open		90.00	90
1994	Wilbur the Pig - T. Suzuki	Open		48.00	48

Bird Collection - R. Nakai, unless otherwise noted

YEAR	ISSUE	EDITION LIMIT	YEAR RETD.	ISSUE PRICE	*QUOTE U.S.$
1986	Bird Bath - N. Mulargia	Closed	1989	54.00	75
1984	Bird Family	Closed	1990	22.00	35
1984	Love Bird	Closed	1988	44.00	65
1986	Love Birds	Closed	1992	54.00	75
1990	Ollie Owl - T. Suzuki	Closed	1993	32.00	40
1983	Owl Standing	Closed	1987	40.00	70
1983	Owl-Large	Closed	1987	44.00	75

*Quotes have been rounded up to nearest dollar

YEAR ISSUE		EDITION LIMIT	YEAR RETD.	ISSUE PRICE	*QUOTE U.S.$
1983	Owl-Small	Closed	1987	22.00	36
1991	Parrot Couple	Closed	1992	90.00	100
1985	Parrot-Extra Large	Closed	1988	300.00	450
1987	Parrot-Large	Closed	1993	130.00	170
1987	Parrot-Small	Closed	1989	30.00	45
1985	Parrot-Small	Closed	1989	100.00	110
1990	Tree Top Owls - T. Suzuki	Closed	1993	96.00	96
1990	Wise Owl - T. Suzuki	Closed	1993	55.00	65
1990	Wise Owl-Small - T. Suzuki	Closed	1993	40.00	65

By The Beautiful Sea Collection - R. Nakai, unless otherwise noted

1992	Baby Seal - T. Suzuki	Open		21.00	21
1991	Beaver	Closed	1996	47.00	47
1992	Cute Crab - T. Suzuki	Open		27.00	32
1988	Dancing Dolphin	Closed	N/A	130.00	130
1993	Extra Large Oyster with Pearl	Closed	1996	75.00	75
1984	Fish	Closed	N/A	36.00	36
1996	Freddy Frog	Open		30.00	30
1996	Frieda Frog	Open		37.00	37
1993	Harbor Lighthouse - N. Mulargia	Open		75.00	79
1988	Hatching Sea Turtle - T. Suzuki	Open		45.00	47
1983	Large Crab	Closed	N/A	20.00	20
1988	Large Island Paradise	Closed	N/A	90.00	90
1988	Large Lighthouse	Closed	1994	150.00	150
1983	Large Oyster	Closed	1994	30.00	30
1983	Mini Oyster	Closed	N/A	12.00	12
1994	Oscar Otter - T. Suzuki	Open		53.00	53
1987	Palm Tree	Closed	N/A	160.00	160
1996	Pelican	Open		65.00	65
1996	Penguin On Cube	Open		48.00	48
1991	Penguin On Cube	Closed	1996	40.00	40
1992	Playful Dolphins - T. Suzuki	Closed	1996	60.00	60
1993	Playful Seal - T. Suzuki	Open		45.00	45
1993	Sailboat	Open		100.00	115
1994	Seal	Closed	1996	47.00	47
1992	Seaside Pelican - T. Suzuki	Closed	1995	55.00	55
1983	Small Crab	Closed	N/A	28.00	28
1988	Small Dolphin	Closed	N/A	55.00	55
1988	Small Island Paradise	Closed	N/A	50.00	50
1988	Small Lighthouse	Open		80.00	80
1983	Small Oyster	Closed	1994	18.00	18
1992	Tropical Fish	Closed	1995	95.00	95
1992	Tuxedo Penguin	Closed	1995	75.00	75
1992	The Whales - T. Suzuki	Closed	1994	60.00	60

By The Lake Collection - R. Nakai, unless otherwise noted

1985	Butterfly Caterpillar	Closed	N/A	40.00	40
1985	Butterfly on Daisy	Closed	N/A	30.00	30
1984	Duck	Closed	N/A	30.00	30
1990	Duck Family	Closed	N/A	70.00	70
1984	Frog & Mushroom	Closed	N/A	46.00	46
1987	King Swan	Closed	N/A	110.00	110
1983	Large Frog	Closed	N/A	30.00	30
1996	Large Love Swans - N. Mulargia	Open		252.00	252
1983	Large Swan	Closed	N/A	44.00	44
1985	Large Swan	Closed	N/A	70.00	70
1987	Large Swan	Closed	1996	70.00	70
1986	Love Swan - N. Mulargia	Closed	N/A	70.00	70
1995	Love Swans - N. Mulargia	Open		83.00	83
1987	Medium Swan	Open		45.00	63
1985	Medium Swan	Closed	N/A	54.00	54
1983	Mini Frog	Closed	N/A	14.00	14
1985	Mini Swan	Open		28.00	29
1983	Small Frog	Closed	N/A	26.00	26
1985	Small Swan	Closed	N/A	44.00	44
1983	Small Swan	Closed	N/A	28.00	28
1987	Small Swan	Open		32.00	47
1990	Swan Family - T. Suzuki	Closed	N/A	70.00	70

Castles and Legends - R. Nakai, unless otherwise noted

1991	Castle In The Sky	Closed	1994	150.00	150
1994	Castle Rainbow Rainbow Mtn. Bs.	Open		1575.00	1575
1994	Castle Royale/Clear Mountain Bs	Open		1300.00	1300
1989	Dragon Baby	Closed	1994	80.00	80
1996	Emerald Castle	Open		105.00	105
1990	I Love You Unicorn - N. Mulargia	Closed	N/A	58.00	58
1987	Ice Castle	Closed	N/A	150.00	150
1988	Imperial Castle	Open		320.00	345
1988	Imperial Ice Castle	Closed	N/A	320.00	320
1993	Large Fantasy Castle	Open		230.00	245
1995	Large Fantasy Coach - N. Mulargia	Open		368.00	368
1989	Magic Fairy	Closed	N/A	40.00	40
1991	Majestic Castle - A. Kato	Open		390.00	390
1993	Medium Fantasy Castle	Open		130.00	142
1995	Medium Fantasy Coach - N. Mulargia	Open		158.00	158
1992	Mini Fantasy Castle - N. Mulargia	Open		40.00	40
1995	Mini Mouse Coach - N. Mulargia	Open		52.00	52
1989	Mini Rainbow Castle	Open		60.00	62
1988	Mystic Castle	Open		90.00	90
1988	Mystic Ice Castle	Closed	N/A	90.00	90
1990	Pegasus - N. Mulargia	Closed	N/A	50.00	50
1987	Rainbow Castle	Open		150.00	184
1990	Rainbow Unicorn - N. Mulargia	Open		50.00	58
1992	Small Fantasy Castle	Open		85.00	95
1995	Small Fantasy Coach - N. Mulargia	Open		100.00	100
1995	Small Mouse Coach - N. Mulargia	Open		95.00	95
1989	Star Fairy	Closed	N/A	65.00	65
1989	Starlight Castle	Closed	1994	155.00	155

YEAR ISSUE		EDITION LIMIT	YEAR RETD.	ISSUE PRICE	*QUOTE U.S.$
1995	Treasure Chest	Open		63.00	63
1989	Unicorn & Friend	Closed	N/A	100.00	100
1990	Unicorn - N. Mulargia	Closed	1994	38.00	38

Clown Collection - R. Nakai, unless otherwise noted

1985	Acrobatic Clown	Closed	N/A	50.00	50
1992	Baby Clown - N. Mulargia	Closed	N/A	30.00	30
1985	Baseball Clown	Closed	N/A	54.00	54
1996	Bo-Bo The Clown - N. Mulargia	Open		53.00	53
1984	Clown	Closed	N/A	42.00	42
1985	Clown On Unicycle	Closed	N/A	54.00	54
1992	Flower Clown - N. Mulargia	Closed	N/A	70.00	70
1985	Golf Clown	Closed	N/A	54.00	54
1985	Juggler	Closed	N/A	54.00	54
1985	Large Clown	Closed	N/A	42.00	42
1985	Large Jack In The Box	Closed	N/A	64.00	64
1985	Small Clown	Closed	N/A	30.00	30
1985	Small Jack In The Box	Closed	N/A	24.00	24
1985	Tennis Clown	Closed	N/A	54.00	54

Decorative Item Collection (Paperweights) - Various

1993	100 mm Diamond - R. Nakai	Open		525.00	525
1996	40 mm Diamond - R. Nakai	Open		48.00	48
1993	50 mm Diamond - R. Nakai	Open		70.00	70
1993	75 mm Diamond - R. Nakai	Open		285.00	285
1990	Baseball - I. Nakamura	Closed	N/A	170.00	170
1995	Boston "Cityscape" Paperweight - R. Nakai	Open		105.00	105
1989	Chicago - I. Nakamura	Open		150.00	150
1996	Crystal Egg And Stand - R. Nakai	Open		83.00	83
1991	Dallas Skyline - I. Nakamura	Open		180.00	180
1988	Empire State - G. Veith	Closed	N/A	120.00	120
1996	Fabulous Fifties Jukebox - N. Mulargia	Open		79.00	79
1990	Fishing - I. Nakamura	Closed	N/A	170.00	170
1990	Golfing - I. Nakamura	Closed	N/A	170.00	170
1992	Heart Clock - R. Nakai	Closed	N/A	100.00	100
1993	Manatee - R. Nakai	Open		125.00	130
1992	Manhattan Reflections - R. Nakai	Open		95.00	95
1995	Med. Boston Skyline Paperweight - R. Nakai	Open		80.00	80
1995	Med. Chicago Skyline Clock Paperweight - R. Nakai	Closed	1996	158.00	158
1994	Med. NY Skyline Paperweight - G. Veith	Open		80.00	80
1995	Med. Philadelphia Skyline Paperweight - R. Nakai	Open		80.00	80
1994	Med. San Francisco Skyline Pwght. - G. Veith	Open		80.00	80
1994	Med. Wash. DC Skyline Paperweight - G. Veith	Open		80.00	80
1988	N.Y. Skyline - G. Veith	Open		100.00	100
1988	Nativity - R. Nakai	Closed	1994	100.00	100
1992	Niagara Falls Pwght. - R. Nakai	Open		85.00	85
1994	NY "Cityscape" Pwght. - G. Veith	Open		105.00	105
1994	NY Dome Paperweight - G. Veith	Closed	1995	75.00	75
1994	NY Skyline Clock Paperweight - R. Nakai	Closed	1996	158.00	158
1995	Philadelphia "Cityscape" Paperweight - R. Nakai	Open		105.00	105
1991	Polar Bear - R. Nakai	Open		98.00	98
1994	S.F. Skyline Clock Paperweight - R. Nakai	Closed	1996	158.00	158
1994	San Francisco "Cityscape" Pwght. - G. Veith	Open		105.00	105
1989	San Francisco - I. Nakamura	Open		150.00	150
1994	San Francisco Dome Paperweight - G. Veith	Closed	1995	75.00	75
1995	San Francisco Skyline Clock Paperweight - R. Nakai	Closed	1996	158.00	158
1992	Small NY - G. Veith	Open		45.00	45
1993	Small San Francisco Skyline	Open		45.00	45
1990	Tennis - I. Nakamura	Closed	N/A	170.00	170
1994	Wash. DC "Cityscape" Paperweight - R. Nakai	Open		105.00	105
1994	Wash. DC Skyline Clock Paperweight - R. Nakai	Closed	1996	158.00	158
1989	Washington - I. Nakamura	Open		150.00	150
1994	Washington DC Dome Paperweight - G. Veith	Closed	1995	75.00	75
1994	Washington Vietnam Memorial Pwt. - R. Nakai	Closed	1996	105.00	105

Fruit Collection - R. Nakai

1985	Large Apple	Open		44.00	68
1991	Large Pineapple	Closed	N/A	42.00	42
1985	Medium Apple	Open		30.00	39
1993	Medium Apple with Red Heart	Open		37.00	39
1991	Medium Pineapple	Closed	N/A	27.00	27
1987	Mini Apple	Open		15.00	16
1985	Pear	Closed	N/A	30.00	30
1996	Pineapple	Open		53.00	53
1985	Small Apple	Open		15.00	15
1993	Small Apple with Red Heart	Open		21.00	22
1991	Small Pineapple	Closed	N/A	16.00	16
1985	Strawberries	Closed	N/A	28.00	28

The Gambler Collection - R. Nakai, unless otherwise noted

1993	Large Rolling Dice	Open		60.00	60
1993	Large Slot Machine - T. Suzuki	Open		83.00	83
1991	Lucky 7	Closed	N/A	50.00	50
1994	Lucky Roll	Open		95.00	95
1993	Medium Rolling Dice	Open		48.00	48
1992	Mini Rolling Dice	Open		32.00	32
1991	Mini Slot Machine	Open		30.00	30

YEAR ISSUE		EDITION LIMIT	YEAR RETD.	ISSUE PRICE	*QUOTE U.S.$
1991	Rolling Dice - T. Suzuki	Closed	N/A	110.00	110
1991	Small Dice	Open		27.00	27
1993	Small Rolling Dice	Closed	1996	40.00	40
1991	Small Slot Machine - T. Suzuki	Open		58.00	58
1994	Super Slot	Open		295.00	295

Holiday Treasure Collection - R. Nakai, unless otherwise noted

1984	Angel	Closed	N/A	28.00	28
1994	Cathedral w/Rainbow Base	Open		104.00	104
1994	Country Church	Open		53.00	53
1994	Country Church w/Rainbow Base	Open		63.00	63
1994	Extra Large Christmas Tree	Open		315.00	315
1996	Frosty	Open		41.00	41
1995	Happy Birthday Cake	Open		63.00	63
1991	Holy Angel Blowing A Trumpet	Open		38.00	38
1991	Holy Angel Holding A Candle - T. Suzuki	Open		38.00	38
1991	Holy Angel Playing A Harp - T. Suzuki	Open		38.00	38
1985	Large Angel	Closed	N/A	30.00	30
1995	Large Angel	Open		53.00	53
1985	Large Christmas Tree	Open		126.00	126
1987	Large Rainbow Christmas Tree	Closed	1995	40.00	40
1985	Mini Angel	Closed	1996	16.00	16
1985	Mini Christmas Tree	Closed	N/A	10.00	10
1986	Nativity - N. Mulargia	Open		150.00	179
1985	Small Christmas Tree	Open		50.00	68
1991	Small Nativity - T. Suzuki	Open		85.00	90
1987	Small Rainbow Christmas Tree	Closed	1993	25.00	25
1984	Snowman	Closed	N/A	38.00	38
1990	Trumpeting Angel	Closed	N/A	60.00	60

Kitty Land Collection - T. Suzuki, unless otherwise noted

1991	Calamity Kitty	Open		60.00	60
1984	Cat - R. Nakai	Closed	N/A	36.00	36
1990	Cat N Mouse	Closed	1996	45.00	45
1992	Country Cat	Open		60.00	62
1990	The Curious Cat	Open		62.00	62
1991	Hello Birdie	Open		65.00	68
1992	Kitten in Basket - C. Kido	Open		35.00	40
1993	Kitty Kare	Closed	1995	70.00	70
1991	Kitty with Butterfly	Closed	N/A	60.00	60
1991	Kitty with Heart	Open		27.00	29
1987	Large Cat with Ball - R. Nakai	Closed	N/A	70.00	70
1991	Large Curious Cat	Open		90.00	90
1993	Large Playful Kitty	Closed	1996	50.00	50
1990	Moonlight Cat - R. Nakai	Closed	1993	100.00	100
1995	Moonlight Kitties	Open		83.00	83
1991	Peekaboo Kitties	Open		65.00	65
1993	Pinky	Closed	1996	50.00	50
1992	Playful Kitty	Open		32.00	32
1989	Rainbow Mini Cat - R. Nakai	Closed	N/A	25.00	25
1991	Rockabye Kitty - R. Nakai	Open		80.00	83
1992	See Saw Pals - A. Kato	Open		40.00	41
1987	Small Cat with Ball - R. Nakai	Closed	1993	32.00	32
1991	Strolling Kitties	Closed	1993	65.00	65

Limited Edition Collection Series - Various

1986	Airplane -T. Suzuki	Closed	1992	400.00	50[illegible]
1995	Classic Motorcycle -T. Suzuki	950		420.00	42[illegible]
1993	Country Gristmill -T. Suzuki	1,250		320.00	34[illegible]
1986	Crucifix - N. Mulargia	Closed	1992	300.00	40[illegible]
1991	Cruise Ship -T. Suzuki	1000		2000.00	210[illegible]
1989	Dream Castle - R. Nakai	500		9000.00	1000[illegible]
1986	The Eiffel Tower -T. Suzuki	2000		1000.00	130[illegible]
1991	Ellis Island - R. Nakai	Closed	1992	450.00	50[illegible]
1996	The Empire State Bldg. - R. Nakai	475		1315.00	131[illegible]
1993	Enchanted Castle - R. Nakai	750		800.00	89[illegible]
1985	Extra Large Empire State Bldg. - R. Nakai	Closed	1992	1000.00	130[illegible]
1989	Grand Castle - R. Nakai	Closed	1996	2500.00	250[illegible]
1995	Independence Hall - R. Nakai	750		370.00	37[illegible]
1987	Large Empire State Bldg. - R. Nakai	2000		650.00	70[illegible]
1987	Large US Capitol Bldg. -T. Suzuki	Closed	1992	1000.00	110[illegible]
1987	Manhattanscape - G. Veith	Closed	1992	1000.00	110[illegible]
1996	Merry-Go-Round - N. Mulargia	750		280.00	28[illegible]
1993	Riverboat - N. Mulargia	350		570.00	60[illegible]
1992	Santa Maria - N. Mulargia	Closed	1993	1000.00	105[illegible]
1988	Small Eiffel Tower -T. Suzuki	2000		500.00	60[illegible]
1989	Space Shuttle Launch -T. Suzuki	Closed	1992	900.00	100[illegible]
1987	Taj Mahal -T. Suzuki	2000		2000.00	210[illegible]
1990	Tower Bridge -T. Suzuki	Closed	1992	600.00	65[illegible]
1993	Victorian House - N. Mulargia	Closed	1996	190.00	19[illegible]
1992	The White House - R. Nakai	200	1993	3000.00	300[illegible]

New York Collection - R. Nakai, unless otherwise noted

1995	Chrysler Building	Open		275.00	27[illegible]
1993	Holiday Empire State Bldg. - N. Mulargia	Open		205.00	20[illegible]
1992	Large Contemp. Empire State Bldg. - A. Kato	Closed	1996	475.00	47[illegible]
1989	Liberty Island - N. Mulargia	Open		75.00	[illegible]
1990	Manhattan Island	Open		240.00	24[illegible]
1992	Med. Contemp. Empire State Bldg.	Open		170.00	1[illegible]
1987	Medium Empire State Bldg.	Open		250.00	25[illegible]
1987	Medium Statue of Liberty	Open		120.00	1[illegible]
1991	Mini Empire State Bldg.	Open		60.00	[illegible]
1992	Mini Empire State Bldg. w/Windows	Open		74.00	[illegible]
1992	Mini Statue Of Liberty	Open		50.00	[illegible]
1992	Small Contemp. Empire State Bldg.	Closed	1996	95.00	[illegible]

74 Collectors' Information Bureau

*Quotes have been rounded up to nearest dollar

Year Issue		Edition Limit	Year Retd.	Issue Price	*Quote U.S.$
1992	Small Contemp. Empire State Bldg. MV	Open		95.00	95
1987	Small Empire State Bldg.	Open		120.00	120
1993	Small Manhattan Island - N. Mulargia	Open		105.00	105
1993	Small Rainbow Contemp. Empire	Open		95.00	95
1987	Small Statue of Liberty - N. Mulargia	Open		50.00	50
1992	Small Twin Towers	Open		130.00	130
1985	The Statue of Liberty	Open		250.00	250
1991	World Trade Center Bldg.	Open		170.00	170

Religious Moment Collection - N. Mulargia, unless otherwise noted

Year Issue		Edition Limit	Year Retd.	Issue Price	*Quote U.S.$
1987	Church - T. Suzuki	Closed	N/A	40.00	40
1987	Cross On Mountain	Closed	N/A	30.00	30
1992	Cross with Rose	Closed	N/A	30.00	30
1987	Crucifix	Closed	N/A	50.00	50
1987	Crucifix On Mountain	Closed	N/A	40.00	40
1987	Face Of Christ - R. Nakai	Closed	N/A	35.00	35
1987	Large Cross On Mountain	Closed	N/A	85.00	85
1992	Peace On Earth - I. Nakamura	Closed	1995	95.00	95
1987	Small Cross	Closed	1993	40.00	40
1987	Star Of David - R. Nakai	Closed	1993	40.00	40

Spring Parade Collection - Various

Year Issue		Edition Limit	Year Retd.	Issue Price	*Quote U.S.$
1990	African Violet - I. Nakamura	Open		32.00	32
1996	American Beauty Rose - N. Mulargia	Open		53.00	53
1992	Barrel Cactus - I. Nakamura	Closed	1995	45.00	45
1991	Blossom Bunny - T. Suzuki	Open		42.00	42
1991	Bunnies On Ice - T. Suzuki	Closed	1996	58.00	58
1991	Bunny Buddy with Carrot - T. Suzuki	Open		32.00	32
1992	Candleholder - N. Mulargia	Closed	1995	125.00	125
1991	Cheep Cheep - T. Suzuki	Open		35.00	35
1990	Crocus - R. Nakai	Closed	N/A	45.00	45
1992	Cute Bunny - T. Suzuki	Closed	1995	38.00	38
1995	Desert Cactus - N. Mulargia	Open		48.00	48
1994	The Enchanted Rose - R. Nakai	Open		126.00	126
1985	Flower Basket - R. Nakai	Closed	1995	36.00	36
1992	Flowering Cactus - I. Nakamura	Closed	1996	58.00	58
1992	Half Dozen Flower Arrangement - N. Mulargia	Closed	1996	20.00	20
1992	Happy Heart - N. Mulargia	Closed	1996	25.00	25
1992	Hummingbird - T. Suzuki	Open		58.00	58
1990	Hyacinth - I. Nakamura	Open		50.00	50
1989	Large Windmill - R. Nakai	Closed	1991	160.00	160
1992	Long Stem Rose - N. Mulargia	Open		35.00	35
1994	Long Stem Rose in Vase - R. Nakai	Open		82.00	82
1992	Loving Hearts - N. Mulargia	Open		35.00	35
1995	Medium Wedding Couple - N. Mulargia	Open		63.00	63
1992	Mini Hummingbird - T. Suzuki	Open		29.00	29
1992	Mini Wedding Couple - N. Mulargia	Open		30.00	30
1995	Pink Rose - R. Nakai	Open		53.00	53
1995	Pink Rose in Vase - R. Nakai	Open		41.00	41
1991	Rainbow Mini Butterfly - R. Nakai	Open		27.00	27
1994	Rainbow Rose - N. Mulargia	Open		82.00	82
1987	Red Rose - R. Nakai	Open		35.00	35
1992	Rose Bouquet - I. Nakamura	Closed	N/A	100.00	100
1987	Small Flower Basket - R. Nakai	Closed	N/A	40.00	40
1996	Small Rose Bouquet - R. Nakai	Open		45.00	45
1989	Small Windmill - R. Nakai	Closed	1993	90.00	90
1993	Songbirds - I. Nakamura	Open		90.00	90
1995	Spring Butterfly - R. Nakai	Open		62.00	62
1989	Spring Chick - R. Nakai	Open		50.00	53
1992	Spring Flowers - T. Suzuki	Open		40.00	40
1996	Water Lily, Medium, AB - R. Nakai	Open		210.00	210
1992	Waterfront Village - N. Mulargia	Open		190.00	190
1989	Wedding Couple - N. Mulargia	Open		75.00	75
1985	Wedding Couple - R. Nakai	Closed	N/A	38.00	38
1987	White Rose - R. Nakai	Closed	N/A	35.00	35

Teddyland Collection - Various

Year Issue		Edition Limit	Year Retd.	Issue Price	*Quote U.S.$
1995	Baby Bear's Christmas - T. Suzuki	Open		48.00	48
1990	Baron Von Teddy - T. Suzuki	Closed	1993	60.00	60
1987	Beach Teddies - N. Mulargia	Open		60.00	60
1992	Billard Buddies - T. Suzuki	Open		70.00	70
1993	Black Jack Teddies - N. Mulargia	Open		97.00	97
1990	Choo Choo Teddy - T. Suzuki	Closed	1993	100.00	100
1991	Christmas Wreath Teddy - T. Suzuki	Closed	1993	70.00	70
1995	CompuBear - N. Mulargia	Open		63.00	63
1996	Cuddly Bear - R. Nakai	Open		48.00	48
1993	Flower Teddy - T. Suzuki	Open		50.00	50
1995	Fly A Kite Teddy - T. Suzuki	Open		41.00	41
1995	Get Well Teddy - R. Nakai	Closed	1996	48.00	48
1989	Golfing Teddies - R. Nakai	Open		100.00	100
1991	Gumball Teddy - T. Suzuki	Closed	1996	63.00	63
1989	Happy Birthday Teddy - R. Nakai	Open		50.00	50
1991	Heart Bear - T. Suzuki	Open		27.00	27
1991	High Chair Teddy - T. Suzuki	Closed	1993	75.00	75
1988	I Love You Teddy - N. Mulargia	Open		50.00	50
1994	I Love You Teddy Couple - N. Mulargia	Open		95.00	95
1995	I Love You Teddy w/lg. Heart - R. Nakai	Open		48.00	48
1992	Ice Cream Teddies - N. Mulargia	Open		55.00	55
1988	Large Bouquet Teddy - N. Mulargia	Closed	N/A	50.00	50
1988	Large Surfing Teddy - R. Nakai	Closed	N/A	80.00	80
1983	Large Teddy Bear - R. Nakai	Closed	N/A	68.00	68
1987	Loving Teddies - N. Mulargia	Open		75.00	75
1991	Luck Of The Irish - R. Nakai	Closed	1993	60.00	60
1983	Medium Teddy Bear - R. Nakai	Closed	N/A	44.00	44
1991	Merry Christmas Teddy - T. Suzuki	Open		55.00	55
1986	Mini Teddy - N. Mulargia	Closed	N/A	15.00	15
1985	Mother and Cub - R. Nakai	Closed	N/A	64.00	64
1990	Mountaineer Teddy - N. Mulargia	Closed	N/A	80.00	80
1991	My Favorite Picture - T. Suzuki	Open		45.00	45
1992	Patriotic Teddy - N. Mulargia	Open		30.00	30
1991	Play It Again Ted - T. Suzuki	Open		65.00	65
1991	Playground Teddy - R. Kido	Closed	N/A	90.00	90
1989	Rainbow Mini Bear - R. Nakai	Closed	N/A	25.00	25
1990	Rainbow Teddies - N. Mulargia	Closed	1993	95.00	95
1990	Rocking Horse Teddy - N. Mulargia	Closed	N/A	80.00	80
1987	Sailing Teddies - N. Mulargia	Open		100.00	100
1991	Santa Bear Christmas - T. Suzuki	Open		70.00	70
1991	Santa Bear Sleighride - T. Suzuki	Open		70.00	70
1991	School Bears - H. Serino	Closed	1993	75.00	75
1991	Scuba Bear - T. Suzuki	Closed	1993	65.00	65
1989	Shipwreck Teddies - N. Mulargia	Closed	1993	100.00	100
1992	Singing Baby Bear - T. Suzuki	Open		55.00	55
1987	Skateboard Teddy - R. Nakai	Closed	1993	30.00	30
1987	Skiing Teddy - R. Nakai	Open		50.00	50
1992	Small Beach Teddies - N. Mulargia	Open		55.00	55
1988	Small Bouquet Teddy - N. Mulargia	Open		35.00	35
1990	Small Loving Teddies - N. Mulargia	Open		60.00	60
1983	Small Teddy Bear - R. Nakai	Closed	N/A	28.00	28
1989	Speedboat Teddies - R. Nakai	Open		90.00	90
1990	Storytime Teddies - T. Suzuki	Open		70.00	70
1987	Surfing Teddy - R. Nakai	Closed	1993	45.00	45
1991	Swinging Teddy - N. Mulargia	Open		100.00	100
1988	Teddies At Eight - N. Mulargia	Open		100.00	100
1988	Teddies With Heart - R. Nakai	Open		45.00	45
1989	Teddy Balloon - R. Nakai	Closed	1993	70.00	70
1994	Teddy Bear - R. Nakai	Open		63.00	63
1987	Teddy Bear Christmas - R. Nakai	Open		100.00	100
1994	Teddy Bear with Rainbow Base - R. Nakai	Open		75.00	75
1988	Teddy Family - N. Mulargia	Closed	1993	50.00	50
1995	Teddy's Self Portrait - T. Suzuki	Open		53.00	53
1987	Teeter Totter Teddies - N. Mulargia	Closed	1993	65.00	65
1988	Touring Teddies - N. Mulargia	Open		90.00	90
1990	Tricycle Teddy - T. Suzuki	Closed	1993	40.00	40
1991	Trim A Tree Teddy - R. Nakai	Closed	1996	50.00	50
1989	Vanity Teddy - R. Nakai	Closed	1993	100.00	100
1989	Windsurf Teddy - R. Nakai	Closed	1993	85.00	85
1988	Winter Teddies - N. Mulargia	Closed	N/A	90.00	90

The Voyage Collection - Various

Year Issue		Edition Limit	Year Retd.	Issue Price	*Quote U.S.$
1995	Amish Buggy - R. Nakai	Open		160.00	160
1995	Amish Buggy w/Wood Base - R. Nakai	Open		190.00	190
1994	Bermuda Rig Sailboat - R. Nakai	Open		105.00	105
1984	Classic Car - T. Suzuki	Closed	N/A	160.00	160
1993	Express Train - N. Mulargia	Closed	1993	95.00	95
1992	Fire Engine - T. Suzuki	Open		100.00	100
1991	Large Cable Car - T. Suzuki	Open		130.00	130
1993	Large San Francisco Cable Car - R. Nakai	Open		59.00	59
1990	Large Train Set - T. Suzuki	Closed	N/A	480.00	480
1984	Limousine - R. Nakai	Closed	N/A	46.00	46
1994	Mainsail Sailboat - R. Nakai	Open		230.00	230
1992	Mini Bi-Plane - T. Suzuki	Open		65.00	65
1992	Mini Cable Car - T. Suzuki	Closed	1996	40.00	40
1995	Mini Cruise Ship - N. Mulargia	Open		105.00	105
1990	Orbiting Space Shuttle - T. Suzuki	Open		300.00	300
1984	Pickup Track - R. Nakai	Closed	N/A	38.00	38
1991	The Rainbow Express - N. Mulargia	Closed	1993	125.00	125
1992	Sailing Ship - N. Mulargia	Open		38.00	38
1991	Schooner - N. Mulargia	Closed	1995	95.00	95
1990	Small Airplane - T. Suzuki	Closed	1993	200.00	200
1991	Small Cable Car - T. Suzuki	Open		70.00	70
1996	Small Classic Motorcycle - T. Suzuki	Open		210.00	210
1994	Small Cruise Ship - T. Suzuki	Open		575.00	575
1991	Small Orbiting Space Shuttle - T. Suzuki	Open		90.00	90
1994	Small Riverboat - N. Mulargia	Open		210.00	210
1993	Small San Francisco Cable Car - R. Nakai	Open		40.00	40
1990	Small Space Shuttle Launch - T. Suzuki	Closed	1996	265.00	265
1990	Small Train Set - T. Suzuki	Open		100.00	100
1994	Spinnaker Sailboat - R. Nakai	Open		265.00	265
1984	Sports Car - T. Suzuki	Closed	N/A	140.00	140
1990	Square Rigger - R. Nakai	Open		250.00	250
1995	Tall Ship - R. Nakai	Open		395.00	395
1984	Touring Car - T. Suzuki	Closed	N/A	140.00	140
1984	Tractor Trailer - R. Nakai	Closed	N/A	40.00	40

Wonders of the World Collection - R. Nakai, unless otherwise noted

Year Issue		Edition Limit	Year Retd.	Issue Price	*Quote U.S.$
1991	Chicago Water Tower w/Base -T. Suzuki	Open		300.00	300
1991	Chicago Water Tower w/o Base -T. Suzuki	Closed	1996	280.00	280
1986	Large Space Needle	Closed	N/A	160.00	160
1990	Le Petit Eiffel -T. Suzuki	Open		240.00	240
1995	The Liberty Bell	Open		160.00	160
1995	Medium Taj Mahal	Open		790.00	790
1993	Sears Tower	Open		150.00	150
1993	Small Capitol Building - N. Mulargia	Open		100.00	100
1986	Small Space Needle - N. Mulargia	Closed	N/A	50.00	50
1995	Small Taj Mahal	Open		215.00	215
1994	Small White House w/Oct. Mirror - N. Mulargia	Open		185.00	185
1986	Taj Mahal	Open		1050.00	1050
1987	U.S. Capitol Building	Open		250.00	250

Dave Grossman Creations

6" Gone With The Wind Series - Unknown

Year Issue		Edition Limit	Year Retd.	Issue Price	*Quote U.S.$
1994	Ashley GWW-102	Open		40.00	40
1994	Rhett GW-104	Open		40.00	40
1994	Scarlett GWW-101	Open		40.00	40

Gone With The Wind Series - Unknown

Year Issue		Edition Limit	Year Retd.	Issue Price	*Quote U.S.$
1993	Belle Waiting GWW-10	Open		70.00	70
1994	Gerald O'Hara GWW-15	Open		70.00	70
1988	Mammy GWW-6	Retrd.		70.00	70
1991	Prissy GWW-8	Open		50.00	50
1993	Rhett & Bonnie GWW-11	Open		80.00	80
1993	Rhett in White Suit GWW-12	Open		70.00	70
1994	Scarlett in Bar B Que Dress GWW-14	Open		70.00	70
1992	Scarlett in Green Dress GWW-9	Open		70.00	70
1987	Tara GWW-5	Retrd.	N/A	70.00	70

Norman Rockwell America Collection - Rockwell-Inspired

Year Issue		Edition Limit	Year Retd.	Issue Price	*Quote U.S.$
1993	After The Prom NRP-916	7,500		75.00	75
1989	Bottom of the Sixth NRC-607	Retrd.	N/A	140.00	140
1989	Doctor and Doll NRP-600	Retrd.	N/A	90.00	60
1989	First Day Home NRC-606	Retrd.	N/A	80.00	60
1989	First Haircut NRC-604	Retrd.	N/A	75.00	75
1989	First Visit NRC-605	Retrd.	N/A	110.00	110
1993	Gone Fishing NRP-915	7,500		65.00	65
1989	Locomotive NRC-603	Retrd.	N/A	110.00	110
1993	Missed NRP-914	7,500		110.00	110
1989	Runaway NRC-610	Retrd.	N/A	140.00	140
1989	Weigh-In NRC-611	Retrd.	N/A	120.00	120

Norman Rockwell America Collection-Lg. Ltd. Edition - Rockwell-Inspired

Year Issue		Edition Limit	Year Retd.	Issue Price	*Quote U.S.$
1989	Bottom of the Sixth NRP-307	Retrd.	N/A	190.00	190
1989	Doctor and Doll NRP-300	Retrd.	N/A	150.00	150
1989	Runaway NRP-310	Retrd.	N/A	190.00	190
1989	Weigh-In NRP-311	Retrd.	N/A	160.00	175

Norman Rockwell America Collection-Miniatures - Rockwell-Inspired

Year Issue		Edition Limit	Year Retd.	Issue Price	*Quote U.S.$
1989	First Day Home MRC-906	Retrd.	N/A	45.00	45
1989	First Haircut MRC-904	Retrd.	N/A	45.00	45

Saturday Evening Post - Rockwell-Inspired

Year Issue		Edition Limit	Year Retd.	Issue Price	*Quote U.S.$
1992	After the Prom NRP-916	Open		75.00	75
1994	Almost Grown Up NRC-609	Open		75.00	75
1993	Baby's First Step NRC-604	Open		100.00	100
1993	Bed Time NRC-606	Open		100.00	100
1990	Bedside Manner NRP-904	Open		65.00	65
1990	Big Moment NRP-906	Retrd.	N/A	100.00	135
1990	Bottom of the Sixth NRP-908	Open		165.00	165
1993	Bride & Groom NRC-605	Open		100.00	100
1991	Catching The Big One NRP-909	Open		75.00	75
1992	Choosin Up NRP-912	Retrd.	N/A	110.00	140-150
1990	Daydreamer NRP-902	Open		55.00	55
1990	Doctor and Doll NRP-907	Retrd.	N/A	110.00	150
1994	For A Good Boy NRC-608	Open		100.00	100
1992	Gone Fishing NRP-915	Open		65.00	65
1991	Gramps NRP-910	Open		85.00	85
1994	Little Mother NRC-607	Open		75.00	75
1992	Locomotive NRC-603	Open		110.00	110
1992	Missed NRP-914	Open		110.00	110
1990	No Swimming NRP-901	Retrd.	N/A	50.00	50
1991	The Pharmacist NRP-911	Open		70.00	70
1990	Prom Dress NRP-903	Retrd.	N/A	60.00	60
1990	Runaway NRP-905	Open		130.00	130
1994	A Visit with Rockwell (100th Aniversary)-NRP-100	1,994		100.00	100

Saturday Evening Post-Miniatures - Rockwell-Inspired

Year Issue		Edition Limit	Year Retd.	Issue Price	*Quote U.S.$
1991	A Boy Meets His Dog BMR-01	Retrd.	N/A	35.00	35
1991	Downhill Daring BMR-02	Retrd.	N/A	40.00	40
1991	Flowers in Tender Bloom BMR-03	Retrd.	N/A	32.00	32
1991	Fondly Do We Remember BMR-04	Retrd.	N/A	30.00	30
1991	In His Spirit BMR-05	Retrd.	N/A	30.00	30
1991	Pride of Parenthood BMR-06	Retrd.	N/A	35.00	35
1991	Sweet Serenade BMR-07	Retrd.	N/A	32.00	32
1991	Sweet Song So Young BMR-08	Retrd.	N/A	30.00	30

*Quotes have been rounded up to nearest dollar

FIGURINES/COTTAGES

Dave Grossman Designs

Lladró-Norman Rockwell Collection Series - Rockwell-Inspired

YEAR ISSUE		EDITION LIMIT	YEAR RETD.	ISSUE PRICE	*QUOTE U.S.$
1982	Court Jester RL-405G	5,000	N/A	600.00	1300
1982	Daydreamer RL-404G	5,000	N/A	450.00	1300-1500
1982	Lladró Love Letter RL-400G	5,000	N/A	650.00	1000-1200
1982	Practice Makes Perfect RL-402G	5,000	N/A	725.00	800-1000
1982	Springtime RL-406G	5,000	N/A	450.00	1200-1500
1982	Summer Stock RL-401G	5,000	N/A	750.00	800-900
1982	Young Love RL-403G	5,000	N/A	450.00	1350-1750

See also Lladró - Norman Rockwell Collection

Norman Rockwell Collection - Rockwell-Inspired

YEAR ISSUE		EDITION LIMIT	YEAR RETD.	ISSUE PRICE	*QUOTE U.S.$
1982	American Mother NRG-42	Retrd.	N/A	100.00	125
1978	At the Doctor NR-29	Retrd.	N/A	108.00	150-275
1979	Back From Camp NR-33	Retrd.	N/A	96.00	120
1973	Back To School NR-02	Retrd.	N/A	20.00	40-45
1975	Barbershop Quartet NR-23	Retrd.	N/A	100.00	1400
1974	Baseball NR-16	Retrd.	N/A	45.00	160
1975	Big Moment NR-21	Retrd.	N/A	60.00	125
1973	Caroller NR-03	Retrd.	N/A	22.50	75
1975	Circus NR-22	Retrd.	N/A	55.00	145
1983	Country Critic NR-43	Retrd.	N/A	75.00	125
1982	Croquet NR-41	Retrd.	N/A	100.00	135
1973	Daydreamer NR-04	Retrd.	N/A	22.50	60
1975	Discovery NR-20	Retrd.	N/A	55.00	175
1973	Doctor & Doll NR-12	Retrd.	N/A	65.00	150-285
1979	Dreams of Long Ago NR-31	Retrd.	N/A	100.00	125
1976	Drum For Tommy NRC-24	Retrd.	N/A	40.00	95
1980	Exasperated Nanny NR-35	Retrd.	N/A	96.00	100
1978	First Day of School NR-27	Retrd.	N/A	100.00	150
1974	Friends In Need NR-13	Retrd.	N/A	45.00	100
1983	Graduate NR-44	Retrd.	N/A	30.00	50
1979	Grandpa's Ballerina NR-32	Retrd.	N/A	100.00	110
1980	Hankerchief NR-36	Retrd.	N/A	110.00	100-110
1973	Lazybones NR-08	Retrd.	N/A	30.00	250
1973	Leapfrog NR-09	Retrd.	N/A	50.00	600-700
1973	Love Letter NR-06	Retrd.	N/A	25.00	60
1973	Lovers NR-07	Retrd.	N/A	45.00	70
1978	Magic Potion NR-28	Retrd.	N/A	84.00	235
1973	Marble Players NR-11	Retrd.	N/A	60.00	400-450
1973	No Swimming NR-05	Retrd.	N/A	25.00	65-145
1977	Pals NR-25	Retrd.	N/A	60.00	120
1986	Red Cross NR-47	Retrd.	N/A	67.00	100
1973	Redhead NR-01	Retrd.	N/A	20.00	210
1980	Santa's Good Boys NR-37	Retrd.	N/A	90.00	100
1973	Schoolmaster NR-10	Retrd.	N/A	55.00	225
1984	Scotty's Home Plate NR-46	Retrd.	N/A	30.00	60
1983	Scotty's Surprise NRS-20	Retrd.	N/A	25.00	50-60
1974	See America First NR-17	Retrd.	N/A	50.00	125
1981	Spirit of Education NR-38	Retrd.	N/A	96.00	110
1974	Springtime '33 NR-14	Retrd.	N/A	30.00	65
1977	Springtime '35 NR-19	Retrd.	N/A	50.00	65
1974	Summertime '33 NR-15	Retrd.	N/A	45.00	65
1974	Take Your Medicine NR-18	Retrd.	N/A	50.00	100
1979	Teacher's Pet NRA-30	Retrd.	N/A	35.00	50
1980	The Toss NR-34	Retrd.	N/A	110.00	150-225
1982	A Visit With Rockwell NR-40	Retrd.	N/A	120.00	100-120
1988	Wedding March NR-49	Retrd.	N/A	110.00	150
1978	Young Doctor NRD-26	Retrd.	N/A	100.00	120
1987	Young Love NR-48	Retrd.	N/A	70.00	120

Norman Rockwell Collection-American Rockwell Series - Rockwell-Inspired

YEAR ISSUE		EDITION LIMIT	YEAR RETD.	ISSUE PRICE	*QUOTE U.S.$
1981	Breaking Home Ties NRV-300	Retrd.	N/A	2000.00	2300
1982	Lincoln NRV-301	Retrd.	N/A	300.00	375
1982	Thanksgiving NRV-302	Retrd.	N/A	2500.00	2650

Norman Rockwell Collection-Boy Scout Series - Rockwell-Inspired

YEAR ISSUE		EDITION LIMIT	YEAR RETD.	ISSUE PRICE	*QUOTE U.S.$
1981	Can't Wait BSA-01	Retrd.	N/A	30.00	50
1981	Good Friends BSA-04	Retrd.	N/A	58.00	65
1981	Good Turn BSA-05	Retrd.	N/A	65.00	100
1982	Guiding Hand BSA-07	Retrd.	N/A	58.00	60
1981	Physically Strong BSA-03	Retrd.	N/A	56.00	150
1981	Scout Is Helpful BSA-02	Retrd.	N/A	38.00	45
1981	Scout Memories BSA-06	Retrd.	N/A	65.00	70
1983	Tomorrow's Leader BSA-08	Retrd.	N/A	45.00	55

Norman Rockwell Collection-Country Gentlemen Series - Rockwell-Inspired

YEAR ISSUE		EDITION LIMIT	YEAR RETD.	ISSUE PRICE	*QUOTE U.S.$
1982	Bringing Home the Tree CG-02	Retrd.	N/A	60.00	75
1982	The Catch CG-04	Retrd.	N/A	50.00	60
1982	On the Ice CG-05	Retrd.	N/A	50.00	60
1982	Pals CG-03	Retrd.	N/A	36.00	45
1982	Thin Ice CG-06	Retrd.	N/A	50.00	60
1982	Turkey Dinner CG-01	Retrd.	N/A	85.00	90

Norman Rockwell Collection-Huck Finn Series - Rockwell-Inspired

YEAR ISSUE		EDITION LIMIT	YEAR RETD.	ISSUE PRICE	*QUOTE U.S.$
1980	Listening HF-02	Retrd.	N/A	110.00	120
1980	No Kings HF-03	Retrd.	N/A	110.00	110
1979	The Secret HF-01	Retrd.	N/A	110.00	130
1980	Snake Escapes HF-04	Retrd.	N/A	110.00	120

Norman Rockwell Collection-Large Limited Editions - Rockwell-Inspired

YEAR ISSUE		EDITION LIMIT	YEAR RETD.	ISSUE PRICE	*QUOTE U.S.$
1975	Baseball NR-102	Retrd.	N/A	125.00	450
1982	Circus NR-106	Retrd.	N/A	500.00	500
1974	Doctor and Doll NR-100	Retrd.	N/A	300.00	1400
1981	Dreams of Long Ago NR-105	Retrd.	N/A	500.00	750
1979	Leapfrog NR-104	Retrd.	N/A	440.00	750
1984	Marble Players NR-107	Retrd.	N/A	500.00	750
1975	No Swimming NR-101	Retrd.	N/A	150.00	550-600
1974	See America First NR-103	Retrd.	N/A	100.00	500-550

Norman Rockwell Collection-Miniatures - Rockwell-Inspired

YEAR ISSUE		EDITION LIMIT	YEAR RETD.	ISSUE PRICE	*QUOTE U.S.$
1984	At the Doctor's NR-229	Retrd.	N/A	35.00	35
1979	Back To School NR-202	Retrd.	N/A	18.00	25
1982	Barbershop Quartet NR-223	Retrd.	N/A	40.00	50
1980	Baseball NR-216	Retrd.	N/A	40.00	50
1982	Big Moment NR-221	Retrd.	N/A	36.00	40
1979	Caroller NR-203	Retrd.	N/A	20.00	25
1982	Circus NR-222	Retrd.	N/A	35.00	40
1979	Daydreamer NR-204	Retrd.	N/A	20.00	30
1982	Discovery NR-220	Retrd.	N/A	35.00	45
1979	Doctor and Doll NR-212	Retrd.	N/A	40.00	40
1984	Dreams of Long Ago NR-231	Retrd.	N/A	30.00	30
1982	Drum For Tommy NRC-224	Retrd.	N/A	25.00	30
1984	First Day of School NR-227	Retrd.	N/A	35.00	35
1980	Friends In Need NR-213	Retrd.	N/A	30.00	40
1979	Lazybones NR-208	Retrd.	N/A	22.00	50
1979	Leapfrog NR-209	Retrd.	N/A	32.00	32
1979	Love Letter NR-206	Retrd.	N/A	26.00	50
1979	Lovers NR-207	Retrd.	N/A	28.00	30
1984	Magic Potion NR-228	Retrd.	N/A	30.00	40
1979	Marble Players NR-211	Retrd.	N/A	36.00	38
1979	No Swimming NR-205	Retrd.	N/A	22.00	30
1984	Pals NR-225	Retrd.	N/A	25.00	25
1979	Redhead NR-201	Retrd.	N/A	18.00	50
1983	Santa On the Train NR-245	Retrd.	N/A	35.00	55
1979	Schoolmaster NR-210	Retrd.	N/A	34.00	45
1980	See America First NR-217	Retrd.	N/A	28.00	50
1980	Springtime '33 NR-214	Retrd.	N/A	24.00	80
1982	Springtime '35 NR-219	Retrd.	N/A	24.00	30
1980	Summertime '33 NR-215	Retrd.	N/A	22.00	25
1980	Take Your Medicine NR-218	Retrd.	N/A	36.00	40
1984	Young Doctor NRD-226	Retrd.	N/A	30.00	50

Norman Rockwell Collection-Pewter Figurines - Rockwell-Inspired

YEAR ISSUE		EDITION LIMIT	YEAR RETD.	ISSUE PRICE	*QUOTE U.S.$
1980	Back to School FP-02	Retrd.	N/A	25.00	25
1980	Barbershop Quartet FP-23	Retrd.	N/A	25.00	25
1980	Big Moment FP-21	Retrd.	N/A	25.00	25
1980	Caroller FP-03	Retrd.	N/A	25.00	25
1980	Circus FP-22	Retrd.	N/A	25.00	25
1980	Doctor and Doll FP-12	Retrd.	N/A	25.00	25
1980	Figurine Display Rack FDR-01	Retrd.	N/A	60.00	60
1980	Grandpa's Ballerina FP-32	Retrd.	N/A	25.00	25
1980	Lovers FP-07	Retrd.	N/A	25.00	25
1980	Magic Potion FP-28	Retrd.	N/A	25.00	25
1980	No Swimming FP-05	Retrd.	N/A	25.00	25
1980	See America First FP-17	Retrd.	N/A	25.00	25
1980	Take Your Medicine FP-18	Retrd.	N/A	25.00	25

Norman Rockwell Collection-Rockwell Club Series - Rockwell-Inspired

YEAR ISSUE		EDITION LIMIT	YEAR RETD.	ISSUE PRICE	*QUOTE U.S.$
1982	Diary RCC-02	Retrd.	N/A	35.00	75
1984	Gone Fishing RCC-04	Retrd.	N/A	30.00	55
1983	Runaway Pants RCC-03	Retrd.	N/A	65.00	75
1981	Young Artist RCC-01	Retrd.	N/A	96.00	105

Norman Rockwell Collection-Select Collection, Ltd. - Rockwell-Inspired

YEAR ISSUE		EDITION LIMIT	YEAR RETD.	ISSUE PRICE	*QUOTE U.S.$
1982	Boy & Mother With Puppies SC-1001	Retrd.	N/A	27.50	28
1982	Father With Child SC-1005	Retrd.	N/A	22.00	22
1982	Football Player SC-1004	Retrd.	N/A	22.00	22
1982	Girl Bathing Dog SC-1006	Retrd.	N/A	26.50	27
1982	Girl With Dolls In Crib SC-1002	Retrd.	N/A	26.50	27
1982	Helping Hand SC-1007	Retrd.	N/A	32.00	32
1982	Lemonade Stand SC-1008	Retrd.	N/A	32.00	32
1982	Save Me SC-1010	Retrd.	N/A	35.00	35
1982	Shaving Lesson SC-1009	Retrd.	N/A	30.00	30
1982	Young Couple SC-1003	Retrd.	N/A	27.50	28

Norman Rockwell Collection-Tom Sawyer Miniatures - Rockwell-Inspired

YEAR ISSUE		EDITION LIMIT	YEAR RETD.	ISSUE PRICE	*QUOTE U.S.$
1983	First Smoke TSM-02	Retrd.	N/A	40.00	45
1983	Lost In Cave TSM-05	Retrd.	N/A	40.00	50
1983	Take Your Medicine TSM-04	Retrd.	N/A	40.00	45
1983	Whitewashing the Fence TSM-01	Retrd.	N/A	40.00	50

Norman Rockwell Collection-Tom Sawyer Series - Rockwell-Inspired

YEAR ISSUE		EDITION LIMIT	YEAR RETD.	ISSUE PRICE	*QUOTE U.S.$
1976	First Smoke TS-02	Retrd.	N/A	60.00	235
1978	Lost In Cave TS-04	Retrd.	N/A	70.00	175
1977	Take Your Medicine TS-03	Retrd.	N/A	63.00	235
1975	Whitewashing the Fence TS-01	Retrd.	N/A	60.00	235

Department 56

All Through The House - Department 56

YEAR ISSUE		EDITION LIMIT	YEAR RETD.	ISSUE PRICE	*QUOTE U.S.$
1992	Aunt Martha With Turkey 9317-3	Closed	1995	27.50	28
1992	Dinner Table 9313-0	Closed	1995	65.00	65
1992	Mr. & Mrs. Bell at Dinner 9314-9, set/2	Closed	1995	40.00	40
1992	Nicholas, Natallie, & Spot The Dog 9315-7, set/3	Closed	1995	45.00	45
1992	Sideboard 9316-5	Closed	1995	45.00	45

Alpine Village Series - Department 56

YEAR ISSUE		EDITION LIMIT	YEAR RETD.	ISSUE PRICE	*QUOTE U.S.$
1987	Alpine Church 6541-2	Closed	1991	32.00	155-195
1992	Alpine Shops 5618-9, set/2 (Metterniche Wurst, Kukuck Uhren)	Open		75.00	60-95
1986	Alpine Village 6540-4, set/5 (Bessor Bierkeller, Gasthof Eisl, Apotheke, E. Staubr Backer, Milch-Kase)	Open		150.00	195
1990	Bahnhof 5615-4	Closed	1993	42.00	60-90
1994	Bakery & Chocolate Shop 5614-6	Open		37.50	38
1988	Grist Mill 5953-6	Open		42.00	45
1987	Josef Engel Farmhouse 5952-8	Closed	1989	33.00	900-1050
1995	Kamm Haus 5617-1	Open		42.00	42
1993	Sport Laden, 5612-0	Open		50.00	50
1991	St. Nikolaus Kirche 5617-0	Open		37.50	38

Christmas In the City Series - Department 56

YEAR ISSUE		EDITION LIMIT	YEAR RETD.	ISSUE PRICE	*QUOTE U.S.$
1989	5607 Park Avenue Townhouse 5977-3	Closed	1992	48.00	75-100
1989	5609 Park Avenue Townhouse 5978-1	Closed	1992	48.00	70-90
1991	All Saints Corner Church 5542-5	Open		96.00	110
1991	Arts Academy 5543-3	Closed	1993	45.00	60-90
1995	Brighton School 5887-6	Open		52.00	52
1994	Brokerage House, 5881-5	Open		48.00	48
1995	Brownstones on the Square 5887-7, set/2 (Beekman House, Pickford Place)	Open		90.00	90
1987	The Cathedral 5962-5	Closed	1990	60.00	320-360
1992	Cathedral Church of St. Mark 5549-2	3,024	1993	120.00	1800-2300
1988	Chocolate Shoppe 5968-4	Closed	1991	40.00	100-130
1987	Christmas In The City 6512-9, set/3	Closed	1990	112.00	425-600
1987	•Bakery 6512-9	Closed	1990	37.50	95-130
1987	•Tower Restaurant 6512-9	Closed	1990	37.50	175-245
1987	•Toy Shop and Pet Store 6512-9	Closed	1990	37.50	185-250
1988	City Hall (small) 5969-2	Closed	1991	65.00	175-225
1988	City Hall (standard) 5969-2	Closed	1991	65.00	150-175
1991	The Doctor's Office 5544-1	Closed	1994	60.00	75-10
1989	Dorothy's Dress Shop 5974-9	12,500	1991	70.00	300-385
1994	First Metropolitan Bank 5882-3	Open		60.00	6
1988	Hank's Market 5970-6	Closed	1992	40.00	65-10
1994	Heritage Museum of Art 5883-1	Open		96.00	9
1991	Hollydale's Department Store 5534-4	Open		75.00	8
1995	Holy Name Church 5887-5	Open		96.00	9
1995	Ivy Terrace Apartments 5887-4	Open		60.00	6
1991	Little Italy Ristorante 5538-7	Closed	1995	50.00	65-9
1987	Palace Theatre 5963-3	Closed	1989	45.00	875-100
1990	Red Brick Fire Station 5536-0	Closed	1995	55.00	60-9
1989	Ritz Hotel 5973-0	Closed	1994	55.00	65-9
1987	Sutton Place Brownstones 5961-7	Closed	1989	80.00	845-95
1992	Uptown Shoppes 5531-0, set/3 (Haberdashery, City Clockworks, Music Emporium)	Open		150.00	15
1988	Variety Store 5972-2	Closed	1990	45.00	150-18
1993	West Village Shops 5880-7, set/2 (Potters' Tea Seller, Spring St. Coffee House)	Open		90.00	9
1990	Wong's In Chinatown 5537-9	Closed	1994	55.00	65-9

Dickens' Village Series - Department 56

YEAR ISSUE		EDITION LIMIT	YEAR RETD.	ISSUE PRICE	*QUOTE U.S.$
1991	Ashbury Inn 5555-7	Closed	1995	55.00	70-9
1987	Barley Bree 5900-5, set/2 (Farmhouse, Barn)	Closed	1989	60.00	375-42
1990	Bishops Oast House 5567-0	Closed	1992	45.00	65-10
1995	Blenham Street Bank, 5833-0	Open		60.00	6
1986	Blythe Pond Mill House 6508-0	Closed	1990	37.00	200-3
1986	By The Pond Mill House 6508-0	Closed	1990	37.00	125-1
1994	Boarding & Lodging School, 5810-6	Open		48.00	4
1993	Boarding and Lodging School, 5809-2 (Christmas Carol Commemorative Piece)	Yr.Iss.	1993	48.00	150-24
1987	Brick Abbey 6549-8	Closed	1989	33.00	375-42
1988	C. Fletcher Public House 5904-8	12,500	1989	35.00	550-6
1986	Chadbury Station and Train 6528-5	Closed	1989	65.00	375-4
1987	Chesterton Manor House 6568-4	7,500	1988	45.00	1550-17
1986	Christmas Carol Cottages 6500-5, set/3	Closed	1995	75.00	120-1
1986	•The Cottage of Bob Cratchit & Tiny Tim 6500-5	Closed	1995	25.00	45-
1986	•Fezziwig's Warehouse 6500-5	Closed	1995	25.00	40-
1986	•Scrooge and Marley Counting House 6500-5	Closed	1995	25.00	40-
1988	Cobblestone Shops 5924-2, set/3	Closed	1990	95.00	360-4
1988	•Booter and Cobbler 5924-2	Closed	1990	32.00	120-1
1988	•T. Wells Fruit & Spice Shop 5924-2	Closed	1990	32.00	90-1
1988	•The Wool Shop 5924-2	Closed	1990	32.00	175-2
1989	Cobles Police Station 5583-2	Closed	1991	37.50	125-1
1988	Counting House & Silas Thimbleton Barrister 5902-1	Closed	1990	32.00	75-1

*Quotes have been rounded up to nearest dolla

YEAR ISSUE		EDITION LIMIT	YEAR RETD.	ISSUE PRICE	*QUOTE U.S. $
1992	Crown & Cricket Inn (Charles Dickens' Signature Series), 5750-9	Yr.Iss.	1992	100.00	175-225
1989	David Copperfield 5550-6, set/3	Closed	1992	125.00	175-225
1989	•Betsy Trotwood's Cottage 5550-6	Closed	1992	42.50	45-70
1989	•Peggotty's Seaside Cottage 5550-6 (green boat)	Closed	1992	42.50	45-75
1989	• Mr. Wickfield Solicitor 5550-6	Closed	1992	42.50	85-115
1989	David Copperfield 5550-6, set/3 with tan boat	Closed	1992	125.00	250-275
1989	Peggotty's Seaside Cottage 5550-6 (tan boat)	Closed	1992	42.50	125-175
1994	Dedlock Arms, 5752-5 (Charles Dickens' Signature Series)	Yr.Iss.	1994	100.00	125-175
1985	Dickens' Cottages 6518-8 set/3	Closed	1988	75.00	900-1100
1985	•Stone Cottage 6518-8	Closed	1988	25.00	400-450
1985	•Thatched Cottage 6518-8	Closed	1988	25.00	175-250
1985	•Tudor Cottage 6518-8	Closed	1988	25.00	350-450
1986	Dickens' Lane Shops 6507-2, set/3	Closed	1989	80.00	550-650
1986	•Cottage Toy Shop 6507-2	Closed	1989	27.00	225-245
1986	•Thomas Kersey Coffee House 6507-2	Closed	1989	27.00	170-220
1986	•Tuttle's Pub 6507-2	Closed	1989	27.00	210-300
1984	Dickens' Village Church (cream) 6516-1	Closed	1989	35.00	275-475
1985	Dickens' Village Church(dark) 6516-1	Closed	1989	35.00	160-200
1985	Dickens' Village Church(green) 6516-1	Closed	1989	35.00	375-475
1985	Dickens' Village Church(tan) 6516-1	Closed	1989	35.00	180-200
1985	Dickens' Village Mill 6519-6	2,500	1986	35.00	4200-5000
1995	Dudden Cross Church 5834-3	Open		45.00	45
1995	Dursley Manor, 5832-9	Open		50.00	50
1991	Fagin's Hide-A-Way 5552-2	Closed	1995	68.00	85
1989	The Flat of Ebenezer Scrooge 5587-5	Open		37.50	38
1994	Giggelswick Mutton & Ham, 5822-0	Open		48.00	48
1996	The Grapes Inn, 5753-4 (Charles Dickens' Signature Series)	Yr.Iss.		120.00	120
1993	Great Denton Mill, 5812-2	Open		50.00	50
1989	Green Gate Cottage 5586-7	22,500	1990	65.00	250-300
1994	Hather Harness 5823-8	Open		48.00	48
1992	Hembleton Pewterer, 5800-9	Closed	1995	72.00	85-100
1988	Ivy Glen Church 5927-7	Closed	1991	35.00	85-120
1995	J.D. Nichols Toy Shop, 5832-8	Open		48.00	48
1987	Kenilworth Castle 5916-1	Closed	1988	70.00	660-700
1992	King's Road Post Office, 5801-7	Open		45.00	45
1993	Kingford's Brewhouse, 5811-4	Open		45.00	45
1990	Kings Road 5568-9, set/2 (Tutbury Printer, C.H. Watt Physician)	Open		72.00	80
1989	Knottinghill Church 5582-4	Closed	1995	50.00	55-95
1995	The Maltings 5833-5	Open		50.00	50
1988	Merchant Shops 5926-9, set/5,	Closed	1993	150.00	235-275
1988	•Geo. Weeton Watchmaker 5926-9	Closed	1993	30.00	40-75
1988	•The Mermaid Fish Shoppe 5926-9	Closed	1993	30.00	55-80
1988	•Poulterer 5926-9	Closed	1993	30.00	50-65
1988	•Walpole Tailors 5926-9	Closed	1993	30.00	40-60
1988	•White Horse Bakery 5926-9	Closed	1993	30.00	50-75
1991	Nephew Fred's Flat 5557-3	Closed	1994	35.00	60-85
1988	Nicholas Nickleby 5925-0, set/2	Closed	1991	72.00	150-200
1988	•Nicholas Nickleby Cottage 5925-0	Closed	1991	36.00	75-95
1988	•Wackford Squeers Boarding School 5925-0	Closed	1991	36.00	80-115
1988	Nickolas Nickleby Cottage 5925-0-misspelled	Closed	1991	36.00	95-125
1988	Nickolas Nickleby set/2, 5925-0-misspelled	Closed	1991	36.00	200-225
1986	Norman Church 6502-1	3,500	1987	40.00	2800-3800
1987	The Old Curiosity Shop 5905-6	Open		32.00	42
1992	Old Michaelchurch, 5562-0	Open		42.00	48
1991	Oliver Twist 5553-0, set/2	Closed	1993	75.00	100-145
1991	•Brownlow House 5553-0	Closed	1993	38.00	55-88
1991	•Maylie Cottage 5553-0	Closed	1993	38.00	50-70
1984	The Original Shops of Dickens' Village, 6515-3, set of 7	Closed	1988	175.00	1200-1400
1984	•Abel Beesley Butcher 6515-3	Closed	1988	25.00	100-150
1984	•Bean And Son Smithy Shop 6515-3	Closed	1988	25.00	170-225
1984	•Candle Shop 6515-3	Closed	1988	25.00	175-225
1984	•Crowntree Inn 6515-3	Closed	1988	25.00	300-350
1984	•Golden Swan Baker 6515-3	Closed	1988	25.00	155-200
1984	•Green Grocer 6515-3	Closed	1988	25.00	150-230
1984	•Jones & Co. Brush & Basket Shop 6515-3	Closed	1988	25.00	275-350
1993	The Pied Bull Inn (Charles Dickens' Signature Series), 5751-7	Closed	1993	100.00	125-200
1994	Portobello Road Thatched Cottages 5824-6, set/3 (Mr. & Mrs. Pickle, Cobb Cottage, Browning Cottage)	Open		120.00	120
1993	Pump Lane Shoppes 5808-4, set/3 (Bumpstead Nye Cloaks & Canes, Lomas Ltd. Molasses, W.M. Wheat Cakes & Puddings)	Open		112.00	112
1989	Ruth Marion Scotch Woolens 5585-9	17,500	1990	65.00	350-450
1995	Sir John Falstaff Inn 5753-3 (Charles Dickens' Signature Series)	Closed	1995	100.00	125-150
1995	Start A Tradition Set 5832-7, set/13 (The Town Square Shops-Faversham Lamps & Oil, Morston Steak and Kidney Pie, The Town Square Carolers Accessory, set/3, 6 Sisal Trees, Bag of Real Plastic Snow, Cobblestone Road)	Open		85.00	85
1989	Theatre Royal 5584-0	Closed	1992	45.00	65-110
1989	Victoria Station 5574-3	Open		100.00	112
1994	Whittlesbourne Church, 5821-1	Open		85.00	85
1995	Wrenbury Shops 5833-1, set/3 (Wrenbury Baker, The Chop Shop, T. Puddlewick Spectacle Shop)	Open		100.00	100

Disney Parks Village Series - Department 56

YEAR ISSUE		EDITION LIMIT	YEAR RETD.	ISSUE PRICE	*QUOTE U.S.$
1994	Disney Parks Family (Accessory), set/3 5354-6	Open		32.50	33
1994	Fire Station 5352-0 Disneyland, CA	Open		45.00	45
1994	Mickey and Minnie (Accessory) 5353-8, set/2	Open		22.50	23
1994	Mickey's Christmas Shop 5350-3, set/2 Disney World, FL	Open		144.00	144
1994	Olde World Antiques Gate (Accessory) 5355-4	Open		15.00	15
1994	Olde World Antiques 5351-1, set/2 Disney World, FL	Open		90.00	90
1995	Silversmith 5352-1	Open		50.00	50
1995	Tinker Bell's Treasures 5352-2	Open		60.00	60

Easter Collectibles - Department 56

YEAR ISSUE		EDITION LIMIT	YEAR RETD.	ISSUE PRICE	*QUOTE U.S.$
1995	Bisque Chick, Large 2464-3	Closed	1996	8.50	10
1995	Bisque Chick, Small, 2465-1	Closed	1996	6.50	8
1993	Bisque Duckling, set	Closed	1993	15.00	26-36
1993	Bisque Duckling, Large 3.5" 7282-6	Closed	1993	8.50	18
1993	Bisque Duckling, Small 2.75" 7281-8	Closed	1993	6.50	15
1994	Bisque Fledgling in Nest, Large 2.75" 2400-7	Closed	1994	6.00	11-16
1994	Bisque Fledgling in Nest, Small 2.5" 2401-5	Closed	1994	5.00	10
1991	Bisque Lamb, set	Closed	1991	12.50	66-78
1991	Bisque Lamb, Large 4" 7392-0	Closed	1991	7.50	26-42
1991	Bisque Lamb, Small 2.5" 7393-8	Closed	1991	5.00	23
1992	Bisque Rabbit, set	Closed	1992	14.00	35-55
1992	Bisque Rabbit, Large 5" 7498-5	Closed	1992	8.00	22-28
1992	Bisque Rabbit, Small 4" 7499-3	Closed	1992	6.00	14-25
1996	Bisque Rabbit, Large 2765-0	Open		8.50	9
1996	Bisque Rabbit, Small 2764-2	Open		7.50	8

Event Piece - Heritage Village Collection Accessory - Department 56

YEAR ISSUE		EDITION LIMIT	YEAR RETD.	ISSUE PRICE	*QUOTE U.S.$
1992	Gate House 5530-1	Closed	1992	22.50	45-75

Little Town of Bethlehem Series - Department 56

YEAR ISSUE		EDITION LIMIT	YEAR RETD.	ISSUE PRICE	*QUOTE U.S.$
1987	Little Town of Bethlehem 5975-7, set/12	Open		150.00	150

Merry Makers - Department 56

YEAR ISSUE		EDITION LIMIT	YEAR RETD.	ISSUE PRICE	*QUOTE U.S.$
1991	Charles The Cellist 9355-6	Closed	1995	19.00	19
1991	Clarence The Concertinist 9353-0	Closed	1995	19.00	19
1991	Frederick The Flutist 9352-1	Closed	1995	19.00	19
1991	Horatio The Hornblower 9351-3	Closed	1995	19.00	19
1991	Martin The Mandolinist 9350-5	Closed	1995	19.00	19
1991	Sidney The Singer 9354-8	Closed	1995	19.00	19

New England Village Series - Department 56

YEAR ISSUE		EDITION LIMIT	YEAR RETD.	ISSUE PRICE	*QUOTE U.S.$
1993	A. Bieler Farm 5648-0, set/2 (Pennsylvania Dutch Farmhouse, Pennsylvania Dutch Barn)	Open		92.00	95
1988	Ada's Bed and Boarding House (lemon yellow) 5940-4	Closed	1991	36.00	275-350
1988	Ada's Bed and Boarding House (pale yellow) 5940-4	Closed	1991	36.00	130-150
1994	Arlington Falls Church, 5651-0	Open		40.00	42
1989	Berkshire House (medium blue) 5942-0	Closed	1991	40.00	150-170
1989	Berkshire House (teal) 5942-0	Closed	1991	40.00	100-125
1993	Blue Star Ice Co., 5647-2	Open		45.00	48
1992	Bluebird Seed and Bulb, 5642-1	Open		48.00	48
1995	Brewster Bay Cottage 5657-0, set/2 (Jeremiah Brewster House, Thomas T. Julian House)	Open		90.00	90
1994	Cape Keag Cannery 5652-9	Open		48.00	48
1990	Captain's Cottage 5947-1	Open		40.00	44
1988	Cherry Lane Shops 5939-0, set/3	Closed	1990	80.00	325-350
1988	•Anne Shaw Toys 5939-0	Closed	1990	27.00	125-185
1988	•Ben's Barbershop 5939-0	Closed	1990	27.00	75-115
1988	•Otis Hayes Butcher Shop 5939-0	Closed	1990	27.00	65-90
1987	Craggy Cove Lighthouse 5930-7	Closed	1994	35.00	55-85
1995	Chowder House 5657-1	Open		40.00	40
1986	Jacob Adams Farmhouse and Barn 6538-2	Closed	1989	65.00	450-625
1989	Jannes Mullet Amish Barn 5944-7	Closed	1992	48.00	85-110
1989	Jannes Mullet Amish Farm House 5943-9	Closed	1992	32.00	95-125
1991	McGrebe-Cutters & Sleighs 5640-5	Closed	1995	45.00	55
1986	New England Village 6530-7, set/7	Closed	1989	170.00	1100-1250
1986	•Apothecary Shop 6530-7	Closed	1989	25.00	90-110
1986	•Brick Town Hall 6530-7	Closed	1989	25.00	175-225
1986	•General Store 6530-7	Closed	1989	25.00	300-375
1986	•Livery Stable & Boot Shop 6530-7	Closed	1989	25.00	125-165
1986	•Nathaniel Bingham Fabrics 6530-7	Closed	1989	25.00	150-175
1986	•Red Schoolhouse 6530-7	Closed	1989	25.00	250-275
1986	•Steeple Church (Original) 6530-7	Closed	1989	25.00	140-180
1988	Old North Church 5932-3	Open		40.00	45
1995	Pierce Boat Works 5657-3	Open		55.00	55
1994	Pigeonhead Lighthouse 5653-7	Open		50.00	50
1990	Shingle Creek House 5946-3	Closed	1994	37.50	45-65
1990	Sleepy Hollow 5954-4, set/3	Closed	1993	96.00	165-200
1990	•Ichabod Crane's Cottage 5954-4	Closed	1993	32.00	35-70
1990	•Sleepy Hollow School 5954-4	Closed	1993	32.00	80-95
1990	•Van Tassel Manor 5954-4	Closed	1993	32.00	45-75
1990	Sleepy Hollow Church 5955-2	Closed	1993	36.00	50-75
1987	Smythe Woolen Mill 6543-9	7,500	1988	42.00	1050-1200
1986	Steeple Church (2nd Version) 6539-0	Closed	1990	30.00	85-110
1992	Stoney Brook Town Hall 5644-8	Closed	1995	42.00	50-80
1987	Timber Knoll Log Cabin 6544-7	Closed	1990	28.00	125-175
1987	Weston Train Station 5931-5	Closed	1989	42.00	255-300
1995	Woodbridge Post Office 5657-2	Open		40.00	40
1992	Yankee Jud Bell Casting 5643-0	Closed	1995	44.00	44-80

North Pole Series - Department 56

YEAR ISSUE		EDITION LIMIT	YEAR RETD.	ISSUE PRICE	*QUOTE U.S.$
1994	Beard Barber Shop 5634-0	Open		27.50	28
1992	Elfie's Sleds & Skates 5625-1	Open		48.00	48
1995	Elfin Forge & Assembly Shop 5638-4	Open		65.00	65
1994	Elfin Snow Cone Works 5633-2	Open		40.00	40
1995	Elves' Trade School 5638-7	Open		50.00	50
1993	Express Depot 5627-8	Open		48.00	48
1991	Neenee's Dolls & Toys 5620-0	Closed	1995	37.50	43-75
1990	North Pole 5601-4, set/2 (Reindeer Barn, Elf Bunkhouse)	Open		70.00	80
1993	North Pole Chapel 5626-0	Open		45.00	45
1994	North Pole Dolls & Santa's Bear Works 5635-9, set/3 (North Pole Dolls, Santa's Bear Works, Entrance)	Open		96.00	96
1992	North Pole Post Office 5623-5	Open		45.00	50
1991	North Pole Shops 5621-9, set/2	Closed	1995	75.00	90-125
1991	•Orly's Bell & Harness Supply	Closed	1995	37.50	45-75
1991	•Rimpy's Bakery	Closed	1995	37.50	45-70
1992	Obbie's Books & Letrinka's Candy 5624-3	Open		70.00	70
1993	Santa's Lookout Tower 5629-4	Open		45.00	48
1995	Santa's Rooming House 5638-6	Open		50.00	50
1993	Santa's Woodworks 5628-6	Open		42.00	45
1990	Santa's Workshop 5600-6	Closed	1993	72.00	400-485
1991	Tassy's Mittens & Hassel's Woolies 5622-7	Closed	1995	50.00	55-85
1995	Tin Soldier Shop 5638-3	Open		42.00	42
1995	Weather & Time Observatory 5638-5	Open		50.00	50

The Original Snow Village Collection - Department 56

YEAR ISSUE		EDITION LIMIT	YEAR RETD.	ISSUE PRICE	*QUOTE U.S.$
1986	2101 Maple 5043-1	Closed	1986	32.00	310-400
1990	56 Flavors Ice Cream Parlor 5151-9	Closed	1992	42.00	88-110
1979	Adobe House 5066-6	Closed	1980	18.00	2100-2800
1992	Airport 5439-9	Open		60.00	60
1992	Al's TV Shop 5423-2	Closed	1995	40.00	50-70
1986	All Saints Church 5070-9	Open		38.00	45
1986	Apothecary 5076-8	Closed	1990	34.00	70-125
1981	Bakery 5077-6	Closed	1983	30.00	240-300
1986	Bakery 5077-6	Closed	1991	35.00	70-95
1982	Bank 5024-5	Closed	1983	32.00	500-675
1981	Barn 5074-1	Closed	1984	32.00	375-500
1984	Bayport 5015-6	Closed	1986	30.00	200-250
1986	Beacon Hill House 5065-2	Closed	1988	31.00	155-180
1995	Beacon Hill Victorian 5485-7	Open		60.00	60
1979	Brownstone 5056-7	Closed	1981	36.00	500-630
1995	Bowling Alley 5485-8	Open		42.00	42
1978	Cape Cod 5013-8	Closed	1980	20.00	380
1994	Carmel Cottage 5466-6	Open		48.00	48
1982	Carriage House 5021-0	Closed	1984	28.00	325-385
1986	Carriage House 5071-7	Closed	1988	29.00	95-125
1987	Cathedral Church 5019-9	Closed	1990	50.00	85-135
1980	Cathedral Church 5067-4	Closed	1981	36.00	2200-3000
1982	Centennial House 5020-2	Closed	1984	32.00	310-400
1983	Chateau 5084-9	Closed	1984	35.00	350-510
1995	Christmas Cove Lighthouse 5483-6	Open		60.00	60
1991	The Christmas Shop 5097-0	Open		37.50	38
1985	Church of the Open Door 5048-2	Closed	1988	34.00	100-150
1988	Cobblestone Antique Shop 5123-3	Closed	1992	36.00	50-80
1994	Coca-Colar Brand Bottling Plant 5469-0	Open		65.00	65
1995	Coca-Colar Brand Corner Drugstore 5484-4	Open		55.00	55
1989	Colonial Church 5119-5	Closed	1992	60.00	45-100
1980	Colonial Farm House 5070-9	Closed	1982	30.00	275-375
1984	Congregational Church 5034-2	Closed	1985	28.00	660
1988	Corner Cafe 5124-1	Closed	1991	37.00	75-100
1981	Corner Store 5076-8	Closed	1983	30.00	200-270
1976	Country Church 5004-7	Closed	1979	18.00	340-375
1979	Countryside Church 5051-8 Meadowland Series	Closed	1980	25.00	760
1979	Countryside Church 5058-3	Closed	1984	27.50	245-340
1989	Courthouse 5144-6	Closed	1993	65.00	140-190
1992	Craftsman Cottage (American Architecture Series), 5437-2	Closed	1995	55.00	60-85
1987	Cumberland House 5024-5	Closed	1995	42.00	55-75
1993	Dairy Barn, 5446-1	Open		55.00	55
1984	Delta House 5012-1	Closed	1986	32.00	220-400
1985	Depot & Train w/2 Train Cars 5051-2	Closed	1988	65.00	95-140
1993	Dinah's Drive-In, 5447-0	Open		45.00	45
1989	Doctor's House 5143-8	Closed	1992	56.00	75-130

FIGURINES/COTTAGES

YEAR ISSUE		EDITION LIMIT	YEAR RETD.	ISSUE PRICE	*QUOTE U.S.$
1991	Double Bungalow, 5407-0	Closed	1994	45.00	50-75
1985	Duplex 5050-4	Closed	1987	35.00	120-185
1995	Dutch Colonial 5485-6 (American Architecture Series)	Open		45.00	45
1981	English Church 5078-4	Closed	1982	30.00	335-400
1981	English Cottage 5073-3	Closed	1982	25.00	290
1983	English Tudor 5033-4	Closed	1985	30.00	220-320
1987	Farm House 5089-0	Closed	1992	40.00	64-100
1994	Federal House (American Architecture Series) 5465-8	Open		50.00	50
1991	Finklea's Finery: Costume Shop 5405-4	Closed	1993	45.00	50-70
1983	Fire Station 5032-6	Closed	1984	32.00	610-700
1987	Fire Station No. 2 5091-1	Closed	1989	40.00	175-200
1994	Fisherman's Nook Cabins 5461-5, set/2, (Fisherman's Nook Bass Cabin, Fisherman's Nook Trout Cabin)	Open		50.00	50
1994	Fisherman's Nook Resort, 5460-7	Open		75.00	75
1982	Flower Shop 5082-2	Closed	1983	25.00	485
1976	Gabled Cottage 5002-1	Closed	1979	20.00	300-400
1982	Gabled House 5081-4	Closed	1983	30.00	350-425
1984	Galena House 5009-1	Closed	1985	32.00	310-400
1978	General Store (tan) 5012-0	Closed	1980	25.00	620-660
1978	General Store (white) 5012-0	Closed	1980	25.00	500
1979	Giant Trees 5065-8	Closed	1982	20.00	300-400
1983	Gingerbread HouseBank (Non-lighted) 5025-3	Closed	1984	24.00	300-400
1994	Glenhaven House 5468-2	Open		45.00	45
1992	Good Shepherd Chapel & Church School 5424-0, set/2	Open		72.00	72
1983	Gothic Church 5028-8	Closed	1986	36.00	250-275
1991	Gothic Farmhouse (American Architecture Series), 5404-6	Open		48.00	48
1983	Governor's Mansion 5003-2	Closed	1985	32.00	275-325
1992	Grandma's Cottage 5420-8	Open		42.00	45
1983	Grocery 5001-6	Closed	1985	35.00	350-400
1992	Hartford House 5426-7	Closed	1995	55.00	55
1984	Haversham House 5008-3	Closed	1987	37.00	210-275
1986	Highland Park House 5063-6	Closed	1988	35.00	100-155
1995	Holly Brothers Garage 5485-4	Open		48.00	48
1988	Home Sweet Home/House & Windmill 5126-8	Closed	1991	60.00	100-130
1978	Homestead 5011-2	Closed	1984	30.00	240-275
1991	Honeymooner Motel 5401-1	Closed	1993	42.00	60-90
1993	Hunting Lodge, 5445-3	Open		50.00	50
1976	The Inn 5003-9	Closed	1979	20.00	380-450
1989	J. Young's Granary 5149-7	Closed	1992	45.00	65-85
1991	Jack's Corner Barber Shop 5406-2	Closed	1994	42.00	50-80
1987	Jefferson School 5082-2	Closed	1991	36.00	150-185
1989	Jingle Belle Houseboat 5114-4	Closed	1991	42.00	95-115
1988	Kenwood House 5054-7	Closed	1990	50.00	110-140
1979	Knob Hill (gold) 5055-9	Closed	1981	30.00	325-400
1979	Knob Hill 5055-9	Closed	1981	30.00	275-400
1981	Large Single Tree 5080-6	Closed	1989	17.00	35-55
1987	Lighthouse 5030-0	Closed	1988	36.00	475-675
1986	Lincoln Park Duplex 5060-1	Closed	1988	33.00	105-130
1979	Log Cabin 5057-5	Closed	1981	22.00	365-500
1984	Main Street House 5005-9	Closed	1986	27.00	235-275
1990	Mainstreet Hardware Store 5153-5	Closed	1993	42.00	60-80
1977	Mansion 5008-8	Closed	1979	30.00	385-550
1988	Maple Ridge Inn 5121-7	Closed	1990	55.00	65-100
1994	Marvel's Beauty Salon 5470-4	Open		37.50	38
1986	Mickey's Diner 5078-4	Closed	1987	22.00	550-675
1979	Mission Church 5062-5	Closed	1980	30.00	1085-1300
1979	Mobile Home 5063-3	Closed	1980	18.00	1825-2500
1990	Morningside House 5152-7	Closed	1992	45.00	40-80
1993	Mount Olivet Church, 5442-9	Open		65.00	65
1976	Mountain Lodge 5001-3	Closed	1979	20.00	360-475
1978	Nantucket 5014-6	Closed	1986	25.00	245-300
1993	Nantucket Renovation 5441-0	Closed	1993	55.00	60-80
1984	New School House 5037-7	Closed	1986	35.00	225-325
1982	New Stone Church 5083-0	Closed	1984	32.00	345-385
1989	North Creek Cottage 5120-9	Closed	1992	45.00	45-75
1991	Oak Grove Tudor 5400-3	Closed	1994	42.00	45-65
1994	The Original Snow Village Starter Set 5462-3 (Shady Oak Church, Sunday School Serenade Accessory, 3 assorted Sisal Trees, 1.5 oz. bag of real plastic snow)	Open		50.00	50
1986	Pacific Heights House 5066-0	Closed	1988	33.00	85-130
1988	Palos Verdes 5141-1	Closed	1990	37.50	70-90
1989	Paramount Theater 5142-0	Closed	1993	42.00	85-125
1984	Parish Church 5039-3	Closed	1986	32.00	300-400
1983	Parsonage 5029-6	Closed	1985	35.00	300-415
1995	Peppermint Porch Day Care 5485-2	Open		45.00	45
1989	Pinewood Log Cabin 5150-0	Closed	1995	37.50	42-90
1982	Pioneer Church 5022-9	Closed	1984	30.00	300-360
1995	Pisa Pizza 5485-1	Open		35.00	35
1985	Plantation House 5047-4	Closed	1987	37.00	88-120
1992	Post Office 5422-4	Closed	1995	35.00	50
1990	Prairie House (American Architecture Series), 5156-0	Closed	1993	42.00	50-80
1992	Print Shop & Village News 5425-9	Closed	1994	37.50	50-75
1990	Queen Anne Victorian (American Architecture Series), 5157-8	Open		48.00	50
1986	Ramsey Hill House 5067-9	Closed	1989	36.00	80-130
1987	Red Barn 5081-4	Closed	1992	38.00	70-90
1988	Redeemer Church 5127-6	Closed	1992	42.00	50-80
1985	Ridgewood 5052-0	Closed	1987	35.00	155-180
1984	River Road House 5010-5	Closed	1987	36.00	220-250
1995	Ryman Auditorium 5485-5	Open		75.00	75

YEAR ISSUE		EDITION LIMIT	YEAR RETD.	ISSUE PRICE	*QUOTE U.S.$
1986	Saint James Church 5068-7	Closed	1988	37.00	132-182
1979	School House 5060-9	Closed	1982	30.00	250-400
1988	Service Station 5128-4	Closed	1991	37.50	175-300
1988	Single Car Garage 5125-0	Closed	1990	22.00	40-80
1994	Skate & Ski Shop 5467-4	Open		50.00	50
1982	Skating Pond 5017-2	Closed	1984	25.00	360-400
1978	Skating Rink, Duck Pond (set) 5015-3	Closed	1979	16.00	1500
1976	Small Chalet 5006-2	Closed	1979	15.00	400-515
1978	Small Double Trees w/ blue birds 5016-1	Closed	1989	13.50	170
1978	Small Double Trees w/ red birds 5016-1	Closed	1989	13.50	35-70
1995	Snow Carnival Ice Palace 5485-0	Open		95.00	95
1987	Snow Village Factory 5013-0	Closed	1989	45.00	125-150
1987	Snow Village Resort Lodge 5092-0	Closed	1989	55.00	125-165
1993	Snowy Hills Hospital, 5448-8	Open		48.00	48
1986	Sonoma House 5062-8	Closed	1988	33.00	125-150
1991	Southern Colonial (American Architecture Series), 5403-8	Closed	1994	48.00	55-80
1990	Spanish Mission Church 5155-1	Closed	1992	42.00	45-90
1987	Springfield House 5027-0	Closed	1990	40.00	55-85
1985	Spruce Place 5049-0	Closed	1987	33.00	225-320
1987	St. Anthony Hotel & Post Office 5006-7	Closed	1989	40.00	95-135
1992	St. Luke's Church 5421-6	Closed	1994	45.00	45-70
1995	Starbucks Coffee 5485-9	Open		48.00	48
1976	Steepled Church 5005-4	Closed	1979	25.00	350-600
1977	Stone Church (10") 5009-6	Closed	1979	35.00	400-650
1979	Stone Church (8") 5059-1	Closed	1980	32.00	900
1980	Stone Mill House 5068-2	Closed	1982	30.00	430-600
1988	Stonehurst House 5140-3	Closed	1994	37.50	40-70
1984	Stratford House 5007-5	Closed	1986	28.00	135-200
1982	Street Car 5019-9	Closed	1984	16.00	330-420
1985	Stucco Bungalow 5045-8	Closed	1986	30.00	385
1984	Summit House 5036-9	Closed	1985	28.00	310-435
1982	Swiss Chalet 5023-7	Closed	1984	28.00	425-485
1979	Thatched Cottage 5050-0 Meadowland Series	Closed	1980	30.00	610-700
1980	Town Church 5071-7	Closed	1982	33.00	350-450
1983	Town Hall 5000-8	Closed	1984	32.00	350-400
1986	Toy Shop 5073-3	Closed	1990	36.00	75-100
1980	Train Station w/ 3 Train Cars 5085-6	Closed	1985	100.00	300-400
1984	Trinity Church 5035-0	Closed	1986	32.00	235-300
1979	Tudor House 5061-7	Closed	1981	25.00	300-400
1983	Turn of the Century 5004-0	Closed	1986	36.00	245-300
1986	Twin Peaks 5042-3	Closed	1986	32.00	340-500
1979	Victorian 5054-2	Closed	1982	30.00	340-440
1983	Victorian Cottage 5002-4	Closed	1984	35.00	300-400
1977	Victorian House 5007-0	Closed	1979	30.00	325-450
1983	Village Church 5026-1	Closed	1984	30.00	425
1991	Village Greenhouse 5402-0	Closed	1995	35.00	55
1988	Village Market 5044-0	Closed	1991	39.00	65-90
1995	Village Police Station 5485-3	Open		48.00	48
1993	Village Public Library, 5443-7	Open		55.00	55
1990	Village Realty 5154-3	Closed	1993	42.00	55-75
1992	Village Station 5438-0	Open		65.00	65
1988	Village Station and Train 5122-5	Closed	1992	65.00	80-130
1992	Village Vet and Pet Shop 5427-5	Closed	1995	32.00	55
1989	Village Warming House 5145-4	Closed	1992	42.00	55-90
1986	Waverly Place 5041-5	Closed	1986	35.00	220-325
1994	Wedding Chapel 5464-0	Open		55.00	55
1985	Williamsburg House 5046-6	Closed	1988	37.00	125-150
1993	Woodbury House, 5444-5	Open		45.00	45
1983	Wooden Church 5031-8	Closed	1985	30.00	250-400
1981	Wooden Clapboard 5072-5	Closed	1984	32.00	200-300

The Original Snow Village Collection Accessories Retired - Department 56

YEAR ISSUE		EDITION LIMIT	YEAR RETD.	ISSUE PRICE	*QUOTE U.S.$
1987	3 Nuns With Songbooks 5102-0	Closed	1988	6.00	120-140
1993	Check It Out Bookmobile 5451-8, set/3	Closed	1995	25.00	27
1992	Early Morning Delivery 5431-3, set/3	Closed	1995	27.50	28
1992	Round & Round We Go! 5433-0, set/2	Closed	1995	18.00	29
1994	Santa Comes To Town, 1995 5477-1	Closed	1995	30.00	30
1990	A Tree For Me 5164-0, set/2	Closed	1995	8.00	9
1989	Village Gazebo 5146-2	Closed	1995	30.00	37
1992	Winter Playground 5436-4	Closed	1995	20.00	22
1988	Apple Girl/Newspaper Boy 5129-2, set/2	Closed	1990	11.00	15-25
1979	Aspen Trees 5052-6, Meadowland Series	Closed	1980	16.00	500
1989	Bringing Home The Tree 5169-1	Closed	1992	15.00	20-30
1989	Calling All Cars 5174-8, set/2	Closed	1991	15.00	25-45
1979	Carolers 5064-1	Closed	1986	12.00	115-130
1987	Caroling Family 5105-5, set/3	Closed	1990	20.00	25-40
1980	Ceramic Car 5069-0	Closed	1986	5.00	50-65
1981	Ceramic Sleigh 5079-2	Closed	1986	5.00	45-65
1987	Children In Band 5104-7	Closed	1989	15.00	20-35
1989	Choir Kids 5147-0	Closed	1992	15.00	15-25
1991	Christmas Cadillac 5413-5	Closed	1994	9.00	15
1987	Christmas Children 5107-1, set/4	Closed	1990	20.00	25-35
1991	Cold Weather Sports 5410-0, set/4	Closed	1994	27.50	35
1991	Come Join The Parade 5411-9	Closed	1992	13.00	10-25
1991	Country Harvest 5415-1	Closed	1993	13.00	20-30
1988	Doghouse/Cat In Garbage Can 5131-4, set/2	Closed	1992	15.00	20-30
1990	Down the Chimney He Goes, 5158-6	Closed	1993	6.50	10-20

YEAR ISSUE		EDITION LIMIT	YEAR RETD.	ISSUE PRICE	*QUOTE U.S.$
1985	Family Mom/Kids, Goose/Girl 5057-1	Closed	1988	11.00	20-45
1987	For Sale Sign 5108-0	Closed	1989	3.50	8-15
1990	Fresh Frozen Fish 5163-2, set/2	Closed	1993	20.00	24-40
1986	Girl/Snowman, Boy 5095-4	Closed	1987	11.00	55-70
1988	Hayride 5117-9	Closed	1990	30.00	55-75
1990	Here We Come A Caroling 5161-6, set/3	Closed	1992	18.00	15-30
1990	Home Delivery 5162-4, set/2	Closed	1992	16.00	25-40
1986	Kids Around The Tree (large) 5094-6	Closed	1990	15.00	45-75
1986	Kids Around The Tree (small) 5094-6	Closed	1990	15.00	40-60
1990	Kids Decorating the Village Sign, 5134-9	Closed	1993	13.00	15-25
1989	Kids Tree House 5168-3	Closed	1991	25.00	40-60
1988	Man On Ladder Hanging Garland 5116-0	Closed	1992	7.50	10-20
1984	Monks-A-Caroling (brown) 5040-7	Closed	1988	6.00	25-50
1983	Monks-A-Caroling (butterscotch) 6459-9	Closed	1984	6.00	70
1992	Nanny and the Preschoolers 5430-5, set/2	Closed	1994	27.50	30-45
1987	Park Bench (green) 5109-8	Closed	1993	3.00	8-15
1987	Praying Monks 5103-9	Closed	1988	6.00	30-50
1985	Santa/Mailbox 5059-8	Closed	1988	11.00	25-55
1988	School Bus, Snow Plow 5137-3, set/2	Closed	1991	16.00	45-55
1988	School Children 5118-7, set/3	Closed	1990	15.00	15-30
1984	Scottie With Tree 5038-5	Closed	1985	3.00	135-175
1979	Sheep, 9 White, 3 Black 5053-4 Meadowland Series	Closed	1980	12.00	400
1986	Shopping Girls w/Packages (large) 5096-2	Closed	1988	11.00	30-50
1986	Shopping Girls w/Packages (small) 5096-2	Closed	1988	11.00	40-55
1985	Singing Nuns 5053-9	Closed	1987	6.00	120-150
1988	Sisal Tree Lot 8183-3	Closed	1991	45.00	105-120
1989	Skate Faster Mom 5170-5	Closed	1991	13.00	15-25
1990	Sleighride 5160-8	Closed	1992	30.00	50-65
1990	Sno-Jet Snowmobile, 5159-4	Closed	1993	15.00	15-30
1987	Snow Kids 5113-6, set/4	Closed	1990	20.00	45-55
1985	Snow Kids Sled, Skis 5056-3	Closed	1987	11.00	42-60
1991	Snowball Fort 5414-3, set/3	Closed	1993	28.00	25-40
1982	Snowman With Broom 5018-0	Closed	1990	3.00	10-20
1989	Statue of Mark Twain 5173-0	Closed	1991	15.00	20-40
1990	SV Special Delivery 5197-7, set/2	Closed	1992	16.00	25-45
1989	Through the Woods 5172-1, set/2	Closed	1991	18.00	25-40
1989	US Mailbox 5179-9	Closed	1990	3.50	10-20
1989	US Special Delivery 5148-9, set/2	Closed	1990	16.00	25-50
1989	Village Birds 5180-2, set/6	Closed	1994	3.50	10-20
1991	Village Greetings 5418-6, set/3	Closed	1994	5.00	8
1991	Village Marching Band 5412-7, set/3	Closed	1992	30.00	45-50
1988	Water Tower 5133-0	Closed	1991	20.00	60-90
1989	Water Tower-John Deer 568-0	Closed	1991	20.00	650-800
1992	We're Going to a Christmas Pageant 5435-6	Closed	1994	15.00	17
1991	Winter Fountain 5409-7	Closed	1993	25.00	45-55
1988	Woodsman & Boy 5130-6, set/2	Closed	1991	13.00	20-35
1988	Woody Station Wagon 5136-5	Closed	1990	6.50	22-35
1991	Wreaths For Sale 5408-9,set/4	Closed	1994	27.50	35

Retired Heritage Village Collection Accessories - Department 56

YEAR ISSUE		EDITION LIMIT	YEAR RETD.	ISSUE PRICE	*QUOTE U.S.$
1991	All Around the Town 5545-0, set/2	Closed	1993	18.00	20-35
1987	Alpine Village Sign 6571-4	Closed	1993	6.00	15-25
1986	Alpine Villagers 6542-0, set/3	Closed	1992	13.00	30-4
1990	Amish Buggy 5949-8	Closed	1992	22.00	25-6
1990	Amish Family 5948-0, set/3	Closed	1992	20.00	25-4
1990	Amish Family, w/Moustache 5948-0, set/3	Closed	1992	20.00	45-6
1991	Baker Elves 5603-0, set/3	Closed	1995	27.50	30-4
1992	The Bird Seller 5803-3, set/3	Closed	1995	25.00	30-5
1987	Blacksmith 5934-0, set/3	Closed	1990	20.00	60-8
1990	Busy Sidewalks 5535-2, set/4	Closed	1992	28.00	35-5
1992	Buying Bakers Bread 5619-7, set/2	Closed	1995	20.00	25-4
1990	Carolers on the Doorstep 5570-0, set/4	Closed	1993	25.00	25-4
1984	Carolers, w/ Lamppost (bl) 6526-9, set/3	Closed	1990	10.00	25-4
1984	Carolers, w/ Lamppost (wh) 6526-9, set/3	Closed	1990	10.00	100-12
1988	Childe Pond and Skaters 5903-0, set/4	Closed	1991	30.00	65-8
1986	Christmas Carol Figures 6501-3, set/3	Closed	1990	12.50	60-8
1987	Christmas in the City Sign, 5960-9	Closed	1993	6.00	1
1992	Churchyard Gate and Fence 5563-8, set/3	Closed	1992	15.00	5
1988	City Bus & Milk Truck 5983-8, set/2	Closed	1991	15.00	20-4
1988	City Newsstand 5971-4, set/4	Closed	1991	25.00	45-6
1987	City People 5965-0, set/5	Closed	1990	27.50	45-5
1987	City Workers 5967-6, set/4	Closed	1988	15.00	40-5
1991	Come into the Inn, 5560-3	Closed	1994	22.00	30-4
1989	Constables 5579-4, set/3	Closed	1991	17.50	55-7
1986	Covered Wooden Bridge 6531-5	Closed	1990	10.00	35-4
1989	David Copperfield Characters 5551-4, set/5	Closed	1992	32.50	30-4
1987	Dickens' Village Sign 6569-2	Closed	1993	6.00	13-
1992	Don't Drop The Presents! 5532-8, set/2	Closed	1995	25.00	25-

*Quotes have been rounded up to nearest dolla

YEAR ISSUE		EDITION LIMIT	YEAR RETD.	ISSUE PRICE	*QUOTE U.S.$
1987	Dover Coach 6590-0	Closed	1990	18.00	60-90
1987	Dover Coach w/o Mustache 6590-0	Closed	1990	18.00	85-110
1989	Farm Animals 5945-5, set/4	Closed	1991	15.00	35-50
1987	Farm People And Animals 5901-3, set/5	Closed	1989	24.00	55-100
1988	Fezziwig and Friends 5928-5, set/3	Closed	1990	12.50	45-55
1991	The Fire Brigade 5546-8, set/2	Closed	1995	20.00	25-35
1991	Fire Truck, "City Fire Dept." 5547-6, set/2	Closed	1995	18.00	28
1992	Harvest Seed Cart 5645-6, set/3	Closed	1995	27.50	30
1989	Heritage Village Sign, 9953-8	Closed	1989	10.00	25-45
1992	Letters for Santa 5604-9, set/3	Closed	1994	30.00	45-55
1986	Lighted Tree With Children & Ladder 6510-2	Closed	1989	35.00	275-335
1987	Maple Sugaring Shed 6589-7, set/3	Closed	1989	19.00	200-245
1991	Market Day 5641-3,set/3	Closed	1993	35.00	30-50
1987	New England Village Sign 6570-6	Closed	1993	6.00	12-20
1986	New England Winter set 6532-3, set/5	Closed	1990	18.00	35-50
1988	Nicholas Nickleby Characters 5929-3, set/4	Closed	1991	20.00	30-45
1992	The Old Puppeteer 5802-5, set/3	Closed	1995	32.00	35-55
1991	Oliver Twist Characters 5554-9, set/3	Closed	1993	35.00	30-46
1988	One Horse Open Sleigh 5982-0	Closed	1993	20.00	25-40
1989	Organ Grinder 5957-9, set/3	Closed	1991	21.00	30-45
1987	Ox Sled (blue pants) 5951-0	Closed	1989	20.00	120-150
1987	Ox Sled (tan pants) 5951-0	Closed	1989	20.00	225-275
1989	Popcorn Vendor 5958-7, set/3	Closed	1992	22.00	25-40
1986	Porcelain Trees 6537-4,set/2	Closed	1992	14.00	35
1994	Postern, 9871-0, (Dickens' Village Ten Year Accessory Anniversary Piece)	Closed	1994	17.50	26
1991	Poultry Market 5559-0, set/3	Closed	1995	32.00	35
1988	Red Covered Bridge, 5987-0	Closed	1994	17.00	25-35
1989	River Street Ice House Cart 5959-5	Closed	1991	20.00	45-55
1989	Royal Coach 5578-6	Closed	1992	55.00	70-80
1988	Salvation Army Band 5985-4, set/6	Closed	1991	24.00	60-75
1990	Santa's Little Helpers 5610-3, set/3	Closed	1993	28.00	45-60
1987	Shopkeepers 5966-8, set/4	Closed	1988	15.00	30-45
1987	Silo And Hay Shed 5950-1	Closed	1989	18.00	125-170
1987	Skating Pond 6545-5	Closed	1990	24.00	70-95
1990	Sleepy Hollow Characters 5956-0, set/3	Closed	1992	27.50	40-50
1986	Sleighride 6511-0	Closed	1990	19.50	40-65
1988	Snow Children 5938-2	Closed	1994	17.00	25-35
1987	Stone Bridge 6546-3	Closed	1990	12.00	60-85
1990	Tis the Season 5539-5	Closed	1994	12.95	15-25
1992	Town Tinker 5646-4, set/2	Closed	1995	24.00	25-35
1991	Toymaker Elves 5602-2, set/3	Closed	1995	27.50	25-40
1990	Trimming the North Pole 5608-1	Closed	1993	10.00	25-28
1989	U.S. Mail Box and Fire Hydrant 5517-4	Closed	1990	5.00	15-25
1989	Village Blvd. 5516-6, set/14	Closed	1993	25.00	46
1987	Village Express Train (electric, black),5997-8	Closed	1988	89.95	260-300
1993	Village Express Van (black), 9951-1	Closed	1993	25.00	125-145
1993	Village Express Van (gold), 9977-5 (promotional)	Closed	1993	N/A	950-1300
1994	Village Express Van-Bachman's, 729-3	Closed	1994	22.50	78
1994	Village Express Van-Bronner's, 737-4	Closed	1994	22.50	45-75
1995	Village Express Van-Canadian 2163-7	Closed	1995	N/A	75-135
1994	Village Express Van-Christmas Dove, 730-7	Closed	1994	25.00	50-75
1994	Village Express Van-European Imports, 739-0	Closed	1994	22.50	60-75
1994	Village Express Van-Fortunoff's, 735-8	Closed	1994	22.50	125-135
1994	Village Express Van-Limited Edition, 733-1	Closed	1994	25.00	75-115
1994	Village Express Van-Lock, Stock & Barrel, 731-5	Closed	1994	22.50	115-135
1994	Village Express Van-North Pole City, 736-6	Closed	1994	25.00	50-70
1995	Village Express Van-Park West 0755-2	Closed	1995	N/A	50-70
1994	Village Express Van-Robert's Christmas Wonderland, 734-0	Closed	1994	22.50	55-75
1994	Village Express Van-Stat's, 741-2	Closed	1994	22.50	50-80
1994	Village Express Van-The Incredible Christmas (Pigeon Forge), 732-3	Closed	1994	24.98	45-80
1994	Village Express Van-The Lemon Tree, 721-8	Closed	1994	30.00	50-75
1994	Village Express Van-William Glen, 738-2	Closed	1994	22.50	45-65
1994	Village Express Van-Windsor Shoppe, 740-4	Closed	1994	25.00	55-75
1988	Village Harvest People 5941-2, set/4	Closed	1991	27.50	20
1989	Village Sign w/Snowman, 5572-7	Closed	1994	10.00	15-30
1992	Village Street Peddlers 5804-1, set/2	Closed	1994	16.00	20-30
1985	Village Train Brighton 6527-7, set/3	Closed	1986	12.00	400-500
1988	Village Train Trestle 5981-1	Closed	1990	17.00	60-80
1987	Village Well And Holy Cross 6547-1, set/2	Closed	1989	13.00	125-155
1989	Violet Vendor/Carolers/Chestnut Vendor 5580-8, set/3	Closed	1992	23.00	30-45
1992	Welcome Home 5533-6, set/3	Closed	1995	27.50	30-50
1988	Woodcutter & Son 5986-2, set/2	Closed	1990	10.00	35-45
1993	Woodsmen Elves 5630-8, set/3	Closed	1995	27.50	40-50

Snowbabies - Department 56

YEAR ISSUE		EDITION LIMIT	YEAR RETD.	ISSUE PRICE	*QUOTE U.S.$
1989	All Fall Down 7984-7, set/4	Closed	1991	36.00	55-85
1990	All Tired Out, waterglobe 7937-5	Closed	1992	55.00	75
1988	Are All These Mine? 7977-4	Open		10.00	13
1995	Are You On My List? 6875-6	Open		25.00	25
1995	Are You On My List?, waterglobe 6879-7	Open		32.50	33
1986	Best Friends 7958-8	Closed	1989	12.00	95-150
1994	Bringing Starry Pines 6862-4	Open		35.00	35
1992	Can I Help, Too? 6806-3	18,500	1992	48.00	65-100
1993	Can I Open it Now? 6838-1 (Event Piece)	Closed	1993	15.00	25-50
1993	Can I Open it Now?, mini music box 7648-1	Closed	1994	20.00	40-60
1986	Catch a Falling Star, waterglobe 7967-7	Closed	1987	18.00	500-600
1986	Climbing on Snowball, Bisque Votive w/Candle 7965-0	Closed	1989	15.00	110-125
1987	Climbing On Tree 7971-5, set/2	Closed	1989	25.00	750-865
1993	Crossing Starry Skies 6834-9	Open		35.00	35
1991	Dancing To a Tune 6808-0, set/3	Closed	1995	30.00	40-60
1987	Don't Fall Off 7968-5	Closed	1990	12.50	85-115
1987	Down The Hill We Go 7960-0	Open		20.00	23
1989	Finding Fallen Stars 7985-5	6,000	1989	32.50	145-185
1991	Fishing For Dreams 6809-8	Closed	1994	28.00	35-45
1992	Fishing For Dreams, waterglobe 6832-2	Closed	1994	32.50	60
1986	Forest Accessory "Frosty Forest" 7963-4, set/2	Open		15.00	20
1988	Frosty Frolic 7981-2	4,800	1989	35.00	700-1000
1989	Frosty Fun 7983-9	Closed	1991	27.50	35-75
1993	Frosty Fun, mini music box 7650-3	Closed	1994	20.00	50
1995	Frosty Pines 76687, set/3	Open		12.50	13
1986	Give Me A Push 7955-3	Closed	1990	12.00	65
1986	Hanging Pair 7966-9	Closed	1989	15.00	145-165
1992	Help Me, I'm Stuck 6817-9	Closed	1994	32.50	45
1989	Helpful Friends 7982-0	Closed	1993	30.00	35-60
1986	Hold On Tight 7956-1	Open		12.00	14
1995	I Can't Find Him 68800	Open		37.50	38
1995	I Found The Biggest Star of All! 6874-8	Open		16.00	16
1993	I Found Your Mittens 6836-5, set/2	Open		30.00	30
1991	I Made This Just For You 6802-0	Open		15.00	15
1992	I Need A Hug 6813-6	Open		20.00	20
1995	I See You! 6878-0, set/2	Open		27.50	28
1995	I'll Hug You Goodnight, waterglobe 68798	Open		32.50	33
1995	I'll Play A Christmas Tune 68801	Open		16.00	16
1991	I'll Put Up The Tree 6800-4	Closed	1995	24.00	25-45
1993	I'll Teach You A Trick 6835-7	Open		24.00	24
1993	I'm Making an Ice Sculpture 6842-0	Open		30.00	30
1986	I'm Making Snowballs 7962-6	Closed	1992	12.00	30-45
1994	I'm Right Behind You! 6852-7	Open		60.00	60
1989	Icy Igloo 7987-1	Open		37.50	38
1991	Is That For Me 6803-9, set/2	Closed	1993	32.50	25-45
1994	Jack Frost...A Touch of Winter's Magic 6854-3	Open		90.00	95
1992	Join The Parade 6824-1	Closed	1994	37.50	48
1992	Just One Little Candle 6823-3	Open		15.00	15
1989	Let It Snow, waterglobe 7992-8	Closed	1993	25.00	35-45
1993	Let's All Chime In! 6845-4, set/2	Closed	1995	37.50	40-55
1994	Let's Go Skating 6860-8	Open		16.50	17
1992	Let's Go Skiing 6815-2	Closed	1994	15.00	20
1994	Lift Me Higher, I Can't Reach 6863-2	Open		75.00	75
1992	Look What I Can Do! 6819-5	Open		16.50	17
1993	Look What I Found 6833-0	Open		45.00	45
1994	Look What I Found, waterglobe 6872-1	Open		32.50	33
1994	Mickey's New Friend 714-5	Retrd.	1995	60.00	200-400
1995	Mush 68805	Open		48.00	48
1993	Now I Lay Me Down to Sleep 6839-0	Open		13.50	14
1992	Over the Milky Way 6828-4	Closed	1995	32.00	60
1995	Parade of Penguins 68804, set/6	Open		15.00	15
1991	Peek-A-Boo, waterglobe 7938-3	Closed	1993	50.00	80
1989	Penguin Parade 7986-3	Closed	1992	25.00	45-70
1993	Penguin Parade, mini music box 7645-5	Closed	1994	20.00	45-60
1994	Pennies From Heaven 6864-0	Open		17.50	18
1994	Planting Starry Pines, waterglobe 6870-5	Open		32.50	33
1991	Play Me a Tune, waterglobe 7936-7	Closed	1993	50.00	55-80
1993	Play Me a Tune, mini music box 7651-1	Closed	1994	20.00	50
1995	Play Me a Tune, music box 68809	Open		37.50	38
1990	Playing Games Is Fun 7947-2	Closed	1993	30.00	25-45
1988	Polar Express 7978-2	Closed	1992	22.00	65-100
1990	Read Me a Story 7945-6	Open		25.00	25
1992	Read Me a Story, waterglobe 6831-4	Open		32.50	33
1993	Reading a Story, mini music box 7649-0	Closed	1994	20.00	45-60
1995	Ring The Bells...It's Christmas! 6876-4	Open		40.00	40
1992	Shall I Play For You? 6820-9	Open		16.50	17
1995	Skate With Me, waterglobe 68799	Open		32.50	33
1995	Snowbabies Animated Skating Pond 7668-6, set/14	Open		60.00	60
1993	Snowbabies Picture Frame, Baby's First Smile 6846-2	Open		30.00	30
1987	Snowbabies Riding Sleds, waterglobe 7975-8	Closed	1988	40.00	700
1986	Snowbaby Holding Picture Frame 7970-7, set/2	Closed	1987	15.00	540-650
1986	Snowbaby Nite-Lite 7959-6	Closed	1989	15.00	275-350
1991	Snowbaby Polar Sign 6804-7	Open		20.00	20
1986	Snowbaby Standing, waterglobe 7964-2	Closed	1987	7.50	445
1987	Snowbaby with Wings, waterglobe 7973-1	Closed	1988	20.00	450-550
1993	So Much Work To Do 6837-3	Open		18.00	18
1993	Somewhere in Dreamland 6840-3	Open		85.00	85
1990	A Special Delivery 7948-0	Closed	1994	15.00	20-35
1992	Starry Pines 6829-2, set/2	Open		17.50	18
1992	Stars-In-A-Row, Tic-Tac-Toe 6822-5	Closed	1995	32.50	45
1994	Stringing Fallen Stars 6861-6	Open		25.00	25
1994	There's Another One!, 6853-5	Open		24.00	24
1991	This Is Where We Live 6805-5	Closed	1994	60.00	65-75
1992	This Will Cheer You Up 6816-0	Closed	1994	30.00	25-55
1988	Tiny Trio 7979-0, set/3	Closed	1990	20.00	150-170
1987	Tumbling In the Snow 7957-0, set/5	Closed	1993	35.00	70-100
1990	Twinkle Little Stars 7942-1, set/2	Closed	1993	37.50	45-60
1992	Wait For Me 6812-8	Closed	1994	48.00	50-70
1991	Waiting For Christmas 6807-1	Closed	1993	27.50	30-45
1993	We Make a Great Pair 6843-8	Open		30.00	30
1990	We Will Make it Shine 7946-4	Closed	1992	45.00	50-90
1994	We'll Plant the Starry Pines 6865-9, set/2	Open		37.50	38
1995	We're Building An Icy Igloo 68802	Open		70.00	70
1995	What Shall We Do Today? 6877-2	Open		32.50	33
1987	When You Wish Upon a Star, music box 7972-3	Closed	1993	30.00	45
1993	Whistle While You Work, music box 6849-7	Closed	1995	32.50	46-60
1993	Where Did He Go? 6841-1	Open		35.00	35
1994	Where Did You Come From? 6856-0	Open		40.00	40
1990	Who Are You? 7949-9	12,500	1991	32.50	110-145
1991	Why Don't You Talk To Me 6801-2	Open		24.00	24
1993	Will it Snow Today? 6844-6	Closed	1995	45.00	45-65
1992	Winken, Blinken, and Nod 6814-4	Open		60.00	65
1987	Winter Surprise 7974-0	Closed	1992	15.00	30-45
1990	Wishing on a Star 7943-0	Closed	1994	22.00	25-45
1992	You Can't Find Me! 6818-7	Open		45.00	45
1992	You Didn't Forget Me 6821-7	Open		32.50	33

Snowbabies Pewter Miniatures - Department 56

YEAR ISSUE		EDITION LIMIT	YEAR RETD.	ISSUE PRICE	*QUOTE U.S.$
1989	All Fall Down 7617-1, set/4	Closed	1993	25.00	35-55
1989	Are All These Mine? 7605-8	Closed	1992	7.00	15-25
1989	Best Friends. 7604-0	Closed	1994	10.00	20
1991	Dancing to a Tune 7630-9, set/3	Closed	1993	18.00	32
1989	Don't Fall Off!, 7603-1	Closed	1994	7.00	10-25
1989	Finding Fallen Stars 7618-0, set/2	Closed	1992	12.50	30-45
1989	Frosty Frolic 7613-9, set/4	Closed	1993	24.00	25-40
1989	Give Me a Push! 7601-5	Closed	1994	7.00	15
1989	Helpful Friends 7608-2, set/4	Closed	1992	13.50	25-35
1991	I Made This Just for You! 7628-7	Closed	1994	7.00	15
1989	Icy Igloo, w/tree 7610-4, set/2	Closed	1992	7.50	22-30
1991	Is That For Me? 7631-7, set/2	Closed	1993	12.50	25
1992	Join the Parade, 7645-7, set/4	Closed	1995	22.50	25-40
1989	Penguin Parade 7616-3, set/4	Closed	1993	12.50	28-35
1990	Playing Games is Fun! 7623-6, set/2	Closed	1993	13.50	25-35
1989	Polar Express 7609-0, set/2	Closed	1992	13.50	30-40
1990	A Special Delivery 7624-4	Closed	1993	7.00	20
1992	This Will Cheer You Up, 7639-2	Closed	1995	13.75	25
1989	Tiny Trio 7615-5, set/3	Closed	1993	18.00	25-40
1989	Tumbling in the Snow! 7614-7, set/5	Closed	1992	30.00	60-75
1990	Twinkle Little Stars 7621-0, set/2	Closed	1993	15.00	20-30
1992	Wait For Me!, 7641-4, set/4	Closed	1995	22.50	25-40
1991	Waiting for Christmas, 7629-5	Closed	1993	13.00	25
1989	Winter Surprise!, 7607-4	Closed	1994	13.50	15-30
1991	Wishing on a Star, 7626-0	Closed	1995	10.00	20
1992	You Didn't Forget Me!, 7643-0, set/3	Closed	1995	17.50	20-30

Village CCP Miniatures - Department 56

YEAR ISSUE		EDITION LIMIT	YEAR RETD.	ISSUE PRICE	*QUOTE U.S.$
1987	Christmas Carol Cottages 6561-7, set/3	Closed	1989	30.00	85-125
1987	•The Cottage of Bob Cratchit & Tiny Tim 6561-7	Closed	1989	10.00	35-50
1987	•Fezziwig's Warehouse 6561-7	Closed	1989	10.00	30-45
1987	•Scrooge/ Marley Countinghouse 6561-7	Closed	1989	10.00	30-40
1987	Dickens' Chadbury Station & Train 6592-7	Closed	1989	27.50	50-80
1987	Dickens' Cottages 6559-5, set/3	Closed	1989	30.00	275-350
1987	•Stone Cottage 6559-5	Closed	1989	10.00	130
1987	•Thatched Cottage 6559-5	Closed	1989	10.00	115-130
1987	•Tudor Cottage 6559-5	Closed	1989	10.00	128
1988	Dickens' Kenilworth Castle 6565-0	Closed	1989	30.00	100-175
1987	Dickens' Lane Shops 6591-9, set/3	Closed	1989	30.00	143
1987	•Cottage Toy Shop 6591-9	Closed	1989	10.00	45
1987	•Thomas Kersey Coffee House 6591-9	Closed	1989	10.00	55
1987	•Tuttle's Pub 6591-9	Closed	1989	10.00	55
1987	Dickens' Village Assorted 6560-9, set/3	Closed	1989	48.00	140

YEAR ISSUE		EDITION LIMIT	YEAR RETD.	ISSUE PRICE	*QUOTE U.S.$
1987	•Blythe Pond Mill House 6560-9	Closed	1989	16.00	40-55
1987	•Dickens Village Church 6560-9	Closed	1989	16.00	50-80
1987	•Norman Church 6560-9	Closed	1989	16.00	120-150
1987	Dickens' Village Assorted 6562-5, set/4	Closed	1989	60.00	300
1987	•Barley Bree Farmhouse 6562-5	Closed	1989	15.00	40-75
1987	•Brick Abbey 6562-5	Closed	1989	15.00	90-125
1987	•Chesterton Manor House 6562-5	Closed	1989	15.00	115-140
1987	•The Old Curiosity Shop 6562-5	Closed	1989	15.00	75-115
1987	Dickens' Village Original 6558-7, set/7	Closed	1989	72.00	300
1987	•Abel Beesley Butcher 6558-7	Closed	1989	12.00	30-50
1987	•Bean and Son Smithy Shop 6558-7	Closed	1989	12.00	35-50
1987	•Candle Shop 6558-7	Closed	1989	12.00	30-50
1987	•Crowntree Inn 6558-7	Closed	1989	12.00	45
1987	•Golden Swan Baker 6558-7	Closed	1989	12.00	25-45
1987	•Green Grocer 6558-7	Closed	1989	12.00	40-50
1987	•Jones & Co Brush & Basket Shop 6558-7	Closed	1989	12.00	45-55
1987	Little Town of Bethlehem 5976-5, set/12	Closed	1989	85.00	180
1988	New England Village Assorted 5937-4, set/6	Closed	1989	85.00	400-500
1988	•Craggy Cove Lighthouse 5937-4	Closed	1989	14.50	160
1988	•Jacob Adams Barn 5937-4	Closed	1989	14.50	70-95
1988	•Jacob Adams Farmhouse 5937-4	Closed	1989	14.50	55-70
1988	•Maple Sugaring Shed 5937-4	Closed	1989	14.50	48-75
1988	•Smythe Wollen Mill 5937-4	Closed	1989	14.50	105
1988	•Timber Knoll Log Cabin 5937-4	Closed	1989	14.50	45
1988	New England Village Original 5935-8, set/7	Closed	1989	72.00	600-800
1988	•Apothecary Shop 5935-8	Closed	1989	10.50	38
1988	•Brick Town Hall 5935-8	Closed	1989	10.50	60-70
1988	•General Store 5935-8	Closed	1989	10.50	80
1988	•Livery Stable & Boot Shop 5935-8	Closed	1989	10.50	40-80
1988	•Nathaniel Bingham Fabrics 5935-8	Closed	1989	10.50	55-70
1988	•Red Schoolhouse 5935-8	Closed	1989	10.50	75-90
1988	•Village Steeple Church 5935-8	Closed	1989	10.50	235-250
1986	Victorian Miniatures, set/2 6564-1	Closed	1987	45.00	275
1986	•Church 6564-1	Closed	1987	22.50	150
1986	•Estate 6564-1	Closed	1987	22.50	175
1986	Victorian Miniatures 6563-3, set/5	Closed	1987	65.00	275
1986	Williamsburg Snowhouse Series, set/6	Closed	1987	60.00	575-650
1986	•Williamsburg Church, White 6566-8	Closed	1987	10.00	125
1986	•Williamsburg House Brown Brick 6566-8	Closed	1987	10.00	60-100
1986	•Williamsburg House, Blue 6566-8	Closed	1987	10.00	60-100
1986	•Williamsburg House, Brown Clapboard	Closed	1987	10.00	60-100
1986	•Williamsburg House, Red 6566-8	Closed	1987	10.00	60-110
1986	•Williamsburg House, White 6566-8	Closed	1987	10.00	85-125

Winter Silhouette - Department 56

1990	Angel Candle Holder w/Candle 6767-9	Closed	1992	32.50	33
1992	Bedtime Stories Waterglobe 7838-7	Closed	1995	30.00	30
1989	Bringing Home The Tree 7790-9, set/4	Closed	1993	75.00	75
1989	Camel w.glass Votive 6766-0	Closed	1993	25.00	25
1987	Carolers 7774-7, set/4	Closed	1993	120.00	150
1991	Chimney Sweep 7799-2	Closed	1993	37.50	55
1989	Father Christmas 7788-7	Closed	1993	50.00	50
1991	Grandfather Clock 7797-6	Closed	1995	27.50	28
1988	Joy To The World 5595-6	Closed	1990	42.00	42
1988	Silver Bells Music Box 8271-6	Closed	1990	75.00	75
1988	Skating Couple 7772-0	Closed	1995	35.00	44
1987	Snow Doves 8215-5, set/2	Closed	1992	60.00	60
1992	Snowy White Deer 7837-9, set/2	Closed	1995	55.00	55
1989	Three Kings Candle Holder 6765-2, set/3	Closed	1992	85.00	85
1991	Town Crier 7800-0	Closed	1994	37.50	50

Disneyana

Disneyana Conventions - Various

1992	1947 Mickey Mouse Plush J20967 - Gund	1,000	1992	50.00	100-150
1992	Big Thunder Mountain A26648 - R. Lee	250	1992	1650.00	3000-3500
1992	Carousel Horse 022482 - PJ's	250	1992	125.00	260-350
1992	Carousel Horse Poster (Lithograph)-A26318 - R. Souders	2,000	1992	25.00	50
1992	Cinderella 022076 - Armani	500	1992	500.00	3300-4500
1992	Cinderella Castle 022077 - John Hine Studio	500	1992	250.00	1100
1992	Cruella DeVil Doll-porcelain 22554 - J. Wols	25	1992	600.00	3000-3500
1992	Disneyana Logo Charger - B. White	25	1992	600.00	2800
1992	Nifty-Nineties Mickey & Minnie 022503 - House of Laurenz	250	1992	650.00	700-850
1992	Pinocchio - R. Wright	250	1992	750.00	1000-2000
1992	Serigraph Diptych Collage (Set/2)-22073 - M. Graves	1,000	1992	900.00	N/A
1992	Steamboat Willie-Resin - M. Delle	500	1992	125.00	1100-1400
1992	Tinker Bell 022075 - Lladró	1,500	1992	350.00	2300-2900
1992	Two Merry Wanderers 022074 - Goebel	1,500	1992	250.00	1100
1992	Walt's Convertible (Cel) - Disney Art Ed.	500	1992	950.00	2300
1993	1947 Minnie Mouse Plush - Gund	1,000	1993	50.00	120
1993	Alice in Wonderland - Malvern	10	1993	8000.00	N/A
1993	Annette Doll - Alexander Doll	1,000	1993	400.00	550
1993	The Band Concert "Maestro Mickey" - Disney Art Ed.	275	1993	2950.00	N/A
1993	The Band Concert-Bronze - B. Toma	25	1993	650.00	2800-3500
1993	Bandleader-Resin - M. Delle	1,500	1993	125.00	225-300
1993	Barbershop Quartet (Lithograph) - C. Boyer	1,000	1993	350.00	600
1993	Disneyland Bandstand Poster - R. Souders	2,000	1993	25.00	55
1993	Dopey - Armani	Retrd.	1993	125.00	190-300
1993	Family Dinner Figurine - C. Boyer	1,000	1993	600.00	1100-1300
1993	Jumper from King Arthur Carousel - PJ's	250	1993	125.00	200-400
1993	Mickey & Pluto Charger - White/Rhodes	25	1993	850.00	3000
1993	Mickey Mouse, the Bandleader - Arribas Brothers	25	1993	700.00	2200-3500
1993	Mickey's Dreams - R. Lee	250	1993	400.00	800-950
1993	Peter Pan - Lladró	2,000	1993	400.00	1000-1500
1993	Sleeping Beauty Castle - John Hine Studio	500	1993	250.00	375-600
1993	Snow White - Armani	2,000	1993	750.00	1000-1800
1993	Two Little Drummers - Goebel	1,500	1993	325.00	450
1993	Walt's Train Celebration - Disney Art Ed.	950	1993	950.00	1800
1994	Ariel - Armani	1,500	1994	750.00	1200-1500
1994	Cinderella/Godmother - Lladró	2,500	1994	875.00	900-1000
1994	Cinderella's Slipper - Waterford	1,200	1994	250.00	500-600
1994	Euro Disney Castle - John Hine Studio	750	1994	250.00	350-500
1994	Jessica & Roger Charger - White/Rhodes	25	1994	2000.00	3000-4000
1994	Mickey Triple Self Portrait - Goebel Miniatures	500	1994	295.00	900-1100
1994	Minnie Be Patient - Goebel	1,500	1994	395.00	450
1994	MM/MN w/House Kinetic - F. Prescott	10	1994	4000.00	N/A
1994	MM/MN/Goofy Limo (Stepin' Out) - Ron Lee	500	1994	500.00	600
1994	Scrooge in Money Bin/Bronze - Carl Barks	100	1994	1800.00	3300
1994	Sleeping Beauty - Malvern	10	1994	5500.00	N/A
1994	Sorcerer Mickey-Bronze - B. Toma	100	1994	1000.00	1850-2100
1994	Sorcerer Mickey-Crystal - Arribas Brothers	50	1994	1700.00	2300-2400
1994	Sorcerer Mickey-Resin - M. Delle	2,000	1994	125.00	220
1994	Studio Poster - R. Souders	1,000	1994	25.00	N/A
1995	Ah, Venice - M. Pierson	100		2600.00	2600
1995	Ariel's Dolphin Ride - Wyland	250		2500.00	2500
1995	Barbershop Quartet - Goebel Miniatures	750	1995	300.00	450-700
1995	Beauty and the Beast - Armani	2,000	1995	975.00	1000-1200
1995	Brave Little Tailor Charger - White/Rhodes	15	1995	2000.00	2850
1995	Celebration-Resin - M. Delle	1,500	1995	125.00	175-250
1995	Donald Duck Mini-Charger - White/Rhodes	1,000	1995	75.00	125-175
1995	Ear Force One - R. Lee	500		600.00	600
1995	Engine No. One - R. Lee	500		650.00	720
1995	Fire Station 105 - Lilliput Lane	501	1995	195.00	450-850
1995	For Father - Goebel	1,500		450.00	550
1995	Grandpa's Boys - Goebel	1,500		340.00	340
1995	Mad Minnie Charger - White/Rhodes	10	1995	2000.00	4000
1995	Memories - B. Toma	200	1995	1200.00	1300-1650
1995	Neat & Pretty Mickey-Crystal - Arribas	50	1995	1700.00	2700-3300
1995	Neat & Pretty Mickey-Resin - M. Delle	2,000	1995	135.00	195
1995	"Night of Stars" Poster - R. Souders	1,000		25.00	25
1995	Plane Crazy - Arribas	50	1995	1750.00	2100
1995	The Prince's Kiss - P Gordon	25	1995	250.00	600
1995	"Proud Pocahontas" Lithogragh - D. Struzan	500	1995	195.00	250
1995	Sheriff of Bullet Valley - Barks/Vought	200	1995	1800.00	2400
1995	Showtime - B. Toma	200		1400.00	2000
1995	Simba - Bolae	200		1500.00	1500
1995	Sleeping Beauty Castle Mirror - Gordon	250		1200.00	1200
1995	Sleeping Beauty Dance - Lladró	1,000	1995	1280.00	1600-2300
1995	Sleeping Beauty's Tiara - Waterford	1,500		250.00	350
1995	Snow White's Apple - Waterford	1,500		225.00	275-350
1995	"Snow White & Friends" Brooch/Pendant	25		1500.00	1500
1995	Thru the Mirror - Barks/Vought	200		2600.00	2900-3500
1995	"Uncle Scrooge" Tile - Barks/Vought	50	1995	900.00	2000

Duncan Royale

Collector Club - Duncan Royale

1991	Today's Nast	Retrd.	1993	80.00	150
1994	Winter Santa	Retrd.	1994	125.00	150
1995	Santa's Gift	Retrd.	1995	100.00	150
1996	Drummer Boy	Yr.Iss.		N/A	N/A

1990 & 1991 Special Event Piece - Duncan Royale

XX	Nast & Music	Retrd.	1993	79.95	100-125

Ebony Collection - Duncan Royale

1996	African American Santa	5,000		125.00	125
1990	Banjo Man	5,000		80.00	80
1993	Ebony Angel	5,000		170.00	170
1991	Female Gospel Singer	5,000		90.00	90
1990	The Fiddler	5,000		90.00	90
1990	Harmonica Man	5,000		80.00	80
1991	Jug Man	5,000		90.00	90
1992	Jug Tooter	5,000		90.00	90
1992	A Little Magic	5,000		80.00	80
1991	Male Gospel Singer	5,000		90.00	90
1996	O' Happy Day (Youth Gospel)	5,000		70.00	71
1996	Pigskin (Youth Football)	5,000		70.00	71
1991	Preacher	5,000		90.00	90
1991	Spoons	5,000		90.00	90

Ebony Collection-Buckwheat - Duncan Royale

1992	O'Tay	5,000		70.00	90
1992	Painter	5,000		80.00	90
1992	Petee & Friend	5,000		90.00	90
1992	Smile For The Camera	5,000		80.00	90

Ebony Collection-Friends & Family - Duncan Royale

1994	Agnes	5,000		100.00	120
1994	Daddy	5,000		120.00	125
1994	Lunchtime	5,000		100.00	100
1994	Millie	5,000		100.00	100
1994	Mommie & Me	5,000		125.00	125

Ebony Collection-Jazzman - Duncan Royale

1992	Bass	5,000		90.00	110
1992	Bongo	5,000		90.00	100
1992	Piano	5,000		130.00	140
1992	Sax	5,000		90.00	100
1992	Trumpet	5,000		90.00	100

Ebony Collection-Jubilee Dancers - Duncan Royale

1993	Bliss	5,000		200.00	200
1993	Fallana	5,000		100.00	100
1993	Keshia	5,000		100.00	100
1993	Lamar	5,000		100.00	100
1993	Lottie	5,000		125.00	125
1993	Wilfred	5,000		100.00	100

Ebony Collection-Special Releases - Duncan Royale

1991	Signature Piece	Open		50.00	50

History of Classic Entertainers - P. Apsit

1987	American	Retrd.	1995	160.00	35
1987	Auguste	Retrd.	1995	220.00	35
1987	Greco-Roman	Retrd.	1995	180.00	35
1987	Grotesque	Retrd.	1995	230.00	35
1987	Harlequin	Retrd.	1995	250.00	35
1987	Jester	Retrd.	1995	410.00	700-80
1987	Pantalone	Retrd.	1995	270.00	30
1987	Pierrot	Retrd.	1995	180.00	22
1987	Pulcinella	Retrd.	1995	220.00	35
1987	Russian	Retrd.	1995	190.00	35
1987	Slapstick	Retrd.	1995	250.00	30
1987	Uncle Sam	Retrd.	1995	160.00	35

History of Classic Entertainers II - P. Apsit

1988	Bob Hope	Retrd.	1995	250.00	250-29
1988	Feste	Retrd.	1995	250.00	25
1988	Goliard	Retrd.	1995	200.00	30
1988	Mime	Retrd.	1995	200.00	30
1988	Mountebank	Retrd.	1995	270.00	30
1988	Pedrolino	Retrd.	1995	200.00	30
1988	Tartaglia	Retrd.	1995	200.00	25
1988	Thomassi	Retrd.	1995	200.00	30
1988	Touchstone	Retrd.	1995	200.00	30
1988	Tramp	Retrd.	1995	200.00	30
1988	White Face	Retrd.	1995	250.00	30
1988	Zanni	Retrd.	1995	200.00	30

History of Classic Entertainers-Special Releases - P. Apsit

1990	Bob Hope-18"	Retrd.	1995	1500.00	170
1990	Bob Hope-6" porcelain	Retrd.	1995	130.00	13
1990	Mime-18"	Retrd.	1995	1500.00	150
1988	Signature Piece	Retrd.	1995	50.00	5

History of Santa Claus I - P. Apsit

1983	Black Peter	Retrd.	1991	145.00	300-45
1983	Civil War	10,000	N/A	145.00	300-45
1983	Dedt Moroz	Retrd.	1989	145.00	450-80
1983	Kris Kringle	Retrd.	1988	165.00	1500-350
1983	Medieval	Retrd.	1988	220.00	1200-240
1983	Nast	Retrd.	1987	90.00	2000-260
1983	Pioneer	Retrd.	1989	145.00	295-49
1983	Russian	Retrd.	1989	145.00	350-52
1983	Soda Pop	Retrd.	1988	145.00	1500-350
1983	St. Nicholas	Retrd.	1989	175.00	1000-280
1983	Victorian	Retrd.	1990	120.00	375-4
1983	Wassail	Retrd.	1991	90.00	275-4

*Quotes have been rounded up to nearest dollar

History of Santa Claus II - P. Apsit

YEAR ISSUE	EDITION LIMIT	YEAR RETD.	ISSUE PRICE	*QUOTE U.S.$
1986 Alsace Angel	10,000		250.00	300
1986 Babouska	10,000		170.00	200
1986 Bavarian	10,000		250.00	300
1986 Befana	10,000		200.00	250
1986 Frau Holda	10,000		160.00	180
1986 Lord of Misrule	10,000		160.00	200
1986 The Magi	10,000		350.00	400
1986 Mongolian/Asian	10,000		240.00	300
1986 Odin	10,000	1996	200.00	250
1986 The Pixie	10,000		140.00	175
1986 Sir Christmas	10,000		150.00	175
1986 St. Lucia	10,000		180.00	225

History of Santa Claus III - Duncan Royale

YEAR ISSUE	EDITION LIMIT	YEAR RETD.	ISSUE PRICE	*QUOTE U.S.$
1990 Druid	10,000	1996	250.00	250
1991 Grandfather Frost & Snow Maiden	10,000		400.00	400
1991 Hoteisho	10,000		200.00	200
1991 Judah Maccabee	10,000		300.00	300
1990 Julenisse	10,000		200.00	200
1991 King Wenceslas	10,000		300.00	300
1991 Knickerbocker	10,000		300.00	300
1991 Samichlaus	10,000		350.00	350
1991 Saturnalia King	10,000	1996	200.00	200
1990 St. Basil	10,000		300.00	300
1990 Star Man	10,000		300.00	300
1990 Ukko	10,000	1996	250.00	250

History of Santa Claus I (6") - P. Apsit

YEAR ISSUE	EDITION LIMIT	YEAR RETD.	ISSUE PRICE	*QUOTE U.S.$
1988 Black Peter-6" porcelain	6,000/yr.		40.00	80
1988 Civil War-6" porcelain	6,000/yr.		40.00	80
1988 Dedt Moroz -6" porcelain	6,000/yr.		40.00	80
1988 Kris Kringle-6" porcelain	6,000/yr.		40.00	80
1988 Medieval-6" porcelain	6,000/yr.		40.00	80
1988 Nast-6" porcelain	6,000/yr.		40.00	80
1988 Pioneer-6" porcelain	6,000/yr.		40.00	80
1988 Russian-6" porcelain	6,000/yr.		40.00	80
1988 Soda Pop-6" porcelain	6,000/yr.		40.00	80
1988 St. Nicholas-6" porcelain	6,000/yr.		40.00	80
1988 Victorian-6" porcelain	6,000/yr.		40.00	80
1988 Wassail-6" porcelain	6,000/yr.		40.00	80

History of Santa Claus II (6") - P. Apsit

YEAR ISSUE	EDITION LIMIT	YEAR RETD.	ISSUE PRICE	*QUOTE U.S.$
1988 Alsace Angel-6" porcelain	6,000/yr		80.00	90
1988 Babouska-6" porcelain	6,000/yr		70.00	80
1988 Bavarian-6" porcelain	6,000/yr		90.00	100
1988 Befana-6" porcelain	6,000/yr		70.00	80
1988 Frau Holda-6" porcelain	6,000/yr		50.00	80
1988 Lord of Misrule-6" porcelain	6,000/yr		60.00	80
1988 Magi-6" porcelain	6,000/yr		130.00	150
1988 Mongolian/Asian-6" porcelain	6,000/yr		80.00	90
1988 Odin-6" porcelain	6,000/yr		80.00	90
1988 Pixie-6" porcelain	6,000/yr		50.00	80
1988 Sir Christmas-6" porcelain	6,000/yr		60.00	80
1988 St. Lucia-6" porcelain	6,000/yr		70.00	80

History of Santa Claus (18") - P. Apsit

YEAR ISSUE	EDITION LIMIT	YEAR RETD.	ISSUE PRICE	*QUOTE U.S.$
1989 Kris Kringle-18"	1,000	1995	1500.00	1500
1989 Medieval-18"	1,000	1995	1500.00	1500
1989 Nast-18"	1,000	1995	1500.00	1500
1989 Russian-18"	1,000	1995	1500.00	1500
1989 Soda Pop-18"	1,000	1995	1500.00	1500
1989 St. Nicholas-18"	1,000	1995	1500.00	1500

History of Santa Claus I -Wood - P. Apsit

YEAR ISSUE	EDITION LIMIT	YEAR RETD.	ISSUE PRICE	*QUOTE U.S.$
1987 Black Peter-8" wood	500	1993	450.00	450
1987 Civil War-8" wood	500	1993	450.00	450
1987 Dedt Moroz-8" wood	500	1993	450.00	450
1987 Kris Kringle-8" wood	500	1993	450.00	450
1987 Medieval-8" wood	500	1993	450.00	1200
1987 Nast-8" wood	500	1993	450.00	1500
1987 Pioneer-8" wood	500	1993	450.00	450
1987 Russian-8" wood	500	1993	450.00	450
1987 Soda Pop-8" wood	500	1993	450.00	850
1987 St. Nicholas-8" wood	500	1993	450.00	700
1987 Victorian-8" wood	500	1993	450.00	450
1987 Wassail-8" wood	500	1993	450.00	450

History Of Santa Claus -Special Releases - Duncan Royale

YEAR ISSUE	EDITION LIMIT	YEAR RETD.	ISSUE PRICE	*QUOTE U.S.$
1992 Nast & Sleigh	5,000		500.00	650
1991 Signature Piece	Open		50.00	50

Painted Pewter Miniatures-Santa 1st Series - Duncan Royale

YEAR ISSUE	EDITION LIMIT	YEAR RETD.	ISSUE PRICE	*QUOTE U.S.$
1986 Black Peter	500		30.00	30
1986 Civil War	500		30.00	30
1986 Dedt Moroz	500		30.00	30
1986 Kris Kringle	500		30.00	30
1986 Medieval	500		30.00	30
1986 Nast	500		30.00	30
1986 Pioneer	500		30.00	30
1986 Russian	500		30.00	30
1986 Soda Pop	500		30.00	30
1986 St. Nicholas	500		30.00	30
1986 Victorian	500		30.00	30
1986 Wassail	500		30.00	30
1986 Set of 12	500		360.00	360-495

Painted Pewter Miniatures-Santa 2nd Series - Duncan Royale

YEAR ISSUE	EDITION LIMIT	YEAR RETD.	ISSUE PRICE	*QUOTE U.S.$
1988 Alsace Angel	500		30.00	30
1988 Babouska	500		30.00	30
1988 Bavarian	500		30.00	30
1988 Befana	500		30.00	30
1988 Frau Holda	500		30.00	30
1988 Lord of Misrule	500		30.00	30
1988 Magi	500		30.00	30
1988 Mongolian	500		30.00	30
1988 Odin	500		30.00	30
1988 Pixie	500		30.00	30
1988 Sir Christmas	500		30.00	30
1988 St. Lucia	500		30.00	30
1988 Set of 12	500		360.00	360-495

Woodland Fairies - Duncan Royale

YEAR ISSUE	EDITION LIMIT	YEAR RETD.	ISSUE PRICE	*QUOTE U.S.$
1988 Almond Blossom	Retrd.	1993	70.00	70
1988 Apple	Retrd.	1994	70.00	70
1988 Calla Lily	Retrd.	1994	70.00	70
1988 Cherry	10,000	1995	70.00	70
1988 Chestnut	10,000	1995	70.00	70
1988 Christmas Tree	Retrd.	1993	70.00	70
1988 Elm	10,000	1995	70.00	70
1988 Guilder Rose	Retrd.	1994	70.00	70
1988 Lime Tree	Retrd.	1993	70.00	70
1988 Mulberry	10,000	1995	70.00	70
1988 Pear Blossom	Retrd.	1993	70.00	70
1988 Pine Tree	10,000	1995	70.00	70
1988 Poplar	10,000	1995	70.00	70
1988 Sycamore	Retrd.	1993	70.00	70

eggspressions! inc.

Christmas Collection - eggspressions

YEAR ISSUE	EDITION LIMIT	YEAR RETD.	ISSUE PRICE	*QUOTE U.S.$
1994 Angel of Hope	250		130.00	130
1994 Angel of Love	250	1995	110.00	110
1994 Beary Blue Christmas	250		98.00	100
1994 Beary Pink Christmas	250		98.00	100
1994 Caroling Mice	250		120.00	120
1994 Christmas Joy	250		104.00	105
1994 O' Holy Night	250		160.00	160
1994 Santas Little Elves	250		130.00	130
1994 Santas Little Sweetheart	100		98.00	100

Hanging Collectibles - eggspressions

YEAR ISSUE	EDITION LIMIT	YEAR RETD.	ISSUE PRICE	*QUOTE U.S.$
1995 Andrea	250		80.00	80
1995 Angel Divine	250		120.00	120
1992 Blue Birds of Happiness	Open		79.00	79
1995 Coo	250		115.00	115
1995 Dawn	250		190.00	190
1995 Father Christmas	250		135.00	135
1992 Golden Crystal	Open		145.00	145
1995 Harvest Fairy	Open		95.00	95
1995 Heavenly	250		120.00	120
1992 Isadora	Open		110.00	130
1995 Jamie	250		80.00	80
1992 Kewpie Doll	Open		99.00	110
1995 Left Behind	250		100.00	100
1992 Love Duet	Open		125.00	140
1992 Love in Flight	Open		95.00	100
1992 McGregor's Garden	Open		98.00	105
1995 Peek N Out	250		55.00	55
1992 Romantique	Open		66.00	75
1995 Santa's Here	250		130.00	130
1995 Shining Star	250		72.00	72
1995 Tara	250		80.00	80
1995 Winter Bunny	250		90.00	90
1992 Winter Colt	Open		104.00	105
1995 Woodland Bunnies	250		120.00	120

Musical Collectibles - eggspressions

YEAR ISSUE	EDITION LIMIT	YEAR RETD.	ISSUE PRICE	*QUOTE U.S.$
1995 First Love	250		190.00	190
1995 Reflections on Ice	250		230.00	230
1995 Royalty	250		170.00	170

Enchantica

Enchantica Collectors Club - Various

YEAR ISSUE	EDITION LIMIT	YEAR RETD.	ISSUE PRICE	*QUOTE U.S.$
1991 Snappa on Mushroom-2101 - A. Bill	Retrd.	1991	Gift	10-150
1991 Rattajack with Snail-2102 - A. Bill	Retrd.	1991	60.00	85
1992 Jonquil-2103 - A. Hull	Retrd.	1992	Gift	75
1992 Ice Demon-2104 - K. Fallon	Retrd.	1992	85.00	150
1992 Sea Dragon-2106 - A. Bill	Retrd.	1993	99.00	275
1993 White Dragon-2107 - A. Bill	Retrd.	1993	Gift	200
1993 Jonquil's Flight-2108 - A. Bill	Retrd.	1993	140.00	300-375
1994 Verratus-2111 - A. Bill	Retrd.	1994	Gift	60
1994 Mimmer-Spring Fairy-2112 - A. Bill	Retrd.	1994	100.00	165
1994 Gorgoyle Cameo piece-2113 - K. Fallon	Retrd.	1994	Gift	10
1995 Destroyer-2116 - A. Hull	Yr.Iss.		100.00	100
1995 Cloudbreaker-2115 - J. Oliver	Yr.Iss.		Gift	N/A

Retired Enchantica Collection - Various

YEAR ISSUE	EDITION LIMIT	YEAR RETD.	ISSUE PRICE	*QUOTE U.S.$
1990 Arangast - Summer Dragon-2026 - K. Fallon	Retrd.	1992	165.00	350
1991 Bledderag, Goblin Twin-2048 - K. Fallon	Retrd.	1993	115.00	175
1988 Blick Scoops Crystals-2015 - A. Bill	Retrd.	1991	47.00	70
1992 Breen - Carrier Dragon-2053 - K. Fallon	Retrd.	1993	156.00	175
1990 Cellandia-Summer Fairy-2029 - K. Fallon	Retrd.	1992	115.00	170
1989 Chuckwalla-2021 - A. Bill	Retrd.	1994	43.00	60
1992 Desert Dragon-2064 - A. Bill	Retrd.	1994	175.00	200
1994 Escape (5th Anniversary)-2110 - A. Bill	Retrd.	1994	250.00	320
1988 Fantazar- Spring Wizard-2016 - A. Bill	Retrd.	1991	132.50	400
1991 Flight to Danger-2044 - K. Fallon	Retrd.	1991	3000.00	6500
1990 Fossfex - Autumn Fairy-2030 - K. Fallon	Retrd.	1992	115.00	200
1991 Furza - Carrier Dragon-2050 - K. Fallon	Retrd.	1993	137.50	200
1988 Gorgoyle - Spring Dragon-2017 - A. Bill	Retrd.	1991	132.50	500
1991 Grawlfang '91 Winter Dragon-2046 - A. Bill	Retrd.	1994	295.00	375
1989 Grawlfang - Winter Dragon-2019 - A. Bill	Retrd.	1991	132.50	600
1988 Hepna Pushes Truck-2014 - A. Bill	Retrd.	1994	47.00	75
1988 Hest Checks Crystals-2013 - A. Bill	Retrd.	1994	47.00	75
1989 Hobba, Hellbenders Twin Son-2023 - A. Bill	Retrd.	1992	69.00	150
1993 Ice Dragon-2109 - A. Bill	Retrd.	1994	95.00	100
1988 Jonquil- Dragons Footprint-2004 - A. Bill	Retrd.	1991	55.00	90
1992 Manu Manu-Peeper-2105 - A. Bill	Retrd.	1993	40.00	60
1991 Ogrod-Ice Troll-2032 - A. Bill	Retrd.	1994	235.00	325
1991 Okra, Goblin Princess-2031 - K. Fallon	Retrd.	1994	105.00	115
1989 Old Yargle-2020 - A. Bill	Retrd.	1994	55.00	75
1992 Olm & Sylphen, Mer-King & Queen-2059 - A. Bill	Retrd.	1994	350.00	450
1990 Orolan-Summer Wizard-2025 - A. Bill	Retrd.	1992	165.00	300
1991 Quillion-Autumn Witch-2045 - A. Bill	Retrd.	1994	205.00	220
1988 Rattajack - Circles-2003 - A. Bill	Retrd.	1993	40.00	70
1988 Rattajack - My Ball-2001 - A. Bill	Retrd.	1993	40.00	70
1988 Rattajack - Please-2000 - A. Bill	Retrd.	1993	40.00	65
1988 Rattajack - Terragon Dreams-2002 - A. Bill	Retrd.	1993	40.00	60
1991 Rattajack-Up & Under-2038 - A. Bill	Retrd.	1994	65.00	70
1991 Samphire-Carrier Dragon-2049 - A. Bill	Retrd.	1994	137.50	175
1988 Snappa Climbs High-2008 - A. Bill	Retrd.	1993	25.00	65
1988 Snappa Finds a Collar-2009 - A. Bill	Retrd.	1992	25.00	60
1988 Snappa Dozes Off-2011 - A. Bill	Retrd.	1993	25.00	60
1988 Snappa Hatches Out-2006 - A. Bill	Retrd.	1991	25.00	60
1991 Snappa Nods Off-2043 - A. Hull	Retrd.	1994	30.00	40
1988 Snappa Plays Ball-2010 - A. Bill	Retrd.	1993	25.00	60
1991 Snappa Posing-2042 - A. Hull	Retrd.	1994	30.00	50
1991 Snappa Tumbles-2047 - A. Hull	Retrd.	1994	30.00	40
1988 Snappa's First Feast-2007 - A. Bill	Retrd.	1993	25.00	60
1991 Snappa-Snowdrift-2041 - A. Hull	Retrd.	1994	30.00	40
1991 Snarlgard - Autumn Dragon-2034 - K. Fallon	Retrd.	1992	337.00	400
1992 Sorren & Gart-2054 - K. Fallon	Retrd.	1994	220.00	350
1992 Spring Wizard and Yim-2060 - A. Bill	Retrd.	1993	410.00	450
1990 The Swamp Demon-2028 - K. Fallon	Retrd.	1992	69.00	95
1988 Tarbet with Sack-2012 - A. Bill	Retrd.	1991	47.00	60
1992 Thrace-Gladiator-2061 - K. Fallon	Retrd.	1993	280.00	350
1992 The Throne Citadel-2063 - J. Woodward	Retrd.	1994	2000.00	2000
1990 Tuatara-Evil Witch-2027 - A. Bill	Retrd.	1994	174.00	185
1989 Vrorst - The Ice Sorcerer-2018 - A. Bill	Retrd.	1991	155.00	650
1991 Waxifrade - Autumn Wizard-2033 - K. Fallon	Retrd.	1992	265.00	400

Enesco Corporation

Cherished Teddies Club - P. Hillman

YEAR ISSUE	EDITION LIMIT	YEAR RETD.	ISSUE PRICE	*QUOTE U.S.$
1995 Cub E. Bear CT001	Yr.Iss.		Gift	30
1995 Mayor Wilson T.Beary CT951	Yr.Iss.		20.00	20
1995 Hilary Hugabear CT952	Yr.Iss.		17.50	18
1996 R. Harrison Hartford-New Membear CT002	Yr.Iss.		Gift	N/A
1996 R. Harrison Hartford-Charter Membear CT102	Yr.Iss.		Gift	N/A
1996 Emily E. Claire CT962	Yr.Iss.		17.50	18
1996 Kurtis D. Claw CT961	Yr.Iss.		17.50	18

Cherished Teddies - P. Hillman

YEAR ISSUE	EDITION LIMIT	YEAR RETD.	ISSUE PRICE	*QUOTE U.S.$
1993 Baby Blocks Displayer-CRT004	Open		40.00	40
1994 Nursery Rhyme Books -CRT013	Open		40.00	40
1996 Sweet Heart Ball Displayer-CRT096	Open		40.00	40
1995 Town Tattler Sign-1995 National Event Piece-CRT109	Yr.Iss.		6.00	6
1996 Park Bench w/Bears 1996 National Event Piece-CRT240	Yr.Iss.		N/A	N/A
1995 Boy Bear Cupid-103551	Suspd.		17.50	33
1995 Girl Bear Cupid-103586	Suspd.		15.00	31

*Quotes have been rounded up to nearest dollar

FIGURINES/COTTAGES

YEAR ISSUE		EDITION LIMIT	YEAR RETD.	ISSUE PRICE	*QUOTE U.S.$
1995	Cupid Boy/Girl Double-103594	Suspd.		25.00	35
1995	Boy Bear Flying Cupid-103608	Open		13.00	25
1995	Girl Bear Flying Cupid-103616	Open		13.00	25
1995	Bear Cupid Girl 2AT-103640	Suspd.		15.00	15
1995	Cupid Baby on Pillow 2 Asst-103659	Suspd.		13.50	14
1995	Margaret "A Cup Full of Love"-103667	Open		20.00	20
1996	Bruno "Step Right Up And Smile"-103713	Open		17.50	18
1996	Claudia "You Take Center Ring With Me"-103721	Open		17.50	18
1995	Hope "Our Love Is Ever-Blooming"-103764	Open		20.00	20
1995	Gail "Catching the First Blooms of Friendship"-103772	Open		20.00	20
1995	Lisa "My Best Is Always You"-103780	Open		20.00	20
1995	Donald "Friends Are Egg-ceptional Blessings"-103799	Open		20.00	20
1995	Bunny "Just In Time For Spring"-103802	Open		13.50	14
1995	Jennifer "Gathering The Blooms of Friendship"-103810	Open		22.50	23
1995	Melissa "Every Bunny Needs A Friend"-103829	Open		20.00	20
1995	Christian "My Prayer Is For You"-103837	Open		18.50	19
1995	Christine "My Prayer Is For You"-103845	Open		18.50	19
1995	Kevin "Good Luck To You"-103896	Open		12.50	13
1996	Wally "You're The Tops With Me"-103934	Open		17.50	18
1996	"Trunk Full of Bear Hugs"-103977	Open		22.50	23
1995	Peter "You're Some Bunny Special-104973	Open		17.50	18
1996	Circus Tent / Rings Display-107700	Open		22.50	23
1995	Sculpted Irish Plaque-110981	Open		13.50	14
1996	Clown on Ball Musical-111430	Open		40.00	40
1995	The Best Is Yet To Come-127949	Open		12.50	14
1995	The Best Is Yet To Come-127957	Open		12.50	14
1995	Kiss The Hurt And Make It Well-127965	Open		15.00	15
1995	Tucker & Travis "We're in This Together"-127973	Open		25.00	25
1995	Allison & Alexandria "Two Friends Mean Twice The Love"-127981	Open		25.00	25
1995	Seth & Sarabeth "We're Beary Good Pals"-128015	Open		25.00	25
1995	Millie, Christy, Dorothy "A. Love Me Tender, B. Take Me To Your Heart, C. Love Me True"-128023	Open		12.50	14
1995	Priscilla & Greta "Our Hearts Belong to You"-128031	19,950		50.00	75-150
1995	Girl Bear on Ottoman Musical-128058	Open		55.00	55
1996	Kittie "You Make Wishes Come True" 1996 Adoption Center Event-131865	Yr.Iss.		17.50	18
1995	Earl "Warm Hearted Friends"-131873	Open		17.50	18
1995	Madeline "A Cup Full of Friendship"-135593	Open		20.00	20
1995	Marilyn "A Cup Full of Cheer"-135682	Open		20.00	20
1995	Maureen "Lucky Friend"-135690	Open		12.50	13
1996	"Seal of Friendship"-137596	Open		10.00	10
1996	Two Boys By Lamp Post Musical-141089	Open		50.00	50
1995	Nickolas "You're At The Top Of My List"-141100	Yr.Iss.		20.00	25-50
1995	Holly "A Cup of Homemade Love"-141119	Open		18.50	19
1995	Ginger "Painting Your Holidays With Love"-141127	Open		22.50	23
1995	Meri "Handsewn Holidays"-141135	Open		20.00	20
1995	Yule "Building a Sturdy Friendship"-141143	Open		22.50	23
1995	Amanda "Here's Some Cheer to Last The Year"-141186	Yr.Iss.		17.50	25-40
1995	Kristen "Hugs of Love And Friendship"-141194	Open		20.00	20
1996	Cheryl & Carl "Wishing You A Cozy Christmas"-141216	Open		25.00	25
1996	Jamie & Ashley "I'm All Wrapped Up In Your Love"-141224	Open		25.00	25
1995	Celeste "An Angel To Watch Over You"-141267	Open		20.00	20
1996	Dina "Bear In Mind, You're Special"-141275	Open		15.00	15
1996	John "Bear In Mind, You're Special"-141283	Open		15.00	15
1996	Rick "Suited Up For The Holidays"-141291	Open		12.50	13
1996	Barbara "Giving Thanks For Our Family"-141305	Open		12.50	13
1995	Pat "Falling For You"-141313	Open		22.50	23
1995	Carrie "The Future 'Beareth' All Things"-141321	Open		18.50	19
1995	Bea "Bee My Friend"-141348	Open		15.00	18
1996	Table With Food / Dog-141542	Open		30.00	30
1995	Santa's Workshop Nightlight-141925	Open		75.00	75
1995	Beary Scary Halloween House-152382	Open		20.00	20
1996	Robert "Love Keeps Me Afloat"-156272	Open		13.50	14
1996	Violet "Blessings Bloom When You Are Near"-156280	Open		15.00	15
1996	Matthew "A Dash of Love Sweetens Any Day!"-156299	Open		15.00	15
1996	Thelma "Cozy Tea For Two"-156302	Open		22.50	23
1996	Tara "You're My Berry Best Friend!"-156310	Open		15.00	15
1996	Ella "Love Grows in My Heart"-156329	Open		15.00	15
1996	Jenna "You're Berry Special To Me"-156337	Open		15.00	15
1996	Tasha "In Grandmother's Attic" 1996 Adoption Center Exclusive-156353	19,960		50.00	50
1996	Debbie "Let's Hear It For Friendship!"-156361	Open		15.00	15
1996	Butch "Can I Be Your Football Hero?"-156388	Open		15.00	15
1996	Laura "Friendship Makes It All Better"-156396	Open		15.00	15
1996	Mindy "Friendship Keeps Me On My Toes"-156418	Open		15.00	15
1996	Linda "ABC And 1-2-3, You're A Friend To Me!"-156426	Open		15.00	15
1996	Robin "You Steal My Heart Away"-156434	Open		17.50	18
1996	Marian "You're The Hero Of My Heart"-156442	Open		20.00	20
1996	Darrel "Love Unveils A Happy Heart"-156450	Open		17.50	18
1996	Darla "My Heart Wishes For You"-156469	Open		20.00	20
1996	Jilly "Won't You Be My Sweetheart?"-156477	Open		17.50	18
1996	Craig & Cheri "Sweethearts Forever"-156485	Open		25.00	25
1996	Bear In Bunny Outfit Resin Egg Dated 1996-156507	Yr.Iss.		8.50	9
1996	Stormi "Hark The Herald Angels Sing"-176001	Yr.Iss.		20.00	20
1996	Erica "Friends Are Always Pulling For You"-176028	Open		22.50	23
1996	Klaus "Bearer of Good Tidings"-176036	Yr.Iss.		20.00	20
1996	Jeffrey "Striking Up Another Year" Dated 1996-176044	Yr.Iss.		17.50	18
1996	Ornaments/Mailsack/North Pole Sign Mini 3 Asst.-176079	Open		15.00	15
1996	Joy "You Always Bring Joy"-176087	Open		15.00	15
1996	Holden "Catchin' The Holiday Spirit"-176095	Open		15.00	15
1996	Noel "An Old Fashioned Noel To You"-176109	Open		15.00	15
1996	Jolene "Dropping You A Holiday Greeting"-176133	Open		20.00	20
1996	Nolan "A String Of Good Tidings"-176141	Open		20.00	20
1996	Pumpkins/Corn Stalk/Scarecrow Mini 3 Asst.-176206	Open		15.00	15
1996	Daniel "You're My Little Pumpkin"-176214	Open		22.50	23
1996	Tabitha "You're The Cat's Meow"-176257	Open		15.00	15
1996	Andy "You Have A Special Place In My Heart"-176265	Open		18.50	19
1996	Nativity Prayer Plaque-176362	Open		13.50	14
1996	Olga "Feel The Peace...Hold The Joy...Share The Love"-182966	Yr.Iss.		50.00	50
1996	Claudette "Our Friendship Is Bon Appetit!"-197254	Open		15.00	15
1996	Kerstin "You're The Swedish of Them All"-197289	Open		15.00	15
1996	Jessica "A Mother's Heart Is Full of Love" GCC Early Introduction-155438A	Yr.Iss.		25.00	25
1996	Machiko "Love Fans A Beautiful Friendship"-202312	Open		15.00	15
1996	Nadia "From Russia, With Love"-202320	Open		15.00	15
1996	Carlos "I Found An Amigo In You"-202339	Open		15.00	15
1996	Lian "Our Friendship Spans Many Miles"-202347	Open		15.00	15
1996	Fernando "You Make Everday A Fiesta"-202355	Open		15.00	15
1996	Rajul "You're The Jewel Of My Heart"-202398	Open		15.00	15
1996	Katrinka "Tulips Blossom With Friendship"-202401	Open		15.00	15
1996	Johann "I'd Climb The Highest Alp For You"-202436	Open		15.00	15
1996	Bob "Our Friendship Is From Sea To Shining Sea"-202444	Open		15.00	15
1996	Lorna "Our Love Is In The Highlands"-202452	Open		15.00	15
1996	Winston "Friendship Is Elementary My Dear"-202878	Open		15.00	15
1996	Preston "Riding Across The Great White North"-216739	Open		15.00	15
1994	Tiny Ted-Bear "God Bless Us Every One"-614777	Open		10.00	10
1994	Jacob Bearly "You Will Be Haunted By Three Spirits"-614785	Open		17.50	18
1994	Gloria "Ghost of Christmas Past," " Garland "Ghost Of Christmas Present", Gabriel "Ghost of Christmas Yet To Come"-614807	Open		55.00	55
1994	Thanksgiving Quilt-617075	Open		12.00	12
1994	Jedediah "Giving Thanks For Friends"-617091	Open		17.50	18
1994	Patience "Happiness Is Homemade"-617105	Open		17.50	18
1994	Phoebe "A Little Friendship Is A Big Blessing"-617113	Retrd.	1995	13.50	35-45
1994	Wylie "I'm Called Little Friend"-617121	Open		15.00	15
1994	Stacie "You Lift My Spirit"-617148	Open		18.50	20
1994	Taylor "Sail The Seas With Me"-617156	Suspd.		15.00	15
1994	Willie "Bears Of A Feather Stay Together"-617164	Open		15.00	15
1994	Winona "Fair Feather Friends"-617172	Open		15.00	15
1994	Breanna "Pumpkin Patch Pals"-617180	Open		15.00	15
1994	Ingrid "Bundled Up With Warm Wishes" Dated 1994-617237	Yr.Iss.		20.00	25-50
1994	Nils "Near And Dear For Christmas"-617245	Suspd.		22.50	28
1994	Ebearneezer Scrooge "Bah Humbug!"-617296	Open		17.50	18
1994	Mrs. Cratchit "A Beary Christmas And Happy New Year!"-617318	Open		18.50	19
1994	Bear Cratchit "And A Very Merry Christmas To You Mr. Scrooge"-617326	Open		17.50	18
1994	Counting House-622788	Open		75.00	75
1994	Eric "Bear Tidings Of Joy"-622796	Open		22.50	25
1994	Sonja "Holiday Cuddles"-622818	Open		20.00	20
1994	Jack & Jill "Our Friendship Will Never Tumble"-624772	Open		30.00	30
1994	Little Jack Horner "I'm Plum Happy You're My Friend"-624780	Open		20.00	23
1994	Little Miss Muffet "I'm Never Afraid With You At My Side"-624799	Open		20.00	20
1994	Little Bo Peep "Looking For A Friend Like You"-624802	Open		22.50	23
1994	Tom, Tom The Piper's Son "Wherever You Go I'll Follow"-624810	Open		20.00	20
1994	Older Son "Child Of Pride"-624829	Open		10.00	10
1994	Young Son "Child of Hope"-624837	Open		9.00	9
1994	Older Daughter "Child Of Love"-624845	Open		10.00	10
1994	Young Daughter "Child Of Kindness"-624853	Open		9.00	9
1994	Mother "A Mother's Love Bears All Things"-624861	Open		20.00	20
1994	Father "A Father Is The Bearer Of Strength"-624888	Open		13.50	14
1994	Billy "Everyone Needs A Cuddle", Betsey "First Step To Love" Bobbie "A Little Friendship To Share"-624896	Open		12.50	13
1994	Boy/Girl in Laundry Basket (Musical)-624926	Open		60.00	60
1994	Bear as Bunny Jointed (Musical)-625302	Open		60.00	60
1994	Betty "Bubblin' Over With Love"-626066	Open		18.50	20
1994	Mary, Mary Quite Contrary "Friendship Blooms With Loving Care"-626074	Open		22.50	23
1994	Bear w/ Goose (Musical) -627445	Open		45.00	45
1994	Bear w/Toy Chest (Musical)-627453	Open		60.00	60
1994	Bear w/Horse (Musical)-628565	Open		150.00	150
1994	Bear w/Rocking Reindeer (Musical)-629618	Open		165.00	165
1994	Wyat "I'm Called Little Running Bear"-629707	Open		15.00	15
1994	Nativity Cow "That's What Friends Are For" -651095	Open		22.50	23
1994	Cratchit's House-651362	Open		75.00	75
1994	Boy/Girl in Sled (Musical)-651435	Open		100.00	100
1994	Baby Boy Jointed (Musical)-699314	Open		60.00	60
1994	Baby Girl Jointed (Musical)-699322	Open		60.00	60
1994	Bride/Groom (Musical)-699349	Open		50.00	50
1995	Cupid Boy Sitting 2 Asst-869074	Suspd.		13.50	14
1995	Cupid Boy/Girl Double 2 Asst-869082	Suspd.		18.50	19
1993	Abigail "Inside We're All The Same"-900362	Suspd.		16.00	35-50
1996	Sign/Bunny/Basket of Strawberries Mini 3 Asst.-900931	Open		3.50	4
1993	Jointed Bear Christmas (Musical)-903337	Suspd.		60.00	60
1993	Alice "Cozy Warm Wishes Coming Your Way" (9")-903620	Suspd.		100.00	100-175
1993	"Friends Like You Are Precious And Few"-904309	Open		30.00	30
1993	Theadore, Samantha & Tyler "Friendship Weathers All Storms" (musical)-904546	Suspd.		170.00	170
1993	Daisy "Friendship Blossoms With Love"-910651	Suspd.		15.00	350-450
1993	Charity "I Found A Friend In Ewe"-910678	Suspd.		20.00	65-120
1993	Henrietta "A Basketful of Wings"-910686	Suspd.		22.50	50-95
1993	Chelsea "Good Friends Are A Blessing" -910694	Retrd.	1995	15.00	200-30
1993	Heidi & David "Special Friends"-910708	Suspd.		25.00	45-5

*Quotes have been rounded up to nearest dollar

YEAR ISSUE		EDITION LIMIT	YEAR RETD.	ISSUE PRICE	*QUOTE U.S. $
1993	Priscilla "Love Surrounds Our Friendship"-910724	Open		15.00	15
1993	Amy "Hearts Quilted With Love"-910732	Open		13.50	15
1993	Timothy "A Friend Is Forever"-910740	Suspd.		15.00	35-45
1993	Molly "Friendship Softens A Bumpy Ride"-910759	Suspd.		30.00	50-75
1993	Marie "Friendship Is A Special Treat"-910767	Open		20.00	20
1993	Michael & Michelle "Friendship Is A Cozy Feeling"-910775	Suspd.		30.00	35-55
1993	"Chalking Up Six Wishes" Age 6-911283	Open		16.50	17
1993	"Color Me Five" Age 5-911291	Open		15.00	15
1993	"Unfolding Happy Wishes Four You" Age 4-911305	Open		15.00	15
1993	"Three Cheers For You" Age 3-911313	Open		15.00	15
1993	"Two Sweet Two Bear" Age 2-911321	Open		13.50	14
1993	"Beary Special One" Age 1-911348	Open		13.50	14
1993	"Cradled With Love" Baby-911356	Open		16.50	17
1993	Tracie & Nicole "Side By Side With Friends"-911372	Open		35.00	35
1993	Robbie & Rachel "Love Bears All Things"-911402	Open		27.50	30
1993	Patrick "Thank You For A Friend That's True"-911410	Open		18.50	20
1993	Patrice "Thank You For The Sky So Blue"-911429	Open		18.50	20
1993	Thomas "Chuggin' Along", Jonathon "Sail With Me", Harrison "We're Going Places"-911739	Open		15.00	18
1993	Freda & Tina "Our Friendship Is A Perfect Blend"- 911747	Open		35.00	35
1993	Miles "I'm Thankful For A Friend Like You"-912751	Open		17.00	18
1993	Gretel "We Make Magic, Me And You"-912778	Open		18.50	20
1993	Gary "True Friendships Are Scarce"-912786	Suspd.		18.50	25
1993	Connie "You're A Sweet Treat"-912794	Suspd.		15.00	15
1993	Prudence "A Friend To Be Thankful For"-912808	Open		17.00	18
1993	Buckey & Brenda "How I Love Being Friends With You"-912816	Retrd.	1995	15.00	75
1993	Mary "A Special Friend Warms The Season"-912840	Open		25.00	25
1993	Nativity (Musical)-912859	Suspd.		60.00	100
1993	"Friendship Pulls Us Through" & "Ewe Make Being Friends Special"-912867	Open		13.50	14
1993	Alice "Cozy Warm Wishes Coming Your Way" Dated 1993-912875	Yr.Iss.		17.50	45-75
1993	Theadore, Samantha & Tyler "Friendship Weathers All Storms (9")-912883	Suspd.		160.00	160
1994	Ronnie "I'll Play My Drum For You"-912905	Open		13.50	14
1993	Carolyn "Wishing You All Good Things"-912921	Suspd.		22.50	23
1993	Hans "Friends In Toyland"-912956	Retrd.	1995	20.00	50-75
1993	Bear Playing w/Train (Musical)-912964	Open		40.00	40
1993	Boy Praying (Musical)-914304	Open		37.50	38
1993	Girl Praying (Musical)-914312	Open		37.50	38
1993	Baby in Cradle (Musical)-914320	Open		60.00	60
1993	Jack January Monthly-914754 (Also available through Hamilton Collection)	Open		15.00	15
1993	Phoebe February Monthly-914762 (Also available through Hamilton Collection)	Open		15.00	15
1993	Mark March Monthly-914770 (Also available through Hamilton Collection)	Open		15.00	15
1993	Alan April Monthly-914789 (Also available through Hamilton Collection)	Open		15.00	15
1993	May May Monthly-914797 (Also available through Hamilton Collection)	Open		15.00	15
1993	June June Monthly-914800 (Also available through Hamilton Collection)	Open		15.00	15
1993	Julie July Monthly-914819 (Also available through Hamilton Collection)	Open		15.00	15
1993	Arthur August Monthly-914827 (Also available through Hamilton Collection)	Open		15.00	15
1993	Seth September Monthly-914835 (Also available through Hamilton Collection)	Open		15.00	15
1993	Oscar October Monthly-914843 (Also available through Hamilton Collection)	Open		15.00	15
1993	Nichole November Monthly-914851 (Also available through Hamilton Collection)	Open		15.00	15
1993	Denise December Monthly-914878 (Also available through Hamilton Collection)	Open		15.00	15
1994	Elizabeth & Ashley "My Beary Best Friend"-916277	Suspd.		25.00	40-60
1994	Victoria "From My Heart To Yours"-916293	Suspd.		16.50	65-130
1994	Kelly "You're My One And Only" -916307	Suspd.		15.00	50-75
1994	Nancy "Your Friendship Makes My Heart Sing"-916315	Suspd.		15.00	40-75
1994	Bear Holding Harp (Musical)-916323	Open		40.00	40
1994	Becky "Springtime Happiness"-916331	Suspd.		20.00	35-65
1994	Courtney "Springtime Is A Blessing From Above"-916390	Suspd.		15.00	65-100
1994	Bessie "Some Bunny Loves You"-916404	Suspd.		15.00	60-85
1994	Faith "There's No Bunny Like You"-916412	Suspd.		20.00	45-65
1994	Henry "Celebrating Spring With You"-916420	Suspd.		20.00	45-65
1994	Sean "Luck Found Me A Friend In You"-916439	Open		12.50	13
1994	Kathleen "Luck Found Me A Friend In You"-916447	Open		12.50	13
1994	Oliver & Olivia "Will You Be Mine?"-916641	Suspd.		25.00	40-80
1992	Camille "I'd Be Lost Without You"-950424	Open		20.00	20
1992	Sara "Lov Ya" Jacki Hugs & Kisses", Karen "Best Buddy"-950432	Open		10.00	10
1992	Katie "A Friend Always Knows When You Need A Hug"-950440	Open		20.00	20
1992	Anna "Hooray For You"-950459	Open		22.50	23
1992	Jasmine " You Have Touched My Heart"-950475	Suspd.		22.50	45-75
1992	Christopher "Old Friends Are The Best Friends" 950483	Open		50.00	50
1992	Zachary "Yesterday's Memories Are Today's Treasures"-950491	Open		30.00	30
1992	Theadore, Samantha & Tyler "Friends Come In All Sizes" -950505	Open		20.00	20
1992	Nathaniel & Nellie "It's Twice As Nice With You"-950513	Open		30.00	30
1992	Jeremy "Friends Like You Are Precious And Few"-950521	Retrd.	1995	15.00	30-65
1992	Benji "Life Is Sweet, Enjoy"-950548	Retrd.	1995	13.50	25-60
1992	Joshua "Love Repairs All"-950556	Open		20.00	20
1992	Blossom & Beth "Friends Are Never Far Apart" w/butterfly-950564	Retrd.	1992	50.00	80-140
1992	Blossom & Beth "Friends Are Never Far Apart"-950564	Open		50.00	50
1992	Mandy "I Love You Just The Way You Are"-950572	Retrd.	1995	15.00	30-175
1992	Beth "Bear Hugs"-950637	Retrd.	1995	17.50	30-60
1992	Couple in Basket/Umbrella (Musical)-950645	Open		60.00	60
1992	Douglas "Let's Be Friends"-950661	Retrd.	1995	20.00	30-75
1992	Maria, Baby & Josh "A Baby Is God's Gift of Love" "Everyone Needs a Daddy"- 950688	Open		35.00	35
1992	Richard "My Gift Is Loving", Edward "My Gift Is Caring", Wilbur"My Gift Is Sharing"-950718	Open		55.00	55
1992	Sammy "Little Lambs Are In My Care"-950726	Open		17.50	18
1992	Jacob "Wishing For Love"-950734	Suspd		22.50	26
1992	Charlie "The Spirit of Friendshiip Warms The Heart"-950742	Suspd		22.50	23
1992	Theadore, Samantha & Tyler "Friendship Weathers All Storms"-950769	Open		20.00	20
1992	Beth "Happy Holidays, Deer Friend"-950807	Suspd.		22.50	40
1992	Bear on Rocking Reindeer (Musical)-950815	Suspd.		60.00	65-80
1992	Signage Plaque-951005	Open		15.00	15
1992	Steven "A Season Filled With Sweetness"-951129	Retrd.	1995	20.00	40-65
1992	Angie "I Brought The Star"-951137	Open		15.00	15
1992	Theadore, Samantha & Tyler (9") "Friends Come In All Sizes"-951196	Open		130.00	130
1992	Creche & Quilt-951218	Open		50.00	50

Cherished Teddies Special Limited Edition - P. Hillman

YEAR ISSUE		EDITION LIMIT	YEAR RETD.	ISSUE PRICE	*QUOTE U.S. $
1993	Teddy & Roosevelt "The Book of Teddies 1903-1993"-624918	Yr.Iss.		20.00	100-175
1993	Holding On To Someone Special-Collector Appreciation Fig.-916285	Yr.Iss.		20.00	200-300
1994	Priscilla Ann "There's No One Like Hue" Collectible Exposition Exclusive available only at Secaucus and South Bend in 1994 and at Long Beach in 1995	Yr.Iss.		24.00	125-200

Cherished Teddies T Is For Teddy - P. Hillman

YEAR ISSUE		EDITION LIMIT	YEAR RETD.	ISSUE PRICE	*QUOTE U.S. $
1995	Bear w/"A" Block-158488A	Open		5.00	5
1995	Bear w/"B" Block-158488B	Open		5.00	5
1995	Bear w/"C" Block-158488C	Open		5.00	5
1995	Bear w/"D" Block-158488D	Open		5.00	5
1995	Bear w/"E" Block-158488E	Open		5.00	5
1995	Bear w/"F" Block-158488F	Open		5.00	5
1995	Bear w/"G" Block-158488G	Open		5.00	5
1995	Bear w/"H" Block-158488H	Open		5.00	5
1995	Bear w/"I" Block-158488I	Open		5.00	5
1995	Bear w/"J" Block-158488J	Open		5.00	5
1995	Bear w/"K" Block-158488K	Open		5.00	5
1995	Bear w/"L" Block-158488L	Open		5.00	5
1995	Bear w/"M" Block-158488M	Open		5.00	5
1995	Bear w/"N" Block-158488N	Open		5.00	5
1995	Bear w/"O" Block-158488O	Open		5.00	5
1995	Bear w/"P" Block-158488P	Open		5.00	5
1995	Bear w/"Q" Block-158488Q	Open		5.00	5
1995	Bear w/"R" Block-158488R	Open		5.00	5
1995	Bear w/"S" Block-158488S	Open		5.00	5
1995	Bear w/"T" Block-158488T	Open		5.00	5
1995	Bear w/"U" Block-158488U	Open		5.00	5
1995	Bear w/"V" Block-158488V	Open		5.00	5
1995	Bear w/"W" Block-158488W	Open		5.00	5
1995	Bear w/"X" Block-158488X	Open		5.00	5
1995	Bear w/"Z" Block-158488Z	Open		5.00	5

Maud Humphrey Bogart Collectors' Club Members Only - M. Humphrey

YEAR ISSUE		EDITION LIMIT	YEAR RETD.	ISSUE PRICE	*QUOTE U.S. $
1991	Friends For Life MH911	Closed	N/A	60.00	65
1992	Nature's Little Helper MH921	Closed	N/A	65.00	60-65
1993	Sitting Pretty MH931	Yr.Iss.		60.00	60

Maud Humphrey Bogart Symbol Of Membership Figurines - M. Humphrey

YEAR ISSUE		EDITION LIMIT	YEAR RETD.	ISSUE PRICE	*QUOTE U.S. $
1991	A Flower For You H5596	Closed	N/A	Unkn.	30
1992	Sunday Best M0002	Closed	N/A	Unkn.	30-53
1993	Playful Companions M0003	Yr.Iss.		Unkn.	Unkn.

Maud Humphrey Bogart - M. Humphrey

YEAR ISSUE		EDITION LIMIT	YEAR RETD.	ISSUE PRICE	*QUOTE U.S. $
1988	Tea And Gossip H1301	Retrd.	N/A	65.00	70-95
1988	Cleaning House H1303	Retrd.	N/A	60.00	55
1988	Susanna H 1305	Retrd.	N/A	60.00	125
1988	Little Chickadees H1306	Retrd.	N/A	65.00	60-65
1988	The Magic Kitten H1308	Retrd.	N/A	66.00	50
1988	Seamstress H1309	Retrd.	N/A	66.00	80
1988	A Pleasure To Meet You H1310	Retrd.	N/A	65.00	80-125
1988	My First Dance H1311	Retrd.	N/A	60.00	100
1988	Sarah H1312	Retrd.	N/A	60.00	245-295
1988	Sealed With A Kiss H1316	Retrd.	N/A	45.00	60
1988	Special Friends H1317	Retrd.	N/A	66.00	70
1988	School Days H1318	Retrd.	N/A	42.50	60
1988	Gift Of Love H1319	Retrd.	N/A	65.00	40
1988	My 1st Birthday H1320	Retrd.	N/A	47.00	47
1989	Winter Fun H1354	Retrd.	N/A	46.00	53
1992	Stars and Stripes Forever 910201	Retrd.	N/A	75.00	80
1993	Playing Mama 5th Anniversary Figurine 915963	Retrd.	N/A	80.00	110
1993	Playing Mama Event Figurine 915963R	Retrd.	N/A	80.00	90-110

Maud Humphrey Bogart Victorian Village - M. Humphrey

YEAR ISSUE		EDITION LIMIT	YEAR RETD.	ISSUE PRICE	*QUOTE U.S. $
1994	Christmas Scene-655457	Open		50.00	50

Memories of Yesterday Society Figurines - M. Attwell

YEAR ISSUE		EDITION LIMIT	YEAR RETD.	ISSUE PRICE	*QUOTE U.S. $
1991	Welcome To Your New Home-MY911	Yr.Iss.		30.00	45
1991	I Love My Friends-MY921	Yr.Iss.		32.50	35
1993	Now I'm The Fairest Of Them All-MY931	Yr.Iss.		35.00	35
1993	A Little Love Song for You-MY941	Yr.Iss.		35.00	35
1994	Wot's All This Talk About Love-MY942	Yr.Iss.		27.50	28
1995	Sharing the Common Thread of Love- MY951	Yr.Iss.		100.00	100
1995	A Song For You From One That's True-MY952	Yr.Iss.		37.50	38
1996	You've Got My Vote-MY961	Yr.Iss.		40.00	40
1996	Peace, Heavenly Peace-MY962	Yr.Iss.		30.00	30

Memories of Yesterday Exclusive Membership Figurine - M. Attwell

YEAR ISSUE		EDITION LIMIT	YEAR RETD.	ISSUE PRICE	*QUOTE U.S. $
1991	We Belong Together-S0001	Yr.Iss.		Gift	35
1992	Waiting For The Sunshine-S0002	Yr.Iss.		Gift	35
1993	I'm The Girl For You-S0003	Yr.Iss.		Gift	40
1994	Blowing a Kiss to a Dear I Miss-S0004	Yr.Iss.		Gift	N/A
1995	Time to Celebrate-S0005	Yr.Iss.		Gift	N/A
1996	Forget-Me-Not!-S0006	Yr.Iss.		Gift	N/A

Memories of Yesterday Exclusive Charter Membership Figurine - M. Attwell

YEAR ISSUE		EDITION LIMIT	YEAR RETD.	ISSUE PRICE	*QUOTE U.S. $
1992	Waiting For The Sunshine-S0102	Yr.Iss.		Gift	N/A
1993	I'm The Girl For You-S0103	Yr.Iss.		Gift	N/A
1994	Blowing a Kiss to a Dear I Miss-S0104	Yr.Iss.		Gift	N/A
1995	Time to Celebrate-S0105	Yr.Iss.		Gift	N/A
1996	Forget-Me-Not!-S0106	Yr.Iss.		Gift	N/A

Memories of Yesterday - M. Attwell

YEAR ISSUE		EDITION LIMIT	YEAR RETD.	ISSUE PRICE	*QUOTE U.S. $
1995	A Friend Like You Is Hard To Find-101176	Open		45.00	45
1995	A Helping Hand For You-101192	Open		40.00	40
1995	Won't You Skate With Me?-134864	5,000		35.00	35
1995	Dear Old Dear, Wish You Were Here-134872	5,000		37.50	38
1995	You're My Sunshine On A Rainy Day-137626	Open		37.50	38
1995	Boo-Boo's Band Set/5-137758	Open		25.00	25
1995	Bedtime Tales-set-153400	2,000		60.00	60
1996	We're In Trouble Now!-162299	7,500		37.50	38
1996	A Basket Full of Love-162582	Open		50.00	50
1996	Just Longing To See You-162620	7,500		27.50	28

*Quotes have been rounded up to nearest dollar

YEAR ISSUE		EDITION LIMIT	YEAR RETD.	ISSUE PRICE	*QUOTE U.S.$
1996	We Are His Children-162639	Open		30.00	30
1996	Just Like Daddy-162698	7,500		27.50	28
1996	How Good of God To Make Us All-164135	5,000		50.00	50
1990	Collection Sign-513156	Closed	1993	7.00	7
1989	Blow Wind, Blow-520012	Open		40.00	40
1990	Hold It! You're Just Swell-520020	Suspd.		50.00	50
1990	Kiss The Place And Make It Well-520039	Suspd.		50.00	50
1989	Let's Be Nice Like We Was Before-520047	Suspd.		50.00	50
1991	Who Ever Told Mother To Order Twins?-520063	Open		33.50	34
1989	I'se Spoken For-520071	Retrd.	1991	30.00	30-50
1993	You Do Make Me Happy-520098	Open		27.50	28
1990	Where's Muvver?-520101	Retrd.	1994	30.00	30
1990	Here Comes The Bride And Groom God Bless 'Em!-520136 (musical)	Suspd.		80.00	80
1989	Daddy, I Can Never Fill Your Shoes-520187	Open		30.00	30
1989	This One's For You, Dear-520195	Suspd.		50.00	50
1989	Should I . . . ?-520209	Suspd.		50.00	50
1990	Luck At Last! He Loves Me-520217	Retrd.	1992	35.00	36-58
1989	Here Comes The Bride-God Bless Her! -9"-520527	2-Yr.	1990	95.00	95-100
1989	We's Happy! How's Yourself?-520616	Retrd.	1991	70.00	85-150
1989	Here Comes The Bride & Groom (musical) God Bless 'Em-520896	Open		50.00	50
1989	The Long and Short of It-522384	Retrd.	1994	32.50	33
1989	As Good As His Mother Ever Made-522392	Open		32.50	32-40
1989	Must Feed Them Over Christmas-522406	Open		38.50	39
1989	Knitting You A Warm & Cozy Winter-522414	Open		37.50	38
1989	Joy To You At Christmas-522449	Open		45.00	45
1989	For Fido And Me-522457	Open		70.00	70
1991	Wishful Thinking-522597	Open		45.00	45
1991	Why Don't You Sing Along?-522600	Retrd.	1995	55.00	55
1995	You Brighten My Day With A Smile-522627	Open		30.00	30
1991	Tying The Knot-522678	Open		60.00	60
1991	Wherever I Am, I'm Dreaming of You-522686	Suspd.		40.00	40
1993	Will You Be Mine?-522694	Open		30.00	30
1991	Sitting Pretty-522708	Retrd.	1993	40.00	50
1993	Here's A Little Song From Me To You Musical-522716	Open		70.00	70
1992	A Whole Bunch of Love For You-522732	Open		40.00	40
1992	I'se Such A Good Little Girl Sometimes-522759	Suspd.		30.00	30
1992	Things Are Rather Upside Down-522775	Suspd.		30.00	30
1991	Pull Yourselves Together Girls, Waists Are In-522783	Open		30.00	30
1993	Bringing Good Luck To You-522791	Open		30.00	30
1995	I Comfort Fido And Fido Comforts Me-522813	5,000		50.00	50
1992	A Kiss From Fido-523119	Suspd.		35.00	35
1994	Bless 'Em!-523127	Open		35.00	35
1994	Bless 'Em!-523232	Open		35.00	35
1990	I'm Not As Backwards As I Looks-523240	Open		32.50	33
1990	I Pray The Lord My Soul To Keep-523259	Open		25.00	25
1990	He Hasn't Forgotten Me-523267	Suspd.		30.00	30
1990	Time For Bed 9"-523275	2-Yr.	1991	95.00	125
1991	Just Thinking 'bout You-523461 (musical)	Suspd.		70.00	70
1992	Now Be A Good Dog Fido-524581	Open		45.00	45
1991	Them Dishes Nearly Done-524611	Open		50.00	50
1995	Join Me For A Little Song-524654	5,000		37.50	38
1990	Let Me Be Your Guardian Angel-524670	Open		32.50	33
1990	A Lapful Of Luck-524689	Open		15.00	15
1990	Not A Creature Was Stirrin'-524697	Suspd.		45.00	45
1990	I'se Been Painting-524700	Suspd.		37.50	38
1992	The Future-God Bless 'Em!-524719	Open		37.50	38
1990	A Dash of Something With Something For the Pot-524727	Open		55.00	55
1991	Opening Presents Is Much Fun!-524735	Suspd.		37.50	38
1992	You'll Always Be My Hero-524743	Open		50.00	50
1990	Got To Get Home For The Holidays-524751(musical)	Retrd.	1994	100.00	100
1990	Hush-A-Bye Baby-524778	Open		80.00	80
1990	The Greatest Treasure The World Can Hold-524808	Open		50.00	50
1993	With A Heart That's True, I'll Wait For You-524816	Open		50.00	50
1994	With A Heart That's True, I'll Wait For You-524816	Open		50.00	50
1990	Hoping To See You Soon-524824	Suspd.		30.00	30
1991	I Must Be Somebody's Darling-524832	Retrd.	1993	30.00	30
1991	We All Loves A Cuddle-524832	Retrd.	1992	30.00	35
1991	He Loves Me -9"-525022	2-Yr.	1992	100.00	100
1993	Now I Lay Me Down To Sleep-525413 (musical)	Suspd.		65.00	65
1992	Making Something Special For You-525472	Open		45.00	45
1991	I'm As Comfy As Can Be-525480	Suspd.		50.00	50
1992	I'm Hopin' You're Missing Me Too-525499	Suspd.		55.00	55
1993	The Jolly Ole Sun Will Shine Again-525502	Retrd.	1994	55.00	55
1991	Friendship Has No Boundaries (Special Understamp)-525545	Yr.Iss.	1991	30.00	30-50
1992	Home's A Grand Place To Get Back To Musical-525553	Retrd.	1995	100.00	100
1991	Give It Your Best Shot-525561	Open		35.00	35
1992	I Pray the Lord My Soul To Keep (musical)-525596	Suspd.		65.00	65
1991	Could You Love Me For Myself Alone?-525618	Retrd.	1994	30.00	30
1996	Whenever I Get A Moment-I Think of You-525626	7,500		37.50	38
1992	Good Night and God Bless You In Every Way!-525634	Suspd.		50.00	50
1992	Five Years Of Memories-525669 (Five Year Anniversary Figurine)	Yr.Iss.	1992	50.00	65
1992	Five Years Of Memories Celebrating Our Five Years 1992-525669A	500		N/A	N/A
1996	Loving You One Stitch At A Time-525677	5,000		50.00	50
1993	May Your Flowers Be Even Better Than The Pictures On The Packets-525685	Open		37.50	38
1995	Let's Sail Away Together-525707	Open		32.50	33
1993	You Won't Catch Me Being A Golf Widow-525715	Open		30.00	30
1995	Good Friends Are Great Gifts-525723	Open		50.00	50
1994	Taking After Mother-525731	Open		40.00	40
1994	Too Shy For Words-525758	Open		50.00	50
1991	Good Morning, Little Boo-Boo-525766	Open		40.00	40
1992	Hurry Up For the Last Train to Fairyland-525863	Suspd.		40.00	40
1992	I'se So Happy You Called-526401	Retrd.	1993	100.00	100
1994	Pleasant Dreams and Sweet Repose-(musical)-526592	Open		80.00	80
1996	Put Your Best Foot Forward-526983	5,000		50.00	50
1994	Bobbed-526991	Retrd.	1995	32.50	33
1996	Can I Keep Her, Mommy?-527025	Open		13.50	14
1992	Time For Bed-527076	Open		30.00	30
1991	S'no Use Lookin' Back Now!-527203	Open		75.00	75
1992	Collection Sign-527300	Open		30.00	30
1993	Having A Wash And Brush Up-527424	Open		35.00	35
1994	Having a Good Ole Laugh-527432	Open		50.00	50
1993	A Bit Tied Up Just Now-But Cheerio-527467	Open		45.00	45
1992	Send All Life's Little Worries Skipping-527505	Open		30.00	30
1994	Don't Wait For Wishes to Come True-Go Get Them!-527645	Open		37.50	38
1993	Hullo! Did You Come By Underground?-527653	Yr.Iss.	1993	40.00	40
1993	Hullo! Did You Come By Underground? Commemorative Issue: 1913-1993 -527653A	500		N/A	N/A
1993	Look Out-Something Good Is Coming Your Way!-528781	Suspd.		37.50	38
1992	Merry Christmas, Little Boo-Boo-528803	Open		37.50	38
1994	Do Be Friends With Me-529117	Open		40.00	40
1994	Good Morning From One Cheery Soul To Another-529141	Open		30.00	30
1994	May Your Birthday Be Bright And Happy-529575	Open		35.00	35
1996	God Bless Our Future-529583	5,000		45.00	45
1993	Strikes Me, I'm Your Match-529656	Open		27.50	28
1993	Wot's All This Talk About Love?-529737	Retrd.	1994	100.00	100
1994	Thank God For Fido-529753	2-Yr.		100.00	100
1994	Making the Right Connection-529907	Yr.Iss.	1994	30.00	30
1994	Still Going Strong-530344	Open		27.50	28
1993	Do You Know The Way To Fairyland?-530379	Open		50.00	50
1996	We'd Do Anything For You, Dear-530905	5,000		50.00	50
1994	Comforting Thoughts-531367	Open		32.50	33
1995	Love To You Always-602752	Open		30.00	30
1995	Wherever You Go, I'll Keep In Touch-602760	Open		30.00	30
1995	Love Begins With Friendship-602914	Open		50.00	50
1994	The Nativity Pageant-602949	Open		90.00	90
1995	May You Have A Big Smile For A Long While-602965	Open		30.00	30
1995	Love To You Today-602973	Open		30.00	30
1996	You Warm My Heart-603007	7,500		35.00	35

Memories of Yesterday A Loving Wish For You - M. Attwell

YEAR ISSUE		EDITION LIMIT	YEAR RETD.	ISSUE PRICE	*QUOTE U.S.$
1995	Happiness Is Our Wedding Wish-135178	Open		25.00	25
1995	A Blessed Day For You-135186	Open		25.00	25
1995	Wishing You A Bright Future-135194	Open		25.00	25
1995	An Anniversary Is Love-135208	Open		25.00	25
1995	A Birthday Wish For You-135216	Open		25.00	25
1995	Bless You, Little One-135224	Open		25.00	25
1996	You Are My Shining Star-164585	Open		25.00	25
1996	You Brighten My Days-164615	Open		25.00	25

Memories of Yesterday Charter 1988 - M. Attwell

YEAR ISSUE		EDITION LIMIT	YEAR RETD.	ISSUE PRICE	*QUOTE U.S.$
1988	Mommy, I Teared It-114480	Open		25.00	40-143
1988	Now I Lay Me Down To Sleep-114499	Open		20.00	25-65
1988	We's Happy! How's Yourself?-114502	Open		40.00	45-60
1988	Hang On To Your Luck!-114510	Open		25.00	27-70
1988	How Do You Spell S-O-R-R-Y?-114529	Retrd.	1990	25.00	50-95
1988	What Will I Grow Up To Be?-114537	Suspd.		40.00	45
1988	Can I Keep Her Mommy?-114545	Retrd.	1995	25.00	27-70
1988	Hush!-114553	Retrd.	1990	45.00	75-125
1988	It Hurts When Fido Hurts-114561	Retrd.	1992	30.00	32-75
1988	Anyway, Fido Loves Me-114588	Suspd.		30.00	32-75
1988	If You Can't Be Good, Be Careful-114596	Retrd.	1993	50.00	55-90
1988	Welcome Santa-114960	Open		45.00	50-100
1988	Special Delivery-114979	Retrd.	1991	30.00	32-70
1988	How 'bout A Little Kiss?-114987	Retrd.	1995	25.00	27-85
1988	Waiting For Santa-114995	Open		40.00	40-50
1988	Dear Santa. . .-115002	Suspd.		50.00	50
1988	I Hope Santa Is Home . . .-115010	Open		30.00	33-45
1988	It's The Thought That Counts-115029	Suspd.		25.00	29-75
1988	Is It Really Santa?-115347	Open		50.00	55-60
1988	He Knows IF You've Been Bad Or Good-115355	Open		40.00	45-75
1988	Now He Can Be Your Friend, Too!-115363	Open		45.00	50-70
1988	We Wish You A Merry Christmas-115371 (musical)	Suspd.		70.00	70
1988	Good Morning Mr. Snowman-115401	Retrd.	1992	75.00	80-170
1988	Mommy, I Teared It, 9"-115924	Retrd.	1990	85.00	140-195

Memories of Yesterday Event Item Only - M. Attwell

YEAR ISSUE		EDITION LIMIT	YEAR RETD.	ISSUE PRICE	*QUOTE U.S.$
1994	I'll Always Be Your Truly Friend-525693	Yr.Iss.		30.00	30
1995	Wrapped In Love And Happiness 602930	Yr.Iss.		35.00	35
1996	A Sweet Treat For You-115126	Yr.Iss.		30.00	30

Memories of Yesterday Exclusive Heritage Dealer Figurine - M. Attwell

YEAR ISSUE		EDITION LIMIT	YEAR RETD.	ISSUE PRICE	*QUOTE U.S.$
1994	Loving Each Other Is The Nicest Thing We've Got- 522430	Yr.Iss.		60.00	60
1991	A Friendly Chat and a Cup of Tea-525510	Yr.Iss.		50.00	100
1993	I'm Always Looking Out For You-527440	Yr.Iss.		55.00	55
1995	A Little Help From Fairyland 529133	1,995		55.00	55
1995	Friendship Is Meant To Be Shared-602922	Yr.Iss.		50.00	50
1996	Tucking My Dears All Safe Away-130095	Yr.Iss.		50.00	50
1996	I Do Like My Holiday Crews-522805	1,996		100.00	100
1996	Peter Pan Collector's Set 174564	1,000		150.00	150

Memories of Yesterday Friendship - M. Attwell

YEAR ISSUE		EDITION LIMIT	YEAR RETD.	ISSUE PRICE	*QUOTE U.S.$
1996	I'll Miss You-179183	Open		25.00	25
1996	I Love You This Much!-179191	Open		25.00	25
1996	Thinking of You-179213	Open		25.00	25
1996	You And Me-179205	Open		25.00	25

Memories of Yesterday Holiday Snapshots - M. Attwell

YEAR ISSUE		EDITION LIMIT	YEAR RETD.	ISSUE PRICE	*QUOTE U.S.$
1995	I'll Help You Mommy 144673	Open		25.00	25
1995	Isn't She Pretty? 144681	Open		25.00	25
1995	I Didn't Mean To Do It 144703	Open		25.00	25
1995	Can I Open Just One? 144711	Open		25.00	25

Memories of Yesterday Memories Of A Special Day - M. Attwell

YEAR ISSUE		EDITION LIMIT	YEAR RETD.	ISSUE PRICE	*QUOTE U.S.$
1994	Monday's Child...-531421	Open		35.00	35
1994	Tuesday's Child...-531448	Open		35.00	35
1994	Wednesday's Child...-531405	Open		35.00	35
1994	Thursday's Child...-531413	Open		35.00	35
1994	Friday's Child...-531391	Open		35.00	35
1994	Saturday's Child...-531383	Open		35.00	35
1994	Sunday's Child...-531480	Open		35.00	35
1994	Collector's Commemorative Edition Set/7, Hand- numbered-528056	1,994		250.00	250

Memories of Yesterday Nativity - M. Attwell

YEAR ISSUE		EDITION LIMIT	YEAR RETD.	ISSUE PRICE	*QUOTE U.S.$
1994	Nativity Set of 4 602949	Open		90.00	90
1995	Innkeeper 602892	Open		27.50	28
1996	Shepherd-602906	Open		27.50	28

Memories of Yesterday Once Upon A Fairy Tale™... - M. Attwell

YEAR ISSUE		EDITION LIMIT	YEAR RETD.	ISSUE PRICE	*QUOTE U.S.$
1992	Mother Goose-526428	18,000		50.00	50
1993	Mary, Mary Quite Contrary-526436	18,000		45.00	45
1993	Little Miss Muffett-526444	18,000		50.00	50
1992	Simple Simon-526452	18,000		35.00	35
1992	Mary Had A Little Lamb-526479	18,000		45.00	45

*Quotes have been rounded up to nearest dollar

YEAR ISSUE		EDITION LIMIT	YEAR RETD.	ISSUE PRICE	*QUOTE U.S.$
1994	Tweedle Dum & Tweedle Dee-526460	10,000		50.00	50

Memories of Yesterday Peter Pan - M. Attwell

YEAR ISSUE		EDITION LIMIT	YEAR RETD.	ISSUE PRICE	*QUOTE U.S.$
1996	John-165441	Open		25.00	25
1996	Michael-165425	Open		30.00	30
1996	Peter Pan-164666	Open		25.00	25
1996	Wendy-164674	Open		25.00	25

Memories of Yesterday Special Edition - M. Attwell

YEAR ISSUE		EDITION LIMIT	YEAR RETD.	ISSUE PRICE	*QUOTE U.S.$
1989	As Good As His Mother Ever Made-522392	9,600		32.50	114-150
1988	Mommy, I Teared It-523488	10,000		25.00	175-325
1990	A Lapful of Luck -525014	5,000		30.00	114-180
1990	Set of Three	N/A		87.50	735

Memories of Yesterday When I Grow Up - M. Attwell

YEAR ISSUE		EDITION LIMIT	YEAR RETD.	ISSUE PRICE	*QUOTE U.S.$
1995	When I Grow Up, I Want To Be A Doctor-102997	Open		25.00	25
1995	When I Grow Up, I Want To Be A Mother-103195	Open		25.00	25
1995	When I Grow Up, I Want To Be A Ballerina-103209	Open		25.00	25
1995	When I Grow Up, I Want To Be A Teacher-103357	Open		25.00	25
1995	When I Grow Up, I Want To Be A Fireman-103462	Open		25.00	25
1995	When I Grow Up, I Want To Be A Nurse-103535	Open		25.00	25
1996	When I Grow Up, I Want To Be A Businessman-164623	Open		25.00	25
1996	When I Grow Up, I Want To Be A Businesswoman-164631	Open		25.00	25

Miss Martha's Collection - M. Holcombe

YEAR ISSUE		EDITION LIMIT	YEAR RETD.	ISSUE PRICE	*QUOTE U.S.$
1993	Erin-Don't Worry Santa Won't Forget Us-307246	Retrd.	1994	55.00	110
1993	Amber-Mr. Snowman! (waterglobe)-310476	Closed	1994	50.00	100
1993	Kekisha-Heavenly Peace Musical-310484	Closed	1994	60.00	120
1993	Whitney-Let's Have Another Party-321559	Closed	1994	45.00	50-90
1993	Megan-My Birthday Cake!-321567	Closed	1994	60.00	100-120
1993	Doug-I'm Not Showin' Off-321575	Closed	1994	40.00	80
1993	Francie-Such A Precious Gift!-321583	Closed	1994	50.00	100
1993	Alicia-A Blessing From God-321591	Closed	1994	40.00	140
1993	Anita-It's For You, Mama!-321605	Closed	1994	45.00	75-90
1994	Jeffrey-Bein' A Fireman Sure Is Hot & Thirsty Work-350206	Closed	1994	40.00	80
1993	Jess-I Can Fly-350516	Retrd.	1994	45.00	90
1993	Ruth-Littlest Angel Figurine-350524	Closed	1994	40.00	80
1993	Stephen-I'll Be The Best Shepherd In The World!-350540	Closed	1994	40.00	80
1993	Jonathon-Maybe I Can Be Like Santa-350559	Closed	1994	45.00	90
1994	Charlotte-You Can Be Whatever You Dream-353191	Closed	1994	40.00	50-80
1992	Lillie-Christmas Dinner!-369373	Retrd.	1993	55.00	110
1992	Eddie-What A Nice Surprise!-369381	Retrd.	1994	50.00	100
1992	Kekisha-Heavenly Peace-421456	Closed	1994	40.00	80
1992	Angela-I Have Wings-421464	Closed	1994	45.00	160
1992	Amber-Mr. Snowman-421472	Retrd.	1993	60.00	110
1992	Mar/Jsh/Christopher-Hush Baby! It's Your B-day! Musical-431362	Closed	1994	80.00	160
1992	Carrie-God Bless America-440035	Closed	1994	45.00	90
1993	Hallie-Sing Praises To The Lord-443166	Retrd.	1993	60.00	80-120
1991	Jana-Plant With Love-443174	Closed	1994	40.00	65-80
1991	Hallie-Sing Praises To The Lord-443182	Closed	1994	37.50	65-95
1992	Belle/Maize-Not Now, Muffin-443204	Retrd.	1993	50.00	100
1991	Sammy/Leisha-Sister's First Day Of School-443190	Retrd.	1993	55.00	70-110
1991	Nate-Hope You Hear My Prayer, Lord-443212	Closed	1994	17.50	55-75
1991	Sadie-They Can't Find Us Here-443220	Retrd.	1993	45.00	85
1992	Patsy-Clean Clothes For Dolly-443239	Retrd.	1993	50.00	100
1991	Dawn-Pretty Please, Mama-443247	Closed	1994	40.00	60-80
1991	Tonya-Hush, Puppy Dear-443255	Closed	1994	50.00	70-100
1991	Jenny/Jeremiah-Birthday Biscuits, With Love...-443263	Retrd.	1993	60.00	85-120
1991	Suzi-Mama, Watch Me!-443271	Retrd.	1993	35.00	45-70
1992	Mattie-Sweet Child-443298	Retrd.	1993	30.00	40-60
1992	Sara Lou-Here, Lammie-443301	Retrd.	1993	50.00	70-100
1992	Angel Tree Topper-446521	Closed	1994	80.00	160
1992	Mar/Jsh/Christopher-Hush, Baby! It's Your B-day Figurine-448354	Closed	1994	55.00	110

Precious Moments Collectors Club Welcome Gift - S. Butcher

YEAR ISSUE		EDITION LIMIT	YEAR RETD.	ISSUE PRICE	*QUOTE U.S.$
1982	But Love Goes On Forever-Plaque-E-0202	Yr.Iss.		Unkn.	65-100
1983	Let Us Call the Club to Order-E-0303	Yr.Iss.		Unkn.	50-60
1984	Join in on the Blessings-E-0404	Yr.Iss.		Unkn.	50-65
1985	Seek and Ye Shall Find-E-0005	Yr.Iss.		Unkn.	55-70
1986	Birds of a Feather Collect Together-E-0006	Yr.Iss.		Unkn.	50-70
1987	Sharing Is Universal-E-0007	Yr.Iss.		Unkn.	40-55
1988	A Growing Love-E-0008	Yr.Iss.		Unkn.	40-50
1989	Always Room For One More-C-0009	Yr.Iss.		Unkn.	50-70
1990	My Happiness-C-0010	Yr.Iss.		Unkn.	57
1991	Sharing the Good News Together-C-0011	Yr.Iss.		Unkn.	35-55
1992	The Club That's Out Of This World-C-0012	Yr.Iss.		Unkn.	30-45
1993	Loving, Caring, and Sharing Along the Way-C-0013	Yr.Iss.		Unkn.	50
1994	You Are the End of My Rainbow-C-0014	Yr.Iss.		Unkn.	50
1995	You're The Sweetest Cookie In The Batch-C-0015	Yr.Iss.		Unkn.	Unkn.
1996	You're As Pretty As A Picture-C-0016	Yr.Iss.		Unkn.	Unkn.

Precious Moments Inscribed Charter Member Renewal Gift - S. Butcher

YEAR ISSUE		EDITION LIMIT	YEAR RETD.	ISSUE PRICE	*QUOTE U.S.$
1981	But Love Goes on Forever-E-0001	Yr.Iss.		Unkn.	130-175
1982	But Love Goes on Forever-Plaque-E-0102	Yr.Iss.		Unkn.	55-100
1983	Let Us Call the Club to Order-E-0103	Yr.Iss.		25.00	55
1984	Join in on the Blessings-E-0104	Yr.Iss.		25.00	50
1985	Seek and Ye Shall Find-E-0105	Yr.Iss.		25.00	45-55
1986	Birds of a Feather Collect Together-E-0106	Yr.Iss.		25.00	30-50
1987	Sharing Is Universal -E-0107	Yr.Iss.		25.00	30-50
1988	A Growing Love-E-0108	Yr.Iss.		25.00	30-50
1989	Always Room For One More-C-0109	Yr.Iss.		35.00	50-55
1990	My Happiness-C-0110	Yr.Iss.		Unkn.	35
1991	Sharing The Good News Together-C-0111	Yr.Iss.		Unkn.	25-45
1992	The Club That's Out Of This World-C-0112	Yr.Iss.		Unkn.	30-45
1993	Loving, Caring, and Sharing Along the Way-C-0113	Yr.Iss.		Unkn.	35-50
1994	You Are the End of My Rainbow -C-0114	Yr.Iss.		Unkn.	45-50
1995	You're The Sweetest Cookie In The Batch-C-0115	Yr.Iss.		Unkn.	Unkn.

Precious Moments Special Edition Members' Only - S. Butcher

YEAR ISSUE		EDITION LIMIT	YEAR RETD.	ISSUE PRICE	*QUOTE U.S.$
1981	Hello, Lord, It's Me Again - PM-811	Yr.Iss.		25.00	375-475
1982	Smile, God Loves You-PM-821	Yr.Iss.		25.00	255-310
1983	Put on a Happy Face-PM-822	Yr.Iss.		25.00	175-275
1983	Dawn's Early Light-PM-831	Yr.Iss.		27.50	80-95
1984	God's Ray of Mercy-PM-841	Yr.Iss.		25.00	65-75
1984	Trust in the Lord to the Finish-PM-842	Yr.Iss.		25.00	80-105
1985	The Lord is My Shepherd -PM-851	Yr.Iss.		25.00	95-125
1985	I Love to Tell the Story-PM-852	Yr.Iss.		27.50	85-95
1986	Grandma's Prayer-PM-861	Yr.Iss.		25.00	90-140
1986	I'm Following Jesus-PM-862	Yr.Iss.		25.00	85-100
1987	Feed My Sheep-PM-871	Yr.Iss.		25.00	40-65
1987	In His Time-PM-872	Yr.Iss.		25.00	60-75
1987	Loving You Dear Valentine-PM-873	Yr.Iss.		25.00	35-55
1987	Loving You Dear Valentine -PM-874	Yr.Iss.		25.00	40-55
1988	God Bless You for Touching My Life-PM-881	Yr.Iss.		27.50	55-65
1988	You Just Can't Chuck A Good Friendship-PM-882	Yr.Iss.		27.50	39-50
1989	You Will Always Be My Choice - PM-891	Yr.Iss.		27.50	30-55
1989	Mow Power To Ya-PM-892	Yr.Iss.		27.50	60-88
1990	Ten Years And Still Going Strong-PM-901	Yr.Iss.		30.00	55
1990	You Are A Blessing To Me -PM-902	Yr.Iss.		30.00	50
1991	One Step At A Time-PM-911	Yr.Iss.		33.00	45-60
1991	Lord, Keep Me In TeePee Top Shape-PM-912	Yr.Iss.		33.00	45
1992	Only Love Can Make A Home -PM-921	Yr.Iss.		30.00	55
1992	Sowing The Seeds of Love -PM-922	Yr.Iss.		30.00	45
1993	His Little Treasure-PM-931	Yr.Iss.		30.00	40
1993	Loving PM-932	Yr.Iss.		30.00	60-80
1994	Caring PM-941	Yr.Iss.		35.00	50
1994	Sharing PM-942	Yr.Iss.		35.00	40-50
1995	You're One In A Million To Me PM-951	Yr.Iss.		35.00	35
1995	Take Time To Pray PM-952	Yr.Iss.		35.00	35
1996	Teach Us To Love One Another PM-961	Yr.Iss.		40.00	40
1996	Our Club Is Soda-licious PM-962	Yr.Iss.		35.00	35

Precious Moments Club 5th Anniversary Commemorative Edition - S. Butcher

YEAR ISSUE		EDITION LIMIT	YEAR RETD.	ISSUE PRICE	*QUOTE U.S.$
1985	God Bless Our Years Together-12440	Yr.Iss.		175.00	300-350

Precious Moments Club 10th Anniversary Commemorative Edition - S. Butcher

YEAR ISSUE		EDITION LIMIT	YEAR RETD.	ISSUE PRICE	*QUOTE U.S.$
1988	The Good Lord has Blessed Us Tenfold-114022	Yr.Iss.		90.00	175-250

Precious Moments Club 15th Anniversary Commemorative Edition - S. Butcher

YEAR ISSUE		EDITION LIMIT	YEAR RETD.	ISSUE PRICE	*QUOTE U.S.$
1993	15 Happy Years Together: What A Tweet-530786	Yr.Iss.		100.00	115
1993	A Perfect Display of 15 Happy Years-127817	Yr.Iss.		100.00	115

Precious Moments - S. Butcher

YEAR ISSUE		EDITION LIMIT	YEAR RETD.	ISSUE PRICE	*QUOTE U.S.$
1983	Sharing Our Season Together -E-0501	Suspd.		50.00	125-175
1983	Jesus is the Light that Shines -E-0502	Suspd.		23.00	50-60
1983	Blessings from My House to Yours-E-0503	Suspd.		27.00	85-105
1983	Christmastime Is for Sharing -E-0504	Retrd.	1990	37.00	80-90
1983	Surrounded with Joy-E-0506	Retrd.	1989	21.00	50-85
1983	God Sent His Son-E-0507	Suspd.		32.50	65-90
1983	Prepare Ye the Way of the Lord -E-0508	Suspd.		75.00	100-130
1983	Bringing God's Blessing to You -E-0509	Suspd.		35.00	70-100
1983	Tubby's First Christmas-E-0511	Suspd.		12.00	32-43
1983	It's a Perfect Boy-E-0512	Suspd.		18.50	45-65
1983	Onward Christian Soldiers-E-0523	Open		24.00	35-59
1983	You Can't Run Away from God -E-0525	Retrd.	1989	28.50	80-110
1983	He Upholdeth Those Who Fall -E-0526	Suspd.		35.00	65-95
1987	His Eye Is On The Sparrow -E-0530	Retrd.	1987	28.50	100-150
1979	Jesus Loves Me-E-1372B	Open		7.00	28-125
1979	Jesus Loves Me-E-1372G	Open		7.00	28-130
1979	Smile, God Loves You-E-1373B	Retrd.	1984	7.00	70-135
1979	Jesus is the Light-E-1373G	Retrd.	1988	7.00	45-125
1979	Praise the Lord Anyhow -E-1374B	Retrd.	1982	8.00	75-130
1979	Make a Joyful Noise-E-1374G	Open		8.00	28-125
1979	Love Lifted Me-E-1375A	Retrd.	1993	11.00	60-125
1979	Prayer Changes Things-E-1375B	Suspd.		11.00	135-215
1979	Love One Another-E-1376	Open		10.00	40-120
1979	He Leadeth Me-E-1377A	Suspd.		9.00	80-135
1979	He Careth For You-E-1377B	Suspd.		9.00	90-105
1979	God Loveth a Cheerful Giver -E-1378	Retrd.	1981	11.00	750-850
1979	Love is Kind-E-1379A	Suspd.		8.00	80-150
1979	God Understands-E-1379B	Suspd.		8.00	90-160
1979	O, How I Love Jesus-E-1380B	Retrd.	1984	8.00	85-175
1979	His Burden Is Light-E-1380G	Retrd.	1984	8.00	80-175
1979	Jesus is the Answer-E-1381	Suspd.		11.50	95-140
1979	We Have Seen His Star-E-2010	Suspd.		8.00	66-144
1979	Come Let Us Adore Him-E-2011	Retrd.	1981	10.00	180-250
1979	Jesus is Born-E-2012	Suspd.		12.00	90-115
1979	Unto Us a Child is Born-E-2013	Suspd.		12.00	88-105
1982	May Your Christmas Be Cozy -E-2345	Suspd.		23.00	70-140
1982	May Your Christmas Be Warm -E-2348	Suspd.		30.00	100-140
1982	Tell Me the Story of Jesus -E-2349	Suspd.		30.00	100-135
1982	Dropping in for Christmas -E-2350	Suspd.		18.00	65-115
1987	Holy Smokes-E-2351	Retrd.	1987	27.00	110-160
1982	O Come All Ye Faithful-E-2353	Retrd.	1986	27.50	75-100
1982	I'll Play My Drum for Him-E-2356	Suspd.		30.00	60-95
1982	I'll Play My Drum for Him-E-2360	Open		16.00	30-40
1982	Christmas Joy from Head to Toe-E-2361	Suspd.		25.00	55-80
1982	Camel Figurine-E-2363	Open		20.00	33-50
1982	Goat Figurine-E-2364	Suspd.		10.00	45-75
1982	The First Noel-E-2365	Suspd.		16.00	60-80
1982	The First Noel-E-2366	Suspd.		16.00	60-70
1982	Bundles of Joy-E-2374	Retrd.	1993	27.50	85-100
1982	Dropping Over for Christmas-E-2375	Retrd.	1991	30.00	70-115
1982	Our First Christmas Together -E-2377	Suspd.		35.00	75-150
1982	3 Mini Nativity Houses & Palm Tree-E-2387	Open		45.00	75-110
1982	Come Let Us Adore Him-E-2395 (11pc. set)	Open		80.00	130-175
1980	Come Let Us Adore Him-E2800 (9 pc. set)	Open		70.00	125-175
1980	Jesus is Born-E-2801	Suspd.		37.00	150-275
1980	Christmas is a Time to Share-E-2802	Suspd.		20.00	60-90
1980	Crown Him Lord of All-E-2803	Suspd.		20.00	60-95
1980	Peace on Earth-E-2804	Suspd.		20.00	118-135
1980	Wishing You a Season Filled w/ Joy-E-2805	Retrd.	1985	20.00	105-130
1984	You Have Touched So Many Hearts-E-2821	Open		25.00	38-52
1984	This is Your Day to Shine -E-2822	Retrd.	1988	37.50	81-100
1984	To God Be the Glory-E-2823	Suspd.		40.00	80-130
1984	To a Very Special Mom-E-2824	Open		27.50	38-57
1984	To a Very Special Sister-E-2825	Open		37.50	55-65
1984	May Your Birthday Be a Blessing-E-2826	Suspd.		37.50	85-140
1984	I Get a Kick Out of You-E-2827	Suspd.		50.00	150-200
1984	Precious Memories-E-2828	Open		45.00	45-70
1984	I'm Sending You a White Christmas-E-2829	Open		37.50	55-60
1984	God Bless the Bride-E-2832	Open		35.00	50-60
1986	Sharing Our Joy Together-E-2834	Suspd.		30.00	52-60

FIGURINES/COTTAGES

YEAR ISSUE		EDITION LIMIT	YEAR RETD.	ISSUE PRICE	*QUOTE U.S.$
1984	Baby Figurines (set of 6)-E-2852	Retrd.	N/A	12.00	105-168
1980	Blessed Are the Pure in Heart-E-3104	Suspd.		9.00	25-45
1980	He Watches Over Us All-E-3105	Suspd.		11.00	52-95
1980	Mother Sew Dear-E-3106	Open		13.00	28-80
1980	Blessed are the Peacemakers -E-3107	Retrd.	1985	13.00	90-140
1980	The Hand that Rocks the Future -E-3108	Suspd.		13.00	60-95
1980	The Purr-fect Grandma-E-3109	Open		13.00	28-75
1980	Loving is Sharing-E-3110B	Retrd.	1993	13.00	60-100
1980	Loving is Sharing-E-3110G	Open		13.00	30-100
1980	Be Not Weary In Well Doing -E-3111	Retrd.	1985	14.00	85-145
1980	God's Speed-E-3112	Retrd.	1983	14.00	65-110
1980	Thou Art Mine-E-3113	Open		16.00	40-65
1980	The Lord Bless You and Keep You E-3114	Open		16.00	45-65
1980	But Love Goes on Forever-E-3115	Open		16.50	38-77
1980	Thee I Love-E-3116	Retrd.	1983	16.50	55-150
1980	Walking By Faith-E-3117	Open		35.00	70-125
1980	Eggs Over Easy-E-3118	Retrd.	1983	12.00	70-125
1980	It's What's Inside that Counts -E-3119	Suspd.		13.00	90-130
1980	To Thee With Love-E-3120	Suspd.		13.00	60-150
1981	The Lord Bless You and Keep You-E-4720	Suspd.		14.00	35-55
1981	The Lord Bless You and Keep You-E-4721	Open		14.00	33-80
1981	Love Cannot Break a True Friendship E-4722	Suspd.		22.50	125-200
1981	Peace Amid the Storm-E-4723	Suspd.		22.50	70-130
1981	Rejoicing with You-E-4724	Open		25.00	45-99
1981	Peace on Earth-E-4725	Suspd.		25.00	75-110
1981	Bear Ye One Another's Burdens-E-5200	Suspd.		20.00	60-105
1981	Love Lifted Me-E-5201	Suspd.		25.00	90-130
1981	Thank You for Coming to My Ade-E-5202	Suspd.		22.50	120-210
1981	Let Not the Sun Go Down Upon Your Wrath-E-5203	Suspd.		22.50	130-175
1981	To A Special Dad-E-5212	Open		20.00	35-79
1981	God is Love-E-5213	Suspd.		17.00	55-104
1981	Prayer Changes Things-E-5214	Suspd.		35.00	100-165
1984	May Your Christmas Be Blessed-E-5376	Suspd.		37.50	75-90
1987	Love is Kind-E-5377	Retrd.	1987	27.50	70-95
1984	Joy to the World-E-5378	Suspd.		18.00	37-50
1984	Isn't He Precious?-E-5379	Open		20.00	30-48
1984	A Monarch is Born-E-5380	Suspd.		33.00	60-75
1984	His Name is Jesus-E-5381	Suspd.		45.00	95-120
1984	For God So Loved the World -E-5382	Suspd.		70.00	115-130
1984	Wishing You a Merry Christmas E-5383	Yr.Iss.		17.00	45
1984	I'll Play My Drum for Him-E-5384	Open		10.00	16-30
1984	Oh Worship the Lord (B)-E-5385	Suspd.		10.00	50-60
1984	Oh Worship the Lord (G)-E-5386	Suspd.		10.00	55-70
1981	Come Let Us Adore Him-E-5619	Suspd.		10.00	30-45
1981	Donkey Figurine-E-5621	Open		6.00	15-30
1981	They Followed the Star-E-5624	Open		130.00	200-270
1981	Wee Three Kings-E-5635	Open		40.00	75-125
1981	Rejoice O Earth-E-5636	Open		15.00	30-70
1981	The Heavenly Light-E-5637	Open		15.00	30-60
1981	Cow with Bell Figurine-E-5638	Open		16.00	30-50
1981	Isn't He Wonderful (B)-E-5639	Suspd.		12.00	50-75
1981	Isn't He Wonderful (G)-E-5640	Suspd.		12.00	65-80
1981	They Followed the Star-E-5641	Suspd.		75.00	175-230
1981	Nativity Wall (2 pc. set)-E-5644	Open		60.00	120-145
1984	God Sends the Gift of His Love-E-6613	Suspd.		22.50	70-150
1982	God is Love, Dear Valentine -E-7153	Suspd.		16.00	22-40
1982	God is Love, Dear Valentine -E-7154	Suspd.		16.00	22-40
1982	Thanking Him for You-E-7155	Suspd.		16.00	60
1982	I Believe in Miracles-E-7156	Suspd.		17.00	90-125
1987	I Believe In Miracles-E-7156R	Retrd.	1992	22.50	65-100
1982	There is Joy in Serving Jesus-E-7157	Retrd.	1986	17.00	50-95
1982	Love Beareth All Things-E-7158	Open		25.00	38-70
1982	Lord Give Me Patience-E-7159	Suspd.		25.00	60-90
1982	The Perfect Grandpa-E-7160	Suspd.		25.00	60-75
1982	His Sheep Am I-E-7161	Suspd.		25.00	55-85
1982	Love is Sharing-E-7162	Suspd.		25.00	150-190
1982	God is Watching Over You -E-7163	Suspd.		27.50	90-120
1982	Bless This House-E-7164	Suspd.		45.00	180-240
1982	Let the Whole World Know -E-7165	Suspd.		45.00	75-120
1983	If God Be for Us, Who Can Be Against Us-E-9239	Suspd.		27.50	55-70
1983	Love is Patient-E-9251	Suspd.		35.00	85-120
1983	Forgiving is Forgetting-E-9252	Suspd.		37.50	75-100
1983	The End is in Sight-E-9253	Suspd.		25.00	75-100
1983	Praise the Lord Anyhow-E-9254	Retrd.	1994	35.00	75-90
1983	Bless You Two-E-9255	Open		21.00	40-50
1983	We are God's Workmanship -E-9258	Open		19.00	33-50
1983	We're In It Together-E-9259	Suspd.		24.00	50-70
1983	God's Promises are Sure-E-9260	Suspd.		30.00	55-75
1983	Seek Ye the Lord-E-9261	Suspd.		21.00	37-50
1983	Seek Ye the Lord-E-9262	Suspd.		21.00	50
1983	How Can Two Walk Together Except They Agree-E-9263	Suspd.		35.00	125-160
1963	Press On-E-9265	Open		40.00	55-100
1973	Animal Collection, Teddy Bear-E-9267A	Suspd.		6.50	21-30
1983	Animal Collection, Dog W/ Slippers-E-9267B	Suspd.		6.50	18-25
1983	Animal Collection, Bunny W/ Carrot-E-9267C	Suspd.		6.50	18-31
1983	Animal Collection, Kitty With Bow-E-9267D	Suspd.		6.50	18-22
1983	Animal Collection, Lamb With Bird-E-9267E	Suspd.		6.50	19-25
1983	Animal Collection, Pig W/ Patches-E-9267F	Suspd.		6.50	18-25
1983	Nobody's Perfect-E-9268	Retrd.	1990	21.00	65-90
1987	Let Love Reign-E-9273	Retrd.	1987	27.50	55-85
1983	Taste and See that the Lord is Good-E-9274	Retrd.	1986	22.50	50-85
1983	Jesus Loves Me-E-9278	Open		9.00	17-34
1983	Jesus Loves Me-E-9279	Open		9.00	17-32
1983	To Some Bunny Special-E-9282A	Suspd.		8.00	18-35
1983	You're Worth Your Weight In Gold-E-9282B	Suspd.		8.00	30
1983	Especially For Ewe-E-9282C	Suspd.		8.00	20-37
1983	Peace on Earth-E-9287	Suspd.		37.50	85-125
1983	Sending You a Rainbow-E-9288	Suspd.		22.50	55-95
1983	Trust in the Lord-E-9289	Suspd.		21.00	62-75
1985	Love Covers All-12009	Suspd.		27.50	48-65
1985	Part of Me Wants to be Good -12149	Suspd.		19.00	55-65
1987	This Is The Day Which The Lord Has Made-12157	Suspd.		20.00	52-75
1985	Get into the Habit of Prayer -12203	Suspd.		19.00	35-45
1985	Miniature Clown-12238A	Open		13.50	19-32
1985	Miniature Clown-12238B	Open		13.50	19-32
1985	Miniature Clown-12238C	Open		13.50	19-32
1985	Miniature Clown-12238D	Open		13.50	19-32
1985	It is Better to Give than to Receive-12297	Suspd.		19.00	175-275
1985	Love Never Fails-12300	Open		25.00	35-57
1985	God Bless Our Home-12319	Open		40.00	55-65
1986	You Can Fly-12335	Suspd.		25.00	55-80
1985	Jesus is Coming Soon-12343	Suspd.		22.50	40-70
1985	Halo, and Merry Christmas-12351	Suspd.		40.00	160-180
1985	May Your Christmas Be Delightful-15482	Suspd.		25.00	35-52
1985	Honk if You Love Jesus-15490	Open		13.00	20-35
1985	Baby's First Christmas-15539	Yr.Iss.		13.00	42-45
1985	Baby's First Christmas-15547	Yr.Iss.		13.00	45
1985	God Sent His Love-15881	Yr.Iss.		17.00	30-78
1986	To My Favorite Paw-100021	Suspd.		22.50	50-65
1987	To My Deer Friend-100048	Open		33.00	50-92
1986	Sending My Love-100056	Suspd.		22.50	40-65
1986	O Worship the Lord-100064	Open		24.00	38-49
1986	To My Forever Friend-100072	Open		33.00	44-80
1987	He's The Healer Of Broken Hearts-100080	Open		33.00	50-59
1987	Make Me A Blessing-100102	Retrd.	1990	35.00	75-110
1986	Lord I'm Coming Home-100110	Open		22.50	33-55
1986	Lord, Keep Me On My Toes-100129	Retrd.	1988	22.50	75-100
1986	The Joy of the Lord is My Strength-100137	Open		35.00	50-89
1986	God Bless the Day We Found You-100145	Suspd.		37.50	85-125
1995	God Bless the Day We Found You(Girl)-100145R	Open		60.00	60
1986	God Bless the Day We Found You-100153	Suspd.		37.50	45-85
1995	God Bless the Day We Found You(Boy)-100153R	Open		60.00	60
1986	Serving the Lord-100161	Suspd.		19.00	65-75
1986	I'm a Possibility-100188	Retrd.	1993	21.00	55-70
1987	The Spirit Is Willing But The Flesh Is Weak-100196	Retrd.	1991	19.00	55-85
1987	The Lord Giveth & the Lord Taketh Away-100226	Retrd.	1995	33.50	40-55
1986	Friends Never Drift Apart-100250	Open		35.00	55-75
1986	Help, Lord, I'm In a Spot-100269	Retrd.	1989	18.50	55-65
1986	He Cleansed My Soul-100277	Open		24.00	38-60
1986	Serving the Lord-100293	Suspd.		19.00	30-55
1987	Scent From Above-100528	Retrd.	1991	19.00	60-80
1986	Brotherly Love-100544	Suspd.		37.00	65-95
1987	No Tears Past The Gate-101826	Open		40.00	70-85
1987	Smile Along The Way-101842	Retrd.	1991	30.00	150-175
1987	Lord, Help Us Keep Our Act Together-101850	Retrd.	1992	35.00	125-155
1986	O Worship the Lord-102229	Open		24.00	38-42
1986	Shepherd of Love-102261	Open		10.00	16-24
1986	Three Mini Animals-102296	Suspd.		13.50	19-30
1986	Wishing You a Cozy Christmas -102342	Yr.Iss.		17.00	39-45
1986	Love Rescued Me-102393	Open		21.00	38-40
1986	Angel of Mercy-102482	Open		19.00	19-40
1986	Sharing our Christmas Together -102490	Suspd.		35.00	65-70
1987	We Are All Precious In His Sight -102903	Yr.Iss.		30.00	65-125
1986	God Bless America-102938	Yr.Iss.		30.00	70-80
1986	It's the Birthday of a King -102962	Suspd.		18.50	35-50
1987	I Would Be Sunk Without You -102970	Open		15.00	20-30
1987	My Love Will Never Let You Go -103497	Open		25.00	38-45
1986	I Believe in the Old Rugged Cross-103632	Open		25.00	35-47
1986	Come Let Us Adore Him -104000 (9 pc. set w/cassette)	Open		95.00	130
1987	With this Ring I...-104019	Open		40.00	65-65
1987	Love Is The Glue That Mends -104027	Suspd.		33.50	55-85
1987	Cheers To The Leader-104035	Open		22.50	30-39
1987	Happy Days Are Here Again-104396	Suspd.		25.00	57-70
1987	A Tub Full of Love-104817	Open		22.50	30-42
1987	Sitting Pretty-104825	Suspd.		22.50	43-60
1987	Have I Got News For You -105635	Suspd.		22.50	35-65
1988	Something's Missing When You're Not Around -105643	Suspd.		32.50	40-75
1987	To Tell The Tooth You're Special-105813	Suspd.		38.50	110-140
1988	Hallelujah Country-105821	Open		35.00	45-65
1987	We're Pulling For You-106151	Suspd.		40.00	60-75
1987	God Bless You Graduate-106194	Open		20.00	33-35
1987	Congratulations Princess-106208	Open		20.00	33-35
1087	Lord Help Me Make the Grade-106216	Suspd.		25.00	49-65
1988	Heaven Bless Your Togetherness-106755	Open		65.00	80-87
1988	Precious Memories-106763	Open		37.50	50-55
1988	Puppy Love Is From Above-106798	Retrd.	1995	45.00	55
1988	Happy Birthday Poppy-106836	Suspd.		27.50	39-49
1988	Sew In Love-106844	Open		45.00	55-80
1987	They Followed The Star-108243	Open		75.00	120
1987	The Greatest Gift Is A Friend-109231	Open		30.00	38-55
1988	Believe the Impossible-109487	Suspd.		35.00	65-110
1988	Happiness Divine-109584	Retrd.	1992	25.00	55-85
1987	Wishing You A Yummy Christmas-109754	Suspd.		35.00	50-70
1987	We Gather Together To Ask The Lord's Blessing-109762	Retrd.	1995	130.00	150-169
1988	Meowie Christmas-109800	Open		30.00	40-50
1987	Oh What Fun It Is To Ride-109819	Open		85.00	110-135
1988	Wishing You A Happy Easter-109886	Open		23.00	33-34
1988	Wishing You A Basket Full Of Blessings-109924	Open		23.00	33
1988	Sending You My Love-109967	Open		35.00	45-60
1988	Mommy, I Love You-109975	Open		22.50	30-34
1987	Love Is The Best Gift of All -110930	Yr.Iss.		22.50	45-39
1988	Faith Takes The Plunge-111155	Open		27.50	40-50
1988	Tis the Season-111163	Open		27.50	35-45
1987	O Come Let Us Adore Him (4 pc. 9" Nativity)-111333	Suspd.		200.00	225-275
1988	Mommy, I Love You-112143	Open		22.50	30-36
1987	A Tub Full of Love-112313	Open		22.50	30-36
1988	This Too Shall Pass-114014	Open		23.00	28-37
1988	Some Bunny's Sleeping-115274	Open		15.00	25-35
1988	Our First Christmas Together-115290	Suspd.		50.00	60-80
1988	Time to Wish You a Merry Christmas-115339	Yr.Iss.		24.00	35-50
1995	Love Blooms Eternal (dated cross series)-127019	Yr.Iss.		35.00	35
1995	Dreams Really Do Come True-128309	Open		37.50	38
1995	Another Year More Grey Hares-128686	Open		17.50	18
1995	Happy Hula Days-128694	Open		30.00	30
1995	I Give You My Love Forever True-129100	Open		70.00	70
1995	He Hath Made Everything Beautiful in His Time-129151	Open		50.00	50
1995	He Covers the Earth With His Beauty-142654	Yr.Iss.		30.00	30
1995	Come Let Us Adore Him-142735 (large nativity)	Open		50.00	50
1995	Come Let Us Adore Him-142743 (small nativity)	Open		35.00	35
1995	Making A Trail to Bethlehem-142751	Open		30.00	30
1995	I'll Give Him My Heart-150088	Open		40.00	40
1995	Soot Yourself To A Merry Christmas-150096	Open		35.00	35
1995	Making Spirits Bright-150118	Open		37.50	38
1996	Standing In The Presence Of The Lord (dated cross series)-163732	Open		37.50	38
1996	Take It To The Lord In Prayer-163767	Open		30.00	30
1996	The Sun Is Always Shining Somewhere-163775	Open		37.50	38
1996	Sewing Seeds of Kindness-163856	Open		37.50	38
1996	It May Be Greener, But It's Just As Hard to Cut-163899	Open		37.50	38
1996	Peace On Earth...Anyway-183342	Yr.Iss.		32.50	33
1996	Angels On Earth-Boy Making Snow Angel-183776	Open		40.00	40
1996	Snowbunny Loves You Like I Do-183792	Open		18.50	19
1996	Sing In Excelsis Deo Tree Topper-183830	Open		125.00	125
1996	Color Your World With Thanksgiving-183857	Open		50.00	50
1996	Shepard/Standing White Lamb/Sitting Black Lamb 3pc. Nativity set -183954	Open		40.00	40
1996	Making a Trail to Bethlehem-Mini Nativity-184004	Open		18.50	19
1996	All Sing His Praises-Large Nativity-184012	Open		32.50	33
1996	Three Kings-Mini Nativity set-213624	Open		55.00	55

*Quotes have been rounded up to nearest dollar

FIGURINES/COTTAGES

YEAR ISSUE		EDITION LIMIT	YEAR RETD.	ISSUE PRICE	*QUOTE U.S. $
1988	Rejoice O Earth-520268	Open		13.00	17-27
1988	Jesus the Savior Is Born-520357	Suspd.		25.00	33-55
1992	The Lord Turned My Life Around-520535	Open		35.00	35
1991	In The Spotlight Of His Grace-520543	Open		35.00	35
1990	Lord, Turn My Life Around-520551	Open		35.00	35-52
1992	You Deserve An Ovation-520578	Open		35.00	35
1989	My Heart Is Exposed With Love-520624	Open		45.00	55-60
1989	A Friend Is Someone Who Cares-520632	Retrd.	1995	30.00	35-55
1989	I'm So Glad You Fluttered Into My Life-520640	Retrd.	1991	40.00	350-500
1995	Wishing You A Happy Bear Hug-520659	Open		27.50	28
1989	Eggspecially For You-520667	Open		45.00	50-60
1989	Your Love Is So Uplifting-520675	Open		60.00	65-79
1989	Sending You Showers Of Blessings-520683	Retrd.	1992	32.50	70-90
1989	Just A LineTo Wish You A Happy Day-520721	Open		65.00	70-79
1989	Friendship Hits The Spot-520748	Open		55.00	60-68
1989	Jesus Is The Only Way-520756	Suspd.		40.00	57-70
1989	Puppy Love-520764	Open		12.50	17-25
1989	Many Moons In Same Canoe, Blessum You-520772	Retrd.	1990	50.00	240-300
1989	Wishing You Roads Of Happiness-520780	Open		60.00	75
1989	Someday My Love-520799	Retrd.	1992	40.00	75-100
1989	My Days Are Blue Without You-520802	Suspd.		65.00	95-145
1989	We Need A Good Friend Through The Ruff Times-520810	Suspd.		35.00	50-60
1989	You Are My Number One-520829	Open		25.00	33-42
1989	The Lord Is Your Light To Happiness-520837	Open		50.00	65
1989	Wishing You A Perfect Choice-520845	Open		55.00	60-67
1989	I Belong To The Lord-520853	Suspd.		25.00	35-50
1990	Heaven Bless You-520934	Open		35.00	30-150
1993	There Is No Greater Treasure Than To Have A Friend Like You -521000	Open		30.00	30
1989	Hello World-521175	Open		15.00	17
1990	That's What Friends Are For-521183	Open		45.00	45-49
1990	Hope You're Up And OnThe Trail Again-521205	Suspd.		35.00	35-45
1993	The Fruit of the Spirit is Love-521213	Yr.Iss.		30.00	30
1996	Enter His Court With Thanksgiving-521221	Open		35.00	35
1991	Take Heed When You Stand-521272	Suspd.		55.00	55-70
1990	Happy Trip-521280	Suspd.		35.00	40-70
1991	Hug One Another-521299	Retrd.	1995	45.00	55
1990	Yield Not To Temptation-521310	Suspd.		27.50	30-50
1990	Faith Is A Victory-521396	Retrd.	1993	25.00	100-185
1990	I'll Never Stop Loving You-521418	Open		37.50	38-53
1991	To A Very Special Mom & Dad-521434	Suspd.		35.00	35-45
1990	Lord, Help Me Stick To My Job-521450	Open		30.00	30-48
1989	Tell It To Jesus-521477	Open		35.00	38-58
1991	There's A Light At The End Of The Tunnel-521485	Open		55.00	55
1991	A Special Delivery-521493	Open		30.00	30
1991	Thumb-body Loves You-521698	Open		55.00	50-65
1996	My Love Blooms For You-521728	Open		50.00	50
1990	Sweep All Your Worries Away-521779	Open		40.00	40-130
1990	Good Friends Are Forever-521817	Open		50.00	55-62
1990	Love Is From Above-521841	Open		45.00	45-59
1989	The Greatest of These Is Love-521868	Suspd.		27.50	45-65
1990	Easter's On Its Way-521892	Open		60.00	65-75
1994	Hoppy Easter Friend-521906	Open		40.00	40-43
1991	Perfect Harmony-521914	Open		55.00	55
1993	Safe In The Arms Of Jesus-521922	Open		30.00	30
1989	Wishing You A Cozy Season-521949	Suspd.		42.50	45-62
1990	High Hopes-521957	Suspd.		30.00	35-50
1991	To A Special Mum-521965	Open		30.00	30-33
1996	Marching To The Beat of Freedom's Drum-521981	Open		35.00	35
1993	To The Apple Of God's Eye-522015	Yr.Iss.		32.50	33
1979	May Your Life Be Blessed With Touchdowns-522023	Open		45.00	50-62
1989	Thank You Lord For Everything-522031	Suspd.		55.00	65-85
1994	Now I Lay Me Down To Sleep-522058	Open		30.00	33
1991	May Your World Be Trimmed With Joy-522082	Open		55.00	55-62
1990	There Shall Be Showers Of Blessings-522090	Open		60.00	70
1992	It's No Yolk When I Say I Love You-522104	Suspd.		60.00	60-75
1989	Don't Let the Holidays Get You Down-522112	Retrd.	1993	42.50	95-125
1989	Wishing You A Very Successful Season-522120	Open		60.00	65-70
1989	Bon Voyage!-522201	Open		75.00	80-105
1989	He Is The Star Of The Morning-522252	Suspd.		55.00	60-75
1989	To Be With You Is Uplifting-522260	Retrd.	1994	20.00	35-50
1991	A Reflection Of His Love-522279	Open		50.00	50
1990	Thinking Of You Is What I Really Like To Do-522287	Open		30.00	30-42
1989	Merry Christmas Deer-522317	Open		50.00	55-70
1996	Sweeter As The Years Go By-522333	Open		60.00	60
1995	Just A Line To Say You're Special-522864	Open		50.00	50
1989	Isn't He Precious-522988	Suspd.		15.00	25-35
1990	Some Bunny's Sleeping-522996	Suspd.		12.00	12-28
1989	Jesus Is The Sweetest Name I Know-523097	Suspd.		22.50	25-36
1991	Joy On Arrival-523178	Open		50.00	50-60
1990	The Good Lord Always Delivers-523453	Open		27.50	28-35
1990	This Day Has Been Made In Heaven-523496	Open		30.00	33-45
1990	God Is Love Dear Valentine-523518	Open		27.50	28-45
1991	I Will Cherish The Old Rugged Cross-523534	Yr.Iss.		27.50	28-40
1992	You Are The Type I Love-523542	Open		40.00	40
1993	The Lord Will Provide-523593	Yr.Iss.		40.00	55
1991	Good News Is So Uplifting-523615	Open		60.00	65
1992	I'm So Glad That God Has Blessed Me With A Friend Like You -523623	Retrd.	1995	50.00	50
1994	I Will Always Be Thinking Of You-523631	Open		45.00	45
1990	Time Heals-523739	Open		37.50	38
1990	Blessings From Above-523747	Retrd.	1994	45.00	50-75
1994	Just Poppin' In To Say Halo-523755	Open		45.00	45
1991	I Can't Spell Success Without You-523763	Suspd.		40.00	40-60
1990	Once Upon A Holy Night-523836	Yr.Iss.		25.00	45
1996	Love Never Leaves A Mother's Arms-523941	Open		40.00	40
1992	My Warmest Thoughts Are You-524085	Open		55.00	60
1991	Good Friends Are For Always-524123	Open		27.50	33
1994	Lord Teach Us to Pray-524158	Yr.Iss.		35.00	35
1991	May Your Christmas Be Merry-524166	Yr.Iss.		27.50	35
1995	Walk In The Sonshine-524212	Open		35.00	35
1991	He Loves Me-524263	Yr.Iss.		35.00	35-65
1992	Friendship Grows When You Plant A Seed-524271	Retrd.	1994	40.00	90-125
1993	May Your Every Wish Come True-524298	Open		50.00	50-60
1991	May Your Birthday Be A Blessing-524301	Open		30.00	33-48
1992	What The World Needs Now-524352	Open		50.00	50
1991	May Only Good Things Come Your Way-524425	Open		30.00	38
1993	Sealed With A Kiss-524441	Open		50.00	55
1993	A Special Chime For Jesus-524468	Yr.Iss.		32.50	33
1994	God Cared Enough To Send His Best-524476	Open		50.00	50
1990	Happy Birthday Dear Jesus-524875	Suspd.		13.50	14-27
1992	It's So Uplifting To Have A Friend Like You-524905	Open		40.00	45
1990	We're Going To Miss You-524913	Open		50.00	50-65
1991	Angels We Have Heard On High-524921	Open		60.00	60
1992	Tubby's First Christmas-525278	Open		10.00	10
1991	It's A Perfect Boy-525286	Open		16.50	17
1993	May Your Future Be Blessed-525316	Open		35.00	38
1992	Ring Those Christmas Bells-525898	Open		95.00	100
1992	Going Home-525979	Open		60.00	60-70
1996	A Prince Of A Guy-526038	Open		35.00	35
1996	Pretty As A Princess-526053	Open		35.00	35
1992	I Would Be Lost Without You -526142	Open		27.50	28
1994	Friends 'Til The Very End -526150	Open		40.00	40
1992	You Are My Happiness-526185	Yr.Iss.		37.50	45-75
1994	You Suit Me to a Tee-526193	Open		35.00	35
1994	Sharing Sweet Moments Together-526487	Open		45.00	45
1991	How Could I Ever Forget You-526924	Open		15.00	17
1996	The Lord Is With You-526835	Open		27.50	28
1991	We Have Come From Afar-526959	Suspd.		17.50	18
1993	Bless-Um You-527335	Open		35.00	35
1992	You Are My Favorite Star-527378	Open		55.00	55
1992	Bring The Little Ones To Jesus-527556	Open		90.00	90-110
1992	God Bless The U.S.A.-527564	Yr.Iss.		32.50	40-50
1993	Tied Up For The Holidays-527580	Yr.Iss.		40.00	40
1993	Bringing You A Merry Christmas-527599	Retrd.	1995	45.00	45
1992	Wishing You A Ho Ho Ho-527629	Open		40.00	40
1992	But The Greatest of These Is Love-527688	Yr.Iss.		27.50	35
1992	Wishing You A Comfy Christmas-527750	Open		30.00	30
1993	I Only Have Arms For You-527769	Open		15.00	16
1992	This Land Is Our Land-527777	Yr.Iss.		35.00	45
1994	Nativity Cart-528072	Open		16.00	16
1994	Have I Got News For You-528137	Open		16.00	17
1994	To a Very Special Sister-528633	Open		60.00	60
1993	America You're Beautiful-528862	Yr.Iss.		35.00	35
1996	My True Love Gave To Me-529723	Open		40.00	40
1993	Ring Out The Good News-529966	Yr.Iss.		27.50	30
1993	Wishing You the Sweetest Christmas-530166	Yr.Iss.		27.50	40
1994	You're As Pretty As A Christmas Tree-530425	Yr.Iss.		27.50	28
1994	Serenity Prayer Girl-530697	Open		35.00	35
1994	Serenity Prayer Boy-530700	Open		35.00	35
1995	We Have Come From Afar-530913	Open		12.00	12
1995	I Only Have Ice For You-530956	Open		27.50	28
1996	I Haven't Seen Much Of You Lately-531057	Open		13.50	14
1995	What The World Needs Is Love-531065	Open		45.00	45
1994	Money Isn't The Only Green Thing Worth Saving-531073	Open		50.00	50
1996	What A Difference You've Made In My Life-531138	Open		50.00	50
1995	Vaya Con Dios (To Go With God)-531146	Open		32.50	33-55
1995	Bless Your Sole-531162	Open		25.00	25
1996	You Deserve a Halo—Thank You-531693	Open		55.00	55
1994	The Lord is Counting on You-531707	Open		32.50	33
1994	Dropping In For The Holidays-531952	Open		40.00	40
1995	Hallelujah For The Cross-532002	Open		35.00	35
1995	Sending You Oceans Of Love-532010	Open		35.00	35
1995	I Can't Bear To Let You Go-532037	Open		50.00	50
1995	Lord Help Me To Stay On Course-532096	Open		35.00	35
1994	The Lord Bless You and Keep You-532118	Open		40.00	45
1994	The Lord Bless You and Keep You-532126	Open		30.00	33
1994	The Lord Bless You and Keep You-532134	Open		30.00	33
1994	Luke 2:10-11-532916	Open		35.00	35
1994	Nothing Can Dampen The Spirit of Caring-603864	Open		35.00	35
1995	A Poppy For You-604208	Open		35.00	35

Precious Moments Anniversary Figurines - S. Butcher

YEAR ISSUE		EDITION LIMIT	YEAR RETD.	ISSUE PRICE	*QUOTE U.S. $
1984	God Blessed Our Years Together With So Much Love And Happiness-E-2853	Open		35.00	50-60
1984	God Blessed Our Year Together With So Much Love And Happiness (1st)-E-2854	Open		35.00	50-60
1984	God Blessed Our Years Together With So Much Love And Happiness (5th)-E-2855	Open		35.00	50-55
1984	God Blessed Our Years Together With So Much Love And Happiness (10th)-E-2856	Open		35.00	50-55
1984	God Blessed Our Years Together With So Much Love And Happiness (25th)-E-2857	Open		35.00	50-65
1984	God Blessed Our Years Together With So Much Love And Happiness (40th)-E-2859	Open		35.00	50-65
1984	God Blessed Our Years Together With So Much Love And Happiness (50th)-E-2860	Open		35.00	50-65
1994	I Still Do-530999	Open		30.00	30
1994	I Still Do-531006	Open		30.00	30

Precious Moments Baby's First - S. Butcher

YEAR ISSUE		EDITION LIMIT	YEAR RETD.	ISSUE PRICE	*QUOTE U.S. $
1984	Baby's First Step-E-2840	Suspd.		35.00	70-95
1984	Baby's First Picture-E-2841	Retrd.	1986	45.00	150-225
1985	Baby's First Haircut-12211	Suspd.		32.50	150-200
1986	Baby's First Trip-16012	Suspd.		32.50	150-275
1989	Baby's First Pet-520705	Suspd.		45.00	50-95
1990	Baby's First Meal-524077	Open		35.00	35-45
1990	Baby's First Word-527238	Open		24.00	24-28
1993	Baby's First Birthday-524069	Open		25.00	25

Precious Moments Birthday Club Figurines - S. Butcher

YEAR ISSUE		EDITION LIMIT	YEAR RETD.	ISSUE PRICE	*QUOTE U.S. $
1986	Fishing For Friends-BC-861	Yr.Iss.		10.00	145-165
1987	Hi Sugar-BC-871	Yr.Iss.		11.00	100-110
1988	Somebunny Cares-BC-881	Yr.Iss.		13.50	50-75
1989	Can't Bee Hive Myself Without You-BC-891	Yr.Iss.		13.50	50-70
1990	Collecting Makes Good Scents-BC-901	Yr.Iss.		15.00	40-60
1990	I'm Nuts Over My Collection-BC-902	Yr.Iss.		15.00	40
1991	Love Pacifies-BC-911	Yr.Iss.		15.00	35-45
1991	True Blue Friends-BC-912	Yr.Iss.		15.00	29-40
1992	Every Man's House Is His Castle-BC-921	Yr.Iss.		16.50	35-45
1993	I Got You Under My Skin-BC-922	Yr.Iss.		16.00	35

*Quotes have been rounded up to nearest dollar

YEAR ISSUE		EDITION LIMIT	YEAR RETD.	ISSUE PRICE	*QUOTE U.S.$
1994	Put a Little Punch In Your Birthday-BC-931	Yr.Iss.		15.00	25
1994	Owl Always Be Your Friend-BC-932	Yr.Iss.		16.00	25
1994	God Bless Our Home-BC-941	Yr.Iss.		16.00	25
1995	Yer A Pel-I-Can Count On-BC-942	Yr.Iss.		16.00	20
1996	There's A Spot In My Heart For You-BC-961	Yr.Iss.		15.00	15

Precious Moments Birthday Club Inscribed Charter Member Renewal Gift - S. Butcher

1987	A Smile's the Cymbal of Joy-B-0102	Yr.Iss.		Unkn.	55-85

Precious Moments Birthday Club Inscribed Charter Membership Renewal Gift - S. Butcher

1988	The Sweetest Club Around-B-0103	Yr.Iss.		Unkn.	50-75
1989	Have A Beary Special Birthday-B-0104	Yr.Iss.		Unkn.	35-65
1990	Our Club Is A Tough Act To Follow-B-0105	Yr.Iss.		Unkn.	40-50
1991	Jest To Let You Know You're Tops-B-0106	Yr.Iss.		Unkn.	45-60
1992	All Aboard For Birthday Club Fun-B-0107	Yr.Iss.		Unkn.	40-55
1994	Happines is Belonging-B-0108	Yr.Iss.		Unkn.	35
1994	Can't Get Enough of Our Club-B-0109	Yr.Iss.		Unkn.	30
1995	Hoppy Birthday-B-0110	Yr.Iss.		Unkn.	Unkn.

Precious Moments Birthday Club Welcome Gift - S. Butcher

1986	Our Club Can't Be Beat-B-0001	Yr.Iss.		Unkn.	85
1987	A Smile's The Cymbal of Joy-B-0002	Yr.Iss.		Unkn.	50-65
1988	The Sweetest Club Around-B-0003	Yr.Iss.		Unkn.	45
1989	Have A Beary Special Birthday-B-0004	Yr.Iss.		Unkn.	30-45
1990	Our Club Is A Tough Act To Follow-B-0005	Yr.Iss.		Unkn.	35
1991	Jest To Let You Know You're Tops-B-0006	Yr.Iss.		Unkn.	40-55
1992	All Aboard For Birthday Club Fun-B-0007	Yr.Iss.		Unkn.	30-40
1994	Happiness Is Belonging-B-0008	Yr.Iss.		Unkn.	30
1994	Can't Get Enough of Our Club-B-0009	Yr.Iss.		Unkn.	Unkn.
1995	Hoppy Birthday-B-0010	Yr.Iss.		Unkn.	Unkn.

Precious Moments Birthday Series - S. Butcher

1988	Friends To The End-104418	Suspd.		15.00	35
1987	Showers Of Blessings-105945	Retrd.	1993	16.00	60-75
1988	Brighten Someone's Day-105953	Suspd.		12.50	30-35
1990	To My Favorite Fan-521043	Suspd.		16.00	30-55
1989	Hello World!-521175	Open		13.50	15-30
1993	Hope You're Over The Hump-521671	Open		16.00	16
1990	Not A Creature Was Stirring-524484	Suspd.		17.00	30-40
1991	Can't Be Without You-524492	Open		16.00	17-29
1991	How Can I Ever Forget You-526924	Open		15.00	15
1992	Let's Be Friends-527270	Open		15.00	15-20
1992	Happy Birdie-527343	Open		8.00	17
1993	Happy Birthday Jesus-530492	Open		20.00	20
1994	Oinky Birthday-524506	Open		13.50	14
1995	Wishing You A Happy Bear Hug-520659	Open		27.50	28

Precious Moments Birthday Train Figurines - S. Butcher

1988	Isn't Eight Just Great-109460	Open		18.50	23
1988	Wishing You Grr-eatness-109479	Open		18.50	23-38
1986	May Your Birthday Be Warm-15938	Open		10.00	16-35
1986	Happy Birthday Little Lamb-15946	Open		10.00	15-39
1986	Heaven Bless Your Special Day-15954	Open		11.00	18-23
1986	God Bless You On Your Birthday-15962	Open		11.00	18-37
1986	May Your Birthday Be Gigantic -15970	Open		12.50	20-38
1986	This Day Is Something To Roar About-15989	Open		13.50	23-40
1986	Keep Looking Up-15997	Open		13.50	23-35
1986	Bless The Days Of Our Youth-16004	Open		15.00	23-38
1992	May Your Birthday Be Mammoth-521825	Open		25.00	25-40
1992	Being Nine Is Just Divine-521833	Open		25.00	25-40

Precious Moments Bless Those Who Serve Their Country - S. Butcher

1991	Bless Those Who Serve Their Country (Navy) 526568	Suspd.		32.50	75-125
1991	Bless Those Who Serve Their Country (Army) 526576	Suspd.		32.50	45-55
1991	Bless Those Who Serve Their Country (Air Force) 526584	Suspd.		32.50	45
1991	Bless Those Who Serve Their Country (Girl Soldier) 527289	Suspd.		32.50	45
1991	Bless Those Who Serve Their Country (Soldier) 527297	Suspd.		32.50	40-65
1991	Bless Those Who Serve Their Country (Marine) 527521	Suspd.		32.50	45

YEAR ISSUE		EDITION LIMIT	YEAR RETD.	ISSUE PRICE	*QUOTE U.S.$
1995	You Will Always Be Our Hero 136271	Yr.Iss.		40.00	40

Precious Moments Bridal Party - S. Butcher

1984	Bridesmaid-E-2831	Open		13.50	22-30
1985	Ringbearer-E-2833	Open		11.00	17-30
1985	Flower Girl-E-2835	Open		11.00	17-25
1984	Groomsman-E-2836	Open		13.50	22-30
1986	Groom-E-2837	Open		13.50	20-40
1985	Junior Bridesmaid-E-2845	Open		12.50	20-30
1987	Bride-E-2846	Open		18.00	25-30
1987	God Bless Our Family (Parents of the Groom)-100498	Open		35.00	50-55
1987	God Bless Our Family (Parents of the Bride)-100501	Open		35.00	50-60
1987	Wedding Arch-102369	Suspd.		22.50	40-55

Precious Moments Calendar Girl - S. Butcher

1988	January-109983	Open		37.50	40-67
1988	February-109991	Open		27.50	38-67
1988	March-110019	Open		27.50	38-50
1988	April-110027	Open		30.00	38-100
1988	May -110035	Open		25.00	30-225
1988	June-110043	Open		40.00	50-112
1988	July-110051	Open		35.00	45-58
1988	August-110078	Open		40.00	45-58
1988	September-110086	Open		27.50	38-40
1988	October-110094	Open		35.00	45-59
1988	November-110108	Open		32.50	38-50
1988	December-110116	Open		27.50	35-75

Precious Moments Clown - S. Butcher

XX	I Get a Bang Out of You-12262	Open		30.00	45-55
1986	Lord Keep Me On the Ball-12270	Open		30.00	45-55
1985	Waddle I Do Without You-12459	Retrd.	1989	30.00	75-110
1986	The Lord Will Carry You Through-12467	Retrd.	1988	30.00	78-110

Precious Moments Commemorative 500th Columbus Anniversary - S. Butcher

1992	This Land Is Our Land-527386	Yr.Iss.		350.00	400-450

Precious Moments Commemorative Easter Seal - S. Butcher

1988	Jesus Loves Me-9" Fig.-104531	1,000		N/A	1800-2000
1987	He Walks With Me-107999	Yr.Iss.		25.00	35-75
1988	Blessed Are They That Overcome-115479	Yr.Iss.		27.50	40-75
1989	Make A Joyful Noise-9" Fig.-520322	1,500		N/A	900-950
1989	His Love Will Shine On You-522376	Yr.Iss.		30.00	50-65
1990	You Have Touched So Many Hearts-9" fig.-523283	2,000		N/A	675-775
1991	We Are God's Workmanship-9" fig.-523879	2,000		N/A	650-725
1990	Always In His Care-524522	Yr.Iss.		30.00	40-55
1992	You Are Such A Purr-fect Friend 9" fig.-526010	2,000		N/A	600-700
1991	Sharing A Gift Of Love-527114	Yr.Iss.		30.00	35-65
1992	A Universal Love-527173	Yr.Iss.		32.50	75
1993	Gather Your Dreams-9" fig.-529680	2,000		N/A	N/A
1993	You're My Number One Friend-530026	Yr.Iss.		30.00	40
1994	It's No Secret What God Can Do-531111	Yr.Iss.		30.00	45
1994	You Are The Rose of His Creation-9" fig.-531243	2,000		N/A	N/A
1995	Take Time To Smell the Flowers-524387	Yr.Iss.		30.00	30
1995	He's Got The Whole World In His Hands-9" fig.-526886	Yr.Iss.		N/A	N/A
1996	He Loves Me 9" fig.-152277	2,000		N/A	N/A
1996	You Can Always Count on Me-526827	Yr.Iss.		30.00	30

Precious Moments Events Figurines - S. Butcher

1988	You Are My Main Event-115231	Yr.Iss.		30.00	45-55
1989	Sharing Begins In The Heart-520861	Yr.Iss.		25.00	60-75
1990	I'm A Precious Moments Fan-523526	Yr.Iss.		25.00	40-50
1990	Good Friends Are Forever-525049	Yr.Iss.		25.00	N/A
1991	You Can Always Bring A Friend-527122	Yr.Iss.		27.50	45-55
1992	An Event Worth Wading For-527319	Yr.Iss.		32.50	30-45
1993	An Event For All Seasons-530158	Yr.Iss.		30.00	50
1994	Memories Are Made of This-529982	Yr.Iss.		30.00	40
1995	Follow Your Heart-528080	Yr.Iss.		30.00	30

Precious Moments Family Christmas Scene - S. Butcher

1985	May You Have the Sweetest Christmas-15776	Suspd.		17.00	40-50
1985	The Story of God's Love-15784	Suspd.		22.50	60-75
1985	Tell Me a Story-15792	Suspd.		10.00	25-40
1985	God Gave His Best-15806	Suspd.		13.00	30-45
1985	Silent Night-15814	Suspd.		37.50	75-120
1986	Sharing Our Christmas Together-102490	Suspd.		40.00	70-80
1989	Have A Beary Merry Christmas-522856	Suspd.		15.00	30-40
1990	Christmas Fireplace-524883	Suspd.		37.50	60-85

YEAR ISSUE		EDITION LIMIT	YEAR RETD.	ISSUE PRICE	*QUOTE U.S.$

Precious Moments Four Seasons - S. Butcher

1985	The Voice of Spring-12068	Yr.Iss.		30.00	200-285
1985	Summer's Joy-12076	Yr.Iss.		30.00	100
1986	Autumn's Praise-12084	Yr.Iss.		30.00	90
1986	Winter's Song-12092	Yr.Iss.		30.00	100-125
1986	Set	Yr.Iss.		120.00	550

Precious Moments Growing In Grace - S. Butcher

1995	Infant Angel With Newspaper-136204	Open		22.50	23
1995	Age 1 Baby With Cake-136190	Open		25.00	25
1995	Age 2 Girl With Blocks-136212	Open		25.00	25
1995	Age 3 Girl With Flowers-136220	Open		25.00	25
1995	Age 4 Girl With Doll-136239	Open		27.50	28
1995	Age 5 Girl With Lunch Box-136247	Open		27.50	28
1995	Age 6 Girl On Bicycle-136255	Open		30.00	30
1996	Age 7 Girl Dressed As Nurse-163740	Open		32.50	33
1996	Age 8 Girl Shooting Marbles-163759	Open		32.50	33
1995	Age 16 Sweet Sixteen Girl Holding Sixteen Roses-136263	Open		45.00	45
1996	Age 9 Girl With Charm Bracelet-183865	Open		30.00	30
1996	Age 10 Girl Bowling-183783	Open		37.50	38

Precious Moments Musical Figurines - S. Butcher

1983	Sharing Our Season Together-E-0519	Retrd.	1986	70.00	117-145
1983	Wee Three Kings-E-0520	Suspd.		60.00	105-130
1983	Let Heaven And Nature Sing-E-2346	Suspd.		55.00	115-135
1982	O Come All Ye Faithful-E-2352	Suspd.		50.00	140-200
1982	I'll Play My Drum For Him-E-2355	Suspd.		45.00	175-225
1979	Christmas Is A Time To Share-E-2806	Retrd.	1984	35.00	140-170
1979	Crown Him Lord Of All-E-2807	Suspd.		35.00	93-110
1979	Unto Us A Child Is Born-E-2808	Suspd.		35.00	95-125
1980	Jesus Is Born-E-2809	Suspd.		35.00	105-135
1980	Come Let Us Adore Him-E-2810	Suspd.		45.00	108-125
1980	Peace On Earth-E-4726	Suspd.		45.00	122-132
1980	The Hand That Rocks The Future-E-5204	Open		30.00	55-85
1980	My Guardian Angel-E-5205	Suspd.		22.50	70-100
1981	My Guardian Angel-E-5206	Suspd.		22.50	80-95
1984	Wishing You A Merry Christmas-E-5394	Suspd.		55.00	80-120
1980	Silent Knight-E-5642	Suspd.		45.00	225-300
1981	Rejoice O Earth-E-5645	Retrd.	1988	35.00	80-125
1981	The Lord Bless You And Keep You-E-7180	Open		55.00	80-100
1981	Mother Sew Dear-E-7182	Open		35.00	55-95
1981	The Purr-fect Grandma-E-7184	Suspd.		35.00	70-100
1981	Love Is Sharing-E-7185	Retrd.	1985	40.00	152-189
1981	Let the Whole World Know-E-7186	Suspd.		60.00	125-190
1985	Lord Keep My Life In Tune (G) (2/set)-12165	Suspd.		50.00	120-140
1984	We Saw A Star-12408	Suspd.		50.00	65-100
1987	Lord Keep My Life In Tune (B) (2/set)-12580	Suspd.		50.00	200-300
1985	God Sent You Just In Time-15504	Retrd.	1989	60.00	90-110
1993	Silent Night-15814	Open		55.00	55-89
1985	Heaven Bless You-100285	Suspd.		45.00	70-78
1986	Our 1st Christmas Together-101702	Retrd.	1992	50.00	97-125
1993	Let's Keep In Touch-102520	Open		85.00	85-115
1993	Peace On Earth-109746	Suspd.		120.00	130
1987	I'm Sending You A White Christmas-112402	Retrd.	1993	55.00	110-135
1987	You Have Touched So Many Hearts-112577	Open		50.00	50-60
1991	Lord Keep My Life In Balance-520691	Suspd.		60.00	68-80
1993	The Light Of The World Is Jesus-521507	Open		65.00	65-87
1992	Do Not Open Till Christmas-522244	Suspd.		75.00	90-130
1992	This Day Has Been Made In Heaven-523682	Open		60.00	60
1993	Wishing You Were Here-526916	Open		100.00	100

Precious Moments Rejoice in the Lord - S. Butcher

1987	Lord Keep My Life In Tune-12165	Suspd.		37.50	85-110
1985	There's a Song in My Heart-12173	Suspd.		11.00	30-48
1985	Happiness is the Lord-12378	Suspd.		15.00	30-40
1985	Lord Give Me a Song-12386	Suspd.		15.00	35-45
1985	He is My Song-12394	Suspd.		17.50	35-45

Precious Moments Sammy's Circus - S. Butcher

1994	Markie-528099	Open		18.50	19
1994	Dusty-529176	Open		22.50	23
1994	Katie-529184	Open		17.00	17
1994	Tippy-529192	Open		12.00	12
1994	Collin-529214	Open		20.00	20
1994	Sammy-529222	Yr.Iss.		20.00	45
1994	Circus Ten-528196 (Nite-Lite)	Open		90.00	90
1994	Jordan-529168	Open		20.00	20
1996	Jennifer-163708	Open		20.00	20

Precious Moments Spring Catalog - S. Butcher

1993	Happiness Is At Our Fingertips-529931	Yr.Iss.	1993	35.00	45-85

88

Collectors' Information Bureau

*Quotes have been rounded up to nearest dollar

YEAR ISSUE		EDITION LIMIT	YEAR RETD.	ISSUE PRICE	*QUOTE U.S.$
1994	So Glad I Picked You As A Friend-524379	Yr.Iss.	1994	40.00	40
1995	Sending My Love Your Way-528609	Yr.Iss.		40.00	40
1996	Have I Toad You Lately That I Love You-521329	Yr.Iss.		30.00	30

Precious Moments Sugartown - S. Butcher

YEAR ISSUE		EDITION LIMIT	YEAR RETD.	ISSUE PRICE	*QUOTE U.S.$
1992	Chapel-529621	Retrd.	1994	85.00	75-175
1992	Christmas Tree-528684	Retrd.	1994	15.00	30
1992	Grandfather-529516	Retrd.	1994	15.00	20-30
1992	Nativity-529508	Retrd.	1994	20.00	35-40
1992	Philip-529494	Retrd.	1994	17.00	35
1992	Aunt Ruth & Aunt Dorothy-529486	Retrd.	1994	20.00	35
1992	Sam Butcher-529567 (1st sign)	Yr.Iss.		22.50	85-150
1993	7 pc. Sam's House Collector's Set-531774	Open		189.00	189
1993	Sam's House Night Light-529605	Open		80.00	85
1993	Fence-529796	Open		10.00	10
1993	Sammy-528668	Open		17.00	17
1993	Katy Lynne-529524	Open		20.00	20
1993	Sam Butcher-529842 (2nd sign)	Yr.Iss.		22.50	45-60
1993	Dusty-529435	Open		17.00	17
1993	Sam's Car-529443	Open		22.50	23
1993	Sugar Town Chapel-530484	Yr.Iss.		17.50	18
1994	Dr. Sam Sugar-530850	Open		17.00	17
1994	Doctor's Office Night Light-529869	Open		80.00	85
1994	Sam's House-530468	Yr.Iss.		17.50	18
1994	Jan-529826	Open		17.00	17
1994	Sugar & Her Dog House-533165	Open		20.00	20
1994	Stork With Baby Sam-529788	Yr.Iss.		22.50	23
1994	Free Christmas Puppies-528064	Open		18.50	19
1994	7 pc. Doctor's Office Collectors Set-529281	Yr.Iss.		189.00	190-225
1994	Leon & Evelyn Mae-529818	Open		20.00	20
1994	Village Town Hall Clock-532908	Open		80.00	85
1995	Sam the Conductor -150169	Yr.Iss.		20.00	20
1995	Train Station Night Light -150150	Open		50.00	50
1995	Railroad Crossing Sign -150177	Open		12.00	12
1995	Tammy and Debbie -531812	Open		22.50	23
1995	Donny -531871	Open		22.50	23
1995	Luggage Cart With Kitten And Tag -150185	Open		13.00	13
1995	6 pc. Train Station Collector Set-750193	Yr.Iss.		190.00	190
1995	Dr. Sugar's Office-530441	Yr.Iss.		17.50	18
1996	Sugar Town Skating Sign-184020	Yr.Iss.		15.00	15
1996	Skating Pond-184047	Open		40.00	40
1996	Mazie-184055	Open		18.50	19
1996	Cocoa-184063	Open		7.50	8
1996	Leroy-184071	Open		18.50	19
1996	Hank and Sharon-184098	Open		25.00	25
1996	Lighted Warming Hut-192341	Yr.Iss.		60.00	60

Precious Moments Sugartown Enhancements - S. Butcher

YEAR ISSUE		EDITION LIMIT	YEAR RETD.	ISSUE PRICE	*QUOTE U.S.$
1994	Lamp Post-529559	Open		8.00	8
1994	Mailbox-531847	Open		5.00	5
1994	Single Tree-533173	Open		10.00	10
1994	Cobble Stone Bridge-533203	Open		17.00	17
1994	Straight Sidewalk-533157	Open		10.00	10
1994	Double Tree-533181	Open		10.00	10
1994	Curved Sidewalk-533149	Open		10.00	10
1995	Street Sign-532185	Open		5.00	5
1995	Dog And Kitten On Park Bench-529540	Open		13.00	13
1995	Bus Stop-150207	Open		8.50	9
1995	Bird Bath-150223	Open		8.50	9
1995	Fire Hydrant-150215	Open		5.00	5
1995	Sugartown Enhancement Pack, set/5-152269	Open		45.00	45
1996	Flag Pole w/Kitten-184136	Open		15.00	15
1996	Tree Night Light-184039	Open		45.00	45
1996	Wooden Barrel Hot Cocoa Stand-184144	Open		15.00	15
1996	Bonfire with Bunnies-184152	Open		10.00	10

Precious Moments To Have And To Hold - S. Butcher

YEAR ISSUE		EDITION LIMIT	YEAR RETD.	ISSUE PRICE	*QUOTE U.S.$
1996	Love Vows To Always Bloom-1st Anniversary Couple With Flowers-129097	Open		70.00	70
996	A Year Of Blessings-1st Anniversary Couple With Cake-163783	Open		70.00	70
996	Each Hour Is Precious With You-5th Anniversary Couple With Clock-163791	Open		70.00	70
996	Ten Years Heart To Heart-10th Anniversary Couple With Pillow-163805	Open		70.00	70
996	A Silver Anniversary To Share-25th Anniversary Couple With Silver Platter-163813	Open		70.00	70
996	Forty Years Of Precious Moments-40th Anniversary Couple With Photo Album-163281	Open		70.00	70
996	Fifty Years As Precious As Gold-50th Anniversary Couple With Gift Box-163848	Open		70.00	70

Precious Moments Two By Two - S. Butcher

YEAR ISSUE		EDITION LIMIT	YEAR RETD.	ISSUE PRICE	*QUOTE U.S.$
993	Noah, Noah's Wife, & Noah's Ark (lighted)-530042	Open		125.00	125-195
993	Sheep (mini double fig.) -530077	Open		10.00	10
1993	Pigs (mini double fig.) -530085	Open		12.00	12
1993	Giraffes (mini double fig.) -530115	Open		16.00	16
1993	Bunnies (mini double fig.) -530123	Open		9.00	9
1993	Elephants (mini double fig.) -530131	Open		18.00	18
1993	Eight Piece Collector's Set -530948	Open		190.00	190
1994	Llamas-531375	Open		15.00	15
1995	Congratulations You Earned Your Stripes-127809	Open		15.00	15
1996	I'd Goat Anywhere With You-163694	Open		10.00	10

Precious Moments You Are Always There For Me - S. Butcher

YEAR ISSUE		EDITION LIMIT	YEAR RETD.	ISSUE PRICE	*QUOTE U.S.$
1996	Mother Kissing Daughter's Owie-163600	Open		50.00	50
1996	Father Helping Son Bat-163627	Open		50.00	50
1996	Sister Consoling Sister-163635	Open		50.00	50

Fenton Art Glass Company

Collectors Club - Fenton

YEAR ISSUE		EDITION LIMIT	YEAR RETD.	ISSUE PRICE	*QUOTE U.S.$
1978	Cranberry Opalescent Baskets w/variety of spot moulds	Yr.Iss.	1978	20.00	75-125
1979	Vasa Murrhina Vases (Variety of colors)	Yr.Iss.	1979	25.00	60-110
1980	Velva Rose Bubble Optic "Melon" Vases	Yr.Iss.	1980	30.00	60-110
1981	Amethyst w/White Hanging Hearts Vases	Yr.Iss.	1981	37.50	130-175
1982	Overlay Baskets in pastel shades (Swirl Optic)	Yr.Iss.	1982	40.00	75-110
1983	Cranberry Opalescent 1 pc. Fairy Lights	Yr.Iss.	1983	40.00	150-295
1984	Blue Burmese w/peloton Treatment Vases	Yr.Iss.	1984	25.00	75-150
1985	Overlay Vases in Dusty Rose w/Mica Flecks	Yr.Iss.	1985	25.00	95
1986	Ruby Iridized Art Glass Vase	Yr.Iss.	1986	30.00	100-195
1987	Dusty Rose Overlay/Peach Blow Interior w/dark blue Crest Vase	Yr.Iss.	1987	38.00	75-95
1988	Teal Green and Milk marble Basket	Yr.Iss.	1988	30.00	75-110
1989	Mulberry Opalescent Basket w/Coin Dot Optic	Yr.Iss.	1989	37.50	100-225
1990	Sea Mist Green Opalescent Fern Optic Basket	Yr.Iss.	1990	40.00	50-75
1991	Rosalene Leaf Basket and Peacock & Dahlia Basket	Yr.Iss.	1991	65.00	95
1992	Blue Bubble Optic Vases	Yr.Iss.	1992	35.00	50-75
1993	Cranberry Opalescent "Jonquil" Basket	Yr.Iss.	1993	35.00	70-110
1994	Cranberry Opalescent Jacqueline Pitcher	Yr.Iss.	1994	55.00	85-135
1994	Rosalene Tulip Vase-1994 Convention Pc.	Yr.Iss.	1994	45.00	110
1995	Fairy Light-Blue Burmese-1995 Convention Pc.	Yr.Iss.	1995	45.00	125

1983 Connoisseur Collection - Fenton

YEAR ISSUE		EDITION LIMIT	YEAR RETD.	ISSUE PRICE	*QUOTE U.S.$
1983	Basket, 9" Vasa Murrhina	1,000	1983	75.00	125
1983	Craftsman Stein, White Satin Carnival	1,500	1983	35.00	50
1983	Cruet/Stopper Vasa Murrhina	1,000	1983	75.00	195
1983	Epergne Set, 5 pc. Burmese	500	1983	200.00	550-795
1983	Vase, 4 1/2" Sculptured Rose Quartz	2,000	1983	32.50	75-95
1983	Vase, 7" Sculptured Rose Quartz	1,500	1983	50.00	120
1983	Vase, 9" Sculptured Rose Quartz	850	1983	75.00	175-220

1984 Connoisseur Collection - Fenton, unless otherwise noted

YEAR ISSUE		EDITION LIMIT	YEAR RETD.	ISSUE PRICE	*QUOTE U.S.$
1984	Basket, 10" Plated Amberina Velvet	1,250	1984	85.00	195
1984	Candy Box w/cover, 3 pc. Blue Burmese	1,250	1984	75.00	200-250
1984	Cane, 18" Plated Amberina Velvet	Yr.Iss.	1984	35.00	125
1984	Top Hat, 8" Plated Amberina Velvet	1,500	1984	65.00	175-195
1984	Vase, 9" Rose Velvet Hndpt. Floral - L. Everson	750	1984	75.00	150-175
1984	Vase, 9" Rose Velvet-Mother/Child	750	1984	125.00	175-225
1984	Vase, Swan, 8" Gold Azure	1,500	1984	65.00	175-225

1985 Connoisseur Collection - Fenton, unless otherwise noted

YEAR ISSUE		EDITION LIMIT	YEAR RETD.	ISSUE PRICE	*QUOTE U.S.$
1985	Basket, 8 1/2" Buremese, Hndpt. - L. Everson	1,250	1985	95.00	175-200
1985	Epergne Set, 4 pc. Diamond Lace Green Opal.	1,000	1985	95.00	150-195
1985	Lamp, 22" Burmese-Butterfly, Hndpt. - L. Everson	350	1985	300.00	595-695
1985	Punch Set, 14 pc. Green Opalescent	500	1985	250.00	295
1985	Vase, 12" Gabrielle Scul. French Opal.	800	1985	150.00	195
1985	Vase, 7 1/2" Burmese-Shell - D. Barbour	950	1985	135.00	250
1985	Vase, 7 1/2" Chrysanthemums/Circlet, Hndpt. - L. Everson	1,000	1985	125.00	150

1986 Connoisseur Collection - Fenton, unless otherwise noted

YEAR ISSUE		EDITION LIMIT	YEAR RETD.	ISSUE PRICE	*QUOTE U.S.$
1986	Basket, Top hat Wild Rose/Teal Overlay	1,500	1986	49.00	110
1986	Boudoir Lamp, Cranberry Pearl	750	1986	145.00	250-295
1986	Cruet/Stopper, Cranberry Pearl	1,000	1986	75.00	250-295
1986	Handled Urn, 13" Cranberry Satin	1,000	1986	185.00	300
1986	Handled Vase, 7" French Royale	1,000	1986	100.00	175
1986	Lamp, 20" Burmese Shells Hndpt. - D. Barbour	500	1986	350.00	600-695
1986	Vanity Set, 4 pc. Blue Ridge	1,000	1986	125.00	250-295
1986	Vase 10 1/2" Danielle Sandcarved - R. Delaney	1,000	1986	95.00	195
1986	Vase, 10 1/2" Misty Morn, Hndpt. - L. Everson	1,000	1986	95.00	195

1987 Connoisseur Collection - Various

YEAR ISSUE		EDITION LIMIT	YEAR RETD.	ISSUE PRICE	*QUOTE U.S.$
1987	Pitcher, 8" Enameled Azure Hndpt.- L. Everson	950	1987	85.00	125
1987	Vase, 7 1/4" Blossom/Bows on Cranberry Hndpt.- D. Barbour	950	1987	95.00	175

1988 Connoisseur Collection - Fenton, unless otherwise noted

YEAR ISSUE		EDITION LIMIT	YEAR RETD.	ISSUE PRICE	*QUOTE U.S.$
1988	Basket, Irid. Teal Cased Vasa Murrhina	2,500	1988	65.00	125-150
1988	Candy, Wave Crest, CranberryHndpt. - L. Everson	2,000	1988	95.00	150-195
1988	Pitcher, Cased Cranberry/ Opal Teal Ring	3,500	1988	60.00	125-150
1988	Vase, 6" Cased Cranberry/Opal Teal/Irid.	3,500	1988	50.00	100-125

1989 Connoisseur Collection - Fenton, unless otherwise noted

YEAR ISSUE		EDITION LIMIT	YEAR RETD.	ISSUE PRICE	*QUOTE U.S.$
1989	Basket, 7" Cranberry w/Crystal Ring Hndpt.- L. Everson	2,500	1989	85.00	100-150
1989	Candy Box, w/cover, Cranberry, Hndpt. - L. Everson	2,500	1989	85.00	150-195
1989	Epergne Set 5 pc., Rosalene	2,000	1989	250.00	400-495
1989	Lamp, 21" Rosalene Satin Hndpt. - L. Everson	1,000	1989	250.00	300-395
1989	Pitcher, Diamond Optic, Rosalene	2,500	1989	55.00	100
1989	Vase, Basketweave, Rosalene	2,500	1989	45.00	85
1989	Vase, Pinch, 8" Vasa Murrhina	2,000	1989	65.00	100

1990-85th Anniversary Collection - Various

YEAR ISSUE		EDITION LIMIT	YEAR RETD.	ISSUE PRICE	*QUOTE U.S.$
1990	Basket, 5 1/2" Trees on Burmese, Hndpt. - Piper /F. Burton	Closed	1990	57.50	110
1990	Basket, 7" Raspberry on Burmese, Hndpt. - L. Everson	Closed	1990	75.00	150-195
1990	Cruet/Stopper Petite Floral on Burmese, Hndpt. - L. Everson	Closed	1990	85.00	150-195
1990	Epergne Set, 2 pc. Pt. Floral on Burmese, Hndpt. - L. Everson	Closed	1990	125.00	200-295
1990	Lamp, 20" Rose Burmese, Hndpt. - Piper/D. Barbour	Closed	1990	250.00	350-450
1990	Lamp, 21" Raspberry on Burmese, Hndpt. - L. Everson	Closed	1990	295.00	450
1990	Vase, 6 1/2" Rose Burmese, Hndpt. - Piper/D. Barbour	Closed	1990	45.00	90
1990	Vase, 9" Trees on Burmese, Hndpt. - Piper/F. Burton	Closed	1990	75.00	150-200
1990	Vase, Fan 6" Rose Burmese, Hndpt. - Piper/D. Barbour	Closed	1990	49.50	95
1990	Water Set, 7 pc. Raspberry on Burmese, Hndpt. - L. Everson	Closed	1990	275.00	500-695

1991 Connoisseur Collection - Various

YEAR ISSUE		EDITION LIMIT	YEAR RETD.	ISSUE PRICE	*QUOTE U.S.$
1991	Basket, Floral on Rosalene, Hndpt. - M. Reynolds	1,500	1991	64.00	100
1991	Candy Box, 3 pc. Favrene - Fenton	1,000	1991	90.00	200
1991	Fish, Paperweight, Rosalene - Fenton	2,000	1991	30.00	60
1991	Lamp, 20" Roses on Burmese, Hndpt. - Piper/F. Burton	500	1991	275.00	450
1991	Vase, 7 1/2" Raspberry on Burmese, Hndpt. - L. Everson	1,500	1991	65.00	100
1991	Vase, Floral on Favrene, Hndpt. - M. Reynolds	850	1991	125.00	350
1991	Vase, Fruit on Favrene, Hndpt. - F. Burton	850	1991	125.00	300-350

1992 Connoisseur Collection - Various

YEAR ISSUE		EDITION LIMIT	YEAR RETD.	ISSUE PRICE	*QUOTE U.S.$
1992	Covered Box, Poppy/Daisy, Hndpt. - F. Burton	1,250	1992	95.00	200
1992	Pitcher, 4 1/2" Berries on Burmese, Hndpt. - M. Reynolds	1,500	1992	65.00	120
1992	Pitcher, 9" Empire on Cranberry, Hndpt. - M. Reynolds	950	1992	110.00	150
1992	Vase, 6 1/2" Raspberry on Burmese, Hndpt. - L. Everson	1,500	1992	45.00	95
1992	Vase, 8" Seascape, Hndpt. - F. Burton	750	1992	150.00	175
1992	Vase, Twining Floral Rosalene Satin, Hndpt. - M. Reynolds	950	1992	110.00	175

1993 Connoisseur Collection - Various

YEAR ISSUE		EDITION LIMIT	YEAR RETD.	ISSUE PRICE	*QUOTE U.S.$
1993	Amphora w/Stand, Favrene, Hndpt. - M. Reynolds	850	1993	285.00	350
1993	Bowl, Ruby Stretch w/Gold Scrolls, Hndpt. - M. Reynolds	1,250	1993	95.00	125
1993	Lamp, Spring Woods Reverse Hndpt. - F. Burton	500	1993	595.00	595
1993	Owl Figurine, 6" Favrene - Fenton	1,500	1993	95.00	125

*Quotes have been rounded up to nearest dollar

YEAR ISSUE		EDITION LIMIT	YEAR RETD.	ISSUE PRICE	*QUOTE U.S.$
1993	Perfume/Stopper, Rose Trellis Rosalene, Hndpt. - F. Burton	1,250	1993	95.00	125
1993	Vase, 9" Gold Leaves Sandcarved on Plum Irid., - M. Reynolds	950	1993	175.00	225
1993	Vase, Victorian Roses Persian Blue Opal., Hndpt. - M. Reynolds	950	1993	125.00	180

1993 Family Signature Collection - Various

YEAR ISSUE		EDITION LIMIT	YEAR RETD.	ISSUE PRICE	*QUOTE U.S.$
1993	Basket, 8 1/2" Lilacs - Bill Fenton	Closed	1993	65.00	90
1993	Vase, 9" Alpine Thistle/Ruby Carnival - Frank M. Fenton	Closed	1993	105.00	175
1993	Vase, 9" Cottage Scene - Shelley Fenton	Closed	1993	90.00	150
1993	Vase, 10" Vintage on Plum - Don Fenton	Closed	1993	80.00	110
1993	Vase, 11" Cranberry Dec. - George Fenton	Closed	1993	110.00	140

1994 Connoisseur Collection - Various

YEAR ISSUE		EDITION LIMIT	YEAR RETD.	ISSUE PRICE	*QUOTE U.S.$
1994	Bowl, 14" Cranberry Cameo Sandcarved - Reynolds/Delaney	500	1994	390.00	390
1994	Clock, 4 1/2" Favrene, Hndpt. - F. Burton	850	1994	150.00	175
1994	Lamp, Hummingbird Reverse, Hndpt. - F. Burton	300	1994	590.00	750
1994	Pitcher, 10" Lattice on Burmese, Hndpt. - F. Burton	750	1994	165.00	225
1994	Vase, 7" Favrene, Hndpt. - M. Reynolds	850	1994	185.00	200
1994	Vase, 8" Plum Opalescent, Hndpt. - M. Reynolds	750	1994	165.00	175
1994	Vase, 11" Gold Amberina, Hndpt. - M. Reynolds	750	1994	175.00	225

1994 Family Signature Collection - Various

YEAR ISSUE		EDITION LIMIT	YEAR RETD.	ISSUE PRICE	*QUOTE U.S.$
1994	Basket, 7 1/2" Lilacs - Shelley Fenton	Closed	1994	65.00	95
1994	Basket, 8" Stiegel Green - Bill Fenton	Closed	1994	60.00	95
1994	Basket, 8 1/2" Ruby Carnival - Tom Fenton	Closed	1994	60.00	95
1994	Basket, 11" Autumn Gold Opal - Frank Fenton	Closed	1994	70.00	90
1994	Candy w/cover, 9 1/2" Autumn Leaves - Don Fenton	Closed	1994	60.00	75
1994	Pitcher, 6 1/2" Cranberry - Frank M. Fenton	Closed	1994	85.00	125
1994	Vase, 9 1/2" Pansies on Cranberry - Bill Fenton	Closed	1994	95.00	125
1994	Vase, 10" Fuchsia - George Fenton	Closed	1994	95.00	125

1995 Connoisseur Collection - M. Reynolds, unless otherwise noted

YEAR ISSUE		EDITION LIMIT	YEAR RETD.	ISSUE PRICE	*QUOTE U.S.$
1995	Amphora w/stand, 10 1/4" Royal Purple, Hndpt.	890	1995	195.00	195
1995	Ginger Jar, 3 Pc. 8 1/2" Favrene, Hndpt.	790	1995	275.00	275
1995	Lamp, 21" Butterfly/Floral Reverse, Hndpt. - F. Burton	300	1995	595.00	595
1995	Pitcher, 9 1/2" Victorian Art Glass, Hndpt.	490	1995	250.00	250
1995	Vase, 7" Aurora Wild Rose, Hndpt.	890	1995	125.00	125

1995 Family Signature Collection - Various

YEAR ISSUE		EDITION LIMIT	YEAR RETD.	ISSUE PRICE	*QUOTE U.S.$
1995	Basket, 8 1/2" Trellis - Lynn Fenton	Closed	1995	85.00	85
1995	Basket, 9 1/2" Coralene Floral - Frank M./Bill Fenton	Closed	1995	75.00	75
1995	Candy w/cover, 9" Red Carnival - Mike Fenton	Closed	1995	65.00	65
1995	Pitcher, 9 1/2" Thistle - Don Fenton	Closed	1995	125.00	125
1995	Vase, 7" Gold Pansies on Cranberry - George Fenton	Closed	1995	75.00	75
1995	Vase, 9" Summer Garden on Spruce - Don Fenton	Closed	1995	85.00	85
1995	Vase, 9 1/2" Golden Flax on Cobalt - Shelley Fenton	Closed	1995	95.00	95

1996 Family Signature Collection - Various

YEAR ISSUE		EDITION LIMIT	YEAR RETD.	ISSUE PRICE	*QUOTE U.S.$
1996	Basket, 8" Mountain Berry - Don Fenton	Closed	1996	85.00	85
1996	Candy Box w/cover Pansies - Shelley Fenton	Closed	1996	65.00	65
1996	Pitcher, 6 1/2" Asters - Lynn Fenton	Closed	1996	70.00	70
1996	Vase, 11" Meadow Beauty - Nancy Fenton	Closed	1996	95.00	95
1996	Vase, 8 1/2" Blush Rose on Opaline - George Fenton	Closed	1996	75.00	75

American Classic Series - M. Dickinson

YEAR ISSUE		EDITION LIMIT	YEAR RETD.	ISSUE PRICE	*QUOTE U.S.$
1986	Jupiter Train on Opal Satin, Lamp, 23"	1,000	1986	295.00	350
1986	Studebaker-Garford Car on Opal Satin, Lamp, 16"	1,000	1986	235.00	300

Christmas - Various

YEAR ISSUE		EDITION LIMIT	YEAR RETD.	ISSUE PRICE	*QUOTE U.S.$
1978	Christmas Morn, Lamp, 16" - M. Dickinson	Yr.Iss.	1978	125.00	250
1978	Christmas Morn, Fairy Light - M. Dickinson	Yr.Iss.	1978	25.00	75
1979	Nature's Christmas, Lamp, 16" - K. Cunningham	Yr.Iss.	1979	150.00	250
1979	Nature's Christmas, Fairy Light - K. Cunningham	Yr.Iss.	1979	30.00	95
1980	Going Home, Lamp, 16" - D. Johnson	Yr.Iss.	1980	165.00	250
1980	Going Home, Fairy Light - D. Johnson	Yr.Iss.	1980	32.50	65
1981	All Is Calm, Lamp, 16" - D. Johnson	Yr.Iss.	1981	175.00	295
1981	All Is Calm, Lamp, 20" - D. Johnson	Yr.Iss.	1981	225.00	295
1981	All Is Calm, Fairy Light - D. Johnson	Yr.Iss.	1981	35.00	65
1982	Country Christmas, Lamp, 16" - R. Spindler	Yr.Iss.	1982	175.00	295
1982	Country Christmas, Lamp, 21" - R. Spindler	Yr.Iss.	1982	225.00	350
1982	Country Christmas, Fairy Light - R. Spindler	Yr.Iss.	1982	35.00	65
1983	Anticipation, Fairy Light - D. Johnson	7,500	1983	35.00	65
1984	Expectation, Lamp, 10 1/2" - D. Johnson	7,500	1984	75.00	275
1984	Expectation, Fairy Light - D. Johnson	7,500	1984	37.50	65
1985	Heart's Desire, Fairy Light - D. Johnson	7,500	1986	37.50	65
1987	Sharing The Spirit, Fairy Light - L. Everson	Yr.Iss.	1987	37.50	65
1987	Cardinal in the Churchyard, Lamp, 18 1/2" - D. Johnson	500	1987	250.00	295
1987	Cardinal in the Churchyard, Fairy Light - D. Johnson	4,500	1987	29.50	95
1988	A Chickadee Ballet, Lamp, 21" - D. Johnson	500	1988	274.00	295
1988	A Chickadee Ballet, Fairy Light - D. Johnson	4,500	1988	29.50	95
1989	Downy Pecker, Lamp, 16" - Chisled Song - D. Johnson	500	1989	250.00	295
1989	Downy Pecker, Fairy Light - Chisled Song - D. Johnson	4,500	1989	29.50	95
1990	A Blue Bird in Snowfall, Lamp, 21" - D. Johnson	500	1990	250.00	295
1990	A Blue Bird in Snowfall, Fairy Light - D. Johnson	4,500	1990	29.50	95
1990	Sleigh Ride, Lamp, 16" - F. Burton	1,000	1990	250.00	295
1990	Sleigh Ride, Fairy Light - F. Burton	3,500	1990	39.00	75
1991	Christmas Eve, Lamp, 16" - F. Burton	1,000	1991	250.00	295
1991	Christmas Eve, Fairy Light - F. Burton	3,500	1991	39.00	95
1992	Family Tradition, Lamp, 20" - F. Burton	1,000	1992	250.00	295
1992	Family Tradition, Fairy Light - F. Burton	3,500	1992	39.00	75
1993	Family Holiday, Lamp, 16" - F. Burton	1,000	1993	265.00	295
1993	Family Holiday, Fairy Light - F. Burton	3,500	1993	39.00	75
1994	Silent Night, Lamp, 16" - F. Burton	500	1994	275.00	325
1994	Silent Night, Fairy Light - F. Burton	1,500	1994	45.00	45
1994	Egg on Stand - F. Burton	1,500	1994	45.00	45
1995	Our Home Is Blessed, Lamp, 21" - F. Burton	500	1995	275.00	275
1995	Our Home Is Blessed, Egg - F. Burton	1,500	1995	45.00	45

Christmas Limited Edition - M. Reynolds

YEAR ISSUE		EDITION LIMIT	YEAR RETD.	ISSUE PRICE	*QUOTE U.S.$
1992	Egg, 3 1/2" Manager Scene on Ruby	2,500	1992	30.00	30
1992	Egg, 3 1/2" Poinsettia on Crystal Irid.	2,500	1992	30.00	30
1993	Egg, 3 1/2" Angel on Green	2,500	1993	35.00	35
1993	Egg, 3 1/2" Woods on White	2,500	1993	35.00	35
1994	Egg, 3 1/2" Magnolia on Gold	1,500	1994	35.00	35
1994	Egg, 3 1/2" Partridge on Ruby	1,500	1994	35.00	35
1995	Egg, 3 1/2" Bow & Holly on Ivory	900	1995	35.00	35
1995	Egg, 3 1/2" Chickadee on Gold	900	1995	35.00	35
1995	Egg, 3 1/2" Iced Poinsettia on Ruby	900	1995	39.50	40
1995	Angel, Radiant-Musical Base	900	1995	85.00	85
1995	Pitcher, Golden Holiday Pine Cones	900	1995	79.00	79

Collectible Eggs - M. Reynolds, unless otherwise noted

YEAR ISSUE		EDITION LIMIT	YEAR RETD.	ISSUE PRICE	*QUOTE U.S.$
1991	Egg, Gold Design/Salem Blue Irid.	1,500	1991	29.50	30
1991	Egg, Partridge/Seamist Green Irid.	1,500	1991	29.50	30
1991	Egg, Poinsettias/Special Milk Glass	1,500	1991	29.50	30
1991	Egg, Shell/Favrene	1,500	1991	35.00	45
1991	Egg, Skater/Ruby	1,500	1991	29.50	30
1991	Egg, Snow Scene/Sp. Milk	1,500	1991	29.50	30
1991	Egg, White Scene/Black	1,500	1991	29.50	30
1992	Egg, Butterflies/Black	2,500	1992	30.00	30
1992	Egg, Croquet/Clear Carnival	2,500	1992	30.00	30
1992	Egg, Floral & Bronze/Special Milk Glass	2,500	1992	30.00	30
1992	Egg, Iris/Seamist Green	2,500	1992	30.00	30
1992	Egg, Pink Floral/Dusty Rose	2,500	1992	30.00	30
1992	Egg, Unicorn/Twilight Blue	2,500	1992	30.00	30
1993	Egg, Cottage/White Opal	2,500	1993	30.00	30
1993	Egg, Fuchsia Floral/White	2,500	1993	30.00	30
1993	Egg, Paisley/Dusty Rose	2,500	1993	30.00	30
1993	Egg, Sandcarved/Black	1,500	1993	35.00	35
1993	Egg, Scrolling Floral/Green - K. Plauche	2,500	1993	30.00	30
1993	Egg, Sea Gulls/Ocean Blue	2,500	1993	30.00	30
1993	Egg, w/gold on Plum - K. Plauche	2,500	1993	35.00	35
1993	Egg, w/gold on Ruby	2,500	1993	30.00	30
1994	Egg, Cascading Floral/Pink - S. Jackson	2,500	1994	32.50	33
1994	Egg, Metallic Floral/Plum - K. Plauche	2,500	1994	32.50	33
1994	Egg, Enameled Flowers/Blue - F. Burton	2,500	1994	37.50	38
1994	Egg, Scrolls/Gold	2,500	1994	32.50	33
1994	Egg, Spring Landscape/Opal - S. Jackson	2,500	1994	32.50	33
1994	Egg, Tulips/Sea Mist - S. Jackson	2,500	1994	32.50	33
1994	Egg, Violets/Milk Pearl - S. Jackson	2,500	1994	32.50	33
1995	Egg, Floral/Blue	2,500	1995	32.50	33
1995	Egg, Floral/Gold	2,500	1995	32.50	33
1995	Egg, Floral/Green	2,500	1995	32.50	33
1995	Egg, Floral/White	2,500	1995	32.50	33
1995	Egg, Hummingbird/Dusty Rose	2,500	1995	35.00	35
1995	Egg, Scene/White	2,500	1995	32.50	33
1995	Egg, Scrolls/Black	2,500	1995	32.50	33
1996	Egg, Honeysuckle - R. Spindler	2,500		37.50	38
1996	Egg, Hummingbird	2,500		37.50	38
1996	Egg, Butterflies - R. Spindler	2,500		37.50	38
1996	Egg, Morning Glories - R. Spindler	2,500		37.50	38
1996	Egg, Lake Scene	2,500		37.50	38
1996	Egg, Jeweled	2,500		37.50	38
1996	Egg, Fish - R. Spindler	2,500		37.50	38

Designer Series - Various

YEAR ISSUE		EDITION LIMIT	YEAR RETD.	ISSUE PRICE	*QUOTE U.S.$
1983	Lighthouse Point, Lamp, 23 1/2", - M. Dickinson	150	1983	350.00	450
1983	Lighthouse Point, Lamp, 25 1/2", - M. Dickinson	150	1983	350.00	575
1983	Down Home, Lamp, 21" - G. Finn	300	1983	300.00	450
1984	Smoke 'N Cinders, Lamp, 16" - M. Dickinson	250	1984	195.00	325
1984	Smoke 'N Cinders, Lamp, 23" - M. Dickinson	250	1984	350.00	400
1984	Majestic Flight, Lamp, 16" - B. Cumberledge	250	1984	195.00	295
1984	Majestic Flight, Lamp, 23 1/2" - B. Cumberledge	250	1984	350.00	450
1985	In Season, Lamp, 16" - M. Dickinson	250	1985	225.00	325
1985	In Season, Lamp, 23" - M. Dickinson	250	1985	295.00	395
1985	Nature's Grace, Lamp, 16" - B. Cumberland	250	1985	225.00	325
1985	Nature's Grace, Lamp, 23" - B. Cumberland	295	1985	295.00	400

Easter Series - M. Reynolds

YEAR ISSUE		EDITION LIMIT	YEAR RETD.	ISSUE PRICE	*QUOTE U.S.$
1995	Fairy Light	Closed	1995	49.00	49

Fenton Miniatures - Fenton

YEAR ISSUE		EDITION LIMIT	YEAR RETD.	ISSUE PRICE	*QUOTE U.S.$
1996	Epergne, 4 1/2" Opaline	Yr.Iss.		35.00	35
1996	Punch Bowl Set, 5" x 3 3/4" high	Closed	1996	59.00	59

Mary Gregory - M. Reynolds

YEAR ISSUE		EDITION LIMIT	YEAR RETD.	ISSUE PRICE	*QUOTE U.S.$
1994	Basket, 7 1/2" Oval	Closed	1994	59.00	59
1995	Basket, 7 1/2" Oval	Closed	1995	65.00	65
1995	Egg on stand, 4" - Butterfly Delight	Closed	1995	37.50	38
1996	Hat Basket on Cranberry, 6 1/2"	2,000		95.00	95
1996	Vase on Cranberry, 9"	1,500		135.00	135

Mouthblown Eggs - M. Reynolds, unless otherwise noted

YEAR ISSUE		EDITION LIMIT	YEAR RETD.	ISSUE PRICE	*QUOTE U.S.$
1991	Egg, 3 1/2" Mother of Pearl	Closed	1991	49.00	4[illegible]
1991	Egg, 4 1/2" Mother of Pearl	Closed	1991	59.00	5[illegible]
1992	Egg, 5" Petal Pink Iridized - F. Burton	Closed	1992	65.00	6[illegible]
1992	Egg, 5" Seamist Green Iridized - F. Burton	Closed	1992	65.00	6[illegible]
1993	Egg, 5" Ocean Blue	Closed	1993	69.00	6[illegible]
1993	Egg, 5" Plum	Closed	1993	69.00	6[illegible]
1994	Egg, 5" Blue - F. Burton	Closed	1994	75.00	7[illegible]
1994	Egg, 5" Rose	Closed	1994	75.00	7[illegible]
1995	Egg, 5" Gold	Closed	1995	75.00	7[illegible]
1995	Egg, 5" Spruce	Closed	1995	75.00	7[illegible]
1996	Egg, 5" Cranberry	Closed	1996	95.00	9[illegible]
1996	Egg, 5" French Opalescent	Closed	1996	75.00	7[illegible]

Valentine's Day Series - Fenton, unless otherwise noted

YEAR ISSUE		EDITION LIMIT	YEAR RETD.	ISSUE PRICE	*QUOTE U.S.$
1992	Basket, 6" Cranberry Opal/Heart Optic	Closed	1992	50.00	8[illegible]
1992	Vase, 4" Cranberry Opal/Heart Optic	Closed	1992	35.00	6[illegible]
1992	Perfume, w/oval stopper Cranberry Opal/Heart Optic	Closed	1992	60.00	9[illegible]
1993	Basket, 7" Caprice Cranberry Opal/Heart Optic	Closed	1993	59.00	8[illegible]
1993	Trinket Box, 5" Cranberry Opal/Heart Optic	Closed	1993	79.00	9[illegible]
1993	Vase, 5 1/2" Melon Cranberry Opal/Heart Optic	Closed	1993	45.00	7[illegible]
1993	Southern Girl, 8", Hndpt. Opal Satin - M. Reynolds	Closed	1993	49.00	9[illegible]
1993	Southern Girl, 8", Rose Pearl Irid.	Closed	1993	45.00	9[illegible]
1994	Basket, 7" Cranberry Opal/Heart Optic	Closed	1994	65.00	9[illegible]
1994	Vase, 5 1/2" Ribbed Cranberry Opal/Heart Optic	Closed	1994	47.50	6[illegible]
1994	Perfume, w/ stopper, 5" Cranberry Opal/Heart Optic	Closed	1994	75.00	1[illegible]
1995	Basket, 8" Melon Cranberry Opal/Heart Optic	Closed	1995	69.00	9[illegible]
1995	Pitcher, 5 1/2" Melon Cranberry Opal/Heart Optic	Closed	1995	69.00	9[illegible]

*Quotes have been rounded up to nearest dolla[illegible]

YEAR ISSUE		EDITION LIMIT	YEAR RETD.	ISSUE PRICE	*QUOTE U.S.$
1995	Perfume, w/ heart stopper, Kristen's Floral Hndpt. - M. Reynolds	2,500	1995	49.00	75
1995	Doll, 7", Kristen's Floral Hndpt. Ivory Satin - M. Reynolds	2,500	1995	49.00	70
1996	Basket, 8" Melon Cranberry Opalescent	Closed	1996	75.00	75
1996	Perfume, 5" Melon Cranberry Opalescent	Closed	1996	95.00	95
1996	Fairy Light, 3 pc. Cranberry Opalescent	Closed	1996	135.00	135
1996	Vanity Set, 4 pc. Tea Rose - M. Reynolds	1,500		250.00	250
1996	Doll, w/Musical Base Tea Rose - M. Reynolds	2,500		55.00	55

Fitz And Floyd, Inc.

Holiday Hamlet®-Accessories - V. Balcou

YEAR ISSUE		EDITION LIMIT	YEAR RETD.	ISSUE PRICE	*QUOTE U.S.$
1993	Blizzard Express Train	Open		95.00	95
1993	Carols in the Snow	Open		30.00	30
1993	Christmas Tree, large	Open		45.00	45
1993	Christmas Tree, small	Open		30.00	30
1994	Hand Car	Open		35.00	35
1993	Silent Night Singers	Closed	1994	30.00	35
1993	Village Sign	Open		40.00	40
1993	Village Square Clock	Open		50.00	50

Holiday Hamlet®-Figurines - V. Balcou

YEAR ISSUE		EDITION LIMIT	YEAR RETD.	ISSUE PRICE	*QUOTE U.S.$
1993	Baby Squirrel	Closed	1995	15.00	30
1993	Bell Choir Bunny	Open		15.00	15
1993	Bell Choir Fox	Open		10.00	10
1994	Blessed Mother/Joseph Players	Open		25.00	25
1993	Christmas Carolers	Open		20.00	20
1993	Christmas Carolers, waterglobe	Open		45.00	45
1993	Christmas Treats	Open		15.00	15
1993	The Conductor	Open		10.00	10
1993	Delivering Gifts	Open		20.00	20
1993	Dollmaker	Open		15.00	15
1993	Dollmaker's Apprentice	Closed	1994	15.00	30
1993	Dr. B. Well	Open		15.00	15
1993	Dr. Quack & Patient	Open		15.00	15
1993	Gathering Apples	Open		15.00	15
1993	Gathering Pine Boughs	Open		10.00	10
1994	Holiday Hamlet, waterglobe	Open		75.00	75
1994	Little Angels	Open		30.00	30
1993	Mr. Grizzly	Open		20.00	20
1994	Mr. Winterberry, Pie Vendor	2,500	1995	25.00	50
1993	Mrs. Grizzly	Open		20.00	20
1993	Nanny Rabbit & Bunnies	Open		20.00	20
1993	Old Royal Elf	Open		20.00	20
1993	The Parson	Open		10.00	10
1993	Pastry Vendor	Open		10.00	10
1994	Poor Shepherds	Open		15.00	15
1994	The Porter	Closed	1995	25.00	25
1994	Proud Mother/Father	Open		20.00	20
1993	Santa Claus	Open		25.00	25
1993	Skaters	Open		20.00	20
1993	Squirrel Family	Closed	1994	15.00	30
1994	Three Wisemen	Open		20.00	20
1993	Tying the Christmas Garland	Closed	1994	20.00	20
1993	Waving Elf	Open		10.00	10
1993	Welcome Banner	Open		20.00	20
1993	Welcoming Elf	Closed	1995	10.00	10

Holiday Hamlet®-Lighted Houses - V. Balcou

YEAR ISSUE		EDITION LIMIT	YEAR RETD.	ISSUE PRICE	*QUOTE U.S.$
1994	Christmas Pageant Stage	Open		75.00	75
1993	Doctor's Office	Open		75.00	75
1993	Dollmaker's Cottage	Open		125.00	125
1993	Holiday Hamlet Chapel	Open		75.00	75
1993	Holiday Manor	Closed	1994	75.00	125
1994	Mr. Winterberry's Pie Shop	2,500	1995	100.00	200-350
1993	Railroad Station	Closed	1994	125.00	300-475
1994	Snowman Supply Hut	Open		65.00	65
1993	Stocking Stuffer's Workshop	Open		45.00	45
1993	Tavern in the Woods	Closed	1995	125.00	200-350
1993	Toymaker's Workshop	Open		45.00	45
1994	Whistlestop Junction Train Stop	Open		65.00	65
1994	World's Best Snowman	Open		55.00	55

Flambro Imports

Emmett Kelly Jr. Members Only Figurine - Undisclosed

YEAR ISSUE		EDITION LIMIT	YEAR RETD.	ISSUE PRICE	*QUOTE U.S.$
1990	Merry-Go-Round	Closed	1990	125.00	400-500
1991	10 Years Of Collecting	Closed	1991	100.00	200
1992	All Aboard	Closed	1992	75.00	200
1993	Ringmaster	Closed	1993	125.00	125
994	Birthday Mail	Closed	1994	100.00	175-225
1995	Salute To Our Vets	Closed	1995	75.00	75
1996	I Love You	Yr.Iss.		95.00	95

EKJ Professionals - Undisclosed

YEAR ISSUE		EDITION LIMIT	YEAR RETD.	ISSUE PRICE	*QUOTE U.S.$
987	Accountant	Retrd.	1994	50.00	100
1991	Barber	Retrd.	1995	50.00	75-100
1988	Bowler	Retrd.	1994	50.00	100
996	Bowler	Open		55.00	55
991	Carpenter	Open		50.00	50
991	The Chef	Retrd.	1994	50.00	100
995	Coach	Open		55.00	55
990	Computer Whiz	Open		50.00	50
987	Dentist	Retrd.	1995	50.00	75-100
996	Dentist	Open		55.00	55
1987	Doctor	Retrd.	1995	50.00	100
1995	Doctor	Open		55.00	55
1987	Engineer	Retrd.	1995	50.00	100
1987	Executive	Open		50.00	50
1996	Farmer	Open		55.00	55
1995	Fireman	Open		55.00	55
1988	Fireman	Retrd.	1994	50.00	75-100
1990	Fisherman	Open		50.00	50
1995	Golfer	Open		55.00	55
1988	Golfer	Open		50.00	50
1990	Hunter	Open		50.00	50
1995	Lawyer	Open		55.00	55
1987	Lawyer	Retrd.	1995	50.00	75-100
1988	Mailman	Retrd.	1995	50.00	100
1996	Mailman	Open		55.00	55
1993	On Maneuvers	Open		50.00	50
1991	Painter	Open		50.00	50
1991	Pharmacist	Open		50.00	50
1990	Photographer	Open		50.00	50
1993	Pilot	Open		50.00	50
1991	Plumber	Retrd.	1994	50.00	100
1995	Policeman	Open		55.00	55
1988	Policeman	Retrd.	1994	50.00	75-100
1990	The Putt	Open		50.00	50
1993	Realtor	Open		50.00	50
1988	Skier	Retrd.	1995	50.00	100
1996	Skier	Open		55.00	55
1987	Stockbrocker	Open		50.00	50
1987	Teacher	Retrd.	1995	50.00	100
1993	Veterinarian	Open		50.00	50

Emmett Kelly Jr. - Undisclosed, unless otherwise noted

YEAR ISSUE		EDITION LIMIT	YEAR RETD.	ISSUE PRICE	*QUOTE U.S.$
1995	20th Anniversary of All Star Circus	5,000	1995	240.00	250
1995	35 Years of Clowning	5,000	1995	240.00	250
1989	65th Birthday Commemorative	1,989	1989	275.00	1200-1600
1993	After The Parade	7,500		190.00	190
1988	Amen	12,000	1991	120.00	350
1996	AmericanCircus Extravaganza	5,000		240.00	240
1991	Artist At Work	7,500		295.00	300-350
1992	Autumn - D. Rust	Retrd.	1996	60.00	100
1983	The Balancing Act	10,000	1985	75.00	700-800
1983	Balloons For Sale	10,000	1985	75.00	600-700
1990	Balloons for Sale II	7,500		250.00	250-300
1986	Bedtime	12,000	1991	98.00	300
1984	Big Business	9,500	1987	110.00	800-900
1990	Convention-Bound	7,500		225.00	230
1986	Cotton Candy	12,000	1987	98.00	375
1996	Daredevil Thrill Motor Show	5,000		240.00	240
1988	Dining Out	12,000	1991	120.00	400
1984	Eating Cabbage	12,000	1986	75.00	475
1985	Emmett's Fan	12,000	1986	80.00	475
1986	The Entertainers	12,000	1991	120.00	150-200
1986	Fair Game	2,500	1987	450.00	1650
1991	Finishing Touch	7,500		245.00	245
1991	Follow The Leader	7,500		200.00	200
1994	Forest Friends	7,500		190.00	190
1983	Hole In The Sole	10,000	1986	75.00	600
1989	Hurdy-Gurdy Man	9,500	1991	150.00	200-350
1985	In The Spotlight	12,000	1989	103.00	400
1993	Kittens For Sale	7,500		190.00	190
1994	Let Him Eat Cake	3,500	1995	300.00	550
1994	The Lion Tamer	7,500		190.00	190
1981	Looking Out To See	12,000	1982	75.00	2400-2700
1986	Making New Friends	9,500	1988	140.00	350
1989	Making Up	7,500	1995	200.00	250-450
1985	Man's Best Friend	9,500	1989	98.00	550-650
1990	Misfortune?	3,500	1989	200.00	500-600
1987	My Favorite Things	9,500	1988	109.00	600-700
1989	No Loitering	7,500	1994	200.00	400
1985	No Strings Attached	9,500	1991	98.00	375
1992	No Use Crying	7,500		200.00	200
1987	On The Road Again	9,500	1991	109.00	450
1988	Over a Barrel	9,500	1991	130.00	250-450
1992	Peanut Butter?	7,500		200.00	200
1984	Piano Player	9,500	1988	160.00	700
1992	Ready-Set-Go	7,500		200.00	200
1987	Saturday Night	7,500	1988	153.00	500-600
1983	Spirit of Christmas I	3,500	1984	125.00	2600
1984	Spirit of Christmas II	3,500	1985	270.00	500-600
1985	Spirit of Christmas III	3,500	1989	220.00	525
1986	Spirit of Christmas IV	3,500	1989	150.00	400-550
1987	Spirit of Christmas V	2,400	1989	170.00	400-550
1988	Spirit of Christmas VI	2,400	1989	194.00	400-600
1990	Spirit of Christmas VII	3,500	1990	275.00	425
1991	Spirit of Christmas VIII	3,500	1992	250.00	350
1993	Spirit of Christmas IX	3,500		200.00	200
1993	Spirit of Christmas X	3,500		200.00	200
1994	Spirit of Christmas XI	3,500	1995	200.00	225-250
1995	Spirit of Christmas XII	3,500		200.00	200
1996	Spirit of Christmas XIII	3,500		200.00	200
1992	Spring - D. Rust	Open		60.00	60
1992	Summer - D. Rust	Open		60.00	60
1981	Sweeping Up	12,000	1982	75.00	1500-1700
1982	The Thinker	15,000	1986	60.00	1100
1987	Toothache	12,000	1995	98.00	125-250
1990	Watch the Birdie	9,500		200.00	225
1982	Wet Paint	15,000	1983	80.00	800
1988	Wheeler Dealer	7,500	1990	160.00	250-300
1982	Why Me?	15,000	1984	65.00	425-600
1992	Winter - D. Rust	Open		60.00	60
1983	Wishful Thinking	10,000	1985	65.00	500-700
1993	World Traveler	7,500		190.00	190

Emmett Kelly Jr. A Day At The Fair - Undisclosed

YEAR ISSUE		EDITION LIMIT	YEAR RETD.	ISSUE PRICE	*QUOTE U.S.$
1990	75 Please	Retrd.	1994	65.00	85-125
1991	Coin Toss	Retrd.	1994	65.00	85-125
1990	Look At You	Retrd.	1994	65.00	85-125
1991	Popcorn!	Retrd.	1994	65.00	85-125
1990	Ride The Wild Mouse	Retrd.	1994	65.00	85-125
1990	Step Right Up	Retrd.	1994	65.00	85-125
1992	Stilt Man	Retrd.	1994	65.00	85-125
1990	The Stilt Man	Retrd.	1994	65.00	85-125
1990	Thanks Emmett	Retrd.	1994	65.00	85-125
1990	Three For A Dime	Retrd.	1994	65.00	85-125
1991	The Trouble With Hot Dogs	Retrd.	1994	65.00	85-125
1990	You Can Do It, Emmett	Retrd.	1994	65.00	85-125
1990	You Go First, Emmett	Retrd.	1994	65.00	85-125

Emmett Kelly Jr. Appearance Figurine - Undisclosed

YEAR ISSUE		EDITION LIMIT	YEAR RETD.	ISSUE PRICE	*QUOTE U.S.$
1992	Now Appearing	Open		100.00	100
1993	The Vigilante	Open		75.00	75

Emmett Kelly Jr. Event Figurine - Undisclosed

YEAR ISSUE		EDITION LIMIT	YEAR RETD.	ISSUE PRICE	*QUOTE U.S.$
1996	EKJ For President	Open		59.00	59

Emmett Kelly Jr. Miniatures - Undisclosed

YEAR ISSUE		EDITION LIMIT	YEAR RETD.	ISSUE PRICE	*QUOTE U.S.$
1994	65th Birthday	Retrd.	1994	70.00	75-95
1996	Amen	Open		35.00	35
1986	Balancing Act	Retrd.	1992	25.00	125
1986	Balloons for Sale	Retrd.	1993	25.00	105
1995	Bedtime	Open		35.00	35
1988	Big Business	Retrd.	1995	35.00	90-100
1989	Cotton Candy	Retrd.	1991	30.00	75
1995	Dining Out	Open		35.00	35
1987	Eating Cabbage	Retrd.	1990	30.00	100
1987	Emmett's Fan	Retrd.	1994	30.00	100
1995	The Entertainers	Open		45.00	45
1994	Fair Game	Open		75.00	75
1986	Hole in the Sole	Retrd.	1989	25.00	100
1995	Hurdy Gurdy Man	Open		40.00	40
1991	In The Spotlight	Numbrd		35.00	85
1986	Looking Out To See	Retrd.	1987	25.00	150-175
1992	Making New Friends	Retrd.	1996	40.00	40
1996	Making Up	Open		55.00	55
1989	Man's Best Friend?	Retrd.	1994	35.00	85
1996	Misfortune	Open		60.00	60
1990	My Favorite Things	Retrd.	1995	45.00	90
1995	No Loitering	Open		50.00	50
1991	No Strings Attached	Numbrd		35.00	35
1992	On the Road Again	Numbrd		35.00	35
1994	Over a Barrel	Open		30.00	30
1992	Piano Player	Numbrd		50.00	50
1990	Saturday Night	Retrd.	1995	50.00	65-100
1988	Spirit of Christmas I	Retrd.	1990	40.00	150
1992	Spirit of Christmas II	Retrd.	1995	50.00	75
1990	Spirit Of Christmas III	Retrd.	1993	50.00	75-125
1993	Spirit of Christmas IV	Numbrd		40.00	40
1994	Spirit of Christmas V	Open		50.00	50
1996	Spirit of Christmas VI	Open		55.00	55
1986	Sweeping Up	Retrd.	1987	25.00	175-200
1986	The Thinker	Retrd.	1991	25.00	75-145
1996	The Toothache	Open		35.00	35
1986	Wet Paint	Retrd.	1993	25.00	125
1996	Wheeler Dealer	Open		65.00	65
1986	Why Me?	Retrd.	1989	25.00	110
1986	Wishful Thinking	Retrd.	1988	25.00	90

Emmett Kelly Jr. Real Rags Collection - Undisclosed

YEAR ISSUE		EDITION LIMIT	YEAR RETD.	ISSUE PRICE	*QUOTE U.S.$
1993	Big Business II	Retrd.	1996	140.00	140
1993	Checking His List	Closed	N/A	100.00	200
1994	Eating Cabbage 2	3,000		100.00	100
1994	A Good Likeness	3,000		120.00	120
1993	Looking Out To See II	Open		100.00	100
1994	On in Two	3,000		100.00	100
1994	Rudolph Has A Red Nose, Too	3,000	1996	135.00	135
1993	Sweeping Up II	Open		100.00	100
1993	Thinker II	Open		120.00	120

Little Emmetts - M. Wu

YEAR ISSUE		EDITION LIMIT	YEAR RETD.	ISSUE PRICE	*QUOTE U.S.$
1996	Balancing Act	Open		25.00	25
1996	Balloons for Sale	Open		25.00	25
1994	Birthday Haul	Open		30.00	30
1995	Dance Lessons	Open		50.00	50
1994	Little Artist Picture Frame	Open		22.00	22
1994	Little Emmett Fishing	Open		35.00	35
1995	Little Emmett Noel, Noel	Open		40.00	40
1994	Little Emmett Shadow Show	Open		40.00	40
1995	Little Emmett Someday	Open		50.00	50
1994	Little Emmett w/Blackboard	Open		30.00	30
1994	Little Emmett, Counting Lession (Musical)	Open		30.00	30
1994	Little Emmett, Country Road (Musical)	Open		35.00	35
1994	Little Emmett, Raindrops (Musical)	Open		35.00	35
1994	Little Emmett, You've Got a Friend (Musical)	Open		33.00	33
1996	Long Distance	Open		50.00	50
1995	Looking Back Musical Waterglobe	Open		75.00	75
1995	Looking Forward Musical Waterglobe	Open		75.00	75
1996	Looking Out To See	Open		25.00	25

YEAR ISSUE		EDITION LIMIT	YEAR RETD.	ISSUE PRICE	*QUOTE U.S.$
1994	Playful Bookends	Open		40.00	40
1996	Sweeping Up	Open		25.00	25
1996	Thinker	Open		25.00	25
1996	Wet Paint	Open		40.00	40
1994	EKJ, Age 1	Open		9.00	9
1994	EKJ, Age 2	Open		9.50	10
1994	EKJ, Age 3	Open		12.00	12
1994	EKJ, Age 4	Open		12.00	12
1994	EKJ, Age 5	Open		15.00	15
1994	EKJ, Age 6	Open		15.00	15
1994	EKJ, Age 7	Open		17.00	17
1994	EKJ, Age 8	Open		21.00	21
1994	EKJ, Age 9	Open		22.00	22
1994	EKJ, Age 10	Open		25.00	25
1996	January-New Years	Open		35.00	35
1996	February-Valentine's Day	Open		30.00	30
1996	March-St. Patrick's Day	Open		40.00	40
1996	April-April Showers	Open		40.00	40
1996	May-May Flowers	Open		45.00	45
1996	June-School Is Out	Open		40.00	40
1996	July-Independence Day	Open		35.00	35
1996	August-Summer Picnic	Open		35.00	35
1996	September-School Is In	Open		34.00	34
1996	October-Pumpkins for Fall & Halloween	Open		45.00	45
1996	November-Thanksgiving	Open		30.00	30
1996	December-Snow Sledding w/Friends	Open		45.00	45

Pleasantville 1893 - J. Berg Victor

1990	1st Church Of Pleasantville	Retrd.	1994	35.00	35
1992	Apothecary/Ice Cream Shop	Open		36.00	36
1992	Ashbey House	Open		40.00	40
1993	Balcomb's Barn	Open		40.00	40
1993	Balcomb's Farm (out buildings)	Open		40.00	40
1993	Balcomb's Farmhouse	Open		40.00	40
1990	The Band Stand	Retrd.	1992	12.00	15
1992	Bank/Real Estate Office	Retrd.	1995	36.00	36
1993	Blacksmith Shop	Open		40.00	40
1991	Court House	Open		36.00	36
1992	Covered Bridge	Retrd.	1995	36.00	36
1990	Department Store	Retrd.	1993	25.00	29
1991	Fire House	Open		40.00	40
1994	Gazebo/Bandstand	Open		25.00	25
1990	The Gerber House	Retrd.	1993	30.00	30
1992	Library	Open		32.00	32
1993	Livery Stable and Residence	Open		40.00	40
1990	Mason's Hotel and Saloon	Open		35.00	35
1991	Methodist Church	Open		40.00	40
1992	Miss Fountains Boarding House	Open		48.00	48
1990	Pleasantville Library	Open		32.00	32
1992	Post Office	Retrd.	1995	40.00	40
1992	Railroad Station	Open		40.00	40
1990	Reverend Littlefield's House	Open		34.00	34
1994	Sacred Heart Catholic Church	Open		40.00	40
1994	Sacred Heart Rectory	Open		40.00	40
1991	School House	Open		36.00	36
1990	Sweet Shoppe & Bakery	Open		40.00	40
1990	Toy Store	Retrd.	1992	30.00	45
1992	Tubbs, Jr. House	Open		40.00	40

Pleasantville 1893 Members Only - J. Berg Victor

1992	Pleasantville Gazette Building	Open		30.00	30

Pocket Dragon Collector Club - R. Musgrave

1991	Collecting Butterflies	Retrd.	1992	Gift	95
1992	The Key to My Heart	Retrd.	1993	Gift	110
1993	Want A Bite?	Retrd.	1994	Gift	55
1993	Bitsy	Retrd.	1994	Gift	N/A
1994	Friendship Pin	Open		Gift	85
1994	Blue Ribbon Dragon	Retrd.	1995	Gift	75
1995	Making Time For You	5/96		Gift	N/A

Pocket Dragon Members Only Pieces - R. Musgrave

1991	A Spot of Tea Won't You Join Us (set)	Retrd.	1992	75.00	265
1991	Wizard's House Print	Retrd.	1993	39.95	65-100
1992	Book Nook	Retrd.	1993	140.00	200
1993	Pen Pals	Retrd.	1994	90.00	135
1994	The Best Seat in the House	Retrd.	1995	75.00	150
1995	Party Time	5/96		75.00	75

Pocket Dragon Appearance Figurines - R. Musgrave

1993	A Big Hug	Retrd.	1994	35.00	50
1994	Packed and Ready	Retrd.	1995	47.00	47
1994	Attention to Detail	Open		24.00	24

Pocket Dragon Christmas Editions - R. Musgrave

1992	A Pocket-Sized Tree	Retrd.	1992	18.95	75-90
1993	Christmas Angel	Retrd.	1993	45.00	65-90
1991	I've Been Very Good	Retrd.	1991	37.50	125
1989	Putting Me on the Tree	Retrd.	1994	52.50	75
1994	Dear Santa	Retrd.	1995	50.00	65
1995	Chasing Snowflakes	Retrd.	1995	35.00	35
1996	Christmas Skates	Yr.Iss.		36.00	36

Pocket Dragons - R. Musgrave

1990	The Apprentice	Retrd.	1994	22.50	45
1989	Attack	Retrd.	1992	45.00	90
1989	Baby Brother	Retrd.	1992	19.50	40
1993	Bath Time	Retrd.	1995	90.00	90
1993	The Book End	Open		90.00	90
1994	A Book My Size	Open		30.00	30
1992	Bubbles	Open		55.00	55
1995	But I am Too Little!	Open		14.50	15
1994	Butterfly Kissess	Open		29.50	30
1994	Candy Cane	Open		55.00	55
1995	Classical Dragon	Open		80.00	80
1994	Coffee Please	Open		24.00	24
1996	D-Pressing	Open		28.00	28
1994	Dance Partner	Open		23.00	23
1992	A Different Drummer	Retrd.	1994	32.50	50
1989	Do I Have To?	Open		45.00	45
1991	Dragons in the Attic	Retrd.	1995	120.00	120
1989	Drowsy Dragon	Open		27.50	28
1995	Elementary My Dear	Open		35.00	35
1989	Flowers For You	Retrd.	1992	42.50	145
1991	Friends	Open		55.00	55
1993	Fuzzy Ears	Open		16.50	17
1989	The Gallant Defender	Retrd.	1992	36.50	95
1989	Gargoyle Hoping For Raspberry Teacakes	Retrd.	1990	139.50	485-600
1994	Gargoyles Just Wanna Have Fun	Open		30.00	30
1989	A Good Egg	Retrd.	1991	36.50	150-165
1995	Hedgehog's Joke	Open		27.00	27
1993	I Ate the Whole Thing	Open		32.50	33
1991	I Didn't Mean To	Open		32.50	33
1991	I'm A Kitty	Retrd.	1993	37.50	55-70
1996	I'm So Pretty	Open		22.50	23
1994	In Trouble Again	Open		35.00	35
1995	It's a Present	Open		21.00	21
1994	It's Dark Out There	Open		45.00	45
1994	It's Magic	Open		31.00	31
1991	A Joyful Noise	Open		16.50	17
1992	The Juggler	Open		32.50	33
1993	Let's Make Cookies	Open		90.00	90
1992	The Library Cat	Retrd.	1994	38.50	65-85
1993	Little Bit (lapel pin)	Open		16.50	17
1993	Little Jewel (brooch)	Retrd.	1994	19.50	30
1994	A Little Security	Open		20.00	20
1989	Look at Me	Retrd.	1990	42.50	175
1992	Mitten Toes	Open		16.50	17
1994	My Big Cookie	Open		35.00	35
1992	Nap Time	Open		15.00	15
1989	New Bunny Shoes	Retrd.	1992	28.50	75
1989	No Ugly Monsters Allowed	Retrd.	1992	47.50	81
1993	Oh Goody!	Open		16.50	17
1990	One-Size-Fits-All	Retrd.	1993	16.50	35
1992	Oops!	Open		16.50	17
1989	Opera Gargoyle	Retrd.	1991	85.00	225
1992	Percy	Retrd.	1994	70.00	105
1991	Pick Me Up	Retrd.	1995	16.50	17
1996	Pillow Fight	3,500		157.00	157
1989	Pink 'n' Pretty	Retrd.	1992	23.90	55
1994	Playing Dress Up	Open		30.00	30
1991	Playing Footsie	Retrd.	1994	16.50	25-30
1989	Pocket Dragon Countersign	Retrd.	1991	50.00	195
1989	The Pocket Minstrel	Retrd.	1991	36.50	125
1996	Pocket Piper	Open		37.00	37
1992	Pocket Posey	Retrd.	1995	16.50	17
1993	Pocket Rider (brooch)	Retrd.	1995	19.50	20
1991	Practice Makes Perfect	Retrd.	1993	32.50	57
1991	Putt Putt	Retrd.	1993	37.50	55
1996	Quartet	Open		80.00	80
1994	Raiding the Cookie Jar	3,500	1995	200.00	200
1993	Reading the Good Parts	Open		70.00	70
1996	Red Ribbon	Open		16.50	17
1991	Scales of Injustice	Open		45.00	45
1989	Scribbles	Retrd.	1994	32.50	45
1989	Sea Dragon	Retrd.	1991	45.00	165
1995	Sees All, Knows All	Open		35.00	35
1989	Sir Nigel Smythebe-Smoke	Retrd.	1993	120.00	150-225
1991	Sleepy Head	Retrd.	1995	37.50	38
1994	Snuggles	Open		35.00	35
1989	Stalking the Cookie Jar	Open		27.50	28
1989	Storytime at Wizard's House	Retrd.	1993	375.00	475
1996	Sweetie Pie	Open		28.00	28
1990	Tag-A-Long	Retrd.	1993	15.00	35
1989	Teddy Magic	Retrd.	1991	85.00	100-145
1995	Telling Secrets	Open		48.00	48
1991	Thimble Foot	Retrd.	1994	38.50	50-85
1991	Tickle	Open		27.50	28
1989	Toady Goldtrayler	Retrd.	1993	55.00	90-110
1993	Treasure	Open		90.00	90
1995	Tumbly	Open		21.00	21
1991	Twinkle Toes	Retrd.	1995	16.50	17
1992	Under the Bed	2,500	1995	450.00	475
1989	Walkies	Retrd.	1992	65.00	165-185
1996	Watcha Doin	Open		22.50	23
1995	Watson	Open		22.50	23
1993	We're Very Brave	Open		37.50	38
1989	What Cookie?	Open		38.50	39
1989	Wizardry for Fun and Profit	Retrd.	1992	375.00	400-600
1993	You Can't Make Me	Open		15.00	15
1989	Your Paint is Stirred	Retrd.	1991	42.50	125
1992	Zoom Zoom	Open		37.50	38

Forma Vitrum

Annual Christmas - B. Job

1995	Confectioner's Cottage 41101	2,500	1995	100.00	100

Coastal Classics - B. Job

1995	Bayside Beacon Lighthouse 21013	Open		65.00	65
1996	Cape Hope Lighthouse 21014	Open		100.00	100
1993	Carolina Lighthouse 21003	Open		65.00	65
1996	Cozy Cottage 21500	Open		70.00	70
1994	Lookout Point Lighthouse 21012	Open		60.00	60
1993	Maine Lighthouse 21002	Open		50.00	50
1993	Michigan Lighthouse 21001	Open		50.00	50
1994	Patriot's Point 29010	Open		70.00	70
1994	Sailor's Knoll Lighthouse 21011	Open		65.00	65

Coastal Heritage - B. Job

1996	Cape Hatteras (NC) 25102	3,867		120.00	120
1995	Cape Neddick (ME) 25002	1,995	1995	140.00	140
1996	Fire Island (NY) 25005	2,996		150.00	150
1995	Marble Head (OH) 25201	1,995	1995	75.00	75
1996	New London (CT) 25004	2,996		145.00	145
1995	North Head (WA) 25302	1,995	1995	100.00	100
1995	Old Point Loma (CA) 25301	1,995	1995	100.00	100
1996	Peggy's Cove (NS) 25501	2,500		75.00	75
1996	Pigeon Point (CA) 25303	2,996		125.00	125
1995	Portland Head (ME) 25003	1,995	1995	140.00	140
1995	Sandy Hook (NJ) 25001	3,759	1995	140.00	140
1996	Split Rock (MN) 25202	2,996		130.00	130
1996	St. Augustine (FL) 25103	2,996		130.00	130
1995	St. Simon's (GA) 25101	1,995	1995	120.00	120

Special Production - B. Job

1993	The Bavarian Church 11503	Retrd.	1994	90.00	125
1994	Gingerbread House 19111	1,020	1994	100.00	175-300
1995	Miller's Mill (Musical) 11304	Open		115.00	115
1993	Pillars of Faith 11504	Retrd.	1994	90.00	135-175

Vitreville™ - B. Job

1993	Breadman's Bakery 11301	Open		70.00	72
1994	Brookview Bed & Breakfast 11303	1,250	1994	295.00	400-485
1993	Candlemaker's Delight 11801	Open		60.00	65
1993	Candymaker's Cottage 11102	Open		65.00	70
1994	Community Chapel 19510	Open		95.00	95
1993	Country Church 11502	12,500	1995	100.00	115
1993	Doctor's Domain 11201	Open		70.00	74
1995	Fire Station 11403	Open		100.00	100
1996	Kramer Building 11404	Open		100.00	100
1994	Maplewood Elementary School 11401	Open		100.00	100
1995	Mayor's Manor 11205	Open		85.00	85
1993	Painter's Place 11202	Open		70.00	74
1993	Pastor's Place 11101	Open		65.00	70
1993	Roofer's Roost 11203	Retrd.	1994	70.00	74
1993	Tailor's Townhouse 11204	Retrd.	1995	70.00	74
1994	Thompson's Drug 11302	5,000	1995	140.00	150-200
1993	Tiny Town Church 11501	Open		95.00	100
1994	Trinity Church 11511	7,000		130.00	130
1994	Vitreville Post Office 11402	Open		90.00	90

Woodland Village™ - B. Job

1993	Badger House 31003	Retrd.	1996	80.00	85
1993	Chipmunk House 31005	Retrd.	1996	80.00	85
1993	Owl House 31004	Retrd.	1996	80.00	85
1993	Rabbit House 31001	Retrd.	1996	90.00	94
1993	Racoon House 31002	Retrd.	1996	80.00	85

Franklin Mint

Joys of Childhood - N. Rockwell

1976	Coasting Along	3,700		120.00	17
1976	Dressing Up	3,700		120.00	17
1976	The Fishing Hole	3,700		120.00	17
1976	Hopscotch	3,700		120.00	17
1976	The Marble Champ	3,700		120.00	17
1976	The Nurse	3,700		120.00	17
1976	Ride 'Em Cowboy	3,700		120.00	17
1976	The Stilt Walker	3,700		120.00	17
1976	Time Out	3,700		120.00	17
1976	Trick or Treat	3,700		120.00	17

Fraser International

Collectors' Society - I. Fraser

1993	Peace Haven	Retrd.	1993	39.95	4
1993	Granny Smith's Cottage	Retrd.	1994	25.00	2
1993	St. Stephen's Church	Retrd.	1994	59.50	6
1994	Granny Mac Gregor's Cottage	7/95		29.95	3
1994	Summer Retreat	Yr.Iss.		34.75	3

Countryside in Miniature Collection - I. Fraser

1988	Acorn Cottage 15	Retrd.	1993	34.00	2
1988	The Barge's Base 58	Retrd.	1993	270.00	27
1991	Belle Cottage 106	Retrd.	1993	17.00	[illegible]
1988	Black Isle Cottage 121	Retrd.	1993	32.00	3
1988	The Blacksmith 09	Retrd.	1993	28.00	2
1988	Bluebell Cottage 04	Retrd.	1991	27.00	2
1988	Boatman's House 91	Retrd.	1993	39.00	3
1988	Bridge House 67	Retrd.	1993	27.00	2
1990	Bull & Bush 100	Retrd.	1993	54.00	[illegible]
1991	But 'N' Ben 104	Retrd.	1993	17.00	[illegible]
1988	Camelot 23 (beige)	Retrd.	1990	44.75	[illegible]
1988	Camelot 23 (gray)	Retrd.	1990	44.75	[illegible]
1988	Camelot 23 (white)	Retrd.	1990	44.75	[illegible]
1990	Castle of Monte Crisco 101	Retrd.	1993	149.75	1

*Quotes have been rounded up to nearest dollar

YEAR ISSUE		EDITION LIMIT	YEAR RETD.	ISSUE PRICE	*QUOTE U.S.$
1988	The Chandlery 31 mold #1	Retrd.	1989	54.00	54
1989	The Chandlery 31 mold #2	Retrd.	1993	54.00	54
1988	Chester House 84	Retrd.	1993	75.00	75
1988	Cornish Cottage 35	Retrd.	1990	57.00	57
1988	Cornish-Tin-Mine 18	Retrd.	1990	35.75	36
1988	Cotswold Cottage 20	Retrd.	1990	39.00	39
1988	Cove Cottage 82	Retrd.	1993	32.00	32
1988	Creel Cottage 83	Retrd.	1993	37.00	37
1988	Crooked House 171	Retrd.	1993	37.00	37
1988	Devon Cottage 64	Retrd.	1993	34.00	34
1988	Drover Cottage 85	Retrd.	1991	22.50	23
1988	Fern Cottage 70	Retrd.	1993	21.00	21
1989	Fisherman's Cottage 30	Retrd.	1993	49.50	50
1988	Fisherman's Wharf 66	Retrd.	1991	89.75	90
1991	Fishers Wynd 110	Retrd.	1993	32.00	32
1991	Follyfoot 112	Retrd.	1993	37.00	37
1988	The Forge 47 mold #1	Retrd.	1988	115.00	115
1988	The Forge 47 mold #2	Retrd.	1993	115.00	115
1988	The Forge on Plinth 48	Retrd.	1993	135.00	135
1991	Grannie's Heiland Home 108	Retrd.	1993	21.00	21
1988	Green Gables 19	Retrd.	1990	39.00	39
1988	Greystone Manor 92	Retrd.	1993	54.00	54
1988	Harbor Base 57	Retrd.	1993	140.00	140
1988	Hawthorn Cottage 01	Retrd.	1993	21.00	21
1990	Heather Lea 97	Retrd.	1993	21.00	21
1988	Highbury House 59	Retrd.	1990	101.75	102
1988	Highland Croft 12 mold #1	Retrd.	1990	32.00	32
1990	Highland Croft mold #2	Retrd.	1990	32.00	32
1988	Highland House 81	Retrd.	1993	63.50	64
1988	Hillview Base 56	Retrd.	1993	137.80	138
1988	The Homestead 34	Retrd.	1993	57.00	57
1988	Honeymoon Cottage 87	Retrd.	1993	25.00	65
1991	Horseshoe Inn 115	Retrd.	1993	39.00	39
1988	Irish Cottage 03	Retrd.	1993	25.00	25
1988	Ivy Mews 60	Retrd.	1993	45.00	45
1991	Kent Oast House 123	Retrd.	1993	37.00	37
1988	Kent Oast House 41	Retrd.	1990	75.00	75
1990	Killarney Cottage 96	Retrd.	1993	63.50	64
1988	Lake View 11	Retrd.	1992	28.00	28
1988	Lavender Lane 24	Retrd.	1993	42.00	42
1991	Lifeboat House 118	Retrd.	1993	54.00	54
1988	Lighthouse 17	Retrd.	1993	32.00	32
1988	Lilac Cottage 13	Retrd.	1990	34.00	34
1990	Linden Lea 98	Retrd.	1993	32.00	32
1991	Meadowsweet Farm 116	Retrd.	1993	39.00	39
1988	Merchant's Court 95	Retrd.	1993	291.00	291
1988	The Mill 06	Retrd.	1993	25.00	25
1988	The Millers 49	Retrd.	1991	129.00	129
1988	The Millers on Plinth 50	Retrd.	1991	159.00	159
1988	Milton Manor 36	Retrd.	1991	57.00	57
1988	Morningside 80	Retrd.	1993	300.00	300
1988	Myrtle Cottage 08	Retrd.	1993	28.00	28
1988	Oak Tree Inn 39	Retrd.	1993	69.50	70
1988	Old Antique Shop 61	Retrd.	1993	42.00	42
1988	Old Brig Inn 79	Retrd.	1993	63.50	64
1988	Old Leonach Cottage 90	Retrd.	1990	41.75	42
1988	Old Market 21	Retrd.	1993	39.00	39
1991	The Parsonage 119	Retrd.	1993	63.50	64
1991	Pebble Cottage 105	Retrd.	1993	17.00	17
1988	Ploughman's Cottage 72	Retrd.	1993	99.50	100
1988	Ploughman's Cottage on Plinth 74	Retrd.	1993	119.50	200
1988	Preston Mill 27	Retrd.	1990	45.00	45
1988	Primrose Cottage 68	Retrd.	1991	33.00	33
1988	Riverside 25	Retrd.	1993	42.00	42
1988	Robert Burns Cottage 26	Retrd.	1990	45.00	45
1991	Rock Cliff 107	Retrd.	1993	17.00	17
1988	Rose Cottage 14	Retrd.	1991	35.75	36
1988	Rowan Cottage 69	Retrd.	1993	21.00	21
1989	Sea View 29	Retrd.	1993	49.50	50
1988	Sheep Farm 16	Retrd.	1993	34.00	34
1988	Shepherd's Cottage 71	Retrd.	1993	99.50	100
1988	Shepherd's Cottage on Plinth 73	Retrd.	1993	119.50	120
1988	Smugglers Cove 05	Retrd.	1993	25.00	25
1988	Snow Church 37	Retrd.	1990	59.75	60
1988	Somerset Cottage 88	Retrd.	1992	32.75	33
1988	Springbank 65	Retrd.	1990	41.75	42
1988	St. Andrews Church 10 mold #1	Retrd.	1990	32.00	32
1990	St. Andrews Church mold #2	Retrd.	1990	32.00	32
1991	St. David's Church 117	Retrd.	1993	42.00	42
1990	St. Georges Church 102	Retrd.	1993	32.00	32
1988	Staging Post 55	Retrd.	1992	389.75	390
1988	Summerside 62	Retrd.	1991	45.00	45
1988	Swan Inn 22	Retrd.	1993	39.00	39
1988	Sweet Hope 07	Retrd.	1993	32.00	32
1988	The Thatchers 51 mold #1	Retrd.	1988	124.00	124
1988	The Thatchers 51 mold #2	Retrd.	1993	124.00	300
1988	The Thatchers on Plinth 52	Retrd.	1993	149.50	150
1991	Tintagel Post Office 122	Retrd.	1993	42.00	42
1988	Tudor Court 53 mold #1	Retrd.	1988	129.00	129
1988	Tudor Court 53 mold #2	Retrd.	1990	129.00	129
1988	Tudor Court on Plinth 54 mold #1	Retrd.	1988	149.50	150
1988	Tudor Court on Plinth 54 mold #2	Retrd.	1990	149.50	250
1988	Tweedale Cottage 89	Retrd.	1991	38.75	39
1991	Village Post Office 114	Retrd.	1993	37.00	37
1988	The Wedding 45 mold #1	Retrd.	1990	115.00	115
1990	The Wedding 45 mold #2	Retrd.	1993	115.00	115
1988	The Wedding on Plinth 46 mold #1	Retrd.	1990	135.00	135
1990	The Wedding on Plinth 46 mold #2	Retrd.	1993	135.00	350
1988	Woodcutters Cottage 63	Retrd.	1991	45.00	45
1988	Yeoman's Cottage 86	Retrd.	1993	25.00	25

Ganz

Back to Basics Collection - C. Thammavongsa

YEAR ISSUE		EDITION LIMIT	YEAR RETD.	ISSUE PRICE	*QUOTE U.S.$
1996	Back to Basics Cabin	Open		25.00	25
1996	Campfire	Open		23.00	23
1996	Camping Out	Open		17.00	17
1996	Canoe Trip	Open		20.00	20
1996	Cub Scout	Open		8.50	9
1996	Family Picnic	Open		25.00	25
1996	Fishing Buddies	Open		23.00	23
1996	Honey Bear	Open		19.00	19
1996	Nature Walk	Open		15.00	15
1996	Sweet Tooth	Open		15.00	15
1996	Under the Stars	Open		12.00	12
1996	Wild Berries	Open		12.00	12

Blazing Spirits Collection - Ganz

1995	Freedom's Foal	Open		75.00	75
1995	Racing The Wind	Open		55.00	55
1995	Wild Stallion	Open		55.00	55

Carnival Classico Collection - Ganz

1995	Columbina	Open		52.00	52
1995	Harlequin	Open		52.00	52
1995	Jester	Open		52.00	52
1995	Pierrot	Open		52.00	52
1995	Spaventa	Open		52.00	52
1995	Tartaglia	Open		52.00	52

Cock-A-Doodle Corners Collection - C.Thammavongsa

1995	Cock-a-Doodle Corners Sign	Open		16.00	16
1995	Coffee Clutch	Open		24.00	24
1995	Country Courting	Open		20.00	20
1995	Follow the Leader	Open		24.00	24
1995	Fresh-Baked	Open		16.50	17
1995	Great Eggspectations	Open		15.00	15
1995	Hen Packed	Open		17.00	17
1995	Home Remedy	Open		21.00	21
1995	Master Craftsman	Open		18.00	18
1995	New Arrival	Open		10.00	10
1995	Organically Grown	Open		22.00	22
1995	Poultry Patrol	Open		16.50	17

Cottage Collectibles Collection - Ganz

1995	Bath Time	Open		17.00	17
1995	Best Friends	Open		16.00	16
1995	Circus Parade	Open		23.00	23
1995	First Love	Open		20.00	20
1995	Goin' Fishin'	Open		16.00	16
1995	Grandma's Treasures	Open		25.00	25
1995	A Job Well Done...	Open		25.00	25
1995	My Favorite Things	Open		16.00	16
1995	Naptime	Open		23.00	23
1995	Play Time	Open		23.00	23
1995	School Days	Open		16.00	16
1995	Tea Time	Open		23.00	23

Cowtown Collection - C.Thammavongsa

1994	Amoolia Steerheart	Open		25.00	25
1995	Bedtime Dairy Tales	Open		19.00	19
1993	Buffalo Bull Cody	Open		15.00	15
1996	Bull Cassidy & The Sundance Calf	Open		20.00	20
1993	Bull Masterson	Open		15.00	15
1993	Bull Rogers	Open		17.00	17
1993	Bull Ruth	Retrd.	1994	13.00	13
1995	Buster Cowtown	Open		15.00	15
1993	Buttermilk & Buttercup	Open		16.00	16
1995	A Calf's Best Friend	Open		12.00	12
1993	Cowlamity Jane	Open		15.00	15
1994	Cowsey Jones & The Cannonbull Express	Open		26.50	27
1993	Daisy Moo	Open		11.00	11
1995	Dracowla	Open		15.00	15
1995	Francowstein	Open		12.50	13
1994	Geronimoo	Open		17.00	17
1993	Gloria Bovine & Rudolph Bullentino	Open		20.00	20
1995	Grandma Mooses	Open		15.00	15
1994	Heiferella	Open		16.50	17
1995	Hicowatha & Moonehaha	Open		18.50	19
1995	Holy Mootrimoony	Open		20.00	20
1995	Jack-Cow-Lantern	Open		11.00	11
1993	Jethro Bovine	Retrd.	1994	15.00	15
1994	King Cowmooamooa	Open		16.50	17
1993	Lil' Orphan Angus	Open		11.00	11
1996	Lone-Wrangler	Open		15.00	15
1994	Ma & Pa Cattle	Open		23.50	24
1993	Moo West	Open		15.00	15
1995	Moother's Li'l Rascow	Open		20.00	20
1993	Old MooDonald	Open		13.50	14
1994	Pocowhantis	Open		16.50	17
1995	Scarecow	Open		11.50	12
1994	Set of Three Cacti	Open		17.00	17
1995	Steershot Annie	Open		16.50	17
1995	Supercow	Open		15.00	15
1994	Tchaicowsky	Open		19.00	19
1996	Tender Loving Cow	Open		12.50	13
1994	Texas Lonesteer	10,000		50.00	50
1995	Will Bull Hickock	Open		17.00	17
1995	Yellowsteer National Park	Open		20.00	20

Cowtown/Christmas Collection - C. Thammavongsa, unless otherwise noted

1994	Billy the Calf	Open		14.00	14
1996	Calf Ton Pickup - Chiemlowski	Open		10.00	10
1994	Christmas Cactus	Open		13.50	14
1995	Ellie-Moo's Angel	Open		11.00	11
1995	Here Comes Santa Cow	Open		17.50	18
1995	John Steere	Open		11.00	11
1995	Milk & Cookies	Open		14.50	15
1995	Moo Claus	Open		17.00	17
1995	Polar Bull	Open		17.50	18
1994	Saint Nicowlas	Open		16.00	16
1994	Santa Cows	Open		18.00	18
1994	Santa's Little Heifer	Open		12.50	13
1996	Snowbull and Friends - Chiemlowski	Open		18.00	18
1995	Twinkle Twinkle Little Steer	Open		12.00	12

Cowtown/Fall, Halloween Collection - C. Thammavongsa, unless otherwise noted

1995	Dracowla	Open		15.00	15
1996	Footbull Jersey - Chiemlowski	Open		10.00	10
1995	Francowstein	Open		12.50	13
1995	Jack-Cow-Lantern	Open		11.00	11
1996	The Mooflowers - Chiemlowski	Open		20.00	20
1995	Scarecow	Open		11.50	12

Cowtown/Valentine Collection - C.Thammavongsa

1994	I Love Moo	Open		15.00	15
1994	Robin Hoof & Maid Mooian	Open		23.00	23
1994	Romecow & Mooliet	Open		22.00	22
1994	Wanted: A Sweetheart	Open		16.00	16

Ferggie Polliwog & Friends Collection - Ganz/B. Lemaire

1996	Band-Aids	Open		15.00	15
1996	Beach Buddies	Open		14.00	14
1996	Frog Prince	Open		15.00	15
1996	Froggie Tales	Open		19.00	19
1996	Hi-Ho Fishy!	Open		19.00	19
1996	The Jitterbug Band	Open		21.00	21
1996	Lawnmower Man	Open		15.00	15
1996	Leap Frog	Open		15.00	15
1996	Lilypad League	Open		17.00	17
1996	Moonlight Serenade	Open		20.00	20
1996	No Fishing! Sign	Open		16.00	16
1996	No Place Like Home	Open		17.00	17

Grandma's Attic Collection - C.Thammavongsa

1995	Balderdash	Open		25.00	25
1995	Bumblebeary	Open		10.00	10
1995	Coco & Jiffy	Open		11.00	11
1995	Crumples & Creampuff	Open		13.50	14
1995	Dilly-Dally	Open		13.50	14
1995	Dumblekin	Open		19.00	19
1995	Jelly-Belly	Open		12.00	12
1995	Molly-Coddle	Open		16.00	16
1995	Prince Fuddle-Duddle & Princess Dazzle	Open		17.00	17
1995	Sprinkles	Open		15.00	15
1995	Tootoo	Open		10.00	10

Grandma's Attic/Easter, Springtime Collection - C.Thammavongsa

1995	Hucklebeary	Open		14.50	15
1995	Lambie-Pie	Open		14.50	15
1995	Slugger	Open		13.00	13

Grandma's Attic/Valentine Collection - C.Thammavongsa

1995	Abracadabra	Open		14.00	14
1995	Cuddles	Open		12.00	12
1995	Skippy and Marmalade	Open		23.00	23
1995	Tickles and Giggles	Open		20.00	20

The Lacewing Fairies Collection - Ganz/B. Lemaire

1995	Lacewing Fairies Sign	Open		10.00	10
1995	Liana & Her Spellbounde Prince	Open		37.00	37
1995	Liana - Spirit of the Woodes	Open		30.00	30
1995	Liana - The Butterflye Maiden	Open		26.50	27
1995	Salina - Enchantress of the Sea	Open		35.00	35
1995	Salina - Midsummer Night's Dreame	Open		36.00	36
1995	Salina - the Faerie Queene	Open		37.00	37

Little Cheesers/Collectors' Club Pieces - C.Thammavongsa

1993	Charter Member	Closed	1994	27.00	27
1994	Fireweed Fox	Closed	1995	15.00	15
1995	Welcome to the Club	5/96		27.00	27
1995	The Invention	5/96		15.00	15

Little Cheesers/Cheeserville Fall - C.Thammavongsa

1995	Bewitched	Open		8.50	9
1995	Candy Bandit	Open		8.50	9
1995	Cornucopia	Open		10.00	10
1995	Peace Offering	Open		8.50	9
1995	Pilgrims	Open		15.50	16
1995	Pumpkin Patch	Open		8.00	8

Little Cheesers/Cheeserville Picnic Collection - G.D.A. Group, unless otherwise noted

1991	Auntie Marigold Eating Cookie	Open		13.00	13

*Quotes have been rounded up to nearest dollar

Ganz
to Ganz

FIGURINES/COTTAGES

YEAR ISSUE		EDITION LIMIT	YEAR RETD.	ISSUE PRICE	*QUOTE U.S.$
1991	Baby Cicely	Retrd.	1995	8.00	8
1991	Baby Truffle	Open		8.00	8
1991	Blossom & Hickory In Love	Open		19.00	19
1995	Cheeserville Tales - C.Thammavongsa	Open		7.50	8
1993	Chuckles The Clown - C.Thammavongsa	Open		16.00	16
1993	Clownin' Around - C.Thammavongsa	Open		10.50	11
1991	Cousin Woody With Bread and Fruit	Open		14.00	14
1991	Fellow With Picnic Hamper	Retrd.	1991	13.00	13
1991	Fellow With Plate Of Cookies	Retrd.	1991	13.00	13
1994	Fiddle-Dee-Dee - C.Thammavongsa	Open		13.00	13
1993	For Someone Special - C.Thammavongsa	Open		13.50	14
1991	Grandmama Thistledown Holding Bread	Open		14.00	14
1991	Grandpapa Thistledown Carrying Basket	Open		13.00	13
1991	Harley Harvestmouse Waving	Open		13.00	13
1991	Harriet Harvestmouse	Retrd.	1993	13.00	13
1995	Hush-A-Bye Baby - C.Thammavongsa	Open		14.00	14
1991	Jenny Butterfield Kneeling	Open		13.00	13
1991	Jeremy Butterfield	Open		13.00	13
1995	Joyful Beginnings - C.Thammavongsa	Open		15.00	15
1991	Lady With Grapes	Retrd.	1991	14.00	14
1993	Little Cheesers Display Plaque - C.Thammavongsa	Open		25.00	25
1991	Little Truffle Eating Grapes	Open		8.00	8
1991	Little Truffle Smelling Flowers	Retrd.	1995	16.50	17
1991	Mama Fixing Sweet Cicely's Hair	Retrd.	1993	16.50	17
1991	Mama With Rolling Pin	Open		13.00	13
1991	Mama Woodsworth With Crate	Retrd.	1992	14.00	14
1991	Marigold Thistledown Picking Up Jar	Open		14.00	14
1991	Medley Meadowmouse w/ Bouquet	Open		13.00	13
1994	Melody Maker - C.Thammavongsa	Retrd.	1995	17.00	17
1994	Ooom-Pah-Pah - C.Thammavongsa	Open		13.00	13
1991	Papa Woodsworth	Open		13.00	13
1991	Picnic Buddies	Open		19.00	19
1995	Picnic with Papa - C.Thammavongsa	Open		14.00	14
1995	Playtime - C.Thammavongsa	Open		14.00	14
1995	Read Me A Story - C.Thammavongsa	Open		15.00	15
1993	The Storyteller - C.Thammavongsa	10,000		25.00	25
1994	Strummin' Away - C.Thammavongsa	Open		13.00	13
1993	Sunday Drive - C.Thammavongsa	Open		40.00	40
1993	Sweet Dreams - C.Thammavongsa	Open		27.50	28
1994	Swingin' Sax - C.Thammavongsa	Open		13.00	13
1991	Violet With Peaches	Open		13.00	13
1994	Washboard Blues - C.Thammavongsa	Open		13.00	13
1994	What a Hoot! - C.Thammavongsa	Open		13.00	13
1993	Willy's Toe-Tappin' Tunes - C.Thammavongsa	Open		15.00	15
1993	Words Of Wisdom - C.Thammavongsa	Open		14.00	14

Little Cheesers/Cheeserville Picnic Collection Accessories - G.D.A. Group

1994	Mayflower Meadow Base	Open		50.00	50

Little Cheesers/Cheeserville Picnic Mini-Food Accessories - G.D.A. Group

1991	Basket Of Apples	Open		2.25	3
1991	Basket Of Peaches	Open		2.00	2
1991	Blueberry Cake	Retrd.	1994	2.50	3
1991	Bread Basket	Open		2.50	3
1991	Candy	Open		2.00	2
1991	Cherry Mousse	Open		2.00	2
1991	Cherry Pie	Retrd.	1991	2.00	2
1991	Chocolate Cake	Open		2.50	3
1991	Chocolate Cheesecake	Open		2.00	2
1991	Doughnut Basket	Open		2.50	3
1991	Egg Tart	Open		1.00	1
1991	Food Basket With Blue Cloth	Retrd.	1994	6.50	7
1991	Food Basket With Green Cloth	Open		7.50	8
1991	Food Basket With Pink Cloth	Retrd.	1994	6.00	6
1991	Food Basket With Purple Cloth	Open		6.00	6
1991	Food Trolley	Retrd.	1991	12.00	12
1991	Hazelnut Roll	Retrd.	1991	2.00	2
1991	Honey Jar	Retrd.	1991	2.00	2
1991	Hot Dog	Open		2.25	3
1991	Ice Cream Cup	Open		2.00	2
1991	Lemon Cake	Retrd.	1991	2.00	2
1991	Napkin In Can	Retrd.	1991	2.00	2
1991	Set Of Four Bottles	Retrd.	1991	10.00	10
1991	Strawberry Cake	Open		2.00	2
1991	Sundae	Open		2.00	2
1991	Wine Glass	Retrd.	1995	1.25	2

Little Cheesers/Cheeserville Picnic Musicals - G.D.A. Group

1994	The Bandstand Base	Open		48.50	49
1991	Blossom & Hickory Musical Jewelry Box	Closed	1992	65.00	65

YEAR ISSUE		EDITION LIMIT	YEAR RETD.	ISSUE PRICE	*QUOTE U.S.$
1991	Mama & Sweet Cicely Waterglobe	Closed	1992	55.00	55
1991	Medley Meadowmouse Waterglobe	Retrd.	1995	47.00	47
1993	Musical "Secret Treasures" Trinket Box	Open		36.00	36
1991	Musical Basket Trinket Box	Open		30.00	30
1991	Musical Floral Trinket Box	Open		32.00	32
1991	Musical Medley Meadowmouse Cookie Jar	Retrd.	1992	75.00	75
1991	Musical Picnic Base	Open		60.00	60
1991	Musical Sunflower Base	Closed	1993	65.00	65
1991	Musical Violet Woodsworth Cookie Jar	Retrd.	1992	75.00	75
1992	Sweet Cicely Musical Doll Basket	Open		85.00	85
1993	Wishing Well Musical	Open		50.00	50

Little Cheesers/Christmas Collection - C. Thammavongsa, unless otherwise noted

1991	Abner Appleton Ringing Bell	Retrd.	1993	14.00	14
1993	All I Want For Christmas - C.Thammavongsa	Open		18.00	18
1994	Angel - C.Thammavongsa	Open		8.00	8
1991	Auntie Blossom With Ornaments	Open		14.00	14
1994	Baby Jesus - C.Thammavongsa	Open		6.50	7
1991	Cheeser Snowman	Retrd.	1994	7.50	8
1993	Christmas Greetings - C.Thammavongsa	Open		16.50	17
1991	Cousin Woody Playing Flute	Open		14.00	14
1994	First Wiseman - C.Thammavongsa	Open		11.00	11
1991	Frowzy Roquefort III Skating	Retrd.	1993	14.00	14
1991	Grandmama & Little Truffle	Retrd.	1993	19.00	19
1991	Grandpapa & Sweet Cicely	Open		19.00	19
1991	Grandpapa Blowing Horn	Retrd.	1994	14.00	14
1991	Great Aunt Rose With Tray	Open		14.00	14
1991	Harley & Harriet Dancing	Retrd.	1993	19.00	19
1991	Hickory Playing Cello	Retrd.	1994	14.00	14
1991	Jenny On Sleigh	Open		16.00	16
1991	Jeremy With Teddy Bear	Open		12.00	12
1994	Joseph - C.Thammavongsa	Open		10.00	10
1995	Joy to the World - C.Thammavongsa	Open		8.00	8
1991	Little Truffle With Stocking	Open		8.00	8
1991	Mama Pouring Tea	Retrd.	1993	14.00	14
1991	Marigold&Oscar Stealing A Christmas Kiss	Open		19.00	19
1994	Mary - C.Thammavongsa	Open		10.00	10
1991	Medley Playing Drum	Open		8.00	8
1991	Myrtle Meadowmouse With Book	Retrd.	1993	14.00	14
1991	Santa Cheeser	Open		13.00	13
1994	Santa's Sleigh - C.Thammavongsa	10,000		22.00	22
1994	Second Wiseman - C.Thammavongsa	Open		11.00	11
1994	Shepherd - C.Thammavongsa	Open		8.50	9
1993	Sleigh Ride - C.Thammavongsa	Retrd.	1995	11.00	11
1995	Tending The Flocks - C.Thammavongsa	Open		9.00	9
1994	Third Wiseman - C.Thammavongsa	Open		10.50	11
1991	Violet With Snowball	Retrd.	1994	8.00	8

Little Cheesers/Christmas Collection Accessories - Various

1993	Candleholder-Santa Cheeser - C.Thammavongsa	Open		19.00	19
1993	Candy Cane - C.Thammavongsa	Open		2.00	2
1994	Christmas Collection Base - C.Thammavongsa	Open		50.00	50
1993	Christmas Gift - C.Thammavongsa	Open		3.00	3
1993	Christmas Stocking - C.Thammavongsa	Open		3.00	3
1991	Christmas Tree	Open		9.00	9
1994	Creche Base - C.Thammavongsa	Open		28.50	29
1993	Gingerbread House - C.Thammavongsa	Open		3.00	3
1993	Ice Pond Base - C.Thammavongsa	Open		5.50	6
1991	Lamp Post	Open		8.50	9
1995	Little Cheeser Tree Topper - C.Thammavongsa	Open		34.00	34
1991	Outdoor Scene Base	Retrd.	1993	35.00	35
1991	Parlor Scene Base	Open		37.50	38
1993	Toy Soldier - C.Thammavongsa	Open		3.00	3
1993	Toy Train - C.Thammavongsa	Open		3.00	3

Little Cheesers/Christmas Collection Musicals - Various

1992	Jenny Butterfield Christmas Waterglobe - GDA/Thammavongsa	Closed	1992	55.00	55
1992	Little Truffle Christmas Waterglobe	Retrd.	1995	45.00	45
1992	Musical Santa Cheeser Roly-Poly	Suspd.		55.00	55
1993	Rotating Round Wood Base "I'll be Home for X'mas" - C.Thammavongsa	Open		30.00	30
1993	Rd. Wood Base "We Wish You a Merry X'mas" - C.Thammavongsa	Open		25.00	25

Little Cheesers/Circus Party Collection - C.Thammavongsa

1995	Balancing Act	Open		8.00	8
1995	Beep-Beep	Open		13.50	14
1995	Cheeserville Choo-Choo	Open		21.00	21
1995	Easy As Cake	Open		15.00	15
1995	Look Ma-No Hands	Open		18.00	18

YEAR ISSUE		EDITION LIMIT	YEAR RETD.	ISSUE PRICE	*QUOTE U.S.$
1995	Woops!	Open		10.50	11

Little Cheesers/Little Hoppers Collection - C.Thammavongsa

1994	Bubble Bath	Open		7.50	8
1994	Let's Play Ball	Open		7.00	7
1994	Somebunny Loves You	Open		7.50	8
1994	Sweet Nothings	Open		15.00	15
1994	Tender Loving Care	Open		10.00	10
1994	Tricycle Built for Two	Open		16.00	16

Little Cheesers/Springtime In Cheeserville Accessories - C.Thammavongsa

1992	April Showers Bring May Flowers	Open		7.50	8
1992	Decorated With Love	Open		7.50	8
1992	For Somebunny Special	Open		7.50	8

Little Cheesers/Springtime In Cheeserville Musicals - GDA/Thammavongsa

1992	Tulips & Ribbons Musical Trinket Box	Closed	1994	28.00	28

Little Cheesers/Springtime In Cheeserville Collection - C.Thammavongsa

1993	Ballerina Sweetheart	Open		10.00	10
1992	A Basket Full Of Joy	Open		16.00	16
1994	Birthday Party	Retrd.	1995	22.00	22
1993	Blossom Has A Little lamb	Open		16.50	17
1993	First Kiss	Open		24.00	24
1993	For My Sweatheart	Open		22.00	22
1993	Friends Forever	Open		22.00	22
1995	Fuzzy Friends	Open		9.00	9
1993	Gently Down The Stream	10,000		27.00	27
1994	Get Well	Open		22.00	22
1993	Gift From Heaven	Open		10.00	10
1994	Hip Hip Hooray	Open		22.00	22
1992	Hippity-Hop. It's Eastertime!	Open		16.00	16
1993	Hugs & Kisses	Open		11.00	11
1993	I Love You	Open		22.00	22
1995	Little Miracles	Open		8.00	8
1993	Playing Cupid	Open		10.00	10
1992	Springtime Delights	Open		12.00	12
1993	Sugar & Spice	Open		24.00	24
1993	Sunday Stroll	Open		22.00	22
1992	A Wheelbarrow Of Sunshine	Open		17.00	17

Little Cheesers/Valentine Collection - C.Thammavongsa

1993	Ballerina Sweetheart	Open		10.00	10
1995	Be My Angel	Open		10.50	11
1993	First Kiss	Open		24.00	24
1993	For My Sweetheart	Open		22.00	22
1993	Friends Forever	Open		22.00	22
1993	Gently Down the Stream	10,000		27.00	27
1993	Hugs & Kisses	Open		11.00	11
1993	I Love You	Open		22.00	22
1995	My L'il Sweetheart	Open		9.00	9
1993	Playing Cupid	Open		10.00	10
1993	Sugar & Spice	Open		24.00	24
1993	Sunday Stroll	Open		22.00	22

Little Cheesers/Wedding Collection - Various

1993	The Big Day - C. Thammavongsa	Open		20.00	20
1992	Blossom Thistledown (bride) - GDA/Thammavongsa	Open		16.00	16
1992	Cousin Woody & Little Truffle - GDA/Thammavongsa	Open		20.00	20
1992	Frowzy Roquefort III w/ Gramophone - GDA/Thammavongsa	Open		20.00	20
1992	Grandmama & Grandpapa Thistledown - GDA/Thammavongsa	Retrd.	1994	20.00	20
1992	Great Aunt Rose Beside Table - GDA/Thammavongsa	Open		20.00	20
1992	Harley & Harriet Harvestmouse - GDA/Thammavongsa	Open		20.00	20
1992	Hickory Harvestmouse (groom) - GDA/Thammavongsa	Open		16.00	16
1992	Jenny Butterfield/Sweet Cicely (bridesmaids) - GDA/Thammavongsa	Retrd.	1995	20.00	2[illegible]
1992	Little Truffle (ringbearer) - GDA/Thammavongsa	Open		10.00	1[illegible]
1992	Mama & Papa Woodsworth Dancing - GDA/Thammavongsa	Open		20.00	2[illegible]
1992	Marigold Thistledown & Oscar Bobbins - GDA/Thammavongsa	Open		20.00	2[illegible]
1992	Myrtle Meadowmouse With Medley - GDA/Thammavongsa	Closed	1992	20.00	2[illegible]
1992	Pastor Smallwood - GDA/Thammavongsa	Open		16.00	1[illegible]
1992	Wedding Procession - GDA/Thammavongsa	Open		40.00	4[illegible]

Little Cheesers/Wedding Collection Accessories - C. Thammavongsa

1993	Banquet Table	Open		14.00	1[illegible]
1993	Gazebo Base	Open		42.00	4[illegible]

Little Cheesers/Wedding Collection Mini-Food Accessories - Various

1992	Bible Trinket Box - GDA/Thammavongsa	Open		16.50	[illegible]
1992	Big Chocolate Cake	Retrd.	1994	4.50	[illegible]
1992	Bride Candleholder - GDA/Thammavongsa	Open		20.00	[illegible]

*Quotes have been rounded up to nearest dollar

YEAR ISSUE		EDITION LIMIT	YEAR RETD.	ISSUE PRICE	*QUOTE U.S.$
1992	Cake Trinket Box - GDA/Thammavongsa	Open		14.00	14
1992	Candles	Open		3.00	3
1992	Cherry Jello	Open		3.00	3
1992	Chocolate Pastry	Retrd.	1992	2.00	2
1992	Chocolate Pudding	Open		2.50	3
1992	Flour Bag	Retrd.	1992	2.00	2
1992	Flower Vase	Retrd.	1994	3.00	3
1992	Fruit Salad	Open		3.00	3
1993	Gooseberry Champagne - C. Thammavongsa	Open		3.00	3
1992	Grass Base - GDA/Thammavongsa	Suspd.		3.50	4
1992	Groom Candleholder - GDA/Thammavongsa	Open		20.00	20
1992	Honey Pot	Open		2.00	2
1992	Ring Cake	Open		3.00	3
1992	Salt Can	Retrd.	1992	2.00	2
1992	Souffle	Retrd.	1992	2.50	3
1992	Soup Pot	Open		3.00	3
1992	Tea Pot Set	Retrd.	1994	3.00	3
1992	Teddy Mouse	Retrd.	1994	2.00	2
1993	Wedding Cake - C. Thammavongsa	Open		4.50	5

Little Cheesers/Wedding Collection Musicals - Various

1993	Blossom & Hickory Musical - C. Thammavongsa	Retrd.	1994	50.00	50
1992	Musical Blossom & Hickory Wedding Waterglobe - GDA/Thammavongsa	Open		55.00	55
1992	Musical Wedding Base - GDA/Thammavongsa	Open		32.00	32
1992	Musical Wooden Base For Wedding Processional	Open		25.00	25
1993	Wh. Musical Wood Base For Gazebo Base "Evergreen" - C. Thammavongsa	Open		25.00	25

Magic of Saint Nicholas Collection - Ganz

1996	Holly Jolly Holidays	Open		60.00	60
1996	Magical Melodies	Open		60.00	60
1996	Twinkling Lights	Open		60.00	60

Perfect Little Place Collection - C.Thammavongsa

1995	All Star Angel	Open		14.00	14
1995	Angel Face	Open		15.00	15
1995	Angel's Food	Open		15.00	15
1996	Bless This Marriage	Open		20.00	20
1995	Divine Intervention	Open		15.00	15
1995	Heaven & Nature	Open		14.00	14
1996	Heaven Makes All Things New	Open		18.00	18
1995	Heavenly Grace	Open		14.00	14
1995	Match Made in Heaven	Open		18.00	18
1995	Paradise	Open		13.00	13
1995	Perfect Little Place	Open		16.00	16
1995	Pray the Lord My Soul to Keep	Open		13.00	13
1995	Ride Like The Wind	Open		15.00	15
1996	Showered With Love	Open		16.00	16
1995	Sweet Sleep, Angel Mild	Open		13.50	14

Perfect Little Place/Christmas Collection - C.Thammavongsa

1996	Angels in the Snow	Open		15.00	15
1995	Bearer of Blessings	Open		17.00	17
1996	Celestial Wonders	Open		17.00	17
1995	A Child is Born	Open		21.00	21
1996	Songs of Praise	Open		17.00	17

Perfect Little Place/Valentine Collection - C.Thammavongsa

1995	Be My Angel	Open		16.00	16
1995	Sweet Innocence	Open		16.00	16
1995	Whispers of Love	Open		21.00	21

Pigsville Accessories - C.Thammavongsa

1995	Bale of Straw	Open		10.00	10
1994	Barn	Open		35.00	35
1995	Outhouse	Open		10.00	10
1994	Silo	Open		15.00	15

Pigsville Collection - C.Thammavongsa, unless otherwise noted

1993	Bakin' at the Beach	Open		11.00	11
1994	Bedtime	Open		9.50	10
1994	Birthday Surprise	Open		9.50	10
1993	Ice Cream Anyone? - G.D.A. Group	Retrd.	1994	9.00	9
1995	Juke Box	Open		12.00	12
1993	Me & My Ice Cream - G.D.A. Group	Retrd.	1994	17.00	17
1996	Melon Patch	Open		11.00	11
1993	Mother Love - G.D.A. Group	Open		13.00	13
1995	Mr. Fix It	Open		14.00	14
1993	Nap Time - G.D.A. Group	Retrd.	1995	11.00	11
1994	Ole Fishing Hole	Open		16.00	16
1995	Open Roads	Open		14.00	14
1993	P.O.P Display Sign	Open		8.00	8
1995	Paradise	Open		10.00	10
1993	Pig at the Beach - G.D.A. Group	Open		9.00	9
1996	Pig Pen Blues	Open		11.00	11
1996	Pig Tails	Open		10.00	10
1995	Piggy Back	Open		10.50	11
1994	Play Ball	Open		11.50	12
1994	Pretty Piglet	Open		8.00	8
1993	Prima Ballerina	Retrd.	1994	11.00	11
1994	Sandcastle	Open		12.00	12
1995	Scrub-A-Dub-Dub	Open		13.50	14
1995	Seeds of Love	Open		14.50	15
1994	Snacktime	Open		11.50	12
1993	Soap Suds - G.D.A. Group	Open		12.00	12
1994	Special Treat	Open		11.50	12
1993	Squeaky Clean - G.D.A. Group	Retrd.	1995	11.00	11
1994	Storytime	Open		13.00	13
1993	Tipsy - G.D.A. Group	Open		9.00	9
1995	Touchdown	Open		11.00	11
1993	True Love	Open		12.00	12
1994	Wedded Bliss	Open		16.00	16
1993	Wee Little Piggy	Open		8.00	8
1996	Yard Work	Open		13.00	13

Pigsville/Christmas Collection - C.Thammavongsa, unless otherwise noted

1996	Christmas Rush - Chiemlowski	Open		14.00	14
1994	Christmas Trimmings	10,000		24.00	24
1995	Dear Santa	Open		10.00	10
1996	Holiday Hog - Chiemlowski	Open		16.00	16
1994	Joy to the World	Open		10.00	10
1994	Let It Snow	Open		12.00	12
1994	Mistletoe Magic	Open		14.00	14
1995	Mrs. Claus	Open		11.00	11
1995	Oh Christmas Tree	Open		10.50	11
1994	Santa Pig	Open		11.00	11
1995	Tucked into Bed	Open		12.00	12
1994	Yuletide Carols	Open		19.00	19

Pigsville/Fall, Halloween Collection - C.Thammavongsa, unless otherwise noted

1995	Apple Bobbing	Open		10.00	10
1995	Giving Thanks	Open		10.00	10
1996	Hell's Angel - Chiemlowski	Open		10.00	10
1996	Hobo Clown - Chiemlowski	Open		10.00	10
1995	Pumpkin Pig	Open		11.00	11
1995	Scarecrow	Open		11.00	11

Pigsville/Valentine Collection - C.Thammavongsa

1995	Barn Dance	Open		14.50	15
1994	Champagne & Roses	Open		14.00	14
1995	The Hayloft	Open		11.00	11
1994	I Love You	Open		9.50	10
1994	I'm All Yours	Open		11.50	12
1995	Lover's Lane	Open		17.00	17
1994	Lovestruck	Open		10.00	10
1995	Popping The Question	Open		10.00	10
1995	Secret Admirer	Open		11.00	11
1995	Serenade	Open		10.50	11
1994	Sweetheart Pig	Open		8.00	8
1994	Together Forever	Open		15.00	15

Portraits of a People Collection - Ganz/B. Galvin

1996	"Crazy Horse" Chief of Oglala Sioux	Open		35.00	35
1996	"Ouanah Parker" Comanche Chief	Open		24.00	24
1996	"Ouray" Ute Chief Round Plaque	Open		15.00	15
1996	"Pontiac" Ottawa Chief Square Plaque	Open		15.00	15
1996	"Sitting Bull"	Open		33.00	33
1996	"Tecumseh" Shawnee Chief	Open		25.00	25
1996	"White Arrow" Cherokee SW	Open		24.00	24
1996	"Winema" (Toby Riddle)	Open		25.00	25
1996	Cheyenne Buffalo-Horn Bonnet	Open		21.00	21

The Precious Steeples Collection - Ganz/L. Sunarth

1995	Display Sign	Open		15.00	15
1995	Florence Cathedral	Open		40.00	40
1995	Notre Dame Cathedral	Open		40.00	40
1995	St. Patrick's Cathedral	Open		40.00	40
1995	St. Paul's Cathedral	Open		40.00	40
1995	St. Peter's Basilica	Open		40.00	40
1995	Westminster Abbey	Open		40.00	40

Trains Gone By Collection - Ganz

1996	C.P. Huntington Train	3,000		70.00	70
1996	C.P. Huntington Train with sound	2,000		85.00	85
1995	Display Sign	Open		24.00	24
1995	The General Train	4,000		70.00	70
1995	The General Train with sound	1,000		85.00	85
1995	New York Central Train	3,000		70.00	70
1995	New York Central Train w/ sound	2,000		85.00	85
1995	Pennsylvania Train	4,000		70.00	70
1995	Pennsylvania Train with sound	1,000		85.00	85
1995	Santa Fe Train with sound	1,000		85.00	85
1995	Santa FeTrain	4,000		70.00	70

Watching Over You Collection - C.Thammavongsa

1995	Angelic Teachings	Open		42.00	42
1996	It Is Written...	Open		40.00	40
1995	New Borne Babe	Open		40.00	40
1995	Sweet Dreams Little One	Open		38.00	38

Watching Over You Collection Musicals - C.Thammavongsa

1996	Sweet Music Fills the Air	Open		60.00	60

Woodland Santas Collection - C.Thammavongsa

1995	Forest Friends	Open		45.00	45
1995	Lake of the Woods	Open		45.00	45
1995	Santa's Sanctuary	Open		41.00	41

Zoological Zodiac Collection - Ganz/B. Lemaire

1996	Aries	Open		25.00	25
1996	Taurus	Open		25.00	25
1996	Gemini	Open		25.00	25
1996	Cancer	Open		25.00	25
1996	Leo	Open		25.00	25
1996	Virgo	Open		25.00	25
1996	Libra	Open		25.00	25
1996	Scorpio	Open		25.00	25
1996	Sagittarius	Open		25.00	25
1996	Capricorn	Open		25.00	25
1996	Aquarius	Open		25.00	25
1996	Pisces	Open		25.00	25

Gartlan USA

Members Only Figurine

1990	Wayne Gretzky-Home Uniform - L. Heyda	N/A	1991	75.00	200-250
1991	Joe Montana-Road Uniform - F. Barnum	N/A	1992	75.00	150-250
1991	Kareem Abdul-Jabbar - L. Heyda	N/A	1993	75.00	175-250
1992	Mike Schmidt - J. Slockbower	N/A	1993	79.00	150-200
1993	Hank Aaron - J. Slockbower	N/A	1994	79.00	100-125
1994	Shaquille O'Neal - L. Cella	N/A	1995	39.95	75-100

Kareem Abdul-Jabbar Sky-Hook Collection - L. Heyda

1989	Kareem Abdul-Jabbar "The Captain"-signed	1,989	1990	175.00	300-550
1989	Kareem Abdul-Jabbar, A/P	100	1990	200.00	550-700
1989	Kareem Abdul-Jabbar, Commemorative	33	1990	275.00	4700-5300

Leave It To Beaver - Noble Studio

1995	Jerry Mathers, (5")	5,000		49.95	50
1995	Jerry Mathers, (7 1/2") signed	1,963		195.00	195
1996	Jerry Mathers, A/P (7 1/2") signed	234		250.00	250

Magic Johnson Gold Rim Collection - Roger

1988	Magic Johnson -"Magic in Motion"	1,737	1989	125.00	500-1000
1988	Magic Johnson A/P-"Magic in Motion", signed	250	1989	175.00	2500
1988	Magic Johnson Commemorative	32	1989	275.00	7500

Mike Schmidt "500th" Home Run Edition - Various

1987	Figurine-signed - Roger	1,987	1988	150.00	750-850
1987	Figurine-signed, A/P - Roger	20	1988	275.00	1400-1700

Plaques - Various

1986	George Brett-"Royalty in Motion", signed - J. Martin	2,000	1987	75.00	275
1987	Mike Schmidt-"Only Perfect", A/P - Paluso	20	1988	200.00	550
1987	Mike Schmidt-"Only Perfect", signed - Paluso	500	1988	150.00	225-400
1985	Pete Rose-"Desire to Win", signed - T. Sizemore	4,192	1986	75.00	325
1986	Reggie Jackson A/P-The Roundtripper, signed - J. Martin	44	1987	175.00	400-475
1986	Reggie Jackson-"The Roundtripper" signed - J. Martin	500	1987	150.00	350-400
1987	Roger Staubach, signed - C. Soileau	1,979	1988	85.00	250-325

Ringo Starr - J. Hoffman

1996	Ringo Starr with drums, (6")	5,000		125.00	125
1996	Ringo Starr, (4")	10,000		49.95	50
1996	Ringo Starr, (8 1/2") A/P signed	250		600.00	600
1996	Ringo Starr, (8 1/2") signed	1,000		350.00	350

Signed Figurines - Various

1991	Al Barlick - V. Bova	1,989	1995	195.00	195
1993	Bob Cousy - L. Heyda	950	1995	150.00	150
1991	Bobby Hull - The Golden Jet - L. Heyda	1,983	1995	250.00	250-300
1992	Bobby Hull, A/P - L. Heyda	300	1994	350.00	400-600
1991	Brett Hull - The Golden Brett - L. Heyda	1,986	1995	250.00	250-300
1992	Brett Hull, A/P - L. Heyda	300	1994	350.00	400-600
1989	Carl Yastrzemski-"Yaz", A/P - L. Heyda	250	1990	150.00	500-800
1989	Carl Yastrzemski-"Yaz" - L. Heyda	1,989	1990	150.00	400
1992	Carlton Fisk - J. Slockbower	1,972	1995	225.00	225
1990	Darryl Strawberry - L. Heyda	2,500	1995	100.00	100
1994	Eddie Matthews - R. Sun	1,978	1995	195.00	200-300
1994	Frank Thomas - D. Carroll	500	1995	225.00	250-300
1990	George Brett - F. Barnum	2,250	1995	225.00	250
1992	Gordie Howe - L. Heyda	2,358	1994	225.00	250-350
1990	Gordie Howe, signed A/P - L. Heyda	250	1994	395.00	395
1992	Hank Aaron - F. Barnum	1,982	1994	225.00	225
1992	Hank Aaron Commemorative w/displ. case - F. Barnum	755	1994	275.00	400
1991	Hull Matched Figurines - L. Heyda	950	1993	500.00	500-700
1989	Joe DiMaggio - L. Heyda	2,214	1990	275.00	1500

YEAR ISSUE		EDITION LIMIT	YEAR RETD.	ISSUE PRICE	*QUOTE U.S.$
1990	Joe DiMaggio- Pinstripe Yankee Clipper - L. Heyda	325	1990	695.00	2600
1990	Joe DiMaggio- Pinstripe Yankee Clipper, A/P - L. Heyda	12	1990	1500.00	4000-8000
1991	Joe Montana - F. Barnum	2,250	1991	325.00	675
1991	Joe Montana, A/P - F. Barnum	250	1991	500.00	700-1100
1989	John Wooden-Coaching Classics - L. Heyda	1,975	1995	175.00	175
1989	John Wooden-Coaching Classics, A/P - L. Heyda	250	1995	350.00	350
1989	Johnny Bench - L. Heyda	1,989	1990	150.00	225
1989	Johnny Bench, A/P - L. Heyda	250	1990	150.00	500-725
1994	Ken Griffey Jr., - J. Slockbower	1,989	1995	225.00	225
1993	Kristi Yamaguchi - K. Ling Sun	950	1995	195.00	195
1990	Luis Aparicio - J. Slockbower	1,984	1995	225.00	225
1991	Monte Irvin - V. Bova	1,973	1995	195.00	195
1991	Negro League, Set/3	950	1995	500.00	500
1985	Pete Rose-"For the Record", signed - H. Reed	4,192	1987	125.00	1100-1500
1992	Ralph Kiner - J. Slockbower	1,975	1995	225.00	225
1991	Rod Carew - Hitting Splendor - J. Slockbower	1,991	1995	225.00	225
1994	Sam Snead - L. Cella	950	1995	225.00	225
1994	Shaquille O'Neal - R. Sun	500	1995	225.00	300-500
1992	Stan Musial - J. Slockbower	1,969	1995	325.00	325
1992	Stan Musial, A/P - J. Slockbower	300	1995	425.00	425
1989	Steve Carlton - L. Heyda	3,290	1992	175.00	225-325
1989	Steve Carlton, A/P - L. Heyda	300	1992	350.00	400-500
1989	Ted Williams - L. Heyda	2,654	1990	295.00	400-800
1989	Ted Williams, A/P - L. Heyda	250	1990	650.00	700-1000
1992	Tom Seaver - J. Slockbower	1,992	1995	225.00	225
1994	Troy Aikman - V. Davila	500	1995	225.00	275-450
1991	Warren Spahn - J. Slockbower	1,973	1995	225.00	275
1989	Wayne Gretzky - L. Heyda	1,851	1989	225.00	600-1000
1989	Wayne Gretzky, A/P - L. Heyda	300	1989	695.00	1800-2300
1990	Whitey Ford - S. Barnum	2,360	1995	225.00	225
1990	Whitey Ford, A/P - S. Barnum	250	1995	350.00	350
1989	Yogi Berra - F. Barnum	2,150	1994	225.00	225
1989	Yogi Berra, A/P - F. Barnum	250	1994	350.00	350

Genesis

Aquatics Collection - K. Cantrell

1994	Ancient Mariner (Sea Turtles)	950		950.00	990
1994	Bringing Up Baby (Humpback Whales)	950		950.00	990
1994	Old Men of the Sea (Sea Otters)	950		990.00	990
1994	Sea Wolves (Killer Whales)	950		950.00	990
1994	Splish Splash (Dolphins)	950		950.00	990

Arctic Collection - K. Cantrell

1995	Arctic Hares	2,500	1995	98.00	98
1995	Arctic Owl	2,500	1995	98.00	98
1995	Arctic Wolves	2,500	1995	98.00	98
1995	Harp Seal	2,500	1995	98.00	98
1995	Polar Bear	2,500	1995	98.00	98

Birds of Prey - K. Cantrell

1994	Bald Eagle	1,250		350.00	350
1994	Great Horned Owl	1,250		350.00	350

The Lighthouse Collection - L. Steorts

1995	Boston Light	2,500		170.00	170
1995	Cape Hatteras	2,500		170.00	170
1996	North Head	2,500		170.00	170
1996	Old Point Loma	2,500		170.00	170

Neptune's Children - K. Cantrell

1995	Neptune's Children	1,250		290.00	290
1995	Tranquil Waters	1,250		290.00	290

Ocean Realm - K. Cantrell

1994	Dolphins	1,250	1996	240.00	250
1994	Humpback Whales	1,250		240.00	250
1994	Manta Ray	1,250		240.00	250
1994	Marlins	1,250		240.00	250
1994	Otters	1,250		240.00	250

River Dwellers - K. Cantrell

1994	Construction Crew	950		990.00	990
1994	Ice Follies	950		890.00	950
1994	Salmon Supper	950		990.00	990

Sea Scapes Collection - K. Cantrell

1996	Exuberant	500		750.00	750
1996	Fluid Motion	500		750.00	750

Special Commission - K. Cantrell

1994	Fragile Planet	950		350.00	350
1995	Heavenly Waters	950		N/A	N/A

Geo. Zoltan Lefton Company

Colonial Village - Lefton

1993	Antiques & Curiosities 00723	Open		50.00	50
1995	Applegate-CVRA Exclusive 01327	Closed	1995	50.00	50
1990	The Ardmore House 07338	Closed	1995	45.00	90
1993	Baldwin's Fine Jewelry 00722	Open		50.00	50
1991	Belle-Union Saloon 07482	Closed	1994	45.00	110
1989	Bijou Theatre 06897	Closed	1990	40.00	250-300
1994	Black Sheep Tavern 01003	Open		50.00	50
1993	Blacksmith 00720	Open		47.00	47
1992	Brenner's Apothecary 07961	Open		45.00	50
1996	The Brookfield 11996	5,500		75.00	75
1994	Brown's Book Shop 01001	Open		50.00	50
1993	Burnside 00717	Open		50.00	50
1989	Capper's Millinery 06904	Suspd.		40.00	95
1988	City Hall 06340	Suspd.		40.00	100
1989	Cobb's Bootery 06903	Suspd.		40.00	140
1990	Coffee & Tea Shoppe 07342	Open		45.00	47
1996	Collectors Set 10740	Open		100.00	100
1989	Cole's Barn 06750	Closed	1994	40.00	150
1995	Colonial Savings and Loan 01321	Open		50.00	50
1995	Colonial Village News 01002	Open		50.00	50
1990	Country Post Office 07341	Closed	1994	45.00	65-150
1992	County Courthouse 00233	Open		45.00	50
1991	Daisy's Flower Shop 07478	Open		45.00	47
1993	Dentist's Office 00724	Open		50.00	50
1993	Doctor's Office 00721	Open		50.00	50
1992	Elegant Lady Dress Shop 00232	Open		45.00	50
1988	Engine Co. No. 5 Firehouse 06342	Open		40.00	50
1996	Fairbanks House 10397	Open		50.00	50
1988	Faith Church 06333	Closed	1991	40.00	125-250
1990	Fellowship Church 07334	Open		45.00	47
1990	The First Church 07333	Open		45.00	47
1988	First Post Office 06343	Open		40.00	50
1996	Franklin College 10393	Open		50.00	50
1988	Friendship Chapel 06334	Closed	1994	40.00	150
1993	Green's Grocery 00725	Open		50.00	50
1988	Greystone House 06339	Closed	1995	40.00	50-85
1989	Gull's Nest Lighthouse 06747	Open		40.00	47
1990	Hampshire House 07336	Open		45.00	50
1990	Hillside Church 11991	Closed	1991	60.00	300-400
1995	Historical Society Museum 01328	Open		50.00	50
1988	House of Blue Gables 06337	Closed	1995	40.00	65
1988	Johnson's Antiques 06346	Closed	1993	40.00	85-175
1993	Joseph House 00718	Open		50.00	50
1993	Kirby House-CVRA Exclusive 00716	Closed	1994	50.00	75-100
1992	Lakehurst House 11992	Closed	1992	55.00	250-335
1996	Lattimore House-CVRA Exclusive 10391	Open		50.00	50
1992	Main St. Church 00230	Open		45.00	50
1989	The Major's Manor 06902	Open		40.00	47
1989	Maple St. Church 06748	Closed	1993	40.00	500-700
1993	Mark Hall 00719	Open		50.00	50
1989	Miller Bros. Silversmiths 06905	Suspd.		40.00	90
1994	Mt. Zion Church 11994	Closed	1994	70.00	75-150
1990	Mulberry Station 07344	Open		50.00	65
1995	Mundt Manor 01008	Open		50.00	50
1988	New Hope Church (Musical) 06470	Closed	N/A	40.00	75-88
1990	The Nob Hill 07337	Closed	1995	45.00	75
1992	Northpoint School 07960	Open		45.00	50
1994	Notfel Cabin 01320	Open		50.00	50
1995	O'Doul's Ice House 01324	Open		50.00	50
1988	Old Time Station 06335	Open		40.00	50
1986	Original Set of 6	Unkn.		210.00	N/A
1986	•Charity Chapel 05895	Closed	1989	35.00	250-325
1986	•King's Cottage 05890	Open		35.00	50
1986	•McCauley House 05892	Closed	1988	35.00	240
1986	•Nelson House 05891	Closed	1989	35.00	250-350
1986	•Old Stone Church 05825	Open		35.00	47
1986	•The Welcome Home 05824	Open		35.00	47
1986	Original Set of 6	Unkn.		210.00	N/A
1986	•Church of the Golden Rule 05820	Open		35.00	50
1986	•General Store 05823	Closed	1988	35.00	300-400
1986	•Lil Red School House 05821	Open		35.00	50
1986	•Penny House 05893	Closed	1988	35.00	275-500
1986	•Ritter House 05894	Closed	1989	35.00	400-650
1986	•Train Station 05822	Closed	1989	35.00	150-200
1995	Patriot Bridge 01325	Open		50.00	50
1990	Pierpont-Smithe's Curios 07343	Closed	1993	45.00	100
1995	Queensgate 01329	Open		50.00	50
1989	Quincy's Clock Shop 06899	Open		40.00	47
1995	Rainy Days Barn 01323	Open		50.00	50
1994	Real Estate Office -CVRA Exclusive 01006	Open		50.00	50
1988	The Ritz Hotel 06341	Suspd.		40.00	100-200
1994	Rosamond 00988	Open		50.00	50
1990	Ryman Auditorium-Special Edition 08010	Open		50.00	55
1992	San Sebastian Mission 00231	Closed	1995	45.00	100
1991	Sanderson's Mill 07927	Open		45.00	47
1990	Ship's Chandler's Shop 07339	Suspd.		45.00	47
1994	Smith and Jones Drug Store 01007	Open		50.00	50
1991	Smith's Smithy 07476	Closed	1991	45.00	200
1994	Springfield 00989	Open		50.00	50
1993	St. James Cathedral 11993	Closed	1993	75.00	150-250
1996	St. Paul's Church 10735	Open		50.00	50
1993	St. Peter's Church w/Speaker 00715	Open		60.00	60
1988	The State Bank 06345	Open		40.00	50
1992	Stearn's Stable 00228	Open		45.00	50
1988	The Stone House 06338	Open		40.00	47
1991	Sweet Shop 07481	Open		45.00	47
1989	Sweetheart's Bridge 06751	Open		40.00	47
1996	Town Hall-Events Only 10390	Yr.Iss.		50.00	50
1991	The Toy Maker's Shop 07477	Open		45.00	47
1988	Trader Tom's Gen'l Store 06336	Open		40.00	47
1996	Treviso House 10392	Open		50.00	50
1990	The Victoria House 07335	Closed	1993	45.00	75-100
1989	Victorian Apothecary 06900	Closed	1991	40.00	150
1991	Victorian Gazebo 07925	Open		45.00	45
1989	The Village Bakery 06898	Open		40.00	47
1989	Village Barber Shop 06901	Open		40.00	47
1986	Village Express 05826	Closed	N/A	27.00	100-145
1992	Village Green Gazebo 00227	Open		22.00	22
1990	Village Hardware 07340	Open		45.00	50
1994	Village Hospital 01004	Open		50.00	50
1992	The Village Inn 07962	Open		45.00	50
1989	Village Library 06752	Open		40.00	47
1988	Village Police Station 06344	Open		40.00	50
1989	Village School 06749	Closed	1991	40.00	300-400
1991	Watt's Candle Shop 07479	Closed	1994	45.00	75-125
1994	White's Butcher Shop 01005	Open		50.00	50
1991	Wig Shop 07480	Suspd.		45.00	75
1992	Windmilll 00229	Open		45.00	47
1995	Wycoff Manor 11995	5,500		75.00	100
1995	Zachary Peters Cabinet Maker 01322	Open		50.00	50

Colonial Village Special Event - Lefton

1995	Bayside Inn 01326	Yr.Iss.		50.00	60

Historic American Lighthouse Collection - Lefton

1995	1716 Boston Lighthouse 08607	7,500	1995	50.00	50
1994	Admirality Head, WA 01126	Open		40.00	40
1992	Assateaque, VA 00137	Open		40.00	40
1995	Barneget, NJ 01333	Open		40.00	40
1993	Big Sable Point, MI 00885	Open		40.00	40
1996	Block Island, RI 10105	Open		50.00	50
1994	Bodie Island, NC 01118	Open		40.00	40
1993	Boston Harbor, MA 00881	Open		40.00	40
1996	Buffalo, NY 10076	Open		40.00	40
1994	Cana Island, WI 01117	Open		40.00	40
1993	Cape Cod, MA 00882	Open		40.00	40
1994	Cape Florida, FL 01125	Open		40.00	40
1992	Cape Hatteras, NC 00133	Open		40.00	40
1992	Cape Henry, VA 00135	Open		40.00	40
1992	Cape Lookout, NC 00134	Open		40.00	40
1994	Cape May, NJ 01013	Closed	1995	40.00	40
1995	Cape May, NJ 01013R	Open		40.00	40
1996	Cape Neddick, ME 10106	Open		47.00	47
1994	Chicago Harbor, IL 01010	Open		40.00	40
1996	Destruction Island, WA 10108	Open		40.00	40
1995	Fire Island, NY 01334	Open		40.00	40
1994	Ft. Gratiot, MI 01123	Open		40.00	40
1993	Gray's Harbor, WA 00880	Open		40.00	40
1994	Heceta Head, OR 01122	Open		40.00	40
1996	Holland Harbor, MI 10104	Open		45.00	45
1995	Jupiter Inlet, FL 01336	Open		40.00	40
1996	Key West, FL 10075	Open		40.00	40
1996	Los Angeles Harbor, CA 10109	Open		45.00	45
1993	Marblehead, OH 00879	Open		40.00	40
1993	Montauk, NY 00884	Open		40.00	40
1994	New London Ledge, CT 01119	Open		40.00	40
1994	Ocracoke, NC 01124	Open		40.00	40
1996	Old Cape Henry, VA 08619	7,500		47.00	47
1994	Old Point Loma, CA 01011	Open		40.00	40
1995	Pigeon Point, CA 01289	Open		40.00	40
1995	Point Betsie, MI 01335	Open		47.00	47
1995	Point Cabrillo, CA 01330	Open		47.00	47
1993	Point Wilson, WA 00883	Open		40.00	40
1995	Ponce De Leon, FL 01332	Open		40.00	40
1994	Portland Head, ME 01121	Open		40.00	40
1996	Pt. Isabel, TX 10074	Open		40.00	40
1992	Sandy Hook, NJ 00132	Open		40.00	40
1994	Split Rock, MN 01009	Open		40.00	40
1994	St. Augustine, FL 01015	Open		40.00	40
1994	St. Simons, GA 01012	Open		40.00	40
1996	Thomas Point, MO 10107	Open		45.00	45
1995	Toledo Harbor, OH 01331	Open		47.00	47
1994	Tybee Island, GA 01014	Open		40.00	40
1992	West Quoddy Head, ME 00136	Open		40.00	40
1993	White Shoal, MI 00878	Open		40.00	40
1994	Yerba Buena, CA 01120	Open		40.00	40

Glynda Turley Prints

Turley - G. Turley

1995	Circle of Friends	4,800		67.00	67
1995	The Courtyard II	4,800		99.00	99
1995	Flowers For Mommy	4,800		85.00	85
1994	Old Mill Stream	4,800		64.00	64
1995	Past Times	4,800		78.00	78
1995	Playing Hookie Again	4,800		83.00	83
1995	Secret Garden II	4,800		95.00	95

Goebel of North America

Co-Boy - G. Skrobek

1981	Al the Trumpet Player	Closed	N/A	45.00	50-7
1987	Bank-Pete the Pirate	Closed	N/A	80.00	125-15
1987	Bank-Utz the Money Bank	Closed	N/A	80.00	100-12
1981	Ben the Blacksmith	Closed	N/A	45.00	50-7
XX	Bert the Soccer Player	Closed	N/A	Unkn.	50-7
1971	Bit the Bachelor	Closed	N/A	16.00	50-7
1972	Bob the Bookworm	Closed	N/A	20.00	50-7
1984	Brad the Clockmaker	Closed	N/A	75.00	125-15
1972	Brum the Lawyer	Closed	N/A	20.00	50-7

*Quotes have been rounded up to nearest dollar

YEAR ISSUE		EDITION LIMIT	YEAR RETD.	ISSUE PRICE	*QUOTE U.S.$
XX	Candy the Baker's Delight	Closed	N/A	Unkn.	50-75
1980	Carl the Chef	Closed	N/A	49.00	50-75
1984	Chris the Shoemaker	Closed	N/A	45.00	50-75
1987	Chuck on His Pig	Closed	N/A	75.00	75
1984	Chuck the Chimney Sweep	Closed	N/A	45.00	50-75
1987	Clock-Conny the Watchman	Closed	N/A	125.00	125-150
1987	Clock-Sepp and the Beer Keg	Closed	N/A	125.00	125-150
1972	Co-Boy Plaque	Closed	N/A	20.00	50-125
XX	Conny the Night Watchman	Closed	N/A	Unkn.	125-150
1980	Doc the Doctor	Closed	N/A	49.00	50-100
XX	Ed the Wine Cellar Steward	Closed	N/A	Unkn.	50-75
1984	Felix the Baker	Closed	N/A	45.00	50-75
1971	Fips the Foxy Fisherman	Closed	N/A	16.00	50-75
1971	Fritz the Happy Boozer	Closed	N/A	16.00	50-75
1981	George the Gourmand	Closed	N/A	45.00	50-75
1980	Gerd the Diver	Closed	N/A	49.00	125-175
1978	Gil the Goalie	Closed	N/A	34.00	50-85
1981	Greg the Gourmet	Closed	N/A	45.00	50-95
1981	Greta the Happy Housewife	Closed	N/A	45.00	50-75
1980	Herb the Horseman	Closed	N/A	49.00	50-100
1984	Herman the Butcher	Closed	N/A	45.00	50-75
1984	Homer the Driver	Closed	N/A	45.00	50-75
XX	Jack the Village Pharmacist	Closed	N/A	Unkn.	50-75
XX	Jim the Bowler	Closed	N/A	Unkn.	50-75
XX	John the Hawkeye Hunter	Closed	N/A	Unkn.	50-75
1972	Kuni the Painter	Closed	N/A	20.00	50-75
XX	Mark-Safety First	Closed	N/A	Unkn.	120
1984	Marthe the Nurse	Closed	N/A	45.00	50-75
XX	Max the Boxing Champ	Closed	N/A	Unkn.	135
1971	Mike the Jam Maker	Closed	N/A	16.00	50-75
1980	Monty the Mountain Climber	Closed	N/A	49.00	50-75
1981	Nick the Nightclub Singer	Closed	N/A	45.00	50-75
1981	Niels the Strummer	Closed	N/A	45.00	50-75
1978	Pat the Pitcher	Closed	N/A	34.00	50-75
1984	Paul the Dentist	Closed	N/A	45.00	50-75
1981	Peter the Accordionist	Closed	N/A	45.00	50-75
XX	Petrl the Village Angler	Closed	N/A	Unkn.	50-75
1971	Plum the Pastry Chef	Closed	N/A	16.00	50-75
1972	Porz the Mushroom Muncher	Closed	N/A	20.00	50-75
1984	Rick the Fireman	Closed	N/A	45.00	50-75
1971	Robby the Vegetarian	Closed	N/A	16.00	85
1984	Rudy the World Traveler	Closed	N/A	45.00	50-75
1971	Sam the Gourmet	Closed	N/A	16.00	50-75
1972	Sepp the Beer Buddy	Closed	N/A	20.00	50-75
1984	Sid the Vintner	Closed	N/A	45.00	50-75
1980	Ted the Tennis Player	Closed	N/A	49.00	95
1971	Tom the Honey Lover	Closed	N/A	16.00	70
1978	Tommy Touchdown	Closed	N/A	34.00	50-75
XX	Toni the Skier	Closed	N/A	Unkn.	50-75
1972	Utz the Banker	Closed	N/A	20.00	50-75
1981	Walter the Jogger	Closed	N/A	45.00	50-75
1971	Wim the Court Supplier	Closed	N/A	16.00	50-75

Co-Boys-Culinary - Welling/Skrobek

1994	Mike the Jam Maker 301050	Open		30.00	30
1994	Plum the Sweets Maker 301052	Open		30.00	30
1994	Robby the Vegetarian 301054	Open		30.00	30
1994	Sepp the Drunkard 301051	Open		30.00	30
1994	Tom the Sweet Tooth 301053	Open		30.00	30

Co-Boys-Professionals - Welling/Skrobek

1994	Brum the Lawyer 301060	Open		30.00	30
1994	Conny the Nightwatchman 301062	Open		30.00	30
1994	Doc the Doctor 301064	Open		30.00	30
1994	John the Hunter 301063	Open		30.00	30
1994	Utz the Banker 301061	Open		30.00	30

Co-Boys-Sports - Welling/Skrobek

1994	Bert the Soccer Player 301059	Open		30.00	30
1994	Jim the Bowler 301057	Open		30.00	30
1994	Petri the Fisherman 301055	Open		30.00	30
1994	Ted the Tennis Player 301058	Open		30.00	30
1994	Toni the Skier 301056	Open		30.00	30

Goebel Figurines - N. Rockwell

1963	Advertising Plaque 218	Closed	N/A	Unkn.	750-1000
1963	Boyhood Dreams (Adventurers between Adventures) 202	Closed	N/A	12.00	350-400
1963	Buttercup Test (Beguiling Buttercup) 214	Closed	N/A	10.00	350-400
1963	First Love (A Scholarly Pace) 215	Closed	N/A	30.00	350-400
1963	His First Smoke 208	Closed	N/A	9.00	350-400
1963	Home Cure 211	Closed	N/A	16.00	350-400
1963	Little Veterinarian (Mysterious Malady) 201	Closed	N/A	15.00	350-400
1963	Mother's Helper (Pride of Parenthood) 203	Closed	N/A	15.00	350-400
1963	My New Pal (A Boy Meets His Dog) 204	Closed	N/A	12.00	350-400
1963	Patient Anglers (Fisherman's Paradise) 217	Closed	N/A	18.00	350-400
1963	She Loves Me (Day Dreamer) 213	Closed	N/A	8.00	350-400
1963	Timely Assistance (Love Aid) 212	Closed	N/A	16.00	350-400

Miniatures-Americana Series - R. Olszewski

1982	American Bald Eagle 661-B	Closed	1989	45.00	240-300
1986	Americana Display 951-D	Open	1995	80.00	105
1989	Blacksmith 667-P	Closed	1989	55.00	120-150
1986	Carrousel Ride 665-B	Closed	1995	45.00	100-150
1985	Central Park Sunday 664-B	Closed	1995	45.00	75
1984	Eyes on the Horizon 663-B	Closed	1995	45.00	80
1981	The Plainsman 660-B	Closed	1989	45.00	200-250
1983	She Sounds the Deep 662-B	Closed	1995	45.00	75
1987	To The Bandstand 666-B	Closed	1995	45.00	75

Miniatures-Bob Timberlake Signature Series - B. Timberlake

1996	Autumn Afternoons Vignette	500		490.00	490

Miniatures-Children's Series - R. Olszewski

1983	Backyard Frolic 633-P	Closed	1995	65.00	100
1980	Blumenkinder-Courting 630-P	Closed	1989	55.00	125-250
1990	Building Blocks Castle (large) 968-D	Closed	1995	75.00	100
1987	Carrousel Days (plain base) 637-P	Closed	1989	85.00	750-815
1987	Carrousel Days 637-P	Closed	1989	85.00	150-230
1988	Children's Display (small)	Closed	1995	45.00	60
1989	Clowning Around 636-P (new style)	Closed	1995	85.00	120-135
1986	Clowning Around 636-P (old style)	Closed	N/A	85.00	165-200
1984	Grandpa 634-P	Closed	1995	75.00	100
1988	Little Ballerina 638-P	Closed	1995	85.00	100-120
1982	Out and About 632-P	Closed	1989	85.00	300
1985	Snow Holiday 635-P	Closed	1995	75.00	100
1981	Summer Days 631-P	Closed	1989	65.00	275-300

Miniatures-Classic Clocks - Larsen

1995	Alexis	2,500		200.00	200
1995	Blinking Admiral	2,500		200.00	200
1995	Play	2,500		250.00	250

Miniatures-Disney-Cinderella - Disney

1991	Anastasia 172-P	Suspd.		85.00	110-150
1991	Cinderella 176-P	Suspd.		85.00	100-175
1991	Cinderella's Coach Display 978-D	Suspd.		95.00	110-160
1991	Cinderella's Dream Castle 976-D	Suspd.		95.00	120-175
1991	Drizella 174-P	Suspd.		85.00	110-150
1991	Fairy Godmother 180-P	Suspd.		85.00	110-150
1991	Footman 181-P	Suspd.		85.00	100-165
1991	Gus 177-P	Suspd.		80.00	100-135
1991	Jaq 173-P	Suspd.		80.00	100-135
1991	Lucifer 175-P	Suspd.		80.00	100-155
1991	Prince Charming 179-P	Suspd.		85.00	110-195
1991	Stepmother 178-P	Suspd.		85.00	100-150

Miniatures-Disney-Peter Pan - Disney

1994	Captain Hook 188-P	Suspd.		160.00	160-200
1992	John 186-P	Suspd.		90.00	120-165
1994	Lost Boy-Fox 191-P	Suspd.		130.00	130-185
1994	Lost Boy-Rabbit 192-P	Suspd.		130.00	130-185
1992	Michael 187-P	Suspd.		90.00	110-150
1992	Nana 189-P	Suspd.		95.00	110-155
1994	Neverland Display 997-D	Suspd.		150.00	150-195
1992	Peter Pan 184-P	Suspd.		90.00	125-200
1992	Peter Pan's London 986-D	Suspd.		125.00	135-200
1994	Smee 190-P	Suspd.		140.00	140-175
1992	Wendy 185-P	Suspd.		90.00	125-175

Miniatures-Disney-Pinocchio - Disney

1991	Blue Fairy 693-P	Suspd.		95.00	120-160
1990	Geppetto's Toy Shop Display 965-D	Suspd.		95.00	125-185
1990	Geppetto/Figaro 682-P	Suspd.		90.00	110-160
1990	Gideon 683-P	Suspd.		75.00	100-150
1990	J. Worthington Foulfellow 684-P	Suspd.		95.00	115-155
1990	Jiminy Cricket 685-P	Suspd.		75.00	100-175
1991	Little Street Lamp Display 964-D	Suspd.		65.00	100-150
1992	Monstro The Whale 985-D	Suspd.		120.00	140-250
1990	Pinocchio 686-P	Suspd.		75.00	100-190
1991	Stromboli 694-P	Suspd.		95.00	120-165
1991	Stromboli's Street Wagon 979-D	Suspd.		105.00	125-195

Miniatures-Disney-Snow White - Disney

1987	Bashful 165-P	Suspd.		60.00	100-150
1991	Castle Courtyard Display 981-D	Suspd.		105.00	115-135
1987	Cozy Cottage Display 941-D	Suspd.		35.00	200-350
1987	Doc 162-P	Suspd.		60.00	110-150
1987	Dopey 167-P	Suspd.		60.00	125-200
1987	Grumpy 166-P	Suspd.		60.00	110-150
1987	Happy 164-P	Suspd.		60.00	100-150
1988	House In The Woods Display 944-D	Suspd.		60.00	120-185
1992	Path In The Woods 996-D	Suspd.		140.00	150-225
1987	Sleepy 163-P	Suspd.		60.00	100-150
1987	Sneezy 161-P	Suspd.		60.00	100-150
1987	Snow White 168-P	Suspd.		60.00	125-200
1990	Snow White's Prince 170-P	Suspd.		80.00	130-165
1992	Snow White's Queen 182-P	Suspd.		100.00	120-185
1992	Snow White's Witch 183-P	Suspd.		100.00	120-185
1990	The Wishing Well Display 969-D	Suspd.		65.00	100-195

Miniatures-Disneyana Convention - R. Olszewski

1995	Barbershop Quartet	750	1995	325.00	325
1994	Mickey Self Portrait	500	1994	295.00	900-1100

Miniatures-Historical Series - R. Olszewski

1985	Capodimonte 600-P (new style)	Suspd.		90.00	150-200
1980	Capodimonte 600-P (old style)	Closed	1987	90.00	385-425
1983	The Cherry Pickers 602-P	Suspd.		85.00	220-250
1990	English Country Garden 970-D	Open		85.00	110
1989	Farmer w/Doves 607-P	Open		85.00	115
1985	Floral Bouquet Pompadour 604-P	Open		85.00	120
1990	Gentleman Fox Hunt 616-P	Suspd.		145.00	170-200
1988	Historical Display 943-D	Open		45.00	65
1981	Masquerade-St. Petersburg 601-P	Closed	1989	65.00	195-250
1987	Meissen Parrot 605-P	Open		85.00	115
1988	Minton Rooster 606-P	7,500		85.00	115
1984	Moor With Spanish Horse 603-P	Open		85.00	115
1992	Poultry Seller 608-G	1,500		200.00	245

Miniatures-Jack & The Beanstalk - R. Olszewski

1994	Beanseller 742-P	5,000		200.00	210
1994	Jack & The Beanstalk Display 999-D	5,000		225.00	260
1994	Jack and the Cow 743-P	5,000		180.00	195
1994	Jack's Mom 741-P	5,000		145.00	180

Miniatures-Mickey Mouse - Disney

1990	Fantasia Living Brooms 972-D	Suspd.		85.00	185-210
1990	The Sorcerer's Apprentice 171-P	Suspd.		80.00	175-200
1990	Set	Suspd.		165.00	450-550

Miniatures-Nativity Collection - R. Olszewski

1992	3 Kings Display 987-D	Open		85.00	105
1992	Balthazar 405-P	Open		135.00	200
1994	Camel & Tender 819292	Open		380.00	395
1992	Caspar 406-P	Open		135.00	200
1994	Final Nativity Display 991-D	Open		260.00	275
1994	Guardian Angel 407-P	Open		200.00	225
1991	Holy Family Display 982-D	Open		85.00	95
1991	Joseph 401-P	Open		95.00	130
1991	Joyful Cherubs 403-P	Open		130.00	185
1992	Melchoir 404-P	Open		135.00	200
1991	Mother/Child 440-P	Open		120.00	155
1994	Sheep & Shepherd 819290	Open		230.00	240
1991	The Stable Donkey 402-P	Open		95.00	130

Miniatures-Nature's Moments - Yenawine

1995	Bathing Beauties	Open		95.00	95
1995	Fish Paradise	Open		110.00	110
1995	Gathering Goodies	Open		95.00	95
1995	Hide and Seek	Open		110.00	110
1995	Penguins Plunge	Open		95.00	95
1995	Polar Playground	Open		110.00	110
1995	Preparing for Flight	Open		80.00	80
1995	Robyn Refresher	Open		95.00	95
1995	Summer Surprise	Open		95.00	95
1995	Touch and Go	Open		95.00	95

Miniatures-Night Before Christmas (1st Edition) - R. Olszewski

1990	Eight Tiny Reindeer 691-P	5,000		110.00	135
1990	Mama & Papa 692-P	5,000		110.00	140
1990	St. Nicholas 690-P	5,000		95.00	125
1990	Sugar Plum Boy 687-P	5,000		70.00	100
1990	Sugar Plum Girl 689-P	5,000		70.00	100
1991	Up To The Housetop 966-D	5,000		95.00	115
1990	Yule Tree 688-P	5,000		90.00	110

Miniatures-Oriental Series - R. Olszewski

1986	The Blind Men and the Elephant 643-P	Suspd.		70.00	125-175
1990	Chinese Temple Lion 646-P	Open		90.00	115-135
1987	Chinese Water Dragon 644-P	Suspd.		70.00	135-175
1990	Empress' Garden Display 967-D	Open		95.00	135
1982	The Geisha 641-P	Suspd.		65.00	150-225
1984	Kuan Yin 640-W (new style)	Suspd.		45.00	125-225
1980	Kuan Yin 640-W (old style)	Closed	1992	40.00	210-330
1987	Oriental Display (small) 945-D	Open		45.00	70
1985	Tang Horse 642-P	Open		65.00	100
1989	Tiger Hunt 645-P	Open		85.00	105

Miniatures-Pendants - R. Olszewski

1986	Camper Bialosky 151-P	Closed	1988	95.00	255-275
1991	Chrysanthemum Pendant 222-P	Open		135.00	155
1991	Daffodil Pendant 221-P	Open		135.00	155
1990	Hummingbird 697-P	Open		125.00	155
1988	Mickey Mouse 169-P	5,000	1989	92.00	285-310
1991	Poinsettia Pendant 223-P	Open		135.00	155
1991	Rose Pendant 220-P	Open		135.00	155

Miniatures-Portrait of America/Saturday Evening Post - N. Rockwell

1989	Bottom Drawer 366-P	7,500	1995	85.00	85
1988	Bottom of the Sixth 365-P	Suspd.		85.00	100-150
1988	Check-Up 363-P	Suspd.		85.00	85-110
1988	The Doctor and the Doll 361-P	Suspd.		85.00	115-150
1991	Home Coming Vignette -Soldier/Mother 990-D	2,000	1995	190.00	225-300
1988	Marbles Champion (Pewter) 362-P	Closed	1995	85.00	85-110
1988	No Swimming (Pewter) 360-P	Closed	1995	85.00	85-110
1988	Rockwell Display (Pewter) 952-D	Closed	1995	80.00	80-100
1988	Triple Self-Portrait (Pewter) 364-P	Suspd.		85.00	150-250

Miniatures-Precious Moments Series I - Goebel

1995	Fields of Friendship-Diorama (display)	Open		135.00	135
1995	God Loveth a Cheerful Giver	Open		70.00	70
1995	His Burden is Light	Open		70.00	70
1995	I'm Sending You a White Christmas	5,000		100.00	100
1995	Love Is Kind	Open		70.00	70
1995	Love One Another	Open		70.00	70

YEAR ISSUE		EDITION LIMIT	YEAR RETD.	ISSUE PRICE	*QUOTE U.S.$
1995	Make a Joyful Noise	Open		70.00	70
1995	Praise the Lord Anyhow	Open		70.00	70
1995	Prayer Changes Things	Open		70.00	70

Miniatures-Special Release-Alice in Wonderland - R. Olszewski

YEAR ISSUE		EDITION LIMIT	YEAR RETD.	ISSUE PRICE	*QUOTE U.S.$
1982	Alice In the Garden 670-P	Closed	1982	60.00	600-650
1984	The Cheshire Cat 672-P	Closed	1984	75.00	400-500
1983	Down the Rabbit Hole 671-P	Closed	1983	75.00	400-425

Miniatures-Special Release-Wizard of Oz - R. Olszewski

YEAR ISSUE		EDITION LIMIT	YEAR RETD.	ISSUE PRICE	*QUOTE U.S.$
1986	The Cowardly Lion 675-P	Closed	1987	85.00	295-325
1992	Dorothy/Glinda 695-P	Closed	1995	135.00	145-165
1992	Good-Bye to Oz Display 980-D	Open		110.00	130-180
1988	The Munchkins 677-P	Closed	1995	85.00	105-140
1987	Oz Display 942-D	Closed	1994	45.00	545-590
XX	Oz Display Set	Closed	1994	410.00	1200-1650
1984	Scarecrow 673-P	Closed	1985	75.00	250-495
1985	Tinman 674-P	Closed	1986	80.00	250-325
1987	The Wicked Witch 676-P	Closed	1995	85.00	115-175

Miniatures-Special Releases - R. Olszewski

YEAR ISSUE		EDITION LIMIT	YEAR RETD.	ISSUE PRICE	*QUOTE U.S.$
1994	Dresden Timepiece 450-P	750		1250.00	1300
1991	Portrait Of The Artist (convention) 658-P	Closed	1991	195.00	450-600
1991	Portrait Of The Artist (promotion) 658-P	Open		195.00	210-250
1992	Summer Days Collector Plaque 659-P	Open		130.00	130-175

Miniatures-The American Frontier Collection - Various

YEAR ISSUE		EDITION LIMIT	YEAR RETD.	ISSUE PRICE	*QUOTE U.S.$
1987	American Frontier Museum Display 947-D - R. Olszewski	Suspd.		80.00	115
1987	The Bronco Buster 350-B - Remington	Suspd.		80.00	130-160
1987	Eight Count 310-B - Pounder	Suspd.		75.00	95
1987	The End of the Trail 340-B - Frazier	Suspd.		80.00	95-150
1987	The First Ride 330-B - Rogers	Suspd.		85.00	105
1987	Grizzly's Last Stand 320-B - Jonas	Suspd.		65.00	85
1987	Indian Scout and Buffalo 300-B - Bonheur	Suspd.		95.00	95-140

Miniatures-Three Little Pigs - R. Olszewski

YEAR ISSUE		EDITION LIMIT	YEAR RETD.	ISSUE PRICE	*QUOTE U.S.$
1991	The Hungry Wolf 681-P	7,500		80.00	110
1991	Little Bricks Pig 680-P	7,500		75.00	110
1989	Little Sticks Pig 678-P	7,500		75.00	110
1990	Little Straw Pig 679-P	7,500		75.00	110
1991	Three Little Pigs House 956-D	7,500		50.00	130

Miniatures-Wildlife Series - R. Olszewski

YEAR ISSUE		EDITION LIMIT	YEAR RETD.	ISSUE PRICE	*QUOTE U.S.$
1985	American Goldfinch 625-P	Open		65.00	100
1986	Autumn Blue Jay 626-P	Suspd.		65.00	125-190
1992	Autumn Blue Jay 626-P (Archive release)	Open		125.00	140
1980	Chipping Sparrow 620-P	Suspd.		55.00	320-415
1987	Country Display (small) 940-D	Open		45.00	70
1990	Country Landscape (large) 957-D	Open		85.00	115
1989	Hooded Oriole 629-P	Open		80.00	105
1990	Hummingbird 696-P	Closed	N/A	85.00	160-180
1987	Mallard Duck 627-P	Open		75.00	110-125
1981	Owl-Daylight Encounter 621-P	Closed	N/A	65.00	325-375
1983	Red-Winged Blackbird 623-P	Closed	N/A	65.00	145-200
1988	Spring Robin 628-P	Closed	N/A	75.00	155-185
1982	Western Bluebird 622-P	Closed	N/A	65.00	165-180
1984	Winter Cardinal 624-P	Closed	N/A	65.00	175-200

Miniatures-Winter Lights - Norrgard

YEAR ISSUE		EDITION LIMIT	YEAR RETD.	ISSUE PRICE	*QUOTE U.S.$
1995	Once Upon a Winter Day	Open		275.00	275

Miniatures-Women's Series - R. Olszewski

YEAR ISSUE		EDITION LIMIT	YEAR RETD.	ISSUE PRICE	*QUOTE U.S.$
1980	Dresden Dancer 610-P	Closed	1989	55.00	250-500
1985	The Hunt With Hounds (new style) 611-P	Closed	N/A	75.00	190-225
1981	The Hunt With Hounds (old style) 611-P	Closed	1984	75.00	335-425
1986	I Do 615-P	Closed	N/A	85.00	195-295
1983	On The Avenue 613-P	Closed	1995	65.00	130
1982	Precious Years 612-P	Closed	N/A	65.00	245-280
1984	Roses 614-P	Closed	1995	65.00	130
1989	Women's Display (small) 950-D	Closed	1995	40.00	65-95

Goebel/M.I. Hummel

M.I. Hummel Collectors Club Exclusives - M. I. Hummel, unless otherwise noted

YEAR ISSUE		EDITION LIMIT	YEAR RETD.	ISSUE PRICE	*QUOTE U.S.$
1977	Valentine Gift 387	Closed	N/A	45.00	400-700
1978	Smiling Through Plaque 690	Closed	N/A	50.00	100-175
1979	Bust of Sister-M.I.Hummel HU-3 - G. Skrobek	Closed	N/A	75.00	200-375
1980	Valentine Joy 399	Closed	N/A	95.00	200-360
1981	Daisies Don't Tell 380	Closed	N/A	80.00	200-300
1982	It's Cold 421	Closed	N/A	80.00	175
1983	What Now? 422	Closed	N/A	90.00	190-280
1983	Valentine Gift Mini Pendant 248-P - R. Olszewski	Closed	N/A	85.00	200-300
1984	Coffee Break 409	Closed	N/A	90.00	150-245
1985	Smiling Through 408/0	Closed	N/A	125.00	275
1986	Birthday Candle 440	Closed	N/A	95.00	200-300
1986	What Now? Mini Pendant 249-P - R. Olszewski	Closed	N/A	125.00	175-300
1987	Morning Concert 447	Closed	N/A	98.00	155-200
1987	Little Cocopah Indian Girl - T. DeGrazia	Closed	N/A	140.00	200-300
1988	The Surprise 431	Closed	N/A	125.00	155-275
1989	Mickey and Minnie - H. Fischer	Closed	N/A	275.00	300-500
1989	Hello World 429	Closed	N/A	130.00	165-195
1990	I Wonder 486	Closed	N/A	140.00	140-200
1991	Gift From A Friend 485	Closed	N/A	160.00	160-250
1991	Miniature Morning Concert w/ Display 269-P - R. Olszewski	Closed	N/A	175.00	175-250
1992	My Wish Is Small 463/0	Closed	N/A	170.00	170-250
1992	Cheeky Fellow 554	Closed	N/A	120.00	125
1993	I Didn't Do It 626	Closed	1995	175.00	175-200
1993	Sweet As Can Be 541	Closed	1995	125.00	125
1994	Little Visitor 563/0	5/96		180.00	180
1994	Little Troubadour 558	5/96		130.00	130
1994	At Grandpa's 621	10,000		1300.00	1300
1994	Miniature Honey Lover Pendant 247-P	5/96		165.00	165
1995	Country Suitor 760	5/97		195.00	195
1995	Strum Along 557	5/97		135.00	135
1995	A Story From Grandma 620	10,000		1300.00	1300

Special Edition Anniversary Figurines For 5/10/15 Year Membership - M.I. Hummel

YEAR ISSUE		EDITION LIMIT	YEAR RETD.	ISSUE PRICE	*QUOTE U.S.$
1990	Flower Girl 548 (5 year)	Open		105.00	135
1990	The Little Pair 449 (10 year)	Open		170.00	200
1991	Honey Lover 312 (15 year)	Open		190.00	220

M.I. Hummel Bavarian Village Collection - M.I. Hummel

YEAR ISSUE		EDITION LIMIT	YEAR RETD.	ISSUE PRICE	*QUOTE U.S.$
1995	Angel's Duet (house)	Open		50.00	50
1995	The Bench and Tree Set (accessory)	Open		25.00	25
1995	Christmas Mail (house)	Open		50.00	50
1995	Company's Coming (house)	Open		50.00	50
1995	The Sled and Pine Tree Set (accessory)	Open		25.00	25
1995	The Village Bakery (house)	Open		50.00	50
1995	The Village Bridge (accessory)	Open		25.00	25
1995	Winter's Comfort (house)	Open		50.00	50
1995	The Wishing Well (accessory)	Open		25.00	25

M.I. Hummel Collectibles Century Collection - M.I. Hummel

YEAR ISSUE		EDITION LIMIT	YEAR RETD.	ISSUE PRICE	*QUOTE U.S.$
1986	Chapel Time 442	Closed	N/A	500.00	1950-2200
1987	Pleasant Journey 406	Closed	N/A	500.00	1950-2050
1988	Call to Worship 441	Closed	N/A	600.00	995
1989	Harmony in Four Parts 471	Closed	N/A	850.00	1350-1950
1990	Let's Tell the World 487	Closed	N/A	875.00	900-1200
1991	We Wish You The Best 600	Closed	N/A	1300.00	1400-1600
1992	On Our Way 472	Closed	N/A	950.00	1100
1993	Welcome Spring 635	Closed	N/A	1085.00	1250
1994	Rock-A-Bye 574	Closed	N/A	1150.00	1200-1300
1995	Strike Up the Band 668	Closed	1995	1200.00	1200
1996	Love's Bounty 751	Yr.Iss.		1200.00	1200

M.I. Hummel Collectibles Christmas Angels - M.I. Hummel

YEAR ISSUE		EDITION LIMIT	YEAR RETD.	ISSUE PRICE	*QUOTE U.S.$
1993	Angel in Cloud 585	Open		25.00	33
1993	Angel with Lute 580	Open		25.00	33
1993	Angel with Trumpet 586	Open		25.00	33
1993	Celestial Musician 578	Open		25.00	33
1993	Festival Harmony with Flute 577	Open		25.00	33
1993	Festival Harmony with Mandolin 576	Open		25.00	33
1993	Gentle Song 582	Open		25.00	33
1993	Heavenly Angel 575	Open		25.00	33
1993	Prayer of Thanks 581	Open		25.00	33
1993	Song of Praise 579	Open		25.00	33

M.I. Hummel Collectibles Figurines - M.I. Hummel

YEAR ISSUE		EDITION LIMIT	YEAR RETD.	ISSUE PRICE	*QUOTE U.S.$
1988	The Accompanist 453	Open		Unkn.	110
XX	Adoration 23/I	Open		Unkn.	380
XX	Adoration 23/III	Open		Unkn.	590
XX	Adventure Bound 347	Open		Unkn.	3960
XX	Angel Duet 261	Open		Unkn.	240
XX	Angel Serenade 214/D/I	Open		Unkn.	100
XX	Angel Serenade with Lamb 83	Open		Unkn.	240
XX	Angel with Accordion 238/B	Open		Unkn.	55
XX	Angel with Lute 238/A	Open		Unkn.	55
XX	Angel With Trumpet 238/C	Open		Unkn.	55
XX	Angelic Song 144	Open		Unkn.	160
1995	The Angler 566	Open		Unkn.	350
1989	An Apple A Day 403	Open		Unkn.	300
XX	Apple Tree Boy 142/3/0	Open		Unkn.	155
XX	Apple Tree Boy 142/I	Open		Unkn.	300
XX	Apple Tree Boy 142/V	Open		Unkn.	1320
XX	Apple Tree Girl 141/3/0	Open		Unkn.	155
XX	Apple Tree Girl 141/I	Open		Unkn.	300
XX	Apple Tree Girl 141/V	Open		Unkn.	1320
1991	Art Critic 318	Open		Unkn.	315
XX	Artist, The 304	Open		Unkn.	270
XX	Auf Wiedersehen 153/0	Open		Unkn.	270
XX	Auf Wiedersehen 153/I	Open		Unkn.	325
XX	Autumn Harvest 355	Open		Unkn.	220
XX	Baker 128	Open		Unkn.	215
XX	Baking Day 330	Open		Unkn.	300
XX	Band Leader 129	Open		Unkn.	220
XX	Band Leader 129/4/0	Open		Unkn.	110
XX	Barnyard Hero 195/2/0	Open		Unkn.	180
XX	Barnyard Hero 195/I	Open		Unkn.	330
XX	Bashful 377	Open		Unkn.	215
1990	Bath Time 412	Open		Unkn.	410
XX	Be Patient 197/2/0	Open		Unkn.	215
XX	Be Patient 197/I	Open		Unkn.	325
XX	Begging His Share 9	Open		Unkn.	275
XX	Big Housecleaning 363	Open		Unkn.	315
XX	Bird Duet 169	Open		Unkn.	155
XX	Bird Watcher 300	Open		Unkn.	240
1989	Birthday Cake 338	Open		Unkn.	155
1994	Birthday Present 341/3/0	Open		140.00	155
XX	Birthday Serenade 218/0	Open		Unkn.	325
XX	Birthday Serenade 218/2/0	Open		Unkn.	190
XX	Blessed Event 333	Open		Unkn.	350
1996	Blossom Time 608	Open		155.00	155
XX	Bookworm 3/I	Open		Unkn.	325
XX	Bookworm 8	Open		Unkn.	240
XX	Boots 143/0	Open		Unkn.	220
XX	Boots 143/I	Open		Unkn.	360
XX	Botanist, The 351	Open		Unkn.	220
XX	Boy with Accordion 390	Open		Unkn.	95
XX	Boy with Horse 239/C	Open		Unkn.	60
XX	Boy with Toothache 217	Open		Unkn.	230
XX	Brother 95	Open		Unkn.	220
1988	A Budding Maestro 477	Open		Unkn.	110
XX	Builder, The 305	Open		Unkn.	270
XX	Busy Student 367	Open		Unkn.	175
XX	Call to Glory 739/I	Open		250.00	275
XX	Carnival 328	Open		Unkn.	240
XX	Celestial Musician 188/0	Open		Unkn.	240
1993	Celestial Musician 188/4/0	Open		Unkn.	100
XX	Celestial Musician 188/I	Open		255.00	255
XX	Chick Girl 57/0	Open		Unkn.	180
XX	Chick Girl 57/2/0	Open		Unkn.	160
XX	Chick Girl 57/I	Open		Unkn.	300
XX	Chicken-Licken 385	Open		Unkn.	310
XX	Chicken-Licken 385/4/0	Open		Unkn.	110
XX	Chimney Sweep 12/2/0	Open		Unkn.	130
XX	Chimney Sweep 12/I	Open		Unkn.	240
1989	Christmas Angel 301	Open		Unkn.	275
XX	Christmas Song 343	Open		Unkn.	240
1996	Christmas Song 343/4/0	Yr.Iss.		115.00	115
XX	Cinderella 337	Open		Unkn.	315
XX	Close Harmony 336	Open		Unkn.	315
1995	Come Back Soon 545	Open		Unkn.	150
XX	Confidentially 314	Open		Unkn.	315
XX	Congratulations 17	Open		Unkn.	220
XX	Coquettes 179	Open		Unkn.	315
1990	Crossroads (Commemorative) 331	10,000		360.00	550-900
XX	Crossroads (Original) 331	Open		Unkn.	440
XX	Culprits 56/A	Open		Unkn.	320
1989	Daddy's Girls 371	Open		Unkn.	250
1996	Delicious 435/3/0	Open		155.00	155
XX	Doctor 127	Open		Unkn.	170
XX	Doll Bath 319	Open		Unkn.	315
XX	Doll Mother 67	Open		Unkn.	230
XX	Easter Greetings 378	Open		Unkn.	220
XX	Easter Time 384	Open		Unkn.	275
1992	Evening Prayer 495	Open		Unkn.	115
XX	Eventide 99	Open		Unkn.	360
XX	A Fair Measure 345	Open		Unkn.	315
XX	Farm Boy 66	Open		Unkn.	250
XX	Favorite Pet 361	Open		Unkn.	315
XX	Feathered Friends 344	Open		Unkn.	300
XX	Feeding Time 199/0	Open		Unkn.	215
XX	Feeding Time 199/I	Open		Unkn.	300
1995	Festival Harmony 693	Open		Unkn.	125
1994	Festival Harmony w/Mandolin 172/4/0	Open		95.00	105
XX	Festival Harmony, w/Flute 173/0	Open		Unkn.	340
XX	Festival Harmony, w/Mandolin 172/0	Open		Unkn.	340
XX	Flower Vendor 381	Open		Unkn.	270
XX	Follow the Leader 369	Open		Unkn.	1320
XX	For Father 87	Open		Unkn.	230
XX	For Mother 257	Open		Unkn.	220
XX	For Mother 257/2/0	Open		Unkn.	130
XX	Forest Shrine 183	Open		Unkn.	585
1993	A Free Flight 569	Open		Unkn.	215
1991	Friend Or Foe 434	Open		Unkn.	240
XX	Friends 136/I	Open		Unkn.	220
XX	Friends 136/V	Open		Unkn.	1320
1993	Friends Together 662/0 (Commemorative)	Open		260.00	300
1993	Friends Together 662/I (Limited)	25,000		475.00	550
XX	Gay Adventure 356	Open		Unkn.	210
1995	Gentle Fellowship (Commemorative) 628	25,000		550.00	550
XX	A Gentle Glow 439	Open		Unkn.	220
XX	Girl with Doll 239/B	Open		Unkn.	60
XX	Girl with Nosegay 239/A	Open		Unkn.	60
XX	Girl with Sheet Music 389	Open		Unkn.	95
XX	Girl with Trumpet 391	Open		Unkn.	95
XX	Going Home 383	Open		Unkn.	340
XX	Going to Grandma's 52/0	Open		Unkn.	290
XX	Good Friends 182	Open		Unkn.	215
XX	Good Hunting 307	Open		Unkn.	270
XX	Good Night 214/C/I	Open		Unkn.	100
XX	Good Shepherd 42	Open		Unkn.	275
XX	Goose Girl 47/0	Open		Unkn.	250
XX	Goose Girl 47/3/0	Open		Unkn.	180
XX	Grandma's Girl 561	Open		Unkn.	160
XX	Grandpa's Boy 562	Open		Unkn.	160
1991	The Guardian 455	Open		Unkn.	180
XX	Guiding Angel 357	Open		Unkn.	95
XX	Happiness 86	Open		Unkn.	145
XX	Happy Birthday 176/0	Open		Unkn.	230

*Quotes have been rounded up to nearest dollar

YEAR ISSUE		EDITION LIMIT	YEAR RETD.	ISSUE PRICE	*QUOTE U.S.$
XX	Happy Birthday 176/I	Open		Unkn.	325
XX	Happy Days 150/0	Open		Unkn.	330
XX	Happy Days 150/2/0	Open		Unkn.	190
XX	Happy Days 150/I	Open		Unkn.	500
XX	Happy Pastime 69	Open		Unkn.	175
XX	Happy Traveller 109/0	Open		Unkn.	155
XX	Hear Ye! Hear Ye! 15/0	Open		Unkn.	220
XX	Hear Ye! Hear Ye! 15/2/0	Open		Unkn.	160
XX	Hear Ye! Hear Ye! 15/I	Open		Unkn.	275
XX	Heavenly Angel 21/0	Open		Unkn.	130
XX	Heavenly Angel 21/0/1/2	Open		Unkn.	240
XX	Heavenly Angel 21/I	Open		Unkn.	275
XX	Heavenly Lullaby 262	Open		Unkn.	200
XX	Heavenly Protection 88/I	Open		Unkn.	470
1995	Hello (Perpetual Calendar) 788A	Open		295.00	295
XX	Hello 124/0	Open		Unkn.	240
XX	Home from Market 198/2/0	Open		Unkn.	160
XX	Home from Market 198/I	Open		Unkn.	230
XX	Homeward Bound 334	Open		Unkn.	360
1990	Horse Trainer 423	Open		Unkn.	240
1989	Hosanna 480	Open		Unkn.	110
1989	I'll Protect Him 483	Open		Unkn.	95
1994	I'm Carefree 633	Open		365.00	410
1989	I'm Here 478	Open		Unkn.	110
1989	In D Major 430	Open		Unkn.	220
XX	In The Meadow 459	Open		Unkn.	220
XX	In Tune 414	Open		Unkn.	310
XX	Is It Raining? 420	Open		Unkn.	280
XX	Joyful 53	Open		Unkn.	130
XX	Joyous News 27/III	Open		Unkn.	240
1995	Just Dozing 451	Open		Unkn.	240
XX	Just Fishing 373	Open		Unkn.	250
XX	Just Resting 112/3/0	Open		Unkn.	160
XX	Just Resting 112/I	Open		Unkn.	310
XX	Kindergartner 467	Open		Unkn.	220
XX	Kiss Me 311	Open		Unkn.	315
XX	Knit One, Purl One 432	Open		Unkn.	125
XX	Knitting Lesson 256	Open		Unkn.	550
1991	Land in Sight 530	30,000		1600.00	1600
XX	Latest News 184	Open		Unkn.	320
XX	Let's Sing 110/0	Open		Unkn.	135
XX	Let's Sing 110/I	Open		Unkn.	180
XX	Letter to Santa Claus 340	Open		Unkn.	360
1993	Little Architect 410/I	Open		Unkn.	330
XX	Little Bookkeeper 306	Open		Unkn.	315
XX	Little Cellist 89/I	Open		Unkn.	230
XX	Little Drummer 240	Open		Unkn.	160
XX	Little Fiddler 2/0	Open		Unkn.	240
XX	Little Fiddler 2/4/0	Open		Unkn.	110
XX	Little Fiddler 4	Open		Unkn.	220
XX	Little Gabriel 32	Open		Unkn.	155
XX	Little Gardener 74	Open		Unkn.	130
XX	Little Goat Herder 200/0	Open		Unkn.	215
XX	Little Goat Herder 200/I	Open		Unkn.	260
XX	Little Guardian 145	Open		Unkn.	160
XX	Little Helper 73	Open		Unkn.	130
XX	Little Hiker 16/2/0	Open		Unkn.	130
XX	Little Hiker 16/I	Open		Unkn.	240
XX	Little Nurse 376	Open		Unkn.	270
XX	Little Pharmacist 322/E	Open		Unkn.	265
XX	Little Scholar 80	Open		Unkn.	230
XX	Little Shopper 96	Open		Unkn.	150
1988	Little Sweeper 171/0	Open		Unkn.	150
XX	Little Sweeper 171/4/0	Open		Unkn.	110
XX	Little Tailor 308	Open		Unkn.	270
XX	Little Thrifty 118	Open		Unkn.	160
XX	Little Tooter 214/H	Open		Unkn.	110
XX	Little Tooter 214/H	Open		Unkn.	135
XX	Lost Stocking 374	Open		Unkn.	155
1995	Lucky Boy (Special Event) 335	25,000		190.00	190
XX	Mail is Here 226	Open		Unkn.	585
1989	Make A Wish 475	Open		Unkn.	220
XX	March Winds 43	Open		Unkn.	170
XX	Max and Moritz 123	Open		Unkn.	240
XX	Meditation 13/0	Open		Unkn.	240
XX	Meditation 13/2/0	Open		Unkn.	155
XX	Merry Wanderer 11/0	Open		Unkn.	215
XX	Merry Wanderer 11/2/0	Open		Unkn.	150
XX	Merry Wanderer 7/0	Open		Unkn.	300
XX	Mischief Maker 342	Open		Unkn.	300
1994	Morning Stroll 375/3/0	Open		170.00	195
XX	Mother's Darling 175	Open		Unkn.	230
XX	Mother's Helper 133	Open		Unkn.	215
XX	Mountaineer 315	Open		Unkn.	230
1991	A Nap 534	Open		Unkn.	130
1996	Nimble Fingers w/wooden bench 758	Open		225.00	225
XX	Not For You 317	Open		Unkn.	265
XX	On Holiday 350	Open		Unkn.	190
XX	On Secret Path 386	Open		Unkn.	270
1989	One For You, One For Me 482	Open		Unkn.	110
1993	One Plus One 556	Open		Unkn.	145
XX	Ooh My Tooth 533	Open		Unkn.	120
XX	Out of Danger 56/B	Open		Unkn.	320
1993	Parade Of Lights 616	Open		Unkn.	275
XX	The Photographer 178	Open		Unkn.	315
1995	Pixie 768	Open		Unkn.	115
XX	Playmates 58/0	Open		Unkn.	180
XX	Playmates 58/2/0	Open		Unkn.	160
XX	Playmates 58/I	Open		Unkn.	300
1994	The Poet 397/I	Open		220.00	250

YEAR ISSUE		EDITION LIMIT	YEAR RETD.	ISSUE PRICE	*QUOTE U.S.$
XX	Postman 119	Open		Unkn.	220
1989	Postman 119/2/0	Open		Unkn.	150
XX	Prayer Before Battle 20	Open		Unkn.	180
1992	The Professor 320	Open		Unkn.	220
1995	Puppy Love Display Plaque 767	Open		Unkn.	265
XX	Retreat to Safety 201/2/0	Open		Unkn.	175
XX	Retreat to Safety 201/I	Open		Unkn.	330
XX	Ride into Christmas 396/2/0	Open		Unkn.	260
XX	Ride into Christmas 396/I	Open		Unkn.	470
XX	Ring Around the Rosie 348	Open		Unkn.	2860
XX	The Run-A-Way 327	Open		Unkn.	275
1992	Scamp 553	Open		Unkn.	120
XX	School Boy 82/0	Open		Unkn.	215
XX	School Boy 82/2/0	Open		Unkn.	155
XX	School Boy 82/II	Open		Unkn.	500
XX	School Boys 170/I	Open		Unkn.	1320
XX	School Girl 81/0	Open		Unkn.	215
XX	School Girl 81/2/0	Open		Unkn.	155
XX	School Girls 177/I	Open		Unkn.	1320
XX	Sensitive Hunter 6/0	Open		Unkn.	215
XX	Sensitive Hunter 6/2/0	Open		Unkn.	160
XX	Sensitive Hunter 6/I	Open		Unkn.	275
XX	Serenade 85/0	Open		Unkn.	145
XX	Serenade 85/4/0	Open		Unkn.	110
XX	Serenade 85/II	Open		Unkn.	500
XX	She Loves Me, She Loves Me Not 174	Open		Unkn.	210
1996	Shepherd Boy 395/0	Open		295.00	295
XX	Shepherd's Boy 64	Open		Unkn.	250
XX	Shining Light 358	Open		Unkn.	95
XX	Sing Along 433	Open		Unkn.	300
XX	Sing With Me 405	Open		Unkn.	340
XX	Singing Lesson 63	Open		Unkn.	135
1995	Sister (Perpetual Calendar) 788B	Open		295.00	295
XX	Sister 98/0	Open		Unkn.	220
XX	Sister 98/2/0	Open		Unkn.	150
XX	Skier 59	Open		Unkn.	220
1990	Sleep Tight 424	Open		Unkn.	240
XX	Smart Little Sister 346	Open		Unkn.	275
XX	Soldier Boy 332	Open		Unkn.	230
XX	Soloist 135	Open		Unkn.	145
XX	Soloist 135/4/0	Open		Unkn.	110
1988	Song of Praise 454	Open		Unkn.	110
1988	Sound the Trumpet 457	Open		Unkn.	110
1988	Sounds of the Mandolin 438	Open		Unkn.	130
XX	Spring Dance 353/0	Open		Unkn.	340
XX	St. George 55	Open		Unkn.	350
XX	Star Gazer 132	Open		Unkn.	225
XX	Stitch in Time 255/4/0	Open		Unkn.	105
XX	Stitch in Time 255/I	Open		Unkn.	315
XX	Stormy Weather 71/2/0	Open		Unkn.	330
XX	Stormy Weather 71/I	Open		Unkn.	495
1992	Storybook Time 458	Open		Unkn.	420
XX	Street Singer 131	Open		Unkn.	210
XX	Surprise 94/3/0	Open		Unkn.	165
XX	Surprise 94/I	Open		Unkn.	315
XX	Sweet Greetings 352	Open		Unkn.	220
XX	Sweet Music 186	Open		Unkn.	220
XX	Telling Her Secret 196/0	Open		Unkn.	325
XX	Thoughtful 415	Open		Unkn.	240
XX	Timid Little Sister 394	Open		Unkn.	470
1995	To Keep You Warm w/ Wooden Chair 759	Open		Unkn.	215
XX	To Market 49/0	Open		Unkn.	315
XX	To Market 49/3/0	Open		Unkn.	175
XX	Trumpet Boy 97	Open		Unkn.	145
1989	Tuba Player 437	Open		Unkn.	290
XX	Tuneful Angel 359	Open		Unkn.	95
1996	A Tuneful Trio	20,000		450.00	450
XX	Umbrella Boy 152/A/0	Open		Unkn.	630
XX	Umbrella Boy 152/A/II	Open		Unkn.	1600
XX	Umbrella Girl 152/B/0	Open		Unkn.	630
XX	Umbrella Girl 152/B/II	Open		Unkn.	1600
XX	Village Boy 51/0	Open		Unkn.	275
XX	Village Boy 51/2/0	Open		Unkn.	155
XX	Village Boy 51/3/0	Open		Unkn.	130
XX	Visiting an Invalid 382	Open		Unkn.	220
XX	Volunteers 50/0	Open		Unkn.	325
XX	Volunteers 50/2/0	Open		Unkn.	240
XX	Waiter 154/0	Open		Unkn.	230
XX	Waiter 154/I	Open		Unkn.	315
1989	Wash Day 321/4/0	Open		Unkn.	110
XX	Wash Day 321/I	Open		Unkn.	315
XX	Watchful Angel 194	Open		Unkn.	340
XX	Wayside Devotion 28/II	Open		Unkn.	450
XX	Wayside Devotion 28/III	Open		Unkn.	600
XX	Wayside Harmony 111/3/0	Open		Unkn.	160
XX	Wayside Harmony 111/I	Open		Unkn.	300
1993	We Come In Peace (Commemorative) 754	Open		385.00	385
XX	We Congratulate 214/E/I	Open		Unkn.	175
XX	We Congratulate 220	Open		Unkn.	165
XX	Weary Wanderer 204	Open		Unkn.	275
1990	What's New? 418	Open		Unkn.	300
XX	Which Hand? 258	Open		Unkn.	215
1992	Whistler's Duet 413	Open		Unkn.	310
XX	Whitsuntide 163	Open		Unkn.	330
1988	A Winter Song 476	Open		Unkn.	120
XX	With Loving Greetings 309	Open		Unkn.	210
XX	Worship 84/0	Open		Unkn.	175

M.I. Hummel Collectibles Figurines Retired - M.I. Hummel

YEAR ISSUE		EDITION LIMIT	YEAR RETD.	ISSUE PRICE	*QUOTE U.S.$
1947	Accordion Boy 185	Closed	1994	Unkn.	200-500
1939	Duet 130	Open	1995	Unkn.	280-2200
1937	Farewell 65 TMK1-5	Closed	1993	Unkn.	250-700
1937	Globe Trotter 79 TMK1-7	Closed	1991	Unkn.	200-500
1937	Lost Sheep 68/0 TMK1-7	Closed	1992	Unkn.	225-300
1955	Lost Sheep 68/2/0 TMK2-7	Closed	1992	7.50	125-300
1935	Puppy Love I TMK1-6	Closed	1988	125.00	300-700
1948	Signs Of Spring 203/2/0 TMK2-6	Closed	1990	120.00	250-900
1948	Signs Of Spring 203/I TMK2-6	Closed	1990	155.00	265-750
1935	Strolling Along 5 TMK1-6	Closed	1989	115.00	265-750

M.I. Hummel Collectibles Madonna Figurines - M.I. Hummel

YEAR ISSUE		EDITION LIMIT	YEAR RETD.	ISSUE PRICE	*QUOTE U.S.$
XX	Flower Madonna, color 10/I/II	Open		Unkn.	470
XX	Madonna with Halo, color 45/I/6	Open		Unkn.	135

M.I. Hummel Collectibles Nativity Components - M. I. Hummel, unless otherwise noted

YEAR ISSUE		EDITION LIMIT	YEAR RETD.	ISSUE PRICE	*QUOTE U.S.$
XX	Ox 214/K/I	Open		Unkn.	75
XX	12-Pc. Set Figs. only, Color, 214/A/M/I, B/I, A/K/I, F/I G/I J/I K/I, L/I, M/I, N/I, O/I, 366/I	Open		Unkn.	1680
XX	Angel Serenade 214/D/I	Open		Unkn.	100
XX	Camel Kneeling - Goebel	Open		Unkn.	275
XX	Camel Lying - Goebel	Open		Unkn.	275
XX	Camel Standing - Goebel	Open		Unkn.	275
XX	Donkey 214/J/0	Open		Unkn.	55
XX	Donkey 214/J/I	Open		Unkn.	75
XX	Flying Angel/color 366/I	Open		Unkn.	135
XX	Good Night 214/C/I	Open		Unkn.	100
XX	Holy Family, 3 Pcs., Color 214/A/M/0, B/0, A/K/0	Open		Unkn.	330
XX	Holy Family, 3 Pcs., Color 214/A/M/I, B/I, A/K/I	Open		Unkn.	440
XX	Infant Jesus 214/A/K/0	Open		Unkn.	45
XX	Infant Jesus 214/A/K/I	Open		Unkn.	70
XX	King, Kneeling 214/M/I	Open		Unkn.	195
XX	King, Kneeling 214M/0	Open		Unkn.	155
XX	King, Kneeling w/ Box 214/N/0	Open		Unkn.	150
XX	King, Kneeling w/Box 214/N/I	Open		Unkn.	175
XX	King, Moorish 214/L/0	Open		Unkn.	165
XX	King, Moorish 214/L/I	Open		Unkn.	200
XX	Lamb 214/O/0	Open		Unkn.	22
XX	Lamb 214/O/I	Open		Unkn.	22
XX	Little Tooter 214/H/0	Open		Unkn.	110
XX	Little Tooter 214/H/I	Open		Unkn.	135
XX	Madonna 214/A/M/0	Open		Unkn.	145
XX	Madonna 214/A/M/I	Open		Unkn.	195
XX	Ox 214/K/0	Open		Unkn.	55
XX	Shepherd Boy 214/G/I	Open		Unkn.	145
XX	Shepherd Kneeling 214/G/0	Open		Unkn.	130
XX	Shepherd Standing 214/F/0	Open		Unkn.	165
XX	Shepherd with Sheep-1 piece 214/F/I	Open		Unkn.	195
XX	Small Camel Kneeling - Goebel	Open		Unkn.	220
XX	Small Camel Lying - Goebel	Open		Unkn.	220
XX	Small Camel Standing - Goebel	Open		Unkn.	220
XX	St. Joseph 214/B/0	Open		Unkn.	145
XX	St. Joseph color 214/B/I	Open		Unkn.	195
XX	Stable only fits12 or 16-pc. HUM214/II Set	Open		Unkn.	110
XX	Stable only, fits 16-piece HUM260 Set	Open		Unkn.	440
XX	Stable only, fits 3-pc. HUM214 Set	Open		Unkn.	50
XX	We Congratulate 214/E/I	Open		Unkn.	175

M.I. Hummel Disneyana Figurines - M.I. Hummel

YEAR ISSUE		EDITION LIMIT	YEAR RETD.	ISSUE PRICE	*QUOTE U.S.$
1995	For Father	1,500		450.00	450
1995	Grandpa's Boys	1,500		340.00	340
1994	Minnie Be Patient	1,500	1994	395.00	425-480
1993	Two Little Drummers	1,500	1993	325.00	450-650
1992	Two Merry Wanderers 022074	1,500	1992	250.00	800-1200

M.I. Hummel First Edition Miniatures - M.I. Hummel

YEAR ISSUE		EDITION LIMIT	YEAR RETD.	ISSUE PRICE	*QUOTE U.S.$
1991	Accordion Boy -37225	Suspd.		105.00	105-135
1989	Apple Tree Boy -37219	Suspd.		115.00	130-200
1990	Baker -37222	Suspd.		100.00	125-150
1992	Bavarian Church (Display) -37370	Closed	N/A	60.00	60-70
1988	Bavarian Cottage (Display) -37355	Closed	N/A	60.00	75-90
1990	Bavarian Marketsquare Bridge(Display) -37358	Closed	N/A	110.00	110-125
1988	Bavarian Village (Display) -37356	Closed	N/A	100.00	105
1991	Busy Student -37226	Suspd.		105.00	130
1990	Cinderella -37223	Suspd.		115.00	120-190
1991	Countryside School (Display) -37365	Closed	N/A	100.00	100-110
1989	Doll Bath -37214	Suspd.		95.00	115
1995	Festival Harmony 173/4/0	Open		100.00	100
1992	Goose Girl -37238	Suspd.		130.00	180-225
1989	Little Fiddler -37211	Suspd.		90.00	125
1989	Little Sweeper -37212	Suspd.		90.00	115-150
1990	Marketsquare Flower Stand (Display) -37360	Closed	N/A	35.00	50-80
1990	Marketsquare Hotel (Display)-37359	Closed	N/A	70.00	90-125
1989	Merry Wanderer -37213	Suspd.		95.00	115-135
1991	Merry Wanderer Dealer Plaque -37229	Closed	N/A	130.00	135
1989	Postman -37217	Suspd.		95.00	125-150
1991	Roadside Shrine (Display)-37366	Closed	N/A	60.00	60
1992	School Boy -37236	Suspd.		120.00	150-180
1991	Serenade -37228	Suspd.		105.00	105-135

*Quotes have been rounded up to nearest dollar

Left Column

YEAR ISSUE	EDITION LIMIT	YEAR RETD.	ISSUE PRICE	*QUOTE U.S.$
1992 Snow-Covered Mountain (Display)-37371	Closed	N/A	100.00	100
1989 Stormy Weather - 37215	Suspd.		115.00	130-180
1992 Trees (Display)-37369	Closed	N/A	40.00	40-50
1989 Visiting an Invalid -37218	Suspd.		105.00	130-160
1990 Waiter - 37221	Suspd.		100.00	115-135
1992 Wayside Harmony -37237	Suspd.		140.00	165-180
1991 We Congratulate - 37227	Suspd.		130.00	130

M.I. Hummel Pen Pals - M.I. Hummel

YEAR ISSUE	EDITION LIMIT	YEAR RETD.	ISSUE PRICE	*QUOTE U.S.$
1995 For Mother 257/5/0	Open		55.00	55
1995 March Winds 43/5/0	Open		55.00	55
1995 One For You, One For Me 482/5/0	Open		55.00	55
1995 Sister 98/5/0	Open		55.00	55
1995 Soloist 135/5/0	Open		55.00	55
1995 Village Boy 151/5/0	Open		55.00	55

M.I. Hummel Tree Toppers - M.I. Hummel

YEAR ISSUE	EDITION LIMIT	YEAR RETD.	ISSUE PRICE	*QUOTE U.S.$
1994 Heavenly Angel 755	Open		450.00	495

M.I. Hummel Vingettes w/Solitary Domes - M.I. Hummel

YEAR ISSUE	EDITION LIMIT	YEAR RETD.	ISSUE PRICE	*QUOTE U.S.$
1992 Bakery Day w/Baker & Waiter 37726	3,000		225.00	225
1992 The Flower Market w/Cinderella 37729	3,000		135.00	135
1993 The Mail Is Here Clock Tower 826504	Open		495.00	575
1995 Ring Around the Rosie Musical 826101	10,000		675.00	675
1992 Winterfest w/Ride Into Christmas 37728	5,000		195.00	195

M.I. Hummel's Temporarily Out of Production (including trademarks) - M.I. Hummel

YEAR ISSUE	EDITION LIMIT	YEAR RETD.	ISSUE PRICE	*QUOTE U.S.$
XX 16-Pc. Set Figs. only, Color, 214/A/M/I, B/I, A/K/I, C/I, D/I, E/I, F/I, G/I, H/I, J/I, K/I, L/I, M/I, N/I, O/I, 366/I	Suspd.		Unkn.	1990
XX 17-Pc. Set Large Color 16 Figs.& Wooden Stable 260 A-R	Suspd.		Unkn.	4540
XX Angel Serenade 260/E	Suspd.		Unkn.	345-445
XX Apple Tree Boy 142/X	Suspd.		Unkn.	17000
XX Apple Tree Girl 141/X	Suspd.		Unkn.	17000
XX Blessed Child 78/I/83	Suspd.		Unkn.	35
XX Blessed Child 78/II/83	Suspd.		Unkn.	50
XX Blessed Child 78/III/83	Suspd.		Unkn.	60
XX Bookworm 3/II	Suspd.		Unkn.	675-1350
XX Bookworm 3/III	Suspd.		Unkn.	1195-2100
XX Celestial Musician 188/I	Suspd.		Unkn.	255-475
XX Christ Child 18	Suspd.		Unkn.	130-325
XX Donkey 260/L	Suspd.		Unkn.	135
XX Festival Harmony, w/Flute 173/II	Suspd.		Unkn.	400-1000
XX Festival Harmony, w/Mandolin 172/II	Suspd.		Unkn.	400-1000
XX Flower Madonna, color 10/III/I	Suspd.		Unkn.	600-750
XX Flower Madonna, white 10/I/W	Suspd.		Unkn.	165-420
XX Flower Madonna, white 10/III/W	Suspd.		Unkn.	470-750
XX Going to Grandma's 52/I	Suspd.		Unkn.	350-900
XX Good Night 260/D	Suspd.		Unkn.	145
XX Goose Girl 47/II	Suspd.		Unkn.	400-1000
XX Happy Traveler 109/II	Suspd.		Unkn.	350-975
XX Hear Ye! Hear Ye! 15/II	Suspd.		Unkn.	375-1500
XX Heavenly Angel 21/II	Suspd.		Unkn.	415-1025
XX Heavenly Protection 88/II	Suspd.		Unkn.	600-900
XX Hello 124/I	Suspd.		Unkn.	175-385
XX Holy Child 70	Suspd.		Unkn.	160-400
XX Hummel Display Plaque 187	Suspd.		Unkn.	125-150
XX Infant Jesus 260/C	Suspd.		Unkn.	120
1985 Jubilee 416 TMK6	Suspd.		200.00	275-380
XX King, Kneeling 260/P	Suspd.		Unkn.	480
XX King, Moorish 260/N	Suspd.		Unkn.	430-500
XX King, Standing 260/O	Suspd.		Unkn.	300-500
XX Little Band 392	Suspd.		Unkn.	250-350
XX Little Cellist 89/II	Suspd.		Unkn.	400-650
XX Little Fiddler 2/I	Suspd.		Unkn.	260-650
XX Little Fiddler 2/II	Suspd.		Unkn.	1100-3000
XX Little Fiddler 2/III	Suspd.		Unkn.	1200-3500
XX Little Tooter 260/K	Suspd.		Unkn.	170-195
XX Lullaby 24/III	Suspd.		Unkn.	450-1800
XX Madonna 260/A	Suspd.		Unkn.	590
XX Madonna Holding Child, color 151/I	Suspd.		Unkn.	115
XX Madonna Holding Child, white 151/W	Suspd.		Unkn.	320
XX Madonna Praying, color 46/III/6	Suspd.		Unkn.	140-400
XX Madonna Praying, white 46/0/W	Suspd.		Unkn.	40-195
XX Madonna Praying, white 46/I/W	Suspd.		Unkn.	70-175
XX Madonna w/o Halo, color 46/I/6	Suspd.		Unkn.	115-300
XX Madonna w/o Halo, white 45/I/W	Suspd.		Unkn.	70-175
XX Madonna w/o Halo, white 46/I/W	Suspd.		Unkn.	70-175
XX Meditation 13/V	Suspd.		Unkn.	1200-5000
XX Meditation, color 13/II	Suspd.		Unkn.	400-4500
XX Merry Wanderer 7/II	Suspd.		Unkn.	850-2200
XX Merry Wanderer 7/III	Suspd.		Unkn.	925-1300
XX Merry Wanderer 7/X	Suspd.		Unkn.	12000-20000
XX Merry Wanderer Stepbase 7/I	Suspd.		Unkn.	360-960
1995 Ooh My Tooth (Special Event) 533	Suspd.		Unkn.	120
XX Ox 260/M	Suspd.		Unkn.	135
XX School Boys 170/III	Suspd.		Unkn.	1600-2000
XX School Girls 177/III	Suspd.		Unkn.	1500-2200
XX Sensitive Hunter 6/II	Suspd.		Unkn.	400-1000
XX Sheep (Lying) 260/R	Suspd.		Unkn.	100

Middle Column

YEAR ISSUE	EDITION LIMIT	YEAR RETD.	ISSUE PRICE	*QUOTE U.S.$
XX Sheep (Standing) w/ Lamb 260/H	Suspd.		Unkn.	110
XX Shepherd Boy, Kneeling 260/J	Suspd.		Unkn.	300
XX Shepherd, Standing 260/G	Suspd.		Unkn.	525
XX Spring Cheer 72	Suspd.		Unkn.	165-500
XX Spring Dance 353/I	Suspd.		Unkn.	500-750
XX St. Joseph 260/B	Suspd.		Unkn.	520
1984 Supreme Protection 364 TMK6	Suspd.		150.00	350
XX Telling Her Secret 196/I	Suspd.		Unkn.	430-800
XX To Market 49/I	Suspd.		Unkn.	300-850
XX Village Boy 51/I	Suspd.		Unkn.	250-650
XX Volunteers 50/I	Suspd.		Unkn.	430-1400
XX We Congratulate 260/F	Suspd.		Unkn.	400
XX Worship 84/V	Suspd.		Unkn.	800-2800

Gorham

(Four Seasons) A Boy And His Dog - N. Rockwell

YEAR ISSUE	EDITION LIMIT	YEAR RETD.	ISSUE PRICE	*QUOTE U.S.$
1972 A Boy Meets His Dog	2,500	1980	200.00	1300-1575
1972 Adventurers Between Adventures	2,500	1980	Set	Set
1972 The Mysterious Malady	2,500	1980	Set	Set
1972 Pride of Parenthood	2,500	1980	Set	Set

(Four Seasons) A Helping Hand - N. Rockwell

1980 Year End Court	2,500	1980	650.00	650-700
1980 Closed For Business	2,500	1980	Set	Set
1980 Swatter's Right	2,500	1980	Set	Set
1980 Coal Seasons Coming	2,500	1980	Set	Set

(Four Seasons) Dad's Boy - N. Rockwell

1981 Ski Skills	2,500	1990	750.00	750-800
1981 In His Spirit	2,500	1990	Set	Set
1981 Trout Dinner	2,500	1990	Set	Set
1981 Careful Aim	2,500	1990	Set	Set

(Four Seasons) Four Ages of Love - N. Rockwell

1974 Gaily Sharing Vintage Times	2,500	1980	300.00	600-1250
1974 Sweet Song So Young	2,500	1980	Set	Set
1974 Flowers In Tender Bloom	2,500	1980	Set	Set
1974 Fondly Do We Remember	2,500	1980	Set	Set

(Four Seasons) Going On Sixteen - N. Rockwell

1978 Chilling Chore	2,500	1980	400.00	650-675
1978 Sweet Serenade	2,500	1980	Set	Set
1978 Shear Agony	2,500	1980	Set	Set
1978 Pilgrimage	2,500	1980	Set	Set

(Four Seasons) Grand Pals - N. Rockwell

1977 Snow Sculpturing	2,500	1980	350.00	1000-1200
1977 Soaring Spirits	2,500	1980	Set	Set
1977 Fish Finders	2,500	1980	Set	Set
1977 Ghostly Gourds	2,500	1980	Set	Set

(Four Seasons) Grandpa and Me - N. Rockwell

1975 Gay Blades	2,500	1980	300.00	800-1000
1975 Day Dreamers	2,500	1980	Set	Set
1975 Goin' Fishing	2,500	1980	Set	Set
1975 Pensive Pals	2,500	1980	Set	Set

(Four Seasons) Life With Father - N. Rockwell

1983 Big Decision	2,500	1990	250.00	250
1983 Blasting Out	2,500	1990	Set	Set
1983 Cheering The Champs	2,500	1990	Set	Set
1983 A Tough One	2,500	1990	Set	Set

(Four Seasons) Me and My Pal - N. Rockwell

1976 A Licking Good Bath	2,500	1980	300.00	1200
1976 Young Man's Fancy	2,500	1980	Set	Set
1976 Fisherman's Paradise	2,500	1980	Set	Set
1976 Disastrous Daring	2,500	1980	Set	Set

(Four Seasons) Old Buddies - N. Rockwell

1984 Shared Success	2,500	1990	250.00	250
1984 Hasty Retreat	2,500	1990	Set	Set
1984 Final Speech	2,500	1990	Set	Set
1984 Endless Debate	2,500	1990	Set	Set

(Four Seasons) Old Timers - N. Rockwell

1982 Canine Solo	2,500	1990	250.00	250
1982 Sweet Surprise	2,500	1990	Set	Set
1982 Lazy Days	2,500	1990	Set	Set
1982 Fancy Footwork	2,500	1990	Set	Set

(Four Seasons) Tender Years - N. Rockwell

1979 New Year Look	2,500	1979	500.00	550-650
1979 Spring Tonic	2,500	1979	Set	Set
1979 Cool Aid	2,500	1979	Set	Set
1979 Chilly Reception	2,500	1979	Set	Set

(Four Seasons) Traveling Salesman - N. Rockwell

1985 Horse Trader	2,500	1985	275.00	250-275
1985 Expert Salesman	2,500	1985	Set	Set
1985 Traveling Salesman	2,500	1985	Set	Set
1985 Country Pedlar	2,500	1985	Set	Set

(Four Seasons) Young Love - N. Rockwell

1973 Downhill Daring	2,500	1973	250.00	1100
1973 Beguiling Buttercup	2,500	1973	Set	Set
1973 Flying High	2,500	1973	Set	Set
1973 A Scholarly Pace	2,500	1973	Set	Set

Right Column

Miniature Christmas Figurines - Various

YEAR ISSUE	EDITION LIMIT	YEAR RETD.	ISSUE PRICE	*QUOTE U.S.$
1979 Tiny Tim - N. Rockwell	Yr.Iss.	1979	15.00	20
1980 Santa Plans His Trip - N. Rockwell	Yr.Iss.	1980	15.00	15
1981 Yuletide Reckoning - N. Rockwell	Yr.Iss.	1981	20.00	20
1982 Checking Good Deeds - N. Rockwell	Yr.Iss.	1982	20.00	20
1983 Santa's Friend - N. Rockwell	Yr.Iss.	1983	20.00	20
1984 Downhill Daring - N. Rockwell	Yr.Iss.	1984	20.00	20
1985 Christmas Santa - T. Nast	Yr.Iss.	1985	20.00	20
1986 Christmas Santa - T. Nast	Yr.Iss.	1986	25.00	25
1987 Annual Thomas Nast Santa - T. Nast	Yr.Iss.	1987	25.00	25

Miniatures - N. Rockwell

YEAR ISSUE	EDITION LIMIT	YEAR RETD.	ISSUE PRICE	*QUOTE U.S.$
1982 The Annual Visit	Closed	1990	50.00	75
1981 At the Vets	Closed	1990	27.50	40
1987 Babysitter	15,000	1990	75.00	75
1981 Beguiling Buttercup	Closed	1990	45.00	45
1985 Best Friends	Closed	1990	27.50	28
1987 Between The Acts	15,000	1990	60.00	60
1981 Boy Meets His Dog	Closed	1990	37.50	38
1984 Careful Aims	Closed	1990	55.00	55
1987 Cinderella	15,000	1990	70.00	75
1981 Downhill Daring	Closed	1990	45.00	75
1985 Engineer	Closed	1990	55.00	55
1981 Flowers in Tender Bloom	Closed	1990	60.00	60
1986 Football Season	Closed	1990	60.00	60
1981 Gay Blades	Closed	1990	45.00	75
1984 Ghostly Gourds	Closed	1990	60.00	60
1984 Goin Fishing	Closed	1990	60.00	60
1986 The Graduate	Closed	1990	30.00	40
1984 In His Spirit	Closed	1990	60.00	60
1986 Lemonade Stand	Closed	1990	60.00	60
1986 Little Angel	Closed	1990	50.00	60
1985 Little Red Truck	Closed	1990	25.00	25
1982 Marriage License	Closed	1990	60.00	75
1987 The Milkmaid	15,000	1990	80.00	85
1986 Morning Walk	Closed	1990	60.00	60
1985 Muscle Bound	Closed	1990	30.00	30
1985 New Arrival	Closed	1990	32.50	35
1986 The Old Sign Painter	Closed	1990	70.00	80
1984 Pride of Parenthood	Closed	1990	50.00	50
1987 The Prom Dress	15,000	1990	75.00	75
1982 The Runaway	Closed	1990	50.00	50
1984 Shear Agony	Closed	1990	60.00	60
1986 Shoulder Ride	Closed	1990	50.00	65
1981 Snow Sculpture	Closed	1990	45.00	70
1985 Spring Checkup	Closed	1990	60.00	60
1987 Springtime	15,000	1990	65.00	75
1987 Starstruck	15,000	1990	75.00	80
1981 Sweet Serenade	Closed	1990	45.00	45
1981 Sweet Song So Young	Closed	1990	55.00	55
1985 To Love & Cherish	Closed	1990	32.50	35
1982 Triple Self Portrait	Closed	1990	60.00	90-150
1983 Trout Dinner	15,000	1990	60.00	60
1982 Vintage Times	Closed	1990	50.00	50
1986 Welcome Mat	Closed	1990	70.00	75
1984 Years End Court	Closed	1990	60.00	60
1981 Young Man's Fancy	Closed	1990	55.00	55

Parasol Lady - Unknown

YEAR ISSUE	EDITION LIMIT	YEAR RETD.	ISSUE PRICE	*QUOTE U.S.$
1991 On the Boardwalk	Closed	1993	95.00	95
1994 Sunday Promenade	Closed	1993	95.00	95
1994 At The Fair	Closed	1993	95.00	95

Rockwell - N. Rockwell

YEAR ISSUE	EDITION LIMIT	YEAR RETD.	ISSUE PRICE	*QUOTE U.S.$
1983 Antique Dealer	7,500	1990	130.00	200
1982 April Fool's (At The Curiosity Shop)	Closed	1990	55.00	100-110
1974 At The Vets	Closed	1990	25.00	85
1974 Batter Up	Closed	1990	40.00	90-235
1975 Boy And His Dog	Closed	1990	38.00	95
1974 Captain	Closed	1990	45.00	95
1984 Card Tricks	7,500	1990	110.00	180
1981 Christmas Dancers	7,500	1990	130.00	195
1988 Confrontation	15,000	1990	75.00	75
1988 Cramming	15,000	1990	80.00	80
1981 Day in the Life Boy II	Closed	1990	75.00	100
1982 A Day in the Life Boy III	Closed	1990	85.00	95
1982 A Day in the Life Girl III	Closed	1990	85.00	150
1988 The Diary	15,000	1990	80.00	80
1988 Dolores & Eddie	15,000	1990	75.00	80
1986 Drum For Tommy	Annual	1986	90.00	N/A
1983 Facts of Life	7,500	1990	110.00	180
1974 Fishing	Closed	1990	50.00	135
1988 Gary Cooper in Hollywood	15,000	1990	90.00	90
1976 God Rest Ye Merry Gentlemen	Closed	1990	50.00	1000-1500
1988 Home for the Holidays	7,500	1990	100.00	100
1976 Independence	Closed	1990	40.00	150
1980 Jolly Coachman	7,500	1990	75.00	175
1982 Marriage License	5,000	1990	110.00	400-600
1976 Marriage License	Closed	1990	50.00	175
1982 Merrie Christmas	7,500	1990	75.00	150
1974 Missing Tooth	Closed	1990	30.00	150
1975 No Swimming	Closed	1990	35.00	175
1976 The Occultist	Closed	1990	50.00	125-180
1975 Old Mill Pond	Closed	1990	45.00	95
1985 The Old Sign Painter	7,500	1990	130.00	210
1985 Puppet Maker	7,500	1990	130.00	130-200
1987 Santa Planning His Annual Visit	7,500	1990	95.00	95
1984 Santa's Friend	7,500	1990	75.00	160

YEAR ISSUE		EDITION LIMIT	YEAR RETD.	ISSUE PRICE	*QUOTE U.S.$
1976	Saying Grace	Closed	1990	75.00	120
1982	Saying Grace	5,000	1990	110.00	500-600
1984	Serenade	7,500	1990	95.00	165
1974	Skating	Closed	1990	37.50	85
1976	Tackled (Ad Stand)	Closed	1990	35.00	150
1982	Tackled (Rockwell Name Signed)	Closed	1990	45.00	100
1974	Tiny Tim	Closed	1990	30.00	100
1982	Triple Self Portrait	5,000	1990	300.00	550
1974	Weighing In	Closed	1990	40.00	150
1981	Wet Sport	Closed	1990	85.00	100

Great American Taylor Collectibles

Great American Collectors' Club - L. Smith, unless otherwise noted

YEAR ISSUE		EDITION LIMIT	YEAR RETD.	ISSUE PRICE	*QUOTE U.S.$
1993	William Claus-USA 700s	Retrd.	1994	35.00	75
1994	Winston-England 716	Retrd.	1995	35.00	60
1995	Timothy Claus-Ireland 717	12/96		35.00	35
1995	Kris Jingle 817 - J. Clement	12/96		70.00	80
1996	Palmer-USA 723	12/97		50.00	50
1996	Big Catch 830 - J. Clement	12/97		60.00	60

Jim Clement Collection - J. Clement

YEAR ISSUE		EDITION LIMIT	YEAR RETD.	ISSUE PRICE	*QUOTE U.S.$
1994	Americana Patriotic Santa 807	Retrd.	1994	20.00	20
1994	Bearded Shorty Santa 812	Retrd.	1994	13.50	16
1994	Big Santa w/Toys 813	12/96		70.00	70
1994	Day After Christmas 809	Retrd.	1995	16.50	17
1995	Doe a Deer 818	12/97		29.00	30
1994	Down the Chimney Santa 814	Retrd.	1995	28.00	30
1994	Golfer Santa 806	Retrd.	1995	28.00	33
1996	Heading South 828	12/98		32.00	32
1995	Ho! Ho! Ho! 819	12/97		11.50	12
1996	Hogan 827	12/98		29.00	29
1995	Mountain Dream 821	12/97		27.00	30
1994	Mr. Egg Santa 802	Retrd.	1995	19.50	22
1994	Mrs. Clement's Santa 808	Retrd.	1994	17.00	17
1994	Night After Christmas 810	12/96		16.50	17
1996	Night Cats 825	12/98		30.00	30
1994	Noah Santa 805	12/96		28.00	30
1996	Radar 826	12/98		13.00	13
1994	Santa High Hat 815	Retrd.	1994	30.00	35
1994	Santa w/Rover 811	12/96		20.00	20
1994	Santa w/Tree 804	Retrd.	1994	15.00	18
1995	Silent Night 820	12/97		29.00	32
1994	Sm. Hobby Horse Santa 803	Retrd.	1995	28.00	33
1996	Ted 829	12/98		29.00	29
1994	Tennis Santa 816	12/96		28.00	29
1995	Visions of Sugar Plums 822	12/97		23.00	25

Lamp Collection - J. Clement

YEAR ISSUE		EDITION LIMIT	YEAR RETD.	ISSUE PRICE	*QUOTE U.S.$
1995	Clementine Cat 55LNKS	12/97		70.00	79
1995	Kris Jingle 817LRS	12/96		99.00	99
1995	Toy Soldier 57LSS	12/97		80.00	80
1995	Uncle Sam 56LRS	12/97		80.00	80

Old World Santas - L. Smith

YEAR ISSUE		EDITION LIMIT	YEAR RETD.	ISSUE PRICE	*QUOTE U.S.$
1988	Jangle Claus-Ireland 335s	Retrd.	1990	20.00	145-160
1988	Hans Von Claus-Germany 337s	Retrd.	1990	20.00	145-160
1988	Ching Chang Claus-China 338s	Retrd.	1990	20.00	145-160
1988	Kris Kringle Claus-Switzerland 339s	Retrd.	1990	20.00	145-160
1988	Jingle Claus-England 336s	Retrd.	1990	20.00	145-160
1989	Rudy Claus-Austria 410s	Retrd.	1991	20.00	130
1989	Noel Claus-Belguim 412s	Retrd.	1991	20.00	130
1989	Pierre Claus-France 414s	Retrd.	1991	20.00	130
1989	Nicholai Claus-Russia 413s	Retrd.	1991	20.00	130
1989	Yule Claus-Germany 411s	Retrd.	1991	20.00	130
1990	Matts Claus-Sweden 430s	Retrd.	1992	20.00	85-105
1990	Vander Claus-Holland 433s	Retrd.	1992	20.00	85-105
1990	Sven Claus-Norway 432s	Retrd.	1992	20.00	85-105
1990	Cedric Claus-England 434s	Retrd.	1992	20.00	85-105
1990	Mario Claus-Italy 431s	Retrd.	1992	20.00	85-105
1991	Mitch Claus-England 437s	Retrd.	1993	25.00	65-80
1991	Samuel Claus-USA 436s	Retrd.	1993	25.00	65-80
1991	Duncan Claus-Scotland 439s	Retrd.	1993	25.00	65-80
1991	Benjamin Claus-Israel 438s	Retrd.	1993	25.00	65-80
1991	Boris Claus-Russia 435s	Retrd.	1993	25.00	65-80
1992	Mickey Claus-Ireland 701s	Retrd.	1994	25.00	55
1992	Jacques Claus-France 702s	Retrd.	1994	25.00	55
1992	Terry Claus-Denmark 703s	Retrd.	1994	25.00	55
1992	José Claus-Spain 704s	Retrd.	1994	25.00	55
1992	Stu Claus-Poland 705s	Retrd.	1994	25.00	55
1993	Otto Claus-Germany 707s	Retrd.	1995	27.50	45
1993	Franz Claus-Switzerland 706s	Retrd.	1995	27.50	45
1993	Bjorn Claus-Sweden 709s	Retrd.	1995	27.50	45
1993	Ryan Claus-Canada 710s	Retrd.	1995	27.50	45
1993	Vito Claus-Italy 708s	Retrd.	1995	27.50	45
1994	Angus Claus-Scotland 713s	12/96		29.00	30
1994	Ivan Claus-Russia 712s	12/96		29.00	30
1994	Desmond Claus-England 715s	12/96		29.00	30
1994	Gord Claus-Canada 714s	12/96		29.00	30
1995	Tomba Claus-South Africa 718s	12/97		29.00	30
1995	Butch Claus-United States 719s	12/97		29.00	30
1995	Lars Claus-Norway 720s	12/97		29.00	30
1995	Stach Claus-Poland 721s	12/97		29.00	30
1995	Raymond Claus-Galapagos Islands 722s	12/97		29.00	30
1996	Gunther-Germany 724s	12/98		30.00	30
1996	Sean-Ireland 725s	12/98		30.00	30
1996	René-France 728s	12/98		30.00	30
1996	Manuel-Mexico 726s	12/98		30.00	30
1996	Zorba-Greece 727s	12/98		30.00	30

Stars & Stripes Collection - J. Clement

YEAR ISSUE		EDITION LIMIT	YEAR RETD.	ISSUE PRICE	*QUOTE U.S.$
1996	American Glory 555	12/98		36.00	36
1996	Flying Sam 553	12/98		29.00	29
1996	Great American Chicken 552	12/98		39.00	39
1996	Small Sam 554	12/98		29.00	29
1996	Tall Sam 551	12/98		39.00	39

Greenwich Workshop

Christensen - J. Christensen

YEAR ISSUE		EDITION LIMIT	YEAR RETD.	ISSUE PRICE	*QUOTE U.S.$
1994	Bird Hunters (Bronze)	50	N/A	4500.00	4500
1990	The Candleman, AP (Bronze)	100	N/A	737.00	4500
1989	The Fish Walker (Bronze)	100	N/A	711.00	4500
1995	Old World Santa	950	1995	295.00	295

McCarthy, Kevin - K. McCarthy

YEAR ISSUE		EDITION LIMIT	YEAR RETD.	ISSUE PRICE	*QUOTE U.S.$
1991	Comanche Rider-Bronze	100	N/A	812.50	813
1991	Pony Express-Bronze	10	N/A	934.00	934
1994	Thunder of Hooves-Bronze	10	N/A	875.00	875

Hallmark Galleries

Kiddie Car Classics - E. Weirick

YEAR ISSUE		EDITION LIMIT	YEAR RETD.	ISSUE PRICE	*QUOTE U.S.$
1994	1936 Steelcraft Lincoln Zephyr by Murray QHG9015	19,500		50.00	50
1995	1937 Steelcraft Auburn Luxury Ed. QHG9021	24,500		65.00	65
1995	1937 Steelcraft Chrysler Airflow by Murray (R) QHG9024	24,500		65.00	65
1992	1940 Murray Airplane QHG9003	14,500	1993	50.00	125-240
1992	1941 Steelcraft Spitfire Airplane QHG9009	19,500		50.00	50
1995	1948 Murray Pontiac QHG9026	Open		50.00	50
1995	1950 Murray Torpedo QHG9020	Open		50.00	50
1992	1953 Murray Dump Truck QHG9012	14,500	1993	48.00	90-150
1992	1955 Murray Champion QHG9008	14,500	1993	45.00	150-200
1992	1955 Murray Dump Truck QHG9011	19,500		48.00	48
1993	1955 Murray Fire Chief QHG9006	19,500		45.00	45
1992	1955 Murray Fire Truck QHG9001	14,500	1993	50.00	160-225
1992	1955 Murray Fire Truck QHG9010	19,500		50.00	50
1993	1955 Murray Ranch Wagon QHG9007	24,500		48.00	48
1992	1955 Murray Red Champion QHG9002	19,500		45.00	45
1995	1955 Murray Royal Deluxe QHG9025	29,500		55.00	55
1992	1955 Murray Tractor and Trailer QHG9004	14,500	1993	55.00	125-195
1994	1956 Garton Dragnet Police Car QHG9016	24,500		50.00	50
1994	1956 Garton Kidillac (Sp. Ed.) QHX9094	Retrd.	1994	50.00	50
1994	1956 GARTON Mark V QHG9022	24,500		45.00	45
1994	1958 Murray Atomic Missile QHG9018	24,500		55.00	55
1995	1959 GARTON Deluxe Kidillac QHG9017	Open		55.00	55
1995	1961 GARTON Casey Jones Locomotive QHG9019	Open		55.00	55
1994	1961 Murray Circus Car QHG90014	24,500		48.00	48
1994	1961 Murray Speedway Pace Car 4500QHG9013	24,500		45.00	45
1995	1962 Murray Super Deluxe Fire Truck QHG9095	Open		55.00	55
1995	1964 GARTON Tin Lizzie QHG9023	Open		50.00	50
1993	1968 Murray Boat Jolly Roger QHG9005	19,500		50.00	50

Tender Touches - E. Seale

YEAR ISSUE		EDITION LIMIT	YEAR RETD.	ISSUE PRICE	*QUOTE U.S.$
1990	Baby Bear in Backpack QEC9863	Retrd.	1991	16.00	60
1988	Baby Raccoon QHG7031	Retrd.	1992	20.00	40
1991	Baby's 1st Riding Rocking Bear QEC9349	Retrd.	1991	16.00	16
1989	Bear Decorating Tree QHG7050	Retrd.	1995	18.00	40
1992	Bear Family Christmas QHG7002	9,500	1995	45.00	80
1990	Bear Graduate QHG7043	Retrd.	1995	15.00	15
1988	Bear w/ Umbrella QHG7029	Retrd.	1994	16.00	35
1990	Bear's Easter Parade QHG7040	Retrd.	1995	23.00	23
1990	Bears Playing Baseball QHG7039	Retrd.	1994	20.00	20
1990	Bears w/ Gift QEC9461	Retrd.	1991	18.00	50-65
1992	Beaver Growth Chart QHG7007	19,500	1995	20.00	20
1992	Beaver w/ Double Bass QHG7058	Retrd.	1995	18.00	18
1990	Beavers w/Tree QHG7052	Retrd.	1994	23.00	23
1989	Birthday Mouse QHG7010	Retrd.	1993	16.00	45
1992	Breakfast in Bed QHG7059	Retrd.	1995	18.00	18
1989	Bride & Groom QHG7009	Retrd.	1994	20.00	40
1992	Building a Pumpkin Man QHG7061	Retrd.	1995	18.00	18
1990	Bunnies Eating Ice Cream QHG7038	Retrd.	1995	20.00	20
1990	Bunnies w/ Slide QHG7016	Retrd.	1994	20.00	20
1990	Bunny Cheerleader QHG7018	Retrd.	1994	16.00	45
1992	Bunny Clarinet QHG7063	Retrd.	1994	16.00	16
1990	Bunny Hiding Valentine QHG7035	Retrd.	1995	16.00	16
1990	Bunny in Boat QHG7021	Retrd.	1994	18.00	40
1989	Bunny in Flowers QHG7012	Retrd.	1992	16.00	30
1991	Bunny in High Chair QHG7054	Retrd.	1995	16.00	16
1990	Bunny Pulling Wagon QHG7008	Retrd.	1994	23.00	23
1990	Bunny w/ Ice Cream QHG7020	Retrd.	1993	15.00	25
1992	Bunny w/ Kite QHG7006	19,500	1995	19.00	19
1991	Bunny w/ Large Eggs QHG7056	Retrd.	1995	16.00	50
1990	Bunny w/ Stocking QEC9416	Retrd.	1990	15.00	25
1992	Chatting Mice QHG7003	19,500	1995	23.00	60
1989	Chipmunk Praying QEC9431	Retrd.	1991	18.00	75
1989	Chipmunk w/Roses QHG7023	Retrd.	1992	16.00	35
1992	Chipmunks w/Album QHG7057	Retrd.	1995	23.00	35
1991	Christmas Bunny Skiing QHG7046	Retrd.	1995	18.00	18
1990	Dad and Son Bears QHG7015	Retrd.	1992	23.00	33
1992	Delightful Fright QHG7067	19,500	1995	23.00	75
1993	Downhill Dash QHG7080	Retrd.	1995	23.00	23
1990	Easter Egg Hunt QEC9866	Retrd.	1991	18.00	28
1993	Easter Stroll QHG7084	Retrd.	1995	21.00	21
1993	Ensemble Chipmunk Kettledrum QHG7087	Retrd.	1994	18.00	18
1991	Father Bear Barbequing QHG7041	Retrd.	1995	23.00	23
1994	Fireman QHG7090	Retrd.	1995	23.00	23
1991	First Christmas Mice @ Piano QEC9357	Retrd.	1991	23.00	23
1992	Fitting Gift QHG7065	Retrd.	1995	23.00	23
1991	Foxes in Rowboat QHG7053	Retrd.	1995	23.00	23
1992	From Your Valentine QHG7071	Retrd.	1995	20.00	20
1993	Garden Capers QHG7078	Retrd.	1995	20.00	20
1994	Golfing QHG7091	Retrd.	1995	23.00	23
1994	Halloween QHG7093	Retrd.	1995	23.00	23
1989	Halloween Trio QEC9714	Retrd.	1990	18.00	130-150
1993	Handling a Big Thirst QHG7076	Retrd.	1995	21.00	21
1994	Happy Campers QHG7092	Retrd.	1995	25.00	25
1994	Jesus, Mary, Joseph QHG7094	Retrd.	1995	23.00	23
1993	Love at First Sight QHG7085	Retrd.	1995	23.00	23
1991	Love-American Gothic-Farmer Raccoons QHG7047	Retrd.	1995	20.00	20
1993	Making A Splash QHG7088	Retrd.	1995	20.00	20
1988	Mice at Tea Party QHG7028	Retrd.	1993	23.00	23
1991	Mice Couple Slow Waltzing QEC9437	Retrd.	1991	20.00	20
1990	Mice in Red Car QEC9886	Retrd.	1991	20.00	30
1988	Mice in Rocking Chair QHG7030	Retrd.	1994	18.00	18
1990	Mice w/Mistletoe QEC9423	Retrd.	1990	20.00	30
1990	Mice w/Quilt QHG7017	Retrd.	1994	20.00	45
1992	Mom's Easter Bonnet QHG7072	Retrd.	1995	18.00	18
1991	Mother Raccoon Reading Bible Stories QHG7042	Retrd.	1994	20.00	20
1989	Mouse at Desk QEC9434	Retrd.	1990	18.00	50
1991	Mouse Couple Sharing Soda QHG7055	Retrd.	1995	23.00	23
1990	Mouse in Pumpkin QEC9473	Retrd.	1991	18.00	35
1992	Mouse Matinee QHG7073	Retrd.	1995	22.00	22
1990	Mouse Nurse QHG7037	Retrd.	1995	15.00	15
1988	Mouse w/Heart QHG7024	Retrd.	1993	18.00	18
1989	Mouse w/Violin QHG7049	Retrd.	1992	16.00	50
1993	Mr. Repair Bear QHG7075	Retrd.	1995	18.00	18
1992	New World, Ahoy! QHG7068	Retrd.	1995	25.00	45
1992	Newsboy Bear QHG7060	Retrd.	1995	16.00	16
1993	The Old Swimming Hole QHG7086	9,500	1995	45.00	80-150
1990	Pilgrim Bear Praying QEC9466	Retrd.	1991	18.00	65
1989	Pilgrim Mouse QEC9721	Retrd.	1990	16.00	95
1993	Playground Go-Round QHG7089	Retrd.	1995	23.00	23
1989	Rabbit Painting Egg QHG7022	Retrd.	1994	18.00	30
1988	Rabbit w/Ribbon QHG7027	Retrd.	1994	15.00	15
1988	Rabbits at Juice Stand QHG7033	Retrd.	1994	23.00	23
1989	Rabbits Ice Skating QEC9391	Retrd.	1991	18.00	28
1988	Rabbits w/Cake QHG7025	Retrd.	1992	20.00	40
1992	Raccoon in Bath QHG7069	Retrd.	1993	18.00	45
1990	Raccoon Mail Carrier QHG7013	Retrd.	1995	16.00	16
1988	Raccoon w/Cake QEC9724	Retrd.	1991	18.00	48
1990	Raccoon Watering Roses QHG7036	Retrd.	1994	20.00	20
1991	Raccoon Witch QHG7045	Retrd.	1994	16.00	35
1988	Raccoons Fishing QHG7034	Retrd.	1994	18.00	18
1992	Raccoons on Bridge QHG7004	19,500	1995	25.00	25
1988	Raccoons Playing Ball QEC9771	Retrd.	1991	18.00	40
1990	Raccoons w/Flag QHG7044	Retrd.	1994	23.00	45
1990	Raccoons w/Wagon QHG7014	Retrd.	1993	23.00	30
1990	Romeo & Juliet Mice QEC9903	Retrd.	1991	25.00	35
1990	Santa in Chimney QHG7051	Retrd.	1994	18.00	18
1989	Santa Mouse in Chair QEC9394	Retrd.	1990	20.00	125
1993	Sculpting Santa QHG7083	Retrd.	1995	20.00	20
1992	Soapbox Racer QHG7005	19,500	1995	23.00	23
1988	Squirrels w/Bandage QHG7032	Retrd.	1993	18.00	18
1992	Stealing a Kiss QHG7066	19,500	1995	23.00	23
1992	Sweet Sharing QHG7062	Retrd.	1995	20.00	20
1992	Swingtime Love QHG7070	Retrd.	1993	21.00	21
1990	Teacher & Student Chipmunks QHG7019	Retrd.	1992	20.00	30
1988	Teacher w/Student QHG7026	Retrd.	1995	18.00	18
1993	Teeter For Two QHG7077	Retrd.	1995	23.00	23
1992	Tender Touches Tree House QHG7001	9,500	1995	55.00	55
1992	Thanksgiving Family Around Table QHG7048	Retrd.	1995	25.00	25
1990	Tucking Baby in Bed QHG7011	Retrd.	1993	18.00	18
1992	Waiting for Santa QHG7064	Retrd.	1995	20.00	20
1993	Woodland Americana-Liberty Mouse QHG7081	Retrd.	1995	21.00	21
1993	Woodland Americana-Patriot George QHG7082	Retrd.	1995	25.00	25
1993	Woodland Americana-Stitching the Stars and Stripes QHG7079	Retrd.	1995	21.00	21

*Quotes have been rounded up to nearest dollar

FIGURINES/COTTAGES

YEAR ISSUE		EDITION LIMIT	YEAR RETD.	ISSUE PRICE	*QUOTE U.S.$
1992	Younger Than Springtime QHG7074	19,500	1995	35.00	50

Tobin Fraley Carousels - T. Fraley

YEAR ISSUE		EDITION LIMIT	YEAR RETD.	ISSUE PRICE	*QUOTE U.S.$
1994	Armour QHG25	4,500	1995	60.00	60
1992	C.W. Parker/1922 QHG5	4,500	1995	30.00	30
1992	C.W. Parker/1922/musical QHG13	4,500	1995	40.00	40
1992	Charles Carmel, circa 1914/musical QHG16	4,500	1995	40.00	40
1992	Charles Carmel/1914 QHG8	4,500	1995	30.00	30
1992	Charles Looff/1915 QHG1	4,500	1995	50.00	50
1992	Charles Looff/1915/musical QHG09	2,500	1995	60.00	60
1994	Floral QHG27	4,500	1995	60.00	60
1994	Indian QHG28	4,500	1995	60.00	60
1992	M.C. Illions & Sons/1910 QHG3	4,500	1995	50.00	50
1992	M.C. Illions & Sons/1910 QHG6	4,500	1995	30.00	30
1992	M.C. Illions & Sons/ 1910/musical QHG11	2,500	1995	60.00	60
1992	M.C. Illions & Sons/ 1910/musical QHG14	4,500	1995	40.00	40
1992	Musical Premier Horse 1QHG21	1,200	1995	275.00	275
1994	Patriot QHG26	4,500	1995	60.00	60
1992	Philadelphia Toboggan Co/1910 QHG7	4,500	1995	30.00	30
1992	Philadelphia Toboggan Co/1910/musical QHG15	4,500	1995	40.00	40
1992	Philadelphia Toboggan Co/1928 QHG2	4,500	1995	50.00	50
1992	Philadelphia Toboggan Co/1928/musical QHG10	2,500	1994	60.00	60
1992	Playland Carousel/musical 1QHG17	1,200	1993	195.00	195
1992	Revolving Brass/Wood Display QHG19	4,500	1995	40.00	40
1992	Stein & Goldstein/1914 QHG4	4,500	1995	50.00	50
1992	Stein & Goldstein/1914/musical QHG12	2,500	1995	60.00	60

Hamilton Collection

American Garden Flowers - D. Fryer

YEAR ISSUE		EDITION LIMIT	YEAR RETD.	ISSUE PRICE	*QUOTE U.S.$
1987	Azalea	15,000		75.00	75
1988	Calla Lilly	15,000		75.00	75
1987	Camelia	9,800		55.00	75
1988	Day Lily	15,000		75.00	75
1987	Gardenia	15,000		75.00	75
1989	Pansy	15,000		75.00	75
1988	Petunia	15,000		75.00	75
1987	Rose	15,000		75.00	75

American Wildlife Bronze Collection - H./N. Deaton

YEAR ISSUE		EDITION LIMIT	YEAR RETD.	ISSUE PRICE	*QUOTE U.S.$
1980	Beaver	7,500		60.00	65
1979	Bobcat	7,500		60.00	75
1979	Cougar	7,500		60.00	125
1980	Polar Bear	7,500		60.00	65
1980	Sea Otter	7,500		60.00	65
1979	White-Tailed Deer	7,500		60.00	105

A Celebration of Roses - N/A

YEAR ISSUE		EDITION LIMIT	YEAR RETD.	ISSUE PRICE	*QUOTE U.S.$
1989	Brandy	Open		55.00	55
1989	Color Magic	Open		55.00	55
1989	Honor	Open		55.00	55
1989	Miss All-American Beauty	Open		55.00	55
1991	Ole'	Open		55.00	55
1990	Oregold	Open		55.00	55
1991	Paradise	Open		55.00	55
1989	Tiffany	Open		55.00	55

Coral Kingdom - N/A

YEAR ISSUE		EDITION LIMIT	YEAR RETD.	ISSUE PRICE	*QUOTE U.S.$
1995	Athena	Open		35.00	35

Freshwater Challenge - M. Wald

YEAR ISSUE		EDITION LIMIT	YEAR RETD.	ISSUE PRICE	*QUOTE U.S.$
1992	Prized Catch	Open		75.00	75
1991	Rainbow Lure	Open		75.00	75
1991	The Strike	Open		75.00	75
1991	Sun Catcher	Open		75.00	75

Gifts of the Ancient Spirits - S. Kehrli

YEAR ISSUE		EDITION LIMIT	YEAR RETD.	ISSUE PRICE	*QUOTE U.S.$
1996	Talesman of Courage	Open		79.00	79

Gone With The Wind-Porcelain Trading Cards - N/A

YEAR ISSUE		EDITION LIMIT	YEAR RETD.	ISSUE PRICE	*QUOTE U.S.$
1995	Fire and Passion	28-day		14.95	15
1995	Scarlett and Her Suitors	28-day		14.95	15
1996	Portrait of Scarlett	28-day		14.95	15
1996	Portrait of Rhett	28-day		14.95	15
1996	The Proposal	28-day		14.95	15

Heroes of Baseball-Porcelain Baseball Cards - N/A

YEAR ISSUE		EDITION LIMIT	YEAR RETD.	ISSUE PRICE	*QUOTE U.S.$
1990	Brooks Robinson	Open		19.50	20
1991	Casey Stengel	Open		19.50	20
1990	Duke Snider	Open		19.50	20
1991	Ernie Banks	Open		19.50	20
1991	Gil Hodges	Open		19.50	20
1991	Jackie Robinson	Open		19.50	20
1991	Mickey Mantle	Open		19.50	20
1990	Roberto Clemente	Open		19.50	20
1991	Satchel Page	Open		19.50	20
1991	Whitey Ford	Open		19.50	20
1990	Willie Mays	Open		19.50	20
1991	Yogi Berra	Open		19.50	20

International Santa - N/A

YEAR ISSUE		EDITION LIMIT	YEAR RETD.	ISSUE PRICE	*QUOTE U.S.$
1995	Alpine Santa	Open		55.00	55
1993	Belsnickel	Open		55.00	55
1995	Dedushka Moroz	Open		55.00	55
1992	Father Christmas	Open		55.00	55
1992	Grandfather Frost	Open		55.00	55
1993	Jolly Old St. Nick	Open		55.00	55
1993	Kris Kringle	Open		55.00	55
1994	Pére Nöel	Open		55.00	55
1992	Santa Claus	Open		55.00	55
1994	Yuletide Santa	Open		55.00	55

Jeweled Carousel - M. Griffin

YEAR ISSUE		EDITION LIMIT	YEAR RETD.	ISSUE PRICE	*QUOTE U.S.$
1995	Sapphire Jumper	Open		55.00	55
1995	Ruby Prancer	Open		55.00	55
1995	Emerald Stander	Open		55.00	55
1995	Amethyst Jumper	Open		55.00	55

Little Friends of the Arctic - N/A

YEAR ISSUE		EDITION LIMIT	YEAR RETD.	ISSUE PRICE	*QUOTE U.S.$
1995	The Young Prince	Open		35.00	35
1995	Princely Fishing	Open		35.00	35
1996	Playful Prince	Open		35.00	35

Little Messengers - P. Parkins

YEAR ISSUE		EDITION LIMIT	YEAR RETD.	ISSUE PRICE	*QUOTE U.S.$
1996	Love Is Patient	Open		29.95	30

Little Night Owls - D.T. Lyttleton

YEAR ISSUE		EDITION LIMIT	YEAR RETD.	ISSUE PRICE	*QUOTE U.S.$
1990	Barn Owl	Open		45.00	45
1991	Barred Owl	Open		45.00	45
1991	Great Grey Owl	Open		45.00	45
1991	Great Horned Owl	Open		45.00	45
1991	Short-Eared Owl	Open		45.00	45
1990	Snowy Owl	Open		45.00	45
1990	Tawny Owl	Open		45.00	45
1991	White-Faced Owl	Open		45.00	45

Masters of the Evening Wilderness - N/A

YEAR ISSUE		EDITION LIMIT	YEAR RETD.	ISSUE PRICE	*QUOTE U.S.$
1994	The Great Snowy Owl	Open		37.50	38
1995	Autumn Barn Owls	Open		37.50	38
1995	Great Grey Owl	Open		37.50	38
1995	Great Horned Owl	Open		37.50	38
1996	Barred Owl	Open		37.50	38
1996	Screech Owl	Open		37.50	38
1996	Burrowing Owl	Open		37.50	38
1996	Eagle Owl	Open		37.50	38

Mystic Spirits - S. Douglas

YEAR ISSUE		EDITION LIMIT	YEAR RETD.	ISSUE PRICE	*QUOTE U.S.$
1995	Spirit of the Wolf	Open		55.00	55
1995	Spirit of the Buffalo	Open		55.00	55
1995	Spirit of the Golden Eagle	Open		55.00	55
1996	Spirit of the Bear	Open		55.00	55
1996	Spirit of the Mountain Lion	Open		55.00	55
1996	Hawk Dancer	Open		55.00	55
1996	Wolf Scout	Open		55.00	55
1996	Spirit of the Deer	Open		55.00	55

Nature's Beautiful Bonds - R. Roberts

YEAR ISSUE		EDITION LIMIT	YEAR RETD.	ISSUE PRICE	*QUOTE U.S.$
1996	A Mother's Vigil	Open		29.95	30
1996	A Moment's Peace	Open		29.95	30
1996	A Warm Embrace	Open		29.95	30

Nature's Majestic Cats - D. Geentz

YEAR ISSUE		EDITION LIMIT	YEAR RETD.	ISSUE PRICE	*QUOTE U.S.$
1995	Tigress and Cubs	Open		55.00	55
1995	Himalayan Snow Leopard	Open		55.00	55
1996	Cougar and Cubs	Open		55.00	55
1996	Pride of the Lioness	Open		55.00	55

Nesting Instincts - R. Willis

YEAR ISSUE		EDITION LIMIT	YEAR RETD.	ISSUE PRICE	*QUOTE U.S.$
1995	By Mother's Side	Open		19.50	20
1995	Learning to Fly	Open		19.50	20
1995	Like Mother, Like Son	Open		19.50	20
1995	A Mother's Pride	Open		19.50	20
1995	Peaceful Perch	Open		19.50	20
1995	Safe and Sound	Open		19.50	20
1995	Under Mother's Wings	Open		19.50	20
1995	A Watchful Eye	Open		19.50	20

Noble American Indian Women - N/A

YEAR ISSUE		EDITION LIMIT	YEAR RETD.	ISSUE PRICE	*QUOTE U.S.$
1994	Falling Star	Open		55.00	55
1995	Lily of the Mohawks	Open		55.00	55
1995	Lozen	Open		55.00	55
1994	Minnehaha	Open		55.00	55
1994	Pine Leaf	Open		55.00	55
1995	Pocahontas	Open		55.00	55
1993	Sacajawea	Open		55.00	55
1993	White Rose	Open		55.00	55

The Noble Swan - G. Granget

YEAR ISSUE		EDITION LIMIT	YEAR RETD.	ISSUE PRICE	*QUOTE U.S.$
1985	The Noble Swan	5,000		295.00	295

Noble Warriors - N/A

YEAR ISSUE		EDITION LIMIT	YEAR RETD.	ISSUE PRICE	*QUOTE U.S.$
1993	Deliverance	Open		135.00	135
1994	Spirit of the Plains	Open		135.00	135
1995	Top Gun	Open		135.00	135
1995	Windrider	Open		135.00	135

The Nolan Ryan Collectors Edition-Porcelain Baseball Cards - N/A

YEAR ISSUE		EDITION LIMIT	YEAR RETD.	ISSUE PRICE	*QUOTE U.S.$
1993	Angels 1972-C #595	Open		19.50	20
1993	Astros 1985-C #7	Open		19.50	20
1993	Mets 1968-C #177	Open		19.50	20
1993	Mets 1969-C #533	Open		19.50	20
1993	Rangers 1990-C #1	Open		19.50	20
1993	Rangers 1992-C #1	Open		19.50	20

North Pole Bears - T. Newsom

YEAR ISSUE		EDITION LIMIT	YEAR RETD.	ISSUE PRICE	*QUOTE U.S.$
1996	All I Want For Christmas	Open		29.95	30
1996	Beary Best Snowman	Open		29.95	30

Ocean Odyssey - W. Youngstrom

YEAR ISSUE		EDITION LIMIT	YEAR RETD.	ISSUE PRICE	*QUOTE U.S.$
1995	Breaching the Waters	Open		55.00	55
1995	Return to Paradise	Open		55.00	55
1995	Riding the Waves	Open		55.00	55
1996	Baja Bliss	Open		55.00	55
1996	Arctic Blue	Open		55.00	55
1996	Splashdown	Open		55.00	55
1996	Free Spirit	Open		55.00	55
1996	Beluga Belles	Open		55.00	55

Princess of the Plains - N/A

YEAR ISSUE		EDITION LIMIT	YEAR RETD.	ISSUE PRICE	*QUOTE U.S.$
1995	Nature's Guardian	Open		55.00	55
1994	Noble Guardian	Open		55.00	55
1994	Snow Princess	Open		55.00	55
1994	Wild Flower	Open		55.00	55
1995	Winter's Rose	Open		55.00	55

Protect Nature's Innocents - R. Manning

YEAR ISSUE		EDITION LIMIT	YEAR RETD.	ISSUE PRICE	*QUOTE U.S.$
1995	African Elephant	Open		14.95	15
1995	Giant Panda	Open		14.95	15
1995	Snow Leopard	Open		14.95	15
1995	Rhinoceros	Open		14.95	15
1996	Orangutan	Open		14.95	15
1996	Key Deer	Open		14.95	15
1996	Bengal Tiger	Open		14.95	15
1996	Pygmy Hippo	Open		14.95	15

Puppy Playtime Sculpture Collection - J. Lamb

YEAR ISSUE		EDITION LIMIT	YEAR RETD.	ISSUE PRICE	*QUOTE U.S.$
1991	Cabin Fever	Open		29.50	30
1991	Catch of the Day	Open		29.50	30
1990	Double Take	Open		29.50	30
1991	Fun and Games	Open		29.50	30
1991	Getting Acquainted	Open		29.50	30
1991	Hanging Out	Open		29.50	30
1991	A New Leash on Life	Open		29.50	30
1991	Weekend Gardner	Open		29.50	30

Puss in Boots - P. Cooper

YEAR ISSUE		EDITION LIMIT	YEAR RETD.	ISSUE PRICE	*QUOTE U.S.$
1993	All Dressed Up	Open		35.00	35
1992	Caught Napping	Open		35.00	35
1994	Daydreamer	Open		35.00	35
1993	Hide'n Go Seek	Open		35.00	35
1993	Sitting Pretty	Open		35.00	35
1992	Sweet Dreams	Open		35.00	35
1994	Tee Time	Open		35.00	35
1993	Tennis Anyone?	Open		35.00	35

Ringling Bros. Circus Animals - P. Cozzolino

YEAR ISSUE		EDITION LIMIT	YEAR RETD.	ISSUE PRICE	*QUOTE U.S.$
1983	Acrobatic Seal	9,800		49.50	50
1983	Baby Elephant	9,800		49.50	55
1983	Miniature Show Horse	9,800		49.50	68
1983	Mr. Chimpanzee	9,800		49.50	50
1984	Parade Camel	9,800		49.50	50
1983	Performing Poodles	9,800		49.50	50
1984	Roaring Lion	9,800		49.50	50
1983	Skating Bear	9,800		49.50	50

Santa Clothtique - Possible Dreams

YEAR ISSUE		EDITION LIMIT	YEAR RETD.	ISSUE PRICE	*QUOTE U.S.$
1992	Checking His List	Open		95.00	95
1993	Last Minute Details	Open		95.00	95
1993	Twas the Nap Before Christmas	Open		95.00	95
1994	Upon the Rooftop	Open		95.00	95
1994	O Tannenbaum!	Open		95.00	95
1995	Baking Christmas Cheer	Open		95.00	95
1995	Santa to the Rescue	Open		95.00	95
1996	Toyshop Tally	Open		95.00	95

Shield of the Mighty Warrior - S. Kehrli

YEAR ISSUE		EDITION LIMIT	YEAR RETD.	ISSUE PRICE	*QUOTE U.S.$
1995	Spirit of the Grey Wolf	Open		45.00	45
1996	Spirit of the Bear	Open		45.00	45

Snuggle Babies - Jacqueline B.

YEAR ISSUE		EDITION LIMIT	YEAR RETD.	ISSUE PRICE	*QUOTE U.S.$
1988	Baby Bears	Open		35.00	35
1988	Baby Bunnies	Open		35.00	35
1989	Baby Chipmunks	Open		35.00	35
1989	Baby Fawns	Open		35.00	35
1988	Baby Foxes	Open		35.00	35
1989	Baby Raccoons	Open		35.00	35
1988	Baby Skunks	Open		35.00	35
1989	Baby Squirrels	Open		35.00	35

Spirit of the Eagle - T. Sullivan

YEAR ISSUE		EDITION LIMIT	YEAR RETD.	ISSUE PRICE	*QUOTE U.S.$
1994	Spirit of Independence	Open		55.00	55
1995	Blazing Majestic Skies	Open		55.00	55
1995	Noble and Free	Open		55.00	55
1995	Proud Symbol of Freedom	Open		55.00	55
1996	Legacy of Freedom	Open		55.00	55
1996	Protector of Liberty	Open		55.00	55

Tropical Treasures - M. Wald

YEAR ISSUE		EDITION LIMIT	YEAR RETD.	ISSUE PRICE	*QUOTE U.S.$
1990	Beaked Coral Butterfly Fish	Open		37.50	38
1990	Blue Girdled Angel Fish	Open		37.50	38
1989	Flag-tail Surgeonfish	Open		37.50	38
1989	Pennant Butterfly Fish	Open		37.50	38
1989	Sail-finned Surgeonfish	Open		37.50	38

*Quotes have been rounded up to nearest dollar

YEAR ISSUE		EDITION LIMIT	YEAR RETD.	ISSUE PRICE	*QUOTE U.S.$
1989	Sea Horse	Open		37.50	38
1990	Spotted Angel Fish	Open		37.50	38
1990	Zebra Turkey Fish	Open		37.50	38

Unbridled Spirits - C. DeHaan

YEAR ISSUE		EDITION LIMIT	YEAR RETD.	ISSUE PRICE	*QUOTE U.S.$
1994	Wild Fury	Open		135.00	135

Visions of Christmas - M. Griffin

YEAR ISSUE		EDITION LIMIT	YEAR RETD.	ISSUE PRICE	*QUOTE U.S.$
1995	Gifts From St. Nick	Open		135.00	135
1994	Mrs. Claus' Kitchen	Open		135.00	135
1993	Santa's Delivery	Open		135.00	135
1993	Toys in Progress	Open		135.00	135

The Way of the Warrior - J. Pyre

YEAR ISSUE		EDITION LIMIT	YEAR RETD.	ISSUE PRICE	*QUOTE U.S.$
1995	One With the Eagle	Open		45.00	45
1996	Star Shooter	Open		45.00	45

Wild Ducks of North America - C. Burgess

YEAR ISSUE		EDITION LIMIT	YEAR RETD.	ISSUE PRICE	*QUOTE U.S.$
1988	American Widgeon	15,000		95.00	95
1988	Bufflehead	15,000		95.00	95
1987	Common Mallard	15,000		95.00	95
1987	Green Winged Teal	15,000		95.00	95
1987	Hooded Merganser	15,000		95.00	95
1988	Northern Pintail	15,000		95.00	95
1988	Ruddy Duck Drake	15,000		95.00	95
1987	Wood Duck	15,000		95.00	95

Wolves of the Wilderness - D. Geenty

YEAR ISSUE		EDITION LIMIT	YEAR RETD.	ISSUE PRICE	*QUOTE U.S.$
1995	A Wolf's Pride	Open		55.00	55
1995	Mother's Watch	Open		55.00	55
1996	Time For Play	Open		55.00	55
1996	Morning Romp	Open		55.00	55

Harbour Lights

Great Lakes Region - Harbour Lights

YEAR ISSUE		EDITION LIMIT	YEAR RETD.	ISSUE PRICE	*QUOTE U.S.$
1992	Buffalo NY 122	5,500		60.00	62
1992	Cana Island WI 119	5,500	1995	60.00	65-120
1996	Charlotte-Genesee NY 165	9,500		77.00	77
1991	Fort Niagara NY 113	5,500	1995	60.00	65-125
1992	Grosse Point IL 120	5,500		60.00	62
1994	Holland (Big Red) MI 142	5,500	1995	60.00	150-215
1992	Marblehead OH 121	5,500	1995	50.00	110-180
1992	Michigan City IN 123	5,500		60.00	62
1992	Old Mackinac Point MI 118	5,500	1995	65.00	115-160
1995	Round Island MI 153	9,500		66.00	85
1991	Sand Island WS 112	5,500		60.00	64
1995	Selkirk NY 157	9,500		75.00	75
1992	Split Rock MI 124 (misspelled)	Closed	1992	60.00	1450-1650
1992	Split Rock MN 124	Retrd.	1995	60.00	110-150
1995	Tawas Pt. MI 152	5,500		75.00	75
1995	Wind Point WS 154	9,500		78.00	78

Great Lighthouses of the World - Harbour Lights

YEAR ISSUE		EDITION LIMIT	YEAR RETD.	ISSUE PRICE	*QUOTE U.S.$
1996	Alcatraz CA 407	9,500		77.00	77
1995	Boston Harbor MA 402	Open		50.00	50
1994	Cape Hatteras NC 401	Open		50.00	50
1996	Cape Lookout NC 405	9,500		64.00	64
1996	Fire Island NY 406	9,500		70.00	70
1996	Mukilteo WA 417	9,500		55.00	55
1995	Portland Head ME 404	Open		50.00	50
1996	Sandy Hook NJ 418	Open		50.00	50
1995	Southeast Block Island RI 403	Open		50.00	50

Gulf Coast Region - Harbour Lights

YEAR ISSUE		EDITION LIMIT	YEAR RETD.	ISSUE PRICE	*QUOTE U.S.$
1995	Biloxi MS 149	5,500		60.00	60
1995	Bolivar TX 146	5,500		70.00	70
1995	New Canal LA 148	5,500		65.00	65
1995	Pensacola FL 150	9,000		80.00	80
1995	Port Isabel TX 147	5,500		65.00	65

Harbour Lights Collector's Society - Harbour Lights

YEAR ISSUE		EDITION LIMIT	YEAR RETD.	ISSUE PRICE	*QUOTE U.S.$
1995	Point Fermin CA 501 (Charter Member Piece)	4/96		80.00	80

Northeast Region - Harbour Lights

YEAR ISSUE		EDITION LIMIT	YEAR RETD.	ISSUE PRICE	*QUOTE U.S.$
1993	Barnegat NJ 139	5,500	1995	60.00	120-180
1991	Boston Harbor MA 117	5,500	1995	60.00	120-150
1995	Brant Point MA 162	9,500		66.00	66
1994	Cape Neddick (Nubble) ME 141	5,500	1995	66.00	120-180
1991	Castle Hill RI 116	5,500		60.00	60
1991	Gt. Captain's Island CT 114	5,500		60.00	66
1995	Highland MA 161	9,500		75.00	75
1992	Minot's Ledge MA 131	5,500		60.00	60
1994	Montauk NY 143	5,500	1995	85.00	170-240
1992	Nauset MA 126	5,500	1995	66.00	120-155
1992	New London Ledge CT 129	5,500	1995	66.00	120-165
1996	Pemaquid ME 164	9,500		90.00	90
1992	Portland Breakwater ME 130	5,500		60.00	60
1992	Portland Head ME 125	5,500	1994	66.00	150-250
1991	Sandy Hook NJ 104	Retrd.	1994	60.00	130-200
1996	Scituate MA 166	9,500		77.00	77
1992	Southeast Block Island RI 128	5,500	1994	71.00	150-225
1991	West Quoddy Head ME 103	5,500	1995	60.00	100-150
1992	Whaleback NH 127	5,500		60.00	60

Southeast Region - Harbour Lights

YEAR ISSUE		EDITION LIMIT	YEAR RETD.	ISSUE PRICE	*QUOTE U.S.$
1994	Assateague VA 145-mold one	988	1994	69.00	300-650
1994	Assateague VA 145-mold two	4,512	1995	69.00	105-135
1996	Bald Head NC 155	9,500		75.00	75
1995	Bodie NC 159	9,500		77.00	77
1996	Cape Canaveral FL 163	9,500		80.00	80
1991	Cape Hatteras NC 102 (w/house)	Retrd.	1991	60.00	2600-3800
1992	Cape Hatteras NC 102R	Retrd.	1993	60.00	450-750
1995	Currituck NC 158	9,500		80.00	80
1993	Hilton Head SC 136	5,500	1994	60.00	110-165
1995	Jupiter FL 151	9,500		77.00	77
1993	Key West FL 134	5,500	1995	60.00	120-140
1993	Ocracoke NC 135	5,500	1995	60.00	120-180
1993	Ponce de Leon FL 132	5,500	1994	60.00	120-175
1993	St. Augustine FL 138	5,500	1994	71.00	145-190
1993	St. Simons GA 137	5,500	1995	66.00	125-160
1993	Tybee GA 133	5,500	1995	60.00	120-145

Special Editions - Harbour Lights

YEAR ISSUE		EDITION LIMIT	YEAR RETD.	ISSUE PRICE	*QUOTE U.S.$
1995	Christmas 1995 - Big Bay Point MI 700	5,000	1995	75.00	125-150
1995	Legacy Light (red) 601	Retrd.	1995	65.00	135-180
1995	Legacy Light 601	Open		65.00	65

Stamp Series - Harbour Lights

YEAR ISSUE		EDITION LIMIT	YEAR RETD.	ISSUE PRICE	*QUOTE U.S.$
1995	Marblehead OH 413	Open		50.00	50
1995	Spectacle Reef MI 410	Open		60.00	60
1995	Split Rock MN 412	Open		60.00	60
1995	St. Joseph MI 411	Open		60.00	60
1995	Thirty Mile Point NY 414	Open		62.00	62
1995	Five Piece Matched Numbered Set 400	5,000		275.00	275

Western Region - Harbour Lights

YEAR ISSUE		EDITION LIMIT	YEAR RETD.	ISSUE PRICE	*QUOTE U.S.$
1991	Admirality Head WA 101(misspelled)	Closed	1994	60.00	120-150
1991	Admiralty Head WA 101	Retrd.	1994	60.00	110-200
1991	Burrows Island OR 108 (misspelled)	Closed	1991	60.00	400-700
1991	Burrows Island WA 108	Retrd.	1994	60.00	120-200
1991	Cape Blanco OR 109	5,500		60.00	60
1996	Cape Meares OR 160	9,500		68.00	68
1991	Coquille River OR 111	1,138	1993	60.00	1800-2300
1994	Diamond Head HI 140	5,500	1995	60.00	120-145
1994	Heceta Head OR 144	5,500		65.00	72
1991	North Head WA 106	5,500		60.00	60
1991	Old Point Loma CA 105	5,500	1995	60.00	120-150
1995	Pt. Arena CA 156	9,500		80.00	80
1991	St. George's Reef CA 115	5,500		60.00	60
1991	Umpqua River OR 107	5,500		60.00	60
1991	Yaquina Head WA 110	5,500		60.00	62

Harmony Kingdom

Hi-Jinx - P. Calvesbert

YEAR ISSUE		EDITION LIMIT	YEAR RETD.	ISSUE PRICE	*QUOTE U.S.$
1994	Antartic Antics	Open		100.00	100
1994	Hold That Line	Open		100.00	100
1994	Mad Dogs and Englishman	Open		100.00	100
1994	Open Mike	Open		100.00	100

Large Treasure Jest - P. Calvesbert

YEAR ISSUE		EDITION LIMIT	YEAR RETD.	ISSUE PRICE	*QUOTE U.S.$
1994	Awaiting A Kiss	Open		50.00	50
1995	Horn A' Plenty	Open		55.00	55
1994	Journey Home	Open		50.00	50
1995	Keeping Current	Open		55.00	55
1994	On A Roll	Open		50.00	50
1994	One Step Ahead	Open		50.00	50
1994	Pen Pals	Open		50.00	50
1994	Pondering	Open		50.00	50
1994	Pride And Joy	Open		50.00	50
1995	Quiet Waters	Open		55.00	55
1995	Standing Guard	Open		55.00	55
1995	Step Aside	Open		55.00	55
1995	Straight From The Hip	Open		55.00	55
1994	Sunnyside Up	Open		50.00	50
1994	Tea For Two	Open		50.00	50

Limited Editions - P. Calvesbert

YEAR ISSUE		EDITION LIMIT	YEAR RETD.	ISSUE PRICE	*QUOTE U.S.$
1996	Noah's Lark	5,000		400.00	400
1995	Unbearables	2,500		400.00	400

Paradoxicals - P. Calvesbert

YEAR ISSUE		EDITION LIMIT	YEAR RETD.	ISSUE PRICE	*QUOTE U.S.$
1995	Paradise Found	Open		35.00	35
1995	Paradise Lost	Open		35.00	35

Small Treasure Jest - P. Calvesbert

YEAR ISSUE		EDITION LIMIT	YEAR RETD.	ISSUE PRICE	*QUOTE U.S.$
1994	40 Winks	Open		30.00	30
1994	All Angles Covered	Open		30.00	30
1994	All Ears	Open		30.00	30
1994	All Tied Up	Open		30.00	30
1995	At Arm's Length	Open		35.00	35
1995	At The Hop	Open		35.00	35
1994	Baby on Board	Open		30.00	30
1994	Back Scratch	Retrd.	1995	30.00	30
1995	Chatelaine	Retrd.	1996	35.00	35
1995	Damnable Plot	Open		35.00	35
1994	Day Dreamer	Open		30.00	30
1995	Den Mothers	Open		35.00	35
1994	Dog Days	Open		30.00	30
1995	Ed's Safari	Open		35.00	35
1995	Family Tree	Open		35.00	35
1995	Fur Ball	Open		35.00	35
1995	Group Therapy	Open		35.00	35
1994	Hammin' It Up	Open		30.00	30
1995	Horse Play	Open		35.00	35
1994	Inside Joke	Open		30.00	30
1994	It's A Fine Day	Open		30.00	30
1995	Jersey Belles	Open		35.00	35
1994	Jonah's Hideaway	Open		30.00	30
1994	Let's Do Lunch	Retrd.	1995	30.00	30
1995	Life's a Picnic	Open		35.00	35
1995	Love Seat	Open		35.00	35
1995	Major's Mousers	Open		45.00	45
1995	Mud Bath	Open		35.00	35
1995	Neighborhood Watch	Open		35.00	35
1994	Of The Same Stripe	Open		30.00	30
1994	Play School	Open		30.00	30
1994	Princely Thoughts	Open		30.00	30
1995	Puddle Huddle	Open		35.00	35
1994	Purrfect Friends	Open		30.00	30
1994	Riminiscence	Open		30.00	30
1994	School's Out	Open		30.00	30
1994	Shell Game	Open		30.00	30
1994	Side Steppin	Open		30.00	30
1995	Sunday Swim	Open		35.00	35
1994	Swamp Song	Open		30.00	30
1995	Sweet Serenade	Open		35.00	35
1994	Teacher's Pet	Open		30.00	30
1995	Tongue And Cheek	Open		35.00	35
1995	Too Much of A Good Thing	Open		35.00	35
1994	Top Banana	Open		30.00	30
1994	Trunk Show	Open		30.00	30
1995	Unbridled & Groomed	Open		35.00	35
1994	Unexpected Arrival	Open		30.00	30
1994	Untouchable	Retrd.	1995	30.00	30
1994	Who'd A Thought	Retrd.	1995	30.00	30
1995	Wise Guys	Open		35.00	35

Hawthorne Architectural Register

Beacons of Freedom (Illuminated) - Unknown

YEAR ISSUE		EDITION LIMIT	YEAR RETD.	ISSUE PRICE	*QUOTE U.S.$
1995	Portland Head Lighthouse	Open		39.90	40
1995	West Quoddy Head	Open		39.90	40

Chestnut Hill Station - K.&H. LeVan

YEAR ISSUE		EDITION LIMIT	YEAR RETD.	ISSUE PRICE	*QUOTE U.S.$
1994	Bicycle Shop	Open		29.90	30
1994	Chestnut Hill Depot	Closed	1994	29.90	30
1993	Parkside Cafe	Open		29.90	30
1993	Wishing Well Cottage	Closed	1994	29.90	30

Concord: The Hometown of American Literature - K.&H. LeVan

YEAR ISSUE		EDITION LIMIT	YEAR RETD.	ISSUE PRICE	*QUOTE U.S.$
1993	Alcott's Orchard House	Closed	1995	34.90	35
1992	Emerson's Old Manse	Closed	1995	34.90	35
1992	Hawthorne's Wayside Retreat	Closed	1995	34.90	35

Currier & Ives: The Art of America - C&I Inspired

YEAR ISSUE		EDITION LIMIT	YEAR RETD.	ISSUE PRICE	*QUOTE U.S.$
1994	American Homestead Winter	Open		29.90	30
1995	A Cold Morning	Open		29.90	30
1995	Early Winter	Open		29.90	30
1995	Feeding the Chickens	Open		29.90	30
1995	The Old Grist Mill	Open		29.90	30
1994	The Snow Storm	Open		29.90	30
1995	Winter Evenings	Open		29.90	30
1995	Winter Moonlight	Open		29.90	30

England of My Dreams - R. Dowding

YEAR ISSUE		EDITION LIMIT	YEAR RETD.	ISSUE PRICE	*QUOTE U.S.$
1994	Mayfair Hill	Closed	1994	59.90	60

The Fairytale Forest - S. Smith

YEAR ISSUE		EDITION LIMIT	YEAR RETD.	ISSUE PRICE	*QUOTE U.S.$
1994	Goldilocks and the Three Bears & figurines	Open		49.80	50
1994	Little Red Riding Hood including figurines	Open		49.80	50

Gone With the Wind (Illuminated) - Unknown

YEAR ISSUE		EDITION LIMIT	YEAR RETD.	ISSUE PRICE	*QUOTE U.S.$
1994	Atlanta Church	Open		39.90	40
1995	Butler Mansion	Open		39.90	40
1994	Kennedy Store	Open		39.90	40
1994	Red Horse Saloon	Open		39.90	40
1993	Tara	Open		39.90	40
1994	Twelve Oaks	Open		39.90	40

Gone With the Wind Collection - K.&H. LeVan

YEAR ISSUE		EDITION LIMIT	YEAR RETD.	ISSUE PRICE	*QUOTE U.S.$
1993	Against Her Will	Open		42.90	43
1994	Alone	Open		45.90	46
1995	Dignity & Respect	Open		45.90	46
1994	Hope for a New Tomorrow	Closed	1995	42.90	43
1994	I Have Done Enough	Open		45.90	46
1994	Kennedy House	Open		45.90	46
1994	Merriweather House	Open		45.90	46
1993	A Message for Captain Butler	Open		42.90	43
1995	Revenge on Shantytown	Open		45.90	46
1993	Rhett Returns	Open		39.90	40
1994	Swept Away	Open		45.90	46
1994	Take Me to Tara	Open		45.90	46
1992	Tara . . .Scarlett's Pride	Closed	1995	39.90	40
1992	Twelve Oaks: The Romance Begins	Closed	1995	39.90	40

Gone With the Wind-Special Edition - Unknown

YEAR ISSUE		EDITION LIMIT	YEAR RETD.	ISSUE PRICE	*QUOTE U.S.$
1994	Burning of Atlanta	10,000		79.95	80
1995	The Butler Mansion	10,000		79.95	80

*Quotes have been rounded up to nearest dollar

Helen Steiner Rice: Windows of Gold - S. Smith

YEAR ISSUE		EDITION LIMIT	YEAR RETD.	ISSUE PRICE	*QUOTE U.S.$
1994	Inspiration Point Lighthouse	Open		39.90	40
1994	Peace of Faith	Open		39.90	40
1994	Winter's Warmth	Open		39.90	40

Hershey, PA: An American Dream Comes True - Unknown

YEAR ISSUE		EDITION LIMIT	YEAR RETD.	ISSUE PRICE	*QUOTE U.S.$
1995	Birthplace of Milton Hershey	Open		34.90	35
1995	Derry Church School	Open		34.90	35

Hometown America - Rockwell Inspired

YEAR ISSUE		EDITION LIMIT	YEAR RETD.	ISSUE PRICE	*QUOTE U.S.$
1993	Evergreen Cottage	Open		34.95	35
1994	Evergreen General Store	Open		39.95	40
1994	Evergreen Valley Church	Open		37.95	38
1993	Evergreen Valley School	Open		34.95	35
1995	Happy Holidays	Open		39.95	40
1993	The Village Bakery	Closed	1994	37.95	38
1994	Waiting For Santa	Closed	1995	39.95	40
1994	Woodcutter's Rest	Open		37.95	38

Hummel's Bavarian Village - M.I. Hummel Inspired

YEAR ISSUE		EDITION LIMIT	YEAR RETD.	ISSUE PRICE	*QUOTE U.S.$
1994	Angel's Duet	Open		49.90	50
1994	The Bakery	Open		49.90	50
1995	Company's Coming	Open		49.90	50
1995	Post Office	Open		49.90	50
1996	School	Open		49.90	50
1996	Shoemaker Shoppe	Open		49.90	50
1996	Train Station	Open		49.90	50
1995	Winter's Comfort	Open		49.90	50

Hummel's Bavarian Village Accessories - Unknown

YEAR ISSUE		EDITION LIMIT	YEAR RETD.	ISSUE PRICE	*QUOTE U.S.$
1996	Large Tree/Sled	Open		24.90	25
1996	Small Tree/Bench	Open		24.90	25
1996	Village Bridge	Open		24.90	25
1996	Wishing Well	Open		24.90	25

Inside Gone With the Wind Collection - K.&H. LeVan

YEAR ISSUE		EDITION LIMIT	YEAR RETD.	ISSUE PRICE	*QUOTE U.S.$
1994	Pride and Passion	Open		39.90	40
1995	Scarlett's Bedroom	Open		39.90	40
1995	Wilke's Library	Open		39.90	40

Kinkade's Candlelight Cottages (Illuminated) - Kinkade-Inspired

YEAR ISSUE		EDITION LIMIT	YEAR RETD.	ISSUE PRICE	*QUOTE U.S.$
1993	Chandler's Cottage	Closed	1994	29.90	30
1993	Olde Porterfield Tea Room	Closed	1994	29.90	30

Kinkade's Candlelight Cottages - Kinkade-Inspired

YEAR ISSUE		EDITION LIMIT	YEAR RETD.	ISSUE PRICE	*QUOTE U.S.$
1994	Candlelit Cottage	Open		29.90	30
1994	Cedar Nooke Cottage	Open		29.90	30
1993	Chandler's Cottage	Open		24.90	25
1994	Merritt's Cottage	Open		27.90	28
1993	Olde Porterfield Tea Room	Open		24.90	25
1994	Seaside Cottage	Open		27.90	28
1993	Swanbrooke Cottage	Open		24.90	25
1994	Sweatheart Cottage	Open		27.90	28

Kinkade's Christmas Memories - Kinkade-Inspired

YEAR ISSUE		EDITION LIMIT	YEAR RETD.	ISSUE PRICE	*QUOTE U.S.$
1995	Home Before Christmas	Open		34.90	35
1995	Home to Grandma's	Open		34.90	35
1995	Homespun Holiday	Open		34.90	35
1995	Olde Porterfield Gift & Shoppe	Open		34.90	35
1995	Silent Night	Open		34.90	35
1995	Warmth of Home	Open		34.90	35

Kinkade's Enchanted Cottages - Kinkade-Inspired

YEAR ISSUE		EDITION LIMIT	YEAR RETD.	ISSUE PRICE	*QUOTE U.S.$
1995	Cottage By the Sea	Open		29.90	30
1995	Heather's Hutch	Open		29.90	30
1995	Julianne's Cottage	Open		29.90	30
1995	McKenna's Cottage	Open		29.90	30
1995	Miller's Cottage	Open		29.90	30
1995	Sweetheart Havencrest	Open		29.90	30

Kinkade's St. Nicholas Square (Illuminated) - Kinkade-Inspired

YEAR ISSUE		EDITION LIMIT	YEAR RETD.	ISSUE PRICE	*QUOTE U.S.$
1994	Evergreen Apothecary	Open		39.90	40
1994	The Firehouse	Open		39.90	40
1994	Holly House Inn	Open		39.90	40
1994	Kringle Brothers	Open		39.90	40
1994	Mrs. C. Bakery	Open		39.90	40
1994	Noel Chapel (free sign in box)	Open		39.90	40
1994	S.C. Toy Maker	Open		39.90	40
1993	Town Hall	Open		39.90	40

On the Water - K.&H. LeVan

YEAR ISSUE		EDITION LIMIT	YEAR RETD.	ISSUE PRICE	*QUOTE U.S.$
1995	Artists Delight	Open		34.90	35
1994	Sunset Cove	Open		34.90	35

P.O. #1, North Pole Collection (Illuminated) - G. Hoover

YEAR ISSUE		EDITION LIMIT	YEAR RETD.	ISSUE PRICE	*QUOTE U.S.$
1995	Santa's Candy Shop	Open		39.90	40
1995	Santa's Gift Wrap Central	Open		39.90	40
1994	Santa's Post Office	Open		39.90	40
1994	Santa's Toy Shoppe with Sign	Open		39.90	40

Peaceable Kingdom - K.&H. LeVan

YEAR ISSUE		EDITION LIMIT	YEAR RETD.	ISSUE PRICE	*QUOTE U.S.$
1993	Squire Boone's Homestead	Open		34.90	35
1994	White Horse Inn	Open		34.90	35

Peppercricket Grove - C. Wysocki

YEAR ISSUE		EDITION LIMIT	YEAR RETD.	ISSUE PRICE	*QUOTE U.S.$
1996	The Black Crow	Open		49.90	50
1996	Budzen's Roadside Food Stand	Open		49.90	50
1995	Peppercricket Farm	Open		44.90	45
1996	Pumpkin Hollow	Open		49.90	50
1995	Virginia's Nest	Open		44.90	45

Rockwell's Four Freedoms (Illuminated) - Rockwell-Inspired

YEAR ISSUE		EDITION LIMIT	YEAR RETD.	ISSUE PRICE	*QUOTE U.S.$
1994	Freedom from Fear: The Rockwell Homestead	Open		39.90	40
1995	Freedom from Want: The Farmhouse	Open		39.90	40
1995	Freedom of Speech: Town Hall	Open		39.90	40
1994	Freedom of Worship: Arlington Church	Open		39.90	40

Rockwell's Heart of Stockbridge (Illuminated) - Rockwell-Inspired

YEAR ISSUE		EDITION LIMIT	YEAR RETD.	ISSUE PRICE	*QUOTE U.S.$
1995	Bell Tower	Open		39.90	40
1995	Church on the Green	Open		39.90	40
1995	Firehouse	Open		39.90	40
1995	Rockwell's Home	Open		39.90	40
1995	Rockwell's Studio	Open		39.90	40

Rockwell's Home for the Holidays - Rockwell-Inspired

YEAR ISSUE		EDITION LIMIT	YEAR RETD.	ISSUE PRICE	*QUOTE U.S.$
1994	Arlington Town Hall	Open		41.90	42
1992	Bringing Home the Christmas Tree	Closed	1994	34.90	35
1992	Carolers In The Church Yard	Open		37.90	38
1992	Christmas Eve at the Studio	Closed	1994	34.90	35
1994	Firestation	Open		41.90	42
1994	A Golden Memory	Open		41.90	42
1994	Howard's Store	Open		39.90	40
1994	Late for the Dance	Open		41.90	42
1993	Letters to Santa	Open		39.90	40
1993	Over the River	Closed	1995	37.90	38
1995	Ready & Waiting	Closed	1995	41.90	42
1993	A Room at the Inn	Open		39.90	40
1993	School's Out	Closed	1994	39.90	40
1993	Three-Day Pass	Open		37.90	38
1994	A White Christmas	Closed	1995	41.90	42

Rockwell's Main Street (Illuminated) - Rockwell-Inspired

YEAR ISSUE		EDITION LIMIT	YEAR RETD.	ISSUE PRICE	*QUOTE U.S.$
1993	The Antique Shop	Open		29.90	30
1993	The Bank	Open		29.90	30
1993	The Country Store	Open		29.90	30
1993	The Library	Open		29.90	30
1993	The Red Lion Inn	Open		29.90	30
1993	Rockwell's Studio	Open		29.90	30
1993	The Town Offices	Open		29.90	30

Rockwell's Neighborhood Collection - Rockwell-Inspired

YEAR ISSUE		EDITION LIMIT	YEAR RETD.	ISSUE PRICE	*QUOTE U.S.$
1994	Fido's New Home	Open		29.90	30
1994	The Lemonade Stand	Open		29.90	30
1994	Sidewalk Speedster	Open		29.90	30

Small Town Christmas - C. Wysocki

YEAR ISSUE		EDITION LIMIT	YEAR RETD.	ISSUE PRICE	*QUOTE U.S.$
1995	Ye Very Olde Fruitcake Shoppe	Open		39.90	40

Stonefield Valley - K.&H. LeVan

YEAR ISSUE		EDITION LIMIT	YEAR RETD.	ISSUE PRICE	*QUOTE U.S.$
1992	Church in the Glen	Closed	1994	37.90	38
1993	Ferryman's Cottage	Closed	1994	39.90	40
1993	Hillside Country Store	Closed	1994	39.90	40
1992	Meadowbrook School	Closed	1994	34.90	35
1993	Parson's Cottage	Closed	1994	37.90	38
1992	Springbridge Cottage	Closed	1994	34.90	35
1994	Valley View Farm	Closed	1994	39.90	40
1992	Weaver's Cottage	Closed	1994	37.90	38

Strolling Through Colonial America - K.&H. LeVan

YEAR ISSUE		EDITION LIMIT	YEAR RETD.	ISSUE PRICE	*QUOTE U.S.$
1992	Captain Lee's Grammar School	Closed	1995	39.90	40
1993	Court House on the Green	Closed	1995	37.90	38
1992	Eastbrook Church	Closed	1995	37.90	38
1993	Everette's Joiner Shop	Closed	1993	39.90	40
1992	Higgins' Grist Mill	Closed	1995	37.90	38
1991	Jefferson's Ordinarie	Closed	1995	34.90	35
1992	Millrace Store	Closed	1995	34.90	35
1992	The Village Smithy	Closed	1993	39.90	40

Tara: The Only Thing Worth Fighting For - K.&H. LeVan

YEAR ISSUE		EDITION LIMIT	YEAR RETD.	ISSUE PRICE	*QUOTE U.S.$
1994	Carriage House	Open		29.90	30
1994	A Dream Remembered	Open		29.90	30
1994	Kitchen & Gateway	Open		29.90	30
1994	Spring House & Hideaway	Closed	1995	29.90	30
1994	The Stable	Open		29.90	30
1994	Tara Mill	Open		29.90	30

Thatcher's Crossing - R. Dowding

YEAR ISSUE		EDITION LIMIT	YEAR RETD.	ISSUE PRICE	*QUOTE U.S.$
1994	Chapel Crossing	Closed	1995	29.90	30
1993	Midsummer's Cottage	Closed	1995	29.90	30
1993	Rose Arbour Cottage	Closed	1994	29.90	30
1994	Woodcutter's Cottage	Closed	1995	29.90	30

Victorian Grove Collection - K.&H. LeVan

YEAR ISSUE		EDITION LIMIT	YEAR RETD.	ISSUE PRICE	*QUOTE U.S.$
1993	Cherry Blossom	Closed	1994	34.90	35
1992	Lilac Cottage	Closed	1995	34.90	35
1992	Rose Haven	Closed	1994	34.90	35

Victoriana - C. Layton

YEAR ISSUE		EDITION LIMIT	YEAR RETD.	ISSUE PRICE	*QUOTE U.S.$
1995	May Cottage	Open		29.90	30

Welcome to Mayberry - Unknown

YEAR ISSUE		EDITION LIMIT	YEAR RETD.	ISSUE PRICE	*QUOTE U.S.$
1994	The Courthouse	Open		39.90	40
1994	Floyd's Barber Shop	Open		39.90	40
1994	Mayberry Methodist Church	Open		39.90	40
1994	Post Office	Open		39.90	40
1994	The Taylor Home	Open		39.90	40
1994	Wally's Gas Station	Open		39.90	40

Welcome to Mayberry Accessories - Unknown

YEAR ISSUE		EDITION LIMIT	YEAR RETD.	ISSUE PRICE	*QUOTE U.S.$
1995	Andy & Barney	Open		21.90	22
1995	Aunt Bee & Opey	Open		21.90	22
1995	Patrol Car & Gas Pumps	Open		21.90	22

Wizard of Oz - Unknown

YEAR ISSUE		EDITION LIMIT	YEAR RETD.	ISSUE PRICE	*QUOTE U.S.$
1995	The Journey Begins	Open		149.50	150

John Hine N.A. Ltd.

David Winter Collectors Guild Exclusives - D. Winter

YEAR ISSUE		EDITION LIMIT	YEAR RETD.	ISSUE PRICE	*QUOTE U.S.$
1987	The Village Scene	Closed	1987	Gift	225-400
1987	Robin Hood's Hideaway	Closed	1987	54.00	200-350
1987	Queen Elizabeth Slept Here	Closed	1987	183.00	200-325
1988	Black Bess Inn	Closed	1988	60.00	100
1988	The Pavillion	Closed	1988	52.00	100-250
1988	Street Scene	Closed	1988	Gift	100-250
1989	Home Guard	Closed	1989	105.00	80-200
1989	Coal Shed	Closed	1989	112.00	100-250
1990	The Plucked Ducks	Closed	1990	Gift	50
1990	The Cobblers Cottage	Closed	1990	40.00	50-65
1990	The Pottery	Closed	1990	40.00	65-125
1990	Cartwright's Cottage	Closed	1990	45.00	100
1991	Pershore Mill	Closed	1991	Gift	40-75
1991	Tomfool's Cottage	Closed	1991	100.00	110
1991	Will-O' The Wisp	Closed	1991	120.00	115-150
1992	Irish Water Mill	Closed	1992	Gift	80
1992	Patrick's Water Mill	Closed	1992	Gift	150-200
1992	Candlemaker's	Closed	1992	65.00	80
1992	Beekeeper's	Closed	1992	65.00	65-100
1993	On The River Bank	Closed	1993	Gift	50-75
1993	Thameside	Closed	1993	79.00	80
1993	Swan Upping Cottage	Closed	1993	69.00	70
1993	Horatio Pernickety's Amorous Intent	9,900	1993	375.00	350
1994	15 Lawnside Road	Closed	1994	Gift	50
1994	While Away Cottage	Closed	1994	70.00	70
1994	Ashe Cottage	Closed	1994	62.00	75
1995	Buttercup Cottage	Closed	1995	60.00	60
1995	The Flowershop	Closed	1995	150.00	150
1995	Gardener's Cottage	Closed	1995	Gift	Gift
1996	Punch Stables	Yr.Iss.		150.00	150
1996	Plough Farmstead	Yr.Iss.		125.00	125

David Winter Special Event Pieces - D. Winter

YEAR ISSUE		EDITION LIMIT	YEAR RETD.	ISSUE PRICE	*QUOTE U.S.$
1992	Birthstone Wishing Well	Closed	1992	40.00	50
1993	Birthday Cottage	Closed	1994	55.00	60-75
1994	Wishing Falls Cottage	Closed	1995	65.00	65
1995	Whisper Cottage	Closed	1995	65.00	65
1996	Primrose Cottage	Yr.Iss.		65.00	65

David Winter Tour Special Event Piece - D. Winter

YEAR ISSUE		EDITION LIMIT	YEAR RETD.	ISSUE PRICE	*QUOTE U.S.$
1993	Arches Thrice	Closed	1993	150.00	100-200

David Winter Appearance Piece - D. Winter

YEAR ISSUE		EDITION LIMIT	YEAR RETD.	ISSUE PRICE	*QUOTE U.S.$
1994	Winter Arch	Closed	1995	N/A	N/A
1995	Grumbleweed's Potting Shed	Closed	1995	99.00	99

David Winter At The Centre of the Village Collection - D. Winter

YEAR ISSUE		EDITION LIMIT	YEAR RETD.	ISSUE PRICE	*QUOTE U.S.$
1983	The Bakehouse	Open		31.40	6
1984	The Chapel	Closed	1992	48.80	8
1985	The Cooper Cottage	Closed	1993	57.90	60-8
1983	The Green Dragon Inn	Open		31.40	60
1982	Ivy Cottage	Closed	1992	22.00	4
1980	Little Market	Closed	1993	28.90	5
1980	Market Street	Open		48.80	9
1984	Parsonage	Open		390.00	56
1980	Rose Cottage	Open		28.90	5
1984	Spinner's Cottage	Closed	1991	28.90	7
1982	The Village Shop	Open		22.00	3
1980	The Wine Merchant	Closed	1993	28.90	5

David Winter British Traditions - D. Winter

YEAR ISSUE		EDITION LIMIT	YEAR RETD.	ISSUE PRICE	*QUOTE U.S.$
1990	Blossom Cottage	Closed	1995	59.00	65-8
1990	The Boat House	Closed	1995	37.50	6
1990	Bull & Bush	Closed	1995	37.50	5
1990	Burns' Reading Room	Closed	1995	31.00	5
1990	Grouse Moor Lodge	Closed	1995	48.00	50-7
1990	Guy Fawkes	Closed	1995	31.00	5
1990	Harvest Barn	Closed	1995	31.00	5
1990	Knight's Castle	Closed	1995	59.00	8
1991	The Printers and The Bookbinders	Closed	1994	120.00	14
1990	Pudding Cottage	Closed	1995	78.00	9
1990	St. Anne's Well	Closed	1995	48.00	55-7
1990	Staffordshire Vicarage	Closed	1995	48.00	55-7
1990	Stonecutters Cottage	Closed	1995	48.00	6

David Winter Cameos - D. Winter

YEAR ISSUE		EDITION LIMIT	YEAR RETD.	ISSUE PRICE	*QUOTE U.S.$
1992	Barley Malt Kilns	Open		12.50	1
1992	Brooklet Bridge	Open		12.50	1
1992	Diorama-Bright	Open		50.00	5
1992	Diorama-Light	Closed	1992	30.00	5
1992	Greenwood Wagon	Open		12.50	1
1992	Lych Gate	Open		12.50	1
1992	Market Day	Open		12.50	1

*Quotes have been rounded up to nearest dollar

YEAR ISSUE		EDITION LIMIT	YEAR RETD.	ISSUE PRICE	*QUOTE U.S.$
1992	One Man Jail	Open		12.50	15
1992	Penny Wishing Well	Open		12.50	15
1992	The Potting Shed	Open		12.50	15
1992	Poultry Ark	Open		12.50	15
1992	The Privy	Open		12.50	15
1992	Saddle Steps	Open		12.50	15
1992	Welsh Pig Pen	Open		12.50	15

David Winter Castle Collection - D. Winter

YEAR ISSUE		EDITION LIMIT	YEAR RETD.	ISSUE PRICE	*QUOTE U.S.$
1995	Bishopsgate	Open		175.00	175
1995	Bishopsgate Premier	3,500		225.00	225
1996	Guinevere's Castle	4,300		299.00	299
1996	Guinevere's Castle Premier	2,200		350.00	350

David Winter Celebration Cottages - D. Winter

YEAR ISSUE		EDITION LIMIT	YEAR RETD.	ISSUE PRICE	*QUOTE U.S.$
1994	Celebration Chapel	Open		75.00	75
1994	Celebration Chapel Premier	3,500		150.00	150
1995	Mother's Cottage	Open		65.00	65
1995	Mother's Cottage Premier	3,500		89.50	90
1994	Spring Hollow	Open		65.00	65
1994	Spring Hollow Premier	3,500		125.00	125
1995	Stork Cottage Boy	Open		65.00	65
1995	Stork Cottage Girl	Open		65.00	65
1994	Sweetheart Haven	Open		60.00	60
1994	Sweetheart Haven Premier	3,500		115.00	115

David Winter Dicken's Christmas - D. Winter

YEAR ISSUE		EDITION LIMIT	YEAR RETD.	ISSUE PRICE	*QUOTE U.S.$
1987	Ebenezer Scrooge's Counting House	Closed	1988	96.90	100-250
1988	Christmas in Scotland & Hogmanay	Closed	1988	100.00	70-100
1989	A Christmas Carol	Closed	1989	135.00	100-200
1990	Mr. Fezziwig's Emporium	Closed	1990	135.00	100-150
1991	Fred's Home: "A Merry Christmas, Uncle Ebenezer saids Scrooge's Nephew Fred, and a Happy New Year.	Closed	1991	145.00	105-200
1992	Scrooge's School	Closed	1992	160.00	120-160
1993	Old Joe's Beetling Shop A Veritable Den of Iniquity!	Closed	1993	175.00	125-175
1994	Scrooge's Family Home	Closed	1994	175.00	175-190
1994	Scrooge's Family Home Premier	Closed	1994	230.00	250
1994	Scrooge's Family Home, Plaque	3,500	1994	125.00	180
1995	Miss Belle's Cottage	Closed	1995	185.00	185
1995	Miss Belle's Cottage Premier	2,200	1995	235.00	235
1995	Miss Belle's Christmas Plaque	4,000	1995	120.00	120

David Winter English Village - D. Winter

YEAR ISSUE		EDITION LIMIT	YEAR RETD.	ISSUE PRICE	*QUOTE U.S.$
1994	Cat & Pipe	Open		53.00	53
1994	Chandlery	Open		53.00	53
1994	Church & Vestry	Open		57.00	57
1994	Constabulary	Open		60.00	60
1994	Crystal Cottage	Open		53.00	53
1994	Engine House	Open		55.00	55
1994	Glebe Cottage	Open		53.00	53
1994	Guardian Castle	8,490	1994	275.00	495
1994	Guardian Castle Premier	1,500	1994	350.00	510-600
1993	The Hall	Open		55.00	55
1993	One Acre Cottage	Open		55.00	55
1994	The Post Office	Open		53.00	53
1994	The Quack's Cottage	Open		57.00	57
1993	The Rectory	Open		55.00	55
1994	The Seminary	Open		57.00	57
1993	The Smithy	Open		50.00	50
1993	The Tannery	Open		50.00	50

David Winter Garden Cottages of England - D. Winter

YEAR ISSUE		EDITION LIMIT	YEAR RETD.	ISSUE PRICE	*QUOTE U.S.$
1995	Spencer Hall Gardens	4,300		395.00	395
1995	Spencer Hall Gardens, Premier	2,200		495.00	495
1995	Willow Gardens	4,300	1995	225.00	225
1995	Willow Gardens, Premier	2,200	1995	299.00	299

David Winter Heart of England Series - D. Winter

YEAR ISSUE		EDITION LIMIT	YEAR RETD.	ISSUE PRICE	*QUOTE U.S.$
1985	The Apothecary Shop	Closed	1995	24.10	50
1985	Blackfriars Grange	Closed	1994	24.10	75
1985	Craftsmen's Cottage	Closed	1995	24.10	40
1985	The Hogs Head Tavern	Closed	1995	24.10	50
1985	Meadowbank Cottages	Closed	1995	24.10	50
1985	The Schoolhouse	Closed	1995	24.10	45
1985	Shirehall	Closed	1995	24.10	50
1985	St. George's Church	Closed	1995	24.10	45
1985	The Vicarage	Closed	1995	24.10	45
1985	The Windmill	Open		37.50	50
1985	Yeoman's Farmhouse	Closed	1995	24.10	40

David Winter In The Country Collection - D. Winter

YEAR ISSUE		EDITION LIMIT	YEAR RETD.	ISSUE PRICE	*QUOTE U.S.$
1983	The Bothy	Open		31.40	60
1982	Brookside Hamlet	Closed	1991	74.80	65-75
1982	Drover's Cottage	Open		22.00	35
1983	Fisherman's Wharf	Open		31.40	60
1994	Guardian Gate	Open		150.00	150
1994	Guardian Gate Premier	3,500	1994	199.00	199
1987	John Benbow's Farmhouse	Closed	1993	78.00	90
1996	Lover's Tryst	Open		125.00	125
1983	Pilgrim's Rest	Closed	1993	48.80	70
1984	Snow Cottage	Closed	1992	24.80	85-115
1986	There was a Crooked House	Open		96.90	155
1996	There was a Narrow House	Open		115.00	115
1984	Tollkeeper's Cottage	Closed	1992	87.00	135

David Winter Irish Collection - D. Winter

YEAR ISSUE		EDITION LIMIT	YEAR RETD.	ISSUE PRICE	*QUOTE U.S.$
1992	Fogartys	Closed	1994	75.00	85
1992	Irish Round Tower	Open		65.00	70
1992	Murphys	Open		100.00	110
1992	O'Donovan's Castle	Open		145.00	170
1991	Only A Span Apart	Closed	1993	80.00	125
1991	Secret Sheben	Closed	1993	70.00	80

David Winter Landowners - D. Winter

YEAR ISSUE		EDITION LIMIT	YEAR RETD.	ISSUE PRICE	*QUOTE U.S.$
1984	Castle Gate	Closed	1992	155.00	245
1982	The Dower House	Closed	1993	22.00	45-55
1988	The Grange	Closed	1989	120.00	800-1000
1985	Squire Hall	Closed	1990	92.30	100-130
1981	Tudor Manor House	Closed	1992	48.80	60

David Winter Main Collection - D. Winter

YEAR ISSUE		EDITION LIMIT	YEAR RETD.	ISSUE PRICE	*QUOTE U.S.$
1983	The Alms Houses	Closed	1987	59.90	225-425
1992	Audrey's Tea Room	Closed	1992	90.00	250-350
1992	Audrey's Tea Shop	Closed	1992	90.00	225-325
1982	Blacksmith's Cottage	Closed	1986	22.00	250-350
1991	Castle in the Air	Open		675.00	710
1981	Castle Keep	Closed	1982	30.00	900-1200
1981	Chichester Cross	Closed	1981	50.00	3200-3700
1980	The Coaching Inn	Closed	1983	165.00	3600
1981	Cornish Cottage	Closed	1986	30.00	850
1983	Cornish Tin Mine	Closed	1989	22.00	85
1983	Cotton Mill	Closed	1989	41.30	400-550
1981	Double Oast	Closed	1982	60.00	3300
1980	Dove Cottage	Closed	1983	60.00	1850
1982	Fairytale Castle	Closed	1989	115.00	250-450
1986	Falstaff's Manor	10,000	1990	242.00	200-275
1980	The Forge	Closed	1983	60.00	1200-1700
1996	Golf Clubhouse	Open		160.00	160
1983	The Haybarn	Closed	1987	22.00	200
1985	Hermit's Humble Home	Closed	1988	87.00	175-300
1984	House of the Master Mason	Closed	1988	74.80	175-200
1982	House on Top	Closed	1988	92.30	360-460
1991	Inglenook Cottage	Open		60.00	75
1988	Jim'll Fixit	Closed	1988	350.00	2850-3250
1994	Kingmaker's Castle	Closed	1994	225.00	225
1980	Little Forge	Closed	1983	40.00	1200-1500
1980	Little Mill	Closed	1980	40.00	1200
1980	Little Mill-remodeled	Closed	1983	Unkn.	1600
1992	Mad Baron Fourthrite's Folly	Closed	1992	275.00	250
1980	Mill House	Closed	1980	50.00	2500
1980	Mill House-remodeled	Closed	1983	50.00	1800
1982	Miner's Cottage	Closed	1987	22.00	140-185
1991	Moonlight Haven	Open		120.00	155
1982	Moorland Cottage	Closed	1987	22.00	130-200
1995	Newtown Millhouse	4,500		195.00	195
1981	The Old Curiosity Shop	Closed	1983	40.00	1200
1980	Quayside	Closed	1985	60.00	1100-1500
1994	Quindene Manor	3,000	1994	695.00	700
1994	Quindene Manor Premier	1,500	1994	850.00	900
1982	Sabrina's Cottage	Closed	1982	30.00	2000-2350
1981	St. Paul's Cathedral	Closed	1982	40.00	1800-2000
1985	Suffolk House	Closed	1989	48.80	65
1980	Three Duck Inn	Closed	1983	60.00	1450
1981	Tythe Barn	Closed	1986	39.30	1450
1981	The Village	Open		362.00	580
1991	The Weaver's Lodgings	Open		65.00	75
1995	Welcome Home Cottage	Closed	1995	99.00	99
1995	Welcome Home Cottage Military	Closed	1995	99.00	99
1982	William Shakespeare's Birthplace (large)	Closed	1984	60.00	1300
1983	Woodcutter's Cottage	Closed	1988	87.00	200-400

David Winter Midlands Collection - D. Winter

YEAR ISSUE		EDITION LIMIT	YEAR RETD.	ISSUE PRICE	*QUOTE U.S.$
1988	Bottle Kilns	Closed	1991	78.00	75
1988	Coal Miner's Row	Open		90.00	120
1988	Derbyshire Cotton Mill	Closed	1994	65.00	90-125
1988	The Gunsmiths	Open		78.00	100
1988	Lacemaker's Cottage	Open		120.00	155
1988	Lock-keepers Cottage	Open		65.00	85

David Winter Porridge Pot Alley - D. Winter

YEAR ISSUE		EDITION LIMIT	YEAR RETD.	ISSUE PRICE	*QUOTE U.S.$
1995	Cob's Bakery	Open		125.00	125
1995	Cob's Bakery Premier	3,500		165.00	165
1995	Porridge Pot Arch	Open		50.00	50
1995	Sweet Dreams	Open		79.00	79
1995	Sweet Dreams Premier	3,500		99.00	99
1995	Tartan Teahouse	Open		99.00	99
1995	Tartan Teahouse Premier	3,500		129.00	129

David Winter Regions Collection - D. Winter

YEAR ISSUE		EDITION LIMIT	YEAR RETD.	ISSUE PRICE	*QUOTE U.S.$
1982	Cotswold Cottage	Open		22.00	35
1982	Cotswold Village	Closed	1990	59.90	75-150
1983	Hertford Court	Closed	1992	87.00	125
1985	Kent Cottage	Open		48.80	110
1981	Single Oast	Closed	1993	22.00	55
1981	Stratford House	Open		47.80	130
1982	Sussex Cottage	Open		22.00	50
1981	Triple Oast (old version)	Closed	1994	59.90	150-250

David Winter Scenes - Cameo Guild, unless otherwise noted

YEAR ISSUE		EDITION LIMIT	YEAR RETD.	ISSUE PRICE	*QUOTE U.S.$
1992	At Rose cottage Vignette - D. Winter	5,000		39.00	39
1992	Daughter - D. Winter	5,000		30.00	30
1992	Father	5,000		45.00	45
1992	Mother	5,000		50.00	50
1992	Son	5,000		30.00	30
1992	At The Bake House Vignette - D. Winter	5,000		35.00	35
1992	Girl Selling Eggs	5,000		30.00	30
1992	Hot Cross Bun Seller	5,000		60.00	60
1992	Lady Customer	5,000		45.00	45
1992	Small Boy And Dog	5,000		45.00	45
1992	Woman At Pump	5,000		45.00	45
1992	At The Bothy Vignette Base - D. Winter	5,000		39.00	39
1992	Farm Hand And Spade	5,000		40.00	40
1992	Farmer And Plough	5,000		60.00	60
1992	Farmer's Wife	5,000		45.00	45
1992	Goose Girl	5,000		45.00	45
1993	Christmas Snow Vignette - D. Winter	5,000		50.00	50
1993	Bob Cratchit And Tiny Tim	5,000		50.00	50
1993	Ebenezer Scrooge	5,000		45.00	45
1993	Fred	5,000		35.00	35
1993	Miss Belle	5,000		35.00	35
1993	Mrs. Fezziwig	5,000		35.00	35
1993	Tom The Street Shoveler	5,000		60.00	60

David Winter Scottish Collection - D. Winter

YEAR ISSUE		EDITION LIMIT	YEAR RETD.	ISSUE PRICE	*QUOTE U.S.$
1986	Crofter's Cottage	Closed	1989	51.00	60-80
1989	Gatekeeper's Cottage	Open		65.00	85
1989	Gillie's Cottage	Open		65.00	85
1989	The House on the Loch	Closed	1994	65.00	75-85
1989	MacBeth's Castle	Open		200.00	260
1982	Old Distillery	Closed	1993	312.00	500
1989	Scottish Crofter's	Open		42.00	65

David Winter Seaside Boardwalk - D. Winter

YEAR ISSUE		EDITION LIMIT	YEAR RETD.	ISSUE PRICE	*QUOTE U.S.$
1995	The Barnacle Theatre	4,500		175.00	175
1995	Dock Accessory	Open		Gift	N/A
1995	The Fisherman's Shanty	Open		110.00	110
1995	Harbour Master's Watch-House	Open		125.00	125
1995	Jolly Roger Tavern	Open		199.00	199
1995	Lodgings and Sea Bathing	Open		165.00	165
1995	Waterfront Market	Open		125.00	125

David Winter Sherwood Forest Collection - D. Winter

YEAR ISSUE		EDITION LIMIT	YEAR RETD.	ISSUE PRICE	*QUOTE U.S.$
1995	Friar Tuck's Sanctum	Open		45.00	45
1995	King Richard's Bower	Open		45.00	45
1995	Little John's Riverloft	Open		45.00	45
1995	Loxley Castle	Open		150.00	150
1995	Maid Marian's Retreat	Open		49.50	50
1995	Much's Mill	Open		45.00	45
1995	Sherwood Forest Diorama	Open		100.00	100
1995	Will Scarlett's Den	Open		49.50	50

David Winter Shires Collection - D. Winter

YEAR ISSUE		EDITION LIMIT	YEAR RETD.	ISSUE PRICE	*QUOTE U.S.$
1993	Berkshire Milking Byre	Closed	1995	38.00	38
1993	Buckinghamshire Bull Pen	Closed	1994	38.00	38
1993	Cheshire Kennels	Closed	1995	36.00	38
1993	Derbyshire Dovecote	Closed	1995	36.00	38
1993	Gloucestershire Greenhouse	Closed	1995	40.00	38
1993	Hampshire Hutches	Closed	1995	34.00	38
1993	Lancashire Donkey Shed	Closed	1995	38.00	38
1993	Oxfordshire Goat Yard	Open	1994	32.00	38
1993	Shropshire Pig Shelter	Closed	1995	32.00	38
1993	Staffordshire Stable	Closed	1995	36.00	38
1993	Wiltshire Waterwheel	Closed	1995	34.00	38
1993	Yorkshire Sheep Fold	Closed	1995	38.00	38

David Winter Tiny Series - D. Winter

YEAR ISSUE		EDITION LIMIT	YEAR RETD.	ISSUE PRICE	*QUOTE U.S.$
1980	Anne Hathaway's Cottage	Closed	1982	Unkn.	750
1980	Cotswold Farmhouse	Closed	1982	Unkn.	450-700
1980	Crown Inn	Closed	1982	Unkn.	600-700
1980	St. Nicholas' Church	Closed	1982	Unkn.	600-900
1980	Sulgrave Manor	Closed	1982	Unkn.	450-700
1980	William Shakespeare's Birthplace	Closed	1982	Unkn.	750

David Winter Welsh Collection - D. Winter

YEAR ISSUE		EDITION LIMIT	YEAR RETD.	ISSUE PRICE	*QUOTE U.S.$
1993	A Bit of Nonsense	Open		50.00	50
1993	Pen-y-Craig	Open		88.00	90
1993	Tyddyn Siriol	Closed	1994	88.00	90
1993	Y' Ddraig Goch	Closed	1994	88.00	90

David Winter West Country Collection - D. Winter

YEAR ISSUE		EDITION LIMIT	YEAR RETD.	ISSUE PRICE	*QUOTE U.S.$
1988	Cornish Engine House	Open		120.00	155
1988	Cornish Harbour	Open		120.00	155
1986	Devon Combe	Closed	1994	73.00	115
1987	Devon Creamery	Open		62.90	110
1986	Orchard Cottage	Closed	1991	91.30	115
1986	Smuggler's Creek	Open		390.00	520
1986	Tamar Cottage	Open		45.30	75

David Winter Winterville Collection - D. Winter

YEAR ISSUE		EDITION LIMIT	YEAR RETD.	ISSUE PRICE	*QUOTE U.S.$
1994	The Christmastime Clockhouse	Open		165.00	165
1994	The Christmastime Clockhouse Premier	3,500	1994	215.00	215
1995	St. Stephen's	5,750		150.00	150
1995	St. Stephen's Premier	1,750	1995	195.00	195
1994	Toymaker	Open		135.00	135
1994	Toymaker Premier	3,500	1994	175.00	175
1995	Winterville Square	Open		75.00	75
1995	Ye Merry Gentlemen's Lodgings	5,750		125.00	125
1995	Ye Merry Gentlemen's Lodgings Premier	1,750	1995	170.00	170

Disneyana Convention - John Hine Studio

YEAR ISSUE		EDITION LIMIT	YEAR RETD.	ISSUE PRICE	*QUOTE U.S.$
1992	Cinderella Castle	500	1992	250.00	1100
1993	Sleeping Beauty Castle	500	1993	250.00	450-800

*Quotes have been rounded up to nearest dollar

YEAR ISSUE		EDITION LIMIT	YEAR RETD.	ISSUE PRICE	*QUOTE U.S.$
1994	Euro Disney Castle	500	1994	250.00	350-450

Father Christmas - J. King

YEAR ISSUE		EDITION LIMIT	YEAR RETD.	ISSUE PRICE	*QUOTE U.S.$
1988	Falling	Closed	N/A	70.00	70
1988	Feet	Closed	N/A	70.00	70
1988	Standing	Closed	N/A	70.00	70

Father Time Clocks - J. Herbert

YEAR ISSUE		EDITION LIMIT	YEAR RETD.	ISSUE PRICE	*QUOTE U.S.$
1995	Captain's Keep	5,000		199.00	199
1991	Castle	Open		110.00	110
1995	Cupid's Clock	Open		55.00	55
1991	Farmhouse	Open		99.00	99
1994	Hokus Pokus	Open		79.90	80
1991	Little Thatched	Open		78.00	78
1991	The Manor	Open		90.00	90
1994	Marshland Castle	Open		99.00	99
1996	Nursery Clock	Open		110.00	110
1994	Riverside Haven	Open		99.00	99
1995	Schoolhouse Clock	Open		55.00	55
1994	Small Farmhouse Clock	Open		79.90	80
1995	A Time To Remember	Open		70.00	70
1991	Treehouse	Open		99.00	99
1995	Tudor Falls	Open		55.00	55
1995	Tudor Hall	Open		55.00	55
1994	Tudor Ruin	Open		94.00	94
1991	Watermill	Open		99.00	99
1991	Windmill	Open		120.00	120

Great British Pubs - M. Cooper

YEAR ISSUE		EDITION LIMIT	YEAR RETD.	ISSUE PRICE	*QUOTE U.S.$
1989	The Bell	Closed	N/A	79.50	100-350
1989	Black Swan	Closed	1990	79.50	100-200
1989	Blue Bell	Closed	N/A	57.50	58
1989	Coach & Horses	Closed	N/A	79.50	80
1989	The Crown Inn	Closed	N/A	79.50	80
1989	Dickens Inn	Closed	N/A	100.00	100
1989	The Feathers	Closed	N/A	200.00	200
1989	The George	Closed	N/A	57.50	58
1989	George Somerset	Closed	N/A	100.00	100
1989	Hawkeshead	Closed	N/A	Unkn.	900
1989	Jamaica Inn	Closed	N/A	39.50	40
1989	King's Arms	Closed	N/A	28.00	28
1989	The Lion	Closed	N/A	57.50	58
1989	Montague Arms	Closed	N/A	57.50	58
1989	Old Bridge House	Closed	N/A	37.50	38
1989	Old Bull Inn	Closed	N/A	87.50	88
1989	The Plough	Closed	N/A	28.00	95
1989	Sherlock Holmes	Closed	N/A	100.00	200
1989	Smith's Arms	Closed	N/A	28.00	28
1989	White Horse	Closed	N/A	39.50	40
1989	White Tower	Closed	N/A	35.00	35
1989	Ye Grapes	Closed	N/A	87.50	88
1989	Ye Olde Spotted Horse	Closed	N/A	79.50	80

Great British Pubs -Yard of Pubs - M. Cooper

YEAR ISSUE		EDITION LIMIT	YEAR RETD.	ISSUE PRICE	*QUOTE U.S.$
1989	Black Friars	Closed	N/A	25.00	25
1989	Dirty Duck	Closed	N/A	25.00	25
1989	The Eagle	Closed	N/A	35.00	35
1989	Falkland Arms	Closed	N/A	25.00	25
1989	The Falstaff	Closed	N/A	35.00	35
1989	George & Pilgrims	Closed	N/A	25.00	25
1989	The Green Man	Closed	N/A	Unkn.	75
1989	Grenadier	Closed	N/A	25.00	25
1989	Lygon Arms	Closed	N/A	35.00	35
1989	Suffolk Bull	Closed	N/A	35.00	35
1989	The Swan	Closed	N/A	35.00	35
1989	Wheatsheaf	Closed	N/A	35.00	35

Heartstrings - S. Kuck

YEAR ISSUE		EDITION LIMIT	YEAR RETD.	ISSUE PRICE	*QUOTE U.S.$
1992	Day Dreaming	Closed	N/A	92.50	93
1992	Hush, It's Sleepytime	Closed	N/A	97.50	98
1992	Taking Tea	Closed	N/A	92.50	93
1992	Watch Me Waltz	Closed	N/A	97.50	98

Mushrooms - C. Lawrence

YEAR ISSUE		EDITION LIMIT	YEAR RETD.	ISSUE PRICE	*QUOTE U.S.$
1989	The Cobblers	Closed	N/A	265.00	265
1989	The Constables	Closed	N/A	200.00	200
1989	The Elders Mushroom	Closed	N/A	175.00	175
1989	The Gift Shop	Closed	N/A	350.00	420
1989	The Ministry	Closed	N/A	185.00	185
1989	The Mush Hospital for Malingerers	Closed	N/A	250.00	250
1989	The Princess Palace	Closed	N/A	600.00	730
1989	Royal Bank of Mushland	Closed	N/A	235.00	235

Santa's Big Day - J. King

YEAR ISSUE		EDITION LIMIT	YEAR RETD.	ISSUE PRICE	*QUOTE U.S.$
1992	Booting Up	Closed	N/A	40.00	40
1992	Feet First	Closed	N/A	55.00	55
1992	Heave Ho!	Closed	N/A	70.00	70
1992	Home Rudolph	Closed	N/A	50.00	50
1992	Ready Boys?	Closed	N/A	80.00	80
1992	Reindeer Breakfast	Closed	N/A	50.00	50
1992	Rest-a-while	Closed	N/A	60.00	60
1992	Santa's Night Ride	Closed	N/A	55.00	55
1992	Tight Fit!	Closed	N/A	55.00	55
1992	Wakey, Wakey!	Closed	N/A	55.00	55
1992	Whoops!	Closed	N/A	60.00	60
1992	Zzzzz...	Closed	N/A	85.00	85

The Shoemaker's Dream - J. Herbert

YEAR ISSUE		EDITION LIMIT	YEAR RETD.	ISSUE PRICE	*QUOTE U.S.$
1991	Baby Booty (blue)	Open		45.00	45
1991	Baby Booty (pink)	Open		45.00	45
1991	Castle Boot	Open		55.00	55
1991	The Chapel	Open		55.00	55
1992	Christmas Boot	Open		55.00	55
1991	The Clocktower Boot	Open		60.00	60
1992	Clown Boot	Open		45.00	45
1991	The Crooked Boot	Open		35.00	35
1991	The Gate Lodge	Open		65.00	65
1992	The Golf Shoe	Open		35.00	40
1991	The Jester Boot	Closed	1994	29.00	29
1991	River Shoe Cottage	Closed	1994	55.00	55
1991	Rosie's Cottage	Closed	1994	40.00	40
1993	Shiver me Timbers	Open		45.00	55
1991	Shoemaker's Palace	Open		50.00	50
1992	The Sports Shoe	Open		35.00	40
1991	Tavern Boot	Open		55.00	55
1992	Upside Down Boot	Open		45.00	45
1991	Watermill Boot	Closed	1994	60.00	60
1993	Wedding Bells	Open		45.00	50
1991	Windmill Boot	Open		65.00	65
1992	Wishing Well Shoe	Open		32.00	35
1993	The Woodcutter's Shoe	Open		40.00	40

Wideman - M. Wideman

YEAR ISSUE		EDITION LIMIT	YEAR RETD.	ISSUE PRICE	*QUOTE U.S.$
1992	Moe's Clubhouse	Closed	1993	40.00	250

Wideman-American Collection - M. Wideman

YEAR ISSUE		EDITION LIMIT	YEAR RETD.	ISSUE PRICE	*QUOTE U.S.$
1989	Band Stand	Closed	1993	90.00	72-90
1989	Barber Shop	Closed	1993	40.00	30
1989	The Blockhouse	Closed	1993	25.00	16-55
1989	Cajun Cottage	Closed	1993	50.00	40
1989	California Winery	Closed	1993	180.00	145-180
1989	Cherry Hill School	Closed	1993	45.00	46-96
1991	Church in the Dale	Closed	1993	130.00	90
1989	Colonial Wellhouse	Closed	1993	15.00	14-30
1991	Desert Storm Tent	Closed	1991	75.00	75-120
1989	Dog House	Closed	1993	10.00	10-15
1991	Fire Station	Closed	1993	160.00	130-200
1989	Forty-Niner Cabin	Closed	1993	50.00	40-60
1989	Garconniere	Closed	1993	25.00	20
1989	The Gingerbread House	Closed	1993	60.00	52-65
1992	Grain Elevator	Closed	1993	110.00	125
1989	Hacienda	Closed	1993	51.00	40-80
1989	Haunted House	Closed	1993	100.00	100-145
1989	Hawaiian Grass Hut	Closed	1992	45.00	45
1991	Joe's Service Station	Closed	1993	90.00	108
1989	King William Tavern	Closed	1993	99.00	80-150
1989	The Kissing Bridge	Closed	1992	50.00	40-50
1989	The Log Cabin	Closed	1993	45.00	40-60
1989	The Maple Sugar Shack	Closed	1993	50.00	40-50
1991	Milk House	Closed	1993	20.00	20
1989	The Mission	Closed	1993	99.00	80-100
1991	Mo At Work	Closed	1991	35.00	35-65
1991	Moe's Diner	Closed	1993	100.00	300-700
1989	The New England Church	Closed	1993	79.00	72-80
1989	New England Lighthouse	Closed	1993	99.00	80-120
1992	News Stand	Closed	1993	30.00	30-72
1989	Octagonal House	Closed	1993	40.00	32-52
1989	The Old Mill	Closed	1993	100.00	80-100
1989	The Opera House	Closed	1992	89.00	72-90
1989	The Out House	Closed	1993	15.00	15-30
1989	Oxbow Saloon	Closed	1993	90.00	65-90
1989	The Pacific Lighthouse	Closed	1993	89.00	80-150
1991	Paul Revere's House	Closed	1992	90.00	72-95
1989	Plantation House	Closed	1993	119.00	90-195
1989	Prairie Forge	Closed	1993	65.00	65-135
1989	Railhead Inn	Closed	1993	250.00	195-250
1989	The River Bell	Closed	1993	99.00	95-120
1989	Seaside Cottage	Closed	1992	225.00	190
1989	Sierra Mine	Closed	1992	120.00	90-120
1989	Sod House	Closed	1992	40.00	25-40
1989	Star Cottage	Closed	1993	30.00	24
1989	Sweetheart Cottage	Closed	1993	45.00	35-45
1992	Telephone Booth	Closed	1993	15.00	30
1989	Tobacconist	Closed	1993	45.00	45
1992	Topper's Drive-In	Closed	1993	120.00	125-145
1989	Town Hall	Closed	1993	129.00	125-150
1989	Tree House	Closed	1993	45.00	45
1992	Village Mercantile	Closed	1993	60.00	70
1989	Wisteria	Closed	1993	15.00	20

Wideman-First Nation Collection - M. Wideman

YEAR ISSUE		EDITION LIMIT	YEAR RETD.	ISSUE PRICE	*QUOTE U.S.$
1993	Elm Bark Longhouse	Closed	1993	56.00	56
1993	The First Nation Collection, set/8	Closed	1993	500.00	1000
1993	Igloo	Closed	1993	60.00	90
1993	Mandan Earth Lodge	Closed	1993	56.00	300
1993	Plains Teepee	Closed	1993	68.00	300
1993	Stilt House	Closed	1993	60.00	60-90
1993	Sweat Lodge	Closed	1993	34.00	100
1993	West Coast Longhouse	Closed	1993	100.00	100
1993	Wigwam	Closed	1993	65.00	300

Woodly Wise - T. Slack

YEAR ISSUE		EDITION LIMIT	YEAR RETD.	ISSUE PRICE	*QUOTE U.S.$
1995	Arbor Stone	Open		55.00	55
1995	Brambly Perch	Open		49.00	49
1995	Chimney Pot Lodge	Open		79.00	79
1995	Crooked Climb	Open		55.00	55
1995	Roundabout	Open		29.00	29
1995	Snow Chapel	2,950		99.00	99
1995	Timberskeep	Open		79.00	79
1995	Water's End	Open		55.00	55
1995	Wendy House	2,950		99.00	99

June McKenna Collectibles, Inc.

7" Limited Edition - J. McKenna

YEAR ISSUE		EDITION LIMIT	YEAR RETD.	ISSUE PRICE	*QUOTE U.S.$
1991	Christmas Bishop	7,500	1993	110.00	145
1993	Christmas Cheer 1st ed.	7,500	1993	120.00	300-400
1993	Christmas Cheer 2nd. ed.	7,500	1995	120.00	120
1990	Christmas Delight	7,500	1992	100.00	100
1988	Christmas Memories	7,500	1991	90.00	220
1992	Christmas Wizard	7,500	1994	110.00	125
1990	Ethnic Santa	7,500	1992	100.00	140
1988	Joyful Christmas	7,500	1991	90.00	150
1989	Old Fashioned Santa	7,500	1991	100.00	150
1989	Santa's Bag of Surprises	7,500	1991	100.00	220

Black Folk Art - J. McKenna

YEAR ISSUE		EDITION LIMIT	YEAR RETD.	ISSUE PRICE	*QUOTE U.S.$
1987	Aunt Bertha - 3D	Closed	1991	36.00	75-100
1983	Black Boy With Watermelon, available in 3 colors	Closed	1988	12.00	75-100
1986	Black Butler	Closed	1989	13.00	75
1983	Black Girl With Watermelon, available in 3 colors	Closed	1988	12.00	80
1984	Black Man With Pig, available in 3 colors	Closed	1988	13.00	100-150
1984	Black Woman With Broom, available in 3 colors	Closed	1988	13.00	125
1989	Delia	Closed	1991	16.00	50
1989	Jake	Closed	1991	16.00	50
1985	Kids in a Tub - 3D	Closed	1990	30.00	110
1985	Kissing Cousins - sill sitter	Closed	1990	36.00	75-125
1990	Let's Play Ball -3D	Closed	1993	45.00	50
1987	Lil' Willie -3D	Closed	1991	36.00	75
1984	Mammie Cloth Doll	Closed	1988	90.00	400-500
1985	Mammie With Kids - 3D	Closed	1990	90.00	125-160
1985	Mammie With Spoon	Closed	1989	13.00	200
1988	Netty	Closed	1991	16.00	50
1984	Remus Cloth Doll	Closed	1988	90.00	350-400
1988	Renty	Closed	1991	16.00	50
1990	Sunday's Best -3D	Closed	1993	45.00	50
1987	Sweet Prissy -3D	Closed	1991	36.00	75
1990	Tasha	Closed	1991	17.00	40
1985	Toaster Cover	Closed	1988	50.00	350
1990	Tyree	Closed	1991	17.00	40
1987	Uncle Jacob- 3D	Closed	1991	36.00	55-70
1985	Watermelon Patch Kids	Closed	1990	24.00	100

Carolers - J. McKenna

YEAR ISSUE		EDITION LIMIT	YEAR RETD.	ISSUE PRICE	*QUOTE U.S.$
1985	Boy Caroler	Closed	1989	36.00	65
1992	Carolers, Grandparents	Closed	1994	70.00	70
1991	Carolers, Man With Girl	Closed	1994	50.00	5
1991	Carolers, Woman With Boy	Closed	1994	50.00	5
1985	Girl Caroler	Closed	1989	36.00	7
1985	Man Caroler	Closed	1989	36.00	6
1985	Woman Caroler	Closed	1989	36.00	6

June McKenna Figurines - J. McKenna

YEAR ISSUE		EDITION LIMIT	YEAR RETD.	ISSUE PRICE	*QUOTE U.S.$
1989	16th Century Santa - 3D, blue	Closed	1991	60.00	175-29
1989	16th Century Santa - 3D, green	Closed	1989	60.00	250-29
1989	17th Century Santa - 3D, red	Closed	1991	70.00	17
1993	Angel Name Plaque	Closed	1994	70.00	10
1983	Boy Rag Doll	Closed	N/A	12.00	300-45
1985	Bride w/o base-3D	Closed	1985	25.00	175-23
1985	Bride-3D	Closed	1987	25.00	20
1993	Children Ice Skaters	Closed	1994	60.00	6
1992	Choir of Angels	Closed	1993	60.00	6
1992	Christmas Santa	Closed	1993	60.00	9
1987	Country Rag Boy (sitting)	Closed	1990	40.00	150-16
1987	Country Rag Girl (sitting)	Closed	1990	40.00	150-16
1985	Father Times - 3D	Closed	1991	40.00	15
1983	Girl Rag Doll	Closed	N/A	12.00	300-45
1993	A Good Night's Sleep	Closed	1995	70.00	7
1985	Groom w/o base-3D	Closed	1985	25.00	175-23
1985	Groom-3D	Closed	1987	25.00	150-20
1989	Jolly Ole Santa - 3D	Closed	1991	44.00	100-20
1986	Little St. Nick -3D	Closed	1990	50.00	175-20
1986	Male Angel	Closed	1986	44.00	1300-170
1988	Mr. Santa - 3D	Closed	1991	44.00	10
1993	Mr. Snowman	Closed	1994	40.00	5
1988	Mrs. Santa - 3D	Closed	1989	50.00	200-25
1987	Name Plaque	Closed	1992	50.00	120-15
1990	Noel - 3D	Closed	1992	50.00	12
1987	Patriotic Santa	Closed	1989	50.00	30
1993	Santa Name Plaque	Closed	1995	70.00	[illegible]
1993	The Snow Family	Closed	1994	40.00	4
1985	Soldier	Closed	1988	40.00	160-22
1992	Taking A Break	Closed	1995	60.00	[illegible]
1984	Tree Topper	Closed	1987	70.00	350-42

Limited Edition - J. McKenna

YEAR ISSUE		EDITION LIMIT	YEAR RETD.	ISSUE PRICE	*QUOTE U.S.$
1988	Bringing Home Christmas	4,000	1990	170.00	275-4
1987	Christmas Eve	4,000	1989	170.00	4
1992	Christmas Gathering	4,000	1996	220.00	2
1991	Coming to Town	4,000	1994	220.00	3
1983	Father Christmas	4,000	1986	90.00	2500-33
1987	Kris Kringle	4,000	1990	350.00	6
1990	Night Before Christmas	1,500	1993	750.00	7
1984	Old Saint Nick	4,000	1986	100.00	800-9
1988	Remembrance of Christmas Past	4,000	1992	400.00	3
1991	Santa's Hot Air Balloon	1,500	1993	800.00	8
1989	Santa's Wardrobe	1,500	1992	750.00	800-10
1989	Seasons Greetings	4,000	1992	200.00	3
1986	Victorian	4,000	1988	150.00	500-9
1990	Wilderness	4,000	1994	200.00	250-3

*Quotes have been rounded up to nearest dolla

Year Issue		Edition Limit	Year Retd.	Issue Price	*Quote U.S. $
1985	Woodland	4,000	1987	140.00	600-975

Limited Edition Flatback - J. McKenna

Year Issue		Edition Limit	Year Retd.	Issue Price	*Quote U.S. $
1991	Bag of Stars	10,000	1993	34.00	40
1993	Bells of Christmas	10,000	1995	40.00	40
1989	Blue Christmas	10,000	1991	32.00	100
1992	Deck The Halls	10,000	1994	34.00	40
1991	Farewell Santa	10,000	1993	34.00	50
1992	Good Tidings	10,000	1994	34.00	40
1990	Medieval Santa	10,000	1992	34.00	60
1988	Mystical Santa	10,000	1991	30.00	100
1990	Old Time Santa	10,000	1992	34.00	60
1993	Santa's Love	10,000	1995	40.00	40
1988	Toys of Joy	10,000	1991	30.00	60-70
1989	Victorian	10,000	1991	32.00	110

Nativity Set - J. McKenna

Year Issue		Edition Limit	Year Retd.	Issue Price	*Quote U.S. $
1988	Nativity - 6 Pieces	6/96		130.00	150
1991	Sheep With Shepherds - 2 Pieces	6/96		60.00	60
1989	Three Wise Men	6/96		60.00	90

Personal Appearance Figurines - J. McKenna

Year Issue		Edition Limit	Year Retd.	Issue Price	*Quote U.S. $
1989	Father Christmas	Closed	1993	30.00	150-200
1990	Old Saint Nick	Closed	1994	30.00	100
1991	Woodland	Closed	1995	35.00	50
1992	Victorian	4-Yr.		35.00	35
1993	Christmas Eve	4-Yr.		35.00	35
1994	Bringing Home Christmas	4-Yr.		35.00	35

Registered Edition - J. McKenna

Year Issue		Edition Limit	Year Retd.	Issue Price	*Quote U.S. $
1991	Checking His List	Closed	1994	230.00	275
1996	Christmas Over Load	Open		260.00	260
1986	Colonial	Closed	1990	150.00	250-350
1992	Forty Winks	Closed	1994	250.00	300
1988	Jolly Ole St. Nick	Closed	1990	170.00	300
1995	Mrs. Santa Down on the Farm	Open		250.00	250
1995	Santa Down on the Farm	Open		260.00	260
1994	Say Cheese, Please	Open		250.00	250
1993	Tomorrow's Christmas	Closed	1995	250.00	250
1990	Toy Maker	Closed	1993	200.00	400
1989	Traditional	Closed	1991	180.00	300
1987	White Christmas	Closed	1987	170.00	1000-1200

Special Limited Edition - J. McKenna

Year Issue		Edition Limit	Year Retd.	Issue Price	*Quote U.S. $
1994	All Aboard-North Pole Express	Open		500.00	500
1995	All Aboard-Toy Car	Closed	1996	250.00	250
1993	Baking Cookies	2,000	1995	450.00	450
1991	Bedtime Stories	2,000	1994	500.00	500
1990	Christmas Dreams	4,000	1992	280.00	350
1990	Christmas Dreams (Hassock)	63	1990	280.00	2000
1996	International Santa	Yr.Iss.		160.00	160
1989	Last Gentle Nudge	4,000	1991	280.00	350-400
1996	North Pole Express-Logging Car	Yr.Iss.		250.00	250
1989	Santa & His Magic Sleigh	4,000	1992	280.00	350-400
1992	Santa's Arrival	2,000	1994	300.00	350
1990	Santa's Reindeer	1,500	1993	400.00	400-450
1995	Show Me The Way	1,000		500.00	500
1990	Up On The Rooftop	4,000	1991	280.00	400
1994	Welcome to the World	2,000	1995	400.00	400

Victorian Limited Edition - J. McKenna

Year Issue		Edition Limit	Year Retd.	Issue Price	*Quote U.S. $
1990	Edward - 3D	1,000	1991	180.00	450
1990	Elizabeth - 3D	1,000	1991	180.00	450
1990	Joseph - 3D	Closed	1991	50.00	50-250
1990	Victoria - 3D	Closed	1991	50.00	50-250

Kurt S. Adler, Inc.

Angel Darlings - N. Bailey

Year Issue		Edition Limit	Year Retd.	Issue Price	*Quote U.S. $
1996	Almost Fits H4765/1	Open		15.00	15
1996	Bottoms Up H4765/6	Open		15.00	15
1996	Buddies H4765/3	Open		15.00	15
1996	Cuddles H4765/5	Open		15.00	15
1996	Dream Builders H4765/4	Open		15.00	15
1996	Peek-A-Boo H4765/2	Open		15.00	15

Christmas Legends - P.F. Bolinger

Year Issue		Edition Limit	Year Retd.	Issue Price	*Quote U.S. $
1994	Aldwyn of the Greenwood J8196	Open		145.00	145
1994	Berwyn the Grand J8198	Open		175.00	175
1995	Bountiful J8234	Open		164.00	164
1994	Caradoc the Kind J8199	Open		70.00	70
1994	Florian of the Berry Bush J8199	Open		70.00	70
1994	Gustave the Gutsy J8199	Open		70.00	70
1995	Luminatus J8241	Open		136.00	136
1994	Silvanus the Cheerful J8197	Open		165.00	165

The Fabriché™ Bear & Friends Series - KSA Design Team

Year Issue		Edition Limit	Year Retd.	Issue Price	*Quote U.S. $
1992	Laughing All The Way J1567	Retrd.	1994	83.00	83
1992	Not A Creature Was Stirring W1534	Open		67.00	67
1993	Teddy Bear Parade W1601	Open		73.00	73

Fabriché™ Angel Series - K.S. Adler

Year Issue		Edition Limit	Year Retd.	Issue Price	*Quote U.S. $
1992	Heavenly Messenger W1584	Retrd.	1994	41.00	41

Fabriché™ Camelot Figure Series - P. Mauk

Year Issue		Edition Limit	Year Retd.	Issue Price	*Quote U.S. $
1994	King Arthur J3372	7,500		110.00	110
1993	Merlin the Magician J7966	7,500		120.00	120
1993	Young Arthur J7967	7,500		120.00	120

Fabriché™ Holiday Figurines - KSA Design Team, unless otherwise noted

Year Issue		Edition Limit	Year Retd.	Issue Price	*Quote U.S. $
1995	All Aboard For Christmas W1679	Open		56.00	56
1994	All Star Santa W1652	Open		56.00	56
1993	All That Jazz W1620	Retrd.	1994	67.00	67
1992	An Apron Full of Love W1582 - M. Rothenberg	Open		75.00	75
1995	Armchair Quarterback W1693	Open		90.00	90
1994	Basket of Goodies W1650	Open		60.00	60
1992	Bringin in the Yule Log W1589 - M. Rothenberg	5,000		200.00	200
1993	Bringing the Gifts W1605	Open		60.00	60
1992	Bundles of Joy W1578	Retrd.	1994	78.00	78
1995	Captain Claus W1680	Open		56.00	56
1994	Checking His List W1643	Open		60.00	60
1993	Checking It Twice W1604	Open		56.00	56
1992	Christmas is in the Air W1590	Retrd.	1995	110.00	125
1995	Diet Starts Tomorrow W1691	Open		60.00	60
1995	Father Christmas W1687	Open		56.00	56
1994	Firefighting Friends W1654	Open		72.00	72
1993	Forever Green W1607	Retrd.	1994	56.00	56
1994	Friendship W1642	Open		65.00	65
1995	Gift From Heaven W1694	Open		60.00	60
1992	He Did It Again J7944 - T. Rubel	Open		160.00	160
1993	Here Kitty W1618 - M. Rothenberg	Retrd.	1994	90.00	125
1994	Ho, Ho, Ho Santa W1632	Open		56.00	56
1994	Holiday Express W1636	Open		100.00	100
1992	Homeward Bound W1568	Open		61.00	65
1992	Hugs and Kisses W1531	Retrd.	1994	67.00	67
1992	I'm Late, I'm Late J7947 - T. Rubel	Retrd.	1995	100.00	100
1992	It's Time To Go J7943 - T. Rubel	Retrd.	1994	150.00	150
1995	Kris Kringle W1685	Open		55.00	55
1994	Mail Must Go Through W1667 - KSA/WRG	Open		110.00	110
1992	Merry Kissmas W1548 - M. Rothenberg	Retrd.	1993	140.00	140
1995	Merry Memories W1735	Open		56.00	56
1994	Merry St. Nick W1641 - Giordano	Open		100.00	100
1995	Mrs. Santa Caroller W1690 - M. Rothenberg	Open		70.00	70
1995	Night Before Christmas W1692 - Wood River Gallery	Open		60.00	60
1994	Officer Claus W1677	Open		56.00	56
1993	Par For The Claus W1603	Open		60.00	60
1994	Peace Santa W1631	Open		60.00	60
1995	Pere Noel W1686	Open		55.00	55
1993	Playtime For Santa W1619	Retrd.	1994	67.00	67
1994	Santa Calls W1678 - W. Joyce	Open		55.00	55
1995	Santa Caroller W1689 - M. Rothenberg	Open		70.00	70
1991	Santa Fiddler W1549 - M. Rothenberg	Retrd.	1992	100.00	100
1992	Santa Steals A Kiss & A Cookie W1581 - M. Rothenberg	Retrd.	1994	150.00	175
1992	Santa's Cat Nap W1504 - M. Rothenberg	Retrd.	1992	98.00	110
1994	Santa's Fishtales W1640	Open		60.00	60
1992	Santa's Ice Capades W1588 - M. Rothenberg	Retrd.	1995	110.00	110
1994	Schussing Claus W1651	Open		78.00	78
1992	St. Nicholas The Bishop W1532	Open		78.00	78
1994	Star Gazing Santa W1656 - M. Rothenberg	Open		120.00	120
1993	Stocking Stuffer W1622	Retrd.	1994	56.00	56
1995	Strike Up The Band W1681	Open		55.00	55
1995	Tee Time W1734	Open		60.00	60
1993	Top Brass W1630	Retrd.	1995	67.00	67
1993	With All The Trimmings W1616	Open		76.00	76
1995	Woodland Santa W1731 - R. Volpi	Open		67.00	67

Fabriché™ Santa at Home Series - M. Rothenberg

Year Issue		Edition Limit	Year Retd.	Issue Price	*Quote U.S. $
1995	Baby Burping Santa W1732	Open		80.00	80
1994	The Christmas Waltz 1635	Open		135.00	135
1995	Family Portrait W1727	Open		140.00	140
1993	Grandpa Santa's Piggyback Ride W1621	7,500		84.00	84
1995	Santa's Horsey Ride W1728	Open		80.00	80
1994	Santa's New Friend W1655	Open		110.00	110

Fabriché™ Santa's Helpers Series - M. Rothenberg

Year Issue		Edition Limit	Year Retd.	Issue Price	*Quote U.S. $
1993	Little Olde Clockmaker W1629	5,000		134.00	134
1992	A Stitch in Time W1591	5,000		135.00	135

Fabriché™ Smithsonian Museum Series - KSA/Smithsonian

Year Issue		Edition Limit	Year Retd.	Issue Price	*Quote U.S. $
1992	Holiday Drive W1556	Retrd.	1995	155.00	155
1993	Holiday Flight W1617	Retrd.	1995	144.00	144
1992	Peace on Earth Angel Treetop W1583	Retrd.	1995	52.00	52
1992	Peace on Earth Flying Angel W1585	Retrd.	1995	49.00	49
1991	Santa On A Bicycle W1527	Retrd.	1994	150.00	150
1995	Toys For Good Boys and Girls W1696	Open		75.00	75

Fabriché™ Thomas Nast Figurines - KSA Design Team

Year Issue		Edition Limit	Year Retd.	Issue Price	*Quote U.S. $
1992	Caught in the Act W1577	Retrd.	1993	133.00	133
1992	Christmas Sing-A-Long W1576	12,000		110.00	110
1993	Dear Santa W1602	Retrd.	1993	110.00	110
1991	Hello! Little One W1552	12,000	1994	90.00	90

Gallery of Angels - KSA Design Team

Year Issue		Edition Limit	Year Retd.	Issue Price	*Quote U.S. $
1994	Guardian Angel M1099	2,000		150.00	150
1994	Unspoken Word M1100	2,000		150.00	150

Halloween - P.F. Bolinger

Year Issue		Edition Limit	Year Retd.	Issue Price	*Quote U.S. $
1996	Dr. Punkinstein HW535	Open		50.00	50
1996	Eat at Drac's HW493	Open		22.00	22
1996	Pumpkin Grumpkin HW494	Open		18.00	18
1996	Pumpkin Plumpkin HW494	Open		18.00	18
1996	Pumpkins Are Us HW534	Open		17.00	17

Helping Hand Santas - P. Bolinger

Year Issue		Edition Limit	Year Retd.	Issue Price	*Quote U.S. $
1996	Harmonious J6509	Open		115.00	115
1996	Noah J6487	Open		56.00	56
1996	Uncle Sam J6488	Open		56.00	56

Ho Ho Ho Gang - P.F. Bolinger

Year Issue		Edition Limit	Year Retd.	Issue Price	*Quote U.S. $
1996	Box of Chocolate J6510	Open		33.00	33
1994	Christmas Goose J8201	Open		22.00	22
1996	Christmas Shopping Santa J6497	Open		22.00	22
1996	Claus-A-Lounger J6478	Open		33.00	33
1995	Cookie Claus J8286	Open		39.00	39
1995	Do Not Disturb J8233	Open		34.00	34
1996	Fire Department North Pole J6508	Open		50.00	50
1996	Fireman Santa J6476	Open		28.00	28
1994	Holy Mackerel J8201	Open		22.00	22
1996	Joy of Cooking J6496	Open		28.00	28
1996	Love Santa J6493	Open		18.00	18
1995	No Hair Day J8287	Open		50.00	50
1996	Noel Roly Poly J6489	Open		20.00	20
1995	North Pole (large) J8237	Open		56.00	56
1995	North Pole (small) J8238	Open		45.00	45
1996	North Pole Pro-Am J6479	Open		28.00	28
1996	On Strike For More Cookies J6506	Open		33.00	33
1996	Police Department North Pole J6507	Open		50.00	50
1996	Policeman Santa J6475	Open		28.00	28
1994	Santa Cob J8203	Retrd.	1995	28.00	28
1996	Save The Reindeer J6498	Open		28.00	28
1996	Some Assembly Required J6477	Open		53.00	53
1994	Surprise J8201	Open		22.00	22
1994	Will He Make It? J8203	Retrd.	1995	28.00	28
1995	Will Work For Cookies J8235	Open		40.00	40
1995	Wishful Thinking J8239	Open		32.00	32

Holly Bearies - H. Adler

Year Issue		Edition Limit	Year Retd.	Issue Price	*Quote U.S. $
1996	Angel Bear J7342	Open		14.00	14
1996	Mother's Day Bear J7318	Open		15.00	15
1996	Teddy Tower J7221	Open		23.00	23

Holly Bearies Calendar Bears - H. Adler

Year Issue		Edition Limit	Year Retd.	Issue Price	*Quote U.S. $
1996	Clairmont, Dempsey & Pete J7215/Jul	Open		16.00	16
1996	Clara & Carnation The Kitty J7215/Oct	Open		16.00	16
1996	Fergus & Fritzi's Frosty Frolic J7215/Jan	Open		16.00	16
1996	Grandma Gladys J7215/Dec	Open		16.00	16
1996	Nicole & Nicholas Sun Bearthing J7215/Aug	Open		16.00	16
1996	Petunia & Nathan Plant Posies J7215/May	Open		16.00	16
1996	Philo's Pot O Gold J7215/Mar	Open		16.00	16
1996	Pinky & Victoria Are Sweeties J7215/Feb	Open		16.00	16
1996	Skeeter & Sigourney Start School J7215/Sep	Open		16.00	16
1996	Sunshine Catching Raindrops J7215/Apr	Open		16.00	16
1996	Thorndike & Filbert Catch Fish J7215/Jun	Open		16.00	16
1996	Thorndike All Dressed Up J7215/Nov	Open		16.00	16

Jim Henson's Muppet Nutcrackers - KSA/JHP

Year Issue		Edition Limit	Year Retd.	Issue Price	*Quote U.S. $
1993	Kermit The Frog H1223	Retrd.	1995	90.00	90

Mickey Unlimited - KSA/Disney

Year Issue		Edition Limit	Year Retd.	Issue Price	*Quote U.S. $
1994	Donald Duck Drummer W1671	Open		45.00	45
1993	Donald Duck H1235	Open		90.00	90
1992	Goofy H1216	Open		78.00	78
1994	Mickey Bandleader W1669	Open		45.00	45
1992	Mickey Mouse Soldier H1194	Open		72.00	72
1992	Mickey Mouse Sorcerer H1221	Open		100.00	100
1993	Mickey Mouse With Gift Boxes W1608	Open		78.00	78
1994	Mickey Santa Nutcracker H1237	Open		90.00	90
1994	Minnie Mouse Soldier Nutcrackers H1236	Open		90.00	90
1994	Minnie With Cymbals W1670	Open		45.00	45
1993	Pinnochio H1222	Open		110.00	110

Old World Santa Series - J. Mostrom

Year Issue		Edition Limit	Year Retd.	Issue Price	*Quote U.S. $
1992	Chelsea Garden Santa W2721	Retrd.	1994	33.50	34
1993	Good King Wenceslas W2928	3,000		134.00	134
1992	Large Black Forest Santa W2717	Retrd.	1994	110.00	110
1992	Large Father Christmas W2719	Retrd.	1994	106.00	106
1993	Medieval King of Christmas W2881	3,000	1994	390.00	390
1992	Mrs. Claus W2714	5,000		37.00	37
1992	Patriotic Santa W2720	3,000	1994	128.00	128
1992	Pere Noel W2723	Retrd.	1994	33.50	34
1992	Small Black Forest Santa W2712	Retrd.	1994	40.00	40
1992	Small Father Christmas W2712	Retrd.	1994	33.50	34
1992	Small Father Frost W2716	Retrd.	1994	43.00	43
1992	Small Grandfather Frost W2718	Retrd.	1994	106.00	106

*Quotes have been rounded up to nearest dollar

Column 1

YEAR ISSUE	EDITION LIMIT	YEAR RETD.	ISSUE PRICE	*QUOTE U.S.$
1992 St. Nicholas W2713	Retrd.	1994	30.00	30
1992 Workshop Santa W2715	5,000		43.00	43

Sesame Street Series - KSA/JHP

1993 Big Bird Fabrich, Figurine J7928	Open		60.00	60
1993 Big Bird Nutcracker H1199	Retrd.	1994	60.00	60

Snow People - P.F. Bolinger

1996 Coola Hula J6430	Open		20.00	20
1996 Snowpoke J6431	Open		28.00	28
1996 Snowy J6429	Open		28.00	28

Steinbach Camelot Smoking Figure Series - KSA/Steinbach

1993 King Arthur ES832	7,500		175.00	175
1992 Merlin The Magician ES830	7,500		150.00	150

Steinbach Nutcracker Collectors' Club - KSA/Steinbach

1995 King Wenceslaus	12/96		225.00	225
1995 The Town Crier	12/96		Gift	N/A

Steinbach Nutcracker American Presidents Series - KSA/Steinbach

1992 Abraham Lincoln ES622	12,000		195.00	225
1993 Ben Franklin ES622	12,000		225.00	225
1992 George Washington ES623	12,000	1994	195.00	500
1993 Teddy Roosevelt ES644	10,000		225.00	225
1996 Thomas Jefferson ES666	7,500		260.00	260

Steinbach Nutcracker Biblical - KSA/Steinbach

1996 Noah ES893	10,000		260.00	260

Steinbach Nutcracker Camelot Series - KSA/Steinbach

1992 King Arthur ES621	Retrd.	1993	195.00	500-1500
1991 Merlin The Magician ES610	Retrd.	1991	185.00	3000-4000
1995 Queen Guenevere ES869	10,000		245.00	245
1994 Sir Galahad ES862	12,000		225.00	225
1993 Sir Lancelot ES638	12,000		225.00	225
1994 Sir Lancelot Smoker ES833	7,500		150.00	150

Steinbach Nutcracker Christmas Legends Series - KSA/Steinbach

1995 1930s Santa Claus ES891	7,500		245.00	245
1993 Father Christmas ES645	7,500		225.00	225
1994 St. Nicholas, The Bishop ES865	7,500		225.00	225

Steinbach Nutcracker Collection - KSA/Steinbach

1991 Columbus ES697	Retrd.	1992	194.00	225
1992 Happy Santa ES601	Open		190.00	220
1984 Oil Sheik	Retrd.	1985	100.00	500

Steinbach Nutcracker Famous Chieftans Series - KSA/Steinbach

1995 Black Hawk ES889	7,500		245.00	245
1993 Chief Sitting Bull ES637	8,500	1995	225.00	250-500
1994 Chief Sitting Bull Smoker ES834	7,500		150.00	150
1994 Red Cloud ES864	8,500		225.00	225

Steinbach Nutcracker Mini Series - KSA/Steinbach

1996 Merlin ES335	15,000		50.00	50
1996 Robin Hood ES338	10,000		50.00	50

Steinbach Nutcracker Tales of Sherwood Forest - KSA/Steinbach

1995 Friar Tuck ES890	7,500		245.00	245
1992 Robin Hood ES863	7,500		225.00	225
1996 Sherif of Nottingham ES892	7,500		260.00	260

Steinbach Nutcracker Three Muskateers - KSA/Steinbach

1996 Aramis ES722	7,500		130.00	130

Visions Of Santa Series - KSA Design Team

1992 Santa Coming Out Of Fireplace J1023	Retrd.	1993	29.00	29
1992 Santa Holding Child J826	Retrd.	1993	24.50	25
1992 Santa Spilling Bag Of Toys J1022	7,500	1994	25.50	26
1992 Santa W/Little Girls On Lap J1024	7,500		24.50	25
1992 Santa W/Sack Holding Toy J827	7,500	1994	24.50	25
1992 Workshop Santa J825	7,500	1994	27.00	27

Zuber Nutcracker Series - KSA/Zuber

1992 The Annapolis Midshipman EK7	5,000	1994	125.00	125
1992 The Bavarian EK16	5,000	1994	130.00	130
1992 Bronco Billy The Cowboy EK1	5,000	1994	125.00	125
1992 The Chimney Sweep EK6	5,000	1993	125.00	125
1992 The Country Singer EK19	5,000	1994	125.00	125
1992 The Fisherman EK17	5,000		125.00	125
1994 The Gardner EK26	2,500		150.00	150
1992 Gepetto, The Toymaker EK9	5,000	1994	125.00	125
1992 The Gold Prospector EK18	5,000	1994	125.00	125
1992 The Golfer EK5	5,000	1994	125.00	125
1993 Herr Drosselmeir Nutcracker EK21	5,000	1995	150.00	300-450
1993 The Ice Cream Vendor EK24	5,000		150.00	150
1992 The Indian EK15	5,000	1994	135.00	135
1994 Jazz Player EK25	2,500		145.00	145
1994 Kurt the Traveling Salesman EK28	2,500	1994	155.00	155
1994 Mouse King EK31	2,500		150.00	150
1993 Napoleon Bonaparte EK23	5,000		150.00	150
1992 The Nor' Easter Sea Captain EK3	5,000		125.00	125
1992 Paul Bunyan The Lumberjack EK2	5,000	1993	125.00	125
1994 Peter Pan EK28	2,500		145.00	145

Column 2

YEAR ISSUE	EDITION LIMIT	YEAR RETD.	ISSUE PRICE	*QUOTE U.S.$
1992 The Pilgrim EK14	5,000	1994	125.00	125
1993 The Pizzamaker EK22	5,000		150.00	150
1994 Scuba Diver EK27	2,500		150.00	150
1994 Soccer Player EK30	2,500		145.00	145
1992 The Tyrolean EK4	5,000	1994	125.00	125
1992 The West Point Cadet w/Canon EK8	5,000	1994	130.00	130

Lalique Society of America

Lalique Society Annual Series - Various

1989 Degas Box 10585 - R. Lalique	Yr.Iss.		295.00	725
1990 Hestia Medallion 61051 - M.C. Lalique	Yr.Iss.		295.00	700
1991 Lily of Valley (perfume bottle) 61053 - R. Lalique	Yr.Iss.		275.00	450
1992 La Patineuse (paperweight) 61054 - M.C. Lalique	Yr.Iss.		325.00	375
1993 Enchantment (figurine) 61055 - M.C. Lalique	Yr.Iss.		395.00	395
1994 Eclipse (perfume bottle) - M.C. Lalique	Yr.Iss.		395.00	395

Lance Corporation

Chilmark MetalART™ The Great Chiefs - J. Slockbower

1992 Chief Joseph	750	1992	975.00	1500-1900
1993 Crazy Horse	750		975.00	975
1992 Geronimo	750		975.00	1300-1850
1993 Sitting Bull	750		1075.00	1075

Chilmark MetalART™ Mickey & Co. On the Road - Staff

1994 Beach Bound	350	1994	350.00	1200-2500
1992 Cruising	350	1992	275.00	2000-3500
1993 Sunday Drive	350	1993	325.00	1500-2500
1993 Matched Numbrd. set/3	350	1993	950.00	8000-9000
1993 Mixed & Matched Numbrd. set/3	350	1993	950.00	5000-8000

Chilmark MetalART™ The Seekers - A. McGrory

1993 Bear Vision	500		1375.00	1375
1992 Buffalo Vision	500	1993	1075.00	1075
1993 Eagle Vision	500		1250.00	1250

Chilmark MetalART™ To The Great Spirit - T. Sullivan

1993 Gray Elk	950		775.00	775
1992 Shooting Star	950	1994	775.00	775
1994 Thunder Cloud	950		775.00	775
1993 Two Eagles	950		775.00	775

Chilmark Pewter Adversaries - F. Barnum

1991 Robert E. Lee	950	1992	350.00	1800
1992 Stonewall Jackson	950	1992	375.00	500
1992 Ulysses S. Grant	950	1992	350.00	600-750
1993 Wm. Tecumseh Sherman	950	1993	375.00	375-750
1993 Set of 4		1993	1450.00	3500-4000

Chilmark Pewter American West - D. Polland, unless otherwise noted

1981 Ambushed	294	1991	2370.00	2700
1987 Appeal to the Great Spirit - F. Barnum	Retrd.	1995	275.00	275
1985 Bear Meet - S. York	Retrd.	1992	500.00	600-800
1983 Bison's Fury - M. Boyett	Retrd.	1995	495.00	495
1982 Blood Brothers - M. Boyett	717	1991	250.00	610-995
1979 Border Rustlers	500	1989	1295.00	1500
1983 Bounty Hunter	264	1987	250.00	300-600
1976 Buffalo Hunt	2,250	1980	300.00	1625
1982 Buffalo Prayer	2,500	1989	95.00	225-400
1990 Buffalo Spirit	2,500	1993	110.00	185
1979 Cavalry Officer - D. LaRocca	500	1985	125.00	400-650
1974 Cheyenne	2,800	1980	200.00	3000
1976 Cold Saddles, Mean Horses	2,800	1986	200.00	800
1974 Counting Coup	2,800	1980	225.00	1600-2000
1979 Cowboy - D. LaRocca	950	1984	125.00	500-750
1974 Crow Scout	3,000	1983	250.00	1000-1700
1978 Dangerous Encounter - B. Rodden	746	1977	475.00	600-950
1985 The Doctor - M. Boyett	Retrd.	1994	750.00	750
1990 Eagle Dancer (deNatura)	614	1993	300.00	300
1981 Enemy Tracks	2,500	1988	225.00	700-725
1984 Flat Out for Red River Station - M. Boyett	2,500	1991	3000.00	4500-7200
1979 Getting Acquainted	950	1988	215.00	800-1100
1985 Horse of A Different Color - S. York	Retrd.	1992	500.00	600-800
1979 Indian Warrior - D. LaRocca	1,186	1988	95.00	400
1982 Jemez Eagle Dancer	2,500	1989	95.00	250-450
1991 Kiowa Princess (deNatura)	444	1993	300.00	300
1982 Last Arrow	2,500	1988	95.00	300-400
1983 Line Rider	2,500	1988	195.00	975
1979 Mandan Hunter	5,000	1985	65.00	780-900
1988 Marauders	Retrd.	1994	850.00	850
1975 Maverick Calf	2,500	1981	250.00	1300-1700
1976 Monday Morning Wash	2,500	1986	200.00	1000
1979 Mountain Man - D. LaRocca	764	1988	95.00	500-650
1983 The Mustanger - D. Polland	Retrd.	1995	425.00	425
1983 Now or Never	693	1991	265.00	800
1975 The Outlaws	2,500	1989	450.00	900-1180
1976 Painting the Town	2,250	1983	300.00	1500-1700
1990 Pequot Wars	950	1990	395.00	1000-1800
1981 Plight of the Huntsman - M. Boyett	950	1987	495.00	850
1985 Postal Exchange - S. York	Retrd.	1992	300.00	400-600
1990 Red River Wars	950	1990	425.00	700-850

Column 3

YEAR ISSUE	EDITION LIMIT	YEAR RETD.	ISSUE PRICE	*QUOTE U.S.$
1976 Rescue	2,500	1980	275.00	1150
1979 Running Battle - B. Rodden	761	1987	400.00	750-900
1990 Running Wolf (deNatura)	720	1993	350.00	350
1982 Sioux War Chief	2,500	1989	95.00	240-480
1991 The Storyteller - D. Polland	Retrd.	1995	150.00	150
1990 Tecumseh's Rebellion	950	1990	350.00	700
1983 Too Many Aces	1,717	1993	400.00	495
1981 U.S. Marshal	1,500	1986	95.00	495
1981 War Party	1,066	1991	550.00	975-1150
1981 When War Chiefs Meet	2,500	1988	300.00	800
1983 The Wild Bunch	285	1987	200.00	225-400
1982 Yakima Salmon Fisherman	2,500	1987	200.00	700
1991 Yellow Boy (deNatura)	460	1993	350.00	350

Chilmark Pewter American West Christmas Special - D. Polland

1991 Merry Christmas Neighbor	1,240	1991	395.00	600
1992 Merry Christmas My Love	819	1992	350.00	350-450
1993 Almost Home	520	1994	375.00	375
1994 Cowboy Christmas	427	1994	250.00	250

Chilmark Pewter American West Event Specials - D. Polland, unless otherwise noted

1991 Uneasy Truce	737	1991	125.00	175-195
1992 Irons In The Fire	612	1992	125.00	125
1994 Bacon 'N' Beans Again?	458	1994	150.00	150
1994 Buffalo Skull - J. Slockbower	Yr. Iss.	1994	125.00	125
1995 Renegade Apache	Closed	1995	150.00	150

Chilmark Pewter American West Redemption Specials - D. Polland, unless otherwise noted

1983 The Chief	2,459	1984	275.00	1400-1900
1984 Unit Colors	1,394	1985	250.00	1200-1700
1985 Oh Great Spirit	3,180	1986	300.00	1000-1300
1986 Eagle Catcher - M. Boyett	1,840	1987	300.00	850-1200
1987 Surprise Encounter - F. Barnum	1,534	1988	250.00	600-800
1988 I Will Fight No More Forever (Chief Joseph)	3,404	1989	350.00	850
1989 Geronimo	1,866	1990	375.00	650-750
1990 Cochise	1,778	1991	400.00	500-600
1991 Crazy Horse	2,067	1992	295.00	600-700
1992 Strong Hearts to the Front	1,252	1993	425.00	600
1993 Sacred Ground Reclaimed	861	1994	495.00	550-650
1994 Horse Breaking	504	1995	395.00	395
1995 The Rainmaker - M. Boyett	Yr.Iss.		350.00	350

Chilmark Pewter Americana - L. Davis

1993 Skeddadlin'	350	1995	2000.00	2000

Chilmark Pewter Cavalry Generals - F. Barnum

1993 George Armstrong Custer	950		375.00	375
1992 J.E.B. Stuart	950	1992	375.00	500
1993 Nathan Bedford Forrest	950		375.00	400-650
1994 Philip Sheridan	950		375.00	375

Chilmark Pewter Civil War - F. Barnum

1993 Abraham Lincoln Bust (Bronze)	50	1993	2000.00	2250
1988 A Father's Farewell	2,500	1994	150.00	275
1988 Johnny Shiloh	2,500	1992	100.00	220-385
1992 Kennesaw Mountain	350	1992	650.00	1500
1992 Parson's Battery	500	1993	495.00	575-800
1987 Pickett's Charge	Retrd.	1994	350.00	450
1987 The Rescue	Retrd.	1995	275.00	310
1987 Saving The Colors	Retrd.	1992	350.00	485-650

Chilmark Pewter Civil War Christmas Specials - F. Barnum

1992 Merry Christmas Yank	810	1992	350.00	500-600
1993 Silent Night	591	1993	350.00	475-600
1994 Christmas Truce	Retrd.	1994	295.00	325-600
1995 Peace on Earth	Retrd.	1995	350.00	350

Chilmark Pewter Civil War Event Specials - F. Barnum

1991 Boots and Saddles	437	1991	95.00	200-450
1992 140th NY Zouave	389	1992	95.00	150-300
1993 Johnny Reb	889	1993	95.00	150-300
1994 Billy Yank	Retrd.	1994	95.00	125
1995 Seaman, CSS Alabama	Retrd.	1995	95.00	95

Chilmark Pewter Civil War Redemption Specials - F. Barnum

1989 Lee To The Rear	1,088	1990	300.00	800-900
1990 Lee And Jackson	1,040	1991	375.00	550-1000
1991 Stonewall Jackson	1,169	1992	295.00	500
1992 Zouaves 1st Manassas	640	1993	375.00	500
1993 Letter to Sarah	Retrd.	1994	395.00	425-600
1994 Angel of Fredericksburg	Retrd.	1995	275.00	275
1995 Rebel Yell	Yr.Iss.		N/A	N/A

Chilmark Pewter Confederates - F. Barnum

1995 The Cavalier (Bronze)	75		1500.00	1500
1995 The Cavalier (Pewter)	750		625.00	625
1993 The Gentleman Soldier (Bronze)	75		1500.00	1500
1993 The Gentleman Soldier (Pewter)	750	1995	625.00	625
1994 Old Jack (Bronze)	75		1500.00	1500
1994 Old Jack (Pewter)	750		625.00	625

Chilmark Pewter Eagles - Various

1991 Cry of Freedom - S. Knight	Suspd.	1993	395.00	395
1981 Freedom Eagle - G. deLodzia	2,500	1983	195.00	750-900
1989 High and Mighty - A. McGrory	Suspd.	1993	185.00	250
1987 Winged Victory - J. Mullican	Suspd.	1993	275.00	275
1982 Wings of Liberty - M. Boyett	950	1986	625.00	625

*Quotes have been rounded up to nearest dollar

Chilmark Pewter Horses - Various

YEAR ISSUE		EDITION LIMIT	YEAR RETD.	ISSUE PRICE	*QUOTE U.S.$
1980	Affirmed - M. Jovine	145	1987	850.00	1275
1980	Born Free - B. Rodden	950	1988	250.00	675
1977	The Challenge - B. Rodden	1,600	1977	175.00	250-300
1981	Clydesdale Wheel Horse - C. Keim	2,808	1989	120.00	430
1978	Paddock Walk - A. Petitto	1,277	1991	85.00	215
1977	Rise and Shine - B. Rodden	1,500	1977	135.00	200
1976	Running Free - B. Rodden	2,500	1977	75.00	300
1976	Stallion - B. Rodden	2,500	1977	75.00	260
1982	Tender Persuasion - J. Mootry	155	1987	950.00	1250
1985	Wild Stallion - D. Polland	179	1988	145.00	350

Chilmark Pewter Kindred Spirits Collection - A. McGrory

YEAR ISSUE		EDITION LIMIT	YEAR RETD.	ISSUE PRICE	*QUOTE U.S.$
1994	Brother Wolf	500	1995	500.00	500
1995	Buffalo Hide	500	1995	750.00	750
1996	Secret Hunter	500	1995	500.00	500

Chilmark Pewter Legacy of Courage - M. Boyett

YEAR ISSUE		EDITION LIMIT	YEAR RETD.	ISSUE PRICE	*QUOTE U.S.$
1983	Along the Cherokee Trace	624	1991	295.00	720
1981	Apache Signals	765	1987	175.00	550-575
1982	Arapaho Sentinel	678	1991	195.00	500
1981	Blackfoot Snow Hunter	984	1988	175.00	650
1981	Buffalo Stalker	1,034	1991	175.00	560
1983	Circling the Enemy	Retrd.	1992	295.00	395
1981	Comanche	1,553	1991	175.00	530-670
1982	Dance of the Eagles	Retrd.	1992	150.00	215
1983	Forest Watcher	658	1991	215.00	540
1981	Iroquois Warfare	1,477	1991	125.00	600
1982	Kiowa Scout	292	1987	195.00	525
1982	Listening For Hooves	883	1991	150.00	400
1982	Mandan Buffalo Dancer	1,494	1991	195.00	450-600
1983	Moment of Truth	1,145	1991	295.00	550-620
1982	Plains Talk-Pawnee	421	1987	195.00	625
1983	Rite of the Whitetail	Retrd.	1992	295.00	400
1982	Shoshone Eagle Catcher	2,500	1985	225.00	1600-2000
1982	The Tracker Nez Perce	686	1988	150.00	575
1981	Unconquered Seminole	1,021	1991	175.00	540
1981	Victor Cheyenne	1,299	1991	175.00	500
1983	A Warrior's Tribute	Retrd.	1992	335.00	635
1983	Winter Hunt	756	1991	295.00	400

Chilmark Pewter Masters of the American West - Various

YEAR ISSUE		EDITION LIMIT	YEAR RETD.	ISSUE PRICE	*QUOTE U.S.$
1985	Bronco Buster (Large) - C. Rousell	766	1989	400.00	400
1986	Buffalo Hunt - A. McGrory	172	1989	550.00	800
1984	Cheyenne (Remington) - C. Rousell	285	1988	400.00	600
1987	Coming Through the Rye - A. McGrory	Retrd.	1995	750.00	750
1986	End of the Trail (lg.) - A. McGrory	Retrd.	1995	450.00	450
1988	End of the Trail (Mini) - A. McGrory	2,500	1992	225.00	325

Chilmark Pewter Mickey & Co. - Staff

YEAR ISSUE		EDITION LIMIT	YEAR RETD.	ISSUE PRICE	*QUOTE U.S.$
1989	"Gold Edition" Hollywood Mickey	Retrd.	1990	200.00	750
1995	California or Bust! (Pewter)	250	1995	1250.00	1750
1989	Hollywood Mickey	Suspd.	1991	165.00	200-300
1994	Lights, Camera, Action (Bronze)	50		3250.00	3250
1994	Lights, Camera, Action (Pewter)	500		1500.00	1500
1994	Mickey on Parade (Bronze)	50	1994	950.00	1500
1994	Mickey on Parade (MetalART))	350	1994	500.00	550-950
994	Mickey on Parade (Pewter)	750		375.00	375
991	Mickey's Carousel Ride	2,500		150.00	160
1992	Minnie's Carousel Ride	2,500		150.00	160
1994	Mouse in a Million (Bronze)	50	1994	1250.00	2000-2500
1994	Mouse in a Million (MetalART))	250	1994	650.00	800-1500
994	Mouse in a Million (Pewter)	500	1994	500.00	600-1200
994	Puttin' on the Ritz (Bronze)	50	1994	2000.00	2200
994	Puttin' on the Ritz (MetalART))	250		1000.00	1000
994	Puttin' on the Ritz (Pewter)	350		750.00	750

Chilmark Pewter Mickey & Co. Annual Christmas Special - Staff

YEAR ISSUE		EDITION LIMIT	YEAR RETD.	ISSUE PRICE	*QUOTE U.S.$
993	Hanging the Stockings	Annual	1993	295.00	350
994	Trimming the Tree	Annual	1994	350.00	350-500
995	Holiday Harmony?	Annual	1995	395.00	395

Chilmark Pewter Mickey & Co. Annual Santa - Staff

YEAR ISSUE		EDITION LIMIT	YEAR RETD.	ISSUE PRICE	*QUOTE U.S.$
993	Checking it Twice	Annual	1993	195.00	300-450
994	Just For You	Annual	1994	265.00	300-450
995	Surprise, Santa!	Annual	1995	225.00	225

Chilmark Pewter Mickey & Co. Annual Special - Staff

YEAR ISSUE		EDITION LIMIT	YEAR RETD.	ISSUE PRICE	*QUOTE U.S.$
994	Bicycle Built For Two	Retrd.	1994	195.00	225-400
995	Riding the Rails	Yr.Iss.		295.00	295

Chilmark Pewter Mickey & Co. Comic Capers - Staff

YEAR ISSUE		EDITION LIMIT	YEAR RETD.	ISSUE PRICE	*QUOTE U.S.$
995	Crack the Whip (Bronze)	50		2000.00	2000
995	Crack the Whip (Pewter)	500		750.00	750
994	Foursome Follies (Bronze)	50	1994	2000.00	2000
994	Foursome Follies (Pewter)	500	1994	750.00	900-1600
994	Matched Numbrd set	500	1994	N/A	3100-3500
994	Un-Matched Numbrd set	500	1994	N/A	2700-2900

Chilmark Pewter Mickey & Co. Generations of Mickey - Staff

YEAR ISSUE		EDITION LIMIT	YEAR RETD.	ISSUE PRICE	*QUOTE U.S.$
987	Antique Mickey	2,500	1990	95.00	800-1600
990	The Band Concert	2,500		185.00	195
990	The Band Concert (Painted)	500	1993	215.00	550
990	Disneyland Mickey	2,500		150.00	160
1989	Mickey's Gala Premiere	2,500		150.00	160
1991	The Mouse-1935	1,200		185.00	195
1991	Plane Crazy-1928	2,500		175.00	185
1989	Sorcerer's Apprentice	2,500	1993	150.00	300-800
1989	Steamboat Willie	2,500	1993	165.00	300-800

Chilmark Pewter Mickey & Co. Mickey and Friends - Staff

YEAR ISSUE		EDITION LIMIT	YEAR RETD.	ISSUE PRICE	*QUOTE U.S.$
1994	Donald (Bronze)	75	1994	325.00	400
1994	Donald (Pewter)	1,500		150.00	150
1994	Goofy (Bronze)	75	1994	375.00	400
1994	Goofy (Pewter)	1,500		175.00	175
1994	Mickey (Bronze)	75	1994	325.00	400
1994	Mickey (Pewter)	1,500		150.00	150
1994	Minnie (Bronze)	75	1994	325.00	400
1994	Minnie (Pewter)	1,500		150.00	150
1994	Pluto (Bronze)	75	1994	325.00	400
1994	Pluto (Pewter)	1,500		150.00	150

Chilmark Pewter Mickey & Co. Sweethearts - Staff

YEAR ISSUE		EDITION LIMIT	YEAR RETD.	ISSUE PRICE	*QUOTE U.S.$
1994	Jitterbugging	500	1994	450.00	700-1100
1995	Mice on Ice	500	1995	425.00	500-700
1994	Rowboat Serenade	500	1994	495.00	700

Chilmark Pewter Mickey & Co. The Sorcerer's Apprentice - Staff

YEAR ISSUE		EDITION LIMIT	YEAR RETD.	ISSUE PRICE	*QUOTE U.S.$
1990	The Whirlpool	Retrd.	1995	225.00	260
1990	The Dream	Retrd.	1995	225.00	240
1990	The Incantation	Retrd.	1995	150.00	175
1990	The Repentant Apprentice	Retrd.	1994	195.00	300-500
1990	The Sorcerer's Apprentice	Retrd.	1995	225.00	240
1990	Matched Numbrd set	Retrd.	1995	225.00	1800-2200

Chilmark Pewter Mickey & Co. Two Wheeling - Staff

YEAR ISSUE		EDITION LIMIT	YEAR RETD.	ISSUE PRICE	*QUOTE U.S.$
1994	Get Your Motor Runnin' (Bronze)	50	1994	1200.00	1400-1800
1994	Get Your Motor Runnin' (MetalART)	950	1994	475.00	800-1200
1994	Head Out on the Highway (Bronze)	50		1200.00	1200
1994	Head Out on the Highway (MetalART)	950		475.00	475
1995	Looking For Adventure (Bronze)	50		1200.00	1200
1995	Looking For Adventure (MetalART)	950		475.00	475

Chilmark Pewter OffCanvas™ - A. T. McGrory

YEAR ISSUE		EDITION LIMIT	YEAR RETD.	ISSUE PRICE	*QUOTE U.S.$
1991	Blanket Signal	350	1993	750.00	850
1990	Smoke Signal	950	1990	345.00	550-700
1990	Vigil	950	1990	345.00	500-700
1990	Warrior	950	1990	300.00	350-600

Chilmark Pewter Sculptures - Various

YEAR ISSUE		EDITION LIMIT	YEAR RETD.	ISSUE PRICE	*QUOTE U.S.$
1981	Budweiser Wagon - Keim/Hazen	890	1989	2000.00	3000
1986	Camelot Chess Set - P. Jackson	Retrd.	1991	2250.00	2250
1979	Carousel - R. Sylvan	950	1983	115.00	115
1980	Charge of the 7th Cavalry - B. Rodden	394	1988	600.00	950
1983	Dragon Slayer - D. LaRocca	290	1988	385.00	500
1985	Moby Dick - J. Royce	Retrd.	1995	350.00	350
1979	Moses - B. Rodden	2,500	1989	140.00	235
1979	Pegasus - R. Sylvan	527	1981	95.00	175
1979	Unicorn - R. Sylvan	2,500	1982	115.00	550

Chilmark Pewter Turning Points - F. Barnum

YEAR ISSUE		EDITION LIMIT	YEAR RETD.	ISSUE PRICE	*QUOTE U.S.$
1994	Clashing Sabers	500	1995	600.00	600
1993	The High Tide	500	1993	600.00	900
1996	Last Resort	500		600.00	600
1995	The Swinging Gate	500		600.00	600

Chilmark Pewter Wildlife - Various

YEAR ISSUE		EDITION LIMIT	YEAR RETD.	ISSUE PRICE	*QUOTE U.S.$
1978	Buffalo - B. Rodden	950	1986	170.00	375-400
1980	Duel of the Bighorns - M. Boyett	137	1987	650.00	1200
1979	Elephant - D. Polland	750	1987	315.00	450-550
1979	Giraffe - D. Polland	414	1981	145.00	145
1979	Kudu - D. Polland	204	1981	160.00	160
1980	Lead Can't Catch Him - M. Boyett	397	1987	645.00	845
1980	Prairie Sovereign - M. Boyett	247	1987	550.00	800
1979	Rhino - D. Polland	142	1981	135.00	135-550
1980	Ruby-Throated Hummingbird - V. Hayton	500	1983	275.00	350
1980	Voice of Experience - M. Boyett	174	1987	645.00	850

Chilmark Pewter/MetalART™ The Medicine Men - D. Polland

YEAR ISSUE		EDITION LIMIT	YEAR RETD.	ISSUE PRICE	*QUOTE U.S.$
1992	False Face (MetalART)	1,000		550.00	550
1992	False Face (pewter)	500	1992	375.00	375

Chilmark Pewter/MetalART™ The Warriors - D. Polland

YEAR ISSUE		EDITION LIMIT	YEAR RETD.	ISSUE PRICE	*QUOTE U.S.$
1995	Keeper of the Eastern Door (pewter)	500		375.00	375
1995	Keeper of the Eastern Door (MetalART)	1,000		500.00	500
1993	Son of the Morning Star (MetalART)	1,000		495.00	495
1993	Son of the Morning Star (pewter)	500	1993	375.00	460
1995	Soul of the Forest (pewter)	500		375.00	375
1995	Soul of the Forest (MetalART)	1,000		500.00	500
1992	Spirit of the Wolf (MetalART)	1,000		500.00	500
1992	Spirit of the Wolf (pewter)	500	1993	350.00	850

Chilmark Polland Collectors Society Annual Redemption Special - Various

YEAR ISSUE		EDITION LIMIT	YEAR RETD.	ISSUE PRICE	*QUOTE U.S.$
1995	Thunder Pipe	Yr.Iss.		395.00	395

See also Polland Studios Collector Society

Chilmark Polland Collectors Society Membership Sculptures - D. Polland

YEAR ISSUE		EDITION LIMIT	YEAR RETD.	ISSUE PRICE	*QUOTE U.S.$
1995	Mystic Medicine Man	Yr.Iss.		Gift	N/A

cp smithshire™ Annual Santa - C. Smith

YEAR ISSUE		EDITION LIMIT	YEAR RETD.	ISSUE PRICE	*QUOTE U.S.$
1993	St. Nicholai	Yr.Iss.	1993	75.00	150
1994	Santa and Nicky	Yr.Iss.	1994	90.00	90
1995	Santa's Endless Journey	Yr.Iss.	1995	70.00	70

cp smithshire™ Event Figurine - C. Smith

YEAR ISSUE		EDITION LIMIT	YEAR RETD.	ISSUE PRICE	*QUOTE U.S.$
1993	Sap	Yr.Iss.	1993	60.00	60
1995	Pied Piper	Yr.Iss.	1995	40.00	40

cp smithshire™ Society Member Only Redemption Specials - C. Smith

YEAR ISSUE		EDITION LIMIT	YEAR RETD.	ISSUE PRICE	*QUOTE U.S.$
1993	Dentzel	Yr.Iss.	1994	90.00	90
1995	Cherni	Yr.Iss.	1995	70.00	70

cp smithshire™ Society Membership Figurines - C. Smith

YEAR ISSUE		EDITION LIMIT	YEAR RETD.	ISSUE PRICE	*QUOTE U.S.$
1993	Fellowship Inn	Yr.Iss.	1994	Gift	N/A
1995	Corey Place	Yr.Iss.	1995	Gift	N/A

cp smithshire™-Gone Home to the Forest - C. Smith

YEAR ISSUE		EDITION LIMIT	YEAR RETD.	ISSUE PRICE	*QUOTE U.S.$
1993	Abraham	Closed	1995	85.00	100
1993	Andrea and Theodora	Closed	1995	80.00	100
1993	Benjamin	Closed	1995	85.00	85
1993	Chipper	Closed	1994	70.00	100
1993	Florence and Lila	Closed	1994	80.00	100
1993	Granny Smith	Closed	1995	60.00	100
1993	Have and Have Not (No Mushroom)	Closed	1993	80.00	160
1993	Heather (No Mushroom)	Closed	1993	50.00	100
1993	Hyde N' Seek	Closed	1994	70.00	70
1993	Jack O' Lantern (No Mushroom)	Closed	1993	75.00	150
1994	Pepe	Closed	1995	85.00	85
1993	Rushmore	Closed	1995	85.00	85
1993	Tyrus	Closed	1995	75.00	75

Hudson Pewter Figures - P.W. Baston, unless otherwise noted

YEAR ISSUE		EDITION LIMIT	YEAR RETD.	ISSUE PRICE	*QUOTE U.S.$
1972	Benjamin Franklin	Closed	1974	15.00	75-100
1969	Betsy Ross	Closed	1971	30.00	100-125
1969	Colonial Blacksmith	Closed	1971	30.00	100-125
1975	Declaration Wall Plaque	100	1975	Unkn.	300-500
1975	The Favored Scholar - P.W. Baston	6	1975	Unkn.	600-1000
1972	George Washington	Closed	1974	15.00	75-100
1969	George Washington (Cannon)	Closed	1971	35.00	75-100
1972	James Madison	Closed	1974	15.00	50-75
1972	John Adams	Closed	1974	15.00	75-100
1969	John Hancock	Closed	1971	15.00	100-125
1975	Lee's Ninth General Order	Closed	1975	Unkn.	300-400
1975	Lincoln's Gettysburg Address	Closed	1975	Unkn.	300-400
1975	Neighboring Pews	6	1975	Unkn.	600-1000
1975	Spirit of '76 - P.W. Baston	12	1975	Unkn.	750-1500
1972	Thomas Jefferson - P.W. Baston	Closed	1974	15.00	75-100
1975	Washington's Letter of Acceptance - P.W. Baston	Closed	1975	Unkn.	300-400
1975	Weighing the Baby - P.W. Baston	6	1975	Unkn.	600-1000

Hudson Pewter Mickey & Co. - Staff

YEAR ISSUE		EDITION LIMIT	YEAR RETD.	ISSUE PRICE	*QUOTE U.S.$
1989	Fantasia	Retrd.	1995	19.00	19
1988	Happy Birthday Mickey	Yr.Iss.	1989	60.00	150
1988	Socerer's Apprentice	Retrd.	1995	25.00	25
1986	Socerer's Apprentice (lg.)	Retrd.	1995	25.00	25
1988	Socerer's Apprentice/Music Train	Retrd.	1995	28.00	28
1990	Socerer's Apprentice/No. 9 Birthday Train	Retrd.	1995	25.00	25
1990	Socerer's Apprentice/No. 9 Birthday Train-painted	Retrd.	1995	27.00	27

Hudson Pewter Mickey & Co. -Registered - Staff

YEAR ISSUE		EDITION LIMIT	YEAR RETD.	ISSUE PRICE	*QUOTE U.S.$
1994	Be My Valentine	Closed	1994	65.00	75-125
1994	Christmas Waltz	Closed	1994	65.00	100-200

Hudson Pewter World of Mickey - Staff

YEAR ISSUE		EDITION LIMIT	YEAR RETD.	ISSUE PRICE	*QUOTE U.S.$
1991	Mouse Waltz	Retrd.	1994	41.00	41
1988	Sweethearts	Retrd.	1993	45.00	45

Pere Noel Collection - C. Smith

YEAR ISSUE		EDITION LIMIT	YEAR RETD.	ISSUE PRICE	*QUOTE U.S.$
1994	Checking His List	3,500		70.00	75
1994	Christ Kindle	3,500		85.00	95
1994	Father Christmas	Closed	1994	150.00	150
1994	Grandfather Frost	3,500		65.00	75
1995	Kriss Kringle	3,500		75.00	75
1994	Pere Noel	3,500		65.00	75
1994	Santa Claus	3,500		75.00	75
1995	Santa McClaus	750		110.00	110
1994	Sinter Klaas	3,500		70.00	75
1995	St. Nikkolo	3,500		65.00	65
1995	Stars & Stripes Santa	3,500		85.00	85

*Quotes have been rounded up to nearest dollar

Sebastian Miniatures Collectors Society - P.W. Baston, unless otherwise noted

YEAR ISSUE		EDITION LIMIT	YEAR RETD.	ISSUE PRICE	*QUOTE U.S.$
1980	S.M.C. Society Plaque ('80 Charter)	11,914	1980	Gift	20-35
1981	S.M.C. Society Plaque	4,957	1981	Gift	20-30
1982	S.M.C. Society Plaque	1,530	1982	Gift	20-30
1983	S.M.C. Society Plaque	1,167	1983	Gift	20-30
1984	S.M.C. Society Plaque	505	1984	Gift	50-75
1984	Self Portrait	Retrd.	1994	Gift	45
1995	Grace - P.W. Baston, Jr.	Annual	1995	Gift	N/A

Sebastian Miniatures Holiday Memories-Member Only - P.W. Baston, Jr.

1990	Thanksgiving Helper	Yr.Iss.	1991	39.50	40
1990	Leprechaun	Yr.Iss.	1991	27.50	35-40
1991	Trick or Treat	Yr.Iss.	1992	25.50	50-75
1993	Father Time	Yr.Iss.	1994	27.50	28
1993	New Year Baby	Yr.Iss.	1994	27.50	28
1994	Look What the Easter Bunny Left Me	Yr.Iss.	1995	27.50	28
1995	On Parade	Yr.Iss.		N/A	N/A

Sebastian Miniatures Member Only - P.W. Baston, Jr.

1989	The Collectors	Yr.Iss.	1990	39.50	40
1992	Christopher Columbus	Yr.Iss.	1993	28.50	29

Sebastian Miniature Figurines - P.W. Baston, Jr.

1991	America Salutes Desert Storm -bronze	Retrd.	1994	26.50	100
1991	America Salutes Desert Storm -painted	350	1991	49.50	200-250
1990	America's Hometown	4,750		34.00	34
1994	Boston Light	3,500		45.00	45
1994	Egg Rock Light	3,500		55.00	55
1992	Firefighter	500	1992	28.00	50
1991	Happy Hood Holidays	2,000	1991	32.50	95-105
1983	Harry Hood	1,000	1983	Unkn.	200-250
1992	I Know I Left It Here Somewhere	1,000		28.50	29
1985	It's Hoods (Wagon)	3,250	1985	N/A	75-100
1994	A Job Well Done	1,000		27.50	28
1993	The Lamplighter	1,000		28.00	28
1994	Nubble Light	3,500		45.00	45
1993	Pumpkin Island Light	3,500		55.00	55
1993	Soap Box Derby	500		45.00	45
1986	Statue of Liberty (AT & T)	1,000	1986	N/A	200-225
1987	White House (Gold, Oval Base)	250	1987	17.00	35-50

Sebastian Miniatures America Remembers - P.W. Baston

1983	Family Feast	4,147	1983	37.50	125-150
1982	Family Fishing	8,734	1982	34.50	50-100
1980	Family Picnic	16,527	1980	29.50	60-100
1981	Family Reads Aloud	21,027	1981	34.50	50-75
1979	Family Sing	7,358	1979	29.50	125-150

Sebastian Miniatures Children At Play - P.W. Baston

1979	Building Days Boy	10,000	1980	19.50	30-50
1979	Building Days Girl	10,000	1980	19.50	30-50
1981	Sailing Days Boy	10,000	1981	19.50	30-50
1981	Sailing Days Girl	10,000	1981	19.50	30-50
1982	School Days Boy	10,000	1982	19.50	40-60
1982	School Days Girl	10,000	1982	19.50	40-60
1978	Sidewalk Days Boy	10,000	1980	19.50	40-60
1978	Sidewalk Days Girl	10,000	1980	19.50	40-60
1980	Snow Days Boy	10,000	1980	19.50	40-60
1980	Snow Days Girl	10,000	1980	19.50	40-60

Sebastian Miniatures Christmas - P.W. Baston, Jr.

1993	Caroling With Santa	1,000		29.00	29
1993	Harmonizing With Santa	1,000		27.00	27
1994	Victorian Christmas Skaters	1,000		32.50	33
1995	Midnight Snacks	1,000		28.50	29

Sebastian Miniatures Exchange Figurines - P.W. Baston, Jr., unless otherwise noted

1984	First Things First	1,267	1985	30.00	45
1987	It's About Time	576	1988	25.00	40
1986	News Wagon	1,422	1987	35.00	45
1983	Newspaper Boy - P.W. Baston	1,708	1984	28.50	60-95
1985	Newstand	1,454	1986	30.00	45

Sebastian Miniatures Firefighter Collection - P.W. Baston, Jr.

1993	Firefighter No. 1	950	1995	48.00	48
1994	Firefighter No. 2	950		48.00	48
1994	Firefighter No. 3	950		48.00	48
1995	Firefighter No. 4	950		48.00	48

Sebastian Miniatures Jimmy Fund - P.W. Baston, Jr., unless otherwise noted

1993	Boy With Ducks	500	1993	27.50	28
1984	Catcher - P.W. Baston	1,872	1984	24.50	35-75
1987	Football Player	1,270	1988	26.50	27
1995	Girl in Riding Outfit	500		28.00	28
1994	Girl on Bench	500	1994	28.00	28
1985	Hockey Player	1,836	1986	24.50	35-50
1988	Santa	500	1988	32.50	33
1983	Schoolboy - P.W. Baston	3,567	1983	24.50	25-35
1986	Soccer Player	1,166	1987	25.00	25

Sebastian Miniatures Private Label - P.W. Baston Jr.

1993	Adams Academy w/ Steeple	75	N/A	100.00	200-225
1993	Adams Academy w/o Steeple	750	N/A	30.00	30

Sebastian Miniatures Shakespearean-Member Only - P.W. Baston, unless otherwise noted

1984	Anne Boleyn	3,897	1984	17.50	35
1984	Henry VIII	4,578	1984	19.50	35
1985	Falstaff	3,357	1985	19.50	35
1985	Mistress Ford	2,836	1985	17.50	35
1986	Juliet	2,620	1986	17.50	35
1986	Romeo	2,853	1986	19.50	35
1987	Countess Olivia	1,893	1987	19.50	35
1987	Malvolio	2,093	1987	21.50	35
1988	Audrey	1,548	1988	22.50	35
1988	Shakespeare - P.W. Baston, Jr.	Retrd.	1989	23.50	35
1988	Touchstone	1,770	1988	22.50	35
1989	Cleopatra	Retrd.	1989	27.00	35
1989	Mark Antony	Retrd.	1989	27.00	35

Sebastian Miniatures Washington Irving-Member Only - P.W. Baston

1980	Rip Van Winkle	12,005	1983	19.50	35
1981	Ichabod Crane	9,069	1983	19.50	35
1981	Dame Van Winkle	11,217	1983	19.50	35
1982	Brom Bones (Headless Horseman)	6,610	1983	22.50	35
1982	Katrina Van Tassel	7,367	1983	19.50	35
1983	Diedrich Knickerbocker	5,528	1983	22.50	35

Legends

Annual Collectors Edition - C. Pardell

1990	The Night Before	500	1991	990.00	2000-2500
1991	Medicine Gift of Manhood	500	1992	990.00	2000
1992	Spirit of the Wolf	500	1992	950.00	2000
1993	Tomorrow's Warrior	500	1993	590.00	1000-1600
1994	Guiding Hand	500	1994	590.00	850-1200
1995	Gift of the Sacred Calf	500	1995	650.00	650-900

Collectors Only - Various

1993	Give Us Peace - C. Pardell	1,250	1993	270.00	370-500
1994	First Born - C. Pardell	1,250	1994	350.00	370-500
1994	River Bandits - K. Cantrell	1,250		350.00	350
1995	Sonata - K. Cantrell	1,250		250.00	290
1995	Daydreams of Manhood - C. Pardell	2,500	1995	390.00	390

American Heritage - D. Edwards

1987	Grizz Country (Bronze)	Retrd.	1990	350.00	350
1987	Grizz Country (Pewter)	Retrd.	1990	370.00	370
1987	Winter Provisions (Bronze)	Retrd.	1990	340.00	340
1987	Winter Provisions (Pewter)	Retrd.	1990	370.00	370
1987	Wrangler's Dare (Bronze)	Retrd.	1990	630.00	630
1987	Wrangler's Dare (Pewter)	Retrd.	1990	660.00	660

American Indian Dance Premier Edition - C. Pardell

1993	Drum Song	750	1995	2800.00	3200-4200
1994	Footprints of the Butterfly	750		1800.00	1990
1994	Image of the Eagle	750		1900.00	2100
1995	Spirit of the Mountain	750		1750.00	1850

American West Premier Edition - C. Pardell

1992	American Horse	950	1995	1300.00	1300
1992	Defending the People	950		1350.00	1450
1991	First Coup	950	1993	1150.00	1500
1993	Four Bears' Challenge	950		990.00	1050
1994	Season of Victory	950		1500.00	1580
1991	Unexpected Rescuer	950	1991	990.00	1400-1700

Animal Dreamer - M. Boyett

1995	Breaking of the War Horse	950		590.00	590
1995	Buffalo Runner	950		550.00	570
1995	He Hunts w/the Eagle Medicine	950		490.00	500
1995	In the Path of the Wolf Spirit	950		490.00	500
1995	Receiving The Cougar Spirit	950		590.00	590

Classic Equestrian Collection - C. Pardell

1988	Lippizzaner (Bronze)	Retrd.	N/A	200.00	200

The Classics Premier Edition - C. Pardell

1995	Indomitable	750		1590.00	1590

Clear Visions - Various

1993	Salmon Falls - W. Whitten	950	1995	950.00	980
1994	Saving Their Skins - C. Pardell	950		1590.00	1630

Culture Covenant Premier Edition - C. Pardell

1995	Each, to the Other	500		1300.00	1350
1995	Our Kind, with All Others	500		1300.00	1350
1994	Our Past, to Our Future	500		1350.00	1450

The Endangered Wildlife Collection - K. Cantrell

1993	Big Pine Survivor	950		390.00	390
1990	Forest Spirit	950	1991	290.00	1500
1991	Mountain Majesty	950		350.00	390
1991	Old Tusker	950		390.00	390
1992	Plains Monarch	950		350.00	390
1994	Prairie Phantom	950		370.00	390
1990	Savannah Prince	950		290.00	350
1993	Silvertip	950		370.00	390
1992	Songs of Autumn	950	1995	390.00	390
1992	Spirit Song	950	1992	350.00	500-1000
1994	Twilight	950		290.00	310
1992	Unchallenged	950		350.00	390

Endangered Wildlife Eagle Series - K. Cantrell

1989	Aquila Libre	2,500	1995	280.00	400-450
1993	Defiance	2,500		350.00	350
1992	Food Fight	2,500		650.00	750
1989	Outpost	2,500	1995	280.00	400-450
1989	Sentinel	2,500	1993	280.00	500-800
1993	Spiral Flight	2,500		290.00	300
1992	Sunday Brunch	2,500		550.00	650
1989	Unbounded	2,500	1994	280.00	400-450

Gallery Editions - Various

1994	Center Fire - W. Whitten	350		2500.00	2600
1994	Mountain Family - D. Lemon	150		7900.00	8300
1993	Over the Rainbow - K. Cantrell	600	1995	2900.00	3100-4100
1993	Over the Rainbow AP - K. Cantrell	Retrd.	1996	4000.00	5000
1992	Resolute - C. Pardell	250	1992	7950.00	12000-15000
1993	Visionary - C. Pardell	350		7500.00	7500
1993	The Wanderer - K. Cantrell	350		3500.00	3700
1996	Wind on Still Water - C. Pardell	350	1996	2500.00	3000-3500

The Great Outdoorsman - C. Pardell

1988	Both Are Hooked (Bronze)	Retrd.	N/A	320.00	320
1988	Both Are Hooked (Pewter)	Retrd.	N/A	320.00	320

Happy Trails Collection - W. Whitten

1994	Cowboy Soul	750	1994	450.00	450

Hidden Images Collection - D. Lemon

1994	In Search of Bear Rock	350	1995	1300.00	1300
1995	Sensed, But Unseen	350	1995	990.00	990
1995	Spirit	350		990.00	990

Indian Arts Collection - C. Pardell

1990	Chief's Blanket	1,500	1992	350.00	700-1000
1990	Indian Maiden	1,500		240.00	240
1990	Indian Potter	1,500		260.00	260
1990	Kachina Carver	1,500	1993	270.00	400-700
1990	Story Teller	1,500	1993	290.00	500-600

Kachina Dancers Collection - C. Pardell

1991	Ahote	2,500		370.00	390
1991	Angakchina	2,500		370.00	390
1994	Deer Kachina	2,500		390.00	390
1994	Eototo	2,500		390.00	390
1991	Hilili	2,500		390.00	390
1993	Koshari	2,500		370.00	390
1991	Koyemsi	2,500		370.00	390
1992	Kwahu	2,500		390.00	390
1993	Mongwa	2,500		390.00	390
1994	Palhik Mana	2,500		390.00	390
1992	Tawa	2,500		390.00	390
1994	Wiharu	2,500		390.00	390

The Legacies Of The West Premier Edition - C. Pardell

1991	Defiant Comanche	950	1991	1300.00	1300-180
1993	Eminent Crow	950	1994	1500.00	150
1994	Enduring	950		1250.00	135
1992	Esteemed Warrior	950	1992	1750.00	2500-350
1990	Mystic Vision	950	1990	990.00	2800-380
1991	No More, Forever	950	1992	1500.00	170
1992	Rebellious	950		1500.00	160
1990	Victorious	950	1990	1275.00	3500-400

The Legendary West Collection - C. Pardell

1992	Beating Bad Odds	2,500		390.00	41
1989	Bustin' A Herd Quitter	2,500		590.00	66
1993	Cliff Hanger	2,500		990.00	105
1992	Crazy Horse	2,500	1992	390.00	900-140
1989	Eagle Dancer	2,500		370.00	41
1993	Hunter's Brothers	2,500		590.00	66
1989	Johnson's Last Fight	2,500	1991	590.00	1200-140
1990	Keeper of Eagles	2,500		370.00	41
1987	Pony Express (Bronze)	2,500	N/A	320.00	320-45
1989	Pony Express (Mixed Media)	2,500		390.00	41
1987	Pony Express (Pewter)	2,500	N/A	320.00	320-45
1989	Sacajawea	2,500	1995	380.00	400-45
1990	Shhh	2,500		390.00	41
1990	Stand of the Sash Wearer	2,500		390.00	41
1989	Tables Turned	2,500		680.00	75
1990	Unbridled	2,500		290.00	29
1991	Warning	2,500		390.00	41
1989	White Feather's Vision	2,500	1991	390.00	1000-130

The Legendary West Premier Edition - C. Pardell

1990	Crow Warrior	750	1990	1225.00	2000-300
1992	The Final Charge	750	1992	1250.00	1500-200
1989	Pursued	750	1989	750.00	2000-400
1988	Red Cloud's Coup	750	1988	480.00	5000-670
1989	Songs of Glory	750	1989	850.00	3500-430
1991	Triumphant	750	1991	1150.00	1700-220

Mystical Quest Collection - D. Medina

1993	Hunter's Quest	950		990.00	10
1994	Peace Quest	950		1150.00	12
1992	Vision Quest	950	1995	990.00	9

*Quotes have been rounded up to nearest dolla

The North & South Collection - W. Whitten

YEAR	ISSUE	EDITION LIMIT	YEAR RETD.	ISSUE PRICE	*QUOTE U.S.$
1993	Brother Against Brother	950	1995	550.00	550
1993	The Noble Heart	950	1995	450.00	450
1994	Stonewall	950	1995	450.00	450
1992	Victory at Hand	950	1995	390.00	390

North American Wildlife - D. Edwards

YEAR	ISSUE	EDITION LIMIT	YEAR RETD.	ISSUE PRICE	*QUOTE U.S.$
1988	Defenders of Freedom (Bronze)	Retrd.	N/A	340.00	340
1988	Defenders of Freedom (Pewter)	Retrd.	N/A	370.00	370
1988	Double Trouble (Bronze)	Retrd.	N/A	300.00	300
1988	Double Trouble (Pewter)	Retrd.	N/A	320.00	320
1988	Downhill Run (Bronze)	Retrd.	N/A	330.00	330
1988	Downhill Run (Pewter)	Retrd.	N/A	340.00	340
1988	Grizzly Solitude (Bronze)	Retrd.	N/A	310.00	310
1988	Grizzly Solitude (Pewter)	Retrd.	N/A	330.00	330
1988	Last Glance (Bronze)	Retrd.	N/A	300.00	300
1988	Last Glance (Pewter)	Retrd.	N/A	320.00	320
1988	The Proud American (Bronze)	Retrd.	N/A	330.00	330
1988	The Proud American (Pewter)	Retrd.	N/A	340.00	340
1988	Ridge Runners (Bronze)	Retrd.	N/A	300.00	300
1988	Ridge Runners (Pewter)	Retrd.	N/A	310.00	310
1988	Sudden Alert (Bronze)	Retrd.	N/A	300.00	300
1988	Sudden Alert (Pewter)	Retrd.	N/A	320.00	320

Oceanic World - D. Medina

YEAR	ISSUE	EDITION LIMIT	YEAR RETD.	ISSUE PRICE	*QUOTE U.S.$
1989	Freedom's Beauty (Bronze)	Retrd.	N/A	330.00	330
1989	Freedom's Beauty (Pewter)	Retrd.	N/A	130.00	130
1989	Together (Bronze)	Retrd.	N/A	140.00	140
1989	Together (Pewter)	Retrd.	N/A	130.00	130

Relics of the Americas - W. Whitten

YEAR	ISSUE	EDITION LIMIT	YEAR RETD.	ISSUE PRICE	*QUOTE U.S.$
1993	Dream Medicine	950		1150.00	1290
1994	Flared Glory	950		1350.00	1350
1995	Walks With Wolves	950		1250.00	1300

Special Commissions - Various

YEAR	ISSUE	EDITION LIMIT	YEAR RETD.	ISSUE PRICE	*QUOTE U.S.$
1988	Alpha Pair (Bronze) - C. Pardell	Retrd.	N/A	330.00	330
1988	Alpha Pair (Mixed Media) - C. Pardell	S/O	N/A	390.00	500-1000
1988	Alpha Pair (Pewter) - C. Pardell	Retrd.	N/A	330.00	330
1991	American Allegiance - D. Edwards	1,250	1996	570.00	625
1995	Father-The Power Within - D. Medina	350		1500.00	1590
1990	Lakota Love Song - C. Pardell	Retrd.	1990	380.00	1950
1987	Mama's Joy (Bronze) - D. Edwards	Retrd.	N/A	200.00	200
1987	Mama's Joy (Pewter) - D. Edwards	Retrd.	N/A	250.00	250
1996	Proud Heritage - K. Cantrell	2,500		290.00	290
1995	Rapture - W. Whitten	350		1750.00	1850
1995	Scent in the Air - K. Cantrell	750		990.00	1050
1991	Symbols of Freedom - K. Cantrell	2,500		490.00	550
1987	Wild Freedom (Bronze) - D. Edwards	Retrd.	N/A	320.00	320
1987	Wild Freedom (Pewter) - D. Edwards	Retrd.	N/A	330.00	330
1992	Yellowstone Bound - K. Cantrell	600	1994	2500.00	3500-4000

Warriors of the Sacred Circle - W. Whitten

YEAR	ISSUE	EDITION LIMIT	YEAR RETD.	ISSUE PRICE	*QUOTE U.S.$
1993	Coup Feather	950	1995	450.00	450
1992	Dog Soldier	950	1995	450.00	450
1992	Peace Offering	950	1995	550.00	550
1994	Traditional Weapons	950	1995	550.00	550
1993	Yellow Boy	950	1995	450.00	450

Way of the Cat Collection - K. Cantrell

YEAR	ISSUE	EDITION LIMIT	YEAR RETD.	ISSUE PRICE	*QUOTE U.S.$
1996	Cat's Cradle	500		790	790
1995	Encounter	500	1995	750.00	1000-1200

Way of the Warrior Collection - C. Pardell

YEAR	ISSUE	EDITION LIMIT	YEAR RETD.	ISSUE PRICE	*QUOTE U.S.$
1991	Clan Leader	1,600	1994	170.00	225
1991	Elder Chief	1,600	1994	170.00	225
1991	Medicine Dancer	1,600	1994	170.00	225
1991	Rite of Manhood	1,600	1994	170.00	225
1991	Seeker of Visions	1,600	1994	170.00	225
1991	Tribal Defender	1,600	1994	170.00	225

Way of the Wolf Collection - K. Cantrell

YEAR	ISSUE	EDITION LIMIT	YEAR RETD.	ISSUE PRICE	*QUOTE U.S.$
1993	Courtship	500	1993	590.00	700-1000
1995	Gossip Column	500		1250.00	1250
1994	Missed by a Hare	500	1994	700.00	1000
1994	Renewal	500	1994	700.00	900-1700
1995	Stink Bomb	500	1995	750.00	750

Western Memories Premier Edition - D. Lemon

YEAR	ISSUE	EDITION LIMIT	YEAR RETD.	ISSUE PRICE	*QUOTE U.S.$
1995	Ole Mossy Horns	500		1450.00	1530
1994	Vacant Thunder	500		1900.00	1990
1995	Winds of Memory	500		1750.00	1850

Wild Realm Collection - C. Pardell

YEAR	ISSUE	EDITION LIMIT	YEAR RETD.	ISSUE PRICE	*QUOTE U.S.$
1988	Fly Fisher (Bronze)	Retrd.	N/A	330.00	330
1988	Fly Fisher (Pewter)	Retrd.	N/A	330.00	330

Wild Realm Premier Edition - C. Pardell

YEAR	ISSUE	EDITION LIMIT	YEAR RETD.	ISSUE PRICE	*QUOTE U.S.$
1989	High Spirit	1,600	1996	870.00	920
1991	Speed Incarnate	1,600	N/A	790.00	790

Lenox Collections

American Fashion - Unknown

YEAR	ISSUE	EDITION LIMIT	YEAR RETD.	ISSUE PRICE	*QUOTE U.S.$
1986	Belle of the Ball	Open		95.00	95
1987	Centennial Bride	Open		95.00	95
1984	First Waltz	Open		95.00	95
1987	Gala at the Whitehouse	Open		95.00	95
1985	Governor's Garden Party	Open		95.00	95
1986	Grand Tour	Open		95.00	95
1992	Royal Reception	Open		95.00	95
1983	Springtime Promenade	Open		95.00	95
1984	Tea at the Ritz	Open		95.00	95

Baby Bears - Unknown

YEAR	ISSUE	EDITION LIMIT	YEAR RETD.	ISSUE PRICE	*QUOTE U.S.$
1991	Polar Bear	Open		45.00	45

Baby Bird Pairs - Unknown

YEAR	ISSUE	EDITION LIMIT	YEAR RETD.	ISSUE PRICE	*QUOTE U.S.$
1992	Chickadee	Closed	1994	64.00	64
1992	Orioles	Closed	1994	64.00	64
1991	Robins	Closed	1994	64.00	64

Breed Puppies - Unknown

YEAR	ISSUE	EDITION LIMIT	YEAR RETD.	ISSUE PRICE	*QUOTE U.S.$
1995	Dachshund	Open		75.00	75

Carousel Animals - Unknown

YEAR	ISSUE	EDITION LIMIT	YEAR RETD.	ISSUE PRICE	*QUOTE U.S.$
1992	Camelot Horse	Open		152.00	152
1990	Carousel Charger	Open		136.00	152
1989	Carousel Circus Horse	Open		136.00	152
1990	Carousel Elephant	Open		136.00	152
1987	Carousel Horse	Open		136.00	152
1990	Carousel Lion	Open		136.00	152
1991	Carousel Polar Bear	Open		152.00	152
1989	Carousel Reindeer	Open		136.00	152
1988	Carousel Unicorn	Open		136.00	152
1992	Christmas Horse 1992	Yr.Iss.	1992	156.00	156
1993	Christmas Horse 1993	Yr.Iss.	1993	156.00	156
1994	Christmas Horse 1994	Yr.Iss.	1994	156.00	156
1994	Midnight Charger	9,500		156.00	156
1993	Nautical Horse	Open		156.00	156
1991	Pride of America	Closed	1991	152.00	152
1993	Rose Prancer	9,500		156.00	156
1993	Statement Horse #1 Victorian Romance	2,500		395.00	395
1994	Statement Horse #2 Ribbons & Roses	2,500		395.00	395
1992	Statement Piece	Open		395.00	395
1992	Tropical Horse	Open		156.00	156
1992	Victorian Romance Horse	Open		156.00	156
1991	Western Horse	Open		152.00	152

Carousels - Unknown

YEAR	ISSUE	EDITION LIMIT	YEAR RETD.	ISSUE PRICE	*QUOTE U.S.$
1995	Carousel Courtship (Spec. Ed.)	5,500		195.00	195
1995	Jeweled Prancer Carousel	Open		154.00	154

Classical Goddesses - Unknown

YEAR	ISSUE	EDITION LIMIT	YEAR RETD.	ISSUE PRICE	*QUOTE U.S.$
1992	Aphrodite	Closed	1994	95.00	95
1992	Aphrodite, Painted	Closed	1994	136.00	136

Crystal Animal Pairs - Unknown

YEAR	ISSUE	EDITION LIMIT	YEAR RETD.	ISSUE PRICE	*QUOTE U.S.$
1994	Lord & Lady, Wolves	Open		76.00	76
1994	Preen & Serene, Cats	Open		76.00	76
1993	Prim & Proper, Cats	Open		76.00	76
1993	Silk & Satin, Rabbits	Open		76.00	76

Crystal Eagles - Unknown

YEAR	ISSUE	EDITION LIMIT	YEAR RETD.	ISSUE PRICE	*QUOTE U.S.$
1994	Soaring Majesty	Open		195.00	195
1995	Wings of the Sun	Open		195.00	195

Doves & Roses - Unknown

YEAR	ISSUE	EDITION LIMIT	YEAR RETD.	ISSUE PRICE	*QUOTE U.S.$
1992	Doves of Honor	Open		119.00	119
1993	Doves of Love	Open		119.00	119
1991	Doves of Peace	Open		95.00	95
1991	Love's Promise	Open		95.00	95

Endangered Baby Animals - Unknown

YEAR	ISSUE	EDITION LIMIT	YEAR RETD.	ISSUE PRICE	*QUOTE U.S.$
1991	Baby Florida Panther	Open		57.00	57
1991	Baby Grey Wolf	Open		57.00	57
1994	Baby Orangatan	Open		58.00	58
1992	Baby Rhinocerous	Open		57.00	57
1994	Bridled Nail-Tailed Wallaby Joey	Open		58.00	58
1994	Burmese Deer	Open		58.50	59
1991	Elephant	Open		57.00	57
1993	Indian Elephant Calf	Open		57.00	57
1990	Panda	Open		39.00	39
1994	Pigmy Hippo	Open		58.00	58
1994	Sumatra Tiger Cub	Open		58.00	58

Exotic Birds - Unknown

YEAR	ISSUE	EDITION LIMIT	YEAR RETD.	ISSUE PRICE	*QUOTE U.S.$
1993	"Plum Headed" Parakeet	Open		49.50	50
1991	Cockatoo	Open		45.00	45

Floral Sculptures - Unknown

YEAR	ISSUE	EDITION LIMIT	YEAR RETD.	ISSUE PRICE	*QUOTE U.S.$
1987	Iris	Open		119.00	136
1988	Magnolia	Open		119.00	136
1988	Peace Rose	Open		119.00	136
1986	Rubrum Lily	Open		119.00	136

Garden Birds - Unknown

YEAR	ISSUE	EDITION LIMIT	YEAR RETD.	ISSUE PRICE	*QUOTE U.S.$
1987	American Goldfinch	Open		39.00	45
1990	Baltimore Oriole	Open		45.00	45
1993	Barn Swallow	Open		45.00	45
1986	Blue Jay	Open		39.00	45
1991	Broadbilled Hummingbird	Open		45.00	45
1987	Cardinal	Open		39.00	45
1988	Cedar Waxwing	Open		39.00	45
1985	Chickadee	Open		39.00	45
1990	Chipping Sparrow	Open		45.00	45
1993	Chipping Sparrow	Open		45.00	45
1994	Christmas Dove	Yr.Iss.		45.00	45
1991	Dark Eyed Junco	Open		45.00	45
1989	Downy Woodpecker	Open		39.00	45
1986	Eastern Bluebird	Open		39.00	45
1994	Female BlueJay	Open		45.00	45
1993	Female Cardinal	Open		45.00	45
1994	Female Chickadee	Open		45.00	45
1993	Female Kinglet	Open		45.00	45
1991	Golden Crowned Kinglet	Open		45.00	45
1988	Hummingbird	Open		39.00	45
1993	Indigo Bunting	Open		45.00	45
1992	Magnificent Hummingbird	Open		45.00	45
1990	Marsh Wren	Open		45.00	45
1993	Mockingbird	Open		45.00	45
1993	Mountain Bluebird	Open		45.00	45
1991	Purple Finch	Open		45.00	45
1994	Purple Martin	Open		45.00	45
1993	Red Winged Blackbird	Open		45.00	45
1987	Red-Breasted Nuthatch	Open		39.00	45
1989	Robin	Open		39.00	45
1991	Rose Grosbeak	Open		45.00	45
1989	Saw Whet Owl	Open		45.00	45
1992	Scarlet Tanger	Open		45.00	45
1993	Statement Piece	Open		45.00	45
1986	Tufted Titmouse	Open		39.00	45
1987	Turtle Dove	Open		39.00	45
1994	Vermillion Flycatcher	Open		45.00	45
1992	Western Meadowlark	Open		45.00	45
1994	Western Tanager	Open		45.00	45
1990	Wood Duck	Open		45.00	45
1993	Yellow Warbler	Open		45.00	45

Garden Flowers - Unknown

YEAR	ISSUE	EDITION LIMIT	YEAR RETD.	ISSUE PRICE	*QUOTE U.S.$
1991	Calla Lily	Open		45.00	45
1991	Camelia	Open		45.00	45
1990	Carnation	Open		45.00	45
1988	Cattleya Orchid	Open		39.00	45
1995	Crocus	Open		39.00	39
1990	Daffodil	Open		45.00	45
1990	Day Lily	Open		45.00	45
1995	Gardenia	Open		39.00	39
1995	Gladiolus	Open		39.00	39
1989	Iris	Open		45.00	45
1995	Keepsake Rose (Statement)	Open		95.00	95
1991	Magnolia	Open		45.00	45
1991	Morning Glory	Open		45.00	45
1988	Parrot Tulip	Open		39.00	39
1991	Poinsettia	Open		39.00	39
1993	Red Rose	Open		45.00	45
1988	Tea Rose	Open		39.00	45

Gentle Majesty - Unknown

YEAR	ISSUE	EDITION LIMIT	YEAR RETD.	ISSUE PRICE	*QUOTE U.S.$
1990	Bear Hug Polar Bear	Open		76.00	76
1991	Keeping Warm (Foxes)	Open		76.00	76
1990	Penguins	Open		76.00	76

Hunters of the Sky - Unknown

YEAR	ISSUE	EDITION LIMIT	YEAR RETD.	ISSUE PRICE	*QUOTE U.S.$
1993	Challenge of the Eagles, Double Eagles	Open		275.00	275
1994	Challenge of the Red Tailed Hawks	Open		295.00	295
1994	Golden Conquerors	Open		295.00	295
1994	Masters of the Wind, Peregian Falcons	Open		295.00	295

International Brides - Unknown

YEAR	ISSUE	EDITION LIMIT	YEAR RETD.	ISSUE PRICE	*QUOTE U.S.$
1992	Japanese Bride, Kiyoshi	Closed	1993	136.00	136
1990	Russian Bride	Closed	1993	136.00	136

International Horse Sculptures - Unknown

YEAR	ISSUE	EDITION LIMIT	YEAR RETD.	ISSUE PRICE	*QUOTE U.S.$
1990	Appaloosa	Open		136.00	136
1988	Arabian Knight	Open		136.00	136
1990	Lippizan	Open		136.00	136
1989	Thoroughbred	Open		136.00	136

International Songbirds - Unknown

YEAR	ISSUE	EDITION LIMIT	YEAR RETD.	ISSUE PRICE	*QUOTE U.S.$
1992	American Goldfinch	Open		152.00	152
1992	European Goldfinch	Open		152.00	152

Jessie Willcox Smith - J.W.Smith

YEAR	ISSUE	EDITION LIMIT	YEAR RETD.	ISSUE PRICE	*QUOTE U.S.$
1991	Feeding Kitty	Closed	1993	60.00	60
1991	Rosebuds	Closed	1993	60.00	60

Kings of the Sky - Unknown

YEAR	ISSUE	EDITION LIMIT	YEAR RETD.	ISSUE PRICE	*QUOTE U.S.$
1991	Defender of Freedom, American Bald Eagle	Closed		234.00	234
1991	Eagle of Glory, Golden Eagle	Open		234.00	234
1994	Eagle of Splendor, American Bald Eagle	Open		252.00	252
1993	Foundation of Freedom	Open		252.00	252
1989	Lord of Skies, American Bald Eagle	Open		195.00	195
1992	Wings of Majesty, American Bald Eagle	Open		252.00	252
1993	Wings of Power, Golden Eagle	Open		252.00	252

*Quotes have been rounded up to nearest dollar

YEAR ISSUE		EDITION LIMIT	YEAR RETD.	ISSUE PRICE	*QUOTE U.S.$
1994	Wings of Pride, Golden Eagle	Open		252.00	252

Legendary Princesses - Unknown

YEAR ISSUE		EDITION LIMIT	YEAR RETD.	ISSUE PRICE	*QUOTE U.S.$
1988	Cinderella	Open		136.00	136
1990	Cleopatra	Open		136.00	136
1994	Fairy Godmother	9,500		156.00	156
1992	Firebird	Open		156.00	156
1994	Frog Princess	Open		156.00	156
1990	Guinevere	Open		136.00	136
1990	Juliet	Open		136.00	136
1993	Little Mermaid, Princess of the Sea	Open		156.00	156
1994	Maid Marion	Open		156.00	156
1991	Peacock Maiden	Open		136.00	136
1991	Pocohontas	9,500	1992	136.00	165
1993	Princes Beauty	Open		156.00	156
1993	Princess and the Pea	Open		156.00	156
1986	Rapunzel	Open		119.00	136
1992	Sheherezade	Open		156.00	156
1986	Sleeping Beauty	Open		119.00	136
1987	Snow Queen	Open		119.00	136
1989	Snow White	Open		136.00	136
1989	Swan Princess	Open		136.00	136

Lenox Baby Book - Unknown

YEAR ISSUE		EDITION LIMIT	YEAR RETD.	ISSUE PRICE	*QUOTE U.S.$
1991	Baby's First Christmas	Closed	1994	57.00	57
1992	Baby's First Portrait	Closed	1994	57.00	57
1990	Baby's First Shoes	Closed	1994	57.00	57
1991	Baby's First Steps	Closed	1994	57.00	57

Lenox Breed Puppies - Unknown

YEAR ISSUE		EDITION LIMIT	YEAR RETD.	ISSUE PRICE	*QUOTE U.S.$
1990	Beagle	Open		76.00	76
1991	Cocker Spaniel	Open		76.00	76
1994	German Shepherd	Open		75.00	75
1995	Labrador Retriever	Open		76.00	76
1992	Poodle	Open		76.00	76

Lenox Sea Animals - Unknown

YEAR ISSUE		EDITION LIMIT	YEAR RETD.	ISSUE PRICE	*QUOTE U.S.$
1994	Adventure of Fur Seals	Open		136.00	136
1991	Dance of the Dolphins	Open		119.00	119
1993	Flight of the Dolphins	Open		119.00	119
1993	Journey of the Whales	Open		136.00	136
1993	Otter Escapade	Open		136.00	136
1994	Penguins at Play	Open		136.00	136
1992	Song of the Whales	Open		136.00	136
1994	Voyage of the Sea Turtles	Open		136.00	136

Life of Christ - Unknown

YEAR ISSUE		EDITION LIMIT	YEAR RETD.	ISSUE PRICE	*QUOTE U.S.$
1992	A Child's Comfort	Open		95.00	95
1992	A Child's Prayer	Open		95.00	95
1993	Children's Adoration	Open		95.00	95
1990	The Children's Blessing	Open		95.00	95
1992	Childrens's Devotion (Painted)	Open		195.00	195
1990	The Good Shepherd	Open		95.00	95
1993	Jesus, The Carpenter	Open		95.00	95
1991	Jesus, The Teacher	9,500		95.00	95
1990	Madonna And Child	Open		95.00	95
1992	Mary & Christ Child (Painted)	Open		195.00	195
1991	The Savior	Open		95.00	95

Miniature Santas Around the World-8" - Unknown

YEAR ISSUE		EDITION LIMIT	YEAR RETD.	ISSUE PRICE	*QUOTE U.S.$
1993	Americana Santa	Open		19.50	20
1993	Bavarian Santa	Open		19.50	20
1994	Befona	Open		19.50	20
1994	Christkindle	Open		19.50	20
1993	Father Christmas	Open		19.50	20
1993	Grandfather Frost	Open		19.50	20
1993	Kris Kringle	Open		19.50	20
1994	Patriotic Santa	Open		19.50	20
1993	Pere Noel	Open		19.50	20
1994	Sanct Herr Nikolaus	Open		19.50	20
1994	Santa Lucia	Open		19.50	20
1994	Sinterklaus	Open		19.50	20
1994	St. Mikulase	Open		19.50	20
1993	St. Nick	Open		19.50	20
1994	Victorian Santa	Open		19.50	20

Mother & Child - Unknown

YEAR ISSUE		EDITION LIMIT	YEAR RETD.	ISSUE PRICE	*QUOTE U.S.$
1991	Afternoon Stroll	7,500		136.00	136
1990	Bedtime Prayers	Open		119.00	119
1986	Cherished Moment	Open		119.00	119
1989	Christening	Open		119.00	119
1991	Evening Lullaby	7,500		136.00	136
1992	Morning Playtime	Open		136.00	136
1988	The Present	Open		119.00	119
1987	Storytime	Open		119.00	119
1986	Sunday in the Park	Open		119.00	119

Nativity - Unknown

YEAR ISSUE		EDITION LIMIT	YEAR RETD.	ISSUE PRICE	*QUOTE U.S.$
1989	Angels of Adoration	Open		136.00	152
1988	Animals of the Nativity	Open		119.00	152
1990	Children of Bethlehem	Open		136.00	152
1986	Holy Family	Open		119.00	136
1988	Shepherds	Open		119.00	152
1991	Standing Camel & Driver	9,500		152.00	152
1987	Three Kings	Open		119.00	152
1991	Townspeople of Bethlehem	Open		136.00	152

Nature's Beautiful Butterflies - Unknown

YEAR ISSUE		EDITION LIMIT	YEAR RETD.	ISSUE PRICE	*QUOTE U.S.$
1991	Adonis	Open		45.00	45
1993	American Painted Lady	Open		45.00	45
1993	Black Swallowtail	Open		45.00	45
1989	Blue Temora	Open		39.00	45
1993	Great Orange Wingtip	Open		45.00	45
1991	Malachite	Open		45.00	45
1990	Monarch	Open		39.00	45
1990	Purple Emperor	Open		45.00	45
1994	Rainforest Dazzler	Open		45.00	45
1990	Yellow Swallowtail	Open		39.00	45

North American Bird Pairs - Unknown

YEAR ISSUE		EDITION LIMIT	YEAR RETD.	ISSUE PRICE	*QUOTE U.S.$
1991	Blue Jay Pairs	Open		119.00	119
1992	Cardinal	Open		119.00	119
1991	Chickadees	Open		119.00	119
1990	Hummingbirds	Open		119.00	119

North American Wildlife - Unknown

YEAR ISSUE		EDITION LIMIT	YEAR RETD.	ISSUE PRICE	*QUOTE U.S.$
1991	White Tailed Deer	Closed	1993	195.00	195

Owls of America - Unknown

YEAR ISSUE		EDITION LIMIT	YEAR RETD.	ISSUE PRICE	*QUOTE U.S.$
1989	Barn Owl	Open		136.00	136
1991	Great Horned Owl	9,500		136.00	136
1990	Screech Owl	Open		136.00	136
1988	Snowy Owl	Open		136.00	136

Parent & Child Bird Pairs - Unknown

YEAR ISSUE		EDITION LIMIT	YEAR RETD.	ISSUE PRICE	*QUOTE U.S.$
1992	Blue Jay Pairs	Open		119.00	119

Porcelain Duck Collection - Unknown

YEAR ISSUE		EDITION LIMIT	YEAR RETD.	ISSUE PRICE	*QUOTE U.S.$
1992	Blue Winged Teal Duck	Open		45.00	45
1991	Mallard Duck	Open		45.00	45
1993	Pintail Duck	Open		45.00	45
1991	Wood Duck	Open		45.00	45

Religious Sculptures - Unknown

YEAR ISSUE		EDITION LIMIT	YEAR RETD.	ISSUE PRICE	*QUOTE U.S.$
1994	Footsteps in the Sand	Open		152.00	152
1993	Last Supper	Open		152.00	152
1992	Moses	Open		95.00	95
1994	Pieta	Open		152.00	152
1995	Praying Hands	Open		95.00	95

Renaissance Nativity - Unknown

YEAR ISSUE		EDITION LIMIT	YEAR RETD.	ISSUE PRICE	*QUOTE U.S.$
1991	Angels	Open		195.00	195
1995	Angels of Harmony	Open		195.00	195
1991	Animals of the Nativity	Open		195.00	195
1993	Camel & Driver	9,500		195.00	195
1994	Children of Bethlehem	9,500		195.00	195
1991	Holy Family	Open		195.00	195
1991	Shepherds of Bethlehem	Open		195.00	195
1991	Three Kings	Open		195.00	195

Santa Claus Collection - Unknown

YEAR ISSUE		EDITION LIMIT	YEAR RETD.	ISSUE PRICE	*QUOTE U.S.$
1991	Americana Santa	Open		136.00	136
1994	Bavarian Santa	Open		136.00	136
1990	Father Christmas	Open		136.00	136
1992	Grandfather Frost	Open		136.00	136
1991	Kris Kringle	Open		136.00	136
1992	Pere Noel	Open		136.00	136
1993	St. Nick	Open		136.00	136
1994	Victorian Santa	Open		136.00	136

Street Crier Collection - Unknown

YEAR ISSUE		EDITION LIMIT	YEAR RETD.	ISSUE PRICE	*QUOTE U.S.$
1991	Belgian Lace Maker	Closed	1993	136.00	136
1990	French Flower Maiden	Closed	1993	136.00	136

Unicorns - Unknown

YEAR ISSUE		EDITION LIMIT	YEAR RETD.	ISSUE PRICE	*QUOTE U.S.$
1995	Celestial Unicorn (Statement #2)	4,500		295.00	295
1993	Eternal Enchantment (Statement #1)	Open		245.00	245
1994	Golden Grace	Open		149.00	149
1995	Love's Celebration (Anniversary/Spec. Ed.)	9,500		136.00	136
1994	Love's Magic	Open		119.00	119
1994	Love's Messenger (Valentine)	Open		119.00	119
1993	Love's Paradise	Open		119.00	119
1993	Love's Pride	Open		119.00	119
1995	Mid-Summer's Night Unicorn (Spec. Ed.)	9,500		149.00	149
1994	Platinum Purity	Open		149.00	149
1994	Royal Court Unicorn	Open		136.00	136
1994	Unicorn of Summer	Open		119.00	119
1992	Yuletide Blessing (Christmas)	Yr.Iss.	1992	119.00	119
1993	Yuletide Magic (Christmas)	Yr.Iss.	1993	119.00	119
1994	Yuletide Splendor (Christmas)	Yr.Iss.	1994	119.00	119

Wildlife of the Seven Continents - Unknown

YEAR ISSUE		EDITION LIMIT	YEAR RETD.	ISSUE PRICE	*QUOTE U.S.$
1988	African Lion	Open		136.00	136
1987	Antarctic Seals	Open		136.00	136
1985	Asian Elephant	Open		120.00	120
1985	Australian Koala	Open		120.00	120
1987	European Red Deer	Open		136.00	136
1984	North American Bighorn Sheep	Open		120.00	120
1986	South American Puma	Open		120.00	120

Woodland Animals - Unknown

YEAR ISSUE		EDITION LIMIT	YEAR RETD.	ISSUE PRICE	*QUOTE U.S.$
1991	Autumn Adventure (Chipmunk)	Open		39.00	39
1993	Autumn Splendor (Fawn)	Open		45.00	45
1992	Daybreak Discovery (Rabbit)	Open		39.00	39
1994	Early Morning Surprise (Fox)	Open		45.00	45
1995	Forest Friends (Statement)	Open		97.00	97
1994	Nature's Reward (Mouse)	Open		45.00	45
1994	Playful Pursuit (Black Bear)	Open		45.00	45
1993	Scent of Spring (Skunk)	Open		45.00	45
1995	Spring Shadow (Ground Hog)	Open		45.00	45
1990	Springtime Skamper (Red Squirrel)	Open		39.00	39
1994	Summer Delight (Chipmunk)	Open		45.00	45
1990	Twilight Mischief (Raccoon)	Open		39.00	39
1994	Woodland Worker (Beaver)	Open		45.00	45

Lilliput Lane Ltd.

Collectors Club Specials - Various

YEAR ISSUE		EDITION LIMIT	YEAR RETD.	ISSUE PRICE	*QUOTE U.S.$
1986	Packhorse Bridge - D. Tate	Retrd.	1987	Gift	700
1986	Packhorse Bridge (dealer) - D. Tate	Retrd.	1987	Gift	450-750
1986	Crendon Manor - D. Tate	Retrd.	1989	285.00	850
1986	Gulliver - Unknown	Retrd.	1986	65.00	325
1987	Little Lost Dog - D. Tate	Retrd.	1988	Gift	225-450
1987	Yew Tree Farm - D. Tate	Retrd.	1988	160.00	230
1988	Wishing Well - D. Tate	Retrd.	1989	Gift	105
1989	Dovecot - D. Tate	Retrd.	1990	Gift	95
1989	Wenlock Rise - D. Tate	Retrd.	1989	175.00	150-200
1990	Cosy Corner - D. Tate	Retrd.	1991	Gift	75-110
1990	Lavender Cottage - D. Tate	Retrd.	1991	50.00	75
1990	Bridle Way - D. Tate	Retrd.	1991	100.00	150-225
1991	Puddlebrook - D. Tate	Retrd.	1992	Gift	60-100
1991	Gardeners Cottage - D. Tate	Retrd.	1992	120.00	175-250
1991	Wren Cottage - D. Tate	Retrd.	1993	13.95	65-110
1992	Pussy Willow - D. Tate	Retrd.	1993	Gift	36-60
1992	Forget-Me-Not - D. Tate	Retrd.	1993	130.00	150-200
1993	The Spinney - Lilliput Lane	Retrd.	1994	Gift	100-125
1993	Heaven Lea Cottage - Lilliput Lane	Retrd.	1994	150.00	250
1993	Curlew Cottage - Lilliput Lane	Retrd.	1995	18.95	50-65
1994	Petticoat Cottage - Lilliput Lane	Retrd.	1995	Gift	70
1994	Woodman's Retreat - Lilliput Lane	Retrd.	1995	135.00	150-200
1995	Thimble Cottage - Lilliput Lane	Retrd.	1996	Gift	N/A
1995	Porlock Down - Lilliput Lane	Retrd.	1996	135.00	135
1996	Wash Day - Lilliput Lane	4/97		Gift	N/A
1996	Meadowsweet Cottage - Lilliput Lane	4/97		N/A	N/A
1996	Nursery Cottage - Lilliput Lane	4/97		N/A	N/A
1996	Winnows - Lilliput Lane	4/97		25.00	25

Anniversary Special - Lilliput Lane

YEAR ISSUE		EDITION LIMIT	YEAR RETD.	ISSUE PRICE	*QUOTE U.S.$
1992	Honeysuckle Cottage	Yr.Iss.	1992	195.00	300-45
1993	Cotman Cottage	Yr.Iss.	1993	220.00	250-35
1994	Watermeadows	Yr.Iss.	1994	189.00	22
1995	Gertrude's Garden	Yr.Iss.	1995	192.00	20
1996	Cruck End	Yr.Iss.		130.00	13

South Bend Dinner Collection - Various

YEAR ISSUE		EDITION LIMIT	YEAR RETD.	ISSUE PRICE	*QUOTE U.S.$
1989	Commemorative Medallion - D. Tate	Retrd.	1989	N/A	130-20
1990	Rowan Lodge - D. Tate	Retrd.	1990	N/A	200-40
1991	Gamekeepers Cottage - D. Tate	Retrd.	1991	N/A	250-40
1992	Ashberry Cottage - D. Tate	Retrd.	1992	N/A	200-40
1993	Magnifying Glass - Lilliput Lane	Retrd.	1993	N/A	N/A

Special Event Collection - Lilliput Lane

YEAR ISSUE		EDITION LIMIT	YEAR RETD.	ISSUE PRICE	*QUOTE U.S.$
1990	Rowan Lodge	Retrd.	1990	50.00	12
1991	Gamekeepers Cottage	Retrd.	1991	75.00	20
1992	Ploughman's Cottage	Retrd.	1992	75.00	7
1993	Aberford Gate	Retrd.	1993	95.00	16
1994	Leagrave Cottage	Retrd.	1994	75.00	7
1995	Vanbrugh Lodge	Retrd.	1995	60.00	6
1996	Amerbly Rose	Yr.Iss.		N/A	N/

American Collection - D. Tate

YEAR ISSUE		EDITION LIMIT	YEAR RETD.	ISSUE PRICE	*QUOTE U.S.$
1984	Adobe Church	Retrd.	1985	22.50	600-90
1984	Adobe Village	Retrd.	1985	60.00	800-150
1984	Cape Cod	Retrd.	1985	22.50	570-91
1984	Country Church	Retrd.	1985	22.50	500-80
1984	Covered Bridge	Retrd.	1985	22.50	1000-200
1984	Forge Barn	Retrd.	1985	22.50	550-66
1984	General Store	Retrd.	1985	22.50	600-100
1984	Grist Mill	Retrd.	1985	22.50	500-78
1984	Light House	Retrd.	1985	22.50	650-80
1984	Log Cabin	Retrd.	1985	22.50	625-100
1984	Midwest Barn	Retrd.	1985	22.50	275-35
1984	San Francisco House	Retrd.	1985	22.50	84
1984	Wallace Station	Retrd.	1985	22.50	40

American Landmark Series - R. Day

YEAR ISSUE		EDITION LIMIT	YEAR RETD.	ISSUE PRICE	*QUOTE U.S.$
1992	16.9 Cents Per Gallon	Open		95.00	9
1995	Afternoon Tea	1,995		495.00	4
1994	Birdsong	Open		85.00	8
1990	Country Church	Retrd.	1992	82.50	1
1989	Countryside Barn	Retrd.	1992	75.00	150-2
1990	Covered Memories	Retrd.	1993	110.00	200-3
1989	Falls Mill	Retrd.	1992	130.00	225-3
1991	Fire House 1	Open		85.00	8
1994	Fresh Bread	Open		95.00	9
1992	Gold Miners' Claim	Open		95.00	9
1990	Great Point Light	Open		45.00	4
1994	Harvest Mill	3,500		395.00	3
1994	Holy Night	Open		170.00	1
1992	Home Sweet Home	Open		95.00	
1990	Hometown Depot	Retrd.	1993	68.00	100-1
1989	Mail Pouch Barn	Retrd.	1993	75.00	100-2
1990	Pepsi Cola Barn	Retrd.	1991	87.00	175-2
1990	Pioneer Barn	Retrd.	1991	30.00	
1991	Rambling Rose	Retrd.	1995	60.00	1
1990	Riverside Chapel	Retrd.	1993	82.50	135-1

*Quotes have been rounded up to nearest dolla

YEAR ISSUE		EDITION LIMIT	YEAR RETD.	ISSUE PRICE	*QUOTE U.S.$
1990	Roadside Coolers	Retrd.	1994	75.00	110-145
1991	School Days	Open		60.00	60
1993	See Rock City	Open		35.00	35
1993	Shave and A Haircut	Open		95.00	95
1990	Sign Of The Times	Open		27.50	35
1993	Simply Amish	Open		110.00	110
1992	Small Town Library	Retrd.	1995	130.00	140
1994	Spring Victorian	Open		170.00	170
1991	Victoriana	Retrd.	1992	295.00	350-650
1992	Winnie's Place	Retrd.	1993	395.00	550-850

Blaise Hamlet Classics - Lilliput Lane

YEAR ISSUE		EDITION LIMIT	YEAR RETD.	ISSUE PRICE	*QUOTE U.S.$
1993	Circular Cottage	Retrd.	1995	95.00	95
1993	Dial Cottage	Retrd.	1995	95.00	95
1993	Diamond Cottage	Retrd.	1995	95.00	95
1993	Double Cottage	Retrd.	1995	95.00	95
1993	Jasmine Cottage	Retrd.	1995	95.00	95
1993	Oak Cottage	Retrd.	1995	95.00	95
1993	Rose Cottage	Retrd.	1995	95.00	145
1993	Sweet Briar Cottage	Retrd.	1995	95.00	95
1993	Vine Cottage	Retrd.	1995	95.00	135

Blaise Hamlet Collection - D. Tate

YEAR ISSUE		EDITION LIMIT	YEAR RETD.	ISSUE PRICE	*QUOTE U.S.$
1989	Circular Cottage	Retrd.	1993	110.00	100-150
1990	Dial Cottage	Retrd.	1995	110.00	100-150
1989	Diamond Cottage	Retrd.	1993	110.00	125-175
1991	Double Cottage	Open		150.00	150
1991	Jasmine Cottage	Retrd.	1996	110.00	120-150
1989	Oak Cottage	Retrd.	1993	110.00	110-150
1991	Rose Cottage	Open		110.00	110
1990	Sweetbriar Cottage	Retrd.	1995	110.00	135-150
1990	Vine Cottage	Retrd.	1995	110.00	135-150

Christmas Church - Lilliput Lane

YEAR ISSUE		EDITION LIMIT	YEAR RETD.	ISSUE PRICE	*QUOTE U.S.$
1996	St. Stephen's Church	Yr.Iss.		100.00	100

Christmas Collection - Various

YEAR ISSUE		EDITION LIMIT	YEAR RETD.	ISSUE PRICE	*QUOTE U.S.$
1992	Chestnut Cottage	Open		35.00	35
1992	Cranberry Cottage	Open		35.00	35
1988	Deer Park Hall - D. Tate	Retrd.	1989	120.00	200-350
1993	The Gingerbread Shop	Open		35.00	35
1992	Hollytree House	Open		35.00	35
1991	The Old Vicarage at Christmas - D. Tate	Retrd.	1992	180.00	200-350
1993	Partridge Cottage	Open		35.00	35
1994	Ring O' Bells	Open		35.00	35
1993	St. Joseph's Church	Open		50.00	50
1994	St. Joseph's School	Open		35.00	35
1989	St. Nicholas Church - D. Tate	Retrd.	1990	130.00	150-250
1994	The Vicarage	Open		35.00	35
1990	Yuletide Inn - D. Tate	Retrd.	1991	145.00	120-150

Christmas Lodge Collection - Lilliput Lane

YEAR ISSUE		EDITION LIMIT	YEAR RETD.	ISSUE PRICE	*QUOTE U.S.$
1993	Eamont Lodge	Retrd.	1993	185.00	250-325
1992	Highland Lodge	Retrd.	1992	180.00	200-300
1995	Kerry Lodge	Retrd.	1995	120.00	120
1994	Snowdon Lodge	Retrd.	1994	175.00	175

Coca Cola Country - R. Day

YEAR ISSUE		EDITION LIMIT	YEAR RETD.	ISSUE PRICE	*QUOTE U.S.$
1996	A Cherry Coke...Just the Prescription	Open		95.00	95
1996	Country Fresh Pickins	Open		150.00	150
1996	Fill'er Up & Check the Oil	Open		125.00	125
1996	Hazards of the Road	Open		50.00	50
1996	Hook, Line & Sinker	Open		95.00	95
1996	We've Got it or They Don't Make it	Open		95.00	95

Countryside Scene Plaques - D. Simpson

YEAR ISSUE		EDITION LIMIT	YEAR RETD.	ISSUE PRICE	*QUOTE U.S.$
1989	Bottle Kiln	Retrd.	1991	49.50	50
1989	Cornish Tin Mine	Retrd.	1991	49.50	50
1989	Country Inn	Retrd.	1991	49.50	50
1989	Cumbrian Farmhouse	Retrd.	1991	49.50	50
1989	Lighthouse	Retrd.	1991	49.50	50
1989	Norfolk Windmill	Retrd.	1991	49.50	50
1989	Oasthouse	Retrd.	1991	49.50	50
1989	Old Smithy	Retrd.	1991	49.50	50
1989	Parish Church	Retrd.	1991	49.50	50
1989	Post Office	Retrd.	1991	49.50	50
1989	Village School	Retrd.	1991	49.50	50
1989	Watermill	Retrd.	1991	49.50	50

Disneyana Convention - R. Day

YEAR ISSUE		EDITION LIMIT	YEAR RETD.	ISSUE PRICE	*QUOTE U.S.$
1995	Fire Station 105	501	1995	195.00	450-850

Dutch Collection - D. Tate

YEAR ISSUE		EDITION LIMIT	YEAR RETD.	ISSUE PRICE	*QUOTE U.S.$
1991	Aan de Amstel	Open		60.00	60
1991	Begijnhof	Open		35.00	35
1991	Bloemenmarkt	Open		60.00	60
1991	De Branderij	Open		55.00	55
1991	De Diamantair	Open		60.00	60
1991	De Pepermolen	Open		35.00	35
1991	De Wolhandelaar	Open		55.00	55
1991	De Zijdewever	Open		60.00	60
1991	Rembrant van Rijn	Open		85.00	85
1991	Rozengracht	Open		50.00	50

English Cottages - D. Tate, unless otherwise noted

YEAR ISSUE		EDITION LIMIT	YEAR RETD.	ISSUE PRICE	*QUOTE U.S.$
1982	Acorn Cottage-Mold 1	Retrd.	1983	30.00	250-350
1983	Acorn Cottage-Mold 2	Retrd.	1987	30.00	60
1982	Anne Hathaway's-Mold 1	Retrd.	1983	40.00	2500
1983	Anne Hathaway's-Mold 2	Retrd.	1984	40.00	400-600
1984	Anne Hathaway's-Mold 3	Retrd.	1988	40.00	375
1989	Anne Hathaway's-Mold 4	Open		130.00	130
1991	Anne of Cleves	Open		250.00	250
1994	Applejack Cottage - Lilliput Lane	Open		35.00	35
1982	April Cottage-Mold 1	Retrd.	1984	Unkn.	350-500
1982	April Cottage-Mold 2	Retrd.	1989	Unkn.	100
1991	Armada House	Open		130.00	130
1989	Ash Nook	Retrd.	1995	47.50	60
1986	Bay View	Retrd.	1988	39.50	90-125
1987	Beacon Heights - Lilliput Lane	Retrd.	1992	125.00	150
1989	Beehive Cottage	Retrd.	1995	72.50	95
1993	Birdlip Bottom - Lilliput Lane	Open		50.00	50
1996	Blue Boar - Lilliput Lane	Open		85.00	85
1992	Bow Cottage	Retrd.	1995	128.00	135
1990	Bramble Cottage	Retrd.	1995	55.00	100
1988	Bredon House	Retrd.	1990	145.00	150-275
1989	The Briary	Retrd.	1995	47.50	60
1982	Bridge House-Mold 1	Retrd.	N/A	15.95	450
1982	Bridge House-Mold 2	Retrd.	1990	15.95	175
1991	Bridge House-Mold 3	Open		20.00	20
1988	Brockbank	Retrd.	1993	58.00	90
1985	Bronte Parsonage	Retrd.	1987	72.00	80
1982	Burnside	Retrd.	1985	30.00	550
1990	Buttercup Cottage	Retrd.	1992	40.00	65
1989	Butterwick	Retrd.	1996	52.50	60
1995	Button Down - Lilliput Lane	Open		30.00	30
1994	Camomile Lawn - Lilliput Lane	Open		90.00	90
1982	Castle Street	Retrd.	1986	130.00	240-350
1993	Cat's Coombe Cottage - Lilliput Lane	Retrd.	1995	95.00	95
1991	Chatsworth View	Retrd.	1996	170.00	170
1995	Cherry Blossom Cottage - Lilliput Lane	Open		95.00	95
1990	Cherry Cottage	Retrd.	1995	33.50	45
1989	Chiltern Mill	Retrd.	1995	87.50	110
1989	Chine Cot-Mold 1	Retrd.	1989	36.00	N/A
1989	Chine Cot-Mold 2	Retrd.	1996	35.00	35
1995	Chipping Combe - Lilliput Lane	3,000		525.00	525
1992	The Chocolate House - Lilliput Lane	Open		90.00	90
1985	Clare Cottage	Retrd.	1993	30.00	63
1993	Cley-next-the-sea - Lilliput Lane	2,500		725.00	725
1987	Clover Cottage	Retrd.	1994	27.50	58
1982	Coach House	Retrd.	1985	100.00	11-1895
1986	Cobblers Cottage - D. Hall	Retrd.	1994	42.00	65
1990	Convent in The Woods	Open		175.00	195
1983	Coopers	Retrd.	1986	15.00	440-825
1996	Cradle Cottage - Lilliput Lane	Open		100.00	100
1994	Creel Cottage - Lilliput Lane	Open		35.00	35
1988	Crown Inn	Retrd.	1992	120.00	120-215
1991	Daisy Cottage	Open		30.00	30
1982	Dale Farm-Mold 1	Retrd.	1986	30.00	1300
1982	Dale Farm-Mold 2	Retrd.	1986	30.00	875
1986	Dale Head	Retrd.	1988	75.00	85-200
1982	Dale House	Retrd.	1986	25.00	840
1992	Derwent-le-Dale - Lilliput Lane	Open		55.00	55
1983	Dove Cottage-Mold 1	Retrd.	1984	35.00	725-1800
1984	Dove Cottage-Mold 2	Retrd.	1988	35.00	55-85
1991	Dovetails	Retrd.	1996	65.00	100
1982	Drapers-Mold 1	Retrd.	1983	15.95	5000
1982	Drapers-Mold 2	Retrd.	1983	15.95	4025
1995	Duckdown Cottage - Lilliput Lane	Open		70.00	70
1994	Elm Cottage - Lilliput Lane	Open		50.00	50
1985	Farriers	Retrd.	1990	40.00	45-65
1991	Farthing Lodge	Open		30.00	30
1992	Finchingfields - Lilliput Lane	Retrd.	1995	82.50	95
1985	Fisherman's Cottage	Retrd.	1989	30.00	60
1989	Fiveways	Retrd.	1995	42.50	55
1991	The Flower Sellers	Retrd.	1996	80.00	110
1987	Four Seasons - M. Adkinson	Retrd.	1991	70.00	125
1993	Foxglove Fields - Lilliput Lane	Open		85.00	85
1996	Fuchsia Cottage - Lilliput Lane	Open		30.00	30
1987	The Gables - Lilliput Lane	Retrd.	1992	145.00	125-225
1996	Gossip Gate - Lilliput Lane	Open		170.00	170
1992	Granny Smiths	Open		45.00	45
1992	Grantchester Meadows - Lilliput Lane	Open		195.00	195
1989	Greensted Church	Retrd.	1995	72.50	95
1994	Gulliver's Gate - Lilliput Lane	Open		35.00	45
1989	Helmere Cottage	Retrd.	1995	65.00	80-125
1992	High Ghyll Farm - Lilliput Lane	Open		250.00	250
1982	Holly Cottage	Retrd.	1988	42.50	85
1987	Holme Dyke	Retrd.	1990	50.00	65
1996	Honey Pot Cottage - Lilliput Lane	Open		60.00	60
1982	Honeysuckle	Retrd.	1987	45.00	200
1991	Hopcroft Cottage	Retrd.	1995	120.00	130
1987	Inglewood	Retrd.	1994	27.50	40
1987	Izaak Waltons Cottage	Retrd.	1989	75.00	80-125
1991	John Barleycorn Cottage	Retrd.	1995	130.00	140
1993	Junk and Disorderly - Lilliput Lane	Open		110.00	110
1987	Keepers Lodge	Retrd.	1988	75.00	75-120
1985	Kentish Oast	Retrd.	1990	55.00	75-125
1990	The King's Arms	Retrd.	1995	450.00	550
1991	Lace Lane	Open		70.00	70
1995	Ladybird Cottage - Lilliput Lane	Open		35.00	35
1982	Lakeside House-Mold 1	Retrd.	1983	40.00	1500
1982	Lakeside House-Mold 2	Retrd.	1986	40.00	810-940
1991	Lapworth Lock	Retrd.	1993	82.50	85
1995	Larkrise - Lilliput Lane	Open		45.00	45
1995	Lazy Days - Lilliput Lane	Open		60.00	60
1994	Lenora's Secret - Lilliput Lane	2,500	1995	350.00	400-450
1995	Little Hay - Lilliput Lane	Open		50.00	50
1996	Little Lupins - Lilliput Lane	Open		40.00	40
1995	Little Smithy - Lilliput Lane	Open		60.00	60
1996	Loxdale Cottage - Lilliput Lane	Open		35.00	35
1987	Magpie Cottage	Retrd.	1990	70.00	100-115
1993	Marigold Meadow - Lilliput Lane	Open		80.00	80
1991	Micklegate Antiques	Open		80.00	80
1995	Milestone Cottage - Lilliput Lane	Open		35.00	35
1983	Millers	Retrd.	1986	15.00	120-200
1983	Miners-Mold 1	Retrd.	1985	15.00	590
1983	Miners-Mold 2	Retrd.	1985	15.00	375-455
1991	Moonlight Cove	Retrd.	1996	60.00	60
1985	Moreton Manor	Retrd.	1989	55.00	65-125
1990	Mrs. Pinkerton's Post Office	Open		70.00	70
1992	The Nutshell - Lilliput Lane	Retrd.	1995	75.00	80
1982	Oak Lodge	Retrd.	1987	40.00	65-100
1992	Oakwood Smithy	Open		300.00	300
1985	Old Curiosity Shop	Retrd.	1989	62.50	100-125
1982	Old Mine	Retrd.	1983	15.95	6500
1993	Old Mother Hubbard's - Lilliput Lane	Open		120.00	120
1982	The Old Post Office	Retrd.	1986	35.00	500
1984	Old School House	Retrd.	1985	25.00	1000-1400
1991	Old Shop at Bignor	Retrd.	1995	215.00	220
1989	Olde York Toll	Retrd.	1991	82.50	125
1994	Orchard Farm Cottage - Lilliput Lane	Open		110.00	110
1985	Ostlers Keep	Retrd.	1991	55.00	75-100
1990	Otter Reach	Open		30.00	30
1991	Paradise Lodge	Retrd.	1996	95.00	95
1988	Pargetters Retreat	Retrd.	1990	75.00	100-150
1991	Pear Tree House	Retrd.	1995	82.50	85
1995	Penny's Post - Lilliput Lane	Open		50.00	50
1990	Periwinkle Cottage	Open		165.00	170
1995	Pipit Toll - Lilliput Lane	Open		50.00	50
1992	Pixie House	Retrd.	1995	55.00	60
1991	The Priest's House	Retrd.	1995	180.00	195
1991	Primrose Hill	Retrd.	1996	46.50	50
1992	Puffin Row	Open		95.00	95
1993	Purbeck Stores - Lilliput Lane	Open		35.00	35
1996	Railway Cottage - Lilliput Lane	Open		60.00	60
1983	Red Lion Inn	Retrd.	1987	125.00	360
1996	Reflections of Jade - Lilliput Lane	3,950		350.00	350
1988	Rising Sun	Retrd.	1992	58.00	84-105
1987	Riverview	Retrd.	1994	27.50	40
1990	Robin's Gate	Retrd.	1996	30.00	55
1996	Rosemary Cottage - Lilliput Lane	Open		70.00	70
1988	Royal Oak	Retrd.	1991	145.00	150-300
1990	Runswick House	Open		55.00	55
1992	Rustic Root House	Open		80.00	80
1995	The Rustlings - Lilliput Lane	Open		95.00	95
1987	Rydal View	Retrd.	1989	220.00	200
1987	Saddlers Inn - M. Adkinson	Retrd.	1989	50.00	70
1994	Saffron House - Lilliput Lane	Open		170.00	170
1985	Sawrey Gill	Retrd.	1992	30.00	125-200
1991	Saxham St. Edmunds	Retrd.	1994	1550.00	1850
1988	Saxon Cottage	Retrd.	1989	245.00	200
1986	Scroll on the Wall	Retrd.	1987	55.00	110-130
1987	Secret Garden - M. Adkinson	Retrd.	1994	145.00	130-200
1988	Ship Inn - Lilliput Lane	Retrd.	1992	210.00	228-325
1988	Smallest Inn	Retrd.	1991	42.50	65
1986	Spring Bank	Retrd.	1991	42.00	50-70
1994	Spring Gate Cottage - Lilliput Lane	Open		95.00	95
1996	St. John the Baptist - Lilliput Lane	Open		75.00	75
1989	St. Lawrence Church	Open		85.00	85
1988	St. Marks	Retrd.	1991	75.00	150-225
1985	St. Mary's Church	Retrd.	1988	40.00	75-125
1989	St. Peter's Cove	Retrd.	1991	1375.00	1500-2500
1993	Stocklebeck Mill - Lilliput Lane	Open		195.00	195
1982	Stone Cottage-Mold 1	Retrd.	1983	40.00	1500
1982	Stone Cottage-Mold 2	Retrd.	1986	40.00	170
1986	Stone Cottage-Mold 3	Retrd.	1986	40.00	200
1987	Stoneybeck	Retrd.	1992	45.00	60-75
1993	Stradling Priory - Lilliput Lane	Open		85.00	85
1990	Strawberry Cottage	Open		35.00	35
1987	Street Scene No. 1 - Unknown	Retrd.	1987	40.00	120
1987	Street Scene No. 2 - Unknown	Retrd.	1987	45.00	120
1987	Street Scene No. 3 - Unknown	Retrd.	1987	45.00	120
1987	Street Scene No. 4 - Unknown	Retrd.	1987	45.00	120
1987	Street Scene No. 5 - Unknown	Retrd.	1987	40.00	120
1987	Street Scene No. 6 - Unknown	Retrd.	1987	40.00	120
1987	Street Scene No. 7 - Unknown	Retrd.	1987	40.00	120
1987	Street Scene No. 8 - Unknown	Retrd.	1987	40.00	120
1987	Street Scene No. 9 - Unknown	Retrd.	1987	45.00	120
1987	Street Scene No. 99 - Unknown	Retrd.	1987	45.00	120
1987	Street Scene Set - Unknown	Retrd.	1987	425.00	800-1000
1990	Sulgrave Manor	Retrd.	1992	120.00	125-195
1987	Summer Haze	Retrd.	1993	90.00	110
1994	Sunnyside - Lilliput Lane	Open		35.00	35
1982	Sussex Mill	Retrd.	1986	25.00	325-450
1988	Swan Inn	Retrd.	1992	120.00	175-225
1994	Sweet Pea Cottage - Lilliput Lane	Open		35.00	35
1988	Swift Hollow	Retrd.	1990	75.00	90
1989	Tanglewood Lodge	Retrd.	1992	97.00	150-200
1987	Tanners Cottage	Retrd.	1992	27.50	45
1994	Teacaddy Cottage - Lilliput Lane	Open		60.00	60
1983	Thatcher's Rest	Retrd.	1988	185.00	250
1986	Three Feathers	Retrd.	1989	115.00	200-250
1991	Tillers Green	Retrd.	1995	60.00	65
1984	Tintagel	Retrd.	1988	39.50	110-170
1994	Tired Timbers - Lilliput Lane	Open		60.00	60

FIGURINES/COTTAGES

YEAR ISSUE		EDITION LIMIT	YEAR RETD.	ISSUE PRICE	*QUOTE U.S.$
1989	Titmouse Cottage	Retrd.	1995	92.50	120
1993	Titwillow Cottage - Lilliput Lane	Open		45.00	45
1983	Toll House	Retrd.	1987	15.00	75-165
1995	Tranquillity	2,500	1995	425.00	425
1983	Troutbeck Farm	Retrd.	1987	125.00	300
1983	Tuck Shop	Retrd.	1986	35.00	650
1986	Tudor Court - Lilliput Lane	Retrd.	1992	260.00	275
1994	Two Hoots - Lilliput Lane	Open		55.00	55
1989	Victoria Cottage	Retrd.	1993	52.50	70
1991	Village School	Open		85.00	85
1983	Warwick Hall-Mold 1	Retrd.	1983	185.00	3000-4000
1983	Warwick Hall-Mold 2	Retrd.	1985	185.00	1300-1800
1985	Watermill	Retrd.	1993	40.00	50-75
1994	Waterside Mill - Lilliput Lane	Open		50.00	50
1987	Wealden House	Retrd.	1990	125.00	140
1992	Wedding Bells - Lilliput Lane	Open		50.00	50
1991	Wellington Lodge	Retrd.	1995	55.00	60
1992	Wheyside Cottage - Lilliput Lane	Open		35.00	35
1989	Wight Cottage	Retrd.	1994	52.50	65
1982	William Shakespeare-Mold 1	Retrd.	1983	55.00	1500-3000
1983	William Shakespeare-Mold 2	Retrd.	1986	55.00	240
1986	William Shakespeare-Mold 3	Retrd.	1989	55.00	215
1989	William Shakespeare-Mold 4	Retrd.	1992	130.00	150
1991	Witham Delph	Retrd.	1994	110.00	120
1983	Woodcutters	Retrd.	1987	15.00	125-150

English Tea Room Collection - Lilliput Lane

1995	Bargate Cottage Tea Room	Open		120.00	120
1995	Bo-Peep Tea Rooms	Open		85.00	85
1995	Grandma Batty's Tea Room	Open		90.00	90
1995	Kendal Tea House	Open		85.00	85
1995	New Forest Teas	Open		120.00	120

Founders Collection - Lilliput Lane

1996	The Almondry	Yr.Iss.		N/A	N/A

Framed English Plaques - D. Tate

1990	Ashdown Hall	Retrd.	1991	59.50	70
1990	Battleview	Retrd.	1991	59.50	70
1990	Cat Slide Cottage	Retrd.	1991	59.50	70
1990	Coombe Cot	Retrd.	1991	59.50	70
1990	Fell View	Retrd.	1991	59.50	70
1990	Flint Fields	Retrd.	1991	59.50	70
1990	Huntingdon House	Retrd.	1991	59.50	70
1990	Jubilee Lodge	Retrd.	1991	59.50	70
1990	Stowside	Retrd.	1991	59.50	70
1990	Trevan Cove	Retrd.	1991	59.50	70

Framed Irish Plaques - D. Tate

1990	Ballyteag House	Retrd.	1991	59.50	70
1990	Crockuna Croft	Retrd.	1991	59.50	70
1990	Pearses Cottages	Retrd.	1991	59.50	70
1990	Shannons Bank	Retrd.	1991	59.50	70

Framed Scottish Plaques - D. Tate

1990	Barra Black House	Retrd.	1991	59.50	70
1990	Fife Ness	Retrd.	1991	59.50	70
1990	Kyle Point	Retrd.	1991	59.50	70
1990	Preston Oat Mill	Retrd.	1991	59.50	70

French Collection - D. Tate

1991	L' Auberge d'Armorique	Open		170.00	170
1991	La Bergerie du Perigord	Open		170.00	170
1991	La Cabane du Gardian	Open		45.00	45
1991	La Chaumiere du Verger	Open		95.00	95
1991	La Maselle de Nadaillac	Open		95.00	95
1991	La Porte Schoenenberg	Open		60.00	60
1991	Le Manoir de Champfleuri	Open		215.00	215
1991	Le Mas du Vigneron	Open		85.00	85
1991	Le Petite Montmartre	Open		95.00	95
1991	Locmaria	Open		50.00	50

German Collection - D. Tate

1992	Alte Schmiede	Open		120.00	120
1987	Das Gebirgskirchlein	Open		120.00	120
1988	Das Rathaus	Open		150.00	150
1992	Der Bücherwurm	Open		100.00	100
1988	Der Familienschrein	Retrd.	1991	52.50	100
1988	Die Kleine Backerei	Retrd.	1994	68.00	80
1987	Haus Im Rheinland	Open		215.00	215
1987	Jaghutte	Open		82.50	85
1987	Meersburger Weinstube	Open		70.00	70
1987	Moselhaus	Open		140.00	150
1987	Nurnberger Burgerhaus	Open		140.00	150
1992	Rosengartenhaus	Open		90.00	90
1987	Schwarzwaldhaus	Open		120.00	120
1992	Strandvogthaus	Open		90.00	90

Historic Castles of England - Lilliput Lane

1994	Bodiam Castle	Open		95.00	95
1994	Castell Coch	Open		120.00	120
1995	Penkill Castles	Open		115.00	115
1994	Stokesay Castle	Open		85.00	85

Irish Cottages - D. Tate

1989	Ballykerne Croft	Retrd.	1996	70.00	70
1987	Donegal Cottage	Retrd.	1992	29.00	60
1989	Hegarty's Home	Retrd.	1992	68.00	75
1989	Kennedy Homestead	Open		30.00	30
1989	Kilmore Quay	Retrd.	1992	68.00	100
1989	Limerick House	Retrd.	1992	110.00	160-170
1989	Magilligans	Open		30.00	30
1989	O'Lacey's Store	Open		60.00	60
1989	Pat Cohan's Bar	Retrd.	1996	85.00	85
1989	Quiet Cottage	Retrd.	1992	72.50	120
1989	St. Columba's School	Open		40.00	40
1989	St. Kevin's Church	Open		55.00	60
1989	St. Patrick's Church	Retrd.	1993	185.00	185
1989	Thoor Ballylee	Retrd.	1992	105.00	160-170

Lakeland Bridge Plaques - D. Simpson

1989	Aira Force	Retrd.	1991	35.00	35
1989	Ashness Bridge	Retrd.	1991	35.00	35
1989	Birks Bridge	Retrd.	1991	35.00	35
1989	Bridge House	Retrd.	1991	35.00	105-120
1989	Hartsop Packhorse	Retrd.	1991	35.00	35
1989	Stockley Bridge	Retrd.	1991	35.00	35

Lakeland Christmas - Lilliput Lane

1995	Langdale Cottage	Open		35.00	35
1995	Patterdale Cottage	Open		35.00	35
1995	Rydal Cottage	Open		35.00	35
1996	All Saints Watermillock	Open		50.00	50
1996	Borrowdale School	Open		35.00	35
1996	Millbeck Cottage	Open		35.00	35

London Plaques - D. Simpson

1989	Big Ben	Retrd.	1991	39.50	40
1989	Buckingham Palace	Retrd.	1991	39.50	40
1989	Piccadilly Circus	Retrd.	1991	39.50	40
1989	Tower Bridge	Retrd.	1991	39.50	40
1989	Tower of London	Retrd.	1991	39.50	40
1989	Trafalgar Square	Retrd.	1991	39.50	40

Scottish Collection - D. Tate, unless otherwise noted

1985	7 St. Andrews Square - A. Yarrington	Retrd.	1986	15.95	85-120
1995	Amisfield Tower - Lilliput Lane	Open		50.00	50
1989	Blair Atholl	Retrd.	1992	275.00	375
1985	Burns Cottage	Retrd.	1988	35.00	70-95
1989	Carrick House	Open		35.00	35
1990	Cawdor Castle	3,000	1992	295.00	300-455
1989	Claypotts Castle	Open		70.00	70
1989	Craigievar Castle	Retrd.	1991	185.00	300-525
1984	The Croft (renovated)	Retrd.	1991	36.00	65-100
1982	The Croft (without sheep)	Retrd.	1984	29.00	800-1250
1989	Culloden Cottage	Open		35.00	35
1992	Culross House	Open		70.00	70
1992	Duart Castle	3,000		450.00	475
1987	East Neuk	Retrd.	1991	29.00	60-75
1993	Edzell Summer House - Lilliput Lane	Open		70.00	70
1990	Eilean Donan	Open		145.00	170
1992	Eriskay Croft	Open		40.00	40
1990	Fishermans Bothy	Open		35.00	35
1990	Glenlochie Lodge	Retrd.	1993	110.00	120
1990	Hebridean Hame	Retrd.	1992	55.00	65-120
1989	Inverlochie Hame	Open		40.00	40
1989	John Knox House	Retrd.	1992	68.00	150-200
1989	Kenmore Cottage	Retrd.	1993	87.00	110
1990	Kinlochness	Retrd.	1993	79.00	85-125
1990	Kirkbrae Cottage	Retrd.	1993	55.00	70-95
1994	Ladybank Lodge - Lilliput Lane	Open		60.00	60
1992	Mair Haven	Open		35.00	35
1985	Preston Mill-Mold 1	Retrd.	1986	45.00	175-200
1986	Preston Mill-Mold 2	Retrd.	1992	62.50	78
1989	Stockwell Tenement	Open		62.50	70

Specials - Various

1985	Bermuda Cottage (3 Colors) - D. Tate	Retrd.	1991	29.00	40-50
1985	Bermuda Cottage (3 Colors)-set - D. Tate	Retrd.	1991	87.00	175-345
1983	Bridge House Dealer Sign - D. Tate	Retrd.	1984	N/A	120-170
1988	Chantry Chapel - D. Tate	Retrd.	1991	N/A	220-265
1983	Cliburn School - D. Tate	Retrd.	1984	Gift	6000-7000
1987	Clockmaker's Cottage - D. Tate	Retrd.	1990	40.00	200-235
1993	Counting House Corner (mounted) - Lilliput Lane	3,093	1993	N/A	N/A
1993	Counting House Corner - Lilliput Lane	3,093	1993	N/A	N/A
1987	Guildhall - D. Tate	Retrd.	1989	N/A	145
1989	Mayflower House - D. Tate	Retrd.	1990	79.50	120-175
1991	Rose Cottage Skirsgill-Mold 1 - Lilliput Lane	200	1991	N/A	700
1991	Rose Cottage Skirsgill-Mold 2 - Lilliput Lane	Retrd.	1991	N/A	250-300
1994	Rose Cottage Skirsgill-Mold 3 - Lilliput Lane	Open		N/A	N/A
1991	Settler's Surprise - Lilliput Lane	Open		135.00	135
1986	Seven Dwarf's Cottage - D. Tate	Retrd.	1986	146.80	500-900
1994	Wycombe Toll House - Lilliput Lane	Retrd.	1994	33.00	240-330

Studley Royal Collection - Lilliput Lane

1994	Banqueting House	5,000		65.00	65
1995	Fountains Abbey	3,500		395.00	395
1994	Octagon Tower	5,000		85.00	85
1994	St. Mary's Church	5,000		115.00	115
1994	Temple of Piety	5,000		95.00	95

Unframed Plaques - D. Tate

1989	Large Lower Brockhampton	Retrd.	1991	120.00	120
1989	Large Somerset Springtime	Retrd.	1991	130.00	130
1989	Medium Cobble Combe Cottage	Retrd.	1991	68.00	68
1989	Medium Wishing Well	Retrd.	1991	75.00	75
1989	Small Stoney Wall Lea	Retrd.	1991	47.50	48
1989	Small Woodside Farm	Retrd.	1991	47.50	48

Village Shop Collection - Various

1995	The Baker's Shop	Open		85.00	85
1995	The Chine Shop	Open		85.00	85
1992	The Greengrocers - D. Tate	Open		80.00	80
1993	Jones The Butcher	Open		80.00	80
1992	Penny Sweets	Open		80.00	80
1993	Toy Shop	Open		80.00	80

Welsh Collection - Various

1986	Brecon Bach - D. Tate	Retrd.	1993	42.00	65
1991	Bro Dawel - D. Tate	Open		30.00	30
1985	Hermitage - D. Tate	Retrd.	1986	30.00	175-300
1987	Hermitage Renovated - D. Tate	Retrd.	1990	42.50	100
1992	St. Govan's Chapel	Open		50.00	50
1991	Tudor Merchant - D. Tate	Open		70.00	70
1991	Ugly House - D. Tate	Open		50.00	50

A Year In An English Garden - Lilliput Lane

1994	Autumn Hues	Open		85.00	85
1995	Spring Glory	Open		85.00	85
1995	Summer Impressions	Open		85.00	85
1994	Winter's Wonder	Open		85.00	85

Lladró

Lladró Collectors Society - Lladró

1985	Little Pals S7600	Closed	1985	95.00	2300-330
1985	LCS Plaque w/blue writing S7601	Closed	N/A	35.00	75-10
1986	Little Traveler S7602	Closed	1986	95.00	1350-180
1987	Spring Bouquets S7603	Closed	1987	125.00	700-100
1988	School Days S7604	Closed	1988	125.00	525-80
1988	Flower Song S7607	Closed	1988	175.00	525-72
1989	My Buddy S7609	Closed	1989	145.00	250-60
1990	Can I Play? S7610	Closed	1990	150.00	375-60
1991	Summer Stroll S7611	Closed	1992	195.00	245-45
1991	Picture Perfect S7612	Closed	1991	350.00	350-70
1992	All Aboard S7619	Closed	1993	165.00	250-50
1993	Best Friend S7620	Closed	1993	195.00	250-37
1994	Basket of Love S7622	Closed	1994	225.00	275-40
1995	10 Year Society Anniversary - Ten and Growing S7635	6/96		395.00	39
1995	Afternoon Promenade S7636	6/96		240.00	24
1995	Now and Forever (10 year membership piece) S7642	N/A		395.00	39
1996	Innocence In Bloom S7644	Yr.Iss.		250.00	25
1996	Where Love Begins w/base S7649	4,000		895.00	89

Lladró Event Figurines - Lladró

1991	Garden Classic L7617G	Closed	1991	295.00	500-75
1992	Garden Song L7618G	Closed	1992	295.00	300-60
1993	Pick of the Litter L7621G	Closed	1993	350.00	375-50
1994	Little Riders L7623P	Closed	1994	250.00	275-35
1995	For A Perfect Performance L7641	Closed	1995	310.00	350-50

Capricho - Lladró

1988	Bust w/ Black Veil & base C1538	Open		650.00	97
1988	Small Bust w/ Veil & base C1539	Open		225.00	45
1987	Orchid Arrangement C1541	Closed	1990	500.00	1700-210
1987	Iris Arrangement C1542	Closed	1990	800.00	1000-150
1987	Fan C1546	Closed	1987	650.00	900-160
1987	Fan C1546.3	Closed	1987	650.00	900-160
1987	Iris with Vase C1551	Closed	1991	110.00	37
1987	Flowers Chest C1572	Open		550.00	90
1987	Flat Basket with Flowers C1575	Closed	1991	450.00	85
1989	White Rosary C1647	Closed	1991	290.00	36
1989	Romantic Lady / Black Veil w/base C1666	Closed	1993	420.00	52
1969	Frosted Angel w/Guitar C4507	Closed	1985	55.00	32
XX	White Bust w/ Veil & base C5927	Open		550.00	86
XX	Special Museum Flower Basket C7606	Closed	1991	N/A	30

Limited Edition - Lladró

1971	Hamlet LL1144	750	1973	125.00	2500-450
1971	Othello and Desdemona LL1145	750	1973	275.00	250
1971	Antique Auto LL1146	750	1975	1000.00	7000-110
1971	Floral LL1184	200	1978	400.00	220
1971	Floral LL1185	200	1974	475.00	180
1971	Floral LL1186	200	1976	575.00	220
1972	Eagles LL1189	750	1978	450.00	32
1972	Sea Birds with Nest LL1194	500	1975	300.00	275
1972	Turkey Group LL1196	350	1982	325.00	180
1972	Peace LL1202	150	1973	550.00	750
1972	Eagle Owl LL1223	750	1983	225.00	10
1972	Hansom Carriage LL1225	750	1975	1450.00	8000-150
1973	Buck Hunters LL1238	800	1976	400.00	30
1973	Turtle Doves LL1240	850	1976	250.00	2300-25
1973	The Forest LL1243	500	1976	625.00	33
1974	Soccer Players LL1266	500	1983	1000.00	75
1974	Man From LaMancha LL1269	1,500	1977	700.00	38
1974	Queen Elizabeth II LL1275	250	1985	3650.00	50
1974	Judge LL1281	1,200	1978	325.00	12
1974	Partridge LL1290G	800	1974	700.00	27
1974	The Hunt LL1308	750	1984	4750.00	69
1974	Ducks at Pond LL1317	1,200	1984	4250.00	57

*Quotes have been rounded up to nearest dolla

YEAR ISSUE		EDITION LIMIT	YEAR RETD.	ISSUE PRICE	*QUOTE U.S.$
976	Impossible Dream LL1318	1,000	1983	1200.00	4400
976	Comforting Baby LL1329	750	1978	350.00	1050
976	Mountain Country Lady LL1330	750	1983	900.00	1700
976	My Baby LL1331	1,000	1981	275.00	900
978	Flight of Gazelles LL1352	1,500	1984	1225.00	3100
978	Car in Trouble LL1375	1,500	1987	3000.00	5250
978	Fearful Flight LL1377	750		7000.00	14500
978	Henry VIII LL 1384	1,200	1993	650.00	1000-1250
981	Venus and Cupid LL1392	750	1993	1100.00	1600-2100
982	First Date w/base LL1393	1,500		3800.00	5900
982	Columbus LL1432G	1,200	1988	535.00	1300-1700
983	Venetian Serenade LL1433	750	1989	2600.00	3900
985	Festival in Valencia w/base LL1457	3,000	1994	1400.00	2350
985	Camelot LL1458	3,000	1994	950.00	1500
985	Napoleon Planning Battle w/base LL1459	1,500	1995	825.00	1450
985	Youthful Beauty w/base LL1461	5,000		750.00	1200
985	Flock of Birds w/base LL1462	1,500		1060.00	1750
985	Classic Spring LL1465	1,500	1995	620.00	975
985	Classic Fall LL1466	1,500	1995	620.00	975
985	Valencian Couple on Horse LL1472	3,000		885.00	1550
985	Coach XVIII Century w/base LL1485	500		14000.00	26000
986	The New World w/base LL1486	4,000		700.00	1350
986	Fantasia w/base LL1487	5,000		1500.00	2700
986	Floral Offering w/base LL1490	3,000		2500.00	4450
986	Oriental Music w/base LL1491	5,000		1350.00	2445
986	Three Sisters w/base LL1492	3,000		1850.00	3250
986	At the Stroke of Twelve w/base LL1493	1,500	N/A	4250.00	6300-7500
986	Hawaiian Festival w/base LL1496	4,000		1850.00	3200
987	A Sunday Drive w/base LL1510	1,000		3400.00	4000
987	Listen to Don Quixote w/base LL1520	750		1800.00	2900
987	A Happy Encounter LL1523	1,500		2900.00	4900
988	Japanese Vase LL1536	750	1989	2600.00	3250
988	Garden Party w/base LL1578	500		5500.00	7250
988	Blessed Lady w/base LL1579	1,000	1991	1150.00	3000
988	Return to La Mancha w/base LL1580	500		6400.00	8350
989	Southern Tea LL1597	1,000	1995	1775.00	2300
989	Kitakami Cruise w/base LL1605	500	N/A	5800.00	7500
989	Mounted Warriors w/base LL1608	500		2850.00	3450
989	Circus Parade w/base LL1609	1,000		5200.00	6550
989	"Jesus the Rock" w/base LL1615	1,000		1175.00	1550
989	Hopeful Group LL1723	1,000	1993	1825.00	1825
991	Valencian Cruise LL1731	1,000		2700.00	2950
991	Venice Vows LL1732	1,500		3755.00	4100
991	Liberty Eagle LL1738	1,500		1000.00	1100
991	Heavenly Swing LL1739	1,000		1900.00	2050
991	Columbus, Two Routes LL1740	1,000	1995	1500.00	1650
991	Columbus Reflecting LL1741	1,000	1994	1850.00	1995
991	Onward! LL1742	1,000	1993	2500.00	2500
991	The Prophet LL1743	300		800.00	875
991	My Only Friend LL1744	200	1993	1400.00	1700-2000
991	Dawn LL1745	N/A	1993	1200.00	2500
991	Champion LL1746	300	1994	1800.00	1950
991	Nesting Doves LL1747	300	1994	800.00	875
991	Comforting News LL1748	300		1200.00	1325
991	Baggy Pants LL1749	300	1994	1500.00	1650
991	Circus Show LL1750	300	1994	1400.00	1525
991	Maggie LL1751	300	1994	900.00	990
991	Apple Seller LL1752	300	1994	900.00	1000-1150
991	The Student LL1753	300		1300.00	1425
991	Tree Climbers LL1754	300	1994	1500.00	1650
991	The Princess And The Unicorn LL1755	1,500	1994	1750.00	1800-2000
1991	Outing In Seville LL1756	500		23000.00	24500
1992	Hawaiian Ceremony LL1757	1,000		9800.00	10250
1992	Circus Time LL1758	2,500		9200.00	9650
1992	Tea In The Garden LL1759	2,000		9500.00	9750
1993	Paella Valenciano w/base LL1762	500		10000.00	10000
1993	Trusting Friends w/base LL1763	350		1200.00	1200
1993	He's My Brother w/base LL1764	350		1500.00	1500
1993	The Course of Adventure LL1765	250		1625.00	1625
1993	Ties That Bind LL1766	250		1700.00	1700
1993	Motherly Love LL1767	250		1330.00	1330
1993	Travellers' Respite w/base LL1768	250		1825.00	1825
1993	Fruitful Harvest LL1769	350		1300.00	1300
1993	Gypsy Dancers LL1770	250		2250.00	2400
1993	Country Doctor w/base LL1771	250		1475.00	1475
1993	Back To Back LL1772	350		1450.00	1450
1993	Mischevous Musician LL1773	350		975.00	1045
1993	A Treasured Moment w/base LL1774	350		950.00	950
1993	Oriental Garden w/base LL1775	750		22500.00	22500
1994	Conquered by Love w/base LL1776	2,500		2850.00	2890
1994	Farewell Of The Samurai w/base LL1777	2,500		3950.00	3950
1994	Pegasus w/base LL1778	1,500		1950.00	1950
1994	High Speed w/base LL1779	1,500		3830.00	3830
1994	Indian Princess w/base LL1780	3,000		1630.00	1630
1994	Allegory of Time LL1781	5,000		1290.00	1290
1994	Circus Fanfare w/base LL1783	1,500		14240.00	14240
1994	Flower Wagon w/base LL1784	3,000		3290.00	3290
1994	Cinderella's Arrival w/base LL1785	1,500		25950.00	25950
1994	Floral Figure w/base LL1788	300		2198.00	2198
1994	Natural Beauty LL1795	500		650.00	650
1994	Floral Enchantment w/base LL1796	300		2990.00	2990
1995	Enchanted Outing w/base LL1797	3,000		3950.00	3950
1995	Far Away Thoughts LL1798	1,500		3600.00	3600
1995	Immaculate Virgin w/base LL1799	2,000		2250.00	2250
1995	To the Rim w/base LL1800	1,500		2475.00	2475
1995	Vision of Peace w/base LL1803	1,500		1895.00	1895
1995	Portrait of a Family w/base LL1805	2,500		1750.00	1750
1995	A Family of Love w/base LL1806	2,500		1750.00	1750
1995	A Dream of Peace w/base LL1807	2,000		1160.00	1160
1996	Noah w/base LL1809	1,200		1720.00	1720
1996	Easter Fantasy w/base LL1810	1,000		3500.00	3500
1996	Moses & The Ten Commandments w/base LL1811	1,200		1860.00	1860
1996	La Menina w/base LL1812	1,000		3850.00	3850
1970	Girl with Guitar LL2016	750	1982	325.00	1800
1970	Madonna with Child LL2018	300	1974	450.00	1750
1971	Oriental Man LL2021	500	1983	500.00	1850
1971	Three Girls LL2028	500	1976	950.00	3500
1971	Eve at Tree LL2029	600	1976	450.00	3000
1971	Oriental Horse LL2030	350	1983	1100.00	3500-5000
1971	Lyric Muse LL2031	400	1982	750.00	2100
1971	Madonna and Child LL2043	300	1974	400.00	1500
1973	Peasant Woman LL2049	750	1977	200.00	1300
1973	Passionate Dance LL2051	500	1975	375.00	4500
1977	St. Theresa LL2061	1,200	1987	387.50	1400-1600
1977	Concerto LL2063	1,200	1988	500.00	1235
1977	Flying Partridges LL2064	1,200	1987	1750.00	4300
1987	Christopher Columbus w/base LL2176	1,000	1994	1000.00	1350
1990	Invincible w/base LL2188	300		1100.00	1250
1993	Flight of Fancy w/base LL2243	300		1400.00	1400
1993	The Awakening w/base LL2244	300		1200.00	1200
1993	Inspired Voyage w/base LL2245	1,000		4800.00	4800
1993	Days of Yore w/base LL2248	1,000		1950.00	2050
1993	Holiday Glow w/base LL2249	1,500		750.00	750
1993	Autumn Glow w/base LL2250	1,500		750.00	750
1993	Humble Grace w/base LL2255	2,000		2150.00	2150
1983	Dawn w/base LL3000	300		325.00	550
1983	Monks w/base LL3001	300	1993	1675.00	2550
1983	Waiting w/base LL3002	125	1991	1550.00	1900
1983	Indolence LL3003	150		1465.00	2100
1983	Venus in the Bath LL3005	N/A	1991	1175.00	1450
1987	Classic Beauty w/base LL3012	500		1300.00	1750
1987	Youthful Innocence w/base LL3013	500		1300.00	1750
1987	The Nymph w/base LL3014	250		1000.00	1450
1987	Dignity w/base LL3015	150		1400.00	1900
1988	Passion w/base LL3016	750		865.00	1200
1988	Muse w/base LL3017	300	1993	650.00	875
1988	Cellist w/base LL3018	300	1993	650.00	875
1988	True Affection w/base LL3019	300		750.00	1025
1989	Demureness w/base LL3020	300	1994	400.00	700
1990	Daydreaming w/base LL3022	500		550.00	775
1990	After The Bath w/base LL3023	300	1991	350.00	1350
1990	Discoveries w/Base LL3024	100		1500.00	1750
1991	Resting Nude LL3025	200	1992	650.00	1000
1991	Unadorned Beauty LL3026	200		1700.00	1850
1994	Ebony w/base LL3027	300		1295.00	1295
1994	Modesty w/base LL3028	300		1295.00	1295
1994	Danae LL3029	300		2880.00	2880
1995	Nude Kneeling LL3030	300		975.00	975
1982	Elk LL3501	500	1987	950.00	1200
1978	Nude with Dove LL3503	1,500	1981	250.00	700-1100
1981	The Rescue LL3504	1,500	1987	2900.00	5000
1978	St. Michael w/base LL3515	1,500		2200.00	4690
1980	Turtle Dove Nest w/base LL3519	1,200	1994	3600.00	6050
1980	Turtle Dove Group w/base LL3520	750		6800.00	11900
1981	Philippine Folklore LL3522	1,500	1995	1450.00	2400
1981	Nest of Eagles w/base LL3523	300	1994	6900.00	11500
1981	Drum Beats/Watusi Queen w/base LL3524	1,500	1994	1875.00	3050
1982	Togetherness LL3527	75	1987	375.00	900
1982	Wrestling LL3528	50	1987	950.00	1125
1983	Companionship w/base LL3529	65		1000.00	1790
1983	Anxiety w/base LL3530	125	1993	1075.00	1875
1983	Victory LL3531	90	1988	1500.00	1800
1983	Plentitude LL3532	50	1988	1000.00	1375
1983	The Observer w/base LL3533	115	1993	900.00	1650
1983	In the Distance LL3534	75	1988	525.00	1275
1983	Slave LL3535	50	1988	950.00	1150
1983	Relaxation LL3536	100	1988	525.00	1000
1983	Dreaming w/base LL3537	250	1994	475.00	1475
1983	Youth LL3538	250	1988	525.00	1120
1983	Dantiness LL3539	100	1988	1000.00	1400
1983	Pose LL3540	100	1988	1250.00	1450
1983	Tranquility LL3541	75	1988	1000.00	1400
1983	Yoga LL3542	125	1991	650.00	900
1983	Demure LL3543	100	1988	1250.00	1700
1983	Reflections w/base LL3544	75		650.00	1050
1983	Adoration LL3545	150	1990	1050.00	1600
1983	African Woman LL3546	50	1988	1300.00	2000
1983	Reclining Nude LL3547	75	1988	650.00	875
1983	Serenity w/base LL3548	300	1993	925.00	1550
1983	Reposing LL3549	80	1988	425.00	575
1983	Boxer w/base LL3550	300	1993	850.00	1450
1983	Bather LL3551	300	1988	975.00	1300
1982	Blue God LL3552	1,500	1994	900.00	1575
1982	Fire Bird LL3553	1,500	1994	800.00	1350
1982	Desert People w/base LL3555	750		1680.00	3100
1982	Road to Mandalay LL3556	750	1989	1390.00	2500
1982	Jesus in Tiberias w/base LL3557	1,200		2600.00	4910
1992	The Reader LL3560	200		2650.00	2815
1993	Trail Boss LL3561M	1,500		2450.00	2595
1993	Indian Brave LL3562M	1,500		2250.00	2250
1994	Saint James The Apostle w/base LL3563	1,000		950.00	950
1994	Gentle Moment w/base LL3564	1,000		1795.00	1835
1994	At Peace w/base LL3565	1,000		1650.00	170
1994	Indian Chief w/base LL3566	3,000		1095.00	1095
1994	Trapper w/base LL3567	3,000		950.00	950
1994	American Cowboy w/base LL3568	3,000		950.00	950
1994	A Moment's Pause w/base LL3569	3,500		1495.00	1635
1994	Ethereal Music w/base LL3570	1,000		2450.00	2500
1994	At The Helm w/base LL3571	3,500		1495.00	1495
1996	Playing the Blues w/base LL3576	1,000		2160.00	2160
1995	Proud Warrior w/base LL3572	3,000		995.00	995
1995	Golgotha w/base LL3773	1, 000		1650.00	1650
1985	Napoleon Bonaparte LL 5338	5,000	1994	275.00	650
1985	Beethoven w/base LL 5339	3,000	1993	760.00	1300
1985	Thoroughbred Horse w/base LL5340	1,000	1993	625.00	1000
1985	I Have Found Thee, Dulcinea LL5341	750	1990	1460.00	2800
1985	Pack of Hunting Dogs w/base LL5342	3,000	1994	925.00	2000
1985	Love Boat w/base LL5343	3,000		825.00	1350
1986	Fox Hunt w/base LL5362	1,000		5200.00	8750
1986	Rey De Copas w/base LL5366	2,000	1993	325.00	600
1986	Rey De Oros w/base LL5367	2,000	1993	325.00	600
1986	Rey De Espadas w/base LL5368	2,000	1993	325.00	600
1986	Rey De Bastos w/base LL5369	2,000	1993	325.00	600
1986	Pastoral Scene w/base LL5386	750	1995	1100.00	2290
1987	Inspiration LL5413	500	1993	1200.00	2100
1987	Carnival Time w/base LL5423	1,000	1993	2400.00	3900
1989	"Pious" LL5541	N/A	1991	1075.00	1550
1989	Freedom LL5602	1,500	1989	875.00	950
1990	A Ride In The Park LL5718	N/A	1991	3200.00	3500
1991	Youth LL5800	500	1993	650.00	725
1991	Charm LL5801	500	1994	650.00	725
1991	New World Medallion LL5808	5,000	1994	200.00	225
1992	The Voyage of Columbus LL5847	7,500	1994	1450.00	1450-1650
1992	Sorrowful Mother LL5849	1,500		1750.00	1850
1992	Justice Eagle LL5863	1,500		1700.00	1840
1992	Maternal Joy LL5864	1,500		1600.00	1700
1992	Motoring In Style LL5884	1,500		3700.00	3850
1992	The Way Of The Cross LL5890	2,000		975.00	1050
1992	Presenting Credentials LL5911	1,500		19500.00	20500
1992	Young Mozart LL5915	2,500	1994	500.00	1000-1600
1993	Jester's Serenade w/base LL5932	3,000		1995.00	2000
1993	The Blessing w/base LL5942	2,000		1345.00	1345
1993	Our Lady of Rocio w/base LL5951	2,000		3500.00	3500
1993	Where to Sir w/base LL5952	1,500		5250.00	5250
1993	Discovery Mug LL5967	1,992	1994	90.00	90
1993	Graceful Moment w/base LL6033	3,000		1475.00	1475
1993	The Hand of Justice w/base LL6033	1,000		1250.00	1250
1992	Tinkerbell LL7518	1,000		350.00	2300-2900
1993	Peter Pan LL7529	3,000		400.00	1000-1500
1994	Cinderella and Fairy Godmother LL7553G	2,500	1994	875.00	900-1000
1995	Abraham Lincoln w/base LL7554	2,500		2190.00	2190
1994	Sleeping Beauty Dance LL7560	1,000	1995	1280.00	1600-2300

Lladró - Lladró

YEAR ISSUE		EDITION LIMIT	YEAR RETD.	ISSUE PRICE	*QUOTE U.S.$
1963	Hunting Dog 308.13	Closed	N/A	N/A	2000
1966	Poodle 325.13	Closed	N/A	N/A	2300
1970	Girl with Pigtails L357.13G	Closed	N/A	N/A	1100
1969	Shepherdess with Goats L1001G	Closed	1987	80.00	675
1969	Shepherdess with Goats L1001M	Closed	1987	80.00	450
1969	Girl's Head L1003G	Closed	1985	150.00	675
1969	Girl's Head L1003M	Closed	1985	150.00	700-900
1969	Pan with Cymbals L1006	Closed	1975	45.00	500-650
1969	Girl With Lamb L1010G	Closed	1993	26.00	200-275
1969	Girl With Pig L1011G	Open		13.00	90
1969	Centaur Girl L1012M	Closed	1989	45.00	375-425
1969	Centaur Boy L1013M	Closed	1989	45.00	400-450
1969	Two Women w/Water Jugs L1014G	Closed	1985	85.00	650
1969	Dove L1015 G	Closed	1994	21.00	105
1969	Dove L1016 G	Closed	1995	36.00	190
1969	Idyl L1017G	Closed	1991	115.00	650
1969	Idyl L1017M	Closed	1991	115.00	550-615
1969	King Gaspar L1018M	Open		345.00	1895
1969	King Melchior L1019M	Open		345.00	1850
1969	King Baltasar L1020M	Open		345.00	1850
1969	Horse Group L1021G	Closed	1975	950.00	1600
1969	Horse Group/All White L1022M	Open		465.00	2100
1969	Flute Player L1025G	Closed	1978	73.00	700
1969	Clown with Concertina L1027G	Closed	1993	95.00	700
1969	Don Quixote w/Stand L1030G	Open		225.00	1450
1969	Sancho Panza L1031G	Closed	1989	65.00	450-550
1969	Old Folks L1033G	Closed	1985	140.00	1400
1969	Old Folks L1033M	Closed	1985	140.00	1400
1969	Shepherdess with Dog L1034	Closed	1991	30.00	225-275
1969	Girl with Geese L1035G	Closed	1995	37.50	180
1969	Girl With Geese L1035M	Closed	1992	37.50	165
1969	Horseman L1037G	Closed	1970	170.00	2500
1969	Girl with Turkeys L1038G	Closed	1978	95.00	650
1969	Violinist and Girl L1039G	Closed	1991	120.00	950-1200
1969	Violinist and Girl L1039M	Closed	1991	120.00	825-1000
1969	Hunters L1048	Closed	1986	115.00	1200-1400
1969	Del Monte (Boy) L1050	Closed	1978	65.00	N/A
1969	Girl with Duck L1052G	Open		30.00	205
1969	Girl with Duck L1052M	Closed	1992	30.00	190
1969	Bird L1053G	Closed	1985	13.00	100

*Quotes have been rounded up to nearest dollar

FIGURINES/COTTAGES

YEAR ISSUE		EDITION LIMIT	YEAR RETD.	ISSUE PRICE	*QUOTE U.S.$
1969	Bird L1054G	Closed	1985	14.00	125
1969	Duck L1056G	Closed	1978	19.00	275
1969	Girl with Pheasant L1055G	Closed	1978	105.00	N/A
1969	Panchito L1059	Closed	1980	28.00	N/A
1969	Deer L1064	Closed	1986	27.50	325
1969	Fox and Cub L1065G	Closed	1985	17.50	400
1969	Basset L1066G	Closed	1981	23.50	500
1969	Old dog L1067G	Closed	1978	40.00	400-500
1969	Afghan (sitting) L1069G	Closed	1985	36.00	575
1969	Beagle Puppy L1070G	Closed	1991	16.50	225-350
1969	Beagle Puppy L1071G	Closed	1992	16.50	225-300
1969	Beagle Puppy L1071M	Closed	1992	16.50	200-250
1969	Beagle Puppy L1072G	Closed	1991	16.50	225-300
1969	Dutch Girl L1077G	Closed	1981	57.50	250-450
1969	Herald L1078G	Closed	1970	110.00	1100
1969	Girl With Brush L1081G	Closed	1985	14.50	300
1969	Girl Manicuring L1082G	Closed	1985	14.50	300
1969	Girl With Doll L1083G	Closed	1985	14.50	300
1969	Girl with Mother's Shoe L1084G	Closed	1985	14.50	300
1969	Little Green-Grocer L1087G	Closed	1981	40.00	375
1969	Girl Seated with Flowers L1088G	Closed	1989	45.00	700
1971	Lawyer (Face) L1089G	Closed	1973	35.00	950
1971	Girl and Gazelle L1091G	Closed	1975	225.00	1200
1971	Satyr with Snail L1092G	Closed	1975	30.00	425
1969	Beggar L1094G	Closed	1981	65.00	400-650
1971	Girl With Hens L1103G	Closed	1981	50.00	375
1971	La Tarantela L1123G	Closed	1975	550.00	2250
1971	Pelusa Clown L1125G	Closed	1978	70.00	875-1150
1971	Clown with Violin L1126G	Closed	1978	71.00	1400
1971	Puppy Love L1127G	Open		50.00	310
1971	Dog in the Basket L1128G	Closed	1985	17.50	450
1971	Faun L1131G	Closed	1972	155.00	1200
1971	Horse L1133G	Closed	1972	115.00	900
1971	Bull L1134G	Closed	1972	130.00	1500
1971	Dog and Snail L1139G	Closed	1981	40.00	270
1971	Girl with Bonnet L1147G	Closed	1985	20.00	275
1971	Girl Shampooing L1148G	Closed	1985	20.00	375
1971	Dog's Head L1149G	Closed	1981	27.50	400
1971	Elephants (3) L1150G	Open		100.00	795
1971	Elephants (2) L1151G	Open		45.00	420
1971	Dog Playing Guitar L1152G	Closed	1978	32.50	375-550
1971	Dog Playing Guitar L1153G	Closed	1978	32.50	400-550
1971	Dog Playing Bass Fiddle L1154G	Closed	1978	36.50	400-550
1971	Dog w/Microphone L1155G	Closed	1978	35.00	400-550
1971	Dog Playing Bongos L1156	Closed	1978	32.50	400-550
1971	Seated Torero L1162G	Closed	1973	35.00	700
1971	Kissing Doves L1169G	Open		32.00	145
1971	Kissing Doves L1169M	Closed	N/A	32.00	150
1971	Kissing Doves L1170G	Closed	1988	25.00	250
1971	Girl With Flowers L1172G	Closed	1993	27.00	350
1971	Girl With Domino L1175G	Closed	1981	34.00	350
1971	Girl With Dice L1176G	Closed	1981	25.00	350
1971	Girl With Ball L1177G	Closed	1981	27.50	350-450
1971	Girl With Accordian L1178G	Closed	1981	34.00	350-450
1971	Clown on Domino L1179G	Closed	1981	34.00	300
1971	Platero and Marcelino L1181G	Closed	1981	50.00	450
1972	Little Girl with Cat L1187G	Closed	1989	37.00	375
1972	Boy Meets Girl L1188G	Closed	1989	310.00	400
1972	Eskimo L1195G	Open		30.00	135
1972	Horse Resting L1203G	Closed	1981	40.00	300-450
1972	Attentive Bear, brown L1204G	Closed	1989	16.00	125
1972	Good Bear, brown L1205G	Closed	1989	16.00	120
1972	Bear Seated, brown L1206G	Closed	1989	16.00	100-125
1972	Attentive Polar Bear, white L1207G	Open		16.00	75
1972	Bear, white L1208G	Open		16.00	75
1972	Bear, white L1209G	Open		16.00	75
1972	Round Fish L1210G	Closed	1981	35.00	450
1972	Girl With Doll L1211G	Closed	1993	72.00	440
1972	Woman Carrying Water L1212G	Closed	1983	100.00	475
1972	Little Jug Magno L1222.3G	Closed	1979	35.00	300
1972	Young Harlequin L1229G	Open		70.00	520
1972	Friendship L1230G	Closed	1991	68.00	475
1972	Friendship L1230M	Closed	1991	68.00	325
1972	Angel with Lute L1231G	Closed	1988	60.00	400
1972	Angel with Clarinet L1232G	Closed	1988	60.00	400
1972	Angel with Flute L1233G	Closed	1988	60.00	400-450
1972	Little Jesus of Prag L1234G	Closed	1978	70.00	725
1973	Christmas Carols L1239G	Closed	1981	125.00	750
1973	Girl with Wheelbarrow L1245G	Closed	1981	75.00	500-650
1973	Caress and Rest L1246G	Closed	1990	50.00	300
1974	Happy Harlequin L1247M	Closed	1983	220.00	800-1200
1974	Honey Lickers L1248G	Closed	1990	100.00	500
1974	The Race L1249G	Closed	1988	450.00	1800-2250
1974	Lovers from Verona L 1250G	Closed	1990	330.00	1300-1600
1974	Pony Ride L1251G	Closed	1979	220.00	1200
1974	Shepherd L1252G	Closed	1981	100.00	N/A
1974	Sad Chimney Sweep L1253G	Closed	1983	180.00	1200
1974	Hamlet and Yorick L1254G	Closed	1983	325.00	1100-1200
1974	Seesaw L1255G	Closed	1993	110.00	575
1974	Mother with Pups L1257G	Closed	1981	50.00	800
1974	Playing Poodles L1258G	Closed	1981	47.50	800
1974	Poodle L1259G	Closed	1985	27.50	300-400
1974	Flying Duck L1263G	Open		20.00	90
1974	Flying Duck L1264G	Open		20.00	90
1974	Flying Duck L1265G	Open		20.00	90
1974	Girl with Ducks L1267G	Closed	1993	55.00	300
1974	Reminiscing L1270G	Closed	1988	975.00	1375
1974	Thoughts L1272G	Open		87.50	3490
1974	Lovers in the Park L1274G	Closed	1993	450.00	1365
1974	Christmas Seller L1276G	Closed	1981	120.00	550-750
1974	Feeding Time L1277G	Closed	1993	120.00	350
1974	Feeding Time L1277M	Closed	N/A	120.00	415

YEAR ISSUE		EDITION LIMIT	YEAR RETD.	ISSUE PRICE	*QUOTE U.S.$
1974	Devotion L1278G	Closed	1990	140.00	475
1974	The Wind L1279M	Open		250.00	250
1974	Playtime L1280G	Closed	1983	110.00	550-700
1974	Afghan Standing L1282G	Closed	1985	45.00	500
1974	Little Gardener L1283G	Open		250.00	785
1974	"My Flowers" L1284G	Open		200.00	550
1974	"My Goodness" L1285G	Closed	1995	190.00	415
1974	Flower Harvest L1286G	Open		200.00	495
1974	Picking Flowers L1287G	Open		170.00	440
1974	Aggressive Duck L1288G	Closed	1995	170.00	475
1974	Good Puppy L1289G	Closed	1985	16.60	225
1974	Victorian Girl on Swing L1297G	Closed	1990	520.00	1650
1974	Birds Resting L1298G	Closed	1985	235.00	975
1974	Birds in Nest L1299G	Closed	1985	120.00	750
1974	Valencian Lady w/Flowers L1304G	Open		200.00	625
1974	"On the Farm" L1306G	Closed	1990	130.00	240
1974	Ducklings L1307G	Open		47.50	150
1974	Girl with Cats L1309G	Open		120.00	310
1974	Girl with Puppies in Basket L1311G	Open		120.00	345
1974	Schoolgirl L1313G	Closed	1990	201.00	600
1974	Girl From Scotland L1315G	Closed	1979	450.00	2800
1976	Collie L1316G	Closed	1981	45.00	400
1976	IBIS L1319G	Open		1550.00	2625
1977	Angel with Tamborine L1320G	Closed	1985	125.00	350-450
1977	Angel with Lyre L1321G	Closed	1985	125.00	475
1977	Angel with Song L1322G	Closed	1985	125.00	475
1977	Angel with Accordian L1323G	Closed	1985	125.00	400
1977	Angel with Mandolin L1324G	Closed	1985	125.00	400
1976	The Helmsman L1325M	Closed	1988	600.00	900-1200
1976	Playing Cards L1327 M, numbered series	Open		3800.00	6600
1977	Dove Group L1335G	Closed	1990	950.00	1600
1977	Blooming Roses L1339G	Closed	1988	325.00	550
1977	Male Jockey L1341G	Closed	1979	120.00	450
1977	Wrath of Don Quixote L1343G	Closed	1990	250.00	800-1000
1977	Derby L1344G	Closed	1985	1125.00	2500
1978	Sacristan L1345G	Closed	1979	385.00	2300
1978	Under the Willow L1346G	Closed	1990	1600.00	2150
1978	Mermaid on Wave L1347G	Closed	1983	425.00	1800
1978	Mermaids Playing L1349G	Closed	1983	Unkn.	3250
1978	In the Gondola L1350G, numbered series	Open		1850.00	3250
1978	Lady with Girl L1353G	Closed	1985	175.00	700
1978	Growing Roses L1354G	Closed	1988	485.00	635
1978	Phyllis L1356G	Closed	1993	75.00	225
1978	Shelley L1357G	Closed	1993	75.00	175
1978	Beth L1358G	Closed	1993	75.00	225
1978	Heather L1359G	Closed	1993	75.00	225
1978	Laura L1360G	Closed	1993	75.00	225
1978	Julia L1361G	Closed	1993	75.00	185
1978	Swinging L1366G	Closed	1988	825.00	1375
1978	Playful Dogs L1367	Closed	1982	160.00	700
1978	Spring Birds L1368G	Closed	1990	1600.00	2500
1978	Anniversary Waltz L1372G	Open		260.00	570
1978	Chestnut Seller L1373G	Closed	1981	800.00	750-900
1978	Waiting in the Park L1374G	Closed	1993	235.00	450
1978	Watering Flowers L1376G	Closed	1990	400.00	1150
1978	Suzy and Her Doll L1378G	Closed	1985	215.00	625
1978	Debbie and Her Doll L1379G	Closed	1985	215.00	600
1978	Cathy and Her Doll L1380G	Closed	1985	215.00	600-800
1978	Medieval Girl L1381G	Closed	1985	11.80	400-600
1978	Medieval Boy L1382G	Closed	1985	235.00	650-700
1978	A Rickshaw Ride L1383G	Open		1500.00	2150
1978	The Brave Knight L1385G	Closed	1988	350.00	750
1981	St. Joseph L1386G	Open		250.00	385
1981	Mary L1387G	Open		240.00	385
1981	Baby Jesus L1388G	Open		85.00	140
1981	Donkey L1389G	Open		95.00	190
1981	Cow L1390G	Open		95.00	190
1982	Holy Mary L1394G, numbered series	Open		1000.00	1475
1982	Full of Mischief L1395G	Open		420.00	825
1982	Appreciation L1396G	Open		420.00	825
1982	Second Thoughts L1397G	Open		420.00	820
1982	Reverie L1398G	Open		490.00	970
1982	Dutch Woman with Tulips L1399G	Closed	1988	750.00	750
1982	Valencian Boy L1400G	Closed	1988	298.00	400
1982	Sleeping Nymph L1401G	Closed	1988	210.00	500-600
1982	Daydreaming Nymph L1402G	Closed	1988	210.00	500-550
1982	Pondering Nymph L1403G	Closed	1988	210.00	525-625
1982	Matrimony L1404G	Open		320.00	585
1982	Illusion L1413G	Open		115.00	260
1982	Fantasy L1414G	Open		115.00	260
1982	Mirage L1415G	Open		115.00	260
1982	From My Garden L1416G	Open		140.00	295
1982	Nature's Bounty L1417G	Closed	1995	160.00	340
1982	Flower Harmony L1418G	Closed	1995	130.00	270
1982	A Barrow of Blossoms L1419G	Open		390.00	675
1982	Born Free w/base L1420G	Open		1520.00	3140
1982	Mariko w/base L1421G	Closed	1995	860.00	1575
1982	Miss Valencia L1422G	Open		175.00	395
1982	King Melchior L1423G	Open		225.00	440
1982	King Gaspar L1424G	Open		265.00	475
1982	King Balthasar L1425G	Open		315.00	585
1982	Male Tennis Player L1426M	Closed	1988	200.00	350
1982	Female Tennis Player L1427M	Closed	1988	200.00	350
1982	Afternoon Tea L1428G	Open		115.00	275
1982	Afternoon Tea L1428M	Open		115.00	275
1982	Winter Wonderland w/base L1429G	Open		1025.00	2125
1982	High Society L1430G	Closed	1993	305.00	750
1982	The Debutante L1431G	Open		115.00	275
1982	The Debutante L1431M	Open		115.00	275

YEAR ISSUE		EDITION LIMIT	YEAR RETD.	ISSUE PRICE	*QUOTE U.S.$
1983	Vows L1434G	Closed	1991	600.00	900
1983	Blue Moon L1435G	Closed	1988	98.00	350
1983	Moon Glow L1436G	Closed	1988	98.00	450-550
1983	Moon Light L1437G	Closed	1988	98.00	375
1983	Full Moon L1438G	Closed	1988	115.00	675
1983	"How Do You Do!" L1439G	Open		185.00	295
1983	Pleasantries L1440G	Closed	1991	960.00	1900
1983	A Litter of Love L1441G	Open		385.00	645
1983	Kitty Confrontation L1442G	Open		155.00	285
1983	Bearly Love L1443G	Open		55.00	120
1983	Purr-Fect L1444G	Open		350.00	615
1983	Springtime in Japan L1445G	Open		965.00	1800
1983	"Here Comes the Bride" L1446G	Open		518.00	995
1983	Michiko L1447G	Open		235.00	460
1983	Yuki L1448G	Open		285.00	550
1983	Mayumi L1449G	Open		235.00	495
1983	Kiyoko L1450G	Open		235.00	495
1983	Teruko L1451G	Open		235.00	495
1983	On the Town L1452G	Closed	1993	220.00	475
1983	Golfing Couple L1453G	Open		248.00	530
1983	Flowers of the Season L1454G	Open		1460.00	2550
1983	Reflections of Hamlet L1455G	Closed	1988	1000.00	1600
1983	Cranes w/base L1456G	Open		1000.00	1950
1985	A Boy and His Pony L1460G	Closed	1988	285.00	800
1985	Carefree Angel with Flute L1463G	Closed	1988	220.00	650
1985	Carefree Angel with Lyre L1464G	Closed	1988	220.00	650
1985	Girl on Carousel Horse L1469G	Open		470.00	935
1985	Boy on Carousel Horse L1470G	Open		470.00	935
1985	Wishing On A Star L1475G	Closed	1988	130.00	375-500
1985	Star Light Star Bright L1476G	Closed	1988	130.00	400
1985	Star Gazing L1477G	Closed	1988	130.00	400
1985	Hawaiian Dancer/Aloha! L1478G	Open		230.00	440
1985	In a Tropical Garden L1479G	Closed	1995	230.00	440
1985	Aroma of the Islands L1480G	Open		260.00	480
1985	Sunning L1481G	Closed	1988	145.00	650
1985	Eve L1482	Closed	1988	145.00	600
1985	Free As a Butterfly L1483G	Closed	1988	145.00	550
1986	Lady of the East w/base L1488G	Closed	1993	625.00	1100
1986	Valencian Children L1489G	Open		700.00	1225
1986	My Wedding Day L1494G	Open		800.00	1495
1986	A Lady of Taste L1495G	Open		575.00	1025
1986	Don Quixote & The Windmill L1497G	Open		1100.00	2050
1986	Tahitian Dancing Girls L1498G	Closed	1995	750.00	1500
1986	Blessed Family L1499G	Open		200.00	395
1986	Ragamuffin L1500G	Closed	1991	125.00	350
1986	Ragamuffin L1500M	Closed	1991	125.00	300
1986	Rag Doll L1501G	Closed	1991	125.00	250-300
1986	Rag Doll L1501M	Closed	1991	125.00	300
1986	Forgotten L1502G	Closed	1991	125.00	300
1986	Forgotten L1502M	Closed	1991	125.00	300
1986	Neglected L1503G	Closed	1991	125.00	375-450
1986	Neglected L1503M	Closed	1991	125.00	300
1986	The Reception L1504G	Closed	1990	625.00	1050
1986	Nature Boy L1505G	Closed	1991	100.00	275
1986	Nature Boy L1505M	Closed	1991	100.00	N/A
1986	A New Friend L1506G	Closed	1991	110.00	275-325
1986	A New Friend L1506M	Closed	1991	110.00	260
1986	Boy & His Bunny L1507G	Closed	1991	90.00	250
1986	Boy & His Bunny L1507M	Closed	1991	90.00	N/A
1986	In the Meadow L1508G	Closed	1991	100.00	175-250
1986	In the Meadow L1508M	Closed	1991	100.00	285
1986	Spring Flowers L1509G	Closed	1991	100.00	250
1986	Spring Flowers L1509M	Closed	1991	100.00	285
1987	Cafe De Paris L1511G	Closed	1995	1900.00	2950
1987	Hawaiian Beauty L1512G	Closed	1990	575.00	1000
1987	A Flower for My Lady L1513G	Closed	1990	1150.00	1750
1987	Gaspar 's Page L1514G	Closed	1990	275.00	300-500
1987	Melchior's Page L1515G	Closed	1990	290.00	650
1987	Balthasar's Page L1516G	Closed	1990	275.00	900-950
1987	Circus Train L1517G	Closed	1994	2900.00	4350
1987	Valencian Garden L1518G	Closed	1991	1100.00	1795
1987	Stroll in the Park L1519G	Open		1600.00	2600
1987	The Landau Carriage L1521G	Open		2500.00	3850
1987	I am Don Quixote! L1522G	Open		2600.00	3950
1987	Valencian Bouquet L1524G	Closed	1991	250.00	400
1987	Valencian Dreams L1525G	Closed	1991	240.00	300-400
1987	Valencian Flowers L1526G	Closed	1991	375.00	550
1987	Tenderness L1527G	Open		260.00	430
1987	I Love You Truly L1528G	Open		375.00	595
1987	Momi L1529G	Closed	1990	275.00	500
1987	Leilani L1530G	Closed	1990	275.00	550
1987	Malia L1531G	Closed	1990	275.00	500
1987	Lehua L1532G	Closed	1990	275.00	600
1987	Not So Fast! L1533G	Open		175.00	265
1988	Little Sister L1534G	Open		180.00	240
1988	Sweet Dreams L1535G	Open		150.00	220
1988	Stepping Out L1537G	Open		230.00	325
1988	Pink Ballet Slippers L1540	Closed	1991	275.00	450-475
1988	White Ballet Slippers L1540.3	Closed	1991	275.00	395
1987	Light Blue Spoon L1548G	Closed	1991	70.00	150
1987	Dark Blue Spoon L1548.1	Closed	1991	70.00	150
1987	White Spoon L1548.3	Closed	1991	70.00	150
1987	Wild Stallions w/base L1566G	Closed	1993	1100.00	1465
1987	Running Free w/base L1567G	Open		1500.00	1600
1987	Grand Dame L1568G	Open		290.00	425
1989	Fluttering Crane L1598G	Open		115.00	145
1989	Nesting Crane L1599G	Open		95.00	115
1989	Landing Crane L1600G	Open		115.00	145
1989	Rock Nymph L1601G	Closed	1995	665.00	795
1989	Spring Nymph L1602G	Closed	1995	665.00	825
1989	Latest Addition L1606G	Open		385.00	480

116 Collectors' Information Bureau

*Quotes have been rounded up to nearest dollar

FIGURINES/COTTAGES

YEAR ISSUE		EDITION LIMIT	YEAR RETD.	ISSUE PRICE	*QUOTE U.S.$
1989	Flight Into Egypt w/base L1610G	Open		885.00	1150
1989	Courting Cranes L1611G	Open		565.00	695
1989	Preening Crane L1612G	Open		385.00	485
1989	Bowing Crane L1613G	Open		385.00	485
1989	Dancing Crane L1614G	Open		385.00	485
1989	Snow Queen Mask No.11 L1645G	Closed	1991	390.00	450
1989	Medieval Cross No.4 L1652G	Closed	1991	250.00	250
1989	Lavender Lady L1667M	Closed	1991	385.00	550
1989	Black Butterfly #3 L1675M	Closed	1991	120.00	185
1989	Pink & Blue Butterfly #7 L1679M	Closed	1991	80.00	140
1989	Quenn Butterfly #14 L1686M	Closed	1991	125.00	200
1989	Small Pink Butterfly #8 L1680M	Closed	1991	72.50	125
1988	Cellist L1700M	Closed	1993	1200.00	1750
1988	Saxophone Player L1701M	Closed	1993	835.00	1840
1988	Boy at the Fair (decorated) L1708M	Closed	1993	650.00	650
1988	Exodus L1709M	Closed	1993	875.00	875
1988	School Boy L1710M	Closed	1993	750.00	750
1988	School Girl L1711M	Closed	1993	950.00	950
1988	Nanny L1714M	Closed	1993	575.00	700
1988	On Our Way Home (decorated) L1715M	Closed	1993	2000.00	2000
1988	Harlequin with Puppy L1716M	Closed	1993	825.00	1000
1988	Harlequin with Dove L1717M	Closed	1993	900.00	1000
1988	Dress Rehearsal L1718M	Closed	1993	1150.00	1150
1989	Back From the Fair L1719M	Closed	1993	1825.00	1825
1990	Sprite w/base L1720G, numbered series	Open		1200.00	1400
1990	Leprechaun w/base L1721G, numrbered series	Open		1200.00	1395
1989	Group Discussion L1722M	Closed	1993	1500.00	1500
1989	Hopeful Group L1723M	Closed	1993	1825.00	1825
1989	Belle Epoque L1724M	Closed	1993	700.00	700
1989	Young Lady w/Parasol L1725M	Closed	1993	950.00	950
1989	Young Lady with Fan L1726M	Closed	1993	750.00	750
1989	Pose L1727M	Closed	1993	725.00	725
1991	Nativity L1730M	Open		725.00	725
1970	Cat L2001G	Closed	1975	27.50	375
1970	Gothic King L2002G	Closed	1975	25.00	450
1970	Gothic Queen L2003G	Closed	1975	25.00	450
1970	Shepherdess with Lamb L2005M	Closed	1981	100.00	710
1970	Water Carrier Girl Lamp L2006M	Closed	1975	30.00	600
1971	Girl with Dog L2013M	Closed	1975	300.00	N/A
1971	Little Eagle Owl L2020M	Closed	1985	15.00	425
1971	Boy/Girl Eskimo L2038.3M	Closed	N/A	100.00	275-455
1974	Setter's Head L2045M	Closed	1981	42.50	550
1974	Magistrates L2052M	Closed	1981	135.00	950
1974	Oriental L2056M	Open		35.00	105
1974	Oriental L2057M	Open		30.00	100
1974	Thailandia L2058M	Open		650.00	1885
1974	Muskateer L2059M	Closed	1981	900.00	2000-3000
1977	Monk L2060M	Open		60.00	145
1977	Day Dream L2062M	Closed	1985	400.00	1300
1977	Dogs-Bust L2067M	Closed	1979	280.00	800
1977	Thai Dancers L2069M	Open		300.00	745
1977	A New Hairdo L2070M	Closed	1991	1060.00	1430
1977	Graceful Duo L2073M	Closed	1994	775.00	1650
1977	Nuns L2075M	Open		90.00	250
1978	Lonely L2076M	Open		72.50	185
1978	Rain in Spain L2077M	Closed	1990	190.00	475-550
1978	Woman L2080M	Closed	1985	625.00	625
1978	Woman L2081M	Closed	1985	550.00	1400
1978	Carmen L2083M	Closed	1981	275.00	625
1978	Don Quixote Dreaming L2084M	Closed	1985	550.00	2050
1978	The Little Kiss L2086M	Closed	1985	180.00	475
1978	Girl in Rocking Chair L2089	Closed	1981	235.00	600
1978	Saint Francis L2090	Closed	1981	565.00	N/A
1978	Holy Virgin L2092M	Closed	1981	200.00	N/A
1978	Girl Waiting L2093M	Closed	1995	90.00	185
1978	Tenderness L2094M	Open		100.00	205
1978	Duck Pulling Pigtail L2095M	Open		110.00	275
1978	Nosy Puppy L2096M	Closed	1993	190.00	400
1978	Laundress L2109M	Closed	1983	325.00	325-650
1980	Marujita with Two Ducks L2113M	Closed	1993	240.00	295
1980	Kissing Father L2114M	Closed	1981	575.00	575
1980	Mother's Kiss L2115M	Closed	1981	575.00	700
1980	The Whaler L2121M	Closed	1988	820.00	1050
1981	Lost in Thought L2125M	Closed	1990	210.00	300
1983	Indian Chief L2127M	Closed	1988	525.00	750
1983	Venus L2128M	Closed	N/A	650.00	1150
1983	Waiting for Santa L2129M	Closed	1985	325.00	600
1983	Egyptian Cat L2130M	Closed	1985	75.00	500
1983	Mother & Son L2131M, numbered series	Open		850.00	1550
1983	Spring Sheperdess L2132M	Closed	1985	450.00	N/A
1983	Autumn Sheperdess L2133M	Closed	1985	285.00	N/A
1984	Nautical Watch L2134M	Closed	1988	450.00	800
1984	Mystical Joseph L2135M	Closed	1988	428.00	700
1984	The King L2136M	Closed	1988	570.00	710
1984	Fairy Ballerina L2137M	Closed	1988	500.00	1250
1984	Friar Juniper L2138M	Closed	1993	160.00	400
1984	Aztec Indian L2139M	Closed	1988	553.00	600
1984	Pepita wth Sombrero L2140M	Open		97.50	200
1984	Pedro with Jug L2141M	Open		100.00	205
1984	Sea Harvest L2142M	Closed	1990	535.00	700
1984	Aztec Dancer L2143M	Closed	1988	463.00	650
1984	Leticia L2144M	Closed	1995	100.00	190
1984	Gabriela L2145M	Closed	1994	100.00	170
1984	Desiree L2146M	Closed	1995	100.00	190
1984	Alida L2147M	Closed	1994	100.00	170
1984	Head of Congolese Woman L2148M	Closed	1988	55.00	500-700
1985	Young Madonna L2149M	Closed	1988	400.00	675

YEAR ISSUE		EDITION LIMIT	YEAR RETD.	ISSUE PRICE	*QUOTE U.S.$
1985	A Tribute to Peace w/base L2150M	Open		470.00	930
1985	A Bird on Hand L2151M	Open		118.00	255
1985	Chinese Girl L2152M	Closed	1990	90.00	200-250
1985	Chinese Boy L2153	Closed	1990	90.00	200-250
1985	Hawaiian Flower Vendor L2154M	Open		245.00	460
1985	Arctic inter L2156M	Open		75.00	145
1985	Eskimo Girl w/Cold Feet L2157M	Open		140.00	285
1985	Pensive Eskimo Girl L2158M	Open		100.00	210
1985	Pensive Eskimo Boy L2159M	Open		100.00	210
1985	Flower Vendor L2160M	Closed	1995	110.00	215
1985	Fruit Vendor L2161M	Closed	1994	120.00	230
1985	Fish Vendor L2162M	Closed	1994	110.00	205
1987	Mountain Shepherd L2163M	Open		120.00	210
1987	My Lost Lamb L2164M	Open		100.00	175
1987	Chiquita L2165M	Closed	1993	100.00	170
1987	Paco L2166M	Closed	1993	100.00	170
1987	Fernando L2167M	Closed	1993	100.00	200
1987	Julio L2168M	Closed	1993	100.00	225
1987	Repose L2169M	Open		120.00	195
1987	Spanish Dancer L2170M	Open		190.00	345
1987	Ahoy Tere L2173M	Open		190.00	325
1987	Andean Flute Player L2174M	Closed	1990	250.00	350
1988	Harvest Helpers L2178M	Open		190.00	265
1988	Sharing the Harvest L2179M	Open		190.00	265
1988	Dreams of Peace w/base L2180M	Open		880.00	1125
1988	Bathing Nymph w/base L2181M	Open		560.00	795
1988	Daydreamer w/base L2182M	Open		560.00	795
1989	Wakeup Kitty L2183M	Closed	1993	225.00	325
1989	Angel and Friend L2184M	Closed	1994	150.00	185
1989	Devoted Reader L2185M	Closed	1994	125.00	160
1989	The Greatest Love L2186M	Open		235.00	320
1989	Jealous Friend L2187M	Closed	1995	275.00	365
1990	Mother's Pride L2189M	Open		300.00	375
1990	To The Well L2190M	Open		250.00	295
1990	Forest Born L2191M	Closed	1991	230.00	450
1990	King Of The Forest L2192M	Closed	N/A	290.00	310
1990	Heavenly Strings L2194M	Closed	1993	170.00	235
1990	Heavenly Sounds L2195M	Closed	1993	170.00	215
1990	Heavenly Solo L2196M	Closed	1993	170.00	235
1990	Heavenly Song L2197M	Closed	1993	175.00	185
1990	A King is Born w/base L2198M	Open		750.00	895
1990	Devoted Friends w/base L2199M	Closed	1995	700.00	895
1990	A Big Hug! L2200M	Open		250.00	310
1990	Our Daily Bread L2201M	Closed	1994	150.00	300
1990	A Helping Hand L2202M	Closed	1993	150.00	185
1990	Afternoon Chores L2203M	Closed	1994	150.00	185
1990	Farmyard Grace L2204M	Closed	1993	180.00	300
1990	Prayerful Stitch L2205M	Closed	1994	160.00	190
1990	Sisterly Love L2206M	Open		300.00	375
1990	What A Day! L2207M	Open		550.00	640
1990	Let's Rest L2208M	Open		550.00	665
1991	Long Dy L2209M	Open		295.00	340
1991	Lazy Day L2210M	Open		240.00	260
1991	Patrol Leader L2212M	Closed	1993	390.00	420
1991	Nature's Friend L2213M	Closed	1993	390.00	420
1991	Seaside Angel L2214M	Open		150.00	165
1991	Friends in Flight L2215M	Open		165.00	180
1991	Laundry Day L2216M	Open		350.00	400
1991	Gentle Play L2217M	Closed	1993	380.00	415
1991	Costumed Couple L2218M	Closed	1993	680.00	750
1992	Underfoot L2219M	Open		360.00	410
1992	Free Spirit L2220M	Closed	1994	235.00	245
1992	Spring Beauty L2221M	Closed	1994	285.00	295
1992	Tender Moment L2222M	Open		400.00	450
1992	New Lamb L2223M	Open		365.00	385
1992	Cherish L2224M	Open		1750.00	1850
1992	FriendlySparrow L2225M	Open		295.00	325
1992	Boy's Best Friend L2226M	Open		390.00	410
1992	Artic Allies L2227M	Open		585.00	615
1992	Snowy Sunday L2228M	Open		550.00	625
1992	Seasonal Gifts L2229M	Open		450.00	475
1992	Mary's Child L2230M	Closed	1994	525.00	550
1992	Afternoon Verse L2231M	Open		580.00	595
1992	Poor Little Bear L2232M	Open		250.00	265
1992	Guess What I Have L2233M	Open		340.00	375
1992	Playful Push L2234M	Open		850.00	875
1993	Adoring Mother L2235M	Open		405.00	440
1993	Frosty Outing L2236M	Open		375.00	410
1993	The Old Fishing Hole L2237M	Open		625.00	640
1993	Learning Together L2238M	Open		500.00	500
1993	Valencian Courtship L2239M	Open		880.00	895
1993	Winged Love L2240M	Closed	1995	285.00	310
1993	Winged Harmony L2241M	Closed	1995	285.00	310
1993	Away to School L2242M	Open		465.00	465
1993	Lion Tamer L2246M	Closed	1995	375.00	375
1993	Just Us L2247M	Closed	1995	650.00	650
1993	Noella L2251M	Open		405.00	420
1993	Waiting For Father L2252M	Open		660.00	660
1993	Noisy Friend L2253M	Open		280.00	280
1993	Step Aside L2254M	Open		280.00	280
1994	Solitude L2256M	Open		398.00	435
1994	Constant Companions L2257M	Open		575.00	625
1994	Family Love L2258M	Open		450.00	485
1994	Little Fisherman L2259M	Open		298.00	330
1994	Artic Friends L2260M	Open		345.00	380
1995	Jesus and Joseph L2294M	Open		550.00	550
1995	Peaceful Rest L2295M	Open		390.00	390
1995	Life's Small Wonders L2296M	Open		370.00	370
1995	Elephants L2297M	Open		875.00	875
1995	Hindu Children L2298M	Open		450.00	450
1995	Poetic Moment L2299M	Open		465.00	465

YEAR ISSUE		EDITION LIMIT	YEAR RETD.	ISSUE PRICE	*QUOTE U.S.$
1995	Emperor L2300M	Open		765.00	765
1995	Empress L2301M	Open		795.00	795
1995	Twilight Years L2302M	Open		385.00	385
1995	Not So Fast L2303M	Open		350.00	350
1995	Love in Bloom L2304M	Open		420.00	420
1995	Fragrant Bouquet L2305M	Open		330.00	330
1995	Hurray Now L2306M	Open		310.00	310
1995	Happy Birthday L2307M	Open		150.00	150
1995	Let's Make Up L2308M	Open		265.00	265
1995	Windblown Girl L2309M	Open		320.00	320
1995	Chit-Chat L2310M	Open		270.00	270
1995	Good Night L2311M	Open		280.00	280
1995	Goose Trying to Eat L2312M	Open		325.00	325
1995	Who's the Fairest L2313M	Open		230.00	230
1995	Breezy Afternoon L2314M	Open		220.00	220
1995	On the Green L2315M	Open		575.00	575
1995	Closing Scene L2316M	Open		560.00	560
1995	Talk to Me L2317M	Open		175.00	175
1995	Taking Time L2318M	Open		175.00	175
1995	A Lesson Shared L2319M	Open		215.00	215
1995	Cat Nap L2320M	Open		265.00	265
1995	All Tuckered Out L2321M	Open		275.00	275
1995	Naptime L2322M	Open		275.00	275
1995	Water Girl L2323M	Open		245.00	245
1995	A Basket of Fun L2324M	Open		320.00	320
1995	Spring Splendor L2325M	Open		440.00	440
1995	Physician L2326M	Open		350.00	350
1995	Sad Sax L2327M	Open		225.00	225
1995	Circus Sam L2328M	Open		225.00	225
1995	Daily Chores L2329M	Open		345.00	345
1996	The Shepherdess L2330	Open		410.00	410
1996	Little Peasant Girl (pink) L2331	Open		155.00	155
1996	Little Peasant Girl (blue) L2332	Open		155.00	155
1996	Little Peasant Girl (white) L2333	Open		155.00	155
1996	Asian Melody L2334	Open		690.00	690
1996	Young Fisherman L2335	Open		225.00	225
1996	Young Water Girl L2336	Open		315.00	315
1996	Virgin of Montserrat w/base L2337	Open		1000.00	1000
1996	Sultan's Dream L2338	Open		700.00	700
1996	The Sultan L2339	Open		480.00	480
1996	Oriental Fantasy w/bow L2340	Open		1350.00	1350
1996	Oriental Fantasy w/brooch L2341	Open		1350.00	1350
1978	Native L3502M	Open		700.00	2450
1978	Letters to Dulcinea L3509M, numbered series	Open		875.00	2175
1978	Horse Heads L3511M	Closed	1990	260.00	700
1978	Girl With Pails L3512M	Open		140.00	285
1978	A Wintry Day L3513M	Closed	1988	525.00	800-1000
1978	Pensive w/ base L3514M	Open		500.00	1050
1978	Jesus Christ L3516M	Closed	1988	1050.00	1450
1978	Nude with Rose w/ base L3517M	Open		225.00	780
1980	Lady Macbeth L3518M	Closed	1981	385.00	700-1200
1980	Mother's Love L3521M	Closed	1990	1000.00	1100
1981	Weary w/ base L3525M	Open		360.00	685
1982	Contemplation w/ base L3526M	Open		265.00	590
1982	Stormy Sea w/base L3554M	Open		675.00	1445
1984	Innocence w/base/green L3558M	Closed	1991	960.00	1650
1984	Innocence w/base/red L3558.3M	Closed	1987	960.00	1200
1985	Peace Offering w/base L3559M	Open		397.00	665
1969	Marketing Day L4502G	Closed	1985	40.00	400
1969	Girl with Lamb L4505G	Open		20.00	125
1969	Boy with Kid L4506M	Closed	1985	22.50	400
1969	Boy with Lambs L4509G	Closed	1981	37.50	275
1969	Girl w/Parasol & Geese L4510G	Closed	1993	40.00	350
1969	Nude L4511M	Closed	1985	45.00	700
1969	Nude L4512G	Closed	1985	44.00	400
1969	Man on Horse L4515G	Closed	1985	180.00	1000
1969	Female Equestrian L4516G	Open		170.00	745
1969	Boy Student L4517G	Closed	1978	57.50	475
1969	Flamenco Dancers L4519G	Closed	1993	150.00	1200
1970	Boy With Dog L4522M	Closed	N/A	25.00	155
1969	Girl With Slippers L4523G	Closed	1993	17.00	100
1969	Girl With Slippers L4523M	Closed	1993	17.00	100
1969	Donkey in Love L4524G	Closed	1985	15.00	350
1969	Donkey in Love L4524M	Closed	1985	15.00	350
1969	Violinist L4527G	Closed	1985	75.00	500
1969	Ballet Lamp L4528G	Closed	1985	120.00	850
1969	Joseph L4533G	Open		60.00	110
1969	Joseph L4533M	Open		60.00	110
1969	Mary L4534G	Open		60.00	85
1969	Mary L4534M	Open		60.00	85
1971	Baby Jesus L4535.3G	Open		60.00	70
1969	Baby Jesus L4535.3M	Open		60.00	70
1969	Angel, Chinese L4536G	Open		45.00	90
1969	Angel, Chinese L4536M	Open		45.00	90
1969	Angel, Black L4537G	Open		13.00	90
1969	Angel, Black L4537M	Open		13.00	90
1969	Angel, Praying L4538G	Open		13.00	90
1969	Angel, Praying L4538M	Open		13.00	90
1969	Angel, Thinking L4539G	Open		13.00	90
1969	Angel, Thinking L4539M	Open		13.00	90
1969	Angel with Horn L4540G	Open		13.00	90
1969	Angel with Horn L4540M	Open		13.00	90
1969	Angel Reclining L4541G	Open		13.00	90
1969	Angel Reclining L4541M	Open		13.00	90
1969	Group of Angels L4542G	Open		31.00	195
1969	Group of Angels L4542M	Open		31.00	195
1969	Geese Group L4549G	Open		28.50	230
1969	Geese Group L4549M	Closed	1992	28.50	230
1969	Flying Dove L4550G	Open		47.50	265
1969	Flying Dove L4550M	Closed	1992	47.50	165

*Quotes have been rounded up to nearest dollar

FIGURINES/COTTAGES

YEAR ISSUE		EDITION LIMIT	YEAR RETD.	ISSUE PRICE	*QUOTE U.S.$
1969	Ducks, Set/3 asst. L4551-3G	Open		18.00	140
1969	Shepherd L4554	Closed	1972	69.00	N/A
1969	Sad Harlequin L4558G	Closed	1993	110.00	575
1969	Waiting Backstage L4559G	Closed	1993	110.00	440
1970	Llama Group 4561G	Closed	1970	55.00	1500
1969	Couple with Parasol L4563G	Closed	1985	180.00	800-1000
1969	Girl with Geese L4568G	Closed	1993	45.00	350
1969	Girl With Turkey L4569G	Closed	1981	28.50	365
1969	Shepherd Resting L4571G	Closed	1981	60.00	475
1969	Girl with Piglets L4572G	Closed	1985	70.00	400
1969	Girl with Piglets L4572M	Closed	1985	70.00	400
1969	Mother & Child L4575G	Open		50.00	265
1969	New Shepherdess L4576G	Closed	1985	37.50	315
1969	New Shepherd L4577G	Closed	1983	35.00	550
1969	Mardi Gras L4580G	Closed	1975	57.50	2000-2500
1969	Girl with Sheep L4584G	Closed	1993	27.00	170
1969	Holy Family L4585G	Closed	1994	18.00	135
1969	Holy Family L4585M	Closed	1994	18.00	135
1969	Madonna L4586G	Closed	1979	32.50	350
1969	White Cockeral L4588G	Closed	1979	17.50	300
1969	Girl with Pitcher L4590G	Closed	1981	47.50	400
1969	Shepherdess w/Basket L4591G	Closed	1993	20.00	275
1969	Lady with Greyhound L4594G	Closed	1981	60.00	800
1969	Fairy L4595G	Closed	1994	27.50	150
1969	Two Horses L4597	Closed	1990	240.00	925-1000
1969	Doctor L4602.3G	Open		33.00	198
1969	Nurse-L4603.3G	Open		35.00	200
1969	Clown with Girl L4605	Closed	1985	160.00	1000
1969	Accordian Player L4606	Closed	1978	60.00	650
1969	Cupid L4607G	Closed	1980	15.00	150
1969	Cook in Trouble L4608	Closed	1985	27.50	650-775
1969	Nuns L4611G	Open		37.50	155
1969	Nuns L4611M	Open		37.50	155
1969	Girl Singer L4612G	Closed	1979	14.00	450
1969	Boy With Cymbals L4613G	Closed	1979	14.00	400
1969	Boy With Guitar L4614G	Closed	1979	19.50	400
1969	Boy with Double Bass L4615G	Closed	1979	22.50	400
1969	Boy With Drum L4616G	Closed	1979	16.50	350
1969	Group of Musicians L4617G	Closed	1979	33.00	500
1969	Clown L4618G	Open		70.00	415
1969	Sea Captain L4621G	Closed	1993	45.00	325
1969	Sea Captain L4621M	Closed	N/A	42.50	300
1969	Old Man with Violin L4622G	Closed	1982	45.00	700
1969	Angel with Child L4635G	Open		15.00	110
1969	Honey Peddler L4638G	Closed	1978	60.00	575
1969	Cow With Pig L4640	Closed	1981	42.50	500
1969	Pekinese L4641G	Closed	1985	20.00	450
1969	Dog L4642	Closed	1981	22.50	425
1969	Skye Terrier L4643G	Closed	1985	15.00	450
1969	Andalucians Group L4647G	Closed	1990	412.00	1400
1969	Valencian Couple on Horseback L4648	Closed	1990	900.00	1000
1969	Madonna Head L4649G	Open		25.00	155
1969	Madonna Head L4649M	Open		25.00	155
1969	Girl with Calla Lillies L4650G	Open		18.00	145
1969	Cellist L4651G	Closed	1978	70.00	650
1969	Happy Travelers L4652	Closed	1978	115.00	650
1969	Orchestra Conductor L4653G	Closed	1979	95.00	850
1969	The Grandfather L4654G	Closed	1979	75.00	950-1100
1969	Horses L4655G	Open		110.00	760
1969	Shepherdess L4660G	Closed	1993	21.00	300
1969	Countryman L4664M	Closed	1979	50.00	500
1969	Girl with Basket L4665G	Closed	1979	50.00	450
1969	Girl with Basket L4665M	Closed	1979	50.00	550
1969	Birds L4667G	Closed	1985	25.00	200
1969	Maja Head L4668G	Closed	1985	50.00	650
1969	Baby Jesus L4670BG	Open		18.00	55
1969	Mary L4671G	Open		33.00	75
1969	St. Joseph L4672G	Open		33.00	90
1969	King Melchior L4673G	Open		35.00	95
1969	King Gaspar L4674G	Open		35.00	95
1969	King Balthasar L4675G	Open		35.00	95
1969	Shepherd with Lamb L4676G	Open		14.00	110
1969	Girl with Rooster L4677G	Open		14.00	90
1969	Shepherdess w/Basket L4678G	Open		13.00	90
1969	Donkey L4679G	Open		36.50	100
1969	Cow L4680G	Open		36.50	90
1970	Girl with Milkpail L4682G	Closed	1991	28.00	325
1970	Hebrew Student L4684G	Closed	1985	33.00	500-650
1970	Hebrew Student L4684M	Closed	1985	33.00	600
1970	Gothic Queen L4689	Closed	1975	20.00	700
1970	Troubadour in Love L4699	Closed	1975	60.00	1000
1970	Dressmaker L4700G	Closed	1993	45.00	500
1970	Mother & Child L4701G	Open		45.00	295
1970	Girl Jewelry Dish L4713G	Closed	1978	30.00	550
1970	Girl Jewelry Dish L4713M	Closed	1978	30.00	550
1970	Lady Empire L4719G	Closed	1979	150.00	850
1970	Girl With Tulips L4720G	Closed	1978	65.00	500
1970	Hamlet L4729G	Closed	1980	85.00	800
1970	Bird Watcher L4730	Closed	1985	35.00	400-500
1971	Small dog L4749	Closed	1985	5.50	175
1971	Romeo and Juliet L4750G	Open		150.00	1250
1971	Doncel With Roses L4757G	Closed	1979	35.00	500
1974	Lady with Dog L4761G	Closed	1993	60.00	400-500
1971	Dentist L4762	Closed	1978	36.00	500-600
1971	Dentist (Reduced) L4762.3G	Closed	1985	30.00	450
1971	Obstetrician L4763G	Closed	1973	47.50	450
1971	Obstetrician L4763.3G	Open		40.00	255
1971	Don Quixote Vase L4770G	Closed	1975	25.00	750
1971	Don Quixote Vase L4770M	Closed	1975	25.00	750
1971	Rabbit L4772G	Open		17.50	135
1971	Rabbit L4773G	Open		17.50	130

YEAR ISSUE		EDITION LIMIT	YEAR RETD.	ISSUE PRICE	*QUOTE U.S.$
1971	Dormouse L4774	Closed	1983	30.00	375
1971	Girl Tennis Player L4798	Closed	1981	50.00	450
1971	Children, Praying L4779G	Open		36.00	195
1971	Children, Praying L4779M	Closed	1992	36.00	153
1971	Boy with Goat L4780	Closed	1978	80.00	600
1972	Japanese Woman L4799	Closed	1975	45.00	500
1972	Gypsy with Brother L4800G	Closed	1979	36.00	400
1972	The Teacher L4801G	Closed	1978	45.00	500
1972	Fisherman L4802G	Closed	1979	70.00	700
1972	Woman with Umbrella L4805G	Closed	1981	100.00	800
1972	Girl with Dog L4806G	Closed	1981	80.00	550
1972	Geisha L4807G	Closed	1993	190.00	475
1972	Wedding L4808G	Open		50.00	190
1972	Wedding L4808M	Open		50.00	190
1972	Going Fishing L4809G	Open		33.00	160
1972	Young Sailor L4810G	Open		33.00	175
1972	Boy with Pails L4811	Closed	1988	30.00	400
1972	Getting Her Goat L4812G	Closed	1988	55.00	450
1972	Girl with Geese L4815G	Closed	1991	72.00	400
1972	Girl with Geese L4815M	Closed	1991	72.00	295
1972	Little Shepherd w/Goat L4817M	Closed	1981	50.00	475
1972	Burro L4821G	Closed	1979	24.00	450
1974	Peruvian Girl with Baby L4822	Closed	1981	65.00	775
1974	Legionary L4823	Closed	1978	55.00	400-500
1972	Male Golfer L4824G	Open		66.00	295
1972	Veterinarian L4825	Closed	1985	48.00	500
1972	Girl Feeding Rabbit L4826G	Closed	1993	40.00	300
1972	Caressing Calf L4827G	Closed	1981	55.00	475
1972	Cinderella L4828G	Open		47.00	245
1975	Swan L4829G	Closed	1983	16.00	400
1972	You and Me L4830G	Closed	1979	112.50	700
1972	Chess Set Pieces L4833.3G	Closed	1985	410	2500
1972	Shepherdess L4835G	Closed	1991	42.00	225-325
1973	Clean Up Time L4838G	Closed	1993	36.00	250-300
1973	Clean Up Time L4838M	Closed	1992	36.00	250
1972	Oriental Flower Arranger/Girl L4840G	Open		90.00	415
1972	Oriental Flower Arranger/Girl L4840M	Open		90.00	515
1974	Girl from Valencia L4841G	Open		35.00	225
1973	Viola Lesson L4842G	Closed	1981	66.00	450
1973	Donkey Ride L4843	Closed	1981	86.00	650
1973	Pharmacist L4844G	Closed	1985	70.00	1650
1973	Classic Dance L4847G	Closed	1985	80.00	600
1973	Feeding The Ducks L4849G	Closed	1995	60.00	270
1973	Feeding The Ducks L4849M	Closed	1992	60.00	250
1973	Aesthetic Pose L4850G	Closed	1985	110.00	650
1973	Lady Golfer L4851M	Closed	1992	70.00	250
1973	Gardner in Trouble L4852	Closed	1981	65.00	500
1974	Cobbler L4853G	Closed	1985	100.00	600
1973	Don Quixote L4854G	Open		40.00	205
1973	Ballerina L4855G	Open		45.00	330
1983	Ballerina, white L4855.3	Closed	1987	110.00	250
1974	Waltz Time L4856G	Closed	1985	65.00	450
1974	Dog L4857G	Closed	1979	40.00	550
1974	Pleasant Encounter L4858M	Closed	1981	60.00	450
1974	Peddler L4859G	Closed	1985	180.00	750
1974	Dutch Girl L4860G	Closed	1985	45.00	250
1974	Horse L4861	Closed	1978	55.00	425
1974	Horse L4862	Closed	1978	55.00	425
1974	Horse L4863	Closed	1978	55.00	400
1974	Embroiderer L4865G	Closed	1994	115.00	700
1974	Girl with Swan and Dog L4866G	Closed	1993	26.00	205
1974	Seesaw L4867G	Open		55.00	350
1974	Girl with Candle L4868G	Open		13.00	90
1974	Girl with Candle L4868M	Closed	1992	13.00	80
1974	Boy Kissing L4869G	Open		13.00	90
1974	Boy Kissing L4869M	Closed	1992	13.00	150-175
1974	Boy Yawning L4870G	Open		13.00	90
1974	Boy Yawning L4870M	Closed	1992	13.00	175
1974	Girl with Guitar L4871G	Open		13.00	90
1974	Girl with Guitar L4871M	Closed	1992	13.00	80
1974	Girl Stretching L4872G	Open		13.00	90
1974	Girl Stretching L4872M	Closed	1992	13.00	80
1974	Girl Kissing L4873G	Open		13.00	90
1974	Girl Kissing L4873M	Closed	1992	13.00	80
1974	Boy & Girl L4874G	Open		25.00	150
1974	Boy & Girl L4874M	Closed	1992	25.00	135
1974	Girl with Jugs L4875G	Closed	1985	40.00	300
1974	Boy Thinking L4876G	Closed	1993	20.00	170
1974	Boy Thinking L4876M	Closed	1992	20.00	120
1974	Boy with Flute L4877G	Closed	1981	60.00	450
1974	Lady with Parasol L4879G	Open		48.00	325
1974	Carnival Couple L4882G	Closed	1995	60.00	300
1974	Lady w/ Young Harlequin L4883G	Closed	1975	100.00	2200
1974	Seraph's Head No.1 L4884	Closed	1985	10.00	100
1974	Seraph's Head No.2 L4885	Closed	1985	10.00	100
1974	Seraph's Head No.3 L4886	Closed	1985	10.00	100
1974	The Kiss L4888G	Closed	1983	150.00	700
1979	Spanish Policeman L4889G	Closed	1991	55.00	400
1976	"My Dog" L4893G	Open		85.00	230
1974	Tennis Player Boy L4894	Closed	1980	75.00	350
1974	Ducks L4895G	Open		45.00	95
1974	Ducks L4895M	Closed	1992	45.00	85
1974	Boy with Snails L4896G	Closed	1979	50.00	400
1974	Boy From Madrid L4898G	Open		55.00	150
1974	Boy From Madrid L4898M	Closed	1992	55.00	130
1974	Boy with Smoking Jacket L4900	Closed	1983	45.00	200
1974	Barrister L4908G	Closed	1985	100.00	585
1974	Girl With Dove L4909G	Closed	1982	70.00	450
1974	Girl With Lantern L4910G	Closed	1990	85.00	300
1974	Young Lady in Trouble L4912G	Closed	1985	110.00	450

YEAR ISSUE		EDITION LIMIT	YEAR RETD.	ISSUE PRICE	*QUOTE U.S.$
1975	Lady with Shawl L4914G	Open		220.00	730
1975	Girl with Pigeons L4915	Closed	1990	110.00	400
1976	Chinese Noblewoman L4916G	Closed	1978	300.00	2000
1974	A Girl at the Pond L4918G	Closed	1985	85.00	350
1976	Gypsy Woman L4919G	Closed	1981	165.00	1100
1974	Country Lass with Dog L4920G	Closed	1995	185.00	495
1974	Country Lass with Dog L4920M	Closed	1992	185.00	495
1974	Chinese Nobleman L4921G	Closed	1978	325.00	495
1974	Windblown Girl L4922G	Open		150.00	375
1974	Lanquid Clown L4924G	Closed	1983	200.00	1500
1974	Sisters L4930	Closed	1981	250.00	625
1974	Children with Fruits L4931G	Closed	1981	210.00	500
1974	Dainty Lady L4934G	Closed	1985	60.00	475
1974	"Closing Scene" L4935G	Open		180.00	520
1983	"Closing Scene"/white L4935.3M	Closed	1987	213.00	265
1974	Spring Breeze L4936G	Open		145.00	410
1976	Baby's Outing L4938G	Open		250.00	725
1977	Missy L4951M	Closed	1985	300.00	600-850
1977	Meditation L4952M	Closed	1979	200.00	N/A
1977	Tavern Drinkers L4956G	Closed	1985	1125.00	3500
1977	Attentive Dogs L4957G	Closed	1981	350.00	1500-2200
1977	Cherub, Puzzled L4959G	Open		40.00	110
1977	Cherub, Smiling L4960G	Open		40.00	110
1977	Cherub, Dreaming L4961G	Open		40.00	110
1977	Cherub, Wondering L4962G	Open		40.00	110
1977	Cherub, Wondering L4962M	Closed	1992	40.00	100
1977	Infantile Candour L4963G	Closed	1979	285.00	1000-1350
1977	Little Red Riding Hood L4965G	Closed	1983	210.00	575
1977	Tennis Player Puppet L4966G	Closed	1985	60.00	250
1977	Soccer Puppet L4967G	Closed	1985	65.00	425
1977	Oympic Puppet L4968	Closed	1983	65.00	800
1977	Cowboy & Sheriff Puppet L4969G	Closed	1985	85.00	650
1977	Skier Puppet L4970G	Closed	1983	85.00	500-900
1977	Hunter Puppet L4971G	Closed	1985	95.00	750
1977	Girl w/Calla Lillies sitting L4972G	Open		65.00	180
1977	Choir Lesson L4973G	Closed	1981	350.00	1850
1977	Dutch Children L4974G	Closed	1981	375.00	1100
1977	Augustina of Aragon L4976G	Closed	1979	475.00	1500-1800
1977	Harlequin Serenade L4977	Closed	1979	185.00	675
1977	Milkmaid w/Wheelbarrow L4979G	Closed	1981	220.00	950
1977	Ironing Time L4981G	Closed	1985	80.00	350
1978	Naughty Dog L4982G	Closed	1995	130.00	250
1978	Gossip L4984G	Closed	1985	260.00	1000
1978	Mimi L4985G	Closed	1980	110.00	650
1978	Attentive Lady L4986G	Closed	1981	635.00	2200
1978	Oriental Spring L4988G	Open		125.00	325
1978	Sayonara L4989G	Open		125.00	300
1978	Chrysanthemum L4990G	Open		125.00	310
1978	Butterfly L4991G	Open		125.00	295
1978	Dancers Resting L4992G	Closed	1983	350.00	850
1978	Gypsy Venders L4993G	Closed	1985	165.00	475
1978	Ready to Go L4996G	Closed	1981	425.00	1500-1700
1978	Don Quixote & Sancho L4998G	Closed	1983	875.00	2900
1978	Reading L5000G	Open		150.00	275
1978	Elk Family L5001G	Closed	1981	550.00	700
1978	Sunny Day L5003G	Closed	1993	193.00	360
1978	Eloise L5005G	Closed	1978	175.00	550
1978	Naughty L5006G	Open		55.00	150
1978	Bashful L5007G	Open		55.00	150
1978	Static-Girl w/Straw Hat L5008G	Open		55.00	150
1978	Curious-Girl w/Straw Hat L5009G	Open		55.00	150
1978	Coiffure-Girl w/Straw Hat L5010G	Open		55.00	150
1978	Trying on a Straw Hat L5011G	Open		55.00	150
1978	Daughters L5013G	Closed	1991	425.00	900
1978	Genteel L5014G	Closed	1981	725.00	2300
1978	Painful Monkey L5018	Closed	1981	135.00	750
1978	Painful Giraffe L5019	Closed	1981	115.00	750
1978	Painful Giraffe L5022G	Closed	1981	95.00	800
1978	Woman With Scarf L5024G	Closed	1985	141.00	450
1980	A Clean Sweep L5025G	Closed	1985	100.00	450
1980	Planning the Day L5026G	Closed	1985	90.00	275
1979	Flower Curtsy L5027G	Open		230.00	470
1980	Flowers in Pot L5028G	Closed	1985	325.00	575
1980	Boy w/Tricycle & Flowers L5029G	Closed	1985	675.00	1200-1350
1980	Wildflower L5030G	Closed	1994	360.00	695
1979	Little Friskies L5032G	Open		108.00	220
1979	Avoiding the Goose L5033G	Closed	1993	160.00	350
1979	Goose Trying To Eat L5034G	Open		135.00	310
1980	Act II w/base L5035G	Open		700.00	1425
1979	Jockey with Lass L5036G	Open		950.00	2240
1980	Sleighride w/base L5037G	Open		585.00	1140
1980	Candid L5039G	Closed	1981	145.00	475
1979	Girl Walking L5040G	Closed	1981	150.00	420-450
1980	Girl Kneeling and Tulips L5041G	Closed	1981	160.00	700
1980	Ladies Talking L5042G	Closed	1983	385.00	575-100
1980	Hind and Baby Deer L5043G	Closed	1981	650.00	3600
1980	Girl with Toy Wagon L5044G	Open		115.00	24
1980	Belinda with Doll L5045G	Closed	1995	115.00	21
1980	Organ Grinder L5046G	Closed	1981	328.00	160
1980	Teacher Woman L5048G	Closed	1981	115.00	550-675
1979	Dancer L5050G	Open		85.00	20
1980	Samson and Delilah L5051G	Closed	1981	350.00	160
1980	Clown and Girl/ At the Circus L5052G	Closed	1985	525.00	125
1980	Festival Time L5053G	Closed	1985	250.00	37
1980	Little Senorita L5054G	Closed	1985	235.00	60
1980	Ship-Boy with Baskets L5055G	Closed	1985	140.00	45
1980	Boy Clown with Clock L5056G	Closed	1985	290.00	85
1980	Boy Clown with Violin and Top Hat L5057G	Closed	1985	270.00	85
1980	Boy Clown w/Concertina L5058G	Closed	1985	290.00	500-60

*Quotes have been rounded up to nearest dollar

YEAR ISSUE		EDITION LIMIT	YEAR RETD.	ISSUE PRICE	*QUOTE U.S.$
1980	Boy Clown w/Saxaphone L5059G	Closed	1985	320.00	600
1980	Girl Clown with Trumpet L5060G	Closed	1985	290.00	550
1980	Girl Bending/March Wind L5061G	Closed	1983	370.00	600
1980	Kristina L5062G	Closed	1985	225.00	400
1980	Dutch Girl With Braids L5063G	Closed	1985	265.00	425-450
1980	Dutch Girl, Hands Akimbo L5064G	Closed	1990	255.00	500
1980	Ingrid L5065G	Closed	1990	370.00	800
1980	Ilsa L5066G	Closed	1990	275.00	600
1981	Snow White with Apple L5067G	Closed	1983	450.00	1500
1980	Fairy Godmother L5068G	Closed	1983	625.00	950-1150
1980	Choir Boy L5070G	Closed	1983	240.00	850
1980	Nostalgia L5071G	Closed	1993	185.00	350
1980	Courtship L5072	Closed	1990	327.00	750
1980	Country Flowers L5073	Closed	1985	315.00	1500
1980	My Hungry Brood L5074G	Open		295.00	415
1980	Little Harlequin "A" L5075G	Closed	1985	217.50	410
1980	Little Harlequin "B" L5076G	Closed	1985	185.00	375
1980	Little Harlequin "C" L5077G	Closed	1985	185.00	500
1980	Teasing the Dog L5078G	Closed	1985	300.00	600
1980	Woman Painting Vase L5079G	Closed	1985	300.00	600-750
1980	Boy Pottery Seller L5080G	Closed	1985	320.00	650-700
1980	Girl Pottery Seller L5081G	Closed	1985	300.00	725
1980	Flower Vendor L5082G	Closed	1985	750.00	1850
1980	A Good Book L5084G	Closed	1985	175.00	350-525
1980	Mother Amabilis L5086G	Closed	1983	275.00	600
1980	Roses for My Mom L5088G	Closed	1988	645.00	1150
1980	Scare-Dy Cat/Playful Cat L5091G	Open		65.00	95
1980	After the Dance L5092G	Closed	1983	165.00	475
1980	A Dancing Partner L5093G	Closed	1983	165.00	500
1980	Ballet First Step L5094G	Closed	1983	165.00	400
1980	Ballet Bowing L5095G	Closed	1983	165.00	300
1989	Her Ladyship, L5097G	Closed	1991	5900.00	6700
1980	Successful Hunt L5098	Closed	1993	5200.00	5200
1982	Playful Tot L5099G	Closed	1985	58.00	265
1982	Cry Baby L5100G	Closed	1985	58.00	275
1982	Learning to Crawl L5101G	Closed	1985	58.00	275-300
1982	Teething L5102G	Closed	1985	58.00	300
1982	Time for a Nap L5103G	Closed	1985	58.00	275
1982	Natalia L5106G	Closed	1985	85.00	350
1982	Little Ballet Girl L5108G	Closed	1985	85.00	400
1982	Little Ballet Girl L5109G	Closed	1985	85.00	400
1982	Dog Sniffing L5110G	Closed	1985	50.00	450-700
1982	Timid Dog L5111G	Closed	1985	44.00	500-600
1982	Play with Me L5112G	Open		40.00	80
1982	Feed Me L5113G	Open		40.00	80
1982	Pet Me L5114G	Open		40.00	80
1982	Little Boy Bullfighter L5115G	Closed	1985	123.00	400
1982	A Victory L5116G	Closed	1985	123.00	400-500
1982	Proud Matador L5117G	Closed	1985	123.00	500
1982	Girl in Green Dress L5118G	Closed	1985	170.00	600
1982	Girl in Bluish Dress L5119G	Closed	1985	170.00	650
1982	Girl in Pink Dress L5120G	Closed	1985	170.00	650
1982	August Moon L5122G	Closed	1993	185.00	350
1982	My Precious Bundle L5123G	Open		150.00	235
1982	Dutch Couple w/Tulips L5124G	Closed	1985	310.00	950
1982	Amparo L5125G	Closed	1990	130.00	330-350
1982	Sewing A Trousseau L5126G	Closed	1990	185.00	400-600
1982	Marcelina L5127G	Closed	1985	255.00	255
1982	Lost Love L5128G	Closed	1988	400.00	700
1982	Jester w/base L5129G	Open		220.00	445
1982	Pensive Clown w/base L5130G	Open		250.00	445
1982	Cervantes L5132G	Closed	1988	925.00	1175
1982	Trophy with Base L5133G	Closed	1983	250.00	650
1982	Girl Soccer Player L5134G	Closed	1983	140.00	575
1982	Billy Football Player L5135G	Closed	1983	140.00	575
1982	Billy Skier L5136G	Closed	1983	140.00	695
1982	Billy Baseball Player L5137G	Closed	1983	140.00	650
1982	A New Doll House L5139G	Closed	1983	185.00	750
1982	Feed Her Son L5140G	Closed	1991	170.00	350
1982	Balloons for Sale L5141G	Open		145.00	250
1982	Comforting Daughter L5142G	Closed	1991	195.00	375
1982	Scooting L5143G	Closed	1988	575.00	850-1000
1982	Amy L5145G	Closed	1985	110.00	1550
1982	"E" is for Ellen L5146G	Closed	1985	110.00	750-1100
1982	Ivez L5147G	Closed	1985	100.00	600
1982	Olivia L5148G	Closed	1985	100.00	375
1982	Ursula L5149G	Closed	1985	100.00	375
1982	Girl's Head L5151G	Closed	1983	380.00	575
1982	Girl's Head L5153G	Closed	1983	475.00	575
1982	First Prize L5154G	Closed	1985	90.00	N/A
1982	Monks at Prayer L5155M	Open		130.00	275
1982	Susan and the Doves L5156G	Closed	1991	203.00	325-360
1982	Bongo Beat L5157G	Open		135.00	230
1982	A Step In Time L5158G	Open		90.00	195
1982	Harmony L5159G	Open		270.00	495
1982	Rhumba L5160G	Open		113.00	185
1982	Cycling To A Picnic L5161G	Closed	1985	2000.00	2800
1982	Mouse Girl/Mindy L5162G	Closed	1985	125.00	500
1982	Bunny Girl/Bunny L5163G	Closed	1985	125.00	450
1982	Cat Girl/Kitty L5164G	Closed	1985	125.00	450
1982	Sancho with Bottle L5165	Closed	1990	100.00	400
1982	Sea Fever L5166M	Closed	1993	130.00	235
1982	Sea Fever L5166G	Closed	1993	130.00	325
1982	Jesus L5167G	Open		130.00	265
1982	King Solomon L5168G	Closed	1985	205.00	750
1982	Abraham L5169G	Closed	1985	155.00	725-750
1982	Moses L5170G	Open		175.00	395
1982	Madonna with Flowers L5171G	Open		173.00	310
1982	Fish A'Plenty L5172G	Closed	1994	190.00	385
1982	Pondering L5173G	Closed	1993	300.00	700
1982	Roaring 20's L5174G	Closed	1993	173.00	350-400
1982	Flapper L5175G	Closed	1995	185.00	375
1982	Rhapsody in Blue L5176G	Closed	1985	325.00	1800
1982	Dante L5177G	Closed	1983	263.00	600
1982	Stubborn Mule L5178G	Closed	1993	250.00	500
1983	Three Pink Roses w/base L5179M	Closed	1990	70.00	110
1983	Dahlia L5180M	Closed	1990	65.00	140
1983	Japanese Camelia w/base L5181M	Closed	1990	60.00	90
1983	White Peony L5182M	Closed	1990	85.00	125
1983	Two Yellow Roses L5183M	Closed	1990	57.50	100
1983	White Carnation L5184M	Closed	1990	65.00	100
1983	Lactiflora Peony L5185M	Closed	1990	65.00	100
1983	Begonia L5186M	Closed	1990	67.50	100
1983	Rhododendrom L5187M	Closed	1990	67.50	190
1983	Miniature Begonia L5188M	Closed	1990	80.00	120
1983	Chrysanthemum L5189M	Closed	1990	100.00	150
1983	California Poppy L5190M	Closed	1990	97.50	180
1985	Predicting the Future L5191G	Closed	1985	135.00	400
1984	Lolita L5192G	Open		80.00	165
1984	Juanita L5193G	Open		80.00	165
1984	Roving Photographer L5194G	Closed	1985	145.00	1400
1983	Say "Cheese!" L5195G	Closed	1990	170.00	600
1983	"Maestro, Music Please!" L5196G	Closed	1988	135.00	500
1983	Female Physician L5197	Open		120.00	260
1984	Boy Graduate L5198G	Open		160.00	290
1984	Girl Graduate L5199G	Open		160.00	285
1984	Male Soccer Player L5200G	Closed	1988	155.00	475
1984	Special Male Soccer Player L5200.3G	Closed	1988	150.00	500
1983	Josefa Feeding Duck L5201G	Closed	1991	125.00	250-300
1983	Aracely with Ducks L5202G	Closed	1991	125.00	250-300
1984	Little Jester L5203G	Closed	1993	75.00	300-325
1984	Little Jester L5203M	Closed	1992	75.00	200-250
1983	Sharpening the Cutlery L5204	Closed	1988	210.00	750
1983	Lamplighter L5205G	Open		170.00	395
1983	Yachtsman L5206G	Closed	1994	110.00	210
1983	A Tall Yarn L5207G	Open		260.00	545
1983	Professor L5208G	Closed	1990	205.00	550-750
1983	School Marm L5209G	Closed	1990	205.00	800-850
1984	Jolie L5210G	Open		105.00	220
1984	Angela L5211G	Open		105.00	220
1984	Evita L5212G	Open		105.00	195
1983	Lawyer L5213G	Open		250.00	570
1983	Architect L5214G	Closed	1990	140.00	450
1983	Fishing w/Gramps w/base L5215G	Open		410.00	850
1983	On the Lake L5216G	Closed	1988	660.00	1000
1983	Spring L5217G	Open		90.00	185
1983	Spring L5217M	Open		90.00	185
1983	Autumn L5218G	Open		90.00	185
1983	Autumn L5218M	Open		90.00	185
1983	Summer L5219G	Open		90.00	185
1983	Summer L5219M	Open		90.00	185
1983	Winter L5220G	Open		90.00	185
1983	Winter L5220M	Open		90.00	185
1983	Sweet Scent L5221G	Open		80.00	145
1983	Sweet Scent L5221M	Open		80.00	145
1983	Pretty Pickings L5222G	Open		80.00	145
1983	Pretty Pickings L5222M	Open		80.00	145
1983	Spring is Here L5223G	Open		80.00	145
1983	Spring is Here L5223M	Open		80.00	145
1984	The Quest L5224G	Open		125.00	295
1984	Male Candleholder L5226	Closed	1985	660.00	1200
1984	Playful Piglets L5228G	Open		80.00	150
1983	Storytime L5229G	Closed	1990	245.00	900
1984	Graceful Swan L5230G	Open		35.00	90
1984	Swan w/Wings Spread L5231G	Open		50.00	125
1983	Playful Kittens L5232G	Open		130.00	280
1984	Charlie the Tramp L5233G	Closed	1991	150.00	750-950
1984	Artistic Endeavor L5234G	Closed	1988	225.00	500-650
1984	Ballet Trio L5235G	Open		785.00	1650
1984	Cat and Mouse L5236G	Open		55.00	98
1984	Cat and Mouse L5236M	Closed	1992	55.00	95
1984	School Chums L5237G	Open		225.00	485
1984	Eskimo Boy with Pet L5238G	Open		55.00	115
1984	Eskimo Boy with Pet L5238M	Closed	1992	55.00	95
1984	Wine Taster L5239G	Open		190.00	395
1984	Lady from Majorca L5240G	Closed	1990	120.00	385
1984	Best Wishes L5244G	Closed	1986	185.00	325
1984	A Thought for Today L5245	Closed	1986	180.00	250
1984	St. Christopher L5246	Closed	1988	265.00	650
1984	Penguin L5247G	Closed	1988	70.00	200
1984	Penguin L5248G	Closed	1988	70.00	200
1984	Penguin L5249G	Closed	1988	70.00	175
1984	Exam Day L5250G	Closed	1994	115.00	210
1984	Torch Bearer L5251G	Closed	1988	100.00	400-500
1984	Dancing the Polka L5252G	Closed	1994	205.00	450
1984	Cadet L5253G	Closed	1984	150.00	550-650
1984	Making Paella L5254G	Closed	1993	215.00	500
1984	Spanish Soldier L5255G	Closed	1988	185.00	475-575
1984	Folk Dancing L5256G	Closed	1990	205.00	475-575
1984	Vase L5257.30	Closed	1988	55.00	200
1984	Vase L5258.30	Closed	1988	55.00	175
1984	Vase L5261.30	Closed	1988	70.00	125
1984	Vase L5262.30	Closed	1988	70.00	125
1984	Centerpiece-Decorated L5265M	Closed	1990	50.00	175
1985	Bust of Lady from Elche L5269M	Closed	1988	432.00	750
1985	Racing Motor Cyclist L5270G	Closed	1988	360.00	675
1985	Gazelle L5271G	Closed	1988	205.00	425-550
1985	Biking in the Country L5272G	Closed	1990	295.00	750
1985	Civil Guard at Attention L5273G	Closed	1988	170.00	500
1985	Wedding Day L5274G	Open		240.00	435
1985	Weary Ballerina L5275G	Closed	1995	175.00	310
1985	Weary Ballerina L5275M	Closed	1992	175.00	310
1985	Sailor Serenades His Girl L5276G	Closed	1988	315.00	950
1985	Pierrot with Puppy L5277G	Open		95.00	160
1985	Pierrot w/Puppy and Ball L5278G	Open		95.00	160
1985	Pierrot with Concertina L5279G	Open		95.00	160
1985	Hiker L5280G	Closed	1988	195.00	425
1985	Nativity Scene "Haute Relief" L5281M	Closed	1988	210.00	450
1985	Over the Threshold L5282G	Open		150.00	290
1985	Socialite of the Twenties L5283G	Open		175.00	340
1985	Glorious Spring L5284G	Open		355.00	710
1985	Summer on the Farm L5285G	Open		235.00	455
1985	Fall Clean-up L5286G	Open		295.00	565
1985	Winter Frost L5287G	Open		270.00	520
1985	Mallard Duck L5288G	Closed	1994	310.00	520
1985	Little Leaguer Exercising L5289	Closed	1990	150.00	450
1985	Little Leaguer, Catcher L5290	Closed	1990	150.00	450
1985	Little Leaguer on Bench L5291	Closed	1990	150.00	450
1985	Love in Bloom L5292G	Open		225.00	425
1985	Mother and Child & Lamb L5299G	Closed	1988	180.00	750
1985	Medieval Courtship L5300G	Closed	1990	735.00	800
1985	Waiting to Tee Off L5301G	Open		145.00	295
1985	Antelope Drinking L5302	Closed	1988	215.00	650
1985	Playing w/Ducks at the Pond L5303G	Closed	1990	425.00	875
1985	Children at Play L5304	Closed	1990	220.00	550
1985	A Visit with Granny L5305G	Closed	1993	275.00	625
1985	Young Street Musicians L5306G	Closed	1988	300.00	1500
1985	Mini Kitten L5307G	Closed	1993	35.00	100
1985	Mini Cat L5308G	Closed	1993	35.00	75
1985	Mini Cocker Spaniel Pup L5309G	Closed	1993	35.00	125-450
1985	Mini Cocker Spaniel L5310G	Closed	1993	35.00	85-150
1985	Mini Puppies L5311G	Closed	1990	65.00	175
1985	Mini Bison Resting L5312G	Closed	1990	50.00	150
1985	Mini Bison Attacking L5313G	Closed	1990	57.50	225
1985	Mini Deer L5314G	Closed	1990	40.00	150
1985	Mini Giraffe L5316G	Closed	1990	50.00	225
1985	Mini Seal Family L5318G	Closed	1990	77.50	275
1985	Wistful Centaur Girl L5319G	Closed	1990	157.00	450
1985	Demure Centaur Girl L5320	Closed	1990	157.00	425
1985	Parisian Lady L5321G	Closed	1995	193.00	325
1985	Viennese Lady L5322G	Closed	1994	160.00	295
1985	Milanese Lady L5323G	Closed	1994	180.00	400
1985	English Lady L5324G	Closed	1994	225.00	475
1985	Ice Cream Vendor L5325G	Closed	1995	380.00	650
1985	The Tailor L5326G	Closed	1988	335.00	900-1300
1985	Nippon Lady L5327G	Open		325.00	575
1985	Lady Equestrian L5328G	Closed	1988	160.00	400
1985	Gentleman Equestrian L5329G	Closed	1988	160.00	525
1985	Concert Violinist L5330G	Closed	1988	220.00	400
1985	Gymnast with Ring L5331	Closed	1988	95.00	295
1985	Gymnast Balancing Ball L5332	Closed	1988	95.00	375
1985	Gymnast Exercising w/Ball L5333G	Closed	1988	95.00	250
1985	Aerobics Push-Up L5334G	Closed	1988	110.00	295
1985	Aerobics Floor Exercies L5335G	Closed	1988	110.00	300
1985	"La Giaconda" L5337G	Closed	1988	110.00	400
1986	A Stitch in Time L5344G	Open		425.00	795
1986	A New Hat L5345G	Closed	1990	200.00	375
1986	Nature Girl L5346G	Closed	1988	450.00	1000
1986	Bedtime L5347G	Open		300.00	545
1986	On The Scent L5348G	Closed	1990	47.50	300
1986	Relaxing L5349G	Closed	1990	47.50	150
1986	On Guard L5350G	Closed	1990	50.00	200
1986	Woe is Me L5351G	Closed	1990	45.00	200
1986	Hindu Children L5352G	Open		250.00	445
1986	Eskimo Riders L5353G	Open		150.00	250
1986	Eskimo Riders L5353M	Open		150.00	250
1986	A Ride in the Country L5354G	Closed	1993	225.00	415
1986	Consideration L5355M	Closed	1988	100.00	225
1986	Wolf Hound L5356G	Closed	1990	45.00	225
1986	Oration L5357G	Open		170.00	295
1986	Little Sculptor L5358G	Closed	1990	160.00	325-400
1986	El Greco L5359G	Closed	1990	300.00	550
1986	Sewing Circle L5360G	Closed	1990	600.00	1250-1400
1986	Try This One L5361G	Open		225.00	385
1986	Still Life L5363G	Open		180.00	395
1986	Litter of Fun L5364G	Open		275.00	465
1986	Sunday in the Park L5365G	Open		375.00	625
1986	Can Can L5370G	Closed	1990	700.00	1200-1400
1986	Family Roots L5371G	Open		575.00	935
1986	Lolita L5372G	Closed	1993	120.00	200-250
1986	Carmencita L5373G	Closed	1993	120.00	200
1986	Pepita L5374G	Closed	1993	120.00	350
1986	Teresita L5375G	Closed	1993	120.00	350
1986	This One's Mine L5376G	Closed	1995	300.00	520
1986	A Touch of Class L5377G	Open		475.00	795
1986	Time for Reflection L5378G	Open		425.00	745
1986	Children's Games L5379G	Closed	1991	325.00	650
1986	Sweet Harvest L5380G	Closed	1990	450.00	915
1986	Serenade L5381	Closed	1990	450.00	625
1986	Lovers Serenade L5382G	Closed	1990	350.00	850
1986	Petite Maiden L5383	Closed	1990	110.00	350
1986	Petite Pair L5384	Closed	1990	225.00	400
1986	Scarecrow & the Lady L5385G	Open		350.00	680
1986	St. Vincent L5387	Closed	1990	190.00	350
1986	Sidewalk Serenade L5388G	Closed	1988	750.00	1100-1300
1986	Deep in Thought L5389G	Closed	1990	170.00	450
1986	Spanish Dancer L5390G	Closed	1990	170.00	450
1986	A Time to Rest L5391G	Closed	1990	170.00	450
1986	Balancing Act L5392G	Closed	1990	35.00	200
1986	Curiosity L5393G	Closed	1990	25.00	150

*Quotes have been rounded up to nearest dollar

FIGURINES/COTTAGES

YEAR ISSUE		EDITION LIMIT	YEAR RETD.	ISSUE PRICE	*QUOTE U.S.$
1986	Poor Puppy L5394G	Closed	1990	25.00	150-175
1986	Valencian Boy L5395G	Closed	1991	200.00	400
1986	The Puppet Painter L5396G	Open		500.00	850
1986	The Poet L5397G	Closed	1988	425.00	900
1986	At the Ball L5398G	Closed	1991	375.00	750
1987	Time To Rest L5399G	Closed	1993	175.00	295
1987	The Wanderer L5400G	Open		150.00	245
1987	My Best Friend L5401G	Closed	1994	150.00	240
1987	Desert Tour L5402G	Closed	1990	950.00	1050
1987	The Drummer Boy L5403G	Closed	1990	225.00	400
1987	Cadet Captain L5404G	Closed	1990	175.00	360
1987	The Flag Bearer L5405G	Closed	1990	200.00	450
1987	The Bugler L5406G	Closed	1990	175.00	375
1987	At Attention L5407G	Closed	1990	175.00	325
1987	Sunday Stroll L5408G	Closed	1990	250.00	600
1987	Courting Time L5409	Closed	1990	425.00	550
1987	Pilar L5410G	Closed	1990	200.00	400
1987	Teresa L5411G	Closed	1990	225.00	430
1987	Isabel L5412G	Closed	1990	225.00	450
1987	Mexican Dancers L5415G	Open		800.00	1195
1987	In the Garden L5416G	Open		200.00	325
1987	Artist's Model L5417	Closed	1990	425.00	475
1987	Short Eared Owl L5418G	Closed	1990	200.00	360
1987	Great Gray Owl L5419G	Closed	1990	190.00	195
1987	Horned Owl L5420G	Closed	1990	150.00	225
1987	Barn Owl L5421G	Closed	1990	120.00	175
1987	Hawk Owl L5422G	Closed	1990	120.00	195-225
1987	Intermezzo L5424	Closed	1990	325.00	550
1987	Studying in the Park L5425G	Closed	1991	675.00	950
1987	Studying in the Park L5425M	Closed	1989	675.00	400-600
1987	One, Two, Three L5426G	Closed	1995	240.00	390
1987	Saint Nicholas L5427G	Closed	1991	425.00	600-700
1987	Feeding the Pigeons L5428	Closed	1990	490.00	700
1987	Happy Birthday L5429G	Open		100.00	155
1987	Music Time L5430G	Closed	1990	500.00	700
1987	Midwife L5431	Closed	1990	175.00	575
1987	Monkey L5432G	Closed	1990	60.00	160-250
1987	Kangaroo L5433G	Closed	1990	65.00	175-300
1987	Miniature Polar Bear L5434G	Open		65.00	110
1987	Cougar L5435G	Closed	1990	65.00	275
1987	Lion L5436G	Closed	1990	50.00	200-300
1987	Rhino L5437G	Closed	1990	50.00	175
1987	Elephant L5438G	Closed	1990	50.00	200
1987	The Bride L5439G	Closed	1995	250.00	425
1987	Poetry of Love L5442G	Open		500.00	865
1987	Sleepy Trio L5443G	Open		190.00	305
1987	Will You Marry Me? L5447G	Closed	1994	750.00	1250
1987	Naptime L5448G	Open		135.00	250
1987	Naptime L5448M	Open		135.00	250
1987	Goodnight L5449	Open		225.00	375
1987	I Hope She Does L5450G	Open		190.00	345
1988	Study Buddies L5451G	Open		225.00	295
1988	Masquerade Ball L5452G	Closed	1993	220.00	375
1988	Masquerade Ball L5452M	Closed	1992	220.00	265
1988	For You L5453G	Open		450.00	640
1988	For Me? L5454G	Open		290.00	395
1988	Bashful Bather L5455G	Open		150.00	190
1988	Bashful Bather L5455M	Closed	1992	150.00	180
1988	New Playmates L5456G	Open		160.00	230
1988	New Playmates L5456M	Closed	1992	160.00	190
1988	Bedtime Story L5457G	Open		275.00	355
1988	Bedtime Story L5457M	Closed	1992	275.00	330
1988	A Barrow of Fun L5460G	Open		370.00	525
1988	A Barrow of Fun L5460M	Closed	1992	370.00	450
1988	Koala Love L5461G	Closed	1993	115.00	200-300
1988	Practice Makes Perfect L5462G	Open		375.00	545
1988	Look At Me! L5465G	Open		375.00	495
1988	Look At Me! L5465M	Closed	1992	375.00	435
1988	"Chit-Chat" L5466G	Open		150.00	198
1988	"Chit-Chat" L5466M	Closed	1992	150.00	180
1988	May Flowers L5467G	Open		160.00	215
1988	May Flowers L5467M	Closed	1992	160.00	190
1988	"Who's The Fairest?" L5468G	Open		150.00	200
1988	"Who's The Fairest?" L5468M	Closed	1992	150.00	180
1988	Lambkins L5469G	Closed	1993	150.00	210
1988	Lambkins L5469M	Closed	1989	150.00	195
1988	Tea Time L5470G	Open		280.00	385
1988	Sad Sax L5471G	Open		175.00	205
1988	Circus Sam L5472G	Open		175.00	205
1988	How You've Grown! L5474G	Open		180.00	250
1988	How You've Grown! L5474M	Closed	1992	180.00	215
1988	A Lesson Shared L5475G	Open		150.00	190
1988	A Lesson Shared L5475M	Closed	1992	150.00	170
1988	St. Joseph L5476G	Open		210.00	270
1988	Mary L5477G	Open		130.00	165
1988	Baby Jesus L5478G	Open		55.00	75
1988	King Melchior L5479G	Open		210.00	265
1988	King Gaspar L5480G	Open		210.00	265
1988	King Balthasar L5481G	Open		210.00	265
1988	Ox L5482G	Open		125.00	175
1988	Donkey L5483G	Open		125.00	175
1988	Lost Lamb L5484G	Open		100.00	140
1988	Shepherd Boy L5485G	Open		140.00	190
1988	Debutantes L5486G	Open		490.00	695
1988	Debutantes L5486M	Closed	1992	490.00	635
1988	Ingenue L5487G	Open		110.00	145
1988	Ingenue L5487M	Closed	1992	110.00	130
1988	Sandcastles L5488G	Closed	1993	160.00	220
1988	Sandcastles L5488M	Closed	1992	160.00	200
1988	Justice L5489G	Closed	1993	675.00	950
1988	Flor Maria L5490G	Open		500.00	635
1988	Heavenly Strings L5491G	Closed	1993	140.00	160
1988	Heavenly Cellist L5492G	Closed	1993	240.00	240
1988	Angel with Lute L5493G	Closed	1993	140.00	160
1988	Angel with Clarinet L5494G	Closed	1993	140.00	160
1988	Angelic Choir L5495G	Closed	1993	300.00	295-475
1988	Recital L5496G	Open		190.00	285
1988	Dress Rehearsal L5497G	Open		290.00	420
1988	Opening Night L5498G	Open		190.00	285
1988	Pretty Ballerina L5499G	Open		190.00	285
1988	Prayerful Moment (blue) L5500G	Open		90.00	110
1988	Time to Sew (blue) L5501G	Open		90.00	110
1988	Time to Sew (white) L5501.3	Closed	1991	90.00	175
1988	Meditation (blue) L5502G	Open		90.00	110
1988	Hurry Now L5503G	Open		180.00	250
1988	Hurry Now L5503M	Closed	1992	180.00	240
1988	Silver Vase No. 20 L5531.4	Closed	1991	1200.00	275
1989	Flowers for Sale L5537G	Open		1200.00	1550
1989	Puppy Dog Tails L5539G	Open		1200.00	1595
1989	An Evening Out L5540G	Closed	1991	350.00	450
1989	Melancholy w/base L5542G	Open		375.00	455
1989	"Hello, Flowers" L5543G	Closed	1993	385.00	545
1989	Reaching the Goal L5546G	Open		215.00	275
1989	Only the Beginning L5547G	Open		215.00	275
1989	Pretty Posies L5548G	Closed	1994	425.00	530
1989	My New Pet L5549G	Open		150.00	185
1989	Serene Moment (blue) L5550G	Closed	1993	115.00	195
1989	Serene Moment (white) L5550.3G	Closed	1991	115.00	195
1989	Serene Moment (white) L5550.3M	Closed	1991	115.00	135
1989	Call to Prayer (blue) L5551G	Closed	1993	100.00	195
1989	Call to Prayer (white) L5551.3G	Closed	1991	100.00	195
1989	Call to Prayer (white) L5551.3M	Closed	1991	100.00	120
1989	Morning Chores (blue) L5552G	Closed	1993	115.00	195
1989	Wild Goose Chase L5553G	Open		175.00	230
1989	Pretty and Prim L5554G	Open		215.00	270
1989	"Let's Make Up" L5555G	Open		215.00	265
1989	Wide Tulip Vase L5560G	Closed	1990	110.00	300
1989	Green Clover Vase L5561G	Closed	1991	130.00	225
1989	Sad Parting L5583G	Closed	1991	375.00	450
1989	Daddy's Girl/Father's Day L5584G	Open		315.00	395
1989	Fine Melody w/base L5585G	Closed	1993	225.00	325
1989	Sad Note w/base L5586G	Closed	1993	185.00	375
1989	Wedding Cake L5587G	Open		595.00	750
1989	Blustery Day L5588G	Closed	1993	185.00	230
1989	Pretty Pose L5589G	Closed	1993	185.00	230
1989	Spring Breeze L5590G	Closed	1993	185.00	230
1989	Garden Treasures L5591G	Closed	1993	185.00	230
1989	Male Siamese Dancer L5592G	Closed	1993	345.00	400
1989	Siamese Dancer L5593G	Closed	1993	345.00	420
1989	Playful Romp L5594G	Open		215.00	270
1989	Joy in a Basket L5595G	Open		215.00	270
1989	A Gift of Love L5596G	Open		400.00	495
1989	Summer Soiree L5597G	Open		150.00	180
1989	Bridesmaid L5598G	Open		150.00	180
1989	Coquette L5599G	Open		150.00	180
1989	The Blues w/base L5600G	Closed	1993	265.00	395
1989	"Ole" L5601G	Open		365.00	460
1989	Close To My Heart L5603G	Open		125.00	165
1989	Spring Token L5604G	Open		175.00	230
1989	Floral Treasures L5605G	Open		195.00	250
1989	Quiet Evening L5606G	Closed	1993	125.00	165
1989	Calling A Friend L5607G	Open		125.00	165
1989	Baby Doll L5608G	Open		150.00	180
1989	Playful Friends L5609G	Closed	1995	135.00	170
1989	Star Struck w/base L5610G	Open		335.00	420
1989	Sad Clown w/base L5611G	Open		335.00	420
1989	Reflecting w/base L5612G	Closed	1994	335.00	420
1989	Startled L5614G	Closed	1991	265.00	425
1989	Bathing Beauty L5615G	Closed	1991	265.00	350-475
1989	Candleholder L5625G	Closed	1990	105.00	125
1989	Candleholder L5626	Closed	1990	90.00	125
1989	Lladró Vase L5631G	Closed	1990	150.00	300-350
1990	Water Dreamer Vase L5633G	Closed	1990	150.00	350
1990	Cat Nap L5640G	Open		125.00	145
1990	The King's Guard w/base L5642G	Closed	1993	950.00	1100
1990	Cathy L5643G	Open		200.00	235
1990	Susan L5644G	Open		190.00	215
1990	Elizabeth L5645G	Open		190.00	215
1990	Cindy L5646G	Open		190.00	215
1990	Sara L5647G	Open		200.00	230
1990	Courtney L5648G	Open		200.00	230
1990	Nothing To Do L5649G	Open		190.00	220
1990	Anticipation L5650G	Closed	1993	300.00	375
1990	Musical Muse L5651G	Open		375.00	440
1989	Marbella Clock L5652	Closed	1994	125.00	235
1989	Avila Clock L5653	Closed	1995	135.00	135
1990	Venetian Carnival L5658G	Closed	1993	500.00	575
1990	Barnyard Scene L5659G	Open		200.00	450
1990	Sunning In Ipanema L5660G	Closed	1993	370.00	475
1990	Traveling Artist L5661G	Closed	1994	250.00	290
1990	May Dance L5662G	Open		170.00	210
1990	Spring Dance L5663G	Open		170.00	300
1990	Giddy Up L5664G	Closed	1994	190.00	230
1990	Hang On! L5665G	Closed	1995	225.00	285
1990	Trino At The Beach L5666G	Closed	1995	390.00	475
1990	Valencian Harvest L5668G	Closed	1993	175.00	350-400
1990	Valencian FLowers L5669G	Closed	1993	370.00	375
1990	Valencian Beauty L5670G	Closed	1993	175.00	325
1990	Little Dutch Gardener L5671G	Closed	1993	400.00	475
1990	Hi There! L5672G	Open		450.00	520
1990	A Quiet Moment L5673G	Open		450.00	520
1990	A Faun And A Friend L5674G	Open		450.00	520
1990	Tee Time L5675G	Closed	1993	280.00	315
1990	Wandering Minstrel L5676G	Closed	1993	270.00	310
1990	Twilight Years L5677G	Open		370.00	420
1990	I Feel Pretty L5678G	Open		190.00	230
1990	In No Hurry L5679G	Closed	1994	550.00	640
1990	Traveling In Style L5680G	Closed	1994	425.00	495
1990	On The Road L5681G	Closed	1991	320.00	450-550
1990	Breezy Afternoon L5682G	Open		180.00	195
1990	Breezy Afternoon L5682M	Open		180.00	195
1990	Beautiful Burro L5683G	Closed	1993	280.00	365
1990	Barnyard Reflections L5684G	Closed	1993	460.00	525
1990	Promenade L5685G	Closed	1994	275.00	325
1990	On The Avenue L5686G	Closed	1994	275.00	325
1990	Afternoon Stroll L5687G	Closed	1994	275.00	350
1990	Dog's Best Friend L5688G	Open		250.00	295
1990	Can I Help? L5689G	Open		250.00	325
1990	Marshland Mates w/base L5691G	Open		950.00	1200
1990	Street Harmonies w/base L5692G	Closed	1993	3200.00	3750
1990	Circus Serenade L5694G	Closed	1994	300.00	375
1990	Concertina L5695G	Closed	1994	300.00	360
1990	Mandolin Serenade L5696G	Closed	1994	300.00	360
1990	Over The Clouds L5697G	Open		275.00	310
1990	Don't Look Down L5698G	Open		330.00	395
1990	Sitting Pretty L5699G	Open		300.00	340
1990	Southern Charm L5700G	Open		675.00	1025
1990	Just A Little Kiss L5701G	Open		320.00	375
1990	Back To School L5702G	Closed	1993	350.00	300-445
1990	Behave! L5703G	Closed	1994	230.00	265
1990	Swan Song L5704G	Closed	1995	350.00	410
1990	The Swan & The Princess L5705G	Closed	1994	350.00	425-450
1990	We Can't Play L5706G	Open		200.00	235
1990	After School L5707G	Closed	1993	280.00	315
1990	My First Class L5708G	Closed	1993	280.00	315
1990	Between Classes L5709G	Closed	1993	280.00	315
1990	Fantasy Friend L5710G	Closed	1993	420.00	495
1990	A Christmas Wish L5711G	Open		350.00	410
1990	Sleepy Kitten L5712G	Open		110.00	130
1990	The Snow Man L5713G	Open		300.00	350
1990	First Ballet L5714G	Open		370.00	420
1990	Mommy, it's Cold! L5715G	Closed	1994	360.00	435-450
1990	Land of The Giants L5716G	Closed	1994	275.00	400
1990	Rock A Bye Baby L5717G	Open		300.00	365
1990	Sharing Secrets L5720G	Open		290.00	335
1990	Once Upon A Time L5721G	Open		550.00	650
1990	Follow Me L5722G	Open		140.00	160
1990	Heavenly Chimes L5723G	Open		100.00	120
1990	Angelic Voice L5724G	Open		125.00	145
1990	Making A Wish L5725G	Open		125.00	145
1990	Sweep Away The Clouds L5726G	Open		125.00	145
1990	Angel Care L5727G	Open		190.00	210
1990	Heavenly Dreamer L5728G	Open		100.00	120
1991	Carousel Charm L5731G	Closed	1994	1700.00	1850
1991	Carousel Canter L5732G	Closed	1994	1700.00	1850
1991	Horticulturist L5733G	Closed	1993	450.00	495
1991	Pilgrim Couple L5734G	Closed	1993	490.00	525
1991	Big Sister L5735G	Open		650.00	685
1991	Puppet Show L5736G	Open		280.00	295
1991	Little Prince L5737G	Closed	1993	295.00	315
1991	Best Foot Forward L5738G	Closed	1994	280.00	305
1991	Lap Full Of Love L5739G	Closed	1995	275.00	295
1991	Alice In Wonderland L5740G	Open		440.00	485
1991	Dancing Class L5741G	Open		340.00	365
1991	Bridal Portrait L5742G	Closed	1995	480.00	560
1991	Don't Forget Me L5743G	Open		150.00	160
1991	Bull & Donkey L5744G	Open		250.00	275
1991	Baby Jesus L5745G	Open		170.00	185
1991	St. Joseph L5746G	Open		350.00	375
1991	Mary L5747G	Open		275.00	295
1991	Shepherd Girl L5748G	Open		150.00	165
1991	Shepherd Boy L5749G	Open		225.00	245
1991	Little Lamb L5750G	Open		40.00	42
1991	Walk With Father L5751G	Closed	1994	375.00	440
1991	Little Virgin L5752G	Closed	1994	295.00	325
1991	Hold Her Still L5753G	Closed	1993	650.00	700
1991	Singapore Dancers L5754G	Closed	1993	950.00	1195
1991	Claudette L5755G	Closed	1993	265.00	350
1991	Ashley L5756G	Closed	1993	265.00	300
1991	Beautiful Tresses L5757G	Closed	1993	725.00	875
1991	Sunday Best L5758G	Open		725.00	785
1991	Presto! L5759G	Closed	1993	275.00	325
1991	Interrupted Nap L5760G	Closed	1995	325.00	350
1991	Out For A Romp L5761G	Closed	1995	375.00	410
1991	Checking The Time L5762G	Closed	1995	560.00	595
1991	Musical Partners L5763G	Closed	1995	625.00	675
1991	Seeds Of Laughter L5764G	Closed	1995	525.00	575
1991	Hats Off To Fun L5765G	Closed	1995	475.00	510
1991	Charming Duet L5766G	Open		575.00	625
1991	First Sampler L5767G	Closed	1995	625.00	680
1991	Academy Days L5768G	Closed	1993	280.00	310
1991	Faithful Steed L5769G	Closed	1994	370.00	395
1991	Out For A Spin L5770G	Closed	1994	390.00	420
1991	The Magic Of Laughter L5771G	Open		950.00	1050
1991	Little Dreamers L5772G	Open		230.00	240
1991	Little Dreamers L5772M	Open		230.00	240
1991	Graceful Offering L5773G	Closed	1995	850.00	895
1991	Nature's Gifts L5774G	Closed	1994	900.00	975
1991	Gift Of Beauty L5775G	Closed	1995	850.00	895
1991	Lover's Paradise L5779G	Open		2250.00	2450
1991	Walking The Fields L5780G	Closed	1993	725.00	795
1991	Not Too Close L5781G	Closed	1994	365.00	450
1991	My Chores L5782G	Closed	1995	325.00	355
1991	Special Delivery L5783G	Closed	1994	525.00	550
1991	A Cradle Of Kittens L5784G	Open		360.00	385
1991	Ocean Beauty L5785G	Open		625.00	665

*Quotes have been rounded up to nearest dollar

YEAR ISSUE		EDITION LIMIT	YEAR RETD.	ISSUE PRICE	*QUOTE U.S. $
1991	Story Hour L5786G	Open		550.00	625
1991	Sophisticate L5787G	Open		185.00	195
1991	Talk Of The Town L5788G	Open		185.00	195
1991	The Flirt L5789G	Open		185.00	195
1991	Carefree L5790G	Open		300.00	325
1991	Fairy Godmother L5791G	Closed	1994	375.00	410
1991	Reverent Moment L5792G	Closed	1994	295.00	320
1991	Precocious Ballerina L5793G	Closed	1995	575.00	625
1991	Precious Cargo L5794G	Closed	1994	460.00	495
1991	Floral Getaway L5795G	Closed	1993	625.00	745
1991	Holy Night L5796G	Closed	1994	330.00	360
1991	Come Out And Play L5797G	Closed	1994	275.00	300
1991	Milkmaid L5798G	Closed	1993	450.00	495
1991	Shall We Dance? L5799G	Closed	1993	600.00	750
1991	Elegant Promenade L5802G	Open		775.00	825
1991	Playing Tag L5804G	Closed	1993	170.00	190
1991	Tumbling L5805G	Closed	1993	130.00	140
1991	Tumbling L5805M	Closed	1992	130.00	140
1991	Tickling L5806G	Closed	1993	130.00	145
1991	Tickling L5806M	Closed	1992	130.00	145
1991	My Puppies L5807G	Closed	1993	325.00	360
1991	Musically Inclined L5810G	Closed	1993	235.00	250
1991	Littlest Clown L5811G	Open		225.00	240
1991	Tired Friend L5812G	Open		225.00	245
1991	Having A Ball L5813G	Open		225.00	240
1991	Curtain Call L5814G	Closed	1994	490.00	520
1991	Curtain Call L5814M	Closed	1994	490.00	520
1991	In Full Relave L5815G	Closed	1994	490.00	520
1991	In Full Relave L5815M	Closed	1994	490.00	520
1991	Prima Ballerina L5816G	Closed	1994	490.00	520
1991	Prima Ballerina L5816M	Closed	1994	490.00	520
1991	Backstage Preparation L5817G	Closed	1994	490.00	520
1991	Backstage Preparation L5817M	Closed	1994	490.00	520
1991	On Her Toes L5818G	Closed	1994	490.00	520
1991	On Her Toes L5818M	Closed	1994	490.00	520
1991	Allegory Of Liberty L5819G	Open		1950.00	2100
1991	Dance Of Love L5820G	Closed	1993	575.00	625
1991	Minstrel's Love L5821G	Closed	1993	525.00	575
1991	Little Unicorn L5826G	Open		275.00	295
1991	Little Unicorn L5826M	Open		275.00	295
1991	I've Got It L5827G	Closed	1995	170.00	180
1991	Next At Bat L5828G	Open		170.00	180
1991	Heavenly Harpist L5830	Yr.Iss.	1991	135.00	150-170
1991	Jazz Horn L5832G	Open		295.00	310
1991	Jazz Sax L5833G	Open		295.00	315
1991	Jazz Bass L5834G	Open		395.00	425
1991	I Do L5835G	Open		165.00	190
1991	Sharing Sweets L5836G	Open		220.00	245
1991	Sing With Me L5837G	Open		240.00	250
1991	On The Move L5838G	Open		340.00	395
1992	A Quiet Afternoon L5843G	Closed	1995	1050.00	1125
1992	Flirtatious Jester L5844G	Open		890.00	925
1992	Dressing The Baby L5845G	Open		295.00	295
1992	All Tuckered Out L5846G	Open		220.00	255
1992	All Tuckered Out L5846M	Open		220.00	255
1992	The Loving Family L5848G	Closed	1994	950.00	985
1992	Inspiring Muse L5850G	Closed	1994	1200.00	1250
1992	Feathered Fantasy L5851G	Open		1200.00	1250
1992	Easter Bonnets L5852G	Closed	1993	265.00	325
1992	Floral Admiration L5853G	Closed	1994	690.00	725
1992	Floral Fantasy L5854G	Closed	1995	690.00	710
1992	Afternoon Jaunt L5855G	Closed	1993	420.00	440
1992	Circus Concert L5856G	Open		570.00	585
1992	Grand Entrance L5857G	Closed	1994	265.00	275
1992	Waiting to Dance L5858G	Closed	1995	295.00	335
1992	At The Ball L5859G	Open		295.00	330
1992	Fairy Garland L5860G	Closed	1995	630.00	650
1992	Fairy Flowers L5861G	Closed	1995	630.00	655
1992	Fragrant Bouquet L5862G	Open		350.00	360
992	Dressing For The Ballet L5865G	Closed	1995	395.00	415
1992	Final Touches L5866G	Closed	1995	395.00	415
1992	Serene Valenciana L5867G	Closed	1994	365.00	385
1992	Loving Valenciana L5868G	Closed	1995	365.00	385
1992	Fallas Queen L5869G	Closed	1995	420.00	440
1992	Olympic Torch w/Fantasy Logo L5870G	Closed	1994	165.00	145
992	Olympic Champion w/Fantasy Logo L5871G	Closed	1994	165.00	145
992	Olympic Pride w/Fantasy Logo L5872G	Closed	1994	165.00	495
992	Modern Mother L5873G	Open		325.00	335
1992	Off We Go L5874G	Closed	1994	365.00	385
992	Angelic Cymbalist L5876	Yr.Iss.	1992	140.00	165
992	Guest Of Honor L5877G	Open		195.00	200
992	Sister's Pride L5878G	Open		595.00	615
992	Shot On Goal L5879G	Open		1100.00	1150
992	Playful Unicorn L5880G	Open		295.00	320
992	Playful Unicorn L5880M	Open		295.00	320
992	Mischievous Mouse L5881G	Open		285.00	295
992	Restful Mouse L5882G	Open		285.00	295
992	Loving Mouse L5883G	Open		285.00	295
992	From This Day Forward L5885G	Open		265.00	285
992	Hippity Hop L5886G	Closed	1995	95.00	95
992	Washing Up L5887G	Closed	1995	95.00	95
992	That Tickles! L5888G	Closed	1995	95.00	105
992	Snack Time L5889G	Closed	1995	95.00	105
992	The Aviator L5891G	Open		375.00	415
992	Circus Magic L5892G	Open		470.00	495
992	Friendship In Bloom L5893G	Closed	1995	650.00	685
992	Precious Petals L5894G	Open		395.00	415
992	Bouquet of Blossoms L5895G	Open		295.00	295

YEAR ISSUE		EDITION LIMIT	YEAR RETD.	ISSUE PRICE	*QUOTE U.S.$
1992	The Loaves & Fishes L5896G	Open		695.00	760
1992	Trimming The Tree L5897G	Open		900.00	925
1992	Spring Splendor L5898G	Open		440.00	450
1992	Just One More L5899G	Open		450.00	495
1992	Sleep Tight L5900G	Open		450.00	495
1992	Surprise L5901G	Open		325.00	335
1992	Easter Bunnies L5902G	Open		240.00	250
1992	Down The Aisle L5903G	Open		295.00	295
1992	Sleeping Bunny L5904G	Open		75.00	75
1992	Attentive Bunny L5905G	Open		75.00	75
1992	Preening Bunny L5906G	Open		75.00	80
1992	Sitting Bunny L5907G	Open		75.00	80
1992	Just A Little More L5908G	Open		370.00	380
1992	All Dressed Up L5909G	Open		440.00	450
1992	Making A Wish L5910G	Open		790.00	825
1992	Swans Take Flight L5912G	Open		2850.00	2950
1992	Rose Ballet L5919G	Open		210.00	215
1992	Swan Ballet L5920G	Open		210.00	215
1992	Take Your Medicine L5921G	Open		360.00	370
1990	Floral Clock L5924	Closed	1995	N/A	165
1990	Garland Quartz Clock L5926	Closed	1995	195.00	195
1992	Jazz Clarinet L5928G	Open		295.00	295
1992	Jazz Drums L5929G	Open		595.00	610
1992	Jazz Duo L5930G	Open		795.00	885
1993	The Ten Commandments w/Base L5933G	Open		930.00	930
1993	The Holy Teacher L5934G	Open		375.00	375
1993	Nutcracker Suite L5935G	Open		620.00	620
1993	Little Skipper L5936G	Open		320.00	320
1993	Riding The Waves L5941G	Open		405.00	405
1993	World of Fantasy L5943G	Closed	1995	295.00	295
1993	The Great Adventure L5944G	Closed	1994	325.00	325
1993	A Mother's Way L5946G	Open		1350.00	1350
1993	General Practitioner L5947G	Open		360.00	360
1993	Physician L5948G	Open		360.00	360
1993	Angel Candleholder w/Lyre L5949G	Open		295.00	315
1993	Angel Candleholder w/Tambourine L5950G	Open		295.00	315
1993	Sounds of Summer L5953G	Open		125.00	142
1993	Sounds of Winter L5954G	Open		125.00	142
1993	Sounds of Fall L5955G	Open		125.00	142
1993	Sounds of Spring L5956G	Open		125.00	142
1993	The Glass Slipper L5957G	Open		475.00	475
1993	Country Ride w/base L5958G	Open		2850.00	2875
1993	It's Your Turn L5959G	Open		365.00	365
1993	On Patrol L5960G	Open		395.00	445
1993	The Great Teacher w/base L5961G	Open		850.00	850
1993	Angelic Melody L5963	Yr.Iss.	1993	145.00	170
1993	The Great Voyage L5964G	Closed	1994	50.00	50
1993	The Clipper Ship w/base L5965M	Open		240.00	250
1993	Flowers Forever w/base L5966G	Open		4150.00	4150
1993	Honeymoon Ride w/base L5968G	Closed	1995	2750.00	2750
1993	A Special Toy L5971G	Open		815.00	815
1993	Before the Dance w/base L5972G	Open		3550.00	3550
1993	Before the Dance w/base L5972M	Open		3550.00	3550
1993	Family Outing w/base L5974G	Open		4275.00	4275
1993	Up and Away w/base L5975G	Open		2850.00	2850
1993	The Fireman L5976G	Open		395.00	445
1993	Revelation w/base (white) L5977G	Closed	1995	310.00	310
1993	Revelation w/base (black) L5978M	Closed	1995	310.00	310
1993	Revelation w/base (sand) L5979M	Closed	1995	310.00	310
1993	The Past w/base (white) L5980G	Closed	1995	310.00	310
1993	The Past w/base (black) L5981M	Closed	1995	310.00	310
1993	The Past w/base (sand) L5982M	Closed	1995	310.00	310
1993	Beauty w/base (white) L5983G	Closed	1995	310.00	310
1993	Beauty w/base (black) L5984M	Closed	1995	310.00	310
1993	Beauty w/base (sand) L5985M	Closed	1995	310.00	310
1993	Sunday Sermon L5986G	Open		425.00	425
1993	Talk to Me L5987G	Open		145.00	165
1993	Taking Time L5988G	Open		145.00	165
1993	A Mother's Touch L5989G	Open		470.00	470
1993	Thoughtful Caress L5990G	Open		225.00	225
1993	Love Story L5991G	Open		2800.00	2800
1993	Unicorn and Friend L5993G	Open		355.00	355
1993	Unicorn and Friend L5993M	Open		355.00	355
1993	Meet My Friend L5994G	Open		695.00	695
1993	Soft Meow L5995G	Open		480.00	515
1993	Bless the Child L5996G	Closed	1994	465.00	465
1993	One More Try L5997G	Open		715.00	715
1993	My Dad L6001G	Closed	1995	550.00	575
1993	Down You Go L6002G	Open		815.00	815
1993	Ready To Learn L6003G	Open		650.00	650
1993	Bar Mitzvah Day L6004G	Open		395.00	430
1993	Christening Day w/base L6005G	Closed	1995	1425.00	1425
1993	Oriental Colonade w/base L6006G	Closed	1995	1875.00	1875
1993	The Goddess & Unicorn w/base L6007G	Open		1675.00	1675
1993	Joyful Event L6008G	Open		825.00	825
1993	Monday's Child (Boy) L6011G	Open		245.00	270
1993	Monday's Child (Girl) L6012G	Open		260.00	290
1993	Tuesday's Child (Boy) L6013G	Open		225.00	250
1993	Tuesday's Child (Girl) L6014G	Open		245.00	270
1993	Wednesday's Child (Boy) L6015G	Open		245.00	270
1993	Wednesday's Child (Girl) L6016G	Open		245.00	270
1993	Thursday's Child (Boy) L6017G	Open		225.00	250
1993	Thursday's Child (Girl) L6018G	Open		245.00	270
1993	Friday's Child (Boy) L6019G	Open		225.00	250
1993	Friday's Child (Girl) L6020G	Open		225.00	250
1993	Saturday's Child (Boy) L6021G	Open		245.00	270
1993	Saturday's Child (Girl) L6022G	Open		245.00	270
1993	Angelic Melody-L5963G	Yr.Iss.	1993	145.00	145-175

YEAR ISSUE		EDITION LIMIT	YEAR RETD.	ISSUE PRICE	*QUOTE U.S.$
1993	Sunday's Child (Boy) L6023G	Open		225.00	250
1993	Sunday's Child (Girl) L6024G	Open		225.00	250
1993	Barnyard See Saw L6025G	Open		500.00	500
1993	My Turn L6026G	Open		515.00	515
1993	Hanukah Lights L6027G	Open		345.00	395
1993	Mazel Tov! L6028G	Open		380.00	395
1993	Hebrew Scholar L6029G	Open		225.00	245
1993	On The Go L6031G	Closed	1995	475.00	485
1993	On The Green L6032G	Open		645.00	645
1993	Monkey Business L6034G	Closed	1994	745.00	745
1993	Young Princess L6036G	Open		240.00	240
1994	Saint James L6084G	Open		310.00	310
1994	Angelic Harmony L6085G	Open		495.00	550
1994	Allow Me L6086G	Open		1625.00	1625
1994	Loving Care L6087G	Open		250.00	270
1994	Communion Prayer (Boy) L6088G	Open		194.00	200
1994	Communion Prayer (Girl) L6089G	Open		198.00	210
1994	Baseball Player L6090G	Open		295.00	310
1994	Basketball Player L6091G	Open		295.00	310
1994	The Prince L6092G	Open		325.00	325
1994	Songbird L6093G	Open		395.00	395
1994	The Sportsman L6096G	Open		495.00	540
1994	Sleeping Bunny W/Flowers L6097G	Open		110.00	110
1994	Attentive Bunny w/Flowers L6098G	Open		140.00	140
1994	Preening Bunny W/Flowers L6099G	Open		140.00	140
1994	Sitting Bunny W/Flowers L6100G	Open		110.00	110
1994	Follow Us L6101G	Open		198.00	215
1994	Mother's Little Helper L6102G	Open		275.00	285
1994	Beautiful Ballerina L6103G	Open		250.00	270
1994	Finishing Touches L6104	Open		240.00	250
1994	Spring Joy L6106G	Open		795.00	795
1994	Football Player L6107	Open		295.00	310
1994	Hockey Player L6108G	Open		295.00	310
1994	Meal Time L6109G	Open		495.00	515
1994	Medieval Maiden L6110G	Open		150.00	165
1994	Medieval Soldier L6111G	Open		225.00	245
1994	Medieval Lord L6112G	Open		285.00	300
1994	Medieval Lady L6113G	Open		225.00	225
1994	Medieval Princess L6114G	Open		245.00	245
1994	Medieval Prince L6115G	Open		295.00	315
1994	Medieval Majesty L6116G	Open		315.00	325
1994	Constance L6117G	Open		195.00	205
1994	Musketeer Portos L6118G	Open		220.00	230
1994	Musketeer Aramis L6119G	Open		275.00	295
1994	Musketeer Dartagnan L6120G	Open		245.00	270
1994	Musketeer Athos L6121G	Open		245.00	270
1994	A Great Adventure L6122	Open		198.00	215
1994	Out For a Stroll L6123G	Open		198.00	215
1994	Travelers Rest L6124G	Open		275.00	295
1994	Angelic Violinist L6126G	Yr.Iss.	1994	150.00	150-170
1994	Sweet Dreamers L6127G	Open		280.00	290
1994	Christmas Melodies L6128G	Open		375.00	385
1994	Little Friends L6129G	Open		225.00	235
1996	Spring Enchantment L6130G	Open		245.00	245
1994	Angel of Peace L6131G	Open		345.00	370
1994	Angel with Garland L6133G	Open		345.00	370
1994	Birthday Party L6134G	Open		395.00	425
1994	Football Star L6135	Open		295.00	295
1994	Basketball Star L6136G	Open		295.00	295
1994	Baseball Star L6137G	Open		295.00	295
1994	Globe Paperweight L6138M	Open		95.00	95
1994	Springtime Friends L6140G	Open		485.00	485
1994	Kitty Cart L6141G	Open		750.00	795
1994	Indian Pose L6142G	Open		475.00	475
1994	Indian Dancer L6143G	Open		475.00	475
1995	Caribbean Kiss L6144G	Open		340.00	340
1994	Heavenly Prayer L6145	Open		675.00	695
1994	Spring Angel L6146G	Open		250.00	265
1994	Fall Angel L6147G	Open		250.00	265
1994	Summer Angel L6148G	Open		220.00	220
1994	Winter Angel L6149G	Open		250.00	265
1994	Playing The Flute L6150G	Open		175.00	190
1994	Bearing Flowers L6151G	Open		175.00	190
1994	Flower Gazer L6152G	Open		175.00	190
1994	American Love L6153G	Open		225.00	225
1994	African Love L6154G	Open		225.00	225
1994	European Love L6155G	Open		225.00	225
1994	Asian Love L6156G	Open		225.00	225
1994	Polynesian Love L6157G	Open		225.00	225
1995	Fiesta Dancer L6163G	Open		285.00	285
1994	Wedding Bells L6164G	Open		175.00	185
1995	Pretty Cargo L6165G	Open		500.00	500
1995	Dear Santa L6166G	Open		250.00	250
1995	Delicate Bundle L6167G	Open		275.00	275
1994	The Apollo Landing L6168G	Closed	1995	450.00	450
1995	Seesaw Friends L6169G	Open		795.00	795
1995	Under My Spell L6170G	Open		195.00	195
1995	Magical Moment L6171G	Open		180.00	180
1995	Coming of Age L6172G	Open		345.00	345
1995	A Moment's Rest L6173G	Open		130.00	130
1995	Graceful Pose L6174G	Open		195.00	195
1995	Graceful Pose L6174M	Open		195.00	195
1995	White Swan L6175G	Open		90.00	90
1995	Communion Bell L6176G	Open		85.00	85
1995	Asian Scholar L6177G	Open		315.00	315
1995	Little Matador L6178G	Open		245.00	245
1995	Peaceful Moment L6179G	Open		385.00	385
1995	Sharia L6180G	Open		235.00	235
1995	Velisa L6181G	Open		180.00	180
1996	Wanda L6182	Open		205.00	205
1995	Preparing For The Sabbath L6183G	Open		385.00	385

*Quotes have been rounded up to nearest dollar

FIGURINES/COTTAGES

YEAR ISSUE		EDITION LIMIT	YEAR RETD.	ISSUE PRICE	*QUOTE U.S.$
1995	For a Better World L6186G	Open		575.00	575
1995	European Boy L6187G	Open		185.00	185
1995	Asian Boy L6188G	Open		225.00	225
1995	African Boy L6189G	Open		195.00	195
1995	Polynesian Boy L6190G	Open		250.00	250
1995	All American L6191G	Open		225.00	225
1995	American Indian Boy L6192G	Open		225.00	225
1995	Summer Serenade L6193G	Open		375.00	375
1995	Summer Serenade L6193M	Open		375.00	375
1995	Carnival Companions L6195G	Open		650.00	650
1995	Seaside Companions L6196G	Open		230.00	230
1995	Seaside Serenade L6197G	Open		275.00	275
1995	Soccer Practice L6198G	Open		195.00	195
1995	In The Procession L6199G	Open		250.00	250
1995	In The Procession L6199M	Open		250.00	250
1995	Bridal Bell L6200G	Open		125.00	125
1995	Cuddly Kitten L6201G	Open		270.00	270
1995	Daddy's Little Sweetheart L6202G	Open		595.00	595
1995	Grace and Beauty L6204G	Open		325.00	325
1995	Grace and Beauty L6204M	Open		325.00	325
1995	Graceful Dance L6205G	Open		340.00	340
1995	Reading the Torah L6208G	Open		535.00	535
1995	The Rabbi L6209G	Open		250.00	250
1995	Gentle Surprise L6210G	Open		125.00	125
1995	New Friend L6211G	Open		120.00	120
1995	Little Hunter L6212G	Open		115.00	115
1995	Lady Of Nice L6213G	Open		198.00	198
1995	Lady Of Nice L6213M	Open		198.00	198
1995	Leo L6214G	Open		198.00	198
1995	Virgo L6215G	Open		198.00	198
1995	Aquarius L6216G	Open		198.00	198
1995	Sagittarius L6217G	Open		198.00	198
1995	Taurus L6218G	Open		198.00	198
1995	Gemini L6219G	Open		198.00	198
1995	Libra L6220G	Open		198.00	198
1995	Aries L6221G	Open		198.00	198
1995	Capricorn L6222G	Open		198.00	198
1995	Pisces L6223G	Open		198.00	198
1995	Cancer L6224G	Open		198.00	198
1995	Scorpio L6225G	Open		198.00	198
1995	Snuggle Up L6226G	Open		170.00	170
1995	Trick or Treat L6227G	Open		250.00	250
1995	Special Gift L6228G	Open		265.00	265
1995	Contented Companion L6229G	Open		195.00	195
1995	Oriental Dance L6230G	Open		198.00	198
1995	Oriental Lantern L6231G	Open		198.00	198
1995	Oriental Beauty L6232G	Open		198.00	198
1995	Chef's Apprentice L6233G	Open		260.00	260
1995	Chef's Apprentice L6233M	Open		260.00	260
1995	The Great Chef L6234G	Open		195.00	195
1995	The Great Chef L6234M	Open		195.00	195
1995	Dinner is Served L6235G	Open		185.00	185
1995	Dinner is Served L6235M	Open		185.00	185
1995	Lady of Monaco L6236G	Open		250.00	250
1995	Lady of Monaco L6236M	Open		250.00	250
1995	The Young Jester-Mandolin L6237G	Open		235.00	235
1995	The Young Jester-Mandolin L6237M	Open		235.00	235
1995	The Young Jester-Trumpet L6238G	Open		235.00	235
1995	The Young Jester-Trumpet L6238M	Open		235.00	235
1995	The Young Jester-Singer L6239G	Open		235.00	235
1995	The Young Jester-Singer L6239M	Open		235.00	235
1995	Graceful Ballet L6240G	Open		795.00	795
1995	Graceful Ballet L6240M	Open		795.00	795
1995	Allegory of Spring L6241G	Open		735.00	735
1995	Allegory of Spring L6241M	Open		735.00	735
1996	Winged Companions L6242G	Open		270.00	270
1996	Winged Companions L6242M	Open		270.00	270
1996	Sweet Symphony L6243	Open		450.00	450
1996	Sunday's Best L6246	Open		370.00	370
1995	Challenge L6247M	Yr.Iss.		350.00	350
1995	Regatta L6248G	Yr.Iss.		695.00	695
1996	Springtime Harvest L6250	Open		760.00	760
1996	Nature's Beauty w/base L6252	Open		770.00	770
1996	Making Rounds L6256	Open		295.00	295
1996	Pierrot in Preparation L6257	Open		195.00	195
1996	Pierrot in Love L6258	Open		195.00	195
1996	Pierrot Rehearsing L6259	Open		195.00	195
1996	Our Lady "Caridid Del Cobre" w/base L6268	Open		1355.00	1355
1996	Diana Goddess of the Hunt w/base L6269	Open		1550.00	1550
1996	Commencement L6270	Open		200.00	200
1996	Cap and Gown L6271	Open		200.00	200
1996	Going Forth L6272	Open		200.00	200
1996	Pharmacist L6273	Open		290.00	290
1996	Daisy L6274	Open		150.00	150
1996	Rose L6275	Open		150.00	150
1996	Iris L6276	Open		150.00	150
1996	Young Mandolin Player L6278	Open		330.00	330
1996	Flowers of Paris L6279	Open		525.00	525
1996	Paris in Bloom L6280	Open		525.00	525
1996	Coqueta L6281G	Open		435.00	435
1996	Coqueta L6281M	Open		435.00	435
1996	Medic L6282G	Open		225.00	225
1996	Medic L6282M	Open		225.00	225
1996	Temis L6283G	Open		435.00	435
1996	Temis L6283M	Open		435.00	435
1996	Quione L6284G	Open		435.00	435
1996	Quione L6284M	Open		435.00	435
1996	Dreams of Aladdin w/base L6285	Open		1440.00	1440
1996	Tennis Champion w/base L6286G	Open		350.00	350
1996	Tennis Champion w/base L6286M	Open		350.00	350
1996	Restless Dove L6287G	Open		105.00	105
1996	Restless Dove L6287M	Open		105.00	105
1996	Taking Flight L6288G	Open		150.00	150
1996	Taking Flight L6288M	Open		150.00	150
1996	Peaceful Dove L6289G	Open		105.00	105
1996	Peaceful Dove L6289M	Open		105.00	105
1996	Proud Dove L6290G	Open		105.00	105
1996	Proud Dove L6290M	Open		105.00	105
1996	Love Nest L6291G	Open		260.00	260
1996	Love Nest L6291M	Open		260.00	260
1996	Little Bear L6299	Open		285.00	285
1996	Rubber Ducky L6300	Open		285.00	285
1996	Care and Tenderness w/base L6301	Open		850.00	850
1996	Thena L6302G	Open		485.00	485
1996	Thena L6302M	Open		485.00	485
1996	Young Nurse L6307	Open		185.00	185
1996	Natural Wonder L6308	Open		220.00	220
1996	Nature's Treasures L6309	Open		220.00	220
1996	Nature's Song L6310	Open		230.00	230
1996	Cupid L6311	Open		200.00	200
1996	Lost in Dreams L6313	Open		420.00	420
1996	Little Sailor Boy L6314	Open		225.00	225
1996	Dreaming of You L6315	Open		1280.00	1280
1996	Making House Calls L6317	Open		260.00	260
1996	Little Distraction L6318	Open		350.00	350
1996	Beautiful Rhapsody L6319	Open		450.00	450
1996	Architect L6320	Open		330.00	330
1996	Virgin of Carmen w/base L6326	Open		1270.00	1270
1996	Blushing Bride L6329G	Open		370.00	370
1996	Blushing Bride L6329M	Open		370.00	370
1996	Refreshing Pause L6330	Open		170.00	170
1996	Bridal Bell L6331	Open		155.00	155
1996	Medieval Chess Set L6333	Open		2120.00	2120
1985	Lladró Plaque L7116	Open		17.50	18
1985	Lladró Plaque L7118	Closed	N/A	17.00	18
1992	Special Torch L7513G	Open		165.00	165
1992	Special Champion L7514G	Open		165.00	165
1992	Special Pride L7515G	Open		165.00	165
1993	Courage L7522G	Open		195.00	200
1994	Dr. Martin Luther King, Jr. L7528G	Open		345.00	345
1994	Spike L7543G	Open		95.00	105
1994	Brutus L7544G	Open		125.00	140
1994	Rocky L7545G	Open		110.00	120
1994	Stretch L7546G	Open		125.00	140
1994	Rex L7547G	Open		125.00	140
1994	Snow White L7555G (Disney-back stamp Theme Park issue)	Closed	N/A	295.00	650-800
1995	16th Century Globe Paperweight	Open		105.00	105
1989	Starting Forward/Lolo L7605G	Closed	1989	125.00	350
1996	By My Side L7645	Open		250.00	250
1996	Chess Board L8036	Open		145.00	145

Lladró Limited Edition Egg Series - Lladró

YEAR ISSUE		EDITION LIMIT	YEAR RETD.	ISSUE PRICE	*QUOTE U.S.$
1993	1993 Limited Edition Egg L6083M	Closed	1993	145.00	150-250
1994	1994 Limited Edition Egg L7532M	Closed	1994	150.00	150-200
1995	1995 Limited Edition Egg L7548M	Closed	1995	150.00	155-175
1996	1996 Limited Edition Egg L7550	Yr.Iss.		155.00	155

Norman Rockwell Collection - Rockwell-Inspired

YEAR ISSUE		EDITION LIMIT	YEAR RETD.	ISSUE PRICE	*QUOTE U.S.$
1982	Lladró Love Letter RL-400G	5,000	N/A	650.00	1000-1200
1982	Summer Stock RL-401G	5,000	N/A	750.00	800-900
1982	Practice Makes Perfect RL-402G	5,000	N/A	725.00	800-1000
1982	Young Love RL-403G	5,000	N/A	450.00	1350-1750
1982	Daydreamer RL-404G	5,000	N/A	450.00	1300-1500
1982	Court Jester RL-405G	5,000	N/A	600.00	1300
1982	Springtime RL-406G	5,000	N/A	450.00	1200-1500

See also Dave Grossman Designs-Lladró Norman Rockwell Collection

Maruri USA

African Safari Animals - W. Gaither

YEAR ISSUE		EDITION LIMIT	YEAR RETD.	ISSUE PRICE	*QUOTE U.S.$
1983	African Elephant	Closed	N/A	3500.00	3500
1983	Black Maned Lion	Closed	N/A	1450.00	1450
1983	Cape Buffalo	Closed	N/A	2200.00	2200
1983	Grant's Zebras, pair	500	1995	1200.00	1200
1981	Nyala	300	1995	1450.00	1450
1983	Sable	Closed	N/A	1200.00	1200
1983	Southern Greater Kudu	Closed	N/A	1800.00	1800
1983	Southern Impala	Closed	N/A	1200.00	1200
1983	Southern Leopard	Closed	1994	1450.00	1450
1983	Southern White Rhino	150		3200.00	3200

American Eagle Gallery - Maruri Studios

YEAR ISSUE		EDITION LIMIT	YEAR RETD.	ISSUE PRICE	*QUOTE U.S.$
1985	E-8501	Closed	1989	45.00	75
1985	E-8502	Open		55.00	65
1985	E-8503	Open		60.00	65
1985	E-8504	Open		65.00	75
1985	E-8505	Closed	1989	65.00	150
1985	E-8506	Open		75.00	90
1985	E-8507	Open		75.00	90
1985	E-8508	Closed	1989	75.00	85
1985	E-8509	Closed	1989	85.00	125
1985	E-8510	Open		85.00	95
1985	E-8511	Closed	1989	85.00	125
1985	E-8512	Open		295.00	325
1987	E-8721	Open		40.00	50
1987	E-8722	Open		45.00	55
1987	E-8723	Closed	1989	55.00	60
1987	E-8724	Open		175.00	195
1989	E-8931	Open		55.00	60
1989	E-8932	Open		75.00	80
1989	E-8933	Open		95.00	95
1989	E-8934	Open		135.00	140
1989	E-8935	Open		175.00	185
1989	E-8936	Open		185.00	195
1991	E-9141 Eagle Landing	Open		60.00	60
1991	E-9142 Eagle w/ Totem Pole	Open		75.00	75
1991	E-9143 Pair in Flight	Open		95.00	95
1991	E-9144 Eagle w/Salmon	Open		110.00	110
1991	E-9145 Eagle w/Snow	Open		135.00	135
1991	E-9146 Eagle w/Babies	Open		145.00	145
1995	E-9551 Eagle	Open		60.00	60
1995	E-9552 Eagle	Open		65.00	65
1995	E-9553 Eagle	Open		75.00	75
1995	E-9554 Eagle	Open		80.00	80
1995	E-9555 Eagle	Open		90.00	90
1995	E-9556 Eagle	Open		110.00	110

Americana - W. Gaither

YEAR ISSUE		EDITION LIMIT	YEAR RETD.	ISSUE PRICE	*QUOTE U.S.$
1981	Grizzley Bear and Indian	Closed	N/A	650.00	650
1982	Sioux Brave and Bison	Closed	N/A	985.00	985

Baby Animals - W. Gaither

YEAR ISSUE		EDITION LIMIT	YEAR RETD.	ISSUE PRICE	*QUOTE U.S.$
1981	African Lion Cubs	1,500	1995	195.00	195
1981	Black Bear Cubs	Closed	N/A	195.00	195
1981	Wolf Cubs	Closed	N/A	195.00	195

Birds of Prey - W. Gaither

YEAR ISSUE		EDITION LIMIT	YEAR RETD.	ISSUE PRICE	*QUOTE U.S.$
1981	Screech Owl	300		960.00	960
1981	American Bald Eagle I	Closed	N/A	165.00	1750
1982	American Bald Eagle II	Closed	N/A	245.00	2750
1983	American Bald Eagle III	Closed	N/A	445.00	1750
1984	American Bald Eagle IV	Closed	N/A	360.00	1750
1986	American Bald Eagle V	Closed	N/A	325.00	1250

Eyes Of The Night - Maruri Studios

YEAR ISSUE		EDITION LIMIT	YEAR RETD.	ISSUE PRICE	*QUOTE U.S.$
1988	Double Barn Owl O-8807	Closed	1993	125.00	130
1988	Double Snowy Owl O-8809	Closed	1993	245.00	250
1988	Single Great Horned Owl O-8803	Closed	1993	60.00	65
1988	Single Great Horned Owl O-8808	Closed	1993	145.00	150
1988	Single Screech Owl O-8801	Closed	1993	50.00	55
1988	Single Screech Owl O-8806	Closed	1993	90.00	95
1988	Single Snowy Owl O-8802	Closed	1993	50.00	55
1988	Single Snowy Owl O-8805	Closed	1993	80.00	85
1988	Single Tawny Owl O-8804	Closed	1993	60.00	65

Gentle Giants - Maruri Studios

YEAR ISSUE		EDITION LIMIT	YEAR RETD.	ISSUE PRICE	*QUOTE U.S.$
1992	Baby Elephant Sitting GG-9252	Open		65.00	65
1992	Baby Elephant Standing GG-9251	Open		50.00	50
1992	Elephant Pair GG-9255	Open		220.00	220
1992	Elephant Pair Playing GG-9253	Open		80.00	80
1992	Mother & Baby Elephant GG-9254	Open		160.00	160

Graceful Reflections - Maruri Studios

YEAR ISSUE		EDITION LIMIT	YEAR RETD.	ISSUE PRICE	*QUOTE U.S.$
1991	Mute Swan w/Baby SW-9152	Closed	1993	95.00	95
1991	Pair-Mute Swan SW-9153	Closed	1993	145.00	145
1991	Pair-Mute Swan SW-9154	Closed	1993	195.00	195
1991	Single Mute Swan SW-9151	Closed	1993	85.00	85

Horses Of The World - Maruri Studios

YEAR ISSUE		EDITION LIMIT	YEAR RETD.	ISSUE PRICE	*QUOTE U.S.$
1993	Arabian HW-9356	Closed	1995	175.00	175
1993	Camargue HW-9354	Closed	1995	150.00	150
1993	Clydesdale HW-9351	Closed	1995	145.00	145
1993	Paint Horse HW-9355	Closed	1995	160.00	160
1993	Quarter Horse HW-9353	Closed	1995	145.00	145
1993	Thoroughbred HW-9352	Closed	1995	145.00	145

Hummingbirds - Maruri Studios

YEAR ISSUE		EDITION LIMIT	YEAR RETD.	ISSUE PRICE	*QUOTE U.S.$
1995	Allen's & Babies w/Rose H-9523	Open		120.00	120
1995	Allen's w/Easter Lily H-9522	Open		95.00	95
1989	Allen's w/Hibiscus H-8906	Open		195.00	195
1989	Anna's w/Lily H-8905	Open		160.00	160
1995	Anna's w/Trumpet Creeper H-9524	Open		130.00	130
1995	Broad-Billed w/Amaryllis H-9526	Open		150.00	150
1989	Calliope w/Azalea H-8904	Open		120.00	120
1989	Ruby-Throated w/Azalea H-8911	Open		75.00	75
1989	Ruby-Throated w/Orchid H-8914	Open		150.00	15
1989	Rufous w/Trumpet Creeper H-8901	Open		70.00	75
1989	Violet-crowned w/Gentian H-8903	Open		90.00	9
1989	Violet-Crowned w/Gentian H-8913	Open		75.00	7
1995	Violet-Crowned w/Iris H-9521	Open		95.00	95
1989	White-eared w/Morning Glory H-8902	Open		85.00	8
1989	White-Eared w/Morning Glory H-8912	Open		75.00	7
1995	White-Eared w/Tulip H-9525	Open		145.00	14

Legendary Flowers of the Orient - Ito

YEAR ISSUE		EDITION LIMIT	YEAR RETD.	ISSUE PRICE	*QUOTE U.S.$
1985	Cherry Blossom	15,000		45.00	5
1985	Chinese Peony	15,000		45.00	5
1985	Chrysanthemum	15,000		45.00	5
1985	Iris	15,000		45.00	5
1985	Lily	15,000		45.00	5
1985	Lotus	15,000		45.00	4
1985	Orchid	15,000		45.00	5
1985	Wisteria	15,000		45.00	5

Majestic Owls of the Night - D. Littleton

YEAR ISSUE		EDITION LIMIT	YEAR RETD.	ISSUE PRICE	*QUOTE U.S.$
1988	Barred Owl	15,000		55.00	5
1987	Burrowing Owl	15,000		55.00	5
1988	Elf Owl	15,000		55.00	5

*Quotes have been rounded up to nearest dollar

National Parks - Maruri Studios

Year Issue		Edition Limit	Year Retd.	Issue Price	*Quote U.S.$
1993	Baby Bear NP-9301	Open		60.00	60
1993	Bear Family NP-9304	Open		160.00	160
1993	Buffalo NP-9306	Open		170.00	170
1993	Cougar Cubs NP-9302	Open		70.00	70
1993	Deer Family NP-9303	Open		120.00	120
1993	Eagle NP-9307	Open		180.00	180
1993	Falcon NP-9308	Open		195.00	195
1993	Howling Wolves NP-9305	Open		165.00	165

North American Game Animals - W. Gaither

Year Issue		Edition Limit	Year Retd.	Issue Price	*Quote U.S.$
1984	White Tail Deer	950		285.00	285

North American Game Birds - W. Gaither

Year Issue		Edition Limit	Year Retd.	Issue Price	*Quote U.S.$
1983	Bobtail Quail, female	Closed	N/A	375.00	375
1983	Bobtail Quail, male	Closed	N/A	375.00	375
1981	Canadian Geese, pair	Closed	N/A	2000.00	2000
1981	Eastern Wild Turkey	Closed	N/A	300.00	300
1982	Ruffed Grouse	Closed	N/A	1745.00	1745
1983	Wild Turkey Hen with Chicks	Closed	N/A	300.00	300

North American Songbirds - W. Gaither

Year Issue		Edition Limit	Year Retd.	Issue Price	*Quote U.S.$
1982	Bluebird	Closed	N/A	95.00	95
1983	Cardinal, female	Closed	N/A	95.00	95
1982	Cardinal, male	Closed	N/A	95.00	95
1982	Carolina Wren	Closed	N/A	95.00	95
1982	Chickadee	Closed	N/A	95.00	95
1982	Mockingbird	Closed	N/A	95.00	95
1983	Robin	Closed	N/A	95.00	95

North American Waterfowl I - W. Gaither

Year Issue		Edition Limit	Year Retd.	Issue Price	*Quote U.S.$
1981	Blue Winged Teal	200		980.00	980
1981	Canvasback Ducks	Closed	1994	780.00	780
1981	Flying Wood Ducks	Closed	N/A	880.00	880
1981	Mallard Drake	Closed	N/A	2380.00	2380
1981	Wood Duck, decoy	950		480.00	480

North American Waterfowl II - W. Gaither

Year Issue		Edition Limit	Year Retd.	Issue Price	*Quote U.S.$
1982	Bufflehead Ducks Pair	1,500		225.00	225
1982	Goldeneye Ducks Pair	Closed	N/A	225.00	225
1983	Loon	Closed	1989	245.00	245
1981	Mallard Ducks Pair	1,500		225.00	225
1982	Pintail Ducks Pair	Closed	1994	225.00	225
1982	Widgeon, female	Closed	N/A	225.00	225
1982	Widgeon, male	Closed	N/A	225.00	225

Polar Expedition - Maruri Studios

Year Issue		Edition Limit	Year Retd.	Issue Price	*Quote U.S.$
1992	Arctic Fox Cubs Playing-P-9223	Open		65.00	65
1990	Baby Arctic Fox-P-9002	Open		50.00	55
1990	Baby Emperor Penguin-P-9001	Open		45.00	50
1992	Baby Harp Seal-P-9221	Open		55.00	55
1990	Baby Harp Seals-P-9005	Open		65.00	70
1992	Emperor Penguins-P-9222	Open		60.00	60
1990	Mother & Baby Emperor Penguins-P-9006	Open		80.00	85
1990	Mother & Baby Harp Seals-P-9007	Open		90.00	95
1990	Mother & Baby Polar Bears-P-9008	Open		125.00	130
1990	Polar Bear Cub Sliding-P-9003	Open		50.00	55
1990	Polar Bear Cubs Playing-P-9004	Open		60.00	65
1992	Polar Bear Family-P-9224	Open		90.00	90
1990	Polar Expedition Sign-PES-001	Open		18.00	18

Precious Panda - Maruri Studios

Year Issue		Edition Limit	Year Retd.	Issue Price	*Quote U.S.$
1992	Lazy Lunch PP-9202	Open		60.00	60
1992	Mother's Cuddle-PP-9204	Open		120.00	120
1992	Snack Time PP-9201	Open		60.00	60
1992	Tug Of War PP-9203	Open		70.00	70

Shore Birds - W. Gaither

Year Issue		Edition Limit	Year Retd.	Issue Price	*Quote U.S.$
1984	Pelican	Closed	N/A	260.00	260
1984	Sand Piper	Closed	N/A	285.00	285

Signature Collection - W. Gaither

Year Issue		Edition Limit	Year Retd.	Issue Price	*Quote U.S.$
1985	American Bald Eagle	Closed	N/A	60.00	60
1985	Canada Goose	Closed	N/A	60.00	60
1985	Hawk	Closed	N/A	60.00	60
1985	Pintail Duck	Closed	N/A	60.00	60
1985	Snow Goose	Closed	N/A	60.00	60
1985	Swallow	Closed	N/A	60.00	60

Songbirds Of Beauty - Maruri Studios

Year Issue		Edition Limit	Year Retd.	Issue Price	*Quote U.S.$
1991	Bluebird w/ Apple Blossom SB-9105	Closed	1994	85.00	85
1991	Cardinal w/ Cherry Blossom SB-9103	Closed	1994	85.00	85
1991	Chickadee w/ Roses SB-9101	Closed	1994	85.00	85
1991	Dbl. Bluebird w/ Peach Blossom SB-9107	Closed	1994	145.00	145
1991	Dbl. Cardinal w/ Dogwood SB-9108	Closed	1994	145.00	145
1991	Goldfinch w/ Hawthorne SB-9102	Closed	1994	85.00	85
1991	Robin & Baby w/ Azalea SB-9106	Closed	1994	115.00	115
1991	Robin w/ Lilies SB-9104	Closed	1994	85.00	85

Special Commissions - W. Gaither

Year Issue		Edition Limit	Year Retd.	Issue Price	*Quote U.S.$
1982	Cheetah	Closed	N/A	995.00	995
1983	Orange Bengal Tiger	240		340.00	340
1981	White Bengal Tiger	240		340.00	340

Studio Collection - Maruri Studios

Year Issue		Edition Limit	Year Retd.	Issue Price	*Quote U.S.$
1990	Majestic Eagles-MS-100	Closed	N/A	350.00	800
1991	Delicate Motion-MS-200	3,500		325.00	325
1992	Imperial Panda-MS-300	3,500		350.00	350
1993	Wild Wings-MS-400	3,500		395.00	450
1994	Waltz of the Dolphins-MS-500	3,500		300.00	300
1995	"Independent Spirit" MS-600	3,500		395.00	395

Stump Animals - W. Gaither

Year Issue		Edition Limit	Year Retd.	Issue Price	*Quote U.S.$
1984	Bobcat	Closed	N/A	175.00	175
1984	Chipmunk	Closed	N/A	175.00	175
1984	Gray Squirrel	1,200	1995	175.00	175
1983	Owl	Closed	N/A	175.00	175
1983	Raccoon	Closed	1989	175.00	175
1982	Red Fox	Closed	N/A	175.00	175

Upland Birds - W. Gaither

Year Issue		Edition Limit	Year Retd.	Issue Price	*Quote U.S.$
1981	Mourning Doves	Closed	N/A	780.00	780

Wings of Love Doves - Maruri Studios

Year Issue		Edition Limit	Year Retd.	Issue Price	*Quote U.S.$
1987	D-8701 Single Dove w/ Forget-Me-Not	Closed	1994	45.00	55
1987	D-8702 Double Dove w/ Primrose	Open		55.00	65
1987	D-8703 Single Dove w/Buttercup	Closed	1994	65.00	70
1987	D-8704 Double Dove w/Daisy	Open		75.00	85
1987	D-8705 Single Dove w/Blue Flax	Closed	1994	95.00	95
1987	D-8706 Double Dove w/Cherry Blossom	Open		175.00	195
1990	D-9021 Double Dove w/Gentian	Open		50.00	55
1990	D-9022 Double Dove w/Azalea	Open		75.00	75
1990	D-9023 Double Dove w/Apple Blossom	Open		115.00	120
1990	D-9024 Double Dove w/Morning Glory	Open		150.00	160

Wonders of the Sea - Maruri Studios

Year Issue		Edition Limit	Year Retd.	Issue Price	*Quote U.S.$
1994	Dolphin WS-9401	Open		70.00	70
1994	Great White Shark WS-9406	Open		90.00	90
1994	Green Sea Turtle WS-9405	Open		85.00	85
1994	Humpback Mother & Baby WS-9409	Open		150.00	150
1994	Manatee & Baby WS-9403	Open		75.00	75
1994	Manta Ray WS-9404	Open		80.00	80
1994	Orca Mother & Baby WS-9410	Open		150.00	150
1994	Sea Otter & Baby WS-9402	Open		75.00	75
1994	Three Dolphins WS-9408	Open		135.00	135
1994	Two Dolphins WS-9407	Open		120.00	120

Michael's Limited

Collectors' Corner - B. Baker

Year Issue		Edition Limit	Year Retd.	Issue Price	*Quote U.S.$
1993	City Cottage (Membership House)-rose/grn.1682	Retrd.	1993	35.00	90
1993	Brian's First House (Redemption House)-red1496	Retrd.	1993	71.00	150-175
1994	Gothic Cottage (Membership Sculpture) 1571	Retrd.	1994	35.00	50-75
1994	Duke of Gloucester Street (Redemption House) 1459	Retrd.	1995	108.00	130
1995	Marie's Cottage-grey (Membership Sculpture) 1942	Retrd.	1996	35.00	35
1995	Welcome Home-brick (Redemption House) 1599	Retrd.	1996	65.00	65
1996	Queen Ann Cottage-rose/blue (Membership Sculpture) 1676	3/97		39.00	39
1996	Oak Street-brick/brown (Redemption House) 1685	9/97		65.00	65

Signing Piece - B. Baker

Year Issue		Edition Limit	Year Retd.	Issue Price	*Quote U.S.$
1995	Joe's Newstand 1348	Yr.Iss.		27.00	27

Brian Baker's Déjà Vu Collection - B. Baker

Year Issue		Edition Limit	Year Retd.	Issue Price	*Quote U.S.$
1988	Adam Colonial Cottage -blue/white 1515	Retrd.	1992	53.00	53
1993	Admiralty Head Lighthouse -white 1532	Retrd.	1995	62.00	62
1992	Alpine Ski Lodge-brown/white 1012	Retrd.	1993	62.00	92
1988	Andulusian Village-white 1060	Retrd.	1993	53.00	63
1992	Angel of the Sea-blue/white 1587	Open		67.00	67
1996	Angel of the Sea-blue/white 1592	Open		69.00	69
1992	Angel of the Sea-mauve/white 1586	Open		67.00	67
1996	Angel of the Sea-mauve/white 1591	Open		69.00	69
1989	Antebellum Mansion-blue/rose 1505	Retrd.	1993	53.00	73
1988	Antebellum Mansion-blue/white 1519	Retrd.	1988	49.00	49
1989	Antebellum Mansion-peach 1506	Retrd.	1991	49.00	56
1988	Antebellum Mansion-peach 1517	Retrd.	1988	49.00	49
1988	Antebellum Mansion -white/green 1518	Retrd.	1988	49.00	49
1994	Barber Shop 1164	Open		53.00	53
1987	Bavarian Church-white 1021	Retrd.	1988	38.00	38
1987	Bavarian Church-yellow 1020	Retrd.	1988	38.00	38
1987	The Bernese Guesthouse -golden br. 1010	Retrd.	1990	49.00	49
1989	Blumen Shop-white/brown 1023	Retrd.	1993	53.00	73
1996	Brick & Brackets-brick 1933	Open		65.00	65
1994	Cabbagetown 1704	Open		65.00	65
1996	Cape Cottage-grey/white 1442	Open		63.00	63
1988	Casa Chiquita-natural 1400	Retrd.	1992	53.00	60
1994	Castle in the Clouds 1090	Retrd.	1995	75.00	85
1993	Charleston Single House -blue/white 1583	Open		60.00	60
1993	Charleston Single House -peach/white 1584	Open		60.00	60
1996	Chateau in the Woods 1683	Yr. Iss.		79.00	79
1994	Christmas at Church 1223	Open		63.00	63
1988	Christmas House-blue 1225	Retrd.	1992	51.00	51
1990	Classic Victorian-blue/white 1555	Retrd.	1994	60.00	80
1990	Classic Victorian-peach 1557	Retrd.	1994	60.00	80
1990	Classic Victorian-rose/blue 1556	Retrd.	1994	60.00	80
1991	Colonial Color-brown 1508	Retrd.	1993	62.00	82
1991	Colonial Cottage-white/bue 1509	Retrd.	1994	59.00	80
1987	Colonial House-blue 1510	Retrd.	1988	49.00	70
1987	Colonial House-wine 1511	Retrd.	1987	40.00	60
1987	Colonial Store-brick 1512	Retrd.	1993	53.00	73
1993	Corner Grocery-brick 1141	Open		67.00	67
1987	The Cottage House-blue 1531	Retrd.	1988	42.00	42
1987	The Cottage House-white 1530	Retrd.	1993	47.00	67
1989	Country Barn-blue 1528	Retrd.	1991	49.00	70
1989	Country Barn-red 1527	Retrd.	1993	53.00	73
1994	Country Bridge 1513	Open		69.00	69
1996	Country Christmas-red 1219	Open		68.00	68
1988	Country Church-white/blue 1522	Retrd.	1994	49.00	50-70
1992	Country Station-blue/rust 1156	Open		64.00	64
1994	Country Store 1435	Open		61.00	61
1994	Craftsman Cottage-cream 1478	Open		56.00	56
1994	Craftsman Cottage-grey 1477	Retrd.	1995	56.00	56
1989	Deja Vu Sign-ivory/brown 1600	Retrd.	1991	21.00	24-29
1992	Deja Vu Sign-ivory/brown 1999	Open		21.00	21
1993	Dinard Mansion-beige/brick 1005	Open		67.00	67
1996	Dixie Landing-white 1740	Open		68.00	68
1994	Ellis Island 1250	Open		62.00	62
1993	Enchanted Cottage-natural 1205	Retrd.	1995	63.00	68
1988	Fairy Tale Cottage-white/brown 1200	Retrd.	1992	46.00	46
1987	The Farm House-beige/blue 1525	Retrd.	1991	49.00	49
1987	The Farm House-spiced tan 1526	Retrd.	1991	49.00	49
1992	Firehouse-brick 1140	Open		60.00	60
1992	Flower Store-tan/green 1145	Open		67.00	67
1988	French Colonial Cottage-beige 1516	Retrd.	1990	42.00	65
1988	Georgian Colonial House -white/blue 1514	Retrd.	1992	53.00	53
1990	Gothic Victorian-blue/mauve 1534	Retrd.	1991	47.00	52-54
1988	Gothic Victorian-peach 1536	Retrd.	1992	51.00	60
1988	Gothic Victorian-sea green 1537	Retrd.	1990	47.00	47
1993	Grandpa's Barn-brown 1498	Open		63.00	63
1988	Hampshire House-brick 1040	Retrd.	1988	49.00	60
1989	Hampshire House-brick 1041	Retrd.	1990	49.00	56
1996	Harbor Sentry-white 1590	Open		59.00	59
1989	Henry VIII Pub-white/brown 1043	Retrd.	1993	56.00	76
1993	Homestead Christmas-red 1224	Retrd.	1995	57.00	57
1987	Hotel Couronne (original)wh./br. 1000	Retrd.	1988	49.00	49
1989	Hotel Couronne-white/brown 1003	Retrd.	1992	55.00	55
1987	Italianate Victorian-brown 1543	Retrd.	1990	52.00	52
1987	Italianate Victorian-lavendar 1550	Retrd.	1988	45.00	45
1987	Italianate Victorian-mauve/blue 1545	Retrd.	1991	49.00	49
1989	Italianate Victorian-peach/teal 1552	Retrd.	1991	51.00	60
1989	Italianate Victorian-rose/blue 1551	Retrd.	1991	51.00	55-58
1987	Italianate Victorian-rust/blue 1544	Retrd.	1988	49.00	49
1987	Japanese House-white/brown 1100	Retrd.	1988	47.00	47
1996	Japanese Tea House -brown/white 1101	Open		59.00	59
1987	The Lighthouse-white 1535	Retrd.	1992	53.00	60
1991	Log Cabin-brown 1501	Retrd.	1994	55.00	75
1992	Looks Like Nantucket-grey 1451	Open		59.00	59
1995	Main Street Cafe-blue 1142	Open		61.00	61
1993	Mansard Lady-blue/rose 1606	Open		64.00	64
1993	Mansard Lady-tan/green 1607	Open		64.00	64
1995	Maple Lane-blue/white 1904	Open		72.00	72
1995	Maple Lane-desert/white 1905	Open		72.00	72
1991	Mayor's Mansion-blue/peach 1585	Retrd.	1994	57.00	77
1996	Meditteranean Ave-cream/tile 1741	Open		65.00	65
1995	Mesa Manor 1733	Open		75.00	75
1994	Mission Dolores (no umbrella) 1435	Retrd.	N/A	47.00	75
1994	Mission Dolores 1435	Open		47.00	47
1993	Monday's Wash-cream/blue 1450	Open		62.00	62
1993	Monday's Wash-white/blue 1449	Open		62.00	62
1995	Mountain Homestead-brown 1401	Open		78.00	78
1994	Mukilteo Lighthouse 1569	Open		55.00	55
1989	Norwegian House-brown 1051	Retrd.	1990	51.00	58
1990	Old Country Cottage-blue 1502	Retrd.	1992	51.00	58
1990	Old Country Cottage-peach 1504	Retrd.	1991	47.00	65
1990	Old Country Cottage-red 1503	Retrd.	1992	51.00	65
1996	Old Glory-brick 1567	Open		59.00	59
1994	The Old School House 1439	Open		61.00	61
1987	Old West General Store -white/grey 1520	Retrd.	1991	50.00	68
1987	Old West General Store -yellow/white 1521	Retrd.	1988	50.00	50
1993	Old West Hotel-cream 1120	Open		62.00	62
1995	Old West Sheriff-red 1125	Open		56.00	56
1995	Old White Church-white 1424	Open		65.00	65
1988	One Room School House-red 1524	Retrd.	1993	53.00	73
1994	Orleans Cottage-white/blue 1447	Open		63.00	63
1994	Orleans Cottage-white/red 1448	Open		63.00	63
1990	Palm Villa-desert/green 1421	Retrd.	1995	54.00	61
1990	Palm Villa-white/blue 1420	Retrd.	1995	54.00	61
1994	Paris by the Bay 1004	Open		55.00	55
1989	Parisian Apartment-beige/blue 1002	Retrd.	1993	53.00	73
1987	Parisian Apartment golden brown 1001	Retrd.	1993	53.00	73
1995	Peggy's Cove Light-white 1533	Open		56.00	56
1996	Pennridge-white/stone 1429	Open		70.00	70
1994	Police Station 1147	Open		55.00	55
1993	Post Office-light green 1146	Open		60.00	60
1987	Queen Ann Victorian -peach/green 1540	Retrd.	1993	53.00	73
1987	Queen Ann Victorian-rose 1541	Retrd.	1993	53.00	73
1987	Queen Ann Victorian-rust/green 1542	Retrd.	1988	49.00	49

*Quotes have been rounded up to nearest dollar

YEAR ISSUE		EDITION LIMIT	YEAR RETD.	ISSUE PRICE	*QUOTE U.S.$
1995	Quiet Afternoon-cream/blue 1623	Open		71.00	71
1995	Quiet Afternoon-rose/blue 1622	Open		71.00	71
1995	River Belle Steamer-white 1092	Open		70.00	70
1994	Riverside Mill 1507	Open		65.00	65
1988	Roeder Gate, Rothenburg -brown 1022	Retrd.	1990	49.00	49
1992	Rose Cottage-grey 1443	Open		59.00	59
1996	Ruby's Watch-blue/white 1630	Open		56.00	56
1996	Ruby's Watch-cream/white 1631	Open		56.00	56
1994	San Francisco Stick-brick/teal 1625	Open		61.00	61
1994	San Francisco Stick-cream/blue 1624	Open		61.00	61
1995	Scenic Route 100-red/green 1426	Open		71.00	71
1995	Scenic Route 100-red/yellow 1425	Open		71.00	71
1996	Seaside Cottage-blue/white1691	Open		64.00	64
1996	Seaside Cottage-rose/white 1690	Open		64.00	64
1988	Second Empire House-sea grn./desert 1539	Retrd.	1991	50.00	50
1988	Second Empire House -white/blue 1538	Retrd.	1993	54.00	74
1993	Smuggler's Cove-grey/brown 1529	Open		72.00	72
1987	Snow Cabin-brown/white 1500	Retrd.	1994	51.00	70
1995	Southern Exposure-cream/rose 1582	Open		62.00	62
1995	Southern Exposure-tan/green 1581	Open		62.00	62
1995	Southern Mansion-brick 1744	Retrd.	1995	79.00	79
1995	St. Nicholas Church-white/blue 1409	Open		56.00	56
1993	Steiner Street-peach/green 1674	Open		63.00	63
1993	Steiner Street-rose/blue 1675	Open		63.00	63
1993	The Stone House-stone/blue 1453	Open		63.00	63
1988	Stone Victorians-browns 1554	Retrd.	1994	56.00	76
1993	Sunday Afternoon-brick 1523	Retrd.	1995	62.00	62
1989	Swedish House-Swed.red 1050	Retrd.	1990	51.00	58
1991	Teddy's Place-teal/rose 1570	Open		61.00	61
1994	Towered Lady-blue/rose 1688	Open		65.00	65
1994	Towered Lady-rose 1689	Open		65.00	65
1992	Tropical Fantasy-blue/coral 1410	Open		67.00	67
1992	Tropical Fantasy-rose/blue 1411	Open		67.00	67
1992	Tropical Fantasy-yellow/teal 1412	Open		67.00	67
1996	Tropical Paradise-white/brown 1115	Open		65.00	65
1995	Tudor Christmas-red brick 1221	Open		67.00	67
1995	Tudor Home-tan brick 1222	Open		67.00	67
1987	Turreted Victorian-beige/blue 1546	Retrd.	1992	55.00	55
1987	Turreted Victorian-peach 1547	Retrd.	1992	55.00	57
1987	Ultimate Victorian-lt. blue/rose 1549	Retrd.	1993	60.00	80
1987	Ultimate Victorian-maroon/slate 1548	Retrd.	1993	60.00	80
1989	Ultimate Victorian-peach/green 1553	Retrd.	1993	60.00	65
1992	Victorian Bay View-cream/teal 1564	Open		63.00	63
1992	Victorian Bay View-rose/blue 1563	Open		63.00	63
1992	Victorian Charm-cream 1588	Open		61.00	61
1992	Victorian Charm-mauve 1589	Open		61.00	61
1990	Victorian Country Estate -desert/br. 1560	Retrd.	1994	62.00	82
1990	Victorian Country Estate -peach/blue 1562	Retrd.	1994	62.00	82
1990	Victorian Country Estate -rose/blue 1561	Retrd.	1994	62.00	82
1991	Victorian Farmhouse -goldenbrown 1565	Retrd.	1994	59.00	90
1995	Victorian Living-clay/white 1927	Open		70.00	70
1995	Victorian Living-teal/tan 1926	Open		70.00	70
1992	Victorian Tower House-blue/maroon 1558	Open		63.00	63
1992	Victorian Tower House -peach/blue 1559	Open		63.00	63
1996	Village Pharmacy-brick 1157	Open		65.00	65
1996	Willow Road-brick 1713	Open		68.00	68
1991	Wind and Roses-brick 1470	Open		63.00	63
1989	Windmill on the Dike -beige/green 1034	Retrd.	1994	60.00	90

Brian Baker's Déjà Vu Collection Accessories - B. Baker

1995	Apple Tree 1317	Open		36.00	36
1996	Autumn Birch 1323	Open		26.00	26
1996	Autumn Flame 1328	Open		29.00	29
1996	Banana Tree 1318	Open		36.00	36
1996	Blue Spruce 1352	Open		24.00	24
1995	Cactus Garden 1334	Open		27.50	28
1995	Coconut Palms 1319	Open		25.00	25
1995	Date Palm 1320	Open		24.00	24
1995	Doghouse 1306	Open		23.00	23
1996	Farm Truck 1357	Open		47.00	47
1996	Forest Fir 1358	Open		24.00	24
1996	Forest Giant 1333	Open		36.00	36
1996	Garden Trellis 1308	Open		24.00	24
1996	Hemlock 1344	Open		24.00	24
1995	House For Sale 1307	Open		24.00	24
1996	Huckleberry's Cat 1343	Open		20.00	20
1995	In The Park 1340	Open		30.00	30
1996	Japanese Bridge 1330	Open		34.00	34
1996	Japanese Pine 1331	Open		36.00	36
1996	Large Blue Spruce 1361	Open		24.00	24
1995	Long Picket Fence 1309	Open		23.00	23
1995	Members Only 1312	Open		46.00	46
1995	Outhouse 1305	Open		26.00	26
1995	Rope Swing 1311	Open		36.00	36
1995	Route 1 1313	Open		28.00	28
1996	Summer Birch 1322	Open		26.00	26
1996	Summer Shade 1327	Open		29.00	29
1996	Tom's Fence 1342	Open		20.00	20
1995	Weeping Willow 1326	Open		39.00	39
1995	Windy Day 1321	Open		35.00	35
1996	Winter Green 1360	Open		24.00	24
1996	Winter Mantel 1351	Open		24.00	24

Limited Editions From Brian Baker - B. Baker

1993	American Classic-rose 1566	Retrd.	1993	99.00	550-595
1987	Amsterdam Canal-brown, S/N 1030	Retrd.	1993	79.00	200
1994	Hill Top Mansion 1598	1,200	1995	97.00	97
1993	James River Plantation-brick 1454	Retrd.	1994	108.00	300-500
1996	London 1045	1,000		119.00	119
1994	Painted Ladies 1190	1,200		125.00	125
1995	Philadelphia-brick 1441	1,500		110.00	110
1994	White Point 1596	700	1996	100.00	150

Midwest of Cannon Falls

Belenes Puig Nativity Collection - J.P. Llobera

1989	Angel 02087-6	Open		50.00	55
1989	Baby Jesus 02085-2	Open		62.00	62
1989	Donkey 02082-1	Open		26.00	26
1989	Joseph 02086-9	Open		62.00	62
1989	Mother Mary 02084-5	Open		62.00	62
1985	Nativity, set/6: Holy Family, Angel, Animals 6 3/4" 00205-6	Open		250.00	250
1989	Ox 02083-8	Open		26.00	26
1990	Resting Camel 04025-6	Open		115.00	115
1986	Sheep, set/3 00475-3	Open		28.00	28
1987	Shepherd & Angel Scene, set/7 06084-1	Open		305.00	305
1989	Shepherd Carrying Lamb 02092-0	Open		56.00	56
1989	Shepherd with Staff 02091-3	Open		56.00	56
1985	Shepherd, set/2 00458-6	Open		110.00	110
1988	Standing Camel 08792-3	Open		115.00	115
1989	Wise Man w/Frankincense 02088-3	Open		66.00	66
1989	Wise Man with Frankincense on Camel 02077-7	Open		155.00	156
1989	Wise Man with Gold 02089-0	Open		66.00	66
1989	Wise Man w/Gold on Camel 02075-3	Open		155.00	156
1989	Wise Man with Myrrh 02090-6	Open		66.00	66
1989	Wise Man w/Myrrh on Camel 02076-0	Open		155.00	156
1985	Wise Men, set/3 00459-3	Open		185.00	185

Cannon Valley Figurines and Accessories - Midwest

1994	Apple Tree, 2 asst. 11484-1	Open		10.00	10
1995	Apple Tree, set/3 12677-6	Open		7.00	7
1996	Battery Operated Mini Light, set/10 16937-7	Open		9.00	9
1996	Border Collie & Sheep, set/3 16677-2	Open		10.00	10
1994	Cannon Valley Sign 11297-7	Open		5.50	6
1994	Chicken, 3 asst. 11299-1	Open		2.00	2
1995	Chickens, 3 asst. 12657-8	Open		3.00	3
1994	Children, 2 asst. 11461-2	Open		5.50	6
1996	Christmas Decoration, set/12 16964-3	Open		10.00	10
1996	Cornstalk 16679-6	Open		5.50	6
1995	Cow with Calf, 2 asst. 12673-8	Open		6.50	7
1994	Cow, 3 asst. 11309-7	Open		5.50	6
1995	Dog by Doghouse 12658-5	Open		5.00	5
1995	Farm Cat 12808-4	Open		5.00	5
1995	Farm Children, 4 asst. 12671-4	Open		7.50	8
1994	Farm Couple, 2 asst. 11458-2	Open		5.50	6
1994	Farm Town Windmill 11306-6	Open		9.50	10
1994	Farm Tractor 11305-9	Open		9.50	10
1995	Farmer with Feed Bag 12672-1	Open		7.50	8
1995	Farmyard Light 12683-7	Open		5.00	5
1996	Fire Fighters, 2 asst. 16674-1	Open		8.00	8
1995	Fire Hydrant 12685-1	Open		3.00	3
1996	Fire Truck 16676-5	Open		13.00	13
1994	Flagpole 11300-4	Retrd.	1994	5.30	6
1996	Gardeners, set/2 16675-8	Open		13.00	13
1995	Grandparents, 2 asst. 12661-5	Open		6.00	6
1995	Gravel Road 12682-0	Open		9.00	9
1996	Hay Rake 16759-5	Open		8.00	8
1994	Hay Wagon and Horse Set 11303-5	Open		19.00	19
1994	Horse, 2 asst. 11485-8	Open		10.00	10
1996	Horse, 2 asst. 16930-8	Open		6.00	6
1994	Mailbox and Water Pump, 2 asst. 11301-1	Retrd.	1995	4.00	4
1995	Mechanic 12660-8	Open		6.00	6
1995	Minister 12674-5	Open		6.00	6
1996	Old Oak Tree 16681-9	Open		11.00	11
1995	Outhouse 12668-4	Open		11.00	11
1995	Parking Meter 12686-8	Open		3.00	3
1995	Picket Fence 13260-9	Open		6.00	6
1994	Pickup Truck 11304-2	Open		12.00	12
1994	Pig and Piglets 11302-8	Open		5.30	6
1995	Pine Tree, set/2 12680-6	Open		7.50	8
1996	Playing Checkers 16680-2	Open		13.00	13
1996	Plow 16761-8	Open		6.50	7
1995	Silo 12667-7	Open		16.00	16
1995	Split Rail Fence 12676-9	Open		2.00	2
1996	Spreader 16760-1	Open		9.00	9
1994	Storekeeper 11459-9	Open		5.50	6
1995	Sunday Best Couple with Children, 2 asst. 12670-7	Open		7.50	8
1994	Teacher and Children, 3 asst. 11460-5	Open		5.50	6
1995	Telephone Pole 12684-4	Open		5.00	5
1996	Tractor 16678-9	Open		9.50	10
1995	Turkey, 2 asst. 12659-2	Open		5.00	5
1995	Water Tower 13116-9	Open		13.00	13
1995	Woody Car 12669-1	Open		12.00	12

Cannon Valley Houses - Midwest

1995	Ace's Garage (lighted) 12665-3	Open		45.00	45
1995	Church (lighted) 12664-6	Open		45.00	45
1995	Dairy Barn (lighted) 12666-0	5,000		49.00	49
1994	Family Farmhouse (lighted) 11292-2	Open		43.00	45
1995	Four Square Farmhouse (lighted) 12662-2	Open		49.00	49
1994	General Store (lighted) 11295-3	Open		43.00	45
1995	Grain Elevator (lighted) 12663-9	Open		45.00	45
1994	Hen House (lighted) 11294-6	Retrd.	1995	33.00	33
1996	Hometown Cafe (lighted) 16669-7	3,500		45.00	45
1994	Little Red Schoolhouse (lighted) 11293-9	Open		43.00	45
1996	Llyod's Barbershop (lighted) 16742-7	Open		45.00	45
1996	Prairie Style Barn (lighted) 16667-3	Open		49.00	49
1994	Red Barn (lighted) 11296-0	Open		43.00	45
1996	Victorian Farmhouse (lighted) 16666-6	Open		45.00	45
1996	Volunteer Fire Department (lighted) 16668-0	Open		49.00	49

Christian Ulbricht "A Christmas Carol" Nutcrackers - C. Ulbricht

1993	Bob Cratchit &Tiny Tim 09577-5	2,500		240.00	250
1996	Ghost of Christmas Past 18299-4	1,500		200.00	200
1994	Ghost of Christmas Present 12041-5	1,500		190.00	200
1996	Ghost of Christmas Yet to Come 17021-2	1,500		190.00	190
1993	Scrooge 09584-3	1,500		210.00	240

Christian Ulbricht "American Folk Hero" Nutcracker Collection - C. Ulbricht

1994	Davy Crockett 12960-9	1,500		190.00	200
1994	Johnny Appleseed 12959-3	1,500		196.00	200
1995	Paul Bunyan 12800-8	1,500		220.00	220
1996	Sacajawea 17018-2	1,000		200.00	200
1996	Wyatt Earp 17019-9	1,000		200.00	200

Christian Ulbricht "Nutcracker Fantasy" Nutcrackers - C. Ulbricht

1991	Clara , 11 1/2" 03657-0	Open		125.00	15[illegible]
1991	Herr Drosselmeyer , 16 1/4" 03656-3	Open		170.00	20[illegible]
1991	Mouse King Nutcracker, 13 1/2" 04510-7	Open		170.00	20[illegible]
1991	Prince, 17" 03665-5	Open		160.00	19[illegible]
1991	Toy Soldier, 14" 03666-2	Open		160.00	19[illegible]

Christian Ulbricht "Traditional Santa Series" Nutcracker - C. Ulbricht

1992	Father Christmas Nutcracker 07094-9	2,500	1992	190.00	50[illegible]
1995	King of Christmas Nutcracker 13665-2	2,500		250.00	25[illegible]
1993	Toymaker Nutcracker 09531-7	2,500		220.00	25[illegible]
1994	Victorian Santa Nutcracker 12961-1	2,500		220.00	25[illegible]

Christian Ulbricht Nutcracker Collection - C. Ulbricht

1995	Biker Nutcracker 13187-9	Open		220.00	22[illegible]
1996	Candyland Santa Nutcracker 17016-8	Open		200.00	20[illegible]
1996	Cinderella Nutcracker 17014-4	Open		200.00	20[illegible]
1995	Clown Nutcracker 13188-6	Open		200.00	20[illegible]
1995	Drummer Nutcracker 12792-6	S/O	N/A	220.00	22[illegible]
1995	Father Time Nutcracker 12794-0	Open		220.00	22[illegible]
1995	Female Health Care Professional Nutcracker 13189-3	Open		200.00	20[illegible]
1995	Female Volleyball Player Nutcracker 13986-8	Open		200.00	20[illegible]
1996	Firefighter Nutcracker 17017-5	Open		200.00	2[illegible]
1996	Fly Fisherman Nutcracker 17022-9	Open		190.00	19[illegible]
1996	Gardening Santa Nutcracker 17025-0	Open		190.00	19[illegible]
1995	Huck Finn Nutcracker 12788-9	S/O	N/A	220.00	22[illegible]
1995	King Nutcracker 13190-9	Open		200.00	20[illegible]
1993	Leprechaun Nutcracker 09110-4	S/O	N/A	170.00	19[illegible]
1995	Moses Nutcracker 13186-2	S/O	N/A	220.00	22[illegible]
1995	Mother Goose Nutcracker 13182-4	Open		220.00	22[illegible]
1993	Mr. Claus Nutcracker 09588-1	2,500		180.00	2[illegible]
1993	Mrs. Claus Nutcracker 09587-4	2,500		180.00	2[illegible]
1995	Nature Santa with Birdhouse Nutcracker 12790-2	S/O	N/A	220.00	22[illegible]
1996	Pied Piper Nutcracker 17026-7	Open		190.00	1[illegible]
1986	Pilgrim, 16 1/2" 00393-0	S/O	N/A	145.00	1[illegible]
1995	Pinocchio Nutcracker 13184-8	S/O	N/A	200.00	2[illegible]
1994	Prince on Rocking Horse Nutcracker 12964-7	S/O	N/A	160.00	1[illegible]
1996	Rock & Roll Singer Nutcracker 17020-5	Open		200.00	2[illegible]
1995	Santa Cookie Baker Nutcracker 13191-6	S/O	N/A	220.00	2[illegible]
1995	Santa Riding Rocking Reindeer Nutcracker 12786-5	Retrd.	1995	200.00	2[illegible]
1995	Santa with Tree Nutcracker 12791-9	S/O	N/A	200.00	2[illegible]
1996	Scarecrow Nutcracker 17023-6	Open		190.00	1[illegible]
1995	Witch Nutcracker 13183-1	Open		220.00	2[illegible]

Cottontail Lane Figurines and Accessories - Midwest

1993	Arbor w/ Fence Set 02188-0	Open		14.00	
1993	Birdbath, Bench & Mailbox, 02184-2	Retrd.	1993	4.00	
1994	Birdhouse, Sundial & Fountain, 3 asst. 00371-8	Open		4.50	
1993	Bridge & Gazebo, 2 asst. 02182-9	Open		11.50	
1996	Bunnies Sitting in Gazebo 15801-2	Open		10.00	
1996	Bunny Band Quartet, set/4 15799-2	Open		16.00	

YEAR ISSUE		EDITION LIMIT	YEAR RETD.	ISSUE PRICE	*QUOTE U.S.$
1995	Bunny Chef, 2 asst. 12433-8	Open		5.00	5
1993	Bunny Child Collecting Eggs, 2 asst. 02880-3	Retrd.	1993	4.20	5
1996	Bunny Children Working in Garden, 2 asst. 15796-1	Open		3.50	4
1995	Bunny Couple at Cafe Table 12444-4	Open		7.00	7
1993	Bunny Couple on Bicycle 02978-7	Retrd.	1993	5.30	6
1995	Bunny Kids at Carrot Juice Stand 12437-6	Open		5.30	6
1994	Bunny Marching Band, 6 asst. 00355-8	Open		4.20	5
1995	Bunny Minister, Soloist, 2 asst. 12434-8	Open		5.00	5
1996	Bunny Picnicking, set/4 15798-5	Open		15.00	15
1995	Bunny Playing Piano 12439-0	Open		5.30	6
1995	Bunny Playing, 2 asst. 12442-0	Open		6.50	7
1995	Bunny Popcorn, Balloon Vendor, 2 asst. 12443-7	Open		6.70	7
1994	Bunny Preparing for Easter, 3 asst. 02971-8	Open		4.20	5
1994	Bunny Shopping Couple, 2 asst. 10362-3	Open		4.20	5
1994	Cobblestone Road 10072-1	Open		9.00	9
1994	Cone-Shaped Tree Set 10369-2	Open		7.50	8
1994	Cottontail Lane Sign 10063-9	Open		5.00	5
1994	Easter Bunny Figure, 2 asst. 00356-5	Open		4.20	5
1994	Egg Stand & Flower Cart, 2 asst. 10354-8	Open		6.00	6
1995	Electric Street Lamppost, set/4 12461-1	Open		25.00	25
1996	Garden Shopkeeper, set/2 15800-5	Open		10.00	10
1996	Garden Table with Potted Plants and Flowers 15802-9	Open		9.00	9
1996	Garden w/Waterfall and Pond 15797-8	Open		15.00	15
1993	Lamppost, Birdhouse & Mailbox, 3 asst. 02187-3	Retrd.	1993	4.50	5
1995	Mayor Bunny and Bunny with Flag Pole, 2 asst. 12441-3	Open		5.50	6
1995	Outdoor Bunny, 3 asst. 12435-2	Open		5.00	5
1994	Policeman, Conductor Bunny, 2 asst.00367-1	Open		4.20	5
1995	Professional Bunny, 3 asst. 12438-3	Open		5.00	5
1995	Street Sign, 3 asst. 12433-8	Open		4.50	5
1993	Strolling Bunny, 2 asst. 02976-3	Retrd.	1993	4.20	5
1995	Strolling Bunny, 2 asst. 12440-6	Open		5.50	6
1994	Sweeper & Flower Peddler Bunny Couple, 2 asst. 00359-6	Open		4.20	5
1994	Topiary Trees, 3 asst. 00346-6	Retrd.	1994	2.50	3
1994	Train Station Couple, 2 asst. 00357-2	Open		4.20	5
1994	Tree & Shrub, 2 asst. 00382-4	Open		5.00	5
1996	Tree with Painted Flowers, set/3 15924-8	Open		20.00	20
1993	Trees, 3 asst. 02194-1	Retrd.	1994	6.20	7
1994	Wedding Bunny Couple, 2 asst. 00347-3	Open		4.20	5

Cottontail Lane Houses - Midwest

YEAR ISSUE		EDITION LIMIT	YEAR RETD.	ISSUE PRICE	*QUOTE U.S.$
1993	Bakery (lighted) 01396-0	Open		43.00	45
1996	Bandshell (lighted) 15753-4	Open		50.00	50
1994	Bed & Breakfast House (lighted) 00337-4	Open		43.00	45
1995	Boutique and Beauty Shop (lighted) 12301-0	Open		45.00	45
1996	Bungalow (lighted) 15752-7	Open		45.00	45
1995	Cafe (lighted) 12303-4	Open		45.00	45
1995	Cathedral (lighted) 12302-7	Open		47.00	47
1994	Chapel (lighted) 00331-2	3,000	1993	43.00	45
1993	Church (lighted) 01385-4	3,000	1993	42.00	140
1992	Confectionary Shop (lighted) 06335-5	Retrd.	1994	43.00	85
1993	Cottontail Inn (lighted) 01394-6	Open		43.00	45
1996	Fire Station w/Figures, set/6 (lighted) 15830-2	5,000		90.00	90
1992	Flower Shop (lighted) 06333-9	Retrd.	1994	43.00	85
1994	General Store (lighted) 00340-4	Open		43.00	45
1993	Painting Studio (lighted) 01395-5	Retrd.	1994	43.00	45
1993	Rose Cottage (lighted) 01386-1	Retrd.	1994	43.00	45
1995	Rosebud Manor (lighted) 12304-1	3,500	1994	45.00	45
1993	Schoolhouse (lighted) 01378-6	Open		43.00	45
1992	Springtime Cottage (lighted) 06329-8	Retrd.	1994	43.00	85
1996	Town Garden Shoppe (lighted) 15751-0	Open		45.00	45
1995	Town Hall (lighted) 12300-3	Open		45.00	45
1994	Train Station (lighted) 00330-5	Open		43.00	45
1992	Victorian House (lighted) 06332-1	Open		43.00	45

Creepy Hollow Figurines and Accessories - Midwest

YEAR ISSUE		EDITION LIMIT	YEAR RETD.	ISSUE PRICE	*QUOTE U.S.$
1994	Black Picket Fence 10685-3	Open		13.50	14
1996	Bone Fence 16961-2	Open		9.50	10
1995	Cemetery Gate 13366-8	Open		16.00	16
1996	Covered Bridge 16664-2	Open		22.00	22
1994	Creepy Hollow Sign 10647-1	Open		5.50	6
1996	Dragon 16936-0	Open		8.50	9
1995	Flying Witch, Ghost, 2 asst. 13362-0	Open		11.00	11
1994	Ghost, 3 asst. 10652-5	Open		6.00	6
1996	Ghostly King 16659-8	Open		8.00	8
1995	Ghoul Usher 13515-0	Open		6.50	7
1995	Ghoulish Organist Playing Organ 13363-7	Open		13.00	13
1995	Grave Digger, 2 asst. 13360-6	Open		10.00	10
1996	Gypsy 16656-7	Open		8.00	8
1996	Gypsy Witch 16655-0	Open		8.00	8
1992	Halloween Sign, 2 asst. 06709-3	Retrd.	1995	6.00	7
1993	Haunted Tree, 2 asst. 05892-3	Open		7.00	7
1996	Headless Horseman 16658-1	Open		11.00	11
1995	Hearse with Monsters 13364-4	Open		15.00	15
1993	Hinged Dracula's Coffin 08545-5	Retrd.	1995	11.00	11
1995	Hinged Tomb 13516-7	Retrd.	1995	15.00	15
1995	Hunchback 13359-0	Open		9.00	9
1996	Inn Keeper 16660-4	Open		7.00	7
1994	Mad Scientist 10646-4	Open		6.00	7
1994	Outhouse 10648-8	Open		7.00	7
1994	Phantom of the Opera 10645-7	Open		6.00	7
1993	Pumpkin Head Ghost 06661-4	Retrd.	1993	5.50	6
1993	Pumpkin Patch Sign, 2 asst. 05898-5	Retrd.	1995	6.50	7
1995	Pumpkin Street Lamp, set/4 13365-1	Open		25.00	25
1993	Resin Skeleton 08651-5	Retrd.	1994	5.50	6
1995	Road of Bones 13371-2	Open		9.00	9
1996	School Teacher 16657-4	Open		8.00	8
1996	Skeleton Butler 16661-1	Open		7.00	7
1994	Street Sign, 2 asst. 10644-0	Open		5.70	6
1995	Street Sign, 3 asst. 13357-6	Open		5.50	6
1995	Theatre Goer, set/2 13358-3	Open		9.00	15
1995	Ticket Seller 13361-3	Open		10.00	10
1994	Tombstone Sign, 3 asst. 10642-6	Open		3.50	4
1993	Trick or Treater, 3 asst. 08591-2	Retrd.	1995	5.50	6
1994	Werewolf 10643-4	Open		6.00	7
1992	Witch 06706-2	Open		6.00	6

Creepy Hollow Houses - Midwest

YEAR ISSUE		EDITION LIMIT	YEAR RETD.	ISSUE PRICE	*QUOTE U.S.$
1995	Bewitching Belfry (lighted) 13355-2	Open		50.00	50
1993	Blood Bank (lighted) 08548-6	Open		40.00	43
1996	Castle (lighted) 16959-9	5,000		50.00	50
1994	Cauldron Cafe (lighted) 10649-5	Open		40.00	43
1992	Dr. Frankenstein's House (lighted) 01621-3	Retrd.	1995	40.00	43
1992	Dracula's Castle (lighted) 01627-5	Retrd.	1995	40.00	43
1995	Funeral Parlor (lighted) 13356-9	Open		50.00	50
1996	Gypsy Wagon (lighted) 16663-5	Open		45.00	45
1993	Haunted Hotel (lighted) 08549-3	Open		40.00	43
1996	Jack-O' Lant-Inn (lighted) 16665-9	Open		45.00	45
1994	Medical Ghoul School (lighted) 10651-8	Open		40.00	43
1992	Mummy's Mortuary (lighted) 01641-1	Retrd.	1995	40.00	43
1994	Phantom's Opera (lighted) 10650-1	Open		40.00	43
1996	School House (lighted) 16662-8	Open		45.00	45
1993	Shoppe of Horrors (lighted) 08550-9	Retrd.	1995	40.00	43
1995	Skeleton Cinema (lighted) 13354-5	5,000	1995	50.00	50
1992	Witches Cove (lighted) 01665-7	Retrd.	1995	40.00	43

Leo R. Smith III Collection - L. R. Smith

YEAR ISSUE		EDITION LIMIT	YEAR RETD.	ISSUE PRICE	*QUOTE U.S.$
1996	Angel of the Morning 18232-1	1,000		48.00	48
1995	Angel w/Lion and Lamb 13990-5	1,500	1995	125.00	125
1995	Circle of Nature Wreath 16120-3	500		200.00	200
1991	Cossack Santa 01092-1	1,700	1993	103.00	130
1993	Dancing Santa 09042-8	5,000	1995	170.00	170
1992	Dreams of Night Buffalo 07999-7	1,062		250.00	270
1991	Fisherman Santa 03311-1	4,000	1995	270.00	290
1993	Folk Angel 05444-4	2,095	1995	145.00	150
1995	Gardening Angel 16118-0	2,500		130.00	130
1994	Gift Giver Santa 12056-9	1,500		180.00	180
1993	Gnome Santa on Deer 05206-8	1,463		270.00	270
1992	Great Plains Santa 08049-8	5,000	1994	270.00	293
1995	Hare Leaping Over the Garden 16121-0	750		100.00	100
1996	Jolly Boatman Santa 17794-5	1,500		180.00	180
1992	Leo Smith Name Plaque 07881-5	5,000		12.00	12
1995	Maize Maiden Angel 13992-9	2,500		45.00	45
1991	Milkmaker 03541-2	5,000	1994	170.00	184
1992	Ms. Liberty 07866-2	5,000	1994	190.00	210
1994	Old-World Santa 12053-8	1,500	1994	75.00	150-200
1995	Orchard Santa 13989-9	1,500		125.00	125
1995	Otter Wall Hanging 16122-7	750		150.00	150
1995	Owl Lady 13988-2	1,000	1995	100.00	105
1991	Pilgrim Man 03313-5	5,000	1994	84.00	125-150
1991	Pilgrim Riding Turkey 03312-8	5,000	1994	230.00	250-327
1991	Pilgrim Woman 03315-9	5,000	1995	84.00	130
1996	Prairie Moon Market 17793-8	750		300.00	300
1993	Santa Fisherman 08979-8	1,748		250.00	300
1996	Santa in Red Convertible 17790-7	2,000		100.00	100
1995	Santa in Sleigh 13987-5	1,500		125.00	125
1992	Santa of Peace 07328-5	5,000	1994	250.00	270
1994	Santa Skier 12054-5	1,500	1995	190.00	200
1996	Snowflake in Nature Santa 17791-4	1,500		125.00	125
1994	Star of the Roundup Cowboy 11966-1	1,500		100.00	100
1991	Stars and Stripes Santa 01743-2	5,000	1994	190.00	200
1995	Sunbringer Santa 13991-2	1,500		125.00	125
1996	SW Bach Santa 17792-1	1,500		125.00	125
1991	Tis a Witching Time 03544-3	609	1991	140.00	1500
1991	Toymaker 03540-5	5,000	1994	120.00	175
1993	Voyageur 09043-5	788		170.00	170
1994	Weatherwise Angel 12055-2	1,500		150.00	150
1995	Wee Willie Santa 13993-6	2,500	1995	50.00	50
1992	Woodland Brave 07867-9	1,500	1993	87.00	250
1991	Woodsman Santa 03310-4	5,000	1995	230.00	250

Ore Mountain "A Christmas Carol" Nutcrackers - Midwest

YEAR ISSUE		EDITION LIMIT	YEAR RETD.	ISSUE PRICE	*QUOTE U.S.$
1993	Bob Cratchit, 09421-1	5,000	1995	120.00	130
1994	Ghost of Christmas Future, 10449-1	1,500	1995	116.00	125
1994	Ghost of Christmas Past, 10447-7	1,500	1995	116.00	125
1993	Ghost of Christmas Present 12041-5	1,500		116.00	200
1994	Marley's Ghost, 10448-4	1,500	1995	116.00	125
1993	Scrooge, 05522-9	2,500	1995	104.00	125

Ore Mountain "Nutcracker Fantasy" Nutcrackers - Midwest

YEAR ISSUE		EDITION LIMIT	YEAR RETD.	ISSUE PRICE	*QUOTE U.S.$
1995	Clara, 12801-5	5,000		125.00	125
1991	Clara, 8" 01254-3	Retrd.	1995	77.00	100
1994	Herr Drosselmeyer, 10456-9	5,000		110.00	125
1988	Herr Drosselmeyer, 14 1/2" 07506-7	Open		75.00	115
1993	The Mouse King, 05350-8	5,000		100.00	125
1988	The Mouse King, 10" 07509-8	Open		60.00	85
1994	Nutcracker Prince, 11001-0	5,000		104.00	125
1988	The Prince, 12 3/4" 07507-4	Open		75.00	105
1988	The Toy Soldier, 11" 07508-1	Open		70.00	95
1995	Toy Soldier, 12804-6	5,000		125.00	125

Ore Mountain Easter Nutcrackers - Midwest

YEAR ISSUE		EDITION LIMIT	YEAR RETD.	ISSUE PRICE	*QUOTE U.S.$
1992	Bunny Painter, 06480-1	Retrd.	1993	77.00	80
1991	Bunny with Egg, 00145-5	Retrd.	1993	77.00	80
1984	March Hare, 00312-1	Retrd.	1993	77.00	80

Ore Mountain Nutcracker Collection - Midwest

YEAR ISSUE		EDITION LIMIT	YEAR RETD.	ISSUE PRICE	*QUOTE U.S.$
1995	American Country Santa, 13195-4	Open		165.00	165
1996	Angel with Candle 17010-6	Open		220.00	220
1994	Annie Oakley, 10464-4	Retrd.	1995	128.00	130
1996	Attorney 17012-0	Open		120.00	120
1995	August the Strong, 13185-5	Open		190.00	190
1995	Barbeque Dad, 13193-0	Open		176.00	176
1994	Baseball Player, 10459-0	Retrd.	1995	111.00	120
1995	Basketball Player, 12784-1	Open		135.00	135
1995	Beefeater, 12797-1	Open		175.00	175
1994	Black Santa, 10460-6	Retrd.	1995	74.00	74
1993	Cat Witch, 09426-6	Retrd.	1995	93.00	93
1994	Cavalier, 12952-4	Open		80.00	95
1994	Cavalier, 12953-1	Open		65.00	77
1994	Cavalier, 12958-6	Open		57.00	65
1996	Chimney Sweep 17043-4	Open		120.00	120
1995	Chimney Sweep, 00326-8	Open		70.00	70
1992	Christopher Columbus, 00152-3	Retrd.	1992	80.00	80
1991	Clown, 03561-0	Retrd.	1994	115.00	118
1994	Confederate Soldier, 12837-4	Open		93.00	105
1996	Count Dracula 17050-2	Open		150.00	150
1989	Country Santa, 09326-9	Retrd.	1995	95.00	150
1996	Cow Farmer 17054-0	Open		120.00	120
1992	Cowboy, 00298-8	Retrd.	1995	97.00	150
1995	Downhill Santa Skier, 13197-8	Open		145.00	145
1996	Drummer 17044-1	Open		120.00	120
1996	East Coast Santa 17047-2	Open		200.00	200
1990	Elf, 04154-3	Retrd.	1993	70.00	73
1996	Emergency Medical Technician 17013-7	Open		140.00	140
1994	Engineer, 10454-5	Retrd.	1995	108.00	108
1992	Farmer, 01109-6	Retrd.	1994	65.00	77
1996	Female Farmer 17011-3	1,000		145.00	145
1993	Fireman with Dog, 06592-1	Open		134.00	140
1989	Fisherman, 09327-6	Retrd.	1995	90.00	100
1996	Frankenstein 17009-0	Open		170.00	170
1994	Gardening Lady, 10450-7	Open		104.00	112
1993	Gepetto Santa, 09417-4	Retrd.	1995	115.00	115
1989	Golfer, 09325-2	Retrd.	1994	85.00	90
1996	Guard 17046-5	Open		120.00	120
1995	Handyman, 12806-0	Open		136.00	137
1996	Harlequin Santa 17174-5	Open		150.00	150
1995	Hockey Player, 12783-4	Open		155.00	155
1995	Hunter Nutcraker 12785-8	Open		136.00	136
1992	Indian, 00195-0	Retrd.	1994	96.00	100
1995	Jack Frost, 12803-9	Open		150.00	150
1995	Jolly St. Nick with Toys, 13709-3	Open		135.00	135
1995	King Richard the Lionhearted, 12798-8	Open		165.00	165
1996	King with Sceptor 17045-8	Open		120.00	120
1995	Law Scholar, 12789-6	Open		127.00	127
1996	Male Farmer 17015-1	1,000		145.00	145
1990	Merlin the Magician, 04207-6	Retrd.	1995	67.00	75
1994	Miner, 10493-4	Retrd.	1995	110.00	120
1994	Nature Lover, 10446-0	Retrd.	1995	112.00	112
1988	Nordic Santa, 08872-2	Retrd.	1995	84.00	110
1996	Northwoods Santa 17048-9	Open		200.00	200
1991	Nutcracker-Maker, 03601-3	Retrd.	1993	62.00	65
1995	Peddler, 12805-3	Open		140.00	140
1995	Pierre Le Chef, 12802-2	Open		147.00	147
1992	Pilgrim, 00188-2	Retrd.	1994	96.00	100
1994	Pinecone Santa, 10461-3	Retrd.	1994	92.00	92
1984	Pinocchio, 00160-8	Open		60.00	68
1995	Pizza Baker, 13194-7	Open		170.00	170
1996	Prince 17038-0	Open		120.00	120
1994	Prince Charming, 10457-6	Retrd.	1994	125.00	130
1994	Pumpkin Head Scarecrow, 10451-1	Open		127.00	140
1994	Regal Prince, 10452-1	Open		140.00	152
1992	Ringmaster, 00196-7	Retrd.	1993	135.00	137
1995	Riverboat Gambler, 12787-2	Open		137.00	137
1995	Royal Lion, 13985-1	Open		130.00	130
1995	Santa at Workbench, 13335-4	Open		130.00	130

*Quotes have been rounded up to nearest dollar

YEAR ISSUE		EDITION LIMIT	YEAR RETD.	ISSUE PRICE	*QUOTE U.S.$
1994	Santa in Nightshirt, 10462-0	Retrd.	1995	108.00	120
1996	Santa One-Man Band Musical 17051-9	Open		170.00	170
1988	Santa w/Tree & Toys, 07666-8	Retrd.	1993	76.00	87
1993	Santa with Animals, 09424-2	Retrd.	1994	117.00	117
1994	Santa with Basket, 10472-9	Open		80.00	100
1992	Santa with Skis, 01305-2	Retrd.	1994	100.00	110
1990	Sea Captain, 04157-4	Retrd.	1994	86.00	95
1994	Snow King, 10470-5	Retrd.	1995	108.00	120
1994	Soccer Player, 10494-1	Open		97.00	107
1994	Sorcerer, 10471-2	Retrd.	1995	100.00	100
1996	Sports Fan 17173-8	Open		120.00	120
1994	Sultan King, 10455-2	Retrd.	1995	130.00	145
1995	Teacher, 13196-1	Open		165.00	165
1994	Toy Vendor, 11987-7	Open		124.00	135
1990	Uncle Sam, 04206-9	Retrd.	1993	50.00	62
1994	Union Soldier, 12836-7	Open		93.00	105
1996	Victorian Santa 17172-1	Open		180.00	180
1992	Victorian Santa, 00187-5	Retrd.	1994	130.00	140
1996	Western 17049-6	Open		250.00	250
1993	White Santa, 09533-1	Retrd.	1995	100.00	100
1990	Windsor Club, 04160-4	Retrd.	1994	85.00	87
1990	Witch, 04159-8	Retrd.	1995	75.00	76
1990	Woodland Santa, 04191-8	Retrd.	1995	105.00	150

Wendt and Kuhn Collection - Wendt/Kuhn

YEAR ISSUE		EDITION LIMIT	YEAR RETD.	ISSUE PRICE	*QUOTE U.S.$
1989	Angel at Piano 09403-7	Open		31.00	37
1983	Angel Brass Musicians, set/6 00470-8	Open		92.00	110
1983	Angel Conductor on Stand 00469-2	Open		21.00	24
1990	Angel Duet in Celestial Stars 04158-1	Retrd.	1994	60.00	63
1983	Angel Percussion Musicians set/6 00443-2	Open		110.00	130
1979	Angel Playing Violin 00403-6	Retrd.	1994	34.00	35
1980	Angel Pulling Wagon 00553-8	Retrd.	1995	43.00	50
1983	Angel String & Woodwind Musicians, set/6 00465-4	Open		108.00	120
1983	Angel String Musicians, set/6 00455-5	Retrd.	1995	105.00	120
1979	Angel Trio, set/3 00471-5	Open		140.00	170
1981	Angel w/Tree & Basket 01190-8	Retrd.	1993	24.00	25
1976	Angel with Sled 02940-4	Retrd.	1994	36.50	38
1981	Angels at Cradle, set/4 01193-5	Open		73.00	80
1996	Angels Bearing Gifts 17039-7	Open		120.00	120
1984	Angels Bearing Toys, set/6 00451-7	Retrd.	1995	97.00	110
1979	Bavarian Moving Van 02854-4	Open		134.00	150
1991	Birdhouse 01209-3	Retrd.	1994	22.50	23
1996	Blueberry Children 17040-3	Open		110.00	110
1991	Boy on Rocking Horse, 2 asst. 01202-4	Retrd.	1994	35.00	36
1994	Busy Elf, 3 asst. 12856-5	Open		22.00	24
1987	Child on Skis, 2 asst. 06083-4	Retrd.	1994	28.00	29
1987	Child on Sled 06085-8	Retrd.	1994	25.50	27
1994	Child with Flowers Set 12947-0	Open		45.00	50
1988	Children Carrying Lanterns Procession, set/6 01213-0	Open		117.00	150
1991	Display Base for Wendt und Kuhn Figures, 12 1/2 x 2" 01214-7	Open		32.00	39
1991	Flower Children, set/6 01213-0	Open		130.00	150
1979	Girl w/Cradle, set/2 01203-1	Retrd.	1994	37.50	40
1979	Girl w/Porridge Bowl 01198-0	Open		29.00	32
1979	Girl w/Scissors 01197-3	Open		25.00	32
1983	Girl w/Wagon 01196-6	Retrd.	1994	27.00	29
1991	Girl with Doll 01200-0	Open		31.50	35
1980	Little People Napkin Rings 6 asst. 03504-7	Open		21.00	25
1988	Lucia Parade Figures, set/3 07667-5	Retrd.	1995	75.00	80
1978	Madonna w/Child 01207-9	Open		120.00	135
1979	Margarita Angels, set/6 02938-1	Open		94.00	110
1983	Margarita Birthday Angels, set/3 00480-7	Retrd.	1995	44.00	53
1979	Pied Piper and Children, set/7 02843-8	Retrd.	1994	120.00	130
1981	Santa w/Angel in Sleigh 01192-8	Retrd.	1995	52.00	60
1976	Santa with Angel 00473-9	Open		50.00	55
1994	Santa with Tree 12942-5	Open		29.00	32
1994	Sun, Moon, Star Set 12943-2	Open		69.00	75
1992	Wendt und Kuhn Display Sign w/ Sitting Angel 07535-7	Open		20.00	23
1991	White Angel with Violin 01205-5	Retrd.	1993	25.50	27

Wendt and Kuhn Collection Music Boxes - Wendt/Kuhn

YEAR ISSUE		EDITION LIMIT	YEAR RETD.	ISSUE PRICE	*QUOTE U.S.$
1978	Angel at Pipe Organ 01929-0	Open		176.00	200
1996	Angel Musicians Music Box 17036-6	Open		260.00	260
1994	Angel Under Stars Crank Music Box 12974-6	300		150.00	190
1991	Angels & Santa Around Tree 01211-6	Open		300.00	330
1996	Children Around Tree Music Box 17037-3	Open		330.00	330
1976	Girl Rocking Cradle 09215-6	Retrd.	1994	180.00	190
1978	Rotating Angels 'Round Cradle 01911-5	Open		270.00	300

Wendt and Kuhn Figurines Candleholders - Wendt/Kuhn

YEAR ISSUE		EDITION LIMIT	YEAR RETD.	ISSUE PRICE	*QUOTE U.S.$
1976	Angel Pair 00472-2	Open		70.00	85
1991	Angel w/Friend 01191-1	Retrd.	1994	33.30	34
1994	Angel w/Wagon 12860-2	Open		35.00	38
1980	Large Angel Pair 01201-7	Retrd.	1994	270.00	277
1996	Orchestra Stand 17042-7	Open		130.00	130
1986	Pair of Angels 01204-8	Retrd.	1994	30.00	32
1987	Santa 06082-7	Retrd.	1994	53.00	54
1991	Small Angel Pair 01195-9	Retrd.	1994	60.00	63
1991	White Angel 01206-2	Retrd.	1994	28.00	29

Museum Collections, Inc.

American Family I - N. Rockwell

YEAR ISSUE		EDITION LIMIT	YEAR RETD.	ISSUE PRICE	*QUOTE U.S.$
1979	Baby's First Step	22,500		90.00	175-200
1980	Birthday Party	22,500		110.00	150
1981	Bride and Groom	22,500		110.00	125
1980	First Haircut	22,500		90.00	150
1980	First Prom	22,500		90.00	135
1980	Happy Birthday, Dear Mother	22,500		90.00	135
1980	Little Mother	22,500		110.00	125
1981	Mother's Little Helpers	22,500		110.00	135
1980	The Student	22,500		110.00	140
1980	Sweet Sixteen	22,500		90.00	125
1980	Washing Our Dog	22,500		110.00	125
1980	Wrapping Christmas Presents	22,500		90.00	125

Christmas - N. Rockwell

YEAR ISSUE		EDITION LIMIT	YEAR RETD.	ISSUE PRICE	*QUOTE U.S.$
1980	Checking His List	Yr.Iss.		65.00	110
1983	High Hopes	Yr.Iss.		95.00	175
1981	Ringing in Good Cheer	Yr.Iss.		95.00	100
1984	Space Age Santa	Yr.Iss.		65.00	100
1982	Waiting for Santa	Yr.Iss.		95.00	110

Classic - N. Rockwell

YEAR ISSUE		EDITION LIMIT	YEAR RETD.	ISSUE PRICE	*QUOTE U.S.$
1984	All Wrapped Up	Closed		65.00	90-95
1980	Bedtime	Closed		65.00	90-95
1984	The Big Race	Closed		65.00	90-95
1983	Bored of Education	Closed		65.00	90-95
1983	Braving the Storm	Closed		65.00	90-95
1980	The Cobbler	Closed		65.00	125
1982	The Country Doctor	Closed		65.00	90-95
1981	A Dollhouse for Sis	Closed		65.00	90-95
1982	Dreams in the Antique Shop	Closed		65.00	90-95
1983	A Final Touch	Closed		65.00	90-95
1980	For A Good Boy	Closed		65.00	125
1984	Goin' Fishin'	Closed		65.00	90-95
1983	High Stepping	Closed		65.00	90-95
1982	The Kite Maker	Closed		65.00	100
1980	Lighthouse Keeper's Daughter	Closed		65.00	125
1980	Memories	Closed		65.00	125
1981	The Music Lesson	Closed		65.00	125
1981	Music Master	Closed		65.00	90-95
1981	Off to School	Closed		65.00	90-95
1981	Puppy Love	Closed		65.00	90-95
1984	Saturday's Hero	Closed		65.00	90-95
1983	A Special Treat	Closed		65.00	90-95
1982	Spring Fever	Closed		65.00	90-95
1980	The Toymaker	Closed		65.00	125
1981	While The Audience Waits	Closed		65.00	85
1983	Winter Fun	Closed		65.00	90-95
1982	Words of Wisdom	Closed		65.00	90-95

Commemorative - N. Rockwell

YEAR ISSUE		EDITION LIMIT	YEAR RETD.	ISSUE PRICE	*QUOTE U.S.$
1985	Another Masterpiece by Norman Rockwell	5,000		125.00	200-250
1981	Norman Rockwell Display	5,000		125.00	200-250
1983	Norman Rockwell, America's Artist	5,000		125.00	200-250
1984	Outward Bound	5,000		125.00	200-250
1986	The Painter and the Pups	5,000		125.00	250
1982	Spirit of America	5,000		125.00	200-250

Old World Christmas

Candleholders - E.M. Merck

YEAR ISSUE		EDITION LIMIT	YEAR RETD.	ISSUE PRICE	*QUOTE U.S.$
1989	Angel 9015	Retrd.	1994	7.50	8
1989	Hummingbird 9013	Retrd.	1994	7.50	8
1989	Nutcracker 9016	Retrd.	1994	7.50	8
1989	Rocking Horse 9011	Retrd.	1994	7.50	8
1989	Santa 9012	Retrd.	1992	7.55	10
1989	Teddy Bear 9014	Retrd.	1994	7.50	8

Collectibles - O.W.C.

YEAR ISSUE		EDITION LIMIT	YEAR RETD.	ISSUE PRICE	*QUOTE U.S.$
1992	Candle Arch with Church 862	Retrd.	1993	28.50	50
1992	Large Seiffener Candle Arch 8616	Retrd.	1994	450.00	495
1992	Weather House 86109	Retrd.	1994	31.50	37

Halloween - E.M. Merck

YEAR ISSUE		EDITION LIMIT	YEAR RETD.	ISSUE PRICE	*QUOTE U.S.$
1988	Black Cat on Wire 9208	Retrd.	1992	8.35	13
1989	Black Cat/Witch with Cart (A) 9251	Retrd.	1994	10.00	12
1989	Cast Iron Scarecrow 9218	Retrd.	1994	32.50	39
1987	Ghost Light 9205	Retrd.	1992	37.00	75
1989	Ghost Votive 9211	Retrd.	1994	8.50	12
1988	Haunted House Waterglobe 9206	Retrd.	1989	22.50	32
1987	Haunted House with Lights 9203	Retrd.	1994	99.50	125-145
1988	Large Pumpkin Bowl 9273	Retrd.	1994	18.50	20
1987	Lighted Ghost Dish 9204	Retrd.	1994	45.00	50
1988	Pumpkin Head on Wire 9207	Retrd.	1992	7.35	12
1987	Pumpkin Light with Ghosts 9201	Retrd.	1994	39.50	45
1987	Pumpkin Light w/Scarecrow 9202	Retrd.	1991	37.00	45
1988	Pumpkin Taper Holder 9272	Retrd.	1992	5.65	9
1988	Pumpkin Votive 9271	Retrd.	1991	8.90	12
1989	Witch on Moon Night Light 9212	Retrd.	1994	37.50	45
1988	Witch Taper Holder 9282	Retrd.	1993	11.00	19
1988	Witch Votive Holder 9281	Retrd.	1994	29.50	350

Night Lights - E.M. Merck

YEAR ISSUE		EDITION LIMIT	YEAR RETD.	ISSUE PRICE	*QUOTE U.S.$
1986	ABC Block 529713	Retrd.	1994	37.00	50
1986	Angel 529703	Retrd.	1992	18.00	97
1990	Father Christmas 529721	Retrd.	1992	45.00	110
1993	Father Christmas w/Toys 529727	Retrd.	1995	65.00	65
1985	Santa 529701	Retrd.	1987	37.00	525
1988	Santa Hugging Tree 529717	Retrd.	1990	42.00	275
1986	Santa in Chimney 529707	Retrd.	1988	37.00	325
1989	Santa on Locomotive 529719	Retrd.	1991	42.00	195
1992	Santa with Nutcracker 529725	Retrd.	1992	45.00	250
1991	Santa with Stocking 529723	Retrd.	1993	45.00	195
1987	Santa with Tree 529715	Retrd.	1989	39.50	255
1986	Snowman 529709	Retrd.	1988	37.00	125
1986	Teddy Bear 529711	Retrd.	1991	37.00	135

Nutcrackers - E.M. Merck, unless otherwise noted

YEAR ISSUE		EDITION LIMIT	YEAR RETD.	ISSUE PRICE	*QUOTE U.S.$
1987	Austrian Musketeer 72048 - K.W.O.	Retrd.	1995	57.50	58
1993	Bohemian Beekeeper 7264	Retrd.	1995	110.00	110
1993	Brandenburger Guard 7250	Retrd.	1994	110.00	125
1987	British Guard 72041 - K.W.O.	Retrd.	1995	60.00	60
1992	Carved Hunter 72213 - O.W.C.	Retrd.	1992	150.00	195
1993	Exceptional Dragon 7231 - K.W.O.	50	1995	995.00	995
1992	Exceptional King 7230	50	1994	950.00	1100
1994	Exceptional Santa 7232 - Merten	Retrd.	1995	995.00	995
1993	Falkensteiner Wizard 7261	Retrd.	1995	110.00	110
1991	Inlaid Natural King 7214 - O.W.C.	Retrd.	1992	150.00	195
1991	Inlaid Natural Muskateer 7225 - O.W.C.	Retrd.	1992	150.00	225
1992	Large Bavarian Duke 72242 - K.W.O.	Retrd.	1995	130.00	130
1992	Large British Guard 72141 - K.W.O.	Retrd.	1994	90.00	95
1992	Large Carved Santa 7223 - K.W.O.	Retrd.	1994	175.00	180
1992	Large Dutch Guard 72140 - K.W.O.	Retrd.	1994	90.00	96
1991	Large Hunter 7228 - K.W.O.	Retrd.	1994	97.50	105
1993	Large King 72033 - K.W.O.	Retrd.	1994	79.95	85
1992	Large Prussian King 72244 - K.W.O.	Retrd.	1994	130.00	135
1992	Large Prussian Sargeant 72145 - K.W.O.	Retrd.	1995	90.00	90
1992	Large Saxon Duke 72241 - K.W.O.	Retrd.	1995	130.00	130
1992	Large Snow Prince 7277	Retrd.	1992	100.00	115
1989	Prussian Corporal 72047 - K.W.O.	Retrd.	1990	42.50	43
1987	Prussian Sergeant 72045 - K.W.O.	Retrd.	1995	60.00	60
1993	Rostocker Pirate 7252	Retrd.	1995	110.00	110
1993	Saalfelder Shepherd 7263	Retrd.	1995	110.00	110
1993	Seiffener Santa 7257	Retrd.	1994	110.00	115
1992	Skier 7294	Retrd.	1992	82.50	83
1993	Teddy Bear 7296	Retrd.	1994	135.00	150
1993	Tegernsee Golfer 7259	Retrd.	1995	135.00	135

Paper Maché - E.M. Merck

YEAR ISSUE		EDITION LIMIT	YEAR RETD.	ISSUE PRICE	*QUOTE U.S.$
1988	52 cm. Father Christmas 9652	Retrd.	1990	175.00	195
1988	Assorted Father Christmas 9615	Retrd.	1989	44.00	50
1989	Assorted Santas 9691	Retrd.	1991	35.00	43
1988	Blue Father Christmas 9602	Retrd.	1988	19.50	27
1988	Father Christmas (A) 9600	Retrd.	1988	19.50	27
1989	Father Christmas 9612	Retrd.	1989	38.50	45
1988	Father Christmas with Gifts 9610	Retrd.	1988	32.50	40
1989	Father Christmas with Pack 9638	Retrd.	1989	40.00	47
1988	Red Father Christmas 9601	Retrd.	1988	19.50	25
1989	Santa in Sleigh 9672	Retrd.	1989	39.50	45
1988	Small Traditional Belznickel 9662	Retrd.	1994	35.00	40
1988	Traditional Belznickel 9661	Retrd.	1994	40.00	50
1988	White Father Christmas 9603	Retrd.	1988	19.50	30
1988	White Father Christmas 9616	Retrd.	1989	50.00	55

Porcelain Christmas - E.M. Merck

YEAR ISSUE		EDITION LIMIT	YEAR RETD.	ISSUE PRICE	*QUOTE U.S.$
1987	Angels, Set/3 9421	Retrd.	1987	15.50	2[illegible]
1988	Bear on Skates Music Box 9492	Retrd.	1988	44.00	50
1988	Bunny on Skies Music Box 9491	Retrd.	1988	44.00	50
1987	Cast Iron Santa 9419	Retrd.	1993	35.00	4[illegible]
1987	Cast Iron Santa on Horse 9418	Retrd.	1993	37.50	48
1987	Four Castles of Germany 9450	Retrd.	1988	31.00	5[illegible]
1995	Mr. C's Roadster 9708	Retrd.	1994	9.95	14
1988	Penguin w/Gifts Music Box 9493	Retrd.	1988	44.00	65
1987	Roly-Poly Santa 9440	Retrd.	1987	27.00	35
1987	Santa Head Night Light 9412	Retrd.	1989	19.00	3[illegible]
1987	Santa Head Stocking Holder 9414	Retrd.	1987	18.00	2[illegible]
1987	Santa Head Votive 9411	Retrd.	1988	10.00	2[illegible]
1987	Santa in Chimney Music Box 9413	Retrd.	1987	44.00	4[illegible]
1988	Santa in Swing 9473	Retrd.	1988	6.25	1[illegible]
1988	Santa on Polar Bear 9471	Retrd.	1988	6.25	1[illegible]
1988	Santa on Teeter-Totter 9475	Retrd.	1988	6.25	1[illegible]
1988	Santa Visiting Igloo 9476	Retrd.	1988	6.25	1[illegible]
1988	Santa Visiting Lighthouse 9472	Retrd.	1988	6.25	1[illegible]
1988	Santa with Angel 9474	Retrd.	1988	6.25	1[illegible]
1995	Swinging into the Season 9705	Retrd.	1994	10.50	1[illegible]

Pyramids - O.W.C., unless otherwise noted

YEAR ISSUE		EDITION LIMIT	YEAR RETD.	ISSUE PRICE	*QUOTE U.S.$
1992	3-Tier Forest 882	Retrd.	1995	225.00	22[illegible]
1992	3-Tier Nativity 883	Retrd.	1995	250.00	25[illegible]
1991	3-Tier Painted Nativity 8818	Retrd.	1993	225.00	26[illegible]
1992	5ft Hand-Carved 884007	Retrd.	1992	1295.00	132[illegible]
1992	6ft Hand-Carved 884006	Retrd.	1992	4000.00	4500-500[illegible]
1991	Camel Caravan 8812	Retrd.	1995	92.50	9[illegible]
1986	Deer w/Tree, Wall Pyramid 88137	Retrd.	1993	65.00	6[illegible]
1992	Detailed Nativity 8851	Retrd.	1993	175.00	19[illegible]
1991	Mini-Pyramid, Angels 8811	Retrd.	1993	22.50	2[illegible]
1992	Mini-Pyramid, Santa 8820	Retrd.	1994	32.50	4[illegible]
1992	Miniature Choir 885	Retrd.	1995	35.00	3[illegible]
1992	Miniature Forest 884	Retrd.	1994	35.00	4[illegible]
1992	Miniature Music Band 886	Retrd.	1993	30.00	3[illegible]
1991	Musical 4-Tier 8815	Retrd.	1991	775.00	8[illegible]
1992	Natural with Deer 8821	Retrd.	1995	65.00	6[illegible]
1992	Santa with Angels 887	Retrd.	1993	175.00	19[illegible]
1991	Santa with Train 8817	Retrd.	1991	62.50	9[illegible]
1992	Small Choir 8879	Retrd.	1993	68.50	7[illegible]
1992	Small Nativity 8822	Retrd.	1995	110.00	1[illegible]

*Quotes have been rounded up to nearest dollar

YEAR ISSUE		EDITION LIMIT	YEAR RETD.	ISSUE PRICE	*QUOTE U.S. $
1992	Small Nativity 889	Retrd.	1993	82.00	90
1991	White 3-Tier 8816	Retrd.	1992	225.00	250
1992	White with Angels 8824	Retrd.	1993	55.00	75

Smoking Men - O.W.C., unless otherwise noted

YEAR ISSUE		EDITION LIMIT	YEAR RETD.	ISSUE PRICE	*QUOTE U.S. $
1992	Alpenhorn Player 7058	Retrd.	1995	70.00	70
1988	Antique Style Coachman 70053 - K.W.O.	Retrd.	1988	28.00	35
1988	Antique Style Cook 70052 - K.W.O.	Retrd.	1989	27.50	33
1986	Artist 7020 - E.M. Merck	Retrd.	1993	55.00	60
1991	Baker 7044	Retrd.	1992	49.50	55
1992	Basket Peddler 7040	Retrd.	1993	130.00	140
1991	Bavarian Hunter 7032	Retrd.	1994	79.50	85
1991	Beer Drinker 7033	Retrd.	1994	67.50	72
1991	Bird Seller 7014	Retrd.	1992	50.00	55
1991	Butcher 7043	Retrd.	1992	49.50	55
1986	Carved Hunter 70100	Retrd.	1991	90.00	97
1992	Carved Hunter 7054	Retrd.	1993	200.00	215
1992	Carved King 7072	Retrd.	1995	68.50	69
1992	Carved Shepherd 7053	Retrd.	1993	150.00	160
1992	Carved Woodsman 7015	Retrd.	1994	67.50	75
1991	Champion Archer 7041	Retrd.	1995	67.50	68
1989	Chimney Sweep 7017 - E.M. Merck	Retrd.	1993	55.00	55
1992	Clock Salesman 7039	Retrd.	1992	275.00	350
1991	Coachman 7057	Retrd.	1992	60.00	72
1991	Cook 7025	Retrd.	1993	55.00	60
1992	Farmer 7026	Retrd.	1993	55.00	60
1992	Farmer with Crate 7023	Retrd.	1994	150.00	155
1992	Father Christmas 70113-1	Retrd.	1989	45.00	60
1986	Father Christmas 702	Retrd.	1994	60.00	63
1991	Father Christmas 7051	Retrd.	1995	80.00	80
1993	Father Christmas 7063	Retrd.	1993	45.00	50
1986	Father Christmas with Toys 7010	Retrd.	1992	60.00	68
1991	Fisherman 7029	Retrd.	1993	55.00	58
1991	Frosty Snowman 703	Retrd.	1993	22.50	31
1991	Gardener 7045	Retrd.	1992	49.50	56
1991	Gardner 7016 - E.M. Merck	Retrd.	1993	55.00	59
1992	Grandma 702622	Retrd.	1993	42.50	48
1985	Grandpa 702615	Retrd.	1993	42.50	46
1986	Hunter 701	Retrd.	1992	30.00	36
1991	Hunter 7018 - E.M. Merck	Retrd.	1993	55.00	60
1992	Hunter with Crate 7021	Retrd.	1994	150.00	155
1991	Ice Skater 7038 - E.M. Merck	Retrd.	1992	60.00	63
1992	Innkeeper 70268	Retrd.	1993	54.00	58
1991	Innkeeper 7037	Retrd.	1995	60.00	60
1992	King 70229 - E.M. Merck	Retrd.	1993	95.00	104
1986	Large Old World Santa 70203	Retrd.	1988	77.50	83
1992	Minstrel 7061	Retrd.	1994	85.00	85
1991	Mountain Climber 7036	Retrd.	1995	67.50	68
1991	Natural Father Christmas 7012	Retrd.	1992	60.00	69
1991	Natural Santa 706	Retrd.	1992	40.00	48
1991	Nightwatchman 7027	Retrd.	1993	55.00	59
1985	Nightwatchman 7034	Retrd.	1993	32.50	41
1986	Old World Santa 70204	Retrd.	1988	42.50	47
1991	Postman 7028	Retrd.	1993	55.00	59
1991	Prussian Soldier 7056	Retrd.	1993	60.00	63
1989	Santa 7086	Retrd.	1992	55.00	61
1991	Santa Claus 705	Retrd.	1993	45.00	51
1992	Santa in Crate 707	Retrd.	1994	165.00	195
1986	Santa Smoker/Candleholder 704	Retrd.	1994	55.00	58
1986	Skier 702616	Retrd.	1992	54.00	62
1992	Skier 7059	Retrd.	1995	59.50	60
1986	Small Old World Santa 70202	Retrd.	1988	37.50	44
1992	Small Santa 7011	Retrd.	1995	37.50	38
1985	Snowman 702621	Retrd.	1991	30.00	38
1991	Snowman on Skis 7092	Retrd.	1992	30.00	39
1988	Snowman with Bird 708	Retrd.	1993	26.00	35
1992	St. Peter 70228	Retrd.	1993	95.00	105
1991	Toy Peddler 7030	Retrd.	1993	60.00	60
1991	Toy Peddler 7055	Retrd.	1993	60.00	66
1992	Toy Peddler 7060	Retrd.	1994	110.00	120
1992	Tyrolian 702613	Retrd.	1993	45.00	50
1992	Witch 70543 - E.M. Merck	Retrd.	1993	49.50	56
1991	Wood Worker 7031	Retrd.	1994	79.50	85
1987	Woodcarver 70043 - K.W.O.	Retrd.	1990	40.00	47
1991	Woodsman 7013	Retrd.	1993	60.00	64
1991	Woodsman 7019 - E.M. Merck	Retrd.	1993	55.00	60

Olszewski Studios

Olszewski Studios - R. Olszewski

YEAR ISSUE		EDITION LIMIT	YEAR RETD.	ISSUE PRICE	*QUOTE U.S. $
1994	The Grand Entrance SM1	1,500	1994	225.00	325
1994	The Grand Entrance A/P SM1	120	1994	450.00	575
1994	Tinker's Treasure Chest SM2	Closed	1994	235.00	450-495
1994	To Be (included w/Treasure Chest) SM3	Closed	1994	Set	Set
1994	The Little Tinker SM4	750	1995	235.00	295
1995	Special Treat SM5	800	1995	220.00	225
1995	Mockingbird	800	1995	230.00	230
1995	Lady With An Urn	1,000	1995	235.00	235
1995	Lady With An Urn A/P	144	1995	470.00	470

Pacific Rim Import Corp.

Bristol Township - P. Sebern, unless otherwise noted

YEAR ISSUE		EDITION LIMIT	YEAR RETD.	ISSUE PRICE	*QUOTE U.S. $
1990	Bedford Manor	Open		30.00	30
1990	Black Swan Millinery	Open		30.00	30
1991	Bridgestone Church	Retrd.	1993	30.00	30
1990	Bristol Books	Open		35.00	35
1995	Bristol Channel Lighthouse	Open		30.00	30
1996	Bristol Somerset Cathedral - Pacific Rim Team	Open		N/A	N/A
1990	Bristol Township Sign	Open		10.00	10
1993	Chesterfield House	Open		30.00	30
1990	Coventry House	Retrd.	1995	30.00	30
1991	Elmstone House	Retrd.	1993	30.00	45
1991	Flower Shop	Open		30.00	30
1993	Foxdown Manor	Open		30.00	30
1990	Geo. Straith Grocer - R. S. Benson	Open		25.00	25
1991	Hardwicke House	Retrd.	1993	30.00	45
1990	High Gate Mill	Open		40.00	40
1990	Iron Horse Livery	Retrd.	1993	30.00	30
1991	Kilby Cottage	Retrd.	1993	30.00	45
1995	King's Gate School	Open		30.00	30
1990	Maps & Charts	Open		25.00	25
1991	Pegglesworth Inn	Retrd.	1995	40.00	40
1990	Queen's Road Church	Open		40.00	40
1994	Shotwick Inn/Surgery	Open		35.00	35
1990	Silversmith	Open		30.00	30
1990	Southwick Church	Open		30.00	30
1994	Surrey Road Church	Open		40.00	40
1990	Trinity Church	Retrd.	1993	30.00	30
1990	Violin Shop	Open		30.00	30
1990	Wexford Manor	Open		25.00	25

Bristol Waterfront - P. Sebern

YEAR ISSUE		EDITION LIMIT	YEAR RETD.	ISSUE PRICE	*QUOTE U.S. $
1992	Admiralty Shipping	Open		30.00	30
1992	Avon Fish Co.	Open		30.00	30
1993	Bristol Point Lighthouse	Open		45.00	45
1994	Bristol Tattler	Open		40.00	40
1992	Chandler	Open		30.00	30
1992	Customs House	Open		40.00	40
1992	Hawke Exports	Open		40.00	40
1993	Lower Quay Chapel	Open		40.00	40
1994	Portshead Lighthouse	Open		30.00	30
1992	Quarter Deck Inn	Open		40.00	40
1992	Regent Warehouse	Open		40.00	40
1993	Rusty Knight Inn	Open		35.00	35

Bunny Toes - Pacific Rim Team, unless otherwise noted

YEAR ISSUE		EDITION LIMIT	YEAR RETD.	ISSUE PRICE	*QUOTE U.S. $
1995	Annie With Strawberries - P. Sebern	Open		15.00	15
1996	Betsy-Celebrate	1,440		15.00	15
1995	Bunny Gazebo	Open		50.00	50
1995	Bunny Toes Sign - P. Sebern	Open		20.00	20
1995	Garden Trellis	Open		30.00	30
1995	Hannah Strolls With Carriage	Open		15.00	15
1995	Hannah With Maximillian	Open		13.00	13
1996	Justin-Stars & Stripes	1,440		15.00	15
1994	Mazie at Play	Open		13.00	13
1994	Phoebe Goes Ballooning	Open		7.00	7
1995	Rustic Garden Accessory Group (6 pcs) - P. Sebern	Open		40.00	40
1994	Sophie Pops Out	Open		7.00	7
1995	Spring Garden Accessory Group (6 pcs) - P. Sebern	Open		40.00	40
1994	Sweethearts (lighted)	Open		50.00	50
1994	Tillie Making a Wreath	Open		13.00	13
1995	Tillie With Her Bike	Open		15.00	15
1995	Timothy With Eggs	Open		13.00	13
1994	Timothy With Flower Cart	Open		17.00	17
1994	Timothy With Tulips	Open		13.00	13
1995	Tommy's Joy Ride - P. Sebern	Open		15.00	15
1994	Wendell at the Mail Box	Open		17.00	17
1995	Wendell Play The Cello	Open		13.00	13
1994	Wendell With Eggs in Hat	Open		13.00	13
1995	Wendell With Flowers	Open		13.00	13
1994	Willis & Skeeter	Open		17.00	17
1995	Willis & Skeeter Gardening	Open		15.00	15
1995	Winifred Paints Eggs	Open		15.00	15
1994	Winifred With Blooms	Open		13.00	13

Bunny Toes Birthday Bunnies - P. Sebern

YEAR ISSUE		EDITION LIMIT	YEAR RETD.	ISSUE PRICE	*QUOTE U.S. $
1995	Anabell Gliding Along	Open		20.00	20
1995	Beth Back to School	Open		20.00	20
1995	Callie Bundle Up	Open		20.00	20
1995	Carly Striking a Pose	Open		20.00	20
1995	Charlotte Best of the Bunch	Open		20.00	20
1995	Chester Sharing With Friends	Open		20.00	20
1995	Christopher & Cory The Best Shot	Open		20.00	20
1995	Dinah Irresistible	Open		20.00	20
1995	Douglas Frosty Friends	Open		20.00	20
1995	Goldie Taking Turns	Open		20.00	20
1995	Harvey Giddy-Up and Go	Open		20.00	20
1995	Jeremy Clear Sailing	Open		20.00	20
1995	Joey Autumn Chores	Open		20.00	20
1995	Maggie Joy of Giving	Open		20.00	20
1995	Molly Sweet Wishes	Open		20.00	20
1995	Nicholas Between Tides	Open		20.00	20
1995	Penelope Wishful Thinking	Open		20.00	20
1995	Phoebe First Outing	Open		20.00	20
1995	Pieter Higher Education	Open		20.00	20
1995	Russel & Robby Sharing the Harvest	Open		20.00	20
1995	Violet Thank You Notes	Open		20.00	20
1995	Wilbur Lazy Daze	Open		20.00	20
1995	Wiley Winter Games	Open		20.00	20
1995	Zachary Waitin' on the Wind	Open		20.00	20

Pemberton & Oakes

Zolan's Children - D. Zolan

YEAR ISSUE		EDITION LIMIT	YEAR RETD.	ISSUE PRICE	*QUOTE U.S. $
1982	Erik and the Dandelion	17,000		48.00	90
1983	Sabina in the Grass	6,800		48.00	115
1985	Tender Moment	10,000		29.00	80
1984	Winter Angel	8,000		28.00	150

PenDelfin

PenDelfin Family Circle Collectors' Club - J. Heap

YEAR ISSUE		EDITION LIMIT	YEAR RETD.	ISSUE PRICE	*QUOTE U.S. $
1993	Herald	Closed	1993	Gift	50
1993	Bosun	Closed	1993	50.00	100
1994	Buttons	Closed	1994	Gift	30
1994	Puffer	Closed	1995	85.00	85
1995	Bellman	Closed	1995	Gift	N/A
1995	Georgie and the Dragon	Closed	1995	125.00	125
1996	Newsie	Yr.Iss.		Gift	N/A
1996	Delia	Yr.Iss.		125.00	125

40th Anniversary Piece - PenDelfin

YEAR ISSUE		EDITION LIMIT	YEAR RETD.	ISSUE PRICE	*QUOTE U.S. $
1994	Aunt Ruby	10,000		275.00	275

Event Piece - J. Heap

YEAR ISSUE		EDITION LIMIT	YEAR RETD.	ISSUE PRICE	*QUOTE U.S. $
1994	Event Piece	2-Yr.		75.00	75
1996	Event Piece	2-Yr.		N/A	N/A

Nursery Rhymes - Various

YEAR ISSUE		EDITION LIMIT	YEAR RETD.	ISSUE PRICE	*QUOTE U.S. $
1956	Little Bo Peep - J. Heap	Retrd.	1959	2.00	N/A
1956	Little Jack Horner - J. Heap	Retrd.	1959	2.00	N/A
1956	Mary Mary Quite Contrary - J. Heap	Retrd.	1959	2.00	N/A
1956	Miss Muffet - J. Heap	Retrd.	1959	2.00	N/A
1956	Tom Tom the Piper's Son - J. Heap	Retrd.	1959	2.00	N/A
1956	Wee Willie Winkie - J. Heap	Retrd.	1959	2.00	N/A

Retired Figurines - Various

YEAR ISSUE		EDITION LIMIT	YEAR RETD.	ISSUE PRICE	*QUOTE U.S. $
1985	Apple Barrel - J. Heap	Retrd.	1992	N/A	15-25
1963	Aunt Agatha - J. Heap	Retrd.	1965	N/A	1500-2000
1955	Balloon Woman - J. Heap	Retrd.	1956	1.00	N/A
1964	Bandstand - J. Heap	Retrd.	N/A	70.00	85
1967	The Bath Tub - J. Heap	Retrd.	1975	4.50	70-100
1955	Bell Man - J. Heap	Retrd.	1956	1.00	N/A
1984	Blossom - D. Roberts	Retrd.	1989	35.00	60-75
1955	Bobbin Woman - J. Heap	Retrd.	1956	N/A	N/A
1964	Bongo - D. Roberts	Retrd.	1987	31.00	75-150
1966	Cakestand - J. Heap	Retrd.	1972	2.00	250-500
1953	Cauldron Witch - J. Heap	Retrd.	1959	3.50	N/A
1959	Cha Cha - J. Heap	Retrd.	1961	N/A	1000-1200
1990	Charlotte - D. Roberts	Retrd.	1992	25.00	75-90
1989	Chirpy - D. Roberts	Retrd.	1992	31.50	60-100
1985	Christmas Set - D. Roberts	2,000	1989	N/A	450-550
1962	Cornish Prayer (Corny) - J. Heap	Retrd.	1965	N/A	500-900
1980	Crocker - D. Roberts	Retrd.	1989	20.00	60-75
1963	Cyril Squirrel - J. Heap	Retrd.	1965	N/A	750-1300
1955	Daisy Duck - J. Heap	Retrd.	1958	N/A	N/A
1956	Desmond Duck - J. Heap	Retrd.	1958	2.50	N/A
1964	Dodger - J. Heap	Retrd.	1996	24.00	28
1955	Elf - J. Heap	Retrd.	1956	1.00	N/A
1954	Fairy Jardiniere - N/A	Retrd.	1958	N/A	N/A
1953	The Fairy Shop - J. Heap	Retrd.	1958	N/A	N/A
1961	Father Mouse (grey) - J. Heap	Retrd.	1966	N/A	500-750
1955	Flying Witch - J. Heap	Retrd.	1956	1.00	N/A
1993	Forty Winks - D. Roberts	Retrd.	1996	57.00	57
1969	The Gallery Series: Wakey, Pieface, Poppet, Robert, Dodger - J. Heap	Retrd.	1971	N/A	200-400
1961	Grand Stand (mold 1) - J. Heap	Retrd.	1969	35.00	400-775
1992	Grand Stand (mold 2)- J. Heap	Retrd.	1996	150.00	150
1960	Gussie - J. Heap	Retrd.	1968	N/A	400
1989	Honey - D. Roberts	Retrd.	1993	40.00	60
1988	Humphrey Go-Kart - J. Heap	Retrd.	1994	70.00	100
1986	Jim-Lad - D. Roberts	Retrd.	1992	22.50	45-75
1985	Jingle - D. Roberts	Retrd.	1992	11.25	25-45
1986	Little Mo - D. Roberts	Retrd.	1994	35.00	43
1961	Lollipop (grey) (Mouse) - J. Heap	Retrd.	1966	N/A	500-700
1960	Lucy Pocket - J. Heap	Retrd.	1967	4.20	300-400
1956	Manx Kitten - J. Heap	Retrd.	1958	2.00	N/A
1955	Margot - J. Heap	Retrd.	1961	2.00	350-550
1967	Maud - J. Heap	Retrd.	1970	N/A	300-550
1961	Megan - J. Heap	Retrd.	1967	3.00	400-500
1956	Midge (Replaced by Picnic Midge) - J. Heap	Retrd.	1965	2.00	300-600
1966	Milk Jug Stand - J. Heap	Retrd.	1972	2.00	250-500
1960	Model Stand - J. Heap	Retrd.	1964	4.00	400-750
1961	Mother Mouse (grey) - J. Heap	Retrd.	1966	N/A	450-800
1965	Mouse House (bronze) - J. Heap	Retrd.	1969	N/A	300-400
1965	Mouse House (stoneware) - J. Heap	Retrd.	N/A	N/A	500-700
1965	Muncher - D. Roberts	Retrd.	1983	26.00	60-100
1981	Nipper - D. Roberts	Retrd.	1989	20.50	75
1955	Old Adam - J. Heap	Retrd.	1956	4.00	N/A
1955	Old Father (remodeled)- J. Heap	Retrd.	1970	50.	700-1000
1957	Old Mother - J. Heap	Retrd.	1978	6.25	550-800
1984	Oliver - D. Roberts	Retrd.	1996	25.00	30
1955	Original Father - J. Heap	Retrd.	1960	50.00	1000-1500
1956	Original Robert - J. Heap	Retrd.	1967	2.50	200-400
1953	Pendle Witch (stoneware) - J. Heap	Retrd.	1957	4.00	800-1200
1967	Phumf - J. Heap	Retrd.	1985	24.00	75
1955	Phynnodderee (Commissioned -Exclusive) - J. Heap	Retrd.	N/A	1.00	N/A
1966	Picnic Basket - J. Heap	Retrd.	1968	2.00	350-600

*Quotes have been rounded up to nearest dollar

YEAR ISSUE		EDITION LIMIT	YEAR RETD.	ISSUE PRICE	*QUOTE U.S.$
1965	Picnic Stand - J. Heap	Retrd.	1985	62.50	150-175
1967	Picnic Table - J. Heap	Retrd.	1972	N/A	250-600
1966	Pieface - D. Roberts	Retrd.	1987	31.00	60-75
1965	Pixie Bods - J. Heap	Retrd.	1967	N/A	N/A
1953	Pixie House - J. Heap	Retrd.	1958	N/A	N/A
1962	Pooch - D. Roberts	Retrd.	1987	24.50	60-75
1958	Rabbit Book Ends - J. Heap	Retrd.	1965	10.00	1500-2000
1954	Rhinegold Lamp - J. Heap	Retrd.	1956	21.00	N/A
1967	Robert w/lollipop - D. Roberts	Retrd.	1979	12.00	100-250
1959	Rocky - J. Heap	Retrd.	N/A	32.00	37
1957	Romeo & Juliet - J. Heap	Retrd.	1959	11.00	N/A
1960	Shiner w/black eye - J. Heap	Retrd.	1967	2.50	300-500
1981	Shrimp Stand - D. Roberts	Retrd.	1994	70.00	80
1985	Solo - D. Roberts	Retrd.	1993	40.00	50-75
1960	Squeezy - J. Heap	Retrd.	1970	2.50	300-550
1957	Tammy - D. Roberts	Retrd.	1987	24.50	75
1987	Tennyson - D. Roberts	Retrd.	1994	35.00	42
1956	Timber Stand - J. Heap	Retrd.	1982	35.00	150-200
1953	Tipsy Witch - J. Heap	Retrd.	1959	3.50	N/A
1955	Toper - J. Heap	Retrd.	1956	1.00	N/A
1971	Totty - J. Heap	Retrd.	1981	21.00	150-250
1959	Uncle Soames - J. Heap	Retrd.	1985	105.00	300-400
1991	Wordsworth - D. Roberts	Retrd.	1993	60.00	75

Polland Studios

Collector Society - D. Polland

YEAR ISSUE		EDITION LIMIT	YEAR RETD.	ISSUE PRICE	*QUOTE U.S.$
1987	I Come In Peace	Closed	1987	35.00	400-600
1987	Silent Trail	Closed	1987	300.00	1300
1987	I Come In Peace, Silent Trail -Matched Numbered Set	Closed	1987	335.00	15-1895
1988	The Hunter	Closed	1988	35.00	545
1988	Disputed Trail	Closed	1988	300.00	700-1045
1988	The Hunter, Disputed Trail -Matched Numbered Set	Closed	1988	335.00	11-1450
1989	Crazy Horse	Closed	1989	35.00	300-470
1989	Apache Birdman	Closed	1989	300.00	700-970
1989	Crazy Horse, Apache Birdman -Matched Numbered Set	Closed	1989	335.00	13-1700
1990	Chief Pontiac	Closed	1990	35.00	420
1990	Buffalo Pony	Closed	1990	300.00	600-800
1990	Chief Pontiac, Buffalo Pony -Matched Numbered Set	Closed	1990	335.00	900-1350
1991	War Drummer	Closed	1991	35.00	330
1991	The Signal	Closed	1991	350.00	730
1991	War Drummer, The Signal -Matched Numbered Set	Closed	1991	385.00	900-1150
1992	Cabinet Sign	Closed	1992	35.00	125
1992	Warrior's Farewell	Closed	1992	350.00	400
1992	Cabinet Sign, Warrior's Farewell -Matched Numbered Set	Closed	1992	385.00	465
1993	Mountain Man	Closed	1993	35.00	125
1993	Blue Bonnets & Yellow Ribbon	Closed	1993	350.00	350-400
1993	Mountain Man, Blue Bonnets & Yellow Ribbon-Matched Numbered Set	Closed	1993	385.00	385
1994	The Wedding Robe	Closed	1995	45.00	45
1994	The Courtship Race	Closed	1995	375.00	375
1994	The Wedding Robe, The Courtside Race-Matched Numbered Set	Closed	1995	385.00	420

See also Lance Corporation Chilmark Pewter Polland Collector Society

Possible Dreams

Santa Claus Network® Collectors Club - Staff

YEAR ISSUE		EDITION LIMIT	YEAR RETD.	ISSUE PRICE	*QUOTE U.S.$
1992	The Gift Giver-805001	Closed	1993	Gift	40
1993	Santa's Special Friend-805050	Closed	1993	59.00	59
1993	Special Delivery-805002	Closed	1994	Gift	N/A
1994	On a Winter's Eve-805051	Closed	1994	65.00	65
1994	Jolly St. Nick-805003	Closed	1995	Gift	N/A
1995	Marionette Santa-805052	Closed	1995	50.00	50
1996	Checking His List-805004	Yr.Iss.		32.00	32

The Citizens of Londonshire® - Unknown

YEAR ISSUE		EDITION LIMIT	YEAR RETD.	ISSUE PRICE	*QUOTE U.S.$
1990	Admiral Waldo-713407	Open		65.00	68
1992	Albert-713426	Closed	1994	65.00	68
1991	Bernie-713414	Open		68.00	71
1992	Beth-713417	Open		35.00	37
1992	Christopher-713418	Open		35.00	37
1992	Countess of Hamlett-713419	Open		65.00	68
1992	David-713423	Open		37.50	39
1992	Debbie-713422	Open		37.50	39
1990	Dianne-713413	Open		33.00	35
1990	Dr. Isaac-713409	Closed	1995	65.00	68
1989	Earl of Hamlett-713400	Closed	1994	65.00	68
1992	Jean Claude-713421	Open		35.00	37
1989	Lady Ashley-713405	Open		65.00	68
1989	Lord Nicholas-713402	Open		72.00	76
1989	Lord Winston of Riverside -713403	Closed	1994	65.00	68
1994	Maggie-713428	Closed	1994	57.00	57
1990	Margaret of Foxcroft-713408	Open		65.00	68
1992	Nicole-713420	Open		35.00	37
1993	Nigel As Santa-713427	Open		53.50	56
1990	Officer Kevin-713406	Closed	1994	65.00	68
1990	Phillip-713412	Open		33.00	35
1992	Rebecca-713424	Open		35.00	37
1992	Richard-713425	Open		35.00	37
1989	Rodney-713404	Open		65.00	68
1991	Sir Red-713415	Closed	1994	72.00	76
1989	Sir Robert-713401	Open		65.00	68
1992	Tiffany Sorbet-713416	Open		65.00	68
1990	Walter-713410	Closed	1994	33.00	35
1990	Wendy-713411	Closed	1994	33.00	35

Clothtique® American Artist Collection™ - Various

YEAR ISSUE		EDITION LIMIT	YEAR RETD.	ISSUE PRICE	*QUOTE U.S.$
1996	The 12 Days of Christmas -15052 - M. Monteiro	Open		48.00	48
1991	Alpine Christmas-15003 - J. Brett	Closed	1994	129.00	135
1992	An Angel's Kiss-15008 - J. Griffith	Closed	1995	85.00	125
1993	A Beacon of Light-15022 - J. Vaillancourt	Closed	1996	60.00	63
1993	A Brighter Day-15024 - J. St. Denis	Open		67.50	70
1994	Captain Claus-15030 - M. Monteiro	Open		77.00	77
1995	Christmas Caller-15035 - J. Vaillancourt	Open		57.50	58
1992	Christmas Company-15011 - T. Browning	Closed	1995	77.00	125
1996	Christmas Light-15055 - D. Wenzel	Open		53.50	54
1996	Christmas Stories-15054 - T. Browning	Open		63.50	64
1994	Christmas Surprise-15033 - M. Alvin	Open		88.00	88
1995	Country Sounds-15042 - M. Monteiro	Open		74.00	74
1996	Dressed For the Holidays-15050 - J. Vaillancourt	Open		27.00	27
1993	Easy Putt-15018 - T. Browning	Closed	1996	110.00	115
1991	Father Christmas-15007 - J. Vaillancourt	Closed	1995	59.50	63
1993	Father Earth-15017 - M. Monteiro	Open		77.00	80
1995	Fresh From The Oven-15051 - M. Alvin	Open		49.00	49
1991	A Friendly Visit-15005 - T. Browning	Closed	1994	99.50	105
1994	The Gentle Craftsman-15031 - J. Griffith	Open		81.00	81
1994	Gifts from the Garden-15032 - J. Griffith	Closed	1996	77.00	77
1995	Giving Thanks-15045 - M. Alvin	Open		45.50	46
1995	A Good Round-15041 - T. Browning	Open		73.00	73
1992	Heralding the Way-15014 - J. Griffith	Closed	1995	72.00	75
1993	Ice Capers-15025 - T. Browning	Open		99.50	105
1993	Just Scooting Along-15023 - J. Vaillancourt	Open		79.50	83
1992	Lighting the Way-15012 - L. Bywaters	Closed	1996	85.00	89
1991	The Magic of Christmas-15001 - L. Bywaters	Closed	1994	132.00	139
1992	Music Makers-15010 - T. Browning	Closed	1995	135.00	155
1993	Nature's Love-15016 - M. Alvin	Closed	1996	75.00	79
1995	A New Suit For Santa-15053 - T. Browning	Open		90.00	90
1996	Not a Creature Was Stirring -15046 - J. Cleveland	Open		44.00	44
1992	Out of the Forest-15013 - J. Vaillancourt	Closed	1995	60.00	68
1995	Patchwork Santa-15039 - J. Cleveland	Open		67.50	68
1992	Peace on Earth-15009 - M. Alvin	Closed	1995	87.50	92
1991	A Peaceful Eve-15002 - L. Bywaters	Closed	1994	99.50	105
1995	Ready For Christmas-15049 - T. Browning	Open		95.00	95
1995	Refuge From The Storm15047 - M. Monteiro	Open		49.00	49
1995	Riding High-15040 - L. Nillson	Open		115.00	115
1994	Santa and Feathered Friend - 15026 - D. Wenzel	Open		84.00	84
1995	Santa and the Ark-15038 - J. Griffith	Open		71.50	72
1992	Santa in Rocking Chair-713090 - M. Monteiro	Closed	1995	85.00	100
1991	Santa's Cuisine-15006 - T. Browning	Closed	1994	138.00	148
1995	Southwest Santa-15043 - V. Wiseman	Open		65.00	65
1994	Spirit of Christmas Past-15036 - J. Vaillancourt	Open		79.00	79
1994	Spirit of Santa-15028 - T. Browning	Open		68.00	68
1995	The Storyteller-15029 - T. Browning	Open		76.00	76
1993	Strumming the Lute-15015 - M. Alvin	Open		79.00	83
1995	Sunflower Santa-15044 - J. Griffith	Open		75.00	75
1994	Tea Time-15034 - M. Alvin	Open		90.00	90
1994	Teddy Love-15037 - J. Griffith	Open		89.00	89
1994	A Touch of Magic-15027 - T. Browning	Open		95.00	95
1991	Traditions-15004 - T. Blackshear	Closed	1994	50.00	75
1993	The Tree Planter-15020 - J. Griffith	Open		79.50	83
1995	Visions of Sugar Plums-15048 - J. Griffith	Open		50.00	50
1993	The Workshop-15019 - T. Browning	Closed	1995	140.00	150

Clothtique® Limited Edition Santas - Unknown

YEAR ISSUE		EDITION LIMIT	YEAR RETD.	ISSUE PRICE	*QUOTE U.S.$
1988	Father Christmas-3001	10,000	1993	240.00	240
1988	Kris Kringle-3002	10,000	1992	240.00	240
1988	Patriotic Santa-3000	10,000	1994	240.00	240
1989	Traditional Santa 40's-3003	10,000	1994	240.00	252

Clothtique® Pepsi® Santa Collection - Various

YEAR ISSUE		EDITION LIMIT	YEAR RETD.	ISSUE PRICE	*QUOTE U.S.$
1994	Holiday Host-3605 - Unknown	Open		62.00	62
1995	Jolly Traveler-3606 - B. Prata	Open		90.00	90
1990	Pepsi Cola Santa 1940's-3601 - Unknown	Open		68.00	74
1992	Pepsi Santa Sitting-3603 - Unknown	Closed	1994	84.00	95
1991	Rockwell Pepsi Santa 1952 -3602 - N. Rockwell	Closed	1994	75.00	82

Clothtique® Santas Collection - Staff, unless otherwise noted

YEAR ISSUE		EDITION LIMIT	YEAR RETD.	ISSUE PRICE	*QUOTE U.S.$
1992	1940's Traditional Santa-713049	Closed	1994	44.00	65
1992	African American Santa-713056	Closed	1995	65.00	68
1993	African-American Santa w/ Doll-713102	Open		40.00	42
1996	Autograph For A Fan-713143	Open		39.00	39
1989	Baby's First Christmas-713042	Closed	1992	42.00	46
1995	Baby's First Noel-713120	Open		62.00	62
1988	Carpenter Santa-713033	Closed	1992	38.00	44
1994	Christmas Cheer-713109	Open		58.00	58
1994	A Christmas Guest-713112	Open		79.00	79
1994	Christmas is for Children-713115	Open		62.00	62
1986	Christmas Man-713027	Closed	1989	34.50	35
1987	Colonial Santa-713032	Closed	1990	38.00	40
1995	Down Hill Santa-713123	Open		66.50	67
1992	Engineer Santa-713057	Closed	1995	130.00	137
1993	European Santa-713095	Open		53.00	55
1989	Exhausted Santa-713043	Closed	1992	60.00	65
1991	Father Christmas-713087	Closed	1993	43.00	47
1995	Finishing Touch-713121	Open		54.70	55
1993	Fireman & Child-713106	Open		55.00	58
1992	Fireman Santa-713053	Closed	1996	60.00	68
1996	For Someone Special-713142	Open		39.00	39
1995	Frisky Friend-713130	Open		45.50	46
1988	Frontier Santa-713034	Closed	1991	40.00	42
1995	Ginger Bread Baker-713135	Open		35.00	35
1994	Good Tidings-713107	Open		51.00	51
1990	Harlem Santa-713046	Closed	1994	46.00	55
1995	Heaven Sent-713138	Open		50.00	50
1993	His Favorite Color-713098	Open		48.00	50
1995	Ho: Ho-Hole in One-713131	Open		43.00	43
1994	Holiday Friend-713110	Open		104.00	10
1995	Home Spun Holidays-713128	Open		49.50	50
1995	Hook Line and Santa-713129	Open		49.70	5
1996	Jumping Jack Santa-713139	Open		45.50	46
1991	Kris Kringle-713088	Closed	1993	43.00	46
1993	A Long Trip-713105	Open		95.00	10
1993	May Your Wishes Come True-713096	Open		59.00	6
1993	The Modern Shopper-713103	Open		40.00	4
1994	A Most Welcome Visitor-713113	Open		63.00	6
1991	Mrs. Claus in Coat -713078	Closed	1995	47.00	7
1989	Mrs. Claus w/doll-713041	Closed	1992	42.00	4
1994	Mrs. Claus-713118	Open		58.00	5
1992	Nicholas-713052	Closed	1994	57.50	6
1994	Our Hero-713116	Open		62.00	6
1989	Pelze Nichol-713039	Closed	1993	40.00	4
1995	Pet Project-713134 - L. Craven	Open		37.00	3
1994	Playmates-713111	Closed	1996	104.00	10
1994	Puppy Love-713117	Open		62.00	6
1988	Russian St. Nicholas-713036	Open		40.00	4
1990	Santa "Please Stop Here"-713045	Closed	1992	63.00	7
1991	Santa Decorating Christmas Tree-713079	Closed	1992	60.00	6
1991	Santa in Bed-713076	Closed	1994	76.00	8
1992	Santa on Motorbike-713054	Closed	1994	115.00	13
1992	Santa on Reindeer-713058	Closed	1995	75.00	8
1992	Santa on Sled-713050	Closed	1994	75.00	7
1992	Santa on Sleigh-713091	Closed	1995	79.00	8
1991	Santa Shelf Sitter-713089	Closed	1995	55.50	6
1990	Santa w/Blue Robe-713048	Closed	1992	46.00	5
1989	Santa w/Embroidered Coat-713040	Closed	1991	43.00	4
1993	Santa w/Groceries-713099	Closed	1996	47.50	5
1986	Santa w/Pack-713026	Closed	1989	34.50	3
1996	Shamrock Santa-713140	Open		41.50	4
1991	Siberian Santa-713077	Closed	1993	49.00	5
1990	Skiing Santa -713047	Closed	1993	62.00	6
1995	Sounds of Christmas-713127	Open		57.50	5
1995	A Special Treat-713122	Open		50.50	5
1988	St. Nicholas-713035	Closed	1991	40.00	4
1995	The Stockings Were Hung-713126	Open		N/A	N/A
1995	Three Alarm Santa-713137	Open		42.50	4
1987	Traditional Deluxe Santa-713030	Closed	1990	38.00	3
1986	Traditional Santa-713028	Closed	1989	34.50	12
1989	Traditional Santa-713038	Closed	1992	42.00	4
1991	The True Spirit of Christmas -713075	Closed	1992	97.00	9
1987	Ukko-713031	Closed	1990	38.00	3
1995	Victorian Evergreen-713125	Open		49.00	4
1995	Victorian Puppeteer-713124	Open		51.50	5
1993	Victorian Santa-713097	Closed	1996	55.50	5
1988	Weihnachtsman-713037	Closed	1991	40.00	4
1994	A Welcome Visit-713114	Open		62.00	6
1990	Workbench Santa-713044	Closed	1993	72.00	7
1994	Yuletide Journey-713108	Open		58.00	5

Clothtique® Saturday Evening Post J. C. Leyendecker - J. Leyendecker

YEAR ISSUE		EDITION LIMIT	YEAR RETD.	ISSUE PRICE	*QUOTE U.S.$
1991	Hugging Santa-3599	Closed	1994	129.00	1
1996	Hugging Santa-3650 (smaller re-issue)	Open		52.50	5
1992	Santa on Ladder-3598	Closed	1995	135.00	1
1996	Santa on Ladder-3651 (smaller re-issue)	Open		59.00	5
1991	Traditional Santa-3600	Closed	1992	100.00	1
1996	Traditional Santa-3652 (smaller re-issue)	Open		66.00	[illegible]

*Quotes have been rounded up to nearest dollar

Clothtique® Saturday Evening Post Norman Rockwell - N. Rockwell

Year Issue		Edition Limit	Year Retd.	Issue Price	*Quote U.S.$
1992	Balancing the Budget-3064	Open		120.00	126
1996	Balancing The Budget-3102 (smaller re-issue)	Open		70.50	71
1989	Christmas "Dear Santa"-3050	Closed	1992	160.00	180
1989	Christmas "Santa with Globe"-3051	Closed	1992	154.00	175
1996	Santa With Globe-3101 (smaller re-issue)	Open		73.00	73
1991	Doctor and Doll-3055	Closed	1995	196.00	206
1991	The Gift-3057	Closed	1996	160.00	168
1991	Gone Fishing-3054	Closed	1995	250.00	263
1991	Gramps at the Reins-3058	Open		290.00	305
1990	Hobo-3052	Open		159.00	167
1990	Love Letters-3053	Open		172.00	180
1991	Man with Geese-3059	Open		120.00	126
1992	Marriage License-3062	Open		195.00	205
1996	Not a Creature was Stirring (smaller re-issue)	Open		44.00	44
1991	Santa Plotting His Course-3060	Open		160.00	168
1992	Santa's Helpers-3063	Closed	1994	170.00	179
1991	Springtime-3056	Closed	1996	130.00	137
1992	Triple Self Portrait-3061	Closed	1995	230.00	250

Clothtique® Signature Series® - Stanley/Chang

Year Issue		Edition Limit	Year Retd.	Issue Price	*Quote U.S.$
1995	Department Store Santa, USA/ Circa 1940s-721001	Open		108.00	108
1995	Father Christmas, England/ Circa 1890s-721002	Open		90.00	90

Crinkle Angels - Staff

Year Issue		Edition Limit	Year Retd.	Issue Price	*Quote U.S.$
1996	Crinkle Angel w/Candle-659405	Open		19.80	20
1996	Crinkle Angel w/Dove-659403	Open		19.80	20
1996	Crinkle Angel w/Harp-659402	Open		19.80	20
1996	Crinkle Angel w/Lamb-659401	Open		19.80	20
1996	Crinkle Angel w/Lantern-659400	Open		19.80	20
1996	Crinkle Angel w/Mandolin-659404	Open		19.80	20

Crinkle Claus - Staff

Year Issue		Edition Limit	Year Retd.	Issue Price	*Quote U.S.$
1995	American Santa-657224	Open		15.50	16
1995	Arctic Santa-615707	Open		15.70	16
1995	Austrian Santa-659103	Open		15.80	16
1995	Bell Shape Santa-659008	Open		23.50	24
1996	Bishop of Maya Plaque-659306	Open		19.90	20
1996	Bishop of Maya-659111	Open		19.90	20
1996	Black Forest Gift Giver Plaque -659302	Open		19.90	20
1996	Black Forest Gift Giver-659114	Open		19.90	20
1996	Buckets of Fruit for Good Girls & Boys-659903	5,000		45.00	45
1995	Candle Stick Santa-659121	Open		15.80	16
1996	Carrying The Torch	Open		19.80	20
1996	Catch of The Day-659504	Open		19.90	20
1996	Celtic Santa Plaque-659305	Open		19.90	20
1996	Celtic Santa-659110	Open		19.90	20
1996	Choo-Choo For The Children-659904	5,000		25.00	25
1995	Christmas Tree Santa-659117	Open		19.90	20
1995	Crescent Moon Santa-659119	Open		19.00	19
1996	Crinkle Claus w/Dome-German Santa-659601	Open		45.00	45
1996	Crinkle Claus w/Dome-Santa/Chimney-659600	Open		45.00	45
1996	Crinkle Claus w/Dome-St. Nicholas-659602	Open		45.00	45
1996	A Crown of Antlers	Open		19.70	20
1996	Dashing Through The Snow -659902	5,000		45.00	45
1996	Display Figurine-965003	Open		11.00	11
1995	English Santa-659100	Open		15.80	16
1996	Feeding His Forest Friends -659905	5,000		27.50	28
1995	Forest Santa-657225	Open		15.50	16
1995	French Santa-659108	Open		15.70	16
1995	German Santa-659105	Open		15.80	16
1995	Hard Boiled Santa-659115	Open		13.70	14
1995	High Hat Santa-657134	Open		13.40	14
1995	Hour Glass Santa-659118	Open		15.00	15
1996	Iceland Visitor Plaque-659303	Open		19.90	20
1996	Iceland Visitor-659112	Open		19.90	20
1995	Italian Santa-659106	Open		15.70	16
1995	Jolly St. Nick-659012	Open		15.00	15
1996	Learned Gentleman	Open		19.80	20
1996	Lighting The Way	Open		19.80	20
1996	Low & Behold	Open		13.90	14
1996	Merry Old England Plaque -659301	Open		19.90	20
1996	Merry Old England-659113	Open		19.90	20
1996	The Music Man	Open		19.80	20
1995	Netherlands Santa-659102	Open		15.70	16
1996	Northland Santa Plaque-659304	Open		19.90	20
1996	Northland Santa-659109	Open		19.90	20
1995	Pine Cone Santa-657226	Open		15.50	16
1996	Rag/Doll Delivery-659906	5,000		34.50	35
1995	Roly Poly Santa 3.5"-657138	Open		12.50	13
1995	Roly Poly Santa 4"-659009	Open		23.00	23
1996	Running Down The List-659901	5,000		33.00	33
1995	Russian Santa 3.5"-659101	Open		15.70	16
1995	Russian Santa 4"-657228	Open		15.50	16
1995	Santa on Bag-657508	Retired	1996	15.00	15
1995	Santa on Roof-659006	Open		28.50	29
1995	Santa Sitting Pretty-659116	Open		13.90	14
1995	Santa w/Book-659010	Open		13.80	14
1995	Santa w/Candy Cane 4.5" -657139	Open		13.00	13
1996	Santa w/Candy Cane 5"-657142	Open		27.00	27
1996	Santa w/Candy Cane 6.5"-657135	Open		17.50	18
1995	Santa w/Cane & Bag-657230	Retired	1996	12.00	12
1995	Santa w/Gifts-657143	Retired	1996	27.00	27
1995	Santa w/Lantern & Bag-657229	Retired	1996	15.50	16
1995	Santa w/Lantern 5"-657136	Open		12.50	13
1995	Santa w/Lantern 5"-657144	Retrd.	1996	27.00	27
1995	Santa w/Noah's Ark-657227	Open		15.50	16
1995	Santa w/Patchwork Bag-657232	Open		19.00	19
1995	Santa w/Stars-657140	Open		14.00	14
1995	Santa w/Teddy Bear-657231	Open		16.00	16
1995	Santa w/Tree-659011	Open		14.20	15
1995	Santa w/Wreath-657141	Retired	1996	16.30	17
1995	Santa's Candy Surprise	Open		27.00	27
1995	Scandinavian Santa-659104	Open		15.80	16
1995	Slimline Santa-657137	Retired	1996	12.00	12
1995	Tall Santa	Open		17.50	18
1995	Tick Tock Santa-659120	Open		15.00	15
1995	Tip Top Santa-659007	Open		23.50	24
1996	To The Rescue	Open		19.90	20
1996	Well Rounded Santa	Open		13.70	14

Crinkle Cousins - Staff

Year Issue		Edition Limit	Year Retd.	Issue Price	*Quote U.S.$
1995	Crinkle Cousin w/Clock-659002	Open		15.50	16
1995	Crinkle Cousin w/Clown-659004	Open		15.50	16
1995	Crinkle Cousin w/Dolls-659003	Open		15.50	16
1995	Crinkle Cousin w/Lantern -659001	Open		15.50	16
1995	Crinkle Cousin w/Teddy-659005	Open		15.50	16

Crinkle Crackers - Staff

Year Issue		Edition Limit	Year Retd.	Issue Price	*Quote U.S.$
1995	Admiral Crinkle Cracker-659212	Open		18.50	19
1995	Captain Crinkle Cracker-659211	Open		13.00	13
1995	Corporal Crinkle Cracker-659214	Open		14.60	15
1995	French Crinkle Cracker-659203	Open		22.00	22
1995	French Lieutenant Crinkle Cracker-659205	Open		13.50	14
1995	General Crinkle Cracker-659213	Open		15.50	16
1995	Lieutenant Crinkle Cracker -659209	Open		26.50	27
1995	Major Crinkle Cracker-659215	Open		14.50	15
1995	Private Crinkle Cracker-659210	Open		15.00	15
1995	Roly Poly French Crinkle Cracker-659204	Open		13.90	14
1995	Roly Poly Russian Crinkle Cracker-659207	Open		13.50	14
1995	Roly Poly Sergeant Crinkle Cracker-659216	Open		13.50	14
1995	Roly Poly U.S. Crinkle Cracker -659201	Open		13.90	14
1995	Russian Crinkle Cracker 4" -659208	Open		13.50	14
1995	Russian Crinkle Cracker 7.75"-659206	Open		29.50	30
1995	U.S. Crinkle Cracker 3.75" -659202	Open		13.50	14
1995	U.S.Crinkle Cracker 7.5"-659200	Open		29.00	29

Crinkle Professionals - Staff

Year Issue		Edition Limit	Year Retd.	Issue Price	*Quote U.S.$
1996	Baseball Player-659507	Open		19.50	20
1996	Doctor-659500	Open		19.50	20
1996	Fireman-659503	Open		19.50	20
1996	Fisherman-659504	Open		19.50	20
1996	Football Player-659506	Open		19.50	20
1996	Golfer-659505	Open		19.50	20
1996	Hockey Player-659508	Open		19.50	20
1996	Policeman-659502	Open		19.50	20
1996	Postman-659501	Open		19.50	20
1996	Soccer Player-659509	Open		19.50	20

The Thickets at Sweetbriar® - B. Ross

Year Issue		Edition Limit	Year Retd.	Issue Price	*Quote U.S.$
1995	Angel Dear-350123	Open		32.00	32
1996	Autumn Peppergrass-350135	Open		31.00	31
1993	The Bride-Emily Feathers -350112	Open		30.00	30
1995	Buttercup-350121	Open		32.00	32
1995	Cecily Pickwick-350125	Open		32.00	32
1995	Clem Jingles-350130	Open		37.00	37
1993	Clovis Buttons-350101	Open		24.15	25
1996	Dainty Whiskers-350136	Open		30.00	30
1996	Goody Pringle-350134	Open		31.00	31
1993	The Groom-Oliver Doone -350111	Closed	1996	30.00	30
1993	Jewel Blossom-350106	Open		36.75	37
1995	Katy Hollyberry-350124	Open		35.00	35
1995	Kris Krinkle-350414	Open		12.50	13
1994	Lady Slipper-350116	Open		20.00	20
1993	Lily Blossom-350105	Closed	1996	36.75	37
1993	Maude Tweedy-350100	Closed	1994	26.25	27
1996	Merry Heart-350131	Open		30.00	30
1994	Morning Dew-350113	Open		30.00	30
1993	Morning Glory-350104	Open		30.45	31
1993	Mr. Claws-350109	Closed	1996	34.00	34
1993	Mrs. Claws-350110	Open		34.00	34
1993	Orchid Beasley-350103	Closed	1996	26.25	27
1995	Parsley Divine-350129	Open		37.00	37
1996	Patience Finney-350133	Open		31.00	31
1993	Peablossom Thorndike-350102	Closed	1994	26.25	27
1995	Penny Pringle-350128	Open		32.00	32
1995	Pittypat-350122	Open		32.00	32
1994	Precious Petals-350115	Open		34.00	34
1993	Raindrop-350108	Open		47.25	48
1995	Riley Pickens-350127	Open		32.00	32
1993	Rose Blossom-350107	Open		36.75	37
1994	Sunshine-350118	Open		33.00	33
1994	Sweetie Flowers-350114	Open		33.00	33
1995	Tillie Lilly-350120	Open		32.00	32
1995	Timmy Evergreen-350126	Open		29.00	29
1996	Velvet Winterberry-350132	Open		30.00	30
1995	Violet Wiggles-350119	Open		32.00	32

Precious Art/Panton

Krystonia Collector's Club - Panton

Year Issue		Edition Limit	Year Retd.	Issue Price	*Quote U.S.$
1989	Pultzr	Retrd.	1990	55.00	500-585
1989	Key	Retrd.	1990	Gift	100-130
1991	Dragons Play	Retrd.	1992	65.00	150-200
1991	Kephrens Chest	Retrd.	1992	Gift	130
1992	Vaaston	Retrd.	1993	65.00	120-220
1992	Lantern	Retrd.	1993	Gift	45-75
1993	Sneaking A Peak	Retrd.	1994	Gift	85
1993	Spreading His Wings	Retrd.	1994	60.00	100-105
1994	All Tuckered Out	Retrd.	1995	65.00	65
1994	Filler-Up	Retrd.	1995	Gift	N/A
1995	Twingnuk	5/96		55.00	55
1995	Kappah Krystal	Retrd.	1996	Gift	N/A
1996	Quinzet	Yr.Iss		38.00	38
1996	Holy Dragons	Yr.Iss		65.00	65
1996	Frobbit	Yr.Iss		Gift	N/A

Fair Maidens - Panton

Year Issue		Edition Limit	Year Retd.	Issue Price	*Quote U.S.$
1994	Faithful Companion	1,000	1994	325.00	325
1995	Safe Passage	1,000		350.00	350

World of Krystonia - Panton

Year Issue		Edition Limit	Year Retd.	Issue Price	*Quote U.S.$
1992	Azael -3811	Retrd.	1995	85.00	85
1989	Babul -1402	Retrd.	1995	25.00	25
1994	Boll-3912	Retrd.	1994	52.00	52
1989	Caught At Last! -1107	Retrd.	1992	150.00	225
1992	Dubious Alliance -1109	Retrd.	1995	195.00	195
1991	Flayla w/Sumbly -1105	Retrd.	1995	104.00	104
1980	Gateway to Krystonia-3301	Retrd.	1994	35.00	75-95
1987	Grackene -1051	Retrd.	1995	50.00	50
1989	Graffyn on Grunch (waterglobe) -9006	Retrd.	1992	42.00	150
1987	Groc -1044	Retrd.	1995	50.00	50
1987	Grumblypeg Grunch -1081	Retrd.	1992	52.00	110
1989	Kephren -2702	Retrd.	1994	56.00	65
1989	Krystonia Sign -701	Retrd.	1993	N/A	35
1987	Large Graffyn on Grumblypeg Grunch -1011	Retrd.	1992	52.00	115
1991	Large Grunch's Toothache -1082	Retrd.	1994	76.00	80
1987	Large Haapf -1901	Retrd.	1991	38.00	100
1987	Large Krak N'Borg -3001	Retrd.	1990	240.00	250-500
1987	Large Moplos -1021	Retrd.	1991	90.00	150-225
1987	Large Myzer -1201	Retrd.	1991	50.00	90-130
1987	Large N' Chakk -2101	Retrd.	1995	140.00	140
1987	Large N'Borg -1092	Retrd.	1994	98.00	140
1988	Large N'Grall -2201	Retrd.	1990	108.00	250
1987	Large Rueggan -1701	Retrd.	1989	55.00	100-200
1987	Large Turfen -1601	Retrd.	1991	50.00	85-100
1987	Large Wodema -1301	Retrd.	1990	50.00	115
1991	Maj-Dron Migration -1108	Retrd.	1994	145.00	155
1988	Medium N'Grall -2202	Retrd.	1994	70.00	80
1988	Medium Rueggan -1702	Retrd.	1993	48.00	70
1987	Medium Stoope -1101	Retrd.	1990	52.00	100-200
1987	Medium Wodema -1302	Retrd.	1993	44.00	85
1992	Mini N' Grall -611	Retrd.	1995	27.00	27
1992	N' Leila-3801	Retrd.	1994	60.00	65
1991	N'Borg-Mini -609	Retrd.	1994	29.00	29
1990	N'Chakk-Mini -607	Retrd.	1994	29.00	29
1990	Owhey (waterglobe) -9004	Retrd.	1995	42.00	100
1987	Owhey -1071	Retrd.	1990	32.00	100-175
1990	Shadra -3401	Retrd.	1994	30.00	65
1987	Small Graffyn/Grunch -1012	Retrd.	1989	45.00	200
1987	Small Groc -1042B	Retrd.	1987	24.00	4600
1987	Small Krak N' Borg -3003	Retrd.	1993	60.00	130-155
1987	Small N' Borg -1091	Retrd.	1989	50.00	200
1987	Small N' Tormet -2602	Retrd.	1993	44.00	65
1988	Small Rueggau -1703	Retrd.	1995	42.00	42
1987	Small Shepf -1152	Retrd.	1990	40.00	85-100
1987	Small Stoope -1102	Retrd.	1995	46.00	46
1988	Small Tulan Captain -2502	Retrd.	1991	44.00	105
1987	Spyke -1061	Retrd.	1993	50.00	85
1989	Stoope (waterglobe) -9003	Retrd.	1991	40.00	156
1988	Tarnhold-Med. -3202	Retrd.	1992	120.00	175
1987	Tarnhold-Small -3203	Retrd.	1995	60.00	60
1988	Tokkel -2401	Retrd.	1995	42.00	42
1992	Zanzibar -3431	Retrd.	1994	45.00	65

Pulaski Furniture, Inc.

Curios Henry Limited Edition Figurine Series - L. Eisen

Year Issue		Edition Limit	Year Retd.	Issue Price	*Quote U.S.$
1996	Jack Russell Terrier	Yr.Iss.		19.95	20

R.R. Creations, Inc.

Collectors' Club - D. Ross

Year Issue		Edition Limit	Year Retd.	Issue Price	*Quote U.S.$
1994	Cape Cod 9400	Retrd.	1994	9.95	10
1995	Grist Mill 9500	Retrd.	1995	11.95	12
1996	Covered Bridge 9600	6/96		13.95	14

*Quotes have been rounded up to nearest dollar

Accessories - D. Ross

YEAR ISSUE		EDITION LIMIT	YEAR RETD.	ISSUE PRICE	*QUOTE U.S.$
1989	4" Brick Fence 8913	Retrd.	1991	3.75	4
1987	4" Corral Fence 8726	Retrd.	1992	3.60	4
1989	4" Fence 8917	Open		3.25	5
1991	4" Fence w/ Tree 9124	Open		7.20	8
1989	8" Brick Fence 8912	Retrd.	1991	3.75	4
1990	Cactus Set/2 9014	Retrd.	1992	2.80	3
1993	Honey Pine Shelf 9333	Open		9.95	12
1990	Large Flag Pole 9017	Open		2.95	4
1989	Large Lamp Post 8911	Open		2.75	5
1990	Mainstreet Sign 9018	Open		2.75	4
1990	Natural Windmill 9019	Retrd.	1992	3.60	4
1991	Oak Tree 9123	Open		3.50	5
1992	Pine Tree 9250	Open		3.50	5
1989	Pine Tree w/Bow other side 8915	Retrd.	1991	3.75	4
1989	Shade Tree 8914	Retrd.	1991	3.75	4
1992	Sisters Sled 9252	Open		5.95	7
1992	Small Flag Pole 9251	Retrd.	1994	2.95	3
1992	Small Lamp Post 9254	Retrd.	1994	2.95	3
1990	Sunflower 9016	Open		2.80	4
1992	Trolley 9255	Retrd.	1994	5.95	6
1987	Welcome Mat 8717	Retrd.	1994	1.80	2
1993	Welcome R.R. Sign 9332	Retrd.	1994	4.50	5
1990	Wheat 9015	Open		2.80	4
1987	Windmill 8725	Open		3.60	4

Amish Accessories - D. Ross

1990	Amish Buggy 9013	Open		4.40	7
1991	Amish Family 9120	Open		4.40	7
1993	Amish Garden 9330	Open		5.95	7
1991	Amish Outhouse 9104	Open		4.25	5
1994	Buggies in a Row 9432	Open		6.50	7
1992	Clothesline 9253	Open		2.95	7
1994	Cows 9434	Open		6.50	7
1994	Milk Cans 9433	Open		6.50	7
1994	No Sunday Sales 9431	Open		3.60	4
1991	Slow Moving Vehicle 9121	Open		2.95	4

Amish Collection Series I - D. Ross

1991	Amish Barn 9102	Retrd.	1994	8.95	11
1991	Amish House 9101	Retrd.	1994	8.95	11
1991	Amish School 9103	Retrd.	1994	8.95	11
1992	Barn Raising 9220	Retrd.	1994	8.95	11
1992	Quilt Shop 9204	Retrd.	1994	8.95	11

Amish Collection Series II - D. Ross

1993	Blacksmith 9329	Retrd.	1995	8.95	11
1993	Harness & Buggy 9331	Retrd.	1995	8.95	11
1993	Troyer Bakery 9328	Retrd.	1995	8.95	11

Amish Collection Series III - D. Ross

1994	Barn 9429	2,500		11.00	11
1994	House 9428	2,500		11.00	11

Amish Collection Series IV - D. Ross

1996	Miller Barn Raising 9605	2,500		14.50	15
1996	Miller House 9604	2,500		13.50	14
1996	Miller School House 9603	2,500		13.50	14

Author Collection Series I - D. Ross

1994	Edgar Allan Poe 9403	2,500		11.00	11
1994	Harriet Beecher Stowe 9404	2,500		11.00	11
1994	Mark Twain 9401	2,500		11.00	11

Christmas Memories Series I - D. Ross

1992	Christmas Chapel 9216	Retrd.	1994	8.95	11
1992	Christmas F Douglass 9218	Retrd.	1994	8.95	11
1992	Daniel Boone 9219	Retrd.	1994	8.95	11

Christmas Memories Series II - D. Ross

1993	Boscobel 9320	Retrd.	1995	8.95	11
1993	Christmas Church 9318	Retrd.	1995	8.95	11
1993	Dell House 9321	Retrd.	1995	8.95	11
1992	Sister Sled 9252	Open		5.95	7

Christmas Memories Series III - D. Ross

1995	Apothecary 9513	2,500		11.00	12
1995	Butcher 9515	2,500		11.00	12
1995	Cobbler 9514	2,500		11.00	12

Colonial Collection Series I - D. Ross

1989	Boot & Shoemaker 8910	Retrd.	1993	8.95	9
1989	Colonial Inn 8903	Retrd.	1993	8.95	9
1989	Easton House 8918	Retrd.	1993	8.95	9
1989	Silversmith 8909	Retrd.	1993	8.95	9
1989	Tavern 8908	Retrd.	1993	8.95	9

Colonial Collection Series II - D. Ross

1989	C.L. Edwards 8901	Retrd.	1994	8.95	11
1989	Dry Good 8904	Retrd.	1994	8.95	11
1989	G. Dressmaker 8920	Retrd.	1994	8.95	11
1989	Kiistner 8902	Retrd.	1994	8.95	11
1989	Town Hall 8906	Retrd.	1994	8.95	11

Court House Collection - D. Ross

1989	Chase Country 8924	Retrd.	1993	8.95	9
1990	Franklin County 9011	Retrd.	1993	8.95	9
1990	Mount Holly 9010	Retrd.	1993	8.95	9

Grandpa's Farm Collection Series I (No Open Window/Printed Both Sides) - D. Ross

YEAR ISSUE		EDITION LIMIT	YEAR RETD.	ISSUE PRICE	*QUOTE U.S.$
1987	Barn 8721	Retrd.	1992	8.95	9
1987	Chicken Coop 8722	Retrd.	1992	6.50	7
1987	Farm House 8720	Retrd.	1992	8.95	9
1987	Outhouse 8724	Retrd.	1992	4.25	5
1987	Wash House 8723	Retrd.	1992	6.00	6

Grandpa's Farm Collection Series II - D. Ross

1993	Chicken Coop 9326	Retrd.	1995	6.50	11
1993	Hofacre House 9323	Retrd.	1995	8.95	11
1993	New Barn 9324	Retrd.	1995	8.95	11
1992	Outhouse 9327	Retrd.	1995	4.25	5
1993	Wash House 9325	Retrd.	1995	6.50	11

Historical Collection Series I - D. Ross

1992	Canfield 9205	Retrd.	1994	8.95	11
1992	Hexagon 9208	Retrd.	1994	8.95	11
1992	Lincoln 9217	Retrd.	1994	8.95	11
1992	Smith-Bly 9201	Retrd.	1994	8.95	11
1992	Susan B. Anthony 9222	Retrd.	1994	8.95	11

Historical Collection Series II - D. Ross

1993	Betsy Ross 9305	Retrd.	1995	8.95	11
1993	Kennedy Home 9308	Retrd.	1995	8.95	11
1993	Stone House 9319	Retrd.	1995	8.95	11

In The Country Series I - D. Ross

1989	Church 8905	Retrd.	1993	8.95	9
1990	Grist Mill 9001	Retrd.	1993	8.95	9
1989	School 8907	Retrd.	1993	8.95	9

In The Country Series II - D. Ross

1993	Country Church 9322	Retrd.	1995	8.95	11
1993	Country Livin' Shop 9307	Retrd.	1995	8.95	11
1993	Toll House 9301	Retrd.	1995	8.95	11

Inn Collection Series I - D. Ross

1994	Black Horse Inn 9411	2,500		11.00	11
1994	Herlong Mansion 9412	2,500		11.00	11
1994	Nathaniel Porter Inn 9410	2,500		11.00	11

Landmark Collection Series I - D. Ross

1994	Locust Grove 9405	2,500		11.00	11
1994	Longfellow 9408	2,500		11.00	11
1994	Melrose 9409	2,500		11.00	11

Lighthouse Collection Series I - D. Ross

1994	Mystic Sea Port 9406	2,500		11.00	11
1994	Old Point Betsie 9402	2,500		11.00	11
1994	Quoddy Head 9407	2,500		11.00	11

Lighthouse Collection Series II - D. Ross

1996	Block Island S.E. 9506	2,500		13.50	14
1996	Boca Grande 9505	2,500		13.50	14
1996	Drumpoint 9504	2,500		13.50	14

Main Street Collection Series I - D. Ross

1989	Barron Theatre 8922	Retrd.	1993	8.95	9
1989	Gas Station 8923	Retrd.	1993	8.95	9
1989	Kingman Firehouse 8919	Retrd.	1993	8.95	9
1990	Library 9007	Retrd.	1993	8.95	9
1989	Myerstown Depot 8921	Retrd.	1993	8.95	9
1990	Santa Fe Depot 9006	Retrd.	1993	8.95	9
1991	Telephone Company 9107	Retrd.	1993	8.95	9

Main Street Collection Series II - D. Ross

1992	Bakery 9212	Retrd.	1994	8.95	11
1992	Bank 9211	Retrd.	1994	8.95	11
1992	Beauty Shop 9209	Retrd.	1994	8.95	11
1991	Chautaqua Hills Jelly 9105	Retrd.	1994	8.95	11
1989	Harrold's Hardware 8925	Retrd.	1994	8.95	11
1992	Oak Brook Fire Co. 9207	Retrd.	1994	8.95	11

On the Square I (No Open Window/Printed Both Sides) - D. Ross

1987	Antique Shop 8708	Retrd.	1992	8.95	9
1987	Bakery 8710	Retrd.	1992	8.95	9
1987	Book Store 8709	Retrd.	1992	8.95	9
1987	Candle Shop 8712	Retrd.	1992	8.95	9
1987	Craft Shop 8711	Retrd.	1992	8.95	9
1988	Flower Shop 8807	Retrd.	1992	8.95	9
1988	Ice Cream Parlor 8806	Retrd.	1992	8.95	9

On the Square II - D. Ross

1993	Antique Shop 9314	Retrd.	1995	8.95	11
1993	Book Store 9309	Retrd.	1995	8.95	11
1993	Candle Shop 9312	Retrd.	1995	8.95	11
1993	Craft Shop 9313	Retrd.	1995	8.95	11
1993	Flower Shop 9311	Retrd.	1995	9.95	11
1993	Ice Cream Shop 9310	Retrd.	1995	9.95	11

Pre-Open Window Series - D. Ross

1990	Adobe House 9005	Retrd.	1992	8.50	9
1991	Faulkner House 9108	Retrd.	1992	8.50	9
1990	Fox Theater 9009	Retrd.	1992	8.50	9
1988	Hardesty House 8808	Retrd.	1992	8.95	9
1991	John Hayes House 9109	Retrd.	1992	11.95	12
1991	Memphis Mansion 9110	Retrd.	1992	8.50	9
1990	Mission 9004	Retrd.	1992	8.50	9
1990	Stone Barn 9003	Retrd.	1992	8.50	9
1990	Stone House 9002	Retrd.	1991	8.50	9
1990	Strater Hotel 9008	Retrd.	1992	8.50	9

Victorian Collection Series I - D. Ross

YEAR ISSUE		EDITION LIMIT	YEAR RETD.	ISSUE PRICE	*QUOTE U.S.$
1992	Chapline 9206	Retrd.	1994	8.95	11
1992	Queen Anne 9203	Retrd.	1994	8.95	11
1991	Victorian Michigan 9106	Retrd.	1994	8.95	11

Wild West Accessories - D. Ross

1996	Gunfighter 9511	Open		6.50	7

Wild West Collection I - D. Ross

1996	Great Western Hotel 9508	2,500		13.50	14
1996	J. Collar Dry Goods 9509	2,500		13.50	14
1996	J.P. Allen Drugstore 9507	2,500		13.50	14
1996	Out Laws 9510	2,500		12.00	12

Williamsburg Collection Series I - D. Ross

1992	Davidson Shop 9213	Retrd.	1994	8.95	11
1992	Orrell House 9214	Retrd.	1994	8.95	11
1992	Tarpley's Shop 9215	Retrd.	1994	8.95	11

Williamsburg Collection Series II - D. Ross

1993	Capitol 9303	Retrd.	1995	8.95	11
1993	Court House 9302	Retrd.	1995	8.95	11
1993	Governors Palace 9304	Retrd.	1995	8.95	11

Rawcliffe Corporation

Baby Bubble Fairies™ - J. deStefano

1992	Turquoise-January	6,700		70.00	7[illegible]
1992	Magenta-February	6,700		70.00	7[illegible]
1992	Blush-March	6,700		70.00	7[illegible]
1992	Chartreuse-April	6,700		70.00	7[illegible]
1992	Violet-May	6,700		70.00	7[illegible]
1992	Coral-June	6,700		70.00	7[illegible]
1992	Saffron-July	6,700		70.00	7[illegible]
1992	Azure-August	6,700		70.00	7[illegible]
1992	Lavender-September	6,700		70.00	7[illegible]
1992	Amber-October	6,700		70.00	7[illegible]
1992	Vermilion-November	6,700		70.00	7[illegible]
1992	Emerald-December	6,700		70.00	7[illegible]

Original Bubble Fairy™ Collection - J. deStefano

1988	Bliss	Open		85.00	8[illegible]
1988	Breeze	Retrd.	1993	85.00	8[illegible]
1988	Echo	Open		85.00	8[illegible]
1988	Luna	Open		145.00	14[illegible]
1988	Meadow	Retrd.	1993	145.00	14[illegible]
1988	Mist	Retrd.	1993	145.00	14[illegible]
1988	Nimbus	Retrd.	1993	85.00	8[illegible]
1988	Sky	Open		145.00	14[illegible]
1988	Sunbeam	Retrd.	1993	85.00	8[illegible]
1988	Twilight	Open		85.00	8[illegible]
1988	Whisper	Open		85.00	8[illegible]
1988	Wishes	Retrd.	1993	85.00	8[illegible]

Reco International

Clown Figurines by John McClelland - J. McClelland

1988	Mr. Cool	9,500		35.00	3[illegible]
1987	Mr. Cure-All	9,500		35.00	3[illegible]
1988	Mr. Heart-Throb	9,500		35.00	3[illegible]
1987	Mr. Lovable	9,500		35.00	3[illegible]
1988	Mr. Magic	9,500		35.00	3[illegible]
1987	Mr. One-Note	9,500		35.00	3[illegible]
1987	Mr. Tip	9,500		35.00	3[illegible]

Faces of Love - J. McClelland

1988	Cuddles	Open		29.50	[illegible]
1988	Sunshine	Open		29.50	[illegible]

Granget Crystal Sculpture - G. Granget

1973	Long Earred Owl, Asio Otus	Retrd.	1974	2250.00	225[illegible]
XX	Ruffed Grouse	Retrd.	1976	1000.00	100[illegible]

Laughables - J. Bergsma

1995	Annie, Geoge & Harry	Open		17.50	[illegible]
1996	Ashley	Open		13.50	[illegible]
1995	Cody & Spot	Open		15.00	[illegible]
1995	Daffodil & Prince	Open		13.50	[illegible]
1995	Daisy & Jeremiah	Open		15.00	[illegible]
1996	Felix & Freddie	Open		15.00	[illegible]
1995	Joey & Jumper	Open		15.00	[illegible]
1996	Jordan & Jessie	Open		15.00	[illegible]
1996	Leo & Lindsey	Open		17.50	[illegible]
1996	Mattie & Quackers	Open		15.00	[illegible]
1995	Merlin & Gemini	Open		15.00	[illegible]
1995	Millie & Mittens	Open		15.00	[illegible]
1996	Nicholas & Chelsea	Yr.iss.		15.00	[illegible]
1995	Patches and Pokey	Open		15.00	[illegible]
1995	Patty & Petunia	Open		16.50	[illegible]
1996	Peter & Polly	Open		17.50	[illegible]
1996	Sammy & Mikey	Open		15.00	[illegible]
1995	Sunny	Open		13.50	[illegible]
1995	Whiskers & Willie	Open		13.50	[illegible]

Porcelains in Miniature by John McClelland - J. McClelland

XX	Alice	10,000		34.50	[illegible]
XX	Autumn Dreams	Open		29.50	[illegible]

*Quotes have been rounded up to nearest dolla[illegible]

YEAR ISSUE		EDITION LIMIT	YEAR RETD.	ISSUE PRICE	*QUOTE U.S.$
XX	The Baker	Open		29.50	30
XX	Batter Up	Retrd.	1993	29.50	30
XX	Center Ice	Open		29.50	30
XX	Cheerleader	Open		29.50	30
XX	Chimney Sweep	10,000		34.50	35
XX	The Clown	Open		29.50	30
XX	Club Pro	Open		29.50	30
XX	Country Lass	Open		29.50	30
XX	Cowboy	Open		29.50	30
XX	Cowgirl	Open		29.50	30
XX	Doc	Open		29.50	30
XX	Dressing Up	10,000		34.50	35
XX	The Farmer	Open		29.50	30
XX	Farmer's Wife	Open		29.50	30
XX	The Fireman	Open		29.50	30
XX	First Outing	Open		29.50	30
XX	First Solo	Open		29.50	30
XX	Highland Fling	7,500		34.50	35
XX	John	10,000		34.50	35
XX	Lawyer	Open		29.50	30
XX	Love 40	Open		29.50	30
XX	The Nurse	Open		29.50	30
XX	The Painter	Open		29.50	30
XX	The Policeman	Open		29.50	30
XX	Quiet Moments	Open		29.50	30
XX	Smooth Smailing	Open		29.50	30
XX	Special Delivery	Open		29.50	30
XX	Sudsie Suzie	Open		29.50	30
XX	Tuck-Me-In	Open		29.50	30
XX	Winter Fun	Open		29.50	30

The Reco Angel Collection - J. McClelland

1986	Adoration	Open		24.00	24
1986	Devotion	Open		15.00	15
1986	Faith	Retrd.	1995	24.00	24
1986	Gloria	Open		12.00	12
1986	Harmony	Retrd.	1994	12.00	12
1986	Hope	Open		24.00	24
1986	Innocence	Open		12.00	12
1986	Joy	Retrd.	1994	15.00	15
1986	Love	Open		12.00	12
1988	Minstral	Retrd.	1995	12.00	12
1986	Peace	Open		24.00	24
1986	Praise	Open		20.00	20
1988	Reverence	Retrd.	1995	12.00	12
1986	Serenity	Open		24.00	24

The Reco Clown Collection - J. McClelland

1985	Arabesque	Open		12.00	13
1985	Bow Jangles	Open		12.00	13
1985	Curly	Open		12.00	13
1987	Disco Dan	Open		12.00	13
1987	Domino	Open		12.00	13
1987	Happy George	Open		12.00	13
1985	Hobo	Open		12.00	13
1987	The Joker	Open		12.00	13
1987	Jolly Joe	Open		12.00	13
1987	Love	Open		12.00	13
1987	Mr. Big	Open		12.00	13
1985	The Professor	Open		12.00	13
1985	Ruffles	Open		12.00	13
1985	Sad Eyes	Open		12.00	13
1985	Scamp	Open		12.00	13
1987	Smiley	Open		12.00	13
1985	Sparkles	Open		12.00	13
1985	Top Hat	Open		12.00	13
1987	Tramp	Open		12.00	13
1987	Twinkle	Open		12.00	13
1985	Whoopie	Open		12.00	13
1985	Winkie	Retrd.	1994	12.00	13
1987	Wistful	Open		12.00	13
1987	Zany Jack	Open		12.00	13

Reco Creche Collection - J. McClelland

1988	Cow	Open		15.00	15
1988	Donkey	Open		16.50	17
1987	Holy Family (3 Pieces)	Open		49.00	49
1988	King/Frankincense	Open		22.50	23
1988	King/Gold	Open		22.50	23
1988	King/Myrrh	Open		22.50	23
1987	Lamb	Open		9.50	10
1987	Shepherd-Kneeling	Open		22.50	23
1987	Shepherd-Standing	Open		22.50	23

Rhodes Studio

Rockwell's Age of Wonder - Rockwell-Inspired

1992	The Birthday Party	Closed	N/A	39.95	40
1991	Hush-A-Bye	Closed	N/A	34.95	35
1991	School Days	Closed	N/A	36.95	37
1991	Splish Splash	Closed	N/A	34.95	35
1991	Stand by Me	Closed	N/A	36.95	37
1991	Summertime	Closed	N/A	39.95	40

Rockwell's Beautiful Dreamers - Rockwell-Inspired

1991	Dear Diary	Closed	N/A	37.95	38
1992	Debutante's Dance	Closed	N/A	42.95	43
1991	Secret Sonnets	Closed	N/A	39.95	40
1991	Sitting Pretty	Closed	N/A	37.95	38
1991	Springtime Serenade	Closed	N/A	39.95	40
1992	Walk in the Park	Closed	N/A	42.95	43

Rockwell's Gems of Wisdom - Rockwell-Inspired

1991	Love Cures All	Closed	N/A	39.95	40
1991	Practice Makes Perfect	Closed	N/A	39.95	40
1991	A Stitch In Time	Closed	N/A	42.95	43

Rockwell's Heirloom Santa Collection - Rockwell-Inspired

1991	Christmas Dream	150-day		49.95	50
1992	Making His List	Closed	N/A	49.95	50
1990	Santa's Workshop	150-day		49.95	50

Rockwell's Hometown - Various

1991	Bell Tower - Rockwell-Inspired	Closed	N/A	36.95	37
1992	The Berkshire Playhouse - Rockwell-Inspired	Closed	N/A	42.95	43
1991	Church On The Green - Rockwell-Inspired	Closed	N/A	39.95	40
1992	Citizen's Hall - Rockwell-Inspired	Closed	N/A	42.95	43
1991	Firehouse - Rockwell-Inspired	Closed	N/A	36.95	37
1991	Greystone Church - Rhodes	Closed	N/A	34.95	35
1992	Mission House - Rockwell-Inspired	Closed	N/A	42.95	43
1992	Old Corner House - Rockwell-Inspired	Closed	1994	42.95	43
1991	Rockwell's Residence - Rhodes	Closed	N/A	34.95	35
1992	Town Hall - Rockwell-Inspired	Closed	N/A	39.95	40

Rockwell's Main Street - Rockwell-Inspired

1990	The Antique Shop	150-day		28.00	150
1991	The Bank	150-day		36.00	36
1990	The Country Store	150-day		32.00	36
1991	The Library	150-day		36.00	36
1991	Red Lion Inn	150-day		39.00	39
1990	Rockwell's Studio	150-day		28.00	85
1990	The Town Offices	150-day		32.00	36

Rick Cain Studios

Collectors Guild - R. Cain

1992	High Point	S/O	1992	82.00	95-125
1992	Visor	Retrd.	1992	Gift	100
1993	Strider	S/O	1993	82.00	105
1993	Star Shadow	Retrd.	1993	Gift	75
1994	Midnight Son	1,225	1994	297.00	500
1994	Arctic Moon II	Retrd.	1994	Gift	75
1995	Family Tree	Yr.Iss.		260.00	260-350
1995	Bonsai	Yr.Iss.		Gift	45-75

Master Series - R. Cain

1986	Aerial Hunter 1114	5,000	1990	70.40	100
1991	Aerial Victor 1707	2,000	1995	115.00	130-175
1986	African Youth 1109	5,000		137.00	137
1991	Alpha Sprout 1601	2,000		99.00	99
1990	Aquarian 1504	2,000		203.00	203
1995	Arctic Heir 1951	2,500		240.00	240
1993	Arctic Moon 1917	2,000	1993	231.00	550-1200
1993	Arctic Son 1927	2,000	1993	275.00	550-900
1988	The Balance 1302	5,000	1992	374.00	515-550
1992	Bathing Hole 1901	2,000	1994	102.00	153-165
1994	Bear Rising 1934	2,000		180.00	200
1988	Blackberry Summer 1201	300	1994	165.00	190
1991	Blossom 1705	2,000		99.00	99
1985	Box Turtle 1101	5,000		66.00	66
1993	Buffalo's Son 1924	2,000		143.00	143
1991	Cain Sign 1600	2,000		55.00	55
1991	Cameo 1700	2,000		154.00	154
1995	Canopy 1959	2,000		250.00	250
1985	Catchmaster 1104	5,000	1990	184.80	325-500
1991	Cheetah 1603	2,000		105.00	105
1990	Dark Feather 1501	2,000	1994	86.00	155
1993	Dark Shadow 1918	900		1650.00	1650
1994	Den Meditation 1943	2,000		375.00	375
1989	Domain 1205	5,000	1992	187.00	255-300
1986	Dragon Sprout 1112	5,000	1990	92.50	300
1987	Dragon Sprout II 1122	5,000		159.00	159
1994	Dragon's Dream 1940	1,500		240.00	300
1987	Dragonflies Dance 1123	5,000	1992	55.00	85
1990	Dual Motion 1503	2,000		185.00	185
1986	Elder 1113	2,500	1993	550.00	750-900
1989	Encompass 1202	5,000		104.00	104
1988	Fair Atlantis 1130	5,000	1993	319.00	375
1990	Falcon Lore 1406	5,000	1992	86.00	155-200
1985	Featherview 1103	5,000	1993	151.80	330
1995	Feet of Clay 1946	2,000		150.00	150
1995	Fire and Ice 1950	2,000		690.00	690
1994	Flight Feathers 1937	1,500		180.00	200
1994	Forest Nimble 1931	2,000		218.00	218
1993	Fountain of Youth 1915	2,000		132.00	132
1994	Four Bears 1933	2,000		1100.00	1100
1988	Guardian 1301	5,000	1995	325.00	370
1987	Habitat 1116	5,000		93.00	93
1989	Hatchling 1205	1,250	1994	85.00	100
1988	Heron Pass 1128	5,000		231.00	231
1991	Highland Voyager 1805	2,000	1995	120.00	150
1987	Innerview 1203	1,500	1994	84.00	95
1994	Ivory Hunter 1939	2,500		160.00	160
1991	Jungle Graces 1706	2,000		110.00	110
1991	La Kimono 1701	2,000		176.00	176
1988	Lady Reflecting 1129	5,000	1995	93.00	105
1992	Leading Wolf 1904	2,000	1992	143.00	450
1987	Liquid Universe 1117	5,000	1995	540.00	615
1993	Little Bears 1921	2,000		220.00	220
1990	Majestic Cradle 1505	900	1995	440.00	500
1986	Marshkeeper 1110	5,000		231.00	231
1993	Medicine Bowl 1920	2,000		220.00	220
1992	Medicine Hawk 1905	2,000		187.00	187
1995	Mergence 1948	2,000		240.00	240
1994	Moon Walk 1930	2,000	1994	198.00	300
1994	Mountain Pass 1938	2,000		180.00	200
1995	Mountain Sketch 1955	2,500		70.00	70
1985	Nightmaster 1105	5,000	1990	184.80	350
1988	Old Man of the Forest 1126	5,000	1992	132.00	200
1988	Orbist 1127	5,000	1992	108.00	150 250
1992	The Pack 1902	2,000	1992	105.50	400
1988	Paradise Found 1124	575	1994	308.00	425
1990	Pathfinder 1403	2,000	1991	101.00	155-200
1994	Pathways 1942	2,500		125.00	125
1990	Pondering 1407	2,000		108.00	108
1992	Power of One 1909	2,000	1995	77.00	95
1992	Prairie Thunder 1903	2,000	1994	110.00	165
1991	Pride 1602	2,000		105.00	105
1992	Radiance 1911	2,000		132.00	132
1994	Rebirth 1928	2,000		180.00	180
1990	Rising Shadow 1408	2,000		187.00	187
1993	Rites of Passage 1916	2,000		165.00	165
1986	Sandmaster 1115	5,000	1995	93.00	105
1990	Scarlett Wing 1404	365	1994	101.00	185
1985	Sea View 1107	5,000	1993	70.40	115
1990	Searchers 1502	2,000	1994	174.00	200-350
1987	Sentinel Crest 1119	5,000	1994	121.00	140-170
1992	Seven Bears 1908	2,000	1993	231.00	385
1995	Snow Pause 1952	2,000		140.00	140
1991	Soft Wave 1604	2,000		121.00	121
1995	Son and Daughters of the Wind 1947	2,000		165.00	165
1993	Speaks to Strangers 1923	2,000		132.00	132
1991	Spirit Dog 1702	2,000	1992	198.00	450-625
1992	Spirit Eagle 1908	2,000	1993	121.00	185
1994	Spirit of the Mountain 1941	2,000		350.00	440
1993	Spirit Totem 1922	2,000	1993	286.00	435-475
1993	Steppin' Wolf 1925	2,000	1993	210.00	315
1995	Taking the Lead 1957	2,500		250.00	250
1987	Teller 1120	5,000	1992	308.00	425
1992	Three Bears 1907	2,000		187.00	187
1991	Thunderbowl 1703	2,000		242.00	242
1985	Tidemaster 1108	2,500	1994	242.00	275
1990	Tropic Array 1405	2,000		100.00	100
1986	Tropical Flame 1111	5,000	1992	209.00	290-350
1989	Universes 1204	5,000	1995	115.00	130
1994	Vision Bear 1935	2,000		250.00	250
1994	Waiting Wolf 1929	2,000	1994	198.00	210-300
1995	Water Dance 1956	2,000		90.00	90
1988	Watercourse Way 1125	5,000		99.00	99
1995	Wedgestone Dragon 1954	2,000		190.00	190
1993	Where Bear 1926	2,000		253.00	253
1986	Wind Horse 1108	5,000	1992	70.00	100-150
1987	Winged Fortress 1118	5,000	1994	363.00	400
1995	Winged Victor 1953	2,500		170.00	170
1993	Wolf Crossing 1914	2,000		715.00	715
1994	Wolf Prince 1932	2,000		325.00	325
1993	Wolf Trail 1919	2,000	1993	121.00	200
1990	Wood Flight 1401	2,000	1992	105.50	150
1993	Wood Song 1912	2,000	1993	143.00	220-320
1985	Woodland Spirit 1102	5,000		165.00	165
1987	Yore Castle 1121	5,000	1992	165.00	225-250

Vision Quest - R. Cain

1992	Alphascape 1900	2,000	1993	210.00	400
1991	Silver Shadow 1606	2,000		176.00	176
1994	Vision Bear 1935	2,000		315.00	315
1995	Vision Ride 1960	2,000		250.00	250
1993	White Vision 1913	2,000		242.00	242

River Shore

Rockwell Single Issues - N. Rockwell

1982	Grandpa's Guardian	9,500	N/A	125.00	195
1981	Looking Out To Sea	9,500	N/A	85.00	200

Roman, Inc.

American Santas Through the Decades - Galleria Lucchese Studios

1994	1800 Cloth-like Santa 7"	Closed	1995	49.50	50
1994	1800 Pencil Santa 8"	Closed	1995	29.50	30
1994	1810 Cloth-like Santa 7"	Closed	1995	49.50	50
1994	1810 Pencil Santa 8"	Closed	1995	29.50	30

Bristol Falls Carolers Society - E. Simonetti

1994	Albert Sinclair	Open		23.50	25
1993	Amos Eleazor Whipple	Open		23.50	25
1994	Caroline Williams	Open		23.50	30
1993	Catherine Lucy Lancaster	Open		23.50	25
1995	Charity and Charles	Open		29.50	30
1993	Chester Adams	Open		23.50	25
1993	Elizabeth Anne Abbot & Stephen	Open		23.50	25
1995	Emily Adams	Open		24.50	25
1994	Jack O'Halloran	Open		23.50	25
1993	James Fisk Cushing	Open		27.50	30
1994	Margaret Louise Winslow Smith	Open		23.50	25

*Quotes have been rounded up to nearest dollar

YEAR ISSUE		EDITION LIMIT	YEAR RETD.	ISSUE PRICE	*QUOTE U.S.$
1994	Mary Beth Lancaster	Open		23.50	25
1994	Mayor Jeremiah Bradshaw Smith	Open		23.50	25
1993	Timothy Palmer	Open		27.50	30

Catnippers - I. Spencer

1985	A Baffling Yarn	15,000		45.00	45
1985	Can't We Be Friends	15,000		45.00	45
1985	A Christmas Mourning	15,000		45.00	50
1985	Flora and Felina	15,000		45.00	50
1985	Flying Tiger-Retired	15,000		45.00	45
1985	The Paw that Refreshes	15,000		45.00	45
1985	Sandy Claws	15,000		45.00	45
1985	A Tail of Two Kitties	15,000		45.00	45

Ceramica Excelsis - Unknown

1978	Assumption Madonna	5,000		56.00	56
1978	Christ Entering Jerusalem	5,000		96.00	96
1978	Christ in the Garden of Gethsemane	5,000		40.00	60
1977	Christ Knocking at the Door	5,000		60.00	60
1980	Daniel in the Lion's Den	5,000		80.00	80
1980	David	5,000		77.00	77
1978	Flight into Egypt	5,000		59.00	90
1983	Good Shepherd	5,000		49.00	49
1978	Guardian Angel with Boy	5,000		69.00	69
1978	Guardian Angel with Girl	5,000		69.00	69
1983	Holy Family	5,000		72.00	72
1978	Holy Family at Work	5,000		96.00	96
1978	Infant of Prague	5,000		37.50	60
1981	Innocence	5,000		95.00	95
1979	Jesus Speaks in Parables	5,000		90.00	90
1983	Jesus with Children	5,000		74.00	74
1981	Journey to Bethlehem	5,000		89.00	89
1983	Kneeling Santa	5,000		95.00	95
1977	Madonna and Child with Angels	5,000		60.00	60
1977	Madonna with Child	5,000		65.00	65
1979	Moses	5,000		77.00	77
1979	Noah	5,000		77.00	77
1981	Sermon on the Mount	5,000		56.00	56
1983	St. Anne	5,000		49.00	49
1983	St. Francis	5,000		59.50	60
1977	St. Francis	5,000		60.00	60
1981	Way of the Cross	5,000		59.00	59
1980	Way to Emmaus	5,000		155.00	155
1977	What Happened to Your Hand?	5,000		60.00	60

A Child's World 1st Edition - F. Hook

1980	Beach Buddies, signed	15,000		29.00	600
1980	Beach Buddies, unsigned	15,000		29.00	450
1980	Helping Hands	Closed	N/A	45.00	85
1980	Kiss Me Good Night	15,000		29.00	40
1980	My Big Brother	Closed	N/A	39.00	200
1980	Nighttime Thoughts	Closed	N/A	25.00	65
1980	Sounds of the Sea	15,000	N/A	45.00	150

A Child's World 2nd Edition - F. Hook

1981	All Dressed Up	15,000		36.00	70
1981	Cat Nap	15,000	N/A	42.00	125
1981	I'll Be Good	15,000	N/A	36.00	80
1981	Making Friends	15,000		42.00	46
1981	The Sea and Me	15,000	N/A	39.00	80
1981	Sunday School	15,000		39.00	70

A Child's World 3rd Edition - F. Hook

1981	Bear Hug	15,000		42.00	45
1981	Pathway to Dreams	15,000		47.00	50
1981	Road to Adventure	15,000		47.00	50
1981	Sisters	15,000	N/A	64.00	75
1981	Spring Breeze	15,000	N/A	37.50	50
1981	Youth	15,000		37.50	40

A Child's World 4th Edition - F. Hook

1982	All Bundled Up	15,000		37.50	40
1982	Bedtime	15,000		35.00	38
1982	Birdie	15,000		37.50	40
1982	Flower Girl	15,000		42.00	45
1982	My Dolly!	15,000		39.00	40
1982	Ring Bearer	15,000		39.00	40

A Child's World 5th Edition - F. Hook

1983	Brothers	15,000		64.00	70
1983	Finish Line	15,000		39.00	42
1983	Handful of Happiness	15,000		36.00	40
1983	He Loves Me...	15,000		49.00	55
1983	Puppy's Pal	15,000		39.00	42
1983	Ring Around the Rosie	15,000		99.00	105

A Child's World 6th Edition - F. Hook

1984	Can I Help?	15,000		37.50	40
1984	Future Artist	15,000		42.00	45
1984	Good Doggie	15,000		47.00	50
1984	Let's Play Catch	15,000		33.00	35
1984	Nature's Wonders	15,000		29.00	31
1984	Sand Castles	15,000		37.50	40

A Child's World 7th Edition - F. Hook

1985	Art Class	15,000		99.00	105
1985	Don't Tell Anyone	15,000		49.00	50
1985	Look at Me!	15,000		42.00	45
1985	Mother's Helper	15,000		45.00	50
1985	Please Hear Me	15,000		29.00	30
1985	Yummm!	15,000		36.00	39

A Child's World 8th Edition - F. Hook

1985	Chance of Showers	15,000		33.00	35
1985	Dress Rehearsal	15,000		33.00	35
1985	Engine	15,000		36.00	40
1985	Just Stopped By	15,000		36.00	40
1985	Private Ocean	15,000		29.00	31
1985	Puzzling	15,000		36.00	40

A Child's World 9th Edition - F. Hook

1987	Hopscotch	15,000		67.50	70
1987	Li'l Brother	15,000		60.00	65

Classic Brides of the Century - E. Williams

1989	1900-Flora	5,000		175.00	175
1989	1910-Elizabeth Grace	5,000		175.00	175
1989	1920-Mary Claire	5,000		175.00	175
1989	1930-Kathleen	5,000		175.00	175
1989	1940-Margaret	5,000		175.00	175
1989	1950-Barbara Ann	5,000		175.00	175
1989	1960-Dianne	5,000		175.00	175
1989	1970-Heather	5,000		175.00	175
1989	1980-Jennifer	5,000		175.00	175
1992	1990-Stephanie Helen	5,000		175.00	175

Divine Servant - M. Greiner Jr.

1993	Divine Servant, pewter sculpture	Open		200.00	200
1993	Divine Servant, porcelain sculpture	Open		59.50	60
1993	Divine Servant, resin sculpture	Open		250.00	250

Fontanini Collectors' Club Member's Only - E. Simonetti

1991	The Pilgrimage	Yr.Iss.	1991	24.95	25
1992	She Rescued Me	Yr.Iss.	1992	23.50	24
1993	Christmas Symphony	Yr.Iss.	1993	13.50	14
1994	Sweet Harmony	Yr.Iss.	1994	13.50	14
1995	Faith: The Fifth Angel	Yr.Iss.	1995	22.50	23

Fontanini Member's Only Nativity Preview - E. Simonetti

1996	Mara	Yr.Iss.		12.50	13

Fontanini Collector Club Renewal Gift - E. Simonetti

1993	He Comforts Me	Yr.Iss.	1993	12.50	13
1994	I'm Heaven Bound	Yr.Iss.	1994	12.50	13
1995	Gift of Joy	Yr.Iss.	1995	12.50	13

Fontanini Collector Club Symbol of Membership - E. Simonetti

1996	Rosannah - Angel of The Roses	Yr.Iss.		Gift	N/A

Fontanini Collector Club Special Event Piece - E. Simonetti

1990	Gideon	Closed	1995	15.00	15
1995	Dominica	7/96		15.00	15

Fontanini Tour Exclusive - E. Simonetti

1995	Luke	Yr.Iss.		15.00	15

Fontanini Collector Club First Year Welcome Gift - E. Simonetti

1990	I Found Him	Closed	1995	Gift	N/A

Fontanini Heirloom Nativity Limited Edition Figurines - E. Simonetti

1994	Abigail & Peter	25,000	1994	29.50	30
1992	Ariel	Retrd.	1992	29.50	30
1995	Gabriela	25,000	1995	18.00	18
1993	Jeshua & Adin	Retrd.	1993	29.50	30
1996	Raphael	Yr.Iss.		18.00	18

Fontanini Retired 5" Collection - E. Simonetti

1985	Aaron	Retrd.	1994	12.50	13
1979	Baby Jesus	Retrd.	1992	11.50	12
1979	Balthazar	Retrd.	1993	11.50	12
1979	Gabriel	Retrd.	1993	11.50	12
1979	Gaspar	Retrd.	1993	11.50	12
1979	Joseph	Retrd.	1992	11.50	12
1979	Josiah	Retrd.	1994	11.50	12
1985	Levi	Retrd.	1994	12.50	13
1979	Mary	Retrd.	1992	11.50	12
1979	Melchior	Retrd.	1993	11.50	12
1985	Miriam	Retrd.	1994	12.50	12

Fontanini Retired 7.5" Collection - E. Simonetti

1979	Baby Jesus	Retrd.	1994	24.50	25
1979	Gabriel	Retrd.	1994	24.50	25
1979	Joseph	Retrd.	1994	24.50	25
1979	Mary	Retrd.	1994	24.50	25

Fontanini, The Collectible Creche - E. Simonetti

1973	10cm., (15 piece Set)	Closed	1992	63.60	89
1973	12cm., (15 piece Set)	Closed	1992	76.50	102
1979	16cm., (15 piece Set)	Closed	1992	178.50	285
1982	17cm., (15 piece Set)	Closed	1992	189.00	305
1973	19cm., (15 piece Set)	Closed	1992	175.50	280
1980	30cm., (15 piece Set)	Closed	1992	670.00	759

Frances Hook's Four Seasons - F. Hook

1984	Winter	12,500		95.00	100
1985	Spring	12,500		95.00	100
1985	Summer	12,500		95.00	100
1985	Fall	12,500		95.00	100

Heartbeats - I. Spencer

1986	Miracle	5,000		145.00	145
1987	Storytime	5,000		145.00	145

Hook - F. Hook

1986	Carpenter Bust	Retrd.	1986	95.00	95
1986	Carpenter Bust-Heirloom Edition	Retrd.	1986	95.00	95
1987	Little Children, Come to Me	15,000		45.00	45
1987	Madonna and Child	15,000		39.50	40
1982	Sailor Mates	2,000		290.00	315
1982	Sun Shy	2,000		290.00	315

Jam Session - E. Rohn

1985	Banjo Player	7,500		145.00	145
1985	Bass Player	7,500		145.00	145
1985	Clarinet Player	7,500		145.00	145
1985	Coronet Player	7,500		145.00	145
1985	Drummer	7,500		145.00	145
1985	Trombone Player	7,500		145.00	145

The Masterpiece Collection - Various

1979	Adoration - F. Lippe	5,000		73.00	73
1981	The Holy Family - G. delle Notti	5,000		98.00	98
1982	Madonna of the Streets - R. Ferruzzi	5,000		65.00	65
1980	Madonna w/Grapes - P. Mignard	5,000		85.00	85

The Museum Collection by Angela Tripi - A. Tripi

1995	The Batter	1,000		95.00	95
1993	Be a Clown	1,000		95.00	95
1994	Blackfoot Woman with Baby	1,000		95.00	95
1991	The Caddie	1,000		135.00	135
1992	Checking It Twice	2,500		95.00	95
1991	Christopher Columbus	1,000		250.00	250
1994	Crow Warrior	1,000		195.00	195
1991	The Fiddler	1,000		175.00	176
1992	Flying Ace	1,000		95.00	95
1993	For My Next Trick	1,000		95.00	95
1992	Fore!	1,000		175.00	175
1992	The Fur Trapper	1,000		175.00	175
1991	A Gentleman's Game	1,000	1994	175.00	175
1992	The Gift Giver	2,500		95.00	95
1994	Iroquois Warrior	1,000		95.00	95
1995	Jesus in Gethsemane	1,000		95.00	95
1993	Jesus, The Good Shepherd	1,000		95.00	95
1992	Justice for All	1,000		95.00	95
1992	Ladies' Day	1,000		175.00	175
1992	Ladies' Tee	1,000		250.00	250
1990	The Mentor	1,000		290.00	291
1994	Native American Chief	1,000		95.00	95
1994	Native American Woman-Cherokee Maiden	1,000		95.00	95
1992	Nativity Set-8 pc.	2,500		425.00	425
1995	Nurse	1,000		95.00	95
1993	One Man Band Clown	1,000		95.00	95
1992	Our Family Doctor	1,000		95.00	95
1995	The Pitcher	1,000		95.00	95
1993	Preacher of Peace	1,000		175.00	175
1992	Prince of the Plains	1,000		175.00	175
1993	Public Protector	1,000		95.00	95
1994	Rhapsody	1,000		95.00	95
1993	Right on Schedule	1,000		95.00	95
1993	Road Show	1,000		95.00	95
1995	The Runner	1,000		95.00	95
1994	Serenade	1,000		95.00	95
1994	Sonata	1,000		95.00	95
1991	St. Francis of Assisi	1,000		175.00	175
1992	The Tannenbaum Santa	2,500		95.00	95
1992	The Tap In	1,000		175.00	175
1995	Teacher	1,000		95.00	95
1991	Tee Time at St. Andrew's	1,000	1993	175.00	175
1992	This Way, Santa	2,500		95.00	95
1992	To Serve and Protect	1,000		95.00	95
1993	Tripi Crucifix-Large	Open		59.00	59
1993	Tripi Crucifix-Medium	Open		35.00	35
1993	Tripi Crucifix-Small	Open		27.50	28

The Richard Judson Zolan Collection - R.J. Zolan

1992	Summer at the Seashore	1,200		125.00	125
1994	Terrace Dancing	1,200		175.00	175

Seraphim Classics™ - Seraphim Studios

1996	Celine - The Morning Star	Open		55.00	55
1994	Cymbeline - Peacemaker	Open		49.50	55
1994	Evangeline - Angel of Mercy	Open		49.50	55
1995	Felcia - Adoring Maiden	Open		49.50	55
1994	Francesca - Loving Guardian	Open		65.00	65
1996	Gabriel - Celestial Messenger	Open		59.50	60
1994	Iris - Rainbow's End	Open		49.50	55
1994	Isabel - Gentle Spirit	Open		49.50	55
1995	Laurice - Wisdom's Child	Open		49.50	55
1994	Lydia - Winged Poet	Open		49.50	55
1996	Mariah - Heavenly Joy	Open		59.50	60
1994	Ophelia - Heart Seeker	Open		49.50	55
1995	Priscilla - Benevolent Guide	Open		49.50	55
1996	Rosalie - Nature's Delight	Open		55.00	55
1995	Sepaphina - Heaven's Helper	Open		49.50	55
1996	Serena - Angel of Peace	Open		65.00	65

Seraphim Classics™ Glitterdome™ - Seraphim Studios

1995	Francesca - Loving Guardian	Open		50.00	50

*Quotes have been rounded up to nearest dollar

Seraphim Classics™ Limited Edition Figurines - Seraphim Studios

YEAR ISSUE	EDITION LIMIT	YEAR RETD.	ISSUE PRICE	*QUOTE U.S.$
1995 Alyssa - Nature's Angel	Closed	1995	145.00	145
1996 Vanessa - Heavenly Maiden	Yr.Iss.		150.00	150

Seraphim Classics™ Musical - Seraphim Studios

YEAR ISSUE	EDITION LIMIT	YEAR RETD.	ISSUE PRICE	*QUOTE U.S.$
1994 Francesca - Loving Guardian	Open		75.00	75
1996 Iris - Rainbow's End	Open		65.00	65

Spencer - I. Spencer

YEAR ISSUE	EDITION LIMIT	YEAR RETD.	ISSUE PRICE	*QUOTE U.S.$
1985 Flower Princess	5,000		195.00	195
1985 Moon Goddess	5,000		195.00	195

Ron Lee's World of Clowns

The Ron Lee Collector's Club Gifts - R. Lee

YEAR ISSUE	EDITION LIMIT	YEAR RETD.	ISSUE PRICE	*QUOTE U.S.$
1987 Hooping It Up CCG1	Closed	N/A	Gift	95
1988 Pudge CCG2	Closed	N/A	Gift	65
1989 Pals CCG3	Closed	N/A	Gift	65
1990 Potsie CCG4	Closed	N/A	Gift	65
1991 Hi! Ya! CCG5	Closed	N/A	Gift	65
1992 Bashful Beau CCG6	Closed	N/A	Gift	65
1993 Lit'l Mate CCG7	Closed	N/A	Gift	65
1994 Chip Off the Old Block CCG8	Closed	N/A	Gift	65
1995 Rock-A-Billy	Closed	N/A	Gift	65

The Ron Lee Collector's Club Renewal Sculptures - R. Lee

YEAR ISSUE	EDITION LIMIT	YEAR RETD.	ISSUE PRICE	*QUOTE U.S.$
1987 Doggin' Along CC1	Yr.Iss.	N/A	75.00	115
1988 Midsummer's Dream CC2	Yr.Iss.	N/A	97.00	140
1989 Peek-A-Boo Charlie CC3	Yr.Iss.	N/A	65.00	125
1990 Get The Message CC4	Yr.Iss.	N/A	65.00	125
1991 I'm So Pretty CC5	Yr.Iss.	N/A	65.00	125
1992 It's For You CC6	Yr.Iss.	N/A	65.00	125
1993 My Son Keven CC7	Yr.Iss.	N/A	70.00	125

Around the World With Hobo Joe - R. Lee

YEAR ISSUE	EDITION LIMIT	YEAR RETD.	ISSUE PRICE	*QUOTE U.S.$
1994 Hobo Joe in Caribbean L412	750	1995	110.00	110
1994 Hobo Joe in Egypt L415	750	1995	110.00	110
1994 Hobo Joe in England L411	750	1995	110.00	110
1994 Hobo Joe in France L407	750	1995	110.00	110
1994 Hobo Joe in Italy L406	750	1995	110.00	110
1994 Hobo Joe in Japan L408	750	1995	110.00	110
1994 Hobo Joe in Norway L413	750	1995	110.00	110
1994 Hobo Joe in Spain L414	750	1995	110.00	110
1994 Hobo Joe in Tahiti L410	750	1995	110.00	110
1994 Hobo Joe in the U.S.A L409	750	1995	110.00	110-125

The Betty Boop Collection - R. Lee

YEAR ISSUE	EDITION LIMIT	YEAR RETD.	ISSUE PRICE	*QUOTE U.S.$
1992 Bamboo Isle BB715	1,500		240.00	240
1992 Boop Oop A Doop BB705	1,500		97.00	97
1992 Harvest Moon BB700	1,500		93.00	93
1992 Max's Cafe BB720	1,500		99.00	99
1992 Spicy Dish BB710	1,500		215.00	215

Center Ring - R. Lee

YEAR ISSUE	EDITION LIMIT	YEAR RETD.	ISSUE PRICE	*QUOTE U.S.$
1994 According To L-431SE	750	1995	125.00	125
1994 Aristocrat L-424SE	750	1995	125.00	125
1994 Barella L-423SE	750	1995	125.00	125-140
1994 Belt-a-Loon L-427SE	750	1995	125.00	125
1994 Boo-Boo L-430SE	750	1995	125.00	125
1994 Bubbles L-422SE	750	1995	125.00	125
1994 Carpetbagger L-421SE	750	1995	125.00	125
1994 Daisy L-417SE	750	1995	125.00	125
1994 Forget-Me-Not L-428SE	750	1995	125.00	125
1994 Glamour Boy L-433SE	750	1995	125.00	125
1994 Hoop-De-Doo L-434SE	750	1995	125.00	125
1994 Hot Dog L-418SE	750	1995	125.00	125
1994 Kandy L-419SE	750	1995	125.00	125
1994 Maid in the USA L-432SE	750	1995	125.00	125-140
1994 Mal-Lett L-426SE	750	1995	125.00	125
1994 Poodles L-420SE	750	1995	125.00	125
1994 Puddles L-416SE	750	1995	125.00	125
1994 Rabbit's Foot L-429SE	750	1995	125.00	125
1994 Ruffles L-435SE	750	1995	125.00	125
1994 Snacks L-425SE	750	1995	125.00	125

The Classics - R. Lee

YEAR ISSUE	EDITION LIMIT	YEAR RETD.	ISSUE PRICE	*QUOTE U.S.$
1991 Huckleberry Hound HB815	2,750	1995	90.00	90
1991 Quick Draw McGraw HB805	2,750	1995	90.00	90
1991 Scooby Doo & Shaggy HB810	2,750	1995	114.00	114
1991 Yogi Bear & Boo Boo HB800	2,750	1995	95.00	95

The Commemorative Collection - R. Lee

YEAR ISSUE	EDITION LIMIT	YEAR RETD.	ISSUE PRICE	*QUOTE U.S.$
1995 April 12th L455	2,500		180.00	180-200
1995 Between Shows L456	2,500		250.00	250-285
1995 Filet of Sole L460	2,500		180.00	200
1995 The Highwayman L457	2,500		165.00	165
1995 Just Plain Tired L459	2,500		195.00	225
1995 Practice Swing...Not!! L458	2,500		180.00	205

The E.T. Collection - R. Lee

YEAR ISSUE	EDITION LIMIT	YEAR RETD.	ISSUE PRICE	*QUOTE U.S.$
1992 E.T. ET100	1,500	1995	94.00	94
1993 Flight ET115	1,500	1995	325.00	325
1993 Friends ET110	1,500	1995	125.00	125
1992 It's Mee...E.T. ET105	1,500	1995	94.00	94

The Flintstones - R. Lee

YEAR ISSUE	EDITION LIMIT	YEAR RETD.	ISSUE PRICE	*QUOTE U.S.$
1991 Bedrock Serenade HB130	2,750		250.00	250
1991 Bogey Buddies HB150	2,750		143.00	143
1991 Buffalo Brothers HB170	2,750		134.00	134
1991 The Flinstones HB100	2,750		410.00	410
1991 Joyride-A-Saurus HB140	2,750		107.00	107
1991 Saturday Blues HB120	2,750		105.00	105
1991 Vac-A-Saurus HB160	2,750		105.00	110
1991 Yabba-Dabba-Doo HB110	2,750		230.00	230

History of Golf - R. Lee

YEAR ISSUE	EDITION LIMIT	YEAR RETD.	ISSUE PRICE	*QUOTE U.S.$
1994 20th Century GTA700	10,000		150.00	150
1994 Age of Chivalry GTA400	10,000		150.00	150
1994 Caesar GTA300	10,000		150.00	150
1994 Dawn of Man GTA100	10,000		150.00	150
1994 New Frontiers GTA800	10,000		150.00	150
1994 Old West GTA600	10,000		150.00	150
1994 The Pharaoh GTA200	10,000		150.00	150
1994 Plymouth GTA500	10,000		150.00	150

Holiday Special - R. Lee

YEAR ISSUE	EDITION LIMIT	YEAR RETD.	ISSUE PRICE	*QUOTE U.S.$
1995 Santa's Other Sleigh L461	750		195.00	195

The Jetsons - R. Lee

YEAR ISSUE	EDITION LIMIT	YEAR RETD.	ISSUE PRICE	*QUOTE U.S.$
1991 4 O'Clock Tea HB550	2,750	1995	203.00	203
1991 Astro: Cosmic Canine HB520	2,750	1995	275.00	275
1991 The Cosmic Couple HB510	2,750	1995	105.00	105
1991 I Rove Roo HB530	2,750	1995	105.00	105
1991 The Jetsons HB500	2,750	1995	500.00	500
1991 Scare-D-Dog HB540	2,750	1995	160.00	160

Musical Clowns in Harmony - R. Lee

YEAR ISSUE	EDITION LIMIT	YEAR RETD.	ISSUE PRICE	*QUOTE U.S.$
1994 Aristocrat L-424	750	1995	175.00	175
1994 Barella L-423	750	1995	175.00	175
1994 Bubbles L-422	750	1995	175.00	175
1994 Carpet Bagger L-421	750	1995	175.00	175
1994 Daisy L-417	750	1995	175.00	175
1994 Hot Dog L-418	750	1995	175.00	175
1994 Kandy L-419	750	1995	175.00	175
1994 Poodles L-420	750	1995	175.00	175
1994 Puddles L-416	750	1995	175.00	175
1994 Snacks L-425	750	1995	175.00	175

The Original Ron Lee Collection-1976 - R. Lee

YEAR ISSUE	EDITION LIMIT	YEAR RETD.	ISSUE PRICE	*QUOTE U.S.$
1976 Alligator Bowling 504	Closed	N/A	15.00	35-78
1976 Bear Fishing 511	Closed	N/A	15.00	35-78
1976 Clown and Dog Act 101	Closed	N/A	48.00	78-140
1976 Clown and Elephant Act 107	Closed	N/A	56.00	85-140
1976 Clown Tightrope Walker 104	Closed	N/A	50.00	82-155
1976 Dog Fishing 512	Closed	N/A	15.00	35-78
1976 Frog Surfing 502	Closed	N/A	15.00	35-78
1976 Hippo on Scooter 505	Closed	N/A	15.00	35-78
1976 Hobo Joe Hitchiking 116	Closed	N/A	55.00	65
1976 Hobo Joe with Balloons 120	Closed	N/A	63.00	90
1976 Hobo Joe with Pal 115	Closed	N/A	63.00	85-170
1976 Hobo Joe with Umbrella 117	Closed	N/A	58.00	65-160
1976 Kangaroos Boxing 508	Closed	N/A	15.00	35-78
1976 Owl With Guitar 500	Closed	N/A	15.00	35-78
1976 Penguin on Snowskis 503	Closed	N/A	15.00	35-78
1976 Pig Playing Violin 510	Closed	N/A	15.00	35-78
1976 Pinky Lying Down 112	Closed	N/A	25.00	145-225
1976 Pinky Sitting 119	Closed	N/A	25.00	145
1976 Pinky Standing 118	Closed	N/A	25.00	145-225
1976 Pinky Upside Down 111	Closed	N/A	25.00	125
1976 Rabbit Playing Tennis 507	Closed	N/A	15.00	35-78
1976 Turtle On Skateboard 501	Closed	N/A	15.00	35-78

The Original Ron Lee Collection-1977 - R. Lee

YEAR ISSUE	EDITION LIMIT	YEAR RETD.	ISSUE PRICE	*QUOTE U.S.$
1977 Bear On Rock 523	Closed	N/A	18.00	30-80
1977 Koala Bear In Tree 514	Closed	N/A	15.00	35-78
1977 Koala Bear On Log 516	Closed	N/A	15.00	35-78
1977 Koala Bear With Baby 515	Closed	N/A	15.00	35-78
1977 Monkey With Banana 521	Closed	N/A	18.00	30-80
1977 Mouse and Cheese 520	Closed	N/A	18.00	30-80
1977 Mr. Penguin 518	Closed	N/A	18.00	39-85
1977 Owl Graduate 519	Closed	N/A	22.00	44-90
1977 Pelican and Python 522	Closed	N/A	18.00	30-80

The Original Ron Lee Collection-1978 - R. Lee

YEAR ISSUE	EDITION LIMIT	YEAR RETD.	ISSUE PRICE	*QUOTE U.S.$
1978 Bobbi on Unicyle 204	Closed	N/A	45.00	65-98
1978 Bow Tie 222	Closed	N/A	67.50	93-215
1978 Butterfly and Flower 529	Closed	N/A	22.00	40-85
1978 Clancy, the Cop 210	Closed	N/A	55.00	72-130
1978 Clara-Bow 205	Closed	N/A	52.00	70-120
1978 Coco-Hands on Hips 218	Closed	N/A	70.00	85-250
1978 Corky, the Drummer Boy 202	Closed	N/A	53.00	85-130
1978 Cuddles 208	Closed	N/A	37.00	55-110
1978 Dolphins 525	Closed	N/A	22.00	40-85
1978 Driver the Golfer 211	Closed	N/A	55.00	200-225
1978 Elephant on Ball 214	Closed	N/A	26.00	42-80
1978 Elephant on Stand 213	Closed	N/A	26.00	42-80
1978 Elephant Sitting 215	Closed	N/A	26.00	42-80
1978 Fancy Pants 224	Closed	N/A	55.00	90-120
1978 Fireman with Hose 216	Closed	N/A	62.00	85-170
1978 Hey Rube 220	Closed	N/A	35.00	53-92
1978 Hummingbird 528	Closed	N/A	22.00	40-85
1978 Jeri In a Barrel 219	Closed	N/A	75.00	110-180
1978 Jocko with Lollipop 221	Closed	N/A	67.50	93-215
1978 Oscar On Stilts 223	Closed	N/A	55.00	90-120
1978 Pierrot Painting 207	Closed	N/A	50.00	80-170
1978 Polly, the Parrot & Crackers 201	Closed	N/A	63.00	100-170
1978 Poppy with Puppet 209	Closed	N/A	60.00	75-140
1978 Prince Frog 526	Closed	N/A	22.00	40-85
1978 Sad Sack 212	Closed	N/A	48.00	62-210
1978 Sailfish 524	Closed	N/A	18.00	40-95
1978 Sea Otter on Back 531	Closed	N/A	22.00	40-85
1978 Sea Otter on Rock 532	Closed	N/A	22.00	40-85
1978 Seagull 527	Closed	N/A	22.00	40-85
1978 Skippy Swinging 239	Closed	N/A	52.00	65-85
1978 Sparky Skating 206	Closed	N/A	55.00	72-260
1978 Tinker Bowing 203	Closed	N/A	37.00	55-110
1978 Tobi-Hands Outstretched 217	Closed	N/A	70.00	98-260
1978 Turtle on Rock 530	Closed	N/A	22.00	40-85

The Original Ron Lee Collection-1979 - R. Lee

YEAR ISSUE	EDITION LIMIT	YEAR RETD.	ISSUE PRICE	*QUOTE U.S.$
1979 Buttons Bicycling 229	Closed	N/A	75.00	110-150
1979 Carousel Horse 232	Closed	N/A	119.00	130-195
1979 Darby Tipping Hat 238	Closed	N/A	35.00	60-140
1979 Darby with Flower 235	Closed	N/A	35.00	60-140
1979 Darby with Umbrella 236	Closed	N/A	35.00	60-140
1979 Darby With Violin 237	Closed	N/A	35.00	60-140
1979 Doctor Sawbones 228	Closed	N/A	75.00	110-150
1979 Fearless Fred in Cannon 234	Closed	N/A	80.00	105-300
1979 Harry and the Hare 233	Closed	N/A	69.00	102-180
1979 Kelly at the Piano 241	Closed	N/A	185.00	285-510
1979 Kelly in Kar 230	Closed	N/A	164.00	210-380
1979 Kelly's Kar 231	Closed	N/A	75.00	90-280
1979 Lilli 227	Closed	N/A	75.00	105-145
1979 Timmy Tooting 225	Closed	N/A	35.00	52-85
1979 Tubby Tuba 226	Closed	N/A	35.00	50

The Original Ron Lee Collection-1980 - R. Lee

YEAR ISSUE	EDITION LIMIT	YEAR RETD.	ISSUE PRICE	*QUOTE U.S.$
1980 Alexander's One Man Band 261	Closed	N/A	N/A	N/A
1980 Banjo Willie 258	Closed	N/A	68.00	85-195
1980 Carousel Horse 248	Closed	N/A	88.00	115-285
1980 Carousel Horse 249	Closed	N/A	88.00	115-285
1980 Chuckles Juggling 244	Closed	N/A	98.00	105-150
1980 Cubby Holding Balloon 240	Closed	N/A	50.00	65-70
1980 Dennis Playing Tennis 252	Closed	N/A	74.00	95-185
1980 Doctor Jawbones 260	Closed	N/A	85.00	110-305
1980 Donkey What 243	Closed	N/A	60.00	92-250
1980 Emile 257	Closed	N/A	43.00	82-190
1980 Happy Waving 255	Closed	N/A	43.00	82-190
1980 Hobo Joe in Tub 259	Closed	N/A	96.00	240
1980 Horse Drawn Chariot 263	Closed	N/A	N/A	N/A
1980 Jaque Downhill Racer 253	Closed	N/A	74.00	90-210
1980 Jingles Telling Time 242	Closed	N/A	75.00	90-190
1980 Jo-Jo at Make-up Mirror 250	Closed	N/A	86.00	125-185
1980 The Menagerie 262	Closed	N/A	N/A	N/A
1980 Monkey 251	Closed	N/A	60.00	85-210
1980 P. T. Dinghy 245	Closed	N/A	65.00	80-190
1980 Peanuts Playing Concertina 247	Closed	N/A	65.00	150-285
1980 Roni Riding Horse 246	Closed	N/A	115.00	180-290
1980 Ruford 254	Closed	N/A	43.00	80-190
1980 Zach 256	Closed	N/A	43.00	82-190

The Original Ron Lee Collection-1981 - R. Lee

YEAR ISSUE	EDITION LIMIT	YEAR RETD.	ISSUE PRICE	*QUOTE U.S.$
1981 Al at the Bass 284	Closed	N/A	48.00	52-112
1981 Barbella 273	Closed	N/A	N/A	N/A
1981 Bojangles 276	Closed	N/A	N/A	N/A
1981 Bosom Buddies 299	Closed	N/A	135.00	90-280
1981 Bozo On Unicycle 279	Closed	N/A	28.00	99-185
1981 Bozo Playing Cymbols 277	Closed	N/A	28.00	99-185
1981 Bozo Riding Car 278	Closed	N/A	28.00	99-185
1981 Carney and Seal Act 300	Closed	N/A	63.00	75-290
1981 Carousel Horse 280	Closed	N/A	88.00	125-290
1981 Carousel Horse 281	Closed	N/A	88.00	125-290
1981 Cashew On One Knee 275	Closed	N/A	N/A	N/A
1981 Elephant Reading 271	Closed	N/A	N/A	N/A
1981 Executive Hitchiking 267	Closed	N/A	23.00	45-110
1981 Executive Reading 264	Closed	N/A	23.00	45-110
1981 Executive Resting 266	Closed	N/A	23.00	45-110
1981 Executive with Umbrella 265	Closed	N/A	23.00	45-110
1981 Harpo 296	Closed	N/A	120.00	190-350
1981 Hobo Joe Praying 298	Closed	N/A	57.00	65-85
1981 Kevin at the Drums 283	Closed	N/A	50.00	92-150
1981 Larry and His Hotdogs 274	Closed	N/A	76.00	90-200
1981 Louie Hitching A Ride 269	Closed	N/A	47.00	58-135
1981 Louie on Park Bench 268	Closed	N/A	56.00	85-160
1981 Louie On Railroad Car 270	Closed	N/A	77.00	95-180
1981 Mickey With Umbrella 291	Closed	N/A	50.00	75-140
1981 Mickey Tightrope Walker 292	Closed	N/A	50.00	75-140
1981 Mickey Upside Down 293	Closed	N/A	50.00	75-140
1981 My Son Darren 295	Closed	N/A	57.00	72-140
1981 Nicky Sitting on Ball 289	Closed	N/A	39.00	48-92
1981 Nicky Standing on Ball 290	Closed	N/A	39.00	48-92
1981 Perry Sitting With Balloon 287	Closed	N/A	37.00	50-95
1981 Perry Standing With Balloon 288	Closed	N/A	37.00	50-95
1981 Pickles and Pooch 297	Closed	N/A	90.00	200-240
1981 Pistol Pete 272	Closed	N/A	76.00	85-180
1981 Rocketman 294	Closed	N/A	77.00	92-150
1981 Ron at the Piano 285	Closed	N/A	46.00	55-110
1981 Ron Lee Trio 282	Closed	N/A	144.00	280-435
1981 Timothy In Big Shoes 286	Closed	N/A	37.00	50-95

The Original Ron Lee Collection-1982 - R. Lee

YEAR ISSUE	EDITION LIMIT	YEAR RETD.	ISSUE PRICE	*QUOTE U.S.$
1982 Ali on His Magic Carpet 335	Closed	N/A	105.00	150-210
1982 Barnum Feeding Bacon 315	Closed	N/A	120.00	160-270
1982 Beaver Playing Accordian 807	Closed	N/A	23.00	35-92
1982 Benny Pulling Car 310	Closed	N/A	190.00	235-360
1982 Burrito Bandito 334	Closed	N/A	150.00	190-260
1982 Buster in Barrel 308	Closed	N/A	85.00	90-120
1982 Camel 818	Closed	N/A	57.00	75-150

*Quotes have been rounded up to nearest dollar

FIGURINES/COTTAGES

YEAR ISSUE		EDITION LIMIT	YEAR RETD.	ISSUE PRICE	*QUOTE U.S.$
1982	Captain Cranberry 320	Closed	N/A	115.00	145-180
1982	Captain Mis-Adventure 703	Closed	N/A	250.00	300-550
1982	Carney and Dog Act 301	Closed	N/A	63.00	75-149
1982	Charlie Chaplain 701	Closed	N/A	230.00	285-650
1982	Charlie in the Rain 321	Closed	N/A	80.00	90-160
1982	Chico Playing Guitar 336	Closed	N/A	70.00	95-180
1982	Clancy, the Cop and Dog 333	Closed	N/A	115.00	140-250
1982	Clarence - The Lawyer 331	Closed	N/A	100.00	140-230
1982	Denny Eating Ice Cream 305	Closed	N/A	39.00	50-170
1982	Denny Holding Gift Box 306	Closed	N/A	39.00	50-170
1982	Denny Juggling Ball 307	Closed	N/A	39.00	50-170
1982	Dog Playing Guitar 805	Closed	N/A	23.00	35-92
1982	Dr. Painless and Patient 311	Closed	N/A	195.00	240-385
1982	Fireman Watering House 303	Closed	N/A	99.00	99-180
1982	Fish With Shoe 803	Closed	N/A	23.00	35-92
1982	Fox In An Airplane 806	Closed	N/A	23.00	35-92
1982	Georgie Going Anywhere 302	Closed	N/A	95.00	275-375
1982	Giraffe 816	Closed	N/A	57.00	75-150
1982	Herbie Balancing Hat 327	Closed	N/A	26.00	40-110
1982	Herbie Dancing 325	Closed	N/A	26.00	40-110
1982	Herbie Hands Outstretched 326	Closed	N/A	26.00	40-110
1982	Herbie Legs in Air 329	Closed	N/A	26.00	40-110
1982	Herbie Lying Down 328	Closed	N/A	26.00	40-110
1982	Herbie Touching Ground 330	Closed	N/A	26.00	40-110
1982	Hobo Joe on Cycle 322	Closed	N/A	125.00	170-280
1982	Horse 819	Closed	N/A	57.00	75-150
1982	Kukla and Friend 316	Closed	N/A	100.00	140-210
1982	Laurel & Hardy 700	Closed	N/A	225.00	290-500
1982	Limousine Service 705	Closed	N/A	330.00	375-750
1982	Lion 817	Closed	N/A	57.00	75-150
1982	Marion With Marrionette 317	Closed	N/A	105.00	135-225
1982	Murphy On Unicycle 337	Closed	N/A	115.00	160-288
1982	Nappy Snoozing 346	Closed	N/A	110.00	125-210
1982	Norman Painting Dumbo 314	Closed	N/A	126.00	150-210
1982	Ostrich 813	Closed	N/A	57.00	75-150
1982	Parrot Rollerskating 809	Closed	N/A	23.00	35-92
1982	Pig Brick Layer 800	Closed	N/A	23.00	35-92
1982	Pinball Pal 332	Closed	N/A	150.00	195-287
1982	Quincy Lying Down 304	Closed	N/A	80.00	92-210
1982	Rabbit With Egg 801	Closed	N/A	23.00	35-92
1982	Reindeer 812	Closed	N/A	57.00	75-150
1982	Robin Resting 338	Closed	N/A	110.00	125-210
1982	Ron Lee Carousel	Closed	N/A	1000.00	12500
1982	Rooster 815	Closed	N/A	57.00	75-150
1982	Rooster With Barbell 808	Closed	N/A	23.00	35-92
1982	Sammy Riding Elephant 309	Closed	N/A	90.00	125-250
1982	Seal Blowing His Horns 804	Closed	N/A	23.00	35-92
1982	Self Portrait 702	Closed	N/A	355.00	2500
1982	Slim Charging Bull 313	Closed	N/A	195.00	265-410
1982	Smokey, the Bear 802	Closed	N/A	23.00	35-92
1982	Steppin' Out 704	Closed	N/A	325.00	390-700
1982	Three Man Valentinos 319	Closed	N/A	55.00	70-120
1982	Tiger 814	Closed	N/A	57.00	75-150
1982	Too Loose-L'Artiste 312	Closed	N/A	150.00	180-290
1982	Tou Tou 323	Closed	N/A	70.00	90-190
1982	Toy Soldier 324	Closed	N/A	95.00	140-270
1982	Turtle With Gun 811	Closed	N/A	57.00	75-150
1982	Two Man Valentinos 318	Closed	N/A	45.00	60-130
1982	Walrus With Umbrella 810	Closed	N/A	23.00	35-92

The Original Ron Lee Collection-1983 - R. Lee

YEAR ISSUE		EDITION LIMIT	YEAR RETD.	ISSUE PRICE	*QUOTE U.S.$
1983	The Bandwagon 707	Closed	N/A	900.00	2000
1983	Beethoven's Fourth Paws 358	Closed	N/A	59.00	110-165
1983	Black Carousel Horse 1001	Closed	N/A	450.00	450-600
1983	Bumbles Selling Balloons 353	Closed	N/A	80.00	170-240
1983	Buster and His Balloons 363	Closed	N/A	47.00	90-125
1983	Captain Freddy 375	Closed	N/A	85.00	425-475
1983	Casey Cruising 351	Closed	N/A	57.00	95-170
1983	Catch the Brass Ring 708	Closed	N/A	510.00	900-1350
1983	Cecil and Sausage 354	Closed	N/A	90.00	200-270
1983	Chef's Cuisine 361	Closed	N/A	57.00	100-110
1983	Chestnut Carousel Horse 1002	Closed	N/A	450.00	700-1100
1983	Cimba the Elephant 706	Closed	N/A	225.00	300-550
1983	Clyde Juggling 339	Closed	N/A	39.00	100-115
1983	Clyde Upside Down 340	Closed	N/A	39.00	100-115
1983	Coco and His Compact 369	Closed	N/A	55.00	145-175
1983	Cotton Candy 377	Closed	N/A	150.00	200-400
1983	Daring Dudley 367	Closed	N/A	65.00	100-200
1983	Door to Door Dabney 373	Closed	N/A	100.00	200-285
1983	Engineer Billie 356	Closed	N/A	190.00	275-550
1983	Flipper Diving 345	Closed	N/A	115.00	200-350
1983	Gazebo 1004	Closed	N/A	750.00	13-1750
1983	Gilbert Tee'd Off 376	Closed	N/A	60.00	225
1983	Hobi in His Hammock 344	Closed	N/A	85.00	175
1983	I Love You From My Heart 360	Closed	N/A	35.00	125
1983	The Jogger 372	Closed	N/A	75.00	120-220
1983	Josephine 370	Closed	N/A	55.00	145-175
1983	Knickers Balancing Feather 366	Closed	N/A	47.00	120-135
1983	The Last Scoop 379	Closed	N/A	175.00	300-475
1983	The Last Scoop 900	Closed	N/A	325.00	300-725
1983	Little Horse - Head Down 342	Closed	N/A	29.00	72
1983	Little Horse - Head Up 341	Closed	N/A	29.00	72
1983	Little Saturday Night 348	Closed	N/A	53.00	200
1983	Lou Proposing 365	Closed	N/A	57.00	120-170
1983	Matinee Jitters 378	Closed	N/A	175.00	200-450
1983	Matinee Jitters 901	Closed	N/A	325.00	355
1983	My Daughter Deborah 357	Closed	N/A	63.00	125-185
1983	No Camping or Fishing 902	Closed	N/A	325.00	350-600
1983	On The Road Again 355	Closed	N/A	220.00	300-650
1983	Riches to Rags 374	Closed	N/A	55.00	200-265
1983	Ride 'em Roni 347	Closed	N/A	125.00	200-375
1983	Rufus and His Refuse 343	Closed	N/A	65.00	160
1983	Say It With Flowers 359	Closed	N/A	35.00	95-110
1983	Singin' In The Rain 362	Closed	N/A	105.00	350
1983	Tatters and Balloons 352	Closed	N/A	65.00	125-200
1983	Teeter Tottie Scottie 350	Closed	N/A	55.00	105-165
1983	Tottie Scottie 349	Closed	N/A	39.00	75-115
1983	Up, Up and Away 364	Closed	N/A	50.00	100-150
1983	White Carousel Horse 1003	Closed	N/A	450.00	700-1100
1983	Wilt the Stilt 368	Closed	N/A	49.00	100-155

The Original Ron Lee Collection-1984 - R. Lee

YEAR ISSUE		EDITION LIMIT	YEAR RETD.	ISSUE PRICE	*QUOTE U.S.$
1984	Baggy Pants 387	Closed	N/A	98.00	250-300
1984	Black Circus Horse 711A	Closed	N/A	305.00	350-520
1984	A Bozo Lunch 390	Closed	N/A	148.00	250-400
1984	Bozo's Seal of Approval 389	Closed	N/A	138.00	200-350
1984	Chestnut Circus Horse 710A	Closed	N/A	305.00	350-520
1984	Give a Dog a Bone 383	Closed	N/A	95.00	95-182
1984	Just For You 386	Closed	N/A	110.00	150-250
1984	Look at the Birdy 388	Closed	N/A	138.00	200-300
1984	Mortimer Fishing 382	Closed	N/A	N/A	N/A
1984	My Fellow Americans 391	Closed	N/A	138.00	250-425
1984	No Camping or Fishing 380	Closed	N/A	175.00	275-450
1984	No Loitering 392	Closed	N/A	113.00	150-250
1984	The Peppermints 384	Closed	N/A	150.00	180-250
1984	Rudy Holding Balloons 713	Closed	N/A	230.00	300-550
1984	Saturday Night 714	Closed	N/A	250.00	600-825
1984	T.K. and OH!! 385	Closed	N/A	85.00	200-325
1984	Tisket and Tasket 393	Closed	N/A	93.00	150-250
1984	Wheeler Sheila 381	Closed	N/A	75.00	175-225
1984	White Circus Horse 709	Closed	N/A	305.00	350-520

The Original Ron Lee Collection-1985 - R. Lee

YEAR ISSUE		EDITION LIMIT	YEAR RETD.	ISSUE PRICE	*QUOTE U.S.$
1985	Bull-Can-Rear-You 422	Closed	N/A	120.00	206
1985	Cannonball 466	Closed	N/A	43.00	83
1985	Catch of the Day 441	Closed	N/A	170.00	305
1985	Clowns of the Caribbean PS101	Closed	N/A	1250.00	2-2800
1985	Dr. Sigmund Fraud 457	Closed	N/A	98.00	190
1985	Dr. Timothy DeCay 459	Closed	N/A	98.00	185
1985	Duster Buster 461	Closed	N/A	43.00	90
1985	The Finishing Touch 409	Closed	N/A	178.00	305
1985	Fred Figures 903	Closed	N/A	175.00	595
1985	From Riches to Rags 374	Closed	N/A	108.00	250
1985	Get the Picture 456	Closed	N/A	70.00	140
1985	Gilbert TeeOd OFF 376	Closed	N/A	63.00	55-63
1985	Giraffe Getting a Bath 428	Closed	N/A	160.00	350-450
1985	Ham Track 451	Closed	N/A	240.00	430
1985	Hi Ho Blinky 462	Closed	N/A	53.00	105
1985	One Wheel Winky 464	Closed	N/A	43.00	83
1985	Pee Wee With Balloons 435	Closed	N/A	50.00	100
1985	Pee Wee With Umbrella 434	Closed	N/A	50.00	100
1985	Policy Paul 904	Closed	N/A	175.00	190
1985	Rosebuds 433	Closed	N/A	155.00	315
1985	Twas the Night Before 408	Closed	N/A	235.00	405
1985	Whiskers Bathing 749	Closed	N/A	305.00	500-800
1985	Whiskers Hitchhiking 745	Closed	N/A	240.00	800
1985	Whiskers Holding Balloons 746	Closed	N/A	265.00	500-800
1985	Whiskers Holding Umbrella 747	Closed	N/A	265.00	500-800
1985	Whiskers On The Bench 750	Closed	N/A	230.00	695-895
1985	Whiskers Sweeping 744	Closed	N/A	240.00	700-850
1985	Yo Yo Stravinsky-Attoney at Law 458	Closed	N/A	98.00	200

The Original Ron Lee Collection-1986 - R. Lee

YEAR ISSUE		EDITION LIMIT	YEAR RETD.	ISSUE PRICE	*QUOTE U.S.$
1986	Bathing Buddies 450	Closed	N/A	145.00	375
1986	Bums Day at the Beach L105	Closed	N/A	97.00	N/A
1986	Captain Cranberry 469	Closed	N/A	140.00	175-335
1986	Christmas Morning Magic L107	Closed	N/A	99.00	N/A
1986	Getting Even 485	Closed	N/A	85.00	125-225
1986	Hari and Hare 454	Closed	N/A	57.00	85-135
1986	High Above the Big Top L112	Closed	N/A	162.00	350
1986	The Last Stop L106	Closed	N/A	99.00	N/A
1986	Most Requested Toy L108	Closed	N/A	264.00	N/A
1986	Puppy Love's Portrait L113	Closed	N/A	168.00	325
1986	Ride 'Em Peanuts 463	Closed	N/A	55.00	70-135
1986	Wet Paint 436	Closed	N/A	80.00	150

The Original Ron Lee Collection-1987 - R. Lee

YEAR ISSUE		EDITION LIMIT	YEAR RETD.	ISSUE PRICE	*QUOTE U.S.$
1987	First & Main L110	Closed	N/A	368.00	775-875
1987	Happines Is L116	Closed	N/A	155.00	185
1987	Heartbroken Harry L101	Closed	N/A	63.00	125-225
1987	Lovable Luke L102	Closed	N/A	70.00	150
1987	Puppy Love L103	Closed	N/A	71.00	150
1987	Show of Shows L115	Closed	N/A	175.00	N/A
1987	Sugarland Express L109	Closed	N/A	342.00	650-895
1987	Would You Like To Ride? L104	Closed	N/A	246.00	350

The Original Ron Lee Collection-1988 - R. Lee

YEAR ISSUE		EDITION LIMIT	YEAR RETD.	ISSUE PRICE	*QUOTE U.S.$
1988	Anchors-A-Way L120	Closed	N/A	195.00	250
1988	Boulder Bay L124	Closed	N/A	700.00	N/A
1988	Bozorina L118	Closed	N/A	95.00	120
1988	Cactus Pete L125	Closed	N/A	495.00	N/A
1988	Dinner for Two L119	Closed	N/A	140.00	N/A
1988	The Fifth Wheel L117	Closed	N/A	250.00	375
1988	Fore! L122	Closed	N/A	135.00	175
1988	New Ron Lee Carousel	Closed	N/A	7000.00	9500
1988	Pumpkuns Galore L121	Closed	N/A	135.00	160-245
1988	To The Rescue L127	Closed	N/A	130.00	160-550
1988	Together Again L126	Closed	N/A	130.00	210
1988	Tunnel of Love L123	Closed	N/A	490.00	600-800
1988	When You're Hot, You're Hot! L128	Closed	N/A	221.00	295

The Original Ron Lee Collection-1989 - R. Lee

YEAR ISSUE		EDITION LIMIT	YEAR RETD.	ISSUE PRICE	*QUOTE U.S.$
1989	The Accountant L173	Closed	N/A	68.00	150-200
1989	The Baseball Player L189	Closed	N/A	72.00	150-200
1989	The Basketball Player L187	Closed	N/A	68.00	150-200
1989	Be Happy L198	Closed	N/A	160.00	195
1989	Be It Ever So Humble L111	Closed	N/A	900.00	950-1250
1989	The Beautician L183	Closed	N/A	68.00	150-200
1989	Beauty Is In The Eye Of L140	Closed	N/A	190.00	250
1989	Birdbrain L206	Closed	N/A	110.00	250
1989	The Bowler L191	Closed	N/A	68.00	150-200
1989	Butt-R-Fly L151	Closed	N/A	47.00	75
1989	Butterflies Are Free L204	Closed	N/A	225.00	250
1989	Candy Apple L155	Closed	N/A	47.00	75
1989	Candy Man L217	Closed	N/A	350.00	350
1989	Catch A Falling Star L148	Closed	N/A	57.00	75
1989	The Chef L178	Closed	N/A	65.00	150-200
1989	The Chiropractor L180	Closed	N/A	68.00	150-200
1989	Circus Little L143	Closed	N/A	990.00	1250
1989	Craps L212	Closed	N/A	530.00	N/A
1989	Dang It L200	Closed	N/A	47.00	N/A
1989	The Dentist L175	Closed	N/A	65.00	150-200
1989	The Doctor L170	Closed	N/A	65.00	150-200
1989	Eye Love You L136	Closed	N/A	68.00	N/A
1989	The Fireman L169	Closed	N/A	68.00	150-200
1989	The Fisherman L194	Closed	N/A	72.00	150-200
1989	The Football Player L186	Closed	N/A	65.00	150-200
1989	Get Well L131	Closed	N/A	79.00	N/A
1989	The Golfer L188	Closed	N/A	72.00	150-200
1989	The Greatest Little Shoe On Earth L210	Closed	N/A	165.00	200-300
1989	Happy Chanakah L162	Closed	N/A	106.00	N/A
1989	Hot Diggity Dog L201	Closed	N/A	47.00	50
1989	The Housewife L181	Closed	N/A	75.00	150-200
1989	Hughie Mungus L144	Closed	N/A	250.00	300-825
1989	I Ain't Got No Money L195	Closed	N/A	325.00	895
1989	I Just Called! L153	Closed	N/A	47.00	75
1989	I Pledge Allegiance L134	Closed	N/A	131.00	150-250
1989	I Should've When I Could've L196	Closed	N/A	325.00	895
1989	I-D-D-D-Do! L215	Closed	N/A	180.00	N/A
1989	If I Were A Rich Man L133	Closed	N/A	315.00	695
1989	If That's Your Drive How's Your Putts L164	Closed	N/A	260.00	N/A
1989	In Over My Head L135	Closed	N/A	95.00	250
1989	Jingles Hitchhiking L209	Closed	N/A	90.00	200
1989	Jingles Holding Balloon L208	Closed	N/A	90.00	200
1989	Jingles With Umbrella L207	Closed	N/A	90.00	175
1989	Just Carried Away L138	Closed	N/A	135.00	230
1989	Just Go! L156	Closed	N/A	47.00	75
1989	The Lawyer 171	Closed	N/A	68.00	150-200
1989	Maestro L132	Closed	N/A	173.00	200
1989	Marcelle L150	Closed	N/A	47.00	N/A
1989	The Mechanic L184	Closed	N/A	68.00	150-200
1989	Memories L197	Closed	N/A	325.00	N/A
1989	Merry Xmas L159	Closed	N/A	94.00	N/A
1989	My Affections L157	Closed	N/A	47.00	75
1989	My First Tree L161	Closed	N/A	92.00	125
1989	My Heart Beats For You L137	Closed	N/A	74.00	125
1989	My Last Chip L213	Closed	N/A	550.00	N/A
1989	My Money's OnThe Bull L142	Closed	N/A	187.00	480
1989	The New Self Portrait L218	Closed	N/A	800.00	2000-3000
1989	No Fishing L130	Closed	N/A	247.00	N/A
1989	Not A Ghost Of A Chance L145	Closed	N/A	195.00	500
1989	The Nurse L168	Closed	N/A	65.00	95
1989	O' Solo Mia L139	Closed	N/A	85.00	90-150
1989	The Optometrist L174	Closed	N/A	65.00	150-200
1989	Over 21 L214	Closed	N/A	550.00	N/A
1989	The Pharmacist L166	Closed	N/A	65.00	N/A
1989	The Photographer L172	Closed	N/A	68.00	150-200
1989	The Plumber L176	Closed	N/A	65.00	150-200
1989	The Policeman L165	Closed	N/A	68.00	100-200
1989	Rain Bugs Me L203	Closed	N/A	225.00	N/A
1989	The Real Estate Lady L185	Closed	N/A	70.00	250
1989	The Real Estate Man L177	Closed	N/A	65.00	150-200
1989	Rest Stop L149	Closed	N/A	47.00	75
1989	The Salesman L167	Closed	N/A	68.00	N/A
1989	Santa's Dilemma L160	Closed	N/A	97.00	250
1989	The Secretary L179	Closed	N/A	65.00	95
1989	The Serenade L202	Closed	N/A	47.00	N/A
1989	Sh-h-h-h! L146	Closed	N/A	210.00	450
1989	She Loves Me Not L205	Closed	N/A	225.00	250
1989	The Skier L193	Closed	N/A	75.00	150-200
1989	Slots Of Luck L211	Closed	N/A	90.00	175
1989	Snowdrifter L163	Closed	N/A	230.00	695
1989	Stormy Weathers L152	Closed	N/A	47.00	N/A
1989	Sunflower L154	Closed	N/A	47.00	75
1989	The Surfer L192	Closed	N/A	72.00	150-200
1989	Tee for Two L141	Closed	N/A	125.00	150
1989	The Tennis Player L190	Closed	N/A	72.00	150-200
1989	Today's Catch L147	Closed	N/A	230.00	350
1989	Two a.m. Blues L199	Closed	N/A	125.00	180-250
1989	The Veterinarian L182	Closed	N/A	72.00	150-200
1989	Wintertime Pals L158	Closed	N/A	90.00	N/A
1989	Wishful Thinking L114	Closed	N/A	230.00	1000-1250
1989	You Must Be Kidding L216	Closed	N/A	N/A	800

The Original Ron Lee Collection-1990 - R. Lee

YEAR ISSUE		EDITION LIMIT	YEAR RETD.	ISSUE PRICE	*QUOTE U.S.$
1990	All Show No Go L238	1,500		285.00	695
1990	The Big Wheel L236	Closed	N/A	240.00	245
1990	Carousel Horse L219	Closed	N/A	150.00	N/A
1990	Carousel Horse L220	Closed	N/A	150.00	N/A
1990	Carousel Horse L221	Closed	N/A	150.00	N/A
1990	Carousel Horse L222	Closed	N/A	150.00	N/A
1990	Fill'er Up L248	Closed	N/A	280.00	300
1990	Flapper Riding Carousel L223	Closed	N/A	190.00	N/A

*Quotes have been rounded up to nearest dollar

FIGURINES/COTTAGES

YEAR	ISSUE	EDITION LIMIT	YEAR RETD.	ISSUE PRICE	*QUOTE U.S.$
1990	Heart of My Heart L246	5,500	1995	55.00	55
1990	Heartbroken Hobo L233	Closed	N/A	116.00	195
1990	Henry 8-3/4 L260	Closed	N/A	37.00	50
1990	Horsin' Around L262	Closed	N/A	37.00	37-50
1990	I Love You L242	5,500	1995	55.00	55
1990	I.Q. Two L253	2,750	1995	33.00	50
1990	Jo-Jo Riding Carousel L226	Closed	N/A	190.00	N/A
1990	Kiss! Kiss! L251	Closed	N/A	37.00	37
1990	L-O-V-E L245	5,500	1995	55.00	55
1990	Loving You L244	5,500		55.00	55
1990	Me Too!! L231	Closed	1995	70.00	70-80
1990	My Heart's on for You L240	5,500	1995	55.00	55
1990	Na! Na! L252	Closed	N/A	33.00	50
1990	New Pinky Lying Down L228	8,500		42.00	42
1990	New Pinky Sitting L230	8,500		42.00	42
1990	New Pinky Standing L229	8,500		42.00	42
1990	New Pinky Upside Down L227	8,500		42.00	42
1990	Paddle L259	2,750	1995	33.00	50
1990	Par Three L232	2,750	1995	144.00	144
1990	Peaches Riding Carousel L224	Closed	N/A	190.00	N/A
1990	Pitch L261	2,750	1995	35.00	50
1990	Push and Pull L249	Closed	N/A	260.00	280
1990	Q.T. Pie L257	2,750	1995	37.00	50
1990	Rascal Riding Carousel L225	Closed	N/A	190.00	N/A
1990	Same To "U" L255	2,750	1995	37.00	50
1990	Scooter L234	Closed	1995	240.00	275
1990	Skiing My Way L239	2,500	1995	400.00	895
1990	Snowdrifter II L250	Closed	N/A	340.00	400-600
1990	Squirt L258	2,750	1995	37.00	50
1990	Stuck on Me L243	5,500	1995	55.00	55
1990	Swinging on a Star L241	5,500	1995	55.00	55
1990	Tandem Mania L235	Closed	N/A	360.00	360
1990	Uni-Cycle L237	Closed	N/A	240.00	245
1990	Watch Your Step L247	2,500		78.00	78
1990	Yo Mama L256	2,750	1995	35.00	50
1990	Your Heaviness L254	2,750	1995	37.00	50

The Original Ron Lee Collection-1991 - R. Lee

YEAR	ISSUE	EDITION LIMIT	YEAR RETD.	ISSUE PRICE	*QUOTE U.S.$
1991	Ain't No Havana L315	500	1995	230.00	230
1991	Anywhere? L269	Closed	N/A	125.00	155
1991	Banjo Willie L293	1,750		90.00	90
1991	Business is Business L266	Closed	1995	110.00	190
1991	Clarence Clarinet L289	1,750	1995	42.00	50
1991	Cruising L265	Closed	N/A	170.00	170-175
1991	Droopy Drummer L290	1,750	1995	42.00	50
1991	Eight Ball-Corner Pocket L311	1,750		224.00	250
1991	Fall L282	1,500		120.00	140
1991	Geronimo L304	1,750		127.00	180
1991	Gilbert's Dilemma L270	Closed	N/A	90.00	125
1991	Give Me Liberty L313	Closed	N/A	155.00	200-250
1991	Happy Birthday Puppy Love L278	Closed	N/A	73.00	85
1991	Harley Horn L291	1,750	1995	42.00	50
1991	Hobi Daydreaming L299	1,750		112.00	112
1991	Hook, Line and Sinker L303	1,750		100.00	60-100
1991	Hot Dawg! L316	500	1995	255.00	255
1991	I'm Singin' In The Rain L268	Closed	N/A	135.00	165
1991	IRS or Bust L285	1,500	1995	122.00	122
1991	Lit'l Snowdrifter L298	1,750		70.00	150
1991	Makin Tracks L283	1,500	1995	142.00	142
1991	Marcelle I L271	2,250	1995	50.00	50
1991	Marcelle II L272	2,250	1995	50.00	100
1991	Marcelle III L273	2,250	1995	50.00	50
1991	Marcelle IV L274	2,250	1995	50.00	50
1991	New Darby Tipping Hat L310	1,250	1995	57.00	57
1991	New Darby with Flower L307	1,250	1995	57.00	57
1991	New Darby with Umbrella L308	1,250	1995	57.00	57
1991	New Darby with Violin L309	1,250	1995	57.00	57
1991	New Harpo L305	1,250	1995	130.00	130
1991	New Toy Soldier L306	1,250	1995	115.00	115
1991	Our Nation's Pride L312	Closed	N/A	150.00	150
1991	Puppy Love Scootin' L275	Closed	N/A	73.00	85
1991	Puppy Love's Free Ride L276	Closed	N/A	73.00	100
1991	Puppy Love's Treat L277	Closed	N/A	73.00	100
1991	Refugee L267	1,750	1995	88.00	88
1991	Sand Trap L301	1,750		100.00	100
1991	Soap Suds Serenade L284	1,750		85.00	85
1991	Spring L280	1,500		95.00	95-110
1991	Strike!!! L302	1,750		76.00	76
1991	Summer L281	1,500	N/A	95.00	125
1991	Surf's Up L300	1,750		80.00	80
1991	TA DA L294	Closed	N/A	220.00	200-295
1991	Tender-Lee L264	1,750	1995	96.00	96
1991	This Won't Hurt L296	1,750	1995	110.00	110
1991	Tootie Tuba L286	1,750	1995	42.00	50
1991	Trash Can Sam L295	1,750	1995	118.00	118
1991	Truly Trumpet L287	1,750	1995	42.00	50
1991	Trusty Trombone L288	1,750	1995	42.00	50
1991	Two For Fore L297	1,750		120.00	120
1991	United We Stand L314	Closed	N/A	150.00	165
1991	The Visit L263	1,750	1995	100.00	100
1991	Winter L279	1,500		115.00	115-125

The Original Ron Lee Collection-1992 - R. Lee

YEAR	ISSUE	EDITION LIMIT	YEAR RETD.	ISSUE PRICE	*QUOTE U.S.$
1992	Baloony L350	2,500		26.00	27
1992	Beats Nothin' L357	1,500		145.00	145
1992	Beau Regards L342	2,500		26.00	27
1992	Big Wheel Kop RLC1005	1,750	1995	65.00	65
1992	Birdy The Hard Way L352	1,750		85.00	85
1992	Bo-Bo Balancing RLC1003	1,750	1995	75.00	75
1992	Break Point L335	2,500		26.00	27
1992	Brokenhearted Huey RLC1006	1,750	1995	65.00	65
1992	Buster Too PC100	1,500	1995	65.00	65
1992	Cannonball RLC1009	1,750	1995	95.00	95
1992	Clar-A-Bow L336	2,500		26.00	27
1992	Cyclin' Around L322	2,500		26.00	27
1992	Dreams L332	2,500		26.00	27
1992	Dudley's Dog Act RLC1010	1,750	1995	75.00	75
1992	Dunkin' L328	2,500		26.00	27
1992	Fish in Pail L358	1,500		130.00	130
1992	Flyin' High L340	2,500		26.00	27
1992	Forget Me Not L341	2,500		26.00	27
1992	Gassing Up RLC1004	1,750	1995	70.00	70
1992	Go Man Go L344	2,500		26.00	27
1992	Handy Standy L321	2,500		26.00	27
1992	Heel's Up L329	2,500		26.00	27
1992	Hi-Five L339	2,500		26.00	27
1992	Hippolong Cassidy L320	Closed	N/A	166.00	140
1992	Howdy L325	2,500		26.00	27
1992	Jo-Jo Juggling RLC1002	1,750	1995	70.00	70
1992	Juggles L347	2,500		26.00	27
1992	Little Pard L349	2,500		26.00	27
1992	Lolly L326	2,500		26.00	27
1992	Love Ya' Baby L355	1,250		190.00	190
1992	Miles PC105	1,500	1995	65.00	65
1992	My Pal L334	2,500		26.00	27
1992	My Portrait L354	Closed	N/A	315.00	315
1992	Myak Kyak L337	2,500		26.00	27
1992	On My Way L348	2,500		26.00	27
1992	Penny Saver L333	2,500		26.00	27
1992	Popcorn & Cotton Candy RLC1001	1,750	1995	70.00	70
1992	Scrub-A- Dub-Dub L319	Closed	N/A	185.00	195
1992	Seven's Up L356	1,250		165.00	165
1992	Shake Jake L324	2,500		26.00	27
1992	Ship Ahoy L345	2,500		26.00	27
1992	Shufflin' L343	2,500		26.00	27
1992	Snowdrifter Blowin' In Wind L317	1,750		77.50	78
1992	Snowdrifter's Special Delivery L318	1,750		136.00	136
1992	Steamer L338	2,500		26.00	27
1992	Stop Cop L331	2,500		26.00	27
1992	Strike Out L323	2,500		26.00	27
1992	Struttin' L346	2,500		26.00	27
1992	Sure-Footed Freddie RLC1007	1,750	1995	80.00	80
1992	To-Tee L327	2,500		26.00	27
1992	Topper PC110	1,500	1995	65.00	65
1992	Twirp Chirp L330	2,500		26.00	27
1992	Vincent Van Clown L353	Closed	N/A	160.00	160
1992	Walking A Fine Line RMB7000	1,750	1995	65.00	65
1992	Webb-ster PC115	1,500	1995	65.00	65
1992	Wrong Hole Clown L351	1,750		125.00	125

The Original Ron Lee Collection-1993 - R. Lee

YEAR	ISSUE	EDITION LIMIT	YEAR RETD.	ISSUE PRICE	*QUOTE U.S.$
1993	Andy Jackson L364	950	1995	87.00	87
1993	Anywhere Warm L398	950		90.00	90
1993	Bellboy L390	950	1995	80.00	80
1993	Blinky Lying Down L384	1,200		45.00	45
1993	Blinky Sitting L383	1,200		45.00	45
1993	Blinky Standing L382	1,200		45.00	45
1993	Blinky Upside Down L385	1,200		45.00	45
1993	Bo-Bo L365	950	1995	95.00	95
1993	Britches L377	750		205.00	205
1993	Bumper Fun L403	750		330.00	330
1993	Buster L368	950	1995	87.00	87
1993	Charkles L381	750	1995	220.00	220
1993	Chattanooga Choo-Choo L374	750		420.00	420
1993	Dave Bomber L360	950	1995	90.00	90
1993	Happy Trails L369	950	1995	90.00	90
1993	Honk Honk L370	950	1995	90.00	90
1993	Hot Buns L376	750		175.00	175
1993	Lollipop L363	950	1995	87.00	90
1993	Merry Go Clown L405	750		375.00	375
1993	Moto Kris L380	750		255.00	255
1993	North Pole L396	950	1995	75.00	75
1993	Piggy Backin' L379	750		205.00	205
1993	Pretzels L372	750		195.00	195
1993	Sailin' L366	950	1995	95.00	95
1993	Scrubs L361	950	1995	87.00	87
1993	Sho-Sho L373	750		115.00	115
1993	Shriner Cop L404	750		175.00	175
1993	Skittles L367	950	1995	95.00	95
1993	Snoozin' L399	950		90.00	90
1993	Soft Shoe L400	750		275.00	275
1993	Sole-Full L375	750		250.00	250
1993	Special Occasion L402	750		280.00	280
1993	Taxi L378	750		470.00	470
1993	Tinker And Toy L359	950	1995	95.00	95
1993	Wagone Hes L371	750		210.00	210
1993	Wanderer L401	750		255.00	255
1993	Yo-Yo L362	950	1995	87.00	87

The Original Ron Lee Collection-1995 - R. Lee

YEAR	ISSUE	EDITION LIMIT	YEAR RETD.	ISSUE PRICE	*QUOTE U.S.$
1995	Bar Mitzvah L463	950		270.00	270
1995	Bat Mitzvah L462	950		270.00	270
1995	Batter Up L465	500		270.00	270
1995	Cimba's Last Stand L466	950		165.00	165
1995	Fillet of Sole L460	750		180.00	180
1995	Fore! Anyone! L464	500		275.00	275
1995	Santa's Other Sleigh L461	750		195.00	195

The Popeye Collection - R. Lee

YEAR	ISSUE	EDITION LIMIT	YEAR RETD.	ISSUE PRICE	*QUOTE U.S.$
1992	Liberty P001	1,750	1995	184.00	184
1992	Men!!! P002	1,750	1995	230.00	230
1992	Oh Popeye P005	1,750	1995	230.00	230
1992	Par Excellence P006	1,750	1995	220.00	220
1992	Strong to The Finish P003	1,750	1995	95.00	95
1992	That's My Boy P004	1,750	1995	145.00	145

Premier Dealer Collection - R. Lee

YEAR	ISSUE	EDITION LIMIT	YEAR RETD.	ISSUE PRICE	*QUOTE U.S.$
1992	Dream On PD002	Closed	N/A	125.00	145
1992	Framed Again PD001	Closed	N/A	110.00	125
1993	Jake-A-Juggling Balls PD008	500		85.00	90
1993	Jake-A-Juggling Clubs PD007	500		85.00	90
1993	Jake-A-Juggling Cylinder PD006	500		85.00	90
1994	Joe's Feline Friend PD009	500		105.00	105
1994	Just Big Enough PD010	500		115.00	115
1992	Moonlighting PD004	Closed	N/A	125.00	125
1992	Nest to Nothing PD003	Closed	N/A	110.00	125
1994	Off The Toe PD011	500		105.00	120
1993	Pockets PD005	500		175.00	175
1994	Storm Warning PD012	500		115.00	115
1994	Trading Places PD013	500		190.00	190

Rocky & Bullwinkle And Friends Collection - R. Lee

YEAR	ISSUE	EDITION LIMIT	YEAR RETD.	ISSUE PRICE	*QUOTE U.S.$
1992	Dudley Do-Right RB610	1,750	1995	175.00	175
1992	KA-BOOM! RB620	1,750	1995	175.00	175
1992	My Hero RB615	1,750	1995	275.00	275
1992	Rocky & Bullwinkle RB600	1,750	1995	120.00	120
1992	The Swami RB605	1,750	1995	175.00	175

The Ron Lee Disney Collection Exclusives - R. Lee

YEAR	ISSUE	EDITION LIMIT	YEAR RETD.	ISSUE PRICE	*QUOTE U.S.$
1993	Aladdin MM560	500		550.00	550
1996	Alice In Wonderland MM840	750		295.00	295
1995	Autopia MM770	750		220.00	220
1992	Bambi MM330	2,750		195.00	195
1990	The Bandleader MM100	Closed	N/A	75.00	75
1992	Beauty & The Beast (shadow box) DIS100	500		1650.00	1650
1994	Beauty & The Beast MM610	800		170.00	170
1992	Big Thunder Mountain MM460	250	1995	1650.00	2000-3000
1992	Captain Hook MM320	2,750		175.00	175
1995	The Carousel MM730	750		125.00	125
1992	Christmas '92 MM420	1,500		145.00	145
1993	Cinderella's Slipper MM510	1,750	1995	115.00	115
1993	Darkwing Duck MM470	1,750		105.00	105
1991	Decorating Donald MM210	2,750		60.00	60
1992	The Dinosaurs MM370	2,750		195.00	195
1991	Dopey MM120	2,750	1995	80.00	80
1996	Dumbo & The Ringmaster MM860	750		195.00	195
1990	Dumbo MM600	2,750		110.00	110
1995	Ear Force One MM790	500	1995	600.00	600
1995	Engine No, One	500		650.00	650
1994	Engine Number One MM690	500	1995	650.00	650
1995	Fantasyland MM780	750		285.00	285
1992	Finishing Touch MM440	1,500		85.00	85
1993	Flying With Dumbo MM530	1,000		330.00	330
1995	Frontierland MM740	750		160.00	160
1992	Genie MM450	2,750		110.00	110
1991	Goofy MM110	2,750		115.00	115
1991	Goofy's Gift MM230	2,750		70.00	70
1994	Grumpy Playing Organ MM590	800	1995	150.00	150
1995	Home Improvements MM820	750		170.00	170
1991	Jiminy's List MM250	2,750		60.00	60
1991	Lady and the Tramp MM280	1,500	1995	295.00	295
1993	Letters to Santa MM550	1,500		170.00	170
1991	Lion Around MM270	2,750		140.00	140
1994	The Lion King MM640	1,750		170.00	170
1992	Litt'l Sorcerer MM340	2,750		57.00	57
1992	Little Mermaid MM310	2,750		230.00	230
1992	Lumiere & Cogsworth MM350	2,750		145.00	145
1995	Main Street MM710	750		120.00	120
1995	The Matterhorn MM750	750		240.00	240
1991	Mickey & Minnie at the Piano MM180	2,750		195.00	195
1991	Mickey's Adventure MM150	2,750		195.00	195
1990	Mickey's Christmas MM400	2,750		95.00	95
1991	Mickey's Delivery MM220	2,750		70.00	70
1993	Mickey's Dream MM520	250	1995	400.00	850
1994	Mickey's Limousine MM650	500	1995	450.00	450
1994	Mickey, Brave Little Tailor MM570	1,750	1995	72.00	72
1991	Minnie Mouse MM170	2,750		80.00	80
1994	Minnie, Brave Little Tailor MM580	1,750	1995	72.00	72
1994	MM/MM/Goofy, Limo	500		500	600
1992	Mrs. Potts & Chip MM360	2,750		125.00	125
1991	Mt. Mickey MM900	2,750		175.00	175
1994	New Tinkerbell MM680	300	1995	99.00	99
1994	Official Conscience MM620	300	1995	65.00	65
1995	The People Mover MM760	750		190.00	190
1990	Pinocchio MM500	2,750	1995	85.00	85
1991	Pluto's Treat MM240	2,750		60.00	60
1994	Pongo & Pups MM670	800	1995	124.00	124
1995	Pooh & The Cookie Jar MM830	750		190.00	190
1996	Pooh In The Honey Tree MM850	750		300.00	300
1995	Reflections MM810	750		99.00	99
1993	Santa's Workshop MM540	1,500		170.00	170
1994	Snow White & Doc MM630	800		135.00	135
1990	Snow White & Grumpy MM800	2,750		140.00	140
1993	Snow White & The Seven Dwarfs (shadow box) DIS200	250		1800.00	1800
1990	The Sorcerer MM200	Closed	N/A	85.00	120
1992	Sorcerer's Apprentice MM290	2,750		125.00	125
1990	Steamboat Willie MM300	2,750	1995	95.00	95
1992	Stocking Stuffer MM410	1,500		63.00	63
1991	The Tea Cup Ride (Disneyland Exclusive) MM260	1,250		225.00	225

*Quotes have been rounded up to nearest dollar

FIGURINES/COTTAGES

YEAR ISSUE		EDITION LIMIT	YEAR RETD.	ISSUE PRICE	*QUOTE U.S.$
1994	Tigger on Rabbit MM660	800	1995	110.00	110
1993	Tinker Bell MM490	1,750	1995	85.00	85
1995	The Topiary MM720	750		145.00	145
1991	Tugboat Mickey MM160	2,750		180.00	180
1991	Two Gun Mickey MM140	2,750		115.00	115
1990	Uncle Scrooge MM700	2,750		110.00	110
1993	Winnie The Pooh MM480	1,750		125.00	125
1992	Winnie The Pooh & Tigger MM390	2,750	1995	105.00	105
1992	Wish Upon A Star MM430	1,500		80.00	80
1991	The Witch MM130	2,750		115.00	115
1992	Workin' Out MM380	2,750		95.00	95
1992	Workin' Out MM380	2,750		95.00	95

The Ron Lee Emmett Kelly, Sr. Collection - R. Lee

YEAR ISSUE		EDITION LIMIT	YEAR RETD.	ISSUE PRICE	*QUOTE U.S.$
1991	Emmett Kelly, Sr. Sign E208	Closed	N/A	110.00	110
1991	God Bless America EK206	Closed	N/A	130.00	250
1991	Help Yourself EK202	Closed	N/A	145.00	350
1991	Love at First Sight EK204	Closed	N/A	197.00	197
1991	My Protege EK207	Closed	N/A	160.00	165
1991	Spike's Uninvited Guest EK203	Closed	N/A	165.00	295
1991	That-A-Way EK201	Closed	N/A	125.00	135
1991	Time for a Change EK205	Closed	N/A	190.00	305

The Ron Lee Looney Tunes Collection - R. Lee

YEAR ISSUE		EDITION LIMIT	YEAR RETD.	ISSUE PRICE	*QUOTE U.S.$
1991	1940 Bugs Bunny LT165	Closed	N/A	85.00	90
1991	Bugs Bunny LT150	Closed	N/A	123.00	125
1991	Daffy Duck LT140	Closed	N/A	80.00	80-85
1991	Elmer Fudd LT125	Closed	N/A	87.00	87-90
1991	Foghorn Leghorn & Henry Hawk LT160	Closed	N/A	115.00	115
1991	Marvin the Martian LT170	Closed	N/A	75.00	75
1991	Michigan J. Frog LT110	Closed	N/A	115.00	115
1991	Mt. Yosemite LT180	850		160.00	160-300
1991	Pepe LePew & Penelope LT145	Closed	N/A	115.00	115
1991	Porky Pig LT115	Closed	N/A	97.00	97-100
1991	Sylvester & Tweety LT135	Closed	N/A	110.00	110-115
1991	Tasmanian Devil LT120	Closed	N/A	105.00	105
1991	Tweety LT155	Closed	N/A	110.00	110-115
1991	Western Daffy Duck LT105	Closed	N/A	87.00	90
1991	Wile E. Coyote & Roadrunner LT175	Closed	N/A	165.00	175
1991	Yosemite Sam LT130	Closed	N/A	110.00	110

The Ron Lee Looney Tunes II Collection - R. Lee

YEAR ISSUE		EDITION LIMIT	YEAR RETD.	ISSUE PRICE	*QUOTE U.S.$
1992	Beep Beep LT220	1,500		115.00	115
1992	Ditty Up LT200	2,750		110.00	110
1992	For Better or Worse LT190	1,500		285.00	285
1992	Leopold & Giovanni LT205	1,500		225.00	225
1992	No Pain No Gain LT210	950		270.00	270
1992	Rackin' Frackin' Varmint LT225	950		260.00	260
1992	Speedy Gonzales LT185	2,750		73.00	73
1992	Van Duck LT230	950		335.00	335
1992	The Virtuosos LT235	950		350.00	350
1992	What The ...? LT195	1,500		240.00	240
1992	What's up Doc? LT215	950		270.00	270

The Ron Lee Looney Tunes III Collection - R. Lee

YEAR ISSUE		EDITION LIMIT	YEAR RETD.	ISSUE PRICE	*QUOTE U.S.$
1992	Bugs Bunny w/ Horse LT245	1,500		105.00	105
1992	Cowboy Bugs LT290	1,500		70.00	70
1992	Daffy Duck w/ Horse LT275	1,500		105.00	105
1992	Elmer Fudd w/ Horse LT270	1,500		105.00	105
1992	Pepe Le Pew w/ Horse LT285	1,500		105.00	105
1992	Porky Pig w/ Horse LT260	1,500		105.00	105
1992	Sylvester w/ Horse LT250	1,500		105.00	105
1992	Tasmanian Devil w/ Horse LT255	1,500		105.00	105
1992	Wile E. Coyote w/ Horse LT280	1,500		105.00	105
1992	Yosemite Sam w/ Horse LT265	1,500		105.00	105

The Ron Lee Looney Tunes IV Collection - R. Lee

YEAR ISSUE		EDITION LIMIT	YEAR RETD.	ISSUE PRICE	*QUOTE U.S.$
1993	Bugs LT330	1,200		79.00	79
1993	A Christmas Carrot LT320	1,200		175.00	175
1993	The Essence of Love LT310	1,200		145.00	145
1993	Martian's Best Friend LT305	1,200		140.00	140
1993	Me Deliver LT295	1,200		110.00	110
1993	Puttin' on the Glitz LT325	1,200		79.00	79
1993	The Rookie LT315	1,200		75.00	75
1993	Yo-Ho-Ho- LT300	1,200		105.00	105

The Ron Lee Looney Tunes V Collection - R. Lee

YEAR ISSUE		EDITION LIMIT	YEAR RETD.	ISSUE PRICE	*QUOTE U.S.$
1994	Bugs LT330	1,200		79.00	79
1994	A Carrot a Day LT350	1,200		85.00	85
1994	Guilty LT345	1,200		80.00	80
1994	Ma Cherie LT340	1,200		185.00	185
1994	No H20 LT355	1,200		160.00	160
1994	Puttin' on the Glitz LT325	1,200		79.00	79
1994	Smashing LT335	1,200		80.00	80
1994	Taz On Ice LT360	1,200		115.00	115

The Ron Lee Looney Tunes VI Collection - R. Lee

YEAR ISSUE		EDITION LIMIT	YEAR RETD.	ISSUE PRICE	*QUOTE U.S.$
1994	Bugs Pharoah LT370	500		130.00	130
1994	Cleopatra's Barge LT400	500		550.00	550
1994	Cruising Down the Nile LT385	500		295.00	295
1994	King Bugs and Friends LT395	500		480.00	480
1994	Ramases & Son LT380	500		230.00	230
1994	Tweety Pharoah LT365	500		110.00	110
1994	Warrior Taz LT375	500		140.00	140
1994	Yosemite's Chariot LT390	500		310.00	310

The Ron Lee Looney Tunes VII Collection - R. Lee

YEAR ISSUE		EDITION LIMIT	YEAR RETD.	ISSUE PRICE	*QUOTE U.S.$
1995	The Baron LT475	750		235.00	235
1995	Daffy Scuba Diving LT470	750		170.00	170
1995	Drive..Drive!! Putt..Putt!! LT450	750		120.00	120
1995	The Great Chase LT485	750		385.00	385
1995	Highway My Way LT460	750		280.00	280
1995	The Hustler LT465	750		397.00	397
1995	Ice Dancing LT440	750		180.00	180
1995	King Pin LT445	750		165.00	165
1995	Slam Dunk LT455	750		190.00	190
1995	Speedy Tweety LT480	750		225.00	225

The Ron Lee Looney Tunes Western Collection - R. Lee

YEAR ISSUE		EDITION LIMIT	YEAR RETD.	ISSUE PRICE	*QUOTE U.S.$
1995	Acme Junction LT435	500		290.00	290
1995	Bwanding Iron LT420	500		210.00	210
1995	Heap Big Chief LT415	500		230.00	230
1995	Lit'l Trooper LT405	500		157.00	157
1995	Roadrunner Express LT425	500		240.00	240
1995	Saturday Serenade LT430	500		255.00	255
1995	Whoa!! LT410	500		215.00	215

The Ron Lee Warner Bros. Collection - R. Lee

YEAR ISSUE		EDITION LIMIT	YEAR RETD.	ISSUE PRICE	*QUOTE U.S.$
1995	Animaniacs WBA100	750		170.00	170
1993	Courtly Gent WB003	1,000		102.00	102
1992	Dickens' Christmas WB400	850		198.00	198
1993	Duck Dodgers WB005	1,000		300.00	300
1993	Gridiron Glory WB002	1,000		102.00	102
1993	Hair-Raising Hare WB006	1,000		300.00	300
1993	Hare Under Par WB001	1,000		102.00	102
1993	Home Plate Heroes WB004	1,000		102.00	102
1991	The Maltese Falcon WB100	Closed	N/A	175.00	175
1995	Pinky And The Brain WB105	750		170.00	170
1991	Robin Hood Bugs WB200	1,000		190.00	190
1992	Yankee Doodle Bugs WB300	850		195.00	195

Shriner Clowns - R. Lee

YEAR ISSUE		EDITION LIMIT	YEAR RETD.	ISSUE PRICE	*QUOTE U.S.$
1994	Bubbles L437	1,750		120.00	120
1994	Helping Hand L436	1,750		145.00	145

Sports & Professionals - R. Lee

YEAR ISSUE		EDITION LIMIT	YEAR RETD.	ISSUE PRICE	*QUOTE U.S.$
1994	The Baseball Player L448	2,500		77.00	77
1994	The Basketball Player L450	2,500		74.00	74
1994	The Chef L441	2,500		74.00	74
1994	The Dentist L446	2,500		70.00	70
1994	The Doctor L439	2,500		70.00	70
1994	The Fireman L444	2,500		90.00	90
1994	The Fisherman L452	2,500		77.00	77
1994	The Football Player L449	2,500		74.00	74
1994	The Golfer L447	2,500		77.00	77
1994	The Hockey Player L454	2,500		80.00	80
1994	The Lawyer L445	2,500		70.00	70
1994	The Nurse L443	2,500		74.00	74
1994	The Pilot L440	2,500		74.00	74
1994	The Policeman L442	2,500		77.00	77
1994	The Skier L453	2,500		77.00	77
1994	The Teacher L438	2,500		70.00	70
1994	The Tennis Player L451	2,500		74.00	74

Superman I - R. Lee

YEAR ISSUE		EDITION LIMIT	YEAR RETD.	ISSUE PRICE	*QUOTE U.S.$
1993	Help Is On The Way SP100	750	1995	280.00	280
1993	Meteor Moment SP115	750	1995	314.00	314
1993	Metropolis SP110	750	1995	320.00	320
1993	Proudly We Wave SP105	750	1995	185.00	185

Superman II - R. Lee

YEAR ISSUE		EDITION LIMIT	YEAR RETD.	ISSUE PRICE	*QUOTE U.S.$
1994	Good and Evil SP135	750	1995	190.00	190
1994	More Powerful SP130	750	1995	420.00	420
1994	Quick Change SP120	750	1995	125.00	125
1994	To The Rescue SP125	750	1995	195.00	195

The Wizard of Oz Collection - R. Lee

YEAR ISSUE		EDITION LIMIT	YEAR RETD.	ISSUE PRICE	*QUOTE U.S.$
1992	The Cowardly Lion WZ425	750		620.00	620
1992	Kansas WZ400	750		550.00	550
1992	The Munchkins WZ405	750		620.00	620
1992	The Ruby Slippers WZ410	750		620.00	620
1992	The Scarecrow WZ415	750		510.00	510
1992	The Tin Man WZ420	750		530.00	530

Wizard of Oz II - R. Lee

YEAR ISSUE		EDITION LIMIT	YEAR RETD.	ISSUE PRICE	*QUOTE U.S.$
1994	The Cowardly Lion WZ445	500		130.00	130
1994	Dorothy WZ430	500		150.00	150
1994	Glinda WZ455	500		225.00	225
1994	The Scarecrow WZ435	500		130.00	130
1994	The Tinman WZ440	500		110.00	110
1994	The Wicked Witch WZ450	500		125.00	125

The Woody Woodpecker And Friends Collection - R. Lee

YEAR ISSUE		EDITION LIMIT	YEAR RETD.	ISSUE PRICE	*QUOTE U.S.$
1992	1940 Woody Woodpecker WL020	1,750		73.00	75
1992	Andy and Miranda Panda WL025	1,750		140.00	150
1992	Birdy for Woody WL005	1,750		117.00	125
1992	Pals WL030	1,750		179.00	190
1992	Peck of My Heart WL010	1,750		370.00	425
1992	Woody Woodpecker WL015	1,750		73.00	73

Royal Doulton

Royal Doulton Collectors' Club - N/A

YEAR ISSUE		EDITION LIMIT	YEAR RETD.	ISSUE PRICE	*QUOTE U.S.$
1980	John Doulton Jug (8 O'Clock) D6656	Yr.Iss.		70.00	125
1981	Sleepy Darling Figure HN2953	Yr.Iss.		100.00	195
1982	Dog of Fo-Flambe	Yr.Iss.		50.00	150
1982	Prized Possessions Figure HN2942	Yr.Iss.		125.00	450
1983	Loving Cup	Yr.Iss.		75.00	150
1983	Springtime HN3033	Yr.Iss.		125.00	325
1984	Sir Henry Doulton Jug D6703	Yr.Iss.		50.00	115
1984	Pride & Joy Figure HN2945	Yr.Iss.		125.00	275
1985	Top of the Hill Plate HN2126	Yr.Iss.		35.00	100
1985	Wintertime Figure HN3060	Yr.Iss.		125.00	225
1986	Albert Sagger Toby Jug	Yr.Iss.		35.00	85
1986	Auctioneer Figure HN2988	Yr.Iss.		150.00	300-350
1987	Collector Bunnykins	Yr.Iss.		40.00	350-450
1987	Summertime Figurine HN3137	Yr.Iss.		140.00	150
1988	Top of the Hill Miniature Figurine HN2126	Yr.Iss.		95.00	125
1988	Beefeater Tiny Jug	Yr.Iss.		25.00	125
1988	Old Salt Tea Pot	Yr.Iss.		135.00	300
1989	Geisha Flambe Figure HN3229	Yr.Iss.		195.00	195
1989	Flower Sellers Children Plate	Yr.Iss.		65.00	70-100
1990	Autumntime Figure HN3231	Yr.Iss.		190.00	195
1990	Jester Mini Figure HN3196	Yr.Iss.		115.00	115
1990	Old King Cole Tiny Jug	Yr.Iss.		35.00	35
1991	Bunny's Bedtime Figure HN3370	Yr.Iss.		195.00	215
1991	Charles Dickens Jug D6901	Yr.Iss.		100.00	125
1991	L'Ambiteuse Figure (Tissot Lady)	Yr.Iss.		295.00	385
1991	Christopher Columbus Jug D6911	Yr.Iss.		95.00	125
1992	Discovery Figure HN3428	Yr.Iss.		160.00	100
1992	King Edward Jug D6923	Yr.Iss.		250.00	260
1992	Master Potter Bunnykins DB131	Yr.Iss.		50.00	110
1992	Eliza Farren Prestige Figure HN3442	Yr.Iss.		335.00	250-325
1993	Barbara Figure	Yr.Iss.		285.00	350-450
1993	Lord Mountbatten L/S Jug	N/A		225.00	225
1993	Punch & Judy Double Sided Jug	2,500		400.00	465
1993	Flambe Dragon HN3552	N/A		260.00	260
1994	Diane HN3604	N/A		250.00	250

Age of Innocence - N. Pedley

YEAR ISSUE		EDITION LIMIT	YEAR RETD.	ISSUE PRICE	*QUOTE U.S.$
1991	Feeding Time HN3373	9,500	1994	245.00	390
1992	First Outing HN3377	9,500	1994	275.00	390
1991	Making Friends HN3372	9,500	1994	270.00	390
1991	Puppy Love HN3371	9,500	1994	270.00	390

Beatrix Potter Figures - Various

YEAR ISSUE		EDITION LIMIT	YEAR RETD.	ISSUE PRICE	*QUOTE U.S.$
1992	And This Pig Had None P3319 - M. Alcock	Open		29.95	33
1971	Appley Dapply P2333 - A. Hallam	Open		29.95	33
1970	Aunt Pettitoes P2276 - A. Hallam	Retrd.	1993	29.95	45-75
1989	Babbity Bumble P2971 - W. Platt	Retrd.	1993	29.95	75
1992	Benjamin Ate a Lettuce Leaf P3317 - M. Alcock	Open		29.95	33
1948	Benjamin Bunny P1105 - A. Gredington	Open		29.95	33
1983	Benjamin Bunny Sat on a Bank P2803 - D. Lyttleton	Open		29.95	33
1975	Benjamin Bunny with Peter Rabbit P2509 - A. Musiankowski	Retrd.	1995	39.95	50
1995	Benjamin Bunny-large size P3403 - M. Alcock	Open		65.00	73
1991	Benjamin Wakes Up P3234 - A. Hughes-Lubeck	Open		29.95	33
1965	Cecily Parsley P1941 - A. Gredington	Retrd.	1993	29.95	45-85
1979	Chippy Hackee P2627 - D. Lyttleton	Retrd.	1993	29.95	49-55
1991	Christmas Stocking P3257 - M. Alcock	Retrd.	1994	65.00	65
1985	Cottontail at Lunchtime P2878 - D. Lyttleton	Open		29.95	33
1970	Cousin Ribby P2284 - A. Hallam	Retrd.	1993	29.95	45-65
1982	Diggory Diggory Delvet P2713 - D. Lyttleton	Open		29.95	33
1995	F.W. Gent-large size P3450 - M. Alcock	Open		65.00	73
1977	Fierce Bad Rabbit P2586 - D. Lyttleton	Open		29.95	33
1954	Flopsy Mopsy and Cottontail P1274 - A. Gredington	Open		29.95	33
1990	Foxy Reading Country News P3219 - A. Hughes-Lubeck	Open		49.95	55
1954	Foxy Whiskered Gentleman P1277 - A. Gredington	Open		29.95	33
1990	Gentleman Mouse Made a Bow P3200 - T. Chawner	Open		29.95	33
1986	Goody and Timmy Tiptoes P2957 - D. Lyttleton	Open		49.95	55
1961	Goody Tiptoes P1675 - A. Gredington	Open		29.95	33
1951	Hunca Munca P1198 - A. Gredington	Open		29.95	33
1992	Hunca Munca Spills the Beads P3288 - M. Alcock	Open		29.95	33
1977	Hunca Munca Sweeping P2584 - D. Lyttleton	Open		29.95	33
1990	Jemema Puddleduck-Foxy Whiskered Gentleman P3193 - T. Chawner	Open		55.00	55
1983	Jemima Puddleduck Made a Feather Nest-P2823 - D. Lyttleton	Open		29.95	33
1948	Jemima Puddleduck P1092 - A. Gredington	Open		29.95	33
1993	Jemima Puddleduck-Large size P3373 - M. Alcock	Open		49.95	73
1988	Jeremy Fisher Digging P3090 - T. Chawner	Retrd.	1994	50.00	75
1950	Jeremy Fisher P1157 - A. Gredington	Open		29.95	33
1995	Jeremy Fisher-large size P3372 - M. Alcock	Open		65.00	73
1990	John Joiner P2965 - G. Tongue	Open		29.95	33
1954	Johnny Townmouse P1276 - A. Gredington	Retrd.	1993	29.95	45-55
1988	Johnny Townmouse with Bag P3094 - T. Chawner	Retrd.	1994	50.00	75
1990	Lady Mouse Made a Curtsy P3220 - A. Hughes-Lubeck	Open		29.95	33
1950	Lady Mouse P1183 - A. Gredington	Open		29.95	33
1977	Little Black Rabbit P2585 - D. Lyttleton	Open		29.95	33
1987	Little Pig Robinson Spying P3031 - T. Chawner	Retrd.	1993	29.95	95

*Quotes have been rounded up to nearest dollar

YEAR ISSUE		EDITION LIMIT	YEAR RETD.	ISSUE PRICE	*QUOTE U.S.$
1991	Miss Dormouse P3251 - M. Alcock	Retrd.	1995	29.95	65
1990	Mittens & Moppet P3197 - T. Chawner	Retrd.	1994	50.00	50
1989	Mother Ladybird P2966 - W. Platt	Open		29.95	33
1973	Mr. Alderman Ptolemy P2424 - G. Tongue	Open		29.95	33
1965	Mr. Benjamin Bunny P1940 - A. Gredington	Open		29.95	33
1979	Mr. Drake Puddleduck P2628 - D. Lyttleton	Open		29.95	33
1974	Mr. Jackson P2453 - A. Hallam	Open		29.95	33
1988	Mr. Tod P3091 - T. Chawner	Retrd.	1993	29.95	95
1965	Mrs. Flopsy Bunny P1942 - A. Gredington	Open		29.95	33
1992	Mrs. Rabbit Cooking P3278 - M. Alcock	Open		29.95	33
1951	Mrs. Rabbit P1200 - A. Gredington	Open		29.95	33
1976	Mrs. Rabbit with Bunnies P2543 - D. Lyttleton	Open		29.95	33
1995	Mrs. Rabbit-large size P3398 - M. Alcock	Open		65.00	73
1951	Mrs. Ribby P1199 - A. Gredington	Open		29.95	33
1948	Mrs. Tittlemouse P1103 - A. Gredington	Retrd.	1993	29.95	45-55
1992	No More Twist P3325 - M. Alcock	Open		29.95	33
1986	Old Mr. Bouncer P2956 - D. Lyttleton	Retrd.	1995	29.95	30
1963	Old Mr. Brown P1796 - A. Hallam	Open		29.95	33
1983	Old Mr. Pricklepin P2767 - N/A	Retrd.	1982	29.95	115-125
1959	Old Woman Who Lived in a Shoe P1545 - C. Melbourne	Open		29.95	33
1983	Old Woman Who Lived in a Shoe, Knitting P2804 - D. Lyttleton	Open		29.95	33
1991	Peter & The Red Handkerchief P3242 - M. Alcock	Open		39.95	43
1995	Peter in Bed P3473 - M. Alcock	Open		39.95	43
1989	Peter Rabbit in the Gooseberry Net P3157 - D. Lyttleton	Retrd.	1995	39.95	50
1948	Peter Rabbit P1098 - A. Gredington	Open		29.95	33
1993	Peter Rabbit-large size P3356 - M. Alcock	Open		65.00	73
1971	Pickles P2334 - N/A	Retrd.	1982	29.95	375-675
1948	Pig Robinson P1104 - A. Gredington	Open		29.95	33
1955	Pigling Bland P1365 - G. Orwell	Open		29.95	33
1991	Pigling Eats Porridge P3252 - M. Alcock	Retrd.	1994	50.00	50
1976	Poorly Peter Rabbit P2560 - D. Lyttleton	Open		29.95	33
1981	Rebeccah Puddleduck P2647 - D. Lyttleton	Open		29.95	33
1992	Ribby and the Patty Pan P3280 - M. Alcock	Open		29.95	33
1974	Sally Henry Penney P2452 - A. Hallam	Retrd.	1993	29.95	65-75
1948	Samuel Whiskers P1106 - A. Gredington	Retrd.	1995	29.95	30
1948	Squirrel Nutkin P1102 - A. Gredington	Open		29.95	33
1961	Tabitha Twitchitt P1676 - A. Gredington	Retrd.	1995	29.95	30
1976	Tabitha Twitchitt with Miss Moppett P2544 - D. Lyttleton	Retrd.	1993	29.95	75-95
1949	Tailor of Gloucester P1108 - A. Gredington	Open		29.95	33
1995	Tailor of Gloucester-large size P3449 - M. Alcock	Open		65.00	73
1948	Tiggy Winkle P1107 - A. Gredington	Open		29.95	33
1985	Tiggy Winkle Takes Tea P2877 - D. Lyttleton	Open		29.95	33
1948	Timmy Tiptoes P1101 - A. Gredington	Open		29.95	33
1949	Timmy Willie P1109 - A. Gredington	Retrd.	1993	29.95	45-195
1986	Timmy Willie Sleeping P2996 - G. Tongue	Open		29.95	33
1948	Tom Kitten P1100 - A. Gredington	Open		29.95	33
1995	Tom Kitten-large size P3405 - M. Alcock	Open		65.00	73
1987	Tom Kitten and Butterfly P3030 - T. Chawner	Retrd.	1994	50.00	50
1987	Tom Thumb P2989 - W. Platt	Open		29.95	33
1955	Tommy Brock P1348 - G. Orwell	Open		29.95	33

British Sporting Heritage - V. Annand

1994	Ascot HN3471	5,000		475.00	475
1993	Henley HN3367	5,000		475.00	475
1995	Wimbledon HN3366	5,000		475.00	475

Bunnykins - Various

1995	Bathtime DB148 - M. Alcock	Open		40.00	40
1987	Be Prepared DB56 - D. Lyttleton	Retrd.	1995	40.00	40
1987	Bed Time DB55 - D. Lyttleton	Open		40.00	40
1991	Bride DB101 - A. Hughes	Open		40.00	40
1987	Brownie DB61 - W. Platt	Retrd.	1993	39.00	65
1990	Cook DB85- W. Platt	Retrd.	1994	35.00	40-65
1995	Easter Greetings - M. Alcock	Open		50.00	50
1988	Father, Mother, Victoria DB68 - M. Alcock	Retrd.	1995	40.00	40
1989	Fireman DB75 - M. Alcock	Open		40.00	40
1990	Fisherman DB84- W. Platt	Retrd.	1993	39.00	75-95
1991	Groom DB102 - M. Alcock	Open		40.00	40
XX	Halloween Bunnykin DB132 - N/A	Open		50.00	50
1983	Happy Birthday DB21 - G. Tongue	Open		40.00	40
1988	Harry DB73 - M. Alcock	Retrd.	1993	34.00	60
1972	Helping Mother DB2 - A Hallam	Retrd.	1993	34.00	55-75
1986	Home Run DB43 - D. Lyttleton	Retrd.	1993	39.00	70-85
1990	Ice Cream DB82 - W. Platt	Retrd.	1993	39.00	60-75
1982	Mr. Bunnykin Easter Parade DB18 - G. Tongue	Retrd.	1993	39.00	65-75
1982	Mrs. Bunnykin Easter Parade DB19 - D. Lyttleton	Retrd.	1995	40.00	40
1989	Nurse DB74 - M. Alcock	Open		35.00	40
1989	Paper Boy DB77 - M. Alcock	Retrd.	1993	39.00	65
1972	Playtime DB8 - A Hallam	Retrd.	1993	34.00	60
1988	Policeman DB69 - M. Alcock	Open		40.00	40
1988	Polly DB71 - M. Alcock	Retrd.	1993	34.00	40-65
1995	Rainy Day DB147 - M. Alcock	Open		40.00	40
1981	Santa Bunnykins DB17 - D. Lyttleton	Retrd.	1995	40.00	40
1987	School Days DB57 - D. Lyttleton	Retrd.	1994	40.00	55
1982	School Master DB60 - W. Platt	Retrd.	1995	40.00	40
1974	Sleepytime DB15 - A. Musiankowski	Retrd.	1993	39.00	65
1972	Sleigh Ride DB4 - A Hallam	Open		40.00	40
1972	Story Time DB9 - A Hallam	Open		35.00	40
1988	Susan DB70 - M. Alcock	Retrd.	1993	34.00	40-60
XX	Sweetheart Bunnykin DB130 - N/A	Open		40.00	40
1988	Tom DB72 - M. Alcock	Retrd.	1993	34.00	45-65
1986	Uncle Sam DB50 - D. Lyttleton	Open		40.00	40
1988	William DB69 - M. Alcock	Retrd.	1993	34.00	40-65

Character Jug of the Year - Various

1991	Fortune Teller D6824 - S. Taylor	Closed	1991	130.00	160-250
1992	Winston Churchill D6907 - S. Taylor	Closed	1992	195.00	195
1993	Vice-Admiral Lord Nelson D6932 - S. Taylor	Closed	1993	225.00	225
1994	Captain Hook - M. Alcock	Closed	1994	235.00	235
1995	Captain Bligh D6967 - S. Taylor	Closed	1995	200.00	235

Character Jugs - Various

1993	Abraham Lincoln - M. Alcock	2,500	1994	190.00	190
1991	Airman, sm. - W. Harper	Open		75.00	75
1995	Alfred Hitchcock D6987 - D. Biggs	Open		200.00	225
1990	Angler, sm. - S. Taylor	Retrd.	1995	82.50	83
1947	Beefeater, lg. - H. Fenton	Open		137.50	150
1947	Beefeater, sm. - H. Fenton	Open		75.00	75
1995	Charles Dickens D6939 - W. Harper	2,500		500.00	500
1989	Clown, lg.- S. Taylor	Retrd.	1995	205.00	205
1991	Columbus, lg.- S. Taylor	Open		137.50	138
1983	D'Artagnan, lg.- S. Taylor	Retrd.	1995	150.00	150
1983	D'Artagnan, sm.- S. Taylor	Retrd.	1995	82.50	83
1991	Equestrian, sm.- S. Taylor	Retrd.	1995	82.50	83
1995	George Washington - M. Alcock	2,500		200.00	225
XX	George Washington, lg. - Unknown	Retrd.	1994	150.00	150
1994	Glenn Miller - M. Alcock	Open		270.00	300
1971	Golfer, lg. - D. Biggs	Retrd.	1995	150.00	150
1993	Graduate-Male, sm.- S. Taylor	Retrd.	1995	85.00	85
1986	Guardsman, lg.- S. Taylor	Open		137.50	150
1986	Gurardsman, sm.- S. Taylor	Open		75.00	83
1990	Guy Fawkes, lg. - W. Harper	Open		137.50	150
1975	Henry VIII, lg. - E. Griffiths	Open		137.50	150
1975	Henry VIII, sm. - E. Griffiths	Open		75.00	83
1991	Jockey, sm.- S. Taylor	Retrd.	1995	82.50	83
1995	Judge and Thief Toby D6988 - S. Taylor	Open		185.00	200
1959	Lawyer, lg. - M. Henk	Open		137.50	150
1959	Lawyer, sm. - M. Henk	Open		75.00	83
1990	Leprechaun, lg. - W. Harper	Open		205.00	225
1990	Leprechaun, sm. - W. Harper	Open		75.00	85
1986	London Bobby, lg.- S. Taylor	Open		137.50	150
1986	London Bobby, sm.- S. Taylor	Open		75.00	83
1952	Long John Silver, lg. - M. Henk	Open		137.50	150
1952	Long John Silver, sm. - M. Henk	Open		75.00	83
1960	Merlin, lg. - G. Sharpe	Open		137.50	150
1960	Merlin, sm. - G. Sharpe	Open		75.00	83
1990	Modern Golfer, sm.- S. Taylor	Open		75.00	83
1955	Rip Van Winkle, lg. - M. Henk	Retrd.	1995	150.00	150
1955	Rip Van Winkle, sm. - M. Henk	Retrd.	1995	82.50	83
1991	Sailor, sm. - W. Harper	Open		75.00	83
1984	Santa Claus, lg. - M. Abberley	Open		137.50	150
1984	Santa Claus, sm. - M. Abberley	Open		75.00	83
1993	Shakespeare, sm. - W. Harper	Open		99.00	107
1973	The Sleuth, lg.- A. Moore	Open		137.50	150
1973	The Sleuth, sm. - A. Moore	Open		75.00	83
1991	Snooker Player, sm.- S. Taylor	Retrd.	1995	82.50	83
1991	Soldier, sm. - W. Harper	Open		75.00	83
1994	Thomas Jefferson - M. Alcock	2,500		200.00	225
XX	Town Crier, lg. - Unknown	Retrd.	1994	170.00	170
1993	Winston Churchill, sm.- S. Taylor	Open		99.00	107
1990	Wizard, lg.- S. Taylor- S. Taylor	Open		175.00	188
1990	Wizard, sm.- S. Taylor	Open		75.00	85
1991	Yeoman of the Guard, lg.- S. Taylor	Open		137.50	150

Character Sculptures - Various

1993	Captain Hook - R. Tabbenor	Open		250.00	269
1994	D' Artagnan - R. Tabbenor	Open		260.00	269
1993	Dick Turpin - R. Tabbenor	Open		250.00	269
1995	Gulliver - D. Biggs	Open		285.00	307
1993	Long John Silver - A. Maslankowski	Open		250.00	269
1994	Pied Piper - A. Maslankowski	Open		260.00	269
1993	Robin Hood - A. Maslankowski	Open		250.00	269

Diamond Anniversary Tinies - N/A

1994	John Barleycorn	2,500	1994	350.00	420
1994	The Cellarer	2,500	1994	set	Set
1994	Dick Turpin	2,500	1994	set	Set
1994	Granny	2,500	1994	set	Set
1994	Jester	2,500	1994	set	Set
1994	Parson Brown	2,500	1994	set	Set

Femmes Fatales - P. Davies

1979	Cleopatra HN2868	750		750.00	1350
1984	Eve HN2466	750		1250.00	1250
1981	Helen of Troy HN2387	750	1993	1250.00	1350
1985	Lucrezia Borgia HN2342	750	1993	1250.00	1250
1982	Queen of Sheba HN2328	750		1250.00	1300-1400
1983	Tz'u-Hsi HN2391	750		1250.00	1250

Figure of the Year - Various

1991	Amy HN3316 - P. Gee	Closed	1991	195.00	400-500
1992	Mary HN3375 - P. Gee	Closed	1992	225.00	375-475
1993	Patricia HN3365 - V. Annand	Closed	1993	250.00	350-475
1994	Jennifer HN3447 - P. Gee	Closed	1994	250.00	290
1995	Deborah - HN3644 - N. Pedley	Closed	1995	225.00	225

The Four Seasons - V. Annand

1993	Springtime HN3477	Open		325.00	350
1994	Summertime HN3478	Open		325.00	350
1993	Autumntime HN3621	Open		325.00	350
1993	Wintertime HN3622	Open		325.00	350

Gainsborough Ladies - P. Gee

1991	Countess of Sefton HN3010	5,000	1994	650.00	650
1991	Hon Frances Duncombe HN3009	5,000	1994	650.00	650-700
1991	Lady Sheffield HN3008	5,000	1994	650.00	650-700
1990	Mary, Countess Howe HN3007	5,000	1994	650.00	650

Great Lovers - R. Jefferson

1994	Robin Hood & Maid Marian HN3111	150		5250.00	5250
1993	Romeo and Juliet HN3113	150		5250.00	5250

Images - Various

1991	Bride & Groom HN3281 - R. Tabbenor	Open		85.00	94
1991	Bridesmaid HN3280 - R. Tabbenor	Open		85.00	94
1993	Brother & Sister HN3460 - A. Hughes	Retrd.	N/A	52.50	107
1991	Brothers HN3191 - E. Griffiths	Open		90.00	107
1981	Family HN2720 - E. Griffiths	Open		187.50	200
1988	First Love HN2747 - D. Tootle	Open		170.00	200
1991	First Steps HN3282 - R. Tabbenor	Open		142.00	200
1993	Gift of Freedom HN3443 - N/A	Open		90.00	107
1989	Happy Anniversary HN3254 - D. Tootle	Open		187.50	200
1981	Lovers HN2762 - D. Tootle	Open		187.50	200
1980	Mother & Daughter HN2841 - E. Griffiths	Open		187.50	200
1993	Our First Christmas HN3452 - N/A	Open		185.00	200
1989	Over the Threshold HN3274 - R. Tabbenor	Open		187.50	200
1983	Sisters HN3018 - P. Parson	Open		90.00	107
1987	Wedding Day HN2748 - D. Tootle	Open		187.50	200

Limited Edition Character Jugs - Various

1992	Abraham Lincoln D6936 - S. Taylor	2,500	1994	190.00	190
1994	Aladdin's Genie D6971 - D. Biggs	1,500	1994	335.00	350
1993	Clown Toby - N/A	3,000	N/A	175.00	175
1993	Elf Miniature D6942 - N/A	2,500	1994	55.00	55
XX	Father Christmas Toby - N/A	3,500	N/A	125.00	125
1990	Henry VIII - N/A	S/O	N/A	150.00	150
1991	Henry VIII - W. Harper	1,991	N/A	395.00	1000-1300
1991	Jester - S. Taylor	2,500	N/A	125.00	150
1994	King & Queen of Diamonds D6969 - J. Taylor	2,500	1994	260.00	275
1992	King Charles I D6917 - W. Harper	2,500	N/A	450.00	495
1994	Leprechaun Toby - N/A	2,500	N/A	150.00	150
1992	Mrs. Claus Miniature D6922 - N/A	2,500	N/A	50.00	55
1993	Napoleon (Lg size) D6941 - S. Taylor	2,000	1994	225.00	225
1994	Oliver Cromwell D6968 - W. Harper	2,500	1994	475.00	475
1991	Santa Claus Miniature D6900 - N/A	5,000	N/A	50.00	55
1988	Sir Francis Drake D6805 - P .Gee	S/O	N/A	N/A	100
XX	Snake Charmer - N/A	2,500	N/A	210.00	230
1994	Thomas Jefferson - N/A	2,500	N/A	200.00	225
1992	Town Crier D6895 - S. Taylor	2,500	N/A	175.00	175
1992	William Shakespeare D6933 - W. Harper	2,500	1994	625.00	635

Limited Editions - Various

1992	Christopher Columbus HN3392 - A. Maslankowski	1,492	N/A	1950.00	1950
1993	Duke of Wellington HN3432 - A. Maslankowski	1,500		1750.00	1750
1994	Field Marshal Montgomery HN3405 - N/A	1,944	N/A	1100.00	1100
1993	General Robert E. Lee HN3404 - R. Tabbenor	5,000	1995	1175.00	1175
1993	Lt. General Ulysses S. Grant HN3403 - R. Tabbenor	5,000	1995	1175.00	1175
1992	Napoleon at Waterloo HN3429 - A. Maslankowski	1,500	N/A	1900.00	1900
1993	Vice Admiral Lord Nelson HN3489 - A. Maslankowski	950		1750.00	1750
1993	Winston S. Churchill HN3433 - A. Maslankowski	5,000		595.00	595

Myths & Maidens - R. Jefferson

1986	Diana The Huntress HN2829	300	N/A	2950.00	3000
1985	Europa & Bull HN2828	300	N/A	2950.00	3000
1984	Juno & Peacock HN2827	300	N/A	2950.00	3000
1982	Lady & Unicorn HN2825	300	N/A	2500.00	2500
1983	Leda & Swan HN2826	300	N/A	2950.00	3000

Prestige Figures - Various

1982	Columbine HN2738 - D. Tootle	Open		1250.00	1350
1982	Harlequin HN2737 - D. Tootle	Open		1250.00	1350

*Quotes have been rounded up to nearest dollar

YEAR ISSUE		EDITION LIMIT	YEAR RETD.	ISSUE PRICE	*QUOTE U.S.$
1964	Indian Brave HN2376 - M. Davis	500	1993	2500.00	5500
1952	Jack Point HN2080 - C.J. Noke	Open		2900.00	3400
1950	King Charles HN2084 - C.J. Noke	Open		2500.00	2500
1964	Matador and Bull HN2324 - M. Davis	Open		21500.00	25200
1952	The Moor HN2082 - C.J. Noke	Open		2500.00	3000
1964	The Palio HN2428 - M. Davis	500	1993	2500.00	6500
1952	Princess Badoura HN2081 - N/A	Open		28000.00	33000
1978	St George and Dragon HN2856 - W.K. Harper	Open		13600.00	14500

Queens of Realm - P. Parsons

1989	Mary, Queen of Scots HN3142	S/O	N/A	550.00	850
1988	Queen Anne HN3141	S/O	N/A	525.00	700
1986	Queen Elizabeth I HN3099	S/O	N/A	495.00	700-900
1987	Queen Victoria HN3125	S/O	N/A	495.00	1100-1300
1987	Set of 4	S/O	N/A	2065.00	3000

Reynolds Collection - P. Gee

1992	Countess Harrington HN3317	5,000	N/A	550.00	595
1993	Countess Spencer HN3320	5,000	N/A	595.00	595
1991	Lady Worsley HN3318	5,000	N/A	550.00	595
1992	Mrs. Hugh Bonfoy HN3319	5,000	N/A	550.00	595

Royal Doulton Figurines - Various

1933	Beethoven - R. Garbe	25	N/A	N/A	6500
1987	Life Boatman HN2764 - W. Harper	Closed	N/A	N/A	225
1975	The Milkmaid HN2057A - L. Harradine	Closed	N/A	N/A	225
1924	Tony Weller HN684 - C. Noke	Closed	N/A	N/A	1800

Royalty - Various

1986	Duchess Of York HN3086 - E. Griffiths	1,500		495.00	750
1981	Duke Of Edinburgh HN2386 - P. Davis	750		395.00	450
1982	Lady Diana Spencer HN2885 - E. Griffiths	1,500		395.00	600
1981	Prince Of Wales HN2883 - E. Griffiths	1,500		395.00	750
1981	Prince Of Wales HN2884 - E. Griffiths	1,500		750.00	1000
1982	Princess Of Wales HN2887 - E. Griffiths	1,500		750.00	1300-1700
1973	Queen Elizabeth II HN2502 - P. Davis	750		N/A	1800
1982	Queen Elizabeth II HN2878 - E. Griffiths	2,500		N/A	450
1992	Queen Elizabeth II, 2nd. Version HN3440 - P. Gee	3,500		460.00	460
1989	Queen Elizabeth, the Queen Mother as the Duchess of York HN3230 - P. Parsons	9,500		N/A	450
1990	Queen Elizabeth, the Queen Mother HN3189 - E. Griffiths	2,500		N/A	450
1980	Queen Mother HN2882 - P. Davis	1,500		650.00	1250

Salvino Inc.

Collector Club Figurines - Salvino

1993	6" Mario Lemieux-Painted Away Uniform (Unsigned)	Closed	N/A	70.00	90
1993	Joe Montana-"KC" Away Uniform (Hand Signed)	Closed	N/A	275.00	275

Boston Celtic Greats - Salvino

1991	Larry Bird	S/O	N/A	285.00	395
1993	Larry Bird (Special Edition)	S/O	N/A	375.00	400-450

Boxing Greats - Salvino

1990	Muhammed Ali	S/O	N/A	250.00	250
1990	Muhammed Ali (Special Edition)	S/O	N/A	375.00	350-700

Brooklyn Dodger - Salvino

1989	Don Drysdale	S/O	N/A	185.00	200-300
1989	Don Drysdale AP	300		200.00	400
1993	Duke Snider	1,000		275.00	275
1990	Roy Campanella	2,000		395.00	350-500
1990	Roy Campanella (Special Edition)	S/O	N/A	550.00	500
1989	Sandy Koufax	S/O	N/A	195.00	225-300
1989	Sandy Koufax AP	500		250.00	400

Collegiate Series - Salvino

1992	Joe Montana	S/O	N/A	275.00	325
1992	OJ Simpson	1,000		275.00	350

Dealer Special Series - Salvino

1992	Joe Namath	S/O	N/A	700.00	700
1992	Mickey Mantle #6	S/O	N/A	700.00	1350
1992	Mickey Mantle #7	S/O	N/A	700.00	1400
1993	Willie Mays	S/O	N/A	700.00	700

Heroes of the Diamond - Salvino

1993	Brooks Robinson	1,000		275.00	275
1992	Mickey Mantle Batting	S/O	N/A	395.00	595-700
1992	Mickey Mantle Batting-Right Hand (Away)	S/O	N/A	545.00	695-995
1992	Mickey Mantle Batting-Right Hand (Home)	S/O	N/A	545.00	895-995
1992	Mickey Mantle Fielding	S/O	N/A	395.00	595-700
1991	Rickey Henderson (Away)	600		275.00	275
1991	Rickey Henderson (Home)	S/O	N/A	275.00	275
1991	Rickey Henderson (Special Edition)	550		375.00	375
1992	Willie Mays New York	750		395.00	395
1992	Willie Mays San Francisco	750		395.00	395

Hockey Greats - Salvino

1991	Mario Lemieux	S/O	N/A	275.00	300-600
1992	Mario Lemieux (Special Editon)	S/O	N/A	285.00	400
1994	Wayne Gretzky	S/O	N/A	395.00	395

NFL Superstar - Salvino

1990	Jim Brown	S/O	N/A	275.00	275-325
1990	Jim Brown (Special Edition)	S/O	N/A	525.00	450-550
1990	Joe Montana	S/O	N/A	275.00	275-325
1990	Joe Montana (Special Edition)	S/O	N/A	395.00	395
1993	Joe Montana 49'er	1,000		275.00	275
1993	Joe Montana Chiefs	450		275.00	400
1990	Joe Namath	2,500		275.00	275
1990	Joe Namath (Special Edition)	500		375.00	375-475
1990	OJ Simpson	1,000		250.00	300-400

Racing Legends - Salvino

1991	AJ Foyt	S/O	N/A	250.00	250
1991	Darrell Waltrip	S/O	N/A	250.00	250
1991	Richard Petty	S/O	N/A	250.00	250
1991	Richard Petty (Special Edition)	S/O	N/A	279.00	350-400
1993	Richard Petty Farewell Tour	2,500		275.00	275

Sarah's Attic, Inc.

Collector's Club Promotion - Sarah's Attic

1991	Diamond 3497	Closed	1992	36.00	100
1991	Ruby 3498	Closed	1992	42.00	150
1992	Christmas Love Santa 3522	Closed	1992	45.00	65
1992	Forever Frolicking Friends 3523	Closed	1992	Gift	75
1992	Love One Another 3561	Closed	1992	60.00	60
1992	Sharing Dreams 3562	Closed	1993	75.00	100
1992	Life Time Friends 3563	Closed	1993	75.00	125
1992	Love Starts With Children 3607	Closed	1993	Gift	75
1993	First Forever Friend Celebration 3903	Closed	1993	50.00	50
1993	Pledge of Allegiance 3749	Closed	1993	45.00	90
1993	Love Starts With Children II 3837	Closed	1994	Gift	65
1993	Gem Wh. Girl w/Basket 3842	Closed	1994	33.00	150
1993	Rocky Bl. Boy w/Marbles 3843	Closed	1994	25.00	65
1994	America Boy 4191	Closed	1994	25.00	25
1994	America Girl 4192	Closed	1994	25.00	25
1994	Forever Friends 4286	Closed	1994	45.00	45
1994	Saturday Night Round Up 4232	Closed	1995	Gift	25
1994	Billy Bob 4233	Closed	1995	38.00	38
1994	Jimmy Dean 4234	Closed	1995	38.00	38
1994	Sally/Jack 4235	Closed	1995	55.00	55
1994	Ellie/T.J. 4236	Closed	1995	55.00	55
1995	Flags in Heaven 4386	Closed	1995	45.00	45
1995	Friends Forever 4444	12/96		60.00	60
1995	Playtime Pals 4446	2/97		65.00	70
1995	Horsin' around 4445	2/97		65.00	65
1996	Abigail 4543	12/96		36.00	36
1996	Aretha 4542	12/96		36.00	36

Angels In The Attic - Sarah's Attic

1989	Abbee-Angel-2336	Closed	1991	10.00	20
1990	Adora Girl Angel Standing 3276	4,000	1990	35.00	125-150
1994	Adora w/Harp 4137	4,000		26.00	26
1991	Angel Adora With Bunny 3390	Closed	1993	50.00	65
1991	Angel Enos With Frog 3391	10,000	1993	50.00	65
1989	Angelica Angel 3201	6,000	1992	25.00	25
1996	Angels on Assignment 4544	12/96		65.00	65
1996	April-Wh. Angel 4514	4,000		40.00	40
1989	Ashbee-Angel 2337	Closed	1991	10.00	25
1991	Bert Angel 3416	1,000	1992	60.00	120
1989	Bevie-Angel 2361	Closed	1990	10.00	10
1990	Billi-Angel 3295	Closed	1991	18.00	22
1993	Blessed is He 3952	1,994	1994	48.00	120
1994	Blessed is He II 4189	2,500		66.00	75
1995	Blessed is He III 4387	4,000		60.00	60
1990	Buster-Angel 3302	Closed	1991	15.00	15
1994	Casey Angel 4245	2,050		32.00	32
1990	Cindi-Angel 3296	Closed	1991	18.00	22
1989	Clyde-Angel 2329	Closed	1991	17.00	20
1992	Contentment 3500	500	1992	100.00	200
1995	Dignity 4330	Open		55.00	55
1992	Enos & Adora-Small 3671	5,000	1993	35.00	60-125
1990	Enos Boy Angel Sitting 3275	4,000	1990	33.00	100
1994	Enos w/Horn 4138	4,000		26.00	26
1993	Faith-Bl. Angel 3953	1,994		40.00	40
1996	Faith-Bl. Angel 4522	3,000		70.00	70
1996	Faith-Wh. Angel 4523	3,000		70.00	70
1989	Floppy-Angel 2330	Closed	1990	10.00	20
1990	Flossy-Angel 3301	Closed	1991	15.00	24
1993	Grace-Wh. Angel 3954	1,994	1995	40.00	40
1989	Gramps Angel 2357	Closed	1990	17.00	40
1989	Grams Angel 2356	Closed	1990	17.00	40
1992	Harmony Angel 3710	3,500	1994	26.00	26
1992	Heavenly Caring 3661	2,500	1993	70.00	90
1992	Heavenly Giving 3663	Closed	1993	70.00	90
1989	Heavenly Guardian 3213	6,000	1990	40.00	40
1992	Heavenly Loving 3664	2,500	1993	70.00	90
1993	Heavenly Peace 3833	2,500	1994	47.00	50
1993	Heavenly Protecting 3795	2,500	1994	40.00	40
1992	Heavenly Sharing 3662	2,500	1993	70.00	90
1993	Heavenly Uniting 3794	2,500	1994	45.00	45
1992	Hope Angel 3659	Closed	1994	40.00	45
1994	Jonathon Angel 4253	2,050		32.00	32
1994	Jovae Angel 4252	2,050		32.00	32
1992	Joy Angel 3711	3,500	1994	26.00	26
1996	Karissa Wh. Angel 4480	1,200	1996	34.00	34
1996	Karita Bl. Angel 4479	1,200	1996	34.00	34
1994	Lacy Angel 4244	2,050		32.00	32
1990	Lena-Angel 3297	Closed	1991	36.00	40
1995	LOL - Baby Bl. Girl 4288	Open		25.00	25
1995	LOL - Beach Wh. Boy 4302	Closed	1995	29.00	29
1995	LOL - Birthday Wh. Girl 4299	Open		29.00	29
1995	LOL - Birthday Bl. Boy 4301	Open		29.00	29
1995	LOL - Birthday Bl. Girl 4290	Open		29.00	29
1995	LOL - Birthday Wh. Boy 4303	Open		29.00	29
1995	LOL - Blk Boy Stocking 4436	Open		18.00	18
1995	LOL - Blk Boy Trumpet 4432	Open		18.00	18
1995	LOL - Blk Girl Wreath 4435	Open		18.00	18
1995	LOL - Bottle Wh. Girl 4306	Closed	1995	29.00	29
1995	LOL - Campfire Wh. Girl 4293	Closed	1995	29.00	29
1995	LOL - Canning Wh. Girl 4297	Closed	1995	29.00	29
1996	LOL - Computer BG 4486	Open		29.00	29
1995	LOL - Computer Bl. Boy 4304	Open		29.00	29
1996	LOL - Computer Wh. Boy 4487	Open		29.00	29
1996	LOL - Computer Wh. Girl 4488	Open		29.00	29
1995	LOL - Fishing Bl. Boy 4300	Open		29.00	29
1995	LOL - Golfing Bl. Boy 4308	Open		29.00	29
1996	LOL - Golfing Wh. Boy 4490	Open		29.00	29
1995	LOL - Growing Bl. Girl 4305	Open		29.00	29
1995	LOL - Happiness Wh. Girl 4291	Open		29.00	29
1995	LOL - Heals Bl. Girl 4292	Open		29.00	29
1995	LOL - Ironing Wh. Girl 4289	Open		29.00	29
1995	LOL - Mechanic Wh. Boy 4298	Closed	1995	29.00	29
1995	LOL - Mowing Bl. Boy 4296	Closed	1995	29.00	29
1995	LOL - Planting Wh. Girl 4287	Open		29.00	29
1995	LOL - Roller Blading Wh. Boy 4309	Open		29.00	29
1995	LOL - Sending Smiles Bl. Girl 4307	Open		29.00	29
1995	LOL - Sewing Bl. Girl 4295	Open		29.00	29
1996	LOL - Sewing Wh. Girl 4489	Open		29.00	29
1995	LOL - Studying Bl. Boy 4294	Open		25.00	25
1995	LOL - Tools Wh. Boy 4310	Closed	1995	29.00	29
1995	LOL - Wh. Boy Wreath 4434	Open		18.00	18
1995	LOL - Wh. Girl Praying 4431	Open		18.00	18
1995	LOL - Wh. Girl Stocking 4433	Open		18.00	18
1995	LOL Mini- Bl. Boy, blue 4383	Open		12.00	12
1995	LOL Mini- Bl. Boy, gold 4382	Open		12.00	12
1995	LOL Mini- Bl. Girl, gold 4378	Open		12.00	12
1995	LOL Mini- Bl. Girl, pink 4379	Open		12.00	12
1995	LOL Mini- Wh. Boy, blue 4385	Open		12.00	12
1995	LOL Mini- Wh. Boy, gold 4384	Open		12.00	12
1995	LOL Mini- Wh. Girl, gold 4380	Open		12.00	12
1995	LOL Mini- Wh. Girl, pink 4381	Open		12.00	12
1995	Louise Angel 4472	2,500		34.00	34
1990	Louise-Angel 3300	Closed	1991	17.00	24
1992	Love 3501	500	1992	80.00	200
1995	Love 4328	Open		40.00	40
1996	May-Bl. Angel 4515	4,000		40.00	40
1992	Noble Angel 3712	3,500	1994	24.00	24
1995	Prayer of Love 4437	500	1995	85.00	170
1992	Priscilla-Angel 3511	5,000	1993	46.00	60
1995	Respect 4329	Open		32.00	32
1993	Risen Christ 3931	1,994	1995	48.00	48
1989	Saint Willie Bill 2360	Closed	1991	30.00	40
1992	Sincerity Angel 3713	3,500	1994	24.00	24
1989	St. Anne 2323	Closed	1991	29.00	32
1989	St. Gabbe 2322	Closed	1991	30.00	33
1990	Trapper-Angel 3299	Closed	1991	17.00	40
1989	Wendall-Angel 2324	Closed	1991	10.00	45
1989	Wilbur-Angel 2327	Closed	1991	10.00	25
1995	Willie Bill Angel 4471	2,500		34.00	34

Beary Adorables Collection - Sarah's Attic

1987	Abbee Bear 2005	Closed	1989	6.00	12
1987	Alex Bear 2003	Closed	1989	10.00	12
1987	Amelia Bear 2004	Closed	1989	8.00	12
1988	Americana Bear 3047	Closed	1990	50.00	75
1992	Andy-Father Bear 3727	3,500	1994	20.00	2[illegible]
1989	Angel Bear 3105	Closed	1990	24.00	25
1988	Arti Boy Bear 6319	Closed	1990	7.00	15
1987	Ashbee Bear 2006	Closed	1989	6.00	12
1990	Bailey 50's Papa Bear 3250	4,000	1991	30.00	3[illegible]
1990	Belinda 50's Girl Bear 3253	4,000	1991	25.00	3[illegible]
1989	Betsy Bear w/Flag 3097	Closed	1990	22.00	4[illegible]
1990	Beulah 50's Mama Bear 3251	4,000	1991	30.00	3[illegible]
1990	Birkey 50's Boy Bear Teddy 3252	4,000	1991	25.00	2[illegible]
1988	Boy Bear Resin Candle 3070	Closed	1989	12.00	1[illegible]
1992	Brandy-Baby Bear 3728	3,500	1994	14.00	1[illegible]
1986	Collectible Bear 2035	Closed	1989	14.00	1[illegible]
1989	Colonial Bear w/Hat 3098	Closed	1990	22.00	4[illegible]
1989	Daisy Bear 3101	Closed	1990	48.00	5[illegible]
1991	Dudley Bear 3355	2,500	1990	32.00	6[illegible]
1988	Ghost Bear 3028	Closed	1989	9.00	2[illegible]
1989	Griswald Bear 3102	Closed	1990	48.00	5[illegible]
1988	Honey Ma Bear 6316	Closed	1990	16.00	2[illegible]
1988	Lefty Bear in Stocking 3049	Closed	1990	70.00	7[illegible]
1995	Love Heals All 4438	Open		28.00	2[illegible]
1992	Mandy-Mother Bear 3726	3,500	1994	20.00	2[illegible]
1988	Marti Girl Bear 6318	Closed	1990	12.00	2[illegible]
1989	Mikey Bear 3104	Closed	1990	26.00	3[illegible]
1996	Mikey-B/W 4528	2,500		60.00	6[illegible]
1996	Mikey-VG 4526	2,500		60.00	6[illegible]
1989	Missy Bear 3103	Closed	1990	26.00	3[illegible]
1996	Missy-B/W 4527	2,500		60.00	6[illegible]
1996	Missy-VG 4525	2,500		60.00	6[illegible]
1996	Proud Bear 4495	2,500		10.00	[illegible]
1988	Rufus Pa Bear 6317	Closed	1990	15.00	2[illegible]
1989	Sammy Boy Bear 3111	Closed	1990	12.00	[illegible]

*Quotes have been rounded up to nearest dollar

YEAR ISSUE		EDITION LIMIT	YEAR RETD.	ISSUE PRICE	*QUOTE U.S.$
1989	Sid Papa Bear 3092	Closed	1990	18.00	25
1989	Sophie Mama Bear 3093	Closed	1990	18.00	25
1989	Spice Bear Crawling 3109	Closed	1990	12.00	15
1989	Sugar Bear Sitting 3112	Closed	1990	12.00	12
1996	You are Special-Bear 4476	5,000		23.00	23
1996	You are Special-Bl. Girl 4477	5,000		29.00	29
1996	You are Special-Wh. Girl 4478	5,000		29.00	29

Black Heritage Collection - Sarah's Attic

YEAR ISSUE		EDITION LIMIT	YEAR RETD.	ISSUE PRICE	*QUOTE U.S.$
1995	Alicia/Yvette on Pew 4410	5,000		50.00	50
1995	Bessie Coleman 4313	2,500		50.00	50
1993	Bessie Gospel Singer 3754	2,500		40.00	40
1995	Bill Pickett 4281	2,500		56.00	56
1991	Bl. Baby Tansy 3388	Closed	1993	40.00	50
1996	Blessed is He IV 4520	2,000		70.00	70
1995	Blessed is She 4312	5,000		50.00	50
1995	Book of Wisdom 4315	4,000		52.00	52
1992	Booker T. Washington 3648	3,000	1993	80.00	100
1992	Boys Night Out 3660	2,000	1994	350.00	450-695
1993	Brewster Clapping Singer 3758	2,500	1995	27.00	27
1990	Brotherly Love 3336	5,000	1991	80.00	175
1992	Buffalo Soldier 3524	5,000	1993	80.00	125
1995	Buffalo Soldier 4285	5,000		65.00	65
1991	Caleb w/ Football 3485	6,000	1993	40.00	55
1991	Caleb w/Vegetables 3375	4,000	1991	50.00	50
1990	Caleb-Lying Down 3232	Closed	1994	23.00	35
1995	Calvin 4319	4,000		28.00	28
1992	Calvin Prayer Time 3510	5,000	1993	46.00	55
1996	Carter 4536	2,500		30.00	30
1993	Carter Woodson 3845	3,000		45.00	45
1996	Cayla 4535	2,500		36.00	36
1995	Charity 4318	4,000		28.00	28
1993	Claudia w/Tamborine Singer 3757	2,500	1995	27.00	27
1994	Coretta Scott King 4178	12/96		60.00	60
1991	Corporal Pervis 3366	8,000	1993	60.00	125
1995	Elroy Praying w/Bible 4411	5,000		25.00	25
1992	Esther w/Butter Churn 3536	Closed	1994	70.00	70
1995	Frederick Douglass 4402	2,500		55.00	55
1993	George Washington Carver 3848	3,000		45.00	45
1987	Gramps 5104	Closed	1988	16.00	100
1987	Grams 5105	Closed	1988	16.00	100
1992	Granny Wynne & Olivia 3535	5,000	1994	85.00	95
1990	Harpster w/Banjo 3257	4,000	1990	60.00	250
1991	Harpster w/Harmonica II 3384	8,000	1993	60.00	125
1992	Harriet Tubman 3687	3,000	1993	60.00	125
1994	Harriet Tubman II 4110	2,500		50.00	50
1991	Hattie Quilting 3483	6,000	1993	60.00	125
1990	Hattie-Knitting 3233	4,000	1990	40.00	75-100
1995	Henry O. Flipper 4403	2,500		55.00	55
1996	Hickory Clown 4485	10,000		29.00	29
1995	Hugs 4185	Open		36.00	36
1996	I Have a Dream-MLK 4540	10,000		65.00	65
1992	Ida B. Wells & Frederick Douglass 3642	3,000	1993	160.00	200
1995	Ida B. Wells and Son 4400	2,500		65.00	65
1996	Jazz Man-Piano 4499	2,000		150.00	150
1993	Jesse Gospel Singer 3755	2,500		40.00	40
1992	Jomo-African Boy 3652	4,000	1994	27.00	27
1992	Kaminda-African Woman 3679	4,000	1994	50.00	50
1995	Kisses 4186	Open		30.00	30
1994	Kitty w/Microphone 4141	2,000		50.00	50
1995	Libby w/Candle 4396	4,000		26.00	26
1994	Libby w/Jacks 4139	4,000		26.00	26
1990	Libby w/Overalls 3259	4,000	1990	36.00	150
1991	Libby w/Puppy 3386	10,000	1993	50.00	70
1995	Lift Your Hearts 4413	5,000		50.00	50
1995	Love 4187	Open		50.00	50
1996	Love of My Life II 4534	2,500		75.00	75
1995	Loving Touch 4314	4,000		66.00	66
1995	Lucas w/Bear 4397	4,000		26.00	26
1991	Lucas w/Dog 3387	10,000	1993	50.00	70
1990	Lucas w/Overalls 3260	4,000	1990	36.00	150
1994	Lucas w/Papers 4140	4,000		26.00	26
1996	Ma Rainey 4500	2,000		50.00	50
1993	Madame CJ Walker 3849	3,000		45.00	45
1995	Martin Luther King Birmingham Jail 4407	12/96		65.00	65
1995	Martin Luther King Wedding 4406	12/96		85.00	85
1994	Martin Luther King, Jr. 4179	12/96		65.00	65
1994	Mary Church Terrell 4122	2,500		50.00	50
1996	Mary Eliza Mahoney 4501	1,000		50.00	50
1993	Mary McLeod Bethune 3847	3,000		45.00	45
1993	Miles Boy Angel 3752	2,500	1995	27.00	40
1992	Miss Lettie-Teacher 3513	6,000	1993	50.00	50
1993	Moriah Girl Angel 3759	2,500	1994	27.00	45
1992	Muffy-Prayer Time 3509	5,000	1993	46.00	55
1992	Music Masters 3533	1,000	1992	300.00	350
1992	Music Masters II 3621	1,000	1994	250.00	300
1994	Music Masters III 4142	2,000		80.00	80
1993	Nat Love Cowboy (Isom Dart) 3792	2,500	1993	45.00	225-350
1994	Nat Love w/Saddle 4121	2,500		60.00	60
1991	Nighttime Pearl 3362	Closed	1993	50.00	65
1991	Nighttime Percy 3363	Closed	1993	50.00	65
1996	Noah's Ark 4529	500		130.00	130
1992	Nurturing with Love-3686	2,000	1993	60.00	60
1995	Old Time Tunes 4317	4,000		54.00	54
1995	Olivia A. D. Washington 4404	2,500		51.00	51
1993	Otis Redding 3793	Closed	1994	70.00	300
1991	Pappy Jake & Susie Mae 3482	6,000	1993	60.00	60
1989	Pappy Jake 3100	Closed	1990	40.00	100
1994	Peaches-Clown 4135	4,000		29.00	29
1990	Pearl-Bl. Girl Dancing 3291	5,000	1992	45.00	75
1990	Percy-Bl. Boy Dancing 3292	5,000	1993	45.00	75
1993	Phillis Wheatley 3846	3,000		45.00	45
1992	Porter 3525	5,000	1993	80.00	125
1991	Portia Quilting 3484	6,000	1993	40.00	40
1990	Portia Reading Book 3256	Closed	1991	30.00	45-65
1991	Portia-Victorian Dress 3373	7,000	1992	35.00	35
1990	Praise the Lord I (Preacher I) 3277	4,000	1991	55.00	150
1991	Praise the Lord II w/Kids 3376	5,000	1994	100.00	100
1993	Praise the Lord III 3753	2,500	1994	44.00	55
1995	Praise the Lord IV 4369	5,000		55.00	55
1994	Pug-Clown 4136	4,000		29.00	29
1989	Quilting Ladies 3099	Closed	1991	90.00	300
1996	Racial Harmony - MLK/JFK 4541	5,000		114.00	114
1992	Rhythm & Blues 3620	5,000	1994	80.00	80
1995	Rosa Parks 4401	6/97		65.00	65
1991	Sadie & Osie Mae 3365	8,000	1993	70.00	70
1996	Sassafras Clown 4484	10,000		29.00	29
1992	Shamba-African Man 3680	4,000	1994	50.00	50
1992	Sojourner Truth 3629	3,000	1993	80.00	100
1995	Stitch of Love 4316	4,000		60.00	60
1990	Susie Mae 3231	Closed	1994	22.00	22
1996	Ta Da - Ballet 4506	3,000		32.00	32
1995	Tuskegee Airman W.W. II 4405	2,500		60.00	60
1991	Uncle Reuben 3389	8,000	1993	70.00	125
1993	Vanessa Gospel Singer (Upside down book) 3756	2,500		40.00	100
1994	W.E.B. DuBois 4123	2,500		60.00	60
1991	Webster-Victorian Suit 3374	7,000	1992	35.00	35
1990	Whoopie & Wooster 3255	4,000	1990	50.00	250
1991	Whoopie & Wooster II 3385	8,000	1993	70.00	95

Classroom Memories - Sarah's Attic

YEAR ISSUE		EDITION LIMIT	YEAR RETD.	ISSUE PRICE	*QUOTE U.S.$
1991	Achieving Our Goals 3417	10,000	1994	80.00	80
1988	Miss Pritchet 6505	Closed	1993	28.00	35

Cookie Kids & Friends - Sarah's Attic

YEAR ISSUE		EDITION LIMIT	YEAR RETD.	ISSUE PRICE	*QUOTE U.S.$
1995	Chip - Wh Boy w/Dog C004	Open		29.50	30
1995	Cookie Kids Displayer C000	Open		20.00	20
1995	Cookie Kids Sign C001	Open		39.00	39
1995	Honey - Bl School Girl C007	Open		29.50	30
1995	Oatie - Bl Boy w/Bike C002	Open		29.50	30
1995	Peanut - Wh Girl w/Dome C005	Open		29.50	30
1995	Sprinkles - Bl Clown Boy C006	Open		29.50	30
1995	Sugar - Bl Girl Baking C003	Open		29.50	30

Cotton Tale Collection - Sarah's Attic

YEAR ISSUE		EDITION LIMIT	YEAR RETD.	ISSUE PRICE	*QUOTE U.S.$
1988	Americana Bunny 3048	Closed	1990	58.00	190
1988	Billi Rabbit 6283	Closed	1990	27.00	35
1987	Bonnie 5727	Closed	1989	30.00	125
1996	Bunny Bun 4510	1,000		60.00	60
1996	Bunny Love 4513	1,500		18.00	18
1991	Chuckles Rabbit 3350	Closed	1993	53.00	53
1988	Cindi Rabbit 6282	Closed	1990	27.00	35
1987	Clyde 5728	Closed	1989	30.00	125
1989	Cookie Rabbit 3078	Closed	1990	29.00	125
1991	Cookie Rabbit 3351	Closed	1993	47.00	47
1994	Cookie-Rabbit Quilting 4196	Closed	1995	40.00	40
1994	Corkey-Rabbit Chair 4197	Closed	1995	30.00	30
1989	Crumb Rabbit 3077	Closed	1990	29.00	35-43
1991	Crumb Rabbit 3352	Closed	1993	53.00	53
1994	Crumb-Rabbit w/Book 4195	Closed	1995	40.00	40
1987	Floppy 5729	Closed	1989	19.00	19
1994	Fluff-Angel Bunny 4199	Closed	1995	19.00	19
1990	Hannah Mom Rabbit 3264	Closed	1992	32.00	32
1993	Hannah w/Muff 3733	Closed	1993	30.00	30
1990	Henry Dad Rabbit w/Pipe 3263	Closed	1992	32.00	32
1993	Henry w/Wreath 3734	Closed	1993	30.00	30
1990	Herbie Boy Rabbit 3265	Closed	1992	22.00	22
1996	Herbie Rabbit 4509	1,500		33.00	33
1993	Herbie Sitting 3736	Closed	1993	25.00	25
1990	Hether Girl Rabbit 3266	Closed	1992	22.00	22
1993	Hether in Sled 3735	Closed	1993	30.00	30
1996	Hether Rabbit 4508	1,500		33.00	33
1996	Jangles Rabbit 4511	1,500		24.00	24
1996	Jingles Rabbit 4512	1,500		24.00	24
1990	Molly Rabbit w/Vest 3240	Closed	1991	75.00	75
1989	Nana Rabbit 3080	Closed	1990	50.00	60-75
1991	Nana Rabbit w/Washboard 3349	Closed	1993	100.00	100
1994	Nana-Rabbit w/Book 4193	Closed	1995	55.00	55
1990	Ollie Rabbit w/Vest 3239	Closed	1991	75.00	150
1989	Papa Rabbit 3079	Closed	1990	50.00	60-75
1991	Papa Rabbit w/Hat 3348	Closed	1993	80.00	80
1994	Papa-Rabbit w/Paper 4194	6/96	1995	55.00	55
1989	Sleepy Rabbit 3088	Closed	1990	16.00	25
1991	Sleepy Rabbit 3353	Closed	1993	35.00	35
1994	Sleepy-Bunny 4198	Closed	1995	23.00	23
1991	Tabitha Victorian Rabbit 3371	Closed	1993	30.00	45
1991	Tessy Victorian Rabbit 3370	Closed	1993	20.00	35
1993	Tessy-Easter 3950	1,994	1995	24.00	24
1989	Thelma Rabbit 3084	Closed	1990	33.00	40
1991	Thelma Victorian Rabbit 3368	Closed	1993	60.00	60
1993	Thelma-Easter 3948	1,994	1995	26.00	26
1989	Thomas Rabbit 3085	Closed	1990	33.00	40
1991	Thomas Victorian Rabbit 3367	Closed	1993	60.00	60
1993	Thomas-Easter 3949	1,994	1995	26.00	26
1991	Toby Victorian Rabbit 3369	Closed	1993	40.00	55
1993	Toby-Easter 3951	1,994	1995	24.00	24
1991	Tucker Victorian Rabbit 3372	Closed	1993	37.00	37
1988	Wendall Mini Rabbit 6268	Closed	1990	8.00	12
1987	Wendall Rabbit 5285	Closed	1989	14.00	25
1988	Wendy Mini Rabbit 6270	Closed	1990	8.00	12
1987	Wendy Rabbit 5286	Closed	1989	15.00	25
1988	Wilbur Mini Rabbit 6269	Closed	1990	8.00	12
1987	Wilbur Rabbit 5287	Closed	1989	13.00	25
1988	Winnie Mini Rabbit 6271	Closed	1990	8.00	8
1986	Winnie Rabbit 2036	Closed	1989	14.00	14
1990	Zeb Pa Rabbit w/Carrots 3217	500	1990	18.00	32
1990	Zeb Sailor Dad 3319	Closed	1992	28.00	32
1990	Zeke Boy Rabbit w/Carrots 3219	500	1990	17.00	32
1990	Zeke Sailor Boy 3321	Closed	1992	26.00	26
1990	Zelda Ma Rabbit w/Carrots 3218	500	1990	18.00	32
1990	Zelda Sailor Mom 3320	Closed	1992	28.00	28
1987	Zoe Girl Rabbit w/Carrots 3220	500	1990	17.00	32
1990	Zoe Sailor Girl 3322	Closed	1992	26.00	26

Daisy Collection - Sarah's Attic

YEAR ISSUE		EDITION LIMIT	YEAR RETD.	ISSUE PRICE	*QUOTE U.S.$
1990	Bomber-Tom 3309	Closed	1993	52.00	57
1990	Jack Boy Ball & Glove 3249	Closed	1993	40.00	44
1993	Jack Boy w/Broken Arm 3970	2,000	1994	30.00	60
1990	Jewel-Julie 3310	Closed	1993	62.00	68
1989	Sally Booba 2344	Closed	1993	40.00	60
1990	Sparky-Mark 3307	Closed	1993	55.00	60
1990	Spike-Tim 3308	Closed	1993	46.00	51
1990	Stretch-Mike 3311	Closed	1993	52.00	57

Dreams of Tomorrow - Sarah's Attic

YEAR ISSUE		EDITION LIMIT	YEAR RETD.	ISSUE PRICE	*QUOTE U.S.$
1994	Annie-Nurse 4128	3,000		33.00	33
1992	Annie-Teacher 3507	6,000	1993	55.00	55
1991	Benjamin w/Drums 3487	10,000	1993	46.00	55
1994	Bernie-Teacher 4132	3,000		38.00	38
1992	Blossom 3502	5,000	1993	50.00	50
1994	Boyd-Basketball 4279	2,000		36.00	36
1994	Boyd-Teacher 4130	3,000		34.00	34
1992	Bubba-Doctor 3506	6,000	1993	60.00	66
1994	Bubba-Fireman 4229	2,000	1995	37.00	37
1994	Bubba-Football 4272	2,000		36.00	36
1992	Bubba-Policeman 3685	3,000	1993	46.00	51
1992	Bud-Fireman 3668	6,000	1993	50.00	55
1994	Bud-Police (blue) 4260	2,000		45.00	45
1994	Bud-Police (brown) 4261	2,000		45.00	45
1994	Calvin-Bl. Golfer 4161	3,000		35.00	35
1994	Calvin-Soccer 4275	2,000		36.00	36
1994	Champ-Soccer 4277	2,000		36.00	36
1993	Champ-Wh. Boy Baseball 3776	Open		32.00	32
1991	Charity Sewing Flags 3486	10,000	1993	46.00	55
1992	Chips-Graduate 3532	6,000	1993	46.00	46
1993	Cody-Cowboy 3886	2,000	1995	30.00	30
1994	Cody-Hockey 4271	2,000	1995	38.00	38
1992	Cricket-Graduate 3531	6,000	1993	46.00	46
1992	Cupcake-Ballerina 3683	3,000	1993	46.00	46
1994	Cupcake-Dentist 4116	3,000		33.00	33
1992	Cupcake-Nurse 3514	6,000	1993	46.00	46
1994	Cupcake-Soccer 4276	2,000		36.00	36
1993	Dana-Wh. Waitress 3779	2,000	1994	34.00	34
1994	Dedication-Wh. Doctor 4111	3,000		38.00	38
1994	Devotion-Bl. Doctor 4112	3,000		33.00	33
1994	Jack Boy-Graduate 3984	3,000		30.00	30
1993	Jack-Boy Wh. Pharmacist 3781	2,000		34.00	34
1994	Joe-Farmer w/Basket 4120	3,000		33.00	33
1994	John-Farmer w/Tractor 4119	3,000		36.00	36
1993	Jojo-Wh. Girl Basketball 3777	Closed	1995	32.00	32
1994	Josh-Hockey 4270	2,000	1995	38.00	38
1993	Josh-Jogger 3887	2,000	1995	25.00	25
1994	Judy-Teacher 4131	3,000		38.00	38
1994	Juliana-Teacher 4129	3,000		34.00	34
1992	Katie-Executive 3665	6,000	1993	46.00	46
1994	Katie-Nurse 3987	3,000		33.00	33
1993	Katie-Pharmacist 3898	2,000		32.00	32
1992	Madge-Farmer 3503	2,500	1993	50.00	50
1992	Marty-Farmer 3504	2,500	1993	50.00	50
1994	Moose-Football 4273	2,000		36.00	36
1993	Noah-Bl. Pharmacist 3780	2,000		34.00	34
1992	Noah-Executive 3508	6,000	1993	46.00	46
1992	Pansy-Ballerina 3682	3,000	1993	46.00	55
1993	Pansy-Bl. Waitress 3778	2,000	1994	40.00	40
1992	Pansy-Nurse 3505	6,000	1993	46.00	51
1993	Pansy-Pharmacist 3899	2,000		32.00	32
1994	Peaches-Dentist 4113	3,000		33.00	33
1994	Pug-Dentist 4114	3,000		33.00	33
1993	Rachel-Photographer 3871	2,000	1995	27.00	32
1994	Sally Booba-Graduate 3983	3,000		30.00	30
1992	Shelby-Executive 3666	6,000	1993	46.00	50
1994	Shelby-Nurse 4127	3,000		33.00	33
1991	Skip-Building Houses 3489	10,000	1993	50.00	50
1994	Spike-Basketball 4278	2,000	1995	36.00	36
1994	Spike-Wh. Golfer 4162	3,000		35.00	35
1991	Susie Painting Train 3488	10,000	1993	46.00	46
1993	Tillie-Girl Basketball 3774	Open		32.00	32
1994	Tillie-Graduate 3985	3,000		30.00	30
1994	Tillie-Nurse 3989	3,000	1995	33.00	33
1996	Tillie-Nurse II 4502	5,000		29.00	29
1993	Tillie-Photographer 3870	2,000		27.00	32
1994	Tillie-Soccer 4274	2,000		36.00	36
1992	Tillie-Teacher 3520	6,000	1993	50.00	50
1992	Twinkie-Doctor 3515	6,000	1993	50.00	50
1993	Twinkie-Pilot 3869	2,000		27.00	35
1992	Twinkie-Policeman 3684	3,000	1993	46.00	46
1994	Twinkie-Wh. Dentist 4115	3,000		33.00	33
1994	Whimpy-Doctor 3988	3,000		33.00	33
1992	Whimpy-Executive 3521	6,000	1993	46.00	46
1994	Whimpy-Fireman 4230	2,000		37.00	37

*Quotes have been rounded up to nearest dollar

FIGURINES/COTTAGES

YEAR ISSUE	EDITION LIMIT	YEAR RETD.	ISSUE PRICE	*QUOTE U.S.$
1993 Willie-Boy Baseball 3775	Open		32.00	32
1994 Willie-Doctor 3990	3,000		33.00	33
1992 Willie-Fireman 3667	6,000	1993	46.00	50
1994 Willie-Graduate 3986	3,000		30.00	30
1993 Willie-Pilot 3868	2,000		27.00	27

Happy Collection - Sarah's Attic

YEAR ISSUE	EDITION LIMIT	YEAR RETD.	ISSUE PRICE	*QUOTE U.S.$
1988 Americana Clown 4025	4,000	1990	80.00	80
1988 Christmas Clown 4026	4,000	1990	88.00	88

Matt & Maggie - Sarah's Attic

YEAR ISSUE	EDITION LIMIT	YEAR RETD.	ISSUE PRICE	*QUOTE U.S.$
1988 Large Matt 3029	4,000	1989	48.00	58
1986 Maggie 2029	4,000	1989	14.00	28
1989 Maggie Bench Sitter 3083	Closed	1990	32.00	42
1986 Maggie Candle Holder 2026	Closed	1987	12.00	12
1987 Maggie on Heart 5145	Closed	1989	9.00	15
1987 Matt & Maggie w/ Bear 5730	100	1987	100.00	150
1986 Matt 2030	Closed	1989	14.00	28
1989 Matt Bench Sitter 3082	Closed	1990	32.00	42
1986 Matt Candle Holder 2025	Closed	1987	12.00	12
1987 Matt on Heart 5144	Closed	1989	9.00	15
1989 Mini Maggie 2314	Closed	1989	6.00	12
1989 Mini Matt 2313	Closed	1989	6.00	12
1988 Small Sitting Maggie 5284	Closed	1989	11.50	35
1988 Small Sitting Matt 5283	Closed	1989	11.50	35
1987 Standing Maggie 2014	Closed	1989	11.00	15
1987 Standing Matt 2013	Closed	1989	11.00	15

Santas Of The Month-Series A - Sarah's Attic

YEAR ISSUE	EDITION LIMIT	YEAR RETD.	ISSUE PRICE	*QUOTE U.S.$
1988 January Wh. Santa	Closed	1990	50.00	135-150
1988 January Bl. Santa	Closed	1990	50.00	200-300
1988 February Wh. Santa	Closed	1990	50.00	135-150
1988 February Bl. Santa	Closed	1990	50.00	200-300
1988 March Wh. Santa	Closed	1990	50.00	135-150
1988 March Bl. Santa	Closed	1990	50.00	200-300
1988 April Wh. Santa	Closed	1990	50.00	135-150
1988 April Bl. Santa	Closed	1990	50.00	200-300
1988 May Wh. Santa	Closed	1990	50.00	135-150
1988 May Bl. Santa	Closed	1990	50.00	200-300
1988 June Wh. Santa	Closed	1990	50.00	135-150
1988 June Bl. Santa	Closed	1990	50.00	200-300
1988 July Wh. Santa	Closed	1990	50.00	175
1988 July Bl. Santa	Closed	1990	50.00	200-300
1988 August Wh. Santa	Closed	1990	50.00	135-150
1988 August Bl. Santa	Closed	1990	50.00	200-300
1988 September Wh. Santa	Closed	1990	50.00	135-150
1988 September Bl. Santa	Closed	1990	50.00	200-300
1988 October Wh. Santa	Closed	1990	50.00	135-150
1988 October Bl. Santa	Closed	1990	50.00	200-300
1988 November Wh. Santa	Closed	1990	50.00	135-150
1988 November Bl. Santa	Closed	1990	50.00	200-300
1988 December Wh. Santa	Closed	1990	50.00	135-150
1988 December Bl. Santa	Closed	1990	50.00	225-375
1988 Mini January Wh. Santa	Closed	1990	14.00	33-35
1988 Mini January Bl. Santa	Closed	1990	14.00	35
1988 Mini February Wh. Santa	Closed	1990	14.00	33-35
1988 Mini February Bl. Santa	Closed	1990	14.00	35
1988 Mini March Wh. Santa	Closed	1990	14.00	33-35
1988 Mini March Bl. Santa	Closed	1990	14.00	35
1988 Mini April Wh. Santa	Closed	1990	14.00	33-35
1988 Mini April Bl. Santa	Closed	1990	14.00	35
1988 Mini May Wh. Santa	Closed	1990	14.00	33-35
1988 Mini May Bl. Santa	Closed	1990	14.00	35
1988 Mini June Wh. Santa	Closed	1990	14.00	33-35
1988 Mini June Bl. Santa	Closed	1990	14.00	35
1988 Mini July Wh. Santa	Closed	1990	14.00	40
1988 Mini July Bl. Santa	Closed	1990	14.00	50
1988 Mini August Wh. Santa	Closed	1990	14.00	33-35
1988 Mini August Bl. Santa	Closed	1990	14.00	35
1988 Mini September Wh. Santa	Closed	1990	14.00	33-35
1988 Mini September Bl. Santa	Closed	1990	14.00	35
1988 Mini October Wh. Santa	Closed	1990	14.00	33-35
1988 Mini October Bl. Santa	Closed	1990	14.00	35
1988 Mini November Wh. Santa	Closed	1990	14.00	33-35
1988 Mini November Bl. Santa	Closed	1990	14.00	35
1988 Mini December Wh. Santa	Closed	1990	14.00	33-35
1988 Mini December Bl. Santa	Closed	1990	14.00	35

Santas Of The Month-Series B - Sarah's Attic

YEAR ISSUE	EDITION LIMIT	YEAR RETD.	ISSUE PRICE	*QUOTE U.S.$
1990 Jan. Santa Winter Fun 7135	Closed	1991	80.00	100
1990 Feb. Santa Cupids Help 7136	Closed	1991	120.00	120
1990 Mar. Santa Irish Delight 7137	Closed	1991	120.00	150
1990 Apr. Santa Spring/Joy 7138	Closed	1991	150.00	150
1990 May Santa Par For Course 7139	Closed	1991	100.00	125
1990 June Santa Graduation 7140	Closed	1991	70.00	70
1990 July Santa God Bless 7141	Closed	1991	100.00	125
1990 August Santa Summers Tranquility 7142	Closed	1991	110.00	130
1990 Sep. Santa Touchdown 7143	Closed	1991	90.00	90
1990 Oct. Santa Seasons Plenty 7144	Closed	1991	120.00	120
1990 Nov. Santa Give Thanks 7145	Closed	1991	100.00	125
1990 Dec. Santa Peace 7146	Closed	1991	120.00	125
1990 January Mrs. Winter Fun 7147	Closed	1991	80.00	100
1990 February Mrs. Cupid's Helper 7148	Closed	1991	110.00	110
1990 March Mrs. Irish Delight7149	Closed	1991	80.00	120
1990 April Mrs. Spring Joy 7150	Closed	1991	110.00	110
1990 May Mrs. Par for the Course 7151	Closed	1991	80.00	100
1990 June Mrs. Graduate 7152	Closed	1991	70.00	100
1990 July Mrs. God Bless America 7153	Closed	1991	100.00	125
1990 August Mrs. Summer Tranquility 7154	Closed	1991	90.00	112
1990 Sept. Mrs. Touchdown 7155	Closed	1991	90.00	100
1990 Oct. Mrs. Seasons of Plenty 7156	Closed	1991	90.00	112
1990 Nov. Mrs. Give Thanks 7157	Closed	1991	90.00	112
1990 Dec. Mrs. Peace 7158	Closed	1991	110.00	137

Santas Of The Month-Series C - Sarah's Attic

YEAR ISSUE	EDITION LIMIT	YEAR RETD.	ISSUE PRICE	*QUOTE U.S.$
1990 Jan. Fruits of Love 3400	Closed	1993	90.00	90
1990 Feb. From The Heart 3401	Closed	1993	90.00	90
1990 Mar. Irish Love 3402	Closed	1993	100.00	100
1990 Apr. Spring Time 3403	Closed	1993	90.00	90
1990 May Caddy Chatter 3404	Closed	1993	100.00	100
1990 June Homerun 3405	Closed	1993	90.00	90
1990 July Celebrate America 3406	Closed	1993	90.00	90
1990 Aug. Fun In The Sun 3407	Closed	1993	90.00	90
1990 Sept. Lessons In Love 3408	Closed	1993	90.00	90
1990 Oct. Masquerade 3409	Closed	1993	120.00	120
1990 Nov. Harvest Of Love 3410	Closed	1993	120.00	120
1990 Dec. A Gift Of Peace 3411	Closed	1993	90.00	90

Santas Of The Month-Series D - Sarah's Attic

YEAR ISSUE	EDITION LIMIT	YEAR RETD.	ISSUE PRICE	*QUOTE U.S.$
1993 Jan. Wh. Wintertime Santa 3881	Closed	1994	35.00	35
1993 Feb. Wh. Valentine Santa 3882	Closed	1994	35.00	35
1993 Mar. Wh. St. Patrick's Santa 3885	Closed	1994	35.00	40
1993 April Wh. Easter Santa 3741	Closed	1994	35.00	35
1993 May Wh. Springtime Santa 3742	Closed	1994	35.00	35
1993 June Wh. Summertime Santa 3743	Closed	1994	35.00	35
1993 July Wh. Americana Santa 3815	Closed	1994	35.00	35
1993 Aug. Wh. Beachtime Santa 3816	Closed	1994	35.00	35
1993 Sept. Wh. Classroom Santa 3817	Closed	1994	35.00	35
1992 Oct. Wh. Halloween Santa 3696	Closed	1994	35.00	35
1992 Nov. Wh. Harvest Santa 3697	Closed	1994	35.00	35
1992 Dec. Wh. Father X-Mas Santa 3698	Closed	1994	35.00	35

Santas Of The Month-Series E - Sarah's Attic

YEAR ISSUE	EDITION LIMIT	YEAR RETD.	ISSUE PRICE	*QUOTE U.S.$
1993 Jan. Bl. Wintertime Santa 3880	Closed	1994	35.00	35
1993 Feb. Bl. Valentine Santa 3883	Closed	1994	35.00	35
1993 March Bl. St. Patrick's Santa 3884	Closed	1994	35.00	35
1993 April Bl. Easter Santa 3746	Closed	1994	35.00	35
1993 May Bl. Springtime Santa 3747	Closed	1994	35.00	35
1993 June Bl. Summertime Santa 3748	Closed	1994	35.00	35
1993 July Bl. Americana Santa 3818	Closed	1994	35.00	35
1993 Aug. Bl. Beachtime Santa 3819	Closed	1994	35.00	35
1993 Sept. Bl. Classroom Santa 3820	Closed	1994	35.00	35
1992 Oct. Bl. Halloween Santa 3729	Closed	1994	35.00	35
1992 Nov. Bl. Harvest Santa 3730	Closed	1994	35.00	35
1992 Dec. Bl. Father X-Mas Santa 3731	Closed	1994	35.00	35

Sarah's Gang Collection - Sarah's Attic

YEAR ISSUE	EDITION LIMIT	YEAR RETD.	ISSUE PRICE	*QUOTE U.S.$
1989 Baby Rachel 2306	Closed	1994	20.00	30
1990 Baby Rachel-Beachtime 3248	Closed	1992	35.00	50
1988 Cupcake 4027	Closed	1994	20.00	25
1995 Cupcake 4346	Open		28.00	28
1989 Cupcake Clown 3144	Closed	1989	21.00	35
1993 Cupcake on Bench 3766	Closed	1994	28.00	28
1987 Cupcake on Heart 5140	Closed	1989	9.00	20
1987 Cupcake w/Rope 5119	Closed	1988	16.00	16
1993 Cupcake w/Snowman 3822	2,500	1994	35.00	40
1989 Cupcake-Americana 2304	Closed	1993	21.00	30
1990 Cupcake-Beachtime 3244	Closed	1992	35.00	53
1990 Cupcake-Devil 3314	Closed	1992	40.00	40
1986 Cupcake-Original 2034	Closed	1988	14.00	20-75
1989 Cupcake-Small School 2309	Closed	1990	11.00	20
1993 Cupcake-Spring 3937	1,994	1995	30.00	30
1993 Katie & Rachel in Chair 3764	Closed	1994	60.00	60
1990 Katie & Whimpy-Beachtime 3243	Closed	1992	60.00	60-75
1988 Katie 4029	Closed	1994	20.00	25
1995 Katie 4344	Open		28.00	28
1987 Katie On Heart 5141	Closed	1989	9.00	20
1992 Katie On Sled 3707	2,500	1994	35.00	35
1987 Katie Sitting 2002	Closed	1987	14.00	20
1989 Katie-Americana 2302	Closed	1993	21.00	25
1991 Katie-Bride 3431	Closed	1994	47.00	52
1986 Katie-Original 2032	Closed	1988	14.00	20
1989 Katie-Small Sailor 2307	Closed	1990	14.00	20
1993 Katie-Spring 3935	1,994	1995	28.00	28
1991 Katie-Thanksgiving 3468	10,000	1993	32.00	32
1990 Katie-Witch 3312	Closed	1992	40.00	50
1991 Peaches-Flower Girl 3438	Closed	1994	40.00	40
1991 Percy-Minister 3440	Closed	1994	50.00	55
1991 Pug-Ringbearer 3439	Closed	1994	40.00	44
1995 Rachel 4348	Open		28.00	28
1993 Rachel in Snowsuit 3823	2,500	1994	25.00	25
1991 Rachel-Americana 3364	Closed	1993	30.00	30
1991 Rachel-Flower Girl 3432	Closed	1994	40.00	43
1990 Rachel-Pumpkin 3318	Closed	1992	40.00	50
1993 Rachel-Spring 3940	1,994	1995	30.00	30
1991 Rachel-Thanksgiving 3474	10,000	1993	32.00	35
1988 Tillie 4032	Closed	1994	20.00	25
1995 Tillie 4342	Open		28.00	28
1991 Tillie Masquerade 3412	Closed	1993	45.00	50
1987 Tillie On Heart 5150	Closed	1989	9.00	20
1992 Tillie On Log 3705	2,500	1994	35.00	35
1986 Tillie Resin Candle 2024	Closed	1987	12.00	12
1993 Tillie w/Bear 3769	Closed	1994	28.00	28
1989 Tillie-Americana 2301	Closed	1993	21.00	25
1996 Tillie-B/W 4530	2,500		75.00	75
1990 Tillie-Beachtime 3247	Closed	1992	35.00	53
1991 Tillie-Bride 3436	Closed	1994	47.00	52
1990 Tillie-Clown 3316	Closed	1992	40.00	50
1986 Tillie-Original 2027	Closed	1988	14.00	20
1989 Tillie-Small Country 2312	Closed	1992	18.00	26
1993 Tillie-Spring 3938	1,994	1995	30.00	30

YEAR ISSUE	EDITION LIMIT	YEAR RETD.	ISSUE PRICE	*QUOTE U.S.$
1991 Tillie-Thanksgiving 3472	10,000	1993	32.00	32
1996 Tillie-Y 4532	2,500		75.00	75
1988 Twinkie 4028	Closed	1994	20.00	20
1995 Twinkie 4347	Open		28.00	28
1989 Twinkie Clown 3145	Closed	1989	19.00	35
1987 Twinkie On Heart 5143	Closed	1989	9.00	20
1993 Twinkie w/Football 3765	Closed	1994	28.00	28
1987 Twinkie w/Pole 5107	Closed	1988	20.00	20
1993 Twinkie w/Snowballs 3821	2,500	1994	35.00	35
1989 Twinkie-Americana 2305	Closed	1993	21.00	25
1990 Twinkie-Beachtime 3245	Closed	1992	35.00	53
1990 Twinkie-Devil 3315	Closed	1992	40.00	50
1991 Twinkie-Minister 3435	Closed	1994	50.00	50
1986 Twinkie-Original 2033	Closed	1988	14.00	20
1989 Twinkie-Small School 2310	Closed	1990	11.00	20
1993 Twinkie-Spring 3936	1,994	1995	28.00	28
1991 Tyler-Ring Bearer 3433	Closed	1994	40.00	44
1988 Whimpy 4030	Closed	1994	20.00	25
1995 Whimpy 4345	Open		28.00	28
1987 Whimpy on Heart 5142	Closed	1989	9.00	20
1987 Whimpy Sitting 2001	Closed	1987	14.00	20
1992 Whimpy w/Book 3708	2,500	1994	35.00	35
1993 Whimpy w/Train 3767	Closed	1994	28.00	28
1989 Whimpy-Americana 2303	Closed	1993	21.00	25
1991 Whimpy-Groom 3430	Closed	1994	47.00	52
1986 Whimpy-Original 2031	Closed	1988	14.00	20
1990 Whimpy-Scarecrow 3313	Closed	1992	40.00	40
1989 Whimpy-Small Sailor 2308	Closed	1990	14.00	20
1993 Whimpy-Spring 3934	1,994	1995	28.00	28
1991 Whimpy-Thanksgiving 3469	10,000	1993	32.00	35
1996 Wille-B/W 4531	2,500		75.00	75
1996 Wille-Y 4533	2,500		75.00	75
1988 Willie 4031	Closed	1994	20.00	25
1995 Willie 4343	Open		28.00	28
1993 Willie Lying w/Pillow 3768	Closed	1994	28.00	28
1987 Willie On Heart 5151	Closed	1989	9.00	20
1986 Willie Resin Candle 2023	Closed	1987	12.00	12
1992 Willie w/Skates 3706	2,500	1994	35.00	35
1989 Willie-Americana 2300	Closed	1993	21.00	30
1990 Willie-Beachtime 3246	Closed	1992	35.00	53
1990 Willie-Clown 3317	Closed	1992	40.00	50
1991 Willie-Groom 3437	Closed	1994	47.00	47
1986 Willie-Original 2028	Closed	1988	14.00	20-75
1989 Willie-Small Country 2311	Closed	1993	18.00	26
1993 Willie-Spring 3939	1,994	1995	28.00	28
1991 Willie-Thanksgiving 3473	10,000	1993	32.00	32

Sarah's Neighborhood Friends - Sarah's Attic

YEAR ISSUE	EDITION LIMIT	YEAR RETD.	ISSUE PRICE	*QUOTE U.S.$
1991 Annie Nativity (Mary) 3419	Closed	1994	30.00	3
1991 Annie w/Flower Basket 3380	Closed	1992	56.00	5
1990 Annie w/Violin 3272	Closed	1992	40.00	4
1991 Babes-Nativity Jesus 3427	Closed	1994	20.00	2
1987 Bevie 5103	Closed	1989	14.00	1
1990 Bubba w/Lantern 3268	Closed	1992	40.00	4
1991 Bubba w/Lemonade Stand 3382	Closed	1992	54.00	10
1991 Bubba-Nativity King 3422	Closed	1994	34.00	3
1991 Bud Nativity (Joseph) 3420	Closed	1994	34.00	3
1990 Bud w/Book 3270	Closed	1992	40.00	4
1991 Bud w/Newspaper 3378	Closed	1992	40.00	4
1995 Chilly & Jingles - Lge 4417	100	1995	80.00	8
1995 Chilly-Snowman 4418	1,000		44.00	4
1991 Dolly Nativity (Jesus) 3418	Closed	1994	20.00	2
1987 Dusty 5106	Closed	1988	19.00	1
1987 Eddie 5337	Closed	1989	14.00	1
1993 Ellie-Girl w/Book 3784	Closed	1993	28.00	2
1993 Emily & Gideon-Small 3670	Closed	1993	40.00	7
1987 Emmy Lou 5112	Closed	1989	14.00	1
1993 Evan-Boy w/Bowl 3785	Closed	1993	28.00	2
1995 Flurry & Boo 4414	1,000		30.00	3
1993 Grams w/Rolling Pin 3782	Closed	1993	50.00	5
1991 Hewett w/Apples 3377	Closed	1992	40.00	4
1990 Hewett w/Drum 3273	Closed	1992	40.00	4
1991 Hewitt-Nativity King 3424	Closed	1994	40.00	4
1989 Jennifer & Max 2319	4,000	1990	57.00	8
1991 Noah-Nativity Jesus 3428	Closed	1994	36.00	3
1991 Pansy Pushing Carriage 3381	Closed	1992	50.00	5
1990 Pansy w/Sled 3269	Closed	1992	35.00	3
1991 Pansy-Nativity Angel 3425	Closed	1994	40.00	4
1987 Patsy-Cheerleader 5120	Closed	1988	19.00	1
1993 Rosie on Crate 3783	Closed	1993	50.00	5
1991 Shelby-Nativity Mary 3429	Closed	1994	30.00	3
1987 Shooter 5110	Closed	1988	20.00	2
1995 Snowy 4416	1,000		30.00	3
1988 Trudy-w/Teacup 3042	Closed	1990	34.00	5
1990 Tyler Victorian Boy 3327	Closed	1992	40.00	4
1990 Weasel w/Cap 3271	Closed	1992	40.00	4
1991 Weasel w/Newspaper 3383	Closed	1992	40.00	4
1991 Weasel-Nativity King 3423	Closed	1994	40.00	4
1988 Willie Bill 5108	Closed	1990	20.00	5

Snowflake Collection - Sarah's Attic

YEAR ISSUE	EDITION LIMIT	YEAR RETD.	ISSUE PRICE	*QUOTE U.S.$
1993 Blizzard Snowman News 3866	4,000	1995	20.00	
1989 Boo Mini Snowman 3200	Closed	1993	6.00	
1993 Bottles Snowman Milkman 3867	4,000	1995	20.00	
1996 Chilly/Snowflake 4482	5,000		32.00	
1992 Christmas Love-Small 3674	5,000	1992	30.00	
1993 Cruiser Snowman on Bike 3865	4,000	1995	23.00	
1992 Crystal Mother Snowman 3721	3,500	1995	20.00	
1989 Flurry 2342	Closed	1993	12.00	
1996 Frilly/Snow Crystal 4483	5,000		36.00	
1990 Old Glory Snowman 3225	4,000	1992	24.00	
1993 Sparkles & Topper on Log 3840	4,000	1995	28.00	

*Quotes have been rounded up to nearest dolla[r]

YEAR ISSUE		EDITION LIMIT	YEAR RETD.	ISSUE PRICE	*QUOTE U.S.$
1992	Sparkles Baby Snowman 3723	3,500	1995	14.00	14
1992	Topper Father Snowman 3722	3,500	1995	20.00	20
1996	Topper/Tabby 4481	5,000		32.00	32
1989	Winter Frolic 3209	Closed	1992	60.00	70

Spirit of America - Sarah's Attic

YEAR ISSUE		EDITION LIMIT	YEAR RETD.	ISSUE PRICE	*QUOTE U.S.$
1994	Asthon-Mother Indian 3977	1,000	1994	40.00	40
1994	Benjamin Franklin 4124	1,776	1994	70.00	70
1988	Betsy Ross 3024	Closed	1992	34.00	40
1991	Bright Sky Mother Indian 3345	Closed	1992	70.00	90-140
1995	Buffalo Bill 4311	2,500	1995	60.00	60
1995	Chief Joseph 4282	2,500	1995	56.00	56
1991	Forever in Our Hearts 3413	10,000	1994	90.00	90
1992	Gray Wolf Father Indian 3692	2,000	1994	46.00	46
1994	Hosteen-Father Indian 3978	1,000	1994	40.00	40
1988	Indian Brave 4007	Closed	1990	10.00	10
1988	Indian Girl 4008	Closed	1990	10.00	10
1991	Iron Hawk Father Indian 3344	Closed	1992	70.00	90-140
1991	Little Dove Girl Indian 3346	Closed	1992	40.00	60-85
1992	Moon Dance Girl Indian 3695	2,000	1994	30.00	30
1992	Morning Flower Indian 3693	2,000	1994	46.00	46
1988	Pilgrim Boy 4009	Closed	1990	12.00	20
1988	Pilgrim Girl 4010	Closed	1990	12.00	24
1992	Red Feather Boy Indian 3694	2,000	1994	30.00	30
1994	Shine-Boy Indian 3980	1,000	1994	25.00	50
1994	Siyah-Girl Indian 3979	1,000	1994	25.00	50
1991	Spotted Eagle Boy Indian 3347	Closed	1992	30.00	45-85

Spirit of Christmas Collection - Sarah's Attic

YEAR ISSUE		EDITION LIMIT	YEAR RETD.	ISSUE PRICE	*QUOTE U.S.$
1995	Ahmad - Nativity 4453	7,500		23.00	23
1995	America Santa 4467	1,776		100.00	100
1995	Angelika - Nativity 4456	7,500		25.00	25
1993	Been Good Santa/Boy 3813	2,500	1994	60.00	60
1990	Bells of Christmas 3326	5,000	1994	35.00	35
1989	Blessed Christmas 2350	7,500	1993	100.00	100
1995	Blessed Family Nativity 4364	5,000		70.00	70
1995	Cherish the Children 4466	1,000		70.00	70
1993	Christine-Christmas 93 3855	Closed	1993	30.00	30
1994	Christine-Christmas 94 4149	Closed	1994	24.00	24
1993	Christmas Bear 3853	Closed	1993	23.00	23
1993	Christmas Holly Santa 3859	Closed	1993	50.00	50
1989	Christmas Joy 3177	6,000	1990	32.00	32
1995	Christmas Joy 4331	2,000		60.00	60
1993	Christmas Proclaim. Love Santa 3860	Closed	1993	50.00	50
1993	Christmas Rabbit 3852	Closed	1993	23.00	23
1990	Christmas Wishes 3325	5,000	1994	50.00	50
1990	Christmas Wonder Santa 3278	3,000	1991	50.00	50
1987	Colonel Santa 3007	Closed	1989	30.00	30
1994	Deck the Halls-Bl. Santa 4159	3,000	1995	30.00	30
1987	Father Snow 2049	Closed	1990	42.00	42
1994	Gift of Christmas-Wh. Santa 4146	2,000		60.00	60
1994	Gift of Love Bl. Santa 4145	2,000		60.00	60
1992	Gifts of Christmas Santa 3677	Closed	1993	90.00	90
1992	Gifts of Love Santa 3678	Closed	1993	90.00	90
1994	Golden Memories Santa 4254	1,000		70.00	70
1988	Ho Ho Santa w/Elf 3053	Closed	1990	84.00	84
1995	Ishamael - Nativity 4454	7,500		23.00	23
1995	Jabari - Nativity 4455	7,500		23.00	23
1993	Jalessa-Christmas 93 3856	Closed	1993	25.00	25
1994	Jalessa-Christmas 94 4154	Closed	1994	28.00	28
1995	Jarrell - Nativity 4452	7,500		23.00	23
1993	Jeb-Christmas 93 3854	Closed	1993	25.00	25
1994	Jeb-Christmas 94 4155	Closed	1994	28.00	30
1993	Jessica-Christmas 93 3858	Closed	1993	25.00	25
1994	Jessica-Christmas 94 4147	Closed	1994	28.00	28
1987	Jingle Bells 2050	Closed	1989	20.00	20
1995	Joah - Nativity 4451	7,500		23.00	23
1995	Joy to the World 4462	1,000		64.00	64
1993	Justin-Christmas 93 3857	Closed	1993	25.00	25
1994	Justin-Christmas 94 4148	Closed	1994	30.00	30
1987	Kris Kringle-Bl. 5860	Closed	1990	100.00	100
1987	Kris Kringle-Wh. 5860	Closed	1990	100.00	100
1995	Lakeisha - Nativity 4450	7,500		25.00	25
1987	Large Santa w/Cane 5124	Closed	1989	27.00	27
1993	Let The Be Peace Santa 3797	2,000	1994	70.00	70
1993	Let There Be Love Santa 3796	2,000	1994	70.00	70
1994	LOL-Christmas 4151	Closed	1994	30.00	35
1987	Long Journey 2051	Closed	1989	19.00	35
1990	Love the Children 3324	5,000	1994	75.00	75
1992	Love the Children-Small 3672	5,000	1993	35.00	35
1987	Mini Santa w/Cane 5123	Closed	1990	8.00	20
1987	Mrs. Claus 5289	Closed	1989	26.00	26
1987	Naughty or Nice 2048	Closed	1989	100.00	100
1993	Oh My! Santa/Girl 3814	2,500		55.00	55
1989	Papa Santa Sitting 3180	Closed	1990	30.00	40
1989	Papa Santa Stocking 3182	Closed	1990	50.00	60
1995	Peace on Earth 4464	1,000		80.00	80
1994	Rejoice-Wh. Santa 4160	3,000	1995	34.00	34
1996	Santa & Friends 4517	1,000		100.00	100
1995	Santa 4429	5,000		45.00	45
1990	Santa Claus Express 3304	4,000	1993	150.00	150
1988	Santa in Chimney 4020	4,000	1990	110.00	150
1987	Santa Sitting 5122	Closed	1988	18.00	18
1991	Santa Tex 3392	500	1990	30.00	75
1995	Santa's Love 4465	1,000		98.00	98
1987	Santa's Workshop 3006	Closed	1990	50.00	100
1994	Sarah Elizabeth Christmas 4150	Closed	1994	27.00	27
1991	Sharing Love Santa 3491	3,000	1993	120.00	140
1989	Silent Night 2343	6,000	1991	33.00	50
1987	Small Santa w/Tree 5125	Closed	1989	14.00	14
1989	Spirit of Christmas Santa 2320	4,000	1993	80.00	80
1996	Spring Treasures 4516	1,000		100.00	100
1987	St. Nick 3005	Closed	1989	28.00	28
1995	Tillie-Caroiing 4461	5,000		26.00	26
1991	Treasures of Love Santa 3490	3,000	1993	140.00	140
1996	USA Santa-Wh. 4496	1,776		100.00	100
1995	Willie-Caroling 4460	5,000		26.00	26
1989	Woodland Santa 2345	7,500	1990	100.00	150

Tender Moments - Sarah's Attic

YEAR ISSUE		EDITION LIMIT	YEAR RETD.	ISSUE PRICE	*QUOTE U.S.$
1995	All Done 4395	3,000		29.00	29
1993	Always & Forever Bl. Wedding 3834	4,000		60.00	60
1996	Betsy 4491	2,500		40.00	40
1992	Bl. Baby Boy 1-2 3518	Closed	1993	50.00	50
1992	Bl. Baby Boy Birth 3516	Closed	1993	50.00	55
1992	Bl. Baby Girl 1-2 3517	Closed	1993	50.00	55
1992	Bl. Baby Girl Birth 3526	Closed	1993	50.00	50
1993	Bl. Boy 3-4/in Wagon 3745	Open		40.00	40
1994	Bl. Boy w/Hobby Horse 4-5 3958	Open		33.00	33
1993	Bl. Girl 3-4/Tricycle 3744	Open		40.00	60
1994	Bl. Girl on Horse 4-5 3957	Open		37.00	37
1993	Bless This Child Wh. Couple 3838	2,500	1994	60.00	60
1996	Breeze 4537	2,000		24.00	24
1996	Bubbles 4503	3,000		35.00	35
1995	Bundle of Joy 4392	3,000		20.00	20
1995	Bundle of Love 4393	3,000		29.00	29
1993	Catch of Love Wh. Men Fishing 3827	4,000	1995	50.00	50
1993	Days to Remember Bl. Men Fishing 3828	4,000	1995	50.00	50
1996	Dinner Time-Boy w/Dog 4507	3,000		32.00	32
1995	Family is Love 4320	4,000	1995	60.00	60
1992	Generations of Love	Closed	1994	293.00	425
1993	Gentle Touch Bl. Girls 3825	2,500	1995	40.00	40
1995	Having Fun 4322	4,000	1995	44.00	44
1993	Joy of Motherhood Bl. Pregnant Woman 3791	1,000	1994	55.00	70
1993	Little Blessing Bl. Couple 3839	2,500	1994	75.00	90
1995	Little Engineer 4389	3,000		25.00	25
1995	Love & Hugs Girl 4255	Open		38.00	38
1993	Love of Life-Bl. Couple 3788	1,000	1993	70.00	75-100
1995	Lullaby 4390	3,000		29.00	29
1995	Me Big Girl 4394	3,000		29.00	29
1996	Misty 4539	2,000		24.00	24
1993	New Beginning Wh. Pregnant Woman 3790	1,000	1994	55.00	55
1996	Peaches 4493	2,500		26.00	26
1995	Precious Dreams 4391	3,000		28.00	28
1993	Promise of Love Wh. Wedding 3835	4,000		60.00	60
1996	Pug 4494	2,500		26.00	26
1995	Remembrance 4470	2,000		100.00	100
1996	Ross 4492	2,500		36.00	36
1993	Special Bl. Boy in Wheelchair 3969	Open		38.00	38
1994	Special Bl. Girl 4126	Open		38.00	38
1993	Special Times Wh. Girls 3826	2,500	1995	40.00	40
1994	Special Wh. Boy 4125	Open		38.00	38
1993	Special Wh. Girl in Wheelchair 3968	Open		38.00	38
1996	Spiritual Guidance-blue 4518	2,000		65.00	65
1996	Spiritual Guidance-gold 4519	2,000		65.00	65
1996	Summer 4538	2,000		24.00	24
1995	Sweet Dreams 4388	3,000		29.00	29
1994	Timeless Knowledge 4323	4,000	1995	47.00	47
1995	Treasured Moments 4321	4,000	1995	70.00	70
1993	True Love-Wh. Couple 3789	1,000	1994	70.00	80
1992	Wh. Baby Boy 1 3527	Closed	1993	60.00	66
1992	Wh. Baby Girl 1 3528	Closed	1993	60.00	65
1992	Wh. Boy 1-2 3530	Closed	1993	60.00	60
1992	Wh. Boy 2-3 3624	Closed	1993	60.00	65
1992	Wh. Boy 3-4 3691	Closed	1993	50.00	50
1994	Wh. Boy w/Fire Truck 4-5 3960	Open		40.00	40
1992	Wh. Girl 1-2 3529	Closed	1993	60.00	60
1992	Wh. Girl 2-3 3623	Closed	1993	60.00	66
1992	Wh. Girl 3-4 3690	Closed	1993	50.00	50
1994	Wh. Girl w/Trunk 4-5 3959	Open		40.00	40
1995	Wow! 4324	4,000	1995	36.00	36
1996	Yakky Jackie 4504	3,000		32.00	32

United Hearts Collection - Sarah's Attic

YEAR ISSUE		EDITION LIMIT	YEAR RETD.	ISSUE PRICE	*QUOTE U.S.$
1992	Adora Angel-May 3632	Closed	1993	50.00	75
1991	Adora Christmas-December 3479	Closed	1992	36.00	60
1991	Annie & Waldo Beach-August 3460	Closed	1992	40.00	40
1991	Barney the Great-October 3466	Closed	1992	40.00	48
1991	Bibi & Biff Clowns-October 3467	Closed	1992	35.00	42
1991	Bibi-Miss Liberty Bear-July 3457	Closed	1992	30.00	36
1991	Bubba Beach-August 3461	Closed	1992	34.00	41
1992	Carrotman-January 3619	Closed	1993	30.00	40
1991	Chilly Snowman-January 3443	Closed	1992	33.00	40
1991	Chuckles-September 3464	Closed	1992	26.00	26
1991	Cookie w/Kitten-September 3462	Closed	1992	28.00	28
1992	Cookie-July 3638	Closed	1993	34.00	34
1991	Crumb on Stool-September 3463	Closed	1992	32.00	39
1992	Crumb-July 3639	Closed	1993	34.00	34
1992	Cupcake-November 3649	Closed	1993	35.00	40
1991	Cupcake-Thanksgiving 3470	Closed	1993	36.00	36
1991	Emily-Springtime May 3452	Closed	1992	53.00	60
1992	Enos Angel-May 3633	Closed	1993	50.00	50
1991	Enos Christmas-December 3480	Closed	1992	36.00	36
1992	Ethan Angel-August 3641	Closed	1993	46.00	60
1991	Gideon-Springtime May 3453	Closed	1992	40.00	43
1992	Herbie-January 3618	Closed	1993	26.00	26
1992	Hether-January 3617	Closed	1993	26.00	26
1991	Hewett w/Leprechaun-March 3448	Closed	1992	56.00	67
1991	Jack Boy Graduation-June 3455	Closed	1992	40.00	40
1992	Katie-September 3643	Closed	1993	35.00	35
1992	Mrs. Claus December 3653	Closed	1993	45.00	45
1991	Noah w/Pot of Gold-March 3447	Closed	1992	36.00	43
1991	Pansy Beach-August 3459	Closed	1992	34.00	41
1991	Papa Barney & Biff-July 3458	Closed	1992	64.00	76
1992	Peaches-October 3647	Closed	1993	30.00	30
1991	Peanut-February 3445	Closed	1992	32.00	32
1991	Prissy w/Shaggy-February 3444	Closed	1992	36.00	36
1992	Pug-October 3646	Closed	1993	47.00	47
1991	Sally Booba Graduation-June 3454	Closed	1992	45.00	50
1992	Santa-December 3654	Closed	1993	45.00	45
1991	Shelby w/Shamrock-March 3446	Closed	1992	36.00	43
1991	Sparky Dog Graduation-June 3456	Closed	1992	16.00	16
1991	Tabitha April 3449	Closed	1992	32.00	32
1992	Tabitha w/Glove-June 3636	Closed	1993	34.00	34
1992	Tessie w/Ball-June 3637	Closed	1993	34.00	34
1991	Tillie-January 3441	Closed	1992	32.00	40
1991	Toby & Tessie-April 3450	Closed	1992	44.00	44
1992	Toby w/Bat-June 3635	Closed	1993	34.00	34
1992	Twinkie-November 3650	Closed	1993	35.00	35
1991	Twinkie-Thanksgiving 3471	Closed	1993	32.00	32
1991	Willie-January 3442	Closed	1992	32.00	40
1992	Willie-September 3644	Closed	1993	35.00	35

Schmid

Lowell Davis Farm Club - L. Davis

YEAR ISSUE		EDITION LIMIT	YEAR RETD.	ISSUE PRICE	*QUOTE U.S.$
1986	The Bride 221001 / 20993	Closed	1987	45.00	450
1987	The Party's Over 221002 / 20994	Closed	1988	50.00	100-190
1988	Chow Time 221003 / 20995	Closed	1989	55.00	85-100
1989	Can't Wait 221004 / 20996	Closed	1990	75.00	125
1990	Pit Stop 221005 / 20997	Closed	1991	75.00	125-150
1991	Arrival Of Stanley 221006 / 20998	Yr.Iss.	1992	100.00	85-100
1991	Don't Pick The Flowers 221007 / 21007	Yr.Iss.	1992	100.00	143
1992	Hog Wild	Yr.Iss.	1993	100.00	100
1992	Check's in the Mail	Yr.Iss.	1993	100.00	100
1993	The Survivor 25371	Yr.Iss.	1994	70.00	70
1993	Summer Days	Yr.Iss.		100.00	100
1994	Dutch Treat	Yr.Iss.		100.00	100
1995	Free Kittens	Yr.Iss.		40.00	40

Lowell Davis Farm Club - L. Davis

YEAR ISSUE		EDITION LIMIT	YEAR RETD.	ISSUE PRICE	*QUOTE U.S.$
1994	Feathering Her Nest	Yr.Iss.		Gift	N/A
1995	After the Rain	Yr.Iss.		Gift	N/A

Lowell Davis Farm Club Renewal Figurine - L. Davis

YEAR ISSUE		EDITION LIMIT	YEAR RETD.	ISSUE PRICE	*QUOTE U.S.$
1986	Thirsty? 892050 / 92050	Yr.Iss.		Gift	85
1987	Cackle Berries 892051 / 92051	Yr.Iss.	1989	Gift	N/A
1988	Ice Cream Churn 892052 / 92052	Yr.Iss.	1990	Gift	50
1990	Not A Sharing Soul 892053 / 92053	Yr.Iss.	1991	Gift	40
1991	New Arrival 892054 / 92054	Yr.Iss.	1992	Gift	40
1992	Garden Toad 92055	Yr.Iss.	1993	Gift	N/A
1993	Luke 12:6 25372	Yr.Iss.	1994	Gift	N/A

Davis Cat Tales Figurines - L. Davis

YEAR ISSUE		EDITION LIMIT	YEAR RETD.	ISSUE PRICE	*QUOTE U.S.$
1982	Company's Coming 25205	Closed	N/A	60.00	225-275
1982	Flew the Coop 25207	Closed	N/A	60.00	300-365
1982	On the Move 25206	Closed	N/A	70.00	550-650
1982	Right Church, Wrong Pew 25204	Closed	N/A	70.00	288-350

Davis Country Christmas Figurines - L. Davis

YEAR ISSUE		EDITION LIMIT	YEAR RETD.	ISSUE PRICE	*QUOTE U.S.$
1995	Bah Humbug	2,500		200.00	200
1987	Blossom's Gift 23554	Closed	N/A	150.00	300
1992	Born on a Starry Night 23559	2,500		225.00	225
1985	Christmas at Fox Fire Farm 23552	Closed	N/A	80.00	275
1986	Christmas at Red Oak 23553	Closed	N/A	80.00	200
1991	Christmas At Red Oak II 23558	Closed	N/A	250.00	250
1984	Country Christmas 23551	Closed	N/A	80.00	450
1988	Cutting the Family Christmas Tree 23555	Closed	N/A	80.00	350
1983	Hooker at Mailbox w/Presents 23550	Closed	N/A	80.00	750
1989	Peter and the Wren 23556	Closed	N/A	165.00	300-450
1994	Visions of Sugar Plums	2,500		250.00	250
1993	Waiting For Mr. Lowell 23606	2,500		250.00	250
1990	Wintering Deer 23557	Closed	N/A	165.00	280

Davis Country Pride - L. Davis

YEAR ISSUE		EDITION LIMIT	YEAR RETD.	ISSUE PRICE	*QUOTE U.S.$
1981	Bustin' with Pride 25202	Closed	N/A	100.00	225-250
1981	Duke's Mixture 25203	Closed	N/A	100.00	160-300
1981	Plum Tuckered Out 25201	Closed	N/A	100.00	950
1981	Surprise in the Cellar 25200	Closed	N/A	100.00	930-1000

Davis Farm Set - L. Davis

YEAR ISSUE		EDITION LIMIT	YEAR RETD.	ISSUE PRICE	*QUOTE U.S.$
1985	Barn 25352	Closed	N/A	47.50	425
1985	Chicken House 25358	Closed	N/A	19.00	45
1985	Corn Crib and Sheep Pen 25354	Closed	N/A	25.00	80
1985	Garden and Wood Shed 25359	Closed	N/A	25.00	65
1985	Goat Yard and Studio 25353	Closed	N/A	32.50	80
1985	Hen House 25356	Closed	N/A	32.50	85
1985	Hog House 25355	Closed	N/A	27.50	85
1985	Main House 25351	Closed	N/A	42.50	100
1985	Privy 25348	Closed	N/A	12.50	35
1985	Remus' Cabin 25350	Closed	N/A	42.50	100
1985	Smoke House 25357	Closed	N/A	12.50	65
1985	Windmill 25349	Closed	N/A	25.00	40

*Quotes have been rounded up to nearest dollar

FIGURINES/COTTAGES

Davis Friends of Mine - L. Davis

YEAR ISSUE		EDITION LIMIT	YEAR RETD.	ISSUE PRICE	*QUOTE U.S.$
1992	Cat and Jenny Wren 23633	5,000		170.00	200
1992	Cat and Jenny Wren Mini Figurine 23634	Open		35.00	35
1989	Sun Worshippers 23620	5,000	1993	120.00	130
1989	Sun Worshippers Mini Figurine 23621	5,000	1993	32.50	33
1990	Sunday Afternoon Treat 23625	5,000	1993	120.00	175-200
1990	Sunday Afternoon Treat Mini Figurine 23626	Closed	1993	32.50	38
1991	Warm Milk 23629	Closed	1993	120.00	200
1991	Warm Milk Mini Figurine 23630	5,000	1993	32.50	38

Davis Little Critters - L. Davis

YEAR ISSUE		EDITION LIMIT	YEAR RETD.	ISSUE PRICE	*QUOTE U.S.$
1992	Charivari 25707	950		250.00	250
1991	Christopher Critter 25514	1,192	1993	150.00	150
1992	Double Yolker 25516	Yr.Iss.		70.00	70
1989	Gittin' a Nibble 25294	Closed	N/A	50.00	57
1991	Great American Chicken Race 25500	2,500		225.00	275
1991	Hittin' The Sack 25510	Closed	N/A	70.00	70
1990	Home Squeezins 25504	Closed	1993	90.00	90
1991	Itiskit, Itasket 25511	Open		45.00	45
1991	Milk Mouse 25503	2,500		175.00	228
1992	Miss Private Time 25517	Yr.Iss.		35.00	35
1990	Outing With Grandpa 25502	2,500	1993	200.00	250
1990	Private Time 25506	Closed	1993	18.00	40
1990	Punkin' Pig 25505	2,500	1993	250.00	300
1991	Punkin' Wine 25501	Closed		100.00	150
1991	Toad Strangler 25509	Closed	N/A	57.00	57
1991	When Coffee Never Tasted So Good 25507	1,250		800.00	800
1992	A Wolf in Sheep's Clothing 25518	Yr.Iss.		110.00	110

Davis Promotional Figurine - L. Davis

YEAR ISSUE		EDITION LIMIT	YEAR RETD.	ISSUE PRICE	*QUOTE U.S.$
1994	Don't Forget Me 227130	N/A	1994	70.00	70
1992	Hen Scratch Prom 225968	N/A	1992	90.00	95
1993	Leapin' Lizard 225969	N/A	1993	80.00	80
1991	Leavin' The Rat Race 225512	N/A	1991	80.00	200
1995	Nasty Stuff 95103	N/A		40.00	40

Davis RFD America - L. Davis

YEAR ISSUE		EDITION LIMIT	YEAR RETD.	ISSUE PRICE	*QUOTE U.S.$
1984	Anybody Home 25239	Closed	N/A	35.00	100
1994	Attic Antics	Open		100.00	100
1982	Baby Blossom 25227	Closed	N/A	40.00	325
1982	Baby Bobs 25222	Closed	N/A	47.50	200-250
1985	Barn Cats 25257	Open		39.50	80
1993	Be My Valentine 27561	Open		35.00	35
1986	Bit Off More Than He Could Chew 25279	Open		15.00	60
1979	Blossom 25032	Closed	N/A	180.00	1800
1982	Blossom and Calf 25326	Closed	N/A	250.00	700-1000
1995	Blossom's Best	750		300.00	300
1987	Bottoms Up 25270	Open	1992	80.00	105
1989	Boy's Night Out 25339	1,500		190.00	225
1982	Brand New Day 25226	Closed	N/A	23.50	150-175
1979	Broken Dreams 25035	Closed	N/A	165.00	1000-1300
1988	Brothers 25286	Closed	1990	55.00	75-100
1984	Catnapping Too? 25247	Closed	1991	70.00	150
1987	Chicken Thief 25338	Closed	N/A	200.00	300
1983	City Slicker 25329	Closed	N/A	150.00	270
1991	Cock Of The Walk 25347	2,500		300.00	300
1986	Comfy? 25273	Open		40.00	80
1994	Companion pc. And Down the Hatch	6 mo.	1994	135.00	135
1994	Companion pc. Open The Lid	6 mo.	1994	135.00	135
1989	Coon Capers 25291	Open		67.50	90
1990	Corn Crib Mouse 25295	Closed	1993	35.00	45
1983	Counting the Days 25233	Closed	1992	40.00	60
1981	Country Boy 25213	Closed	N/A	37.50	250-375
1985	Country Cousins 25266	Open		42.50	80
1982	Country Crook 25280	Closed	N/A	37.50	350
1985	Country Crooner 25256	Open		25.00	45
1984	Country Kitty 25246	Closed	N/A	52.00	115-125
1979	Country Road 25030	Closed	N/A	100.00	900
1984	Courtin' 25220	Closed	N/A	45.00	125
1980	Creek Bank Bandit 25038	Closed	N/A	37.50	400
1995	Cussin' Up a Storm	Open		45.00	45
1993	Don't Open Till Christmas 27562	Open		35.00	35
1992	Don't Play With Fire 25319	Open		120.00	120
1985	Don't Play with Your Food 25258	Closed	1992	28.50	100
1981	Double Trouble 25211	Closed	N/A	35.00	475
1981	Dry as a Bone 25216	Closed	N/A	45.00	275-325
1993	Dry Hole 25374	Open		30.00	30
1987	Easy Pickins 25269	Closed	1990	45.00	85
1983	Fair Weather Friend 25236	Closed	N/A	25.00	75
1983	False Alarm 25237	Closed	N/A	65.00	150-185
1989	Family Outing 25289	Open		45.00	60
1985	Feelin' His Oats 25275	1,500		150.00	260
1990	Finder's Keepers 25299	Open		39.50	45
1991	First Offense 25304	Closed	1993	70.00	75
1994	First Outing	Open		65.00	65
1988	Fleas 25272	Open		20.00	24
1980	Forbidden Fruit 25022	Closed	N/A	25.00	150
1990	Foreplay 25300	Closed	1993	59.50	80
1979	Fowl Play 25033	Closed	N/A	100.00	275-325
1992	Free Lunch 25321	Open		85.00	85
1993	The Freeloaders 95042	1,250		230.00	230
1985	Furs Gonna Fly 25335	1,500		145.00	240
1987	Glutton for Punishment 25268	Closed	1991	95.00	160
1988	Goldie and Her Peeps 25283	Open		25.00	37
1984	Gonna Pay for His Sins 25243	Open		27.50	55
1980	Good, Clean Fun 25020	Closed	1989	40.00	125
1984	Gossips 25248	Closed	N/A	110.00	200
1992	The Grass is Always Greener 25367	Open		195.00	195
1991	Gun Shy 25305	Closed	1993	70.00	70
1990	Hanky Panky 25298	Closed	1993	65.00	80-100
1993	Happy Birthday My Sweet 27560	Open		35.00	35
1988	Happy Hour 25287	Open		57.50	75-100
1983	Happy Hunting Ground 25330	Closed	N/A	160.00	235
1984	Headed Home 25240	Closed	1991	25.00	50
1992	Headed South 25327	Open		45.00	45
1991	Heading For The Persimmon Grove 25306	Closed	1993	80.00	80
1994	Helpin Himself	Open		65.00	65
1983	Hi Girls, The Name's Big Jack 25328	Closed	N/A	200.00	380
1981	Hightailing It 25214	Closed	N/A	50.00	375-500
1983	His Eyes Are Bigger Than His Stomach 25332	Closed	N/A	235.00	350
1984	His Master's Dog 25244	Closed	N/A	45.00	150
1994	Hittin The Trail	1,250		250.00	250
1985	Hog Heaven 25336	1,500		165.00	260-450
1992	The Honeymoon's Over 25370	1,950		300.00	300
1984	Huh? 25242	Closed	1989	40.00	90-160
1993	I'm Thankful For You 27563	Open		35.00	35
1982	Idle Hours 25230	Closed	N/A	37.50	225-300
1993	If You Can't Beat Em Join Em 25379	1,750		250.00	250
1979	Ignorance is Bliss 25031	Closed	N/A	165.00	1300
1988	In a Pickle 25284	Open		40.00	50
1980	Itching Post 25037	Closed	N/A	30.00	75-115
1993	King of The Mountain 25380	750		500.00	500
1991	Kissin' Cousins 25307	Closed	1993	80.00	80
1990	The Last Straw 25301	Open		125.00	180
1989	Left Overs 25290	Open		90.00	105
1983	Licking Good 25234	Closed	N/A	35.00	200-250
1990	Little Black Lamb (Baba) 25297	Closed	1993	30.00	38
1990	Long Days, Cold Nights 25344	2,500	1993	175.00	190
1991	Long, Hot Summer 25343	1,950		250.00	250
1985	Love at First Sight 25267	Closed	1992	70.00	115
1984	Mad As A Wet Hen 25334	Closed	N/A	185.00	700-800
1987	Mail Order Bride 25263	Closed	1991	150.00	185-260
1983	Makin' Tracks 25238	Closed	1989	70.00	125
1988	Making a Bee Line 25274	Closed	1990	75.00	125
1994	Mama Can Willie Stay For Supper	1,250		200.00	200
1983	Mama's Prize Leghorn 25235	Closed	N/A	55.00	125
1986	Mama? 25277	Closed	1991	15.00	45
1989	Meeting of Sheldon 25293	Closed	1992	120.00	150
1980	Milking Time 25023	Closed	N/A	20.00	240
1988	Missouri Spring 25278	Closed	1992	115.00	175
1982	Moon Raider 25325	Closed	N/A	190.00	325
1989	Mother Hen 25292	Open		37.50	50
1982	Moving Day 25225	Closed	N/A	43.50	325
1992	My Favorite Chores 25362	1,500		750.00	750
1980	New Day 25025	Closed	N/A	20.00	165
1989	New Friend 25288	Open		45.00	60
1993	No Hunting 25375	1,000		95.00	95
1988	No Private Time 25316	Closed	N/A	200.00	300
1994	Not a Happy Camper	Open		75.00	75
1994	Oh Mother What is it?	1,000		250.00	250
1992	OH Sheeeit . . . 25363	Open		120.00	120
1993	Oh Where is He Now 95041	1,250		250.00	250
1984	One for the Road 25241	Open		37.50	60-70
1987	The Orphans 25271	Open		50.00	95
1985	Out-of-Step 25259	Open		45.00	90
1985	Ozark Belle 25264	Closed	1990	35.00	70
1992	Ozark's Vittles 25318	Open		60.00	60
1984	Pasture Pals 25245	Closed	1990	52.00	130
1994	Pecking Order	Open		200.00	200
1993	Peep Show 25376	Open		35.00	35
1988	Perfect Ten 25282	Closed	1990	95.00	175
1990	Piggin' Out 25345	Closed	N/A	190.00	250
1984	Prairie Chorus 25333	Closed	N/A	135.00	1000-1500
1981	Punkin' Seeds 25219	Closed	N/A	225.00	1200-1750
1994	Qu'est - Ceque C'est?	Open		200.00	200
1985	Renoir 25261	Closed	1991	45.00	75
1981	Rooted Out 25217	Closed	1989	45.00	85-115
1992	Safe Haven 25320	Open		95.00	95
1988	Sawin' Logs 25260	Open		85.00	105
1981	Scallawags 25221	Closed	N/A	65.00	150
1992	School Yard Dogs 25369	Open		100.00	100
1990	Seein' Red (Gus w/shoes) 25296	Closed	1993	35.00	47
1992	She Lay Low 25364	Open		120.00	120
1993	Sheep Sheerin Time 25388	1,200		500.00	500
1982	A Shoe to Fill 25229	Closed	N/A	37.50	150-175
1979	Slim Pickins 25034	Closed	N/A	165.00	525-700
1992	Snake Doctor 25365	Open		70.00	70
1991	Sooieee 25360	1,500		350.00	350
1981	Split Decision 25210	Closed	N/A	45.00	175-325
1995	Sticks and Stones	Open		30.00	30
1983	Stirring Up Trouble 25331	Closed	N/A	160.00	250
1980	Strawberry Patch 25021	Closed	1989	25.00	95
1982	Stray Dog 25223	Closed	N/A	35.00	75
1981	Studio Mouse 25215	Closed	N/A	60.00	360
1980	Sunday Afternoon 25024	Closed	N/A	22.50	225-250
1993	Sweet Tooth 25373	Open		60.00	60
1982	Thinking Big 25231	Closed	N/A	35.00	70-90
1985	Too Good to Waste on Kids 25262	Open		70.00	130
1982	Treed 25327	Closed	N/A	155.00	320
1989	A Tribute to Hooker 25340	Closed	N/A	180.00	215-300
1993	Trick or Treat 27565	Open		35.00	35
1990	Tricks Of The Trade 25346	Closed	N/A	300.00	300-375
1987	Two in the Bush 25337	Closed	N/A	150.00	320
1994	Two Timer	Open		95.00	95
1982	Two's Company 25224	Closed	N/A	43.50	200
1981	Under the Weather 25212	Closed	1991	25.00	85
1995	Uninvited Caller	Open		35.00	35
1981	Up To No Good 25218	Closed	N/A	200.00	850-950
1982	Waiting for His Master 25281	Closed	N/A	50.00	300
1994	Warmin'	1,250		270.00	270
1991	Washed Ashore 25308	Closed	1993	70.00	75
1982	When Mama Gets Mad 25228	Closed	N/A	37.50	300-375
1987	When the Cat's Away 25276	Open		40.00	60
1988	When Three Foot's a Mile 25315	Closed	N/A	230.00	300
1980	Wilbur 25029	Closed	N/A	100.00	585
1985	Will You Still Respect Me in the Morning 25265	Open		35.00	75
1988	Wintering Lamb 25317	Closed	N/A	200.00	250
1988	Wishful Thinking 25285	Open		55.00	70
1983	Woman's Work 25232	Closed	1989	35.00	95
1989	Woodscolt 25342	Closed	N/A	300.00	380
1993	You're a Basket Full of Fun 27564	Open		35.00	35

Davis Route 66 - L. Davis

YEAR ISSUE		EDITION LIMIT	YEAR RETD.	ISSUE PRICE	*QUOTE U.S.$
1992	Fresh Squeezed? (w/ wooden base) 25609	350		600.00	600
1992	Fresh Squeezed? 25608	2,500		450.00	450
1992	Going To Grandma's 25619	Open		80.00	80
1993	Home For Christmas 25621	Open		80.00	80
1991	Just Check The Air 25600	350	1995	700.00	1500
1991	Just Check The Air 25603	2,500		550.00	550
1993	Kickin' Himself 25622	Open		80.00	80
1991	Little Bit Of Shade 25602	Open		100.00	100
1991	Nel's Diner 25601	350	1995	700.00	1700
1991	Nel's Diner 25604	2,500		550.00	550
1992	Quiet Day at Maple Grove 25618	Open		130.00	175
1992	Relief 25605	Open		80.00	80
1993	Summer Days 25607	Yr.Iss.		100.00	100
1992	Welcome Mat (w/ wooden base) 25606	1,500		400.00	400-500
1992	What Are Pals For? 25620	Open		100.00	100

Davis Special Edition Figurines - L. Davis

YEAR ISSUE		EDITION LIMIT	YEAR RETD.	ISSUE PRICE	*QUOTE U.S.$
1983	The Critics 23600	Closed	N/A	400.00	900-1300
1989	From A Friend To A Friend 23602	1,200		750.00	1700
1985	Home from Market 23601	Closed	N/A	400.00	1500
1992	Last Laff 23604	1,200		900.00	1000
1990	What Rat Race? 23603	1,200		800.00	1025

Davis Uncle Remus - L. Davis

YEAR ISSUE		EDITION LIMIT	YEAR RETD.	ISSUE PRICE	*QUOTE U.S.$
1981	Brer Bear 25251	Closed	N/A	80.00	900-1200
1981	Brer Coyote 25255	Closed	N/A	80.00	500
1981	Brer Fox 25250	Closed	N/A	70.00	900-950
1981	Brer Rabbit 25252	Closed	N/A	85.00	200
1981	Brer Weasel 25254	Closed	N/A	80.00	70
1981	Brer Wolf 25253	Closed	N/A	85.00	50

Don Polland Figurines I - D. Polland

YEAR ISSUE		EDITION LIMIT	YEAR RETD.	ISSUE PRICE	*QUOTE U.S.$
1983	Challenge	2,000	1989	275.00	60
1983	Dangerous Moment	2,000	1989	250.00	35
1986	Down From The High Country	2,250	1989	225.00	29
1983	Downed	2,500	1989	250.00	60
1986	Eagle Dancer	2,500	1989	170.00	29
1983	Escape	2,500	1989	175.00	65
1983	Fighting Bulls	2,500	1989	200.00	60
1983	The Great Hunt	350	1989	3750.00	375
1983	Hot Pursuit	2,500	1989	225.00	55
1983	The Hunter	2,500	1989	225.00	50
1986	Plains Warrior	1,250	1989	350.00	55
1986	Running Wolf-War Chief	2,500	1989	170.00	29
1986	Second Chance	2,000	1989	125.00	65
1983	A Second Chance	2,000	1989	350.00	65
1986	Shooting the Rapids	2,500	1989	195.00	49
1986	War Trophy	2,250	1989	225.00	50
1983	Young Bull	2,750	1989	125.00	25

Sebastian Studios

Large Ceramastone Figures - P.W. Baston

YEAR ISSUE		EDITION LIMIT	YEAR RETD.	ISSUE PRICE	*QUOTE U.S.$
1963	Abraham Lincoln Toby Jug	Closed	N/A	Unkn.	600-100
1963	Anne Boleyn	Closed	N/A	Unkn.	600-100
1940	Basket	Closed	N/A	Unkn.	300-40
1973	Blacksmith	Closed	N/A	Unkn.	300-40
1940	Breton Man	Closed	N/A	Unkn.	1000-150
1940	Breton Woman	Closed	N/A	Unkn.	1000-150
1973	Cabinetmaker	Closed	N/A	Unkn.	300-4
1940	Candle Holder	Closed	N/A	Unkn.	300-40
1940	Caroler	Closed	N/A	Unkn.	300-40
1973	Clockmaker	Closed	N/A	Unkn.	600-10
1964	Colonial Boy	Closed	N/A	Unkn.	600-10
1964	Colonial Girl	Closed	N/A	Unkn.	600-10
1964	Colonial Man	Closed	N/A	Unkn.	600-10
1964	Colonial Woman	Closed	N/A	Unkn.	600-10
1963	David Copperfield	Closed	N/A	Unkn.	600-10
1965	The Dentist	Closed	N/A	Unkn.	600-10
1963	Dora	Closed	N/A	Unkn.	600-10
1963	George Washington Toby Jug	Closed	N/A	Unkn.	600-10
1966	Guitarist	Closed	N/A	Unkn.	600-10
1963	Henry VIII	Closed	N/A	Unkn.	600-10
1940	Horn of Plenty	Closed	N/A	Unkn.	300-4
1964	IBM Father	Closed	N/A	Unkn.	600-10
1964	IBM Mother	Closed	N/A	Unkn.	600-10
1964	IBM Photographer	Closed	N/A	Unkn.	600-10
1964	IBM Son	Closed	N/A	Unkn.	600-10
1964	IBM Woman	Closed	N/A	Unkn.	600-10
1967	Infant of Prague	Closed	N/A	Unkn.	600-10
1956	Jell-O Cow Milk Pitcher	Closed	N/A	Unkn.	175-2
1940	Jesus	Closed	N/A	Unkn.	300-4

*Quotes have been rounded up to nearest dolla

YEAR ISSUE		EDITION LIMIT	YEAR RETD.	ISSUE PRICE	*QUOTE U.S.$
1963	John F. Kennedy Toby Jug	Closed	N/A	Unkn.	600-1000
1940	Lamb	Closed	N/A	Unkn.	300-400
1947	Large Victorian Couple	Closed	N/A	Unkn.	600-1000
1940	Mary	Closed	N/A	Unkn.	600-1000
1963	Mending Time	Closed	N/A	Unkn.	600-1000
1975	Minuteman	Closed	N/A	Unkn.	600-1000
1978	Mt. Rushmore	Closed	N/A	Unkn.	400-500
1965	N.E. Home For Little Wanderers	Closed	N/A	Unkn.	600-1000
1939	Paul Revere Plaque	Closed	N/A	Unkn.	400-500
1973	Potter	Closed	N/A	Unkn.	300-400
XX	Santa Fe...All The Way	Closed	N/A	Unkn.	600-1000
XX	St. Francis (Plaque)	Closed	N/A	Unkn.	600-1000
1965	Stanley Music Box	Closed	N/A	Unkn.	300-500
1958	Swift Instrument Girl	Closed	N/A	Unkn.	500-750
1963	Tom Sawyer	Closed	N/A	Unkn.	600-1000
1959	Wasp Plaque	Closed	N/A	Unkn.	500-750
1948	Woody at Three	Closed	N/A	Unkn.	600-1000

Sebastian Miniatures - P.W. Baston

YEAR ISSUE		EDITION LIMIT	YEAR RETD.	ISSUE PRICE	*QUOTE U.S.$
1956	77th Bengal Lancer (Jell-O)	Closed	N/A	Unkn.	600-1000
1942	Accordion	Closed	N/A	Unkn.	325-375
1952	Aerial Tramway	Closed	N/A	Unkn.	300-600
1959	Alcoa Wrap PS	Closed	N/A	Unkn.	350-400
1959	Alexander Smith Weaver	Closed	N/A	Unkn.	350-425
1956	Alike, But Oh So Different	Closed	N/A	Unkn.	300-350
1957	Along the Albany Road PS	Closed	N/A	Unkn.	600-1000
1940	Ann Stvyvesant	Closed	N/A	Unkn.	75-100
1940	Annie Oakley	Closed	N/A	Unkn.	75-100
1956	Arthritic Hands (J & J)	Closed	N/A	Unkn.	600-1000
XX	Babe Ruth	Closed	N/A	Unkn.	600-1000
1952	Baby (Jell-O)	Closed	N/A	Unkn.	525-600
1939	Benjamin Franklin	Closed	N/A	Unkn.	75-100
1962	Big Brother Bob Emery	Closed	N/A	Unkn.	600-1000
1953	Blessed Julie Billart	Closed	N/A	Unkn.	400-500
1962	Blue Belle Highlander	Closed	N/A	Unkn.	200-250
1954	Bluebird Girl	Closed	N/A	Unkn.	400-450
XX	Bob Hope	Closed	N/A	Unkn.	600-1000
1957	Borden's Centennial (Elsie the Cow)	Closed	N/A	Unkn.	600-1000
1971	Boston Gas Tank	Closed	N/A	Unkn.	300-500
1953	Boy Jesus in the Temple	Closed	N/A	Unkn.	350-400
1949	Boy Scout Plaque	Closed	N/A	Unkn.	300-350
1940	Buffalo Bill	Closed	N/A	Unkn.	75-100
1961	Bunky Knudsen	Closed	N/A	Unkn.	600-1000
1954	Campfire Girl	Closed	N/A	Unkn.	400-450
1955	Captain Doliber	Closed	N/A	Unkn.	300-350
1968	Captain John Parker	Closed	N/A	Unkn.	300-350
1951	Carl Moore (WEEI)	Closed	N/A	Unkn.	200-300
1951	Caroline Cabot (WEEI)	Closed	N/A	Unkn.	200-350
940	Catherine LaFitte	Closed	N/A	Unkn.	75-100
958	CBS Miss Columbia PS	Closed	N/A	Unkn.	600-1000
951	Charles Ashley (WEEI)	Closed	N/A	Unkn.	200-350
951	Chief Pontiac	Closed	N/A	Unkn.	400-700
951	Chiquita Banana	Closed	N/A	Unkn.	350-400
951	Christopher Columbus	Closed	N/A	Unkn.	250-300
958	Cliquot Club Eskimo PS	Closed	N/A	Unkn.	10-2300
957	Colonial Fund Doorway PS	Closed	N/A	Unkn.	600-1000
958	Commodore Stephen Decatur	Closed	N/A	Unkn.	125-175
958	Connecticut Bank & Trust	Closed	N/A	Unkn.	225-275
939	Coronado	Closed	N/A	Unkn.	75-100
939	Coronado's Senora	Closed	N/A	Unkn.	75-100
X	Coronation Crown	Closed	N/A	Unkn.	600-1000
942	Cymbals	Closed	N/A	Unkn.	325-375
954	Dachshund (Audiovox)	Closed	N/A	Unkn.	300-350
947	Dahl's Fisherman	Closed	N/A	Unkn.	150-175
940	Dan'l Boone	Closed	N/A	Unkn.	75-100
953	Darned Well He Can	Closed	N/A	Unkn.	300-350
955	Davy Crockett	Closed	N/A	Unkn.	225-275
939	Deborah Franklin	Closed	N/A	Unkn.	75-100
948	Democratic Victory	Closed	N/A	Unkn.	350-500
963	Dia-Mel Fat Man	Closed	N/A	Unkn.	375-400
947	Dilemma	Closed	N/A	Unkn.	275-300
967	Doc Berry of Berwick (yellow shirt)	Closed	N/A	Unkn.	300-350
941	Doves	Closed	N/A	Unkn.	600-1000
947	Down East	Closed	N/A	Unkn.	125-150
942	Drum	Closed	N/A	Unkn.	325-375
941	Ducklings	Closed	N/A	Unkn.	600-1000
949	Dutchman's Pipe	Closed	N/A	Unkn.	175-225
951	E. B. Rideout (WEEI)	Closed	N/A	Unkn.	200-350
X	Eagle Plaque	Closed	N/A	Unkn.	1000-1500
956	Eastern Paper Plaque	Closed	N/A	Unkn.	350-400
940	Elizabeth Monroe	Closed	N/A	Unkn.	150-175
956	Elsie the Cow Billboard	Closed	N/A	Unkn.	600-1000
949	Emmett Kelly	Closed	N/A	Unkn.	200-300
949	Eustace Tilly	Closed	N/A	Unkn.	750-1500
939	Evangeline	Closed	N/A	Unkn.	100-125
952	The Fat Man (Jell-O)	Closed	N/A	Unkn.	525-600
952	The Favored Scholar	Closed	N/A	Unkn.	200-300
959	Fiorello LaGuardia	Closed	N/A	Unkn.	125-175
947	First Cookbook Author	Closed	N/A	Unkn.	125-150
952	The First House, Plimoth Plantation	Closed	N/A	Unkn.	150-195
947	Fisher Pair PS	Closed	N/A	Unkn.	400-1000
959	Fleischman's Margarine PS	Closed	N/A	Unkn.	225-325
939	Gabriel	Closed	N/A	Unkn.	100-125
966	Gardener Man	Closed	N/A	Unkn.	250-300
966	Gardener Women	Closed	N/A	Unkn.	250-300
966	Gardeners (Thermometer)	Closed	N/A	Unkn.	300-400
949	Gathering Tulips	Closed	N/A	Unkn.	225-250
972	George & Hatchet	Closed	N/A	Unkn.	400-450
1939	George Washington	Closed	N/A	Unkn.	35-75
1949	Giant Royal Bengal Tiger	Closed	N/A	Unkn.	1000-1500
1959	Giovanni Verrazzano	Closed	N/A	Unkn.	125-175
1955	Giraffe (Jell-O)	Closed	N/A	Unkn.	350-375
1956	Girl on Diving Board	Closed	N/A	Unkn.	400-450
1951	Great Stone Face	Closed	N/A	Unkn.	600-1000
1956	The Green Giant	Closed	N/A	Unkn.	400-500
1956	H.P. Hood Co. Cigar Store Indian	Closed	N/A	Unkn.	600-1000
1958	Hannah Duston PS	Closed	N/A	Unkn.	250-325
1940	Hannah Penn	Closed	N/A	Unkn.	100-150
1959	Harvard Trust Co. Town Crier	Closed	N/A	Unkn.	350-400
1958	Harvard Trust Colonial Man	Closed	N/A	Unkn.	275-325
1948	A Harvey Girl	Closed	N/A	Unkn.	250-300
1959	Henry Hudson	Closed	N/A	Unkn.	125-175
1965	Henry Wadsworth Longfellow	Closed	N/A	Unkn.	275-325
1953	Holgrave the Daguerrotypist	Closed	N/A	Unkn.	200-250
1954	Horizon Girl	Closed	N/A	Unkn.	400-450
1942	Horn	Closed	N/A	Unkn.	325-375
1955	Horse Head PS	Closed	N/A	Unkn.	350-375
1947	Howard Johnson Pieman	Closed	N/A	Unkn.	300-450
1957	IBM 305 Ramac	Closed	N/A	Unkn.	400-450
1939	Indian Maiden	Closed	N/A	Unkn.	100-125
1939	Indian Warrior	Closed	N/A	Unkn.	100-125
1960	The Infantryman	Closed	N/A	Unkn.	600-1000
1951	The Iron Master's House	Closed	N/A	Unkn.	350-500
1958	Jackie Gleason	Closed	N/A	Unkn.	600-1000
1963	Jackie Kennedy Toby Jug	Closed	N/A	Unkn.	600-1000
1940	James Monroe	Closed	N/A	Unkn.	150-175
1957	Jamestown Church	Closed	N/A	Unkn.	400-450
1957	Jamestown Ships	Closed	N/A	Unkn.	350-475
1940	Jean LaFitte	Closed	N/A	Unkn.	75-100
1951	Jesse Buffman (WEEI)	Closed	N/A	Unkn.	200-350
1939	John Alden	Closed	N/A	Unkn.	35-50
1963	John F. Kennedy Toby Jug	Closed	N/A	Unkn.	600-1000
1940	John Harvard	Closed	N/A	Unkn.	125-150
1940	John Smith	Closed	N/A	Unkn.	75-150
1958	Jordan Marsh Observer	Closed	N/A	Unkn.	175-275
1948	Jordan Marsh Observer	Closed	N/A	Unkn.	150-175
1951	Jordon Marsh Observer Rides the A.W. Horse	Closed	N/A	Unkn.	300-325
1951	Judge Pyncheon	Closed	N/A	Unkn.	175-225
1954	Kernel-Fresh Ashtray	Closed	N/A	Unkn.	400-450
XX	The King	Closed	N/A	Unkn.	600-1000
1941	Kitten (Sitting)	Closed	N/A	Unkn.	600-1000
1941	Kitten (Sleeping)	Closed	N/A	Unkn.	600-1000
1953	Lion (Jell-O)	Closed	N/A	Unkn.	350-375
1966	Little George	Closed	N/A	Unkn.	350-450
1956	Lost in the Kitchen (Jell-O)	Closed	N/A	Unkn.	350-375
1942	Majorette	Closed	N/A	Unkn.	325-375
1952	Marblehead High School Plaque	Closed	N/A	Unkn.	200-300
1939	Margaret Houston	Closed	N/A	Unkn.	75-100
1960	Marine Memorial	Closed	N/A	Unkn.	300-400
1949	The Mark Twain Home in Hannibal, MO	Closed	N/A	Unkn.	600-1000
1972	Martha & the Cherry Pie	Closed	N/A	Unkn.	350-400
1939	Martha Washington	Closed	N/A	Unkn.	35-75
1948	Mary Lyon	Closed	N/A	Unkn.	250-300
1960	Masonic Bible	Closed	N/A	Unkn.	300-400
1966	Massachusetts SPCA	Closed	N/A	Unkn.	250-350
1957	Mayflower PS	Closed	N/A	Unkn.	300-325
1949	Menotomy Indian	Closed	N/A	Unkn.	175-250
1961	Merchant's Warren Sea Capt.	Closed	N/A	Unkn.	200-250
1960	Metropolitan Life Tower PS	Closed	N/A	Unkn.	350-400
1956	Michigan Millers PS	Closed	N/A	Unkn.	200-275
1951	Mit Seal	Closed	N/A	Unkn.	350-425
1954	Moose (Jell-O)	Closed	N/A	Unkn.	350-375
1951	Mother Parker (WEEI)	Closed	N/A	Unkn.	200-350
1947	Mr. Beacon Hill	Closed	N/A	Unkn.	50-75
1950	Mr. Obocell	Closed	N/A	Unkn.	75-125
1948	Mr. Rittenhouse Square	Closed	N/A	Unkn.	150-175
1948	Mr. Sheraton	Closed	N/A	Unkn.	400-500
1947	Mrs. Beacon Hill	Closed	N/A	Unkn.	50-75
1940	Mrs. Dan'l Boone	Closed	N/A	Unkn.	75-100
1940	Mrs. Harvard	Closed	N/A	Unkn.	125-150
1956	Mrs. Obocell	Closed	N/A	Unkn.	400-450
1948	Mrs. Rittenhouse Square	Closed	N/A	Unkn.	150-175
1959	Mrs. S.O.S.	Closed	N/A	Unkn.	300-350
1958	Mt. Vernon	Closed	N/A	Unkn.	400-500
1957	Nabisco Buffalo Bee	Closed	N/A	Unkn.	600-1000
1957	Nabisco Spoonmen	Closed	N/A	Unkn.	600-1000
1948	Nathaniel Hawthorne	Closed	N/A	Unkn.	175-200
1950	National Diaper Service	Closed	N/A	Unkn.	250-300
1963	Naumkeag Indian	Closed	N/A	Unkn.	225-275
1952	Neighboring Pews	Closed	N/A	Unkn.	200-300
1956	NYU Grad School of Bus. Admin. Bldg.	Closed	N/A	Unkn.	300-350
1951	The Observer & Dame New England.	Closed	N/A	Unkn.	325-375
1952	Old Powder House	Closed	N/A	Unkn.	250-300
1953	Old Put Enjoys a Licking	Closed	N/A	Unkn.	300-350
1955	Old Woman in the Shoe (Jell-O)	Closed	N/A	Unkn.	500-600
1957	Olde James Fort	Closed	N/A	Unkn.	250-300
XX	Ortho Gynecic	Closed	N/A	Unkn.	600-1000
1967	Ortho-Novum	Closed	N/A	Unkn.	600-1000
1952	Our Lady of Good Voyage	Closed	N/A	Unkn.	200-250
1954	Our Lady of Laleche	Closed	N/A	Unkn.	300-350
1965	Panti-Legs Girl PS	Closed	N/A	Unkn.	250-300
1949	Patrick Henry	Closed	N/A	Unkn.	100-125
1949	Paul Bunyan	Closed	N/A	Unkn.	150-250
1966	Paul Revere Plaque (W.T. Grant)	Closed	N/A	Unkn.	300-350
1941	Peacock	Closed	N/A	Unkn.	600-1000
1956	Permacel Tower of Tape Ashtray	Closed	N/A	Unkn.	600-1000
1960	Peter Stvyvesant	Closed	N/A	Unkn.	125-175
1940	Peter Stvyvesant	Closed	N/A	Unkn.	75-100
1941	Pheasant	Closed	N/A	Unkn.	600-1000
1950	Phoebe, House of 7 Gables	Closed	N/A	Unkn.	150-175
1940	Pocohontas	Closed	N/A	Unkn.	75-150
1961	Pope John 23rd	Closed	N/A	Unkn.	400-450
1965	Pope Paul VI	Closed	N/A	Unkn.	400-500
1956	Praying Hands	Closed	N/A	Unkn.	250-300
1947	Prince Philip	Closed	N/A	Unkn.	200-300
1947	Princess Elizabeth	Closed	N/A	Unkn.	200-300
1939	Priscilla	Closed	N/A	Unkn.	35-50
1951	Priscilla Fortesue (WEEI)	Closed	N/A	Unkn.	200-350
1946	Puritan Spinner	Closed	N/A	Unkn.	500-1000
1953	R.H. Stearns Chestnut Hill Mall	Closed	N/A	Unkn.	225-275
1954	Rabbit (Jell-O)	Closed	N/A	Unkn.	350-375
1956	Rarical Blacksmith	Closed	N/A	Unkn.	300-500
1948	Republican Victory	Closed	N/A	Unkn.	600-1000
1954	Resolute Ins. Co. Clipper PS	Closed	N/A	Unkn.	300-325
1956	Robin Hood & Friar Tuck	Closed	N/A	Unkn.	400-500
1956	Robin Hood & Little John	Closed	N/A	Unkn.	400-500
1958	Romeo & Juliet	Closed	N/A	Unkn.	400-500
1941	Rooster	Closed	N/A	Unkn.	600-1000
1958	Salem Savings Bank	Closed	N/A	Unkn.	250-300
1939	Sam Houston	Closed	N/A	Unkn.	75-100
1955	Santa (Jell-O)	Closed	N/A	Unkn.	500-600
1949	Sarah Henry	Closed	N/A	Unkn.	100-125
1946	Satchel-Eye Dyer	Closed	N/A	Unkn.	125-150
1953	The Schoolboy of 1850	Closed	N/A	Unkn.	350-400
1952	Scottish Girl (Jell-O)	Closed	N/A	Unkn.	350-375
1954	Scuba Diver	Closed	N/A	Unkn.	400-450
1962	Seaman's Bank for Savings	Closed	N/A	Unkn.	300-350
1951	Seb. Dealer Plaque (Marblehead)	Closed	N/A	Unkn.	300-350
1955	Second Bank-State St. Trust PS	Closed	N/A	Unkn.	300-325
1941	Secrets	Closed	N/A	Unkn.	600-1000
1938	Shaker Lady	Closed	N/A	Unkn.	50-100
1938	Shaker Man	Closed	N/A	Unkn.	50-100
1959	Siesta Coffee PS	Closed	N/A	Unkn.	600-1000
1951	Sir Frances Drake	Closed	N/A	Unkn.	250-300
1948	Sitzmark	Closed	N/A	Unkn.	175-200
1948	Slalom	Closed	N/A	Unkn.	175-200
1960	Son of the Desert	Closed	N/A	Unkn.	200-275
1957	Speedy Alka Seltzer	Closed	N/A	Unkn.	600-1000
1952	St. Joan d'Arc	Closed	N/A	Unkn.	300-350
1961	St. Jude Thaddeus	Closed	N/A	Unkn.	400-500
1954	St. Pius X	Closed	N/A	Unkn.	400-475
1952	St. Sebastian	Closed	N/A	Unkn.	300-350
1953	St. Teresa of Lisieux	Closed	N/A	Unkn.	225-275
1965	State Street Bank Globe	Closed	N/A	Unkn.	250-300
1954	Stimalose (Men)	Closed	N/A	Unkn.	600-1000
1954	Stimalose (Woman)	Closed	N/A	Unkn.	175-200
1952	Stork (Jell-O)	Closed	N/A	Unkn.	425-525
1960	Supp-Hose Lady	Closed	N/A	Unkn.	300-500
1941	Swan	Closed	N/A	Unkn.	600-1000
1954	Swan Boat Brooch-Enpty Seats	Closed	N/A	Unkn.	600-1000
1954	Swan Boat Brooch-Full Seats	Closed	N/A	Unkn.	600-1000
1948	Swedish Boy	Closed	N/A	Unkn.	250-500
1948	Swedish Girl	Closed	N/A	Unkn.	250-500
XX	Sylvania Electric-Bulb Display	Closed	N/A	Unkn.	600-1000
1952	Tabasco Sauce	Closed	N/A	Unkn.	400-500
1956	Texcel Tape Boy	Closed	N/A	Unkn.	350-425
1949	The Thinker	Closed	N/A	Unkn.	175-250
1956	Three Little Kittens (Jell-O)	Closed	N/A	Unkn.	375-400
1947	Tollhouse Town Crier	Closed	N/A	Unkn.	125-175
1961	Tony Piet	Closed	N/A	Unkn.	600-1000
1966	Town Lyne Indian	Closed	N/A	Unkn.	600-1000
1971	Town Meeting Plaque	Closed	N/A	Unkn.	350-400
1942	Tuba	Closed	N/A	Unkn.	325-375
1949	Uncle Mistletoe	Closed	N/A	Unkn.	250-300
1970	Uncle Sam in Orbit	Closed	N/A	Unkn.	350-400
1968	Watermill Candy Plaque	Closed	N/A	Unkn.	600-1000
1952	Weighing the Baby	Closed	N/A	Unkn.	200-300
1954	Whale (Jell-O)	Closed	N/A	Unkn.	350-375
1940	William Penn	Closed	N/A	Unkn.	100-150
1954	William Penn	Closed	N/A	Unkn.	175-225
1939	Williamsburg Governor	Closed	N/A	Unkn.	75-100
1939	Williamsburg Lady	Closed	N/A	Unkn.	75-100
1962	Yankee Clipper Sulfide	Closed	N/A	Unkn.	600-1000

Seymour Mann, Inc.

Bunny Musical Figurines - Kenji

YEAR ISSUE		EDITION LIMIT	YEAR RETD.	ISSUE PRICE	*QUOTE U.S.$
1991	Bunny In Teacup MH-781	Open		25.00	25
1991	Bunny In Teapot MH-780	Open		25.00	25

Cat Musical Figurines - Kenji

YEAR ISSUE		EDITION LIMIT	YEAR RETD.	ISSUE PRICE	*QUOTE U.S.$
1990	Bride/Groom Cat MH-738	Closed	1995	37.50	38
1991	Brown Cat in Bag	Closed	1995	30.00	30
1987	Brown Cat in Bag MH-617B/6	Closed	1995	30.00	30
1991	Brown Cat in Hat	Closed	1995	35.00	35
1988	Brown Cat in Hat MH-634B/6	Closed	1995	35.00	35
1991	Brown Cat in Teacup	Closed	1995	30.00	30
1987	Brown Cat in Teacup MH-600VGB16	Closed	1995	30.00	30
1987	Cat in Garbage Can MH-490	Closed	1995	35.00	35
1987	Cat in Rose Teacup MH-600VG	Closed	1995	30.00	30
1990	Cat Asleep MH-735	Closed	1995	17.50	18
1990	Cat Calico in Easy Chair MH-743VG	Closed	1995	27.50	28
1991	Cat in Bag	Closed	1995	30.00	30
1991	Cat in Bag	Closed	1995	30.00	30

*Quotes have been rounded up to nearest dollar

YEAR ISSUE	EDITION LIMIT	YEAR RETD.	ISSUE PRICE	*QUOTE U.S.$
1987 Cat in Bag MH-614	Closed	1995	30.00	30
1987 Cat in Bag MH-617	Closed	1995	30.00	30
1989 Cat in Basinet MH-714	Closed	1995	35.00	35
1989 Cat in Basket MH-713B	Closed	1995	35.00	35
1991 Cat in Basket MH-768	Closed	1995	35.00	35
1991 Cat in Bootie	Closed	1995	35.00	35
1990 Cat in Bootie MH-728	Closed	1995	35.00	35
1990 Cat in Dress MH-751VG	Closed	1995	37.50	38
1989 Cat in Flower MH-709	Closed	1995	35.00	35
1991 Cat in Garbage Can	Closed	1995	35.00	35
1989 Cat in Gift Box Musical MH-732	Closed	1995	40.00	40
1991 Cat in Hat	Closed	1995	35.00	35
1991 Cat in Hat Box	Closed	1995	35.00	35
1988 Cat in Hat Box MH-634	Closed	1995	35.00	35
1988 Cat in Hat MH-634B	Closed	1995	35.00	35
1991 Cat in Rose Teacup	Closed	1995	30.00	30
1989 Cat in Shoe MH-718	Closed	1995	30.00	30
1991 Cat in Teacup	Closed	1995	30.00	30
1987 Cat in Teacup MH-600VGG	Closed	1995	30.00	30
1991 Cat in Teapot Brown	Closed	1995	30.00	30
1987 Cat in Teapot Brown MH-600VGB	Closed	1995	30.00	30
1989 Cat in Water Can Musical MH-712	Closed	1995	35.00	35
1991 Cat Momma MH-758	Closed	1995	35.00	35
1989 Cat on Basket MH-713	Closed	1995	35.00	35
1990 Cat on Gift Box Music MH-740	Closed	1995	40.00	40
1990 Cat on Pillow MH-731	Closed	1995	17.50	18
1991 Cat on Tipped Garbage Can	Closed	1995	35.00	35
1987 Cat on Tipped Garbage Can MH-498	Closed	1995	35.00	35
1990 Cat Sailor in Rocking Boat MH-734	Closed	1995	45.00	45
1990 Cat w/Bow on Pink Pillow MH-741P	Closed	1995	33.50	34
1989 Cat w/Coffee Cup Musical MH-706	Closed	1995	35.00	35
1990 Cat w/Parrot Musical MH-730	Closed	1995	37.50	38
1989 Cat w/Swing Musical MH-710	Closed	1995	35.00	35
1991 Cat Watching Butterfly MH-784	Closed	1995	17.50	18
1991 Cat Watching Canary MH-783	Closed	1995	25.00	25
1991 Cat With Bow on Pink Pillow MH-741P	Closed	1995	33.50	34
1991 Cats Ball Shape	Closed	1995	25.00	25
1985 Cats Ball Shape MH-303A/G	Closed	1995	25.00	25
1990 Cats Graduation MH-745	Closed	1995	27.50	28
1989 Cats in Basket XMAS-664	Closed	1995	7.50	8
1991 Cats w/Ribbon	Closed	1995	30.00	30
1986 Cats w/Ribbon MH-481A/C	Closed	1995	30.00	30
1991 Family Cat MH-770	Closed	1995	35.00	35
1991 Grey Cat in Bootie	Closed	1995	35.00	35
1990 Grey Cat in Bootie MH-728G/6	Closed	1995	35.00	35
1991 Kitten Picking Tulips MH-756	Closed	1995	40.00	40
1990 Kitten Trio in Carriage MH-742	Closed	1995	37.50	38
1991 Kittens w/Balls of Yarn	Closed	1995	30.00	30
1987 Kittens w/Balls of Yarn MH-612	Closed	1995	30.00	30
1991 Musical Bear	Closed	1995	27.50	28
1987 Musical Bear MH-602	Closed	1995	27.50	28
1991 Revolving Cat with Butterfly MH-759	Closed	1995	40.00	40
1991 Teapot Cat	Closed	1995	30.00	30
1987 Teapot Cat MH-631	Closed	1995	30.00	30
1987 Valentine Cat in Bag Musical MH-600	Closed	1995	33.50	34
1987 Valentine Cat in Teacup MH-600VLT	Closed	1995	33.50	34

Christmas Collection - Various

YEAR ISSUE	EDITION LIMIT	YEAR RETD.	ISSUE PRICE	*QUOTE U.S.$
1991 2 Tone Stone Church MER-360B - J. White	Closed	1993	35.00	35
1986 Antique Santa Musical XMAS-364 - J. White	Closed	1987	20.00	20
1990 Antique Shop Lite Up House MER-376 - J. White	Closed	1993	27.50	28
1991 Apothecary Lite Up CJ-128 - Jaimy	Closed	1993	33.50	34
1990 Bakery Lite Up House MER-373 - J. White	Closed	1993	27.50	28
1991 Beige Church Lite Up House MER-360A - Jaimy	Closed	1993	35.00	35
1990 Bethlehem Lite Up Set 3 CP-59893 - J. White	Closed	1993	120.00	120
1991 Boy and Girl on Bell CJ-132 - Jaimy	Closed	1993	13.50	14
1991 Boy on Horse CJ-457 - Jaimy	Closed	1993	6.00	6
1990 Brick Church Lite Up House MER-360C - J. White	Closed	1993	35.00	35
1991 Carolers Under Lamppost CJ-114A - Jaimy	Closed	1993	7.50	8
1989 Cat in Teacup Musical XMAS-600 - J. White	Closed	1992	30.00	30
1990 Cathedral Lite Up House MER-362 - J. White	Closed	1993	37.50	38
1991 Church Lite Up MER-410 - J. White	Closed	1993	17.50	18
1990 Church Lite Up House MER-310 - J. White	Closed	1993	27.50	28
1991 Church w/Blue Roof Lite Up House MER-360E - J. White	Closed	1993	35.00	35
1991 Covered Bridge CJ-101 - Jaimy	Closed	1993	27.50	28
1990 Deep Gold Church Lite Up House MER-360D - J. White	Closed	1993	35.00	35
1990 Double Store Lite Up House MER-311 - J. White	Closed	1993	27.50	28
1991 Elf w/Doll House CB-14 - E. Mann	Closed	1993	30.00	30
1991 Elf w/Hammer CB-11 - E. Mann	Closed	1993	30.00	30
1991 Elf w/Reindeer CJ-422 - Jaimy	Closed	1993	9.00	9
1991 Elf w/Rocking Horse CB-10 - E. Mann	Closed	1993	30.00	30
1991 Elf w/Teddy Bear CB-12 - E. Mann	Closed	1993	30.00	30
1991 Emily's Toys CJ-127 - Jaimy	Closed	1993	35.00	35
1991 Father and Mother w/Daughter CJ-133 - Jaimy	Closed	1993	13.50	14
1991 Father Christmas CJ-233	Closed	1993	33.50	34
1991 Father Christmas w/Holly CJ-239	Closed	1993	35.00	35
1991 Fire Station CJ-129 - Jaimy	Closed	1993	50.00	50
1990 Fire Station Lite Up House XMS-1550C - E.Mann	Closed	1993	25.00	25
1991 Four Men Talking CJ-138 - Jaimy	Closed	1993	27.50	28
1991 Gift Shop Lite Up CJ-125 - Jaimy	Closed	1993	33.50	34
1991 Girls w/Instruments CJ-131 - Jaimy	Closed	1993	13.50	14
1990 Grist Mill Lite Up House MER-372 - J. White	Closed	1993	27.50	28
1991 Horse and Coach CJ-207 - Jaimy	Closed	1993	25.00	25
1990 Inn Lite Up House MER-316 - J. White	Closed	1993	27.50	28
1986 Jumbo Santa/Toys XMAS-38 - J. White	Closed	1987	45.00	45
1991 Kids Building Igloo CJ-137 - Jaimy	Closed	1993	13.50	14
1991 Lady w/Dogs CJ-208 - Jaimy	Closed	1993	13.50	14
1990 Leatherworks Lite Up House MER-371 - J. White	Closed	1993	27.50	28
1990 Library Lite Up House MER-317 - J. White	Closed	1993	27.50	28
1990 Light House Lite Up House MER-370 - J. White	Closed	1993	27.50	28
1991 Man w/Wheelbarrow CJ-134 - Jaimy	Closed	1993	13.50	14
1990 Mansion Lite Up House MER-319 - J. White	Closed	1993	27.50	28
1991 Mr/Mrs Santa Musical CJ-281 - Jaimy	Closed	1993	37.50	38
1990 New England Church Lite Up House MER-375 - J. White	Closed	1993	27.50	28
1990 New England General Store Lite Up House MER-377 - J. White	Closed	1993	27.50	28
1991 Newsboy Under Lamppost CJ-144B - Jaimy	Closed	1993	15.00	15
1991 Old Curiosity Lite Up CJ-201 - Jaimy	Closed	1993	37.50	38
1991 Playhouse Lite Up CJ-122 - Jaimy	Closed	1993	50.00	50
1991 Public Library Lite Up CJ-121 - Jaimy	Closed	1993	45.00	45
1990 Railroad Station Lite Up House MER-374 - J. White	Closed	1993	27.50	28
1991 Reindeer Barn Lite Up House CJ-421 - Jaimy	Closed	1993	55.00	55
1991 Restaurant Lite Up House MER-354 - J. White	Closed	1993	27.50	28
1990 Roly Poly Santa 3 Asst. CJ-253/4/7 - Jaimy	Closed	1993	17.50	18
1991 Santa Cat Roly Poly CJ-252	Closed	1993	17.50	18
1991 Santa Fixing Sled CJ-237	Closed	1993	35.00	35
1991 Santa In Barrel Waterball CJ-243 - Jaimy	Closed	1993	33.50	34
1989 Santa in Sled w/Reindeer CJ-3 - Jaimy	Closed	1992	25.00	25
1991 Santa In Toy Shop CJ-441 - Jaimy	Closed	1993	33.50	34
1989 Santa Musicals CJ-1/4 - Jaimy	Closed	1992	27.50	28
1990 Santa on Chimney Musical CJ-212 - Jaimy	Closed	1993	33.50	34
1989 Santa on Horse CJ-33A - Jaimy	Closed	1992	33.50	34
1990 Santa on See Saw TR-14 - E. Mann	Closed	1993	30.00	30
1991 Santa On Train CJ-458 - Jaimy	Closed	1993	6.00	6
1991 Santa On White Horse CJ-338 - E. Mann	Closed	1993	33.50	34
1991 Santa Packing Bag CJ-210 - Jaimy	Closed	1993	33.50	34
1990 Santa Packing Bag CJ-210 - Jaimy	Closed	1993	33.50	34
1991 Santa Packing Bag CJ-236 - Jaimy	Closed	1993	35.00	35
1991 Santa Sleeping Musical CJ-214 - Jaimy	Closed	1993	30.00	30
1991 Santa w/Bag and List CJ-431 - Jaimy	Closed	1993	33.50	34
1991 Santa w/Deer Musical CJ-21R - Jaimy	Closed	1993	33.50	34
1991 Santa w/Girl Waterball CJ-241 - Jaimy	Closed	1993	33.50	34
1991 Santa w/Lantern Musical CJ-211 - Jaimy	Closed	1993	33.50	34
1990 Santa w/List CJ-23 - Jaimy	Closed	1993	27.50	28
1989 Santa w/List CJ-23 - Jaimy	Closed	1992	27.50	28
1991 Santa w/List CJ-23R - Jaimy	Closed	1993	27.50	28
1990 School Lite Up House MER-320 - J. White	Closed	1993	27.50	28
1991 The Skaters CJ-205 - Jaimy	Closed	1993	25.00	25
1991 Snowball Fight CJ-124B - Jaimy	Closed	1993	25.00	25
1991 Soup Seller Waterball CJ-209 - Jaimy	Closed	1993	25.00	25
1991 Stone Cottage Lite Up CJ-100 - Jaimy	Closed	1993	37.50	38
1991 Stone House Lite Up CJ-102 - Jaimy	Closed	1993	45.00	45
1991 The Story Teller CJ-204 - Jaimy	Closed	1993	20.00	20
1991 Teddy Bear On Wheels CB-42 - E. Mann	Closed	1993	25.00	25
1991 Three Ladies w/Food CJ-136 - Jaimy	Closed	1993	13.50	14
1990 Town Hall Lite Up House MER-315 - J. White	Closed	1993	27.50	28
1991 The Toy Seller CJ-206 - Jaimy	Closed	1993	13.50	14
1991 Toy Store Lite Up House MER-355 - J. White	Closed	1993	27.50	28
1991 Trader Santa Musical CJ-442 - Jaimy	Closed	1993	30.00	30
1991 Train Set MER-378 - J. White	Closed	1993	25.00	25
1985 Trumpeting Angel w/Jesus XMAS-527 - J. White	Closed	1987	40.00	40
1991 Two Old Men Talking CJ-107 - Jaimy	Closed	1993	13.50	14
1991 Village Mill Lite Up CJ-104 - Jaimy	Closed	1993	30.00	30
1991 Village People CJ-116A - Jaimy	Closed	1993	60.00	60
1985 Virgin w/Christ Musical XMAS-528 - J. White	Closed	1987	33.50	34
1991 Woman w/Cow CJ-135 - Jaimy	Closed	1993	15.00	15
1991 Ye Olde Town Tavern CJ-130 - Jaimy	Closed	1993	45.00	45

Christmas In America - Various

YEAR ISSUE	EDITION LIMIT	YEAR RETD.	ISSUE PRICE	*QUOTE U.S.$
1990 Cart With People - E. Mann	Closed	1992	25.00	38
1988 Doctor's Office Lite Up - E. Mann	Closed	1990	27.50	28
1991 New England Church Lite Up House MER-375 - J. White	Closed	1992	27.50	28
1991 New England General Store Lite Up House MER-377 - J. White	Closed	1992	27.50	28
1989 Santa in Sleigh - E. Mann	Closed	1993	25.00	4
1988 Set/3, Capitol, White House, Mt. Vernon - E. Mann	Closed	1990	75.00	15

Christmas Village - L. Sciola

YEAR ISSUE	EDITION LIMIT	YEAR RETD.	ISSUE PRICE	*QUOTE U.S.$
1991 Away, Away	Closed	1993	30.00	3
1991 Counsil House	Closed	1993	60.00	6
1991 Curiosity Shop	Closed	1993	45.00	4
1991 Emily's Toys	Closed	1993	45.00	4
1991 The Fire Station	Closed	1993	60.00	6
1991 On Thin Ice	Closed	1993	30.00	3
1991 The Playhouse	Closed	1993	60.00	6
1991 Public Library	Closed	1993	50.00	5
1991 Scrooge/Marley's Counting House	Closed	1993	45.00	4
1991 Story Teller	Closed	1993	20.00	2
1991 Ye Old Gift Shoppe	Closed	1993	50.00	5

Dickens Collection - Various

YEAR ISSUE	EDITION LIMIT	YEAR RETD.	ISSUE PRICE	*QUOTE U.S.$
1990 Black Swan Inn Lite Up XMS-7000E - J. White	Closed	1993	30.00	3
1990 Cratchit Family MER-121 - J. White	Closed	1993	37.50	3
1991 Cratchit's Lite Up House CJ-200 - Jaimy	Closed	1993	37.50	
1991 Cratchit/Tiny Tim Musical CJ-117 - Jaimy	Closed	1993	33.50	
1990 Cratchit/Tiny Tim Musical MER-105 - J. White	Closed	1993	33.50	
1989 Cratchits Lite Up XMS-7000A - J. White	Closed	1991	30.00	
1989 Fezziwigs Lite Up XMS-7000C - J. White	Closed	1991	30.00	
1989 Gift Shoppe Lite Up XMS-7000D - J. White	Closed	1991	30.00	
1990 Hen Poultry Lite Up XMS-7000H - J. White	Closed	1993	30.00	
1991 Scrooge Musical CJ-118 - Jaimy	Closed	1993	30.00	
1991 Scrooge/Marley Counting House CJ-202 - Jaimy	Closed	1993	37.50	
1989 Scrooge/Marley Lite Up XMS-7000B - J. White	Closed	1991	30.00	
1990 Tea and Spice Lite Up XMS-7000F - J. White	Closed	1993	30.00	
1990 Waite Fish Store Lite Up XMS-7000G - J. White	Closed	1993	30.00	

Gingerbread Christmas Collection - J. Sauerbrey

YEAR ISSUE	EDITION LIMIT	YEAR RETD.	ISSUE PRICE	*QUOTE U.S.$
1991 Gingerbread Angel CJ-411	Closed	1993	7.50	
1991 Gingerbread Church Lite Up House CJ-403	Closed	1993	65.00	
1991 Gingerbread House CJ-416	Closed	1993	7.50	
1991 Gingerbread House Lite Up CJ-404	Closed	1993	65.00	
1991 Gingerbread Man CJ-415	Closed	1993	7.50	
1991 Gingerbread Mansion Lite Up CJ-405	Closed	1993	70.00	
1991 Gingerbread Mouse/Boot CJ-409	Closed	1993	7.50	
1991 Gingerbread Mrs. Claus CJ-414	Closed	1993	7.50	
1991 Gingerbread Reindeer CJ-410	Closed	1993	7.50	
1991 Gingerbread Rocking Horse Music CJ-460	Closed	1993	33.50	
1991 Gingerbread Santa CJ-408	Closed	1993	7.50	
1991 Gingerbread Sleigh CJ-406	Closed	1993	7.50	
1991 Gingerbread Snowman CJ-412	Closed	1993	7.50	
1991 Gingerbread Swan Musical CJ-462	Closed	1993	33.50	
1991 Gingerbread Sweet Shop Lite Up House	Closed	1993	60.00	
1991 Gingerbread Teddy Bear Music CJ-461	Closed	1993	33.50	
1991 Gingerbread Toy Shop Lite Up House CJ-402	Closed	1993	60.00	
1991 Gingerbread Tree CJ-407	Closed	1993	7.50	
1991 Gingerbread Village Lite Up House CJ-400	Closed	1993	60.00	

Victorian Christmas Collection - Various

YEAR ISSUE	EDITION LIMIT	YEAR RETD.	ISSUE PRICE	*QUOTE U.S.$
1991 Antique Shop Lite Up House MER-353 - J. White	Closed	1993	27.50	
1991 Beige Church Lite Up House MER-351 - J. White	Closed	1993	35.00	
1991 Book Store Lite Up House MER-351 - J. White	Closed	1993	27.50	
1991 Church Lite Up House MER-350 - J. White	Closed	1993	37.50	
1991 Country Store Lite Up House MER-356 - J. White	Closed	1993	27.50	
1993 Couple Against Wind CJ-420 - Jaimy	Closed	1994	15.00	

Year	Issue	Edition Limit	Year Retd.	Issue Price	*Quote U.S.$
1991	Inn Lite Up House MER-352 - J. White	Closed	1993	27.50	28
1991	Little Match Girl CJ-419 - Jaimy	Closed	1993	9.00	9
1990	Toy/Doll House Lite Up MER-314 - J. White	Closed	1993	27.50	28
1990	Two Boys w/Snowman CJ-106 - Jaimy	Closed	1993	12.00	12
1990	Victorian House Lite Up House MER-312 - J. White	Closed	1993	27.50	28
1990	Yarn Shop Lite Up House MER-313 - J. White	Closed	1993	27.50	28

Wizard Of Oz - 40th Anniversary - E. Mann

Year	Issue	Edition Limit	Year Retd.	Issue Price	*Quote U.S.$
1979	Dorothy, Scarecrow, Lion, Tinman	Closed	1981	7.50	45
1979	Dorothy, Scarecrow, Lion, Tinman, Musical	Closed	1981	12.50	75

Shelia's Collectibles

Shelia's Collectors' Society - S. Thompson

Year	Issue	Edition Limit	Year Retd.	Issue Price	*Quote U.S.$
1993	Anne Peacock House SOC01	Retrd.	1994	16.00	100
1993	Susan B. Anthony CGA93	Retrd.	1994	Gift	100
1993	Anne Peacock House Print	Retrd.	1994	Gift	N/A
1994	Seaview Cottage SOC02	Retrd.	1995	17.00	72
1994	Helen Keller's Birthplace-Ivy Green CGA94	Retrd.	1995	Gift	40-75
1994	Collector's Society T-Shirt	Retrd.	1995	Gift	N/A
1995	Pink Lady SOC03	6/96		20.00	20
1995	Red Cross CGA95	Retrd.	1996	Gift	N/A
1995	Collector's Society T-Shirt & Collector's Society Pin	Retrd.	1996	Gift	N/A
1996	Tinker Toy House SOC04	6/97		20.00	N/A
1996	Tatman House CGA96	4/97		Gift	N/A
1996	Tinker Toy House Ornament	4/97		Gift	N/A

Accessories - S. Thompson

Year	Issue	Edition Limit	Year Retd.	Issue Price	*Quote U.S.$
1994	Amish Quilt Line COL12	Retrd.	1994	18.00	25-45
1993	Apple Tree COL09	Retrd.	1996	12.00	16
1996	Autumn Tree ACC09	Open		14.00	14
1996	Barber Gazebo ACC05	Open		13.00	13
1993	Dogwood Tree COL08	Retrd.	1996	12.00	16
1992	Fence 5" COL04	Retrd.	1993	9.00	25
1992	Fence 7" COL05	Retrd.	1995	10.00	25
1995	Flower Garden ACC02	Open		13.00	30-50
1994	Formal Garden COL13	Retrd.	1994	18.00	35
1992	Gazebo W/Victorian Lady COL02	Retrd.	1995	11.00	15-25
1996	Grazing Cows ACC04	Open		12.00	12
1992	Lake With Swan COL06	Retrd.	1993	11.00	20-30
1992	Oak Bower COL03	Retrd.	1993	11.00	25-50
1996	Palm Tree ACC07	Open		14.00	14
1995	Real Estate Sign ACC03	Open		12.00	12
1996	Sailboat ACC06	Open		12.00	12
1996	Spring Tree ACC10	Open		14.00	14
1996	Summertime Picket Fence ACC08	Open		12.00	12
1994	Sunrise At 80 Meeting COL10	Retrd.	1994	18.00	25-35
1992	Tree With Bush COL07	Retrd.	1996	10.00	12-18
1994	Victorian Arbor COL11	Retrd.	1994	18.00	25-35
1995	Wisteria Arbor ACC01	Open		12.00	12
1992	Wrought Iron Gate With Magnolias COL01	Retrd.	1993	11.00	20-50

American Barns - S. Thompson

Year	Issue	Edition Limit	Year Retd.	Issue Price	*Quote U.S.$
1995	Casey Barn BAR04	Open		18.00	18
1995	Mail Pouch Barn BAR03	Open		18.00	18
1995	Pennsylvania Dutch Barn AP BAR02	Retrd.	1995	20.00	40
1995	Pennsylvania Dutch Barn BAR02	Retrd.	1996	18.00	20-35
1994	Rock City Barn AP BAR01	Retrd.	1994	20.00	20-40
1994	Rock City Barn BAR01	Open		18.00	18

Amish Village - S. Thompson

Year	Issue	Edition Limit	Year Retd.	Issue Price	*Quote U.S.$
1994	Amish Barn (renovated) AMS04II	Open		17.00	17
1993	Amish Barn AMS04	Open		17.00	17
1993	Amish Barn, AP AMS04	Retrd.	1993	20.00	40
1994	Amish Buggy (renovated) AMS05II	Open		12.00	12
1993	Amish Buggy AMS05	Open		12.00	12
1993	Amish Buggy, AP AMS05	Retrd.	1993	16.00	25-35
1994	Amish Home (renovated) AMS01II	Open		17.00	17
1993	Amish Home AMS01	Open		17.00	17
1993	Amish Home, AP AMS01	Retrd.	1993	20.00	25-35
1994	Amish School (renovated) AMS02II	Open		15.00	15
1993	Amish School AMS02	Open		15.00	15
1993	Amish School, AP AMS02	Retrd.	1993	20.00	25-35
1994	Covered Bridge (renovated) AMS03II	Open		16.00	16
1993	Covered Bridge AMS03	Open		16.00	16
1993	Covered Bridge, AP AMS03	Retrd.	1993	20.00	25-35
1995	Roadside Stand AMS06	Open		17.00	17
1995	Roadside Stand, AP AMS06	Retrd.	1995	24.00	30-40

Atlanta - S. Thompson

Year	Issue	Edition Limit	Year Retd.	Issue Price	*Quote U.S.$
1995	Fox Theatre ATL06	Open		19.00	19
1995	Hammond's House ATL05	Open		18.00	18
1995	Swan House ATL03	Open		18.00	18
1995	Tullie Smith House ATL01	Open		17.00	17
1995	Victorian Playhouse ATL02	Open		17.00	17
1995	Wren's Nest ATL04	Open		19.00	19

Charleston - S. Thompson

Year	Issue	Edition Limit	Year Retd.	Issue Price	*Quote U.S.$
1994	#2 Meeting Street (renovated) CHS06II	Open		16.00	16
1991	#2 Meeting Street CHS06	Open		15.00	15
1990	90 Church St. CHS17	Retrd.	1993	12.00	50
1994	Ashe House (renovated) CHS51II	Open		16.00	16
1993	Ashe House CHS51	Open		16.00	16
1991	Beth Elohim Temple CHS20	Retrd.	1993	15.00	22-35
1994	The Citadel (renovated) CHS22II	Open		16.00	16
1993	The Citadel CHS22	Open		16.00	16
1993	City Hall (No banner) CHS21	Retrd.	1993	15.00	115
1993	City Hall (without Spuleto colors) CHS21	Retrd.	1993	15.00	200
1993	City Hall CHS21	Retrd.	1993	15.00	80-150
1991	City Market (closed gates) CHS07	Retrd.	1991	15.00	25-65
1991	City Market (open gates) CHS07	Open		15.00	15
1994	City Market (renovated) CHS07II	Open		15.00	15
1994	College of Charleston (renovated) CHS40II	Retrd.	1996	16.00	19-25
1993	College of Charleston CHS40	Retrd.	1996	16.00	25
1993	College of Charleston, AP CHS40	Retrd.	1993	20.00	36
1992	Dock Street Theater (chimney) CHS08	Retrd.	1993	15.00	30-65
1991	Dock Street Theater (no chimney) CHS08	Retrd.	1992	15.00	65
1994	Edmonston-Alston (renovated) CHS04II	Retrd.	1995	16.00	50
1991	Edmonston-Alston CHS04	Retrd.	1995	15.00	50
1990	Exchange Building CHS15	Retrd.	1994	15.00	25-50
1990	Heyward-Washington House CHS02	Retrd.	1993	15.00	25-50
1994	John Rutledge House Inn (renovated) CHS50II	Open		16.00	16
1993	John Rutledge House Inn CHS50	Open		16.00	16
1991	Magnolia Plantation House (beige curtains) CHS03	Retrd.	1996	16.00	21
1994	Magnolia Plantation House (renovated) CHS03II	Retrd.	1996	16.00	21
1991	Magnolia Plantation House (white curtains) CHS03	Retrd.	1996	16.00	16
1990	Manigault House CHS01	Retrd.	1993	15.00	25-45
1990	Middleton Plantation CHS19	Retrd.	1991	9.00	150-200
1990	Pink House CHS18	Retrd.	1993	12.00	15-35
1990	Powder Magazine CHS16	Retrd.	1991	9.00	125-225
1994	Single Side Porch (renovated) CHS30II	Open		16.00	16
1993	Single Side Porch CHS30	Open		16.00	16
1993	Single Side Porch, AP CHS30	Retrd.	1993	20.00	36
1990	St. Michael's Church CHS14	Retrd.	1994	15.00	25-40
1994	St. Philip's Church (renovated) CHS05II	Retrd.	1996	15.00	18-25
1991	St. Philip's Church CHS05	Retrd.	1996	15.00	25
1991	St. Phillip's Church (misspelling Phillips) CHS05	Retrd.	1996	15.00	15

Charleston Battery - S. Thompson

Year	Issue	Edition Limit	Year Retd.	Issue Price	*Quote U.S.$
1996	22 South Battery CHB01	Open		19.00	19
1996	22 South Battery, AP CHB01	109		24.00	40
1996	24 South Battery CHB02	Open		19.00	19
1996	24 South Battery, AP CHB02	99		24.00	40
1996	26 South Battery CHB03	Open		19.00	19
1996	26 South Battery, AP CHB03	74		24.00	40
1996	28 South Battery CHB04	Open		19.00	19
1996	28 South Battery, AP CHB04	74		24.00	40

Charleston Gold Seal - S. Thompson

Year	Issue	Edition Limit	Year Retd.	Issue Price	*Quote U.S.$
1988	90 Church St. CHS17	Retrd.	1990	9.00	50
1988	CHS31 Rainbow Row-rust	Retrd.	1990	9.00	N/A
1988	CHS32 Rainbow Row-tan	Retrd.	1990	9.00	N/A
1988	CHS33 Rainbow Row-cream	Retrd.	1990	9.00	N/A
1988	CHS34 Rainbow Row-green	Retrd.	1990	9.00	N/A
1988	CHS35 Rainbow Row-lavender	Retrd.	1990	9.00	N/A
1988	CHS36 Rainbow Row-pink	Retrd.	1990	9.00	N/A
1988	CHS37 Rainbow Row-blue	Retrd.	1990	9.00	N/A
1988	CHS38 Rainbow Row-lt. yellow	Retrd.	1990	9.00	N/A
1988	CHS39 Rainbow Row-lt. pink	Retrd.	1990	9.00	N/A
1988	Exchange Building CHS15	Retrd.	1990	9.00	N/A
1988	Middleton Plantation CHS19	Retrd.	1990	9.00	150
1988	Pink House CHS18	Retrd.	1990	9.00	36
1988	Powder Magazine CHS16	Retrd.	1990	9.00	250
1988	St. Michael's Church CHS14	Retrd.	1990	9.00	N/A

Charleston II - S. Thompson

Year	Issue	Edition Limit	Year Retd.	Issue Price	*Quote U.S.$
1995	Boone Hall Plantation CHS56	Open		18.00	18
1995	Boone Hall Plantation, AP CHS56	Retrd.	1995	24.00	40
1994	Drayton House CHS52	Open		18.00	18
1994	Drayton House, AP CHS52	Retrd.	1994	24.00	40-75
1996	Huguenot Church CHS58	Open		19.00	19
1996	Huguenot Church, AP CHS58	95		24.00	40
1996	Magnolia Garden CHS57	Open		19.00	19
1995	O'Donnell's Folly CHS55	Open		18.00	18
1995	O'Donnell's Folly, AP CHS55	Retrd.	1995	24.00	45
1996	Sotille CHS59	Open		19.00	19
1996	Sotille, AP CHS59	98		24.00	40

Charleston Rainbow Row - S. Thompson

Year	Issue	Edition Limit	Year Retd.	Issue Price	*Quote U.S.$
1990	CHS31 Rainbow Row-rust	Retrd.	1993	9.00	40
1990	CHS32 Rainbow Row-cream	Retrd.	1993	9.00	20-35
1990	CHS33 Rainbow Row-tan	Retrd.	1993	9.00	25
1990	CHS34 Rainbow Row-green	Retrd.	1993	9.00	23
1990	CHS35 Rainbow Row-lavender	Retrd.	1993	9.00	33
1990	CHS36 Rainbow Row-pink	Retrd.	1993	9.00	23-35
1990	CHS37 Rainbow Row-blue	Retrd.	1993	9.00	23-40
1990	CHS38 Rainbow Row-lt. yellow	Retrd.	1993	9.00	40
1990	CHS39 Rainbow Row-lt. pink	Retrd.	1993	9.00	25
1993	CHS41 Rainbow Row-aurora	Open		13.00	13
1994	CHS41II Rainbow Row-aurora (renovated)	Open		13.00	13
1993	CHS42 Rainbow Row-off-white	Open		13.00	13
1994	CHS42II Rainbow Row-off-white (renovated)	Open		13.00	13
1993	CHS43 Rainbow Row-cream	Open		13.00	13
1994	CHS43II Rainbow Row-cream (renovated)	Open		13.00	13
1993	CHS44 Rainbow Row-green	Open		13.00	13
1994	CHS44II Rainbow Row-green (renovated)	Open		13.00	13
1993	CHS45 Rainbow Row-lavender	Open		13.00	13
1994	CHS45II Rainbow Row-lavender (renovated)	Open		13.00	13
1993	CHS46 Rainbow Row-pink	Open		13.00	13
1994	CHS46II Rainbow Row-pink (renovated)	Open		13.00	13
1993	CHS47 Rainbow Row-blue	Open		13.00	13
1994	CHS47II Rainbow Row-blue (renovated)	Open		13.00	13
1993	CHS48 Rainbow Row-yellow	Open		13.00	13
1994	CHS48 Rainbow Row-yellow (renovated)	Open		13.00	13
1993	CHS49 Rainbow Row-gray	Open		13.00	13
1994	CHS49II Rainbow Row-gray (renovated)	Open		13.00	13
1993	Rainbow Row Sign	Retrd.	N/A	12.50	20

Dicken's Village - S. Thompson

Year	Issue	Edition Limit	Year Retd.	Issue Price	*Quote U.S.$
1991	Butcher Shop XMS03	Retrd.	1993	15.00	30
1991	Evergreen Tree XMS08	Retrd.	1993	11.00	20-40
1991	Gazebo & Carolers XMS06	Retrd.	1993	12.00	17-40
1991	Scrooge & Marley's Shop XMS01	Retrd.	1993	15.00	25-50
1991	Scrooge's Home XMS05	Retrd.	1993	15.00	20-40
1991	Toy Shoppe XMS04	Retrd.	1993	15.00	30-40
1991	Victorian Apartment Building XMS02	Retrd.	1993	15.00	30-40
1992	Victorian Church XMS09	Retrd.	1993	15.00	25-50
1991	Victorian Skaters XMS07	Retrd.	1993	12.00	15-40
1992	Set	Retrd.	1993	125.00	175-190

Galveston - S. Thompson

Year	Issue	Edition Limit	Year Retd.	Issue Price	*Quote U.S.$
1995	Beissner House GLV04	Open		18.00	18
1995	Dancing Pavillion GLV03	Open		18.00	18
1995	Frenkel House GLV01	Open		18.00	18
1995	Reymershoffer House GLV02	Open		18.00	18

Ghost House Series - S. Thompson

Year	Issue	Edition Limit	Year Retd.	Issue Price	*Quote U.S.$
1995	Gaffos House GHO04	Open		19.00	19
1994	Inside-Outside House GHO01	Retrd.	1996	18.00	25
1994	Inside-Outside House, AP GHO01	Retrd.	1994	20.00	30-40
1994	Pirates' House GHO02	Retrd.	1996	18.00	20-40
1994	Pirates' House, AP GHO02	Retrd.	1994	20.00	25-40
1995	Red Castle GHO03	Open		19.00	19

Gone with the Wind - S. Thompson

Year	Issue	Edition Limit	Year Retd.	Issue Price	*Quote U.S.$
1995	Aunt Pittypat's GWW03	Open		24.00	24
1995	Aunt Pittypat's, AP GWW03	Retrd.	1995	30.00	40
1995	General Store GWW04	Open		24.00	24
1995	General Store, AP GWW04	Retrd.	1995	30.00	40
1995	Loew's Grand GWW05	Retrd.	1995	24.00	26
1996	Silhouette GWW06	Open		16.00	16
1995	Loew's Grand, AP GWW05	Retrd.	1995	30.00	25-75
1995	Tara GWW01	Open		24.00	24
1995	Tara, AP GWW01	Retrd.	1995	30.00	25-75
1995	Twelve Oaks GWW02	Open		24.00	24
1995	Twelve Oaks, AP GWW02	Retrd.	1995	30.00	40
1995	Set of 5, AP	Retrd.	1995	150.00	250

Inventor Series - S. Thompson

Year	Issue	Edition Limit	Year Retd.	Issue Price	*Quote U.S.$
1993	Ford Motor Company (green) INV01	Retrd.	1993	17.00	25-45
1993	Ford Motor Company (grey) INV01	Retrd.	1994	17.00	25
1993	Ford Motor Company, AP INV01	Retrd.	1993	20.00	40
1993	Menlo Park Laboratory (cream) INV02	Retrd.	1993	16.00	25-45
1993	Menlo Park Laboratory (grey) INV02	Retrd.	1994	16.00	25
1993	Menlo Park Laboratory, AP INV02	Retrd.	1993	20.00	24
1993	Noah Webster House INV03	Retrd.	1994	15.00	25
1993	Noah Webster House, AP INV03	Retrd.	1993	20.00	24-35
1993	Wright Cycle Shop INV04	Retrd.	1994	17.00	25
1993	Wright Cycle Shop, AP INV04	Retrd.	1993	20.00	24-35

Jazzy New Orleans Series - S. Thompson

Year	Issue	Edition Limit	Year Retd.	Issue Price	*Quote U.S.$
1994	Beauregard-Keys House JNO04	Retrd.	1996	18.00	20
1994	Beauregard-Keys House, AP JNO04	Retrd.	1994	20.00	45
1994	Gallier House JNO02	Open		18.00	18
1994	Gallier House, AP JNO02	Retrd.	1994	20.00	50
1994	La Branche Building JNO01	Open		18.00	18
1994	La Branche Building, AP JNO01	Retrd.	1994	20.00	50
1994	LePretre House JNO03	Open		18.00	18
1994	LePretre House, AP JNO03	Retrd.	1994	20.00	50

Key West - S. Thompson

Year	Issue	Edition Limit	Year Retd.	Issue Price	*Quote U.S.$
1995	Artist House KEY06	Open		19.00	19
1995	Artist House, AP KEY06	Retrd.	1995	24.00	40
1995	Eyebrow House KEY01	Open		18.00	18
1995	Eyebrow House, AP KEY01	Retrd.	1995	24.00	40
1995	Hemingway House KEY07	Open		19.00	19
1995	Hemingway House, AP KEY07	Retrd.	1995	24.00	40
1995	Illingsworth Gingerbread House KEY05	Open		19.00	19
1995	Illingsworth Gingerbread House, AP KEY05	Retrd.	1995	24.00	40
1995	Shotgun House KEY03	Open		17.00	17
1995	Shotgun House, AP KEY03	Retrd.	1995	24.00	40
1995	Shotgun Sister KEY04	Open		17.00	17
1995	Shotgun Sister, AP KEY04	Retrd.	1995	24.00	40
1995	Southernmost House KEY02	Open		19.00	19

YEAR ISSUE		EDITION LIMIT	YEAR RETD.	ISSUE PRICE	*QUOTE U.S.$
1995	Southernmost House, AP KEY02	Retrd.	1995	24.00	40

Ladies By The Sea - S. Thompson

YEAR ISSUE		EDITION LIMIT	YEAR RETD.	ISSUE PRICE	*QUOTE U.S.$
1996	Abbey II LBS01	Open		19.00	19
1996	Abbey II, AP LBS01	93		24.00	40
1996	Centennial Cottage LBS02	Open		19.00	19
1996	Centennial Cottage, AP LBS02	94		24.00	24
1996	Hall Cottage LBS04	Open		19.00	19
1996	Hall Cottage, AP LBS04	108		24.00	24
1996	Heart Blossom LBS03	Open		19.00	19
1996	Heart Blossom, AP LBS03	107		24.00	24

Lighthouse Series - S. Thompson

YEAR ISSUE		EDITION LIMIT	YEAR RETD.	ISSUE PRICE	*QUOTE U.S.$
1991	Anastasia Lighthouse (burgundy) FL103	Retrd.	1991	15.00	25
1991	Anastasia Lighthouse (red) FL103	Retrd.	1994	15.00	35
1993	Assateague Island Light LTS07	Open		17.00	17
1994	Assateague Island Light, AP LTS07	Retrd.	1994	20.00	40
1995	Cape Hatteras Light LTS09	Open		17.00	17
1995	Cape Hatteras Light, AP LTS09	Retrd.	1995	24.00	40
1991	Cape Hatteras Lighthouse NC103	Retrd.	1994	15.00	35
1994	Charleston Light (renovated) LTS01	Retrd.	1995	15.00	25
1993	Charleston Light LTS01	Retrd.	1995	15.00	25
1993	New London Ledge Light LTS08	Retrd.	1996	17.00	20
1994	New London Ledge Light, AP LTS08	Retrd.	1994	20.00	40-75
1993	Round Island Light LTS06	Open		17.00	17
1994	Round Island Light, AP LTS06	Retrd.	1994	20.00	40
1990	Stage Harbor Lighthouse NEW06	Retrd.	1993	15.00	70-115
1993	Thomas Point Light LTS05	Open		17.00	17
1994	Thomas Point Light, AP LTS05	Retrd.	1994	20.00	45
1990	Tybee Lighthouse SAV07	Retrd.	1994	15.00	25-45

Limited Edition American Gothic - S. Thompson

YEAR ISSUE		EDITION LIMIT	YEAR RETD.	ISSUE PRICE	*QUOTE U.S.$
1993	Gothic Revival Cottage ACL01	Retrd.	1993	20.00	25-45
1993	Mele House ACL04	Retrd.	1993	20.00	43
1993	Perkins House ACL02	Retrd.	1993	20.00	45
1993	Rose Arbor ACL05	Retrd.	1993	14.00	25-45
1993	Roseland Cottage ACL03	Retrd.	1993	20.00	30
1993	Set of 5	Retrd.	1993	94.00	140

Limited Edition Mail-Order Victorians (Barber Houses) - S. Thompson

YEAR ISSUE		EDITION LIMIT	YEAR RETD.	ISSUE PRICE	*QUOTE U.S.$
1994	Brehaut House ACL09	3,300	1994	24.00	30-40
1994	Goeller House ACL08	3,300	1994	24.00	31-45
1994	Henderson House ACL07	3,300	1994	24.00	30-50
1994	Titman House ACL06	3,300	1994	24.00	33-40
1994	Set of 4	3,300	1994	96.00	100-145

Limited Pieces - S. Thompson

YEAR ISSUE		EDITION LIMIT	YEAR RETD.	ISSUE PRICE	*QUOTE U.S.$
1991	Bridgetown Library NJ102	Retrd.	N/A	16.00	25
1993	Comly-Rich House XXX01	Retrd.	N/A	12.00	25-75
1991	Delphos City Hall OH101	Retrd.	N/A	15.00	125
1991	Historic Burlington County Clubhouse NJ101	Retrd.	N/A	16.00	N/A
1991	Mark Twain Boyhood Home MO101	Retrd.	N/A	15.00	N/A
1990	Newton County Court House GA101	Retrd.	N/A	16.00	200

Mackinac - S. Thompson

YEAR ISSUE		EDITION LIMIT	YEAR RETD.	ISSUE PRICE	*QUOTE U.S.$
1996	Amberg Cottage MAK01	Open		19.00	19
1996	Amberg Cottage, AP MAK01	102		24.00	40
1996	Anne Cottage MAK02	Open		19.00	19
1996	Anne Cottage, AP MAK02	95		24.00	40
1996	Rearick Cottage MAK03	Open		19.00	19
1996	Rearick Cottage, AP MAK03	103		24.00	40
1996	Windermere Hotel MAK04	Open		19.00	19
1996	Windermere Hotel, AP MAK04	105		24.00	40

Martha's Vineyard - S. Thompson

YEAR ISSUE		EDITION LIMIT	YEAR RETD.	ISSUE PRICE	*QUOTE U.S.$
1994	Alice's Wonderland (renovated) MAR08II	Open		16.00	16
1993	Alice's Wonderland MAR08	Open		16.00	16
1993	Alice's Wonderland, AP MAR08	Retrd.	1993	20.00	30
1995	Blue Cottage MAR13	Open		17.00	17
1995	Blue Cottage, AP MAR13	Retrd.	1995	24.00	30-40
1994	Campground Cottage (renovated) MAR07II	Retrd.	1995	16.00	16
1993	Campground Cottage MAR07	Retrd.	1995	16.00	25-75
1993	Campground Cottage, AP MAR07	Retrd.	1993	20.00	30
1994	Gingerbread Cottage-grey (renovated) MAR09II	Retrd.	1996	16.00	18
1993	Gingerbread Cottage-grey AP MAR09	Retrd.	1993	20.00	30
1993	Gingerbread Cottage-grey MAR09	Retrd.	1996	16.00	25
1995	Trails End MAR11	Open		17.00	17
1995	Trails End, AP MAR11	Retrd.	1995	24.00	30-40
1995	White Cottage MAR12	Open		17.00	17
1995	White Cottage, AP MAR12	Retrd.	1995	24.00	30-40
1994	Wood Valentine (renovated) MAR10II	Open		16.00	16
1993	Wood Valentine MAR10	Open		16.00	16
1993	Wood Valentine, AP MAR10	Retrd.	1993	20.00	30-40

New England - S. Thompson

YEAR ISSUE		EDITION LIMIT	YEAR RETD.	ISSUE PRICE	*QUOTE U.S.$
1991	Faneuil Hall NEW09	Retrd.	1993	15.00	25-75
1990	Longfellow's House NEW01	Retrd.	1993	15.00	25-50
1990	Malden Mass. Victorian Inn NEW05	Retrd.	1992	10.00	60-100
1990	Martha's Vineyard Cottage-blue/mauve MAR06	Retrd.	1993	15.00	30-75
1990	Martha's Vineyard Cottage-blue/orange MAR05	Retrd.	1993	15.00	50
1990	Motif #1 Boathouse NEW02	Retrd.	1993	15.00	20-70
1990	Old North Church NEW04	Retrd.	1993	15.00	25-85
1990	Paul Revere's Home NEW03	Retrd.	1993	15.00	25-85
1991	President Bush's Home NEW07	Retrd.	1993	15.00	40-95
1991	Wedding Cake House NEW08	Retrd.	1993	15.00	25-70

North Carolina - S. Thompson

YEAR ISSUE		EDITION LIMIT	YEAR RETD.	ISSUE PRICE	*QUOTE U.S.$
1990	Josephus Hall House NC101	Retrd.	1993	15.00	50
1990	Presbyterian Bell Tower NC102	Retrd.	1993	15.00	50
1991	The Tryon Palace NC104	Retrd.	1993	15.00	25-75

Old-Fashioned Christmas - S. Thompson

YEAR ISSUE		EDITION LIMIT	YEAR RETD.	ISSUE PRICE	*QUOTE U.S.$
1994	Conway Scenic Railroad Station OFC04	Open		18.00	18
1994	Conway Scenic Railroad Station, AP OFC04	Retrd.	1994	20.00	40-50
1994	Dwight House OFC02	Retrd.	1996	18.00	25
1994	Dwight House, AP OFC02	Retrd.	1994	20.00	50-85
1994	General Merchandise OFC03	Open		18.00	18
1994	General Merchandise, AP OFC03	Retrd.	1994	20.00	40-50
1994	Old First Church OFC01	Open		18.00	18
1994	Old First Church, AP OFC01	Retrd.	1994	20.00	40-50
1994	Set of 4 1994 AP	Retrd.	1994	80.00	199
1995	Christmas Inn OFC05	Open		18.00	18
1995	Town Square Tree OFC06	Open		18.00	18

Painted Ladies I - S. Thompson

YEAR ISSUE		EDITION LIMIT	YEAR RETD.	ISSUE PRICE	*QUOTE U.S.$
1990	The Abbey LAD08	Retrd.	1992	10.00	115-150
1990	Atlanta Queen Anne LAD07	Retrd.	1992	10.00	150-200
1990	Cincinnati Gothic LAD05	Retrd.	1992	10.00	75-125
1990	Colorado Queen Anne LAD04	Retrd.	1992	10.00	75-125
1990	Illinois Queen Anne LAD06	Retrd.	1991	10.00	385-450
1990	San Francisco Italianate-yellow LAD03	Retrd.	1992	10.00	125-150
1990	San Francisco Stick House-blue LAD02	Retrd.	1991	10.00	60-80
1990	San Francisco Stick House-yellow LAD01	Retrd.	1991	10.00	85-125
1990	Painted Ladies I Sign	Retrd.	N/A	12.50	20

Painted Ladies II - S. Thompson

YEAR ISSUE		EDITION LIMIT	YEAR RETD.	ISSUE PRICE	*QUOTE U.S.$
1994	Cape May Gothic (renovated) LAD13II	Retrd.	1995	16.00	35
1992	Cape May Gothic LAD13	Retrd.	1995	15.00	25-35
1994	Cape May Victorian Pink House (renovated) LAD16II	Retrd.	1996	16.00	20
1992	Cape May Victorian Pink House LAD16	Retrd.	1996	15.00	22
1994	The Gingerbread Mansion (renovated) LAD09II	Retrd.	1994	16.00	25-35
1992	The Gingerbread Mansion LAD09	Retrd.	1993	15.00	20-35
1994	Morningstar Inn (renovated) LAD15II	Retrd.	1994	16.00	25-35
1992	Morningstar Inn LAD15	Retrd.	1994	15.00	25-35
1994	Pitkin House (renovated) LAD10II	Retrd.	1996	16.00	20
1992	Pitkin House LAD10	Retrd.	1996	15.00	20
1994	Queen Anne Townhouse (renovated) LAD12II	Retrd.	1994	16.00	35
1992	Queen Anne Townhouse LAD12	Retrd.	1994	15.00	25-35
1994	The Victorian Blue Rose (renovated) LAD14II	Retrd.	1996	16.00	20
1992	The Victorian Blue Rose LAD14	Retrd.	1996	15.00	21
1994	The Young-Larson House (renovated) LAD11II	Retrd.	1996	16.00	20
1992	The Young-Larson House LAD11	Retrd.	1996	15.00	20

Painted Ladies III - S. Thompson

YEAR ISSUE		EDITION LIMIT	YEAR RETD.	ISSUE PRICE	*QUOTE U.S.$
1994	Cape May Green Stockton Row (renovated) LAD20II	Retrd.	1995	16.00	25
1993	Cape May Green Stockton Row LAD20	Retrd.	1995	16.00	25
1994	Cape May Linda Lee (renovated) LAD17II	Retrd.	1996	16.00	20
1993	Cape May Linda Lee LAD17	Retrd.	1996	16.00	20
1994	Cape May Pink Stockton Row (renovated)LAD19II	Open		16.00	16
1993	Cape May Pink Stockton Row LAD19	Open		16.00	16
1994	Cape May Tan Stockton Row (renovated)LAD18II	Open		16.00	16
1993	Cape May Tan Stockton Row LAD18	Open		16.00	16
1996	Cream Stockton LAD22	Open		19.00	19
1996	Cream Stockton, AP LAD22	101		24.00	24
1995	Steiner Cottage LAD21	Open		17.00	17
1995	Steiner Cottage, AP LAD21	Retrd.	1995	24.00	40

Panaramic Lights - S. Thompson

YEAR ISSUE		EDITION LIMIT	YEAR RETD.	ISSUE PRICE	*QUOTE U.S.$
1996	Jeffrys Hook Light PLH02	Open		19.00	19
1996	Jeffrys Hook Light, AP PLH02	97		24.00	40
1996	New Canal Light PLH03	Open		19.00	19
1996	New Canal Light, AP PLH03	104		24.00	40
1996	Quoddy Head Light PLH04	Open		19.00	19
1996	Quoddy Head Light, AP PLH04	102		24.00	40
1996	Split Rock Light PLH01	Open		19.00	19
1996	Split Rock Light, AP PLH01	105		24.00	40

Philadelphia - S. Thompson

YEAR ISSUE		EDITION LIMIT	YEAR RETD.	ISSUE PRICE	*QUOTE U.S.$
1990	"Besty" Ross House (misspelling) PHI03	Retrd.	1990	15.00	20-45
1990	Betsy Ross House PHI03	Retrd.	1993	15.00	35-75
1990	Carpenter's Hall PHI01	Retrd.	1993	15.00	35
1990	Elphreth's Alley PHI05	Retrd.	1993	15.00	30-65
1990	Graff House PHI07	Retrd.	1993	15.00	35-75
1990	Independence Hall PHI04	Retrd.	1993	15.00	35-75
1990	Market St. Post Office PHI02	Retrd.	1993	15.00	35
1990	Old City Hall PHI08	Retrd.	1993	15.00	25-35
1990	Old Tavern PHI06	Retrd.	1993	15.00	33

Plantations - S. Thompson

YEAR ISSUE		EDITION LIMIT	YEAR RETD.	ISSUE PRICE	*QUOTE U.S.$
1995	Farley PLA04	Retrd.	1996	18.00	18
1995	Farley, AP PLA04	Retrd.	1995	24.00	40-65
1995	Longwood PLA02	Open		19.00	19
1995	Longwood, AP PLA02	Retrd.	1995	24.00	30-40
1995	Merry Sherwood PLA03	Open		18.00	18
1995	Merry Sherwood, AP PLA03	Retrd.	1995	24.00	30-40
1995	San Francisco PLA01	Open		19.00	19
1995	San Francisco, AP PLA01	Retrd.	1995	24.00	40-50

San Francisco - S. Thompson

YEAR ISSUE		EDITION LIMIT	YEAR RETD.	ISSUE PRICE	*QUOTE U.S.$
1995	Brandywine SF101	Open		18.00	18
1995	Brandywine, AP SF101	Retrd.	1995	24.00	30-40
1995	Eclectic Blue SF103	Open		19.00	19
1995	Eclectic Blue, AP SF103	Retrd.	1995	24.00	40-50
1995	Edwardian Green SF104	Open		18.00	18
1995	Edwardian Green, AP SF104	Retrd.	1995	24.00	30-40
1995	Queen Rose SF102	Open		19.00	19
1995	Queen Rose, AP SF102	Retrd.	1995	24.00	30-40

Savannah - S. Thompson

YEAR ISSUE		EDITION LIMIT	YEAR RETD.	ISSUE PRICE	*QUOTE U.S.$
1990	Andrew Low Mansion SAV02	Retrd.	1994	15.00	35-60
1996	Asendorf SAV13	Open		19.00	1
1996	Asendorf, AP SAV13	100		24.00	24
1994	Catherdral of St. John (renovated) SAV09II	Retrd.	1995	16.00	35-45
1992	Catherdral of St. John SAV09	Retrd.	1995	16.00	40-9
1994	Chestnut House SAV11	Open		18.00	1
1994	Chestnut House, AP SAV11	Retrd.	1994	24.00	7
1990	Davenport House SAV03	Retrd.	1994	15.00	30-7
1990	Herb House SAV05	Retrd.	1993	15.00	30-85
1994	Juliette Low House (renovated) SAV04II	Open		15.00	1
1990	Juliette Low House (w/logo) SAV04	Open		15.00	1
1990	Juliette Low House (w/o logo) SAV04	Retrd.	1990	15.00	10
1995	Mercer House SAV12	Open		18.00	1
1995	Mercer House, AP SAV12	Retrd.	1995	24.00	40-7
1990	Mikve Israel Temple SAV06	Retrd.	1994	15.00	35-8
1994	Olde Pink House (renovated) SAV01II	Retrd.	1996	15.00	2
1990	Olde Pink House SAV01	Retrd.	1996	15.00	35-4
1994	Owens Thomas House (renovated) SAV10II	Retrd.	1996	16.00	25-3
1993	Owens Thomas House AP SAV10	Retrd.	1993	20.00	7
1993	Owens Thomas House SAV10	Retrd.	1996	16.00	30-4
1990	Savannah Gingerbread House I SAV08	Retrd.	1990	15.00	265-30
1990	Savannah Gingerbread House II SAV08	Retrd.	1992	15.00	37

Signing Only Pieces - S. Thompson

YEAR ISSUE		EDITION LIMIT	YEAR RETD.	ISSUE PRICE	*QUOTE U.S.$
1994	Star Barn SOP01	Retrd.	1994	24.00	6
1995	Shelia's Real Estate Office SOP02	Retrd.	1995	20.00	4

South Carolina - S. Thompson

YEAR ISSUE		EDITION LIMIT	YEAR RETD.	ISSUE PRICE	*QUOTE U.S.$
1991	All Saints' Church SC105	Retrd.	1993	15.00	45-5
1990	The Governer's Mansion (misspelling) SC102	Retrd.	1990	15.00	
1994	The Governor's Mansion (renovated) SC102II	Retrd.	1995	15.00	3
1990	The Governor's Mansion SC102	Retrd.	1995	15.00	3
1994	The Hermitage (renovated) SC101II	Retrd.	1995	15.00	2
1990	The Hermitage SC101	Retrd.	1995	15.00	25-3
1994	The Lace House (renovated) SC103II	Retrd.	1995	15.00	
1990	The Lace House SC103	Retrd.	1995	15.00	40-5
1994	The State Capitol (renovated) SC104II	Retrd.	1994	15.00	50-7
1991	The State Capitol SC104	Retrd.	1994	15.00	3

South Carolina Ladies - S. Thompson

YEAR ISSUE		EDITION LIMIT	YEAR RETD.	ISSUE PRICE	*QUOTE U.S.$
1996	Cinnamon Hill SCL04	Open		19.00	
1996	Cinnamon Hill, AP SCL04	93		24.00	4
1996	Davis-Johnsey House SCL02	Open		19.00	
1996	Davis-Johnsey House, AP SCL02	104		24.00	4
1996	Inman House SCL01	Open		19.00	
1996	Inman House, AP SCL01	107		24.00	4
1996	Montgomery House SCL03	Open		19.00	
1996	Montgomery House, AP SCL03	105		24.00	

St. Augustine - S. Thompson

YEAR ISSUE		EDITION LIMIT	YEAR RETD.	ISSUE PRICE	*QUOTE U.S.$
1991	Anastasia Lighthousekeeper's House FL104	Retrd.	1993	15.00	35-
1991	Mission Nombre deDios FL105	Retrd.	1993	15.00	30-
1991	Old City Gates FL102	Retrd.	1993	15.00	
1991	The "Oldest House" FL101	Retrd.	1993	15.00	30-

Texas - S. Thompson

YEAR ISSUE		EDITION LIMIT	YEAR RETD.	ISSUE PRICE	*QUOTE U.S.$
1990	The Alamo TEX01	Retrd.	1993	15.00	150-2
1990	Mission Concepcion TEX04	Retrd.	1993	15.00	50-
1990	Mission San Francisco TEX03	Retrd.	1993	15.00	35-
1990	Mission San Jose' TEX02	Retrd.	1993	15.00	40-
1990	Texas Sign	Retrd.	N/A	12.50	

Victorian Springtime - S. Thompson

YEAR ISSUE		EDITION LIMIT	YEAR RETD.	ISSUE PRICE	*QUOTE U.S.$
1993	Heffron House VST03	Retrd.	1996	17.00	
1993	Heffron House, AP VST03	Retrd.	1993	20.00	30-
1993	Jacobsen House VST04	Retrd.	1996	17.00	
1993	Jacobsen House, AP VST04	Retrd.	1993	20.00	30-
1993	Ralston House VST01	Retrd.	1996	17.00	25-
1993	Ralston House, AP VST01	Retrd.	1993	20.00	
1993	Sessions House VST02	Retrd.	1996	17.00	25-
1993	Sessions House, AP VST02	Retrd.	1993	20.00	
1993	Set of 4, AP	Retrd.	1993	100.00	

Victorian Springtime II - S. Thompson

YEAR	ISSUE	EDITION LIMIT	YEAR RETD.	ISSUE PRICE	*QUOTE U.S.$
1995	Dragon House VST07	Open		18.00	18
1995	Dragon House, AP VST07	Retrd.	1995	24.00	40
1995	E.B. Hall House VST08	Open		19.00	19
1995	E.B. Hall House, AP VST08	Retrd.	1995	24.00	40
1995	Gibney Home VST09	Open		18.00	18
1995	Gibney Home, AP VST09	Retrd.	1995	24.00	40
1995	Ray Home VST05	Open		18.00	18
1995	Ray Home, AP VST05	Retrd.	1995	24.00	40
1995	Victoria VST06	Open		18.00	18
1995	Victoria, AP VST06	Retrd.	1995	24.00	40

Victorian Springtime III - S. Thompson

YEAR	ISSUE	EDITION LIMIT	YEAR RETD.	ISSUE PRICE	*QUOTE U.S.$
1996	Clark House VST14	Open		19.00	19
1996	Clark House, AP VST14	96		24.00	40
1996	Goodwill House VST13	Open		19.00	19
1996	Goodwill House, AP VST13	88		24.00	40
1996	Queen-Anne Mansion VST12	Open		19.00	19
1996	Queen-Anne Mansion, AP VST12	103		24.00	40
1996	Sheppard House VST11	Open		19.00	19
1996	Sheppard House, AP VST11	98		24.00	40
1996	Urfer House VST10	Open		19.00	19
1996	Urfer House, AP VST10	71		24.00	40

Washington D.C. - S. Thompson

YEAR	ISSUE	EDITION LIMIT	YEAR RETD.	ISSUE PRICE	*QUOTE U.S.$
1992	Cherry Trees DC005	Retrd.	1993	12.00	35-50
1992	Library of Congress DC002	Retrd.	1993	16.00	35-50
1991	National Archives DC001	Retrd.	1993	16.00	30-60
1991	Washington Monument DC004	Retrd.	1993	16.00	30-60
1992	White House DC003	Retrd.	1993	16.00	100-200
1992	Set of 5	Retrd.	1993	76.00	250-375

West Coast Lighthouse Series - S. Thompson

YEAR	ISSUE	EDITION LIMIT	YEAR RETD.	ISSUE PRICE	*QUOTE U.S.$
1995	East Brother Light WCL01	Open		19.00	19
1995	East Brother Light, AP WCL01	Retrd.	1995	24.00	40
1995	Mukilteo Light WCL02	Open		18.00	18
1995	Mukilteo Light, AP WCL02	Retrd.	1995	24.00	40
1995	Point Fermin Light WCL04	Open		18.00	18
1995	Point Fermin Light, AP WCL04	Retrd.	1995	24.00	40
1995	Yaquina Bay Light WCL03	Open		18.00	18
1995	Yaquina Bay Light, AP WCL03	Retrd.	1995	24.00	40

Williamsburg - S. Thompson

YEAR	ISSUE	EDITION LIMIT	YEAR RETD.	ISSUE PRICE	*QUOTE U.S.$
1990	Apothecary WIL09	Retrd.	1994	12.00	25
1994	Bruton Parish Church (renovated) WIL13II	Open		15.00	15
1992	Bruton Parish Church WIL13	Open		15.00	15
1995	Capitol WIL15	Open		18.00	18
1995	Capitol, AP WIL15	Retrd.	1995	24.00	30-40
1994	Courthouse (renovated) WIL11II	Retrd.	1995	15.00	20
1990	Courthouse WIL11	Retrd.	1995	15.00	21
1990	The Golden Ball Jeweler WIL07	Retrd.	1994	12.00	25
1994	Governor's Palace (renovated) WIL04II	Open		15.00	15
1990	Governor's Palace WIL04	Open		15.00	15
1994	Homesite (renovated) WIL12II	Retrd.	1996	15.00	15
1990	Homesite WIL12	Retrd.	1996	15.00	15
1994	King's Arm Tavern (renovated) WIL10II	Retrd.	1995	15.00	25-35
1990	King's Arm Tavern WIL10	Retrd.	1995	15.00	25
1990	Milliner WIL06	Retrd.	1994	12.00	25
1990	Nicolson Shop WIL08	Retrd.	1994	12.00	25
1990	The Printing Offices WIL05	Retrd.	1993	12.00	20-40
1995	Raleigh Tavern WIL14	Open		18.00	18
1995	Raleigh Tavern, AP WIL14	Retrd.	1995	24.00	30-40

Shube's Manufacturing, Inc.

Busts - P. Sedlow

YEAR	ISSUE	EDITION LIMIT	YEAR RETD.	ISSUE PRICE	*QUOTE U.S.$
1995	General Grant	750		380.00	380
1995	General Lee	750		380.00	380
1995	Kennedy	750		380.00	380
1995	Lincoln	750		380.00	380

Fantasy - Various

YEAR	ISSUE	EDITION LIMIT	YEAR RETD.	ISSUE PRICE	*QUOTE U.S.$
1992	Behold - P. Sedlow	2,500		280.00	280
1987	Castle - N/A	Retrd.	1992	N/A	N/A
1992	Crystal Fortress - Sedlow/Wimberly	2,500		480.00	480
1987	Dragon - N/A	Retrd.	1992	N/A	N/A
1991	Dragon Lord - P. Sedlow	4,500		330.00	330
1991	Guardian of the Crystal - D. Wimberly	2,500		870.00	870
1990	Immortal Power - R. Gonzales	3,500		280.00	280
1991	Keeper of the Fire Lamp - P. Sedlow	4,500		330.00	330
1992	Pinnacle - P. Sedlow	Retrd.	1995	280.00	280
1991	Winged Splendor - P. Sedlow	4,500		420.00	420
1989	Wizard - N/A	Retrd.	1992	N/A	N/A
1991	Wizards Spell - P. Sedlow	4,500		330.00	330

Frontier - P. Sedlow

YEAR	ISSUE	EDITION LIMIT	YEAR RETD.	ISSUE PRICE	*QUOTE U.S.$
1991	High Desert Ambush	Retrd.	1995	550.00	550
1991	Summit Confrontation	Retrd.	1995	480.00	480

Great Chiefs and Leaders - P. Sedlow

YEAR	ISSUE	EDITION LIMIT	YEAR RETD.	ISSUE PRICE	*QUOTE U.S.$
1992	Chief Joseph	2,500		240.00	240
1992	CrazyHorse	2,500		240.00	240
1992	Geronimo	2,500		240.00	240
1992	Quanna Parker	2,500		240.00	240
1992	Red Cloud	2,500		240.00	240
1992	Sitting Bull	2,500		240.00	240

Limited Edition Figurine - N/A

YEAR	ISSUE	EDITION LIMIT	YEAR RETD.	ISSUE PRICE	*QUOTE U.S.$
1990	Entrancing Carousel	4,500		240.00	240

Native American - Various

YEAR	ISSUE	EDITION LIMIT	YEAR RETD.	ISSUE PRICE	*QUOTE U.S.$
1993	Battleground - P. Sedlow	900		380.00	380
1991	Blood Bros - P. Sedlow	4,500		330.00	330
1994	End of the Trail (classic pewter) - P. Sedlow	500		800.00	800
1994	End of the Trail - P. Sedlow	250		650.00	650
1994	Heritage (classic pewter) - P. Sedlow	300		380.00	380
1994	Heritage - P. Sedlow	700		480.00	480
1991	Moon Bear (diamond cut) - P. Sedlow	3,500		750.00	750
1991	Moon Bear - P. Sedlow	3,500		680.00	680
1990	Noble Flight - R. Gonzales	Retrd.	1995	240.00	240
1994	Offering (classic pewter) - P. Sedlow	250		650.00	650
1994	Offering (diamond cut) - P. Sedlow	250		870.00	870
1994	Offering - P. Sedlow	1,200		800.00	800
1994	Old Enemies (classic pewter) - M. Phelps	250		550.00	550
1994	Old Enemies (diamond cut) - M. Phelps	250		330.00	330
1994	Old Enemies - M. Phelps	1,200		700.00	700
1994	Pueblo Dancer (classic pewter) - M. Phelps	350		280.00	280
1994	Pueblo Dancer - M. Phelps	750		380.00	380
1990	Saga on the Plains - P. Sedlow	4,500		430.00	430
1995	Scout - P. Sedlow	750		170.00	170
1994	Sitting Bull (classic pewter) - P. Sedlow	300		1500.00	1500
1992	Sitting Bull (classic pewter) - P. Sedlow	400		170.00	170
1994	Sitting Bull - P. Sedlow	500		2000.00	2000
1993	Smoke Signal - P. Sedlow	900		380.00	380
1994	Traditional Dancer (classic pewter) - M. Phelps	350		280.00	280
1994	Traditional Dancer - M. Phelps	750		380.00	380
1993	Victorious - P. Sedlow	900		380.00	380
1990	Whitewater Rush - P. Sedlow	4,500		430.00	430

Wildlife - Various

YEAR	ISSUE	EDITION LIMIT	YEAR RETD.	ISSUE PRICE	*QUOTE U.S.$
1990	American Eagle - D. Wimberly	S/O	1995	430.00	430
1990	Bugling Monarch (diamond cut) - D. Wimberly	4,500		280.00	280
1990	Bugling Monarch - D. Wimberly	4,500		240.00	240
1993	Catch of the Day (classic pewter) - P. Sedlow	450		240.00	240
1993	Catch of the Day (diamond cut) - P. Sedlow	2,500		330.00	330
1993	Catch of the Day - P. Sedlow	2,500		280.00	280
1991	Dancers of the Land (diamond cut) - D. Wimberly	4,500		480.00	480
1991	Dancers of the Land - D. Wimberly	4,500		430.00	430
1990	Duel - P. Sedlow	Retrd.	1995	280.00	280
1990	Family Frolic - H. Freidland	Retrd.	1992	N/A	N/A
1993	Freedom's Cry (classic pewter) - P. Sedlow	450		280.00	280
1993	Freedom's Cry (diamond cut) - P. Sedlow	1,800		380.00	380
1993	Freedom's Cry - P. Sedlow	1,800		330.00	330
1994	Lobo - P. Sedlow	750		240.00	240
1990	Master of the Night - P. Sedlow	Retrd.	1995	330.00	330
1991	Morning Solitude - D. Wimberly	Retrd.	1995	330.00	330
1993	Night Song (diamond cut) - P. Sedlow	1,800		430.00	430
1993	Night Song - P. Sedlow	1,800		380.00	380
1993	Soaring Spirit (classic pewter) - D. Wimberly	450		330.00	330
1993	Soaring Spirit (diamond cut) - D. Wimberly	1,800		430.00	430
1993	Soaring Spirit - D. Wimberly	1,800		380.00	380
1990	Unbridled Majesty - P. Sedlow	Retrd.	1992	N/A	N/A
1993	Warhorse (diamond cut) - P. Sedlow	1,800		430.00	430
1993	Warhorse - P. Sedlow	1,800		380.00	380

Sports Impressions/Enesco

Collectors' Club Members Only - Various

YEAR	ISSUE	EDITION LIMIT	YEAR RETD.	ISSUE PRICE	*QUOTE U.S.$
1990	The Mick-Mickey Mantle 5000-1	Yr.Iss.	N/A	75.00	200
1991	Rickey Henderson-Born to Run 5001-11	Yr.Iss.	N/A	49.95	50
1991	Nolan Ryan-300 Wins 5002-01	Yr.Iss.	N/A	125.00	125
1991	Willie, Mickey & Duke plate 5003-04	Yr.Iss.	N/A	39.95	40
1992	Babe Ruth 5006-11	Yr.Iss.	N/A	40.00	40
1992	Walter Payton 5015-01	Yr.Iss.	N/A	50.00	50
1993	The 1927 Yankees plate - R.Tanenbaum	Yr.Iss.	N/A	60.00	75

Collectors' Club Symbol of Membership - Sports Impressions

YEAR	ISSUE	EDITION LIMIT	YEAR RETD.	ISSUE PRICE	*QUOTE U.S.$
1991	Mick/7 plate 5001-02	Yr.Iss.	N/A	Gift	70
1992	USA Basketball team plate 5008-30	Yr.Iss.	N/A	Gift	N/A
1993	Nolan Ryan porcelain card	Yr.Iss.	N/A	Gift	25

Baseball Superstar Figurines - Sports Impressions

YEAR	ISSUE	EDITION LIMIT	YEAR RETD.	ISSUE PRICE	*QUOTE U.S.$
1988	Al Kaline	2,500	N/A	90.00	125
1988	Andre Dawson	2,500	N/A	90.00	125-200
1988	Bob Feller	2,500	N/A	90.00	125-200
1992	Cubs Ryne Sandberg Home 1118-23	975	1993	150.00	195
1987	Don Mattingly	Closed	N/A	90.00	250
1987	Don Mattingly (Franklin glove variation)	Closed	N/A	90.00	750
1989	Duke Snider	2,500	N/A	90.00	125
1994	Giants Barry Bonds (signed) 1160-46	975	1995	150.00	150
1992	Johnny Bench (hand signed) 1126-23	975	1994	150.00	150
1988	Jose Canseco	Closed	N/A	90.00	125-200
1987	Keith Hernandez	2,500	N/A	90.00	125-200
1989	Kirk Gibson	Closed	N/A	90.00	125-200
1987	Mickey Mantle	Closed	N/A	90.00	175-295
1996	Mickey Mantle "The Greatest Switch Hitter" (hand signed) 1228-46 - T. Treadway	975		395.00	500
1990	Nolan Ryan	Closed	N/A	50.00	50
1992	Nolan Ryan Figurine/plate/stand 1134-31	500	1994	260.00	260
1990	Nolan Ryan Kings of K	Closed	N/A	125.00	125
1990	Nolan Ryan Mini	Closed	N/A	50.00	50
1990	Nolan Ryan Supersize	Closed	N/A	250.00	250
1993	Oakland A's Reggie Jackson (signed) 1048-46	975	1994	150.00	150
1993	Rangers Nolan Ryan (signed) 1127-46	975	1994	175.00	175
1994	Rangers Nolan Ryan (signed) Farewell 1161-49	975	1994	150.00	250
1990	Ted Williams	Closed	N/A	90.00	475-625
1987	Wade Boggs	Closed	N/A	90.00	150-225
1989	Will Clark	Closed	N/A	90.00	125-250
1993	Yankees Mickey Mantle (signed) 1038-46	975	1993	195.00	350

Basketball Superstar Figurines - Sports Impressions

YEAR	ISSUE	EDITION LIMIT	YEAR RETD.	ISSUE PRICE	*QUOTE U.S.$
1993	Julius Erving 76ers (hand signed) 4102-46	975	1994	150.00	150
1993	Julius Erving 76ers (hand signed) 4102-61	76	1994	295.00	295

Football Superstar Figurines - Sports Impressions

YEAR	ISSUE	EDITION LIMIT	YEAR RETD.	ISSUE PRICE	*QUOTE U.S.$
1993	Gale Sayers Bears (hand signed) 3029-23	975	1994	150.00	150
1992	John Unitas Colts (hand signed) 3016-23	975	1994	150.00	150
1993	Kenny Stabler Raiders (hand signed) 3026-23	975	1994	150.00	150
1993	Walter Payton Bears (hand signed) 3028-23	975	1994	150.00	150

NASCAR - Sports Impressions

YEAR	ISSUE	EDITION LIMIT	YEAR RETD.	ISSUE PRICE	*QUOTE U.S.$
1995	Bill Elliott (hand signed) 8100-46	975		150.00	150

Plaques - Various

YEAR	ISSUE	EDITION LIMIT	YEAR RETD.	ISSUE PRICE	*QUOTE U.S.$
1995	Life of a Legend Mickey Mantle 1228-71 - T. Fogarty	Open		40.00	40
1995	Profiles in Courage Mickey Mantle 1231-62 - M. Petronella	Open		40.00	40

Swarovski America Limited

Collectors Society Editions - Various

YEAR	ISSUE	EDITION LIMIT	YEAR RETD.	ISSUE PRICE	*QUOTE U.S.$
1987	Togetherness-The Lovebirds - Schreck/Stocker	Yr.Iss.	1987	150.00	2500-4000
1988	Sharing-The Woodpeckers - A. Stocker	Yr.Iss.	1988	165.00	1200-1900
1988	Mini Cactus	Yr.Iss.	1988	Gift	200-300
1989	Amour-The Turtledoves - A. Stocker	Yr.Iss.	1989	195.00	750-1150
1989	SCS Key Chain	Yr.Iss.	1989	Gift	55-125
1990	Lead Me-The Dolphins - M. Stamey	Yr.Iss.	1990	225.00	950-1600
1990	Mini Chaton	Yr.Iss.	1990	Gift	50-100
1991	Save Me-The Seals - M. Stamey	Yr.Iss.	1991	225.00	400-750
1991	Dolphin Brooch	Yr.Iss.	1991	75.00	125-200
1991	SCS Pin	Yr.Iss.	1991	Gift	80-100
1992	Care For Me - The Whales - M. Stamey	Yr.Iss.	1992	265.00	375-1000
1992	SCS Pen	Yr.Iss.	1992	Gift	30-70
1992	5th Anniversary Edition-The Birthday Cake - G. Stamey	Yr.Iss.	1992	85.00	125-275
1993	Inspiration Africa-The Elephant - M. Zendron	Yr.Iss.	1993	325.00	975-1300
1993	Elephant Brooch	Yr.Iss.	1993	85.00	85-150
1993	Leather Luggage Tag	Yr.Iss.	1993	Gift	25
1994	Inspiration Africa-The Kudu - M. Stamey	Yr.Iss.	1994	295.00	400-700
1994	Leather Double Picture Frame	Yr.Iss.	1994	Gift	20
1995	Inspiration Africa-The Lion - A. Stocker	Yr.Iss.	1995	325.00	400-500
1995	Centenary Swan Brooch	Yr.Iss.	1995	125.00	125-175
1995	Miniature Crystal Swan	Yr.Iss.	1995	Gift	75
1996	Fabulous Creatures-The Unicorn - M. Zendron	Yr.Iss.		325.00	325

Swarovski Silver Crystal Worldwide Limited Editions - A. Stocker

YEAR	ISSUE	EDITION LIMIT	YEAR RETD.	ISSUE PRICE	*QUOTE U.S.$
1995	Eagle	10,000	1995	1750.00	5500-8500

African Wildlife - Various

YEAR	ISSUE	EDITION LIMIT	YEAR RETD.	ISSUE PRICE	*QUOTE U.S.$
1995	Baby Elephant - M. Zendron	Open		155.00	155
1994	Cheetah - M. Stamey	Open		275.00	275
1989	Elephant-Small - A. Stocker	Open		50.00	65

Among Flowers And Foliage - C. Schneiderbauer

YEAR	ISSUE	EDITION LIMIT	YEAR RETD.	ISSUE PRICE	*QUOTE U.S.$
1992	Bumblebee	Open		85.00	85
1994	Butterfly on Leaf	Open		75.00	85

*Quotes have been rounded up to nearest dollar

YEAR ISSUE		EDITION LIMIT	YEAR RETD.	ISSUE PRICE	*QUOTE U.S.$
1995	Dragonfly	Open		85.00	85
1992	Hummingbird	Open		195.00	210

Barnyard Friends - Various

1993	Mother Goose - A. Stocker	Open		75.00	75
1993	Tom Gosling - A. Stocker	Open		37.50	38
1993	Dick Gosling - A. Stocker	Open		37.50	38
1993	Harry Gosling - A. Stocker	Open		37.50	38
1984	Medium Pig - M. Schreck	Open		35.00	55
1988	Mini Chicks (Set/3) - G. Stamey	Open		35.00	45
1987	Mini Hen - G. Stamey	Open		35.00	45
1982	Mini Pig - M. Schreck	Open		16.00	30
1987	Mini Rooster - G. Stamey	Open		35.00	55

Beauties of the Lake - Various

1983	Drake-Mini - M. Schreck	Open		20.00	45
1994	Frog - G. Stamey	Open		49.50	50
1989	Mallard-Giant - M. Stamey	Open		2000.00	4500
1986	Standing Duck-Mini - A. Stocker	Open		22.00	38
1977	Swan-Large - M. Schreck	Open		55.00	95
1995	Swan-Maxi - A. Hirzinger	Open		4500.00	4500
1977	Swan-Medium - M. Schreck	Open		44.00	85
1989	Swan-Small - M. Schreck	Open		35.00	50
1986	Swimming Duck-Mini - A. Stocker	Open		16.00	38

Centenary Edition - A. Hirzinger

1995	Centenary Swan	Yr.Iss.	1995	150.00	150

Commemorative Single Issues - Team

1990	Elephant,(Introduced by Swarovski America as a commemorative item during Design Celebration/January '90 in Walt Disney World)	Closed	N/A	125.00	850-1050
1993	Elephant,(Introduced by Swarovski America as a commemorative item during Design Celebration/January '93 in Walt Disney World)	Open		150.00	150

Crystal Melodies - M. Zendron

1993	Grand Piano	Open		250.00	260
1992	Harp	Open		175.00	210
1992	Lute	Open		125.00	140

Decorative Items For The Desk (Paperweights) - M. Schreck

1990	Chaton-Giant 7433NR180000	Open		4500.00	4500
1987	Chaton-Large 7433NR80	Open		190.00	260
1987	Chaton-Small 7433NR50	Open		50.00	65
1987	Pyramid-Small Crystal Cal. 7450NR40095	Open		100.00	125
1987	Pyramid-Small Vitrail Med. 7450NR40087	Open		100.00	125

Endangered Species - Various

1993	Baby Panda - A. Stocker	Open		24.50	25
1993	Mother Panda - A. Stocker	Open		120.00	125
1991	Kiwi - M. Stamey	Open		37.50	45
1987	Koala - A. Stocker	Open		50.00	65
1989	Mini Koala - A. Stocker	Open		35.00	45
1992	Mother Beaver - A. Stocker	Open		110.00	125
1992	Sitting Baby Beaver - A. Stocker	Open		47.50	50
1993	Mother Kangaroo with Baby - G. Stamey	Open		95.00	95
1981	Turtle-Giant - M. Schreck	Open		2500.00	4500
1977	Turtle-Large - M. Schreck	Open		48.00	75
1977	Turtle-Small - M. Schreck	Open		35.00	50

Exquisite Accents - Various

1995	Angel - A. Stocker	Open		210.00	210
1980	Birdbath - M. Schreck	Open		150.00	210
1987	Birds' Nest - Team	Open		90.00	125
1987	Dinner Bell-Medium - M. Schreck	Open		80.00	95
1987	Dinner Bell-Small - M. Schreck	Open		60.00	65
1995	The Orchid-pink - M. Stamey	Open		140.00	140
1995	The Orchid-yellow - M. Stamey	Open		140.00	140
1992	The Rose - M. Stamey	Open		150.00	155

Feathered Friends - Various

1995	Baby Lovebirds - A. Stocker	Open		155.00	155
1995	Dove - E. Mair	Open		55.00	55
1993	Pelican - A. Hirzinger	Open		37.50	38

Game of Kings - M. Schreck

1984	Chess Set	Open		950.00	1375

Horses on Parade - M. Zendron

1993	White Stallion	Open		250.00	260

In A Summer Meadow - Various

1994	Field Mice (Set/3) - A. Stocker	Open		42.50	45
1991	Field Mouse - A. Stocker	Open		47.50	50
1985	Hedgehog-Large - M. Schreck	Open		120.00	140
1985	Hedgehog-Medium - M. Schreck	Open		70.00	85
1987	Hedgehog-Small - M. Schreck	Open		50.00	55
1995	Ladybug - E. Mair	Open		29.50	30
1988	Mini Sitting Rabbit - A. Stocker	Open		35.00	45
1988	Mother Rabbit - A. Stocker	Open		60.00	75
1992	Sparrow - C. Schneiderbauer	Open		29.50	30
1982	Butterfly - Team	Open		44.00	85
1986	Mini Butterfly - Team	Open		16.00	45

Kingdom Of Ice And Snow - Various

1986	Large Polar Bear - A. Stocker	Open		140.00	210
1986	Mini Baby Seal - A. Stocker	Open		30.00	45
1984	Mini Penguin - M. Schreck	Open		16.00	38
1995	Sir Penguin - A. Stocker	Open		85.00	85

Our Candleholders - Various

1987	Star-Large 7600NR143	Open		250.00	375
1989	Star-Medium 7600NR143001	Open		200.00	260
1985	Water Lily-Large 7600NR125 - M. Schreck	Open		200.00	375
1983	Water Lily-Medium 7600NR123 - M. Schreck	Open		150.00	260
1985	Water Lily-Small 7600NR124 - M. Schreck	Open		100.00	175

Our Woodland Friends - Various

1981	Bear-Large - M. Schreck	Open		75.00	95
1985	Bear-Mini - M. Schreck	Open		16.00	55
1987	Fox - A. Stocker	Open		50.00	75
1988	Mini Running Fox - A. Stocker	Open		35.00	45
1988	Mini Sitting Fox - A. Stocker	Open		35.00	45
1989	Mushrooms - A. Stocker	Open		35.00	45
1983	Owl-Giant - M. Schreck	Open		1200.00	2000
1979	Owl-Large - M. Schreck	Open		90.00	125
1979	Owl-Mini - M. Schreck	Open		16.00	30
1995	Owlet - A. Hirzinger	Open		45.00	45
1994	Roe Deer Fawn - E. Mair	Open		75.00	75
1985	Squirrel - M. Schreck	Open		35.00	55

Pets' Corner - Various

1993	Beagle Playing - A. Stocker	Open		49.50	50
1990	Beagle Puppy - A. Stocker	Open		40.00	50
1992	Poodle - A. Stocker	Open		125.00	140
1990	Scotch Terrier - A. Stocker	Open		60.00	75
1991	Sitting Cat - M. Stamey	Open		75.00	85
1993	Sitting Poodle - A. Stocker	Open		85.00	85
1995	Tomcat - A. Hirzinger	Open		45.00	45

South Sea - Various

1987	Blowfish-Mini - Team	Open		22.00	30
1986	Blowfish-Small - Team	Open		35.00	55
1991	Butterfly Fish - M. Stamey	Open		150.00	175
1995	Dolphin - M. Stamey	Open		210.00	210
1988	Open Shell w/Pearl - M. Stamey	Open		120.00	175
1993	Sea Horse - M. Stamey	Open		85.00	85
1995	Shell - M. Stamey	Open		45.00	45
1995	Starfish - M. Stamey	Open		29.50	30
1995	Conch - M. Stamey	Open		29.50	30
1995	Maritime Trio (Shell, Starfish, Conch) - M. Stamey	Open		104.00	104
1993	Three South Sea Fish - M. Stamey	Open		135.00	140

Sparkling Fruit - Various

1991	Apple - M. Stamey	Open		175.00	185
1995	Grapes - Team	Open		375.00	375
1991	Pear - M. Stamey	Open		175.00	185
1981	Pineapple-Giant /Gold - M. Schreck	Open		1750.00	3250
1981	Pineapple-Large /Gold - M. Schreck	Open		150.00	260
1986	Pineapple-Small /Gold - M. Schreck	Open		55.00	85

When We Were Young - Various

1988	Locomotive - G. Stamey	Open		150.00	155
1990	Petrol Wagon - G. Stamey	Open		75.00	95
1988	Tender - G. Stamey	Open		55.00	55
1993	Tipping Wagon - G. Stamey	Open		95.00	95
1988	Wagon - G. Stamey	Open		85.00	95
1990	Airplane - A. Stocker	Open		135.00	155
1993	Kris Bear - M. Zendron	Open		75.00	75
1995	Kris Bear on Skates - M. Zendron	Open		75.00	75
1994	Replica Cat	Open		37.50	38
1994	Replica Hedgehog	Open		37.50	38
1994	Replica Mouse	Open		37.50	38
1994	Starter Set	Open		112.50	113
1994	Sailboat - G. Stamey	Open		195.00	210
1991	Santa Maria - G. Stamey	Open		375.00	375
1994	Rocking Horse - G. Stamey	Open		125.00	125
1995	Train-Mini - G. Stamey	Open		125.00	125

Retired Candleholders - Various

XX	Candleholder 7600NR101	Retrd.	1982	23.00	75-200
XX	Candleholder 7600NR102	Retrd.	1987	35.00	75-135
XX	Candleholder 7600NR103	Retrd.	1988	40.00	100-150
XX	Candleholder 7600NR104	Retrd.	1988	95.00	200-250
XX	Candleholder 7600NR106	Retrd.	1986	85.00	250
XX	Candleholder 7600NR107	Retrd.	1986	100.00	250-345
XX	Candleholder 7600NR109	Retrd.	1986	37.00	100
XX	Candleholder 7600NR110	Retrd.	1987	40.00	110
XX	Candleholder 7600NR111	Retrd.	1986	100.00	250
XX	Candleholder 7600NR112	Retrd.	1986	75.00	225-300
XX	Candleholder 7600NR114	Retrd.	1986	37.00	150-225
XX	Candleholder 7600NR115	Retrd.	1987	185.00	375-450
XX	Candleholder 7600NR116	Retrd.	1986	350.00	850-1200
XX	Candleholder 7600NR119	Retrd.	1989	N/A	350-385
XX	Candleholder 7600NR122	Retrd.	1988	85.00	150-250
XX	Candleholder 7600NR127	Retrd.	1987	65.00	150-275
XX	Candleholder 7600NR128	Retrd.	1987	100.00	200
XX	Candleholder 7600NR129	Retrd.	1987	120.00	250-300
XX	Candleholder 7600NR130	Retrd.	1986	275.00	750-1000
XX	Candleholder 7600NR131 (Set/6)	Retrd.	N/A	43.00	450-595
XX	Candleholder 7600NR138	Retrd.	1987	160.00	400
XX	Candleholder 7600NR139	Retrd.	1987	140.00	260
XX	Candleholder 7600NR140	Retrd.	1987	120.00	375
XX	Candleholder-Baroque 7600NR121	Retrd.	1987	150.00	250-330
XX	Candleholder-European Style 7600NR103	Retrd.	1991	N/A	450-600
XX	Candleholder-European Style 7600NR108	Retrd.	1990	N/A	425
XX	Candleholder-European Style 7600NR141	Retrd.	1991	N/A	450-500
XX	Candleholder-European Style 7600NR142	Retrd.	1990	N/A	250-400
XX	Candleholder-Global-Kg. Sz. 7600NR135	Retrd.	1989	50.00	105-200
XX	Candleholder-Global-Lg. 600NR134	Retrd.	1991	40.00	75-90
XX	Candleholder-Global-Med. (2) 7600NR133	Retrd.	1991	40.00	75-110
XX	Candleholder-Global-Sm. (4) 7600NR132	Retrd.	1990	60.00	160
1990	Candleholder-Neo-Classic-Lg. 7600NR144090 - A. Stocker	Retrd.	1993	220.00	265-650
1990	Candleholder-Neo-Classic-Med. 7600NR144080 - A. Stocker	Retrd.	1993	190.00	210-350
1990	Candleholder-Neo-Classic-Sm. 7600NR144070 - A. Stocker	Retrd.	1993	170.00	205-500
XX	Candleholder-Pineapple 7600NR136G	Retrd.	1987	150.00	275
XX	Candleholder-Pineapple 7600NR136R	Retrd.	1987	150.00	275
XX	Candleholder-w/Flowers-Lg. 7600NR137	Retrd.	1991	150.00	250-350
XX	Candleholder-w/Flowers-Sm. 7600NR120	Retrd.	1987	60.00	250-330
XX	Candleholder-w/Leaves-Sm. 7600NR126	Retrd.	1987	100.00	175-325

Retired - Various

1992	Angel 6475NR000009	Retrd.	1994	65.00	75-130
XX	Apple Photo Stand-Kg. Sz. (Gold) 7504NR060G	Retrd.	1989	120.00	350-525
XX	Apple Photo Stand-Kg. Sz. (Rhodium) 7504NR060R - M. Schreck	Retrd.	1989	120.00	425-475
XX	Apple Photo Stand-Lg. 7504NR050R	Retrd.	1987	80.00	150-300
XX	Apple Photo Stand-Lg. (Gold) 7504NR050G	Retrd.	1991	80.00	200-250
XX	Apple Photo Stand-Sm. (Gold) 7504NR030G	Retrd.	1991	40.00	150-200
XX	Apple Photo Stand-Sm. 7504NR030R	Retrd.	1987	40.00	150-200
XX	Ashtray 7461NR100	Retrd.	1991	45.00	200-250
XX	Ashtray 7501NR061	Retrd.	1981	45.50	1000-1200
XX	Bear-Giant Size 7637NR112 - M. Schreck	Retrd.	1988	125.00	1350-1650
XX	Bear-Kg Sz 7637NR92 - M. Schreck	Retrd.	1987	95.00	1200-1750
1984	Bear-Mini 7670NR32 - M. Schreck	Retrd.	1989	16.00	130-185
1982	Bear-Sm 7637NR054000 - M. Schreck	Retrd.	1995	44.00	85
1992	Beaver-Baby Lying 7616NR000003 - A. Stocker	Retrd.	1995	47.50	50
1985	Bee (Gold) 7553NR100	Retrd.	1989	200.00	1250-1760
1985	Bee (Rhodium) 7553NR200	Retrd.	1987	200.00	1800-2100
XX	Beetle Bottle Opener (Gold) 7505NR76	Retrd.	1984	80.00	950-1500
XX	Beetle Bottle Opener (Rhodium) 7505NR76	Retrd.	1984	80.00	800-1000
1984	Blowfish-Lg. 7644NR41	Retrd.	1992	40.00	100-150
1985	Butterfly (Gold) 7551NR100	Retrd.	1989	200.00	850-950
1985	Butterfly (Rhodium) 7551NR200	Retrd.	1987	200.00	1300-1700
XX	Butterfly-Mini 7671NR30	Retrd.	1989	16.00	75-100
XX	Cardholders-Lg. , Set/4 -7403NR30095	Retrd.	1990	45.00	250-500
XX	Cardholders-Sm., Set/4-7403NR20095	Retrd.	1990	25.00	175-275
1977	Cat-Lg 7634NR70 - M. Schreck	Retrd.	1992	44.00	70-90
19XX	Cat-Medium 7634NR52	Retrd.	1987	38.00	275-450
1982	Cat-Mini 7659NR31 - M. Schreck	Retrd.	1992	16.00	35-70
1981	Chess Set/Wooden Board 7550NR432032	Retrd.	1987	950.00	1200
XX	Chicken-Mini 7651NR20	Retrd.	1989	16.00	40-80
XX	Cigarette Box 7503NR050	Retrd.	1982	136.00	2500
XX	Cigarette Holder 7463NR062	Retrd.	1991	85.00	165-250
1991	City Gates 7474NR000023 - G. Stamey	Retrd.	1995	95.00	95-120
1991	City Tower 7474NR000022 - G. Stamey	Retrd.	1995	37.50	40-65
1984	Dachshund-Lg. 7641NR75 - M. Schreck	Retrd.	1992	48.00	90-125
XX	Dachshund-Mini 7672NR42 - A. Stocker	Retrd.	1989	20.00	75-100
1987	Dachshund-Mini 7672NR042000 - A. Stocker	Retrd.	1995	20.00	50
1981	Dinner Bell-Lg. 7467NR071000 - M. Schreck	Retrd.	1992	80.00	135-150
XX	Dog (standing) 7635NR70	Retrd.	1991	44.00	70-100
XX	Duck-Lg 7653NR75	Retrd.	1987	44.00	215-275
XX	Duck-Medium 7653NR55	Retrd.	1988	38.00	75-110
XX	Duck-Mini 7653NR45	Retrd.	1989	16.00	50-90
XX	Elephant 7640NR55	Retrd.	1990	90.00	150-245
1988	Elephant-Lg. 7640NR060000 - A. Stocker	Retrd.	1995	70.00	100-225
1984	Falcon Head-Lg. 7645NR100 - M. Schreck	Retrd.	1992	600.00	1000-1250

*Quotes have been rounded up to nearest dollar

YEAR ISSUE		EDITION LIMIT	YEAR RETD.	ISSUE PRICE	*QUOTE U.S.$
1986	Falcon Head-Sm. 7645NR45 - M. Schreck	Retrd.	1992	60.00	105-130
1984	Frog (black eyes) 7642NR48 - M. Schreck	Retrd.	1992	30.00	90-125
1984	Frog (clear eyes) 7642NR48 - M. Schreck	Retrd.	1992	30.00	125-225
XX	Grapes-Large 7550NR30015	Retrd.	1989	250.00	1000-1200
1985	Grapes-Med. 7550NR20029	Retrd.	1995	300.00	375-470
1985	Grapes-Sm. 7550NR20015	Retrd.	1995	200.00	260-345
XX	Hedgehog-Kg. Sz. 7630NR60 - M. Schreck	Retrd.	1987	98.00	350-550
XX	Hedgehog-Lg. 7630NR50 - M. Schreck	Retrd.	1987	65.00	155-250
XX	Hedgehog-Med. 7630NR40 - M. Schreck	Retrd.	1987	44.00	100-155
XX	Hedgehog-Sm. 7630NR30 - M. Schreck	Retrd.	1987	38.00	300-440
1988	Hippopotamus 7626NR65 - A. Stocker	Retrd.	1993	70.00	95-140
1989	Hippopotamus-Sm. 7626NR055000 - A. Stocker	Retrd.	1995	70.00	75-95
1991	Holy Family w/Arch 7475NR001	Retrd.	1994	250.00	225-350
1985	Hummingbird (Gold) 7552NR100	Retrd.	1989	200.00	950-1350
1985	Hummingbird (Rhodium) 7552NR200	Retrd.	1987	200.00	1800
1990	Kingfisher 7621NR000001 - M. Stamey	Retrd.	1993	75.00	110-160
1991	Kitten 7634NR028000 - M. Stamey	Retrd.	1995	47.50	50-60
XX	Lighter 7462NR062	Retrd.	1991	160.00	200-250
XX	Lighter 7500NR050	Retrd.	1982	160.00	2300
1986	Mallard 7647NR80 - M. Schreck	Retrd.	1995	80.00	140-155
XX	Mouse-Kg. Sz. 7631NR60 - M. Schreck	Retrd.	1987	95.00	500-800
XX	Mouse-Lg. 7631NR50 - M. Schreck	Retrd.	1987	69.00	175-275
1976	Mouse-Med. 7631NR040000 - M. Schreck	Retrd.	1995	48.00	85
XX	Mouse-Mini 7655NR23	Retrd.	1989	16.00	55-70
XX	Mouse-Sm. 7631NR30 - M. Schreck	Retrd.	1992	35.00	55-90
1989	Old Timer Automobile 7473NR000001 - G. Stamey	Retrd.	1995	130.00	155
1989	Owl 7621NR000003 - M. Stamey	Retrd.	1993	70.00	110-155
1979	Owl-Sm. 7636NR046000 - M. Schreck	Retrd.	1995	59.00	85
1989	Parrot 7621NR000004 - M. Stamey	Retrd.	1993	70.00	110-160
1987	Partridge 7625NR50 - A. Stocker	Retrd.	1991	85.00	100-145
1984	Penguin-Lg. 7643NR085000 - M. Schreck	Retrd.	1995	44.00	95
XX	Picture Frame/Oval 7505NR75G	Retrd.	1990	90.00	225-290
XX	Picture Frame/Square 7506NR60G	Retrd.	1990	100.00	250
XX	Pig-Lg. 7638NR65 - M. Schreck	Retrd.	1987	50.00	225-300
1985	Pineapple/Rhodium-Giant 7507NR26002 - M. Schreck	Retrd.	1987	1750.00	3500
1982	Pineapple/Rhodium-Lg. 7507NR105002 - M. Schreck	Retrd.	1987	150.00	250-475
1987	Pineapple/Rhodium-Sm. 7507NR060002 - M. Schreck	Retrd.	1987	55.00	135-165
XX	Pprwgt-Atomic-Crystal Cal 7454NR60095	Retrd.	1985	80.00	600-1200
XX	Pprwgt-Atomic-Vitrl Med. 7454NR60087	Retrd.	1985	80.00	650-800
XX	Pprwgt-Barrel-Crystal Cal 7453NR60095	Retrd.	1989	80.00	175
XX	Pprwgt-Barrel-Vitrl Med. 7453NR60087	Retrd.	1989	80.00	175
XX	Pprwgt-Carousel-Crystal Cal 7451NR60095	Retrd.	1985	80.00	650-1075
XX	Pprwgt-Carousel-Vitrl Med. 7451NR60087	Retrd.	1985	80.00	750-1200
1982	Pprwgt-Cone Crystal Cal 7452NR60095 - M. Schreck	Retrd.	1993	80.00	125-300
1982	Pprwgt-Cone Vitrl Med. 7452NR60087 - M. Schreck	Retrd.	1993	80.00	150-195
1981	Pprwgt-Egg 7458NR63069 - M. Schreck	Retrd.	1993	60.00	75-150
XX	Pprwgt-Geometric 7432NR57002N	Retrd.	1991	75.00	140-165
XX	Pprwgt-Octron-Crystal Cal 7456NR41	Retrd.	1992	75.00	160-170
XX	Pprwgt-Octron-Vitrl Med. 7456NR41087	Retrd.	1992	75.00	100-165
XX	Pprwgt-One Ton 7495NR65	Retrd.	1991	75.00	140
XX	Pprwgt-Rd.-Berm Blue 7404NR30MM	Retrd.	N/A	15.00	200-400
XX	Pprwgt-Rd.-Berm Blue 7404NR40MM	Retrd.	N/A	20.00	200-400
XX	Pprwgt-Rd.-Berm Blue 7404NR50MM	Retrd.	N/A	40.00	300
XX	Pprwgt-Rd.-Crystal Cal 7404NR30095/30MM	Retrd.	1989	15.00	50-70
XX	Pprwgt-Rd.-Crystal Cal 7404NR40095/40MM	Retrd.	1989	20.00	70-95
XX	Pprwgt-Rd.-Crystal Cal 7404NR50095/50MM	Retrd.	1989	40.00	100-200
XX	Pprwgt-Rd.-Crystal Cal 7404NR60095/60MM	Retrd.	1989	50.00	150-250
XX	Pprwgt-Rd.-Green 7404NR30	Retrd.	N/A	15.00	200-400
XX	Pprwgt-Rd.-Green 7404NR40	Retrd.	N/A	20.00	200-400
XX	Pprwgt-Rd.-Green 7404NR50	Retrd.	N/A	40.00	300-500
XX	Pprwgt-Rd.-Sahara 7404NR30	Retrd.	1983	15.00	200-400
XX	Pprwgt-Rd.-Sahara 7404NR40	Retrd.	1982	20.00	215
XX	Pprwgt-Rd.-Sahara 7404NR50	Retrd.	1983	40.00	300-500
XX	Pprwgt-Rd.-Vitrl Med. 7404NR30087/30MM	Retrd.	1989	15.00	75
XX	Pprwgt-Rd.-Vitrl Med. 7404NR40087/40MM	Retrd.	1989	20.00	50
XX	Pprwgt-Rd.-Vitrl Med. 7404NR50087/50MM	Retrd.	1989	40.00	125
XX	Pprwgt-Rd.-Vitrl Med. 7404NR60087/60MM	Retrd.	1989	50.00	150
1987	Pyramid-Lg.-Crystal Cal 7450NR50095 - M. Schreck	Retrd.	1994	90.00	200-250
1987	Pyramid-Lg.-Vitrl Med. 7450NR50087 - M. Schreck	Retrd.	1994	90.00	165-265
XX	Rabbit-Lg. 7652NR45	Retrd.	1988	38.00	150-225
XX	Rabbit-Mini 7652NR20	Retrd.	1989	16.00	65-110
1988	Rabbit-Mini Lying 7678NR030000 - A. Stocker	Retrd.	1995	35.00	45
1988	Rhinoceros 7622NR70 - A. Stocker	Retrd.	1993	70.00	110-130
1990	Rhinoceros-Sm. 7622NR060000 - A. Stocker	Retrd.	1995	70.00	75-95
XX	Salt and Pepper Shakers 7508NR068034	Retrd.	1989	80.00	250-360
XX	Schnapps Glasses, Set/6-7468NR039000	Retrd.	1991	150.00	250-345
1985	Seal-Large 7646NR085000 - M. Schreck	Retrd.	1995	44.00	85-130
1992	Shepherd 7475NR000007	Retrd.	1994	65.00	65-110
1990	Silver Crystal City-Cathedral 7474NR000021 - G. Stamey	Retrd.	1995	95.00	120-140
1990	Silver Crystal City-Houses I& II (Set/2) 7474NR100000 - G. Stamey	Retrd.	1995	75.00	75-95
1990	Silver Crystal City-Houses III & IV (Set/2) 7474NR200000 - G. Stamey	Retrd.	1995	75.00	85-115
1990	Silver Crystal City-Poplars (Set/3) 7474NR020003 - G. Stamey	Retrd.	1995	40.00	60
1986	Snail 7648NR030000 - M. Stamey	Retrd.	1995	35.00	55
1991	South Sea Shell 7624NR72000 - M. Stamey	Retrd.	1995	110.00	120-145
XX	Sparrow-Lg. 7650NR32	Retrd.	1988	38.00	110-140
1979	Sparrow-Mini 7650NR20 - M. Schreck	Retrd.	1992	16.00	45-125
XX	Swan-Mini 7658NR27 - M. Schreck	Retrd.	1989	16.00	120-150
XX	Table Magnifyer (no chain) 7510NR01G	Retrd.	1984	70.00	750
XX	Table Magnifyer (no chain) 7510NR01R	Retrd.	1984	80.00	550
XX	Table Magnifyer (with chain) 7510NR01R	Retrd.	1984	80.00	990
1989	Toucan 7621NR000002 - M. Stamey	Retrd.	1993	70.00	105-150
1993	Town Hall 7474NR000027 - G. Stamey	Retrd.	1995	135.00	135-200
XX	Treasure Box (Heart/Butterfly)7465NR52/100	Retrd.	1991	80.00	150-195
XX	Treasure Box (Heart/Flower)7465NR52	Retrd.	1989	80.00	155-200
XX	Treasure Box (Oval/Butterfly)7466NR063100	Retrd.	1989	80.00	225-260
XX	Treasure Box (Oval/Flower) 7466NR063000	Retrd.	1991	80.00	175
XX	Treasure Box (Round/Butterfly) 7464NR50/100	Retrd.	1989	80.00	175-275
XX	Treasure Box (Round/Flower) 7464NR50	Retrd.	1991	80.00	135-165
XX	Turtle-King Sz. 7632NR75 - M. Schreck	Retrd.	1988	58.00	200-250
XX	Vase 7511NR70	Retrd.	1991	50.00	105-180
1989	Walrus 7620NR100000 - M. Stamey	Retrd.	1994	120.00	150
1988	Whale 7628NR80 - M. Stamey	Retrd.	1992	70.00	130-160
1992	Wise Men (Set/3) 7475NR200000	Retrd.	1994	175.00	185-220

The Tudor Mint Inc.

Arthurian Legend - M. Locker, unless otherwise noted

YEAR ISSUE		EDITION LIMIT	YEAR RETD.	ISSUE PRICE	*QUOTE U.S.$
1990	3200 Merlin	Open		18.60	34
1990	3201 Into Merlin's Care Mold 1	Closed	N/A	25.40	175-225
1990	3201 Into Merlin's Care Mold 2	Closed	1993	25.40	50-75
1990	3202 Excaliber - M.L./R.G.	Open		18.60	34
1990	3203 Camelot	Open		25.40	42
1990	3204 King Arthur - M.L./R.G.	Open		18.60	34
1990	3205 Queen Guinevere	Open		18.60	34
1990	3206 Sir Percival & the Grail	Closed	1993	18.60	125-200
1990	3207 Morgan Le Fey	Open		25.40	42
1990	3208 Sir Lancelot	Open		25.40	42
1992	3209 Vigil of Sir Galahad - A. Slocombe	Open		31.45	42
1992	3210 Sir Mordred - R. Gibbons	Open		23.70	34
1992	3211 Return of Excalibur	Open		23.70	34
1993	3212 Sir Gawain - A. Slocombe	Open		25.40	34
1993	3213 King Arthur/Sir Bedevere	Open		33.90	42

Dark Secrets - Various

YEAR ISSUE		EDITION LIMIT	YEAR RETD.	ISSUE PRICE	*QUOTE U.S.$
1994	6201 Dark Secrets - A. Slocombe	Open		84.90	112
1994	6202 Guardian of the Skulls - R. Gibbons	Open		30.18	40
1994	6203 The Skull Gateway - M. Locker	Open		33.90	44
1994	6204 The Tortured Skull - M. Locker	Open		33.90	44
1994	6205 The Serpent of the Skulls - S. Darnley	Open		33.90	44
1994	6206 The Altar of the Skulls - M. Locker	Open		25.40	36
1994	6207 The Skull Master - R. Gibbons	Open		33.90	44
1994	6208 The Vampire of the Skulls - A. Slocombe	Open		25.40	36
1994	6209 The Chamber of the Skulls - A. Slocombe	Open		101.90	142
1994	6210 The Guardian of the Demons - M. Locker	Open		30.18	40
1994	6211 The Ice Demon - S. Darnley	Open		25.40	36
1994	6212 The Demon of the Pit - S. Darnley	Open		25.40	36
1994	6213 The Demon of the Night - M. Locker	Open		25.40	36
1994	6214 The Demon of the Catacombs - R. Gibbons	Open		25.40	36
1994	6215 The Demon Slayer - M. Locker	Open		25.40	36
1994	6216 The Demon Jailer - S. Darnley	Open		25.40	36
1994	6217 The Chamber of the Demons - A. Slocombe	Open		101.90	142
1994	6218 The Guardian of Skeletons - R. Gibbons	Open		30.51	42
1994	6219 The Vigil of the Skeleton - R. Gibbons	Open		25.40	36
1994	6220 The Forgotten Skeleton - R. Gibbons	Open		30.51	42
1994	6221 The Prisoners of the Sword - A. Slocombe	Open		30.51	42
1994	6222 The Executioner - M. Locker	Open		30.51	42
1994	6223 The Finder of the Treasure - A. Slocombe	Open		25.40	36
1994	6224 The Skeleton Warrior - S. Darnley	Open		30.51	42
1994	6225 The Chamber of Skeletons - A. Slocombe	Open		101.90	142

Dinosaur Collection - Various

YEAR ISSUE		EDITION LIMIT	YEAR RETD.	ISSUE PRICE	*QUOTE U.S.$
1993	6001 Pteranodon - M. Locker	Closed	1994	25.40	50-70
1993	6002 Triceratops - A. Slocombe	Closed	1994	25.40	50-70
1993	6003 Stegosaurus - A. Slocombe	Closed	1994	25.40	50-70
1993	6004 Brontosaurus - M. Locker	Closed	1994	25.40	50-70
1993	6005 Tyrannosaurus Rex - A. Slocombe	Closed	1994	25.40	50-70
1993	6006 Spinosaurus - R. Gibbons	Closed	1994	25.40	50-70

Hobbit Collection - A. Slocombe, unless otherwise noted

YEAR ISSUE		EDITION LIMIT	YEAR RETD.	ISSUE PRICE	*QUOTE U.S.$
1991	5001 Bilbo Baggins - R. Gibbons	Open		23.70	38
1991	5002 Gandalf	Open		42.41	64
1991	5003 Thorn Oakenshield - R. Gibbons	Closed	1992	23.70	50-80
1991	5004 The Great Goblin - R. Gibbons	Closed	1993	23.70	55
1991	5005 Gollum	Open		29.75	46
1991	5006 Beorn	Closed	1992	42.41	85
1991	5007 The Elven King	Closed	1992	29.75	70-85
1991	5008 Smaug the Dragon	Closed	1993	93.41	200
1991	5009 Bard - M. Locker	Closed	1992	23.70	100
1991	5010 'Good Morn.' at Bag End - R. Gibbons	Closed	1993	67.90	150
1991	5011 Moon Letters	Closed	1992	93.41	150-200
1991	5012 Finding the 'Precious' - R. Gibbons	Closed	1992	67.90	155
1991	5013 The Capture of Bilbo	Closed	1992	67.90	150-200
1991	5014 'Riddles in the Dark'	Closed	1992	56.01	150
1991	5015 Escape From the Wargs - R. Gibbons	Closed	1992	67.90	150-200
1991	5016 Barrels Out of Bond - M. Locker	Closed	1992	67.90	150-200
1991	5017 The 'Courage of the Bilbo'	Closed	1992	56.01	150
1991	5018 Prisoner of Elven King	Closed	1992	67.90	150
1991	5019 The Enchanted Door - M. Locker	Closed	1992	93.41	200-250
1991	5020 The Wrath of Beorn - M. Locker	Closed	1992	67.90	150-185
1991	5021 Journey's End - R. Gibbons	Closed	1993	67.90	150
1991	5022 The Troll's Clearing - R. Gibbons	Closed	1992	251.51	750-1000
1991	5023 Burglar Steals Smaug's	Closed	1993	254.91	750-1000
1991	5024 Farewell, King Under Mt. - M. Locker	Closed	1992	254.91	750-1000

Lord of the Rings - Various

YEAR ISSUE		EDITION LIMIT	YEAR RETD.	ISSUE PRICE	*QUOTE U.S.$
1992	5025 Frodo Baggins - R. Gibbons	Open		25.40	38
1992	5026 Bilbo's Tale - M. Locker	Open		25.40	38
1992	5027 Gimli the Dwarf - M. Locker	Open		25.40	38
1992	5028 Sam Gamgee - R. Gibbons	Open		25.40	38
1992	5029 Aragorn (Strider) - A. Slocombe	Open		25.40	38
1992	5030 An Orc - R. Gibbons	Closed	1994	30.51	60
1992	5031 Legolas the Elf - A. Slocombe	Open		30.51	46
1992	5032 The Mirror of Galadriel - R. Gibbons	Open		30.51	46
1992	5033 Saruman - A. Slocombe	Closed	1994	43.78	80
1992	5034 The Balrog - R. Gibbons	Open		67.90	100
1992	5035 Gandalf & Shadowfax - M. Locker	Open		67.90	100
1992	5036 A Black Rider - A. Slocombe	Open		67.90	100
1992	5037 Pippin - A. Slocombe	Closed	1994	25.40	48
1992	5038 Merry - A. Slocombe	Closed	1994	25.40	48
1992	5039 Boromir - R. Gibbons	Closed	1994	25.40	48
1992	5040 Treebeard (Fangorn) - R. Gibbons	Closed	1994	43.78	65

Myth & Magic Club - Various

YEAR ISSUE		EDITION LIMIT	YEAR RETD.	ISSUE PRICE	*QUOTE U.S.$
1990	9001 The Quest For the Truth - R.G./M.L.	Closed	1991	84.90	675
1991	9002 The Game of Strax - R. Gibbons	Closed	1991	25.40	550
1991	9003 The Well of Aspirations - A. Slocombe	Closed	1992	84.90	800
1992	9004 Playmates - R. Gibbons	Closed	1992	28.80	100-175
1992	9005 Friends - A. Slocombe	Closed	1993	32.20	100-175
1992	9006 The Enchanted Pool - R. Gibbons	Closed	1993	84.90	150-225
1993	9007 The Mystical Encounter - A. Slocombe	Closed	1994	33.58	60-85
1994	9008 Keeper of the Dragons - R. Gibbons	Closed	1994	84.90	125

*Quotes have been rounded up to nearest dollar

YEAR ISSUE		EDITION LIMIT	YEAR RETD.	ISSUE PRICE	*QUOTE U.S.$
1994	9009 The Crystal Shield - M. Locker	Closed	1995	44.00	63
1994	9010 Battle for the Crystal - A. Slocombe	Closed	1995	108.00	130
1995	9011 Starstruck - S. Darnley	Open		44.00	44
1990	CC01 The Protector - R. Gibbons	Closed	1991	Gift	450
1991	CC02 The Jovial Wizard - M. Locker	Closed	1992	Gift	270
1992	CC03 Dragon of Destiny - R. Gibbons	Closed	1993	Gift	175-200
1993	CC04 Dragon of Methtintdour - A. Slocombe	Closed	1994	Gift	80-100
1994	CC05 The Dreamy Dragon - M. Locker	Closed	1995	Gift	50
1995	CC06 The Regal Dragon - A. Slocombe	6/95		Gift	N/A
1996	9012 Cauldron of Fire - A. Slocombe	Yr.Iss.		108.00	108

Myth & Magic One Year Only Piece - R. Gibbons, unless otherwise noted

YEAR ISSUE		EDITION LIMIT	YEAR RETD.	ISSUE PRICE	*QUOTE U.S.$
1993	OY93 The Flying Dragon - A. Slocombe	Closed	1993	67.90	375
1994	OY94 Dragon of Underworld - R. Gibbons	Closed	1994	70.55	375
1995	OY95 Guardian of the Crystal - A. Slocombe	Closed	1995	84.90	110-160
1996	OY96 The Enchanted Dragon - J. Watson	Yr.Iss.		114.00	114

Myth & Magic Promotion - Various

YEAR ISSUE		EDITION LIMIT	YEAR RETD.	ISSUE PRICE	*QUOTE U.S.$
1993	3601 Dactrius - R.G./M.L./A.S.	Closed	1993	67.90	495
1994	3603 Vexius - A. Slocombe	Closed	1994	70.55	122
1995	3606 Viamphe - M. Locker	Closed	1995	73.42	110
1995	3607 Quargon - A. Slocombe	Closed	1995	26.32	50

Myth & Magic Colleggtibles - R. Gibbons

YEAR ISSUE		EDITION LIMIT	YEAR RETD.	ISSUE PRICE	*QUOTE U.S.$
1996	1049 The Protector	Open		38.00	38
1996	1050 The Supreme Dragon	Open		38.00	38
1996	1051 The Family of Dragons	Open		38.00	38
1996	1052 The Dragon of Justice	Open		38.00	38
1996	1053 The Paternal Dragon	Open		38.00	38
1996	1054 The Sleepy Lizards	Open		38.00	38
1996	1055 The Castle of Unicorns	Open		38.00	38
1996	1056 The Fairy Rider	Open		38.00	38
1996	1057 The Leaping Pegasus	Open		38.00	38
1996	1058 The Fairy Glade	Open		38.00	38
1996	1059 The Damsel & Unicorn	Open		38.00	38
1996	1060 The Wizard's Cauldron	Open		38.00	38

Myth & Magic Extravaganza Study - Various

YEAR ISSUE		EDITION LIMIT	YEAR RETD.	ISSUE PRICE	*QUOTE U.S.$
1992	3600 Sauria - A. Slocombe	Closed	1992	33.90	700
1993	3602 Deinos - R. Gibbons	Closed	1993	33.90	600
1994	3604 Lithia - M. Locker	Closed	1994	31.92	32
1995	3608 Imperia - S. Darnley	Closed	1995	41.25	42

Myth & Magic Large - Various

YEAR ISSUE		EDITION LIMIT	YEAR RETD.	ISSUE PRICE	*QUOTE U.S.$
1990	3300 The Dragon Master - R. Gibbons	7,500		297.50	404
1990	3301 The Magical Encounter - R. Gibbons	Open		30.50	42
1990	3302 The Keeper of the Magic - R. Gibbons	Closed	1995	59.40	110-130
1990	3303 Summoning the Elements - R. Gibbons	Closed	1993	59.40	300-465
1990	3304 Sorceror's Apprentice - R. Gibbons	Closed	1991	59.40	465
1990	3305 The Nest of Dragons - M. Locker	Closed	1993	59.40	175-225
1990	3306 Meeting of the Unicorns - M. Locker	Open		59.40	86
1990	3307 Sentinels at the Portal - R. Gibbons	Closed	1991	59.40	465
1990	3308 The VII Seekers of Knowledge - M. Locker	7,500		297.50	404
1990	3309 Le Morte D'Arthur - A. Slocombe	Open		84.90	122
1990	3310 The Magical Vision - A. Slocombe	Closed	1995	84.90	110-185
1990	3311 The Dance of the Dolphins - R. Gibbons	1,537	1993	297.50	500
1991	3312 Altar of Enlightenment - M. Locker	Open		84.90	122
1991	3313 Power of the Crystal - A. Slocombe	3,500		595.00	595
1992	3314 The Awakening - J. Pickering	Closed	1995	64.50	110-130
1992	3315 The Crystal Dragon - A. Slocombe	Open		101.90	122
1992	3318 The Gathering of the Unicorns - A.S./R.G.	5,000		314.50	110-185
1993	3319 The Invocation - M. Locker	Closed	1995	84.90	153
1993	3320 The Fighting Dragons - A. Slocombe	Open		67.90	86
1993	3321 The Playful Dolphins - M. Locker	Open		56.95	68
1993	3322 The Dragon of Darkness - A. Slocombe	Open		67.90	90
1994	3323 The Destroyer of the Crystal - S. Darnley	Open		84.90	114
1994	3324 A Tranquil Moment - M. Locker	Open		84.90	114
1994	3325 Great Earth Dragon - R. Gibbons	Open		101.90	136
1995	3326 The Great Sun Dragon - A. Slocombe	Open		136.00	136
1995	3327 The Great Moon Dragon - R. Gibbons	Open		136.00	136
1995	3328 The Great Sea Dragon - M. Locker	Open		136.00	136

Myth & Magic Miniatures - R. Gibbons, unless otherwise noted

YEAR ISSUE		EDITION LIMIT	YEAR RETD.	ISSUE PRICE	*QUOTE U.S.$
1989	3500 The Incantation	Closed	1991	8.42	100
1989	3501 The Book of Spells - R.G./M.L.	Closed	1995	8.42	23
1989	3502 The Enchanted Castle	Closed	1993	8.42	28
1989	3503 The Cauldron of Light - M.L./R.G	Open		8.42	12
1989	3504 The Winged Serpent	Closed	1995	8.42	23
1989	3505 The White Witch - R.G./M.L.	Closed	1991	8.42	83
1989	3506 The Master Wizard	Closed	1995	8.42	23
1989	3507 The Guardian Dragon	Open		8.42	12
1989	3508 The Unicorn	Open		8.42	12
1989	3509 Pegasus	Open		8.42	12
1989	3510 The Castle of Dreams	Closed	1993	8.42	38
1989	3511 The Light of Knowledge - R.G./M.L.	Closed	1991	8.42	25-80
1990	3512 The Siren	Closed	1991	8.42	160
1990	3513 The Crystal Queen	Closed	1992	8.76	28-50
1990	3514 The Astronomer - R.G./M.L.	Closed	1991	8.76	50-100
1990	3515 The Alchemist - R.G./M.L.	Closed	1991	8.76	50-100
1990	3516 The Minotaur	Closed	1991	8.76	150
1990	3517 The Grim Reaper - R.G./M.L.	Closed	1995	8.76	23
1990	3518 The Castle of Souls	Closed	1993	8.76	41
1990	3519 The Dragon Gateway	Closed	1995	8.76	23
1990	3520 The Dragon Rider - R.G./M.L.	Closed	1991	8.76	150
1990	3521 The Dragon's Kiss	Closed	1992	8.76	55
1990	3522 The Witch & Familiar	Closed	1991	8.76	240
1990	3523 The Oriental Dragon - R.G./M.L.	Closed	1993	8.76	30
1990	3524 The Reborn Dragon	Open		8.76	12
1990	3525 The Fire Dragon - R.G./M.L.	Closed	1994	8.76	28
1990	3526 The Giant Sorceror - R.G./M.L.	Closed	1991	8.76	120
1990	3527 The Wizard of Light	Closed	1994	8.76	28
1990	3528 Keeper of the Treasure	Closed	1992	8.76	82
1990	3529 The Old Hag	Closed	1991	8.76	240
1991	3530 Mother Nature	Closed	1994	9.44	25
1991	3531 The Earth Wizard - R.G./M.L.	Closed	1992	9.44	74
1991	3532 The Fire Wizard	Closed	1994	9.44	27
1991	3533 The Water Wizard	Closed	1992	9.44	14
1991	3534 The Air Wizard	Closed	1992	9.44	70
1991	3535 The Dragon of the Lake	Closed	1994	9.44	35
1991	3536 The Dragon's Spell - R.G./M.L.	Closed	1991	9.44	14
1991	3537 Merlin - M. Locker	Open		9.44	12
1991	3538 Excalibur - M.L./R.G.	Closed	1993	9.44	25
1991	3539 Camelot - M. Locker	Open		9.44	12
1991	3540 King Arthur - M.L./R.G.	Open		9.44	12
1991	3541 Queen Guinevere - M. Locker	Closed	1993	9.44	30
1992	3542 Dragon of the Forest	Closed	1995	10.11	23
1992	3543 Dragon of the Moon	Closed	1995	10.11	23
1992	3544 Wizard of Winter	Closed	1995	10.11	23
1992	3545 Dragon of Wisdom	Closed	1995	10.11	23
1992	3546 Dragon of the Sun - M. Locker	Closed	1995	10.11	23
1992	3547 Dragon of the Clouds - M. Locker	Closed	1995	10.11	23
1993	3548 Moon Wizard - A. Slocombe	Open		10.62	12
1993	3549 Unicorn of Light - A. Slocombe	Open		10.62	12
1993	3550 Return of Excalibur - M. Locker	Closed	1994	10.62	25
1993	3551 Magical Encounter	Open		10.62	12
1993	3552 Ice Dragon - A. Slocombe	Closed	1995	10.62	23
1993	3553 Sleepy Dragon - M. Locker	Open		10.62	12
1994	3554 Keeper of the Skulls	Open		10.80	12
1994	3555 The Dark Dragon - A. Slocombe	Open		10.80	12
1994	3556 Protector of the Young - M.L./R.G.	Open		10.80	12
1994	3557 Dragon of Light - R.G./A.S.	Open		10.80	12
1994	3558 Unicorns of Freedom	Open		10.80	12
1994	3559 Defender of the Crystal	Open		10.80	12
1995	3560 The Loving Dragons - N/A	Open		12.00	12
1995	3561 The Wizard of the Lake - N/A	Open		12.00	12
1995	3562 The Hatch Wings - N/A	Open		12.00	12
1995	3563 The Dragon of the Treasure - N/A	Open		12.00	12
1995	3564 The Armoured Dragon - N/A	Open		12.00	12
1995	3565 The Sword Master - N/A	Open		12.00	12
1996	3566 The Dragon of the Ice Crystals - S. Riley	Open		14.00	14
1996	3567 The Mischievous Dragon - S. Riley	Open		14.00	14
1996	3568 The Summoner of Light S. Riley	Open		14.00	14
1996	3569 The Proud Pegasus - S. Riley	Open		14.00	14
1996	3570 The Crystal Unicorn - S. Riley	Open		14.00	14
1996	3571 The Majestic Dragon - S. Riley	Open		14.00	14
1996	3572 The Celtic Dragon - H. Coventry	Open		14.00	14
1996	3573 The Dragon Warrior - H. Coventry	Open		14.00	14
1996	3574 The Dragon Thief - J. Watson	Open		14.00	14
1996	3575 The Crystal Serpent - S. Riley	Open		14.00	14
1996	3576 The Dragon's Nest - J. Watson	Open		14.00	14
1996	3577 The Guardian of Light - J. Watson	Open		14.00	14

Myth & Magic Standard - R. Gibbons, unless otherwise noted

YEAR ISSUE		EDITION LIMIT	YEAR RETD.	ISSUE PRICE	*QUOTE U.S.$
1989	3001 The Incantation	Open		16.90	34
1989	3002 The Siren	Closed	1995	16.90	40-60
1989	3003 The Evil of Greed	Closed	1989	16.90	325
1989	3004 The Book of Spells - M. Locker	Open		16.90	34
1989	3005 The Enchanted Castle	Closed	1991	16.90	90
1989	3006 The Cauldron of Light - M.L./R.G.	Open		16.90	34
1989	3007 The Winged Serpent	Closed	1991	16.90	100
1989	3008 The White Witch - M. Locker	Closed	1991	16.90	85-100
1989	3009 The Master Wizard	Closed	1993	16.90	85
1989	3010 The Infernal Demon	Closed	1989	16.90	375
1989	3011 The Warrior Knight Mold 1	Closed	N/A	16.90	375-425
1989	3011 The Warrior Knight Mold 2	Closed	1990	16.90	375
1989	3012 The Deadly Combat	Closed	1989	16.90	375
1989	3013 The Old Hag Mold 1	Closed	N/A	16.90	375
1989	3013 The Old Hag Mold 2	Closed	1990	16.90	200-250
1989	3014 The Crystal Queen	Closed	1993	16.90	90
1989	3015 The Astronomer - M. Locker	Closed	1990	16.90	375
1989	3016 The Pipes of Pan	Closed	1990	16.90	200
1989	3017 Mischievous Goblin	Closed	1990	16.90	200
1989	3018 The Gorgon Medusa - R.G./M.L.	Closed	1990	16.90	200
1989	3019 The Alchemist - M. Locker	Closed	1990	16.90	200
1989	3020 The Merman - M. Locker	Closed	1990	16.90	200
1989	3021 The Guardian Dragon	Closed	1995	16.90	60-90
1989	3022 The Minotaur	Closed	1991	16.90	200
1989	3023 The Grim Reaper	Open		16.90	34
1989	3024 The Unicorn	Open		16.90	34
1989	3027 The Castle of Souls	Closed	1995	22.00	66-88
1989	3028 The Dragon Gateway	Closed	1995	22.00	66-90
1989	3029 The Dragon Rider - M. Locker	Closed	1995	16.90	50
1989	3030 The Dragon's Kiss Mold 1 - M. Locker	Closed	N/A	16.90	100
1989	3030 The Dragon's Kiss Mold 2 - M. Locker	Closed	1993	16.90	82
1989	3031 The Witch and Familiar	Closed	1990	16.90	240
1989	3032 The Oriental Dragon Mold 1 - M. Locker	Closed	N/A	16.90	600
1989	3032 The Oriental Dragon Mold 2 - M. Locker	Closed	N/A	16.90	480
1989	3032 The Oriental Dragon Mold 3 - M. Locker	Closed	1993	16.90	295
1989	3033 The Reborn Dragon	Open		16.90	34
1989	3034 The Fire Dragon - M. Locker	Closed	1993	16.90	90
1989	3035 The Giant Sorceror	Closed	1993	16.90	90
1989	3036 The Wizard of Light	Closed	1995	16.90	60-88
1989	3037 The Light of Knowledge - M. Locker	Closed	1991	16.90	165
1989	3038 Pegasus	Open		16.90	34
1990	3039 The Earth Wizard	Closed	1991	18.60	100
1990	3040 The Fire Wizard	Closed	1994	18.60	90
1990	3041 The Water Wizard	Closed	1991	18.60	100
1990	3042 The Air Wizard	Closed	1991	18.60	100
1990	3043 Mother Nature	Open		18.60	34
1990	3044 The Dragon of the Lake	Closed	1993	26.10	100-140
1990	3045 The Dragon's Spell	Closed	1992	18.60	100
1990	3046 The Keeper of the Treasure	Closed	1995	18.60	60-88
1990	3047 George & the Dragon	Closed	1990	18.60	550
1990	3048 Dragon of the Sea	Closed	1993	18.60	88
1990	3049 Dragon of the Forest	Closed	1994	18.65	88
1990	3050 Dragon of Wisdom	Open		18.60	34
1990	3051 Spirits of the Forest	Closed	1995	18.60	66-88
1990	3052 Virgin and Unicorn	Closed	1993	26.10	88
1991	3053 The Wizard of Autumn	Open		22.00	34
1991	3054 The Wizard of Winter	Open		22.00	34
1991	3055 The Wizard of Spring - A. Slocombe	Closed	1995	22.00	60-88
1991	3056 The Wizard of Summer	Open		22.00	34
1991	3057 The Dragon of the Moon	Open		22.00	34
1991	3058 The Sun Dragon - M. Locker	Open		22.00	34
1991	3059 Dragon of the Clouds - M. Locker	Open		22.00	34
1991	3060 The Spirited Pegasus	Closed	1994	22.00	88
1991	3061 The Castle of Spires - A. Slocombe	Closed	1993	29.75	100
1991	3062 The Castle in the Clouds - A. Slocombe	Closed	1992	22.00	88
1991	3063 The Moon Wizard - A. Slocombe	Open		22.00	3
1991	3064 Dragon of the Stars - M. Locker	Closed	1995	29.75	60-8
1991	3065 The Sorceress of Light - M. Locker	Closed	1994	22.00	8
1991	3066 The Jewelled Dragon - A. Slocombe	Closed	1995	22.00	60-8
1991	3067 Old Father Time - M. Locker	Closed	1993	29.75	10
1991	3068 Runelore	Open		29.75	4
1992	3069 The Fairy Queen - A. Slocombe	Closed	1993	23.70	8
1992	3070 The Dragon Queen - A. Slocombe	Open		32.20	4
1992	3071 The Ice Dragon - A. Slocombe	Open		23.70	3
1992	3072 The Sleepy Dragon - M. Locker	Open		23.70	3
1992	3073 Unicorn of Light - A. Slocombe	Open		23.70	3
1992	3074 Starspell - M. Locker	Open		23.70	3
1992	3075 The Visionary	Open		32.20	4
1992	3076 The Crystal Spell - M. Locker	Closed	1995	23.70	60-9
1992	3077 Unicorn Rider - A. Slocombe	Open		23.70	3

*Quotes have been rounded up to nearest dollar

YEAR ISSUE		EDITION LIMIT	YEAR RETD.	ISSUE PRICE	*QUOTE U.S. $
1992	3078 The Loremaker - A. Slocombe	Open		23.70	34
1992	3079 Dragon's Enchantress - A. Slocombe	Closed	1994	32.20	88
1992	3080 The Leaf Spirit	Closed	1994	23.70	90
1992	3081 The Wizard of the Future	Open		23.70	34
1992	3082 The Swamp Dragon - A. Slocombe	Open		23.70	34
1992	3083 The Dragon of the Skulls	Open		23.70	34
1992	3084 The DarkDragon-A.Slocombe	Open		23.70	34
1992	3085 The Dragon of Light - R.G./A.S.	Open		23.70	34
1993	3092 The Fountain of Light - A. Slocombe	Closed	1995	25.00	60-88
1993	3093 The Dawn of the Dragon - R. Gibbons	Open		25.00	34
1993	3094 The Dragon of Prehistory	Closed	1995	25.00	60-88
1993	3095 Defender of the Crystal - A. Slocombe	Open		25.00	34
1993	3096 Rising of the Phoenix - M. Locker	Closed	1995	25.00	60-88
1993	3097 The Protector of Young - M. Locker	Open		25.00	34
1993	3098 The Unicorns of Freedom - A. Slocombe	Open		25.00	34
1993	3099 The Keeper of the Skulls	Open		33.60	42
1993	3100 The Wizard of the Serpents - M. Locker	Open		25.00	34
1993	3101 The Loving Dragons - M. Locker	Open		25.00	34
1993	3102 The Sword Master - A. Slocombe	Open		25.00	34
1993	3103 Dragon of Mystery - M. Locker	Open		25.00	34
1994	3104 The Wizard of the Skies - M. Locker	Open		25.40	36
1994	3105 The Dragon of the Treasure - A. Slocombe	Open		25.40	36
1994	3106 The Wizard of the Lake	Open		25.40	36
1994	3107 Banishing the Dragon - S. Darnley	Open		25.40	36
1994	3108 The Dragon's Castle	Open		25.40	44
1994	3109 The Mystical Traveller - M. Locker	Open		25.40	36
1994	3110 The Armoured Dragon - S. Darnley	Open		25.40	36
1994	3111 The Hatchlings - S. Darnley	Open		25.40	36
1994	3112 Dragon of Ice Crystals - A. Slocombe	Open		30.50	42
1994	3113 Mischievous Dragon - S. Darnley	Open		25.40	36
1994	3114 The Crystal Unicorn - S. Darnley	Open		30.50	42
1994	3115 Summoner of Light - M. Locker	Open		30.50	42
1994	3116 The Majestic Dragon - A. Slocombe	Open		30.50	42
1994	3117 The Proud Pegasus	Open		25.40	36
1995	3118 The Dragon Warrior - S. Darnley	Open		40.00	42
1995	3119 The Crystal Serpent - M. Locker	Open		54.00	54
1995	3120 The Dragon of the Deep - M. Locker	Open		34.00	34
1995	3121 The Celtic Dragon - A. Slocombe	Open		42.00	42
1995	3122 The Unicorn of Justice - A. Slocombe	Open		34.00	34
1995	3123 The Dragon King - M. Locker	Open		64.00	64
1995	3124 The Castle of Light	Open		34.00	34
1995	3125 The Dragon's Nest - A. Slocombe	Open		42.00	42
1995	3126 The Mischievous Dragonets	Open		42.00	42
1995	3127 The Guardian of Light	Open		54.00	54
1995	3128 The Dragon Thief	Open		42.00	42
1995	3129 The Earth Dragon	Open		54.00	54
1995	3130 The Studious Dragon - A. Slocombe	Open		42.00	42
1995	3131 Finding the Dragonets - M. Locker	Open		34.00	34
1995	3132 Learning to Fly	Open		34.00	34
1995	3133 The Wizard's Best Friend	Open		34.00	34
1995	3134 Reflections - M. Locker	Open		42.00	42
1995	3135 The Lord of the Wizards - A. Slocombe	Open		42.00	42
1995	3136 The Solar Dragon - S. Darnley	Open		54.00	54
1995	3137 The Lunar Dragon	Open		54.00	54
1995	3138 Wizard Mountain	Open		28.00	28
1995	3139 The Crystal Chalice	Open		32.00	32
1995	3140 The Wizard's Scroll - A. Slocombe	Open		28.00	28
1995	3141 The Magic Glade - S. Darnley	Open		32.00	32
1995	3142 The Magic Staff - M. Locker	Open		28.00	28
1995	3143 The Wrong Spell - M. Locker	Open		32.00	32
1996	3144 The Sea Dragon - S. Riley	Open		35.00	35
1996	3145 The First Born - J. Watson	Open		35.00	35
1996	3146 Way Out Dragon - H. Coventry	Open		35.00	35
1996	3147 Dragons At Play - H. Coventry	Open		46.00	46
1996	3148 The Nursery - H. Coventry	Open		35.00	35
1996	3149 Snoozing Wizard - H. Coventry	Open		35.00	35
1996	3150 The Fairy Princess - H. Coventry	Open		46.00	46
1996	3151 Follow Me Kids! - H. Coventry	Open		35.00	35
1996	3152 Don't Push Me! - S. Riley	Open		35.00	35

United Design Corp.

Angels Collection - D. Newburn, unless otherwise noted

YEAR ISSUE		EDITION LIMIT	YEAR RETD.	ISSUE PRICE	*QUOTE U.S.$
1993	Angel of Flight AA-032 - K. Memoli	10,000		100.00	100
1993	Angel w/ Birds AA-034	10,000	1995	75.00	75
1994	Angel w/ Book AA-058	10,000		84.00	84
1994	Angel w/ Christ Child AA-061 - K. Memoli	10,000		84.00	84
1993	Angel w/ Lilies AA-033	10,000	1996	80.00	80
1993	Angel w/ Lilies, Crimson AA-040	10,000		80.00	80
1992	Angel, Lamb & Critters AA-021 - S. Bradford	10,000		90.00	95
1992	Angel, Lion & Lamb AA-020 - K. Memoli	10,000	1994	135.00	245-300
1994	Angel, Roses and Bluebirds AA-054	10,000		65.00	65
1993	Autumn Angel AA-035	10,000	1996	70.00	70
1993	Autumn Angel, Emerald AA-041	10,000	1996	70.00	70
1995	Celestial Guardian Angel AA-069 - S. Bradford	10,000		120.00	120
1991	Christmas Angel AA-003 - S. Bradford	10,000	1994	125.00	125
1991	Classical Angel AA-005 - S. Bradford	10,000		79.00	79
1994	Dreaming of Angels AA-060 - K. Memoli	10,000		120.00	120
1994	Earth Angel AA-059 - S. Bradford	10,000		84.00	84
1991	The Gift AA-009 - S. Bradford	2,500	1991	135.00	500
1992	The Gift '92 AA-018 - S. Bradford	3,500	1992	140.00	295
1993	The Gift '93 AA-037 - S. Bradford	3,500	1993	120.00	200-250
1994	The Gift '94 AA-057	5,000	1994	140.00	175
1995	The Gift '95 AA-067	5,000	1995	140.00	140
1995	Guardian Angel, Lion & Lamb AA-083 - S. Bradford	10,000		165.00	165
1995	Guardian Angel, Lion & Lamb, lt. AA-068 - S. Bradford	10,000		165.00	165
1994	Harvest Angel AA-063 - S. Bradford	10,000		84.00	84
1991	Heavenly Shepherdess AA-008 - S. Bradford	10,000		99.00	99
1992	Joy To The World AA-016	10,000	1996	90.00	95
1995	A Little Closer to Heaven AA-081 - K. Memoli	10,000		230.00	230
1995	A Little Closer to Heaven, lt. AA-085 - K. Memoli	10,000		230.00	230
1993	Madonna AA-031 - K. Memoli	10,000		100.00	100
1991	Messenger of Peace AA-006 - S. Bradford	10,000		75.00	79
1992	Peaceful Encounter AA-017	10,000		100.00	100
1995	Starlight Starbright AA-066	10,000		70.00	70
1991	Trumpeter Angel AA-004 - S. Bradford	10,000		99.00	99
1992	Winter Angel AA-019	10,000		75.00	75
1991	Winter Rose Angel AA-007 - S. Bradford	10,000	1994	65.00	65

Backyard Birds™ - Various

YEAR ISSUE		EDITION LIMIT	YEAR RETD.	ISSUE PRICE	*QUOTE U.S.$
1994	Allen's on Pink Flowers BB-044 - P.J. Jonas	Open		22.00	22
1994	Allen's on Purple Morning Glory BB-051 - P.J. Jonas	Open		22.00	22
1989	Baltimore Oriole BB-024 - S. Bradford	Open		19.50	22
1989	Blue Jay BB-026 - S. Bradford	Open		19.50	22
1989	Blue Jay, Baby BB-027 - S. Bradford	Open		15.00	15
1990	Bluebird (Upright) BB-031 - S. Bradford	Open		20.00	20
1988	Bluebird BB-009 - S. Bradford	Open		15.00	21
1988	Bluebird Hanging BB-017 - S. Bradford	Retrd.	1990	11.00	17
1988	Bluebird, Small BB-001 - S. Bradford	Open		10.00	11
1994	Broadbill on Blue Morning Glory BB-053 - P.J. Jonas	Open		22.00	22
1994	Broadbill on Trumpet Vine BB-043 - P.J. Jonas	Open		22.00	22
1994	Broadbill on Yellow Fuscia BB-055 - P.J. Jonas	Open		22.00	22
1994	Broadbill Pair on Yellow Flowers BB-048 - P.J. Jonas	Open		30.00	30
1988	Cardinal Hanging BB-018 - S. Bradford	Retrd.	1990	11.00	11
1988	Cardinal, Female BB-011 - S. Bradford	Open		15.00	17
1988	Cardinal, Male BB-013 - S. Bradford	Open		15.00	18
1988	Cardinal, Small BB-002 - S. Bradford	Open		10.00	11
1990	Cedar Waxwing Babies BB-033 - S. Bradford	Open		22.00	22
1990	Cedar Waxwing BB-032 - S. Bradford	Open		20.00	20
1988	Chickadee BB-010 - S. Bradford	Open		15.00	18
1988	Chickadee Hanging BB-019 - S. Bradford	Retrd.	1990	11.00	11
1988	Chickadee, Small BB-003 - S. Bradford	Open		10.00	11
1990	Evening Grosbeak BB-034 - S. Bradford	Open		22.00	22
1989	Goldfinch BB-028 - S. Bradford	Open		16.50	20
1989	Hoot Owl BB-025 - S. Bradford	Open		15.00	20
1988	Humingbird BB-012 - S. Bradford	Open		15.00	18
1988	Hummingbird Female, Small BB-005 - S. Bradford	Retrd.	1991	10.00	10
1988	Hummingbird Flying, Small BB-004 - S. Bradford	Open		10.00	11
1988	Hummingbird Sm., Hanging BB-022 - S. Bradford	Retrd.	1990	11.00	11
1988	Hummingbird, Lg., Hanging BB-023 - S. Bradford	Retrd.	1990	15.00	15
1990	Indigo Bunting BB-036 - S. Bradford	Open		20.00	20
1990	Indigo Bunting, Female BB-039 - S. Bradford	Open		20.00	20
1994	Magnificent Pair on Trumpet Vine BB-046 - P.J. Jonas	Open		30.00	30
1990	Nuthatch, White-throated BB-037 - S. Bradford	Open		20.00	20
1990	Painted Bunting BB-040 - S. Bradford	Open		20.00	20
1990	Painted Bunting, Female BB-041 - S. Bradford	Open		20.00	20
1990	Purple Finch BB-038 - S. Bradford	Open		20.00	20
1988	Red-winged Blackbird BB-014 - S. Bradford	Retrd.	1991	15.00	17
1988	Robin Babies BB-008 - S. Bradford	Open		15.00	19
1988	Robin Baby, Small BB-006 - S. Bradford	Open		10.00	11
1988	Robin BB-015 - S. Bradford	Open		15.00	21
1988	Robin Hanging BB-020 - S. Bradford	Retrd.	1990	11.00	11
1990	Rose Breasted Grosbeak BB-042 - S. Bradford	Open		20.00	20
1994	Rubythroat on Pink Fuscia BB-054 - P.J. Jonas	Open		22.00	22
1994	Rubythroat on Red Morning Glory BB-052 - P.J. Jonas	Open		22.00	22
1994	Rubythroat on Thistle BB-049 - P.J. Jonas	Open		16.50	17
1994	Rubythroat on Yellow Flowers BB-045 - P.J. Jonas	Open		22.00	22
1994	Rubythroat Pair on Pink Flowers BB-047 - P.J. Jonas	Open		30.00	30
1989	Saw-Whet Owl BB-029 - S. Bradford	Open		15.00	18
1988	Sparrow BB-016 - S. Bradford	Open		15.00	17
1988	Sparrow Hanging BB-021 - S. Bradford	Retrd.	1990	11.00	11
1988	Sparrow, Small BB-007 - S. Bradford	Open		10.00	11
1989	Woodpecker BB-030 - S. Bradford	Open		16.50	20

Easter Bunny Family™ - D. Kennicutt

YEAR ISSUE		EDITION LIMIT	YEAR RETD.	ISSUE PRICE	*QUOTE U.S.$
1994	All Hidden SEC-045	Retrd.	1996	24.50	25
1989	Auntie Bunny SEC-008	Retrd.	1992	20.00	23
1992	Auntie Bunny w/Cake SEC-033R	Retrd.	1994	20.00	22
1991	Baby in Buggy, Boy SEC-027R	Retrd.	1994	20.00	22
1991	Baby in Buggy, Girl SEC-029R	Retrd.	1994	20.00	22
1994	Babysitter SEC-049	Open		24.50	25
1994	Bath Time SEC-044	Open		24.50	25
1995	Bed Time SEC-057	Open		24.00	24
1992	Boy Bunny w/Large Egg SEC-034R	Retrd.	1994	20.00	22
1991	Bubba In Wheelbarrow SEC-021	Retrd.	1993	20.00	20
1990	Bubba w/Wagon SEC-016	Retrd.	1993	16.50	18
1988	Bunnies, Basket Of SEC-001	Retrd.	1991	13.00	18
1991	Bunny Boy w/Basket SEC-025	Retrd.	1993	20.00	20
1988	Bunny Boy w/Duck SEC-002	Retrd.	1991	13.00	18
1988	Bunny Girl w/Hen SEC-004	Retrd.	1991	13.00	18
1989	Bunny w/Prize Egg SEC-010	Retrd.	1993	19.50	20
1988	Bunny, Easter SEC-003	Retrd.	1991	15.00	18
1993	Christening Day SEC-040	Retrd.	1995	20.00	22
1989	Ducky w/Bonnet, Blue SEC-015	Retrd.	1992	10.00	12
1989	Ducky w/Bonnet, Pink SEC-014	Retrd.	1992	10.00	12
1996	Easter Bunny In Evening Clothes-SEC-064	Open		20.00	20
1992	Easter Bunny w/Back Pack SEC-030	Open		20.00	22
1990	Easter Bunny w/Crystal SEC-017	Retrd.	1995	23.00	25
1993	Easter Bunny, Chocolate Egg SEC-041	Retrd.	1996	23.00	25
1995	Easter Cookies SEC-052	Open		24.00	24
1989	Easter Egg Hunt SEC-012	Retrd.	1995	16.50	22
1996	Easter Pageant - SEC-059	Open		17.00	17
1996	Easter Parade - SEC-063	Open		25.00	25
1993	Egg Roll SEC-036	Open		23.00	25
1991	Fancy Find SEC-028	Retrd.	1995	20.00	22
1996	First Kiss - SEC-061	Open		20.00	20
1995	First Outing SEC-054	Open		19.00	19
1994	First Steps SEC-048	Open		24.50	25
1994	Gift Carrot SEC-046	Open		22.00	22
1993	Girl Bunny w/Basket SEC-039	Open		20.00	22
1992	Girl Bunny w/Large Egg SEC-035R	Retrd.	1994	20.00	22
1993	Grandma & Quilt SEC-037	Open		23.00	25
1992	Grandma w/ Bible SEC-031	Retrd.	1996	20.00	22
1996	Grandma's Dress Makers Form-1996-SEC-066	Yr.Iss.		25.00	25
1992	Grandpa w/Carrots SEC-032R	Retrd.	1994	20.00	22
1996	Grandpa w/Sunflowers - SEC-065	Open		20.00	20
1990	Hen w/Chick SEC-018	Retrd.	1992	23.00	23
1994	Large Prize Egg SEC-047	Open		22.00	22
1989	Little Sis w/Lolly SEC-009	Retrd.	1992	14.50	18
1993	Lop Ear Dying Eggs SEC-042	Open		23.00	25
1996	Lop Girl w/Gift Box - SEC-060	Open		20.00	20
1991	Lop-Ear w/Crystal SEC-022	Open		23.00	25
1993	Mom Storytime SEC-043	Open		20.00	22
1996	Mom w/Chocolate Egg - SEC-062	Open		25.00	25
1990	Momma Making Basket SEC-019	Retrd.	1992	23.00	23

*Quotes have been rounded up to nearest dollar

YEAR ISSUE		EDITION LIMIT	YEAR RETD.	ISSUE PRICE	*QUOTE U.S.$
1990	Mother Goose SEC-020	Retrd.	1992	16.50	20
1991	Nest of Bunny Eggs SEC-023	Open		17.50	22
1995	Printing Lessons SEC-053	Open		19.00	19
1995	Quality Inspection SEC-055	Open		19.00	19
1988	Rabbit, Grandma SEC-005	Retrd.	1991	15.00	20
1988	Rabbit, Grandpa SEC-006	Retrd.	1991	15.00	20
1988	Rabbit, Momma w/Bonnet SEC-007	Retrd.	1991	15.00	20
1989	Rock-A-Bye Bunny SEC-013	Retrd.	1995	20.00	25
1993	Rocking Horse SEC-038	Retrd.	1996	20.00	22
1989	Sis & Bubba Sharing SEC-011	Retrd.	1996	22.50	25
1995	Spring Flying SEC-058	Open		19.00	19
1995	Team Work SEC-051	Open		24.00	24
1995	Two in a Basket SEC-056	Open		24.00	24
1991	Victorian Auntie Bunny SEC-026	Retrd.	1993	20.00	20
1991	Victorian Momma SEC-024	Retrd.	1993	20.00	20
1994	Wheelbarrow SEC-050	Open		24.50	25

Easter Bunny Family™ Babies - D. Kennicutt

YEAR ISSUE		EDITION LIMIT	YEAR RETD.	ISSUE PRICE	*QUOTE U.S.$
1995	Baby in Basket SEC-815	Open		8.00	8
1994	Baby on Blanket, Naptime SEC-807	Open		6.50	7
1996	Baby w/Diaper & Bottle, Blue - SEC-825	Open		8.00	8
1996	Baby w/Diaper & Bottle, Pink - SEC-817	Open		8.00	8
1996	Baby w/Diaper & Bottle, Yellow - SEC-824	Open		8.00	8
1995	Basket of Carrots SEC-812	Open		8.00	8
1994	Boy Baby w/Blocks SEC-805	Open		6.50	7
1994	Boy w/Baseball Bat SEC-801	Open		6.50	7
1996	Boy w/Baseball Mitt - SEC-822	Open		8.00	8
1994	Boy w/Basket and Egg SEC-802	Open		6.50	7
1996	Boy w/Big Teddy - SEC-819	Open		8.00	8
1995	Boy w/Butterfly SEC-814	Open		8.00	8
1994	Boy w/Stick Horse SEC-803	Open		6.50	7
1996	Boy w/Train Engine - SEC-816	Open		8.00	8
1996	Dress Up Girl - SEC-821	Open		8.00	8
1996	Egg Delivery - SEC-823	Open		8.00	8
1995	Gift Egg SEC-808	Open		8.00	8
1996	Girl w/Apron Full - SEC-820	Open		8.00	8
1994	Girl w/Big Egg SEC-806	Open		6.50	7
1994	Girl w/Blanket SEC-800	Open		6.50	7
1996	Girl w/Book - SEC-818	Open		8.00	8
1994	Girl w/Toy Rabbit SEC-804	Open		6.50	7
1995	Hostess SEC-810	Open		8.00	8
1995	Lop Ear & Flower Pot SEC-809	Open		8.00	8
1995	Spring Flowers SEC-813	Open		8.00	8
1995	Tea Party SEC-811	Open		8.00	8

Legend of Santa Claus™ - L. Miller, unless otherwise noted

YEAR ISSUE		EDITION LIMIT	YEAR RETD.	ISSUE PRICE	*QUOTE U.S.$
1992	Arctic Santa CF-035 - S. Bradford	7,500		90.00	100-140
1988	Assembly Required CF-017	7,500	1994	79.00	120
1991	Blessed Flight CF-032 - K. Memoli	7,500	1994	159.00	300
1987	Checking His List CF-009	15,000	1994	75.00	120
1989	Christmas Harmony CF-020 - S. Bradford	7,500	1992	85.00	130
1992	The Christmas Tree CF-038	7,500	1995	90.00	90
1993	Dear Santa CF-046 - K. Memoli	7,500	1996	170.00	170
1995	Dear Santa, Vict. CF-063	10,000		170.00	170
1987	Dreaming Of Santa CF-008 - S. Bradford	15,000	1988	65.00	325
1992	Earth Home Santa CF-040 - S. Bradford	7,500		135.00	140
1986	Elf Pair CF-005	10,000	1992	60.00	130
1988	Father Christmas CF-018 - S. Bradford	7,500	1993	75.00	115
1991	For Santa CF-029	7,500		99.00	135
1990	Forest Friends CF-025	7,500	1993	90.00	110
1995	Getting Santa Ready CF-056	10,000		170.00	170
1989	Hitching Up CF-021	7,500	1993	90.00	110
1995	Into the Wind CF-061	10,000		140.00	140
1995	Into the Wind, Vict. CF-062	10,000		140.00	140
1993	Jolly St. Nick CF-045 - K. Memoli	7,500		130.00	130
1993	Jolly St. Nick, Victorian CF-050 - K. Memoli	7,500		120.00	120
1986	Kris Kringle CF-002	10,000	1991	60.00	160
1992	Letters to Santa CF-036	7,500	1995	125.00	130
1988	Load 'Em Up CF-016 - S. Bradford	7,500	1990	79.00	350
1987	Loading Santa's Sleigh CF-010	15,000	1993	100.00	110
1992	Loads of Happiness CF-041 - K. Memoli	7,500	1996	100.00	110
1994	Long Stocking Dilemma, Victorian CF-055 - K. Memoli	7,500		170.00	170
1994	Longstocking Dilemma CF-052 - K. Memoli	7,500		170.00	170
1987	Mrs. Santa CF-006 - S. Bradford	15,000	1991	60.00	195
1993	The Night Before Christmas CF-043	7,500	1996	100.00	100
1993	Northwoods Santa CF-047 - S. Bradford	7,500	1996	100.00	100
1987	On Santa's Knee-CF007 - S. Bradford	15,000	1994	65.00	120
1990	Puppy Love CF-024	7,500	1994	100.00	220
1989	A Purr-Fect Christmas CF-019 - S. Bradford	7,500	1994	95.00	135
1991	Reindeer Walk CF-031 - K. Memoli	7,500		150.00	165
1995	The Ride CF-057	10,000		130.00	130
1986	Rooftop Santa CF-004 - S. Bradford	10,000	1991	65.00	170
1990	Safe Arrival CF-027 - Memoli/Jonas	7,500	1996	150.00	175
1992	Santa and Comet CF-037	7,500	1995	110.00	110
1992	Santa and Mrs. Claus CF-039 - K. Memoli	7,500		150.00	150
1992	Santa and Mrs. Claus, Victorian CF-042 - K. Memoli	7,500		135.00	140
1986	Santa At Rest CF-001	10,000	1988	70.00	600
1991	Santa At Work CF-030	7,500	1995	99.00	110
1987	Santa On Horseback CF-011 - S. Bradford	15,000	1990	75.00	295
1994	Santa Riding Dove CF-053	7,500		120.00	120
1986	Santa With Pups CF-003 - S. Bradford	10,000	1988	65.00	570
1993	Santa's Friends CF-044	7,500	1996	100.00	100
1995	Santa, Dusk & Dawn CF-060	10,000		150.00	150
1988	St. Nicholas CF-015	7,500	1992	75.00	135
1994	Star Santa w/ Polar Bear CF-054 - S. Bradford	7,500		130.00	130
1995	Starlight Express CF-059	10,000		170.00	170
1994	The Story of Christmas CF-051 - K. Memoli	10,000		180.00	180
1993	Victorian Lion & Lamb Santa CF-048 - S. Bradford	7,500		100.00	100
1990	Victorian Santa CF-028 - S. Bradford	7,500	1992	125.00	285-400
1991	Victorian Santa w/ Teddy CF-033 - S. Bradford	7,500		150.00	160
1990	Waiting For Santa CF-026 - S. Bradford	7,500	1995	100.00	130

Legend Of The Little People™ - L. Miller

YEAR ISSUE		EDITION LIMIT	YEAR RETD.	ISSUE PRICE	*QUOTE U.S.$
1989	Adventure Bound LL-002	Retrd.	1993	35.00	50
1989	Caddy's Helper LL-007	Retrd.	1993	35.00	50
1991	The Easter Bunny's Cart LL-020	Retrd.	1994	45.00	50
1991	Fire it Up LL-023	Retrd.	1994	50.00	55
1990	Fishin' Hole LL-012	Retrd.	1994	35.00	50
1989	A Friendly Toast LL-003	Retrd.	1993	35.00	50
1990	Gathering Acorns LL-014	Retrd.	1994	100.00	100
1991	Got It LL-021	Retrd.	1994	45.00	50
1990	Hedgehog In Harness LL-010	Retrd.	1994	45.00	50
1990	Husking Acorns LL-008	Retrd.	1994	60.00	65
1991	It's About Time LL-022	Retrd.	1994	55.00	60
1990	A Little Jig LL-018	Retrd.	1994	45.00	50
1990	A Look Through The Spyglass LL-015	Retrd.	1994	40.00	50
1989	Magical Discovery LL-005	Retrd.	1993	45.00	50
1990	Ministral Magic LL-017	Retrd.	1994	45.00	50
1990	A Proclamation LL-013	Retrd.	1994	45.00	55
1989	Spring Water Scrub LL-006	Retrd.	1993	35.00	50
1990	Traveling Fast LL-009	Retrd.	1994	45.00	50
1989	Treasure Hunt LL-004	Retrd.	1993	45.00	50
1991	Viking LL-019	Retrd.	1994	45.00	50
1989	Woodland Cache LL-001	Retrd.	1993	35.00	50
1990	Woodland Scout LL-011	Retrd.	1994	40.00	50
1990	Writing The Legend LL-016	Retrd.	1994	35.00	65

Lil' Doll™ - Various

YEAR ISSUE		EDITION LIMIT	YEAR RETD.	ISSUE PRICE	*QUOTE U.S.$
1992	Clara & The Nutcracker LD-017 - D. Newburn	Retrd.	1994	35.00	35
1991	The Nutcracker LD-006 - P.J. Jonas	Retrd.	1994	35.00	35

Music Makers™ - Various

YEAR ISSUE		EDITION LIMIT	YEAR RETD.	ISSUE PRICE	*QUOTE U.S.$
1991	A Christmas Gift MM-015 - D. Kennicutt	Retrd.	1993	59.00	59
1991	Crystal Angel MM-017 - D. Kennicutt	Retrd.	1993	59.00	59
1991	Dashing Through The Snow MM-013 - D. Kennicutt	Retrd.	1993	59.00	59
1989	Evening Carolers MM-005 - D. Kennicutt	Retrd.	1993	69.00	69
1989	Herald Angel MM-011 - S. Bradford	Retrd.	1993	79.00	79
1991	Nutcracker MM-024 - P.J. Jonas	Retrd.	1994	69.00	69
1991	Peace Descending MM-025 - P.J. Jonas	Retrd.	1993	69.00	69
1991	Renaissance Angel MM-028 - P.J. Jonas	Retrd.	1994	69.00	69
1989	Santa's Sleigh MM-004 - L. Miller	Retrd.	1993	69.00	69
1991	Teddy Bear Band #2 MM-023 - D. Kennicutt	Retrd.	1994	90.00	90
1989	Teddy Bear Band MM-012 - S. Bradford	Retrd.	1993	99.00	100
1989	Teddy Drummers MM-009 - D. Kennicutt	Retrd.	1993	69.00	69
1991	Teddy Soldiers MM-018 - D. Kennicutt	Retrd.	1994	69.00	84
1991	Victorian Santa MM-026 - L. Miller	Retrd.	1993	69.00	69

Party Animals™ - L. Miller, unless otherwise noted

YEAR ISSUE		EDITION LIMIT	YEAR RETD.	ISSUE PRICE	*QUOTE U.S.$
1992	Democratic Donkey ('92) - K. Memoli	Retrd.	1994	20.00	20
1984	Democratic Donkey ('84) - D. Kennicutt	Retrd.	1986	14.50	16
1986	Democratic Donkey ('86)	Retrd.	1988	14.50	15
1988	Democratic Donkey ('88)	Retrd.	1990	14.50	16
1990	Democratic Donkey ('90) - D. Kennicutt	Retrd.	1992	16.00	16
1984	GOP Elephant ('84)	Retrd.	1986	14.50	16
1986	GOP Elephant ('86)	Retrd.	1988	14.50	15
1988	GOP Elephant ('88)	Retrd.	1990	14.50	16
1990	GOP Elephant ('90) - D. Kennicutt	Retrd.	1992	16.00	16
1992	GOP Elephant ('92) - K. Memoli	Retrd.	1994	20.00	20

PenniBears™ - P.J. Jonas

YEAR ISSUE		EDITION LIMIT	YEAR RETD.	ISSUE PRICE	*QUOTE U.S.$
1992	After Every Meal PB-058	Retrd.	1994	22.00	22
1992	Apple For Teacher PB-069	Retrd.	1994	24.00	24
1989	Attic Fun PB-019	Retrd.	1992	20.00	40
1989	Baby Hugs PB-007	Retrd.	1992	20.00	35
1991	Baking Goodies PB-043	Retrd.	1993	26.00	30
1989	Bathtime Buddies PB-023	Retrd.	1992	20.00	25
1992	Batter Up PB-066	Retrd.	1994	22.00	22
1991	Bear Footin' it PB-037	Retrd.	1993	24.00	24
1992	Bear-Capade PB-073	Retrd.	1994	22.00	22
1991	Bearly Awake PB-033	Retrd.	1993	22.00	25
1989	Beautiful Bride PB-004	Retrd.	1992	20.00	35
1993	Big Chief Little Bear PB-088	12/96		28.00	28
1989	Birthday Bear PB-018	Retrd.	1992	20.00	40
1991	Boo Hoo Bear PB-050	Retrd.	1994	22.00	22
1990	Boooo Bear PB-025	Retrd.	1993	20.00	22
1991	Bountiful Harvest PB-045	Retrd.	1994	24.00	24
1989	Bouquet Boy PB-003	Retrd.	1992	20.00	45
1989	Bouquet Girl PB-001	Retrd.	1992	20.00	45
1991	Bump-bear-Crop PB-035	Retrd.	1993	26.00	30
1991	Bunny Buddies PB-042	Retrd.	1993	22.00	25
1989	Butterfly Bear PB-005	Retrd.	1992	20.00	45-50
1990	Buttons & Bows PB 012	Retrd.	1992	20.00	45
1992	Christmas Cookies PB-075	Retrd.	1994	22.00	22
1991	Christmas Reinbear PB-046	Retrd.	1994	28.00	28
1992	Cinderella PB-056	Retrd.	1994	22.00	22
1992	Clowning Around PB-065	Retrd.	1994	22.00	22
1989	Cookie Bandit PB-006	Retrd.	1992	20.00	30
1990	Count Bearacula PB-027	Retrd.	1993	22.00	24
1991	Country Lullabye PB-036	Retrd.	1993	24.00	25
1990	Country Quilter PB-030	Retrd.	1993	22.00	30
1990	Country Spring PB-013	Retrd.	1992	20.00	45
1991	Curtain Call PB-049	Retrd.	1994	24.00	24
1992	Decorating The Wreath PB-076	Retrd.	1994	22.00	22
1989	Doctor Bear PB-008	Retrd.	1992	20.00	30
1992	Downhill Thrills PB-070	Retrd.	1994	24.00	24
1990	Dress Up Fun PB-028	Retrd.	1993	22.00	30
1992	Dust Bunny Roundup PB-062	Retrd.	1994	22.00	22
1992	First Prom PB-064	Retrd.	1994	22.00	22
1990	Garden Path PB-014	Retrd.	1992	20.00	45-50
1993	Getting 'Round On My Own PB-085	12/96		26.00	26
1990	Giddiap Teddy PB-011	Retrd.	1992	20.00	35
1991	Goodnight Little Prince PB-041	Retrd.	1993	26.00	30
1991	Goodnight Sweet Princess PB-040	Retrd.	1993	26.00	30
1993	Gotta Try Again PB-082	12/96		24.00	24
1989	Handsome Groom PB-015	Retrd.	1992	20.00	40
1993	Happy Birthday PB-084	12/96		26.00	26
1993	A Happy Camper PB-077	12/96		28.00	28
1991	Happy Hobo PB-051	Retrd.	1994	26.00	26
1989	Honey Bear PB-002	Retrd.	1992	20.00	45
1992	I Made It Boy PB-061	Retrd.	1994	22.00	22
1992	I Made It Girl PB-060	Retrd.	1994	22.00	22
1989	Lazy Days PB-009	Retrd.	1992	20.00	25
1992	Lil' Devil PB-071	Retrd.	1994	24.00	24
1991	Lil' Mer-teddy PB-034	Retrd.	1993	24.00	24
1992	Lil' Sis Makes Up PB-074	Retrd.	1994	22.00	22
1993	Little Bear Peep PB-083	12/96		24.00	24
1993	Making It Better PB-087	12/96		24.00	24
1993	May Joy Be Yours PB-080	12/96		24.00	24
1993	My Forever Love PB-078	12/96		28.00	28
1989	Nap Time PB-016	Retrd.	1992	20.00	22
1989	Nurse Bear PB-017	Retrd.	1992	20.00	35
1992	On Your Toes PB-068	Retrd.	1994	24.00	24
1989	Petite Mademoiselle PB-010	Retrd.	1992	20.00	40
1991	Pilgrim Provider PB-047	Retrd.	1994	32.00	32
1992	Pot O' Gold PB-059	Retrd.	1994	22.00	22
1992	Puddle Jumper PB-057	Retrd.	1994	24.00	24
1989	Puppy Bath PB-020	Retrd.	1992	20.00	25
1989	Puppy Love PB-021	Retrd.	1992	20.00	25
1993	Rest Stop PB-079	12/96		24.00	24
1992	Sandbox Fun PB-063	Retrd.	1994	22.00	22
1990	Santa Bear-ing Gifts PB-031	Retrd.	1993	24.00	30
1993	Santa's Helper PB-081	12/96		28.00	28
1990	Scarecrow Teddy PB-029	Retrd.	1993	24.00	25
1992	Smokey's Nephew PB-055	Retrd.	1994	22.00	22
1990	Sneaky Snowball PB-026	Retrd.	1993	20.00	25
1989	Southern Belle PB-024	Retrd.	1992	20.00	35
1992	Spanish Rose PB-053	Retrd.	1994	24.00	24
1990	Stocking Surprise PB-032	Retrd.	1993	22.00	26
1993	Summer Belle PB-086	12/96		24.00	24
1991	Summer Sailing PB-039	Retrd.	1993	26.00	30
1991	Sweet Lil 'Sis PB-048	Retrd.	1994	22.00	22
1991	Sweetheart Bears PB-044	Retrd.	1993	28.00	30
1992	Tally Ho! PB-054	Retrd.	1994	22.00	22
1992	Touchdown PB-072	Retrd.	1994	22.00	22
1989	Tubby Teddy PB-022	Retrd.	1992	20.00	22
1991	A Wild Ride PB-052	Retrd.	1994	26.00	26
1992	Will You Be Mine? PB-067	Retrd.	1994	22.00	22
1991	Windy Day PB-038	Retrd.	1993	24.00	24

PenniBears™ Collector's Club Members Only Editions - P.J. Jonas

YEAR ISSUE		EDITION LIMIT	YEAR RETD.	ISSUE PRICE	*QUOTE U.S.$
1990	1990 First Collection PB-C90	Retrd.	1990	26.00	125
1991	1991 Collecting Makes Cents PB-C91	Retrd.	1991	26.00	75
1992	1992 Today's Pleasures, Tomorrow's Treasures PB-C92	Retrd.	1992	26.00	100
1993	1993 Chalkin Up Another Year PB-C93	Retrd.	1993	26.00	35
1994	1994 Artist's Touch-Collector's Treasure PB-C94	Retrd.	1994	26.00	26

Storytime Rhymes & Tales - H. Henriksen

YEAR ISSUE		EDITION LIMIT	YEAR RETD.	ISSUE PRICE	*QUOTE U.S.$
1991	Humpty Dumpty SL-008	Retrd.	1993	64.00	64
1991	Little Jack Horner SL-007	Retrd.	1993	50.00	50
1991	Little Miss Muffet SL-006	Retrd.	1993	64.00	64
1991	Mistress Mary SL-002	Retrd.	1993	64.00	64

*Quotes have been rounded up to nearest dollar

YEAR ISSUE		EDITION LIMIT	YEAR RETD.	ISSUE PRICE	*QUOTE U.S.$
1991	Mother Goose SL-001	Retrd.	1993	64.00	64
1991	Owl & Pussy Cat SL-004	Retrd.	1993	100.00	100
1991	Simple Simon SL-003	Retrd.	1993	90.00	90
1991	Three Little Pigs SL-005	Retrd.	1993	100.00	100

Teddy Angels™ - P.J. Jonas

YEAR ISSUE		EDITION LIMIT	YEAR RETD.	ISSUE PRICE	*QUOTE U.S.$
1995	Bruin & Bluebirds "Nurture nature." BA-013	Open		19.00	19
1995	Bruin Making Valentines "Holidays start within the heart." BA-012	Open		15.00	15
1995	Bruin With Harp Seal "Make your corner of the world a little warmer." BA-021	Open		15.00	15
1995	Bunny's Picnic "Make a feast of friendship." BA-007	Open		19.00	19
1995	Casey & Honey Reading "Friends are the best recipe for relaxation." BA-023	Open		15.00	15
1995	Casey Tucking Honey In "There is magic in the simplest things we do." BA-008	Open		19.00	19
1995	Cowboy Murray "Have a Doo Da Day." BA-002	Open		19.00	19
1995	Honey "Love gives our hearts wings." BA-014	Open		13.00	13
1995	Ivy & Blankie "Nothing is as comfortable as an old friend." BA-003	Open		13.00	13
1995	Ivy In Garden "Celebrate the little things." BA-009	Open		15.00	15
1995	Ivy With Locket "You're always close at heart." BA-028	Open		13.00	13
1995	Murray & Little Bit "Imagination can take you anywhere." BA-004	Open		19.00	19
1995	Murray Mending Bruin "Everybody needs a helping hand." BA-005	Open		15.00	15
1995	Murray With Angel "I believe in you, too." BA-022	Open		22.00	22
1995	Nicholas With Stars "Dreams are never too far away to catch." BA-024	Open		15.00	15
1995	Old Bear "Always remember your way home." BA-011	Open		19.00	19
1995	Old Bear & Little Bit Gardening "The well-watered garden produces a great harvest." BA-026	Open		15.00	15
1995	Old Bear & Little Bit Reading "Love to learn and learn to love." BA-006	Open		15.00	15
1995	Rufus Helps Bird "We could all use a little lift." BA-027	Open		15.00	15
1995	Sweetie "Come tell me all about it." - BA-001	Open		15.00	15
1995	Sweetie With Kitty Cats "Always close-knit." BA-025	Open		15.00	15
1995	Tilli & Murray "Friendship is a bridge between hearts." BA-010	Open		15.00	15

Teddy Angels™ Christmas - P.J. Jonas

YEAR ISSUE		EDITION LIMIT	YEAR RETD.	ISSUE PRICE	*QUOTE U.S.$
1995	Casey "You're a bright & shining star." BA-019	Open		13.00	13
1995	Ivy "Enchantment glows in winter snows." BA-020	Open		13.00	13
1995	Sweetie & Santa Bear "Tis the season of surprises." BA-016	Open		22.00	22
1995	Tilli & Doves "A wreath is a circle of love." BA-015	Open		19.00	19

WACO Products Corp.

Melody In Motion/Collector's Society - S. Nakane, unless otherwise noted

YEAR ISSUE		EDITION LIMIT	YEAR RETD.	ISSUE PRICE	*QUOTE U.S.$
1992	Amazing Willie the One-Man Band 07152	Retrd.	1994	130.00	250-300
1992	Willie The Conductor	Retrd.	1994	Gift	35
1993	Charmed Bunnies	Retrd.	1993	Gift	45
1993	Willie The Collector 07170	Retrd.	1995	200.00	200
1994	Springtime	Retrd.	1994	Gift	45
1995	Best Friends	Retrd.	1995	Gift	45
1996	Willie The Entertainer 07199	Yr. Iss.		200.00	200
1996	'86 Santa Replica - K. Maeda	Yr. Iss.		Gift	N/A

Melody In Motion - S. Nakane, unless otherwise noted

YEAR ISSUE		EDITION LIMIT	YEAR RETD.	ISSUE PRICE	*QUOTE U.S.$
1985	Willie The Trumpeter 07000	Open		90.00	175
1985	Willie The Hobo (Memories) 07001	2,500	1985	90.00	175
1985	Willie The Hobo (Show Me...) 07001	Retrd.	1996	90.00	175
1985	Willie The Whistler (Show Me...) 07002	2,500	1985	90.00	175
1985	Willie The Whistler (Memories) 07002	Open		90.00	175
1985	Salty 'N' Pepper 07010	Retrd.	1992	90.00	400
1986	The Cellist 07011	Retrd.	1995	100.00	180
1986	Santa Claus 1986 07012	20,000	1986	100.00	2500
1986	The Guitarist 07013	Retrd.	1994	100.00	200
1986	The Fiddler 07014	Retrd.	1995	100.00	160
1987	Lamppost Willie 07051	Open		85.00	150
1987	The Organ Grinder 07053	Retrd.	1994	100.00	200
1987	Violin Clown 07055	Retrd.	1992	85.00	200
1987	Clarinet Clown 07056	Retrd.	1991	85.00	300
1987	Saxophone Clown 07057	Retrd.	1991	85.00	250
1987	Accordion Clown 07058	Retrd.	1991	85.00	250
1987	Santa Claus 1987 07060	16,000	1987	110.00	700-2000
1987	Balloon Clown 07061	Open		85.00	150
1987	The Carousel (1st Edition) 07065	Retrd.	1993	190.00	260
1987	Madame Violin 07075	Retrd.	1991	130.00	130
1987	Madame Mandolin 07076	Retrd.	1994	130.00	130
1987	Madame Cello 07077	Retrd.	1991	130.00	130
1987	Madame Flute 07078	Retrd.	1992	130.00	130
1987	Madame Harpsichord 07080	Retrd.	1991	130.00	130
1987	Madame Lyre 07081	Retrd.	1994	130.00	130
1988	Madame Harp 07079	Open		130.00	130
1988	Spotlight Clown Cornet 07082	Retrd.	1992	120	125-200
1988	Spotlight Clown Banjo 07083	Retrd.	1992	120.00	200
1988	Spotlight Clown Trombone 07084	Retrd.	1992	120.00	200
1988	Spotlight Clown Bingo 07085	Open		130.00	160
1988	Spotlight Clown Tuba 07086	Retrd.	1992	120.00	200
1988	Spotlight Clown Bass 07087	Retrd.	1994	130.00	160
1988	Peanut Vendor 07088	Retrd.	1994	140.00	200
1988	Ice Cream Vendor 07089	Retrd.	1994	140.00	200
1988	Santa Claus 1988 07090	12,000	1988	130.00	1000
1989	Clockpost Willie 07091	Open		150.00	220
1989	Santa Claus 1989 (Willie) 07092	12,000	1989	130.00	N/A
1989	Lull'aby Willie 07093	Retrd.	1992	170.00	170
1989	The Grand Carousel 07094	Retrd.	1995	3000.00	3000
1989	Grandfather's Clock 07096	Retrd.	1994	200.00	295
1990	Santa Claus 1990 07097	12,000	1990	150.00	200-225
1990	Shoemaker 07130	3,700	1993	110.00	200
1990	Blacksmith 07131	3,700	1993	110.00	200
1990	Woodchopper 07132	3,700	1993	110.00	200
1990	Accordion Boy 07133	4,100	1992	120.00	200
1990	Hunter 07134	Retrd.	1994	110.00	150
1990	Robin Hood 07135 - C. Johnson	2,000	1991	180.00	350
1990	Little John 07136 - C. Johnson	2,000	1992	180.00	300
1990	Clockpost Willie II (European) 07140	Retrd.	1990	N/A	N/A
1990	Clockpost Clown 07141	Open		220.00	220
1990	Lull' A Bye Willie II (European) 07142	Retrd.	1990	N/A	N/A
1991	The Carousel (2nd Edition) 07065	Retrd.	1995	240.00	350
1991	Victoria Park Carousel 07143	Open		300.00	360
1991	Hunter Timepiece 07144	Retrd.	1994	250.00	320
1991	Santa Claus 1991 07146	7,000	1991	150.00	160
1992	Wall Street Willie 07147	Open		180.00	240
1991	Willie The Fisherman 07148	Open		150.00	200
1992	King of Clowns Carousel 07149	Open		740.00	850
1992	Golden Mountain Clock 07150	Open		250.00	280
1992	Santa Claus 1992 07151	11,000	1992	160.00	180
1992	Dockside Willie 07153	Open		160.00	190
1993	Wild West Willie 07154	Open		175.00	200
1993	Alarm Clock Post 07155	Open		N/A	N/A
1993	Lamplight Willie 07156	Open		220.00	220
1993	Madame Cello Player, glaze 07157	200	1993	170.00	170
1993	Madame Flute, glaze 07158	200	1993	170.00	170
1993	Madame Harpsichord, glaze	200	1993	170.00	170
1993	Madame Harp, glaze	150	1993	190.00	190
1993	Santa Claus 1993 Coke 07161	6,000	1993	180.00	225
1993	Wall Street (Japanese) 07162	Retrd.	1993	N/A	N/A
1993	Santa Claus 1993 (European) 07163	1,000	1993	N/A	N/A
1993	Willie The Golfer - Alarm 07164	Retrd.	1995	240.00	240
1993	The Artist 07165	Open		240.00	240
1993	Heartbreak Willie 07166	Open		180.00	190
1993	South of the Border 07167	Open		180.00	180
1993	When I Grow Up 07171	Open		200.00	200
1994	Low Press Job-Alarm 07168	Retrd.	1995	240.00	240
1994	Day's End-Alarm 07169	Open		240.00	240
1994	Santa '94 Coca-Cola 07174	9,000	1994	190.00	225
1994	Smooth Sailing 07175	Open		200.00	200
1994	Santa Claus 1994 (European) 07176	700	1994	N/A	N/A
1994	The Longest Drive 07177	Open		150.00	150
1994	Happy Birthday Willie 07178	Open		170.00	170
1994	Chattanooga Choo Choo 07179	Open		180.00	190
1994	Jackpot Willie 07180	Open		180.00	190
1994	Caroler Boy 07189	10,000		172.00	180
1994	Caroler Girl 07190	10,000		172.00	180
1994	Willie the Yodeler 07192	Open		158.00	160
1994	Willie the Golfer- Clock 07264	Open		240.00	240
1994	Day's End-Clock 07269	Open		240.00	240
1995	Campfire Cowboy 07172	Retrd.	1995	180.00	180
1995	Blue Danube Carousel 07173	Open		280.00	300
1995	Willie the Conductor (10th Anniversary) 07181	10,000		220.00	220
1995	Coca-Cola Norman Rockwell 07194	Open		194.00	200
1995	Santa Claus '95 07195	6,000	1995	190.00	190
1995	Gaslight Willie 07197	Open		190.00	190
1995	Coca Cola Polar Bear 07198	6,000		180.00	180
1995	Low Pressure Job-Clock 07268	Open		240.00	240
1995	Willie The Fireman 07271	1,500		200.00	200
1996	The Candy Factory-I Love Lucy 07203 - Willingham/Maeda	Open		250.00	250
1996	Willie On The Road 07204 - K. Maeda	Open		180.00	180
1996	Marionette Clown 07205 - K. Maeda	Open		200.00	200
1996	Willie the Racer 07206 - K. Maeda	Open		180.00	180
1996	Willie the Organ Grinder 07207	3,000		200.00	200
1996	Willie the Champion 07209 - K. Maeda	Open		180.00	180

Walnut Ridge Collectibles

Autumn Figurines - K. Bejma

YEAR ISSUE		EDITION LIMIT	YEAR RETD.	ISSUE PRICE	*QUOTE U.S.$
1991	Pilgrim Set-400	Open		80.00	80
1991	Pumpkin, set/3-404	Open		22.00	22
1991	Turkey-small-401	Open		20.00	20

Cat Figurines - K. Bejma

YEAR ISSUE		EDITION LIMIT	YEAR RETD.	ISSUE PRICE	*QUOTE U.S.$
1993	Basket of Kittens-309	Open		70.00	70
1991	Calico Cat-306	Open		40.00	40
1991	Goodrich Cat-300	Open		50.00	50
1994	Tabby Cat-310	Open		50.00	50
1991	Tiny Cat-304	Open		24.00	24

Christmas Figurines - K. Bejma

YEAR ISSUE		EDITION LIMIT	YEAR RETD.	ISSUE PRICE	*QUOTE U.S.$
1988	Belsnickle-102	Open		32.00	32
1988	Belsnickle-104	12/96		48.00	48
1988	Belsnickle-105	12/96		32.00	32
1989	Belsnickle-124	12/96		30.00	30
1991	Belsnickle-140	12/96		40.00	40
1994	Belsnickle-176	12/96		28.00	28
1988	Belsnickle-mini-116	Open		22.00	22
1994	Belsnickle/Tree-174	Open		32.00	32
1994	Children on Sled-172	Open		48.00	48
1995	Crying Snowman-189	Open		44.00	44
1994	Father Christmas-175	Open		28.00	28
1992	Father Christmas-large-161	Open		270.00	270
1988	Father Christmas/Apples-122	12/96		48.00	48
1988	Father Christmas/Bag-114	12/96		34.00	34
1993	Father Christmas/Bag-163	12/96		38.00	38
1994	Father Christmas/Bag-166	Open		30.00	30
1994	Father Christmas/Bag-178	12/96		42.00	42
1988	Father Christmas/Basket-100R	12/96		120.00	120
1988	Father Christmas/Basket-100W	12/96		120.00	120
1994	Father Christmas/Girl/Doll-165	Open		52.00	52
1993	Father Christmas/Holly-164	Open		52.00	52
1990	Father Christmas/Toys/Switch-136	12/96		120.00	120
1991	Gnome/Rabbit-148	12/96		32.00	32
1990	Jolly St. Nick-135	12/96		52.00	52
1994	Primitive Snowman-173	Open		32.00	32
1990	Rocking Santa-129	12/96		36.00	36
1992	Santa/Horse-small-158	Open		24.00	24
1991	Santa/Walking Stick-152	12/96		56.00	56
1994	Snowflake Belsnickle-177	Open		36.00	36
1994	Snowman & Boy-181	Open		34.00	34
1993	Snowman with Scarf-162	Open		28.00	28
1995	Snowman with Twig Arms-188	Open		32.00	32
1990	Snowman-127	12/96		32.00	32
1994	Snowman-large-182	Open		44.00	44
1990	Snowman-medium-131	Open		28.00	28
1991	Snowman-small-139	12/96		22.00	22
1992	Snowman/Twigs-156	Open		30.00	30
1995	Tall Tree-190	Open		28.00	28
1992	Tree Set-160	Open		44.00	44
1994	Walking Santa-180	12/96		90.00	90

Easter Figurines - K. Bejma

YEAR ISSUE		EDITION LIMIT	YEAR RETD.	ISSUE PRICE	*QUOTE U.S.$
1991	Bavarian Rabbit Set-226	Open		90.00	90
1996	Bunny in Shamrocks-268	Open		52.00	52
1996	Bunny with Carrots on Base-272	Open		48.00	48
1995	Bunny with Colored Eggs-263	Open		28.00	28
1990	Bunny/Acorns/Carrots-202	Open		32.00	32
1991	Bunny/Basket-227	12/96		26.00	26
1993	Bunny/Cabbage-233	Open		24.00	24
1994	Chick with Egg-257	Open		48.00	48
1994	Chicks, set/3 -260	Open		64.00	64
1995	Country Rabbit-large-265	Open		70.00	70
1996	Farmer Rabbit w/Carrots-270	Open		56.00	56
1992	Folksy/Rabbit-231	Open		48.00	48
1994	Hatching Chick-259	Open		20.00	20
1993	Hatching Rabbit-234	Open		34.00	34
1995	Hiking Bunny w/Egg Basket-262	Open		28.00	28
1994	Lady Vendor Rabbit-256	Open		42.00	42
1994	Laying Sheep-245	Open		44.00	44
1995	Meadow Rabbit-266	Open		90.00	90
1991	Mother Rabbit/Basket-215	12/96		48.00	48
1990	Mother Rabbit/Six Babies-200	Open		120.00	120
1990	Mother/Bowl of Eggs-207	12/96		30.00	30
1993	Mr. Rabbit/Two Children-244	12/96		44.00	44
1994	Professor Rabbit/Chicks-236	Open		30.00	30
1990	Rabbit Holding Basket-220	12/96		50.00	50
1994	Rabbit Holding Carrot-253	Open		52.00	52
1994	Rabbit in Flower Garden-246	Open		64.00	64
1996	Rabbit on Scooter-271	Open		44.00	44
1991	Rabbit Riding Rooster-209	Open		36.00	36
1996	Rabbit w/Ferns and Lillies-269	Open		120.00	120
1994	Rabbit with Basket-255	Open		52.00	52
1994	Rabbit with Vest-254	Open		38.00	38
1991	Rabbit/Basket Eggs-224	Open		46.00	46
1991	Rabbit/Basket/Bow-225	Open		46.00	46
1994	Rabbit/Hat/Stick-239	Open		28.00	28
1990	Rabbit/Holding Basket-203	Open		30.00	30
1990	Rabbit/Umbrella-208	12/96		30.00	30
1994	Rabbits on See-Saw-252	Open		44.00	44
1990	Running Rabbit-205	Open		32.00	32
1990	Sitting Bunny-204	12/96		24.00	24
1995	Sitting Bunny-261	Open		24.00	24
1990	Sitting Bunny-large-216	Open		68.00	68
1994	Sitting Rabbit-251	Open		36.00	36
1993	Sitting Rabbit-large-235	Open		44.00	44
1994	Squirrel on Pinecone-249	Open		40.00	40
1994	Standing Chick-258	Open		24.00	24
1994	Standing Rabbit-237	12/96		44.00	44
1990	Standing Sheep-211	12/96		36.00	36
1996	Tan Rabbit w/Basket on Back-267	Open		90.00	90
1990	Two Rabbits/Basket-219	Open		52.00	52
1994	Wheelbarrow Rabbit-250	Open		44.00	44
1995	Woodland Rabbit-264	Open		48.00	48

Gossamer Wings - K. Bejma

YEAR ISSUE		EDITION LIMIT	YEAR RETD.	ISSUE PRICE	*QUOTE U.S.$
1994	Addie-167	Open		40.00	40
1995	Alexandra-183	Open		54.00	54
1996	Deborah-192	Open		50.00	50
1994	Elizabeth-170	Open		52.00	52

*Quotes have been rounded up to nearest dollar

FIGURINES/COTTAGES

YEAR ISSUE		EDITION LIMIT	YEAR RETD.	ISSUE PRICE	*QUOTE U.S.$
1996	Gabriella-194	Open		64.00	64
1994	Hannah-169	Open		50.00	50
1995	Julia-184	Open		38.00	38
1996	Kathleen-193	Open		56.00	56
1995	Lucia-187	Open		62.00	62
1995	Lydia-185	Open		58.00	58
1994	Meghan-168	Open		46.00	46
1996	Olivia-196	Open		56.00	56
1995	Tatiana-186	Open		58.00	58
1996	Thomas-195	Open		64.00	64
1996	Victoria-191	Open		54.00	54

Herr Belsnickle Collection - K. Bejma

1993	Herr Dieter-807	Open		90.00	90
1993	Herr Franz-805	Open		90.00	90
1993	Herr Fritz-803	Open		100.00	100
1993	Herr Gottfried-806	Open		90.00	90
1994	Herr Gregor-818	Open		90.00	90
1993	Herr Gunther-809	Open		70.00	70
1993	Herr Heinrich-810	Open		60.00	60
1993	Herr Hermann-813	Open		48.00	48
1995	Herr Johann-820	Open		230.00	230
1993	Herr Karl-801	Open		150.00	150
1993	Herr Klaus-800	Open		180.00	180
1993	Herr Ludwig-811	Open		60.00	60
1993	Herr Nicholas-802	Open		130.00	130
1993	Herr Oskar-816	Open		44.00	44
1993	Herr Peter-815	Open		44.00	44
1993	Herr Reiner-812	Open		60.00	60
1994	Herr Rudolph-819	Open		230.00	230
1995	Herr Rutger-822	Open		150.00	150
1995	Herr Sebastian-821	Open		70.00	70
1994	Herr Viktor-817	Open		64.00	64
1993	Herr Wilhelm-804	Open		100.00	100
1993	Herr Willi-814	Open		44.00	44
1993	Herr Wolfgang-808	Open		70.00	70

Limited Edition Collector's Series - K. Bejma

1995	Downhill Racer-618	2,500		48.00	48
1994	Egg Cottage-603	1,500		80.00	80
1994	Egyptian Egg/Rabbits-600	1,500		48.00	48
1995	Happy Christmas-622	2,000		50.00	50
1995	Hareratio-613	1,500		42.00	42
1994	Hemlocks And Holly-610	750		260.00	260
1996	Hitching a Ride-625	750		44.00	44
1995	Holiday Sledding-620	2,500		52.00	52
1994	Holy Night-612	750		250.00	250
1995	Jacqueline-614	1,500		48.00	48
1995	Jeffrey-615	1,500		48.00	48
1994	Keeping Secrets-605	3,500		52.00	52
1994	Kimbra-609	10,000		24.00	24
1996	Life is but a Dream-627	1,000		42.00	42
1994	Lite The Way-604	3,500		52.00	52
1995	Magnolias in Bloom-616	1,500		90.00	90
1994	Miles To Go-607	10,000		52.00	52
1995	O' Tannenbaum-621	1,500		56.00	56
1995	Père Noel-619	1,500		90.00	90
1994	Rabbits At Home Egg-602	1,500		80.00	80
1996	Robin Tracks-624	1,000		48.00	48
1995	Santa Express-617	2,000		56.00	56
1994	Shhh...-606	5,000		44.00	44
1994	Silent Night-611	750		120.00	120
1995	St. Nick's Visit-623	750		380.00	380
1994	Strolling Rabbits Egg-601	1,500		80.00	80
1994	Up On The Rooftop-608	5,000		56.00	56
1996	Violets for Mary-626	500		64.00	64

Nativity Collection - K. Bejma

1995	Elephant	Open		120.00	120
1995	Group I Stable, Joseph, Mary, Baby Jesus, Angel	Open		324.00	324
1995	Group II Wise Men, set/3	Open		190.00	190
1995	Group III Shepards and Wanderer, set/4	Open		190.00	190
1995	Group IV Farm Animals, Sheep/2, Goat, Donkey, Cow	Open		130.00	130
1995	Laying Camel	Open		120.00	120
1995	Standing Camel	Open		120.00	120

Walt Disney

Walt Disney Collectors Society - Disney Studios

1993	Jiminy Cricket Kit	Closed	1993	Gift	175-250
1993	Jiminy Cricket 4" /wheel	Closed	1993	Gift	150-225
1993	Jiminy Cricket/clef	Closed	1993	Gift	125-200
1993	Brave Little Tailor 7 1/4"	Closed	1994	160.00	250-350
1994	Cheshire Cat 4 3/4"/clef	Closed	1994	Gift	95-135
1994	Cheshire Cat 4 3/4"/flower	Closed	1994	Gift	85-115
1994	Pecos Bill 9 1/2"	Closed	1994	650.00	650-750
1994	Admiral Duck 6 1/4"	Closed	1995	165.00	200-250
1995	Dumbo	Closed	1995	Gift	75-95
1995	Cruella De Vil 10 1/4"	Closed	1995	250.00	250
1995	Dumbo Ornament	Closed	1995	20.00	20
1995	Slue Foot Sue 41075	Closed	1995	695.00	695
1996	Winnie the Pooh 41091	Yr.Iss.		Gift	N/A
1996	Princess Minnie 41095	Yr.Iss.		165.00	165
1996	Winnie the Pooh Ornament 41096	Yr.Iss.		25.00	25

Classics Collection-Special Event - Disney Studios

1993	Flight of Fancy 3" 41051	Closed	1994	35.00	40-65
1994	Mr. Smee 5" 41062	Closed	1995	90.00	90-115
1994	Mr. Smee 5" 41062 (teal stamp)	Closed	1995	90.00	110-125
1995	Lucky 41080	Closed	1995	40.00	50-75
1995	Wicked Witch 41084	3/96		130.00	130

Classics Collection-3 Caballeros - Disney Studios

1995	Amigo Donald 7" 41076	Open		180.00	180
1995	Amigo Jose 7" 41077	Open		180.00	180
1995	Amigo Panchito 7" 41078	Open		180.00	180

Classics Collection-Bambi - Disney Studios

1992	Bambi 6" 41033	Open		195.00	195
1992	Bambi 6" 41033/wheel	Closed	1992	195.00	225-275
1992	Bambi & Flower 6" 41010	10,000	1993	298.00	425-495
1992	Field Mouse-not touching 5 3/5" 41012	7,500	1993	195.00	1300-1750
1992	Field Mouse-touching 5 3/5" 41012	7,500	1993	195.00	1100-1350
1992	Flower 3"41034	Open		78.00	78
1992	Flower 3"41034/wheel	Closed	1992	78.00	125-155
1992	Friend Owl 8 3/5" 41011	Open		195.00	195
1992	Friend Owl 8 3/5" 41011/wheel	Closed	1992	195.00	170-220
1992	Thumper 3" 41013	Open		55.00	55
1992	Thumper 3" 41013/wheel	Closed	1992	55.00	60-75
1992	Thumper's Sisters 3 3/5" 41014	Open		69.00	69
1992	Thumper's Sisters 3 3/5" 41014/wheel	Closed	1992	69.00	75-90
1992	Bambi-Opening Title 41015	Open		29.00	29
1992	Bambi-Opening Title 41015/wheel	Closed	1992	29.00	35-45

Classics Collection-Cinderella - Disney Studios

1993	A Dress For Cinderelly 41030/wheel & clef	5,000	1993	800.00	1800-2300
1992	Birds With Sash 6 2/5" 41005	Closed	1994	149.00	155-190
1992	Chalk Mouse 3 2/5" 41006	Closed	1994	65.00	75-90
1992	Cinderella 6" 41000/clef	Closed	1993	195.00	295-400
1992	Cinderella 6" 41000/wheel	Closed	1992	195.00	350-375
1995	Cinderella & The Prince 41079	Open		275.00	275
1992	Cinderella, Lucifer, Bruno, Set/3/wheel & clef	Closed	1993	333.00	475-600
1992	Gus 3 2/5" 41007	Closed	1994	65.00	85-115
1992	Bruno 4 2/5" 41002/wheel & clef	Closed	1993	69.00	85-125
1992	Jaq 4 1/5" 41008	Closed	1994	65.00	80-115
1992	Lucifer 2 3/5" 41001/wheel & clef	Closed	1993	69.00	85-135
1992	Needle Mouse 5 4/5" 41004	Closed	1994	69.00	75-95
1992	Sewing Book 41003	Closed	1994	69.00	75-90
1992	Sewing Book 41003/no mark	Closed	1994	69.00	90
1992	Cinderella-Opening Title 41009	Open		29.00	29
1992	Cinderella-Opening Title-Technicolor 41009	Closed	1993	29.00	40-50
1992	Cinderella-Opening Title - Technicolor 41009/wheel	Closed	1993	29.00	35-40

Classics Collection-Fantasia - Disney Studios

1993	Blue Centaurette-Beauty in Bloom 7 1/2" 41041	Retrd.	1995	195.00	200-235
1992	Broom, 5 4/5" 41017	Retrd.	1995	75.00	100-110
1992	Broom, w/water spots 5 4/5" 41017/wheel	Closed	1992	75.00	130-165
1996	Ben Ali Gator 7 1/2" 41118	Open		185.00	185
1994	Hop Low 2 3/4" 41067	Open		35.00	35
1996	Hyacinth Hippo 5 1/2" 41117	Open		195.00	195
1993	Love's Little Helpers 8" 41042	Retrd.	1995	290.00	290-325
1994	Mushroom Dancer-Medium 4 1/4" 41068	Open		50.00	50
1994	Mushroom Dancer-Medium 4 1/4" 41068/teal stamp	Closed	1994	50.00	50-65
1994	Mushroom Dancer-Large 4 3/4" 41058	Open		60.00	60
1994	Mushroom Dancer-Large 4 3/4" 41058/teal stamp	Closed	1994	60.00	60-90
1993	Pink Centaurette-Romantic Reflections 7 1/2" 41040	Retrd.	1995	175.00	200-225
1992	Sorcerer Mickey 5 1/8" 41016	Retrd.	1995	195.00	215-250
1992	Fantasia-Opening Title 41018	Open		29.00	29
1992	Fantasia-Opening Title-blank 41018	Closed	1994	29.00	35-45
1992	Fantasia-Opening Title - Technicolor 41018	Closed	1993	29.00	35-45

Classics Collection-Holiday Series - Disney Studios

1995	Presents For My Pals 41086	12/95		150.00	150

Classics Collection-Lady and The Tramp - Disney Studios

1996	Lady 4 1/2" 41089	Open		120.00	120
1996	Tramp 1/2" 41090	Open		100.00	100
1996	Lady and the Tramp-Opening Title 41099	Open		29.00	29

Classics Collection-Mr. Duck - Disney Studios

1993	Donald & Daisy 6 3/5" 41024/clef	5,000	1993	298.00	450-675
1993	Donald & Daisy 6 3/5" 41024/wheel	5,000	1993	298.00	650-800
1993	Mr. Duck Steps Out-Opening Title 41023	Open		29.00	29
1993	Mr. Duck Steps Out-Opening Title 41023/clef	Closed	1993	29.00	35
1993	Nephew Duck-Dewey 4" 41025	Open		65.00	65
1993	Nephew Duck-Dewey 4" 41025/wheel	Closed	1993	65.00	80-100
1993	Nephew Duck-Huey 4" 41049	Open		65.00	65
1993	Nephew Duck-Huey 4" 41049/clef	Closed	1993	65.00	80-90
1993	Nephew Duck-Louie 4" 41050	Open		65.00	65
1993	Nephew Duck-Louie 4" 41050/clef	Closed	1993	65.00	80-90
1994	With Love From Daisy 6 1/4" 41060	Open		180.00	180

Classics Collection-Peter Pan - Disney Studios

1993	Captain Hook 8" 41044	Open		275.00	275
1993	Captain Hook 8" 41044/clef	Closed	1994	275.00	700-785
1993	The Crocodile 6 1/4" 41054	Open		315.00	315
1993	Peter Pan 7 1/2" 41043	Open		165.00	165
1993	Peter Pan 7 1/2"41043/clef	Closed	1994	165.00	220-275
1993	Tinkerbell 5" 41045/clef	12,500	1994	215.00	425-650
1993	Tinkerbell 5" 41045/flower	12,500	1994	215.00	360-420
1993	Peter Pan-Opening Title 41047	Open		29.00	29
1993	Peter Pan-Opening Title 41047/clef	Closed	1994	29.00	40

Classics Collection-Pocahontas - Disney Studios

1996	Pocahontas 6 1/2" 41098	5/96		225.00	225

Classics Collection-Snow White - Disney Studios

1994	Snow White 8 1/4" 41063/flower	Closed	1994	165.00	220-260
1994	Snow White 8 1/4" 41063	Open		165.00	165
1995	Bashful 5" 91069	Open		95.00	95
1995	Doc 5 1/4" 41071	Open		95.00	95
1995	Dopey 5" 41074	Open		95.00	95
1995	Grumpy 7 3/4" 41065	Open		180.00	180
1995	Happy 5 1/2" 41064	Open		125.00	125
1995	Sleepy 3 1/4" 41066	Open		95.00	95
1995	Sneezy 4 1/2" 41073	Open		90.00	90
1995	Snow White-Opening Title 41083	Open		29.00	29

Classics Collection-Song of the South - Disney Studios

1996	Brer Bear 7 1/2" 41112	Open		175.00	175
1996	Brer Fox 4" 41101	Open		120.00	120
1996	Brer Rabbit 4 3/4" 41103	Open		150.00	150
1996	Song of the South-Opening Title 41104	Open		29.00	29

Classics Collection-Symphony Hour - Disney Studios

1993	Clarabelle 6 4/5" 41027/wheel	Closed	1993	198.00	240-265
1993	Clarabelle 6 4/5"41027	Open		198.00	198
1994	Clara Cluck 41061	Open		185.00	185
1993	Goofy 6 4/5" 41026/wheel	Closed	1993	198.00	1200-1650
1993	Goofy 6 4/5" 41026	Open		198.00	198
1996	Donald Duck 8 1/4" 41105	Open		225.00	225
1993	Horace 6 4/5" 41028	Open		198.00	198
1993	Horace 6 4/5" 41028/wheel	Closed	1993	198.00	200-215
1993	Mickey Conductor 7 3/8" 41029	Open		185.00	185
1993	Mickey Conductor 7 3/8" 41029/wheel	Closed	1993	185.00	225-260
1993	Symphony Hour-Opening Title 41031	Open		29.00	29
1993	Symphony Hour-Opening Title 41031/clef	Closed	1993	29.00	35-45

Classics Collection-The Delivery Boy - Disney Studios

1992	Delivery Boy-Opening Title 41019	Open		29.00	29
1992	Delivery Boy-Opening Title 41019/clef	Closed	1993	29.00	35-50
1992	Mickey 6" 41020	Open		125.00	135
1992	Mickey 6" 41020/wheel	Closed	1992	125.00	150-175
1992	Minnie 6" 41021	Open		125.00	135
1992	Minnie 6" 41021/wheel	Closed	1992	125.00	140-200
1992	Pluto (raised letters) 3 3/5" 41022/wheel	Closed	1992	125.00	265-350
1992	Pluto 3 3/5" 41022	Open		125.00	125
1992	Pluto 3 3/5" 41022/wheel	Closed	1992	125.00	150-170

Classics Collection-The Reluctant Dragon - Disney Studios

1996	The Reluctant Dragon 7" 41072	7,500		695.00	695

Classics Collection-Three Little Pigs - Disney Studios

1993	Big Bad Wolf (short tooth) 41039 1st version	S/O	1994	295.00	800-950
1993	Big Bad Wolf 41039	7,500	1994	295.00	650-900
1993	Fiddler Pig 4 1/2" 41038	Open		75.00	75
1993	Fiddler Pig 4 1/2" 41038/clef	Closed	1993	75.00	80-95
1993	Fifer Pig 4 1/2" 41037	Open		75.00	75
1993	Fifer Pig 4 1/2" 41037/clef	Closed	1993	75.00	80-95
1993	Practical Pig 4 1/2" 41036	Open		75.00	75
1993	Practical Pig 4 1/2" 41036/clef	Closed	1993	75.00	80-95
1993	Three Little Pigs-Opening Title 41046	Open		29.00	30-4
1993	Three Little Pigs-Opening Title 41046/clef	Closed	1993	29.00	3

Classics Collection-Tribute Series - Disney Studios

1995	Pals Forever 41085	Closed	1995	175.00	220-275

Disney's Enchanted Places - Disney Studios

1996	Fiddler Pig's Stick House 41204	Open		85.00	8
1996	Fifer Pig's Straw House 41205	Open		85.00	8
1996	Geppetto's Toy Shop 41207	Open		150.00	15
1996	Practical Pig's Brick House 41206	Open		115.00	11
1995	Seven Dwarf's Cottage 41200	Open		180.00	18
1995	Seven Dwarf's Jewel Mine 41203	Open		190.00	19
1995	White Rabbit's House 41202	Open		175.00	17
1995	Woodcutter's Cottage 41201	Open		170.00	17

Disney's Enchanted Places Miniatures - Disney Studios

1996	Briar Rose 41214	Open		50.00	5
1996	Dopey 41215	Open		50.00	5
1996	Fiddler Pig 41224	Open		50.00	5
1996	Fifer Pig 41223	Open		50.00	5
1996	Pinocchio 41217	Open		50.00	5
1996	Practical Pig 41216	Open		50.00	5
1996	Snow White 41212	Open		50.00	5
1996	The White Rabbit 41213	Open		50.00	5

*Quotes have been rounded up to nearest dollar

Wee Forest Folk

Animals - A. Petersen, unless otherwise noted

YEAR	ISSUE	EDITION LIMIT	YEAR RETD.	ISSUE PRICE	*QUOTE U.S.$
1974	Baby Hippo H-2	Closed	1977	7.00	N/A
1978	Beaver Wood Cutter BV-1 - W. Petersen	Closed	1980	8.00	400-500
1974	Miss and Baby Hippo H-3	Closed	1977	15.00	N/A
1973	Miss Ducky D-1	Closed	1977	6.00	N/A
1974	Miss Hippo H-1	Closed	1977	8.00	N/A
1977	Nutsy Squirrel SQ-1 - W. Petersen	Closed	1977	3.00	N/A
1979	Turtle Jogger TS-1	Closed	1980	4.00	N/A

Bears - A. Petersen

YEAR	ISSUE	EDITION LIMIT	YEAR RETD.	ISSUE PRICE	*QUOTE U.S.$
1978	Big Lady Bear BR-4	Closed	1980	7.50	N/A
1977	Blueberry Bears BR-1	Closed	1982	8.75	500-700
1977	Boy Blueberry Bear BR-3	Closed	1982	4.50	300-550
1977	Girl Blueberry Bear BR-2	Closed	1982	4.25	300-550
1978	Traveling Bear BR-5	Closed	1980	8.00	400-750

Book / Figurine - W. Petersen

YEAR	ISSUE	EDITION LIMIT	YEAR RETD.	ISSUE PRICE	*QUOTE U.S.$
1988	Tom & Eon BK-1	Suspd.	1991	45.00	200-250

Bunnies - A. Petersen, unless otherwise noted

YEAR	ISSUE	EDITION LIMIT	YEAR RETD.	ISSUE PRICE	*QUOTE U.S.$
1977	Batter Bunny B-9	Closed	1982	4.50	300-550
1973	Broom Bunny B-6	Closed	1978	9.50	N/A
1972	Double Bunnies B-1	Closed	1980	4.25	N/A
1972	Housekeeping Bunny B-2	Closed	1980	4.50	N/A
1973	Market Bunny B-8	Closed	1977	9.00	N/A
1973	Muff Bunny B-7	Closed	1977	9.00	N/A
1973	The Professor B-4	Closed	1980	4.75	N/A
1980	Professor Rabbit B-11 - W. Petersen	Closed	1981	14.00	N/A
1973	Sir Rabbit B-3 - W. Petersen	Closed	1980	4.50	N/A
1973	Sunday Bunny B-5	Closed	1978	4.75	N/A
1977	Tennis Bunny BS-1	Closed	1980	3.75	300-400
1985	Tiny Easter Bunny B-12 - D. Petersen	Closed	1992	25.00	85
1978	Wedding Bunnies B-10 - W. Petersen	Closed	1981	12.50	700-1000

Cinderella Series - A. Petersen

YEAR	ISSUE	EDITION LIMIT	YEAR RETD.	ISSUE PRICE	*QUOTE U.S.$
1988	Cinderella's Slipper (w/Prince) C-1	Closed	1989	62.00	200-250
1989	Cinderella's Slipper C-1a	Closed	1994	32.00	95
1988	Cinderella's Wedding C-5	Closed	1994	62.00	150-175
1989	The Fairy Godmother C-7	Closed	1994	69.00	175
1988	Flower Girl C-6	Closed	1994	22.00	75-85
1988	The Flower Girls C-4	Closed	1994	42.00	95-115
1988	The Mean Stepmother C-3	Closed	1994	32.00	90-140
1988	The Ugly Stepsisters C-2	Closed	1994	62.00	125-150

Fairy Tale Series - A. Petersen

YEAR	ISSUE	EDITION LIMIT	YEAR RETD.	ISSUE PRICE	*QUOTE U.S.$
1980	Red Riding Hood & Wolf FT-1	Closed	1982	29.00	900-1400
1980	Red Riding Hood FT-2	Closed	1982	13.00	400-600

Forest Scene - A. Petersen, unless otherwise noted

YEAR	ISSUE	EDITION LIMIT	YEAR RETD.	ISSUE PRICE	*QUOTE U.S.$
1988	Woodland Serenade FS-1 - W. Petersen	Closed	1995	125.00	250-350

Foxes - A. Petersen

YEAR	ISSUE	EDITION LIMIT	YEAR RETD.	ISSUE PRICE	*QUOTE U.S.$
1978	Barrister Fox FX-3	Closed	1980	7.50	600-850
1977	Dandy Fox FX-2	Closed	1979	6.00	450-500
1977	Fancy Fox FX-1	Closed	1979	4.75	350-475

Frogs - A. Petersen, unless otherwise noted

YEAR	ISSUE	EDITION LIMIT	YEAR RETD.	ISSUE PRICE	*QUOTE U.S.$
1977	Frog Friends F-3 - W. Petersen	Closed	1981	5.75	400-600
1974	Frog on Rock F-2	Closed	1977	6.00	N/A
1977	Grampa Frog F-5 - W. Petersen	Closed	1981	6.00	700-900
1974	Prince Charming F-1 - W. Petersen	Closed	1977	7.50	N/A
1978	Singing Frog F-6	Closed	1979	5.50	N/A
1977	Spring Peepers F-4	Closed	1979	3.50	N/A

Limited Edition - A. Petersen, unless otherwise noted

YEAR	ISSUE	EDITION LIMIT	YEAR RETD.	ISSUE PRICE	*QUOTE U.S.$
1981	Beauty and the Beast BB-1 - W. Petersen	Closed	1981	89.00	2500-6000
1985	Helping Hand LTD-2	Closed	1985	62.00	500-750
1984	Postmouster LTD-1 - W. Petersen	Closed	1984	46.00	500-750
1987	Statue in the Park LTD-3 - W. Petersen	Closed	1987	93.00	700-950
1988	Uncle Sammy LTD-4	Closed	1988	85.00	225-295

Mice - A. Petersen, unless otherwise noted

YEAR	ISSUE	EDITION LIMIT	YEAR RETD.	ISSUE PRICE	*QUOTE U.S.$
1988	Aloha! M-158	Closed	1994	32.00	85
1982	Arty Mouse M-71	Closed	1991	19.00	75-175
1985	Attic Treasure M-126	Closed	1995	42.00	100-150
1977	Baby Sitter M-19	Closed	1981	5.75	350-500
1982	Baby Sitter M-66	Closed	1993	23.50	85-115
1981	Barrister Mouse M-57	Closed	1982	16.00	600-800
1987	Bat Mouse M-154	Closed	1994	25.00	85
1982	Beach Mousey M-76	Closed	1993	19.00	95-125
1981	Blue Devil M-61	Closed	N/A	12.50	125-175
1982	Boy Sweetheart M-81	Closed	1982	13.50	350-500
1975	Bride Mouse M-9	Closed	1978	4.00	N/A
1978	Bridge Club Mouse M-20	Closed	1979	6.00	600-800
1978	Bridge Club Mouse Partner M-21	Closed	1979	6.00	600-800
1984	Campfire Mouse M-109 - W. Petersen	Closed	1986	26.00	300-450
1981	The Carolers M-63	Closed	1981	29.00	400-600
1980	Carpenter Mouse M-49	Closed	1981	15.00	600-800
1983	Chief Geronimouse M-107a	Closed	1995	21.00	70-100
1978	Chief Nip-a-Way Mouse M-26	Closed	1981	7.00	500-700
1987	Choir Mouse M-147 - W. Petersen	Closed	1990	23.00	50-115
1979	Chris-Miss M-32	Closed	1982	9.00	250-395
1979	Chris-Mouse M-33	Closed	1982	9.00	250-395
1983	Christmas Morning M-92	Closed	1987	35.00	200-350
1983	Clown Mouse M-98	Closed	1984	22.00	300-400
1986	Come & Get It! M-141	Closed	1988	34.00	125-150
1985	Come Play! M-131	Closed	1991	18.00	65-100
1980	Commo-Dormouse M-42 - W. Petersen	Closed	1981	14.00	600-950
1978	Cowboy Mouse M-25	Closed	1981	6.00	550-850
1981	Doc Mouse & Patient M-55 - W. Petersen	Closed	1981	14.00	400-600
1987	Don't Cry! M-149	Closed	1990	33.00	85-125
1986	Down the Chimney M-143	Closed	1988	48.00	250-300
1987	Drummer M-153b - W. Petersen	Closed	1989	29.00	50-75
1989	Elf Tales M-163	Closed	1995	48.00	95
1985	Family Portrait M-127	Closed	1987	54.00	225-350
1976	Fan Mouse M-10	Closed	1979	5.75	N/A
1974	Farmer Mouse M-5	Closed	1979	3.75	N/A
1983	First Christmas M-93	Closed	1986	16.00	225-350
1984	First Day of School M-112	Closed	1985	27.00	250-550
1986	First Haircut M-137 - W. Petersen	Closed	1992	58.00	175-225
1980	Fishermouse M-41	Closed	1981	16.00	550-750
1981	Flower Girl M-53	Closed	1983	15.00	300-350
1979	Gardener Mouse M-37	Closed	1981	12.00	600-800
1983	Get Well Soon! M-96	Closed	1983	15.00	375-450
1974	Good Knight Mouse M-4 - W. Petersen	Closed	1977	7.50	N/A
1981	Graduate Mouse M-58	Closed	1988	15.00	85-115
1992	Greta M-169b	Closed	1993	35.00	75-95
1992	Hans M-169a	Closed	1993	35.00	75-95
1990	Hans & Greta M-169	Closed	1992	64.00	125-150
1983	Harvest Mouse M-104 - W. Petersen	Closed	1984	23.00	250-350
1992	High on the Hog M-186	Closed	1995	52.00	95-125
1976	June Belle M-13	Closed	1979	4.25	N/A
1977	King "Tut" Mouse TM-1	Closed	1979	4.50	450-600
1982	Lamplight Carolers M-86	Closed	1987	35.00	250-350
1982	Little Fire Chief M-77 - W. Petersen	Closed	1984	29.00	375-650
1982	Little Sledders M-85	Closed	1985	24.00	200-350
1982	Littlest Angel M-88	Closed	1986	15.00	95-115
1987	Littlest Witch M-156	Closed	1993	24.00	75-100
1981	Lone Caroler M-64	Closed	1981	15.50	400-600
1993	Lord & Lady Mousebatten M-195	Closed	1995	85.00	150
1976	Mama Mouse with Baby M-18	Closed	1979	6.00	350-450
1987	Market Mouse M-150 - W. Petersen	Closed	1993	49.00	120-150
1972	Market Mouse M-1a	Closed	1978	4.25	N/A
1976	May Belle M-12	Closed	1980	4.25	250-550
1983	Merry Chris-Miss M-90	Closed	1985	17.00	250-375
1983	Merry Chris-Mouse M-91	Closed	1985	16.00	250-395
1972	Miss Mouse M-1	Closed	1978	4.25	N/A
1972	Miss Mousey M-2	Closed	1978	4.00	N/A
1972	Miss Mousey w/ Bow Hat M-2b	Closed	1979	4.25	N/A
1972	Miss Mousey w/ Straw Hat M-2a	Closed	1980	4.25	250-350
1973	Miss Nursey Mouse M-3	Closed	1980	4.00	N/A
1980	Miss Polly Mouse M-46	Closed	1984	23.00	275-375
1982	Miss Teach & Pupil M-73	Closed	1984	29.50	350-575
1980	Miss Teach M-45	Closed	1980	18.00	500-700
1982	Moon Mouse M-78	Closed	1984	15.50	350-650
1981	Mother's Helper M-52	Closed	1983	11.00	250-300
1979	Mouse Artiste M-39	Closed	1981	12.50	350-500
1979	Mouse Ballerina M-38	Closed	1979	12.50	700-900
1983	Mouse Call M-97 - W. Petersen	Closed	1983	24.00	400-800
1979	Mouse Duet M-29	Closed	1982	25.00	550-700
1986	Mouse on Campus M-139 - W. Petersen	Closed	1988	25.00	125
1979	Mouse Pianist M-30	Closed	1984	17.00	300-600
1985	Mouse Talk M-130	Closed	1993	44.00	115-150
1979	Mouse Violinist M-31	Closed	1984	9.00	250-350
1976	Mouse with Muff M-16	Closed	1977	9.00	N/A
1979	Mousey Baby M-34	Closed	1982	9.50	300-350
1981	Mousey Express M-65	Closed	1993	22.00	100-150
1983	Mousey's Cone M-100	Closed	1994	22.00	75-100
1983	Mousey's Dollhouse M-102	Closed	1985	30.00	325-425
1988	Mousey's Easter Basket M-160	Closed	N/A	32.00	85-150
1982	Mousey's Teddy M-75	Closed	1985	29.00	350-475
1976	Mrs. Mousey M-15	Closed	1978	4.00	N/A
1976	Mrs. Mousey w/ Hat M-15a	Closed	1979	4.25	N/A
1980	Mrs. Tidy M-51	Closed	1981	19.50	325-400
1980	Mrs. Tidy and Helper M-50	Closed	1981	24.00	450-600
1976	Nightie Mouse M-14	Closed	1979	4.75	400-500
1981	Nurse Mousey M-54	Closed	1982	14.00	350-500
1982	Office Mousey M-68	Closed	1984	23.00	375-650
1983	Pack Mouse M-106 - W. Petersen	Closed	1984	19.00	300-400
1985	Pageant Shepherds M-122	Closed	1985	35.00	200-275
1985	Pageant Wiseman M-121	Closed	1985	58.00	200-275
1981	Pearl Knit Mouse M-59	Closed	1985	20.00	200-275
1984	Pen Pal Mousey M-114	Closed	1985	26.00	275-375
1993	Peter Pumpkin Eater M-190	Closed	1995	98.00	110-175
1984	Peter's Pumpkin M-118	Closed	1992	19.00	85-125
1980	Photographer Mouse M-48 - W. Petersen	Closed	1981	23.00	500-800
1978	Picnic Mice M-23 - W. Petersen	Closed	1979	7.25	500-700
1985	Piggy-Back Mousey M-129 - W. Petersen	Closed	1986	28.00	300-400
1978	Pirate Mouse M-27	Closed	1979	6.50	800-1000
1980	Pirate Mouse M-47 - W. Petersen	Closed	1981	16.00	700-1000
1990	Polly's Parasol M-170	Closed	1993	39.00	95-145
1982	Poorest Angel M-89	Closed	1986	15.00	100-130
1984	Prudence Pie Maker M-119	Closed	1992	18.50	75-125
1977	Queen "Tut" Mouse TM-2	Closed	1979	4.50	450-600
1979	Raggedy and Mouse M-36	Closed	1981	12.00	350-500
1987	The Red Wagon M-151 - W. Petersen	Closed	1991	54.00	175-250
1979	Rock-a-bye Baby Mouse M-35	Closed	1981	17.00	350-500
1983	Rocking Tot M-103	Closed	1990	19.00	70-100
1983	Rope 'em Mousey M-108	Closed	1984	19.00	300-400
1980	Santa Mouse M-43	Closed	1985	12.00	200-350
1984	Santa's Trainee M-116 - W. Petersen	Closed	1984	36.50	400-550
1982	Say "Cheese" M-72 - W. Petersen	Closed	1983	15.50	300-400
1981	School Marm Mouse M-56	Closed	1981	19.50	500-700
1978	Secretary Miss Pell M-22	Closed	1981	4.50	375-425
1976	Shawl Mouse M-17	Closed	1977	9.00	N/A
1987	Skeleton Mousey M-157	Closed	1993	27.00	75-100
1982	Snowmouse & Friend M-84	Closed	1985	23.50	375-450
1985	Sunday Drivers M-132 - W. Petersen	Closed	1994	58.00	250-300
1986	Sweet Dreams M-136	Closed	1992	58.00	150-185
1982	Sweethearts M-79	Closed	1982	26.00	400-500
1982	Tea for Two M-74	Closed	1984	26.00	350-450
1976	Tea Mouse M-11	Closed	1979	5.75	500-650
1984	Tidy Mouse M-113	Closed	1985	38.00	500-600
1978	Town Crier Mouse M-28	Closed	1979	10.50	1000
1984	Traveling Mouse M-110	Closed	1987	28.00	250-325
1987	Trumpeter M-153a - W. Petersen	Closed	1989	29.00	65
1987	Tuba Player M-153c - W. Petersen	Closed	1989	29.00	65
1992	Tuckered Out! M-136a	Closed	1993	46.00	100-200
1975	Two Mice with Candle M-7	Closed	1979	4.50	450-550
1975	Two Tiny Mice M-8	Closed	1979	4.50	350-500
1986	Waltzing Matilda M-135 - W. Petersen	Closed	1993	48.00	115-150
1983	Wash Day M-105	Closed	1984	23.00	400-550
1978	Wedding Mice M-24 - W. Petersen	Closed	1981	7.50	500-800
1982	Wedding Mice M-67 - W. Petersen	Closed	1993	29.50	115-150
1980	Witch Mouse M-44	Closed	1983	12.00	350
1984	Witchy Boo! M-120	Closed	1995	21.00	38
1974	Wood Sprite M-6a	Closed	1978	4.00	N/A
1974	Wood Sprite M-6b	Closed	1978	4.00	N/A
1974	Wood Sprite M-6c	Closed	1978	4.00	N/A

Minutemice - A. Petersen, unless otherwise noted

YEAR	ISSUE	EDITION LIMIT	YEAR RETD.	ISSUE PRICE	*QUOTE U.S.$
1974	Concordian On Drum with Glasses MM-4	Closed	1977	9.00	N/A
1974	Concordian Wood Base w/Hat MM-4b	Closed	1977	8.00	N/A
1974	Concordian Wood Base w/Tan Coat MM-4a	Closed	1977	7.50	N/A
1974	Little Fifer on Drum MM-5b	Closed	1977	8.00	N/A
1974	Little Fifer on Drum w/Fife MM-5	Closed	1977	8.00	N/A
1974	Little Fifer on Wood Base MM-5a	Closed	1977	8.00	N/A
1974	Mouse Carrying Large Drum MM-3	Closed	1977	8.00	N/A
1974	Mouse on Drum w/Black Hat MM-2	Closed	1977	9.00	N/A
1974	Mouse on Drum with Fife MM-1	Closed	1977	9.00	N/A
1974	Mouse on Drum with Fife Wood Base MM-1a	Closed	1977	9.00	N/A

Moles - A. Petersen

YEAR	ISSUE	EDITION LIMIT	YEAR RETD.	ISSUE PRICE	*QUOTE U.S.$
1978	Mole Scout MO-1	Closed	1980	4.25	300-500

Mouse Sports - A. Petersen, unless otherwise noted

YEAR	ISSUE	EDITION LIMIT	YEAR RETD.	ISSUE PRICE	*QUOTE U.S.$
1975	Bobsled Three MS-1	Closed	1977	12.00	N/A
1985	Fishin' Chip MS-14 - W. Petersen	Closed	1992	46.00	200-275
1981	Golfer Mouse MS-10	Closed	1984	15.50	350-400
1977	Golfer Mouse MS-7	Closed	1980	5.25	400-500
1984	Land Ho! MS-12	Closed	1987	36.50	150-300
1976	Mouse Skier MS-3	Closed	1979	4.25	300-400
1975	Skater Mouse MS-2	Closed	1980	4.50	300-400
1980	Skater Mouse MS-8	Closed	1983	16.50	250-550
1977	Skating Star Mouse MS-6	Closed	1979	3.75	250-350
1980	Skier Mouse (Early Colors) MS-9	Closed	1983	13.00	225-400
1984	Tennis Anyone? MS-13	Closed	1988	18.00	125-150
1976	Tennis Star MS-4	Closed	1978	3.75	N/A
1976	Tennis Star MS-5	Closed	1981	3.75	N/A

Owls - A. Petersen, unless otherwise noted

YEAR	ISSUE	EDITION LIMIT	YEAR RETD.	ISSUE PRICE	*QUOTE U.S.$
1975	Colonial Owls O-4	Closed	1977	11.50	N/A
1979	Grad Owl O-5 - W. Petersen	Closed	1979	4.25	N/A
1980	Graduate Owl (On Books) O-6 - W. Petersen	Closed	1980	12.00	400-600
1974	Mr. and Mrs. Owl O-1	Closed	1981	6.00	500-600
1974	Mr. Owl O-3	Closed	1981	3.25	300-400
1974	Mrs. Owl O-2	Closed	1981	3.00	300-400

Piggies - A. Petersen

YEAR	ISSUE	EDITION LIMIT	YEAR RETD.	ISSUE PRICE	*QUOTE U.S.$
1978	Boy Piglet/ Picnic Piggy P-6	Closed	1981	4.00	250-300
1978	Girl Piglet/Picnic Piggy P-5	Closed	1981	4.00	250-300
1981	Holly Hog P-11	Closed	1981	25.00	400-600
1978	Jolly Tar Piggy P-3	Closed	1979	4.50	300-350
1978	Miss Piggy School Marm P-1	Closed	1979	4.50	300-600
1980	Nurse Piggy P-10	Closed	1981	15.50	300-400
1978	Picnic Piggies P-4	Closed	1981	7.75	400-600
1980	Pig O' My Heart P-9	Closed	1981	12.00	300-400
1978	Piggy Baker P-2	Closed	1981	4.50	300-350
1980	Piggy Ballerina P-7	Closed	1981	15.50	300-500
1978	Piggy Jogger PS-1	Closed	1981	4.50	400-600
1980	Piggy Policeman P-8	Closed	1981	17.50	300-500

Raccoons - A. Petersen

YEAR	ISSUE	EDITION LIMIT	YEAR RETD.	ISSUE PRICE	*QUOTE U.S.$
1978	Bird Watcher Raccoon RC-3	Closed	1981	6.50	600-800
1977	Hiker Raccoon RC-2	Closed	1980	4.50	500-700
1977	Mother Raccoon RC-1	Closed	1980	4.50	400-600
1978	Raccoon Skater RCS-1	Closed	1980	4.75	400-600
1978	Raccoon Skier RCS-2	Closed	1980	6.00	400-600

*Quotes have been rounded up to nearest dollar

FIGURINES/COTTAGES/GRAPHICS

Rats - A. Petersen, unless otherwise noted

YEAR ISSUE		EDITION LIMIT	YEAR RETD.	ISSUE PRICE	*QUOTE U.S.$
1975	Doc Rat R-2 - W. Petersen	Closed	1980	5.25	500-700
1975	Seedy Rat R-1	Closed	1977	5.25	N/A

Robin Hood Series - A. Petersen

YEAR ISSUE		EDITION LIMIT	YEAR RETD.	ISSUE PRICE	*QUOTE U.S.$
1990	Friar Tuck RH-3	Closed	1994	32.00	60-95
1990	Maid Marion RH-2	Closed	1994	32.00	60-95
1990	Robin Hood RH-1	Closed	1994	37.00	60-95

Single Issues - A. Petersen, unless otherwise noted

YEAR ISSUE		EDITION LIMIT	YEAR RETD.	ISSUE PRICE	*QUOTE U.S.$
1980	Cave Mice - W. Petersen	Closed	N/A	N/A	550-800
1972	Party Mouse in Plain Dress	Closed	N/A	N/A	N/A
1972	Party Mouse in Polka-Dot Dress	Closed	N/A	N/A	N/A
1972	Party Mouse in Sailor Suit	Closed	N/A	N/A	N/A
1972	Party Mouse with Bow Tie	Closed	N/A	N/A	N/A
1980	Screech Owl - W. Petersen	Closed	1982	N/A	N/A

Tiny Teddies - D. Petersen

YEAR ISSUE		EDITION LIMIT	YEAR RETD.	ISSUE PRICE	*QUOTE U.S.$
1984	Boo Bear T-3	Suspd.		20.00	75-150
1987	Christmas Teddy T-10	Suspd.		26.00	75-125
1984	Drummer Bear T-4	Suspd.		22.00	75-125
1988	Hansel & Gretel Bears @ Witch's House T-11	Suspd.		175.00	75-125
1986	Huggy Bear T-8	Suspd.		26.00	75-125
1984	Little Teddy T-1	Closed	1986	20.00	75-125
1989	Momma Bear T-12	Suspd.		27.00	100-150
1985	Ride 'em Teddy! T-6	Suspd.		32.00	95-150
1984	Sailor Teddy T-2	Suspd.		20.00	75-125
1984	Santa Bear T-5	Suspd.		27.00	95-125
1985	Seaside Teddy T-7	Suspd.		28.00	75-125
1983	Tiny Teddy TT-1	Closed	1983	16.00	N/A
1987	Wedding Bears T-9	Suspd.		54.00	150-200

Wind in the Willows - A. Petersen, unless otherwise noted

YEAR ISSUE		EDITION LIMIT	YEAR RETD.	ISSUE PRICE	*QUOTE U.S.$
1982	Badger WW-2	Closed	1983	18.00	300-500
1982	Mole WW-1	Closed	1983	18.00	300-400
1982	Ratty WW-4	Closed	1983	18.00	300-500
1982	Toad WW-3 - W. Petersen	Closed	1983	18.00	300-400

GRAPHICS

American Artists

Fred Stone - F. Stone

YEAR ISSUE		EDITION LIMIT	YEAR RETD.	ISSUE PRICE	*QUOTE U.S.$
1979	Affirmed, Steve Cauthen Up	750	N/A	100.00	600
1988	Alysheba	950	N/A	195.00	650
1992	The American Triple Crown I, 1948-1978	1,500		325.00	325
1993	The American Triple Crown II, 1937-1946	1,500		325.00	325
1993	The American Triple Crown III, 1919-1935	1,500		225.00	225
1983	Andalusian, The	750	N/A	150.00	350
1981	Arabians, The	750	N/A	115.00	525
1989	Battle For The Triple Crown	950	N/A	225.00	650
1980	The Belmont-Bold Forbes	500	N/A	100.00	375
1991	Black Stallion	1,500		225.00	250
1988	Cam-Fella	950	N/A	175.00	350
1981	Contentment	750	N/A	115.00	525
1992	Dance Smartly-Pat Day Up	950	N/A	225.00	325
1995	Dancers, canvas litho	350		375.00	375
1995	Dancers, print	Open		60.00	60
1983	The Duel	750	N/A	150.00	400
1985	Eternal Legacy	950	N/A	175.00	950
1980	Exceller-Bill Shoemaker	500	N/A	90.00	800
1990	Final Tribute- Secretariat	1,150	N/A	265.00	1300
1987	The First Day	950	N/A	175.00	225
1991	Forego	1,150		225.00	250
1986	Forever Friends	950	N/A	175.00	725
1985	Fred Stone Paints the Sport of Kings (Book)	750	N/A	265.00	750
1980	Genuine Risk	500	N/A	100.00	700
1991	Go For Wand-A Candle in the Wind	1,150		225.00	225
1986	Great Match Race-Ruffian & Foolish Pleasure	950	N/A	175.00	375
1995	Holy Bull, canvas litho	350		375.00	375
1995	Holy Bull, litho	1,150		225.00	225
1981	John Henry-Bill Shoemaker Up	595	N/A	160.00	1500
1985	John Henry-McCarron Up	750	N/A	175.00	500-750
1995	Julie Krone - Colonial Affair	1,150		225.00	225
1985	Kelso	950	N/A	175.00	750
1980	The Kentucky Derby	750	N/A	100.00	650
1980	Kidnapped Mare-Franfreluche	750	N/A	115.00	575
1987	Lady's Secret	950	N/A	175.00	425
1982	Man O'War "Final Thunder"	750	N/A	175.00	2500-3100
1979	Mare and Foal	500	N/A	90.00	500
1979	The Moment After	500	N/A	90.00	350
1986	Nijinski II	950	N/A	175.00	275
1984	Northern Dancer	950	N/A	175.00	625
1982	Off and Running	750	N/A	125.00	250-350
1990	Old Warriors Shoemaker-John Henry	1,950	N/A	265.00	595
1979	One, Two, Three	500	N/A	100.00	1000
1980	The Pasture Pest	500	N/A	100.00	875
1979	Patience	1,000	N/A	90.00	1200
1989	Phar Lap	950	N/A	195.00	275
1982	The Power Horses	750	N/A	125.00	250
1987	The Rivalry-Alysheba & Bet Twice	950	N/A	195.00	550
1979	The Rivals-Affirmed & Alydar	500	N/A	90.00	500
1983	Ruffian-For Only a Moment	750	N/A	175.00	1100
1983	Secretariat	950	N/A	175.00	995-1200
1989	Shoe Bald Eagle	950	N/A	195.00	675
1981	The Shoe-8,000 Wins	395	N/A	200.00	7000
1980	Spectacular Bid	500	N/A	65.00	350-400
1995	Summer Days, canvas litho	350		375.00	375
1995	Summer Days, litho	1,150		225.00	225
XX	Sunday Silence	950	N/A	195.00	425
1981	The Thoroughbreds	750	N/A	115.00	425
1983	Tranquility	750	N/A	150.00	525
1984	Turning For Home	750	N/A	150.00	425
1982	The Water Trough	750	N/A	125.00	575

Anheuser-Busch, Inc.

Anheuser-Busch - H. Droog

YEAR ISSUE		EDITION LIMIT	YEAR RETD.	ISSUE PRICE	*QUOTE U.S.$
1994	Gray Wolf Mirror N4570	2,500		135.00	150

Armani

Wall Art - G. Armani

YEAR ISSUE		EDITION LIMIT	YEAR RETD.	ISSUE PRICE	*QUOTE U.S.$
1994	Abiding Love 105A	675		475.00	475
1994	Abiding Love A/P 111A	25	1995	675.00	675
1994	The Embrace 103A	675	1995	475.00	475
1994	The Embrace A/P 109A	25	1995	675.00	675
1994	La Pieta 102A	675		475.00	475
1994	La Pieta A/P 108A	25	1995	675.00	675
1994	Lady w/Mirror 101A	675		475.00	475
1994	Lady w/Mirror A/P 107A	25	1995	675.00	675
1994	Lady w/Peacock 100A	675		475.00	475
1994	Lady w/Peacock A/P 106A	25	1995	675.00	675
1994	Wind Song 104A	675		475.00	475
1994	Wind Song A/P 110A	25	1995	675.00	675

Artaffects

Perillo - G. Perillo

YEAR ISSUE		EDITION LIMIT	YEAR RETD.	ISSUE PRICE	*QUOTE U.S.$
1980	Babysitter, S/N	3,000		45.00	125-350
1988	By the Stream, S/N	950		100.00	125
1985	Chief Crazy Horse, S/N	950		125.00	450
1982	Chief Pontiac, S/N	950		75.00	100
1985	Chief Sitting Bull, S/N	500		125.00	350
1982	Hoofbeats, S/N	950		100.00	150
1982	Indian Style, S/N	950		75.00	100
1986	Learning His Ways, S/N	325		150.00	250
1982	Lonesome Cowboy, S/N	950		75.00	150
1978	Madonna of the Plains, S/N	500		125.00	200-600
1977	Madre, S/N	500		125.00	350
1988	Magnificent Seven, S/N	950		125.00	125
1982	Maria, S/N	550		150.00	350
1985	Marigold, S/N	500		125.00	150-450
1983	The Moment Poster, S/N	495		20.00	60
1984	Navajo Love, S/N	300		125.00	700
1984	Out of the Forest, S/N	Unkn.		Unkn.	450
1990	The Pack, S/N	950		150.00	200
1982	Papoose, S/N	950		125.00	125
1981	Peaceable Kingdom, S/N	950		100.00	375-800
1986	The Pout, S/N	325		150.00	200-450
1980	Puppies, S/N	3,000		45.00	200
1986	The Rescue, S/N	325		150.00	200-550
1985	Secretariat, S/N	950		125.00	150
1979	Sioux Scout and Buffalo Hunt, matched set	500		150.00	250-850
1978	Snow Pals, S/N	500		125.00	150-550
1982	Tender Love, S/N	950		75.00	125-450
1982	Tinker, S/N	3,000		45.00	100-350
1986	War Pony, S/N	325		150.00	150
1985	Whirlaway, S/N	950		125.00	150

Circle Fine Art

Rockwell - N. Rockwell

YEAR ISSUE		EDITION LIMIT	YEAR RETD.	ISSUE PRICE	*QUOTE U.S.$
XX	American Family Folio	200		Unkn.	17500
XX	The Artist at Work	130		Unkn.	3500
XX	At the Barber	200		Unkn.	4900
XX	Autumn	200		Unkn.	3500
XX	Autumn/Japon	25		Unkn.	3600
XX	Aviary	200		Unkn.	4200
XX	Barbershop Quartet	200		Unkn.	4200
XX	Baseball	200		Unkn.	3600
XX	Ben Franklin's Philadelphia	200		Unkn.	3600
XX	Ben's Belles	200		Unkn.	3500
XX	The Big Day	200		Unkn.	3400
XX	The Big Top	148		Unkn.	2800
XX	Blacksmith Shop	200		Unkn.	6300
XX	Bookseller	200		Unkn.	2700
XX	Bookseller/Japon	25		Unkn.	2750
XX	The Bridge	200		Unkn.	3100
XX	Cat	200		Unkn.	3400
XX	Cat/Collotype	200		Unkn.	4000
XX	Cheering	200		Unkn.	3600
XX	Children at Window	200		Unkn.	3600
XX	Church	200		Unkn.	3400
XX	Church/Collotype	200		Unkn.	4000
XX	Circus	200		Unkn.	2650
XX	County Agricultural Agent	200		Unkn.	3900
XX	The Critic	200		Unkn.	4650
XX	Day in the Life of a Boy	200		Unkn.	6200
XX	Day in the Life of a Boy/Japon	25		Unkn.	6500
XX	Debut	200		Unkn.	3600
XX	Discovery	200		Unkn.	5900
XX	Doctor and Boy	200		Unkn.	9400
XX	Doctor and Doll-Signed	200		Unkn.	11900
XX	Dressing Up/Ink	60		Unkn.	4400
XX	Dressing Up/Pencil	200		Unkn.	3700
XX	The Drunkard	200		Unkn.	3600
XX	The Expected and Unexpected	200		Unkn.	3700
XX	Family Tree	200		Unkn.	5900
XX	Fido's House	200		Unkn.	3600
XX	Football Mascot	200		Unkn.	3700
XX	Four Seasons Folio	200		Unkn.	13500
XX	Four Seasons Folio/Japon	25		Unkn.	14000
XX	Freedom from Fear-Signed	200		Unkn.	6400
XX	Freedom from Want-Signed	200		Unkn.	6400
XX	Freedom of Religion-Signed	200		Unkn.	6400
XX	Freedom of Speech-Signed	200		Unkn.	6400
XX	Gaiety Dance Team	200		Unkn.	4300
XX	Girl at Mirror-Signed	200		Unkn.	8400
XX	The Golden Age	200		Unkn.	3500
XX	Golden Rule-Signed	200		Unkn.	4400
XX	Golf	200		Unkn.	3600
XX	Gossips	200		Unkn.	5000
XX	Gossips/Japon	25		Unkn.	5100
XX	Grotto	200		Unkn.	3400
XX	Grotto/Collotype	200		Unkn.	4000
XX	High Dive	200		Unkn.	3400
XX	The Homecoming	200		Unkn.	3700
XX	The House	200		Unkn.	3700
XX	Huck Finn Folio	200		Unkn.	35000
XX	Ichabod Crane	200		Unkn.	6700
XX	The Inventor	200		Unkn.	4100
XX	Jerry	200		Unkn.	4700
XX	Jim Got Down on His Knees	200		Unkn.	4500
XX	Lincoln	200		Unkn.	11400
XX	Lobsterman	200		Unkn.	5500
XX	Lobsterman/Japon	25		Unkn.	5750
XX	Marriage License	200		Unkn.	6900
XX	Medicine	200		Unkn.	3400
XX	Medicine/Color Litho	200		Unkn.	4000
XX	Miss Mary Jane	200		Unkn.	4500
XX	Moving Day	200		Unkn.	3900
XX	Music Hath Charms	200		Unkn.	4200
XX	My Hand Shook	200		Unkn.	4500
XX	Out the Window	200		Unkn.	3400
XX	Out the Window/ Collotype	200		Unkn.	4000
XX	Outward Bound-Signed	200		Unkn.	7900
XX	Poor Richard's Almanac	200		Unkn.	24000
XX	Prescription	200		Unkn.	4900
XX	Prescription/Japon	25		Unkn.	5000
XX	The Problem We All Live With	200		Unkn.	4500
XX	Puppies	200		Unkn.	3700
XX	Raliegh the Dog	200		Unkn.	3900
XX	Rocket Ship	200		Unkn.	3650
XX	The Royal Crown	200		Unkn.	3500
XX	Runaway	200		Unkn.	3800
XX	Runaway/Japon	200		Unkn.	570
XX	Safe and Sound	200		Unkn.	380
XX	Saturday People	200		Unkn.	3300
XX	Save Me	200		Unkn.	3600
XX	Saying Grace-Signed	200		Unkn.	740
XX	School Days Folio	200		Unkn.	1400
XX	Schoolhouse	200		Unkn.	450
XX	Schoolhouse/Japon	25		Unkn.	465
XX	See America First	200		Unkn.	565
XX	See America First/Japon	25		Unkn.	610
XX	Settling In	200		Unkn.	360
XX	Shuffelton's Barbershop	200		Unkn.	740
XX	Smoking	200		Unkn.	340
XX	Smoking/Collotype	200		Unkn.	400
XX	Spanking	200		Unkn.	340
XX	Spanking/ Collotype	200		Unkn.	400
XX	Spelling Bee	200		Unkn.	650
XX	Spring	200		Unkn.	350
XX	Spring Flowers	200		Unkn.	520
XX	Spring/Japon	25		Unkn.	360
XX	Study for the Doctor's Office	200		Unkn.	600
XX	Studying	200		Unkn.	360
XX	Summer	200		Unkn.	350
XX	Summer Stock	200		Unkn.	490
XX	Summer Stock/Japon	25		Unkn.	500
XX	Summer/Japon	25		Unkn.	360
XX	The Teacher	200		Unkn.	340
XX	Teacher's Pet	200		Unkn.	360
XX	The Teacher/Japon	25		Unkn.	350
XX	The Texan	200		Unkn.	370
XX	Then For Three Minutes	200		Unkn.	450
XX	Then Miss Watson	200		Unkn.	450
XX	There Warn't No Harm	200		Unkn.	450
XX	Three Farmers	200		Unkn.	36
XX	Ticketseller	200		Unkn.	42
XX	Ticketseller/Japon	25		Unkn.	44
XX	Tom Sawyer Color Suite	200		Unkn.	300
XX	Tom Sawyer Folio	200		Unkn.	265
XX	Top of the World	200		Unkn.	42
XX	Trumpeter	200		Unkn.	39
XX	Trumpeter/Japon	25		Unkn.	41
XX	Two O'Clock Feeding	200		Unkn.	36
XX	The Village Smithy	200		Unkn.	35
XX	Welcome	200		Unkn.	35
XX	Wet Paint	200		Unkn.	38
XX	When I Lit My Candle	200		Unkn.	45
XX	White Washing	200		Unkn.	34
XX	Whitewashing the Fence/Collotype	200		Unkn.	40
XX	Window Washer	200		Unkn.	48
XX	Winter	200		Unkn.	35
XX	Winter/Japon	25		Unkn.	36

*Quotes have been rounded up to nearest dolla

YEAR	ISSUE	EDITION LIMIT	YEAR RETD.	ISSUE PRICE	*QUOTE U.S. $
XX	Ye Old Print Shoppe	200		Unkn.	3500
XX	Your Eyes is Lookin'	200		Unkn.	4500

Cross Gallery, Inc.

Bandits & Bounty Hunters - P.A. Cross

YEAR	ISSUE	EDITION LIMIT	YEAR RETD.	ISSUE PRICE	*QUOTE U.S. $
1996	Bandits	865		225.00	225
1994	Bounty Hunter	865		225.00	225

The Gift - P.A. Cross

YEAR	ISSUE	EDITION LIMIT	YEAR RETD.	ISSUE PRICE	*QUOTE U.S. $
1989	B' Achua Dlubh-bia Bii Noskiiyahi The Gift, Part II	S/O	1989	225.00	650
1993	The Gift, Part III	S/O	1993	225.00	350-1000

Half Breed Series - P.A. Cross

YEAR	ISSUE	EDITION LIMIT	YEAR RETD.	ISSUE PRICE	*QUOTE U.S. $
1989	Ach-hua Dlubh: (Body Two), Half Breed	S/O	1989	190.00	1450
1989	Ach-hua Dlubh: (Body Two), Half Breed II	S/O	1989	225.00	800-1100
1990	Ach-hua Dlubh: (Body Two), Half Breed III	S/O	1990	225.00	850
1995	Ach-hua Dlubh: (Body Two), Half Breed IV	865		225.00	225

Limited Edition Original Graphics - P.A. Cross

YEAR	ISSUE	EDITION LIMIT	YEAR RETD.	ISSUE PRICE	*QUOTE U.S. $
1991	Bia-A-Hoosh (A Very Special Woman), Stone Lithograph	S/O	1991	500.00	500
1987	Caroline, Stone Lithograph	S/O	1987	300.00	600
1988	Maidenhood Hopi, Stone Lithograph	S/O	1988	950.00	1150
1990	Nighteyes, I, Serigraph	S/O	1990	225.00	425
1989	The Red Capote, Serigraph	S/O	1989	750.00	1150
1989	Rosapina, Etching	74		1200.00	1200
1991	Wooltalkers, Serigraph	275		750.00	750

Limited Edition Prints - P.A. Cross

YEAR	ISSUE	EDITION LIMIT	YEAR RETD.	ISSUE PRICE	*QUOTE U.S. $
1991	Ashpahdua Hagay Ashae-Gyoke (My Home & Heart Is Crow)	S/O	1991	225.00	225-350
1983	Ayla-Sah-Xuh-Xah (Pretty Colours, Many Designs)	S/O	1983	150.00	450
1990	Baape Ochia (Night Wind, Turquoise)	S/O	1990	185.00	370
1990	Biaachee-itah Bah-achbeh (Medicine Woman Scout)	S/O	1990	225.00	525
1984	Blue Beaded Hair Ties	S/O	1984	85.00	330
1991	The Blue Shawl	S/O	1991	185.00	275
1987	Caroline	S/O	1987	45.00	145
1989	Chey-ayjeh: Prey	S/O	1989	190.00	325-600
1988	Dance Apache	S/O	1988	190.00	360
1987	Dii-tah-shteh Ee-wihza-ahook (A Coat of much Value)	S/O	1987	90.00	740
1989	The Dreamer	S/O	1989	190.00	600
1987	The Elkskin Robe	S/O	1987	190.00	640
1990	Eshte	S/O	1990	185.00	200
1986	Grand Entry	S/O	1986	85.00	85
1983	Isbaaloo Eetshiileehcheek (Sorting Her Beads)	S/O	1983	150.00	1750
1990	Ishia-Kahda #1 (Quiet One)	S/O	1990	185.00	400
1988	Ma-a-luppis-she-La-dus (She is above everything, nothing can touch her)	S/O	1988	190.00	525
1984	Profile of Caroline	S/O	1984	85.00	185
1986	The Red Capote	S/O	1986	150.00	850
1987	The Red Necklace	S/O	1987	90.00	210
1989	Teesa Waits To Dance	S/O	1989	135.00	180
1984	Thick Lodge Clan Boy: Crow Indian	475		85.00	85
1987	Tina	S/O	1987	45.00	110
1985	The Water Vision	S/O	1985	150.00	325
1984	Whistling Water Clan Girl: Crow Indian	S/O	1984	85.00	85
1993	Winter Girl Bride	1,730		225.00	225
1986	Winter Morning	S/O	1986	185.00	1450
1986	The Winter Shawl	S/O	1986	150.00	1600

Miniature Line - P.A. Cross

YEAR	ISSUE	EDITION LIMIT	YEAR RETD.	ISSUE PRICE	*QUOTE U.S. $
1991	BJ	S/O	1995	80.00	80
1993	Braids	447		80.00	80
1993	Daybreak	447		80.00	80
1991	The Floral Shawl	S/O	1995	80.00	80
1991	Kendra	S/O	1995	80.00	80
1993	Ponytails	447		80.00	80
1993	Sundown	447		80.00	80
1991	Watercolour Study #2 For Half Breed	S/O	1995	80.00	80

The Painted Ladies' Suite - P.A. Cross

YEAR	ISSUE	EDITION LIMIT	YEAR RETD.	ISSUE PRICE	*QUOTE U.S. $
1992	Acoria (Crow; Seat of Honor)	S/O	1995	185.00	185
1992	Avisola	S/O	1995	185.00	185
1992	Dah-say (Crow; Heart)	S/O	1995	185.00	185
1992	Itza-chu (Apache; The Eagle)	S/O	1995	185.00	185
1992	Kel'hoya (Hopi; Little Sparrow Hawk)	S/O	1995	185.00	185
1992	The Painted Ladies	S/O	1992	225.00	1200
1996	Sus(h)gah-daydus(h) (Crow; Quick)	447		185.00	185
1996	Tze-go-juni (Chiricahua Apache)	447		185.00	185

Star Quilt Series - P.A. Cross

YEAR	ISSUE	EDITION LIMIT	YEAR RETD.	ISSUE PRICE	*QUOTE U.S. $
1988	The Quilt Makers	S/O	1988	190.00	1200
1986	Reflections	S/O	1986	185.00	865
1985	Winter Warmth	S/O	1985	150.00	900-1215

Wolf Series - P.A. Cross, unless otherwise noted

YEAR	ISSUE	EDITION LIMIT	YEAR RETD.	ISSUE PRICE	*QUOTE U.S. $
1990	Agnjnaug Amaguut;Inupiag (Women With Her Wolves)	S/O	1993	325.00	350-750
1993	Ahmah-ghut, Tuhtu-loo; Eelahn-nuht Kah-auhk (Wolves and Caribou; My Furs and My Friends)	1,050		255.00	255
1989	Biagoht Eecuebeh Hehsheesh-Checah: (Red Ridinghood and Her Wolves), Gift I	S/O	1989	225.00	1500-2500
1996	Chedah	865		225.00	225
1985	Dii-tah-shteh Bii-wik; Chedah-bah liidah (My Very Own Protective Covering; Walks w/the Wolf Woman)	S/O	1985	185.00	3275
1996	The Healer - J. Geshick	250		795.00	795
1987	The Morning Star Gives Long Otter His Hoop Medicine Power	S/O	1987	190.00	1800-2500

Flambro Imports

Emmett Kelly Jr. Lithographs - B. Leighton-Jones

YEAR	ISSUE	EDITION LIMIT	YEAR RETD.	ISSUE PRICE	*QUOTE U.S. $
1995	All Star Circus	2 Yr.		150.00	150
1994	EKJ 70th Birthday Commemorative	1,994		150.00	150
1994	I Love You	2 Yr.		90.00	90
1994	Joyful Noise	2 Yr.		90.00	90
1994	Picture Worth 1,000 Words	2 Yr.		90.00	90

Gartlan USA

Lithograph - Various

YEAR	ISSUE	EDITION LIMIT	YEAR RETD.	ISSUE PRICE	*QUOTE U.S. $
1986	George Brett-"The Swing" - J. Martin	2,000		85.00	200
1991	Joe Montana - M. Taylor	500	1994	495.00	600-700
1989	Kareem Abdul Jabbar-The Record Setter - M. Taylor	1,989	1993	85.00	395
1991	Negro League 1st World Series (print) - Unknown	1,924	1993	109.00	125
1987	Roger Staubach - C. Soileau	1,979	1992	85.00	200-300

Glynda Turley Prints

Turley - Canvas - G. Turley

YEAR	ISSUE	EDITION LIMIT	YEAR RETD.	ISSUE PRICE	*QUOTE U.S. $
1992	Courtyard II	200		140.00	140
1994	Courtyard III	350		140.00	140
1988	Elegance	350		130.00	130
1991	Floral Fancy	150		130.00	130
1992	Flower Garden	350		130.00	130
1990	Garden Room	250		130.00	130
1992	The Garden Wreath II	200		130.00	130
1994	The Garden Wreath III	350		140.00	140
1994	Georgia Sweet	350		140.00	140
1992	Grand Glory I	350		160.00	160
1992	Grand Glory II	350		160.00	160
1995	Grand Glory III	350		160.00	160
1995	Grand Glory IV	350		160.00	160
1992	In Full Bloom	200		160.00	160
1992	In Full Bloom	200	N/A	160.00	160
1994	In Full Bloom II	350		160.00	160
1988	Iris Basket II	350		130.00	130
1990	Iris Basket III	50		130.00	130
1991	Iris Basket IV	25		130.00	130
1989	Iris Parade	350		130.00	130
1988	La Belle IV	25		130.00	130
1995	Mabry In Spring	350		160.00	160
1992	Old Mill Stream	350	N/A	130.00	130
1993	Old Mill Stream II	350	N/A	130.00	130
1994	Old Mill Stream III	350		190.00	190
1988	Once Upon A Time	200		130.00	130
1989	Petals In Pink	100		190.00	190
1989	Pretty Pickings I	350		130.00	130
1989	Pretty Pickings II	300		130.00	130
1989	Pretty Pickings III	100		130.00	130
1993	Primrose Lane II	300		130.00	130
1995	Remember When	350		190.00	190
1991	Secret Garden	350		130.00	130
1994	Secret Garden II	350		130.00	130
1991	Simply Southern	350		160.00	160
1992	Southern Sunday	200		140.00	140
1995	Southern Sunday II	350		190.00	190
1993	A Southern Tradition II	350		190.00	190
1994	A Southern Tradition IV	350		190.00	190
1993	Spring's Promise II	300		130.00	130
1988	Spring's Return	350		130.00	130
1995	Summer in Victoria	350		130.00	130
1994	Summer Stroll	350		160.00	160
1990	Sweet Nothings	350		130.00	130

Turley - Print - G. Turley

YEAR	ISSUE	EDITION LIMIT	YEAR RETD.	ISSUE PRICE	*QUOTE U.S. $
1995	Almost An Angel	7,500		56.00	56
1995	Almost An Angel A/P	50		84.00	84
1986	Attic Curiosity	2,000	N/A	15.00	15
1986	Attic Curiosity A/P	50	N/A	25.00	25
1986	Busy Bodies I	2,000	N/A	25.00	25
1986	Busy Bodies I A/P	50	N/A	40.00	40
1986	Busy Bodies II	2,000	N/A	25.00	25
1986	Busy Bodies II A/P	50	N/A	40.00	40
1986	Callie And Company	2,000	N/A	30.00	30
1986	Callie And Company A/P	50	N/A	50.00	50
1987	Callie And Company II	3,000	N/A	30.00	30
1987	Callie And Company II A/P	50	N/A	50.00	50
1988	Calling On Callie	5,000		30.00	30
1988	Calling On Callie A/P	50		45.00	45
1990	Childhood Memories I	3,500		30.00	30
1990	Childhood Memories I A/P	50		45.00	45
1990	Childhood Memories II	3,500		30.00	30
1990	Childhood Memories II A/P	50		45.00	45
1988	Circle of Friends	5,000		25.00	25
1988	Circle Of Friends A/P	50	N/A	40.00	40
1990	The Coming Out Party	3,500		35.00	35
1991	The Courtyard	2,500	N/A	47.00	47
1991	The Courtyard A/P	50	N/A	70.50	71
1992	The Courtyard II	2,500	N/A	50.00	50
1992	The Courtyard II A/P	50		75.00	75
1994	The Courtyard III A/P	50		91.50	92
1990	Dear To My Heart	3,500		35.00	35
1990	Dear To My Heart A/P	50		52.50	53
1988	Elegance	5,000		30.00	30
1988	Elegance A/P	50		45.00	45
1986	A Family Affair	2,500	N/A	25.00	25
1986	A Family Affair A/P	50	N/A	40.00	40
1984	Feeding Time	1,000	N/A	50.00	50
1984	Feeding Time A/P	50	N/A	75.00	75
1984	Feeding Time II	1,000	N/A	25.00	25
1984	Feeding Time II A/P	50	N/A	40.00	40
1987	Fence Row Gathering	3,000	N/A	30.00	30
1987	Fence Row Gathering A/P	50	N/A	50.00	50
1988	Fence Row Gathering II	5,000	N/A	30.00	30
1988	Fence Row Gathering II A/P	50	N/A	50.00	50
1991	Floral Fancy	3,500	N/A	40.00	40
1991	Floral Fancy A/P	50		60.00	60
1992	The Flower Garden	2,500		43.00	43
1992	The Flower Garden A/P	50		64.50	65
1986	Flowers And Lace	3,000	N/A	25.00	25
1986	Flowers And Lace A/P	50	N/A	40.00	40
1988	Flowers For Mommy	5,000	N/A	25.00	25
1988	Flowers For Mommy A/P	50	N/A	40.00	40
1990	Forever Roses	3,500		30.00	30
1990	Forever Roses A/P	50		45.00	45
1987	The Garden Gate	3,000	N/A	30.00	30
1987	The Garden Gate A/P	50	N/A	50.00	50
1990	Garden Room	3,500	N/A	40.00	40
1991	The Garden Wreath	2,500	N/A	47.00	47
1991	The Garden Wreath A/P	50	N/A	60.00	60
1992	The Garden Wreath II	2,500	N/A	50.00	50
1992	The Garden Wreath II A/P	50	N/A	75.00	75
1994	The Garden Wreath III	5,000		61.00	61
1994	The Garden Wreath III A/P	50		91.50	92
1994	Georgia Sweet	2,500		50.00	50
1994	Georgia Sweet A/P	50		75.00	75
1995	Glynda's Garden	7,500		73.00	73
1995	Glynda's Garden A/P	50		109.50	110
1993	Grand Glory I	2,500	N/A	53.00	53
1992	Grand Glory I A/P	50		79.50	80
1993	Grand Glory II	2,500	N/A	53.00	53
1992	Grand Glory II A/P	50		79.50	80
1995	Grand Glory III	7,500		65.00	65
1995	Grand Glory III A/P	50		97.50	98
1995	Grand Glory IV	7,500		65.00	65
1995	Grand Glory IV A/P	50		97.50	98
1984	Heading Home I	1,000	N/A	25.00	25
1984	Heading Home I A/P	50	N/A	40.00	40
1984	Heading Home II	1,000	N/A	25.00	25
1984	Heading Home II A/P	50	N/A	40.00	40
1984	Heading Home III	1,000	N/A	25.00	25
1984	Heading Home III A/P	50	N/A	40.00	40
1987	Heart Wreath	3,000	N/A	25.00	25
1987	Heart Wreath A/P	50	N/A	40.00	40
1988	Heart Wreath II	3,500	N/A	25.00	25
1988	Heart Wreath II A/P	50	N/A	40.00	40
1989	Heart Wreath III	3,500	N/A	25.00	25
1989	Heart Wreath III A/P	50	N/A	40.00	40
1987	Hollyhocks	3,000	N/A	30.00	30
1987	Hollyhocks A/P	50	N/A	50.00	50
1990	Hollyhocks II	3,500	N/A	25.00	25
1990	Hollyhocks II A/P	50	N/A	60.00	60
1995	Hollyhocks III	7,500		69.00	69
1995	Hollyhocks III A/P	50		103.50	104
1992	In Full Bloom	2,500	N/A	53.00	53
1992	In Full Bloom A/P	50	N/A	79.50	80
1994	In Full Bloom II	3,500	N/A	65.00	65
1994	In Full Bloom II A/P	50		97.50	98
1995	In Full Bloom III	7,500		64.00	64
1995	In Full Bloom III A/P	50		96.00	96
1984	In One Ear And Out The Other	950	N/A	50.00	50
1984	In One Ear And Out The Other A/P	50	N/A	75.00	75
1987	Iris Basket	3,000	N/A	30.00	30
1987	Iris Basket A/P	50	N/A	50.00	50
1988	Iris Basket II	3,500	N/A	30.00	30
1988	Iris Basket II A/P	50	N/A	50.00	50
1990	Iris Basket III	3,500	N/A	35.00	35
1990	Iris Basket III A/P	50	N/A	52.50	53
1991	Iris Basket IV	2,500		35.00	35
1991	Iris Basket IV A/P	50		52.50	53
1989	Iris Parade	3,500		35.00	35
1989	Iris Parade A/P	50		52.50	53
1985	La Belle	750	N/A	25.00	25
1985	La Belle A/P	50	N/A	40.00	40
1986	La Belle II	2,000	N/A	25.00	25
1986	La Belle II A/P	50	N/A	40.00	40
1986	La Belle III	3,500	N/A	25.00	25
1986	La Belle III A/P	50	N/A	40.00	40
1988	La Belle IV	5,000	N/A	30.00	30

GRAPHICS

YEAR ISSUE	EDITION LIMIT	YEAR RETD.	ISSUE PRICE	*QUOTE U.S.$
1988 La Belle IV A/P	50	N/A	50.00	50
1995 Little Red River	7,500		73.00	73
1995 Little Red River A/P	50		109.50	110
1995 Mabry In Spring	7,500		65.00	65
1995 Mabry In Spring A/P	50		97.50	98
1987 Mauve Iris I	3,000	N/A	10.00	10
1987 Mauve Iris I A/P	50	N/A	25.00	25
1987 Mauve Iris II	3,000	N/A	10.00	10
1987 Mauve Iris II A/P	50	N/A	25.00	25
1983 Now I Lay Me	1,000	N/A	50.00	50
1983 Now I Lay Me A/P	50	N/A	75.00	75
1989 Old Favorites	3,500	N/A	35.00	35
1989 Old Favorites A/P	50	N/A	52.50	53
1988 Old Friends	5,000	N/A	30.00	30
1988 Old Friends A/P	50	N/A	50.00	50
1992 Old Mill Stream	2,500	N/A	40.00	40
1992 Old Mill Stream A/P	50		60.00	60
1993 Old Mill Stream II	2,500	N/A	43.00	43
1993 Old Mill Stream II A/P	50		64.50	65
1994 Old Mill Stream III	3,500	N/A	69.00	69
1994 Old Mill Stream III A/P	50		103.50	104
1988 Once Upon A Time	5,000	N/A	30.00	30
1988 Once Upon A Time A/P	50		45.00	45
1988 Past Times	5,000	N/A	30.00	30
1988 Past Times A/P	50	N/A	50.00	50
1988 Peeping Tom	5,000	N/A	35.00	35
1988 Peeping Tom A/P	50	N/A	55.00	55
1989 Petals In Pink	3,500	N/A	30.00	30
1989 Petals In Pink A/P	50	N/A	79.50	80
1987 Playing Hookie	3,000	N/A	30.00	30
1987 Playing Hookie A/P	50	N/A	50.00	50
1988 Playing Hookie Again	5,000	N/A	30.00	30
1988 Playing Hookie Again A/P	50	N/A	50.00	50
1988 The Porch	5,000	N/A	30.00	30
1988 The Porch A/P	50	N/A	50.00	50
1989 Pretty Pickings I	3,500	N/A	30.00	30
1989 Pretty Pickings I A/P	50		45.00	45
1989 Pretty Pickings II	3,500		35.00	35
1989 Pretty Pickings II A/P	50		52.50	53
1989 Pretty Pickings III	3,500		30.00	30
1989 Pretty Pickings III A/P	50		45.00	45
1991 Primrose Lane	3,500	N/A	40.00	40
1991 Primrose Lane A/P	50	N/A	60.00	60
1993 Primrose Lane II	2,500	N/A	43.00	43
1993 Primrose Lane II A/P	50		64.50	65
1995 Remember When	7,500		73.00	73
1995 Remember When A/P	50		109.50	110
1983 Sad Face Clown	950	N/A	50.00	50
1983 Sad Face Clown A/P	50	N/A	75.00	75
1991 Secret Garden	3,500	N/A	40.00	40
1991 Secret Garden A/P	50		60.00	60
1994 Secret Garden II A/P	50		79.50	80
1991 Simply Southern	3,500	N/A	53.00	53
1991 Simply Southern A/P	50	N/A	79.50	80
1985 Snips N Snails	750	N/A	25.00	25
1985 Snips N Snails A/P	50	N/A	40.00	40
1992 Southern Sunday	2,500	N/A	50.00	50
1992 Southern Sunday A/P	50		75.00	75
1995 Southern Sunday II	7,500		73.00	73
1995 Southern Sunday II A/P	50		109.50	110
1993 A Southern Tradition II	3,500	N/A	60.00	60
1993 A Southern Tradition II A/P	50	N/A	90.00	90
1994 A Southern Tradition IV	5,000	N/A	69.00	69
1994 A Southern Tradition IV A/P	50		103.50	104
1988 A Special Time	5,000	N/A	30.00	30
1988 A Special Time A/P	50		45.00	45
1993 Spring's Promise II	2,500		43.00	43
1993 Spring's Promise III A/P	50		64.50	65
1988 Spring's Return	5,000		35.00	35
1988 Spring's Return A/P	50		52.50	53
1983 Stepping Out	1,000	N/A	50.00	50
1983 Stepping Out A/P	50	N/A	75.00	75
1985 Sugar N Spice	750	N/A	25.00	25
1985 Sugar N Spice A/P	50	N/A	40.00	40
1987 A Summer Day	3,000	N/A	30.00	30
1987 A Summer Day A/P	50	N/A	50.00	50
1995 Summer In Victoria	7,500		53.00	53
1995 Summer In Victoria A/P	50		79.50	80
1994 Summer Stroll	3,500	N/A	65.00	65
1994 Summer Stroll A/P	50		97.50	98
1990 Sweet Nothings	3,500		40.00	40
1990 Sweet Nothings A/P	50		60.00	60
1987 Victorian Bouquet	3,500	N/A	25.00	25
1987 Victorian Bouquet A/P	50	N/A	40.00	40
1989 Victorian Bouquet II	3,500		25.00	25
1986 White Iris	2,000	N/A	25.00	25
1986 White Iris A/P	50	N/A	40.00	40
1987 Wild Roses	3,000	N/A	30.00	30
1987 Wild Roses A/P	50	N/A	50.00	50
1990 Wild Roses II	3,500		35.00	35
1990 Wild Roses II A/P	50		52.50	53

Greenwich Workshop

Ballantyne - Ballantyne

YEAR ISSUE	EDITION LIMIT	YEAR RETD.	ISSUE PRICE	*QUOTE U.S.$
1995 John's New Pup	850		150.00	150
1995 Kate and Her Fiddle	850		150.00	150

Bama - J. Bama

YEAR ISSUE	EDITION LIMIT	YEAR RETD.	ISSUE PRICE	*QUOTE U.S.$
1993 Art of James Bama Book w/ Chester Medicine Crow Fathers Flag Print	2,500	N/A	345.00	345
1981 At a Mountain Man Wedding	1,500	N/A	145.00	275
1981 At Burial Gallager and Blind Bill	1,650	N/A	135.00	150
1988 Bittin' Up-Rimrock Ranch	1,250	N/A	195.00	500-1000
1992 Blackfeet War Robe	1,000		195.00	195
1995 Blackfoot Ceremonial Headdress	200		850.00	850
1987 Buck Norris-Crossed Sabres Ranch	1,000	N/A	195.00	850
1990 Buffalo Bill	1,250	N/A	210.00	210
1993 The Buffalo Dance	1,000		195.00	195
1991 Ceremonial Lance	1,250		225.00	225
1996 Cheyene Split Horn Headdress	200		850.00	850
1994 Cheyenne Dog Soldier	1,000		225.00	225
1991 Chuck Wagon	1,000		225.00	225
1975 Chuck Wagon in the Snow	1,000	N/A	50.00	1000
1992 Coming' Round the Bend	1,000		195.00	195
1978 Contemporary Sioux Indian	1,000	N/A	75.00	1600
1995 A Cowboy Named Anne	1,000		185.00	185
1992 Crow Cavalry Scout	1,000		195.00	195
1977 A Crow Indian	1,000	N/A	65.00	125
1982 Crow Indian Dancer	1,250		150.00	150
1988 Crow Indian From Lodge Grass	1,250		225.00	225
1988 Dan-Mountain Man	1,250	N/A	195.00	195
1983 The Davilla Brothers-Bronc Riders	1,250		145.00	145
1983 Don Walker-Bareback Rider	1,250	N/A	85.00	85
1991 The Drift on Skull Creek Pass	1,500		225.00	225
1979 Heritage	1,500	N/A	75.00	300
1978 Indian at Crow Fair	1,500	N/A	75.00	75
1988 Indian Wearing War Medicine Bonnet	1,000	N/A	225.00	225
1980 Ken Blackbird	1,500	N/A	95.00	95
1974 Ken Hunder, Working Cowboy	1,000	N/A	55.00	800
1989 Little Fawn-Cree Indian Girl	1,250	N/A	195.00	195
1979 Little Star	1,500	N/A	80.00	1000
1993 Magua-"The Last of the Mohicans"	1,000		225.00	225
1993 Making Horse Medicine	1,000		225.00	225
1978 Mountain Man	1,000	N/A	75.00	400-600
1980 Mountain Man 1820-1840 Period	1,500	N/A	115.00	350
1979 Mountain Man and His Fox	1,500	N/A	90.00	450
1982 Mountain Man with Rifle	1,250	N/A	135.00	350
1978 A Mountain Ute	1,000	N/A	75.00	600
1992 Northern Cheyene Wolf Scout	1,000		195.00	195
1981 Old Arapaho Story-Teller	1,500	N/A	135.00	135
1980 Old Saddle in the Snow	1,500	N/A	75.00	150
1980 Old Sod House	1,500	N/A	80.00	400-500
1981 Oldest Living Crow Indian	1,500	N/A	135.00	135
1993 On the North Fork of the Shoshoni	1,000		195.00	195
1990 Paul Newman as Butch Cassidy & Video	2,000		250.00	250
1981 Portrait of a Sioux	1,500	N/A	135.00	135
1979 Pre-Columbian Indian with Atlatl	1,500	N/A	75.00	75
1991 Ready to Rendezvous	1,000		225.00	225
1995 Ready to Ride	1,000		185.00	185
1990 Ridin' the Rims	1,250	N/A	210.00	210
1991 Riding the High Country	1,250		225.00	225
1978 Rookie Bronc Rider	1,000	N/A	75.00	125
1976 Sage Grinder	1,000	N/A	65.00	1600
1980 Sheep Skull in Drift	1,500	N/A	75.00	1600
1974 Shoshone Chief	1,000	N/A	65.00	650
1982 Sioux Indian with Eagle Feather	1,250	N/A	150.00	150
1992 Sioux Subchief	1,000		195.00	195
1994 Slim Warren, The Old Cowboy	1,000		125.00	125
1983 Southwest Indian Father & Son	1,250		145.00	145
1977 Timber Jack Joe	1,000	N/A	65.00	600
1988 The Volunteer	1,500		225.00	225
1987 Winter on Trout Creek	1,000	N/A	150.00	500
1981 Winter Trapping	1,500	N/A	150.00	500
1980 Young Plains Indian	1,500	N/A	125.00	1500
1990 Young Sheepherder	1,500		225.00	225

Bean - A. Bean

YEAR ISSUE	EDITION LIMIT	YEAR RETD.	ISSUE PRICE	*QUOTE U.S.$
1993 Conrad Gordon and Bean:The Fantasy	1,000		385.00	385
1987 Helping Hands	850		150.00	150
1995 Houston, We Have a Problem	1,000		500.00	500
1988 How It Felt to Walk on the Moon	850	N/A	150.00	150
1992 In Flight	850		385.00	385
1994 In The Beginning Apollo 25 C/S	1,000	N/A	450.00	1000

Blackshear - T. Blackshear

YEAR ISSUE	EDITION LIMIT	YEAR RETD.	ISSUE PRICE	*QUOTE U.S.$
1994 Beauty and the Beast	1,000		225.00	225
1993 Hero Frederick Douglass	746		20.00	20
1993 Hero Harriet Tubman	753		20.00	20
1993 Hero Martin Luther King, Jr.	762		20.00	20
1993 Heroes of Our Heritage Portfolio	5,000		35.00	35
1995 Intimacy	550		850.00	850
1995 Night in Day	850		195.00	195
1994 Swansong	1,000		175.00	175

Blake - B. Blake

YEAR ISSUE	EDITION LIMIT	YEAR RETD.	ISSUE PRICE	*QUOTE U.S.$
1995 The Old Double Diamond	850		175.00	175
1994 West of the Moon	650		195.00	195

Blossom - C. Blossom

YEAR ISSUE	EDITION LIMIT	YEAR RETD.	ISSUE PRICE	*QUOTE U.S.$
1987 After the Last Drift	950		145.00	145
1984 Ah Your Majesty	N/A	N/A	45.00	45
1985 Allerton on the East River	650	N/A	145.00	145
1988 Black Rock	950		150.00	150
1984 December Moonrise	650	N/A	135.00	135
1984 December Moonrise (remarqued)	25	N/A	175.00	175
1990 Ebb Tide	950		175.00	175
1983 First Out	450	N/A	90.00	90
1983 First Out (remarqued)	25	N/A	190.00	190
1987 Gloucester Mackeral Seiners	950		145.00	145
1989 Harbor Light	950		165.00	165
1988 Heading Home	950	N/A	150.00	250
1985 Off Palmer Land	850		145.00	145
1992 Port of Call	850		175.00	175
1986 Potomac By Moonlight	950	N/A	145.00	145
1987 San Francisco-Eve of the Gold Rush	950		150.00	150
1992 Silhouette	850		175.00	175
1986 Southport @ Twilight	950		145.00	145
1985 Tranquil Dawn	650		95.00	95
1994 Traveling in Company	850		175.00	175
1994 Traveling in Company, Remarque	100		415.00	415
1992 Windward	950		175.00	175
1986 Winter Dawn @ Boston Wharf	850		85.00	85

Bralds - B. Bralds

YEAR ISSUE	EDITION LIMIT	YEAR RETD.	ISSUE PRICE	*QUOTE U.S.$
1995 Bag Ladies	2,500	1995	150.00	250-350

Bullas - W. Bullas

YEAR ISSUE	EDITION LIMIT	YEAR RETD.	ISSUE PRICE	*QUOTE U.S.$
1995 The Big Game	1,500		95.00	95
1993 Billy the Pig	850		95.00	172
1995 The Chimp Shot	1,000		95.00	95
1994 Clucks Unlimited	850		95.00	95
1995 The Consultant	1,000		95.00	95
1994 Court of Appeals	850	1995	95.00	95
1995 Dog Byte	1,000		95.00	95
1994 Ductor	850		95.00	95
1995 fowl ball...	1,500		95.00	95
1994 Fridays After Five	850		95.00	95
1995 Legal Eagles	1,000		95.00	95
1993 Mr. Harry Buns	850	N/A	95.00	95
1993 Our Ladies of the Front Lawn	850		95.00	95
1993 The Pale Prince	850		110.00	110
1993 Sand Trap Pro	850		95.00	95
1993 Some Set of Buns	850		95.00	95
1995 tennis, anyone?	1,000		95.00	95
1993 Wine-Oceros	850		95.00	95
1993 You Rang, Madam?	850		95.00	114

Christensen - J. Christensen

YEAR ISSUE	EDITION LIMIT	YEAR RETD.	ISSUE PRICE	*QUOTE U.S.$
1989 The Annunciation	850	N/A	175.00	175
1995 Balancing Act	3,500	N/A	185.00	185
1996 The Bassonist	2,500		125.00	125
1990 The Burden of the Responsible Man	850	N/A	145.00	800-1200
1991 The Candleman	850	N/A	160.00	260
1993 College of Magical Knowledge	4,500	N/A	185.00	220-325
1993 College of Magical Knowledge, remarque	500	N/A	252.50	32
1991 Diggery Diggery Dare-Etching	75	N/A	210.00	46
1994 Evening Angels	4,000	N/A	195.00	19
1994 Evening Angels w/Art Furnishings Frame	200	N/A	800.00	80
1989 Fantasies of the Sea-poster	Open		35.00	3
1995 Fishing	2,500	N/A	145.00	14
1993 Getting it Right	4,000	N/A	185.00	18
1985 The Gift For Mrs. Claus	3,500	N/A	80.00	41
1991 Jack Be Nimble-Etching	75	N/A	210.00	42
1986 Jonah	850	N/A	95.00	20
1991 Lawrence and a Bear	850	N/A	145.00	25
1987 Low Tech-Poster	Open		35.00	3
1991 Man in the Moon-Etching	75	N/A	210.00	450-60
1988 The Man Who Minds the Moon	850	N/A	145.00	65
1991 Mother Goose-Etching	75	N/A	210.00	45
1987 Old Man with a Lot on His Mind	850	N/A	85.00	380-56
1986 Olde World Santa	3,500	N/A	80.00	42
1992 The Oldest Angel	850	N/A	125.00	48
1991 Once Upon a Time	1,500	N/A	175.00	107
1991 Once Upon a Time, remarque	500	N/A	220.00	115
1996 One Light	1,500		125.00	12
1991 Pelican King	850	N/A	115.00	24
1991 Peter Peter Pumpkin Eater-Etching	75	N/A	210.00	450-60
1995 Piscatorial Percussionist	3,000	N/A	125.00	12
1992 The Reponsible Woman	2,500	N/A	175.00	1
1990 Rhymes & Reasons w/Booklet	Open		150.00	24
1990 Rhymes & Reasons w/Booklet, remarque	500	N/A	208.00	3
1993 The Royal Music Barque	2,750	N/A	375.00	37
1992 The Royal Processional	1,500	N/A	185.00	34
1992 The Royal Processional, remarque	500	N/A	252.50	6
1993 The Scholar	3,250	N/A	125.00	4
1995 Serenade For an Orange Cat	3,000	N/A	125.00	12
1987 The Shakespearean Poster	Open		35.00	
1995 Sisters of the Sea	2,000	N/A	195.00	1
1994 Six Bird Hunters-Full Camouflage 3	4,662	N/A	165.00	1
1994 Sometimes the Spirit Touches w/book	3,600	N/A	195.00	3
1991 Three Blind Mice-Etching	75	N/A	210.00	4
1991 Three Wise Men of Gotham-Etching	75	N/A	210.00	4
1991 Tweedle Dee & Tweedle Dum-Etching	75	N/A	210.00	4
1994 Two Angels Discussing Botticelli	2,950	N/A	145.00	1
1990 Two Sisters	650	N/A	325.00	3
1987 Voyage of the Basset w/Journal	850	N/A	225.00	12
1993 Waiting for the Tide	2,250	N/A	150.00	1
1988 The Widows Mite	850	N/A	145.00	25
1986 Your Plaice, or Mine?	850	N/A	125.00	1

*Quotes have been rounded up to nearest dolla

ombes - S. Combes

YEAR ISSUE		EDITION LIMIT	YEAR RETD.	ISSUE PRICE	*QUOTE U.S. $
92	African Oasis	650	N/A	375.00	500
81	Alert	1,000	N/A	95.00	95
87	The Angry One	850		95.00	95
88	Bushwhacker	850	N/A	145.00	145
83	Chui	275	N/A	250.00	250
88	Confrontation	850		145.00	145
88	The Crossing	1,250	N/A	245.00	245
94	Disdain	850		110.00	110
80	Facing the Wind	1,500	N/A	75.00	75
93	Fearful Symmetry	850	N/A	110.00	110
95	Golden Silhouette	950		175.00	175
90	The Guardian (Silverback)	1,000		185.00	185
92	The Hypnotist	1,250		145.00	145
94	Indian Summer	950		175.00	175
80	Interlude	1,500	N/A	85.00	85
95	Jungle Phantom	950		175.00	175
91	Kilimanjaro Morning	850		185.00	185
81	Leopard Cubs	1,000	N/A	95.00	95
92	Lookout	1,250		95.00	95
80	Manyara Afternoon	1,500	N/A	75.00	250
89	Masai-Longonot, Kenya	850		145.00	145
92	Midday Sun (Lioness & Cubs)	850		125.00	125
89	Mountain Gorillas	550	N/A	135.00	135
95	Mountain Myth	950		175.00	175
95	Pride	950		175.00	175
80	Serengeti Monarch	1,500	N/A	85.00	85
95	Serious Intent	950		175.00	175
95	Siberian Winter	950		175.00	175
88	Simba	850		125.00	125
95	Snow Tracker	950		175.00	175
80	Solitary Hunter	1,500	N/A	75.00	75
90	Standoff	850	N/A	375.00	375
91	Study in Concentration	850	N/A	185.00	225
87	Tall Shadows	850	N/A	150.00	425
85	Tension at Dawn	825	N/A	145.00	1000
85	Tension at Dawn, remarque	25	N/A	275.00	1200
89	The Watering Hole	850		225.00	225
86	The Wildebeest Migration	450	N/A	350.00	1700

rowley - D. Crowley

YEAR ISSUE		EDITION LIMIT	YEAR RETD.	ISSUE PRICE	*QUOTE U.S. $
81	Afterglow	1,500		110.00	110
92	Anna Thorne	650		160.00	160
80	Apache in White	1,500	N/A	85.00	85
79	Arizona Mountain Man	1,500	N/A	85.00	85
80	Beauty and the Beast	1,500	N/A	85.00	85
92	Colors of the Sunset	650		175.00	175
79	Desert Sunset	1,500	N/A	75.00	75
78	Dorena	1,000	N/A	75.00	75
94	The Dreamer	650		150.00	150
81	Eagle Feathers	1,500	N/A	95.00	95
88	Ermine and Beads	550	N/A	85.00	85
89	The Gunfighters	3,000	N/A	35.00	35
81	The Heirloom	1,000	N/A	125.00	125
82	Hopi Butterfly	275		350.00	350
78	Hudson's Bay Blanket	1,000	N/A	75.00	75
80	The Littlest Apache	275	N/A	325.00	850
94	Plumes and Ribbons	650		160.00	160
79	Security Blanket	1,500	N/A	65.00	65
81	Shannandoah	275	N/A	325.00	325
78	The Starquilt	1,000	N/A	65.00	500
86	The Trapper	550		75.00	75

awson - J. Dawson

YEAR ISSUE		EDITION LIMIT	YEAR RETD.	ISSUE PRICE	*QUOTE U.S. $
92	The Attack (Cougars)	850		175.00	175
93	Berry Contented	850		150.00	150
93	Berry Contented (Remarque)	100		235.00	235
94	The Face Off (Right & Left Panel)	850		150.00	150
93	Looking Back	850		110.00	110
93	Otter Wise	850		150.00	150
93	Taking a Break	850	N/A	150.00	150

oolittle - B. Doolittle

YEAR ISSUE		EDITION LIMIT	YEAR RETD.	ISSUE PRICE	*QUOTE U.S. $
983	Art of Camouflage, signed	2,000	1983	55.00	300
980	Bugged Bear	1,000	1980	85.00	3500-4000
987	Calling the Buffalo	8,500	1987	245.00	1000-1500
983	Christmas Day, Give or Take a Week	4,581	1983	80.00	1500
988	Doubled Back	15,000	1988	245.00	1500
992	Eagle Heart	48,000	1992	285.00	285
982	Eagle's Flight	1,500	1982	185.00	4000
983	Escape by a Hare	1,500	1983	80.00	700
984	Forest Has Eyes, The	8,544	1984	175.00	4000-5200
980	Good Omen, The	1,000	1980	85.00	4500
987	Guardian Spirits	13,238	1987	295.00	1200-1500
990	Hide and Seek (Composite & Video)	25,000	1990	1200.00	1500
984	Let My Spirit Soar	1,500	1984	195.00	5000
979	Pintos	1,000	1979	65.00	10000
993	Prayer for the Wild Things	65,000	1993	325.00	225
983	Runs With Thunder	1,500	1983	150.00	1800
983	Rushing War Eagle	1,500	1983	150.00	1500
991	Sacred Circle (Print & Video)	40,192	1991	325.00	350-500
989	Sacred Ground	69,996	1989	265.00	1000
987	Season of the Eagle	36,548	1987	245.00	975
991	The Sentinel	35,000	1991	275.00	775
981	Spirit of the Grizzly	1,500	1981	150.00	4100
995	Spirit Takes Flight	48,000		225.00	225
986	Two Bears of the Blackfeet	2,650	1986	225.00	1200
985	Two Indian Horses	12,253	1985	225.00	4250-4800
1995	Two More Indian Horses	48,000	1995	225.00	400-700
1981	Unknown Presence	1,500	1981	135.00	3200
1992	Walk Softly (Chapbook)	40,192	1992	225.00	225
1994	When The Wind Had Wings	57,500	1994	325.00	325
1986	Where Silence Speaks, Doolittle The Art of Bev Doolittle	3,500	1986	650.00	3000
1980	Whoo !?	1,000	1980	75.00	1800-2000
1993	Wilderness? Wilderness!	50,000	1993	65.00	65
1985	Wolves of the Crow	2,650	1985	225.00	2000
1981	Woodland Encounter	1,500	1981	145.00	11000

Ferris - K. Ferris

YEAR ISSUE		EDITION LIMIT	YEAR RETD.	ISSUE PRICE	*QUOTE U.S.$
1990	The Circus Outbound	1,000		225.00	225
1991	Farmer's Nightmare	850		185.00	185
1991	Linebacker in the Buff	1,000		225.00	225
1983	Little Willie Coming Home	1,000	N/A	145.00	1900
1994	Real Trouble	1,000		195.00	195
1995	Schweinfurt Again	1,000		195.00	195
1982	Sunrise Encounter	1,000	N/A	145.00	145
1993	A Test of Courage	850		185.00	185
1991	Too Little, Too Late w/Video	1,000		245.00	245

Frederick - R. Frederick

YEAR ISSUE		EDITION LIMIT	YEAR RETD.	ISSUE PRICE	*QUOTE U.S.$
1990	Autumn Leaves	1,250	N/A	175.00	175
1989	Barely Spring	1,500		165.00	165
1994	Beeline (C)	1,000		195.00	195
1987	Before the Storm (Diptych)	550	N/A	350.00	950
1991	Breaking the Ice	2,750	N/A	235.00	235
1989	Colors of Home	1,500	N/A	165.00	225
1995	Drifters	850		175.00	175
1985	Early Evening Gathering	475	N/A	325.00	355
1992	An Early Light Breakfast	1,750	N/A	235.00	235
1990	Echoes of Sunset	1,750	N/A	235.00	650
1987	Evening Shadows (White-Tail Deer)	1,500	N/A	125.00	125
1992	Fast Break	2,250		235.00	235
1992	Fire and Ice (Suite of 2)	1,750		175.00	175
1984	First Moments of Gold	825	N/A	145.00	170
1984	First Moments of Gold, remarque	25	N/A	172.50	185
1984	From Timber's Edge	850	N/A	125.00	140-165
1989	Gifts of the Land #2	500	N/A	150.00	150
1988	Gifts of the Land w/Wine & Wine Label	500	N/A	150.00	150
1988	Glimmer of Solitude	1,500		145.00	145
1993	Glory Days	1,750		115.00	115
1986	Great Horned Owl	1,250	N/A	115.00	135
1995	High Country Harem	1,000		185.00	185
1985	High Society	950	N/A	115.00	300
1991	The Long Run	1,750	N/A	235.00	300
1991	The Long Run, AP	200	N/A	167.50	300
1985	Los Colores De Chiapas	950	N/A	85.00	85
1994	The Lost World	1,000		175.00	175
1985	Misty Morning Lookout	950	N/A	145.00	145
1984	Misty Morning Sentinel	850	N/A	125.00	145
1989	Monarch of the North	2,000		150.00	150
1990	Morning Surprise	1,750	N/A	165.00	165
1991	Morning Thunder	1,750	N/A	185.00	250
1988	The Nesting Call	2,500		150.00	150
1988	The Nesting Call, remarque	1,000	N/A	165.00	165
1993	New Heights	1,950		195.00	195
1987	Northern Light	1,500	N/A	165.00	165
1986	Out on a Limb	1,250	N/A	145.00	350
1993	Point of View	1,000		235.00	235
1992	Rain Forest Rendezvous	1,500	N/A	225.00	225
1988	Rim Walk	1,500	N/A	90.00	100
1988	Shadows of Dusk	1,500	N/A	165.00	165
1990	Silent Watch (High Desert Museum)	2,000	N/A	35.00	35
1994	Snow Pack	1,000		175.00	175
1992	Snowstorm	1,750		195.00	195
1990	Snowy Reflections (Snowy Egret)	1,500		150.00	150
1986	Sounds of Twilight	1,500	N/A	135.00	200
1991	Summer's Song (Triptych)	2,500		225.00	225
1993	Temple of the Jaguar	1,500		225.00	225
1988	Timber Ghost w/Mini Wine Label	3,000	N/A	150.00	175
1994	Tropic Moon	850		165.00	165
1987	Tundra Watch (Snowy Owl)	1,500	N/A	145.00	145
1994	Way of the Caribou	1,235		235.00	235
1987	Winter's Brilliance (Cardinal)	1,500	N/A	135.00	140
1986	Winter's Call	1,250	N/A	165.00	600
1986	Winter's Call Raptor, AP	100	N/A	165.00	600
1987	Woodland Crossing (Caribou)	1,500	N/A	145.00	145
1988	World of White	2,500	N/A	150.00	150

Gurney - J. Gurney

YEAR ISSUE		EDITION LIMIT	YEAR RETD.	ISSUE PRICE	*QUOTE U.S.$
1992	Birthday Pageant	2,500	N/A	60.00	60
1992	Birthday Pageant, remarque	300	N/A	275.00	425
1995	Cottage Reflections	3,000		195.00	195
1991	Dinosaur Boulevard	2,000	N/A	125.00	125
1991	Dinosaur Boulevard, remarque	250	N/A	196.00	650
1990	Dinosaur Parade	1,995	1995	125.00	125
1990	Dinosaur Parade, remarque	150	N/A	130.00	2000
1992	Dream Canyon	N/A	N/A	125.00	125
1992	Dream Canyon, remarque	150	N/A	196.00	300
1993	The Excursion	3,500		175.00	175
1993	Garden of Hope	3,500		175.00	175
1990	Morning in Treetown	1,500	N/A	175.00	260
1993	Palace in the Clouds	3,500	N/A	175.00	175
1993	Ring Riders	2,500	N/A	175.00	175
1995	Rumble & Mist	2,500		175.00	175
1990	Seaside Romp	1,000	N/A	175.00	290
1992	Skyback Print w/Dinotopia Book	3,500	N/A	295.00	295
1994	Small Wonder	3,299	N/A	75.00	75
1994	Steep Street	3,500		95.00	95
1991	Waterfall City	3,000	N/A	125.00	125
1991	Waterfall City, remarque	250	N/A	186.00	400
1995	The World Beneath Collectors' Book w/ print	3,000		195.00	195

Gustafson - S. Gustafson

YEAR ISSUE		EDITION LIMIT	YEAR RETD.	ISSUE PRICE	*QUOTE U.S.$
1995	The Alice in Wonderland Suite	4,000		195.00	195
1994	Frog Prince	3,500	1994	125.00	450
1993	Goldilocks and the Three Bears	3,500	1993	125.00	300
1995	Hansel & Gretel	3,000		125.00	125
1993	Humpty Dumpty	3,500	1993	125.00	125
1995	Jack in the Beanstalk	3,500		125.00	125
1993	Little Red Riding Hood	3,500	1993	125.00	165
1994	Pat-A-Cake	4,000	1994	125.00	125
1995	Rumplestiltskin	2,750		125.00	125
1993	Snow White & the Seven Dwarfs	3,500	1993	165.00	250-400
1995	Touched by Magic	4,000		185.00	185

Hartough - L. Hartough

YEAR ISSUE		EDITION LIMIT	YEAR RETD.	ISSUE PRICE	*QUOTE U.S.$
1995	14th Hole, St. Andrews	850	1995	225.00	225
1995	7th Hole Pebble Beach Golf Links	850		225.00	225

Johnson - J. Johnson

YEAR ISSUE		EDITION LIMIT	YEAR RETD.	ISSUE PRICE	*QUOTE U.S.$
1994	Moose River	650		175.00	175
1994	Sea Treasures	650		125.00	125
1994	Winter Thaw	650		150.00	150
1993	Wolf Creek	550	N/A	165.00	200

Kennedy - S. Kennedy

YEAR ISSUE		EDITION LIMIT	YEAR RETD.	ISSUE PRICE	*QUOTE U.S.$
1988	After Dinner Music	2,500	N/A	175.00	250
1995	Alaskan Malamute	1,000		125.00	125
1992	Aurora	2,250	N/A	195.00	195
1991	A Breed Apart	2,750	N/A	225.00	225
1992	Cabin Fever	2,250		175.00	175
1988	Distant Relations	950	N/A	200.00	400
1988	Eager to Run	950	N/A	200.00	1700
1990	Fish Tales	5,500	N/A	225.00	225
1991	In Training	3,350	N/A	165.00	165
1991	In Training, remarque	150	N/A	215.50	216
1995	The Lesson	1,000		125.00	125
1993	Midnight Eyes	1,750		125.00	125
1993	Never Alone	2,250		225.00	225
1993	Never Alone, remarque	250	N/A	272.50	273
1990	On the Edge	4,000		225.00	225
1995	On the Heights	850		175.00	175
1994	Quiet Time Companions -Samoyed	1,000		125.00	125
1994	Quiet Time Companions -Siberian Husky	1,000	N/A	125.00	125
1994	Silent Observers	1,250	N/A	165.00	265
1989	Snowshoes	4,000	N/A	185.00	185
1994	Spruce and Fur	1,500		165.00	165
1995	Standing Watch	850		175.00	175
1993	The Touch	1,500		115.00	115
1989	Up a Creek	2,500	N/A	185.00	285

Kodera - C. Kodera

YEAR ISSUE		EDITION LIMIT	YEAR RETD.	ISSUE PRICE	*QUOTE U.S.$
1986	The A Team (K10)	850		145.00	145
1995	A.M. Sortie	1,000		225.00	225
1991	Darkness Visible (Stealth)	2,671	N/A	40.00	40
1987	Fifty Years a Lady	550	N/A	150.00	500
1988	The Great Greenwich Balloon Race	1,000		145.00	145
1990	Green Light-Jump!	650	N/A	145.00	200
1992	Halsey's Surprise	850		95.00	95
1994	Last to Fight	1,000		225.00	225
1995	Lonely Flight to Destiny	1,000	1995	347.00	347
1992	Looking For Nagumo	1,000		225.00	225
1992	Memphis Belle/Dauntless Dotty	1,250		245.00	245
1990	A Moment's Peace	1,250		150.00	150
1988	Moonlight Intruders	1,000		125.00	125
1995	Only One Survived	1,000		245.00	245
1989	Springtime Flying in the Rockies	550	N/A	95.00	95
1992	Thirty Seconds Over Tokyo	1,000	N/A	275.00	275
1991	This is No Drill w/Video	1,000		225.00	225
1994	This is No Time to Lose an Engine	850		150.00	150
1994	Tiger's Bite	850		150.00	150
1987	Voyager: The Skies Yield	1,500		225.00	225

Landry - P. Landry

YEAR ISSUE		EDITION LIMIT	YEAR RETD.	ISSUE PRICE	*QUOTE U.S.$
1993	The Antique Shop	1,250	N/A	125.00	125
1992	Apple Orchard	1,250		150.00	150
1992	Aunt Martha's Country Farm	1,500	N/A	185.00	300
1995	Autumn Market	1,000		185.00	185
1987	Bluenose Country	550	N/A	115.00	175
1992	Boardwalk Promenade	1,250		175.00	175
1989	A Canadian Christmas	1,250		125.00	125
1989	Cape Cod Welcome Cameo	850	N/A	75.00	300
1990	The Captain's Garden	1,000	N/A	165.00	350
1993	Christmas at Mystic Seaport	2,000		125.00	125
1992	Christmas at the Flower Market	2,500		125.00	125
1994	Christmas Carousel Pony	2,000		125.00	125
1990	Christmas Treasures	2,500		165.00	165
1992	Cottage Garden	1,250	N/A	160.00	160
1995	Cottage Reflections	850		135.00	135
1994	An English Cottage	850		150.00	150
1994	Flower Barn	1,000		175.00	175
1988	Flower Boxes	550	N/A	75.00	225
1991	Flower Market	1,500	N/A	185.00	800
1990	Flower Wagon	1,500	N/A	165.00	175

*Quotes have been rounded up to nearest dollar

GRAPHICS

YEAR ISSUE		EDITION LIMIT	YEAR RETD.	ISSUE PRICE	*QUOTE U.S.$
1994	Flowers For Mary Hope	1,250		165.00	165
1995	Harbor Garden	1,000		160.00	160
1993	Hometown Parade	1,250		165.00	165
1995	Lantern Skaters	1,500		135.00	135
1990	Morning Papers	1,250	N/A	135.00	200
1994	Morning Walk	850		135.00	135
1991	Nantucket Colors	1,500		150.00	150
1993	Paper Boy	1,500		150.00	150
1993	A Place in the Park	1,500		185.00	185
1984	Regatta	500	N/A	75.00	135
1984	Regatta, remarque	50	N/A	97.50	145
1990	Seaside Carousel	1,500	N/A	165.00	200
1988	Seaside Cottage	550	N/A	125.00	125
1986	Seaside Mist	450	N/A	85.00	300
1985	The Skaters	500		75.00	75
1985	The Skaters, remarque	50	N/A	97.50	98
1995	Spring Song	2,500		145.00	145
1991	Summer Concert	1,500		195.00	195
1989	Summer Garden	850	N/A	125.00	400
1995	Summer Mist (Fine Art Original Lithograph)	550		750.00	900
1992	Sunflowers	1,250	N/A	125.00	125
1991	The Toymaker	1,500	N/A	165.00	165
1991	Victorian Memories	1,500	N/A	150.00	150

Lovell - T. Lovell

YEAR ISSUE		EDITION LIMIT	YEAR RETD.	ISSUE PRICE	*QUOTE U.S.$
1988	The Battle of the Crater	1,500	N/A	225.00	225
1988	Berdan's Sharpshooters -Gettysburg	1,500		225.00	225
1986	Blackfeet Wall	450	N/A	325.00	325
1981	Carson's Boatyard	1,000		150.00	150
1985	Chiricahua Scout	650		90.00	90
1981	The Deceiver	1,000		150.00	150
1990	Dry Goods and Molasses	1,000		225.00	225
1981	Fires Along the Oregon Trail	1,000	N/A	150.00	150
1993	The Handwarmer	1,000		225.00	225
1988	The Hunter	1,000		150.00	150
1982	Invitation to Trade	1,000	N/A	150.00	150
1989	The Lost Rag Doll	1,000		225.00	225
1988	Mr. Bodmer's Music Box	5,000		40.00	40
1975	The Mud Owl's Warning	1,000	N/A	150.00	150
1988	North Country Rider	2,500		95.00	95
1976	Quicksand at Horsehead	1,000		150.00	150
1976	Shotgun Toll	1,000		150.00	150
1983	Sugar in The Coffee	650	N/A	165.00	165
1987	Surrender at Appomattox	1,000	N/A	225.00	225
1992	Target Practice	2,000		25.00	25
1976	Time of Cold-Maker	1,000		150.00	150
1989	Union Fleet Passing Vicksburg	1,500		225.00	225
1982	Walking Coyote & Buffalo Orphans	650	N/A	165.00	165
1982	The Wheelsoakers	1,000		150.00	150
1984	Winter Holiday	850		95.00	95
1989	Youth's Hour of Glory	1,500		175.00	175

Lyman - S. Lyman

YEAR ISSUE		EDITION LIMIT	YEAR RETD.	ISSUE PRICE	*QUOTE U.S.$
1990	Among The Wild Brambles	1,750	1990	185.00	185
1985	Autumn Gathering	850	N/A	115.00	115
1985	Bear & Blossoms (C)	850	N/A	75.00	450
1987	Canadian Autumn	1,500	1987	165.00	300
1995	Cathedral Snow	4,000		245.00	245
1989	Color In The Snow (Pheasant)	1,500	N/A	165.00	300
1991	Dance of Cloud and Cliff	1,500	1991	225.00	225
1991	Dance of Water and Light	3,000	1991	225.00	225
1983	Early Winter In The Mountains	850	N/A	95.00	350
1987	An Elegant Couple (Wood Ducks)	1,000	N/A	125.00	125
1991	Embers at Dawn	3,500	1991	225.00	1150
1983	End Of The Ridge	850	N/A	95.00	450
1990	Evening Light	2,500	1990	225.00	1550
1995	Evening Star w/collector's edition book	9,500	1995	195.00	370
1993	Fire Dance	8,500	1993	235.00	400
1984	Free Flight	850		70.00	70
1987	High Creek Crossing	1,000	N/A	165.00	850
1989	High Light	1,250	1989	165.00	300
1986	High Trail At Sunset	1,000	N/A	125.00	420
1988	The Intruder	1,500	N/A	150.00	150
1993	Lake of the Shining Rocks	2,250	1993	235.00	250
1992	Lantern Light Print w Firelight Chapbook	10,000	1993	195.00	195
1989	Last Light of Winter	1,500	1989	175.00	900
1995	Midnight Fire	8,500		245.00	245
1994	Moon Fire	7,500	1994	245.00	525-650
1987	Moon Shadows	1,500	N/A	135.00	135
1994	Moonlit Flight on Christmas Night	2,750	1994	165.00	250
1986	Morning Solitude	850	N/A	115.00	600
1990	A Mountain Campfire	1,500	1990	195.00	2050-2200
1994	New Kid on the Rock	2,250		185.00	185
1987	New Territory (Grizzly & Cubs)	1,000	N/A	135.00	135
1984	Noisy Neighbors	675	N/A	95.00	500
1984	Noisy Neighbors, remarque	25	N/A	127.50	1800
1994	North Country Shores	3,000	1994	225.00	225
1983	The Pass	850	N/A	95.00	550
1989	Quiet Rain	1,500	N/A	165.00	700
1988	The Raptor's Watch	1,500	N/A	150.00	500
1988	Return Of The Falcon	1,500	N/A	150.00	200
1993	Riparian Riches	2,500	1993	235.00	250
1992	River of Light (Geese)	2,950	N/A	225.00	225
1991	Secret Watch (Lynx)	2,250		150.00	150
1990	Silent Snows	1,750	N/A	210.00	210
1988	Snow Hunter	1,500	N/A	135.00	135
1986	Snowy Throne (C)	850	N/A	85.00	300
1993	The Spirit of Christmas	2,750	1993	165.00	250

YEAR ISSUE		EDITION LIMIT	YEAR RETD.	ISSUE PRICE	*QUOTE U.S.$
1995	Thunderbolt	7,000		235.00	235
1987	Twilight Snow (C)	950	N/A	85.00	150
1988	Uzumati: Great Bear of Yosemite	1,750	N/A	150.00	600
1992	Warmed by the View	8,500	1992	235.00	325
1992	Wilderness Welcome	8,500	N/A	235.00	450-550
1992	Wildflower Suite (Hummingbird)	2,250		175.00	175
1992	Woodland Haven	2,500	N/A	195.00	255

Marris - B. Marris

YEAR ISSUE		EDITION LIMIT	YEAR RETD.	ISSUE PRICE	*QUOTE U.S.$
1987	Above the Glacier	850	N/A	145.00	145
1986	Best Friends	850	N/A	85.00	300
1994	Big Gray's Barn and Bistro	1,000		125.00	125
1989	Bittersweet	1,000	N/A	135.00	135
1990	Bugles and Trumpets!	1,000	N/A	175.00	175
1992	The Comeback	1,250		175.00	175
1991	Cops & Robbers	1,000	N/A	165.00	165
1988	Courtship	850	N/A	145.00	145
1995	Dairy Queens	1,000		125.00	125
1995	The Dartmoor Ponies	1,000		165.00	165
1987	Desperados	850	N/A	135.00	135
1991	End of the Season	1,000		165.00	165
1985	The Fishing Lesson	1,000		145.00	145
1995	The Gift	1,000		125.00	125
1987	Honey Creek Whitetales	850	N/A	145.00	145
1985	Kenai Dusk	1,000	N/A	145.00	900
1994	Lady Marmalade's Bed & Breakfast	1,000		125.00	125
1990	Mom's Shadow	1,000		165.00	165
1994	Moonshine	1,000		95.00	95
1989	New Beginnings	1,000	N/A	175.00	400
1990	Of Myth and Magic	1,500	N/A	175.00	175
1986	Other Footsteps	950		75.00	75
1989	The Playgroud Showoff	850	N/A	165.00	165
1992	Security Blanket	1,250		175.00	175
1993	Spring Fever	1,000		165.00	165
1991	The Stillness (Grizzly & Cubs)	1,000	N/A	165.00	165
1992	Sun Bath	1,000		95.00	95
1992	To Stand and Endure	1,000	N/A	195.00	275
1991	Under the Morning Star	1,500		175.00	175
1988	Waiting For the Freeze	1,000	N/A	125.00	125
1995	Where Best Friends Are Welcome	850	1996	95.00	95

McCarthy, Frank - F. McCarthy

YEAR ISSUE		EDITION LIMIT	YEAR RETD.	ISSUE PRICE	*QUOTE U.S.$
1984	After the Dust Storm	1,000	N/A	145.00	145
1982	Alert	1,000	N/A	135.00	135
1984	Along the West Fork	1,000	N/A	175.00	200
1995	Ambush at the Ancient Rocks	1,000		225.00	225
1978	Ambush, The	1,000	N/A	125.00	300
1982	Apache Scout	1,000	N/A	165.00	165
1988	Apache Trackers (C)	1,000	N/A	95.00	95
1992	The Art of Frank McCarthy	10,418	N/A	60.00	60
1982	Attack on the Wagon Train	1,400	N/A	150.00	150
1977	The Beaver Men	1,000	N/A	75.00	400
1980	Before the Charge	1,000	N/A	115.00	200
1978	Before the Norther	1,000	N/A	90.00	325
1990	Below The Breaking Dawn	1,250	N/A	225.00	225
1994	Beneath the Cliff (Petraglyphs)	1,500		295.00	295
1989	Big Medicine	1,000	N/A	225.00	400
1983	Blackfeet Raiders	1,000	N/A	90.00	300
1992	Breaking the Moonlit Silence	650	N/A	375.00	300-375
1986	The Buffalo Runners	1,000	N/A	195.00	170
1980	Burning the Way Station	1,000	N/A	125.00	350
1993	By the Ancient Trails They Passed	1,000	N/A	245.00	245
1989	Canyon Lands	1,250	N/A	225.00	225
1982	The Challenge	1,000	N/A	175.00	300
1995	Charge of the Buffalo Soldiers	1,000	1995	195.00	195
1985	Charging the Challenger	1,000	N/A	150.00	550
1991	The Chase	1,000		225.00	225
1986	Children of the Raven	1,000	N/A	185.00	550
1987	Chiricahua Raiders	1,000	N/A	165.00	200
1977	Comanche Moon	1,000	N/A	75.00	250
1992	Comanche Raider-Bronze	100		812.50	813
1986	Comanche War Trail	1,000	N/A	165.00	170
1989	The Coming Of The Iron Horse	1,500	N/A	225.00	225
1989	The Coming Of The Iron Horse (Print/Pewter Train Special Publ. Ed.)	100	N/A	1500.00	1600-2150
1981	The Coup	1,000	N/A	125.00	250
1981	Crossing the Divide (The Old West)	1,500	N/A	850.00	700
1984	The Decoys	450	N/A	325.00	500
1977	Distant Thunder	1,500	N/A	75.00	600
1989	Down From The Mountains	1,500	N/A	245.00	245
1986	The Drive (C)	1,000	N/A	95.00	95-175
1977	Dust Stained Posse	1,000	N/A	75.00	700
1985	The Fireboat	1,000	N/A	175.00	200
1994	Flashes of Lighting-Thunder of Hooves	550		435.00	435
1987	Following the Herds	1,000	N/A	195.00	250
1980	Forbidden Land	1,000	N/A	125.00	125
1978	The Fording	1,000	N/A	75.00	300
1987	From the Rim	1,000	N/A	225.00	225
1981	Headed North	1,000	N/A	150.00	225
1992	Heading Back	1,000		225.00	200-225
1995	His Wealth	850		225.00	225
1990	Hoka Hey: Sioux War Cry	1,250		225.00	225
1987	The Hostile Land	1,000	N/A	225.00	235
1976	The Hostiles	1,000	N/A	75.00	400
1984	Hostiles, signed	1,000	N/A	55.00	55
1974	The Hunt	1,000	N/A	75.00	575
1988	In Pursuit of the White Buffalo	1,500	N/A	225.00	600
1992	In the Land of the Ancient Ones	1,250	N/A	245.00	245
1983	In The Land Of The Sparrow Hawk People	1,000	N/A	165.00	180
1987	In The Land Of The Winter Hawk	1,000	N/A	225.00	225

YEAR ISSUE		EDITION LIMIT	YEAR RETD.	ISSUE PRICE	*QU
1978	In The Pass	1,500	N/A	90.00	
1985	The Last Crossing	550	N/A	350.00	
1989	The Last Stand: Little Big Horn	1,500	N/A	225.00	
1984	Leading the Charge, signed	1,000	N/A	55.00	
1974	Lone Sentinel	1,000		55.00	
1979	The Loner	1,000	N/A	75.00	
1974	Long Column	1,000		75.00	
1985	The Long Knives	1,000	N/A	175.00	
1989	Los Diablos	1,250	N/A	225.00	
1995	Medicine Man	850		165.00	
1983	Moonlit Trail	1,000	N/A	90.00	
1992	Navajo Ponies Comanchie Warriors	1,000		225.00	
1978	Night Crossing	1,000	N/A	75.00	
1974	The Night They Needed a Good Ribbon Man	1,000	N/A	65.00	
1977	An Old Time Mountain Man	1,000	N/A	65.00	
1990	On The Old North Trail (Triptych)	650	N/A	550.00	
1979	On the Warpath	1,000	N/A	75.00	
1983	Out Of The Mist They Came	1,000	N/A	165.00	
1990	Out Of The Windswept Ramparts	1,250		225.00	
1976	Packing In	1,000	N/A	65.00	
1991	Pony Express	1,000		225.00	
1979	The Prayer	1,500	N/A	90.00	
1991	The Pursuit	650	N/A	550.00	
1981	Race with the Hostiles	1,000	N/A	135.00	
1987	Red Bull's War Party	1,000	N/A	165.00	
1979	Retreat to Higher Ground	2,000	N/A	90.00	
1975	Returning Raiders	1,000	N/A	75.00	
1980	Roar of the Norther	1,000	N/A	90.00	
1977	Robe Signal	850	N/A	60.00	
1988	Saber Charge	2,250		225.00	225
1984	The Savage Taunt	1,000	N/A	225.00	
1985	Scouting The Long Knives	1,400	N/A	195.00	
1993	Shadows of Warriors (3 Print Suite)	1,000		225.00	
1994	Show of Defiance	1,000		195.00	
1993	Sighting the Intruders	1,000		225.00	
1978	Single File	1,000	N/A	75.00	
1976	Sioux Warriors	650	N/A	55.00	
1975	Smoke Was Their Ally	1,000	N/A	75.00	
1980	Snow Moon	1,000	N/A	115.00	
1995	Splitting the Herd	550		465.00	
1986	Spooked	1,400	N/A	195.00	
1981	Surrounded	1,000	N/A	150.00	195-
1975	The Survivor	1,000	N/A	65.00	
1980	A Time Of Decision	1,150	N/A	125.00	
1978	To Battle	1,000	N/A	75.00	
1985	The Traders	1,000	N/A	195.00	
1980	The Trooper	1,000	N/A	90.00	
1988	Turning The Leaders	1,500	N/A	225.00	
1983	Under Attack	5,676	N/A	125.00	
1981	Under Hostile Fire	1,000	N/A	150.00	
1975	Waiting for the Escort	1,000	N/A	75.00	
1976	The Warrior	650	N/A	55.00	
1982	The Warriors	1,000	N/A	150.00	
1984	Watching the Wagons	1,400	N/A	175.00	
1995	The Way of the Ancient Migrations	1,250		245.00	
1987	When Omens Turn Bad	1,000	N/A	165.00	
1992	When the Land Was Theirs	1,000		225.00	
1992	Where Ancient Ones Had Hunted	1,000	N/A	245.00	
1992	Where Others Had Passed	1,000	N/A	245.00	
1986	Where Tracks Will Be Lost	550	N/A	350.00	
1982	Whirling He Raced to Meet the Challenge	1,000	N/A	175.00	
1991	The Wild Ones	1,000	N/A	225.00	
1990	Winter Trail	1,500	N/A	235.00	
1993	With Pistols Drawn	1,000		195.00	

Mitchell - D. Mitchell

YEAR ISSUE		EDITION LIMIT	YEAR RETD.	ISSUE PRICE	*QU
1994	Bonding Years	550		175.00	
1993	Country Church	550		175.00	
1995	Innocence	1,000		150.00	
1995	Let Us Pray	850		175.00	
1993	Psalms 4:1	550	N/A	195.00	
1992	Rowena	550	N/A	195.00	

Mo Da-Feng - M. Da-Feng

YEAR ISSUE		EDITION LIMIT	YEAR RETD.	ISSUE PRICE	*QU
1990	Family Boat	888		235.00	
1993	First Journey	650		150.00	
1989	Fishing Hut	888		235.00	
1994	Ocean Mist	850		150.00	

Parker, E. - E. Parker

YEAR ISSUE		EDITION LIMIT	YEAR RETD.	ISSUE PRICE	*QU
1995	The Glorious 4th	850		150.00	
1995	A Visit From St. Nicholas	850		125.00	

Parker, R. - R. Parker

YEAR ISSUE		EDITION LIMIT	YEAR RETD.	ISSUE PRICE	*QU
1995	The Breakfast Club	850		125.00	
1995	Coastal Morning	850		195.00	
1995	Evening Solitude	850		195.00	
1994	Forest Flight	850		195.00	
1994	Grizzlies at the Falls	850		225.00	
1994	Morning Flight	4,000		20.00	
1995	Tea For Two	850		125.00	

Phillips - W. Phillips

YEAR ISSUE		EDITION LIMIT	YEAR RETD.	ISSUE PRICE	*QU
1982	Advantage Eagle	1,000	N/A	135.00	
1992	Alone No More	850		195.00	
1988	America on the Move	1,500	N/A	185.00	
1994	Among the Columns of Thor	1,000		295.00	
1993	And Now the Trap	850		175.00	
1986	Changing of the Guard	500		100.00	

GRAPHICS

YEAR ISSUE		EDITION LIMIT	YEAR RETD.	ISSUE PRICE	*QUOTE U.S. $
1993	Chasing the Daylight	850		185.00	185
1994	Christmas Leave When Dreams Come True	1,500	N/A	185.00	230
1986	Confrontation at Beachy Head	1,000		150.00	150
1991	Dauntless Against a Rising Sun	850	N/A	195.00	195
1995	The Dream Fulfilled	1,750		195.00	195
1991	Fifty Miles Out	1,000		175.00	175
1983	The Giant Begins to Stir	1,250	N/A	185.00	1800
1990	Going in Hot w/Book	1,500		250.00	250
1985	Heading For Trouble	1,000	N/A	125.00	250
1984	Hellfire Corner	1,225	N/A	185.00	500
1984	Hellfire Corner, remarque	25	N/A	225.80	800
1990	Hunter Becomes the Hunted w/video	1,500		265.00	265
1992	I Could Never Be So Lucky Again	850	N/A	295.00	750
1993	If Only in My Dreams	1,000	N/A	175.00	400
1984	Into the Teeth of the Tiger	975	N/A	135.00	1000
1984	Into the Teeth of the Tiger, remarque	25	N/A	167.50	2000
1994	Into the Throne Room of God w/book "The Glory of Flight"	750	N/A	195.00	400
1991	Intruder Outbound	1,000		225.00	225
1991	Last Chance	1,000	N/A	165.00	225
1985	Lest We Forget	1,250	N/A	195.00	195
1994	Lethal Encounter	1,000		225.00	225
1988	The Long Green Line	3,500		185.00	185
1992	The Long Ride Home (P-51D)	850	N/A	195.00	195
1991	Low Pass For the Home Folks, BP	1,000	N/A	175.00	175
1986	Next Time Get 'Em All	1,500	N/A	225.00	300
1989	No Empty Bunks Tonight	1,500	N/A	165.00	165
1989	No Flying Today	1,500		185.00	185
1989	Over the Top	1,000		165.00	165
1985	The Phantoms and the Wizard	850	N/A	145.00	800
1992	Ploesti: Into the Fire and Fury	850		195.00	195
1987	Range Wars	1,000		160.00	160
1987	Shore Birds at Point Lobos	1,250	N/A	175.00	175
1989	Sierra Hotel	1,250	N/A	175.00	175
1995	Summer of '45	1,750		195.00	195
1987	Sunward We Climb	1,000		175.00	175
1983	Those Clouds Won't Help You Now	625	N/A	135.00	300
1983	Those Clouds Won't Help You Now, remarque	25	N/A	275.00	325
1987	Those Last Critical Moments	1,250	N/A	185.00	300
1993	Threading the Eye of the Needle	1,000		195.00	195
1986	Thunder in the Canyon	1,000	N/A	165.00	650
1990	A Time of Eagles	1,250		245.00	245
1989	Time to Head Home	1,500		165.00	165
1986	Top Cover for the Straggler	1,000	N/A	145.00	210
1983	Two Down, One to Go	3,000	N/A	15.00	15
1982	Welcome Home Yank	1,000	N/A	135.00	850
1993	When Prayers are Answered	850		245.00	245
1991	When You See Zeros, Fight Em'	1,000		N/A	200

Reynolds - J. Reynolds

YEAR ISSUE		EDITION LIMIT	YEAR RETD.	ISSUE PRICE	*QUOTE U.S. $
1994	Arizona Cowboys	850	N/A	195.00	225
1994	Cold Country, Hot Coffee	1,000		185.00	185
1994	The Henry	850	N/A	195.00	195
1995	Mystic of the Plains	1,000		195.00	195
1994	Quiet Place	1,000	N/A	185.00	185
1994	Spring Showers	1,000		225.00	225
1996	The Summit	950		195.00	195

Simpkins - J. Simpkins

YEAR ISSUE		EDITION LIMIT	YEAR RETD.	ISSUE PRICE	*QUOTE U.S. $
1994	All My Love	850		125.00	125
1993	Angels	850		225.00	225
1994	Gold Falls	1,750		195.00	195
1995	Mrs. Tenderhart	1,000		175.00	175
1995	Pavane in Gold	2,500		175.00	175
1994	Reverence For Life w/border & card	750	N/A	175.00	335
1994	Reverence For Life w/frame	100	N/A	600.00	600
1995	Where Love Resides (Premiere Ed.)	1,000		450.00	450
1995	Where Love Resides (Studio Ed.)	1,000		225.00	225

Smith - T. Smith

YEAR ISSUE		EDITION LIMIT	YEAR RETD.	ISSUE PRICE	*QUOTE U.S. $
1992	The Challenger	1,300		185.00	185
1995	The Refuge	1,000		245.00	245

Terpning - H. Terpning

YEAR ISSUE		EDITION LIMIT	YEAR RETD.	ISSUE PRICE	*QUOTE U.S. $
1992	Against the Coldmaker	1,000	1992	195.00	195
1993	The Apache Fire Makers	1,000	1993	235.00	235
1993	Army Regulations	1,000		235.00	235
1987	Blackfeet Among the Aspen	1,000	1987	225.00	300
1985	Blackfeet Spectators	475	1985	350.00	1100
1988	Blood Man	1,250	1988	95.00	365
1982	CA Set Pony Soldiers/Warriors	1,000	1982	200.00	400
1985	The Cache	1,000		175.00	175
1992	Capture of the Horse Bundle	1,250		235.00	235
1982	Chief Joseph Rides to Surrender	1,000	1982	150.00	3000
1986	Comanche Spoilers	1,000		195.00	195
1990	Cree Finery	1,000		225.00	225
1983	Crossing Medicine Lodge Creek	1,000	1983	150.00	550
1994	Crow Camp, 1864	1,000	1994	235.00	235
1984	Crow Pipe Holder	1,000		150.00	150
1991	Digging in at Sappa Creek MW	650	1991	375.00	375
1994	The Feast	1,850	1994	245.00	245
1992	Four Sacred Drummers	1,000	1992	225.00	225
1988	Hope Springs Eternal-Ghost Dance	2,250		225.00	400
1994	Isdzan-Apache Woman	1,000	1994	175.00	175
1991	The Last Buffalo	1,000		225.00	225
1991	Leader of Men	1,250	1991	235.00	235
1984	The Long Shot, signed	1,000	1984	55.00	55
1984	Medicine Man of the Cheyene	450	1984	350.00	3000
1993	Medicine Pipe	1,000	1993	150.00	175
1985	One Man's Castle	1,000		150.00	150
1995	Opening the Sacred Bundle	550	1995	850.00	850
1983	Paints	1,000	1983	140.00	250
1992	Passing Into Womanhood	650	1992	375.00	500
1987	The Ploy	1,000	1987	195.00	1250
1992	Prairie Knights	1,000	1992	225.00	225
1996	Prairie Shade	1,000		225.00	225
1987	Preparing for the Sun Dance	1,000	1987	175.00	270
1988	Pride of the Cheyene	1,250		195.00	195
1993	Profile of Wisdom	1,000		175.00	175
1989	Scout's Report	1,250		225.00	225
1985	The Scouts of General Crook	1,000	1985	175.00	250
1988	Search For the Pass	1,000	1988	225.00	270
1982	Search For the Renegades	1,000	1982	150.00	150
1989	Shepherd of the Plains Cameo	1,250		125.00	125
1982	Shield of Her Husband	1,000	1982	150.00	900
1983	Shoshonis	1,250	1983	85.00	225
1985	The Signal	1,250	1985	90.00	650
1981	Sioux Flag Carrier	1,000	1981	125.00	125
1981	Small Comfort	1,000	1981	135.00	450
1993	Soldier Hat	1,000		235.00	235
1981	The Spectators	1,000	1981	135.00	250
1994	Spirit of the Rainmaker	1,500		235.00	235
1983	Staff Carrier	1,250	1983	90.00	700
1986	Status Symbols	1,000	1986	185.00	1450
1981	Stones that Speak	1,000	1981	150.00	1000
1989	The Storyteller w/Video & Book	1,500	1989	950.00	950
1992	The Strength of Eagles	1,250		235.00	235
1988	Sunday Best	1,250		195.00	195
1995	Talking Robe	1,250		235.00	235
1990	Telling of the Legends	1,250	1990	225.00	900
1986	Thunderpipe and the Holy Man	550	1986	350.00	550
1995	Trading Post at Chadron Creek	1,000		225.00	225
1991	Transferring the Medicine Shield	850	1991	375.00	1500
1981	The Victors	1,000	1981	150.00	750
1985	The Warning	1,650	1985	175.00	500
1986	Watching the Column	1,250	1986	90.00	90
1990	When Careless Spelled Disaster	1,000	1990	225.00	350
1987	Winter Coat	1,250	1987	95.00	95
1996	With Mother Earth	1,250		245.00	245
1984	Woman of the Sioux	1,000	1984	165.00	1100

Townsend - B. Townsend

YEAR ISSUE		EDITION LIMIT	YEAR RETD.	ISSUE PRICE	*QUOTE U.S. $
1994	Autumn Hillside	1,000		175.00	175
1993	Dusk	1,250		195.00	195
1995	Gathering of the Herd	1,000		195.00	195
1993	Hailstorm Creek	1,250		195.00	195
1994	Mountain Light	1,000		195.00	195
1992	Open Ridge	1,500	N/A	225.00	225
1993	Out of the Shadows	1,500		195.00	195
1992	Riverbend	1,000	N/A	185.00	335

Weiss - J. Weiss

YEAR ISSUE		EDITION LIMIT	YEAR RETD.	ISSUE PRICE	*QUOTE U.S. $
1995	All Is Well	1,250		165.00	165
1984	Basset Hound Puppies	1,000	N/A	65.00	65
1988	Black Labrador Head Study Cameo	1,000		90.00	90
1984	Cocker Spaniel Puppies	1,000	N/A	75.00	265
1992	Cuddle Time	850		95.00	95
1993	A Feeling of Warmth	1,000	N/A	165.00	300
1994	Forever Friends	1,000	1994	95.00	200
1983	Golden Retriever Puppies	1,000	N/A	65.00	600
1988	Goldens at the Shore	850	N/A	145.00	500
1995	I Didn't Do It	1,250		125.00	125
1982	Lab Puppies	1,000	N/A	65.00	65
1992	No Swimming Lessons Today	1,000		140.00	140
1984	Old English Sheepdog Puppies	1,000	N/A	65.00	240
1993	Old Friends	1,000	1993	95.00	200
1986	One Morning in October	850	N/A	125.00	340
1985	Persian Kitten	1,000	N/A	65.00	65
1982	Rebel & Soda	1,000	N/A	45.00	90
1991	Wake Up Call	850		165.00	165
1988	Yellow Labrador Head Study Cameo	1,000		90.00	90

Williams - B.D. Williams

YEAR ISSUE		EDITION LIMIT	YEAR RETD.	ISSUE PRICE	*QUOTE U.S. $
1993	Avant Garde S&N	500	N/A	60.00	60
1993	Avant Garde unsigned	2,603	N/A	30.00	30

Wootton - F. Wootton

YEAR ISSUE		EDITION LIMIT	YEAR RETD.	ISSUE PRICE	*QUOTE U.S. $
1990	Adlertag, 15 August 1940 & Video	1,500	N/A	245.00	245
1993	April Morning:France, 1918	850		245.00	245
1983	The Battle of Britain	850	N/A	150.00	350
1988	Encounter with the Red Baron	850	N/A	165.00	165
1985	Huntsmen and Hounds	650		115.00	115
1982	Knights of the Sky	850	N/A	165.00	400
1993	Last Combat of the Red Baron	850		185.00	185
1992	The Last of the First F. Wooten	850		235.00	235
1994	Peenemunde	850		245.00	245
1986	The Spitfire Legend	850	N/A	195.00	195

Wysocki - C. Wysocki

YEAR ISSUE		EDITION LIMIT	YEAR RETD.	ISSUE PRICE	*QUOTE U.S. $
1987	'Twas the Twilight Before Christmas	7,500	N/A	95.00	150
1988	The Americana Bowl	3,500		295.00	295
1983	Amish Neighbors	1,000	N/A	150.00	1200
1989	Another Year At Sea	2,500	N/A	175.00	500
1983	Applebutter Makers	1,000	N/A	135.00	600
1987	Bach's Magnificat in D Minor	2,250	N/A	150.00	700
1991	Beauty And The Beast	2,000	N/A	125.00	125
1990	Belly Warmers	2,500		150.00	195-200
1984	Bird House Cameo	1,000	N/A	85.00	450
1985	Birds of a Feather	1,250	N/A	145.00	400
1989	Bostonians And Beans (PC)	6,711	N/A	225.00	650-750
1979	Butternut Farms	1,000	N/A	75.00	1000
1980	Caleb's Buggy Barn	1,000	N/A	80.00	300
1984	Cape Cod Cold Fish Party	1,000	N/A	150.00	150
1986	Carnival Capers	620		200.00	200
1981	Carver Coggins	1,000	N/A	145.00	900
1989	Christmas Greeting	11,000	N/A	125.00	100
1982	Christmas Print, 1982	2,000	N/A	80.00	700
1984	Chumbuddies, signed	1,000		55.00	55
1985	Clammers at Hodge's Horn	1,000	N/A	150.00	1500
1983	Commemorative Print, 1983	2,000	N/A	55.00	55
1983	Commemorative Print, 1984	2,000		55.00	55
1984	Commemorative Print, 1985	2,000		55.00	55
1985	Commemorative Print, 1986	2,000		55.00	55
1984	Cotton Country	1,000	N/A	150.00	200
1983	Country Race	1,000	N/A	150.00	400
1986	Daddy's Coming Home	1,250	N/A	150.00	1200
1987	Dahalia Dinalhaven Makes a Dory Deal	2,250	N/A	150.00	250
1986	Dancing Pheasant Farms	1,750	N/A	165.00	400
1980	Derby Square	1,000	N/A	90.00	1100
1986	Devilbelly Bay	1,000	N/A	145.00	300
1986	Devilstone Harbor/An American Celebration (Print & Book)	3,500	N/A	195.00	400
1989	Dreamers	3,000		175.00	350
1992	Ethel the Gourmet	10,179	N/A	150.00	375
1979	Fairhaven by the Sea	1,000	N/A	75.00	700
1988	Feathered Critics	2,500		150.00	150
1979	Fox Run	1,000	N/A	75.00	1600
1984	The Foxy Fox Outfoxes the Fox Hunters	1,500	N/A	150.00	600
1992	Frederick the Literate	6,500	N/A	150.00	2100-2500
1989	Fun Lovin' Silly Folks	3,000	N/A	185.00	300
1984	The Gang's All Here	Open		65.00	65
1984	The Gang's All Here, remarque	250		90.00	90
1992	Gay Head Light	2,500		165.00	165
1986	Hickory Haven Canal	1,500	N/A	165.00	1000
1988	Home Is My Sailor	2,500	N/A	150.00	150
1985	I Love America	2,000		20.00	20
1990	Jingle Bell Teddy and Friends	5,000		125.00	125
1980	Jolly Hill Farms	1,000	N/A	75.00	750
1986	Lady Liberty's Independence Day Enterprising Immigrants	1,500	N/A	140.00	300
1992	Love Letter From Laramie	1,500		150.00	150
1989	The Memory Maker	2,500		165.00	165
1985	Merrymakers Serenade	1,250	N/A	135.00	135
1986	Mr. Swallobark	2,000	N/A	145.00	1200
1982	The Nantucket	1,000	N/A	145.00	400
1981	Olde America	1,500	N/A	125.00	650
1981	Page's Bake Shoppe	1,000	N/A	115.00	450
1983	Plum Island Sound, signed	1,000	N/A	55.00	55
1983	Plum Island Sound, unsigned	Open	N/A	40.00	40
1981	Prairie Wind Flowers	1,000	N/A	125.00	1600
1992	Proud Little Angler	2,750	N/A	150.00	250
1994	Remington w/Book-Heartland	15,000		195.00	195
1990	Robin Hood	2,000		165.00	165
1991	Rockland Breakwater Light	2,500		165.00	280
1985	Salty Witch Bay	475	N/A	350.00	2400
1991	Sea Captain's Wife Abiding	1,500	N/A	150.00	150
1979	Shall We?	1,000	N/A	75.00	1000
1982	Sleepy Town West	1,500	N/A	150.00	500
1984	Storin' Up	450	N/A	325.00	1000
1982	Sunset Hills, Texas Wildcatters	1,000	N/A	125.00	150
1984	Sweetheart Chessmate	1,000	N/A	95.00	1200
1983	Tea by the Sea	1,000	N/A	145.00	1500
1993	The Three Sisters of Nauset, 1880	2,500	N/A	165.00	350
1984	A Warm Christmas Love	3,951	N/A	80.00	350
1990	Wednesday Night Checkers	2,500		175.00	175
1991	West Quoddy Head Light, Maine	2,500		165.00	165
1990	Where The Bouys Are	2,750	N/A	175.00	200
1991	Whistle Stop Christmas	5,000		125.00	125
1980	Yankee Wink Hollow	1,000	N/A	95.00	1300
1987	Yearning For My Captain	2,000	N/A	150.00	260
1987	You've Been So Long at Sea, Horatio	2,500	N/A	150.00	200

Guildhall, Inc.

DeHaan - C. DeHaan

YEAR ISSUE		EDITION LIMIT	YEAR RETD.	ISSUE PRICE	*QUOTE U.S. $
1992	73º In Amarillo...Yesterday	925		140.00	140
1993	Appeasing The Water People	925		150.00	150
1993	As The Buffalo Leave	925		150.00	150
1983	Crossin' Horse Creek	650		100.00	625
1992	Crossing At The Big Trees	925		140.00	200
1990	Crow Autumn	925		135.00	250
1987	Crow Ceremonial Dress	750		100.00	175
1989	Crows	800		135.00	525
1991	The Encounter	925		140.00	300
1990	Escape	925		135.00	200
1979	Foggy Mornin' Wait	650		75.00	2525
1981	Forgin' The Keechi	650		85.00	725
1993	Goosed	925		150.00	150
1990	High Plains Drifters	925		140.00	200
1985	Horsemen of the West (Suite of 3)	650		145.00	975
1984	Jake	650		100.00	600
1985	Keechi Country	750		100.00	375
1983	Keep A Movin' Dan	750		85.00	125
1989	Kentucky Blue	750		125.00	575
1986	The Loner (with matching buckle)	750		145.00	425

*Quotes have been rounded up to nearest dollar

YEAR ISSUE		EDITION LIMIT	YEAR RETD.	ISSUE PRICE	*QUOTE U.S.$
1981	MacTavish	650		75.00	1000
1986	Moon Dancers	750		100.00	165
1988	Mornin' Gather	750		100.00	350
1987	Murphy's Law	750		100.00	225
1986	The Mustangers	750		100.00	400
1982	O' That Strawberry Roan	750		85.00	125
1985	Oklahoma Paints	750		100.00	425
1990	The Pipe Carrier	925		140.00	175
1991	The Prideful Ones (Set/2)	925		150.00	200
1989	The Quarter Horse	800		125.00	325
1993	The Return	925		150.00	150
1983	Ridin' Ol' Paint	750		85.00	625
1986	The Searchers	650		100.00	375
1992	Silent Trail Talk	925		140.00	175
1987	Snow Birds	750		100.00	350
1984	Spooked	650		95.00	1825
1988	Stage To Deadwood	750		100.00	275
1991	Sundance	925		140.00	175
1987	Supremacy	750		100.00	175
1981	Surprise Encounter	750		85.00	475
1980	Texas Panhandle	650		75.00	1525
1985	Up the Chisholm	750		85.00	125
1989	Village Markers	750		125.00	525
1990	War Cry	925		135.00	275
1988	Water Breakin'	750		125.00	600

Hadley House

Capser - M. Capser

YEAR ISSUE		EDITION LIMIT	YEAR RETD.	ISSUE PRICE	*QUOTE U.S.$
1993	Briar and Brambles	999		100.00	100
1992	Comes the Dawn	600		100.00	100
1994	Dashing Through the Snow	999		100.00	100
1994	Down the Lane	Open		30.00	30
1995	Enchanted Waters	999		100.00	100
1995	Grapevine Estates	999		100.00	100
1994	The Lifting Fog	Open		30.00	30
1995	Mariner's Point	999		100.00	100
1994	Nappin'	999		100.00	100
1994	A Night's Quiet	999		100.00	100
1995	On Gentle Wings	999		100.00	100
1993	Pickets & Vines	999	1994	100.00	100
1992	Reflections	600	1993	100.00	100
1993	Rock Creek Spring	999		80.00	80
1994	September Blush	999		100.00	100
1992	Silence Unbroken	600		100.00	100
1993	Skyline Serenade	600	1993	100.00	100
1995	Spring Creek Fever	999		100.00	100
1993	A Summer's Glow	999		60.00	60
1994	A Time For Us	999		125.00	125
1994	To Search Again	Open		30.00	30
1992	The Watch	600	1993	100.00	150
1994	The Way Home	Open		30.00	30
1993	Whispering Wings	1,500	1994	100.00	100

Franca - O. Franca

YEAR ISSUE		EDITION LIMIT	YEAR RETD.	ISSUE PRICE	*QUOTE U.S.$
1988	The Apache	950	1990	70.00	175
1990	Blue Navajo	1,500	1991	125.00	210
1990	Blue Tranquility	999	1990	100.00	100
1988	Cacique	950	1990	70.00	175
1990	Cecy	1,500	1992	125.00	225
1990	Destiny	999	1990	100.00	100
1991	Early Morning	3,600		125.00	225
1993	Evening In Taos	4,000		80.00	80
1988	Feathered Hair Ties	600	1988	80.00	300
1990	Feathered Hair Ties II	999	1990	100.00	300
1991	The Lovers	2,400	1991	125.00	900
1991	The Model	1,500	1991	125.00	400
1992	Navajo Daydream	3,600	1993	175.00	425
1989	Navajo Fantasy	999	1989	80.00	150
1992	Navajo Meditating	4,000		80.00	125
1992	Navajo Reflection	4,000	1992	80.00	225
1990	Navajo Summer	999	1988	100.00	240
1991	Olympia	1,500	1991	125.00	250
1989	Pink Navajo	999	1989	80.00	250
1988	The Red Shawl	600	1990	80.00	300
1991	Red Wolf	1,500	1991	125.00	225
1990	Santa Fe	1,500	1991	125.00	300
1988	Sitting Bull	950	1990	70.00	250
1988	Slow Bull	950	1990	70.00	250
1990	Turqoise Necklace	999	1990	100.00	450
1990	Wind Song	999	1990	100.00	425
1992	Wind Song II	4,000	1992	80.00	150
1989	Winter	999	1989	80.00	220
1989	Young Warrior	999	1989	80.00	425

Hanks - S. Hanks

YEAR ISSUE		EDITION LIMIT	YEAR RETD.	ISSUE PRICE	*QUOTE U.S.$
1994	All Gone Awry	2,000		150.00	150
1994	All In a Row	2,000	1994	150.00	150
1995	A Captive Audience	1,500		150.00	150
1995	Cat's Lair	1,500		150.00	150
1993	Catching The Sun	999	1993	150.00	500
1992	Conferring With the Sea	999	1993	125.00	500
1990	Contemplation	999		100.00	150
1995	Country Comfort	999		100.00	100
1995	Drip Castles	4,000		30.00	30
1991	Duet	999	1993	150.00	800
1990	Emotional Appeal	999		150.00	225
1993	Gathering Thoughts	1,500	1995	150.00	150
1992	An Innocent View	999	1992	150.00	600
1994	The Journey Is The Goal	1,500	1995	150.00	150
1995	Kali	Open		25.00	25
1993	Little Black Crow	1,500		150.00	150
1994	Michaela and Friends/Book	2,500		200.00	200
1993	The New Arrival	1,500		150.00	200
1995	Pacific Sanctuary	1,500		150.00	150
1993	Peeking Out	Open		40.00	40
1993	Places I Remember	1,500		150.00	150
1990	Quiet Rapport	999		150.00	300
1993	A Sense of Belonging	1,500		150.00	150
1995	Small Miracle	1,500		125.00	125
1992	Sometimes It's the Little Things	999		125.00	225
1994	Southwestern Bedroom	999		150.00	180-225
1992	Stepping Stones	999	1993	150.00	170-200
1991	Sunday Afternoon	Open		40.00	40
1992	Things Worth Keeping	999	1991	125.00	2000
1993	The Thinkers	1,500		150.00	150
1994	Water Lilies In Bloom	750		295.00	295
1993	When Her Blue Eyes Close	999		100.00	100
1994	Where The Light Shines Brightest	1,500		150.00	150
1991	A World For Our Children	999	1992	125.00	2000

Hulings - C. Hulings

YEAR ISSUE		EDITION LIMIT	YEAR RETD.	ISSUE PRICE	*QUOTE U.S.$
1990	Ancient French Farmhouse	999		150.00	225
1989	Chechaquene-Morocco Market Square	999	1993	150.00	250
1992	Cuernavaca Flower Market	580		225.00	225
1988	Ile de la Cite-Paris	580	1990	150.00	225
1990	The Lonely Man	999	1993	150.00	150
1988	Onteniente	580	1989	150.00	425
1991	Place des Ternes	580	1991	195.00	700
1989	Portuguese Vegetable Woman	999	1993	85.00	85
1994	The Red Raincoat	580		225.00	225
1990	Spanish Shawl	999	1994	125.00	125
1993	Spring Flowers	580		225.00	225
1992	Sunday Afternoon	580		195.00	275
1988	Three Cats on a Grapevine	580	1989	65.00	225
1993	Washday In Provence	580		225.00	225

Redlin - T. Redlin

YEAR ISSUE		EDITION LIMIT	YEAR RETD.	ISSUE PRICE	*QUOTE U.S.$
1981	1981 MN Duck Stamp Print	7,800	1981	125.00	150
1982	1982 MN Trout Stamp Print	960	1982	125.00	600
1983	1983 ND Duck Stamp Print	3,438	1983	135.00	150
1984	1984 Quail Conservation	1,500	1984	135.00	135
1985	1985 MN Duck Stamp	4,385	1985	135.00	135
1985	Afternoon Glow	960	1985	150.00	1600
1979	Ageing Shoreline	960	1979	40.00	375
1981	All Clear	960	1981	150.00	300
1994	America, America	29,500		250.00	250
1994	And Crown Thy Good w/Brotherhood	29,500		250.00	250
1977	Apple River Mallards	Retrd.	1977	10.00	100
1981	April Snow	960	1981	100.00	450
1989	Aroma of Fall	6,800	1989	200.00	1500-1800
1987	Autumn Afternoon	4,800	1987	100.00	700
1993	Autumn Evening	29,500		250.00	250
1980	Autumn Run	960	1980	60.00	400
1983	Autumn Shoreline	Retrd.	1983	50.00	200
1978	Back from the Fields	720	1978	40.00	250-400
1985	Back to the Sanctuary	960	1986	150.00	500
1978	Backwater Mallards	720	1978	40.00	1000
1983	Backwoods Cabin	960	1983	150.00	900
1990	Best Friends (AP)	570	1993	1000.00	1500
1982	The Birch Line	960	1982	100.00	500
1984	Bluebill Point (AP)	240	1984	300.00	650
1988	Boulder Ridge	4,800		150.00	150
1980	Breaking Away	960	1980	60.00	430
1985	Breaking Cover	960	1985	150.00	500
1981	Broken Covey	960	1981	100.00	525
1985	Brousing	960	1985	150.00	800
1994	Campfire Tales	29,500		250.00	250
1988	Catching the Scent	2,400		200.00	200
1986	Changing Seasons-Autumn	960	1986	150.00	425
1987	Changing Seasons-Spring	960	1987	200.00	475
1984	Changing Seasons-Summer	960	1984	150.00	1400
1986	Changing Seasons-Winter	960	1986	200.00	600
1985	Clear View	1,500	1985	300.00	600
1980	Clearing the Rail	960	1980	60.00	650-850
1984	Closed for the Season	960	1984	150.00	300
1979	Colorful Trio	960	1979	40.00	800
1991	Comforts of Home	22,900	N/A	175.00	800
1986	Coming Home	2,400	1986	100.00	1800
1992	The Conservationists	29,500		175.00	175
1988	Country Neighbors	4,800	1988	150.00	600
1980	Country Road	960	1980	60.00	650-745
1987	Deer Crossing	2,400	1987	200.00	1000
1985	Delayed Departure	1,500	1985	150.00	500-1000
1980	Drifting	960	1980	60.00	400
1987	Evening Chores (print & book)	2,400	1988	400.00	775-1000
1985	Evening Company	960	1985	150.00	500
1983	Evening Glow	960	1983	150.00	2400
1987	Evening Harvest	960	1987	200.00	1400
1982	Evening Retreat (AP)	300	1982	400.00	3000
1990	Evening Solitude	9,500	1990	200.00	800
1983	Evening Surprise	960	1983	150.00	1000
1990	Evening With Friends	19,500	1991	225.00	1500
1990	Family Traditions	Retrd.	1993	80.00	100
1979	Fighting a Headwind	960	1979	30.00	350
1991	Flying Free	14,500		200.00	200
1993	For Amber Waves of Grain	29,500		250.00	250
1993	For Purple Mountains Majesty	29,500		250.00	250
1995	From Sea to Shining Sea	29,500		250.00	250
1994	God Shed His Grace on Thee	29,500		250.00	250
1987	Golden Retreat (AP)	500	1986	800.00	2000
1995	Harvest Moon Ball	9,500	1995	275.00	500
1986	Hazy Afternoon	2,560	1986	200.00	850
1990	Heading Home	Retrd.	1993	80.00	200
1983	Hidden Point	960	1983	150.00	600
1981	High Country	960	1981	100.00	600
1981	Hightailing	960	1981	75.00	300
1980	The Homestead	960	1980	60.00	640
1988	Homeward Bound	Retrd.	1993	70.00	150
1989	Homeward Bound	Retrd.	1994	80.00	250
1988	House Call	6,800	1990	175.00	1000
1991	Hunter's Haven (A/P)	1,000	N/A	175.00	1000
1989	Indian Summer	4,800	1989	200.00	600-725
1980	Intruders	960	1980	60.00	310
1982	The Landing	Retrd.	1982	30.00	80
1981	The Landmark	960	1981	100.00	400
1984	Leaving the Sanctuary	960	1984	150.00	475
1994	Lifetime Companions	29,500		250.00	25
1988	Lights of Home	9,500	1988	125.00	85
1979	The Loner	960	1979	40.00	300
1990	Master of the Valley	6,800		200.00	20
1988	The Master's Domain	2,400	1988	225.00	80
1988	Moonlight Retreat (A/P)	530	N/A	1000.00	160
1979	Morning Chores	960	1979	40.00	135
1984	Morning Glow	960	1984	150.00	140
1981	Morning Retreat (AP)	240	N/A	400.00	300
1989	Morning Rounds	6,800	1992	175.00	60
1991	Morning Solitude	12,107	1991	250.00	60
1984	Night Harvest	960	1984	150.00	100
1985	Night Light	1,500	1985	300.00	60
1986	Night Mapling	960	1986	200.00	55
1995	A Night on the Town	29,500		150.00	15
1980	Night Watch	2,400	1980	60.00	100
1984	Nightflight (AP)	360	1984	600.00	220
1982	October Evening	960	1982	100.00	100
1989	Office Hours	6,800	1991	175.00	100
1992	Oh Beautiful for Spacious Skies	29,500		250.00	25
1978	Old Loggers Trail	720	1978	40.00	950-120
1983	On the Alert	960	1983	125.00	40
1977	Over the Blowdown	Retrd.	1977	20.00	10
1978	Over the Rushes	720	1978	40.00	45
1981	Passing Through	960	1981	100.00	22
1983	Peaceful Evening	960	1983	100.00	35
1991	Pleasures of Winter	24,500	1992	150.00	40
1986	Prairie Monuments	960	1986	200.00	70
1988	Prairie Morning	4,800	1988	150.00	50
1984	Prairie Skyline	960	1984	150.00	60
1983	Prairie Springs	960	1983	150.00	32
1987	Prepared for the Season	Retrd.	1994	70.00	10
1990	Pure Contentment	9,500	1989	150.00	60
1978	Quiet Afternoon	720	1978	40.00	57
1988	Quiet of the Evening	4,800	1988	150.00	70
1982	Reflections	960	1982	100.00	60
1985	Riverside Pond	960	1985	150.00	52
1984	Rural Route	960	1984	150.00	35
1983	Rushing Rapids	960	1983	125.00	4
1980	Rusty Refuge I	960	1980	60.00	6
1981	Rusty Refuge II	960	1980	100.00	70
1984	Rusty Refuge III	960	1984	150.00	60
1985	Rusty Refuge IV	960	1985	150.00	60
1980	Secluded Pond	960	1980	60.00	2
1982	Seed Hunters	960	1982	100.00	57
1985	Sharing Season I	Retrd.	1993	60.00	1
1986	Sharing Season II	Retrd.	1993	60.00	1
1981	Sharing the Bounty	960	1981	100.00	15
1994	Sharing the Evening	29,500		175.00	1
1987	Sharing the Solitude	2,400	1987	125.00	9
1986	Silent Flight	960	1986	150.00	3
1980	Silent Sunset	960	1980	60.00	7
1984	Silent Wings Suite (set of 4)	960	1984	200.00	7
1981	Soft Shadows	960	1984	100.00	3
1989	Special Memories (AP)	570		1000.00	10
1982	Spring Mapling	960	1982	100.00	6
1981	Spring Run-Off	1,700	1981	125.00	4
1980	Spring Thaw	960	1980	60.00	4
1980	Squall Line	960	1980	60.00	3
1978	Startled	720	1978	30.00	7
1986	Stormy Weather	1,500	1986	200.00	5
1992	Summertime	24,900		225.00	2
1984	Sundown	960	1984	300.00	5
1986	Sunlit Trail	960	1986	150.00	3
1984	Sunny Afternoon	960	1984	150.00	7
1987	That Special Time	2,400	1987	125.00	700-10
1987	Together for the Season	Open		70.00	1
1995	Total Comfort	9,500	1995	275.00	2
1986	Twilight Glow	960	1986	200.00	7
1988	Wednesday Afternoon	6,800	1989	175.00	9
1990	Welcome to Paradise	14,500	1990	150.00	7
1985	Whistle Stop	960	1985	150.00	5
1979	Whitecaps	960	1979	40.00	5
1982	Whitewater	960	1982	100.00	4
1982	Winter Haven	500	1982	85.00	8
1977	Winter Snows	Retrd.	1977	20.00	1
1984	Winter Windbreak	960	1984	150.00	7
1992	Winter Wonderland	29,500	1993	150.00	4

Imperial Graphics, Ltd.

Chang - L. Chang

YEAR ISSUE		EDITION LIMIT	YEAR RETD.	ISSUE PRICE	*QUOTE U.S.$
1988	Egrets with Lotus S/N	1,950		10.00	
1988	Flamingos with Catail S/N	1,950		10.00	

*Quotes have been rounded up to nearest dolla

Irvine - G. Irvine

YEAR ISSUE	EDITION LIMIT	YEAR RETD.	ISSUE PRICE	*QUOTE U.S.$
1995 Pansies	Open		8.00	8
1995 Violets	Open		8.00	8

Lee - H.C. Lee

YEAR ISSUE	EDITION LIMIT	YEAR RETD.	ISSUE PRICE	*QUOTE U.S.$
1988 Blue Bird of Paradise S/N	950		35.00	35
1988 Cat & Callas S/N	1,950		30.00	30
1990 Double Red Hibiscus S/N	1,950		16.00	16
1988 Hummingbird I S/N	1,950		16.00	16
1988 Hummingbird II S/N	1,950		16.00	16
1990 Maroon & Mauve Peonies S/N	950		60.00	60
1990 Maroon & Peach Peonies S/N	950		60.00	60
1990 Maroon Peony S/N	2,950		20.00	20
1990 Peacock w/Tulip & Peony S/N	1,950		105.00	105
1990 Peonies & Butterflies S/N	2,950		40.00	40
1990 Pink Peony S/N	2,950		20.00	20
1990 Single Red Hibiscus S/N	1,950		16.00	16
1988 White Bird of Paradise S/N	950		35.00	35
1988 White Peacocks w/Peonies S/N	950		65.00	65

Liu - Celestial Symphony Series - L. Liu

YEAR ISSUE	EDITION LIMIT	YEAR RETD.	ISSUE PRICE	*QUOTE U.S.$
1995 Flute Interlude S/N	5,500		40.00	40
1995 French Horn Melody S/N	5,500		40.00	40
1995 Piano Sonata S/N	5,500		40.00	40
1995 Violin Concerto S/N	5,500		40.00	40

Liu - Celestial Symphony Series Unframed Canvas Transfers - L. Liu

YEAR ISSUE	EDITION LIMIT	YEAR RETD.	ISSUE PRICE	*QUOTE U.S.$
1995 Flute Interlude S/N	300		145.00	145
1995 French Horn Melody S/N	300		145.00	145
1995 Piano Sonata S/N	300		145.00	145
1995 Violin Concerto S/N	300		145.00	145

Liu - L. Liu

YEAR ISSUE	EDITION LIMIT	YEAR RETD.	ISSUE PRICE	*QUOTE U.S.$
1989 Abundance of Lilies (poster)	Open		30.00	30
XX Afternoon Nap S/N	1,000		45.00	45
XX Aiming High S/N	950	N/A	65.00	65
1994 Allen's Hummingbird w/Columbine S/N	3,300	1994	30.00	30
1987 Amaryllis S/N	1,950	N/A	16.00	16
1993 Anna's Hummingbird w/Fuchsia S/N	3,300	1993	30.00	30
XX At Peace S/N	950	N/A	45.00	45
1989 Autumn Melody S/N	1,950	1993	45.00	45
1990 Azalea Path S/N	2,500	N/A	85.00	85
1990 Azalea w/Dogwood S/N	2,500	N/A	55.00	55
1988 Baby Bluebirds S/N	1,950	N/A	16.00	16
1990 Baby Bluebirds w/Plum Tree S/N	2,500	N/A	18.00	18
1988 Baby Chickadees S/N	1,950	N/A	16.00	16
1990 Baby Chickadees w/Pine Tree S/N	2,500	N/A	18.00	18
XX Basket of Begonias S/N	2,500	N/A	40.00	40
1993 Basket of Calla Lilies S/N	3,300	1994	50.00	50
1991 Basket of Grapes & Raspberries S/N	2,500	N/A	25.00	25
1993 Basket of Hydrangi A/P	50		65.00	65
1993 Basket of Hydrangi S/N	3,300	1995	50.00	50
1989 Basket of Irises & Lilacs S/N	1,950	N/A	45.00	45
1993 Basket of Magnolias S/N	3,300	1993	50.00	50
1993 Basket of Orchids S/N	3,300		50.00	50
1992 Basket of Pansies & Lilacs S/N	2,950	N/A	50.00	50
XX Basket of Pansies S/N	2,500	N/A	40.00	40
1991 Basket of Peonies S/N	2,500	N/A	40.00	40
1992 Basket of Roses & Hydrangeas S/N	2,950	N/A	50.00	50
1991 Basket of Roses S/N	2,500	N/A	40.00	40
1991 Basket of Strawberries & Grapes A/P	50		35.00	35
1991 Basket of Strawberries & Grapes S/N	2,500	N/A	25.00	25
1991 Basket of Sweet Peas S/N	2,500		25.00	25
1989 Basket of Tulips & Lilacs S/N	1,950	N/A	45.00	45
1991 Basket of Wild Roses S/N	2,500	N/A	25.00	25
1991 Baskets of Primroses A/P	50		35.00	35
1991 Baskets of Primroses S/N	2,500	N/A	25.00	25
1986 Bearded Irises S/N	1,950	N/A	45.00	45
XX Begonia w/Ribbon S/N	2,500	N/A	16.00	16
1994 Berries & Cherries S/N	3,500		30.00	30
XX Blue & Peach Irises S/N	1,950	N/A	35.00	35
XX Blue Bird of Paradise S/N	950		35.00	35
XX Blue Peacock S/N	950	N/A	65.00	65
1990 Bluebirds & Dandelion S/N	2,500	N/A	40.00	40
XX Bluebirds S/N	950	N/A	35.00	35
1986 Bluebirds w/Plum Blossoms S/N	1,950	N/A	35.00	35
1988 Bluebirds w/Rhododendrons S/N	1,950		40.00	40
1990 Bouquet of Peonies S/N	2,500	N/A	50.00	50
1990 Bouquet of Poppies S/N	2,500	N/A	50.00	50
1992 Bouquet of Roses A/P	50		25.00	25
1992 Bouquet of Roses S/N	2,950	1994	20.00	20
1992 Breath of Spring S/N	2,950		135.00	135
1993 Broad-Billed HB w/Petunias S/N	3,300		30.00	30
1995 Burgundy Irises w/Foxgloves S/N	5,500		60.00	60
XX Butterfly & Morning Glories S/N	950	N/A	35.00	35
XX Butterfly & Poppies S/N	950	N/A	35.00	35
1995 Butterfly Garden I S/N	5,500		50.00	50
1995 Butterfly Garden II S/N	5,500		50.00	50
1994 Butterfly Kisses S/N	3,500		50.00	50
1990 Butterfly w/Clematis A/P	50		55.00	55
1990 Butterfly w/Clematis S/N	2,500	1994	40.00	40
1990 Butterfly w/Wild Rose S/N	2,500	1993	40.00	40
1987 Calla Lily S/N	1,950		35.00	35
1994 Calliope Hummingbird w/Trumpet Vine S/N	3,300		30.00	30
1990 Cardinal & Queen Anne's Lace S/N	2,500	1994	40.00	40
XX Cardinal S/N	950	N/A	35.00	35
XX Cat & Callas S/N	950		30.00	30
XX Cat & Hummer S/N	1,000		45.00	45
1989 Cherries & Summer Bouquet S/N	2,500	N/A	45.00	45
1993 Cherub Orchestra S/N	3,300	1994	80.00	80
1991 Cherubim w/Ivy S/N	2,500	1993	20.00	20
XX Chickadees S/N	950	N/A	35.00	35
1988 Chickadees w/Cherry Blossoms S/N	1,950		40.00	40
1992 Conservatory A/P	50		110.00	110
1992 Conservatory S/N	2,950	1994	80.00	80
1987 Daylily S/N	1,950	N/A	35.00	35
1989 Daylily w/Hummingbird S/N	2,500	N/A	18.00	18
1987 Dogwood S/N	1,950	N/A	30.00	30
XX Double Red Hibiscus S/N	1,950		16.00	16
1986 The Dreamer S/N	950		65.00	65
1991 Dried-Floral Bouquet S/N	2,500		25.00	25
1991 The Drying Room S/N	2,500		75.00	75
1992 Early Spring S/N	2,950	1993	85.00	85
1988 Eastern Black Swallowtail w/Milkweed S/N	1,950		45.00	45
1991 Egret's w/Queen Anne's Lace S/N	2,500	1995	60.00	60
1992 Entryway S/N	2,950		40.00	40
1993 Fairy Ballet S/N	3,300		80.00	80
1986 Fall S/N	950		35.00	35
1994 Fancy Fiddle S/N	5,500	1994	80.00	80
1988 Feathered Harmony S/N	1,950	N/A	60.00	60
1991 Field of Irises A/P	50		115.00	115
1991 Field of Irises S/N	2,500	1994	85.00	85
1989 First Landing S/N	1,950	N/A	16.00	16
1991 Floral Arch S/N	2,500		25.00	25
1988 Floral Symphony S/N	1,950	N/A	95.00	95
XX Flying Free S/N	950	N/A	45.00	45
1990 Forest Azalea S/N	2,500	N/A	55.00	55
1992 Forest Stream S/N	2,950	1995	85.00	85
1992 Fountain S/N	2,950		40.00	40
1986 Free Flight I -Rust Butterfly S/N	950		60.00	60
1986 Free Flight II -Pink Butterfly S/N	950		60.00	60
1989 Fritillaries w/ Violet S/N	2,500		18.00	18
1989 Fruit & Spring Basket S/N	1,500	N/A	45.00	45
1988 Garden Blossoms I S/N	1,950	N/A	35.00	35
1988 Garden Blossoms II S/N	1,950	N/A	35.00	35
1991 Garden Peonies S/N	2,500		60.00	60
1986 Garden Poppies S/N	2,000		45.00	45
1991 Garden Poppies S/N	2,500		60.00	60
1992 Garden Seat S/N	2,950		40.00	40
1991 The Gathering S/N	2,500	N/A	75.00	75
1988 Harmonious Flight S/N	1,950		50.00	50
1994 Heavenly Tulips S/N	3,300	1994	80.00	80
1987 Herons & Irises S/N	1,950		65.00	65
1987 Hibiscus & Hummer S/N	1,950	1995	45.00	45
1988 Hummingbird & Hollyhock S/N	1,950	N/A	40.00	40
XX Hummingbird & Columbine S/N	950	N/A	35.00	35
1989 Hummingbird & Floral I S/N	2,500	1994	35.00	35
1989 Hummingbird & Floral II S/N	2,500	1994	35.00	35
XX Hummingbird & Hibiscus S/N	950	N/A	45.00	45
XX Hummingbird & Trumpet Vine S/N	950	N/A	35.00	35
XX Hummingbird I A/P	50		16.00	16
XX Hummingbird II A/P	50		16.00	16
1988 Hummingbirds & Iris S/N	1,950	N/A	40.00	40
1989 Hydrangea Bouquet S/N	2,500		30.00	30
1989 Innocents S/N	1,950		16.00	16
1993 Iris Garden II S/N	3,300	1994	105.00	105
XX Iris Garden S/N	1,950	N/A	45.00	45
1989 Iris Profusion (poster)	Closed	1995	30.00	30
XX Iris S/N	950	N/A	45.00	45
1987 Iris S/N	1,950	N/A	16.00	16
1991 Irises in Bloom S/N	2,500	N/A	85.00	85
1992 Ivy & Fragrant Flowers S/N	3,300	1993	60.00	60
1992 Ivy & Honeysuckle S/N	3,300	1993	50.00	50
1992 Ivy & Sweetpea A/P	50		65.00	65
1992 Ivy & Sweetpea S/N	3,300	1994	50.00	50
1988 Kingfisher & Iris S/N	1,950		45.00	45
XX Kingfisher & Lotus S/N	950	N/A	45.00	45
1986 Kingfisher S/N	950		35.00	35
1995 Lilac Breezes S/N	5,500		80.00	80
1986 Lily Pond S/N	950		35.00	35
1987 Lily S/N	1,950	N/A	16.00	16
1994 Love Notes S/N	5,500	1994	80.00	80
1995 Magnolia Path S/N	5,500		135.00	135
1987 Magnolia S/N	1,950	N/A	30.00	30
1995 Magnolias & Day Lilies S/N	5,500		80.00	80
1995 Magnolias & Hydrangeas S/N	5,500		80.00	80
XX Maroon & Mauve Peonies A/P	50		60.00	60
XX Maroon & Peach Peonies A/P	50		60.00	60
XX Maroon Peony S/N	2,950		20.00	20
1986 Mauve Veiltail S/N	950		35.00	35
1994 Mermaid Callas S/N	5,500		80.00	80
XX Misty Valley S/N	1,950		45.00	45
1990 Mixed Irises I S/N	2,500	N/A	50.00	50
1990 Mixed Irises II S/N	2,500	N/A	50.00	50
1988 Moonlight Splendor S/N	1,950	N/A	60.00	60
1987 Morning Glories & Hummer S/N	1,950	N/A	45.00	45
1989 The Morning Room S/N	2,500	N/A	95.00	95
1987 Motherlove S/N	1,950	N/A	45.00	45
1987 Motif Orientale S/N	1,950	N/A	95.00	95
1994 Mystic Bouquet S/N	3,300		80.00	80
XX Nature's Retreat A/P	25	1995	435.00	435
1995 Nature's Retreat S/N	5,500		145.00	145
1986 Nuthatch w/Dogwood S/N	1,950	N/A	35.00	35
1992 Old Stone House S/N	2,950		50.00	50
1986 Opera Lady S/N	950	N/A	95.00	95
1989 Orange Tip & Blossoms S/N	2,500		18.00	18
XX Orchid S/N	950	N/A	45.00	45
1989 Oriental Screen S/N	2,500	N/A	95.00	95
1988 Painted Lady w/Thistle S/N	1,950		45.00	45
1988 Pair of Finches S/N	1,950	N/A	35.00	35
1992 Palladian Windows S/N	2,950	1993	80.00	80
1990 Pansies & Ivy S/N	2,500	N/A	18.00	18
1992 Pansies & Lilies of the Valley S/N	2,950	1993	20.00	20
1992 Pansies & Sweet Peas S/N	2,950	1994	20.00	20
1991 Pansies in a Basket S/N	2,500	N/A	25.00	25
1993 Pansies w/Blue Stardrift A/P	50		35.00	35
1993 Pansies w/Blue Stardrift S/N	2,950	1995	25.00	25
1993 Pansies w/Daisies S/N	2,950		25.00	25
XX Pansies w/Ribbon S/N	2,500	N/A	16.00	16
1991 Pansies w/Sweet Pea S/N	2,500	N/A	16.00	16
1991 Pansies w/Violets S/N	2,500	N/A	16.00	16
1987 Parenthood S/N	1,950	N/A	45.00	45
1992 Patio S/N	2,950		40.00	40
1993 Peach & Purple Irises S/N	3,300	1994	50.00	50
1993 Peach & Yellow Roses S/N	3,300		50.00	50
1986 Peach Veiltail S/N	950		35.00	35
1994 Peaches & Fruits S/N	3,500		30.00	30
1991 Peacock Duet-Serigraph S/N	325		550.00	550
1987 Peacock Fantasy S/N	950		65.00	65
1991 Peacock Solo-Serigraph S/N	325		550.00	550
XX Peacock w/Tulip & Peony S/N	1,950		105.00	105
1988 Peonies & Azaleas S/N	1,950	N/A	35.00	35
XX Peonies & Butterflies S/N	2,950		40.00	40
1988 Peonies & Forsythia S/N	1,950	N/A	35.00	35
1988 Peonies & Waterfall S/N	1,950	N/A	65.00	65
1993 Peonies S/N	3,300	1995	30.00	30
1990 Petunias & Ivy S/N	2,500		18.00	18
1989 Phlox w/Hummingbird S/N	2,500		18.00	18
XX Pink Peony S/N	2,950		20.00	20
1990 Potted Beauties S/N	2,500		105.00	105
1995 Purple Irises w/Foxgloves S/N	5,500		60.00	60
1991 Putti w/Column S/N	2,500		20.00	20
1990 Quiet Moment S/N	2,500	N/A	105.00	105
1989 Romantic Abundance S/N	1,950	N/A	95.00	95
1989 Romantic Garden (poster)	Open		35.00	35
1994 Romantic Reflection S/N	5,950		145.00	185
1993 Rose Bouquet w/Tassel S/N	3,300	1995	25.00	25
1994 Rose Fairies S/N	5,500		80.00	80
1989 Roses & Lilacs S/N	2,500		30.00	30
1992 Roses & Violets A/P	50		25.00	25
1992 Roses & Violets S/N	2,950	1993	20.00	20
1993 Roses in Bloom S/N	3,300	1995	105.00	105
1990 Royal Garden S/N	1,950		95.00	95
1990 Royal Retreat S/N	1,950	N/A	95.00	95
1995 Ruby Throated Hummingbird w/Hibiscus S/N	5,800		40.00	40
1993 Rufous Hummingbird w/Foxgloves S/N	3,300	1993	30.00	30
XX Single Red Hibiscus S/N	1,950		16.00	16
1988 Snapdragon S/N	1,950	N/A	16.00	16
1987 Solitude S/N	1,950	N/A	60.00	60
1993 Southern Magnolia S/N	3,300	1995	30.00	30
XX Spring Blossoms I S/N	1,950		45.00	45
XX Spring Blossoms II S/N	1,950		45.00	45
1989 Spring Bouquet (poster)	Closed	1995	30.00	30
1989 Spring Bouquet (poster-signed)	Closed	1995	45.00	45
1994 Spring Conservatory S/N	3,300		105.00	105
XX Spring Duet S/N	1,950	N/A	60.00	60
1986 Spring Fairy S/N	950		35.00	35
1990 Spring Floral S/N	2,500	N/A	105.00	105
XX Spring Forest S/N	2,500	N/A	75.00	75
1995 Spring Garden S/N	5,500		125.00	125
1986 Spring S/N	950		35.00	35
XX Spring Song S/N	1,950		60.00	60
1986 Spring Tulips S/N	1,950	N/A	45.00	45
1989 Spring Tulips S/N	2,500	N/A	45.00	45
XX Stream w/Blossoms S/N	1,950		45.00	45
1992 Study for a Breath of Spring S/N	2,950		105.00	105
XX Summer Garden S/N	2,500	N/A	75.00	75
1986 Summer Glads S/N	1,950	N/A	45.00	45
1986 Summer Lace w/Blue Chicory S/N	1,950	N/A	45.00	45
1987 Summer Lace w/Chicadees S/N	950	N/A	65.00	65
1986 Summer Lace w/Chickadees II S/N	1,950	N/A	65.00	65
1986 Summer Lace w/Daisies S/N	1,950	N/A	45.00	45
1987 Summer Lace w/Dragon Fly S/N	950	N/A	45.00	45
1987 Summer Lace w/Lady Bug S/N	950	N/A	45.00	45
1989 Summer Rose S/N	2,500	N/A	45.00	45
1986 Summer S/N	950		35.00	35
1987 Swans & Callas S/N	1,950	1994	65.00	65
1991 Swans w/Daylilies S/N	2,500	1993	60.00	60
1989 Swans w/Dogwood S/N	1,950	N/A	65.00	65
1995 Sweet Bounty S/N	5,500		80.00	80
1994 Sweet Delight S/N	3,500		50.00	50
1988 Sweet Pea Floral S/N	1,950	N/A	16.00	16
XX Sweet Pea w/Ribbon S/N	2,500	N/A	16.00	16
1986 Three Little Deer S/N	950		35.00	35
1987 Togetherness S/N	1,950	N/A	60.00	60
1988 Trio of Sparrows S/N	1,950	N/A	35.00	35
1993 Tulip Bouquet w/Tassel A/P	50		35.00	35
1993 Tulip Bouquet w/Tassel S/N	3,300	1995	25.00	25
1987 Tulips S/N	1,950	N/A	16.00	16
1993 Two Burgundy Irises S/N	3,300	1994	50.00	50
XX Two Peach Irises S/N	1,950	N/A	35.00	35
1990 Two White Irises S/N	2,500	N/A	40.00	40
1992 Victorian Pavilion S/N	2,950		50.00	50
1992 Vintage Bouquet S/N	2,950	1994	135.00	135

*Quotes have been rounded up to nearest dollar

YEAR ISSUE		EDITION LIMIT	YEAR RETD.	ISSUE PRICE	*QUOTE U.S.$
1993	Violet Crowned HB w/Morning Glories S/N	3,300		30.00	30
XX	Violets w/Ribbon A/P	50		22.00	22
XX	Violets w/Ribbon S/N	2,500	N/A	16.00	16
XX	Waterfall I S/N	950	N/A	60.00	60
XX	Waterfall II S/N	950	N/A	60.00	60
XX	Waterfall w/Blossoms S/N	1,950	N/A	65.00	65
1989	Waterfall w/Dogwood S/N	1,950		45.00	45
1989	Waterfall w/White & Pink Dogwood S/N	1,950		45.00	45
1990	White & Blue Irises S/N	2,500	N/A	40.00	40
1993	White & Burgundy Roses A/P	50		65.00	65
1993	White & Burgundy Roses S/N	3,300	1995	50.00	50
XX	White Bird of Paradise S/N	950		35.00	35
1995	White Eared Hummingbird w/Hydrangea S/N	5,800		40.00	40
XX	White Peacock S/N	950	N/A	65.00	65
XX	White Peacocks w/Peonies S/N	950		65.00	65
1991	Wild Flowers w/Single Butterfly S/N	2,500		50.00	50
1991	Wild Flowers w/Two Butterflies S/N	2,500		50.00	50
1986	Winter S/N	950		35.00	35
1993	Woodland Path S/N	3,300	1994	135.00	135
1993	Woodland Steps S/N	3,300	1995	85.00	85
1993	Woodland View A/P	50		115.00	115
1993	Woodland View S/N	3,300	1995	85.00	85
XX	Woodpecker S/N	950	N/A	35.00	35
1995	Wreath of Lilies S/N	5,500		55.00	55
1995	Wreath of Pansies S/N	5,500		55.00	55
1994	Wreath of Peonies S/N	3,500		55.00	55
1994	Wreath of Roses S/N	3,500	1995	55.00	55

Liu - The Music Room - L. Liu

1991	The Music Room I S/N	2,500	N/A	135.00	135
1992	The Music Room II-Nutcracker S/N	4,500	1993	200.00	200
1994	The Music Room III-Composer's Retreat S/N	5,500	1994	145.00	145
1995	The Music Room IV-Swan Melody S/N	6,500		150.00	150

Liu - Unframed Canvas Transfers - L. Liu

1993	Basket of Calla Lilies S/N	300	1995	195.00	195
1993	Basket of Magnolias S/N	300	1995	195.00	195
1993	Cherub Orchestra S/N	300	1995	295.00	295
1992	Conservatory S/N	300	1995	295.00	295
1993	Fairy Ballet S/N	300	1995	295.00	295
1994	Fancy Fiddle S/N	300		295.00	295
1993	Iris Garden II S/N	300	1995	395.00	395
1995	Lilac Breezes A/P	25		355.00	355
1995	Lilac Breezes S/N	300		295.00	295
1994	Love Notes S/N	300		295.00	295
1995	Magnolia Path A/P	25		455.00	455
1995	Magnolia Path S/N	300		395.00	395
1994	Mermaid Callas S/N	300		295.00	295
1995	Nature's Retreat S/N	300		395.00	395
1992	Old Stone House S/N	300	1995	195.00	195
1992	Palladian Windows S/N	300	1995	295.00	295
1994	Romantic Reflection S/N	500		395.00	395
1994	Rose Fairies S/N	300		295.00	295
1993	Roses in Bloom S/N	300	1995	395.00	395
1994	Spring Conservatory S/N	300	1995	395.00	395
1995	Spring Garden A/P	25		435.00	435
1995	Spring Garden S/N	300		395.00	395
1995	Sweet Bounty A/P	25		355.00	355
1995	Sweet Bounty S/N	300		295.00	295
1992	Victorian Pavillion S/N	300	1995	195.00	195
1992	Vintage Bouquet S/N	300	1995	395.00	395
1993	Woodland Path S/N	300	1995	495.00	495

Liu - Unframed Canvas Transfers The Music Room - L. Liu

1991	The Music Room S/N	300	N/A	395.00	395
1992	The Music Room II-Nutcracker S/N	300	N/A	395.00	395
1994	The Music Room III-Composer's Retreat S/N	300	1994	395.00	395
1995	Music Room IV - Swan Melody S/N	300		425.00	425
1995	Music Room IV A/P	25		485.00	485

McDonald - M. McDonald

1988	Amaryllis Dancer S/N	1,000		55.00	55
1988	Lily Queen S/N	1,000		55.00	55

John Hine N.A. Ltd.

Rambles - A. Wyatt

1989	Blue Tit	Closed	N/A	33.00	33
1989	Bluebell Cottage	Closed	N/A	50.00	50
1989	Castle Street	Closed	N/A	42.00	42
1989	Frog	Closed	N/A	33.00	33
1989	Garden Gate	Closed	N/A	59.90	60
1989	Hedgerow	Closed	N/A	59.90	60
1989	Kingfisher	Closed	N/A	33.00	33
1989	Lobster Pot	Closed	N/A	50.00	50
1989	Otter's Holt	Closed	N/A	50.00	50
1989	Puffin Rock	Closed	N/A	50.00	50
1989	Riverbank	Closed	N/A	59.90	60
1989	Shirelarm	Closed	N/A	42.00	42
1989	St. Mary's Church	Closed	N/A	42.00	42
1989	Summer Harvest	Closed	N/A	59.90	60
1989	The Swan	Closed	N/A	42.00	42
1989	Two for Joy	Closed	N/A	59.90	60
1989	Waters Edge	Closed	N/A	59.90	60
1989	Wren	Closed	N/A	33.00	33

Lightpost Publishing

Kinkade Member's Only Collectors' Society - T. Kinkade

YEAR ISSUE		EDITION LIMIT	YEAR RETD.	ISSUE PRICE	*QUOTE U.S.$
1992	Skater's Pond	Closed	N/A	295.00	400-600
1992	Morning Lane	Closed	N/A	Gift	100
1994	Collector's Cottage I	Closed	1995	315.00	360-500
1994	Painter of Light Book	Closed	1995	Gift	50-80
1995	Lochavan Cottage	Closed	1995	295.00	400
1995	Gardens Beyond Autumn Gate-pencil sketch	Closed	1995	Gift	100
1996	Julianne's Cottage-Keepsake Box	12/96		Gift	60

Kinkade-Archival Paper/Canvas-Combined Edition-Framed - T. Kinkade

1989	Blue Cottage (Paper)	Retrd.	1993	125.00	350
1989	Blue Cottage (Canvas)	Retrd.	1993	495.00	1500
1990	Moonlit Village (Paper)	Closed	N/A	225.00	1100-1200
1990	Moonlit Village (Canvas)	Closed	N/A	595.00	2700-3500
1986	New York, 1932 (Paper)	Closed	N/A	225.00	1750
1986	New York, 1932 (Canvas)	Closed	N/A	595.00	3500-3800
1989	Skating in the Park (Paper) S/N	750	1994	225.00	1200-1500
1989	Skating in the Park (Canvas) S/N	750	1994	595.00	1500-2500

Kinkade-Canvas Editions-Framed - T. Kinkade

YEAR ISSUE		EDITION LIMIT	YEAR RETD.	ISSUE PRICE	*QUOTE U.S.$
1991	Afternoon Light, Dogwood A/P	98	1991	595.00	2100-2500
1991	Afternoon Light, Dogwood S/N	980	N/A	495.00	1900-2200
1992	Amber Afternoon A/P	595	1992	715.00	1100-1400
1992	Amber Afternoon S/N	980	N/A	695.00	1000-1300
1994	Autumn at Ashley's Cottage A/P	395		590.00	600-800
1994	Autumn at Ashley's Cottage S/N	3,950		440.00	450-650
1991	The Autumn Gate A/P	200	N/A	695.00	3300-3800
1991	The Autumn Gate R/P	Retrd.	1992	695.00	3300-4200
1991	The Autumn Gate S/N	980	N/A	595.00	3100-3600
1995	Autumn Lane A/P	295		800.00	800-900
1995	Autumn Lane G/P	1,240		750.00	800
1995	Autumn Lane S/N	2,950		650.00	650
1994	Beacon of Hope A/P	275	1994	765.00	900-1300
1994	Beacon of Hope S/N	2,750	1994	615.00	725-1100
1996	Beginning of a Perfect Day A/P	295		1025.00	1025
1996	Beginning of a Perfect Day G/P	740		1240.00	1240
1996	Beginning of a Perfect Day S/N	2,950		1090.00	1090
1993	Beside Still Waters A/P	400	N/A	745.00	1200-1700
1993	Beside Still Waters G/P	490	N/A	745.00	1200-1700
1993	Beside Still Waters S/N	1,280	N/A	595.00	1100-1500
1995	Beside Still Waters S/P	Retrd.	N/A	N/A	2500
1993	Beyond Autumn Gate A/P	600	1993	915.00	3500-3800
1993	Beyond Autumn Gate G/P	500	N/A	915.00	3500-3900
1993	Beyond Autumn Gate S/N	1,750	N/A	815.00	3200-3600
1995	Beyond Autumn Gate S/P	Retrd.	N/A	N/A	4000
1993	The Blessings of Autumn A/P	300	1994	715.00	915-1200
1993	The Blessings of Autumn G/P	250	1994	715.00	915-1300
1993	The Blessings of Autumn S/N	1,250	1994	615.00	815-1200
1994	The Blessings of Spring A/P	275	1994	665.00	775-900
1994	The Blessings of Spring G/P	685	1994	665.00	800-1000
1994	The Blessings of Spring S/N	2,750	1994	515.00	625-800
1995	Blessings of Summer A/P	495		1015.00	1070
1995	Blessings of Summer G/P	1,240		965.00	965
1995	Blessings of Summer S/N	4,950		865.00	920
1995	Blossom Bridge A/P	295		730.00	730
1995	Blossom Bridge G/P	740		685.00	685
1995	Blossom Bridge S/N	2,950		580.00	580
1992	Blossom Hill Church A/P	200	1994	695.00	815-1200
1992	Blossom Hill Church R/P	Retrd.	1993	695.00	1000-1400
1992	Blossom Hill Church S/N	980	1994	595.00	715-1100
1991	Boston A/P	50	N/A	595.00	2300-2800
1991	Boston S/N	550	N/A	495.00	2000-2300
1992	Broadwater Bridge A/P	200	N/A	595.00	2100-2400
1992	Broadwater Bridge G/P	200	N/A	645.00	2100-2500
1992	Broadwater Bridge S/N	980	N/A	495.00	1900-2200
1995	Brookside Hideaway A/P	395	1995	695.00	795-1000
1995	Brookside Hideaway G/P	990	1995	695.00	800-1100
1995	Brookside Hideaway S/N	3,950		545.00	580
1991	Carmel, Delores Street and the Tuck Box Tea Room A/P	200	1992	745.00	3100-3400
1991	Carmel, Delores Street and the Tuck Box Tea Room R/P	Retrd.	1992	745.00	3200-3600
1991	Carmel, Delores Street and the Tuck Box Tea Room S/N	980	1992	645.00	2300-3100
1989	Carmel, Ocean Avenue A/P	Closed	N/A	795.00	6500-7500
1989	Carmel, Ocean Avenue S/N	Closed	N/A	645.00	4000-6000
1991	Cedar Nook Cottage R/P	200	1991	295.00	700-800
1991	Cedar Nook Cottage S/N	1,960	1991	195.00	315-415
1990	Chandler's Cottage S/N	Closed	N/A	495.00	2300-3000
1992	Christmas At the Ahwahnee A/P	200		615.00	730
1992	Christmas At the Ahwahnee S/N	980		515.00	580
1990	Christmas Cottage 1990 A/P	Closed	1990	295.00	2300-2600
1990	Christmas Cottage 1990 S/N	Closed	N/A	295.00	1600-2200
1990	Christmas Eve A/P	200	1991	495.00	1000-1500
1990	Christmas Eve R/P	Retrd.	1991	495.00	1800
1990	Christmas Eve S/N	980	N/A	395.00	800-1800
1994	Christmas Memories A/P	345	N/A	695.00	800-1100
1994	Christmas Memories G/P	860		695.00	800-1000
1994	Christmas Memories S/N	3,450	N/A	545.00	650-850
1994	Christmas Tree Cottage A/P	395		590.00	615
1994	Christmas Tree Cottage G/P	990		590.00	615
1994	Christmas Tree Cottage S/N	3,950		440.00	465
1992	Cottage-By-The-Sea A/P	200	1992	695.00	1600-2200
1992	Cottage-By-The-Sea G/P	200	N/A	745.00	1600-2300
1992	Cottage-By-The-Sea S/N	980	N/A	595.00	1400-1800
1992	Country Memories A/P	200	1992	495.00	800-1000
1992	Country Memories G/P	200		545.00	665
1992	Country Memories S/N	980	N/A	395.00	700-950
1994	Creekside Trail A/P	198	1994	840.00	840
1994	Creekside Trail G/P	500		840.00	840
1994	Creekside Trail S/N	1,984		690.00	690
1994	Days of Peace A/P	198		840.00	840
1994	Days of Peace G/P	500		840.00	840
1994	Days of Peace S/N	1,984		690.00	690
1995	Deer Creek Cottage A/P	295		615.00	615
1995	Deer Creek Cottage G/P	740		565.00	565
1995	Deer Creek Cottage S/N	2,950		465.00	465
1994	Dusk in the Valley A/P	198		840.00	840
1994	Dusk in the Valley G/P	500		840.00	840
1994	Dusk in the Valley S/N	1,984		690.00	690
1994	Emerald Isle Cottage A/P	275	1994	665.00	765-800
1994	Emerald Isle Cottage G/P	685		665.00	665
1994	Emerald Isle Cottage S/N	2,750		515.00	580
1993	End of a Perfect Day I A/P	400	N/A	615.00	2200-2300
1993	End of a Perfect Day I G/P	300	N/A	665.00	2200-2400
1993	End of a Perfect Day I S/N	1,250	N/A	515.00	1800-2000
1995	End of a Perfect Day I S/P	Retrd.	N/A	N/A	2450
1994	End of a Perfect Day II A/P	275	1994	765.00	1400-2200
1994	End of a Perfect Day II G/P	685	1994	765.00	1400-2200
1994	End of a Perfect Day II S/N	2,750	1995	615.00	1200-2000
1995	End of a Perfect Day III A/P	495	1995	1145.00	1145-1500
1995	End of a Perfect Day III G/P	1,240		1145.00	1245
1995	End of a Perfect Day III S/N	4,950		995.00	1055
1989	Entrance to the Manor House A/P	Closed	N/A	595.00	2000-2500
1989	Entrance to the Manor House S/N	Closed	N/A	495.00	1700-2000
1989	Evening at Merritt's Cottage A/P	Closed	N/A	595.00	2700-3000
1989	Evening at Merritt's Cottage S/N	Closed	N/A	495.00	2500-3000
1992	Evening at Swanbrooke Cottage Thomashire A/P	Closed	N/A	595.00	2000-2800
1992	Evening at Swanbrooke Cottage Thomashire G/P	Closed	N/A	645.00	2000-2900
1992	Evening at Swanbrooke Cottage Thomashire S/N	Closed	N/A	495.00	1900-2400
1992	Evening Carolers A/P	200		415.00	505
1992	Evening Carolers G/P	200		415.00	505
1992	Evening Carolers S/N	1,960		315.00	355
1995	Evening in the Forest A/P	495		695.00	730
1995	Evening in the Forest G/P	1,250		645.00	680
1995	Evening in the Forest S/N	4,950		545.00	580
1993	Fisherman's Wharf San Francisco A/P	275	1993	1065.00	1200-1600
1993	Fisherman's Wharf San Francisco G/P	550	N/A	1065.00	1200-1600
1993	Fisherman's Wharf San Francisco S/N	2,750	N/A	965.00	1100-1300
1991	Flags Over The Capitol A/P	200	N/A	695.00	715-1000
1991	Flags Over The Capitol R/P	Retrd.	N/A	695.00	1000-1300
1991	Flags Over The Capitol S/N	980		595.00	690
1993	The Garden of Promise A/P	300	N/A	715.00	1200-1800
1993	The Garden of Promise G/P	400	N/A	715.00	1700-1900
1993	The Garden of Promise S/N	1,250	1994	615.00	1000-1700
1995	The Garden of Promise S/P	Retrd.	N/A	N/A	3000
1992	The Garden Party A/P	200		595.00	650
1992	The Garden Party G/P	200		595.00	615
1992	The Garden Party S/N	980		495.00	580
1994	Gardens Beyond Autumn Gate S/N	Closed	1996	1025.00	1025-1200
1993	Glory of Evening A/P	400	1993	365.00	515-700
1993	Glory of Evening G/P	490		365.00	415
1993	Glory of Evening S/N	1,980	1994	315.00	415-600
1993	Glory of Morning A/P	400	1993	365.00	515-700
1993	Glory of Morning G/P	490	1993	365.00	515-700
1993	Glory of Morning S/N	1,980	1994	315.00	415-600
1993	Glory of Winter A/P	300		715.00	715-765
1993	Glory of Winter G/P	250		715.00	840
1993	Glory of Winter S/N	1,250		615.00	690
1995	Golden Gate Bridge, San Francisco A/P	395		1240.00	1240
1995	Golden Gate Bridge, San Francisco G/P	990		1190.00	1190
1995	Golden Gate Bridge, San Francisco S/N	3,950		1090.00	1090
1994	Guardian Castle A/P	475		1015.00	1070
1994	Guardian Castle G/P	1,190		1015.00	1070
1994	Guardian Castle S/N	4,750		865.00	920
1993	Heather's Hutch A/P	400	1993	515.00	665-900
1993	Heather's Hutch G/P	300	N/A	515.00	665-900
1993	Heather's Hutch S/N	1,250	N/A	415.00	600-900
1994	Hidden Arbor A/P	375		665.00	730
1994	Hidden Arbor G/P	685		665.00	730
1994	Hidden Arbor S/N	3,750		515.00	580
1990	Hidden Cottage I A/P	100	N/A	595.00	2500-4000
1990	Hidden Cottage I S/N	500	N/A	495.00	2300-3700
1993	Hidden Cottage II A/P	400	1993	615.00	800-1000
1993	Hidden Cottage II G/P	400	1995	665.00	800-1100
1993	Hidden Cottage II S/N	1,480	1994	515.00	700-1000
1994	Hidden Gazebo A/P	240	1994	665.00	800-1200
1994	Hidden Gazebo G/P	600	1994	665.00	800-1200
1994	Hidden Gazebo S/N	2,400	1994	515.00	900
1991	Home For The Evening A/P	200	1994	295.00	700-1000
1991	Home For The Evening S/N	980	N/A	195.00	550-700
1991	Home For The Holidays A/P	200	1991	695.00	2200-3000
1991	Home For The Holidays R/P	N/A	1991	695.00	3200-3500
1991	Home For The Holidays S/N	980	N/A	595.00	1600-2500
1992	Home is Where the Heart Is A/P	200	N/A	695.00	2100-2200
1992	Home is Where the Heart Is G/P	200	N/A	695.00	2100-2200
1992	Home is Where the Heart Is S/N	980	N/A	595.00	1900
1993	Homestead House A/P	300		715.00	715
1993	Homestead House G/P	250		715.00	840
1993	Homestead House S/N	1,250	1995	615.00	715
1995	Hometown Chapel A/P	495		1045.00	1100
1995	Hometown Chapel G/P	1,240		995.00	1050
1995	Hometown Chapel S/N	4,950		895.00	95

*Quotes have been rounded up to nearest dollar

YEAR ISSUE		EDITION LIMIT	YEAR RETD.	ISSUE PRICE	*QUOTE U.S.$
1995	Hometown Memories I A/P	495	1995	1015.00	1015-1100
1995	Hometown Memories I G/P	1,240		1015.00	1020
1995	Hometown Memories I S/N	4,950		865.00	920
1992	Julianne's Cottage A/P	200	N/A	495.00	1800-2000
1992	Julianne's Cottage G/P	200	N/A	545.00	1900-2100
1992	Julianne's Cottage S/N	980	N/A	395.00	1500-1800
1993	Lamplight Brooke A/P	400	1994	715.00	1900-2400
1993	Lamplight Brooke G/P	330	1994	715.00	1900-2500
1993	Lamplight Brooke S/N	1,650	1994	615.00	1600-2200
1994	Lamplight Inn A/P	275	1994	765.00	900-1100
1994	Lamplight Inn G/P	685	1994	765.00	900-1100
1994	Lamplight Inn S/N	2,750	1994	615.00	715-815
1993	Lamplight Lane A/P	200	N/A	695.00	3200-3700
1993	Lamplight Lane G/P	200	1994	695.00	3200-3800
1993	Lamplight Lane S/N	980	N/A	595.00	3000-3600
1995	Lamplight Lane S/P	Retrd.	N/A	N/A	2700-3000
1995	Lamplight Village A/P	495	1995	800.00	900-1100
1995	Lamplight Village G/P	1,240		800.00	900
1995	Lamplight Village S/N	4,950	1995	650.00	750-1000
1995	A Light in the Storm A/P	395	1995	800.00	800
1995	A Light in the Storm G/P	1,240		750.00	750
1995	A Light in the Storm S/N	3,950		650.00	650
1995	The Lights of Home S/N	2,500		195.00	195
1996	Lilac Gazebo A/P	295		615.00	615
1996	Lilac Gazebo G/P	740		615.00	615
1996	Lilac Gazebo S/N	2,950		465.00	465
1991	The Lit Path A/P	200	1991	395.00	415-495
1991	The Lit Path R/P	Retrd.	1991	395.00	395-495
1991	The Lit Path S/N	1,960	1994	195.00	315
1995	Main Street Celebration A/P	125	1995	800.00	800
1995	Main Street Celebration S/N	1,250		650.00	650
1995	Main Street Courthouse A/P	125	1995	800.00	800
1995	Main Street Courthouse S/N	1,250		650.00	690
1995	Main Street Matinee A/P	125	1995	800.00	800
1995	Main Street Matinee S/N	1,250		650.00	690
1995	Main Street Trolley A/P	125	1995	800.00	800
1995	Main Street Trolley S/N	1,250		650.00	690
1991	McKenna's Cottage A/P	100		595.00	730
1991	McKenna's Cottage R/P	200	N/A	615.00	615
1991	McKenna's Cottage S/N	980	1995	495.00	615-715
1992	Miller's Cottage, Thomashire A/P	200	N/A	595.00	1000-1300
1992	Miller's Cottage, Thomashire G/P	200	N/A	595.00	1000-1400
1992	Miller's Cottage, Thomashire S/N	980	1994	495.00	900-1500
1994	Moonlight Lane I A/P	240	1995	665.00	665
1994	Moonlight Lane I G/P	600		665.00	665
1994	Moonlight Lane I S/N	2,400		515.00	580
1992	Moonlit Sleigh Ride A/P	200	1995	395.00	505
1992	Moonlit Sleigh Ride S/N	1,960	1994	295.00	315-500
1995	Morning Dogwood A/P	495		645.00	675
1995	Morning Dogwood G/P	1,240		645.00	645
1995	Morning Dogwood S/N	4,950		495.00	525
1995	Morning Glory Cottage A/P	495		695.00	730
1995	Morning Glory Cottage G/P	1,240		645.00	680
1995	Morning Glory Cottage S/N	4,950		545.00	580
1990	Morning Light A/P	N/A	N/A	695.00	2000-2300
1992	Olde Porterfield Gift Shoppe A/P	200	1995	595.00	615-915
1992	Olde Porterfield Gift Shoppe G/P	200		595.00	615
1992	Olde Porterfield Gift Shoppe S/N	980	1994	495.00	515-750
1991	Olde Porterfield Tea Room A/P	200	N/A	595.00	1300-1700
1991	Olde Porterfield Tea Room R/P	Retrd.	1991	595.00	1200-1900
1991	Olde Porterfield Tea Room S/N	980	N/A	495.00	1100-1500
1991	Open Gate, Sussex A/P	100	1994	295.00	415
1991	Open Gate, Sussex R/P	Retrd.	1992	295.00	500-600
1991	Open Gate, Sussex S/N	980	1994	195.00	315-450
1993	Paris, City of Lights A/P	600	1994	765.00	1600-2200
1993	Paris, City of Lights G/P	600	N/A	815.00	1900-2300
1993	Paris, City of Lights S/N	1,980	N/A	695.00	1400-1800
1994	Paris, Eiffel Tower A/P	275	1994	945.00	1200-1600
1994	Paris, Eiffel Tower G/P	685	1995	945.00	1400-1600
1994	Paris, Eiffel Tower S/N	2,750	1994	795.00	800-1245
1995	Petals of Hope A/P	395		730.00	730
1995	Petals of Hope G/P	990		680.00	680
1995	Petals of Hope S/N	3,950		580.00	580
1994	The Power & The Majesty A/P	275		765.00	840
1994	The Power & The Majesty G/P	685		765.00	840
1994	The Power & The Majesty S/N	2,750		615.00	690
1991	Pye Corner Cottage A/P	200		295.00	395
1991	Pye Corner Cottage R/P	Retrd.	N/A	295.00	395
1991	Pye Corner Cottage S/N	1,960		195.00	245
1990	Rose Arbor A/P	Closed	N/A	595.00	1900-2400
1990	Rose Arbor S/N	Closed	N/A	495.00	1500-2000
1996	Rose Gate A/P	295		615.00	615
1996	Rose Gate G/P	740		615.00	615
1996	Rose Gate S/N	2,950		465.00	465
1994	San Francisco Market Street A/P	750	1994	945.00	945-1045
1994	San Francisco Market Street G/P	1,875		945.00	945-1045
1994	San Francisco Market Street S/N	7,500		795.00	800-900
1992	San Francisco, Nob Hill (California St.) A/P	Closed	N/A	715.00	4200-5400
1992	San Francisco, Nob Hill (California St.) P/P	Closed	N/A	815.00	5500-5900
1992	San Francisco, Nob Hill (California St.) S/N	Closed	N/A	645.00	4000-5200
1989	San Francisco, Union Square A/P	Closed	N/A	795.00	5000-6000
1989	San Francisco, Union Square S/N	Closed	N/A	595.00	5000-5500
1992	Silent Night A/P	200	N/A	495.00	1100-1300
1992	Silent Night G/P	200	N/A	495.00	1100-1300
1992	Silent Night S/N	980	N/A	395.00	1000-1100
1995	Simpler Times I A/P	345		840.00	840
1995	Simpler Times I G/P	870		790.00	790
1995	Simpler Times I S/N	3,450		690.00	690
1990	Spring At Stonegate A/P	50	N/A	395.00	515
1990	Spring At Stonegate S/N	550	1995	295.00	415
1994	Spring in the Alps A/P	198		725.00	730
1994	Spring in the Alps G/P	500		725.00	730
1994	Spring in the Alps S/N	1,984		575.00	580
1993	St. Nicholas Circle A/P	420	1995	715.00	915-1100
1993	St. Nicholas Circle G/P	350	1995	715.00	915-1100
1993	St. Nicholas Circle S/N	1,750	1994	615.00	750-950
1995	Stepping Stone Cottage A/P	295		840.00	840
1995	Stepping Stone Cottage G/P	740		840.00	840
1995	Stepping Stone Cottage S/N	2,950		690.00	690
1993	Stonehearth Hutch A/P	300	N/A	515.00	695-1000
1993	Stonehearth Hutch G/P	300	1994	515.00	695-1000
1993	Stonehearth Hutch S/N	1,650	N/A	415.00	450-850
1993	Studio in the Garden A/P	400		515.00	615
1993	Studio in the Garden G/P	600		515.00	600
1993	Studio in the Garden S/N	1,480		415.00	465
1992	Sunday at Apple Hill A/P	200	1993	595.00	1200-1400
1992	Sunday at Apple Hill G/P	200	N/A	595.00	1200-1500
1992	Sunday at Apple Hill S/N	980	1993	495.00	1100-1400
1993	Sunday Outing A/P	200	N/A	595.00	1100-1500
1993	Sunday Outing G/P	200	N/A	595.00	1100-1500
1993	Sunday Outing S/N	980	N/A	495.00	1000-1400
1992	Sweetheart Cottage I A/P	200	1992	595.00	1300-1500
1992	Sweetheart Cottage I G/P	200	N/A	595.00	1300-1500
1992	Sweetheart Cottage I S/N	980	N/A	495.00	1200-1400
1993	Sweetheart Cottage II A/P	400	1993	695.00	1450-1700
1993	Sweetheart Cottage II G/P	490	N/A	745.00	1400-1700
1993	Sweetheart Cottage II S/N	980	N/A	595.00	1200-1500
1994	Sweetheart Cottage III A/P	165	1994	765.00	865-1300
1994	Sweetheart Cottage III G/P	410	1994	765.00	865-1300
1994	Sweetheart Cottage III S/N	1,650	1994	615.00	650-1150
1992	Victorian Christmas I A/P	200	1992	695.00	2000-2900
1992	Victorian Christmas I G/P	200	1992	695.00	2600-2900
1992	Victorian Christmas I S/N	980	1992	595.00	2400-2600
1993	Victorian Christmas II A/P	400	1994	715.00	1700-2000
1993	Victorian Christmas II G/P	300	1994	715.00	1700-2000
1993	Victorian Christmas II S/N	1,650	1994	615.00	1400-1800
1994	Victorian Christmas III A/P	395	1994	800.00	800
1994	Victorian Christmas III G/P	990		800.00	800
1994	Victorian Christmas III S/N	3,950	1995	650.00	650-900
1995	Victorian Christmas IV S/N	2,330	1995	650.00	650
1991	Victorian Evening	Closed	1993	495.00	1300-1500
1992	Victorian Garden A/P	200	1993	895.00	2500-2800
1992	Victorian Garden G/P	200	1993	895.00	2500-2800
1992	Victorian Garden S/N	980	1993	795.00	2300-2600
1993	Village Inn A/P	400		615.00	730
1993	Village Inn G/P	400		615.00	730
1993	Village Inn S/N	1,200	1994	515.00	615-800
1994	The Warmth of Home A/P	345		590.00	615
1994	The Warmth of Home G/P	860		590.00	615
1994	The Warmth of Home S/N	3,450		440.00	465
1992	Weathervane Hutch A/P	200	1995	395.00	515-800
1992	Weathervane Hutch G/P	200		395.00	415
1992	Weathervane Hutch S/N	1,960	1992	295.00	415-700
1996	Winsor Manor A/P	395		840.00	840
1996	Winsor Manor G/P	990		840.00	840
1996	Winsor Manor S/N	3,950		690.00	690
1993	Winter's End A/P	400		715.00	840
1993	Winter's End G/P	490		715.00	840
1993	Winter's End S/N	1,450		615.00	690
1991	Woodman's Thatch A/P	200	1995	295.00	500-700
1991	Woodman's Thatch R/P	200	N/A	295.00	500-700
1991	Woodman's Thatch S/N	1,960	1994	195.00	300-450
1992	Yosemite A/P	200		695.00	840
1992	Yosemite G/P	200		695.00	840
1992	Yosemite S/N	980		595.00	690

Kinkade-Premium Paper-Unframed - T. Kinkade

YEAR ISSUE		EDITION LIMIT	YEAR RETD.	ISSUE PRICE	*QUOTE U.S.$
1991	Afternoon Light, Dogwood A/P	98	N/A	295.00	500-1000
1991	Afternoon Light, Dogwood S/N	980	N/A	185.00	350-750
1992	Amber Afternoon S/N	980		225.00	265
1994	Autumn at Ashley's Cottage A/P	245		335.00	395
1994	Autumn at Ashley's Cottage S/N	2,450		185.00	195
1991	The Autumn Gate S/N	980	1994	225.00	500-1000
1995	Autumn Lane A/P	285		400.00	400
1995	Autumn Lane S/N	2,850		250.00	250
1994	Beacon of Hope S/N	2,750		235.00	265
1996	Beginning of a Perfect Day A/P	285		475.00	475
1996	Beginning of a Perfect Day S/N	2,850		325.00	325
1993	Beside Still Waters S/N	1,280	1994	185.00	400-600
1993	Beyond Autumn Gate S/N	1,750	1994	285.00	500-1000
1985	Birth of a City S/N	Closed	N/A	150.00	900-1300
1993	The Blessings of Autumn S/N	1,250		235.00	265
1994	The Blessings of Spring A/P	275		345.00	370
1994	The Blessings of Spring S/N	2,750		195.00	220
1995	Blessings of Summer A/P	485		450.00	450
1995	Blessings of Summer S/N	4,850		300.00	300
1995	Blossom Bridge S/N	2,850		205.00	205
1992	Blossom Hill Church S/N	980		225.00	265
1991	Boston S/N	550	1994	175.00	350-850
1992	Broadwater Bridge S/N	980	1994	225.00	400-800
1995	Brookside Hideaway A/P	385		355.00	355
1995	Brookside Hideaway S/N	3,850		205.00	220
1991	Carmel, Delores Street and the Tuck Box Tea Room S/N	980	1994	275.00	500-1100
1989	Carmel, Ocean Avenue S/N	Closed	N/A	225.00	1500-2500
1990	Chandler's Cottage S/N	Closed	N/A	125.00	1000-1500
1992	Christmas At the Ahwahnee S/N	980	1995	175.00	220
1990	Christmas Cottage 1990 S/N	Closed	N/A	95.00	350-600
1991	Christmas Eve S/N	980	1995	125.00	185
1994	Christmas Tree Cottage A/P	295		335.00	395
1994	Christmas Tree Cottage S/N	2,950		185.00	195
1992	Cottage-By-The-Sea S/N	980	N/A	250.00	500-900
1992	Country Memories S/N	980		185.00	195
1994	Creekside Trail A/P	198		425.00	425
1994	Creekside Trail S/N	1,984		275.00	275
1984	Dawson S/N	Closed	N/A	150.00	1200-1600
1994	Days of Peace A/P	198		425.00	425
1994	Days of Peace S/N	1,984		275.00	275
1995	Deer Creek Cottage A/P	285		335.00	335
1995	Deer Creek Cottage S/N	2,850		185.00	185
1994	Dusk in the Valley A/P	198		425.00	425
1994	Dusk in the Valley S/N	1,984		275.00	275
1994	Emerald Isle Cottage A/P	275		345.00	355
1994	Emerald Isle Cottage S/N	2,750		195.00	220
1993	End of a Perfect Day I S/N	1,250	1994	195.00	500-900
1994	End of a Perfect Day II A/P	275		385.00	435
1994	End of a Perfect Day II S/N	2,750		235.00	300
1995	End of a Perfect Day III A/P	485		475.00	475
1995	End of a Perfect Day III S/N	4,850		325.00	345
1989	Entrance to the Manor House	Closed	N/A	125.00	800-1000
1989	Evening at Merritt's Cottage	Closed	N/A	125.00	1000-1200
1992	Evening at Swanbrooke Cottage, S/N	Closed	1994	250.00	600-1100
1995	Evening in the Forest A/P	485		355.00	355
1995	Evening in the Forest S/N	4,850		205.00	205
1985	Evening Service S/N	Closed	N/A	90.00	700-1100
1991	Flags Over The Capitol S/N	1,991		195.00	265
1993	The Garden of Promise S/N	1,250	1994	235.00	500
1992	The Garden Party S/N	980		175.00	220
1994	Gardens Beyond Autumn Gate S/N	Closed	1996	325.00	325
1993	Glory of Winter S/N	1,250		235.00	265
1995	Golden Gate Bridge, San Francisco A/P	385		475.00	475
1995	Golden Gate Bridge, San Francisco S/N	3,850		325.00	325
1994	Guardian Castle A/P	275		450.00	450
1994	Guardian Castle G/P	685		450.00	450
1994	Guardian Castle S/N	2,750		300.00	320
1993	Heather's Hutch S/N	1,250		175.00	195
1994	Hidden Arbor S/N	2,750	N/A	195.00	195
1993	Hidden Cottage II S/N	1,480		195.00	195
1990	Hidden Cottage S/N	550	N/A	125.00	1000-1500
1994	Hidden Gazebo A/P	275		345.00	355
1994	Hidden Gazebo, S/N	2,400	1995	195.00	195
1991	Home For The Evening S/N	Closed	N/A	100.00	200-300
1991	Home For The Holidays S/N	980	1994	225.00	500
1992	Home is Where the Heart Is, S/N	980	1994	225.00	500-800
1993	Homestead House S/N	1,250		235.00	265
1995	Hometown Memories I A/P	485		450.00	470
1995	Hometown Memories I S/N	4,850		300.00	320
1992	Julianne's Cottage S/N	Closed	N/A	185.00	400-550
1993	Lamplight Brook S/N	1,650	1995	235.00	300-400
1994	Lamplight Inn A/P	275	1995	385.00	415
1994	Lamplight Inn S/N	2,750		235.00	265
1993	Lamplight Lane S/N	Closed	N/A	225.00	500-900
1995	Lamplight Village A/P	485		400.00	415
1995	Lamplight Village S/N	4,850		250.00	265
1995	A Light in the Storm A/P	385		415.00	415
1995	A Light in the Storm S/N	3,850		265.00	265
1995	The Lights of Home A/P	250		225.00	225
1996	Lilac Gazebo A/P	285		335.00	335
1996	Lilac Gazebo S/N	2,850		185.00	185
1995	Main Street Celebration A/P	195		400.00	400
1995	Main Street Celebration S/N	1,950		250.00	250
1995	Main Street Courthouse A/P	195		400.00	400
1995	Main Street Courthouse S/N	1,950		250.00	250
1995	Main Street Matinee A/P	195		400.00	400
1995	Main Street Matinee S/N	1,950		250.00	250
1995	Main Street Trolley A/P	195		400.00	400
1995	Main Street Trolley S/N	1,950		250.00	250
1991	McKenna's Cottage S/N	980		150.00	220
1992	Miller's Cottage S/N	980	1995	175.00	300-400
1994	Moonlight Lane I A/P	240		345.00	345
1994	Moonlight Lane I S/N	2,400		195.00	195
1985	Moonlight on the Riverfront S/N	Closed	N/A	150.00	1800
1995	Morning Dogwood A/P	485		345.00	345
1995	Morning Dogwood S/N	4,850		195.00	205
1995	Morning Glory Cottage A/P	485		355.00	355
1995	Morning Glory Cottage S/N	4,850		205.00	205
1986	New York, 6th Avenue S/N	Closed	N/A	150.00	1700-2000
1992	Olde Porterfield Gift Shoppe S/N	980		175.00	195
1991	Olde Porterfield Tea Room S/N	980	N/A	150.00	200-500
1991	Open Gate, Sussex S/N	980		100.00	115
1993	Paris, City of Lights S/N	1,980	1995	285.00	295-495
1994	Paris, Eiffel Tower A/P	275		445.00	445
1994	Paris, Eiffel Tower S/N	2,750		295.00	310
1995	Petals of Hope A/P	385		355.00	355
1995	Petals of Hope S/N	3,850		205.00	205
1984	Placerville, 1916 S/N	Closed	N/A	90.00	1800-2800
1994	The Power & The Majesty A/P	275		385.00	385
1994	The Power & The Majesty S/N	2,750		235.00	265
1988	Room with a View S/N	Closed	N/A	150.00	800-1000
1990	Rose Arbor S/N	Closed	1994	125.00	350-700
1996	Rose Gate A/P	285		335.00	335
1996	Rose Gate S/N	2,850		185.00	185
1994	San Francisco Market Street A/P	750		525.00	550
1994	San Francisco Market Street S/N	7,500		375.00	400
1986	San Francisco, 1909 S/N	Closed	N/A	150.00	1900-2500
1993	San Francisco, Fisherman's Wharf S/N	2,750	1995	305.00	305

*Quotes have been rounded up to nearest dollar

YEAR ISSUE		EDITION LIMIT	YEAR RETD.	ISSUE PRICE	*QUOTE U.S.$
1992	San Francisco, Nob Hill (California St.) S/N	Closed	N/A	275.00	1800-2800
1989	San Francisco, Union Square S/N	Closed	N/A	225.00	2000-3000
1992	Silent Night S/N	980	1994	175.00	375
1995	Simpler Time I A/P	335		400.00	400
1995	Simpler Time I S/N	3,350		250.00	250
1990	Spring At Stonegate S/N	550	N/A	95.00	175-275
1994	Spring in the Alps A/P	198		375.00	375
1994	Spring in the Alps S/N	1,984		225.00	225
1993	St. Nicholas Circle S/N	1,750	1995	235.00	265
1995	Stepping Stone Cottage A/P	285		400.00	400
1995	Stepping Stone Cottage S/N	2,850		250.00	250
1993	Stonehearth Hutch S/N	1,650	1995	175.00	195
1993	Studio in the Garden S/N	980	1995	175.00	175
1992	Sunday At Apple Hill, S/N	980	1994	175.00	400-500
1993	Sunday Outing S/N	980	1995	175.00	205-295
1992	Sweetheart Cottage I S/N	980	1995	150.00	250-400
1993	Sweetheart Cottage II S/N	980	1994	150.00	400-600
1993	Sweetheart Cottage III A/P	165	1995	385.00	400
1993	Sweetheart Cottage III S/N	1,650		235.00	265
1992	Victorian Christmas I S/N	980	N/A	235.00	500-800
1993	Victorian Christmas II S/N	1,650		235.00	250
1994	Victorian Christmas III S/N	2,950	1995	250.00	250
1995	Victorian Christmas IV S/N	750	1995	250.00	250
1991	Victorian Evening, S/N	Retrd.	1993	150.00	250-450
1992	Victorian Garden, S/N	980	1994	275.00	500-1000
1993	Village Inn S/N	1,200		195.00	220
1994	The Warmth of Home A/P	245		335.00	345
1994	The Warmth of Home S/N	2,450		185.00	195
1996	Winsor Manor A/P	385		400.00	400
1996	Winsor Manor S/N	3,850		250.00	250
1993	Winter's End S/N	875		235.00	265
1992	Yosemite S/N	980	1995	225.00	265

Lightpost Publishing/ Recollections

American Heroes Collection-Framed - Recollections

YEAR ISSUE		EDITION LIMIT	YEAR RETD.	ISSUE PRICE	*QUOTE U.S.$
1992	Abraham Lincoln	7,500		150.00	150
1993	Babe Ruth	2,250	1996	95.00	95
1993	Ben Franklin	1,000		95.00	95
1994	Dwight D. Eisenhower	Open		30.00	30
1994	Eternal Love (Civil War)	1,861		195.00	195
1994	Franklin D. Roosevelt	Open		30.00	30
1992	George Washington	7,500		150.00	150
1994	George Washington	Open		30.00	30
1992	John F. Kennedy	7,500		150.00	150
1994	John F. Kennedy	Open		30.00	30
1992	Mark Twain	7,500		150.00	150
1994	A Nation Divided	1,000		150.00	150
1993	A Nation United	1,000		150.00	150

Cinema Classics Collection - Recollections

YEAR ISSUE		EDITION LIMIT	YEAR RETD.	ISSUE PRICE	*QUOTE U.S.$
1993	As God As My Witness Classic Clip	Closed	1995	40.00	40
1994	Attempted Deception Classic Clip	Open		30.00	30
1994	A Chance Meeting Classic Clip	Open		30.00	30
1993	A Dream Remembered Classic Clip	Closed	1995	40.00	40
1993	The Emerald City Classic Clip	Closed	1995	40.00	40
1993	Follow the Yellow Brick Road Classic Clip	Closed	1995	40.00	40
1993	Frankly My Dear Classic Clip	Closed	1995	40.00	40
1994	The Gift Classic Clip	Open		30.00	30
1993	Gone With the Wind-Movie Ticket Classic Clip	2,000		40.00	40
1994	If I Only Had a Brain Classic Clip	Open		30.00	30
1994	If I Only Had a Heart Classic Clip	Open		30.00	30
1994	If I Only Had the Nerve Classic Clip	Open		30.00	30
1993	The Kiss Classic Clip	Closed	1995	40.00	40
1993	Not A Marrying Man	12,500		150.00	150
1993	Over The Rainbow	7,500		150.00	150
1994	The Proposal Classic Clip	Open		30.00	30
1993	The Ruby Slippers Classic Clip	Closed	1995	40.00	40
1993	Scarlett & Her Beaux	12,500		150.00	150
1994	There's No Place Like Home Classic Clip	Open		30.00	30
1993	We're Off to See the Wizard Classic Clip	Closed	1995	40.00	40
1993	You Do Waltz Divinely	12,500		195.00	195
1993	You Need Kissing	12,500		195.00	195

The Elvis Collection - Recollections

YEAR ISSUE		EDITION LIMIT	YEAR RETD.	ISSUE PRICE	*QUOTE U.S.$
1994	Celebrity Soldier/Regular G.I.	Open		30.00	30
1994	Dreams Remembered/Dreams Realized	Open		30.00	30
1994	Elvis the King	2,750		195.00	195
1994	Elvis the Pelvis	2,750		195.00	195
1994	The King/The Servant	Open		30.00	30
1994	Lavish Spender/Generous Giver	Open		30.00	30
1994	Professional Artist/Practical Joker	Open		30.00	30
1994	Public Image/Private Man	Open		30.00	30
1994	Sex Symbol/Boy Next Door	Open		30.00	30
1994	To Elvis with Love	2,750		195.00	195
1994	Vulgar Showman/Serious Musician	Open		30.00	30

Gone With the Wind - Recollections

YEAR ISSUE		EDITION LIMIT	YEAR RETD.	ISSUE PRICE	*QUOTE U.S.$
1995	Final Parting Classic Clip	Open		30.00	30
1995	A Parting Kiss Classic Clip	Open		30.00	30
1995	The Red Dress Classic Clip	Open		30.00	30
1995	Sweet Revenge Classic Clip	Open		30.00	30

The Wizard of Oz - Recollections

YEAR ISSUE		EDITION LIMIT	YEAR RETD.	ISSUE PRICE	*QUOTE U.S.$
1995	Glinda the Good Witch	Open		30.00	30
1995	Toto	Open		30.00	30
1995	The Wicked Witch	Open		30.00	30
1995	The Wizard	Open		30.00	30

Marty Bell

Members Only Collectors Club - M. Bell

YEAR ISSUE		EDITION LIMIT	YEAR RETD.	ISSUE PRICE	*QUOTE U.S.$
1991	Little Thatch Twilight	Closed	1992	288.00	350
1991	Charter Rose, The	Closed	1992	Gift	N/A
1992	Candle At Eventide	Closed	1993	Gift	N/A
1992	Blossom Lane	Closed	1993	288.00	288-395
1993	Laverstoke Lodge	Closed	1994	328.00	328
1993	Chideock Gate	Closed	1994	Gift	N/A
1994	Hummingbird Hill	Closed	1995	320.00	450-495
1994	The Hummingbird	Closed	1995	Gift	N/A
1995	The Bluebird Victorian	Closed	1996	320.00	340
1995	The Bluebird	Closed	1996	Gift	N/A
1996	Goldfinch Garden	Yr.Iss.		220.00	220
1996	The Goldfinch	Yr.Iss.		Gift	N/A

America the Beautiful - M. Bell

YEAR ISSUE		EDITION LIMIT	YEAR RETD.	ISSUE PRICE	*QUOTE U.S.$
1993	Jones Victorian	750	1994	400.00	1300
1995	The Tuck Box Tea Room, Carmel	500	1995	456.00	1295
1993	Turlock Spring	500	1995	700.00	750

Christmas - M. Bell

YEAR ISSUE		EDITION LIMIT	YEAR RETD.	ISSUE PRICE	*QUOTE U.S.$
1989	Fireside Christmas	500	1989	136.00	750
1990	Ready For Christmas	700	1990	148.00	495
1991	Christmas in Rochester	900	1991	148.00	275-350
1992	McCoy's Toy Shoppe	900	1992	148.00	350
1993	Christmas Treasures	900	1993	200.00	200
1994	Rocky Mountain Christmas	750	1994	400.00	424
1995	Tuck Box Christmas	750	1995	250.00	250

England - M. Bell

YEAR ISSUE		EDITION LIMIT	YEAR RETD.	ISSUE PRICE	*QUOTE U.S.$
1987	Alderton Village	500	1988	235.00	650
1990	Arbor Cottage	900	1990	130.00	150-250
1993	Arundel Row	750	1995	130.00	138
1991	Bay Tree Cottage, Rye	1,100	1992	230.00	230-520
1981	Bibury Cottage	500	1988	280.00	800-1000
1981	Big Daddy's Shoe	700	1989	64.00	150-300
1988	The Bishop's Roses	900	1989	220.00	695
1989	Blush of Spring	1,200	1990	96.00	120-160
1988	Bodiam Twilight	900	1991	520.00	900-1100
1988	Brendon Hills Lane	900	1995	304.00	318
1992	Briarwood	217	1993	220.00	220
1993	Broadway Cottage	750	1995	330.00	350
1987	Broughton Village	900	1988	128.00	400-500
1984	Brown Eyes	312	1993	296.00	296
1990	Bryants Puddle Thatch	900	1990	130.00	150-295
1986	Burford Village Store	500	1988	106.00	595
1981	Castle Combe Cottage	500	1988	230.00	895
1993	The Castle Tearoom	900	1993	88.00	88
1987	The Chaplains Garden	500	1987	235.00	1000-2000
1991	Childswickham Morning	305	1993	396.00	396
1987	Chippenham Farm	500	1988	120.00	300-900
1988	Clove Cottage	900	1988	128.00	500
1988	Clover Lane Cottage	1,800	1988	272.00	800
1991	Cobblestone	1,200	1995	374.00	404
1993	Coln St. Aldwyn's	1,000	1995	730.00	1200-1400
1986	Cotswold Parish Church	500	1988	98.00	1500-2000
1988	Cotswold Twilight	900	1988	128.00	200-495
1991	Cozy Cottage	900	1991	130.00	130
1982	Crossroads Cottage	S/O	1987	38.00	200
1992	Devon Cottage	900	1995	374.00	404
1991	Devon Roses	1,200	1991	78.00	195-500
1991	Dorset Roses	1,200	1991	96.00	195
1987	Dove Cottage Garden	900	1990	260.00	304-495
1987	Driftstone Manor	500	1988	440.00	1500-1800
1987	Ducksbridge Cottage	500	1988	400.00	2000
1987	Eashing Cottage	900	1988	120.00	200-400
1992	East Sussex Roses (Archival)	1,200	1993	184.00	184
1985	Fiddleford Cottage	500	1986	78.00	1950
1988	Friday Street Lane	1,800	1992	280.00	600
1989	The Game Keeper's Cottage	900	1989	560.00	1800-2000
1992	Garlands Flower Shop	900	1992	220.00	220
1988	Ginger Cottage	1,800	1988	320.00	550-800
1989	Glory Cottage	911	1993	96.00	96
1989	Goater's Cottage	900	1991	368.00	400-560
1990	Gomshall Flower Shop	900	1990	396.00	2900-3300
1987	Halfway Cottage	900	1988	260.00	300-500
1992	Hollybush	1,200	1994	560.00	795
1991	Horsham Farmhouse	1,200	1995	180.00	200
1986	Housewives Choice	500	1987	98.00	750-1000
1988	Icomb Village Garden	900	1988	620.00	1300-1500
1988	Jasmine Thatch	900	1991	272.00	495
1989	Larkspur Cottage	900	1989	220.00	495
1985	Little Boxford	500	1987	78.00	300-900
1991	Little Timbers	900	1992	130.00	130
1987	Little Tulip Thatch	500	1988	120.00	400-700
1990	Little Well Thatch	950	1990	130.00	150-250
1990	Longparish Cottage	900	1991	368.00	650
1990	Longstock Lane	900	1990	130.00	295
1986	Lorna Doone Cottage	500	1987	380.00	7000-8000
1990	Lower Brockhampton Manor	900	1990	640.00	1800
1988	Lullabye Cottage	900	1988	220.00	300-400
1987	May Cottage	900	1988	120.00	200-699
1988	Meadow School	816	1993	220.00	350
1985	Meadowlark Cottage	500	1987	78.00	450-699
1987	Millpond, Stockbridge, The	500	1987	120.00	1100
1987	Morning Glory Cottage	500	1988	120.00	450-599
1988	Morning's Glow	1,800	1989	280.00	320-650
1988	Murrle Cottage	1,800	1988	320.00	450-650
1983	Nestlewood	500	1987	300.00	2500
1989	Northcote Lane	1,160	1993	88.00	88
1989	Old Beams Cottage	900	1990	368.00	650
1988	Old Bridge, Grasmere	453	1993	640.00	640
1990	Old Hertfordshire Thatch	900	1990	396.00	2000
1993	Old Mother Hubbard's Cottage	2-Yr.	1995	230.00	250
1989	Overbrook	827	1993	220.00	350
1992	Pangbourne on Thames	900	1994	304.00	675
1984	Penshurst Tea Rooms (Archival)	1,000	1988	335.00	950
1984	Penshurst Tea Rooms (Canvas)	500	1987	335.00	1500-3600
1989	Pride of Spring	1,200	1990	96.00	200-400
1988	Rodway Cottage	900	1989	694.00	700-1500
1989	Rose Bedroom, The	515	1993	388.00	388
1990	Sanctuary	900	1992	220.00	450
1982	Sandhills Cottage	S/O	1987	38.00	38
1988	Sandy Lane Thatch	375	1993	380.00	500
1982	School Lane Cottage	S/O	1987	38.00	38
1993	Selborne Cottage	750	1995	300.00	318
1988	Shere Village Antiques	900	1988	272.00	304-699
1981	Spring in the Santa Ynez	500	1991	400.00	1100
1991	Springtime at Scotney	1,200	1992	730.00	950-1200
1989	St. Martin's Ashurst	243	1993	344.00	344
1990	Summer's Garden	900	1991	78.00	400-800
1985	Summers Glow	500	1987	98.00	600-1000
1987	Sunrise Thatch	900	1988	120.00	200-300
1985	Surrey Garden House	500	1986	98.00	850-1499
1985	Sweet Pine Cottage	500	1987	78.00	350-1499
1988	Sweet Twilight	900	1988	220.00	350-600
1990	Sweetheart Thatch	900	1993	220.00	375
1991	Tea Time	900	1991	130.00	300
1982	Thatchcolm Cottage	S/O	1987	38.00	38
1989	The Thimble Pub	641	1993	344.00	344
1993	Tithe Barn Cottage	900	1995	368.00	398
1991	Upper Chute	900	1991	496.00	1200
1987	The Vicar's Gate	500	1988	110.00	700-900
1987	Wakehurst Place	900	1988	480.00	1750
1987	Well Cottage, Sandy Lane	500	1988	440.00	650-1500
1991	Wepham Cottage	1,200	1991	396.00	1200
1984	West Kington Dell	500	1988	215.00	650
1992	West Sussex Roses (Archival)	1,200	1993	184.00	184
1990	Weston Manor	900	1995	694.00	742
1987	White Lilac Thatch	900	1988	260.00	400-700
1992	Wild Rose Cottage	155	1993	248.00	248
1985	Windsong Cottage	500	1987	156.00	350-799
1991	Windward Cottage, Rye	1,100	1991	228.00	895
1986	York Garden Shop	500	1988	98.00	250-999

Mill Pond Press

Bateman - R. Bateman

YEAR ISSUE		EDITION LIMIT	YEAR RETD.	ISSUE PRICE	*QUOTE U.S.$
1982	Above the River-Trumpeter Swans	950	1984	200.00	850
1984	Across the Sky-Snow Geese	950	1985	220.00	800
1980	African Amber-Lioness Pair	950	1980	175.00	500
1979	Afternoon Glow-Snowy Owl	950	1979	125.00	600
1990	Air, The Forest and The Watch	42,558	N/A	325.00	350
1984	Along the Ridge-Grizzly Bears	950	1984	200.00	1000
1984	American Goldfinch-Winter Dress	950	1984	75.00	150
1979	Among the Leaves-Cottontail Rabbit	950	1980	75.00	1000
1980	Antarctic Elements	950	1980	125.00	150
1991	Arctic Cliff-White Wolves	13,000	1991	325.00	325
1982	Arctic Evening-White Wolf	950	1982	185.00	1200
1980	Arctic Family-Polar Bears	950	1980	150.00	1500
1992	Arctic Landscape-Polar Bear	5,000	N/A	345.00	345
1992	Arctic Landscape-Polar Bear-Premier Ed.	450		800.00	800
1982	Arctic Portrait-White Gyrfalcon	950	1982	175.00	20
1985	Arctic Tern Pair	950	1985	175.00	20
1981	Artist and His Dog	950	1983	150.00	450
1980	Asleep on Hemlock-Screech Owl	950	1980	125.00	450
1991	At the Cliff-Bobcat	12,500	1991	325.00	325
1992	At the Feeder-Cardinal	950	1992	125.00	15
1987	At the Nest-Secretary Birds	950	1987	290.00	29
1982	At the Roadside-Red-Tailed Hawk	950	1984	185.00	65
1980	Autumn Overture-Moose	950	1980	245.00	180
1980	Awesome Land-American Elk	950	1980	245.00	210
1989	Backlight-Mute Swan	950	1989	275.00	50
1983	Bald Eagle Portrait	950	1983	185.00	28
1982	Baobab Tree and Impala	950	1986	245.00	30
1980	Barn Owl in the Churchyard	950	1981	125.00	80
1989	Barn Swallow and Horse Collar	950	N/A	225.00	22
1982	Barn Swallows in August	950	N/A	245.00	42
1992	Beach Grass and Tree Frog	1,250		345.00	35
1985	Beaver Pond Reflections	950	1985	185.00	18
1984	Big Country, Pronghorn Antelope	950	1985	185.00	18
1986	Black Eagle	950	1986	200.00	20
1993	Black Jaguar-Premier Edition	450		850.00	120
1986	Black-Tailed Deer in the Olympics	950	1986	245.00	24
1986	Blacksmith Plover	950	1986	185.00	18
1991	Bluebird and Blossoms	4,500		235.00	23
1991	Bluebird and Blossoms-Prestige Ed.	450		625.00	62
1980	Bluffing Bull-African Elephant	950	1981	135.00	120
1981	Bright Day-Atlantic Puffins	950	1985	175.00	87
1989	Broad-Tailed Hummingbird Pair	950	1989	225.00	22
1980	Brown Pelican and Pilings	950	1980	165.00	150
1979	Bull Moose	950	1979	125.00	80
1978	By the Tracks-Killdeer	950	1980	75.00	90
1983	Call of the Wild-Bald Eagle	950	1983	200.00	25
1985	Canada Geese Family(stone lithograph)	260	1985	350.00	120

*Quotes have been rounded up to nearest dollar

GRAPHICS

YEAR ISSUE		EDITION LIMIT	YEAR RETD.	ISSUE PRICE	*QUOTE U.S.$
1985	Canada Geese Over the Escarpment	950	1985	135.00	175
1986	Canada Geese With Young	950	1986	195.00	195
1981	Canada Geese-Nesting	950	1981	295.00	2400
1993	Cardinal and Sumac	2,510	N/A	235.00	235
1988	Cardinal and Wild Apples	12,183	1988	235.00	235
1989	Catching The Light-Barn Owl	2,000	1990	295.00	295
1988	Cattails, Fireweed and Yellowthroat	950	1988	235.00	235
1989	Centennial Farm	950	1989	295.00	295
1988	The Challenge-Bull Moose	10,671		325.00	325
1980	Chapel Doors	950	1985	135.00	375
1986	Charging Rhino	950	1986	325.00	650
1982	Cheetah Profile	950	1985	245.00	400
1978	Cheetah With Cubs	950	1980	95.00	450
1988	Cherrywood with Juncos	950	1988	245.00	245
1990	Chinstrap Penguin	810	1991	150.00	150
1992	Clan of the Raven	950	1992	235.00	500
1981	Clear Night-Wolves	950	1981	245.00	5500
1988	Colonial Garden	950	1988	245.00	245
1987	Continuing Generations-Spotted Owls	950	1987	525.00	750
1991	Cottage Lane-Red Fox	950	1991	285.00	250
1984	Cougar Portrait	950	1984	95.00	250
1979	Country Lane-Pheasants	950	1981	85.00	600
1981	Courting Pair-Whistling Swans	950	1981	245.00	300
1981	Courtship Display-Wild Turkey	950	1981	175.00	175
1980	Coyote in Winter Sage	950	1980	245.00	3600
1992	Cries of Courtship-Red Crowned Cranes	950	1992	350.00	550
1980	Curious Glance-Red Fox	950	1980	135.00	900
1986	Dark Gyrfalcon	950	1986	225.00	325
1993	Day Lilies and Dragonflies	1,250		345.00	345
1982	Dipper By the Waterfall	950	1985	165.00	650
1989	Dispute Over Prey	950		325.00	325
1989	Distant Danger-Raccoon	1,600	1989	225.00	225
1984	Down for a Drink-Morning Dove	950	1985	135.00	275
1978	Downy Woodpecker on Goldenrod Gall	950	1979	50.00	1425
1988	Dozing Lynx	950	1988	335.00	1750
1986	Driftwood Perch-Striped Swallows	950	1986	195.00	195
1983	Early Snowfall-Ruffed Grouse	950	1985	195.00	225
1983	Early Spring-Bluebird	950	1984	185.00	700
1981	Edge of the Ice-Ermine	950	1981	175.00	475
1982	Edge of the Woods-Whitetail Deer, w/Book	950	1983	745.00	1200
1991	Elephant Cow and Calf	950	1991	300.00	300
1986	Elephant Herd and Sandgrouse	950	1986	235.00	235
1991	Encounter in the Bush-African Lions	950	1991	295.00	300
1987	End of Season-Grizzly	950	1987	325.00	600
1991	Endangered Spaces-Grizzly	4,008	1991	325.00	350
1985	Entering the Water-Common Gulls	950	1986	195.00	200
1986	European Robin & Hydrangeas	950	1986	130.00	275
1989	Evening Call-Common Loon	950	1989	235.00	500
1980	Evening Grosbeak	950	1980	125.00	750
1983	Evening Idyll-Mute Swans	950	1984	245.00	650
1981	Evening Light-White Gyrfalcon	950	1981	245.00	1000
1979	Evening Snowfall-American Elk	950	1980	150.00	1200
1987	Everglades	950	1987	360.00	360
1980	Fallen Willow-Snowy Owl	950	1980	200.00	950
1987	Farm Lane and Blue Jays	950	1987	225.00	450
1986	Fence Post and Burdock	950	1987	130.00	130
1991	Fluid Power-Orca	290		2500.00	2500
1980	Flying High-Golden Eagle	950	1980	150.00	1100
1982	Fox at the Granary	950	1985	165.00	250
1982	Frosty Morning-Blue Jay	950	1982	185.00	1000
1982	Gallinule Family	950		135.00	135
1981	Galloping Herd-Giraffes	950	1981	175.00	1200
1985	Gambel's Quail Pair	950	1985	95.00	350
1982	Gentoo Penguins & Whale Bones	950	1986	205.00	500
1983	Ghost of the North-Great Gray Owl	950	1983	200.00	2200
1982	Golden Crowned Kinglet and Rhododendron	950	1982	150.00	2400
1979	Golden Eagle	950	1981	150.00	250
1985	Golden Eagle Portrait	950	1987	115.00	175
1989	Goldfinch In the Meadow	1,600	1989	150.00	200
1983	Goshawk and Ruffed Grouse	950	1984	185.00	600
1988	Grassy Bank-Great Blue Heron	950	1988	285.00	285
1981	Gray Squirrel	950	1981	180.00	750
1979	Great Blue Heron	950	1980	125.00	1300
1987	Great Blue Heron in Flight	950	1987	295.00	450
1988	Great Crested Grebe	950	1988	135.00	135
1987	Great Egret Preening	950	1987	315.00	650
1983	Great Horned Owl in the White Pine	950	1983	225.00	575
1987	Greater Kudu Bull	950	1987	145.00	145
1993	Grizzly and Cubs	2,250		335.00	400
1991	Gulls on Pilings	1,950		265.00	265
1988	Hardwood Forest-White-Tailed Buck	630	1988	300.00	1800
1988	Harlequin Duck-Bull Kelp-Executive Ed.	623	1988	550.00	550
1988	Harlequin Duck-Bull Kelp-Gold Plated	950	1988	300.00	300
1980	Heron on the Rocks	950	1980	75.00	300
1981	High Camp at Dusk	950	1985	245.00	350
1979	High Country-Stone Sheep	950	1982	125.00	325
1987	High Kingdom-Snow Leopard	950	1987	325.00	650
1990	Homage to Ahmed	290		3300.00	3300
1984	Hooded Mergansers in Winter	950	1984	210.00	500
1984	House Finch and Yucca	950	1984	95.00	175
1986	House Sparrow	950	1986	125.00	250
1987	House Sparrows and Bittersweet	950	1987	220.00	400
1986	Hummingbird Pair Diptych	950	1986	330.00	475
1987	Hurricane Lake-Wood Ducks	950		135.00	200
1981	In for the Evening	950	1981	150.00	2000
1994	In His Prime-Mallard	950	N/A	195.00	250
1984	In the Brier Patch-Cottontail	950	1985	165.00	350
1986	In the Grass-Lioness	950	1986	245.00	245
1985	In the Highlands-Golden Eagle	950	1985	235.00	350
1985	In the Mountains-Osprey	950	1987	95.00	150
1992	Intrusion-Mountain Gorilla	2,250		325.00	325
1990	Ireland House	950	1990	265.00	265
1985	Irish Cottage and Wagtail	950	1990	175.00	175
1992	Junco in Winter	1,250	1992	185.00	185
1990	Keeper of the Land	290		3300.00	3300
1993	Kestrel and Grasshopper	1,250		335.00	335
1979	King of the Realm	950	1979	125.00	600
1987	King Penguins	950	1987	130.00	135
1981	Kingfisher and Aspen	950	1981	225.00	850
1980	Kingfisher in Winter	950	1981	175.00	1000
1980	Kittiwake Greeting	950	1980	75.00	375
1981	Last Look-Bighorn Sheep	950	1986	195.00	225
1987	Late Winter-Black Squirrel	950	1987	165.00	165
1981	Laughing Gull and Horseshoe Crab	950	1981	125.00	125
1982	Leopard Ambush	950	1986	245.00	500
1988	Leopard and Thomson Gazelle Kill	950	1988	275.00	275
1985	Leopard at Seronera	950	1985	175.00	280
1980	Leopard in a Sausage Tree	950	1980	150.00	1750
1984	Lily Pads and Loon	950	1984	200.00	1600
1987	Lion and Wildebeest	950	1987	265.00	265
1980	Lion at Tsavo	950	1983	150.00	275
1978	Lion Cubs	950	1981	125.00	400
1987	Lioness at Serengeti	950	1987	325.00	325
1985	Lions in the Grass	950	1985	265.00	1250
1981	Little Blue Heron	950	1981	95.00	275
1982	Lively Pair-Chickadees	950	1982	160.00	400
1983	Loon Family	950	1983	200.00	750
1990	Lunging Heron	1,250	1990	225.00	225
1978	Majesty on the Wing-Bald Eagle	950	1979	150.00	2650
1988	Mallard Family at Sunset	950	1988	235.00	235
1986	Mallard Family-Misty Marsh	950	1986	130.00	175
1986	Mallard Pair-Early Winter	41,740	1986	135.00	200
1985	Mallard Pair-Early Winter 24K Gold	950	1986	1650.00	2000
1986	Mallard Pair-Early Winter Gold Plated	7,691	1986	250.00	375
1989	Mangrove Morning-Roseate Spoonbills	2,000	1989	325.00	325
1991	Mangrove Shadow-Common Egret	1,250		285.00	285
1993	Marbled Murrelet	55	1993	1200.00	1200
1986	Marginal Meadow	950	1986	220.00	220
1979	Master of the Herd-African Buffalo	950	1980	150.00	2250
1984	May Maple-Scarlet Tanager	950	1984	175.00	750
1982	Meadow's Edge-Mallard	950	1982	175.00	750
1982	Merganser Family in Hiding	950	1982	200.00	625
1994	Meru Dusk-Lesser Kudu	950		135.00	135
1989	Midnight-Black Wolf	25,352	1989	325.00	1750
1980	Mischief on the Prowl-Raccoon	950	1980	85.00	350
1980	Misty Coast-Gulls	950	1980	135.00	400
1984	Misty Lake-Osprey	950	1985	95.00	300
1981	Misty Morning-Loons	950	1981	150.00	1500
1986	Moose at Water's Edge	950	1986	130.00	260
1990	Morning Cove-Common Loon	950	1990	165.00	165
1985	Morning Dew-Roe Deer	950	1985	175.00	175
1983	Morning on the Flats-Bison	950	1983	200.00	350
1984	Morning on the River-Trumpeter Swans	950	1984	185.00	400
1990	Mossy Branches-Spotted Owl	4,500	1990	300.00	400
1990	Mowed Meadow	950	1990	190.00	190
1986	Mule Deer in Aspen	950	1986	175.00	225
1983	Mule Deer in Winter	950	1983	200.00	275
1988	Muskoka Lake-Common Loons	2,500	1988	265.00	400
1989	Near Glenburnie	950		265.00	265
1983	New Season-American Robin	950	1983	200.00	450
1986	Northern Reflections-Loon Family	8,631	1986	255.00	2000
1985	Old Whaling Base and Fur Seals	950	1985	195.00	450
1987	Old Willow and Mallards	950	1987	325.00	400
1980	On the Alert-Chipmunk	950	1980	60.00	500
1993	On the Brink-River Otters	1,250		345.00	345
1985	On the Garden Wall	950	1985	115.00	300
1985	Orca Procession	950	1985	245.00	2525
1981	Osprey Family	950	1981	245.00	300
1983	Osprey in the Rain	950	1983	110.00	500
1987	Otter Study	950	1987	235.00	500
1981	Pair of Skimmers	950	1981	150.00	150
1988	Panda's At Play (stone lithograph)	160	1988	400.00	1500
1994	Path of the Panther	1,950		295.00	295
1984	Peregrine and Ruddy Turnstones	950	1985	200.00	350
1985	Peregrine Falcon and White-Throated Swifts	950	1985	245.00	550
1987	Peregrine Falcon on the Cliff-Stone Litho	525	1988	350.00	350
1983	Pheasant in Cornfield	950	1983	200.00	350
1988	Pheasants at Dusk	950	1988	325.00	600
1982	Pileated Woodpecker on Beech Tree	950	1982	175.00	1000
1990	Pintails in Spring	9,651	1989	135.00	300
1982	Pioneer Memories-Magpie Pair	950	1982	175.00	250
1987	Plowed Field-Snowy Owl	950	1987	145.00	400
1990	Polar Bear	290	1990	3300.00	3300
1982	Polar Bear Profile	950	1982	210.00	2350
1982	Polar Bears at Bafin Island	950	1982	245.00	875
1990	Power Play-Rhinoceros	950	1990	320.00	320
1980	Prairie Evening-Short-Eared Owl	950	1983	150.00	150
1994	Predator Portfolio/Black Bear	950		475.00	475
1992	Predator Portfolio/Cougar	950		465.00	465
1993	Predator Portfolio/Grizzly	950		475.00	475
1993	Predator Portfolio/Polar Bear	950		485.00	485
1993	Predator Portfolio/Wolf	950	N/A	475.00	475
1988	Preening Pair-Canada Geese	950	1988	235.00	235
1987	Pride of Autumn-Canada Goose	15,294	1987	135.00	245
1986	Proud Swimmer-Snow Goose	950	1986	185.00	185
1989	Pumpkin Time	950		195.00	195
1982	Queen Anne's Lace and American Goldfinch	950	1982	150.00	900
1984	Ready for Flight-Peregrine Falcon	950	1984	185.00	500
1982	Ready for the Hunt-Snowy Owl	950	1982	245.00	550
1993	Reclining Snow Leopard	1,250		335.00	335
1988	Red Crossbills	950	1988	125.00	125
1984	Red Fox on the Prowl	950	1984	245.00	800
1982	Red Squirrel	950	1982	175.00	350
1986	Red Wolf	950	1986	250.00	300
1981	Red-Tailed Hawk by the Cliff	950	1981	245.00	550
1981	Red-Winged Blackbird &Rail Fence	950	1981	195.00	225
1984	Reeds	950	1984	185.00	450
1986	A Resting Place-Cape Buffalo	950	1986	265.00	265
1986	Resting Place-Cape Buffalo	950		265.00	265
1987	Rhino at Ngoro Ngoro	950	1988	325.00	325
1993	River Otter-North American Wilderness	350		325.00	500
1993	River Otters	290		1500.00	1500
1986	Robins at the Nest	950	1986	185.00	225
1987	Rocky Point-October	950	1987	195.00	400
1980	Rocky Wilderness-Cougar	950	1980	175.00	1100
1990	Rolling Waves-Lesser Scaup	3,330		125.00	125
1993	Rose-breasted Grosbeak	290		450.00	450
1981	Rough-Legged Hawk in the Elm	950	1991	175.00	175
1981	Royal Family-Mute Swans	950	1981	245.00	1100
1983	Ruby Throat and Columbine	950	1983	150.00	2200
1987	Ruddy Turnstones	950	1987	175.00	175
1994	Salt Spring Sheep	1,250		235.00	235
1981	Sarah E. with Gulls	950	1981	245.00	2600
1993	Saw Whet Owl and Wild Grapes	950		185.00	185
1991	The Scolding-Chickadees & Screech Owl	12,500		235.00	235
1991	Sea Otter Study	950	1991	150.00	150
1993	Shadow of the Rain Forest	9,000	1993	345.00	400
1981	Sheer Drop-Mountain Goats	950	1981	245.00	2800
1988	Shelter	950	1988	325.00	1000
1992	Siberian Tiger	4,500		325.00	325
1984	Smallwood	950	1985	200.00	500
1990	Snow Leopard	290	1990	2500.00	2500
1985	Snowy Hemlock-Barred Owl	950	1985	245.00	245
1994	Snowy Nap-Tiger	950	1994	185.00	400
1994	Snowy Owl	150	N/A	265.00	750
1987	Snowy Owl and Milkweed	950	1987	235.00	750
1983	Snowy Owl on Driftwood	950	1983	245.00	750
1983	Spirits of the Forest	950	1984	170.00	2500
1986	Split Rails-Snow Buntings	950	1986	220.00	220
1980	Spring Cardinal	950	1980	125.00	400
1982	Spring Marsh-Pintail Pair	950	1982	200.00	350
1980	Spring Thaw-Killdeer	950	1980	85.00	150
1982	Still Morning-Herring Gulls	950	1982	200.00	250
1987	Stone Sheep Ram	950	1987	175.00	175
1985	Stream Bank June	950	1986	160.00	175
1984	Stretching-Canada Goose	950	1984	225.00	3000
1985	Strutting-Ring-Necked Pheasant	950	1985	225.00	450
1985	Sudden Blizzard-Red-Tailed Hawk	950	1985	245.00	550
1990	Summer Morning Pasture	950	1990	175.00	175
1984	Summer Morning-Loon	950	1984	185.00	1200
1986	Summertime-Polar Bears	950	1986	225.00	250
1979	Surf and Sanderlings	950	1980	65.00	450
1981	Swift Fox	950	1981	175.00	350
1986	Swift Fox Study	950	1986	115.00	150
1987	Sylvan Stream-Mute Swans	950	1987	125.00	125
1984	Tadpole Time	950	1985	135.00	550
1988	Tawny Owl In Beech	950		325.00	325
1992	Tembo (African Elephant)	1,550		350.00	350
1984	Tiger at Dawn	950	1984	225.00	1800
1983	Tiger Portrait	950	1983	130.00	500
1988	Tree Swallow over Pond	950	1988	290.00	290
1991	Trumpeter Swan Family	290		2500.00	2500
1985	Trumpeter Swans and Aspen	950	1985	245.00	550
1979	Up in the Pine-Great Horned Owl	950	1981	150.00	300
1980	Vantage Point	950	1980	245.00	1200
1993	Vigilance	9,500		330.00	330
1989	Vulture And Wildebeest	550		295.00	295
1981	Watchful Repose-Black Bear	950	1981	245.00	550
1985	Weathered Branch-Bald Eagle	950	1985	115.00	300
1991	Whistling Swan-Lake Erie	1,950		325.00	375
1980	White Encounter-Polar Bear	950	1980	245.00	3750
1990	White on White-Snowshoe Hare	950	1990	195.00	590
1982	White World-Dall Sheep	950	1982	200.00	500
1985	White-Breasted Nuthatch on a Beech Tree	950	1985	175.00	300
1980	White-Footed Mouse in Wintergreen	950	1980	60.00	650
1982	White-Footed Mouse on Aspen	950	1983	90.00	180
1992	White-Tailed Deer Through the Birches	10,000		335.00	335
1984	White-Throated Sparrow & Pussy Willow	950	1984	150.00	650
1991	Wide Horizon-Tundra Swans	2,862		325.00	350
1991	Wide Horizon-Tundra Swans Companion	2,862		325.00	325
1986	Wildbeest	950		185.00	185
1982	Willet on the Shore	950	N/A	125.00	225
1979	Wily and Wary-Red Fox	950	1979	125.00	1100
1984	Window into Ontario	950	1984	265.00	1500
1983	Winter Barn	950	1984	170.00	400
1979	Winter Cardinal	950	1979	75.00	3550
1992	Winter Coat	1,250		245.00	245

*Quotes have been rounded up to nearest dollar

YEAR ISSUE		EDITION LIMIT	YEAR RETD.	ISSUE PRICE	*QUOTE U.S.$
1985	Winter Companion	950	1985	175.00	600
1980	Winter Elm-American Kestrel	950	1980	135.00	600
1986	Winter in the Mountains-Raven	950	1987	200.00	200
1981	Winter Mist-Great Horned Owl	950	1981	245.00	900
1980	Winter Song-Chickadees	950	1980	95.00	800
1984	Winter Sunset-Moose	950	1984	245.00	2200
1992	Winter Trackers	4,500	1992	335.00	335
1981	Winter Wren	950	1981	135.00	250
1983	Winter-Lady Cardinal	950	1983	200.00	1400
1979	Winter-Snowshoe Hare	950	1980	95.00	1200
1987	Wise One, The	950	1987	325.00	700
1979	Wolf Pack in Moonlight	950	1979	95.00	2600
1994	Wolf Pair in the Snow	290		795.00	795
1994	Wolverine Porfolio	950		275.00	275
1983	Wolves on the Trail	950	1983	225.00	700
1985	Wood Bison Portrait	950	1985	165.00	200
1983	Woodland Drummer-Ruffed Grouse	950	1984	185.00	250
1981	Wrangler's Campsite-Gray Jay	950	1981	195.00	750
1979	Yellow-Rumped Warbler	950	1980	50.00	400
1978	Young Barn Swallow	950	1979	75.00	700
1983	Young Elf Owl-Old Saguaro	950	1983	95.00	400
1991	Young Giraffe	290		850.00	850
1989	Young Kittiwake	950		195.00	195
1988	Young Sandhill-Cranes	950	1988	325.00	325
1989	Young Snowy Owl	950	1990	195.00	195

Brenders - C. Brenders

YEAR ISSUE		EDITION LIMIT	YEAR RETD.	ISSUE PRICE	*QUOTE U.S.$
1986	The Acrobat's Meal-Red Squirrel	950	1989	65.00	275
1988	Apple Harvest	950	1989	115.00	350
1989	The Apple Lover	1,500	1990	125.00	275
1987	Autumn Lady	950	1989	150.00	375
1991	The Balance of Nature	1,950		225.00	225
1993	Black Sphinx	950		235.00	235
1986	Black-Capped Chickadees	950	1989	40.00	450
1990	Blond Beauty	1,950	1990	185.00	185
1986	Bluebirds	950	1989	40.00	200-300
1988	California Quail	950	1989	95.00	350-400
1991	Calm Before the Challenge -Moose	1,950	1991	225.00	225
1987	Close to Mom	950	1988	150.00	1500
1993	Collectors Group (Butterfly Collections)	290		375.00	375
1986	Colorful Playground-Cottontails	950	1989	75.00	475
1989	The Companions	18,036	1989	200.00	900-1250
1994	Dall Sheep Portrait	950		115.00	115
1992	Den Mother-Pencil Sketch	2,500	1992	135.00	135
1992	Den Mother-Wolf Family	25,000	1992	250.00	400
1986	Disturbed Daydreams	950	1989	95.00	425
1987	Double Trouble-Raccoons	950	1988	120.00	500-750
1993	European Group (Butterfly Collections)	290		375.00	375
1993	Exotic Group (Butterfly Collections)	290		375.00	375
1989	Forager's Reward-Red Squirrel	1,250	1989	135.00	135
1988	Forest Sentinel-Bobcat	950	1988	135.00	500
1990	Full House-Fox Family	20,106	1990	235.00	400
1990	Ghostly Quiet-Spanish Lynx	1,950	1990	200.00	200
1986	Golden Season-Gray Squirrel	950	1987	85.00	450-525
1986	Harvest Time-Chipmunk	950	1989	65.00	150-250
1988	Hidden In the Pines-Immature Great Hor	950	1988	175.00	1500
1988	High Adventure-Black Bear Cubs	950	1989	105.00	375
1988	A Hunter's Dream	950	1988	165.00	850
1993	In Northern Hunting Grounds	1,750		375.00	375
1992	Island Shores-Snowy Egret	2,500		250.00	250
1987	Ivory-Billed Woodpecker	950	1989	95.00	500
1988	Long Distance Hunters	950	1988	175.00	2250
1989	Lord of the Marshes	1,250	1989	135.00	175
1986	Meadowlark	950	1989	40.00	150
1989	Merlins at the Nest	1,250	1989	165.00	300-375
1985	Mighty Intruder	950	1989	95.00	275
1987	Migration Fever-Barn Swallows	950	1989	150.00	295
1990	The Monarch is Alive	4,071	1990	265.00	400
1993	Mother of Pearls	5,000		275.00	275
1990	Mountain Baby-Bighorn Sheep	1,950		165.00	165
1987	Mysterious Visitor-Barn Owl	950	1989	150.00	250
1993	Narrow Escape-Chipmunk	1,750		150.00	150
1991	The Nesting Season-House Sparrow	1,950	1991	195.00	200-250
1989	Northern Cousins-Black Squirrels	950	1989	150.00	250
1984	On the Alert-Red Fox	950	1986	95.00	475
1990	On the Old Farm Door	1,500	1990	225.00	450
1991	One to One-Gray Wolf	10,000	1991	245.00	450
1992	Pathfinder-Red Fox	5,000	1992	245.00	375
1984	Playful Pair-Chipmunks	950	1987	60.00	400
1994	Power and Grace	2,500	1994	265.00	265
1989	The Predator's Walk	1,250	1989	150.00	375
1992	Red Fox Study	1,250	1992	125.00	125
1994	Riverbank Kestrel	2,500		225.00	225
1988	Roaming the Plains-Pronghorns	950	1989	150.00	150
1986	Robins	950	1989	40.00	125
1993	Rocky Camp-Cougar Family	5,000		275.00	275
1993	Rocky Camp-Cubs	950		225.00	225
1992	Rocky Kingdom-Bighorn Sheep	1,750		255.00	255
1991	Shadows in the Grass-Young Cougars	1,950	1991	235.00	235
1990	Shoreline Quartet-White Ibis	1,950		265.00	265
1984	Silent Hunter-Great Horned Owl	950	1987	95.00	450
1984	Silent Passage	950	1988	150.00	495
1990	Small Talk	1,500	1990	125.00	150-250
1992	Snow Leopard Portrait	1,750	1993	150.00	150
1990	Spring Fawn	1,500	1990	125.00	300
1990	Squirrel's Dish	1,950		110.00	110

YEAR ISSUE		EDITION LIMIT	YEAR RETD.	ISSUE PRICE	*QUOTE U.S.$
1989	Steller's Jay	1,250	1989	135.00	175
1991	Study for One to One	1,950		120.00	200
1993	Summer Roses-Winter Wren	1,500	1993	250.00	350
1989	The Survivors-Canada Geese	1,500	1989	225.00	850-950
1994	Take Five-Canadian Lynx	1,500		245.00	245
1988	Talk on the Old Fence	950	1988	165.00	550
1990	A Threatened Symbol	1,950	1990	145.00	300
1994	Tundra Summit-Arctic Wolves	6,061	1994	265.00	325
1984	Waterside Encounter	950	1987	95.00	1000
1987	White Elegance-Trumpeter Swans	950	1989	115.00	390
1993	White Wolves-North American Wilderness Portfolio	350		325.00	475
1988	Witness of a Past-Bison	950	1990	110.00	110
1992	Wolf Scout #1	2,500	1992	105.00	105
1992	Wolf Scout #2	2,500	1992	105.00	105
1991	Wolf Study	950	1991	125.00	125
1987	Yellow-Bellied Marmot	950	1989	95.00	425
1989	A Young Generation	1,250	1989	165.00	375-425

Calle - P. Calle

YEAR ISSUE		EDITION LIMIT	YEAR RETD.	ISSUE PRICE	*QUOTE U.S.$
1981	Almost Home	950	1981	150.00	150
1991	Almost There	950	1991	165.00	165
1989	And A Good Book For Company	950	1990	135.00	190
1993	And A Grizzly Claw Necklace	750		150.00	150
1981	And Still Miles to Go	950	1981	245.00	300
1981	Andrew At The Falls	950	1981	150.00	175
1989	The Beaver Men	950		125.00	125
1984	A Brace for the Spit	950	1985	110.00	275
1980	Caring for the Herd	950	1981	110.00	110
1985	The Carrying Place	950	1990	195.00	195
1984	Chance Encounter	950	1986	225.00	300
1981	Chief High Pipe (Color)	950	1981	265.00	275
1980	Chief High Pipe (Pencil)	950	1980	75.00	165
1980	Chief Joseph-Man of Peace	950	1980	135.00	150
1990	Children of Walpi	350		160.00	160
1990	The Doll Maker	950		95.00	95
1982	Emerging from the Woods	950	1987	110.00	110-160
1981	End of a Long Day	950	1981	150.00	150-190
1984	Fate of the Late Migrant	950	1985	110.00	300
1983	Free Spirits	950	1985	195.00	325
1983	Free Trapper Study	550	1985	75.00	125-300
1981	Fresh Tracks	950	1981	150.00	165
1981	Friend of Foe	950		125.00	125
1981	Friends	950	1987	150.00	150
1985	The Frontier Blacksmith	950		245.00	245
1989	The Fur Trapper	550		75.00	175
1982	Generations in the Valley	950	1987	245.00	245
1985	The Grandmother	950	1987	400.00	400
1989	The Great Moment	950		350.00	350
1992	Hunter of Geese	950		125.00	125
1993	I Call Him Friend	950		235.00	235
1983	In Search of Beaver	950	1983	225.00	600
1991	In the Beginning . . . Friends	1,250	1993	250.00	250
1987	In the Land of the Giants	950	1988	245.00	780
1990	Interrupted Journey	1,750	1991	265.00	265
1990	Interrupted Journey-Prestige Ed.	290	1991	465.00	465
1987	Into the Great Alone	950	1988	245.00	600
1981	Just Over the Ridge	950	1982	245.00	325
1980	Landmark Tree	950	1980	125.00	225
1991	Man of the Fur Trade	550		110.00	110
1984	Mountain Man	550	1988	95.00	250-550
1993	Mountain Man-North American Wilderness Portfolio	350		325.00	N/A
1989	The Mountain Men	300	1989	400.00	400
1989	Navajo Madonna	650		95.00	95
1988	A New Day	950		150.00	150
1981	One With The Land	950	1981	245.00	325
1992	Out of the Silence	2,500		265.00	265
1992	Out of the Silence-Prestige	290		465.00	465
1981	Pause at the Lower Falls	950	1981	110.00	125
1980	Prayer to the Great Mystery	950	1980	245.00	400
1982	Return to Camp	950	1982	245.00	400
1991	The Silenced Honkers	1,250		250.00	250
1980	Sioux Chief	950	1980	85.00	85-140
1986	Snow Hunter	950	1988	150.00	250-410
1980	Something for the Pot	950	1980	175.00	1000
1990	Son of Sitting Bull	950		95.00	95
1985	Storyteller of the Mountains	950	1985	225.00	575
1983	Strays From the Flyway	950	1983	195.00	250-340
1981	Teton Friends	950	1981	150.00	200
1991	They Call Me Matthew	950		125.00	125
1992	Through the Tall Grass	950		175.00	175
1988	Trapper at Rest	550		95.00	95
1982	Two from the Flock	950	1982	245.00	400
1980	View from the Heights	950	1980	245.00	350
1988	Voyageurs and Waterfowl...Constant	950	1988	265.00	265
1980	When Snow Came Early	950	1980	85.00	250-340
1984	When Trails Cross	950	1984	245.00	750
1991	When Trails Grow Cold	2,500		265.00	265
1991	When Trails Grow Cold-Prestige Ed.	290	1991	465.00	465-600
1994	When Trappers Meet	750		165.00	165
1989	Where Eagles Fly	1,250	1990	265.00	265
1989	A Winter Feast	1,250	1989	265.00	265
1989	A Winter Feast-Prestige Ed.	290	1989	465.00	465
1981	Winter Hunter (Color)	950	1981	245.00	725
1980	Winter Hunter (Pencil)	950	1980	65.00	450
1983	A Winter Surprise	950	1984	195.00	800

Cross - T. Cross

YEAR ISSUE		EDITION LIMIT	YEAR RETD.	ISSUE PRICE	*QUOTE U.S.$
1994	April	750		55.00	55
1994	August	750		55.00	55
1993	Ever Green	750		135.00	135
1993	Flame Catcher	750	1993	185.00	185
1993	Flicker, Flash and Twirl	525		165.00	165
1994	July	750		55.00	55
1994	June	750		55.00	55
1994	March	750		55.00	55
1994	May	750		55.00	55
1992	Shell Caster	750	1993	150.00	150
1993	Sheperds of Magic	750		135.00	135
1993	Spellbound	750		85.00	85
1994	Spring Forth	750		145.00	145
1992	Star Weaver	750	1993	150.00	150
1994	Summer Musings	750		145.00	145
1993	The Summons...And Then They Are One	750	1993	195.00	195
1994	When Water Takes to Air	750		135.00	135
1993	Wind Sifter	750	1993	150.00	150

Daly - J. Daly

YEAR ISSUE		EDITION LIMIT	YEAR RETD.	ISSUE PRICE	*QUOTE U.S.$
1990	The Big Moment	1,500		125.00	125
1991	Cat's Cradle-Prestige Edition	950		450.00	450
1994	Catch of My Dreams	4,500		45.00	45
1994	Childhood Friends	950		110.00	110
1990	Confrontation	1,500	1992	85.00	85
1990	Contentment	1,500	1990	95.00	300
1992	Dominoes	1,500		155.00	155
1992	Favorite Gift	2,500	1992	175.00	175
1987	Favorite Reader	950	1990	85.00	85
1986	Flying High	950	1988	50.00	350
1992	The Flying Horse	950		325.00	325
1993	Good Company	1,500		155.00	155
1992	Her Secret Place	1,500	1992	135.00	250
1991	Home Team: Zero	1,500		150.00	150
1991	Homemade	1,500	1992	125.00	125
1990	Honor and Allegiance	1,500	1993	110.00	110
1990	The Ice Man	1,500	1992	125.00	125
1992	The Immigrant Spirit	5,000		125.00	125
1992	The Immigrant Spirit-Prestige Edi.	950		125.00	125
1989	In the Doghouse	1,500	1990	75.00	300
1990	It's That Time Again	1,500		120.00	120
1992	Left Out	1,500		110.00	110
1989	Let's Play Ball	1,500	1991	75.00	150
1990	Make Believe	1,500	1990	75.00	125
1994	Mud Mates	950		150.00	150
1994	My Best Friends	950		85.00	85
1991	A New Beginning	5,000		125.00	125
1993	The New Citizen	5,000		125.00	125
1993	The New Citizen-Prestige Edition	950		125.00	125
1987	Odd Man Out	950	1988	85.00	85
1988	On Thin Ice	950	1993	95.00	95
1991	Pillars of a Nation-Charter Ed.	20,000		175.00	200
1992	Playmates	1,500	1992	155.00	350
1990	Radio Daze	1,500		150.00	150
1983	Saturday Night	950	1985	85.00	1125
1990	The Scholar	1,500	N/A	110.00	110
1993	Secret Admirer	1,500		150.00	150
1994	Slugger	950		75.00	75
1982	Spring Fever	950	1988	85.00	750
1993	Sunday Afternoon	1,500		150.00	150
1988	Territorial Rights	950	1990	85.00	85
1989	The Thief	1,500	1990	95.00	175
1989	The Thorn	1,500	1990	125.00	125
1988	Tie Breaker	950	1990	95.00	95
1991	Time-Out	1,500	1993	125.00	125
1993	To All a Good Night	1,500		160.00	160
1992	Walking the Rails	1,500		175.00	175
1993	When I Grow Up	1,500		175.00	175
1994	Wind-Up, The	950		75.00	75
1988	Wiped Out	1,250	1990	125.00	125

Morrissey - D. Morrissey

YEAR ISSUE		EDITION LIMIT	YEAR RETD.	ISSUE PRICE	*QUOTE U.S.$
1994	The Amazing Time Elevator	950		195.00	195
1993	Charting the Skies	1,250	1993	195.00	195
1993	Charting the Skies-Caprice Ed.	550	1993	375.00	375
1993	Draft of a Dream	175	1993	250.00	250
1993	Draft of Dream	175		250.00	250
1994	The Dreamer's Trunk	1,500		195.00	195
1993	Drifting Closer	1,250		175.00	175
1993	The Mystic Mariner	750	1993	150.00	250
1993	The Redd Rocket	1,250		175.00	375
1994	The Redd Rocket-Pre-Flight	950	1993	110.00	110
1992	The Sandman's Ship of Dreams	750	1993	150.00	150
1994	Sighting off the Stern	950		135.00	135
1993	Sleeper Flight	1,250	1993	195.00	195
1993	The Telescope of Time	5,000		195.00	195

Olsen - G. Olsen

YEAR ISSUE		EDITION LIMIT	YEAR RETD.	ISSUE PRICE	*QUOTE U.S.$
1993	Airship Adventures	750		150.00	150
1993	Angels of Christmas	750	1993	135.00	135
1993	Dress Rehearseal	750	1993	165.00	620
1993	The Fraternity Tree	750		195.00	195
1994	Little Girls Will Mothers Be	750	N/A	135.00	135
1994	Mother's Love	750	1994	165.00	165
1994	Summerhouse	750		165.00	165

Seerey-Lester - J. Seerey-Lester

YEAR ISSUE		EDITION LIMIT	YEAR RETD.	ISSUE PRICE	*QUOTE U.S.$
1994	Abandoned	950		175.00	175
1986	Above the Treeline-Cougar	950	1986	130.00	175
1986	After the Fire-Grizzly	950	1990	95.00	95
1986	Along the Ice Floe-Polar Bears	950		200.00	200
1987	Alpenglow-Artic Wolf	950	1987	200.00	275
1987	Amboseli Child-African Elephant	950		160.00	16[illegible]

*Quotes have been rounded up to nearest dollar

YEAR ISSUE		EDITION LIMIT	YEAR RETD.	ISSUE PRICE	*QUOTE U.S. $
1984	Among the Cattails-Canada Geese	950	1985	130.00	425
1984	Artic Procession-Willow Ptarmigan	950	1988	220.00	600
1990	Artic Wolf Pups	290		500.00	500
1987	Autumn Mist-Barred Owl	950	1987	160.00	225
1987	Autumn Thunder-Muskoxen	950		150.00	150
1985	Awakening Meadow-Cottontail	950		50.00	50
1992	Banyan Ambush- Black Panther	950	1992	235.00	400
1984	Basking-Brown Pelicans	950	1988	115.00	125
1988	Bathing-Blue Jay	950		95.00	95
1987	Bathing-Mute Swan	950	1992	175.00	175
1989	Before The Freeze-Beaver	950		165.00	165
1990	Bittersweet Winter-Cardinal	1,250	1990	150.00	275
1992	Black Jade	1,950	1992	275.00	275
1992	Black Magic-Panther	750	1992	195.00	195
1993	Black Wolf-North American Wilderness	350		325.00	N/A
1984	Breaking Cover-Black Bear	950	N/A	130.00	130
1987	Canyon Creek-Cougar	950	1987	195.00	450
1992	The Chase-Snow Leopard	950		200.00	200
1994	Child of the Outback	950		175.00	175
1985	Children of the Forest-Red Fox Kits	950	1985	110.00	150
1985	Children of the Tundra-Artic Wolf Pup	950	1985	110.00	225
1988	Cliff Hanger-Bobcat	950		200.00	200
1984	Close Encounter-Bobcat	950	1989	130.00	190
1988	Coastal Clique-Harbor Seals	950		160.00	160
1986	Conflict at Dawn-Heron & Osprey	950	1989	130.00	130
1983	Cool Retreat-Lynx	950	1988	85.00	100
1986	Cottonwood Gold-Baltimore Oriole	950		85.00	85
1985	Cougar Head Study	950		60.00	60
1989	Cougar Run	950	1989	185.00	350-450
1994	The Courtship	950		175.00	175
1993	Dark Encounter	3,500	N/A	200.00	200
1990	Dawn Majesty	1,250	1991	185.00	185
1987	Dawn on the Marsh-Coyote	950		200.00	200
1985	Daybreak-Moose	950		135.00	135
1991	Denali Family-Grizzly Bear	950	1991	195.00	195
1986	Early Arrivals-Snow Buntings	950		75.00	75
1983	Early Windfall-Gray Squirrels	950		85.00	85
1988	Edge of the Forest-Timber Wolves	950	1988	500.00	700
1989	Evening Duet-Snowy Egrets	1,250		185.00	185
1991	Evening Encounter-Grizzly & Wolf	1,250		185.00	185
1988	Evening Meadow-American Goldfinch	950		150.00	150
1991	Face to Face	1,250		200.00	200
1985	Fallen Birch-Chipmunk	950	1985	60.00	250
1985	First Light-Gray Jays	950	1985	130.00	200
1983	First Snow-Grizzly Bears	950	1984	95.00	250
1987	First Tracks-Cougar	950		150.00	150
1989	Fluke Sighting-Humback Whales	950	1989	185.00	185
1993	Freedom I	350		500.00	500
1993	Frozen Moonlight	2,500	1993	225.00	225
1985	Gathering-Gray Wolves, The	950	1987	165.00	350
1989	Gorilla	290	1989	400.00	600
1993	Grizzly Impact	950		225.00	225
1990	Grizzly Litho	290	1990	400.00	600
1989	Heavy Going-Grizzly	950	1989	175.00	300
1986	Hidden Admirer-Moose	950	1986	165.00	275
1988	Hiding Place-Saw-Whet Owl	950		95.00	95
1989	High and Mighty-Gorilla	950	1989	185.00	375
1986	High Country Champion-Grizzly	950	1986	175.00	275
1984	High Ground-Wolves	950	1984	130.00	325
1987	High Refuge-Red Squirrel	950		120.00	120
1984	Icy Outcrop-White Gyrfalcon	950	1986	115.00	200
1987	In Deep-Black Bear Cub	950		135.00	135
1990	In Their Presence	1,250		200.00	200
1985	Island Sanctuary-Mallards	950	1987	95.00	175
1986	Kenyan Family-Cheetahs	950		130.00	130
1986	Lakeside Family-Canada Geese	950		75.00	75
1988	Last Sanctuary-Florida Panther	950	1993	175.00	175
1983	Lone Fisherman-Great Blue Heron	950	1985	85.00	300
1993	Loonlight	1,500		225.00	225
1986	Low Tide-Bald Eagles	950		130.00	130
1987	Lying in Wait-Arctic Fox	950		175.00	175
1984	Lying Low-Cougar	950	1986	85.00	450
1991	Monsoon-White Tiger	950	1994	195.00	195
1991	Moonlight Chase-Cougar	1,250		195.00	195-220
1988	Moonlight Fishermen-Raccoons	950	1990	175.00	175
1988	Moose Hair	950		165.00	165
1988	Morning Display-Common Loons	3,395	1988	135.00	300
1986	Morning Forage-Ground Squirrel	950	1988	75.00	75
1993	Morning Glory-Bald Eagle	1,250	N/A	225.00	225
1984	Morning Mist-Snowy Owl	950	1988	95.00	95-180
1990	Mountain Cradle	1,250		200.00	300
1988	Night Moves-African Elephants	950		150.00	150
1990	Night Run-Artic Wolves	1,250	1990	200.00	250
1993	Night Specter	1,250		195.00	195
1986	Northwoods Family-Moose	950		75.00	75
1987	Out of the Blizzard-Timber Wolves	950	1987	215.00	350
1992	Out of the Darkness	290		200.00	200
1987	Out of the Mist-Grizzly	950	1990	200.00	200
1991	Out on a Limb-Young Barred Owl	950		185.00	185
1991	Panda Trilogy	950		375.00	375
1993	Phantoms of the Tundra	950		235.00	235
1984	Plains Hunter-Prairie Falcon	950		95.00	95
1990	The Plunge-Northern Sea Lions	1,250		200.00	200
1986	Racing the Storm-Artic Wolves	950	1986	200.00	350
1987	Rain Watch-Belted Kingfisher	950		125.00	125
1993	The Rains-Tiger	950		225.00	225
1992	Ranthambhore Rush	950		225.00	225
1983	The Refuge-Raccoon	950	1983	85.00	300
1992	Regal Majesty	290		200.00	200
1985	Return to Winter-Pintails	950	1990	135.00	135
1983	River Watch-Peregrine Falcon	950		85.00	85
1988	Savana Siesta-African Lions	950		165.00	165
1990	Seasonal Greeting-Cardinal	1,250		150.00	150
1993	Seeking Attention	950		200.00	200
1991	Sisters-Artic Wolves	1,250		185.00	185
1989	Sneak Peak	950		185.00	185
1986	Snowy Excursion-Red Squirrel	950		75.00	75
1988	Snowy Watch-Great Gray Owl	950		175.00	175
1989	Softly, Softly-White Tiger	950	1989	220.00	490
1991	Something Stirred (Bengal Tiger)	950		195.00	195
1988	Spanish Mist-Young Barred-Owl	950		175.00	175
1984	Spirit of the North-White Wolf	950	1986	130.00	185
1990	Spout	290		500.00	500
1989	Spring Flurry-Adelie Penguins	950		185.00	185
1986	Spring Mist-Chickadees	950	1986	105.00	150
1990	Suitors-Wood Ducks	3,313	1989	135.00	135
1990	Summer Rain-Common Loons	4,500	1990	200.00	200
1990	Summer Rain-Common Loons (Prestige)	450		425.00	425
1987	Sundown Alert-Bobcat	950		150.00	150
1985	Sundown Reflections-Wood Ducks	950		85.00	85
1990	Their First Season	1,250	1990	200.00	200
1990	Togetherness	1,250		125.00	185
1986	Treading Thin Ice-Chipmunk	950		75.00	75
1988	Tundra Family-Arctic Wolves	950		200.00	200
1985	Under the Pines-Bobcat	950	1986	95.00	275
1989	Water Sport-Bobcat	950	1989	185.00	185
1990	Whitetail Spring	1,250	1990	185.00	185
1988	Winter Grazing-Bison	950		185.00	185
1986	Winter Hiding-Cottontail	950		75.00	75
1983	Winter Lookout-Cougar	950	1985	85.00	500
1986	Winter Perch-Cardinal	950	1986	85.00	175
1985	Winter Rendezvous-Coyotes	950	1985	140.00	225
1988	Winter Spirit-Gray Wolf	950		200.00	200
1987	Winter Vigil-Great Horned Owl	950	1990	175.00	175
1993	Wolong Whiteout	950		225.00	225
1986	The Young Explorer-Red Fox Kit	950		75.00	75

Smith - D. Smith

YEAR ISSUE		EDITION LIMIT	YEAR RETD.	ISSUE PRICE	*QUOTE U.S. $
1993	African Ebony-Black Leopard	1,250		195.00	195
1992	Armada	950		195.00	195
1993	Catching the Scent-Polar Bear	950		175.00	175
1994	Curious Presence-Whitetail Deer	950		195.00	195
1991	Dawn's Early Light-Bald Eagles	950		185.00	185
1993	Echo Bay-Loon Family	1,150		185.00	250
1992	Eyes of the North	2,500		225.00	225
1993	Guardians of the Den	1,500		195.00	350
1991	Icy Reflections-Pintails	500		250.00	250
1992	Night Moves-Cougar	950		185.00	185
1994	Parting Reflections	950		185.00	185
1993	Shrouded Forest-Bald Eagle	950		150.00	950
1991	Twilight's Calling-Common Loons	950	1991	175.00	300
1993	What's Bruin	1,750		185.00	275

New Masters Publishing

Bannister - P. Bannister

YEAR ISSUE		EDITION LIMIT	YEAR RETD.	ISSUE PRICE	*QUOTE U.S. $
1982	Amaryllis	500	N/A	285.00	1900
1988	Apples and Oranges	485	N/A	265.00	600
1982	April	300	N/A	200.00	1100
1984	April Light	950	N/A	150.00	600
1978	Bandstand	250	N/A	75.00	450
1991	Celebration	662	N/A	350.00	700
1989	Chapter One	485	N/A	265.00	1300
1991	Crossroads	485	N/A	295.00	590
1993	Crowning Glory	485	N/A	265.00	265
1992	Crystal Bowl	485	N/A	265.00	265
1989	Daydreams	485	N/A	265.00	530
1993	Deja Vu	663	N/A	265.00	265
1983	The Duchess	500	N/A	250.00	1800
1980	Dust of Autumn	200	N/A	200.00	1225
1981	Easter	300	N/A	260.00	950
1982	Emily	500	N/A	285.00	800
1980	Faded Glory	200	N/A	200.00	1225
1984	The Fan Window	950	N/A	195.00	450
1987	First Prize	950	N/A	115.00	175
1988	Floribunda	485	N/A	265.00	550
1994	From Russia With Love	950	N/A	165.00	165
1980	Gift of Happiness	200	N/A	200.00	2000
1980	Girl on the Beach	200	N/A	200.00	1200
1990	Good Friends	485	N/A	265.00	750
1988	Guinevere	485	N/A	265.00	1000
1993	Into The Woods	485	N/A	265.00	265
1982	Ivy	500	N/A	285.00	700
1982	Jasmine	500	N/A	285.00	650
1981	Juliet	300	N/A	260.00	5000
1990	Lavender Hill	485	N/A	265.00	625
1992	Love Letters	485	N/A	265.00	265
1988	Love Seat	485	N/A	230.00	500
1989	Low Tide	485	N/A	265.00	550
1982	Mail Order Brides	500	N/A	325.00	2300
1984	Make Believe	950	N/A	150.00	600
1989	March Winds	485	N/A	265.00	530
1983	Mementos	950	N/A	150.00	1400
1982	Memories	500	N/A	235.00	500
1992	Morning Mist	485	N/A	265.00	265
1981	My Special Place	300	N/A	260.00	1850
1982	Nuance	500	N/A	235.00	470
1994	Once Upon A Time	950	N/A	265.00	265
1983	Ophelia	950	N/A	150.00	675
1989	Peace	485	N/A	265.00	1100
1981	Porcelain Rose	300	N/A	260.00	2000
1982	The Present	500	N/A	260.00	800
1986	Pride & Joy	950	N/A	150.00	300
1991	Pudding & Pies	485	N/A	265.00	265
1987	Quiet Corner	950	N/A	115.00	300
1989	The Quilt	485	N/A	265.00	900
1993	Rambling Rose	485	N/A	265.00	265
1981	Rehearsal	300	N/A	260.00	1850
1990	Rendezvous	485	N/A	265.00	650
1984	Scarlet Ribbons	950	N/A	150.00	325
1980	Sea Haven	300	N/A	260.00	1100
1990	Seascapes	485	N/A	265.00	550
1987	September Harvest	950	N/A	150.00	300
1980	The Silver Bell	200	N/A	200.00	2000
1990	Sisters	485	N/A	265.00	950
1990	Songbird	485	N/A	265.00	550
1991	String of Pearls	485	N/A	265.00	850
1988	Summer Choices	300	N/A	250.00	800
1991	Teatime	485	N/A	295.00	600
1980	Titania	350	N/A	260.00	900
1991	Wildflowers	485	N/A	295.00	590
1983	Window Seat	950	N/A	150.00	600

Past Impressions

Maley - A. Maley

YEAR ISSUE		EDITION LIMIT	YEAR RETD.	ISSUE PRICE	*QUOTE U.S. $
1989	Alexandria	750	1994	125.00	125
1989	Beth	750	1994	125.00	125
1991	Between Friends	750		275.00	275
1988	The Boardwalk	Closed	N/A	250.00	340
1990	Cafe Royale	750		275.00	275
1989	Catherine	750	1994	125.00	125
1992	Circle of Love	500		250.00	250
1988	Day Dreams	Closed	N/A	200.00	350-450
1992	An Elegant Affair	500		260.00	260
1989	English Rose	Closed	N/A	250.00	285
1990	Evening Performance	750		150.00	150
1990	Festive Occasion	Closed	N/A	250.00	250
1984	Glorious Summer	Closed	N/A	150.00	725
1990	Gracious Era	750		275.00	275
1995	Grand Entrance	500		250.00	250
1989	In Harmony	750	1995	250.00	250
1992	Intimate Moment	750		250.00	250
1988	Joys of Childhood	Closed	N/A	250.00	250
1995	The Letter	500		250.00	250
1967	Love Letter	Closed	N/A	200.00	300-550
1995	The New Carriage	500		100.00	100
1994	New Years Eve	500		250.00	250
1988	Opening Night	Closed	N/A	250.00	2000
1994	Parisian Beauties	500		275.00	275
1985	Passing Elegance	Closed	N/A	150.00	750
1987	The Promise	Closed	N/A	200.00	315
1993	Rags and Riches	500		250.00	250
1994	The Recital	500		275.00	275
1990	Romantic Engagement	750		275.00	275
1984	Secluded Garden	Closed	N/A	150.00	970
1985	Secret Thoughts	Closed	N/A	150.00	850
1993	Sleigh Bells	500		260.00	260
1991	Summer Carousel	750		200.00	200
1994	Summer Elegance	500		275.00	275
1990	Summer Pastime	Closed	N/A	250.00	250
1995	Summer Romance	500		250.00	250
1991	Sunday Afternoon	750		275.00	275
1986	Tell Me	Closed	N/A	150.00	850
1988	Tranquil Moment	Closed	N/A	250.00	315
1989	Victoria	750	1994	125.00	125
1988	Victorian Trio	Closed	N/A	250.00	340
1994	Visiting The Nursery	500		250.00	250
1992	A Walk in the Park	500		260.00	260
1991	Winter Carousel	750		200.00	200
1989	Winter Impressions	750		250.00	315
1986	Winter Romance	Closed	N/A	150.00	650

Pemberton & Oakes

Canvas Replicas - D. Zolan

YEAR ISSUE		EDITION LIMIT	YEAR RETD.	ISSUE PRICE	*QUOTE U.S. $
1992	Quiet Time	Retrd.	N/A	18.80	50
1992	September Girl	Retrd.	N/A	18.80	40
1992	Summer Garden	Retrd.	N/A	18.80	45

Canvas Transfer - D. Zolan

YEAR ISSUE		EDITION LIMIT	YEAR RETD.	ISSUE PRICE	*QUOTE U.S. $
1992	Daisy Days	Retrd.	N/A	24.20	45
1993	It's Grandma & Grandpa	Retrd.	N/A	24.20	45
1993	Spring Duet	Retrd.	N/A	24.40	45

Grandparents Day-Miniature Lithographs - D. Zolan

YEAR ISSUE		EDITION LIMIT	YEAR RETD.	ISSUE PRICE	*QUOTE U.S. $
1992	Letter to Grandma	Retrd.	N/A	35.00	41

Membership-Miniature Lithographs - D. Zolan

YEAR ISSUE		EDITION LIMIT	YEAR RETD.	ISSUE PRICE	*QUOTE U.S. $
1992	Brotherly Love	Retrd.	N/A	18.00	68
1993	New Shoes	Retrd.	N/A	18.00	42
1993	Country Walk	Retrd.	N/A	22.00	40
1994	Enchanted Forest	Retrd.	N/A	22.00	40

*Quotes have been rounded up to nearest dollar

Miniature Replicas of Oils - D. Zolan

YEAR ISSUE		EDITION LIMIT	YEAR RETD.	ISSUE PRICE	*QUOTE U.S.$
1990	Brotherly Love	Retrd.	N/A	24.40	77
1991	Crystal's Creek	Retrd.	N/A	24.40	45
1990	Daddy's Home	Retrd.	N/A	24.40	71
1992	It's Grandma & Grandpa	Retrd.	N/A	24.40	41
1992	Mother's Angels	Retrd.	N/A	24.40	40
1992	Touching the Sky	Retrd.	N/A	24.40	37

Quiet Moments-Miniature Lithographs - D. Zolan

1993	Birthday Greetings	Retrd.	N/A	22.00	42
1993	Country Kitten	Retrd.	N/A	22.00	42
1993	Crystal's Creek	Retrd.	N/A	22.00	43
1992	One Summer Day	Retrd.	N/A	22.00	40

Single Issues-Miniature Lithographs - D. Zolan

1993	A Christmas Prayer 1993	Retrd.	N/A	35.00	42
1993	Daddy's Home	Retrd.	N/A	22.00	50
1993	First Kiss	Retrd.	N/A	22.00	45-80
1994	A Gift for Laurie	Retrd.	N/A	22.00	40
1993	Letter To Grandma	Retrd.	N/A	22.00	42
1994	Rodeo Girl	Retrd.	N/A	35.00	42
1991	Tender Moment	Retrd.	N/A	35.00	75

Zolan's Children-Lithographs - D. Zolan

1989	Almost Home	Retrd.	N/A	98.00	255
1991	Autumn Leaves	Retrd.	N/A	98.00	120
1993	The Big Catch	Retrd.	N/A	98.00	130
1989	Brotherly Love	Retrd.	N/A	98.00	295
1982	By Myself	Retrd.	N/A	98.00	230
1989	Christmas Prayer	Retrd.	N/A	98.00	175-225
1990	Colors of Spring	Retrd.	N/A	98.00	175-240
1990	Crystal's Creek	Retrd.	N/A	98.00	175
1989	Daddy's Home	Retrd.	N/A	98.00	310
1988	Day Dreamer	Retrd.	N/A	35.00	130
1992	Enchanted Forest	Retrd.	N/A	98.00	110-135
1982	Erik and the Dandelion	Retrd.	N/A	98.00	400
1990	First Kiss	Retrd.	N/A	98.00	240
1991	Flowers for Mother	Retrd.	N/A	98.00	160
1993	Grandma's Garden	Retrd.	N/A	98.00	135
1989	Grandma's Mirror	Retrd.	N/A	98.00	140-195
1990	Laurie and the Creche	Retrd.	N/A	98.00	115-165
1989	Mother's Angels	Retrd.	N/A	98.00	175-240
1992	New Shoes	Retrd.	N/A	98.00	150
1989	Rodeo Girl	Retrd.	N/A	98.00	160
1984	Sabina in the Grass	Retrd.	N/A	98.00	625
1988	Small Wonder	Retrd.	N/A	98.00	250
1989	Snowy Adventure	Retrd.	N/A	98.00	205
1991	Summer Suds	Retrd.	N/A	98.00	140-175
1989	Summer's Child	Retrd.	N/A	98.00	225
1986	Tender Moment	Retrd.	N/A	98.00	275
1988	Tiny Treasures	Retrd.	N/A	150.00	215
1987	Touching the Sky	Retrd.	N/A	98.00	175-225
1988	Waiting to Play	Retrd.	N/A	35.00	135
1988	Winter Angel	Retrd.	N/A	98.00	230

Zolan's Children-Miniature Lithographs - D. Zolan

1992	Colors of Spring	Retrd.	N/A	35.00	40
1992	Forest & Fairytales	Retrd.	N/A	22.00	42
1992	The Little Fisherman	Retrd.	N/A	35.00	43
1991	Morning Discovery	Retrd.	N/A	35.00	55

Reco International

Fine Art Canvas Reproduction - J. McClelland

1990	Beach Play	350		80.00	80
1991	Flower Swing	350		100.00	100
1991	Summer Conversation	350		80.00	80

Limited Edition Print - S. Kuck

1986	Ashley	500		85.00	150
1985	Heather	Retrd.	1987	75.00	150
1984	Jessica	Retrd.	1986	60.00	400

McClelland - J. McClelland

XX	I Love Tammy	500		75.00	100
XX	Just for You	300		155.00	155
XX	Olivia	300		175.00	175
XX	Reverie	300		110.00	110
XX	Sweet Dreams	300		145.00	145

Roman, Inc.

Abble Williams - A. Williams

1988	Mary, Mother of the Carpenter	Closed	N/A	100.00	100

The Discovery of America Miniature Art Print - I. Spencer

1991	The Discovery of America	Open		2.00	2

Divine Servant - M. Greiner Jr.

1993	Divine Servant, print of drawing	Open		35.00	35
1994	Divine Servant, print of painting	Closed	1994	150.00	150
1994	Divine Servant, print of painting	Closed	1994	75.00	75
1994	Divine Servant, print of painting w/remarque	Closed	1994	75.00	75
1994	Divine Servant, print of painting w/remarque	Closed	1994	150.00	150

Fishers of Men - M. Greiner, Jr.

1994	Fishers of Men 8x10	Open		10.00	10
1994	Fishers of Men 11x14	Open		20.00	20
1994	Fishers of Men 16x20	Open		35.00	35

Hook - F. Hook

1982	Bouquet	1,200		70.00	350
1981	The Carpenter	Closed	1981	100.00	1000
1981	The Carpenter (remarque)	Closed	1981	100.00	3000
1982	Frolicking	1,200		60.00	350
1982	Gathering	1,200		60.00	350-450
1982	Little Children, Come to Me	1,950		50.00	500
1982	Little Children, Come to Me, remarque	50		100.00	500
1982	Posing	1,200		70.00	350
1982	Poulets	1,200		60.00	350
1982	Surprise	1,200		50.00	350

Portraits of Love - F. Hook

1988	Expectation	2,500		25.00	25
1988	In Mother's Arms	2,500		25.00	25
1988	My Kitty	2,500		25.00	25
1988	Remember When...	2,500		25.00	25
1988	Sharing	2,500		25.00	25
1988	Sunkissed Afternoon	2,500		25.00	25

Schmid

Ferrandiz Lithographs - J. Ferrandiz

1983	Friendship	460	1983	165.00	450
1983	Friendship, remarque	15	1983	1200.00	2300
1982	He Seems to Sleep	450	1982	150.00	700
1982	He Seems to Sleep, remarque	25	1982	300.00	3200
1981	Heart of Seven Colors	600	1981	100.00	395
1981	Heart of Seven Colors, remarque	75	1981	175.00	1300
1982	Mirror of the Soul	225	1982	150.00	425
1982	Mirror of the Soul, remarque	35	1982	250.00	2400
1980	Most Precious Gift	425	1980	125.00	1200
1980	Most Precious Gift, remarque	50	1980	225.00	2800
1980	My Star	675	1980	100.00	650
1980	My Star, remarque	75	1980	175.00	1800
1982	Oh Small Child	450	1982	125.00	495
1982	Oh Small Child, remarque	50	1982	225.00	1450
1982	On the Threshold of Life	425	1982	150.00	450
1982	On the Threshold of Life, remarque	50	1982	275.00	1350
1982	Riding Through the Rain	900	1982	165.00	350
1982	Riding Through the Rain, remarque	100	1982	300.00	950
1982	Spreading the Word	675	1982	125.00	190-250
1982	Spreading the Word, remarque	75	1982	225.00	1075
1984	Star in the Teapot	410	1984	165.00	165
1984	Star in the Teapot, remarque	15	1984	1200.00	2100

V.F. Fine Arts

Kuck - S. Kuck

1994	'95 Angel Collection, S/N	750	1995	198.00	198
1995	'96 Angel Collection, S/N	750		198.00	198
1993	Best Friend, proof	250	N/A	175.00	225
1993	Best Friends, Canvas Transfer	250	N/A	500.00	600
1993	Best Friends, S/N	2,500	N/A	145.00	150
1994	Best of Days, S/N	750	1994	160.00	175
1989	Bundle of Joy, S/N	1,000	1989	125.00	250
1993	Buttons & Bows, proof	95	N/A	125.00	150
1993	Buttons & Bows, S/N	950	N/A	95.00	125
1990	Chopsticks, proof	150	1991	120.00	150
1990	Chopsticks, remarque	25	1991	160.00	200
1990	Chopsticks, S/N	1,500	1990	80.00	95
1995	Christmas Magic, S/N	950		80.00	80
1987	The Daisy, proof	90	1988	40.00	175
1987	The Daisy, S/N	900	1988	30.00	125
1989	Day Dreaming, proof	90	1989	225.00	250
1989	Day Dreaming, remarque	50	1989	300.00	395
1989	Day Dreaming, S/N	900	1989	150.00	200
1994	Dear Santa, S/N	950	1994	95.00	125
1992	Duet, Canvas Framed	500	1994	255.00	325
1992	Duet, proof	95	N/A	175.00	200
1992	Duet, S/N	950	N/A	125.00	135
1988	First Recital, proof	25	1988	250.00	750
1988	First Recital, remarque	25	1988	400.00	1000
1988	First Recital, S/N	150	1988	200.00	500
1990	First Snow, proof	50	1990	150.00	250
1990	First Snow, remarque	25	1990	200.00	350
1990	First Snow, S/N	500	1990	95.00	150
1987	The Flower Girl, proof	90	1987	50.00	125
1987	The Flower Girl, S/N	900	1987	40.00	95
1994	Garden Memories, Canvas Transfer	250	N/A	500.00	500
1994	Garden Memories, S/N	2,500	N/A	145.00	175
1991	God's Gift, proof	150	N/A	150.00	175
1991	God's Gift, S/N	1,500	1993	95.00	125
1993	Good Morning, Canvas	250	1993	500.00	500
1993	Good Morning, proof	50	N/A	175.00	200
1993	Good Morning, S/N	2,500	N/A	145.00	165
1995	Homecoming, proof	95	1995	172.50	173
1995	Homecoming, S/N	1,150	1995	125.00	125
1989	Innocence, proof	90	1989	225.00	275
1989	Innocence, remarque	50	1989	300.00	395
1989	Innocence, S/N	900	1989	150.00	220
1992	Joyous Day, Canvas Transfer	250	N/A	250.00	295
1992	Joyous Day, proof	120	N/A	175.00	200
1992	Joyous Day, S/N	1,200	1993	125.00	150
1988	The Kitten, proof	50	1988	150.00	1000
1988	The Kitten, remarque	25	1988	250.00	1200
1988	The Kitten, S/N	350	1988	120.00	1000
1990	Le Beau, proof	150	1990	120.00	225
1990	Le Beau, remarque	25	1990	160.00	275
1990	Le Beau, S/N	1,500	1990	80.00	175
1987	Le Papillion, proof	35	1990	110.00	175
1987	Le Papillion, remarque	7	1990	150.00	250
1987	Le Papillion, S/N	350	1990	90.00	150
1990	Lilly Pond, color remarque	125	1990	500.00	500
1990	Lilly Pond, proof	75	1990	200.00	200
1990	Lilly Pond, S/N	750	1990	150.00	150
1988	Little Ballerina, proof	25	1988	150.00	350
1988	Little Ballerina, remarque	25	1988	225.00	450
1988	Little Ballerina, S/N	150	1988	110.00	275
1987	The Loveseat, proof	90	1987	40.00	150
1987	The Loveseat, S/N	900	1987	30.00	100
1991	Memories, S/N	5,000	1991	195.00	250
1987	Mother's Love, proof	12	1987	225.00	1200
1987	Mother's Love, S/N	150	1987	195.00	750
1988	My Dearest, proof	50	1988	200.00	900
1988	My Dearest, remarque	25	1988	325.00	1200
1988	My Dearest, S/N	350	1988	160.00	700
1995	Night Before Christmas, S/N	1,150		95.00	95
1995	Playful Kitten	950	1995	95.00	95
1989	Puppy, proof	50	1989	180.00	500
1989	Puppy, remarque	50	1989	240.00	750
1989	Puppy, S/N	500	1989	120.00	400
1987	A Quiet Time, proof	90	1987	50.00	100
1987	A Quiet Time, S/N	900	1987	40.00	75
1987	The Reading Lesson, proof	90	1987	70.00	200
1987	The Reading Lesson, S/N	900	1987	60.00	150
1995	Rhapsody & Lace	1,150		95.00	100
1989	Rose Garden, proof	50	1989	150.00	400
1989	Rose Garden, remarque	50	1989	200.00	500
1989	Rose Garden, S/N	500	1989	95.00	390
1986	Silhouette, proof	25	1987	90.00	250
1986	Silhouette, S/N	250	1987	80.00	200
1989	Sisters, proof	90	1989	150.00	550
1989	Sisters, remarque	50	1989	200.00	650
1989	Sisters, S/N	900	1988	95.00	300
1989	Sonatina, proof	90	1989	225.00	700
1989	Sonatina, remarque	50	1989	300.00	850
1989	Sonatina, S/N	900	1989	150.00	400
1986	Summer Reflections, proof	90	1987	70.00	300
1986	Summer Reflections, S/N	900	1987	60.00	250
1986	Tender Moments, proof	50	1986	80.00	300
1986	Tender Moments, S/N	500	1986	70.00	200
1993	Thinking of You, Canvas Transfer	250	1993	500.00	500
1993	Thinking of You, S/N	2,500	N/A	145.00	175
1988	Wild Flowers, proof	50	1988	175.00	300
1988	Wild Flowers, remarque	25	1988	250.00	400
1988	Wild Flowers, S/N	350	1988	160.00	250
1992	Yesterday, Canvas Framed	550	N/A	195.00	200
1992	Yesterday, proof	95	N/A	150.00	150
1992	Yesterday, S/N	950	N/A	95.00	95

PLATES

Ace Product Management Group, Inc.

Good Times Together - B. Otero

1995	Road Trip 99276-95Z	10,000		32.00	32

Harley-Davidson Collector Christmas Plates - Ace

1984	1909 V-Twin 99133-85Z	8,500	1984	19.95	20
1985	Perfect Tree 99134-86Z	8,500	1985	22.50	2
1986	Mainstreet 99136-87Z	8,500	1986	24.95	2
1987	Joy Of Giving 99133-88Z	8,500	1987	24.95	2
1988	Home For The Holidays 99134-89Z	8,500	1988	29.95	3
1989	29 Days Till Xmas 99134-90Z	8,500	1989	34.95	3
1990	Rural Delivery 99134-91Z	8,500	1990	34.95	3
1991	Skating Party 99138-92Z	8,500	1991	34.95	3
1992	A Surprise Visit 99135-93Z	9,500	1992	38.00	3
1993	Christmas Vacation 99287-94Z	9,500	1993	38.00	3

Harley-Davidson Collector Pewter Decade Series Plates - Ace

1992	Birth Of Legend-1900's 99139-92Z	3,000	1992	120.00	12
1993	Growth Of Sport-1910's 99129-94Z	3,000	1993	125.00	12
1994	Roaring Into The 20's-1920's 99136-95Z	3,000		130.00	13
1995	Growing Stronger With Time-1930's 99294-96Z	3,000		132.00	13

Harley-Davidson Collector Pewter Plates - Ace

1988	Winter Gathering 99139-89ZP	3,000	1988	74.95	7
1989	1989 Plate 99139-90ZP	3,000	1989	89.95	9
1990	Spring Races 99136-91ZP	3,000	1990	99.95	10
1990	Summer Tradition 99139-91ZP	3,000	1990	99.95	10

Holiday Memories Christmas Plates - B. Otero

1984	Under The Mistletoe 99090-95Z	15,000	1994	38.00	3
1995	Late Arrival 99415-96Z	15,000	1995	38.00	3

American Artists

The Best of Fred Stone-Mares & Foals Series (6 1/2") - F. Stone

1991	Patience	19,500		25.00	25-3
1992	Water Trough	19,500		25.00	2
1992	Pasture Pest	19,500		25.00	2
1992	Kidnapped Mare	19,500		25.00	2
1993	Contentment	19,500		25.00	2
1993	Arabian Mare & Foal	19,500		25.00	2

*Quotes have been rounded up to nearest dollar

YEAR	ISSUE	EDITION LIMIT	YEAR RETD.	ISSUE PRICE	*QUOTE U.S.$
1994	Diamond in the Rough	19,500		25.00	25
1995	The First Day	19,500		25.00	25

Famous Fillies Series - F. Stone

YEAR	ISSUE	EDITION LIMIT	YEAR RETD.	ISSUE PRICE	*QUOTE U.S.$
1987	Lady's Secret	9,500		65.00	90
1988	Ruffian	9,500		65.00	85
1988	Genuine Risk	9,500		65.00	90
1992	Go For The Wand	9,500		65.00	80-90

Fred Stone Classic Series - F. Stone

YEAR	ISSUE	EDITION LIMIT	YEAR RETD.	ISSUE PRICE	*QUOTE U.S.$
1986	The Shoe-8,000 Wins	9,500		75.00	85-100
1986	The Eternal Legacy	9,500		75.00	95
1988	Forever Friends	9,500		75.00	85
1989	Alysheba	9,500		75.00	75-95

Gold Signature Series - F. Stone

YEAR	ISSUE	EDITION LIMIT	YEAR RETD.	ISSUE PRICE	*QUOTE U.S.$
1990	Secretariat Final Tribute, signed	4,500		150.00	375
1990	Secretariat Final Tribute, unsigned	7,500		75.00	75
1991	Old Warriors, signed	4,500		150.00	425
1991	Old Warriors, unsigned	7,500		75.00	75

Gold Signature Series II - F. Stone

YEAR	ISSUE	EDITION LIMIT	YEAR RETD.	ISSUE PRICE	*QUOTE U.S.$
1991	Northern Dancer, double signature	1,500		175.00	250
1991	Northern Dancer, single signature	3,000		150.00	150
1991	Northern Dancer, unsigned	7,500		75.00	75
1991	Kelso, double signature	1,500		175.00	175
1991	Kelso, single signature	3,000		150.00	150
1991	Kelso, unsigned	7,500		75.00	75

Gold Signature Series III - F. Stone

YEAR	ISSUE	EDITION LIMIT	YEAR RETD.	ISSUE PRICE	*QUOTE U.S.$
1992	Dance Smartly-Pat Day, Up, double signature	1,500		175.00	175
1992	Dance Smartly-Pat Day, Up, single signature	3,000		150.00	150
1992	Dance Smartly-Pat Day, Up, unsigned	7,500		75.00	75
1993	American Triple Crown-1937-1946, signed	2,500		195.00	195
1993	American Triple Crown-1937-1946, unsigned	7,500		75.00	75
1993	American Triple Crown-1948-1978, signed	2,500		195.00	195
1993	American Triple Crown-1948-1978, unsigned	7,500		75.00	175
1994	American Triple Crown-1919-1935, signed	2,500		95.00	95
1994	American Triple Crown-1919-1935, unsigned	7,500		75.00	75

Gold Signature Series IV - F. Stone

YEAR	ISSUE	EDITION LIMIT	YEAR RETD.	ISSUE PRICE	*QUOTE U.S.$
1995	Julie Krone - Colonial Affair	7,500		75.00	75
1995	Julie Krone - Colonial Affair, signed	2,500		150.00	150

The Horses of Fred Stone - F. Stone

YEAR	ISSUE	EDITION LIMIT	YEAR RETD.	ISSUE PRICE	*QUOTE U.S.$
1982	Patience	9,500		55.00	200
1982	Arabian Mare and Foal	9,500		55.00	175
1982	Safe and Sound	9,500		55.00	125
1983	Contentment	9,500		55.00	125

Mare and Foal Series - F. Stone

YEAR	ISSUE	EDITION LIMIT	YEAR RETD.	ISSUE PRICE	*QUOTE U.S.$
1986	Water Trough	12,500		49.50	160
1986	Tranquility	12,500		49.50	65
1986	Pasture Pest	12,500		49.50	130
1987	The Arabians	12,500		49.50	55

Mare and Foal Series II - F. Stone

YEAR	ISSUE	EDITION LIMIT	YEAR RETD.	ISSUE PRICE	*QUOTE U.S.$
1989	The First Day	Open		35.00	35
1989	Diamond in the Rough	Retrd.		35.00	35

Racing Legends - F. Stone

YEAR	ISSUE	EDITION LIMIT	YEAR RETD.	ISSUE PRICE	*QUOTE U.S.$
1989	Phar Lap	9,500		75.00	75
1989	Sunday Silence	9,500		75.00	75
1990	John Henry-Shoemaker	9,500		75.00	75

Sport of Kings Series - F. Stone

YEAR	ISSUE	EDITION LIMIT	YEAR RETD.	ISSUE PRICE	*QUOTE U.S.$
1984	Man O'War	9,500		65.00	125-150
1984	Secretariat	9,500		65.00	295
1985	John Henry	9,500		65.00	200
1986	Seattle Slew	9,500		65.00	65

The Stallion Series - F. Stone

YEAR	ISSUE	EDITION LIMIT	YEAR RETD.	ISSUE PRICE	*QUOTE U.S.$
1983	Black Stallion	19,500		49.50	150
1983	Andalusian	19,500		49.50	150

Anheuser-Busch, Inc.

1992 Olympic Team Series - A-Busch, Inc.

YEAR	ISSUE	EDITION LIMIT	YEAR RETD.	ISSUE PRICE	*QUOTE U.S.$
1991	1992 Olympic Team Winter Plate N3180	Retrd.	1994	35.00	35
1992	1992 Olympic Team Summer Plate N3122	Retrd.	1994	35.00	35

Archives Plate Series - D. Langeneckert

YEAR	ISSUE	EDITION LIMIT	YEAR RETD.	ISSUE PRICE	*QUOTE U.S.$
1992	1893 Columbian Exposition N3477	25-day		27.50	28
1992	Ganymede N4004	25-day		27.50	28
1995	Budweiser's Greatest Triumph Plate N5195	25-day		27.50	28
1995	Mirror of Truth Plate N5196	25-day		27.50	28

Civil War Series - D. Langeneckert

YEAR	ISSUE	EDITION LIMIT	YEAR RETD.	ISSUE PRICE	*QUOTE U.S.$
1992	General Grant N3478	Retrd.	1994	45.00	45-99
1993	General Robert E. Lee N3590	Retrd.	1994	45.00	45-99
1993	President Abraham Lincoln N3591	Retrd.	1994	45.00	45-99

Collector Edition Series - M. Urdahl

YEAR	ISSUE	EDITION LIMIT	YEAR RETD.	ISSUE PRICE	*QUOTE U.S.$
1995	"This Bud's For You" N4945	25-day		27.50	28

Holiday Plate Series - Various

YEAR	ISSUE	EDITION LIMIT	YEAR RETD.	ISSUE PRICE	*QUOTE U.S.$
1989	Winters Day N2295 - B. Kemper	Retrd.	N/A	30.00	65-80
1990	An American Tradition N2767 - S. Sampson	Retrd.	N/A	30.00	30-40
1991	The Season's Best N3034 - S. Sampson	25-day		30.00	30
1992	A Perfect Christmas N3440 - S. Sampson	25-day		27.50	28
1993	Special Delivery N4002 - N. Koerber	Retrd.		27.50	30-80
1994	Hometown Holiday N4572 - B. Kemper	25-day		27.50	28
1995	Lighting the Way Home N5215 - T. Jester	25-day		27.50	28

Man's Best Friend Series - M. Urdahl

YEAR	ISSUE	EDITION LIMIT	YEAR RETD.	ISSUE PRICE	*QUOTE U.S.$
1990	Buddies N2615	Retrd.	N/A	30.00	40-75
1990	Six Pack N3005	Retrd.	N/A	30.00	35-45
1992	Something's Brewing N3147	Retrd.	1994	30.00	30
1993	Outstanding in Their Field N4003	25-day		27.50	28

Anna-Perenna Porcelain

American Silhouettes Family Series - P. Buckley Moss

YEAR	ISSUE	EDITION LIMIT	YEAR RETD.	ISSUE PRICE	*QUOTE U.S.$
1982	Family Outing	5,000		75.00	95
1982	John and Mary	5,000		75.00	95
1984	Homemakers Quilting	5,000		75.00	85-195
1983	Leisure Time	5,000		75.00	85

American Silhouettes Valley Series - P. Buckley Moss

YEAR	ISSUE	EDITION LIMIT	YEAR RETD.	ISSUE PRICE	*QUOTE U.S.$
1982	Frosty Frolic	5,000		75.00	85-95
1984	Hay Ride	5,000		75.00	85
1983	Sunday Ride	5,000		75.00	85-100
1983	Market Day	5,000		75.00	120

American Silhouettes-Childrens Series - P. Buckley Moss

YEAR	ISSUE	EDITION LIMIT	YEAR RETD.	ISSUE PRICE	*QUOTE U.S.$
1981	Fiddlers Two	5,000		75.00	95
1982	Mary With The Lambs	5,000		75.00	85
1983	Ring-Around-the-Rosie	5,000		75.00	200
1983	Waiting For Tom	5,000		75.00	175

Annual Christmas Plate - P. Buckley Moss

YEAR	ISSUE	EDITION LIMIT	YEAR RETD.	ISSUE PRICE	*QUOTE U.S.$
1984	Noel, Noel	5,000		67.50	325
1985	Helping Hands	5,000		67.50	100-150
1986	Night Before Christmas	5,000		67.50	75-100
1987	Christmas Sleigh	5,000		75.00	95
1988	Christmas Joy	7,500		75.00	75
1989	Christmas Carol	7,500		80.00	95
1990	Christmas Eve	7,500		80.00	80
1991	The Snowman	7,500		80.00	80
1992	Christmas Warmth	7,500		85.00	85
1993	Joy to the World	7,500		85.00	85

The Celebration Series - P. Buckley Moss

YEAR	ISSUE	EDITION LIMIT	YEAR RETD.	ISSUE PRICE	*QUOTE U.S.$
1986	Wedding Joy	5,000		100.00	200-350
1987	The Christening	5,000		100.00	175
1988	The Anniversary	5,000		100.00	120-190
1990	Family Reunion	5,000		100.00	150

Uncle Tad's Cats - T. Krumeich

YEAR	ISSUE	EDITION LIMIT	YEAR RETD.	ISSUE PRICE	*QUOTE U.S.$
1979	Oliver's Birthday	5,000		75.00	200
1980	Peaches & Cream	5,000		75.00	100
1981	Princess Aurora	5,000		80.00	100
1981	Walter's Window	5,000		80.00	120

ANRI

ANRI Father's Day - Unknown

YEAR	ISSUE	EDITION LIMIT	YEAR RETD.	ISSUE PRICE	*QUOTE U.S.$
1972	Alpine Father & Children	Closed	1972	35.00	100
1973	Alpine Father & Children	Closed	1973	40.00	95
1974	Cliff Gazing	Closed	1974	50.00	100
1975	Sailing	Closed	1975	60.00	90

ANRI Mother's Day - Unknown

YEAR	ISSUE	EDITION LIMIT	YEAR RETD.	ISSUE PRICE	*QUOTE U.S.$
1972	Alpine Mother & Children	Closed	1972	35.00	50
1973	Alpine Mother & Children	Closed	1973	40.00	50
1974	Alpine Mother & Children	Closed	1974	50.00	55
1975	Alpine Stroll	Closed	1975	60.00	65
1976	Knitting	Closed	1976	60.00	65

Christmas - J. Malfertheiner, unless otherwise noted

YEAR	ISSUE	EDITION LIMIT	YEAR RETD.	ISSUE PRICE	*QUOTE U.S.$
1971	St. Jakob in Groden	6,000	1971	37.50	65
1972	Pipers at Alberobello	6,000	1972	45.00	75
1973	Alpine Horn	6,000	1973	45.00	390
1974	Young Man and Girl	6,000	1974	50.00	95
1975	Christmas in Ireland	6,000	1975	60.00	60
1976	Alpine Christmas	6,000	1976	65.00	190
1977	Legend of Heligenblut	6,000	1977	65.00	91
1978	Klockler Singers	6,000	1978	80.00	80
1979	Moss Gatherers - Unknown	6,000	1979	135.00	177
1980	Wintry Churchgoing - Unknown	6,000	1980	165.00	165
1981	Santa Claus in Tyrol - Unknown	6,000	1981	165.00	200
1982	The Star Singers - Unknown	6,000	1982	165.00	165
1983	Unto Us a Child is Born - Unknown	6,000	1983	165.00	310
1984	Yuletide in the Valley - Unknown	6,000	1984	165.00	170
1985	Good Morning, Good Cheer	6,000	1985	165.00	165
1986	A Groden Christmas	6,000	1986	165.00	200
1987	Down From the Alps	6,000	1987	195.00	250
1988	Christkindl Markt	6,000	1988	220.00	230
1989	Flight Into Egypt	6,000	1989	275.00	275
1990	Holy Night	6,000	1990	300.00	300

Disney Four Star Collection - Disney Studios

YEAR	ISSUE	EDITION LIMIT	YEAR RETD.	ISSUE PRICE	*QUOTE U.S.$
1989	Mickey Mini Plate	5,000	1989	40.00	65
1990	Minnie Mini Plate	5,000	1990	40.00	95
1991	Donald Mini Plate	5,000	1991	50.00	55

Ferrandiz Christmas - J. Ferrandiz

YEAR	ISSUE	EDITION LIMIT	YEAR RETD.	ISSUE PRICE	*QUOTE U.S.$
1972	Christ In The Manger	4,000	1972	35.00	230
1973	Christmas	4,000	1973	40.00	225
1974	Holy Night	4,000	1974	50.00	100
1975	Flight into Egypt	4,000	1975	60.00	95
1976	Tree of Life	4,000	1976	60.00	85
1977	Girl with Flowers	4,000	1977	65.00	185
1978	Leading the Way	4,000	1978	77.50	180
1979	The Drummer	4,000	1979	120.00	175
1980	Rejoice	4,000	1980	150.00	160
1981	Spreading the Word	4,000	1981	150.00	150
1982	The Shepherd Family	4,000	1982	150.00	150
1983	Peace Attend Thee	4,000	1983	150.00	150

Ferrandiz Mother's Day Series - J. Ferrandiz

YEAR	ISSUE	EDITION LIMIT	YEAR RETD.	ISSUE PRICE	*QUOTE U.S.$
1972	Mother Sewing	3,000	1972	35.00	200
1973	Alpine Mother & Child	3,000	1973	40.00	150
1974	Mother Holding Child	3,000	1974	50.00	150
1975	Dove Girl	3,000	1975	60.00	150
1976	Mother Knitting	3,000	1976	60.00	200
1977	Alpine Stroll	3,000	1977	65.00	125
1978	The Beginning	3,000	1978	75.00	150
1979	All Hearts	3,000	1979	120.00	170
1980	Spring Arrivals	3,000	1980	150.00	165
1981	Harmony	3,000	1981	150.00	150
1982	With Love	3,000	1982	150.00	150

Ferrandiz Wooden Birthday Plates - J. Ferrandiz

YEAR	ISSUE	EDITION LIMIT	YEAR RETD.	ISSUE PRICE	*QUOTE U.S.$
1972	Boy	Unkn.	1972	15.00	150
1972	Girl	Unkn.	1972	15.00	160
1973	Boy	Unkn.	1973	20.00	200
1973	Girl	Unkn.	1973	20.00	150
1974	Boy	Unkn.	1974	22.00	160
1974	Girl	Unkn.	1974	22.00	160

Ferrandiz Wooden Wedding Plates - J. Ferrandiz

YEAR	ISSUE	EDITION LIMIT	YEAR RETD.	ISSUE PRICE	*QUOTE U.S.$
1972	Boy and Girl Embracing	Closed	1972	40.00	150
1973	Wedding Scene	Closed	1973	40.00	150
1974	Wedding	Closed	1974	48.00	150
1975	Wedding	Closed	1975	60.00	150
1976	Wedding	Closed	1976	60.00	90-150

Armstrong's

Classic Memory Collection - R. Skelton

YEAR	ISSUE	EDITION LIMIT	YEAR RETD.	ISSUE PRICE	*QUOTE U.S.$
1995	The Donut Dunker (signed)	1,000		375.00	375

Commemorative Issues - R. Skelton

YEAR	ISSUE	EDITION LIMIT	YEAR RETD.	ISSUE PRICE	*QUOTE U.S.$
1983	70 Years Young (10 1/2")	15,000		85.00	85-100
1984	Freddie the Torchbearer (8 1/2")	15,000		62.50	63
1994	Red & His Friend	160		700.00	1200

Freedom Collection of Red Skelton - R. Skelton

YEAR	ISSUE	EDITION LIMIT	YEAR RETD.	ISSUE PRICE	*QUOTE U.S.$
1990	The All American, (signed)	1,000		195.00	300
1990	The All American	9,000		62.50	63-85
1991	Independence Day? (signed)	1,000		195.00	200
1991	Independence Day?	9,000		62.50	63
1992	Let Freedom Ring, (signed)	1,000		195.00	200
1992	Let Freedom Ring	9,000		62.50	63
1993	Freddie's Gift of Life, (signed)	1,000		195.00	200
1993	Freddie's Gift of Life	9,000		62.50	63

Happy Art Series - W. Lantz

YEAR	ISSUE	EDITION LIMIT	YEAR RETD.	ISSUE PRICE	*QUOTE U.S.$
1981	Woody's Triple Self-Portrait, Signed	1,000		100.00	150
1981	Woody's Triple Self-Portrait	9,000		39.50	40
1983	Gothic Woody, Signed	1,000		100.00	150
1983	Gothic Woody	9,000		39.50	40
1984	Blue Boy Woody, Signed	1,000		100.00	150
1984	Blue Boy Woody	9,000		39.50	40

The Signature Collection - R. Skelton

YEAR	ISSUE	EDITION LIMIT	YEAR RETD.	ISSUE PRICE	*QUOTE U.S.$
1986	Anyone for Tennis?	9,000		62.50	65
1986	Anyone for Tennis? (signed)	1,000		125.00	450
1987	Ironing the Waves	9,000		62.50	65
1987	Ironing the Waves (signed)	1,000		125.00	300
1988	The Cliffhanger	9,000		62.50	65
1988	The Cliffhanger (signed)	1,000		150.00	300
1988	Hooked on Freddie	9,000		62.50	65
1988	Hooked on Freddie (signed)	1,000		175.00	250

Sports - Schenken

YEAR	ISSUE	EDITION LIMIT	YEAR RETD.	ISSUE PRICE	*QUOTE U.S.$
1985	Pete Rose h/s (10 1/4")	1,000		100.00	275
1985	Pete Rose u/s (10 1/4")	10,000		45.00	75

*Quotes have been rounded up to nearest dollar

PLATES

Armstrong's/Crown Parlan

YEAR ISSUE		EDITION LIMIT	YEAR RETD.	ISSUE PRICE	*QUOTE U.S.$

Freddie The Freeloader - R. Skelton

1979	Freddie in the Bathtub	10,000		60.00	200
1980	Freddie's Shack	10,000		60.00	75
1981	Freddie on the Green	10,000		60.00	60
1982	Love that Freddie	10,000		60.00	60

Freddie's Adventures - R. Skelton

1982	Captain Freddie	15,000		60.00	65
1982	Bronco Freddie	15,000		60.00	60
1983	Sir Freddie	15,000		62.50	63
1984	Gertrude and Heathcliffe	15,000		62.50	65

Artaffects

Club Member Limited Edition Redemption Offerings - G. Perillo

1992	The Pencil	Yr. Iss.		35.00	75
1992	Studies in Black & White (Set /4)	Yr. Iss.		75.00	100
1993	Watcher of the Wilderness	Yr. Iss.		60.00	60

America's Indian Heritage - G. Perillo

1987	Cheyenne Nation	10-day		24.50	45
1988	Arapaho Nation	10-day		24.50	45
1988	Kiowa Nation	10-day		24.50	45
1988	Sioux Nation	10-day		24.50	45
1988	Chippewa Nation	10-day		24.50	45
1988	Crow Nation	10-day		24.50	45
1988	Nez Perce Nation	10-day		24.50	45
1988	Blackfoot Nation	10-day		24.50	45

Chieftains I - G. Perillo

1979	Chief Sitting Bull	7,500		65.00	325
1979	Chief Joseph	7,500		65.00	110
1980	Chief Red Cloud	7,500		65.00	120
1980	Chief Geronimo	7,500		65.00	85
1981	Chief Crazy Horse	7,500		65.00	150

Chieftains II - G. Perillo

1983	Chief Pontiac	7,500		70.00	110
1983	Chief Victorio	7,500		70.00	85
1984	Chief Tecumseh	7,500		70.00	85
1984	Chief Cochise	7,500		70.00	85
1984	Chief Black Kettle	7,500		70.00	110

Council of Nations - G. Perillo

1992	Strength of the Sioux	14-day		29.50	35
1992	Pride of the Cheyenne	14-day		29.50	35
1992	Dignity of the Nez Perce	14-day		29.50	35
1992	Courage of the Arapaho	14-day		29.50	35
1992	Power of the Blackfoot	14-day		29.50	35
1992	Nobility of the Algonquin	14-day		29.50	35
1992	Wisdom of the Cherokee	14-day		29.50	35
1992	Boldness of the Seneca	14-day		29.50	35

Indian Bridal - G. Perillo

1990	Yellow Bird (6 1/2")	14-day		25.00	25
1990	Autumn Blossom (6 1/2")	14-day		25.00	25
1990	Misty Waters (6 1/2")	14-day		25.00	25
1990	Sunny Skies (6 1/2")	14-day		25.00	25

Indian Nations - G. Perillo

1983	Blackfoot	7,500		140.00	350
1983	Cheyenne	7,500		set	Set
1983	Apache	7,500		set	Set
1983	Sioux	7,500		set	Set

March of Dimes: Our Children - G. Perillo

| 1989 | A Time to Be Born | 150-day | | 29.00 | 40 |

Mother's Love - G. Perillo

1988	Feelings	Yr.Iss.		35.00	55
1989	Moonlight	Yr.Iss.		35.00	65
1990	Pride & Joy	Yr.Iss.		39.50	50
1991	Little Shadow	Yr.Iss.		39.50	45

Motherhood Series - G. Perillo

1983	Madre	10,000		50.00	75
1984	Madonna of the Plains	3,500		50.00	75
1985	Abuela	3,500		50.00	75
1986	Nap Time	3,500		50.00	75

Native American Christmas - G. Perillo

| 1993 | The Little Shepherd | Annual | | 35.00 | 55 |
| 1994 | Joy to the World | Annual | | 45.00 | 45 |

Nature's Harmony - G. Perillo

1982	The Peaceable Kingdom	12,500		100.00	125-200
1982	Zebra	12,500		50.00	50
1982	Bengal Tiger	12,500		50.00	60
1983	Black Panther	12,500		50.00	70
1983	Elephant	12,500		50.00	80

North American Wildlife - G. Perillo

1989	Mustang	14-day		29.50	35-55
1989	White-Tailed Deer	14-day		29.50	35
1989	Mountain Lion	14-day		29.50	35
1990	American Bald Eagle	14-day		29.50	35
1990	Timber Wolf	14-day		29.50	35

1990	Polar Bear	14-day		29.50	35
1990	Buffalo	14-day		29.50	35-55
1990	Bighorn Sheep	14-day		29.50	35

Perillo Christmas - G. Perillo

1987	Shining Star	Yr.Iss.		29.50	75
1988	Silent Light	Yr.Iss.		35.00	65
1989	Snow Flake	Yr.Iss.		35.00	65
1990	Bundle Up	Yr.Iss.		39.50	65
1991	Christmas Journey	Yr.Iss.		39.50	40

Portraits of American Brides - R. Sauber

1986	Caroline	10-day		29.50	40-85
1986	Jacqueline	10-day		29.50	45
1987	Elizabeth	10-day		29.50	45
1987	Emily	10-day		29.50	45
1987	Meredith	10-day		29.50	50
1987	Laura	10-day		29.50	45
1987	Sarah	10-day		29.50	45
1987	Rebecca	10-day		29.50	65

Pride of America's Indians - G. Perillo

1986	Brave and Free	10-day		24.50	50
1986	Dark-Eyed Friends	10-day		24.50	30
1986	Noble Companions	10-day		24.50	35
1987	Kindred Spirits	10-day		24.50	35
1987	Loyal Alliance	10-day		24.50	55
1987	Small and Wise	10-day		24.50	40
1987	Winter Scouts	10-day		24.50	40
1987	Peaceful Comrades	10-day		24.50	40

The Princesses - G. Perillo

1982	Lily of the Mohawks	7,500		50.00	175
1982	Pocahontas	7,500		50.00	100
1982	Minnehaha	7,500		50.00	100
1982	Sacajawea	7,500		50.00	100

Proud Young Spirits - G. Perillo

1990	Protector of the Plains	14-day		29.50	45
1990	Watchful Eyes	14-day		29.50	55
1990	Freedom's Watch	14-day		29.50	35-45
1990	Woodland Scouts	14-day		29.50	35-45
1990	Fast Friends	14-day		29.50	35-45
1990	Birds of a Feather	14-day		29.50	50
1990	Prairie Pals	14-day		29.50	35-45
1990	Loyal Guardian	14-day		29.50	35

Special Issue - G. Perillo

1981	Apache Boy	5,000		95.00	175
1983	Papoose	3,000		100.00	125
1983	Indian Style	17,500		50.00	50
1984	The Lovers	Closed	N/A	50.00	100
1984	Navajo Girl	3,500		95.00	175
1986	Navajo Boy	3,500		95.00	175

The Thoroughbreds - G. Perillo

1984	Whirlaway	9,500		50.00	125-250
1984	Secretariat	9,500		50.00	350
1984	Man o' War	9,500		50.00	150
1984	Seabiscuit	9,500		50.00	150

The Young Chieftains - G. Perillo

1985	Young Sitting Bull	5,000		50.00	75-100
1985	Young Joseph	5,000		50.00	75-100
1986	Young Red Cloud	5,000		50.00	75-100
1986	Young Geronimo	5,000		50.00	75-100
1986	Young Crazy Horse	5,000		50.00	75-100

Artists of the World

Celebration Series - T. DeGrazia

1993	The Lord's Candle	5,000		39.50	45-75
1993	Pinata Party	5,000		39.50	45-75
1993	Holiday lullaby	5,000		39.50	45-75
1993	Caroling	5,000		39.50	45-75

Children (Signed) - T. DeGrazia

1978	Los Ninos, signed	500		100.00	1500-2200
1978	White Dove, signed	500		100.00	450-700
1978	Flower Girl, signed	500		100.00	450-700
1979	Flower Boy, signed	500		100.00	450-700
1980	Little Cocopah Girl, signed	500		100.00	450-650
1981	Beautiful Burden, signed	500		100.00	450-650
1981	Merry Little Indian, signed	500		100.00	450-650

Children - T. DeGrazia

1976	Los Ninos	5,000		35.00	1100-1550
1977	White Dove	5,000		40.00	150-300
1978	Flower Girl	9,500		45.00	250-350
1979	Flower Boy	9,500		45.00	250-350
1980	Little Cocopah	9,500		50.00	125-200
1981	Beautiful Burden	9,500		50.00	150-200
1982	Merry Little Indian	9,500		55.00	150-200
1983	Wondering	10,000		60.00	160
1984	Pink Papoose	10,000		65.00	125
1985	Sunflower Boy	10,000		65.00	125

Children at Play - T. DeGrazia

1985	My First Horse	15,000		65.00	100-125
1986	Girl With Sewing Machine	15,000		65.00	95-125
1987	Love Me	15,000		65.00	95-125

1988	Merrily, Merrily, Merrily	15,000		65.00	95-125
1989	My First Arrow	15,000		65.00	95-125
1990	Away With My Kite	15,000		65.00	95-125

Children Mini-Plates - T. DeGrazia

1980	Los Ninos	5,000		15.00	300
1981	White Dove	5,000		15.00	100
1982	Flower Girl	5,000		15.00	100
1982	Flower Boy	5,000		15.00	100
1983	Little Cocopah Indian Girl	5,000		15.00	100
1983	Beautiful Burden	5,000		20.00	100
1984	Merry Little Indian	5,000		20.00	100
1984	Wondering	5,000		20.00	100
1985	Pink Papoose	5,000		20.00	100
1985	Sunflower Boy	5,000		20.00	100

Children of the Sun - T. DeGrazia

1987	Spring Blossoms	150-day		34.50	60-125
1987	My Little Pink Bird	150-day		34.50	60-125
1987	Bright Flowers of the Desert	150-day		37.90	60-125
1988	Gifts from the Sun	150-day		37.90	60-125
1988	Growing Glory	150-day		37.90	60-125
1988	The Gentle White Dove	150-day		37.90	60-125
1988	Sunflower Maiden	150-day		39.90	60-125
1989	Sun Showers	150-day		39.90	60-125

Floral Fiesta - T. DeGrazia

1994	Little Flower Vendor	5,000		39.50	40-7
1994	Flowers For Mother	5,000		39.50	40-7
1995	Floral Innocence	5,000		39.50	40-7
1995	Floral Bouquet	5,000		39.50	40-7

Holiday (Signed) - T. DeGrazia

1976	Festival of Lights, signed	500		100.00	600-85
1977	Bell of Hope, signed	500		100.00	450-70
1978	Little Madonna, signed	500		100.00	450-75
1979	The Nativity, signed	500		100.00	500-55
1980	Little Pima Drummer, signed	500		100.00	450-55
1981	A Little Prayer, signed	500		100.00	450-50
1982	Blue Boy, signed	96		100.00	450-40

Holiday - T. DeGrazia

1976	Festival of Lights	9,500		45.00	200-40
1977	Bell of Hope	9,500		45.00	125-30
1978	Little Madonna	9,500		45.00	125-35
1979	The Nativity	9,500		50.00	29
1980	Little Pima Drummer	9,500		50.00	125-20
1981	A Little Prayer	9,500		55.00	125-20
1982	Blue Boy	10,000		60.00	125-20
1983	Heavenly Blessings	10,000		65.00	13
1984	Navajo Madonna	10,000		65.00	13
1985	Saguaro Dance	10,000		65.00	12

Holiday Mini-Plates - T. DeGrazia

1980	Festival of Lights	5,000		15.00	25
1981	Bell of Hope	5,000		15.00	9
1982	Little Madonna	5,000		15.00	9
1982	The Nativity	5,000		15.00	9
1983	Little Pima Drummer	5,000		15.00	9
1983	Little Prayer	5,000		20.00	2
1984	Blue Boy	5,000		20.00	2
1984	Heavenly Blessings	5,000		20.00	2
1985	Navajo Madonna	5,000		20.00	2
1985	Saguaro Dance	5,000		20.00	2

Special Release - T. DeGrazia

| 1996 | Wedding Party | 5,000 | | 49.50 | |

Western - T. DeGrazia

1986	Morning Ride	5,000		65.00	75-1
1987	Bronco	5,000		65.00	90-1
1988	Apache Scout	5,000		65.00	90-1
1989	Alone	5,000		65.00	90-1

Bareuther

Christmas - H. Mueller, unless otherwise noted

1967	Stiftskirche	10,000		12.00	
1968	Kapplkirche	10,000		12.00	
1969	Christkindlesmarkt	10,000		12.00	
1970	Chapel in Oberndorf	10,000		12.50	
1971	Toys for Sale - From Drawing By L. Richter	10,000		12.75	
1972	Christmas in Munich	10,000		14.50	
1973	Sleigh Ride	10,000		15.00	
1974	Black Forest Church	10,000		19.00	
1975	Snowman	10,000		21.50	
1976	Chapel in the Hills	10,000		23.50	
1977	Story Time	10,000		24.50	
1978	Mittenwald	10,000		27.50	
1979	Winter Day	10,000		35.00	
1980	Mittenberg	10,000		37.50	
1981	Walk in the Forest	10,000		39.50	
1982	Bad Wimpfen	10,000		39.50	
1983	The Night before Christmas	10,000		39.50	
1984	Zeil on the River Main	10,000		42.50	
1985	Winter Wonderland	10,000		42.50	
1986	Christmas in Forchheim	10,000		42.50	
1987	Decorating the Tree	10,000		42.50	
1988	St. Coloman Church	10,000		52.50	
1989	Sleigh Ride	10,000		52.50	80

YEAR ISSUE		EDITION LIMIT	YEAR RETD.	ISSUE PRICE	*QUOTE U.S. $
1990	The Old Forge in Rothenburg	10,000		52.50	53
1991	Christmas Joy	10,000		56.50	57
1992	Market Place in Heppenheim	10,000		59.50	60
1993	Winter Fun	10,000		59.50	60
1994	Coming Home For Christmas	10,000		59.50	60

Belleek

Christmas - Unknown

YEAR ISSUE		EDITION LIMIT	YEAR RETD.	ISSUE PRICE	*QUOTE U.S. $
1970	Castle Caldwell	7,500	1970	25.00	70-85
1971	Celtic Cross	7,500	1971	25.00	60
1972	Flight of the Earls	7,500	1972	30.00	35
1973	Tribute To Yeats	7,500	1973	38.50	40
1974	Devenish Island	7,500	1974	45.00	190
1975	The Celtic Cross	7,500	1975	48.00	80
1976	Dove of Peace	7,500	1976	55.00	55
1977	Wren	7,500	1977	55.00	55

Holiday Scenes in Ireland - Unknown

YEAR ISSUE		EDITION LIMIT	YEAR RETD.	ISSUE PRICE	*QUOTE U.S. $
1991	Traveling Home	7,500		75.00	75
1992	Bearing Gifts	7,500		75.00	75
1994	The Ice Skaters	7,500		75.00	75

Berlin Design

Christmas - Unknown

YEAR ISSUE		EDITION LIMIT	YEAR RETD.	ISSUE PRICE	*QUOTE U.S. $
1970	Christmas in Bernkastel	4,000		14.50	125
1971	Christmas in Rothenburg	20,000		14.50	45
1972	Christmas in Michelstadt	20,000		15.00	55
1973	Christmas in Wendlestein	20,000		20.00	55
1974	Christmas in Bremen	20,000		25.00	53
1975	Christmas in Dortland	20,000		30.00	35
1976	Christmas in Augsburg	20,000		32.00	75
1977	Christmas in Hamburg	20,000		32.00	32
1978	Christmas in Berlin	20,000		36.00	85
1979	Christmas in Greetsiel	20,000		47.50	60
1980	Christmas in Mittenberg	20,000		50.00	55
1981	Christmas Eve In Hahnenklee	20,000		55.00	55
1982	Christmas Eve In Wasserberg	20,000		55.00	50
1983	Christmas in Oberndorf	20,000		55.00	65
1984	Christmas in Ramsau	20,000		55.00	55
1985	Christmas in Bad Wimpfen	20,000		55.00	59
1986	Christmas Eve in Gelnhaus	20,000		65.00	65
1987	Christmas Eve in Goslar	20,000		65.00	65
1988	Christmas Eve in Ruhpolding	20,000		65.00	90
1989	Christmas Eve in Friedechsdadt	20,000		80.00	80
1990	Christmas Eve in Partenkirchen	20,000		80.00	80
1991	Christmas Eve in Allendorf	20,000		80.00	80

Bing & Grondahl

American Christmas Heritage Collection - C. Magadini

YEAR ISSUE		EDITION LIMIT	YEAR RETD.	ISSUE PRICE	*QUOTE U.S. $
1996	The Statue of Liberty	Yr.Iss.		47.50	48

Centennial Anniversary Commemoratives - Various

YEAR ISSUE		EDITION LIMIT	YEAR RETD.	ISSUE PRICE	*QUOTE U.S. $
1995	Centennial Plaquettes: Series of 10 5" plates featuring B&G motifs: 1895, 1905, 1919, 1927, 1932, 1945, 1954, 1967, 1974, 1982	Yr.Iss.	1995	250.00	250
1995	Centennial Plate: Behind the Frozen Window - F.A. Hallin	10,000	1995	39.50	40
1995	Centennial Platter: Towers of Copenhagen - J. Nielsen	7,500	1995	195.00	195

Centennial Collection - Various

YEAR ISSUE		EDITION LIMIT	YEAR RETD.	ISSUE PRICE	*QUOTE U.S. $
1991	Crows Enjoying Christmas - D. Jensen	Annual	1991	59.50	60
1992	Copenhagen Christmas - H. Vlugenring	Annual	1992	59.50	60
1993	Christmas Elf - H. Thelander	Annual	1993	59.50	60
1994	Christmas in Church - H. Thelander	Annual	1994	59.50	60
1995	Behind The Frozen Window - A. Hallin	Annual	1995	59.50	60

Children's Day Plate Series - Various

YEAR ISSUE		EDITION LIMIT	YEAR RETD.	ISSUE PRICE	*QUOTE U.S. $
1985	The Magical Tea Party - C. Roller	Annual	1985	24.50	25
1986	A Joyful Flight - C. Roller	Annual	1986	26.50	55
1986	The Little Gardeners - C. Roller	Annual	1987	29.50	75
1988	Wash Day - C. Roller	Annual	1988	34.50	45
1989	Bedtime - C. Roller	Annual	1989	37.00	60
1990	My Favorite Dress - S. Vestergaard	Annual	1990	37.00	75
1991	Fun on the Beach - S. Vestergaard	Annual	1991	45.00	60
1992	A Summer Day in the Meadow - S. Vestergaard	Annual	1992	45.00	60-75
1993	The Carousel - S. Vestergaard	Annual	1993	45.00	55-60
1994	The Little Fisherman - S. Vestergaard	Annual	1994	45.00	46
1995	My First Book - S. Vestergaard	Annual	1995	45.00	45
1996	The Little Racers - S. Vestergaard	Annual		45.00	45

Christmas - Various

YEAR ISSUE		EDITION LIMIT	YEAR RETD.	ISSUE PRICE	*QUOTE U.S. $
1895	Behind The Frozen Window - F.A. Hallin	Annual	1895	.50	5000-5500
1896	New Moon - F.A. Hallin	Annual	1896	.50	2200-2500
1897	Sparrows - F.A. Hallin	Annual	1897	.75	1200-1700
1898	Roses and Star - F. Garde	Annual	1898	.75	800-975
1899	Crows - F. Garde	Annual	1899	.75	1200-2000
1900	Church Bells - F. Garde	Annual	1900	.75	1300-1600
1901	Three Wise Men - S. Sabra	Annual	1901	1.00	450-540
1902	Gothic Church Interior - D. Jensen	Annual	1902	1.00	450-800
1903	Expectant Children - M. Hyldahl	Annual	1903	1.00	250-450
1904	Fredericksberg Hill - C. Olsen	Annual	1904	1.00	150-225
1905	Christmas Night - D. Jensen	Annual	1905	1.00	150-210
1906	Sleighing to Church - D. Jensen	Annual	1906	1.00	115-155
1907	Little Match Girl - E. Plockross	Annual	1907	1.00	135-185
1908	St. Petri Church - P. Jorgensen	Annual	1908	1.00	80-105
1909	Yule Tree - Aarestrup	Annual	1909	1.50	100-135
1910	The Old Organist - C. Ersgaard	Annual	1910	1.50	100-115
1911	Angels and Shepherds - H. Moltke	Annual	1911	1.50	75-115
1912	Going to Church - E. Hansen	Annual	1912	1.50	85-125
1913	Bringing Home the Tree - T. Larsen	Annual	1913	1.50	90-105
1914	Amalienborg Castle - T. Larsen	Annual	1914	1.50	85-110
1915	Dog Outside Window - D. Jensen	Annual	1915	1.50	130-170
1916	Sparrows at Christmas - P. Jorgensen	Annual	1916	1.50	70-90
1917	Christmas Boat - A. Friis	Annual	1917	1.50	85
1918	Fishing Boat - A. Friis	Annual	1918	1.50	90
1919	Outside Lighted Window - A. Friis	Annual	1919	2.00	70-100
1920	Hare in the Snow - A. Friis	Annual	1920	2.00	75-90
1921	Pigeons - A. Friis	Annual	1921	2.00	60-85
1922	Star of Bethlehem - A. Friis	Annual	1922	2.00	60-90
1923	The Ermitage - A. Friis	Annual	1923	2.00	65-95
1924	Lighthouse - A. Friis	Annual	1924	2.50	80-90
1925	Child's Christmas - A. Friis	Annual	1925	2.50	90-115
1926	Churchgoers - A. Friis	Annual	1926	2.50	80-115
1927	Skating Couple - A. Friis	Annual	1927	2.50	95
1928	Eskimos - A. Friis	Annual	1928	2.50	55-95
1929	Fox Outside Farm - A. Friis	Annual	1929	2.50	90-100
1930	Town Hall Square - H. Flugenring	Annual	1930	2.50	100-130
1931	Christmas Train - A. Friis	Annual	1931	2.50	90-108
1932	Life Boat - H. Flugenring	Annual	1932	2.50	70-95
1933	Korsor-Nyborg Ferry - H. Flugenring	Annual	1933	3.00	77-96
1934	Church Bell in Tower - H. Flugenring	Annual	1934	3.00	65-90
1935	Lillebelt Bridge - O. Larson	Annual	1935	3.00	75-140
1936	Royal Guard - O. Larson	Annual	1936	3.00	77
1937	Arrival of Christmas Guests - O. Larson	Annual	1937	3.00	80-110
1938	Lighting the Candles - I. Tjerne	Annual	1938	3.00	150-250
1939	Old Lock-Eye, The Sandman - I. Tjerne	Annual	1939	3.00	150-250
1940	Christmas Letters - O. Larson	Annual	1940	4.00	165-275
1941	Horses Enjoying Meal - O. Larson	Annual	1941	4.00	200-300
1942	Danish Farm - O. Larson	Annual	1942	4.00	115-215
1943	Ribe Cathedral - O. Larson	Annual	1943	5.00	175-200
1944	Sorgenfri Castle - O. Larson	Annual	1944	5.00	100-150
1945	The Old Water Mill - O. Larson	Annual	1945	5.00	120-180
1946	Commemoration Cross - M. Hyldahl	Annual	1946	5.00	80-100
1947	Dybbol Mill - M. Hyldahl	Annual	1947	5.00	100-175
1948	Watchman - M. Hyldahl	Annual	1948	5.50	75-120
1949	Landsoldaten - M. Hyldahl	Annual	1949	5.50	70-80
1950	Kronborg Castle - M. Hyldahl	Annual	1950	5.50	110-150
1951	Jens Bang - M. Hyldahl	Annual	1951	6.00	90
1952	Thorsvaldsen Museum - B. Pramvig	Annual	1952	6.00	80-120
1953	Snowman - B. Pramvig	Annual	1953	7.50	80-115
1954	Royal Boat - K. Bonfils	Annual	1954	7.00	90-145
1955	Kaulundorg Church - K. Bonfils	Annual	1955	8.00	90-150
1956	Christmas in Copenhagen - K. Bonfils	Annual	1956	8.50	125-250
1957	Christmas Candles - K. Bonfils	Annual	1957	9.00	140-175
1958	Santa Claus - K. Bonfils	Annual	1958	9.50	105-125
1959	Christmas Eve - K. Bonfils	Annual	1959	10.00	110-155
1960	Village Church - K. Bonfils	Annual	1960	10.00	175
1961	Winter Harmony - K. Bonfils	Annual	1961	10.50	70-115
1962	Winter Night - K. Bonfils	Annual	1962	11.00	60-120
1963	The Christmas Elf - H. Thelander	Annual	1963	11.00	70-130
1964	The Fir Tree & Hare - H. Thelander	Annual	1964	11.50	50
1965	Bringing Home the Tree - H. Thelander	Annual	1965	12.00	50
1966	Home for Christmas - H. Thelander	Annual	1966	12.00	50
1967	Sharing the Joy - H. Thelander	Annual	1967	13.00	55
1968	Christmas in Church - H. Thelander	Annual	1968	14.00	40
1969	Arrival of Guests - H. Thelander	Annual	1969	14.00	30
1970	Pheasants in Snow - H. Thelander	Annual	1970	14.50	25
1971	Christmas at Home - H. Thelander	Annual	1971	15.00	20
1972	Christmas in Greenland - H. Thelander	Annual	1972	16.50	25
1973	Country Christmas - H. Thelander	Annual	1973	19.50	25
1974	Christmas in the Village - H. Thelander	Annual	1974	22.00	25
1975	Old Water Mill - H. Thelander	Annual	1975	27.50	40
1976	Christmas Welcome - H. Thelander	Annual	1976	27.50	40
1977	Copenhagen Christmas - H. Thelander	Annual	1977	29.50	40
1978	Christmas Tale - H. Thelander	Annual	1978	32.00	47
1979	White Christmas - H. Thelander	Annual	1979	36.50	49
1980	Christmas in Woods - H. Thelander	Annual	1980	42.50	49
1981	Christmas Peace - H. Thelander	Annual	1981	49.50	50
1982	Christmas Tree - H. Thelander	Annual	1982	54.50	55
1983	Christmas in Old Town - H. Thelander	Annual	1983	54.50	55
1984	The Christmas Letter - E. Jensen	Annual	1984	54.50	75
1985	Christmas Eve at the Farmhouse - E. Jensen	Annual	1985	54.50	75
1986	Silent Night, Holy Night - E. Jensen	Annual	1986	54.50	75
1987	The Snowman's Christmas Eve - E. Jensen	Annual	1987	59.50	77
1988	In the Kings Garden - E. Jensen	Annual	1988	64.50	70
1989	Christmas Anchorage - E. Jensen	Annual	1989	59.50	71
1990	Changing of the Guards - E. Jensen	Annual	1990	64.50	71
1991	Copenhagen Stock Exchange - E. Jensen	Annual	1991	69.50	70
1992	Christmas At the Rectory - J. Steensen	Annual	1992	69.50	75-100
1993	Father Christmas in Copenhagen - J. Nielsen	Annual	1993	69.50	70
1994	A Day At The Deer Park - J. Nielsen	Annual	1994	72.50	75
1995	The Towers of Copenhagen - J. Nielsen	Annual	1995	72.50	75
1996	Winter at the Old Mill - J. Nielsen	Yr.Iss.		74.50	75

Christmas In America - J. Woodson

YEAR ISSUE		EDITION LIMIT	YEAR RETD.	ISSUE PRICE	*QUOTE U.S. $
1986	Christmas Eve in Williamsburg	Annual	1986	29.50	125-150
1987	Christmas Eve at the White House	Annual	1987	34.50	35
1988	Christmas Eve at Rockefeller Center	Annual	1988	34.50	55
1989	Christmas In New England	Annual	1989	37.00	55
1990	Christmas Eve at the Capitol	Annual	1990	39.50	55
1991	Christmas Eve at Independence Hall	Annual	1991	45.00	55
1992	Christmas in San Francisco	Annual	1992	47.50	55
1993	Coming Home For Christmas	Annual	1993	47.50	48
1994	Christmas Eve In Alaska	Annual	1994	47.50	60
1995	Christmas Eve in Mississippi	Annual	1995	47.50	48

Christmas in America Anniversary Plate - J. Woodson

YEAR ISSUE		EDITION LIMIT	YEAR RETD.	ISSUE PRICE	*QUOTE U.S. $
1991	Christmas Eve in Williamsburg	Annual	1991	69.50	75
1995	The Capitol - J. Woodson	Annual	1995	74.50	75

Jubilee-5 Year Cycle - Various

YEAR ISSUE		EDITION LIMIT	YEAR RETD.	ISSUE PRICE	*QUOTE U.S. $
1915	Frozen Window - F.A. Hallin	Annual	1915	Unkn.	190-225
1920	Church Bells - F. Garde	Annual	1920	Unkn.	60
1925	Dog Outside Window - D. Jensen	Annual	1925	Unkn.	160-300
1930	The Old Organist - C. Ersgaard	Annual	1930	Unkn.	225
1935	Little Match Girl - E. Plockross	Annual	1935	Unkn.	450
1940	Three Wise Men - S. Sabra	Annual	1940	Unkn.	1800
1945	Amalienborg Castle - T. Larsen	Annual	1945	Unkn.	100
1950	Eskimos - A. Friis	Annual	1950	Unkn.	100
1955	Dybbol Mill - M. Hyldahl	Annual	1955	Unkn.	210
1960	Kronborg Castle - M. Hyldahl	Annual	1960	25.00	100
1965	Chruchgoers - A. Friis	Annual	1965	25.00	105
1970	Amalienborg Castle - T. Larsen	Annual	1970	30.00	30
1975	Horses Enjoying Meal - O. Larson	Annual	1975	40.00	60
1980	Yule Tree - Aarestrup	Annual	1980	60.00	60
1985	Lifeboat at Work - H. Flugenring	Annual	1985	65.00	80
1990	The Royal Yacht Dannebrog - J. Bonfils	Annual	1990	95.00	80-95
1995	Centennial Platter - J. Nielsen	7,500	1995	195.00	195

Mother's Day - Various

YEAR ISSUE		EDITION LIMIT	YEAR RETD.	ISSUE PRICE	*QUOTE U.S. $
1969	Dogs & Puppies - H. Thelander	Annual	1969	9.75	400-500
1970	Bird and Chicks - H. Thelander	Annual	1970	10.00	45
1971	Cat and Kitten - H. Thelander	Annual	1971	11.00	15
1972	Mare and Foal - H. Thelander	Annual	1972	12.00	20
1973	Duck & Ducklings - H. Thelander	Annual	1973	13.00	20
1974	Bear and Cubs - H. Thelander	Annual	1974	16.50	20
1975	Doe and Fawns - H. Thelander	Annual	1975	19.50	20
1976	Swan Family - H. Thelander	Annual	1976	22.50	23
1977	Squirrel & Young - H. Thelander	Annual	1977	23.50	27
1978	Heron and Young - H. Thelander	Annual	1978	24.50	30
1979	Fox and Cubs - H. Thelander	Annual	1979	27.50	32
1980	Woodpecker & Young - H. Thelander	Annual	1980	29.50	30
1981	Hare and Young - H. Thelander	Annual	1981	36.50	38
1982	Lioness and Cubs - H. Thelander	Annual	1982	39.50	40
1983	Raccoon & Young - H. Thelander	Annual	1983	39.50	45
1984	Stork & Nestlings - H. Thelander	Annual	1984	39.50	48
1985	Bear and Cubs - H. Thelander	Annual	1985	39.50	45
1986	Elephant with Calf - H. Thelander	Annual	1986	39.50	40-55
1987	Sheep w/Lambs - H. Thelander	Annual	1987	42.50	75-85
1988	Crested Plover & Young - H. Thelander	Annual	1988	47.50	61
1988	Lapwing Mother with Chicks - H. Thelander	Annual	1988	49.50	90
1989	Cow With Calf - H. Thelander	Annual	1989	49.50	55
1990	Hen with Chicks - L. Jensen	Annual	1990	52.50	70-85
1991	The Nanny Goat and her Two Frisky Kids - L. Jensen	Annual	1991	54.50	100
1992	Panda With Cubs - L. Jensen	Annual	1992	59.50	65-90
1993	St. Bernard Dog and Puppies - A. Therkelsen	Annual	1993	59.50	85-105
1994	Cat with Kittens - A. Therkelsen	Annual	1994	59.50	85
1995	Hedgehog w/Young - A. Therkelsen	Annual	1995	59.50	95
1996	Koala with Young - A. Therkelsen	Annual		59.50	60

Mother's Day Jubilee-5 Year Cycle - Thelander

YEAR ISSUE		EDITION LIMIT	YEAR RETD.	ISSUE PRICE	*QUOTE U.S. $
1979	Dog & Puppies	Yr.Iss.	1979	55.00	55
1984	Swan Family	Yr.Iss.	1984	65.00	65
1989	Mare & Colt	Yr.Iss.	1989	95.00	110
1994	Woodpecker & Young	Yr.Iss.	1994	95.00	95

Olympic - Unknown

YEAR ISSUE		EDITION LIMIT	YEAR RETD.	ISSUE PRICE	*QUOTE U.S. $
1972	Munich, Germany	Closed	1972	20.00	15-25
1976	Montreal, Canada	Closed	1976	29.50	60
1980	Moscow, Russia	Closed	1980	43.00	89
1984	Los Angeles, USA	Closed	1984	45.00	259
1988	Seoul, Korea	Closed	1988	60.00	65
1992	Barcelona, Spain	Closed	1992	74.50	75

Santa Around the World - H. Hansen

YEAR ISSUE		EDITION LIMIT	YEAR RETD.	ISSUE PRICE	*QUOTE U.S. $
1995	Santa in Greenland	Yr.Iss.	1995	74.50	75

*Quotes have been rounded up to nearest dollar

Column 1

YEAR ISSUE		EDITION LIMIT	YEAR RETD.	ISSUE PRICE	*QUOTE U.S.$
1996	Santa in Egypt	Yr.Iss.		74.50	75

Statue of Liberty - Unknown

| 1985 | Statue of Liberty | 10,000 | 1985 | 60.00 | 80 |

The Bradford Exchange/Russia

The Nutcracker - N. Zaitseva

1993	Marie's Magical Gift	95-day		39.87	40
1993	Dance of Sugar Plum Fairy	95-day		39.87	40
1993	Waltz of the Flowers	95-day		39.87	40
1993	Battle With the Mice King	95-day		39.87	40

The Bradford Exchange/United States

Alice in Wonderland - S. Gustafson

1993	The Mad Tea Party	95-day		29.90	95
1993	The Cheshire Cat	95-day		29.90	30
1994	Croquet with the Queen	95-day		29.90	30

America's Favorite Classic Cars - D. Everhart

1993	1957 Corvette	Closed	1995	54.00	75
1993	1956 Thunderbird	Closed	1995	54.00	125
1994	1957 Bel Air	Closed	1995	54.00	54
1994	1965 Mustang	Closed	1995	54.00	54

Baskets of Love - A. Isakov

| 1993 | Andrew and Abbey | 95-day | | 29.90 | 30 |
| 1993 | Cody and Courtney | 95-day | | 29.90 | 30 |

Carousel Daydreams - Unknown

| 1995 | Swept Away | Closed | 1996 | 39.90 | 40 |

Chosen Messengers - G. Running Wolf

| 1994 | The Pathfinders | 95-day | | 29.90 | 40 |
| 1994 | The Overseers | 95-day | | 29.90 | 30 |

A Christmas Carol - L. Garrison

1993	God Bless Us Everyone	95-day		29.90	45
1993	Ghost of Christmas Present	95-day		29.90	40
1994	A Merry Christmas to All	95-day		29.90	45
1994	A Visit From Marley's Ghost	95-day		29.90	30

Christmas Memories - J. Tanton

1993	A Winter's Tale	95-day		29.90	30
1993	Finishing Touches	95-day		29.90	48
1993	Welcome to Our Home	95-day		29.90	30
1993	Christmas Celebration	95-day		29.90	30

Dog Days - J. Gadamus

| 1993 | Sweet Dreams | 95-day | | 29.90 | 30 |

Family Circles - R. Rust

1993	Great Gray Owl Family	95-day		29.90	30
1994	Great Horned Owl Family	95-day		29.90	30
1994	Barred Owl Family	95-day		29.90	30

Field Pup Follies - L. Kaatz

1994	Sleeping on the Job	Closed	1995	29.90	30
1994	Hat Check	Closed	1995	29.90	30
1994	Fowl Play	Closed	1995	29.90	30
1994	Tackling Lunch	Closed	1996	29.90	30

Footsteps of the Brave - H. Schaare

1993	Noble Quest	95-day		24.90	25
1993	At Storm's Passage	95-day		24.90	25
1993	With Boundless Vision	95-day		27.90	28
1993	Horizons of Destiny	95-day		27.90	28
1993	Path of His Forefathers	95-day		27.90	28
1993	Soulful Reflection	95-day		29.90	30
1993	The Reverent Trail	95-day		29.90	30
1994	At Journey's End	95-day		34.90	35

Heirloom Memories - A. Pech

1994	Porcelain Treasure	95-day		29.90	32
1994	Rhythms in Lace	95-day		29.90	33
1994	Pink Lemonade Roses	95-day		29.90	50
1994	Victorian Romance	95-day		29.90	30

Hideaway Lake - R. Rust

| 1993 | Rusty's Retreat | 95-day | | 34.90 | 35 |
| 1993 | Fishing For Dreams | 95-day | | 34.90 | 35 |

Immortals of the Diamond - C. Jackson

| 1994 | The Sultan of Swat | Closed | 1996 | 39.90 | 40 |
| 1995 | Pride of the Yankees | Closed | 1996 | 39.90 | 40 |

In A Hidden Garden - T. Clausnitzer

1993	Curious Kittens	95-day		29.90	30
1994	Through Eyes of Blue	95-day		29.90	30
1994	Amber Gaze	95-day		29.90	30
1994	Fascinating Find	95-day		29.90	30

Keepsakes of the Heart - C. Layton

1993	Forever Friends	95-day		29.90	33
1993	Afternoon Tea	95-day		29.90	40
1993	Riding Companions	95-day		29.90	30
1993	Sentimental Sweethearts	95-day		29.90	45

Column 2

Kingdom of the Unicorn - M. Ferraro

1993	The Magic Begins	95-day		29.90	39
1993	In Crystal Waters	95-day		29.90	60
1993	Chasing a Dream	95-day		29.90	52
1993	The Fountain of Youth	95-day		29.90	45

Lena Liu's Beautiful Gardens - Inspired by L. Liu

1994	Iris Garden	Closed	1995	34.00	34
1994	Peony Garden	Closed	1996	34.00	34
1994	The Rose Garden	Closed	1996	39.00	39

Little Bandits - C. Jagodits

1993	Handle With Care	95-day		29.90	60
1993	All Tied Up	95-day		29.90	30
1993	Everything's Coming Up Daisies	95-day		32.90	47

Me & My Shadow - J. Welty

1994	Easter Basset	95-day	1995	29.90	30
1994	Giddyup	95-day	1995	29.90	30
1994	A Golden Moment	95-day	1995	29.90	30
1994	Perfect Timing	95-day	1995	29.90	30

Native American Legends: Chiefs of Destiny - C. Jackson

| 1994 | Sitting Bull | Closed | 1996 | 39.90 | 40 |
| 1994 | Chief Joseph | Closed | 1996 | 39.90 | 40 |

New Horizons - R. Copple

| 1993 | Building For a New Generation | 95-day | | 29.90 | 45 |

Notorious Disney Villains - Disney Studios

1993	The Wicked Queen	95-day		29.90	30
1994	Maleficent	95-day		29.90	30
1994	Ursella	95-day		29.90	30
1994	Cruella De Vil	95-day		29.90	30

Panda Bear Hugs - W. Nelson

1994	Loving Advice	Closed	1995	39.00	39
1994	A Playful Interlude	Closed	1995	39.00	39
1994	A Taste of Life	Closed	1995	39.00	39

Peace on Earth - D. Geisness

1993	Winter Lullaby	95-day		29.90	30
1994	Heavenly Slumber	95-day		29.90	30
1994	Sweet Embrace	95-day		32.90	33
1994	Woodland Dreams	95-day		32.90	33

Practice Makes Perfect - L. Kaatz

| 1994 | What's a Mother to Do? | 95-day | | 29.90 | 30 |
| 1994 | The Ones That Got Away | 95-day | | 29.90 | 30 |

Sacred Circle - K. Randle

| 1993 | Before the Hunt | 95-day | | 29.90 | 45 |

Sovereigns of the Sky - G. Dieckhoner

1994	Spirit of Freedom	Closed	1995	39.00	39
1994	Spirit of Pride	Closed	1995	39.00	39
1994	Spirit of Valor	Closed	1995	44.00	44
1994	Spirit of Majesty	Closed	1995	44.00	44
1995	Spirit of Glory	Closed	1996	44.00	44

Sovereigns of the Wild - D. Grant

| 1993 | The Snow Queen | 95-day | | 29.90 | 60 |
| 1994 | Let Us Survive | 95-day | | 29.90 | 30 |

Tale of Peter Rabbit & Benjamin Bunny - R. Akers

| 1994 | A Pocket Full of Onions | Closed | 1996 | 39.00 | 39 |
| 1994 | Beside His Cousin | | 5/96 | 39.00 | 39 |

That's What Friends Are For - A. Isakov

| 1994 | Friends Are Forever | 95-day | | 29.90 | 30 |

Thomas Kinkade's Illuminated Cottages - T. Kinkade

1994	The Flagstone Path	Closed	1996	34.90	35
1995	The Garden Walk	Closed	1996	34.90	35
1995	Cherry Blossom Hideaway		5/96	34.90	35

Thundering Waters - F. Miller

1994	Niagara Falls	95-day		34.90	45
1994	Lower Falls, Yellowstone	95-day		34.90	70
1994	Bridal Veil Falls	95-day		34.90	60

Trains of the Great West - K. Randle

1993	Moonlit Journey	95-day		29.90	45
1993	Mountain Hideaway	95-day		29.90	30
1993	Early Morning Arrival	95-day		29.90	50
1994	The Snowy Pass	95-day		29.90	30

Untamed Spirits - P. Weirs

1994	Wild Hearts	95-day		29.90	40
1994	Breakaway	95-day		29.90	50
1994	Forever Free	95-day		29.90	30
1994	Distant Thunder	95-day		29.90	30

Vanishing Paradises - G. Dieckhoner

1993	The Rainforest	95-day		29.90	30
1993	The Panda's World	95-day		29.90	30
1993	Splendors of India	95-day		29.90	30
1993	An African Safari	95-day		29.90	30

Column 3

A Visit from St. Nick - C. Jackson

| 1995 | Twas the Night Before Christmas | | 5/96 | 49.00 | 49 |

A Visit to Brambly Hedge - J. Barklem

1994	Summer Story	Closed	1995	39.90	40
1994	Spring Story	Closed	1995	39.90	40
1994	Autumn Story	Closed	1995	39.90	40
1994	Winter Story	Closed	1995	39.90	40

Winnie the Pooh - C. Jackson

| 1994 | Time For a Little Something | Closed | 1996 | 39.90 | 40 |
| 1995 | Bouncing Tiggers Do Best | Closed | 1996 | 39.90 | 40 |

The World of the Eagle - J. Hansel

1994	Sentinel of the Night	95-day		29.90	48
1994	Silent Guard	95-day		29.90	55
1994	Night Flyer	95-day		32.90	33
1995	Midnight Duty	95-day		32.90	55

Cavanagh Group Intl.

Coca-Cola Brand Heritage Collection - Various

1995	Boy Fishing - N. Rockwell	5,000		60.00	65
1995	Good Boys and Girls - Sundblom	2,500	1995	60.00	60
1995	Hilda Clark with Roses - CGI	5,000		60.00	65
1996	Travel Refreshed - Sundblom	Open		60.00	60

Dave Grossman Creations

Emmett Kelly Plates - B. Leighton-Jones

1986	Christmas Carol	Yr.Iss.		20.00	40
1987	Christmas Wreath	Yr.Iss.		20.00	22
1988	Christmas Dinner	Yr.Iss.		20.00	4
1989	Christmas Feast	Yr.Iss.		20.00	3
1990	Just What I Needed	Yr.Iss.		24.00	3
1991	Emmett The Snowman	Yr.Iss.		25.00	4
1992	Christmas Tunes	Yr.Iss.		25.00	3
1993	Downhill-Christmas Plate	Yr.Iss.		30.00	3
1994	Holiday Skater EKP-94	Yr.Iss.		30.00	3

Saturday Evening Post Collection - Rockwell-Inspired

1991	Downhill Daring BRP-91	Yr.Iss.		25.00	2
1991	Missed BRP-101	Yr.Iss.		25.00	2
1992	Choosin Up BRP-102	Yr.Iss.		25.00	2

Dave Grossman Designs

Norman Rockwell Collection - Rockwell-Inspired

1979	Leapfrog NRP-79	Retrd.		50.00	5
1980	Lovers NRP-80	Retrd.		60.00	6
1981	Dreams of Long Ago NRP-81	Retrd.		60.00	6
1982	Doctor and Doll NRP-82	Retrd.		65.00	9
1983	Circus NRP-83	Retrd.		65.00	6
1984	Visit With Rockwell NRP-84	Retrd.		65.00	6
1980	Christmas Trio RXP-80	Retrd.		75.00	
1981	Santa's Good Boys RXP-81	Retrd.		75.00	2
1982	Faces of Christmas RXP-82	Retrd.		75.00	7
1983	Christmas Chores RXP-83	Retrd.		75.00	
1984	Tiny Tim RXP-84	Retrd.		75.00	
1980	Back To School RMP-80	Retrd.		24.00	
1981	No Swimming RMP-81	Retrd.		25.00	2
1982	Love Letter RMP-82	Retrd.		27.00	
1983	Doctor and Doll RMP-83	Retrd.		27.00	
1984	Big Moment RMP-84	Retrd.		27.00	
1979	Butterboy RP-01	Retrd.		40.00	
1982	American Mother RGP-42	Retrd.		45.00	
1983	Dreamboat RGP-83	Retrd.		24.00	
1978	Young Doctor RDP-26	Retrd.		50.00	

Norman Rockwell Collection-Boy Scout Plates - Rockwell-Inspired

1981	Can't Wait BSP-01	Retrd.		30.00	
1982	Guiding Hand BSP-02	Retrd.		30.00	
1983	Tomorrow's Leader BSP-03	Retrd.		30.00	

Norman Rockwell Collection-Huck Finn Plates - Rockwell-Inspired

1979	Secret HFP-01	Retrd.		40.00	
1980	Listening HFP-02	Retrd.		40.00	
1980	No Kings HFP-03	Retrd.		40.00	
1981	Snake Escapes HFP-04	Retrd.		40.00	

Norman Rockwell Collection-Tom Sawyer Plates - Rockwell-Inspired

1975	Whitewashing the Fence TSP-01	Retrd.		26.00	
1976	First Smoke TSP-02	Retrd.		26.00	
1977	Take Your Medicine TSP-03	Retrd.		26.00	
1978	Lost in Cave TSP-04	Retrd.		26.00	

Delphi

The Beatles '67-'70 - D. Sivavec

1992	Sgt. Pepper the 25th Anniversary	150-day		27.75	
1992	All You Need is Love	150-day		27.75	
1993	Magical Mystery Tour	150-day		30.75	
1993	Hey Jude	150-day		30.75	
1993	Abbey Road	150-day		30.75	
1993	Let It Be	150-day		30.75	

The Beatles Collection - N. Giorgio

YEAR ISSUE		EDITION LIMIT	YEAR RETD.	ISSUE PRICE	*QUOTE U.S. $
1991	The Beatles, Live In Concert	150-day		24.75	40
1991	Hello America	150-day		24.75	45
1991	A Hard Day's Night	150-day		27.75	50
1992	Beatles '65	150-day		27.75	45
1992	Help	150-day		27.75	60
1992	The Beatles at Shea Stadium	150-day		29.75	30
1992	Rubber Soul	150-day		29.75	30
1992	Yesterday and Today	150-day		29.75	30

Commemorating The King - M. Stutzman

1993	The Rock and Roll Legend	95-day		29.75	50
1993	Las Vegas, Live	95-day		29.75	45
1993	Blues and Black Leather	95-day		29.75	50
1993	Private Presley	95-day		29.75	30
1993	Golden Boy	95-day		29.75	30
1993	Screen Idol	95-day		29.75	30
1993	Outstanding Young Man	95-day		29.75	30
1993	The Tiger: Faith, Spirit & Discipline	95-day		29.75	30

Dream Machines - P. Palma

1988	'56 T-Bird	150-day		24.75	25
1988	'57 'Vette	150-day		24.75	25
1989	'58 Biarritz	150-day		27.75	28
1989	'56 Continental	150-day		27.75	28
1989	'57 Bel Air	150-day		27.75	50
1989	'57 Chrysler 300C	150-day		27.75	30

Elvis on the Big Screen - B. Emmett

1992	Elvis in Loving You	150-day		29.75	45
1992	Elvis in G.I. Blues	150-day		29.75	75
1992	Viva Las Vegas	150-day		32.75	70
1993	Elvis in Blue Hawaii	150-day		32.75	40
1993	Elvis in Jailhouse Rock	150-day		32.75	40
1993	Elvis in Spinout	150-day		34.75	40
1993	Elvis in Speedway	150-day		34.75	35
1993	Elvis in Harum Scarum	150-day		34.75	35

The Elvis Presley Hit Parade - N. Giorgio

1992	Heartbreak Hotel	150-day		29.75	30
1992	Blue Suede Shoes	150-day		29.75	30
1992	Hound Dog	150-day		32.75	33
1992	Blue Christmas	150-day		32.75	33
1992	Return to Sender	150-day		32.75	33
1993	Teddy Bear	150-day		34.75	35
1993	Always on My Mind	150-day		34.75	35
1993	Mystery Train	150-day		34.75	35
1993	Blue Moon of Kentucky	150-day		34.75	35
1993	Wear My Ring Around Your Neck	150-day		36.75	37
1993	Suspicious Minds	150-day		36.75	37
993	Peace in the Valley	150-day		36.75	37

Elvis Presley: In Performance - B. Emmett

1990	'68 Comeback Special	150-day		24.75	53
1991	King of Las Vegas	150-day		24.75	55
991	Aloha From Hawaii	150-day		27.75	55
991	Back in Tupelo, 1956	150-day		27.75	65
991	If I Can Dream	150-day		27.75	55
991	Benefit for the USS Arizona	150-day		29.75	50
991	Madison Square Garden, 1972	150-day		29.75	60
991	Tampa, 1955	150-day		29.75	50
991	Concert in Baton Rouge, 1974	150-day		29.75	45
992	On Stage in Wichita, 1974	150-day		31.75	47
992	In the Spotlight: Hawaii, '72	150-day		31.75	45
992	Tour Finale: Indianapolis 1977	150-day		31.75	40

Elvis Presley: Looking At A Legend - B. Emmett

988	Elvis at/Gates of Graceland	150-day		24.75	85
989	Jailhouse Rock	150-day		24.75	80
989	The Memphis Flash	150-day		27.75	60
989	Homecoming	150-day		27.75	55
990	Elvis and Gladys	150-day		27.75	65
990	A Studio Session	150-day		27.75	45
990	Elvis in Hollywood	150-day		29.75	60
990	Elvis on His Harley	150-day		29.75	70
990	Stage Door Autographs	150-day		29.75	55
991	Christmas at Graceland	150-day		32.75	70
991	Entering Sun Studio	150-day		32.75	50
991	Going for the Black Belt	150-day		32.75	45
991	His Hand in Mine	150-day		32.75	75
991	Letters From Fans	150-day		32.75	60
991	Closing the Deal	150-day		34.75	55
992	Elvis Returns to the Stage	150-day		34.75	55

abulous Cars of the '50's - G. Angelini

993	'57 Red Corvette	95-day		24.75	45
993	'57 White T-Bird	95-day		24.75	85
993	'57 Blue Belair	95-day		27.75	37
993	'59 Cadillac	95-day		27.75	35
993	'56 Lincoln Premier	95-day		27.75	52
994	'59 Red Ford Fairlane	95-day		27.75	40

n the Footsteps of the King - D. Sivavec

993	Graceland: Memphis, Tenn.	95-day		27.75	41
994	Elvis' Birthplace: Tupelo, Miss	95-day		29.75	45
994	Day Job: Memphis, Tenn.	95-day		32.75	40
994	Flying Circle G. Ranch: Walls, Miss.	95-day		32.75	33
994	The Lauderdale Courts	95-day		32.75	33

YEAR ISSUE		EDITION LIMIT	YEAR RETD.	ISSUE PRICE	*QUOTE U.S.$
1995	Patriotic Soldier	95-day		34.75	35

Indiana Jones - V. Gadino

1989	Indiana Jones	150-day		24.75	25-35
1989	Indiana Jones and His Dad	150-day		24.75	40
1990	Indiana Jones/Dr. Schneider	150-day		27.75	30
1990	A Family Discussion	150-day		27.75	50
1990	Young Indiana Jones	150-day		27.75	50
1991	Indiana Jones/The Holy Grail	150-day		27.75	50

Legends of Baseball - Various

1992	Babe Ruth: The Called Shot - B. Benger	150-day		24.95	30
1992	Lou Gehrig: The Luckiest Man - J. Barson	150-day		24.75	25
1993	Ty Cobb: The Georgia Peach - J. Barson	150-day		27.95	28
1993	Cy Young: The Perfect Game - J. Barson	150-day		27.75	28
1993	Roger Hornsby: .424 Season - J. Barson	150-day		27.75	28
1993	Honus Wagner: Flying Dutchman - J. Barson	150-day		29.75	30
1993	Jimmie Fox: The Beast - J. Barson	150-day		29.75	30
1993	Walter Johnson: The Shutout - J. Barson	150-day		29.75	30
1993	Tris Speaker: The Gray Eagle - J. Barson	150-day		29.75	30
1994	Christy Matthewson: 1905 W. Series - J. Barson	150-day		31.75	32
1994	Mel Ott: Master Melvin - J. Barson	150-day		31.75	32
1994	Lefty Grove: His Greatest Season - J. Barson	150-day		31.75	32
1994	Shoeless Joe Jackson: Where Triples Go to Die - J. Barson	150-day		31.75	32
1995	Pie Traynor: Pittsburgh Champ - J. Barson	150-day		33.75	32
1995	Mickey Cochrane: Black Mike - J. Barson	150-day		33.75	32
1995	Grover Alexander - J. Barson	150-day		33.75	32

The Magic of Marilyn - C. Notarile

1992	For Our Boys in Korea, 1954	150-day		24.75	35
1992	Opening Night	150-day		24.75	35
1993	Rising Star	150-day		27.75	35
1992	Stopping Traffic	150-day		27.75	28
1992	Strasberg's Student	150-day		27.75	28
1993	Photo Opportunity	150-day		29.75	30
1993	Shining Star	150-day		29.75	30
1993	Curtain Call	150-day		29.75	30

The Marilyn Monroe Collection - C. Notarile

1989	Marilyn Monroe/7 Year Itch	150-day		24.75	80
1990	Diamonds/Girls Best Friend	150-day		24.75	77-90
1991	Marilyn Monroe/River of No Return	150-day		27.75	80
1992	How to Marry a Millionaire	150-day		27.75	87
1992	There's No Business/Show Business	150-day		27.75	60-75
1992	Marilyn Monroe in Niagra	150-day		29.75	75
1992	My Heart Belongs to Daddy	150-day		29.75	50
1992	Marilyn Monroe as Cherie in Bus Stop	150-day		29.75	60-80
1992	Marilyn Monroe in All About Eve	150-day		29.75	50-75
1992	Marilyn Monroe in Monkey Business	150-day		31.75	55
1992	Marilyn Monroe in Don't Bother to Knock	150-day		31.75	87
1992	Marilyn Monroe in We're Not Married	150-day		31.75	75

Portraits of the King - D. Zwierz

1991	Love Me Tender	150-day		27.75	45
1991	Are You Lonesome Tonight?	150-day		27.75	55
1991	I'm Yours	150-day		30.75	45
1991	Treat Me Nice	150-day		30.75	50
1992	The Wonder of You	150-day		30.75	32
1992	You're a Heartbreaker	150-day		32.75	33
1992	Just Because	150-day		32.75	33
1992	Follow That Dream	150-day		32.75	33

Take Me Out To The Ballgame - D. Henderson

1993	Wrigley Field: The Friendly Confines	95-day		29.75	30
1993	Yankee Stadium: House that Ruth Built	95-day		29.75	30
1993	Fenway Park: Home of the Green Monster	95-day		32.75	33
1993	Briggs Stadium: Home of the Tigers	95-day		32.75	33
1993	Comiskey Park: Home of the White Sox	95-day		32.75	33
1994	Cleveland Stadium: Home of the Indians	95-day		34.75	35
1994	Memorial Stadium: Home of the Orioles	95-day		34.75	35
1994	County Stadium: Home of the 1957 Champions	95-day		34.75	35
1994	Ebbets Field: Home of the Dodgers	95-day		34.75	35

Take Me Out to the Ballgame - D. Henderson

1995	Shibe Park	95-day		36.75	37

Department 56

A Christmas Carol - R. Innocenti

YEAR ISSUE		EDITION LIMIT	YEAR RETD.	ISSUE PRICE	*QUOTE U.S.$
1991	The Cratchit's Christmas Pudding 5706-1	18,000	1991	60.00	60-80
1992	Marley's Ghost Appears To Scrooge 5721-5	18,000	1992	60.00	65
1993	The Spirit of Christmas Present 5722-3	18,000	1993	60.00	60
1994	Visions of Christmas Past 5723-1	18,000	1994	60.00	60

Dickens' Village - Department 56

1987	Dickens' Village Porcelain Plates, 5917-0 set/4	Closed	1990	140.00	220

Duncan Royale

History of Santa Claus I - S. Morton

1985	Medieval	Retrd.	N/A	40.00	75
1985	Kris Kringle	Retrd.	N/A	40.00	75
1985	Pioneer	10,000	N/A	40.00	40
1986	Russian	Retrd.	N/A	40.00	65
1986	Soda Pop	Retrd.	N/A	40.00	75
1986	Civil War	10,000	N/A	40.00	40
1986	Nast	Retrd.	N/A	40.00	75
1987	St. Nicholas	Retrd.	N/A	40.00	75
1987	Dedt Moroz	10,000	N/A	40.00	45
1987	Black Peter	10,000	N/A	40.00	60
1987	Victorian	Retrd.	N/A	40.00	45
1987	Wassail	Retrd.	N/A	40.00	45
XX	Collection of 12 Plates	Retrd.	N/A	480.00	480

Edna Hibel Studios

Allegro - E. Hibel

1978	Plate & Book	7,500		120.00	150

Arte Ovale - E. Hibel

1980	Takara, gold	300		1000.00	4200
1980	Takara, blanco	700		450.00	1200
1980	Takara, cobalt blue	1,000		595.00	2350
1984	Taro-kun, gold	300		1000.00	2700
1984	Taro-kun, blanco	700		450.00	825
1984	Taro-kun, cobalt blue	1,000		995.00	1050

Christmas Annual - E. Hibel

1985	The Angels' Message	Yr.Iss.		45.00	220
1986	Gift of the Magi	Yr.Iss.		45.00	275
1987	Flight Into Egypt	Yr.Iss.		49.00	250
1988	Adoration of the Shepherds	Yr.Iss.		49.00	175
1989	Peaceful Kingdom	Yr.Iss.		49.00	165
1990	The Nativity	Yr.Iss.		49.00	125

David Series - E. Hibel

1979	Wedding of David & Bathsheba	5,000		250.00	650
1980	David, Bathsheba & Solomon	5,000		275.00	425
1982	David the King	5,000		275.00	295
1982	David the King, cobalt A/P	25		275.00	1200
1984	Bathsheba	5,000		275.00	295
1984	Bathsheba, cobalt A/P	100		275.00	1200

Edna Hibel Holiday - E. Hibel

1991	The First Holiday	Yr.Iss.		49.00	85
1991	The First Holiday, gold	1,000		99.00	150
1992	The Christmas Rose	Yr.Iss.		49.00	70
1992	The Christmas Rose, gold	1,000		99.00	125

Eroica - E. Hibel

1990	Compassion	10,000		49.50	65
1992	Darya	10,000		49.50	50

Famous Women & Children - E. Hibel

1980	Pharaoh's Daughter & Moses, gold	2,500		350.00	625
1980	Pharaoh's Daughter & Moses, cobalt blue	500		350.00	1350
1982	Cornelia & Her Jewels, gold	2,500		350.00	495
1982	Cornelia & Her Jewels, cobalt blue	500		350.00	350
1982	Anna & The Children of the King of Siam, gold	2,500		350.00	495
1982	Anna & The Children of the King of Siam, colbalt blue	500		350.00	1350
1984	Mozart & The Empress Marie Theresa, gold	2,500		350.00	395
1984	Mozart & The Empress Marie Theresa, cobalt blue	500		350.00	975

Flower Girl Annual - E. Hibel

1985	Lily	15,000		79.00	150-275
1986	Iris	15,000		79.00	225
1987	Rose	15,000		79.00	175
1988	Camellia	15,000		79.00	165
1989	Peony	15,000		79.00	100
1992	Wisteria	15,000		79.00	90

International Mother Love French - E. Hibel

1985	Yvette Avec Ses Enfants	5,000		125.00	225
1991	Liberte, Egalite, Fraternite	5,000		95.00	95

*Quotes have been rounded up to nearest dollar

Edna Hibel Studios to Edwin M. Knowles

YEAR ISSUE		EDITION LIMIT	YEAR RETD.	ISSUE PRICE	*QUOTE U.S.$
International Mother Love German - E. Hibel					
1982	Gesa Und Kinder	5,000		195.00	195
1983	Alexandra Und Kinder	5,000		195.00	195
March of Dimes: Our Children Our Future - E. Hibel					
1990	A Time To Embrace	150-day		29.00	29
Mother and Child - E. Hibel					
1973	Colette & Child	15,000		40.00	725
1974	Sayuri & Child	15,000		40.00	425
1975	Kristina & Child	15,000		50.00	400
1976	Marilyn & Child	15,000		55.00	400
1977	Lucia & Child	15,000		60.00	350
1981	Kathleen & Child	15,000		85.00	275
Mother's Day - E. Hibel					
1992	Molly & Annie	Yr.Iss.		39.00	75
1992	Molly & Annie, gold	2,500		95.00	150
1992	Molly & Annie, platinum	500		275.00	275
Mother's Day Annual - E. Hibel					
1984	Abby & Lisa	Yr.Iss.		29.50	300-400
1985	Erica & Jamie	Yr.Iss.		29.50	200-250
1986	Emily & Jennifer	Yr.Iss.		29.50	150-300
1987	Catherine & Heather	34.50		34.50	200
1988	Sarah & Tess	Yr.Iss.		34.90	175
1989	Jessica & Kate	Yr.Iss.		34.90	100
1990	Elizabeth, Jorday & Janie	Yr.Iss.		36.90	95
1991	Michele & Anna	Yr.Iss.		36.90	65
1992	Olivia & Hildy	Yr.Iss.		39.90	80
Museum Commemorative - E. Hibel					
1977	Flower Girl of Provence	12,750		175.00	425
1980	Diana	3,000		350.00	395
Nobility Of Children - E. Hibel					
1976	La Contessa Isabella	12,750		120.00	425
1977	Le Marquis Maurice Pierre	12,750		120.00	225
1978	Baronesse Johanna-Maryke Van Vollendam Tot Marken	12,750		130.00	175
1979	Chief Red Feather	12,750		140.00	200
Nordic Families - E. Hibel					
1987	A Tender Moment	7,500		79.00	95
Oriental Gold - E. Hibel					
1975	Yasuko	2,000		275.00	3000
1976	Mr. Obata	2,000		275.00	2100
1978	Sakura	2,000		295.00	1800
1979	Michio	2,000		325.00	1500
Scandinavian Mother & Child - E. Hibel					
1987	Pearl & Flowers	7,500		55.00	225
1989	Anemone & Violet	7,500		75.00	95
1990	Holly & Talia	7,500		75.00	85
To Life Annual - E. Hibel					
1986	Golden's Child	5,000		99.00	200-275
1987	Triumph! Everyone A Winner	19,500		55.00	60
1988	The Whole Earth Bloomed as a Sacred Place	15,000		85.00	85
1989	Lovers of the Summer Palace	5,000		65.00	75
1992	People of the Fields	5,000		49.00	49
Tribute To All Children - E. Hibel					
1984	Giselle	19,500		55.00	95
1984	Gerard	19,500		55.00	95
1985	Wendy	19,500		55.00	75-125
1986	Todd	19,500		55.00	125
The World I Love - E. Hibel					
1981	Leah's Family	17,500		85.00	175-200
1982	Kaylin	17,500		85.00	375
1983	Edna's Music	17,500		85.00	195
1983	O' Hana	17,500		85.00	195

Edwin M. Knowles

YEAR ISSUE		EDITION LIMIT	YEAR RETD.	ISSUE PRICE	*QUOTE U.S.$
Aesop's Fables - M. Hampshire					
1988	The Goose That Laid the Golden Egg	150-day		27.90	30
1988	The Hare and the Tortoise	150-day		27.90	30
1988	The Fox and the Grapes	150-day		30.90	35
1989	The Lion And The Mouse	150-day		30.90	37
1989	The Milk Maid And Her Pail	150-day		30.90	32
1989	The Jay And The Peacock	150-day		30.90	32
American Innocents - Marsten/Mandrajji					
1986	Abigail in the Rose Garden	100-day		19.50	20
1986	Ann by the Terrace	100-day		19.50	25
1986	Ellen and John in the Parlor	100-day		19.50	20
1986	William on the Rocking Horse	100-day		19.50	45
The American Journey - M. Kunstler					
1987	Westward Ho	150-day		29.90	30
1988	Kitchen With a View	150-day		29.90	30
1988	Crossing the River	150-day		29.90	30
1988	Christmas at the New Cabin	150-day		29.90	30
Americana Holidays - D. Spaulding					
1978	Fourth of July	Yr.Iss.		26.00	26

YEAR ISSUE		EDITION LIMIT	YEAR RETD.	ISSUE PRICE	*QUOTE U.S.$
1979	Thanksgiving	Yr.Iss.		26.00	26
1980	Easter	Yr.Iss.		26.00	26
1981	Valentine's Day	Yr.Iss.		26.00	26
1982	Father's Day	Yr.Iss.		26.00	26
1983	Christmas	Yr.Iss.		26.00	26
1984	Mother's Day	Yr.Iss.		26.00	27
Amy Brackenbury's Cat Tales - A. Brackenbury					
1987	A Chance Meeting: White American Shorthairs	150-day		21.50	30
1987	Gone Fishing: Maine Coons	150-day		21.50	40
1988	Strawberries and Cream: Cream Persians	150-day		24.90	40
1988	Flower Bed: British Shorthairs	150-day		24.90	25
1988	Kittens and Mittens: Silver Tabbies	150-day		24.90	25
1988	All Wrapped Up: Himalayans	150-day		24.90	45
Annie - W. Chambers					
1983	Annie and Sandy	100-day		19.00	25
1983	Daddy Warbucks	100-day		19.00	19
1983	Annie and Grace	100-day		19.00	19
1984	Annie and the Orphans	100-day		21.00	21
1985	Tomorrow	100-day		21.00	21
1986	Annie and Miss Hannigan	100-day		21.00	21
1986	Annie, Lily and Rooster	100-day		24.00	30
1986	Grand Finale	100-day		24.00	25
Baby Owls of North America - J. Thornbrugh					
1991	Peek-A-Whoo:Screech Owls	150-day		27.90	37
1991	Forty Winks: Saw-Whet Owls	150-day		29.90	40
1991	The Tree House: Northern Pygmy Owls	150-day		30.90	45
1991	Three of a Kind: Great Horned Owls	150-day		30.90	35
1991	Out on a Limb: Great Gray Owls	150-day		30.90	45
1991	Beginning to Explore: Boreal Owls	150-day		32.90	50
1992	Three's Company: Long Eared Owls	150-day		32.90	45
1992	Whoo's There: Barred Owl	150-day		32.90	50
Backyard Harmony - J. Thornbrugh					
1991	The Singing Lesson	150-day		27.90	38
1991	Welcoming a New Day	150-day		27.90	45
1991	Announcing Spring	150-day		30.90	60
1992	The Morning Harvest	150-day		30.90	45
1992	Spring Time Pride	150-day		30.90	60
1992	Treetop Serenade	150-day		32.90	60
1992	At The Peep Of Day	150-day		32.90	40
1992	Today's Discoveries	150-day		32.90	35
Bambi - Disney Studios					
1992	Bashful Bambi	150-day		34.90	40
1992	Bambi's New Friends	150-day		34.90	60
1992	Hello Little Prince	150-day		37.90	50-60
1992	Bambi's Morning Greetings	150-day		37.90	60
1992	Bambi's Skating Lesson	150-day		37.90	100
1993	What's Up Possums?	150-day		37.90	38
Beauty and the Beast - Disney Studios					
1993	Love's First Dance	150-day		29.90	30
1993	A Blossoming Romance	150-day		29.90	30
1993	Warming Up	150-day		32.90	33
1993	Learning to Love	150-day		32.90	33
1993	Papa's Workshop	150-day		32.90	33
1993	Be Our Guest	150-day		34.90	35
1993	Belle's Favorite Story	150-day		34.90	35
1993	A Mismatch	150-day		34.90	35
1994	A Spot of Tea	150-day		34.90	35
1994	Enchanté, Cherie	150-day		34.90	35
1994	A Gift for Belle	150-day		34.90	35
1994	The Spell is Broken	150-day		34.90	35
Biblical Mothers - E. Licea					
1983	Bathsheba and Solomon	Yr.Iss.		39.50	40
1984	Judgment of Solomon	Yr.Iss.		39.50	40
1984	Pharaoh's Daughter and Moses	Yr.Iss.		39.50	40
1985	Mary and Jesus	Yr.Iss.		39.50	40
1985	Sarah and Isaac	Yr.Iss.		44.50	45
1986	Rebekah, Jacob and Esau	Yr.Iss.		44.50	45
Birds of the Seasons - S. Timm					
1990	Cardinals In Winter	150-day		24.90	40
1990	Bluebirds In Spring	150-day		24.90	30
1991	Nuthatches In Fall	150-day		27.90	28
1991	Baltimore Orioles In Summer	150-day		27.90	30
1991	Blue Jays In Early Fall	150-day		27.90	45
1991	Robins In Early Spring	150-day		27.90	30
1991	Cedar Waxwings in Fall	150-day		29.90	60
1991	Chickadees in Winter	150-day		29.90	55
Call of the Wilderness - K. Daniel					
1991	First Outing	150-day		29.90	50
1991	Howling Lesson	150-day		29.90	100
1991	Silent Watch	150-day		32.90	55
1991	Winter Travelers	150-day		32.90	55
1992	Ahead of the Pack	150-day		32.90	55
1992	Northern Spirits	150-day		34.90	50
1992	Twilight Friends	150-day		34.90	50
1992	A New Future	150-day		34.90	35
1992	Morning Mist	150-day		36.90	37
1992	The Silent One	150-day		36.90	37

YEAR ISSUE		EDITION LIMIT	YEAR RETD.	ISSUE PRICE	*QUOT U.S
Carousel - D. Brown					
1987	If I Loved You	150-day		24.90	25
1988	Mr. Snow	150-day		24.90	25
1988	The Carousel Waltz	150-day		24.90	25
1988	You'll Never Walk Alone	150-day		24.90	25
Casablanca - J. Griffin					
1990	Here's Looking At You, Kid	150-day		34.90	3
1990	We'll Always Have Paris	150-day		34.90	4
1991	We Loved Each Other Once	150-day		37.90	3
1991	Rick's Cafe Americain	150-day		37.90	4
1991	A Franc For Your Thoughts	150-day		37.90	5
1991	Play it Sam	150-day		37.90	6
China's Natural Treasures - T.C. Chiu					
1992	The Siberian Tiger	150-day		29.90	4
1992	The Snow Leopard	150-day		29.90	4
1992	The Giant Panda	150-day		32.90	3
1992	The Tibetan Brown Bear	150-day		32.90	4
1992	The Asian Elephant	150-day		32.90	5
1992	The Golden Monkey	150-day		34.90	5
Christmas in the City - A. Leimanis					
1992	A Christmas Snowfall	150-day		34.90	3
1992	Yuletide Celebration	150-day		34.90	5
1993	Holiday Cheer	150-day		34.90	6
1993	The Magic of Christmas	150-day		34.90	6
Cinderella - Disney Studios					
1988	Bibbidi, Bobbidi, Boo	150-day		29.90	6
1988	A Dream Is A Wish Your Heart Makes	150-day		29.90	6
1989	Oh Sing Sweet Nightingale	150-day		32.90	5
1989	A Dress For Cinderelly	150-day		32.90	8
1989	So This Is Love	150-day		32.90	6
1990	At The Stroke Of Midnight	150-day		32.90	6
1990	If The Shoe Fits	150-day		34.90	6
1990	Happily Ever After	150-day		34.90	3
Classic Fairy Tales - S. Gustafson					
1991	Goldilocks and the Three Bears	150-day		29.90	5
1991	Little Red Riding Hood	150-day		29.90	
1991	The Three Little Pigs	150-day		32.90	
1991	The Frog Prince	150-day		32.90	
1992	Jack and the Beanstalk	150-day		32.90	
1992	Hansel and Gretel	150-day		34.90	
1992	Puss in Boots	150-day		34.90	
1992	Tom Thumb	150-day		34.90	
Classic Mother Goose - S. Gustafson					
1992	Little Miss Muffet	150-day		29.90	
1992	Mary had a Little Lamb	150-day		29.90	
1992	Mary, Mary, Quite Contrary	150-day		29.90	
1992	Little Bo Peep	150-day		29.90	
The Comforts of Home - H. Hollister Ingmire					
1992	Sleepyheads	150-day		24.90	
1992	Curious Pair	150-day		24.90	
1993	Mother's Retreat	150-day		27.90	
1993	Welcome Friends	150-day		27.90	
1993	Playtime	150-day		27.90	
1993	Feline Frolic	150-day		29.90	
1993	Washday Helpers	150-day		29.90	
1993	A Cozy Fireside	150-day		29.90	
Cozy Country Corners - H. H. Ingmire					
1990	Lazy Morning	150-day		24.90	
1990	Warm Retreat	150-day		24.90	
1991	A Sunny Spot	150-day		27.90	
1991	Attic Afternoon	150-day		27.90	
1991	Mirror Mischief	150-day		27.90	
1991	Hide and Seek	150-day		29.90	
1991	Apple Antics	150-day		29.90	
1991	Table Trouble	150-day		29.90	
Csatari Grandparent - J. Csatari					
1980	Bedtime Story	100-day		18.00	
1981	The Skating Lesson	100-day		20.00	
1982	The Cookie Tasting	100-day		20.00	
1983	The Swinger	100-day		20.00	
1984	The Skating Queen	100-day		22.00	
1985	The Patriot's Parade	100-day		22.00	
1986	The Home Run	100-day		22.00	
1987	The Sneak Preview	100-day		22.00	
The Disney Treasured Moments Collection - Disney Studios					
1992	Cinderella	150-day		29.90	
1992	Snow White and the Seven Dwarves	150-day		29.90	
1993	Alice in Wonderland	150-day		32.90	
1993	Sleeping Beauty	150-day		32.90	
1993	Peter Pan	150-day		32.90	
1993	Pinocchio	150-day		34.90	
1993	The Jungle Book	150-day		34.90	
1994	Beauty & The Beast	150-day		34.90	
Ency. Brit. Birds of Your Garden - K. Daniel					
1985	Cardinal	100-day		19.50	
1985	Blue Jay	100-day		19.50	
1985	Oriole	100-day		22.50	

YEAR	ISSUE	EDITION LIMIT	YEAR RETD.	ISSUE PRICE	*QUOTE U.S.$
1986	Chickadees	100-day		22.50	30
1986	Bluebird	100-day		22.50	25
1986	Robin	100-day		22.50	30
1986	Hummingbird	100-day		24.50	30
1987	Goldfinch	100-day		24.50	30
1987	Downy Woodpecker	100-day		24.50	35
1987	Cedar Waxwing	100-day		24.90	35

Fantasia: (The Sorcerer's Apprentice) Golden Anniversary - Disney Studios

YEAR	ISSUE	EDITION LIMIT	YEAR RETD.	ISSUE PRICE	*QUOTE U.S.$
1990	The Apprentice's Dream	150-day		29.90	60
1990	Mischievous Apprentice	150-day		29.90	70
1991	Dreams of Power	150-day		32.90	55
1991	Mickey's Magical Whirlpool	150-day		32.90	50
1991	Wizardry Gone Wild	150-day		32.90	45
1991	Mickey Makes Magic	150-day		34.90	60
1991	The Penitent Apprentice	150-day		34.90	47
1992	An Apprentice Again	150-day		34.90	50

Father's Love - B. Bradley

YEAR	ISSUE	EDITION LIMIT	YEAR RETD.	ISSUE PRICE	*QUOTE U.S.$
1984	Open Wide	100-day		19.50	20
1984	Batter Up	100-day		19.50	20
1985	Little Shaver	100-day		19.50	20
1985	Swing Time	100-day		22.50	23

Field Puppies - L. Kaatz

YEAR	ISSUE	EDITION LIMIT	YEAR RETD.	ISSUE PRICE	*QUOTE U.S.$
1987	Dog Tired-The Springer Spaniel	150-day		24.90	45-60
1987	Caught in the Act-The Golden Retriever	150-day		24.90	45-60
1988	Missing/Point/Irish Setter	150-day		27.90	35
1988	A Perfect Set-Labrador	150-day		27.90	40-50
1988	Fritz's Folly-German Shorthaired Pointer	150-day		27.90	35-42
1988	Shirt Tales: Cocker Spaniel	150-day		27.90	40-51
1989	Fine Feathered Friends-English Setter	150-day		29.90	37
1989	Command Performance/ Wiemaraner	150-day		29.90	35

Field Trips - L. Kaatz

YEAR	ISSUE	EDITION LIMIT	YEAR RETD.	ISSUE PRICE	*QUOTE U.S.$
1990	Gone Fishing	150-day		24.90	25
1991	Ducking Duty	150-day		24.90	25
1991	Boxed In	150-day		27.90	28
1991	Pups 'N Boots	150-day		27.90	28
1991	Puppy Tales	150-day		27.90	28
1991	Pail Pals	150-day		29.90	35
1991	Chesapeake Bay Retrievers	150-day		29.90	32
1991	Hat Trick	150-day		29.90	30

First Impressions - J. Giordano

YEAR	ISSUE	EDITION LIMIT	YEAR RETD.	ISSUE PRICE	*QUOTE U.S.$
1991	Taking a Gander	150-day		29.90	40
1991	Two's Company	150-day		29.90	35
1991	Fine Feathered Friends	150-day		32.90	45
1991	What's Up?	150-day		32.90	40
1991	All Ears	150-day		32.90	65
1992	Between Friends	150-day		32.90	40

The Four Ancient Elements - G. Lambert

YEAR	ISSUE	EDITION LIMIT	YEAR RETD.	ISSUE PRICE	*QUOTE U.S.$
1984	Earth	75-day		27.50	28
1984	Water	75-day		27.50	28
1985	Air	75-day		29.50	30
1985	Fire	75-day		29.50	40

Frances Hook Legacy - F. Hook

YEAR	ISSUE	EDITION LIMIT	YEAR RETD.	ISSUE PRICE	*QUOTE U.S.$
1985	Fascination	100-day		19.50	20
1985	Daydreaming	100-day		19.50	20
1986	Discovery	100-day		22.50	23
1986	Disappointment	100-day		22.50	23
1986	Wonderment	100-day		22.50	23
1987	Expectation	100-day		22.50	23

Free as the Wind - M. Budden

YEAR	ISSUE	EDITION LIMIT	YEAR RETD.	ISSUE PRICE	*QUOTE U.S.$
1992	Skyward	150-day		29.90	55
1992	Aloft	150-day		29.90	60
1992	Airborne	150-day		32.90	40
1993	Flight	150-day		32.90	50
1993	Ascent	150-day		32.90	45
1993	Heavenward	150-day		32.90	33

Friends I Remember - J. Down

YEAR	ISSUE	EDITION LIMIT	YEAR RETD.	ISSUE PRICE	*QUOTE U.S.$
1983	Fish Story	97-day		17.50	18
1984	Office Hours	97-day		17.50	18
1985	A Coat of Paint	97-day		17.50	18
1985	Here Comes the Bride	97-day		19.50	20
1985	Fringe Benefits	97-day		19.50	20
1986	High Society	97-day		19.50	20
1986	Flower Arrangement	97-day		21.50	22
1986	Taste Test	97-day		21.50	22

Friends of the Forest - K. Daniel

YEAR	ISSUE	EDITION LIMIT	YEAR RETD.	ISSUE PRICE	*QUOTE U.S.$
1987	The Rabbit	150-day		24.50	35
1987	The Raccoon	150-day		24.50	35
1987	The Squirrel	150-day		27.90	28
1988	The Chipmunk	150-day		27.90	28
1988	The Fox	150-day		27.90	28
1988	The Otter	150-day		27.90	28

Garden Secrets - B. Higgins Bond

YEAR	ISSUE	EDITION LIMIT	YEAR RETD.	ISSUE PRICE	*QUOTE U.S.$
993	Nine Lives	150-day		24.90	50
993	Floral Purr-fume	150-day		24.90	70
993	Bloomin' Kitties	150-day		24.90	60

YEAR	ISSUE	EDITION LIMIT	YEAR RETD.	ISSUE PRICE	*QUOTE U.S.$
1993	Kitty Corner	150-day		24.90	55
1993	Flower Fanciers	150-day		24.90	25
1993	Meadow Mischief	150-day		24.90	25
1993	Pussycat Potpourri	150-day		24.90	25
1993	Frisky Business	150-day		24.90	25

Gone with the Wind - R. Kursar

YEAR	ISSUE	EDITION LIMIT	YEAR RETD.	ISSUE PRICE	*QUOTE U.S.$
1978	Scarlett	100-day		21.50	175-185
1979	Ashley	100-day		21.50	85
1980	Melanie	100-day		21.50	40
1981	Rhett	100-day		23.50	35
1982	Mammy Lacing Scarlett	100-day		23.50	50-80
1983	Melanie Gives Birth	100-day		23.50	55
1984	Scarlet's Green Dress	100-day		25.50	45
1985	Rhett and Bonnie	100-day		25.50	70-95
1985	Scarlett and Rhett: The Finale	100-day		29.50	50

Great Cats Of The Americas - L. Cable

YEAR	ISSUE	EDITION LIMIT	YEAR RETD.	ISSUE PRICE	*QUOTE U.S.$
1989	The Jaguar	150-day		29.90	45
1989	The Cougar	150-day		29.90	35
1989	The Lynx	150-day		32.90	33
1990	The Ocelot	150-day		32.90	33
1990	The Bobcat	150-day		32.90	33
1990	The Jaguarundi	150-day		32.90	35
1990	The Margay	150-day		34.90	35
1991	The Pampas Cat	150-day		34.90	35

Heirlooms And Lace - C. Layton

YEAR	ISSUE	EDITION LIMIT	YEAR RETD.	ISSUE PRICE	*QUOTE U.S.$
1989	Anna	150-day		34.90	45
1989	Victoria	150-day		34.90	60
1990	Tess	150-day		37.90	75
1990	Olivia	150-day		37.90	105
1991	Bridget	150-day		37.90	105
1991	Rebecca	150-day		37.90	90

Hibel Christmas - E. Hibel

YEAR	ISSUE	EDITION LIMIT	YEAR RETD.	ISSUE PRICE	*QUOTE U.S.$
1985	The Angel's Message	Yr.Iss.		45.00	45
1986	The Gifts of the Magi	Yr.Iss.		45.00	45
1987	The Flight Into Egypt	Yr.Iss.		49.00	49
1988	Adoration of the Shepherd	Yr.Iss.		49.00	50-60
1989	Peaceful Kingdom	Yr.Iss.		49.00	49
1990	Nativity	Yr.Iss.		49.00	65

Home Sweet Home - R. McGinnis

YEAR	ISSUE	EDITION LIMIT	YEAR RETD.	ISSUE PRICE	*QUOTE U.S.$
1989	The Victorian	150-day		39.90	40
1989	The Greek Revival	150-day		39.90	40
1989	The Georgian	150-day		39.90	40
1990	The Mission	150-day		39.90	40

It's a Dog's Life - L. Kaatz

YEAR	ISSUE	EDITION LIMIT	YEAR RETD.	ISSUE PRICE	*QUOTE U.S.$
1992	We've Been Spotted	150-day		29.90	30
1992	Literary Labs	150-day		29.90	30
1993	Retrieving Our Dignity	150-day		32.90	33
1993	Lodging a Complaint	150-day		32.90	33
1993	Barreling Along	150-day		32.90	33
1993	Play Ball	150-day		34.90	35
1993	Dogs and Suds	150-day		34.90	35
1993	Paws for a Picnic	150-day		34.90	35

J. W. Smith Childhood Holidays - J. W. Smith

YEAR	ISSUE	EDITION LIMIT	YEAR RETD.	ISSUE PRICE	*QUOTE U.S.$
1986	Easter	97-day		19.50	21
1986	Thanksgiving	97-day		19.50	20
1986	Christmas	97-day		19.50	20
1986	Valentine's Day	97-day		22.50	23
1987	Mother's Day	97-day		22.50	23
1987	Fourth of July	97-day		22.50	23

Jerner's Less Travelled Road - B. Jerner

YEAR	ISSUE	EDITION LIMIT	YEAR RETD.	ISSUE PRICE	*QUOTE U.S.$
1988	The Weathered Barn	150-day		29.90	30
1988	The Murmuring Stream	150-day		29.90	30
1988	The Covered Bridge	150-day		32.90	33
1989	Winter's Peace	150-day		32.90	33
1989	The Flowering Meadow	150-day		32.90	33
1989	The Hidden Waterfall	150-day		32.90	33

Jewels of the Flowers - T.C. Chiu

YEAR	ISSUE	EDITION LIMIT	YEAR RETD.	ISSUE PRICE	*QUOTE U.S.$
1991	Sapphire Wings	150-day		29.90	35
1991	Topaz Beauties	150-day		29.90	55
1991	Amethyst Flight	150-day		32.90	35
1991	Ruby Elegance	150-day		32.90	45
1991	Emerald Pair	150-day		32.90	50
1991	Opal Splendor	150-day		34.90	40
1992	Pearl Luster	150-day		34.90	60
1992	Aquamarine Glimmer	150-day		34.90	35

Keepsake Rhymes - S. Gustafson

YEAR	ISSUE	EDITION LIMIT	YEAR RETD.	ISSUE PRICE	*QUOTE U.S.$
1992	Humpty Dumpty	150-day		29.90	35
1993	Peter Pumpkin Eater	150-day		29.90	85
1993	Pat-a-Cake	150-day		29.90	70
1993	Old King Cole	150-day		29.90	60

The King and I - W. Chambers

YEAR	ISSUE	EDITION LIMIT	YEAR RETD.	ISSUE PRICE	*QUOTE U.S.$
1984	A Puzzlement	150-day		19.50	20
1985	Shall We Dance?	150-day		19.50	30
1985	Getting to Know You	150-day		19.50	20
1985	We Kiss in a Shadow	150-day		19.50	20

Lady and the Tramp - Disney Studios

YEAR	ISSUE	EDITION LIMIT	YEAR RETD.	ISSUE PRICE	*QUOTE U.S.$
1992	First Date	150-day		34.90	70
1992	Puppy Love	150-day		34.90	70

YEAR	ISSUE	EDITION LIMIT	YEAR RETD.	ISSUE PRICE	*QUOTE U.S.$
1992	Dog Pound Blues	150-day		37.90	38
1992	Merry Christmas To All	150-day		37.90	50
1993	Double Siamese Trouble	150-day		37.90	38
1993	Ruff House	150-day		39.90	40
1993	Telling Tails	150-day		39.90	40
1993	Moonlight Romance	150-day		39.90	40

Lincoln Man of America - M. Kunstler

YEAR	ISSUE	EDITION LIMIT	YEAR RETD.	ISSUE PRICE	*QUOTE U.S.$
1986	The Gettysburg Address	150-day		24.50	25-30
1987	The Inauguration	150-day		24.50	25
1987	The Lincoln-Douglas Debates	150-day		27.50	28
1987	Beginnings in New Salem	150-day		27.90	28
1988	The Family Man	150-day		27.90	28
1988	Emancipation Proclamation	150-day		27.90	28

The Little Mermaid - Disney Studio Artists

YEAR	ISSUE	EDITION LIMIT	YEAR RETD.	ISSUE PRICE	*QUOTE U.S.$
1993	A Song From the Sea	95-day		29.90	30
1993	A Visit to the Surface	95-day		29.90	30
1993	Daddy's Girl	95-day		32.90	33
1993	Underwater Buddies	95-day		32.90	33
1993	Ariel's Treasured Collection	95-day		32.90	33
1993	Kiss the Girl	95-day		32.90	33
1994	Fireworks at First Sight	95-day		34.90	35
1994	Forever Love	95-day		34.90	35

Living with Nature-Jerner's Ducks - B. Jerner

YEAR	ISSUE	EDITION LIMIT	YEAR RETD.	ISSUE PRICE	*QUOTE U.S.$
1986	The Pintail	150-day		19.50	25
1986	The Mallard	150-day		19.50	35
1987	The Wood Duck	150-day		22.50	35
1987	The Green-Winged Teal	150-day		22.50	40
1987	The Northern Shoveler	150-day		22.90	25
1987	The American Widgeon	150-day		22.90	40
1987	The Gadwall	150-day		24.90	35
1988	The Blue-Winged Teal	150-day		24.90	35

Majestic Birds of North America - D. Smith

YEAR	ISSUE	EDITION LIMIT	YEAR RETD.	ISSUE PRICE	*QUOTE U.S.$
1988	The Bald Eagle	150-day		29.90	30-40
1988	Peregrine Falcon	150-day		29.90	30
1988	The Great Horned Owl	150-day		32.90	33
1989	The Red-Tailed Hawk	150-day		32.90	33
1989	The White Gyrfalcon	150-day		32.90	33
1989	The American Kestral	150-day		32.90	33
1990	The Osprey	150-day		34.90	35
1990	The Golden Eagle	150-day		34.90	35

Mary Poppins - M. Hampshire

YEAR	ISSUE	EDITION LIMIT	YEAR RETD.	ISSUE PRICE	*QUOTE U.S.$
1989	Mary Poppins	150-day		29.90	50
1989	A Spoonful of Sugar	150-day		29.90	50
1990	A Jolly Holiday With Mary	150-day		32.90	37
1990	We Love To Laugh	150-day		32.90	45
1991	Chim Chim Cher-ee	150-day		32.90	39
1991	Tuppence a Bag	150-day		32.90	50

Mickey's Christmas Carol - Disney Studios

YEAR	ISSUE	EDITION LIMIT	YEAR RETD.	ISSUE PRICE	*QUOTE U.S.$
1992	Bah Humbug	150-day		29.90	40
1992	What's So Merry About Christmas?	150-day		29.90	50
1993	God Bless Us Every One	150-day		32.90	63
1993	A Christmas Surprise	150-day		32.90	33
1993	Yuletide Greetings	150-day		32.90	33
1993	Marley's Warning	150-day		34.90	35
1993	A Cozy Christmas	150-day		34.90	35
1993	A Christmas Feast	150-day		34.90	35

Musical Moments From the Wizard of Oz - K. Milnazik

YEAR	ISSUE	EDITION LIMIT	YEAR RETD.	ISSUE PRICE	*QUOTE U.S.$
1993	Over the Rainbow	95-day		29.90	50
1993	We're Off to See the Wizard	95-day		29.90	50
1993	Munchkin Land	95-day		29.90	30
1993	If I Only Had a Brain	95-day		29.90	30
1993	Ding Dong The Witch is Dead	95-day		29.90	30
1993	The Lullabye League	95-day		29.90	30
1994	If I Were King of the Forest	95-day		29.90	30
1994	Merry Old Land of Oz	95-day		29.90	30

My Fair Lady - W. Chambers

YEAR	ISSUE	EDITION LIMIT	YEAR RETD.	ISSUE PRICE	*QUOTE U.S.$
1989	Opening Day at Ascot	150-day		24.90	25
1989	I Could Have Danced All Night	150-day		24.90	25
1989	The Rain in Spain	150-day		27.90	28
1989	Show Me	150-day		27.90	28
1990	Get Me To/Church On Time	150-day		27.90	28
1990	I've Grown Accustomed/Face	150-day		27.90	40

Nature's Child - M. Jobe

YEAR	ISSUE	EDITION LIMIT	YEAR RETD.	ISSUE PRICE	*QUOTE U.S.$
1990	Sharing	150-day		29.90	31
1990	The Lost Lamb	150-day		29.90	30
1990	Seems Like Yesterday	150-day		32.90	40
1990	Faithful Friends	150-day		32.90	36
1990	Trusted Companion	150-day		32.90	50
1991	Hand in Hand	150-day		32.90	50

Nature's Garden - C. Decker

YEAR	ISSUE	EDITION LIMIT	YEAR RETD.	ISSUE PRICE	*QUOTE U.S.$
1994	Peaceful Harmony	95-day		34.90	35
1993	Springtime Friends	95-day		29.90	30
1993	A Morning Splash	95-day		29.90	30
1993	Flury of Activity	95-day		32.90	33
1993	Hanging Around	95-day		32.90	33
1993	Tiny Twirling Treasures	95-day		32.90	33
1994	Peaceful Harmony	95-day		29.90	30

*Quotes have been rounded up to nearest dollar

Nature's Nursery - J. Thornbrugh

YEAR ISSUE		EDITION LIMIT	YEAR RETD.	ISSUE PRICE	*QUOTE U.S.$
1992	Testing the Waters	150-day		29.90	50
1993	Taking the Plunge	150-day		29.90	45
1993	Race Ya Mom	150-day		29.90	46
1993	Time to Wake Up	150-day		29.90	50
1993	Hide and Seek	150-day		29.90	45
1993	Piggyback Ride	150-day		29.90	30

Not So Long Ago - J. W. Smith

YEAR ISSUE		EDITION LIMIT	YEAR RETD.	ISSUE PRICE	*QUOTE U.S.$
1988	Story Time	150-day		24.90	25
1988	Wash Day for Dolly	150-day		24.90	30
1988	Suppertime for Kitty	150-day		24.90	30
1988	Mother's Little Helper	150-day		24.90	30

Oklahoma! - M. Kunstler

YEAR ISSUE		EDITION LIMIT	YEAR RETD.	ISSUE PRICE	*QUOTE U.S.$
1985	Oh, What a Beautiful Mornin'	150-day		19.50	25
1986	Surrey with the Fringe on Top'	150-day		19.50	25
1986	I Cain't Say No	150-day		19.50	25
1986	Oklahoma	150-day		19.50	25

The Old Mill Stream - C. Tennant

YEAR ISSUE		EDITION LIMIT	YEAR RETD.	ISSUE PRICE	*QUOTE U.S.$
1990	New London Grist Mill	150-day		39.90	40
1991	Wayside Inn Grist Mill	150-day		39.90	45
1991	Old Red Mill	150-day		39.90	40
1991	Glade Creek Grist Mill	150-day		39.90	40

Old-Fashioned Favorites - M. Weber

YEAR ISSUE		EDITION LIMIT	YEAR RETD.	ISSUE PRICE	*QUOTE U.S.$
1991	Apple Crisp	150-day		29.90	75
1991	Blueberry Muffins	150-day		29.90	65
1991	Peach Cobbler	150-day		29.90	98
1991	Chocolate Chip Oatmeal Cookies	150-day		29.90	200

Once Upon a Time - K. Pritchett

YEAR ISSUE		EDITION LIMIT	YEAR RETD.	ISSUE PRICE	*QUOTE U.S.$
1988	Little Red Riding Hood	150-day		24.90	25
1988	Rapunzel	150-day		24.90	25
1988	Three Little Pigs	150-day		27.90	30
1989	The Princess and the Pea	150-day		27.90	30
1989	Goldilocks and the Three Bears	150-day		27.90	35
1989	Beauty and the Beast	150-day		27.90	50

Pinocchio - Disney Studios

YEAR ISSUE		EDITION LIMIT	YEAR RETD.	ISSUE PRICE	*QUOTE U.S.$
1989	Gepetto Creates Pinocchio	150-day		29.90	55-65
1990	Pinocchio And The Blue Fairy	150-day		29.90	80
1990	It's an Actor's Life For Me	150-day		32.90	60
1990	I've Got No Strings On Me	150-day		32.90	50
1991	Pleasure Island	150-day		32.90	50
1991	A Real Boy	150-day		32.90	55

Portraits of Motherhood - W. Chambers

YEAR ISSUE		EDITION LIMIT	YEAR RETD.	ISSUE PRICE	*QUOTE U.S.$
1987	Mother's Here	150-day		29.50	30
1988	First Touch	150-day		29.50	30

Precious Little Ones - M. T. Fangel

YEAR ISSUE		EDITION LIMIT	YEAR RETD.	ISSUE PRICE	*QUOTE U.S.$
1988	Little Red Robins	150-day		29.90	30
1988	Little Fledglings	150-day		29.90	30
1988	Saturday Night Bath	150-day		29.90	33
1988	Peek-A-Boo	150-day		29.90	32

Proud Sentinels of the American West - N. Glazier

YEAR ISSUE		EDITION LIMIT	YEAR RETD.	ISSUE PRICE	*QUOTE U.S.$
1993	Youngblood	150-day		29.90	55
1993	Cat Nap	150-day		29.90	70
1993	Desert Bighorn-Mormon Ridge	150-day		32.90	55
1993	Crown Prince	150-day		32.90	65

Purrfect Point of View - J. Giordano

YEAR ISSUE		EDITION LIMIT	YEAR RETD.	ISSUE PRICE	*QUOTE U.S.$
1992	Unexpected Visitors	150-day		29.90	30
1992	Wistful Morning	150-day		29.90	50
1992	Afternoon Catnap	150-day		29.90	50
1992	Cozy Company	150-day		29.90	40

Pussyfooting Around - C. Wilson

YEAR ISSUE		EDITION LIMIT	YEAR RETD.	ISSUE PRICE	*QUOTE U.S.$
1991	Fish Tales	150-day		24.90	25
1991	Teatime Tabbies	150-day		24.90	25
1991	Yarn Spinners	150-day		24.90	30
1991	Two Maestros	150-day		24.90	32

Romantic Age of Steam - R.B. Pierce

YEAR ISSUE		EDITION LIMIT	YEAR RETD.	ISSUE PRICE	*QUOTE U.S.$
1992	The Empire Builder	150-day		29.90	35
1992	The Broadway Limited	150-day		29.90	75
1992	Twentieth Century Limited	150-day		32.90	55
1992	The Chief	150-day		32.90	33
1992	The Crescent Limited	150-day		32.90	33
1993	The Overland Limited	150-day		34.90	35
1993	The Jupiter	150-day		34.90	35
1993	The Daylight	150-day		34.90	35

Santa's Christmas - T. Browning

YEAR ISSUE		EDITION LIMIT	YEAR RETD.	ISSUE PRICE	*QUOTE U.S.$
1991	Santa's Love	150-day		29.90	45
1991	Santa's Cheer	150-day		29.90	45
1991	Santa's Promise	150-day		32.90	65
1991	Santa's Gift	150-day		32.90	75
1992	Santa's Surprise	150-day		32.90	60
1992	Santa's Magic	150-day		32.90	55

Season For Song - M. Jobe

YEAR ISSUE		EDITION LIMIT	YEAR RETD.	ISSUE PRICE	*QUOTE U.S.$
1991	Winter Concert	150-day		34.90	43
1991	Snowy Symphony	150-day		34.90	50
1991	Frosty Chorus	150-day		34.90	70
1991	Silver Serenade	150-day		34.90	70

Seasons of Splendor - K. Randle

YEAR ISSUE		EDITION LIMIT	YEAR RETD.	ISSUE PRICE	*QUOTE U.S.$
1992	Autumn's Grandeur	150-day		29.90	45
1992	School Days	150-day		29.90	40
1992	Woodland Mill Stream	150-day		32.90	65
1992	Harvest Memories	150-day		32.90	55
1992	A Country Weekend	150-day		32.90	65
1993	Indian Summer	150-day		32.90	60

Shadows and Light: Winter's Wildlife - N. Glazier

YEAR ISSUE		EDITION LIMIT	YEAR RETD.	ISSUE PRICE	*QUOTE U.S.$
1993	Winter's Children	150-day		29.90	55
1993	Cub Scouts	150-day		29.90	65
1993	Little Snowman	150-day		29.90	50
1993	The Snow Cave	150-day		29.90	50

Singin' In The Rain - M. Skolsky

YEAR ISSUE		EDITION LIMIT	YEAR RETD.	ISSUE PRICE	*QUOTE U.S.$
1990	Singin' In The Rain	150-day		32.90	35
1990	Good Morning	150-day		32.90	34
1991	Broadway Melody	150-day		32.90	45
1991	We're Happy Again	150-day		32.90	50

Sleeping Beauty - Disney Studios

YEAR ISSUE		EDITION LIMIT	YEAR RETD.	ISSUE PRICE	*QUOTE U.S.$
1991	Once Upon A Dream	150-day		39.90	50
1991	Awakened by a Kiss	150-day		39.90	100
1991	Happy Birthday Briar Rose	150-day		42.90	50
1992	Together At Last	150-day		42.90	55

Small Blessings - C. Layton

YEAR ISSUE		EDITION LIMIT	YEAR RETD.	ISSUE PRICE	*QUOTE U.S.$
1992	Now I Lay Me Down to Sleep	150-day		29.90	40
1992	Bless Us O Lord For These, Thy Gifts	150-day		29.90	45
1992	Jesus Loves Me, This I Know	150-day		32.90	48
1992	This Little Light of Mine	150-day		32.90	60
1992	Blessed Are The Pure In Heart	150-day		32.90	33
1993	Bless Our Home	150-day		32.90	33

Snow White and the Seven Dwarfs - Disney Studios

YEAR ISSUE		EDITION LIMIT	YEAR RETD.	ISSUE PRICE	*QUOTE U.S.$
1991	The Dance of Snow White/Seven Dwarfs	150-day		29.90	60
1991	With a Smile and a Song	150-day		29.90	45
1991	A Special Treat	150-day		32.90	50
1992	A Kiss for Dopey	150-day		32.90	55
1992	The Poison Apple	150-day		32.90	55
1992	Fireside Love Story	150-day		34.90	55
1992	Stubborn Grumpy	150-day		34.90	55
1992	A Wish Come True	150-day		34.90	60
1992	Time To Tidy Up	150-day		34.50	70
1993	May I Have This Dance?	150-day		36.90	60
1993	A Surprise in the Clearing	150-day		36.50	37
1993	Happy Ending	150-day		36.90	37

Songs of the American Spirit - H. Bond

YEAR ISSUE		EDITION LIMIT	YEAR RETD.	ISSUE PRICE	*QUOTE U.S.$
1991	The Star Spangled Banner	150-day		29.90	30
1991	Battle Hymn of the Republic	150-day		29.90	45
1991	America the Beautiful	150-day		29.90	40
1991	My Country 'Tis of Thee	150-day		29.90	50

Sound of Music - T. Crnkovich

YEAR ISSUE		EDITION LIMIT	YEAR RETD.	ISSUE PRICE	*QUOTE U.S.$
1986	Sound of Music	150-day		19.50	20
1986	Do-Re-Mi	150-day		19.50	20
1986	My Favorite Things	150-day		22.50	23
1986	Laendler Waltz	150-day		22.50	25
1987	Edelweiss	150-day		22.50	23
1987	I Have Confidence	150-day		22.50	23
1987	Maria	150-day		24.90	25
1987	Climb Ev'ry Mountain	150-day		24.90	30

South Pacific - E. Gignilliat

YEAR ISSUE		EDITION LIMIT	YEAR RETD.	ISSUE PRICE	*QUOTE U.S.$
1987	Some Enchanted Evening	150-day		24.50	25
1987	Happy Talk	150-day		24.50	25
1987	Dites Moi	150-day		24.90	25
1988	Honey Bun	150-day		24.90	25

Stately Owls - J. Beaudoin

YEAR ISSUE		EDITION LIMIT	YEAR RETD.	ISSUE PRICE	*QUOTE U.S.$
1989	The Snowy Owl	150-day		29.90	55
1989	The Great Horned Owl	150-day		29.90	51
1990	The Barn Owl	150-day		32.90	35
1990	The Screech Owl	150-day		32.90	35
1990	The Short-Eared Owl	150-day		32.90	33
1990	The Barred Owl	150-day		32.90	35
1990	The Great Grey Owl	150-day		34.90	35
1991	The Saw-Whet Owl	150-day		34.90	35

The Story of Christmas by Eve Licea - E. Licea

YEAR ISSUE		EDITION LIMIT	YEAR RETD.	ISSUE PRICE	*QUOTE U.S.$
1987	The Annunciation	Yr.Iss.		44.90	50
1988	The Nativity	Yr.Iss.		44.90	50
1989	Adoration Of The Shepherds	Yr.Iss.		49.90	53
1990	Journey Of The Magi	Yr.Iss.		49.90	50
1991	Gifts Of The Magi	Yr.Iss.		49.90	55
1992	Rest on the Flight into Egypt	Yr.Iss.		49.90	65

Sundblom Santas - H. Sundblom

YEAR ISSUE		EDITION LIMIT	YEAR RETD.	ISSUE PRICE	*QUOTE U.S.$
1989	Santa By The Fire	Closed		27.90	30
1990	Christmas Vigil	Closed		27.90	45
1991	To All A Good Night	Closed		32.90	70
1992	Santa's on His Way	Closed		32.90	70

A Swan is Born - L. Roberts

YEAR ISSUE		EDITION LIMIT	YEAR RETD.	ISSUE PRICE	*QUOTE U.S.$
1987	Hopes and Dreams	150-day		24.50	25
1987	At the Barre	150-day		24.50	25
1987	In Position	150-day		24.50	25
1988	Just For Size	150-day		24.50	45

Sweetness and Grace - J. Welty

YEAR ISSUE		EDITION LIMIT	YEAR RETD.	ISSUE PRICE	*QUOTE U.S.$
1992	God Bless Teddy	150-day		34.90	4
1992	Sunshine and Smiles	150-day		34.90	6
1992	Favorite Buddy	150-day		34.90	4
1992	Sweet Dreams	150-day		34.90	6

Thomas Kinkade's Enchanted Cottages - T. Kinkade

YEAR ISSUE		EDITION LIMIT	YEAR RETD.	ISSUE PRICE	*QUOTE U.S.$
1993	Fallbrooke Cottage	95-day		29.90	3
1993	Julianne's Cottage	95-day		29.90	3
1993	Seaside Cottage	95-day		29.90	3
1993	Sweetheart Cottage	95-day		29.90	3
1993	Weathervane Cottage	95-day		29.90	3
1993	Rose Garden Cottage	95-day		29.90	3

Thomas Kinkade's Garden Cottages of England - T. Kinkade

YEAR ISSUE		EDITION LIMIT	YEAR RETD.	ISSUE PRICE	*QUOTE U.S.$
1991	Chandler's Cottage	150-day		27.90	60-10
1991	Cedar Nook Cottage	150-day		27.90	45-7
1991	Candlelit Cottage	150-day		30.90	50-7
1991	Open Gate Cottage	150-day		30.90	40-7
1991	McKenna's Cottage	150-day		30.90	45-8
1991	Woodsman's Thatch Cottage	150-day		32.90	45-7
1992	Merritt's Cottage	150-day		32.90	60-9
1992	Stonegate Cottage	150-day		32.90	60-9

Thomas Kinkade's Home for the Holidays - T. Kinkade

YEAR ISSUE		EDITION LIMIT	YEAR RETD.	ISSUE PRICE	*QUOTE U.S.$
1991	Sleigh Ride Home	150-day		29.90	50-7
1991	Home to Grandma's	150-day		29.90	45-7
1991	Home Before Christmas	150-day		32.90	50-9
1991	The Warmth of Home	150-day		32.90	60-8
1992	Homespun Holiday	150-day		32.90	55-8
1992	Hometime Yuletide	150-day		34.90	50-8
1992	Home Away From Home	150-day		34.90	75-10
1992	The Journey Home	150-day		34.90	50-7

Thomas Kinkade's Home is Where the Heart Is - T. Kinkade

YEAR ISSUE		EDITION LIMIT	YEAR RETD.	ISSUE PRICE	*QUOTE U.S.$
1992	Home Sweet Home	150-day		29.90	60-12
1992	A Warm Welcome Home	150-day		29.90	60-8
1992	A Carriage Ride Home	150-day		32.90	50-
1993	Amber Afternoon	150-day		32.90	35-
1993	Country Memories	150-day		32.90	90-1
1993	The Twilight Cafe	150-day		34.90	50-
1993	Our Summer Home	150-day		34.90	40-
1993	Hometown Hospitality	150-day		34.90	40-

Thomas Kinkade's Thomashire - T. Kinkade

YEAR ISSUE		EDITION LIMIT	YEAR RETD.	ISSUE PRICE	*QUOTE U.S.$
1992	Olde Porterfield Tea Room	150-day		29.90	45-
1992	Olde Thomashire Mill	150-day		29.90	50-
1992	Swanbrook Cottage	150-day		32.90	65-14
1992	Pye Corner Cottage	150-day		32.90	70-
1993	Blossom Hill Church	150-day		32.90	40-
1993	Olde Garden Cottage	150-day		32.90	50-

Thomas Kinkade's Yuletide Memories - T. Kinkade

YEAR ISSUE		EDITION LIMIT	YEAR RETD.	ISSUE PRICE	*QUOTE U.S.$
1992	The Magic of Christmas	150-day		29.90	75-1
1992	A Beacon of Faith	150-day		29.90	45-
1993	Moonlit Sleighride	150-day		29.90	60-1
1993	Silent Night	150-day		29.90	50-
1993	Olde Porterfield Gift Shoppe	150-day		29.90	80-
1993	The Wonder of the Season	150-day		29.90	80-
1993	A Winter's Walk	150-day		29.90	
1993	Skater's Delight	150-day		32.90	

Tom Sawyer - W. Chambers

YEAR ISSUE		EDITION LIMIT	YEAR RETD.	ISSUE PRICE	*QUOTE U.S.$
1987	Whitewashing the Fence	150-day		27.50	
1987	Tom and Becky	150-day		27.90	
1987	Tom Sawyer the Pirate	150-day		27.90	
1988	First Pipes	150-day		27.90	

Under Mother's Wing - J. Beaudoin

YEAR ISSUE		EDITION LIMIT	YEAR RETD.	ISSUE PRICE	*QUOTE U.S.$
1992	Arctic Spring: Snowy Owls	150-day		29.90	
1992	Forest's Edge: Great Gray Owls	150-day		29.90	
1992	Treetop Trio: Long-Eared Owls	150-day		32.90	
1992	Woodland Watch: Spotted Owls	150-day		32.90	
1992	Vast View: Saw Whet Owls	150-day		32.90	
1992	Lofty-Limb: Great Horned Owl	150-day		34.90	
1993	Perfect Perch: Barred Owls	150-day		34.90	
1993	Happy Home: Short-Eared Owl	150-day		34.90	

Upland Birds of North America - W. Anderson

YEAR ISSUE		EDITION LIMIT	YEAR RETD.	ISSUE PRICE	*QUOTE U.S.$
1986	The Pheasant	150-day		24.50	
1986	The Grouse	150-day		24.50	
1987	The Quail	150-day		27.50	
1987	The Wild Turkey	150-day		27.50	
1987	The Gray Partridge	150-day		27.50	
1987	The Woodcock	150-day		27.90	

Windows of Glory - J. Welty

YEAR ISSUE		EDITION LIMIT	YEAR RETD.	ISSUE PRICE	*QUOTE U.S.$
1993	King of Kings	95-day		29.90	
1993	Prince of Peace	95-day		29.90	
1993	The Messiah	95-day		32.90	
1993	The Good Shepherd	95-day		32.90	
1993	The Light of the World	95-day		32.90	
1993	The Everlasting Father	95-day		32.90	

Wizard of Oz - J. Auckland

YEAR ISSUE		EDITION LIMIT	YEAR RETD.	ISSUE PRICE	*QUOTE U.S.$
1977	Over the Rainbow	100-day		19.00	
1978	If I Only Had a Brain	100-day		19.00	
1978	If I Only Had a Heart	100-day		19.00	
1978	If I Were King of the Forest	100-day		19.00	
1979	Wicked Witch of the West	100-day		19.00	
1979	Follow the Yellow Brick Road	100-day		19.00	

*Quotes have been rounded up to nearest dolla

YEAR	ISSUE	EDITION LIMIT	YEAR RETD.	ISSUE PRICE	*QUOTE U.S. $
1979	Wonderful Wizard of Oz	100-day		19.00	55
1980	The Grand Finale	100-day		24.00	55

Wizard of Oz: A National Treasure - R. Laslo

YEAR	ISSUE	EDITION LIMIT	YEAR RETD.	ISSUE PRICE	*QUOTE U.S. $
1991	Yellow Brick Road	150-day		29.90	50
1992	I Haven't Got a Brain	150-day		29.90	50
1992	I'm a Little Rusty Yet	150-day		32.90	50
1992	I Even Scare Myself	150-day		32.90	50
1992	We're Off To See the Wizard	150-day		32.90	50
1992	I'll Never Get Home	150-day		34.90	60
1992	I'm Melting	150-day		34.90	65
1992	There's No Place Like Home	150-day		34.90	35

Yesterday's Innocents - J. Wilcox Smith

YEAR	ISSUE	EDITION LIMIT	YEAR RETD.	ISSUE PRICE	*QUOTE U.S. $
1992	My First Book	150-day		29.90	30
1992	Time to Smell the Roses	150-day		29.90	50
1993	Hush, Baby's Sleeping	150-day		32.90	40
1993	Ready and Waiting	150-day		32.90	60

Enchantica

Retired Enchantica Collection - Various

YEAR	ISSUE	EDITION LIMIT	YEAR RETD.	ISSUE PRICE	*QUOTE U.S. $
992	Winter Dragon-Grawlfang-2200 - J. Woodward	Retrd.	1993	50.00	75
992	Spring Dragon-Gorgoyle-2201 - J. Woodward	Retrd.	1993	50.00	75
993	Summer Dragon-Arangast-2202 - J. Woodward	Retrd.	1993	50.00	75
993	Autumn Dragon-Snarlgard-2203 - J. Woodward	Retrd.	1993	50.00	75
992	Cave Dragon-2065 - A. Bill	Retrd.	1994	200.00	225
991	Snappa Caught Napping-2039 - A. Hull	Retrd.	1994	39.50	60

Enesco Corporation

Barbie-Bob Mackie JC Penney Exclusive - Enesco

YEAR	ISSUE	EDITION LIMIT	YEAR RETD.	ISSUE PRICE	*QUOTE U.S. $
995	Queen of Hearts Barbie-11276	7,500	1995	30.00	30

Barbie-FAO Schwarz Exclusive - Enesco

YEAR	ISSUE	EDITION LIMIT	YEAR RETD.	ISSUE PRICE	*QUOTE U.S. $
994	Silver Screen Barbie-128805	3,600	1995	30.00	30
995	Circus Star Barbie-150339	3,600	1995	30.00	30

Barbie-Glamour - Enesco

YEAR	ISSUE	EDITION LIMIT	YEAR RETD.	ISSUE PRICE	*QUOTE U.S. $
996	Here Comes The Bride, 1966-170984	Open		30.00	30

Barbie-Great Eras - Enesco

YEAR	ISSUE	EDITION LIMIT	YEAR RETD.	ISSUE PRICE	*QUOTE U.S. $
996	Gibson Girl Barbie-171468	10,000		30.00	30
996	1920's Flapper Barbie-174777	10,000		30.00	30

Barbie-Happy Holiday - Enesco

YEAR	ISSUE	EDITION LIMIT	YEAR RETD.	ISSUE PRICE	*QUOTE U.S. $
994	Happy Holidays Barbie, 1994-115088	5,000	1994	30.00	100-150
995	Happy Holidays Barbie, 1995-143154	Yr.Iss.	1995	30.00	30
995	Happy Holidays Barbie, 1988-154180	Yr.Iss.	1995	30.00	30

Barbie-Hollywood Legends - Enesco

YEAR	ISSUE	EDITION LIMIT	YEAR RETD.	ISSUE PRICE	*QUOTE U.S. $
996	Barbie As Scarlett O'Hara in Green Velvet-171085	10,000	1995	30.00	35

Barbie-Nostalgic - Enesco

YEAR	ISSUE	EDITION LIMIT	YEAR RETD.	ISSUE PRICE	*QUOTE U.S. $
993	35th Anniversary Barbie-655112	5,000	1994	30.00	30
994	Barbie Solo In The Spotlight, 1959-114383	5,000	1995	30.00	45
996	Barbie Enchanted Evening, 1960-175587	5,000	1995	30.00	30

Cherished Teddies - P. Hillman

YEAR	ISSUE	EDITION LIMIT	YEAR RETD.	ISSUE PRICE	*QUOTE U.S. $
995	Jack/Jill Nursery Rhyme-114901	Open		35.00	35
995	Mary/Lamb Nursery Rhyme-128902	Open		35.00	35
995	Old King Cole Nursery Rhyme-135437	Open		35.00	35
995	Girl in Green Dress Dtd 95-141550	Yr.Iss.		35.00	35

Memories of Yesterday Dated Plate Series - Various

YEAR	ISSUE	EDITION LIMIT	YEAR RETD.	ISSUE PRICE	*QUOTE U.S. $
993	Look Out-Something Good Is Coming Your Way!-530298 - S. Butcher	Yr.Iss.		50.00	50
994	Pleasant Dreams and Sweet Repose-528102 - M. Atwell	Yr.Iss.		50.00	50
995	Join Me For a Little Song-134880 - M. Attwell	Yr.Iss.		50.00	50

Precious Moments Beauty of Christmas Collection - S. Butcher

YEAR	ISSUE	EDITION LIMIT	YEAR RETD.	ISSUE PRICE	*QUOTE U.S. $
994	You're as Pretty as a Christmas Tree-530409	Yr.Iss.		50.00	50
995	He Covers the Earth With His Beauty-142670	Yr.Iss.		50.00	50

Precious Moments Christmas Blessings - S. Butcher

YEAR	ISSUE	EDITION LIMIT	YEAR RETD.	ISSUE PRICE	*QUOTE U.S. $
990	Wishing You A Yummy Christmas-523801	Yr.Iss.		50.00	50
991	Blessings From Me To Thee -523860	Yr.Iss.		50.00	55
992	But The Greatest of These Is Love-527742	Yr.Iss.		50.00	50
993	Wishing You the Sweetest Christmas-530204	Yr.Iss.		50.00	50

Precious Moments Christmas Collection - S. Butcher

YEAR	ISSUE	EDITION LIMIT	YEAR RETD.	ISSUE PRICE	*QUOTE U.S.$
1981	Come Let Us Adore Him-E-5646	15,000		40.00	48-60
1982	Let Heaven and Nature Sing-E-2347	15,000		40.00	40
1983	Wee Three Kings-E-0538	15,000		40.00	40
1984	Unto Us a Child Is Born-E-5395	15,000		40.00	40

Precious Moments Christmas Love Series - S. Butcher

YEAR	ISSUE	EDITION LIMIT	YEAR RETD.	ISSUE PRICE	*QUOTE U.S.$
1986	I'm Sending You a White Christmas-101834	Yr.Iss.		45.00	55
1987	My Peace I Give Unto Thee-102954	Yr.Iss.		45.00	90
1988	Merry Christmas Deer-520284	Yr.Iss.		50.00	55
1989	May Your Christmas Be A Happy Home-523003	Yr.Iss.		50.00	55

Precious Moments Inspired Thoughts Series - S. Butcher

YEAR	ISSUE	EDITION LIMIT	YEAR RETD.	ISSUE PRICE	*QUOTE U.S.$
1985	Love One Another-E-5215	15,000		40.00	66
1982	Make a Joyful Noise-E-7174	15,000		40.00	40
1983	I Believe In Miracles-E-9257	15,000		40.00	40
1984	Love is Kind-E-2847	15,000		40.00	40

Precious Moments Joy of Christmas Series - S. Butcher

YEAR	ISSUE	EDITION LIMIT	YEAR RETD.	ISSUE PRICE	*QUOTE U.S.$
1982	I'll Play My Drum For Him-E-2357	Yr.Iss.		40.00	90-93
1983	Christmastime is for Sharing-E-0505	Yr.Iss.		40.00	60-75
1984	The Wonder of Christmas-E-5396	Yr.Iss.		40.00	45
1985	Tell Me the Story of Jesus-15237	Yr.Iss.		40.00	90-115

Precious Moments Mother's Day Series - S. Butcher

YEAR	ISSUE	EDITION LIMIT	YEAR RETD.	ISSUE PRICE	*QUOTE U.S.$
1994	Thinking of You Is What I Really Like to Do-531766	Yr.Iss.		50.00	50
1995	He Hath Made Everything Beautiful In His Time-129151	Yr.Iss.		50.00	50
1996	Of All The Mothers I Have Known There's None As Precious As My Own-163716	Yr.Iss.		50.00	50

Precious Moments Mother's Love Series - S. Butcher

YEAR	ISSUE	EDITION LIMIT	YEAR RETD.	ISSUE PRICE	*QUOTE U.S.$
1981	Mother Sew Dear-E-5217	15,000		40.00	50
1982	The Purr-fect Grandma-E-7173	15,000		40.00	40
1983	The Hand that Rocks the Future-E-9256	15,000		40.00	40
1984	Loving Thy Neighbor-E-2848	15,000		40.00	40

Precious Moments Open Editions - S. Butcher

YEAR	ISSUE	EDITION LIMIT	YEAR RETD.	ISSUE PRICE	*QUOTE U.S.$
1982	Our First Christmas Together-E-2378	Suspd.		30.00	45-55
1981	The Lord Bless You and Keep You-E-5216	Suspd.		30.00	40-45
1982	Rejoicing with You-E-7172	Suspd.		30.00	40
1983	Jesus Loves Me-E-9275	Suspd.		30.00	45-48
1983	Jesus Loves Me-E-9276	Suspd.		30.00	45-48
1994	Bring The Little Ones To Jesus-531359	Yr.Iss.		50.00	50
1996	You Have Touched So Many Hearts-151114	Yr.Iss.		35.00	35
1996	Peace On Earth...Anyway-183377	Yr.Iss.		50.00	50

Precious Moments The Four Seasons Series - S. Butcher

YEAR	ISSUE	EDITION LIMIT	YEAR RETD.	ISSUE PRICE	*QUOTE U.S.$
1985	The Voice of Spring-12106	Yr.Iss.		40.00	110-120
1985	Summer's Joy-12114	Yr.Iss.		40.00	85-110
1986	Autumn's Praise-12122	Yr.Iss.		40.00	53
1986	Winter's Song-12130	Yr.Iss.		40.00	58

Ernst Enterprises/Porter & Price, Inc.

A Beautiful World - S. Morton

YEAR	ISSUE	EDITION LIMIT	YEAR RETD.	ISSUE PRICE	*QUOTE U.S.$
1981	Tahitian Dreamer	Retrd.	1987	27.50	30
1982	Flirtation	Retrd.	1987	27.50	30
1984	Elke of Oslo	Retrd.	1987	27.50	30

Classy Cars - S. Kuhnly

YEAR	ISSUE	EDITION LIMIT	YEAR RETD.	ISSUE PRICE	*QUOTE U.S.$
1982	The 26T	Retrd.	1990	24.50	25
1982	The 31A	Retrd.	1990	24.50	25
1983	The Pickup	Retrd.	1990	24.50	25
1984	Panel Van	Retrd.	1990	24.50	25

Commemoratives - S. Morton

YEAR	ISSUE	EDITION LIMIT	YEAR RETD.	ISSUE PRICE	*QUOTE U.S.$
1981	John Lennon	Retrd.	1988	39.50	100-150
1982	Elvis Presley	Retrd.	1988	39.50	75-125
1982	Marilyn Monroe	Retrd.	1988	39.50	100
1983	Judy Garland	Retrd.	1988	39.50	70
1984	John Wayne	Retrd.	1988	39.50	95

Elvira - S. Morton

YEAR	ISSUE	EDITION LIMIT	YEAR RETD.	ISSUE PRICE	*QUOTE U.S.$
1988	Night Rose	90-day		29.50	45
1988	Red Velvet	90-day		29.50	35
1988	Mistress of the Dark	90-day		29.50	35

Elvis Presley - S. Morton

YEAR	ISSUE	EDITION LIMIT	YEAR RETD.	ISSUE PRICE	*QUOTE U.S.$
1987	The King	Retrd.	1991	39.50	90
1987	Loving You	Retrd.	1991	39.50	90
1987	Early Years	Retrd.	1991	39.50	90
1987	Tenderly	Retrd.	1991	39.50	90
1988	Forever Yours	Retrd.	1991	39.50	90
1988	Rockin in the Moonlight	Retrd.	1991	39.50	90
1988	Moody Blues	Retrd.	1991	39.50	60-85
1988	Elvis Presley	Retrd.	1991	39.50	75
1989	Elvis Presley-Special Request	Retrd.	1991	150.00	250-300

Hollywood Greats - S. Morton

YEAR	ISSUE	EDITION LIMIT	YEAR RETD.	ISSUE PRICE	*QUOTE U.S.$
1981	Henry Fonda	Retrd.	1988	29.95	60
1981	John Wayne	Retrd.	1988	29.95	100
1981	Gary Cooper	Retrd.	1988	29.95	30
1982	Clark Gable	Retrd.	1988	29.95	65
1984	Alan Ladd	Retrd.	1988	29.95	40-60

Hollywood Walk of Fame - S. Morton

YEAR	ISSUE	EDITION LIMIT	YEAR RETD.	ISSUE PRICE	*QUOTE U.S.$
1989	Jimmy Stewart	Retrd.	1992	39.50	45
1989	Elizabeth Taylor	Retrd.	1992	39.50	45
1989	Tom Selleck	Retrd.	1992	39.50	45
1989	Joan Collins	Retrd.	1992	39.50	45
1990	Burt Reynolds	Retrd.	1992	39.50	50
1990	Sylvester Stallone	Retrd.	1992	39.50	45

The Republic Pictures Library - S. Morton

YEAR	ISSUE	EDITION LIMIT	YEAR RETD.	ISSUE PRICE	*QUOTE U.S.$
1991	Showdown With Laredo	28-day		37.50	38
1991	The Ride Home	28-day		37.50	38
1991	Attack at Tarawa	28-day		37.50	38
1991	Thoughts of Angelique	28-day		37.50	38
1992	War of the Wildcats	28-day		37.50	38
1992	The Fighting Seabees	28-day		37.50	38
1992	The Quiet Man	28-day		37.50	38
1992	Angel and the Badman	28-day		37.50	38
1993	Sands of Iwo Jima	28-day		37.50	38
1993	Flying Tigers	28-day		37.50	38
1993	The Tribute (12")	28-day		97.50	98
1994	The Tribute (8 1/4") AP	9,500		35.00	35

Seems Like Yesterday - R. Money

YEAR	ISSUE	EDITION LIMIT	YEAR RETD.	ISSUE PRICE	*QUOTE U.S.$
1981	Stop & Smell the Roses	Retrd.	1988	24.50	30
1982	Home by Lunch	Retrd.	1988	24.50	35
1982	Lisa's Creek	Retrd.	1988	24.50	25
1983	It's Got My Name on It	Retrd.	1988	24.50	30
1983	My Magic Hat	Retrd.	1988	24.50	25
1984	Little Prince	Retrd.	1988	24.50	25

Star Trek - S. Morton

YEAR	ISSUE	EDITION LIMIT	YEAR RETD.	ISSUE PRICE	*QUOTE U.S.$
1984	Mr. Spock	Retrd.	1989	29.50	60-150
1985	Dr. McCoy	Retrd.	1989	29.50	60-95
1985	Sulu	Retrd.	1989	29.50	60-90
1985	Scotty	Retrd.	1989	29.50	60-100
1985	Uhura	Retrd.	1989	29.50	65-95
1985	Chekov	Retrd.	1989	29.50	65-90
1985	Captain Kirk	Retrd.	1989	29.50	70-150
1985	Beam Us Down Scotty	Retrd.	1989	29.50	60-80
1985	The Enterprise	Retrd.	1989	39.50	80-150

Star Trek: Commemorative Collection - S. Morton

YEAR	ISSUE	EDITION LIMIT	YEAR RETD.	ISSUE PRICE	*QUOTE U.S.$
1987	The Trouble With Tribbles	Retrd.	1989	29.50	100-175
1987	Mirror, Mirror	Retrd.	1989	29.50	170
1987	A Piece of the Action	Retrd.	1989	29.50	75-175
1987	The Devil in the Dark	Retrd.	1989	29.50	90-165
1987	Amok Time	Retrd.	1989	29.50	75-175
1987	The City on the Edge of Forever	Retrd.	1989	29.50	100-150
1987	Journey to Babel	Retrd.	1989	29.50	100-125
1987	The Menagerie	Retrd.	1989	29.50	100-150

Turn of The Century - R. Money

YEAR	ISSUE	EDITION LIMIT	YEAR RETD.	ISSUE PRICE	*QUOTE U.S.$
1981	Riverboat Honeymoon	Retrd.	1987	35.00	40
1982	Children's Carousel	Retrd.	1987	35.00	40
1984	Flower Market	Retrd.	1987	35.00	35
1985	Balloon Race	Retrd.	1987	35.00	35

Women of the West - D. Putnam

YEAR	ISSUE	EDITION LIMIT	YEAR RETD.	ISSUE PRICE	*QUOTE U.S.$
1979	Expectations	Retrd.	1986	39.50	40
1981	Silver Dollar Sal	Retrd.	1986	39.50	40
1982	School Marm	Retrd.	1986	39.50	40
1983	Dolly	Retrd.	1986	39.50	40

Fairmont

Famous Clowns - R. Skelton

YEAR	ISSUE	EDITION LIMIT	YEAR RETD.	ISSUE PRICE	*QUOTE U.S.$
1976	Freddie the Freeloader	10,000		55.00	400
1977	W. C. Fields	10,000		55.00	100
1978	Happy	10,000		55.00	80
1979	The Pledge	10,000		55.00	65

Spencer Special - I. Spencer

YEAR	ISSUE	EDITION LIMIT	YEAR RETD.	ISSUE PRICE	*QUOTE U.S.$
1978	Hug Me	10,000		55.00	150
1978	Sleep Little Baby	10,000		65.00	125

Fenton Art Glass Company

American Classic Series - M. Dickinson

YEAR	ISSUE	EDITION LIMIT	YEAR RETD.	ISSUE PRICE	*QUOTE U.S.$
1986	Jupiter Train on Opal Satin	5,000	1986	75.00	75
1986	Studebaker-Garford Car on Opal Satin	5,000	1986	75.00	75

American Craftsman Carnival - Fenton

YEAR	ISSUE	EDITION LIMIT	YEAR RETD.	ISSUE PRICE	*QUOTE U.S.$
1970	Glassmaker	Closed	1970	10.00	50-60
1971	Printer	Closed	1971	10.00	50-60
1972	Blacksmith	Closed	1972	10.00	50-60
1973	Shoemaker	Closed	1973	10.00	50-60
1974	Pioneer Cooper	Closed	1974	11.00	50-60
1975	Paul Revere (Patriot & Silversmith)	Closed	1975	12.50	50-60
1976	Gunsmith	Closed	1976	13.50	50-60
1977	Potter	Closed	1977	15.00	50-60
1978	Wheelwright	Closed	1978	15.00	50-60

*Quotes have been rounded up to nearest dollar

Column 1

YEAR ISSUE		EDITION LIMIT	YEAR RETD.	ISSUE PRICE	*QUOTE U.S.$
1979	Cabinetmaker	Closed	1979	15.00	50-60
1980	Tanner	Closed	1980	16.50	50-60
1981	Housewright	Closed	1981	17.50	50-60

Artist Series - Various

1982	After The Snow (3 1/4") - D. Johnson	15,000	1982	14.50	15
1983	Winter Chapel (3 1/4") - D. Johnson	15,000	1984	15.00	15
1985	Flying Geese (3 1/4") - D. Johnson	15,000	1985	15.00	15
1986	The Hummingbird (3 1/4") - D. Johnson	15,000	1986	15.00	15
1987	Out in the Country (3 1/4") - L. Everson	15,000	1987	15.00	15
1988	Serenity (3 1/4") - F. Burton	5,000	1988	16.50	17
1989	Househunting (3 1/4") - D. Barbour	5,000	1989	16.50	17

Childhood Treasurers Series - Various

1983	Teddy Bear (3 1/4") - D. Johnson	15,000	1983	15.00	15
1984	Hobby Horse (3 1/4") - L. Everson	15,000	1984	15.00	15
1985	Clown (3 1/4") - L. Everson	15,000	1985	17.50	18
1986	Playful Kitten (3 1/4") - L. Everson	15,000	1986	15.00	15
1987	Frisky Pup (3 1/4") - D. Barbour	15,000	1987	15.00	15
1988	Castles in the Air (3 1/4") - D. Barbour	5,000	1988	16.50	17
1989	A Child's Cuddly Friend (3 1/4") - D. Johnson	5,000	1989	16.50	17

Christmas - Various

1979	Nature's Christmas - K. Cunningham	Yr.Iss.	1979	35.00	35
1980	Going Home - D. Johnson	Yr.Iss.	1980	38.50	39
1981	All Is Calm - D. Johnson	Yr.Iss.	1981	42.50	43
1982	Country Christmas - R. Spindler	Yr.Iss.	1982	42.50	43
1983	Anticipation - D. Johnson	7,500	1983	45.00	45
1984	Expectation - D. Johnson	7,500	1984	50.00	50
1985	Heart's Desire - D. Johnson	7,500	1986	50.00	50
1987	Sharing The Spirit - L. Everson	Yr.Iss.	1987	50.00	50
1987	Cardinal in the Churchyard - D. Johnson	4,500	1987	39.50	40
1988	A Chickadee Ballet - D. Johnson	4,500	1988	39.50	40
1989	Downy Pecker - Chisled Song - D. Johnson	4,500	1989	39.50	40
1990	A Blue Bird in Snowfall - D. Johnson	4,500	1990	39.50	40
1990	Sleigh Ride - F. Burton	3,500	1990	45.00	45
1991	Christmas Eve - F. Burton	3,500	1991	45.00	45
1992	Family Tradition - F. Burton	3,500	1992	49.00	49
1993	Family Holiday - F. Burton	3,500	1993	49.00	49
1994	Silent Night - F. Burton	1,500	1994	65.00	65
1995	Our Home Is Blessed - F. Burton	1,500	1995	65.00	65

Christmas In America - Fenton

1970	Little Brown Church in the Vale, Bradford, IA, Blue Satin	Closed	1970	12.50	15
1970	Little Brown Church in the Vale, Bradford, IA, Carnival	Closed	1970	12.50	15
1970	Little Brown Church in the Vale, Bradford, IA, White Satin	Closed	1970	12.50	15
1971	The Old Brick Church, Isle of Wight County, VA, Blue Satin	Closed	1971	12.50	15
1971	The Old Brick Church, Isle of Wight County, VA, Carnival	Closed	1971	12.50	15
1971	The Old Brick Church, Isle of Wight County, VA, White Satin	Closed	1971	12.50	15
1972	The Two Horned Church, Marietta, OH, Blue Satin	Closed	1972	12.50	15
1972	The Two Horned Church, Marietta, OH, Carnival	Closed	1972	12.50	15
1972	The Two Horned Church, Marietta, OH, White Satin	Closed	1972	12.50	15
1973	St. Mary's in the Mountain, Virginia City, NV, Blue Satin	Closed	1973	12.50	15
1973	St. Mary's in the Mountain, Virginia City, NV, Carnival	Closed	1973	12.50	15
1973	St. Mary's in the Mountain, Virginia City, NV, White Satin	Closed	1973	12.50	15
1974	The Nation's Church, Philadelphia, PA, Blue Satin	Closed	1974	13.50	15
1974	The Nation's Church, Philadelphia, PA, Carnival	Closed	1974	13.50	15
1974	The Nation's Church, Philadelphia, PA, White Satin	Closed	1974	13.50	15
1975	Birthplace of Liberty, Richmond, VA, Blue Satin	Closed	1975	13.50	15
1975	Birthplace of Liberty, Richmond, VA, Carnival	Closed	1975	13.50	15
1975	Birthplace of Liberty, Richmond, VA, White Satin	Closed	1975	13.50	15
1976	The Old North Church, Boston, MA, Blue Satin	Closed	1976	15.00	15
1976	The Old North Church, Boston, MA, Carnival	Closed	1976	15.00	15
1976	The Old North Church, Boston, MA, White Satin	Closed	1976	15.00	15
1977	San Carlos Borromeo de Carmelo, Carmel, CA, Blue Satin	Closed	1977	15.00	15
1977	San Carlos Borromeo de Carmelo, Carmel, CA, Carnival	Closed	1977	15.00	15
1977	San Carlos Borromeo de Carmelo, Carmel, CA, White Satin	Closed	1977	15.00	15
1978	The Church of Holy Trinity, Philadelphia, PA, Blue Satin	Closed	1978	15.00	15
1978	The Church of Holy Trinity, Philadelphia, PA, Carnival	Closed	1978	15.00	15
1978	The Church of Holy Trinity, Philadelphia, PA, White Satin	Closed	1978	15.00	15

Column 2

YEAR ISSUE		EDITION LIMIT	YEAR RETD.	ISSUE PRICE	*QUOTE U.S.$
1979	San Jose Y Miguel de Aguayo, San Antonio, TX, Blue Satin	Closed	1979	15.00	15
1979	San Jose Y Miguel de Aguayo, San Antonio, TX, Carnival	Closed	1979	15.00	15
1979	San Jose Y Miguel de Aguayo, San Antonio, TX, White Satin	Closed	1979	15.00	15
1980	Christ Church, Alexandria, VA, Blue Satin	Closed	1980	16.50	17
1980	Christ Church, Alexandria, VA, Carnival	Closed	1980	16.50	17
1980	Christ Church, Alexandria, VA, White Satin	Closed	1980	16.50	17
1981	San Xavier Del Bac, Tucson, AZ, Blue Satin	Closed	1981	18.50	19
1981	San Xavier Del Bac, Tucson, AZ, Carnival	Closed	1981	18.50	19
1981	San Xavier Del Bac, Tucson, AZ, White Satin	Closed	1981	18.50	19
1981	San Xavier Del Bac, Tucson, AZ, Florentine	Closed	1981	25.00	25

Designer Series - Various

1983	Lighthouse Point - M. Dickinson	1,000	1983	65.00	65
1983	Down Home - G. Finn	1,000	1983	65.00	65
1984	Smoke 'N Cinders - M. Dickinson	1,250	1984	65.00	65
1984	Majestic Flight - B. Cumberledge	1,250	1984	65.00	65
1985	In Season - M. Dickinson	1,250	1985	65.00	65
1985	Nature's Grace - B. Cumberland	1,250	1985	65.00	65
1985	Statue of Liberty - S. Bryan	1,250	1985	65.00	65
1986	Statue of Liberty - S. Bryan	1,250	1986	65.00	65

Easter Series - M. Reynolds

| 1995 | Covered Hen & Egg | 950 | 1995 | 95.00 | 95 |

Mary Gregory - M. Reynolds

| 1994 | Plate w/stand, 9" | Closed | 1994 | 65.00 | 65 |
| 1995 | Plate w/stand, 9" | Closed | 1995 | 65.00 | 65 |

Mother's Day Series - Fenton, unless otherwise noted

1971	Madonna w/Sleeping Child, Carnival	Closed	1971	10.75	15
1971	Madonna w/Sleeping Child, Blue Satin	Closed	1971	10.75	15
1972	Madonna of the Goldfinch, Carnival	Closed	1972	12.50	15
1972	Madonna of the Goldfinch, Blue Satin	Closed	1972	12.50	15
1972	Madonna of the Goldfinch, White Satin	Closed	1972	12.50	15
1973	The Small Cowper Madonna, Carnival	Closed	1973	12.50	15
1973	The Small Cowper Madonna, Blue Satin	Closed	1973	12.50	15
1973	The Small Cowper Madonna, White Satin	Closed	1973	12.50	15
1974	Madonna of the Grotto, Carnival	Closed	1974	13.50	15
1974	Madonna of the Grotto, Blue Satin	Closed	1974	13.50	15
1974	Madonna of the Grotto, White Satin	Closed	1974	13.50	15
1975	Taddei Madonna, Blue Satin	Closed	1975	13.50	15
1975	Taddei Madonna, Carnival	Closed	1975	13.50	15
1975	Taddei Madonna, White Satin	Closed	1975	13.50	15
1976	The Holly Night, Cardinal	Closed	1976	13.50	15
1976	The Holly Night, Blue Satin	Closed	1976	13.50	15
1976	The Holly Night, White Satin	Closed	1976	13.50	15
1977	Madonna & Child w/Pomegrantate, Carnival	Closed	1977	15.00	15
1977	Madonna & Child w/Pomegrantate, Blue Satin	Closed	1977	15.00	15
1977	Madonna & Child w/Pomegrantate, White Satin	Closed	1977	15.00	15
1978	The Madonnina, Cardinal	Closed	1978	15.00	15
1978	The Madonnina, Blue Satin	Closed	1978	15.00	15
1978	The Madonnina, White Satin	Closed	1978	15.00	15
1979	Madonna of the Rose Hedge, Carnival	Closed	1979	15.00	15
1979	Madonna of the Rose Hedge, Blue Satin	Closed	1979	15.00	15
1979	Madonna of the Rose Hedge, White Satin	Closed	1979	15.00	15
1979	Madonna of the Rose Hedge, Ruby Carnival	Closed	1979	35.00	35
1980	New Born - L. Everson	Closed	1980	28.50	29
1981	Gentle Fawn - L. Everson	Closed	1981	32.50	33
1982	Nature's Awakening - L. Everson	Closed	1982	35.00	35
1983	Where's Mom - L. Everson	Closed	1983	35.00	35
1984	Precious Panda - L. Everson	Closed	1984	35.00	35
1985	Mother's Little Lamb - L. Everson	Closed	1985	35.00	35
1990	Mother Swan - L. Everson	Closed	1990	45.00	50
1991	Mother's Watchful Eye - M. Reynolds	Closed	1991	45.00	50
1992	Let's Play With Mom - M. Reynolds	Closed	1992	49.50	50
1993	Mother Deer - M. Reynolds	Closed	1993	49.50	50
1994	Loving Puppy - M. Reynolds	Closed	1994	49.50	50

Flambro Imports

Emmett Kelly Jr. Plates - Various

1983	Why Me? Plate I - C. Kelly	10,000		40.00	450
1984	Balloons For Sale Plate II - C. Kelly	10,000		40.00	350
1985	Big Business Plate III - C. Kelly	10,000		40.00	350
1986	And God Bless America IV - C. Kelly	10,000		40.00	325
1988	Tis the Season - D. Rust	10,000		50.00	125-150
1989	Looking Back - 65th Birthday - D. Rust	6,500		50.00	125-150

Column 3

YEAR ISSUE		EDITION LIMIT	YEAR RETD.	ISSUE PRICE	*QUOTE U.S.$
1991	Winter - D. Rust	10,000		30.00	30
1992	Spring - D. Rust	10,000		30.00	30
1992	Summer - D. Rust	10,000		30.00	30
1992	Autumn - D. Rust	10,000		30.00	30
1993	Santa's Stowaway - D. Rust	10,000		30.00	30
1994	70th Birthday Commemorative - D. Rust	5,000		30.00	30
1995	All Wrapped Up in Christmas - Undis.	5,000		30.00	30

Fountainhead

As Free As The Wind - M. Fernandez

| 1989 | As Free As The Wind | Unkn. | | 295.00 | 300-600 |

The Wings of Freedom - M. Fernandez

| 1985 | Courtship Flight | 2,500 | | 250.00 | 1300-1500 |
| 1986 | Wings of Freedom | 2,500 | | 250.00 | 1300-1500 |

Ganz

Watching Over You Collection - C. Thammavongsa

| 1996 | Wings of the Wind | Open | | 40.00 | 40 |

Gartlan USA

Club Gift

1989	Pete Rose, Plate (8 1/2") - B. Forbes	Closed	1990	Gift	125-150
1990	Al Barlick, Plate (8 1/2") - M. Taylor	Closed	1991	Gift	110
1991	Joe Montana (8 1/2") - M. Taylor	Closed	1992	Gift	125-175
1992	Ken Griffey Jr., Plate (8 1/2") - M. Taylor	Closed	1993	Gift	70-90
1993	Gordie Howe, Plate (8 1/2") - M. Taylor	Closed	1994	Gift	50-70
1994	Shaquille O'Neal, Plate (8 1/2") - M. Taylor	Closed	1995	Gift	65-100

Bob Cousy - M. Taylor

1994	Signed Plate (10 1/4")	950	1995	175.00	200
1994	Plate (8 1/2")	10,000		30.00	30
1994	Plate (3 1/4")	Open		15.00	15

Brett & Bobby Hull - M. Taylor

1992	Hockey's Golden Boys (10 1/4") signed by both	950	1995	250.00	475
1992	Hockey's Golden Boys (8 1/2")	10,000		30.00	30
1992	Hockey's Golden Boys (3 1/4")	Open		15.00	15

Carl Yastrzemski - M. Taylor

1993	Signed Plate (10 1/4")	950	1995	175.00	225
1993	Plate (8 1/2")	10,000		30.00	30
1993	Plate (3 1/4")	Open		15.00	15

Carlton Fisk - M. Taylor

1993	Signed Plate (10 1/4")	950	1995	175.00	250
1993	Plate (8 1/2")	5,000		30.00	30
1993	Plate (3 1/4")	Open		15.00	15

Darryl Strawberry - M. Taylor

1991	Signed Plate (10 1/4")	2,500	1995	150.00	150
1991	Plate (8 1/2")	10,000	1995	40.00	40
1991	Plate (3 1/4")	Retrd.	1995	15.00	15

George Brett Gold Crown Collection - J. Martin

| 1986 | George Brett "Baseball's All Star" (3 1/4") | Open | | 12.95 | 15-20 |
| 1986 | George Brett "Baseball's All Star" (10 1/4") signed | 2,000 | 1988 | 100.00 | 200 |

Gordie Howe - M. Taylor

1993	Signed Plate (10 1/4")	2,358	1995	150.00	250
1993	Signed Plate (8 1/2")	10,000		30.00	30
1993	Signed Plate (3 1/4")	Open		15.00	15

Joe Montana - M. Taylor

1991	Signed Plate (10 1/4")	2,250	1991	125.00	335-395
1991	Signed Plate (10 1/4") A/P	250	1991	195.00	400-450
1991	Plate (8 1/2")	10,000		30.00	50
1991	Plate (3 1/4")	Open		15.00	15

John Wooden - M. Taylor

1990	Signed Plate (10 1/4")	1,975	1995	150.00	150
1990	Plate (8 1/2")	10,000		30.00	30
1990	Plate (3 1/4")	Retrd.	1995	15.00	15

Johnny Bench - M. Taylor

| 1989 | Signed Plate (10 1/4") | 1,989 | 1991 | 100.00 | 200 |
| 1989 | Plate (3 1/4") | Open | | 15.00 | 15 |

Kareem Abdul-Jabbar Sky-Hook Collection - M. Taylor

| 1989 | Kareem Abdul-Jabbar "Path of Glory" (10 1/4"), signed | 1,989 | 1991 | 100.00 | 225-295 |
| 1989 | Plate (3 1/4") | Closed | 1993 | 16.00 | 30 |

Ken Griffey Jr. - M. Taylor

1992	Signed Plate (10 1/4")	1,989	1995	150.00	350
1992	Plate (8 1/2")	10,000		30.00	30
1992	Plate (3 1/4")	Open		15.00	15

PLATES

Kristi Yamaguchi - M. Taylor

YEAR	ISSUE	EDITION LIMIT	YEAR RETD.	ISSUE PRICE	*QUOTE U.S. $
1993	Signed Plate (10 1/4")	950	1995	150.00	200
1993	Plate (8 1/2")	5,000		30.00	30
1993	Plate (3 1/4")	Open		15.00	15

Leave It To Beaver - M. Taylor

YEAR	ISSUE	EDITION LIMIT	YEAR RETD.	ISSUE PRICE	*QUOTE U.S. $
1995	Jerry Mathers, (10 1/4") signed	1,963		125.00	125
1996	Jerry Mathers, (10 1/4") A/P signed	234		175.00	175
1995	Jerry Mathers, (8 1/4")	10,000		39.95	40
1995	Jerry Mathers, (3 1/4") miniature	Open		14.95	15

Luis Aparicio - M. Taylor

YEAR	ISSUE	EDITION LIMIT	YEAR RETD.	ISSUE PRICE	*QUOTE U.S. $
1991	Signed Plate (10 1/4")	1,984	1995	150.00	200
1991	Plate (8 1/2")	10,000		30.00	30
1991	Plate (3 1/4")	Open		15.00	15

Magic Johnson Gold Rim Collection - R. Winslow

YEAR	ISSUE	EDITION LIMIT	YEAR RETD.	ISSUE PRICE	*QUOTE U.S. $
1987	Magic Johnson "The Magic Show" (10 1/4"), signed	1,987	1988	100.00	495-595
1987	Magic Johnson "The Magic Show" (3 1/4")	Closed	1993	14.50	25-35

Mike Schmidt "500th" Home Run Edition - C. Paluso

YEAR	ISSUE	EDITION LIMIT	YEAR RETD.	ISSUE PRICE	*QUOTE U.S. $
1987	Mike Schmidt "Power at the Plate" (10 1/4"), signed	1,987	1988	100.00	395-495
1987	Mike Schmidt "Power at the Plate" (3 1/4")	Open		14.50	19
1987	Mike Schmidt A/P	56	1988	150.00	150

Pete Rose Diamond Collection - Forbes

YEAR	ISSUE	EDITION LIMIT	YEAR RETD.	ISSUE PRICE	*QUOTE U.S. $
1988	Pete Rose "The Reigning Legend" (10 1/4"), signed	950	1989	195.00	250-300
1988	Pete Rose "The Reigning Legend" (10 1/4"), signed A/P	50	1989	300.00	395
1988	Pete Rose "The Reigning Legend"(3 1/4")	Open		14.50	15

Pete Rose Platinum Edition - T. Sizemore

YEAR	ISSUE	EDITION LIMIT	YEAR RETD.	ISSUE PRICE	*QUOTE U.S. $
1985	Pete Rose "The Best of Baseball"(3 1/4")	Open		12.95	15-20
1985	Pete Rose "The Best of Baseball"(10 1/4")	4,192	1988	100.00	385

Ringo Starr - M. Taylor

YEAR	ISSUE	EDITION LIMIT	YEAR RETD.	ISSUE PRICE	*QUOTE U.S. $
1996	Ringo Starr, (10 1/4") signed	1,000		225.00	225
1996	Ringo Starr, (10 1/4") A/P signed	250		400.00	400
1996	Ringo Starr, (8 1/4")	10,000		29.95	30
1996	Ringo Starr, (3 1/4") miniature	Open		14.95	15

Rod Carew - M. Taylor

YEAR	ISSUE	EDITION LIMIT	YEAR RETD.	ISSUE PRICE	*QUOTE U.S. $
1992	Signed Plate (10 1/4")	950	1995	150.00	175
1992	Plate (8 1/2")	10,000		30.00	30
1992	Plate (3 1/4")	Open		15.00	15

Roger Staubach Sterling Collection - C. Soileau

YEAR	ISSUE	EDITION LIMIT	YEAR RETD.	ISSUE PRICE	*QUOTE U.S. $
1987	Roger Staubach (3 1/4" diameter)	Open		12.95	15-20
1987	Roger Staubach (10 1/4" diameter) signed	1,979	1990	100.00	125-195

Sam Sneed - M. Taylor

YEAR	ISSUE	EDITION LIMIT	YEAR RETD.	ISSUE PRICE	*QUOTE U.S. $
1994	Signed Plate (10 1/4")	950	1995	100.00	200
1994	Plate (8 1/2")	5,000		30.00	30
1994	Plate (3 1/4")	Open		15.00	15

Tom Seaver - M. Taylor

YEAR	ISSUE	EDITION LIMIT	YEAR RETD.	ISSUE PRICE	*QUOTE U.S. $
1993	Signed Plate (10 1/4")	1,992	1995	150.00	300
1993	Signed Plate (8 1/2")	10,000		30.00	30
1993	Signed Plate (3 1/4")	Open		15.00	15

Troy Aikman - M. Taylor

YEAR	ISSUE	EDITION LIMIT	YEAR RETD.	ISSUE PRICE	*QUOTE U.S. $
1994	Signed Plate (10 1/4")	1,993	1995	225.00	225
1994	Plate (8 1/2")	10,000		30.00	30
1994	Plate (3 1/4")	Open		14.95	15

Wayne Gretzky - M. Taylor

YEAR	ISSUE	EDITION LIMIT	YEAR RETD.	ISSUE PRICE	*QUOTE U.S. $
1989	Plate (10 1/4"), signed by Gretzky and Howe	1,851	1989	225.00	225-350
1989	Plate (10 1/4") A/P, signed by Gretzky and Howe	300	1989	300.00	450-575
1989	Plate (8 1/2")	10,000		45.00	45-50
1989	Plate (3 1/4")	Open		15.00	15

Whitey Ford - M. Taylor

YEAR	ISSUE	EDITION LIMIT	YEAR RETD.	ISSUE PRICE	*QUOTE U.S. $
1991	Signed Plate (10 1/4")	2,360	1995	150.00	150
1991	Plate (8 1/2")	10,000	1995	30.00	30
1991	Plate (3 1/4")	Retrd.	1995	15.00	15

Yogi Berra - M. Taylor

YEAR	ISSUE	EDITION LIMIT	YEAR RETD.	ISSUE PRICE	*QUOTE U.S. $
1991	Signed Plate (10 1/4")	2,150	1995	150.00	175
1991	Plate (8 1/2")	10,000		30.00	30
1991	Plate (3 1/4")	Open		15.00	15

Georgetown Collection, Inc.

Children of the Great Spirit - C. Theroux

YEAR	ISSUE	EDITION LIMIT	YEAR RETD.	ISSUE PRICE	*QUOTE U.S. $
1993	Buffalo Child	35-day		29.95	30
1993	Winter Baby	35-day		29.95	30

Goebel/M.I. Hummel

M.I. Hummel Annual Figural Christmas Plates - M.I. Hummel

YEAR	ISSUE	EDITION LIMIT	YEAR RETD.	ISSUE PRICE	*QUOTE U.S. $
1995	Festival Harmony w/Flute 693	Open		125.00	125
1996	Christmas Song 692	Open		130.00	130

M.I. Hummel Club Exclusive-Celebration - M.I. Hummel

YEAR	ISSUE	EDITION LIMIT	YEAR RETD.	ISSUE PRICE	*QUOTE U.S. $
1986	Valentine Gift (Hum 738)	Closed		90.00	90-120
1987	Valentine Joy (Hum 737)	Closed		98.00	90-120
1988	Daisies Don't Tell (Hum 736)	Closed		115.00	115-130
1989	It's Cold (Hum 735)	Closed		120.00	120-150

M.I. Hummel Collectibles Anniversary Plates - M.I. Hummel

YEAR	ISSUE	EDITION LIMIT	YEAR RETD.	ISSUE PRICE	*QUOTE U.S. $
1975	Stormy Weather 280	Closed		100.00	75-120
1980	Spring Dance 281	Closed		225.00	50-100
1985	Auf Wiedersehen 282	Closed		225.00	250

M.I. Hummel Collectibles-Annual Plates - M.I. Hummel

YEAR	ISSUE	EDITION LIMIT	YEAR RETD.	ISSUE PRICE	*QUOTE U.S. $
1971	Heavenly Angel 264	Closed		25.00	600-875
1972	Hear Ye, Hear Ye 265	Closed		30.00	40-80
1973	Glober Trotter 266	Closed		32.50	120-200
1974	Goose Girl 267	Closed		40.00	78
1975	Ride into Christmas 268	Closed		50.00	80
1976	Apple Tree Girl 269	Closed		50.00	80-90
1977	Apple Tree Boy 270	Closed		52.50	80-108
1978	Happy Pastime 271	Closed		65.00	83
1979	Singing Lesson 272	Closed		90.00	100
1980	School Girl 273	Closed		100.00	100
1981	Umbrella Boy 274	Closed		100.00	100
1982	Umbrella Girl 275	Closed		100.00	150-175
1983	The Postman 276	Closed		108.00	200-250
1984	Little Helper 277	Closed		108.00	108
1985	Chick Girl 278	Closed		110.00	110
1986	Playmates 279	Closed		125.00	165
1987	Feeding Time 283	Closed		135.00	395
1988	Little Goat Herder 284	Closed		145.00	100-120
1989	Farm Boy 285	Closed		160.00	130-150
1990	Shepherd's Boy 286	Closed		170.00	250
1991	Just Resting 287	Closed		196.00	125-170
1992	Wayside Harmony 288	Closed		210.00	270
1993	Doll Bath 289	Closed		210.00	350
1994	Doctor 290	Closed		225.00	250
1995	Come Back Soon 291	Yr.Iss.		250.00	250

M.I. Hummel Four Seasons - M.I. Hummel

YEAR	ISSUE	EDITION LIMIT	YEAR RETD.	ISSUE PRICE	*QUOTE U.S. $
1996	Winter Melody 296	Yr.Iss.		195.00	195

M.I. Hummel-Friends Forever - M.I. Hummel

YEAR	ISSUE	EDITION LIMIT	YEAR RETD.	ISSUE PRICE	*QUOTE U.S. $
1992	Meditation 292	Open		180.00	195
1993	For Father 293	Open		195.00	195
1994	Sweet Greetings 294	Open		205.00	205
1995	Surprise 295	Open		210.00	210

M.I. Hummel-Little Music Makers - M.I. Hummel

YEAR	ISSUE	EDITION LIMIT	YEAR RETD.	ISSUE PRICE	*QUOTE U.S. $
1984	Little Fiddler 744	Closed		30.00	75
1985	Serenade 741	Closed		30.00	30-70
1986	Soloist 743	Closed		35.00	35-70
1987	Band Leader 742	Closed		40.00	40-70

M.I. Hummel-The Little Homemakers - M.I. Hummel

YEAR	ISSUE	EDITION LIMIT	YEAR RETD.	ISSUE PRICE	*QUOTE U.S. $
1988	Little Sweeper (Hum 745)	Closed		45.00	45
1989	Wash Day (Hum 746)	Closed		50.00	50
1990	A Stitch in Time (Hum 747)	Closed		50.00	50
1991	Chicken Licken (Hum 748)	Closed		70.00	70

Gorham

(Four Seasons) A Boy and His Dog Plates - N. Rockwell

YEAR	ISSUE	EDITION LIMIT	YEAR RETD.	ISSUE PRICE	*QUOTE U.S. $
1971	Boy Meets His Dog	Annual	1971	50.00	225
1971	Adventures Between Adventures	Annual	1971	Set	Set
1971	The Mysterious Malady	Annual	1971	Set	Set
1971	Pride of Parenthood	Annual	1971	Set	Set

(Four Seasons) A Helping Hand Plates - N. Rockwell

YEAR	ISSUE	EDITION LIMIT	YEAR RETD.	ISSUE PRICE	*QUOTE U.S. $
1979	Year End Court	Annual	1979	100.00	100-125
1979	Closed for Business	Annual	1979	Set	Set
1979	Swatter's Rights	Annual	1979	Set	Set
1979	Coal Season's Coming	Annual	1979	Set	Set

(Four Seasons) Dad's Boys Plates - N. Rockwell

YEAR	ISSUE	EDITION LIMIT	YEAR RETD.	ISSUE PRICE	*QUOTE U.S. $
1980	Ski Skills	Annual	1980	135.00	90-135
1980	In His Spirits	Annual	1980	Set	Set
1980	Trout Dinner	Annual	1980	Set	Set
1980	Careful Aim	Annual	1980	Set	Set

(Four Seasons) Four Ages of Love - N. Rockwell

YEAR	ISSUE	EDITION LIMIT	YEAR RETD.	ISSUE PRICE	*QUOTE U.S. $
1973	Gaily Sharing Vintage Time	Annual	1973	60.00	165
1973	Flowers in Tender Bloom	Annual	1973	Set	Set
1973	Sweet Song So Young	Annual	1973	Set	Set
1973	Fondly We Do Remember	Annual	1973	Set	Set

(Four Seasons) Going on Sixteen Plates - N. Rockwell

YEAR	ISSUE	EDITION LIMIT	YEAR RETD.	ISSUE PRICE	*QUOTE U.S. $
1977	Chilling Chore	Annual	1977	75.00	95
1977	Sweet Serenade	Annual	1977	Set	Set
1977	Shear Agony	Annual	1977	Set	Set
1977	Pilgrimage	Annual	1977	Set	Set

(Four Seasons) Grand Pals Four Plates - N. Rockwell

YEAR	ISSUE	EDITION LIMIT	YEAR RETD.	ISSUE PRICE	*QUOTE U.S. $
1976	Snow Sculpturing	Annual	1976	70.00	120
1976	Soaring Spirits	Annual	1976	Set	Set
1976	Fish Finders	Annual	1976	Set	Set
1976	Ghostly Gourds	Annual	1976	Set	Set

(Four Seasons) Grandpa and Me Plates - N. Rockwell

YEAR	ISSUE	EDITION LIMIT	YEAR RETD.	ISSUE PRICE	*QUOTE U.S. $
1974	Gay Blades	Annual	1974	60.00	90
1974	Day Dreamers	Annual	1974	Set	Set
1974	Goin' Fishing	Annual	1974	Set	Set
1974	Pensive Pals	Annual	1974	Set	Set

(Four Seasons) Landscapes - N. Rockwell

YEAR	ISSUE	EDITION LIMIT	YEAR RETD.	ISSUE PRICE	*QUOTE U.S. $
1980	Summer Respite	Annual	1980	45.00	80
1981	Autumn Reflection	Annual	1981	45.00	65
1982	Winter Delight	Annual	1982	50.00	63
1983	Spring Recess	Annual	1983	60.00	60

(Four Seasons) Life with Father Plates - N. Rockwell

YEAR	ISSUE	EDITION LIMIT	YEAR RETD.	ISSUE PRICE	*QUOTE U.S. $
1982	Big Decision	Annual	1982	100.00	100
1982	Blasting Out	Annual	1982	Set	Set
1982	Cheering the Champs	Annual	1982	Set	Set
1982	A Tough One	Annual	1982	Set	Set

(Four Seasons) Me and My Pals Plates - N. Rockwell

YEAR	ISSUE	EDITION LIMIT	YEAR RETD.	ISSUE PRICE	*QUOTE U.S. $
1975	A Lickin' Good Bath	Annual	1975	70.00	115
1975	Young Man's Fancy	Annual	1975	Set	Set
1975	Fisherman's Paradise	Annual	1975	Set	Set
1975	Disastrous Daring	Annual	1975	Set	Set

(Four Seasons) Old Buddies Plates - N. Rockwell

YEAR	ISSUE	EDITION LIMIT	YEAR RETD.	ISSUE PRICE	*QUOTE U.S. $
1983	Shared Success	Annual	1983	115.00	115
1983	Endless Debate	Annual	1983	Set	Set
1983	Hasty Retreat	Annual	1983	Set	Set
1983	Final Speech	Annual	1983	Set	Set

(Four Seasons) Old Timers Plates - N. Rockwell

YEAR	ISSUE	EDITION LIMIT	YEAR RETD.	ISSUE PRICE	*QUOTE U.S. $
1981	Canine Solo	Annual	1981	100.00	100
1981	Sweet Surprise	Annual	1981	Set	Set
1981	Lazy Days	Annual	1981	Set	Set
1981	Fancy Footwork	Annual	1981	Set	Set

(Four Seasons) Tender Years Plates - N. Rockwell

YEAR	ISSUE	EDITION LIMIT	YEAR RETD.	ISSUE PRICE	*QUOTE U.S. $
1978	New Year Look	Annual	1978	100.00	100-125
1978	Spring Tonic	Annual	1978	Set	Set
1978	Cool Aid	Annual	1978	Set	Set
1978	Chilly Reception	Annual	1978	Set	Set

(Four Seasons) Young Love Plates - N. Rockwell

YEAR	ISSUE	EDITION LIMIT	YEAR RETD.	ISSUE PRICE	*QUOTE U.S. $
1972	Downhill Daring	Annual	1972	60.00	100-180
1972	Beguiling Buttercup	Annual	1972	Set	Set
1972	Flying High	Annual	1972	Set	Set
1972	A Scholarly Pace	Annual	1972	Set	Set

American Artist - R. Donnelly

YEAR	ISSUE	EDITION LIMIT	YEAR RETD.	ISSUE PRICE	*QUOTE U.S. $
1976	Apache Mother & Child	9,800	1980	25.00	56

Barrymore - Barrymore

YEAR	ISSUE	EDITION LIMIT	YEAR RETD.	ISSUE PRICE	*QUOTE U.S. $
1971	Quiet Waters	15,000	1980	25.00	25
1972	San Pedro Harbor	15,000	1980	25.00	25
1972	Nantucket, Sterling	1,000	1972	100.00	100
1972	Little Boatyard, Sterling	1,000	1972	100.00	145

Bas Relief - N. Rockwell

YEAR	ISSUE	EDITION LIMIT	YEAR RETD.	ISSUE PRICE	*QUOTE U.S. $
1981	Sweet Song So Young	Undis.	1984	100.00	100
1981	Beguiling Buttercup	Undis.	1984	62.50	70
1982	Flowers in Tender Bloom	Undis.	1984	100.00	100
1982	Flying High	Undis.	1984	62.50	65

Boy Scout Plates - N. Rockwell

YEAR	ISSUE	EDITION LIMIT	YEAR RETD.	ISSUE PRICE	*QUOTE U.S. $
1975	Our Heritage	18,500	1980	19.50	40
1976	A Scout is Loyal	18,500	1990	19.50	55
1977	The Scoutmaster	18,500	1990	19.50	60
1977	A Good Sign	18,500	1990	19.50	50
1978	Pointing the Way	18,500	1990	19.50	50
1978	Campfire Story	18,500	1990	19.50	25
1980	Beyond the Easel	18,500	1990	45.00	45

Charles Russell - C. Russell

YEAR	ISSUE	EDITION LIMIT	YEAR RETD.	ISSUE PRICE	*QUOTE U.S. $
1980	In Without Knocking	9,800	1990	38.00	75
1981	Bronc to Breakfast	9,800	1990	38.00	50-75
1982	When Ignorance is Bliss	9,800	1990	45.00	75-115
1983	Cowboy Life	9,800	1990	45.00	100

China Bicentennial - Gorham

YEAR	ISSUE	EDITION LIMIT	YEAR RETD.	ISSUE PRICE	*QUOTE U.S. $
1972	1776 Plate	18,500	1980	17.50	35
1976	1776 Bicentennial	8,000	1980	17.50	35

Christmas - N. Rockwell

YEAR	ISSUE	EDITION LIMIT	YEAR RETD.	ISSUE PRICE	*QUOTE U.S. $
1974	Tiny Tim	Annual	1974	12.50	30
1975	Good Deeds	Annual	1975	17.50	20-30
1976	Christmas Trio	Annual	1976	19.50	30
1977	Yuletide Reckoning	Annual	1977	19.50	45
1978	Planning Christmas Visit	Annual	1978	24.50	30
1979	Santa's Helpers	Annual	1979	24.50	25
1980	Letter to Santa	Annual	1980	27.50	32
1981	Santa Plans His Visit	Annual	1981	29.50	30
1982	Jolly Coachman	Annual	1982	29.50	30
1983	Christmas Dancers	Annual	1983	29.50	35

*Quotes have been rounded up to nearest dollar

PLATES

YEAR ISSUE	EDITION LIMIT	YEAR RETD.	ISSUE PRICE	*QUOTE U.S.$
1984 Christmas Medley	17,500	1984	29.95	30
1985 Home For The Holidays	17,500	1985	29.95	30
1986 Merry Christmas Grandma	17,500	1986	29.95	65
1987 The Homecoming	17,500	1987	35.00	35
1988 Discovery	17,500	1988	37.50	45

Christmas/Children's Television Workshop - Unknown

1981 Sesame Street Christmas	Annual	1981	17.50	18
1982 Sesame Street Christmas	Annual	1982	17.50	18
1983 Sesame Street Christmas	Annual	1983	19.50	20

Encounters, Survival and Celebrations - J. Clymer

1982 A Fine Welcome	7,500	1983	50.00	75
1983 Winter Trail	7,500	1984	50.00	125
1983 Alouette	7,500	1984	62.50	63
1983 The Trader	7,500	1984	62.50	63
1983 Winter Camp	7,500	1984	62.60	75
1983 The Trapper Takes a Wife	7,500	1984	62.50	63

Gallery of Masters - Various

1971 Man with a Gilt Helmet - Rembrandt	10,000	1975	50.00	50
1972 Self Portrait with Saskia - Rembrandt	10,000	1975	50.00	50
1973 The Honorable Mrs. Graham - Gainsborough	7,500	1975	50.00	50

Gorham Museum Doll Plates - Gorham

1984 Lydia	5,000	1984	29.00	125
1984 Belton Bebe	5,000	1984	29.00	55
1984 Christmas Lady	7,500	1984	32.50	33
1985 Lucille	5,000	1985	29.00	35
1985 Jumeau	5,000	1985	29.00	35

Julian Ritter - J. Ritter

1977 Christmas Visit	9,800	1977	24.50	29
1978 Valentine, Fluttering Heart	7,500	1978	45.00	45

Julian Ritter, Fall In Love - J. Ritter

1977 Enchantment	5,000	1977	100.00	100
1977 Frolic	5,000	1977	set	Set
1977 Gutsy Gal	5,000	1977	set	Set
1977 Lonely Chill	5,000	1977	set	Set

Julian Ritter, To Love a Clown - J. Ritter

1978 Awaited Reunion	5,000	1978	120.00	120
1978 Twosome Time	5,000	1978	120.00	120
1978 Showtime Beckons	5,000	1978	120.00	120
1978 Together in Memories	5,000	1978	120.00	120

Leyendecker Annual Christmas Plates - J. C. Leyendecker

1988 Christmas Hug	10,000	1988	37.50	50

Moppet Plates-Anniversary - Unknown

1976 Anniversary	20,000	1977	13.00	13

Moppet Plates-Christmas - Unknown

1973 Christmas	Annual	1973	10.00	35
1974 Christmas	Annual	1974	12.00	12
1975 Christmas	Annual	1975	13.00	13
1976 Christmas	Annual	1976	13.00	15
1977 Christmas	Annual	1977	13.00	14
1978 Christmas	Annual	1978	13.00	10
1979 Christmas	Annual	1979	12.00	12
1980 Christmas	Annual	1980	12.00	12
1981 Christmas	Annual	1981	12.00	12
1982 Christmas	Annual	1982	12.00	12
1983 Christmas	Annual	1983	12.00	12

Moppet Plates-Mother's Day - Unknown

1973 Mother's Day	Annual	1973	10.00	30
1974 Mother's Day	Annual	1974	12.00	20
1975 Mother's Day	Annual	1975	13.00	15
1976 Mother's Day	Annual	1976	13.00	15
1977 Mother's Day	Annual	1977	13.00	15
1978 Mother's Day	Annual	1978	10.00	10

Pastoral Symphony - B. Felder

1982 When I Was a Child	7,500	1983	42.50	50
1982 Gather the Children	7,500	1983	42.50	50
1984 Sugar and Spice	7,500	1985	42.50	50
XX He Loves Me	7,500	1985	42.50	50

Pewter Bicentennial - R. Pailthorpe

1971 Burning of the Gaspee	5,000	1971	35.00	35
1972 Boston Tea Party	5,000	1972	35.00	35

Presidential - N. Rockwell

1976 John F. Kennedy	9,800	1976	30.00	65
1976 Dwight D. Eisenhower	9,800	1976	30.00	35

Remington Western - F. Remington

1973 A New Year on the Cimarron	Annual	1973	25.00	35-50
1973 Aiding a Comrade	Annual	1973	25.00	30-125
1973 The Flight	Annual	1973	25.00	30-95
1973 The Fight for the Water Hole	Annual	1973	25.00	30-125
1975 Old Ramond	Annual	1975	20.00	35-60
1975 A Breed	Annual	1975	20.00	35-65
1976 Cavalry Officer	5,000	1976	37.50	60-75
1976 A Trapper	5,000	1976	37.50	60-75

Silver Bicentennial - Various

1972 1776 Plate - Gorham	500	1972	500.00	500
1972 Burning of the Gaspee - R. Pailthorpe	750	1972	500.00	500
1973 Boston Tea Party - R. Pailthorpe	750	1973	550.00	575

Single Release - N. Rockwell

1974 The Golden Rule	Annual	1974	12.50	30
1975 Ben Franklin	Annual	1975	19.50	35

Single Release - F. Quagon

1976 The Black Regiment 1778	7,500	1978	25.00	58

Single Release - N. Rockwell

1974 Weighing In	Annual	1974	12.50	80-99
1976 The Marriage License	Numbrd	1985	37.50	52-75
1978 Triple Self Portrait Memorial	Annual	1978	37.50	95
1980 The Annual Visit	Annual	1980	32.50	70
1981 Day in Life of Boy	Annual	1981	50.00	80
1981 Day in Life of Girl	Annual	1981	50.00	80-108

Time Machine Teddies Plates - B. Port

1986 Miss Emily, Bearing Up	5,000	1986	32.50	50
1987 Big Bear, The Toy Collector	5,000	1987	32.50	45
1988 Hunny Munny	5,000	1988	37.50	40

Vermeil Bicentennial - Gorham

1972 1776 Plate	250	1972	750.00	800

Hackett American

Sports - Various

1981 Reggie Jackson h/s - Paluso	Retrd.	N/A	100.00	1065
1983 Steve Garvey h/s - Paluso	Retrd.	N/A	100.00	150-250
1983 Nolan Ryan h/s - Paluso	Retrd.	N/A	100.00	825
1983 Tom Seaver h/s - Paluso	3,272	N/A	100.00	350
1984 Steve Carlton h/s - Paluso	Retrd.	N/A	100.00	275
1985 Willie Mays h/s - Paluso	Retrd.	N/A	125.00	350-445
1985 Whitey Ford h/s - Paluso	Retrd.	N/A	125.00	295
1985 Hank Aaron h/s - Paluso	Retrd.	N/A	125.00	350-445
1985 Sandy Koufax h/s - Paluso	1,000	N/A	125.00	300-500
1985 H. Killebrew d/s - Paluso	Retrd.	N/A	125.00	200-360
1985 E. Mathews d/s - Paluso	Retrd.	N/A	125.00	225-300
1986 T. Seaver 300 d/s - Paluso	1,200	N/A	125.00	250
1986 Roger Clemens d/s - Paluso	Retrd.	N/A	125.00	600-900
1986 Reggie Jackson d/s - Paluso	Retrd.	N/A	125.00	395
1986 Wally Joyner d/s - Paluso	Retrd.	N/A	125.00	295
1986 Don Sutton d/s (great events) - Paluso	300	N/A	125.00	250
XX Gary Carter d/s - Simon	Retrd.	N/A	125.00	175
1985 Dwight Gooden u/s - Simon	Retrd.	N/A	55.00	85
XX Arnold Palmer h/s - Alexander	Retrd.	N/A	125.00	225
XX Gary Player h/s - Alexander	Retrd.	N/A	125.00	350
1983 Reggie Jackson h/s - Alexander	Retrd.	N/A	125.00	695
1983 Reggie Jackson, proof - Alexander	Retrd.	N/A	250.00	1695
1986 Joe Montana d/s - Alexander	Retrd.	N/A	125.00	595

Hadley House

American Memories Series - T. Redlin

1987 Coming Home	9,500		85.00	85
1988 Lights of Home	9,500	1994	85.00	150
1989 Homeward Bound	9,500		85.00	85
1991 Family Traditions	9,500		85.00	85

Annual Christmas Series - T. Redlin

1991 Heading Home	9,500	1994	65.00	225
1992 Pleasures Of Winter	19,500		65.00	125
1993 Winter Wonderland	19,500		65.00	125
1994 Almost Home	19,500		65.00	125
1995 Sharing the Evening	45-day		29.95	30

Country Doctor Collection - T. Redlin

1995 Wednesday Afternoon	45-day		29.95	30
1995 Office Hours	45-day		29.95	30
1995 House Calls	45-day		29.95	30
1995 Morning Rounds	45-day		29.95	30

Glow Series - T. Redlin

1985 Evening Glow	5,000	1986	55.00	325-450
1985 Morning Glow	5,000	1986	55.00	150-250
1985 Twilight Glow	5,000	1988	55.00	125-150
1988 Afternoon Glow	5,000	1989	55.00	100

Lovers Collection - O. Franca

1992 Lovers	9,500		50.00	50

Navajo Visions Suite - O. Franca

1993 Navajo Fantasy	9,500		50.00	50
1993 Young Warrior	9,500		50.00	50

Navajo Woman Series - O. Franca

1990 Feathered Hair Ties	5,000	1994	50.00	50
1991 Navajo Summer	5,000		50.00	50
1992 Turquoise Necklace	5,000		50.00	50
1993 Pink Navajo	5,000		50.00	50

Retreat Series - T. Redlin

1987 Morning Retreat	9,500	1988	65.00	120
1987 Evening Retreat	9,500	1989	65.00	120
1988 Golden Retreat	9,500	1989	65.00	120
1989 Moonlight Retreat	9,500	1993	65.00	85

Seasons - T. Redlin

1994 Autumn Evening	45-day		29.95	30
1995 Spring Fever	45-day		29.95	30
1995 Summertime	45-day		29.95	30
1995 Wintertime	45-day		29.95	30

That Special Time - T. Redlin

1991 Evening Solitude	9,500	1994	65.00	95
1991 That Special Time	9,500	1993	65.00	95
1992 Aroma of Fall	9,500	1994	65.00	95
1993 Welcome To Paradise	9,500		65.00	65

Tranquility - O. Franca

1994 Blue Navajo	9,500		50.00	50
1994 Blue Tranquility	9,500		50.00	50
1994 Navajo Meditating	9,500		50.00	50
1995 Navajo Reflection	9,500		50.00	50

Wildlife Memories - T. Redlin

1994 Best Friends	19,500		65.00	65
1994 Comforts of Home	19,500		65.00	65
1994 Pure Contentment	19,500		65.00	65
1994 Sharing in the Solitude	19,500		65.00	65

Windows to the Wild - T. Redlin

1990 Master's Domain	9,500		65.00	65
1991 Winter Windbreak	9,500		65.00	65
1992 Evening Company	9,500		65.00	65
1994 Night Mapling	9,500		65.00	65

Hamilton Collection

All in a Day's Work - J. Lamb

1994 Where's the Fire?	28-day		29.50	30
1994 Lunch Break	28-day		29.50	30
1994 Puppy Patrol	28-day		29.50	30
1994 Decoy Delivery	28-day		29.50	30
1994 Budding Artist	28-day		29.50	30
1994 Garden Guards	28-day		29.50	30
1994 Saddling Up	28-day		29.50	30
1995 Taking the Lead	28-day		29.50	30

America's Greatest Sailing Ships - T. Freeman

1988 USS Constitution	14-day		29.50	40
1988 Great Republic	14-day		29.50	40
1988 America	14-day		29.50	45
1988 Charles W. Morgan	14-day		29.50	40
1988 Eagle	14-day		29.50	48
1988 Bonhomme Richard	14-day		29.50	40
1988 Gertrude L. Thebaud	14-day		29.50	45
1988 Enterprise	14-day		29.50	36

The American Civil War - D. Prechtel

1990 General Robert E. Lee	14-day		37.50	75
1990 Generals Grant and Lee At Appomattox	14-day		37.50	50
1990 General Thomas "Stonewall" Jackson	14-day		37.50	55
1990 Abraham Lincoln	14-day		37.50	60
1991 General J.E.B. Stuart	14-day		37.50	50
1991 General Philip Sheridan	14-day		37.50	60
1991 A Letter from Home	14-day		37.50	60
1991 Going Home	14-day		37.50	45
1992 Assembling The Troop	14-day		37.50	75
1992 Standing Watch	14-day		37.50	75

The American Wilderness - M. Richter

1995 Gray Wolf	28-day		29.95	30
1995 Silent Watch	28-day		29.95	30
1995 Moon Song	28-day		29.95	30
1995 Silent Pursuit	28-day		29.95	30
1996 Still of the Night	28-day		29.95	30

Andy Griffith - R. Tanenbaum

1992 Sheriff Andy Taylor	28-day		29.50	45
1992 A Startling Conclusion	28-day		29.50	45
1993 Mayberry Sing-a-long	28-day		29.50	30
1993 Aunt Bee's Kitchen	28-day		29.50	30
1993 Surprise! Surprise!	28-day		29.50	30
1993 An Explosive Situation	28-day		29.50	30
1993 Meeting Aunt Bee	28-day		29.50	30
1993 Opie's Big Catch	28-day		29.50	30

The Angler's Prize - M. Susinno

1991 Trophy Bass	14-day		29.50	30
1991 Blue Ribbon Trout	14-day		29.50	30
1991 Sun Dancers	14-day		29.50	30
1991 Freshwater Barracuda	14-day		29.50	30
1991 Bronzeback Fighter	14-day		29.50	30
1991 Autumn Beauty	14-day		29.50	30
1992 Old Mooneyes	14-day		29.50	30
1992 Silver King	14-day		29.50	30

Beauty Of Winter - N/A

1992 Silent Night	28-day		29.50	30
1993 Moonlight Sleighride	28-day		29.50	30

*Quotes have been rounded up to nearest dollar

The Best Of Baseball - R. Tanenbaum

YEAR ISSUE		EDITION LIMIT	YEAR RETD.	ISSUE PRICE	*QUOTE U.S. $
1993	The Legendary Mickey Mantle	28-day		29.50	30
1993	The Immortal Babe Ruth	28-day		29.50	30
1993	The Great Willie Mays	28-day		29.50	30
1993	The Unbeatable Duke Snider	28-day		29.50	30
1993	The Extraordinary Lou Gehrig	28-day		29.50	30
1993	The Phenomenal Roberto Clemente	28-day		29.50	30
1993	The Remarkable Johnny Bench	28-day		29.50	30
1993	The Incredible Nolan Ryan	28-day		29.50	30
1993	The Exceptional Brooks Robinson	28-day		29.50	30
1993	The Unforgettable Phil Rizzuto	28-day		29.50	30
1995	The Incomparable Reggie Jackson	28 day		29.50	30

Bialosky® & Friends - P./A.Bialosky

YEAR ISSUE		EDITION LIMIT	YEAR RETD.	ISSUE PRICE	*QUOTE U.S. $
1992	Family Addition	28-day		29.50	33
1993	Sweetheart	28-day		29.50	30
1993	Let's Go Fishing	28-day		29.50	30
1993	U.S. Mail	28-day		29.50	30
1993	Sleigh Ride	28-day		29.50	30
1993	Honey For Sale	28-day		29.50	30
1993	Breakfast In Bed	28-day		29.50	36
1993	My First Two-Wheeler	28-day		29.50	30

Big Cats of the World - D. Manning

YEAR ISSUE		EDITION LIMIT	YEAR RETD.	ISSUE PRICE	*QUOTE U.S. $
1989	African Shade	14-day		29.50	30
1989	View from Above	14-day		29.50	30
1990	On The Prowl	14-day		29.50	30
1990	Deep In The Jungle	14-day		29.50	30
1990	Spirit Of The Mountain	14-day		29.50	30
1990	Spotted Sentinel	14-day		29.50	30
1990	Above the Treetops	14-day		29.50	30
1990	Mountain Dweller	14-day		29.50	30
1992	Jungle Habitat	14-day		29.50	30
1992	Solitary Sentry	14-day		29.50	30

Bundles of Joy - B. P. Gutmann

YEAR ISSUE		EDITION LIMIT	YEAR RETD.	ISSUE PRICE	*QUOTE U.S. $
1988	Awakening	14-day		24.50	75-99
1988	Happy Dreams	14-day		24.50	60-125
1988	Tasting	14-day		24.50	50
1988	Sweet Innocence	14-day		24.50	40-85
1988	Tommy	14-day		24.50	35
1988	A Little Bit of Heaven	14-day		24.50	75
1988	Billy	14-day		24.50	45
1988	Sun Kissed	14-day		24.50	30

Butterfly Garden - P. Sweany

YEAR ISSUE		EDITION LIMIT	YEAR RETD.	ISSUE PRICE	*QUOTE U.S. $
1987	Spicebush Swallowtail	14-day		29.50	45
1987	Common Blue	14-day		29.50	38
1987	Orange Sulphur	14-day		29.50	35
1987	Monarch	14-day		29.50	38
1987	Tiger Swallowtail	14-day		29.50	35
1987	Crimson Patched Longwing	14-day		29.50	38
1988	Morning Cloak	14-day		29.50	35
1988	Red Admiral	14-day		29.50	38

The Call of the North - J. Tift

YEAR ISSUE		EDITION LIMIT	YEAR RETD.	ISSUE PRICE	*QUOTE U.S. $
1993	Winter's Dawn	28-day		29.50	30
1994	Evening Silence	28-day		29.50	30
1994	Moonlit Wilderness	28-day		29.50	30
1994	Silent Snowfall	28-day		29.50	30
1994	Snowy Watch	28-day		29.50	30
1994	Sentinels of the Summit	28-day		29.50	30
1994	Arctic Seclusion	28-day		29.50	30
1994	Forest Twilight	28-day		29.50	30
1994	Mountain Explorer	28-day		29.50	30
1994	The Cry of Winter	28-day		29.50	30

Call to Adventure - R. Cross

YEAR ISSUE		EDITION LIMIT	YEAR RETD.	ISSUE PRICE	*QUOTE U.S. $
1993	USS Constitution	28-day		29.50	30
1993	The Bounty	28-day		29.50	30
1994	Bonhomme Richard	28-day		29.50	30
1994	Old Nantucket	28-day		29.50	30
1994	Golden West	28-day		29.50	30
1994	Boston	28-day		29.50	30
1994	Hannah	28-day		29.50	30
1994	Improvement	28-day		29.50	30
1995	Anglo-American	28-day		29.50	30
1995	Challenge	28-day		29.50	30

Cameo Kittens - Q. Lemonds

YEAR ISSUE		EDITION LIMIT	YEAR RETD.	ISSUE PRICE	*QUOTE U.S. $
1993	Ginger Snap	28-day		29.50	30
1993	Cat Tails	28-day		29.50	30
1993	Lady Blue	28-day		29.50	30
1993	Tiny Heart Stealer	28-day		29.50	30
1993	Blossom	28-day		29.50	30
1994	Whisker Antics	28-day		29.50	30
1994	Tiger's Temptation	28-day		29.50	30
1994	Scout	28-day		29.50	30
1995	Timid Tabby	28-day		29.50	30

A Child's Best Friend - B. P. Gutmann

YEAR ISSUE		EDITION LIMIT	YEAR RETD.	ISSUE PRICE	*QUOTE U.S. $
1985	In Disgrace	14-day		24.50	90-195
1985	The Reward	14-day		24.50	60-125
1985	Who's Sleepy	14-day		24.50	90-125
1985	Good Morning	14-day		24.50	75
1985	Sympathy	14-day		24.50	55
1985	On the Up and Up	14-day		24.50	75-125
1985	Mine	14-day		24.50	90
1985	Going to Town	14-day		24.50	90-125

A Child's Christmas - J. Ferrandiz

YEAR ISSUE		EDITION LIMIT	YEAR RETD.	ISSUE PRICE	*QUOTE U.S. $
1995	Asleep in the Hay	28-day		29.95	30
1995	Merry Little Friends	28-day		29.95	30
1995	Love is Warm All Over	28-day		29.95	30
1995	Little Shepard Family	28-day		29.95	30
1995	Life's Little Blessings	28-day		29.95	30
1995	Happiness is Being Loved	28-day		29.95	30
1995	My Heart Belongs to You	28-day		29.95	30
1996	Lil' Dreamers	28-day		29.95	30

Childhood Reflections - B.P. Gutmann

YEAR ISSUE		EDITION LIMIT	YEAR RETD.	ISSUE PRICE	*QUOTE U.S. $
1991	Harmony	14-day		29.50	75
1991	Kitty's Breakfast	14-day		29.50	40
1991	Friendly Enemies	14-day		29.50	40-70
1991	Smile, Smile, Smile	14-day		29.50	40
1991	Lullaby	14-day		29.50	40
1991	Oh! Oh! A Bunny	14-day		29.50	50-85
1991	Little Mother	14-day		29.50	35
1991	Thank You, God	14-day		29.50	40

Children of the American Frontier - D. Crook

YEAR ISSUE		EDITION LIMIT	YEAR RETD.	ISSUE PRICE	*QUOTE U.S. $
1986	In Trouble Again	10-day		24.50	35
1986	Tubs and Suds	10-day		24.50	27
1986	A Lady Needs a Little Privacy	10-day		24.50	38
1986	The Desperadoes	10-day		24.50	27
1986	Riders Wanted	10-day		24.50	30
1987	A Cowboy's Downfall	10-day		24.50	25
1987	Runaway Blues	10-day		24.50	25
1987	A Special Patient	10-day		24.50	38

Civil War Generals - M. Gnatek

YEAR ISSUE		EDITION LIMIT	YEAR RETD.	ISSUE PRICE	*QUOTE U.S. $
1994	Robert E. Lee	28-day		29.50	30
1994	J.E.B. Stewart	28-day		29.50	30
1994	Joshua L. Chamberlain	28-day		29.50	30
1994	George Armstrong Custer	28-day		29.50	30
1994	Nathan Bedford Forrest	28-day		29.50	30
1994	James Longstreet	28-day		29.50	30
1995	Thomas "Stonewall" Jackson	28-day		29.50	30
1995	Confederate Heroes	28-day		29.50	30

Classic American Santas - G. Hinke

YEAR ISSUE		EDITION LIMIT	YEAR RETD.	ISSUE PRICE	*QUOTE U.S. $
1993	A Christmas Eve Visitor	28-day		29.50	30
1994	Up on the Rooftop	28-day		29.50	30
1994	Santa's Candy Kitchen	28-day		29.50	30
1994	A Christmas Chorus	28-day		29.50	30
1994	An Exciting Christmas Eve	28-day		29.50	30
1994	Rest Ye Merry Gentlemen	28-day		29.50	30
1994	Preparing the Sleigh	28-day		29.50	30
1994	The Reindeer's Stable	28-day		29.50	30
1994	He's Checking His List	28-day		29.50	30

Classic Corvettes - M. Lacourciere

YEAR ISSUE		EDITION LIMIT	YEAR RETD.	ISSUE PRICE	*QUOTE U.S. $
1994	1957 Corvette	28-day		29.50	30
1994	1963 Corvette	28-day		29.50	30
1994	1968 Corvette	28-day		29.50	30
1994	1986 Corvette	28-day		29.50	30
1995	1967 Corvette	28-day		29.50	30
1995	1953 Corvette	28-day		29.50	30
1995	1962 Corvette	28-day		29.50	30
1995	1990 Corvette	28-day		29.50	30

Classic Sporting Dogs - B. Christie

YEAR ISSUE		EDITION LIMIT	YEAR RETD.	ISSUE PRICE	*QUOTE U.S. $
1989	Golden Retrievers	14-day		24.50	60
1989	Labrador Retrievers	14-day		24.50	60
1989	Beagles	14-day		24.50	40
1989	Pointers	14-day		24.50	30
1989	Springer Spaniels	14-day		24.50	40
1990	German Short-Haired Pointers	14-day		24.50	55
1990	Irish Setters	14-day		24.50	40
1990	Brittany Spaniels	14-day		24.50	48

Classic TV Westerns - K. Milnazik

YEAR ISSUE		EDITION LIMIT	YEAR RETD.	ISSUE PRICE	*QUOTE U.S. $
1990	The Lone Ranger and Tonto	14-day		29.50	60-100
1990	Bonanza™	14-day		29.50	50-75
1990	Roy Rogers and Dale Evans	14-day		29.50	60
1991	Rawhide	14-day		29.50	60-75
1991	Wild Wild West	14-day		29.50	60-75
1991	Have Gun, Will Travel	14-day		29.50	60-75
1991	The Virginian	14-day		29.50	60-75
1991	Hopalong Cassidy	14-day		29.50	60-75

Cloak of Visions - A. Farley

YEAR ISSUE		EDITION LIMIT	YEAR RETD.	ISSUE PRICE	*QUOTE U.S. $
1994	Visions in a Full Moon	28-day		29.50	30
1994	Protector of the Child	28-day		29.50	30
1995	Spirits of the Canyon	28-day		29.50	30
1995	Freedom Soars	28-day		29.50	30
1995	Mystic Reflections	28-day		29.50	30
1995	Staff of Life	28-day		29.50	30
1995	Springtime Hunters	28-day		29.50	30

Coral Paradise - H. Bond

YEAR ISSUE		EDITION LIMIT	YEAR RETD.	ISSUE PRICE	*QUOTE U.S. $
1989	The Living Oasis	14-day		29.50	45
1990	Riches of the Coral Sea	14-day		29.50	30
1990	Tropical Pageantry	14-day		29.50	40
1990	Caribbean Spectacle	14-day		29.50	35
1990	Undersea Village	14-day		29.50	36
1990	Shimmering Reef Dwellers	14-day		29.50	36
1990	Mysteries of the Galapagos	14-day		29.50	33
1990	Forest Beneath the Sea	14-day		29.50	30

Cottage Puppies - K. George

YEAR ISSUE		EDITION LIMIT	YEAR RETD.	ISSUE PRICE	*QUOTE U.S. $
1993	Little Gardeners	28-day		29.50	30
1993	Springtime Fancy	28-day		29.50	30
1993	Endearing Innocence	28-day		29.50	30
1994	Picnic Playtime	28-day		29.50	30
1994	Lazy Afternoon	28-day		29.50	30
1994	Summertime Pals	28-day		29.50	30
1994	A Gardening Trio	28-day		29.50	30
1994	Taking a Break	28-day		29.50	30

Council Of Nations - G. Perillo

YEAR ISSUE		EDITION LIMIT	YEAR RETD.	ISSUE PRICE	*QUOTE U.S. $
1991	Strength of the Sioux	28-day		29.50	30
1992	Pride of the Cheyenne	28-day		29.50	30
1992	Dignity of the Nez Parce	28-day		29.50	30
1992	Courage of the Arapaho	28-day		29.50	30
1992	Power of the Blackfoot	28-day		29.50	30
1992	Nobility of the Algonqui	28-day		29.50	30
1992	Wisdom of the Cherokee	28-day		29.50	30
1992	Boldness of the Seneca	28-day		29.50	45

Country Garden Cottages - E. Dertner

YEAR ISSUE		EDITION LIMIT	YEAR RETD.	ISSUE PRICE	*QUOTE U.S. $
1992	Riverbank Cottage	28-day		29.50	36
1992	Sunday Outing	28-day		29.50	30
1992	Shepherd's Cottage	28-day		29.50	30
1993	Daydream Cottage	28-day		29.50	30
1993	Garden Glorious	28-day		29.50	30
1993	This Side of Heaven	28-day		29.50	30
1993	Summer Symphony	28-day		29.50	30
1993	April Cottage	28-day		29.50	30

Country Kitties - G. Gerardi

YEAR ISSUE		EDITION LIMIT	YEAR RETD.	ISSUE PRICE	*QUOTE U.S. $
1989	Mischief Makers	14-day		24.50	45
1989	Table Manners	14-day		24.50	36
1989	Attic Attack	14-day		24.50	40
1989	Rock and Rollers	14-day		24.50	45
1989	Just For the Fern of It	14-day		24.50	45
1989	All Washed Up	14-day		24.50	50
1989	Stroller Derby	14-day		24.50	39
1989	Captive Audience	14-day		24.50	50

A Country Season of Horses - J.M. Vass

YEAR ISSUE		EDITION LIMIT	YEAR RETD.	ISSUE PRICE	*QUOTE U.S. $
1990	First Day of Spring	14-day		29.50	40
1990	Summer Splendor	14-day		29.50	35
1990	A Winter's Walk	14-day		29.50	35
1990	Autumn Grandeur	14-day		29.50	30
1990	Cliffside Beauty	14-day		29.50	30
1990	Frosty Morning	14-day		29.50	30
1990	Crisp Country Morning	14-day		29.50	30
1990	River Retreat	14-day		29.50	30

A Country Summer - N. Noel

YEAR ISSUE		EDITION LIMIT	YEAR RETD.	ISSUE PRICE	*QUOTE U.S. $
1985	Butterfly Beauty	10-day		29.50	36
1985	The Golden Puppy	10-day		29.50	30
1986	The Rocking Chair	10-day		29.50	36
1986	My Bunny	10-day		29.50	33
1988	The Piglet	10-day		29.50	30
1988	Teammates	10-day		29.50	30

Curious Kittens - B. Harrison

YEAR ISSUE		EDITION LIMIT	YEAR RETD.	ISSUE PRICE	*QUOTE U.S. $
1990	Rainy Day Friends	14-day		29.50	50-75
1990	Keeping in Step	14-day		29.50	36
1991	Delightful Discovery	14-day		29.50	36
1991	Chance Meeting	14-day		29.50	36
1991	All Wound Up	14-day		29.50	36
1991	Making Tracks	14-day		29.50	36
1991	Playing Cat and Mouse	14-day		29.50	36
1991	A Paw's in the Action	14-day		29.50	36
1992	Little Scholar	14-day		29.50	36
1992	Cat Burglar	14-day		29.50	36

Daughters Of The Sun - K. Thayer

YEAR ISSUE		EDITION LIMIT	YEAR RETD.	ISSUE PRICE	*QUOTE U.S. $
1993	Sun Dancer	28-day		29.50	30
1993	Shining Feather	28-day		29.50	30
1993	Delighted Dancer	28-day		29.50	30
1993	Evening Dancer	28-day		29.50	30
1993	A Secret Glance	28-day		29.50	30
1993	Chippewa Charmer	28-day		29.50	30
1994	Pride of the Yakima	28-day		29.50	30
1994	Radiant Beauty	28-day		29.50	30

Dear to My Heart - J. Hagara

YEAR ISSUE		EDITION LIMIT	YEAR RETD.	ISSUE PRICE	*QUOTE U.S. $
1990	Cathy	14-day		29.50	30-60
1990	Addie	14-day		29.50	30
1990	Jimmy	14-day		29.50	30
1990	Dacy	14-day		29.50	30
1990	Paul	14-day		29.50	30
1991	Shelly	14-day		29.50	30
1991	Jenny	14-day		29.50	30
1991	Joy	14-day		29.50	30

Dolphin Discovery - D. Queen

YEAR ISSUE		EDITION LIMIT	YEAR RETD.	ISSUE PRICE	*QUOTE U.S. $
1995	Sunrise Reverie	28-day		29.50	30
1995	Dolphin's Paradise	28-day		29.50	30
1995	Coral Cove	28-day		29.50	30
1995	Undersea Journey	28-day		29.50	30
1995	Dolphin Canyon	28-day		29.50	30
1995	Coral Garden	28-day		29.50	30

*Quotes have been rounded up to nearest dollar

PLATES

YEAR ISSUE		EDITION LIMIT	YEAR RETD.	ISSUE PRICE	*QUOTE U.S.$
1996	Dolphin Duo	28-day		29.50	30
1996	Underwater Tranquility	28-day		29.50	30

Dreamsicles - K. Haynes

YEAR ISSUE		EDITION LIMIT	YEAR RETD.	ISSUE PRICE	*QUOTE U.S.$
1994	The Flying Lesson	28-day		19.50	20
1995	By the Light of the Moon	28-day		19.50	20
1995	The Recital	28-day		19.50	20
1995	Heavenly Pirouettes	28-day		19.50	20
1995	Blossoms and Butterflies	28-day		19.50	20
1995	Love's Shy Glance	28-day		19.50	20
1996	Wishing Upon a Star	28-day		19.50	20
1996	Rainy Day Friends	28-day		19.50	20

Dreamsicles Special Friends - K. Haynes

YEAR ISSUE		EDITION LIMIT	YEAR RETD.	ISSUE PRICE	*QUOTE U.S.$
1995	A Hug From the Heart	28-day		29.95	30
1995	Heaven's Little Helper	28-day		29.95	30
1995	Bless Us All	28-day		29.95	30
1996	Love's Gentle Touch	28-day		29.95	30
1996	The Best Gift of All	28-day		29.95	30

Drivers of Victory Lane - R. Tanenbaum

YEAR ISSUE		EDITION LIMIT	YEAR RETD.	ISSUE PRICE	*QUOTE U.S.$
1994	Bill Elliott	28-day		29.50	30
1994	Jeff Gordon	28-day		29.50	30
1994	Rusty Wallace	28-day		29.50	30
1995	Geoff Bodine	28-day		29.50	30
1995	Dale Earnhardt	28-day		29.50	30

Easyriders - M. Lacourciere

YEAR ISSUE		EDITION LIMIT	YEAR RETD.	ISSUE PRICE	*QUOTE U.S.$
1995	American Classic	28-day		29.95	30
1995	Symbols of Freedom	28-day		29.95	30

Elvis Remembered - S. Morton

YEAR ISSUE		EDITION LIMIT	YEAR RETD.	ISSUE PRICE	*QUOTE U.S.$
1989	Loving You	90-day		37.50	100-155
1989	Early Years	90-day		37.50	55-75
1989	Tenderly	90-day		37.50	70-125
1989	The King	90-day		37.50	120-150
1989	Forever Yours	90-day		37.50	100
1989	Rockin in the Moonlight	90-day		37.50	100-150
1989	Moody Blues	90-day		37.50	100
1989	Elvis Presley	90-day		37.50	100-175

Enchanted Seascapes - J. Enright

YEAR ISSUE		EDITION LIMIT	YEAR RETD.	ISSUE PRICE	*QUOTE U.S.$
1993	Sanctuary of the Dolphin	28-day		29.50	30
1994	Rhapsody of Hope	28-day		29.50	30
1994	Oasis of the Gods	28-day		29.50	30
1994	Sphere of Life	28-day		29.50	30
1994	Edge of Time	28-day		29.50	30
1994	Sea of Light	28-day		29.50	30
1994	Lost Beneath the Blue	28-day		29.50	30
1994	Blue Paradise	28-day		29.50	30
1995	Morning Odyssey	28-day		29.50	30
1995	Paradise Cove	28-day		29.50	30

English Country Cottages - M. Bell

YEAR ISSUE		EDITION LIMIT	YEAR RETD.	ISSUE PRICE	*QUOTE U.S.$
1990	Periwinkle Tea Room	14-day		29.50	45
1991	Gamekeeper's Cottage	14-day		29.50	75
1991	Ginger Cottage	14-day		29.50	60
1991	Larkspur Cottage	14-day		29.50	45
1991	The Chaplain's Garden	14-day		29.50	33
1991	Lorna Doone Cottage	14-day		29.50	45
1991	Murrle Cottage	14-day		29.50	36
1991	Lullabye Cottage	14-day		29.50	30

Eternal Wishes of Good Fortune - Shuho

YEAR ISSUE		EDITION LIMIT	YEAR RETD.	ISSUE PRICE	*QUOTE U.S.$
1983	Friendship	10-day		34.95	35
1983	Purity and Perfection	10-day		34.95	35
1983	Illustrious Offspring	10-day		34.95	35
1983	Longevity	10-day		34.95	35
1983	Youth	10-day		34.95	35
1983	Immortality	10-day		34.95	35
1983	Marital Bliss	10-day		34.95	35
1983	Love	10-day		34.95	35
1983	Peace	10-day		34.95	35
1983	Beauty	10-day		34.95	35
1983	Fertility	10-day		34.95	35
1983	Fortitude	10-day		34.95	35

Exotic Tigers of Asia - K. Ottinger

YEAR ISSUE		EDITION LIMIT	YEAR RETD.	ISSUE PRICE	*QUOTE U.S.$
1995	Lord of the Rainforest	28-day		29.50	30
1995	Snow King	28-day		29.50	30
1995	Ruler of the Wetlands	28-day		29.50	30
1996	Majestic Vigil	28-day		29.50	30
1996	Keeper of the Jungle	28-day		29.50	30
1996	Eyes of the Jungle	28-day		29.50	30
1996	Sovereign Ruler	28-day		29.50	30

Farmyard Friends - J. Lamb

YEAR ISSUE		EDITION LIMIT	YEAR RETD.	ISSUE PRICE	*QUOTE U.S.$
1992	Mistaken Identity	28-day		29.50	30
1992	Little Cowhands	28-day		29.50	30
1993	Shreading the Evidence	28-day		29.50	30
1993	Partners in Crime	28-day		29.50	30
1993	Fowl Play	28-day		29.50	30
1993	Follow The Leader	28-day		29.50	36
1993	Pony Tales	28-day		29.50	30
1993	An Apple A Day	28-day		29.50	30

Favorite American Songbirds - D. O'Driscoll

YEAR ISSUE		EDITION LIMIT	YEAR RETD.	ISSUE PRICE	*QUOTE U.S.$
1989	Blue Jays of Spring	14-day		29.50	36
1989	Red Cardinals of Winter	14-day		29.50	36
1989	Robins & Apple Blossoms	14-day		29.50	36
1989	Goldfinches of Summer	14-day		29.50	36
1990	Autumn Chickadees	14-day		29.50	36
1990	Bluebirds and Morning Glories	14-day		29.50	36
1990	Tufted Titmouse and Holly	14-day		29.50	30
1991	Carolina Wrens of Spring	14-day		29.50	30

Favorite Old Testament Stories - S. Butcher

YEAR ISSUE		EDITION LIMIT	YEAR RETD.	ISSUE PRICE	*QUOTE U.S.$
1994	Jacob's Dream	28-day		35.00	35
1995	The Baby Moses	28-day		35.00	35
1995	Esther's Gift To Her People	28-day		35.00	35
1995	A Prayer For Victory	28-day		35.00	35
1995	Where You Go, I Will Go	28-day		35.00	35
1995	A Prayer Answered, A Promise Kept	28-day		35.00	35
1996	Joseph Sold Into Slavery	28-day		35.00	35
1996	Daniel In the Lion's Den	28-day		35.00	35
1996	Noah And The Ark	28-day		35.00	35

The Fierce And The Free - F. McCarthy

YEAR ISSUE		EDITION LIMIT	YEAR RETD.	ISSUE PRICE	*QUOTE U.S.$
1992	Big Medicine	28-day		29.50	30
1993	Land of the Winter Hawk	28-day		29.50	30
1993	Warrior of Savage Splendor	28-day		29.50	30
1994	War Party	28-day		29.50	30
1994	The Challenge	28-day		29.50	30
1994	Out of the Rising Mist	28-day		29.50	30
1994	The Ambush	28-day		29.50	35
1994	Dangerous Crossing	28-day		29.50	30

Forging New Frontiers - J. Deneen

YEAR ISSUE		EDITION LIMIT	YEAR RETD.	ISSUE PRICE	*QUOTE U.S.$
1994	The Race is On	28-day		29.50	30
1994	Big Boy	28-day		29.50	30
1994	Cresting the Summit	28-day		29.50	30
1994	Spring Roundup	28-day		29.50	30
1994	Winter in the Rockies	28-day		29.50	30
1994	High Country Logging	28-day		29.50	30
1994	Confrontation	28-day		29.50	30
1994	A Welcome Sight	28-day		29.50	30

A Garden Song - M. Hanson

YEAR ISSUE		EDITION LIMIT	YEAR RETD.	ISSUE PRICE	*QUOTE U.S.$
1994	Winter's Splendor	28-day		29.50	30
1994	In Full Bloom	28-day		29.50	30
1994	Golden Glories	28-day		29.50	30
1995	Autumn's Elegance	28-day		29.50	30
1995	First Snowfall	28-day		29.50	30
1995	Robins in Spring	28-day		29.50	30
1995	Summer's Glow	28-day		29.50	30
1995	Fall's Serenade	28-day		29.50	30
1996	Sounds of Winter	28-day		29.50	30
1996	Springtime Haven	28-day		29.50	30

Glory of Christ - C. Micarelli

YEAR ISSUE		EDITION LIMIT	YEAR RETD.	ISSUE PRICE	*QUOTE U.S.$
1992	The Ascension	48-day		29.50	30
1992	Jesus Teaching	48-day		29.50	30
1993	Last Supper	48-day		29.50	30
1993	The Nativity	48-day		29.50	30
1993	The Baptism of Christ	48-day		29.50	30
1993	Jesus Heals the Sick	48-day		29.50	30
1994	Jesus Walks on Water	48-day		29.50	30
1994	Descent From the Cross	48-day		29.50	30

Glory of the Game - T. Fogarty

YEAR ISSUE		EDITION LIMIT	YEAR RETD.	ISSUE PRICE	*QUOTE U.S.$
1994	"Hank Aaron's Record-Breaking Home Run"	28-day		29.50	30
1994	"Bobby Thomson's Shot Heard 'Round the World"	28-day		29.50	30
1994	1969 Miracle Mets	28-day		29.50	30
1995	Reggie Jackson: Mr. October	28-day		29.50	30
1995	Don Larsen's Perfect World	28-day		29.50	30
1995	Babe Ruth's Called Shot	28-day		29.50	30
1995	Wille Mays: Greatest Catch	28-day		29.50	30
1995	Bill Mazeroski's Series	28-day		29.50	30

The Golden Age of American Railroads - T. Xaras

YEAR ISSUE		EDITION LIMIT	YEAR RETD.	ISSUE PRICE	*QUOTE U.S.$
1991	The Blue Comet	14-day		29.50	40-50
1991	The Morning Local	14-day		29.50	50-60
1991	The Pennsylvania K-4	14-day		29.50	80
1991	Above the Canyon	14-day		29.50	50-90
1991	Portrait in Steam	14-day		29.50	50-75
1991	The Santa Fe Super Chief	14-day		29.50	105
1991	The Big Boy	14-day		29.50	60
1991	The Empire Builder	14-day		29.50	60
1992	An American Classic	14-day		29.50	33
1992	Final Destination	14-day		29.50	36

Golden Discoveries - L. Budge

YEAR ISSUE		EDITION LIMIT	YEAR RETD.	ISSUE PRICE	*QUOTE U.S.$
1995	Boot Bandits	28-day		29.95	30
1995	Hiding the Evidence	28-day		29.95	30
1995	Decoy Dilemma	28-day		29.95	30
1995	Fishing for Dinner	28-day		29.95	30
1996	Lunchtime Companions	28-day		29.95	30
1996	Friend or Foe?	28-day		29.95	30

Golden Puppy Portraits - P. Braun

YEAR ISSUE		EDITION LIMIT	YEAR RETD.	ISSUE PRICE	*QUOTE U.S.$
1994	Do Not Disturb!	28-day		29.50	30
1995	Teething Time	28-day		29.50	30
1995	Table Manners	28-day		29.50	30
1995	A Golden Bouquet	28-day		29.50	30
1995	Time For Bed	28-day		29.50	30
1995	Bathtime Blues	28-day		29.50	30
1996	Spinning a Yarn	28-day		29.50	30
1996	Partytime Puppy	28-day		29.50	30

Good Sports - J. Lamb

YEAR ISSUE		EDITION LIMIT	YEAR RETD.	ISSUE PRICE	*QUOTE U.S.$
1990	Wide Retriever	14-day		29.50	55
1990	Double Play	14-day		29.50	36
1990	Hole in One	14-day		29.50	45
1990	The Bass Masters	14-day		29.50	40
1990	Spotted on the Sideline	14-day		29.50	36
1990	Slap Shot	14-day		29.50	45
1991	Net Play	14-day		29.50	45
1991	Bassetball	14-day		29.50	36
1992	Boxer Rebellion	14-day		29.50	36
1992	Great Try	14-day		29.50	39

Great Fighter Planes Of World War II - R. Waddey

YEAR ISSUE		EDITION LIMIT	YEAR RETD.	ISSUE PRICE	*QUOTE U.S.$
1992	Old Crow	14-day		29.50	30
1992	Big Hog	14-day		29.50	30
1992	P-47 Thunderbolt	14-day		29.50	30
1992	P-40 Flying Tiger	14-day		29.50	30
1992	F4F Wildcat	14-day		29.50	30
1992	P-38F Lightning	14-day		29.50	30
1993	F6F Hellcat	14-day		29.50	30
1993	P-39M Airacobra	14-day		29.50	30
1995	Memphis Belle	14-day		29.50	30
1995	The Dragon and His Tail	14-day		29.50	30

Great Mammals of the Sea - Wyland

YEAR ISSUE		EDITION LIMIT	YEAR RETD.	ISSUE PRICE	*QUOTE U.S.$
1991	Orca Trio	14-day		35.00	45
1991	Hawaii Dolphins	14-day		35.00	43
1991	Orca Journey	14-day		35.00	43
1991	Dolphin Paradise	14-day		35.00	45
1991	Children of the Sea	14-day		35.00	60
1991	Kissing Dolphins	14-day		35.00	39
1991	Islands	14-day		35.00	60
1991	Orcas	14-day		35.00	45

The Greatest Show on Earth - F. Moody

YEAR ISSUE		EDITION LIMIT	YEAR RETD.	ISSUE PRICE	*QUOTE U.S.$
1981	Clowns	10-day		30.00	45
1981	Elephants	10-day		30.00	30-60
1981	Aerialists	10-day		30.00	30
1981	Great Parade	10-day		30.00	30
1981	Midway	10-day		30.00	30
1981	Equestrians	10-day		30.00	30
1982	Lion Tamer	10-day		30.00	30
1982	Grande Finale	10-day		30.00	30

Growing Up Together - P. Brooks

YEAR ISSUE		EDITION LIMIT	YEAR RETD.	ISSUE PRICE	*QUOTE U.S.$
1990	My Very Best Friends	14-day		29.50	36
1990	Tea for Two	14-day		29.50	30
1990	Tender Loving Care	14-day		29.50	30
1990	Picnic Pals	14-day		29.50	30
1991	Newfound Friends	14-day		29.50	30
1991	Kitten Caboodle	14-day		29.50	30
1991	Fishing Buddies	14-day		29.50	30
1991	Bedtime Blessings	14-day		29.50	30

The Historic Rails - T. Xaras

YEAR ISSUE		EDITION LIMIT	YEAR RETD.	ISSUE PRICE	*QUOTE U.S.$
1995	Harper's Ferry	28-day		29.95	30
1995	Horseshoe Curve	28-day		29.95	30
1995	Kentucky's Red River	28-day		29.95	30
1995	Sherman Hill Challenger	28-day		29.95	30
1996	New York Central's 4-6-4 Hudson	28-day		29.95	30

The I Love Lucy Plate Collection - J. Kritz

YEAR ISSUE		EDITION LIMIT	YEAR RETD.	ISSUE PRICE	*QUOTE U.S.$
1989	California, Here We Come	14-day		29.50	95-195
1989	It's Just Like Candy	14-day		29.50	150-175
1990	The Big Squeeze	14-day		29.50	100-175
1990	Eating the Evidence	14-day		29.50	200-300
1990	Two of a Kind	14-day		29.50	125-175
1991	Queen of the Gypsies	14-day		29.50	95-110
1992	Night at the Copa	14-day		29.50	75-100
1992	A Rising Problem	14-day		29.50	95-150

Japanese Floral Calendar - Shuho/Kage

YEAR ISSUE		EDITION LIMIT	YEAR RETD.	ISSUE PRICE	*QUOTE U.S.$
1981	New Year's Day	10-day		32.50	40
1982	Early Spring	10-day		32.50	40
1982	Spring	10-day		32.50	40
1982	Girl's Doll Day Festival	10-day		32.50	40
1982	Buddha's Birthday	10-day		32.50	40
1982	Early Summer	10-day		32.50	40
1982	Boy's Doll Day Festival	10-day		32.50	40
1982	Summer	10-day		32.50	33
1982	Autumn	10-day		32.50	40
1983	Festival of the Full Moon	10-day		32.50	33
1983	Late Autumn	10-day		32.50	33
1983	Winter	10-day		32.50	33

The Jeweled Hummingbirds - J. Landenberger

YEAR ISSUE		EDITION LIMIT	YEAR RETD.	ISSUE PRICE	*QUOTE U.S.$
1989	Ruby-throated Hummingbirds	14-day		37.50	45
1989	Great Sapphire Wing Hummingbirds	14-day		37.50	45
1989	Ruby-Topaz Hummingbirds	14-day		37.50	45
1989	Andean Emerald Hummingbirds	14-day		37.50	45
1989	Garnet-throated Hummingbirds	14-day		37.50	45
1989	Blue-Headed Sapphire Hummingbirds	14-day		37.50	45
1989	Pearl Coronet Hummingbirds	14-day		37.50	45
1989	Amethyst-throated Sunangels	14-day		37.50	45

Kitten Classics - P. Cooper

YEAR ISSUE		EDITION LIMIT	YEAR RETD.	ISSUE PRICE	*QUOTE U.S.$
1985	Cat Nap	14-day		29.50	3[illegible]
1985	Purrfect Treasure	14-day		29.50	3[illegible]

*Quotes have been rounded up to nearest dollar

YEAR	ISSUE	EDITION LIMIT	YEAR RETD.	ISSUE PRICE	*QUOTE U.S.$
1985	Wild Flower	14-day		29.50	30
1985	Birdwatcher	14-day		29.50	30
1985	Tiger's Fancy	14-day		29.50	33
1985	Country Kitty	14-day		29.50	33
1985	Little Rascal	14-day		29.50	30
1985	First Prize	14-day		29.50	30

The Last Warriors - C. Ren

YEAR	ISSUE	EDITION LIMIT	YEAR RETD.	ISSUE PRICE	*QUOTE U.S.$
1993	Winter of '41	28-day		29.50	30
1993	Morning of Reckoning	28-day		29.50	30
1993	Twilights Last Gleaming	28-day		29.50	30
1993	Lone Winter Journey	28-day		29.50	30
1994	Victory's Reward	28-day		29.50	30
1994	Solitary Hunter	28-day		29.50	30
1994	Solemn Reflection	28-day		29.50	30
1994	Confronting Danger	28-day		29.50	30
1995	Moment of Contemplation	28-day		29.50	30
1995	The Last Sunset	28-day		29.50	30

The Legend of Father Christmas - V. Dezerin

YEAR	ISSUE	EDITION LIMIT	YEAR RETD.	ISSUE PRICE	*QUOTE U.S.$
1994	The Return of Father Christmas	28-day		29.50	30
1994	Gifts From Father Christmas	28-day		29.50	30
1994	The Feast of the Holiday	28-day		29.50	30
1995	Christmas Day Visitors	28-day		29.50	30
1995	Decorating the Tree	28-day		29.50	30
1995	The Snow Sculpture	28-day		29.50	30
1995	Skating on the Pond	28-day		29.50	30
1995	Holy Night	28-day		29.50	30

Legendary Warriors - M. Gentry

YEAR	ISSUE	EDITION LIMIT	YEAR RETD.	ISSUE PRICE	*QUOTE U.S.$
1995	White Quiver and Scout	28-day		29.95	30
1995	Lakota Rendezvous	28-day		29.95	30
1995	Crazy Horse	28-day		29.95	30
1995	Sitting Bull's Vision	28-day		29.95	30
1996	Crazy Horse	28-day		29.95	30
1996	Sitting Bull's Vision	28-day		29.95	30
1996	Noble Surrender	28-day		29.95	30
1996	Sioux Thunder	28-day		29.95	30
1996	Eagle Dancer	28-day		29.95	30

A Lisi Martin Christmas - L. Martin

YEAR	ISSUE	EDITION LIMIT	YEAR RETD.	ISSUE PRICE	*QUOTE U.S.$
1992	Santa's Littlest Reindeer	28-day		29.50	30
1993	Not A Creature Was Stirring	28-day		29.50	30
1993	Christmas Dreams	28-day		29.50	30
1993	The Christmas Story	28-day		29.50	30
1993	Trimming The Tree	28-day		29.50	30
1993	A Taste Of The Holidays	28-day		29.50	30
1993	The Night Before Christmas	28-day		29.50	30
1993	Christmas Watch	28-day		29.50	30
1995	Christmas Presence	28-day		29.50	30
1995	Nose to Nose	28-day		29.50	30

Little Fawns of the Forest - R. Manning

YEAR	ISSUE	EDITION LIMIT	YEAR RETD.	ISSUE PRICE	*QUOTE U.S.$
1995	In the Morning Light	28-day		29.95	30
1995	Cool Reflections	28-day		29.95	30
1995	Nature's Lesson	28-day		29.95	30
1996	A Friendship Blossoms	28-day		29.95	30

Little Ladies - M.H. Bogart

YEAR	ISSUE	EDITION LIMIT	YEAR RETD.	ISSUE PRICE	*QUOTE U.S.$
1989	Playing Bridesmaid	14-day		29.50	75-125
1990	The Seamstress	14-day		29.50	60-100
1990	Little Captive	14-day		29.50	45
1990	Playing Mama	14-day		29.50	60-100
1990	Susanna	14-day		29.50	35
1990	Kitty's Bath	14-day		29.50	55-100
1990	A Day in the Country	14-day		29.50	45-100
1991	Sarah	14-day		29.50	45
1991	First Party	14-day		29.50	55
1991	The Magic Kitten	14-day		29.50	50

The Little Rascals - Unknown

YEAR	ISSUE	EDITION LIMIT	YEAR RETD.	ISSUE PRICE	*QUOTE U.S.$
1985	Three for the Show	10-day		24.50	30
1985	My Gal	10-day		24.50	30
1985	Skeleton Crew	10-day		24.50	25
1985	Roughin' It	10-day		24.50	45
1985	Spanky's Pranks	10-day		24.50	25
1985	Butch's Challenge	10-day		24.50	25
1985	Darla's Debut	10-day		24.50	25
1985	Pete's Pal	10-day		24.50	25

Little Shopkeepers - G. Gerardi

YEAR	ISSUE	EDITION LIMIT	YEAR RETD.	ISSUE PRICE	*QUOTE U.S.$
1990	Sew Tired	14-day		29.50	30
1991	Break Time	14-day		29.50	30
1991	Purrfect Fit	14-day		29.50	30
1991	Toying Around	14-day		29.50	36
1991	Chain Reaction	14-day		29.50	45
1991	Inferior Decorators	14-day		29.50	36
1991	Tulip Tag	14-day		29.50	36
1991	Candy Capers	14-day		29.50	36

Lore Of The West - L. Danielle

YEAR	ISSUE	EDITION LIMIT	YEAR RETD.	ISSUE PRICE	*QUOTE U.S.$
1993	A Mile In His Mocassins	28-day		29.50	30
1993	Path of Honor	28-day		29.50	30
1993	A Chief's Pride	28-day		29.50	30
1994	Pathways of the Pueblo	28-day		29.50	30
1994	In Her Seps	28-day		29.50	30
1994	Growing Up Brave	28-day		29.50	30
1994	Nomads of the Southwest	28-day		29.50	30
1994	Sacred Spirit of the Plains	28-day		29.50	30
1994	We'll Fight No More	28-day		29.50	30

YEAR	ISSUE	EDITION LIMIT	YEAR RETD.	ISSUE PRICE	*QUOTE U.S.$
1994	The End of the Trail	28-day		29.50	30

Love's Messengers - J. Grossman

YEAR	ISSUE	EDITION LIMIT	YEAR RETD.	ISSUE PRICE	*QUOTE U.S.$
1995	To My Love	28-day		29.50	30
1995	Cupid's Arrow	28-day		29.50	30
1995	Love's Melody	28-day		29.50	30
1995	A Token of Love	28-day		29.50	30
1995	Harmony of Love	28-day		29.50	30
1996	True Love's Offering	28-day		29.95	30
1996	Love's In Bloom	28-day		29.95	30
1996	To My Sweetheart	28-day		29.95	30

The Lucille Ball (Official) Commemorative Plate - M. Weistling

YEAR	ISSUE	EDITION LIMIT	YEAR RETD.	ISSUE PRICE	*QUOTE U.S.$
1993	Lucy	28-day		37.50	150-225

Madonna And Child - Various

YEAR	ISSUE	EDITION LIMIT	YEAR RETD.	ISSUE PRICE	*QUOTE U.S.$
1992	Madonna Della Sedia - R. Sanzio	28-day		37.50	38
1992	Virgin of the Rocks - L. DaVinci	28-day		37.50	38
1993	Madonna of Rosary - B. E. Murillo	28-day		37.50	38
1993	Sistine Madonna - R. Sanzio	28-day		37.50	38
1993	Virgin Adoring Christ Child - A. Correggio	28-day		37.50	38
1993	Virgin of the Grape - P. Mignard	28-day		37.50	38
1993	Madonna del Magnificat - S. Botticelli	28-day		37.50	38
1993	Madonna col Bambino - S. Botticelli	28-day		37.50	38

The Magical World of Legends & Myths - J. Shalatain

YEAR	ISSUE	EDITION LIMIT	YEAR RETD.	ISSUE PRICE	*QUOTE U.S.$
1993	A Mother's Love	28-day		35.00	35
1993	Dreams of Pegasus	28-day		35.00	35
1994	Flight of the Pegasus	28-day		35.00	45
1994	The Awakening	28-day		35.00	35
1994	Once Upon a Dream	28-day		35.00	45
1994	The Dawn of Romance	28-day		35.00	35
1994	The Astral Unicorn	28-day		35.00	45
1994	Flight into Paradise	28-day		35.00	35
1995	Pegasus in the Stars	28-day		35.00	35
1995	Unicorn of the Sea	28-day		35.00	35

Majestic Birds of Prey - C.F. Riley

YEAR	ISSUE	EDITION LIMIT	YEAR RETD.	ISSUE PRICE	*QUOTE U.S.$
1983	Golden Eagle	12,500		55.00	55
1983	Coopers Hawk	12,500		55.00	55
1983	Great Horned Owl	12,500		55.00	55
1983	Bald Eagle	12,500		55.00	60
1983	Barred Owl	12,500		55.00	60
1983	Sparrow Hawk	12,500		55.00	60
1983	Peregrine Falcon	12,500		55.00	60
1983	Osprey	12,500		55.00	60

Majesty of Flight - T. Hirata

YEAR	ISSUE	EDITION LIMIT	YEAR RETD.	ISSUE PRICE	*QUOTE U.S.$
1989	The Eagle Soars	14-day		37.50	48
1989	Realm of the Red-Tail	14-day		37.50	40
1989	Coastal Journey	14-day		37.50	45
1989	Sentry of the North	14-day		37.50	48
1989	Commanding the Marsh	14-day		37.50	38
1990	The Vantage Point	14-day		29.50	45
1990	Silent Watch	14-day		29.50	48
1990	Fierce and Free	14-day		29.50	45

Man's Best Friend - L. Picken

YEAR	ISSUE	EDITION LIMIT	YEAR RETD.	ISSUE PRICE	*QUOTE U.S.$
1992	Special Delivery	28-day		29.50	30
1992	Making Waves	28-day		29.50	30
1992	Good Catch	28-day		29.50	30
1993	Time For a Walk	28-day		29.50	45
1993	Faithful Friend	28-day		29.50	45
1993	Let's Play Ball	28-day		29.50	30
1993	Sitting Pretty	28-day		29.50	30
1993	Bedtime Story	28-day		29.50	30
1993	Trusted Companion	28-day		29.50	30

Mike Schmidt - R. Tanenbaum

YEAR	ISSUE	EDITION LIMIT	YEAR RETD.	ISSUE PRICE	*QUOTE U.S.$
1994	The Ultimate Competitor: Mike Schmidt	28-day		29.50	30
1995	A Homerun King	28-day		29.50	30
1995	An All Time, All Star	28-day		29.50	30
1995	A Career Retrospective	28-day		29.50	30

Milestones in Space - D. Dixon

YEAR	ISSUE	EDITION LIMIT	YEAR RETD.	ISSUE PRICE	*QUOTE U.S.$
1994	Moon Landing	28-day		29.50	30
1995	Space Lab	28-day		29.50	30
1995	Maiden Flight of Columbia	28-day		29.50	30
1995	Free Walk in Space	28-day		29.50	30
1995	Lunar Rover	28-day		29.50	30
1995	Handshake in Space	28-day		29.50	30

Mixed Company - P. Cooper

YEAR	ISSUE	EDITION LIMIT	YEAR RETD.	ISSUE PRICE	*QUOTE U.S.$
1990	Two Against One	14-day		29.50	36
1990	A Sticky Situation	14-day		29.50	36
1990	What's Up	14-day		29.50	30
1990	All Wrapped Up	14-day		29.50	36
1990	Picture Perfect	14-day		29.50	30
1991	A Moment to Unwind	14-day		29.50	33
1991	Ole	14-day		29.50	33
1991	Picnic Prowlers	14-day		29.50	30

Murals From The Precious Moments Chapel - S. Butcher

YEAR	ISSUE	EDITION LIMIT	YEAR RETD.	ISSUE PRICE	*QUOTE U.S.$
1995	The Pearl of Great Price	28-day		35.00	35
1995	The Good Samaritan	28-day		35.00	35
1996	The Prodigal Son	28-day		35.00	35

YEAR	ISSUE	EDITION LIMIT	YEAR RETD.	ISSUE PRICE	*QUOTE U.S.$
1996	The Good Shepherd	28-day		35.00	35

Mystic Warriors - C. Ren

YEAR	ISSUE	EDITION LIMIT	YEAR RETD.	ISSUE PRICE	*QUOTE U.S.$
1992	Deliverance	28-day		29.50	30
1992	Mystic Warrior	28-day		29.50	35
1992	Sun Seeker	28-day		29.50	30
1992	Top Gun	28-day		29.50	30
1992	Man Who Walks Alone	28-day		29.50	30
1992	Windrider	28-day		29.50	30
1992	Spirit of the Plains	28-day		29.50	30
1993	Blue Thunder	28-day		29.50	30
1993	Sun Glow	28-day		29.50	30
1993	Peace Maker	28-day		29.50	30

Native American Legends - A. Biffignandi

YEAR	ISSUE	EDITION LIMIT	YEAR RETD.	ISSUE PRICE	*QUOTE U.S.$
1996	Peace Pipe	28-day		29.95	30
1996	Feather-Woman	28-day		29.95	30
1996	Spirit of Serenity	28-day		29.95	30

Nature's Majestic Cats - M. Richter

YEAR	ISSUE	EDITION LIMIT	YEAR RETD.	ISSUE PRICE	*QUOTE U.S.$
1993	Siberian Tiger	28-day		29.50	30
1993	Himalayan Snow Leopard	28-day		29.50	30
1993	African Lion	28-day		29.50	30
1994	Asian Clouded Leopard	28-day		29.50	30
1994	American Cougar	28-day		29.50	30
1994	East African Leopard	28-day		29.50	30
1994	African Cheetah	28-day		29.50	30
1994	Canadian Lynx	28-day		29.50	30

Nature's Nighttime Realm - G. Murray

YEAR	ISSUE	EDITION LIMIT	YEAR RETD.	ISSUE PRICE	*QUOTE U.S.$
1992	Bobcat	28-day		29.50	30
1992	Cougar	28-day		29.50	30
1993	Jaguar	28-day		29.50	30
1993	White Tiger	28-day		29.50	30
1993	Lynx	28-day		29.50	30
1993	Lion	28-day		29.50	30
1993	Snow Leopard	28-day		29.50	30
1993	Cheetah	28-day		29.50	30

Nature's Quiet Moments - R. Parker

YEAR	ISSUE	EDITION LIMIT	YEAR RETD.	ISSUE PRICE	*QUOTE U.S.$
1988	A Curious Pair	14-day		37.50	38
1988	Northern Morning	14-day		37.50	38
1988	Just Resting	14-day		37.50	38
1989	Waiting Out the Storm	14-day		37.50	38
1989	Creekside	14-day		37.50	38
1989	Autumn Foraging	14-day		37.50	38
1989	Old Man of the Mountain	14-day		37.50	38
1989	Mountain Blooms	14-day		37.50	38

Noble American Indian Women - D. Wright

YEAR	ISSUE	EDITION LIMIT	YEAR RETD.	ISSUE PRICE	*QUOTE U.S.$
1989	Sacajawea	14-day		29.50	30-45
1990	Pocahontas	14-day		29.50	30-45
1990	Minnehaha	14-day		29.50	35
1990	Pine Leaf	14-day		29.50	45
1990	Lily of the Mohawk	14-day		29.50	30
1990	White Rose	14-day		29.50	35
1991	Lozen	14-day		29.50	30
1991	Falling Star	14-day		29.50	35

Noble Owls of America - J. Seerey-Lester

YEAR	ISSUE	EDITION LIMIT	YEAR RETD.	ISSUE PRICE	*QUOTE U.S.$
1986	Morning Mist	15,000		55.00	55
1987	Prairie Sundown	15,000		55.00	55
1987	Winter Vigil	15,000		55.00	55
1987	Autumn Mist	15,000		75.00	75
1987	Dawn in the Willows	15,000		55.00	55
1987	Snowy Watch	15,000		60.00	60
1988	Hiding Place	15,000		55.00	55
1988	Waiting for Dusk	15,000		55.00	55

Nolan Ryan - R. Tanenbaum

YEAR	ISSUE	EDITION LIMIT	YEAR RETD.	ISSUE PRICE	*QUOTE U.S.$
1994	The Strikeout Express	28-day		29.50	45
1994	Birth of a Legend	28-day		29.50	30
1994	Mr. Fastball	28-day		29.50	30
1994	Million-Dollar Player	28-day		29.50	30
1994	27 Seasons	28-day		29.50	30
1994	Farewell	28-day		29.50	30
1994	The Ryan Express	28-day		29.50	30

Norman Rockwell's Saturday Evening Post Baseball - N. Rockwell

YEAR	ISSUE	EDITION LIMIT	YEAR RETD.	ISSUE PRICE	*QUOTE U.S.$
1992	100th Year of Baseball	Open		19.50	20
1993	The Rookie	Open		19.50	20
1993	The Dugout	Open		19.50	20
1993	Bottom of the Sixth	Open		19.50	20

North American Ducks - R. Lawrence

YEAR	ISSUE	EDITION LIMIT	YEAR RETD.	ISSUE PRICE	*QUOTE U.S.$
1991	Autumn Flight	14-day		29.50	36
1991	The Resting Place	14-day		29.50	30
1991	Twin Flight	14-day		29.50	30
1992	Misty Morning	14-day		29.50	30
1992	Springtime Thaw	14-day		29.50	30
1992	Summer Retreat	14-day		29.50	30
1992	Overcast	14-day		29.50	30
1992	Perfect Pintails	14-day		29.50	30

North American Gamebirds - J. Killen

YEAR	ISSUE	EDITION LIMIT	YEAR RETD.	ISSUE PRICE	*QUOTE U.S.$
1990	Ring-necked Pheasant	14-day		37.50	38
1990	Bobwhite Quail	14-day		37.50	45
1990	Ruffed Grouse	14-day		37.50	38
1990	Gambel Quail	14-day		37.50	42
1990	Mourning Dove	14-day		37.50	45

*Quotes have been rounded up to nearest dollar

YEAR ISSUE		EDITION LIMIT	YEAR RETD.	ISSUE PRICE	*QUOTE U.S.$
1990	Woodcock	14-day		37.50	45
1991	Chukar Partridge	14-day		37.50	45
1991	Wild Turkey	14-day		37.50	45

North American Waterbirds - R. Lawrence

YEAR ISSUE		EDITION LIMIT	YEAR RETD.	ISSUE PRICE	*QUOTE U.S.$
1988	Wood Ducks	14-day		37.50	50
1988	Hooded Mergansers	14-day		37.50	50
1988	Pintails	14-day		37.50	40
1988	Canada Geese	14-day		37.50	40
1989	American Widgeons	14-day		37.50	54
1989	Canvasbacks	14-day		37.50	55
1989	Mallard Pair	14-day		37.50	60
1989	Snow Geese	14-day		37.50	45

The Nutcracker Ballet - S. Fisher

YEAR ISSUE		EDITION LIMIT	YEAR RETD.	ISSUE PRICE	*QUOTE U.S.$
1978	Clara	28-day		19.50	36
1979	Godfather	28-day		19.50	20
1979	Sugar Plum Fairy	28-day		19.50	45
1979	Snow Queen and King	28-day		19.50	40
1980	Waltz of the Flowers	28-day		19.50	20
1980	Clara and the Prince	28-day		19.50	45

Official Honeymooner's Commemorative Plate - D. Bobnick

YEAR ISSUE		EDITION LIMIT	YEAR RETD.	ISSUE PRICE	*QUOTE U.S.$
1993	The Official Honeymooner's Commemorative Plate	28-day		37.50	125-225

The Official Honeymooners Plate Collection - D. Kilmer

YEAR ISSUE		EDITION LIMIT	YEAR RETD.	ISSUE PRICE	*QUOTE U.S.$
1987	The Honeymooners	14-day		24.50	100-200
1987	The Hucklebuck	14-day		24.50	100-195
1987	Baby, You're the Greatest	14-day		24.50	90-200
1988	The Golfer	14-day		24.50	110-220
1988	The TV Chefs	14-day		24.50	100-120
1988	Bang! Zoom!	14-day		24.50	80-110
1988	The Only Way to Travel	14-day		24.50	90-120
1988	The Honeymoon Express	14-day		24.50	125-200

On Wings of Eagles - J. Pitcher

YEAR ISSUE		EDITION LIMIT	YEAR RETD.	ISSUE PRICE	*QUOTE U.S.$
1994	"By Dawn's Early Light"	28-day		29.50	30
1994	Winter's Majestic Flight	28-day		29.50	30
1994	Over the Land of the Free	28-day		29.50	30
1995	Free Flight	28-day		29.50	30
1995	Morning Majesty	28-day		29.50	30
1995	Soaring Free	28-day		29.50	30

Our Cherished Seas - S. Barlowe

YEAR ISSUE		EDITION LIMIT	YEAR RETD.	ISSUE PRICE	*QUOTE U.S.$
1992	Whale Song	48-day		37.50	38
1992	Lions of the Sea	48-day		37.50	38
1992	Flight of the Dolphins	48-day		37.50	38
1992	Palace of the Seals	48-day		37.50	38
1993	Orca Ballet	48-day		37.50	38
1993	Emperors of the Ice	48-day		37.50	38
1993	Sea Turtles	48-day		37.50	38
1993	Splendor of the Sea	48-day		37.50	38

Petals and Purrs - B. Harrison

YEAR ISSUE		EDITION LIMIT	YEAR RETD.	ISSUE PRICE	*QUOTE U.S.$
1988	Blushing Beauties	14-day		24.50	55
1988	Spring Fever	14-day		24.50	38
1988	Morning Glories	14-day		24.50	45
1988	Forget-Me-Not	14-day		24.50	36
1989	Golden Fancy	14-day		24.50	30
1989	Pink Lillies	14-day		24.50	30
1989	Summer Sunshine	14-day		24.50	55
1989	Siamese Summer	14-day		24.50	55

Portraits of Jesus - W. Sallman

YEAR ISSUE		EDITION LIMIT	YEAR RETD.	ISSUE PRICE	*QUOTE U.S.$
1994	Jesus, The Good Shepherd	28-day		29.50	30
1994	Jesus in the Garden	28-day		29.50	30
1994	Jesus, Children's Friend	28-day		29.50	30
1994	The Lord's Supper	28-day		29.50	30
1994	Christ at Dawn	28-day		29.50	30
1994	Christ at Heart's Door	28-day		29.50	30
1994	Portrait of Christ	28-day		29.50	30
1994	Madonna and Christ Child	28-day		29.50	30

Portraits of the Bald Eagle - J. Pitcher

YEAR ISSUE		EDITION LIMIT	YEAR RETD.	ISSUE PRICE	*QUOTE U.S.$
1993	Ruler of the Sky	28-day		37.50	38
1993	In Bold Defiance	28-day		37.50	38
1993	Master Of The Summer Skies	28-day		37.50	38
1993	Spring's Sentinel	28-day		37.50	38

Portraits of the Wild - J. Meger

YEAR ISSUE		EDITION LIMIT	YEAR RETD.	ISSUE PRICE	*QUOTE U.S.$
1994	Interlude	28-day		29.50	30
1994	Winter Solitude	28-day		29.50	30
1994	Devoted Protector	28-day		29.50	30
1994	Call of Autumn	28-day		29.50	30
1994	Watchful Eyes	28-day		29.50	30
1994	Babies of Spring	28-day		29.50	30
1994	Rocky Mountain Grandeur	28-day		29.50	30
1995	Unbridled Power	28-day		29.50	30
1995	Moonlight Vigil	28-day		29.50	30

Precious Moments Bible Story - S. Butcher

YEAR ISSUE		EDITION LIMIT	YEAR RETD.	ISSUE PRICE	*QUOTE U.S.$
1990	Come Let Us Adore Him	28-day		29.50	30
1992	They Followed The Star	28-day		29.50	30
1992	The Flight Into Egypt	28-day		29.50	30
1992	The Carpenter Shop	28-day		29.50	30
1992	Jesus In The Temple	28-day		29.50	30
1992	The Crucifixion	28-day		29.50	30
1993	He Is Not Here	28-day		29.50	30

Precious Moments Classics - S. Butcher

YEAR ISSUE		EDITION LIMIT	YEAR RETD.	ISSUE PRICE	*QUOTE U.S.$
1993	God Loveth A Cheerful Giver	28-day		35.00	35
1993	Make A Joyful Noise	28-day		35.00	35
1994	Love One Another	28-day		35.00	35
1994	You Have Touched So Many Hearts	28-day		35.00	35
1994	Praise the Lord Anyhow	28-day		35.00	35
1994	I Believe in Miracles	28-day		35.00	35
1994	Good Friends Are Forever	28-day		35.00	35
1994	Jesus Loves Me	28-day		35.00	35
1995	Friendship Hits the Spot	28-day		35.00	35
1995	To My Deer Friend	28-day		35.00	35

Precious Moments Plates - T. Utz

YEAR ISSUE		EDITION LIMIT	YEAR RETD.	ISSUE PRICE	*QUOTE U.S.$
1979	Friend in the Sky	28-day		21.50	50
1980	Sand in her Shoe	28-day		21.50	27
1980	Snow Bunny	28-day		21.50	18
1980	Seashells	28-day		21.50	38
1981	Dawn	28-day		21.50	27
1982	My Kitty	28-day		21.50	36

Precious Moments Words of Love - S. Butcher

YEAR ISSUE		EDITION LIMIT	YEAR RETD.	ISSUE PRICE	*QUOTE U.S.$
1995	Your Friendship Is Soda-licious	28-day		35.00	35
1996	Your Love Is So Uplifting	28-day		35.00	35
1996	Love Is From Above	28-day		35.00	35
1996	Love Lifted Me	28-day		35.00	35

Precious Portraits - B. P. Gutmann

YEAR ISSUE		EDITION LIMIT	YEAR RETD.	ISSUE PRICE	*QUOTE U.S.$
1987	Sunbeam	14-day		24.50	36-49
1987	Mischief	14-day		24.50	30
1987	Peach Blossom	14-day		24.50	36
1987	Goldilocks	14-day		24.50	30
1987	Fairy Gold	14-day		24.50	36-45
1987	Bunny	14-day		24.50	30

The Prideful Ones - C. DeHaan

YEAR ISSUE		EDITION LIMIT	YEAR RETD.	ISSUE PRICE	*QUOTE U.S.$
1994	Village Markers	28-day		29.50	30
1994	His Pride	28-day		29.50	30
1994	Appeasing the Water People	28-day		29.50	30
1994	Tribal Guardian	28-day		29.50	30
1994	Autumn Passage	28-day		29.50	30
1994	Winter Hunter	28-day		29.50	30
1994	Silent Trail Break	28-day		29.50	30
1994	Water Breaking	28-day		29.50	30
1994	Crossing at the Big Trees	28-day		29.50	30
1995	Winter Songsinger	28-day		29.50	30

Princesses of the Plains - D. Wright

YEAR ISSUE		EDITION LIMIT	YEAR RETD.	ISSUE PRICE	*QUOTE U.S.$
1993	Prairie Flower	28-day		29.50	30
1993	Snow Princess	28-day		29.50	30
1993	Wild Flower	28-day		29.50	30
1993	Noble Beauty	28-day		29.50	30
1993	Winter's Rose	28-day		29.50	30
1993	Gentle Beauty	28-day		29.50	30
1994	Nature's Guardian	28-day		29.50	30
1994	Mountain Princess	28-day		29.50	30
1995	Proud Dreamer	28-day		29.50	30
1995	Spring Maiden	28-day		29.50	30

Proud Indian Families - K. Freeman

YEAR ISSUE		EDITION LIMIT	YEAR RETD.	ISSUE PRICE	*QUOTE U.S.$
1991	The Storyteller	14-day		29.50	50
1991	The Power of the Basket	14-day		29.50	36
1991	The Naming Ceremony	14-day		29.50	30
1992	Playing With Tradition	14-day		29.50	30
1992	Preparing the Berry Harvest	14-day		29.50	30
1992	Ceremonial Dress	14-day		29.50	30
1992	Sounds of the Forest	14-day		29.50	30
1992	The Marriage Ceremony	14-day		29.50	30
1993	The Jewelry Maker	14-day		29.50	30
1993	Beautiful Creations	14-day		29.50	30

Proud Innocence - J. Schmidt

YEAR ISSUE		EDITION LIMIT	YEAR RETD.	ISSUE PRICE	*QUOTE U.S.$
1994	Desert Bloom	28-day		29.50	30
1994	Little Drummer	28-day		29.50	30
1995	Young Archer	28-day		29.50	30
1995	Morning Child	28-day		29.50	30
1995	Wise One	28-day		29.50	30
1995	Sun Blossom	28-day		29.50	30
1995	Laughing Heart	28-day		29.50	30
1995	Gentle Flower	28-day		29.50	30

The Proud Nation - R. Swanson

YEAR ISSUE		EDITION LIMIT	YEAR RETD.	ISSUE PRICE	*QUOTE U.S.$
1989	Navajo Little One	14-day		24.50	50
1989	In a Big Land	14-day		24.50	40
1989	Out with Mama's Flock	14-day		24.50	25
1989	Newest Little Sheepherder	14-day		24.50	38
1989	Dressed Up for the Powwow	14-day		24.50	30
1989	Just a Few Days Old	14-day		24.50	30
1989	Autumn Treat	14-day		24.50	30
1989	Up in the Red Rocks	14-day		24.50	25

Puppy Playtime - J. Lamb

YEAR ISSUE		EDITION LIMIT	YEAR RETD.	ISSUE PRICE	*QUOTE U.S.$
1987	Double Take-Cocker Spaniels	14-day		24.50	75
1987	Catch of the Day-Golden Retrievers	14-day		24.50	45
1987	Cabin Fever-Black Labradors	14-day		24.50	45
1987	Weekend Gardener-Lhasa Apsos	14-day		24.50	36
1987	Getting Acquainted-Beagles	14-day		24.50	36
1987	Hanging Out-German Shepherd	14-day		24.50	45
1987	New Leash on Life-Mini Schnauzer	14-day		24.50	45
1987	Fun and Games-Poodle	14-day		24.50	36

Quiet Moments Of Childhood - D. Green

YEAR ISSUE		EDITION LIMIT	YEAR RETD.	ISSUE PRICE	*QUOTE U.S.$
1991	Elizabeth's Afternoon Tea	14-day		29.50	45
1991	Christina's Secret Garden	14-day		29.50	36
1991	Eric & Erin's Storytime	14-day		29.50	30
1992	Jessica's Tea Party	14-day		29.50	33
1992	Megan & Monique's Bakery	14-day		29.50	36
1992	Children's Day By The Sea	14-day		29.50	30
1992	Jordan's Playful Pups	14-day		29.50	33
1992	Daniel's Morning Playtime	14-day		29.50	30

The Quilted Countryside: A Signature Collection by Mel Steele - M. Steele

YEAR ISSUE		EDITION LIMIT	YEAR RETD.	ISSUE PRICE	*QUOTE U.S.$
1991	The Old Country Store	14-day		29.50	36
1991	Winter's End	14-day		29.50	36
1991	The Quilter's Cabin	14-day		29.50	45
1991	Spring Cleaning	14-day		29.50	36
1991	Summer Harvest	14-day		29.50	36
1991	The Country Merchant	14-day		29.50	36
1992	Wash Day	14-day		29.50	30
1992	The Antiques Store	14-day		29.50	33

Remembering Norma Jeane - F. Accornero

YEAR ISSUE		EDITION LIMIT	YEAR RETD.	ISSUE PRICE	*QUOTE U.S.$
1994	The Girl Next Door	28-day		29.50	39
1994	Her Day in the Sun	28-day		29.50	39
1994	A Star is Born	28-day		29.50	35
1994	Beauty Secrets	28-day		29.50	35
1995	In the Spotlight	28-day		29.50	30
1995	Bathing Beauty	28-day		29.50	30
1995	Young & Carefree	28-day		29.50	30
1995	Free Spirit	28-day		29.50	30
1995	A Country Girl at Heart	28-day		29.50	30
1996	Hometown Girl	28-day		29.50	30

The Renaissance Angels - L. Bywaters

YEAR ISSUE		EDITION LIMIT	YEAR RETD.	ISSUE PRICE	*QUOTE U.S.$
1994	Doves of Peace	28-day		29.50	30
1994	Angelic Innocence	28-day		29.50	30
1994	Joy to the World	28-day		29.50	30
1995	Angel of Faith	28-day		29.50	30
1995	The Christmas Star	28-day		29.50	30
1995	Trumpeter's Call	28-day		29.50	30
1995	Harmonious Heavens	28-day		29.50	30
1995	The Angels Sing	28-day		29.50	30

Rockwell Home of the Brave - N. Rockwell

YEAR ISSUE		EDITION LIMIT	YEAR RETD.	ISSUE PRICE	*QUOTE U.S.$
1981	Reminiscing	18,000		35.00	53
1981	Hero's Welcome	18,000		35.00	53
1981	Back to his Old Job	18,000		35.00	53
1981	War Hero	18,000		35.00	35
1982	Willie Gillis in Church	18,000		35.00	53
1982	War Bond	18,000		35.00	35
1982	Uncle Sam Takes Wings	18,000		35.00	75
1982	Taking Mother over the Top	18,000		35.00	35

Romance of the Rails - D. Tutwiler

YEAR ISSUE		EDITION LIMIT	YEAR RETD.	ISSUE PRICE	*QUOTE U.S.$
1994	Starlight Limited	28-day		29.50	30
1994	Portland Rose	28-day		29.50	30
1994	Orange Blossom Special	28-day		29.50	30
1994	Morning Star	28-day		29.50	30
1994	Crescent Limited	28-day		29.50	30
1994	Sunset Limited	28-day		29.50	30
1994	Western Star	28-day		29.50	30
1995	Sunrise Limited	28-day		29.50	30
1995	The Blue Bonnett	28-day		29.50	30
1995	The Pine Tree Limited	28-day		29.50	

Romantic Castles of Europe - D. Sweet

YEAR ISSUE		EDITION LIMIT	YEAR RETD.	ISSUE PRICE	*QUOTE U.S.$
1990	Ludwig's Castle	19,500		55.00	55
1991	Palace of the Moors	19,500		55.00	55
1991	Swiss Isle Fortress	19,500		55.00	55
1991	The Legendary Castle of Leeds	19,500		55.00	55
1991	Davinci's Chambord	19,500		55.00	55
1991	Eilean Donan	19,500		55.00	55
1992	Eltz Castle	19,500		55.00	55
1992	Kylemore Abbey	19,500		55.00	55

Romantic Flights of Fancy - Q. Lemonds

YEAR ISSUE		EDITION LIMIT	YEAR RETD.	ISSUE PRICE	*QUOTE U.S.$
1994	Sunlit Waltz	28-day		29.50	30
1994	Morning Minuet	28-day		29.50	30
1994	Evening Solo	28-day		29.50	30
1994	Summer Sonata	28-day		29.50	30
1995	Twilight Tango	28-day		29.50	30
1995	Sunset Ballet	28-day		29.50	30

Romantic Victorian Keepsake - J. Grossman

YEAR ISSUE		EDITION LIMIT	YEAR RETD.	ISSUE PRICE	*QUOTE U.S.$
1992	Dearest Kiss	28-day		35.00	35
1992	First Love	28-day		35.00	35
1992	As Fair as a Rose	28-day		35.00	35
1992	Springtime Beauty	28-day		35.00	35
1992	Summertime Fancy	28-day		35.00	35
1992	Bonnie Blue Eyes	28-day		35.00	35
1992	Precious Friends	28-day		35.00	35
1994	Bonnets and Bouquets	28-day		35.00	3
1994	My Beloved Teddy	28-day		35.00	3
1994	A Sweet Romance	28-day		35.00	3

Santa Takes a Break - T. Newsom

YEAR ISSUE		EDITION LIMIT	YEAR RETD.	ISSUE PRICE	*QUOTE U.S.$
1995	Santa's Last Stop	28-day		29.95	3
1995	Santa's Railroad	28-day		29.95	3
1995	A Jolly Good Catch	28-day		29.95	3

*Quotes have been rounded up to nearest dollar

YEAR	ISSUE	EDITION LIMIT	YEAR RETD.	ISSUE PRICE	*QUOTE U.S.$
1995	Simple Pleasures	28-day		29.95	30

The Saturday Evening Post - N. Rockwell

YEAR	ISSUE	EDITION LIMIT	YEAR RETD.	ISSUE PRICE	*QUOTE U.S.$
1989	The Wonders of Radio	14-day		35.00	45
1989	Easter Morning	14-day		35.00	60
1989	The Facts of Life	14-day		35.00	45
1990	The Window Washer	14-day		35.00	45
1990	First Flight	14-day		35.00	54
1990	Traveling Companion	14-day		35.00	35
1990	Jury Room	14-day		35.00	35
1990	Furlough	14-day		35.00	35

Scenes of An American Christmas - B. Perry

YEAR	ISSUE	EDITION LIMIT	YEAR RETD.	ISSUE PRICE	*QUOTE U.S.$
1994	I'll Be Home for Christmas	28-day		29.50	30
1994	Christmas Eve Worship	28-day		29.50	30
1994	A Holiday Happening	28-day		29.50	30
1994	A Long Winter's Night	28-day		29.50	30
1994	The Sounds of Christmas	28-day		29.50	30
1994	Dear Santa	28-day		29.50	30
1995	An Afternoon Outing	28-day		29.50	30
1995	Winter Worship	28-day		29.50	30

Seasons of the Bald Eagle - J. Pitcher

YEAR	ISSUE	EDITION LIMIT	YEAR RETD.	ISSUE PRICE	*QUOTE U.S.$
1991	Autumn in the Mountains	14-day		37.50	45
1991	Winter in the Valley	14-day		37.50	38
1991	Spring on the River	14-day		37.50	38
1991	Summer on the Seacoast	14-day		37.50	38

Sharing Life's Most Precious Memories - S. Butcher

YEAR	ISSUE	EDITION LIMIT	YEAR RETD.	ISSUE PRICE	*QUOTE U.S.$
1995	Thee I Love	28-day		35.00	35
1995	The Joy of the Lord Is My Strength	28-day		35.00	35
1995	May Your Every Wish Come True	28-day		35.00	35
1996	I'm So Glad That God	28-day		35.00	35
1996	Heaven Bless You	28-day		35.00	35

Sharing the Moments - S. Butcher

YEAR	ISSUE	EDITION LIMIT	YEAR RETD.	ISSUE PRICE	*QUOTE U.S.$
1995	You Have Touched So Many Hearts	28-day		35.00	35
1996	Friendship Hits The Spot	28-day		35.00	35
1996	Jesus Love Me	28-day		35.00	35

Single Issues - T. Utz

YEAR	ISSUE	EDITION LIMIT	YEAR RETD.	ISSUE PRICE	*QUOTE U.S.$
1983	Princess Grace	21-day		39.50	45

Small Wonders of the Wild - C. Frace

YEAR	ISSUE	EDITION LIMIT	YEAR RETD.	ISSUE PRICE	*QUOTE U.S.$
1989	Hideaway	14-day		29.50	45
1990	Young Explorers	14-day		29.50	36
1990	Three of a Kind	14-day		29.50	75
1990	Quiet Morning	14-day		29.50	36
1990	Eyes of Wonder	14-day		29.50	30
1990	Ready for Adventure	14-day		29.50	30
1990	Uno	14-day		29.50	45
1990	Exploring a New World	14-day		29.50	30

Spirit of the Mustang - C. DeHaan

YEAR	ISSUE	EDITION LIMIT	YEAR RETD.	ISSUE PRICE	*QUOTE U.S.$
1995	Winter's Thunder	28-day		29.95	30
1995	Moonlit Run	28-day		29.95	30
1995	Morning Reverie	28-day		29.95	30
1995	Autumn Respite	28-day		29.95	30
1996	Spring Frolic	28-day		29.95	30

Sporting Generation - J. Lamb

YEAR	ISSUE	EDITION LIMIT	YEAR RETD.	ISSUE PRICE	*QUOTE U.S.$
1991	Like Father, Like Son	14-day		29.50	40
1991	Golden Moments	14-day		29.50	45
1991	The Lookout	14-day		29.50	35
1992	Picking Up The Scent	14-day		29.50	30
1992	First Time Out	14-day		29.50	36
1992	Who's Tracking Who	14-day		29.50	30
1992	Springing Into Action	14-day		29.50	30
1992	Point of Interest	14-day		29.50	30

STAR TREK® : 25th Anniversary Commemorative - T. Blackshear

YEAR	ISSUE	EDITION LIMIT	YEAR RETD.	ISSUE PRICE	*QUOTE U.S.$
1991	STAR TREK 25th Anniversary Commemorative Plate	14-day		37.50	200-225
1991	SPOCK	14-day		35.00	150-180
1991	Kirk	14-day		35.00	140-170
1992	McCoy	14-day		35.00	45-60
1992	Uhura	14-day		35.00	45
1992	Scotty	14-day		35.00	55
1993	Sulu	14-day		35.00	50
1993	Chekov	14-day		35.00	48
1994	U.S.S. Enterprise NCC-1701	14-day		35.00	50-75

STAR TREK® : Captain James T. Kirk Autographed Wall Plaque - N/A

YEAR	ISSUE	EDITION LIMIT	YEAR RETD.	ISSUE PRICE	*QUOTE U.S.$
1995	Captain James T. Kirk	5,000		195.00	195

STAR TREK® : Captain Jean-Luc Picard Autographed Wall Plaque - N/A

YEAR	ISSUE	EDITION LIMIT	YEAR RETD.	ISSUE PRICE	*QUOTE U.S.$
1994	Captain Jean-Luc Picard	5,000		195.00	100-200

STAR TREK® : Deep Space 9 - M. Weistling

YEAR	ISSUE	EDITION LIMIT	YEAR RETD.	ISSUE PRICE	*QUOTE U.S.$
1994	Commander Benjamin Sisko	28-day		35.00	35
1994	Security Chief Odo	28-day		35.00	35
1994	Major Kira Nerys	28-day		35.00	35
1994	Space Station	28-day		35.00	35
1994	Proprietor Quark	28-day		35.00	35
1995	Doctor Julian Bashir	28-day		35.00	35
1995	Lieutenant Jadzia Dax	28-day		35.00	35
1995	Chief Miles O'Brien	28-day		35.00	35

STAR TREK® : First Officer Spock® Autographed Wall Plaque - N/A

YEAR	ISSUE	EDITION LIMIT	YEAR RETD.	ISSUE PRICE	*QUOTE U.S.$
1994	First Officer Spock®	2,500		195.00	195

STAR TREK® : The Movies - M. Weistling

YEAR	ISSUE	EDITION LIMIT	YEAR RETD.	ISSUE PRICE	*QUOTE U.S.$
1994	STAR TREK IV: The Voyage Home	28-day		35.00	35
1994	STAR TREK II: The Wrath of Khan	28-day		35.00	35
1994	STAR TREK VI: The Undiscovered Country	28-day		35.00	35
1995	STAR TREK III: The Search For Spock	28-day		35.00	35
1995	STAR TREK V: The Final Frontier	28-day		35.00	35
1996	Triumphant Return	28-day		35.00	35

STAR TREK® : The Next Generation - T. Blackshear

YEAR	ISSUE	EDITION LIMIT	YEAR RETD.	ISSUE PRICE	*QUOTE U.S.$
1993	Captain Jean-Luc Picard	28-day		35.00	35
1993	Commander William T. Riker	28-day		35.00	35
1994	Lieutenant Commander Data	28-day		35.00	35
1994	Lieutenant Worf	28-day		35.00	35
1994	Counselor Deanna Troi	28-day		35.00	35
1995	Dr. Beverly Crusher	28-day		35.00	35
1995	Lieutenant Commander Laforge	28-day		35.00	35
1996	Ensign W. Crusher	28-day		35.00	35

STAR TREK® : The Next Generation The Episodes - K. Birdsong

YEAR	ISSUE	EDITION LIMIT	YEAR RETD.	ISSUE PRICE	*QUOTE U.S.$
1994	The Best of Both Worlds	28-day		35.00	35
1994	Encounter at Far Point	28-day		35.00	35
1995	Unification	28-day		35.00	35
1995	Yesterday's Enterprise	28-day		35.00	35
1995	All Good Things	28-day		35.00	35
1995	Descent	28-day		35.00	35
1996	Relics	28-day		35.00	35
1996	Redemption	28-day		35.00	35
1996	The Big Goodbye	28-day		35.00	35

STAR TREK® : The Spock® Commemorative Wall Plaque - N/A

YEAR	ISSUE	EDITION LIMIT	YEAR RETD.	ISSUE PRICE	*QUOTE U.S.$
1993	Spock® STAR TREK VI The Undiscovered Country	2,500		195.00	195

STAR TREK® : The Voyagers - K. Birdsong

YEAR	ISSUE	EDITION LIMIT	YEAR RETD.	ISSUE PRICE	*QUOTE U.S.$
1994	U.S.S. Enterprise NCC-1701	28-day		35.00	35
1994	U.S.S. Enterprise NCC-1701-D	28-day		35.00	35
1994	Klingon Battlecruiser	28-day		35.00	35
1994	Romulan Warbird	28-day		35.00	35
1994	U.S.S. Enterprise NCC-1701-A	28-day		35.00	35
1995	Ferengi Marauder	28-day		35.00	35
1995	Klingon Bird of Prey	28-day		35.00	35
1995	Triple Nacelled U.S.S. Enterprise	28-day		35.00	35
1995	Cardassian Galor Warship	28-day		35.00	35
1995	U.S.S. Excelsior	28-day		35.00	35

STAR TREK® Generations - K. Birdsong

YEAR	ISSUE	EDITION LIMIT	YEAR RETD.	ISSUE PRICE	*QUOTE U.S.$
1996	The Ultimate Confrontation	28-day		35.00	35
1996	Kirk's Final Voyage	28-day		35.00	35

Star Wars 10th Anniversary Commemorative - T. Blackshear

YEAR	ISSUE	EDITION LIMIT	YEAR RETD.	ISSUE PRICE	*QUOTE U.S.$
1990	Star Wars 10th Anniversary Commemorative Plates	14-day		39.50	100-145

Star Wars Plate Collection - T. Blackshear

YEAR	ISSUE	EDITION LIMIT	YEAR RETD.	ISSUE PRICE	*QUOTE U.S.$
1987	Hans Solo	14-day		29.50	75-120
1987	R2-D2 and Wicket	14-day		29.50	75-150
1987	Luke Skywalker and Darth Vader	14-day		29.50	75-150
1987	Princess Leia	14-day		29.50	90-100
1987	The Imperial Walkers	14-day		29.50	90
1987	Luke and Yoda	14-day		29.50	100
1988	Space Battle	14-day		29.50	200-345
1988	Crew in Cockpit	14-day		29.50	100-225

Star Wars Space Vehicles - S. Hillios

YEAR	ISSUE	EDITION LIMIT	YEAR RETD.	ISSUE PRICE	*QUOTE U.S.$
1995	Millenium Falcon	28-day		35.00	35
1995	TIE Fighters	28-day		35.00	35
1995	Red Five X-Wing Fighters	28-day		35.00	35
1995	Imperial Shuttle	28-day		35.00	35
1995	STAR Destroyer	28-day		35.00	35
1996	Snow Speeders	28-day		35.00	35
1996	B-Wing Fighter	28-day		35.00	35

Star Wars Trilogy - M. Weistling

YEAR	ISSUE	EDITION LIMIT	YEAR RETD.	ISSUE PRICE	*QUOTE U.S.$
1993	Star Wars	28-day		37.50	50-75
1993	The Empire Strikes Back	28-day		37.50	50-65
1993	Return Of The Jedi	28-day		37.50	65-75

Symphony of the Sea - R. Koni

YEAR	ISSUE	EDITION LIMIT	YEAR RETD.	ISSUE PRICE	*QUOTE U.S.$
1995	Fluid Grace	28-day		29.95	30
1995	Dolphin's Dance	28-day		29.95	30
1995	Orca Ballet	28-day		29.95	30
1995	Moonlit Minuet	28-day		29.95	30
1995	Sailfish Serenade	28-day		29.95	30
1995	Starlit Waltz	28-day		29.95	30
1995	Sunset Splendor	28-day		29.95	30
1995	Coral Chorus	28-day		29.95	30

Those Delightful Dalmations - N/A

YEAR	ISSUE	EDITION LIMIT	YEAR RETD.	ISSUE PRICE	*QUOTE U.S.$
1995	You Missed a Spot	28-day		29.95	30
1995	Here's a Good Spot	28-day		29.95	30

Timeless Expressions of the Orient - M. Tsang

YEAR	ISSUE	EDITION LIMIT	YEAR RETD.	ISSUE PRICE	*QUOTE U.S.$
1990	Fidelity	15,000		75.00	95
1991	Femininity	15,000		75.00	75
1991	Longevity	15,000		75.00	75
1991	Beauty	15,000		55.00	55
1992	Courage	15,000		55.00	55

Treasured Days - H. Bond

YEAR	ISSUE	EDITION LIMIT	YEAR RETD.	ISSUE PRICE	*QUOTE U.S.$
1987	Ashley	14-day		29.50	60
1987	Christopher	14-day		24.50	45
1987	Sara	14-day		24.50	30
1987	Jeremy	14-day		24.50	30-45
1987	Amanda	14-day		24.50	45
1988	Nicholas	14-day		24.50	45
1988	Lindsay	14-day		24.50	45
1988	Justin	14-day		24.50	45

A Treasury of Cherished Teddies - P. Hillman

YEAR	ISSUE	EDITION LIMIT	YEAR RETD.	ISSUE PRICE	*QUOTE U.S.$
1994	Happy Holidays, Friend	28-day		29.50	30
1995	A New Year with Old Friends	28-day		29.50	30
1995	Valentines For You	28-day		29.50	30
1995	Friendship is in the Air	28-day		29.50	30
1995	Showers of Friendship	28-day		29.50	30
1996	Friendship is in Bloom	28-day		29.50	30
1996	Planting the Seeds of Friendship	28-day		29.50	30
1996	A Day in the Park	28-day		29.50	30
1996	Smooth Sailing	28-day		29.50	30
1996	School Days	28-day		29.50	30

Unbridled Spirit - C. DeHaan

YEAR	ISSUE	EDITION LIMIT	YEAR RETD.	ISSUE PRICE	*QUOTE U.S.$
1992	Surf Dancer	28-day		29.50	30
1992	Winter Renegade	28-day		29.50	30
1992	Desert Shadows	28-day		29.50	30
1993	Painted Sunrise	28-day		29.50	30
1993	Desert Duel	28-day		29.50	30
1993	Midnight Run	28-day		29.50	30
1993	Moonlight Majesty	28-day		29.50	30
1993	Autumn Reverie	28-day		29.50	30
1993	Blizzard's Peril	28-day		29.50	30
1993	Sunrise Surprise	28-day		29.50	30

Under the Sea - C. Bragg

YEAR	ISSUE	EDITION LIMIT	YEAR RETD.	ISSUE PRICE	*QUOTE U.S.$
1993	Tales of Tavarua	28-day		29.50	30
1993	Water's Edge	28-day		29.50	30
1994	Beauty of the Reef	28-day		29.50	30
1994	Rainbow Reef	28-day		29.50	30
1994	Orca Odyssey	28-day		29.50	30
1994	Rescue the Reef	28-day		29.50	30
1994	Underwater Dance	28-day		29.50	30
1994	Gentle Giants	28-day		29.50	30
1995	Undersea Enchantment	28-day		29.50	30
1995	Penguin Paradise	28-day		29.50	30

Undersea Visions - J. Enright

YEAR	ISSUE	EDITION LIMIT	YEAR RETD.	ISSUE PRICE	*QUOTE U.S.$
1995	Secret Sanctuary	28-day		29.95	30
1995	Temple of Treasures	28-day		29.95	30
1996	Temple Beneath the Sea	28-day		29.95	30
1996	Lost Kingdom	28-day		29.95	30
1996	Mysterious Ruins	28-day		29.95	30

Utz Mother's Day - T. Utz

YEAR	ISSUE	EDITION LIMIT	YEAR RETD.	ISSUE PRICE	*QUOTE U.S.$
1983	A Gift of Love	N/A		27.50	38
1983	Mother's Helping Hand	N/A		27.50	28
1983	Mother's Angel	N/A		27.50	28

Vanishing Rural America - J. Harrison

YEAR	ISSUE	EDITION LIMIT	YEAR RETD.	ISSUE PRICE	*QUOTE U.S.$
1991	Quiet Reflections	14-day		29.50	45
1991	Autumn's Passage	14-day		29.50	45
1991	Storefront Memories	14-day		29.50	30
1991	Country Path	14-day		29.50	36
1991	When the Circus Came To Town	14-day		29.50	36
1991	Covered in Fall	14-day		29.50	45
1991	America's Heartland	14-day		29.50	33
1991	Rural Delivery	14-day		29.50	33

Victorian Christmas Memories - J. Grossman

YEAR	ISSUE	EDITION LIMIT	YEAR RETD.	ISSUE PRICE	*QUOTE U.S.$
1992	A Visit from St. Nicholas	28-day		29.50	30
1993	Christmas Delivery	28-day		29.50	30
1993	Christmas Angels	28-day		29.50	30
1992	With Visions of Sugar Plums	28-day		29.50	30
1993	Merry Olde Kris Kringle	28-day		29.50	30
1993	Grandfather Frost	28-day		29.50	30
1993	Joyous Noel	28-day		29.50	30
1993	Christmas Innocence	28-day		29.50	30
1993	Dreaming of Santa	28-day		29.50	30
1993	Mistletoe & Holly	28-day		29.50	30

Victorian Playtime - M. H. Bogart

YEAR	ISSUE	EDITION LIMIT	YEAR RETD.	ISSUE PRICE	*QUOTE U.S.$
1991	A Busy Day	14-day		29.50	50
1992	Little Masterpiece	14-day		29.50	30
1992	Playing Bride	14-day		29.50	55
1992	Waiting for a Nibble	14-day		29.50	30
1992	Tea and Gossip	14-day		29.50	30
1992	Cleaning House	14-day		29.50	30
1992	A Little Persuasion	14-day		29.50	30
1992	Peek-a-Boo	14-day		29.50	30

*Quotes have been rounded up to nearest dollar

Warrior's Pride - C. DeHaan

YEAR ISSUE		EDITION LIMIT	YEAR RETD.	ISSUE PRICE	*QUOTE U.S.$
1994	Crow War Pony	28-day		29.50	30
1994	Running Free	28-day		29.50	30
1994	Blackfoot War Pony	28-day		29.50	30
1994	Southern Cheyenne	28-day		29.50	30
1995	Shoshoni War Ponies	28-day		29.50	30
1995	A Champion's Revelry	28-day		29.50	30
1995	Battle Colors	28-day		29.50	30
1995	Call of the Drums	28-day		29.50	30

The West of Frank McCarthy - F. McCarthy

1991	Attacking the Iron Horse	14-day		37.50	60
1991	Attempt on the Stage	14-day		37.50	45
1991	The Prayer	14-day		37.50	54
1991	On the Old North Trail	14-day		37.50	48
1991	The Hostile Threat	14-day		37.50	45
1991	Bringing Out the Furs	14-day		37.50	45
1991	Kiowa Raider	14-day		37.50	45
1991	Headed North	14-day		37.50	45

Wilderness Spirits - P. Koni

1994	Eyes of the Night	28-day		29.95	30
1995	Howl of Innocence	28-day		29.95	30
1995	Midnight Call	28-day		29.95	30
1995	Breaking the Silence	28-day		29.95	30
1995	Moonlight Run	28-day		29.95	30
1995	Sunset Vigil	28-day		29.95	30
1995	Sunrise Spirit	28-day		29.95	30
1996	Valley of the Wolf	28-day		29.95	30

Winged Reflections - R. Parker

1989	Following Mama	14-day		37.50	38
1989	Above the Breakers	14-day		37.50	38
1989	Among the Reeds	14-day		37.50	38
1989	Freeze Up	14-day		37.50	38
1989	Wings Above the Water	14-day		37.50	38
1990	Summer Loon	14-day		29.50	30
1990	Early Spring	14-day		29.50	30
1990	At The Water's Edge	14-day		29.50	30

Winter Rails - T. Xaras

1992	Winter Crossing	28-day		29.50	30
1993	Coal Country	28-day		29.50	30
1993	Daylight Run	28-day		29.50	30
1993	By Sea or Rail	28-day		29.50	30
1993	Country Crossroads	28-day		29.50	30
1993	Timber Line	28-day		29.50	30
1993	The Long Haul	28-day		29.50	30
1993	Darby Crossing	28-day		29.50	30
1995	East Broad Top	28-day		29.50	30
1995	Landsdowne Station	28-day		29.50	30

Winter Wildlife - J. Seerey-Lester

1989	Close Encounters	15,000		55.00	55
1989	Among the Cattails	15,000		55.00	55
1989	The Refuge	15,000		55.00	55
1989	Out of the Blizzard	15,000		55.00	55
1989	First Snow	15,000		55.00	55
1989	Lying In Wait	15,000		55.00	55
1989	Winter Hiding	15,000		55.00	55
1989	Early Snow	15,000		55.00	55

Wizard of Oz Commemorative - T. Blackshear

1988	We're Off to See the Wizard	14-day		24.50	180-225
1988	Dorothy Meets the Scarecrow	14-day		24.50	75-150
1989	The Tin Man Speaks	14-day		24.50	125-175
1989	A Glimpse of the Munchkins	14-day		24.50	75-175
1989	The Witch Casts A Spell	14-day		24.50	100-175
1989	If I Were King Of The Forest	14-day		24.50	100-175
1989	The Great and Powerful Oz	14-day		24.50	125-175
1989	There's No Place Like Home	14-day		24.50	150-175

Wizard of Oz-Fifty Years of Oz - T. Blackshear

1989	Fifty Years of Oz	14-day		37.50	150-250

Wizard of Oz-Portraits From Oz - T. Blackshear

1989	Dorothy	14-day		29.50	125-200
1989	Scarecrow	14-day		29.50	100-150
1989	Tin Man	14-day		29.50	105-175
1990	Cowardly Lion	14-day		29.50	125-175
1990	Glinda	14-day		29.50	100-150
1990	Wizard	14-day		29.50	100-150
1990	Wicked Witch	14-day		29.50	175-300
1990	Toto	14-day		29.50	175-300

The Wonder Of Christmas - J. McClelland

1991	Santa's Secret	28-day		29.50	30
1991	My Favorite Ornament	28-day		29.50	30
1991	Waiting For Santa	28-day		29.50	30
1993	The Caroler	28-day		29.50	30

Woodland Babies - P. Manning

1995	Hollow Hideaway	28-day		29.95	30
1995	A Springtime Adventure	28-day		29.95	30
1995	Amber Eyes	28-day		29.95	30
1996	Peaceful Dreams	28-day		29.95	30
1996	Cozy Nest	28-day		29.95	30

Woodland Encounters - G. Giordano

1991	Want to Play?	14-day		29.50	30
1991	Peek-a-boo!	14-day		29.50	30
1991	Lunchtime Visitor	14-day		29.50	33
1991	Anyone for a Swim?	14-day		29.50	36
1991	Nature Scouts	14-day		29.50	36
1991	Meadow Meeting	14-day		29.50	33
1991	Hi Neighbor	14-day		29.50	30
1992	Field Day	14-day		29.50	36

The World Of Zolan - D. Zolan

1992	First Kiss	28-day		29.50	50
1992	Morning Discovery	28-day		29.50	40
1993	The Little Fisherman	28-day		29.50	45
1993	Letter to Grandma	28-day		29.50	50
1993	Twilight Prayer	28-day		29.50	60
1993	Flowers for Mother	28-day		29.50	50

Year Of The Wolf - A. Agnew

1993	Broken Silence	28-day		29.50	30
1993	Leader of the Pack	28-day		29.50	30
1993	Solitude	28-day		29.50	30
1994	Tundra Light	28-day		29.50	30
1994	Guardians of the High Country	28-day		29.50	30
1994	A Second Glance	28-day		29.50	30
1994	Free as the Wind	28-day		29.50	30
1994	Song of the Wolf	28-day		29.50	30
1995	Lords of the Tundra	28-day		29.50	30
1995	Wilderness Companions	28-day		29.50	30

Young Lords of The Wild - M. Richter

1994	Siberian Tiger Club	28-day		29.95	30
1995	Snow Leopard Cub	28-day		29.95	30
1995	Lion Cub	28-day		29.95	30
1995	Clouded Leopard Cub	28-day		29.95	30
1995	Cougar Cub	28-day		29.95	30
1995	Leopard Cub	28-day		29.95	30
1995	Cheetah Cub	28-day		29.95	30

Hamilton/Boehm

Award Winning Roses - Boehm

1979	Peace Rose	15,000		45.00	100
1979	White Masterpiece Rose	15,000		45.00	75
1979	Tropicana Rose	15,000		45.00	63
1979	Elegance Rose	15,000		45.00	63
1979	Queen Elizabeth Rose	15,000		45.00	63
1979	Royal Highness Rose	15,000		45.00	63
1979	Angel Face Rose	15,000		45.00	63
1979	Mr. Lincoln Rose	15,000		45.00	63

Gamebirds of North America - Boehm

1984	Ring-Necked Pheasant	15,000		62.50	63
1984	Bob White Quail	15,000		62.50	63
1984	American Woodcock	15,000		62.50	63
1984	California Quail	15,000		62.50	63
1984	Ruffed Grouse	15,000		62.50	63
1984	Wild Turkey	15,000		62.50	63
1984	Willow Partridge	15,000		62.50	63
1984	Prairie Grouse	15,000		62.50	63

Hummingbird Collection - Boehm

1980	Calliope	15,000		62.50	80
1980	Broadbilled	15,000		62.50	63
1980	Rufous Flame Bearer	15,000		62.50	80
1980	Broadtail	15,000		62.50	63
1980	Streamertail	15,000		62.50	80
1980	Blue Throated	15,000		62.50	80
1980	Crimson Topaz	15,000		62.50	63
1980	Brazilian Ruby	15,000		62.50	80

Owl Collection - Boehm

1980	Boreal Owl	15,000		45.00	65-85
1980	Snowy Owl	15,000		45.00	85
1980	Barn Owl	15,000		45.00	85
1980	Saw Whet Owl	15,000		45.00	85
1980	Great Horned Owl	15,000		45.00	85
1980	Screech Owl	15,000		45.00	85
1980	Short Eared Owl	15,000		45.00	85
1980	Barred Owl	15,000		45.00	85

Water Birds - Boehm

1981	Canada Geese	15,000		62.50	75
1981	Wood Ducks	15,000		62.50	63
1981	Hooded Merganser	15,000		62.50	87
1981	Ross's Geese	15,000		62.50	63
1981	Common Mallard	15,000		62.50	63
1981	Canvas Back	15,000		62.50	63
1981	Green Winged Teal	15,000		62.50	63
1981	American Pintail	15,000		62.50	63

Haviland

Twelve Days of Christmas - R. Hetreau

1970	Partridge	30,000		25.00	54
1971	Two Turtle Doves	30,000		25.00	25
1972	Three French Hens	30,000		27.50	28
1973	Four Calling Birds	30,000		28.50	30
1974	Five Golden Rings	30,000		30.00	30
1975	Six Geese a'laying	30,000		32.50	33
1976	Seven Swans	30,000		38.00	38
1977	Eight Maids	30,000		40.00	40
1978	Nine Ladies Dancing	30,000		45.00	67
1979	Ten Lord's a'leaping	30,000		50.00	50
1980	Eleven Pipers Piping	30,000		55.00	65
1981	Twelve Drummers	30,000		60.00	60

Haviland & Parlon

Christmas Madonnas - Various

1972	By Raphael - Raphael	5,000		35.00	42
1973	By Feruzzi - Feruzzi	5,000		40.00	78
1974	By Raphael - Raphael	5,000		42.50	43
1975	By Murillo - Murillo	7,500		42.50	43
1976	By Botticelli - Botticelli	7,500		45.00	45
1977	By Bellini - Bellini	7,500		48.00	48
1978	By Lippi - Lippi	7,500		48.00	53
1979	Madonna of The Eucharist - Botticelli	7,500		49.50	112

Hutschenreuther

The Glory of Christmas - W./C. Hallett

1982	The Nativity	25,000		80.00	125
1983	The Annunciation	25,000		80.00	115
1984	The Shepherds	25,000		80.00	100
1985	The Wiseman	25,000		80.00	100

Gunther Granget - G. Granget

1972	American Sparrows	5,000		50.00	150
1972	European Sparrows	5,000		30.00	65
1973	American Kildeer	2,250		75.00	90
1973	American Squirrel	2,500		75.00	75
1973	European Squirrel	2,500		35.00	50
1974	American Partridge	2,500		75.00	90
1975	American Rabbits	2,500		90.00	90
1976	Freedom in Flight	5,000		100.00	100
1976	Wrens	2,500		100.00	110
1976	Freedom in Flight, Gold	200		200.00	20
1977	Bears	2,500		100.00	10
1978	Foxes' Spring Journey	1,000		125.00	200

Imperial Ching-te Chen

Beauties of the Red Mansion - Z. HuiMin

1986	Pao-chai	115-day		27.92	5
1986	Yuan-chun	115-day		27.92	6
1987	Hsi-feng	115-day		30.92	3
1987	Hsi-chun	115-day		30.92	4
1988	Miao-yu	115-day		30.92	5
1988	Ying-chun	115-day		30.92	5
1988	Tai-yu	115-day		32.92	5
1988	Li-wan	115-day		32.92	5
1988	Ko-Ching	115-day		32.92	4
1988	Hsiang-yun	115-day		34.92	3
1989	Tan-Chun	115-day		34.92	4
1989	Chiao-chieh	115-day		34.92	3

Blessings From a Chinese Garden - Z. Song Mao

1988	The Gift of Purity	175-day		39.92	4
1989	The Gift of Grace	175-day		39.92	4
1989	The Gift of Beauty	175-day		42.92	4
1989	The Gift of Happiness	175-day		42.92	4
1990	The Gift of Truth	175-day		42.92	4
1990	The Gift of Joy	175-day		42.92	4

Flower Goddesses of China - Z. HuiMin

1991	The Lotus Goddess	175-day		34.92	3
1991	The Chrysanthemum Goddess	175-day		34.92	3
1991	The Plum Blossom Goddess	175-day		37.92	4
1991	The Peony Goddess	175-day		37.92	5
1991	The Narcissus Goddess	175-day		37.92	6
1991	The Camellia Goddess	175-day		37.92	

The Forbidden City - S. Fu

1990	Pavilion of 10,000 Springs	150-day		39.92	
1990	Flying Kites/Spring Day	150-day		39.92	
1990	Pavilion/Floating Jade Green	150-day		42.92	4
1991	The Lantern Festival	150-day		42.92	
1991	Nine Dragon Screen	150-day		42.92	
1991	The Hall of the Cultivating Mind	150-day		42.92	
1991	Dressing the Empress	150-day		45.92	
1991	Pavilion of Floating Cups	150-day		45.92	

Garden of Satin Wings - J. Xue-Bing

1992	A Morning Dream	115-day		29.92	
1993	An Evening Mist	115-day		29.92	
1993	A Garden Whisper	115-day		29.92	
1993	An Enchanting Interlude	115-day		29.92	

Legends of West Lake - J. Xue-Bing

1989	Lady White	175-day		29.92	
1990	Lady Silkworm	175-day		29.92	
1990	Laurel Peak	175-day		29.92	
1990	Rising Sun Terrace	175-day		32.92	
1990	The Apricot Fairy	175-day		32.92	
1990	Bright Pearl	175-day		32.92	
1990	Thread of Sky	175-day		34.92	
1991	Phoenix Mountain	175-day		34.92	35
1991	Ancestors of Tea	175-day		34.92	
1991	Three Pools Mirroring/Moon	175-day		36.92	
1991	Fly-In Peak	175-day		36.92	
1991	The Case of the Folding Fans	175-day		36.92	

*Quotes have been rounded up to nearest dolla

Maidens of the Folding Sky - J. Xue-Bing

YEAR	ISSUE	EDITION LIMIT	YEAR RETD.	ISSUE PRICE	*QUOTE U.S. $
1992	Lady Lu	175-day		29.92	35
1992	Mistress Yang	175-day		29.92	45
1992	Bride Yen Chun	175-day		32.92	80
1993	Parrot Maiden	175-day		32.92	80

Scenes from the Summer Palace - Z. Song Mao

YEAR	ISSUE	EDITION LIMIT	YEAR RETD.	ISSUE PRICE	*QUOTE U.S. $
1988	The Marble Boat	175-day		29.92	32
1988	Jade Belt Bridge	175-day		29.92	32
1989	Hall that Dispels the Clouds	175-day		32.92	33
1989	The Long Promenade	175-day		32.92	35
1989	Garden/Harmonious Pleasure	175-day		32.92	35
1989	The Great Stage	175-day		32.92	33
1989	Seventeen Arch Bridge	175-day		34.92	35
1989	Boaters on Kumming Lake	175-day		34.92	35

International Silver

Bicentennial - M. Deoliveira

YEAR	ISSUE	EDITION LIMIT	YEAR RETD.	ISSUE PRICE	*QUOTE U.S. $
1972	Signing Declaration	7,500		40.00	310
1973	Paul Revere	7,500		40.00	160
1974	Concord Bridge	7,500		40.00	115
1975	Crossing Delaware	7,500		50.00	80
1976	Valley Forge	7,500		50.00	65
1977	Surrender at Yorktown	7,500		50.00	60

John Hine N.A. Ltd.

David Winter Plate Collection - M. Fisher

YEAR	ISSUE	EDITION LIMIT	YEAR RETD.	ISSUE PRICE	*QUOTE U.S. $
1991	A Christmas Carol	10,000	1993	30.00	35-60
1991	Cotswold Village Plate	10,000	1993	30.00	35-60
1992	Chichester Cross Plate	10,000	1993	30.00	35-60
1992	Little Mill Plate	10,000	1993	30.00	35-60
1992	Old Curiosity Shop	10,000	1993	30.00	35-60
1992	Scrooge's Counting House	10,000	1993	30.00	35-60
1993	Dove Cottage	10,000		30.00	35
1993	Little Forge	10,000		30.00	35

KPM-Royal Berlin

Christmas - Unknown

YEAR	ISSUE	EDITION LIMIT	YEAR RETD.	ISSUE PRICE	*QUOTE U.S. $
1969	Christmas Star	5,000		28.00	380
1970	Three Kings	5,000		28.00	300
1971	Christmas Tree	5,000		28.00	290
1972	Christmas Angel	5,000		31.00	300
1973	Christ Child on Sled	5,000		33.00	280
1974	Angel and Horn	5,000		35.00	180
1975	Shepherds	5,000		40.00	165
1976	Star of Bethlehem	5,000		43.00	140
1977	Mary at Crib	5,000		46.00	100
1978	Three Wise Men	5,000		49.00	54
1979	The Manger	5,000		55.00	55
1980	Shepherds in Fields	5,000		55.00	55

Lalique Society of America

Annual - M. Lalique

YEAR	ISSUE	EDITION LIMIT	YEAR RETD.	ISSUE PRICE	*QUOTE U.S. $
1965	Deux Oiseaux (Two Birds)	2,000		25.00	1300
1966	Rose de Songerie (Dream Rose)	5,000		25.00	115
1967	Ballet de Poisson (Fish Ballet)	5,000		25.00	100
1968	Gazelle Fantaisie (Gazelle Fantasy)	5,000		25.00	75
1969	Papillon (Butterfly)	5,000		30.00	50
1970	Paon (Peacock)	5,000		30.00	60
1971	Hibou (Owl)	5,000		35.00	70
1972	Coquillage (Shell)	5,000		40.00	75
1973	Petit Geai (Jayling)	5,000		42.50	100
1974	Sous d'Argent (Silver Pennies)	5,000		47.50	95
1975	Duo de Poisson (Fish Duet)	5,000		50.00	140
1976	Aigle (Eagle)	5,000		60.00	90

Lance Corporation

American Expansion (Hudson Pewter) - P.W. Baston

YEAR	ISSUE	EDITION LIMIT	YEAR RETD.	ISSUE PRICE	*QUOTE U.S. $
975	Spirit of '76 (6" Plate)	4,812	1975	27.50	100-120
1975	American Independence	18,462	N/A	Unkn.	100-125
1975	American Expansion	2,250	N/A	Unkn.	50-75
1975	The American War Between the States	825	N/A	Unkn.	150-200

Sebastian Plates - P.W. Baston

YEAR	ISSUE	EDITION LIMIT	YEAR RETD.	ISSUE PRICE	*QUOTE U.S. $
978	Motif No. 1	4,878	1985	75.00	50-75
979	Grand Canyon	2,492	1985	75.00	50-75
980	Lone Cypress	718	1985	75.00	150-175
980	In The Candy Store	9,098	1985	39.50	40
981	The Doctor	7,547	1985	39.50	40
983	Little Mother	2,710	1985	39.50	40
984	Switching The Freight	706	1985	42.50	80-100

Lenox Collections

Adventures of the Deep Plate Collection - Unknown

YEAR	ISSUE	EDITION LIMIT	YEAR RETD.	ISSUE PRICE	*QUOTE U.S. $
994	Let's Play	Open		39.50	40
994	A New Day	Open		39.50	40
994	Shining On	Open		39.50	40
994	Polar Strollers	Open		39.50	40
994	New Birth	Open		39.50	40
1994	Gratitude	Open		39.50	40
1994	After Hours	Open		39.50	40
1994	Sea of Joy	Open		39.50	40

American Wildlife - N. Adams

YEAR	ISSUE	EDITION LIMIT	YEAR RETD.	ISSUE PRICE	*QUOTE U.S. $
1982	Red Foxes	9,500		65.00	65
1982	Ocelots	9,500		65.00	65
1982	Sea Lions	9,500		65.00	65
1982	Raccoons	9,500		65.00	65
1982	Dall Sheep	9,500		65.00	65
1982	Black Bears	9,500		65.00	65
1982	Mountain Lions	9,500		65.00	65
1982	Polar Bears	9,500		65.00	65
1982	Otters	9,500		65.00	65
1982	White Tailed Deer	9,500		65.00	65
1982	Buffalo	9,500		65.00	65
1982	Jack Rabbits	9,500		65.00	65

Amish Life Plates - D. Patterson

YEAR	ISSUE	EDITION LIMIT	YEAR RETD.	ISSUE PRICE	*QUOTE U.S. $
1994	Barn Raising	Open		39.50	40
1994	Country Kids	Open		39.50	40

Annual Christmas Plates - Various

YEAR	ISSUE	EDITION LIMIT	YEAR RETD.	ISSUE PRICE	*QUOTE U.S. $
1992	Sleigh - Unknown	Yr.Iss.	1992	75.00	75
1993	Midnight Sleighride - L. Bywater	90-day	1993	119.00	119

Arctic Wolves - J. VanZyle

YEAR	ISSUE	EDITION LIMIT	YEAR RETD.	ISSUE PRICE	*QUOTE U.S. $
1993	Far Country Crossing	90-day	1994	29.90	30
1993	Cry of the Wild	90-day	1994	29.90	30
1993	Nightwatch	90-day	1994	29.90	30
1993	Midnight Renegade	90-day	1994	29.90	30
1993	On the Edge	90-day	1994	29.90	30
1993	Picking Up the Trail	90-day	1994	29.90	30

Big Cats of the World - Q. Lemonds

YEAR	ISSUE	EDITION LIMIT	YEAR RETD.	ISSUE PRICE	*QUOTE U.S. $
1993	Black Panther	Open		39.50	40
1993	Chinese Leopard	Open		39.50	40
1993	Cougar	Open		39.50	40
1993	Bobcat	Open		39.50	40
1993	White Tiger	Open		39.50	40
1993	Tiger	Open		39.50	40
1993	Lion	Open		39.50	40
1993	Snow Leopard	Open		39.50	40

Birds of the Garden - W. Mumm

YEAR	ISSUE	EDITION LIMIT	YEAR RETD.	ISSUE PRICE	*QUOTE U.S. $
1992	Spring Glory, Cardinals	Open		39.50	40
1993	Sunbright Songbirds, Goldfinch	Open		39.50	40
1993	Bluebirds Haven, Bluebirds	Open		39.50	40
1993	Blossoming Bough, Chickadees	Open		39.50	40
1993	Jewels of the Garden, Hummingbirds	Open		39.50	40
1993	Indigo Meadow, Indigo Buntings	Open		39.50	40
1993	Scarlet Tanagers	Open		39.50	40

Boehm Birds - E. Boehm

YEAR	ISSUE	EDITION LIMIT	YEAR RETD.	ISSUE PRICE	*QUOTE U.S. $
1970	Wood Thrush	Yr.Iss.	1970	35.00	100
1971	Goldfinch	Yr.Iss.	1971	35.00	50
1972	Mountain Bluebird	Yr.Iss.	1972	37.50	45
1973	Meadowlark	Yr.Iss.	1973	50.00	50
1974	Rufous Hummingbird	Yr.Iss.	1974	45.00	50
1975	American Redstart	Yr.Iss.	1975	50.00	50
1976	Cardinals	Yr.Iss.	1976	53.00	53
1977	Robins	Yr.Iss.	1977	55.00	55
1978	Mockingbirds	Yr.Iss.	1978	58.00	58
1979	Golden-Crowned Kinglets	Yr.Iss.	1979	65.00	95
1980	Black-Throated Blue Warblers	Yr.Iss.	1980	80.00	112
1981	Eastern Phoebes	Yr.Iss.	1981	92.50	100

Boehm Woodland Wildlife - E. Boehm

YEAR	ISSUE	EDITION LIMIT	YEAR RETD.	ISSUE PRICE	*QUOTE U.S. $
1973	Racoons	Yr.Iss.	1973	50.00	50
1974	Red Foxes	Yr.Iss.	1974	52.50	53
1975	Cottontail Rabbits	Yr.Iss.	1975	58.50	59
1976	Eastern Chipmunks	Yr.Iss.	1976	62.50	63
1977	Beaver	Yr.Iss.	1977	67.50	68
1978	Whitetail Deer	Yr.Iss.	1978	70.00	70
1979	Squirrels	Yr.Iss.	1979	76.00	76
1980	Bobcats	Yr.Iss.	1980	82.50	83
1981	Martens	Yr.Iss.	1981	100.00	150
1982	River Otters	Yr.Iss.	1982	100.00	180

Cat Family Portrait - G. Coheleach

YEAR	ISSUE	EDITION LIMIT	YEAR RETD.	ISSUE PRICE	*QUOTE U.S. $
1994	Cougars	Open		39.50	40
1994	Lynx	Open		39.50	40
1994	Tigers	Open		39.50	40
1994	Snow Leopard	Open		39.50	40

Children of the Sun & Moon - D. Crowley

YEAR	ISSUE	EDITION LIMIT	YEAR RETD.	ISSUE PRICE	*QUOTE U.S. $
1993	Desert Blossom	Open		39.50	40
1993	Shy One	Open		39.50	40
1993	Feathers & Furs	Open		39.50	40
1994	Little Flower	Open		39.90	40
1994	Daughter of the Sun	Open		39.90	40
1994	Red Feathers	Open		39.90	40
1994	Stars in Her Eyes	Open		39.90	40
1994	Indigo Girl	Open		39.90	40

Crystal Hunter - Unknown

YEAR	ISSUE	EDITION LIMIT	YEAR RETD.	ISSUE PRICE	*QUOTE U.S. $
1994	Crystal Tiger	Open		39.50	40
1994	Dreamscape	Open		39.50	40
1994	Crystal Domain	Open		39.50	40
1994	Heart of Crystal	Open		39.50	40

Cubs of the Big Cats - Q. Lemonds

YEAR	ISSUE	EDITION LIMIT	YEAR RETD.	ISSUE PRICE	*QUOTE U.S. $
1993	Jaquar Cub	90-day	1994	29.90	30

Darling Dalmations - L. Picken

YEAR	ISSUE	EDITION LIMIT	YEAR RETD.	ISSUE PRICE	*QUOTE U.S. $
1993	Three Alarm Fire	90-day	1994	29.90	30
1993	All Fired Up	90-day	1994	29.90	30
1993	Fire Brigade	90-day	1994	29.90	30
1993	Pup in Boots	90-day	1994	29.90	30
1993	Caught in the Act	90-day	1994	29.90	30
1993	Please Don't Pick the Flowers	90-day	1994	29.90	30

Dolphins of the Seven Seas - J. Holderby

YEAR	ISSUE	EDITION LIMIT	YEAR RETD.	ISSUE PRICE	*QUOTE U.S. $
1993	Bottlenose Dolphins	Open		39.50	40

Eagle Conservation - R. Kelley

YEAR	ISSUE	EDITION LIMIT	YEAR RETD.	ISSUE PRICE	*QUOTE U.S. $
1993	Soaring the Peaks	Open		39.50	40
1993	Solo Flight	Open		39.50	40
1993	Northern Heritage	Open		39.50	40
1993	Lone Sentinel	Open		39.50	40
1993	River Scout	Open		39.50	40
1993	Eagles on Mt. McKinley	Open		39.50	40
1993	Daybreak on River's Edge	Open		39.50	40
1993	Northwood's Legend	Open		39.50	40

Enchanted World of the Unicorn - R. Sanderson

YEAR	ISSUE	EDITION LIMIT	YEAR RETD.	ISSUE PRICE	*QUOTE U.S. $
1992	Hidden Glade of Unicorn	90-day	1993	29.90	30
1992	Secret Garden of Unicorn	90-day	1993	29.90	30
1993	Joyful Meadow of Unicorn	90-day	1994	29.90	30
1993	Misty Hills of Unicorn	90-day	1994	29.90	30
1993	Tropical Paradise of Unicorn	90-day	1994	29.90	30
1993	Springtime Pasture of Unicorn	90-day	1994	29.90	30

English Country Cats - A. Mortimer

YEAR	ISSUE	EDITION LIMIT	YEAR RETD.	ISSUE PRICE	*QUOTE U.S. $
1994	Pepper & Ginger	Open		39.50	40
1994	Bluebell & Sage	Open		39.50	40
1994	Bib & Tucker	Open		39.50	40
1994	Calico & Cosmos	Open		39.50	40
1994	Peaches & Cream	Open		39.50	40
1994	Buttons & Buster	Open		39.50	40
1994	Sweet Prince & Pansy	Open		39.50	40
1994	Felix & Oscar	Open		39.50	40

Garden Bird Plate Collection - Unknown

YEAR	ISSUE	EDITION LIMIT	YEAR RETD.	ISSUE PRICE	*QUOTE U.S. $
1988	Chickadee	Open		48.00	48
1988	Bluejay	Open		48.00	48
1989	Hummingbird	Open		48.00	48
1991	Dove	Open		48.00	48
1991	Cardinal	Open		48.00	48
1992	Goldfinch	Open		48.00	48

Great Castles of the World - Unknown

YEAR	ISSUE	EDITION LIMIT	YEAR RETD.	ISSUE PRICE	*QUOTE U.S. $
1994	Neuschwanstein	Open		39.50	40
1994	Alcazar de Segovia	Open		39.50	40
1994	Chateau de Chambord	Open		39.50	40
1994	Houses of Parliment	Open		39.50	40
1994	West Minster	Open		39.50	40
1994	Taj Mahal	Open		39.50	40
1994	St. Basil	Open		39.50	40

Great Cats of the World - G. Coheleach

YEAR	ISSUE	EDITION LIMIT	YEAR RETD.	ISSUE PRICE	*QUOTE U.S. $
1993	Siberian Tiger	Open		39.50	40
1993	Lion	Open		39.50	40
1993	Lioness	Open		39.50	40
1993	Snow Leopard	Open		39.50	40
1993	White Tiger	Open		39.50	40
1993	Jaquar	Open		39.50	40
1993	Cougar	Open		39.50	40
1993	Chinese Leopard	Open		39.50	40
1994	Puma	Open		39.50	40

Heaven Sent - Lenox

YEAR	ISSUE	EDITION LIMIT	YEAR RETD.	ISSUE PRICE	*QUOTE U.S. $
1994	Cherubs in Clouds	Open		39.50	40
1994	Heaven's Messengers	Open		39.50	40
1994	Angel Blues	Open		39.50	40

I Love Labradors - L. Picken

YEAR	ISSUE	EDITION LIMIT	YEAR RETD.	ISSUE PRICE	*QUOTE U.S. $
1994	Little Helpers	Open		39.50	40
1994	Rookie of the Year	Open		39.50	40
1994	Catch of the Day	Open		39.50	40
1994	Just Ducky	Open		39.50	40

International Victorian Santas - R. Hoover

YEAR	ISSUE	EDITION LIMIT	YEAR RETD.	ISSUE PRICE	*QUOTE U.S. $
1992	Kris Kringle	90-day	1993	39.50	40
1993	Father Christmas	90-day	1994	39.50	40
1994	Grandfather Frost	90-day	1995	39.50	40
1995	American Santa Claus	90-day	1995	39.50	40

Kimble Barnyard - Kimble

YEAR	ISSUE	EDITION LIMIT	YEAR RETD.	ISSUE PRICE	*QUOTE U.S. $
1994	Statement Plate 1	Open		39.50	40
1994	Statement Plate 2	Open		39.50	40

Kimble Cats - Kimble

YEAR	ISSUE	EDITION LIMIT	YEAR RETD.	ISSUE PRICE	*QUOTE U.S. $
1994	Happy Cat	Open		39.50	40
1994	Welcome Cat	Open		39.50	40
1994	Fat Cat	Open		39.50	40
1994	Taffy Cat	Open		39.50	40
1994	Cool Cat	Open		39.50	40
1994	Proper Cats	Open		39.50	40

*Quotes have been rounded up to nearest dollar

Column 1

YEAR ISSUE		EDITION LIMIT	YEAR RETD.	ISSUE PRICE	*QUOTE U.S.$
1994	Happy Family Cats	Open		39.50	40
1994	Lucky Cat	Open		39.50	40

King of the Plains - S. Combes
1994	Tsava Elephant	Open		39.90	40
1994	Guardian	Open		39.90	40
1994	Rainbow Trail	Open		39.90	40
1994	African Ancients	Open		39.90	40
1994	Protecting the Flanks	Open		39.90	40
1994	The Last Elephant	Open		39.90	40
1994	End of the Line	Open		39.90	40
1994	Sparring Bulls	Open		39.90	40

Land of Buffalo - T. Lovell
1994	Fire in Buffalo Grass	Open		39.50	40
1994	Four Times to the Sun	Open		39.50	40
1994	Listening for the Drums	Open		39.50	40
1994	Finishing Touch	Open		39.50	40
1994	Long Ago Creature	Open		39.50	40
1994	The Wolf Man	Open		39.50	40
1994	War Bonnet Ceremony	Open		39.50	40
1994	The Gift	Open		39.50	40

Larry Chandler Puppy Portraits - L. Chandler
1994	Smoky	Open		39.50	40
1994	Dutch	Open		39.50	40
1994	Custard	Open		39.50	40
1994	Ebony & Ivory	Open		39.50	40

Life of Christ - J. Fuentes DeFalamanca
1994	Holy Family	Open		39.50	40
1994	Baptism	Open		39.50	40
1994	Crucifixion	Open		39.50	40
1994	Last Supper	Open		39.50	40
1994	Jesus the Good Shepherd	Open		39.50	40
1994	Agony in the Garden	Open		39.50	40
1994	Ascension	Open		39.50	40
1994	Resurrection	Open		39.50	40

Loveable Labs - L. Chandler
1994	Photo Labs	Open		39.50	40
1994	Space Labs	Open		39.50	40
1994	Dental Labs	Open		39.50	40
1994	Science Labs	Open		39.50	40

Magic of Christmas - L. Bywaters
1993	Santa of the Northen Forest	Open		39.50	40
1993	Santa's Gift of Peace	Open		39.50	40
1993	Gifts For All	Open		39.50	40
1994	Coming Home	Open		39.50	40
1994	Santa's Sentinels	Open		39.50	40
1994	Wonder of Wonders	Open		39.50	40
1994	A Berry Merry Christmas	Open		39.50	40

Magnificent Dolphins of the 7 Seas - J. Holderby
| 1994 | Bottlenose Dophin | Open | | 39.50 | 40 |
| 1994 | Dolphins in Ruins | Open | | 39.50 | 40 |

Miracles of Christ - M. Weistling
| 1994 | Wedding at Canna | Open | | 39.50 | 40 |
| 1994 | Walking on Water | Open | | 39.50 | 40 |

Moonlight Fantasy - B. Chall
1994	Moonlight Highway	Open		39.50	40
1994	Moonlight Enchantment	Open		39.50	40
1994	Moonlight Voyager	Open		39.50	40
1994	Orca Moon	Open		39.50	40

Mumm-Birds in Snow - W. Mumm
1994	Cardinals in Winter	Open		39.50	40
1994	Chickadees	Open		39.50	40
1994	Juncos	Open		39.50	40

Nature's Collage - C. McClung
1992	Cedar Waxwing, Among The Berries	Open		34.50	35
1992	Gold Finches, Golden Splendor	Open		34.50	35
1993	Bluebirds, Summer Interlude	90-day	1994	39.50	40
1993	Chickadees, Rose Morning	90-day	1994	39.50	40
1993	Bluejays, Winter Song	90-day	1994	39.50	40
1993	Cardinals, Spring Courtship	90-day	1994	39.50	40
1993	Hummingbirds, Jeweled Glory	90-day	1994	39.50	40
1993	Indigo Buntings, Indigo Evening	90-day	1994	39.50	40

Nature's Nestlings - C. McClung
1994	Golden Moments	Open		39.50	40
1994	New Beginnings	Open		39.50	40
1994	Precious Treasures	Open		39.50	40
1994	Morning Song	Open		39.50	40
1994	Goldfinches	Open		39.50	40
1994	Cardinals	Open		39.50	40
1994	Wren Family	Open		39.50	40
1994	Cardinal Family	Open		39.50	40

Owls of North America - L. Laffin
| 1993 | Spirit of the Arctic, Snowy Owl | Open | | 39.50 | 40 |

Pierced Nativity - Unknown
1993	Holy Family	Open		45.00	45
1994	Three Kings	Open		45.00	45
1994	Heralding Angels	Open		45.00	45

Column 2

YEAR ISSUE		EDITION LIMIT	YEAR RETD.	ISSUE PRICE	*QUOTE U.S.$
1994	Shepherds	Open		45.00	45

Pierced Religious Plates - Unknown
| 1994 | Pierced Pieta | Open | | 39.50 | 40 |

Royal Cats of Guy Coheleach - G. Coheleach
1994	Afternoon Shade	Open		39.50	40
1994	Jungle Jaquar	Open		39.50	40
1994	Rocky Mountain Puma	Open		39.50	40
1994	Rocky Refuge	Open		39.50	40
1994	Siesta	Open		39.50	40
1994	Ambush in the Snow	Open		39.50	40
1994	Lion in Wait	Open		39.50	40
1994	Cat Nap	Open		39.50	40

Spirit of the Navajo - Unknown
1994	Navajo Hug	Open		39.50	40
1994	Six Days Old	Open		39.50	40
1994	Jewel	Open		39.50	40
1994	The Sentinel	Open		39.50	40
1994	Never Alone	Open		39.50	40
1994	Windy but Warm	Open		39.50	40
1994	Ride to the Song	Open		39.50	40
1994	Girl Holding Puppy	Open		39.50	40

Spirits of the Sky - M. Fields
1994	Soul of the Wolf	Open		39.50	40
1994	Spirit Riders	Open		39.50	40
1994	Medicine Woman	Open		39.50	40
1994	Spirit Lovers	Open		39.50	40
1994	Spirit 8	Open		39.50	40

Victorian Santas - D. Morgan
1994	Kris Kringle	Open		39.50	40
1994	Father Christmas	Open		39.50	40
1994	Grandfather Frost	Open		39.50	40
1994	American Santa	Open		39.50	40
1994	Victorian Santa	Open		39.50	40
1994	97 Santa	Open		39.50	40
1994	Belsnickle	Open		39.50	40
1994	The Magic Never Ends	Open		39.50	40
1994	Checking His List	Open		39.50	40
1994	Twas the Night	Open		39.50	40

Whale Conservation - J. Holderby
| 1993 | Orca | Open | | 39.50 | 40 |

Wilderness Solitude - T. Doughty
1994	Snowy Haven	Open		39.50	40
1994	Midnight Lookout	Open		39.50	40
1994	Old Homestead	Open		39.50	40

Wreaths of the Month - Unknown
| 1994 | Winter Greetings-December | Open | | 39.50 | 40 |
| 1994 | Spring Blessings-May | Open | | 39.50 | 40 |

Lightpost Publishing
Kinkade-Thomas Kinkade Signature Collection - T. Kinkade
1991	Chandler's Cottage	2,500		49.95	50-75
1991	Cedar Nook	2,500		49.95	40-75
1991	Sleigh Ride Home	2,500		49.95	50-75
1991	Home To Grandma's	2,500		49.95	52-75

Lilliput Lane Ltd.
American Landmarks Collection - R. Day
| 1990 | Country Church | 5,000 | | 35.00 | 35 |
| 1990 | Riverside Chapel | 5,000 | | 35.00 | 35 |

The Best Loved Cottages of Lilliput Lane (bas-relief) - Lilliput Lane
1996	Cotman Cottage	Open		55.00	55
1996	Paradise Lodge	Open		55.00	55
1996	Rose Cottage	Open		55.00	55

Lladró
Lladró Plate Collection - Lladró
1993	The Great Voyage L5964G	Open		50.00	50
1993	Looking Out L5998G	Open		38.00	38
1993	Swinging L5999G	Open		38.00	38
1993	Duck Plate L6000G	Open		38.00	38
1994	Friends L6158	Open		32.00	32
1994	Apple Picking L6159M	Open		32.00	32
1994	Turtledove L6160	Open		32.00	32
1994	Flamingo L6161M	Open		32.00	32

March of Dimes
Our Children, Our Future - Various
1989	A Time for Peace - D. Zolan	150-day		29.00	36
1989	A Time To Love - S. Kuck	150-day		29.00	40
1989	A Time To Plant - J. McClelland	150-day		29.00	32
1989	A Time To Be Born - G. Perillo	150-day		29.00	35
1990	A Time To Embrace - E. Hibel	150-day		29.00	55
1990	A Time To Laugh - A. Williams	150-day		29.00	32

Column 3

YEAR ISSUE		EDITION LIMIT	YEAR RETD.	ISSUE PRICE	*QUOTE U.S.$

Marigold
Sport - Carreno
1989	Mickey Mantle-handsigned		Retrd.	100.00	800
1909	Mickey Mantlo-unsigned		Retrd.	60.00	100
1989	Joe DiMaggio-handsigned		Retrd.	100.00	1475
1989	Joe DiMaggio f/s (blue sig.)		Retrd.	60.00	195
1990	Joe DiMaggio AP-handsigned		Retrd.	N/A	2695

Maruri USA
Eagle Plate Series - W. Gaither
| 1984 | Free Flight | Closed | 1993 | 150.00 | 150-198 |

Museum Collections, Inc.
American Family I - N. Rockwell
1979	Baby's First Step	9,900		28.50	48
1979	Happy Birthday Dear Mother	9,900		28.50	45
1979	Sweet Sixteen	9,900		28.50	35
1979	First Haircut	9,900		28.50	60
1979	First Prom	9,900		28.50	35
1979	Wrapping Christmas Presents	9,900		28.50	35
1979	The Student	9,900		28.50	35
1979	Birthday Party	9,900		28.50	35
1979	Little Mother	9,900		28.50	35
1979	Washing Our Dog	9,900		28.50	35
1979	Mother's Little Helpers	9,900		28.50	35
1979	Bride and Groom	9,900		28.50	35

American Family II - N. Rockwell
1980	New Arrival	22,500		35.00	50-55
1980	Sweet Dreams	22,500		35.00	38
1980	Little Shaver	22,500		35.00	40
1980	We Missed You Daddy	22,500		35.00	38
1980	Home Run Slugger	22,500		35.00	38
1980	Giving Thanks	22,500		35.00	55
1980	Space Pioneers	22,500		35.00	35
1980	Little Salesman	22,500		35.00	38
1980	Almost Grown up	22,500		35.00	38
1980	Courageous Hero	22,500		35.00	38
1981	At the Circus	22,500		35.00	35
1981	Good Food, Good Friends	22,500		35.00	38

Christmas - N. Rockwell
1979	Day After Christmas	Yr.Iss		75.00	75
1980	Checking His List	Yr.Iss		75.00	75
1981	Ringing in Good Cheer	Yr.Iss		75.00	75
1982	Waiting for Santa	Yr.Iss		75.00	75
1983	High Hopes	Yr.Iss		75.00	75
1984	Space Age Santa	Yr.Iss		55.00	55

Norman Rockwell Gallery
Norman Rockwell Centennial - Rockwell Inspired
| 1993 | The Toymaker | Closed | | 39.90 | 60 |
| 1993 | The Cobbler | Closed | | 39.90 | 60 |

Rockwell's Christmas Legacy - Rockwell Inspired
1992	Santa's Workshop	Closed		49.90	60
1993	Making a List	Closed		49.90	60
1993	While Santa Slumbers	Closed		54.90	70
1993	Visions of Santa	Closed		54.90	80

Pemberton & Oakes
Adventures of Childhood Collection - D. Zolan
1989	Almost Home		Retrd.	19.60	50
1989	Crystal's Creek		Retrd.	19.60	40
1989	Summer Suds		Retrd.	22.00	35-40
1990	Snowy Adventure		Retrd.	22.00	40
1991	Forests & Fairy Tales		Retrd.	24.40	35

The Best of Zolan in Miniature - D. Zolan
1985	Sabina		Retrd.	12.50	17
1986	Erik and Dandelion		Retrd.	12.50	16
1986	Tender Moment		Retrd.	12.50	
1986	Touching the Sky		Retrd.	12.50	
1987	A Gift for Laurie		Retrd.	12.50	
1987	Small Wonder		Retrd.	12.50	

Childhood Discoveries (Miniature) - D. Zolan
1990	Colors of Spring		Retrd.	14.40	
1990	Autumn Leaves		Retrd.	14.40	
1991	Enchanted Forest		Retrd.	16.60	
1991	Just Ducky		Retrd.	16.60	
1991	Rainy Day Pals		Retrd.	16.60	
1992	Double Trouble		Retrd.	16.60	36
1990	First Kiss		Retrd.	14.40	50
1993	Peppermint Kiss		Retrd.	16.60	
1995	Tender Hearts		19-day	16.60	

Childhood Friendship Collection - D. Zolan
1986	Beach Break		Retrd.	19.00	
1987	Little Engineers		Retrd.	19.00	45
1988	Tiny Treasures		Retrd.	19.00	30
1988	Sharing Secrets		Retrd.	19.00	40
1988	Dozens of Daisies		Retrd.	19.00	
1990	Country Walk		Retrd.	19.00	

*Quotes have been rounded up to nearest dollar

Children and Pets - D. Zolan

YEAR ISSUE	EDITION LIMIT	YEAR RETD.	ISSUE PRICE	*QUOTE U.S.$
1984 Tender Moment	Retrd.		19.00	60-73
1984 Golden Moment	Retrd.		19.00	45
1985 Making Friends	Retrd.		19.00	45
1985 Tender Beginning	Retrd.		19.00	45
1986 Backyard Discovery	Retrd.		19.00	40
1986 Waiting to Play	Retrd.		19.00	45

Children at Christmas - D. Zolan

YEAR ISSUE	EDITION LIMIT	YEAR RETD.	ISSUE PRICE	*QUOTE U.S.$
1981 A Gift for Laurie	Retrd.		48.00	75
1982 Christmas Prayer	Retrd.		48.00	50-90
1983 Erik's Delight	Retrd.		48.00	68
1984 Christmas Secret	Retrd.		48.00	50-66
1985 Christmas Kitten	Retrd.		48.00	60-75
1986 Laurie and the Creche	Retrd.		48.00	75

Christmas (Miniature) - D. Zolan

YEAR ISSUE	EDITION LIMIT	YEAR RETD.	ISSUE PRICE	*QUOTE U.S.$
993 Snowy Adventure	Retrd.		16.60	30
1994 Candlelight Magic	19-day		16.60	25

Christmas - D. Zolan

YEAR ISSUE	EDITION LIMIT	YEAR RETD.	ISSUE PRICE	*QUOTE U.S.$
1991 Candlelight Magic	Retrd.		24.80	35

Companion to Brotherly Love - D. Zolan

YEAR ISSUE	EDITION LIMIT	YEAR RETD.	ISSUE PRICE	*QUOTE U.S.$
989 Sisterly Love	Retrd.		22.00	40-50

Easter (Miniature) - D. Zolan

YEAR ISSUE	EDITION LIMIT	YEAR RETD.	ISSUE PRICE	*QUOTE U.S.$
991 Easter Morning	Retrd.		16.60	45

Father's Day (Miniature) - D. Zolan

YEAR ISSUE	EDITION LIMIT	YEAR RETD.	ISSUE PRICE	*QUOTE U.S.$
994 Two of a Kind	Retrd.		16.60	36

Father's Day - D. Zolan

YEAR ISSUE	EDITION LIMIT	YEAR RETD.	ISSUE PRICE	*QUOTE U.S.$
986 Daddy's Home	Retrd.		19.00	120

Grandparent's Day - D. Zolan

YEAR ISSUE	EDITION LIMIT	YEAR RETD.	ISSUE PRICE	*QUOTE U.S.$
990 It's Grandma & Grandpa	Retrd.		24.40	40
993 Grandpa's Fence	Retrd.		24.40	45

Heirloom Ovals - D. Zolan

YEAR ISSUE	EDITION LIMIT	YEAR RETD.	ISSUE PRICE	*QUOTE U.S.$
992 My Kitty	Retrd.		18.80	47

March of Dimes: Our Children, Our Future - D. Zolan

YEAR ISSUE	EDITION LIMIT	YEAR RETD.	ISSUE PRICE	*QUOTE U.S.$
989 A Time for Peace	Retrd.		29.00	40-50

Members Only Single Issue (Miniature) - D. Zolan

YEAR ISSUE	EDITION LIMIT	YEAR RETD.	ISSUE PRICE	*QUOTE U.S.$
990 By Myself	Retrd.		14.40	62
993 Summer's Child	Retrd.		16.60	43
994 Little Slugger	10-day		16.60	37

Membership (Miniature) - D. Zolan

YEAR ISSUE	EDITION LIMIT	YEAR RETD.	ISSUE PRICE	*QUOTE U.S.$
987 For You	Retrd.		12.50	102
988 Making Friends	Retrd.		12.50	75
989 Grandma's Garden	Retrd.		12.50	72
990 A Christmas Prayer	Retrd.		14.40	54
991 Golden Moment	Retrd.		15.00	47
992 Brotherly Love	Retrd.		15.00	60-90
993 New Shoes	Retrd.		17.00	40
994 My Kitty	19-day		Gift	34

Moments To Remember (Miniature) - D. Zolan

YEAR ISSUE	EDITION LIMIT	YEAR RETD.	ISSUE PRICE	*QUOTE U.S.$
992 Just We Two	Retrd.		16.60	45
992 Almost Home	Retrd.		16.60	25
993 Tiny Treasures	Retrd.		16.60	27
993 Forest Friends	Retrd.		16.60	30

Mother's Day (Miniature) - D. Zolan

YEAR ISSUE	EDITION LIMIT	YEAR RETD.	ISSUE PRICE	*QUOTE U.S.$
990 Flowers for Mother	Retrd.		14.40	40
992 Twilight Prayer	Retrd.		16.60	30
993 Jessica's Field	Retrd.		16.60	30
994 One Summer Day	Retrd.		16.60	48

Mother's Day - D. Zolan

YEAR ISSUE	EDITION LIMIT	YEAR RETD.	ISSUE PRICE	*QUOTE U.S.$
988 Mother's Angels	Retrd.		19.00	40-75

Nutcracker II - Various

YEAR ISSUE	EDITION LIMIT	YEAR RETD.	ISSUE PRICE	*QUOTE U.S.$
981 Grand Finale - S. Fisher	Retrd.		24.40	36
982 Arabian Dancers - S. Fisher	Retrd.		24.40	68
983 Dew Drop Fairy - S. Fisher	Retrd.		24.40	40
984 Clara's Delight - S. Fisher	Retrd.		24.40	45
985 Bedtime for Nutcracker - S. Fisher	Retrd.		24.40	45
986 The Crowning of Clara - S. Fisher	Retrd.		24.40	36
987 Dance of the Snowflakes - D. Zolan	Retrd.		24.40	50-70
988 The Royal Welcome - R. Anderson	Retrd.		24.40	47
989 The Spanish Dancer - M. Vickers	Retrd.		24.40	45

Plaques - D. Zolan

YEAR ISSUE	EDITION LIMIT	YEAR RETD.	ISSUE PRICE	*QUOTE U.S.$
991 New Shoes	Retrd.		18.80	40
992 Grandma's Garden	Retrd.		18.80	30-50
992 Small Wonder	Retrd.		18.80	36
992 Easter Morning	Retrd.		18.80	25-35

Plaques-Single Issues - D. Zolan

YEAR ISSUE	EDITION LIMIT	YEAR RETD.	ISSUE PRICE	*QUOTE U.S.$
991 Flowers for Mother	Retrd.		16.80	30

Single Issue - D. Zolan

YEAR ISSUE	EDITION LIMIT	YEAR RETD.	ISSUE PRICE	*QUOTE U.S.$
993 Winter Friends	Retrd.		18.80	45

Single Issue Bone China (Miniature) - D. Zolan

YEAR ISSUE	EDITION LIMIT	YEAR RETD.	ISSUE PRICE	*QUOTE U.S.$
1992 Window of Dreams	Retrd.		18.80	35

Single Issue Day to Day Spode - D. Zolan

YEAR ISSUE	EDITION LIMIT	YEAR RETD.	ISSUE PRICE	*QUOTE U.S.$
1991 Daisy Days	Retrd.		48.00	55

Single Issues (Miniature) - D. Zolan

YEAR ISSUE	EDITION LIMIT	YEAR RETD.	ISSUE PRICE	*QUOTE U.S.$
1986 Backyard Discovery	Retrd.		12.50	107
1986 Daddy's Home	Retrd.		12.50	820
1989 Sunny Surprise	Retrd.		12.50	66
1989 My Pumpkin	Retrd.		14.40	45-70
1991 Backyard Buddies	Retrd.		16.60	40
1991 The Thinker	Retrd.		16.60	40
1993 Quiet Time	Retrd.		16.60	60
1994 Little Fisherman	19-day		16.60	30

Special Moments of Childhood Collection - D. Zolan

YEAR ISSUE	EDITION LIMIT	YEAR RETD.	ISSUE PRICE	*QUOTE U.S.$
1988 Brotherly Love	Retrd.		19.00	45-75
1988 Sunny Surprise	Retrd.		19.00	40-50
1989 Summer's Child	Retrd.		22.00	45
1990 Meadow Magic	Retrd.		22.00	35
1990 Cone For Two	Retrd.		24.60	36
1990 Rodeo Girl	Retrd.		24.60	35

Tenth Anniversary - D. Zolan

YEAR ISSUE	EDITION LIMIT	YEAR RETD.	ISSUE PRICE	*QUOTE U.S.$
1988 Ribbons and Roses	Retrd.		24.40	30-45

Thanksgiving (Miniature) - D. Zolan

YEAR ISSUE	EDITION LIMIT	YEAR RETD.	ISSUE PRICE	*QUOTE U.S.$
1993 I'm Thankful Too	Retrd.		16.60	37

Thanksgiving - D. Zolan

YEAR ISSUE	EDITION LIMIT	YEAR RETD.	ISSUE PRICE	*QUOTE U.S.$
1981 I'm Thankful Too	Retrd.		19.00	50-75

Times To Treasure Bone China (Miniature) - D. Zolan

YEAR ISSUE	EDITION LIMIT	YEAR RETD.	ISSUE PRICE	*QUOTE U.S.$
1993 Little Traveler	Retrd.		16.60	35
1993 Garden Swing	Retrd.		16.60	29
1994 Summer Garden	19-day		16.60	30
1994 September Girl	19-day		16.60	30

Wonder of Childhood - D. Zolan

YEAR ISSUE	EDITION LIMIT	YEAR RETD.	ISSUE PRICE	*QUOTE U.S.$
1982 Touching the Sky	Retrd.		19.00	40
1983 Spring Innocence	Retrd.		19.00	45
1984 Winter Angel	Retrd.		22.00	50
1985 Small Wonder	Retrd.		22.00	48
1986 Grandma's Garden	Retrd.		22.00	45
1987 Day Dreamer	Retrd.		22.00	40

Yesterday's Children (Miniature) - D. Zolan

YEAR ISSUE	EDITION LIMIT	YEAR RETD.	ISSUE PRICE	*QUOTE U.S.$
1994 Little Friends	19-day		16.60	40
1994 Seaside Treasures	19-day		16.60	35

Zolan's Children - D. Zolan

YEAR ISSUE	EDITION LIMIT	YEAR RETD.	ISSUE PRICE	*QUOTE U.S.$
1978 Erik and Dandelion	Retrd.		19.00	255
1979 Sabina in the Grass	Retrd.		22.00	250
1980 By Myself	Retrd.		24.00	55
1981 For You	Retrd.		24.00	36

Pickard

Mother's Love - I. Spencer

YEAR ISSUE	EDITION LIMIT	YEAR RETD.	ISSUE PRICE	*QUOTE U.S.$
1980 Miracle	7,500		95.00	95
1981 Story Time	7,500		110.00	110
1982 First Edition	7,500		115.00	115
1983 Precious Moment	7,500		120.00	145

Symphony of Roses - I. Spencer

YEAR ISSUE	EDITION LIMIT	YEAR RETD.	ISSUE PRICE	*QUOTE U.S.$
1982 Wild Irish Rose	10,000		85.00	95
1983 Yellow Rose of Texas	10,000		90.00	100-110
1984 Honeysuckle Rose	10,000		95.00	135
1985 Rose of Washington Square	10,000		100.00	175

Reco International

Amish Traditions - B. Farnsworth

YEAR ISSUE	EDITION LIMIT	YEAR RETD.	ISSUE PRICE	*QUOTE U.S.$
1994 Golden Harvest	95-day		29.50	30
1994 Family Outing	95-day		29.50	30
1994 The Quilting Bee	95-day		29.50	30
1995 Last Day of School	95-day		29.50	30

Barefoot Children - S. Kuck

YEAR ISSUE	EDITION LIMIT	YEAR RETD.	ISSUE PRICE	*QUOTE U.S.$
1987 Night-Time Story	Retrd.	1994	29.50	40
1987 Golden Afternoon	14-day		29.50	40
1988 Little Sweethearts	Retrd.	1995	29.50	40
1988 Carousel Magic	14-day		29.50	60
1988 Under the Apple Tree	Retrd.	1995	29.50	40
1988 The Rehearsal	Retrd.	1995	29.50	40
1988 Pretty as a Picture	Retrd.	1993	29.50	45
1988 Grandma's Trunk	Retrd.	1993	29.50	45

Becky's Day - J. McClelland

YEAR ISSUE	EDITION LIMIT	YEAR RETD.	ISSUE PRICE	*QUOTE U.S.$
1985 Awakening	90-day		24.50	29
1985 Getting Dressed	Retrd.	1988	24.50	29
1986 Breakfast	Retrd.	1987	27.50	35
1986 Learning is Fun	Retrd.	1988	27.50	28
1986 Muffin Making	Retrd.	1989	27.50	28
1986 Tub Time	Retrd.	1989	27.50	35
1986 Evening Prayer	Retrd.	1990	27.50	28

Birds of the Hidden Forest - G. Ratnavira

YEAR ISSUE	EDITION LIMIT	YEAR RETD.	ISSUE PRICE	*QUOTE U.S.$
1994 Macaw Waterfall	96-day		29.50	30
1994 Paradise Valley	96-day		29.50	30
1995 Toucan Treasure	96-day		29.50	30

Bohemian Annuals - Factory Artist

YEAR ISSUE	EDITION LIMIT	YEAR RETD.	ISSUE PRICE	*QUOTE U.S.$
1974 1974	Retrd.	1975	130.00	155
1975 1975	Retrd.	1976	140.00	160
1976 1976	Retrd.	1978	150.00	160

Castles & Dreams - J. Bergsma

YEAR ISSUE	EDITION LIMIT	YEAR RETD.	ISSUE PRICE	*QUOTE U.S.$
1992 The Birth of a Dream	48-day		29.50	30
1992 Dreams Come True	48-day		29.50	30
1993 Believe In Your Dreams	48-day		29.50	30
1994 Follow Your Dreams	48-day		29.50	30

A Childhood Almanac - S. Kuck

YEAR ISSUE	EDITION LIMIT	YEAR RETD.	ISSUE PRICE	*QUOTE U.S.$
1985 Fireside Dreams-January	Retrd.	1991	29.50	45-49
1985 Be Mine-February	Retrd.	1992	29.50	45
1986 Winds of March-March	Retrd.	1994	29.50	40
1985 Easter Morning-April	Retrd.	1992	29.50	55
1985 For Mom-May	Retrd.	1992	29.50	45
1985 Just Dreaming-June	Retrd.	1992	29.50	40
1985 Star Spangled Sky-July	Retrd.	1995	29.50	45
1985 Summer Secrets-August	Retrd.	1991	29.50	53
1985 School Days-September	Retrd.	1991	29.50	60
1986 Indian Summer-October	Retrd.	1991	29.50	45
1986 Giving Thanks-November	Retrd.	1995	29.50	45-49
1985 Christmas Magic-December	Retrd.	1995	35.00	70

A Children's Christmas Pageant - S. Kuck

YEAR ISSUE	EDITION LIMIT	YEAR RETD.	ISSUE PRICE	*QUOTE U.S.$
1986 Silent Night	Retrd.	1987	32.50	55
1987 Hark the Herald Angels Sing	Retrd.	1988	32.50	45
1988 While Shepherds Watched...	Retrd.	1990	32.50	33
1989 We Three Kings	Yr.Iss.		32.50	35

The Children's Garden - J. McClelland

YEAR ISSUE	EDITION LIMIT	YEAR RETD.	ISSUE PRICE	*QUOTE U.S.$
1993 Garden Friends	120-day		29.50	32
1993 Tea for Three	120-day		29.50	30
1993 Puppy Love	120-day		29.50	30

Christening Gift - S. Kuck

YEAR ISSUE	EDITION LIMIT	YEAR RETD.	ISSUE PRICE	*QUOTE U.S.$
1995 God's Gift	Open		29.90	30

The Christmas Series - J. Bergsma

YEAR ISSUE	EDITION LIMIT	YEAR RETD.	ISSUE PRICE	*QUOTE U.S.$
1990 Down The Glistening Lane	14-day		35.00	39
1991 A Child Is Born	14-day		35.00	35
1992 Christmas Day	14-day		35.00	35
1993 I Wish You An Angel	14-day		35.00	35

Christmas Wishes - J. Bergsma

YEAR ISSUE	EDITION LIMIT	YEAR RETD.	ISSUE PRICE	*QUOTE U.S.$
1994 I Wish You Love	75-day		29.50	30
1995 I Wish You Joy	75-day		29.50	30

Days Gone By - S. Kuck

YEAR ISSUE	EDITION LIMIT	YEAR RETD.	ISSUE PRICE	*QUOTE U.S.$
1983 Sunday Best	Retrd.	1984	29.50	40
1983 Amy's Magic Horse	Retrd.	1985	29.50	50-70
1984 Little Anglers	Retrd.	1985	29.50	27
1984 Afternoon Recital	Retrd.	1985	29.50	50
1984 Little Tutor	Retrd.	1985	29.50	30
1985 Easter at Grandma's	Retrd.	1985	29.50	30
1985 Morning Song	Retrd.	1986	29.50	30
1985 The Surrey Ride	Retrd.	1987	29.50	75

Dresden Christmas - Factory Artist

YEAR ISSUE	EDITION LIMIT	YEAR RETD.	ISSUE PRICE	*QUOTE U.S.$
1971 Shepherd Scene	Retrd.	1978	15.00	50
1972 Niklas Church	Retrd.	1978	15.00	25
1973 Schwanstein Church	Retrd.	1978	18.00	35
1974 Village Scene	Retrd.	1978	20.00	30
1975 Rothenburg Scene	Retrd.	1978	24.00	30
1976 Village Church	Retrd.	1978	26.00	35
1977 Old Mill	Retrd.	1978	28.00	30

Dresden Mother's Day - Factory Artist

YEAR ISSUE	EDITION LIMIT	YEAR RETD.	ISSUE PRICE	*QUOTE U.S.$
1972 Doe and Fawn	Retrd.	1979	15.00	20
1973 Mare and Colt	Retrd.	1979	16.00	25
1974 Tiger and Cub	Retrd.	1979	20.00	23
1975 Dachshunds	Retrd.	1979	24.00	28
1976 Owl and Offspring	Retrd.	1979	26.00	30
1977 Chamois	Retrd.	1979	28.00	30

The Enchanted Norfin Trolls - C. Hopkins

YEAR ISSUE	EDITION LIMIT	YEAR RETD.	ISSUE PRICE	*QUOTE U.S.$
1993 Troll Maiden	75-day		19.50	20
1993 The Wizard Troll	75-day		19.50	20
1993 The Troll and His Dragon	75-day		19.50	20
1994 Troll in Shinning Armor	75-day		19.50	20
1994 Minstrel Troll	75-day		19.50	20
1994 If Trolls Could Fly	75-day		19.50	20
1994 Chef le Troll	75-day		19.50	20
1994 Queen of Trolls	75-day		19.50	20

The Flower Fairies Year Collection - C.M. Barker

YEAR ISSUE	EDITION LIMIT	YEAR RETD.	ISSUE PRICE	*QUOTE U.S.$
1990 The Red Clover Fairy	14-day		29.50	30
1990 The Wild Cherry Blossom Fairy	14-day		29.50	30
1990 The Pine Tree Fairy	14-day		29.50	30
1990 The Rose Hip Fairy	14-day		29.50	30

Four Seasons - J. Poluszynski

YEAR ISSUE	EDITION LIMIT	YEAR RETD.	ISSUE PRICE	*QUOTE U.S.$
1973 Spring	Retrd.	1975	50.00	75

*Quotes have been rounded up to nearest dollar

Column 1

YEAR ISSUE		EDITION LIMIT	YEAR RETRD.	ISSUE PRICE	*QUOTE U.S.$
1973	Summer	Retrd.	1975	50.00	75
1973	Fall	Retrd.	1975	50.00	75
1973	Winter	Retrd.	1975	50.00	75

Friends For Keeps - S. Kuck
| 1996 | Puppy Love | 95-day | | 29.95 | 30 |
| 1996 | Gone Fishing | 95-day | | 29.95 | 30 |

Furstenberg Christmas - Factory Artist
1971	Rabbits	Retrd.	1977	15.00	30
1972	Snowy Village	Retrd.	1977	15.00	20
1973	Christmas Eve	Retrd.	1977	18.00	35
1974	Sparrows	Retrd.	1977	20.00	30
1975	Deer Family	Retrd.	1977	22.00	30
1976	Winter Birds	Retrd.	1977	25.00	25

Furstenberg Deluxe Christmas - E. Grossberg
1971	Wise Men	Retrd.	1974	45.00	45
1972	Holy Family	Retrd.	1974	45.00	45
1973	Christmas Eve	Retrd.	1974	60.00	65

Furstenberg Easter - Factory Artist
1971	Sheep	Retrd.	1973	15.00	150
1972	Chicks	Retrd.	1975	15.00	60
1973	Bunnies	Retrd.	1976	16.00	80
1974	Pussywillow	Retrd.	1976	20.00	33
1975	Easter Window	Retrd.	1977	22.00	30
1976	Flower Collecting	Retrd.	1977	25.00	25

Furstenberg Mother's Day - Factory Artist
1972	Hummingbirds, Fe	Retrd.	1974	15.00	45
1973	Hedgehogs	Retrd.	1974	16.00	40
1974	Doe and Fawn	Retrd.	1974	20.00	30
1975	Swans	Retrd.	1976	22.00	23
1976	Koala Bears	Retrd.	1976	25.00	30

Furstenberg Olympic - J. Poluszynski
| 1972 | Munich | Retrd. | 1972 | 20.00 | 75 |
| 1976 | Montreal | Retrd. | 1976 | 37.50 | 38 |

Games Children Play - S. Kuck
1979	Me First	Retrd.	1983	45.00	50
1980	Forever Bubbles	Retrd.	1983	45.00	48
1981	Skating Pals	Retrd.	1983	45.00	48
1982	Join Me	10,000		45.00	45

Gardens of Beauty - D. Barlowe
1988	English Country Garden	14-day		29.50	30
1988	Dutch Country Garden	14-day		29.50	30
1988	New England Garden	14-day		29.50	30
1988	Japanese Garden	14-day		29.50	30
1989	Italian Garden	14-day		29.50	30
1989	Hawaiian Garden	14-day		29.50	30
1989	German Country Garden	14-day		29.50	30
1989	Mexican Garden	14-day		29.50	30
1992	Colonial Splendor	48-day	1994	29.50	30

Gift of Love Mother's Day Collection - S. Kuck
| 1993 | Morning Glory | Retrd. | 1994 | 65.00 | 65 |
| 1994 | Memories From The Heart | Retrd. | 1994 | 65.00 | 65 |

The Glory Of Christ - C. Micarelli
1992	The Ascension	48-day		29.50	30
1993	Jesus Teaching	48-day		29.50	30
1993	The Last Supper	48-day		29.50	30
1993	The Nativity	48-day		29.50	30
1993	The Baptism Of Christ	48-day		29.50	30
1993	Jesus Heals The Sick	48-day		29.50	30
1994	Jesus Walks On Water	48-day		29.50	30
1994	Descent From The Cross	48-day		29.50	30

God's Own Country - I. Drechsler
1990	Daybreak	14-day		30.00	30
1990	Coming Home	14-day		30.00	30
1990	Peaceful Gathering	14-day		30.00	30
1990	Quiet Waters	14-day		30.00	30

The Grandparent Collector's Plates - S. Kuck
| 1981 | Grandma's Cookie Jar | Yr.Iss. | | 37.50 | 38 |
| 1981 | Grandpa and the Dollhouse | Yr.Iss. | | 37.50 | 38 |

Great Stories from the Bible - G. Katz
1987	Moses in the Bulrushes	14-day	1994	29.50	35
1987	King Saul & David	14-day	1994	29.50	35
1987	Moses and the Ten Commandments	14-day	1994	29.50	38
1987	Joseph's Coat of Many Colors	14-day	1994	29.50	35
1988	Rebekah at the Well	14-day	1994	29.50	35
1988	Daniel Reads the Writing on the Wall	14-day	1994	29.50	35
1988	The Story of Ruth	14-day	1994	29.50	35
1988	King Solomon	14-day	1994	29.50	35

Guardians Of The Kingdom - J. Bergsma
1990	Rainbow To Ride On	Retrd.	1993	35.00	37
1990	Special Friends Are Few	17,500		35.00	35
1990	Guardians Of The Innocent Children	17,500		35.00	38
1990	The Miracle Of Love	17,500		35.00	37
1991	The Magic Of Love	17,500		35.00	35
1991	Only With The Heart	17,500		35.00	35
1991	To Fly Without Wings	17,500		35.00	35

Column 2

YEAR ISSUE		EDITION LIMIT	YEAR RETRD.	ISSUE PRICE	*QUOTE U.S.$
1991	In Faith I Am Free	17,500		35.00	35

Haven of the Hunters - H. Roe
| 1994 | Eagle's Castle | 96-day | | 29.50 | 30 |
| 1994 | Sanctuary of the Hawk | 96-day | | 29.50 | 30 |

Hearts And Flowers - S. Kuck
1991	Patience	120-day		29.50	40
1991	Tea Party	120-day		29.50	58
1992	Cat's In The Cradle	120-day		32.50	45
1992	Carousel of Dreams	120-day		32.50	40
1992	Storybook Memories	120-day		32.50	50
1993	Delightful Bundle	120-day		34.50	35
1993	Easter Morning Visitor	120-day		34.50	35
1993	Me and My Pony	120-day		34.50	35

In The Eye of The Storm - W. Lowe
1991	First Strike	120-day		29.50	35
1992	Night Force	120-day		29.50	35
1992	Tracks Across The Sand	120-day		29.50	30
1992	The Storm Has Landed	120-day		29.50	30

J. Bergsma Mother's Day Series - J. Bergsma
1990	The Beauty Of Life	14-day		35.00	35
1992	Life's Blessing	14-day		35.00	35
1993	My Greatest Treasures	14-day		35.00	35
1994	Forever In My Heart	14-day		35.00	35

King's Christmas - Merli
1973	Adoration	Retrd.	1974	100.00	265
1974	Madonna	Retrd.	1975	150.00	250
1975	Heavenly Choir	Retrd.	1976	160.00	235
1976	Siblings	Retrd.	1978	200.00	225

King's Flowers - A. Falchi
1973	Carnation	Retrd.	1974	85.00	130
1974	Red Rose	Retrd.	1975	100.00	145
1975	Yellow Dahlia	Retrd.	1976	110.00	162
1976	Bluebells	Retrd.	1977	130.00	165
1977	Anemones	Retrd.	1979	130.00	175

King's Mother's Day - Merli
1973	Dancing Girl	Retrd.	1974	100.00	225
1974	Dancing Boy	Retrd.	1975	115.00	250
1975	Motherly Love	Retrd.	1976	140.00	225
1976	Maiden	Retrd.	1978	180.00	200

Kingdom of the Great Cats - P. Jepson
| 1995 | Out of the Mist | 36-day | | 29.50 | 30 |
| 1995 | Summit Sanctuary | 36-day | | 29.50 | 30 |

Kittens 'N Hats - S. Somerville
1994	Opening Night	48-day		29.50	30
1994	Sitting Pretty	48-day		29.50	30
1995	Little League	48-day		29.50	30

Little Angel Plate Collection - S. Kuck
| 1994 | Angel of Charity | 95-day | | 29.50 | 30 |
| 1994 | Angel of Joy | 95-day | | 29.50 | 30 |

Little Professionals - S. Kuck
1982	All is Well	Retrd.	1983	39.50	43-65
1983	Tender Loving Care	Retrd.	1985	39.50	50-75
1984	Lost and Found	Retrd.	1995	39.50	45
1985	Reading, Writing and...	Retrd.	1989	39.50	45

Magic Companions - J. Bergsma
1994	Believe in Love	48-day		29.50	30
1994	Imagine Peace	48-day		29.50	30
1995	Live in Harmony	48-day		29.50	30
1995	Trust in Magic	48-day		29.50	30

March of Dimes: Our Children, Our Future - Various
| 1989 | A Time to Love (2nd in Series) - S. Kuck | Retrd. | 1993 | 29.00 | 45 |
| 1989 | A Time to Plant (3rd in Series) - J. McClelland | 150-day | 1993 | 29.00 | 50 |

Marmot Christmas - Factory Artist
1970	Polar Bear, Fe	Retrd.	1971	13.00	60
1971	Buffalo Bill	Retrd.	1972	16.00	55
1972	Boy and Grandfather	Retrd.	1973	20.00	50
1971	American Buffalo	Retrd.	1973	14.50	35
1973	Snowman	Retrd.	1974	22.00	45
1974	Dancing	Retrd.	1975	24.00	30
1975	Quail	Retrd.	1976	30.00	40
1976	Windmill	Retrd.	1978	40.00	40

Marmot Father's Day - Factory Artist
| 1970 | Stag | Retrd. | 1970 | 12.00 | 100 |
| 1971 | Horse | Retrd. | 1972 | 12.50 | 40 |

Marmot Mother's Day - Factory Artist
1972	Seal	Retrd.	1973	16.00	60
1973	Bear with Cub	Retrd.	1974	20.00	140
1974	Penguins	Retrd.	1975	24.00	50
1975	Raccoons	Retrd.	1976	30.00	45
1976	Ducks	Retrd.	1977	40.00	40

The McClelland Children's Circus Collection - J. McClelland
| 1982 | Tommy the Clown | Retrd. | 1973 | 29.50 | 49 |

Column 3

YEAR ISSUE		EDITION LIMIT	YEAR RETRD.	ISSUE PRICE	*QUO U.
1982	Katie, the Tightrope Walker	Retrd.	1975	29.50	
1983	Johnny the Strongman	Retrd.	1976	29.50	
1984	Maggie the Animal Trainer	100-day	1978	29.50	

Memories of Childhood - C. Getz
1994	Teatime with Teddy	75-day		29.50	
1995	Bases Loaded	75-day		29.50	
1996	Mommy's Little Helper	75-day		29.50	

Memories Of Yesterday - M. Attwell
1993	Hush	Open		29.50	
1993	Time For Bed	Open		29.50	
1993	I'se Been Painting	Open		29.50	
1993	Just Looking Pretty	Open		29.50	
1994	Give it Your Best Shot	Open		29.50	
1994	I Pray The Lord My Soul to Keep	Open		29.50	
1994	Just Thinking About You	Open		29.50	
1994	What Will I Grow Up To Be	Open		29.50	

Moments At Home - S. Kuck
1995	Moments of Caring	95-day		29.90	
1995	Moments of Tenderness	95-day		29.90	
1995	Moments of Friendship	95-day		29.90	
1995	Moments of Sharing	95-day		29.90	
1995	Moments of Love	95-day		29.90	

Moser Christmas - Factory Artist
1970	Hradcany Castle	Retrd.	1971	75.00	
1971	Karlstein Castle	Retrd.	1972	75.00	
1972	Old Town Hall	Retrd.	1973	85.00	
1973	Karlovy Vary Castle	Retrd.	1974	90.00	

Moser Mother's Day - Factory Artist
1971	Peacocks	Retrd.	1971	75.00	
1972	Butterflies	Retrd.	1972	85.00	
1973	Squirrels	Retrd.	1973	90.00	

Mother Goose - J. McClelland
1979	Mary, Mary	Retrd.	1979	22.50	75-
1980	Little Boy Blue	Retrd.	1980	22.50	
1981	Little Miss Muffet	Yr.Iss.		24.50	
1982	Little Jack Horner	Retrd.	1982	24.50	
1983	Little Bo Peep	Yr.Iss.		24.50	
1984	Diddle, Diddle Dumpling	Yr.Iss.		24.50	
1985	Mary Had a Little Lamb	Yr.Iss.		27.50	
1986	Jack and Jill	Retrd.	1988	27.50	

Mother's Day Collection - S. Kuck
1985	Once Upon a Time	Retrd.	1987	29.50	50
1986	Times Remembered	Yr.Iss.		29.50	
1987	A Cherished Time	Yr.Iss.		29.50	
1988	A Time Together	Yr.Iss.		29.50	

Noble and Free - Kelly
1994	Gathering Storm	95-day		29.50	
1994	Protected Journey	95-day		29.50	
1994	Moonlight Run	95-day		29.50	

The Nutcracker Ballet - C. Micarelli
1989	Christmas Eve Party	14-day	1994	35.00	
1990	Clara And Her Prince	14-day		35.00	
1990	The Dream Begins	14-day		35.00	
1991	Dance of the Snow Fairies	14-day	1994	35.00	
1992	The Land of Sweets	14-day		35.00	
1992	The Sugar Plum Fairy	14-day		35.00	

Oscar & Bertie's Edwardian Holiday - P.D. Jackson
1991	Snapshot	48-day		29.50	
1992	Early Rise	48-day		29.50	
1992	All Aboard	48-day		29.50	
1992	Learning To Swim	48-day		29.50	

Our Cherished Seas - S. Barlowe
1991	Whale Song	48-day		37.50	
1991	Lions of the Sea	48-day		37.50	
1991	Flight of the Dolphins	48-day		37.50	
1992	Palace of the Seals	48-day		37.50	
1992	Orca Ballet	48-day		37.50	
1993	Emperors of the Ice	48-day		37.50	
1993	Turtle Treasure	48-day		37.50	
1993	Splendor of the Sea	48-day		37.50	

Plate Of The Month Collection - S. Kuck
1990	January	28-day		25.00	
1990	February	28-day		25.00	
1990	March	28-day		25.00	
1990	April	28-day		25.00	
1990	May	28-day		25.00	
1990	June	28-day		25.00	
1990	July	28-day		25.00	
1990	August	28-day		25.00	
1990	September	28-day		25.00	
1990	October	28-day		25.00	
1990	November	28-day		25.00	
1990	December	28-day		25.00	

Precious Angels - S. Kuck
1995	Angel of Grace	95-day		29.90	
1995	Angel of Happiness	95-day		29.90	
1995	Angel of Hope	95-day		29.90	
1995	Angel of Laughter	95-day		29.90	

YEAR ISSUE	EDITION LIMIT	YEAR RETD.	ISSUE PRICE	*QUOTE U.S. $
995 Angel of Love	95-day		29.90	30
995 Angel of Peace	95-day		29.90	30
995 Angel of Sharing	95-day		29.90	30
995 Angel of Sunshine	95-day		29.90	30

he Premier Collection - J. McClelland

991 Love	7,500		75.00	75

remier Collection - S. Kuck

991 Puppy	Retrd.	1993	95.00	125-150
991 Kitten	Retrd.	1992	95.00	150-200
92 La Belle	7,500		95.00	95
992 Le Beau	7,500		95.00	95

oyal Mother's Day - Factory Artist

970 Swan and Young	Retrd.	1971	12.00	80
71 Doe and Fawn	Retrd.	1972	13.00	55
72 Rabbits	Retrd.	1973	16.00	40
973 Owl Family	Retrd.	1974	18.00	40
74 Duck and Young	Retrd.	1975	22.00	40
75 Lynx and Cubs	Retrd.	1976	26.00	40
76 Woodcock and Young	Retrd.	1978	27.50	33
77 Koala Bear	Retrd.	1978	30.00	30

oyale - Factory Artist

69 Apollo Moon Landing	Retrd.	1969	30.00	80

oyale Christmas - Factory Artist

69 Christmas Fair	Retrd.	1970	12.00	125
70 Vigil Mass	Retrd.	1971	13.00	110
71 Christmas Night	Retrd.	1972	16.00	50
72 Elks	Retrd.	1973	16.00	45
73 Christmas Down	Retrd.	1974	20.00	38
74 Village Christmas	Retrd.	1975	22.00	60
75 Feeding Time	Retrd.	1976	26.00	35
76 Seaport Christmas	Retrd.	1977	27.50	30
77 Sledding	Retrd.	1978	30.00	30

oyale Father's Day - Factory Artist

70 Frigate Constitution	Retrd.	1971	13.00	80
71 Man Fishing	Retrd.	1972	13.00	35
72 Mountaineer	Retrd.	1973	16.00	55
73 Camping	Retrd.	1974	18.00	45
74 Eagle	Retrd.	1975	22.00	35
75 Regatta	Retrd.	1976	26.00	35
76 Hunting	Retrd.	1977	27.50	33
77 Fishing	Retrd.	1978	30.00	30

oyale Game Plates - Various

72 Setters - J. Poluszynski	Retrd.	1974	180.00	200
73 Fox - J. Poluszynski	Retrd.	1975	200.00	250
74 Osprey - W. Schiener	Retrd.	1976	250.00	250
75 California Quail - W. Schiener	Retrd.	1976	265.00	265

oyale Germania Christmas Annual - Factory Artist

70 Orchid	Retrd.	1971	200.00	650
71 Cyclamen	Retrd.	1972	200.00	325
72 Silver Thistle	Retrd.	1973	250.00	290
73 Tulips	Retrd.	1974	275.00	310
74 Sunflowers	Retrd.	1975	300.00	320
75 Snowdrops	Retrd.	1976	450.00	500

oyale Germania Crystal Mother's Day - Factory Artist

71 Roses	Retrd.	1971	135.00	650
72 Elephant and Youngster	Retrd.	1972	180.00	250
73 Koala Bear and Cub	Retrd.	1973	200.00	225
74 Squirrels	Retrd.	1974	240.00	250
75 Swan and Young	Retrd.	1975	350.00	360

ndra Kuck Mothers' Day - S. Kuck

95 Home is Where the Heart Is	48-day		35.00	35
96 Dear To The Heart	48-day		35.00	35

culpted Heirlooms - S. Kuck

96 Best Friends (sculpted plate)	24-mo.		29.95	30

ongs From The Garden - G. Ratnavira

96 Love Song	76-day		29.95	30

e Sophisticated Ladies Collection - A. Fazio

85 Felicia	21-day		29.50	33
85 Samantha	21-day	1994	29.50	33
85 Phoebe	21-day	1994	29.50	33
85 Cleo	21-day		29.50	33
86 Cerissa	21-day	1994	29.50	33
86 Natasha	21-day	1994	29.50	33
86 Bianka	21-day	1994	29.50	33
86 Chelsea	21-day	1994	29.50	33

ecial Occasions by Reco - S. Kuck

88 The Wedding	Open		35.00	35
89 Wedding Day (6 1/2")	Open		25.00	25
90 The Special Day	Open		25.00	25

ecial Occasions-Wedding - C. Micarelli

91 From This Day Forward (9 1/2")	Open		35.00	35
91 From This Day Forward (6 1/2")	Open		25.00	25
91 To Have And To Hold (9 1/2")	Open		35.00	35
91 To Have And To Hold (6 1/2")	Open		25.00	25

Sugar and Spice - S. Kuck

YEAR ISSUE	EDITION LIMIT	YEAR RETD.	ISSUE PRICE	*QUOTE U.S.$
1993 Best Friends	95-day		29.90	30
1993 Sisters	95-day		29.90	30
1994 Little One	95-day		32.90	33
1994 Teddy Bear Tales	95-day		32.90	33
1994 Morning Prayers	95-day		32.90	33
1995 First Snow	95-day		34.90	35
1994 Garden of Sunshine	95-day		34.90	35
1995 A Special Day	95-day		34.90	35

Tidings Of Joy - S. Kuck

1992 Peace on Earth	Retrd.	1995	35.00	50
1993 Rejoice	N/A		35.00	50
1994 Noel	Retrd.	1995	35.00	50

Totems of the West - J. Bergsma

1994 The Watchmen	96-day		29.50	30
1995 Peace At Last	96-day		29.50	30
1995 Never Alone	96-day		35.00	35

Town And Country Dogs - S. Barlowe

1990 Fox Hunt	36-day		35.00	35
1991 The Retrieval	36-day		35.00	35
1991 Golden Fields (Golden Retriever)	36-day		35.00	35
1993 Faithful Companions (Cocker Spaniel)	36-day		35.00	35

Trains of the Orient Express - R. Johnson

1993 The Golden Arrow-England	N/A		29.50	30
1994 Austria	N/A		29.50	30
1994 Bavaria	N/A		29.50	30
1994 Rumania	N/A		29.50	30
1994 Greece	N/A		29.50	30
1994 Frankonia	N/A		29.50	30
1994 Turkey	N/A		29.50	30
1994 France	N/A		29.50	30

Treasured Songs of Childhood - J. McClelland

1987 Twinkle, Twinkle, Little Star	Retrd.	1990	29.50	30
1988 A Tisket, A Tasket	150-day	1991	29.50	30
1988 Baa, Baa, Black Sheep	Retrd.	1991	32.90	33
1989 Round The Mulberry Bush	150-day		32.90	35
1989 Rain, Rain Go Away	Retrd.	1993	32.90	33
1989 I'm A Little Teapot	Retrd.	1993	32.90	33
1989 Pat-A-Cake	150-day		34.90	35
1990 Hush Little Baby	150-day		34.90	35

Up, Up And Away - P. Alexander

1996 Rally At The Grand Canyon	76-day		29.95	30

Vanishing Animal Kingdoms - S. Barlowe

1986 Rama the Tiger	21,500		35.00	40-50
1986 Olepi the Buffalo	21,500		35.00	35
1987 Coolibah the Koala	21,500		35.00	42
1987 Ortwin the Deer	21,500		35.00	39
1987 Yen-Poh the Panda	21,500		35.00	40
1988 Mamakuu the Elephant	21,500		35.00	59

Victorian Christmas - S. Kuck

1995 Dear Santa	72-day		35.00	35
1996 Night Before Christmas	72-day		35.00	35

Victorian Mother's Day - S. Kuck

1989 Mother's Sunshine	Retrd.	1990	35.00	45-85
1990 Reflection Of Love	Retrd.	1991	35.00	50-80
1991 A Precious Time	Retrd.	1992	35.00	45-75
1992 Loving Touch	Retrd.	1993	35.00	45-49

Western - E. Berke

1974 Mountain Man	Retrd.		165.00	165

Women of the Plains - C. Corcilius

1994 Pride of a Maiden	36-day		29.50	30
1995 No Boundaries	36-day		29.50	30
1995 Silent Companions	36-day		35.00	35

The Wonder of Christmas - J. McClelland

1991 Santa's Secret	48-day		29.50	50
1992 My Favorite Ornament	48-day		29.50	55
1992 Waiting For Santa	48-day		29.50	55
1993 Candlelight Christmas	Retrd.	1995	29.50	55

The World of Children - J. McClelland

1977 Rainy Day Fun	10,000	1977	50.00	50
1978 When I Grow Up	15,000	1978	50.00	55
1979 You're Invited	15,000	1979	50.00	55
1980 Kittens for Sale	15,000	1980	50.00	55

River Shore

Baby Animals - R. Brown

1979 Akiku	20,000		50.00	80
1980 Roosevelt	20,000		50.00	90
1981 Clover	20,000		50.00	65
1982 Zuela	20,000		50.00	65

Famous Americans - Rockwell-Brown

1976 Brown's Lincoln	9,500		40.00	40
1977 Rockwell's Triple Self-Portrait	9,500		45.00	45

YEAR ISSUE	EDITION LIMIT	YEAR RETD.	ISSUE PRICE	*QUOTE U.S.$
1978 Peace Corps	9,500		45.00	45
1979 Spirit of Lindbergh	9,500		50.00	50

Little House on the Prairie - E. Christopherson

1985 Founder's Day Picnic	10-day		29.50	50
1985 Women's Harvest	10-day		29.50	45
1985 Medicine Show	10-day		29.50	45
1985 Caroline's Eggs	10-day		29.50	45
1985 Mary's Gift	10-day		29.50	45
1985 A Bell for Walnut Grove	10-day		29.50	45
1985 Ingall's Family	10-day		29.50	45
1985 The Sweetheart Tree	10-day		29.50	45

Norman Rockwell Single Issue - N. Rockwell

1979 Spring Flowers	17,000		75.00	145
1980 Looking Out to Sea	17,000		75.00	195
1982 Grandpa's Guardian	17,000		80.00	80
1982 Grandpa's Treasures	17,000		80.00	80

Puppy Playtime - J. Lamb

1987 Double Take	14-day		24.50	32-35
1988 Catch of the Day	14-day		24.50	25
1988 Cabin Fever	14-day		24.50	25
1988 Weekend Gardener	14-day		24.50	25
1988 Getting Acquainted	14-day		24.50	25
1988 Hanging Out	14-day		24.50	25
1988 A New Leash On Life	14-day		24.50	30
1987 Fun and Games	14-day		24.50	30

Rockwell Four Freedoms - N. Rockwell

1981 Freedom of Speech	17,000		65.00	80-99
1982 Freedom of Worship	17,000		65.00	80
1982 Freedom from Fear	17,000		65.00	65
1982 Freedom from Want	17,000		65.00	65

Rockwell Society

Christmas - N. Rockwell

1974 Scotty Gets His Tree	Yr.Iss.		24.50	45-100
1975 Angel with Black Eye	Yr.Iss.		24.50	40
1976 Golden Christmas	Yr.Iss.		24.50	35
1977 Toy Shop Window	Yr.Iss.		24.50	25-75
1978 Christmas Dream	Yr.Iss.		24.50	25
1979 Somebody's Up There	Yr.Iss.		24.50	25
1980 Scotty Plays Santa	Yr.Iss.		24.50	25
1981 Wrapped Up in Christmas	Yr.Iss.		25.50	27
1982 Christmas Courtship	Yr.Iss.		25.50	30
1983 Santa in the Subway	Yr.Iss.		25.50	30
1984 Santa in the Workshop	Yr.Iss.		27.50	28
1985 Grandpa Plays Santa	Yr.Iss.		27.90	28
1986 Dear Santy Claus	Yr.Iss.		27.90	30
1987 Santa's Golden Gift	Yr.Iss.		27.90	30
1988 Santa Claus	Yr.Iss.		29.90	30
1989 Jolly Old St. Nick	Yr.Iss.		29.90	35
1990 A Christmas Prayer	Yr.Iss.		29.90	40
1991 Santa's Helpers	Yr.Iss.		32.90	33
1992 The Christmas Surprise	Yr.Iss.		32.90	35
1993 The Tree Brigade	Yr.Iss.		32.90	40
1994 Christmas Marvel	Yr.Iss.		32.90	73
1995 Filling The Stockings	Yr.Iss.		32.90	33

Colonials-The Rarest Rockwells - N. Rockwell

1985 Unexpected Proposal	150-day		27.90	28
1986 Words of Comfort	150-day		27.90	28
1986 Light for the Winter	150-day		30.90	31
1987 Portrait for a Bridegroom	150-day		30.90	31
1987 The Journey Home	150-day		30.90	31
1987 Clinching the Deal	150-day		30.90	31
1988 Sign of the Times	150-day		32.90	33
1988 Ye Glutton	150-day		32.90	33

Coming Of Age - N. Rockwell

1990 Back To School	150-day		29.90	45
1990 Home From Camp	150-day		29.90	50
1990 Her First Formal	150-day		32.90	65
1990 The Muscleman	150-day		32.90	33
1990 A New Look	150-day		32.90	35
1991 A Balcony Seat	150-day		32.90	33
1991 Men About Town	150-day		34.90	35
1991 Paths of Glory	150-day		34.90	35
1991 Doorway to the Past	150-day		34.90	40
1991 School's Out!	150-day		34.90	60

Heritage - N. Rockwell

1977 Toy Maker	Yr.Iss.		14.50	80-100
1978 Cobbler	Yr.Iss.		19.50	40-50
1979 Lighthouse Keeper's Daughter	Yr.Iss.		19.50	25-35
1980 Ship Builder	Yr.Iss.		19.50	20-45
1981 Music maker	Yr.Iss.		19.50	25-40
1982 Tycoon	Yr.Iss.		19.50	35
1983 Painter	Yr.Iss.		19.50	20
1984 Storyteller	Yr.Iss.		19.50	20
1985 Gourmet	Yr.Iss.		19.50	20
1986 Professor	Yr.Iss.		22.90	23
1987 Shadow Artist	Yr.Iss.		22.90	25
1988 The Veteran	Yr.Iss.		22.90	23
1988 The Banjo Player	Yr.Iss.		22.90	25
1990 The Old Scout	Yr.Iss.		24.90	25
1991 The Young Scholar	Yr.Iss.		24.90	30
1991 The Family Doctor	Yr.Iss.		27.90	50-60

*Quotes have been rounded up to nearest dollar

PLATES

YEAR ISSUE		EDITION LIMIT	YEAR RETD.	ISSUE PRICE	*QUOTE U.S.$
1992	The Jeweler	Yr.Iss.		27.90	45-60
1993	Halloween Frolic	Yr.Iss.		27.90	52
1994	The Apprentice	Yr.Iss.		29.90	30

Innocence and Experience - N. Rockwell

1991	The Sea Captain	150-day		29.90	30
1991	The Radio Operator	150-day		29.90	30
1991	The Magician	150-day		32.90	35
1992	The American Heroes	150-day		32.90	35

A Mind of Her Own - N. Rockwell

1986	Sitting Pretty	150-day		24.90	30
1987	Serious Business	150-day		24.90	28
1987	Breaking the Rules	150-day		24.90	30
1987	Good Intentions	150-day		27.90	28
1988	Second Thoughts	150-day		27.90	28
1988	World's Away	150-day		27.90	28
1988	Kiss and Tell	150-day		29.90	30
1988	On My Honor	150-day		29.90	30

Mother's Day - N. Rockwell

1976	A Mother's Love	Yr.Iss.		24.50	40-65
1977	Faith	Yr.Iss.		24.50	48
1978	Bedtime	Yr.Iss.		24.50	30
1979	Reflections	Yr.Iss.		24.50	25
1980	A Mother's Pride	Yr.Iss.		24.50	25
1981	After the Party	Yr.Iss.		24.50	25
1982	The Cooking Lesson	Yr.Iss.		24.50	30
1983	Add Two Cups and Love	Yr.Iss.		25.50	28
1984	Grandma's Courting Dress	Yr.Iss.		25.50	26
1985	Mending Time	Yr.Iss.		27.50	28
1986	Pantry Raid	Yr.Iss.		27.90	28
1987	Grandma's Surprise	Yr.Iss.		29.90	30
1988	My Mother	Yr.Iss.		29.90	32
1989	Sunday Dinner	Yr.Iss.		29.90	30
1990	Evening Prayers	Yr.Iss.		29.90	30
1991	Building Our Future	Yr.Iss.		32.90	33
1991	Gentle Reassurance	Yr.Iss.		32.90	33
1992	A Special Delivery	Yr.Iss.		32.90	35

Rockwell Commemorative Stamps - N. Rockwell

1994	Triple Self Portrait	95-day		29.90	30
1994	Freedom From Want	95-day		29.90	30
1994	Freedom From Fear	95-day		29.90	30
1995	Freedom of Speech	95-day		29.90	30
1995	Freedom of Worship	95-day		29.90	30

Rockwell on Tour - N. Rockwell

1983	Walking Through Merrie Englande	150-day		16.00	16
1983	Promenade a Paris	150-day		16.00	16
1983	When in Rome	150-day		16.00	16
1984	Die Walk am Rhein	150-day		16.00	16

Rockwell's American Dream - N. Rockwell

1985	A Young Girl's Dream	150-day		19.90	20
1985	A Couple's Commitment	150-day		19.90	27
1985	A Family's Full Measure	150-day		22.90	30
1986	A Mother's Welcome	150-day		22.90	25
1986	A Young Man's Dream	150-day		22.90	30
1986	The Musician's Magic	150-day		22.90	25
1987	An Orphan's Hope	150-day		24.90	26
1987	Love's Reward	150-day		24.90	30

Rockwell's Golden Moments - N. Rockwell

1987	Grandpa's Gift	150-day		19.90	30
1987	Grandma's Love	150-day		19.90	35
1988	End of day	150-day		22.90	40
1988	Best Friends	150-day		22.90	23
1989	Love Letters	150-day		22.90	23
1989	Newfound Worlds	150-day		22.90	23
1989	Keeping Company	150-day		24.90	25
1989	Evening's Repose	150-day		24.90	25

Rockwell's Light Campaign - N. Rockwell

1983	This is the Room that Light Made	150-day		19.50	20
1984	Grandpa's Treasure Chest	150-day		19.50	20
1984	Father's Help	150-day		19.50	20
1984	Evening's Ease	150-day		19.50	20
1984	Close Harmony	150-day		21.50	22
1984	The Birthday Wish	150-day		21.50	22

Rockwell's Rediscovered Women - N. Rockwell

1984	Dreaming in the Attic	100-day		19.50	30
1984	Waiting on the Shore	100-day		22.50	23
1984	Pondering on the Porch	100-day		22.50	23
1984	Making Believe at the Mirror	100-day		22.50	23-30
1984	Waiting at the Dance	100-day		22.50	23
1984	Gossiping in the Alcove	100-day		22.50	23
1984	Standing in the Doorway	100-day		22.50	25-35
1984	Flirting in the Parlor	100-day		22.50	25-35
1984	Working in the Kitchen	100-day		22.50	33
1984	Meeting on the Path	100-day		22.50	23
1984	Confiding in the Den	100-day		22.50	23
1984	Reminiscing in the Quiet	100-day		22.50	23
XX	Complete Collection	100-day		267.00	267

Rockwell's The Ones We Love - N. Rockwell

1988	Tender Loving Care	150-day		19.90	25
1989	A Time to Keep	150-day		19.90	25
1989	The Inventor And The Judge	150-day		22.90	30

YEAR ISSUE		EDITION LIMIT	YEAR RETD.	ISSUE PRICE	*QUOTE U.S.$
1989	Ready For The World	150-day		22.90	30
1989	Growing Strong	150-day		22.90	30
1990	The Story Hour	150-day		22.90	35
1990	The Country Doctor	150-day		24.90	25
1990	Our Love of Country	150-day		24.90	25
1990	The Homecoming	150-day		24.90	25
1991	A Helping Hand	150-day		24.90	25

Rockwell's Treasured Memories - N. Rockwell

1991	Quiet Reflections	150-day		29.90	30
1991	Romantic Reverie	150-day		29.90	30
1991	Tender Romance	150-day		32.90	33
1991	Evening Passage	150-day		32.90	33
1991	Heavenly Dreams	150-day		32.90	34
1991	Sentimental Shores	150-day		32.90	34

Roman, Inc.

Abbie Williams Collection - A. Williams

1991	Legacy of Love	Open		29.50	30
1991	Bless This Child	Open		29.50	30

Catnippers - I. Spencer

1986	Christmas Mourning	9,500		34.50	35
1992	Happy Holidaze	9,500		34.50	35

A Child's Play - F. Hook

1982	Breezy Day	30-day		29.95	39
1982	Kite Flying	30-day		29.95	39
1984	Bathtub Sailor	30-day		29.95	35
1984	The First Snow	30-day		29.95	35

A Child's World - F. Hook

1980	Little Children, Come to Me	15,000		45.00	49

Fontanini Annual Christmas Plate - E. Simonetti

1986	A King Is Born	Yr.Iss.		60.00	60
1987	O Come, Let Us Adore Him	Yr.Iss.		60.00	65
1988	Adoration of the Magi	Yr.Iss.		70.00	75
1989	Flight Into Egypt	Yr.Iss.		75.00	85

Frances Hook Collection-Set I - F. Hook

1982	I Wish, I Wish	15,000		24.95	35-39
1982	Baby Blossoms	15,000		24.95	35-39
1982	Daisy Dreamer	15,000		24.95	35-39
1982	Trees So Tall	15,000		24.95	35-39

Frances Hook Collection-Set II - F. Hook

1983	Caught It Myself	15,000		24.95	25
1983	Winter Wrappings	15,000		24.95	25
1983	So Cuddly	15,000		24.95	25
1983	Can I Keep Him?	15,000		24.95	25

Frances Hook Legacy - F. Hook

1985	Fascination	100-day		19.50	35-39
1985	Daydreaming	100-day		19.50	35-39
1985	Discovery	100-day		22.50	35-39
1985	Disappointment	100-day		22.50	35-39
1985	Wonderment	100-day		22.50	35-39
1985	Expectation	100-day		22.50	35-39

God Bless You Little One - A. Williams

1991	Baby's First Birthday (Girl)	Open		29.50	30
1991	Baby's First Birthday (Boy)	Open		29.50	30
1991	Baby's First Smile	Open		19.50	20
1991	Baby's First Word	Open		19.50	20
1991	Baby's First Step	Open		19.50	20
1991	Baby's First Tooth	Open		19.50	20

The Ice Capades Clown - G. Petty

1983	Presenting Freddie Trenkler	30-day		24.50	25

The Lord's Prayer - A. Williams

1986	Our Father	10-day		24.50	25
1986	Thy Kingdom Come	10-day		24.50	25
1986	Give Us This Day	10-day		24.50	25
1986	Forgive Our Trespasses	10-day		24.50	34
1986	As We Forgive	10-day		24.50	25
1986	Lead Us Not	10-day		24.50	25
1986	Deliver Us From Evil	10-day		24.50	25
1986	Thine Is The Kingdom	10-day		24.50	25

The Love's Prayer - A. Williams

1988	Love Is Patient and Kind	14-day		29.50	30
1988	Love Is Never Jealous or Boastful	14-day		29.50	30
1988	Love Is Never Arrogant or Rude	14-day		29.50	30
1988	Love Does Not Insist on Its Own Way	14-day		29.50	30
1988	Love Is Never Irritable or Resentful	14-day		29.50	30
1988	Love Rejoices In the Right	14-day		29.50	30
1988	Love Believes All Things	14-day		29.50	30
1988	Love Never Ends	14-day		29.50	30

The Magic of Childhood - A. Williams

1985	Special Friends	10-day		24.50	35
1985	Feeding Time	10-day		24.50	35
1985	Best Buddies	10-day		24.50	35
1985	Getting Acquainted	10-day		24.50	35
1986	Last One In	10-day		24.50	35

YEAR ISSUE		EDITION LIMIT	YEAR RETD.	ISSUE PRICE	*QUOTE U.S.$
1986	A Handful Of Love	10-day		24.50	35
1986	Look Alikes	10-day		24.50	35
1986	No Fair Peeking	10-day		24.50	35

March of Dimes: Our Children, Our Future - A. Williams

1990	A Time To Laugh	150-day		29.00	39-4

The Masterpiece Collection - Various

1979	Adoration - F. Lippe	5,000		65.00	65
1980	Madonna with Grapes - P. Mignard	5,000		87.50	88
1981	The Holy Family - G. Delle Notti	5,000		95.00	95
1982	Madonna of the Streets - R. Ferruzzi	5,000		85.00	85

Millenium™ Series - Various

1992	Silent Night - Morcaldo/Lucchesi	Closed	1992	49.50	5
1993	The Annunciation - Morcaldo/Lucchesi	5,000	1993	49.50	5
1994	Peace On Earth - Morcaldo/Lucchesi	5,000	1994	49.50	5
1995	Cause of Our Joy - A. Lucchesi	7,500		49.50	5
1996	Prince of Peace - A. Lucchesi	15,000		49.50	5

Precious Children - A. Williams

1993	Bless Baby Brother	N/A		29.50	3
1993	Blowing Bubbles	N/A		29.50	3
1993	Don't Worry, Mother Duck	N/A		29.50	3
1993	Treetop Discovery	N/A		29.50	3
1993	The Tea Party	N/A		29.50	3
1993	Mother's Little Angel	N/A		29.50	3
1993	Picking Daisies	N/A		29.50	3
1993	Let's Say Grace	N/A		29.50	3

Pretty Girls of the Ice Capades - G. Petty

1983	Ice Princess	30-day		24.50	2

Promise of a Savior - Unknown

1993	An Angel's Message	95-day		29.90	3
1993	Gifts to Jesus	95-day		29.90	3
1993	The Heavenly King	95-day		29.90	3
1993	Angels Were Watching	95-day		29.90	3
1993	Holy Mother & Child	95-day		29.90	3
1993	A Child is Born	95-day		29.90	3

The Richard Judson Zolan Collection - R.J. Zolan

1992	The Butterfly Net	100-day		29.50	3
1994	The Ring	100-day		29.50	3
1994	Terrace Dancing	100-day		29.50	3

Roman Memorial - F. Hook

1984	The Carpenter	Closed	1984	100.00	1

Sepaphim Collection by Faro - Faro

1994	Rosalyn - Rarest of Heaven	7,200	1995	65.00	6
1995	Helena - Heaven's Herald	7,200		65.00	6
1996	Flora - Flower of Heaven	7,200		65.00	6

Single Releases - A. Williams

1987	The Christening	Open		29.50	3
1990	The Dedication	Open		29.50	3
1990	The Baptism	Open		29.50	3

The Sweetest Songs - I. Spencer

1986	A Baby's Prayer	30-day		39.50	4
1986	This Little Piggie	30-day		39.50	4
1988	Long, Long Ago	30-day		39.50	4
1989	Rockabye	30-day		39.50	4

Tender Expressions - B. Sargent

1992	Thoughts of You Are In My Heart	100-day		29.50	

Rorstrand

Christmas - G. Nylund

1968	Bringing Home the Tree	Annual	N/A	12.00	300-3
1969	Fisherman Sailing Home	Annual	N/A	13.50	
1970	Nils with His Geese	Annual	N/A	13.50	
1971	Nils in Lapland	Annual	N/A	15.00	
1972	Dalecarlian Fiddler	Annual	N/A	15.00	20-
1973	Farm in Smaland	Annual	N/A	16.00	
1974	Vadslena	Annual	N/A	19.00	
1975	Nils in Vastmanland	Annual	N/A	20.00	
1976	Nils in Uapland	Annual	N/A	20.00	43-
1977	Nils in Varmland	Annual	N/A	29.50	
1978	Nils in Fjallbacka	Annual	N/A	32.50	
1979	Nils in Vaestergoetland	Annual	N/A	38.50	
1980	Nils in Halland	Annual	N/A	55.00	
1981	Nils in Gotland	Annual	N/A	55.00	
1982	Nils at Skansen	Annual	N/A	47.50	
1983	Nils in Oland	Annual	N/A	42.50	
1984	Angerman land	Annual	N/A	42.50	
1985	Nils in Jamtland	Annual	N/A	42.50	
1986	Nils in Karlskr	Annual	N/A	42.50	
1987	Dalsland, Forget-Me-Not	Annual	N/A	47.50	
1988	Nils in Halsingland	Annual	N/A	55.00	
1989	Nils Visits Gothenborg	Annual		60.00	
1990	Nils in Kvikkjokk	Annual	N/A	75.00	
1991	Nils in Medelpad	Annual	N/A	85.00	
1992	Gastrikland, Lily of the Valley	Annual	N/A	92.50	
1993	Orebro Castle in Narkes	Annual		92.50	
1994	Gripsholm Castle Sodermanland	Annual		92.50	

*Quotes have been rounded up to nearest dolla

YEAR ISSUE		EDITION LIMIT	YEAR RETD.	ISSUE PRICE	*QUOTE U.S. $
1995	Nils in Hårjedalen	Annual		92.50	93

Rosenthal

Christmas - Unknown

YEAR ISSUE		EDITION LIMIT	YEAR RETD.	ISSUE PRICE	*QUOTE U.S. $
1910	Winter Peace	Annual		Unkn.	550
1911	Three Wise Men	Annual		Unkn.	325
1912	Stardust	Annual		Unkn.	255
1913	Christmas Lights	Annual		Unkn.	235
1914	Christmas Song	Annual		Unkn.	350
1915	Walking to Church	Annual		Unkn.	180
1916	Christmas During War	Annual		Unkn.	240
1917	Angel of Peace	Annual		Unkn.	200
1918	Peace on Earth	Annual		Unkn.	200
1919	St. Christopher with Christ Child	Annual		Unkn.	225
1920	Manger in Bethlehem	Annual		Unkn.	325
1921	Christmas in Mountains	Annual		Unkn.	200
1922	Advent Branch	Annual		Unkn.	200
1923	Children in Winter Woods	Annual		Unkn.	200
1924	Deer in the Woods	Annual		Unkn.	200
1925	Three Wise Men	Annual		Unkn.	200
1926	Christmas in Mountains	Annual		Unkn.	195
1927	Station on the Way	Annual		Unkn.	200
1928	Chalet Christmas	Annual		Unkn.	185
1929	Christmas in Alps	Annual		Unkn.	225
1930	Group of Deer Under Pines	Annual		Unkn.	225
1931	Path of the Magi	Annual		Unkn.	225
1932	Christ Child	Annual		Unkn.	185
1933	Thru the Night to Light	Annual		Unkn.	190
1934	Christmas Peace	Annual		Unkn.	190
1935	Christmas by the Sea	Annual		Unkn.	190
1936	Nurnberg Angel	Annual		Unkn.	195
1937	Berchtesgaden	Annual		Unkn.	195
1938	Christmas in the Alps	Annual		Unkn.	195
1939	Schneekoppe Mountain	Annual		Unkn.	195
1940	Marien Chruch in Danzig	Annual		Unkn.	250
1941	Strassburg Cathedral	Annual		Unkn.	250
1942	Marianburg Castle	Annual		Unkn.	300
1943	Winter Idyll	Annual		Unkn.	300
1944	Wood Scape	Annual		Unkn.	300
1945	Christmas Peace	Annual		Unkn.	400
1946	Christmas in an Alpine Valley	Annual		Unkn.	240
1947	Dillingen Madonna	Annual		Unkn.	985
1948	Message to the Shepherds	Annual		Unkn.	875
1949	The Holy Family	Annual		Unkn.	185
1950	Christmas in the Forest	Annual		Unkn.	185
1951	Star of Bethlehem	Annual		Unkn.	450
1952	Christmas in the Alps	Annual		Unkn.	195
1953	The Holy Light	Annual		Unkn.	195
1954	Christmas Eve	Annual		Unkn.	195
1955	Christmas in a Village	Annual		Unkn.	195
1956	Christmas in the Alps	Annual		Unkn.	195
1957	Christmas by the Sea	Annual		Unkn.	195
1958	Christmas Eve	Annual		Unkn.	195
1959	Midnight Mass	Annual		Unkn.	195
1960	Christmas in a Small Village	Annual		Unkn.	195
1961	Solitary Christmas	Annual		Unkn.	225
1962	Christmas Eve	Annual		Unkn.	195
1963	Silent Night	Annual		Unkn.	195
1964	Christmas Market in Nurnberg	Annual		Unkn.	225
1965	Christmas Munich	Annual		Unkn.	185
1966	Christmas in Ulm	Annual		Unkn.	275
1967	Christmas in Reginburg	Annual		Unkn.	185
1968	Christmas in Bremen	Annual		Unkn.	195
1969	Christmas in Rothenburg	Annual		Unkn.	220
1970	Christmas in Cologne	Annual		Unkn.	175
1971	Christmas in Garmisch	Annual		42.00	100
1972	Christmas in Franconia	Annual		50.00	95
1973	Lubeck-Holstein	Annual		77.00	105
1974	Christmas in Wurzburg	Annual		85.00	100

Nobility of Children - E. Hibel

YEAR ISSUE		EDITION LIMIT	YEAR RETD.	ISSUE PRICE	*QUOTE U.S. $
1976	La Contessa Isabella	12,750		120.00	120
1977	La Marquis Maurice-Pierre	12,750		120.00	120
1978	Baronesse Johanna	12,750		130.00	140
1979	Chief Red Feather	12,750		140.00	180

Oriental Gold - E. Hibel

YEAR ISSUE		EDITION LIMIT	YEAR RETD.	ISSUE PRICE	*QUOTE U.S. $
1976	Yasuko	2,000		275.00	650
1977	Mr. Obata	2,000		275.00	500
1978	Sakura	2,000		295.00	400
1979	Michio	2,000		325.00	375

Wiinblad Christmas - B. Wiinblad

YEAR ISSUE		EDITION LIMIT	YEAR RETD.	ISSUE PRICE	*QUOTE U.S. $
1971	Maria & Child	Undis.		100.00	750
1972	Caspar	Undis.		100.00	290
1973	Melchior	Undis.		125.00	335
1974	Balthazar	Undis.		125.00	300
1975	The Annunciation	Undis.		195.00	195
1976	Angel with Trumpet	Undis.		195.00	195
1977	Adoration of Shepherds	Undis.		225.00	225
1978	Angel with Harp	Undis.		275.00	295
1979	Exodus from Egypt	Undis.		310.00	310
1980	Angel with Glockenspiel	Undis.		360.00	360
1981	Christ Child Visits Temple	Undis.		375.00	375
1982	Christening of Christ	Undis.		375.00	375

Royal Copenhagen

Christmas - Various

YEAR ISSUE		EDITION LIMIT	YEAR RETD.	ISSUE PRICE	*QUOTE U.S. $
1908	Madonna and Child - C. Thomsen	Annual	1908	1.00	3000-4000
1909	Danish Landscape - S. Ussing	Annual	1909	1.00	200-240
1910	The Magi - C. Thomsen	Annual	1910	1.00	100-180
1911	Danish Landscape - O. Jensen	Annual	1911	1.00	125-200
1912	Christmas Tree - C. Thomsen	Annual	1912	1.00	100-200
1913	Frederik Church Spire - A. Boesen	Annual	1913	1.50	140-165
1914	Holy Spirit Church - A. Boesen	Annual	1914	1.50	175-225
1915	Danish Landscape - A. Krog	Annual	1915	1.50	165-210
1916	Shepherd at Christmas - R. Bocher	Annual	1916	1.50	115-140
1917	Our Savior Church - O. Jensen	Annual	1917	2.00	115-160
1918	Sheep and Shepherds - O. Jensen	Annual	1918	2.00	110-180
1919	In the Park - O. Jensen	Annual	1919	2.00	115-135
1920	Mary and Child Jesus - G. Rode	Annual	1920	2.00	120-170
1921	Aabenraa Marketplace - O. Jensen	Annual	1921	2.00	80-180
1922	Three Singing Angels - E. Selschau	Annual	1922	2.00	75-95
1923	Danish Landscape - O. Jensen	Annual	1923	2.00	95
1924	Sailing Ship - B. Olsen	Annual	1924	2.00	130
1925	Christianshavn - O. Jensen	Annual	1925	2.00	120
1926	Christianshavn Canal - R. Bocher	Annual	1926	2.00	145-175
1927	Ship's Boy at Tiller - B. Olsen	Annual	1927	2.00	140-175
1928	Vicar's Family - G. Rode	Annual	1928	2.00	140
1929	Grundtvig Church - O. Jensen	Annual	1929	2.00	115-140
1930	Fishing Boats - B. Olsen	Annual	1930	2.50	135-145
1931	Mother and Child - G. Rode	Annual	1931	2.50	145-175
1932	Frederiksberg Gardens - O. Jensen	Annual	1932	2.50	115-130
1933	Ferry and the Great Belt - B. Olsen	Annual	1933	2.50	195-225
1934	The Hermitage Castle - O. Jensen	Annual	1934	2.50	200-325
1935	Kronborg Castle - B. Olsen	Annual	1935	2.50	310-450
1936	Roskilde Cathedral - R. Bocher	Annual	1936	2.50	200-300
1937	Main Street Copenhagen - N. Thorsson	Annual	1937	2.50	250-340
1938	Round Church in Osterlars - H. Nielsen	Annual	1938	3.00	440
1939	Greenland Pack-Ice - S. Nielsen	Annual	1939	3.00	450-600
1940	The Good Shepherd - K. Lange	Annual	1940	3.00	350-550
1941	Danish Village Church - T. Kjolner	Annual	1941	3.00	499
1942	Bell Tower - N. Thorsson	Annual	1942	4.00	450-600
1943	Flight into Egypt - N. Thorsson	Annual	1943	4.00	650-750
1944	Danish Village Scene - V. Olson	Annual	1944	4.00	300-400
1945	A Peaceful Motif - R. Bocher	Annual	1945	4.00	375-600
1946	Zealand Village Church - N. Thorsson	Annual	1946	4.00	275
1947	The Good Shepherd - K. Lange	Annual	1947	4.50	350-500
1948	Nodebo Church - T. Kjolner	Annual	1948	4.50	260-300
1949	Our Lady's Cathedral - H. Hansen	Annual	1949	5.00	200-340
1950	Boeslunde Church - V. Olson	Annual	1950	5.00	250-340
1951	Christmas Angel - R. Bocher	Annual	1951	5.00	300-440
1952	Christmas in the Forest - K. Lange	Annual	1952	5.00	175
1953	Frederiksberg Castle - T. Kjolner	Annual	1953	6.00	160-200
1954	Amalienborg Palace - K. Lange	Annual	1954	6.00	180-250
1955	Fano Girl - K. Lange	Annual	1955	7.00	250-350
1956	Rosenborg Castle - K. Lange	Annual	1956	7.00	210-270
1957	The Good Shepherd - H. Hansen	Annual	1957	8.00	130-160
1958	Sunshine over Greenland - H. Hansen	Annual	1958	9.00	100-175
1959	Christmas Night - H. Hansen	Annual	1959	9.00	160-180
1960	The Stag - H. Hansen	Annual	1960	10.00	150-185
1961	Training Ship - K. Lange	Annual	1961	10.00	200-230
1962	The Little Mermaid - Unknown	Annual	1962	11.00	200-310
1963	Hojsager Mill - K. Lange	Annual	1963	11.00	50-100
1964	Fetching the Tree - K. Lange	Annual	1964	11.00	50-70
1965	Little Skaters - K. Lange	Annual	1965	12.00	45-74
1966	Blackbird - K. Lange	Annual	1966	12.00	38
1967	The Royal Oak - K. Lange	Annual	1967	13.00	38
1968	The Last Umiak - K. Lange	Annual	1968	13.00	38
1969	The Old Farmyard - K. Lange	Annual	1969	14.00	38
1970	Christmas Rose and Cat - K. Lange	Annual	1970	14.00	36
1971	Hare In Winter - K. Lange	Annual	1971	15.00	25
1972	In the Desert - K. Lange	Annual	1972	16.00	30
1973	Train Homeward Bound - K. Lange	Annual	1973	22.00	30
1974	Winter Twilight - K. Lange	Annual	1974	22.00	28
1975	Queen's Palace - K. Lange	Annual	1975	27.50	30
1976	Danish Watermill - S. Vestergaard	Annual	1976	27.50	30
1977	Immervad Bridge - K. Lange	Annual	1977	32.00	30
1978	Greenland Scenery - K. Lange	Annual	1978	35.00	30
1979	Choosing Christmas Tree - K. Lange	Annual	1979	42.50	75
1980	Bringing Home the Tree - K. Lange	Annual	1980	49.50	50
1981	Admiring Christmas Tree - K. Lange	Annual	1981	52.50	80
1982	Waiting for Christmas - K. Lange	Annual	1982	54.50	75
1983	Merry Christmas - K. Lange	Annual	1983	54.50	75
1984	Jingle Bells - K. Lange	Annual	1984	54.50	75
1985	Snowman - K. Lange	Annual	1985	54.50	90
1986	Christmas Vacation - K. Lange	Annual	1986	54.50	85
1987	Winter Birds - S. Vestergaard	Annual	1987	59.50	80
1988	Christmas Eve in Copenhagen - S. Vestergaard	Annual	1988	59.50	90
1989	The Old Skating Pond - S. Vestergaard	Annual	1989	59.50	95
1990	Christmas at Tivoli - S. Vestergaard	Annual	1990	64.50	200
1991	The Festival of Santa Lucia - S. Vestergaard	Annual	1991	69.50	100
1992	The Queen's Carriage - S. Vestergaard	Annual	1992	69.50	80
1993	Christmas Guests - S. Vestergaard	Annual	1993	69.50	100
1994	Christmas Shopping - S. Vestergaard	Annual	1994	72.50	80
1995	Christmas at the Manor House - S. Vestergaard	Annual	1995	72.50	75
1996	Lighting the Street Lamps - S. Vestergaard	Annual		74.50	75

Royal Devon

Rockwell Christmas - N. Rockwell

YEAR ISSUE		EDITION LIMIT	YEAR RETD.	ISSUE PRICE	*QUOTE U.S. $
1975	Downhill Daring	Yr.Iss.		24.50	30
1976	The Christmas Gift	Yr.Iss.		24.50	35
1977	The Big Moment	Yr.Iss.		27.50	50
1978	Puppets for Christmas	Yr.Iss.		27.50	28
1979	One Present Too Many	Yr.Iss.		31.50	32
1980	Gramps Meets Gramps	Yr.Iss.		33.00	33

Rockwell Mother's Day - N. Rockwell

YEAR ISSUE		EDITION LIMIT	YEAR RETD.	ISSUE PRICE	*QUOTE U.S. $
1975	Doctor and Doll	Yr.Iss.		23.50	50
1976	Puppy Love	Yr.Iss.		24.50	104
1977	The Family	Yr.Iss.		24.50	85
1978	Mother's Day Off	Yr.Iss.		27.00	35
1979	Mother's Evening Out	Yr.Iss.		30.00	32
1980	Mother's Treat	Yr.Iss.		32.50	35

Royal Doulton

Christmas Plates - N/A

YEAR ISSUE		EDITION LIMIT	YEAR RETD.	ISSUE PRICE	*QUOTE U.S. $
1993	Royal Doulton-Together For Christmas	Closed	N/A	45.00	45
1993	Royal Albert-Sleighride	Closed	N/A	45.00	45

Family Christmas Plates - N/A

YEAR ISSUE		EDITION LIMIT	YEAR RETD.	ISSUE PRICE	*QUOTE U.S. $
1991	Dad Plays Santa	Closed	1991	60.00	60

Royal Worcester

Birth Of A Nation - P.W. Baston

YEAR ISSUE		EDITION LIMIT	YEAR RETD.	ISSUE PRICE	*QUOTE U.S. $
1972	Boston Tea Party	10,000		45.00	140-275
1973	Paul Revere	10,000		45.00	140-250
1974	Concord Bridge	10,000		50.00	140
1975	Signing Declaration	10,000		65.00	140
1976	Crossing Delaware	10,000		65.00	140
1977	Washington's Inauguration	1,250		65.00	140

Currier and Ives Plates - P.W. Baston

YEAR ISSUE		EDITION LIMIT	YEAR RETD.	ISSUE PRICE	*QUOTE U.S. $
1974	Road in Winter	5,570		59.50	55-100
1975	Old Grist Mill	3,200		59.50	55-100
1976	Winter Pastime	1,500		59.50	55-125
1977	Home to Thanksgiving	546		59.50	200-250

Kitten Classics - P. Cooper

YEAR ISSUE		EDITION LIMIT	YEAR RETD.	ISSUE PRICE	*QUOTE U.S. $
1985	Cat Nap	14-day		29.50	36
1985	Purrfect Treasure	14-day		29.50	30
1985	Wild Flower	14-day		29.50	30
1985	Birdwatcher	14-day		29.50	30
1985	Tiger's Fancy	14-day		29.50	33
1985	Country Kitty	14-day		29.50	33
1985	Little Rascal	14-day		29.50	30
1986	First Prize	14-day		29.50	30

Kitten Encounters - P. Cooper

YEAR ISSUE		EDITION LIMIT	YEAR RETD.	ISSUE PRICE	*QUOTE U.S. $
1987	Fishful Thinking	14-day		29.50	30-54
1987	Puppy Pal	14-day		29.50	36
1987	Just Ducky	14-day		29.50	36
1987	Bunny Chase	14-day		29.50	30
1987	Flutter By	14-day		29.50	30
1987	Bedtime Buddies	14-day		29.50	30
1988	Cat and Mouse	14-day		29.50	33
1988	Stablemates	14-day		29.50	48

Schmid

Christmas - B. Hummel

YEAR ISSUE		EDITION LIMIT	YEAR RETD.	ISSUE PRICE	*QUOTE U.S. $
1971	Angel	Annual		15.00	20
1972	Angel With Flute	Annual		15.00	15
1973	The Nativity	Annual		15.00	60
1974	The Guardian Angel	Annual		18.50	19
1975	Christmas Child	Annual		25.00	25
1976	Sacred Journey	Annual		27.50	28
1977	Herald Angel	Annual		27.50	28
1978	Heavenly Trio	Annual		32.50	33
1979	Starlight Angel	Annual		38.00	38
1980	Parade Into Toyland	Annual		45.00	45
1981	A Time To Remember	Annual		45.00	45
1982	Angelic Procession	Annual		45.00	49
1983	Angelic Messenger	Annual		45.00	45
1984	A Gift from Heaven	Annual		45.00	48
1985	Heavenly Light	Annual		45.00	45

*Quotes have been rounded up to nearest dollar

YEAR ISSUE		EDITION LIMIT	YEAR RETD.	ISSUE PRICE	*QUOTE U.S.$
1986	Tell The Heavens	Annual		45.00	45
1987	Angelic Gifts	Annual		47.50	48
1988	Cheerful Cherubs	Annual		53.00	60
1989	Angelic Musician	Annual		53.00	53
1990	Angel's Light	Annual		53.00	53
1991	Message From Above	Annual		60.00	60
1992	Sweet Blessings	Annual		65.00	65

Davis Cat Tales Plates. - L. Davis

YEAR ISSUE		EDITION LIMIT	YEAR RETD.	ISSUE PRICE	*QUOTE U.S.$
1982	Right Church, Wrong Pew	12,500		37.50	90
1982	Company's Coming	12,500		37.50	90
1982	On the Move	12,500		37.50	90
1982	Flew the Coop	12,500		37.50	90

Davis Christmas Plates - L. Davis

YEAR ISSUE		EDITION LIMIT	YEAR RETD.	ISSUE PRICE	*QUOTE U.S.$
1983	Hooker at Mailbox With Present	7,500		45.00	130
1984	Country Christmas	7,500		45.00	75
1985	Christmas at Foxfire Farm	7,500		45.00	150
1986	Christmas at Red Oak	7,500		45.00	50-75
1987	Blossom's Gift	7,500		47.50	100
1988	Cutting the Family Christmas Tree	7,500		47.50	65
1989	Peter and the Wren	7,500		47.50	75
1990	Wintering Deer	7,500		47.50	48
1991	Christmas at Red Oak II	7,500		55.00	75
1992	Born On A Starry Night	7,500		55.00	55
1993	Waiting For Mr. Lowell	5,000		55.00	55
1994	Visions of Sugarplums	5,000		55.00	55
1995	Bah Humbug	5,000		55.00	55

Davis Country Pride Plates - L. Davis

YEAR ISSUE		EDITION LIMIT	YEAR RETD.	ISSUE PRICE	*QUOTE U.S.$
1981	Surprise in the Cellar	7,500		35.00	175-225
1981	Plum Tuckered Out	7,500		35.00	70
1981	Duke's Mixture	7,500		35.00	190
1982	Bustin' with Pride	7,500		35.00	75

Davis Red Oak Sampler - L. Davis

YEAR ISSUE		EDITION LIMIT	YEAR RETD.	ISSUE PRICE	*QUOTE U.S.$
1986	General Store	5,000		45.00	175
1987	Country Wedding	5,000		45.00	125
1989	Country School	5,000		45.00	75
1990	Blacksmith Shop	5,000		52.50	53

Davis Special Edition Plates - L. Davis

YEAR ISSUE		EDITION LIMIT	YEAR RETD.	ISSUE PRICE	*QUOTE U.S.$
1983	The Critics	12,500		45.00	60-145
1984	Good Ole Days Privy Set 2	5,000		60.00	80-125
1986	Home From Market	7,500		55.00	145

Disney Annual - Disney Studios

YEAR ISSUE		EDITION LIMIT	YEAR RETD.	ISSUE PRICE	*QUOTE U.S.$
1983	Sneak Preview	20,000		22.50	23
1984	Command Performance	20,000		22.50	23
1985	Snow Biz	20,000		22.50	23
1986	Tree For Two	20,000		22.50	23
1987	Merry Mouse Medley	20,000		25.00	25
1988	Warm Winter Ride	20,000		25.00	25
1989	Merry Mickey Claus	20,000		32.50	60
1990	Holly Jolly Christmas	20,000		32.50	33
1991	Mickey and Minnie's Rockin' Christmas	20,000		37.00	37

Disney Christmas - Disney Studios

YEAR ISSUE		EDITION LIMIT	YEAR RETD.	ISSUE PRICE	*QUOTE U.S.$
1973	Sleigh Ride	Annual		10.00	275
1974	Decorating The Tree	Annual		10.00	70
1975	Caroling	Annual		12.50	15
1976	Building A Snowman	Annual		13.00	15
1977	Down The Chimney	Annual		13.00	20
1978	Night Before Christmas	Annual		15.00	25
1979	Santa's Suprise	15,000		17.50	32
1980	Sleigh Ride	15,000		17.50	33
1981	Happy Holidays	15,000		17.50	25
1982	Winter Games	15,000		18.50	25

Disney Mother's Day - Disney Studios

YEAR ISSUE		EDITION LIMIT	YEAR RETD.	ISSUE PRICE	*QUOTE U.S.$
1974	Flowers For Mother	Annual		10.00	45
1975	Snow White & Dwarfs	Annual		12.50	50
1976	Minnie Mouse	Annual		13.00	25
1977	Pluto's Pals	Annual		13.00	18
1978	Flowers For Bambi	Annual		15.00	40
1979	Happy Feet	10,000		17.50	20
1980	Minnie's Surprise	10,000		17.50	30
1981	Playmates	10,000		17.50	35
1982	A Dream Come True	10,000		18.50	40

Disney Special Edition Plates - Disney Studios

YEAR ISSUE		EDITION LIMIT	YEAR RETD.	ISSUE PRICE	*QUOTE U.S.$
1978	Mickey Mouse At Fifty	15,000		25.00	65-100
1980	Happy Birthday Pinocchio	7,500		17.50	25-60
1981	Alice in Wonderland	7,500		17.50	18
1982	Happy Birthday Pluto	7,500		17.50	39
1982	Goofy's Golden Jubilee	7,500		18.50	29
1987	Snow White Golden Anniversary	5,000		47.50	90
1988	Mickey Mouse & Minnie Mouse 60th	10,000		50.00	95-125
1989	Sleeping Beauty 30th Anniversary	5,000		80.00	95
1990	Fantasia-Sorcerer's Apprentice	5,000		59.00	59-99
1990	Pinocchio's Friend	Annual		25.00	25
1990	Fantasia Relief Plate	20,000		25.00	39

Ferrandiz Beautiful Bounty Porcelain Plates - J. Ferrandiz

YEAR ISSUE		EDITION LIMIT	YEAR RETD.	ISSUE PRICE	*QUOTE U.S.$
1982	Summer's Golden Harvest	10,000		40.00	40
1982	Autumn's Blessing	10,000		40.00	40
1982	A Mid-Winter's Dream	10,000		40.00	43
1982	Spring Blossoms	10,000		40.00	40

Ferrandiz Music Makers Porcelain Plates - J. Ferrandiz

YEAR ISSUE		EDITION LIMIT	YEAR RETD.	ISSUE PRICE	*QUOTE U.S.$
1981	The Flutist	10,000		25.00	29
1981	The Entertainer	10,000		25.00	29
1982	Magical Medley	10,000		25.00	29
1982	Sweet Serenade	10,000		25.00	32

Ferrandiz Porcelain Christmas Plates - J. Ferrandiz

YEAR ISSUE		EDITION LIMIT	YEAR RETD.	ISSUE PRICE	*QUOTE U.S.$
1972	Christ in the Manger	Unkn.		30.00	179
1973	Christmas	Unkn.		30.00	229

The Littlest Night - B. Hummel

YEAR ISSUE		EDITION LIMIT	YEAR RETD.	ISSUE PRICE	*QUOTE U.S.$
1993	The Littlest Night	Annual		25.00	25

Mother's Day - B. Hummel

YEAR ISSUE		EDITION LIMIT	YEAR RETD.	ISSUE PRICE	*QUOTE U.S.$
1972	Playing Hooky	Annual		15.00	15
1973	Little Fisherman	Annual		15.00	33
1974	Bumblebee	Annual		18.50	20
1975	Message of Love	Annual		25.00	29
1976	Devotion For Mother	Annual		27.50	30
1977	Moonlight Return	Annual		27.50	29
1978	Afternoon Stroll	Annual		32.50	33
1979	Cherub's Gift	Annual		38.00	38
1980	Mother's Little Helpers	Annual		45.00	52
1981	Playtime	Annual		45.00	52
1982	The Flower Basket	Annual		45.00	48
1983	Spring Bouquet	Annual		45.00	54
1984	A Joy to Share	Annual		45.00	45
1985	A Mother's Journey	Annual		45.00	45
1986	Home From School	Annual		45.00	55
1988	Young Reader	Annual		52.50	81
1989	Pretty as a Picture	Annual		53.00	75
1990	Mother's Little Athlete	Annual		53.00	53
1991	Soft & Gentle	Annual		55.00	55

Peanuts Christmas - C. Schulz

YEAR ISSUE		EDITION LIMIT	YEAR RETD.	ISSUE PRICE	*QUOTE U.S.$
1972	Snoopy Guides the Sleigh	Annual		10.00	45
1973	Christmas Eve at Doghouse	Annual		10.00	85
1974	Christmas At Fireplace	Annual		10.00	45
1975	Woodstock and Santa Claus	Annual		12.50	19
1976	Woodstock's Christmas	Annual		13.00	20
1977	Deck The Doghouse	Annual		13.00	19
1978	Filling the Stocking	Annual		15.00	35
1979	Christmas at Hand	15,000		17.50	45
1980	Waiting for Santa	15,000		17.50	50
1981	A Christmas Wish	15,000		17.50	30
1982	Perfect Performance	15,000		18.50	40

Peanuts Special Edition Plate - C. Schulz

YEAR ISSUE		EDITION LIMIT	YEAR RETD.	ISSUE PRICE	*QUOTE U.S.$
1976	Bi-Centennial	Unkn.		13.00	30

Peanuts Valentine's Day Plates - C. Schulz

YEAR ISSUE		EDITION LIMIT	YEAR RETD.	ISSUE PRICE	*QUOTE U.S.$
1977	Home Is Where the Heart is	Unkn.		13.00	33
1978	Heavenly Bliss	Unkn.		13.00	30
1979	Love Match	Unkn.		17.50	28
1980	From Snoopy, With Love	Unkn.		17.50	25
1981	Hearts-A-Flutter	Unkn.		17.50	20
1982	Love Patch	Unkn.		17.50	18

Peanuts World's Greatest Athlete - C. Schulz

YEAR ISSUE		EDITION LIMIT	YEAR RETD.	ISSUE PRICE	*QUOTE U.S.$
1982	Go Deep	10,000		17.50	25
1982	The Puck Stops Here	10,000		17.50	23
1982	The Way You Play The Game	10,000		17.50	20
1982	The Crowd Went Wild	10,000		17.50	18

Raggedy Ann Annual Plates - Unknown

YEAR ISSUE		EDITION LIMIT	YEAR RETD.	ISSUE PRICE	*QUOTE U.S.$
1980	The Sunshine Wagon	10,000		17.50	80-100
1981	The Raggedy Shuffle	10,000		17.50	28-75
1982	Flying High	10,000		18.50	19
1983	Winning Streak	10,000		22.50	23
1984	Rocking Rodeo	10,000		22.50	23

Raggedy Ann Bicentennial Plate - Unknown

YEAR ISSUE		EDITION LIMIT	YEAR RETD.	ISSUE PRICE	*QUOTE U.S.$
1976	Bicentennial Plate	Unkn.		13.00	30-60

Raggedy Ann Christmas Plates - Unknown

YEAR ISSUE		EDITION LIMIT	YEAR RETD.	ISSUE PRICE	*QUOTE U.S.$
1975	Gifts of Love	Unkn.		12.50	45
1976	Merry Blades	Unkn.		13.00	38
1977	Christmas Morning	Unkn.		13.00	23
1978	Checking the List	Unkn.		15.00	20
1979	Little Helper	Unkn.		17.50	20

Raggedy Ann Valentine's Day Plates - Unknown

YEAR ISSUE		EDITION LIMIT	YEAR RETD.	ISSUE PRICE	*QUOTE U.S.$
1978	As Time Goes By	Unkn.		13.00	25
1979	Daisies Do Tell	Unkn.		17.50	20

Seymour Mann, Inc.

Connoisseur Collection - M. Bernini

YEAR ISSUE		EDITION LIMIT	YEAR RETD.	ISSUE PRICE	*QUOTE U.S.$
1995	Bluebird CLT-13	25,000		50.00	50
1995	Canary CLT-10	25,000		50.00	50
1995	Cardinal CLT-7	25,000		50.00	50
1995	Dove Duo CLT-1	25,000		50.00	50
1995	Hummingbird Duo CLT-4	25,000		50.00	50
1995	Pink Rose CLT-70	25,000		50.00	50
1995	Robin CLT-16	25,000		50.00	50
1995	Swan Duo CLT-50	25,000		50.00	50

Sports Impressions/Enesco

Gold Edition Plates - Various

YEAR ISSUE		EDITION LIMIT	YEAR RETD.	ISSUE PRICE	*QUOTE U.S.$
XX	A's Jose Canseco Gold (10 1/4") 1028-04 - J. Canseco	2,500	N/A	125.00	125
1990	Andre Dawson - R. Lewis	Closed		150.00	150
1988	Brooks Robinson - R. Simon	Closed		125.00	225
1987	Carl Yastrzemski - R. Simon	Closed		125.00	175
1992	Chicago Bulls '92 World Champions - C. Hayes	Closed		150.00	150
1993	Chicago Bulls 1993 World Championship Gold (10 1/4") 4062-04 - B. Vann	1,993	1994	150.00	150
1987	Darryl Strawberry #1 - R. Simon	Closed		125.00	125
1989	Darryl Strawberry #2 - T. Fogerty	Closed		125.00	125
1986	Don Mattingly - B. Johnson	Closed		125.00	125
1991	Dream Team (1st Ten Chosen) - L. Salk	Closed		150.00	300
1992	Dream Team - R.Tanenbaum	Closed		150.00	175
1992	Dream Team 1992 (8 1/2") 5507-03 - C. Hayes	7,500	1994	60.00	300-395
1992	Dream Team 1992 Gold (10 1/4") 5509-04 - R. Tanenbaum	1,992	1994	150.00	150
1991	Hawks Dominique Wilkins - J. Catalano	Closed		150.00	195
1990	Joe Montana 49ers - J. Catalano	Closed		150.00	195
1990	Joe Montana 49ers Gold (10 1/4") 3000-04 - J. Catalano	1,990	1991	150.00	150
1986	Keith Hernandez - R. Simon	Closed		125.00	175
1991	Lakers Magic Johnson - W.C. Mundy	Closed		150.00	225
1991	Larry Bird - J. Catalano	Closed		150.00	195
1986	Larry Bird - R. Simon	Closed		125.00	200
1988	Larry Bird - R. Simon	Closed		125.00	275
1990	Living Triple Crown - R. Lewis	Closed		150.00	150-225
1993	Magic Johnson (4042-04) - R.Tanenbaum	Closed		150.00	150
1988	Magic Johnson - R. Simon	Closed		125.00	225
1993	Magic Johnson - T. Fogerty	Closed		150.00	175
1991	Magic Johnson Lakers Gold (10 1/4") 4007-04 - C.W. Mundy	1,991	1991	150.00	175
1992	Magic Johnson Lakers Gold (10 1/4") 4042-04 - R. Tanenbaum	1,992	1994	150.00	150
1991	Magic Johnson Lakers Platinum (8 1/2") 4007-03 - M. Petronella	5,000	1992	60.00	60
1989	Mantle Switch Hitter - J. Catalano	Closed		150.00	295-325
1990	Michael Jordan - J. Catalano	Closed		150.00	275-325
1991	Michael Jordan - J. Catalano	Closed		150.00	195
1992	Michael Jordan - R.Tanenbaum	Closed		150.00	175
1993	Michael Jordan - T. Fogerty	Closed		150.00	200
1992	Michael Jordan Bulls (10 1/4") 4032-04 - R. Tanenbaum	1,991	1992	150.00	275-325
1993	Michael Jordan Bulls Gold (10 1/4") 4046-04 - T. Fogarty	2,500	1993	150.00	150
1991	Michael Jordan Gold (10 1/4") 4002-04 - J. Catalano	1,991	1992	150.00	150
1991	Michael Jordan Platinum (8 1/2") 4002-03 - M. Petronella	1,991	1993	60.00	95
1995	Mickey Mantle "My Greatest Year 1956" 1229-04 - B. Vann	1,956		100.00	100
1991	Mickey Mantle 7 - B. Simon	Closed		150.00	195
1986	Mickey Mantle At Night - R. Simon	Closed		125.00	250
1995	Mickey Mantle double plate set 176923 - T. Treadway	2,401		75.00	75
1987	Mickey, Willie, & Duke - R. Simon	Closed		150.00	800-1000
1992	NBA 1st Ten Chosen Gold (10 1/4") 5501-04 - L. Salk	1,992	1992	150.00	295-395
1992	NBA 1st Ten Chosen Platinum (8 1/2") (blue) 5502-03 - J. Catalano	7,500	1993	60.00	125
1992	NBA 1st Ten Chosen Platinum (8 1/2") (red) 5503-03 - C.W. Mundy	7,500	1993	60.00	95
1990	Nolan Ryan 300 - J. Catalano	Closed		150.00	175
1990	Nolan Ryan 300 Gold 1091-04 - T. Fogarty	1,990	1992	150.00	150
1995	Profiles in Courage Mickey Mantle 1231-03 - M. Petronella	Open		30.00	30
1990	Rickey Henderson - R. Lewis	Closed		150.00	150
XX	Roberto Clemente 1090-03 - R. Lewis	10,000	N/A	75.00	75
1993	Shaquille O'Neal Gold (10 1/4") 4047-04 - T. Fogarty	2,500	1994	150.00	150
1987	Ted Williams (signed) - R. Simon	Closed		125.00	450-550
1990	Tom Seaver - R. Lewis	Closed		150.00	150
1986	Wade Boggs - B. Johnson	Closed		125.00	150
1989	Will Clark - J. Catalano	Closed		125.00	150
1988	Yankee Tradition - J. Catalano	Closed		150.00	175-225

The Tudor Mint Inc.

Collector Plates - J. Mulholland

YEAR ISSUE		EDITION LIMIT	YEAR RETD.	ISSUE PRICE	*QUOTE U.S.$
1992	4401 Meeting of Unicorns	Closed	1993	27.10	79
1992	4402 Cauldron of Light	Closed	1993	27.10	79
1992	4403 The Guardian Dragon	Closed	1993	27.10	79
1992	4404 The Dragon's Nest	Closed	1993	27.10	79

V-Palekh Art Studios

Russian Legends - Various

YEAR ISSUE		EDITION LIMIT	YEAR RETD.	ISSUE PRICE	*QUOTE U.S.$
1988	Ruslan and Ludmilla - G. Lubimov	195-day		29.87	30-45
1988	The Princess/Seven Bogatyrs - A. Kovalev	195-day		29.87	35-45
1988	The Golden Cockerel - V. Vleshko	195-day		32.87	35
1988	Lukomorya - R. Belousov	195-day		32.87	35

*Quotes have been rounded up to nearest dollar

YEAR	ISSUE	EDITION LIMIT	YEAR RETD.	ISSUE PRICE	*QUOTE U.S.$
1989	Fisherman and the Magic Fish - N. Lopatin	195-day		32.87	35
1989	Tsar Saltan - G. Zhiryakova	195-day		32.87	35
1989	The Priest and His Servant - O. An	195-day		34.87	35
1990	Stone Flower - V. Bolshakova	195-day		34.87	40
1990	Sadko - E. Populor	195-day		34.87	45
1990	The Twelve Months - N. Lopatin	195-day		36.87	80
1990	Silver Hoof - S. Adeyanor	195-day		36.87	65
1990	Morozko - N. Lopatin	195-day		36.87	60

Villeroy & Boch

Flower Fairy - C. Barker

YEAR	ISSUE	EDITION LIMIT	YEAR RETD.	ISSUE PRICE	*QUOTE U.S.$
1979	Lavender	21-day		35.00	125
1980	Sweet Pea	21-day		35.00	125
1980	Candytuft	21-day		35.00	89
1981	Heliotrope	21-day		35.00	75
1981	Blackthorn	21-day		35.00	75
1981	Appleblossom	21-day		35.00	95

Russian Fairytales Maria Morevna - B. Zvorykin

YEAR	ISSUE	EDITION LIMIT	YEAR RETD.	ISSUE PRICE	*QUOTE U.S.$
1982	Maria Morevna and Tsarevich Ivan	27,500		70.00	85
1982	Koshchey Carries Off Maria Morevna	27,500		70.00	70
1982	Tsarevich Ivan and the Beautiful Castle	27,500		70.00	90

Russian Fairytales The Firebird - B. Zvorykin

YEAR	ISSUE	EDITION LIMIT	YEAR RETD.	ISSUE PRICE	*QUOTE U.S.$
1981	In Search of the Firebird	27,500		70.00	75
1981	Ivan and Tsarevna on the Grey Wolf	27,500		70.00	70
1981	The Wedding of Tsarevna Elena the Fair	27,500		70.00	100

Russian Fairytales The Red Knight - B. Zvorykin

YEAR	ISSUE	EDITION LIMIT	YEAR RETD.	ISSUE PRICE	*QUOTE U.S.$
1981	The Red Knight	27,500		70.00	40-70
1981	Vassilissa and Her Stepsisters	27,500		70.00	45-77
1981	Vassilissa is Presented to the Tsar	27,500		70.00	56-75

Villeroy & Boch - B. Zvorykin

YEAR	ISSUE	EDITION LIMIT	YEAR RETD.	ISSUE PRICE	*QUOTE U.S.$
1980	The Snow Maiden	27,500		70.00	100
1981	Snegurochka at the Court of Tsar Berendei	27,500		70.00	45-70
1981	Snegurochka and Lei, the Shepherd Boy	27,500		70.00	44-70

W.S. George

Alaska: The Last Frontier - H. Lambson

YEAR	ISSUE	EDITION LIMIT	YEAR RETD.	ISSUE PRICE	*QUOTE U.S.$
1991	Icy Majesty	150-day		34.50	34
1991	Autumn Grandeur	150-day		34.50	35
1992	Mountain Monarch	150-day		37.50	40
1992	Down the Trail	150-day		37.50	38
1992	Moonlight Lookout	150-day		37.50	60
1992	Graceful Passage	150-day		39.50	66
1992	Arctic Journey	150-day		39.50	70
1992	Summit Domain	150-day		39.50	60

Along an English Lane - M. Harvey

YEAR	ISSUE	EDITION LIMIT	YEAR RETD.	ISSUE PRICE	*QUOTE U.S.$
1993	Summer's Bright Welcome	95-day		29.50	52
1993	Greeting the Day	95-day		29.50	55
1993	Friends and Flowers	95-day		29.50	60
1993	Cottage Around the Bend	95-day		29.50	30

America the Beautiful - H. Johnson

YEAR	ISSUE	EDITION LIMIT	YEAR RETD.	ISSUE PRICE	*QUOTE U.S.$
1988	Yosemite Falls	150-day		34.50	35
1989	The Grand Canyon	150-day		34.50	30
1989	Yellowstone River	150-day		37.50	38
1989	The Great Smokey Mountains	150-day		37.50	38
1990	The Everglades	150-day		37.50	38
1990	Acadia	150-day		37.50	40
1990	The Grand Tetons	150-day		39.50	40
1990	Crater Lake	150-day		39.50	40

America's Pride - R. Richert

YEAR	ISSUE	EDITION LIMIT	YEAR RETD.	ISSUE PRICE	*QUOTE U.S.$
1992	Misty Fjords	150-day		29.50	50
1992	Rugged Shores	150-day		29.50	40
1992	Mighty Summit	150-day		32.50	45
1993	Lofty Reflections	150-day		32.50	60
1993	Tranquil Waters	150-day		32.50	55
1993	Mountain Majesty	150-day		34.50	40
1993	Canyon Climb	150-day		34.50	45
1993	Golden Vista	150-day		34.50	35

Art Deco - M. McDonald

YEAR	ISSUE	EDITION LIMIT	YEAR RETD.	ISSUE PRICE	*QUOTE U.S.$
1989	A Flapper With Greyhounds	150-day		39.50	45
1990	Tango Dancers	150-day		39.50	60
1990	Arriving in Style	150-day		39.50	60
1990	On the Town	150-day		39.50	70

Bear Tracks - J. Seerey-Lester

YEAR	ISSUE	EDITION LIMIT	YEAR RETD.	ISSUE PRICE	*QUOTE U.S.$
1992	Denali Family	150-day		29.50	40
1993	Their First Season	150-day		29.50	45
1993	High Country Champion	150-day		29.50	45
1993	Heavy Going	150-day		29.50	50
1993	Breaking Cover	150-day		29.50	50
1993	Along the Ice Flow	150-day		29.50	30

Beloved Hymns of Childhood - C. Barker

YEAR	ISSUE	EDITION LIMIT	YEAR RETD.	ISSUE PRICE	*QUOTE U.S.$
1988	The Lord's My Shepherd	150-day		29.50	40
1988	Away In a Manger	150-day		29.50	40
1989	Now Thank We All Our God	150-day		32.50	33
1989	Love Divine	150-day		32.50	33
1989	I Love to Hear the Story	150-day		32.50	35
1989	All Glory, Laud and Honour	150-day		32.50	35
1990	All People on Earth Do Dwell	150-day		34.50	35
1990	Loving Shepherd of Thy Sheep	150-day		34.50	35

A Black Tie Affair: The Penguin - C. Jagodits

YEAR	ISSUE	EDITION LIMIT	YEAR RETD.	ISSUE PRICE	*QUOTE U.S.$
1992	Little Explorer	150-day		29.50	50
1992	Penguln Parade	150-day		29.50	50
1992	Baby-Sitters	150-day		29.50	45
1993	Belly Flopping	150-day		29.50	55

Blessed Are The Children - W. Rane

YEAR	ISSUE	EDITION LIMIT	YEAR RETD.	ISSUE PRICE	*QUOTE U.S.$
1990	Let the/Children Come To Me	150-day		29.50	45
1990	I Am the Good Shepherd	150-day		29.50	45
1991	Whoever Welcomes/Child	150-day		32.50	45
1991	Hosanna in the Highest	150-day		32.50	35
1991	Jesus Had Compassion on Them	150-day		32.50	50
1991	Blessed are the Peacemakers	150-day		34.50	55
1991	I am the Vine, You are the Branches	150-day		34.50	50
1991	Seek and You Will Find	150-day		34.50	35

Bonds of Love - B. Burke

YEAR	ISSUE	EDITION LIMIT	YEAR RETD.	ISSUE PRICE	*QUOTE U.S.$
1989	Precious Embrace	150-day		29.50	30
1990	Cherished Moment	150-day		29.50	30
1991	Tender Caress	150-day		32.50	35
1992	Loving Touch	150-day		32.50	35
1992	Treasured Kisses	150-day		32.50	40
1994	Endearing Whispers	150-day		32.50	55

The Christmas Story - H. Garrido

YEAR	ISSUE	EDITION LIMIT	YEAR RETD.	ISSUE PRICE	*QUOTE U.S.$
1992	Gifts of the Magi	150-day		29.50	45
1993	Rest on the Flight into Egypt	150-day		29.50	30
1993	Journey of the Magi	150-day		29.50	30
1993	The Nativity	150-day		29.50	30
1993	The Annunciation	150-day		29.50	30
1993	Adoration of the Shepherds	150-day		29.50	30

Classic Waterfowl: The Ducks Unlimited - L. Kaatz

YEAR	ISSUE	EDITION LIMIT	YEAR RETD.	ISSUE PRICE	*QUOTE U.S.$
1988	Mallards at Sunrise	150-day		36.50	40
1988	Geese in the Autumn Fields	150-day		36.50	50
1989	Green Wings/Morning Marsh	150-day		39.50	40
1989	Canvasbacks, Breaking Away	150-day		39.50	40
1989	Pintails in Indian Summer	150-day		39.50	40
1990	Wood Ducks Taking Flight	150-day		39.50	40
1990	Snow Geese Against November Skies	150-day		41.50	42
1990	Bluebills Coming In	150-day		41.50	42

Columbus Discovers America: The 500th Anniversary - J. Penalva

YEAR	ISSUE	EDITION LIMIT	YEAR RETD.	ISSUE PRICE	*QUOTE U.S.$
1992	Under Full Sail	150-day		29.50	30
1992	Ashore at Dawn	150-day		29.50	35
1992	Columbus Raises the Flag	150-day		32.50	35
1992	Bringing Together Two Cultures	150-day		32.50	47
1992	The Queen's Approval	150-day		32.50	33
1992	Treasures From The New World	150-day		32.50	90

Country Bouquets - G. Kurz

YEAR	ISSUE	EDITION LIMIT	YEAR RETD.	ISSUE PRICE	*QUOTE U.S.$
1991	Morning Sunshine	150-day		29.50	45
1991	Summer Perfume	150-day		29.50	50
1991	Warm Welcome	150-day		32.50	50
1991	Garden's Bounty	150-day		32.50	65

Country Nostalgia - M. Harvey

YEAR	ISSUE	EDITION LIMIT	YEAR RETD.	ISSUE PRICE	*QUOTE U.S.$
1989	The Spring Buggy	150-day		29.50	30
1989	The Apple Cider Press	150-day		29.50	40
1989	The Vintage Seed Planter	150-day		29.50	35
1989	The Old Hand Pump	150-day		32.50	50
1990	The Wooden Butter Churn	150-day		32.50	45
1990	The Dairy Cans	150-day		32.50	33
1990	The Forgotten Plow	150-day		34.50	35
1990	The Antique Spinning Wheel	150-day		34.50	40

Critic's Choice: Gone With The Wind - P. Jennis

YEAR	ISSUE	EDITION LIMIT	YEAR RETD.	ISSUE PRICE	*QUOTE U.S.$
1991	Marry Me, Scarlett	150-day		27.50	50-75
1991	Waiting for Rhett	150-day		27.50	50-60
1991	A Declaration of Love	150-day		30.50	50
1991	The Paris Hat	150-day		30.50	50-60
1991	Scarlett Asks a Favor	150-day		30.50	55
1992	Scarlett Gets Her Way	150-day		32.50	45
1992	The Smitten Suitor	150-day		32.50	45
1992	Scarlett's Shopping Spree	150-day		32.50	40
1992	The Buggy Ride	150-day		32.50	50-75
1992	Scarlett Gets Down to Business	150-day		34.50	40
1993	Scarlett's Heart is with Tara	150-day		34.50	45
1993	At Cross Purposes	150-day		34.50	50

A Delicate Balance: Vanishing Wildlife - G. Beecham

YEAR	ISSUE	EDITION LIMIT	YEAR RETD.	ISSUE PRICE	*QUOTE U.S.$
1992	Tomorrow's Hope	95-day		29.50	45
1993	Today's Future	95-day		29.50	45
1993	Present Dreams	95-day		32.50	40
1993	Eyes on the New Day	95-day		32.50	33

Dr. Zhivago - G. Bush

YEAR	ISSUE	EDITION LIMIT	YEAR RETD.	ISSUE PRICE	*QUOTE U.S.$
1990	Zhivago and Lara	150-day		39.50	40
1991	Love Poems For Lara	150-day		39.50	40
1991	Zhivago Says Farewell	150-day		39.50	45
1991	Lara's Love	150-day		39.50	55

The Elegant Birds - J. Faulkner

YEAR	ISSUE	EDITION LIMIT	YEAR RETD.	ISSUE PRICE	*QUOTE U.S.$
1988	The Swan	150-day		32.50	33
1988	Great Blue Heron	150-day		32.50	33
1989	Snowy Egret	150-day		32.50	36
1989	The Anhinga	150-day		35.50	36
1989	The Flamingo	150-day		35.50	36
1990	Sandhill and Whooping Crane	150-day		35.50	36

Enchanted Garden - E. Antonaccio

YEAR	ISSUE	EDITION LIMIT	YEAR RETD.	ISSUE PRICE	*QUOTE U.S.$
1993	A Peaceful Retreat	95-day		24.50	25
1993	Pleasant Pathways	95-day		24.50	25
1993	A Place to Dream	95-day		24.50	25
1993	Tranquil Hideaway	95-day		24.50	25

Eyes of the Wild - D. Pierce

YEAR	ISSUE	EDITION LIMIT	YEAR RETD.	ISSUE PRICE	*QUOTE U.S.$
1993	Eyes in the Mist	95-day		29.50	60
1993	Eyes in the Pines	95-day		29.50	40
1993	Eyes on the Sly	95-day		29.50	55
1993	Eyes of Gold	95-day		29.50	30
1993	Eyes of Silence	95-day		29.50	30
1993	Eyes in the Snow	95-day		29.50	30
1993	Eyes of Wonder	95-day		29.50	30
1994	Eyes of Strength	95-day		29.50	30

The Faces of Nature - J. Kramer Cole

YEAR	ISSUE	EDITION LIMIT	YEAR RETD.	ISSUE PRICE	*QUOTE U.S.$
1992	Canyon of the Cat	150-day		29.50	55
1992	Wolf Ridge	150-day		29.50	60
1993	Trail of the Talisman	150-day		29.50	60
1993	Wolfpack of the Ancients	150-day		29.50	30
1993	Two Bears Camp	150-day		29.50	30
1993	Wintering With the Wapiti	150-day		29.50	30
1993	Within Sunrise	150-day		29.50	30
1993	Wambli Okiye	150-day		29.50	30

The Federal Duck Stamp Plate Collection - N. Anderson

YEAR	ISSUE	EDITION LIMIT	YEAR RETD.	ISSUE PRICE	*QUOTE U.S.$
1990	The Lesser Scaup	150-day		27.50	35
1990	Mallard	150-day		27.50	45
1990	Canvasbacks	150-day		30.50	42
1991	Pintails	150-day		30.50	35
1991	Wigeons	150-day		30.50	35
1991	Cinnamon Teal	150-day		32.50	33
1991	Fulvous Wistling Duck	150-day		32.50	50
1991	The Redheads	150-day		32.50	45
1991	Snow Goose	150-day		32.50	35

Feline Fancy - H. Ronner

YEAR	ISSUE	EDITION LIMIT	YEAR RETD.	ISSUE PRICE	*QUOTE U.S.$
1993	Globetrotters	95-day		34.50	40
1993	Little Athletes	95-day		34.50	50
1993	Young Adventurers	95-day		34.50	50
1993	The Geographers	95-day		34.50	50

Field Birds of North America - D. Bush

YEAR	ISSUE	EDITION LIMIT	YEAR RETD.	ISSUE PRICE	*QUOTE U.S.$
1991	Winter Colors: Ring-Necked Pheasant	150-day		39.50	45
1991	In Display: Ruffed Goose	150-day		39.50	45
1991	Morning Light: Bobwhite Quail	150-day		42.50	60
1991	Misty Clearing: Wild Turkey	150-day		42.50	80
1992	Autumn Moment: American Woodcock	150-day		42.50	45
1992	Season's End: Willow Ptarmigan	150-day		42.50	55

Floral Fancies - C. Callog

YEAR	ISSUE	EDITION LIMIT	YEAR RETD.	ISSUE PRICE	*QUOTE U.S.$
1993	Sitting Softly	95-day		34.50	45
1993	Sitting Pretty	95-day		34.50	35
1993	Sitting Sunny	95-day		34.50	35
1993	Sitting Pink	95-day		34.50	35

Flowers From Grandma's Garden - G. Kurz

YEAR	ISSUE	EDITION LIMIT	YEAR RETD.	ISSUE PRICE	*QUOTE U.S.$
1990	Country Cuttings	150-day		24.50	45
1990	The Morning Bouquet	150-day		24.50	40
1991	Homespun Beauty	150-day		27.50	40
1991	Harvest in the Meadow	150-day		27.50	40
1991	Gardener's Delight	150-day		27.50	50
1991	Nature's Bounty	150-day		27.50	60
1991	A Country Welcome	150-day		29.50	55
1991	The Springtime Arrangement	150-day		29.50	50

Flowers of Your Garden - V. Morley

YEAR	ISSUE	EDITION LIMIT	YEAR RETD.	ISSUE PRICE	*QUOTE U.S.$
1988	Roses	150-day		24.50	30
1988	Lilacs	150-day		24.50	70
1988	Daisies	150-day		27.50	35
1988	Peonies	150-day		27.50	28
1988	Chrysanthemums	150-day		27.50	28
1989	Daffodils	150-day		27.50	28
1989	Tulips	150-day		29.50	30
1989	Irises	150-day		29.50	30

Garden of the Lord - C. Gillies

YEAR	ISSUE	EDITION LIMIT	YEAR RETD.	ISSUE PRICE	*QUOTE U.S.$
1992	Love One Another	150-day		29.50	30
1992	Perfect Peace	150-day		29.50	30
1992	Trust In the Lord	150-day		32.50	33
1992	The Lord's Love	150-day		32.50	33
1992	The Lord Bless You	150-day		32.50	33
1992	Ask In Prayer	150-day		34.50	35
1993	Peace Be With You	150-day		34.50	35
1993	Give Thanks To The Lord	150-day		34.50	35

*Quotes have been rounded up to nearest dollar

Gardens of Paradise - L. Chang

YEAR ISSUE		EDITION LIMIT	YEAR RETD.	ISSUE PRICE	*QUOTE U.S.$
1992	Tranquility	150-day		29.50	50
1992	Serenity	150-day		29.50	55
1993	Splendor	150-day		32.50	53
1993	Harmony	150-day		32.50	33
1993	Beauty	150-day		32.50	33
1993	Elegance	150-day		32.50	33
1993	Grandeur	150-day		32.50	33
1993	Majesty	150-day		32.50	33

Gentle Beginnings - W. Nelson

1991	Tender Loving Care	150-day		34.50	45
1991	A Touch of Love	150-day		34.50	50
1991	Under Watchful Eyes	150-day		37.50	50
1991	Lap of Love	150-day		37.50	85
1002	Happy Together	150-day		37.50	60
1992	First Steps	150-day		37.50	75

Glorious Songbirds - R. Cobane

1991	Cardinals on a Snowy Branch	150-day		29.50	35
1991	Indigo Buntings and/Blossoms	150-day		29.50	30
1991	Chickadees Among The Lilacs	150-day		32.50	33
1991	Goldfinches in/Thistle	150-day		32.50	33
1991	Cedar Waxwing/Winter Berries	150-day		32.50	34
1991	Bluebirds in a Blueberry Bush	150-day		34.50	35
1991	Baltimore Orioles/Autumn Leaves	150-day		34.50	50
1991	Robins with Dogwood in Bloom	150-day		34.50	50

The Golden Age of the Clipper Ships - C. Vickery

1989	The Twilight Under Full Sail	150-day		29.50	30
1989	The Blue Jacket at Sunset	150-day		29.50	30
1989	Young America, Homeward	150-day		32.50	33
1990	Flying Cloud	150-day		32.50	33
1990	Davy Crocket at Daybreak	150-day		32.50	35
1990	Golden Eagle Conquers Wind	150-day		32.50	35
1990	The Lightning in Lifting Fog	150-day		34.50	35
1990	Sea Witch, Mistress/Oceans	150-day		34.50	35

Gone With the Wind: Golden Anniversary - H. Rogers

1988	Scarlett and Her Suitors	150-day		24.50	55-90
1988	The Burning of Atlanta	150-day		24.50	50-90
1988	Scarlett and Ashley After the War	150-day		27.50	65
1988	The Proposal	150-day		27.50	70-90
1989	Home to Tara	150-day		27.50	45
1989	Strolling in Atlanta	150-day		27.50	40-55
1989	A Question of Honor	150-day		29.50	40-65
1989	Scarlett's Resolve	150-day		29.50	45-65
1989	Frankly My Dear	150-day		29.50	50-70
1989	Melane and Ashley	150-day		32.50	35-45
1990	A Toast to Bonnie Blue	150-day		32.50	50-58
1990	Scarlett and Rhett's Honeymoon	150-day		32.50	45-70

Gone With the Wind: The Passions of Scarlett O'Hara - P. Jennis

1992	Fiery Embrace	150-day		29.50	65
1992	Pride and Passion	150-day		29.50	75
1992	Dreams of Ashley	150-day		32.50	75
1992	The Fond Farewell	150-day		32.50	60
1992	The Waltz	150-day		32.50	75
1992	As God Is My Witness	150-day		34.50	60
1993	Brave Scarlett	150-day		34.50	55
1993	Nightmare	150-day		34.50	35
1993	Evening Prayers	150-day		34.50	35
1993	Naptime	150-day		36.50	37
1993	Dangerous Attraction	150-day		36.50	37
1994	The End of An Era	150-day		36.50	37

Grand Safari: Images of Africa - C. Fracé

1992	A Moment's Rest	150-day		34.50	35
1992	Elephant's of Kilimanjaro	150-day		34.50	50
1992	Undivided Attention	150-day		37.50	45
1993	Quiet Time in Samburu	150-day		37.50	50
1993	Lone Hunter	150-day		37.50	38
1993	The Greater Kudo	150-day		37.50	38

Heart of the Wild - G. Beecham

1991	A Gentle Touch	150-day		29.50	35
1992	Mother's Pride	150-day		29.50	50
1992	An Afternoon Together	150-day		32.50	55
1992	Quiet Time?	150-day		32.50	50

Hollywood's Glamour Girls - E. Dzenis

1989	Jean Harlow-Dinner at Eight	150-day		24.50	35
1990	Lana Turner-Postman Ring Twice	150-day		29.50	30
1990	Carol Lombard-The Gay Bride	150-day		29.50	30
1990	Greta Garbo-In Grand Hotel	150-day		29.50	30

Hometown Memories - H.T. Becker

1993	Moonlight Skaters	150-day		29.50	30
1993	Mountain Sleigh Ride	150-day		29.50	60
1993	Heading Home	150-day		29.50	30
1993	A Winter Ride	150-day		29.50	30

Last of Their Kind: The Endangered Species - W. Nelson

1988	The Panda	150-day		27.50	53
1989	The Snow Leopard	150-day		27.50	50
1989	The Red Wolf	150-day		30.50	50
1989	The Asian Elephant	150-day		30.50	31
1990	The Slender-Horned Gazelle	150-day		30.50	31
1990	The Bridled Wallaby	150-day		30.50	31
1990	The Black-Footed Ferret	150-day		33.50	34
1990	The Siberian Tiger	150-day		33.50	45
1991	The Vicuna	150-day		33.50	34
1991	Przewalski's Horse	150-day		33.50	34

Lena Liu's Basket Bouquets - L. Liu

1992	Roses	150-day		29.50	45
1992	Pansies	150-day		29.50	40
1992	Tulips and Lilacs	150-day		32.50	60
1992	Irises	150-day		32.50	50
1992	Lilies	150-day		32.50	60
1992	Parrot Tulips	150-day		32.50	45
1992	Peonies	150-day		32.50	45
1993	Begonias	150-day		32.50	33
1993	Magnolias	150-day		32.50	33
1993	Calla Lilies	150-day		32.50	33
1993	Orchids	150-day		32.50	33
1993	Hydrangeas	150-day		32.50	33

Lena Liu's Flower Fairies - L. Liu

1993	Magic Makers	95-day		29.50	30
1993	Petal Playmates	95-day		29.50	30
1993	Delicate Dancers	95-day		32.50	33
1993	Mischief Masters	95-day		32.50	33
1993	Amorous Angels	95-day		32.50	33
1993	Winged Wonders	95-day		34.50	35
1993	Miniature Mermaids	95-day		34.50	35
1993	Fanciful Fairies	95-day		34.50	35

Lena Liu's Hummingbird Treasury - L. Liu

1992	The Ruby-Throated Hummingbird	150-day		29.50	60
1992	Anna's Hummingbird	150-day		29.50	30
1992	Violet-Crowned Hummingbird	150-day		32.50	33
1992	The Rufous Hummingbird	150-day		32.50	33
1993	White-Eared Hummingbird	150-day		32.50	33
1993	Broad-Billed Hummingbird	150-day		34.50	35
1993	Calliope Hummingbird	150-day		34.50	35
1993	The Allen's Hummingbird	150-day		34.50	35

Little Angels - B. Burke

1992	Angels We Have Heard on High	150-day		29.50	45
1992	O Tannenbaum	150-day		29.50	50
1993	Joy to the World	150-day		32.50	100
1993	Hark the Herald Angels Sing	150-day		32.50	50
1993	It Came Upon a Midnight Clear	150-day		32.50	55
1993	The First Noel	150-day		32.50	33

A Loving Look: Duck Families - B. Langton

1990	Family Outing	150-day		34.50	35
1991	Sleepy Start	150-day		34.50	35
1991	Quiet Moment	150-day		37.50	40
1991	Safe and Sound	150-day		37.50	40
1991	Spring Arrivals	150-day		37.50	40
1991	The Family Tree	150-day		37.50	50

The Majestic Horse - P. Wildermuth

1992	Classic Beauty: Thoroughbred	150-day		34.50	45
1992	American Gold: The Quarterhorse	150-day		34.50	50
1992	Regal Spirit: The Arabian	150-day		34.50	60
1992	Western Favorite: American Paint Horse	150-day		34.50	70

Melodies in the Mist - A. Sakhavarz

1993	Early Morning Rain	95-day		34.50	35
1993	Among the Dewdrops	95-day		34.50	35
1993	Feeding Time	95-day		37.50	38
1993	The Garden Party	95-day		37.50	38
1993	Unpleasant Surprise	95-day		37.50	38
1993	Spring Rain	95-day		37.50	38

Memories of a Victorian Childhood - Unknown

1992	You'd Better Not Pout	150-day		29.50	30
1992	Sweet Slumber	150-day		29.50	55
1992	Through Thick and Thin	150-day		32.50	45
1992	An Armful of Treasures	150-day		32.50	65
1993	A Trio of Bookworms	150-day		32.50	55
1993	Pugnacious Playmate	150-day		32.50	65

Nature's Legacy - J. Sias

1990	Blue Snow at Half Dome	150-day		24.50	30
1991	Misty Morning/Mt. McKinley	150-day		24.50	25
1991	Mount Ranier	150-day		27.50	30
1991	Havasu Canyon	150-day		27.50	28
1991	Autumn Splendor in the Smoky Mts.	150-day		27.50	35
1991	Winter Peace in Yellowstone Park	150-day		29.50	30
1991	Golden Majesty/Rocky Mountains	150-day		29.50	35
1991	Radiant Sunset Over the Everglades	150-day		29.50	30

Nature's Lovables - C. Fracé

1990	The Koala	150-day		27.50	35
1991	New Arrival	150-day		27.50	40
1991	Chinese Treasure	150-day		27.50	28
1991	Baby Harp Seal	150-day		30.50	40
1991	Bobcat: Nature's Dawn	150-day		30.50	35
1991	Clouded Leopard	150-day		32.50	35
1991	Zebra Foal	150-day		32.50	45
1991	Bandit	150-day		32.50	45

Nature's Playmates - C. Fracé

1991	Partners	150-day		29.50	40
1991	Secret Heights	150-day		29.50	45
1991	Recess	150-day		32.50	45
1991	Double Trouble	150-day		32.50	40
1991	Pals	150-day		32.50	40
1992	Curious Trio	150-day		34.50	50
1992	Playmates	150-day		34.50	50
1992	Surprise	150-day		34.50	50-70
1992	Peace On Ice	150-day		36.50	75
1992	Ambassadors	150-day		36.50	70

Nature's Poetry - L. Liu

1989	Morning Serenade	150-day		24.50	40
1989	Song of Promise	150-day		24.50	40
1990	Tender Lullaby	150-day		27.50	35
1990	Nature's Harmony	150-day		27.50	35
1990	Gentle Refrain	150-day		27.50	30
1990	Morning Chorus	150-day		27.50	35
1990	Melody at Daybreak	150-day		29.50	30
1991	Delicate Accord	150-day		29.50	30
1991	Lyrical Beginnings	150-day		29.50	30
1991	Song of Spring	150-day		32.50	40
1991	Mother's Melody	150-day		32.50	40
1991	Cherub Chorale	150-day		32.50	50

On Golden Wings - W. Goebel

1993	Morning Light	95-day		29.50	50
1993	Early Risers	95-day		29.50	30
1993	As Day Breaks	95-day		32.50	33
1993	Daylight Flight	95-day		32.50	33
1993	Winter Dawn	95-day		32.50	33
1994	First Light	95-day		34.50	35

On Gossamer Wings - L. Liu

1988	Monarch Butterflies	150-day		24.50	35
1988	Western Tiger Swallowtails	150-day		24.50	40
1988	Red-Spotted Purple	150-day		27.50	50
1988	White Peacocks	150-day		27.50	50
1989	Eastern Tailed Blues	150-day		27.50	35
1989	Zebra Swallowtails	150-day		29.50	30
1989	Red Admirals	150-day		29.50	30

On the Wing - T. Humphrey

1992	Winged Splendor	150-day		29.50	30
1992	Rising Mallard	150-day		29.50	40
1992	Glorious Ascent	150-day		32.50	50
1992	Taking Wing	150-day		32.50	45
1992	Upward Bound	150-day		32.50	40
1993	Wondrous Motion	150-day		34.50	50
1993	Springing Forth	150-day		34.50	50
1993	Graceful Climb	150-day		34.50	50

On Wings of Snow - L. Liu

1991	The Swans	150-day		34.50	40
1991	The Doves	150-day		34.50	50
1991	The Peacocks	150-day		37.50	50
1991	The Egrets	150-day		37.50	55
1991	The Cockatoos	150-day		37.50	65
1992	The Herons	150-day		37.50	40

Our Woodland Friends - C. Brenders

1989	Fascination	150-day		29.00	29
1990	Beneath the Pines	150-day		29.50	32
1990	High Adventure	150-day		32.50	33
1990	Shy Explorers	150-day		32.50	40
1991	Golden Season:Gray Squirrel	150-day		32.50	35
1991	Full House Fox Family	150-day		32.50	45
1991	A Jump Into Life: Spring Fawn	150-day		34.50	35
1991	Forest Sentinel:Bobcat	150-day		34.50	40

Paw Prints: Baby Cats of the Wild - C. Fracé

1992	Morning Mischief	95-day		29.50	45
1993	Togetherness	95-day		29.50	50
1993	The Buddy System	95-day		32.50	3
1993	Nap Time	95-day		32.50	3

Petal Pals - L. Chang

1992	Garden Discovery	150-day		24.50	2
1992	Flowering Fascination	150-day		24.50	2
1993	Alluring Lilies	150-day		24.50	2
1993	Springtime Oasis	150-day		24.50	2
1993	Blossoming Adventure	150-day		24.50	2
1993	Dancing Daffodils	150-day		24.50	2
1993	Summer Surprise	150-day		24.50	2
1993	Morning Melody	150-day		24.50	2

Poetic Cottages - C. Valente

1992	Garden Paths of Oxfordshire	150-day		29.50	5
1992	Twilight at Woodgreen Pond	150-day		29.50	5
1992	Stonewall Brook Blossoms	150-day		32.50	4
1992	Bedfordshire Evening Sky	150-day		32.50	5
1993	Wisteria Summer	150-day		32.50	3
1993	Wiltshire Rose Arbor	150-day		32.50	3
1993	Alderbury Gardens	150-day		32.50	3
1993	Hampshire Spring Splendor	150-day		32.50	3

Portraits of Christ - J. Salamanca

1991	Father, Forgive Them	150-day		29.50	7

Collectors' Information Bureau

*Quotes have been rounded up to nearest dollar

YEAR ISSUE		EDITION LIMIT	YEAR RETD.	ISSUE PRICE	*QUOTE U.S.$
1991	Thy Will Be Done	150-day		29.50	50
1991	This is My Beloved Son	150-day		32.50	45
1991	Lo, I Am With You	150-day		32.50	55
1991	Become as Little Children	150-day		32.50	60
1991	Peace I Leave With You	150-day		34.50	50
1992	For God So Loved the World	150-day		34.50	55
1992	I Am the Way, the Truth and the Life	150-day		34.50	50
1992	Weep Not For Me	150-day		34.50	50
1992	Follow Me	150-day		34.50	60

Portraits of Exquisite Birds - C. Brenders

1990	Backyard Treasure/Chickadee	150-day		29.50	30
1990	The Beautiful Bluebird	150-day		29.50	30
1991	Summer Gold: The Robin	150-day		32.50	33
1991	The Meadowlark's Song	150-day		32.50	33
1991	Ivory-Billed Woodpecker	150-day		32.50	33
1991	Red-Winged Blackbird	150-day		32.50	33

Purebred Horses of the Americas - D. Schwartz

1989	The Appalosa	150-day		34.50	35
1989	The Tenessee Walker	150-day		34.50	35
1990	The Quarterhorse	150-day		37.50	38
1990	The Saddlebred	150-day		37.50	45
1990	The Mustang	150-day		37.50	39
1990	The Morgan	150-day		37.50	65

Rare Encounters - J. Seerey-Lester

1993	Softly, Softly	95-day		29.50	55
1993	Black Magic	95-day		29.50	40
1993	Future Song	95-day		32.50	65
1993	High and Mighty	95-day		32.50	60
1993	Last Sanctuary	95-day		32.50	33
1993	Something Stirred	95-day		34.50	35

Romantic Gardens - C. Smith

1989	The Woodland Garden	150-day		29.50	30
1989	The Plantation Garden	150-day		29.50	30
1990	The Cottage Garden	150-day		32.50	33
1990	The Colonial Garden	150-day		32.50	33

Romantic Harbors - C. Vickery

1993	Advent of the Golden Bough	95-day		34.50	40
1993	Christmas Tree Schooner	95-day		34.50	60
1993	Prelude to the Journey	95-day		37.50	50
1993	Shimmering Light of Dusk	95-day		37.50	40

Romantic Roses - V. Morley

1993	Victorian Beauty	95-day		29.50	30
1993	Old-Fashioned Grace	95-day		29.50	30
1993	Country Charm	95-day		32.50	33
1993	Summer Romance	95-day		32.50	33
1993	Pastoral Delight	95-day		32.50	33
1993	Springtime Elegance	95-day		34.50	35
1993	Vintage Splendor	95-day		34.50	35
1994	Heavenly Perfection	95-day		34.50	35

Scenes of Christmas Past - L. Garrison

1987	Holiday Skaters	150-day		27.50	40
1988	Christmas Eve	150-day		27.50	35
1989	The Homecoming	150-day		30.50	31
1990	The Toy Store	150-day		30.50	31
1991	The Carollers	150-day		30.50	31
1992	Family Traditions	150-day		32.50	45
1993	Holiday Past	150-day		32.50	70
1994	A Gathering of Faith	150-day		32.50	85

The Secret World Of The Panda - J. Bridgett

1990	A Mother's Care	150-day		27.50	30
1991	A Frolic in the Snow	150-day		27.50	28
1991	Lazy Afternoon	150-day		30.50	31
1991	A Day of Exploring	150-day		30.50	31
1991	A Gentle Hug	150-day		32.50	35
1991	A Bamboo Feast	150-day		32.50	70

Soaring Majesty - C. Fracé

1991	Freedom	150-day		29.50	35
1991	The Northern Goshhawk	150-day		29.50	40
1991	Peregrine Falcon	150-day		32.50	33
991	Red-Tailed Hawk	150-day		32.50	33
1991	The Ospray	150-day		32.50	35
1991	The Gyrfalcon	150-day		34.50	40
1991	The Golden Eagle	150-day		34.50	40
1992	Red-Shouldered Hawk	150-day		34.50	35

Sonnets in Flowers - G. Kurz

992	Sonnet of Beauty	150-day		29.50	40
992	Sonnet of Happiness	150-day		34.50	45
1992	Sonnet of Love	150-day		34.50	35
992	Sonnet of Peace	150-day		34.50	55

The Sound of Music: Silver Anniversary - V. Gadino

991	The Hills are Alive	150-day		29.50	35
992	Let's Start at the Very Beginning	150-day		29.50	35
992	Something Good	150-day		32.50	50
992	Maria's Wedding Day	150-day		32.50	50

Spirit of Christmas - J. Sias

990	Silent Night	150-day		29.50	37
991	Jingle Bells	150-day		29.50	30

YEAR ISSUE		EDITION LIMIT	YEAR RETD.	ISSUE PRICE	*QUOTE U.S.$
1991	Deck The Halls	150-day		32.50	40
1991	I'll Be Home For Christmas	150-day		32.50	45
1991	Winter Wonderland	150-day		32.50	35
1991	O Christmas Tree	150-day		32.50	35

Spirits of the Sky - C. Fisher

1992	Twilight Glow	150-day		29.50	40
1992	First Light	150-day		29.50	40
1992	Evening Glimmer	150-day		32.50	75
1992	Golden Dusk	150-day		32.50	40
1993	Sunset Splendor	150-day		32.50	33
1993	Amber Flight	150-day		34.50	35
1993	Winged Radiance	150-day		34.50	35
1993	Day's End	150-day		34.50	35

Symphony of Shimmering Beauties - L. Liu

1991	Iris Quartet	150-day		29.50	50
1991	Tulip Ensemble	150-day		29.50	35
1991	Poppy Pastorale	150-day		32.50	43
1991	Lily Concerto	150-day		32.50	55
1991	Peony Prelude	150-day		32.50	45
1991	Rose Fantasy	150-day		34.50	50
1991	Hibiscus Medley	150-day		34.50	40
1992	Dahlia Melody	150-day		34.50	50
1992	Hollyhock March	150-day		34.50	40
1992	Carnation Serenade	150-day		36.50	45
1992	Gladiolus Romance	150-day		36.50	55
1992	Zinnia Finale	150-day		36.50	37

Tis the Season - J. Sias

1993	A World Dressed in Snow	95-day		29.50	40
1993	A Time for Tradition	95-day		29.50	45
1993	We Shall Come Rejoining	95-day		29.50	45
1993	Our Family Tree	95-day		29.50	30

Tomorrow's Promise - W. Nelson

1992	Curiosity: Asian Elephants	150-day		29.50	45
1992	Playtime Pandas	150-day		29.50	40
1992	Innocence: Rhinos	150-day		32.50	65
1992	Friskiness: Kit Foxes	150-day		32.50	45

Touching the Spirit - J. Kramer Cole

1993	Running With the Wind	95-day		29.50	60
1993	Kindred Spirits	95-day		29.50	50
1993	The Marking Tree	95-day		29.50	50
1993	Wakan Tanka	95-day		29.50	65
1993	He Who Watches	95-day		29.50	30
1993	Twice Traveled Trail	95-day		29.50	30
1993	Keeper of the Secret	95-day		29.50	30
1993	Camp of the Sacred Dogs	95-day		29.50	30

A Treasury of Songbirds - R. Stine

1995	Alluring Daylight	150-day		34.50	35
1995	Sapphire Dawn	150-day		34.50	35
1992	Springtime Splendor	150-day		29.50	48
1992	Morning's Glory	150-day		29.50	50
1992	Golden Daybreak	150-day		32.50	45
1992	Afternoon Calm	150-day		32.50	50
1992	Dawn's Radiance	150-day		32.50	50
1993	Scarlet Sunrise	150-day		34.50	35
1993	Sapphire Dawn	150-day		34.50	35
1993	Alluring Daylight	150-day		34.50	35

The Vanishing Gentle Giants - A. Casay

1991	Jumping For Joy	150-day		32.50	35
1991	Song of the Humpback	150-day		32.50	35
1991	Monarch of the Deep	150-day		35.50	40
1991	Travelers of the Sea	150-day		35.50	65
1991	White Whale of the North	150-day		35.50	65
1991	Unicorn of the Sea	150-day		35.50	40

Victorian Cat - H. Bonner

1990	Mischief With The Hatbox	150-day		24.50	42
1991	String Quartet	150-day		24.50	50
1991	Daydreams	150-day		27.50	35
1991	Frisky Felines	150-day		27.50	40
1991	Kittens at Play	150-day		27.50	45
1991	Playing in the Parlor	150-day		29.50	50
1991	Perfectly Poised	150-day		29.50	50
1992	Midday Repose	150-day		29.50	60

Victorian Cat Capers - Various

1992	Who's the Fairest of Them All? - F. Paton	150-day		24.50	65
1992	Puss in Boots - Unknown	150-day		24.50	60
1992	My Bowl is Empty - W. Hepple	150-day		27.50	35
1992	A Curious Kitty - W. Hepple	150-day		27.50	35
1992	Vanity Fair - W. Hepple	150-day		27.50	30
1992	Forbidden Fruit - W. Hepple	150-day		29.50	50
1993	The Purr-fect Pen Pal - W. Hepple	150-day		29.50	35
1993	The Kitten Express - W. Hepple	150-day		29.50	40

Wild Innocents - C. Fracé

1993	Reflections	95-day		29.50	45
1993	Spiritual Heir	95-day		29.50	45
1993	Lion Cub	95-day		29.50	50
1993	Sunny Spot	95-day		29.50	30

Wild Spirits - T. Hirata

1992	Solitary Watch	150-day		29.50	40

YEAR ISSUE		EDITION LIMIT	YEAR RETD.	ISSUE PRICE	*QUOTE U.S.$
1992	Timber Ghost	150-day		29.50	50
1992	Mountain Magic	150-day		32.50	33
1993	Silent Guard	150-day		32.50	33
1993	Sly Eyes	150-day		32.50	33
1993	Mighty Presence	150-day		34.50	35
1993	Quiet Vigil	150-day		34.50	35
1993	Lone Vanguard	150-day		34.50	35

Wings of Winter - D. Rust

1992	Moonlight Retreat	150-day		29.50	30
1993	Twilight Serenade	150-day		29.50	30
1993	Silent Sunset	150-day		29.50	30
1993	Night Lights	150-day		29.50	30
1993	Winter Haven	150-day		29.50	30
1993	Full Moon Companions	150-day		29.50	30
1993	White Night	150-day		29.50	30
1993	Winter Reflections	150-day		29.50	30

Winter's Majesty - C. Fracé

1992	The Quest	150-day		34.50	40
1992	The Chase	150-day		34.50	40
1993	Alaskan Friend	150-day		34.50	55
1993	American Cougar	150-day		34.50	35
1993	On Watch	150-day		34.50	35
1993	Solitude	150-day		34.50	35

Wonders Of The Sea - R. Harm

1991	Stand By Me	150-day		34.50	35
1991	Heart to Heart	150-day		34.50	35
1991	Warm Embrace	150-day		34.50	45
1991	A Family Affair	150-day		34.50	35

The World's Most Magnificent Cats - C. Fracé

1991	Fleeting Encounter	150-day		24.50	40
1991	Cougar	150-day		24.50	55
1991	Royal Bengal	150-day		27.50	30
1991	Powerful Presence	150-day		27.50	45
1991	Jaguar	150-day		27.50	40
1991	The Clouded Leopard	150-day		29.50	45
1991	The African Leopard	150-day		29.50	40
1991	Mighty Warrior	150-day		29.50	50
1992	The Cheetah	150-day		31.50	45
1992	Siberian Tiger	150-day		31.50	55

Waterford Wedgwood USA

Bicentennial - Unknown

1972	Boston Tea Party	Annual		40.00	40
1973	Paul Revere's Ride	Annual		40.00	115
1974	Battle of Concord	Annual		40.00	55
1975	Across the Delaware	Annual		40.00	105
1975	Victory at Yorktown	Annual		45.00	53
1976	Declaration Signed	Annual		45.00	45

Wedgwood Christmas - Various

1969	Windsor Castle - T. Harper	Annual		25.00	200
1970	Trafalgar Square - T. Harper	Annual		30.00	50
1971	Picadilly Circus - T. Harper	Annual		30.00	50
1972	St. Paul's Cathedral - T. Harper	Annual		35.00	45
1973	Tower of London - T. Harper	Annual		40.00	90
1974	Houses of Parliament - T. Harper	Annual		40.00	40
1975	Tower Bridge - T. Harper	Annual		45.00	45
1976	Hampton Court - T. Harper	Annual		50.00	50
1977	Westminister Abbey - T. Harper	Annual		55.00	60
1978	Horse Guards - T. Harper	Annual		60.00	60
1979	Buckingham Palace - Unknown	Annual		65.00	65
1980	St. James Palace - Unknown	Annual		70.00	70
1981	Marble Arch - Unknown	Annual		75.00	75
1982	Lambeth Palace - Unknown	Annual		80.00	90
1983	All Souls, Langham Palace - Unknown	Annual		80.00	80
1984	Constitution Hill - Unknown	Annual		80.00	80
1985	The Tate Gallery - Unknown	Annual		80.00	80
1986	The Albert Memorial - Unknown	Annual		80.00	150
1987	Guildhall - Unknown	Annual		80.00	85
1988	The Observatory/Greenwich - Unknown	Annual		80.00	90
1989	Winchester Cathedral - Unknown	Annual		88.00	88

STEINS

Ace Product Management Group, Inc.

Harley-Davidson Decade Series - Ace

1993	Birth Of A Legend-1900's 99282-94Z	3,000	1995	180.00	180
1993	Birth Of A Legend-1900's (Signaure) 99712-94Z	500	1995	275.00	275
1994	Growth Of A Sport-1910's 99283-95Z	3,000	1995	180.00	180
1994	Growth Of A Sport-1910's (Signature) 99285-95Z	500	1995	285.00	285
1995	Roaring Into The 20's-1920's 99295-96Z	500		285.00	285
1995	Roaring Into The 20's-1920's (Signature) 99291-96Z	3,000		185.00	185
1993	8 Ltr Stein 99716-94Z	100	1993	875.00	875

Anheuser-Busch, Inc.

Anheuser-Busch Collectors Club - Various

YEAR ISSUE		EDITION LIMIT	YEAR RETD.	ISSUE PRICE	*QUOTE U.S.$
1995	Budweiser Clydesdales at the Bauernhof - A. Leon	Yr.Iss.	1996	Gift	35-50
1995	The Brew House Clock Tower - D. Thompson	Retrd.	1996	150.00	150
1996	The World's Largest Brewer - A. Leon	Yr.Iss.		Gift	35-50
1996	King - A Regal Spirit - D. Thompson	4/97		100.00	100

A & Eagle Historical Trademark Series-Giftware Edition - Various

YEAR ISSUE		EDITION LIMIT	YEAR RETD.	ISSUE PRICE	*QUOTE U.S.$
1992	A & Eagle Trademark I (1872) CS201, tin	Retrd.	N/A	31.00	45-60
1993	A & Eagle Trademark I (1872) CS191, boxed	Retrd.	N/A	22.00	30-45
1993	A & Eagle Trademark II (1890s) CS218, tin	Retrd.	N/A	24.00	40-50
1994	A & Eagle Trademark II (1890s) CS219, boxed	Retrd.	N/A	24.00	30-50
1994	A & Eagle Trademark III (1900s) CS238, tin	20,000	1994	28.00	40-52
1995	A & Eagle Trademark III (1900s) CS240, boxed	30,000	1995	25.00	25-30
1995	A & Eagle Trademark IV (1930s) CS255, tin	20,000		30.00	30
1996	A & Eagle Trademark IV (1930s) CS271, boxed	30,000		27.00	27

Anheuser-Busch Founder Series-Premier Collection - A-Busch, Inc.

YEAR ISSUE		EDITION LIMIT	YEAR RETD.	ISSUE PRICE	*QUOTE U.S.$
1993	Adophus Busch CS216	10,000		180.00	180
1994	August A. Busch, Sr. CS229	10,000	1996	220.00	220
1995	Adolphus Busch III CS265	10,000		220.00	220

Archives Series-Collector Edition - Various

YEAR ISSUE		EDITION LIMIT	YEAR RETD.	ISSUE PRICE	*QUOTE U.S.$
1992	1893 Columbian Exposition CS169 - D. Langeneckert	75,000	1995	35.00	35-45
1993	Ganymede CS190 - D. Langeneckert	Retrd.	1995	35.00	50-75
1994	Budweiser's Greatest Triumph CS222 - D. Langeneckert	75,000	1996	35.00	35-60
1995	Mirror of Truth Stein CS252 - D. Langeneckert	75,000		35.00	35

Birds of Prey Series-Premier Edition - P. Ford

YEAR ISSUE		EDITION LIMIT	YEAR RETD.	ISSUE PRICE	*QUOTE U.S.$
1991	American Bald Eagle CS164	25,000	1995	125.00	125-155
1992	Peregrine Falcon CS183	25,000		125.00	125
1994	Osprey CS212	Retrd.	1994	135.00	350-430
1995	Great Horned Owl CS264	25,000		137.00	137

Bud Label Series-Giftware Edition - A-Busch, Inc.

YEAR ISSUE		EDITION LIMIT	YEAR RETD.	ISSUE PRICE	*QUOTE U.S.$
1989	Budweiser Label CS101	Retrd.	1995	14.00	15-25
1990	Antique Label II CS127	Retrd.	N/A	14.00	15-25
1991	Bottled Beer III CS136	Retrd.	1995	15.00	15-22
1995	Budweiser Label Stein CS282	Open		19.50	20

Budweiser Military Series-Giftware Edition - M. Watts

YEAR ISSUE		EDITION LIMIT	YEAR RETD.	ISSUE PRICE	*QUOTE U.S.$
1994	Army CS224	Retrd.	1995	19.00	25-35
1994	Air Force CS228	Open		19.00	19
1995	Budweiser Salutes the Navy CS243	Open		19.50	20
1995	Marines stein CS256	Open		22.00	22

Budweiser Racing Series - H. Droog

YEAR ISSUE		EDITION LIMIT	YEAR RETD.	ISSUE PRICE	*QUOTE U.S.$
1993	Budweiser Racing Team CS194	Retrd.	1995	19.00	19
1993	Bill Elliott CS196	25,000	1995	150.00	95-150
1993	Bill Elliott, Signature Edition, CS196SE	1,500	1995	295.00	195-295

Civil War Series-Premier Edition - D. Langeneckert

YEAR ISSUE		EDITION LIMIT	YEAR RETD.	ISSUE PRICE	*QUOTE U.S.$
1992	General Grant CS181	25,000	1995	150.00	150
1993	General Robert E. Lee CS188	25,000	1995	150.00	150
1993	President Abraham Lincoln CS189	25,000	1995	150.00	150

Classic Series - A-Busch, Inc.

YEAR ISSUE		EDITION LIMIT	YEAR RETD.	ISSUE PRICE	*QUOTE U.S.$
1988	1st Edition CS93	Retrd.	N/A	34.95	145-175
1989	2nd Edition CS104	Retrd.	N/A	54.95	95-115
1990	3rd Edition CS113	Retrd.	N/A	65.00	45-85
1991	4th Edition CS130	Retrd.	N/A	75.00	40-80

Clydesdales Holiday Series - Various

YEAR ISSUE		EDITION LIMIT	YEAR RETD.	ISSUE PRICE	*QUOTE U.S.$
1980	1st-Budweiser Champion Clydesdales CS19 - A-Busch, Inc.	Retrd.	N/A	9.95	95-135
1981	1st-Budweiser Champion Clydesdales CS19A - A-Busch, Inc.	Retrd.	N/A	N/A	195-250
1981	2nd-Snowy Woodland CS50 - A-Busch, Inc.	Retrd.	N/A	9.95	195-250
1982	3rd-50th Anniversary CS57 - A-Busch, Inc.	Retrd.	N/A	9.95	75-95
1983	4th-Cameo Wheatland CS58 - A-Busch, Inc.	Retrd.	N/A	9.95	30
1984	5th-Covered Bridge CS62 - A-Busch, Inc.	Retrd.	N/A	9.95	15
1985	6th-Snow Capped Mountains CS63 - A-Busch, Inc.	Retrd.	N/A	9.95	15-20
1986	7th-Traditional Horses CS66 - A-Busch, Inc.	Retrd.	N/A	9.95	30-40
1987	8th-Grant's Farm Gates CS70 - A-Busch, Inc.	Retrd.	N/A	9.95	15
1988	9th-Cobblestone Passage CS88 - A-Busch, Inc.	Retrd.	N/A	9.95	15
1989	10th-Winter Evening CS89 - A-Busch, Inc.	Retrd.	N/A	12.95	15
1990	11th-An American Tradition, CS112, 1990 - S. Sampson	Retrd.	N/A	13.50	14
1990	11th-An American Tradition, CS112-SE, 1990 - S. Sampson	Retrd.	N/A	50.00	50-75
1991	12th-The Season's Best, CS133, 1991 - S. Sampson	Retrd.	N/A	14.50	15
1991	12th-The Season's Best, CS133-SE Signature Edition, 1991 - S. Sampson	Retrd.	N/A	50.00	40-50
1992	13th-The Perfect Christmas, CS167, 1992 - S. Sampson	Retrd.	N/A	14.50	15
1992	13th-The Perfect Christmas, CS167-SE Signature Edition, 1992 - S. Sampson	Open		50.00	40-50
1993	14th-Special Delivery, CS192, 1993 - N. Koerber	Retrd.	N/A	15.00	20
1993	14th-Special Delivery, CS192-SE Signature Edition, 1993 - N. Koerber	Retrd.	N/A	60.00	95-125
1994	15th-Hometown Holiday, CS211, 1994 - B. Kemper	Retrd.	1994	14.00	15
1994	15th-Hometown Holiday, CS211-SE Signature Edition, 1994 - B. Kemper	Retrd.	N/A	65.00	85-125
1995	16th-Lighting the Way Home, CS263 - T. Jester	Open		17.00	17
1995	16th-Lighting the Way Home, CS263-SE Signature Edition - T. Jester	10,000	1995	75.00	75-95

Clydesdales Series-Giftware Edition - A-Busch, Inc.

YEAR ISSUE		EDITION LIMIT	YEAR RETD.	ISSUE PRICE	*QUOTE U.S.$
1987	World Famous Clydesdales CS74	Retrd.	N/A	9.95	20-25
1988	Mare & Foal CS90	Retrd.	N/A	11.50	20-45
1989	Parade Dress CS99	Retrd.	N/A	11.50	45-75
1991	Training Hitch CS131	Retrd.	N/A	13.00	20-25
1992	Clydesdales on Parade CS161	Retrd.	N/A	16.00	20-25
1994	Proud and Free CS223	Open		17.00	17

Collector Edition - J. Tull

YEAR ISSUE		EDITION LIMIT	YEAR RETD.	ISSUE PRICE	*QUOTE U.S.$
1994	Budweiser World Cup Stein CS230	25,000	1994	40.00	40-55

Discover America Series-Collector Edition - A-Busch, Inc.

YEAR ISSUE		EDITION LIMIT	YEAR RETD.	ISSUE PRICE	*QUOTE U.S.$
1990	Nina CS107	100,000	1995	40.00	35-50
1991	Pinta CS129	100,000	1995	40.00	35-50
1992	Santa Maria CS138	100,000	1995	40.00	35-50

Endangered Species Series-Collector Edition - B. Kemper

YEAR ISSUE		EDITION LIMIT	YEAR RETD.	ISSUE PRICE	*QUOTE U.S.$
1989	Bald Eagle CS106 (First)	Retrd.	N/A	24.95	275-425
1990	Asian Tiger CS126 (Second)	Retrd.	N/A	27.50	55-75
1991	African Elephant CS135 (Third)	100,000	1995	29.00	30-40
1992	Giant Panda CS173 (Fourth)	100,000	1996	29.00	33
1993	Grizzly CS199 (Fifth)	100,000		29.50	30
1994	Gray Wolf Stein CS226 (Sixth)	100,000		29.50	30
1995	Cougar Stein CS253 (Seventh)	100,000		32.00	32
1996	Gorilla Stein CS283 (Eighth)	100,000		32.00	32

Giftware Edition - A-Busch, Inc.

YEAR ISSUE		EDITION LIMIT	YEAR RETD.	ISSUE PRICE	*QUOTE U.S.$
1992	1992 Rodeo CS184	Retrd.	N/A	18.00	20
1993	Bud Man Character Stein CS213	Retrd.	1996	45.00	40-50
1994	"Fore!" Budweiser Golf Bag Stein CS225	Retrd.	1995	16.00	16
1994	"Walking Tall" Budweiser Cowboy Boot Stein CS251	Open		17.50	18
1995	"Play Ball" Baseball Mitt stein CS244	Open		18.00	18
1995	Billiards stein CS278	Open		24.00	24

Historical Landmark Series - A-Busch, Inc.

YEAR ISSUE		EDITION LIMIT	YEAR RETD.	ISSUE PRICE	*QUOTE U.S.$
1986	Brew House CS67 (First)	Retrd.	N/A	19.95	25-40
1987	Stables CS73 (Second)	Retrd.	N/A	19.95	25-40
1988	Grant Cabin CS83 (Third)	Retrd.	N/A	19.95	45-65
1988	Old School House CS84 (Fourth)	Retrd.	N/A	19.95	25

Horseshoe Series - A-Busch, Inc.

YEAR ISSUE		EDITION LIMIT	YEAR RETD.	ISSUE PRICE	*QUOTE U.S.$
1986	Horseshoe CS68	Retrd.	N/A	14.95	35-40
1987	Horsehead CS76	Retrd.	N/A	16.00	35-45
1987	Horseshoe CS77	Retrd.	N/A	16.00	40-75
1987	Horsehead CS78	Retrd.	N/A	14.95	45-75
1988	Harness CS94	Retrd.	N/A	16.00	55-75

Hunter's Companion Series-Collector Edition - Various

YEAR ISSUE		EDITION LIMIT	YEAR RETD.	ISSUE PRICE	*QUOTE U.S.$
1993	Labrador Retriever CS195 - L. Freeman	50,000	1996	32.50	35-45
1994	The Setter Stein CS205 - S. Ryan	50,000		32.50	33
1995	The Golden Retreiver Stein CS248 - S. Ryan	50,000		34.00	34
1996	Beagle Stein CS272 - S. Ryan	50,000		35.00	35

Limited Edition Series - A-Busch, Inc.

YEAR ISSUE		EDITION LIMIT	YEAR RETD.	ISSUE PRICE	*QUOTE U.S.$
1985	Ltd. Ed. I Brewing & Fermenting CS64	Retrd.	N/A	29.95	150-225
1986	Ltd. Ed. II Aging & Cooperage CS65	Retrd.	N/A	29.95	50-75
1987	Ltd. Ed. III Transportation CS71	Retrd.	N/A	29.95	35-50
1988	Ltd. Ed. IV Taverns & Public Houses CS75	Retrd.	N/A	29.95	25-35
1989	Ltd. Ed.V Festival Scene CS98	Retrd.	N/A	34.95	25-35

Logo Series Steins-Giftware Edition - A-Busch, Inc.

YEAR ISSUE		EDITION LIMIT	YEAR RETD.	ISSUE PRICE	*QUOTE U.S.$
1990	Budweiser CS143	Retrd.	N/A	16.00	16
1990	Bud Light CS144	Retrd.	N/A	16.00	16
1990	Michelob CS145	Retrd.	N/A	16.00	16
1990	Michelob Dry CS146	Retrd.	N/A	16.00	16
1990	Busch CS147	Retrd.	N/A	16.00	16
1990	A&Eagle CS148	Retrd.	N/A	16.00	16
1990	Bud Dry CS156	Open		16.00	16

Marine Conservation Series-Collector Edition - B. Kemper

YEAR ISSUE		EDITION LIMIT	YEAR RETD.	ISSUE PRICE	*QUOTE U.S.$
1994	Manatee Stein CS203	25,000		33.50	30-40
1995	Great White Shark Stein CS247	25,000		39.50	35-40

Octoberfest Series-Giftware Edition - A-Busch, Inc.

YEAR ISSUE		EDITION LIMIT	YEAR RETD.	ISSUE PRICE	*QUOTE U.S.$
1991	1991 Octoberfest N3286	25,000	N/A	19.00	25-30
1992	1992 Octoberfest CS185	35,000		16.00	16
1993	1993 Octoberfest CS202	35,000	N/A	18.00	18

Olympic Centennial Collection - A-Busch, Inc.

YEAR ISSUE		EDITION LIMIT	YEAR RETD.	ISSUE PRICE	*QUOTE U.S.$
1995	1996 U.S. Olympic Team "Gymnastics" Stein CS262	10,000		85.00	85
1995	1996 U.S. Olympic Team "Track & Field" Stein CS246	10,000		85.00	85
1995	Centennial Olympic Games Giftware Stein CS266	Open		25.00	25
1995	Collector's Edition Official Centennial Olympics Games Stein CS259	12/96		50.00	50

Olympic Team Series 1992-Collector Edition - A-Busch, Inc.

YEAR ISSUE		EDITION LIMIT	YEAR RETD.	ISSUE PRICE	*QUOTE U.S.$
1991	1992 Winter Olympic Stein CS162	25,000	N/A	85.00	45-85
1992	1992 Summer Olympic Stein CS163	Retrd.	1994	85.00	45-90
1992	1992 U.S.Olympic Stein CS168	50,000	N/A	16.00	19

Porcelain Heritage Series-Premier Edition - Various

YEAR ISSUE		EDITION LIMIT	YEAR RETD.	ISSUE PRICE	*QUOTE U.S.$
1990	Berninghaus CS105 - Berninghaus	Retrd.	1994	75.00	50-80
1991	After The Hunt CS155 - A-Busch, Inc.	Retrd.	1994	100.00	75-100
1992	Cherub CS182 - D. Langeneckert	25,000	1996	100.00	75-100

Sea World Series-Collector Edition - A-Busch, Inc.

YEAR ISSUE		EDITION LIMIT	YEAR RETD.	ISSUE PRICE	*QUOTE U.S.$
1992	Killer Whale CS186	25,000	1996	100.00	60-100
1992	Dolphin CS187	22,500	1996	90.00	60-90

Specialty Steins - A-Busch, Inc.

YEAR ISSUE		EDITION LIMIT	YEAR RETD.	ISSUE PRICE	*QUOTE U.S.$
1975	Bud Man CS1	Retrd.	N/A	N/A	325-465
1976	A&Eagle CS2	Retrd.	N/A	N/A	150-250
1976	A&Eagle Lidded CSL2 (Reference CS28)	Retrd.	N/A	N/A	175-275
1976	Katakombe CS3	Retrd.	N/A	N/A	250-300
1976	Katakombe Lidded CSL3	Retrd.	N/A	N/A	275-400
1976	German Tavern Scene CS4	Retrd.	N/A	N/A	60-100
1975	Senior Grande Lidded CSL4	Retrd.	N/A	N/A	525-650
1975	German Pilique CS5	Retrd.	N/A	N/A	350-425
1976	German Pilique Lidded CSL5	Retrd.	N/A	N/A	400-500
1976	Senior Grande CS6	Retrd.	N/A	N/A	450-700
1975	German Tavern Scene CSL6	Retrd.	N/A	N/A	250
1975	Miniature Bavarian CS7	Retrd.	N/A	N/A	250-300
1976	Budweiser Centennial Lidded CSL7	Retrd.	N/A	N/A	350-450
1976	U.S. Bicentennial Lidded CSL8	Retrd.	N/A	N/A	375-450
1976	Natural Light CS9	Retrd.	N/A	N/A	175-200
1976	Clydesdales Hofbrau Lidded CSL9	Retrd.	N/A	N/A	225-325
1976	Blue Delft CS11	Retrd.	N/A	N/A	2000-2400
1976	Clydesdales CS12	Retrd.	N/A	N/A	200-275
1976	Budweiser Centennial CS13	Retrd.	N/A	N/A	300-450
1976	U.S. Bicentennial CS14	Retrd.	N/A	N/A	275-425
1976	Clydesdales Grants Farm CS15	Retrd.	N/A	N/A	200-275
1976	German Cities (6 assorted) CS16	Retrd.	N/A	N/A	1800-2000
1976	Americana CS17	Retrd.	N/A	N/A	350-500
1976	Budweiser Label CS18	Retrd.	N/A	N/A	300
1980	Budweiser Ladies (4 assorted) CS20	Retrd.	N/A	N/A	1500-2000
1977	Budweiser Girl CS21	Retrd.	N/A	N/A	350-45
1976	Budweiser Centennial CS22	Retrd.	N/A	N/A	300-425
1977	A&Eagle CS24	Retrd.	N/A	N/A	300-350
1976	A&Eagle Barrel CS26	Retrd.	N/A	N/A	110-175
1976	Michelob CS27	Retrd.	N/A	N/A	135-180
1976	A&Eagle Lidded CS28 (Reference CSL2)	Retrd.	N/A	N/A	195-30
1976	Clydesdales Lidded CS29	Retrd.	N/A	N/A	200-30
1976	Coracao Decanter Set (7 piece) CS31	Retrd.	N/A	N/A	500-70
1976	German Wine Set (7 piece) CS32	Retrd.	N/A	N/A	425-50
1976	Clydesdales Decanter CS33	Retrd.	N/A	N/A	1100-120
1976	Holanda Brown Decanter Set (7 piece) CS34	Retrd.	N/A	N/A	35
1976	Holanda Blue Decanter Set (7 piece) CS35	Retrd.	N/A	N/A	50
1976	Canteen Decanter Set (7 piece) CS36	Retrd.	N/A	N/A	N/A
1976	St. Louis Decanter CS37	Retrd.	N/A	N/A	40
1976	St. Louis Decanter Set (7 piece) CS38	Retrd.	N/A	N/A	1050-120
1980	Wurzburger Hofbrau CS39	Retrd.	N/A	N/A	275-40
1980	Budweiser Chicago Skyline CS40	Retrd.	N/A	N/A	125-15
1978	Busch Gardens CS41	Retrd.	N/A	N/A	250-35
1980	Oktoberfest— "The Old Country" CS42	Retrd.	N/A	N/A	250-40
1980	Natural Light Label CS43	Retrd.	N/A	N/A	150-22
1980	Busch Label CS44	Retrd.	N/A	N/A	17
1980	Michelob Label CS45	Retrd.	N/A	N/A	50-10
1980	Budweiser Label CS46	Retrd.	N/A	N/A	50-12
1981	Budweiser Chicagoland CS51	Retrd.	N/A	N/A	40-5
1981	Budweiser Texas CS52	Retrd.	N/A	N/A	50-6
1981	Budweiser California CS56	Retrd.	N/A	N/A	5
1983	Budweiser San Francisco CS59	Retrd.	N/A	N/A	17

*Quotes have been rounded up to nearest dollar

YEAR ISSUE	EDITION LIMIT	YEAR RETD.	ISSUE PRICE	*QUOTE U.S. $
1984 Budweiser Olympic Games CS60	Retrd.	N/A	N/A	20
1983 Bud Light Baron CS61	Retrd.	N/A	N/A	35-55
1987 Santa Claus CS79	Retrd.	N/A	N/A	70-80
1987 King Cobra CS80	Retrd.	N/A	N/A	225
1987 Winter Olympic Games, Lidded CS81	Retrd.	N/A	49.95	65-75
1988 Budweiser Winter Olympic Games CS85	Retrd.	N/A	24.95	25
1988 Summer Olympic Games, Lidded CS91	Retrd.	N/A	54.95	30-55
1988 Budweiser Summer Olympic Games CS92	Retrd.	N/A	54.95	25
1988 Budweiser/ Field&Stream Set (4 piece) CS95	Retrd.	N/A	69.95	225-325
1989 Bud Man CS100	Retrd.	N/A	29.95	45
1990 Baseball Cardinal Stein CS125	Retrd.	N/A	30.00	25-35
1991 Bevo Fox Stein CS160	Retrd.	1994	250.00	200-250
1992 Budweiser Racing-Elliot/Johnson N3553 - M. Watts	Retrd.	1995	19.00	25-35

Sports History Series-Giftware Edition - A-Busch, Inc.

YEAR ISSUE	EDITION LIMIT	YEAR RETD.	ISSUE PRICE	*QUOTE U.S. $
1990 Baseball, America's Favorite Pastime CS124	Retrd.	N/A	20.00	25-35
1990 Football, Gridiron Legacy CS128	Retrd.	N/A	20.00	25
1991 Auto Racing, Chasing The Checkered Flag CS132	100,000	1995	22.00	22
1991 Basketball, Heroes of the Hardwood CS134	100,000		22.00	22
1992 Golf, Par For The Course CS165	100,000	1995	22.00	22
1993 Hockey, Center Ice CS209	100,000		22.00	22

Sports Legend Series-Collector Edition - Various

YEAR ISSUE	EDITION LIMIT	YEAR RETD.	ISSUE PRICE	*QUOTE U.S. $
1991 Babe Ruth CS142 - A-Busch	50,000	1995	85.00	65-85
1992 Jim Thorpe CS171 - M. Caito	50,000	1995	85.00	65-85
1993 Joe Louis CS206 - M. Caito	Retrd.	1994	85.00	75-100

St. Patrick's Day Series-Giftware Edition - A-Busch, Inc.

YEAR ISSUE	EDITION LIMIT	YEAR RETD.	ISSUE PRICE	*QUOTE U.S. $
1991 1991 St. Patrick's Day CS109	Retrd.	N/A	15.00	45-60
1992 1992 St. Patrick's Day CS166	100,000	N/A	15.00	15
1993 1993 St. Patrick's Day CS193	Retrd.	N/A	15.30	25-40
1994 Luck O' The Irish CS210	Retrd.	1995	18.00	18
1995 1995 St. Patrick's Day CS242	Open		19.00	19
1996 "Horseshoe" 1996 St. Patrick's Day Stein CS269	Open		19.50	20

Anheuser-Busch, Inc./Gerz Meisterwerke

American Heritage Collection - Gerz

YEAR ISSUE	EDITION LIMIT	YEAR RETD.	ISSUE PRICE	*QUOTE U.S. $
1993 John F. Kennedy Stein-GM-4	10,000		220.00	220

Gerz Collectorwerke - Various

YEAR ISSUE	EDITION LIMIT	YEAR RETD.	ISSUE PRICE	*QUOTE U.S. $
1993 The Dugout-GL1 - A-Busch, Inc.	10,000		110.00	110
1994 Winchester Stein-GL2 - A-Busch, Inc.	10,000	N/A	120.00	120
1995 "Saturday Evening Post" Christmas Stein GL5 - J.C. Leyendecker	5,000		105.00	105

Gerz Meisterwerke Collection - A-Busch, Inc.

YEAR ISSUE	EDITION LIMIT	YEAR RETD.	ISSUE PRICE	*QUOTE U.S. $
1994 Norman Rockwell-Triple Self Portrait GM6	5,000		250.00	250
1994 Mallard Stein GM7	5,000		220.00	220
1994 Winchester "Model 94" Centennial Stein GM10	5,000		150.00	150
1995 Giant Panda Stein GM-8	3,500		210.00	210
1995 Rosie the Riveter Stein GM-9	5,000		165.00	165

Gerz Meisterwerke First Hunt Series - P. Ford

YEAR ISSUE	EDITION LIMIT	YEAR RETD.	ISSUE PRICE	*QUOTE U.S. $
1992 Golden Retriever GM-2	10,000		150.00	150
1994 Springer Spaniel GM-5	10,000		170.00	170
1995 Pointer Stein GM-16	10,000		190.00	190
1995 Labrador Stein GM-17	10,000		190.00	190

Gerz Saturday Evening Post Collection - J.C. Leyendecker

YEAR ISSUE	EDITION LIMIT	YEAR RETD.	ISSUE PRICE	*QUOTE U.S. $
1993 Santa's Mailbag GM-1	Retrd.		195.00	250
1993 Santa's Helper GM-3	7,500		200.00	200
1994 "All I Want For Christmas" GM-13	5,000		220.00	220
1995 Fourth of July Stein GM-15	5,000		180.00	180

Artaffects

Perillo Steins - G. Perillo

YEAR ISSUE	EDITION LIMIT	YEAR RETD.	ISSUE PRICE	*QUOTE U.S. $
1989 Buffalo Hunt	5,000		125.00	125
1991 Hoofbeats	5,000		125.00	125

CUI/Carolina Collection/Dram Tree

Classic Car Series - Various

YEAR ISSUE	EDITION LIMIT	YEAR RETD.	ISSUE PRICE	*QUOTE U.S. $
1992 1957 Chevy - G. Geivette	Retrd.		100.00	100
1993 Classic T-Birds - K. Eberts	6,950		100.00	100

Ducks Unlimited - Various

YEAR ISSUE	EDITION LIMIT	YEAR RETD.	ISSUE PRICE	*QUOTE U.S. $
1987 Wood Duck Edition I - K. Bloom	Retrd.		80.00	200
1988 Mallard Edition II - M. Bradford	Retrd.		80.00	125
1989 Canvasbacks Edition III - L. Barnicle	Retrd.		80.00	100
1990 Pintails Edition IV - R. Plasschaert	Retrd.		80.00	90
1991 Canada Geese Edition V - J. Meger	20,000		80.00	80

Ducks Unlimited Classic Decoy Series - D. Boncela

YEAR ISSUE	EDITION LIMIT	YEAR RETD.	ISSUE PRICE	*QUOTE U.S.$
1992 1930's Bert Graves Mallard Decoys Edition I	Retrd.		100.00	100

Elvis Presley Deluxe Series - Unknown

YEAR ISSUE	EDITION LIMIT	YEAR RETD.	ISSUE PRICE	*QUOTE U.S.$
1993 Comeback Special-25th Anniversary	1,968		130.00	130
1994 Life of Elvis Deluxe	1,977		130.00	130
1994 Elvis: Aloha from Hawaii Deluxe	1,973		130.00	130

Federal Duck Stamp - Various

YEAR ISSUE	EDITION LIMIT	YEAR RETD.	ISSUE PRICE	*QUOTE U.S.$
1990 Lesser Scaup Edition I - N. Anderson	6,950		80.00	80
1991 Black Bellied Whistling Duck Edition II - J. Hautman	6,950		80.00	80
1992 King Eiders Edition III - N. Howe	Retrd.		80.00	80
1993 Spectacled Eiders - J. Hautman	6,950		80.00	80
1993 50th Anniversary Commemorative - W.C. Morris	6,950		85.00	85
1994 Canvasbacks - B. Miller	6,950		80.00	80

Great American Achievements - CUI

YEAR ISSUE	EDITION LIMIT	YEAR RETD.	ISSUE PRICE	*QUOTE U.S.$
1986 First Successful Flight Edition I	Retrd.		10.95	75-95
1987 The Model T Edition II	Retrd.		12.95	30-55
1988 First Transcontinental Railway Edition III	Retrd.		15.95	28-55
1989 The First River Steamer Edition IV	Retrd.		25.00	25
1990 Man's First Walk on the Moon Edition V	Retrd.		25.00	25

The History of Billiards - Various

YEAR ISSUE	EDITION LIMIT	YEAR RETD.	ISSUE PRICE	*QUOTE U.S.$
1993 1694 Louis XIV - Trouvian	Retrd.		39.50	40
1993 1745 Ich Mache Nur Colle - Unknown	Retrd.		39.50	40
1993 1823 Indifference - D. Egerton	Retrd.		39.50	40
1993 1859 First Major Stake Match - Unknown	Retrd.		39.50	40
1993 1875 Grand Union Hotel, Saratoga NY - Unknown	Retrd.		39.50	40
1993 1905 Untitled Print - M. Neuman	Retrd.		39.50	40

Quarterback Legends - CUI

YEAR ISSUE	EDITION LIMIT	YEAR RETD.	ISSUE PRICE	*QUOTE U.S.$
1992 Hall of Fame - John Unitas Edition I	4,950		175.00	175
1992 Hall of Fame - Y.A. Tittle Edition II	4,950		175.00	175
1992 Hall of Fame - Bart Starr	4,950		175.00	175
1992 Hall of Fame - Otto Graham	Retrd.		175.00	175

Still the King - Various

YEAR ISSUE	EDITION LIMIT	YEAR RETD.	ISSUE PRICE	*QUOTE U.S.$
1992 Elvis Presley Postage Stamp - Unknown	Retrd.		60.00	60
1993 '68 Comeback Special - CUI	45-day		60.00	60
1994 Gates of Graceland - Unknown	45-day		60.00	60
1994 Elvis in the Army - Unknown	45-day		65.00	65
1994 Elvis: Aloha from Hawaii - Unknown	45-day		65.00	65
1994 Elvis in Las Vegas - Unknown	45-day		65.00	65

Stroh Bavaria Collection - CUI

YEAR ISSUE	EDITION LIMIT	YEAR RETD.	ISSUE PRICE	*QUOTE U.S.$
1990 Dancers Edition I - Bavaria I	Retrd.		45.00	45
1990 Dancers Pewter Figure Edition I - Bavaria I	Retrd.		70.00	70
1991 Barrel Pusher Edition II - Bavaria II	Retrd.		45.00	45
1991 Barrel Pusher Pewter Edition II - Bavaria II	Retrd.		70.00	70
1992 The Aging Cellar-Edition III	Retrd.		45.00	45
1992 The Aging Cellar-Pewter Edition III	Retrd.		70.00	70
1993 Bandwagon Street Party-Pewter Edition II	Retrd.		70.00	70
1993 Bandwagon Street Party-Edition IV	Retrd.		45.00	45

Stroh Heritage Collection - CUI

YEAR ISSUE	EDITION LIMIT	YEAR RETD.	ISSUE PRICE	*QUOTE U.S.$
1984 Horsedrawn Wagon - Heritage I	Retrd.		11.95	15-25
1985 Kirn Inn Germany - Heritage II	Retrd.		12.95	15-22
1986 Lion Brewing Company - Heritage III	Retrd.		13.95	25-35
1987 Bohemian Beer - Heritage IV	Retrd.		14.95	19-22
1988 Delivery Vehicles - Heritage V	Retrd.		25.00	25
1989 Fire Brewed - Heritage V I	Retrd.		16.95	19

Hadley House

Annual Christmas Series - T. Redlin

YEAR ISSUE	EDITION LIMIT	YEAR RETD.	ISSUE PRICE	*QUOTE U.S.$
1994 Almost Home	45-day		39.95	40
1995 Winter Wonderland	45-day		39.95	40

Hamilton Collection

The STAR TREK® Tankard Collection - T. Blackshear

YEAR ISSUE	EDITION LIMIT	YEAR RETD.	ISSUE PRICE	*QUOTE U.S.$
1994 SPOCK	Open		49.50	50
1995 Kirk	Open		49.50	50
1995 McCoy	Open		49.50	50
1995 Uhura	Open		49.50	50
1995 Scotty	Open		49.50	50
1995 Sulu	Open		49.50	50
1995 Chekov	Open		49.50	50
1995 U.S.S. Enterprise NCC-1701	Open		49.50	50

Warriors of the Plains Tankards - G. Stewart

YEAR ISSUE	EDITION LIMIT	YEAR RETD.	ISSUE PRICE	*QUOTE U.S.$
1992 Thundering Hooves	Open		125.00	125
1995 Warrior's Choice	Open		125.00	125
1995 Healing Spirits	Open		125.00	125
1995 Battle Grounds	Open		125.00	125

Sports Impressions/Enesco

Baseball Steins - Various

YEAR ISSUE	EDITION LIMIT	YEAR RETD.	ISSUE PRICE	*QUOTE U.S.$
1990 Nolan Ryan Rangers - R. Lewis	Closed	N/A	30.00	30
1990 Life Of A Legend Mickey Mantle - T. Fogarty	Closed	N/A	30.00	30
1990 Kings of K - J. Catalano	Closed	N/A	30.00	30
1990 Rangers Nolan Ryan 300th Win - J. Catalano	Closed	N/A	30.00	30
1995 Life of a Legend Mickey Mantle (17 oz.) 1228-72 - T. Fogarty	Open		15.00	15

Football Steins - J. Catalano

YEAR ISSUE	EDITION LIMIT	YEAR RETD.	ISSUE PRICE	*QUOTE U.S.$
1990 Dan Marino	2,500	N/A	30.00	30
1991 Jim Kelly	2,500	N/A	30.00	30
1990 Joe Montana 49ers 3000-06	2,500	1992	30.00	30
1991 Troy Aikman Cowboys 3008-06	2,500	1993	30.00	30

*Quotes have been rounded up to nearest dollar

❖ Collectors' Information Bureau ❖

DIRECTORY TO SECONDARY MARKET DEALERS

The C.I.B. Directory to Secondary Market Dealers is designed to put you in touch with secondary market experts who are in the business of making it easier for you to buy and sell retired collectibles. Together, they have a wealth of knowledge about the field of collectibles and are eager to help you enjoy your hobby even more.

HOW TO USE THIS DIRECTORY

We've organized this directory to make it easy for you to find the dealer you need. Each dealer is listed alphabetically by state. They are also listed in the Directory Index on pages D11 and 12 according to their specialty.

LOCATING DEALERS BY THEIR SPECIALTY

Each dealer has been assigned a locator number in the top right-hand corner of their listing. This number will come in handy when you are looking for a dealer who is an expert in a particular line or company. For example, if you are looking for a dealer to help you buy or sell a Department 56 piece, just turn to the index and look up the Department 56 listing. The numbers you find next to the listing are the locator numbers of the dealers who specialize in Department 56. Once you've found the numbers, look over the individual dealer listings and begin contacting the dealers who most appeal to you.

LOCATING DEALERS BY STATE

Though most dealers are accustomed to doing business on a national basis, you may want to start by contacting dealers closer to home. That's why we've also organized the dealers by state. Within each state listing, dealers are organized in alphabetical order by business name.

LET'S GET STARTED!

Now that you know how to use the directory, you may want to take a moment or two to turn to pages 4-5 and learn the answers to the "10 MOST FREQUENTLY ASKED QUESTIONS ABOUT BUYING AND SELLING LIMITED EDITION COLLECTIBLES." These questions have come to us from collectors like you who want to know more about buying and selling on the secondary market. We've gathered the answers from our panel of secondary market experts. Hopefully, they'll give you the background you need to make the most out of your secondary market transactions!

ABBREVIATIONS

Amex = American Express	MOY = Memories of Yesterday
Dept. 56 = Department 56	WFS = Wee Forest Folk
EKJ = Emmett Kelly, Jr.	Byers' = Byers' Choice
Ltd. = Limited	

AZ — CRYSTAL WORLD — 1
2743 North Campbell Avenue
Tucson, AZ 85719

Phone: (602) or (520) 326-5990
Hours: T-F: 10:30-6:00, Sat: 11:00-3:00

Services: We buy/sell appraise, engrave, design and repair crystal. Brokerage fee applicable. Visa, MasterCard and check.

Lines: Authorized Swarovski/SCS retailer, Crystal World, Austrian faceted sculptures, Abelman Art Glass ltd. edition clowns, Krystonia.

Noteworthy: In business for over 25 years, we specialize in cut glass, paperweights, custom engraving on wedding and anniversary gifts, corporate presentation awards and trophies expertly created. Attention Swarovski collectors: we pay your membership fee. Now you can purchase your investment collectibles with confidence. All crystal professionally inspected, evaluated and graded for mint condition by William Threm, master glass engraver. Complete crystal showroom of exquisite cut glass and art glass from around the world. We offer repairing on Steuben, Baccarat, Lalique, Waterford, etc. Appraisal services and expert advice of future crystal investments.

AZ — SWAN SEEKERS NETWORK — 2
4118 East Vernon Avenue
Phoenix, AZ 85008-2333

Phone: (602) 957-6294
Fax: (602) 957-1631
Hours: M-F: 9:00-5:00 MST

Services: A mail order buy/sell exchange where each seller sets his/her own price. 24 hour phone and fax.

Lines: Swarovski

Noteworthy: Swarovski enthusiast Maret Webb A.I.A. conceived Swan Seekers Network in 1989. Their services offer an unbiased view of the secondary market and the broad spectrum of Swarovski items available. Over 2,800 collectors, insurance adjusters, and retailers from 38 countries have sought out Swan Seekers to date. They publish *Swan Seekers News*, the first independent publication for Swarovski collectors, and *Swan Seekers Marketplace*, a comprehensive listing of retired Swarovski items available for purchase. Subscription cost is $28/yr. USA or $34/yr. foreign. They are honored to serve as advisor to CIB, Warman's and Schroeder's price guides.

AZ — WHAT THE DICKENS — 3
2885 W. Ribera Place
Tucson, AZ 85742

Phone: (520) 297-7019
Hours: M-F: 9:00-9:00, Sat: 10:00-2:00

Services: Consignments. Buy/sell trade publication offering subscriptions. 10% commission charged to buyer. 10% commission on trades split between traders. Call for details. Visa/MasterCard, Discover. All sales handled personally and items are UPS insured. Appraisal for Department 56 and Disney pieces.

Lines: Department 56: Villages, Snowbabies, Winter Silhouette, Lite-Ups, Cold Cast Porcelain; Disney, Swarovski, Lladro, and Hummel.

Noteworthy: Owners Kenneth and Judith Isaacson have been collectors of Dickens Village and Snowbabies since 1990, which led to the birth of the secondary market brokerage service in 1991. The Isaacsons have expanded their service to include Disney and many other fine collectibles. The Isaacsons can be found at most major secondary market shows for Department 56 and Disney.

CA — CAROUSEL COLLECTIBLES EXCHANGE — 4
6359 Galletta Drive
Newark, CA 94560

Phone: (510) 795-0609
On line: CARCOLEXCH@AOL.com
Fax: (510) 742-8123
Hours: Anytime (Closed Sundays)

Services: Locator and listing service for retired and limited edition collectibles. Personal checks, cashiers checks or Money Orders.

Lines: Armani, Swarovski, Boyds, Wee Forest Folk, Byers' Choice, Walt Disney Classics, Cherished Teddies, Precious Moments, Hallmark, Simpich, C. Radko, Lladro, and Hamilton. Plates by Disney Studios, Kaatz, Gustafson, Chiu, B.P Gutmann, Wyland, Bell, Cooper, Gerardi, T. Redlin, Kuck, Bergsma, and Red Skelton.

Noteworthy: Carousel Collectibles also does categorical research on specific types of collectibles. (i.e. Exotic birds, Endangered species, Campbells' Kids, Disney's Lady and The Tramp and others).

CA — COLLECTOR'S WORLD — 5
2249 Honolulu Ave.
Montrose, CA 91020

Phone: (800) 366-7890 (818) 248-9451
Fax: (818) 248-0439
Hours: M-Sat: 10:00-5:30

Services: Limited consignments. Buy outright. Call for details.

Lines: All God's Children, Armani, Chilmark, David Winter, DeGrazia, Dennis Patrick Lewan, Disney Classics, G. Harvey, Jack Terry, Jan Hagara, Hummel, T. Kinkade, Legends, Lilliput, Lladro, Lowell Davis, Marty Bell, Maud Humphrey, Memories of Yesterday, Robert Olszewski, Swarovski, Tom Clark Gnomes, Wee Forest Folk.

Noteworthy: Collector's World has over 20 years of experience in servicing both novice and experienced collectors alike in obtaining hard-to-find retired, discontinued, or limited production items. They stock a large inventory of secondary market items in their normal lines and have worldwide connections in locating specific items. They maintain their own large active "want" to buy and sell computerized collector listings.

CA — CRYSTAL REEF — 6
P.O. Box 8084
Foster City, CA 94404

Phone: (415) 312-8265
Hours: M-Sat: 9:00-7:00, 24hr. Message Service

Services: Secondary market service. Occasionally buy outright. Dealer inquiries welcome. No cost, no obligation listing. Very low brokerage rates. Quoted price is the price to the buyer, commission fees included. Layaway available. Personal checks, money orders, Visa, MasterCard, and American Express accepted.

Lines: Pocket Dragons, Swarovski, Disney Classics and Disneyana, Wee Forest Folk, R. John Wright, Steiff, Tom Clark Gnomes, Lilliput, David Winter, Robert Olszewski, Armani, Lladro, Cherished Teddies, Animation Art.

Noteworthy: Crystal Reef, a Christian owned & operated organization, was established in 1991, and has grown to become one of the largest secondary market exchanges in North America with international listings. Guest speaker at collectible conventions. CIB panel member.

CA — FLASH COLLECTIBLES — 7
560 N. Moorpark Road, Suite 287
Thousand Oaks, CA 91360

Phone: (800) 266-2337 (805) 499-9222
Fax: (805) 376-5541
Hours: M-F: 10:00-5:00, 24-hour answering service

Services: Buy outright. Consignment and trades. Search service.

Lines: Budweiser, Anheuser-Busch, Strohs, Old Style, Miller, Hamms, Pabst, Coors and Lone Star; steins and plates. Brewery and Coca Cola banks by Ertl and Spec Cast, German steins.

Noteworthy: Flash Collectibles started as a part time business in 1971. By 1973, owners Doug and Natalie Marks were totally consumed by the antique and collectibles "bug" and opened their first store called The Antique Co. In 1984, the Marks discovered the Anheuser-Busch collectible steins. In 1986, the firm moved to their current location & changed their name to Flash Collectibles. Specializing in mail order beer steins, they offer a free brochure listing their current stock of over 1,000 beer steins. Also featured are movie stills, and an exceptionally large collection of full-color original fruit and vegetable labels.

CA — THE FRAME GALLERY — 8
305 Third Avenue
Chula Vista, CA 91910

Phone: (619) 422-1700
Fax: (619) 422-5860
Hours: M-F: 10:00-5:30, Sat: 10:00-5:00

Services: Specializes in searching for hard-to-find collectibles. Does not buy outright. Call for details.

Lines: All collector plates. Also prints, figurines, crystal, & pewter, including Snowbabies, Perillo, Disney Classics, Kinkade, Olszewski, Autographed photos, Swarovski, Hummels, Rockwell, Kevin Francis.

Noteworthy: The Frame Gallery began as a framing shop, but soon collectors began coming to the store for advice on the art of framing different collectibles. Before long, mother-daughter team Margaret and Jan introduced collectibles to their store. Today, they are a redemption center for Kinkade, Disney Classics, Lilliput, Krystonia, Pocket Dragons, Myth & Magic, and Hantel Miniatures. They also carry artists' work of local scenes - of particular interest to tourists.

CA — JULIET'S COLLECTIBLES — 9
44060 Margarita Road
Temecula, CA 92592-2746

Phone: (909) 693-1410
Fax: (909) 693-1412
Hours: T-Sat: 10:00-5:30, evenings by appt.

Services: Buy outright, consignment, 90 day layaway. Free shipping in the continental U.S.

Lines: All God's Children, Hummel, Sarah's Attic, Wee Forest Folk, Kinkade, Lena Liu, Sandra Kuck, D. Zolan, G. Harvey, Alan Maley.

Noteworthy: Juliet's Collectibles was opened in 1967 by Juliet Anne Boysen. The store has one of the largest selections of All God's Children retired pieces to be found in California, including most of the Father Christmas pieces and a large selection of Sarah's Attic. They are a redemption center for Precious Moments, Sarah's Attic, G. Harvey, Hummel. They print a quarterly newsletter which collectors can receive just by calling the store. Open houses are hosted when either an artist or a representative comes to the store. Customer service is a most important part of Juliet Anne Boysen's policy.

CA — RYSTAD'S LIMITED EDITIONS — 10
1013 Lincoln Avenue
San Jose, CA 95125

Phone: (408) 279-1960
Fax: (408) 279-1960
Hours: T-Sat: 10:00-5:00

Services: Buy outright. Buy/sell brokerage.

Lines: Red Skelton, Rockwell, Hamilton, Hummel, David Winter, Ashton-Drake, Zolan, Noritake, Lenox, All God's Children, Goebel Miniatures, Bradford, Department 56: Snowbabies, Disney Classics, Royal Copenhagen, Bing & Grondahl, Kinkade, Marty Bell, all plates.

Noteworthy: Dean Rystad started in the collectibles mail order business in 1967. In 1978 Rystad opened a store, which today features 85% collector plates. The store showcases more than 3,000 plates at any given time. Rystad's specialty is in locating back issues of collectibles. His track record is about 98% of requests. He also offers an appraisal service. Rystad's is a redemption center for most collector clubs. A new gallery was added recently to feature Red Skelton, Thomas Kinkade, Marty Bell, Sandra Kuck, and Jack Terry.

CT — BABE'S BEARS AND DOLLS — 11
32 Walnut Street
Seymour, CT 06483

Phone: (203) 888-6141
Fax: (203) 881-1672
Hours: By appointment. Telephone or fax 24 hours. If answered by machine, please leave message & they'll get back to you.

Services: Buy outright, cash, credit card, checks. Layaways and shipping available.

Lines: Nabor Kids dolls, Robert Raikes Bears and dolls, Limited Edition Beverly Port bears by Gorham. Call for other collectibles they carry.

Noteworthy: Babe's Bears is owned and operated by Jeanette Spinelli and husband Carl, affectionately known as Babe and Papa Bear. Babe, Papa Bear, along with their children, travel to secondary market shows up and down the east coast. There is something for collectors of all ages, from children to adult.

FL — THE CHRISTMAS PALACE — 12
10600 N.W. 77 Ave.
Hialeah Gardens, FL 33016

Phone: (305) 558-5352
Fax: (305) 558-6718
Hours: M-Sat: 10-7, Sun: 11-6 Off Season
M-Sat: 10-9, Sun: 10-7 In Season

Services: No consignments, buy outright. Call for details. Free shipping anywhere in the United States for orders over $50. All major credit cards accepted. No sales tax outside of Florida.

Lines: Department 56: Villages, Snowbabies, Snow Bunnies, Swarovski, Walt Disney Classics, Precious Moments, Armani, Boyds Bears, Ebony Visions by Willits.

Noteworthy: Since 1989, The Christmas Palace has become one of the top collectors' stores in the country. They are one of the largest Department 56 dealers (Gold Key status). Redemption center for all listed lines.

FL — DISNEYANA/MARTHA'S EXCHANGE — 13
3961 Kiawa Drive
Orlando, FL 32837

Phone: (407) 438-5634 (Disneyana)
Phone: (407) 438-4869 (Martha's)
Fax: (407) 438-8372
Hours: M-F: 9:00-6:00

Services: 10% commission to both buyer and seller. Subscriptions to the Disneyana Exchange or Martha's Exchange Newsletters available.
Lines: **(Disneyana Exchange):** Walt Disney Classics, Disneyana Convention, Animation Art, watches, Disney Store merchandise, Vintage memorabilia. **(Martha's Exchange):** Dept. 56, Disney, D. Winter, Wee Forest Folk, Swarovski, Armani, Lladro, Chilmark.
Noteworthy: The Disneyana Exchange started in 1993 as a break-off of Martha's Exchange which has been in business for eight years. They are currently the largest Disney secondary market in the country and actively work with over 500 Disney dealers in the world.

FL — KATHY'S HALLMARK — 16
7709 Seminole Mall
Seminole, FL 34642

Phone: (813) 392-2459
Fax: (813) 392-2459 (call first)
Hours: M-Sat: 10:00-9:00, Sun: Noon-5:00

Services: Buy and sell outright or trade. Visa, MasterCard, Amex, and Discover accepted. Ship UPS.
Lines: Collector plates, Swarovski, Star Trek, Department 56, Star Wars, Precious Moments dolls, Barbie, Hallmark and Enesco Ornaments, Kiddie Car Classics, Hummel, Dreamsicles, Ashton-Drake dolls, Precious Moments.
Noteworthy: Redemption center for Precious Moments, Hummel, Swarovski, Dreamsicles, Hallmark, Cherished Teddies. Call Jack for collector plate information.

FL — DONNA'S COLLECTIBLES EXCHANGE — 14
163 Long Leaf Pine Circle
Sanford, FL 32773

Phone: (800) 480-5105
Fax: (407) 323-7747
Hours: M-F: 11:00 AM-8:00 PM EST

Services: Secondary Market Buy & Sell free listing exchange. Dealers welcome. Accept Visa & MasterCard.
Lines: ANRI, Armani, Barbies, Boyds Bearstones, Folkstones & Plushes, Byers', Charming Tails, Cherished Teddies, Dept. 56, WFF, C. Radko, D. Winter, EKJ, Forma Vitrum, Kinkade, Snowbabies, Kiddie Car Classics, Tender Touches & Merry Miniatures, Mickey & Co., Harbour Lights, Hummel, JP Editions, Lefton, Lilliput, L. Davis, Maud Humphrey, Muffy's, Raikes, Sarah's Attic, Tom Clark Gnomes, Swarovski, Disney Classics & Convention, Disney Classic Videos,
Noteworthy: Donna's Collectibles Exchange is strictly a mail-order business. We send out current listings on request.

FL — A RETIRED COLLECTION — 17
550 Harbor Cove Circle
Longboat Key, FL 34228-3544

Phone: (800) 332-8594 (941) 387-0102 (FL)
On Line: LladroLady@aol.com, or
         Home Page: http://www.hkproducts.com/lladro-lady
Fax: (941) 383-8865
Hours: Mail Order: 8:00-8:00 daily. Visits by appointment.

Services: Buy & sell exchange. Occasionally buy outright. Dealers welcome. Accept Visa, MasterCard, Amex & Discover. Free layaway plan.
Lines: Lladro
Noteworthy: A Retired Collection, specializing in Lladro, was established in 1992 by Janet Gale Hammer. A free Newsletter/Stock List is published bi-monthly. Just call or fax to be added to the master mailing list. Janet keeps current on Lladro secondary market activities by attending auctions in CA and FL and is a charter member of the Tampa Bay/Sarasota Chapter group and a CIB panel member.

FL — HEIRLOOMS OF TOMORROW — 15
2178-1/2 NE 123rd Street
North Miami, FL 33181

Phone: (800) 544-2-BUY (305) 899-0920
Hours: M-W& F: 9:30-6:00, Thurs: 9:30-8:00, Sat: 9-5:00

Services: Buy outright. Commission. Collectors send a typed list divided into buy and sell.
Lines: ANRI, Hibel, Lladro, Goebel Mini, David Winter, Hummel, Armani, Swarovski, Department 56, Cabbage Patch, Legends, Bradford, Krystonia, Sarah's Attic, Precious Moments, M.O.Y., Chilmark, Disney Classics, Lilliput Lane, Lowell Davis, cp smithshire, Caithness, Ashton-Drake dolls, Thomas Kinkade, Olszewski, Kuck, Sandridge.
Noteworthy: With over 16 years of experience and literally thousands of items, Heirlooms of Tomorrow is considered one of South Florida's foremost one-stop collectible shops. The store is owned and operated by Pearl Finkelstein, who is an avid collector. They have a booming mail order business, and care is taken to ensure that collectibles will arrive safely, as they are shipped worldwide.

ID — THREE C's GIFT GALLERY — 18
350 N. Milwaukee - 1009
Boise, ID 83788

Phone: (800) 847-3302
Fax: (208) 884-1111
Hours: M-F: 10:00-9:00, Sat: 10:00-7:00, Sun: 11:00-6:00

Services: All major credit cards accepted. Layaway available.
Lines: Walt Disney Classics, Swarovski, David Winter, Thomas Kinkade, Armani, Chilmark, Legends, Snowbabies, M.I. Hummel, Wee Forest Folk, Selkirk Glass.
Noteworthy: Redemption center for Walt Disney Classics, David Winter, Swarovski, Lilliput Lane, M.I. Hummel, Armani, Chilmark, Legends, and Thomas Kinkade.

IL — THE CRYSTAL CONNECTION — 19
507 W. Wolf Road
Peoria, IL 61614-2054

Phone: (800) 692-0708: order / (309) 692-2221: info
Fax: (309) 692-2221 (24-hr. fax line)
Hours: M-F: 4:00-9:00, Sat-Sun: 10:00-5:00
(24-hr. answering machine)

Services: Buy/sell listing brokerage service and appraisals. Accept checks, money orders and Visa or MasterCard.
Lines: Swarovski Silver Crystal
Noteworthy: The Crystal Connection is the world's leading authority on Swarovski crystal and also the publisher of the *Crystal News*, a newsletter dedicated to the joy of collecting Swarovski crystal. It is registered with the Better Business Bureau and is a regular CIB panel member. The owner, Robin Yaw is a fully accredited member of the prestigious International Society of Appraisers and the first appraiser in the world to specialize in Swarovski crystal. He has appeared a number of times as a panel "expert" for CIB and on Swarovski's "Ask The Expert" seminars.

IL — EILENE'S TREASURES — 20
P.O. Box 285
Virden, IL 62690

Phone: (217) 965-3648
Hours: 9:00AM-8:00 PM

Services: Buy outright. Layaways available. Fair prices. Satisfaction guaranteed.
Lines: Precious Moments, suspended and retired: figurines, bells, ornaments, plates; Memories of Yesterday figurines and ornaments, Hallmark Ornaments, Enesco Treasury Ornaments.
Noteworthy: Eilene Kruse is an expert on Precious Moments marks, as she purchased many early pieces with original marks. She then expanded her business to include other Enesco lines and Hallmark ornaments. Eilene attends four to five ornament and collectible shows in the Illinois area and publishes a price list which is available upon request.

IL — EUROPEAN IMPORTS & GIFTS — 21
Oak Mill Mall, 7900 North Milwaukee
Niles, IL 60714

Phone: (847) 967-5253
Fax: (847) 967-0133
Hours: M-F: 10:00-8:00, Sat: 10:00-5:30, Sun: Noon-5:00

Services: No consignments. Buy outright; mail a complete listing. Ships free anywhere in U.S. for purchases over $75. Call for details.
Lines: Annalee, ANRI, Armani, Ashton-Drake, Bradford plates, Byers' Choice, Cairn Gnomes, Chilmark, Lowell Davis, Dept. 56, Disney Classics, Duncan Royale, Goebel Miniatures, Hamilton dolls and plates, Lizzie High, M.I. Hummel, EKJ, Krystonia, S. Kuck, Legends, Lilliput Lane, Lladro, Memories of Yesterday, Michael's Limited, All God's Children, Rockwell, Precious Moments, Royal Doulton, Sandicast, Sports Impressions, Swarovski, Enesco's Treasury of Christmas ornaments, United Design, WACO, Wee Forest Folk, David Winter, Madame Alexander Dolls.
Noteworthy: Since 1966, European Imports has grown to one of the largest collectible showcases in the U.S. NALED member.

IN — GRAHAM'S CRACKERS — 22
5981 E. 86th Street
Indianapolis, IN 46250

Phone: (800) 442-5727 (317) 842-5727
Fax: (317) 577-7777
Hours: M-Sat: 10:00-9:00 PM, Sun: Noon-5:00

Services: Buy retired pieces outright. Call for details. Hosts many artist appearances and special events throughout the year. Special orders our specialty!
Lines: Department 56, German Nutcrackers, Lilliput Lane, Mary Englebreit, Walt Disney Classics, David Winter, Possible Dreams, Harbour Lights, Sarah's Attic, Precious Moments, Christopher Radko, Boyds Bears, Cherished Teddies, Byers' Choice, Lizzie High, Hummel, Rick Cain, Old World Christmas. Over 90 lines!
Noteworthy: Opened in 1986, now over 20,000 square feet - a Collector's Paradise. Specializes in personal service, exquisite collectibles, collector clubs and seasonal merchandise for EVERY holiday. Interested collectors may call to have their name included on the mailing list.

IN — MARKER'S HUMMELS — 23
P.O. Box 66
603 W. South Street
Bremen, IN 46506

Phone: (219) 546-3111
Hours: M-Sat: 10:00-6:00

Services: Buy and sell outright. No consignment.
Lines: M.I. Hummel figurines only.
Noteworthy: Marker's has been specializing in Hummel figurines for over 20 years. They stock current figurines for the beginning collector as well as Crown, Full Bee, and stylized trademarks. Marker's also maintains a stock of rare Hummel figurines which includes internationals. They have a close working relationship with Goebel because of their many trips to Germany, and the staff will be glad to asnwer any questions about Hummels or Goebel. Marker's recommends a visit to the Donald Stephens Museum in the O'Hare Convention Center to see some of the rare Hummel figurines they can provide for your collection.

IN — ROSE MARIE'S — 24
1119 Lincoln Avenue
Evansville, IN 47714

Phone: (800) 637-5734 (812) 423-7557
Fax: (812) 423-7578
Hours: M-Th & Sat: 10:00-5:00, F: 10:00-7:00.
Nov. & Dec. M-F: 10:00-7:00, Sat: 10:00-5:00, Sun: Noon-5

Services: Buy/sell exchange. Listed price plus 10%. Accept Visa, Mastercard, Amex, & Discover. Fully guaranteed. Dealers welcome.
Lines: All Dept. 56, Disney Classics, M.I. Hummel, Lladro, Armani, Swarovski and many more.
Noteworthy: Looking for a way to aid her missionary sons, Rose Marie Hillenbrand began by selling a few exquisite pieces from a restored wardrobe in her living room in 1958. Today, over 35 years later, Rose Marie's specializes in assisting the collector in gift giving and in the acquisition of fine collectibles. The store services and supports over 35 collector clubs. ***Notice to all Collector Club Members, "We pay your club dues for you."** Call for details.

LA — DICKENS' EXCHANGE, INC. — 25
5150 Highway 22, Suite C-9
Mandeville, LA 70471

Phone: (504) 845-1954
Fax: (504) 845-1873
Hours: M-F: 9:00-5:30, Sat: 10:00-2:00

Services: 10% commission paid by purchaser on consignment listings. Exchange sells outright-no commissions. Call for details.
Lines: Department 56: Snow Village, Dickens Village, Christmas in the City, New England, Alpine, Little Town of Bethlehem, North Pole, Cold Cast Porcelains, Snowbabies and accessories.
Noteworthy: Lynda Blankenship began as a collector of Department 56 collectibles. Eventually this led to the publishing of *The Dickens' Exchange*, a reliable source for Department 56 news and a thriving exchange. Today, Lynda publishes a 32-page newsletter which boasts over 12,000 subscribers! She describes her newsletter as a place for collectors to meet and share their hobby. She is also the author of "Willage Mania," a 300-page color book for Dept. 56 collectors and co-author of "Display Mania."

MA — FOSTERS' — 26
100 Pleasant Street
South Weymouth, MA 02190

Phone: (800) 439-3546 (617) 337-3546
Fax: (617) 331-6277
Hours: M-Sat: 10:00-5:00, Sun: Noon-5:00

Services: Consignment. Some outright buying. Call for details. Visa, MasterCard, Discover, and American Express accepted. Fosters' will ship anywhere and has a 30 day layaway plan.
Lines: Byers' Choice Carolers, June McKenna Santas, Cat's Meow, Steiff bears.
Noteworthy: **They are a club redemption center for Cat's Meow, Radko, Lizzie High, McKenna, Gund, Steiff, and Possible Dreams.** For over 25 years Fosters' has been a family run business, located 15 miles south of Boston in the historical village of South Weymouth. They pride themselves on having the largest year-round display of Byers' Choice Carolers on the East coast with an in-store museum of Carolers. Fosters' is a very unique store featuring fine collectibles, country home accessories and furniture.

MA — LINDA'S ORIGINALS & THE YANKEE CRAFTSMEN — 27
220 Rt. 6A
Brewster, MA 02631

Phone: (800) 385-4758 (508) 385-4758
Fax: (508) 385-7935
Hours: Daily: 9:30-9:00 PM - Summer
Daily: 9:30-5:00 PM - Winter

Services: Buy/Sell outright, take consignment & take **no** added commissions. Free shipping with $50 purchase, free layaway & newsletter.
Lines: Byers' Choice, Harbour Lights, Swarovski, Forma Vitrum, Disney Classics, D. Winter, Lilliput, Department 56, Snowbabies, Michael's Limited, Shelia's, Lizzie High, Christopher Radko, Cairn Gnomes, Cat's Meow, Lladro, T. Kinkade, Wee Forest Folk.
Noteworthy: Located on Cape Cod, they feature one of the largest collections of Byers' Choice collections in the country. Enter to win a 1991 Byers' Choice Apple Lady with any purchase of their Byers' Collection or win a Tinkerbell from their Disney Classics Collection.

MA — NEW ENGLAND COLLECTIBLES EXCHANGE — 28
201 Pine Avenue
Clarksburg, MA 01247

Phone: (800) 854-6323 (413) 663-3643
Hours: M-F: 3:00-9:00 EST, Anytime Weekends

Services: Subscribers receive nine newsletters a year which include listings by artist of retired pieces, "wanted" listings, and artists to meet on tour. Buyers pay 15% commission plus shipping costs.
Lines: ANRI, Barbie, Boyds, Byers' Choice, Cat's Meow, Cherished Teddies, Chilmark, Daddy's Long Legs, Dept. 56, Disney Classics, Harbour Lights, Hummel, June McKenna, Lee Sievers, Lefton, Lilliput, lithos, Maurice Wideman, Miss Martha, N. Rockwell, Precious Moments, R. Griffin, Ron Lee, Shelia's, Swarovski, T. Wolfe, T.Clark.
Noteworthy: Established in 1992, Bob Dorman developed the NECE with the rules of courteous, honest, fair, and confidential personal service to all buyers and sellers. They ship insured to collectors worldwide.

MI — BONNIE'S HALLMARK — 29
108 N. Mitchell Street
Cadillac, MI 49601

Phone: (800) 968-6260 (616) 775-4282
Fax: (616) 775-7499
Hours: M-Sat: 8:30-9:00 PM, Sun & Holidays: 10:00-6:00

Services: Buy/sell exchange, locator service. Ship UPS, layaways. Free gift wrapping. Accept major credit cards.
Lines: Hallmark Keepsake Ornaments, Enesco Treasury Ornaments, Disney Classics, Hummel, Sarah's Attic, Tom Clark Gnomes, Department 56, All God's Children, Cherished Teddies, Memories of Yesterday, Lilliput Lane, Harbor Lights, Precious Moments, Charming Tails, Kiddie Car Classics.
Noteworthy: Gold Crown Hallmark store. Redemption center for Precious Moments, Tom Clark Gnomes, Memories of Yesterday, All God's Children, Sarah's Attic, Hummel, Department 56, Cherished Teddies, Disney Classics and more. Extensively stocked.

MI — DEPARTMENT 56 RETIREES — 30
Harry & June McGowan
6576 Balmoral Terrace
Clarkston, MI 48346

Phone: (810) 623-6664
Fax: (810) 623-6104
Hours: Retired - flexible - daily shipping year round.

Services: Buy outright, creating faster delivery since "what is on our price list is in our possesion." No added commission. Visa and MasterCard sales. Ship daily. Free shipping on orders over $300.
Lines: Department 56: Dickens Village, Christmas in the City, New England, Alpine, North Pole, and some Snow Village, Snowbabies (regular and mini), Disney Classics, and Lilliput Lane.
Noteworthy: We publish one newsletter per year announcing our annual home show (6th anniversary this year). The entry fee proceeds benefit children from the Oakland County Child Village, Salvation Army, Knights of Columbus and Neighbor to Neighbor.

MI — HOUSE OF COLLECTIBLES — 31
15425 Hall Road
Macomb, MI 48044

Phone: (810) 247-2000
Hours: M: 10:00-6:00, Th: 10:00-8:00, Sat: 10:00-5:00,
Sunday: seasonal

Services: Consignments and outright buys. Call for details.

Lines: Precious Moments, Swarovski, Department 56: Snow Village, Heritage Village, and Snowbabies, Disney Classics, Boyd's, Shelia's, Cherished Teddies, Margaret Furlong, Fenton, Knickerbocker Dolls and Bears, Steinbach, Armani, Kinkade, Memories of Yesterday, David Winter, Lilliput Lane, Hummel, Bradford plates, Ashton-Drake, Harbour Lights, Annalee, Belsnickle, Seraphim Classic, Dreamsicle, Olszewski, All God's Children.

Noteworthy: Specializing in Precious Moments secondary market. Established in 1984. Redemption center for clubs. Hosts local chapter Precious Moments Club "Friends Forever." Distinguished Service Retailer for Enesco and Silver Key for Department 56.

MI — RETIRED FIGURINE EXCHANGE — 32
8170 Cooley Lake Road
White Lake, MI 48386

Phone: (800) 893-4494 (810) 360-4155
Hours: M-W: 10-8, Th-F: 10-6, Sat: 10-6, Noon: 12-4

Services: Have large stock of items in store. Accept some consignments. Buy outright. Exchange and locator service.

Lines: Disney Classics, Swarovski, Precious Moments, Lladro, Ron Lee, Cherished Teddies, Royal Doulton, M.I. Hummel, Royal Copenhagen, Dahl Jensen, Royal Worcester, Possible Dreams, Norman Rockwell, Krystonia, Pendelfin, Kevin Francis, Leo Smith, Creepy Hollow, Snowbabies, Department 56, Barbie.

Noteworthy: Owners Stewart and Arlene Richardson have been dealing in antiques and collectibles for 12 years. They have an extensive background in Royal Doulton, M.I. Hummel, and Precious Moments, and belong to several collectors clubs. In 1993 the Richardsons opened a store selling secondary market figurines. It features a showroom with over 3,000 figurines in stock.

MI — SOMETHING SPECIAL, GIFTS SOMETHING SPECIAL, TOO — 33
85 & 97 Kercheval
Grosse Pointe Farms, MI 48236

Phone: (313) 886-4341
Fax: (313) 886-9505
Hours: M-Sat: 10:00-5:30, Th: 10:00-7:00

Services: 15% commission added to collector's price. Locator service. UPS shipping available. Accept Visa, MasterCard, American Express, and Discover.

Lines: Department 56, Harbour Lights, Michael's, Shelia's, Christopher Radko, Vitreville.

Noteworthy: Original store established in 1983. Second store in 1993. Department 56 Gold Key dealer.

MN — COLLECTORS GALLERY — 34
7150 Valley Creek Plaza #212
Woodbury, MN 55125

Phone: (800) 878-7868 (612) 738-8351
Fax: (612) 738-6760
Hours: M-F: 10:00-9:00, Sat: 10:00-6:00, Sun: Noon-5:00

Services: Buy/sell/trade. Consignment service. Visa, MasterCard, Discover.

Lines: Department 56, Hummel, Lladro, Precious Moments, David Winter, Swarovski, Lilliput Lane, Armani, Kinkade, JP Editions, Disney Classics, Legends.

Noteworthy: We service all collectors clubs. "Largest inventory of new and retired collectibles in the upper Midwest." We also carry current collectibles - David Winter Gold Premier, Precious Moments DSR, Lladro Millenium, Swarovski Premier, Department 56 Village Key, Legends Preferred, Cherished Teddies Adoption Center, Kinkade Premier.

MO — HERITAGE VILLAGE COLLECTION EXCHANGE — 35
3273 139th Avenue NW
Andover, MN 55304

Phone: (612) 323-3570
Hours: Open daily 24 hours (collectors may leave message)

Services: Buy/sell/trade, locator service.

Lines: Dept. 56: Dickens, New England, Alpine, Christmas in the City, North Pole Villages & Accessories, Snowbabies, Cherished Teddies.

Noteworthy: The Heritage Village Collection Exchange has been in the secondary market business since 1990. Owners Ron and Kathy Jacobs enjoy attending trade shows throughout the United States. They own and display the Dickens' Village pieces and accessories along with Bachman's Hometown series, the North Pole, and Little Town of Bethlehem collections. Kathy enjoys dealing and visiting with all the friendly and enthusiastic collectors she meets. The Heritage Village Collection Exchange offers immediate shipping and layaway on many pieces and accessories.

MO — HOLIDAY MELODY — 36
#9 South Tenth St.
Columbia, MO 65201

Phone: (573) 442-0298
Fax: (573) 449-8557
Hours: T-Sat: 10:00-5:30, (Mail order and walk-ins.)
Holiday expanded 7 days

Services: Buy outright. No consignments. Commission for swap and sell transactions. Publish bimonthly newsletter. Call for details.

Lines: Christopher Radko, Polonaise, Old World Christmas, Patricia Breen, Boyds Bears, Cherished Teddies, Precious Moments, Harbour Lights, Forma Vitrum, Amish Heritage, Ebony Visions, Possible Dreams, Shelia's, Eddie Walker, Leo R. Smith, and Anheuser-Busch steins.

Noteworthy: Publisher of *The Collector's Melody*, comprehensive European Glass Ornament Newsletter since 1994. Club redemption center for all lines carried.

MO — JERDÓN — 37
311 S. Main
Carthage, MO 64836

Phone: (800) 503-9844 (417) 358-3343
Hours: M-Sat: 10:00-5:00, Other hours by appointment.

Services: Buy outright. Limited brokerage.
Lines: Precious Moments, Lowell Davis, Cybis, Ispanky, ANRI, Shelia's, Boyds, Lefton, Harmony Kingdom, Country Artists, Armani, Lilliput Lane.
Noteworthy: Located halfway between Sam Butcher's Precious Moments Chapel and Lowell Davis' Red Oak II in Carthage, MO. Jerdón is a block-long store, sitting across from one of the most beautiful courthouses in the country. Owner Gerri Green handles private liquidation of estates and private collections. She works with individuals nationwide and handles many of their secondary market transactions by phone. The staff are members of the American Society of Appraisers. They utilize the Collectors' Information Bureau's Price Guide, whose values help the firm establish a fair and accurate price for buyers and sellers.

MT — THE SHIP'S BELL — 38
101 E. 6th Ave.
Helena, MT 59601

Phone: (406) 443-4470
Fax: (406) 442-1800
Hours: M-F: 11:00-5:30, Sat: 11:00-4:00 MNT

Services: Available for current and past issues. Payment in money order or certified checks get immediate shipment whereas personal checks have to clear. You can also order through E-mail: AOL - ShirleyLou.
Lines: Bradford, Hamilton, Reco, M.I. Hummel, Ernst, Perillo, Villeroy & Boch, Christian Bell, Winston/Rolland, Redlin, Lowell Davis, Ashton Drake dolls and more.
Noteworthy: Established in 1973, authorized Bradford and Reco dealer. Large plate gallery featured, in addition to other collectible lines. Secondary market specialists for the lines listed above and they welcome all other inquiries as well. Shirley DeWolf and her staff pride themselves on adding a personal touch, as they work with each and every collector.

NC — CALLAHAN'S OF CALABASH — 39
9973 Beach Drive
Calabash, NC 28467

Phone: (800) 344-3816
Hours: Daily: 9:00-10:00 PM - Summer
Daily: 9:00-9:00 PM - Winter

Services: Price list available. Items taken on consignment with a 15% commission fee added to the selling price.
Lines: As a Department 56 "Gold Key" dealer, Callahan's specialty is Department 56 Villages, accessories, and Snowbabies. They also offer a secondary market for Wee Forest Folk and a growing Christopher Radko market.
Noteworthy: Come visit their 26,000 square foot shopping extravaganza, featuring the 2,000 sq. ft. award winning Department 56 room. In 1996, as a Rising Star Dealer, they are proud to introduce their Christopher Radko Room.

NC — THE GREAT AMERICAN BREWERY SHOPPE — 40
128 N. Main Street
Salisbury, NC 28144

Phone: (704) 642-1345
Fax: (704) 642-1377
Hours: T-Sat: 11:00-6:00

Services: Buy, sell, and trade. Mail order available. MasterCard and Visa accepted.
Lines: Anheuser-Busch, Coca-Cola, Coors, Hamm's, Miller, Pabst, Strohs, mirrors, neons, and steins. Brewery banks, cars, pins, and trucks. Liquor advertising and decanters by Jim Beam, McCormick, Wild Turkey, etc.
Noteworthy: Their store is 3,000 square feet, housing the largest selection of new and old Budweiser advertising, steins, and toys. Easy access off I-85, exit 76 B. Downtown historic Salisbury.

NC — REPLACEMENTS LTD. — 41
1089 Knox Road
P.O. Box 26029
Greensboro, NC 27420

Phone: (800) REPLACE (800 737-5223)
Fax: (910) 697-3100
Showroom Hours: Daily: 8:00 AM-9:00 PM
Phone Hours: Daily: 8:00 AM-10:00 PM

Services: Buy/sell outright. MasterCard & Visa accepted. Layaway.
Lines: Lladro, M.I. Hummel, Royal Doulton, Royal Copenhagen, Bing & Grondahl, Boehm, Hutschenreuther, Lenox, Wallace, Gorham, Reed & Barton, Waterford, Towle, Orrefors, Lalique, Bradford collector plates, ornaments, and figurines.
Noteworthy: Founded in 1981 by Bob Page, Replacements, Ltd. is the world's largest supplier of discontinued and active china, crystal, and flatware. Replacements, Ltd. stocks 3.2 million pieces of tableware and collectibles in over 62,000 patterns. The company features many major collector lines. They offer free daily tours of their warehouse & offices.

NJ — ALISA'S INTERNATIONAL DOLL ART — 42
1328 River Ave. Suite 300
Lakewood, NJ 08701

Phone: (908) 864-0466
Hours: M-F: 8:00 AM-7:00 PM, Sat: 9:00-1:00

Services: Does not buy outright. Up to 5-month layaway. Small deposit on dolls ordered. Sells to dealers. 24 hour answering service. Satisfaction guaranteed.
Lines: Lynn & Michael Roche, Annette Himstedt, Yolanda Bello, Dolls by Jerri, Georgetown Dolls, Paul Crees, Jan McLean, Grossle-Schmidt, Sabine Esche, Disney, Dept. 56 Snowbabies, Swarovski, Kinkade & Hibel lithos, limited edition Barbie dolls & Barbie ornaments, one-of-a-kind limited edition international doll art.
Noteworthy: Alisa's Dolls is strictly a mail order business, started by doll collector turned businesswoman, Alisa Benaresh. Alisa, a doll collector herself for over 27 years, began her business in 1988. She is considered a secondary market expert in dolls starting from the early 80's. Alisa specializes in exclusive one-of-a-kind dolls by world famous artists and offers individualized attention to her customers.

NY — COLLECTIBLY YOURS — 43
80 E Route 59
Spring Valley, NY 10977

Phone: (914) 425-9244
Hours: T-Sat: 10:00-6:00, Sun. by chance. Holiday hours.

Services: Buy outright. Occasionally considers consignment. Visa, MasterCard, Discover. No appraisals.
Lines: Swarovski, Precious Moments, Lladro, Hummel, Wee Forest Folk, Memories of Yesterday, Cherished Teddies, Enesco Treasury Ornaments, All God's Children, Bradford and Hamilton plates, Disney Classics, Thomas Kinkade, Lowell Davis, Lilliput Lane, David Winter, Sports Impressions. Department 56: All villages, accessories, Snowbabies, Merry Makers. Dolls: Yolanda Bello, Annette Himstedt, Ashton-Drake, Cabbage Patch, Robin Woods, Dolls by Jerri, Gorham, Wakeen, Georgetown, Hamilton, North American Bear, Virginia Turner, Wendy Lawton.
Noteworthy: Extensive selection of dolls. Department 56 Gold Key dealer, Kinkade Premier Center, NALED, GCC (Gift Creation Concepts).

NY — THE LIMITED EDITION — 44
"The Gift And Collectible Authority"
2170 Sunrise Highway
Merrick, NY 11566

Phone: (800) 645-2864 (516) 623-4400
Fax: (516) 867-3701
Hours: M-Sat: 10:00-6:00, Fri until 9:00 PM

Services: No consignments. Buy outright. Mail your list with asking price. Visa, MasterCard, American Express, Discover.
Lines: Annalee, Cherished Teddies, Collector Plates, David Winter, Department 56 Villages & Snowbabies, Disney Classics, EKJ, Lladro, Hummel, Precious Moments, Swarovski.
Noteworthy: Over the past 21 years, The Limited Edition has become one of the most important sources of primary and secondary market collectibles in the country. The Limited Edition has a very knowledgeable and caring sales staff. All purchases are recorded on computer so collectors can be informed of new releases, retired items, limited editions, special offers and more. The Limited Edition is a member of GAA, BBB, NALED, and GCC.

NY — A WORK OF ART — 45
12 Legion Drive
Valhalla, NY 10595

Phone: (914) 948-4655
Fax: (800) 311-1330
Hours: M-F: 9:00 - 6:30
Telephone & Fax 24 hours

Services: Buy and sell outright, buy and sell listing service to thousands of collectors. All dealers welcome. Accept Visa, Mastercard, American Express, Discover, and other Novus cards.
Lines: Publishes *A Work of Art* solely about the Lladro secondary market. They are considered to be the expert in the Lladro secondary market, consulting with the CIB and other collectible magazines regarding Lladro. Worldwide access to the retired Lladro market.
Noteworthy: David and Joan Lewis have been Lladro collectors since 1974. They have been in business since 1989 and are the primary instrument in getting information out to Lladro collectors.

OH — GLASS ORNAMENT EXCHANGE — 46
4226 Deepwood Lane
Cincinnati, OH 45245-1718

Phone: (800) 58-RADKO (513) 752-3434 (OH)
Fax: (513) 752-5253
Hours: 24 hour Service

Services: The Glass Ornament Exchange is a free listing service. If they don't have an ornament listed, they keep a search file. Once the ornament is found, the buyer has the opportunity to buy with no obligation. Visa/MasterCard accepted.
Lines: Christopher Radko, Patricia Breen, Polonaise, Old World, many others.
Noteworthy: Glass Ornament Exchange is the largest glass ornament listing agent in the United States. They specialize in Christopher Radko, Patricia Breen, and many others. Currently there are over 1,000 ornaments listed - with Radko's dating back to 1987. Call today for more information.

OK — SHIRLEY'S GIFTS, INC. — 47
1021 W. Broadway
Ardmore, OK 73401

Phone: (800) 537-2116 (405) 223-2116
Hours: M-Sat: 10:00-6:00

Services: Buy/Sell. All major credit cards accepted. Freight-free shipping available.
Lines: Disney Classics, Swarovski, Chilmark, Lefton, Hummel, Dept. 56, Cherished Teddies, Boyds Bears & Dollstones, Precious Moments, Calico Kittens, Shelia's, Lizzie High, Pocket Dragons, Madame Alexander, Tom Clark, Tim Wolfe, Lee Sievers, Armani, Kinkade, Genesis, Byers' Choice, EKJ, All God's Children, M. Furlong, Dreamsicles, Possible Dreams, Cottontail Lane, Patchville Bunnies, Seraphim Angels, Fontanini, Forma Vitrum, nutcrackers, and more.
Noteworthy: The store is now a Key Dealer for Cairn Studios, a Showcase Dealer for Department 56, a premier dealer for Swarovski, Charter dealer for Lefton. Shirley's is a redemption center for most collectibles and hosts collector events throughout the year.

OK — WINTER IMAGES — 48
3008 Hilltop
Muskogee, OK 74403

Phone: (918) 683-3488
Fax: (918) 683-2325
Hours: Evenings and Weekends

Services: Secondary market exchange, listing retired pieces to buy or sell. Major credit cards accepted. If paying by check, prefer money order or certified check. Order is held for one week if paid by personal check.
Lines: David Winter, Precious Moments, Hummel, Hallmark, Lowell Davis, Swarovski, Lladro, DeGrazia, Disney, Department 56, Lilliput Lane, Enesco, Rockwell and others.
Noteworthy: Home owned and run business founded in 1992. Will provide appraisals for valuation of collections. Business prides itself on personalized services to its customers. Will help locate any collectible item.

OR — CHRISTMAS TREASURES — 49
52959 McKenzie Highway
Blue River, OR 97413

Phone: (800) 820-8189 (541) 822-3516
Fax: (541) 822-3516
Hours: Daily: 9:00-7:00 (PST)

Services: Retail and secondary market. Credit cards accepted. Items bought outright as needed. Newletters and lists available.
Lines: Dept. 56, Byers' Choice, Old World Christmas ornaments and Santa Lights, Christopher Radko, Hallmark, Roman Seraphim Angels, Duncan Royale Santas, Boyds Bears, History of Angels, Melody In Motion Santas, Steinbach Nutcrackers, Christmas Reproduction Memories of Santa, Muffy Vanderbear, V.I.B. and Raikes Christmas Bears, Raggedy Ann and Andy L.T.D. by Applause and old Knickerbockers, Possible Dreams Santas.
Noteworthy: Christmas Treasures brings you the most treasured items for gift giving and collecting. Experience the Old World charm all through the year. "If we don't stock it, we can usually get it."

OR — LITAMI SALE IMPORTS (LITA) — 50
15565 Eilers Road
Aurora, OR 97002

Phone: (503) 678-1622
Fax: (503) 266-2973
Hours: Showroom open by appointment

Services: Buy and sell outright. Layaway available.
Lines: ANNETTE HIMSTEDT DOLLS, STEINBACH AND ULBRICHT NUTCRACKERS (ltd. ed. and regular stock). Exclusive dealer of Himstedt dolls. 20-22 different Himstedt dolls available at all times. 4 or 5 of the same doll are available, each uniquely shaded and therefore slightly different.
Noteworthy: Born and raised in Europe, Lita Sale has developed personal relationships with Ulbricht, Steinbach, and Himstedt. When German doll artist Annette Himstedt decided to export dolls to the U.S., Lita opened an importing company & showroom. Through trips to the New York Toy Fair and the International Toy Fair in Nuremberg, Germany, and visits to artists' homes, studios, and factories, Lita is constantly adding to her inventory of Limited Collectibles.

PA — BOB LAMSON BEER STEINS, INC. — 51
509 N. 22nd Street
Allentown, PA 18104

Phone: (800) 435-8611 (215) 435-8611
Hours: M-F: 9:00-9:00, Sat: 10:00-4:00

Services: Buy/sell/trade. Terms available upon request for larger purchases. Please inquire.
Lines: Anheuser-Busch, Michelob, Budweiser, Bud Light, Coors, Strohs, Miller, Heineken, steins and related collectibles with beer affiliations.
Noteworthy: Incorporated in 1990, Bob Lamson Beer Steins, Inc. is owned and operated solely by the Lamson family. The company has a retail store located in Allentown, Pennsylvania, and also ships orders to every state in the nation and to Canada. Collectors should call with any additional questions they have regarding the company. Anheuser-Busch Collectors Club Redemption Center.

PA — CRAYON SOUP — 52
King of Prussia Plaza
King of Prussia, PA 19406

Phone: (800) 552-3760 (610) 265-2446 (610) 265-0458
Fax: (610) 265-2979
Hours: M-Sat: 10:00-9:30, Sun: 11:00-6:00

Services: Buy outright.
Lines: All God's Children, Lladro, Department 56: Heritage Village and Accessories, Snowbabies, Lilliput Lane, Emmett Kelly Jr., David Winter, Precious Moments, PenDelfin, Sarah's Attic, Swarovski, Steinbach Nutcrackers, M.I. Hummel, Memories of Yesterday, Maud Humphrey, Norman Rockwell, Olszewski, Anheuser and German Gentz steins, Limoges Boxes.
Noteworthy: The formation of Crayon Soup in 1982 was a natural, considering that the owners Joe and Trish Zawislack had already been collecting for 30 years. They have over 700 Hummels in stock. Crayon Soup hosts 40 collector events including artist appearances and organizes in-store collector clubs. Information on new and retired products and collector clubs is available free of charge.

PA — LIGHTHOUSE TRADING COMPANY — 53
112 Elio Circle
Limerick, PA 19468

Phone: (610) 409-9336
Fax: (610) 409-9336
Hours: Mail order: M-F: 5-10 PM, Sat-Sun: 10-5
24-hr. answering service

Services: Buy/sell. Secondary market service. Occasionally buy outright. Dealers welcome. Layaway plan.
Lines: Harbour Lights
Noteworthy: Lighthouse Trading Company is owned and operated by Matt Rothman. He keeps current in Harbour Lights and other popular collectibles, offering a personalized secondary market service for collectors to buy and sell their collectibles. Matt has had articles published in national collectible publications and is a contributing Collectors' Information Bureau panel member.

PA — WORLDWIDE COLLECTIBLES AND GIFTS — 54
P.O. Box 158 2 Lakeside Avenue
Berwyn, PA 19312-0158

Phone: (800) 222-1613 (610) 644-2442
Fax: (610) 889-9549
Hours: M-Sat: 10:00-5:00

Services: No consignments. Call for specific quotes. Prompt payment on all items purchased. Prompt delivery on items ordered.
Lines: Swarovski, Lladro, Department 56, Disney Classics, M.I. Hummel, David Winter, Duncan Royale, Steiff, collector plates, bells, collector club pieces and many others.
Noteworthy: Worldwide Collectibles is a full service company established in 1975. They deal in current and secondary market pieces and maintain a large inventory on all lines carried. **A 64-page mail order catalog available free, upon request.** The Worldwide staff is actively involved with major insurers for replacement and estimate valuation purposes. Appraisals and references are available on request.

TN — CLASSIC ENDEAVORS — 55

349 Southshore Drive
Greenback, TN 37742

Phone: (423) 856-8100
Fax: (423) 856-8001
Hours: M-F: 10:00-5:00 EST

Services: 20% added to the seller's price. Seller will receive 80% of the transaction. No hidden charges. Printed price lists available on request. Price lists include commission. No surprises. Accept Visa and MasterCard with no added usage charges.

Lines: Specializes in Walt Disney Classic Collection and Disneyana convention limited editions. Strong secondary market activity in Harbour Lights, also Kinkade (canvas editions only) & Forma Vitrum.

Noteworthy: Classic Endeavors, a secondary exchange, formed in 1994 with their business motto "An Informed Collector is a Happy Collector," is dedicated to providing information to help the collector complete his collection, be it for enjoyment or investment. Every purchase inspected thoroughly before shipment.

VA — MEMORIES IN MOTION — 58

114 Clark Ave.
Elkton, VA 22827

Phone: (540) 298-9234
Hours: Mail order: 6:00 PM - 10:00 PM EST

Services: Price list available. Accept Visa / MasterCard. Ship worldwide. Buy outright when needed, refer and sell to other dealers. Call for details.

Lines: Hallmark Ornaments (including Star Trek and Barbie), Cherished Teddies, some Barbie dolls.

Noteworthy: Memories In Motion is mail order only. It was started by Bobbie Ann Horne in 1990, from her home in the beautiful Shenandoah Valley of Virginia. Memories In Motion serves clients around the world. Bobbie Ann is a charter member of the Hallmark Ornament Collector's Club, serves as a consultant to Hallmark Stores, and donates large quantities of ornaments to local charities. Easy to talk with, she serves her clients with honesty and warmth. Says Bobbie Ann, "My specialty is pleasing clients, and I'm not satisfied unless you are."

TX — AMANDA'S FINE GIFTS — 56

265 Central Park Mall
San Antonio, TX 78216-5506

Phone: (800) 441-4458 (210) 525-0412
Hours: M-Sat: 10:00-9:00, Sun: Noon-6:00

Services: Consignments. Buy outright. Layaway. Redemption center for Lladro, Disney, Swarovski, Ron Lee, M.I. Hummel, Lalique, and Armani collector clubs. Appraisal Service for insurance purposes.

Lines: Lladro, Swarovski, M.I. Hummel, Tom Clark, Ron Lee, Armani, Chilmark, Lowell Davis, Bossons, Disney.

Noteworthy: Barry Harris developed a deep appreciation for Lladro artwork, which eventually led to the purchase of Amanda's Fine Gifts in 1983. Realizing the great potential for offering Lladro artwork and information to collectors, Barry and his staff have become known as experts in the field. The largest Lladro dealer in the southwest, Amanda's has welcomed Lladro family members to the store for artist appearances. Other guests have included Don Polland, Tom Clark, Ron Lee, Michael Boyett, Armani, and M.I. Hummel artists.

WA — THE SECOND HAND NEWS™ — 59

8712 NE 57th Street
Vancouver, WA 98662

Phone: (800) 925-1532
Fax: (360) 896-1925
Hours: 24 hour answering service

Services: Publishes a newsletter six times per year for secondary market collector plates with separate sections for "Plates for Sale" and "Plates Wanted." Subscriptions are $20 a year in the USA, $25 a year foreign and includes 50 free plate listings per issue. Readers interested in buying or selling a listed plate contact the listing party directly to negotiate a deal. Sample copies are $3.

Lines: Hamilton, Bradford, Lenox, Enesco, Schmid, Princeton Galleries, Franklin Mint, Goebel, Hallmark, Pemberton & Oakes, Reco, Marty Bell, Rockwell Society, Disney, etc.

Noteworthy: *The Second Hand News™* was founded in 1993 to enable plate lovers to buy, sell, or trade secondary market plates directly with one another, without paying a broker's fee or commissions.

TX — ANTIQUE HAVEN — 57

Route 1, Box 60
Stanton, TX 79782

Phone: (800) 299-3480 (915) 458-3480
Hours: M-Sat: 9:00-5:00

Services: 10 month layaway. Ship freight free in U.S. Major credit cards accepted. Buy outright. Consignment. Quarterly newsletter

Lines: All God's Children, Miss Martha's Collection, Endearing Memories, Tom Clark Gnomes, Lee Sievers, Tim Wolfe, Cat's Meow, Daddy's Long Legs, Cherished Teddies, Fenton, Disney Classics, Lowell Davis, Maud Humphrey.

Noteworthy: Located 12 miles east of Midland, TX and 5 miles west of Stanton on N. Access Road of Interstate Hwy 20, mile marker 151, Antique Haven, in exsistence for 29 years, is second generation owned by Vanita and Jerry Waid. They carry European and American antiques, glassware, candles, and many gift items and accessories in addition to specializing in the secondary market and collectibles. They are also a redemption center for many collectible lines.

WI — WEMAS OF WISCONSIN, INC. — 60

FORMERLY COTTAGE PARK LTD.
P.O. Box 71
Greendale, WI 53129

Phone: (414) 427-1959
Fax: (414) 427-4468
Hours: M-Sat: 9:00-4:30 CST

Services: No consignments. Buy outright if not in our inventory. We accept all major credit cards. Free shipping. 6 month layaway available. All items in mint condition.

Lines: David Winter, Lilliput Lane, Malcom Cooper Pubs, Department 56 (Dickens and Signature Series), and Harbour Lights.

Noteworthy: In 1980, Dick and Syl Maslowski entered the giftware business and became a secondary market dealer in 1985. Today, this establishment hosts in-store events, including artist appearances to promote the collectibles hobby. The store is a redemption center for David Winter, Harbour Lights, Dreamsicles, and Cherished Teddies collector clubs.